TROUBLESHOOTING, MAINTAINING, & REPAIRING PCS

FOURTH EDITION

STEPHEN J. BIGELOW

Osborne/**McGraw-Hill**

Berkeley / New York / St. Louis / San Francisco / Auckland / Bogotá
Hamburg / London / Madrid / Mexico City / Milan / Montreal / New Delhi
Panama City / Paris / São Paulo / Singapore / Sydney / Tokyo / Toronto

Osborne/**McGraw-Hill**
2600 Tenth Street
Berkeley, California 94710
U.S.A.

For information on translations or book distributors outside the U.S.A., or to arrange bulk purchase discounts for sales promotions, premiums, or fund-raisers, please contact Osborne/**McGraw-Hill** at the above address.

Troubleshooting, Maintaining, & Repairing PCs, Fourth Edition

1234567890 DOC DOC 019876543210

Book P/N 0-07-212684-1 and CD P/N 0-07-212685-X
parts of
ISBN 0-07-212686-8

Publisher
Brandon A. Nordin

Vice President and Associate Publisher
Scott Rogers

Acquisitions Editor
Michael Sprague

Project Editor
Madhu Prasher

Copy Editors
Judith Brown
Barbara Brodnitz
Carl Wikander

Proofreaders
Laurie Stewart
Carol Burbo
Pamela Vevea

Indexer
Valerie Robbins

Computer Designers
Michelle Galicia
Gary Corrigan

Illustrator
Robert Hansen

Series Design
Michelle Galicia

This book was composed with Corel VENTURA™ Publisher.

CONTENTS AT A GLANCE

CONTENTS

CST CERTIFICATION

The Computer Service Technician (CST) certification program was initiated in 1998 by the ETA-I. It has since gained popularity as the standard computer certification program for electronics technicians. The CST certification examination consists of 50 questions and covers nine (9) basic areas related to personal computer maintenance, repair, upgrading, and troubleshooting. The areas of competencies tested include:

- Microprocessor architecture and operational characteristics
- Video display systems
- Memory
- Bus architectures
- Hard drive installation and troubleshooting
- Printers
- I/O hardware characteristics
- Networking—basic features of LANs, network protocols
- Network operating systems

Certified ETA-I examiners at various locations in the United States, Canada, and other countries administer the CST examinations. The fee for the exam, as well as recertification after four years, is $50.00. Information regarding ETA-I certifications, local test sites, exam results, and recertification may be obtained from the Electronics Technicians Association—International headquarters by calling one of the following numbers: 800-288-3824 or 765-653-4301. Or you can visit the ETA-I Web site at www.eta-sda.com.

Disclaimer and Cautions

It is important that you read and understand the following information. Please read it carefully!

Personal Risk and Limits Of Liability

The repair of personal computers and their peripherals involves some amount of personal risk. Use extreme caution when working with AC and high-voltage power sources. Every reasonable effort has been made to identify and reduce areas of personal risk. You are instructed to read this book carefully *before* attempting the procedures discussed. If you are uncomfortable following the procedures that are outlined in this book, do *not* attempt them—refer your service to qualified service personnel.

Neither the author, the publisher, nor anyone directly or indirectly connected with the publication of this book AND ACCOMPANYING COMPUTER SOFTWARE shall make any warranty EITHER EXPRESSED OR IMPLIED, with regard to this material, including, but not limited to, the implied warranties of quality, merchantability, and fitness for any particular purpose. Furthermore, neither the author,

Virus Warning

Although the software included with this book was thoroughly checked for viruses before publication, you are *strongly* advised to inspect all new software, including this book's companion software, for the presence of computer viruses *before* executing the software. Antivirus software can be obtained through commercial and shareware sources. Neither the author, publisher, nor anyone directly or indirectly connected with this book assume any liability whatsoever for incidental or consequential damages, financial loss, or material loss resulting from the occurrence of computer viruses on your system or network. You use this software at your own risk.

Vendor Warning

The products, materials, equipment, manufacturers, service providers, and distributors listed and presented in this book are shown for reference purposes only. Their mention and use in this book shall not be construed as an endorsement of any individual or organization, nor the quality of their products or services, nor their performance or business integrity. The author, publisher, and anyone directly or indirectly associated with the production of this book expressly disclaim all liability whatsoever for any financial or material losses or incidental or consequential damages that might occur from contacting or doing business with any such organization or individual.

INTRODUCTION: A BOOK FOR CHANGING TIMES

It used to be that when a PC failed, it wound up sitting on a test bench surrounded by a battalion of test equipment. An experienced technician would be hovering over the PC, logic probe or test leads in hand. They relied on their knowledge of electronics and microprocessor operations to track the problem to a faulty chip or passive component that could then be replaced with relatively simple soldering tools. There were few add-ons or peripherals to worry about, and only a few MB of memory to work with. The few expansion devices that did exist were often plagued by compatibility problems and proprietary interfaces.

Well, times certainly *have* changed. Today's PC is largely a collection of very inexpensive subassemblies—most of which are now manufactured in the Pacific Rim—and assembled in high volumes at factories around the world. The diverse array of peripherals that are now available (i.e. tape drives, CD-ROMs, video accelerators, DVD-ROMs, pointing devices, and so on) enjoy a remarkable level of hardware compatibility using well-established interface schemes (i.e. AGP, SCSI, UDMA/66, USB, or PCI). The labor cost involved in a component-level repair today is usually more expensive than the cost of a replacement assembly. There is little doubt that the day of component-level PC repair is over.

However, PCs still fail, and they fail in ways that continue to exhaust even the most patient mind. When you realize that there are now well over 100 million PCs in operation (and growing at an astonishing rate each year), you can see that *effective* troubleshooting requires more than simply an arbitrary swapping of boards and drives. Now, more than ever, efficient and cost-effective troubleshooting requires an understanding of PC hardware and operating systems, along with a keen knowledge of symptoms and diagnostics. Setting up, optimizing, and upgrading a PC are three other important areas that demand the attention of today's technician.

INSIDE THIS EDITION

This book is intended for the modern computer enthusiast, working technician, or PC student. It is not designed to explain computer theory—there are already plenty of theory books out there. Instead, this book is designed to be a hands-on desktop (or workbench) reference for PC repair, maintenance, and upgrading. This book concentrates on the symptoms and problem areas that occur in every area of the modern PC, as well as proper *diagnosis* of problems. Online resources are included for almost every chapter, making the book ideal for classroom or home study. Previous editions have been extremely popular, but this fourth edition is packed with improvements, just a few of which are highlighted below:

- This fourth edition continues to expand much of the troubleshooting and reference information throughout previous editions of the book, and adds 7 new chapters and 2 new appendices. There are more than 2000 symptoms and solutions completely updated and revised (compared to about 1500 in the Millennium Edition). Many chapters have been rewritten, and all have been reviewed and revised.

- Each chapter includes a number of Web addresses for further study. This should give the book an added value for classroom instruction, and as an aid to self-paced study.
- The diagnostic CD included with the Millennium Edition has been completely updated with the DLS Diagnostic CD III containing over 120 ready-to-go shareware diagnostics and utilities, most of which run under Windows 95/98.
- The DLS Technician's Certificate III has been completely updated and revised to 300 questions. This offers a new technology/troubleshooting challenge for all readers—even those that have taken previous versions of the exam.

This book is meant to be a lifeline and a resource to help you repair your PC, keep it running, and get the most out of it. You'll find more than 2000 PC problems fully detailed and explained. There are references to hundreds more POST and diagnostic codes to help you identify even the most obscure problems. But the support you'll find here goes far beyond these book pages. You'll find an entire CD-ROM full of over 120 *power-tools*—shareware and freeware diagnostics and utilities designed to help you identify even the peskiest PC problems. This is one of the only PC hardware books to bundle so many Windows 95/98 diagnostic software products with the text.

SUBSCRIBE TO THE PC TOOLBOX

Many readers also complain that PC books suffer from a limited "life-span." All too often, a book is dated as soon as it gets on bookstore shelves. You can avoid this kind of "technical obsolescence" by subscribing to our #1 newsletter, *The PC Toolbox*™—to stay informed of the latest hands-on service articles, optimization techniques, and find the answers to your PC questions. Even if you don't fix computers for a living, a subscription can save you hundreds of dollars in shop costs. You can find the ad and order form for *The PC Toolbox*™ at the back of this book.

TEST YOUR KNOWLEDGE

Worried about keeping yourself employable? Go for the Dynamic Learning Systems *Technician's Certificate III*. You can take the electronic *DLS Technician's Examination* included on the CD-ROM as Appendix J; if you pass you will receive a high-quality certificate showing your mastery of the material in this book. But the certificate is not just for framing—readers who successfully complete the examination are much better prepared to tackle the industry-recognized A+ examination, and even move on to acquire CST certification through the ETA (Electronic Technician's Association).

I'M INTERESTED IN YOUR SUCCESS

I've taken a lot of time and effort to see that this edition is the most comprehensive and understandable book on PC/peripheral repair available. If you have any questions or comments about the book, please don't hesitate to contact me.

—Stephen J. Bigelow

FAQ: GETTING THE MOST FROM THIS BOOK

GENERAL BOOK INFORMATION

Q I have a question or comment about the book. How can I contact you?

A We welcome any questions or comments regarding this book. Feel free to send an e-mail through our Web site at **http://www.dlspubs.com**. It may take a few days to respond depending on our mail volume. If you'd prefer to contact us by mail: Dynamic Learning Systems, PO Box 402, Leicester, MA 01524-0402 USA. Our fax number is 508-892-1482.

Q Do you help folks troubleshoot their PCs? Do you offer any kind of technical or telephone support?

A The answer to your question is "yes and no." Yes, we *do* welcome troubleshooting questions through our Web site at **http://www.dlspubs.com**, by fax, or by mail (see our contact information above). However, we do *not* run a live tech support hotline. Inquiries are gladly answered, but *only* on a time-available basis. It may take several days or longer to research and formulate a reply (depending on our mail volume). As a result, we cannot provide emergency troubleshooting help, or respond to immediate requests for advice. We reserve the right to refuse or reject inquiries at our discretion.

Q What a long title! Just what *is* the difference between troubleshooting, maintaining, and repairing? Aren't they all the same?

A No, they're not the same, but they're close—it's really a matter of semantics. "Troubleshooting" is a process of determining the problem, "Maintaining" is an ongoing activity focusing on keeping the PC running smoothly, and "Repairing" is the actual fixing of the problem.

Q What new material does this book have that your first edition did not?

A This edition of the book is a substantial improvement over previous editions with over 2000 symptoms and more than 120 shareware/freeware utilities (most for Windows 95/98), many chapters have been expanded and updated, and a number of new chapters have been added. See the "Contents at a Glance" section.

Q I see a lot of cryptic "http" and/or "www" references used at the ends of each chapter and in tables and text throughout the book. What are these designations, and how do I use them?

A There are "universal resource locators" (or URLs), which point to Internet Web pages containing extra details and information from manufacturers or organizations. You can usually "jump" from each site to other related sites as well, expanding your access to information over the Internet.

Q I'm a college instructor and I want to use this book for my class. What resources do you have here for students and instructors?

A You'll find a number of topic-related Web sites listed at the end of each chapter. We've also updated the DLS Technician's Certificate III to 300 questions. *The PC Toolbox*™ subscriptions are available to all readers, and you'll find MONITORS and PRINTERS utilities right on the Companion CD, along with over 120 other software utilities.

Q I want to recommend this as the standard PC course textbook for my school, and we often plan lectures with excerpts from the book. Do I need to request permissions each time we take an excerpt?

A Qualified educational institutions that use the book must make a single request in writing using the institution's letterhead stating what you want to excerpt. You'll get a prompt reply, which entitles you to use excerpts from the book subject to the following limitations: you can't post excerpts online; you can't sell excerpts to students; and you can't distribute excerpts electronically (i.e. downloadable text files).

USING THE BOOK PRODUCTIVELY

Q I've been trying to access a Web site you listed in the book, but I keep getting an error saying that there's "no such site" or that the Web browser can't connect. What good is that?

A This is a fair complaint, but it is also a reality of today's Internet. Although we've made every effort to provide current contact information, it's not always possible to stay "up to the minute" with the fast and furious changes taking place on the Internet. Web sites appear, change URLs, and sometimes disappear with little or no warning. Unfortunately, there is little that can be done about this issue except to try cross-referencing the desired company or contact through a search engine like Yahoo, Alta Vista, or Excite.

Q You said I could download a patch or update from a manufacturer's Web site, but I've been searching this Web site for hours and I still can't find a trace of the patch or update. What can I do now?

A Web sites are a mixed blessing—they can change dynamically with up-to-the-minute information, but needed information and important support resources can also disappear without a trace at the whim of a webmaster. If you cannot track down a patch or update file from a particular manufacturer's Web site, we can only suggest that you e-mail the webmaster or technical support department (there's almost always an e-mail link through a Web site) and inquire directly with them. They may direct you to the proper Web page URL, another Web site, an FTP site, a BBS, or some other resource that may allow you to obtain the desired file.

Q I want to certify my knowledge in PC technology and repair. What kind of certifications should I pursue?

A There are several options available to new technicians: start by taking the DLS Technician's Certificate III (see the following section). This is an inexpensive and informal option for testing and fine-tuning your troubleshooting knowledge. The next step up is the A+ exam, which is an industry-recognized certification that employers look at when evaluating a new candidate. There are also other prime industry certifications such as CST certification (sponsored by the ETA), which you should seriously consider as your career expands.

Q I'm pretty new to PCs and I want to make sure that I don't mess up my system. How can I protect myself from making mistakes?

A The best way to protect yourself from "messing up" your system is to make a complete backup of everything on the hard drive(s) before proceeding with a repair or upgrade.

Q I use this book for a lot of troubleshooting, but is there any way to track down symptoms fast instead of paging through the entire book?

A We've taken steps to simplify your reference of symptoms. See the "Symptoms at a Glance" section of the book.

Q Is there any way to find topics quickly without wading through the "Table of Contents"?

A We've taken steps to simplify your reference of the book's contents. See the "Contents at a glance" section of the book.

Q Why aren't there any anti-virus programs on the accompanying CD? There are so many.

A While there is a great deal of anti-virus software available, it often grows obsolete quickly. As a result, the decision was made to avoid anti-virus software on the companion CD. Instead, you'll find URLs pointing to a wealth of anti-virus shareware available for download, as well as links to major commercial anti-virus products. Hopefully, this will help you get the most from your anti-virus strategy.

THE BOOK'S COMPANION CD

Q What's on the CD?

A We've really pulled out all the stops to bring you a value-packed CD. There are over 120 completely new programs for diagnostics and utilities, along with our own commercial products: MONITORS and PRINTERS.

Q I don't understand how to install/use a particular software product. Can I call you for support?

A No! Aside from the MONITORS and PRINTERS utilities (which ARE Dynamic Learning Systems products), neither Dynamic Learning Systems nor Osborne/McGraw-Hill can provide technical support for any of the software on the DLS Diagnostic CD III. If you have any questions about installing or using a piece of software that is not answered in the product's documentation, you must refer to the author of the particular software for support or product registration.

Q My DLS Diagnostic CD III is missing or damaged. Can I get another from you? How can I get another?

A Osborne/McGraw-Hill is the publisher of the book and the CD; Dynamic Learning Systems does not provide warranty or replacement service for the CD. You'll need to return the book to your place of purchase for a new book/CD, or contact Osborne/McGraw-Hill's Customer Support department as instructed in the CD's warranty page at the end of the book.

Q I've seen so much about computer viruses lately. How do I know that the programs and documents on the companion CD are virus-free?

A First, every program has been checked for viruses using current anti-virus software before being compressed and mastered to the Companion CD. But don't take our word for it! Be sure to check all software (from any source) with a current virus checker before executing it for the first time. You can unzip a program without risk of infection, but be sure to check the decompressed files before launching the actual program.

Q How do I use the software on the CD?

A See Appendix A for general guidelines on installing a program to hard disk or floppy. If you still cannot get the program installed or running, you must refer to the respective program author.

Q I tried one of the programs from the CD on my system, but the program won't work. What's wrong?

A It is possible that the particular utility you are using is not compatible with the PC you're using it on, or the combination of hardware installed in the PC. Try a different utility, or check with the program author to see if there is an update or patch that can help you overcome the problem.

Q Shareware costs money to register. You don't expect me to register everything that's on this CD do you?

A Absolutely not! Shareware works on the "try before you buy" principle, so the idea is that you can use the software on your CD for a limited period of time to see if it works for you. If you choose to continue using the software (and want the benefits provided when you register the software), then you should consider registering the software. You may register as many or as few programs as you wish depending on your needs.

Q I can't decompress the MONITORS and PRINTERS programs on the CD. Why not?

A Unlike the other software on this CD, the MONITORS and PRINTERS utilities are *not* shareware—they are fully-functional commercial software products that have been included on the CD, but have been encrypted. To use MONITORS or PRINTERS, you need to buy the "unlock code" from Dynamic Learning Systems at 508-892-1475 (see the order form at the back of the book).

THE DLS TECHNICIAN'S CERTIFICATE III

Q I want to take the A+ test. Will this exam help me to take the A+ exam successfully?

A Yes—although the DLS Technician's Certificate III exam is not a direct reflection of the A+ exam, we've received a great deal of positive feedback from readers who have taken the A+ exam after passing the DLS Technician's Certificate exam, and found that the exam HAS made the A+ exam easier.

Q What is the DLS Technician's Certificate III exam, and why should I take it?

A The DLS Technician's Certificate III is the next generation exam from Dynamic Learning Systems designed to aid PC enthusiasts and technicians in learning the issues involved in PC technology, troubleshooting, and maintenance. If you're serious about troubleshooting, consider taking the exam, especially as a "tune-up" for the A+ exam.

Q How much does it cost, and what do I get?

A The A+ exam is a 300-question multiple choice troubleshooting test. There is a one-time processing fee of $50.00 to grade the exam and generate your certificate. If you fail the exam, you can retake it again as many times as necessary for no additional fee. When you pass the exam, you'll receive your graded test, along with a certificate suitable for framing.

Q What if I fail the exam?

A No problem; you'll get a new set of answer sheets, and you can try again until you pass. There are no additional fees to re-take the exam.

Q What's different between the previous exam and this one?

A This third generation of the DLS Technician's Certificate exam uses 300 multiple-choice questions—overall, the exam has been revised to keep pace with advances in PC technology.

Q I've already taken a previous DLS Technician's Certificate exam. Why should I take this test too?

A You'll find that there are many new questions and issues covered by the exam, which has been completely rewritten to keep pace with the advances in PC technology. If you've already taken the exam from an older edition of the book, you can test your knowledge and keep it current for a very reasonable price.

THE PC TOOLBOX NEWSLETTER

Q What is the newsletter all about? What does it cover?

A *The PC Toolbox*™ newsletter is a bi-monthly (6 issues/year) newsletter focusing on trouble-shooting all aspects of the PC and peripherals. You'll find this to be an exceptional supplement to the book.

Q I'm interested in *The PC Toolbox*™ newsletter. Is there any way I can get a sample copy to look over before I choose to subscribe?

A Yes, we're always pleased to send along a complimentary copy for individual reviews. All we need is a brief request mailed, faxed, or e-mailed to Dynamic Learning Systems with your full name, mailing address, and daytime telephone number. Please help us conserve resources by limiting your request to one per person. Remember that if you choose to subscribe, every subscription is backed by a 90-day unconditional money-back guarantee.

Q I teach at a college/university, and I'm interested in purchasing a number of subscriptions for my class. Do you offer any discounts?

A Yes, Dynamic Learning Systems can provide a quantity of newsletters to qualified educational organizations on either a "one-time" basis (for free), or on an ongoing basis (for a nominal charge). Submit your request on official institution letterhead via mail or fax. Be sure to indicate the desired quantity, shipping information, and your direct contact information. Dynamic Learning Systems will respond promptly with a quote.

PLACING ORDERS WITH DYNAMIC LEARNING SYSTEMS

Q I'm interested in ordering software or a subscription to *The PC Toolbox*™ newsletter, but I live outside of the U.S. What are the prices for international orders?

A The prices listed in this book are global—there are no surcharges or extra fees for orders placed from outside of the U.S. However, all payments must be in U.S. dollars (USD).

Q Do you take American Express?

A No, Dynamic Learning Systems only accepts Visa or MasterCard purchases at this time. If you do not have a credit card, you may mail your order form (see the order form in the back of the book) along with a check or money order made out to Dynamic Learning Systems.

Q How long does it take to receive my order(s)?

A It depends on *how* you order. Dynamic Learning Systems processes all orders within 48 hours, and ships all newsletters and software via first-class mail (for domestic U.S. orders), or air mail (for all orders placed outside of the U.S.). The general delivery guidelines are below:

- Mail orders placed from within the U.S. — 2 weeks
- Fax/phone orders placed from within the U.S. — 1 week
- Mail orders placed within the western hemisphere — 3 weeks
- Fax orders placed within the western hemisphere — 2 weeks
- Mail orders placed from outside of the western hemisphere — 4 weeks
- Fax orders placed from outside of the western hemisphere — 3 weeks

Q I'm uncomfortable sending a check or money order for a lot of money. How do I know the order will get to you promptly?

A We get this question a lot, especially from customers outside of the U.S. If you have any question at all about your mail service to Dynamic Learning Systems, you should send the order as a "Registered" letter (your local post office can assist you with this). This requires a signature from the DLS employee who receives the order, and provides proof that the order was received.

ABOUT THE AUTHOR

Stephen J. Bigelow is the founder and president of Dynamic Learning Systems, a technical writing, research, and publishing company specializing in electronic and PC service topics. Bigelow is the author of 15 feature-length books for TAB/McGraw-Hill, and more than 100 major articles for mainstream electronics magazines such as *Popular Electronics*, *Electronics NOW*, *Circuit Cellar INK*, and *Electronic Service & Technology*. Bigelow is a contributing columnist for *Computer Currents* (the "Computer Advisor" column) and is a regular online instructor for PC building, repair, and A+ courses at SmartPlanet (www.smartplanet.com). Bigelow is also the editor and publisher of *The PC Toolbox*™, a premier PC service newsletter for computer enthusiasts and technicians. He is an Electrical Engineer with a BS EE from Central New England College in Worcester, MA. You may contact the author at the address below:

Dynamic Learning Systems
PO Box 402
Leicester, MA 01524-0402 USA

http://www.dlspubs.com

SYMPTOMS AT A GLANCE

1

AN INSIDE LOOK AT DESKTOPS AND TOWERS

CHAPTER AT A GLANCE

In order to upgrade or troubleshoot a PC effectively, technicians must be familiar with the general mechanical and physical aspects of the PC. They must be able to disassemble the unit quickly (without causing damage to the case or internal assemblies in the process), then accurately identify each subassembly, expansion board, and connector. Once diagnosis and repair have been completed, the technician must be able to reassemble the PC and its enclosures (again without damaging assemblies or enclosures). This chapter is designed to provide you with a guided tour of the typical desktop and tower PCs (Figure 1-1), point out the various operating subassemblies, and offer a series of assembly guidelines.

FIGURE 1-1 A selection of PC enclosures (Computer cases designed and manufactured by Olson metal products, Seguin, TX)

Under the Hood

The first step will be to take a look at the generic components you'll expect to find in a desktop or tower system. Figure 1-2 illustrates an exposed view of a desktop PC. Although it may look crowded at first glance, you'll see that there are actually only a handful of subassemblies to deal with. With a little practice, identifying various assemblies should become almost automatic. An average tower system is illustrated in Figure 1-3. With few exceptions, desktop and tower PCs incorporate seven key items: the enclosure, the power supply, the motherboard, a floppy disk drive, a hard disk drive, a video adapter, and a drive controller. The following sections detail each item. Feel free to skip directly to related chapters later in the book for more detailed definitions and discussion.

ENCLOSURE

The *enclosure* is the most obvious and least glamorous element of a PC. Yet, the enclosure serves some very important functions. First, the enclosure (such as the generic Baby AT case of Figure 1-4) forms the mechanical foundation (or *chassis*) of every PC. Every other subassembly is bolted securely to this chassis. Second, the chassis is electrically grounded through the power supply. Grounding prevents the buildup or discharge of static electricity from damaging other subassemblies. Whenever you work inside

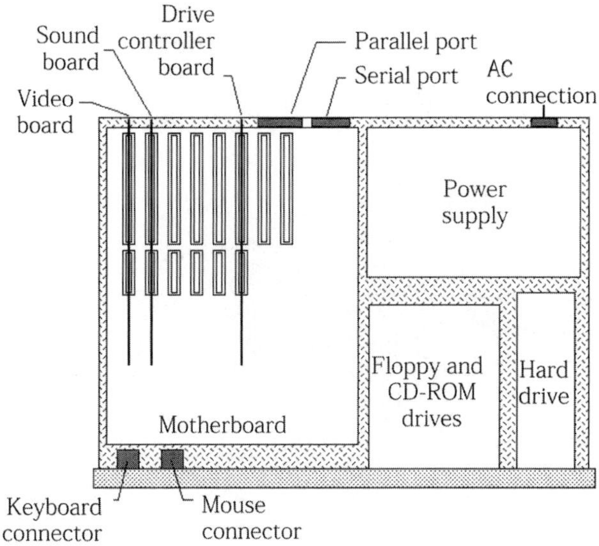

FIGURE 1-2 Layout of a typical desktop PC

a PC, be sure to use a properly grounded antistatic wrist strap to prevent electrostatic discharge from your body from accidentally damaging circuitry inside the system. If you do not have an antistatic wrist strap handy, you can discharge yourself on the PC's metal chassis as long as the power supply is plugged in. However, since you are *strongly* urged to protect yourself by unplugging the power supply AC, do *not* rely on the chassis to discharge you. Grounding also prevents a serious shock or fire hazard if live AC should come in contact with the metal case.

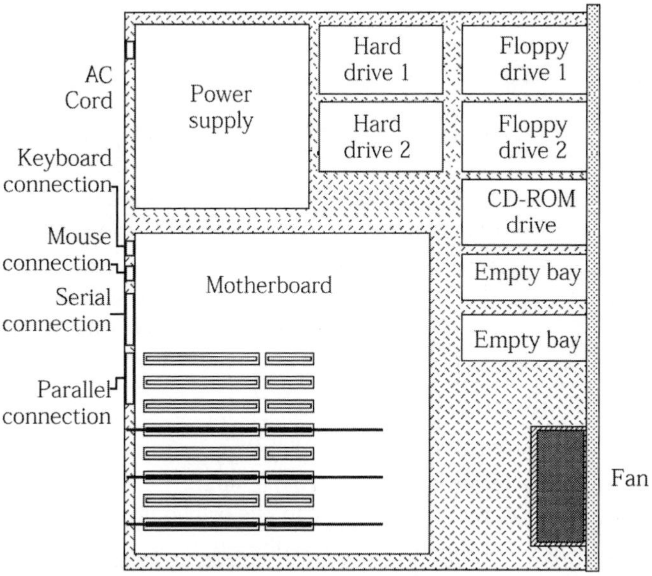

FIGURE 1-3 Layout of a typical tower PC

1

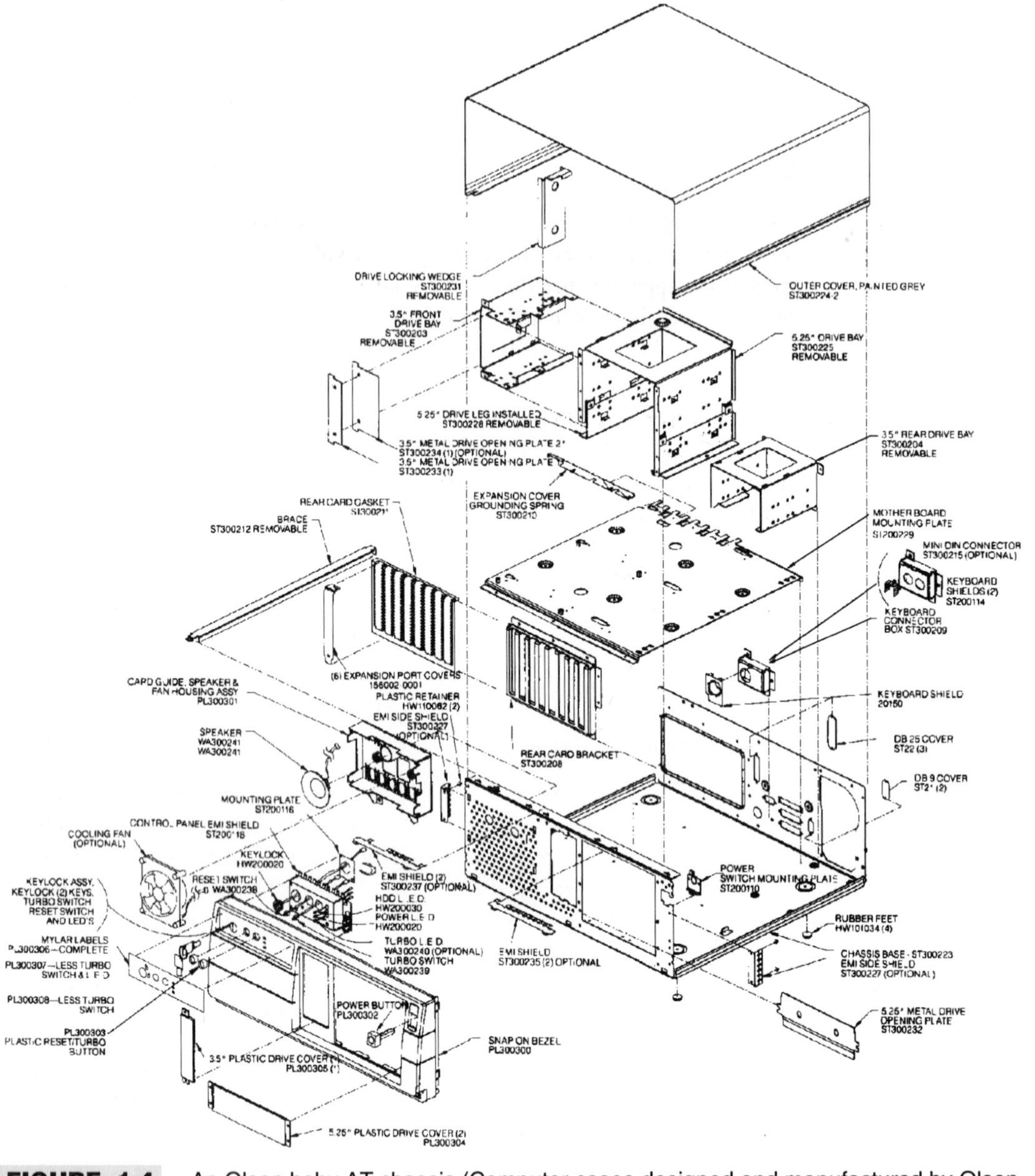

FIGURE 1-4 An Olson baby AT chassis (Computer cases designed and manufactured by Olson metal products, Seguin, TX)

The enclosure also limits the PC's expansion capacity. Average-sized desktop enclosures typically offer room for motherboards with six to eight expansion slots, and provide space for three or four drives—two drives mounted in front openings (or external drive bays) and one or two drives mounted inside the PC (in internal drive bays). An average-sized enclosure such as this allows a fair amount of space to expand the system as your customer's needs change. Unfortunately, the push toward smaller PCs has led to the use of smaller, more confined enclosures. Small (or *low-profile*) desktop enclosures restrict the size of the motherboard, which results in fewer expansion slots (usually four to six) and allows room for only one to three drives.

The great advantage to *tower* enclosures is their larger physical size. Towers usually offer four or five external drive bays, as well as three or four internal bays. To accommodate such expandability, a large power supply (300–350 watts) is often included. Tower cases can also fit larger motherboards, which tend to support a greater number of expansion slots. The higher power demands of a tower system result in greater heat generation. Towers compensate for heat by providing one or more internal fans to force air into the enclosure. If a second internal fan is included, it generally works in conjunction with the first fan to exhaust heated air. For example, you'll often find tower systems with two fans—one in the lower front to force in cooler air and one in the upper rear to exhaust heated air. If only one fan is used, it will usually be located in the upper rear of the chassis to exhaust heated air.

POWER SUPPLY

The power supply is the silver box that is usually located in the rear right quarter of a desktop enclosure. AC enters the supply through the AC line cord connected at the rear of the enclosure. A supply then produces a series of DC outputs that power the motherboard and drives. The importance of a power supply is easy enough to understand, but its implications for system integrity and expandability may not be as obvious.

Power supplies sustain a great deal of electrical stress in normal everyday operation. The conversion of AC into DC results in substantial heat, which is why so many power supplies are equipped with a cooling fan. Surges, spikes, and other anomalies that plague AC power distribution (especially in underdeveloped regions of the world) also find their way into PC power supplies where damage can occur. The quality of a power supply's components and design dictates how long it will last in operation. A quality supply will resist power problems and tolerate the rigors of normal operation, but a substandard supply can fail spontaneously after only a few months of operation. When replacing or upgrading a power supply, be sure to choose a reliable model.

Power supplies also limit a system's expandability. Every element used in the PC requires a certain amount of power (marked *W* or "watts"). The supply must be capable of producing enough power to adequately meet the system's demand. An underpowered supply (typical in low-profile systems) or a supply overloaded by excessive expansion (which frequently occurs in tower systems) may not be able to support the power needs of the system. Inadequate power results in very strange system behavior such as unpredictable system lockups, random memory faults, or disk access problems. When replacing a power supply, make certain that the new supply can provide at *least* as much power as the supply being replaced. When upgrading a supply, choose a supply that offers at least 50 watts *more* than the original supply.

> Power supply assemblies are generally regarded as extremely safe because it is virtually impossible to come into contact with exposed high-energy circuitry. Still, exercise care and common sense whenever working with a running power supply.

MOTHERBOARD

The *motherboard* (also known as the *main board*, *system board*, *backplane board*, or *planar board*) holds the majority of a computer's processing power. As a minimum, a motherboard contains the system CPU, math coprocessor (now routinely built into the CPU), clock/timing circuits, RAM, cache, BIOS ROM, serial port(s), parallel port, and expansion slots. Each portion of the motherboard is tied together with interconnecting logic circuitry. Most current motherboards also include the circuitry to handle drive and video interfaces (a few also supply sound features). You can identify the motherboard easily, as shown in Figure 1-5. It is the single large printed circuit board located just off the enclosure's base. As you might

FIGURE 1-5 A dual Pentium Pro motherboard assembly

expect, it is the motherboard more than any other element of the PC that defines the performance (and performance *limitations*) of any given computer system. This is the reason why motherboard upgrades are so popular, and often provide such stunning improvements to a PC. Let's sort motherboard limitations into the following nine categories:

CPU Type A CPU is responsible for processing each instruction and virtually all of the data needed by the computer (whether the instruction is for BIOS, the operating system, or an application). The type of CPU limits the PC's overall processing power. For example, a PC with a Pentium III CPU runs Windows 98 much faster than a PC with a "classic" Pentium CPU. As another example, an AMD K6-2 processor with its "3DNow" instruction set will generally handle graphics-intensive 3DNow-enabled applications better than a classic Pentium CPU.

CPU Speed Even when using CPUs from the same family, clock speed (measured in MHz) affects performance. For example, a PC with a Pentium III 500MHz CPU will run faster than a PC with a Pentium III 350MHz CPU.

CPU Upgrade Potential Since CPUs have a finite processing limit, it follows that upgrading the CPU will improve system processing. While this is great in theory, you can't just place any old CPU in the CPU socket or slot and expect the motherboard to work. Any motherboard is limited to using a handful of current CPU versions. For example, Intel's AN430TX motherboard supports Pentium processors at 90, 100, 120, 133, 150, 166, and 200MHz, as well as Pentium MMX processors running at 166, 200, and 233MHz. By comparison, Intel's newer NX440LX motherboard supports Pentium II microprocessors operating at 233, 266, and 300MHz. Changing the processor type and speed requires changes in several of the motherboard's jumper settings.

Memory Slots The sheer amount of memory that can be added to the motherboard will indirectly affect system performance because of a reduced dependence on virtual memory (a swap file on the hard drive). Memory is added in the form of SIMMs (Single In-line Memory Modules) or DIMMs (Dual In-line Memory Modules). Motherboards that can accept more (or larger-capacity) memory modules will support more memory. It is not uncommon today to find motherboards that will support 768MB to 1.5GB of RAM (equal to the storage capacity of older hard drives).

Memory Types The type of memory will also have an effect on motherboard (and system) performance. Faster memory will improve system performance. DRAM remains the slowest type of PC memory and is usually employed in older systems or video boards. EDO RAM is faster than ordinary DRAM and is commonplace in Pentium PCs. SDRAM is measurably faster than EDO RAM and is now typical in high-to-mid-range PC applications. RDRAM is an emerging memory type that should gain broad acceptance in the next few years. It is not necessary for you to understand what these memory types are yet—just understand that memory performance and system performance *are* related.

Cache Memory Traditional RAM is much slower than a CPU—so slow that the CPU must insert pauses (or *wait states*) in order for memory to catch up. *Cache* is a technique of improving memory performance by keeping a limited amount of frequently used information in *very* fast cache RAM. If the needed information is found, the CPU reads the cache at full speed (and performance is improved because less time is wasted). By making the cache larger, it is possible to hold more of the frequently used data. Older motherboards employed from 128KB to 256KB of cache. Current motherboards use 512KB to 1MB of cache RAM (though Pentium II/III systems include cache in the CPU itself).

Chipsets A *chipset* is a set of highly optimized, tightly interrelated ICs which, taken together, handle virtually all of the support functions required for a motherboard. As new CPUs and hardware features are crammed into a PC, new chipsets must be developed to implement those functions. For example, the Intel 430HX chipset supports the Pentium CPU and EDO RAM. Intel's 430VX chipset supports use of the Pentium CPU, the Universal Serial Bus, and SDRAM. By comparison, the Intel 440LX chipset supports the Pentium II CPU, an Accelerated Graphics Port, SDRAM, and an Ultra DMA-33 drive interface. Newer chipsets support the latest PC features and functions.

System BIOS The BIOS ROM contained on the motherboard also limits the system's capabilities, although such limits are not always drastic or obvious. BIOS is a set of small programs recorded onto ROM ICs that allow the operating system (such as MS-DOS or Windows) to interact with memory and the various drives and devices in the system. Although the BIOS versions produced today are generally quite uniform, older BIOS ICs may not support some of the new features we now expect from computers. For example, many systems using i286-based motherboards do not support the format process for 3.5-inch 1.44MB floppy disk drives directly as newer systems do, or your BIOS may not support new bootable CD-ROM drives (using the "El Torito" standard). Overcoming BIOS limitations is often a matter of upgrading the BIOS program or upgrading the motherboard entirely.

Expansion Slots Each motherboard offers a fixed number of expansion slots. The number of expansion slots limits the number of features and devices that can be added to the system. Internal modems, scanner boards, video boards, drive controller boards, sound boards, network cards, and SCSI controllers are only some of the devices competing for expansion space in your PC. The fewer slots that are available, the less a system can be expanded. The type of expansion slots also influences expandability and performance. Classical motherboard designs offer a mix of 8-bit XT and 16-bit ISA slots. Late-model 486 and some early Pentium motherboards have added several slots to accommodate enhanced expansion technologies such as the VL bus for improved video boards (and a second VL slot may be available for an improved drive or network adapter). Today, motherboards typically incorporate three to five PCI slots for high-performance network or drive controller boards, and an AGP slot for a high-performance video accelerator card. There may be one or two 16-bit ISA slots to support older "legacy" devices.

DRIVES

The modern PC would be entirely useless without long-term, high-volume storage, as well as the ability to transfer files between PCs. *Drives* represent a variety of devices used for storing or retrieving relatively large amounts of information. Floppy disk drives (FDDs), hard disk drives (HDDs), and CD-ROM drives are the three most popular drive types for desktop and tower PCs, although Iomega Zip drives (resembling 3.5-inch floppy drives) and tape drives are occasionally found. CD recorders, rewriters, and DVD-ROM drives are now common in current PCs. Even PC Card "drives" are finding their way into desktop/tower systems. Figure 1-6 illustrates the standard profile for each drive.

Drives are typically located in the front right quarter of the desktop enclosure. Each drive is secured into an available drive bay within the enclosure. There are two types of drive bays that you should be familiar with: internal and external. The external drive bay allows a drive to be mounted facing the outside world. Floppy, CD-ROM, CD-R, CD-RW, DVD-ROM, PC Card, and tape drives rely on the availability of external drive bays. After all, what good is the drive if you can't insert or remove the media? On the other hand, hard disk drives use nonremovable media. This means the drive can be mounted in an internal (or nonaccessible) bay. A typical desktop PC offers two external and two internal bays. The external bays usually hold a 3.5-inch FDD and a CD-ROM. The internal drive bay(s) are typically reserved for one or two hard drives. Larger desktop cases may offer additional external bays. Tower cases can easily support

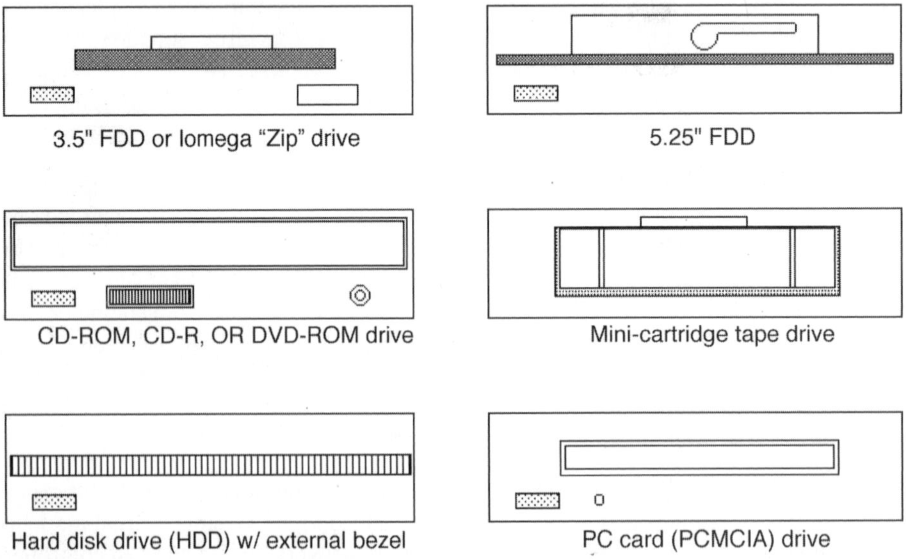

FIGURE 1-6 The front appearance of typical PC drives

a full range of external drives mounted along the upper front of the enclosure. A tower's internal drive bays can handle another three or four hard drives.

Floppy Disk Drives (FDDs) Floppy disks have gone through several incarnations (5.25-inch 360KB, 5.25-inch 1.2MB, 3.5-inch 720KB, and 3.5-inch 1.44MB) since they first appeared in the IBM PC. But in spite of its limited storage capacity, the floppy drive remains the traditional PC drive that is universally accepted in virtually every PC manufactured since 1982. Floppy disks use only one light to indicate drive activity.

Iomega Zip Drives Combining magnetic and optical storage technologies, Iomega has developed a 3.5-inch drive capable of storing up to 250MB on a single Zip disk. Over the last few years, the Zip drive has proven to be an inexpensive and handy storage system—so much so that some PC manufacturers now include Zip drives as standard equipment in their new systems. At first glance, the Zip disk and drive could easily be mistaken for a floppy disk drive.

CD-ROM Drives Originally developed for the music industry as a digital replacement for aging phonographs, the CD-ROM quickly found a place in modern PCs where a laser is used to read an optical disc. One optical disc can store up to 650MB of programs, data, or other media such as Kodak photos and digital audio. Although their storage capacity is now dated when compared to multigigabyte hard drives, CD-ROM drives are standard equipment in all modern PCs. CD-ROM drives use a load/eject button, a volume control (to adjust CD audio), and a single activity light.

Tape Drives Tape drives offer a significant amount of storage capacity using relatively inexpensive tape media. However, tape devices are slow, hot, and noisy, so they have largely been relegated to occasional system backup chores. Tape drives use two lights: one as a power indicator and another as a drive activity light.

Hard Disk Drives (HDDs) The hard drive is truly the icon of the personal computer. Magnetic storage technology has evolved at a staggering pace, and the slow 100–200MB hard drives of years ago have been replaced by lightning-fast 30–40+GB hard drives. The hard drive has provided the PC industry with huge, fast, reliable, and quiet storage mechanisms for just pennies per megabyte. This upward spiral of hard drive capacity shows no signs of slowing. Hard drives are standard equipment on all PCs and are the preferred boot device for quick loading of even the largest operating systems. The hard drive typically uses only one light to indicate drive activity.

CD-R and CD-RW Drives CDs have been around for years, but recording your own CD has been prohibited by proprietary (and hideously expensive) hardware and software. In the last few years, CD recorder (CD-R) drives have plummeted in price. While hardly standard equipment, the combination of falling prices, improved reliability, more extensive PC resources (such as RAM, hard drive space, and faster CPUs), and good intuitive Windows 95/98 authoring software has made CD-R drives an attractive option for such tasks as software backups, file archiving, and software product prototyping. More recently, CD rewritable (CD-RW) drives have become popular upgrade options for the PC—allowing users to record and rewrite CDs with the same ease as writing a floppy disk. CD-R and CD-RW drives use a load/eject button, drive activity light, and volume control. They also sport a second activity light to show when the drive is writing.

DVD-ROM Drives The DVD drive represents the next step in the evolution of optical storage for the PC. DVD discs can offer up to 17GB of storage on a single disc the size of a CD (yet are backward compatible with almost all existing CD-ROM standards). They are an ideal medium for the distribution of audio and video multimedia (when combined with a PCI MPEG-2 decoder board), as well as unimaginable volumes of data. The first generations of DVD drives, which appeared in mid-1997, only *read* DVD discs, but upcoming iterations of DVD (known as DVD-R and DVD-RAM) will be able to record blank DVD discs. DVD-ROM drives use a load/eject button, a volume control (to adjust CD audio), and a single activity light.

PC Card Drives With the explosive growth of portable computers, the use of desktop PC Card (formerly referred to as *PCMCIA cards*) "drives" is increasing to support the easy transfer of files between laptop and desktop systems. At first glance, the PC Card drive looks much like a 3.5-inch floppy drive, though the card opening is thicker and narrower. The term drive is a bit of a misnomer here because the PC Card drive is entirely electronic—there are no moving parts except for the electrical card connector and a simple card ejection mechanism. PC Card drives are relatively rare and are most often encountered on PC platforms used for data acquisition (such as downloading images from digital cameras) or postprocessing from remote data-gathering PCs. A mechanical lever ejects the PC Card, and a single light is used to indicate drive activity.

EXPANSION BOARDS

While many PCs today incorporate video, sound, and FDD/HDD controller circuitry directly on the motherboard, those circuits can often be disabled when expansion boards are used. In fact, many such "integrated" controllers are eventually disabled so that video and drive systems can be upgraded with more advanced expansion boards. In most cases, you should expect to find at least a video board plugged into an expansion slot. The video board will often be accompanied by an FDD/HDD controller board. Of course, there will probably be additional boards in the system (such as modems, network cards, video capture or videoconferencing systems, or other devices). This part of the chapter is intended to help you identify each category of expansion board on sight.

Video Boards

Video adapter circuits (whether implemented on the motherboard or on an expansion board) are designed to convert raw graphic data traveling over the system bus into pixel data that can be displayed by a monitor. Without the monitor attached, however, the video adapter can only be identified through its video port connector. Figure 1-7 compares the four major generations of video adapters: MDA, CGA, EGA, and VGA. Keep in mind that the illustrations shown in Figure 1-7 are typical examples—some video board designs (especially high-end video boards) may not follow these layouts exactly.

The Monochrome Display Adapter (MDA) is the oldest video adapter board, and few are still in service. MDA boards are noted for their use of a 25-pin parallel port included with the 9-pin video connector. You might find MDA boards used in classic IBM PC/XTs or compatible systems. The Color Graphics Adapter (CGA) is roughly the same vintage as MDA and is the first graphics adapter to introduce color to PC displays. A CGA board can often be identified by a round RCA-type feature connector located just above a 9-pin video connector. Like the MDA boards, CGA is long-since obsolete, and many of the older systems that used CGA boards have been scrapped or have been upgraded to later video systems. The Enhanced Graphics Adapter (EGA) offers more colors and higher display resolution than CGA. You can identify an EGA board by its small bank of DIP switches located above two RCA-type feature connectors and a 9-pin video connector.

The Video Graphics Array (VGA) board marked a departure from previous video systems. VGA abandoned logic-level video signals (on/off signaling) in favor of analog video levels. Thus, primary colors could be "mixed" together to provide many more color combinations than ever before—up to 262,144 possible colors for ordinary VGA. You can easily identify a VGA connector as a 15-pin high-density connector (15 pins stuffed into a 9-pin shell). SVGA (or Super VGA) extends the capabilities of VGA by add-

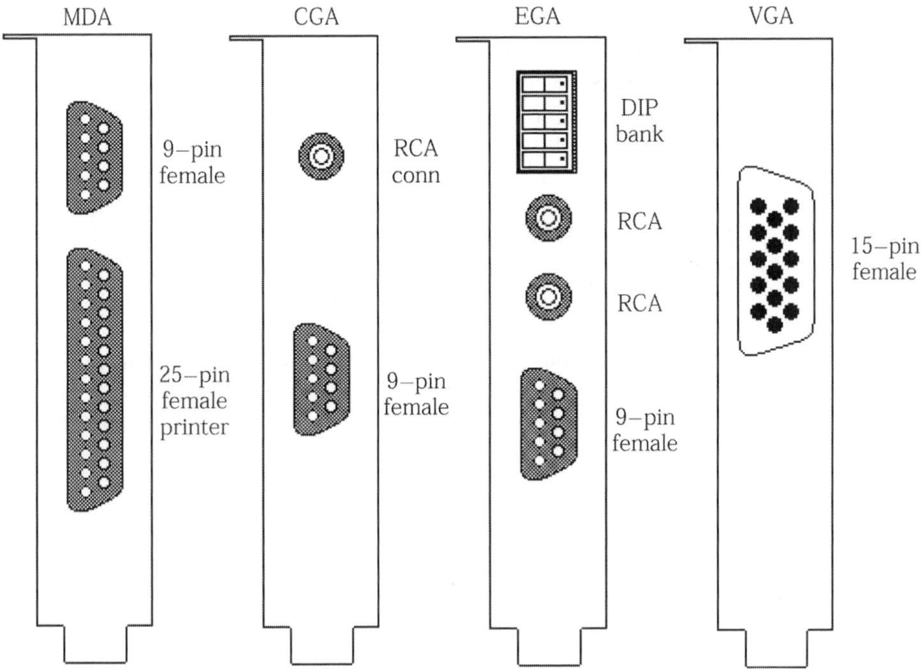

FIGURE 1-7 Comparison of typical video board layouts

1

ing more resolutions and color depths, allowing as many as 16 million colors (known as *true color* mode) to be displayed at one time. Table 1-1 compares the common resolutions and color depths for a typical SVGA video board.

TABLE 1-1 TYPICAL VIDEO RESOLUTION AND PIXEL DEPTH

RESOLUTION	BITS/PIXEL (2MB)	BITS/PIXEL (4MB)	BITS/PIXEL (8MB)
640 × 480	8, 16, 24, 32	8, 16, 24, 32	8, 16, 24, 32
800 × 600	8, 16, 24, 32	8, 16, 24, 32	8, 16, 24, 32
1024 × 768	8, 16	8, 16, 24, 32	8, 16, 24, 32
1152 × 864	8, 16	8, 16, 24, 32	8, 16, 24, 32
1280 × 1024	8	8, 16, 24	8, 16, 24, 32
1600 × 1200	8	8, 16	8, 16, 24

NOTE: 8 bits/pixel = 256 colors
16 bits/pixel = 65,536 colors (high color mode)
24 bits/pixel = 16M colors (true color mode)
32 bits/pixel = 4B colors (usually reserved for scanning)

Drive Adapters

The term *drive adapter* is usually applied to the floppy drive controller, UDMA/EIDE/IDE drive controller, and tape drive accelerator boards. As a rule, SCSI adapters are not classified as drive adapters because a SCSI adapter can handle other peripherals besides drives. Drive controllers are easily identified by tracing drive signal cables from the particular drive back to the supporting controller.

Note the signal *headers* that connect to the individual ribbon cables. The 34-pin header is marked "FDD," or "floppy," and is always connected to the floppy drive(s). The 40-pin headers are marked "UDMA" and "EIDE," respectively, or "HDD1" and "HDD2," and are always connected to UDMA/EIDE hard drives. The first hard drive port is often designed for UDMA drives, and the second hard drive port is designed for older EIDE drives (though many new controllers support UDMA drives on both drive ports).

> If there is only one hard drive port on the controller (marked "HDD" or "hard"), chances are very good that the controller is an older IDE-only controller board. Do not attempt to use EIDE drives on IDE ports. The 40-pin interface will work (and you won't damage the drive), but you cannot partition and format the full capacity of the drive without drive overlay software such as EZ-Drive.

You should also be able to identify proprietary drive adapters—most notably for early (non-IDE) CD-ROM drives. The earliest CD-ROM adapters used stand-alone controller boards, but these were quickly replaced by one or more proprietary controller ports built right into popular sound boards like the Creative Labs Sound Blaster series. Note that there are often several connectors: a 44-pin connector for a Mitsumi CD-ROM, a 36-pin connector for a Sony CD-ROM, and a 44-pin interface for a Creative-brand CD-ROM. You would then use a jumper to select the desired port, depending on which CD-ROM came packaged with the sound board.

The real trick comes with 40-pin CD-ROM interfaces. It's impossible to tell by sight whether the port is IDE or proprietary. Still, you can employ the following rule. Older sound boards with a 40-pin CD-ROM interface are almost always proprietary, and the port will often share space with other proprietary interfaces nearby. Newer sound boards with a 40-pin CD-ROM interface sitting by itself (with no other proprietary ports nearby) are almost always standard IDE.

> An IDE interface on a sound board is a "true" IDE port and should support any other IDE drives (including older IDE hard drives or IDE tape backups) without problems.

SCSI Adapters

The Small-Computer System Interface (SCSI) offers impressive expandability by allowing all SCSI-compatible devices (SCSI hard drives, SCSI CD-ROMs, SCSI tape drives, SCSI scanners, etc.) to be connected together over the same daisy-chained cable. There are several ways to detect the presence of a SCSI adapter. First, you will see a screen message generated by the SCSI adapter BIOS when the PC initializes. You can also confirm the presence of a SCSI adapter by identifying the interconnecting cables. Internally, SCSI cables are 50-pin or 68-pin ribbon cables. Figure 1-8 illustrates a SCSI adapter with a 50-pin SCSI header. Since many SCSI adapters can handle both internal and external devices, the adapter will have an external 50-pin D-type connector available. If the SCSI adapter also includes a 34-pin header, the adapter is providing a standard floppy drive port. You may need to disable any such floppy port since there is probably a working floppy port elsewhere in the system (for example, on the motherboard or drive controller board).

Ports and Modems

PCs are rarely any use in a vacuum—they must be able to communicate with devices in the outside world. PC communication is accomplished through the use of parallel or serial ports, and you should recognize

FIGURE 1-8 A typical SCSI controller board (© 1995 Future Domain Corporation. Reprinted with permission)

1

such ports on sight. Traditionally, *parallel* ports allow the PC to drive printers, but with improvements in parallel port performance, new peripherals are available that can operate through a parallel port (such as parallel port tape drives, hard drives, and CD-ROM drives). Such devices are particularly handy when they must be moved between several machines. A parallel port is implemented as a 25-pin (female) connector (Figure 1-9). While older PCs included parallel ports as part of the MDA video board (Figure 1-7) or as a stand-alone expansion board, virtually all current PCs incorporate at least one parallel port directly on the motherboard.

Given the tremendous appeal of inexpensive online resources such as AOL and the Internet, serial communication has evolved substantially over the last decade. As a result, you will likely find one or two *serial* ports located on the PC, as shown in Figure 1-9. Older PCs typically implement a single serial (or RS-232) port as a 25-pin D-type (male) connector. *Do not confuse this with 25-pin D-type female connectors that are used for parallel ports!* Since most serial communication can be accomplished with far fewer than 25 pins, most PC manufacturers now use a 9-pin D-type male connector instead of the 25-pin D-type male connector. Newer systems offer two 9-pin D-type male serial ports directly on the motherboard. When implemented on a stand-alone expansion board, you will often find a 9-pin D-type male serial port combined with a 25-pin D-type female parallel port.

To communicate over a telephone line, serial signals must be translated into tones that can be carried within the frequency bandwidth of an ordinary voice telephone line. Returning signals must also be decoded into serial logic levels. The device that performs this PC-to-telephone line interface is called a *modem*. External modems are stand-alone devices that attach to an available serial port. Internal modems, however, are quite popular, and combine the circuitry for a serial port and modem on a single expansion

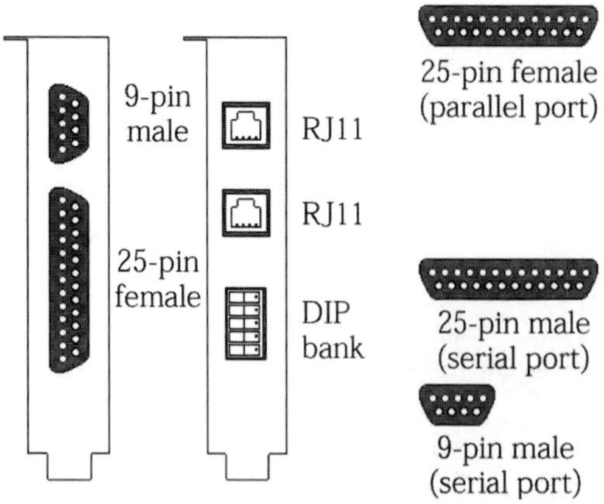

FIGURE 1-9 Comparison of typical video board layouts

board. You can usually identify an internal modem board by its two RJ11 (phone jack) connectors. Note that one jack is for the telephone line itself, while the second connector is a feed-through, which can be connected to any standard telephone.

Sound Boards

The acceptance of sound boards in everyday PCs has been simply staggering. What started as a novel means of moving beyond the limitations of PC speakers has quickly evolved into a low-cost, CD-quality stereo playback/recording system. Even business applications routinely embrace sound cards for presentations and simple speech recognition tasks. Sound cards are firmly established as an essential part of every PC used for educational, game, and multimedia applications. Fortunately, sound boards are relatively easy to recognize, as shown in Figure 1-10.

The clues here are three miniature jacks on the sound card. The *line input* jack allows prerecorded sound (such as output from tape player, CD player, or synthesizer) to be digitized and recorded by the sound board. The *microphone input* supports recording from an ordinary 600 ohm microphone. The *stereo output* is the main output for the board where digitized voice and music files are reproduced. An output can drive amplified speakers or an interim stereo amplifier deck. Keep in mind that your particular sound board may have slightly different features (and older sound cards such as a classic Sound Blaster may also offer a manual volume control knob). You will also note that the sound board offers a 15-pin D-type female connector. This feature connector is designed to serve double duty as either a *joystick port* (a.k.a. *game port*) or a *MIDI interface*.

MPEG Decoder Boards

Although a DVD-ROM drive requires a standard interface (SCSI or EIDE) for normal programs and data, DVD video and audio do not use this data path. There are two reasons for this. First, the data required to reproduce real-time video and audio would bog down even the fastest PC when transferred across a standard drive interface. Second, video and audio data are highly compressed using MPEG standards, so even if the PC wasn't bogged down by the compressed data, the decompression process would load down the system with processing overhead. In order to play DVD audio and video, DVD-ROM drives typically recommend a stand-alone, hardware-based MPEG-2 decoder board such as the one in Figure 1-11. The MPEG-2 decoder board works independently of the drive controller system, video system, and sound system.

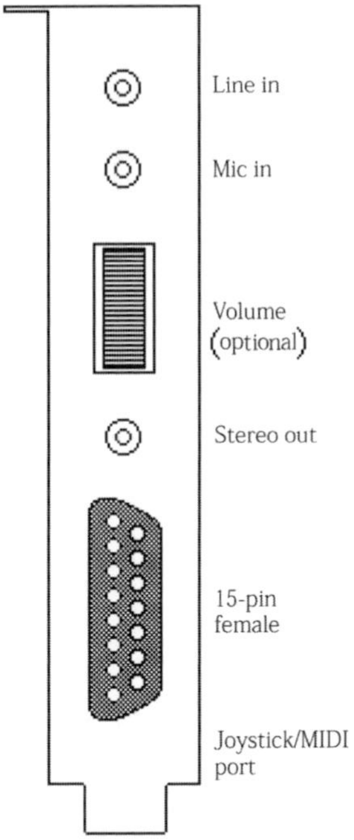

FIGURE 1-10 Layout of a typical sound board

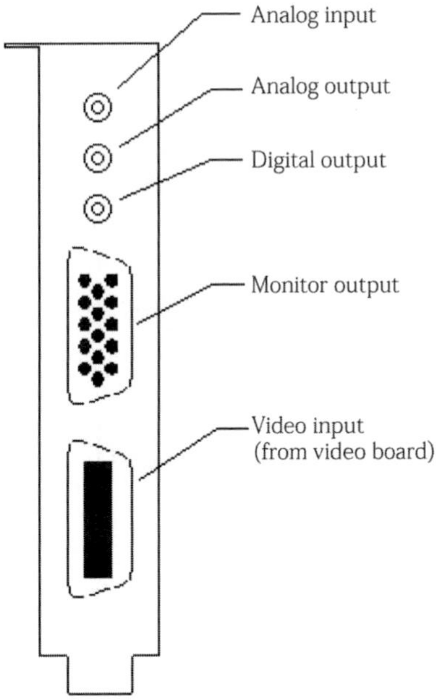

FIGURE 1-11 Layout of a typical MPEG-2 decoder board

There are five major connections on the MPEG-2 decoder board: an analog input jack, an analog output jack, a digital output jack, a monitor connector, and a video input connector. The *analog input* is rarely (if ever) used in normal operations, but it may be handy for mixing in an auxiliary audio signal to the decoder board. The *analog output* signal provides the master audio signal that is fed to the line input of your existing sound board. The advantage of using a line input is that you don't need a volume control on the decoder board. Instead, you can set the line input volume through your sound board's mixer applet. When you play a DVD video, any audio will continue to play through your sound board and speakers. The *digital output* is intended to drive an external Dolby Digital device, so you will probably not be using the digital output in most basic PC setups.

The MPEG-2 decoder board will now drive your VGA/SVGA monitor through the *monitor* connector. This is important because the decoded video stream is converted to RGB information and fed to the monitor directly. This avoids having to pass the video data across the PCI bus to your video card. The normal output from your video card is looped from your video board to the decoder card, so while the decoder board is idle, your normal video signal is just passed through the MPEG-2 board to the monitor.

Given the increasing processing power found in current systems, DVD video can often be played using software decoders rather than a hardware-based MPEG-2 decoder board. However, a decoder card should still be considered for best system performance.

Joystick Adapters

The use of PC games and simulators often requires the use of an analog joystick. Joysticks are connected to one of two 15-pin D-type female connectors on the joystick adapter (or game port). Figure 1-12 illus-

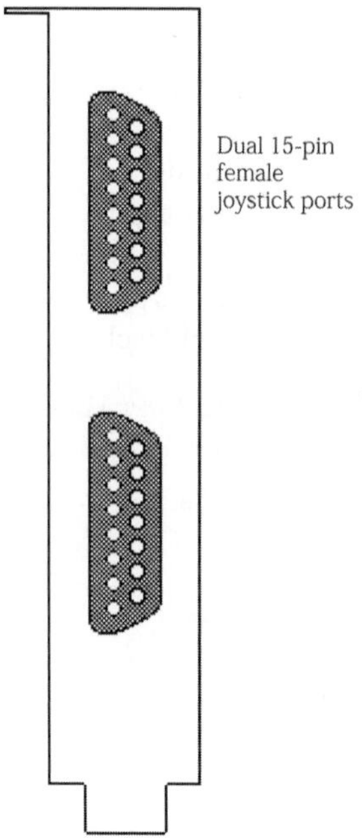

FIGURE 1-12 Layout of a dual game-port board

trates the typical layout for a joystick adapter. Since two connectors are usually included, an adapter can support two analog joysticks. Another hallmark of a joystick adapter is its small size—typically an 8-bit (or *half-slot*) board.

Notes for Disassembly and Reassembly

All too often, the mechanics of PC repair—taking the system apart and putting it back together again—are overlooked or treated as an afterthought. As you saw in the first part of this chapter, PC assemblies are not terribly complicated, but a careless or rushed approach to the repair can do more harm than good. Lost parts and collateral damage to the system are certain ways to lose a customer (and perhaps open yourself to legal recourse). The following section outlines a set of considerations that can help ensure a speedy, top-quality repair effort.

THE VALUE OF DATA

It is a fact of modern computing that the data contained on a customer's hard drive(s) is usually more valuable than the PC hardware itself. If your customer is an entrepreneur or corporate client, you can expect that the system contains valuable accounting, technical, reference, design, or operations information that is vital to their business. As a consequence, you should make it a priority to protect yourself from any potential liability issues connected with your customer's data. Even if the drives are causing the problem, a customer may hold you responsible if you are unable to restore or recover his precious information. Start a consistent regimen of written and oral precautions. Such precautions should include (but are not limited to):

- Always advise your customers to back up their systems regularly. Before customers bring in their systems, advise them to perform a complete backup of their drives, if possible.
- Always advise your customers to check (or verify) their backups—a backup is useless if it can't be restored.
- When customers deliver a system for repair, be sure they sign a work order. Work orders should give you authority and permission to work on the customer's system, outline such things as your hourly rate and labor minimums for evaluation and service, and show all applicable disclaimers. Your work order should include a strong disclaimer expressly relieving you of any and all liability for the contents of any magnetic media (such as hard drives) in the system. If you attempt data recovery, the disclaimer should also disclaim any warranty or guarantee of results. That way, you're not liable if you are unable to recover vital files. Since liability issues vary from state to state and country to country, a local attorney can advise you on specific wording.

OPENING THE SYSTEM

Most desktop and tower systems use a metal chassis covered by a painted metal cover or shroud that is secured with a series of screws. There are often nine screws—two on either side of the enclosure, and five at the rear of the chassis. While this pattern covers many of the desktop PCs in service, you are likely to encounter a number of variations. You may find that instead of bolting screws in from the sides, the screws may be bolted in from the bottom. There may also be more or fewer screws in the rear of the chassis. Only on rare occasions will you find screws used to secure the enclosure at its front, because the molded plastic housing found on most desktop PCs does not accommodate screws without spoiling the finished look.

Tower cases are a bit different. The metal shroud also uses about nine screws—all secured from the rear. The bottom and front edges of the enclosure are typically bent inward to interlock with the chassis when seated properly. This approach allows the entire enclosure to fit securely along the whole chassis while using a minimum of screws. Enclosures that do not interlock, however, may require screws along the bottom and front edges. As a general rule, PC enclosure manufacturers tend to minimize the use of visible screws in order to enhance a seamless appearance—this is why most screws are relegated to the back chassis.

There are three factors to keep in mind when removing screws and other mounting hardware. First, be extremely careful not to mark or gouge the painted metal enclosure. Customers are rightfully possessive of their PC investment, and putting a scratch or dent in an enclosure is tantamount to dinging their new car.

(A reputation for carelessness is very bad for business.) Be equally careful of the enclosure after removing and setting it aside. Second, store the screws in a safe, organized place. The old egg carton trick may seem cliché, but it really does work. Of course, you are free to use plastic bags or organizer boxes as well—the idea here is to keep screws and other hardware off the work surface (unless you enjoy picking them up off the floor). Third, take note of each screw as you remove it, and keep groups of screws separated. This allows you to put the right screws back into the corresponding locations. Since most enclosures use screws of equal size and length, this is rarely an issue at this phase of disassembly. But as you dismantle other subassemblies for upgrade or repair, keeping track of hardware becomes an important concern.

Use care when sliding the enclosure off the chassis. Metal inserts or reinforcements welded to the cover can easily catch on ribbon cables or other wiring. This can result in damage to the cable, and damage to whatever the cable is attached to. The rule here is simple: *force nothing!* If you encounter any resistance at all, stop and search for the obstruction carefully: it's faster to clear an obstruction than to replace a damaged cable.

CLOSING THE SYSTEM

After your repair or upgrade is complete, you will need to close the system. Before sliding the enclosure back into place, however, make it a point to check the PC carefully. Make sure that every subassembly is installed and secured into place with the proper screws and hardware—leftover parts are *unacceptable*. A little care in organizing and sorting hardware during disassembly really pays off here. Remember to reattach power and signal cables as required. Each cable must be installed properly and completely (in its correct orientation). Take time to route each signal cable with care and avoid jamming the cables into the system haphazardly. Careless cable runs stand a good chance of being caught and damaged by the enclosure during reassembly or the next time the system needs to be disassembled. Properly routed cables also reduce the chance of signal problems (such as noise or crosstalk) that can result in unstable long-term operation. Also check the installation of any auxiliary cables such as CD-ROM sound cables, the speaker cable, and the keylock cable.

Once the system components are reassembled securely, you can apply power to the PC and run final diagnostics to test the system. When the system checks properly, you can slide the enclosure into place (being careful not to damage any cables or wiring) and secure the enclosure with its full complement of screws.

TIPS FOR WORKING INSIDE A DESKTOP OR TOWER PC

Whether you're troubleshooting, upgrading, or building your own PC from scratch, there's no doubt that you'll get plenty of hands-on time inside desktop and tower PCs. Unfortunately, many potential problems can be overlooked (or even caused) while working inside a PC. The following tips should help you make the most of your PC experience and minimize the chances of collateral problems:

- Be extremely careful of any sharp edges along the metal cover or inside the metal chassis itself. Case manufacturers often save costs by omitting such production steps as removing burrs and dulling sharp edges.

- Make sure the chassis assembly is tight. All chassis are not created equal. Some stand solid as a house, while others can seem to sway freely. Take note of the chassis condition, and tighten the chassis if necessary.
- Watch your vents and fans for good air flow. Make sure the fan blades, grills, and any intake and exhaust filters are kept clean. Check to see that all fans are working.
- Watch for dust and debris. When you're examining the enclosure, check for accumulations of dust or other debris. Dust is generally a thermal insulator and electrical conductor, and can easily block the flow of air inside a chassis, so it is important to avoid accumulations of dust and debris wherever possible.
- Choose a new chassis with care. Replacing a chassis (or building a new PC from scratch) is an exciting but time-consuming effort; so plan for adequate expansion in terms of drive bays, expansion slot openings, power supply capacity, and drive power cables.
- Go with standardized cases, power supplies, and motherboards. New PC systems have largely abandoned the use of AT-style cases (such as baby AT or full AT) in favor of ATX or NLX versions. As you'll see in the following sections, standard dimensioning ensures that cases, motherboards, and power supplies will all fit together.
- Keep drives mounted snugly. All PC drives (whether in an internal or external drive bay) should be mounted with at least four screws. Fewer screws can allow the drive to vibrate, and this can shorten the drive's working life. Make sure that all four screws are in place and secure, but do not overtighten the screws. Overtightening can actually warp a drive's internal frame and cause premature failures as well.
- Be careful when mounting the motherboard. Under no circumstances should you ever flex a motherboard, or install it in such a way that it is uneven. See that no metal edges or standoffs touch the motherboard, and the motherboard should not sit flush against any part of the PC chassis.
- Check your cables closely. There are myriad of cables inside a PC. Make it a point to check the installation and routing of each cable. Each end of a cable should be installed evenly and completely. Cables should be run (where possible) to minimize any interruptions to air flow.
- Check your expansion boards. Whenever you're working inside a PC, make sure that any expansion boards inside the system are inserted evenly and completely into their bus slots. Often, exchanging external cables can accidentally wiggle a card loose, resulting in possible system problems. Also see that each expansion board is secured with a screw in the PC chassis.
- Check your memory devices. While you're in the system, take a look at the memory devices. Make sure that each SIMM or DIMM is clipped securely into place (especially if you're replacing or upgrading memory). If your motherboard uses COAST (cache-on-a-stick) modules for cache RAM, also see that the COAST module is installed properly.
- Check the CPU heat sink/fan. Chances are that your CPU is fitted with a heat sink/fan assembly. Check to see that the heat sink is attached securely to the CPU, and verify that the fan portion of the assembly is working once the system is powered up. The CPU itself should also be mounted securely into place.

Standardized Form Factors

Traditional PC chassis have always been somewhat of a hit-or-miss proposition. You'd choose cases, power supplies, and motherboards, and hope that everything would fit properly. All too often, screw holes wouldn't line up, and you'd be forced to return assemblies, or "kluge" the assemblies together—aligning as many screw holes as possible and ignoring, clipping, or removing standoffs outright. Over the last few years, the PC industry has come together to develop a set of standard dimensions for key PC components (cases, motherboards, and power supplies). The three current standards are known as LPX, ATX, and NLX. This part of the chapter looks at these standards in more detail.

> The use of new form factors does not have any bearing on the capabilities or performance of any new PC. Only the dimensions of the motherboard, case, and power supply are affected.

LPX FORM FACTOR

The Low-Profile Extended (or LPX) form factor proved to be the PC industry's first major step beyond AT and baby AT–style motherboards. Developed jointly by Intel and Western Digital some years ago, the LPX specification covers the physical layout, power requirements, and electrical issues for such motherboards. A standard LPX motherboard has the same *maximum* dimensions as a baby AT board: no more than 8.5 inches wide by 13 inches long (Figure 1-13). It also shares the same baby AT mounting hole arrangements.

The LPX approach does not support expansion cards on the motherboard. Instead, it uses a riser card inserted into a single board slot, and any cards added into the system attach to the riser card. LPX power connectors are the same as the original IBM AT power connectors: two 6-pin connectors attached to the motherboard (usually labeled P8 and P9). The LPX format also provides a strict series of I/O ports arranged from left to right across the back of a board:

- VGA monitor connector
- Parallel port
- Two serial ports
- PS/2-style mouse port
- PS/2-style keyboard port

> Later variations in LPX design may alter the placement of external connectors, substitute two Universal Serial Bus (USB) interfaces in place of serial connectors, and perhaps even add local area network (LAN) and sound connectors.

In addition, an LPX motherboard typically provides two IDE drive controllers, a floppy disk controller, and 72-pin SIMM sockets. The LPX riser card slot conforms to the older EISA standard (both physi-

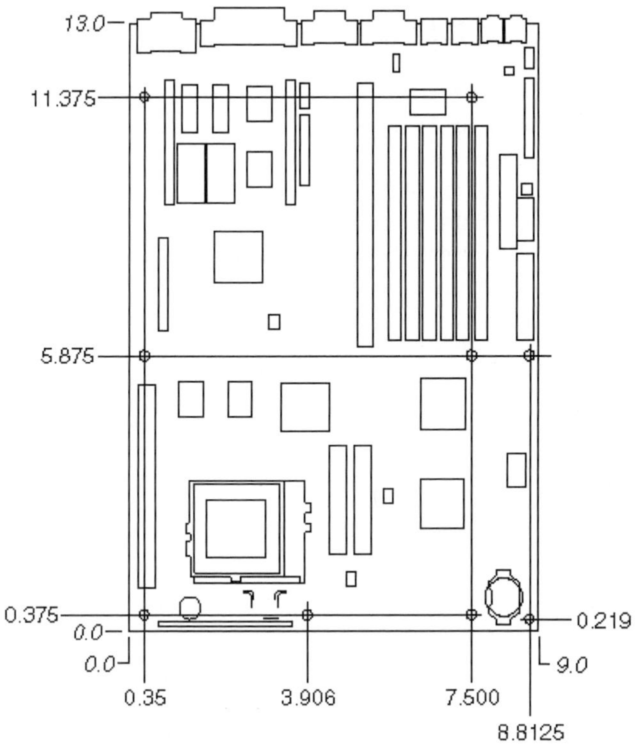

FIGURE 1-13 Image of LPX motherboard

cally and electronically), but LPX is generally compatible with newer high-performance expansion architectures like PCI. As a result, it's not uncommon to find LPX riser cards offering ISA and PCI slots for expansion devices.

LPX was embraced widely by popular PC makers such as AST, Compaq, Digital, Dell, Gateway, Hewlett-Packard, IBM, NCR, NEC, Packard-Bell, and Zenith, and LPX-type motherboards have been produced up to the introduction of Pentium II processors. The main problem with LPX was its proprietary use of riser cards. Riser cards need to meet the LPX physical and electrical connector standard—but that's the extent of LPX standardization. Otherwise, every computer manufacturer was free to choose its own riser card layout (the number of slots, the type of slots ([ISA or PCI]), the distance of the slots from the top of the LPX connector, and the size of the riser card). Table 1-2 illustrates the known compatibility issues with major LPX system manufacturers.

TABLE 1-2 COMMON NONSTANDARD LPX ISSUES

BRAND/MODEL	NONSTANDARD FEATURE(S)
AST Advantage (before Socket 5)	LPX physical connector
AST Bravo LC, Bravo LC CX, Bravo MS-L, Bravo MS-T	LPX physical connector
Compaq DeskPro (All)	LPX physical connector
DEC Celebris and Venturis 4xx and 5xx, DECpc LPV+	LPX physical connector
DEC Starion 200/300	Riser w/ 5 ISA slots; connector may be ISA
DEC Starion 200i/300i (Trio 32)	Riser w/ ISA, PCI, shared; connector may be standard
DEC Starion 400/500 (C&T 63400)	Riser w/ 2 ISA, PCI, shared; connector appears nonstandard
DEC Starion 400i thru 900i (Trio 32)	Riser w/ 3 ISA, PCI, shared; connector may be standard
DEC Starion 910 thru 920 (Trio 32)	Riser w/ 8-bit, 2 ISA, PCI, shared; connector may be standard
DEC Starion 930 thru 942 and 2001 (64-bit)	Riser w/ 8-bit, 2 ISA, PCI, shared; connector may be standard
Dell Optiplex 4xx/L	Board mounting uses two screws, oblong holes; wires that connect board to front panel of case
Gateway 2000 486 low-profile (ISA & PCI)	LPX physical connector
IBM PC350	LPX physical connector
NCR 3000 series	LPX physical connector, motherboard mounting holes, power supply connector
Packard-Bell PB600 motherboard	Non-Intel board; connector order is VGA, keyboard, mouse, (Axcel 461CDT) serial, parallel
Packard-Bell 386s and 486s	Connectors sometimes in different order on rear of case; some LPX riser cards have an ISA bus connector, but the card slots are placed closer to the rear of the computer case

As a consequence of this weak standardization, riser cards are rarely interchangeable among various cases (often even for the same manufacturer), and this made it extremely difficult to replace and upgrade LPX motherboards. Eventually, the PC industry abandoned LPX in favor of ATX and NLX form factors.

ATX FORM FACTOR

The version 2.03 ATX form factor (Figure 1-14) represents the most popular and well-established effort to standardize the major assemblies of a PC. In addition to the use of well-established mounting holes, the ATX approach makes several key improvements to the layout of a system. The CPU is relocated to a position on the motherboard that will not interfere with the use of full-length expansion boards (a common

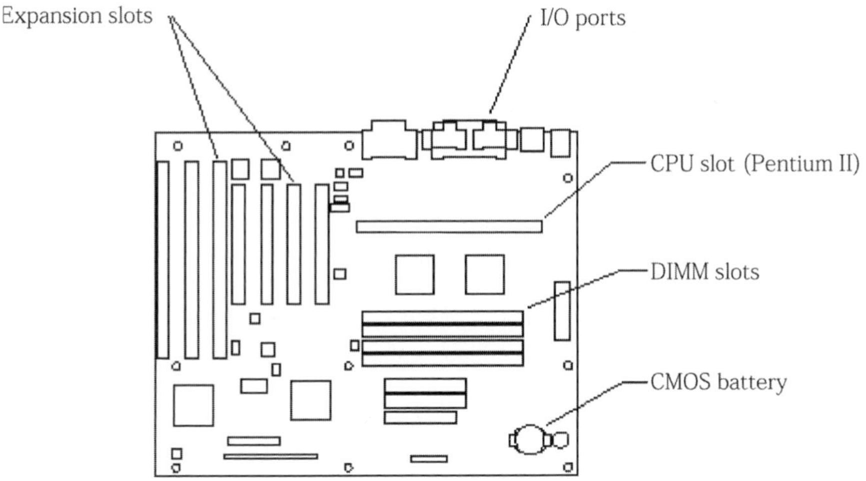

FIGURE 1-14 Layout of an ATX motherboard

complaint of baby/full AT motherboard users). Since full-length cards can now be used in all the slots, it isn't necessary to shuffle expansion cards around to avoid interfering with the CPU. The CPU itself can also be upgraded without having to remove expansion cards. SIMM and DIMM connectors are also located away from drive bays and expansion slots for easier access. The use of rear I/O ports (Figure 1-15) and

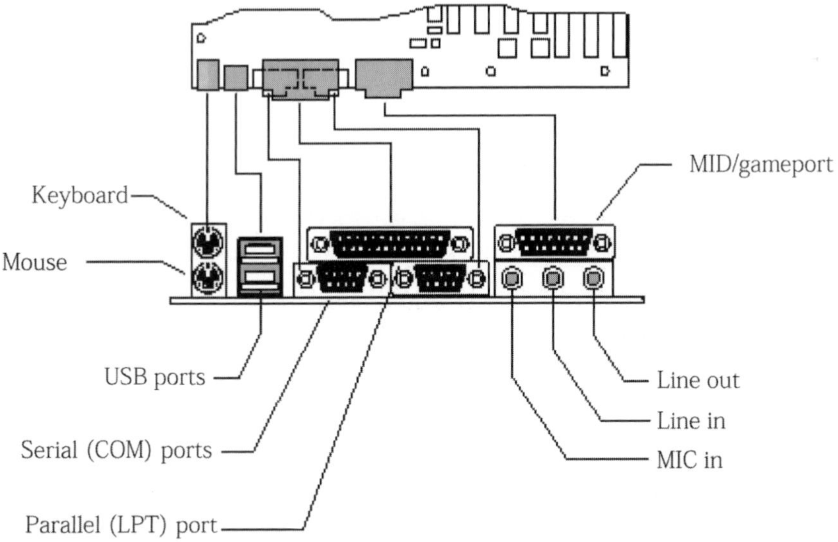

FIGURE 1-15 Layout of an ATX I/O port panel

front panel connections has been standardized on the ATX motherboard, which simplifies case design and reduces the wiring on the motherboard. Integrated drive controller connections are now located closer to the drive bays to reduce drive cable lengths and reduce clutter. The ATX power supply provides power (including a native 3.3 volts) through a single 20-pin cable rather than the two 6-pin cables used in traditional baby/full AT systems. Finally, the ATX case design is configured to be cooled by a single fan located in the ATX power supply. This not only simplifies the case and reduces power demands, but it makes the system quieter.

ATX Motherboard Sizes A full-size ATX board is 12 inches wide by 9.6 inches deep (305mm × 244mm). The Mini-ATX board is 11.2 inches by 8.2 inches (284mm × 208mm). The microATX form factor is the newest iteration of ATX and allows for motherboards down to 9.6 inches by 9.6 inches (244mm × 244mm). Designers have attempted to use as many mounting holes as possible from older baby/full AT–style motherboards to allow existing chassis to use ATX motherboards with a minimum of modification (though it's certainly preferable to use an ATX case with ATX motherboards). Figure 1-16 illustrates a comparison between a full AT motherboard, a baby AT motherboard, and a full-size ATX motherboard.

When using a microATX motherboard, it may be necessary to use a small form factor power supply (SFX Power Supply) if the system is to be built into a low-profile chassis.

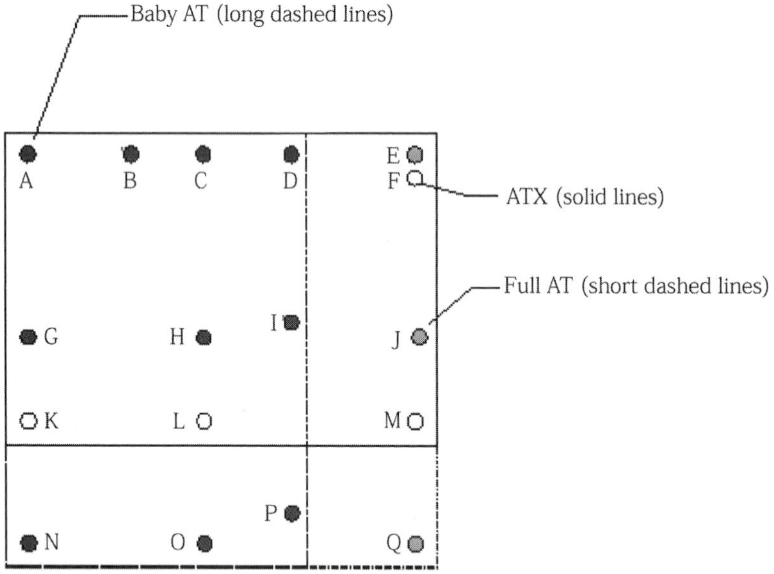

FIGURE 1-16 Comparison of full AT, baby AT, and ATX mountings

ATX Motherboard Connectors Aside from the board size and placement of mounting holes, an ATX motherboard is also characterized by the general placement of various connectors. The list below outlines the major connectors:

- Expansion slots (PCI/ISA) are located at the rear left of the motherboard.
- The power input connector is placed along the right edge of the board (near the CPU).
- Drive signal connectors are located along the front edge of the board near the drive bays.
- Front panel I/O connectors (the power switch and LED) are located along the front edge of the board, usually to the right of the expansion slots.
- Back panel I/O connectors (COM ports, parallel port, USB port, etc.) are all located on a single panel to the right rear of the motherboard. There is no single accepted layout for ATX connections, so you may find that different ATX motherboards offer unique I/O port layouts.
- Memory module connectors are located between the CPU and expansion slots or between the CPU and drive signal connectors (usually visible on inspection).
- The CPU is usually located on the right side of the motherboard in front of the back panel I/O connectors.

ATX Power Supply An ATX power supply is about 6.1 inches long, 5.7 inches wide, and 3.5 inches deep—roughly equivalent to a PS/2 power supply footprint. The supply must generate the four traditional PC voltage levels (+5V, –5V, +12V, –12V), as well as a 3.3V level to better support low-voltage logic being used in modern PCs. Power is provided to the motherboard through a single 20-pin connector. A single exhaust fan assembly located in the supply must be capable of maintaining a minimum air flow of 23CFM.

ATX Case The only real distinguishing characteristic of an ATX case is the rear opening corresponding to the motherboard's back panel I/O connector plate. You may need to obtain an I/O shield that matches the layout of your specific motherboard's I/O ports.

1

NLX FORM FACTOR

The version 1.2 NLX form factor (Figure 1-17) is one of the newest dimensioning specifications for modern PCs. NLX is specifically designed to accommodate low-profile PC systems while providing superior management for heat control and easy maintainability. The key to the NLX configuration is not the motherboard, but a riser board (similar in nature to the LPX form factor). The vertical riser board connects directly to the power supply (not the motherboard) and holds all of the expansion boards horizontally. The riser board also holds the drive cable connectors (floppy connectors and hard drive connectors), which previously resided on the motherboard. This means that the NLX motherboard has no cables to be attached or removed when servicing the NLX system. An NLX motherboard can simply be undocked from the system's riser card, and another one can be installed in a matter of moments. A wide area for back panel I/O connectors is provided on the rear of the NLX motherboard, which allows for a large variety of high-end ports such as TV, sound, game ports, and so on. NLX motherboards are also some of the first to support the AGP (Accelerated Graphics Port) for better graphics performance on PCs. The CPU is placed

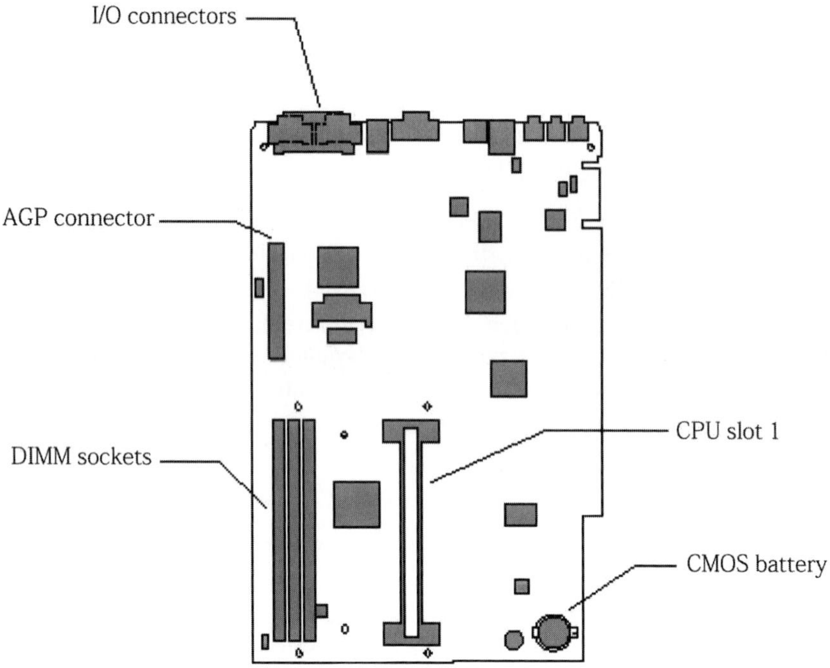

FIGURE 1-17 Layout of an NLX motherboard

toward the front of the NLX motherboard (close to the fan) to ensure better system cooling. You can get a better view of the NLX riser, motherboard, and back panel in Figure 1-18.

NLX Motherboard Sizes NLX motherboards are not as straightforward as ATX units. The NLX specification defines motherboards of 9.0 inches by 13.6 inches (maximum) and 8.0 inches by 10.0 inches (minimum). This means an NLX motherboard might run *anywhere* between these two sizes, and an NLX case must be able to support all possible sizes, though the typical NLX motherboard dimensions will be as follows (in inches):

- 8.0 × 10.0
- 9.0 × 10.0
- 8.0 × 11.2
- 9.0 × 11.2
- 8.0 × 13.6
- 9.0 × 13.6

NLX Motherboard Connectors Perhaps the most noticeable difference between an NLX motherboard and other motherboards is the apparent lack of expansion board connectors and drive port connectors

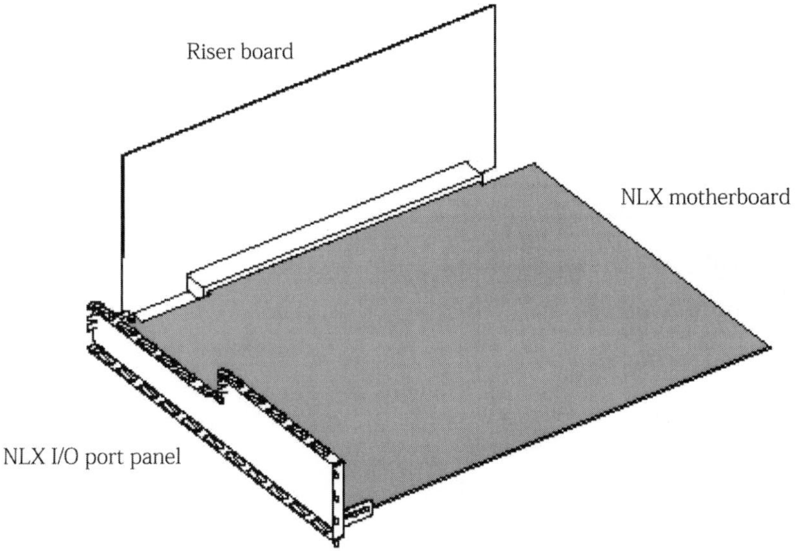

FIGURE 1-18 View of NLX riser, motherboard, and back panel

that have been implemented on the riser card. You'll also note the presence of a 340-pin card edge connector that interfaces to the riser card. The list below outlines the disposition of important connections:

- Expansion slots (PCI/ISA) are located on the riser card in a horizontal orientation.
- The power input connector is attached to the riser card.
- Drive signal connectors are attached to the riser card.
- Back panel I/O connectors (COM ports, parallel port, USB port, etc.) are all located on a single panel to the right rear of the motherboard. This back panel occupies the entire rear of the motherboard.
- Memory module connectors are typically located somewhere between the CPU and expansion slots, or behind the CPU toward the rear of the motherboard.
- The CPU is usually located on the left front of the motherboard in direct proximity to an NLX case intake fan.
- The AGP connector is located along the left side of the motherboard several inches from the left rear corner of the motherboard.

NLX Power Supply An NLX power supply uses the same dimensions as an ATX power supply (about 6.1 inches long, 5.7 inches wide, and 3.5 inches deep). The supply must generate the four traditional PC voltage levels (+5V, –5V, +12V, –12V), as well as a 3.3V level to better support low-voltage logic being used in modern PCs. Power is provided to the riser card through a single 20-pin connector. A single exhaust fan assembly located in the supply must be capable of maintaining a minimum air flow of 23CFM.

NLX Case The only distinguishing characteristic of an NLX case is the long rear opening corresponding to the motherboard's back panel I/O connector plate. There may also be hinged access or other provision to ease the installation or replacement of NLX motherboards. An additional inlet fan is located in the front left part of the chassis to aid in cooling the CPU.

Further Study

AGP Implementers' Forum: **http://www.agpforum.org/**

Amtrade Products: **www.amtrade.com**

ATX information: **www.teleport.com/~atx/**

Enlight: **www.enlightcorp.com.tw**

Fong Kai Industrial: **www.fkusa.com**

Intel chipsets: **http://developer.intel.com/design/pcisets/**

Intel's AN430TX motherboard: **http://developer.intel.com/design/motherbd/an/index.htm**

Intel's NX440LX motherboard: **http://developer.intel.com/design/motherbd/nx/index.htm**

InWin Development: **www.in-win.com**

Iomega: **http://www.iomega.com**

microATX information: **http://www.teleport.com/~microatx/**

NLX information: **www.teleport.com/~nlx/**

ProCase: **www.procase.com.tw/68.htm**

The Intel AGP Web site: **http://developer.intel.com/pc-supp/platform/agfxport/**

2

AN INSIDE LOOK AT MONITORS

CHAPTER AT A GLANCE

The ability to display images and information has evolved right along with CPUs, memory, hard drive space, and all of the other computer attributes that we associate with PC performance. Although the essential principles of a monitor have remained virtually unchanged, the small, drab monochrome displays of just a decade ago have been almost entirely replaced by flicker-free, high-resolution monitors capable of producing photo-realistic color images (Figure 2-1). Today's monitor is more than just an output device—it has become our window into the complex virtual world created by computers. This chapter shows you what is inside the typical color monitor and provides some guidelines for monitor disassembly and reassembly.

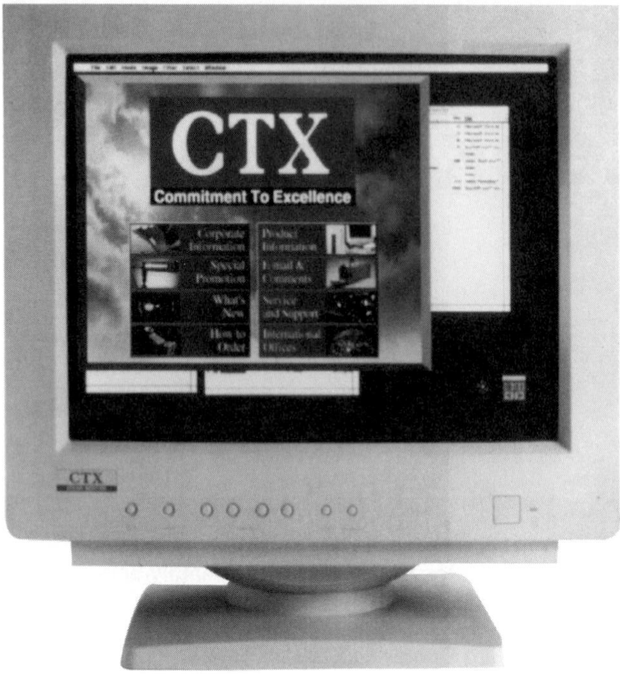

FIGURE 2-1 A modern PC monitor (CTX International Inc.)

Monitor Assembly

As you can see from Figure 2-2, a typical computer monitor is not terribly complicated. Compared to notebook computers and low-profile desktop systems, the monitor assembly is spacious. This is not an accident—monitors require substantial amounts of energy for operation. Much of this energy is dissipated as heat. Extra space prevents a buildup of heat from damaging the monitor's circuitry, and heat is allowed to escape through ventilation slots in the enclosure. Another reason for ample enclosure space is to ensure ample high-voltage insulation. Some monitors generate up to 30kV during normal operation (sometimes more for very large monitors), and normal plastic-wire insulation is hardly sufficient to ensure safety. High-voltage insulation and plenty of unobstructed space keep high voltage from arcing to other circuits. The typical monitor can be broken down into five sections: the enclosure, the CRT, a CRT drive board (or video drive board), a raster drive board, and a power supply.

ENCLOSURE

Monitor enclosures are built as two pieces. The front enclosure (*3* on Figure 2-2) is used to mount the CRT and degaussing coil. This is bolted to a frame (*12*), which forms the base of the monitor. Once other circuit boards are attached to the frame, the rear enclosure (*17*) forms a shroud over almost all of the monitor. In most cases, the rear enclosure can be freed by removing four screws (*18*). A few monitor enclosures are held together by plastic latches in addition to screws. If the rear enclosure does not slide away easily, suspect the presence of snap-in latches or extra screws installed into the frame from the bottom.

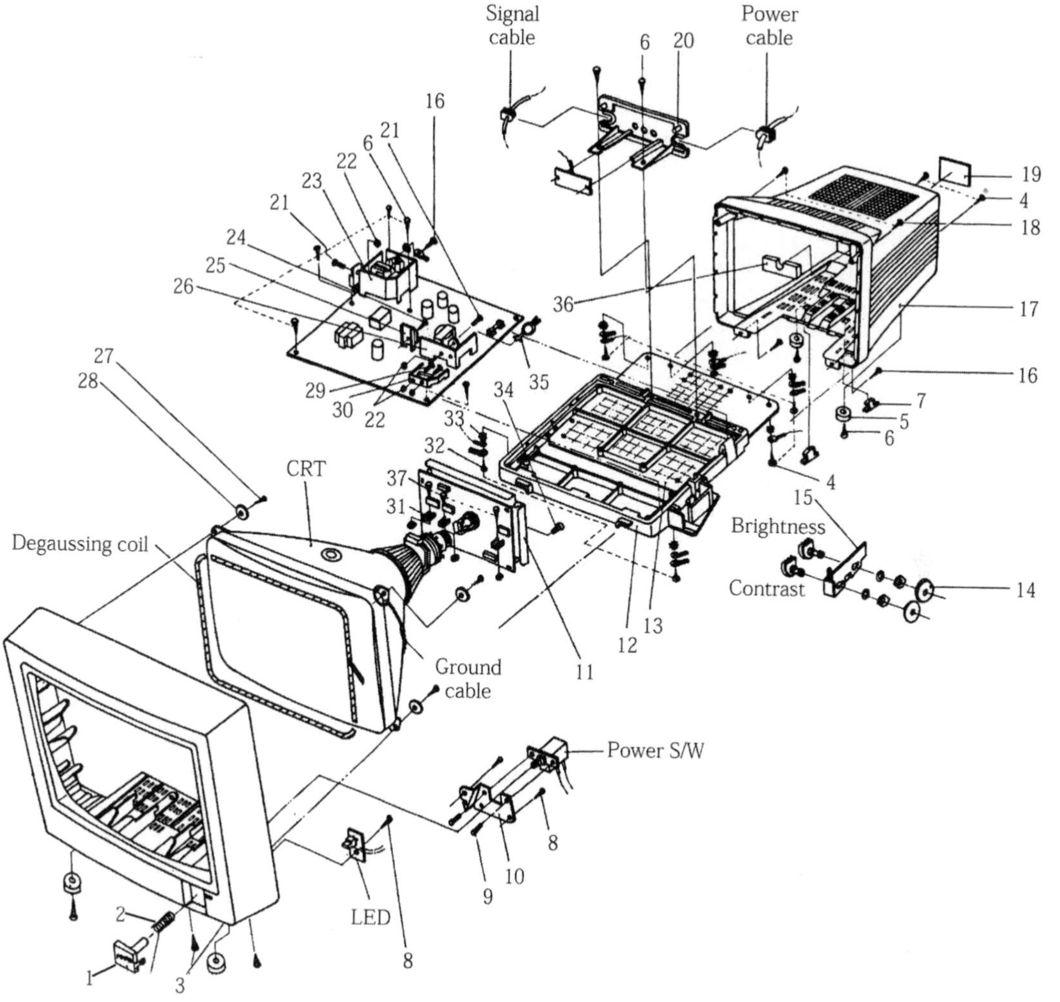

FIGURE 2-2 Exploded diagram of a Tandy VGM200 monitor (Tandy Corp.)

CRT

Although color monitors rely on extra video circuitry to process color signals, it is the design and construction of the CRT itself (*CRT* in Figure 2-2) that really makes color monitors possible. The basic principles of a color CRT (Figure 2-3) are very similar to a monochrome monitor: electrons "boil" off the cathode and are accelerated toward the phosphor-coated front face by a high positive potential. Color CRTs use three cathodes and video control grids—one for each primary color. Control (brightness), screen, and focus grids serve the same purpose as they do in monochrome CRTs. The *control grid* regulates the overall brightness of the electron beams, the *screen grid* begins accelerating the electron beams toward the front screen, and the *focus grid* narrows the beams. Once the electron beams are focused, vertical and horizontal deflection coils (or deflection yokes) apply magnetic force to direct the beams around the screen.

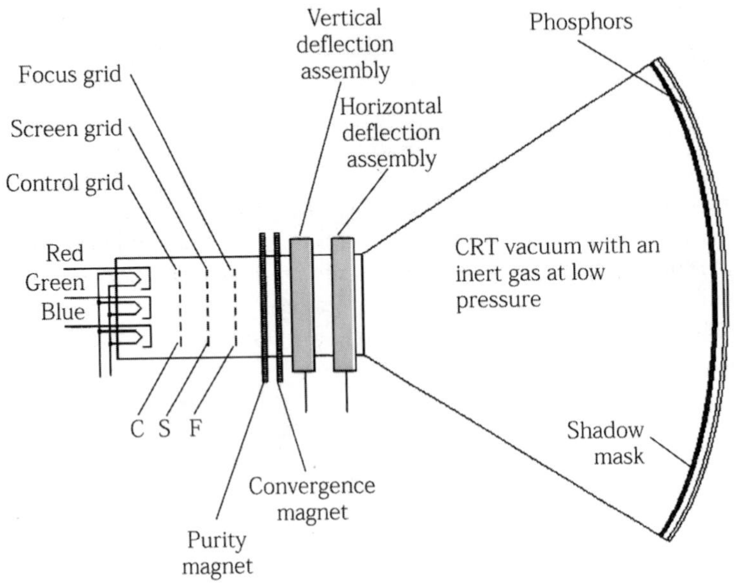

FIGURE 2-3 Diagram of a typical color CRT assembly

You will notice a *shadow mask* added to the color CRT. A shadow mask is a thin plate of metal that contains thousands of microscopic perforations—one perforation for each screen pixel. The mask is placed in close proximity to the phosphor face. There is also a substantial difference in the screen phosphors. Where a monochrome CRT uses a homogeneous layer of phosphor across the entire face, a color CRT uses phosphor *triads*, as shown in Figure 2-4. (Note that the distance between the shadow mask and phosphor screen is shown greatly exaggerated.) Red, green, and blue phosphor dots are arranged in sets such that the red, green, and blue electron beams will strike the corresponding phosphor. In actual opera-

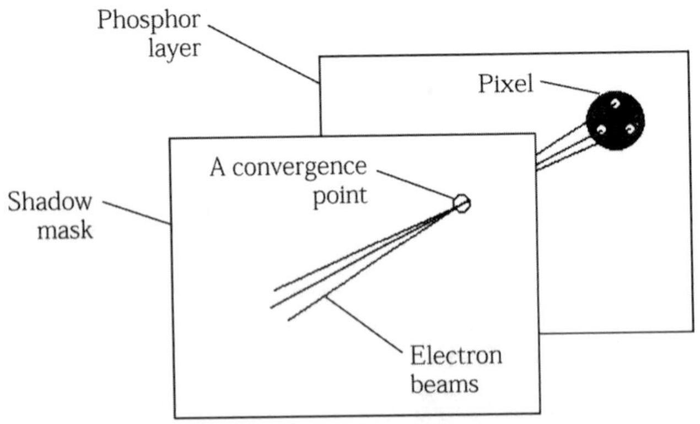

FIGURE 2-4 The relationship of a shadow mask and color phosphors

tion, the color dots are so close together that each triad appears as a single point (or pixel). A *degaussing coil* (shown in Figure 2-2) mounted in front of the CRT works to keep the shadow mask demagnetized.

Color CRTs must also be more precise in how the three electron beams are directed around the screen. Since there are now three phosphors instead of one, it is critical that each electron beam strike only its corresponding phosphor color, not adjoining phosphors. This is known as *color purity*. A *purity magnet* added to the CRT yoke helps to adjust fine beam positioning. By using a shadow mask, the electron beams are only allowed to reach the phosphors where there are holes in the mask. Also remember that each of the three electron beams must converge at each hole in the shadow mask. A *convergence magnet* added to the CRT yoke adjusts beam convergence in the display center (known as *static convergence*), while a convergence coil driven by the raster circuitry optimizes beam convergence at the edges of the display (known as *dynamic convergence*). It is this delicate balance of purity and convergence adjustments—as well as the presence of a shadow mask—that gives today's color monitors such rich, precise color.

CRT DRIVE BOARD

The CRT drive board (*31* in Figure 2-2) attaches directly to the CRT pins through a circular connector. Control (brightness), screen, and focus grid voltages are applied to the CRT through this board. The CRT drive board also contains the red, green, and blue video amplifiers and drivers. Since more CRT drive circuitry is needed for a color monitor than for a monochrome monitor, the CRT drive board for a color monitor is usually much larger than that of a monochrome monitor. Once the monitor is unplugged and discharged, make sure that this board is attached evenly and securely to the CRT. It is the CRT drive circuit that regulates the strength of each electron beam by adjusting signal strength on the corresponding video control grid in the CRT. The CRT drive circuit must convert a small video signal (usually no more than 0.7 volts) into a signal large enough to drive the CRT (typically around 50 volts). For color monitors with three analog video lines, three separate video drive circuits are required.

Problems can strike the CRT drive circuits in a number of ways, but there are clues to help guide your way. If the display should disappear, but the raster remains (*raster* is that dim haze you see by turning up the monitor's brightness), the video signal may have failed at the video adapter board in your PC. If there is suddenly not enough (or far too much) red, green, or blue in the displayed image, the corresponding DAC (digital-to-analog converter) on the video adapter may have failed, or the corresponding CRT drive circuit in the monitor may have broken down. Try a monitor that you know is working properly. If the correct image appears, you know the video adapter is producing the desired output, and the original monitor is probably defective. If no display appears on the good monitor, suspect the video adapter board in your PC. If the screen is black, suffers from fixed brightness (with or without video input), or loses focus, one or more grids in the CRT may have shorted and failed.

RASTER DRIVE BOARD

The main raster board contains the vertical raster, horizontal raster, and high-voltage circuits that actually drive the CRT and direct the electron beam(s) around the screen. Depending on the design of your particular monitor, the raster board may contain part or all of the power supply circuit as well, along with some microcontroller-driven circuitry to operate on-screen monitor adjustments. Just about all monitors mount the raster board directly to the frame horizontally below the CRT neck. This assembly can be difficult to remove since it is obstructed by the CRT neck and yoke, as well as the interconnecting wiring that connects to the power supply, front panel controls, and flyback transformer.

The vertical drive circuit is used to operate the vertical deflection yoke. This is accomplished with a vertical sweep oscillator, which is little more than a free-running oscillator set to run at 60, 70, 75, or 85Hz (perhaps more, depending on the design of the particular monitor). When the oscillator is triggered, it produces a sawtooth wave. The start of the sawtooth wave corresponds to the top of the screen, while the end of the sawtooth wave corresponds to the bottom of the screen. When the sawtooth cycle is complete, there is a blank period for blanking and retrace. One vertical sweep will be accomplished in less than 1/60th of a second.

Trouble with the vertical drive circuit usually strikes the vertical output driver circuit. If part of the driver should fail, either the upper or lower half of the image will disappear. If the entire driver should fail, the screen image will compress to a straight horizontal line in the center of the screen (there would be no vertical deflection, only horizontal deflection). Another problem is vertical oversweep, which elongates the picture to the extent where it wraps back on itself in the lower portion of the screen. The area where the vertical image oversweeps will appear with a whitish haze and is typically the fault of the vertical oscillator circuit.

The horizontal drive circuit is the second part of the color monitor's raster circuit, and it is designed to operate the horizontal deflection yoke. This is accomplished with a horizontal oscillator, which is little more than a free-running oscillator set to run at a frequency between 15kHz and 95kHz. For example, a classic CGA monitor will typically use a horizontal sweep frequency of about 15.75kHz, but a current high-resolution (1600 × 1200) monitor may run as high as 93.7kHz. Table 2-1 illustrates the typical relationships between resolution and vertical/horizontal drive frequencies. The actual oscillator may be based on a transistor, but is usually designed around an integrated circuit, which is more stable at the higher frequencies that are needed. When a horizontal synchronization trigger pulse is received from the video adapter board, the oscillator is forced to fire. When the oscillator is triggered, it produces a square wave. The start of the square wave corresponds to the left side of the screen. When the cycle is complete, there is a blank period for blanking and retrace. At an operating frequency of 31.5kHz, one horizontal sweep will be accomplished in about 31.7µS.

Trouble with the horizontal drive circuit usually strikes the horizontal output drive circuit since that is the circuit that sustains the greatest stress in the monitor. If the drive circuit should fail, the entire image will disappear since high-voltage generation will also be affected. Unfortunately, a fault in the horizontal oscillator will also result in an image loss since high-voltage generation depends on a satisfactory horizontal pulse. If the horizontal oscillator or amplifier fails, high-voltage fails as well, and the image

TABLE 2-1 RELATIONSHIP BETWEEN VERTICAL AND HORIZONTAL DRIVE FREQUENCIES

VIDEO STANDARD	RESOLUTION	HORIZ. FREQ.	VERT. FREQ.
IBM/VGA	640 × 400	31.5kHz	70Hz
IBM/VGA	640 × 480	31.5kHz	60Hz
VESA/75	640 × 480	37.5kHz	75Hz
VESA/85	640 × 480	43.3kHz	85Hz
VESA/75	800 × 600	46.9kHz	75Hz
VESA/85	800 × 600	53.7kHz	85Hz
VESA/75	1024 × 768	60.0kHz	75Hz
VESA/85	1024 × 768	68.6kHz	85Hz
VESA/75	1280 × 1024	80.0kHz	75Hz
VESA/75	1600 × 1200	93.7kHz	75Hz

becomes too faint to see. This makes troubleshooting horizontal problems a bit more difficult than troubleshooting vertical problems.

The high-voltage system is actually part of the horizontal drive circuit. A monitor's power supply generates relatively low voltages (usually not much higher than 140 volts). This means that the high positive potential needed to excite the CRT's anode is *not* developed in the power supply. Instead, the 15kV to 30kV or more needed to power a CRT anode is generated from the horizontal output. The amplified, high-frequency pulse signal generated by the horizontal driver circuit is provided to the primary winding of a device known as the *flyback transformer* (or FBT). It is the FBT that produces the high voltage. The principle is similar to the ignition system used in automobiles.

POWER SUPPLY

The power supply is typically a hand-sized assembly that converts AC into several DC voltage levels (usually +135, +20, +12, +6.3, and +87 volts DC) that will be needed by other monitor circuits. The AC itself may be filtered and fused by a separate small assembly near the monitor's base. If there is no stand-alone power supply board in your particular monitor, the supply is probably incorporated into the raster board. As you saw earlier, the only voltage that is *not* produced in the power supply is the high-voltage source. A stand-alone power supply is typically mounted vertically to the frame. The metal frame not only provides a rigid mounting platform, but it serves as a chassis common and helps to contain RF signals generated by the monitor.

Working with On-Screen Controls

PC monitors have traditionally been analog devices with manually adjusted controls for configuring proper operation. However, as monitor sizes, viewing areas, and resolutions continue to increase, users demand more control over the image's appearance. The use of microcontrollers in large modern monitors allows many display adjustments to be made through the front control panel, which otherwise would require a tedious and time-consuming internal alignment. Such changes can then be easily saved in the monitor's internal memory. Since adjustments can be set for major resolutions independently, the monitor can "remember" your optimum display configuration for your most frequently used display modes—there is almost no tinkering with the monitor each time you change a screen mode. On-screen controls are listed through a series of icons that indicate the general action of each control. Figure 2-5 illustrates some of the most popular icons for basic on-screen monitor adjustments.

BASIC CONTROLS

The basic on-screen controls may seem overwhelming at first glance—that's understandable because most PC users never get to use more than brightness and contrast knobs. Still, the basic controls are designed to help you set the overall image position and quality for your current display mode.

> Some of these adjustments can cause severe image distortion if set improperly. Before making any adjustments (beyond contrast and brightness), be sure to note the starting level of each adjustment or find the "factory default" button, which can restore default levels automatically.

Horizontal Size Also called *H-size*, this makes the image fatter or thinner. If the image is too wide (where one or both ends are "lost" beyond the edges of the display area), you can use the H-size control to pull the image inside the display area.

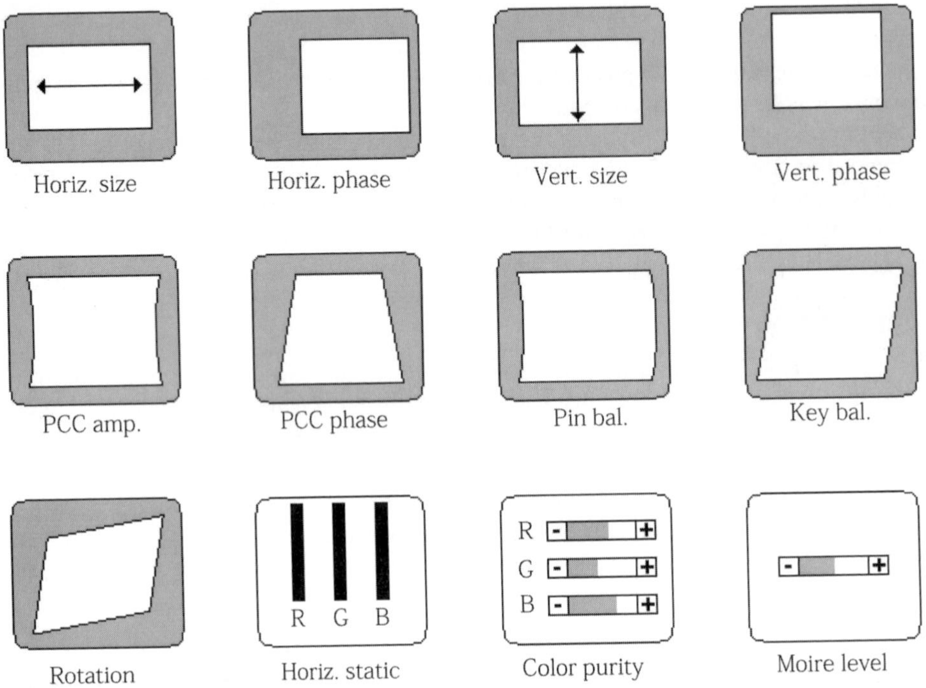

FIGURE 2-5 Basic on-screen monitor adjustments

Horizontal Phase Also called *H-phase* or *H-posi*, this control lets you position the image left or right in the display area. For example, if the image is too far to the right, use H-phase to shift the image to the left. You may use H-phase and H-size alternately to size the image properly.

Vertical Size Also called *V-size*, this makes the image taller or shorter. If the image is too tall (where one or both ends are "lost" beyond the top and bottom of the display area), you can use the V-size control to pull the image inside the display area.

Vertical Phase Also called *V-phase* or *V-posi*, this control lets you position the image higher or lower in the display area. For example, if the image is too low, use V-phase to shift the image upward. You may use V-phase and V-size alternately to size the image properly.

PCC Amp This is also known as the *pincushion adjustment*. Use this control to straighten the left and right sides of the image. If the PCC control is set too low, the image will bow outward. If the PCC control is set too high, the image will draw inward. Ideally, the sides of the image should be straight.

PCC Phase This is also known as *trapezoidal adjustment*. Use this control to make the image perfectly rectangular. If the adjustment is set too low, the top of the image may be narrower than the bottom. If the adjustment is set too high, the top of the image may be wider than the bottom.

Pin Balance This is also known as the *curvature adjustment*. Use this adjustment also to straighten the image. If the control is too high, the image may curve to the left. If the control is too low, the image may curve to the right. Note that this is not a pincushion (PCC amp) adjustment because the left and right sides of the image are being affected in the same direction.

Key Balance This may also be referred to as a *slant control* or *tilt adjustment*. Use this adjustment also to straighten the image. If the control is set too high, the top of the image may be pulled right, and the bottom of the image may be pulled left. If the control is set too low, the top of the image may be pulled left, and the bottom of the image may be pulled right.

Rotation This may also be referred to as the *twist adjustment*. This control affects the rotation of the entire image in the display. Ideally, the image should appear straight in the display—the two bottom corners of the image should be exactly the same distance from the desk.

Horizontal Static This is an adjustment of color alignment. Use this control to adjust the alignment of the red, green, and blue electron beams.

Color Purity You may also see this called *color balance*. Ideally, white should be a "pure" white—containing the same amounts of red, green, and blue. However, age may affect CRT color guns and video driver levels, so you can tweak the RGB settings to restore color purity.

Moire Level *Moire* is a form of distortion that occurs when certain conditions of resolution, dot pitch, screen size, and image coloring are met. The moire pattern usually appears as wavy or elliptical patterns in the display. Use this control to adjust the amount of moire distortion that may appear in an image.

ADVANCED CONTROLS

The advanced on-screen image adjustments are often quite similar to the basic adjustments, but advanced adjustments allow more precise and subtle corrections—especially in the corners of an image, which are the most difficult to set correctly. Figure 2-6 highlights the advanced controls that you'll encounter most frequently.

Vertical Linearity This is also called *V-lin*. Linearity is the geometric "correctness" of the display. For example, if there is an image of small colored boxes the same size throughout, each box should appear to be the same size. If not, linearity might be a problem. This control adjusts linearity in the vertical direction.

2

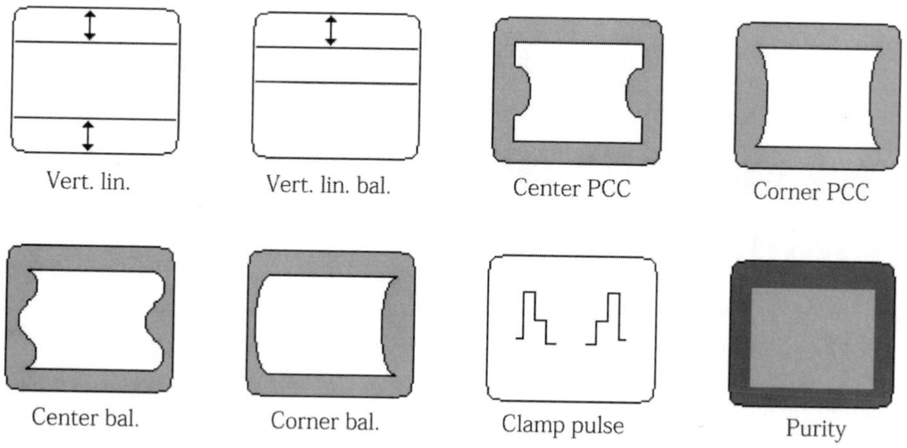

FIGURE 2-6 Advanced on-screen monitor adjustments

Vertical Linearity Balance Also called *V-lin balance*, this control effectively centers the linearity of the display's vertical axis. For example, it may be necessary to shift the linearity balance when changing linearity in order to avoid making uniform linearity changes across the entire display.

Center PCC Also called *center pincushion*, this is a precision adjustment that allows you to tweak the pincushion adjustment near the vertical center of the image, instead of across the entire left and right sides of the image. This adjustment should only be used when there is limited pincushioning around the middle of the image.

Corner PCC Also called *corner pincushion*, this is a precision adjustment that allows you to tweak the pincushion adjustment near the corners of the image, instead of across the entire left and right sides of the image. This adjustment should only be used when there is limited pincushioning around the edges of the image.

Center Balance This feature (similar to pin balance) adjusts the curvature of the left and right sides of the display near the vertical center of the image, instead of across the entire image. Use this adjustment to correct minor curvature in the center of the image.

Corner Balance This feature (similar to pin balance) adjusts the curvature of the left and right sides of the display at the corners of the image, instead of across the entire image. Use this adjustment to correct minor curvature at the corners of the image.

Clamp Pulse Position This feature is not needed with RGB inputs such as those provided by your 15-pin video cable, but may be needed when using Sync-on-Green signals through a BNC connector. Clamp pulse controls allow you to eliminate the excessive green or white background that can occur when using Sync-on-Green or external sync signals at the monitor.

Purity This feature allows you to adjust the color purity, or color uniformity, of the display. Do not adjust this level unless it is absolutely necessary. This is sometimes referred to as the monitor's *color temperature* setting.

Power Management This option can be used to disable the power management (a.k.a. "Energy Star") features of your monitor. When disabled, the monitor will *not* power-down after a given period of system inactivity.

Degaussing This feature allows you to manually degauss the monitor if you notice unusual screen discoloration. Use this feature with extreme caution, and only on an as-needed basis.

Notes on Monitor Disassembly and Reassembly

The process of monitor disassembly is remarkably straightforward. In most cases, only the rear enclosure must be removed to expose the entire inner workings of the monitor. The rear enclosure itself is typically held in place with only four screws (there may be additional screws inserted at the bottom). On some occasions, you may also encounter a number of plastic latches, but this is rare. After removing the rear enclosure, you will see the bell and neck of the CRT, the CRT drive board, the raster board, and the power supply (if a separate supply is used).

The computer monitor operates with exposed voltages that are potentially lethal! This makes monitors unusually dangerous in the hands of novice or inexperienced troubleshooters. Make sure that the monitor is *unplugged* and allowed several minutes to discharge before reaching into the assembly. Do not operate the monitor without its X-ray and RF shields in place (if applicable). It is also advisable to work with a second person nearby.

You should take note of any metal shrouds or coverings that are included with the monitor assembly. Metal shielding serves two very important purposes. First, the oscillators and amplifiers in a monitor produce radio-frequency (RF) signals that have the potential to interfere with radio and TV reception. The presence of metal shields or screens helps to attenuate any such interference, so always make it a point to replace shields securely before testing or operating the monitor. Second, large CRTs (larger than 17 inches) use *very* high voltages (30kV or more) at the CRT anode. With such high potentials, X-radiation becomes a serious concern. CRTs with lower anode voltages can usually contain X-rays with lead in the CRT glass. Metal shields are added to the larger CRTs as supplemental shielding in order to stop X-rays from escaping the monitor enclosure. When X-ray shielding is removed, it is vital that it be replaced *before* the monitor is tested and returned to service. X-ray shields will usually be clearly marked when you remove the monitor's rear cover.

DISCHARGING THE CRT

Before removing any wiring or boards from the monitor, it is important to be sure that the CRT is fully discharged. Even though unplugging the monitor will prevent AC and high-voltage electrocution, there may still be enough high-voltage charge stored in the CRT to provide a fair kick to the careless. Make sure the monitor is turned off, and allow several minutes for the AC supply to discharge. Use a regular-blade screwdriver with a heavy-duty alligator clip attached between the screwdriver shaft and the metal chassis. *Gently* insert the screwdriver blade under the high-voltage anode cap, as shown in Figure 2-7. You will probably hear a mild crackle as the CRT is grounded. *Do not rotate the screwdriver or force it in the CRT.* Remember that the CRT is still a glass assembly, and excessive force can damage it easily. Once the crackling noise stops, remove the screwdriver and unplug the monitor's AC cord. The assembly should now be safe to work on.

2

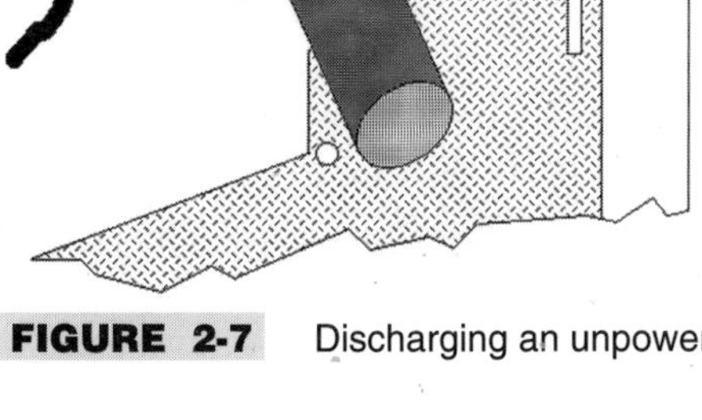

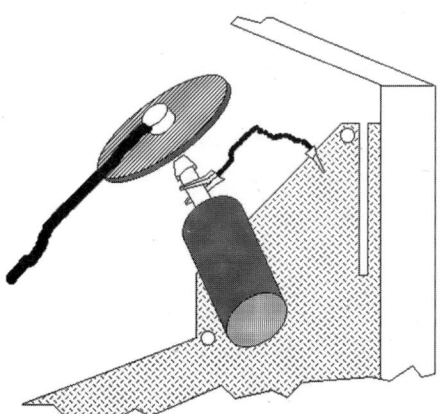

FIGURE 2-7 Discharging an unpowered CRT before servicing

REMOVING SUBASSEMBLIES

Removing boards is often a simple matter. The CRT drive board is simply plugged into the CRT through a circular connector. Rock the video board back and forth gently to pull it away from the CRT. The raster board is typically mounted to the frame with several screws. After the screws are removed, the raster board should be free. When removing any board, be sure to make a careful note of each connector's location and orientation. A CRT is held in place with a metal bracket bolted to the front enclosure. Unfortunately, replacing the CRT usually means removing the video and raster boards along with the frame. If you must place the monitor (or front enclosure alone) facedown onto a work surface, be sure to use a layer of soft towels or foam to prevent scratches to the front enclosure or CRT.

REPLACING SUBASSEMBLIES

The most important rule to remember when exchanging a board or CRT is to use an *exact* replacement part. Monitors are precisely timed, high-energy systems, so "close" doesn't count. An improper replacement assembly may cause the monitor to malfunction, or it may work only for a limited amount of time. When reassembling a monitor, be extremely careful of the wiring interconnecting each board and the CRT. Be sure that all wiring and connectors are installed properly and completely. Loose connectors can cause erratic or intermittent operation. Pay close attention to wire paths—do not allow wiring to be pinched under boards or against the metal chassis. Finally, make it a point to reinstall any RF or X-ray shielding that may have been removed during the repair.

> Remember that a monitor may need to be realigned after completing a repair.

TIPS FOR WORKING WITH A MONITOR

Of all the PC peripherals, monitors are perhaps the most potentially dangerous in careless hands. The tips listed below will help you protect yourself from injury and get the most working life from your monitor investment:

- For best monitor images, always keep the 15-pin video cable secured to the video adapter board. Also avoid using monitor cable extensions, which can cause image ghosting.
- Use simple ammonia-based cleaners to clean the monitor case, but never spray cleaner onto the monitor, only onto the cleaning cloth.
- CRT coatings (such as antiglare coatings) can be extremely sensitive to chemicals, so never use any sort of cleaner other than demineralized water to clean the CRT. Remember to wet the cleaning cloth, not the CRT.
- Monitors use convection for cooling. Be sure to keep all of the vent openings on the monitor case unobstructed and free of dust and debris. Vacuum any accumulations of dust within the monitor.
- When working on a monitor, always use a soft pillow or plush towel to cushion the CRT and avoid scratches.
- Monitors can contain potentially dangerous voltages. Be sure to keep the monitor turned off and unplugged before working inside it. Discharge the CRT's high-voltage anode before performing any service.
- Do not use metal tools when working inside a monitor, especially when attempting to make alignments.
- When reassembling a monitor, be extremely careful to avoid damaging wiring and connectors.

- Monitors (especially large monitors) are extremely sensitive to the influences of magnetic fields. Be sure to keep any motorized or magnetic devices well clear of the monitor. Even unshielded multimedia speakers can adversely affect the monitor.
- Monitors are particularly heavy devices, so be very careful when lifting a monitor. Lift from the knees, not from the back. Hold the CRT face toward your chest.

Further Study

Anatek Corporation: **http://www.anatekcorp.com**

CTX: **http://www.ctxintl.com/**

NEC: **http://www.nec.com**

Sony: **http://www.ita.sel.sony.com/support/displays/**

Viewsonic: **http://www.viewsonic.com/desk/desk.htm**

3

AN INSIDE LOOK AT OPERATING SYSTEMS AND THE BOOT PROCESS

CHAPTER AT A GLANCE

As a technician, it is vital for you to understand the relationship between PC hardware and software. In the early days of computers, hardware was typically the center of attention. Since early software was written for a specific computer (such as a DEC PDP system or IBM Vax), and early computers were very limited in their storage and processing capacity, software often arrived as an afterthought. (We still see software development lagging behind hardware advances to this day.) With the introduction of personal computers in the mid-1970s, designers realized that a wide selection of software would be needed to make PCs attractive. Instead of writing software specifically for particular machines, a uniform environment would be needed to manage system resources and launch applications. In this way, applications would be *portable* between systems whose hardware resources would otherwise be incompatible. This uniform applications environment became known as the *operating system* (or *OS*). When IBM designed the PC, they chose to license a simple command-line–based operating system from a fledgling company called Microsoft—and the rest is history.

Although this book is dedicated to dealing with PC hardware (since it is the hardware that "breaks"), you must realize that the operating system has a profound effect on PC resources and how those resources are allocated to individual software applications. This is especially true of the more sophisticated operating systems such as Windows 95/98/NT, Linux, and OS/2. Every good technician is sensitive to the fact that problems with an OS will result in problems with PC performance. This chapter explains the relationship between PC hardware and software, illustrates some of the major features found in typical operating systems, and walks you through a typical PC boot process.

The PC Hierarchy

Before we dig into the operating system itself, you should understand the complex (and often frustrating) relationship between computer hardware and software. This relationship is often expressed as a *hierarchy* shown in the diagram of Figure 3-1. Each layer in the hierarchy serves a very specific function in PC operation. There are four levels to this hierarchy: the hardware, the BIOS, the OS, and the application(s).

HARDWARE

As you might expect, hardware forms the core of a PC hierarchy—there is no computer without the hardware. The hardware includes all of the circuits, drives, expansion boards, power supplies, peripheral devices, and their interconnecting wiring or cables. This extends not only to the PC itself, but also to monitors, keyboards, pointing devices, printers, and so on. By sending digital information to various ports or addresses in memory, it is possible to manipulate almost anything attached to the system CPU. Unfortunately, controlling PC hardware is a difficult process that requires an intimate knowledge of a PC's electronic architecture. How is it that Microsoft can sell an operating system that works on an i286-based AT, as well as on a new Pentium III system? Since each PC manufacturer designs their circuitry (especially motherboard circuitry) differently, it is virtually impossible to create a universal operating system without

3

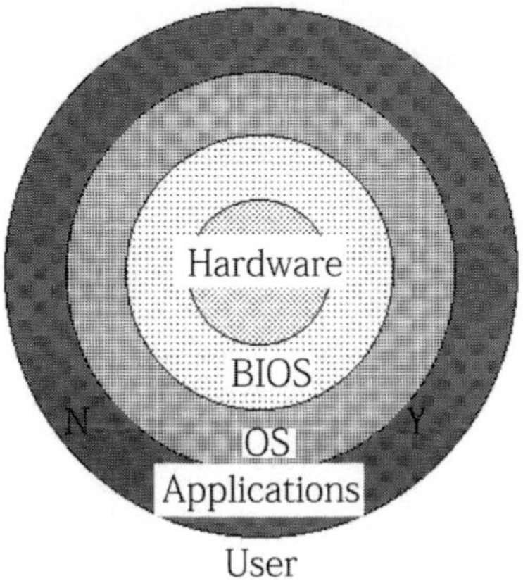

FIGURE 3-1 A standard PC hierarchy

some sort of interface between the one standard OS and the myriad variations of hardware in the marketplace. This interface is accomplished by the *Basic Input/Output System* (*BIOS*).

BIOS

Simply put, a BIOS is a set of small programs (or *system services*) that are designed to operate each major PC subsystem (video, disk, keyboard, etc.). Each of these system services is invoked by a set of standard calls—originally developed by IBM—which are made from the operating system. When the operating system requests a standard BIOS service, the particular BIOS program will perform the appropriate function tailored to the particular hardware. Thus, each motherboard design requires its own BIOS. Using this methodology, BIOS acts as a glue that allows diverse (and older) hardware to operate with a single uniform OS. In addition to system services, the BIOS runs a power-on self-test (POST) program each time the PC is initialized. POST checks the major subsystems before attempting to load an operating system.

Since BIOS is specific to each motherboard design, BIOS resides on the motherboard in the form of a read-only memory (ROM) IC, although newer systems employ electrically rewritable (or *flash*) ROMs that allow the BIOS to be updated without having to replace the BIOS ROM IC. You may see BIOS referred to as *firmware* rather than software because it is software permanently recorded on an IC. As you might imagine, the efficiency and accuracy of BIOS code will have a profound impact on the overall operation of a PC: better BIOS routines will result in superior system performance, while clumsy, inefficient BIOS routines can easily bog a system down. *Bugs* (software errors) in BIOS can have very serious consequences for the system (such as lost files and system lockups).

OPERATING SYSTEM

The operating system serves two important functions in the modern PC. First, an OS interacts with and provides an extension to the BIOS. This extension provides applications with a rich selection of high-level file handling and disk control functions. It is this large number of disk-related functions that added the term "disk" to "operating system" and gave us *disk operating system*, or *DOS*. When an application needs to perform disk access or file handling, it is the OS layer that performs most of the work. By providing access to a library of frequently used functions through the OS, application programs can be written without the need to incorporate the code for such complex functions into each application itself. In actual operation, the OS and BIOS work closely together to give an application easy access to system resources.

Second, an OS forms an environment (or *shell*) through which applications can be executed, and provides a user interface allowing you and your customers to interact with the PC. MS-DOS uses a keyboard-driven, command-line interface signified by the command-line prompt (such as C:>_), which we have become so familiar with. By contrast, the Windows family of operating systems provides a graphical user interface (GUI) relying on symbols, icons, and dialog boxes that are selected with a mouse or other pointing device.

APPLICATIONS

Ultimately, the aim of a computer is to execute applications (such as games, word processors, spreadsheets). An OS loads and allows the user to launch the desired application(s). As the application requires system resources during run time, it will make an appropriate call to the OS or BIOS, which in turn will access the needed function and return any needed information to the calling application. The actual dynamics of such an exchange are more complex than described here, but you get the general idea. Now that you have read an overview of the typical PC hierarchy and understand how each layer interacts with one another, it is time to take a closer look at the OS layer itself.

Understanding Popular OS Features

There are many different operating systems written for today's computers. The range and sophistication of operating systems span the entire spectrum of features and complexity—some are large, complex, commercial giants (such as Windows 95/98, Windows 2000, and Windows NT), while others are small, freely distributed packages (such as FreeBSD). Other operating systems are tailored for such features as real-time operation, true or high-performance multitasking, or networking. New specialized operating systems are regularly being introduced to support particular systems such as process control, manufacturing, or other mission-critical needs. Table 3-1 offers a partial listing of today's available operating systems. As a technician, you should understand the important features of today's operating systems and why one OS might be selected over another. The following sections offer some highlights of the major commercial operating systems offered by Microsoft and IBM.

TABLE 3-1 PARTIAL LIST OF CONTEMPORARY OPERATING SYSTEMS

OPERATING SYSTEM	PURPOSE/EMPHASIS	FURTHER STUDY
A/UX	Unix variant	http://jagubox.gsfc.nasa.gov/aux/
AROS	Replacement for Amiga OS	http://194.52.182.14/
BeOS	Mac/Pentium/Alpha OS	http://www.be.com/
CHORUS	For communication devices	http://www.chorus.com/
Coherent UNIX	UNIX variant	comp.os.coherent
CP/M	Precursor to DOS	comp.os.cpm
CTOS	Networking OS	www.dogstar.com/Sirius/Menu/TechLibrary.NewsletterExcerpts.html
DR-DOS v6.0	DOS from Novell	http://support.novell.com/Ftp/Updates/dsktop/drdos60/Date0.html
FreeBSD	Free UNIX variant	http://www.freebsd.org/
GEOS	OS from GeoWorks	http://users.bergen.org/~edwdig/geos/
GNU	Free UNIX variant	http://www.delorie.com/gnu/
Grasshopper	OS for persistent systems	http://www.gh.cs.su.oz.au/Grasshopper/index.html
Helios	Real-time embedded OS	http://www.perihelion.co.uk/spg.html
HP/UX 10.x	UNIX variant from HP	http://eigen.ee.ualberta.ca/
IBM OS/2 v4.x	Commercial GUI OS from IBM	http://www-4.ibm.com/software/os/warp/
Inferno	Networking OS	http://207.121.184.224/
Linux	Free UNIX variant	http://www.linux.org/
LynxOS	Real-time OS	comp.os.lynx
Mach 4.x	Small multiprocessor OS	www.cs.cmu.edu/afs/cs.cmu.edu/project/mach/public/www/mach.html
Macintosh OS 8	OS for Mac systems	http://www.apple.com/macos/
Macintosh OS 9	OS for Mac systems	http://www.apple.com/macos/
Mac OS X	Server OS for Apple computers	http://www.apple.com/macosx/server/
MacMinix	Minix variant for Mac systems	http://www.pliner.com/macminix/

3

TABLE 3-1 PARTIAL LIST OF CONTEMPORARY OPERATING SYSTEMS *(CONTINUED)*

OPERATING SYSTEM	PURPOSE/EMPHASIS	FURTHER STUDY
Magic Cap	Communication-based OS	http://www.genmagic.com/MagicCap/index.html
Minix	Small free UNIX variant	http://www.cs.vu.nl/~ast/minix.html
MkLinux	Mach-based Linux for Apple computers	http://www.mklinux.apple.com/
MS-DOS v6.x	Commercial DOS from Microsoft	http://www.microsoft.com/kb/default.asp
Multics	Time-sharing OS	ftp://ftp.stratus.com/pub/vos/multics/tvv/multics.html
NetBSD 1.2	Free UNIX variant	http://www.netbsd.org/
NetWare v4.x	Networking OS from Novell	http://www.novell.com/intranetware/products/
NetWare v5.x	Networking OS from Novell	http://www.novell.com/netware5/index.html
NeXTStep	Networking OS	http://www.omnigroup.com/Documentation/NEXTSTEP/Guide.html
Novell-DOS v7.0	DOS version from Novell	http://www.novell.ru:8080/Ftp/Updates/dsktop/ndos7/Alpha0.html
OpenStep 4.0	Open platform OS	http://www.stepwise.com/
OSF/1	DEC OS for Alpha	http://wsspinfo.cern.ch/file/osfsp
PC-DOS v7.0 (2000)	DOS version from IBM	http://www-4.ibm.com/software/os/dos/index.html
Plan9	Distributed computing OS	http://www.ecf.toronto.edu/plan9/
QNX	Real-time OS	http://www.qnx.com/
Rhapsody	Mac OS	http://www.stepwise.com/
SCO UNIX	UNIX variant from SCO	http://www.sco.com/
Solaris 2.5	UNIX variant from Sun	http://www.lafayette.edu/~mulligaj/SUN/
UNIX	The classic workstation OS	http://www.unix.digital.com/
UnixWare	UNIX variant from SCO	http://www.sco.com/
VMS (OpenVMS)	The classic mainframe OS	http://www.levitte.org/~ava/index.htmlx
Windows 95	Commercial GUI PC OS	http://www.microsoft.com/products/prodref/426_ov.htm
Windows 98	Commercial GUI PC OS	http://www.microsoft.com/windows98/
Windows 2000	Commercial networking OS	http://www.microsoft.com/windows/professional/
Windows CE	Version for handheld PCs	http://www.microsoft.com/products/prodref/120_ov.htm
Windows NT v4.0	Commercial networking OS	http://www.microsoft.com/products/prodref/428_ov.htm
X Window System	UNIX variant	http://www.rahul.net/kenton/xsites.html
Xinu	Multitasking OS	http://willow.canberra.edu.au/~chrisc/xinu.html

MS-DOS 6.22

MS-DOS 6.22 is the last stand-alone command-line operating system designed by Microsoft for the PC, and is generally considered to be one of the most versatile and reliable DOS-type OSs ever released by Microsoft. There are numerous safety features and enhancements designed to provide the safest possible computing environment of any MS-DOS version. The most notable features are outlined below, and Table 3-2 highlights the system requirements for MS-DOS 6.22 and other popular operating systems.

- *DriveSpace and DoubleGuard*: DriveSpace integrates disk compression into the operating system supporting both hard disks and floppy disks. DriveSpace includes DoubleGuard safety checking, which protects data by verifying data integrity before writing to the disk.
- *MemMaker*: This memory-optimization program is designed to free conventional memory by moving device drivers and memory-resident programs from conventional memory into the upper memory area (UMA).
- *Backup*: This is a utility for backing up your hard disk drive. MS-DOS 6.22 includes a version of Backup for both DOS and Windows 3.1x.
- *Anti-Virus*: This utility can identify and remove more than 1000 different computer viruses. MS-DOS 6.22 includes a version of Anti-Virus for both DOS and Windows 3.1x.
- *Undelete*: The Undelete feature allows you to recover deleted files. MS-DOS 6.22 includes a version of Undelete for both DOS and Windows 3.1x.
- *ScanDisk*: MS-DOS 6.22 includes a more current version of ScanDisk (limited to FAT16) that detects, diagnoses, and repairs disk errors on uncompressed drives and DriveSpace-compressed drives. ScanDisk can repair file system errors (such as cross-linked files and lost clusters) and physical disk errors.
- *MultiConfig*: You can use this utility to define more than one configuration in your CONFIG.SYS file. If your CONFIG.SYS file defines multiple configurations, MS-DOS displays a menu that enables you to choose the configuration you want to use each time you boot the computer.
- *Interactive start*: This feature gives you the ability to bypass startup commands when you turn on your computer by pressing the F8 key. This allows you to choose which CONFIG.SYS and AUTOEXEC.BAT commands MS-DOS should carry out.

TABLE 3-2 COMPARISON OF SYSTEM REQUIREMENTS FOR MAJOR OPERATING SYSTEMS

FEATURE	DOS	WINDOWS 95	WINDOWS 98	WINDOWS NT	WINDOWS 2000*
PC Platform	Any	486/25MHz	486/66MHz	486/25MHz Alpha, MIPS R4X00, PowerPC	Pentium 166
RAM	1024KB	8MB	16MB	16–32MB	64MB
Install drive	1.44MB	CD-ROM	CD-ROM	CD-ROM	CD-ROM
Hard drive	6MB	40–45MB	250MB	110MB	250MB
Display	Mono text	VGA	VGA	VGA	VGA
Mouse	Optional	Required	Required	Required	Required

** These are preliminary requirements that may change prior to the introduction of Windows 2000.*

3

- *Defrag*: MS-DOS 6.22 includes a later version of Defrag that reorganizes files on your hard disk to minimize the time it takes your computer to access them.
- *SmartDrive*: The SmartDrive program included with MS-DOS 6.22 speeds up your computer by using a disk cache that stores information being read from your hard disk or CD-ROM drive. SmartDrive can also be set to cache information being written to your hard disk.
- *Interlink*: This feature enables you to easily transfer files between computers. With Interlink and a cable, you can access information on another computer without using floppy disks to copy data from one computer to another.

PC-DOS 7.0

PC-DOS is IBM's answer to MS-DOS. Early versions of PC-DOS were actually licensed to IBM from Microsoft, but the two giants eventually parted company, and IBM continued the development of PC-DOS under their own banner. Today, PC-DOS 7.0 is roughly equivalent in features and performance to MS-DOS 6.22, including disk compression, antivirus software, and limited networking features. System requirements are about the same, but PC-DOS 7.0 includes PCMCIA support, a DOS file update feature (to keep files synchronized between PCs), and a high-level programming language called REXX.

- *Improved utilities*: There are numerous enhancements to DOS and Windows utilities, including Central Point's Backup utility, Phoenix Technology's PCMCIA support utility, and the RAMBoost Memory Optimizer.
- *Anti-Virus*: PC-DOS 7.0 includes IBM Anti-Virus, which checks for more than 2100 viruses.
- *Stacker*: Stacker 4.0 disk compression delivers an excellent mix of compression and performance.
- *File update*: A new PC-DOS file update feature automatically synchronizes files between your desktop and notebook PCs so they're always up-to-date.
- *REXX*: PC-DOS 7.0 includes a new integrated REXX high-level programming language.

WINDOWS 95

Microsoft released Windows 95 in August 1995 as the major upgrade to Windows 3.1x. Windows 95 was designed to offer superior performance while taking advantage of emerging PC hardware such as plug-and-play, power conservation, PCI bus architecture, and so on. Windows 95 runs most Windows 3.1x and DOS programs, but also supports improved features like a built-in uninstaller, dial-up networking, multitasking, and long file names. Though aging and no longer available preinstalled on new computers, Windows 95 is still the operating system used on a large number of personal computers.

- *Taskbar*: The Taskbar acts as a home base where you can start programs (with the Start button) and keep track of what programs have been launched. You can use the Taskbar to switch between programs as needed for convenient multitasking.
- *Windows Explorer*: The traditional File Manager of earlier Windows versions has been replaced by Windows Explorer for browsing through and managing your files, drives, and network connections.
- *Active right mouse button*: Use the right mouse button to accomplish many common tasks quickly and easily. Click almost anything in Windows 95 with your right mouse button to see a context-sensitive menu of options.
- *Long file names*: Windows 95 supports long file names (up to 250 characters) to make your files and folders easier to organize and find. File names can now have sensible titles.

- *Shortcuts*: You can create links for easy access to important files, folders, drives, programs, or Web sites.
- *Multitasking*: Windows 95 offers improved multitasking capabilities that truly allow the system to handle multiple tasks simultaneously without system interruptions.
- *Plug-and-play*: This feature allows you to insert the card for a hardware device into your computer, and Windows automatically recognizes and sets up the hardware for you.
- *Dial-up networking*: This feature allows easy access to online resources (such as the Internet) and supports communication between connected PCs.

OS/2 WARP 4.X

OS/2 Warp has long been IBM's premier OS. Originally codeveloped with Microsoft, OS/2 development continued in-house after IBM and Microsoft ceased their cooperative ventures. OS/2 is a GUI-based operating system capable of running most Windows and DOS software, as well as native OS/2 applications in a true multitasking environment. OS/2 Warp 4.x focuses on network operations and connectivity—including built-in Internet applications—and offers an advantage over competing operating systems with its use of voice input controls. In spite of these advantages, OS/2 is noted for a surprising lack of hardware support. For example, it can be surprisingly difficult to find suitable OS/2 drivers for devices such as CD-ROM drives and sound boards.

- *Software compatibility*: OS/2 runs DOS and most Windows 3.1x applications, along with native OS/2 and Java applications. OS/2 also supports TrueType, OpenGL, OpenDOC, Open32, and plug-and-play.
- *Connectivity*: OS/2 is particularly noted for its strong network connectivity.
- *Reliability*: A true multitasking environment is well suited to critical applications, and OS/2 is relatively crash-proof when compared to Windows 95 and NT.
- *Systems management*: OS/2 offers powerful system management features, including DMI (Desktop Management Interface) support.
- *Speech recognition*: OS/2 includes VoiceType for OS/2 Warp speech recognition software.

WINDOWS CE

Windows CE is designed to serve as an operating system for a broad range of communications, entertainment, and mobile-computing devices. It also enables new types of non-PC business and consumer devices that can communicate with each other, share information with Windows-based PCs, and connect to the Internet (for example, wallet PCs, digital information pagers, cellular smart phones, DVD players, and Internet Web phones). The first handheld PC products based on Windows CE began shipping in November 1996. It is important to note that Windows CE is released strictly as an OEM product and cannot be purchased through retail channels.

- *Companion applications*: The Windows CE operating system supports Windows CE–based companion applications that share or synchronize information with their counterparts for Windows.
- *Internet Explorer*: Windows CE includes a version of Internet Explorer that offers built-in Web access for many types of communications, entertainment, and mobile-computing devices.
- *Windows development environment*: The Windows CE development environment supports a comprehensive and expandable subset of Win32 APIs, and uses familiar off-the-shelf development tools. The hope is that this will ensure a strong aftermarket for Windows CE applications.

- *Communication with Windows-based PCs*: Windows CE can seamlessly synchronize, communicate, and exchange information with Windows-based PCs.

WINDOWS NT (WORKSTATION)

Windows NT represents Microsoft's emphasis on business communication and networking. While the look and feel of Windows NT may seem quite similar to Windows 95, NT incorporates a powerful suite of networking and Internet-related features backed up by detailed security, cryptography, and system policies configurations. Windows NT also abandons DOS-mode support. There is no doubt that Windows NT represents one of the most complex and versatile operating systems now in service for business and networking environments.

- *Management and control*: Windows NT includes remote management and troubleshooting tools, and allows administrators to implement policies and standards for systemwide desktop configurations.
- *Windows NT Explorer*: This is the Windows NT tool for browsing and managing files, drives, and network connections. It displays your computer's contents as a hierarchy, or tree, allowing you to see the contents of each drive, folder, and network connection.
- *Task Manager*: An integrated tool for managing applications and tasks, the Task Manager maintains detailed information on each application and process running on the desktop. It also provides an effective way to terminate applications and processes that are not responding.
- *Internet Explorer*: Windows NT Workstation comes with Internet Explorer, which gives you full support to explore the Internet.
- *Peer Web Services (PWS)*: This feature enables easy publication of personal Web pages, and lets systems share that Web information over intranets. It's also ideal for developing, testing, and staging Web applications and content.
- *Client support for PPTP*: Point-to-Point Tunneling Protocol provides a secure path for using public data networks (such as the Internet) to create virtual private networks. PPTP allows you to safely transmit confidential communications over the Internet.
- *WINS and DNS integration*: Windows NT takes advantage of the integration between Windows Internet Name Service (WINS) and Domain Name System (DNS) to provide a form of dynamic DNS that makes it easier to connect to network resources.
- *Client support for NDS*: Windows NT Workstation includes an improved version of Client Services for NetWare that supports Novell NetWare Directory Services (NDS). This enables users to log on to Novell NetWare 4.x servers running DNS to access files and print resources.
- *Dial-up networking multilink channel aggregation*: Dial-up networking now provides channel aggregation that enables users to combine all available dial-up lines to achieve higher transfer speeds. For example, you can combine two or more PPP ISDN B channels to achieve speeds of up to 128KB.
- *Windows messaging client*: This is a universal e-mail inbox that you can use with many different e-mail systems. It includes full Messaging API (MAPI) 1.0 support. You can send, receive, organize, and store e-mail and file system objects.
- *System policies and user profiles*: System policies are used to provide a standardized, controlled desktop environment for users. User profiles contain all user-definable settings and can be stored on a Windows NT Server, so users can receive the same desktop regardless of their location.
- *Setup Manager*: This Windows NT utility assists administrators in creating installation scripts and reduces the time and effort of deploying Windows NT.

- *Dial-up networking*: Improved dial-up networking provides the ability to easily and automatically dial-up on demand.
- *Hardware profiles*: Windows NT hardware profiles allow you to have different computer settings depending on the environment in which a computer is being used, and they make it easier to use computers in different configurations (such as docked and undocked laptop configurations).
- *Multimedia APIs*: Windows NT supports the multimedia APIs found in Windows 95: DirectDraw, DirectInput, DirectPlay, and DirectSound. Supporting these APIs allows developers to create games and other applications for both platforms simultaneously.
- *Telephony APIs*: Telephony API (TAPI) integrates telephones and PCs. Using the TAPI interface, communications applications can ask for access to a modem or telephone device, allowing them to be shared.
- *Cryptography APIs*: Windows NT includes a set of encryption APIs that allows developers to easily create applications that work securely over nonsecure networks (such as the Internet).
- *Distributed Component Object Model (DCOM)*: Windows NT provides the infrastructure that allows DCOM applications (also known as *Network OLE*) to communicate across networks without needing to redevelop applications.

WINDOWS 98

With the many new hardware standards and features being developed for the PC, Windows 95 became increasingly hard-pressed to make the fullest use of system resources. Windows 98 (previously code-named "Memphis") builds on Windows 95 by adding a rich suite of refinements and improvements to a full 32-bit operating system. New wizards, utilities, and resources work proactively to keep systems running more smoothly. Performance is faster for many common tasks such as application loading, system startup, and shutdown. Full integration with the Internet's World Wide Web aids online work and system versatility. After numerous delays, Windows 98 was finally released in June 1998, and an upgrade containing a year's worth of learning and improvements named "Windows 98 Second Edition" (or "Windows 98 SE") was released in September 1999. Microsoft is currently working on another upgrade in a project code-named "Millennium." This should be the last release of a Microsoft operating system based on the Windows 98 kernel. The following notes outline some of the improved and added features in Windows 98.

- *Disk Defragmenter Optimization wizard*: This new wizard uses the process of disk defragmentation to increase the speed with which your most frequently used applications run.
- *System Information tool*: This utility provides extensive information on the system hardware and software environment. Many of the new troubleshooting, repair, and report utilities are available from the System Information utility through the Tools menu.
- *System Configuration utility*: This utility allows for the fine-tuning of the Windows 98 startup and shutdown. Individual items in AUTOEXEC.BAT, CONFIG.SYS, SYSTEM.INI, WIN.INI, and the Startup folder can be enabled or disabled to troubleshoot conflicts or problems. It replaces and vastly improves on Windows 95 Sysedit.
- *Windows 98 Report tool*: Available under Tools in the System Information utility, this program allows you to submit a problem report to Microsoft. It automatically includes the information about your system that the Microsoft technicians need to examine the problem.
- *Windows System Update*: This feature helps you ensure that you're using the latest drivers and file systems available. The new Web-based service scans your system to determine what hardware and software you have installed, then compares that information to a back-end database to determine

whether there are newer drivers or system files available. If there are newer drivers or system files, the service can automatically install the drivers.

- *System File Checker*: This utility provides an easy way to verify that the Windows 98 system files (*.dll, *.com, *.vxd, *.drv, *.ocx, *.inf, *.hlp, etc.) have not been modified or corrupted. The utility also provides an easy mechanism for restoring the original versions of system files that have changed.
- *System Troubleshooter*: This utility automates the routine troubleshooting steps used by support personnel and users when diagnosing issues with the Windows configuration. The troubleshooters are designed to address specific areas and devices. You can find the troubleshooters listed under the Help utility.
- *Dr. Watson*: Windows 98 includes an enhanced version of the Dr. Watson utility. When a software fault occurs (such as a general protection fault or system hang), Dr. Watson will intercept it and indicate what software failed (and why). Dr. Watson also collects detailed information about the state of your system at the time the fault occurred. A Log file is created and can be used by a technician to troubleshoot the problem. Dr. Watson does not run by default; it must be started manually or from a shortcut placed in the Startup folder.
- *Backup*: A new backup applet supports SCSI tape devices and makes backing up your data easier and more versatile.
- *Faster shutdown*: The time it takes to shut down the system has been dramatically reduced in Windows 98.
- *Broadcast architecture*: With a TV tuner board installed, Windows 98 allows a PC to receive and display television and other data distributed over the broadcast networks, including enhanced television programs (which combine standard television with HTML information related to the programs).
- *Support for new hardware*: Windows 98 provides support for an array of innovations that have occurred in computer hardware over the last few years. Some of the major hardware standards supported by Windows 98 include Universal Serial Bus (USB), IEEE 1394, Accelerated Graphics Port (AGP), Advanced Configuration and Power Interface (ACPI), and Digital Video Disc (DVD).
- *Display configuration enhancements*: Display setting enhancements provide support for dynamically changing screen resolution and color depth. Adapter refresh rates can also be set with most newer display driver chipsets.
- *Windows Media Player*: Windows 98 supports a new media-streaming architecture called ActiveMovie that delivers high-quality video playback of popular media types including MPEG audio, WAV audio, MPEG video, AVI video, and Apple QuickTime video. The Media Player supports many popular audio, video, and combined media file formats. Updated Media Players are available for download from Microsoft.
- *Support for Intel MMX processors*: Windows 98 provides support for software that uses the Pentium Multimedia Extensions (MMX) for fast audio and video support on the next generation of Pentium processor.
- *FAT32*: This improved version of the FAT file system allows disks over two gigabytes to be formatted as a single drive. FAT32 also uses smaller clusters than FAT drives, resulting in a more efficient use of space on large disks.
- *Power management improvements*: Windows 98 includes support for the Advanced Configuration and Power Interface (ACPI), and support for the Advanced Power Management (APM) 1.2 extensions, including disk spindown, PCMCIA modem power down, and resume on ring.

- *Multiple display support*: This feature allows you to use multiple monitors and/or multiple graphics adapters on a single PC.
- *Remote Access Server*: Windows 98 includes all of the components necessary to enable your desktop to act as a dial-up server. This allows dial-up clients to remotely connect to a Windows 98 machine for local resource access.
- *PCMCIA enhancements*: There have been several enhancements to Windows 98 for PCMCIA support, including support for PC Card32 (CardBus) for implementing high-bandwidth applications such as video capture and 100Mbps networking. There is also support for PC Cards that operate at 3.3 volts and for multifunction PC Cards (such as LAN and modem, or SCSI and sound) to operate on a single physical PC Card.
- *Support for Infrared Data Association (IrDA) 3.0*: Windows 98 supports IrDA for wireless connectivity, which means users can easily connect to peripheral devices or other PCs without using connecting cables. Infrared-equipped laptop or desktop computers have the capability of networking, transferring files, and printing wirelessly with other IrDA-compatible infrared devices.
- *Dial-up networking improvements*: The dial-up networking included with Windows 98 has been updated to support features like dial-up scripting and support for multilink channel aggregation, which enables users to combine all available dial-up lines to achieve higher transfer speeds.
- *Support for PPTP*: The Point-to-Point Tunneling Protocol provides a way to use public data networks (such as the Internet) to create virtual private networks connecting client PCs with servers. PPTP offers protocol encapsulation to support multiple protocols via TCP/IP connections and data encryption for privacy, making it safer to send information over nonsecure networks.
- *Internet connection sharing (for Windows 98 SE)*: This feature enables you to configure your home computer network to share a single connection to the Internet.
- *Distributed Component Object Model (DCOM)*: Windows 98 (and Windows NT 4.0) provides the infrastructure that allows DCOM applications (the technology formally known as *Network OLE*) to communicate across networks without needing to redevelop applications.
- *Support for NetWare Directory Services (NDS)*: Windows 98 includes Client Services for NetWare that support Novell NetWare Directory Services (NDS). This enables Windows 98 users to log on to Novell NetWare 4.x servers running NDS to access files and print resources.

WINDOWS 2000

Released in February 2000, Windows 2000 is the successor to Windows NT and is intended for high-end business workstations and servers. Windows 2000 is a true 32-bit operating system (no DOS support) and also contains code to support 64-bit operations. Windows 2000 is divided into four versions targeted for different workplace requirements. Windows 2000 Professional is intended for desktop or workstation use and replaces Windows NT Workstation in the Microsoft product line. Windows 2000 Server Standard Edition supersedes NT Server, intended for use in general-purpose network server environments found in small-to-medium businesses. Windows 2000 Advanced Server is intended for use in mission-critical environments of any medium-to-large business, including Internet Service Providers (ISPs). These last two versions replace Windows NT Server and Windows NT Server-Enterprise Edition. A third (even more powerful) server version named Windows 2000 Datacenter Server released in the middle of the year.

The publicized goal of Microsoft is eventually to integrate the personal (Windows 98) and business (Windows 2000) versions of Windows into a single product line (code-named "Neptune"), with every version using the same basic operating system files. Windows 98, including Millenium Edition and any other improvements, may be the last Windows operating system able to run 16-bit and DOS programs.

Windows 2000 Professional includes all the features of Windows NT Workstation with some additions and improvements. The added features are meant to combine the ease-of-use of Windows 98 with the stability, speed, and security of Windows NT.

- *Active Directory*: This is the integral directory service within Windows 2000. It improves manageability, enables security, and extends the compatibility between Windows 2000 and other operating systems.
- *Group Policy*: This feature allows an administrator to define and control the state of computers and/or users in an organization. The effect of Group Policy may be adjusted using memberships in security groups.
- *Intellimirror desktop management*: This feature allows users to work at any station on a network and maintain their personal desktop settings, application data, and documents. Intellimirror gives administrators the ability to automatically distribute software (including remote operating system installation). Administrators can also remotely control desktop configuration and maintenance.
- *Personalized Start menu*: Windows 2000 tracks programs and files launched from Start | Programs. After the first six sessions, it alters the Programs menu to show just the most used items. The other entries are collapsed and available by clicking on the double arrows displayed. Windows 2000 continues to monitor file use and make adjustments to the Start | Programs menu.
- *Index Server*: This utility runs in the background and creates an index of the contents of the local hard drive or files on a network (if connected). It includes the ability to select what directories and file properties to index. Index Server can operate locally or across a network to improve speed and accuracy, and search results can be ranked according to relevance.
- *Windows Installer*: The Installer allows for easier program installation and reduces problems caused by replacing shared DLL files with different versions during the install process. Windows Installer allows applications to examine existing DLL files in order to keep common files already installed. It also allows for adding program components at a later time and can be used to repair damaged applications. The Windows Installer needs cooperative applications, so software publishers must write programs with MSI scripts that take advantage of Installer features.
- *Network Connection wizard*: A Network Connections folder in My Computer replaces the Network Settings item in the NT 4.0 Control Panel. Clicking on the Make New Connection icon opens Windows 2000's Network Connection wizard. The wizard guides you through fewer steps than were required in NT 4.0 to create a new connection. When used with Windows 2000 Server's Active Directory, the operating system also adds a series of new management functions designed to simplify running a network.
- *Open/Save/Save As dialogs*: Windows 2000 provides an Outlook-like directory tree displayed to the left of the Open or Save dialog box allowing for quick and easy navigation to different folders on the hard drive.
- *Windows 2000 Explorer*: The Explorer in Windows 2000 includes all the individual customizable features of Windows 98 Explorer. Added improvements include enabling Thumbnail View on all files instead of on a folder-by-folder basis, customized Windows Explorer toolbars, and Folder Options in Control Panel with a new streamlined Folder Options dialog.

- *SMP support*: Symmetric Multiprocessing allows for multiple processors in the different versions of Windows 2000. The Professional and Standard Server editions support two processors, while the most advanced server edition can support up to eight processors.
- *Plug-and-play*: Windows 2000 is compatible with current plug-and-play standards. This includes support for the latest busses (such as USB, IEEE 1394 or "FireWire," and AGP) and other devices, including DVD players, scanners, and digital cameras.
- *Hardware wizard*: The Hardware wizard gives you a single, simple interface for dealing with many hardware issues. The options include the ability to add, configure, remove, troubleshoot, and upgrade the peripherals that you use.
- *64-bit ready*: Microsoft has enabled the Windows 2000 code base to be 64-bit ready and is working toward delivering a full-featured 64-bit operating system in 2000 (this will be fully compatible with existing 32-bit applications). The goal is to take full advantage of Intel's 64-bit "Merced" processor when it is released.
- *Internet Explorer 5.x*: The latest Microsoft browser is fully integrated in the Windows 2000 Professional edition.

A Closer Look at MS-DOS

The operating system provides I/O resources to application programs, as well as an environment that can be used to execute programs or interact with the operating system. To accomplish these two tasks, MS-DOS uses three files: IO.SYS, MSDOS.SYS, and COMMAND.COM. Note that the myriad of other files shipped with MS-DOS are technically not part of the operating system itself, but are instead a library of utilities intended to help you optimize and maintain the system. The following sections examine each of the three core MS-DOS files in more detail. Keep in mind that loading and running an operating system properly relies on adequate processing, memory, and disk system resources.

IO.SYS

The IO.SYS file provides many of the low-level routines (or *drivers*) that interact with BIOS. Some versions of IO.SYS are customized by original equipment manufacturers (OEMs) to supplement the particular BIOS for their system. However, OS customization is rare today because it leads to system incompatibilities. In addition to low-level drivers, IO.SYS contains a system initialization routine. The entire contents of the file (except for the system initialization routine) are kept in low memory throughout system operation. IO.SYS is a file assigned with a hidden-file attribute, so you will not see the file when searching a bootable disk with an ordinary DIR command. Although Microsoft uses the file name IO.SYS, other OS makers may use a different name. For example, the corresponding file name in IBM's PC-DOS is IBMBIO.COM.

In order for a disk (floppy or hard disk) to be bootable under MS-DOS 3.x or 4.x, IO.SYS must be the first file in the disk directory, and it must occupy at least the first available cluster on the disk (usually cluster 2). This is the disk's *OS volume boot sector*. Of course, subsequent clusters containing IO.SYS can be placed anywhere in the disk, just like any other ordinary file. MS-DOS 5.x and later versions eliminate this requirement and allow IO.SYS to be placed in any root directory location anywhere on the disk. When disk access begins during the boot process, the bootable drive's boot sector is read, which loads IO.SYS into memory and gives it control of the system. Once IO.SYS is running, the boot process can continue, as you will learn later in this chapter. If this file is missing or corrupt, you will see some type of boot failure message, or the system may lock up.

MSDOS.SYS

The core of MS-DOS versions up through 6.22 is the MSDOS.SYS file, which is listed second in the boot disk's directory and is the second file to be loaded during the boot process. It contains the routines that handle OS disk and file access. Like IO.SYS, the MSDOS.SYS file is loaded into low memory where it resides throughout the system's operation. If the file is missing or corrupt, you will see some kind of boot failure message, or the system may lock up.

IO.SYS AND MSDOS.SYS VARIATIONS UNDER WINDOWS 95/98

With the introduction of Windows 95 (and continued with Windows 98), the classical DOS files have been redesigned to streamline the boot process. Windows 95/98 places all of the functions found in IO.SYS and MSDOS.SYS into a single hidden file called IO.SYS (this file may be renamed WINBOOT.SYS if you start the PC with a previous OS). Most of the options formerly set with entries in the CONFIG.SYS file are now incorporated into Windows 95/98's IO.SYS. The settings that are selected with IO.SYS can be superseded by entries in a CONFIG.SYS file, but the defaults used with IO.SYS are listed below:

dos=high	DOS components are automatically loaded into high memory.
himem.sys	The real-mode memory manager is loaded.
ifshlp.sys	The file system enhancement utility is loaded.
setver.exe	The MS-DOS version utility is loaded.
files=60	File handle buffers are allocated.
lastdrive=z	This specifies the last drive letter available for assignment.
buffers=30	File buffers are allocated.
stacks=9,256	Stack frames are created.
shell=command.com	This sets the desired command processor.
fcbs=4	This sets the maximum number of file control blocks.

Few of the default settings in IO.SYS are really needed by Windows 95/98, but they are included to provide a level of backward compatibility with preexisting system configurations.

The MSDOS.SYS file has also been dramatically altered under Windows 95/98. Whereas older versions of MS-DOS relied on MSDOS.SYS for disk and file code, all of that functionality has been worked into IO.SYS. MSDOS.SYS under Windows 95/98 is now little more than a text INI file that is used to configure the boot properties of Windows and list important paths to key Windows files (including the registry).

ADJUSTING MSDOS.SYS UNDER MS-DOS 7.X

Windows 95 and Windows 98 essentially eliminate the function of the MSDOS.SYS file—replacing it instead with a text file used to tailor the startup process. Normally, there is little need to access the MSDOS.SYS file, but you may be faced with the need to adjust the Windows 95/98 boot process. This part of the chapter takes you inside the MSDOS.SYS file for MS-DOS 7.x (Windows 9x) and illustrates the various options you can use to enhance the Windows 9x platform. A typical example of an MSDOS.SYS file is shown in Figure 3-2.

```
[Paths]
WinDir=C:\WINDOWS
WinBootDir=C:\WINDOWS
HostWinBootDrv=C

[Options]
BootMulti=1
BootGUI=1
;
;The following lines are required for compatibility with other programs.
;Do not remove them (MSDOS.SYS needs to be >1024 bytes).
;xxxxxxxxxxxxxxxxxxxxxxxxxxxxxxxxxxxxxxxxxxxxxxxxxxxxxxxxxxxxxxxxxxxxxa
;xxxxxxxxxxxxxxxxxxxxxxxxxxxxxxxxxxxxxxxxxxxxxxxxxxxxxxxxxxxxxxxxxxxxxb
;xxxxxxxxxxxxxxxxxxxxxxxxxxxxxxxxxxxxxxxxxxxxxxxxxxxxxxxxxxxxxxxxxxxxxc
;xxxxxxxxxxxxxxxxxxxxxxxxxxxxxxxxxxxxxxxxxxxxxxxxxxxxxxxxxxxxxxxxxxxxxd
;xxxxxxxxxxxxxxxxxxxxxxxxxxxxxxxxxxxxxxxxxxxxxxxxxxxxxxxxxxxxxxxxxxxxxe
;xxxxxxxxxxxxxxxxxxxxxxxxxxxxxxxxxxxxxxxxxxxxxxxxxxxxxxxxxxxxxxxxxxxxxf
;xxxxxxxxxxxxxxxxxxxxxxxxxxxxxxxxxxxxxxxxxxxxxxxxxxxxxxxxxxxxxxxxxxxxxg
;xxxxxxxxxxxxxxxxxxxxxxxxxxxxxxxxxxxxxxxxxxxxxxxxxxxxxxxxxxxxxxxxxxxxxh
;xxxxxxxxxxxxxxxxxxxxxxxxxxxxxxxxxxxxxxxxxxxxxxxxxxxxxxxxxxxxxxxxxxxxxi
;xxxxxxxxxxxxxxxxxxxxxxxxxxxxxxxxxxxxxxxxxxxxxxxxxxxxxxxxxxxxxxxxxxxxxj
;xxxxxxxxxxxxxxxxxxxxxxxxxxxxxxxxxxxxxxxxxxxxxxxxxxxxxxxxxxxxxxxxxxxxxk
;xxxxxxxxxxxxxxxxxxxxxxxxxxxxxxxxxxxxxxxxxxxxxxxxxxxxxxxxxxxxxxxxxxxxxl
;xxxxxxxxxxxxxxxxxxxxxxxxxxxxxxxxxxxxxxxxxxxxxxxxxxxxxxxxxxxxxxxxxxxxxm
;xxxxxxxxxxxxxxxxxxxxxxxxxxxxxxxxxxxxxxxxxxxxxxxxxxxxxxxxxxxxxxxxxxxxxn
;xxxxxxxxxxxxxxxxxxxxxxxxxxxxxxxxxxxxxxxxxxxxxxxxxxxxxxxxxxxxxxxxxxxxxo
;xxxxxxxxxxxxxxxxxxxxxxxxxxxxxxxxxxxxxxxxxxxxxxxxxxxxxxxxxxxxxxxxxxxxxp
;xxxxxxxxxxxxxxxxxxxxxxxxxxxxxxxxxxxxxxxxxxxxxxxxxxxxxxxxxxxxxxxxxxxxxq
;xxxxxxxxxxxxxxxxxxxxxxxxxxxxxxxxxxxxxxxxxxxxxxxxxxxxxxxxxxxxxxxxxxxxxr
;xxxxxxxxxxxxxxxxxxxxxxxxxxxxxxxxxxxxxxxxxxxxxxxxxxxxxxxxxxxxxxxxxxxxxs
Network=1
```

FIGURE 3-2 A look inside the MSDOS.SYS file

3

> Notice that MSDOS.SYS must be longer than 1024 bytes in length. Otherwise, Windows 95/98 will fail to load. Do not alter or remove the *X* lines in MSDOS.SYS.

There are two main sections to the MSDOS.SYS file: the [Paths] section, and the [Options] section. The paths define the directory paths to major Windows file areas, while the options allow you to configure many of the available attributes used to boot a Windows 95/98 system. The paths and options are listed below:

[PATHS]	
WinDir=	Indicates the location of the Windows 9x directory specified during setup.
WinBootDir=	Indicates the location of the necessary startup files. The default is the directory specified during the setup process (C :\WINDOWS).
HostWinBootDrv=c	Indicates the location of the boot drive root directory.
[OPTIONS]	
BootMulti=	Enables dual-boot capabilities. The default is 0. Setting this value to 1 allows the user to start MS-DOS by pressing F4, or by pressing F8 to use the Windows Startup menu.
BootGUI=	Enables automatic graphical startup into Windows 9x. The default is 1.

[OPTIONS]	
BootMenu=	Enables automatic display of the Windows 9x Startup menu (the user must press F8 in Windows 95, or press and hold the CTRL key in Windows 98 to see the menu). The default is 0. Setting this value to 1 eliminates the need to press F8 to see the menu.
BootKeys=	Enables the startup option keys (F5, F6, and F8). The default is 1.
BootWin=	Enables Windows 9x as the default operating system. Setting this value to 0 disables Windows 9x as the default (useful only with MS-DOS version 5 or 6.x on the computer). The default is 1.
BootDelay=n	Sets the initial startup delay to *n* seconds (default is 2). A BootKeys=0 entry disables the delay. The only purpose of the delay is to give the user sufficient time to press F8 after the "Starting Windows" message appears.
BootFailSafe=	Enables Safe mode for system startup. The default is 0.
BootMenuDefault=#	Sets the default menu item on the Windows Startup menu; the default is 3 for a computer with no networking components and 4 for a networked computer.
BootMenuDelay=#	Sets the number of seconds to display the Windows Startup menu before running the default menu item. The default is 30 seconds.
Logo=	Enables display of the Windows 9x logo. The default is 1. Setting this value to 0 also avoids hooking a variety of interrupts that can create incompatibilities with certain memory managers from other vendors.
BootWarn=	Enables the Safe mode startup warning. The default is 1.
DblSpace=	Enables automatic loading of DBLSPACE.BIN. The default is 1.
DrvSpace=	Enables automatic loading of DRVSPACE.BIN. The default is 1.
DoubleBuffer=	Enables loading of a double-buffering driver for a SCSI controller. The default is 0. Setting this value to 1 enables double-buffering (if required by the SCSI controller).
LoadTop=	Enables the loading of COMMAND.COM or DRVSPACE.BIN at the top of 640KB memory. The default is 1. Set this value to 0 with Novell NetWare or any software that makes assumptions about what is used in specific memory areas.
Network=	Enables "Safe Mode with Networking" as a menu option. The default is 1 for computers with networking installed. This value should be 0 if network software components are not installed.

If Windows 95 is installed in its own directory, the earlier version of MS-DOS is preserved on the hard disk. If you set BootMulti=1 in MSDOS.SYS, you can start the earlier version of MS-DOS by pressing F4 when starting Windows 95. Windows 98 offers the same feature.

COMMAND.COM

The COMMAND.COM file serves as the MS-DOS shell and command processor. This is the program that you are interacting with at the command-line prompt. COMMAND.COM is the third file loaded when a PC boots, and it is stored in low memory along with IO.SYS and MSDOS.SYS. The number of commands that you have available depends on the version of MS-DOS in use. MS-DOS uses two types of commands in normal operation: resident and transient.

Resident commands (also called *internal commands*) are procedures that are coded directly into COMMAND.COM. As a result, resident commands execute almost immediately when called from the command line. CLS and DIR are two typical resident commands. *Transient commands* (also called *external commands*) represent a broader and more powerful group of commands. However, transient commands are not loaded with COMMAND.COM. Instead, the commands are available as small COM or EXE utility files in the DOS directory (such as DEBUG and EMM386). Transient commands must be loaded from the disk and executed each time they are needed. By pulling out complex commands as separate utilities, the size of COMMAND.COM can be kept relatively small. The transient (external) commands for MS-DOS are shown in Table 3-3, and the resident (internal) commands for MS-DOS are listed in Table 3-4.

TABLE 3-3 INDEX OF EXTERNAL/TRANSIENT MS-DOS COMMANDS

COMMAND	2.0	2.1	3.0 3.1	3.2	3.3	4.0	5.0	6.0	6.2	6.21 6.22	7.0 7.1
APPEND					*	*	*	*	*	*	
ASSIGN	*	*	*	*	*	*	*				
ATTRIB			*	*	*	*	*	*	*	*	*
BACKUP	*	*	*	*	*	*	*				
BASIC	*	*	*	*							
BASICA	*	*	*	*							
CHKDSK	*	*	*	*	*	*	*	*	*	*	*
CHOICE								*	*	*	*
COMMAND	*	*	*	*	*	*	*	*	*	*	*
COMP	*	*	*	*	*	*					
DBLSPACE								*	*		
DEBUG	*	*	*	*	*	*	*	*	*	*	*
DEFRAG								*	*	*	*
DELTREE								*	*	*	*
DISKCOMP	*	*	*	*	*	*	*	*	*	*	
DISKCOPY	*	*	*	*	*	*	*	*	*	*	*
DOSKEY							*	*	*	*	*
DOSSHELL						*	*	*			
DOSSWAP							*	*			
DRVSPACE										*	*
EDIT							*	*	*	*	*
EDLIN	*	*	*	*	*	*	*				
EMM386							*	*	*	*	*
EXE2BIN		*	*	*	*	*	*				
EXPAND							*	*	*	*	*
FASTHELP								*	*	*	
FASTOPEN					*	*	*	*	*	*	
FC					*	*	*	*	*	*	*
FDISK	*	*	*	*	*	*	*	*	*	*	*
FILESYS						*					
FIND	*	*	*	*	*	*	*	*	*	*	*
FORMAT	*	*	*	*	*	*	*	*	*	*	*
GRAFTABL			*	*	*	*	*				
GRAPHICS	*	*	*	*	*	*	*	*	*	*	
GWBASIC					*	*					

TABLE 3-3 INDEX OF EXTERNAL/TRANSIENT MS-DOS COMMANDS *(CONTINUED)*

COMMAND	2.0	2.1	3.0 3.1	3.2	3.3	4.0	5.0	6.0	6.2	6.21 6.22	7.0 7.1
HELP							*	*	*	*	
IFSFUNC						*					
INTERLNK								*	*	*	
INTERSVR								*	*	*	
JOIN				*	*	*	*				
KEYB					*	*	*	*	*	*	*
KEYBFR			*	*							
KEYBGR			*	*							
KEYBIT			*	*							
KEYBSP			*	*							
KEYBUK			*	*							
LABEL			*	*	*	*	*	*	*	*	*
LINK	*	*	*	*	*	*					
LOADFIX							*	*	*	*	*
MEM						*	*	*	*	*	*
MEMMAKER								*	*	*	
MIRROR							*				
MODE	*	*	*	*	*	*	*	*	*	*	*
MORE	*	*	*	*	*	*	*	*	*	*	*
MOVE								*	*	*	*
MSBACKUP								*	*	*	
MSCDEX								*	*	*	
MSD								*	*	*	
MWAV								*	*	*	
MWAVTSR								*	*	*	
MWBACKUP								*	*	*	
MWUNDEL								*	*	*	
NLSFUNC					*	*	*	*	*	*	*
POWER								*	*	*	
PRINT	*	*	*	*	*	*	*	*	*	*	
QBASIC							*	*	*	*	
RECOVER	*	*	*	*	*	*	*				
REPLACE			*		*	*	*	*	*	*	
RESTORE	*	*	*	*	*	*	*	*	*	*	
SCANDISK									*	*	*
SELECT			*	*	*	*					
SETVER							*	*	*	*	*
SHARE			*	*	*	*	*	*	*	*	
SIZER								*	*	*	

TABLE 3-3 INDEX OF EXTERNAL/TRANSIENT MS-DOS COMMANDS *(CONTINUED)*

COMMAND	2.0	2.1	3.0 3.1	3.2	3.3	4.0	5.0	6.0	6.2	6.21 6.22	7.0 7.1
SMARTDRV								*	*	*	*
SMARTMON								*	*		
SORT	*	*	*	*	*	*	*	*	*	*	*
SUBST				*	*	*	*	*	*	*	*
SYS	*	*	*	*	*	*	*	*	*	*	*
TREE	*	*	*	*	*	*	*	*	*	*	*
UNDELETE							*	*	*	*	
UNFORMAT							*	*	*	*	
VSAFE								*	*	*	
XCOPY					*	*	*	*	*	*	*

TABLE 3-4 INDEX OF INTERNAL/RESIDENT MS-DOS COMMANDS

COMMAND	2.0	2.1	3.0	3.1	3.2	3.3	4.X	5.X	6.X	7.X
CD/CHDIR	*	*	*	*	*	*	*	*	*	*
CHCP							*	*	*	*
CLS	*	*	*	*	*	*	*	*	*	*
COPY	*	*	*	*	*	*	*	*	*	*
CTTY	*	*	*	*	*	*	*	*	*	*
DATE	*	*	*	*	*	*	*	*	*	*
DEL/ERASE	*	*	*	*	*	*	*	*	*	*
DIR	*	*	*	*	*	*	*	*	*	*
EXIT			*	*	*	*	*	*	*	*
EXPAND								*	*	
LOADHIGH/LH								*	*	*
MD/MKDIR	*	*	*	*	*	*	*	*	*	*
PATH	*	*	*	*	*	*	*	*	*	*
PROMPT	*	*	*	*	*	*	*	*	*	*
RD/RMDIR	*	*	*	*	*	*	*	*	*	*
REN/RENAME	*	*	*	*	*	*	*	*	*	*
SET	*	*	*	*	*	*	*	*	*	*
TIME	*	*	*	*	*	*	*	*	*	*
TYPE	*	*	*	*	*	*	*	*	*	*
VER			*	*	*	*	*	*	*	*
VERIFY	*	*	*	*	*	*	*	*	*	*
VOL	*	*	*	*	*	*	*	*	*	*

3

RECOGNIZING AND DEALING WITH OS PROBLEMS

Since the operating system is an integral part of the PC, any problems with using or upgrading the OS can adversely affect system operation. Software does not fail like hardware—once software is loaded and running, it will not eventually break down from heat or physical stress. Unfortunately, software is hardly perfect. Upgrading from one OS to another can upset the system's operation, and bugs in the operating system can result in an unforeseen operation that might totally destroy a system's reliability.

Virtually all versions of operating systems have bugs in them, especially in early releases. In most cases, such bugs are found in the transient commands that are run from the command line rather than in the three core files (IO.SYS, MSDOS.SYS, and COMMAND.COM) Even the latest stand-alone version of MS-DOS (6.22) has endured several incarnations since its initial release as 6.0. As a technician, you should be sensitive to the version of DOS (and Windows) being used by your customer. Whenever the customer complains of trouble using a DOS utility (such as BACKUP or EMM386) or complains of difficulties using particular software under DOS, one of your first steps should be to ensure that the version in use is appropriate. If it has been updated, you should try the new release. Remember that a software fault can manifest itself as a hardware problem—that is, the hardware may malfunction or refuse to respond. Check with the OS maker to find their newest releases and fixes. Microsoft maintains an extensive Web site for the support of their operating systems. Check in regularly to find error reports and upgrades. If your customer is using Windows 98, check the Windows Help file for a troubleshooter that deals with the error or the device that is causing the problem.

Another concern for technicians is dealing with old versions of an OS. Remember that part of the task of an OS is to manage system resources (disk space, memory, etc.). New OS versions such as MS-DOS 5.0 and later do a much better job of disk and memory management than MS-DOS 4.x and earlier. Should you recommend an upgrade to your customer? As a general rule, any MS-DOS version older than 5.0 is worth upgrading to MS-DOS 6.22, especially if your customer is planning to keep or upgrade the PC. If the MS-DOS version is 5.0 or later, the only good reason to upgrade would be to take advantage of advanced utilities such as MemMaker or DoubleSpace, which have been refined and included with MS-DOS 6.22. If the PC hardware will support an upgrade to Windows 95 or Windows 98, it should also be considered as a potential OS upgrade.

The Boot Process

Computer initialization is a *process*, not an event. From the moment power is applied until the system sits idle at the command-line prompt or graphical desktop, the PC boot process is a sequence of predictable steps that verify the system and prepare it for operation. By understanding each step in system initialization, you can develop a real appreciation for the way that hardware and software relate to one another. You also stand a much better chance of identifying and resolving problems when a system fails to boot properly. This part of the chapter provides a step-by-step review of a typical PC boot process.

APPLYING POWER

PC initialization starts when you turn the system on. When all output voltages from the power supply are valid, the supply generates a Power Good (PG) logic signal. It can take between 100ms and 500ms for the supply to generate a PG signal. When the motherboard timer IC receives the PG signal, the timer stops forcing a Reset signal to the CPU. At this point, the CPU starts processing.

THE BOOTSTRAP

The very first operation performed by a CPU is to fetch an instruction from address FFFF:0000h. Since this address is almost at the end of available ROM space, the instruction is almost always a jump command (JMP) followed by the actual BIOS ROM starting address. By making all CPUs start at the same point, the BIOS ROM can then send program control anywhere in the particular ROM (and each ROM *is* usually different). This initial search of address FFFF:0000h and the subsequent redirection of the CPU is traditionally referred to as the *bootstrap* in which the PC "pulls itself up by its bootstraps," or gets itself going. Today, we have shortened the term to *boot* and have broadened its meaning to include the entire initialization process.

CORE TESTS

The core tests are part of the overall power-on self-test (POST) sequence, which is the most important use of a system BIOS during initialization. As you might expect, allowing the system to initialize and run with flaws in the motherboard, memory, or drive systems can have catastrophic consequences for files in memory or on disk. To insure system integrity, a set of hardware-specific self-test routines checks the major motherboard components and identifies the presence of any other specialized BIOS ICs in the system (drive controller BIOS, video BIOS, SCSI BIOS, etc.).

BIOS starts with a test of the motherboard hardware such as the CPU, math coprocessor, timer ICs, direct memory access (DMA) controllers, and interrupt (IRQ) controllers. If an error is detected in this early phase of testing, a series of beeps (or *beep codes*) are produced. By knowing the BIOS manufacturer and the beep code, you can determine the nature of the problem. Chapter 19 deals with beep and error codes in more detail. Beep codes are used because the video system has not been initialized.

Next, BIOS looks for the presence of a video ROM between memory locations C000:0000h through C780:000h. In just about all systems, the search will reveal a video BIOS ROM on a video adapter board plugged into an available expansion slot. If a video BIOS is found, its contents are evaluated with a checksum test. If the test is successful, control is transferred to the video BIOS, which loads and initializes the video adapter. When initialization is complete, you will see a cursor on the screen, and control returns to the system BIOS. When no external video adapter BIOS is located, the system BIOS will provide an initialization routine for the motherboard's video adapter, and a cursor will also appear. Once the video system initializes, you are likely to see a bit of text on the display identifying the system or video BIOS ROM maker and revision level. If the checksum test fails, you will see an error message such as "C000 ROM Error" or "Video ROM Error." Initialization will usually halt right there.

Now that the video system is ready, system BIOS will scan memory from C800:0000h through DF80:0000h in 2KB increments to search for any other ROMs that might be on other adapter cards in the system. If other ROMs are found, their contents are tested and run. As each supplemental ROM is executed, it will show manufacturer and revision ID information. In some cases, a supplemental (or *adapter*) ROM may alter an existing BIOS ROM routine. For example, an Ultra DMA/33 drive controller board with its own on-board ROM will replace the motherboard's older drive routines. When a ROM fails the checksum test, you will see an error message such as "XXXX ROM Error." The XXXX indicates the segment address where the faulty ROM was detected. When a faulty ROM is detected, system initialization will usually halt.

POST

BIOS then checks the memory location at 0000:0472h. This address contains a flag that determines whether the initialization is a cold start (power first applied) or a warm start (reset button or CTRL+ALT+DEL key combination). A value of 1234h at this address indicates a warm start, in which case the POST routine is skipped. If any other value is found at that location, a cold start is assumed, and the full POST routine will be executed.

The full POST checks many of the other higher-level functions on the motherboard, memory, keyboard, video adapter, floppy drive, math coprocessor, printer port, serial port, hard drive, and other subsystems. There are dozens of tests performed by the POST. When an error is encountered, the single-byte POST code is written to I/O port 80h where it may be read by a POST code reader. In other cases, you may see an error message on the display (and system initialization will halt). Keep in mind that POST codes and their meanings will vary slightly between BIOS manufacturers. If the POST completes successfully, the system will respond with a single beep from the speaker. Chapter 19 covers I/O port POST codes.

FINDING THE OS

The system now needs to load an operating system (usually DOS or Windows 9x). The first step here is to have the BIOS search for a DOS volume boot sector (VBS) on the A: drive. If there is no disk in the drive, you will see the drive light illuminate briefly, and then BIOS will search the next drive in the boot order (usually drive C:). If there is a disk in drive A:, BIOS will load sector 1 (head 0 cylinder 0) from the disk's DOS volume boot sector into memory starting at 0000:7C00h. There are a number of potential problems when attempting to load the VBS. Otherwise, the first program in the directory (IO.SYS) will begin to load, followed by MSDOS.SYS.

- If the first byte of the DOS VBS is less than 06h (or if the first byte is greater than or equal to 06h, and the next nine words of the sector contain the same data pattern), you will see an error message similar to "Diskette boot record error."
- If IO.SYS and MSDOS.SYS are not the first two files in the directory (or some other problem is encountered in loading), you'll see an error such as "Non-system disk or disk error."
- If the boot sector on the floppy disk is corrupt and cannot be read (DOS 3.3 or earlier), you'll probably get a "Disk boot failure" message.

If the OS cannot be loaded from any floppy drive, the system will search the first fixed drive (hard drive). Hard drives are a bit more involved than floppy disks. BIOS loads sector 1 (head 0 cylinder 0) from the hard drive's master partition boot sector (called the *master boot sector*, or *MBS*) into memory starting at 0000:7C00h, and the last two bytes of the sector are checked. If the final two bytes of the master partition boot sector are not 55h and AAh, respectively, the boot sector is invalid, and you will see an error message similar to "No boot device available," and system initialization will halt. Other systems may depict the error differently or attempt to load ROM BASIC. If the BIOS attempts to load ROM BASIC, and there is no such feature in the BIOS, you'll see a "ROM BASIC error" message.

Otherwise, the disk will search for and identify any extended partitions (up to 24 total partitions). Once any extended partitions have been identified, the drive's original boot sector will search for a boot indicator byte marking a partition as active and bootable. If none of the partitions are marked as bootable (or if more than one partition is marked bootable), a disk error message will be displayed such as "Invalid partition table." Some older BIOS versions may attempt to load ROM BASIC, but will generate an error message in most cases anyway.

When an active bootable partition is found in the master partition boot sector, the DOS volume boot sector (VBS) from the bootable partition is loaded into memory and tested. If the DOS volume boot sector cannot be read, you will see an error message similar to "Error loading operating system." When the DOS volume boot sector *does* load, the last two bytes are tested for a signature of 55h and AAh, respectively. If these signature bytes are missing, you will see an error message such as "Missing operating system." Under either error condition, system initialization will halt.

After the signature bytes are identified, the DOS volume boot sector (now in memory) is executed as if it were a program. This "program" checks the root directory to ensure that IO.SYS and MSDOS.SYS (or IBMBIO.COM and IBMDOS.COM) are available. In older MS-DOS versions, IO.SYS and MSDOS.SYS have to be the first two directory entries. If the DOS volume boot sector was created with MS-DOS 3.3 or earlier and the two startup files are not the first two files in the directory (or there is an error in loading the files), the system will produce an error code such as "Non-System disk or disk error." If the boot sector is corrupt, you may see a message like "Disk boot failure."

LOADING THE OS

If no problems are detected in the disk's DOS volume boot sector, IO.SYS (or IBMBIO.COM) is loaded and executed. If Windows 95/98 is on the system, IO.SYS may be renamed WINBOOT.SYS, which will be executed instead. IO.SYS contains extensions to BIOS that start low-level device drivers for such things as the keyboard, printer, and block devices. Remember that IO.SYS also contains initialization code that is only needed during system startup. A copy of this initialization code is placed at the top of conventional memory, which takes over initialization. The next step is to load MSDOS.SYS (or IBMDOS.COM), which is loaded such that it overlaps the part of IO.SYS containing the initialization code. MSDOS.SYS (the MS-DOS kernel) is then executed to initialize base device drivers, detect system status, reset the disk system, initialize devices such as the printer and serial port, and set up system default parameters. The MS-DOS essentials are now loaded, and control returns to the IO.SYS/WINBOOT.SYS initialization code in memory.

> Remember that for Windows 95/98 systems, IO.SYS (or WINBOOT.SYS) combines the functions of IO.SYS and MSDOS.SYS.

ESTABLISHING THE ENVIRONMENT

If a CONFIG.SYS file is present, it is opened and read by IO.SYS/WINBOOT.SYS. The DEVICE statements are processed first in the order they appear, and then INSTALL statements are processed in the order they appear. A SHELL statement is handled next. If no SHELL statement is present, the COMMAND.COM processor is loaded. When COMMAND.COM is loaded, it overwrites the initialization code left over from IO.SYS (which is now no longer needed). Under Windows 9x, COMMAND.COM is loaded only if an AUTOEXEC.BAT file is present in order to process the AUTOEXEC.BAT statements. Finally, all other statements in CONFIG.SYS are processed, and WINBOOT.SYS also looks for the SYSTEM.DAT registry file.

When an AUTOEXEC.BAT file is present, COMMAND.COM (which now has control of the system) will load and execute the batch file. After batch file processing is complete, the familiar DOS prompt will appear. If there is no AUTOEXEC.BAT in the root directory, COMMAND.COM will request the current DATE and TIME, then show the DOS prompt. You may now launch applications or use any available OS commands. AUTOEXEC.BAT may also call a shell (such as Windows 3.1x) or start an application. Under Windows 95/98, IO.SYS/WINBOOT.SYS automatically loads HIMEM.SYS, IFSHLP.SYS, and SETVER.EXE, then loads the WIN.COM kernel to officially start Windows 9x.

CREATING A DOS BOOT DISK

The most persistent problem with PC troubleshooting is that it can be difficult to boot a system successfully, especially if there are hard drive problems. This makes it particularly important to have a bootable floppy disk on hand. There are two means of creating a boot disk: automatically through an existing Windows 9x platform, or manually through a DOS 6.22 platform. In either case, you're going to need access to a running PC with an operating system similar to the version you plan to install on the new PC.

Windows 95/98

Windows 95 and Windows 98 come with an automatic Startup Disk maker. If you have access to a Windows 9x system, use the following procedure to create a DOS 7.x startup disk:

1. Label a blank disk and insert it into your floppy drive.
2. Click on Start | Settings | Control Panel.
3. Double-click on the Add/Remove Programs icon.
4. Select the Startup Disk tab.
5. Click on Create Disk.
6. The utility will remind you to insert a disk, then prepare the disk automatically. When the preparation is complete, test the disk.

The preparation process takes several minutes and will copy the following files to your disk; ATTRIB, CHKDSK, COMMAND, DEBUG, DRVSPACE.BIN, EDIT, FDISK, FORMAT, REGEDIT, SCANDISK, SYS, and UNINSTAL. All of these files are DOS 7.x–based files, so you can run them from the A: prompt.

The Startup disk made with the Windows 98 Startup Disk utility is much more powerful and useful. The major difference between the disk made by Windows 95 and the one made by Windows 98 is that the Windows 98 disk will include the generic drivers for your CD-ROM. If you want a Windows 95 Startup disk with CD-ROM support, you will have to add the real mode (DOS) drivers yourself. In addition, Windows 98 compresses a lot of utilities into a CAB file, EBD.CAB. Windows 98 creates a Ramdrive in memory and then expands the files in EBD.CAB to the Ramdrive. Without the compressed file, there would not be enough room on a single floppy disk to contain all the startup files, drivers, and utilities.

> The Windows 95 FDISK utility has been reported to have a bug that can cause problems when creating more than one partition on the same drive. Later releases of Windows 95 (such as OSR 2) claim to have corrected this issue, but if you encounter problems with FDISK, use the DOS 6.22 version.

DOS 6.22

If you don't have access to a system with Windows 95/98 already, you'll need to make a boot disk manually, using DOS 6.22 utilities. Create a bootable disk by using the SYS feature, as shown here:

```
C:\DOS\> SYS A:
```

Or use the FORMAT command to make a bootable disk, like this:

```
C:\DOS\> FORMAT A: /S
```

Once the disk is bootable, copy the following DOS utilities (usually from the DOS directory): FDISK, FORMAT, SYS, MEM, DEFRAG, SCANDISK, EDIT, HIMEM, EMM386, and EDIT. You may not need all of these utilities, but it can be handy to have them on hand in case you need to check a disk or memory.

Windows 9x Maintenance Tips

Troubleshooting individual devices and subsystems is covered in their respective chapters, but it is useful to note some general setup and maintenance issues with Windows 9x here. A careful installation followed by a routine maintenance schedule will prevent a lot of problems for you and your customers.

The SETUP.TXT file in the \Win9x folder on your Windows 9x CD contains an extensive list of setup error messages, problems, and resolutions. Most problems occur when upgrading an existing system that has numerous peripherals and programs already installed. This increases the chances for conflicts, setup errors, and failures. Upgrading or installing a new operating system over an old one also increases the chances for an error.

The SETUP.TXT file also contains directions on how to prepare the computer system for Windows 9x installation. The idea is to simplify the system hardware and software as much as possible before installing Windows 9x. The best way to avoid setup errors and achieve a good installation is to start with a freshly formatted hard drive on a system with as few peripherals attached as possible. This is generally referred to as a *clean* install. You can follow this policy even with the "Upgrade" version of Windows 98. (Simply run Setup on the freshly formatted hard drive and insert your Windows 95 CD when the Setup program requests proof of ownership for a previous version of Windows.)

Once Windows 9x is installed and operating smoothly, it's a good idea to set up a regular schedule for the maintenance programs included with Windows 9x. The basic maintenance programs included with Windows 9x are ScanDisk and Disk Defragmenter (a.k.a. Defrag). Running these programs on a regular basis can not only prevent some file system problems, but also warn you far enough in advance of more serious problems so you have time to catch and fix the trouble before permanent data loss occurs.

ScanDisk can be run in Standard or Thorough mode. Standard mode checks files and folders for errors. Thorough mode adds an extensive check of the hard disk surface to the file and folder check; so Thorough testing requires a great deal more time than Standard testing. This should be scheduled at a time when the computer is not in use. (Any activity on the drive being scanned will cause ScanDisk to restart the file and folder check.) After 10 restarts, ScanDisk stops and a dialog box asks if you want to continue, so it is best to run a Thorough test when nothing will cause restarts.

> You might need the Windows Plus pack or another utility to schedule running programs under Windows 95.

Windows 98 includes a third general maintenance utility named Disk Cleanup. This program will find and remove useless files that accumulate over time, such as TMP temp files, Internet Cache files, and other unnecessary program files. Windows 98 allows you to schedule these and other programs to run at any time you set. You can use Maintenance wizard or Scheduled Tasks to establish a suite of regular maintenance times and help keep the computer systems under your supervision running smoothly. Preventive maintenance is a good way to establish a reputation of reliability.

Further Study

IBM: **http://www-4.ibm.com/software/os/warp/**

Microsoft: **http://www.microsoft.com**

Microsoft Support: **http://support.microsoft.com/support/**

Microsoft Troubleshooters: **http://support.microsoft.com/support/tshoot/**

Novell: **http://www.novell.com**

V Communications (System Commander): **http://www.v-com.com**

4

ARRANGING THE PRESERVICE CHECKOUT

CHAPTER AT A GLANCE

As a PC technician, you must understand a basic rule of business: time is money. Whether you are the boss or work for someone else, the ability to identify and isolate a PC or peripheral fault quickly and decisively is a critical element to your success. It requires a keen eye, some common sense, and a little bit of intuition. It also requires an understanding of the troubleshooting process and a reliable plan of action. You see, even though the number of PC configurations and setups is virtually unlimited, the methodology used to approach each repair is always about the same. This chapter is intended to illustrate the concepts of basic troubleshooting and show you how to apply a suite of cause-and-effect relationships that will help you narrow the problem down before you even take a screwdriver to the enclosure. By applying a consistent technique, you can shave precious time from every repair.

The Universal Troubleshooting Process

Regardless of how complex your particular computer or peripheral device may be, a dependable troubleshooting procedure can be broken down into the four basic steps illustrated in Figure 4-1: define your symptoms, identify and isolate the potential source (or location) of your problem, replace the suspected subassembly, and retest the unit thoroughly to be sure that you have solved the problem. If you have not solved the problem, start again from step 1. This is a universal procedure that you can apply to *any* sort of troubleshooting, not just for personal computer equipment.

DEFINE YOUR SYMPTOMS

When a PC breaks down, the cause may be as simple as a loose wire or connector, or as complicated as an IC or subassembly failure. Before you open your toolbox, you must have a firm understanding of all the symptoms. Think about the symptoms carefully, for example:

- Is the disk or tape inserted properly?
- Is the power or activity LED lit?
- Does this problem occur only when the computer is tapped or moved?

By recognizing and understanding your symptoms, it can be much easier to trace a problem to the appropriate assembly or component. Take the time to write down as many symptoms as you can. This note taking may seem tedious now, but once you have begun your repair, a written record of symptoms and circumstances will help to keep you focused on the task at hand. It will also help to jog your memory if you must explain the symptoms to someone else at a later date. As a professional troubleshooter, you must often log problems or otherwise document your activities anyway.

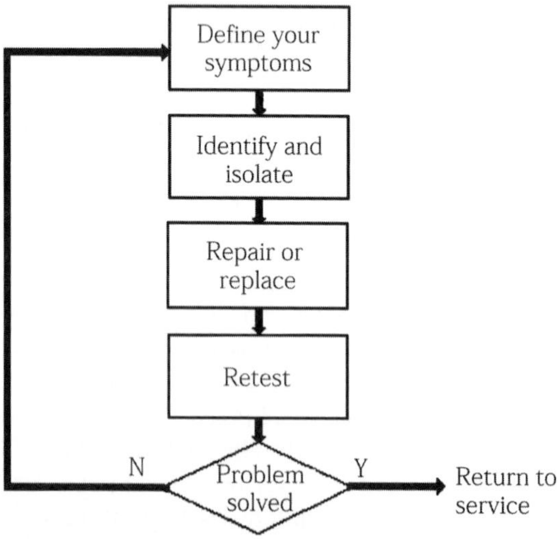

FIGURE 4-1 The universal troubleshooting procedure

IDENTIFY AND ISOLATE

Before you try to isolate a problem within a piece of computer hardware, you must first be sure that it is the equipment itself that is causing the problem. In many circumstances, this will be fairly obvious, but there may be situations that appear ambiguous (for example, there is no power, no DOS prompt). Always remember that a PC works because of an intimate mingling of hardware and software. A faulty or improperly configured piece of software can cause confusing system errors. Chapter 3 touched on some of the problems that can occur with operating systems.

When you are confident that the failure lies in your system's hardware, you can begin to identify possible problem areas. Since this book is designed to deal with subassembly troubleshooting, start your diagnostics there. The troubleshooting procedures throughout this book will guide you through the major sections of today's popular PC components and peripherals to aid you in deciding which subassembly may be at fault. When you have identified a potential problem area, you can begin the actual repair process and swap the suspect subassembly.

REPAIR OR REPLACE

Since computers and their peripherals are designed as collections of subassemblies, it is almost always easier to replace a subassembly outright than to troubleshoot the subassembly to its component level. Even if you had the time, documentation, and test equipment to isolate a defective component, many complex parts are proprietary, so it is highly unlikely that you would be able to obtain replacement components without a significant hassle. The labor and frustration factor involved in such an endeavor is often just as expensive as replacing the entire subassembly to begin with (perhaps even more expensive). On the other hand, manufacturers and their distributors often stock a selection of subassemblies and supplies. Keep in mind that you may need to know the manufacturer's part number for the subassembly in order to obtain a new one.

During a repair, you may reach a roadblock that requires you to leave your equipment for a day or two, or maybe longer. This generally happens after an order has been placed for new parts, and you are waiting for those parts to come in. Make it a point to reassemble your system as much as possible before leaving it. Gather any loose parts in plastic bags, seal them shut, and mark them clearly. If you are working with electronic circuitry, make sure to use good-quality antistatic boxes or bags for storage. Partial reassembly (combined with careful notes) will help you remember how the unit goes together later on.

Another problem with the fast technological progress we enjoy is that parts rarely stay on the shelf long. That video board you bought last year is no longer available, is it? How about that 4x CD-ROM drive you put in some time back? Today there's something newer and faster in its place. When a PC fails and you need to replace a broken device, chances are that you'll need to upgrade simply because you cannot obtain an identical replacement device. From this standpoint, upgrading is often a proxy of troubleshooting and repair.

RETEST

When a repair is finally complete, the system must be reassembled carefully before testing it. All guards, housings, cables, and shields must be replaced before final testing. If symptoms persist, you will have to reevaluate the symptoms and narrow the problem to another part of the equipment. If normal operation is restored (or greatly improved), test the computer's various functions. When you can verify that your symptoms have stopped during actual operation, the equipment may be returned to service. As a general rule, it is wise to let the system run for at least 24 hours in order to ensure that the replacement subassembly will not fail prematurely. This is known as letting the system *burn-in*.

Check your CD for the utilities "Performance 95" (PERFORMN.ZIP), "SANDRA Standard" (SAN420.ZIP), and "Bench32" (BENCH32.ZIP).

Don't be discouraged if the equipment still malfunctions. Perhaps you missed a jumper setting or DIP switch, or maybe software settings and device drivers need to be updated to accommodate the replacement subassembly. If you get stuck, simply walk away, clear your head, and start again by defining your current symptoms. Never continue with a repair if you are tired or frustrated—tomorrow is another day. Even the most experienced troubleshooters get overwhelmed from time to time. You should also realize that there may be more than one bad assembly to deal with. Remember that a PC is just a collection of assemblies, and each assembly is a collection of parts. Normally, everything works together, but when one assembly fails, it may cause one or more interconnected assemblies to fail as well.

The Spare Parts Dilemma

Once a problem is isolated, technicians face another problem: the availability of spare parts. Novice technicians often ask what kinds and quantity of spare parts they should keep on hand. The best answer to give here is, simply, none at all. The reason for this somewhat drastic answer is best explained by the two realities of PC service: parts are always changing, and inventory costs money.

PARTS ARE ALWAYS CHANGING

After almost 20 years, the PC is in its seventh CPU generation (with devices such as the AMD Athlon). As a result, a new generation matures every 24 to 36 months (although the newer generations have been arriving in 18 to 24 months). Even so-called standardized products such as CD-ROM drives have proliferated in different speeds and versions (from 8x to 50x and faster). Once production stops for a drive or board, stock rarely remains for very long. You see, even if you know what the problem is, the chances of your locating an exact replacement part are often quite slim if the part is over two years old. Note the word "exact"—this is the key word in PC repair. This is the reason why so many repairs involve an upgrade. For example, why replace a failed EGA board with another EGA board when you can install a state-of-the-art video card (which is typically fully compatible) for the same price or less? Choosing the right parts to stock is like hitting a moving target, so don't bother.

INVENTORY COSTS MONEY

Financial considerations also play a big role in choosing parts. For computer enthusiasts or novice technicians tinkering in their spare time, the expense and space demands required for inventory are simply out of the question. For more serious repair businesses, the expense of inventory can burden the bottom line. And what happens if you don't actually use a part? After a while, you're stuck with an "antique."

A BETTER STRATEGY

Unless you are in the business of selling replacement parts and upgrade components yourself, don't waste your money and space stocking parts that are going to be obsolete in less than 24 months. Rather than worry about stocking parts yourself, work to cultivate new vendors and develop your contacts with computer parts stores and superstores that specialize in PC parts and subassemblies. Let *them* stock the parts for you. Since parts stores generally have an inside line with distributors and manufacturers, parts that they do not stock can often be ordered for you. Even many reputable mail-order firms can provide parts in under 48 hours with today's delivery services.

Benchmarking the PC

We all know that today's personal computers are capable of astounding performance. If you doubt that, consider any of the current 3D games like Quake III or Unreal. However, it is often important to quantify the performance of a system. Just saying that a PC is faster than another system is simply not enough. We must often apply a number to that performance in order to measure the improvements offered by an upgrade, or to objectively compare the performance of various systems. *Benchmarks* are used to test and report the performance of a PC by running a set of well-defined tasks on the system. A benchmark program has several different uses in the PC industry depending on what your needs are:

- *System comparisons*: Benchmarks are often used to compare a system to one or more competing machines (or to compare a newer system to older machines). Just flip through any issue of *PC Magazine* or *Byte*, and you'll see a flurry of PC ads all quoting numerical performance numbers backed up by benchmarks. You may also run a benchmark to establish the overall performance of a new system before making a purchase decision.
- *Upgrade improvements*: Benchmarks are frequently used to gauge the value of an upgrade. By running the benchmark before and after the upgrade process, you can get a numerical assessment of just how much that new CPU, RAM, drive, or motherboard may have improved (or hindered) system performance.
- *Diagnostics*: Benchmarks sometimes have a role in system diagnostics. Systems that are performing poorly can be benchmarked as key components are checked or reconfigured. This helps the technician isolate and correct performance problems far more reliably than simple observations.

4

AVOIDING BENCHMARK PROBLEMS

One of the most serious problems encountered with benchmarks is the integrity of their numbers. You've probably heard that "statistics can lie," and the same thing is true of benchmarks. In order for benchmarks to provide you with reliable results, there are some precautions that you must take:

- *Note the complete system configuration*. When you run a benchmark and achieve a result, be sure to note the entire system configuration (CPU, RAM, cache, OS version, etc.). The benchmark may yield vastly different numbers on different configurations of the same system.
- *Run the same benchmark on every system*. Benchmarks are still software, and the way benchmark code is written can impact the way it produces results on a given computer. Often, two different versions of the same benchmark will yield two different results. When you use benchmarks for comparisons between systems, be sure to use the same program and version number.
- *Minimize hardware differences between hardware platforms*. A computer is an assembly of many interdependent subassemblies (motherboard, drive controllers, drives, CPU, etc.), but when a benchmark is run to compare a difference between systems, that difference can be masked by other elements in the system. For example, suppose you're using a benchmark to test the hard drive data transfer on two systems. Different hard drives and drive controllers will yield different results (that's expected). However, even if you're using identical drives and controllers, other differences between the systems (such as BIOS versions, TSRs, OS differences, or motherboard chipsets) can also influence different results.
- *Run the benchmarks under the same load*. The results generated by a benchmark do not guarantee that same level of performance under real-world applications. This was one of the flaws of early computer

benchmarking—small, tightly written benchmark code resulted in artificially high performance, but the system still performed poorly when real applications were used. Use benchmarks that make use of (or simulate) actual programs, or otherwise simulate your true workload.

OBTAINING BENCHMARKS

Benchmarks have been around since the earliest computers, and there are now a vast array of benchmark products to measure all aspects of the PC, as well as more specialized issues such as networking, real-time systems, and UNIX (or other operating system) platforms. Table 4-1 highlights a cross-section of computer benchmarks for your reference. In many cases, the table includes a URL or FTP site where you can either obtain source code for the benchmark or download the complete benchmark program. The benchmarks shown in bold with a * are described in more detail below.

Today, Ziff-Davis and CMP publish a suite of freeware benchmark utilities that have become standard tools for end users and technicians alike.

TABLE 4-1 INDEX OF COMPUTER BENCHMARKS

BENCHMARK	DESCRIPTION/PURPOSE	SOURCE/APPLET AVAILABILITY
007 (ODBMS)	Designed to simulate a CAD/CAM environment	ftp.cs.wisc.edu/007
3D WinBench 99*	PC 3D system benchmark	http://www1.zdnet.com/zdbop/3dwinbench/3dwinbench.html
3D-Bench	PC 3D graphics benchmark	http://www.sysopt.com/3dbench.html http://www.sysopt.com/cbench.html
AIM	Overall performance and multitasking throughput	—
Audio WinBench 99*	Sound subsystem performance benchmark	http://www1.zdnet.com/zdbop/auwinbench/auwinbench.html
BatteryMark 3.0*	Mobile PC battery benchmark	http://www1.zdnet.com/zdbop/battmark/battmark.html
Bonnie	Bottleneck checking	—
Busperf	PC bus performance benchmark	http://www.sysopt.com/pub/busperf.zip
Byte	UNIX performance	—
CacheChk	PC cache checking benchmark	http://www.sysopt.com/cachk4.html
CD WinBench 99*	CD subsystem performance benchmark	http://www1.zdnet.com/zdbop/cdwinbench/cdwinbench.html
CompTest	General PC benchmark	ftp://oak.oakland.edu/SimTel/msdos/sysinfo/ctest259.zip
CPU2	Floating-point benchmark (UNIX/VMS)	ftp://swedishchef.lerc.nasa.gov/drlabs/cpu/ (select cpu2.unix.tar.Z or cpu2.vms.tar.Z)
Dhrystone MIPS	Short test for system programming	ftp.nosc.mil/pub/aburto
Fhourstones	Integer-only benchmark	ftp.nosc.mil:pub/aburto/c4.shar
Flops	MFLOP rating benchmark	ftp.nosc.mil/pub/aburto
Hanoi	Recursive function benchmark	ftp.nosc.mil/pub/aburto

TABLE 4-1 INDEX OF COMPUTER BENCHMARKS *(CONTINUED)*

BENCHMARK	DESCRIPTION/PURPOSE	SOURCE/APPLET AVAILABILITY
Hartstone	Real-time benchmark	ftp.sei.cmu.edu/pub/hartstone
Heapsort	Array sorting benchmark	ftp.nosc.mil/pub/aburto
IOBENCH	Multistream benchmark	—
IOZONE	Read/write test	—
JMark 1.01*	PC Java virtual machine benchmark	http://www8.zdnet.com/pcmag/pclabs/bench/benchjm.htm
Khornerstone	Multipurpose benchmark	—
LFK (Livermore Loops)	General performance testing	netlib.att.com/netlib/benchmark/livermore
LINPACK	Algebraic processing	netlib.att.com/netlib/benchmark/linpack
Matrix Multiply	Matrix multiplication benchmark	ftp.nosc.mil/pub/aburto
MUSBUS	—	monu1.cc.monash.edu.au/pub/musbus.sh
NAS Kernels	Computational fluid dynamics	ftp.cs.wisc.edu/wwt/Misc/NAS
NetBench 6.0*	PC networking benchmark	http://www1.zdnet.com/zdbop/netbench/netbench.html
Netperf	Networking performance	ftp://ftp.cup.hp.com/dist/networking/benchmarks
Nettest	Networking performance	—
Nhfsstone	File server performance	—
PERFECT	—	—
RhosettaStone	—	eos.arc.nasa.gov
ServerBench 4.1*	PC network server benchmark	http://www1.zdnet.com/zdbop/svrbench/svrbench.html
Sieve of Eratosthenes	Integer testing	otis.stanford.edu/pub/benchmarks/c/small/sieve.c
SLALOM	—	tantalus.al.iastate.edu/pub/Slalom/
SPEC	CPU-intensive benchmarks	ftp.nosc.mil/pub/aburto
SSBA	UNIX performance	ftp.inria.fr:/system/benchmark/SSBA/ssba1.22F.tar.Z
Stanford	Compares RISC/CISC	—
SYSmark	App/OS-based benchmark	—
TFFTDP	FFT benchmark	ftp.nosc.mil/pub/aburto
TPC A/B/C	POS benchmark	—
ttcp	TCP/UDP performance	—
VidSpeed	PC video benchmark	http://www.sysopt.com/pub/vidspd40.zip
WebBench 3.0*	PC Internet browser benchmark	http://www1.zdnet.com/zdbop/webbench/webbench.html
Whetstone	Floating-point benchmark	netlib.att.com/netlib/benchmark/whetstone
WinBench 99*	PC subsystem benchmarks	http://www1.zdnet.com/zdbop/winbench/winbench.html
Winstone 99*	Overall Windows 95/NT benchmark	http://www1.zdnet.com/zdbop/winstone/winstone.html

4

TABLE 4-1 INDEX OF COMPUTER BENCHMARKS *(CONTINUED)*

BENCHMARK	DESCRIPTION/PURPOSE	SOURCE/APPLET AVAILABILITY
Wintach	Windows benchmark	ftp://ftp.winsite.com/pub/pc/win3/util/wintch12.zip
WinTune 98*	Overall PC Windows 95 benchmark	http://www.winmag.com/software/wt.htm
WPI Benchmark	General benchmarks	wpi.wpi.edu
Xstone	General benchmarks	netcom.com/pub/micromed/uploads/xstones.summary.z

Use caution when exploring the benchmarks of Table 4-1. Many classic benchmarks will no longer work on today's PC platforms, or they may require specialized hardware configurations. As a general rule, stay with the end-user benchmarks highlighted with an asterisk and detailed below.

Audio WinBench 99 The Audio WinBench 99 benchmark will take you deep into the heart of your PC's sound system by offering objective and subjective tests to measure CPU usage, hardware voices, 3D positioning, and more. Audio WinBench 99 measures the performance of a PC's audio subsystem, which includes the sound card and its driver, the processor, the DirectSound and DirectSound 3D software, and the speakers. You'll need DirectX 6 (which includes DirectSound and DirectSound3D) to run all the Audio WinBench 99 tests.

Winstone 99 Winstone 99 is a system-level, application-based benchmark that measures a PC's overall performance when running today's top-selling Windows-based 32-bit applications on Windows 95, Windows 98, or Windows NT (High-End Winstone runs only on NT). Winstone runs real 32-bit business suites, moving applications through a series of scripted activities, and uses the time a PC takes to complete those activities to produce its performance scores. Winstone's tests don't mimic what these programs do; they run actual application code. (The CD-ROM that contains Winstone also contains all the files and application portions the benchmark needs to run.)

The new Business Winstone marks a dramatic shift in Winstone performance. Business Winstone 99 now tests with the most popular office suites in the marketplace (such as Corel WordPerfect Suite 8, Lotus SmartSuite, and Microsoft Office 97) rather than individual applications. Multiple applications remain open within each suite and switch tasks between those applications and Netscape Navigator. The new High-End Winstone 99 focuses on hot spots where demanding users tend to have to wait on their PCs. Its seven specialized applications include Microstation SE, Adobe Photoshop, and Sonic Foundry's SoundForge. There are also new tests to showcase the potential of dual-processor systems.

WinBench 99 Version 1.1 of WinBench 99 is a more hardware-oriented utility that provides a detailed measure of graphics, disk, processor, CD-ROM, and video-playback performance under Windows 95/98 and Windows NT. WinBench produces two graphics WinMark 99 scores that reflect performance of a machine's graphics subsystem: the business graphics WinMark 99 score, which reflects performance when running the typical business applications, and the high-end graphics WinMark 99 score, which reflects performance when running the corresponding test applications. WinBench also tests disk-subsystem performance, producing a business disk WinMark 99 score and a high-end disk WinMark 99 score.

WinBench 99 also provides a score (known as CPUmark99) indicating the speed of a processor subsystem. WinBench 99 includes CD-ROM tests based on a profile of several of today's most popular Windows CD-ROMs (including sequential-read tests, access-time tests, and CPU utilization tests). There are a variety of CD video-playback tests that report performance when replaying a number of video clips.

3D WinBench 99 Version 1.2 of 3D WinBench 99 is a specialized benchmarking utility that measures the performance of a 3D graphics subsystem (including the Direct3D software, the monitor, the graphics adapter, the graphics driver, and the bus used to carry information from the graphics adapter to and from the processor subsystem). You can use 3D WinBench 99 to test hardware graphics adapters, drivers, and the value of processor enhancement technologies such as MMX. Remember that 3D WinBench 99 does not work with Windows NT because NT doesn't support hardware acceleration of the Windows Direct3D interface. Also note that you'll need DirectX 6 or later in order to run the 3D benchmark tests.

BatteryMark 3.0 BatteryMark 3.0 uses a combination of hardware and software to measure the battery life of notebook computers under real-world conditions (the ZDigit II device is no longer needed if the system supports ACPI). BatteryMark exercises different 32-bit software workload engines for processor, disk, and graphics tasks. BatteryMark mixes these workloads together and adds periodic breaks in the work that reflect the way users pause while working. BatteryMark 2.0 works with Windows 95, Windows 98, Windows NT, and Windows 2000.

CD WinBench 99 CD WinBench 99 measures the performance of a PC's CD-ROM subsystem (which includes the CD drive, controller, and driver, and the system processor). You need to run this benchmark from the CD WinBench 99 CD-ROM while it's spinning in your system's CD drive. Version 1.1 of CD WinBench 99 includes numerous bug fixes.

NetBench 6.0 NetBench 6.0 is the benchmark test for checking the performance of network file servers. NetBench provides a way to measure, analyze, and predict how a file server will handle network file I/O requests from 32-bit Windows clients. It monitors the response of the server as multiple clients request data and reports the server's total throughput. To test application servers, you should use the ServerBench utility instead. Version 6.0 of NetBench supports new response time measures for NetBench clients that show how long a server takes to respond to each client's requests. There is also support for the 32-bit Windows client only for Windows 95, Windows 98, or Windows NT. (There is no support for 16-bit Windows, DOS, or Mac OS clients.)

ServerBench 4.1 ServerBench 4.1 is the latest version of Ziff-Davis's standard benchmark for measuring the performance of servers in a true client-server environment. ServerBench clients make requests of an application that runs on the server, and the server's ability to service those requests is reported in transactions per second. ServerBench 4.1 runs on IBM's OS/2 Warp Server, Microsoft's Windows NT Server (for both Digital Alpha and x86-compatible processors), Novell's NetWare, Sun's Solaris (32-bit SPARC and x86), Linux, and SCO's OpenServer and UnixWare 2.1. To test network file servers, use the NetBench utility instead.

WebBench 3.0 WebBench 3.0 is the Ziff-Davis benchmark test for checking performance of Web server hardware and software. Standard test suites produce two overall scores for the server: requests per second and throughput (as measured in bytes per second). WebBench includes static testing (which involves only HTML pages) and dynamic testing (including CGI executables, Internet Server API libraries, and Netscape Server API dynamic link libraries).

Version 3.0 includes support for SSL 2.0/3.0 (including new e-commerce suites that let you test the secure-transaction features of Web servers). There is also a WSAPI plug-in that you can use to test Mac OS–based Web servers like WebSTAR and WebTen. Finally, it supports CGI executables for Mac OS X (Rhapsody) and Solaris on X86, which means you can now run dynamic workloads (including our new e-commerce test suites) on these platforms.

JMark 1.01 JMark 1.01 is a suite of 11 synthetic benchmark tests for evaluating the performance of Java virtual machines. The JMark 1.01 suite simulates a number of important tests of Java functionality. It includes Java versions of a number of classic benchmark test algorithms, as well as tests designed to measure graphics performance in a GUI environment. You can download JMark 1.01 from Ziff-Davis, or run the tests online within your browser.

WinTune 98 WinTune 98 for Windows 95/98 is a fairly recent benchmark entry from CMP, the publishers of *Windows Magazine*. WinTune 98 is an overall benchmark to measure Windows 95/98 performance. It has a fast user interface that allows the program to load much faster than the earlier versions, and it now supports testing of the latest Pentium II/III systems. WinTune 98 tests video systems on the fastest new computers at full-screen resolution. In addition, you can use WinTune 98 to test the system while it's online (if your system uses IE 3.02 or later). Of course, you may download and install an offline version for individual system testing.

Viruses and Computer Service

Few developments in the personal computer field have caused more concern and alarm than the computer virus. Although viruses do not physically damage computer hardware, they can irrevocably destroy vital data, disable your PC (or shut down a network), and propagate to other systems through networks, disk swapping, and online services. Even though virus infiltration is generally regarded as rare, responsible PC technicians will always protect themselves (and their customers) by checking the system for viruses before and after using their diagnostic disks on the PC. A careful process of virus isolation can detect viruses on the customer's system before any hardware-level work is done. Virus isolation tactics also prevent your diagnostic disks from becoming infected and subsequently transferring the virus to other systems (for which you might be legally liable). This part of the chapter outlines a virus screening procedure for PCs.

COMPUTER VIRUSES EXPLAINED

There have been many attempts to define a computer virus, and most definitions have a great deal of technical merit. For the purposes of this book, however, we can consider a *virus* to be some length of computer code (a program or program fragment) that performs one or more, often destructive, functions and replicates itself wherever possible to other disks and systems. Since viruses generally want to escape detection, they may often hide by copying themselves as hidden, system, or read-only files. However, this only prevents casual detection. More elaborate viruses affect the boot sector code on floppy and hard disks or attach themselves to other executable programs. Each time the infected program is executed, the virus has a chance to wreak havoc. Still other viruses infect the partition table. Most viruses exhibit a code sequence that can be detected. Many virus scanners work by checking the contents of memory and disk files for such virus *signatures*. As viruses become more complex, however, they are using encryption techniques to escape detection. Encryption changes the virus signature each time the virus replicates itself, and for a well-designed virus, this can make detection extremely difficult.

Just as a biological virus is an unwanted (and sometimes deadly) organism in a body, "viral" code in software can lead to a slow, agonizing death for your customer's data. In actual practice, few viruses *immediately* crash a system (with notable exceptions such as the much-publicized Michelangelo virus). Most viruses make only small changes each time they are executed, creating a pattern of chronic problems. This slow manifestation gives viruses a chance to replicate and infect backups and floppy disks, which are frequently swapped, thus infecting other systems.

> Frequent system backups are an effective protection against computer viruses because you can restore files damaged by viruses. Even if the backup is infected, the infected files can often be cleaned once they are restored from the backup.

THE TELL-TALE SIGNS

Viruses are especially dangerous since you are rarely made aware of their presence until it is too late and the damage is already done. However, there are a number of behaviors that might suggest the presence of a virus in your system. Once again, remember that one of the best protections against viruses (or other drive failures) is to maintain regular backups of your data. None of these symptoms alone guarantees the presence of a virus (there are other reasons why such symptoms can occur), but when symptoms do surface, it is always worth running an antivirus checker just to be safe. The following symptoms are typical of virus activity:

- *The hard drive is running out of disk space for no apparent reason.* Some viruses multiply by attaching copies of themselves to EXE and COM files, often multiple times. This increases the file size of infected files (sometimes dramatically) and consumes more disk space. If left unchecked, files can grow until the disk runs short of space. However, disk space can also be gobbled up by many CAD, graphics, and multimedia applications such as video capture systems. Be aware of what kind of applications are on the disk.
- *You notice that various EXE and COM programs have increased in size for no reason.* This is a classic indicator of a virus at work. In actual practice, few rational people make it a habit to keep track of file sizes, but dates can be a giveaway. For example, if most of the files in a subdirectory are dated six months ago when the package was installed, but the main EXE file is dated yesterday, it's time to run that virus checker.
- *You notice substantial hard drive activity but were not expecting it.* It is hardly unusual to see the drive indicator LED register activity when programs are loaded and run. In disk-intensive systems such as Windows 98 or NT, you should expect to see extensive drive activity due to swap file operation. However, you should not expect to see regular or substantial disk activity when the system is idle. If the drive runs for no apparent reason—especially under MS-DOS—run the virus checker.
- *System performance has slowed down noticeably.* This symptom is usually coupled with low drive space, and it may very well be the result of a filled and fragmented disk such as those found in systems that deal with CAD and multimedia applications. Run the virus checker first. If no virus is detected, try eliminating any unneeded files and defragment the drive completely.
- *Files have been lost or corrupted for no apparent reason, or there are an unusual number of access problems.* Under ordinary circumstances, files should not be lost or corrupted on a hard drive. Even though bad sectors will crop up on extremely rare occasions, you should expect the drive to run properly. Virus infiltration can interrupt the flow of data to and from the drives and result in file errors. Such errors may occur randomly, or they may be quite consistent. You may see error messages such as "Error in .EXE file." Regular errors may even simulate a drive failure. Try running a virus checker

before running ScanDisk or other diagnostic. Inadequate power problems can also have an effect on drive reliability.

- *The system locks up frequently or without explanation.* Faulty applications and corrupted files can freeze a system. Memory and motherboard problems can also result in system lockups. Although viruses rarely manifest themselves this way, it is possible that random or consistent system lockups may suggest a virus (or virus damage to key files).
- *There are unexplained problems with system memory or memory allocation.* Although there may be one or more memory defects, it is quite common for viruses to exist in memory where other files can be infected. In some cases, this can affect the amount of free memory available to other applications. You may see error messages such as "Program too big to fit in memory." If you are having trouble with free memory or memory allocation, run a virus checker that performs a thorough memory check. If the system checks clear of viruses, you can run diagnostics to check the memory.

ANTIVIRUS SOFTWARE

In the race between good and evil, it is evil that usually has the head start. As a result, antivirus detection and elimination packages are constantly trying to keep up with new viruses and their variations (in addition to dealing with more than 45,000 viruses that have already been identified). This leads to an important conclusion about antivirus software: they all quickly become obsolete. Even though first-class shareware and commercial packages can be quite comprehensive, they must all be updated frequently. Some of the most notable antivirus products are found in Symantec's Norton Anti-Virus (NAV) and VirusScan from Network Associates. If you use MS-DOS 6.0 or later, you already own Microsoft Anti-Virus (MSAV).

Another important factor in antivirus programs is their inability to successfully remove all viruses from executable (EXE) files. Files with a .COM extension are simply reflections of memory, but EXE files contain header information that is easily damaged by a virus (and are subsequently unrecoverable). It is always worth trying to eliminate the virus—if the EXE header is damaged, you've lost nothing in the attempt, and you can reload the damaged EXE file from a backup or its original distribution disks if necessary. Remember that there is no better protection against viruses and other hardware faults than keeping regular backups. It is better to restore an infected backup and clean it, than to forego backups entirely.

STERILIZING YOUR SHOP

Sterilization starts by assuming that *all* machines coming in for service are infected with a virus. You should assume the possibility of an infection even if the complaint is something innocent (for example, the keyboard is "acting up"). This part of the chapter shows you how to create antivirus work disks that will be used to boot and check the systems brought in for service. Guard your master antivirus disks by placing them somewhere away from the shop. That way they won't be infected accidentally. *Immediately write-protect your work disks!* Also, be ready to discard your work disks frequently. Replacing a 20-cent work disk is much cheaper than having to scan and clean every disk in your shop. If the antivirus software, DOS, and the DISKCOPY program can all fit, you should use double-density disks rather than high-density disks. Double-density disks can be used in high-density drives (but not vice versa).

Routine, preservice virus scanning makes good sense. It will save time by detecting virus-related problems right away. You won't waste time disassembling cabinets and troubleshooting hardware. Also, eliminating viruses is much easier than reformatting or replacing the hard drive (a devastating choice if your customer has no current backup). Reformatting a hard drive on a system with a virus may not solve the problem, which may result in a call back. On the other hand, *not* wiping out your customer's entire drive is a sure way to make a friend. Finally, preservice virus checking is quick—the computer is on the bench anyway. Sticking in a disk and turning on the computer is all the labor required.

> The procedure below assumes that your floppy disk drive is A:, your main hard drive is C:, and your CD-ROM drive (if installed) is D:. If your particular system is configured differently, please substitute the correct drive letters.

1. Start at the DOS command line. You should exit Windows 95/98 to the DOS prompt before proceeding.
2. Ensure your system is virus free. Run a current virus checker that checks for the most important types of viruses, including memory-resident viruses. Once the system is clean, you can proceed.
3. Format ten (10) floppy disks as bootable (system) disks. If your disks are totally blank, use the FORMAT command as shown here:

   ```
   C:\DOS\> format a:
   ```

   Next, make the disks bootable by transferring system files. Use the SYS command to make the disks bootable, as shown here:

   ```
   C:\DOS\> sys a:
   ```

   If you purchase your disks preformatted, simply use the SYS command.
4. Test a disk. Reboot your computer and see that the system will boot successfully to the A: DOS prompt. If so, you have created simple boot disks (you need only test one disk), but there are other steps required to complete a virus-checking disk.
5. Copy the virus checker to your first bootable floppy disk. Virus checkers are typically self-contained, single-file tools such as Norton's NAV.EXE, Microsoft's MSAV.EXE, or the shareware tool FPROT.EXE. Copy the necessary executable file(s) to your disk.
6. Create an AUTOEXEC.BAT file that will start the virus checker. Ideally, you want the virus checker to start automatically, so create a simple AUTOEXEC.BAT file that will start the virus checker. For example, MSAV.EXE could use a command line such as:

   ```
   a:\msav.exe
   ```

   You might also add command-line arguments to streamline the virus checker even further. Save the AUTOEXEC.BAT file to your floppy disk.
7. Test the disk again. Reboot the system with your master antivirus floppy disk. The system should boot clean—with no drivers or TSRs loaded that might confuse the virus checker—and the antivirus program should load. Depending on exactly which virus checker and command-line options you choose, the checker may run through a complete scan automatically, or you may have to start testing manually from the program's menu.
8. Duplicate the original disk to the other work disks. Use the DOS DISKCOPY command to duplicate your original virus-checking disk to the other nine disks you have prepared. You may have to swap back and forth between the source (original) and target (new) disks several times. When the new disk is done, DISKCOPY will ask if you want to repeat the procedure.
9. Mark the disks carefully. You have just created a batch of antivirus work disks. They should be immediately write-protected and kept together as a set.

> Step 3 above instructs you to create 10 copies of the virus-checking software. Even though the disks are exclusively for your use, and you will only use one disk at a time, this kind of multiple duplication may violate the license agreement for your antivirus software. Be sure your license allows multiple copies of the software before proceeding.

Using the Virus Work Disks

Whenever a PC comes in for service, use one of your antivirus work disks to boot and check the system first, before trying a boot disk or diagnostic disk. Professionals always create antivirus disks in batches because the disks are disposable. That is, if a virus is detected and cleaned, the disk that detected the infection should be destroyed, and you should boot the system with a new work disk to locate any other instances of the same virus, or any different viruses. This may seem radical, but it is cheap insurance against cross-contamination of the disk. Once a system is booted with a work disk and checks clean, you can put that work disk away and boot the system again with a diagnostic or boot disk as required. It is also advisable to check the PC for viruses again once the repair is complete.

Problems with Antivirus Tools

The protocol outlined above should help to protect you (and your customer) from virus attacks. Still, there are two situations where trouble can occur. First, viruses are proliferating with the aid of powerful new programming languages and vast avenues of distribution such as the Internet. You will need to update your virus work disks regularly with the very latest antivirus software and signature updates. Too often, technicians buy an antivirus package and continue to use it for years. The software certainly remains adept at detecting the viruses it was designed for, but it does not take into account the many new strains that crop up regularly. As a result, older virus checkers may allow newer viruses to pass undetected.

Second, technicians tend to get cheap with their floppy disks. If a work disk detects and eliminates a virus, it should be considered contaminated, and you should throw it away. Start again with a fresh work disk. Continue checking and eradicating viruses until the system checks clean. The 20 cents or so that the disk is worth is not worth the risk of contracting the virus.

Quick-Start Bench Testing

Of the many problems that can plague the PC, perhaps the most troubling occur during startup, when the computer fails to start at all or does not start completely. Startup problems make it almost impossible to use diagnostics or other utilities that we depend on to help isolate problems. With the advent of graphics-oriented operating systems such as Windows 95/98, there are even more difficulties that can develop. This part of the chapter offers you a series of possible quick-start explanations for full and partial system failures.

THE SYSTEM DOESN'T START AT ALL

SYMPTOM 4-1 **There is no power light, and you cannot hear any cooling fan**

Chances are that there is insufficient power to the computer. Use a voltmeter and confirm that there is adequate AC voltage at the wall outlet. Check the AC cord next—it may be loose or disconnected. See that the power switch is turned on and connected properly. Check the power supply fuse(s). The main fuse may have opened. Replace any failed fuse.

> If you replace a main fuse and the fuse continues to fail, you may have a serious fault in the power supply. Try replacing the power supply.

SYMPTOM 4-2 **There is no power light, but you hear the cooling fan running** This usually means that some level of AC power is reaching the system. Use a voltmeter and confirm that there is adequate AC voltage at the wall outlet. Unusually low AC voltages (such as during brownout conditions) can cause the power supply to malfunction. Verify that the power supply cables are attached properly and securely to the motherboard. Use a voltmeter to verify that each output from the power supply is correct. (Table 4-2 illustrates the proper voltage levels at each wire color.) If any output is very low or

TABLE 4-2 PINOUTS OF ATX AND BABY AT POWER CONNECTORS

ATX POWER CONNECTOR

COLOR	VOLTAGE	PIN
Orange	+3.3 VDC	1
Orange	+3.3 VDC	2
Black	GND	3
Red	+5 VDC	4
Black	GND	5
Red	+5 VDC	6
Black	GND	7
Gray	PwrOK	8
Purple	+5VStandby	9
Yellow	+12 VDC	10
Orange	+3.3 VDC	11
Brown	3.3V sense	11
Blue	–12 VDC	12
Black	GND	13
Green	PS-ON	14
Black	GND	15
Black	GND	16
Black	GND	17
White	–5 VDC	18
Red	+5 VDC	19
Red	+5 VDC	20

BABY AT POWER CONNECTORS

COLOR	VOLTAGE	PIN
Orange	PwrOK	1 (P8)
Red	+5 VDC	2 (P8)
Yellow	+12 VDC	3 (P8)
Blue	–12 VDC	4 (P8)
Black	GND	5 (P8)
Black	GND	6 (P8)
Black	GND	1 (P9)
Black	GND	2 (P9)
White	–5 VDC	3 (P9)
Red	+5 VDC	4 (P9)
Red	+5 VDC	5 (P9)
Red	+5 VDC	6 (P9)

4

absent (especially the +5 volt output), replace the power supply. Finally, use a voltmeter and verify that the Power Good (or PwrOK) signal is +5 volts. If this signal is below 1.0 volts, it may inhibit the CPU from running by forcing a continuous Reset condition. Since the Power Good signal is generated by the power supply, try replacing the power supply.

SYMPTOM 4-3 The power light is on, but there is no apparent system activity Check the power supply voltages. Use a voltmeter to verify that each output from the power supply is correct. Table 4-2 lists the proper voltage for each wire color. If any output is very low or absent (especially the +5 volt output), replace the power supply. Use a voltmeter and verify that the Power Good signal is +5 volts. If this signal is below 1.0 volts, it may inhibit the CPU from running by forcing a continuous Reset condition. Since the Power Good signal is generated by the power supply, try replacing the power supply.

Check to see that the CPU is cool, that the heat-sink/fan assembly is fitted correctly, and that the CPU itself is inserted properly and completely into its socket. Check the CPU socket. If the CPU is seated in a ZIF (Zero Insertion Force) socket, make sure the socket's tension lever is closed and locked into place. For Pentium II/III processors, verify that the retention mechanism is secure. Next, check the expansion boards and make sure that all are seated properly. Any boards that are not secured properly or that are inserted unevenly, can short bus signals and prevent the PC from starting. Check the motherboard for shorts. Inspect the motherboard at every metal standoff and see that no metal traces are being shorted against a standoff or screw. You may want to free the motherboard and see if the system starts. If it does, use nonconductive spacers (such as a small piece of manila folder) to insulate the motherboard from each metal standoff. If the system still fails to start (and all voltages from the power supply are correct), replace the motherboard.

THE SYSTEM STARTS BUT WON'T INITIALIZE

SYMPTOM 4-4 The power light is on, but you hear two or more beeps There is no video. Check the video board first. Video problems can easily halt the initialization process. Turn off and unplug the PC; then make sure your video board is inserted completely into its expansion slot. Consider the beep code itself—a catastrophic fault has been detected in the power-on self-test (POST) before the video system could be initialized. BIOS makers use different numbers and patterns of beeps to indicate failures. You can determine the exact failure by finding the BIOS maker (usually marked on the motherboard BIOS IC), then finding the error message in Chapter 19. In the majority of cases, the fault will be traced to the CPU, RAM, motherboard circuitry, video controller, or drive controller.

SYMPTOM 4-5 The power light is on, but the system hangs during initialization Video may be active, but there may be no text in the display. The power-on self-test (POST) has detected a fault and is unable to continue with the initialization process. BIOS makers mark the completion of each POST step by writing single-byte hexadecimal completion codes to port 80h. Turn off and unplug the PC, and then insert a POST board to read the completion codes. Reboot the computer and find the last code to be written before the initialization stops—that is the likely point of failure. You can determine the meaning of that POST code by finding the BIOS maker (usually displayed in the initial moments of power-up), then locating the corresponding error message in Chapter 19. Note that without a POST board available, it will be extremely difficult to identify the problem.

SYMPTOM 4-6 You see a message indicating a CMOS setup problem The system parameters entered into CMOS RAM do not match the hardware configuration found during the POST. Enter your setup routine. If you are working on an older system (early i386 and i286 systems), you will probably need to boot the PC from a setup disk. If there is no setup disk available, you may be able to find a suitable routine at one of the sites at **oak.oakland.edu:/SimTel/msdos/at** or **ftp.uu.net:/systems/msdos/simtel/at**.

Review each entry in the CMOS setup—especially things like drive parameters and installed memory—and make sure that the CMOS entries accurately reflect the actual hardware installed on your system. If not, correct the error(s), save your changes, and reboot the system. Finally, test the CMOS battery. See if CMOS RAM will hold its contents by turning off the PC, waiting several minutes, then rebooting the PC. If setup problems persist and you find that the values you entered have been lost, change the CMOS backup battery.

SYMPTOM 4-7 **You see no drive light activity** The boot drive cannot be located. The most frequent cause of drive problems is power connections. Inspect the 4-pin power cable and see that it is attached properly and completely to the drive. Check the power supply voltages next. Use a voltmeter and verify that the +5 and +12 voltage levels (especially +12 volts) are correct at the 4-pin connector. If either voltage is low or absent, replace the power supply. Locate the wide ribbon cable that connects to the drive and make sure it is attached correctly and completely at the drive and controller ends. Look for any scrapes or nicks along the cable that might cause problems. Start the CMOS setup. If you are working on an older system (early i386 and i286 systems), you will probably need to boot the PC from a setup disk. If there is no setup disk available, you may be able to find a suitable routine at **oak.oakland.edu:/SimTel/msdos/at** or **ftp.uu.net:/systems/msdos/simtel/at**.

Check the CMOS setup next. Review the drive parameters entered in the CMOS setup, and make sure that the CMOS entries accurately reflect the actual boot drive installed on your system. If not, correct the error(s), save your changes, and reboot the system. Also make sure that the drive controller board is installed properly and completely in its expansion slot, and see that any jumpers are set correctly. Try booting the system from your boot floppy. If the system successfully boots to the A: prompt, your problem is limited to the hard drive system. Now try switching to the C: drive. If the drive responds (and you can access its information), there may be a problem with the boot sector. Try a package like PC Tools or Norton Utilities to try and fix the boot sector. If you can't access the hard drive, try a diagnostic to check the drive controller and drive. Check for boot sector viruses. A boot sector virus can render the hard drive unbootable. If you haven't checked for viruses yet, use your antivirus work disk now, and focus on boot sector problems. If you cannot determine the problem at this point, try replacing the drive with a known-good working drive. Remember that you will have to change the CMOS setup parameters to accommodate the new drive. If all else fails, try a new drive controller board.

SYMPTOM 4-8 **The drive light remains on continuously** The boot drive cannot be located. This typically happens if the signal cable is inserted backwards at one end. In most cases, this type of problem happens after replacing a drive or upgrading a controller. Make sure the cable is inserted in the correct orientation at both the drive and controller ends. If you cannot determine the problem at this point, try replacing the drive with a known-good working drive. Remember that you will have to change the CMOS setup parameters to accommodate the new drive. If all else fails, try a new drive controller board.

SYMPTOM 4-9 **You see normal system activity, but there is no video** Make sure the monitor is plugged in and turned on. This type of oversight is really more common than you might think. Make sure the monitor works (you may want to try the monitor on a known-good system). If the monitor fails on a known-good system, replace the monitor. Next, trace the monitor cable to its connection at the video board, and verify that the connector is inserted securely. Check the video board. It is possible that the video board has failed. If the problem persists, replace the video board.

THE SYSTEM STARTS BUT CRASHES/REBOOTS INTERMITTENTLY

SYMPTOM 4-10 **The system randomly crashes/reboots for no apparent reason** Check for viruses first. Some viruses (especially memory-resident viruses) can cause the PC to crash or reboot unexpectedly. If you haven't run your virus checker yet, do so now. Check the power supply cables, and verify that they are attached properly and securely to the motherboard. Use a voltmeter to verify that each output from the power supply is correct, as outlined in Table 4-2. If any output is low (especially the +5 volt output), replace the power supply.

With all power off, check to see that the CPU is cool, that the heat-sink/fan assembly is fitted correctly, and that the CPU itself is inserted properly and completely into its socket. If the CPU overheats, it will stall, taking the entire system with it. If the CPU is seated in a ZIF (Zero Insertion Force) socket, make sure the socket's tension lever is closed and locked into place. For Pentium II/III processors, verify that the retention mechanism is secure. Also make sure that all SIMMs/DIMMs are seated properly in their holders and locked into place. You may try removing each module, cleaning the contacts, and reinstalling the SIMMs/DIMMs.

Make sure that all expansion boards are seated properly. Any boards that are not secured properly, or that are inserted unevenly, can short bus signals and cause spurious reboots. If you've recently installed new expansion hardware, make sure there are no hardware conflicts between interrupts, DMA channels, or I/O addresses. Inspect the motherboard at every metal standoff and see that no metal traces are being shorted against a standoff or screw. You may want to free the motherboard and see if the crashes or reboots go away. If so, use nonconductive spacers (such as a small piece of manila folder) to insulate the motherboard from each metal standoff. If the system continues to crash or reboot (and all voltages from the power supply are correct), replace the motherboard.

AFTER AN UPGRADE

SYMPTOM 4-11 **The system fails to boot, freezes during boot, or freezes during operation for no apparent reason** This is the classic sign of a hardware conflict. A PC is designed with a limited number of resources (memory, I/O addresses, interrupt [IRQ] lines, DMA channels, etc.). For the PC to function properly, each device added to the system must use its own unique resources. For example, no two devices can use the same IRQ, DMA, or I/O resources. When such an overlap of resources occurs, the PC can easily malfunction and freeze. Unfortunately, it is virtually impossible to predict when the malfunction will occur, so a conflict can manifest itself early (any time during the boot process), or later (after DOS is loaded) while an application is running.

Resolving a conflict is not difficult, but it requires patience and attention to detail. Examine the upgrade and its adapter board and check the IRQ, DMA, and I/O address settings of other boards in the system. Make sure the upgrade hardware is set to use resources that are not in use by other devices already in the system. For example, some motherboards offer built-in video controller circuits. Before another video adapter can be added to the system, the motherboard video adapter must be disabled—usually with a single motherboard jumper. Some sophisticated adapter boards (especially high-end video adapters and video capture boards) require the use of extra memory space. If memory exclusions are needed, be sure the appropriate entries are made in CONFIG.SYS and AUTOEXEC.BAT files. If memory exclusions are not followed, multiple devices may attempt to use the same memory space, which will result in a conflict.

SYMPTOM 4-12 **The system fails to recognize its upgrade device** Even if the hardware is installed in a system correctly, the PC may not recognize the upgrade device(s) without the proper software loaded. A great example of this is the CD-ROM drive. It is a simple matter to install the drive (and a controller card if necessary), but the PC will not even recognize the drive unless the low-level CD-ROM device driver is added to CONFIG.SYS and the MS-DOS CD-ROM driver (MSCDEX) is included in AUTOEXEC.BAT. If the PC is running in a stable fashion, but it does not recognize the expansion hardware, make sure you have loaded all required software correctly.

If you are mixing and matching existing subassemblies from new and old systems, make sure that each device is fully compatible with the PC. Incompatibilities between vintages and manufacturers can lead to operational problems. For example, adding a 3.5-inch floppy drive to an i286 AT system can result in problems because the older BIOS could not format 3.5-inch high-density (1.44MB) floppy disks. A DOS utility (such as DRIVER.SYS) is needed to correct this deficiency.

It is also possible that the upgrade device may simply be defective or installed incorrectly. Open the system and double-check your installation. Pay particular attention to any cables, connectors, or drive jumpers. When you confirm that the hardware and software installation is correct, suspect a hardware defect. Try the upgrade in another system if possible. If the problem persists when you attempt the upgrade on another PC, one or more elements of the upgrade hardware are probably defective. Return it to the vendor for a prompt refund or replacement. If the upgrade works on another system, the original system may be incompatible with the upgrade, or you may have missed a jumper or DIP switch setting on the motherboard.

SYMPTOM 4-13 **One or more applications fail to function as expected after an upgrade** This is not uncommon among video adapter and sound board upgrades. Often, applications are configured to work with various sets of hardware. When that hardware is altered, the particular application(s) may no longer run properly (this is especially true under Windows). The best way to address this problem is to check and change the hardware configuration for each affected application. Most DOS applications come with a setup utility. Under Windows 95/98, you can access system configuration settings through the System icon under the Control Panel (a.k.a. the Device Manager).

WINDOWS 95/98 BOOT SYMPTOMS

SYMPTOM 4-14 **The Windows 95/98 boot drive is no longer bootable after restoring data with the DOS Backup utility** This happens frequently when a replacement drive is installed and you attempt to restore the Windows 95/98 backup data. Unfortunately, the DOS version of Backup is not configured to restore system files. Start Backup and restore your root directory with System Files, Hidden Files, and Read Only Files checked. Next, boot the system from an MS-DOS 6.x upgrade setup disk 1, or a Windows 95/98 startup disk, and then use the SYS command to make the hard drive bootable, as shown here:

```
A:\> sys c:
```

You should then be able to restore the remainder of your files. When backing up a Windows 95/98 system, your best approach is to use the Windows Backup program. Once the new drive is installed, partitioned, and formatted, install a new copy of Windows 95/98, start Windows Backup, and then restore the remaining files to the drive.

SYMPTOM 4-15 Windows 95/98 will not boot, and ScanDisk reports bad clusters that it cannot repair This is a problem encountered with Western Digital hard drives. If your WD drive fails in this way, you can recover the drive, but you will lose all information on it. Back up as much information from the drive as possible before proceeding:

1. Download the Western Digital service files WDATIDE.EXE and WD_CLEAR.EXE from WD at **http://www.wdc.com/**. You can also get these files from AOL by typing the keyword WDC.
2. Copy these files to a clean boot floppy disk.
3. Boot to DOS from a clean disk (no CONFIG.SYS or AUTOEXEC.BAT files), and run WD_CLEAR.EXE. This utility clears all data on the media (and destroys all data).
4. Next, run the WDATIDE.EXE utility to perform a comprehensive surface scan.
5. Repartition and reformat the drive; then restore your data.

SYMPTOM 4-16 You see a "Bad or missing <filename>" error on startup A file used by Windows 95/98 during startup has probably become corrupt. Locate the file mentioned in the error message. If you can find the file, erase it and try reinstalling it from the original Windows 95/98 installation CD.

SYMPTOM 4-17 Windows 95/98 reports damaged or missing files, or a "VxD error" During startup, Windows 95/98 depends on several key files being available. If a key file is damaged or missing, Windows will not function properly (if it loads at all). Run Windows setup again and select the Verify option in Safe Recovery to replace the missing or damaged file(s). Otherwise, you may need to reinstall Windows from scratch.

SYMPTOM 4-18 After installing Windows 95/98, you can't boot from a different drive The Windows setup program checks all hard disks to find just one that contains the 80h designator in the DriveNumber field of a boot sector. Windows 95/98 will typically force the first drive to be bootable and prevent other drives from booting. However, there are two ways to correct the problem after Windows 95/98 is installed:

- Use the version of FDISK included with Windows 95/98 to set the primary active partition.
- Use a disk editor utility to change a disk's DriveNumber field so that you can boot from that hard disk.

SYMPTOM 4-19 Windows 95/98 registry files are missing There are two registry files: USER.DAT and SYSTEM.DAT. They are also backed up automatically as USER.DA0 and SYSTEM.DA0. If a DAT file is missing, Windows 95/98 will automatically load the corresponding DA0 file. If both the DAT and DA0 registry files are missing or corrupt, Windows 95/98 will start in the Safe Mode, offering to restore the registry. However, this cannot be accomplished without a backup. Either restore the registry files from a tape or floppy disk backup, or run Windows setup to create a new registry. Unfortunately, restoring an old registry or creating a new registry from scratch will reload programs and re-add hardware to restore the system to its original state—a long and difficult procedure. Use the following DOS procedure to back up the registry files to a floppy disk:

```
attrib -r -s -h system.da?
attrib -r -s -h user.da?
copy system.da? A:\
copy user.da? A:\
```

```
attrib +r +s +h system.da?
attrib +r +s +h user.da?
```

SYMPTOM 4-20 During the Windows 95/98 boot, you get an "Invalid System Disk" error This often happens in the first reboot during Windows setup, or when you boot from the startup disk. When you a see a message such as "Invalid system disk. Replace the disk, and then press any key," there may be several possible problems. First, your disk may be infected with a boot sector virus. Run your antivirus work disk and check closely for boot sector viruses. Windows setup may also fail if there is antivirus software running as a TSR, or your BIOS has enabled boot sector protection. Make sure that any boot sector protection is turned off before installing Windows 95/98. Check for disk overlay software (Windows 95/98 may not detect overlay software such as Disk Manager, EZ-Drive, or DrivePro), and overwrite the master boot record (MBR). See the documentation that accompanies your particular management software for recovering the MBR. To reinstall the Windows 95/98 system files, follow the steps below:

1. Boot the system using the Windows 95/98 emergency boot disk.
2. At the DOS command prompt, type the following lines:

```
c:
cd\windows\command
attrib c:\msdos.sys -h -s -r
ren c:\msdos.sys c:\msdos.xxx
a:
sys c:
del c:\msdos.sys
ren c:\msdos.xxx c:\msdos.sys
attrib c:\msdos.sys +r +s +h
```

3. Remove the emergency boot disk and reboot the system.

SYMPTOM 4-21 Windows 95/98 will not install on a compressed drive You are probably using an old version of the compression software that Windows 95/98 does not recognize. Although Windows 95/98 should be compatible with all versions of SuperStor, it does require version 2.0 or later of Stacker. Make sure your compression software is recent, and see that there is enough free space on the host drive to support Windows 95/98 installation. If you have the PlusPack for Windows 95/98, you should be able to install DriveSpace 3 for best Windows support.

SYMPTOM 4-22 The drive indicates that it is in "MS-DOS compatibility mode" For some reason, Windows 95/98 is using a real-mode (DOS) driver instead of a protected-mode (32-bit) driver. Make sure that any software related to the hard drive (especially hard disk drivers) are using the protected-mode versions. Windows 95/98 should install equivalent protected-mode software, but you may need to contact the drive manufacturer and obtain the latest Windows 95/98 drivers. If you are using Disk Manager, make sure you're using version 6.0 or later. You can get the latest patch (DMPATCH.EXE) from the Ontrack Web site at **http://www.ontrack.com/**. Finally, check your motherboard BIOS. Windows 95/98 may use DOS compatibility mode on large EIDE hard disks (hard disks with more than 1024 cylinders) in some computers. This may occur because of an invalid drive geometry translation in the system ROM BIOS that prevents the protected-mode IDE device driver from being loaded. Contact your system manufacturer for information about obtaining an updated BIOS.

SYMPTOM 4-23 Disabling protected-mode disk driver(s) hides the partition table when FDISK is used As with Symptom 4-22, there are problems preventing 32-bit operation of your hard drive(s). Do not use the "Disable all 32-bit protected-mode disk drivers" option. Instead, upgrade your motherboard BIOS to a later version.

SYMPTOM 4-24 You cannot achieve 32-bit disk access under Windows 95/98 If the Windows 95/98 system refuses to allow 32-bit disk access, there may be a conflict between the motherboard CMOS setup entries and the BIOS on your EIDE controller. For example, if both BIOS have settings for Logical Block Addressing (or LBA), make sure only one entry is in use.

SYMPTOM 4-25 Windows 95/98 does not recognize a new device In some cases, Windows 95/98 is unable to recognize a new device. When this happens, check to see if there is a hardware conflict between the device and other devices in the system. (You can see conflicts represented in the Device Manager with small yellow exclamation marks.) Also make sure that any necessary drivers have been installed properly. If problems continue, remove the new device through your Device Manager, and reinstall it through the Add New Hardware wizard. (Or perform a full reboot and allow Windows to redetect the device at start time.)

SYMPTOM 4-26 Windows 95/98 malfunctions when installed over Disk Manager Disk Manager should typically be compatible with Windows 95/98, but there are some points to keep in mind. Check your Disk Manager version first. If you are using Disk Manager, make sure that you're using version 6.0 or later. You can get the latest patch (DMPATCH.EXE) from the Ontrack Web site at **http://www.ontrack.com/**. Check the slave drive with Disk Manager. Although the Windows 95/98 file system is supposed to work properly with a slave drive only using Disk Manager, there are some circumstances where problems can occur:

- When a Windows 3.1x virtual driver replaces the Windows 95 protected-mode driver (such as WDCDRV.386)
- When the cylinder count in CMOS for the slave drive is greater than 1024 cylinders
- When the motherboard CMOS settings for the slave drive are set to autodetect

SYMPTOM 4-27 You have problems using a manufacturer-specific hard disk driver (such as Western Digital's FastTrack driver WDCDRV.386) for 32-bit access under Windows 95/98 Generally speaking, Windows 95/98 has 32-bit protected-mode drivers for a wide variety of EIDE devices. In actual practice, you should not need a manufacturer-specific driver. If Windows 95/98 has not removed all references to the driver from SYSTEM.INI, you should edit the file and remove those references manually; then reboot the system. Be sure to make a backup copy of SYSTEM.INI before editing it.

TIPS FOR SLOW WINDOWS STARTUPS

Windows 95/98 is a complex operating system, and it takes time to load the many components and drivers required to make it run. However, there are some circumstances that can make Windows really drag. If it seems that your Windows 98 system is taking an unusually long time to start, follow the tips below to help streamline your setup.

Shut down unneeded programs The first thing to do is examine what programs you're launching at startup and decide whether you really need them. Remember that programs can be launched from the Startup folder (under the Start menu), from the RUN= and LOAD= lines of your WIN.INI file, or from entries in the registry. Under Windows 95 you'd have to check each of these locations manually, but Windows 98 has a convenient one-stop location to tweak them all (Figure 4-2). Just click Start, select Run, and then type **MSCONFIG**. Under the Startup tab you'll see all the programs you are launching. By clearing the check box next to any item, you'll prevent it from running at startup.

Disable real-time virus scanning Many of today's antivirus utilities offer real-time scanning for viruses. Unfortunately, since the scanner loads at startup, it can seriously impact performance because it must scan every program file as it is being loaded into memory. If you're willing to accept a bit less virus protection, you can accelerate your boot times by turning off real-time scanning; instead, schedule a task to run a standard virus scan at least once a day. Not only will this shorten boot times, but it will make your system faster during any disk access.

Don't check the floppy drive Among its many other startup checks, Windows 98 checks to see if you've added or changed floppy drives each time the system starts up. Chances are that you'll never reconfigure your floppy, so tell Windows to stop checking it. Click Start, highlight Settings, select Control Panel, and then double-click the System icon. Click the Performance tab, click the File System button, and then select the Floppy Disk tab. Clear the check box marked "Search for new floppy disk drives each time your computer starts." Apply your changes and try rebooting the computer.

Check your network settings Network settings are often a cause of slow boot times. One common problem occurs when a network card has the TCP/IP protocol loaded and is set to obtain an IP address from a DHCP server, but no server is available. The PC will wait up to a minute for an answer from the server before it continues booting. Click Start, highlight Settings, select the Control Panel, and double-click the Network icon. (Don't make changes if you're on a company network that is supported by a network administrator. Check with the administrator first.)

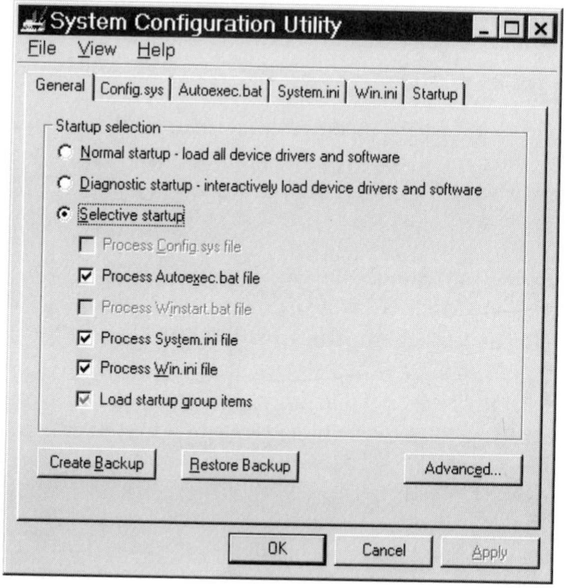

FIGURE 4-2 The MSCONFIG utility

If you're not using TCP/IP on your local network (only for ISP dial-up), then just remove the binding between the network card and the TCP/IP protocol. You'll see this in the Network dialog as a line that reads "TCP/IP -> (network card name)." Select that item and click Remove. If you are using TCP/IP on your local network, you either need to have a DHCP server running on the network or use manually assigned IP addresses. For most small networks of Windows 98 systems, manually assigned addresses work fine. For each PC on the network, give it a unique IP number in a sequence such as 10.0.0.1, 10.0.0.2, 10.0.0.3, and so on. You set this number in the Network dialog. Select the entry "TCP/IP -> (network card name)" and click Properties. On the IP Address tab, choose "Specify an IP address" and enter the unique IP number that you've chosen for this system. For the subnet mask, try using **255.0.0.0** for all systems.

Tweak your CMOS setup Check your CMOS setup routine for options that can speed your system's boot time. Enabling options such as Quick Boot or Quick POST and shortening drive initialization delays can shave a few seconds off the system's POST process. You'll also get a faster boot sequence if the system can boot directly from the C: drive rather than first checking for a floppy. (This also prevents viruses from infecting your system via a boot floppy.)

Examine the boot log You may be faced with a problematic hardware component or software driver. These can be a bit difficult to diagnose, but the BOOTLOG.TXT feature can help. This allows you to generate a boot log that indicates each step in the boot process. You'll need to access the Windows startup menu, which will give you the option to generate a boot log. After the BIOS has completed its POST, hold down the CTRL key. The boot menu should appear. (If the Windows 98 logo appears instead, you probably didn't press the CTRL key soon enough.)

From the boot menu, select a "logged startup." Once Windows has finished booting up, the file BOOTLOG.TXT will be in the root of your C: drive, and you can view this file with Notepad. On a normal system, it's unusual to have any step in the boot process take more than a second or two. Large delays (10 or 20 seconds) usually indicate some sort of problem with a driver or its associated hardware.

To help you make sense of the BOOTLOG.TXT file, try the Boot Log Analyzer utility (BLA.ZIP) on your companion CD.

TIPS FOR WINDOWS STARTUP PROBLEMS

It's bad enough when Windows takes a long time to load, but when Windows fails to start at all, it may be difficult (or impossible) to use diagnostics and Windows tools to correct the problem. This part of the chapter outlines a suite of tips that can help you track down and correct serious startup faults.

Try the Safe Mode One of your first options is to try starting Windows 98 in the Safe Mode. Hold down the CTRL key right after the BIOS finishes its POST (but before Windows starts to load). You should get a Startup menu of options to select from. Choose Safe Mode from the menu and allow Windows to boot. If the boot is successful, right-click My Computer and select Properties; then click the Device Manager tab. If any hardware is malfunctioning, it will be shown there with a yellow exclamation point. (You can also use Device Manager to disable hardware manually and see if that lets you boot normally.) If you cannot boot Windows to the Safe Mode, chances are there's a serious hardware problem in the system.

Check for disk errors If you cannot start Windows due to a disk error, it may be that the drive's power or signal cable has become loose. Check the cables and see that the drive is receiving adequate power. Try booting from a floppy disk. If you can reach a DOS prompt from a boot disk, the system hard drive may be defective.

Use the Automatic Skip Driver agent If your system crashes or hangs during the startup process, Windows 98 tries to avoid crashing again by skipping the operation that it "thinks" caused the problem. This is the Automatic Skip Driver (ASD) agent. However, the ASD may cause other problems (such as disabling some of your hardware) when a driver is skipped. To see if Windows is skipping any boot-up operations on your system, select Start, choose Run, and type **ASD**. If everything is okay, you'll receive a dialog with the message "There are no current ASD critical operation failures on this machine." If your system has had boot problems, they will be listed in this dialog. You can put a check next to any or all of the skipped drivers to have Windows 98 retry them the next time you boot. After you boot the system again, run ASD and see if the function was disabled again; if so, you may have a problem with that hardware (or your BIOS).

Check for missing files If you see the message "a file needed by Windows is missing" during a boot cycle, it's often due to a poor uninstallation of an application. This can sometimes occur when you uninstall and then immediately reinstall an application without rebooting first. Take a look at the name of the missing file and see if it yields any clue to the application that might be causing the problem. Then try to uninstall, reboot, and reinstall that application. If the offending file relates to an application that you no longer need, you can use RegEdit to find and delete the registry keys that refer to the file. (Be sure you have good backups before trying this.) As a last resort, you may need to reinstall Windows to fix this problem cleanly.

Windows Protection Errors In some cases, Windows may refuse to boot, returning the message "Windows Protection Error. You need to restart your computer." At this point, you're stuck unless you boot from a floppy disk. One cause in Windows 95 is a problem between SmartDrive and a large number of installed device drivers. If you see something about "initializing IOS" in the error message, try booting from a floppy, find the file SMARTDRV.EXE (usually in the Windows directory), and rename it to SMARTDRV.BAD. Now try booting the system from the hard drive again.

There is also a known problem in Windows 95 that affects AMD K6 processors running at 350MHz or higher speeds, and this will sometimes give a Windows protection error message. (You can refer to Microsoft's document Q192841 for more detailed information and a patch file.) Other solutions to Windows Protection Errors can be identified in Microsoft's document Q149962.

Other startup problems You can refer to the Microsoft Web site to learn about numerous other startup problems:

Q143053: Mouse Systems Driver May Cause Windows Protection Error

Q186351: Norton Anti Virus 4.0 May Cause Windows Protection Error

Q186844: "Windows Protection Error" with EZ-SCSI 4.0 and Easy-CD Pro 95

Q175930: Illegal Operations or Access Violations When Starting Windows

Q141898: Windows 95/98 Boots Directly to "Shut Down" Screen

Q187524: MS-DOS Based Program Starts When You Start Your Computer

Further Study

Symantec: **http://www.symantec.com**

Network Associates: **http://www.networkassociates.com/**

IBM setup routines: **oak.oakland.edu:/SimTel/msdos/at** or **ftp.uu.net:/systems/msdos/simtel/at**

Ontrack Software: **http://www.ontrack.com/**

Ziff-Davis benchmark site: **http://www8.zdnet.com/pcmag/pclabs/bench/**

Benchmarking newsgroup: **comp.benchmarks**

5

BACKUP GUIDE

CHAPTER AT A GLANCE

Few events are as frightening or disturbing as losing your valuable data. It really doesn't make much difference *how* it happens—virus damage, drive failure, sabotage, user error, an improper software installation, or old age are all equally effective at disabling your computer and rendering your data inaccessible. There are myriad of preventive maintenance tools and data recovery tactics available, but regardless of manufacturers' claims, all of those recovery techniques have limitations, especially when the drive fails outright. The only certain means of protecting your valuable data is to back up your system. This chapter covers some important backup considerations, offers some guidelines for preparing backups, and explains the major limitations and pitfalls of backup strategies.

Backup Considerations

Although it is not terribly expensive or difficult to start a backup regimen, it is hardly a trivial concern. Whether protecting your system against data loss or archiving unused applications and data, proper backups depend on understanding the needs of the particular system being backed up. One of the most common misconceptions about backups is that they are used solely for the purpose of protecting data. True, the threat of data loss is a major factor in any backup strategy, but there are other advantages of backups as well.

For example, backups are often used to archive older or unused files. Let's face it, even the largest hard drive will eventually run short of space. Older applications and work files can be off-loaded through a backup, then erased from the hard drive, thus freeing valuable drive space. Backups also play an important role in periodic drive maintenance. As magnetic media ages, the sector and track IDs decay slowly. In extreme cases, the ID data may become irretrievable and result in the loss of an application or its data. By maintaining timely backups, a drive can be low-level formatted (using a formatting program designed for the particular drive) to rewrite sector and track ID information, then reloaded from a most recent backup. The "refreshed" drive may then continue providing years of trouble-free service. Effective backups also demand a variety of other considerations:

- *Consider the backup frequency.* How often should a backup be performed? This is one of the most perplexing questions surrounding tape backups, and the answer is different depending on who you talk to. The most common yardstick is need: if you can't afford to lose what you've got, back it up. While this may be effective for individual PC owners, it is not quite so simple to evaluate the backup needs of business and professional users. In such cases, need should be based on the value of data contained in the PC and how often it changes. For example, a graphic design or desktop publishing firm may need to back up every week or two. On the other hand, a busy order-entry system would probably be best served making daily backups.
- *Consider the most effective type of backup.* Traditionally, there are three different types of backups: total, selective, and modified. The *total backup* is just as the name implies: all files and directories on the specified drive are saved to the backup device. Total backups provide the best protection of data, and files can be restored selectively, but total backups take the longest to complete. *Selective backups* allow you to back up only desired files or directories. This is particularly handy for archival purposes, or if the majority of new data on the system is limited to a number of known directories. Selective backups also take less time than total backups (depending on the number of files selected). *Modified backups* (also known as *differential backups*) copy only the files that were changed since the last backup. This is the fastest but least flexible type of backup. It is often a combination of these strategies that provides the best level of data protection.
- *Consider the hardware and media requirements.* There are many means of producing backups. Floppy disk, magneto-optical disks such as the Iomega Zip drive, tape drives (in all their variations), and optical disks such as CD-Rs or CD-RWs are just a few of the available options. Some years ago, floppy disks were often used for backups. Today, however, it would take thousands of disks to perform a total backup of one contemporary hard drive. Disks are still used for small groups of files (such as DTP files, graphics, and data files) that are considered "work in progress," but they are hardly useful for serious backup work. On the other side of the scale, magneto-optical (MO) devices provide tremendous storage capacity, but their price and sophistication are often best suited for busy networks and high-end workstations. For the individual PC or a small network, tape drives or CD-R/CD-RW drives generally provide the best cost/performance trade-off. A single low-end tape drive can back up

as much as 2GB on one tape, and more expensive drives can hold over 8GB. In most installations, a tape drive will provide more than adequate backup power.

- *Get the media preformatted.* If you've ever had to format a box of floppy disks, you know what a cumbersome, time-consuming process it can be. Tapes are even more difficult to deal with. A typical minicartridge can take up to one hour to format. While this may not be a problem for individual users who back up infrequently, business users may have trouble committing hours of PC time to tape formatting. Use factory-formatted media wherever possible. Even though preformatted media may cost a bit more, the savings in time is often well worth it.
- *Consider where to store the backups.* Since backups can serve a number of practical purposes, it is important to plan where the backups will be kept and who will have access to them. Again, individuals who use their PC for casual applications can probably keep their backup tape in a desk drawer or filing cabinet without a second thought. For businesses and busy professional systems, the problem becomes a bit more complicated. One of the key reasons for backups is disaster recovery, so the backup should be protected from disaster. Often, this means securing backups in a fire-proof safe or fire-proof file cabinet in another room away from the original system—sometimes away from the site of business entirely. Another reason for this concern is security—you would not want confidential files falling into the wrong hands. In many companies, backup, restoration, and security are assigned to authorized individuals.
- *Consider compression.* Data compression is an excellent means of expanding the capacity of a tape. If your backup software provides the capability of tape compression, use it. There may be a small penalty in reading or writing speed, but the extra capacity is usually worth it.
- *Consider manual versus automatic backups.* If you run your system for regular, prolonged periods of time, automatic backups can be configured with a scheduler feature of most backup software (or the Task Manager feature of Windows 98). This makes it possible to save desired files at regular times while remaining virtually transparent to the user. Businesses with extensive computer time can usually take advantage of automatic backups. Individuals who use PCs inconsistently are probably best served with manual backups. Keep in mind that tape drives require routine cleaning, so automatic backups should also include periods of downtime for regular scheduled cleanings.

Tape Rotation Tactics

Tape cartridges are the most common medium for backup systems. Although the number of backups you perform per week or per month will depend entirely on the amount of activity on your system or network, backup integrity is limited by the tapes themselves. By using more than one tape as part of your backup regimen, you will not find yourself writing over a current backup (potentially disastrous if the backup process is interrupted). Tape rotation helps to ensure that data is protected and integral at all times.

TWO TAPES

The two-tape strategy is generally considered to be the most rudimentary strategy—ideal for individual or infrequent PC users. There are usually two variations with this strategy. The most common implementation is simply to make full backups, alternating the tapes each time. For example, tape A is reformatted and used for a backup on March 1, tape B is reformatted and used on April 1, then tape A is reformatted and reused for a complete backup on May 1, and so on. This approach guarantees that you are never overwriting a current backup. An alternative strategy is to create a total backup on tape A, then make modified backups on tape B as needed.

THREE TAPES

The three-tape cycle is frequently used for small offices or home offices where a limited number of files are changing from day to day. The process is easy to understand if you look at it over a one-week period. On Monday, make a complete backup on tape A. Tuesday through Friday, make modified (a.k.a. incremental) backups on tape B. (Each modified backup should have its own tape volume.) The next week, make a total backup on tape C, and store tape A in a secure location off-site. Erase or reformat tape B, and use it for modified backups throughout the week. On Monday of the subsequent week, store tape C off-site, and return tape A to be erased or reformatted for a new complete backup. Thus, tapes A and C are alternated each week for complete system backups, while tape B remains on-site for daily modified backups.

If you are not using the system enough to justify daily maintenance, try a weekly approach. Use tape A for a total backup on the first of the month, and then use tape B for modified backups once a week during the month (or whenever important new files must be protected). The first of the next month, perform a total backup on tape C, and store tape A in a secure location off-site. Erase tape B and reuse it for modified backups throughout the month. On the first of the third month, move tape C off-site, erase tape A and perform a complete backup; then erase tape B and use it for modified backups. This way, tapes A and C are alternated the first of every month rather than the first of every week.

SIX TAPES

The six-tape rotation is intended for businesses and busy offices where important files are changed and updated daily. Start the week by erasing or reformatting tapes A and F, then creating total backups on both tapes. Store tape F in a secure location off-site. Use tapes B, C, D, and E to perform modified (incremental) backups on Tuesday through Friday. On the subsequent Monday, tapes A and F would be erased and backed up once again. Each day through the week, the tape designated for that particular day would be erased and saved with a modified backup.

TEN TAPES

When you need to maintain weekly and monthly off-site archives of on-going work, you can use a ten-tape rotation cycle (which is really just an adjustment to the six-tape cycle). By adding four more tapes to the six-tape cycle, you can create a total backup the first of every week, then store those weekly backups off-site. For example, on the first Monday of the month, a total backup is made on tapes A and F (just as in the six-tape rotation), and tape F is stored off-site. On Tuesday through Friday, tapes B, C, D, and E hold modified backups of each day. Tape F becomes the archive of week 1. The next week, total backups are made on tapes A and G, while tapes B, C, D, and E provide modified backups. Tape G would be the archive for week 2. The third week, tapes A and H would be the total backups, and tape H would archive the third week. Tapes A and I would hold total backups on the fourth week, so tape I would archive the fourth week. Finally, tape J would be used as a total backup on the last day of the month. Although this process is overkill for many businesses, it may come in handy for businesses that require long-term archives of their work (for example, government contractors).

Backup Limitations

Although backups are usually considered to be a cost-effective form of data archiving and a reliable means of data protection, they are hardly perfect. There are a whole array of limitations that can adversely affect your backup efforts (or those of your customer). This part of the chapter is designed to illustrate the pitfalls to look out for when planning and executing backups.

- *Irregular or inconsistent backups*. This is probably the single most troublesome problem when implementing a backup strategy. In order to be effective, backups must be performed regularly. All too often, users make some initial backups on schedule, but fail to follow through with subsequent backups. Before long, the backups that *were* made fall so far out of date that they become useless. When trouble occurs, the investment in equipment and media just does not pay off. Make it a point to implement regular backups and follow through with them consistently.
- *Poorly labeled and stored backups*. This problem is typical of large tape rotations. Often, tapes and other backup media are left strewn around an office or department with little or no record of what is on them. Effective backup strategies demand that each tape be marked and identified clearly so that no one will accidentally discard or overwrite it. Groups of tapes should always be kept together in a drawer or on a shelf the same way you would organize volumes of books. It's hard enough to keep regular backups without having to search for the tapes and guess which ones to use. Make it a point to keep tapes (and all magnetic media) away from telephones, monitors, power supplies, excessive heat, extreme cold, and all forms of moisture.
- *Inadequate disaster preparation*. Here's another real impediment to successful backups. Too often, businesses invest serious money in backup equipment, only to leave the tapes sitting on top of the backed-up system. If you rely on backups to store your vital files, those tapes should be stored in a location that is reasonably safe from disasters such as fire, flood, theft, or sabotage. Often, a fire-proof safe or file cabinet will perform quite well. The same concern is true for off-site storage.
- *Inadequate testing and maintenance*. Some businesses are so preoccupied with performing a backup that they do not check to confirm that the backup is any good. When trouble strikes, they are horrified to find that the backup either lacks vital files, is unreadable, or does not restore properly, leaving the backup virtually useless. After a backup is made, it should be tested using a "compare" or "verify" function of the backup software to check the tape contents against the disk files. This takes a bit longer, but it need not be done each time a backup is made. When errors are indicated, it usually means that the drive is failing or has not been routinely cleaned as required. Try cleaning the backup drive as recommended by the manufacturer, and perform the backup again. Every so often, it may be worth testing your backup capability with a "backup drill."
- *Inadequate attention to the media*. Like floppy disk, tapes are magnetic media. Unfortunately, magnetic media do not last forever. One of the big problems with frequent backups is that users mistake backup or compare errors as a problem with the drive or backup software, when it is actually the tape that has worn out. As a general rule, plan on replacing your tapes at least once a year. If you are performing frequent backups, plan on replacing your tapes even more frequently. Tape life is also dependent on tape quality—high-quality tapes last longer than low-quality tapes. It is often more prudent to spend a bit more for a reliable, good-quality tape than to save a little money on a low-cost tape, only to find that the tape wears out much sooner, or loses data when it's needed.

Making the Most of Microsoft Backup

There are numerous backup utilities available today, but Microsoft includes a version of Backup with each copy of Windows 95 and Windows 98. Backup is generally regarded as a basic end-user utility, but there are some important issues to remember when installing and using Backup. This part of the chapter outlines the essentials for using Backup and covers many of the most common Backup problems.

GUIDELINES FOR USING BACKUP

When using Backup, it's important that you remember the following points; otherwise, you may encounter problems setting up or using Backup for Windows 95.

Tape Drive Support The Backup program supports the following QIC-40, QIC-80, and QIC-3010 tape backup units made by the following companies (and connected to the primary floppy disk controller): Colorado Memory Systems (CMS), Conner, Iomega, and Wangtek (in "hardware phantom mode" or "Drive B sharing mode"). Backup also supports CMS QIC-40, QIC-80, and QIC-3010 tape drives connected to a parallel port. However, the following drives are *not* compatible with Backup:

- Drives connected to a secondary floppy disk controller (or to a floppy accelerator card)
- Archive drives
- Irwin AccuTrak tapes (and other Irwin drives)
- Mountain drives
- QIC Wide tapes (Backup supports QIC Wide drives using QIC 80 tapes)
- QIC 3020 drives
- SCSI tape drives
- Summit drives
- Proprietary tape drive controllers of any type
- Travan drives

> Some floppy controller–driven tape backup units may require firmware (BIOS) revisions to work properly with the Backup program.

FC-20 Tape Controller Support Backup does not support proprietary controller cards for tape drives. Similar unsupported controllers include FC-10 and FC-15 controllers, and controllers from Iomega.

Using Other Backup Sets Backup can restore data from backup sets created by third-party DOS-based or Windows 3.1–based tape backup programs. However, the third-party tape backup program must conform to the QIC standard for implementing compression. Unfortunately, Backup cannot restore data sets created by earlier versions of Backup.

Backup Types Backup supports full and incremental backup sets, but does not support differential backups. To enable incremental backup, click Options on Backup's Settings menu, and then click the Incremental option button on the Backup tab.

Restoring Without Windows Backup requires Windows. If you're reinstalling Windows for any reason, you need at least a minimum install (including Backup). Then you can use the Backup utility to restore your backup set.

Registry Errors When Restoring Files When restoring just one or two files from a backup set, you may receive a message such as "There may have been an error restoring the registry. Your computer may not work properly," even though you chose not to restore the registry. This message appears when you restore files from the "Full System Backup Set" collection, which is intended to be used only to perform a full system backup or restore. The Full System Backup Set collection contains the files necessary to restore your Windows configuration to its original state. Keep this backup set in a safe place in case your hard disk partition or the Windows folder is damaged, and create separate backup sets for backing up other data.

Tape Drive Detection Tape drive detection is performed by Microsoft Backup when it loads. Backup does not rely on the operating system for information about tape drive units attached to the system, so it is not necessary for your tape drive to be listed in Device Manager.

INSTALLING BACKUP

Although the Backup utility is included with Windows 95/98, it is not installed by default when Windows is installed. Instead, you'll need to install Backup manually from the Windows installation CD. Follow these steps to install Backup:

1. Open Control Panel, and then double-click the Add/Remove Programs icon.
2. On the Windows Setup tab, click Disk Tools (or System Tools), and then click Details.
3. Click the Backup check box to select it, and then click OK.
4. Click OK again. The installation process will proceed automatically.

BACKING UP AND RESTORING

Using Microsoft Backup is not a terribly complicated process, but a few guidelines might make the procedure a bit easier. Use the steps below when creating a backup set:

1. Click Start, highlight Programs, select Accessories, highlight System Tools, and then click Backup.
2. Click the Backup tab.
3. Create a backup set. (A *backup set* is an index of the files you plan to back up.) The first time you run Backup, a Full System Backup Set is created. This set includes every file on your hard disk.
4. To create a smaller set of selected files, use the Select Files To Backup dialog. Each drive, folder, and file has a check box next to it. If a check appears in a given box, that file, folder, or the contents of the selected drive will be backed up. If a check appears in a check box with a dark background, some items in the folder or drive (but not everything) will be backed up.
5. Click Next Step.
6. In the "Select a destination for the backup" window, click the desired destination for your backup. If you have a supported tape backup drive that is detected by Backup, it appears at the bottom of the "Select a destination for the backup" window. If you do not have a tape drive (or your tape drive is not detected), you can select a floppy disk drive or a location on your hard disk.

> You can also back up your files to a network drive by mapping a drive letter to the network destination where you want to back up your files. If you have mapped a drive letter to a network drive, Backup shows it in the "Select a destination for the backup" window.

7 Click Start Backup and allow the process to proceed. If you have created a new backup set, you are prompted to name it. Backup will inform you when the operation is finished.

You can use the steps below to restore your backup set:

1. Click Start, highlight Programs, select Accessories, highlight System Tools, and then click Backup.
2. Click the Restore tab.
3. In the Restore From window, select the drive or folder where the backup is stored. In the Backup Set window, select the backup set that you need to restore, and then click Next Step.
4. Click the check boxes by the files you want to restore (a check will appear in the check box), or clear the check boxes for any files you do not want to restore.
5. Click Start Restore and allow the process to proceed. Backup will inform you when the operation is finished.

RESTORING EARLIER BACKUP SETS

It is important to remember that the Backup utility included with Windows 95 cannot restore files that were saved with an earlier version of Backup (the versions of Backup included with DOS versions 5.0 and 6.x). In order to restore files saved with earlier versions of Backup, you must use the RESTORE.EXE or MSBACKUP.EXE utility located on the Windows 95 CD. Before using RESTORE.EXE or MSBACKUP.EXE, refer to the LFNBK.TXT file in the \admin\apptools\lfnback folder on your Windows CD.

To restore files saved with the Backup program included in DOS 5.0, use the RESTORE.EXE program located in the \other\oldmsdos folder on your Windows 95 CD. To run this program, copy it to a folder on your hard drive, and then run it from a command prompt (making sure to use the appropriate syntax). For detailed information about the RESTORE.EXE program, type the following line:

```
restore /?
```

If you receive the error message "Incorrect DOS version" when you try to use RESTORE.EXE, type the following line to modify the version table:

```
setver restore.exe 6.22
```

After you type this line, restart your computer and try to run RESTORE.EXE again.

To restore files created with the backup program included in DOS 6.x, use the MSBACKUP.EXE utility located in the \other\oldmsdos\msbackup folder on your Windows 95 CD. To run this program, copy all the files from the folder on that CD to a folder on your hard drive. Double-click the MSBACKUP.EXE file in Windows Explorer to start it. For detailed information about the MSBACKUP.EXE program, start the program and click Restore on the Help menu.

TROUBLESHOOTING NOTES ON MICROSOFT BACKUP

Backup offers most Windows 95/98 users a simple and convenient tool for backing up their important files or day-to-day work. Although Backup is compatible with a wide range of drives, it is certainly not foolproof. When you encounter problems with Backup, check the following tips before diving into the troubleshooting issues in the next section.

Tape Drive Not Detected When you cannot get Backup to recognize a specific tape drive, verify that the drive is compatible with Backup. See the above section on Tape Drive Support for a list of drives not compatible with Backup.

Problems Restoring Files File restoration problems are often the result of drive maintenance and system (or OS) configuration issues. Use the tips below to help troubleshoot file problems:

- Clean the read/write heads.
- Set your computer to a slower speed (disable the "turbo" mode).
- Try to restore the files in Safe Mode. If the tape backup drive requires a protected-mode driver, it will not work in Safe Mode. For example, Colorado Trakker drives do not work in Safe Mode because the VCOMM driver doesn't load.
- Try to restore the files on a different computer.
- Verify that there is enough swap file space on your hard drive.

Network Backup/Restore Problems This problem is usually related to the network or network configuration rather than the Backup utility. If you can't back up or restore files through a network, try a different network protocol, or try to copy a large file across the network with the XCOPY command. You may also need to disconnect the PC from its network and backup/restore files locally.

Tape Cannot Be Formatted Formatting problems are usually the result of defective tapes, incompatible formats, or OS driver conflicts:

- See that you're using a compatible tape format. For example, you cannot format a 3010 tape in a QIC-80 drive, and you cannot format a QIC-80 Wide tape in a QIC-80 drive.
- The tape may be bad or worn out. Try to format a different tape. Do not try to format bulk-erased tapes.
- Try to format the tape in Windows 95 Safe Mode. If the tape backup drive requires a protected-mode driver, it will not work in Safe Mode. For example, Colorado Trakker drives do not work in Safe Mode because the VCOMM driver doesn't load.
- There may be a video DMA conflict (typically encountered on older PCs). Minimize the progress indicator. If formatting still fails, change the video resolution to 640×480×16 colors. If problems persist, try formatting the tape in a full-screen DOS command prompt session. (If this works, use Device Manager to look for a DMA conflict between the video card and the floppy drive controller.)

The Tape Despools If your tapes frequently despool, the end-of-tape (EOT) sensor in your tape drive may be dirty or damaged. This prevents the drive from accurately determining when the end of the tape has been reached. Many drive manufacturers recommend cleaning the end-of-tape sensor after every eight hours of drive operation, when excessive dust or other debris accumulates on the sensor, or when a tape used in the drive becomes despooled. For specific cleaning information, refer to the documentation that came with your drive.

Tape Comparison Fails This almost always means that the tape has failed. Try a known-good or good-quality tape.

Cannot Access the Tape Drive (and Backup Stops Responding) If Backup is unable to access the tape drive and appears to stop responding, there may be a resource conflict between IDE devices in your computer. For example, your SyQuest removable drive may be configured to use the same resources as your tape drive. Use the Device Manager to check for hardware conflicts in the system.

Colorado Trakker Tape Backup Issues If you're experiencing random Backup problems with a Trakker tape drive on a parallel port, make sure the parallel port is not configured in the computer's CMOS setup as an ECP or EPP port. If it is, reconfigure the port to a standard parallel port.

Iomega QIC-80 Tape Backup Issues Iomega suggests that these drives require new drivers from Iomega (**www.iomega.com**). You may also need to verify that the following line exists in the CONFIG.SYS file:

```
buffers=30
```

Miscellaneous Suggestions If you continue to have problems with Backup, try some of the tips below:

- Clean the tape drive carefully (especially the read/write heads).
- Verify that all of the power connections and signal cables are securely and properly attached.
- Verify that any jumpers on the drive (and drive controller) are set in a compatible mode for your system.
- If you have an internal tape drive, position it as far as possible from the hard disk. If you have an external tape drive, position it as far as possible from the monitor.

BACKUP SYMPTOMS

SYMPTOM 5-1 **Backup has trouble spanning multiple disks when backing up to a removable media drive under Windows 95** When you're using Backup to store files to a removable disk (other than floppy disks), Backup doesn't prompt you to insert a second disk. If the entire backup doesn't fit on one disk, you'll receive an error such as "Errors occurred during this operation—do you want to view them now?" The incomplete backup volume on the first disk is damaged and cannot be restored.

This is a limitation of the Backup utility. Although Backup does support the use of removable disk drives (Bernoulli and SyQuest drives), it does not support performing backups that span multiple disks. Backup can span multiple disks only on floppy disk drives connected to the primary floppy drive controller. When you're using Backup to store files to a removable disk, perform only backups that fit on one disk. Large backups that require more than one disk should be broken into smaller backups, each of which fits on one disk.

SYMPTOM 5-2 **Backup performance appears poor under Windows 95** Performing a backup operation through Backup may take (significantly) longer than you expect. This poor backup performance might also be accompanied by diminished hard drive performance while you perform other tasks in Windows 95. There are several important factors that can affect backup performance.

First, check your available memory. A lack of available memory is typically caused by having too many programs open at the same time, or by not having enough physical RAM installed in the computer. Close all running programs before starting the backup process. If that does not improve performance, remove all programs from the Startup folder and from the "load=" and "run=" lines of your WIN.INI file. If performance remains poor after restarting Windows, try adding more RAM to the system.

Also check for DOS Compatibility Mode. Double-click the System icon in Control Panel, and then click the Performance tab. If the Performance tab in System properties shows that one or more of the hard drives are operating in DOS Compatibility Mode, resolve this problem as soon as possible to improve performance in Backup.

Check the hard drive performance. Even if your hard drives are not stuck in DOS Compatibility Mode, Backup performance may be affected by overall drive performance. If you're using an IDE-type hard drive, its performance may be affected by another device on the same controller channel (such as tape drives and CD-ROMs). Move the slower device(s) to a separate IDE controller channel.

Update any compression software. When using disk compression on an older (slower) computer, hard drive performance may suffer. If you're using third-party disk compression software that employs real-mode drivers to access your compressed drives, you may be able to improve performance by replacing the real-mode driver with a protected-mode driver.

Check and correct any file fragmentation. Badly fragmented hard disks can affect the performance of Backup (as well as the performance of other tasks in Windows 95). Click the Start button, highlight Programs, point to Accessories, point to System Tools, and then click Disk Defragmenter. Run Defrag to reorganize the files on your hard drive(s).

Finally, check the tape for defects. Backup can detect and avoid unusable sectors on a tape, but the process that it uses for this type of checking can be time consuming. If you suspect that performance problems in Backup are caused by unusable sectors on a tape, try using a new tape, or use a tape that you know does not contain bad sectors.

SYMPTOM 5-3 **You encounter problems restoring a Windows 95 backup set under Windows 98** This occurs when you try to use the Windows 98 Backup tool to restore an individual file from a Windows 95 Backup set. The restored file may be damaged, and the resulting file may be 0 bytes. This can happen when you try to restore an individual file from a multiple-file backup set that spans more than one disk or tape. This is caused by design differences between Windows 98 and Windows 95 in the implementation of the QIC tape format. To work around this problem, you'll need to restore the entire Windows 95 backup set, and then delete any of the other restored files that you do not want. You may wish to check the Microsoft Web site to see if there is a patch or update to the Windows 98 Backup utility that will correct this problem.

SYMPTOM 5-4 **The HP Colorado Backup utility doesn't detect your tape drive under Windows 98** When you try to use the HP Colorado Backup for Windows 95 software under Windows 98, Colorado Backup does not detect your tape drive, even though your tape drive is listed in Device Manager. This might happen if Microsoft Backup is currently installed (or has been installed in the past). Backup makes subtle changes to the registry. You'll need to remove unneeded files and correct the changes to the registry. To utilize Colorado Backup software instead of Microsoft Backup, uninstall Microsoft Backup first; then reinstall Colorado Backup from scratch by following the steps below.

> Be sure to make a complete backup of your registry files (as well as the RegEdit utility) to your emergency boot disk. If you make a mistake editing the registry, you can install the original files from your boot floppy.

1. Click Start, highlight Settings, and then click Control Panel.
2. Double-click Add/Remove Programs, and then click the Windows Setup tab.
3. Click on System Tools (not the check box); then click Details.

4 Click the Backup check box to clear it, click OK, click OK again, and then click Yes to restart your computer.

5 Delete or rename the following files (if they exist):

PNPWPROP.DLL in Windows\System

PNPWRENU.DLL in Windows\System

PNPWFDC.INF in Windows\Inf

PNPWIDE.INF in Windows\Inf

PNPWPPT.INF in Windows\Inf

PNPWTAPE.INF in Windows\Inf

PNPWTAPE.CAT in Windows

6 Use the registry editor (RegEdit) to delete the following registry keys (if they exist):

```
HKEY_LOCAL_MACHINE\System\CurrentControlSet\Services\Class\Tape
HKEY_LOCAL_MACHINE\System\CurrentControlSet\Services\Class\TapeController
HKEY_LOCAL_MACHINE\System\CurrentControlSet\Services\Class\TapeDetection
```

7 Restart your computer.

8 Now check Device Manager to verify that the Windows 98 tape icons and drivers no longer exist. Remove them if they are present.

9 Reinstall the Colorado Backup software and test it to see if the problem is resolved. (Your tape drive should be detected properly.)

> Microsoft Backup is not installed by default in Windows 98. If Backup is installed in Windows 95 before you install Windows 98, Backup is upgraded to the Windows 98 version automatically.

SYMPTOM 5-5 **When starting Backup under Windows 98, you receive a driver installation error** The exact error may appear similar to "Driver already installed Ref 00-02-00-00-0000." After Backup starts, you may receive another error message such as "No device found." Chances are that the backup devices in your computer will not work correctly, and running the Add New Hardware wizard will probably not correctly detect your backup device(s). In most cases, the problem is caused when Seagate Direct Tape Access (version 2.0 or 3.0) is installed on your computer. Uninstall the Seagate Direct Tape Access (version 2.0 or 3.0) software, or uninstall Microsoft Backup for Windows 98. To uninstall Backup:

1 Click Start, highlight Settings, click Control Panel, and then double-click Add/Remove Programs.

2 Click the Windows Setup tab, click on System Tools (not the check box), click Details, click the Backup check box to clear it, and then click OK.

3 Follow the instructions on the screen to finish uninstalling Backup.

SYMPTOM 5-6 **You cannot restore from multiple tapes if one or more tapes are damaged** For example, when you try to use Microsoft Backup for Windows 98 to restore files from a backup that spans multiple tapes, you may receive an error message that says the backup media are damaged. If you then click OK or Cancel, the restore process stops, and you are not prompted to insert the next tape. This trouble occurs when one of the backup tapes is damaged. To circumvent this problem, manually restore the files on each tape:

1. Click Start, highlight Programs, point to Accessories, point to System Tools, and then click Backup.
2. Insert one of the tapes from your backup set into the tape drive, and then click Refresh on the Restore tab. Note that you cannot restore damaged files from the tape.
3. When you receive a message that says your backup spans multiple tapes, click No.
4. From the list of files on that tape, highlight the files you want to restore, and then click Start. Repeat this process with each tape in the set until you restore all the files you want, and then quit Backup.

SYMPTOM 5-7 **Backup cannot identify a "removable media" drive as a backup device** You'd normally click the Where To Back Up box in Microsoft Backup for Windows 98 to view your backup devices, but you notice that your removable media drives do not appear on the list. Note that "removable media" includes devices such as floppy drives, Zip drives, Jazz drives, and so on. This problem occurs because the removable media drive is recognized as a regular drive with a drive letter (such as a hard disk) rather than a backup device (like a tape drive). If you want to back up to removable media, click File in the Where To Back Up box when you make a backup.

> If your PC only has a removable media drive for backup use, you receive a message stating there are no backup devices when you start Backup for the first time. When you're prompted to use Add New Hardware to find a backup device (or to continue without looking for a backup device), click No.

SYMPTOM 5-8 **Windows 98 runs poorly when backing up a large number of files** When you're backing up a very large number of files to a tape drive (or other large-capacity devices)— or you're comparing an existing backup to the original files on the hard drive—Windows 98 may appear to run slowly. This problem typically occurs if you back up a large number of files (2000 to 3000+ files) while the backup software is configured to perform a comparison. A comparison will check the files on the tape versus the original files on the hard drive. This problem may also occur when you're comparing a set of files that had been backed up previously. This problem is known to occur with the Onstream 30GB digital drive.

This problem is caused by a fault in the Windows 98 protected-mode disk cache (VCACHE.VXD). The error occurs when the maximum value used to track the age of blocks in the cache has been exceeded. If this occurs while the protected-mode disk cache tries to free the oldest blocks to make room for new data, it takes a long time for the operation to finish. Windows will run slowly (and continues to do so until the computer is restarted). You can download and install an updated version of VCACHE.VXD (version 4.10.2183, dated 4/7/99).

SYMPTOM 5-9 **You see a Windows 98 error message such as "You have restored a good registry"** When you start your computer, you may receive the following error message: "You have restored a good registry. Windows found an error in your system files and restored a recent backup of the files to fix the problem." When you restart your computer, you may receive the error message again. This problem can occur if the registry backup file you're trying to restore is damaged (or if the "damage" flag in the current registry file is not being reset by the Registry Checker utility). To fix this problem, run the Registry Checker tool using the **/fix** and **/opt** switches:

1. Start your computer to the Safe Mode command prompt.
2. At the DOS prompt, type **scanreg /fix** and press ENTER. The **/fix** switch causes the Registry Checker tool to repair any damaged portions of the registry.
3. Press ENTER after the Registry Checker tool finishes repairing the registry.
4. At the DOS prompt, type **scanreg /opt** and press ENTER. The **/opt** switch causes the Registry Checker tool to optimize the registry by removing unused space.
5. Restart your computer.
6. If the problem persists, try restoring a different registry backup file using the **/restore** switch.

SYMPTOM 5-10 **You encounter "Out of Memory" errors when running SCANREG.EXE under Windows 98** When you run Registry Checker (SCANREG.EXE) with the **/fix** or **/restore** switch, you may receive an "Out of Memory" error message. You may also receive this error message when SCANREG.EXE creates a backup copy of the registry (during Windows startup). This error may occur with less than 340KB of free conventional memory. When you try to launch SCANREG.EXE with the **/fix** or **/restore** switch, more than 340KB of free conventional memory may be required, depending on the size of the registry. Increase the free conventional memory to more than 340KB. The easiest way to do this is to reboot the computer to the Safe Mode command prompt; then run SCANREG.EXE with the appropriate switch(es).

SYMPTOM 5-11 **You encounter errors when using Backup under Windows 95/98** When you use Backup to create a full system backup (or a backup that includes the \Windows folder), a status box may indicate that errors occurred during the backup. When you click Report to view the backup report, you may see the following error messages:

```
Error: C:\WINDOWS\Cookies\index.dat - busy
Error: C:\WINDOWS\History\index.dat - busy
Error: C:\WINDOWS\Temporary Internet Files\index.dat - busy
Warning: C:\WINDOWS\Cookies\index.dat was busy during backup. It cannot be
restored or compared.
Warning: C:\WINDOWS\History\index.dat was busy during backup. It cannot be
restored or compared.
Warning: C:\WINDOWS\Temporary Internet Files\index.dat was busy during
backup. It cannot be restored or compared.
```

This problem can occur because the INDEX.DAT files that are in each of these locations are open if Internet Explorer (IE) is running. Since IE is part of the Windows 98 graphical user interface, these files are always open and therefore cannot be backed up. This also happens in Windows 95 if you're running IE when you run Backup (or if IE 4.0 or 4.01 is installed on your computer and you have enabled the Windows Desktop Update feature).

> The INDEX.DAT files are re-created each time IE starts, so it's not necessary to back up these files—all other files that you've selected are successfully backed up.

SYMPTOM 5-12 **An error occurs while writing data to the backup drive under Windows 98** When you attempt to back up data using Backup, you may receive an error message such as:

```
An error occurred while writing the backup data. The end of the media was
approached unexpectedly. (08-22-07-01-0000)
```

This problem occurs if you compress a floppy disk or removable media using DriveSpace, then try to back up more data than there is space available on the compressed disk. Backup does not prompt you to insert another blank disk or media as expected. Do not use DriveSpace if you want to back up your data on more than one blank disk or removable media.

SYMPTOM 5-13 A backup is generated when Backup for Windows 98 completes its process When you back up files or folders located on a password-protected network system, you may receive the following error message:

```
Backup complete - error reported
```

You may see errors when you view the backup log,

```
Error: \\<share> - accessed denied
Error: \\<share> - could not be accessed
```

where <share> is the name of the network share. This problem can occur because Backup doesn't prompt you for a password to access a password-protected network system. Connect to the network system and enter your password before you try to back up files or folders.

SYMPTOM 5-14 When backing up to tape under Windows 98, you get a media error When you use Backup to read a backup tape, you may receive an error such as:

```
The media is not supported by this product - please insert another media.
```

Using a different tape generates the same error message. The error message may occur with any operation that attempts to read the tape.

The error occurs if the tape drive fails to support the Quick File Access format (or QFA), also known as *media partitioning*. Backup requires that the tape drive support QFA. The QFA format allows tapes to be divided into a large data partition and a small directory partition. The directory partition holds information about each of the backup sets on the tape and can also be used to store the exact block address of each file on the tape. This feature allows for fast file retrieval with the tape drive.

SYMPTOM 5-15 The tape backup drive is not detected Although Microsoft Backup is a handy tool, it has rather limited compatibility with tape drives. If Backup reports that it cannot detect your drive, make sure your tape drive is compatible. You can check the Help file in your version of Backup for a current listing of compatible drives.

SYMPTOM 5-16 You encounter problems restoring files with Backup No backup has value unless it can be restored, and PC users often forget to test their backup. The only thing worse than losing your work, is discovering that your backup is inaccessible. If Backup reports trouble restoring your files, there are some steps you can take to address the problem:

- *Clean the drive.* If the drive's read/write heads are dirty, it will not be able to read the tape reliably, and errors will result. This should not damage the tape or its contents, but will make restoring difficult until the heads are cleaned. Refer to the drive's particular cleaning instructions and clean the heads. (This is good routine maintenance anyway.)

- *Use a slower tape speed.* Some parallel ports become sensitive when the PC is operating in its turbo mode. Often, the tape drive is forced to work much harder, pulling the tape back and forth across the heads (an undesirable behavior called *shoeshining*). If your backup or restoration process appears to be taking an unusually long time, try either disabling the PC's turbo mode or reconfiguring the parallel port to compatibility mode. This does not seem to be an issue with floppy interface tape drives.
- *Try the Windows 95 Safe Mode.* Some drivers may interfere with the proper restoration of tape files. Try restarting Windows 95 in the Safe Mode and restoring files then. Note that if the tape drive requires a protected-mode driver (such as Colorado Trakker's VCOMM file), the tape drive will not work in the Safe Mode.
- *Check your drive space.* Make sure there is enough space on your hard drive. File restoration under Windows 95 involves the use of a swap file. Since the swap file size can change dynamically under Windows 95, the swap file can grow to be quite large (depending on the number of files involved). If there is very limited drive space, free some space and try again.

SYMPTOM 5-17 **You find that there are problems formatting your tapes** Like any magnetic media, you must format a tape before using it to store files. Today, many common tapes are available already formatted, but if the drive does not recognize the format (or you have trouble formatting the tape yourself), here are some things to consider:

- *Check your tape standard.* Remember that you cannot format a 3010 tape in a QIC-80 drive, and you cannot format a QIC-80 Wide tape in a QIC-80 drive. Make sure you are using the right tape in the drive.
- *Try a different tape.* If you have trouble formatting or working with a particular tape (but similar tapes behave correctly), it may be worn out or otherwise defective. Throw the tape away; it is not worth trying to reuse.

> Do not attempt to reuse the tape by degaussing it (a.k.a. "bulk erasing"). This will not restore a worn tape or repair damage to it. If data is subsequently written to bad blocks, it may render your backup unusable.

- *Try the Windows 95 Safe Mode.* Some drivers may interfere with the proper operation of the drive. Start Windows 95 in the Safe Mode and try formatting the tape then. Note that if the tape drive requires a protected-mode driver, the tape drive will not work in the Safe Mode.
- *Check for hardware conflicts.* This is typical in floppy interface tape drive installations. There may be a conflict between the video board and floppy drive controller. Start the format operation and minimize the progress indicator. If problems persist, change the video mode to 640×480×16. If problems continue, try formatting in a full-screen DOS session. Use the Device Manager to look for conflicts between the video board and floppy drive controller.

SYMPTOM 5-18 **You find that tape comparisons fail** After a backup has been completed, Backup (and most other tape backup utilities) allows you to perform a comparison that checks the tape contents against your original files. This is how you know the data is good. When you encounter errors in comparison, it also means you will probably have trouble restoring from the tape later on. Comparison errors almost always mean that data was lost writing to the tape or that the tape itself is defective (for example, a bad block is encountered). First, clean the tape drive read/write heads, and then check the comparison again. If the problem persists, try creating another backup now that the heads have been cleaned. If the problem still continues, the tape itself is probably worn out (or is otherwise defective) and should be replaced.

SYMPTOM 5-19 **There is a serious error in the memory manager** When Backup attempts to perform a backup, restore, or compare operation, you may receive an important error message that typically reads like this:

```
Microsoft Backup has encountered a serious error in the Memory Manager.
Quit and restart Backup, and then try again.
```

This error message contains the word "serious" because the potential causes for this problem all demand your careful consideration:

- *Suspect incompatible device drivers.* If you have recently installed a new application or updated any of your system drivers, you may be faced with an incompatible device driver or memory-resident program being loaded through your AUTOEXEC.BAT, CONFIG.SYS, SYSTEM.INI, or WIN.INI file. Try starting Windows 95/98 in the Safe Mode. If the problem disappears, locate and correct the conflicting driver(s)—usually the last change you made to the system before the problem occurred.
- *Check your Windows swap file.* This error may also be caused if the swap file is damaged. Check the swap file's condition by opening the Control Panel, selecting the System icon, selecting the Performance page, and clicking on Virtual Memory. Click on "Let me specify my own virtual memory settings," and then select the Disable Virtual Memory box. Select OK and restart the computer. Next, go into the Virtual Memory dialog again and select "Let Windows manage my virtual memory settings." Then click OK. This should re-create your swap file and set it to automatic control under Windows 95.

> You cannot select the Disable Virtual Memory box on a PC with only 8MB of RAM. If your computer has only 8MB of RAM, restart your computer to the command prompt, delete any SWP file in the Windows folder, and then restart your computer and create a new swap file.

- *Suspect your tape or drive.* The particular tape drive may be malfunctioning or incompatible with Backup. (The backup tape itself may also be damaged or improper for the drive.)
- *Reinstall Backup.* One or more files under Microsoft Backup may be corrupt. To ensure that your installation is correct, open your Control Panel, select the Add/Remove Programs icon, click the Windows Setup page, select Disk Tools, and then click Details. Find the entry for Backup and clear its check box; then click OK. Restart the PC if necessary. This removes Backup from your PC. Next, go to the Backup check box again and reselect it; then click OK. This will reinstall the Backup application.

Making the Most of Backup Exec

Another popular backup application is Seagate's Backup Exec utility. With Backup Exec, you can create and test emergency recovery disks, which allow you to recover files without having to first reinstall the operating system or backup software. This is a powerful advantage when it becomes necessary to recover your system from a catastrophic loss. Backup Exec also supports many QIC and SCSI backup devices. This part of the chapter is intended to highlight some features of Backup Exec and identify some potential problems that you should keep in mind.

CREATING EMERGENCY RECOVERY DISKS

Backup Exec's Emergency Restore feature enables you to rebuild the operating system and the latest "Selected Files" backup without having to reinstall the operating system or the backup software. Your entire local drive can be restored using the emergency recovery (ER) disks and a backup of your drive. The first time Backup Exec launches, you are prompted to create ER disks. The ER disks enable you to restore your files even if Windows will not start. You may use the following procedure to create ER disks.

> If you do not create ER disks the first time Backup Exec launches, you may do so later by choosing Emergency Diskettes from the Tools menu.

> You cannot use the File option for Emergency Recovery. Instead, you must use a backup device when creating your ER disks. If you installed a new backup device since you created your ER disks, you must create new ER disks to accompany your new backup device.

1. With Backup Exec running, select Emergency Diskettes from the Tools menu.
2. If you have more than one backup device, your backup devices appear on the Tools menu under Emergency Diskettes. Select the device you want to use to store your local drive and registry files. You may need to select the correct DOS ASPI drivers at this time (for SCSI backup drives).
3. Follow the on-screen instructions.
4. A message appears when the ER disks are complete.

> The Emergency Recovery feature of Backup Exec will not restore a dual boot system (such as Windows 98 and NT). Also, Emergency Recovery will not restore data to a compressed hard drive. If you have used a disk compression program to increase the capacity of your hard drive, you may not be able to restore your data. Emergency Recovery may run out of space on the hard drive before your data is fully recovered.

TESTING EMERGENCY RECOVERY DISKS

After you create your ER disks, it is highly recommended that you test them. This is particularly important if your backup device requires a DOS driver.

1. Insert ER disk 1 into the floppy drive.
2. Restart your computer. The README.ER file appears. After reading the text, press ALT+F, and then press X to exit the editor.
3. Insert ER disk 2.
4. To start the recovery process, type **RESTORE** and press ENTER.
5. Insert your media containing the backup sets you want to recover, and press ENTER.
6. If prompted, select the specific backup set to recover. (The backup set is selected automatically if your media contain only one backup set.)
7. If your backup set is password protected, you are prompted to enter your password. Type your password and press ENTER.

8 Ensure all of your selections are correct before continuing. If they are, then you have verified that Emergency Recovery will be able to read data from the media in case of an actual emergency. If you see any error messages during this process, there is a problem communicating with the backup device. Most likely the problem is a missing DOS driver that is required for your backup device (or incorrect command-line parameters for the driver).

USING EMERGENCY RECOVERY

The Emergency Recovery process enables you to recover from hard disk failure and should be used in emergency situations only. Before using Emergency Recovery, decide whether another recovery method can be implemented instead. For example, if the problem appears to be a Windows 95/98 system problem (such as a corrupt registry), try to recover as suggested by the operating system instructions. Otherwise, you should go ahead and use your ER disks:

1. Insert ER disk 1 into the floppy drive.
2. Turn on your computer.
3. If necessary, you may prepare your hard disk using FDISK, FORMAT, and SYS, all located on ER disk 1.

> If you alter your drives by using FDISK (or another partition utility), you must reboot with ER disk 1 prior to using the FORMAT and SYS utilities (or continuing with Emergency Recovery).

4. Insert ER disk 2. At the command prompt, type **RESTORE**.
5. If prompted, select your specific backup device. (The backup device is selected automatically if only one device is connected to your computer.)
6. Insert the media containing your backup sets to be recovered, and press ENTER.
7. If prompted, select the most recent "All Selected Files" (Full) backup set to recover. (The backup set is selected automatically if your media contain only one backup set.)
8. If the backup set is password protected, you are prompted to enter the password. Type your password and press ENTER.
9. Select the drive volume where you want to recover your data.
10. Ensure that all of your selections are correct before proceeding; then press ENTER.

The Emergency Recovery process now begins restoring the Windows 95/98 file system on your selected drive. If your selected backup set spans two or more media, you are prompted to insert the next medium in the sequence after all the current files are recovered. When the recovery is complete, a summary of the recovery process appears. This summary includes the number of files selected and the number actually recovered. If these numbers are different, refer to the RESTORE.RPT file for a listing of what files could not be recovered. Press ENTER to close the summary and return to DOS.

> If you want to recover other backup sets or drive volumes, run the RESTORE.EXE program again. When you're finished restoring files, remove the ER disk from the floppy drive and restart your computer. It may be necessary to reboot your computer more than once if any hardware has changed in your system since your backup was made.

CONFLICTS WITH OTHER BACKUP PROGRAMS

Although Backup Exec is generally regarded as a stable and reliable utility, there are drivers from other backup programs (or Windows 3.1 applications) that may conflict with it. In order to troubleshoot problems with Backup Exec, it may be necessary to disable suspect driver files before you can begin. Note the following driver files that are known to cause problems:

device=cmswtape.386	Colorado Backup for Windows
device=cmsdtape.386	Colorado Backup for DOS
device=vfintd.386	Backup Exec, Conner, Iomega, and Norton Backup
device=cpbvxd.386	Central Point Backup
device=symevnt.386	Symantec Norton Utilities
device=adw30.386	After Dark screen savers
device=awdos.386	PC Anywhere for DOS
device=vpcaw.386	PC Anywhere for Windows
device=fastback.386	Fastback Backup
device=irw286.drv	Irwin Eztape Backup
device=novabkp.386	Novastor Backup
device=virwt.386	Irwin EZtape Backup

You can use the steps below to disable suspect drivers:

1. Make a copy of your SYSTEM.INI file (in your Windows folder) and name the copy SYSTEMBKUP.INI. (This provides a copy of your original file.)
2. Click Start, and then click Run.
3. Type **system.ini** and click OK. The SYSTEM.INI file will open in Notepad.
4. In the [386Enh] section of your SYSTEM.INI file, type a semicolon (;) at the beginning of the driver file line(s) that you need to disable.
5. Save the modified SYSTEM.INI file and restart your computer.

If the problem persists, use the steps below to disable other potential problem programs:

1. Make a copy of your WIN.INI file (in your Windows folder) and name the copy WINBKUP.INI. (This provides a copy of your original file.)
2. Click Start, and then click Run.
3. Type **win.ini** and click OK. The WIN.INI file will open in Notepad.
4. Type a semicolon (;) at the beginning of the "load=" and "run=" lines of any files that need to be disabled; then save the updated file.
5. Restart your computer and run Backup Exec.

If you're using a SCSI backup device, try disabling any real-mode drivers loading in CONFIG.SYS:

1. Click Start, then click Run.
2. Type **sysedit.exe** and click OK.
3. Click on the CONFIG.SYS window.

4. Type **rem** at the beginning of each line that contains a real-mode driver. For example:

```
rem device=c:\aspi\aspi4dos.sys
```

5. Save the CONFIG.SYS file.
6. Restart your computer and run Backup Exec.

BACKUP EXEC SYMPTOMS

SYMPTOM 5-20 The system locks up immediately after Backup Exec is installed In most cases, there may be conflicts between Backup Exec and other applications. You can try disabling possible conflicting programs:

1. Press CTRL+ALT+DEL to display the Close Program dialog box. (The only application that must be running is the Explorer.)
2. Close other applications by highlighting the desired application and clicking the End Task button.
3. If all applications have been disabled and Backup Exec is still not responding, rename (using the .OLD extension) any Backup Exec drivers not being used.

SYMPTOM 5-21 Backup Exec locks up when displaying a selection Files in your Recycle Bin may be conflicting with other files on your hard drive. Delete the files in your Recycle Bin before using Backup Exec. Click the right mouse button on the Recycle Bin located on the desktop, and select Empty Recycle Bin.

SYMPTOM 5-22 The tape controller is not responding during backup, compare, or restore If you have an internal QIC backup device that is attached to the floppy disk controller, use the Device Manager to verify that there are no extra backup device entries. If there are, you should delete additional backup device entries:

1. Right-click the My Computer icon and select Properties.
2. Click the Device Manager tab.
3. Locate the Tape Drive Controller section. If you find an entry in this section that has an *X* on the icon, remove it by selecting the item and clicking the Remove button.
4. Restart Windows 95/98.

If the problem continues and you are using a high-speed controller (a.k.a. accelerator card), make sure that the settings on the card match those reported by the Device Manager.

SYMPTOM 5-23 There is a DMA conflict during backup or compare You may need to reduce the data transfer speed used in your system:

1. Go to Device Manager and double-click the "backup device" item.
2. Select the "backup device" and click Properties.
3. Select the Settings tab and disable "high speed burst mode," "concurrent video update," and "concurrent hard disk access" settings.
4. Reduce the transfer rate to its lowest setting (500 Kb/Sec).

If you still have a DMA conflict problem, use the lowest resolution setting available on your video card. If this corrects the problem, contact your video card or computer manufacturer for available driver updates for Windows 95/98.

SYMPTOM 5-24 **You receive an error such as "media not formatted or unreadable"** You may need to disable the high-speed burst transfer option under your system properties:

1. Right-click the My Computer icon and select Properties.
2. Click the Device Manager tab in your System Properties dialog.
3. Click the plus (+) sign next to your "backup device type" to expand the entries, and then double-click your backup device.
4. Click the Settings tab in the Properties dialog.
5. Uncheck the "High speed burst transfers" option and click OK.
6. Restart your computer.

Further Study

@Backup: **http://www.atbackup.com/VID101.4.571554.0/**

BACKUP Data Protection Agency: **http://members.aol.com/backupdpa/index.htm**

Micro Solutions: **http://www.micro-solutions.com**

Microsoft (Backup): **http://www.microsoft.com**

PowerQuest: **http://www.powerquest.com**

Seagate: **http://www.seagate.com**

Symantec: **http://www.symantec.com**

6

BATTERIES

CHAPTER AT A GLANCE

Of all the elements in a PC, few are as overlooked and ignored as the battery. Batteries play an important role in all PCs by maintaining the system's configuration data while main AC power is turned off. (Just imagine how inconvenient it would be to reenter the entire system setup in CMOS before being able to use the system each time.) For portable systems such as notebook and sub-notebook PCs, battery packs also provide main power for the entire system. This chapter outlines the technologies and operating characteristics of today's battery families and illustrates a selection of battery-related problems that can plague a PC.

A Battery Primer

The battery is perhaps the most common and dependable source of power ever developed. This electrochemical device uses two dissimilar metals (called *electrodes*) that are immersed or encapsulated in a chemical catalyst (or *electrolyte*). The chemical reaction that takes place in a battery causes a voltage differential to be developed across its electrodes. When a battery is attached to a circuit, the battery provides current. The more current required by a load, the faster a chemical reaction will occur. As the chemical reaction continues, electrodes are consumed. As a result of this chemical consumption, the battery will eventually wear out. It is important to realize that a *battery* and a *cell* are not necessarily the same. A cell is the basic element of a battery, but a battery may be made up of several individual cells.

For some batteries, the chemical reaction is irreversible. When the battery is dead, it must be discarded. These are known as nonrechargeable (or *primary*) batteries. Most PCs use small primary-type batteries to sustain the contents of CMOS RAM. However, some types of batteries can be recharged. By applying current to the battery from an external source (a battery charger), the expended chemical reaction can be almost entirely reversed. Such rechargeable batteries are referred to as *secondary* batteries. Rechargeable batteries are used to supply main power for all mobile computers.

BATTERY RATINGS

Batteries carry two important ratings: cell voltage and ampere-hours (Ah). *Cell voltage* refers to the cell's working voltage. Most everyday cells operate around +1.5 Vdc, but can range from +1.2 Vdc to +3.0 Vdc (or more) depending on the particular battery chemistry in use. The *ampere-hour* rating is a bit more involved, but it reflects the energy storage capacity of a battery. A large Ah rating suggests a high-capacity battery; a low rating, a low capacity.

As an example, suppose your battery is rated for 2.0 Ah. Ideally, you should be able to draw 2 amps from the battery for 1 hour before it is exhausted. However, you should also be able to draw 1 amp for 2 hours, 0.5 amps for 4 hours, 0.1 amps for 20 hours, and so on. Keep in mind that the ampere-hour relationship is not always precisely linear. Higher current loads may shorten battery life to less than that expected by the ampere-hour rating, while small loads may allow slightly more battery life than expected. Regardless of the ampere-hour rating, all batteries have an upper current limit—attempting to draw excess current can destroy the battery (causing it to rupture and leak caustic chemicals). Physically large batteries can usually supply more current (and last longer) than smaller batteries. Another way to express a battery's energy capacity is in watt-hours per kilogram (Wh/kg) or watt-hours per pound (Wh/lb). For example, a 1 kg battery rated at 60 Wh could provide 60W of power for 1 hour, 30W of power for 2 hours, 10W of power for 6 hours, and so on.

CHARGING

In its simplest sense, *charging* is the replacement of electrical energy to batteries whose stored chemical energy has been discharged. By applying an electrical current to a discharged battery over a given period of time, it is possible to cause a chemical recombination at the battery's electrodes that will restore most of the battery's spent potential. Essentially, you must back-feed the battery at a known, controlled rate.

> Recharging only works for secondary cells such as nickel-cadmium, nickel metal-hydride, or lithium-ion batteries. Attempting to recharge a primary battery will quickly destroy it.

Before you dive into an overview of charging circuits and troubleshooting, you must understand the concept of C. The term *C* designates the normal current capacity of a battery (in amperes). In most circumstances, the value of C is the same as the ampere-hour current level. For example, a battery rated for 1300 mAh (1.30 Ah) would be considered to have a C value of 1.30 amps. A battery rated for 700 mAh (0.70 Ah) would have a C of 0.70 amps. Charging rates are based upon fractions or multiples of C.

To charge a battery, you must apply a reverse voltage that will cause the appropriate amount of charging current to flow back into the battery. Ideally, the battery should be charged at a rate of 0.1C. For batteries with a C of 500 mA (0.5A), 0.1C would be 50 mA (0.05A). At 0.1C, the battery could be left connected in the charger indefinitely without damage. Low-current charge rates such as 0.1C are sometimes referred to as a *slow charge* or *trickle charge*. Slow charging produces the least physical or thermal stress within a battery and ensures the maximum possible number of charge/discharge cycles.

Many current secondary batteries can be charged well above the 0.1C rate. The *quick charge* approach uses current levels of 0.3C (three times the rate of a slow charge) to recharge the battery in 4 to 6 hours. For a battery with a C of 600 mA (0.60A), the 0.1C charging rate would be 60 mA (0.06A), but the quick charge rate would be 180 mA (0.18A). However, the quick charging process runs the risk of overcharging a battery. Once a battery is fully recharged, additional current at or above the quick charge rate causes temperature and pressure buildups within the cell(s). In extreme cases, a severely overcharged battery may rupture and be destroyed. When quick charging, the 0.3C charging rate should be used only long enough to restore the bulk of a battery's energy. The rate should be reduced to 0.1C (or less) for continuous operation (a.k.a. trickle charging).

New nickel-cadmium (NiCd) and nickel metal-hydride (NiMH) battery designs allow for an even faster charge of 1 hour. The *1-hour charge* uses a rate of 1.5C—1.5 times the amount of current the battery is intended to provide. A battery with a C of 1400 mA (1.40A) would use a 1-hour charge rate of 2100 mA (2.10A). Remember that only specially designed secondary cells can be safely charged in 1 hour or less. With 1-hour charging, current control and timing become critical issues. The battery charging current must be reduced as soon as the battery approaches its full charge, or catastrophic battery failure will almost certainly result. Rapid charging causes substantial temperature and pressure increases that eventually take their toll on a battery's working life. You should expect the working life of any battery to be curtailed when it is regularly operated in a 1-hour charge mode.

The *constant-current charger* is designed to automatically compensate for changes in battery terminal voltage in order to maintain charging current at a constant level. Constant-current charging is very efficient, but it is not adjustable. If the charger were set to deliver substantial charging currents, the battery pack could charge quickly, but the pack could eventually be damaged by overcharging. The charger could be set to a lower level for safe charging (perhaps 0.1C), but the low charging rate means very long charge times for a battery pack (10 hours or more). Such limitations make constant-current chargers ill suited for use in mobile computers. Instead, constant-current chargers are typically used in stand-alone battery pack charging units.

A more effective approach for portable computers is a *variable-current* (constant-voltage) scheme. When a battery is deeply discharged and its terminal voltage is low, there will be a substantial difference between the power supply source and battery voltage level. This difference results in a sizable current flow to the battery. Charging usually starts around the 0.5C to 0.3C rate for fast charge operation. As the battery takes on a charge, its terminal voltage increases. Higher battery voltage reduces the difference between the supply and battery—current flow into the battery decreases. When the battery pack reaches full charge, there is almost no voltage difference between the charger and battery, so only a small amount of current trickles into the battery. Current flow may reach levels as low as 0.05C.

Storing Batteries

At some point, you'll probably need to store unused batteries for some period of time. Remember that the chemical process that makes batteries work will always continue regardless of whether the battery is installed or not. This means your battery will eventually go dead even if you don't use it. You can extend your battery's shelf life by reducing its temperature. Typically, this means storing your batteries in the refrigerator (in a vapor-proof container to prevent drying the battery's electrolyte due to the low humidity). The cold will slow the chemical reaction and keep the battery "fresh" much longer. Just remember to remove the battery from the refrigerator and allow it to stabilize at room temperature for at least 24 hours before using it.

CMOS Backup Batteries

When IBM released its PC/AT in the early 1980s, one of the many design changes over the older PC/XT was the elimination of DIP switches used to set the system configuration. Instead of discrete physical switches, PC designers chose to set system parameters using bit sequences stored in small areas of low-power static RAM. Since it is necessary to maintain the contents of this RAM even when system power is off, designers chose to use RAM chips based on Complementary Metal Oxide Semiconductor (CMOS) fabrication. This memory became known as CMOS RAM. CMOS RAM can be maintained for years using only a single small battery or battery pack incorporated onto the motherboard (Figure 6-1), called a CMOS backup battery. All motherboards require a CMOS backup battery.

FIGURE 6-1 A Rayovac Computer Clock battery (Courtesy of Rayovac, Corp.)

Mobile computers such as IBM's ThinkPad series often employ additional batteries to serve as a standby power source. These *standby batteries* are rechargeable battery packs frequently used to supplement the main battery in mobile computers. Traditionally, you'd need to shut down a laptop and replace a main battery pack, then reboot the system in order to keep working. If the main battery pack failed, you'd lose any work in progress (and perhaps corrupt important files). With a standby power source, the system can automatically enter a "suspend" mode where almost no power is used, but files and data can be kept active in memory. You can then replace the main battery and leave the suspend mode to keep working without the time and trouble to reboot and reload your applications. If the main battery should fail, the standby batteries can keep your work intact for up to several days until you can exchange the main battery pack or find an AC outlet for a battery eliminator.

LITHIUM BATTERIES

Lithium/manganese-dioxide (Li/MnO_2 or simply "lithium") batteries are commonly employed as CMOS backup batteries. Lithium batteries use a layer of lithium as the anode, a specially formulated manganese-dioxide alloy as the cathode, and a conductive organic electrolyte. Depending on the overall size and shape of the cell, a lithium battery can supply +3.0 Vdc at up to 330 Wh/kg of energy density. Lithium cells also offer a five-year shelf life with almost no loss of power. Although their energy density is quite high, lithium cells offer only low ampere-hour ratings between 70 mAh (0.70 Ah) and 1300 mAh (1.30 Ah). Limited Ah ratings allow lithium cells to maintain an almost constant output voltage over a long working life.

The classical type of lithium battery is the *coin cell*. The typical coin cell is designed in two halves, with a lithium anode at the top and a manganese-dioxide cathode layer on the bottom. Both halves are separated by a thin membrane containing a conductive electrolyte. The finished electrochemical assembly is then packaged into a small metal can. The lid forms the negative electrode, while the side walls and bottom of the coin form the positive electrode. The lid is physically isolated from the rest of the metal can by a thin insulating grommet—thus, the coin cell is not sealed. A grommet keeps moisture and contaminants out, yet will allow any pressure buildup to escape the battery.

6

BACKUP BATTERY REPLACEMENT

Battery life has a finite limit. Eventually, all backup batteries will discharge to the point where they can no longer sustain the system. When the battery finally does fail, CMOS information is lost. The next time you attempt to turn on the PC, the system will generate an error code or message indicating that the system configuration does not match the CMOS setup information. The loss of a CMOS setup suddenly leaves a system disabled until new (and correct) CMOS information is entered. This presents a serious problem for most PC users, since few users bother to back up or record their CMOS setup. As you might imagine, it then becomes an exercise in frustration to load the setup routine and reconstruct the system setup from scratch.

Fortunately, there are two things you can do to avoid this problem. First, make it a point to routinely replace the backup battery every two years (no more than three years). If you change the backup battery for a customer, note the battery part number and replacement date on a sticker, and then place the sticker inside the PC enclosure (you might also note the next replacement date on your customer's bill). Second, back up the system CMOS entries *before* replacing the battery. You can note the entries on paper and tape the page inside the enclosure, or you can use a shareware utility to back up CMOS contents as a disk file. CMOS backup as a disk file is quick and easy, and the file can be restored in a matter of seconds. A backup utility is especially handy when there is no setup disk available for the system being worked on. Make it a point to keep the backup current, as system parameters change. Otherwise, you would be restoring information that is no longer valid.

The actual process of backup battery replacement is simply a matter of removing the old battery and inserting a new one. Since the battery is often located prominently on the motherboard, it is possible to replace a backup battery with system power applied (this lets the system maintain its CMOS settings). However, working inside a "hot" system is against the safety protocols that we have established for this book, so be sure to record the CMOS settings on floppy disk or paper first; then power-down and unplug the PC before opening it. Replace the battery; then restart the PC and reload the CMOS settings from disk or paper. Replacing the backup battery in a notebook or sub-notebook PC is sometimes easier since the battery is usually accessible from a small panel on the bottom enclosure. (You do not have to disassemble the notebook enclosures to replace the battery.) Even with easy access, you should make it a point to remove power before replacing the battery.

> If you act quickly when replacing the CMOS backup battery, there may be enough of a latent charge in CMOS RAM to keep the contents intact for several minutes. However, each motherboard is designed differently, and there is no guarantee how long CMOS RAM contents may remain intact once the battery is removed. Always be prepared to restore CMOS settings from scratch before removing the CMOS backup battery.

TROUBLESHOOTING BACKUP BATTERY PROBLEMS

Lithium CMOS backup batteries are typically rugged and reliable devices whose greatest threat is simply old age. Since lithium cells are the primary type, they cannot be recharged, so they must be replaced periodically. Under most circumstances, only a few symptoms account for the majority of backup battery problems. In a few cases, you may find a motherboard that employs a nickel-cadmium (rechargeable) battery. In that case, the backup battery is recharged whenever the system is running. The problem with NiCd backup batteries is that NiCd has a very short shelf life, so you must run the system periodically in order to keep the backup battery charged. Otherwise, you may lose your CMOS data just letting the system sit idle.

Checking the CMOS Backup Battery

It is usually a simple matter to check the CMOS backup battery. Power-down the system and expose the motherboard. Locate the CMOS backup battery and find the two battery terminals leading from the battery to the motherboard. Measure the voltage between those two terminals—they should read between 2.5 to 3.7 Vdc. If the backup battery voltage is correct, there may be a software program or motherboard failure. If the backup battery reads low, replace the battery. If the battery discharges again quickly, a problem on the motherboard is shorting the CMOS backup battery.

> Do not remove the CMOS backup battery from the motherboard in order to check it. This will clear your CMOS configuration and make it difficult for the system to boot until the CMOS settings are restored.

SYMPTOM 6-1 **You see an error such as "System hardware does not match CMOS configuration"** For some reason(s), the BIOS has identified different hardware than that listed in the CMOS setup, or the CMOS RAM contents have been lost. Start by checking your CMOS RAM contents through the CMOS setup routine. Make sure the CMOS setup is configured properly. (Configuration errors can happen frequently when a new drive or RAM is added to the system.) Remember to save your changes to CMOS RAM before exiting the setup routine. If the CMOS RAM contents won't hold, check the battery connector to see that the battery is secure. A loose or corroded battery connector may effectively "disconnect" the battery—even if the battery is working perfectly. If the CMOS RAM contents still won't hold, replace the CMOS backup battery outright. When replacing the battery, be sure to install the new battery in the proper orientation and verify that it is secure in its connector.

> The error in Symptom 6-1 often happens when RAM is added to the system, even though there is no entry for installed RAM anywhere in the CMOS setup. Try to "exit saving changes," though you may not have actually changed any settings.

SYMPTOM 6-2 **You notice corrosion from the CMOS battery on the battery holder and motherboard** This frequently occurs with older motherboards (i386 and i486 vintage motherboards) that have been stored for prolonged periods. The battery has ruptured and electrolyte has leaked onto the holder or onto the motherboard itself. Battery chemicals are very caustic to metals, and chances are that any traces or solder connections that have come in contact with the battery leakage have been ruined. Unfortunately, this also means the motherboard has been ruined and must be replaced.

> If you're planning to remove and store a motherboard for any period of time, take a PRINTSCREEN of all CMOS setup pages before removing the motherboard; then store the old motherboard with the battery removed. You may place the battery in a small, heavy-gauge plastic bag at the bottom of the motherboard's antistatic box. When resurrecting the motherboard later, you can replace the battery and restore the CMOS settings from your printed record.

SYMPTOM 6-3 **The system configuration is lost intermittently** A lithium battery generally produces a stable output voltage until the very end of its operating life. When the battery finally dies, it tends to be a permanent event. When a system loses its setup configuration without warning, but seems to hold the configuration once it is restored, a loose or intermittent connection is suggested. Turn the PC off and unplug it. Check the battery and make sure it is inserted correctly and completely in its holder. A coin cell should fit snugly. If the cell is loose, gently tighten the holder's prongs to hold the cell more securely. Make sure to remove any corrosion or debris that may be interfering with the contacts. High-quality electrical contact cleaner on a moistened swab is particularly effective at cleaning contacts. When the battery is attached by a short cable, see that the cable is not broken or frayed, and make sure it is inserted properly into its receptacle. If problems persist, replace the CMOS backup battery.

SYMPTOM 6-4 **The backup battery is going dead frequently** This is a rare and perplexing problem that is often difficult to detect because it may only manifest itself several times a year. Ideally, a lithium coin cell should last for several years (perhaps three years or more). A lithium or alkaline battery pack can last five years or more. When a system loses its setup more than once a year due to battery failures, it is likely that an error in the motherboard design is draining the backup batteries faster than normal. Unfortunately, the only way to be sure is to replace the motherboard with a different or updated version. Before suggesting this option to your customer, you may wish to contact technical support for the original motherboard manufacturer and find out if similar cases have been reported. If so, find out if there is a fix or correction that will rectify the problem. (In this case, it may be necessary to return the motherboard to the manufacturer for corrective action.)

SYMPTOM 6-5 **You see a "161" error or message indicating that the system battery is dead** Depending on the particular system you are working with, there may also be a message indicating that the CMOS setup does not match the system configuration. In either case, the backup battery has probably failed and should be replaced. Remember to turn off the system before replacing the battery. Once the backup battery is replaced, restart the system. You will likely receive a message that the CMOS setup does not match the system configuration. Restore the configuration from paper notes or a file backup. The system should now function normally.

Mobile Batteries

Besides providing power to back up the system's configuration, batteries supply main power for notebook and sub-notebook computers when operating away from AC. Such power is typically provided from a battery pack installed from the bottom or side of the computer. The requirements for battery packs are ever-more stringent: packs have to provide as much power for as long as today's technology will allow, yet be as light and small as possible. Further, today's battery packs must be quickly rechargeable and offer a long working life through hundreds of recharging cycles. The three battery technologies best suited to these requirements are nickel-cadmium, nickel metal-hydride, and lithium-ion.

NICKEL-CADMIUM

The NiCd battery is one of the most cost-effective power sources in mass production today. Large NiCd battery packs have been widely used in mobile computers (primarily laptops and notebooks) as a main power source. Since NiCd cells can be manufactured in almost limitless shapes and sizes, they are ideal for systems requiring unusual battery configurations. Although NiCd batteries initially cost more than primary batteries, they can be recharged often—usually recovering their initial cost many times over.

Nickel-cadmium batteries are secondary (rechargeable) devices using an anode of nickel hydroxide and a cathode consisting of a specially formulated cadmium compound. The electrolyte is made of potassium hydroxide. NiCd cells can supply up to +1.2 Vdc each with ampere hour ratings from 500 mAh (0.50 Ah) to 2300 mAh (2.30 Ah). Energy densities in NiCd cells can approach 50 Wh/kg (23 Wh/lb). Respectable ampere-hour ratings allow NiCd cells to supply sizable amounts of current, but their inherently low energy density means that NiCds must be recharged fairly often.

The NiCd *memory effect* is a unique phenomenon that is not entirely understood. In operation, a NiCd battery can develop a "memory," which serves to limit either the capacity or terminal voltage of a cell. As you might expect, either limit can result in problems with the battery. *Voltage memory* is generally caused by prolonged charging over a period of weeks and months. High ambient temperatures and high charging currents can accelerate this condition. In effect, the battery is charged for so long, or at such a high rate or temperature, that the efficiency of the electrochemical reaction is impaired. As a result, the battery suffers from low terminal voltage.

The *memory capacity* problem is probably more widely recognized and is usually expressed as the loss of a NiCd's ability to deliver its full power capacity. The generally accepted cause of capacity problems is frequent partial battery discharge, followed by a full recharge. Over several such cycles, the battery "learns" that only a portion of its capacity is used. This renders the battery unable to deliver a full discharge when needed. Although the chemical reason for memory capacity is not fully understood, it is believed to be caused by oxidation reactions that temporarily coat the electrodes with nonreactive chemical compounds. Fortunately, the memory effect is usually temporary and can usually be cleared by forcing the battery through several full discharge/recharge cycles. If you are in the habit of using your notebook or laptop PC until you receive low-battery warnings, you will probably not have to worry about NiCd memory problems. It is interesting to note that the newer lithium-ion batteries do not seem to suffer from memory problems.

NiCd cells also have a very limited charged life when sitting idle. While alkaline and lithium cells can hold close to their original charge for years, NiCds will lose approximately 25 percent to 35 percent of their remaining charge each *month*. After several months of inactivity, a NiCd battery pack will need to be recharged before use. As a general rule, you should fully recharge any new or rarely used NiCd battery or battery pack prior to use. Today, NiCd batteries have largely been phased out of mobile computer use in favor of NiMH and Li-ion batteries.

NICKEL METAL-HYDRIDE

Nickel metal-hydride (NiMH) batteries are a somewhat newer type of rechargeable battery designed to offer substantially greater energy density than NiCd cells for mobile computer applications. Since their introduction in 1990, NiMH cells have already undergone some substantial improvements and cost reductions that have made them the dominant type of battery for mobile computers.

NiMH batteries are remarkably similar in construction and operating principles to NiCds. A positive electrode of nickel-hydroxide remains the same as that used in NiCds, but the negative electrode replaces cadmium with a metal-hydroxide alloy. When combined with a uniquely formulated electrolyte, NiMH cells are rated to provide at least 40 percent more capacity than similarly sized NiCd cells. NiMH batteries can provide +1.2 Vdc with discharge ratings from 800 mAh (0.80 Ah) to more than 2400 mAh (2.40 Ah) at continuous discharge currents of 9A or more. Energy densities can exceed 80 Wh/kg (38.1 Wh/lb). This means a NiMH battery can power a laptop and support additional features (such as a larger active-matrix color display) for longer periods of time. NiMH batteries also seem to suffer the memory effects that plague NiCd batteries, but not to the same extent. Keep in mind that NiMH has a fairly short shelf life (often a matter of days); so you'll need to keep your NiMH batteries fully charged before traveling.

LITHIUM-ION AND ZINC-AIR

Lithium-ion (Li-ion) batteries are a relatively recent development, but they are now readily available for the current generation of mobile computers. The formulation of the Li-ion battery allows 20 percent to 30 percent more running time than a similarly sized NiMH battery (at about 115 Wh/kg) and retains a charge for a long time while on the shelf. Li-ion batteries are also free of the memory effects found in NiCd and NiMH batteries and will last through well over 800 recharge cycles. Li-ion batteries represent the newest generation of "smart" batteries because status information on the battery's remaining charge can be communicated to the host system for an accurate determination of running time.

Zinc-air batteries are another recent development in mobile battery design, and the batteries now appearing in the field offer almost twice the energy density of Li-ion batteries (at a whopping 220 Wh/kg). In actual practice, however, zinc-air batteries have proven extremely large and heavy. They are also quite expensive. These factors have kept zinc-air batteries out of most small mobile systems. Still, the high energy potential of zinc-air will keep development active. Over the next few years, Li-ion and zinc-air batteries should continue to be the major power sources for mobile systems.

IDENTIFYING NICD AND NIMH BATTERIES

Although it is often difficult to distinguish between a NiCd and NiMH battery pack at first glance, there are some tips that might help you tell the difference. NiCd battery packs typically use three metal contacts (a slightly longer "negative" contact bridges contacts in the laptop and indicates the presence of the battery to the system). By comparison, NiMH battery packs are newer and "smarter" than NiCd packs, so the NiMH packs will typically include a type and temperature sensing contact located near the positive terminal of the battery pack. The firmware of some laptops will not begin charging the battery pack if the battery temperature is over 104°F (or if the temperature rises above 140°F while charging).

IDENTIFYING A RESERVE BATTERY

Many current laptop designs employ a *reserve battery*, which powers the system for a few minutes—allowing the main battery to be replaced without having to shut down the system or connect to AC power. In most cases, the internal reserve battery is a pack of four half-length AA-size, 270 mAh, NiCd batteries in an in-line stack. When fully charged, this pack can power the system for about eight minutes before being fully discharged. In operation, the reserve battery is permitted to support the computer for two to three minutes at the most before forcing a system shutdown.

Rechargeable Battery Guidelines

Rechargeable batteries are reliable and robust devices, but a number of guidelines need to be observed in order to get the most from them:

- *Plan on charging the battery before use.* For safety reasons, rechargeable batteries are typically shipped in a discharged state. You will need to prepare (or "condition") your battery pack (according to the manufacturer's instructions) before placing the battery pack into common use.
- *Cycle the battery pack as recommended.* Rechargeable batteries generally need to be *cycled* (fully charged and discharged) as many as five times before they will perform at full load capacity.
- *New batteries may fool a status indicator.* A new battery may cause the battery status indicator on your computer to indicate a dead or low battery condition. If this happens, try letting the battery charge in the system overnight so that the PC's charging circuit might synchronize with the battery pack. If you have trouble using battery packs with a certain make and model of mobile PC, the system's BIOS may be at fault. (Check with the system maker for a BIOS upgrade.)
- *Store the battery carefully.* When the battery pack is not in use, remove it from the system and store it in a cool, dry place.
- *Never short-circuit the battery terminals.* Although some battery packs are protected by internal self-resetting fuses, short circuits can still cause considerable damage to the battery. Use extreme care when packing spare batteries with other equipment during transit or storage.
- *Handle the battery pack carefully.* Do not drop, hit, or abuse the battery pack in any way. Not only might this damage the battery's internal cells, but a break in the casing may release electrolyte or expose cell contents. This material is corrosive and can damage circuitry in the PC.
- *Check for excessive heat.* It is perfectly normal for a battery pack to become warm to the touch when charging or discharging. However, if the battery pack gets over 50°C or 122°F, there may be a problem with the charging circuit. If you're using a stand-alone battery charger, do not leave the battery connected to the charger; this can overcharge the battery and shorten its life.
- *Keep an eye on your running time.* Running time depends on the power demands of your system components and the way the computer is used. Changing screen types and adding accessories will often shorten actual run times. After 300 to 500 recharges, a shortened run time may indicate that the battery needs to be replaced.

Battery Charging and Replacement Guidelines

For best results with rechargeable batteries, use the following guidelines:

- Remember that AC adapters are generally designed for specific laptops in order to handle the specific power requirements of the laptop and its add-on devices (such as a Dell Token Ring Advanced Port

Replicator). This means you typically cannot mix and match AC adapters. Be sure to use only the AC adapter intended for your laptop model.

- Each time the computer is connected to AC power (or a battery is installed in a computer that is connected to AC power), the computer checks the battery's charge. The AC adapter then charges the battery (if needed) and reserve battery, then maintains the battery's charge.
- For lithium-ion battery packs with built-in charge indicators, you can check the battery's charge by clicking the Battery Test button. For a fully charged battery pack, all the indicators should light up. Otherwise, the number of indicators lit will correspond to the amount of battery power remaining. For example, if there are five LEDs, each LED represents 20 percent of the battery's capacity. If one of the battery cells is shorted, you'll probably see a blinking indicator for that cell (the battery pack should be replaced).
- Do not attempt to replace the main battery while running on battery power without first placing the computer in battery-swap (reserve battery) or "suspend-to-disk" mode. Otherwise, a loss of data will probably result.
- Today, an AC adapter requires about 1.25–1.5 hours to charge a battery if the computer is off. The battery charges in 2.75–3 hours if the computer is on.
- For maximum battery performance, charge the battery only at normal room temperature.
- The battery starts charging immediately. The corresponding battery indicator lights while the battery is being charged and turns off when the cycle is complete.
- If a battery indicator blinks while the AC adapter is connected to the computer, the battery may be defective or installed improperly. Check the documentation for your particular laptop and verify that you're seeing the correct charging indicator.

CONSERVING MOBILE BATTERY POWER

Battery life is affected by the current drawn by a computer—greater current draw results in shorter battery life and lower draw, in longer life. A large portion of battery troubleshooting consists of ensuring that your system setup is adequate. The following guidelines should help you to optimize battery life. Table 6-1 illustrates typical settings for power conservation.

- Special power modes like suspend or hibernation use very little power and should be selected when you'll be away from the running laptop for any period of time.
- Any unnecessary devices in the laptop should be removed or disabled. For example, you may not need that PCMCIA modem card or sound card during that flight cross-country, so remove the card. If you can *disable* unneeded devices (shut down power to the built-in infra-red communication unit), that will also save substantial power.
- Using the lowest screen brightness that you are comfortable with by adjusting the display's brightness and contrast control(s) will conserve battery life.
- LCD backlights gobble up substantial amounts of power, so set a short timeout interval for the backlight (one or two minutes is often a good selection).
- A setting with light characters and images on a dark background generally consumes less power than dark characters or images on a light background. Try setting your screen mode to a "light on dark" configuration. If you're using Windows 95, select a dark color scheme.

TABLE 6-1 RECOMMENDED POWER-SAVING SETTINGS

FOR THIS FEATURE...	CONFIGURE THE SYSTEM TO...
Power button mode	Standby/Resume
PM Control	Battery
Power Savings	Maximum Battery Life
Sleep Timeout	2 Minutes
Standby Timeout	10 Minutes
Hard Disk Timeout	2 Minutes
Video Timeout	4 Minutes
Audio Timeout	2 Minutes
Battery Low Standby	Enabled
Auto Dim With Battery Only	On
Cooling control	Silence

- The hard disk drive is another major power user—not only by spinning, but during spinup as well. Select a moderate timeout interval for the hard drive (not so long that it spins forever, and not so short that it is constantly starting). Otherwise, you will waste more power constantly spinning up the drive than you save by turning it off. Also, constant starting and stopping can reduce the life expectancy of the drive.
- RAM consumes much less power than hard drives, so try setting up a disk cache or RAM disk to reduce the number of disk accesses. This allows the hard drive to shut down fairly quickly and not require access for a relatively long period of time.
- Microprocessor speed can be a serious drain on battery power. If your laptop computer allows you to select processor speed, use the slowest speed possible for all but the most demanding applications. Most word processors and conventional DOS utility software runs just fine with slower processor speeds.
- Most mobile batteries have trouble retaining their full charge capacity when left unused for prolonged periods of time. For example, IBM tests suggest that after a one-year shelf life at room temperature, a Li-ion battery retained 95 percent of its original capacity (about 90 percent for NiMH). If you purchase several batteries for a mobile computer, be sure to alternate the use of each battery.

RECOGNIZING RECHARGEABLE BATTERY FAILURES

Rechargeable batteries can and do fail eventually. The process of discharge and recharge generates physical stress in the battery that eventually wears it out. As a rule of thumb, a NiCd battery will last from about three to five years (through 500 to 1500 complete charge cycles). NiMH and lithium-ion batteries generally last somewhat longer. However, proper charging in a cool environment can extend battery life much further. (Up to as much as 10,000 complete charge cycles have been reported.) Over the life of a rechargeable battery, microscopic "whiskers" of conductive compounds develop between the electrodes. Ultimately, these deposits work to short-circuit the battery from inside. Although "zapping" techniques have been developed using brief surges of current to remove these deposits, such techniques are very risky since the battery stands a good chance of exploding. Another failure mode is the premature loss of liquid electrolyte during high-current or high-temperature charging. Improperly designed "quick-charge" chargers can drive a battery so hard that electrolyte starts to corrode the battery's pressure relief vent. If the vent is damaged or frozen in the open position, electrolyte will continue to evaporate, and the battery will fail.

TROUBLESHOOTING MOBILE BATTERY PROBLEMS

When discussing batteries as main power sources, not only are the batteries or battery pack involved, but a host of other circuitry is included as well (such as battery charging, battery protection, and power management circuits). As a result, you should understand that problems running or charging the battery may be originating *outside* of the battery compartment itself. Since batteries power notebook and sub-notebook systems, trouble may be on the motherboard (where most charging and power management functions are located).

Check the Battery Pack

When the battery refuses to take or hold a charge, it will often be necessary for you to verify the integrity of your mobile battery. The following steps outline the procedure:

- Power-down the laptop or notebook computer and remove the battery pack according to the instructions for your particular system.
- Once the battery pack is removed, measure the voltage between battery terminals. If there are more than two terminals (as in Figure 6-2 for an IBM ThinkPad battery), be sure to measure across the proper two terminals. For the example of Figure 6-2, you would measure across pins 1 and 4. If you read 0 Vdc, the battery pack is defective and should be replaced.

> The remaining pins on the battery pack are used for thermal sensors and other communication between the mobile PC and the battery.

- If the voltage across the battery terminals is less than the optimum value (usually less than +11.0 Vdc), the battery pack has been discharged through self-discharge (being left on the shelf) or use in the PC. Recharge the battery pack. If the voltage is *still* less than what the fully charged voltage should be after recharging, replace the battery pack.
- If the voltage is more than +11.0 Vdc, measure the resistance between the thermal sensor and ground terminals (pins 3 and 4 in Figure 6-2). The resistance should be about 4 kOhms to 30 kOhms. If the resistance is not correct, the thermal sensor has failed. This can make it impossible to charge the battery properly, so replace the battery pack.
- If the resistance is correct, the battery charging circuit has probably failed.

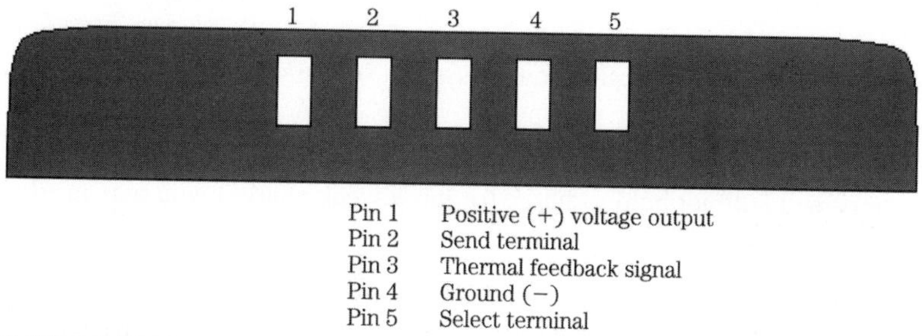

FIGURE 6-2 Battery terminals for an IBM ThinkPad battery pack

Recalibrate the Battery

Today's "smart" lithium-ion batteries are designed to communicate with your laptop system and provide the system with vital information about the amount of charge that remains in the battery pack. This feature allows you to monitor the amount of charge (or running time) left on your battery. In order to provide the proper information to your laptop, a battery must be calibrated so that it "knows" the difference between a full charge and an empty charge.

When your laptop goes into a standby mode prematurely and without warning (for example, while you're typing or watching a DVD video), it's possible that the battery has "forgotten" the difference between a full and empty charge. When this occurs, the battery may need to be recalibrated. The steps below outline a general procedure, but check with your laptop maker for more specific details:

- Power up your notebook.
- Start the laptop's CMOS setup routine.
- Check the Advanced or Power Management menus and locate a "Battery Calibrate" or "Recalibrate" feature. (Some laptops refer to this function as "Recalibrate Gas Gauge.")
- Press ENTER. A screen opens prompting you to start the recalibration program.
- Press ENTER to start discharging the battery. A message appears indicating the amount of time the discharge process will take.

> If you're connected to AC power, you'll be prompted to disconnect the AC power adapter. (After you have disconnected the AC power, the discharge process should start automatically.)

- When the battery has been fully discharged, the notebook will turn itself off.
- You can now fully charge the battery, and the laptop's battery meter should display an accurate status of your battery's charge level.

SYMPTOM 6-6 **You cannot deep discharge the main battery on your laptop** Often, early laptop systems needed to "deep discharge" the main battery when battery life became shorter. This feature was designed to help correct the memory problem encountered with NiCd and NiMH batteries. Some laptops (such as the Dell Latitude LX or Latitude M) provide a deep discharge feature. Try the following procedure:

- Reboot your system and enter the CMOS setup. Select Power Management Control from the main menu.
- Check for a submenu in Power Management Control, and then select the Deep Discharge option and enable it.
- Save your changes and reboot the system again. When the system reboots, it will be in deep discharge mode, which means it is using battery power as quickly as possible. Now allow the system to run on battery power until it powers off.
- Recharge the battery fully, and then repeat the process. (You may need to repeat this process as many as three times.) If your battery will still not hold a charge (or has a weak charge), you may need to replace the battery pack.

Use extreme caution when employing this tactic. Some batteries may not tolerate this deep discharge process very well, and battery damage may result. Check with the laptop maker to see if deep discharging is permitted (or if an alternative deep discharge process is recommended).

SYMPTOM 6-7 **The battery pack does not charge** In this type of situation, the computer may run fine from the AC-powered supply, and the system may very well run from its onboard battery when the AC-powered supply is removed. However, the battery pack does not appear to charge when the AC supply is connected and running. Without a charge, the battery will eventually go dead. Remember that some computers will not recharge their battery packs while the system is on—the computer may have to be turned off with the AC supply connected in order for the battery pack to charge. Refer to the user manual for your particular system to review the correct charging protocol.

Your clue to the charging situation comes from the computer's battery status indicator. Most notebook/laptop systems incorporate a multicolor LED or an LCD status bar to show battery information. For example, the LED may be red when the small-computer is operating from its internal battery. A yellow color may appear when the AC-powered supply is connected to indicate the battery is charging. The LED may turn green when the battery is fully charged. If the battery status indicator fails to show a charging color when the AC-powered supply is being used, that is often a good sign of trouble. Table 6-2 lists the status indicators for an IBM ThinkPad. (Check the user manual for your particular computer.)

Check the battery pack with all computer power off. Make sure that the battery pack is inserted properly and completely into its compartment. Also check any cabling and connectors that attach the battery pack to the charging circuit. Loose or corroded connectors, as well as faulty cable wiring, can prevent energy from the AC-powered supply from reaching the battery. Reseat any loose connectors, and reattach any loose wiring that you may find.

After you are confident of your connections, you should trace charging voltage from the AC-powered supply to the battery terminals. If charging voltage does not reach the battery, the battery can never charge. Set your multimeter to measure DC voltage (probably in the 10 Vdc to 20 Vdc range), and measure the voltage across your battery pack. You should read some voltage below the pack's rated voltage because the battery pack is somewhat discharged. Now, connect the computer's AC-powered supply and measure voltage across your battery pack again. If charging voltage is available to the battery, your voltage reading should climb above the battery pack's rated voltage. If charging still does not seem to take place, try replacing the battery pack, which may be worn out or damaged. If charging voltage is not available to your battery pack, the charging circuit is probably faulty. Replace the charging circuit. Since the charging circuit is typically located on the motherboard, it may be necessary to replace the entire motherboard assembly.

SYMPTOM 6-8 **The system does not run on battery power, but runs properly from main (AC) power** This symptom usually suggests that your computer runs fine whenever the AC-powered supply is being used, but the system will not run from battery power alone. The system may or

TABLE 6-2 STATUS INDICATORS FOR AN IBM THINKPAD COMPUTER

MODE	COLOR	MEANING
Charging	Green	Battery fully charged
	Orange	Battery charging
	Blinking orange	Battery needs charging
Conservation	Green	Computer is in suspend mode
	Blinking green	Computer is entering suspend mode or hibernation mode, or resuming normal operation
Status	Green	Power on

may not initialize depending on the extent of the problem. Before you disassemble the computer or attempt any sort of repair, make sure that you have a fully charged battery pack in the system. Remove the battery pack and measure the voltage across its terminals. You should read approximately the battery voltage marked on the pack. A measurably lower voltage may indicate that the battery is not fully charged. Try a different battery pack, or try to let the battery pack recharge. The charging process may take several hours on older systems, but newer small-computer battery systems can charge in an hour or so.

When you have a fully charged battery, check to be sure that it is inserted completely and connected properly. Inspect any wiring and connectors that attach the battery pack to its load circuit. Faulty wiring, corroded connections, or loose connectors can cut off the battery pack entirely. At this point, it is safe to assume that battery power is not reaching the laptop circuit(s). In this event, the battery charging/protection circuit may be defective and should be replaced. If the circuit is incorporated into the motherboard, the motherboard should be replaced.

SYMPTOM 6-9 **Your laptop no longer has a Standby option on the Shutdown menu** You notice that the "plug" icon (rather than the "battery" icon) always appears in the system tray while using battery power. In virtually all cases, you'll need to reinstall the laptop's Advanced Power Management feature:

1. Shut down all running applications.
2. Click Start, highlight Settings, select Control Panel, and then double-click the System icon.
3. Click the Device Manager tab, and then click on the View Devices by Type radio button.
4. Click the plus (+) next to System Devices, select Advanced Power Management, select Remove, and then click OK. Restart the system when prompted to do so.
5. Once the system has rebooted, click Start, highlight Settings, select Control Panel, and then double-click the Add New Hardware icon.
6. Click Next to search for new hardware. Click Next again to search for any new plug-and-play devices. The system may find new hardware (and list the items). If Advanced Power Management Support is not listed, then select Yes for Windows to search for your new hardware. Then click Next to begin the search.
7. Once device detection is finished, select Details—it should find Advanced Power Management Support.
8. Select Finish to begin the installation. The system will prompt you to insert your Windows 98 CD. After the necessary files are installed, you'll be prompted to reboot the system. Once the system has rebooted, the system will find the APM Battery Slot.
9. After the system finishes booting, click Start, select Shut Down, and you should see Standby as one of the shutdown options. Switch from AC power to battery power, and the plug icon should change to a battery icon.

SYMPTOM 6-10 **The system suffers from a short battery life** Today's mobile computers are designed to squeeze up to six hours of operation (or more) from every charge. Most systems get at least two hours from a charge. Short battery life can present a perplexing problem—especially if you do a great deal of computing on the road. All other computer functions are assumed to be normal.

Begin your investigation by inspecting the battery pack itself. Check for any damaged batteries. Make sure the battery pack is inserted properly into the computer, and see that its connections and wiring are clean and intact. Try replacing the battery pack. Keep in mind that rechargeable batteries do not last forever. Typical NiCd packs are usually good for about 800 cycles, NiMH packs are often suitable for 500 cycles, and Li-ion packs are usually rated for 1200 cycles. Fast-charge battery packs are subject to the greatest abuse and can suffer the shortest life spans. It is possible that one or more cells in the battery pack have failed. The battery pack may also have developed the memory problem discussed earlier. Try several cycles of completely discharging and recharging the pack. If the problem remains, replace the battery pack.

The computer's configuration itself can largely determine the amount of running time available from each charge. The CPU, the display (and its backlight), the hard drive, floppy drive/CD-ROM drive access—each of these items consumes substantial amounts of power. Many mobile computers are designed to shut down each major power consumer after some preset period of disuse. For example, an LCD screen may shut off if there is no keyboard activity after two minutes, or the hard drive may stop spinning after three minutes if there is no hard drive access, and so on. Even reducing CPU clock speed during periods of inactivity will reduce power consumption. The amount of time required before shutdown can usually be adjusted through setup routines in the computer or through the operating system. See the "Conserving Mobile Battery Power" section earlier in the chapter.

SYMPTOM 6-11 **The battery pack becomes extremely hot during charging** As you learned earlier in the chapter, current must be applied to a battery from an external source in order to restore battery charge. When a battery receives *significant* charging current (during or after the charging process), its temperature will begin to rise. Temperature rise continues as long as current is applied. If high charging current continues unabated, battery temperature may climb high enough to actually damage the cells. Even under the best circumstances, prolonged high-temperature conditions can shorten the working life of a battery pack. Today's high-current charging circuits must be carefully controlled to ensure a full, rapid battery charge, but prevent excessive temperature rise and damage.

Battery packs or compartments are fitted with a *thermistor* (a temperature-sensitive resistor). When the battery pack is fully charged, the thermistor responds to the subsequent temperature increase and signals charging circuitry to reduce or stop its charging current. In this way, temperature is used to detect when full charge has been reached. It is normal for most battery packs to become a bit warm during the charging process—especially packs that use fast-charge currents. However, the cell(s) should not give off an obnoxious odor or become too hot to touch. Hot batteries are likely to be damaged. In many cases, the thermistor (or the thermistor's signal conditioning circuitry) has failed and is no longer shutting down charge current. Try another battery pack. If the new pack also becomes very hot, the fault is in the charging circuit, which should be replaced. If the new pack remains cooler, the fault is probably in the original battery pack.

6

SYMPTOM 6-12 **After several days of disuse, your laptop may not power up properly** This may happen regardless of whether you use the AC adapter or battery. You find that the battery shows a full charge. The system may have failed to detect (or misdetected) the available power. With the system powered off, unplug the AC adapter from the back of the computer, and remove the battery from the case so that both power sources are removed. Then replace the battery and AC adapter cord before turning the unit on. Your laptop should power-up normally.

SYMPTOM 6-13 **Your laptop locks up if you hot- or warm-swap a CD-ROM module with a battery** This lockup is caused by system detection problems. If a CD-ROM drive is detected by Windows 95 at boot time, and then at some point that drive is removed, the operating system is not made aware of this (and will attempt to poll the device when My Computer is opened). At this point the operating system will continue to wait for a response from the device until it times out. This can take anywhere from four to six minutes, during which the system appears to be locked up. Swapping the CD-ROM is currently not supported by Windows 95 CD-ROM drivers.

SYMPTOM 6-14 **A "battery problem" indicator comes on and will not go out** This is a known problem on the Gateway Solo 2300/9100 and other systems, and it is almost always caused by a problem with the BIOS. Generally, a BIOS upgrade will correct the problem and allow the computer to communicate properly with the "smart" battery. Once the BIOS is upgraded, be sure to charge the battery to 100 percent. If the battery indicator light still turns red, it should only last four to five seconds, and then return to orange (charging) or green (charged fully).

SYMPTOM 6-15 **The computer quits without producing a low-battery warning** Computers are rarely subtle in regard to low-power warnings. Once a battery pack falls below a certain voltage threshold, the computer initiates a series of unmistakable audible (and sometimes visual) cues that tell you there are only minutes of power remaining. Such a warning affords you a last-minute opportunity to save your work and switch over to AC power if possible. If you choose to ignore a low-power warning, the system will soon reach a minimum working level and crash on its own—whether you like it or not.

Mobile computers measure their battery voltage levels constantly. A custom IC on the motherboard is typically given the task of watching over battery voltage. When voltage falls below a fixed preset level, the detector IC produces a logic alarm signal. The alarm, in turn, drives an interrupt to the CPU, or passes the signal to a power management IC, which then deals with the CPU or system controller. Once the alarm condition reaches the CPU, the computer typically initiates a series of tones, flashes a "power" LED, or sometimes both (see Table 6-2).

Most PCs produce at least one beep during initialization in order to test the internal speaker. If you do not hear this beep, the speaker or its driving circuit may be damaged. Try replacing the speaker; then try replacing the motherboard. When an audible beep is heard during initialization, there is probably a fault in the computer's battery detection or power management circuits. Try cleaning the battery contacts first; then try replacing the laptop's motherboard.

SYMPTOM 6-16 **Your battery indicator displays a zero percent charge, even though the battery has been fully charged** After attempting to charge a laptop's battery, the battery may display a status of zero percent (and may not accept a charge). This typically occurs only after the battery has been left completely discharged for an extended period of time, or after a fully charged battery has been left completely out of a computer for a period of several months or more. This issue is often avoided by regularly charging the battery. For example, seat or reseat the battery and A/C adapter as necessary, and (with the computer plugged into the adapter) allow the battery to charge up to approximately 100 percent. Here are some tips to resolve the issue:

- Verify that the latest version of the computer's BIOS is installed on the system.
- Reseat the battery and A/C adapter to ensure a good connection.
- If your laptop uses battery monitoring/conditioning software, be sure to install the latest version (which can typically be downloaded directly from the laptop manufacturer).
- If the battery still shows zero percent (or does not accept a charge), the battery may be defective and needs to be replaced.

Battery Recycling

Most types of batteries use metals and electrolyte chemicals that are harmful to the environment. As a consequence, many states and provinces have enacted legislation prohibiting the dumping or discarding of batteries (especially lead-acid, NiCd, and alkaline). NiMH and lithium batteries are somewhat less toxic, but can also often be recycled. To support a cleaner environment, many vendors who sell PC batteries are accepting returns of the old defective batteries, which are recycled. For example, IBM supports the Reusable Battery Recycling Center (at 770-984-0708). Another major battery vendor, 1-800-Batteries, also accepts returns (at 408-879-1930). Before purchasing new batteries, verify that the vendor will accept your spent batteries; if not, contact your local town recycling center to see if it takes exhausted batteries.

Further Study

Battery Network: **http://www.battnet.com/**

Direct Power: **http://www.dpp.com/index.html**

1-800-Batteries: **http://www.800batteries.com/index2.html**

Duracell: **http://www.duracell.com/**

Electrochem: **http://www.greatbatch.com/combat-specs.html**

Energizer: **http://www.energizer.com/**

Fedco: **http://www.fedcoelectronics.com/home.tmpl**

GS Battery: **http://www.gsbattery.com/index.html**

Tadiran: **http://www.tadiranbat.com/**

Rayovac: **http://www.rayovac.com/**

Varta: **http://www.varta.com/index.html**

7

BIOS

CHAPTER AT A GLANCE

Although every personal computer uses the same essential subassemblies, each subassembly is designed a bit differently. This is especially true of the processing components (chipsets and controllers) contained on a motherboard. This is understandable given the tremendous speed at which PC components and technology are advancing. Unfortunately, such dramatic variations in hardware make it difficult to use a single standard operating system. Instead of tailoring an operating system (and applications) to specific computers, a Basic Input/Output System (BIOS) is added on ROM ICs to provide an interface between the raw PC hardware and the standardized operating system. BIOS gives an OS access to a standard set of functions. As a result, every system uses a slightly different BIOS, but each BIOS contains the same set of functions that provide the interface for an OS. This chapter explains the internal workings of a typical BIOS, illustrates some means of identifying BIOS versions, and shows you the many features that a modern BIOS must support.

Of course, BIOS is not limited solely to the motherboard (although most BIOS versions carry enough routines to support video and drive controller operations in addition to other motherboard features). But what happens when a new video card is developed that the system BIOS does not know how to work with, or an advanced drive controller board becomes available? A common practice in computer design is to include a BIOS ROM for major subsystems such as video and drive control. One of the early steps of system initialization is to check for the presence of other valid BIOS ROMs located in upper memory (between 640KB and 1024KB). These are usually referred to as *expansion* or *adapter* BIOS. When another BIOS is located, it is also checksum tested and used by the PC. In general, a PC may be fitted with up to six or more BIOS ROMs, such as:

- System (motherboard) BIOS
- Video adapter firmware (BIOS)
- Drive controller firmware (BIOS)
- Network adapter board BIOS
- Modem card firmware (BIOS)
- SCSI adapter BIOS

A Look Inside Motherboard BIOS

The typical BIOS ROM occupies 128KB of space in the system's upper memory area (UMA), from E0000h to FFFFFh (within the PC's first MB of memory). Contrary to popular belief, BIOS is not a single program, but an arsenal of individual programs—most quite small. In general, BIOS contains three sections, as shown in Figure 7-1: the power-on self-test (POST), the CMOS setup routine, and the system services routines. The particular section of BIOS code that is executed depends on the computer's state and its activities at any given moment.

POST

Although many novice technicians are aware that POST checks the system, few are aware that POST actually manages the entire system startup. The power-on self-test handles virtually all of the initialization activities for a PC. POST performs a low-level diagnostic and reliability test of the main processing components, including ROM programs and system RAM. It tests the CPU, initializes the motherboard's chipset, checks the 128 bytes of CMOS for system configuration data, and sets up an index of interrupt vectors for the CPU from 0000h to 02FFh. POST then sets up a BIOS Stack Area from 0300h to 03FFh, loads the BIOS Data Area (BDA) in low memory 0400h to 04FFh, detects any optional equipment (adapter BIOS ROMs) in the system, and proceeds to boot the operating system.

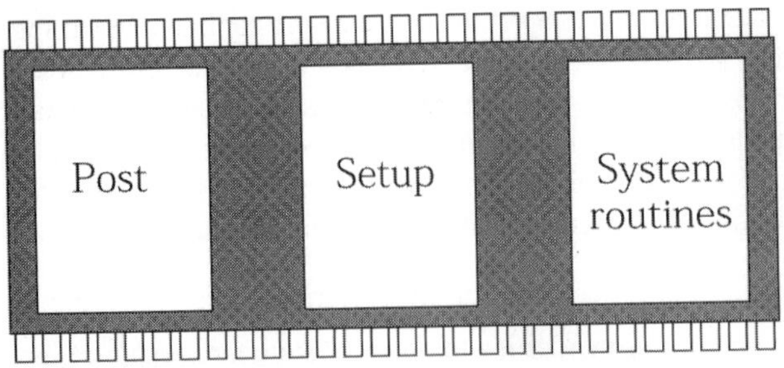

FIGURE 7-1 Main sections of a typical BIOS

SETUP

The hardware configuration for any given computer is maintained in a small amount of CMOS RAM, and a CMOS setup routine is required in order for you to access the system's configuration. Older i286 and i386 systems provided the CMOS setup routine as a separate utility included with the system on a floppy disk. In most cases, the "setup disk" was promptly misplaced or discarded. Starting with late-model i386 and later systems, the CMOS setup routine has been integrated into the motherboard BIOS itself. The actual CMOS setup program can vary tremendously between system manufacturers and motherboards, so there is no single standard for which settings can be controlled, or where those entries are located.

Many Compaq systems place the setup routine on a "diagnostic partition" on the hard drive. If the drive fails (or is repartitioned), the diagnostic partition may be lost, and it may be impossible to adjust the system's configuration until the diagnostic partition is restored.

SYSTEM SERVICE ROUTINES

The *system services* (also referred to as *BIOS services*) are a set of individual functions that form the layer between hardware and the operating system. Services are called through the use of interrupts. An *interrupt* essentially causes the CPU to stop whatever it is working on and sends program control to another address in memory, which usually starts a subroutine designed specifically to deal with the particular interrupt. When the interrupt handling routine is complete, the CPU's original state is restored, and control is returned to where the PC left off before the interrupt occurred. A wide range of interrupts can attract the attention of a CPU, and interrupts can be produced from three major sources: the CPU itself, a hardware condition, and a software condition.

Interrupts produced by the CPU itself (known as *processor interrupts*) are often the result of an unusual, unexpected, or erroneous program result. For example, if a program tries to divide a number by zero, the CPU will generate INT 00h, which causes a "Divide by zero" error message. There are five processor interrupts (00h to 04h).

The *hardware interrupts* are generated when a device is in need of the CPU's attention to perform a certain task. Hardware interrupts are invoked by asserting a logic level on a physical interrupt request (IRQ) line. The CPU suspends its activities and executes the interrupt handling routine. When the interrupt handler is finished, the CPU resumes normal operation. For example, each time a keyboard key is pressed, the keyboard buffer asserts a logic line corresponding to INT 09h (IRQ 1). This invokes a keyboard handling routine. PC/AT-compatible systems typically provide 16 hardware interrupts (IRQ 0 to IRQ 15), which correspond to INT 08h to 0Fh and 70h to 77h, respectively.

Software interrupts are generated when a hardware device must be checked or manipulated by the PC. The "print screen" function is a prime example of a software interrupt. When the PRINTSCREEN button is pressed on the keyboard, an INT 05h is generated. The interrupt routine dumps the contents of its video character buffer to the printer port.

BIOS Features

PC technology is constantly advancing in CPUs, chipsets, memory, video, drives, and so on. As the hardware continues to advance, the BIOS must also advance to keep pace with the resources emerging on today's systems. As a result, it is important for you to recognize the key features included in a modern BIOS. You do not need to understand the details of each feature right now, but you should at least recognize a current BIOS by reviewing its feature set. While many of the items listed in a BIOS feature set may seem a bit incidental, the core features of a modern BIOS can be broken down into a number of major areas:

- *CPU support* BIOS should support a rich range of CPUs, preferably from various CPU makers such as Intel, AMD, and Cyrix. Look for Pentium, Pentium MMX, Pentium Pro, Pentium II, Pentium III, and AMD "Athlon" support (though one BIOS will probably not support all of these CPU families).
- *Chipset support* The BIOS should support the latest chipset families (such as Intel's 440BX chipset). Chipset support is critical because it is the chipset that allows motherboard designers to implement other features such as USB and advanced memory.
- *Memory support* The BIOS should be able to autosize and support the most modern forms of memory (such as SDRAM or even RAMBUS). Memory error checking (such as "parity" and "ECC") should also be supported. Modern BIOS can support up to 4GB of RAM, though the system's motherboard may not handle that much.
- *Power management support* The BIOS should be fully compliant with the Advanced Configuration and Power Interface (ACPI) specification (revision 1.0 or later), and support APM BIOS specifications through version 1.2 or later. Power management is vitally important for mobile systems and is widely used in desktop/tower systems to reduce energy waste. The BIOS should also support DPMS (Display Power Management System) for monitors and other display devices.
- *Drive support* The BIOS must support large EIDE/Ultra-ATA hard drives (over 1024 cylinders) with very fast data transfer modes such as PIO Modes 0-4, Ultra-DMA/33, and Ultra-DMA/66.
- *PC 99 support* The BIOS should be compliant with the current Microsoft PC 99 BIOS requirements.
- *I^2O support* The BIOS may support I^2O (Intelligent I/O), which allows the dynamic assignment of ports and resources for I/O devices in the PC.
- *Boot versatility support* The BIOS should be able to boot from a number of different drives and include the BIOS Boot Specification for Initial Program Load (IPL) devices. This currently supports booting from up to four IDE-type drives (including CD-ROM drives), SCSI drives, and network cards. Support for removable media drives (such as Iomega Zip or SyQuest drives) is an advantage.
- *Plug-and-play support* The BIOS must detect and configure PnP devices during POST. The BIOS also communicates with Windows 95/98 to determine system resources. Support of Microsoft's AML permits compatibility with PnP capability in future Windows operating systems (such as Windows 2000).

7

- *Parallel port support* The BIOS should support a full range of parallel port modes, including Standard Parallel Port (SPP or "compatibility" mode), bidirectional mode, Enhanced Capabilities Port (ECP), and Enhanced Parallel Port (EPP).
- *PCI and AGP support* The BIOS must support Intel's Peripheral Component Interconnect (PCI) bus specification (version 2.1 or later), including PCI-to-PCI and PCI-to-ISA bridging. The BIOS must also support the Advanced Graphics Port (AGP).
- *USB support* The BIOS should support both Universal and Open HCI standards. It should maintain full core compatibility and provide legacy support for USB hardware and multilayered USB hubs. You may also find support for USB II (high-speed USB) in the very newest BIOS versions.
- *Antivirus protection* The BIOS should offer the option of virus protection. As a minimum, the BIOS should prevent changes to the master boot record (often a sign of virus activity).

Whether you're trying to learn the capabilities of your current BIOS or planning a BIOS upgrade, you can learn a lot about a BIOS and its features by studying the BIOS ID codes. This part of the chapter explains several means of identifying popular BIOS versions and will help you to understand the information encoded in the BIOS ID string.

AMI BIOS AND AMI BIOS PLUS

Various versions of American Megatrends firmware (AMI BIOS and AMI BIOS Plus) have been sold from 1986 through 1990. The ID string identifies the BIOS type, the BIOS release date, and the keyboard BIOS revision level, for example:

```
AAAA-BBBB-DDMMYY-Kx
```

- **AAAA**—*BIOS type* This includes chipset identification codes.
- **BBBB**—*AMI customer reference number* This code identifies the motherboard manufacturer that AMI tailored the BIOS for. (See Table 7-1 to reference the motherboard maker.)
- **DDMMYY**—*BIOS release date* The code is in day/month/year format.
- **Kx**—*Keyboard BIOS* This indicates the revision level of the keyboard BIOS code.

AMI HI-FLEX BIOS

The more recent AMI Hi-Flex BIOS family provides a three-line BIOS identification string. This yields much more detailed information about the BIOS and its capabilities. The first line appears at the bottom left of the screen during boot-up. You can see the second and third lines by pressing the INS key during the moments following power-on. This Hi-Flex BIOS ID string has the following format:

```
A#-BBBB-CCCCCC-DDDDDDDD-EEEEEE-FFFFFFFF-G
HHH-I-JJJJ-KK-LL-MMMM-NN-OO-PPP
QQQ-R-SSSS-TT-UU-VVVV-WW-XX-YY-Z
```

- **A**—*CPU type* This code identifies the CPU vintage, where 0 = 8086 (or 8088), 2 = 80286, 3 = 80386, and 4 = 80486.
- **#**—*BIOS size* This code tells the size of the BIOS chip, where 0 = 64KB, and 1 = 128KB.

TABLE 7-1 AMI BIOS VERSIONS TAILORED FOR INDIVIDUAL MOTHERBOARD MANUFACTURERS

CODE	CUSTOMER
1101	Sunlogix, Inc.
1102	Soyo Technology Co., Ltd.
1105	Autocomputer Co., Ltd.
1106	Dynasty Computer Inc.
1107	DataExpert Corp.
1108	Chaplet Systems, Ltd.
1109	Fair Friend Enterprise Co., Ltd.
1111	Paoku P&C Co., Ltd.
1112	Aquarius Systems, Ltd.
1113	Micro Leader Enterprises Corp.
1114	Iwill Corp.
1115	Senor Science Co., Ltd.
1116	Chicony Electronics Co., Ltd.
1117	A-Trend Technology Co., Ltd.
1120	Unicorn Computer Corp.
1121	First International Computer, Ltd.
1122	Micro-Star Computer Corp.
1123	Magtron Technology Co., Ltd.
1124	Tekram Technology Co., Ltd.
1126	Chuntex Electronic Co., Ltd.
1128	Chaintech Computer Co., Ltd.
1130	Pai Jung Electronic Ind. Co., Ltd.
1131	Elitegroup Computer Co., Ltd.
1132	Dkine Enterprise Co., Ltd.
1133	Seritech Enterprise Co., Ltd.
1135	Acer Inc.
1136	Sun's Electronics Co., Ltd.
1138	Win Win Electronic Co., Ltd.
1140	Angine, Ltd.
1141	Nuseed Technology, Inc.
1142	Firich Enterprises Co., Ltd.
1143	Crete Systems, Inc.
1144	Vista Technology Co., Ltd.
1146	Taste Corp.
1147	Integrated Technology Express, Inc.
1150	Achitec Corporation, Ltd.
1151	Accos Enterprise Co., Ltd.
1152	Top-Thunder Technology Co., Ltd.
1154	San Li Technology Co, Ltd.
1156	Technica House, Inc.
1158	Hi-Com Industrial Co., Ltd.
1159	Twinhead International Corp.
1161	Monterey International Corp.
1163	Softek Systems Co., Ltd.
1165	Mercury Computer Corp.
1169	Micro-Star International Co., Ltd.
1170	Taiwan Igel Co., Ltd.
1171	Shing Yunn Electronics Enterprise Corp.
1176	Sigma Computer Corp.
1178	Clevo Co.
1188	Quanta Computer, Inc.
1195	GNS Technologies, Inc.
1196	Universal Scientific Industrial Co., Ltd.
1197	Golden Way Electronic Corp.
1199	Giga-Byte Technology Co., Ltd.
1201	New Tech International Co., Ltd.
1203	Sunrex Technology Corp.
1204	Bestek Computer Co., Ltd.
1209	Puretek Industrial Co., Ltd.
1210	Rise Computer, Inc.
1211	Diamond Flower Electric Instrument Co., Ltd.
1214	Rever Computer, Inc.
1218	Elite Computer Co., Ltd.
1223	Biostar Microtech International Corp.
1225	Yunglin Technology Corp.
1234	Leadman Electronic Co., Ltd.
1241	Mustek Corp.
1242	Amptek Technology Co., Ltd.
1244	Flytech Technology Co., Ltd.
1246	Cosmotech Computer Corp.
1247	ABIT Computer Corp.
1256	Lucky Star Technology Co., Ltd.
1258	Four Star Computer Co., Ltd.
1259	GVC Corp.
1262	Arima Computer Corp.
1266	Modula Tech Co., Ltd.

TABLE 7-1 AMI BIOS VERSIONS TAILORED FOR INDIVIDUAL MOTHERBOARD MANUFACTURERS *(CONTINUED)*

CODE	CUSTOMER	CODE	CUSTOMER
1271	Tidal Technologies, Inc.	1462	Arche Technologies, Inc.
1273	Ufo Computer Co., Ltd.	1470	Flexus Computer Technology, Inc.
1274	Full Yes Industrial Corp.	1472	Datacom Technology Co., Ltd.
1276	Jet Way Information Co., Ltd.	1484	Mitac International Corp.
1277	Tarng Bow Co., Ltd.	1490	Great Tek Corp.
1281	EFA Corp.	1491	President Technology, Inc.
1283	Advance Creative Computer Corp.	1493	Artdex Computer Corp.
		1494	Pro Team Computer Corp.
1284	Lung Hwa Electronics Co., Ltd.	1500	Netcom Co., Ltd.
1291	Taiwan Mycomp Co., Ltd.	1503	Up Right Tech Co., Ltd.
1292	AsusTek Computer Inc.	1514	Wuu Lin Electronics Co., Ltd.
1297	DD&TT Enterprise, Inc.	1519	Epox Computer Co., Ltd.
1301	Taken Corp.	1526	Eagle Computer Technology Co., Ltd.
1304	Dual Enterprises Corp.		
1309	Protronic Enterprises Corp.	1531	Force System, Inc.
1317	New Comm Technology Co., Ltd.	1540	BCM Computers Co., Ltd.
1318	Unitron, Inc.	1546	Golden Horse Computer Co., Ltd.
1343	Holco Enterprise Co., Ltd.	1549	CT Continental Corp.
1346	Snobol Industrial Corp.	1564	Random Technology, Inc.
1351	Singdak Electronic Co., Ltd.	1576	Jetta Computers Co., Ltd.
1353	J-Bond Computer Systems Corp.	1585	Gleem Industries Co, Ltd.
1354	Protech Systems Co., Ltd.	1588	Boser Technology Co., Ltd.
1367	Coxswain Technology Co., Ltd.	1593	Advantech Co., Ltd.
1371	Adi Corp.	1608	Consolidated Marketing Corp.
1373	Silicon Integrated Systems Corp.	1612	Datavan International Corp.
1379	Win Technologies Co., Ltd.	1617	Honotron Corp.
1391	Aten International Co., Ltd.	1618	Union Genius Computer Co., Ltd.
1392	ACC Taiwan, Inc.	1621	New Paradise Enterprise Co. Ltd.
1393	Plato Technology Co., Ltd.	1622	RPT Intergroups International Ltd.
1396	Tatung Co.	1628	Digital Equipment International Ltd.
1398	Spring Circle Computer, Inc.	1630	Iston Computer Corp.
1404	Alptech Logic Products, Inc.	1647	Lantic, Inc.
1421	Well Join Industry Co., Ltd.	1652	ASE Technologies, Inc.
1422	Labway Computer Co., Ltd.	1655	Kingston Technology, Inc.
1437	Hsing Tech Enterprise Co., Ltd.	1656	Storage System, Inc.
1440	Great Electronics Corp.	1658	Macrotek International Corp.
1451	Ecel Systems Corp.	1666	Cast Technology, Inc.
1452	United Hitech Corp.	1671	Cordial Far East Corp.
1453	Kaimei Electronic Corp.	1672	Lapro Corp.
1461	Hedonic Computer Co., Ltd.	1675	Advanced Scientific Corp.

TABLE 7-1 AMI BIOS VERSIONS TAILORED FOR INDIVIDUAL MOTHERBOARD MANUFACTURERS *(CONTINUED)*

CODE	CUSTOMER
1685	High Ability Computer Co., Ltd. (Hsien, Taiwan)
1691	Gain Technology Co., Ltd.
1707	Chaining Computer & Communication Co.
1708	E-San Electronic Co., Ltd.
1719	Taiwan Turbo Technology Co., Ltd.
1720	Fantas Technology Co., Ltd.
1723	NTK Computer, Inc.
1727	Tripod Technology Corp.
1737	Ay Ruey International Co., Ltd.
1739	Jetpro Infotech Co., Ltd.
1743	Mitac, Inc.
1762	Ansoon Technology Co.
1770	Acer, Inc.
1771	Toyen Computer Co., Ltd.
1774	Acer Sertek, Inc.
1776	Joss Technology Ltd.
1780	Acrosser Technology Co., Ltd.
1783	Efar Microsystems, Inc.
1788	Systex Corp.
1792	U-Board Computerize Ltd.
1794	CMT Taiwan, Inc.
1796	J&J Technology Co., Ltd.
1801	Palit Microsystems, Inc.
1806	Interplanetary Information Co., Ltd.
1807	Expert Electronic Corp.
1810	Elechands International Co., Ltd.
1815	Powertech Electronic Co., Ltd.
1820	Ovis Enterprises Co., Ltd.
1823	Inlog Micro Systems Co., Ltd.
1826	TerComputer Technologies Corp.
1827	Anpro, Inc.
1828	Axiom Technology Co., Ltd.
1840	New Union H.K. Ltd.
1845	PC Direct Technology Co., Ltd.
1846	Garnet International Corp.
1847	Brain Power Co.
1850	HTR Asia Pacific, Inc.
1853	Veridata Electronics, Inc.
1856	Smart D&M Technology Co., Ltd.
1867	Lih Rong Electronic Enterprise Co., Ltd.
1868	Soyo Technology Co., Ltd.
1879	Aeontech International Co., Ltd.
1881	Manufacturing Technology Resources
1888	Seal International Corp.
1889	Rock Technology Co., Ltd.
1906	Freedom Data Technology Co., Ltd.
1914	Aquarius Systems, Inc.
1917	Source of Computer Co., Ltd.
1918	Lanner Electronics, Inc.
1920	Ipex ITG International Ltd.
1924	Join, Inc.
1926	Kou Sheng Computer Co., Ltd.
1927	Seahill Technology Co., Ltd.
1928	Nexcom International Co., Ltd.
1929	CAM Enterprise, Inc.
1931	AAEON Technology Co., Ltd.
1932	Kuei Hao Industrial Co., Ltd.
1933	ASMT Corp.
1934	Silver Bally, Inc.
1935	Prodisti Co., Ltd.
1936	Codegen Technology Co., Ltd.
1937	Orientech Electronics Corp.
1938	Project Information Co., Ltd.
1939	Arbor Technology Corp.
1940	SunTop Computer Systems Corp.
1941	Funtech Entertainment Corp.
1942	Sunflower Systems, Inc.
1943	Needs System Development Co., Ltd.
1945	Norm Advanced Technology Corp.
1947	Ten Yun Co., Ltd.
1948	Beneon Corp.
1949	National Advantages Computer Inc.
1950	Mits Technology Co.
1951	Macromate Corp.
1953	Orlycon Enterprise Co., Ltd.
1954	Chung Yu Electronics, Co., Ltd.

TABLE 7-1 AMI BIOS VERSIONS TAILORED FOR INDIVIDUAL MOTHERBOARD MANUFACTURERS *(CONTINUED)*

CODE	CUSTOMER	CODE	CUSTOMER
1955	Yamashita Systems Corp.	1974	Green Taiwan Computer Co., Ltd.
1957	High Large Corp.	1975	Supertone Electronic Co., Ltd.
1958	Young Micro Systems	1977	AT&T Taiwan Telecommunications Co.
1959	Fast Fame Computer Co., Ltd.	1978	Winco Electronic Co., Ltd.
1960	Acqutek Corp.	1980	Teryang Systems Co., Ltd.
1961	Deson Trade, Inc.	1981	Nexcom International Co., Ltd.
1962	Astra Communication Corp.	1982	China Semiconductor Corp.
1963	Dimensions Electronics Co., Ltd.	1985	Top Union Electronics Corp.
1964	Micron Design Technology, Ltd.	1986	DMP Electronics Co., Ltd.
1965	Cantta Enterprises Co., Ltd.	1988	Concierge Co., Ltd.
1968	Khi Way Enterprise Co., Ltd.	1989	Atherton Technology Co., Ltd.
1969	Gemlight Computer Ltd.	1990	Expen Tech Electronics Co., Ltd.
1970	Mat Technologies Ltd. (Advanced Technology Corp.)	1994	Japan Cere'Bro Computers Inc. (CBR)
		1996	Ikon Technologies Corp.
1973	Fugu Tech Enterprise Co., Ltd.	1998	Chang Tseng Corp.

- **BBBB**—*BIOS version number* This is the main version number, which you would use to identify the BIOS currently on the system.
- **CCCCCC**—*AMI customer reference number* This code identifies the motherboard manufacturer that AMI tailored the BIOS for. (See Table 7-1 to reference the motherboard maker.)
- **DDDDDDDD**—*AMIBCP settings* This is a set of eight logical "flags" that define several key operating parameters of the BIOS (0 = no, 1 = yes):
  1. Halt on error during POST.
  2. Initialize CMOS RAM at every boot.
  3. Keyboard controller output pin 23, 24 blocked.
  4. Mouse support in BIOS and keyboard controller.
  5. Wait for in case of POST error.
  6. Display floppy error during POST.
  7. Display video error during POST.
  8. Display keyboard error during POST.
- **EEEEEE**—*BIOS release date* This is given in day/month/year format.
- **FFFFFFFF**—*BIOS type* This includes chipset identification codes.
- **G**—*Keyboard BIOS* This indicates the revision level of the keyboard BIOS code.

Line 2 of the BIOS ID string generally provides information about the keyboard controller and keyboard clock. This information is of a lower priority, but it provides interesting information about the operations and performance of the keyboard.

- **HHH**—*KBC pin* This indicates the keyboard controller pin for clock switching.
- **I**—*Clock switching* This flag indicates the clock switching through chipset registers (0 = no, 1 = yes).
- **JJJJ**—*High port address* This is the port address used to switch the clock high.
- **KK**—*High data value* This is the data value used to switch the clock high.
- **LL**—*High mask value* This is the mask value used to switch the clock high.
- **MMMM**—*Low port address* This is the port address used to switch the clock low.
- **NN**—*Low data value* This is the data value used to switch the clock low.
- **OO**—*Low mask value* This is the mask value used to switch the clock low.
- **PPP**—*Turbo switch* This is the keyboard controller pin for the system's "turbo" switch.

Line 3 of the BIOS ID string typically provides information about the cache system and a few more details about the keyboard controller. As with line 2, this information is of a lower priority, but it provides additional interesting information about the operations and performance of the system cache.

- **QQQ**—*Cache control* This entry identifies the keyboard controller pin for cache control.
- **R**—*Cache through registers* This selects cache control through chipset registers (0 = no, 1 = yes).
- **SSSS**—*Enable cache port address* This is the port address for enabling cache control.
- **TT**—*Enable cache data value* This is the data value for enabling cache control.
- **UU**—*Enable cache mask value* This is the mask value for enabling cache control.
- **VVVV**—*Disable cache port address* This is the port address for disabling cache control.
- **WW**—*Disable cache data value* This is the data value for disabling cache control.
- **XX**—*Disable cache mask value* This is the mask value for disabling cache control.
- **YY**—*Reset pin* This indicates the keyboard controller pin for 82335 reset.
- **Z**—*BIOS modification number* This represents the specific modification number of the BIOS version.

AWARD BIOS

Award generally provides a great deal of information in their BIOS ID strings, including a product group, bus/topology, processor, chipset, hardware and driver option support, firmware options, media type, and release data. The typical Award BIOS ID format is

```
ABC-DEF-GG-HH-I
```

- **A**—*Product group* This flag indicates the type of product represented (1 = BIOS, 2 = BIOS, 3 = software on floppy disk, 6 = Award/OEM, 7 = socket services, 8 = card services, 9 = OEM card manufacturing kit).

7

- **B**—*Bus system or topology* This flag represents the principal bus type in use by the motherboard (1 = ISA, 2 = PS/2, 3 = video, 4 = other, 5 = EISA, 6 = SCSI, 7 = PCMCIA, 8 = SCSI/CAM, 9 = SCSI/CAMkit, A = ISA/PCI, B = EISA/PCI).
- **C**—*Processor* This flag denotes the motherboard's class of processor (1 = 8086/8088, 2 = 80286, 3 = 80386, 4 = 80486, 5 = Pentium, 6 = Cyrix386, 7 = Cyrix486, 8 = 386SL, 9 = 386SX, A = 42, B = 80C51SL, E = EGA, V = VGA).
- **D**—*Chipset* This flag indicates the particular chipset in use by the system. Table 7-2 lists the most typical chipsets that you can expect.
- **E**—*Hardware and driver support* This flag denotes the hardware and drivers supported with the BIOS. Table 7-3 lists the options for this entry.

TABLE 7-2 AWARD BIOS CHIPSETS

CODE	CHIPSET
C	Seat
D	VLSI Topcat/Intel 340
E	TI TACT83000
F	C&T Scat
G	VLSI
H	UMC 82C380
I	SiS
J	WinBond
K	HT 12
L	C&T Peak
M	ACC 82021
N	Eteq
O	TI 82411 Snake
P	WD 7600
Q	C&T PeakDM
R	Forex
S	Hong Kong Technology
T	ACC 2036
U	OPTi WB/PI
V	Elite
W	Headland 131
X	UMC 82C480
Y	ACC 2046
Z	Mosel 400
IF THE "PRODUCT GROUP" = 2:	
1	VLSI Scamp
2	OPTi NB
3	Symphony

CODE	CHIPSET
IF THE "PRODUCT GROUP" = 2: *(CONT.)*	
4	OPTi 496/497
5	HTK 320
6	AMD286 ZX
7	HTK 420
8	VLSI 82C486
9	OPTi 498
A	NEC XT
B	C&T
C	VLSI Scamp II
D	Intel HxC
E	PicoPower
F	VLSI 82C480
G	Acer 1419
H	VLSI 82C481
I	HT25
J	Intel Saturn
K	Intel Mercury
L	C&T 4021
IF THE "PRODUCT GROUP" = 3:	
0	Databook TM8200
1	Mustang BL1
2	Fujitsu MB86301
3	Label 365SL
4	Scamp 311L
5	Intel PHIC
6	Intel 82365SL

- **F**—*Firmware options* This index lists the firmware options supported by the BIOS. Table 7-4 lists the firmware options for Award BIOS.
- **GG**—*Custom* This entry is reserved for Award's exclusive use.
- **HH**—*Media type* This entry indicates the type of media on which the BIOS is provided. Table 7-5 lists the available media types for Award BIOS.
- **I**—*Release type* This entry lists the type of BIOS release you're using (0 = Label, 1 = Master, 2 = Evaluation, 3 = Beta, and 4 = Special).

TABLE 7-3 AWARD BIOS HARDWARE AND DRIVER SUPPORT

CODE	HARDWARE/DRIVER
0	None
1	C&T 82C307 Integrated Cache/DRAM Controller
2	C&T 82C605 or 82C606 Peripherals Controller
3	Austek 201 Cache Controller
4	Intel 82385/82385SX/82396SX Cache Controller
5	Not used
6	Intel 8242 Keyboard Controller
7	C&T 82C307 + 82C605 or 82C606
8	C&T 82C601 Peripherals Controller
9	Not used
A	Intel 82385 Cache + 8242 Keyboard Controller
B	Intel 82341 or VLSI 82C106 I/O controller + 82077 FDC
C	Austek 202/202SX Cache Controller
D	Intel 82341 I/O + 82385 Cache Controller
E	Weitek 3167 or 4167 + Cyrix EMC87 Math coprocessor
F	Intel 82C8 Cache Controller
G	Intel 82340 + 82341 I/O + 82C8 Cache Controller
H	Intel 82341 or VLSI 82C106 + WD 37C65 FDC
I	Intel 82341 or VLSI 82C106 + 82077 FDC + Austek 202
J	Intel 8242 + C&T 82C601 Peripheral Controller
K	Austek 152 Cache Controller
L	C&T 82C711 Peripheral Controller
M	Intel 487SX Math coprocessor
N	NSC PC87310 I/O controller
O	OPTi 82C491 WriteBack chipset
P	OPTi 82C491 WB chipset + C&T 82C711
Q	ACC 3221 Data Processor
R	Intel 82077SL Peripheral Controller
S	VLSI 425 Cache Controller
T	NSC PC87311 Super I/O

7

TABLE 7-4 AWARD BIOS FIRMWARE OPTIONS

CODE	FIRMWARE	CODE	FIRMWARE
0	None	F	Mouse, PWord, and EXSetup
1	EMS	G	Mouse, PWord, and EMS
2	EXSetup	H	Advanced Setup
3	Virus	I	Mouse and PWord
4	EMX and EXSetup	J	Mouse and EMS
5	PScan	K	Novell and Mouse
6	PWord	L	Novell
7	PWord and EXSetup	M	Novell and PWord
8	PWord and EMS	N	Novell, PWord, and EXSetup
9	PWord, EMS, and EXSetup	O	Novell, EXSetup, and Mouse
A	PWord and PScan	P	Novell, PWord, EXSetup, Mouse, and PScan
B	PWord, EXSetup, and PScan	Q	1024 Cylinders
C	EXSetup and PScan	R	1024 Cylinders and EXSetup
D	Mouse	S	1024 Cylinders, PWord, and EXSetup
E	Mouse and EXSetup	T	1024 Cylinders, Mouse, and EXSetup

TABLE 7-5 AWARD BIOS MEDIA TYPES

CODE	MEDIA TYPE	CODE	MEDIA TYPE
00	Bin/Hex 5.25-inch 360K	61	1xROM 27128
01	Bin/Hex 5.25-inch 1.2M	62	1xROM 27256
02	Bin/Hex 3.5-inch 720K	63	1xROM 27512
03	Bin/Hex 3.5-inch 1.44M	64	1xROM 27010
30	Source 5.25-inch 360K	6A	1xROM 8742
31	Source 5.25-inch 1.2M	70	2xROM 2764
32	Source 3.5-inch 720K	71	2xROM 27128
33	Source 3.5-inch 1.44M	72	2xROM 27256
40	1xPROM 2764	73	2xROM 27512
41	1xPROM 27128	74	2xROM 27010
42	1xPROM 27256	7A	2xROM 8742
43	1xPROM 27512	80	1xMask 8042
44	1xPROM 27010	84	1xPLCC 8742
4A	1xPROM 8742	A0	PAL
50	2xPROM 2764	B0	Pack
51	2xPROM 27128	C0	PCA (hardware)
52	2xPROM 27256	D0	Kit
53	2xPROM 27512	E0	Source listing
54	2xPROM 27010	E1	Manual set
60	1xROM 2764		

MICROID RESEARCH (MR BIOS)

The MR BIOS identification string is located at the top right corner of the Summary screen (and all or most of the Setup screens). The code directly relates to a specific motherboard model and manufacturer, as shown in Table 7-6. For example, a code of ACER309 means the MR BIOS was designed for an Acer/ALI M1209 motherboard using a Cyrix 486SLC processor.

A code of xxxx3xx indicates a 386-type CPU, and a code of xxxx4xx indicates a 486-type CPU.

TABLE 7-6 MR BIOS ID STRINGS

CODE	DESCRIPTION
ACER300	Acer/ALI M1209
ACER301	Acer/ALI M1209
ACER304	Acer/ALI M1209
ACER305	Acer/ALI M1209
ACER306	Acer/ALI M1209
ACER307	Acer/ALI M1209
ACER308	Acer/ALI M1209—Cyrix 486SLC
ACER309	Acer/ALI M1209—Cyrix 486SLC
ACER30C	Acer/ALI M1209—Cyrix 486SLC
ACER30D	Acer/ALI M1209—Cyrix 486SLC
ACER30E	Acer/ALI M1209—Cyrix 486SLC
ACER30F	Acer/ALI M1209—Cyrix 486SLC
ACER310	Acer/ALI M1217
ACER311	Acer/ALI M1217
ACER314	Acer/ALI M1217
ACER315	Acer/ALI M1217
ACER316	Acer/ALI M1217
ACER317	Acer/ALI M1217
ACER318	Acer/ALI M1217—Cyrix 486SLC
ACER319	Acer/ALI M1217—Cyrix 486SLC
ACER31C	Acer/ALI M1217—Cyrix 486SLC
ACER31D	Acer/ALI M1217—Cyrix 486SLC
ACER31E	Acer/ALI M1217—Cyrix 486SLC
ACER31F	Acer/ALI M1217—Cyrix 486SLC
C&T_300	Chips & Technologies CS8230
C&T_304	Chips & Technologies CS8230
C&T_305	Chips & Technologies CS8230
C&T_308	Chips & Technologies CS8230
C&T_309	Chips & Technologies CS8230

TABLE 7-6 MR BIOS ID STRINGS *(CONTINUED)*

CODE	DESCRIPTION
CNTQ400	Contaq 82C591/82C592 WriteBack
CNTQ404	Contaq 82C591/82C592 WriteBack
CNTQ405	Contaq 82C591/82C592 WriteBack
CNTQ406	Contaq 82C591/82C592 WriteBack
CNTQ407	Contaq 82C591/82C592 WriteBack
CNTQ410	Contaq 82C596 WriteBack
CNTQ411	Contaq 82C596 WriteBack
CNTQ412	Contaq 82C596 WriteBack
EFAR400	Efar Microsystems 82EC495 WriteBack
EFAR401	Efar Microsystems 82EC495 WriteBack—82C711 Combo I/O
EFAR402	Efar Microsystems 82EC495 WriteBack—PC87310 Super I/O
EFAR404	Efar Microsystems 82EC495 WriteBack
EFAR405	Efar Microsystems 82EC495 WriteBack
EFAR406	Efar Microsystems 82EC495 WriteBack
EFAR407	Efar Microsystems 82EC495 WriteBack
EFAR408	Efar Microsystems 82EC495 WriteBack—82C711 Combo I/O
EFAR409	Efar Microsystems 82EC495 WriteBack—82C711 Combo I/O
EFAR40A	Efar Microsystems 82EC495 WriteBack—82C711 Combo I/O
EFAR40B	Efar Microsystems 82EC495 WriteBack—82C711 Combo I/O
EFAR40C	Efar Microsystems 82EC495 WriteBack—PC87310 Super I/O
EFAR40D	Efar Microsystems 82EC495 WriteBack—PC87310 Super I/O
EFAR40E	Efar Microsystems 82EC495 WriteBack—PC87310 Super I/O
EFAR40F	Efar Microsystems 82EC495 WriteBack—PC87310 Super I/O
EFAR410	Efar Microsystems 82EC798 WriteBack
EFAR411	Efar Microsystems 82EC798 WriteBack—82C711 Combo I/O
EFAR412	Efar Microsystems 82EC798 WriteBack—PC87310 Super I/O
EFAR414	Efar Microsystems 82EC798 WriteBack
EFAR415	Efar Microsystems 82EC798 WriteBack
EFAR416	Efar Microsystems 82EC798 WriteBack
EFAR417	Efar Microsystems 82EC798 WriteBack
EFAR418	Efar Microsystems 82EC798 WriteBack—82C711 Combo I/O
EFAR419	Efar Microsystems 82EC798 WriteBack—82C711 Combo I/O
EFAR41A	Efar Microsystems 82EC798 WriteBack—82C711 Combo I/O
EFAR41B	Efar Microsystems 82EC798 WriteBack—82C711 Combo I/O
EFAR41C	Efar Microsystems 82EC798 WriteBack—PC87310 Super I/O
EFAR41D	Efar Microsystems 82EC798 WriteBack—PC87310 Super I/O
EFAR41E	Efar Microsystems 82EC798 WriteBack—PC87310 Super I/O
EFAR41F	Efar Microsystems 82EC798 WriteBack—PC87310 Super I/O
EFAR41G	Efar Microsystems 82EC798 WriteBack—Cyrix 486DLC
EFAR41H	Efar Microsystems 82EC798 WriteBack—Cyrix 486DLC—82C711 Combo I/O

TABLE 7-6 MR BIOS ID STRINGS *(CONTINUED)*

CODE	DESCRIPTION
EFAR41J	Efar Microsystems 82EC798 WriteBack—Cyrix 486DLC—PC87310 Super I/O
EFAR41K	Efar Microsystems 82EC798 WriteBack—Cyrix 486DLC
EFAR41L	Efar Microsystems 82EC798 WriteBack—Cyrix 486DLC
EFAR41M	Efar Microsystems 82EC798 WriteBack—Cyrix 486DLC
EFAR41N	Efar Microsystems 82EC798 WriteBack—Cyrix 486DLC
EFAR41P	Efar Microsystems 82EC798 WriteBack—Cyrix 486DLC—82C711 Combo I/O
EFAR41Q	Efar Microsystems 82EC798 WriteBack—Cyrix 486DLC—82C711 Combo I/O
EFAR41R	Efar Microsystems 82EC798 WriteBack—Cyrix 486DLC—82C711 Combo I/O
EFAR41S	Efar Microsystems 82EC798 WriteBack—Cyrix 486DLC—82C711 Combo I/O
EFAR41T	Efar Microsystems 82EC798 WriteBack—Cyrix 486DLC—PC87310 Super I/O
EFAR41U	Efar Microsystems 82EC798 WriteBack—Cyrix 486DLC—PC87310 Super I/O
EFAR41V	Efar Microsystems 82EC798 WriteBack—Cyrix 486DLC—PC87310 Super I/O
EFAR41W	Efar Microsystems 82EC798 WriteBack—Cyrix 486DLC—PC87310 Super I/O
EFAR41X	Efar Microsystems 82EC798 WriteBack—Cyrix 486DLC
ELIT320	Elite Microelectronics Eagle Rev. A1
ELIT324	Elite Microelectronics Eagle Rev. A1
ELIT325	Elite Microelectronics Eagle Rev. A1
ELIT420	Elite Microelectronics Eagle Rev. A1
ELIT424	Elite Microelectronics Eagle Rev. A1
ELIT425	Elite Microelectronics Eagle Rev. A1
ELIT426	Elite Microelectronics Eagle Rev. A1
ELIT427	Elite Microelectronics Eagle Rev. A1
ETEQ301	Eteq Microsystems 82C491/82C493 Bobcat Rev. A
ETEQ303	Eteq Microsystems 82C491/82C492 Cougar Rev. B, C
ETEQ304	Eteq Microsystems 82C491/82C492 Cougar Rev. B, C
ETEQ305	Eteq Microsystems 82C491/82C492 Cougar Rev. B, C
ETEQ311	Eteq Microsystems 82C491/82C493 Bobcat Rev. A
ETEQ314	Eteq Microsystems 82C491/82C493 Bobcat Rev. A
ETEQ315	Eteq Microsystems 82C491/82C493 Bobcat Rev. A
ETEQ321	Eteq Microsystems 82C4901/82C4902 Bengal WriteBack
ETEQ324	Eteq Microsystems 82C4901/82C4902 Bengal WriteBack
ETEQ325	Eteq Microsystems 82C4901/82C4902 Bengal WriteBack
ETEQ421	Eteq Microsystems 82C4901/82C4902 Bengal WriteBack
ETEQ428	Eteq Microsystems 82C4901/82C4902 Bengal WriteBack
ETEQ429	Eteq Microsystems 82C4901/82C4902 Bengal WriteBack
ETEQ401	Eteq Microsystems 82C491/82C493 Bobcat Rev. A
ETEQ403	Eteq Microsystems 82C491/82C492 Cougar Rev. B, C
ETEQ404	Eteq Microsystems 82C491/82C492 Cougar Rev. B, C
ETEQ405	Eteq Microsystems 82C491/82C492 Cougar Rev. B, C

7

TABLE 7-6 MR BIOS ID STRINGS *(CONTINUED)*

CODE	DESCRIPTION
HDK_200	EverTech 286 Hedaka
HDK_210	EverTech 286 Hedaka—built-in EMS
FORX300	Forex 36C300/200 [36C300/46C402] WriteThru
FORX303	Forex 36C300/200 [36C300/46C402] WriteThru
FORX320	Forex 36C311 Single Chip 386SX with Cache
FORX323	Forex 36C311 Single Chip 386SX with Cache
FORX410	Forex 46C411/402 WriteThru
FORX413	Forex 46C411/402 WriteThru
FORX418	Forex 46C411/402 WriteThru
FORX419	Forex 46C411/402 WriteThru
FORX420	Forex 46C521 WriteBack or Forex 46C421A/422 WriteBack
FORX421	Forex 46C521 WriteBack or Forex 46C421A/422 WriteBack
FORX422	Forex 46C521 WriteBack or Forex 46C421A/422 WriteBack
FORX423	Forex 46C521 WriteBack or Forex 46C421A/422 WriteBack
FORX424	Forex 46C521 WriteBack or Forex 46C421A/422 WriteBack
FORX425	Forex 46C521 WriteBack or Forex 46C421A/422 WriteBack
FORX426	Forex 46C521 WriteBack or Forex 46C421A/422 WriteBack
FORX427	Forex 46C521 WriteBack or Forex 46C421A/422 WriteBack
FORX428	Forex 46C521 WriteBack or Forex 46C421A/422 WriteBack
FORX429	Forex 46C521 WriteBack or Forex 46C421A/422 WriteBack
FTDI400	FTDI 82C3480 WriteBack/WriteThru
FTDI401	FTDI 82C3480 WriteBack/WriteThru with 82C711 Combo I/O
FTDI402	FTDI 82C3480 WriteBack/WriteThru with PC87310 Super I/O
FTDI408	FTDI 82C3480 WriteBack/WriteThru
FTDI409	FTDI 82C3480 WriteBack/WriteThru with 82C711 Combo I/O
FTDI40A	FTDI 82C3480 WriteBack/WriteThru with PC87310 Super I/O
HKT_301	Hong Kong Technology HK3000 (Phoenix 8242 Keyboard Controller)
HKT_302	Hong Kong Technology HK3000 (MR BIOS 8042 Keyboard Controller)
HT12200	Headland Technologies HT12/HT12+
HT12201	Headland Technologies HT12/HT12+
HT12202	Headland Technologies HT12/HT12+
HT12210	Headland Technologies HT12/HT12+ with built-in EMS
HT12211	Headland Technologies HT12/HT12+ with built-in EMS
HT22300	Headland Technologies HT22/HT18C
HT22302	Headland Technologies HT22/HT18C
HT22303	Headland Technologies HT22/HT18C
HT2230A	Headland Technologies HT22/HT18C with 82C711 Combo I/O

TABLE 7-6 MR BIOS ID STRINGS *(CONTINUED)*

CODE	DESCRIPTION
HT2230B	Headland Technologies HT22/HT18C with PC87310 Super I/O
HT2230C	Headland Technologies HT22/HT18C with 82C711 Combo I/O
HT2230D	Headland Technologies HT22/HT18C with PC87310 Super I/O
HT2230E	Headland Technologies HT22/HT18C with 82C711 Combo I/O
HT2230F	Headland Technologies HT22/HT18C with PC87310 Super I/O
HT32300	Headland Technologies HT320 Shasta
HT32302	Headland Technologies HT320 Shasta
HT32303	Headland Technologies HT320 Shasta
HT3230A	Headland Technologies HT320 Shasta with 82C711 Combo I/O
HT3230B	Headland Technologies HT320 Shasta with PC87310 Super I/O
HT3230C	Headland Technologies HT320 Shasta with 82C711 Combo I/O
HT3230D	Headland Technologies HT320 Shasta with PC87310 Super I/O
HT3230E	Headland Technologies HT320 Shasta with 82C711 Combo I/O
HT3230F	Headland Technologies HT320 Shasta with PC87310 Super I/O
HT34400	Headland Technologies HT340 Shasta
HT34408	Headland Technologies HT340 Shasta
HT34409	Headland Technologies HT340 Shasta
HT3440A	Headland Technologies HT340 Shasta with 82C711 Combo I/O
HT3440B	Headland Technologies HT340 Shasta with PC87310 Super I/O
HT3440C	Headland Technologies HT340 Shasta with 82C711 Combo I/O
HT3440D	Headland Technologies HT340 Shasta with PC87310 Super I/O
HT3440E	Headland Technologies HT340 Shasta with 82C711 Combo I/O
HT3440F	Headland Technologies HT340 Shasta with PC87310 Super I/O
MOSL400	Mosel MS400 Single Chip
MOSL403	Mosel MS400 Single Chip
MOSL404	Mosel MS400 Single Chip
MOSL410	Mosel MS400 Single Chip with 82C711 Combo I/O
MOSL413	Mosel MS400 Single Chip with 82C711 Combo I/O
MOSL415	Mosel MS400 Single Chip with 82C711 Combo I/O
MXIC300	Micronix MX83C305/306 (with built-in 8KB cache)
MXIC302	Micronix MX83C305/306 (with built-in 8KB cache)
MXIC303	Micronix MX83C305/306 (with built-in 8KB cache)
MXIC304	Micronix MX83C305/306 (with built-in 8KB cache)
MXIC305	Micronix MX83C305/306 (with built-in 8KB cache)
MXIC308	Micronix MX83C305/306 (with built-in 8KB cache)
MXIC30A	Micronix MX83C305/306 (with built-in 8KB cache)
MXIC30B	Micronix MX83C305/306 (with built-in 8KB cache)
MXIC30C	Micronix MX83C305/306 (with built-in 8KB cache)
MXIC30D	Micronix MX83C305/306 (with built-in 8KB cache)

TABLE 7-6 MR BIOS ID STRINGS *(CONTINUED)*

CODE	DESCRIPTION
OPTI306	OPTi 82C381 WriteThru
OPTI308	OPTi 82C381 WriteThru
OPTI309	OPTi 82C381 WriteThru
OPTI315	OPTi 82C281 SxPW Single-Chip Posted-Write
OPTI316	OPTi 82C281 SxPW Single-Chip Posted-Write
OPTI319	OPTi 82C281 SxPW Single-Chip Posted-Write with 82C711 Combo I/O
OPTI31A	OPTi 82C281 SxPW Single-Chip Posted-Write with PC87310 Super I/O
OPTI31K	OPTi 82C281 SxPW Single-Chip Posted-Write
OPTI31L	OPTi 82C281 SxPW Single-Chip Posted-Write
OPTI31M	OPTi 82C281 SxPW Single-Chip Posted-Write with 82C711 Combo I/O
OPTI31N	OPTi 82C281 SxPW Single-Chip Posted-Write with 82C711 Combo I/O
OPTI31P	OPTi 82C281 SxPW Single-Chip Posted-Write with PC87310 Super I/O
OPTI31Q	OPTi 82C281 SxPW Single-Chip Posted-Write with PC87310 Super I/O
OPTI317	OPTi 82C283 SxPI Single Chip
OPTI318	OPTi 82C283 SxPI Single Chip
OPTI31B	OPTi 82C283 SxPI Single Chip with 82C711 Combo I/O
OPTI31C	OPTi 82C283 SxPI Single Chip with PC87310 Super I/O
OPTI31D	OPTi 82C283 SxPI Single Chip
OPTI31E	OPTi 82C283 SxPI Single Chip
OPTI31F	OPTi 82C283 SxPI Single Chip with 82C711 Combo I/O
OPTI31G	OPTi 82C283 SxPI Single Chip with 82C711 Combo I/O
OPTI31H	OPTi 82C283 SxPI Single Chip with PC87310 Super I/O
OPTI31J	OPTi 82C283 SxPI Single Chip with PC87310 Super I/O
OPTI324	OPTi 82C391 WriteBack Rev. A & Rev. B
OPTI32B	OPTi 82C391 WriteBack Rev. A & Rev. B with 82C711 Combo I/O
OPTI32C	OPTi 82C391 WriteBack Rev. A & Rev. B with PC87310 Super I/O
OPTI32E	OPTi 82C391 WriteBack Rev. A & Rev. B
OPTI32F	OPTi 82C391 WriteBack Rev. A & Rev. B
OPTI32G	OPTi 82C391 WriteBack Rev. A & Rev. B
OPTI32H	OPTi 82C391 WriteBack Rev. A & Rev. B
OPTI32J	OPTi 82C391 WriteBack Rev. A & Rev. B with 82C711 Combo I/O
OPTI32K	OPTi 82C391 WriteBack Rev. A & Rev. B with 82C711 Combo I/O
OPTI32L	OPTi 82C391 WriteBack Rev. A & Rev. B with 82C711 Combo I/O
OPTI32M	OPTi 82C391 WriteBack Rev. A & Rev. B with 82C711 Combo I/O
OPTI32P	OPTi 82C391 WriteBack Rev. A & Rev. B with PC87310 Super I/O
OPTI32Q	OPTi 82C391 WriteBack Rev. A & Rev. B with PC87310 Super I/O
OPTI32R	OPTi 82C391 WriteBack Rev. A & Rev. B with PC87310 Super I/O
OPTI32S	OPTi 82C391 WriteBack Rev. A & Rev. B with PC87310 Super I/O
OPTI330	OPTi 82C496/497 DxPI Rev. A & Rev. B
OPTI331	OPTi 82C496/497 DxPI Rev. A & Rev. B with 82C711 Combo I/O
OPTI332	OPTi 82C496/497 DxPI Rev. A & Rev. B with PC87310 Super I/O

TABLE 7-6 MR BIOS ID STRINGS *(CONTINUED)*

CODE	DESCRIPTION
OPTI334	OPTi 82C496/497 DxPI Rev. A & Rev. B
OPTI335	OPTi 82C496/497 DxPI Rev. A & Rev. B
OPTI336	OPTi 82C496/497 DxPI Rev. A & Rev. B
OPTI337	OPTi 82C496/497 DxPI Rev. A & Rev. B
OPTI338	OPTi 82C496/497 DxPI Rev. A & Rev. B with 82C711 Combo I/O
OPTI339	OPTi 82C496/497 DxPI Rev. A & Rev. B with 82C711 Combo I/O
OPTI33A	OPTi 82C496/497 DxPI Rev. A & Rev. B with 82C711 Combo I/O
OPTI33B	OPTi 82C496/497 DxPI Rev. A & Rev. B with 82C711 Combo I/O
OPTI33C	OPTi 82C496/497 DxPI Rev. A & Rev. B with PC87310 Super I/O
OPTI33D	OPTi 82C496/497 DxPI Rev. A & Rev. B with PC87310 Super I/O
OPTI33E	OPTi 82C496/497 DxPI Rev. A & Rev. B with PC87310 Super I/O
OPTI33F	OPTi 82C496/497 DxPI Rev. A & Rev. B with PC87310 Super I/O
OPTI340	OPTi 82C291 SxWB Single-Chip WriteBack
OPTI341	OPTi 82C291 SxWB Single-Chip WriteBack with 82C711 Combo I/O
OPTI342	OPTi 82C291 SxWB Single-Chip WriteBack with PC87310 Super I/O
OPTI344	OPTi 82C291 SxWB Single-Chip WriteBack
OPTI345	OPTi 82C291 SxWB Single-Chip WriteBack
OPTI346	OPTi 82C291 SxWB Single-Chip WriteBack
OPTI347	OPTi 82C291 SxWB Single-Chip WriteBack
OPTI348	OPTi 82C291 SxWB Single-Chip WriteBack with 82C711 Combo I/O
OPTI349	OPTi 82C291 SxWB Single-Chip WriteBack with 82C711 Combo I/O
OPTI34A	OPTi 82C291 SxWB Single-Chip WriteBack with 82C711 Combo I/O
OPTI34B	OPTi 82C291 SxWB Single-Chip WriteBack with 82C711 Combo I/O
OPTI34C	OPTi 82C291 SxWB Single-Chip WriteBack with PC87310 Super I/O
OPTI34D	OPTi 82C291 SxWB Single-Chip WriteBack with PC87310 Super I/O
OPTI34E	OPTi 82C291 SxWB Single-Chip WriteBack with PC87310 Super I/O
OPTI34F	OPTi 82C291 SxWB Single-Chip WriteBack with PC87310 Super I/O
OPTI406	OPTi 82C481 WriteThru
OPTI408	OPTi 82C481 WriteThru
OPTI409	OPTi 82C481 WriteThru
OPTI424	OPTi 82C491 WriteBack (original)
OPTI428	OPTi 82C491 WriteBack Rev. A & Rev. B
OPTI42B	OPTi 82C491 WriteBack Rev. A & Rev. B with 82C711 Combo I/O
OPTI42C	OPTi 82C491 WriteBack Rev. A & Rev. B with PC87310 Super I/O
OPTI42E	OPTi 82C491 WriteBack Rev. A & Rev. B
OPTI42F	OPTi 82C491 WriteBack Rev. A & Rev. B
OPTI42G	OPTi 82C491 WriteBack Rev. A & Rev. B
OPTI42H	OPTi 82C491 WriteBack Rev. A & Rev. B
OPTI42J	OPTi 82C491 WriteBack Rev. A & Rev. B with 82C711 Combo I/O
OPTI42K	OPTi 82C491 WriteBack Rev. A & Rev. B with 82C711 Combo I/O
OPTI42L	OPTi 82C491 WriteBack Rev. A & Rev. B with 82C711 Combo I/O

7

TABLE 7-6 MR BIOS ID STRINGS *(CONTINUED)*

CODE	DESCRIPTION
OPTI42M	OPTi 82C491 WriteBack Rev. A & Rev. B with 82C711 Combo I/O
OPTI42P	OPTi 82C491 WriteBack Rev. A & Rev. B with PC87310 Super I/O
OPTI42Q	OPTi 82C491 WriteBack Rev. A & Rev. B with PC87310 Super I/O
OPTI42R	OPTi 82C491 WriteBack Rev. A & Rev. B with PC87310 Super I/O
OPTI42S	OPTi 82C491 WriteBack Rev. A & Rev. B with PC87310 Super I/O
OPTI430	OPTi 82C496/497 DxPI Rev. A & Rev. B
OPTI431	OPTi 82C496/497 DxPI Rev. A & Rev. B with 82C711 Combo I/O
OPTI432	OPTi 82C496/497 DxPI Rev. A & Rev. B with PC87310 Super I/O
OPTI434	OPTi 82C496/497 DxPI Rev. A & Rev. B
OPTI435	OPTi 82C496/497 DxPI Rev. A & Rev. B
OPTI436	OPTi 82C496/497 DxPI Rev. A & Rev. B
OPTI437	OPTi 82C496/497 DxPI Rev. A & Rev. B
OPTI438	OPTi 82C496/497 DxPI Rev. A & Rev. B with 82C711 Combo I/O
OPTI439	OPTi 82C496/497 DxPI Rev. A & Rev. B with 82C711 Combo I/O
OPTI43A	OPTi 82C496/497 DxPI Rev. A & Rev. B with 82C711 Combo I/O
OPTI43B	OPTi 82C496/497 DxPI Rev. A & Rev. B with 82C711 Combo I/O
OPTI43C	OPTi 82C496/497 DxPI Rev. A & Rev. B with PC87310 Super I/O
OPTI43D	OPTi 82C496/497 DxPI Rev. A & Rev. B with PC87310 Super I/O
OPTI43E	OPTi 82C496/497 DxPI Rev. A & Rev. B with PC87310 Super I/O
OPTI43F	OPTi 82C496/497 DxPI Rev. A & Rev. B with PC87310 Super I/O
OPTI450	OPTi 82C498 DxWB WriteBack
OPTI451	OPTi 82C498 DxWB WriteBack with 82C711 Combo I/O
OPTI452	OPTi 82C498 DxWB WriteBack with PC87310 Super I/O
OPTI454	OPTi 82C498 DxWB WriteBack
OPTI455	OPTi 82C498 DxWB WriteBack
OPTI456	OPTi 82C498 DxWB WriteBack
OPTI457	OPTi 82C498 DxWB WriteBack
OPTI458	OPTi 82C498 DxWB WriteBack with 82C711 Combo I/O
OPTI459	OPTi 82C498 DxWB WriteBack with 82C711 Combo I/O
OPTI45A	OPTi 82C498 DxWB WriteBack with 82C711 Combo I/O
OPTI45B	OPTi 82C498 DxWB WriteBack with 82C711 Combo I/O
OPTI45C	OPTi 82C498 DxWB WriteBack with PC87310 Super I/O
OPTI45D	OPTi 82C498 DxWB WriteBack with PC87310 Super I/O
OPTI45E	OPTi 82C498 DxWB WriteBack with PC87310 Super I/O
OPTI45F	OPTi 82C498 DxWB WriteBack with PC87310 Super I/O
OPTI470	OPTi 82C495SxLC
OPTI471	OPTi 82C495SxLC with 82C711 Combo I/O
OPTI472	OPTi 82C495SxLC with PC87310 Super I/O
OPTI474	OPTi 82C495SxLC
OPTI475	OPTi 82C495SxLC
OPTI476	OPTi 82C495SxLC

TABLE 7-6 MR BIOS ID STRINGS *(CONTINUED)*

CODE	DESCRIPTION
OPTI477	OPTi 82C495SxLC
OPTI478	OPTi 82C495SxLC with 82C711 Combo I/O
OPTI479	OPTi 82C495SxLC with 82C711 Combo I/O
OPTI47A	OPTi 82C495SxLC with 82C711 Combo I/O
OPTI47B	OPTi 82C495SxLC with 82C711 Combo I/O
OPTI47C	OPTi 82C495SxLC with PC87310 Super I/O
OPTI47D	OPTi 82C495SxLC with PC87310 Super I/O
OPTI47E	OPTi 82C495SxLC with PC87310 Super I/O
OPTI47F	OPTi 82C495SxLC with PC87310 Super I/O
OPTI47G	OPTi 82C495SxLC
OPTI47H	OPTi 82C495SxLC with 82C711 Combo I/O
OPTI47J	OPTi 82C495SxLC with PC87310 Super I/O
OPTI47K	OPTi 82C495SxLC
OPTI47L	OPTi 82C495SxLC
OPTI47M	OPTi 82C495SxLC
OPTI47N	OPTi 82C495SxLC
OPTI47P	OPTi 82C495SxLC with 82C711 Combo I/O
OPTI47Q	OPTi 82C495SxLC with 82C711 Combo I/O
OPTI47R	OPTi 82C495SxLC with 82C711 Combo I/O
OPTI47S	OPTi 82C495SxLC with 82C711 Combo I/O
OPTI47T	OPTi 82C495SxLC with PC87310 Super I/O
OPTI47U	OPTi 82C495SxLC with PC87310 Super I/O
OPTI47V	OPTi 82C495SxLC with PC87310 Super I/O
OPTI47W	OPTi 82C495SxLC with PC87310 Super I/O
OPTI480	OPTi 82C499 DxSC Single Chip
OPTI481	OPTi 82C499 DxSC Single Chip with 82C711 Combo I/O
OPTI482	OPTi 82C499 DxSC Single Chip with PC87310 Super I/O
OPTI484	OPTi 82C499 DxSC Single Chip
OPTI485	OPTi 82C499 DxSC Single Chip
OPTI486	OPTi 82C499 DxSC Single Chip
OPTI487	OPTi 82C499 DxSC Single Chip
OPTI488	OPTi 82C499 DxSC Single Chip with 82C711 Combo I/O
OPTI489	OPTi 82C499 DxSC Single Chip with 82C711 Combo I/O
OPTI48A	OPTi 82C499 DxSC Single Chip with 82C711 Combo I/O
OPTI48B	OPTi 82C499 DxSC Single Chip with 82C711 Combo I/O
OPTI48C	OPTi 82C499 DxSC Single Chip with PC87310 Super I/O
OPTI48D	OPTi 82C499 DxSC Single Chip with PC87310 Super I/O
OPTI48E	OPTi 82C499 DxSC Single Chip with PC87310 Super I/O
OPTI48F	OPTi 82C499 DxSC Single Chip with PC87310 Super I/O
OPTI48G	OPTi 82C499 DxSC Single Chip
OPTI48H	OPTi 82C499 DxSC Single Chip with 82C711 Combo I/O

TABLE 7-6 MR BIOS ID STRINGS *(CONTINUED)*

CODE	DESCRIPTION
OPTI48J	OPTi 82C499 DxSC Single Chip with PC87310 Super I/O
OPTI48K	OPTi 82C499 DxSC Single Chip
OPTI48L	OPTi 82C499 DxSC Single Chip
OPTI48M	OPTi 82C499 DxSC Single Chip
OPTI48N	OPTi 82C499 DxSC Single Chip
OPTI48P	OPTi 82C499 DxSC Single Chip with 82C711 Combo I/O
OPTI48Q	OPTi 82C499 DxSC Single Chip with 82C711 Combo I/O
OPTI48R	OPTi 82C499 DxSC Single Chip with 82C711 Combo I/O
OPTI48S	OPTi 82C499 DxSC Single Chip with 82C711 Combo I/O
OPTI48T	OPTi 82C499 DxSC Single Chip with PC87310 Super I/O
OPTI48U	OPTi 82C499 DxSC Single Chip with PC87310 Super I/O
OPTI48V	OPTi 82C499 DxSC Single Chip with PC87310 Super I/O
OPTI48W	OPTi 82C499 DxSC Single Chip with PC87310 Super I/O
OPTI48Z	OPTi 82C499 DxSC Single Chip with PC87311/312 Super I/O
OPTI490	OPTi 82C495 SLC
OPTI491	OPTi 82C495 SLC with 82C711 Combo I/O
OPTI492	OPTi 82C495 SLC with PC87310 Super I/O
OPTI493	OPTi 82C495 SLC
OPTI494	OPTi 82C495 SLC with 82C711 Combo I/O
OPTI495	OPTi 82C495 SLC with PC87310 Super I/O
OPTI496	OPTi 82C495 SLC
OPTI497	OPTi 82C495 SLC with 82C711 Combo I/O
OPTI498	OPTi 82C495 SLC with PC87310 Super I/O
OPTI499	OPTi 82C495 SLC
OPTI49A	OPTi 82C495 SLC with 82C711 Combo I/O
OPTI49B	OPTi 82C495 SLC with PC87310 Super I/O
OPTI4A0	OPTi 82C801 SCWB2 Single-Chip WriteBack
OPTI4A1	OPTi 82C801 SCWB2 Single-Chip WriteBack with 82C711 Combo I/O
OPTI4A2	OPTi 82C801 SCWB2 Single-Chip WriteBack with PC87310 Super I/O
OPTI4A3	OPTi 82C801 SCWB2 Single-Chip WriteBack with PC87311 Super I/O
OPTI500	OPTi 586 VHP Pentium Chipset
PKDM301	Chips & Technologies CS82310 PEAKset DM Rev-0
PKDM304	Chips & Technologies CS82310 PEAKset DM Rev-0
PKDM305	Chips & Technologies CS82310 PEAKset DM Rev-0
PKDM311	Chips & Technologies CS82310 PEAKset DM Rev-0—82C711 Combo I/O
PKDM314	Chips & Technologies CS82310 PEAKset DM Rev-0—82C711 Combo I/O
PKDM315	Chips & Technologies CS82310 PEAKset DM Rev-0—82C711 Combo I/O
PKDM321	Chips & Technologies CS82310 PEAKset DM Rev-B1
PKDM322	Chips & Technologies CS82310 PEAKset DM Rev-B1
PKDM323	Chips & Technologies CS82310 PEAKset DM Rev-B1

TABLE 7-6 MR BIOS ID STRINGS *(CONTINUED)*

CODE	DESCRIPTION
PKDM324	Chips & Technologies CS82310 PEAKset DM Rev-B1
PKDM325	Chips & Technologies CS82310 PEAKset DM Rev-B1
PKDM331	Chips & Technologies CS82310 PEAKset DM Rev-B1—82C711 Combo I/O
PKDM332	Chips & Technologies CS82310 PEAKset DM Rev-B1—82C711 Combo I/O
PKDM333	Chips & Technologies CS82310 PEAKset DM Rev-B1—82C711 Combo I/O
PKDM334	Chips & Technologies CS82310 PEAKset DM Rev-B1—82C711 Combo I/O
PKDM335	Chips & Technologies CS82310 PEAKset DM Rev-B1—82C711 Combo I/O
PKDM420	Chips & Technologies CS82310 PEAKset DM Rev-B1
PKDM421	Chips & Technologies CS82310 PEAKset DM Rev-B1
PKDM424	Chips & Technologies CS82310 PEAKset DM Rev-B1
PKDM425	Chips & Technologies CS82310 PEAKset DM Rev-B1
PKDM428	Chips & Technologies CS82310 PEAKset DM Rev-B1
PKDM429	Chips & Technologies CS82310 PEAKset DM Rev-B1
PKDM430	Chips & Technologies CS82310 PEAKset DM Rev-B1—82C711 Combo I/O
PKDM431	Chips & Technologies CS82310 PEAKset DM Rev-B1—82C711 Combo I/O
PKDM434	Chips & Technologies CS82310 PEAKset DM Rev-B1—82C711 Combo I/O
PKDM435	Chips & Technologies CS82310 PEAKset DM Rev-B1—82C711 Combo I/O
PKDM438	Chips & Technologies CS82310 PEAKset DM Rev-B1—82C711 Combo I/O
PKDM439	Chips & Technologies CS82310 PEAKset DM Rev-B1—82C711 Combo I/O
SARC302	SARC RC2016A Rev. A3 (standard)
SARC306	SARC RC2016A Rev. A3 with built-in EMS
SARC30A	SARC RC2016A Rev. A3 Cyrix
SARC30E	SARC RC2016A Rev. A3 Cyrix, with built-in EMS
SCAT300	Chips & Technologies 82C236 SCATsx
SCAT304	Chips & Technologies 82C236 SCATsx
SCAT305	Chips & Technologies 82C236 SCATsx
SIS_303	SiS 85C310/320/330 Rabbit Rev. A, B & C
SIS_306	SiS 85C310/320/330 Rabbit Rev. A, B & C
SIS_307	SiS 85C310/320/330 Rabbit Rev. A, B & C
SIS_308	SiS 85C310/320/330 Rabbit Rev. A, B & C
SIS_309	SiS 85C310/320/330 Rabbit Rev. A, B & C
SIS_400	SiS 85C460 & 85C461V Single Chip
SIS_404	SiS 85C460 & 85C461V Single Chip
SIS_405	SiS 85C460 & 85C461V Single Chip
SLGC301	SysLogic 386 non-cache

7

TABLE 7-6 MR BIOS ID STRINGS *(CONTINUED)*

CODE	DESCRIPTION
SLGC302	SysLogic 386 with cache
SLGC304	SysLogic 386 non-cache
SLGC305	SysLogic 386 non-cache
SLGC306	SysLogic 386 with cache
SLGC307	SysLogic 386 with cache
SLGC401	SysLogic 486 no external cache
SLGC404	SysLogic 486 no external cache
SLGC405	SysLogic 486 no external cache
STD_286	Generic 286 (TTL/Discrete Logic)
STD_202	Generic 286 (TTL/Discrete Logic)
STD_203	Generic 286 (TTL/Discrete Logic)
STD_386	Generic 386 (TTL/Discrete Logic)
STD_302	Generic 386 (TTL/Discrete Logic)
STD_303	Generic 386 (TTL/Discrete Logic)
STD_486	Generic 486 (TTL/Discrete Logic)
STD_408	Generic 486 (TTL/Discrete Logic)
STD_409	Generic 486 (TTL/Discrete Logic)
SYML401	Symphony Labs SL82C46x Haydn Rev. 1.1
SYML402	Symphony Labs SL82C46x Haydn Rev. 1.1 with 82C711 Combo I/O
SYML403	Symphony Labs SL82C46x Haydn Rev. 1.1 with PC87310 Super I/O
SYML404	Symphony Labs SL82C46x Haydn Rev. 1.1
SYML405	Symphony Labs SL82C46x Haydn Rev. 1.1
SYML406	Symphony Labs SL82C46x Haydn Rev. 1.1 with 82C711 Combo I/O
SYML407	Symphony Labs SL82C46x Haydn Rev. 1.1 with 82C711 Combo I/O
SYML408	Symphony Labs SL82C46x Haydn Rev. 1.1 with PC87310 Super I/O
SYML409	Symphony Labs SL82C46x Haydn Rev. 1.1 with PC87310 Super I/O
SYML411	Symphony Labs SL82C46x Haydn Rev. 1.2
SYML412	Symphony Labs SL82C46x Haydn Rev. 1.2 with 82C711 Combo I/O
SYML413	Symphony Labs SL82C46x Haydn Rev. 1.2 with PC87310 Super I/O
SYML414	Symphony Labs SL82C46x Haydn Rev. 1.2
SYML415	Symphony Labs SL82C46x Haydn Rev. 1.2
SYML416	Symphony Labs SL82C46x Haydn Rev. 1.2 with 82C711 Combo I/O
SYML417	Symphony Labs SL82C46x Haydn Rev. 1.2 with 82C711 Combo I/O
SYML418	Symphony Labs SL82C46x Haydn Rev. 1.2 with PC87310 Super I/O
SYML419	Symphony Labs SL82C46x Haydn Rev. 1.2 with PC87310 Super I/O
TACT300	Texas Instruments TACT83000 Tiger non-cache

TABLE 7-6 MR BIOS ID STRINGS *(CONTINUED)*

CODE	DESCRIPTION
TACT302	Texas Instruments TACT83000 Tiger with Intel 82385 cache
TACT303	Texas Instruments TACT83000 Tiger with Austek cache
TACT30A	Texas Instruments TACT83000 Tiger non-cache
TACT30B	Texas Instruments TACT83000 Tiger non-cache
TACT30C	Texas Instruments TACT83000 Tiger with Austek cache
TACT30D	Texas Instruments TACT83000 Tiger with Austek cache
TACT30E	Texas Instruments TACT83000 Tiger with Intel 82385 cache
TACT30F	Texas Instruments TACT83000 Tiger with Intel 82385 cache
TACT400	Texas Instruments TACT83000 Tiger no external cache
TACT40A	Texas Instruments TACT83000 Tiger no external cache
TACT40B	Texas Instruments TACT83000 Tiger no external cache
UMC_301	UMC 82C48x WriteBack Rev. 0
UMC_302	UMC 82C48x WriteBack Rev. A & Rev. B
UMC_304	UMC 82C48x WriteBack Rev. A & Rev. B
UMC_310	UMC 82C330 Twinstar
UMC_314	UMC 82C330 Twinstar
UMC_315	UMC 82C330 Twinstar
UMC_401	UMC 82C48x WriteBack Rev. 0
UMC_402	UMC 82C48x WriteBack Rev. A & Rev. B
UMC_403	UMC 82C48x WriteBack Rev. A & Rev. B
UMC_404	UMC 82C48x WriteBack Rev. A & Rev. B
UMC_405	UMC 82C48x WriteBack Rev. A & Rev. B
UMC_406	UMC 82C48x WriteBack Rev. A & Rev. B
UMC_407	UMC 82C48x WriteBack Rev. A & Rev. B
UMC_40A	UMC 82C48x WriteBack Rev. B
UMC_40B	UMC 82C48x WriteBack Rev. B
UMC_40C	UMC 82C48x WriteBack Rev. B
UMC_40D	UMC 82C48x WriteBack Rev. B
UMC_40E	UMC 82C48x WriteBack Rev. B
UMC_40F	UMC 82C48x WriteBack Rev. B
UMC_40G	UMC 82C48x WriteBack Rev. A & Rev. B
UMC_410	UMC 82C491 Single Chip
VLSI301	VLSI Technology 386 Topcat—Intel 82340 non-cache
VLSI302	VLSI Technology 386 Topcat—Intel 82340 non-cache with 82C106 IPC
VLSI312	VLSI Technology 386 Topcat—Intel 82340 with 82385 cache and 82C106 IPC
VLSI401	VLSI Technology 386 Topcat—Intel 82340
VLSI402	VLSI Technology 386 Topcat—Intel 82340 with 82C106 IPC
VLSI404	VLSI Technology 386 Topcat—Intel 82340 with 82C106 IPC

7

IDENTIFYING YOUR BIOS CHIP

There may also be times when it becomes necessary to identify the flash BIOS chip itself in order to replace the chip or more closely identify the motherboard. The most obvious sign of a BIOS chip is the presence of a sticker carrying the name of a known BIOS maker such as AMI, Award, Phoenix, MR BIOS, and so on. When you gently peel back the sticker, you can determine the characteristics of your flash BIOS chip from the part number. Table 7-7 identifies many of the most popular flash chips.

> Anything without a quartz window that doesn't have a 28 or 29 as the preceding digits of the part number is most likely a standard ROM chip that cannot be reprogrammed.

TABLE 7-7 FLASH BIOS PART NUMBERS

PART NUMBER	FLASH CHIP
27Cxxx	With window—EPROM—read-only, requires programmer to write and UV to erase
28Cxxx	EEPROM—Not flash memory
28EE011	SST 5 volt flash ROM
28F001BX-B	Intel 12 volt flash ROM
28F001BX-T	Intel 12 volt flash ROM
28F010	Fujitsu 12 volt flash ROM (or ISSI 12 volt flash ROM)
28F010	Intel 12 volt flash ROM
29EE010	SST 5 volt flash ROM
29LVxxx	3 volt flash memory (rare)
A28F010	Intel 12 volt flash ROM
Am28F010	AMD 12 volt flash ROM
Am28F010A	AMD 12 volt flash ROM
Am29F010	AMD 5 volt flash ROM
AT28C010	Atmel 5 volt flash ROM
AT28MC010	Atmel 5 volt flash ROM
AT29C010	Atmel 5 volt flash ROM
AT29LC010	Atmel 5 volt flash ROM
AT29MC010	Atmel 5 volt flash ROM
CAT28F010	Catalyst 12 volt flash ROM
CAT28F010I	Catalyst 12 volt flash ROM
CAT28F010V5	Catalyst 5 volt flash ROM
CAT28F010V5I	Catalyst 5 volt flash ROM
DQ28C010	SEEQ 5 volt flash ROM
DQ47F010	SEEQ 12 volt flash ROM
DQ48F010	SEEQ 12 volt flash ROM
DQM28C010A	SEEQ 5 volt flash ROM
DYM28C010	SEEQ 5 volt flash ROM
HN28F101	Hitachi 12 volt flash ROM
HN29C010	Hitachi 12 volt flash ROM

TABLE 7-7 FLASH BIOS PART NUMBERS *(CONTINUED)*

PART NUMBER	FLASH CHIP
HN29C010B	Hitachi 12 volt flash ROM
HN58C1000	Hitachi 5 volt flash ROM
HN58C1001	Hitachi 12 volt flash ROM
HN58V1001	Hitachi 12 volt flash ROM
KM29C010	Samsung 5 volt flash ROM
M28F010	SGS-Thomson 12 volt flash ROM
M28F1001	SGS-Thomson 12 volt flash ROM
M5M28F101FP	Mitsubishi 12 volt flash ROM
M5M28F101P	Mitsubishi 12 volt flash ROM
M5M28F101RV	Mitsubishi 12 volt flash ROM
M5M28F101VP	Mitsubishi 12 volt flash ROM
MSM28F101	OKI 12 volt flash ROM
MX28F1000	MXIC 12 volt flash ROM
PH29EE010	SST ROM Chip—flashable
TMS28F010	Texas Instruments 12 volt flash ROM
TMS29F010	Texas Instruments 5 volt flash ROM
W27F010	Winbond 12 volt flash ROM
W29EE011	Winbond 5 volt flash ROM
X28C010	XICOR 5 volt flash ROM
X28C010I	XICOR 5 volt flash ROM
XM28C010	XICOR 5 volt flash ROM

BIOS and Boot Sequences

The next step in understanding the BIOS is to recognize how it boots—the series of steps that take a PC from power-on to the point where it's loading an operating system. Although every BIOS follows a similar pattern of steps, each BIOS is written a bit differently and may have more or fewer steps than comparable BIOS versions. This part of the chapter looks at the boot sequences for several popular BIOS versions.

AMERICAN MEGATRENDS

American Megatrends (AMI) is renowned for their BIOS, PC diagnostics, and motherboards. AMI BIOS performs a fairly comprehensive suite of 24 steps in order to check and initialize the PC. The general AMI BIOS POST procedure is listed below.

1. *Disable the NMI* BIOS disables the nonmaskable interrupt line to the CPU. A failure here suggests a problem with the CMOS RAM IC or its associated circuitry.
2. *Power-on delay* The system resets the soft and hard reset bits. A fault here indicates a problem with the keyboard controller IC or system clock generator IC.
3. *Initialize chipsets* BIOS initializes any particular motherboard chipsets (such as the Intel or VIA chipsets) that may be present in the system. A problem here may be caused by the BIOS, the clock generator IC, or the chipset itself.

4 *Reset determination* The system reads the reset bits in the keyboard controller to determine whether a hard or soft reset (cold or warm boot) is required. A failure here may be caused by the BIOS or keyboard controller IC.

5 *BIOS ROM checksum* The system performs a checksum test of ROM contents and adds a factory preset value that should make the total equal to 00h. If this total does not equal 00h, the BIOS ROM is defective.

6 *Keyboard test* A command is sent to the 8042 (keyboard controller), which performs a test and sets a buffer space for commands. After the buffer is defined, the BIOS sends a command byte, writes data to the buffer, checks the high order bits (Pin 23) of the internal keyboard controller, and issues a No Operation (NOP) command. A fault here is likely the keyboard controller IC.

7 *CMOS shutdown check* BIOS tests the shutdown byte in CMOS RAM, calculates the CMOS checksum, and updates the CMOS diagnostic byte. The system then initializes a small CMOS area in conventional memory and updates the date and time. A problem here is likely in the RTC/CMOS IC, or the CMOS backup battery.

8 *Controller disable* BIOS now disables the DMA and IRQ controller ICs before proceeding. A fault at this point suggests trouble in the respective controller.

9 *Disable video* BIOS disables the video controller IC. If this procedure fails, the trouble is probably in the video adapter board.

10 *Detect memory* The system proceeds to check the amount of memory available. BIOS measures system memory in 64KB blocks. A problem here may be in the memory IC(s).

11 *PIT test* BIOS tests the programmable interrupt timer (PIT) vital for memory refresh. A problem with the PIT test may reflect a fault in the PIT IC or in the RTC IC.

12 *Check memory refresh* BIOS now uses the PIT to try refreshing memory. A failure indicates a problem with the PIT IC.

13 *Check low address lines* The system checks the first 16 address lines controlling the first 64KB of RAM. A problem with this test typically means a fault in an address line.

14 *Check low 64KB RAM* The system now checks the first 64KB of system RAM. This is vital since this area must hold information that is critical for system initialization. A problem here is usually the result of a bad RAM IC.

15 *Initialize support ICs* BIOS proceeds to initialize the programmable interrupt timer (PIT), the programmable interrupt controller (PIC), and the direct memory access (DMA) ICs. A fault here would be located in one of those locations.

16 *Load INT vector table* BIOS loads the system's interrupt vector table into the first 2KB of system RAM.

17 *Check the keyboard controller (KBC)* BIOS reads the keyboard controller buffer at I/O port 60h. A problem here indicates a fault in the keyboard controller IC.

18 *Video tests* The system checks for the type of video adapter in use, then tests and initializes the video memory and adapter. A problem with this test typically indicates a fault with the video memory or adapter, respectively. After a successful video test, the video system will be operational.

19 *Load the BDA* The system now loads the BIOS data area (BDA) into conventional memory.

20 *Test memory* BIOS checks all memory below 1MB. A problem here is typically the fault of one or more RAM ICs, the keyboard controller IC, or a bad data line.

21 *Check DMA registers* BIOS performs a register-level check of the DMA controller(s) using binary test patterns. A problem here is often due to a failure of the DMA IC(s).

22 *Check the keyboard* The system performs a final check of the keyboard interface. An error at this point is usually the fault of the keyboard.

23 *Perform high-level tests* This step involves a whole suite of tests that check such high-level devices as the floppy and hard disks, serial adapters, parallel adapters, mouse adapter, and so on. The number and complexity of these tests vary with the BIOS version. When an error occurs, a corresponding text message will be displayed. If the system hardware does not match the setup shown in the CMOS setup, a corresponding error code will be displayed.

24 *Load the OS* At this point, BIOS triggers INT 19h, which is the routine that loads an operating system. An error here generally results in an error message such as "Non-system disk."

AWARD SOFTWARE

Award is another popular and well-established BIOS maker whose products can be found in a wide range of PCs spanning almost every generation. The procedure outlined below is generally found with Award BIOS v4.2 and later.

1 *Test the CPU* The BIOS checks the error flags in the CPU, then performs a register test by writing and reading bit patterns. Failure here is normally due to the CPU or clock chip.

2 *Initialize support chips* Video is disabled along with parity/DMA and NMI; then the PIT/PIC and DMA chips are initialized. Failure at this point is normally due to the PIT or DMA chips.

3 *Initialize the keyboard* The keyboard and keyboard controller (KBC) are initialized. Problems here are due to keyboard connection faults or a failure of the KBC chip.

4 *ROM BIOS test* A checksum is performed on the ROM BIOS. Failure here is normally due to the ROM BIOS chip, which would normally be reprogrammed or replaced.

5 *CMOS RAM test* A test of the CMOS chip is performed (which should also detect a bad battery). Trouble here is due to either the CMOS chip or the CMOS backup battery.

6 *Memory test* The first 356KB of memory is tested with any diagnostic routines in the chipsets. A fault at this point is normally due to defective memory chips, SIMMs, or DIMMs.

7 *Cache initialization* Any cache external to the main chipset is activated. Failure to control the cache here is normally caused by a fault in the cache controller or cache chips.

8 *Initialize the vector table* Interrupt vectors are initialized, and the interrupt table is installed into low memory. Failure here is normally caused by the BIOS or a fault in low memory.

9 *CMOS RAM checksum* The CMOS RAM is checksum tested. (BIOS defaults are loaded if the CMOS RAM checksum is invalid.) When trouble occurs here, it may be necessary to replace the CMOS RAM chip.

10 *Keyboard initialization* The keyboard is initialized, and the Num Lock is set On. Check the keyboard or keyboard controller (KBC) if you have problems here.

11 *Video circuit test* The video adapter circuit is tested and initialized.

12 *Video memory test* Memory is tested on Mono and CGA adapters (if installed). Check the adapter card if trouble occurs here.

13 *DMA controller test* The DMA controllers and page registers are tested. Check the DMA chips when problems occur here.

14 *PIC tests* The 8259 PIC chips are tested.

15 *EISA mode test* A checksum is performed on the extended data area of CMOS where EISA information is stored. If the test passes, the EISA adapter is initialized.

16 *Enable EISA slots* Slots 0–15 (for EISA adapters) are enabled if the test passes.

17 *Check memory size* Memory addresses above 265KB are written to in 64KB blocks, and any addresses found are initialized. If a bit is bad, the entire block containing it (and those above it) will not be seen. Replace any defective memory chips, SIMMs, or DIMMs.

18 *Memory test* A read/write test is performed on memory over 256KB. A failure would be due to bad bit in RAM, and the defective memory chip, SIMM, or DIMM should be replaced.

19 *Check EISA memory* This checks memory on any adapters initialized previously. If there are problems here, check the memory chips/devices on those adapters.

20 *Mouse initialization* This checks for a mouse and installs the appropriate interrupt vectors if one is found. Check the mouse adapter if there is a problem.

21 *Cache initialization* The cache controller is initialized (if present).

22 *Shadow RAM setup* Any shadow RAM that is present (according to the CMOS setup) is enabled.

23 *Floppy test* Test and initialize the floppy controller and drive.

24 *Hard drive test* Test and initialize the hard disk controller and drive. If there is trouble here, there may be an improper setup, a bad controller, or a defective hard drive.

25 *Serial/parallel port test* Any serial and parallel ports found at the proper addresses are initialized.

26 *Initialize math coprocessor* The MCP is initialized if found.

27 *Boot speed* This sets the default speed at which the computer boots.

28 *POST loop* A reboot occurs if the "loop pin" is set. (This is used only for manufacturing purposes.)

29 *Security* The system will ask for a password (if one has been configured). If this does not happen, check the CMOS data or the CMOS RAM chip. For example, a CMOS password may be cleared if the CMOS backup battery is removed.

30 *Write to CMOS RAM* The BIOS tries to write the CMOS values from setup to CMOS RAM. Failure here is normally due to an invalid CMOS configuration.

31 *Initialize adapter ROM(s)* Any adapter ROMs between C800h and EFFFh are initialized. The ROM will do an internal test before giving back control to the system ROM. Failure here is normally due to the adapter ROM or the attached hardware, which should be replaced.

32 *Set up the time* This sets the CMOS time to the value located at 40h of the BIOS data area (BDA).

33 *Boot the system* Control is given to the Int 19 boot loader.

PHOENIX TECHNOLOGIES

Phoenix Technologies is one of the premier BIOS manufacturers for IBM-compatible PCs and is known for its extensive POST and versatility with OEMs. A typical Phoenix BIOS performs essentially the same steps as an AMI BIOS, but there are several variations, as shown below.

1 *Check the CPU* The registers and control lines of the CPU are checked. Any problems will usually be the result of a faulty CPU or clock IC.

2 *Test CMOS RAM* The CMOS IC is tested. A fault is usually due to a failure of the RTC/CMOS IC.

3 *BIOS ROM checksum* A checksum is performed on the BIOS ROM. If the calculated checksum does not match the factory-set value, an error is generated. A checksum problem is typically the result of a faulty BIOS ROM. Try replacing the BIOS ROM.

4 *Test chipset(s)* The system checks any chipsets (such as the Intel or VIA chipsets) for proper operation with the BIOS. A problem here is typically due to a fault in the chipset. Replace the motherboard.

5 *Test PIT* The programmable interrupt timer (PIT) is tested to ensure that all interrupt requests are handled properly. A problem here indicates that the PIT IC is defective.

6 *Test DMA* The direct memory access (DMA) controller is tested next. A fault at this point is typically caused by the CPU, the DMA IC, or an address line problem.

7 *Test base 64KB memory* BIOS checks the lowest 64KB of system RAM. A problem here is due to a fault in memory or an address line problem.

8 *Check serial and parallel ports* The system checks the presence of serial and parallel port hardware, and I/O data areas are assigned for any devices found.

9 *Test PIC* The programmable interrupt controller (PIC) is tested to see that proper interrupt levels can be generated. A problem here is typically due to a fault in the PIC IC.

10 *Check keyboard controller (KBC)* The keyboard controller IC is tested for proper operation. When a problem occurs, the keyboard controller is probably defective.

11 *Verify CMOS data* Data within the CMOS is checked for validity. If the extended area returns a failure, CMOS data has probably been set up incorrectly. However, continuous failures typically represent a faulty RTC/CMOS IC.

12 *Verify video system* Video RAM is tested; then the video controller is located, tested, and initialized. A fault is usually the result of a defective video controller. If the controller is located on an expansion board, try replacing the video board.

13 *Test RTC* The real-time clock (RTC) is tested next, and each frequency output is verified. A problem here is usually due to a fault in the RTC, PIT, or system crystal.

14 *Test CPU in protected mode* The CPU is switched to protected mode and returned to POST at the point indicated in CMOS RAM offset 0Fh. When this step fails, the CPU, keyboard controller IC, CMOS IC, or address line(s) may be at fault.

15 *Verify PIC 2* Counter number 2 is tested on the PIC IC. If this test fails, the PIC IC is probably defective.

16 *Check NMI* The NMI is checked to be sure it is active. A problem here often indicates trouble with the CMOS IC, but could also reflect problems in the BIOS ROM, PIC IC, or CPU.

17 *Check the keyboard* The keyboard buffer and controller are checked.

18 *Check the mouse* BIOS initializes the mouse (if present) through the keyboard controller. A fault is usually caused in the mouse adapter circuit.

19 *Check system RAM* All remaining system RAM is tested in 64KB blocks. Trouble usually means a defective memory IC.

20 *Test disk controller* Fixed and floppy disk controllers are checked using standard BIOS calls. Problems here are usually the result of defective controllers or faulty drives. If the controllers are installed on expansion boards, you can try replacing the respective expansion board.

21 *Set shadow RAM areas* The system looks at CMOS to find which ROM(s) will be shadowed into RAM. Problems here are often due to a faulty adapter ROM or problems in RAM.

22 *Check extended ROMs* BIOS looks for signatures of 55AAh in memory, which indicate the presence of additional ROMs. The system then performs a checksum test on each ROM. A problem with this step generally indicates trouble with the extended ROM or related adapter circuitry.

23 *Test cache controller* The external cache controller IC is tested. A problem is usually due to a fault in the cache controller IC itself or to a defect in cache memory.

24 *Test CPU cache* The internal cache present in the CPU is tested. A problem here is almost always due to a CPU fault.

25 *Check hardware adapters* BIOS proceeds to check the high-level subsystems such as the video system, floppy disk, hard disk, I/O adapters, serial ports, and parallel ports. Problems usually reflect a fault with the respective adapter or an invalid CMOS setup.

26 *Load the OS* At this point, BIOS triggers INT 19h, which is the routine that loads an operating system. An error here generally results in an error message such as "Non-system disk."

BIOS Shortcomings and Compatibility Issues

No matter how much time and effort are put into BIOS code development, there are still many times when BIOS can come up short (especially in the newest, state-of-the-art systems). Before you start troubleshooting, you should have an understanding of the places where BIOS is weakest.

DEVICE DRIVERS

As you might expect, no BIOS can possibly address *every* piece of hardware in the PC marketplace or keep pace with the rapid advances of those devices that a BIOS does support. As a result, PC designers have devised a way to augment BIOS through the use of *device drivers*. Traditional CD-ROMs are an excellent example. There are a number of CD-ROM designs in use today, and each CD-ROM and its corresponding controller board use their own circuitry to operate the drive and interface it to the PC bus. Neither the CD-ROM application, DOS, or BIOS are capable of identifying the drive or interface. To get around this, a low-level device driver is loaded into conventional memory from disk once the PC initializes. The low-level device driver translates a set of standard DOS calls into the instructions necessary to operate the adapter and drive. An extension of DOS (MSCDEX for MS-DOS-based systems) is also loaded into memory *after* the low-level driver. The DOS extension works seamlessly with MSDOS.SYS to provide applications with a standard set of software interrupt CD-ROM services. Generally speaking, device drivers all interface hardware to the operating system and serve to supplement the BIOS. Video, SCSI, and network adapters all make use of device drivers at some level.

> The newest BIOS versions do identify and support bootable CD-ROM drives that adhere to the El Torito standard.

"FLASH" LAZINESS

The broad acceptance of "flash" memory allows BIOS to be reprogrammed "in-system" through the use of a downloadable program. There is no need to open the PC or to exchange BIOS ICs. This offers BIOS makers a great deal of versatility in the development of new BIOS, but it can also foster an attitude of laziness. Given the astounding speed at which new developments are proliferating, BIOS makers are under a great deal of pressure to create ever-more powerful and diverse BIOS. With traditional BIOS, programmers needed to create solid, well-tested code—because replacing thousands of BIOS ICs in the field is an expensive and cumbersome task. Now that BIOS updates can be quickly downloaded directly from the Internet, BIOS programmers can sometimes take the "release it now and patch it later" attitude. As a rule, BIOS code is still quite solid, but you should be aware that the potential for BIOS problems and oversights is now much higher than in years past.

BIOS SHADOWING

Another problem with BIOS chips is their inherently slow speed. BIOS is typically recorded onto flash ROM chips. (Older BIOS used conventional ROM ICs or other programmable ROM chips.) These read-only devices are necessary because BIOS data must be maintained even when power is removed. Unfortunately, permanent storage ICs such as these have hideously slow access times (150nS to 200nS) when compared to the fast RAM used in today's PCs (50nS to 70nS). When you consider that the services stored in a BIOS ROM are used almost continuously, it is easy to see that each delay is additive—the net result is an overall reduction in PC performance.

To overcome this limitation, it would be necessary to accelerate the access time of BIOS ROM. However, this is not too likely given the current state of semiconductor technology, so PC designers do the next best thing—*ROM shadowing*. The process of shadowing basically copies ROM contents from the BIOS chip into available RAM in the upper memory area (UMA). Once the copy is complete, the system will work from the *copy* rather than the original. This allows BIOS routines to take advantage of faster RAM. Not only system BIOS, but all BIOS can be shadowed. (Video BIOS is particularly popular for shadowing.) ROM shadowing can typically be turned on or off through the CMOS setup routine.

> Not all BIOS can be successfully shadowed. Shadowing problems can cause erratic system behavior and lockups. Whenever you encounter problems configuring a system, you should always try stabilizing the system by shutting down all shadowing options. You can restore shadowing options later and observe if system problems return.

DIRECT CONTROL

In the race to wring every last clock-tick of performance from a PC, even the most elegantly written BIOS is simply too slow for high-performance applications. If the application could work with PC hardware *directly*, system performance (especially disk and video subsystems) could be substantially improved. Writing directly to hardware is hardly new—pre-IBM PCs relied on direct application control. The use of BIOS was included by IBM to ensure that variations in PC hardware would remain compatible with operating system and application software. As it turns out, today's PC hardware functions are remarkably standardized (even though the actual components can vary dramatically). With this broad base of relatively standard features, software developers are reviving the direct control approach and ignoring the use of BIOS services in favor of drivers or routines written into the application. For example, a powerful 3D accelerator such as the 3Dfx Voodoo 3 works with drivers only and does not involve any BIOS routines. The trouble with this approach is that direct hardware control may not work on all system configurations, and any changes to the system hardware (such as upgrade or replacement parts) may cause the PC to malfunction when the particular application or driver is executed.

BIOS BUGS

As with all software-based products, BIOS code is subject to accidental errors or omissions (software bugs). When BIOS is developed, it is replicated by the thousands and purchased by motherboard manufacturers who incorporate the BIOS into their motherboards. If a bug is present in the BIOS, the system will typically lock up or crash unexpectedly, or during a certain operation. Since the same BIOS may be used in several motherboards, the bug may not manifest itself in all cases. As one example, some users of AMI BIOS (dated 04/09/90 or earlier) reported problems with the keyboard controller when running Windows or OS/2. As you can imagine, BIOS bugs are particularly frustrating. If an application contains a bug, you can turn the application off. Unfortunately, you cannot turn the BIOS off; so the only way to correct a bug in BIOS is to update the BIOS IC, "flash" the BIOS with an updated BIOS file, or replace the entire motherboard.

When investigating a customer complaint for a PC, you may wish to check with the BIOS manufacturer (through technical support, fax-back service, or their Web site) and find out if there have been any problems with the BIOS when used in the particular motherboard (for example, a given Phoenix BIOS version in a particular Intel motherboard). If your symptoms match other symptoms that have been reported, a quick BIOS upgrade may save the day for your customer.

THE YEAR 2000 (Y2K) PROBLEM

The turn of the century is here, and with it comes a perplexing problem with file dates. Traditional operating systems and applications use two-digit year designations (1998 would be shown as "98"). The problem is that not all PC hardware or applications are suitable to move into the new century because they cannot properly handle the rollover of year designations, such as "00" for 2000, "01" for 2001, and so on. This is known as the "year 2000 (or Y2K) problem."

As far as the PC hardware is concerned, Y2K problems are with the real-time clock (RTC) and its relation to the internal DOS clock device driver (CLOCK$), which is actually a counter and not a real clock at all. You can verify whether your system has an RTC problem by setting the date and time to 11:57 p.m. (or 23:57) on December 31, 1999, and leaving the machine running to see what happens when it reaches 2000. DOS copes with the problem quite easily, but if you turn the power off and reboot, you might see a system date starting somewhere in 1900 or 1980. The date 01/01/1980 is usually set if your CMOS contents are lost.

The reason for this discrepancy is the interaction between the RTC and DOS clocks. The RTC is part of the CMOS RAM chip that maintains the system BIOS settings and is kept intact by a backup battery. Some of the older RTC chips cannot keep track of the centuries by themselves, so a byte is used in the CMOS to do the job instead. Also, the RTC timing components are "trimmed" at the factory to a certain tolerance (typically plus or minus 20 seconds a month), which will only be adhered to if the desired operating environment (temperature and humidity) is maintained.

By contrast, the DOS device driver (CLOCK$) only interrogates the RTC (via the BIOS) when the machine starts, then proceeds to ignore it as long as the PC is running. The date supplied is converted to the number of days since January 1, 1980, and the number of seconds since midnight of the current day. The number of seconds since midnight is stored in the counter by the BIOS, and when DOS needs to read the clock, the BIOS is called to read the counter, and the number of ticks is converted back to seconds. If the counter goes past midnight, it is reset to zero by the BIOS, and the first call after that is told that the day has advanced. As a result, if more than 24 hours have elapsed between calls, there is no way that DOS can tell which day it is.

> Have you wondered why there is often a time difference between your watch and your PC at the end of the day? The system clock has to compete for attention with other devices and is often reprogrammed by games or other applications that use it for their own timing purposes. Being interrupt driven, the system clock's accuracy depends on system activity.

As DOS operates between 1980 and 2099, it can figure out that 00 equates to 2000 (although DOS may have problems if the RTC specifically hands it a date of 1900 or any other incompatible date). In practice, the BIOS converts the date as well, and some correct the time automatically at boot and supply DOS with 2000 instead of a hardware date of 1900. However, other BIOS cannot produce a date later than 1999 (for example, Award BIOS 4.5G prior to November 1995 can only accept dates between 1994 and 1999).

Most new BIOS and RTC versions (released after 1996) are designed to deal with the year 2000 properly. But you will need to test older systems for rollover capability—especially now that the year 2000 is here. If your owner's manual doesn't mention this issue (and you can't call the computer manufacturer for clarification), try these steps:

1. Set the time on your computer to three minutes before midnight (23:57:00) and the date to December 31, 1999.
2. Turn your computer off and wait for five minutes.
3. Turn your computer on, booting from a clean floppy disk (DOS only with no CONFIG.SYS or AUTOEXEC.BAT files). Check the date.
4. If the date is correct, you're all set.
5. If the date is incorrect, try entering the correct date in CMOS setup (remember to exit saving your changes). Then reboot the system. If the new dates hold after adjusting the CMOS setup, you're all set.
6. If the date is still incorrect after a reboot, or you find that you need to reset the system date every day, you'll need to upgrade the system BIOS.
7. If the date problems persist after upgrading the BIOS, you may need a new RTC (or upgrade the motherboard).

> Even if the BIOS and RTC are functioning properly for Y2K service, the operating system and applications may also need to be patched to support dates after January 1, 2000.

BIOS Troubleshooting

You've got to be familiar with the myriad of error messages that a system can generate. Each time you start the PC, the power-on self-test (POST) initiates a comprehensive series of tests to verify the computer's hardware. Traditionally, the POST generates two types of error messages: beep codes and POST codes. Beep codes are generated through the PC speaker before the video system has properly initialized. POST codes are single-byte hexadecimal characters written to I/O port 80h (or other I/O port) as each POST test is started. You can read the POST code using a POST reader card. By matching the beep code or POST code to your particular BIOS, you can determine the exact fault. (See Chapter 19 for a comprehensive set of error codes.)

The problem with beep codes and POST codes is their cryptic nature—you need a detailed code listing in order to match the code to the fault. However, current generations of BIOS and operating systems are starting to employ more user-friendly error messages. By displaying complete error messages (rather than simple codes), a great deal of guesswork is removed from the troubleshooting process. Remember that BIOS error messages are designed to *enhance* (rather than replace) beep and POST codes. You should also note that unlike beep codes and POST codes, many BIOS error messages are not fatal—that is, the system will continue to run after the error has been generated.

SYMPTOM 7-1 **8042 Gate—A20 Error** There is a fault using gate A20 to access memory over 1MB. One or more SIMMs/DIMMs may be loose, or the keyboard controller (KBC) may have failed. Check that each of the SIMMs/DIMMs is installed securely. Try replacing the keyboard controller (if possible), or replace the entire motherboard if necessary.

SYMPTOM 7-2 **Address line short** There is a serious problem with the memory address decoding circuitry on your motherboard. In some cases, this may be a spontaneous error that can be cleared by turning the system off for a few seconds and rebooting. If the problem persists, you should replace the motherboard outright.

SYMPTOM 7-3 **BIOS ROM checksum error—System halted** The checksum of the BIOS code in the BIOS chip is incorrect. This is a *fatal* problem indicating that the BIOS code may have become corrupt. If your BIOS includes a "boot block," you may be able to boot to a floppy disk and try "reflashing" the BIOS. If your system is unable to boot, you'll need to replace the motherboard BIOS chip outright before the system will initialize.

SYMPTOM 7-4 **C: (or D:) drive error** The system cannot detect drive C: or D:. The hard disk "type" is probably set incorrectly in the CMOS setup, or the disk may not be connected or formatted properly. Check the CMOS setup and reconnect the hard drive. You may need to repartition and reformat the drive.

SYMPTOM 7-5 **C: (or D:) drive failure** The drive was detected, but it failed to respond properly. This is more serious than a drive error and generally means that the drive is defective. Double-check the drive signal cable, and replace the drive if necessary.

SYMPTOM 7-6 **Cache memory bad, do not enable cache** POST has determined that your cache memory is defective. Do *not* attempt to enable the cache in your system. You should replace the cache RAM at your earliest opportunity. Until then, you may notice a decline in system performance. If you're using a Pentium II/III CPU where the L2 cache is integrated into the CPU cartridge itself, try replacing the CPU.

SYMPTOM 7-7 **CMOS battery failed** The CMOS battery is no longer functional. You will need to replace the CMOS battery as soon as possible. If you haven't yet lost CMOS contents, take a PRINTSCREEN of each CMOS setup page immediately to record the setup configuration; then power-down the system and install a new battery.

SYMPTOM 7-8 **CMOS battery state low** The CMOS battery power is getting low. Make it a point to record your CMOS settings as soon as possible, and then replace the CMOS battery promptly.

SYMPTOM 7-9 **CMOS checksum error—defaults loaded** CMOS RAM has become corrupt, so the CMOS checksum is incorrect. The system loads the default equipment configuration in an effort to ensure that the system can start. This error may have been caused by a weak battery. Check the CMOS backup battery and replace if necessary.

SYMPTOM 7-10 **CMOS display type mismatch** The video type indicated in CMOS RAM is not the one detected by the BIOS. Check your CMOS setup and make sure the correct video type is selected (usually VGA). Remember to save your changes before exiting and rebooting. Also verify that there is no conflict between an integrated video adapter (on the motherboard) and a video adapter card in your system.

SYMPTOM 7-11 **CMOS memory size mismatch** The amount of memory recorded in the CMOS setup configuration does not match the memory detected by the POST. If you have added new memory, start your CMOS setup and make the appropriate corrections (or simply save changes and reboot, even though you change nothing). If you've made no changes to the system, try rebooting the computer. If the error appears again, some of your memory may have failed. Try a systematic replacement to locate the defective SIMM/DIMM.

SYMPTOM 7-12 **CMOS system options not set** The values stored in CMOS RAM are either corrupt or nonexistent. Check your CMOS backup battery and replace it if necessary. Enter the CMOS setup routine and reload any missing or corrupted entries. Remember to save your changes before exiting and rebooting.

SYMPTOM 7-13 **CPU at "nnn"** The running speed of the CPU is displayed (where "nnn" is the speed in MHz). This is not an error, but a measurement. If the displayed speed is known to be different from the actual clock speed, you should check the motherboard's clock settings and multipliers, or suspect an error in BIOS speed detection. (You may need to update the BIOS to achieve an accurate measurement.)

7

SYMPTOM 7-14 **Data error** The floppy disk or hard drive that you are accessing cannot read the data. One or more sectors on the disk may be corrupted. If you are using DOS, run the CHKDSK or ScanDisk utility to check the file structure of the floppy or hard disk drive. If you find errors, rerun the utility to correct those errors. Keep in mind that it may be necessary to reload any applications or data files that were subject to file structure problems.

SYMPTOM 7-15 **Decreasing available memory** An error has been detected in memory, and the available memory is being reduced below the point at which the fault was detected. Either a SIMM/DIMM has failed, or one or more SIMMs/DIMMs may be improperly seated. Try reinstalling your memory modules, or replace them outright.

SYMPTOM 7-16 **Diskette drive 0 (or 1) seek failure** Your floppy drive was unable to seek to the desired track. A cable may be loose, or the CMOS setup information may not match your actual floppy drive hardware. Check and correct your CMOS setup, check your signal cable, and replace the floppy drive if necessary.

SYMPTOM 7-17 **Diskette read failure** This may also be displayed as a "Diskette boot failure." The system was unable to read from a floppy disk. This is usually due to dirty read/write heads, a loose signal cable, or a defective floppy disk. Try cleaning the read/write heads, try a different disk, check/replace the floppy signal cable, and replace the floppy drive outright if necessary.

SYMPTOM 7-18 **Diskette subsystem reset failed** The PC was unable to access the floppy drive system. The disk drive controller may be faulty. Make sure that the drive controller is seated properly in its bus slot (if you're using a stand-alone drive controller) and that all cables are attached securely. Try the drive controller in another slot, and replace the drive controller if necessary.

SYMPTOM 7-19 **Display switch is set incorrectly** Some motherboards provide a display switch that can be set to either monochrome or color. This message indicates the switch is set to a different setting than indicated in CMOS setup. Determine which video setting is correct, and then either turn off the system and change the motherboard jumper, or enter CMOS setup and change the video selection.

SYMPTOM 7-20 **DMA (or DMA #1 or DMA #2) error** A serious fault has occurred in the DMA controller system of your motherboard. In virtually all cases, the motherboard will have to be replaced (unless you can replace the DMA controller).

SYMPTOM 7-21 **DMA bus timeout** A device has driven the bus signal for more than 7.8 microseconds. This may be a random fault, but chances are that a DMA-dependent device in the PC has failed (such as your sound card or Ultra-DMA drive controller). Try removing expansion devices first. Otherwise, replace the motherboard.

SYMPTOM 7-22 **Drive not ready** No floppy disk is in the drive. Make sure the valid disk is secure in the drive before continuing. Try another known-good disk.

SYMPTOM 7-23 **EISA CMOS checksum failure** The checksum for your EISA CMOS RAM is bad. This means the CMOS RAM is defective or the backup battery is exhausted. Try replacing the backup battery first. If the problem persists, replace the CMOS RAM chip (or the entire motherboard).

SYMPTOM 7-24 **EISA CMOS not operational** A read/write failure occurred in extended CMOS RAM. Either the CMOS RAM backup battery has died, or the CMOS RAM chip itself has failed. Try replacing the CMOS backup battery. If the problem persists, replace the CMOS RAM chip (or the entire motherboard).

SYMPTOM 7-25 **EISA configuration is not complete** The slot configuration information stored in the EISA CMOS RAM is incomplete. When this error appears, the system will boot in ISA mode, which allows you to run the EISA Configuration Utility (ECU). Run the ECU and finish configuring the system; then save your changes and reboot.

SYMPTOM 7-26 **Enable/disable expansion board** One of your EISA expansion boards suffered a nonmaskable interrupt (NMI). You can press E to enable that board, or press D to disable it. This allows the system to finish booting. If the problem persists, try replacing the suspect expansion board.

SYMPTOM 7-27 **Expansion board not ready at slot "X"** Your EISA BIOS cannot find the expansion board assigned to slot "X." Verify that the expansion board is in the correct slot and is seated properly. If the problem persists, try replacing the expansion board or moving it to another available slot.

SYMPTOM 7-28 **Floppy disk controller failure** There is a problem with the floppy drive system—either the floppy drive or drive controller has failed. Check the floppy drive controller first, and make sure it's seated properly in its bus slot. Try a different bus slot. Check that all the drive cables are secure. Make sure that the floppy drive is receiving power. Try a new drive controller, and try a different floppy drive if necessary.

SYMPTOM 7-29 **Floppy disk(s) fail** The PC cannot find or initialize the floppy drive controller or the floppy drive itself. Make sure the drive controller is installed correctly. (You might try a different expansion slot.) If no floppy drives are installed, be sure the "Diskette Drive" entries in CMOS setup are set to "none" or "not installed."

SYMPTOM 7-30 **Hard disk configuration error** The system could not initialize the hard drive in the expected way. This is often due to an incorrect configuration in the CMOS setup. Make sure the correct hard drive geometry is entered for the drive (or try autodetecting the drive). If the drive was partitioned with different parameters, you may need to duplicate those parameters in order to access the drive. If the problem persists, try replacing the hard drive.

SYMPTOM 7-31 **Hard disk controller failure** There is a problem with the hard drive system—either the hard drive or drive controller has failed. Check the drive controller first, and make sure it's seated properly in its bus slot. Try a different bus slot. Check that all the drive cables are secure. Make sure that the hard drive is spinning up. Try a new drive controller, and try a different hard drive if necessary.

SYMPTOM 7-32 **Hard disk(s) diagnosis fail** Your BIOS may run specific disk diagnostic routines. This type of message appears if one or more hard disks return an error when those diagnostics are run. In most cases, the drive itself is installed improperly, or is defective. Check the drive installation, and replace the drive if necessary.

SYMPTOM 7-33 **Hard disk failure** The hard drive failed initialization, which usually suggests that the drive has failed. Make sure the drive signal cable is attached properly, and see that the drive spins up. Then replace the hard drive if necessary.

SYMPTOM 7-34 **Hard disk drive read failure** The drive cannot read from the hard drive, which usually suggests that the drive has failed. Make sure the drive signal cable is attached properly, and see that the drive spins up. Then replace the hard drive if necessary.

SYMPTOM 7-35 **Incompatible Processor: CPU0 (or CPU1) is B0 step or below** You have installed an old version of a CPU that is not supported by the BIOS. In a single-microprocessor system, CPU0 refers to the system board microprocessor; in a dual-microprocessor system, it refers to the *secondary* microprocessor on the add-in card. The CPU1 message appears only on a dual-microprocessor system and *always* refers to the system board microprocessor. Replace the microprocessor with a current version of the microprocessor.

SYMPTOM 7-36 **Incompatible Processor: Cache sizes different** This message appears for a dual-microprocessor system if the CPUs use different L2 cache sizes. Replace one of the microprocessors to make the L2 cache sizes match.

SYMPTOM 7-37 **Insert Bootable Media** The BIOS cannot find a bootable media. Insert a bootable floppy disk or bootable CD, or switch to a known-good bootable drive.

SYMPTOM 7-38 **INTR #1 (or INTR #2) error** A serious fault has occurred with your interrupt controller (PIC) on the motherboard. In virtually all cases, the motherboard will have to be replaced entirely.

SYMPTOM 7-39 **Invalid Boot Diskette** The BIOS can read the disk in floppy drive A:, but cannot boot the system from it. Use another known-good boot disk, or try booting from a different drive.

SYMPTOM 7-40 **Invalid configuration information—please run SETUP program** The system configuration information in your CMOS setup does not match the hardware configuration detected by the POST. Enter the CMOS setup program and correct the system configuration information. Remember to save your changes before exiting and rebooting.

SYMPTOM 7-41 **Invalid configuration information for slot "X"** The configuration information for the EISA board in slot "X" is not correct, which usually means that the system has been reconfigured without running the EISA Configuration Utility (ECU). Run the ECU, being sure to configure the system properly and save your changes.

SYMPTOM 7-42 **I/O Card Parity Error at xxxxx** An expansion card has failed. If the address can be determined, it is displayed as "xxxxx." If not, the message is I/O Card Parity Error ????. In either case, you'll need to find and replace the defective expansion card.

SYMPTOM 7-43 **Keyboard clock line failure** The BIOS has not detected the keyboard clock signal when testing the keyboard. Often, the keyboard connector is loose, or the keyboard is defective. Check the keyboard cable, and try another keyboard if necessary. If the problem persists, the keyboard controller (KBC) may have failed. Try replacing the keyboard controller chip, or replace the entire motherboard.

SYMPTOM 7-44 **Keyboard controller failure** This may also be denoted as a "keyboard interface error." The keyboard controller on the motherboard is not responding as expected. Start by checking the keyboard connection, and try a different keyboard. If the problem persists, the keyboard controller (KBC) may have failed. Try replacing the keyboard controller IC, or replace the entire motherboard.

SYMPTOM 7-45 **Keyboard data line failure** The BIOS has not detected the keyboard data signal when testing the keyboard. Often, the keyboard connector is loose, or the keyboard is defective. Check the keyboard cable, and try another keyboard if necessary. If the problem persists, the keyboard controller may have failed. Try replacing the keyboard controller (KBC) chip, or replace the entire motherboard.

SYMPTOM 7-46 **Keyboard error or no keyboard present** The system cannot initialize the keyboard. Make sure the keyboard is attached correctly, and see that no keys are pressed during POST. To purposely configure the system without a keyboard (for example, if you're setting up a server), you can configure the CMOS setup to ignore the keyboard.

SYMPTOM 7-47 **Keyboard is locked out—unlock the key** If your system comes fitted with a key lock switch, make sure the switch is set to the "unlocked" position. If there is no key lock switch (or the switch is set properly), one or more keys may be pressed or shorted on the keyboard. Try a new keyboard.

SYMPTOM 7-48 **Keyboard stuck key failure** In almost all cases, this is a keyboard problem. POST has determined that one or more keys on the keyboard are stuck. Make sure that nothing is resting on the keyboard, and see that no paper clips or staples have fallen into the keyboard. Try a different keyboard.

SYMPTOM 7-49 **Memory address line failure at <address>, read <value> expecting <value>** An error has occurred in the address decoding circuitry used in memory. In many cases, one or more SIMMs/DIMMs may be improperly seated. Check that all SIMMs/DIMMs are installed correctly. If the problem continues, try systematic replacement to locate a defective memory module. If you cannot find a defective SIMM/DIMM, the problem is likely to be elsewhere on the motherboard. Replace the motherboard.

SYMPTOM 7-50 Memory data line failure at <address>, read <value> expecting <value> An error has been encountered in memory. In virtually all cases, one or more SIMMs/DIMMs may be faulty or improperly seated. Make sure that every SIMM/DIMM is seated correctly, and try a systematic replacement to locate a defective memory module.

SYMPTOM 7-51 Memory double word logic failure at <address>, read <value> expecting <value> An error has been encountered in memory. In virtually all cases, one or more SIMMs/DIMMs may be faulty or improperly seated. Make sure that every SIMM/DIMM is seated correctly, and try a systematic replacement to locate a defective memory module.

SYMPTOM 7-52 Memory odd/even logic failure at <address>, read <value> expecting <value> An error has been encountered in memory. In virtually all cases, one or more SIMMs/DIMMs may be faulty or improperly seated. Make sure that every SIMM/DIMM is seated correctly, and try a systematic replacement to locate a defective memory module.

SYMPTOM 7-53 Memory parity failure at <address>, read <value> expecting <value> An error has been encountered in memory. In virtually all cases, one or more SIMMs/DIMMs may be faulty or improperly seated. Make sure that every SIMM/DIMM is seated correctly, and try a systematic replacement to locate a defective memory module.

SYMPTOM 7-54 Memory write/read failure at <address>, read <value> expecting <value> An error has been encountered in memory. In virtually all cases, one or more SIMMs/DIMMs may be faulty or improperly seated. Make sure that every SIMM/DIMM is seated correctly, and try a systematic replacement to locate a defective memory module.

SYMPTOM 7-55 Memory size in CMOS invalid The amount of memory recorded in the CMOS setup configuration does not match the memory detected by the POST. If you have added new memory, start your CMOS setup and make the appropriate corrections. If you've made no changes to the system, try rebooting the computer. If the error appears again, some of your memory may have failed. Try a systematic replacement to locate a defective SIMM or DIMM.

SYMPTOM 7-56 Memory verify error at <address> This suggests an error verifying a value already written to memory, which almost always indicates a bad memory device. Use the <address> location along with your system's memory map to locate the defective memory devices, or systematically replace your SIMMs/DIMMs until the defective memory device is found.

SYMPTOM 7-57 No boot device available The computer cannot find a viable floppy disk or hard drive—typically because the drives have not been entered properly into CMOS. Enter the CMOS setup program and configure the proper drive information. You should also verify that your floppy disk or hard drive has been prepared as "bootable." You may need to repartition and/or reformat the hard drive.

SYMPTOM 7-58 No boot sector on hard-disk drive The PC is refusing to boot from the hard drive. This is usually because the drive is not configured properly. Check the CMOS setup and verify that the correct drive information has been entered (or select autodetect). Also make sure to partition the drive with an active bootable partition, and format it as a bootable device. If the problem continues, try replacing the hard drive.

SYMPTOM 7-59 **No timer tick interrupt** The interrupt timer on the motherboard has failed. This is a *fatal* error that will probably require you to replace the motherboard.

SYMPTOM 7-60 **Non-system disk or disk error** The disk in drive A: (or your hard drive) does not have a bootable operating system installed on it. If you're booting from a floppy drive, make the disk bootable. If you're booting from a hard drive, make sure that the drive is partitioned and formatted for bootable operation.

SYMPTOM 7-61 **Not a boot diskette** There is no operating system on the floppy disk. Boot the computer with a disk that contains an operating system.

SYMPTOM 7-62 **Off-board parity error** There is a parity error in memory installed in an expansion slot (for example, a SIMM on the video adapter). The format is OFF BOARD PARITY ERROR ADDR (HEX) = (XXXX), where XXXX is the hex address where the error occurred. Chances are that the memory installed at the error address has failed.

SYMPTOM 7-63 **On-board parity error** There is a parity error in memory installed on the motherboard in one of the SIMM/DIMM slots. The format is ON BOARD PARITY ERROR ADDR (HEX) = (XXXX), where XXXX is the hex address where the error occurred. Chances are that the memory installed at the error address has failed.

SYMPTOM 7-64 **Override enabled—defaults loaded** If the system cannot boot using the current CMOS configuration for any reason, the BIOS can override the current configuration using a set of defaults designed for the most stable, minimal-performance system operations. The CMOS may be ignored if the CMOS RAM checksum is wrong or if a critical piece of CMOS information is missing that would otherwise cause a fatal error.

SYMPTOM 7-65 **Parity error** A parity error has occurred in system memory at an unknown address. Chances are that a memory module has failed. Try a systematic check-and-replace approach to isolate the defective memory component.

SYMPTOM 7-66 **Plug-and-Play configuration error** The system has encountered a problem in trying to configure one or more expansion cards. Start the CMOS setup routine and check that any PnP options have been set correctly. If any configuration utilities are included with your particular system, try running those utilities to resolve any configuration issues.

SYMPTOM 7-67 **Press TAB to show POST screen** Some system OEMs (such as Acer) may replace the normal BIOS POST display with their own proprietary display—usually a graphic logo. When the BIOS displays this message, the operator is able to switch between the OEM display and the default POST display. This can be helpful for troubleshooting purposes.

SYMPTOM 7-68 **Primary master hard disk fail** POST detects an error in the primary ("master") hard drive on the primary EIDE controller channel. Double-check the drive's installation, jumpering, and cable connections. Otherwise, replace the drive outright.

SYMPTOM 7-69 **Primary slave hard disk fail** POST detects an error in the secondary ("slave") hard drive on the primary EIDE controller channel. Double-check the drive's installation, jumpering, and cable connections. Otherwise, replace the drive outright.

SYMPTOM 7-70 **Resuming from disk** Award BIOS (and other BIOS versions) offers a save-to-disk feature for notebook computers. This message may appear when the operator restarts the system after a save-to-disk shutdown. You will almost never find this type of message on a desktop or tower system.

SYMPTOM 7-71 **Secondary master hard disk fail** POST detects an error in the primary ("master") hard drive on the secondary IDE controller channel. Double-check the drive's installation, jumpering, and cable connections. Otherwise, replace the drive outright.

SYMPTOM 7-72 **Secondary slave hard disk fail** POST detects an error in the secondary ("slave") hard drive on the secondary IDE controller channel. Double-check the drive's installation, jumpering, and cable connections. Otherwise, replace the drive outright.

SYMPTOM 7-73 **Should be empty but EISA board found** A valid EISA board ID was found in a slot that was configured as having no board installed. This is normally due to an improper system configuration, so run the EISA Configuration Utility (ECU) and reconfigure the system properly. Remember to save any changes and reboot the system.

SYMPTOM 7-74 **Should have EISA board but none found** The board installed in a given EISA slot is not responding to the expected ID request (or no board ID has been found in the indicated slot at all). This is normally due to an improper system configuration, so run the EISA Configuration Utility (ECU) and reconfigure the system properly. Remember to save any changes and reboot the system.

SYMPTOM 7-75 **Shutdown failure** There is a serious fault on the motherboard—usually associated with the CMOS RAM/RTC function. In most cases, you'll need to replace the motherboard outright.

SYMPTOM 7-76 **System halted—press CTRL+ALT+DEL to reboot** This error indicates the current boot attempt has been aborted, and the system must be rebooted. In most cases, the system files on the boot drive have been damaged, or the boot drive itself has failed. Try booting from another drive (such as a floppy disk). You may need to repartition and reformat the boot drive as a bootable device, or replace the boot drive outright.

SYMPTOM 7-77 **Terminator/processor card not installed** This is an error that occurs with dual-CPU systems when neither a "terminator" card nor a secondary microprocessor card is installed in the secondary card connector. Make sure either a terminator card or a secondary microprocessor card is installed in the connector. Install the appropriate card and start the system again.

SYMPTOM 7-78 **Time of day clock stopped** The real-time clock (RTC) has stopped. The CMOS battery may be dead (or almost dead). Enter the CMOS setup and correct the date and time. If the trouble continues, try replacing the CMOS backup battery.

SYMPTOM 7-79 **Time or date in CMOS is invalid** The time or date displayed in the CMOS setup does not match the system clock. This can happen often under Windows 95/98 or other operating systems that can "desynchronize" the system clock. Enter the CMOS setup utility and correct the date and time. If the problem reoccurs, you may be able to determine a specific application that is causing the problem.

SYMPTOM 7-80 **Timer chip counter 2 failed** There is a serious fault on the motherboard—probably due to a failure of a programmable interrupt timer (or PIT). In most cases, you'll need to replace the motherboard outright.

SYMPTOM 7-81 **Unexpected interrupt in protected-mode** An interrupt has occurred unexpectedly. Loose or poorly inserted SIMMs/DIMMs can cause such a problem, so start by checking and reinstalling the SIMMs/DIMMs. A faulty keyboard controller (KBC) can also result in interrupt problems. Try replacing the keyboard controller if possible, or replace the entire motherboard.

SYMPTOM 7-82 **Warning—Thermal Probes failed** This error is usually found in Pentium Pro systems with one or two thermal probes. At system startup, the BIOS has detected that one or both of the thermal probes in the computer are not operational. You can continue to use the system, but be aware that the temperature probe(s) are disabled—a processor overheat condition will not shut down the system. You will probably have to replace the motherboard to correct this fault.

> The Pentium Pro has a built-in thermocouple that halts microprocessor operation if the CPU exceeds its rated temperature.

SYMPTOM 7-83 **Warning—Temperature is too high** During system startup, the BIOS has detected that one or both microprocessors are overheated. This can happen if you try to restart the system too soon after a thermal shutdown. After displaying this message, the BIOS halts the processes and turns off the system. Let the system cool down before attempting to restart it.

SYMPTOM 7-84 **Wrong board in slot "X"** This is typically an EISA system error when the board's ID does not match the ID stored in the EISA nonvolatile memory. Run the EISA Configuration Utility to reconfigure your device layout and save any system changes.

PCI ERROR MESSAGES

SYMPTOM 7-85 **Bad PnP serial ID checksum** The serial ID checksum of a plug-and-play card is invalid. Try reconfiguring or replacing the offending expansion card.

SYMPTOM 7-86 **Floppy disk controller resource conflict** The floppy disk controller has requested a resource that is already in use by another device. Try reconfiguring or freeing the resources that are requested by the PnP system.

SYMPTOM 7-87 **NVRAM checksum error, NVRAM cleared** The extended system configuration data (ESCD) was reinitialized because of an NVRAM checksum error. Try rerunning the ISA Configuration Utility (ICU). If the problem persists, replace the NVRAM IC, or replace the motherboard entirely.

SYMPTOM 7-88 **NVRAM cleared by jumper** The "Clear CMOS" jumper on the motherboard has been moved to the "Clear" position, and the system has been initialized. CMOS RAM and ESCD have been cleared and now must be reconfigured/reloaded with the necessary data.

SYMPTOM 7-89 **NVRAM data invalid, NVRAM cleared** Invalid data has been found in the ESCD (which may mean that you have changed devices in the system). When this message is displayed, the BIOS has already rewritten the ESCD with current configuration data. Try rebooting the system once again, or enter the CMOS setup and save and exit, even though you may not change anything.

SYMPTOM 7-90 **Parallel port resource conflict** The parallel port requested a resource that is already in use by another device. Try reconfiguring or freeing the resources requested by the PnP system.

SYMPTOM 7-91 **PCI error log is full** More than 15 PCI conflict errors have been detected, and no additional PCI errors can be logged. Deal with the PCI errors already contained in the log in order to reduce the total number of errors and address subsequent errors.

SYMPTOM 7-92 **PCI I/O port conflict** Two devices have requested the same I/O address, resulting in a conflict. Try reconfiguring or freeing the I/O resources needed to allow both devices to be configured properly.

SYMPTOM 7-93 **PCI IRQ conflict** Two devices have requested the same IRQ, resulting in a conflict. Try reconfiguring or freeing the IRQs needed to allow both devices to be configured properly.

SYMPTOM 7-94 **PCI memory conflict** Two devices have requested the same memory range resources, resulting in a conflict. Try reconfiguring or freeing the memory ranges needed to allow both devices to be configured properly.

SYMPTOM 7-95 **Primary boot device not found** The designated primary boot device (a hard disk drive, floppy disk drive, or CD-ROM drive) could not be found. Check the installation and configuration of each possible boot device.

SYMPTOM 7-96 **Primary IDE controller resource conflict** The primary IDE controller has requested a resource that is already in use by another device. Try reconfiguring or freeing the resources that are needed to allow the IDE controller to operate.

SYMPTOM 7-97 **Primary input device not found** The designated primary input device such as the keyboard or mouse (or other device if input is redirected) could not be found. Check the installation and configuration of all your input devices. Make sure that the input devices are also enabled in the CMOS setup.

SYMPTOM 7-98 **Secondary IDE controller resource conflict** The secondary IDE controller has requested a resource that is already in use by another device. Try reconfiguring or freeing the resources that are needed to allow the IDE controller to operate.

SYMPTOM 7-99 **"Static device resource conflict" or "System board device resource conflict"** A non-plug-and-play (or legacy) ISA card has requested a resource that is already in use. Try reconfiguring the ISA card to use other resources, or try freeing the resources needed by the ISA card.

OTHER BIOS SYMPTOMS

In actual practice, you cannot "fix" a BIOS chip, but you must be able to identify possible problems with BIOS versions and incompatibilities (especially when trying to use the newest operating systems and hardware). When you find such a problem, you'll need to flash the BIOS with an updated version or replace the troublesome BIOS chip outright. This part of the chapter highlights a number of common BIOS-related problems that you may encounter.

SYMPTOM 7-100 **Norton Utilities 8 reports poor disk performance with MR BIOS** You may notice that Norton 8 identifies changes in the disk controller and suggests that disk performance may measure artificially high, but you find that disk performance is reported with a much lower result. This is a problem with the way Norton 8 interacts with certain versions of MR BIOS. Version 3.2 and later use slightly different coding that corrects this reporting problem. You may consider upgrading your version of MR BIOS, or update your version of Norton Utilities.

SYMPTOM 7-101 **Norton Utilities 9 reports problems on the disk when using MR BIOS** After installing some versions of MR BIOS, there have been a few reports that NDD95 will misdiagnose your disk with a problem (even though ScanDisk reports the drive to be working perfectly). If this occurs, do not use NDD95 to correct the problem—this may damage your disk's file system. Instead, uninstall and reinstall Norton Utilities.

According to Microid Research, most NDD95 problems have been traced to the CMOS date being reset after running the flash loader utility. The flash loader intentionally clears the CMOS RAM to assure a clean startup with the newly installed MR BIOS. Be sure to reenter the date (especially the century part of the year) after flashing MR BIOS into the computer. Beginning with version 3.26, the MR BIOS flash loader carefully avoids clearing the CMOS date.

SYMPTOM 7-102 **After partitioning and formatting a drive under MR BIOS, the drive is not recognized on other systems** You may also find this problem when reflashing the original system BIOS back over the MR BIOS that you're using. This is not a problem with MR BIOS. Instead, the trouble is with the version of FDISK included with Windows 95. The latest version of FDISK supplied with Windows 95 supports three new partition types that are written to partition table entries on the hard disk:

- *Type 0Eh* The same as type 06h (primary DOS), but uses BIOS INT13 extensions to get hard disk parameters
- *Type 0Fh* The same as type 05h (extended DOS), but uses BIOS INT13 extensions to get hard disk parameters
- *Type 0Ch* A FAT32 partition using BIOS INT13 extensions to get hard disk parameters
- *Type 0Bh* A FAT32 partition that does *not* use BIOS INT13 extensions to get hard disk parameters

MR BIOS supports INT 13h extensions, and when you partition your hard drive under MR BIOS, FDISK will use type 0Eh or 0Fh as a partition type. When you boot from the drive, the OS reads this partition type byte and uses the BIOS INT 13 extensions to get the hard disk parameters. As long as you don't change this setup, everything works fine.

However, if you use this partitioned hard drive with another BIOS that does *not* support INT 13 extensions, the operating system expects to access the hard disk parameters using the BIOS INT 13 extensions. Since your other version of the BIOS does not support this, the operating system cannot boot. According to Microid Research, this is not a problem with MR BIOS only. They claim to have re-created this problem on motherboards using BIOS from other vendors besides MR BIOS.

The recommended solution is to boot from a floppy disk, switch to the hard drive, back up the hard drive, and then repartition the drive using FDISK from the system where you intend to use the hard drive. You can also use Windows 95 FDISK with the **/X** switch, which forces FDISK to use older partition types. After you repartition and reformat the drive, reload your operating system and restore your files.

SYMPTOM 7-103 **You cannot use two PCI devices simultaneously in slots 1 and 5** This is a known issue with Tyan S1470 Titan XV motherboards and MR BIOS. The problem is generally not the BIOS, but rather the device drivers used to communicate with the PCI devices in slots 1 and 5. This problem is due to the PCI bus architecture, which only provides four IRQ pins on the PCI bus. In the case of two PCI cards in slots 1 and 5, both slots are hardwired to use the same PCI IRQ. The BIOS is properly configuring both PCI cards to use the same IRQ—unfortunately, many device drivers are not properly written to handle the sharing of a PCI IRQ between different devices. You should contact the manufacturer of the PCI cards involved in order to obtain the latest drivers. If the problem persists after installing updated drivers, you may be able to work around the problem by rearranging the PCI cards. You may be able to place lower-priority devices in slot 5.

SYMPTOM 7-104 **You notice that you frequently get memory/stack errors when using Windows 95 with certain BIOS versions** In virtually all cases, this problem is caused by odd memory timings in your particular BIOS version. It may be possible to update the BIOS to a more current version, but you may be able to work around the problem by adjusting the CMOS setup with the following value(s).

Under the Cache menu:

- Set **WaitStates** to 1.
- Set **SRAM Burst** to a "3-1-1" pattern.

Under the Chipset menu:

- Set **I/O Recoverys** to 1.
- Set **VLB-XXX's** to 1.

Under the PCI Bus menu:

- Set **Latency** to 64 (or as close as possible).

Your particular CMOS setup may offer other or additional options. If you have trouble making the adjustments described above, try selecting the "BIOS Defaults" or "Startup Defaults" for your CMOS setup. This should establish the maximum system reliability, though performance may be degraded a bit.

SYMPTOM 7-105 **Windows 95 will not boot with Intel Advanced/MN (Morrison) motherboards when using MR BIOS** In other cases, the motherboard's Crystal 4232 sound system may not function. This is a known problem on some HP Pavilion systems that use the Advanced/MN motherboard. Microid Research reports that certain OEM versions of Windows 95 may not boot properly, and the integrated sound system may not function properly with retail versions of Windows 95. You'll need to correct this problem by updating the BIOS with a later version that contains the initialization code for the Crystal 4232 sound system. You can identify such a motherboard with the Intel BIOS ID such as 1.00.xx.BT0x. Also check for the presence of an integrated sound system by verifying that the speaker cables attach to the motherboard rather than a sound card in an expansion slot.

If you still have trouble with the sound system, try installing the latest drivers for the Crystal 4232 sound system. You can get the Windows 95 drivers from **ftp://ftp.cirrus.com/pub/drivers/audio/b95us250.zip**, but later versions may also be available at this time. Other drivers can be found at **http://www.cirrus.com/drivers/audiodrv**.

SYMPTOM 7-106 **You cannot use MR BIOS with the Adaptec 2940 1.2 BIOS** You notice that the adapter works on other systems. This is a problem with older versions of MR BIOS. All MR BIOS versions prior to version 3.20 are incompatible with the BIOS used with Adaptec's AHA 2940 controller using v.1.2 BIOS. MR BIOS generates an incorrect adapter ROM image in shadow RAM, which causes the system to crash. MR BIOS version 3.20 (and later) now overcomes this problem. Update your MR BIOS to the latest version, or avoid the use of Adaptec 2940 cards with that v.1.2 BIOS.

SYMPTOM 7-107 **You encounter warm-boot problems with MR BIOS systems using Adaptec 2940 1.21 BIOS** All MR BIOS versions prior to 3.22 may have spurious warm-boot (CTRL+ALT+DEL) failures when the system includes an Adaptec 2940 card using the AHA 2940 v.1.21 BIOS. While trying to fix a memory-related bug in v.1.20, the Adaptec v.1.21 BIOS searches for a clear 128KB block of memory before performing its initialization. If it cannot find such a region, it generates a memory error on the monitor, and the system halts. In most cases, it's best to update the Adaptec BIOS to a later version, or replace the SCSI adapter with another model.

SYMPTOM 7-108 **The parallel port fails diagnostics when in the bidirectional mode** In most cases, this type of problem occurs with the National Semiconductor Super I/O chip's parallel port (though it may occur with other I/O chip makers), and it is usually due to the way BIOS handles the port's setup. This is a known issue with National's Super I/O chip and MR BIOS versions prior to 3.19. In the standard parallel port (or SPP) mode, you should have pseudo-bidirectional capability, but instead it is strictly an output port. If your application requires bidirectional capability, you'll need to change its mode to that particular setting through the CMOS setup. You'll need to update your MR BIOS version to 3.19 or later, in which all four parallel port modes (SPP, bidirectional, EPP, and ECP) have been made available in the CMOS setup.

Considering a BIOS Upgrade

You might wonder why it would even be necessary to bother with an upgrade. Ideally, a BIOS ROM should be viable for the life of a PC. While this is true in a majority of situations, there are two compelling reasons to undertake a BIOS upgrade. First, a newer BIOS can add support for drives and devices that are not currently supported, or require device drivers or TSRs. Two recent examples of this are the addition of bootable CD-ROM drives (using the El Torito standard) and the bootable LS-120 drives. Placing support on a BIOS ROM means that there is one less device driver demanding space in your conventional memory. This factor used to be considered most important for older systems (i386 and slower i486-based PCs), but with the addition of so many new hardware devices, even new PCs are prime candidates for BIOS upgrades. Second (and maybe even more important), BIOS ROM is fundamentally a piece of *software*. Like all software, there are sometimes defects or oversights (bugs) that cause problems with system operations. This is especially true when the same core BIOS code is "OEMed" into a variety of motherboards. For example, some motherboards may require a BIOS upgrade to better support the main chipset in use or to properly identify non-Intel CPUs. Bugs and compatibility problems virtually demand a BIOS upgrade.

RECOGNIZING BIOS PROBLEMS

Unfortunately, diagnosing a BIOS bug is not a simple task. There are no diagnostics to check BIOS operations. BIOS manufacturers rarely publicize their errors, so there is no centralized index of symptoms that you can refer to that suggest a faulty BIOS or incompatibility. However, BIOS problems tend to fall into several categories that might alert you to the *possibility* of BIOS trouble. You can then address the symptoms with the system or motherboard manufacturer directly.

- *There is trouble with Windows 3.1, Windows 95, or Windows 98.* This is a problem typically found on older systems that appeared before the broad introduction of Windows 3.x and is usually related to drive access or keyboard operation problems. Some versions of BIOS intended to enhance Windows can cause certain older motherboard designs to crash or hang up intermittently. When the drives and keyboard check properly (and work just fine under DOS), a BIOS upgrade may be in order. You may also have to replace the keyboard controller IC. Note that BIOS upgrades may no longer be available for older systems. When this occurs, you'll need to upgrade the motherboard outright.
- *There is trouble with floppy disk support.* Random disk errors may occur when a 720KB disk is used in a 1.44MB drive, or the 1.44MB drive may be unable to format 1.44MB disks. Once again, this symptom is seen most frequently on older PCs (1988–1991) when 1.44MB floppy drives were becoming commonplace in PCs. Floppy drive problems may be coupled with the mouse configuration.
- *There is trouble with ATA (IDE) support.* The ATA drive interface standard (also known as Integrated Drive Electronics, or IDE) came to prominence in late 1989 and early 1990. Due to their unique timing requirements, early IDE devices were susceptible to such errors as data corruption, failure to boot, and so on. By Q2 of 1990, most BIOS versions had streamlined their IDE support. When you encounter difficulties installing an ordinary IDE drive in an older PC, check its BIOS date. If the date is 1989 or earlier, consider a BIOS upgrade.
- *There is no ATA-2 (EIDE) or Ultra-ATA (Ultra-DMA/33) support.* The mid-1990s saw hard drives move beyond 528MB and employ advanced data transfer modes. The use of large, fast hard drives using the ATA-2 interface standard (called Enhanced IDE, or EIDE) required a BIOS that could "translate" more than 1024 cylinders and employ Logical Block Addressing when accessing the hard drive. Systems sold prior to the Pentium 133MHz processor (before 1995) will need a BIOS upgrade to support large hard drives, though new drive controllers will often provide their own onboard BIOS to overcome this problem. It is also possible to use "overlay software" such as Disk Manager or EZ-Drive to correct this issue.

  Current PCs provide support for Ultra-ATA hard drives that can support data transfer modes up to 66Mbps (called Ultra-DMA/66 or UDMA/66). Both the hard drive, drive controller, and BIOS must be capable of supporting Ultra-ATA in order to wring the highest performance from the drive. Otherwise, performance will fall back to lower data transfer speeds. If your current system does not support Ultra-ATA, you may be able to use a BIOS upgrade to support an Ultra-ATA hard drive, or upgrade the drive controller to one with a suitable onboard BIOS.
- *You can't successfully support hard drive partitions over 2GB, 4GB, or 8GB.* This is a symptom indirectly related to drive controller support. Even though ATA-2 supports hard drives beyond 8GB in size using Logical Block Addressing (LBA), many BIOS makers have cut corners—limiting their BIOS to supporting only far smaller hard drives. There seem to be two distinct generations of this problem. The first seems to kick in around 2GB, and the second seems to occur around the 4GB or 8GB point. In many cases, the drive will seem to partition properly, but the system will hang up during the reboot after using FDISK. You will need a BIOS upgrade (or a new drive controller) to correct this problem.
- *There is trouble with network support.* In some circumstances, the PC will not work properly when integrated into a Novell NetWare system (or other network). This is often due to the inability of older Novell versions to work with PC "user-defined" drive types. ROM shadowing usually has to be enabled to allow user-defined drive types—unfortunately, not all older motherboard chipsets supported ROM shadowing. BIOS versions later than 1990 have generally corrected this problem.

- *There is trouble with one or both serial ports.* Older BIOS problems often manifest themselves as COM port difficulties under DOS or Windows (often when a mouse is installed). If the serial port circuitry checks properly under diagnostics, suspect a BIOS bug. Check with the BIOS manufacturer to find out if an upgrade or patch file is available.
- *You cannot disable onboard features to employ upgraded expansion devices.* Most current PC designs typically incorporate a number of key features (such as a video adapter and drive controller) directly on the motherboard. This provides the user with a distinct cost savings. To upgrade that existing controller, you'd need to disable it on the motherboard before installing the upgraded device—otherwise a hardware conflict would result. Unfortunately, many motherboards in the marketplace do not properly disable existing controllers. The result is that you cannot upgrade the particular feature. In some cases, a BIOS upgrade will be adequate to correct this problem. In other cases, this is a flaw in the design of the motherboard that will require you to replace the motherboard outright.
- *The system does not identify the particular CPU or bus speed properly.* Classic 486 motherboards used a jumper to "select" the installed CPU, but Pentium and later systems use the CPUID feature incorporated into most new CPUs. In many cases, a BIOS is released before the motherboard has been tested with non-Intel CPUs (such as AMD or Cyrix chips). When these non-Intel CPUs are employed on the motherboard, the BIOS cannot identify them, or it identifies them incorrectly as Intel CPUs. When the system does not identify the CPU or bus speed at startup, chances are you need a BIOS upgrade.
- *Key system features are not supported.* This often occurs in the very latest motherboard designs when the BIOS does not adequately support the features handled in the chipset. Typical examples of this are USB problems, SDRAM support or performance issues, or plug-and-play trouble. A BIOS upgrade should usually correct the problem, but be sure to check with the motherboard or system maker first to verify that a BIOS upgrade will be enough to correct the problem by itself.
- *You note BIOS checksum errors in the POST.* Normally, the POST scans all BIOS chips located in the memory space and calculates a checksum for each one. That unique checksum is then compared against the checksum stored in the BIOS chip itself. If the two checksums match, the BIOS is assumed good, and the boot process can continue. Otherwise, an error is flagged. A BIOS checksum error is almost always fatal, and a new BIOS chip is required to correct the problem.

There is no need to upgrade a BIOS indiscriminately. Only attempt a BIOS upgrade to correct a specific problem or facilitate features that are not previously supported.

GATHERING INFORMATION

The BIOS upgrade process is not terribly difficult, but success depends on obtaining the correct replacement or upgrade. To ensure that you order (or download) the proper BIOS, it is important to collect some information about the system. In most cases, the following five specifications should help ensure an accurate upgrade:

- PC make and model.
- Motherboard manufacturer and CPU (motherboard chipset also if possible).
- Make and version of existing BIOS (shown on the display during initialization).
- Part number of the ROM IC itself. (You may have to peel back the ROM label.)
- Make, model, and part numbers of main motherboard chipset(s) (if any).

When you consider how closely BIOS is related to PC hardware, you can understand why this information is necessary. Today, virtually all PC BIOS is recorded on flash chips, which can be reprogrammed in the field. If you find that you must replace the actual BIOS chip (due to a BIOS failure or corrupted flash process), upgrades can usually be purchased from a BIOS maker or the original system manufacturer. For your own protection, though, place orders only with firms that offer a reasonable return policy (in the event that the new BIOS does not work as expected).

Performing the Upgrade

There are several methods of incorporating a BIOS upgrade into your PC, and in all cases, the proper solution will rely on an understanding of the options available to you. For the purposes of this book, there are four solutions available to a technician: (1) using a BIOS patch, (2) replacing the BIOS chip, (3) "burning" a new EPROM, and (4) "flashing" the BIOS. The solution you choose will depend on the age of the particular machine.

USING A BIOS PATCH

As distracting and unsettling as a BIOS problem may be, few BIOS problems are fatal. Since device drivers and TSRs can serve to supplement a BIOS, they can also support shortfalls in BIOS operation. By adding a corrective file to CONFIG.SYS, AUTOEXEC.BAT, or your Windows 95/98 system, many BIOS problems can be at least abated without even opening the PC enclosure. As just one example, an AMI BIOS error concerning a problem with COM2 can be corrected by adding the FIFO-OFF.COM file to AUTOEXEC.BAT. Another example is the use of a driver to enable the cache in a Cyrix CPU to enhance its performance. While this tactic will not "repair" the problem entirely, a corrective routine can at least allow the system to work until a suitable BIOS upgrade becomes available. To find patches and corrective files for a BIOS, you will need to search the online resources for your particular BIOS manufacturer.

REPLACING THE BIOS CHIP

Replacing the BIOS chip(s) outright is the classic solution for many older PC designs. Traditional ROMs are 28- or 32-pin *dual in-line* (DIP) devices. IBM PC/XT, PC/AT (i286), (i386), and many i486-based motherboards use traditional DIP ROM ICs. Fast i486 and Pentium-based motherboards use a socket-mounted *plastic-leaded chip carrier* (PLCC) IC for BIOS. While today's PCs and expansion products make extensive use of surface-mount ICs and other components, BIOS devices are the single remaining element still implemented in DIP or PLCC sockets. PC/XT systems use a single ROM to supply a 32KB BIOS, most PC/AT systems use two ROMs to supply a 64KB BIOS, and newer i486 and Pentium-based systems incorporate a 128KB or 256KB BIOS on a single ROM. You can obtain updated ROMs from the motherboard's manufacturer or from one of the BIOS vendors listed at the end of this chapter. (In a few cases, you may be able to obtain updates directly from the BIOS manufacturer.)

Before proceeding with a BIOS upgrade, remove all power from the PC and disconnect the AC line cord. Remove the outer enclosure and locate the BIOS ROM(s) on the motherboard. Remember to use an antistatic wrist strap to prevent accidental static discharge from damaging the motherboard. Pay particular attention to the orientation (or *keying*) of pin 1. When more than one IC is involved, also note which ROM is "even" and which one is "odd." Remove DIP ICs carefully. You can use a DIP removal tool, or rock the IC gently from its socket using the wide edge of a regular screwdriver. Be extremely careful when removing DIP ICs—you may have to put them back if things go wrong. *Gentle* is definitely better here. A specialized removal tool will be needed to remove PLCC devices.

You should be equally cautious when installing new DIP ICs. If those 28 or 32 little pins are not inserted evenly and straight, they will bend—and *break*. PLCCs are a bit more forgiving since there are no leads to bend, but make sure to install ICs completely. Before restoring power, make sure the ICs are inserted in their proper orientation. If the ICs are installed in an orientation opposite from the one intended, you may damage the ROM. If the system fails to initialize, the IC(s) may not be inserted completely, or you may have transposed the "even" and "odd" ROMs. Double-check your work if necessary. Depending on your particular upgrade, you may also find yourself replacing the motherboard's keyboard controller chip.

BURNING NEW EPROMS

If you handle a large number of BIOS upgrades and have access to PC-based EPROM programming equipment, you can program (or burn) your own ROMs. The term EPROM stands for "erasable programmable read-only memory," so given the proper BIOS data, you can translate the contents of a BIOS disk file to a physical IC. (You might call this "BIOS-while-u-wait.") EPROM programming equipment is not terribly expensive and can be obtained from any full-service electronics catalog store, but a good model with PC compatibility can easily run over $500. As you might expect, this kind of workbench BIOS requires a bit of technical skill and is certainly not a worthwhile endeavor for the occasional PC hobbyist.

However, the ability to burn your own EPROMs does offer some unique advantages for an enterprising technician. Knowledgeable technicians versed in machine language can actually customize the BIOS (by adding new hard drive parameters to the hard drive table). You can also create backup copies of older BIOS for systems that may no longer be in production, as well as other BIOS for video or drive systems. Of course, modifying a BIOS can have unforeseen consequences for a system—mistakes and errors will disable or crash the PC. Fortunately, you are not altering the *original* BIOS ROM, so you can always restore the original IC.

> Altering or duplicating BIOS code may violate the copyright of the BIOS manufacturer. A BIOS should only be duplicated or modified for the benefit of your individual customers.

It is a simple matter to back up your BIOS contents to a disk file. All you need is the DOS DEBUG utility on a simple bootable floppy disk. The typical DEBUG BIOS backup procedure is illustrated below:

```
C:\> DEBUG                  ;start the DEBUG utility
- N BIOSBACK.ROM            ;name the backup file
- R BX                      ;alter the CPU's BX register
BX 0000                     ;from zero
:1                          ;to one (this indicates a 64KB file)
- M F000:0 FFFF CS:0        ;move BIOS data in preparation for recording
- W 0                       ;write the file from offset 0
Writing 10000 bytes         ;10000h = 64KB
- Q                         ;quit DEBUG
```

This procedure will save the entire 64KB data segment from F000:0000h to F000:FFFFh as a disk file. If the BIOS in your particular system is 128KB (usually starting at E000:0000h), replace the starting address in the "move" command. You can also back up other ROMs to disk, but you must know the starting address and size of the ROM. For example, a ROM that starts at D400:0000h and is 16KB long can be backed up with a procedure such as this:

```
C:\> DEBUG                  ;start the DEBUG utility
- N TEST.ROM                ;choose a name for the file
```

```
- R CX                    ;alter the CPU's CX register (for short
                           transfers)
CX 0000                   ;from zero
:4000                     ;to 4000h (16KB)
- M D400:0 3FFF CS:0      ;move BIOS data in preparation of recording
- W 0                     ;write the file from offset 0
Writing 04000 bytes       ;4000h = 16KB
- Q                       ;quit DEBUG
```

FLASHING THE BIOS

Flash BIOS represents the current class of BIOS ROM ICs that have typically been included in PCs since the era of fast i486 systems; so your Pentium/MMX, Pentium II, or Pentium III–based PCs will almost certainly have a flash BIOS chip. A flash BIOS is essentially an electrically erasable programmable read-only memory (EEPROM)—that is, the IC can be erased and reprogrammed right on the motherboard. Rather than worry about warehousing and shipping new BIOS ICs, a BIOS or motherboard manufacturer can provide the updated BIOS code and "flash loader" utility as a downloadable file. The name of the file is typically coupled to only a particular motherboard. For example, updating the flash BIOS on an AMI Atlas ISA/PCI Pentium motherboard requires a file named S721P.ROM. If this file name is not used, the BIOS will not be reprogrammed. The AMI Excalibur PCI-II ISA/PCI Pentium motherboard requires the file name S722P.ROM, and so on. When attempting a flash procedure, follow the points below:

- First, you *must* have a flash BIOS chip in the computer (see Table 7-7). If the chip does not use flash technology, you won't be able to reprogram it.
- Make a complete backup of your system hard drive(s) *first*—just in case there are drive problems with the new BIOS after the flash process is complete.
- Make a complete record of all CMOS setup settings before flashing the BIOS. Since the flash loader utility will often clear the CMOS RAM anyway, you'll need to restore or tweak the CMOS setup again after performing the flash upgrade. Pay particular attention to the hard drive geometry settings and other drive configurations.
- Record the current BIOS version number and/or release date, and verify that you do not already have this version running on your system. (It's pointless to try flashing your system with the same BIOS version.)
- When downloading the flash file (usually several BIOS data files, a flash loader utility, and brief documentation all compressed into a single ZIP file), be certain to download only the flash package for your exact PC make and model.

Downloading and flashing the incorrect BIOS upgrade can render your computer unbootable, forcing you to restore the original BIOS or replace the physical BIOS IC.

- Create a clean bootable floppy disk with any version of DOS, or as a Windows 95/98 startup disk.
- Copy the downloaded ZIP file containing your flash package to the floppy disk, and decompress the ZIP file into its constituent files (usually an EXE file as the flashing utility, a BIN or ROM file as the new BIOS data file, and one or more TXT files as the documentation).

Never attempt to flash a BIOS by running the flash utility from a hard drive. Proceed from the floppy drive only.

- You may need to set the "Flash Enable" jumper on your particular motherboard. If so, turn off the PC, locate this jumper (refer to the documentation for your system), and set it to the "program" position.
- Reboot the PC and start your CMOS setup to verify that the PC will boot from the floppy drive first. This is usually indicated as a "Boot Order" or "Boot Sequence" of A:/C:.
- Once the PC boots clean from the bootable disk, start the flash loader utility with a command such as

```
A:\> awdflash
```

- When the flash loader program starts, it may ask you for the name of the BIN or ROM file you wish to use as an upgrade. Type the exact name of this file when prompted to do so. In some cases, the flash utility will automatically use the only available source file.
- Many flash loader utilities will ask you to back up your current BIOS. If you have this opportunity, please do make a backup copy of the current BIOS before proceeding. Enter the file name to save, and proceed. In some cases, the flash loader program will assign a backup file name automatically (for example, BACKUP.BIN).
- You will then be asked if you are sure you wish to continue. Answer yes.
- Once the flash process begins, you'll usually see a progress indicator at the bottom of the display that will keep track of the flashing process.

It is *critical* that you do not power-down or reset the PC while the flash process is proceeding. Doing so will interrupt the flash process and leave your BIOS corrupt and *unrecoverable*.

- When the progress indicator has stopped (or the flash process has otherwise concluded), you'll probably see a message such as "Please cycle power or reset this machine."
- Turn your computer completely off. Your new BIOS is installed and is ready to use.
- If you had to set a "Flash Enable" jumper on the motherboard, reset it now to the "protected" position before restoring power to the PC.
- Remove the bootable disk from the system.
- Restart the computer now. The new BIOS version will be shown on the display screen. You're done with the BIOS upgrade.
- In virtually all cases, you'll need to enter your CMOS setup immediately and restore your CMOS setup parameters (such as your drive types) before you can utilize the PC.

If there is an error at any point in the reprogramming process, you may hear one or more beeps. Table 7-8 outlines the beeps and descriptions for AMI flash BIOS. These are not beep codes as described in Chapter 19, but flash BIOS procedural errors. Keep in mind that the flash BIOS procedures outlined here may vary for your particular system.

THE KEYBOARD CONTROLLER

The keyboard controller is a remarkably important element of the PC. In addition to handling system interaction with the keyboard, it manages the A20 gate. It is the A20 gate that allows modern CPUs to operate in the protected mode and address memory above 1MB. Some keyboard controllers also serve to select CPU clock speed. Since the keyboard controller contains a small amount of onboard ROM, the controller may become outdated or suffer from software defects just like any other BIOS element. Keyboard controller problems often manifest themselves under early versions of Windows or OS/2. As a result, it

TABLE 7-8 AMI FLASH PROGRAMMING BEEP MESSAGES

BEEPS	MEANING
None	No error; successful completion
Continuous single beep	No floppy disk in drive A:
Five beeps	Needed ROM program not present on floppy disk
Seven beeps	Floppy read error
Six beeps	BIOS file size error
Eight beeps	The expected flash EEPROM is not present
Continuous two beeps	Problem erasing the flash EEPROM
Continuous three beeps	Problem programming the flash EEPROM
Continuous four beeps	BIOS is not able to reset the CPU

may be necessary to replace the keyboard controller IC along with BIOS ROM ICs, but this is no longer a common issue.

UPGRADING MODEM FIRMWARE

As PC communication pushes the limits of classical telephone system technologies, modem makers often release modems before new standards are finalized. When new standards finally emerge, users can often make use of enhanced speeds and modem capabilities by updating the modem's firmware. For example, many K56flex or X2 (both 56Kbps modems) can be updated to the ITU V.90 standard. You can use a technique similar to that used for your motherboard's BIOS to update your modem's firmware.

> Before you upgrade a modem, make sure your Internet Service Provider (ISP) has upgraded their servers to V.90. If your ISP has not upgraded their servers, do not upgrade your modem. If you upgrade before your ISP does, you will be limited to modem speeds of 33.6Kbps and below. If this happens, reflash your modem to the previous version.

Download the complete flash update kit for your exact modem model from the manufacturer's Web site. (You may need to check your modem's firmware version first.) For example, you'd update a Diamond Multimedia SupraExpress 56I SP modem with the V90_208X.EXE file. Open (unzip) the flash update kit and review the specific instructions according to your operating system. In most cases, you can update the modem's BIOS through Windows 95/98 without having to leave the Windows environment. You can use the following procedure to check your modem firmware through Windows 95/98:

1. Click Start, highlight Programs, select Accessories, and choose HyperTerminal. If you're using Windows 98, try Start, highlight Programs, select Accessories, choose Communications, and then select HyperTerminal.
2. Click the HYPERTRM icon.
3. When you're asked to enter a name, type **TEST** and click OK.
4. When you're asked for a phone number, type **1234**. (It doesn't matter what this number is.) Make sure the correct modem is selected in the "Connect using" box, and then click OK.
5. When the Connect screen appears, click Cancel.

6 Now at the terminal screen, type **ATZ** and press ENTER. You should see a response of "OK."

7 Type **ATi92** and press ENTER, and you will see an entry such as "SUPxxxx"—this would be your modem's model number.

8 Type **Ati3** and press ENTER. This should display the modem's firmware version.

9 Exit HyperTerminal. (It's OK to close the connection.)

UPDATING VIDEO FIRMWARE

Video systems are not typically updated, but it's not uncommon to find firmware updates in order to correct hardware incompatibilities or firmware bugs in the very newest generations of video and 3D accelerators. For example, the Diamond Multimedia Viper V550 can be updated with BIOS version 195CBIOS.EXE. You can use a technique similar to that used for your motherboard's BIOS to update your video card's firmware:

1. Make a bootable floppy.
2. Insert the blank floppy in the A: drive.
3. At the DOS command prompt, type **Format A: /S**.
4. Extract all files from the 195CBIOS.EXE file to your A: drive.
5. Reboot using the floppy disk. This will start the flash loader and begin the update process.
6. When the process is complete, remove the floppy disk and reboot the system.

UPGRADING DRIVE FIRMWARE

It's rather rare to update the firmware in a drive (such as a CD-ROM or hard drive), but there are times when a firmware update may be necessary to correct a firmware bug or tweak a drive's performance or features. For example, Western Digital has developed a firmware update to reduce the mechanical noise associated with Western Digital's "wear leveling" feature. This firmware update is applicable to **WD Caviar models AC11200, AC22000, AC22500, AC33200, AC34000, AC34300, and AC35100**. The firmware update will only reduce the noise associated with wear leveling and will not affect the performance of the wear leveling feature.

Download the firmware update file. (For example, download the WDOVRLY4.EXE utility for the WD update mentioned above.)

1. Copy the firmware update file to a bootable floppy disk.
2. Restart the system with the floppy disk in the drive, and run the utility from your A: prompt.
3. Once the firmware update software starts, it will detect which drives are available—and whether they need to be updated. Allow the utility to update any drives that require service.
4. Turn off your system after the upgrade is complete; then restart the system to allow the new firmware to take effect.

BOOT BLOCK RECOVERY

Not every BIOS upgrade goes as well as expected. You may flash the wrong version, power may be interrupted, or you may encounter problems with other drivers or TSRs running on the system. So what happens when there's a problem? Normally, a bad BIOS upgrade will leave your system unbootable, and this would require you to replace the BIOS chip outright. More recently, system BIOS has been designed with a *boot block* area that is protected from being overwritten during a flash process. If the flash process is interrupted, you can use the boot block to at least start the system. Once the system boots from the boot block, you can restore the original BIOS file, or try reloading the BIOS upgrade. The boot block recovery procedure for an Intel Classic R motherboard is described below.

Before recovering the boot block, you'll need a recovery disk for your BIOS. In most cases, a recovery disk is made before the flash process is started. If you do not have a recovery disk, you'll need to create one using an image file from the BIOS maker's Web site. For example, you can use the INTELRD.EXE file for the Classic R motherboard from **http://www.firmware.com/support/recovery**. If there is a working BIOS present, the system can also be booted from this disk to flash the BIOS on this disk into the flash chip.

1. Turn off and unplug the system.
2. Move the boot block jumper to the enable position. You may also need to set the flash chip's write-protect jumper.
3. Insert the recovery disk. If you did not create a recovery disk when you tried flashing the BIOS, check for a recovery "image file" from the BIOS maker.
4. Now turn the system on.
5. After a few seconds, the floppy drive's light will come on.
6. About 20 or 30 seconds later, the speaker will beep once to indicate that the flash process has started.
7. The disk access light will remain on, but there will be nothing on the display.
8. After another 45 to 60 seconds, the speaker will beep twice to indicate that the process has finished. (The disk drive light may remain on.)
9. Turn the system off and remove the disk.
10. Reset the system's boot block jumper (and the flash chip's write-protect jumper if necessary).
11. Turn the system on and enter the CMOS setup to restore the system's configuration.

If you encounter more than two beeps (for example, four long low beeps), there may be no disk in the drive (or the disk drive may not be installed properly). If any disk besides a valid recovery disk is used, no action will be taken.

BIOS Upgrade Troubleshooting

Ideally, a BIOS upgrade can be accomplished quickly and easily, and upgrades are rarely plagued by problems. However, BIOS upgrade problems can and do occur, and they can be quite serious under the right circumstances. This part of the chapter looks at a series of common BIOS upgrade symptoms and solutions.

SYMPTOM 7-109 **The flash loader utility refuses to run** This is a known problem with BIOS flash utilities that have been customized for particular motherboards. Chances are that the flash loader was designed to run on a different motherboard. For example, the MR BIOS ZIP file includes a flash loader that was specifically customized for certain Intel motherboards—the file name of that flash loader will resemble the BIOS image file name (with the .BIO extension)—but other generic motherboards will typically use ZIP files that contain either 29C010.EXE or 28F010.EXE (or both) flash loaders.

In most cases, the flash loader (whether it's custom or generic) attempts to qualify the flash ROM in your computer as a type that it's able to program. If not, an error message to that effect is displayed, and the flash loader aborts. When this happens, you should check that a "flash-protect" jumper is set correctly to permit flash operations. If your motherboard is set for flashing, but the flash loader utility refuses to run, chances are that you're trying to install a BIOS upgrade that is not intended for your specific motherboard. Verify that you've downloaded the correct BIOS update and flash loader utility. Do not attempt to "force" a flash update by using other flash loader utilities.

SYMPTOM 7-110 **You receive an "erase chip failure" when trying to run a flash loader** The flash BIOS chip must be erased *before* the new BIOS code can be programmed into the chip. The flash loader program is reporting that it cannot erase the flash chip, which may happen for several reasons.

The flash chip's voltage setting may be set to a different voltage than the chip requires. For example, most flash BIOS chips are 12 volts, but some manufacturers deliberately set the flash voltage setting on the motherboard to 5 volts. This acts like a "write protect" for the BIOS chip, which means you cannot reprogram the BIOS without *first* setting the voltage jumper back to 12 volts. (This also protects you from certain viruses, such as the CIH Virus, that would try to erase the BIOS and effectively "kill" your computer.) Consult your motherboard's manual for the location and settings of your "flash voltage" and "write-protect" jumpers.

In other cases, the motherboard's manufacturer may have installed a flash BIOS chip that the flash loader cannot erase. Verify that you've downloaded the correct flash loader and BIOS update file for your particular motherboard. You may need to download and use a different flash loader. If there is no alternate flash loader utility for your motherboard, it will be necessary to replace the BIOS chip outright.

SYMPTOM 7-111 **You receive a "flash chip not supported" error when trying to run a flash loader** The flash loader utility must first check the type of flash chip that is currently installed on the motherboard, then determine whether the flash loader can read and write to the flash chip safely. When you encounter this error, the flash loader is indicating that it does not recognize the type of flash chip currently installed on the motherboard. Verify that you've downloaded the correct flash loader and BIOS update file for your particular motherboard. You may need to download and use a different flash loader. If there is no alternate flash loader utility for your motherboard, it will be necessary to replace the BIOS chip outright.

SYMPTOM 7-112 **After installing a new BIOS, the system now asks for a password** Your BIOS stores the configuration data for your system in the CMOS RAM/real-time clock chip that is installed on the motherboard. The data values for the new BIOS (and the way that data is arranged) may differ from your original BIOS data configuration since new commands and features are added to newer versions of the BIOS. The first time you turn on the computer after installing the new BIOS, your new BIOS is reading the old data configuration and mistakenly thinks that a password is set.

To correct this problem, you must clear the old configuration data from your CMOS RAM chip. Some motherboards offer a "Clear CMOS" or "Clear Password" jumper located near the CMOS RAM/RTC chip. When this jumper is set and the system is booted, you can erase the CMOS data (or just the password, depending on which jumper is available to you). Turn off the PC and reset those jumpers to their original positions; then restart the system directly to the CMOS setup and reconfigure each of the system's setup values. (Or simply select the BIOS Defaults option to load a set of basic parameters into your CMOS setup.)

SYMPTOM 7-113 **After flashing the BIOS and reloading the system setup, the system refuses to recognize your drives** This is almost always due to unforeseen motherboard updates that the BIOS was not designed for. During the course of a production run, a motherboard manufacturer may make a design change that may be as simple as a wiring trace change, or as complex as changing the components used on the motherboard. For example, when the Super I/O chip of the motherboard has been changed, the BIOS can no longer initialize and "talk" to the IDE controllers—in effect, this cuts off your hard drives. In most cases, you'll need to contact the motherboard maker and determine whether a new BIOS chip is available to replace the existing BIOS chip.

SYMPTOM 7-114 **After installing a new BIOS, you cannot print under DOS or Windows** Chances are that the new BIOS has defaulted the printer port to "standard" mode (or SPP), which is inadequate for your particular printer. You'll need to enter the CMOS setup and change the parallel port mode setting to EPP or ECP, and verify that your LPT1 port is set to address 378h. Save your changes and reboot the system.

SYMPTOM 7-115 **You cannot flash a MR BIOS version on a Super Micro motherboard** Super Micro motherboards normally use a 28F001 flash chip, which contains a boot block loader. The boot block loader not only functions as a boot loader for BIOS recovery, but also contains the standard jump vector used during normal boot-up. In order to use MR BIOS on this type of motherboard, you must overwrite this boot block with MR BIOS boot code. However, the boot block portion of the flash chip is write protected and cannot be flashed. You can update the flash chip using the Super Micro flash loader because it only updates the non-boot-block portion of the flash chip. To update the motherboard to MR BIOS, you'll need to use the new flash loader from MR BIOS that is specifically designed to work around this boot block issue:

1. Run the MRSUPER2 flash loader.
2. Select the Backup option to create a backup copy of original BIOS code.
3. When your backup is complete, select the Update option and specify the correct MR BIOS flash update. Allow the update to proceed.
4. After updating, power-off the system and set jumper J37 to 2-3. This jumper should remain in this position even when updating the flash to future revisions of MR BIOS.

To restore your original Super Micro BIOS from a backup file after MR BIOS is installed:

1. Run the MRSUPER2 flash loader.
2. Select the Update option and specify the appropriate file name for the Super Micro backup BIOS file. Allow the update to proceed.
3. After updating, power-off the system and set jumper J37 to 1-2.

SYMPTOM 7-116 **The PC does not boot after upgrading the BIOS** This is a classic problem that frequently haunts technicians. When you've replaced the physical BIOS chip(s), double-check the chip(s) for proper orientation and installation. Make sure that all of the pins are inserted into the socket and that none of the DIP pins have been bent under the chip's body. If you're replacing "even and odd" BIOS chips, make sure you have not accidentally transposed the even and odd chip locations. If the problem persists, try replacing the original BIOS chips. If the original chips work, you may have defective or improper replacement chips.

If you've flashed the BIOS, chances are that your problem is a little stickier. You've either flashed the wrong BIOS version, or the flash process failed for some reason. In either case, there's nothing you can do except to replace the BIOS IC (you'll need to contact the system or motherboard manufacturer for a replacement) or restore the original BIOS from the boot block.

SYMPTOM 7-117 **You accidentally reset or power-down the PC during a BIOS flash, and now the PC won't start** The great weakness of flash BIOS is that it cannot be interrupted once the flash process is underway—otherwise, the BIOS will be left partially programmed and totally corrupted. Your only course of action here is to replace the BIOS IC outright (you'll need to contact the system or motherboard manufacturer for a replacement) or restore the original BIOS from the boot block.

SYMPTOM 7-118 **The BIOS upgrade proceeded properly, but now the system behaves erratically, or other errors appear** There are several potential causes here. Most of the time, you've either flashed the wrong BIOS version (probably for a system using an *almost* identical motherboard), or the BIOS became corrupted during the flash process. If you made a backup copy of the original BIOS file during the flash process, repeat the process and restore the original BIOS version. If the system works, you can verify that you downloaded the correct flash file (and repeat the upgrade if possible). If you cannot restore the original BIOS, or the problems persist, replace the BIOS chip. If the problem occurs when replacing physical chips, chances are that you've installed the BIOS for the wrong PC or motherboard, and you'll need to replace the original BIOS chip(s) until you get the proper replacements.

SYMPTOM 7-119 **The BIOS upgrade proceeded properly, but system performance seems poor** This is a frequent (but little-discussed) complaint with BIOS upgrades. In many cases, a new BIOS will require you to restore or tweak your CMOS setup for proper performance. If you recorded your original CMOS setup contents before attempting your upgrade, you can enter the CMOS setup and compare the current settings to the original ones. Chances are that one or more performance-oriented settings have been disabled. Here are some points for quick tweaking. (Remember that not all of these features may be available in all BIOS versions.) For fastest booting:

- Set the "Boot Sequence" to C:/A:.
- Set the "Boot Up Floppy Drive Seek" to DISABLED.
- Set the "Boot Up System Speed" to HIGH.
- Set the "Quick Power-on Self Test" to ENABLED.

For highest overall system performance:

- Enable all shadowing unless you are using an adapter that absolutely requires that shadowing be disabled for a specified address. Video shadow will increase the video speed.
- Set "Auto Configuration" to DISABLE.
- Reduce all of the memory timings to their minimum values.
- Enable the "Turbo Read Lead Off."
- Enable the "Speculative Lead Off."
- Enable the "Turn Around Insertion."
- Increase the ISA speed by setting ISA Clock to PCICLK/3.
- Lower 8- and 16-bit recovery times to 1 (one) each.
- Set the "System BIOS Cacheable" to ENABLE.
- Set the "Video BIOS Cacheable" to ENABLE.
- L2 Cache Cacheable Size—If you are installing 64MB of RAM or more, set to 512MB (64MB is the default).

- Pipeline Cache Timing—Set to FASTEST if there is only 256KB total pipeline cache (FASTER is the default).

> When tweaking BIOS settings in the CMOS setup, be sure to change only one parameter at a time; then retest the system's performance each time.

SYMPTOM 7-120 **You see a message such as "Update ESCD Successfully" on boot up** This is not really an error, but more of an informational message. The ESCD (extended system configuration data) is a method that the BIOS uses to store resource information for both PnP and non-PnP devices. The reason it shows this message is because the system has at least one ISA card in it, and it is running Windows 95/98. The ESCD boot-up sequence arranged by Windows 95/98 is different from the ESCD boot-up sequence arranged by the BIOS. So on boot-up, the system BIOS will attempt to update the ESCD. This will in no way affect system performance.

SYMPTOM 7-121 **You just upgraded the BIOS, and now you can't boot from the A: drive** Otherwise, the A: drive seems to be working normally. In virtually all cases, the updated BIOS defaulted the CMOS setup to a "Boot Sequence" of C:/A: instead of A:/C:, so the system isn't even checking the floppy drive at startup. Start your CMOS setup and tweak the "Boot Sequence" to A:/C:. Then save your changes and try the system again. Also verify that you actually have a working bootable floppy disk in the drive.

SYMPTOM 7-122 **You get a message that reads "Incompatible BIOS translation detected—unable to load disk overlay"** This typically happens when you upgrade a BIOS to support Logical Block Addressing (LBA), but the hard drive in your system is already using overlay software such as Disk Manager. Since overlay software and LBA are usually incompatible, you'll either need to disable LBA in the CMOS setup, or remove the overlay software from the hard drive. Since you probably upgraded the BIOS to support LBA anyway, chances are that you'll want to remove the overlay software:

1. Back up the hard drive before proceeding.
2. Boot the system from a bootable floppy disk.
3. Run FDISK and delete all partitions on the hard drive.
4. Reboot and check with FDISK to be sure that all the partitions on the drive have been removed.
5. You can repartition and reformat the drive, then restore your files from a backup.

If you cannot remove all partitions from the hard drive with FDISK, you can use the procedure below to erase the master boot record (MBR) on the hard drive. You'll need the DEBUG utility on your bootable disk before proceeding.

```
A:\> debug
F 200 L200 0
a 100
mov ax,301
mov bx,200
mov cx,1
```

```
mov dx,0080        ;Note: use 0081 for second fixed disk
int 13
int 3
(enter a blank line here)
G=100
q
```

The drive should now have no partitions on it. Reboot and use FDISK to partition the drive, and use FORMAT to reformat each partition. You can then restore the operating system and recover files from your backup.

Further Study

American Megatrends: **http://www.megatrends.com**

Award: **http://www.award.com**

Hardware IC newsgroup: **comp.sys.ibm.pc.hardware.chips**

IBM SurePath BIOS page: **http://www.surepath.ibm.com/**

Micro Firmware: **http://www.firmware.com**

Microid Research (Mr. BIOS): **http://www.mrbios.com/**

Phoenix Technologies: **http://www.phoenix.com/**

SystemSoft: **http://www.systemsoft.com**

Unicore: **http://www.unicore.com**

Wim's BIOS page: **http://www.ping.be/bios/bios.shtml**

Year 2000 reference: **http://www.year2000.com (or http://www.sbhs.com/y2k)**

8

BUSSES

CHAPTER AT A GLANCE

When it was first introduced, the IBM PC was no gem. It was a slow, clunky contraption with virtually no system resources (memory, interrupts, DMA channels, etc.). Yet, the IBM PC ushered in the personal computer era that we know today. Certainly, it was not speed or efficiency that brought IBM systems to the forefront of technology. Instead, it was a revolutionary (and rather risky) concept called *open architecture*. Rather than designing a computer and being the sole developer of proprietary add-on devices (as so many other computer manufacturers were at the time), IBM chose to incorporate only the essential processing elements on the motherboard, and leave many of the other functions to add-on devices (a.k.a. expansion boards) that could be plugged into standardized bus connectors. The use of so-called expansion busses made the PC extraordinarily versatile since a system could be configured according to the devices that were added. This chapter is intended to familiarize you with the six major bus types found in IBM-type PCs: ISA, EISA, MCA, VL, PCI, and AGP.

Industry Standard Architecture (ISA)

The venerable *Industry Standard Architecture* (ISA) shown in Figure 8-1 is the first open system bus architecture used for IBM-type personal computers. Any manufacturer was welcome to use the architecture for a small licensing fee. Since there were no restrictions placed on the use of ISA busses (also referred to simply as "PC busses"), they were duplicated in every IBM-compatible clone that followed. Not only did the use of a standardized bus pave the way for thousands of manufacturers to produce compatible PCs and expansion devices, but it also helped to support the use of standardized operating systems and applications software. Both an 8-bit and 16-bit version of the ISA bus are available, although all motherboards manufactured since the mid-1980s have abandoned the 8-bit XT version in favor of the faster, more flexible 16-bit AT version.

8-BIT ISA

Use of the 8-bit XT bus started in 1982. The 8-bit ISA bus consists of a single card edge connector with 62 contacts. The bus provides 8 data lines and 20 address lines, which allow the board to reside within the XT's 1MB of conventional memory. The bus also supports connections for 6 interrupts (IRQ2–IRQ7) and 3 DMA channels (DMA0–DMA2). The XT bus runs at the system speed of 4.77MHz. Although the bus itself is relatively simple, IBM failed to publish specific timing relationships for data, address, and control signals. This ambiguity left early manufacturers to find the proper timing relationships by trial and error.

Although each connector on the bus is supposed to work the same way, early PCs designed with eight expansion slots required any card inserted in the eighth slot (the slot closest to the power supply) to provide a special "card selected" signal on pin B8. Timing requirements for the eighth slot are also tighter. Contrary to popular belief, the eighth slot has nothing to do with the IBM expansion chassis. The demands of slot 8 were to support a keyboard/timer adapter board for IBM's special configuration called the 3270PC. Most XT clones did not adhere to this "eighth slot" peculiarity.

Knowing the XT Signals

Table 8-1 shows the pinout for both an XT and AT ISA bus configuration. The Oscillator pin provides the 14.3MHz system oscillator signal to the expansion bus, while the Clock pin supplies the 4.77MHz system clock signal. When the PC needs to be reset, the RESET DRV pin drives the whole system into a reset

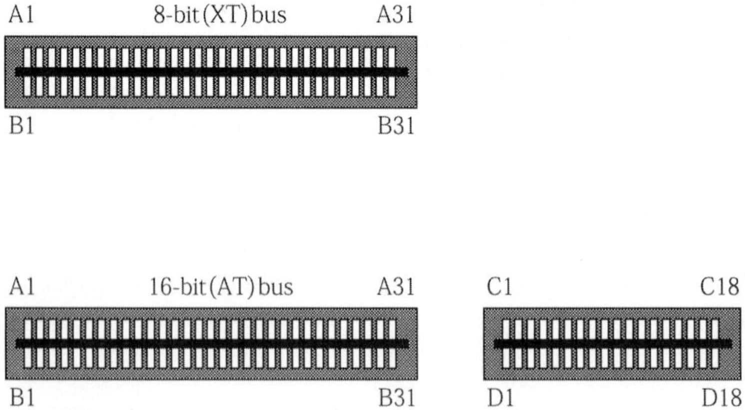

FIGURE 8-1 Diagram of 8-bit and 16-bit ISA slots

TABLE 8-1 ISA 8-BIT BUS PINOUT

SIGNAL	PIN	PIN	SIGNAL
Ground	B1	A1	I/O Channel Check
Reset	B2	A2	Data Bit 7
+5 Vdc	B3	A3	Data Bit 6
IRQ 2	B4	A4	Data Bit 5
-5 Vdc	B5	A5	Data Bit 4
DRQ 2	B6	A6	Data Bit 3
-12 Vdc	B7	A7	Data Bit 2
- Card Selected	B8	A8	Data Bit 1
+12 Vdc	B9	A9	Data Bit 0
Ground	B10	A10	I/O Channel Ready
- SMEMW	B11	A11	AEN
- SMEMR	B12	A12	Address Bit 19
- I/O W	B13	A13	Address Bit 18
- I/O R	B14	A14	Address Bit 17
- DACK 3	B15	A15	Address Bit 16
DRQ 3	B16	A16	Address Bit 15
- DACK 1	B17	A17	Address Bit 14
DRQ 1	B18	A18	Address Bit 13
- REFRESH	B19	A19	Address Bit 12
Clock (4.77MHz)	B20	A20	Address Bit 11
IRQ 7	B21	A21	Address Bit 10
IRQ 6	B22	A22	Address Bit 9
IRQ 5	B23	A23	Address Bit 8
IRQ 4	B24	A24	Address Bit 7
IRQ 3	B25	A25	Address Bit 6
- DACK 2	B26	A26	Address Bit 5
T/C	B27	A27	Address Bit 4
BALE	B28	A28	Address Bit 3
+5 Vdc	B29	A29	Address Bit 2
Oscillator (14.3MHz)	B30	A30	Address Bit 1
Ground	B31	A31	Address Bit 0

state. The 20 address pins (0–19) connect an expansion board to the system's address bus; when address signals are valid, the Address Latch Enable (ALE) signal indicates that the address may now be decoded. The eight data lines (0–7) connect the board to the system's data bus.

Signal labels marked with a minus sign (-) such as "- REFRESH" indicate what's known as "active low logic," where the signal is "true" when the logic level is "low."

The -I/O Channel Check (-IOCHCK) line flags the motherboard when errors occur on the expansion board. Note that the minus sign (-) preceding the signal indicates that the signal uses active-low logic. The

I/O Channel Ready is active when an addressed expansion board is ready. If this pin is logic 0, the CPU will extend the bus cycle by inserting wait states. The six hardware interrupts (IRQ2 to IRQ7) are used by the expansion board to demand the CPU's attention. Interrupts 0 and 1 are not available to the bus since they handle the highest priorities of the timer chip and keyboard. The -I/O Read (-I/O R) and -I/O Write (-I/O W) lines indicate that the CPU or DMA controller wants to transfer data to or from the data bus. The -Memory Read (-MEMR) and -Memory Write (-MEMW) signals tell the expansion board that the CPU or DMA controller is going to read or write data to main memory.

The XT bus supplies three DMA Requests (DRQ1 to DRQ3) so that an expansion board can transfer data to or from memory. DMA requests must be held until the corresponding -DMA Acknowledge (-DACK1 to -DACK3) signals become true. If the Address Enable (AEN) signal is true, the DMA controller is controlling the bus for a data transfer. Finally, the Terminal Count (T/C) signal provides a pulse when the DMA transfer is completed.

16-BIT ISA

The limitations of the 8-bit ISA bus were soon obvious. With a floppy drive and hard drive taking up two of the six available interrupts, COM3 and COM4 taking up another two interrupts (IRQ3 and IRQ4), and an LPT port taking up IRQ7, competition for the remaining interrupt was fierce. Of the three DMA channels available, the floppy and hard drives take two, so only one DMA channel remains available. Only 1MB of address space is addressable, and 8 data bits form a serious bottleneck for data transfers. It would have been a simple matter to start from scratch and design an entirely new bus, but that would have rendered the entire installed base of XT systems obsolete.

The next logical step in bus evolution came in 1984/85 with the introduction of the 80286 in IBM's PC/AT. System resources were added to the bus while still allowing XT boards to function in the expanded bus. The result became what we know today as the 16-bit AT bus. Instead of a different bus connector, the original 62-pin connector was left intact, and an extra 36-pin connector was added, designated "C" and "D," as shown in Table 8-2. An extra 8 data bits are added to bring the total data bus to 16 bits. Five interrupts and four DMA channels are included. Four more address lines are also provided, in addition to several more control signals. Clock speed is increased on the AT bus to 8.33MHz. It is important to note that although XT boards should *theoretically* work with an AT bus, not all older XT expansion boards will work on the AT bus.

TABLE 8-2 ISA 16-BIT (AT) BUS PINOUT

SIGNAL	PIN	PIN	SIGNAL
Ground	B1	A1	- I/O Channel Check
Reset	B2	A2	Data Bit 7
+5 Vdc	B3	A3	Data Bit 6
IRQ 9	B4	A4	Data Bit 5
-5 Vdc	B5	A5	Data Bit 4
DRQ 2	B6	A6	Data Bit 3
-12 Vdc	B7	A7	Data Bit 2
- 0 WAIT	B8	A8	Data Bit 1
+12 Vdc	B9	A9	Data Bit 0
Ground	B10	A10	- I/O Channel Ready

TABLE 8-2 ISA 16-BIT (AT) BUS PINOUT *(CONTINUED)*

SIGNAL	PIN	PIN	SIGNAL
- SMEMW	B11	A11	AEN
- SMEMR	B12	A12	Address Bit 19
- I/O W	B13	A13	Address Bit 18
- I/O R	B14	A14	Address Bit 17
- DACK 3	B15	A15	Address Bit 16
DRQ 3	B16	A16	Address Bit 15
- DACK 1	B17	A17	Address Bit 14
DRQ 1	B18	A18	Address Bit 13
- REFRESH	B19	A19	Address Bit 12
Clock (8.33MHz)	B20	A20	Address Bit 11
IRQ 7	B21	A21	Address Bit 10
IRQ 6	B22	A22	Address Bit 9
IRQ 5	B23	A23	Address Bit 8
IRQ 4	B24	A24	Address Bit 7
IRQ 3	B25	A25	Address Bit 6
- DACK 2	B26	A26	Address Bit 5
T/C	B27	A27	Address Bit 4
BALE	B28	A28	Address Bit 3
+5 Vdc	B29	A29	Address Bit 2
Oscillator (14.3MHz)	B30	A30	Address Bit 1
Ground	B31	A31	Address Bit 0
Key	Key	Key	Key
- MEM CS16	D1	C1	
- I/O CS16	D2	C2	Address Bit 23
IRQ 10	D3	C3	Address Bit 22
IRQ 11	D4	C4	Address Bit 21
IRQ 12	D5	C5	Address Bit 20
IRQ 15	D6	C6	Address Bit 19
IRQ 14	D7	C7	Address Bit 18
- DACK 0	D8	C8	Address Bit 17
DRQ 0	D9	C9	- MEM R
- DACK 5	D10	C10	- MEM W
DRQ 5	D11	C11	Data Bit 8
- DACK 6	D12	C12	Data Bit 9
DRQ 6	D13	C13	Data Bit 10
- DACK 7	D14	C14	Data Bit 11
DRQ 7	D15	C15	Data Bit 12
+5 Vdc	D16	C16	Data Bit 13
- MASTER	D17	C17	Data Bit 14
Ground	D18	C18	Data Bit 15

Knowing the AT Signals

The -System Bus High Enable (-SBHE) is active when the upper 8 data bits are being used. If the upper 8 bits are not being used (there is an XT board in the AT slot), -SBHE will be inactive. If the expansion board requires 16-bit access to memory locations, it must return an active -MEM CS16 signal. If the expansion board requires 16-bit access to an I/O location, it must make the -I/O CS16 signal active. The -Memory Read (-MEMR) and -Memory Write (-MEMW) signals provided by an expansion board tell the CPU or DMA controller that memory access is needed up to 16MB. The -SMEMR and -SMEMW signals only indicate memory access for the first 1MB. The -MASTER signal can be used by expansion boards that are able to take control of the bus through use of a DMA channel. It is interesting to note that small, highly integrated AT systems are available for embedded systems and dedicated applications.

Potential Problems Mixing 8-Bit and 16-Bit ISA Boards

ISA 16-bit architecture was developed on the foundation of IBM's original 8-bit XT bus. By extending the original XT bus rather than redesigning an expansion bus from scratch, IBM was able to develop their AT so that it would accommodate new, more sophisticated 16-bit expansion boards while still being backward compatible with the installed base of 8-bit boards. For the most part, this strategy worked quite well—the ISA bus remains a prominent feature of today's PCs. However, there is a potential problem with the ISA bus when inserting 8-bit and 16-bit adapters that both use ROM residing in the same memory region. Such a problem generally results in trouble with the 8-bit board.

To understand how this problem arises, you should be familiar with the ISA bus pinout shown in Table 8-2. There is an initial 62-pin connector (A1 through A31 and B1 through B31), followed by the extended 36-pin connector (C1 through C18 and D1 through D18). Notice that Address Bits 17, 18, and 19 are repeated on pins C8, C7, and C6. When a 16-bit board is inserted in the system, those repeated address lines indicate that a memory access is about to occur somewhere within 128KB of the address signals on A17, A18, and A19. (The lower 17 address lines—A0 to A16—specify *exactly* where in that 128KB range the access will take place.) If a 16-bit expansion board has memory (such as a video BIOS ROM or hard drive controller ROM) within the 128KB range about to be accessed, it uses the -MEM CS16 or -I/O CS16 line to tell the system that its memory is ready for access in 16-bit transfers. If the system receives no response from either of these lines, data is transferred in 8-bit sections.

The problem here is that 8-bit boards may also have memory within that 128KB range, but since they cannot detect the three extra address lines, the board cannot respond to the system. If a 16-bit board tells the system to proceed with a 16-bit data transfer, but there is also an 8-bit board in that same address range, the 8-bit board will be forced to receive 16-bit data transfers. As you might expect, this is quite impossible for an 8-bit board, so the 8-bit board will appear to malfunction. Since most expansion boards reserve their ROM addresses for the 128KB block between 768KB and 896KB (C0000h to DBFFFh, sometimes called the *ROM Reserve*), this is where most problems reside.

It is important for you to understand that this problem does not refer to a hardware conflict. The ROM locations of the 8-bit and 16-bit boards can certainly *not* overlap at any point. As you might realize, however, it is possible to have several different ROMs contained within the same 128KB of system memory. If one such ROM is on a 16-bit board and one is on an 8-bit board, the 8-bit board will likely malfunction due to the way 16-bit boards handle ISA bus operation. Correcting such a problem is generally a matter of replacing the 8-bit board with a 16-bit version. It might also be possible to disable the 8-bit ROM using an onboard jumper, and then use the motherboard BIOS ROM instead.

Extended Industry Standard Architecture (EISA)

The *Extended ISA* (or EISA) bus (Figure 8-2) is a 32-bit bus developed in 1988/89 to address the continuing need for greater speed and performance from expansion peripherals caused by the use of 80386 and 80486 CPUs. It also did not make sense to leave the entire 32-bit bus market to IBM's MicroChannel Architecture (MCA) bus. Even though the bus works at 8.33MHz, the 32-bit data path doubles data throughput between a motherboard and expansion board. Unlike the MCA bus, however, EISA ensures backward compatibility with existing ISA peripherals and PC software. The EISA bus is designed to be fully compatible with ISA boards, as shown in the pinout of Table 8-3. The EISA bus switches automatically between 16-bit ISA and 32-bit EISA operation using a second row of card edge connectors and the -EX32 and -EX16 lines. Thus, EISA boards have access to all of the signals available to ISA boards, as well as the second row of EISA signals.

As with the MCA bus, EISA supports arbitration for bus mastering and automatic board configuration, which simplifies the installation of new boards. The EISA bus can access 15 interrupt levels and 7 DMA channels. To maintain backward compatibility with ISA expansion boards, however, there is no direct bus support for video or audio as there is with the MCA bus. Since the EISA bus clock runs at the same 8.33MHz rate as ISA, the potential data throughput of an EISA board is roughly twice that of ISA boards. EISA systems are used as network servers, workstations, and high-end PCs of the late 1980s/early 1990s. Although EISA systems have proliferated farther than MCA systems, EISA was typically regarded as the high-end standard of its day for systems such as network servers (never really filtering down to low-cost consumer systems).

Knowing the EISA Signals

The EISA bus uses 30 address lines (Addr. 2 to Addr. 31). The lower two address lines (A0 and A1) are decoded by the Byte Enable lines (-BE0 to -BE3). Data bits 0 to 15 are taken from the ISA portion of the bus, but the upper 16 data lines are provided by (Data 16 to Data 31). The Memory/ -I/O (M/ -I/O) signal determines whether a memory or I/O bus cycle is being performed, while the Write/ -Read (W/ -R) line defines whether the access is for reading or writing. When an EISA device is allowed to complete a bus cycle, the EISA Ready (EXRDY) line is used to insert wait states. When the motherboard is providing

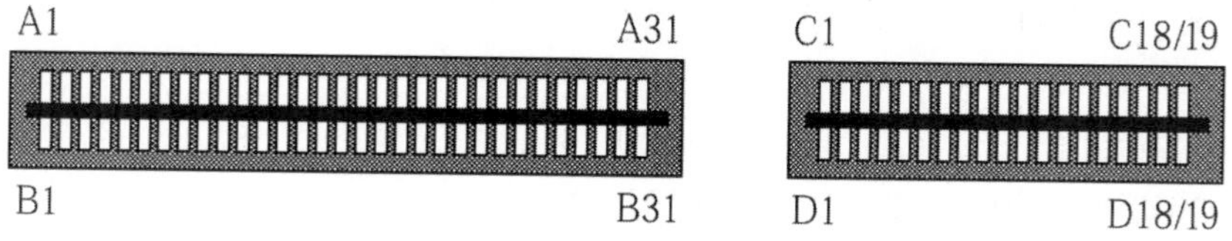

FIGURE 8-2 Diagram of a 32-bit EISA slot

TABLE 8-3 EISA 16/32-BIT BUS PINOUT

32 BIT	16 BIT	PIN	PIN	16 BIT	32 BIT
Ground	Ground	B1	A1	- I/O Channel Check	- CMD
+5 Vdc	Reset	B2	A2	Data Bit 7	- START
+5 Vdc	+5 Vdc	B3	A3	Data Bit 6	EXRDY
Reserved	IRQ 9	B4	A4	Data Bit 5	- EX32
Reserved	-5 Vdc	B5	A5	Data Bit 4	Ground
Key	DRQ 2	B6	A6	Data Bit 3	Key
Reserved	-12 Vdc	B7	A7	Data Bit 2	- EX16
Reserved	-0 WAIT	B8	A8	Data Bit 1	- SLBURST
+12 Vdc	+12 Vdc	B9	A9	Data Bit 0	- MSBURST
M -I/O	Ground	B10	A10	- I/O Channel Ready	W -R
- LOCK	- SMEMW	B11	A11	AEN	Ground
Reserved	- SMEMR	B12	A12	Address Bit 19	Reserved
Ground	- I/O W	B13	A13	Address Bit 18	Reserved
Reserved	- I/O R	B14	A14	Address Bit 17	Reserved
- BE3	- DACK 3	B15	A15	Address Bit 16	Ground
Key	DRQ 3	B16	A16	Address Bit 15	Key
- BE2	- DACK 1	B17	A17	Address Bit 14	- BE1
- BE0	DRQ 1	B18	A18	Address Bit 13	- Addr. 31
Ground	- REFRESH	B19	A19	Address Bit 12	Ground
+5 Vdc	Clock (8.33MHz)	B20	A20	Address Bit 11	- Addr. 30
- Addr. 29	IRQ 7	B21	A21	Address Bit 10	- Addr. 28
Ground	IRQ 6	B22	A22	Address Bit 9	- Addr. 27
- Addr. 26	IRQ 5	B23	A23	Address Bit 8	- Addr. 25
- Addr. 24	IRQ 4	B24	A24	Address Bit 7	Ground
Key	IRQ 3	B25	A25	Address Bit 6	Key
Addr. 16	- DACK 2	B26	A26	Address Bit 5	Addr. 15
Addr. 14	T/C	B27	A27	Address Bit 4	Addr. 13
+5 Vdc	BALE	B28	A28	Address Bit 3	Addr. 12
+5 Vdc	+5 Vdc	B29	A29	Address Bit 2	Addr. 11
Ground	Osc. (14.3MHz)	B30	A30	Address Bit 1	Ground
Addr. 10	Ground	B31	A31	Address Bit 0	Addr. 9
Key	Key	Key	Key	Key	Key
Addr. 8	- MEM CS16	D1	C1	- SBHE	Addr. 7
Addr. 6	- I/O CS16	D2	C2	Address Bit 23	Ground
Addr. 5	IRQ 10	D3	C3	Address Bit 22	Addr. 4
+5 Vdc	IRQ 11	D4	C4	Address Bit 21	Addr. 3
Addr. 2	IRQ 12	D5	C5	Address Bit 20	Ground
Key	IRQ 15	D6	C6	Address Bit 19	Key
Data 16	IRQ 14	D7	C7	Address Bit 18	Data 17
Data 18	- DACK 0	D8	C8	Address Bit 17	Data 19
Ground	DRQ 0	D9	C9	- MEM R	Data 20

TABLE 8-3 EISA 16/32-BIT BUS PINOUT *(CONTINUED)*

32 BIT	16 BIT	PIN	PIN	16 BIT	32 BIT
Data 21	- DACK 5	D10	C10	- MEM W	Data 22
Data 23	DRQ 5	D11	C11	Data Bit 8	Ground
Data 24	- DACK 6	D12	C12	Data Bit 9	Data 25
Ground	DRQ 6	D13	C13	Data Bit 10	Data 26
Data 27	- DACK 7	D14	C14	Data Bit 11	Data 28
Key	DRQ 7	D15	C15	Data Bit 12	Key
Data 29	+5 Vdc	D16	C16	Data Bit 13	Ground
+5 Vdc	- MASTER	D17	C17	Data Bit 14	Data 30
+5 Vdc	Ground	D18	C18	Data Bit 15	Data 31
- MAKx	-----	D19	C19	-----	- MREQx

exclusive access to an EISA board, the -Locked Cycle (-LOCK) signal is true. If an EISA board can run in 32-bit mode, the -EISA 32 bit Device (-EX32) signal is true, but if the board can only run in 16-bit mode, the -EISA 16 bit Device (-EX16) signal is true.

The -Master Burst (-MSBURST) signal is activated by the EISA bus master, which informs the EISA bus controller that a burst transfer cycle will commence, thus doubling the bus transfer rate. When an external device must send a data burst, it activates the -Slave Burst (-SLBURST) line. An external device requests control of the EISA bus using the -Master Request (-MREQ) line. If the bus arbitrator decides that the requester can control the bus, a -Master Acknowledge (-MACK) signal is sent to the requesting device. A -Command (-CMD) signal is sent to synchronize the EISA bus cycle with the system clock, while the -Start (-START) signal helps to coordinate the system clock with the beginning of an EISA bus cycle. Finally, the Bus Clock (BCLK) is provided at 8.33MHz.

Configuring an EISA System

There's an added wrinkle when working with EISA systems: each EISA slot must be configured through software. Whenever adding, removing, or upgrading an EISA device, you'll need to run an EISA Configuration Utility (or ECU) to configure each EISA slot. If you don't have an ECU handy, you may be able to download ECU v.3 from Micro Computer Systems at **http://www.mcsdallas.com/mcs/ecuv3.htm**.

MCA Bus Operations

With the introduction and widespread use of 32-bit microprocessors such as the Intel 80386 and 80486, the 16-bit ISA bus faced a serious data throughput bottleneck. Passing a 32-bit word across the expansion bus in two 16-bit halves presented a serious waste of valuable processing time. Not only was data and CPU speed an issue, but video and audio systems in PCs had also been improving—and demanding an increasing share of bus bandwidth. By early 1987, IBM concluded that it was time to lay the ISA bus to rest and unleash an entirely new bus structure, which it dubbed the *MicroChannel Architecture* (MCA). IBM incorporated the MCA bus into their PS/2 series of personal computers and also in their System/6000 workstations. This part of the chapter shows you the layout and operations of the MCA bus.

MICROCHANNEL ARCHITECTURE

All things considered, IBM's MicroChannel bus was a revolutionary—and superior—design. One of the most substantial advantages is a reduction in electrical noise due to a radical rearrangement of bus signals. Unlike the ISA or EISA bus (which had only a few ground lines), the MCA bus provides an electrical ground every fourth pin. Superior grounding and the corresponding reduction in electrical interference also meant that the MCA bus can operate at higher frequencies than XT or AT busses (10MHz as opposed to 8.33MHz for ISA/EISA). The MCA bus also offers extended performance in data and addressing. You already know that an MCA bus can work with up to 32 bits of data. However, the bus also has an increased number of address lines (32 instead of 24). This increases the amount of directly addressable memory from 16MB to 4GB.

The MCA bus also brings sound and video to the bus. A single analog audio channel is added to the 8-bit bus segment. The audio channel can handle voice and music and is intended to be almost as good as FM radio (roughly about 50Hz to 10kHz). Since the audio channel is available to all expansion devices, the signal can be exchanged and processed among each device independently. A VGA video extension is also provided with the MCA bus. This allows expansion video boards to be installed and work *in concert* with the VGA circuitry already existing on the MCA motherboard. An 8-bit video data bus and all necessary synchronization signals are available to an expansion board. Typically, only one video extension connector is included on an MCA motherboard.

Still more advances include such features as matched memory cycles, burst and streaming data modes, data multiplexing, and a first venture into bus mastering. A *matched memory cycle* is supported with a small expansion connector. When a device is capable of sustaining matched memory transfers, the typical memory transfer cycle of 250nS is increased 25 percent to only 187nS. The *burst* data transfer mode allows data to be transferred in blocks without the intervention of a CPU (unlike ordinary data transfers, which require multiple CPU cycles for each transfer). The *streaming* data transfer mode allows even faster transfers during bus-mastering operation. Using a *data multiplexing* technique, the MCA bus can accomplish 64-bit data transfers by multiplexing the upper 32 data bits on the 32 idle address lines. Finally, the MCA bus supports *bus mastering*—a technique that allows other devices besides the main CPU to take control of the system busses to accomplish their respective tasks (a technique that the PCI bus now depends on for peak performance).

Although MCA offers many tangible enhancements over the ISA bus, computer users refused to abandon their hardware and software investment in order to scramble for limited MCA-compatible peripherals to fill their needs. As a result, the MCA bus has never become the new standard that IBM hoped it would be. Though there are very few "true" PS/2 systems remaining in service, you may still encounter older PS/2s in many home and school environments.

MCA Layout

The layout for an MCA bus slot is shown in Figure 8-3. Note that there are up to three segments to the bus connector: an 8-bit portion, a 16-bit portion, and a 32-bit portion. There is also an auxiliary video extension connector that is usually available on only one slot. The first thing you should realize about the MCA bus is that it is physically much smaller than an ISA or EISA bus; as a result, it is totally incompatible with ISA or EISA expansion products.

The pinout for a 16-bit MCA slot is shown in Table 8-4. This is the primary type of MCA connector that combines video and audio signals in the expansion bus. The connection itself can be divided into three sections: the video section (pins xV00 to xV10), the 8-bit section (pins 1 to 45), and the 16-bit section (pins 48 to 58). Power, ground, and interrupt lines are easy to spot, but most other signals are new. The

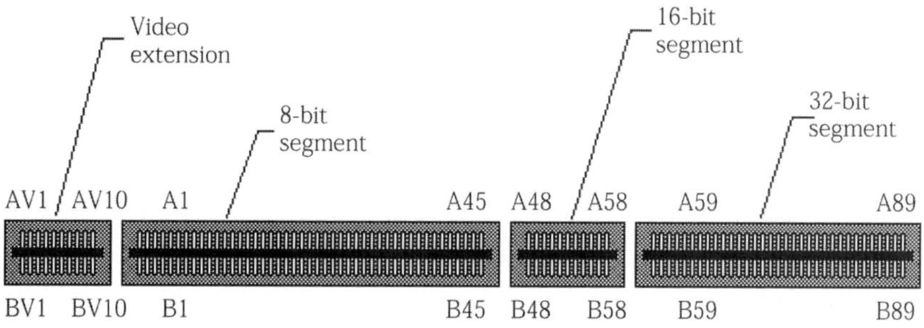

FIGURE 8-3 Various portions of an MCA bus

signal pinout for a 32-bit MCA slot is shown in Table 8-5. The 32-bit bus replaces the video section with a smaller matched memory control section (pins xM4 to xM1), but 8-bit and 16-bit sections remain the same. The 32-bit MCA slot also includes a 32-bit section (pins 59 to 89).

TABLE 8-4 MCA 16-BIT BUS PINOUT

SIGNAL	PIN	PIN	SIGNAL
ESYNC	BV10	AV10	VSYNC
Ground	BV9	AV9	HSYNC
P5	BV8	AV8	BLANK
P4	BV7	AV7	Ground
P3	BV6	AV6	P6
Ground	BV5	AV5	EDCLK
P2	BV4	AV4	DCLK
P1	BV3	AV3	Ground
P0	BV2	AV2	P7
Ground	BV1	AV1	EVIDEO
Key	Key	Key	Key
AUDIO Ground	B1	A1	- CD Setup
AUDIO	B2	A2	MADE 24
Ground	B3	A3	Ground
Oscillator (14.3MHz)	B4	A4	Address Bit 11
Ground	B5	A5	Address Bit 10
Address Bit 23	B6	A6	Address Bit 9
Address Bit 22	B7	A7	+5 Vdc
Address Bit 21	B8	A8	Address Bit 8
Ground	B9	A9	Address Bit 7
Address Bit 20	B10	A10	Address Bit 6
Address Bit 19	B11	A11	+5 Vdc
Address Bit 18	B12	A12	Address Bit 5
Ground	B13	A13	Address Bit 4

TABLE 8-4 MCA 16-BIT BUS PINOUT *(CONTINUED)*

SIGNAL	PIN	PIN	SIGNAL
Address Bit 17	B14	A14	Address Bit 3
Address Bit 16	B15	A15	+5 Vdc
Address Bit 15	B16	A16	Address Bit 2
Ground	B17	A17	Address Bit 1
Address Bit 14	B18	A18	Address Bit 0
Address Bit 13	B19	A19	+12 Vdc
Address Bit 12	B20	A20	- ADL
Ground	B21	A21	- PREEMPT
- IRQ 9	B22	A22	- BURST
- IRQ 3	B23	A23	-12 Vdc
- IRQ 4	B24	A24	ARB 00
Ground	B25	A25	ARB 01
- IRQ 5	B26	A26	ARB 02
- IRQ 6	B27	A27	-12 Vdc
- IRQ 7	B28	A28	ARB 03
Ground	B29	A29	ARB/ - GNT
Reserved	B30	A30	- TC
Reserved	B31	A31	+5 Vdc
- CHCK	B32	A32	- SO
Ground	B33	A33	- S1
- CMD	B34	A34	M/ -I/O
CHRDYRTN	B35	A35	+12 Vdc
- CD SFDBK	B36	A36	CD CHRDY
Ground	B37	A37	Data Bit 0
Data Bit 1	B38	A38	Data Bit 2
Data Bit 3	B39	A39	+5 Vdc
Data Bit 4	B40	A40	Data Bit 5
Ground	B41	A41	Data Bit 6
CHRESET	B42	A42	Data Bit 7
Reserved	B43	A43	Ground
Reserved	B44	A44	- DS 16 RTN
Ground	B45	A45	- REFRESH
Key	Key	Key	Key
Key	Key	Key	Key
Data Bit 8	B48	A48	+5 Vdc
Data Bit 9	B49	A49	Data Bit 10
Ground	B50	A50	Data Bit 11
Data Bit 12	B51	A51	Data Bit 13
Data Bit 14	B52	A52	+12 Vdc
Data Bit 15	B53	A53	Reserved

TABLE 8-4 MCA 16-BIT BUS PINOUT *(CONTINUED)*

SIGNAL	PIN	PIN	SIGNAL
Ground	B54	A54	- SBHE
- IRQ 10	B55	A55	- CD DS 16
- IRQ 11	B56	A56	+5 Vdc
- IRQ 12	B57	A57	- IRQ 14
Ground	B58	A58	- IRQ 15
Reserved	B59	A59	Reserved
Reserved	B60	A60	Reserved

TABLE 8-5 MCA 32-BIT BUS PINOUT

SIGNAL	PIN	PIN	SIGNAL
Ground	BM4	AM4	Reserved
Reserved	BM3	AM3	- MMC CMD
- MMCR	BM2	AM2	Ground
Reserved	BM1	AM1	- MMC
AUDIO Ground	B1	A1	-CD Setup
AUDIO	B2	A2	MADE 24
Ground	B3	A3	Ground
Oscillator (14.3MHz)	B4	A4	Address Bit 11
Ground	B5	A5	Address Bit 10
Address Bit 23	B6	A6	Address Bit 9
Address Bit 22	B7	A7	+5 Vdc
Address Bit 21	B8	A8	Address Bit 8
Ground	B9	A9	Address Bit 7
Address Bit 20	B10	A10	Address Bit 6
Address Bit 19	B11	A11	+5 Vdc
Address Bit 18	B12	A12	Address Bit 5
Ground	B13	A13	Address Bit 4
Address Bit 17	B14	A14	Address Bit 3
Address Bit 16	B15	A15	+5 Vdc
Address Bit 15	B16	A16	Address Bit 2
Ground	B17	A17	Address Bit 1
Address Bit 14	B18	A18	Address Bit 0
Address Bit 13	B19	A19	+12 Vdc
Address Bit 12	B20	A20	- ADL
Ground	B21	A21	- PREEMPT
- IRQ 9	B22	A22	- BURST
- IRQ 3	B23	A23	-12 Vdc
- IRQ 4	B24	A24	ARB 00
Ground	B25	A25	ARB 01

TABLE 8-5 MCA 32-BIT BUS PINOUT *(CONTINUED)*

SIGNAL	PIN	PIN	SIGNAL
- IRQ 5	B26	A26	ARB 02
- IRQ 6	B27	A27	-12 Vdc
- IRQ 7	B28	A28	ARB 03
Ground	B29	A29	ARB/ - GNT
Reserved	B30	A30	- TC
Reserved	B31	A31	+5 Vdc
- CHCK	B32	A32	- SO
Ground	B33	A33	- S1
- CMD	B34	A34	M/ - I/O
CHRDYRTN	B35	A35	+12 Vdc
- CD SFDBK	B36	A36	CD CHRDY
Ground	B37	A37	Data Bit 0
Data Bit 1	B38	A38	Data Bit 2
Data Bit 3	B39	A39	+5 Vdc
Data Bit 4	B40	A40	Data Bit 5
Ground	B41	A41	Data Bit 6
CHRESET	B42	A42	Data Bit 7
Reserved	B43	A43	Ground
Reserved	B44	A44	- DS 16 RTN
Ground	B45	A45	- REFRESH
Key	Key	Key	Key
Key	Key	Key	Key
Data Bit 8	B48	A48	+5 Vdc
Data Bit 9	B49	A49	Data Bit 10
Ground	B50	A50	Data Bit 11
Data Bit 12	B51	A51	Data Bit 13
Data Bit 14	B52	A52	+12 Vdc
Data Bit 15	B53	A53	Reserved
Ground	B54	A54	- SBHE
- IRQ 10	B55	A55	- CD DS 16
- IRQ 11	B56	A56	+5 Vdc
- IRQ 12	B57	A57	- IRQ 14
Ground	B58	A58	- IRQ 15
Reserved	B59	A59	Reserved
Reserved	B60	A60	Reserved
Reserved	B61	A61	Ground
Reserved	B62	A62	Reserved
Ground	B63	A63	Reserved
Data Bit 16	B64	A64	Reserved
Data Bit 17	B65	A65	+12 Vdc

TABLE 8-5 MCA 32-BIT BUS PINOUT *(CONTINUED)*

SIGNAL	PIN	PIN	SIGNAL
Data Bit 18	B66	A66	Data Bit 19
Ground	B67	A67	Data Bit 20
Data Bit 22	B68	A68	Data Bit 21
Data Bit 23	B69	A69	+5 Vdc
Reserved	B70	A70	Data Bit 24
Ground	B71	A71	Data Bit 25
Data Bit 27	B72	A72	Data Bit 26
Data Bit 28	B73	A73	+5 Vdc
Data Bit 29	B74	A74	Data Bit 30
Ground	B75	A75	Data Bit 31
- BE 0	B76	A76	Reserved
- BE 1	B77	A77	+12 Vdc
- BE 2	B78	A78	- BE 3
Ground	B79	A79	- DC 32 RTN
TR 32	B80	A80	- CD DS 32
Address Bit 24	B81	A81	+5 Vdc
Address Bit 25	B82	A82	Address Bit 26
Ground	B83	A83	Address Bit 27
Address Bit 29	B84	A84	Address Bit 28
Address Bit 30	B85	A85	+5 Vdc
Address Bit 31	B86	A86	Reserved
Ground	B87	A87	Reserved
Reserved	B88	A88	Reserved
Reserved	B89	A89	Ground

8

Knowing the MCA Signals

Enable Synchronization (ESYNC) controls VGA signals (VSYNC, HSYNC, and BLANK) on the motherboard. When ESYNC is true, the Vertical Synchronization (VSYNC) pulses and Horizontal Synchronization (HSYNC) and Blanking (BLANK) signals control the display. An independent 8-bit video data bus (P0 to P7) supports 256 colors on the VGA display. VGA timing signals are controlled by the Enable Data Clock (EDCLK) and Data Clock (DCLK) signals. The Enable Video (EVIDEO) signal switches control of the palette bus, allowing an external video adapter to provide signals on P0 to P7. Audio (AUDIO) and Audio Signal Ground (Audio GROUND) allow the expansion board to send tone signals to the motherboard speaker.

There are 32 address bits (Address Bit 0 to Address Bit 31), 11 interrupts, and 32 data bits (Data Bit 0 to Data Bit 31). The -Address Latch (-ADL) signal is true when a valid address exists on the address lines. A -Channel Check (-CHCK) signal flags the motherboard when an error is detected on the expansion board. When data on the data bus is valid, the -Command (-CMD) is true. The Channel Ready Return (CHRDYRTN) signal is sent to the motherboard when the addressed expansion board I/O channel is ready. A Channel Reset (CHRESET) signal can be used to reset all expansion boards. The -Card Setup

(-CDSETUP) instructs an addressed board to perform a setup. The Memory Address Enable 24 (MADE24) line activates address line 24. The Channel Ready (CHRDY) line ensures that the addressed board is idle after completing its access. When -Burst (-BURST) is true, the system bus will execute a burst cycle.

The -Data Size 16 Return (-DS16RTN) and -Data Size 32 Return (-DS32RTN) tell the motherboard whether the board is running at a 16- or 32-bit bus width. The System Byte High Enable (SBHE) signal is true when the upper 16 data bits are being used, but the Card Data Size 16 (CDDS16) signal is true when only 16 data bits are being used. If all 32 bits of data are being transferred, the -Card Data Size 32 (-CDDS32) signal is true. When the main memory is being refreshed, the -Refresh (-REF) line is true. This allows any dynamic memory on expansion boards to be refreshed as well. The Memory/ -I/O (M/ -I/O) signal defines whether the expansion board is accessing a memory or I/O location. Signals -S0 and -S1 carry the status of a MicroChannel bus.

The -Preempt (-PREEMPT) signal is true when a bus arbitration cycle begins. The Arbitration signals ARB00 to ARB03 indicate (in BCD) which of the 16 possible bus masters has won arbitration. The Arbitration/ -Grant (ARB/ -GNT) is high when the bus is in arbitration and low when bus control has been granted. When a DMA transfer has finished, the Terminal Count (TC) signal is true. -Byte Enable signals 0 to 3 (-BE0 to -BE3) indicate which 4 bytes of a 32-bit data bus are transferring data. When an external bus master is a 32-bit device, the Translate 32 (TR32) line is true. The -MMCR, -MMCCMD, and -MMC lines are matched memory control signals.

PS/2 REFERENCE AND DIAGNOSTIC DISKS

MicroChannel (a.k.a. PS/2) computers require the use of a *reference* (or startup) *disk* whenever configuring the system or exchanging MCA cards in their bus slots. Each time you add, remove, or exchange an MCA card, you'll need to run the reference disk in order to configure the system properly. However, reference disks are often among the first items to be misplaced as a PC is sold or passed from owner to owner. When servicing a PS/2 system, you may easily find yourself without a reference disk. Fortunately, the reference disks for many PS/2 systems (along with a variety of diagnostic disks) can be downloaded from the IBM FTP site. Table 8-6 highlights the most popular FTP download addresses. Download the file to an empty directory on the hard drive, and then decompress the file. This will usually result in several individual files, with specific instructions for creating a reference/startup disk.

> For files with a .TG0 extension, you will also need to download Teleget—a utility that will extract TG0 files: **ftp://ftp.pc.ibm.com/pub/pccbbs/os2_fixes/tgsfx.com**.

Clearing a 55sx Password

For PS/2 55sx systems, a password will prevent the reference disk from running. You'll need to clear the CMOS RAM (including the password). Ordinarily, you can remove the CMOS backup battery and allow the memory to clear. But for 55sx systems, you can use the speaker cable to clear the CMOS RAM:

1. Turn off your system.
2. Unplug the speaker cable from the riser card and plug it in upside down.
3. Turn it back on, wait for memory to count, and listen for the beep.
4. Turn the system off, and plug the speaker cable right side up again.
5. The password will be cleared when you power-up the system again.

TABLE 8-6 FTP ADDRESSES FOR PS/2 REFERENCE AND DIAGNOSTIC DISKS

MODEL	ADDRESS
PS/2 25	ftp://ftp.pc.ibm.com/pub/pccbbs/refdisks/25start.tg0
PS/2 25 - 286	ftp://ftp.pc.ibm.com/pub/pccbbs/refdisks/rs25286a.tg0
PS/2 30	ftp://ftp.pc.ibm.com/pub/pccbbs/refdisks/30start.exe
PS/2 30 - 286	ftp://ftp.pc.ibm.com/pub/pccbbs/refdisks/mod30286.exe
PS/2 35/40	ftp://ftp.pc.ibm.com/pub/pccbbs/refdisks/3540st.exe
PS/2 50/50z/60	ftp://ftp.pc.ibm.com/pub/pccbbs/refdisks/rf5060a.exe
PS/2 53	ftp://ftp.pc.ibm.com/pub/pccbbs/refdisks/rf9553a.exe (reference disk)
PS/2 53	ftp://ftp.pc.ibm.com/pub/pccbbs/refdisks/rd9553a.exe (diagnostic disk)
PS/2 55sx/65sx	ftp://ftp.pc.ibm.com/pub/pccbbs/refdisks/rf5565a.exe
PS/2 56/57 - 386	ftp://ftp.pc.ibm.com/pub/pccbbs/refdisks/rf855657.exe
PS/2 56/57 - 486	ftp://ftp.pc.ibm.com/pub/pccbbs/refdisks/rf955657.exe
PS/2 P70 (portable)	ftp://ftp.pc.ibm.com/pub/pccbbs/refdisks/rfp70a.exe
PS/2 70/80	ftp://ftp.pc.ibm.com/pub/pccbbs/refdisks/rf7080a.exe
PS/2 P75 (portable)	ftp://ftp.pc.ibm.com/pub/pccbbs/refdisks/rfp75a.exe
PS/2 76/77	ftp://ftp.pc.ibm.com/pub/pccbbs/refdisks/rf7677a.exe (reference disk)
PS/2 76/77	ftp://ftp.pc.ibm.com/pub/pccbbs/refdisks/rd7677a.exe (diagnostic disk)
PS/2 76/77 (I or S)	ftp://ftp.pc.ibm.com/pub/pccbbs/refdisks/7677ref.exe (reference disk)
PS/2 76/77 (I or S)	ftp://ftp.pc.ibm.com/pub/pccbbs/refdisks/7677diag.exe (diagnostic disk)
PS/2 85 (9585)	ftp://ftp.pc.ibm.com/pub/pccbbs/pc_servers/9585rf.exe (reference disk)
PS/2 85 (9585)	ftp://ftp.pc.ibm.com/pub/pccbbs/pc_servers/9585rd.exe (diagnostic disk)
PS/2 90/95 (type 1)	ftp://ftp.pc.ibm.com/pub/pccbbs/pc_servers/rf90951a.exe
PS/2 90/95 (type 2)	ftp://ftp.pc.ibm.com/pub/pccbbs/pc_servers/rf90952a.exe
PS/2 90/95 (type 3)	ftp://ftp.pc.ibm.com/pub/pccbbs/pc_servers/rf90953a.exe
PS/2 90/95 (type 4)	ftp://ftp.pc.ibm.com/pub/pccbbs/pc_servers/rf90954a.exe
PS/2 90/95 (all)	ftp://ftp.pc.ibm.com/pub/pccbbs/pc_servers/rd9095a.exe (diagnostic disk)

Dealing with PS/2 "165" Errors (ADF Files)

When running the PS/2 reference disk, you'll need to have an ADF file for each MCA board in the system. If you encounter a "165" error when running autoconfigure with the reference disk, chances are that the ADF file for one or more MCA devices in the system is missing from the reference disk. Check with the driver software that came with the particular MCA card. (Its floppy disk may contain the needed ADF file.)

If you have IBM-brand MCA cards in the system, you can obtain current ADFs (Adapter Description Files) directly from IBM. Download the ALLFILES.TXT file from **ftp://ftp.pc.ibm.com/pub/pccbbs/allfiles.txt** and locate the ADF file for your particular device(s). You can then navigate the FTP site and obtain the ADF file (usually somewhere under **ftp://ftp.pc.ibm.com/pub/pccbbs/**).

If you're using third-party MicroChannel cards, you'll need to contact each particular manufacturer and download the current ADF file from their technical support areas or FTP sites. One very good source for ADF files for older, non-IBM MicroChannel cards is at NCR's Web site (**http://www3.ncr.com/support/pc/pcdesc/library/adfs.shtml**). You should also check Peter H. Wendt's Web site (**http://members.aol.com/mcapage0/mcaindex.htm**) for free software that will identify MicroChannel controllers and give you the ADF file name. The site also has a large library of ADF files for download.

VL Bus Operations

The demands of data transfer across the expansion bus have continued to evolve faster than the throughput of classical ISA/EISA bus architectures allow. The volumes of data required by graphical user interfaces (such as Microsoft's Windows) presented serious challenges to conventional video adapter and memory design of the late 1980s and early 1990s. Early in 1992, the Video Electronics Standards Association (VESA) proposed a new local bus standard called the *VESA Local* bus (or VL bus—also dubbed the *Video Local* bus) intended to improve the performance of graphics and video subsystems. In general terms, a *local bus* is a pathway that allows peripherals to access the system's main memory quickly. For the VL bus, such improved access means higher data throughput and performance for video information approaching the bus speed of the CPU itself. By using a stand-alone bus for video, ISA or EISA busses can be implemented for backward system compatibility—that is, users could upgrade to a VL-capable motherboard and VL bus graphics card, but all other peripherals and software remain compatible.

VL BUS CONFIGURATION AND SIGNALS

Of course, the path to a standard local bus was not an easy one. In 1991 and 1992, a few chipset suppliers and manufacturers implemented nonstandard high-performance I/O busses. For example, some OPTi chipsets were designed to support an *OPTi local* bus. Unfortunately, the OPTi local bus was supported by only a handful of manufacturers, and since the OPTi approach was specific to their chipsets, few (if any) I/O cards were ever actually developed for these busses, and few manufacturers provided them. Consequently, OPTi and other proprietary busses met the same fate as all other nonstandardized approaches in the PC industry—they disappeared. However, the failure of proprietary local bus designs did not prevent industry acceptance of a standard VL bus design developed by the Video Electronics Standards Association in late 1992. By placing the VL extension connectors in-line with standard ISA connectors, the VL board can also serve as an ISA board, but with far higher data throughput.

The essential advantage of a VL bus is direct access to the CPU's main busses. This allows a VL device to rapidly transfer the large quantities of data that are vital for high-performance video under Windows (and now Windows 95/98). Further, the VL bus operates at 386/486 motherboard bus speeds (25–33MHz) rather than a fixed 8.3MHz like the ISA bus. As a result, faster CPU speed will result in faster bus speed. Unfortunately, this is where the advantages end.

While virtually direct connection to the CPU may seem like a real asset, there are also some serious drawbacks that you should understand. Processor dependence ultimately became a distinct disadvantage for the VL bus. Since higher processor speed results in higher bus capacitance, VL signals can lose reliability at high CPU clock frequencies (above 33MHz or so). Further, the processor signals were intended to attach to only a few chips (like the RAM controller) and have very precise timing rules. In fact, each type of Intel i486 chip (486SX, 486DX, 486DX2, and 486DX4) has slightly different timing requirements. When additional loads are added by including multiple VL bus connectors and multiple local-bus chips, all sorts of undesirable things can happen. The two most likely problems are data glitches due to slowed processor bus signals and out-of-spec timing for different I/O cards with different loading characteristics.

> I mention i486-type CPUs in this section because the VL bus had largely fallen into disuse by the time Pentium processors arrived. You will only rarely (if ever) find a Pentium or later motherboard fitted with VL bus slots.

Although the VL specification does not list an upper frequency limit, the potential load problems discussed above dictate a practical limit. With a clock speed of 33MHz, a VL motherboard should be able to support two VL devices reliably. At 40MHz, only one VL device should be used. Above 40MHz, the chances of unreliable operation with even one VL device become substantial. If you find yourself working on a fast VL system with random system errors, see if the problem goes away when the VL device(s) are removed (and replaced with ISA equivalents if necessary).

Another problem is the lack of concurrency. For a PCI bus, the CPU can continue operating when a PCI device takes control of the system busses. VL architecture also allows for bus mastering operation, but when a VL device takes control of the bus, the CPU must be stopped. While this is technically not a defect, it clearly limits the performance of high-end devices (such as SCSI controllers) that might attempt to use a VL architecture. Finally, there are several other disadvantages to the VL bus. It is a +5 Vdc architecture (whereas PCI can support +3.3 Vdc). Unlike PCI, there is no autoconfiguration capability in the VL bus (jumpers and DIP switches are required), so plug-and-play operation is not supported. Today, the VL bus is considered obsolete, and it will be extremely difficult to locate VL-based replacement devices (such as motherboards, video cards, and controllers). When replacing a defective VL device, it may be necessary to upgrade the system to a PCI-based platform.

VL Bus Layout

The VL bus uses a 116-pin card edge connector with small contacts (similar in appearance to MicroChannel contacts), as shown in Figure 8-4. The most recent VL bus release (2.0) offers a 32-bit data path with a maximum data throughput of about 130MB/sec. The pinout for a VL bus is illustrated in Table 8-7. One of the most interesting things to note about the VL bus is that it is an extension to the standard ISA/EISA bus. The two right connectors are standard 16-bit ISA bus connectors. It is the two rightmost connectors that provide the VL compatibility. The long VL connector portion provides the 32-bit VL support. This is different from the PCI bus, which does not use any part of the ISA bus.

Knowing the VL Signals

The Data/ -Command (D/ -C) signal tells whether information on the bus is data or a command. Clock signals from the CPU are provided through the Local Bus Clock (LCLK) line. Memory/ -I/O (M/ -I/O) distinguishes between memory and I/O access, while the Write/ -Read (W/ -R) signal differentiates between read or write operations. The -Byte Enable lines (-BE0 to -BE7) indicate which 8-bit bytes of the data bus are being transferred. A -Reset signal (-RESET) will initialize the VL device. The -Ready Return (-RDYRTN) line indicates that the VL bus is free for access. Data bus width is determined by the -Local Bus Size 16 (-LBS16) signal.

Accessing the VL bus is a process of arbitration—much like the arbitration that takes place on an MCA or EISA bus. Each VL device is defined by its own ID number (ID0 to ID4). The -Local Bus Ready (-LRDY), -Local Bus Device (-LDEV), -Local Bus Request (-LREQ), and -Local Bus Grant (-LGNT) lines are used to negotiate for control of the VL bus. In most cases, there is only one VL device on the bus, but arbitration must be performed to ensure proper access to memory.

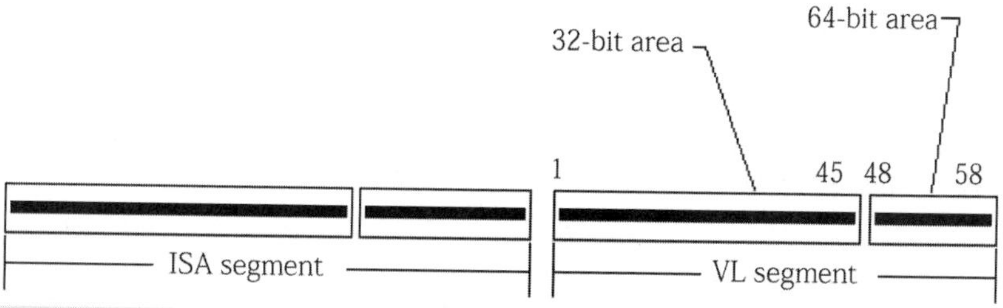

FIGURE 8-4 Simplified drawing of a VL card and bus

TABLE 8-7 VL BUS PINOUT (REV. 2.0)

PIN	DESCRIPTION	PIN	DESCRIPTION
A01	Data 00	B01	Data 01
A02	Data 02	B02	Data 03
A03	Data 04	B03	Ground
A04	Data 06	B04	Data 05
A05	Data 08	B05	Data 07
A06	Ground	B06	Data 09
A07	Data 10	B07	Data 11
A08	Data 12	B08	Data 13
A09	+Vcc	B09	Data 15
A10	Data 14	B10	Ground
A11	Data 16	B11	Data 17
A12	Data 18	B12	+Vcc
A13	Data 20	B13	Data 19
A14	Ground	B14	Data 21
A15	Data 22	B15	Data 23
A16	Data 24	B16	Data 25
A17	Data 26	B17	Ground
A18	Data 28	B18	Data 27
A19	Data 30	B19	Data 29
A20	+Vcc	B20	Data 31
A21	Address 31	B21	Address 30
A22	Ground	B22	Address 28
A23	Address 29	B23	Address 26
A24	Address 27	B24	Ground
A25	Address 25	B25	Address 24
A26	Address 23	B26	Address 22
A27	Address 21	B27	+Vcc
A28	Address 19	B28	Address 20
A29	Ground	B29	Address 18
A30	Address 17	B30	Address 16
A31	Address 15	B31	Address 14
A32	+Vcc	B32	Address 12
A33	Address 13	B33	Address 10
A34	Address 11	B34	Address 8
A35	Address 9	B35	Ground
A36	Address 7	B36	Address 6
A37	Address 5	B37	Address 4
A38	Ground	B38	-WBAK
A39	Address 3	B39	-BE 0
A40	Address 2	B40	+Vcc

TABLE 8-7 VL BUS PINOUT (REV. 2.0) *(CONTINUED)*

PIN	DESCRIPTION	PIN	DESCRIPTION
A41	n/c	B41	-BE 1
A42	-RESET	B42	-BE 2
A43	D/ -C	B43	Ground
A44	M/ -I/O	B44	-BE 3
A45	W/ -R	B45	-ADS
Key	Key	Key	Key
A48	-RDYRTN	B48	-LRDY
A49	Ground	B49	-LDEV
A50	IRQ 9	B50	-LREQ
A51	-BRDY	B51	Ground
A52	-BLAST	B52	-LGNT
A53	ID 0	B53	+Vcc
A54	ID 1	B54	ID 2
A55	Ground	B55	ID 3
A56	LCLK	B56	ID 4
A57	+Vcc	B57	n/c
A58	-LBS16	B58	-LEADS

8

VL-SPECIFIC ISSUES

Although the VL-bus is generally considered to be a sound (but dated) bus architecture, there are some perplexing issues that sometimes crop up on the workbench. The two major issues to contend with are bus speed and VL device types.

- *Bus speed* The VL bus is linked to the CPU clock speed. This was fine when CPUs ran at 33MHz or less, but the VL bus wasn't intended to support higher clock speeds. Clock speeds higher than 33MHz (often activated when a late-model i486 motherboard was upgraded with an OverDrive processor) could cause signal degradation, and the VL device(s) would malfunction. Whenever you encounter difficulty on a VL motherboard, always verify that the bus speed is 33MHz or less. Note that a single well-designed VL board can often run up to 40MHz (sometimes 50MHz on a precious few platforms), but this is extremely rare and should never be expected.
- *Multiple VL devices* The VL bus was originally intended as a single-slot architecture (primarily for high-performance graphic accelerators of the day). When designers expanded the role of VL and added more VL slots, the potential for signal degradation increased. More than two VL devices often cause problems on VL motherboards (especially at system clock speeds over 33MHz).

PCI Bus Operations

By the late 1980s, the proliferation of 32-bit CPUs and graphics-intensive operating systems made it painfully obvious that the 8.33MHz ISA bus was no longer satisfactory. The PC industry began to develop alternative architectures for improved performance. Two architectures emerged: VL and PCI. Although the VL bus seemed more straightforward, there were some serious limitations that had to be overcome. Perhaps most important is the VL bus dependence on CPU speed. Another problem is that the VL standard is voluntary, and not all manufacturers adhere to VESA specifications completely. In mid-1992, Intel and a comprehensive consortium of manufacturers introduced the *Peripheral Component Interconnect* (PCI) bus. Where the VL bus was designed specifically to enhance PC video systems, the 188-pin PCI bus looked to the future of CPUs (and PCs in general) by providing a bus architecture that also supports peripherals such as hard drive controllers, network adapters, and so on. This part of the chapter describes the layout and operations of the PCI bus.

PCI BUS CONFIGURATION AND SIGNALS

PCI is a 33MHz fixed-frequency bus architecture capable of transferring data at 132MB/sec—a great improvement over the 5MB/sec transfer rate of the standard ISA bus. Another key advantage of the PCI bus is that it has automatic configuration capabilities for switchless/jumperless peripherals. Autoconfiguration (the heart of plug-and-play) will take care of all addresses, interrupt requests, and DMA assignments used by a PCI peripheral. Table 8-8 lists the features of a PCI bus.

The PCI bus supports *linear bursts*, which is a method of transferring data that insures the bus is continually filled with data. The peripheral devices expect to receive data from the system main memory in a linear address order. This means that large amounts of data are read from or written to a single address, which is then incremented for the next byte in the stream. The linear burst is one of the unique aspects of the PCI bus since it will perform both burst reads and burst writes. In short, it will transfer data on the bus *every* clock cycle. This doubles the PCI throughput compared to busses without linear burst capabilities.

The devices designed to support PCI have low *access latency*, reducing the time required for a peripheral to be granted control of the bus after requesting access. For example, an Ethernet controller card connected to a LAN has large data files from the network coming into its buffer. Waiting for access to the bus, the Ethernet is unable to transfer the data to the CPU quickly enough to avoid a buffer overflow—forcing it to temporarily store the file's contents in extra RAM. Since PCI-compliant devices support faster access times, the Ethernet card can promptly send data to the CPU.

The PCI bus supports bus mastering, which allows one of a number of intelligent peripherals to take control of the bus in order to accelerate a high-throughput, high-priority task. PCI architecture also sup-

TABLE 8-8 FEATURES OF A PCI BUS ARCHITECTURE

PERFORMANCE FEATURES INCLUDE	PERFORMANCE FEATURES INCLUDE
Data bursting as normal operating mode—both read and write	Synchronous, 8–33MHz (132MB/sec) operation
Linear burst ordering	Variable length, linear bursting (both read and write)
Concurrency support (deadlock, buffering solutions)	Parity on address, data, command signals
Low latency guarantees for real-time devices	Concurrency/pipelining support
Access-oriented arbitration (not time slice)	Initialization hooks for auto-configuration
Supports multiple loads (PCI boards) at 33MHz	Arbitration supported
Error detection and reporting	64-bit extension transparently compatible with 32 bit
Multimaster and peer-to-peer communication	CMOS drivers, TTL voltage levels
32-bit multiplexed, processor independent	5-V and 3.3-V compatible

ports concurrency—a technique that ensures the microprocessor operates simultaneously with these masters, instead of waiting for them. As one example, concurrency allows the CPU to perform floating-point calculations on a spreadsheet while an Ethernet card and the LAN have control of the bus. Finally, PCI was developed as a dual-voltage architecture. Normally, the bus is a +5 Vdc system like other busses. However, the bus can also operate in a +3.3 Vdc (low-voltage) mode.

PCI Bus Layout

The layout for a PCI bus slot is shown in Figure 8-5. Note that there are two major segments to the +5 Vdc–version connector. A +3.3 Vdc–version connector adds a key in the 12/13 positions to prevent accidental insertion of a +5 Vdc PCI board into a +3.3 Vdc slot. Similarly, the +5 Vdc slot is keyed in the 50/51 position to prevent placing a +3.3 Vdc board into a +5 Vdc slot. The pinout for a PCI bus is shown in Table 8-9.

Knowing the PCI Signals

To reduce the number of pins needed in the PCI bus, data and address lines are multiplexed together (Adr./Dat 0 to Adr./Dat 63). It is also interesting to note that PCI is the first bus standard designed to support a low-voltage (+3.3 Vdc) logic implementation. On inspection, you will see that +5 Vdc and +3.3 Vdc implementations of the PCI bus place their physical key slots in different places so that the two implementations are *not* interchangeable. The Clock (CLOCK) signal provides timing for the PCI bus only and can be adjusted from DC (0Hz) to 33MHz. Asserting the -Reset (-RST) signal will reset all PCI devices. Since the 64-bit data path uses 8 bytes, the Command/ -Byte Enable signals (C/ -BE0 to C/ -BE7) define which bytes are transferred. Parity across the Address/Data and Byte Enable lines is represented with a Parity (PAR) or 64 Bit Parity (PAR64) signal. Bus mastering is initiated by the -Request (-REQ) line and granted after approval using the -Grant (-GNT) line.

When a valid PCI bus cycle is in progress, the -Frame (-FRAME) signal is true. If the PCI bus cycle is in its final phase, -Frame will be released. The -Target Ready (-TRDY) line is true when an addressed device is able to complete the data phase of its bus cycle. An -Initiator Ready (-IRDY) signal indicates that valid data is present on the bus (or the bus is ready to accept data). The -FRAME, -TARGET READY, and -INITIATOR READY signals are all used together. A -Stop (-STOP) signal is asserted by a target asking a master to halt the current data transfer. The ID Select (IDSEL) signal is used as a chip select signal during board configuration read and write cycles. The -Device Select (-DEVSEL) line is both an input and an output. As an input, -DEVSEL indicates whether a device has assumed control of the current bus transfer. As an output, -DEVSEL shows that a device has identified itself as the target for the current bus transfer.

There are four interrupt lines (-INTA to -INTD). When the full 64-bit data mode is being used, an expansion device will initiate a -64 Bit Bus Request (-REQ 64) and await a -64 Bit Bus Acknowledge (-ACK64) signal from the bus controller. The -Bus Lock (-LOCK) signal is an interface control used to ensure use of

8

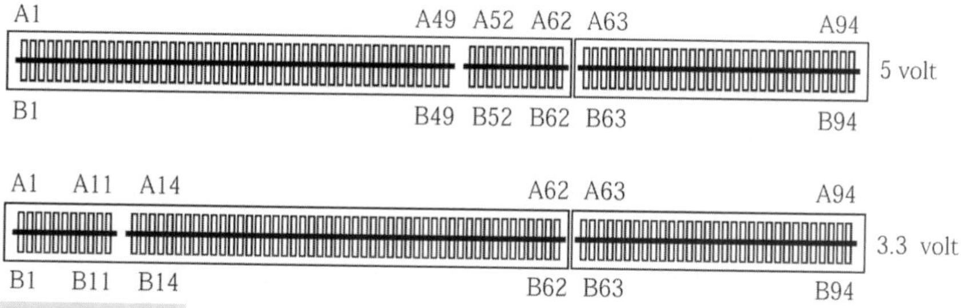

FIGURE 8-5 PCI local bus diagrams

TABLE 8-9 PCI BUS PINOUT—5 VOLT AND 3.3 VOLT (REV. 2.0)

5 VOLT	3.3 VOLT	PIN	PIN	3.3 VOLT	5 VOLT
-12 Vdc	-12 Vdc	B1	A1	- TRST	- TRST
TCK	TCK	B2	A2	+12 Vdc	+12 Vdc
Ground	Ground	B3	A3	TMS	TMS
TDO	TDO	B4	A4	TDI	TDI
+5 Vdc	+5 Vdc	B5	A5	+5 Vdc	+5 Vdc
+5 Vdc	+5 Vdc	B6	A6	- INTA	- INTA
- INTB	- INTB	B7	A7	- INTC	- INTC
- INTD	- INTD	B8	A8	+5 Vdc	+5 Vdc
- PRSNT1	- PRSNT1	B9	A9	Reserved	Reserved
Reserved	Reserved	B10	A10	+3.3 Vdc (I/O)	+5 Vdc
- PRSNT2	- PRSNT2	B11	A11	Reserved	Reserved
Ground	Key	B12	A12	Key	Ground
Ground	Key	B13	A13	Key	Ground
Reserved	Reserved	B14	A14	Reserved	Reserved
Ground	Ground	B15	A15	- RST	- RST
Clock	Clock	B16	A16	+3.3 Vdc	+5 Vdc
Ground	Ground	B17	A17	- GNT	- GNT
- REQ	- REQ	B18	A18	Ground	Ground
+5 Vdc	+3.3 Vdc	B19	A19	Reserved	Reserved
Adr/Dat 31	Adr/Dat 31	B20	A20	Adr/Dat 30	Adr/Dat 30
Adr/Dat 29	Adr/Dat 29	B21	A21	+3.3 Vdc	+5 Vdc
Ground	Ground	B22	A22	Adr/Dat 28	Adr/Dat 28
Adr/Dat 27	Adr/Dat 27	B23	A23	Adr/Dat 26	Adr/Dat 26
Adr/Dat 25	Adr/Dat 25	B24	A24	Ground	Ground
+5 Vdc	+3.3 Vdc	B25	A25	Adr/Dat 24	Adr/Dat 24
C/ - BE3	C/ - BE3	B26	A26	IDSEL	IDSEL
Adr/Dat 23	Adr/Dat 23	B27	A27	+3.3 Vdc	+5 Vdc
Ground	Ground	B28	A28	Adr/Dat 22	Adr/Dat 22
Adr/Dat 21	Adr/Dat 21	B29	A29	Adr/Dat 20	Adr/Dat 20
Adr/Dat 19	Adr/Dat 19	B30	A30	Ground	Ground
+5 Vdc	+3.3 Vdc	B31	A31	Adr/Dat 18	Adr/Dat 18
Adr/Dat 17	Adr/Dat 17	B32	A32	Adr/Dat 16	Adr/Dat 16
C/ - BE2	C/ - BE2	B33	A33	+3.3 Vdc	+5 Vdc
Ground	Ground	B34	A34	- FRAME	- FRAME
- IRDY	- IRDY	B35	A35	Ground	Ground
+5 Vdc	+3.3 Vdc	B36	A36	- TRDY	- TRDY
- DEVSEL	- DEVSEL	B37	A37	Ground	Ground
Ground	Ground	B38	A38	- STOP	- STOP
- LOCK	- LOCK	B39	A39	+3.3 Vdc	+5 Vdc
- PERR	- PERR	B40	A40	SDONE	SDONE

TABLE 8-9 PCI BUS PINOUT—5 VOLT AND 3.3 VOLT (REV. 2.0) *(CONTINUED)*

5 VOLT	3.3 VOLT	PIN	PIN	3.3 VOLT	5 VOLT
+5 Vdc	+3.3 Vdc	B41	A41	- SBO	- SBO
- SERR	- SERR	B42	A42	Ground	Ground
+5 Vdc	+3.3 Vdc	B43	A43	PAR	PAR
C/ - BE1	C/ - BE1	B44	A44	Adr/Dat 15	Adr/Dat 15
Adr/Dat 14	Adr/Dat 14	B45	A45	+3.3 Vdc	+5 Vdc
Ground	Ground	B46	A46	Adr/Dat 13	Adr/Dat 13
Adr/Dat 12	Adr/Dat 12	B47	A47	Adr/Dat 11	Adr/Dat 11
Adr/Dat 10	Adr/Dat 10	B48	A48	Ground	Ground
Ground	Ground	B49	A49	Adr/Dat 9	Adr/Dat 9
Key	Ground	B50	A50	Ground	Key
Key	Ground	B51	A51	Ground	Key
Adr/Dat 8	Adr/Dat 8	B52	A52	C/ - BE0	C/ - BE0
Adr/Dat 7	Adr/Dat 7	B53	A53	+3.3 Vdc	+5 Vdc
+5 Vdc	+3.3 Vdc	B54	A54	Adr/Dat 6	Adr/Dat 6
Adr/Dat 5	Adr/Dat 5	B55	A55	Adr/Dat 4	Adr/Dat 4
Adr/Dat 3	Adr/Dat 3	B56	A56	Ground	Ground
Ground	Ground	B57	A57	Adr/Dat 2	Adr/Dat 2
Adr/Dat 1	Adr/Dat 1	B58	A58	Adr/Dat 0	Adr/Dat 0
+5 Vdc	+3.3 Vdc	B59	A59	+3.3 Vdc	+5 Vdc
- ACK64	- ACK64	B60	A60	- REQ64	- REQ64
+5 Vdc	+5 Vdc	B61	A61	+5 Vdc	+5 Vdc
+5 Vdc	+5 Vdc	B62	A62	+5 Vdc	+5 Vdc
Key	Key	Key	Key	Key	Key
Key	Key	Key	Key	Key	Key
Reserved	Reserved	B63	A63	Ground	Ground
Ground	Ground	B64	A64	C/ - BE7	C/ - BE7
C/ - BE6	C/ - BE6	B65	A65	C/ - BE5	C/ - BE5
C/ - BE4	C/ - BE4	B66	A66	+3.3 Vdc	+5 Vdc
Ground	Ground	B67	A67	PAR64	PAR64
Adr/Dat 63	Adr/Dat 63	B68	A68	Adr/Dat 62	Adr/Dat 62
Adr/Dat 61	Adr/Dat 61	B69	A69	Ground	Ground
+5 Vdc	+3.3 Vdc	B70	A70	Adr/Dat 60	Adr/Dat 60
Adr/Dat 59	Adr/Dat 59	B71	A71	Adr/Dat 58	Adr/Dat 58
Adr/Dat 57	Adr/Dat 57	B72	A72	Ground	Ground
Ground	Ground	B73	A73	Adr/Dat 56	Adr/Dat 56
Adr/Dat 55	Adr/Dat 55	B74	A74	Adr/Dat 54	Adr/Dat 54
Adr/Dat 53	Adr/Dat 53	B75	A75	+3.3 Vdc	+5 Vdc
Ground	Ground	B76	A76	Adr/Dat 52	Adr/Dat 52
Adr/Dat 51	Adr/Dat 51	B77	A77	Adr/Dat 50	Adr/Dat 50
Adr/Dat 49	Adr/Dat 49	B78	A78	Ground	Ground

8

TABLE 8-9 PCI BUS PINOUT—5 VOLT AND 3.3 VOLT (REV. 2.0) *(CONTINUED)*

5 VOLT	3.3 VOLT	PIN	PIN	3.3 VOLT	5 VOLT
+5 Vdc	+3.3 Vdc	B79	A79	Adr/Dat 48	Adr/Dat 48
Adr/Dat 47	Adr/Dat 47	B80	A80	Adr/Dat 46	Adr/Dat 46
Adr/Dat 45	Adr/Dat 45	B81	A81	Ground	Ground
Ground	Ground	B82	A82	Adr/Dat 44	Adr/Dat 44
Adr/Dat 43	Adr/Dat 43	B83	A83	Adr/Dat 42	Adr/Dat 42
Adr/Dat 41	Adr/Dat 41	B84	A84	+3.3 Vdc	+5 Vdc
Ground	Ground	B85	A85	Adr/Dat 40	Adr/Dat 40
Adr/Dat 39	Adr/Dat 39	B86	A86	Adr/Dat 38	Adr/Dat 38
Adr/Dat 37	Adr/Dat 37	B87	A87	Ground	Ground
+5 Vdc	+3.3 Vdc	B88	A88	Adr/Dat 36	Adr/Dat 36
Adr/Dat 35	Adr/Dat 35	B89	A89	Adr/Dat 34	Adr/Dat 34
Adr/Dat 33	Adr/Dat 33	B90	A90	Ground	Ground
Ground	Ground	B91	A91	Adr/Dat 32	Adr/Dat 32
Reserved	Reserved	B92	A92	Reserved	Reserved
Reserved	Reserved	B93	A93	Ground	Ground
Ground	Ground	B94	A94	Reserved	Reserved

the bus by a selected expansion device. Error reporting is performed by -Primary Error (-PERR) and -Secondary Error (-SERR) lines. Cache memory and JTAG support are also provided on the PCI bus.

AGP Bus Operations

One of the remarkable advantages of the PC is its ability to "visualize" information. Whether you're graphing out your spreadsheet data for a corporate report, or slashing your way through the latest dungeon, the PC's video system continues to improve in color depth and resolutions. All of this video information requires a tremendous amount of data. Not only does this data require memory, but it also needs a lot of bandwidth to pass that data to the video card. The Accelerated Graphics Port (or AGP) opens a freeway for graphics information that is especially well suited for 3D applications.

For example, the fast floating-point performance of today's CPUs can smooth the drawing of 3D meshes and animation effects and add depth to a 3D scene. The next step is to add lifelike realism. To do this, the PC must render a 3D image by adding textures, alpha-blended transparencies, texture-mapping, lighting, and other effects. AGP technology accelerates graphics performance by providing a dedicated high-speed bus for the movement of large blocks of 3D texture data between the PC's graphics controller and system memory. In practice, AGP enables a hardware-accelerated graphics controller to execute texture maps directly from system RAM (instead of caching them in the relatively limited local video memory). It also helps speed the flow of decoded video from the CPU to the graphics controller. In addition, off-loading this tremendous data overhead from the PCI bus leaves PCI free to handle drive data transfers and other controllers.

High bandwidth is the key to AGP's power. The 66MHz AGP interface is positioned between the PC's chipset and graphics controller, as shown in Figure 8-6. This architecture significantly increases the

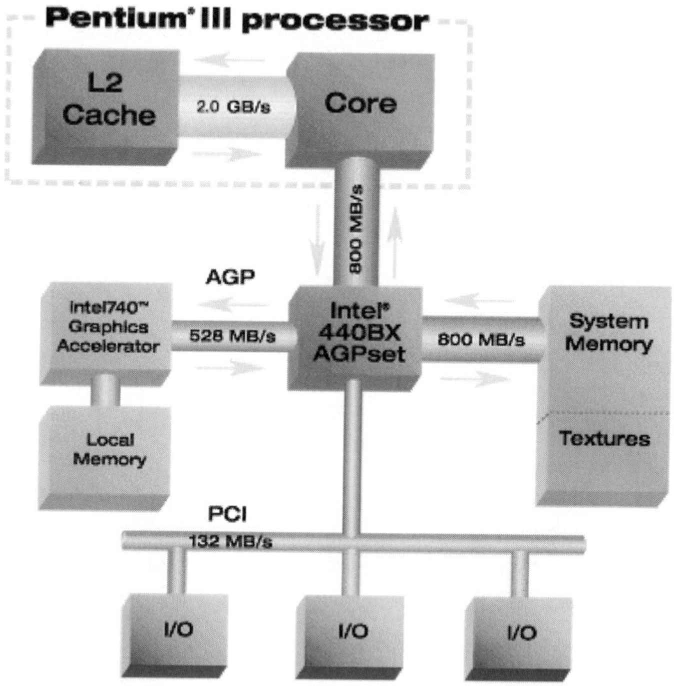

FIGURE 8-6 Block diagram of the AGP interface (Courtesy of Intel Corporation)

bandwidth available to a graphics accelerator. In its basic form, AGP offers a bandwidth of 266MB/s (twice the bandwidth of PCI). This is referred to as "AGP 1X." With advanced data handling techniques, 2 bytes can be passed on every AGP clock for a bandwidth of 532MB/s (known as "AGP 2X"). Further refinements to AGP data handling and the introduction of new chipsets allow 4 bytes to be passed on every AGP clock for a bandwidth of more than 1GB/s (called "AGP 4X").

AGP SIMILARITIES TO PCI

The 32-bit AGP bus gets its roots in the PCI local bus specification, but makes some significant improvements and additions intended to optimize AGP for high-performance 3D graphics. The most notable difference is the clock speed. PCI uses a fixed 33MHz bus, but AGP ups the clock speed to 66MHz. Other major differences include

- Deeply pipelined memory read and write operations. This hides memory access latency.
- Demultiplexing of address and data on the bus, allowing almost 100 percent bus efficiency.
- New AC timing for the 3.3V electrical specification that provides for one (AGP 1X) or two (AGP 2X) data transfers per 66MHz clock cycle, allowing for real data throughput in excess of 500MB/s.
- A new low-voltage electrical specification that allows four (AGP 4X) data transfers per 66MHz clock cycle, providing real data throughput of over 1GB/s.
- The bus slot defined for AGP uses a new connector body (for electrical signaling reasons) that is not compatible with the PCI connector, so PCI and AGP boards are not mechanically interchangeable.

AGP LAYOUT

The AGP bus is a low-profile 132-pin connector intended to be used on ATX- and NLX-style motherboards (though many current AT and baby AT motherboards will include an AGP bus). There are three variations of the AGP bus: 3.3V (Figure 8-7), Universal (Figure 8-8), and 1.5V (Figure 8-9). The signal layout (Table 8-10) is very similar between all three versions, but the key locations are different. As a result, 3.3V and 1.5V AGP cards are not interchangeable.

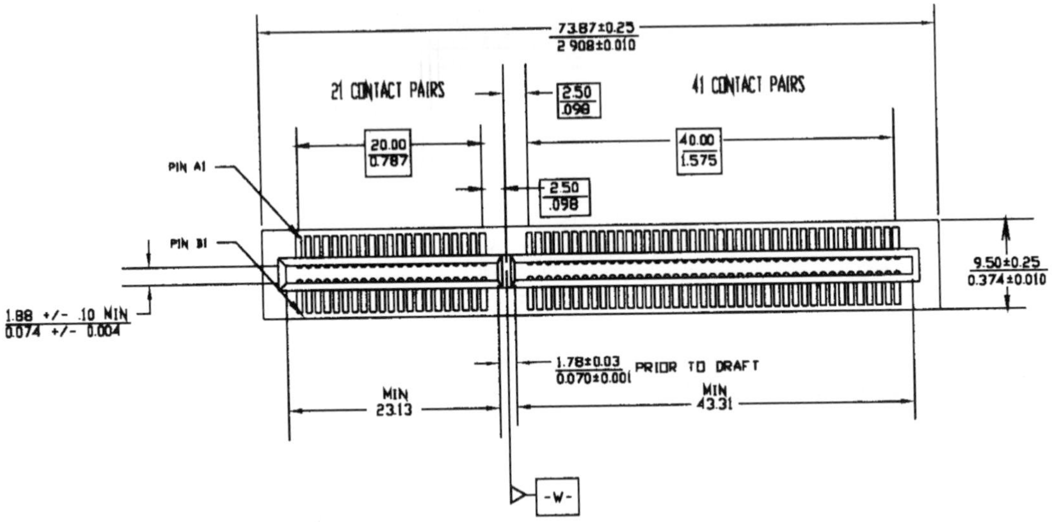

FIGURE 8-7 3.3V AGP bus connector

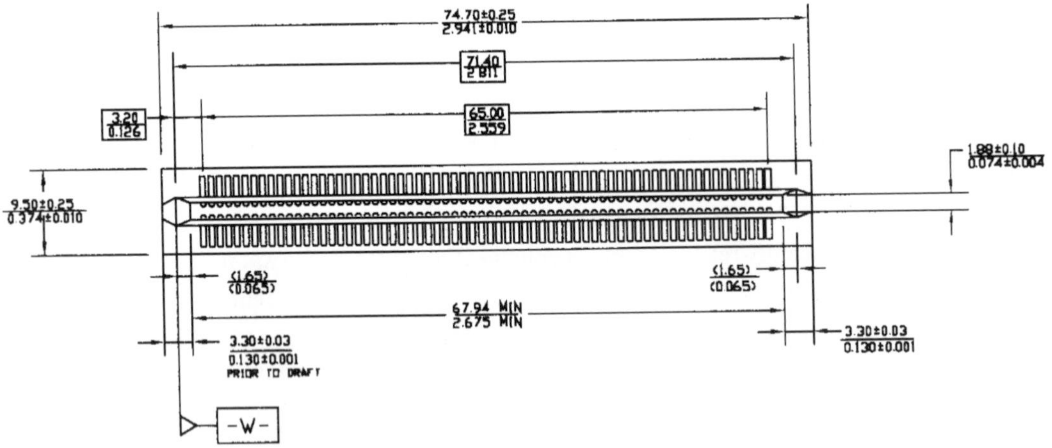

FIGURE 8-8 Universal AGP bus connector

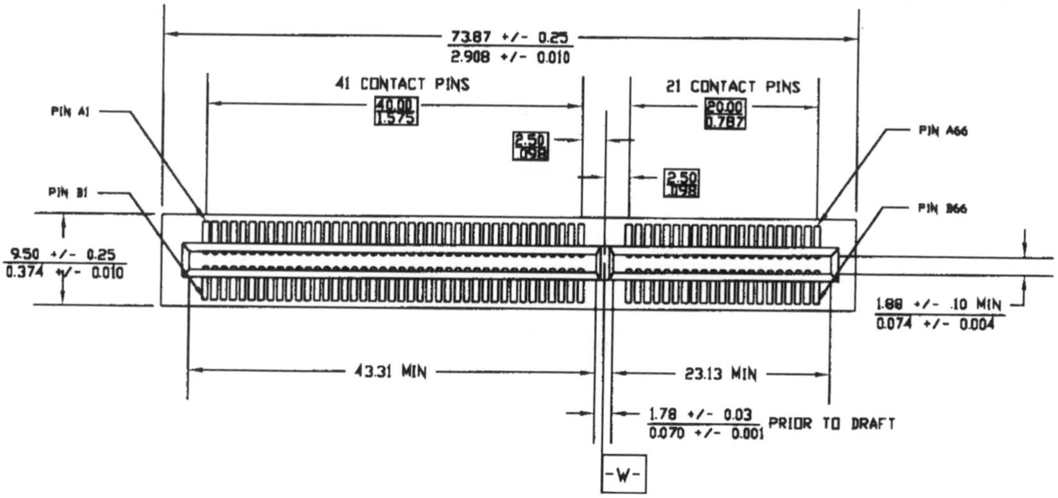

FIGURE 8-9 1.5V AGP bus connector

TABLE 8-10 AGP BUS PINOUT—3.3V, UNIVERSAL, AND 1.5V

	3.3 VOLT		UNIVERSAL		1.5 VOLT	
PIN	**B**	**A**	**B**	**A**	**B**	**A**
1	OVRCNT#	12V	OVRCNT#	12V	OVRCNT#	12V
2	5.0V	TYPEDET#	5.0V	TYPEDET#	5.0V	TYPEDET#
3	5.0V	Reserved	5.0V	Reserved	5.0V	Reserved
4	USB+	USB-	USB+	USB-	USB+	USB-
5	GND	GND	GND	GND	GND	GND
6	INTB#	INTA#	INTB#	INTA#	INTB#	INTA#
7	CLK	RST#	CLK	RST#	CLK	RST#
8	REQ#	GNT#	REQ#	GNT#	REQ#	GNT#
9	VCC3.3	VCC3.3	VCC3.3	VCC3.3	VCC3.3	VCC3.3
10	ST0	ST1	ST0	ST1	ST0	ST1
11	ST2	Reserved	ST2	Reserved	ST2	Reserved
12	RBF#	PIPE#	RBF#	PIPE#	RBF#	PIPE#
13	GND	GND	GND	GND	GND	GND
14	Reserved	Reserved	Reserved	WBF#	Reserved	WBF#
15	SBA0	SBA1	SBA0	SBA1	SBA0	SBA1
16	VCC3.3	VCC3.3	VCC3.3	VCC3.3	VCC3.3	VCC3.3
17	SBA2	SBA3	SBA2	SBA3	SBA2	SBA3
18	SB_STB	Reserved	SB_STB	SB_STB#	SB_STB	SB_STB#
19	GND	GND	GND	GND	GND	GND
20	SBA4	SBA5	SBA4	SBA5	SBA4	SBA5

TABLE 8-10 AGP BUS PINOUT—3.3V, UNIVERSAL, AND 1.5V *(CONTINUED)*

	3.3 VOLT		UNIVERSAL		1.5 VOLT	
PIN	B	A	B	A	B	A
21	SBA6	SBA7	SBA6	SBA7	SBA6	SBA7
22	KEY	KEY	Reserved	Reserved	Reserved	Reserved
23	KEY	KEY	GND	GND	GND	GND
24	KEY	KEY	3.3Vaux	Reserved	3.3Vaux	Reserved
25	KEY	KEY	VCC3.3	VCC3.3	VCC3.3	VCC3.3
26	AD31	AD30	AD31	AD30	AD31	AD30
27	AD29	AD28	AD29	AD28	AD29	AD28
28	VCC3.3	VCC3.3	VCC3.3	VCC3.3	VCC3.3	VCC3.3
29	AD27	AD26	AD27	AD26	AD27	AD26
30	AD25	AD24	AD25	AD24	AD25	AD24
31	GND	GND	GND	GND	GND	GND
32	AD_STB1	Reserved	AD_STB1	AD_STB1	AD_STB1	AD_STB1#
33	AD23	C/BE3#	AD23	C/BE3#	AD23	C/BE3#
34	Vddq3.3	Vddq3.3	Vddq	Vddq	Vddq1.5	Vddq1.5
35	AD21	AD22	AD21	AD22	AD21	AD22
36	AD19	AD20	AD19	AD20	AD19	AD20
37	GND	GND	GND	GND	GND	GND
38	AD17	AD18	AD17	AD18	AD17	AD18
39	C/BE2#	AD16	C/BE2#	AD16	C/BE2#	AD16
40	Vddq3.3	Vddq3.3	Vddq	Vddq	Vddq1.5	Vddq1.5
41	IRDY#	FRAME#	IRDY#	FRAME#	IRDY#	FRAME#
42	3.3Vaux	Reserved	3.3Vaux	Reserved	KEY	KEY
43	GND	GND	GND	GND	KEY	KEY
44	Reserved	Reserved	Reserved	Reserved	KEY	KEY
45	VCC3.3	VCC3.3	VCC3.3	VCC3.3	KEY	KEY
46	DEVSEL#	TRDY#	DEVSEL#	TRDY#	DEVSEL#	TRDY#
47	Vddq3.3	STOP#	Vddq	STOP#	Vddq1.5	STOP#
48	PERR#	PME#	PERR#	PME#	PERR#	PME#
49	GND	GND	GND	GND	GND	GND
50	SERR#	PAR	SERR#	PAR	SERR#	PAR
51	C/BE1#	AD15	C/BE1#	AD15	C/BE1#	AD15
52	Vddq3.3	Vddq3.3	Vddq	Vddq	Vddq1.5	Vddq1.5
53	AD14	AD13	AD14	AD13	AD14	AD13
54	AD12	AD11	AD12	AD11	AD12	AD11
55	GND	GND	GND	GND	GND	GND
56	AD10	AD9	AD10	AD9	AD10	AD9
57	AD8	C/BE0#	AD8	C/BE0#	AD8	C/BE0#
58	Vddq3.3	Vddq3.3	Vddq	Vddq	Vddq1.5	Vddq1.5
59	AD_STB0	Reserved	AD_STB0	AD_STB0#	AD_STB0	AD_STB0#
60	AD7	AD6	AD7	AD6	AD7	AD6

TABLE 8-10 AGP BUS PINOUT—3.3V, UNIVERSAL, AND 1.5V *(CONTINUED)*

	3.3 VOLT		UNIVERSAL		1.5 VOLT	
PIN	**B**	**A**	**B**	**A**	**B**	**A**
61	GND	GND	GND	GND	GND	GND
62	AD5	AD4	AD5	AD4	AD5	AD4
63	AD3	AD2	AD3	AD2	AD3	AD2
64	Vddq3.3	Vddq3.3	Vddq	Vddq	Vddq1.5	Vddq1.5
65	AD1	AD0	AD1	AD0	AD1	AD0
66	Reserved	Reserved	Vrefcg	Vrefgc	Vrefcg	Vrefgc

The AGP connector is not hot unpluggable. Be sure that the system and motherboard power is off. Unplugging an AGP card with power at the connector may cause irreparable damage to the card and/or system boards.

All 3.3V cards leave TYPEDET# open.

Knowing the AGP Signals

The PIPE# request is asserted by the current master to indicate that a full width request is to be queued by the target. The master queues one request with each rising edge of CLK while PIPE# is asserted. When PIPE# is deasserted, no new requests are queued across the AD bus. The SideBand Address port (SBA[7 through 0]) provides an additional bus to pass requests (address and command) to the target from the master. SBA[7 through 0] are outputs from the master and an input to the target. This port is ignored by the target until enabled.

The Read Buffer Full signal (RBF#) indicates whether the master is ready to accept previously requested low-priority read data. When RBF# is asserted, the arbiter is not allowed to initiate the return of low priority read data to the master. A "Write Buffer Full" signal (WBF#) indicates whether the master is ready to accept data from the core logic. When WBF# is asserted, the core logic arbiter is not allowed to initiate a transaction to provide data.

The Status bus (ST[2 through 0]) provides information from the arbiter to the master on what it may do. ST[2 through 0] signals only have meaning to the master when its GNT# is asserted. When GNT# is deasserted, these signals have no meaning and must be ignored. The master may enqueue A.G.P. Requests by asserting PIPE# or start a PCI transaction by asserting FRAME#. ST[2 through 0] signals are always output from the core logic and input to the master.

The AD Bus Strobe 0 signal (AD_STB0) provides timing for the 2x data transfer mode on address lines AD[15 through 00]. The agent that is providing data drives this signal. The AD Bus Strobe 0 compliment (AD_STB0#, along with AD_STB0) provide timing for the 4x data transfer mode on address lines AD[15 through 00]. The agent that is providing data drives this signal. The AD Bus Strobe 1 signal (AD_STB1) provides timing for the 2x data transfer mode on address lines AD[31 through 16]. The agent that is providing data drives this signal. The AD Bus Strobe 1 compliment (AD_STB1#, along with AD_STB1) provide timing for the 4x data transfer mode on address lines AD[31 through 16]. The agent that is providing data drives this signal.

The SideBand Strobe signal (SB_STB) provides timing for SBA[7 through 0] (when supported) and is always driven by the AGP master. When the SideBand Strobes have been idle, a synch cycle needs to be performed before a request can be queued. The SideBand Strobe compliment (SB_STB#, along with SB_STB#) provides timing for SBA[7 through 0] signals (when supported) when 4x timing is supported and is always driven by the AGP master.

Clock (CLK) provides timing for AGP and PCI control signals. The USB Positive Differential Data Line (USB+) is used to send USB data and control packets to external peripheral devices. The USB Negative Differential Data Line (USB-) is used to send USB data and control packets to external peripheral devices. The USB Overcurrent Indicator (OVRCNT#) is low when too much current has been taken from the 5-volt power supply (Vbus) line on the bus connector. Otherwise, the line is at a level between 2.4 volts and Vddq. The Power Management Event signal (PME#) is not used by the AGP protocol, but is used by the PCI target interface when being power managed by the operating system. The Type Detect signal (TYPEDET#) indicates whether the interface is 1.5 volt or 3.3 volt.

CONFIGURING AN AGP SYSTEM

The AGP bus requires a 66MHz clock. This clock is developed from the motherboard's front side bus clock (noted "FSB" or the "CPU clock"). When the motherboard is operated at 66MHz, your AGP bus can use this clock directly. When the motherboard is operated at 100MHz or higher, it will have to be divided down in order to achieve 66MHz. Normally, you can adjust this divisor (1:1 or 2:3) using a jumper on the motherboard, or directly through the CMOS setup. Be sure that you configure the system correctly depending on the clock speed. If the divisor is set to 2:3 when the system clock is 66MHz, you will be *underclocking* the AGP bus. On the other hand, if the divisor is set to 1:1 when the system clock is 100MHz, you will be *overclocking* the AGP bus.

General Bus Troubleshooting

In most cases, you will not be *troubleshooting* a bus—after all, the bus is little more than a passive connector. However, the major signals that exist on a bus can provide you with important clues about the system's operation. The most effective bus troubleshooting tool available to you is a POST board (such as the ones discussed in Chapter 19). Many POST boards are equipped with a number of LEDs that display power status, along with important timing and control signals. If one or more of those LEDs is missing, a fault has likely occurred somewhere on the motherboard. Keep in mind that the vast majority of POST boards are designed for the ISA bus. You can plug a POST board (with a built-in logic probe capable of 33MHz operation or more) into an ISA connector, then use the logic probe to test key signals.

- *Voltage* Use your multimeter and check each voltage level on the PCI bus. You should be able to find -12 Vdc and +5 Vdc regardless of whether the bus is standard or low voltage. For a low-voltage bus, you should also be able to find a +3.3 Vdc supply. If any of these supply levels are low or absent, troubleshoot or replace the power supply.
- *CLOCK* The Clock signal provides timing signals for the expansion device. It can be adjusted between DC (0Hz) and 33MHz (or higher). If this signal is absent, the expansion board will probably not run. Check the clock generating circuitry on the motherboard, or replace the motherboard outright.
- *RST* The Reset line can be used to reinitialize the expansion device. This line should not be active for more than a few moments after power is applied, or after a warm reset is initiated.

> PCI and AGP busses are highly dependent on a myriad of settings in the CMOS setup. Always check for proper CMOS configuration whenever you encounter trouble with PCI or AGP devices or bus performance.

Another point to consider is that bus connectors are mechanical devices—as a result, they do not last forever. If you or your customer are in the habit of removing and inserting boards frequently, it is likely that the metal "fingers" providing contact will wear and result in unreliable connections. Similarly, inserting a board improperly (or with excessive force) can break the connector. In extreme cases, even the motherboard can be damaged. The first rule of board replacement is *always try removing and reinserting the suspect board.* It is not uncommon for oxides to develop on board and slot contacts that may eventually degrade signal quality. By removing the board and reinserting it, you can wipe off any oxides or dust and possibly improve the connections.

The second rule of board replacement is *always try a board in another expansion slot before replacing it.* This way, a faulty bus slot can be ruled out before suffering the expense of a new board. Keep in mind that many current motherboards have a limited number of PCI slots and only one AGP slot—the remainder are ISA slots. If a bus slot proves defective, there is little that a technician can do except:

- Block the slot and inform the customer that it is damaged and should not be used.
- Replace the damaged bus slot connector (a tedious and time-consuming task) and pass the labor expense on to the customer.
- Replace the motherboard outright (also a rather expensive option).

Further Study

AGP: **http://www.agpforum.org/**

CompactPCI Home Page: **http://www.compactpci.com/**

General Technics: **http://gtweb.net/mi151.html** (MicroChannel Sound Card)

IBM PS/2 Reference Disks: **ftp://ftp.pc.ibm.com/pub/pccbbs/refdisks/**

Indelible Blue: **http://www.indelible-blue.com/** (MicroChannel add-on boards)

Intel's AGP site: **http://developer.intel.com/technology/agp/**

Intel's AGP interface specification:
ftp://download.intel.com/technology/agp/downloads/agp20.pdf

Micro Computer Systems: **http://www.mcsdallas.com/mcs/ecuv3.htm** (ECU - EISA Config Util v.3.)

PC2 Consulting: **http://www.pc2.com/**

PCI Special Interest Group Home Page: **http://www.pcisig.com/**

PS/2 Parts: **http://www.can.ibm.com/parts/catalogue/indexes/ps2indx.htm**

Small PCI: **http://www.pcisig.com/current/smallpci/**

VESA (Video Electronics Standards Organization): **http://www.vesa.org**

Vintage PCs: **http://www.can.ibm.com/helpware/vintage.html**

USENET Newsgroup(s): **comp.sys.ibm.ps2.hardware**

9

CD-ROM, CD-R, AND CD-RW DRIVES

CHAPTER AT A GLANCE

The *compact disc* (or CD) first appeared in the commercial marketplace in early 1982. Sony and Philips developed the CD as a joint venture and envisioned it as a reliable, high-quality replacement for aging phonograph technology. With the introduction of the audio CD, designers demonstrated that huge amounts of information can be stored simply and very inexpensively on common, nonmagnetic media. Unlike previous recording media, the CD recorded data in *digital* form through the use of physical "pits" and "lands" in the disc. The digital approach allowed excellent stereo sound quality that does not degrade each time the disc is played. This optical storage technology also found its way into the PC and has evolved over the last 15 years into a complete family of reliable high-volume storage devices: the CD-ROM, CD writer (or CD-R), and CD rewriter (or CD-RW). This chapter examines the basics of these technologies, offers some handy installation guidelines, and covers a wealth of troubleshooting issues.

The CD-ROM Drive

The CD-ROM drive that we know today has its origins in digital audio recording, but was quickly adapted for the PC by designers who saw CDs as a natural solution for all types of computer information (including text, graphics, programs, video clips, and audio files). Although the CD-ROM drive can only read data—it cannot write—the CD-ROM is known for its low cost, reliability, and broad media compatibility. In fact, the CD-ROM proved so popular that it quickly became standard equipment on both desktop and mobile PC systems. This part of the chapter outlines the elements of CD-ROM drives (Figure 9-1) and technologies, and offers a suite of troubleshooting information.

FIGURE 9-1 A Smart and Friendly CD-R 4006 (Courtesy of Smart and Friendly)

CD Media

CDs are mass produced by stamping the pattern of pits and lands onto a molded polycarbonate disc (known as a *substrate*). It is this stamping process (much like the stamping used to produce vinyl records) that places the data on the disc. But the disc is not yet readable—there are finish steps that must be performed to transform a clear plastic disc into viable, data-carrying media. The clear polycarbonate disc is given a silvered (reflective) coating so that it will reflect laser light. Silvering coats all parts of the disc side (pits and lands) equally. After silvering, the disc is coated with a tough, scratch-resistant lacquer that seals the disc from the elements (especially oxygen, which will oxidize and ruin the reflective coating). Finally, a label can be silk-screened onto the finished disc before it is tested and packaged. Figure 9-2 illustrates each of these layers in a cross-sectional diagram.

CD DATA

CDs are not segregated into concentric tracks and sectors as magnetic media is. Instead, CDs are recorded as a single, continuous spiral track running from the spindle to the lead-out area. Figure 9-3 shows an example of the spiral pattern as it might be recorded on a CD. The inset illustrates the relationship between the pits and lands. Each pit is about 0.12 μm (micrometers) deep and 0.6 μm wide. Pits and lands may range from 0.9 μm to 3.3 μm in length. There are approximately 1.6 μm between each iteration of the spiral. Given these microscopic dimensions, a CD-ROM disc offers about 16,000 tracks per inch (tpi).

During playback, CDs use a highly focused laser beam and laser detector to sense the presence or absence of pits. Figure 9-4 illustrates the reading behavior. The laser/detector pair is mounted on a carriage that follows the spiral track across the CD. A laser is directed at the underside of the CD where it penetrates more than 1 mm of clear plastic before shining on the reflective surface. When laser light strikes a land, the light is reflected toward the detector, which, in turn, produces a very strong output signal. As laser light strikes a pit, the light is slightly out of focus. As a result, most of the incoming laser energy is scattered away in all directions, so very little output signal is generated by the detector. As with floppy and hard drives, it is the *transition* from pit to land (and back again) that corresponds to binary levels, not the presence or absence of a pit or land. The analog light signal returned by the detector must be converted to logic levels and decoded. A process known as *eight-to-fourteen modulation* (EFM) is very common with CD-ROMs.

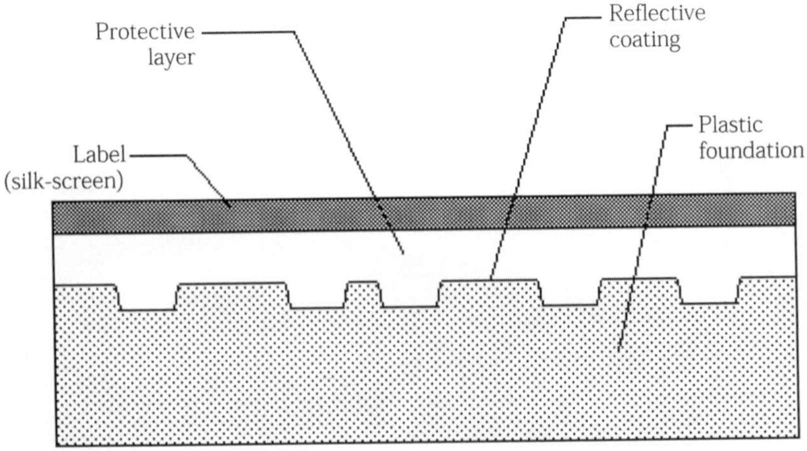

FIGURE 9-2 Cross-section of common CD media

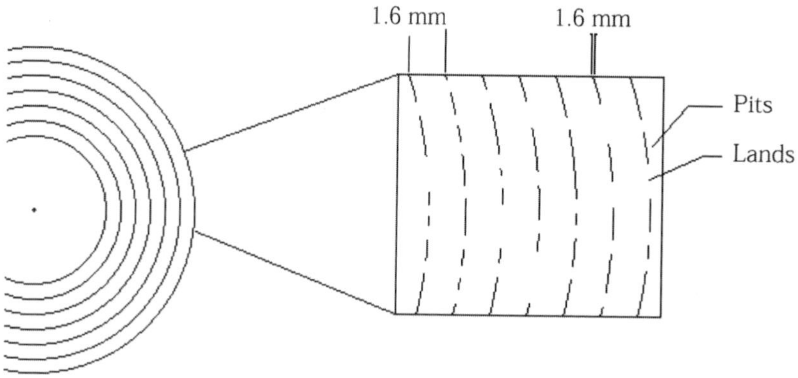

FIGURE 9-3 Close-up of a CD spiral track pattern

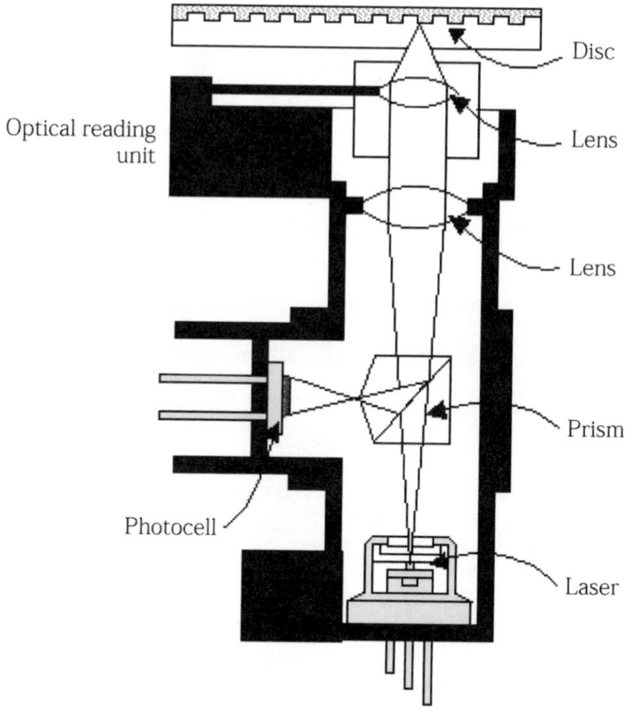

FIGURE 9-4 Reading a typical compact disc

EFM AND DATA STORAGE

A complex decoding process is necessary to convert this arcane sequence of pits and lands into meaningful binary information. The technique of eight-to-fourteen modulation is used with CD-ROMs. For hard disk drives, techniques such as *2,7 RLL encoding* can be used to place a large number of bits into a limited number of flux transitions. The same is true for CDs using EFM. User data, error correction information, address information, and synchronization patterns are all contained in a bit stream represented by pits and lands.

Magnetic media encodes bits as flux *transitions*, not the discrete orientation of any magnetic area. The same concept holds true with CD-ROMs where binary 1s and 0s do not correspond to pits or lands. A binary 1 is represented wherever a transition (pit-to-land or land-to-pit) occurs. The length of a pit or land represents the number of binary 0s. Figure 9-5 illustrates this concept. The eight-to-fourteen encoding technique equates each byte (8 bits) with a 14-bit sequence (called a *symbol*), where each binary 1 must be separated by at least two binary 0s. Table 9-1 shows part of the eight-to-fourteen conversion. Three bits are added to merge each 14-bit symbol together.

A CD-ROM *frame* is composed of 24 synchronization bits, 14 control bits, 24 of the 14-bit data symbols you saw previously, and 8 complete 14-bit error correction (EC) symbols. Keep in mind that each symbol is separated by an additional 3 merge bits, bringing the total number of bits in the frame to 588. Thus, 24 bytes of data are represented by 588 bits on a CD-ROM expressed as a number of pits and lands. There are 98 frames in a data *block*, so each block carries [98×24] 2048 bytes (2352 with error correction, synchronization, and address bytes). The basic CD-ROM can deliver 153.6KB of data (75 blocks) per second to its host controller.

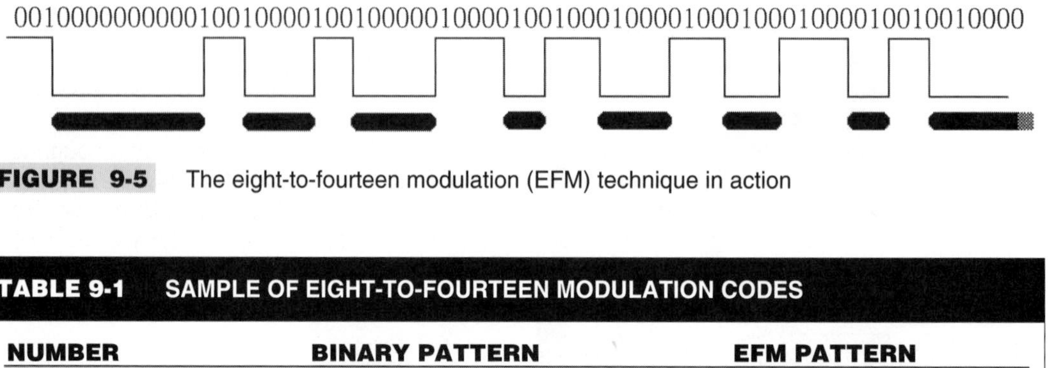

FIGURE 9-5 The eight-to-fourteen modulation (EFM) technique in action

TABLE 9-1 SAMPLE OF EIGHT-TO-FOURTEEN MODULATION CODES

NUMBER	BINARY PATTERN	EFM PATTERN
0	00000000	01001000100000
1	00000001	10000100000000
2	00000010	10010000100000
3	00000011	10001000100000
4	00000100	01000100000000
5	00000101	00000100010000
6	00000110	00010000100000
7	00000111	00100100000000
8	00001000	01001001000000
9	00001001	10000001000000
10	00001010	10010001000000

Remember that the CD-ROM disc is recorded as one continuous spiral track running around the disc, so ordinary sector and track ID information that we associate with magnetic disks does not apply very well. Instead, information is divided in terms of 0 to 59 *minutes*, and 0 to 59 *seconds* recorded at the beginning of each block. A CD-ROM (like an audio CD) can hold up to 79 *minutes* of data. However, many CD-ROMs tend to limit this to 60 minutes since the last 14 minutes of data are encoded in the outer 5 mm of disc space, which is the most difficult to manufacture and keep clean in everyday use. There are 270,000 blocks of data in 60 minutes. At 2048 data bytes per block, the disc's capacity is 552,950,000 bytes (553MB). If all 79 minutes are used, 681,984,000 bytes (681MB) will be available in 333,000 blocks. Most CD-ROMs run between 553MB and 650MB in normal production.

CARING FOR COMPACT DISCS

A compact disc is a remarkably reliable long-term storage media. (Conservative expectations place the life estimates of a current CD at about 100 years.) However, the longevity of a CD is affected by its storage and handling. A faulty CD can cause file and data errors that you might otherwise interpret as a defect in the drive itself. Below are some tips to help protect and maintain the disc itself:

- *Don't bend the disc.* Polycarbonate is a forgiving material, but you risk cracking or snapping (and thus ruining) the disc.
- *Don't heat the disc.* Remember, the disc is plastic. Leaving it by a heater or on the dashboard of your car will cause melting.
- *Don't scratch the disc.* Laser wavelengths have a tendency to "look past" minor scratches, but a major scratch can cause problems. Be especially careful of circular scratches (one that follows the spiral track). A circular scratch can easily wipe out entire segments of data, which would be unrecoverable.
- *Don't use chemicals on the disc.* Chemicals containing solvents such as ammonia, benzene, acetone, carbon tetrachloride, or chlorinated cleaning solvents can easily damage the disc's plastic surface.

Eventually, a buildup of excessive dust or fingerprints can interfere with the laser beam enough to cause disc errors. When this happens, the disc can be cleaned easily using a dry, soft, lint-free cloth. Hold the disc from its edges and wipe radially (from hub to edge). *Do not wipe in a circular motion.* For stubborn stains, moisten the cloth in a bit of fresh isopropyl alcohol. (Do not use water.) Place the cleaned disc in a caddie or jewel case for transport and storage.

General CD Standards and Characteristics

Like so many other PC peripheral devices, the early CD-ROM faced a serious problem of industry standardization. Just recording the data to a CD is not enough—the data must be recorded in a way that any CD-ROM drive can read. Standards for CD-ROM data and formats were developed by consortiums of influential PC manufacturers and interested CD-ROM publishers. Ultimately, this kind of industrywide cooperation has made the CD-ROM one of the most uniform and standardized peripherals in the PC market. With the broad introduction of CD recorders and rewriters into the marketplace, it is also important for you to understand the major concepts and operations of CD recorders. This part of the chapter explains many of the key ideas needed to master the three CD drive families.

HIGH SIERRA

In 1984 (before the general release of CD-ROM), the PC industry realized that there must be a standard method of reading a disc's VTOC (Volume Table of Contents)—otherwise, the CD-ROM market would become extremely fragmented as various (incompatible) standards vied for acceptance. PC manufacturers, prospective CD publishers, and software developers met at the High Sierra Hotel in Lake Tahoe, California, to begin developing just such a uniform standard. By 1986, the CD-ROM standard file format (dubbed the High Sierra format) was accepted and approved. High Sierra remained the standard for several years, but has since been replaced by ISO 9660.

ISO 9660

High Sierra was certainly a workable format, but it was primarily a domestic U.S. development. When placed before the International Standards Organization (ISO), High Sierra was tweaked and refined to meet international needs. After international review, High Sierra was absorbed (with only a few changes) into the ISO 9660 standard. Although many technicians refer to High Sierra and ISO 9660 interchangeably, you should understand that the two standards are not the same. For the purposes of this book, ISO 9660 is the current CD-ROM and CD-R file format. All CD-ROM drives can read ISO 9660 discs, and all CD recorders are capable of recording a disc in the ISO 9660 format.

By adhering to ISO 9660, CD-ROM drive makers can write software drivers (and use MSCDEX under DOS) to enable a PC to read the disc's VTOC. ISO 9660 also allows a CD-ROM disc to be accessed by any computer system and CD-ROM drive that follows the standard. Of course, just because a disc is recognized does not mean that it can be used. For example, an ISO 9660–compliant Mac can access an ISO 9660 MPC disc, but the files on the disc cannot be used by the Mac.

CD-ROM STANDARDS ("BOOKS")

When Philips and Sony defined the proprietary standards that became CD audio, CD-ROM, and so on, the documents were bound in different-colored covers. By tradition, each color now represents a different level of standardization. Red Book (a.k.a. Compact Disc Digital Audio Standard: CEI IEC 908) defines the media, recording and mastering process, and the player design for CD audio. When you listen to your favorite audio CD, you are enjoying the benefits of the Red Book standard. CDs conforming to Red Book standards will usually have the words "digital audio" printed below the disc logo. Today, Red Book audio may be combined with programs and other PC data on the same disc.

The Yellow Book standard (ISO 10149:1989) makes CD-ROM possible by defining the additional error correction data needed on the disc, and detection hardware and firmware needed in the drive. When a disc conforms to Yellow Book, it will usually be marked "data storage" beneath the disc logo. Mode 1 Yellow Book is the typical operating mode that supports computer data. Mode 2 Yellow Book (also known as the XA format) supports compressed audio data and video/picture data. The Yellow Book standards build on the Red Book, so virtually all CD-ROM drives are capable of playing back CD audio discs.

The Orange Book (a.k.a. Recordable Compact Disc Standard) is the key to CD recorders and serves to extend the basic Red and Yellow Book standards by providing specifications for recordable products such as (Part 1) magneto-optical (MO) drives, and (Part 2) write-once CD-R drives. The Green Book standard defines an array of supplemental standards for data recording and provides an outline for a specific computer system that supports CD-I (compact disc–interactive). Interactive kiosks and information systems using CD-I discs are based on Green Book standards. Blue Book is the standard for laser discs and their players. The White Book standards define CD-ROM video.

THE MULTISPEED DRIVE

The Red Book standard defines CD audio as a stream of data that flows from the player mechanism to the amplifier (or other audio manipulation circuit) at a rate of 150KB/sec. This data rate was chosen to take music off the disc for truest reproduction. When the Yellow Book was developed to address CD-ROMs, this basic data rate was carried over. Designers soon learned that computer data can be transferred much faster than Red Book audio information, so the multispeed (or multispin) drive was developed to work with Red Book audio at the normal 150KB/sec rate, but run faster for Yellow Book data in order to multiply the data throughput.

The first common multispeed drives available were 2X drives. By running at 2X the normal data transfer speed, data throughput can be doubled from 150KB/sec to 300KB/sec. If Red Book audio is encountered, the drive speed drops back to 150KB/sec. Increased data transfer rates make a real difference in CD-ROM performance, especially for data-intensive applications such as audio/video clips. CD-ROM drives with 4X transfer speed (600KB/sec) can transfer data four times faster than a Red Book drive. Table 9-2 lists the average data rates for current CD-ROM drives.

TABLE 9-2 DATA TRANSFER RATES FOR CD-ROM DRIVES

	DATA TRANSFER RATES					
SPEED	CD-ROM (MODE 1)	CD-ROM (MODE 2)	CD-I XA (FORM 2)	2048 BYTES/ BLOCK	2336 BYTES/ BLOCK	2324 BYTES/ BLOCK
1X	153.6KB/s	(0.15MB/s)	175.2KB/s	(0.17MB/s)	174.3KB/s	(0.17MB/s)
2X	307.2KB/s	(0.3MB/s)	350.4KB/s	(0.35MB/s)	348.6KB/s	(0.34MB/s)
4X	614.4KB/s	(0.61MB/s)	700.8KB/s	(0.70MB/s)	697.2KB/s	(0.69MB/s)
6X	921.6KB/s	(0.92MB/s)	1051.2KB/s	(1.05MB/s)	1045.8KB/s	(1.04MB/s)
8X	1200KB/s	(1.2MB/s)	1401.6KB/s	(1.40MB/s)	1394.4KB/s	(1.39MB/s)
10X	1500KB/s	(1.5MB/s)	1752.0KB/s	(1.75MB/s)	1743.0KB/s	(1.74MB/s)
12X	1800KB/s	(1.8MB/s)	2102.4KB/s	(2.10MB/s)	2091.6KB/s	(2.09MB/s)
14X	2100KB/s	(2.1MB/s)	2452.8KB/s	(2.45MB/s)	2440.2KB/s	(2.44MB/s)
16X	2400KB/s	(2.4MB/s)	2803.2KB/s	(2.80MB/s)	2788.8KB/s	(2.78MB/s)
18X	2700KB/s	(2.7MB/s)	3153.6KB/s	(3.15MB/s)	3137.4KB/s	(3.13MB/s)
20X	3000KB/s	(3.0MB/s)	3504.0KB/s	(3.50MB/s)	3486.0KB/s	(3.48MB/s)
22X	3300KB/s	(3.3MB/s)	3854.4KB/s	(3.85MB/s)	3834.6KB/s	(3.83MB/s)
24X	3600KB/s	(3.6MB/s)	4204.8KB/s	(4.20MB/s)	4183.2KB/s	(4.18MB/s)
28X	4200KB/s	(4.2MB/s)	4905.6KB/s	(4.90MB/s)	4880.4KB/s	(4.88MB/s)
32X	4800KB/s	(4.8MB/s)	5606.4KB/s	(5.60MB/s)	5577.6KB/s	(5.57MB/s)
36X	5400KB/s	(5.4MB/s)	6307.2KB/s	(6.30MB/s)	6274.8KB/s	(6.27MB/s)
40X	6000KB/s	(6.0MB/s)	7008.0KB/s	(7.00MB/s)	6972.0KB/s	(6.97MB/s)

THE MPC

One of the most fundamental problems in writing software for PCs is the tremendous variability in the possible hardware and software configurations of individual machines. The selection of CPUs, motherboard chipsets, operating system versions, available memory, graphics resolutions, drive space, and other peripherals makes the idea of a standard PC almost meaningless. Most software developers in the PC market establish a base (or minimal) PC configuration to ensure that a product will run properly in a minimal machine. CD-ROM multimedia products have intensified these performance issues because of the unusually heavy demands posed by real-time audio and graphics. Microsoft has assembled some of the largest PC manufacturers to create the Multimedia Personal Computer (or MPC) standard. By adhering to the MPC specification, software developers and consumers can anticipate the minimal capacity needed to run multimedia products.

> Appendix B outlines the broader standards for a "PC 99–compliant" computer system.

CD-ROM CACHING

The limiting factor of a CD-ROM is its data transfer rate. Even a fast multispin CD-ROM takes a fairly substantial amount of time to load programs and files into memory, and this causes system delays during CD-ROM access. If the PC could *predict* the data needed from a CD and load that data into RAM or virtual memory (on the hard drive) during background operations, the effective performance of a CD-ROM drive could be enhanced dramatically. CD-ROM caching utilities provide a "look-ahead" ability that enables CD-ROMs to continue transferring information in anticipation of use.

However, real-mode (DOS) CD-ROM caching is a mixed blessing. The utilities required for caching (such as SmartDrive) must reside in conventional memory (or be loaded into upper memory). In systems that are already strained by the CD-ROM drivers and other device drivers that have become so commonplace on PC platforms, adding a cache may prohibit some large DOS programs from running. Keep this in mind when evaluating CD-ROM caches for yourself or your customers.

> Windows 95/98 discontinues the use of SmartDrive in favor of its own internal protected-mode caching features. If you're using Windows 95/98, you may optimize the CD-ROM cache through the File System Properties dialog. Click on Start, Settings, Control Panel, and then double-click on the System icon. Select the Performance tab, and click the File System button; then select the CD-ROM tab. You can then optimize the CD-ROM cache size and access pattern for your drive.

BOOTABLE CD-ROM (EL TORITO)

Traditionally, CD-ROM drives have not been bootable devices. Since the CD-ROM drive needs software drivers, the PC always had to boot first in order to load the drivers. This invariably required a bootable hard drive or floppy drive. When building a new system, this required you to boot from a floppy disk, install DOS and the CD-ROM drivers, and then pop in your Windows 95/98 CD for setup. In early 1995, the so-called El Torito standard was finalized, which provides the hardware and software specifications needed to implement a bootable CD-ROM. You need three elements to implement a bootable CD-ROM:

- A bootable CD-ROM drive mechanism (almost always fitted with a UDMA or EIDE interface).
- A BIOS version that supports the bootable CD-ROM (now standard on almost all new motherboards).
- A CD with boot code and an operating system on it. If you don't already have a bootable (or system) CD, see "Creating a Bootable CD" later in this chapter.

CD-ROM Construction

Now that you have an understanding of CD-ROM media and standards, it is time to review a drive in some detail. CD-ROM/CD-R/CD-RW drives are impressive pieces of engineering. The drive must be able to accept standard-sized discs from a variety of sources (each disc may contain an assortment of unknown surface imperfections). The drive must then spin the disc at a constant linear velocity (CLV)—that is, the disc speed varies inversely with the tracking radius. As tracking approaches the disc edge, disc speed slows, and vice versa. Keep in mind that CLV is different from the constant angular velocity (CAV) method used by floppy and hard drives, which move the media at a constant speed. The purpose of CLV is to ensure that CD data is read at a constant *rate*. A drive must be able to follow the spiral data path on a spinning CD-ROM accurately to within less than 1 μm along the disc's radius. The drive electronics must be able to detect and correct any unforeseen data errors in real time, operate reliably over a long working life, and be available for a low price that computer users have come to expect.

CD-ROM MECHANICS

You can begin to appreciate how a CD drive achieves its features by reviewing the exploded diagram of Figure 9-6. At the center of the drive is a cast aluminum or rigid stainless steel frame assembly. As with other drives, the frame is the single primary structure for mounting the drive's mechanical and electronic components. The front bezel, lid, volume control, and eject button attach to the frame, providing the drive with its clean cosmetic appearance, and offering a fixed reference slot for CD insertion and removal. Keep in mind that many drives use a sliding tray, so the front bezel (and the way it is attached) will not be the same for every drive.

> Although the laser type and drive electronics are somewhat different, the physical descriptions and electronic details for CD-ROM drives are also generally true for CD-R and CD-RW drives.

9

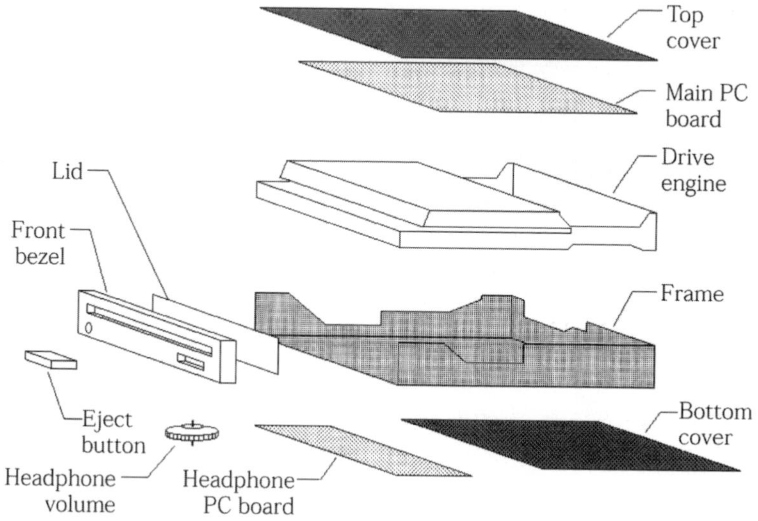

FIGURE 9-6 Exploded diagram of a CD-ROM drive

The drive's electronics package has been split into several PC board assemblies: the main PCB, which handles drive control and interfacing, and the headphone PCB, which simply provides an audio amplifier and jack for headphones. The bulk of the drive's actual physical work, however, is performed by a main CD subassembly called a *drive engine*, which is often manufactured by only a few companies. As a result, many of the diverse CD-ROM drives on the market actually use identical "engines" to hold/eject, spin, and read the disk. This interchangeability is part of the genius of CD-ROM drives—a single subassembly performs 80 percent of the work. Sony, Philips, and Toshiba are the major manufacturers of CD-ROM engines, but other companies such as IBM and Ikka have also been known to produce engines.

A typical drive engine is shown in Figure 9-7. The upper view of the engine features a series of mechanisms that accept, clamp, and eject the disk. The foundation of this engine is the BC-7C assembly. It acts as a subframe on which everything else is mounted. Notice that the subframe is shock-mounted with four rubber feet to cushion the engine from minor bumps and ordinary handling. Even with such mounting, a CD-ROM drive is a fragile mechanism. The slider assembly, loading chassis assembly, and the cover shield provide the mechanical action needed to accept the disk and clamp it into place over the drive spindle, as well as free the disk and eject it on demand. A number of levers and oil dampers serve to provide a slow, smooth mechanical action when motion takes place. A motor/gear assembly drives the load/unload mechanics.

The serious work of spinning and reading a disk is handled *under* the engine, as shown in Figure 9-8. A spindle motor is mounted on the subframe and connected to a spindle motor PC board. A thrust retainer helps keep the spindle motor turning smoothly. The most critical part of the CD engine is the optical device containing the 780 nm (nanometer) 0.6mW gallium aluminum arsenide (GaAlAs) laser diode and detector, along with the optical focus and tracking components. The optical device slides along two guide rails and shines through an exposed hole in the subframe. This combination of device mounting and guide rails is called a *sled*.

CD-R and CD-RW drives will typically use lasers with different characteristics, though you may not be able to distinguish between a CD-ROM, CD-R, or CD-RW engine at first glance.

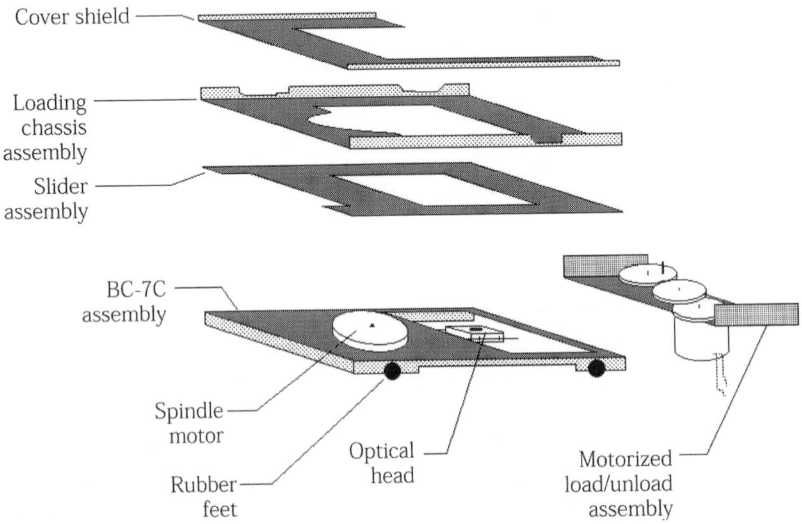

FIGURE 9-7 Exploded diagram of a CD drive engine

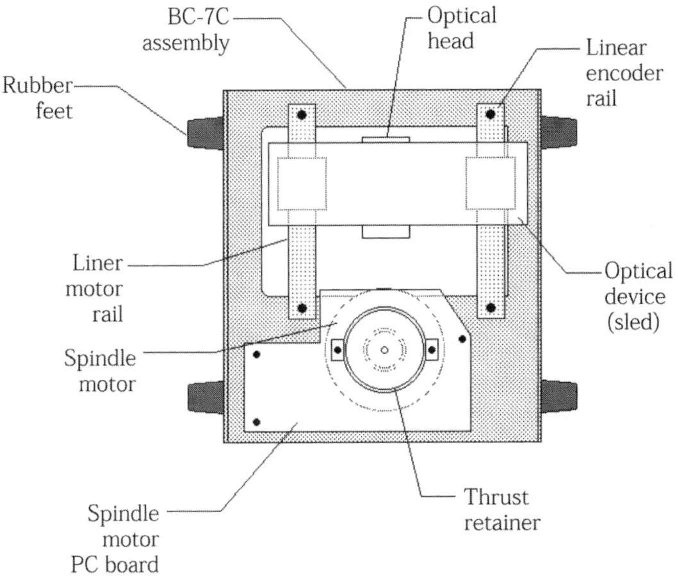

FIGURE 9-8 Underside view of a typical BC-7C assembly

A sled must be made to follow the spiral data track along the disc. While floppy disks (using clearly defined concentric tracks) can easily make use of a stepping motor to position the head assembly, a CD drive ideally requires a *linear motor* to act much like the voice coil motor used to position hard drive R/W heads. By altering the signal that drives a sled motor and constantly measuring and adjusting the sled's position, a sled can be made to track very smoothly along a disc—free from the sudden, jerky motion of stepping motors. Some CD drives still use stepping motors with an extremely fine-pitch lead screw to position the sled. The drive's main PC board is responsible for managing these operations.

9

CD-ROM ELECTRONICS

The electronics package used in a typical CD-ROM drive is illustrated in Figure 9-9. The electronics package can be divided into two major areas: the controller section and the drive section. The controller section is dedicated to the peripheral interface—its connection to the drive controller board. Much of the reason for a CD-ROM's electronic sophistication can be traced to the controller section. Notice that the controller circuitry shown in Figure 9-9 is dedicated to handling a SCSI interface, though most CD-ROM drives today offer a UDMA or EIDE drive interface that will support a CD-ROM right along with your existing hard drive(s). This allows the unit's "intelligence" to be located right in the drive itself. You need only connect the drive to a system-level interface board such as a SCSI host adapter or IDE-type drive controller (such as an IDE, EIDE, or UDMA controller) and set the drive's device identification to establish a working system.

The drive section's electronics will manage the CD-ROM's physical operations (load/unload, spin the disc, move the sled, etc.), as well as data decoding (EFM) and error correction. Drive circuitry converts an analog output from the laser diode into an EFM signal, which is, in turn, decoded into binary data and CIRC (Cross-Interleaved Reed-Solomon Code) information. A drive controller IC and servo proces-

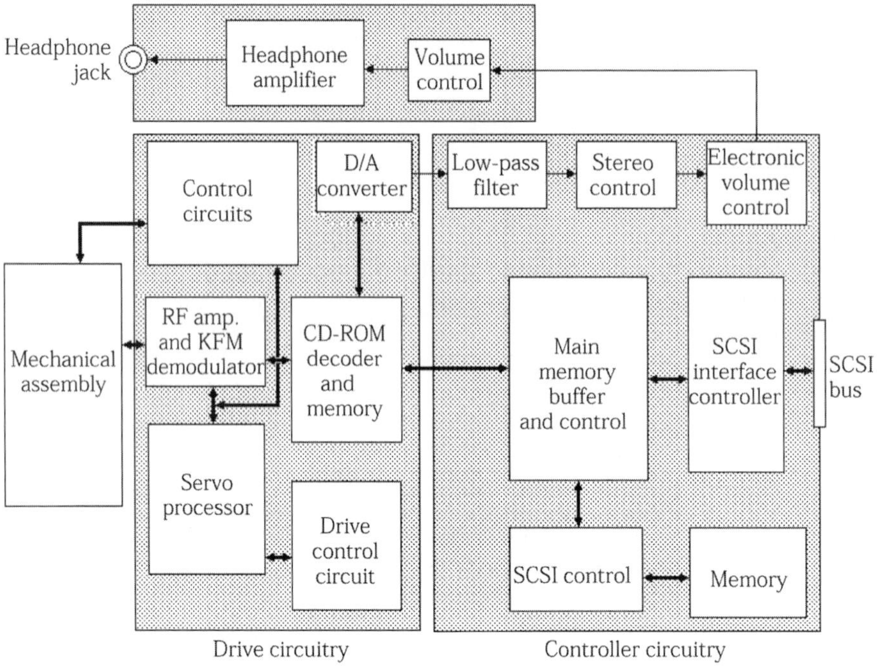

FIGURE 9-9 Electronics block diagram for a typical CD-ROM drive

sor IC are responsible for directing laser focus, tracking, sled motor control (and feedback), spindle motor control (and feedback), and loading/unloading motor control.

When it comes to CD drive electronics, you should certainly treat the diagram of Figure 9-9 as a guideline rather than as an absolute. There are quite a few different iterations of drive electronics and interfaces: some manufacturers use SCSI interfaces, but most systems use the UDMA or EIDE system-level interface, and several manufacturers implement proprietary interfaces. (In some cases, these are often subtle, nonstandard variations of SCSI or IDE interfaces.) Obtain the manufacturer's service data wherever possible for specific information on your particular drive.

Understanding the Software

Hardware alone is not enough to implement a CD-ROM, CD-R, or CD-RW drive. In an ideal world, BIOS and DOS/Windows would provide the software support to handle the drive (such as for hard drives), but in practice, the variations between CD-ROM designs and interfaces make it impractical to provide low-level BIOS services. Manufacturers provide a hardware-specific device driver used to communicate with the CD-ROM and interface. An MS-DOS extension (MSCDEX) provides file handling and logical drive letter support. This part of the chapter explains the operations and features of real-mode CD-ROM device drivers and MSCDEX.

> This software discussion deals with real-mode software operating under DOS. If you're using a CD-ROM under Windows95/98, you can skip these discussions. Windows 95/98 does not use MSCDEX and will install a protected-mode driver for the CD-ROM (either a "native" Windows driver, or one directly from the drive maker).

DEVICE DRIVERS

A low-level device driver allows programs to access the CD-ROM, CD-R, or CD-RW drive properly at the register (hardware) level. Since most drives are designed differently, they require similar but different device drivers. If you change or upgrade the drive at any point, the device driver must be upgraded as well. A typical real-mode device driver uses a .SYS extension and is enabled by adding its command line to the PC's CONFIG.SYS file, for example:

```
DEVICE=HITACHIA.SYS /D:MSCD000 /N:1 /P:300
```

> The DEVICE command may be replaced by the DEVICEHIGH command if you have available space in the upper memory area (UMA).

A CD device driver will typically have three command-line switches associated with it. These parameters are needed to ensure that the driver installs properly. For the example command line shown above, the /D switch is the name used by the driver when it is installed in the system's device table. This name must be unique, and it must be matched by the /D switch in the MSCDEX.EXE command line (covered later). The /N switch is the number of CD-ROM drives attached to the interface card. The default is 1 (which is typical for most general-purpose systems). Finally, the /P switch is the I/O port address where the drive's adapter card resides. As you might expect, the port address should match the port address on the physical interface. If there is no /P switch, the default is 0300h.

There's an additional wrinkle when using SCSI-based CD recorders. This means the PC must be fitted with a SCSI host adapter and configured with a real-mode ASPI driver in order to allow the SCSI adapter to interface to the drive. (This is also true if you're using a SCSI CD-ROM drive.) A typical ASPI driver entry might appear in CONFIG.SYS like this:


```
DEVICE=C:\SCSI\ASPIPPA3.SYS /L=001
```

> If there are no SCSI hard drives in the system, the SCSI adapter's onboard BIOS ROM can usually be disabled.

> Again, if the SCSI drive is being enabled under Windows 95/98, you will use a protected-mode driver to run the SCSI host adapter. However, you may still need a real-mode driver for the SCSI host adapter if you're using the SCSI adapter to operate other devices under DOS.

MSCDEX.EXE

MS-DOS was developed in a time when no one anticipated that large files would be accessible to a PC, and it is severely limited in the file sizes that it can handle. With the development of CD-ROMs, Microsoft created an extension to MS-DOS that allows software publishers to access 650MB CDs in a standard way—the Microsoft CD-ROM Extensions (MSCDEX). As with most software, MSCDEX offers some vital features (and a few limitations), but it is required by a vast majority of CD-ROM and CD-R products when you're working in DOS. Obtaining MSCDEX is not a problem—it is generally provided on the same disk containing the CD-ROM's low-level device driver. New versions of MSCDEX can be obtained from the Microsoft Web site (**www.microsoft.com**).

In actual operation, MSCDEX is loaded in the AUTOEXEC.BAT file. It should be loaded after any mouse driver and before any MENU, SHELL, DOSSHELL, or WIN line. It should also be loaded before any BAT file is started. Keep in mind that if a BAT file loads a network, MSCDEX must be included in the batch file after the network driver. Further, MSCDEX must be loaded after that network driver with the /S (share) switch in order to hook into the network driver chain. If you want to use the MS-DOS drive caching software (SmartDrive) to buffer the CD-ROM drive(s), load MSCDEX before SmartDrive. The MSCDEX /M (number of buffers) switch can be set to 0 when using SmartDrive. If you find that SmartDrive is interfering with MPC applications like Video for Windows, you can load SmartDrive before MSCDEX and set the /M switch for at least 2. When loading MSCDEX, remember that the MSCDEX /D switch must match the /D label used in the low-level driver. Otherwise, MSCDEX will not load. If SETVER is loaded in the CONFIG.SYS file, be sure to use the latest version of MSCDEX.

Although the vast majority of CD-ROM bundles include installation routines that automate the installation process for the low-level driver and MSCDEX, you should understand the various command-line switches (shown in Table 9-3) that make MSCDEX operate. Understanding these switches may help you to overcome setup problems.

TABLE 9-3 MSCDEX COMMAND-LINE SWITCHES

SWITCH	DESCRIPTION	PURPOSE
/D:x	Device name	The label used by the low-level device driver when it loads. MSCDEX must match this label in order for the device driver and MSCDEX to work together. A typical label is MSCD000.
/M:x	Buffers allocated	The number of 2KB buffers allocated to the CD-ROM drives. There are typically eight buffers (16KB) for a single drive and four buffers for each additional drive. This number can be set to 1 or 2 if conventional memory space is at a premium.
/L:x	Drive letter	This is the optional drive letter for the CD-ROM. If this is not specified, the drive will be automatically assigned to the first available letter (usually D:). There must be a LASTDRIVE= entry in CONFIG.SYS to use a letter higher than the default letter. When choosing a letter for the LASTDRIVE entry, do not use Z—otherwise, network drives may not install after MSCDEX.
/N	Verbose option	This switch forces MSCDEX to show memory usage statistics on the display each time the system boots.
/S	Share option	This switch is used with CD-ROM installations in network systems.
/K	Kanji option	Instructs MSCDEX to use Kanji (Japanese) file types on the CD if present.
/E	Expanded memory	Allows MSCDEX to use expanded memory for buffers. There must be an expanded memory driver running (such as EMM386.EXE) with enough available space to use it.

CD-ROM Installation and Replacement

CD-ROM drives are generally easy devices to install or replace. Most are installed as "master" devices located on the secondary IDE drive controller channel, though a few will coexist as "slave" devices alongside a hard drive or other drive device. The most important issue to remember is that the BIOS will not support the CD-ROM directly (even if the BIOS identifies the CD-ROM at boot time). You'll need real-mode drivers for the CD-ROM under DOS, or protected-mode drivers for the CD-ROM under Windows. This part of the chapter covers the guidelines needed to install a basic internal IDE-type CD-ROM.

SELECT JUMPER CONFIGURATIONS

An IDE-type CD-ROM drive may be installed as a master or slave device on any hard drive controller channel. These master/slave settings are handled through one or two jumpers located on the rear of the drive (next to the 40-pin signal cable connector). One of your first decisions when planning an installation should be to decide the drive's configuration:

- If you're installing the CD-ROM as the first drive on the secondary drive controller channel, it must be jumpered as the master device.
- If you're installing the CD-ROM drive alongside another drive (on either the primary or secondary drive controller channel), the CD-ROM must be jumpered as the slave device.

> Refer to the documentation that accompanies your particular CD-ROM drive in order to determine the exact master/slave jumper settings. If you do not have the drive documentation handy, check the drive manufacturer's Web site for online information.

ATTACH CABLES AND MOUNT THE DRIVE

Follow these steps:

1. Turn off and unplug the PC; then remove the outer cover to expose the computer's drive bays.
2. Attach one end of the 40-pin drive interface cable to the drive controller connector on your motherboard (or drive controller card). Remember to align pin 1 on the cable (the side of the cable with the blue or red stripe) with pin 1 on the drive controller connector.
3. Locate an available drive bay for the CD-ROM drive. Remove the plastic housing covering the drive bay, and then slide the drive inside. Locate the four screw holes needed to mount the drive. In some cases, you may need to attach "mounting rails" to the drive so that the drive will be wide enough to fit in the drive bay. In virtually all cases, you should mount a tray-driven CD-ROM drive horizontally (though caddy-loaded CD-ROM drives may be mounted vertically).
4. Attach the 40-pin signal cable and the 4-pin power connector to the new drive, and then bolt the drive securely into place. Do not overtighten the screws since this may damage the drive. If you do not have an available 4-pin power connector, you may use an appropriate Y-splitter if necessary to split power from another drive (preferably the floppy drive).
5. Attach the small 4-pin CD-audio signal cable from the CD-ROM to the CD-audio input connector on your sound card. This connection allows you to play music CDs directly through your sound

card. Verify that the CD-audio cable is compatible with your sound card (otherwise you may need a specialized cable from the sound card's manufacturer).

CONFIGURE THE CMOS SETUP

Although the CD-ROM does require driver support, recent motherboard designs can identify the ATAPI IDE CD-ROM drive in BIOS, so you should configure your computer's BIOS to accept the drive if possible (through the CMOS setup).

1. Turn the computer on. As your computer starts up, watch for a message that describes how to run the CMOS setup (for example, "Press F1 for Setup"). Press the appropriate key to start the CMOS setup program.
2. Select the "hard drive settings" menu, and choose the drive location occupied by the CD-ROM drive (for example, "primary slave," "secondary slave," or "secondary master," depending on how you've physically jumpered and installed the drive).
3. Select "automatic drive detection" if available. This option will automatically identify the new drive. If your BIOS does not provide automatic drive detection, select "none" or "not installed" for the CD-ROM, and rely on drivers only.
4. Save the settings and exit the CMOS setup program. Your computer will automatically reboot.

REASSEMBLE THE COMPUTER

Double-check all of your signal and power cables to verify that they are secure; then tuck the cables gently into the computer's chassis. Check that there are no loose tools, screws, or cables inside the chassis. Now reattach the computer's outer housing(s).

INSTALL THE SOFTWARE

In order to complete your CD-ROM installation, you'll need to install the software drivers that accompanied the drive on floppy disk or CD. Windows 95/98 systems will generally detect the presence of the new CD-ROM and prompt you for the protected-mode drivers automatically. Under DOS, you may need to run an "installer" routine that will add the real-mode drivers to your system and update your CONFIG.SYS and AUTOEXEC.BAT files to load those drivers. If there's no real-mode installer, you'll need to update your startup files manually. (See the earlier section "Understanding the Software.") After you install the drivers and reboot the system, the CD-ROM should be ready for use.

Troubleshooting CD-ROM Drives

Though the majority of CD-ROM problems are due to software or setup problems, the drives themselves are delicate and unforgiving devices. Considering that their prices have plummeted to the point where they are virtually disposable devices, there is little economic sense in attempting a lengthy repair. When a fault occurs in the drive or in its adapter board, your best course is typically to replace the defective drive outright.

> The companion CD contains a number of CD-ROM testing/caching utilities. Check out CDANALYZ.ZIP and CDCHECK.ZIP.

GENERAL SYMPTOMS

SYMPTOM 9-1 **The drive has trouble accepting or rejecting a CD** This problem is typical of motorized CD-ROM drives where the disc is accepted into a slot, or placed in a motorized tray, so you don't see this issue in caddy-type CD-ROM drives.

- *Check for obstructions.* Before performing any disassembly, check the assembly through the CD tray for any obvious obstructions. If there is nothing obvious, expose the assembly and check each linkage and motor drive gear very carefully. Carefully remove or free any obstruction. Be gentle when working around the load/unload assembly. Notice how it is shock-mounted in four places.
- *Replace the CD-ROM drive.* If the problem persists, there is most likely a problem in the tray motor or mechanism. Your best course is to replace the CD-ROM drive outright.

SYMPTOM 9-2 **Optical read head does not seek (a.k.a. drive "seek" error)** An optical head is used to identify pits and lands along a CD-ROM and to track the spiral data pattern as the head moves across the disk. The optical head must move very slowly and smoothly to ensure accurate tracking. Head movement is accomplished using a linear stepping motor (or *linear actuator*) to shift the optical assembly in microscopic increments—head travel appears perfectly smooth to the unaided eye. Check the drive for any damaged parts or obstructions. When the optical head fails to seek, the easiest and fastest fix is simply to replace the CD-ROM mechanism outright.

SYMPTOM 9-3 **Disc cannot be read** This type of problem may result in a DOS-level "sector not found" or "drive not ready" error.

- *Clean the CD and drive optics.* Check the CD itself to ensure that it is the right format, inserted properly, and physically clean. Cleanliness is very important to a CD. Although the laser will often "look past" any surface defects in a disc, the presence of dust or debris on a disc surface can produce serious tracking (and read) errors. Try a different disc to confirm the problem. If a new or different disc reads properly, the trouble may indeed be in (or *on*) the original disc itself. The disc must not only be clean, but the head optics must also be clear. Gently dust or clean the head optics as suggested by your drive's particular manufacturer.
- *Check the cables.* Examine the power connector and signal cable between the drive and its controller board. Be sure the cable is connected correctly and completely.
- *Replace the CD-ROM drive.* Either the drive's optical head or electronics are defective. Your best course here is to try replacing the drive. If problems persist on a drive with a proprietary interface, replace the adapter board.

SYMPTOM 9-4 **The disc does not turn** You may not hear the disc "spin up" for access. The disc must turn at a constant linear velocity (CLV), which is directed and regulated by the spindle motor.

- *Check for obstructions.* If the disc is not spinning during access, check to be sure that the disc is seated properly and is not jammed or obstructed.
- *Recheck the drive's installation.* Before beginning a repair, review your drive installation and setup carefully to ensure that the drive is properly configured for operation on your system. If the computer does not recognize the CD drive (you may get a message such as "invalid drive specification"), there may be a setup or configuration problem. (Either the low-level device driver or MSCDEX may not have loaded properly.)

- *Clean the drive optics.* If your particular drive provides you with instructions for cleaning the optical head aperture, perform that cleaning operation and try the drive again. A fouled optical head can sometimes upset spindle operation.
- *Replace the CD-ROM drive.* If the drive's "Activity LED" comes on when drive access is attempted but the disc still doesn't turn (you may also see a corresponding DOS error message), the drive spindle system is probably defective.

SYMPTOM 9-5 **The optical head cannot focus its laser beam** To compensate for the minute fluctuations in disc flatness, the optical head mounts its objective lens into a small focusing mechanism that is little more than a miniature voice coil actuator. The lens does not have to move very much at all to maintain precise focus. If focus is out or not well maintained, the laser detector may produce erroneous signals. This may result in DOS drive error messages.

If random but consistent DOS errors appear, check the disc to be sure that it is *optically* clean—dust and fingerprints can result in serious access problems. Try another disc. If a new disc continues to perform badly, try cleaning the optical aperture with clean (photography-grade) air. When problems persist, the optical system is probably damaged or defective. Try replacing the CD-ROM drive mechanism outright.

SYMPTOM 9-6 **Audio is not being played by the sound card** In most cases, there is a problem with the CD-audio connection or system mixer setting.

- *Check the CD.* Double-check to verify that the CD you're trying to play actually contains Red Book audio. (Don't try to "play" data CDs.)
- *Check the headphone output.* Try playing the music CD with a set of headphones attached to the CD-ROM drive. If there is no audio from the headphone jack, adjust the volume control. If there is still no music, the drive is probably defective and should be replaced.
- *Check the sound card and mixer.* Try playing WAV or MIDI files through the sound card and verify that the card's volume setting is adequate. If you cannot play any sounds at all, there may be a problem with the sound card or its drivers rather than with the CD-ROM drive. Open the sound card's mixer applet and verify that the CD-audio channel volume is enabled and turned up to an appropriate level.
- *Check the CD-audio cable.* Verify that the CD-audio cable is appropriate for your sound card and CD-ROM drive, and see that it's attached securely at both ends. Try another CD-audio cable.

SYMPTOM 9-7 **There is no audio being generated by the drive** Normally you can listen to CD-audio using the drive's headphone jack. Check your headphones on another stereo and see that the headphones are working. Also adjust the headphone volume using the small dial located on the front of the CD-ROM drive. If the problem persists and no audio is being generated, the headphone amplifier circuit in the CD-ROM is probably defective and should be replaced.

SYMPTOM 9-8 **You see a "Wrong DOS version" error message when attempting to load MSCDEX** You are running MS-DOS 4, 5, or 6 with a version of MSCDEX that does not support it. The solution is then to change to the correct version of MSCDEX. The version compatibility for MSCDEX is shown below:

- v1.01 14,913 bytes (No ISO 9660 support—High Sierra support only)
- v2.00 18,307 bytes (High Sierra and ISO 9660 support for DOS 3.1–3.3)
- v2.10 19,943 bytes (DOS 3.1–3.3 and 4.0—DOS 5.x support provided with SETVER)

- v2.20 25,413 bytes (same as above with Win 3.x support—changes in audio support)
- v2.21 25,431 bytes (DOS 3.1–5.0 support with enhanced control under Win 3.1)
- v2.22 25,377 bytes (DOS 3.1–6.0 and higher with Win 3.1 support)
- v2.23 25,361 bytes (DOS 3.1–6.2 and Win 3.1 support—supplied with MS-DOS 6.2)

When using MS-DOS 5.x to 6.1, you will need to add the SETVER utility to CONFIG.SYS in order to use MSCDEX v2.10 or v2.20 properly (for example, DEVICE = C:\DOS\SETVER.EXE). SETVER is used to tell programs that they are running under a different version of DOS than DOS 5.0. This is important since MSCDEX (v2.10 and v2.20) refuses to work with DOS versions higher than 4.0. SETVER is used to fool MSCDEX into working with higher versions of DOS. In some versions of DOS 5.0 (such as Compaq DOS 5.0), you will need to add an entry to SETVER for MSCDEX (for example, SETVER MSCDEX.EXE 4.00). This entry modifies SETVER without changing the file size or date.

SYMPTOM 9-9 **You cannot access the CD-ROM drive letter under DOS** The drive is probably available under Windows 95/98. You may see an error message such as "Invalid drive specification." This is typically a problem with the CD-ROM drivers. The MS-DOS extension MSCDEX has probably not loaded. Switch to the DOS subdirectory and use the MEM /C function to check the loaded drivers and TSRs. If you see the low-level driver and MSCDEX displayed in the driver list, check the CD-ROM hardware. Make sure the signal cable between the drive and drive controller is inserted properly and completely. If problems persist, try replacing the drive controller.

If you do not see the low-level driver and MSCDEX shown in the driver list, inspect your CONFIG.SYS and AUTOEXEC.BAT files. Check that the drivers are included in the startup files to begin with. Make sure that the label used in the /D switch is the same for both the low-level driver and MSCDEX. If the label is not the same, MSCDEX will not load. If you are using MS-DOS 5.0, be sure the SETVER utility is loaded. You could also try updating MSCDEX to v2.30 or later.

SYMPTOM 9-10 **You see an error when trying to load the low-level CD-ROM driver** Check that you are using the proper low-level device driver for your CD-ROM drive. If you are swapping the drive or drive controller board, you probably need to load a new driver. If the driver fails to load with original hardware, the drive controller board may have failed, or its jumper settings may not match those in the driver's command-line switches. Check the signal cable running between the drive and adapter board. If the cable is crimped or scuffed, try replacing the cable. Next, try replacing the adapter board. If problems persist, try replacing the CD-ROM drive mechanism itself.

SYMPTOM 9-11 **You see an error such as "Not ready reading from drive D:"** Check that a suitable disc is inserted in the drive and that the drive is closed properly. Make sure the low-level device driver and MSCDEX are loaded correctly. If the drivers do not load, there may be a problem with the drive controller board (or drive mechanism itself). Also check that the data cable between the drive and adapter is connected properly and completely. If problems persist, suspect a weakness in the PC power supply (especially if the system is heavily loaded or upgraded, or if there is a Y-splitter cable feeding the CD-ROM). Try a larger supply in the system. If problems persist, replace the CD-ROM drive. If a new drive does not correct the problem, try a different drive controller.

SYMPTOM 9-12 **SmartDrive is not caching the CD-ROM properly in DOS** The version of SmartDrive supplied with DOS 6.2x provides three forms of caching, although older forms of SmartDrive (such as the ones distributed with Windows 3.1, DOS 6.0 and 6.1) will not adequately cache

CD-ROM drives. The BUFFERS statement also does not help caching. So if you are looking to SmartDrive for a CD-ROM cache, you should be using the version distributed with DOS 6.2x. You should also set BUFFERS=10,0 in the CONFIG.SYS file, and the SmartDrive command line should come *after* MSCDEX. When using SmartDrive, you can change the buffers setting in the MSCDEX command line (/M) to 0, which allows you to save 2KB per buffer.

> SmartDrive is not used by Windows 95/98, which employs its own CD caching scheme. Try disabling SmartDrive when running under Windows 95/98.

SYMPTOM 9-13 After installing the CD-ROM drivers, the system reports significantly less available RAM This is usually a caching issue with CD-ROM driver software, and you may need to adjust the CD-ROM driver software accordingly. This type of problem has been documented with Teac CD-ROM drives and CORELCDX.COM software. If the software offers a command-line switch to change the amount of XMS allocated, reduce the number to 512 or 256. Check with tech support for your particular drive for the exact command-line switch settings.

SYMPTOM 9-14 The CD-ROM drivers will not install properly on a drive using compression software This is usually because you booted from a floppy disk and attempted to install drivers without loading the compression software first. Before doing anything else, check the loading order—allow your system to boot from the hard drive before installing the CD-ROM drivers. This allows the compression software to assign all drive letters. As an alternative, boot from a compression-aware floppy disk. If you must boot the system from a floppy disk, make sure the disk is configured to be fully compatible with the compression software being used.

SYMPTOM 9-15 You see an error indicating that the CD-ROM drive is not found This type of problem may also appear as loading problems with the low-level driver. There are several possible reasons why the drive hardware cannot be found.

- *Check the power connector.* Make sure the 4-pin power connector is inserted properly and completely. If the drive is being powered by a Y-connector, make sure any interim connections are secure. Use a voltmeter and measure the +5-volt (pin 4) and +12-volt (pin 1) levels. If either voltage (especially the +12-volt supply) is unusually low or absent, replace the power supply.
- *Check the signal connector.* See that the drive's signal interface cable is connected securely at both the drive and controller. If the cable is visibly worn or damaged, try a new one.
- *Check for hardware conflicts.* Inspect the drive controller card (especially if it's a proprietary controller) and make sure the adapter's IRQ, DMA, and I/O address settings are correct. They must also match with the command-line switches used with the low-level driver. If the controller is for a CD-ROM alone, you may also try installing the controller in a different bus slot.
- *Check the SCSI bus.* If your CD-ROM uses a SCSI interface, make sure that the SCSI bus cable is properly terminated at both ends.
- *Replace the drive/controller.* If problems persist, replace the drive controller first; then replace the CD-ROM drive if necessary.

SYMPTOM 9-16 In a new installation, the driver fails to load successfully for the proprietary interface card In almost all cases, the proprietary interface card (or drive controller) has been configured improperly. Check the drive controller card first, and verify that the interface card is configured with the correct IRQ, DMA, and I/O address settings; then check for hardware conflicts with other devices in the system. In some cases, you may simply enter the drive maker (such as Teac) as the interface type during driver installation. Make sure the interface is set properly for the system and your particular drive. Check the driver's command line next—the driver's command-line switches should correctly reflect the drive adapter's configuration.

SYMPTOM 9-17 The CD-ROM driver loads, but you see an error such as "CDR101" (drive not ready) or "CDR103" (CDROM disk not HIGH SIERRA or ISO) You are using a very old version of the low-level driver or MSCDEX. Check your driver version (it may be outdated). Contact the drive manufacturer's tech support (or Web site) and see that you have the very latest version of their low-level driver. For very old drives, there may also be a later generic driver available. Check your version of MSCDEX next. Since low-level drivers are often bundled with MSCDEX, you may also be stuck with an old version of MSCDEX. You can usually download a current version of MSCDEX from the same place you get an updated low-level driver, or download it from Microsoft at **www.microsoft.com**.

SYMPTOM 9-18 You are having trouble setting up more than one CD-ROM drive You must be concerned about hardware and software issues. Check the drive controller first. Make sure the drive controller will support more than one CD-ROM on the same channel. (Most standard or nonproprietary controllers should.) If not, you will have to install another drive controller to support the new CD-ROM drive. Low-level drivers present another problem since you will need to have *another* copy of a low-level driver loaded in CONFIG.SYS—one for each drive. Make sure that the command-line switches for each driver match the hardware settings of the corresponding drive adapter. Finally, check your copy of MSCDEX. You need only one copy of MSCDEX in AUTOEXEC.BAT, but the /D: switch must appear twice—once for *each* drive ID.

SYMPTOM 9-19 Your CD-ROM drive refuses to work with an IDE port It may very well be that the drive uses a nonstandard or proprietary port (other than IDE). You must connect the CD-ROM drive to a compatible drive adapter, so try replacing the drive adapter board with the correct type. If the drive is proprietary, it will not interface to a regular IDE port. It may be necessary to purchase a drive adapter specifically for the CD-ROM drive. As an alternative, you might choose to upgrade the CD-ROM drive to a model that will use a standard IDE-type controller.

SYMPTOM 9-20 You cannot get the CD-ROM drive to run properly when mounted vertically CD-ROM drives with motorized drive trays generally cannot be mounted vertically—disc tracking simply will not work correctly. The only CD-ROM drives that can be mounted vertically are those with caddies, but you should check with those manufacturers before proceeding with vertical mounting.

SYMPTOM 9-21 The SCSI CD-ROM drive refuses to work when connected to an Adaptec SCSI interface Other SCSI drives are working fine. This is a common type of problem among SCSI adapters, and it is particularly recognized with Adaptec boards because of their great popularity. In most cases, the Adaptec drivers are the wrong version for your adapter, or they're corrupted. Try turning off Sync Negotiations on the Adaptec SCSI interface, and reboot the system. Your SCSI drivers may also be buggy or outdated. Check with Adaptec technical support (**www.adaptec.com**) to determine whether there are later drivers that you should use instead.

SYMPTOM 9-22 You see a "No drives found" error when the CD-ROM driver line is executed in CONFIG.SYS In most cases, the driver command-line switches do not match the hardware configuration of the drive controller, or your low-level driver may be missing or corrupt.

- *Check the CD-ROM driver.* Open CONFIG.SYS into a word processor and see that the low-level driver has a complete and accurate command line. See that any command-line switches are set correctly. Also verify that the driver referenced in the command line is actually present on the hard drive.
- *Check the MSCDEX driver.* Open AUTOEXEC.BAT into a word processor and see that the MSCDEX command line is accurate and complete. Also confirm that any MSCDEX command-line switches are set correctly. You might try updating your version of MSCDEX.
- *Check your CD-ROM cache.* If you are using SmartDrive with DOS 6.0 or later, try adding the /U switch to the end of your SmartDrive command line in AUTOEXEC.BAT.
- *Check for hardware conflicts.* Make sure that there are no other hardware devices in the system that may be conflicting with the CD-ROM drive controller. If problems persist, replace the drive controller, or replace the CD-ROM drive if necessary.

SYMPTOM 9-23 **The LCD on your CD-ROM displays an error code** Even without knowing the particular meaning of every possible error message, you can be assured that most CD-based error messages can be traced to the following causes (in order of ease):

- *Bad caddy* The CD caddy is damaged or inserted incorrectly. The CD may also be inserted into the caddy improperly. With a motorized tray, the CD may be inserted improperly.
- *Bad mounting* The drive is mounted improperly, or mounting screws are shorting out the drive's electronics.
- *Bad power* Check the +12 and +5 volts powering the CD-ROM drive. Low power may require a new or larger supply. Remove any Y-splitter that may be tapping the drive's power.
- *Bad drive* Internal diagnostics have detected a fault in the CD-ROM drive. Try replacing the drive.
- *Bad drive controller* Drive diagnostics have detected a fault in the drive controller. Try replacing the drive controller or SCSI adapter (whichever interface you're using).

SYMPTOM 9-24 **When a SCSI CD-ROM drive is connected to a SCSI adapter, the system hangs when the SCSI BIOS loads** In most cases, the CD-ROM drive supports plug-and-play, but the SCSI controller's BIOS does not. Disable the SCSI BIOS through a jumper on the controller (or remove the SCSI BIOS IC entirely) and use a SCSI driver in CONFIG.SYS instead. You may need to download a low-level SCSI driver from the adapter manufacturer.

> If there are other SCSI drives on the adapter that rely on the SCSI BIOS (such as SCSI hard drives), it may not be possible to disable the SCSI BIOS. In that case, a separate SCSI controller may be needed.

SYMPTOM 9-25 **You see an error such as "Unable to detect ATAPI IDE CD-ROM drive, device driver not loaded"** You have a problem with the configuration of your IDE/EIDE controller hardware. Check the signal cable first, and make sure the 40-pin signal cable is attached properly between the drive and controller. IDE CD-ROM drives are typically installed on a secondary 40-pin IDE port. Make sure that there is no device in the system using the same IRQ or I/O address as your secondary IDE port. Finally, make sure that any command-line switches for the low-level driver in CONFIG.SYS correspond to the controller's hardware settings.

SYMPTOM 9-26 **The CD-ROM drive door will not open once the 40-pin IDE signal cable is connected** You should only need power to operate the drive door. If the door stops when the signal cable is attached, there are some possible problems to check.

- *Check the power connector*. Make sure that both +5 volts and +12 volts are available at the power connector. See that the power connector is attached securely to the back of the CD-ROM drive.
- *Check the IDE signal cable*. The 40-pin signal cable is probably reversed at either the drive or controller. Try a different signal cable. Also make sure that the 40-pin IDE drive is plugged into a "true" IDE port, not a proprietary (non-IDE 40-pin) port.
- *Replace the CD-ROM drive*. If problems persist, try a known-good CD-ROM drive.

SYMPTOM 9-27 **You are using an old CD-ROM and can play CD audio, but you cannot access directories or other computer data from a CD** Older proprietary CD-ROM drives often used two low-level drivers—one for audio and one for data. You probably have only one of the drivers installed. Check your low-level drivers first, and see that any necessary low-level drivers are loaded in the CONFIG.SYS file. Also see that any command-line switches are set properly. Some older sound boards with integrated proprietary CD-ROM drive controllers may not work properly with the drivers required for your older CD-ROM drive. You may have to alter the proprietary controller's IRQ, DMA, or I/O settings (and update the driver's command-line switches) until you find a combination that lets the driver and controller work together.

SYMPTOM 9-28 **An IDE CD-ROM is not detected on a 486 PCI motherboard** This is a known problem when using Aztech CD-ROM drives and 486 PCI motherboards with SIS 82C497 chipsets. The motherboard bus noise is far too high, and this results in the misinterpretation of the IDE interface handshaking signals (namely DASP and PDIAG). As a consequence, the CD-ROM drive sometimes (or always) is not detected. You may be able to resolve this problem by connecting the IDE CD-ROM drive as a slave device to the hard disk, though you may need to slow the hard drive's data transfer mode to accommodate the slower CD-ROM drive.

SYMPTOM 9-29 **You notice that Matsushita CD-ROM drives are misdetected as "Matshita"** This occurs under Windows 95, Windows 95 OSR2, and Windows 98. This is a problem with the CD-ROM drive itself. It returns "Matshita" (instead of "Matsushita") as the device description when enumerated by Windows. You'll need to check with Matsushita for a firmware upgrade, driver fix, or other corrective options. You may also choose to replace the CD-ROM drive outright.

SYMPTOM 9-30 **An IDE CD-ROM is not detected when "slaved" to an IBM hard drive** This is a known problem with Aztech IDE CD-ROM drives and IBM Dala 3450 hard drives. The pulse width for the drive detection signal (DASP) is not long enough for the CD-ROM to identify itself properly. This results in the improper detection of an Aztech IDE CD-ROM. You should make the CD-ROM drive a master device on its own IDE channel, or (if possible) upgrade the CD-ROM drive's firmware to utilize more reliable timing. If the CD-ROM manufacturer has no firmware upgrades available, and you cannot reconfigure the CD-ROM on another IDE channel, you'll need to replace the CD-ROM *or* the hard drive.

SYMPTOM 9-31 **The CD-ROM drive will not read or run CD Plus or Enhanced CD titles** This is a known problem with Acer CD-ROM models 625A, 645A, 655A, 665A, 525E, 743E, 747E, and 767E. The CD Plus (or Enhanced CD) titles use a nonstandard data format released and supported by Sony. The new format is for interactive CD titles that incorporate video clips and music, and the data structures on these CDs cannot be recognized by these CD-ROM drive models. In this case, you'll need to upgrade the CD-ROM drive outright to a newer model that can accommodate newer file types.

SYMPTOM 9-32 **You notice that the LED indicator on the CD-ROM is always on** The drive seems to be working properly. This is not necessarily a problem. Some CD-ROM drive models (such as the Acer 600 series) use the LED indicator as a "Ready" light instead of a "Busy" light. Whenever a CD is loaded in the drive, the LED will be lit and will remain lit whether the drive is being accessed or not. This feature tells the user whether a CD-ROM disc is currently loaded in the drive by simply checking the LED. There may be a jumper on the CD-ROM drive that allows you to switch the indicator light from "Ready" mode to "Busy" mode.

SYMPTOM 9-33 **The drive vibrates or makes a great deal of noise with certain CD and CD-R discs** This is almost always due to an unbalanced disc in high-speed (12X and faster) CD-ROM drives. A disc may become unbalanced from improper silk-screening or the application of a label. When that unbalanced disc is rotated at high speeds, the entire drive tends to vibrate. (Often this vibration resonates inside the case, making the sound seem even louder.) Make sure that each disc used in the drive is evenly marked or labeled. If the problem seems to occur on all discs, verify that the drive itself is mounted securely to the chassis.

SYMPTOM 9-34 **The system locks up when using a Panasonic "Big 5" CD-ROM drive under Windows 95** This trouble is known to occur if you're using IDE bus-mastering drivers with the Panasonic "Big 5" five-disc CD-ROM changer (model SQ-TC510N). The Panasonic drive will require new firmware to overcome this problem, so contact Panasonic to update the device with the latest firmware revision. To avoid this problem in the meantime, remove the CD-ROM changer from your system.

WINDOWS-RELATED SYMPTOMS

SYMPTOM 9-35 **The front-panel controls of your SCSI CD-ROM drive do not appear to work under Windows 95/98** Those same controls appear to work fine in DOS. Windows 95/98 uses SCSI commands to poll removable media devices every two seconds in order to see if there has been a change in status. Since SCSI commands to the CD-ROM generally have higher priority than front-panel controls, the front-panel controls may appear to be disabled under Windows 95/98. Try pressing the front-panel controls repeatedly. You may be able to correct this issue by disabling the CD-ROM polling under Windows 95/98.

SYMPTOM 9-36 **You cannot change the CD-ROM drive letter under Windows 95/98** You need to change the drive's settings under the Device Manager:

1. Open the Control Panel and select the System icon.
2. Once the System Properties dialog opens, click on the Device Manager page.
3. Locate the entry for the CD-ROM. Click on the + sign to expand the list of CD-ROM devices.
4. Double-click on the desired CD-ROM.
5. Once the CD-ROM drive's Properties dialog appears, choose the Settings page.
6. Locate the current drive letter assignment box and enter the new drive designation. Multiple letters are needed only when a SCSI device is implementing LUN addressing (multidisc changers).
7. Click on the OK button to save your changes.
8. Click on the OK button to close the Device Manager.
9. A System Settings Change window should appear. Click on the Yes button to reboot the system so that the changes can take effect, or click on the No button so that you can make more changes to

other CD-ROMs before rebooting the system. Changes will not become effective until the system is rebooted.

SYMPTOM 9-37 **You installed Windows 95/98 from a CD-ROM disc using DOS drivers, but when you removed the real-mode CD-ROM drivers from CONFIG.SYS, the CD-ROM no longer works** You need to enable protected-mode drivers by running the Add New Hardware wizard from the Control Panel:

1. Boot Windows 95/98 using the real-mode drivers for your CD-ROM and its interface.
2. Open the Control Panel and select the Add New Hardware icon.
3. Proceed to add new hardware, but do not let Windows 95/98 attempt to autodetect the new hardware. Use the floppy disk with protected-mode drivers for the new installation.
4. When the new software is installed, Windows 95/98 will tell you that it must reboot before the hardware will be available—*do not reboot yet.*
5. Open a word processor such as Notepad, and edit the CONFIG.SYS and AUTOEXEC.BAT files to "REMark" out the real-mode drivers for your CD and the reference to MSCDEX.
6. Shut down Windows 95/98, and then power-down the system.
7. Check to be sure the CD-ROM interface is set to use the resources assigned by Windows 95/98 (not necessary if the interface is PnP or a standard IDE-type controller).
8. Reboot the system. Your protected-mode drivers should now load normally.

SYMPTOM 9-38 **Your CD-ROM drive's "parallel port-to-SCSI" interface worked with Windows 3.1x, but does not work under Windows 95/98** This problem is typical of the NEC CD-EPPSCSI01 interface and is usually due to a problem with the driver's assessment of your parallel port type (bidirectional, unidirectional, or enhanced parallel port).

- *Cold boot the computer.* Since typical parallel-port-to-SCSI interfaces get their power from the SCSI device, the external drive must be powered up first.
- *Check the CMOS setup.* Start your CMOS setup routine first and see what mode your parallel port is set to operate in. Make sure it is set to a mode that is compatible with your parallel port drive.
- *Check the MSCDEX driver.* Update your version of MSCDEX if necessary. Change the MSCDEX command line in AUTOEXEC.BAT to load from the C:\WINDOWS\CONTROL\ directory, and remove the /L:x parameter from the end of the MSCDEX command line (if present).
- *Check the device drivers.* If you're using real-mode drivers for the interface, place a switch at the end of the interface's command line that tells the driver what mode your parallel port is operating in. For example, the Trantor T358 driver (MA358.SYS) uses the following switches (yours will probably be different):

  /m02—For unidirectional mode (also known as standard or output only)
  /m04—For bidirectional mode (also known as PS/2 mode)
  /m08—For enhanced mode

- *Disable the real-mode drivers.* Remove or REMark out any references to the interface's real-mode drivers in CONFIG.SYS, and then remove or disable the MSCDEX command line in AUTOEXEC.BAT. Start Windows 95/98, open the Control Panel, select the System icon, and then choose the Device Manager page. Find the SCSI adapter settings and expand the SCSI Controllers branch of the device tree. Select the device identification line for your parallel-port-to-SCSI interface; then click on the Properties

9

button. Click on the Settings page. In the Adapter Settings dialog box, type in the same parameter that would have been used if you were using real-mode drivers. Click on the OK button to save your changes; then select Yes to reboot the system.

- *Check/replace the adapter itself.* If problems persist, check the technical support for your parallel-port-to-SCSI adapter, and see if there are any known problems with your particular setup, or any updated drivers available for download.

SYMPTOM 9-39 You see a message such as "CD-ROM can run, but results may not be as expected" This simply means that Windows 95/98 is using real-mode drivers. If protected-mode drivers are available for the CD-ROM drive, you should use those instead. You may download and install protected-mode drivers from the CD-ROM manufacturer's Web site.

SYMPTOM 9-40 The CD-ROM works fine in DOS or Windows 3.1x, but sound or video appears choppy under Windows 95/98 Several factors can affect CD-ROM performance under Windows 95:

- *Install the latest protected-mode drivers.* Windows 95 performance (and stability) is severely degraded by real-mode drivers, so start by removing or disabling any real-mode drivers. Try installing the protected-mode drivers for your CD-ROM drive instead. If protected-mode drivers are not available for your drive, consider upgrading the CD-ROM hardware.
- *Avoid real-mode applications under Windows 95/98.* Real-mode applications that are run under Windows 95/98 can cripple a system's performance. Try exiting any DOS or Windows 3.1x applications that may be running on the Windows 95/98 desktop. Also exit unneeded Windows 95/98 applications since additional applications take a toll on processing power. Try exiting any Windows 95 applications that may be running in the background.
- *Free "wasted" resources.* Try rebooting the system to ensure that Windows 95/98 has the maximum amount of resources available before running your CD-ROM application.

SYMPTOM 9-41 You can't read a video CD-I disc in Windows 95 using any ATAPI/IDE CD-ROM drive The built-in ATAPI driver in Windows 95 cannot read raw data in 32-bit disk access mode. Note that such symptoms can also happen to any ATAPI/IDE-compatible CD-ROM as long as it is using the built-in ATAPI driver in Windows 95. You should update the CD-ROM's ATAPI driver to a current manufacturer-specific version. As another alternative, you can use the following procedure:

1. Disable the 32-bit disk access feature of Windows 95.
2. Under the Windows 95 desktop, click Start and choose Settings and Control Panel.
3. Click on System icon and select the Performance option.
4. Choose File System and select the Troubleshooting option.
5. At the Troubleshooting dialog, click on "Disable all 32-bit disk access."
6. Edit AUTOEXEC.BAT and append the following line (where <path> is the path name of your Windows 95 software):

```
C:\<path>\COMMAND\MSCDEX.EXE /D:MSCD000
```

SYMPTOM 9-42 You cannot play CD-audio on a particular CD-ROM under Windows 95 Replacing the CD-ROM resolves the problem. This is a known incompatibility issue with Acer 525E CD-ROM drives and Windows 95. (This does not affect the integrity of programs and data.) Windows 95 will mute the CD audio on this and many other brands of double speed IDE CD-ROMs. If you cannot obtain a patch directly from Microsoft or the CD-ROM manufacturer, your only alternative is to replace the CD-ROM drive.

SYMPTOM 9-43 **After upgrading to Windows 98, you notice multiple CD-ROM letters** You may see up to four CD-ROM drives displayed in My Computer and/or Windows Explorer, even though you have only one CD-ROM drive in the computer. This problem is known to occur with NEC 4X4, 4X6, 4X8, or 4X16 CD-ROM drives if you've installed the NEC Single CD tool in your previous version of Windows. To correct the problem, simply reinstall the NEC Single CD tool under Windows 98 using the disc included with your NEC 4X CD-ROM drive. You may also wish to download and install the latest versions of that software (and the CD-ROM drivers).

SYMPTOM 9-44 **After upgrading to Windows 98, you encounter problems with the CD-ROM and hard drive** Once the upgrade to Windows 98 is complete, the following symptoms may occur:

- You cannot access your CD-ROM drive.
- Hard disks connected to the IDE-type controller are forced to use DOS Compatibility Mode.
- Another drive appears in My Computer and/or Windows Explorer that is about 13MB in size.

This is a known problem when Helix Hurricane for Windows 95 (by Helix Software) is installed on your computer. To correct this issue, you'll need to remove Hurricane, using its uninstall tool. (You may be able to patch or update Hurricane, but you'll need to contact the program manufacturer.) Restart your computer, and use the Startup menu to boot to the Windows 98 "Safe Mode Command Prompt Only." Run the uninstall tool in the folder where Hurricane is installed. If the uninstall tool is not available, you can disable Hurricane manually:

1. Use a text editor (such as Notepad) to open the AUTOEXEC.BAT file.
2. Disable the line containing QWATCH.COM in the AUTOEXEC.BAT file by REMarking out that command line.
3. Save and close the AUTOEXEC.BAT file.
4. Use a text editor to open the SYSTEM.INI file.
5. Disable the following lines in the [386Enh] section of SYSTEM.INI by placing a semicolon (;) at the beginning of each line:

```
device=<path>\arpl.386
device=<path>\Winsa.386
device=<path>\Winguard.386
device=<path>\vxmsems.386
device=<path>\windrv.386
device=<path>\vcache16.386
device=<path>\vsectd.386
device=<path>\heapx.386
```

6. Now change the following lines in the [Boot] section of SYSTEM.INI from

```
system.drv=<path>\sysdrv.drv
```

to

```
system.drv=System.drv
```

and from

```
display.drv=<path>\winsa256.drv
```

to

```
display.drv=Pnpdrvr.drv.
```

> If your original display driver was not PNPDRVR.DRV, start Windows in the Safe Mode and change the display driver to the appropriate version.

7 Save and close the SYSTEM.INI file; then reboot the computer.

SYMPTOM 9-45 **Your CD-ROM changer doesn't work after upgrading to Windows 98** This is a known problem with the AST Advantage 828 computer with a CD-ROM changer. After upgrading to Windows 98, a single CD-ROM drive may be displayed in Device Manager (and the CD-ROM changer may be displayed as "Unknown Hardware" under the Other Devices entry). This problem will occur if the SmartCD Manager software is installed on an AST system with a Torisan (Sanyo) CDR-C36 6X three-disc CD-ROM changer. The SCDMGRT3.VXD file located in the \Windows\System\Iosubsys folder will typically prevent Windows 98 from detecting the CD-ROM changer. To correct this problem, you'll need to move the SCDMGRT3.VXD file into a different folder. You may also check for an updated version of SCDMGRT3.VXD from AST or Sanyo.

SYMPTOM 9-46 **Your SmartCD Manager software does not work under Windows 98** After upgrading to Windows 98, you may find that your Torisan (Sanyo) three-disc CD-ROM drive now has three separate drive letters assigned to it. This problem may occur even though the SmartCD Manager program has assigned only one drive letter to this device. The problem occurs because Windows 98 replaces the CDVSD.VXD and TORISAN3.VXD files included with the SmartCD Manager program, and the updated versions of these files are not compatible with your SmartCD Manager software. To correct this problem, simply reinstall the SmartCD Manager program.

SYMPTOM 9-47 **The "auto insert notification" feature prevents a system's "automatic suspend" modes from working** Many current computers include power management features that place the computer in a suspended power state (a.k.a. power-down mode) after a given period of inactivity. If the "auto insert notification" option is enabled for IDE-type CD-ROM drives when power management is also enabled, the computer may not suspend automatically. This typically occurs because some IDE-type CD-ROM drives use the "ATA GET MEDIA STATUS" command method for polling. But a power management system will detect the action as "drive activity." Since a drive then appears to be in use, the power management system will not power-down the system. (This is a known issue with Windows 95 OSR2.) You can work around this issue by disabling the "auto insert notification" option for affected drives.

As a more permanent fix, you may also download and install the REMIDEUP.EXE file from Microsoft's Web site. This update will install the following file update: ESDI_506.PDR version 4.00.956 (dated 5/14/96). Of course, later versions of the file should also work.

SYMPTOM 9-48 **The computer locks up while browsing a CD-ROM** This often occurs under Windows 95/98 after installing a Hewlett-Packard CD-RW drive in some Compaq Deskpro computers. Your computer may halt when you try to use My Computer or Windows Explorer to view the CD-RW drive. In most circumstances, this type of problem is driver related. When dealing with Compaq systems, Compaq uses a custom device driver file named CPQDFVS.VXD. This file is located in the \Windows\System\Iosubsys folder, and it can lock up the computer when you try to read from the CD-RW drive. To work around this problem for the Compaq, delete or rename the CPQDFVS.VXD file. To correct this issue on a more permanent basis, contact Compaq for a patch or update to the CPQDFVS.VXD file.

SYMPTOM 9-49 You cannot read Rock Ridge CD-ROM extensions under Windows This occurs because Windows 95 and 98 are simply not designed to support the Rock Ridge CD-ROM extensions. Rock Ridge is a means of storing POSIX file system extensions on a CD-ROM, but Windows 95/98 uses the Joliet file system (which allows for deep subdirectories and long file names) instead of the Rock Ridge CD-ROM format. If you need to read Rock Ridge–formatted CD-ROMs in Windows 95/98, configure real-mode driver support for the CD-ROM using the Windows 95/98 version of MSCDEX.EXE in AUTOEXEC.BAT, and the DOS device drivers (provided by the CD-ROM drive manufacturer) in CONFIG.SYS.

SYMPTOM 9-50 Under Windows 98, an Alps DC544 CD-ROM changer appears as four individual CD-ROM drives in My Computer or Windows Explorer This problem occurs because the ALPSTRAY.EXE program does not work correctly in Windows 98. To work around this issue, use the Alps DC544 CD-ROM changer as if it were four different CD-ROM drives. As a more permanent fix, check with Alps for an updated ALPSTRAY.EXE file.

SYMPTOM 9-51 The Pioneer DR-UA124X CD-ROM drive disables your IDE channel under Windows 95/98 You may see a yellow exclamation point next to an IDE port in your Device Manager. This problem frequently occurs when you have a Pioneer CD-ROM drive (such as the DR-UA124X) installed on your computer, and you cannot access the CD-ROM drive connected to that IDE port. The Pioneer DR-UA124X CD-ROM drive's firmware causes this issue. You'll need to reenable real-mode support for the drive. Use any text editor (such as Notepad) to open the AUTOEXEC.BAT file. Find the MSCDEX command line, and remove the "REM" statement at the beginning of that line. Save your changes and restart the computer. As an alternative, contact Pioneer for a firmware update or exchange.

SYMPTOM 9-52 Your Toshiba Tecra 750 locks up when Windows 98 starts This is a known issue with Toshiba Tecra PCs with CD-ROM drives, and it can occur if all of the following conditions exist:

- The computer uses an IDE-type CD-ROM drive.
- The IDE controller that is operating the CD-ROM drive is using the driver shipped with Windows 98.
- You enable direct memory access (DMA) support for the CD-ROM drive.

This problem is caused by the IDE chipset used in Toshiba Tecra 750 computers. You may be able to correct this trouble by installing the Toshiba drivers rather than using the native Windows drivers:

1. Turn off the computer.
2. Physically remove the CD-ROM drive from the computer.
3. Restart the computer.
4. Install the Toshiba drivers for the IDE controller. (If you don't have the drivers on a floppy disk already, download them from Toshiba's Web site.)

9

5 Shut down the computer.
6 Put the CD-ROM drive back into the computer.
7 Restart your computer.
8 Windows should start normally and redetect the CD-ROM drive.

SYMPTOM 9-53 When loading an audio CD in the drive, you receive a "no disc loaded" error This problem can occur under Windows 95 or 98 and is typically caused when the MCI CD audio driver is not installed. You'll need to verify that the CD audio device driver is enabled:

1 Open the Control Panel and double-click on the Multimedia icon.
2 On the Advanced or Devices tab, double-click Media Control Devices.
3 Double-click CD Audio Device (Media Control).
4 Verify that the Use This Media Control Device entry is selected.

If the driver is enabled (but you still receive the error message), try removing and reinstalling the device. To accomplish this, click Remove on the General tab in your CD Audio Device (Media Control) properties, and then follow these steps:

1 Open the Control Panel and double-click the Add New Hardware icon.
2 Click Next, click No, and then click Next.
3 In the Hardware Types box, click Sound, Video, and Game Controllers, and then click Next.
4 In the Manufacturers box, click Microsoft MCI.
5 In the Models box, click CD Audio Device (Media Control).
6 Click Next, click Finish, and then restart your computer.

SYMPTOM 9-54 You get poor performance from a CD-based program under Windows 95/98 When running a program that accesses a CD-ROM, you may notice that the program is not performing very well. You may notice slow data transfer in a business or reference program, or skipping (choppy audio or video) in a multimedia program. In many cases, this problem crops up when the Supplemental Cache Size and/or Optimize Access Pattern For settings are not configured correctly for your particular CD-ROM drive. Optimize your CD-ROM settings as follows:

1 Click Start, highlight Settings, click Control Panel, and double-click the System icon.
2 On the Performance tab, click File System; then click the CD-ROM tab.
3 Move the Supplemental Cache Size slider to the right to allocate more memory (RAM) for caching data from the CD-ROM drive, or to the left to allocate less RAM for caching data. (Many multimedia programs perform better with a smaller cache because these programs tend not to reuse data.)
4 For reading continuous data (such as AVI files), use a higher setting in the Optimize Access Pattern For box. For reading random data, increase the Supplemental Cache Size setting, and decrease the Optimize Access Pattern For setting.
5 Click OK, then click Close. Restart the PC when prompted to do so.

SYMPTOM 9-55 You cannot access a CD-ROM on an Acer 91 Pentium-based PC under Windows 95/98 After you upgrade an Acer computer from an earlier version of Windows to Windows 95/98, you may find that the CD-ROM drive is not detected, or 32-bit disk and file access are not available. These problems may also occur when you upgrade an Acer computer to Windows 95/98. This issue occurs when the CD-ROM drive is connected to a CMD CSA-6400E PCI IDE controller—the CMD640X.SYS real-mode driver used with Acer computers is designed to work in Windows 3.1 and does not work in Windows 95/98. To correct this problem, install the Windows 95/98 version of the CMD CSA-6400E PCI IDE driver, or download the self-extracting file CMDWIN95.EXE from Acer's Web site (**www.acer.com/aac/win95/upgrades/ftp.htm**).

> If you use the CMD 6400 PCI controller's protected-mode driver, 32-bit disk and file access is functional, but the CD-ROM drive is not detected. If you use the CMD 6400 PCI controller real-mode driver CMD640X.SYS, the CD-ROM drive is detected, but 32-bit disk and file access is not available.

> All Acer computer systems with a part number starting with "91.AA043" or "91.AA260" (using the CMD CSA-6400E PCI IDE controller and a Maxtor 7546AT hard disk) running Windows 95/98 will exhibit this problem.

SYMPTOM 9-56 **You cannot access a CD-ROM drive under Windows 95/98** When you try to access your CD-ROM drive in Windows, you may encounter one of the following symptoms:

- You cannot run executable (EXE) files.
- You cannot view complete directory listings.
- You get a "Device not found" error message.

These problems will develop if you're using an older version of the MSCDEX.EXE file, which is not compatible with Windows 95/98. This commonly occurs when you install certain real-mode CD-ROM drivers—an older version of the MSCDEX.EXE file is copied to the hard disk, and the AUTOEXEC.BAT file is updated to utilize this older file. Modify the AUTOEXEC.BAT file manually to address the correct version of MSCDEX.EXE:

1. Use any text editor (such as Notepad) to open the AUTOEXEC.BAT file.
2. Locate the MSCDEX command line; then modify the line to read

   ```
   <drive>:\<windows>\command\mscdex.exe <parameters>
   ```

   where <drive> is the drive letter where the Windows folder is located, <windows> is the name of the folder where Windows is installed, and <parameters> are the parameters from the original command line. Make sure to use all the parameters exactly as they are used in the original line.
3. Save and then close the AUTOEXEC.BAT file.
4. Restart your computer.

SYMPTOM 9-57 **A Sony CD-ROM drive is not detected during Windows 95/98 setup** This problem can occur when the Sony CD-ROM drive is attached to a Media Vision sound card. Setup searches for Sony CD-ROM drives at several base I/O addresses, but a Sony CD-ROM drive attached to a Media Vision sound card is not in the range of addresses that setup checks. As a result, setup retains the existing real-mode drivers for the CD-ROM drive, but this often reduces system performance. You can get around this problem by setting up the Sony CD-ROM drive in Windows manually:

1. Click the Start button, highlight Settings, and click Control Panel.

2 Double-click the Add New Hardware icon, and then click the Next button.
3 Click the No option button, and then click Next.
4 Click CD-ROM Controllers, and then click Next.
5 In the Manufacturers box, click Sony. In the Models box, click Sony Proprietary CD-ROM Controller, and then click Next.
6 Click Next, and then click Finish.
7 When you are prompted to restart your computer, click No.
8 Click the Start button, highlight Settings, and then click Control Panel.
9 Double-click the System icon.
10 On the Device Manager tab, double-click the CD-ROM Controllers entry, and then double-click Sony Proprietary CD-ROM Controller.
11 Click the Resources tab.
12 In the Settings Based On box, click Basic Configuration 0.
13 Click the Use Automatic Settings check box to clear it.
14 Use the Change Settings button to modify the resources to match the CD-ROM drive's settings.
15 Click OK.
16 Restart your computer when you're prompted to do so.

> To verify that the CD-ROM drive is set up correctly, check it in Device Manager to see that no problems are reported in the Device Status box. Also, make sure that you can read a CD-ROM in the CD-ROM drive.

SYMPTOM 9-58 **The system locks up while copying data from the CD-ROM under Windows 95/98** When you are copying a large directory structure from a CD-ROM drive to a local hard disk, your computer may lock up (forcing you to reboot). This problem is typically caused by the CD-ROM "read-ahead" feature. The feature can cause the CD-ROM drive controller to be driven faster than it was designed to be. To prevent this problem, reduce the read-ahead caching level for your CD-ROM:

1 Click the Start button, highlight Settings, and then click Control Panel.
2 Double-click the System icon.
3 On the Performance tab, click File System, and then click the CD-ROM tab.
4 In the Optimize Access Pattern For box, click the setting that matches the CD-ROM drive you're using. Click OK, and then restart the computer when you are prompted to.
5 If the problem persists, repeat this process, selecting a lower read-ahead value (or select No Read-Ahead).

SYMPTOM 9-59 **Two CD-ROM drive letters appear in My Computer under Windows 95/98** When you use My Computer or Windows Explorer, two CD-ROM drives may be displayed (even though you have only one CD-ROM drive in your computer). When you try to access either CD-ROM drive, your computer may lock up. This trouble can occur if you have both the real-mode CD-ROM device drivers and the Windows 95/98 CD-ROM device drivers installed. To resolve this problem, use the System Configuration Editor (SYSEDIT.EXE) to disable the real-mode CD-ROM device drivers:

1. Click Start, click Run, type **sysedit** in the Open box, and then click OK.
2. Select the AUTOEXEC.BAT file, locate the line that loads the real-mode CD-ROM device drivers, and then type **rem** followed by a space at the beginning of the line. For example:

   ```
   rem c:\windows\command\mscdex.exe /d:mscd001
   ```

3. Select the CONFIG.SYS file, locate the line that loads the real-mode CD-ROM device drivers, and then type **rem** followed by a space at the beginning of the line. For example:

   ```
   rem device=c:\cdrom\cdrom.sys /d:mscd001
   ```

4. On the File menu, click Exit.
5. Click Yes when you're prompted to save the CONFIG.SYS and AUTOEXEC.BAT files.
6. Restart your computer.

SYMPTOM 9-60 The CD-ROM refuses to run automatically under Windows 95/98 when a disc is inserted This may occur even when the "auto insert notification" feature is enabled. In most cases, the trouble is caused by an incorrect value in the registry. To resolve this problem, use the registry editor to locate the following key:

```
HKEY_CURRENT_USER\Software\Microsoft\Windows\CurrentVersion\Policies\
Explorer\NoDriveTypeAutoRun
```

Then modify the value for the "NoDriveTypeAutoRun" key to **0000 95 00 00 00** (or **0x95** in REGEDT32.EXE). After you make this change, quit the registry editor and restart your computer.

SYMPTOM 9-61 A CD-ROM icon appears for a hard drive under Windows 95 OSR2 or Windows 98 When you attempt to review your drives through My Computer, your hard disk icon may appear as a CD-ROM icon. If you double-click the CD-ROM icon in My Computer, you may receive an error message such as "Cannot find autorun.exe." This problem can occur if the AUTORUN.INF file has been located in the root folder of your hard disk. To correct the problem, rename the AUTORUN.INF file to AUTORUN.OLD:

1. Click Start, point to Find, and then click Files Or Folders.
2. In the Named box, type **autorun.inf**, and then click Find Now.
3. Right-click on AUTORUN.INF in the list of found files, and then click Properties.
4. Click the Read-Only check box to clear it, and then click OK.
5. Right-click on AUTORUN.INF in the list of found files, and then click Rename.
6. Type **autorun.old**, and then press ENTER.
7. Restart your computer.

SYMPTOM 9-62 You receive an error such as "CD-ROM cache acceleration file is invalid" under Windows 98 This kind of problem is typically encountered when using Quarterdeck SpeedyROM version 1.0 under Windows 98. Also, even though SpeedyROM may offer to reconstruct this file, you may continue to receive the same error message whenever you restart your computer. This trouble is generally caused when your computer's BIOS is configured to use a "fast reboot" feature. To correct this issue, disable the "fast reboot" feature in your computer's CMOS setup.

Your BIOS may use a term other than "fast reboot" to identify the feature, so refer to your system's documentation for more CMOS setup details.

INSTALLATION-RELATED SYMPTOMS

SYMPTOM 9-63 **The computer does not initialize** This symptom assumes that you have proper power connected to the computer and that the power switch is on. If the system's power light comes on, but there is no system activity (or the system begins its memory test and initialization, but freezes or hangs up), there may be a problem with the drive's adapter board. Turn off all power to the system, open the computer, and check again to see that the adapter board and all available expansion boards are inserted properly and completely. Also double-check the board's configuration to be sure that its base I/O address, IRQ line, or DMA channel does not conflict with other devices that may be present in your system. You may have to remove the adapter board to check its configuration settings. Finally, double-check the data cable running between the drive and adapter board. If one end of the cable is reversed, the confused flow of data may be enough to freeze some computer designs—it really depends on your adapter board and computer—but it is always worth a second look.

If you are unable to resolve the problem with the new drive installed, try disabling the drive by removing the adapter board and data cable. You may leave the actual CD-ROM, CD-R, or CD-RW drive in its drive bay, but you should also disconnect the drive's power cable. If the system then initializes normally (although you will see errors when the system tries to load the drive's device drivers), you will know the problem lies in your drive installation. Try a new drive adapter.

SYMPTOM 9-64 **The computer fails to recognize the new CD-ROM, CD-R, or CD-RW drive** The typical causes of this problem relate to the device drivers that must be loaded to support your drive—one or more device drivers may not be loading properly. If a driver fails to load or loads improperly, the drive will not operate properly (if at all). Check that the Microsoft MSCDEX.EXE device driver is installed in your system and that it is located in the path called out in your AUTOEXEC.BAT file. If the driver is in a different path, adjust the calling line in AUTOEXEC.BAT. If the driver is not found, copy the driver to the location called out in AUTOEXEC.BAT, or reinstall the CD-ROM/CD-R/CD-RW device driver software from scratch. If you make any changes, be sure to reboot your computer to effect the change.

Next, check that the manufacturer's drive-specific device driver (usually with a .SYS extension) is installed in the system and that it is located in the path called out in your CONFIG.SYS file. If the driver is in a different path, adjust the calling line in CONFIG.SYS. If the driver is not found, copy the driver to the location called out in CONFIG.SYS, or reinstall the CD-ROM/CD-R/CD-RW device driver software from scratch. If you make any changes, be sure to reboot your computer to effect the change. When dealing with drivers, the command-line switches for both drivers must match in order to address the drive properly. Check the command-line switches for the low-level driver and MSCDEX.

There may also be a problem with your drive's host adapter board. Turn off all power to the system, open the computer, and check again to see that the adapter board and all available expansion boards are inserted properly and completely. Double-check the board's configuration to be sure that its base I/O address, IRQ line, or DMA channel does not conflict with other devices that may be present in your system. You may have to remove the adapter board to check its configuration settings.

SYMPTOM 9-65 **The drive will not read a CD correctly** As a sanity check, make sure that a CD is indeed inserted in the drive in its proper orientation (usually silk-screen side *up*). Also make sure that the CD in the drive is the right kind of disc. For example, an audio CD cannot be accessed for programs and data files like a computer-compatible CD. Try accessing the disc a number of times before giving up. Try removing and reinserting the disc several times as well—inexpensive drives do not always center the disc very well.

Once you know the disc is appropriate and installed correctly, the problem may be in the adapter board or the data cable. There may be a problem with your drive's host adapter board. Turn off all power to the system, open the computer, and check again to see that the adapter board and all available expansion boards are inserted properly and completely. Double-check the data cable running between the drive and adapter board. If the cable is loose, or one end of the cable is reversed, data will not flow properly from drive to adapter. Double-check the board's configuration to be sure that its base address, interrupt line, or DMA channel does not conflict with other devices that may be present in your system. You may have to remove the adapter board to check its configuration settings.

SYMPTOM 9-66 **The drive is recognized, but no audio is produced** Remember that a CD-ROM, CD-R, or CD-RW drive is generally a data-only device—the analog signals produced by CD audio must be routed to a sound board. Make sure that the thin, four-wire audio cable is connected between the drive and the sound board. Adjust the sound board's volume control to achieve an adequate output. You could also plug in at the drive's headphone jack. Adjust the drive's headphone volume control for an adequate output. If your amplifier/speakers are not producing sound from the sound board, try using headphones in the drive's headphone jack. If there is sound from the headphones but none from the sound board, the sound board may be faulty, or the cable carrying the audio signal to the sound board may be disconnected or faulty. If the audio is absent under Windows 95/98, check to see that the necessary driver(s) are installed under the Control Panel.

SYMPTOM 9-67 **You see the following message when attempting to list a directory: Not ready reading drive [drive letter]:** There is a communication problem between the SCSI host controller and the CD-ROM, CD-R, or CD-RW drive caused by an undesirable SCSI ID for the drive or excessive bus speed at the ISA bus. Your first step should be to power-down the computer and check that the drive is connected properly to the SCSI host controller. Also make sure that the CD is inserted into the drive with the right side facing up. If problems continue, change the drive's switch settings to select a new SCSI device number. Reboot the computer and try the directory listing again. If the error message persists, you might need to try several different SCSI device ID numbers. If a new SCSI number does not correct the trouble, the bus speed of the computer may be at fault. ISA bus speed should generally not exceed 8.33MHz, so take the computer out of its "turbo" or high-speed mode and try the directory again.

SYMPTOM 9-68 **You see the following message when attempting to list a directory: CDROM not High Sierra or ISO 9660 format** This error code (or if your bundled software's SCSI test program fails to detect a host adapter) suggests a memory conflict in your system—more than one device is attempting to use the same memory address(es). Conflicts are typically caused by expanded memory managers (EMM386, QEMM, 386MAX, etc.). Check your CONFIG.SYS file for the presence of a valid memory manager. You should see a device driver line such as

```
device=c:\qemm\qemm386.sys
device=c:\dos\emm386.exe
```

Try adding parameters to your memory managers that will *exclude* the addresses used by your SCSI host adapter. You need to know the active addresses of the SCSI host adapter card from the settings of its configuration switches. Each setting should define a range of addresses (CC00 to CDFF, C800 to C9FF,

9

DC00 to DDFF, D800 to D9FF, etc.). Refer to the documentation for your SCSI host adapter for more information. Once you know the address range of your adapter, add exclusion parameters to your CONFIG.SYS file as shown here (where *aaaa* and *bbbb* are hexadecimal addresses):

```
device=c:\qemm\qemm386.sys [parameters] exclude=aaaa-bbbb
device=c:\dos\emm386.exe [parameters] x=aaaa-bbbb
```

Reboot the computer and try the CD-ROM, CD-R, or CD-RW drive again. Other possible sources of conflict exist in the use of memory shadowing or disk caching, which are enabled through your system CMOS setup program. Access your CMOS setup and set all "disk caching," "BIOS shadow," "Shadow RAM," "Video BIOS Shadow," or any "shadow" options to the DISABLE condition. Reboot the computer and try the drive again.

Last-ditch sources of conflict can occur in the various computer peripherals (such as your 16-bit video card, modem card, scanner card, etc.). If your SCSI host adapter address range overlaps the address(es) of any other board, your system can encounter problems. Check the address settings of each installed peripheral, move that peripheral's address out of range of the SCSI controller, and modify the address (if necessary) in the peripheral's setup or configuration program. As a check, you may wish to simply remove the peripheral to see if the problem goes away. Once you make a change, reboot the computer and try the drive again.

SYMPTOM 9-69 You see the following message during initialization: No SCSI host adapter(s) detected Your system cannot find the SCSI host controller board. This may be due to faulty I/O, IRQ, or DMA settings on the host controller itself, or a memory conflict in hardware or software. Begin your investigation by powering down the computer and checking the host controller's resource settings. Use your documentation for the host controller and carefully verify each jumper or dip switch setting. A missing or improperly configured jumper can render the controller inoperative. Reset the controller board if necessary; then reboot the computer.

If the problem persists (or if you cannot find faulty controller settings), you may be encountering trouble due to memory conflicts. Possible sources of conflict exist in the use of memory shadowing or disk caching, which are enabled through your system CMOS setup program. Access your CMOS setup and set all "disk caching," "BIOS shadow," "Shadow RAM," "Video BIOS Shadow," or any "shadow" options to the DISABLE condition. Reboot the computer and try the CD-ROM, CD-R, or CD-RW drive again.

Sources of conflict can also occur in various computer peripherals (your video card, modem card, scanner card, etc.). If your SCSI host adapter address range overlaps the address(es) of any other board, your system can encounter problems. Check the address settings of each installed peripheral, move that peripheral's address out of range of the SCSI controller, and modify the address (if necessary) in the peripheral's setup or configuration program. As a check, you may wish to simply remove the peripheral to see if the problem goes away. Once you make a change, reboot the computer and try the drive again. Finally, if the system simply refuses to acknowledge the SCSI controller, you may wish to try replacing the SCSI host controller.

SYMPTOM 9-70 You see the following message during initialization: No xxxCD functions in use First, make sure the external CD-ROM, CD-R, or CD-RW drive is powered on before the computer starts to initialize. The CD drive must be available to the SCSI host controller in order for the CD-ROM/CD-R device driver MSCDEX to be loaded into memory. If the drive is turned on as expected and the MSCDEX driver will not load, check to see that the device driver is listed in the AUTOEXEC.BAT file similarly to

```
C:\SCSI\MSCDEX /D:xxxCD /M:10 /L:[drive letter]
```

or:

```
C:\CDMENU\MSCDEX /D:xxxCD /M:10 /L:[drive letter]
```

If your AUTOEXEC.BAT file is set up as expected, check to be sure that the CD device driver (MSCDEX in this case) is actually present in the desired subdirectory. If the driver is missing (even if it is present in the wrong subdirectory), the driver will not load. Copy the driver to the appropriate subdirectory, or change the path specification to the driver in the AUTOEXEC.BAT file. It is also generally recommended that your calling line appear *first* in the AUTOEXEC.BAT file. If the problem persists, try moving the calling line to the first line. Reboot the computer and try the drive again.

The CD-R Drive

While CD-ROM drives bring a great deal of reliable storage potential to the PC, it has only recently been possible to *record* CDs on the desktop. The technology required to create audio and computer CDs has traditionally been terribly complex and expensive, and limited by PC computing power of the day. Since the early 1990s, CD recorder (or CD-R) technology has steadily become more reliable and economical. CD recorders allow huge files, databases, and multimedia presentations to be developed and distributed with ease. Today, virtually any Pentium PC (or later) with a SCSI or UDMA interface and 1GB or more of hard drive space can support a CD-R drive for under $400. This part of the chapter explains the issues of CD-R technology and troubleshooting.

CD-R MEDIA VARIATIONS

Recordable media looks very similar to the "pressed" CD media illustrated in Figure 9-2, but with two important variations. First, the polycarbonate CD-R substrate is preformed with a track spiral into which data will be written during the recording process. The substrate is then coated with a greenish or bluish translucent layer and backed with a reflective layer of gold before protective lacquer is applied over the gold. These translucent and gold layers allow the recorded pits and lands to be read back after the recording is complete.

"ORANGE BOOK CERTIFIED" MEDIA

The Orange Book (Part II) is the primary specification for CD-R media, and all CD-R media should meet the Orange Book criteria for recordability and playback. Philips and Sony (the originators of the Orange Book specification) provide Orange Book certification of CD-R media. CD-R media that is not "Orange Book certified" should generally be avoided.

MULTISESSION CDS

One of the problems with recording early CDs was that once the CD was written, it could not be appended. This means if 123MB of data is written to a 650MB disc, the remaining 527MB of storage potential on the disc is lost. CD developers sought a means of adding new data to a CD that has been previously recorded. This *multisession* capability means a CD can be written in terms of sessions, and subsequent sessions can be linked to previous sessions—allowing the CD to be systematically filled.

A CD recorder that supports multisession recording can write a disc that will have multiple sessions linked together—each session containing its own lead-in, program, and lead-out areas. In effect, each session is treated as a different CD. Any multisession-capable CD-ROM can access the data in any session. By comparison, a "pressed" CD-ROM or a CD-R written in "Disc-at-Once" mode contains only one lead-in area, program area, and lead-out area.

> Some older CD-ROM drives that are not multisession capable can only read the first session of a multisession disc.

FIXATION VS. FINALIZATION

Each session written to a disc (whether multisession or single session) must be "fixed" before the session can be read. *Fixation* is the process of writing the session's lead-in and lead-out information to the disc. This process finishes a writing session and creates a table of contents. Fixation is required before a CD-ROM or CD audio player can play the disc. Discs that are "fixated for append" can have additional sessions recorded later (each with their own session lead-in and lead-out), creating a multisession disc. When a disc is *finalized*, the absolute lead-in and lead-out for the entire disc is written, along with information that tells the reader not to look for subsequent sessions. This final table of contents (TOC) conforms to the ISO 9660 file standard.

DISC-AT-ONCE

Disc-at-Once is a CD writing mode that requires data to be written continuously without any interruptions, until the entire data set is transferred to the CD-R. The complete lead-in, program, and lead-out are written in a single writing process. All of the information to be recorded needs to be staged on the computer's hard disk prior to recording in the Disc-at-Once mode. Recording in the Disc-at-Once mode eliminates the linking, run-in, and run-out blocks associated with multisession and packet recording modes (which often are interpreted as uncorrectable errors during the glass mastering process).

> Disc-at-Once mode is usually preferred for discs that are sent to a CD-ROM replication facility when CD-R is the source media.

TRACK-AT-ONCE

The *Track-at-Once* writing mode is the key to multisession capability and allows a session to be written in a number of discrete write events, called *tracks* because the written sessions contain complete tracks of information. The disc may be removed from the writer and read in another writer (given the proper software) before the session is fixated.

INCREMENTAL AND PACKET WRITING

Track-at-Once writing is a form of incremental write, which mandates a minimum track length of 300 blocks and a maximum of 99 tracks per disc. A track written "at once" has 150 blocks of overhead for run-in, run-out, pregap, and linking purposes. On the other hand, *packet write* is a method whereby several write events are allowed *within* a track, thus reducing the demands of overhead data. Each writing packet is bounded by seven blocks of data: four for run-in, two for run-out, and one for linking.

CARING FOR RECORDABLE CDS

As a rule, recordable CDs are as rugged and reliable as ordinary "pressed" CDs. Still, you should follow some additional rules in the careful handling and storage of recordable media:

- *Maintain a comfortable environment.* Don't expose recordable discs to sunlight or other strong light for long periods of time. Also avoid high heat and humidity, which can damage the physical disc. Always keep blank or recorded media in clean jewel cases for best protection.
- *Don't write on the disc.* Don't use alcohol-based pens to write on discs—the ink may eventually eat through the top (lacquer) surface and damage your data. Also don't use ballpoint or other sharp-tipped pens because you may scratch right through the lacquer surface and damage the reflective gold layer (and ruin your data).
- *Don't use labels on the disc.* Don't put labels on discs unless the labels are *expressly* designed for recordable CDs. The glue may eat through the lacquer surface just as some inks do, and/or the label may unbalance the disc and cause problems in reading it back or recording subsequent sessions. Never try to remove a label—you might tear off the lacquer and some of the reflecting surface.
- *Watch your media quality.* Many different brands of recordable CD media are now available in the marketplace. Quality varies from brand to brand (and even from batch to batch within a given brand). If you have repeated problems that can be traced to the blank media you are using, try using a different brand or even a different batch of the same brand.
- *Don't use Kodak Photo CDs.* Avoid the use of Kodak Photo CDs on everyday CD recorders. Kodak Photo CDs are designed to be used only with Kodak Photo CD professional workstations. Although the discs are inexpensive, they have a protection bit that prevents them from being written on many CD recorders. When you attempt to write these discs on the recorders that recognize the protection bit, you will receive an error message.

Creating a Bootable CD

With the acceptance of the El Torito standard for IDE CD-ROM drives, it is now possible to boot your PC from a CD and load an operating system without a floppy or hard drive. The problem is in obtaining bootable CDs to begin with. Many new computers are being sold with a system disc, which can boot and load an operating system, but it is rare for users to bring in their bootable CDs with the system when service is required. If you have a CD-R drive and some readily available software tools, you can make a bootable CD yourself. This part of the chapter discusses the procedure used to create a bootable CD. Before you can create a bootable CD, you will need a system (or access to a system) with the following hardware and software tools:

- An El Torito–capable IDE or SCSI CD-ROM drive (with their standard IDE/SCSI interfaces).
- An El Torito–capable motherboard or SCSI adapter BIOS that supports booting from bootable CDs.
- A hexadecimal editor utility. If you have Norton Utilities (version 8.0 or Windows 95), the DISKEDIT.EXE utility is preferred.
- A bootable floppy disk (from MS-DOS 6.2x or a Windows 95/98 startup disk). You may also use a bootable hard drive.
- A hard disk drive with ample speed and space to hold an ISO 9660 image file for the bootable CD. A SCSI disk is preferred, but a fast UDMA or EIDE hard drive will also work. There should be at least 650MB of free space on the HDD for the image file.

- A CD-R drive (UDMA, EIDE, or SCSI).
- Any CD-R software that can make an ISO 9660 image file. For example, you could use Adaptec's Easy CD Pro for Windows 95/98.
- A blank CD-R disc (remember that you can't make a multisession CD bootable).

> Creating a bootable CD is a rather lengthy and sophisticated procedure that requires some knowledge of editing hexadecimal files and creating ISO image files. You may choose to seek the advice and guidance of more experienced personnel before proceeding on your own.

In order to boot from a CD, there must be a "Boot Volume Descriptor" (or BVD) located at sector 17 of the CD. The BVD is a string of hex codes. Somewhere in those hex codes, there must be a series of 4 bytes that list the starting address of the "Booting Catalog" (or BC). The BC is another set of hex codes that describe several different aspects of the CD. Again, there must be a sequence of 4 bytes that indicate the starting address of a bootable image file.

The actual process of making a bootable CD consists of roughly five steps. First, we'll make an image file of the bootable floppy (or hard) disk with the hex editor. We'll name the file OSBOOT.IMG. Next, we'll make a booting catalog file, which we'll name BOOTCAT.BIN. Third, we'll make an ISO 9660 image file that contains these two files as well as other files and directories to be written to the CD. We'll edit the ISO file using the hex editor. Finally, we'll burn that ISO 9660 image file to the blank CD-R disc.

MAKE THE BOOTABLE IMAGE FILE

Before making a bootable image file of your floppy (or hard) disk, pay particular attention to your CD-ROM drivers. If you create a bootable CD *without* the CD-ROM drivers and MSCDEX, you'll simply create an image of the A: (or C:) drive. This will allow you to boot from the CD, but the other files and directories on the CD will not be accessible because the CD-ROM drivers will not be loaded. You must include the CD-ROM drivers if you wish the other (nonbooting) files on the CD to be available after the boot process has finished. In fact, some more experienced technicians have developed a multiboot menu in CONFIG.SYS that allows them to select low-level CD-ROM drivers for many possible drives. (This allows the same bootable CD to be accessible on many different drives.) If you're using Norton's DISKEDIT.EXE, follow the steps below to create an image file:

1. Select Object, then Drive, then A: (or B: or C:, depending on what bootable disk you care to take an image from).
2. Select Object, Physical Sector, and OK.
3. Select Tools, Write Object to, and then choose To a File.
4. Enter the file name (for example, OSBOOT.IMG), and then select Yes to save the file.

> Remember that the actual file used to boot the CD is just an image of another bootable drive. The other files "outside" the bootable image file (after the CD has booted) can only be found after the CD-ROM drivers have been loaded by an appropriate CONFIG.SYS and AUTOEXEC.BAT file.

MAKE A BOOTING CATALOG FILE

The next step is to create a booting catalog file. There is no tool to do this automatically, so you'll have to handle this manually. Create a hex file (we'll call it BOOTCAT.BIN) using your hex editor. The file should be 2048 bytes long. Use DISKEDIT (or your own hex editor) to edit the BOOTCAT.BIN file like this:

```
01 00 00 00 00 00 00 00 00 00 00 00 00 00 00 00
00 00 00 00 00 00 00 00 00 00 00 00 AA 55 55 AA
88 02 00 00 00 00 01 00 BB
```

The rest of this file must be filled with hex 00. The last "BB" in the file has no meaning and will be changed later. We're just using it to mark the place where the OSBOOT.IMB file address should go.

CREATE THE ISO 9660 IMAGE FILE

Now we must create an ISO 9660–compatible file that contains our booting catalog, the bootable image file, and any other files and directories we want to be on the bootable CD. You can use virtually any CD-R authoring software you wish (for example, Easy CD Pro for Windows 95/98). Most CD-R authoring software now uses a drag-and-drop interface for defining the files that will be placed on the CD. The order in which files are dragged and dropped into the workspace is the order in which they will be written. Make the booting catalog (BOOTCAT.BIN) your first file on the CD-R; then make the bootable image file (OSBOOT.IMG) your second file on the CD-R. After that, you can simply drag and drop any other files and directories that will be written on the CD.

> Some technicians have reported that placing the booting catalog and bootable image file at the end of the CD-R will still work with SCSI CD-ROM drives, but not with IDE CD-ROM drives; but placing the files at the beginning of the CD-R should work in all cases.

Once you have all the desired files defined for the new bootable CD, go ahead and generate the ISO 9660 image file to your hard drive. (Keep in mind that there must be sufficient space on the hard drive to hold the entire image file—up to 650MB.)

MODIFY THE ISO 9660 IMAGE FILE

This is perhaps the trickiest part of the process because you'll use your hex editor to modify the ISO 9660 image file before burning the file to a blank CD-R disc. Start DISKEDIT.EXE (or whatever other hex editor you're using), and then load the image file you just created. Depending on the amount of material you added to the image file, it can be quite lengthy.

1. *Find the ASCII string in "BOOTCAT."* Put your active cursor at the *B*, and then move the cursor up two lines and right one space. Write down the next 4 bytes. For example, if you move the cursor and the next 4 bytes read 15 00 00 00, then write down "15 00 00 00" on a sheet of paper for later use.
2. *Find the ASCII string in "OSBOOT."* Put your active cursor at the *O*, and then move the cursor up two lines and right one space. Write down the next 4 bytes. For example, if you move the cursor and the next 4 bytes read 16 00 00 00, then write down "16 00 00 00" on a sheet of paper for later use.
3. *Find the hex string "AA 55 55 AA."* It is located in the sector occupied by the BOOTCAT.BIN file. You will find a "BB" (where you placed it) in the third row of this sector. From this place, fill in the 4 bytes obtained from finding the "OSBOOT" ASCII string (16 00 00 00). For example, the line that reads

   ```
   88 02 00 00 00 00 01 00 BB 00 00 00
   ```

   should be changed to:

   ```
   88 02 00 00 00 00 01 00 16 00 00 00
   ```

That "02" in the second byte of this row means it's a 1.44MB floppy bootable image. If you use other media for the bootable image, change it to 01 for a 1.2MB floppy disk, 02 for a 1.44MB floppy disk, 03 for a 2.88MB floppy disk, or 04 for a hard disk.

4 *Edit sector 17 of the ISO file.* Go back to the beginning (sector 0) of this ISO image file, and then press PAGE DOWN to offset 34816 (decimal)—this is the beginning of sector 17. Replace the hex codes from the beginning of this sector with the following:

```
00 43 44 30 30 31 01 45 4C 20 54 4F 52 49 54 4F
20 53 50 45 43 49 46 49 43 41 54 49 4F 4E 00 00
00 00 00 00 00 00 00 00 00 00 00 00 00 00 00 00
00 00 00 00 00 00 00 00 00 00 00 00 00 00 00 00
00 00 00 00 00 00 00 BB
```

The ASCII area should now read ".CD001.EL TORITO SPECIFICATION." Notice the "BB" in the fifth row from the beginning of this sector. It's the beginning place to put the address codes of BOOTCAT.BIN. From this place, fill in the 4 bytes obtained from finding the "BOOTCAT" ASCII string (15 00 00 00). For example, the line that reads

```
00 00 00 00 00 00 00 BB 00 00 00
```

should be changed to:

```
00 00 00 00 00 00 00 15 00 00 00
```

The rest of this sector (ended at offset 36863) should be replaced by "00."

BURN THE ISO FILE TO CD-R

At this point, use your CD-R authoring tool to "burn" the modified ISO 9660 image file to the CD-R disc. The writing process may take several minutes to as much as an hour depending on the amount of programs and data being transferred to the disc. If you want extra safety, have the authoring software test the writing process for proper data transfer before starting to write.

TEST THE BOOTABLE CD

For an IDE-type CD-ROM, you only have to change the setting of booting sequence in BIOS to "CDROM, C:, A:," and then reboot the PC with the bootable CD in the CD-ROM drive. For SCSI CD-ROM drives, the booting sequence of the motherboard BIOS should be changed to "SCSI, IDE." If the BIOS doesn't have this option, you'll just have to temporarily set all the IDE HDD entries to "none" or "not installed." Next, enter the BIOS setting of your SCSI card. For example, in Adaptec's AHA 2940U, go into Advanced Configuration Options, and enable the options Host Adapter BIOS (Configuration Utility Reserve BIOS Space) and BIOS Support for Bootable CD-ROM. Then reboot the PC with the bootable CD in the drive.

Upgrading CD-R/CD-RW Firmware

You may be able to update the firmware used in your CD-R or CD-RW drive. This may be necessary to correct bugs or fix drive compatibility problems with the system. The following steps offer a guide that you can refer to when upgrading CD-R/CD-RW firmware.

> The steps below are based on an internal Plextor SCSI CD-R drive. You should always refer to the Web page or README file that accompanies the new firmware download. Be sure to download the correct firmware version for your drive—installing the wrong firmware can permanently disable the drive.

1. Power-off your system completely.
2. Locate the CD-R drive and place its flash jumper in the flash upgrade position.
3. Make sure the power cable and the signal cable (SCSI or IDE) are still connected.
4. Power-on your system and boot "clean" to a command-line prompt.
5. Make sure the CD-R appears in program mode. For an internal Plextor SCSI CD-R, you'll see that all four LEDs on the front panel of the drive are blinking.
6. When the system comes up, execute the new firmware program (such as FIRM412.EXE), which you may receive or download from the manufacturer, and use the new firmware (*.BIN) file.
7. When the EXE application starts, specify the location of the BIN file.
8. Click the Update button to begin the flash process.
9. When the Update button becomes highlighted again, the flash process is complete.
10. Power-off the system and reset the CD-R drive's flash jumper to its original position.
11. Power-on the system normally.

Troubleshooting CD-R Drives

CD recorders present some special problems for the typical PC. Many high-performance CD-R units use the SCSI interface in order to handle more consistent data transfer from the system to the drive. Installing a CD-R may require the addition (and expense) of a SCSI host adapter and associated driver software. CD recording demands a substantial commitment of hard drive space—perhaps as much as 1GB—in order to create an image file for recording. (An *image file* basically converts the data to be recorded into the pits and lands that must be encoded to the blank disc.) So if you're tight on drive space, you may also need another hard drive to support the CD-R. Finally, CD-Rs require a constant and uninterrupted flow of data during the recording process. If the CD-R data buffer empties, the recording process will halt, and your blank CD will be ruined. This means you'll need fast hard drives and a high-performance interface (such as PIO Mode 4 or UDMA). This part of the chapter explains some of the problems associated with installing and using a CD-R and illustrates a series of troubleshooting symptoms and solutions.

CD RECORDING ISSUES

Writing data to a recordable CD is a complex process that demands a great deal from your PC's hardware and software. Most of this complexity is hidden by the power of the CD authoring program, but there are a number of important factors that you should be aware of that can influence the success of CD recording. This part of the chapter covers the principal issues involved in CD recording.

File Sizes

The sheer *amount* of data being written to the CD is less important than the individual file sizes. The recorder may have trouble locating and opening small files quickly enough to send them smoothly to the CD recorder, whereas fewer large files are typically problem free.

System Interruptions

Any interruption in the flow of data is fatal to CD recording, so make sure your CONFIG.SYS and AUTOEXEC.BAT files do not load any TSR utilities that may periodically interrupt the computer's drive operations. Utilities such as screen savers, calendar alarms or reminders, and incoming faxes are just a few features that will interrupt disc writing. If the PC is part of a network, you should temporarily disable network sharing so that no one tries to access the files you're writing to the CD.

The Hard Disk

The hard drive is a critical component of the CD-R system because you must transfer data from the HDD to the CD-R at a rate adequate to keep the recorder's buffer filled. There are three major issues when considering your hard drive: speed, file fragmentation, and thermal calibration.

- *Speed* In order to write a virtual image file to a compact disc, the hard disk from which you are writing must have a transfer rate fast enough to keep the CD-R drive buffer full. This usually means an average hard disk access time of 19ms or less. It would also help to use a high-performance drive interface such as Ultra-DMA/33, Ultra-DMA/66, or SCSI-3.
- *Fragmentation* This issue is also related to speed. Searching all over a very fragmented hard disk for image file data can cause drive operations to slow down. In many cases, a badly fragmented hard drive cannot support CD-R operations. Be sure to defragment your hard drive before creating an image file.
- *Thermal calibration* All hard disks periodically perform an automatic thermal calibration to ensure proper performance. Calibration interrupts hard disk operations for as much as 1.5 seconds. Some hard disks "force" a calibration at fixed intervals (even if the disk is in use), causing interruptions that are fatal to CD writing. This problem is worse when the image file is large, and the writing process takes longer. If you can select a new hard drive to support CD-R operations, choose a drive with "intelligent" thermal calibration (which postpones recalibration until the drive is idle).

CD Recorder Speed

Typical CD recorders are capable of writing at twice or four times the standard writing/playback speed of 150KB/sec (75 sectors/sec). Recording speed is simply a matter of how fast the bits are inscribed by the laser on the disc surface. It has nothing to do with how fast you read them back or how much data you can fit on the disc. However, higher recording speeds can accomplish a writing process in a shorter period of time. Faster recording speeds are certainly a time-saver, but it also means that larger recording buffers are required (and those buffers empty faster). As a consequence, faster recorders will demand a faster hard drive and interface to support data transfer. In most cases, "buffer underrun" problems can often be corrected by slowing down the recording process rather than upgrading the drive system.

When you write a real ISO image file from hard disk to CD, speed is rarely a problem because the image is already one gigantic file. The files and structures are already in order and divided into CD-ROM sectors, so it is only necessary to stream data off the hard drive to the CD recorder. When you write from a virtual image, things get trickier because a virtual image is little more than a list. The CD authoring program must consult the virtual image database to find out where each file should go in the image and where each file is actually stored on hard disk. The authoring software must then open the file and divide it into CD-ROM sectors—all the while sending data to the CD recorder in a smooth, continuous stream. Locating and opening each file is often the more time-consuming part of the recording process (which is why on-the-fly writing is more difficult when you have many small files).

CD Recorder Buffer

All CD recorders have a small amount of onboard buffer memory. The CD recorder's buffer helps to ensure that there is always data ready to be written because extra data is stored as it arrives from the computer. The size of the buffer is critical to trouble-free writing—a slowdown or interruption in the transfer of data from the computer will not interrupt writing so long as the buffer is not completely emptied. The larger the buffer, the more safety margin you have in case of interruptions. If your CD recorder has a very small buffer and your hard disk is slow, you may find it difficult (or impossible) to write virtual images on-the-fly to CD. When this occurs, you can make a real ISO image file on the hard disk and record to CD from that, use a faster hard disk subsystem, or upgrade your CD recorder's buffer (if possible).

> If you want to write a virtual image on-the-fly to CD, and you have a slow hard disk, it is generally safest to write at 1x speed. Otherwise, create a real ISO image file first and record from that. In most situations where your hardware configuration is adequate (a fast, defragmented hard disk, few small files, and a good-sized CD recorder buffer), you can successfully write virtual images straight to CD. However, it's always best to test first and create a real ISO image file only if necessary.

TYPICAL COMPATIBILITY PROBLEMS

Even when CDs record perfectly, it is not always possible to read them correctly in other drives. The following sections highlight three common compatibility issues.

Problems Reading Recordable CDs

Recordable CDs frequently cannot be read in older CD-ROM drives. If the CD can be read when used on the CD-R but *not* on a standard CD-ROM drive, check the disc recording utility to make sure that the session containing the data you just wrote is *closed*—CD-ROM drives cannot read data from a session that is not closed.

If your recorded disc is ejected, if you receive an error message, or if you have any random problems accessing files from the recorded disc, the problem may be that your CD-ROM drive is not well calibrated to read recorded CDs. Try the disc on another CD-ROM drive, or upgrade the CD-ROM drive itself.

If you recorded the disc using DOS file names, but there are difficulties in reading back the recorded CD with DOS or Windows, it may be that you have an older version of MSCDEX (before version 2.23) on your system. Check your MSCDEX version, and update it if necessary.

Problems Reading Multisession CDs

If you can only see data recorded in the first session on the CD—but not in subsequent sessions—it may be that the disc was recorded in CD-ROM (Mode 1) format, while your multisession CD-ROM drive only recognizes CD-ROM XA (Mode 2) multisession CDs. If this happens, you may need to re-record the disc in the correct mode. Of course, your CD-ROM drive must support multisession operation in the first place. If you can only see data recorded in the last session, you may have forgotten to link your new data with data previously recorded on the CD. Refer to the instructions for your CD recorder and review the suggested steps required to create a multisession CD.

CD-ROM Drive Incompatibility with Recordable CDs

It may seem that you write a CD without trouble, and can read it properly on your CD-R, but when you put the disc in a standard CD-ROM drive, the disc is ejected. You may also see error messages such as "No CD-ROM" or "Drive not ready," or you may have random problems accessing some files or directories. You may also find that the problems disappear when reading the CD on a different CD-ROM drive.

At first, you may suspect a problem with the original CD-ROM drive, but this may be due to compatibility problems with some CD-ROM drives (especially older ones) and recorded CDs. Some CD-ROM drive lasers are not calibrated to read recordable CDs (often the surface is different from that of factory-pressed CDs). If your CD-ROM drive reads mass-produced (silver) CDs but not recordable CDs, check with the CD-ROM drive manufacturer to determine whether this is the problem. In some cases, a drive upgrade may be available, and this will resolve the problem.

> The combination of blank disc brand and CD recorder can also make a difference. Use blank CD media that has been recommended by the CD-R manufacturer.

TYPICAL MULTISESSION CD ISSUES

You may encounter older CD-ROM drives that have trouble reading multisession CDs. Multisession discs are recorded according to the Orange Book (Part II) standard, which states that sessions can be written in either the CD-ROM or CD-ROM XA format. A fully compliant multisession CD-ROM drive should always be able to access the last session on a disc regardless of its format.

Unfortunately, there have been misunderstandings and misinterpretations of the Orange Book standard, but to understand the problem, you need to know a bit of history. Multisession recording was first used by Kodak for their "Photo CD" initiative. One roll of film does not fill up a Photo CD, so when you take your disc and a new roll of film for new Photo CD processing, the new photos are added in a "new session." This new session is linked to previous sessions so that you can see all the photos on the disc—no matter how many sessions they are recorded in.

Kodak chose the CD-ROM XA standard for its Photo CD format for reasons that had nothing to do with the Orange Book standard. But since Photo CD was the first reason that CD-ROM drive manufacturers had to create multisession drives, many assumed that the Kodak approach to multisession (CD-ROM XA) was the *only* approach. They accordingly wrote software drivers that assume a multisession disc must also be XA. When one of these drivers sees a disc that is not XA, it assumes that the disc is also not multisession, and it tells the CD-ROM drive to read only the first session on the disc. The result is that a multisession disc is read as if it were a single-session disc, and you see only the data in the first session.

CD-ROM drive manufacturers have generally resolved this glitch in newer drives and drivers (in 8X CD-ROM and later drives), but if you record a multisession disc in CD-ROM format, you may find that some older drives—even if specified as a multisession drive—may not read beyond the first session on the disc. If you need to share multisession discs with others, you should test to see which format their CD-ROM drives can handle. To be on the safe side, write your disc in the CD-ROM XA format. A more permanent fix is to upgrade the older CD-ROM to a model that is fully multisession compliant.

> You cannot mix formats on the same disc—a multisession disc containing both CD-ROM and CD-ROM XA sessions would be unreadable on most drives.

BUFFER UNDERRUNS

CD writing is a real-time process that must run constantly at the selected recording speed *without interruptions*. Most of the time, your computer will pass data to the CD-R faster than it is needed. This keeps the CD-R's buffer constantly filled with a reserve of data waiting to be written, so small slowdowns or interruptions in the flow of data from the computer will not interrupt the writing process. The CD-R's internal buffer stores this extra data as it arrives to help maintain a steady flow of data to the writing laser.

The size of the buffer is critical to trouble-free writing. Remember that a slowdown or interruption in the transfer of data from the computer will not stop a writing cycle so long as the buffer is not *completely* emptied. The larger the buffer, the more safety margin you have in case of interruptions. A buffer underrun error means that for some reason the flow of data from hard disk to CD-R was interrupted long enough for the CD recorder's buffer to be emptied, and writing was halted. If this occurs during an actual write operation (rather than a prewriting test), your recordable disc may be ruined. The following checklists cover many of the typical issues that may trigger a buffer underrun.

Hard Disk Issues

- *"Dumb" thermal recalibration* Disable thermal recalibration on the drive before writing, or allow one hour or so for the system temperature to stabilize before writing.
- *Excessive file fragmentation* Defragment the drive with Defrag before "burning" a CD.
- *Insufficient free space* The CD-R will almost certainly require some amount of temporary workspace on the hard drive. If there is insufficient free space on the hard drive, you may need to free additional space by offloading unneeded files or upgrading the drive itself.
- *Too many small files* When recording on-the-fly, many small files may present too much of a load on your data transfer system, so try making an ISO image file first.
- *Damaged files* Damaged or corrupted files will often cause errors that will interrupt the flow of data. Run ScanDisk and Defrag to locate any possible file system problems before recording.
- *Recording files in use* Make sure that no files to be recorded are currently in use by any application.

Hardware Issues

- *Slow hard drives* Older hard drives may not support data transfer speeds high enough to keep the CD-R buffer filled. If you use slow hard drives, make an ISO image file first rather than writing on-the-fly.
- *Burst data transfers* Source devices that operate in "burst" data transfer modes may have difficulty keeping the CD-R buffer filled. Try disabling the burst mode. This may slow the overall data transfer, but may even out the flow of data, making it easier to keep the buffer filled.
- *CD-R controller configuration* Verify that the IDE or SCSI controller operating the CD-R is configured for optimum performance (use bus master drivers for IDE controllers).
- *Sync problems* Certain combinations of drives and controllers may not synchronize data properly. Check that you're using the recommended hardware devices for proper CD-R operation.
- *Outdated device drivers* Verify that you're using the latest device drivers for the CD-R, controller, and other related devices in the system.
- *Slow computer speed* Systems older than 486 platforms may simply be too old to support the data transfer needs of a CD-R. Verify that your system meets the minimum system requirements for your particular CD-R model.
- *CD-R quality* Be sure to use good-quality CD-R discs that are recommended by the CD-R manufacturer. Dirty, old, or scratched discs may not function.

Memory-Resident Software Issues

CD-R systems may encounter buffer underrun problems when the following types of software are at work on your system. You may wish to systematically disable the following software types:

- Antivirus software
- Screen saver software
- System agent software

- Scheduler software
- TSR (Terminate and Stay Resident) software
- Network software
- System sounds
- Animated icons or utilities
- Any program that may activate on its own

Windows 95/98 Issues

- *Insufficient virtual memory* Adjust your virtual memory settings to use at least 32MB of RAM for virtual memory.
- *Disable "auto insert notification"* If you have more than 16MB of RAM, disable "auto insert notification" for the CD-ROM.
- *Change the system's role* If you have more than 16MB of RAM, change the hard drive's "Typical Role" to Network Server.

Tips to Avoid Buffer Underruns

- Always set audio discs to write at 1X.
- Change the DMA transfer rate for the drive controller card being used. (Select the fastest data transfer rate available for your system and drives.)
- Defragment your hard drives at least once a week to prevent files from being scattered across the hard drive.
- Disable or remove all software in the computer except the operating system, the recording software, and the drivers for your source devices and CD-R.
- Disc-to-disc copying generally requires a SCSI-2, fully ASPI-compliant CD-ROM drive (at least 4X). Copying audio requires a source CD-ROM drive that supports digital audio extraction.
- Do not record across a network—copy the desired files to your local hard drive first.
- Do not try to copy empty directories, zero-byte files, or files that may be in use by the system at the time.
- For best results use SCSI-2 (or faster) source devices.
- In any operating system, always use the newest drivers from your SCSI controller card manufacturer.
- Log out of any networks if possible (including Windows for Workgroups and/or Microsoft Network).
- Make sure your hard drive does Smart Thermal Recalibration—it won't recalibrate if the drive is being used.
- Make sure your SCSI controller card is fully ASPI-compliant.
- More than 10,000 very small files should be written to an ISO image first, or recorded at 1X if possible, in order to ease data transfer demands.
- Record at a slower speed (such as 2X rather than 4X).
- The temporary directory should always have space free at least twice the size of the largest file you are recording.
- Try a different hard disk and/or high-quality gold recordable disc.

- With DOS 6.22 or below and a source hard disk 1GB or larger, partitions should be kept smaller than 1GB so that hard disk cluster size is 16KB instead of 32Kb.
- Write an ISO image to the hard disk first (if you have enough hard drive space).

GENERAL CD-R SYMPTOMS

CD recorders are subject to a large number of potential errors during operation. Many typical recording errors are listed below. In most cases, the error is not terribly complex and can be corrected in just a few minutes once the nature of the problem is understood. Keep in mind that the error message is dependent on the CD recorder software in use, so your actual error messages may vary.

For basic CD-related issues, refer to the CD-ROM troubleshooting information earlier in this chapter.

SYMPTOM 9-71 **Absorption control error <xxx>** This error most often means that there is a slight problem writing to a recordable disc—perhaps caused by a smear or speck of dust. It does not *necessarily* mean that your data has not been correctly recorded. A sector address is usually given so that you can (if you wish) verify the data in and around that sector. When writing is completed, try cleaning the disc gently (on the nonlabel side) with a lint-free cloth. If the error occurs again, try a new disc.

SYMPTOM 9-72 **Application code error** This error typically occurs when you try to write Kodak recordable CDs (Photo CDs) on non-Kodak CD recorders. These discs have a protection bit that is recognized only by the Kodak CD-R—all other recorders will not record these discs. In this case, you'll need to use standard blank CDs.

SYMPTOM 9-73 **Bad ASPI open** The CD-R ASPI driver is bad or missing, and the SCSI CD-R cannot be found. Check the installation of your CD-R drive and SCSI adapter; then check the driver installation. Try reinstalling the SCSI driver(s).

SYMPTOM 9-74 **Buffer underrun at sector <xxx>** Once an image file is generated, CD writing is a real-time process that must run constantly at the selected recording speed—*without interruptions*. The CD recorder's buffer is constantly filled with data from the hard drive that is waiting to be written. This "buffering" action ensures that small slowdowns or interruptions in the flow of data from the computer do not interrupt the writing process. A "buffer underrun" message indicates that the flow of data from hard disk to CD recorder was interrupted long enough for the CD recorder's buffer to be emptied, and writing was halted. If this occurs during an actual write operation rather than a test, your CD may be damaged.

To avoid buffer underruns, you should remove as much processing load as possible from the system. For example, make sure that no screen savers or other Terminate and Stay Resident (TSR) programs are active. (They can momentarily interrupt operations.) Close as many open windows as possible. See that your working hard disk cannot be accessed via a network.

For SCSI CD-R drives, the CD recorder's position in the SCSI chain—or the cable length between the computer and CD recorder—may cause data slowdowns. Try connecting the CD recorder as the first peripheral in the SCSI chain (if not done already), and use a shorter SCSI cable (if possible) between the CD recorder and the SCSI host adapter.

SYMPTOM 9-75 **Current disc already contains a closed audio session** Under the Red Book standard for audio CDs, all audio tracks must be written in a *single* session. If you add audio tracks in more than one session, playback results will be unpredictable. Most CD-ROM drives will play back all audio tracks on a CD even if they are recorded in several different sessions, but most home and car CD players can only play back the tracks in the *first* session. If you continue and record audio in a different session, you may have problems reading subsequent audio sessions.

SYMPTOM 9-76 **Current disc contains a session that is not closed** In actual practice, CD-ROM drives can only read back one data track per session, so avoid recording another data track in an open session. Be sure to close the session before writing additional data to the disc.

SYMPTOM 9-77 **Currently selected source CD-ROM drive or CD recorder cannot read audio in digital format** This is more of a warning than a fault. Reading audio tracks in "digital format" is not the same as playing the music, and few CD-ROM drives are able to read audio tracks in digital format (only Red Book format). You may need to copy the music data from the CD to the hard drive first, then post-process the digital audio data through the application used to make the new CD.

SYMPTOM 9-78 **Data overrun/underrun** The SCSI host adapter has reported an error that is almost always caused by improper termination or a bad SCSI cable. Recheck the installation of your SCSI adapter, cabling, and termination. You may also need to reduce the processing overhead needed by unused applications. Refer to the "Buffer Underruns" section earlier in this chapter for more details.

SYMPTOM 9-79 **Destination disc is smaller than the source disc** This error commonly occurs when you're trying to duplicate an existing CD to the CD-R. There is not enough room on the recordable CD to copy the source CD. Try recording to a blank CD-R disc. Use 74-minute media instead of 60-minute media. Some CDs cannot be copied due to the TOC (table of contents) overhead in CD recorders, and also due to the calibration zone overhead. You may need to break up the source CD between two or more different CD-R discs.

SYMPTOM 9-80 **Disc already contains tracks and/or sessions that are incompatible with the requested operation** This error appears if you are trying to add data in a format that is different from the data format already on the disc. For example, you'll see this type of error when trying to add a CD-ROM XA session to a disc that already contains a standard CD-ROM session. A disc containing multiple formats is *unreadable*, so you are not allowed to record the different session type.

SYMPTOM 9-81 **Disc write-protected** You are attempting to write to a CD-R disc that has already been closed. Do not try writing to discs that are closed—instead, use a fresh blank disc for writing.

SYMPTOM 9-82 **Error 175-xx-xx-xx** This error code often indicates a buffer underrun. See the earlier section "Buffer Underruns."

SYMPTOM 9-83 **Error 220-01-xx-xx** This error code often indicates that some of your software cannot communicate with a SCSI device—possibly because your SCSI bus was reset. In many cases, this is caused by conflicts between real-mode and protected-mode SCSI drivers working in a Windows 95/98 system. Try REMming out any real-mode SCSI drivers in your CONFIG.SYS file. (The protected-mode drivers provided for Windows 95/98 should be sufficient on their own.) You may need to download and install updated protected-mode drivers for the SCSI host adapter and CD-R drive (as well as other SCSI devices that may be installed).

SYMPTOM 9-84 **Error 220-06-xx-xx** This error code often indicates a SCSI selection timeout error, which suggests a SCSI setup problem—usually with the SCSI host adapter. Contact your SCSI host adapter manufacturer for detailed installation and testing instructions. You may need to adjust the SCSI BIOS setup or update the SCSI drivers in your system.

SYMPTOM 9-85 **Error reading the Table of Contents (TOC) or Program Memory Area (PMA) from the disc** This recordable disc is defective or has been damaged (probably during a previous write operation or the current write operation). Do not try writing to this disc. Unfortunately, there is very little you can do here except to discard the defective disc. Try a fresh, good-quality disc instead.

SYMPTOM 9-86 **General protection fault** This type of problem has been identified with the Adaptec AHAr-152x family of SCSI host adapters and is caused by outdated driver software. You can solve this problem by upgrading to version 3.1 (or later) of Adaptec's EZ-SCSI software. If you're not using Adaptec software, check that you have current drivers for whatever SCSI adapter you're using.

SYMPTOM 9-87 **Invalid logical block address** This error message usually means that the CD mastering software has requested a data block from the hard disk which either does not exist or is illegal—this may suggest a corrupted hard disk or damaged ISO file. Exit the CD mastering software and run ScanDisk and Defrag to check and reorganize your hard drive. You may need to rebuild an ISO file or reload damaged files from a backup.

SYMPTOM 9-88 **Last two blocks stripped** This message appears when copying a track to hard disk if the track you are reading was created as multisession compliant (following the Orange Book standard). This is because a multisession track is always followed by two run-out blocks. These are included in the count of the total size (in blocks) of the track, but do not contain data and cannot be read back. This message appears to alert you in case you notice that you got two blocks fewer than were reported for the Read Length. Don't panic—you haven't lost any data.

SYMPTOM 9-89 **"MSCDEX" errors are being encountered** Early versions of MSCDEX (prior to v.2.23) had problems with file names containing "illegal" ASCII characters such as a hyphen (-). If a directory contains a file name with an illegal ASCII character, you can still see all the files by doing a directory check (DIR) from DOS, or you can open the illegally named file. However, one or more files listed *after* the illegal one may not be accessible or may give errors. You should update MSCDEX to the latest available version. As an alternative, you may REM out the real-mode driver and MSCDEX command lines in your startup files and allow Windows 95/98 to rely exclusively on protected-mode drivers.

SYMPTOM 9-90 **DOS or Windows cannot find the CD-R drive** There are several possible reasons why the CD-R drive cannot be found by software. First, turn off the computer and wait at least 15 seconds. Make sure the IDE or SCSI adapter card is firmly seated and secured to the computer case. The IDE or SCSI adapter must also be properly configured. Check the IDE or SCSI cable and see that it is properly attached to the adapter and drive. Turn on the computer. If problems persist, make sure the correct IDE or SCSI drivers are installed and any command-line switches are set correctly.

SYMPTOM 9-91 **No write data (buffer empty)** The flow of data to the CD-R drive must be extremely reliable so that its working buffer is never empty when it prepares to write a block of information to disc. This message indicates that the flow of data from the hard disk to the CD recorder has been interrupted (similar to the "buffer underrun" error).

- *Check for processing overhead.* Ensure that no screen savers, other TSR utilities, or unneeded open windows are active, which might momentarily interrupt operations. Your working hard disk should not be accessible over a network.

- *Check the SCSI setup*. The SCSI CD recorder's position in the SCSI chain, or the length of cabling between the SCSI adapter and CD recorder, may also cause data slowdowns. Try connecting the CD recorder as the first device in the SCSI chain (you may need to reterminate the SCSI chain), and keep the SCSI cable as short as possible.
- *Check the file caching*. Windows 3.1x requires the use of a RAM cache to manage the flow of data. SmartDrive (the caching utility supplied with Windows 3.1x) is necessary for writing virtual images on-the-fly to CD. However, when writing a real ISO image from hard disk to CD, it may cause a buffer underrun. If a buffer underrun occurs during testing or writing of a real ISO 9660 image under Windows 3.1x, exit to the DOS shell and type the following:

```
smartdrv x-
```

where *x* is the letter of the hard drive from which you will write the ISO image. This disables SmartDrive for the specified drive so that CD writing can proceed smoothly.

SYMPTOM 9-92 **Read file error** A file referenced by the virtual image database cannot be located or accessed. Make sure the suspect file is not being used by you or by someone else on a network. The file may also be damaged or corrupt, so exit the CD-R application and run ScanDisk and Defrag to check the file system for problems. You may need to reload damaged files from a backup.

SYMPTOM 9-93 **Selected disc image file was not prepared for the current disc** This type of error message occurs if you prepared the disc image file for a blank CD, but are now trying to record it to a CD already containing data (or vice versa). In either case, you would wind up writing a CD that couldn't be read at all because the CD addresses calculated for the disc image are wrong for that actual CD. If you are given the option of writing anyway, select No to abort because it is very unlikely that the writing operation would yield a readable CD. Retry the operation with a known-blank CD-R disc.

SYMPTOM 9-94 **Selected disc track is longer than the image file** The disc verify process fails immediately because the source ISO 9660 image file and the actual ISO 9660 track on CD are not the same size. The disc track is actually longer than the image file, which could indicate a defective CD-R drive. Retry the operation with a good-quality CD-R disc. If the problem persists, you might try replacing the CD-R drive.

SYMPTOM 9-95 **Selected disc track is shorter than the image file** The disc verify process fails immediately because the source ISO 9660 image file and the actual ISO 9660 track on CD are not the same size. The disc track is actually shorter than the image file, which could indicate a defective CD-R drive. Retry the operation with a good-quality CD-R disc. If the problem persists, you might try replacing the CD-R drive.

SYMPTOM 9-96 **The "disc in" light on the drive does not blink after you turn on the computer** In virtually all cases, there is no power reaching the CD-R drive. For internal CD-R drives, make sure the computer's four-pin power cable is properly connected to the CD-R drive unit. For external CD-R drives, make sure the power cord is properly connected to the back of the CD-R drive unit, and is plugged into a grounded power outlet. Make sure the power switch on the back of the drive is on. Refer to your CD-R drive's installation guide for more detailed information.

SYMPTOM 9-97 **Write emergency** This error occurs if the drive is interrupted during a write action. It is commonly seen when writing Red Book audio, but can also occur with data recordings. For example, one typical reason for a write emergency is dust particles that cause the laser to jump off track. In most cases, the CD-R disc is ruined, and you'll need to retry the write process with a good-quality disc.

SYMPTOM 9-98 The CD-R is recognized by Windows 95/98, but it will not function as a normal CD-ROM drive The drive appears normally in the Windows 95/98 Device Manager. The driver that is operating the CD-R drive may not allow the drive to function as a normal CD-ROM reader. For example, this is a known problem with the Philips CDD2000 CD-R. Check to see if there is an updated Windows 95/98 CD-R driver that can overcome this limitation. If not, you may need to replace the CD-R drive with an upgraded model whose drivers *do* support CD-ROM–type functionality on the CD-R drive.

SYMPTOM 9-99 You cannot read CD-R (gold) discs in some ordinary CD-ROM drives This is a very complex issue because there are a number of important factors that affect the way a CD is read.

- *Check the laser calibration.* Some older CD-ROM drive lasers are not calibrated to read recordable discs (whose recorded surface is slightly different from that of "pressed" discs). If your CD-ROM drive reads mass-produced (silver) CDs but not recordable CDs, check with the CD-ROM drive manufacturer to determine whether laser calibration is the problem. You may be able to return the CD-ROM drive for factory recalibration, or replace the CD-ROM drive with a newer model that is better calibrated for reading both CD-ROM and CD-R discs.
- *Check the CD-ROM compatibility.* Fast CD-ROM drive operations may be another problem. In order for some CD-ROM models to work as fast as they do, they must perform unconventional operations such as a laser calibration in the lead-out area to determine the approximate position of several tracks. With some CD recorders, the session lead-out is not recorded correctly, and this can cause problems with gold disc compatibility.
- *Check the CD-R software.* The CD-R authoring software can be a problem. Any authoring software can sometimes produce incorrect tracks due to bugs or recording glitches. A good way to check whether incompatibility problems lie with the originating software is to test the same gold disc on several CD-ROM drives. If one drive is capable of reading the gold disc back correctly, chances are that the problem was *not* in the recording process. If no drives can read the CD-R disc, then the disc may have been damaged in the recording process.
- *Update or disable MSCDEX.* Consider your version of MSCDEX. Although MSCDEX (the Microsoft extension for reading CD-ROMs) will allow non-ISO legal characters in file names, versions of MSCDEX *prior* to 2.23 have a problem in dealing with file names that contain the hyphen. If a directory contains a file name with a hyphen in it, you will be able to see all the files by using the DIR command from DOS. But any files listed *after* the file with the illegal name are not accessible—when trying to open them, you will get a "file not found" message. MSCDEX 2.23 appears to have fixed this bug. You may also REM out the real-mode drivers and MSCDEX command lines in your startup files and rely on protected-mode drivers under Windows 95/98.

SYMPTOM 9-100 You encounter "buffer miscompare" errors when using a SCSI host adapter diagnostic utility In many cases, you likely have a DMA channel conflict with another card (or device) in the system. Check the settings of every card or device that uses an IRQ, DMA channel, or I/O port address, and compare these settings to the ones used for the SCSI host adapter. If there is a DMA conflict, change the DMA channel on the SCSI card to an unused channel.

Another possibility is that you're dealing with a motherboard that doesn't support bus mastering (not all PC's support bus mastering). For example, a Gateway 2000 P5-133 only has one bus mastering slot, which is normally occupied by the video adapter. If the SCSI adapter (such as an Adaptec AHA-1535 card) is installed in a non-bus-mastering slot in this machine, the system may freeze when trying to access a CD from the CD-R drive. It may be necessary to upgrade the motherboard to access additional bus mastering slots.

SYMPTOM 9-101 **You encounter a "servo tracking error" when writing a CD** A "servo tracking error" message is reported by the CD-R drive when it is unable to record to the media (the blank disc)—this is similar to when a needle skips on a phonograph. There is a microscopic groove imprinted on the surface of each CD-R disc that guides the laser during writing. There are a number of reasons why a servo tracking error might occur.

- *Check for defective media.* Defective media can include a bad disc, a bad lot of discs, or an unsupported brand of media. (Not all CD-R disc media work the same on all CD-R drives.) For example, the Pinnacle Micro RCD-1000/5020/5040 series drives support the following disc brands: DOT, Taiyo Yuden, Mitsubishi, Sony, 3M, TDK, Verbatim, and Kodak Infoguard. Make sure you're using a blank disc that's certified to work with your particular drive, and try another disc (or disc brand) if necessary.
- *Check the data you're recording.* Verify that the amount of data you are trying to record does not exceed the capacity of the disc. Your recording software will usually prevent you from making that mistake, but it has no way of adjusting for previously failed sessions or bad blocks on the media. This can cause the software to incorrectly calculate the remaining free space, which will differ from what is *actually* free.
- *Clean the drive and disc.* There may be a dirty lens within the drive that prevents the laser from focusing on the surface of the media. Use a can of compressed air to blow out the inside of the drive through the front access door or tray.
- *Check for excessive temperature.* A servo tracking error may also occur if the ambient temperature inside the drive itself is too high. If your drive is external, remove the filter from the back of the drive and use compressed air to clean it out. Confirm that the cooling fan works when the unit is powered on—if not, the drive may need to be replaced. If your drive is internal, verify that it receives enough air circulation by removing the computer's case, letting the drive cool off for a while, and then rerunning the recording session. If the problem persists, replace the drive.

SYMPTOM 9-102 **You notice frequent "pops" or "clicks" between CD audio tracks** This is almost always a result of your particular CD recording software. The pops or clicks heard between tracks on CD digital audio (CD-DA) discs are caused when recording without using the Disc-at-Once option. When you select the Disc-at-Once option in the authoring software, the laser will remain powered on between each track (and run-in/run-out blocks are written without interruption). Keep in mind that the Disc-at-Once feature is not currently available on some software packages, so check the manual of your CD authoring software to see if it has this feature—if not, you may have an outdated or "lite" version, which will require an upgrade. For example, the Disc-at-Once feature is available with Easy-CD Pro version 1.1.409 and later (but not in Easy-CD 95). By comparison, Corel CD Creator does not support true Disc-at-Once, even as late as version 2.01.079.

Another possible cause for pops between tracks occurs when a WAV file is created improperly (or it is corrupt). Some early shareware audio editing software had problems saving WAV files properly, and bugs caused pops to occur between tracks (and at other various points throughout a song). These WAV files were corrupted by the editing software.

The most recent problem with WAV files is the use of "extended information." Some WAV editing software packages allow the user to save the WAV file in an extended WAV format, as well as the standard WAV format. If extended information is included in the WAV file (author name, date, etc.), this will cause a pop to occur when played back through a standard audio CD player. Make sure you can save a WAV file without this extra information to avoid the problem.

SYMPTOM 9-103 **On your home stereo, the disc will not repeat play after the last track** When you set your home stereo CD player to "repeat playback" after the last track, the CD playback simply stops—it will not repeat. Some audio CD players cannot play back a "burned" audio disc properly if there are B0h and C0h pointers in the disc's table of contents. B0h and C0h pointers are used to point to the next session, and they are created on discs written using the Track-at-Once (or multisession) option. CDs written using Disc-at-Once do not contain these pointers because there are no subsequent sessions. If you would like to have a disc that is fully compatible with audio CD, use the Disc-at-Once option during recording.

SYMPTOM 9-104 **You cannot access a CD-R after upgrading to Windows 98** You may find this happens most frequently with Philips CDD200 or HO 4020I CD-R drives, and it is almost always due to problems with Corel CD Creator 2.0 being present on your system. There are two means of correcting this problem. First, uninstall Corel CD Creator and install other CD authoring software (such as Adaptec Easy CD Creator Pro), which should be better able to support the CD-R drive. If you cannot replace the CD authoring software, check with the CD-R maker to see if there is a firmware upgrade available for the CD-R drive.

SYMPTOM 9-105 **When upgrading to Windows 95/98, you receive a "fatal exception 0E" error** While you are installing Windows and setup restarts your computer for the last time, you may see a "blue screen" error such as:

```
A fatal exception 0E has occurred at 0028:C02A0201 in VXD IOS(04)+00001FC9
```

This problem can typically occur if Corel CD Creator 2.0 is installed on your computer. Windows 95/98 is known to be incompatible with the CDRASPI.VXD file installed by Corel CD Creator 2.0. You can work around this problem by renaming the CDRASPI.VXD file:

1 Start Windows 95/98 in the Safe Mode.
2 Click Start, highlight Find, and then click "Files or Folders."
3 In the Named box, type **cdraspi.vxd**, and then click Find Now.
4 In the list of found files, right-click the cdraspi.vxd file, and then click Rename.
5 Type a new name for the cdraspi.vxd file (such as **cdraspi.old**), and then press ENTER.
6 Restart your computer normally.

SYMPTOM 9-106 **You receive a "Windows protection" error with EZ-SCSI 4.0 and Easy CD Pro 95** After you install the Adaptec EZ-SCSI 4.0 and the Adaptec Easy-CD Pro 95 programs under Windows 98, you may receive the following error message:

```
Windows Protection Error: You need to restart your computer.
```

You may be able to use Windows, but you may not be able to use the EZ-SCSI 4.0 and Easy CD Pro 95 programs. You'll need to restart Windows 98 in the Safe Mode and remove (uninstall) both EZ-SCSI 4.0 and Easy CD Pro 95. Check with Adaptec for updated versions of both programs.

9

SYMPTOM 9-107 **You receive an error when recording an audio track under four seconds** If you try to record an audio track or WAV file that is less than four seconds long, you will get a message indicating that a certain track cannot be written because it is less than four seconds long. Do not use WAV files of less than four seconds. The audio standard for compact disc (Red Book) does not allow for audio files of less than four seconds. Make the audio file longer and try recording it again.

SYMPTOM 9-108 **You get poor audio quality from the CD-R** Changes in recording speed (from 4X to 2X to 1X) have little or no effect on the quality of the recording. Most current CD authoring software allows the use of IDE-style CD-ROM devices as "source drives" for copying audio CDs (Red Book or CD-DA). The digital audio extraction (or DAE) test will pass, yet the copy process results in poor audio quality. Program and data CDs usually copy without problems. In virtually all cases, the problem is the source CD-ROM drive.

Use the source CD-ROM drive to extract a troublesome audio CD track to the hard disk as a WAV file (name it CDTEST.WAV). Now use the CD-R to extract the same audio track to the hard disk as a WAV file (name it WTEST.WAV). Play the two WAV files from the hard drive and compare them. If the CDTEST.WAV file contains the same clicks/pops as you encountered during recording, yet the CD-R is producing clean WAV files, then your source drive is not producing quality digital audio extraction. There are three ways around this problem:

- Use the CD-R as the source *and* destination. (Check the CD-R manual and CD authoring software for detailed instructions on how to do this.)
- Purchase a new CD-ROM drive guaranteed to support high-speed DAE.
- Use the CD authoring software settings to slow down the DAE rate. For example, in Easy CD Creator, the DAE rate is found under Tools, Options, and Advanced tab. You can experiment by extracting tracks as WAV files after making those changes, and test their quality by playing them from the hard drive.

The CD-RW Drive

CD recording offers a powerful tool for backing up important files or archiving completed work. Recording also makes it possible to distribute projects or multimedia presentations on simple and inexpensive media. The problem with CD recording is that it's a one-time deal—once the media is written, it cannot be erased or rewritten. Within the last several years, rewritable CD technology (or CD-RW) has developed a lot of interest by allowing specialized optical CD media to be written, erased, then rewritten with the ease of a floppy disk. Such capability allows CD rewriters to be used for large local file storage (rather than simple archiving). Almost any Pentium PC (or later) with a SCSI or UDMA interface can support a CD-RW drive. This part of the chapter outlines the important points of CD-RW technology and troubleshooting.

UNDERSTANDING CD-RW CONCEPTS

The ISO 9660 file system has long been the established standard in CD-ROM and CD recording. (By comparison, Mac systems use the HFS approach.) In fact, ISO 9660 is one of the key elements that propelled CD-ROM drives to the status of "standard equipment" on the PC by the early 1990s. With the broad introduction of CD-RW drives, however, ISO 9660 has been replaced by the *Universal Data Format* (or simply UDF) file system. This section of the chapter offers some essential background on UDF and explains how the use of UDF affects the compatibility of CD-RW discs with existing CD-ROM and CD-RW drives.

Let's start with some perspective on ISO 9660. The ISO 9660 file system grew out of the original High Sierra file system of the late 1980s. All the files read on your CD-ROM or recorded on your CD-R use the ISO 9660 format. Both Windows and Mac operating systems can read ISO 9660 discs because they provide built-in ISO 9660 readers—the reader is totally transparent to the end user.

While ISO 9660 is just fine for existing CD-ROM and CD-R drives, it is really not sufficient to support the new generation of CD-RW drives and the emergence of DVD drives. CD-RW drives require that files be added incrementally (one file at a time) without a waste of overhead space and that individual files can be erased "at will" to make room on a disc. In addition, DVD drives require a file system that can support drives at least 4GB in size. These demands are well beyond the scope of ISO 9660.

UDF addresses all of these concerns by providing a format that can add and erase individual files as needed, as well as support the large disc space promised by DVD. Another advantage of UDF is its cross-platform compatibility—a UDF disc can be read by both a Mac and Windows platform. For example, a file could be written using a Mac, then read back on a Windows PC. The UDF file format is also able to maintain Mac file attributes (such as icons, resource forks, and file types), where ISO 9660 cannot do this.

Working with UDF

The DirectCD technology used with CD-RW drives reads and writes to the CD-RW disc using the UDF format. If you're working on a PC with a CD-RW drive (or plan on installing one yourself), chances are that you'll be using a DirectCD applet to invoke UDF on that disc. There are currently two versions of UDF. UDF 1.02 is the version used on current DVD-ROM and DVD-Video discs. UDF 1.5 is a superset of 1.02 that adds support for CD-R and CD-RW drives. If you're using DirectCD under Windows 95/98, chances are that you're using UDF 1.5.

Disc Capacity Under UDF

An important issue to keep in mind when using DirectCD is that you never get the same data capacity from a CD-RW disc that you do from a CD-R disc under ISO 9660. Traditional CD-Rs under ISO 9660 can provide a full 650MB from a blank 74-minute disc. By comparison, UDF demands a certain amount of recording overhead that reduces the overall amount of data that can be recorded on a CD-R or CD-RW disc. In normal operation, you can fit up to 493MB on a CD-RW disc under DirectCD. For a CD-R disc under DirectCD, you can generally fit up to 618MB.

UDF and Disc Compatibility

There's only one little problem with UDF—Windows 95 does not support it natively. The DirectCD drivers installed with a CD-RW drive will allow Windows 95 to read UDF discs in a CD-RW drive, but using DirectCD (UDF) discs in other drives is a little trickier. When DirectCD begins writing data to a disc, it opens a session. Before any CD-ROM drive can read a disc, the session must be closed.

When you eject a disc from a CD-RW drive using the DirectCD applet, you can choose to close the disc to ISO 9660. If you do not close the disc to ISO 9660 when you eject it, you cannot read it on a CD-ROM drive—you must read it on a CD-R or CD-RW drive fitted with DirectCD. This is a limitation of CD-ROM drives, not the DirectCD software. Table 9-4 outlines the compatibility of UDF discs.

> Windows 98 SE (and subsequent versions of Windows) with DVD support should fully support UDF.

If you close the disc to UDF, you can still read the UDF format, but you'll need a Multi-Read CD-ROM drive and a UDF reader utility. For example, when you install Adaptec's UDF Reader in your

TABLE 9-4 UDF DISC COMPATIBILITY

DISC TYPE	PLAYBACK ON...			
	CD-ROM or Multi-Read CD player	CD-ROM	CD-R	CD-RW
CD-R	Yes	Yes	Yes	Yes
CD-RW	No	Yes[1]	Yes[1,2]	Yes

NOTES: 1 A UDF reader utility may be required.
2 If it reads CD-RW discs.

system, you should be able to read your closed session CD-R and CD-RW discs on CD-ROM drives regardless of whether they are ISO 9660 or UDF.

Multi-Read CD-ROM Drives

UDF reader utilities are designed to support the new generation of Multi-Read CD-ROM drives. Multi-Read is a specification developed and endorsed by the Optical Storage Technology Association (OSTA) and accepted by the industry at large. Most new CD-ROM drives on the market today (manufactured after mid-1997) are Multi-Read compatible. To be Multi-Read compliant, a CD-ROM drive must be able to

- Read CD-RW discs
- Read packet-written discs (both CD-R and CD-RW)
- Support the operating system to utilize UDF 1.5 (or later)

> There are some non-Multi-Read CD-ROM drives that can read UDF-formatted CD-R media, but not CD-RW media, using an appropriate UDF reader utility.

UDF Readers

A UDF reader enables Multi-Read CD-ROM drives to read closed-session UDF-formatted CD-R and CD-RW media under Windows 95/98 and the Macintosh operating system. The UDF reader for Windows is called "UDF Reader Driver,, and the UDF reader for Mac OS is called "UDF Volume Access." UDF readers are particularly useful if you're using DirectCD to *record* data to a CD-RW disc because you will then be able to read the CD-RW disc in a Multi-Read CD-ROM drive. Without a UDF reader, you could only read the UDF disc in another CD-RW drive using DirectCD. Since UDF is designed to be a cross-platform file format, UDF readers also allow you to interchange UDF-formatted discs between Mac and Windows systems.

Most companies that develop DirectCD software (such as Adaptec) already offer UDF reader utilities free of charge. You can download the Adaptec UDF reader from the Adaptec Web site at **www.adaptec.com**, or specifically from their patch/upgrade Web page at **http://www.adaptec.com/support/files/upgrades.html**. For more information, you could also send e-mail to Adaptec at **udfreader@adaptec.com**.

UDF Reader Compliance

Since UDF is intended to provide a universal file interchange format, any UDF reader utility *should* be able to read all UDF 1.5 formatted media (media formatted with DirectCD). However, there is no independent third-party organization to test for UDF compliance, so there is no guarantee that all media claiming to be UDF formatted will be readable by every UDF reader under all conditions.

If you have trouble reading a UDF disc with one particular reader utility, you might wish to try another reader utility.

UDF and Audio CDs

A popular use of CD-R and CD-RW discs has been to record music for playback on an ordinary CD player (for example, copying vinyl LPs to CD). While this is a tried-and-true process for CD-R discs recorded under ISO 9660, this will not work with UDF discs recorded with DirectCD. Audio files recorded under UDF will not work when played back in a commercial CD player. But audio files played back on a CD-R or CD-RW drive under DirectCD should work normally.

Windows 98 and UDF

While Windows 95 does not provide direct support for UDF, information gleaned from Microsoft and Adaptec suggests that Windows 98 will support UDF 1.02 for DVD-ROM and DVD-Video discs. However, preliminary results indicate that Windows 98 may not provide native support for UDF 1.5, so DirectCD software and UDF readers may still be required after Windows 98 is installed. Windows 98 SE may not require a separate UDF reader.

> Mac OS 8.1 already supports UDF 1.02.

Using DirectCD

There are some simple rules to follow when preparing and working with CD-RW drives. Preparing new discs, writing data, adding data, erasing data, ejecting the disc, and recovering damaged discs are the most typical procedures that you'll need to master. This part of the chapter outlines these essential steps—though you should refer to your CD-RW user's manual for specific information.

PREPARING A DATA CD

Use the following steps to start DirectCD and prepare a blank CD-RW disc for reading and writing data:

1 Start the computer—insert a blank CD-RW disc in the CD-RW drive. After a few seconds, a screen will appear with the message "Please select the type of CD you wish to create." If the DirectCD Disc Ready window appears, the disc has already been prepared, and you can start writing data to it immediately.

> If no screen appears after about 15 seconds, the disc may not be blank, it may have an unreadable format, or the "auto insert notification" option may be disabled.

2 Select the option "Click here to create a data CD that will be accessible through a drive letter." (Use this as you would a floppy drive.) The Format Disc screen appears.

3 If you're formatting a CD-R disc, click Next on the Format Disc screen.

4 If you're formatting a CD-RW disc, you can choose between two formatting options—click the Advanced button that appears on the Format Disc screen. When the next screen appears, select either Fast Format or Full Format, and click OK.

> It's often easier to select the Fast Format option, which lets you start writing to the CD-RW disc almost immediately (while the disc is formatted in the background). A Full Format requires you to wait about an hour until the formatting is complete before you can write to the disc.

5. When the Name Your Disc screen appears, type a name for the disc and click Finish. Disc formatting begins. When the DirectCD Disc Ready window appears, the formatting is complete.
6. Click OK. The DirectCD disc is ready for you to write data to it.

WRITING DATA TO A DIRECTCD DISC

Once your CD is formatted as a DirectCD disc, you can write data to it in several different ways:

- Drag and drop files from Windows Explorer right onto the CD-RW icon.
- Select Save As from a Windows 95/98/NT application File menu, and select the drive letter of your CD-RW.
- Use the Send To command.
- Use the MS-DOS command prompts from a DOS window in Windows 95/98/NT.

EJECTING A DIRECTCD DISC

DirectCD gives you several formatting options when you eject a DirectCD disc from the CD-RW drive. The options depend on what kind of disc DirectCD detects in the drive and how you want to use the disc. To eject a DirectCD disc, follow these steps:

1. Push the Eject button on the front of the CD-RW drive, or right-click on the CD icon on the taskbar and select Eject from the drop-down list box. The Eject Disc screen appears.
2. Carefully read the text that appears on the screen, and (if options are presented) select the option you require.
3. Click Finish to eject the disc from the CD-RW drive.

ERASING A DIRECTCD DISC

If you're using CD-RW discs, you can actually erase files from the disc and use the recovered space to write new files. However, if you delete files from a CD-R disc, the files become invisible to the file system (Windows Explorer), but the space they occupy is not made available for other files. So deleting files from a CD-R disc will not increase the available free space on the disc. To erase the contents of a DirectCD disc, follow these steps:

1. While in Windows Explorer, select the file(s) you want to erase.
2. Select Delete from the File menu.
3. Click Yes to confirm that you want to erase the files from the disc.
4. DirectCD erases the selected file(s) from the disc.

FIXING AN UNREADABLE DISC

If no window appears on the screen (after about 15 seconds) when you insert a disc in the CD-RW drive, the disc may have an unreadable format. DirectCD has a ScanDisc application that may be able to recover data on the disc and allow you to write to it and read from it again. Follow these steps to use ScanDisc:

1. Double-click the CD icon on the right side of the Windows taskbar. If the disc is unreadable, the ScanDisc window will appear.
2. Read the text in the window, and then click the ScanDisc button.
3. Wait while ScanDisc repairs the disc. A message will appear on the screen when ScanDisc is finished.

CARING FOR REWRITABLE CDS

As a rule, rewritable CDs are as rugged and reliable as ordinary "pressed" CDs. Still, you should follow the same guidelines with Caring for Recordable CDs as well as:

- *Don't use Kodak Photo CDs.* Avoid the use of Kodak Photo CDs on everyday CD recorders. Kodak Photo CDs are designed to be used only with Kodak Photo CD professional workstations. Although the discs are inexpensive, they have a protection bit that prevents them from being written on many CD recorders. When you attempt to write these discs on the recorders that recognize the protection bit, you will receive an error message.
- *Be careful when dealing with power issues.* If you lose power while writing to your CD-RW (or if you exit an application or press CTRL+ALT+DEL) while writing to CD, you may be able to salvage your rewritable CD if you follow the steps below:
    1. Leave the CD in the drive—do not open the tray.
    2. Turn the machine off, and then turn it back on.
    3. Reenter the application you were using.

Once the application tries to access the CD-RW drive, the recovery operation will make it appear that the last session is there. However, only a part of the CD's directory may be there, and your rewritable CD is still usable if you can read that directory. Repeat the entire copy operation to make sure your files are copied successfully.

Troubleshooting CD-RW Drives

Although UDF and CD-RW drives are now well-established industry standards, there are still a number of compatibility problems and operating issues that technicians may eventually need to address. This part of the chapter examines a selection of UDF issues and CD-RW problems.

> For basic CD and recording issues, refer to the previous parts of this chapter for CD-ROM and CD-R troubleshooting information.

TROUBLESHOOTING TIPS

CD-RW drives are not terribly complicated devices to troubleshoot, but they can present some peculiar problems for technicians and do-it-yourselfers. Before you attempt to troubleshoot a CD-RW issue with your system, take a moment to work through the checklist below:

- Verify that your system meets the minimum requirements for your CD-RW drive. If not, the system may fail to run properly (if at all).
- Make sure the computer is plugged in and that each device has power. Connect any devices that are not receiving power.

- Turn off the computer's power, wait 15–20 seconds, and then reboot the system. This can clear some software conflicts.
- Repeat the operation with a different (known-good) CD.
- Make sure you're using the right type of CD for the task at hand.
- Check the README file that came with the CD-RW drive for any last-minute compatibility or performance notes that might be present with your system. Also check the CD-RW drive maker's Web site for the latest drivers and firmware upgrades.
- If the problem(s) occur with power management, disable your PC's power management modes.

GENERAL SYMPTOMS

SYMPTOM 9-109 **The CD-ROM drive or CD audio player refuses to read CD-RW discs** This is a common problem that depends on the age of the CD-ROM drive itself. Older CD-ROM drives (manufactured before mid- to late 1997) are probably not Multi-Read/UDF compatible and cannot read UDF-formatted discs at all. CD audio players also cannot read UDF discs. If your CD-ROM is not Multi-Read compliant, you'll need to upgrade to a Multi-Read compliant model, or record your discs (especially audio discs) in a conventional ISO 9660 format using the CD-RW or CD-R drive.

CD-ROM drives manufactured after mid- to late 1997 will probably offer Multi-Read capability, but still may not be able to read a UDF-formatted disc without the assistance of a UDF reader utility. In most cases, you can obtain a free UDF reader from the company (such as Adaptec) providing the DirectCD software.

SYMPTOM 9-110 **A backup disc will not run properly** DirectCD is not suitable for making backup copies of game or application discs where the application must run from the CD. This is because DirectCD uses a different method of writing data to disc (a.k.a. packet writing) than any discs produced with the ISO 9660 format. Packet-written (UDF) discs cannot be read by many standard CD-ROM drives or game machines. The only way to work around this sort of problem is to make a backup copy of the disc to CD-R using other recording software (such as Easy CD Creator for Windows 95/98 or Adaptec Toast for the Mac).

> Keep in mind that some games and commercial application discs use forms of copy protection that recording software cannot work around or "break." Also remember that you cannot copy commercial software because of copyright restrictions.

SYMPTOM 9-111 **You cannot "see" a second session reading a CD-RW disc from a CD-ROM drive** First make sure you're trying to read the disc on a newer Multi-Read-compatible CD-ROM drive (along with a UDF reader utility if necessary). Try ejecting the CD and reinserting it in the drive. Then refresh the screen by selecting My Computer from inside Windows Explorer and pressing F5. Finally, try reading the disc from the CD-RW drive (or from another suitable CD-ROM drive). If another drive can read the disc, the problem is likely to be with the suspect CD-ROM drive. If the disc cannot be read in any drive, the problem is likely to be with the disc itself. (Try re-recording the disc.)

You cannot read a multisession disc created with DirectCD under DOS or Windows 3.1x—there are no drivers to support UDF on these operating systems. If the disc was not recorded with DirectCD (that is, ISO 9660) and you cannot read it under DOS or Windows 3.1x, make sure that your copy of MSCDEX (located in the AUTOEXEC.BAT file) is version 2.23. You can download the latest version of MSCDEX from the Microsoft Web site at **www.microsoft.com**.

SYMPTOM 9-112 **You receive an error such as "CD-RW is not under Direct CD control"** You'll typically notice this problem under Windows 95/98 when you attempt to erase, format, or copy data to a CD-RW. This type of problem is most frequently encountered when using a Ricoh CD-RW drive and Adaptec Direct CD software. The problem can occur when the CD-RW drive uses older firmware (such as a Ricoh CD-RW drive with v.2.03 firmware or earlier), or if you're using Adaptec DirectCD 2.0 or earlier. Try updating the drive's firmware and CD authoring software.

SYMPTOM 9-113 **The CD-RW media cannot be used when the UDF format is interrupted** If power is lost while formatting a CD-RW disc, the disc will become unusable in any application, and fail if another format is attempted. To correct this issue, use the DirectCD Full Erase feature to wipe the disc; then try the format operation again.

SYMPTOM 9-114 **Files recorded in a second session do not appear** If the files that you recorded in a second session do not appear when you try to read the disc in a CD-ROM drive, try the following tips:

- Try ejecting and reinserting the CD.
- Refresh the file list by selecting the CD-RW icon in My Computer or Windows Explorer and then pressing F5.
- Check the drive. CD-RW discs can be used only in CD-RW drives or newer Multi-Read CD-ROMs.
- Try reading the CD in other CD-ROM drives. If other drives are able to read the disc, the problem is probably with the original CD-ROM drive.

SYMPTOM 9-115 **Your computer loses power while writing a CD-RW disc, and now the disc is inaccessible** If you lose power while writing to your CD (the CD-RW's drive light is on) or if you press CTRL+ALT+DEL while writing to a CD, you'll interrupt the disc. But you may be able to salvage your disc. Leave your CD-RW disc in the drive, but don't open the CD tray. Turn your computer off and cycle the power back on. Then restart the utility that you were using.

Once the DirectCD utility tries to access the CD-RW drive/disc again, the recovery operation will make it appear that the last session is there, but actually only a *part* of the CD's directory may be there. Your recordable CD is still usable if you can read the directory. Just repeat the entire copy operation to make sure your files are copied to the rewritable CD.

SYMPTOM 9-116 **You receive a "buffer underrun" error when you're writing in CD-R mode** CD recordable devices require an uninterrupted data stream from the hard drive to write successfully to a CD. A "buffer underrun" message appears when the data stream is interrupted. This can occur if another program interrupts the writing process (or if the CD-RW drive's write speed is set too high for the speed at which the hard drive is running). Here are some tips to deal with buffer underrun errors. (See the section "Buffer Underrun" earlier in this chapter for more detailed information.)

- Use the CD authoring software's Test option to ensure that the write speed is appropriate for your computer.
- Try recording at a lower speed (such as 4X, 2X, or 1X).
- Do not use hard drive compression software—buffer underruns may be caused by this type of software.

- Exit any other background programs before writing data to the CD.
- Disable your computer's power-management feature.
- Run ScanDisk and Defrag on your hard drive. These programs improve access times to the hard drive.
- Do not run other programs that could interrupt the writing process. Log off any networks, disable the fax modem software, screen saver, or other programs (such as TSRs) that may automatically send messages to your computer while writing data to the CD.
- Make sure the hard drive has enough temporary directory space. The space free should be at least twice the size of the largest file that you are recording.
- Do not copy empty folders (files with a zero byte size) or files that are in current use.

SYMPTOM 9-117 **There is no DirectCD window after inserting a new CD-RW disc** Verify that the CD-RW drive's DirectCD software and utilities have been installed properly. If the DirectCD window doesn't appear on the screen after you insert a new disc, follow these steps:

1. Wait a moment—it can take up to 15 seconds for the DirectCD window to appear.
2. If the rewritable disc is already formatted, you can "force" the window by clicking Start on the taskbar, choosing Programs, and then selecting Create a CD.
3. To prepare a CD with Easy CD Creator or DirectCD, the disc must be blank. (You may have inserted a disc that is already formatted.) Remove the disc and insert a good-quality blank one.
4. The disc may have an unreadable format. DirectCD has a ScanDisk utility that may be able to recover data on the disc. Simply double-click the CD icon on the Windows taskbar. Start ScanDisk and allow the process to run. A message will appear when ScanDisk is finished.

SYMPTOM 9-118 **The CD-RW drive doesn't show up in My Computer or Windows Explorer** In effect, the drive is "disconnected" from the rest of the system. There are many possible problems that can cause this kind of behavior.

- *Refresh Windows Explorer.* If the drive doesn't appear in Explorer, click View from the top menu, and then click Refresh. You might also try rebooting the computer (from a cold start) so that the PnP BIOS might recognize the CD-RW drive.
- *Check the drive power.* Make sure the drive's power connector is attached securely. Test the power by opening and closing the drive tray using the Eject button.
- *Check the signal cable.* Make sure the drive's SCSI or IDE signal cable is oriented properly and secured between the drive and drive controller.
- *Check the drive jumpers.* Chances are that you installed the CD-RW as a master IDE device. Verify that the drive jumpers are set properly, and see that any other drive on that channel has been rejumpered as a slave drive. If you're using a SCSI CD-RW drive, see that the SCSI ID for the CD-RW is unique and that the SCSI chain is properly connected and terminated.
- *Check the drivers.* Verify that the latest CD-RW drivers and utility software are installed.
- *Replace the drive.* If problems persist, try another CD-RW drive, or reconfigure the drive so that it is alone on its controller channel (disconnect the slave IDE drive).

SYMPTOM 9-119 **The device that is sharing the IDE signal cable with your CD-RW drive no longer responds** In most cases, that other drive was accidentally disconnected or unpowered when the new CD-RW drive was installed.

- *Check the cables.* Turn off and unplug your computer; then make sure the power cables are securely attached to both drives. You can verify power to the drives by observing their power LEDs, or by ejecting their disk trays. Also verify that the SCSI or IDE signal cable is oriented properly and connected securely at both drives. When using a SCSI controller, verify that the SCSI chain is properly terminated.
- *Check the IDE jumpers.* The master/slave relationship of the drives may also be an issue. If you installed the CD-RW drive as a slave device, try reconfiguring the devices so that the CD-RW drive is the master. For example, when using a CD-RW drive with Sony or Goldstar CD-ROMs, try configuring the CD-RW drive as the master, and set the CD-ROM as the slave.
- *Replace the suspect device.* Try the suspect drive by itself (disconnect the CD-RW drive). If the suspect drive returns to normal, there may be a conflict between the CD-RW drive and the other device. You may need to separate the two devices to different drive controller channels. If the problem persists, try replacing the suspect device.

SYMPTOM 9-120 You receive an error message when double-clicking on the CD-RW icon There are several possible issues that are typically caused by the drive's inability to read the disc. Here are a few things to check:

- There is no CD in the CD-RW drive. Insert a good-quality CD and try reading again.
- After inserting a CD, you need to wait a moment to let the CD-RW drive read the disc information.. When the LED on the front of the drive stops flashing and stays green, click on the CD-RW drive's icon again.
- The CD may be in the tray upside down or a little off center. Try reinserting the CD—the disc label should be facing up.
- You may be trying to read from a blank recordable CD. Copy some information to the disc and try reading it again.

SYMPTOM 9-121 You receive an "invalid media" error when trying to boot from the CD-RW In many newer PC platforms, it is possible to boot from a CD-RW drive rather than a floppy or hard drive. An "invalid media" error from the CD-RW drive generally means that the disc doesn't contain the bootstrap files needed to begin the boot process and load your operating system. Chances are that the disc itself isn't bootable. Use a bootable CD (such as a "system rescue" disc or an OS disc such as Windows NT).

If you need to work around this problem, simply remove the disc from the CD-RW. During boot, the BIOS will skip the CD-RW and move directly to the next drive in the boot order (the hard drive). If you want to prevent your system from checking the CD-RW at boot time, go into the system's CMOS setup and change the boot order so that the CD-RW is not included. For example, you might change the boot order to "A:/C:" or "C:/A:".

SYMPTOM 9-122 You cannot copy directly from a CD-ROM drive to the CD-RW drive This is a very common problem that is almost always caused by inadequate hardware capabilities. Here are the major issues to check:

- *Check the source drive.* The source drive (typically a CD-ROM) must support the extremely fast data transfers found in late-model ATAPI EIDE or SCSI-2 drives. If you're copying audio CDs, the source drive must be capable of digital audio extraction (DAE). It may be necessary to upgrade the source drive or drive controller in order to support faster data transfers.

- *Check the drive arrangement.* If you're using an IDE-type source and CD-RW drive, make sure the source and destination drives are not on the same IDE controller channel. You may need to reconfigure your drives so that the source and destination drives are split on separate controller channels.
- *Check the CD itself.* Some CDs have a copy-prevention feature (or other features) that do not allow a CD-to-CD copy. If that's the case, it may not be possible to copy that particular disc.

> Make sure you only copy material that belongs to you, or you have written permission to copy. Otherwise, you may be violating international copyright laws.

SYMPTOM 9-123 **Audio from the CD-RW drive is poor or absent** Whenever you have trouble with CD audio from a CD-ROM, CD-R, or CD-RW drive, try listening to the audio using a set of headphones plugged into the headset connector on the drive's front panel. If you cannot hear the audio (and volume adjustments don't help), the drive is probably defective and should be replaced. If you hear the audio normally, the problem is likely in the PC's sound system:

- *Check the CD audio cable.* Make sure the audio cable is completely plugged into the sound card and into the CD-RW drive. If you already have a CD-ROM or other drive providing CD audio to the sound card, you cannot connect the CD-RW's audio cable unless you remove the current CD audio cable, or use a sound card with more than one CD audio port.
- *Check the mixer applet.* Make sure the CD audio channel is not muted in the mixer software, and see that the CD audio level is turned up adequately. You may need to update the sound card's drivers or application software if the sound system is not currently supporting CD audio.
- *Check the sound file quality.* If the problem is with WAV file playback from the disc, try listening to the WAV files from your hard drive. If the problem persists, the problem is with poor WAV recordings (not with the CD-RW drive or sound card). If the WAV files sound correct from the hard drive (but not from the CD), the problem may be poor recording to the CD. It may be necessary to re-record the disc using updated recording software.

SYMPTOM 9-124 **Video playback is choppy from a CD-RW drive** This is generally not a problem with the CD-RW drive, but rather with the system's ability to handle streaming audio/video data from a CD. Your best solution is typically to reduce the system's processing overhead in order to provide more processing power to the video playback software (for example, Windows Media Player).

- Shut down any background applications, TSRs, or screen savers.
- Reduce the size of your video playback window.
- Download and install the latest versions of DirectX, your video drivers, and your multimedia player (for example, Windows Media Player).
- Many CD-RW drives tend to be rather slow (4X/2X), and this may interfere with data transfers on older systems. Try playing the video from another faster drive such as your system's CD-ROM drive.
- If problems persist, you may need to make one or more hardware upgrades to improve your system's multimedia playback capability (such as a faster video card, more system RAM, and a faster CPU).

SYMPTOM 9-125 **Your CD-ROM drive cannot "see" a second (or subsequent) session recorded on discs from a CD-RW drive** There are several possible issues that can occur when reading multisession discs created on a CD-RW drive with DirectCD software.

- *Reinsert the disc.* Start by ejecting and reinserting the disc. This allows the drive to redetect the disc and try reading its sessions once again. You should also try refreshing the display—select the My Computer icon in Windows Explorer, and then press F5.
- *Check the drive.* CD-RW discs can only be used in CD-RW drives or newer Multi-Read CD-ROMs (compatible with the UDF file system). If you're trying to read the disc on an older CD-ROM that is not Multi-Read compliant, you may need to upgrade the CD-ROM to a newer version.
- *Check your operating system.* Multisession CDs created with DirectCD cannot be read in DOS or Windows 3.x. Make sure you're in Windows 95, Windows 98, or some other UDF-compliant operating system.

SYMPTOM 9-126 You cannot get an application to "find" a CD in the CD-RW drive This is almost always a problem with the application itself rather than the drive. Many programs (such as CD-based games) look only for the first logical drive letter assigned to a CD-ROM drive or CD-RW drive. For example, if a CD-ROM drive is assigned to D:\ and the CD-RW drive is assigned to E:\, the program will probably look for the CD only in drive D:\ and will not see the CD in drive E:\. If you want to use the CD-RW drive with such programs, reassign the drive letters to make the CD-RW drive precede the CD-ROM drive:

1. For Windows 95/98, click Start, highlight Settings, and then click Control Panel. Double-click the System icon. Select the Device Manager tab and double-click the CD-ROM entry.
2. Double-click on the CD-ROM drive, and then click the Settings tab. Under Reserved drive letters, select the drive letter *after* the existing letter (for both start and end drive letter), and click OK.
3. Now double-click on the CD-RW drive entry, and click the Settings tab. Under Reserved drive letters, select the drive letter *before* the current one, and click OK.

9

Further Study

AcerOpen: **http://www.acercomponents.com/POL_CD-Drives.htm**

Adaptec: **http://www.adaptec.com/cdrec/** (CD Creator 2.x and Adaptec's Easy CD Creator Deluxe 3.0)

Aztech: **http://www.aztech.com.sg/c&t/spec_cd.htm**

CDR Publisher: **http://www.cdr1.com**

CeQuadrat: **http://www.cequadrat.com/** (WinOnCD 3.0 software)

Creative Labs: **http://www.creaf.com**

Diamond Multimedia: **http://www.diamondmm.com**

El Torito specification: **http://www.ptltd.com/techs/specs.html**

Hewlett-Packard: **http://www.hp.com**

HiVal: **http://www.hival.com**

NEC: **http://www.nec.com**

Philips: **http://www.pps.philips.com**

Pinnacle Micro: **http://www.pinnaclemicro.com/**

Plextor: **http://www.plextor.com**

Smart and Friendly: **http://www.smartandfriendly.com**

Teac America: **http://www.teac.com/dsp/dsp.htm**l

CD-RELATED NEWSGROUPS

alt.cd-rom

alt.cd-rom.reviews

comp.publish.cdrom.hardware

comp.publish.cdrom.multimedia

comp.publish.cdrom.software

comp.sys.ibm.pc.hardware.cd-rom

10

CHIPSETS

CHAPTER AT A GLANCE

In the early days of the PC, motherboards (and pretty much every other device) were designed and built with discrete logic gates. If you were around in the days of the PC/XT and PC/AT, you probably remember the huge motherboards packed with over 150 to 200 individual ICs. Discrete ICs demanded a lot of power and took up lots of room. It didn't take designers long to realize that standard functions of the PC (such as floppy drive interface circuits, DMA controllers, and programmable interrupt controllers) could easily be integrated into application-specific ICs (or ASICs). With the use of these custom-made chips, PCs were able to drop their chip count, reduce construction costs, and reduce power requirements.

But there are also performance advantages to such high levels of integration. Combining a PC's sophisticated logic circuitry onto a few chips dramatically shortens the signal paths and allows the circuit to operate at higher speeds. By optimizing the signal paths within the chip itself, performance could be improved even further. Designers quickly saw that they could integrate all the core logic needed to facilitate a complete state-of-the-art PC in just a few highly integrated chips. Since these chips were specifically designed to be used as a *set* on the motherboard, they were dubbed the *chipset* (Figure 10-1).

Today, chipsets play a leading role in the design and fabrication of modern personal computers. Whereas early motherboards could use hundreds of ICs, you'd be hard-pressed to find more than 20 ICs on a current motherboard. In fact, chipsets are so important that new chipsets must often be developed to support each new computer technology or processor. For example, you'll find that Intel's 820 chipset supports features such as RDRAM, AGP 4X, and Ultra DMA/66, but the venerable 440BX Pentium II/III chipset does not. As a result, motherboards with a 440BX chipset would have to be replaced with a motherboard using the 820 chipset before those features would be available. Ultimately, the overall features and capabilities of your PC are largely defined by the motherboard chipset (sometimes called the computer's *core logic*). This chapter is intended to identify many of the current chipsets in use today and familiarize you with their principal features.

FIGURE 10-1 An Intel 440LX chipset (Intel Corporation)

If you're looking for detailed technical information about today's chipsets, you can usually download the complete technical manual from the chipset manufacturer's Web site (usually in Adobe Acrobat's PDF format). Table 10-1 provides the URLs for downloading many of today's chipset manuals. Table 10-2 outlines the chipsets covered in this chapter and explains their functions.

TABLE 10-1 DETAILED CHIPSET MANUALS AND TECHNICAL INFORMATION

ALi M1531 Intel, Cyrix, AMD Socket 7	http://www.acerlabs.com/eng/product/core/m1531.htm
ALi M1541 Intel, Cyrix, AMD Socket 7	http://www.acerlabs.com/eng/product/core/m1541.htm
ALi M1621 Pentium II chipset	http://www.acerlabs.com/eng/product/core/m1621.htm
ALi M1631 Pentium II chipset	http://www.acerlabs.com/eng/product/core/m1631.htm
ALi M1543c Southbridge chipset	http://www.acerlabs.com/eng/product/core/m1543c.htm
AMD 750 chipset	http://www.amd.com/products/cpg/athlon/chipset.html
AMD 640 chipset	http://www.amd.com/K6/k6docs/pdf/21090.pdf
Intel 840 Pentium III, III Xeon chipset	http://developer.intel.com/design/chipsets/datashts/298020.htm
Intel 820 Pentium III chipset	http://developer.intel.com/design/chipsets/datashts/290630.htm
Intel 810E Celeron, Pentium III chipset	http://developer.intel.com/design/chipsets/datashts/290676.htm
Intel 810 Celeron, Pentium III chipset	http://developer.intel.com/design/chipsets/datashts/290656.htm
Intel 440 MX Celeron chipset	http://developer.intel.com/design/chipsets/datashts/245052.htm
Intel 440 EX Celeron chipset	http://developer.intel.com/design/chipsets/datashts/290616.htm
Intel 440 BX Pentium II, III chipset	http://developer.intel.com/design/chipsets/datashts/290633.htm
Intel 450 NX Pentium II, III Xeon chipset	http://developer.intel.com/design/chipsets/datashts/243771.htm
Intel 440 ZX Pentium II, III chipset	http://developer.intel.com/design/chipsets/datashts/290650.htm
Intel 430 FX Pentium chipset	http://developer.intel.com/design/pcisets/datashts/290518.htm
Intel 430 HX Pentium chipset	http://developer.intel.com/design/chipsets/datashts/290551.htm
Intel 430 VX Pentium chipset	http://developer.intel.com/design/pcisets/datashts/290553.htm
Intel 430 TX Pentium chipset	http://developer.intel.com/design/chipsets/datashts/290559.htm
Intel 450 GX/KX Pentium Pro chipset	http://developer.intel.com/design/chipsets/datashts/290523.htm
Intel 440FX Pentium Pro chipset	http://developer.intel.com/design/chipsets/datashts/290549.htm

TABLE 10-1 DETAILED CHIPSET MANUALS AND TECHNICAL INFORMATION *(CONTINUED)*

Intel 440LX Pentium Pro chipset	http://developer.intel.com/design/chipsets/440lx/
Intel 430MX mobile Pentium chipset	http://developer.intel.com/design/chipsets/440mx/ index.htm
VIA VT8371 AMD Athlon 133MHz chipset	http://www.viatech.com/products/prodkx133.htm
VIA VT82C693A Intel 133MHz chipset	http://www.via.com.tw/pdf/productinfo/693A.pdf
VIA VT82C693 Celeron Pentium II chipset	http://www.viatech.com/pdf/productinfo/693.pdf
VIA VT82C691 Pentium II chipset	http://www.viatech.com/pdf/productinfo/691.pdf
VIA VT82C686A chipset	http://www.via.com.tw/pdf/productinfo/686a.pdf
VIA VT8501 Super 7 AGP chipset	http://www.viatech.com/pdf/productinfo/501.pdf
VIA VT82C598 chipset	http://www.viatech.com/pdf/productinfo/598.pdf
VIA VT82C590 Apollo VP2	http://www.via.com.tw/vp2586a.pdf
VIA VT82C595	http://www.via.com.tw/595.pdf
VIA VT82C586B	http://www.via.com.tw/586b.pdf
VIA VT82C580 Apollo VPX	http://www.via.com.tw/vpx586a.pdf
VIA VT82C580 Apollo VPX/97	http://www.via.com.tw/580vpx.pdf
VIA VT82C580 Apollo VP-1	http://www.via.com.tw/apollovp.pdf
VIA VT82C570M Apollo VP Master	http://www.via.com.tw/apollovp.pdf
VIA VT82C496 Pluto	http://www.via.com.tw/496pluto.pdf
SiS 630 Pentium II chipset	http://216.122.33.119/products/pentium2/630.htm
SiS 620 Pentium II AGP chipset	http://216.122.33.119/products/pentium2/620.htm
SiS chipset family	http://216.122.33.119/products/products.htm
OPTi Vendetta	ftp://ftp.opti.com/pub/chipsets/system/vendetta/ index.htm

TABLE 10-2 SUMMARY OF MOTHERBOARD CHIPSET COMPONENTS

CHIPSET DESIGNATION	COMPONENT	#NEEDED	FUNCTION
ALi Aladdin Pro III	M1631	1	System controller
	M1543C	1	PCI/ISA/IDE/USB controller
ALi Aladdin Pro	M1621	1	System controller
	M1533	1	PCI/ISA/IDE/USB controller
ALi Aladdin-5M+	M1541	1	System controller
	M1533	1	PCI/ISA/IDE/USB controller
ALi Aladdin IV	M1531B	1	System controller
	M1533	1	PCI/ISA/IDE/USB controller
AMD 750	AMD 751	1	System controller
	AMD 756	1	Peripheral bus controller
AMD-640	AMD-640	1	System controller
	AMD-645	1	Peripheral bus controller
Intel 840	82840	1	Memory controller hub
	82803	1	Memory repeater hub RDRAM

TABLE 10-2 SUMMARY OF MOTHERBOARD CHIPSET COMPONENTS *(CONTINUED)*

CHIPSET DESIGNATION	COMPONENT	#NEEDED	FUNCTION
	82804	1	Memory repeater hub SDRAM
	82806	1	64-bit PCI controller
	82801	1	Integrated controller hub
	82802	1	Firmware hub
Intel 820	82820	1	Memory controller hub
	82820DP	1	Memory controller hub, dual processor
	82801	1	I/O controller hub
	82802	1	Firmware hub
	82380AB	1	PCI-ISA bridge
Intel 810e	82810E	1	Memory controller hub
	82801	1	Integrated controller hub
	82802	1	Firmware hub
Intel 810	82810	1	Graphics memory controller hub
	82801	1	Integrated controller hub
	82802	1	Firmware hub
Intel 440 ZX	82443ZX	1	System AGP controller
	82371AB&EB	1	PCI ISA IDE Xcelerator (PIIX4&E)
Intel 440 EX	82443EX	1	System AGP controller
	82371AB	1	PCI ISA IDE Xcelerator (PIIX4)
Intel 440 BX	82443BX	1	AGP host bridge controller
	82371AB	1	PCI ISA IDE Xcelerator (PIIX4)
Intel 430 VX (Triton II*)	82437VX	1	System controller
	82371SB	1	PCI ISA IDE Xcelerator (PIIX3)
	82438VX	2	Data path unit
Intel 430 TX	82439TX	1	System controller
	82371AB	1	PCI ISA IDE Xcelerator (PIIX4)
Intel 430 HX (Triton II*)	82439HX	1	System controller
	82371SB	1	PCI I/O IDE Xcelerator (PIIX3)
Intel 430 FX (Triton*)	82437FX	1	System controller
	82371FB	1	ISA bridge, PCI/ISA/IDE Xcelerator (PIIX)
	82438FX	2	Data path unit
Intel 430 MX	82437MX	1	System controller
	82438MX	2	Data path units
	82371MX	1	PCI I/O IDE Xcelerator (MPIIX)
Intel 440 FX (Natoma*)	82441FX	1	PCI and memory controller
	82442FX	1	Data bus accelerator
	82371SB	1	PCI ISA IDE Xcelerator (PIIX3)
Intel 450 KX (Orion*)	82451KX	4	Memory interface component
	82452KX	1	Data path unit
	82453KX	1	Data controller

TABLE 10-2 SUMMARY OF MOTHERBOARD CHIPSET COMPONENTS *(CONTINUED)*

CHIPSET DESIGNATION	COMPONENT	#NEEDED	FUNCTION
	82454KX	1 or 2	PCI bridge
Intel 450 GX (Orion*)	82451GX	4	Memory interface component
	82452GX	1	Data path unit
	82453GX	1	Data controller
	82454GX	1 or 2	PCI bridge
Intel 440 LX	82443LX	1	PCI AGP system controller
	82371AB	1	PCI ISA IDE Xcelerator (PIIX4)
VIA KX133 ATHLON	VT8371	1	System controller
	VT82C686A	1	PCI/ISA/IDE/USB controller
VIA KX133 PRO	VT82C693A	1	System controller
	VT82C686A	1	PCI/ISA/IDE/USB controller
VIA Apollo Pro Plus	VT82C693	1	System controller
	VT82C686A	1	PCI/ISA/IDE/USB controller
VIA Apollo Pro	VT82C691	1	System controller
	VT82C686A	1	PCI/ISA/IDE/USB controller
Via MVP4	VT8501	1	AGP System controller
	VT82C686A	1	PCI/ISA/IDE/USB controller
VIA Apollo MVP3	VT82C598MVP	1	System controller
	VT82C686A	1	PCI/ISA/IDE/USB controller
VIA Apollo P6	VT82C685VP	1	System controller
	VT82C586	1	PCI/ISA/IDE/USB controller
	VT82C687	1	Memory controller
VIA Apollo VP3	VT82C597	1	System controller
	VT82C586B	1	PCI/IDE/USB controller
VIA Apollo VP2/97	VT82C595	1	System controller
	VT82C586B	1	PCI/IDE/USB controller
VIA Apollo VPX/97	VT82C585VPX	1	System controller
	VT82C586B	1	PCI/ISA/IDE/USB controller (PC97)
or	VT82C586A	1	PCI/ISA/IDE/USB controller (non-97)
	VT82C587VP	2	Share frame buffers
VIA Apollo VP-1	VT82C585VP	1	System controller
	VT82C586	1	PCI/IDE/ISA/USB controller
	VT82C587VP	2	Share frame buffers
VIA Apollo Master	VT82C575M	1	System controller
	VT82C576M	1	PCI/ISA/IDE controller
	VT82C577M	2	Frame buffers
	VT82C416	1	Support controller
SiS 5597 (Jedi)	5597	1	Integrated system controller
SiS 5596	5596	1	System controller
	5513	1	USB controller

TABLE 10-2 SUMMARY OF MOTHERBOARD CHIPSET COMPONENTS *(CONTINUED)*

CHIPSET DESIGNATION	COMPONENT	#NEEDED	FUNCTION
SiS 5571 (Trinity)	5571	1	Integrated system controller
SiS 551X	5511	1	System controller
	5512	1	Bus controller
	5513	1	USB controller
SiS 85C49X (486)	85C496	1	System controller
	85C497	1	Bus controller
OPTi Discovery	82C650	1	System Controller
	82C651	1	Bus controller
	82C652	1	Auxiliary PCI bus controller
OPTi Vendetta	82C750	1	Integrated system controller
OPTi Fire Star	82C700	1	Integrated system controller

Typical chipset function designations:

- AGP: Accelerated Graphics Port
- APIC: Advance Programmable Interrupt Controller
- DBX: Data Bus Accelerator
- DC: Data Controller
- DP: Data Path
- DPU: Data Path Unit
- IB: ISA Bridge
- MIC: Memory Interface Component
- PB: PCI Bridge
- PIIX: PCI ISA IDE Xcelerator
- PMC: PCI and Memory Controller
- PRMC: Power Management Controller
- SC: System Controller
- SMBA: Shared Memory Buffer Architecture
- UMA: Unified Memory Architecture
- USBC: Universal Serial Bus Controller

*Note that Intel chipset code names are strictly unofficial, and Intel does not even acknowledge the use of code names.

The companion CD offers a utility called DR. HARDWARE for the detection of core logic chipsets. Look for the file name DRHW25E.EXE on your CD.

There is a tremendous rivalry between the major chipset manufacturers. This chapter does not advocate the use of any given chipset (or manufacturer) over another, or attempt to make product recommendations. This chapter merely familiarizes you with the features of each chipset and allows you to make objective assessments of system capabilities based upon the particular core logic in use.

ALi Chipsets

Within the last several years, Acer Laboratories, Inc. (or simply ALi) had their very existence challenged by the introduction of the Intel TX chipset. The TX chipset represented Intel's entry into the low-cost/low-end chipset market—a market that provided the foundation for manufacturers such as ALi and VIA. ALi has survived by providing a less than cutting edge—even lower cost—chip solution for motherboard and systems manufacturers' needs. ALi has attempted to reduce buyers' costs even further by including a video/3D graphics engine in some of their chipset products while still supporting modern features like USB, UDMA/33, and PC100 memory.

ALI ALADDIN IV CHIPSET

The ALi Aladdin IV chipset is a continuation of the venerable Aladdin series. The Aladdin IV can be a combination of either the M1531 system controller and the M1533 peripheral bus controller, or the M1531(B) system controller and the M1543 peripheral bus controller. The main improvements in the Aladdin IV are in the M1531(B) chip, which handles 64Mbit SDRAM support and more cacheable RAM region support—otherwise the features are the same for both chip combinations.

The ALi Aladdin IV is designed as a low-cost chipset to support the Socket 7 system architecture. This includes support for Pentium-class Intel, Cyrix, and AMD processors at bus speeds from 50MHz to 83.3MHz and split voltages (for processors with MMX features). The Aladdin IV provides the option of either 64MB cache RAM with 8-bit tag SRAM, or 512MB cache memory with 11-bit tag SRAM. Memory type support from FPM to SDRAM (at 3.3V to 5V operation) allows some versatility in memory choice and still provides for support of faster, newer standards. The Aladdin IV contains 8 RAS lines for up to 1GB of RAM support. Additional support for features like ACPI, USB, bus mastering, and UDMA/33 keep the Aladdin IV chipset competitive (you can find major features summarized in Table 10-3), but this chipset is designed mainly for affordability, not performance.

ALI ALADDIN 5M+ CHIPSET

The Aladdin 5M+ is a fifth-generation (Pentium-class) chipset from ALi. It is also a two-chip solution that provides a combination of system performance and low system cost. The chipset comprises the M1541 system controller and either the M1533 peripheral bus controller or the M1543 peripheral bus controller. Like the Aladdin IV, the Aladdin 5M+ supports all Socket 7 processors. The Aladdin 5M+ supports the same features as the IV with some additions and improvements, including support for AGP 2X, a 100MHz bus speed, and power management features that support Microsoft's On Now technology OS (Table 10-4). The Aladdin 5M+ also offers processor feature support including the Cyrix M1 and M2 "linear wrap" mode and AMD's K6 "write allocation."

ALI ALADDIN PRO CHIPSET

The Aladdin Pro is ALi's entry-level offering for the Pentium II system market. The Aladdin Pro employs various techniques to improve the memory and I/O throughput to match up with the advanced super-scalar, super-pipelined Pentium II-class processors. It provides parity protection over the PCI bus, along with independent EC and ECC protection in memory to improve reliability and performance (a powerful feature for network servers). To support the 3D graphics functions, the chipset supports both a 66MHz graphics bus and 1x/2x AGP.

TABLE 10-3 ALI ALADDIN IV CHIPSET FEATURES AT A GLANCE

- Supports all Intel, Cyrix, TI, and AMD 586-class CPUs with bus speeds of 83.3MHz, 75MHz, 66MHz, 60MHz, and 50MHz at 3.3V/2.5V
- Supports “linear wrap” mode for Cyrix M1 and M2
- Supports “Pseudo Synchronous” PCI bus access
- Supports pipelined-burst (PB) SRAM cache size of 256KB, 512KB, or 1MB
- Cacheable memory up to 64MB with 8-bit Tag SRAM, or up to 512MB with 11-bit Tag SRAM
- Supports 3.3V or 5V FPM/EDO/SDRAM DIMMs
- Supports 64Mbit (16M*4, 8M*8, 4M*16) technology DRAMs
- Supports “Error Checking and Correction” (ECC) and parity checking for DRAM
- Fully synchronous 25/30/33MHz 3.3V/5V tolerant PCI v.2.1 interface
- Includes a PCI bus arbiter supporting five PCI masters
- PCI-to-DRAM bandwidth up to 133MB/sec
- Enhanced Power Management including ACPI support, PCI bus CLKRUN functions, dynamic clock stop, suspend to DRAM, and self-refresh during Suspend

TABLE 10-4 ALI ALADDIN 5M+ CHIPSET FEATURES AT A GLANCE

- Supports all 3.3V/2.5V socket 7 processors with bus speeds at 100MHz, 83.3MHz, 75MHz, 66MHz, 60MHz, and 50MHz
- Supports “linear wrap” mode for Cyrix M1 and M2
- Supports “write allocation” feature for AMD K6
- Supports “pseudo synchronous” PCI bus access
- Supports pipelined-burst (PB) SRAM cache size of 256KB, 512KB, or 1MB
- Cacheable memory up to 512MB with 10-bit Tag SRAM when using 512KB L2 cache, or 1GB when using 256KB L2 cache
- Supports 3.3V or 5V FPM/EDO/SDRAM DIMMs
- Supports 64Mbit (16M*4, 8M*8, 4M*16) technology DRAMs
- Supports “Error Checking and Correction” (ECC) and parity checking for DRAM
- Supports four single-sided DIMMs based on x4 DRAMs
- Supports four single and double-sided DIMMs based on x8 and x16 DRAMs
- Synchronous/Pseudo Synchronous 25/30/33MHz 3.3V/5V tolerance PCI v.2.1 interface
- Includes a PCI bus arbiter supporting five PCI masters and an AGP master
- PCI-to-DRAM bandwidth up to 133MB/sec
- Enhanced Power Management including ACPI support, PCI bus CLKRUN functions, dynamic clock stop, suspend to DRAM, power-on Suspend, Suspend to Disk, and self-refresh during Suspend
- Supports the Accelerated Graphics Port (AGP) 1.0 interface with AGP66MHz PCI protocol and AGP 1X and 2X sideband functions

The Aladdin Pro includes a data path with multiport buffers for improved data acceleration and an external I/O APIC controller to support multiple Pentium II processors (another important feature for servers). For the memory subsystem, the "pipelined" memory cycle design helps overcome precharge latency and refresh cycle delays. Support for USB and UDMA/33 (Table 10-5) round out the Aladdin Pro package of the M1621 system controller combined with either the M1533 or the M1543 peripheral bus controller. However, the support is missing for accepted standards such as IEEE 1394 FireWire and UDMA/66.

ALI ALADDIN PRO III CHIPSET

Acer Laboratories combines the M1631 AGP/PCI/3D graphics system controller with any of four ALi "Southbridge" (or I/O controllers) chips to create the Aladdin Pro III package. The chipset supports the Pentium II processor interface in Slot 1 of Socket 370 configuration (Table 10-6). The Pro III supports system bus speeds from 66MHz to 133MHz (the current Intel top speed). The Aladdin Pro III will also support up to 1.5GB of EDO, SDRAM, or VC-SDRAM main memory.

The Aladdin Pro III is designed to improve system performance with memory and I/O throughput. The pipelined memory cycle design helps reduce the effects of memory latency and refresh cycles. For the I/O subsystem, deep data-in/out buffers hide the latency for PCI-initiated master reads and writes. Programmable data-in buffer controls can be tuned to optimize the PCI-to-memory transfer rate for different memory configurations and PCI device characteristics. The chipset complies with the PCI 2.2 specification (including flexible PCI latency control). This allows the PCI latency to be adjusted to achieve the best system performance. The Aladdin Pro III can support up to five PCI masters. It is also possible to support more PCI masters depending on the layout arrangement, impedance load, and the quality of the motherboard.

Power management features of the chipset include power-on suspend, suspend to disk, PCI bus CLKRUN, and dynamic clock stop. This provides desktop systems with a very flexible power management configuration control.

The built-in 3D graphics engine supports both UMA and non-UMA 64-bit frame buffer architecture. It includes a 128-bit 3D processor that processes two pixels per clock cycle. This enables single-pass multitexturing and delivers a 180 million pixels-per-second fill rate. The twin-texel 32-bit color pipeline, 24-bit Z, and 8-bit stencil buffer enhances performance and allows developers to write standards-based applications with improved visual effects and realism. Video performance is also addressed with support for the AGP 1.0 specification.

TABLE 10-5 ALI ALADDIN PRO CHIPSET FEATURES AT A GLANCE

- Supports all 60, 66, and 100MHz CPU bus Intel Pentium II ("Deschutes") processors
- Includes a 256-byte buffer for CPU-to-Memory write and a 128-byte buffer for CPU-to-Memory read
- Memory support includes FPM or EDO (up to 2GB) and SDRAM (up to 1GB)
- Supports ECC to provide single-bit error correction and multiple-bit error detection
- Supports mix of SDRAM, EDO DRAM, and Page Mode DRAM
- Supports 4Mbit, 16Mbit, 64Mbit, 128Mbit, and 256Mbit DRAM technologies
- PCI v.2.1 bus support for up to five PCI masters (excluding PCI-to-ISA bridge) and parity protection on all PCI bus signals
- AGP v.1.0 support for 1X and 2X AGP modes

TABLE 10-6 LI ALADDIN PRO III CHIPSET FEATURES AT A GLANCE

- Supports Pentium II processors using a host bus frequency of 66, 100, or 133MHz
- Supports EDO, SDRAM, and VC-SDRAM up to 1.5GB
- Supports symmetrical and asymmetrical DRAM addressing
- Supports 4Mbit, 16Mbit, 64Mbit, 128Mbit, and 256Mbit DRAM technologies
- Supports ECC, which offers single-bit error correction and multiple-bit error detection
- PCI v.2.2 bus support includes synchronous clock mode between the processor bus and PCI bus
- Supports up to 6 PCI masters (excluding the PCI-to-ISA bridge) with parity protection on all PCI bus signals
- Includes an advanced 3D/2D graphic engine with 100 percent hardware triangle setup and a twin texel 32-bit graphic pipeline
- Optimized Direct3D acceleration for DirectX 5.0 and DirectX 6.0, and optimized for DirectX 6.0 and OpenGL support
- Video system supports both SGRAM and SDRAM
- Video acceleration for DirectShow, MPEG-1, MPEG-2, and Indeo Video
- Power management features include power-on suspend, suspend to disk, PCI bus CLKRUN, and dynamic clock stop

> Currently, the literature for the Aladdin Pro III only lists support for the Pentium II processor. There is no mention of the Celeron or Pentium III, even though diagrams show the Socket 370 interface.

AMD Chipsets

AMD (Advanced Micro Devices) is certainly no stranger to the CPU arena, but it is a relative newcomer to the chipset market. Traditionally, AMD relied on other chipset makers to support its line of CPUs (the 5x85, K5, K6, K6-2, and K6-3). However, not all chipset makers provided the optimum support for AMD's products. As a consequence, AMD has developed the 640 chipset for use with their K6 and K6-2 CPU. In addition, the introduction of AMD's Athlon processor required AMD to develop a supporting chipset if the company wanted the widest possible acceptance of the Athlon's unique architecture. The result is the AMD 750 chipset, currently regarded as one of the most stable and best-performing chipsets for the Athlon.

AMD 640 CHIPSET

The AMD 640 chipset features two devices: the AMD 640 system controller and the AMD 645 peripheral bus controller. (Refer to Table 10-2 for a comparison of chipset designations.) Working together, these chips can deliver numerous high-performance features that accelerate multimedia applications (especially those designed for MMX-type processors). The AMD 640 system controller has been optimized to accelerate AMD-K6 processor transactions, and it also incorporates support for SDRAM (Synchronous DRAM)—the most recent development in the evolution of main system memory. The AMD 645 peripheral bus controller features support for Ultra DMA/33, which allows the ATA/IDE interface to provide a 33MB/s data transfer rate. System performance is further increased with "Type F" DMA, which provides a 5x improvement over standard DMA transfers. Type F DMA reduces the system bus requirements for

DMA transfers, providing the CPU with greater access to the ISA bus (less of a bottleneck during data transfers). Perhaps most important for AMD, the 640 chipset is backward compatible with existing AMD and Intel CPUs.

MORE ON THE AMD 640 SYSTEM CONTROLLER

The AMD-640 system controller (the "Northbridge" chip) features the 64-bit Socket 7 interface, integrated write-back cache controller, system memory controller, and PCI bus controller. The Socket 7 interface has been optimized for the AMD-K6 processor—providing 3-1-1-1 transfer timing for both read and write transactions from PBSRAM (Pipeline Burst Static RAM) at 66MHz. The memory controller features a data buffering design that uses four cache lines (16 quad words, or QW) of processor-to-DRAM or cache-to-DRAM write buffering with concurrent write-back capability to accelerate write-back and write-miss cycles. The integrated PCI bus controller features concurrent processor and PCI operation through a 5-double word (or DW) posted write buffer design. PCI concurrency with DRAM or cache memory is achieved through a 48-double word post write buffer and 26-double word prefetch buffer.

The AMD 640 design also uses byte-merging, which optimizes processor-to-PCI throughput and reduces PCI bus traffic by converting consecutive processor addresses into burst PCI cycles. The controller minimizes PCI initiator read latency and DRAM access using techniques like snoop ahead, snoop filtering, forwarding cache write-backs to the PCI initiator, and merging L1 write-backs into the PCI-posted write buffers. The integrated PCI controller supports enhanced PCI bus commands such as Memory-Read-Line, Memory-Read-Multiple, and Memory-Write-Invalidate. These features allow a PCI initiator to achieve the full 133Mbps burst transfer rate. The integrated PCI bus controller is fully compatible with the PCI Local Bus Specification (revision 2.1). Table 10-7 offers the AMD 640 chipset features at a glance.

MORE ON THE AMD 645 PERIPHERAL BUS CONTROLLER

The AMD 645 peripheral bus controller (the "Southbridge" chip) features an integrated ISA bus controller, enhanced master mode PCI EIDE controller with Ultra DMA/33 technology, ACPI-compatible Power Management Unit, USB controller, PS2-compatible keyboard/mouse controller, and real-time clock (RTC) with extended 256-byte CMOS RAM. The on-chip EIDE controller has a dual-channel DMA engine with capability of interlaced dual-channel commands. High-bandwidth PCI transfers are achieved by an enhanced 16 double-word data FIFO with full scatter and gather capability. The integrated USB controller features a root hub with two ports having 18-level-deep data FIFOs and built-in physical

TABLE 10-7 AMD 640 CHIPSET FEATURES AT A GLANCE

- Optimized for the AMD-K6 processor
- Provides SDRAM, EDO RAM, and FPM RAM support
- Offers PCI concurrency
- Supports Ultra-DMA/33
- Includes "data path units"
- Includes PS/2 keyboard/mouse controller
- Includes RTC
- Backward compatible with other AMD and non-AMD processors
- Offers USB support
- Supports ACPI
- Includes plug-and-play support

layer transceivers. The USB controller also offers backward compatibility with legacy keyboard and PS/2 mouse support. The AMD 645 peripheral bus controller meets Windows 95/98 plug-and-play requirements with steerable PCI interrupts, ISA interrupts, and DMA channels. The integrated power management unit complies with ACPI and APM, and provides dedicated input pins for external modem ring indication and power-on, five general-purpose I/O pins with option for I^2C port, and 16 general-purpose pins that can be programmed as inputs or outputs.

AMD 750 Chipset

The AMD 750 is a highly integrated system chipset that offers the features and enhanced performance needed to support the AMD Athlon processor (and other Athlon-compatible processors when they become available). The AMD 750 chipset consists of the AMD 751 system controller and the AMD 756 peripheral bus controller.

The AMD 751 system controller includes a front side bus (FSB) that supports three 200MHz channels, a 32-bit PCI 2.2-compliant bus interface at 33MHz supporting up to six masters, and a 66MHz AGP 2.0-compliant interface to support the AGP 2X data transfer mode. Currently the AMD 751 system controller is designed to support up to 768MB of PC100 SDRAM DIMMs using 16Mbit, 64Mbit, and 128Mbit memory technologies. The 200MHz FSB includes a high-performance point-to-point system bus capability with synchronous clocking for high-speed data transfers (up to 1.6GB/s at 200MHz). The combination of the 200MHz system bus and the AMD 750 chipset enables high throughput between system components like CPU-to-memory, CPU-to-AGP, CPU-to-PCI, AGP-to-memory, and PCI-to-memory. This provides measurably improved performance for 3D video and multimedia applications that require high-speed data transfers and calculations.

The AMD 756 peripheral bus controller adds PCI-ISA bridge support, bus master IDE control with UDMA/33 and UDMA/66 support, USB support, and includes the keyboard/mouse controller. Current standards for plug-and-play and power management are supplied by the AMD 756 chip. These features enable AMD 750–based systems to be Microsoft PC99 compliant. Table 10-8 lists more highlights for the AMD 750 chipset.

10

TABLE 10-8 AMD 750 CHIPSET FEATURES AT A GLANCE

- Designed to be used in PC99-compliant systems
- 200MHz AMD-K7 (a.k.a. Athlon) host channel
- Supports UDMA/66
- AGP 2X
- USB (four-port OHCI)
- Supports up to 768MB of ECC-compliant PC100 SDRAM
- PCI 2.2 compliant with support for six PCI masters
- PCI-to-ISA bridge
- Plug-and-play support
- Advanced Power Management (ACPI 1.0 and APM 1.2 compliant)
- Keyboard/mouse controller

Intel Chipsets

Intel Corporation provided the 8086 CPU that went into the first PC and has often led the way in CPU development ever since. Though competitors like AMD and Cyrix are narrowing the performance gap (especially AMD with its Athlon processor), Intel has remained competitive with the fastest high-performance CPUs like the Pentium II and Pentium III. Since Intel is normally the first to release new CPUs, it is also ideally positioned to develop the chipsets to complement those CPUs. Intel is also a frequent collaborator with Microsoft in the proposal of new industry initiatives (such as ACPI and AGP), so the company often has a powerful head start in supporting those initiatives. As you'll see below, Intel offers a wide range of chipsets.

INTEL 840 PENTIUM III XEON CHIPSET

The Intel 840 chipset is the high-performance (workstation) member of the 800-series chipset family. In addition to the basic 82801 and 82802 support chips, the 840 utilizes the 82840 memory controller hub (or MCH). This chip provides AGP graphics 2X and 4X support, dual RDRAM memory channels, and multiple PCI segments for high-performance I/O performance. The 840 is more versatile than its 810E and 820 counterparts due to its ability to support three additional components that may be used with the standard core 800 components: the 82806, the 82803, and 82804.

The 64-bit 82806 PCI controller hub (P64H) supports 64-bit PCI slots at speeds of either 33MHz or 66MHz. The P64H connects directly to the MCH using Intel's "accelerated hub architecture"—providing a dedicated path for high-performance I/O. For systems requiring high RDRAM capacity, an 82803 RDRAM memory repeater hub (MRH-R) may be utilized. The MRH-R converts each memory channel into two memory channels for expanded memory capacity. For systems requiring high SDRAM capacity, an 82804 SDRAM memory repeater hub (MRH-S) may be utilized. The MRH-S efficiently translates the RDRAM protocol into SDRAM-based signals for system memory flexibility.

Chip combinations provide for SDRAM, RDRAM support, bandwidth doubling on the processor, AGP, USB, and PCI busses and dual processor support to provide the highest possible performance. This chipset supports processors using a 133MHz system bus, and hard drives using UDMA/66 technology. Future performance enhancements can be implemented through BIOS code changes if BIOS suppliers comply with Intel's Modular BIOS specifications. Table 10-9 compares the most recent Intel chipsets.

INTEL 820 PENTIUM II/III CHIPSET

Intel continued its development of the 800-series chipset without the integrated video. The next member of the 800 family was the Intel 820 chipset with features designed to support mainstream and performance systems. It includes the 800-series support for the "modular BIOS," which is flash upgradable as features are added to the chipset. Using the same two support chips as the Intel 810E chipset (the 82801 I/O controller hub and the 82802 firmware hub), the 820 adds either the 82820 or the 82820DP (dual processor) memory controller hub. Intended as a "long life" platform chipset solution in the rapidly changing PC market, the accelerated hub architecture of the 820 allows Intel to enhance and update components without forcing system changes. The plan is to use this capability to maintain support for the fastest Pentium III processors all the way into 2001.

Although current SDRAM DIMMs are supported, achieving top performance for the 820 chipset depends on the emerging RAMBUS DRAM technology (delivering the potential bandwidth of 1.6GB/s needed to optimize Pentium III and AGP performance). RDRAM allows more open memory pages,

TABLE 10-9 INTEL PENTIUM II/III AND CELERON CHIPSET FEATURES AT A GLANCE

CHIPSET	INTEL 840	INTEL 820	INTEL 810E	440 BX	440 ZX
Processor	Pentium III/Xeon	Pentium II/III	Pentium II/III	Pentium II/III	Pentium II/III
			Celeron (810 only)		Celeron (ZX x66 only)
Voltage	AGTL+	AGTL+	AGTL+	GTL+	GTL+
Dual CPUs	Yes	Yes	No	Yes	No
Refresh	RDRAM active	N/A	CAS-before-RAS	CAS-before-RAS	CAS-before-RAS
Memory Support	64/128/256Mbit	64/128/256Mbit	16/64/128Mbit	N/A	N/A
Max Memory Size	8GB	1GB	512MB	1GB	256MB
Memory Types	PC100 (SDRAM)	SDRAM	PC100 (SDRAM)	SDRAM	SDRAM
	PC600 (RDRAM)	RDRAM			
	PC800 (RDRAM)				
ECC/Parity	Yes	Yes	N/A	Yes	No
PCI Support	PCI 2.2	PCI 2.1	PCI 2.2	PCI 2.1	PCI 2.1
Concurrent PCI	Yes	Yes	Yes	Yes	Yes
AGP	Yes (1X/2X/4X)	Yes (1X/2X/4X)	Yes (Integrated)	Yes (1X/2X)	Yes (1X/2X)
MTT	Yes	Yes	Dyn. Int. Arb.	Yes	Yes
Bridge Type	ICH	ICH	ICH	PIIX4E	PIIX4E
USB Support	Yes	Yes	Yes	Yes	Yes
IDE Support	Yes (UDMA/66)	Yes (UDMA/66)	Yes (UDMA/66)	Yes (UDMA/33)	Yes (UDMA/33)
RTC		Yes	Yes	Yes	Yes
Power Mgt.	SMM & ACPI	SMM & ACPI	SMM & ACPI	SMM & ACPI	SMM & ACPI
I/O Mgt.	SMBus & GPIO	SMBus & GPIO	SMBus & GPIO	SMBus & GPIO	SMBus & GPIO

increasing the opportunity for page hits and better memory access. RDRAM and the 820 chipset are designed to enable what Intel has termed "constant computing." This is the ability to perform numerous functions in the background without impairing foreground performance. The 820 chipset supports RDRAM technology in its current state and provides for two memory sockets and 512MB of system memory. Continued RDRAM development should increase this amount to 1GB.

The 820 uses three integrated busses to reduce interference problems and increase data transfer rates. The Direct RAMBUS (memory) interface, internal hub interface, and LPC bus interface allows the doubling of bandwidth and data transfer rates. In addition, performance is improved with support for AGP 4X, UDMA/66, and a 133MHz system bus. AGP 4X graphics support offers the same direct connection to the memory controller and twice the graphics bandwidth of AGP 2X (achieving transfer rates in excess of 1GB/s). The architecture of the 820 chipset features a direct pipeline for audio and video data, and the new architecture allows for concurrent data transfer streams over the CPU, PCI, USB, and AGP busses. Table 10-9 lists features of the 820 chipset.

INTEL 810(E) PENTIUM II/III AND CELERON CHIPSET

Intel began competing in the low-cost, integrated video chipset market with the introduction of the 810 chipset (dubbed the "Camino"). This is a three-chip solution including the 82810 graphics memory controller hub (GMCH), the 82801 integrated controller hub (ICH), and an 82802 firmware hub. The technology included in the 810 chipset is designed to enhance performance of the Intel Pentium II/III and Celeron processors. The chipset builds on the 440BX AGP technology and includes additional features to provide improved graphics at a lower cost. Two-dimensional and 3D graphics can be optimized if software that takes advantage of "Intel Graphics Technology" becomes available.

The 82810 chip is the core of the 810 chipset, with built-in control of memory and graphics that optimizes system memory arbitration in a way that is similar to AGP technology. The 82810 graphics memory controller hub (GMCH) uses "Direct AGP" to provide 2D and 3D effects and images, and integrated "Hardware Motion Compensation" to improve soft-DVD video quality. Traditional TVs and digital flat panel displays can be used through a digital video output port. RAM memory support allows use of up to 512MB of PC100 memory. Dynamic Video Memory Technology (DVMT) provides efficient memory utilization and Direct AGP, though the operating system must use Intel software drivers and support Intel's intelligent memory arbiter to implement graphics applications.

The 82801 I/O controller hub (ICH) uses "Intel Accelerated Hub Architecture" to make a direct connection from the graphics and memory to the integrated Audio Codec 97 (AC97) controller, the IDE controllers, dual USB ports, and PCI add-on cards. The Accelerated Hub Architecture provides twice the bandwidth of the PCI bus at 266MB/s, which allows better data transfer from the I/O controller to the memory controller. True UDMA/66 and PCI Rev. 2.2 support are provided by the Intel 810 chipset.

The 82802 firmware hub (FWH) is the third member of the set. It stores system BIOS and video BIOS, eliminating a redundant nonvolatile memory component. Originally, the 810 chipset had a delayed introduction (and received some bad reviews). Intel continued development of the 800-series chipset minus the integrated AGP video system. By the time Intel was able to make the 810 chipset available, PC133 memory on a 133MHz bus forced Intel to quickly make some improvements to the 810—dubbed the Intel 810E. The Intel 810E chipset includes all the features of the 810, with added support for faster speeds. You can compare the features of the 810 and 810E chipsets in Table 10-9.

INTEL 440 BX PENTIUM II/III CHIPSET

The Intel 440 BX was the last and most powerful X-series chipset before Intel decided the new Camino chipset architecture needed a new naming method. The 440 BX consists of the 82443BX AGP host bridge controller (Northbridge) and the 82371EB (PIIX4E) PCI-ISA peripheral bus controller (Southbridge). The chipset supports both 66MHz and 100MHz processor bus speeds, which support a wide range of Pentium II or Pentium III processors. Dual processors are also supported with full Symmetric Multiprocessor Protocol (SMP). The Intel 440 BX was the first 100MHz chipset designed for use in Pentium II mobile systems and the first one optimized for Pentium III performance in 3D and video applications.

Memory support is provided through an integrated DRAM controller allowing for up to four SDRAM DIMMs for a total of 1GB of memory (if registered DIMMs are used). The 440 BX enables "open page architecture" supporting multiple SDRAM pages to improve 3D performance. Additional video features include AGP 2X, AGP sideband, and AGP-specific data buffering support. The chipset enables concurrent CPU, AGP, and PCI transactions to main memory.

The PIIX4E controller in this chipset provides PC98 ACPI power management support that allows use of the 440 BX in mobile systems. The chip is PCI v.2.1 compliant to support PCI-to-ISA bridges in both 3.3V and 5V 33MHz configurations. It includes the enhanced DMA controller, interrupt controller, and timer functions. The USB host interface has support for two USB ports, and the integrated IDE controller supports up to UDMA/33.

The Intel 440 BX chipset is presented as UDMA/66 compatible, but this does not mean that the chipset supports UDMA/66. It means you can use a UDMA/66 hard drive in a 440 BX chipset system, but transfer speeds will be limited to the UDMA/33 standard. Table 10-9 lists the features of an Intel 440 BX chipset.

INTEL 440 ZX PENTIUM II/III AND CELERON CHIPSET

Consisting of the 82443ZX system controller and 82371EB (PIIX4E) peripheral bus controller, the 440 ZX chipset was designed to be a lower-cost alternative to the 440 BX chipset (see Table 10-9). By eliminating dual processor support, cutting maximum memory support to 256MB, and dropping the support for ECC, Intel hoped this chipset would attract manufacturers producing low-cost Pentium II/III systems. Intel even included a 66MHz version of the 440 ZX for Celeron support. However, the ZX has not proven as popular as Intel hoped. PC manufacturers producing a 100MHz Pentium II/III system wanted some of the features eliminated in the 440 ZX, and instead used the 440 BX chipset. Manufacturers producing a 66MHz Celeron system already had the respected 440 LX chipset available at a lower cost.

INTEL 430 VX PENTIUM CHIPSET

The Intel 430 VX chipset is found in rather late-model Pentium-based PCs designed for low-end or end-user applications (such as multimedia, games, and personal productivity software). The 430 VX chipset integrates support for the Universal Serial Bus (USB) standard, so home users can add a wide variety of plug-and-play digital input devices such as mice, keyboards, joysticks, scanners, and cameras. The 430 VX supports concurrent PCI architecture, which maximizes system performance with simultaneous activity on the CPU, PCI, and ISA busses. This generally improves video and audio performance for multimedia applications and allows more high-speed peripherals in the systems without impacting the performance of the PCI bus. Improved EDO memory support, faster timing, and support for Synchronous DRAM (SDRAM) are also included. Memory support also allows the Shared Memory Buffer Architecture (SMBA) option. The Intel 430VX PCIset consists of the 82437VX system controller, two 82438VX data paths, and the 82371SB PCI ISA IDE Xcelerator (PIIX3).

Although the 430 VX is generally considered to be a good performer, some features are noticeably absent. There is no support for multiple CPUs and no support for ECC. The chipset will handle up to 128MB of RAM (but only 64MB are cacheable). RAM timing is also a bit slower than the 430 HX, so 430 TX systems tend to be a bit slower, even when SDRAM is installed. Table 10-10 outlines the features of the 430 VX chipset.

INTEL 430 TX PENTIUM CHIPSET

The 430 TX chipset optimizes the capabilities of the Intel Pentium processor with MMX technology (Pentium MMX) and has found dual duty in both desktop and mobile PCs. Reduced power consumption enables new applications by delivering mobile-style power management to the desktop. The 430 TX chipset features Dynamic Power Management Architecture (DPMA)—extending the battery life of mobile computers and enabling new power-efficient desktop models. Support for the Advanced Configuration and Power Interface (ACPI) also improves power management.

The 430 TX also supports the Ultra-DMA disk drive protocol with the enhancements required for faster performance of multimedia applications. For higher memory throughput, the chipset supports Synchronous DRAM (or a mix of SDRAM and EDO RAM). Concurrent PCI support is available for the first time in a mobile PCI chipset, enabling faster and smoother video and audio performance. There is also support for the Universal Serial Bus (USB). With the "outside the box" plug-and-play capabilities of USB, the 430 TX chipset helps the integration of multimedia, I/O peripherals, and digital imaging devices.

The 430 TX also implements a full System Management Bus (SMBus) host controller with three-wire interface, through which the system can communicate with simple monitoring controllers. For example, "Smart Battery" devices can provide information to the power management charging system via the SMBus. The user can then be informed of the current battery state, along with an accurate prediction of the available operating time (or remaining time to fully charge the battery). Table 10-10 lists the features of the 430 TX.

The 430 TX chipset is a two-chip solution consisting of the 82439TX system controller and the 82371AB PCI ISA IDE Xcelerator. The 430 TX forms a Host-to-PCI bridge, provides the second level (L2) cache control, and offers a full 64-bit data path to main memory. The system controller integrates the cache and main memory DRAM control functions and provides bus control for transfers between the

TABLE 10-10 INTEL PENTIUM/MMX CHIPSET FEATURES AT A GLANCE

CHIPSET	430 VX	430 TX	430 HX	430 FX	430 MX
Processor	Pentium	Pentium	Pentium	Pentium	Pentium
Voltage	3.3V(I/O)	3.3V(I/O)	3.3V(I/O)	3.3V(I/O)	3.3V(I/O)
Dual CPUs	No	No	Yes	No	No
Refresh	CAS-before-RAS	CAS-before-RAS	CAS-before-RAS	RAS Only	CAS-before-RAS
RAS Lines	5	6	8	5	4
64Mbit Support	No	Yes	Yes	No	No
Max Memory Size	128MB	256MB	512MB	128MB	128MB
Memory Types	SDRAM/EDO/FPM	SDRAM/EDO/FPM	EDO/FPM	EDO/SPM	EDO/SPM
SDRAM (CL=2)	6-1-1-1	6-1-1-1	N/A	N/A	N/A
EDO (66MHz)	6-2-2-2	5-2-2-2	5-2-2-2	7-2-2-2	7-2-2-2
MA Buffers	Integrated	Integrated	Integrated	External	External
ECC/Parity	No	No	Yes	No	No
L2 Cache Type	Async, DRAM, Pburst	Pburst	Pburst	Async, Burst, Pburst	Async, Burst, Pburst
Cacheability	64MB	64MB	512MB	64MB	64MB
PCI Support	PCI 2.1	PCI 2.1	PCI 2.1	PCI 2.0	PCI 2.0
Concurrent PCI	Yes	Yes	Yes	No	No
MTT	Yes	Yes	Yes	No	No
SMBA Support	Yes	No	No	No	No
Bridge Type	PIIX3	PIIX4	PIIX3	PIIX	MPIIX
USB Support	Yes	Yes	Yes	No	No
IDE Support	BMIDE	Ultra DMA	BMIDE	BMIDE	Normal IDE
RTC	External	Integrated	External	External	External
Power Mgt.	N/A	ACPI	N/A	N/A	SMI, APM
I/O Mgt.	N/A	SM Bus/GPIO	N/A	N/A	N/A

CPU, cache, main memory, and the PCI bus. The L2 cache controller supports write-back cache for cache sizes of 256KB and 512KB (cacheless designs are also supported).

INTEL 430 HX PENTIUM CHIPSET

The venerable 430 HX chipset (unofficially dubbed "Triton II") is perhaps the most well known and well respected Pentium chipset ever produced. With uncompromising EDO RAM timing, the 430 HX matches the performance of an asynchronous L2 cache-based system (without the cache). It supports 64Mbit DRAM and offers eight RAS lines (for up to 512MB of system memory). Memory address buffers are built into the system controller. Integrated deep-posting and FIFO buffers enable concurrent activity on both sides of the system controller and data paths for improved CPU utilization. ECC and parity memory support are integrated into the chipset, along with dual CPU support. The 430 HX supports concurrent PCI architecture and the Universal Serial Bus (USB). The 430 HX chipset consists of the 82439HX system controller and the 82371SB PCI I/O IDE Xcelerator (PIIX3). Table 10-10 lists the features of the 430 HX.

INTEL 430 FX PENTIUM CHIPSET

The 430 FX chipset (or "Triton" as it is unofficially known) was the first Intel Pentium chipset to become extremely successful—so successful, in fact, that it is largely deemed to be the undoing of other competitors such as ETEQ, UMC, and others. It was also the first x86-type chipset using EDO RAM (and is responsible for EDO now being a standard RAM type). Although the 430 FX is now obsolete, it is still considered to be a decent performer. Table 10-10 lists the specifications for the 430 FX chipset.

The 430 FX chipset consists of the 82437FX system controller, two 82438FX data paths, and the 82371FB PCI ISA IDE Xcelerator (or PIIX). The chipset forms a Host-to-PCI bridge, provides second level (L2) cache control, and supports a full 64-bit data path to main memory. The system controller integrates the cache and main memory DRAM control functions and provides bus control for transfers between the CPU, cache, main memory, and the PCI bus. The L2 cache controller supports a write-back cache for cache sizes of 256KB and 512KB (cacheless designs are also supported). Cache memory can be implemented with either standard, burst, or pipelined burst SRAMs. An external Tag RAM is used for the address tag, and an internal Tag RAM handles the cache line status bits. The system controller supports up to 128MB of main memory. An optimized PCI interface allows the CPU to sustain a high bandwidth to the graphics frame buffer at all frequencies. Using the "snoop ahead" feature, the system controller allows PCI masters to achieve full PCI bandwidth. The data paths provide the connections between the CPU/cache, main memory, and PCI bus.

INTEL 430 MX MOBILE PENTIUM CHIPSET

The 430 MX chipset is the first of Intel's complete mobile chipset solutions for the Pentium processor. The 430 MX employs many architectural innovations developed for the 430 FX chipset designed for desktop computers, and was designed for such uses as ProShare, high-speed Ethernet, and audio/graphic-intensive applications. The 430 MX chipset is ideally suited for any application that requires a faster bus (from 25MHz to 33MHz) for greater performance. See Table 10-10 for detailed specifications.

The 430 MX supports EDO RAM and pipelined burst SRAM. Its architecture provides greater than 100MB/s PCI data streaming. The highly integrated Mode 4 local bus IDE controller improves the operation of fast hard drives. In addition, its integrated plug-and-play port makes systems easier to use and increases performance by transforming ISA motherboard peripherals into pseudo-PCI devices. As a mobile chipset, the 430 MX benefits from Advanced Power Management (APM) support.

The 430 MX chipset consists of the 82437MX system controller, two 82438MX data paths, and the 82371MX PCI I/O IDE Xcelerator (or MPIIX). The 430 MX forms a Host-to-PCI bridge, provides the second level (L2) cache control, and supports a full 64-bit data path to main memory. The 82371MX MPIIX provides the bridge between the PCI bus and the ISA-like Extended I/O expansion bus. In addition, the 82371MX has an IDE interface that supports two IDE devices, providing an interface for IDE hard disks and CD-ROM drives. The MPIIX integrates many common I/O functions found in ISA-based PC systems—a seven-channel DMA controller, two 82C59 interrupt controllers, an 8254 timer/counter, Intel SMM power management support, and control logic for NMI generation. Chip select decoding is provided for the BIOS, real-time clock, and keyboard controller. Edge/level interrupts and interrupt steering are supported for PCI plug-and-play compatibility.

INTEL 440 FX PENTIUM PRO/II CHIPSET

The 440 FX chipset (unofficially referred to as the "Natoma" chipset) is a highly integrated solution for supporting Pentium II and Pentium Pro processors in mainstream business systems. This second-generation chipset optimizes system performance for 32-bit application software in 32-bit operating system environments, and will support multiple CPUs. Based on concurrent PCI architecture, the 440 FX chipset includes a multitransaction timer (MTT) for enhanced video transfer and higher frame rates, and a passive release mechanism for improved MPEG and audio performance. There is also enhanced write performance for full utilization of write buffers (to improve host-based processing applications) and PCI delayed transactions to ensure CPU-to-ISA write control compatibility with the PCI 2.1 specification.

The 440 FX chipset is slated for compact designs implemented in a four-layer board (in either the ATX, baby AT, or LPX form factors). The chipset supports up to 1GB maximum memory size using flexible memory options, including EDO RAM. Memory is further enhanced with ECC support. The 440 FX also utilizes the PIIX3, allowing motherboards to use the same I/O subsystems as those used with the 430 HX and 430 VX. Universal Serial Bus (USB) support allows for plug-and-play connectivity "outside the box," and Bus Master IDE (BMIDE) handles access for fast hard drives. Table 10-11 lists the features of a 440 FX chipset, which consists of the 82441FX PCI and memory controller, the 82442FX data bus accelerator, and the 82371SB PCI ISA IDE Xcelerator (or PIIX3).

INTEL 450 GX/KX PENTIUM PRO CHIPSET

The 450 GX chipset (known unofficially as the "Orion" chipset) is designed to support Pentium Pro processor servers and scientific systems—especially those that use multiple CPUs (up to four). By comparison, the 450 KX (also sometimes referred to as "Orion") is aimed at designers of workstations and high-performance desktops with one or two CPUs. In actual practice, the 450 GX/KX chipsets are rarely used because of the many features the chipsets lack. Neither supports concurrent PCI, USB, or any form of I/O management. When compared with other contemporary chipsets, the 450 GX/KX are simply not as competitive as the more recent 440 FX chipset. Table 10-11 highlights the features of the 450 GX/KX chipset.

INTEL 440 LX PENTIUM II CHIPSET

The 440 LX chipset is the first in a series of AGP (Accelerated Graphics Port) chipsets from Intel designed to optimize the performance of a Pentium II processor. This was seen as a major new computing platform for small business, large business, and home users alike. The 440 LX chipset with AGP extends the system bandwidth to the graphics controller and optimizes the system bandwidth and concurrency with the

TABLE 10-11 INTEL PENTIUM PRO/II CHIPSET FEATURES AT A GLANCE

CHIPSET	440 FX	450 GX	450 KX
Processor	Pentium Pro, Pentium II	Pentium Pro	Pentium Pro
Voltage	GTL+	GTL+	GTL+
Dual CPUs	Yes	Up to Quad Processor	Yes
Refresh	RAS only or CAS-before-RAS	CAS-before-RAS	CAS-before-RAS
RAS Lines	8	16	8
64Mbit Support	Yes	Yes	Yes
Max Memory Size	1GB	8GB	1GB
Memory Types	EDO/FPM/BEDO	FPM	FPM
Memory Interleave	No	4-way, 2-way, non	2-way, non
ECC/Parity	Yes	Yes*	Yes*
PCI Support	PCI 2.1	PCI 2.0	PCI 2.0
Concurrent PCI	Yes	N/A	N/A
MTT	Yes	No	No
SMBA Support	No	No	No
Bridge Type	PIIX3	Not Included	Not Included
USB Support	Yes	N/A**	N/A**
IDE Support	BMIDE	N/A***	N/A***
RTC	External	N/A	N/A
Power Mgt.	SMM	SMM	SMM
I/O Mgt.	N/A	N/A	N/A

NOTES: * ECC only on memory and parity on host bus.
** Some motherboard implementations include the 82371SB, which is capable of USB.
*** Some motherboard implementations include the 82371FB, which is capable of bus master IDE.

implementation of Quad Port Acceleration (QPA). QPA provides four-port concurrent arbitration of the processor bus, graphics bus, PCI bus, and SDRAM.

The 440 LX chipset also offers advanced power management and fast resume from powered-down states through Advanced Configuration and Power Interface (ACPI). This enables local power-down operation, with remote wake-up for off-hours maintenance. Application performance for 3D graphics is also improved. AGP gives PCs the ability to handle memory-intensive 3D graphics applications, providing the faster performance and enabling larger textures out of main memory, which results in more lifelike detail in images.

The 82443LX PCI AGP system controller integrates a Host-to-PCI bridge, optimized DRAM controller and data path, and an Accelerated Graphics Port (AGP) interface into a single chip. The I/O subsystem portion of the 440 LX is the 82371AB, which provides an ISA bridge, a PCI ISA IDE Xcelerator (PIIX4), and USB controller. Table 10-12 lists the features of the 440 LX chipset.

TABLE 10-12 INTEL 440 LX PENTIUM II CHIPSET FEATURES AT A GLANCE

CHIPSET	440 LX
Processor	Pentium II
Voltage	GTL+
Dual CPUs	Yes
DRAMRefresh	CAS-before-RAS
RAS Lines	8
64Mbit Support	Yes
Max. Memory Size	1GB EDO, 512MB SDRAM
Memory Types	EDO/SDRAM
Memory Interleave	No
ECC/Parity	Yes
PCI Support	PCI 2.1
Concurrent PCI	Yes
AGP compliant	Yes
1x Support	Yes
2x Support	Yes
PIPE	Yes
SEA	Yes
MTT	Yes
SMBA Support	No
Bridge Type	PIIX4
USB Support	Yes
IDE Support	BMIDE & Ultra DMA/33
RTC	Integrated
Power Mgt.	SMM & ACPI
I/O Mgt.	SMBus/GP10

VIA Chipsets

Founded in 1987, VIA is perhaps the greatest threat to Intel's dominance of the chipset market. Their line of Apollo chipsets has provided an effective alternative for the support of Intel Pentium/MMX/Pro, AMD K5 and K6, and Cyrix 6x86 and M2 CPUs. VIA chipsets are generally recognized as full-featured, high-performance solutions that are used on many motherboards. VIA also produces a selection of network and peripheral controller ICs for computer applications.

VIA APOLLO PRO 133 CHIPSET

The VIA Apollo Pro 133 meets the PC133 standard—increasing the speed of the system and memory busses from 100MHz to 133MHz. The 133MHz memory interface supports the wide range of PC133 memory devices now on the market, and support for VCM/133 and HSDRAM technologies expands the memory performance capabilities of the chipset (Table 10-13). A 133MHz-capable front side bus delivers a clear upgrade path to future generation 133MHz processor types. Ultra-ATA/66 provides speedier HDD throughput that boosts overall system performance.

The VT82C693A system controller and the VT82C596B peripheral bus controller combine to provide the features of the VIA Apollo Pro 133 chipset. All Slot 1 and Socket 370 Intel processors are supported. The 133MHz FSB combines with UDMA/66 support to provide high-speed data transfers and boost overall system performance.

The Apollo Pro 133 continues support for 66/100/133 CPU bus and memory settings, and is highly scalable. The latest VIA chipset to support an asynchronous memory bus architecture, the Apollo Pro 133 provides the option of 66/100 or 100/133MHz CPU and memory bus combinations. Rounding out the feature set are all currently available mainstream features, including AGP 2x, USB, ACPI, and more.

VIA APOLLO KX133 CHIPSET

The VIA Apollo KX133 is designed for use with AMD Athlon-based high-performance desktop systems. It supports current and emerging computer technologies, including AGP 4X, PC133, a 200MHz front side bus (FSB), and UDMA/66. This chipset was the first to support AGP 4X—a standard that users hope will finally show significant improvement over PCI and AGP 2X implementations. The Apollo KX133 supports the AMD Athlon 200MHz bus—the fastest processor bus yet for desktop PCs. This architecture provides twice the bus throughput of current-generation 100MHz Pentium III-based systems. Table 10-14 lists the features of the KX133 chipset.

VIA APOLLO PRO PLUS CHIPSET

The VIA Apollo Pro Plus is designed for Slot 1/Socket 370 mobile and desktop PC systems. To provide a high level of flexibility for motherboard and system designers, the Apollo Pro Plus incorporates the full range of core logic technologies, including advanced system power management techniques for both desktop and mobile PC applications, PC100 SDRAM, AGP 2x mode, and multiple CPU/DRAM timing configurations (Table 10-15). The VIA Apollo Pro Plus consists of two devices. The VT82C693 combines with the new VT82C596A (a Southbridge chip) with a full set of mobile power management features for high-performance, power-conscious desktop and mobile designs. Side-by-side comparison with the VIA Apollo Pro shows the major difference in the Pro Plus is support for Socket 370 Celeron processors.

VIA APOLLO PRO CHIPSET

The VIA Apollo Pro is a high-performance chipset for Slot 1 mobile and desktop PC systems. To provide the greatest flexibility for motherboard and system designers, the Apollo Pro incorporates a suite of core logic technologies, including advanced system power management capability for both desktop and mobile PC applications, PC100 SDRAM, AGP 2x mode, and multiple CPU/DRAM timing configurations. The Apollo Pro supports a mixing of 100MHz and 66MHz memory to preserve users' memory

TABLE 10-13 VIA APOLLO PRO 133 CHIPSET FEATURES AT A GLANCE

- System bus speeds up to 133MHz
- VCM/HSDRAM Support
- ATA-66
- Asynchronous Architecture

TABLE 10-14 VIA APOLLO KX133 CHIPSET FEATURES AT A GLANCE

- Supports AGP 4X
- Supports the EV-6 200MHz front side bus
- Supports the PC133 133MHz memory bus
- Includes VCM/HSDRAM support
- Supports Ultra-ATA/66

investment. Memory can be used in different speed and size configurations up to 1GB total. The chipset is AGP 1.0 and PCI 2.1 compliant, and supports up to five PCI masters. Support for concurrent CPU and AGP access provides improved video performance. Disk data transfer speed supported is UDMA/33.

The VIA Apollo Pro is available in two configurations. For mobile and power-conscience desktop computers, the chipset combines the VT82C691 system controller with the VT82C596 Southbridge chip, providing a full set of mobile power management features (Table 10-16). For cost-effective, high-performance desktop designs, the VT82C691 can also be configured with the VT82C586B Southbridge.

VIA APOLLO MVP4 CHIPSET

The Apollo MVP4 is an advanced System Multimedia Architecture (SMA) PC core logic chipset for Socket 7 systems. The VIA Apollo MVP4 is a combination of the widely successful VIA Apollo MVP3 and a high-performance 2D/3D graphics controller. The VT8501 Northbridge chip paired with the new VIA VT82C686 Super Southbridge create the MVP4—designed to provide a low-cost, full-featured chipset for desktop and mobile PCs. System costs are also reduced by the integrated AGP 2.0–compliant

TABLE 10-15 VIA APOLLO PRO PLUS CHIPSET FEATURES AT A GLANCE

- Supports all Slot 1 (Pentium II/III) and Socket 370 (Celeron) processors
- AGP/PCI/ISA mobile and "deep green" PC ready
- Supports the 66/100MHz CPU external bus speed (450MHz CPUs and above)
- AGP v1.0 and PCI 2.1 compliant
- Supports SideBand Addressing (SBA) mode
- Concurrent CPU and AGP access
- Supports FPM, EDO, and SDRAM
- Different DRAM types may be used in mixed combinations
- Supports eight banks up to 1GB DRAM
- Supports up to five PCI masters
- PC98-Compatible Mobile Power Management—supports both ACPI (Advanced Configuration and Power Interface) and legacy (APM) power management
- USB v.1.0 and Intel Universal HCI v.1.1 compatible
- Windows 95/98 and plug-and-play BIOS compliant
- Supports ATAPI-compliant devices, including DVD devices
- Integrated USB Controller, Ultra-DMA-33 master mode, and EIDE controller

TABLE 10-16 VIA APOLLO PRO CHIPSET FEATURES AT A GLANCE

- Supports all Slot-1 (Pentium II) and Socket-8 (PentiumPro) processors
- AGP/PCI/ISA mobile and "deep green" PC ready
- 66/100MHz CPU external bus speed (450MHz CPUs and above)
- AGP v1.0 and PCI 2.1 compliant
- Supports SideBand Addressing (SBA) mode
- Concurrent CPU and AGP access
- Supports FPM, EDO, and SDRAM
- Different DRAM types may be used in mixed combinations
- Supports eight banks up to 1GB DRAM
- Supports up to five PCI masters
- PC98-Compatible Mobile Power Management—supports both ACPI (Advanced Configuration and Power Interface) and legacy (APM) power management
- USB v.1.0 and Intel Universal HCI v.1.1 compatible
- Windows 95/98 and plug-and-play BIOS compliant
- Supports ATAPI-compliant devices, including DVD devices
- Integrated USB Controller, Ultra-DMA/33 master mode, and EIDE controller

2D/3D AGP graphics controller. The controller incorporates a 64-bit 2D/3D graphics engine and video accelerator with advanced DVD video and optional TV output capability.

The VIA Apollo MVP4 includes performance feature support for PC100 memory for use on a 100MHz front side bus and UDMA/33, and UDMA/66 (Table 10-17). USB support for peripheral add-on devices and ACPI power management features round out the basic MVP4 VIA chipset.

TABLE 10-17 VIA APOLLO MVP4 CHIPSET FEATURES AT A GLANCE

- Integrated advanced 2D/3D AGP graphics with setup engine and DVD hardware acceleration
- 100MHz front side/memory bus
- Advanced ECC memory controller supports up to 768MB PC100 SDRAM, Virtual Channel SDRAM, EDO, and FPM
- Compatible with all Socket 7 processors
- Synchronous/Asynchronous AGP/PCI/memory operation
- 66/75/83/95/100MHz front side bus capabilities
- Integrated AC97 2.0 support
- Integrated Super I/O chip, including FDC, parallel port, serial port, and IR port
- Voltage, temperature, and fan speed hardware monitoring
- UDMA/33 and UDMA/66
- Advanced mobile PC power management
- Supports ATAPI-compliant devices, including DVD devices
- USB
- ACPI
- Compatible with all VIA Socket 7 and Slot 1 Northbridge chips

VIA APOLLO P6 CHIPSET

VIA's VT82C680 Apollo P6 is a high-performance energy-efficient chipset for PCI/ISA desktop and notebook PC systems based on 64-bit Intel Pentium Pro processors. The chipset supports multiple Pentium Pro configurations (based on Intel GTL+), and handles up to 66MHz external CPU bus speed. The chipset also supports the Pentium Pro CPU multiphase protocols for split transactions and eight level deep in-order queue for optimal CPU throughput. The DRAM and PCI bus are also independently powered so that each of the busses can be run at 3.3V or 5V (the ISA bus always runs at 5V). The main features of the Apollo P6 chipset are listed in Table 10-18.

VIA APOLLO VP3 CHIPSET

The Apollo VP3 is a high-performance, two-chip chipset for the implementation of AGP, PCI, and ISA bus architectures in desktop and notebook PC systems based on 64-bit Socket 7 CPUs (including Intel Pentium and Pentium MMX, AMD K5 and K6, and Cyrix/IBM 6x86 and 6x86MX processors). The Apollo VP3 chipset consists of the VT82C597 system controller and the VT82C586B PCI-to-ISA bridge. The VT82C597 system controller provides superior performance between the CPU, optional synchronous cache, DRAM, AGP bus, and the PCI bus with pipelined, burst, and concurrent operation. The VT82C597 complies with the Accelerated Graphics Port Specification 1.0 and features a 66MHz master system bus. It is interesting to note that the VP3 chipset is one of the few that provide AGP support for non-Pentium Pro processors. The key features for the chipset are shown in Table 10-19.

VIA APOLLO VP2 CHIPSET

Although now dated, the two-chip VIA Apollo VP2/97 was the industry's most highly integrated, high-performance Socket 7–compliant chipset. With ECC, Microsoft PC-97 compliance, SDRAM, 512MB DRAM, and 2MB cache support, the VP2/97 offers remarkable versatility for Intel Pentium, Pentium MMX, Cyrix/IBM 6x86 and 6x86MX, and AMD K5 and K6 MMX processors.

The Apollo VP2/97 builds on the VIA VT82C580VP Apollo VP (widely recognized as a leading Socket 7 chipset). Additional performance-related features include a fast DRAM controller with support for SDRAM, EDO, BEDO, and FPM DRAM types in mixed combinations with 32/64-bit data bus widths and row and column addressing, a deeper buffer with enhanced performance, an intelligent PCI bus controller with concurrent PCI master/CPU/IDE operations, and zero-wait-state PCI master and slave burst transfer rates. The Apollo VP2/97 features the VIA VT82C586B PCI-IDE controller chip, which supports ACPI/OnNow, Ultra-DMA/33, and USB technologies. Table 10-20 lists the main features of the chipset.

TABLE 10-18 VIA APOLLO P6 CHIPSET FEATURES AT A GLANCE

- Highly integrated three-chip solution
- Fast DRAM controller
- Intelligent PCI bus controller
- Enhanced master mode PCI IDE controller
- Plug-and-play controller with two Windows 95-compliant plug-and-play ports
- Integrated USB interface with hub and dual function ports
- Integrated power management providing normal, doze, sleep suspend and conserve modes
- GTL+ bus driver/receiver compatible with Intel fast DRAM controller specifications
- Up to 1GB of banked DRAM

TABLE 10-19 VIA APOLLO VP3 CHIPSET FEATURES AT A GLANCE

- PC-97 compatible using VT82C586B with ACPI power management
- Includes Ultra-DMA/33, EIDE, USB, and Keyboard/PS2-mouse interfaces
- Includes RTC/CMOS on-chip
- Supports 64-bit Socket 7 CPUs, 64-bit system memory, 32-bit PCI, and 32-bit AGP interfaces
- 3.3V and sub-3.3V interface to CPU
- 3.3V (5V tolerant) DRAM, AGP, and PCI interface
- AGP v1.0 compliant
- PCI busses are synchronous to host CPU bus
- 33MHz operation on the primary PCI bus
- 66MHz PCI operation on the AGP bus
- Concurrent CPU and AGP access
- Supports FPM RAM, EDO RAM, and SDRAM

VIA APOLLO VPX/97 CHIPSET

In its day, the VIA VT82C580VPX Apollo VPX/97 core logic chipset was a high-performance four-chip solution for Socket 7 main boards supporting Intel Pentium, Pentium MMX, Cyrix/IBM 6x86 and 6x86MX, and AMD K5 and K6 MMX processors. To enable proper implementation of the Cyrix/IBM 6x86 200+ processor, the chipset features an asynchronous CPU bus that operates at either 66MHz or 75MHz speeds. Apollo VPX/97 also supports the Cyrix/IBM linear burst mode.

The Apollo VPX/97 features a fast DRAM controller with support for SDRAM, EDO, BEDO, and FPM DRAM types in mixed combinations of 32- or 64-bit data bus widths. Additional features include a deeper buffer with enhanced performance, an intelligent PCI bus controller with concurrent PCI master/CPU/IDE operations, and zero-wait-state PCI master and slave burst transfer rates. There is support for up to 2MB of L2 cache, and up to 512MB of DRAM. The VIA Apollo VPX/97 features the VIA VT82C586B PCI-IDE controller chip, which complies with the Microsoft PC97 industry standard by supporting ACPI/OnNow, Ultra-DMA/33, and USB technologies. Table 10-21 lists the key features of the Apollo VPX/97.

TABLE 10-20 VIA APOLLO VP2 CHIPSET FEATURES AT A GLANCE

- PC97 compliance includes an extension to ACPI/OnNow
- Integrated Universal Serial Bus controller
- Enhanced master mode PCI IDE controller with extension to Ultra-DMA/33
- Support for up to 512MB DRAM with ECC
- DRAM controller with FPM/EDO/SDRAM support in mixed combinations of 32-bit or 64-bit data bus widths
- Intelligent PCI bus controller offering concurrent PCI master/CPU/IDE operations, and zero-wait-state PCI master and slave burst transfer rates
- Integrated Keyboard Controller (KBC) and real-time clock (RTC)
- Supports Pentium, Pentium MMX, Cyrix 6x86 and M2, and AMD K5 and K6 MMX
- Advanced cache controller with burst synchronous cache SRAM support up to 2MB
- Plug-and-play controller and PCI-to-ISA bridge

TABLE 10-21 VIA APOLLO VPX/97 CHIPSET FEATURES AT A GLANCE

- Asynchronous CPU bus, which is operational at either 66/75MHz
- PC97 compliance includes extension to ACPI/OnNow
- Integrated Universal Serial Bus controller
- Enhanced master mode PCI IDE controller with extension to Ultra-DMA/33
- Support for up to 512MB DRAM
- DRAM controller with FPM/EDO/SDRAM support in mixed combinations with 32-bit or 64-bit data bus widths
- Intelligent PCI bus controller offering concurrent PCI master/CPU/IDE operations, and zero-wait-state PCI master and slave burst transfer rates
- Integrated Keyboard Controller (KBC) and real-time clock (RTC)
- Supports the Pentium, Pentium MMX, Cyrix 6x86 and M2, and AMD K5 and K6 MMX
- Advanced cache controller with burst synchronous cache SRAM supports up to 2MB
- Integrated plug-and-play controller and PCI-to-ISA bridge
- Multiple processor support

VIA APOLLO VP-1 CHIPSET

Now obsolete, the VT82C580VP Apollo VP-1 is a four-chip solution for PCI/ISA desktop and notebook PCs based on Pentium, AMD K5x86, and Cyrix 6x86 CPUs. Apollo VP-1 features functions designed to bypass conventional board-level bottlenecks, including burst and normal EDO RAM, FPM RAM, and SDRAM support, burst SRAM and cache module support, and an onboard dual-channel enhanced master mode PCI IDE controller that supports up to four Enhanced IDE (EIDE) devices. The VIA Apollo VP-1 chipset consists of one VT82C585VP system controller, a VT82C586 PCI/IDE/ISA/USB controller, and two VT82C587VP share frame buffers. The features of the VP-1 are listed in Table 10-22.

VIA APOLLO MASTER CHIPSET

The obsolete VT82C570M Apollo Master is an older chipset for PCI/ISA desktop PCs based on Intel Pentium, AMD K5x86, and Cyrix 6x86 CPUs. The VIA Apollo Master consists of a VT82C575M system controller, a VT82C576M PCI/ISA/IDE controller, two VT82C577M frame buffers, and a VT82C416 support IC. There are few features that would now be considered advanced, but Table 10-23 lists the main features.

TABLE 10-22 VIA APOLLO VP-1 CHIPSET FEATURES AT A GLANCE

- PCI/ISA “Green PC” ready
- Integrated Universal Serial Bus support and intelligent PCI Bus controller
- Unified Memory Architecture includes SDRAM and BEDO support
- Fast DRAM Controller with support for various DRAM modes (32-bit or 64-bit data width)
- Enhanced master mode IDE controller with support for up to four devices
- Integrated Cache Controller
- Shared Frame Buffers
- Integrated plug-and-play controller and Power Management Unit
- Integrated PCI-to-ISA bridge

TABLE 10-23 VIA APOLLO MASTER CHIPSET FEATURES AT A GLANCE

- PCI/ISA "Green" chipset
- Fast DRAM Controller
- Master mode PCI bus controller
- Enhanced master mode PCI IDE controller supports up to four devices
- Windows 95 plug-and-play compliant
- Power Management Unit
- Supports Intel Pentium, AMD K5, and Cyrix 6x86 CPUs
- Synchronous ISA bus controller

SiS Chipsets

SiS is another major manufacturer of chipsets that support core logic (motherboards) as well as mobile PCs and multimedia applications. Although SiS is a bit behind VIA and Intel in chipset development, the company is rather unique in the inclusion of video accelerator hardware into the chipset (particularly in later products). This makes SiS chipsets particularly appealing to entry-level PCs, where minimizing cost is very important. Since SiS products are not as widely used as other chipsets, you'll find summaries of SiS chipset features in the following tables:

- SiS5597 chipset: Table 10-24
- SiS5596 chipset: Table 10-25
- SiS5571 chipset: Table 10-26
- SiS551X chipset: Table 10-27
- SiS85C49X chipset: Table 10-28

TABLE 10-24 SIS5597 CHIPSET FEATURES AT A GLANCE

- Single-chip solution with the 5597 ("Jedi" chip)
- Pentium/PCI/ISA low-cost core logic with integrated VGA controller
- 64-bit PCI/Host graphic and video accelerator
- Meets PC-97 and ACPI requirements
- PCI Burst Write
- Supports the Universal Serial Bus
- Integrated Direct-Draw hardware accelerator
- 85Hz vertical refresh rate

TABLE 10-25 SIS5596 CHIPSET FEATURES AT A GLANCE

- Two-chip solution with the 5596 and 5513
- Pentium low-cost core logic with integrated VGA controller
- Supports Intel Pentium CPUs (and other compatible CPUs) at 66/60/50MHz
- Integrated high-performance video/graphics accelerator
- Integrated L2 cache controller supporting up to 1MB of L2 cache
- Integrated high-performance DRAM controller (FPM and EDO RAM)
- Supports up to 512MB of main system memory
- Integrated PCI bus support
- Supports super-high-resolution graphic modes up to 1280×1024
- Supports a "virtual screen" up to 2048×2048
- Microsoft Video for Windows compliant

TABLE 10-26 SIS5571 CHIPSET FEATURES AT A GLANCE

- Pentium/PCI/ISA high-performance core logic
- Single-chip solution with the 5571 (Trinity chip)
- Supports Intel Pentium CPUs (and other compatible CPUs) at 66/60/50MHz
- Integrated L2 Cache Controller supporting up to 1MB of L2 cache
- Integrated high-performance DRAM controller supporting up to 384MB of main system memory
- Concurrent CPU and PCI operations
- Integrated post-write buffers and read prefetch buffers to increase system performance
- Supports five external PCI masters
- Includes an enhanced PCI IDE Master/Slave controller
- Integrated Universal Serial Bus controller
- ISA-compatible and Fast Type F DMA cycles supported

TABLE 10-27 SIS551X CHIPSET FEATURES AT A GLANCE

- Pentium/PCI/ISA core logic
- A three-chip solution with the 5511, 5512, and 5513
- Supports Intel Pentium CPUs (and other compatible CPUs) at 66/60/50MHz
- Integrated second level (L2) cache controller
- Integrated DRAM controller
- Provides high-performance PCI arbiter and integrated PCI bridge
- Supports the full 64-bit Pentium data bus
- Provides 32-bit Interface to the PCI bus
- Includes enhanced DMA functions and integrated interrupt controllers
- Integrated Keyboard Controller(KBC) and real-time clock (RTC)
- Includes a fast PCI IDE Master/Slave controller
- Includes a USB Interface
- On-board plug-and-play support

TABLE 10-28 SIS85C49X CHIPSET FEATURES AT A GLANCE

- 486 PCI/ISA core logic chipset
- A two-chip solution using the 85C496 and 85C497
- Supports the Intel 486 (and other compatible CPUs) at 50/40/33/25MHz
- Includes an L2 cache controller and DRAM controller
- Supports VESA Bus Specification Rev 2.0p
- Supports PCI Bus Specification Rev 2.0
- Supports up to four external PCI masters

OPTi Chipsets

Founded in 1989, OPTi is a well-known supplier of core logic and multimedia chipsets to manufacturers of desktop and mobile computer products worldwide. Although the chipsets by Intel and VIA have pushed OPTi into the background, the company continues to produce some respected motherboard chipsets.

OPTI DISCOVERY CHIPSET

The OPTi Discovery chipset (82C650/651) provides a highly integrated solution for a wide range of fully compatible, high-performance PC platforms based on the Intel Pentium Pro processor. The Discovery chipset contains two chips, the 82C650 system controller and the 82C651 bus controller (and an optional third chip—the 82C652—that provides an auxiliary PCI bus that can be used as the AGP port). It provides 64-bit core logic, integrated PCI (revision 2.1), support for a second Host-to-PCI device (the 82C652), support for all popular memory technologies, sophisticated power management features, as well as optional support for Unified Memory Architecture (UMA) and the Accelerated Graphics Port (AGP). The deep buffers and several levels of pipelining minimize system-level latencies and maximize/sustain throughputs for all the major subsystems. Support for parity/ECC protection provides enhanced levels of fault tolerance to greatly improve the reliability of the system.

10

OPTI VENDETTA CHIPSET

The OPTi Vendetta (82C750) single-chip core logic unit provides a highly integrated solution for high-performance PC platforms. It supports the Intel 3.3V Pentium, Cyrix 6x86, and AMD 5K86. In addition to supporting a wide range or platform designs, the 82C750 feature set also includes audio and one game port functionality, Common Architecture support, isolated primary/secondary Ultra-DMA IDE support, and dual USB ports. This makes the Vendetta an ideal choice for multimedia-based end-user systems.

FIRESTAR CHIPSET

OPTi's FireStar single-chip core logic combines high-performance features with space-saving design that is ideal for mobile applications. This solution is based on the Intel 3.3V and 2.5V (split voltage) Pentium MMX, Cyrix M2, and AMD K6 processors. FireStar also allows FPM DRAM, EDO DRAM, or Synchronous DRAM (SDRAM) as options when designing the system. The highly concurrent cycles and deep buffering features of FireStar also improve the system's performance. For power management applications, FireStar offers power-saving modes for extended battery life and provides true CPU temperature monitoring. In STPGNT mode, CPU power consumption can be reduced by 80 percent. In STPCLK mode, CPU power consumption can be reduced by as much as 99 percent. FireStar also features advanced fail-safe thermal management, full peripheral activity tracking and power-off control, Advanced Configuration and Power Interface (ACPI) support, and Advanced Power Management (APM), as well as "suspend to memory" and "suspend to disk" power management options.

Further Study

ALi: **http://www.acerlabs.com/**

AMD: **http://www.amd.com**

Intel: **http://www.intel.com/design/chipsets/**

VIA: **http://www.via.com.tw/**

SiS: **http://www.sis.com.tw/**

OPTi: **http://www.opti.com**

VLSI: **http://www.vlsi.com**

11

CMOS

CHAPTER AT A GLANCE

With the introduction of their PC/AT computer, IBM abandoned the configuration DIP switches that had been used for the PC/XT. Rather than limit the system's configuration options, IBM chose to store the system's setup parameters in a small, low-power RAM IC called the CMOS RAM. (In actual practice, CMOS RAM is typically combined on the same IC with the real-time clock, or RTC.) In effect, the discrete switches of the XT were replaced with logical "switches" of each CMOS bit. (After all, a bit can be high or low, just as a switch can be on or off.) When an AT-type computer starts, its system attributes—stored in the CMOS RAM—are read by the BIOS. BIOS then uses those attributes during normal system operation. As a result, it is vitally important that the correct settings be used when configuring a system. Otherwise, system problems may result. This chapter explains a broad selection of CMOS parameters in detail, then provides some guidelines for proper CMOS optimization and battery maintenance.

Many PC enthusiasts (and even experienced technicians) use the terms *BIOS* and *CMOS* interchangeably. However, BIOS and CMOS RAM are not the same thing—though the two are intimately related. BIOS refers to the firmware instructions located on the BIOS ROM, while CMOS refers to the low-power RAM that is holding the system's setup parameters. BIOS reads the CMOS RAM into main memory at start time and provides the setup routine that allows you to change the contents of CMOS, but the CMOS RAM/RTC device is a totally different chip.

What CMOS Does

In simplest terms, CMOS RAM is nothing more than some amount of very low-power static RAM. Older CMOS RAM devices offered 64 bytes, and later implementations provide an extra 64 bytes (128 bytes total). The latest motherboards use 512 bytes or more to store the CMOS setup along with ESCD (Extended System Configuration Data) information needed by the PC's plug-and-play (PnP) system. For the purposes of this book, we will consider a basic 128-byte CMOS system. Since RAM is naturally lost when system power is removed, a battery is added to the PC, which continues to provide power to the CMOS RAM (and RTC). It is this CMOS battery backup that keeps the date, time, and system parameters intact until you turn the system on again. Of course, if the battery should fail, the system will lose its date, time, and *all* of its setup parameters. Many a tear has been shed trying to reconstruct lost system parameters by trial and error. You will learn about CMOS backup techniques later in this chapter.

THE CMOS MAP

To truly appreciate the importance of CMOS RAM, you should understand the contents of a typical CMOS RAM IC, as shown in Table 11-1. You will find that a standard 128-byte ISA-compatible CMOS is divided into four fairly distinct sections: 16 bytes of real-time clock data [00h-0Fh], 32 bytes of ISA configuration data [10h-2Fh], 16 bytes of BIOS-specific configuration data [30h-3Fh], and 64 bytes of extended CMOS data [40h-7Fh]. Additional CMOS RAM is typically used as the ESCD (and is inaccessible through the typical CMOS setup).

TABLE 11-1 A TYPICAL CMOS RAM MAP

OFFSET	DESCRIPTION	
00h	RTC Seconds. Contains the seconds value of current time.	
01h	RTC Seconds Alarm. Contains the seconds value for the RTC alarm.	
02h	RTC Minutes. Contains the minutes value of current time.	
03h	RTC Minutes Alarm. Contains the minutes value for the RTC alarm.	
04h	RTC Hours. Contains the hours value of current time.	
05h	RTC Hours Alarm. Contains the hours value for the RTC alarm.	
06h	RTC Day of Week. Contains the current day of the week.	
07h	RTC Date Day. Contains day value of current date.	
08h	RTC Date Month. Contains month value of current date.	
09h	RTC Date Year. Contains year value of current date.	
0Ah	Status Register A. Various bits that define the following:	
	Bit 7	Update progress flag

TABLE 11-1 A TYPICAL CMOS RAM MAP *(CONTINUED)*

OFFSET	DESCRIPTION	
	Bit 6-4	Time base frequency setting
	Bit 3-0	Interrupt rate selection
0Bh	Status Register B. Various bits that define the following:	
	Bit 7	Halt cycle to set clock
	Bit 6	Periodic interrupt disable/enable
	Bit 5	Alarm interrupt disable/enable
	Bit 4	Update ended interrupt disable/enable
	Bit 3	Square wave rate disable/enable
	Bit 2	Date and time format (BCD/binary)
	Bit 1	Hour mode (12/24)
	Bit 0	Daylight savings disable/enable
0Ch	Status Register C. Read-only flags indicating system status conditions.	
0Dh	Status Register D. Valid CMOS RAM flag on bit 7 (battery condition flag).	
0Eh	Diagnostic Status Flags. Various bits that define the following:	
	Bit 7	RTC IC power invalid/valid
	Bit 6	CMOS RAM checksum invalid/valid
	Bit 5	CMOS RAM configuration mismatch/match
	Bit 4	CMOS RAM memory size mismatch/match
	Bit 3	Hard disk C: initialization failed/passed
	Bit 2	Time status is invalid/valid
	Bit 1-0	Reserved—should be 0
0Fh	CMOS Shutdown Status. Allows the CPU to reset after switching from protected- to real-mode addressing. The shutdown code is written here so that after reset, the CPU will know the reason for the reset.	
	00h	Normal POST execution
	01h	Chipset initialization for return to real mode
	02h-03h	Internal BIOS use
	04h	Jump to bootstrap code
	05h	User-defined shutdown. Jump to pointer at 40:67h. Interrupt controller and math coprocessor are initialized.
	06h	Jump to pointer at 40:67h
	07h	Return to INT 15 function 87h
	08h	Return to POST memory test
	09h	INT 18 function 87h block move shutdown request
	0Ah	User-defined shutdown. Jump to pointer at 40:67h. Interrupt controller and math coprocessor are not initialized.
10h	Floppy Drive Type. Defines drives A: and B:.	
	Bits 7-4	Drive A: type
	0h	No drive
	1h	360KB drive
	2h	1.2MB drive

11

TABLE 11-1 A TYPICAL CMOS RAM MAP *(CONTINUED)*

OFFSET	DESCRIPTION	
	3h	730KB drive
	4h	1.44MB drive
	5h	2.88MB drive
	Bits 3-0	Drive B: type
	0h	No drive
	1h	360KB drive
	2h	1.2MB drive
	3h	730KB drive
	4h	1.44MB drive
	5h	2.88MB drive
11h	System Configuration Settings. Various bits that define the following:	
	Bit 7	Mouse support disable/enable
	Bit 6	Memory test above 1MB disable/enable
	Bit 5	Memory test tick sound disable/enable
	Bit 4	Memory parity error check disable/enable
	Bit 3	Setup utility trigger display disable/enable
	Bit 2	Hard disk type 47 RAM area (0:300h or upper 1KB of DOS area)
	Bit 1	Wait for F1 if any error message disable/enable
	Bit 0	System boot-up with NumLock (off/on)
12h	Hard Disk Type ID.	
	Bits 7-4	Hard disk drive C: type
	0000h	No drive installed
	0001h	Type 1
		...
	1110h	Type 14
	1111h	Type 16-47 (defined later in 1Ah)
	Bits 3-0	Hard disk drive D: type
	0000h	No drive installed
	0001h	Type 1
		...
	1110h	Type 14
	1111h	Type 16-47 (defined later in 19h)
13h	Typematic Parameters.	
	Bit 7	Typematic rate programming disabled/enabled
	Bits 6-5	Typematic rate delay
	Bits 4-2	Typematic rate
14h	Equipment Parameters. Lists a selection of equipment parameters.	
	Bits 7-6	Number of floppy drives
	00h	No drives

TABLE 11-1 A TYPICAL CMOS RAM MAP *(CONTINUED)*

OFFSET	DESCRIPTION	
	01h	One drive
	10h	Two drives
	Bits 5-4	Monitor type
	00h	Not CGA or MDA
	01h	40x25 CGA
	10h	80x25 CGA
	11h	MDA
	Bit 3	Display adapter installed/not installed
	Bit 2	Keyboard installed/not installed
	Bit 1	Math coprocessor installed/absent
	Bit 0	Always set to 1
15h	Base Memory (in 1KB increments)—least significant byte	
16h	Base Memory (in 1KB increments)—most significant byte	
17h	Extended Memory (in 1KB increments)—least significant byte	
18h	Extended Memory (in 1KB increments)—most significant byte	
19h	Hard Disk C: Type (16-46)	
	10h to 2Eh	Type 16 to 46, respectively
1Ah	Hard Disk D: Type (16-46)	
	10h to 2Eh	Type 16 to 46, respectively
1Bh	User-Defined Drive C: Number of cylinders—least significant byte	
1Ch	User-Defined Drive C: Number of cylinders—most significant byte	
1Dh	User-Defined Drive C: Number of heads	
1Eh	User-Defined Drive C: Write precomp. cylinder—least significant byte	
1Fh	User-Defined Drive C: Write precomp. cylinder—most significant byte	
20h	User-Defined Drive C: Control byte	
21h	User-Defined Drive C: Landing zone—least significant byte	
22h	User-Defined Drive C: Landing zone—most significant byte	
23h	User-Defined Drive C: Number of sectors	
24h	User-Defined Drive D: Number of cylinders—least significant byte	
25h	User-Defined Drive D: Number of cylinders—most significant byte	
26h	User-Defined Drive D: Number of heads	
27h	User-Defined Drive D: Write precomp. cylinder—least significant byte	
28h	User-Defined Drive D: Write precomp. cylinder—most significant byte	
29h	User-Defined Drive D: Control byte	
2Ah	User-Defined Drive D: Landing zone—least significant byte	
2Bh	User-Defined Drive D: Landing zone—most significant byte	
2Ch	User-Defined Drive D: Number of sectors	
2Dh	System Operational Flags.	
	Bit 7	Weitek processor present/absent
	Bit 6	Floppy drive seek at boot enable/disable

TABLE 11-1 A TYPICAL CMOS RAM MAP *(CONTINUED)*

OFFSET	DESCRIPTION	
	Bit 5	System boot sequence (C: then A: / A: then C:)
	Bit 4	System boot CPU speed high/low
	Bit 3	External cache enable/disable
	Bit 2	Internal cache enable/disable
	Bit 1	Fast Gate A20 operation enable/disable
	Bit 0	Turbo switch function enable/disable
2Eh	Standard CMOS Checksum—most significant byte	
2Fh	Standard CMOS Checksum—least significant byte	
30h	Extended Memory Found by BIOS—least significant byte	
31h	Extended Memory Found by BIOS—most significant byte	
32h	Century Byte. BCD value for century of current date.	
33h	Information Flags. Various bytes that define the following:	
	Bit 7	BIOS length (64KB/128KB)
	Bits 6-1	Reserved—should be set to 0
	Bit 0	POST cache test passed/failed
34h	BIOS and Shadow Option Flags.	
	Bit 7	Boot sector virus protection disabled/enabled
	Bit 6	Password checking option disabled/enabled
	Bit 5	Adapter ROM shadow C800h (16KB) disabled/enabled
	Bit 4	Adapter ROM shadow CC00h (16KB) disabled/enabled
	Bit 3	Adapter ROM shadow D000h (16KB) disabled/enabled
	Bit 2	Adapter ROM shadow D400h (16KB) disabled/enabled
	Bit 1	Adapter ROM shadow D800h (16KB) disabled/enabled
	Bit 0	Adapter ROM shadow DC00h (16KB) disabled/enabled
35h	BIOS and Shadow Option Flags.	
	Bit 7	Adapter ROM shadow E000h (16KB) disabled/enabled
	Bit 6	Adapter ROM shadow E400h (16KB) disabled/enabled
	Bit 5	Adapter ROM shadow E800h (16KB) disabled/enabled
	Bit 4	Adapter ROM shadow EC00h (16KB) disabled/enabled
	Bit 3	System ROM shadow F000h (64KB) disabled/enabled
	Bit 2	Video ROM shadow C000h (16KB) disabled/enabled
	Bit 1	Video ROM shadow C400h (16KB) disabled/enabled
	Bit 0	Numeric processor test disabled/enabled
36h	Chipset-Specific Information.	
37h	Password Seed and Color Option. Variables used for password control.	
	Bits 7-4	Password seed (do not change)
	Bits 3-0	Setup screen color palette
	07h	White on black
	70h	Black on white
	17h	White on blue

TABLE 11-1 A TYPICAL CMOS RAM MAP *(CONTINUED)*

OFFSET	DESCRIPTION	
	20h	Black on green
	30h	Black on turquoise
	47h	White on red
	57h	White on magenta
	60h	Black on brown
38h-3Dh	Encrypted Password (do not change)	
3Eh	MSB of Extended CMOS Checksum	
3Fh	LSB of Extended CMOS Checksum	
40h	Model Number Byte	
41h	1st serial number byte	
42h	2nd serial number byte	
43h	3rd serial number byte	
44h	4th serial number byte	
45h	5th serial number byte	
46h	6th serial number byte	
47h	CRC Byte	
48h	Century Byte	
49h	Date Alarm	
4Ah	Extended Control Register 4A	
4Bh	Extended Control Register 4B	
4Ch-4Dh	Reserved	
4Eh	RTC Address—2	
4Fh	RTC Address—3	
50h	Extended RAM Address—LSB	
51h	Extended RAM Address—MSB	
52h	Reserved	
53h	Extended Ram Data Port	
54h-5Dh	Reserved	
5Eh	RTC Write Counter	
5Fh-7Fh	Reserved	

11

Configuring the CMOS Setup

As you might expect, CMOS data does not simply materialize out of the ether—it must be entered manually (initially by the system manufacturer, and later by you or your customers) through a setup routine. Early AT-compatible PCs relied on a disk-based setup utility—that is, you needed to boot the computer from a floppy disk containing the CMOS setup utility. The great danger with a setup disk is that the disk may fail and leave you without a setup disk, or you may lose the setup disk as the system changes hands or falls into disuse. If you find yourself with a setup disk, be sure to make a backup copy of it as soon as possible. Late-model 386 and subsequent systems abandon the use of setup disks and incorporate the setup utility onto the BIOS chip. When the setup routine is resident in the system, you can usually access the setup during system initialization by pressing one or more keys simultaneously (such as DEL or CTRL+F1). This part of the chapter is intended to familiarize you with the options found in current CMOS setup programs and illustrate the typical defaults.

> Keep in mind that the listings of CMOS setup features found in this chapter are compiled from a number of different sources. Your own CMOS setup may offer more or fewer options to choose from depending on your BIOS maker and vintage.

ENTERING CMOS SETUP

The first trick in configuring your CMOS setup is to launch the setup utility in the first place. BIOS manufacturers are rarely consistent when it comes to accessing the setup utility. In most cases, you can only launch setup in the first few moments after the system boots—just after the memory test is finished, but before the operating system starts to load. A note on the display will usually indicate the correct key or key combination such as:

```
Press <F1> to enter Setup…
```

> Some BIOS versions allow these setup entry messages to be turned off through the CMOS setup, so you may not even see a message displayed on the monitor. However, the setup routine should still be accessible.

Unfortunately, there are about as many key combinations as there are BIOS makers, and knowing the proper key combinations for every system can be an exercise in frustration. Table 11-2 lists the known key combinations for many popular BIOS and system types. When you're stuck and cannot enter CMOS with any of the key combinations in Table 11-2, you might be able to "force" the CMOS setup routine by causing a configuration change (such as removing a DIMM or two). This sometimes causes a CMOS configuration error and allows you to proceed to the setup routine.

> Some new motherboard designs allow access to CMOS setup to be disabled through a motherboard jumper. If you absolutely cannot access the setup using a proper key combination or a forced configuration change, check the motherboard to see if the setup access jumper has been disabled.

TABLE 11-2 TYPICAL CMOS SETUP KEY SEQUENCES

BIOS/SYSTEM	KEY OR KEY SEQUENCE
AMI BIOS	DEL key during the POST
Award BIOS	CTRL+ALT+ESC
DTK BIOS	ESC key during the POST
IBM PS/2 BIOS	CTRL+ALT+INS after CTRL+ALT+DEL
Phoenix BIOS	CTRL+ALT+ESC or CTRL+ALT+S
ALR PC	F2 (for PCI systems) or CTRL+ALT+ESC (for non-PCI systems)
Compaq PCs	F10
Gateway 2000 PC	F1
Sony PC	F3 while the PC is starting (you see the Sony logo), then F1

Of course, if you have a 286 or early 386 model PC sitting on your workbench, you'll need a setup disk to load the CMOS setup utility. If you actually *have* a setup disk for the system, consider yourself lucky—they are usually the first things to be lost. If you need a setup utility, you may be able to download a suitable third-party freeware utility from **oak.oakland.edu:/SimTel/msdos/at** or **ftp.uu.net:/systems/msdos/simtel/at.**

If you find yourself working with a GRiD system, you can probably get a setup utility from **http://support.tandy.com/grid.html** or **http://www.ast.com/americas/files.htm**.

For IBM PS/2 systems, you can get a setup utility from the IBM site at **http://www.pc.ibm.com/files.html**.

Finally, setup utilities for Panasonic computers are available on the Web at **http://www.panasonic.com/host/support/**.

BASIC CMOS OPTIMIZATION TACTICS

As PCs have continued to evolve, the ever-increasing variety of memory types, busses, PC technology initiatives, and system architectures has forced BIOS makers to provide more and more entries in the CMOS setup. Today, there are dozens of possible setup entries in any given BIOS—each yielding hundreds of potential combinations. This variety makes it very difficult to select the optimum settings for a system. However, if you're really just interested in getting the most from your setup, the following points may come in handy:

- *Check the basics.* Make sure that all standard CMOS settings correspond to the installed components of your system. For instance, you should verify the date, time, available memory (if possible), hard disks, and floppy disks. (See "Configuring the Standard CMOS Setup" below.)
- *Enable all system cache.* Make sure that all your cache memory (both internal and external) is enabled. Of course, you must have internal (L1) and external (L2) cache memory present in the system, which is always the case for systems less than five years old. (See "Configuring the Advanced CMOS Setup" below.)
- *Minimize RAM wait-states.* Make sure the wait-state values used for your main system RAM are set at the minimum possible. You must be careful here because if values are *too* low, your system may freeze (hang up). For more information, check out "Configuring the Advanced Chipset Setup" below.
- *Enable ROM shadowing.* As a minimum, you should shadow your video and system ROM. On older systems, this may improve performance significantly. Newer systems (with faster "flash" ROM devices) may not benefit as much from shadowing. (See "Configuring the Advanced CMOS Setup" below.)
- *Enable power management.* Make sure to employ the power management features supported by your BIOS. Proper power management will conserve electricity and can extend the working life of many of the system components. (See "Configuring Power Management" below.)
- *Optimize drive access.* Hard disk data transfer speeds are a major bottleneck for system performance. Use the fastest data transfer protocol that your hard disk system will support (for example, PIO mode 4 or Ultra-DMA/33). Remember that both the drive and drive controller must support the chosen data transfer protocol. If the hard drive system supports Bus Mastering IDE (BMIDE), you may consider using that to improve drive performance on multitasking or disk-intensive systems.
- *Go with the BIOS defaults.* With modern systems, it's often not necessary to reenter every CMOS setup parameter from scratch. Suitable default settings are now typically incorporated into the BIOS

itself, so you can get a system running without messing with individual entries. (You just need to enter the drives properly.) You can find this as a "Select BIOS Defaults" option in your CMOS setup main menu. BIOS defaults will generally not optimize your system's performance, but they will get you out of a tough spot when you have trouble after changing one or more settings.

DEALING WITH "HIDDEN" BIOS SETTINGS

Although today's BIOS has more options than ever, there's no guarantee that you'll be able to access every available option through the CMOS setup. In some cases, there may be "hidden" settings that you cannot see in the CMOS setup (and such hidden settings cannot be altered). This can be a major impairment since many settings such as DRAM timings and cache settings can have a serious impact on PC performance. In actual practice, the settings still exist, but they are masked—often because the PC maker doesn't trust you to modify the settings. There are several tools that you can use to view and modify hidden system settings.

- *AMI BIOS* A programmer by the name of Robert Muchsel has written a program called AMI Setup (v.2.99) that will allow you to access and change the hidden settings of your AMI BIOS. The program works with AMI's High Flex BIOS versions—as well as with AMI WinBIOS. The shareware version has excellent documentation to assist you in your optimization efforts. If you need help on what a particular setting affects, take a look at the long list of BIOS options presented in the following sections. You can download AMI Setup 2.99 from **ftp://ftp.cdrom.com/pub/simtelnet/msdos/sysutl/amis2990.zip**.
- *Non-AMI BIOS* For systems that do not use an AMI BIOS (MR BIOS, Award, Phoenix, etc.), you can use the more generic CTCHIPZ utility available from **http://www.sysopt.com/pub/ctchip34.zip**. As with AMI Setup, the CTCHIPZ utility checks and accesses "undocumented" system settings. The one wrinkle with CTCHIPZ is that you'll need to know which chipset your system uses in order to select the correct configuration (CFG) file for your particular system. Check the documentation for CTCHIPZ in order to find the correct CFG file name.

> The CTCHIPZ program can be a bit tricky to comprehend and use since it's in German. You can find an English translation for the documentation at **http://www.sysopt.com/ctdocs.html**.

CONFIGURING THE STANDARD CMOS SETUP

The standard CMOS setup usually comprises one screen of basic data about your system's date, time, and attached devices (primarily floppy and hard drives). It is important for you to get this data correct because the system will refuse to boot unless it is aware of all the drives installed.

Assign IRQ for VGA When enabled, this option causes the system to assign an IRQ for the video card in order to speed the transfer of data between the CPU and video card. This option must be enabled if your video card requires bus mastering (as do the Matrox Mystique cards with 3D graphics features). By disabling this option, you'll free up an IRQ for use elsewhere in the system.

Date and Time Use these settings to change the date and time of the system clock.

> RTC devices are notoriously inaccurate. Depending on the quality of the motherboard, you should expect to lose (or gain) several seconds per month. You should periodically check the date and time, and correct it as necessary.

Daylight Saving When enabled, this feature allows the RTC to automatically adapt to the daylight saving scheme (which is removing one hour on the last Sunday of October and adding one hour on the last Sunday of April). As a rule, this can be enabled. Otherwise, you'll need to correct for daylight saving manually.

Floppy Drive A: Set this entry to reflect the type of floppy drive installed for drive A:. In most cases, the drive will be 1.44MB 3.5-inch floppy, though a few systems may use a 2.88MB 3.5-inch floppy. Older systems may use 720KB 3.5-inch, 1.2MB 5.25-inch, or even 360KB 5.25-inch floppy drives.

Floppy Drive B: Set this entry to reflect the type of floppy drive installed for drive B:. The typical selections for a floppy drive are shown above.

Halt On This entry tells the BIOS which errors to skip during the POST. For example, if you want the BIOS POST to continue whether or not it gets an error on a missing keyboard, set this option to "All, but keyboard."

Hard Disk C: This number is the BIOS drive table number of your primary (master) hard drive. In virtually all cases today, this number is 47 (User Defined), which means that you must specify the drive specs according to your hard drive manual. Otherwise, you can typically autodetect the drive parameters. SCSI drives in the C: position should be set to "none" or "not installed." If you cannot autodetect the drive, there are typically six parameters that define your hard drive:

- *Cyl* The number of cylinders (tracks) on your hard disk.
- *Heads* The number of heads in the hard disk.
- *WPre* This setting specifies the cylinder where Write Precompensation begins, and uses additional energy to write the "compensated" cylinders. Today, WPcom is essentially useless. Set it either to –1 or the maximum number of cylinders on the drive. For EIDE/IDE hard drives, it is not necessary to enter a WPcom cylinder.
- *LZ* This setting specifies the cylinder used as the landing zone for older drives without an "autoparking" feature. Today, LZ is essentially useless. Set it either to 0 or the maximum number of cylinders on the drive.
- *Sect/Trk* This setting specifies the number of sectors per track (or SPT). It is often 17 for MFM drives and 26 for RLL drives. Modern types of drives use "Zoned Recording," and the number of sectors per track will vary (increasing on the outer tracks). There is usually one "translation number" provided for the drive.
- *Size* The total drive size is automatically calculated according the number of cylinders, heads, and sectors entered above. The number is given in MB according to the formula (Hds*Cyl*Sect*512)/1048.

Hard Disk D: This number is the BIOS drive table number of your secondary (slave) hard drive. In virtually all cases today, this number is 47 (User Defined), which means that you must specify the drive specs according to your hard drive manual. Otherwise, you can typically autodetect the drive parameters. SCSI drives set to the D: position should be set to "none" or "not installed." If you cannot autodetect the drive, the six parameters that define your hard drive are listed above.

> If your drive controller supports four hard drives, you may find an additional two hard drive entries (such as Hard Disk E: and Hard Disk F:). These would be a "secondary master" and "secondary slave" drive.

> When installing two drives on the same channel, be sure to set the drive's master/slave jumpers properly.

HDD Delay Some hard drives require several seconds in order to be identified correctly. With fast boots, there may not be enough time to identify the hard drive properly. This setting allows you to artificially delay the boot-up so the drive may be initialized. You can select from several possible time options. To keep your boot speed as fast as possible, be sure to select the lowest possible delay.

Keyboard This sets whether or not a keyboard is attached. In virtually all cases, the proper entry is "installed." If "not installed," the BIOS will pass the keyboard test in the POST, allowing a PC to boot without a keyboard *without* the BIOS producing a keyboard error (most commonly encountered in file servers, printer servers, etc.).

OS Select for DRAM > 64MB If you're using OS/2, select the OS/2 option. If you're using DOS or Windows, select Non-OS/2. Generally, Non-OS/2 is selected.

PCI/VGA Palette Snoop This option must be enabled if any ISA card installed in the PC requires VGA palette snooping. For example, an MPEG card can be synchronized with the PCI VGA system. However, few (if any) modern cards require palette snooping, so this option is generally left disabled.

Primary Display This entry specifies the general type of display you are using. The most frequent selection for older systems is VGA/PGA/EGA, though current systems shorten this to simply VGA. If you have an older black/white display, select Mono or Hercules. If your video adapter card is text only, select MDA.

Quick Power-On Self-Test If you have hard drives that initialize quickly, you may be able to speed your boot time even more by selecting the Quick POST. When enabled, the BIOS will shorten or skip some items during the POST (such as no memory count). This option is normally disabled to allow the normal POST routine.

Swap Floppy Drives When enabled, this option allows you to reverse the A: and B: floppy drive assignments. Normally, this option is disabled because few systems have more than one floppy drive.

Translation Mode IDE drives below 528MB are typically set as CHS (cylinder/head/sector) addressing, while EIDE, Fast-ATA and Ultra-ATA drives use LBA (logical block addressing) instead.

> If you alter a drive's translation mode *after* the drive has been partitioned and formatted, the data contained on the drive will be inaccessible. You'll need to repartition and reformat the drive.

CONFIGURING THE ADVANCED CMOS SETUP

The advanced CMOS setup contains the settings needed to tweak your boot characteristics and optimize the performance of memory and cache. Most of the options found here are not *vital* to the system's proper operation, but can help you tailor the system to your particular tastes and needs.

Above 1 MB Memory Test Enable this feature if you want the system to check the memory above 1MB for errors. The HIMEM.SYS driver for DOS 6.2 verifies the XMS anyway, so the test would be redundant in this case. In most cases, all memory is tested by the BIOS. But for faster boot performance, leave the feature disabled.

Adapter ROM Shadow C800, 16K This feature enables shadowing for other adapter ROMs at C800h (such as SCSI or network controller BIOS) that may be in the system. If there are no other adapter devices in the system, keep this feature disabled.

Adapter ROM Shadow CC00, 16K This feature enables shadowing for other adapter ROMs that may be in the system at CC00h. This feature is often disabled by default because some hard drive adapters use the CC00h address.

Adapter ROM Shadow D000, 16K This feature enables shadowing for other adapter ROMs that may be in the system at D000h. This is the default address for most network adapters, so it should usually be disabled unless there is a network adapter in the system, or some other known device with ROM at D000h.

Adapter ROM Shadow D400, 16k This feature enables shadowing for other adapter ROMs that may be in the system at D400h. Since some special controllers (such as controllers that support four floppy drives) often use this space, the default is often set disabled.

Adapter ROM Shadow D800, 16K This feature enables shadowing for other adapter ROMs that may be in the system at D800h. The default is often disabled unless there is a known ROM in the system at that address.

Adapter ROM Shadow DC00, 16K This feature enables shadowing for other adapter ROMs that may be in the system at DC00h. The default is often disabled unless there is a known ROM in the system at that address.

Adapter ROM Shadow E000, 16K This feature enables shadowing for other adapter ROMs that may be in the system at E000h. The default is often disabled unless there is a known ROM in the system at that address.

Adapter ROM Shadow E400, 16K This feature enables shadowing for other adapter ROMs that may be in the system at E400h. The default is often disabled unless there is a known ROM in the system at that address.

Adapter ROM Shadow E800, 16K This feature enables shadowing for other adapter ROMs that may be in the system at E800h. The default is often disabled unless there is a known ROM in the system at that address.

Adapter ROM Shadow EC00, 16K This feature enables shadowing for other adapter ROMs that may be in the system at EC00h. The default is often disabled unless there is a known ROM in the system at that address. SCSI adapter BIOS ROMs are often set to this address.

> Some recent forms of SCSI controllers use writable addresses and should not be shadowed or cached. Check for such warnings or cautions in the SCSI controller manual before attempting to shadow the SCSI BIOS ROM.

Boot Sector Virus Protection This well-established feature in all current BIOS versions provides a warning whenever any software attempts to write to the disk's boot sector, which is a main target for computer viruses. You can generally keep this feature enabled unless you're installing a new operating system (like Windows 95/98) that needs to write to the boot sector during installation. You can disable the boot sector virus protection before installing the OS, then reenable the feature afterward.

External Cache Memory This feature allows you to enable or disable the external (L2) cache in the system. If there is L2 cache in the system, make sure this feature is enabled for best performance. (Virtually all 486 and Pentium-type systems use L2 cache on the motherboard, but Pentium II/III CPUs include L2 cache right in the processor cartridge.) If there is no L2 cache, keep this feature disabled. Enabling the L2 cache when there is no cache in the system may cause the PC to lock up.

Fast Gate A20 Option This relates to the first 64KB of extended memory (A0 to A19) known as the *high memory area* (or HMA). This option controls the use of the A20 address line to access memory above 1MB. Normally, all RAM access above 1MB is handled through the A20 gate in the keyboard controller chip (8042 or 8742). In virtually all cases, this option should be enabled. Disabling this option may make it impossible to access memory over 1MB.

Floppy Drive Seek at Boot This feature selects whether a floppy drive will be checked at boot time. Keep this feature disabled for faster booting and reduced damage to floppy R/W heads. Enable this feature if you want to boot from a floppy disk (important for "booting clean" and running diagnostic utilities).

> Disabling the floppy drive, changing the system boot sequence, and setting a CMOS password are good techniques for adding some security to a PC.

Hard Disk Type 47 RAM Area This selection allows you to choose the location of the Type 47 HDD data area in memory. The BIOS has to place the HD type 47 data somewhere in memory. You can choose between DOS memory or the I/O address space at 0:300h. DOS memory is valuable (you only have 640KB to work with), so you should try to use the I/O space instead. However, there may be some peripheral, such as a sound card or network card, that needs this area too. Note that this feature is redundant if BIOS is shadowed (except possibly for very old BIOS).

Internal Cache Memory This feature allows you to enable or disable the internal (L1) cache in the CPU. If there is L1 cache in the system (all 486-Pentium- and Pentium II/III–type CPUs use L1 cache), make sure this feature is enabled for best performance. If there is no L1 cache (or you have reason to believe that the CPU's L1 cache is damaged), keep this feature disabled. Enabling the L1 cache when there is no cache in the CPU may cause the PC to lock up. This feature may also be presented as "CPU Internal Cache."

> Some CMOS setup utilities combine the cache control into a single entry such as "Cache Memory" and allow you to select Disabled, Internal Cache Only, or Both Enabled.

Memory Parity Error Check This feature controls the parity checking of your system's memory. Parity checking can help improve the integrity of data in memory. When enabled, parity checking will generate an error such as "PARITY ERROR AT 0AB5:00BE SYSTEM HALTED" if an error is detected. Otherwise, errors in memory will go undetected—possibly corrupting and crashing the system. If you're using parity memory on the system, go ahead and enable parity checking. If you're using any nonparity memory on your system, parity checking must be disabled.

> Besides being caused by data errors, parity errors can also be caused by insufficient wait-states or by mixing slower memory with faster memory components.

Memory Test Tick Sound When enabled, this feature generates a sequence of audible tones (or "ticks") as the memory test executes. It also provides an audible confirmation of your CPU clock speed/turbo switch setting. The idea is that an experienced user can hear if something is wrong with the system just by the tick sound pattern. However, since PCs now have much more memory than before, this setting is not used that frequently. If the noise is annoying, disable the test. If you cannot hear the test when it's enabled, check the speaker.

Numeric Processor Test This feature will test the math coprocessor. All 486DX and later CPUs use a built-in coprocessor, and this test should be enabled (otherwise, the coprocessor function may not be enabled). 486SX, 486DLC, 486SLC, and all older CPUs use a separate math coprocessor, and you should set this feature depending on whether a coprocessor is present or not.

Password Checking Option This option controls whether a password is used to access the system, or access the CMOS setup, or both. When enabled, you'll need to set a password, then enter the appropriate password(s) as required. Always remember to note your password(s) in a safe place, and change your passwords frequently. If you forget a password, or encounter a system with a password option in place, see the section "CMOS Password Troubleshooting" at the end of this chapter.

Shadow Memory Cacheable *Shadowing* is the process of copying ROM to RAM. Once the ROM contents are copied into RAM, its performance can often be increased even further by making that RAM space cacheable. You can enable this feature to cache shadow memory, or disable it to prevent caching of shadow memory. Shadow caching is usually a good idea for DOS and Windows-based platforms and should be enabled. But Linux and other UNIX-like operating systems will not benefit from this feature, and it can remain disabled.

System Boot Sequence This feature controls the order in which system drives are checked for an operating system. A:, C: is the typical sequence, but C:, A: can be selected for faster booting. Modern BIOS also supports booting from other items such as the CD-ROM (if it meets the El Torito bootable CD-ROM specification) and SCSI drives (even while UDMA/EIDE/IDE drives are in the system).

System Boot-up CPU Speed This is commonly referred to as the "turbo mode" and allows you to specify what processor speed the system will boot to. The typical settings are High and Low. High speed is recommended for best performance, but if you encounter booting problems, you should try the Low speed.

System Boot-up NumLock This specifies whether you want the NUMLOCK key to be activated at boot-up. You are free to keep this feature enabled or disabled as your personal taste dictates.

System ROM Shadow F000, 64K Memory hidden in the "I/O hole" of 0x0A0000h to 0x0FFFFFh may be used to shadow the system ROM, where the contents of the motherboard BIOS ROM are copied into RAM, and the faster RAM copy is used instead. It is generally recommended to enable this feature, though systems with faster "flash" motherboard BIOS may not see as much performance benefit. You should disable motherboard ROM shadowing if you need to update a flash motherboard BIOS or if you're using some memory-resident utility to shadow the BIOS. Note that motherboard ROM shadowing may also cause some operating systems (other than DOS or Windows) or applications to lock up.

Turbo Switch Function This feature enables or disables the turbo switch. This setting is now rarely used in modern systems because PCs are always run at their top speed. (There is no need to slow down a PC artificially.) If there is a turbo switch in the system, keep this feature enabled. Otherwise, disable this feature.

Typematic Rate This is how fast the key will repeat (in characters per second or CPS). A typical setting is 15 CPS.

Typematic Rate Delay This sets the initial delay (in mS) before a key starts repeating. (This is how long you've got to press a key *before* it starts repeating.) A setting of 500 mS (0.5s) is recommended.

Typematic Rate Programming This feature enables the typematic rate programming of the keyboard, which determines how a keyboard will respond if a key is held down. If enabled, a key will repeat automatically if it is held down. If disabled, the key will not repeat. This feature is often disabled.

> Not all keyboards support typematic rate programming, and this feature must be disabled if the keyboard doesn't support it.

Video ROM Shadow C000, 32K Memory hidden in the "I/O hole" of 0x0A0000h to 0x0FFFFFh may be used to shadow video ROM, where the contents of the video ROM are copied into RAM, and the faster RAM copy is used instead. It is generally recommended to enable this feature, though systems with faster "flash" video BIOS may not see as much performance benefit. You should disable video ROM shadowing if you need to update a flash video BIOS or if you're using a memory-resident utility to shadow the video BIOS. Note that video ROM shadowing may also cause some operating systems or applications to lock up.

Wait for <F1> If Any Error If enabled, the system will halt and wait for F1 keyboard input before proceeding. If disabled, the system will simply continue after displaying an error message without waiting for any keyboard input. Disable the feature if you want the system to operate as a server (without a keyboard). Otherwise, you can enable the feature.

Weitek Coprocessor This feature is normally found on older 386 motherboards from a period when Weitek coprocessors were popular. This high-performance coprocessor has two to three times the performance of the comparable Intel coprocessors. Weitek uses some RAM address space, so memory from this region must be remapped elsewhere. If you have a 386 system with a Weitek unit, enable the feature. If you do not have a Weitek unit, disable the feature. This setting is normally found on 386 motherboards, so don't worry about it on later systems.

CONFIGURING THE INTEGRATED PERIPHERALS SETUP

Typical motherboards now incorporate many diverse ports, including parallel port, serial port, USB, and drive controllers. Traditionally, this meant motherboard jumpers to enable the ports, but now most motherboard designs use the CMOS setup to control and configure each port.

Primary PIO This function allows IDE drives to transfer several sectors at a time. Several modes are possible. Mode 0 means one sector at a time. Mode 1 uses no interrupts. Mode 2 means sectors are transferred in a single burst. Mode 3 means 32-bit instructions at up to 11.1 MB/sec. Mode 4 offers 16.6 MB/sec. Mode 5 is a fairly unique mode that supports up to 20 MB/sec. The standard PIO mode for most drives today is PIO mode 4. Many BIOS versions offer a setting that will automatically make the best decision for your drive. Data transfer modes must be set for each drive.

IDE DMA Normally this is set to Auto. Enable this feature if your drives are UDMA capable. Windows 98 can configure this feature for you.

On-Chip PCI ID This feature is used either to enable or disable your onboard IDE controllers if such controllers are integrated into your motherboard chipset. If you wish to use a stand-alone drive controller card, you may need to disable this feature.

SMART A few BIOS versions offer the option to enable or disable a hard disk's SMART (Self-Monitoring Analysis and Reporting Technology) capability. SMART is used to detect and report impending disk problems. Some utilities use this technology to make disk diagnostics. Chances are that this feature (if available) will be disabled by default. If you know that the drive supports SMART, you can try enabling it.

USB Controller If your computer has one or more USB ports, use this setting to enable or disable your motherboard's onboard USB controller.

FDD Controller Use this feature to enable or disable your motherboard's onboard floppy disk controller. You probably want this feature enabled unless you're using a separate drive controller card and do not need the integrated floppy controller.

Serial Port This feature is used to disable a serial port (or to specify IRQ and I/O port addresses for the hardware). Normally your serial (COM) ports are enabled, but you can disable the serial port(s) if necessary.

Parallel Port This feature is used either to disable or enable a parallel port, as well as change the parallel port mode (such as standard, bidirectional, ECP, or EPP). Use ECP mode if possible since that will support faster data transfers between the system and other parallel port devices.

CONFIGURING THE ADVANCED CHIPSET SETUP

The core logic (or *chipset*) is responsible for providing many of the advanced features that we take for granted in today's PCs. As a consequence, there are a tremendous number of variables involved in the proper configuration of a chipset. This part of the CMOS setup allows you to tweak the performance of your chipset (namely, memory operations, memory refresh options, data bus performance, cache enhancements, etc.).

> The advanced chipset setup requires a more detailed understanding of chipset operation and features, and should be attempted only by experienced technicians. Incorrect chipset configurations can easily impair system performance. Remember *always* to record your original CMOS setup settings before changing any parameters.

16-Bit I/O Recovery Time This is an additional delay time inserted after every 16-bit operation. This is sometimes needed to support older 16-bit devices, and the value is added to the minimum delay inserted after every AT bus cycle.

16-Bit Memory, I/O Wait-State This entry lists the number of wait-states inserted with 16-bit memory and I/O operations. Too many wait-states will reduce bus performance, and too few wait-states can cause bus errors and system lockups.

8-Bit Memory, I/O Wait-State This entry lists the number of wait-states inserted with 8-bit memory and I/O operations. Too many wait-states will reduce bus performance, and too few wait-states can cause bus errors and system lockups.

Alternate Bit in Tag RAM Tag bits are used to determine the state of the information that is stored in the L2 (external) cache. The level of error determination is set with this option. If you use the Write Back caching method, use the "7+1" setting to receive best results. Otherwise, use the "8+0" setting.

AT Bus Clock Selection (or AT Bus Clock Source) This selects a division of the CPU clock (or system clock) so it can approximate the ISA/EISA bus clock of 8.33MHz. The settings are in terms of CLK/*x*, (or CLKIN/*x* and CLK2/*x*), where *x* may have values like 2, 3, 4, or 5. CLK represents your bus processor speed. For example, 486DX33, 486DX2/66, and 486DX3/99 all use a 33MHz bus speed and should have a divider value of 4 for an ISA speed of 8.25MHz. For 286 and 386 processors, CLK is half the speed of the CPU. Here are some typical settings:

- *CLK/2* All 286 and 386 systems
- *CLK/3* SX/DX16, DX20, DX25, DX2/50, DX4/100
- *CLK/4* SX/DX33, DX2/66, DX3/99
- *CLK/5* DX40, DX2/80
- *CLK/6* DX50, DX2/100
- *CLK/7* 60MHz bus
- *CLK/8* 66MHz bus

The bus speed doesn't have to be precisely 8.33MHz, but that's what to shoot for. An improper setting may cause significant decrease in performance. If the divider is too high, the ISA bus speed will be too low (below 8.33MHz), and the ISA devices will perform poorly. If the divider is too low, the ISA bus speed will be too high (above 8.33MHz), and the ISA devices may malfunction.

AT Cycle Wait-State This entry indicates the number of wait-states inserted whenever an operation is performed with the AT bus. You may need some additional wait-states if old ISA cards are used, especially if they are used together with fast adapter cards. Too many wait-states will reduce bus performance, and too few wait-states can cause bus errors and system lockups.

Automatic Configuration When enabled, this feature allows the BIOS to automatically set the settings in the advanced chipset setup (clock divider, wait states, etc.). If you're uncertain about configuring the advanced chipset features, keep this feature enabled. Disable this feature if you're going to make manual changes to the chipset setup. You may have to disable this feature when some highly specialized adapter cards are used in the system.

Burst Copy-Back Option This option may be enabled or disabled. When enabled, and a read from the memory to the processor results in a "cache miss," the chipset will try a second read (when the data transfers in burst mode).

Burst Refresh When enabled, this feature performs several refresh cycles at once. This feature can normally be enabled unless your system uses an unusual memory type or configuration.

Burst SRAM Cycle This lets you specify the timing of the burst mode read and write cycles to and from the external cache memory (L2). The typical options are 4-1-1-1 and 3-1-1-1, so choose the lowest setting that works well with your system.

Burst Write When enabled, the processor will write to the cache in bursts, which can make caching more efficient. When disabled, the CPU will not write to the cache in bursts.

Bus Mode This feature selects the clock mode that is used to drive the bus. In synchronous mode, the CPU clock is used to drive the bus. In asynchronous mode, the ATCLK is used. In most cases, the synchronous mode is selected.

Cacheable RAM Address Range Chipsets usually allow memory to be cached only up to 16MB or 32MB. This is to limit the number of memory address bits that need to be saved in the cache together with its contents. Set this entry to the lowest possible value. For example, if you only have 4MB of RAM, select 4MB—don't enter 16MB if you only have 8MB installed.

Cache Read Option (Often Called the "SRAM Read Wait-State" or "Cache Read Hit Burst") This specifies the number of clocks needed to load four 32-bit words into a CPU internal cache (typically specified as clocks per word). A timing of 2-1-1-1 indicates 5 clocks to load the four words, which is the theoretical minimum for current high-end CPUs (486DX, Pentium, Pentium II/III, and later). This timing determines the number of wait-states for the cache RAM in normal and burst transfers (the latter for 486 systems only). Timing of 4-1-1-1 is usually recommended, but the faster the timing that a computer can support, the better.

Cache Timing Control This option sets the timing parameters for reading/writing to cache. The typical selections are fast, medium, normal, and turbo.

Cache Wait-State This feature is used to introduce additional wait-states for cache operations. Like conventional memory, fewer wait-states will result in better cache performance (but will demand faster cache). An entry of 0 will give the optimal performance, but 1 wait-state may be required for bus speeds higher than 33MHz.

Cache Write Option This is the same as "Cache Read Option," but is used to control cache write timing.

CAS-Before-RAS When enabled, this option reduces refresh cycles and power consumption.

CAS Width in Read Cycle This feature expresses the number of wait-states for the CPU to read DRAM. Lower figures are better for system performance.

Concurrent Refresh This feature enables both the processor and the refresh hardware to have access to the memory at the same time. If this feature is disabled, the processor has to wait until the refresh hardware has finished, and this can slow system performance slightly. Many systems enable concurrent refresh by default.

CPU Write Back Cache When enabled, the system will use "write back" caching. If disabled, the system will use "write through" caching.

Decoupled Refresh Option This feature enables the ISA bus and the RAM to refresh separately. Because refreshing the ISA bus is a slower process, separating the refresh cycles this way causes less strain on the CPU. This option is often enabled.

DMA Clock Source This entry indicates the source of the DMA clock, which is used for DMA transfers. This setting will affect DMA performance for any peripheral using DMA (such as floppy, tape, network, and SCSI adapters). The maximum is 5MHz.

DMA Wait-States This entry lists the number of wait-states inserted before Direct Memory Access (DMA) is attempted. Lower numbers (fewer wait-states) result in better DMA performance.

DRAM Burst at 4 Refresh This is a slight variation of Burst Refresh, where the refresh is occurring in bursts of four. This feature can normally be enabled.

DRAM CAS Timing Delay DRAM is organized into rows and columns, and is accessed through strobe lines. The CPU activates a RAS (Row Access Strobe) line to find the row containing the required data; then a CAS (Column Access Strobe) line specifies the column. As a result, RAS and CAS signals are used to identify a location in a DRAM chip. When using slow RAM, it may be necessary to introduce a delay into the CAS timing. The default is no CAS delay.

DRAM Refresh Method This feature selects the refresh method used for RAM. The options are RAS Only and CAS-before-RAS. Most current systems use CAS-before-RAS timing by default.

E0000 ROM Belongs to ATBUS This entry indicates whether the E0000h area (upper memory) belongs to the motherboard DRAM or to the AT bus. For most systems, enabled (yes) is recommended.

Extended DMA Registers With a standard AT type of computer, DMA support is only provided for the first 16MB of system RAM. With this feature enabled, DMA support will be extended for up to 4GB of RAM. In most cases, this feature can be left disabled.

Extended I/O Decode The normal range of I/O addresses is 0–0x3FFh using only 10 address bits. With this feature enabled, the system will support a 16-bit I/O-address bus allowing a 64KB I/O space. Most motherboards or I/O adapters can be decoded by only 10 address bits, so this feature can usually be left disabled.

Fast AT Cycle When enabled, this feature may speed up data transfer rates with ISA cards (and can have an important effect on ISA video boards).

Fast Cache Read/Write Allows enhanced cache performance through memory interleaving techniques. Enable this feature if you have two banks of cache (64KB or 256KB).

Fast Decode Enable This refers to some hardware that monitors the commands sent to the keyboard controller chip. The original AT used special codes not processed by the keyboard itself to control the switching of the 286 processor back from protected mode to real mode. The 286 itself had no hardware to do this, so the CPU actually had to be reset to switch back. PC makers added a few logic chips to monitor the commands sent to the keyboard controller chip, and when the "reset CPU" code was detected, the logic chips did an immediate reset. This "fast decode" of the keyboard reset command allowed OS/2 and Windows to switch between real and protected modes faster, and allowed much better performance. You will generally find this entry on 286 and early 386 systems, since newer processors *do* have hardware instructions for switching between modes.

If you find this entry on a current system, the "Fast Decode Enable" command is probably defined a bit differently. The design of the original AT bus made it very difficult to mix 8-bit and 16-bit RAM or ROM within the same 128KB block of high address space. An 8-bit BIOS ROM on a VGA card forced all other peripherals using the C000h–DFFFh range to use 8 bits as well. By doing an "early decode" of the high address lines along with the 8/16-bit select flag, the I/O bus could then use mixed 8- and 16-bit peripherals. In both cases, you should probably have this feature enabled.

Fast Page Mode DRAM When enabled, this feature speeds up memory access for FPM DRAM. When memory access occurs in the same memory "page," the overhead of RAS and CAS sequences are not necessary, and memory performance is improved.

Hidden Refresh This feature allows the RAM refresh memory cycles to take place in memory banks not used by your CPU at this time, instead of with the normal refresh cycles that are executed every time the interrupt DRQ0 is called (every 15 mS). There are typically three types of refresh schemes: cycle steal, cycle stretch, or hidden refresh. *Cycle steal* actually steals a clock cycle from the CPU to do the refresh.

Cycle stretch delays a cycle from the processor to do the refresh (since it only occurs every 4 mS or so, it's an improvement from cycle steal). *Hidden refresh* simply refreshes idle memory banks. Most systems enable hidden refresh by default, but some memory supports hidden refresh better than others. Try hidden refresh, but if the computer crashes or locks up, disable the hidden refresh.

Hi-Speed Refresh (or Fast Refresh) When enabled, this feature causes refresh cycles to occur at higher frequencies in order to accomplish a refresh cycle in a shorter period. When combined with features like Burst Refresh, the overall system performance can improve. Not all types of memory can support Fast Refresh, and it uses more power than Slow Refresh.

IDE 32-Bit Transfer When enabled, the read/write performance of the hard disk is faster. When disabled, only 16-bit data transfers are possible. Enable this feature if possible.

IDE DMA Transfer Mode This defines the means by which DMA transfers are executed. The three typical settings are Disabled, Type B (for EISA), and Standard (for PCI). Standard is the fastest, but may cause problems with IDE CD-ROMs. The standard type is Type F.

IDE Multi-Block Mode (also called IDE Block Mode) This feature enables IDE drives to transfer several sectors per interrupt. Six modes are possible:

- Mode 0 (standard mode transferring a single sector at a time)
- Mode 1 (no interrupts)
- Mode 2 (sectors are transferred in a single burst)
- Mode 3 (speeds up to 11.1 MB/s—sometimes abbreviated as "32-bit mode")
- Mode 4 (up to 16.7 MB/s)
- Mode 5 (up to 20 MB/s—not used in actual drive implementations)

The important attribute for block mode is the number of sectors per interrupt. The maximum number of sectors per interrupt is often (but not always) related to the drive's buffer size. If this setting is not set properly, communication with COM ports may not work. If the block size (sectors/interrupt) is set too large, you may experience serial port overruns and CRC errors. To fix this, decrease the block size, or disable block mode altogether.

IDE Multiple Sector Mode When IDE DMA Transfer Mode is enabled, this feature sets the number of sectors per burst (with a maximum of 64). Problems may occur with COM ports if this setting is configured improperly.

I/O Recovery Time The I/O recovery time is the number of wait-states to be inserted between two consecutive I/O operations (generally specified as a two-number pair such as 5/3). The first number is the number of wait-states to insert for an 8-bit operation; the second is the number of wait-states for a 16-bit operation. In general, this feature can be disabled. If the AT Bus Clock is running fast (over 8.33MHz), or you're using slow peripherals, it may be necessary to enable I/O Recovery Time starting with a value like 5/3.

> A few BIOS versions specify an "I/O Setup Time" (or "AT Bus (I/O) Command Delay"). It is specified similarly to I/O Recovery Time, but is a delay before *starting* an I/O operation rather than a delay *between* I/O operations.

Interleave Mode When enabled, the system will use an interleaved approach to access system memory. If the motherboard is not designed to support interleaved memory (or uses an advanced form of high-performance memory), this option should be disabled.

ISA IRQs This entry informs the PCI cards of IRQs used by ISA cards so that the PCI cards will not attempt to assign those legacy resources. If you have no ISA devices in your system, make sure that no IRQs are reserved.

Keyboard Reset Control This feature enables the CTRL+ALT+DEL warm reboot. Disable this feature if you want to prohibit this kind of warm reboot.

Memory Read Wait-State (or "DRAM Read Wait-States") The CPU is often much faster than RAM, and it is necessary to introduce wait-states to allow the slower RAM to "catch up" to the CPU. Each wait-state effectively adds 30 nS or RAM speed. Fewer wait-states result in better system performance, and the ideal number of wait-states is 0 (though 1 wait-state is typically required). The number of wait-states necessary is approximately (RamSpeed[ns]+10)*Clock[MHz]/1000–2. If there are too many wait-states, system performance will suffer. If there are too few wait-states, parity errors and system crashes will occur.

Memory Remapping This feature remaps the memory used by the BIOS (A0000h to FFFFFh or 384KB) above the 1MB limit. If enabled, you cannot shadow video and system BIOS. In many cases, you should set this feature to disabled.

Memory Write Wait-State (or "DRAM Write Wait-States") This is the same as Memory Read Wait-State, but it applies to RAM writing.

> Some BIOS versions combine memory read/write wait-state options as the "DRAM Wait-States." In this case, the number of read and write wait-states must be equal.

Non-Cacheable Block-1 Base Enter the base address of the area you don't want to cache. It must be a multiple of the Non-Cacheable Block-1 Size selected below. When disabled, set this to 0KB.

Non-Cacheable Block-2 Base This is the same as Non-Cacheable Block-1 Base, and is usually set to 0KB.

Non-Cacheable Block-1 Size The non-cacheable region is intended for a memory-mapped I/O device that isn't supposed to be cached. For example, some video cards can present all video memory at 15MB to 16MB so software doesn't have to bank-switch. If the non-cacheable region covers actual RAM memory you are using, expect a significant performance decrease for accesses to that area. If the non-cacheable region covers only nonexistent memory addresses, there should be no performance hit. If you are using devices that should not be cached, enable this feature to set aside some memory from caching. Otherwise, you can leave this entry disabled.

Non-Cacheable Block-2 Size This is the same function as Non-Cacheable Block-1 Size, and is normally left disabled.

RAS Active Time This is the amount of time a RAS signal can be kept open for multiple accesses. Higher figures will improve system performance.

RAS Precharge Time This is the time interval during which the Row Address Strobe (RAS) signal to DRAM is held low for normal read and write cycles. This is the minimum interval between completing one read or write and starting another from the same (non-page mode) DRAM. Advanced techniques such as memory interleaving or the use of page mode DRAM are often used to avoid this delay. The RAS Precharge value is typically about the same as the RAM access time. For a 33MHz CPU, an entry of 4 is a good choice, while lower values should be selected for slower speeds.

RAS-to-CAS Delay Time This is the amount of time a CAS is performed after a RAS. Lower figures are better for system performance, but some DRAM will not support low figures.

Refresh RAS Active Time This is the amount of active time needed for Row Address Strobe during refresh. Lower entries are usually better.

Refresh Value The lower this value is, the better the performance.

Single ALE Enable Address Latch Enable (ALE) is an ISA Bus Signal (Pin B28) that indicates that a valid address is posted on the bus, and this bus is used to communicate with 8- and 16-bit peripheral cards. Some chipsets can support an enhanced mode in which multiple ALE assertions may be made during a single bus cycle. Single ALE Enable enables or disables this capability. Since this feature may slow the video bus if enabled, it is generally set as disabled (no).

Slow Memory Refresh Divider If you can extend the refresh cycles of your system (using techniques like Slow Refresh), you can free more CPU time, and system performance improves. This feature allows you to select a divider that slows the refresh cycles. If you slow the refresh too much, you'll get parity errors and system crashes.

Slow Refresh This option reduces the frequency of RAM refresh. This increases system performance slightly due to the reduced contention between the CPU and refresh circuitry, but not all RAM types necessarily support these reduced refresh rates (in which case you will get parity errors and system crashes). Many systems enable the Slow Refresh by default.

> Here's a tip for mobile PC users—refresh cycles take power, so using Slow Refresh to reduce the number of refresh cycles can save power.

Staggered Refresh When enabled, refresh is performed on memory banks sequentially. This results in less power consumption and less interference between memory banks. Many systems enable Staggered Refresh by default.

Tag Ram Includes Dirty When enabled, the cache is not replaced during cycles, simply overwritten. This results in a performance increase. However, the maximum range of cacheable memory is cut in half because a bit is needed as a "dirty bit" tag. In general, you can leave this feature disabled unless you have little system RAM.

Video BIOS Area Cacheable This feature can enable or disable caching the video BIOS. Caching the video BIOS can often enhance video performance, but with many of today's accelerated video cards, it may be necessary to prevent caching.

CONFIGURING PLUG-AND-PLAY/PCI

Plug-and-play (PnP) and the PCI (Peripheral Component Interconnect) bus are two tightly related features designed to ease the configuration burden of PC devices and provide those devices with a high-performance bus capable of working directly with the CPU and main memory. However, plug-and-play and

PCI features must be configured properly in BIOS in order to ensure trouble-free operation. This part of the chapter explains the options used to configure PCI slots and PnP behavior.

Action When W_Buffer Full This feature sets the behavior of the system when the write buffer is full. By default, the system will immediately retry (rather than wait for it to be emptied).

AT/ISA bus clock frequency This is the AT bus speed in a PCI system. Select a divisor that will give you a bus speed closest to 8.33MHz (depending on the speed of the PCI bus).

Base I/O Address This entry lists the base of the I/O address range from which the PCI device resource requests are satisfied.

Base Memory Address This entry lists the base of the 32-bit memory address range from which the PCI device resource requests are satisfied.

Burst Copy-Back Option When this feature is enabled, if a cache miss occurs, the chipset will initiate a second, burst cache line fill from main memory to the cache—the goal being to maintain the status of the cache.

Byte Merge Support (a Variation of Byte Merging) Eight- or 16-bit data traveling from the CPU to the PCI bus is held in a buffer where it is accumulated, or merged, into 32-bit data, giving faster overall performance. In this case, enabling this feature means that CPU-PCI writes are buffered.

Byte Merging This feature allows writes to sequential memory addresses to be merged into one PCI-to-memory operation, which increases performance for older applications that write to video memory in bytes rather than words. This feature is not supported well on all PCI video cards. Enable this feature unless you encounter graphics problems.

Configuration Mode This entry sets the method by which information about legacy cards is conveyed to the system:

- *Use ICU* The BIOS depends on information provided by plug-and-play software (such as the Configuration Manager or ISA Configuration Utility). Only select this if you have the utilities needed.
- *Use Setup Utility* The BIOS depends on information provided in the CMOS setup routine—don't use configuration utilities.

CPU Burst Write Assembly The Intel 450GX/KX Orion chipset maintains four posted write buffers. When this feature is enabled, the chipset can assemble long PCI bursts from the data held in them. By default, the feature is disabled.

CPU Dynamic-Fast-Cycle This feature gives you faster access to the ISA bus. When the CPU issues a bus cycle, the PCI bus examines the command to determine whether a PCI agent claims it. If not, then an ISA bus cycle is initiated. The Dynamic-Fast-Cycle then allows for faster access to the ISA bus by decreasing the latency (or delay) between the original CPU command and the beginning of the ISA cycle.

CPU Line Read This feature enables or disables (default) full CPU line reads.

CPU Line Read Multiple A line read means that the CPU is reading a full cache line. When a cache line is full it holds 32 bytes (eight DWORDS) of data. Because the line is full, the system knows exactly how much data it will be reading and doesn't need to wait for an end-of-data signal, freeing it to do other things. When this feature is enabled, the system is allowed to read more than one full cache line at a time. The default is disabled.

CPU Line Read Prefetch When this feature is enabled, the system is allowed to prefetch the next read instruction and initiate the next process.

CPU Master DEVSEL# Timeout When the CPU initiates a master cycle using an address (target) that has not been mapped to PCI/VESA or ISA space, the system will monitor the DEVSEL (device select) pin for a period of time to see if any device claims the cycle. This entry allows you to determine how long the system will wait before timing out. Choices are 3 PCICLK, 4 PCICLK, 5 PCICLK, and 6 PCICLK (default).

CPU Master Fast Interface This entry enables or disables what is known as a "fast back-to-back" interface when the CPU operates as a bus master. When enabled, consecutive reads/writes are interpreted as the CPU high-performance burst mode.

CPU Master Post-W/R Buffer When the CPU operates as a bus master for either memory access or I/O, this entry controls its ability to use a high-speed posted write buffer. Choices are N/A, 1, 2, and 4 (default).

CPU Master Post-WR Burst Mode When the CPU operates as a bus master for either memory access or I/O, this entry controls its ability to use a high-speed burst mode for posted writes to a buffer.

CPU Memory Sample Point This feature allows you to select the cycle check point (which is where memory decoding and cache hit/miss checking takes place). Each selection indicates that the check takes place at the end of a CPU cycle, with one wait-state indicating more time for checking to take place than zero wait-states. A longer check time allows for greater stability at the expense of some performance.

CPU/PCI Post Write Delay This is the delay time before the CPU writes data into the PCI bus.

CPU/PCI Write Phase This feature determines the turnaround between the address and data phases of the CPU master to PCI slave writes. Choices are 1 LCLK (default) or 0 LCLK.

CPU Pipelined Function This feature allows the system controller to signal the CPU for a new memory address even before all data transfers for the current cycle are complete. This results in increased data throughput. The default is usually disabled, so pipelining is off. Enabled means that address pipelining is active.

CPU Read Multiple Prefetch A prefetch occurs during a process (such as reading from the PCI bus or memory) when the chipset peeks at the next instruction and actually begins the next read. The Intel 450GX/KX Orion chipset has four read lines. A multiple prefetch means the chipset can initiate more than one prefetch during a process. By default, the feature is disabled.

CPU-to-PCI Burst Memory Write When enabled, back-to-back sequential CPU memory write cycles to PCI are translated to PCI burst memory write cycles. Otherwise, each single write to PCI will have an associated FRAME# sequence. Keeping this feature enabled is best for performance, but some nonstandard PCI cards (such as VGA adapters) may have problems.

CPU-to-PCI POST/BURST Data from the CPU to the PCI bus can be posted (buffered by the controller) and/or burst. This entry sets the methods used:

- *POST/CON.BURST* Posting and bursting supported (default)
- *NONE/NONE* Neither supported
- *POST/NONE* Posting but not bursting supported

CPU-to-PCI Post Memory Write This feature enables up to four double words (Dwords) of data to be posted to PCI. Otherwise, not only is buffering disabled, but completion of CPU writes is limited. (The CPU write does not complete until the PCI transaction completes.) Keeping this feature enabled is best for performance.

CPU-to-PCI Read Buffer (Sometimes Called "PCI-to-CPU Write Buffer") When enabled, up to four double words (DW) can be read from the PCI bus without interrupting the CPU. When disabled, a write buffer is not used, and the CPU read cycle will not be completed until the PCI bus signals that it is ready to receive the data. Enabling the buffer is best for system performance.

CPU-to-PCI Read-Burst When enabled (on), the PCI bus will interpret CPU read cycles as the PCI burst protocol, meaning that back-to-back sequential CPU memory read cycles addressed to the PCI will be translated into fast PCI burst memory cycles. Performance is improved, but some nonstandard PCI adapters (such as VGA adapters) may experience problems.

CPU-to-PCI Read-Line When enabled (on), more time will be allocated for data setup with faster CPUs. This feature may only be required if you add an Intel OverDrive processor to your 486-class system.

CPU-to-PCI Write Buffer Same as CPU-to-PCI Read Buffer, only for writing.

CPU-to-PCI Write Posting The Intel 450GX/KX Orion chipset maintains its own internal read and write buffers, which are used to help compensate for the speed differences between the CPU and the PCI bus. When this feature is enabled, writes from the CPU to the PCI bus will be buffered. When disabled (default), the writes will not be buffered, and the CPU will be forced to wait until the write is completed.

Delay for SCSI/HDD (Sometimes Called "SCSI Boot Delay") This is the length of time (in seconds) that the BIOS will wait for the SCSI hard disk to be ready for operation. If the hard drive is not ready, the PCI SCSI BIOS might not detect the hard drive correctly. The range is from 0–60 seconds.

DMA Line Buffer This feature allows DMA data to be stored in a buffer so PCI bus operations are not interrupted. Disabled means that the line buffer for DMA is in single-transaction mode. Enabled allows it to operate in an 8-byte transaction mode for greater efficiency. This feature should be enabled for best system performance.

DMA Line Buffer Mode This feature allows DMA data to be stored in a buffer so as not to interrupt the PCI bus. When the Standard mode is selected, the line buffer is in single-transaction mode. When the Enhanced mode is selected, the feature allows it to operate in 8-byte transaction mode.

E8000 32K Accessible This 64KB area of upper memory is used for BIOS purposes on PS/2s, 32-bit operating systems, and plug-and-play. This setting allows the second 32KB page to be used for other purposes when not needed (in the same way that the first 32KB page of the F range is usable after boot-up has finished).

Enable Master This feature enables the selected device as a PCI bus master and checks whether the card is capable of performing as a PCI master.

Fast Back-to-Back When this feature is enabled, the PCI bus will interpret CPU read cycles as the PCI burst protocol, meaning that back-to-back sequential CPU memory read cycles addressed to the PCI will be translated into the fast PCI burst memory cycles. By default the feature is enabled.

FRAMEJ Generation When the PCI-VL bus bridge is acting as a PCI master and receiving data from the CPU, a fast CPU-to-PCI buffer will be enabled if this selection is also enabled. Using the buffer allows the CPU to complete a write, even though the data has not been delivered to the PCI bus. This reduces the number of CPU cycles involved and speeds overall processing:

- Normal Buffering not employed (Default)
- Fast Buffer used for CPU-to-PCI writes

HCLK PCICLK This entry allows you to set the host CLK/PCI CLK divider. The options are AUTO, 1-1, 1-1.5.

IBC DEVSEL# Decoding This feature allows you to set the type of decoding used by the ISA Bridge Controller (IBC) to determine which device to select. The longer the decoding cycle, the better chance the IBC has to correctly decode the commands. Choices are Fast, Medium, and Slow (default).

IDE Buffer for DOS and Windows When enabled, this feature provides IDE read-ahead and posted-write buffers, so you can increase throughput to and from IDE devices by buffering reads and writes. However, this feature may actually slow older devices, so it should be disabled.

IDE Master (Slave) PIO Mode This option changes the IDE data transfer speed: Mode 0–4, or Auto. Rather than have the BIOS issue commands to effect transfers to or from the disk drive, PIO allows the BIOS to tell the controller what it wants, and then lets the controller and the CPU perform the complete task by themselves. Modes 1–4 are available for EIDE systems, but set to Auto for an automatic configuration.

11

I/O Cycle Post-Write When this feature is enabled (default), data being written during an I/O cycle will be buffered for faster performance.

I/O Cycle Recovery When enabled, the PCI bus will be allowed a recovery period for back-to-back I/O (which slows back-to-back data transfers). It's like adding wait-states to the PCI bus, so disable this feature (default) for best performance.

I/O Recovery Period This feature sets the length of time for the I/O Cycle Recovery—a programmed delay that allows the PCI bus to exchange data with the slower ISA bus without data errors. The range is from 0–1.75 microseconds in 0.25 microsecond intervals.

IRQ 3–IRQ 15 These entries are used to list what IRQs are in use (or reserved) by ISA legacy cards. If you don't use specific IRQs, set the respective entries to Available. Otherwise, set Used by ISA Card, which means that nothing else can use it.

IRQ Line If you have installed a device requiring an IRQ service into the given PCI slot, use this entry to inform the PCI bus which IRQ it should initiate. Choices range from IRQ 3 through IRQ 15.

ISA Linear Frame Buffer This feature enables a buffer if you use an ISA card that features a linear frame buffer (for example, a second video card for AutoCAD). The buffer address will be set automatically.

ISA Master Line Buffer ISA master buffers are designed to isolate the slower ISA I/O operations from the PCI bus for better performance. Keeping this feature disabled means the buffer for ISA master transaction is in single mode. Enabling this feature means it is in 8-byte mode, which increases the ISA master's performance.

ISA Shared Memory Size This option sets a block of system memory that will not be shadowed. This feature should normally be disabled unless you have an ISA card that uses the upper memory area. If you enable this feature, you'll also need to configure the following:

- *ISA Shared Memory Base Address* Enter the base address here. If you choose 64K, you can only choose D000h or below.

ISA VGA Frame Buffer Size (or "ISA LFB Size") This feature allows you to use a VGA frame buffer and 16MB of RAM at the same time—the system will allow access to the graphics card through a "hole" in its own memory map. In other words, access to addresses within this hole will be directed to the ISA bus instead of main memory. This feature should be set to disabled unless you're using an ISA card with more than 64KB of memory that needs to be accessed by the CPU, *and* you are not using the plug-and-play utilities. If you have less than 8MB of memory, or use MS-DOS, this feature will be ignored.

Keyboard Controller Clock This entry sets the speed of the keyboard controller (PCICLKI = PCI bus speed). Typical options are

- *7.16 MHz* Default
- *PCICLKI/2* 1/2 PCICLKI
- *PCICLKI/3* 1/3 PCICLKI
- *PCICLKI/4* 1/4 PCICLKI

Latency for CPU-to-PCI Write This is the delay time before a CPU writes data to the PCI bus.

Latency from ADS# Status This feature allows you to configure how long the CPU waits for the Address Data Status (ADS). It determines the CPU-to-PCI POST write speed. When set to 3T, this is 5T for each double word. With 2T (default), it is 4T per double word. For a quad word (Qword) PCI memory write, the rate is 7T (2T) or 8T (3T). The default should be correct, but if you add a faster CPU to your system, you may find it necessary to increase it. The choices are 3T (three CPU clocks) or 2T (two CPU clocks—the default.

Latency Timer (PCI Clocks) This entry controls the length of time an agent on the PCI bus can hold the bus when another device has requested it. Since the PCI bus runs faster than the ISA bus, the PCI bus must be slowed during interactions with it. This setting allows you to define how long the PCI bus will delay for a transaction between the given PCI slot and the ISA bus. This number depends on the PCI master device in use, and ranges from 0 to 255. The default is often 66, but 40 is a good place to start. Smaller values result in faster access to the bus (with better response times), but bandwidth and data throughput become lower. Normally, you'd leave this setting alone unless you're working with latent-sensitive devices (for example, audio cards or network cards with small buffers).

Latency Timer Value This is the maximum number of PCI bus clocks that the master may burst. A longer latency time gives the CPU more of a chance to control the bus.

LDEV# Check Point The VESA local device (LDEV#) check point is where the VL bus device decodes the bus commands and checks for errors, within the bus cycle itself:

- *0* Bus cycle point T1 (default)
- *1* During the first T2
- *2* During second T2
- *3* During third T2

LDEVJ Check Point Delay This feature allows you to select how much time is allocated for checking bus cycle commands. These commands must be decoded to determine whether a local bus device access signal (LDEVJ) is being sent, or an ISA device is being addressed. Increasing the delay increases stability (especially in the VESA subsystem) while very slightly degrading the performance of the ISA subsystem. Settings are in terms of the feedback clock rate (FBCLK2) used in the cache/memory control interface:

- *1 FBCLK2* One clock
- *2 FBCLK2* Two clocks (default)
- *3 FBCLK2* Three clocks

Local Memory Check Point This entry allows you to select between two techniques for decoding and error checking local bus writes to DRAM during a memory cycle:

- *Slow* Extra wait-state; better checking (default)
- *Fast* No extra wait-state used

M1445RDYJ to CPURDYJ This feature determines whether the PCI Ready signal is to be synchronized by the CPU clock's ready signal or bypassed (default).

Master Arbitration Protocol This is the method by which the PCI bus determines which bus master device gains access to the bus.

Master IOCHRDY When this feature is enabled, it allows the system to monitor for a VESA master request to generate an I/O channel ready (IOCHRDY) signal.

Master Retry Timer This feature sets how long the CPU master will attempt a PCI cycle before the cycle is unmasked (terminated). The choices are measured in PCICLKs with the PCI timer. Values are 10 (default), 18, 34, or 66 PCICLKs.

Max. Burstable Range This feature sets the size of the maximum range of contiguous memory that can be addressed by a burst from the PCI bus. Longer burst durations should improve performance.

Memory Hole Size This entry defines the size of the memory hole. Options are 1MB, 2MB, 4MB, 8MB, and disabled. These are the amounts below 16MB that are assigned to the AT bus and reserved for ISA cards.

Memory Hole Start Address This entry defines where the memory hole starts. The selections are from 1MB to 15MB. This entry is not used if the memory hole is disabled.

Memory Map Hole Start/End Address This entry determines where the hole starts, and depends on the ISA LFB Size. If you can change it, the base address should be 16MB, minus the buffer size. See "ISA VGA Frame Buffer Size."

Memory Start Address This feature is for devices with their own memory, which use part of the CPU's memory address space. It allows you to determine the starting point in memory where PCI device memory will be mapped.

Multimedia Mode This feature enables or disables palette snooping for multimedia cards.

Onbooard PCI/SCSI BIOS You should enable this feature if your system motherboard has a built-in SCSI controller attached to the PCI bus, and you want to boot from it.

Parity When enabled, this feature allows parity checking of PCI devices.

PCI Arbiter Mode Devices gain access to the PCI bus through arbitration. There are two modes: mode 1 (default) and mode 2. The idea is to minimize the time it takes to gain control of the bus and move data. Generally, mode 1 should be sufficient, but try mode 2 if you encounter problems with PCI bus access.

PCI Arbit. Rotate Priority Typically, the system manages (or arbitrates) access to the PCI bus on a first-come-first-served basis. When priority is rotated, once a device gains control of the bus, it is assigned the lowest priority and every other device is moved up one in the priority queue. This helps to prevent any one device from monopolizing the PCI bus.

PCI Bursting When this feature is enabled, consecutive writes from the CPU will be regarded as a PCI burst cycle. This feature should normally be enabled.

PCI Bus Parking This is a sort of bus mastering—a device parking on the PCI bus has full control of the bus for a short time. This feature improves performance when that device is being used, but excludes others. Try enabling this feature with network cards and hard disk controllers.

PCI CLK This feature determines whether the PCI clock is tightly synchronized with the CPU clock, or is asynchronous. If your CPU, motherboard, and PCI bus are running at multiple speeds of each other (for example, Pentium 120, 60MHz, and 30MHz PCI bus), choose to synchronize.

PCI Clock Frequency This entry allows you to set the clock rate for the PCI bus, which can operate between 0MHz and 33MHz. CPUCLK/3 means the PCI bus is operating at 11MHz (33/3 = 11). The typical entries are

- *CPUCLK/1.5* CPU speed/1.5 (default)
- *CPUCLK/3* CPU speed/3
- *14MHz* 14MHz
- *CPUCLK/2* CPU speed/2

PCI Concurrency When enabled, this means that more than one PCI device can be active at a time. With Intel chipsets, it allocates memory bus cycles to a PCI controller while an ISA operation (such as bus mastered DMA) is taking place, which normally requires constant attention. This involves turning on additional read and write buffering in the chipset. The PCI bus can also obtain access cycles for small data transfers without the delays caused by renegotiating bus access for each part of the transfer; so the feature is meant to improve performance and consistency.

PCI Cycle Cache Hit This option defines how the cache is refreshed during PCI operation. Normal refresh will produce a cache refresh during normal PCI cycles. Fast refresh will produce a cache refresh without a PCI cycle for CAS. Fast performance is usually better.

PCI Device, Slot 1/2/3 This feature enables I/O and memory cycle decoding for PCI slots. There are three options: Enable (enables the device as a slave PCI device), En Master (enables the device as a master PCI device), and Use Default Latency Timer. If this is enabled (yes), you don't need to set the Latency Timer value.

PCI Dynamic Decoding When this feature is enabled, the system can remember the PCI command that has just been requested. If subsequent commands fall within the same address space, the cycle will be automatically interpreted as a PCI command.

PCI IDE 2nd Channel Disable this feature if you're not using the second channel on the PCI IDE card. This frees up IRQ 15. Otherwise, you will lose IRQ 15 on the ISA slots.

PCI (IDE) Bursting This is similar to PCI Bursting, but this one enables burst mode access to video memory over the PCI bus. The CPU provides the first address, and consecutive data is transferred at one word per clock. The device must support burst mode.

PCI IDE IRQ Map To This option allows you to configure your system to the type of IDE disk controller. An ISA device is assumed. If you have a PCI IDE controller, this setting allows you to specify which slot has the controller and which PCI INT# (A, B, C, or D) is associated with the connected hard drives. Note that this refers to the hard disk rather than individual partitions. Since each IDE controller supports two drives, you can select the INT# for each. Also note that the primary channel has a lower interrupt than the secondary channel. There are four modes:

- *PCI-Auto* If the IDE is detected by the BIOS on one of the PCI slots, the appropriate INT# channel will be assigned to IRQ 14.
- *PCI-Slot X* If the IDE is not detected, you can manually select the slot.
- *Primary IDE INT#, Secondary IDE INT#* This assigns two INT# channels for primary and secondary channels (if supported).
- *ISA* This option assigns no IRQs to PCI slots. Use this mode for PCI IDE cards that connect IRQs 14 and 15 directly from an ISA slot using a table from a legacy paddle board.

PCI IDE Prefetch Buffers This feature allows you to enable or disable a set of prefetch buffers in the PCI IDE controller. You may need to disable this feature with an operating system (like Windows NT) that doesn't use the BIOS to access the hard disk, and doesn't disable interrupts when completing a programmed I/O operation. Disabling also prevents errors with faulty PCI-IDE interface chips that can corrupt data on the hard disk (as can happen with true 32-bit operating systems). You can usually leave this feature disabled.

PCI I/O Start Address The I/O devices make themselves accessible by occupying an address space. This allows you to make additional room for older ISA devices by defining the I/O start address for the PCI devices.

PCI IRQ Activated By This lists the method by which the PCI bus recognizes an IRQ request (Level or Edge). Use the default entries unless advised otherwise by your PCI device manufacturer, or if you have a PCI device that only recognizes one of these methods.

PCI-ISA BCLK Divider This entry allows you to set the PCI bus CLK/ISA bus CLK divider. The options are AUTO, PCICLK1/3, PCICLK1/2, and PCICLK1/4.

PCI Master Accesses Shadow RAM This feature enables the shadowing of a ROM on a PCI master for better performance.

PCI Master Burst Mode When a PCI device operates as a bus master for either memory access or I/O, this entry controls its use of a high-speed burst mode for posted writes to a buffer.

PCI Master DEVSEL# Timeout When a PCI device initiates a master cycle using an address (target) that has not been mapped to PCI/VESA or ISA space, the system will monitor the DEVSEL (device select) pin for a period of time to see if any device claims the cycle. This entry allows you to determine how long the system will wait before timing out. Choices are 3 PCICLK, 4 PCICLK (default), 5 PCICLK, and 6 PCICLK.

PCI Master Fast Interface This feature enables or disables what is known as a "fast back-to-back" interface when a PCI device operates as a bus master. When enabled, consecutive reads/writes are interpreted as the PCI high-performance burst mode.

PCI Master Latency This option sets the time that a PCI master can control the bus. If your PCI master controls the bus for too long, there is less time for the CPU to control it. A longer latency time gives the CPU more time to control the PCI bus.

PCI Master Post-W/R Buffer When a PCI device operates as a bus master for either memory access or I/O, this entry controls its use of a high-speed posted write buffer. Choices are N/A, 1, 2, and 4 (default).

PCI Master Timing Mode This entry gives you the ability to choose between two timing modes: 0 (default) and 1.

PCI Post-Write Fast When this feature is enabled (default), data being written during a PCI cycle will be buffered for faster performance.

PCI Preempt Timer This entry sets the length of time before one PCI master preempts another when a service request has been pending. Typical entries are

- *Disabled* No preemption (default)
- *260 LCLKs* Preempt after 260 LCLKs
- *132 LCLKs* Preempt after 132 LCLKs
- *68 LCLKs* Preempt after 68 LCLKs
- *36 LCLKs* Preempt after 36 LCLKs
- *20 LCLKs* Preempt after 20 LCLKs
- *12 LCLKs* Preempt after 12 LCLKs
- *5 LCLKs* Preempt after 5 LCLKs

PCI Pre-Snoop Pre-snooping is a technique by which a PCI master can continue to burst to the local memory until a 4K page boundary is reached rather than just a line boundary. This feature can be enabled.

PCI Slot x INTx Use this entry to assign PCI interrupts (INT#s) to specific PCI slots.

- *Edge/Level Select* Once an interrupt is assigned with PCI Slot x INTx, this option programs PCI IRQs to single-edge or logic level triggering modes. Most PCI cards use level triggering, while most ISA cards use edge triggering. However, try selecting edge triggering for PCI IDE.

PCI Streaming Data is typically moved to and from memory and between devices in discrete chunks of limited sizes, because the CPU is involved. On the PCI bus, data can be "streamed"—that is, much larger chunks can be moved without the CPU being used. This feature should be enabled for best performance.

PCI-to-CPU Write Pending This feature sets the behavior of the system when the write buffer is full. By default, the system will immediately retry (but you can set it to wait for the buffer to be emptied before retrying).

PCI-to-DRAM Buffer When enabled, this feature improves PCI to DRAM performance by allowing data to be stored if a destination is busy. Buffers are needed for this feature because the PCI bus is separate from the CPU.

PCI-to-ISA Write Buffer When enabled, the system will temporarily write data to a buffer so the CPU is not interrupted. When disabled, the memory write cycle for the PCI bus will be direct to the slower ISA bus. As a result, keeping this feature enabled is best for performance.

PCI/VGA Palette Snoop This feature alters the VGA palette setting while graphic signals pass through the feature connector of the PCI VGA card, and are processed by the MPEG card. VGA snooping is used by multimedia video devices (such as video capture boards) to look ahead at the video controller (VGA device) to see what color palette is currently in use. Enable this feature if you have MPEG connections through the VGA feature connector. (This means you can adjust PCI/VGA palettes.) Otherwise, go ahead and disable the feature.

PCI Write-Byte-Merge (Sometimes Called "CPU-to-PCI Byte Merge") When enabled, this allows data sent from the CPU to the PCI bus to be held in a buffer. The chipset will then write the data in the buffer to the PCI bus when appropriate.

Post Write CAS Active This is the pulse width of the CAS# signal when the PCI master writes to DRAM.

Preempt PCI Master Option When this feature is enabled, PCI bus operations can be preempted by certain system operations, such as DRAM refresh, and so on. Otherwise, they can take place concurrently.

Primary Frame Buffer When this feature is enabled, the system can use unreserved memory as a primary frame buffer. Unlike the VGA frame buffer, this would reduce overall available RAM for applications. The default is usually disabled.

Residence of VGA Card This option lists whether the VGA card resides on a PCI or VL bus. Today, the default is PCI.

Slot X Using INT# This entry selects an interrupt (INT#) channel for a PCI slot, and there are four (A, B, C, and D) for each one—that is, each PCI bus slot supports interrupts A, B, C, and D. INT#A is allocated automatically, and you would only use #B, #C, and #D if the PCI card needs to use more than one (PCI) interrupt service. For example, select #D if your PCI card needs four interrupts. Often, it is simplest to use the Auto mode.

Snoop Ahead This feature is only applicable if the cache is enabled. When enabled, PCI bus masters can monitor the VGA palette registers for direct writes and translate them into PCI burst protocol for greater speed, which can enhance the performance of multimedia video.

Snoop Filter (or "Cache Snoop Filter") This feature saves the need for multiple inquiries to the same line if it was checked previously. When enabled, cache snoop filters ensure data integrity (cache coherency) while reducing the snoop frequency to a minimum.

State Machines The chipset uses four state machines to manage specific CPU and/or PCI operations. Each can be thought of as a highly optimized process center designed to handle specific operations. Generally, each operation involves a master device and the bus it wishes to employ. The four state machines are CPU master to CPU bus (CC), CPU master to PCI bus (CP), PCI master to PCI bus (PP), and PCI master to CPU bus (PC). Each state machine has the following settings:

- *Address 0 WS* This refers to the length of time the system will delay while the transaction address is decoded. When enabled, there will be no delay.
- *Data Write 0 WS* The length of time the system will delay while data is being written to the target address. When enabled, there will be no delay.
- *Data Read 0 WS* The length of time the system will delay while data is being read from the target address. When enabled, there will be no delay.

Stop CPU when PCI Flush When this feature is enabled, the CPU will be stopped when the PCI bus is being flushed of data. Disabling this feature (default) allows the CPU to continue processing, giving somewhat greater system performance.

Stop CPU at PCI Master When this feature is enabled, the CPU will be stopped when the PCI bus master is operating on the bus. Disabling this feature (default) allows the CPU to continue processing, giving somewhat greater system performance.

Use Default Latency Timer Value This option determines whether the default value for the latency timer will be loaded, or the succeeding latency timer value will be used. If yes is selected (default), no further programming is needed for the latency timer value.

VESA Master Cycle ADSJ This feature allows you to increase the length of time the VESA master has in order to decode bus commands. Typical choices are Normal (default) and Long.

VGA 128K Range Attribute When this feature is enabled, it allows the chipset to apply features like CPU-to-PCI Byte Merge and CPU-to-PCI Prefetch to be applied to VGA memory range A0000H–BFFFFH. When enabled, the VGA receives CPU-to-PCI functions. When disabled, the system retains the standard VGA interface.

VGA Performance Mode When this feature is enabled, the VGA memory range of A0000–B0000 will use a special set of performance features. This feature has little or no effect using video modes beyond the standard VGA most commonly used for Windows, OS/2, UNIX, and so on, but this memory range is heavily used by games such as DOOM.

VGA Type This entry is used when the video BIOS is being shadowed. The BIOS uses this information to determine which bus to use. Choices are Standard (default), PCI, and ISA/VESA.

Video Palette Snoop This feature controls how a PCI graphics card can "snoop" write cycles to an ISA video card's color palette registers. *Snooping* essentially means interfering with a device. This is a powerful performance option, so only disable it if (1) an ISA card connects to a PCI graphics card through a VESA connector, (2) the ISA card connects to a color monitor, and (3) the ISA card uses the RAMDAC on the PCI card, and palette snooping (RAMDAC shadowing) is not operative on the PCI card.

Xth Available IRQ This feature selects (or maps) an IRQ for one of the available INT#s (A, B, C, or D). There are eleven selections (3, 4, 5, 6, 7, 9, 10, 11, 12, 14, 15). The "1st available IRQ" means the BIOS will assign this IRQ to the first PCI slots (order is 1, 2, 3, 4), and so on. N/A means the particular IRQ has been assigned to the ISA bus and is therefore not available to a PCI slot.

CONFIGURING POWER MANAGEMENT

Energy is expensive, and in a world of dwindling energy reserves and escalating energy demands, PCs are often required to work longer hours and pack in more features, yet be energy efficient. Today's PCs use far less energy than their early counterparts—largely because there are fewer components, but also because PCs employ a wide range of energy-saving techniques designed to reduce power demands as the system remains idle for a time. (These are collectively known as "green PCs.") Most power management features are selectable through the CMOS setup. This part of the chapter illustrates how to deal with typical power management features.

Doze Timer This feature sets the time delay before the system will reduce 80 percent of its activity. Ten to 20 minutes is usually the preferred time.

Green Timer of Main Board This feature allows you to set the time before a CPU of an idle system will shut down. The usual options are Disabled, or a time interval ranging from 1 to 15 minutes. As a rule, 5 to 10 minutes is recommended.

11

HDD Standby Timer This feature sets the time after which the hard disk of an HDD idle system (no HDD access) will shut down (or spin down). Ten to 20 minutes is usually the preferred time.

Modem Use IRQ Enter the IRQ assigned to the modem on your system (if any). If there is activity on the selected IRQ, the system will "awaken." This allows features such as "wake on ring."

PM Control by APM If disabled, the system BIOS will ignore APM when managing the system power. When enabled, system BIOS will wait for an APM prompt before it enters any power management mode (such as doze, standby, or suspend). If APM is installed and there is a task running (even the timer has timed out), the APM will not prompt the BIOS to put the system into any power-saving mode.

Power Management Scheme This allows you to define the amount of power management taking place in the system:

- *Disabled* Global power management will be disabled.
- *User Define* Users can define their own power management settings.
- *Min Saving* Predefined timer values are used such that all timers are in their maximum value.
- *Max Saving* Predefined timer values are used such that all timers are in their minimum value.

PM Wake-Up Events You can specify which events will wake the system and take it out of power-saving mode. When an event is disabled, the event's activity will not affect the PM timers or wake up the system. When an event is enabled, the specified activity will reset the PM timers and wake up the system. For example, if you have a modem on IRQ3, you can turn on IRQ3 as a wake-up event, so an interrupt from the modem can wake up the system. Conversely, you may wish to turn off IRQ12 (the PS/2 mouse) as a wake-up event, so that accidentally brushing the mouse does not awaken the system. By default, keyboard activity is the typical wake-up event.

Standby Timer This feature sets the time delay before the system will reduce 92 percent of its activity. Thirty to 45 minutes is usually the preferred time.

Suspend Switch This setting is used for enabling or disabling the "hardware suspend" switch on the motherboard. If your motherboard has a hardware suspend switch, enabling this option activates the suspend switch, and disabling this option deactivates the suspend switch.

Suspend Timer This feature sets the time after which the system goes into the most inactive state possible (which is 99 percent). Once this state is entered, the system will require a warm-up period so that the CPU, hard disk, and monitor may go online. The preferred time is usually 45 to 60 minutes.

System Slow Down This feature will slow the CPU clock dramatically after the timer has elapsed—reducing CPU heating and saving a great deal of power. A time anywhere from 30 to 60 minutes is usually acceptable.

Video Off Option This selects how power management modes will turn off the display.

- *Always on* System BIOS will never turn off the display
- *Suspend off* Display is off when system is in suspend mode
- *Susp, Stby off* Display is off when system is in standby or suspend mode
- *All modes off* Display is off when system is in doze, standby, or suspend mode

Making Use of Autoconfiguration

Virtually all current motherboards now provide an autoconfiguration option—taking most of BIOS setup problems out of the technician's hands. In the majority of cases, an autoconfigured BIOS will work just fine. But you must remember that autoconfiguration is not an optimization of the system's setup, but rather a set of efficient settings that should insure a working system. You will have to disable this setting if you want to tweak the CMOS setup yourself (otherwise your settings will be ignored). If you're stuck with CMOS settings, you should be able to get the system running by using system defaults. There are two levels of default you can work with: BIOS defaults and power-on defaults.

BIOS DEFAULTS

BIOS defaults may not be (and usually aren't) tuned for your particular motherboard or chipset, but they give a reasonable chance of getting the system to boot. The BIOS default settings are also a good place to start fine-tuning your system. BIOS defaults can also recover your setup if you enter completely unacceptable values in CMOS setup and the system refuses to boot. Of course, you'll have to start optimizing all over again.

POWER-ON DEFAULTS

When powering up the system, the BIOS puts the system into the most conservative state possible—turbo off, all caches disabled, all wait-states set to maximum, and so on. This ensures that you can always enter CMOS setup. This mode is particularly useful if the settings returned by BIOS defaults fail. If the system still refuses to boot, there is a serious hardware issue with the motherboard (or elsewhere in the system) that you will need to address first.

Backing Up CMOS RAM

Taken all together, CMOS settings are hardly intuitive—determining the proper settings for optimum system performance requires an understanding of each CMOS variable and a detailed knowledge of the individual system. Unfortunately, most end users (and many technicians) are not familiar enough with the intricacies of any given PC or the meaning of each setup entry, to adequately reconstruct the CMOS setup should the backup battery ever fail. When the battery does fail (it *will* eventually), it may take an unprepared user (or unfortunate technician) hours to rediscover settings that otherwise could be entered in a matter of minutes. This is the real tragedy—with just a few minutes of advance planning, CMOS contents can be backed up with complete safety. There are two methods of backing up CMOS contents: hard copy backup, and file backup.

Hard copy backup is just as the name implies—CMOS contents are recorded on paper, which is filed away or taped to the inside of the PC enclosure. The simplest method of hard copy backup is to connect the PC to a printer and capture a PRINTSCREEN of each data screen. This provides a fast, simple, and permanent record. On the other hand, it may take several minutes to restore the configuration.

File backup is a fairly new alternative that uses a small utility to copy CMOS RAM contents to a data file (usually on floppy disk), then restore the file to CMOS RAM addresses later as needed. Shareware utilities such as CMOS_RAM (available for download at **www.zdnet.com**) are ideal for this kind of support. When saving a CMOS RAM file, be sure to save it to a floppy disk, since losing CMOS contents will often disable the hard drive. The advantage of a backup file is speed—CMOS contents can be restored in a matter of moments.

> Regardless of which technique you use to record your CMOS settings, it is important to back up the CMOS each time you alter the PC's configuration (for example, after adding a new hard drive). Otherwise, the record will no longer reflect the current state of your system.

CMOS Maintenance and Troubleshooting

Although it is very rare for CMOS RAM/RTC devices to fail, there *are* many circumstances where CMOS contents may be lost or corrupted, and system performance may be compromised by a poorly configured CMOS setup. Beyond the traditional beep and POST codes that suggest a CMOS problem (Chapter 19), or the more recent BIOS error messages (Chapter 7), there are a wide range of PC symptoms that can indicate an improperly or incompletely configured CMOS. This part of the chapter identifies a series of symptoms that can suggest CMOS setup problems and offers suggestions for corrective action.

TYPICAL CMOS-RELATED SYMPTOMS

SYMPTOM 11-1 **Changes to CMOS are not saved after rebooting the PC** In virtually all cases, you have exited the CMOS setup routine incorrectly. This is a very common oversight (especially given the proliferation of different BIOS versions and CMOS setup routines). Try making your changes again; then be sure to "Save Then Exit and Reboot" from the setup utility's main menu.

SYMPTOM 11-2 **The system appears to be performing poorly** The system must also be stable—if it crashes frequently, or certain devices refuse to work, you may be dealing with a system conflict in hardware or software. Use a diagnostic tool such as MSD (in DOS) or the Device Manager (in Windows 95/98) to help identify possible points of conflict.

If the system is free of hardware or software conflicts, you can focus on performance. "Performance" is often a subjective evaluation and should first be verified using a benchmark test compared to other similar PCs (identical systems if possible). If you find that your particular system is performing below its optimum level, suspect a CMOS setup problem. In some cases, the CMOS RAM may have been loaded with its "power-on" or "autoconfiguration" defaults. While defaults almost always allow the system to function, they rarely offer top performance. Check the advanced CMOS and chipset setup pages (particularly the memory, cache, and bus-speed-related entries). Refer to the "Basic CMOS Optimization Tactics" section toward the beginning of the chapter.

SYMPTOM 11-3 **CMOS mismatch errors occur** These errors occur when the PC equipment found during the POST does not match equipment listed in CMOS. In most cases, the CMOS backup battery has failed and should be replaced. You can then load the CMOS defaults and tweak the setup as necessary to optimize the system (an easy task if you've got a record of the CMOS settings). Otherwise, refer to the "Basic CMOS Optimization Tactics" section earlier in the chapter.

> If you've cleared the CMOS setup (using a "clear" jumper on the motherboard), be sure that you've reset the jumper so as not to continue clearing the CMOS RAM.

SYMPTOM 11-4 **Some drives are not detected during boot** This happens most often with hard drives or other devices in the Basic CMOS setup page. In some cases, the device simply may not be listed or entered properly. (For example, you may have forgotten to enter your newly installed hard drive or floppy drive in the CMOS setup.) In other cases, the drive may need more time to initialize at boot time. Try increasing the "boot delay," or disabling any "quick boot" feature that might be in use.

SYMPTOM 11-5 **The system boots from the hard drive, even though there is a bootable floppy disk in the drive** Note that the system still boots and runs properly. The floppy disk is fully accessible (if not, check the floppy drive, power, and signal cables). This type of issue is usually not a problem, but due instead to an improper *boot sequence*. Most BIOS versions allow the PC to search through several different drives to locate an operating system, and will boot from the first suitable drive where an operating system is found. Chances are that your boot sequence is set to "C: A:," where the C: drive is checked first. Since the C: drive is connected and functional, the A: drive will simply be ignored. To boot from the A: drive, you'll need to change the boot sequence to something like "A: C:." Remember to save any changes before exiting the CMOS setup.

SYMPTOM 11-6 **Power management features are not available** First, make sure your BIOS supports power management to begin with. Modern PC power management is typically handled by a combination of BIOS and the operating system (for example, APM under Windows 95, or ACPI under Windows 98). However, power management must be supported by BIOS and enabled under the CMOS setup in order for the operating system to make use of it. If you can't use power management (or it is not available in the Windows 95/98 Device Manager under System Devices), it probably isn't enabled in the CMOS setup. Check the Power Management page of your CMOS setup (or the Advanced Chipset Setup), and make sure that power management features are enabled. You may also want to review and adjust the various device timeouts as required. When you restart the operating system, you should then be able to configure the corresponding power management features.

SYMPTOM 11-7 **PnP support is not available, or PnP devices do not function properly** First, make sure your BIOS supports plug-and-play (PnP) standards to begin with. If not, you'll need to employ a DOS ISA configuration utility (or ICU) to support any PnP devices in the system. Also make sure that you're using an operating system that supports PnP (such as Windows 95/98).

If you can't get support for PnP devices, make sure PnP support is enabled in the CMOS setup, and verify that PnP-related settings (such as "Configuration Mode" or "IRQ3-IRQ15") are all configured properly. If necessary, try loading the BIOS defaults for your CMOS setup, which *should* give you baseline PnP support if your BIOS and OS support it. Be sure to record your original CMOS settings before attempting to load defaults.

SYMPTOM 11-8 **Devices in some PCI slots are not recognized or not working properly** First, make sure your motherboard supports PCI (Peripheral Component Interconnect) slots, and verify that there is in fact at least one PCI adapter board in the system. There are simply a proliferation of PCI-related configuration settings in the PnP/PCI area of a CMOS setup, so it is extremely difficult to suggest any one probable oversight. If you cannot get PCI devices to work (or work properly), try loading the BIOS defaults for your CMOS setup, which *should* give you baseline PCI support. Be sure to record your original CMOS settings before attempting to load defaults. If your motherboard was designed early during the development of PnP, you may need a BIOS upgrade to provide adequate PnP support.

SYMPTOM 11-9 **You cannot enter CMOS setup, even though the correct key combination is used** Make sure you're pressing that key combination quickly enough—many BIOS versions only allow a few moments during POST to enter CMOS setup. Once the operating system begins to load, you'll need to reboot. Also verify that you are *in fact* using the correct key or key combination. It is also possible that access to CMOS setup has been disabled through a motherboard jumper. Refer to the documentation for your particular motherboard and locate the "CMOS access" jumper. The jumper (if it exists) should be in the position that allows access.

> Careful that you don't accidentally confuse this access jumper with the "CMOS clear" jumper—the two serve completely different purposes.

SYMPTOM 11-10 **The system crashes or locks up frequently** There are many reasons for a PC to crash or lock up—everything from a hardware fault to a bad driver to a software bug can interfere with normal system operation. Before you check the CMOS setup, run a DOS diagnostic to verify that the system hardware is performing properly, and check that there is no hardware conflict in the system. Then check the Device Manager and look for any signs of conflicting or inoperative devices (marked with yellow or red exclamation marks). If the system runs properly when DOS is booted "clean" or Windows 95/98 is started in the Safe Mode, there may be a buggy or conflicting driver (or TSR) that is interfering with system operation.

If problems persist, there may be any of several different problems in the CMOS setup. Typical oversights include insufficient wait-states, memory speed mismatches (such as mixing 60 ns and 70 ns memory), and enabling cache (L1 or L2) when there is no such cache in the system. Review your system configuration very carefully. It is also possible that shadowing and snooping features can interfere with system operation. Try systematically disabling video ROM shadowing, motherboard ROM shadowing, and other shadowing options. Then try disabling video palette snoop and other snooping or "pre-snoop" options.

If problems still continue, try loading the BIOS defaults into CMOS. The defaults should ensure some level of hardware stability, but you'll still need to optimize the CMOS setup manually for best performance.

SYMPTOM 11-11 **COM ports don't work** Assuming that the COM ports are installed and configured properly, operating problems can sometimes be traced to "IDE Block Mode" or "IDE Multiple Sector Mode" issues. Try disabling the "Block Mode" or "Multiple Sector Mode," or scale back the block mode to a lower level.

SYMPTOM 11-12 **The RTC doesn't keep proper time over a month** This is a very common problem for real-time clock (RTC) units. RTCs are notoriously inaccurate devices anyway—often straying by as much as several minutes per month. Some "third tier" RTCs (or units burdened by heavy interrupt activity) may be off by more than several minutes per week (or even more). In practice, very little can be done to correct this kind of poor time keeping other than to replace the motherboard with one using a better-quality RTC (hardly an economical solution), or use a time-correcting utility that compensates for the RTC's drift.

SYMPTOM 11-13 **The RTC doesn't keep time while system power is off** Time seems to be maintained while system power is on, but the RTC appears to stop while the system is turned off. This is often a classic sign of CMOS backup battery failure. Since the RTC usually takes a bit more power than the CMOS RAM—and CMOS RAM can be maintained by a latent change—this kind of "clock stall" is often the first sign that the CMOS battery is failing. Record your CMOS setup and replace the CMOS battery at your earliest opportunity.

SYMPTOM 11-14 **You see an "Invalid System Configuration Data" error** This type of error often means there is a problem with the Extended System Configuration Data (also called the ESCD). This is a storage space for the configuration data in a plug-and-play system. Once you have configured your system properly, the plug-and-play BIOS uses your ESCD to load the same configuration from one boot to the next. If this error message is displayed, take these steps:

1. Go into Setup and find a field labeled "Reset configuration data."
2. Set this field to "yes."
3. Save and exit the CMOS setup program. The system restarts and clears the ESCD during POST.
4. Run whatever PnP configuration tool is appropriate for your system:
   - If you have Windows 95/98 (a plug-and-play operating system), just restart your computer. Windows 95/98 will automatically configure your system and load the ESCD with the new data.
   - If you don't have Windows 95/98, run the DOS ICU (ISA Configuration Utility) to reset the ESCD.

SYMPTOM 11-15 You encounter "CMOS checksum" errors after updating a flash BIOS Flashing a BIOS IC will typically require you to clear the CMOS setup and reconfigure the setup again from scratch. Most current motherboards offer a "Clear CMOS" jumper that can be used to wipe out all the CMOS settings. This is sometimes referred to as a "CMOS clear" or "CMOS NVRAM clear." Try clearing the CMOS RAM; then load the BIOS defaults. At that point, the errors should stop, and you may need to optimize the CMOS setup entries in order to tweak the system. If you documented the original CMOS setup entries with PRINTSCREEN before upgrading the BIOS, you should be able to reset key entries in a matter of minutes. Remember to save your changes when exiting.

SYMPTOM 11-16 You notice that only some CMOS setup entries are corrupted when running a particular application This kind of error sometimes happens with several games and other programs on the market that access memory locations used by CMOS RAM and the BIOS Data Area (BDA), which are shadowed into the upper memory area (UMA). This can alter or corrupt at least some CMOS locations. One solution is to contact the program maker and see if there is a patch or fix that will prevent CMOS access. Another solution to this problem is to *exclude* the C000h to CFFFh range in the EMM386 device line in your CONFIG.SYS file. This prevents programs from accessing the section of memory that the BIOS uses for shadowing. Here is an example:

```
DEVICE=C:\DOS\EMM386.EXE X=C000-CFFF
```

CMOS PASSWORD TROUBLESHOOTING

Passwords are usually regarded as a necessary evil—a means of keeping out the malicious and the curious. However, passwords also cause their share of problems. As systems are passed from person to person or department to department, passwords often become lost or forgotten. This means the system won't start. The trick with all system passwords (passwords that must be entered before the operating system loads) is that they are stored in CMOS RAM along with the rest of the system's settings. If you can clear the CMOS RAM, you can effectively disable the CMOS password protection. Still, simply "clearing" the CMOS RAM is not always an acceptable solution because the myriad of CMOS settings are almost impossible to restore without a great deal of tweaking. The following tips will help you deal with unwanted CMOS passwords.

11

Does Anybody Know the Password? Check with friends, colleagues, supervisors—someone might know the password. This will save you a lot of hassle, and you can always disable the password in CMOS setup once you're "in." If you're using an AMI BIOS and the password feature has been enabled (but no new password has been entered), try "AMI." For Award BIOS, you can try "BIOSTAR" or "AWARD_SW." There's no guarantee such defaults will work, but it's worth a try.

Check for a "Password Clear" Jumper Crack open the case and take a look at the motherboard. There's probably a jumper that will clear the password *without* wiping out the entire CMOS setup. In some cases, the jumper is even marked "clear password" (so much for security). If you can find such a jumper, set it, and then boot the system. After the system boots, power-down and reset the jumper. Your password should now be clear, while leaving the CMOS settings intact.

Force a Configuration Change Try taking out a SIMM or DIMM and power-up the PC. In many cases, the BIOS will recognize the configuration change and generate an error such as "CMOS mismatch—Press F1 for Setup." This gets you into CMOS where you can disable the password without clearing the CMOS RAM entirely. You'll have to save your changes and reboot. Keep in mind that when you finally replace that SIMM/DIMM, you'll probably see another CMOS error—just go back into CMOS and do a quick correction. Keep in mind that newer BIOS versions are getting smarter and may still require the password before the CMOS setup routine will start, but it's worth a shot.

Clear the CMOS RAM There's no doubt that this is your *least* desirable choice. There are several ways to clear the CMOS. Look for a motherboard jumper that says "CMOS clear" or some similar marking. Set the jumper and power-up the system. When you see a message indicating that CMOS is clear, or that default settings have been loaded, power-down the PC and reset the jumper (the password should now be gone). You can then restart the PC and reconfigure your CMOS setup from scratch.

If you're using an AMI, Award, or Phoenix BIOS (and can't find the proper jumper), you can use the DOS DEBUG utility on a "clean" bootable floppy disk. Start DEBUG and use the following commands for an AMI BIOS (don't try this through a DOS window):

```
C:\DEBUG
-O 70 17
-O 71 17
Q
```

If you're using a Phoenix BIOS, try the following DEBUG commands:

```
C:\DEBUG
-O 70 FF
-O 71 17
Q
```

As another option, you can remove the CMOS battery and wait for the CMOS RAM to clear. As a rule, you should wait for at least 30 minutes, but I've seen CMOS RAM hold a latent charge for days. To accelerate the process, you can short a 10 kΩ resistor across the empty battery terminals (be sure to turn the power off *first*). If that doesn't work, you can use the same resistor to short the CMOS RAM power pins directly, as shown in Table 11-3. Again, remember that all system power should be *off* before you do this.

TABLE 11-3 LIST OF CMOS RAM/RTC POWER PINS

BRAND	PART	SHORT PIN NUMBERS
Benchmarq	BQ3258S	12 and 20
Benchmarq	BQ3287AMT	12 and 21
Benchmarq	BQ3287MT	Cannot clear (replace the IC)
C&T	P82C206	12 and 32
Dallas	DS1287	Cannot clear (replace the IC)
Dallas	DS1287A	12 and 21
Dallas	DS12885S	12 and 20
Hitachi	HD146818AP	12 and 24
Motorola	MC146818AP	12 and 24
OPTi	F82C206	3 and 26
Samsung	KS82C6818A	12 and 24

Once your CMOS RAM is clear, you will need to restore the setup (probably starting with defaults). After the CMOS is restored, be sure to take a PRINTSCREEN of each setup page and keep the copies with the PC's documentation.

CMOS BATTERY MAINTENANCE

Ordinarily, the RTC/CMOS IC requires no maintenance. However, the backup battery will need to be replaced on a fairly regular basis (often every few years). Before replacing the battery (or battery pack), be sure that you have a valid CMOS backup—either on paper or floppy disk. Turn off system power, unplug the system, and remove the battery. This will cause the CMOS RAM IC to eventually lose its contents—it may take moments, or hours, depending on the CMOS RAM chip. Recycle the original battery and install the new one according to the system manufacturer's instructions. Secure the new battery and restart the system. When the system boots, go directly to the CMOS setup routine and restore each setting. If you have CMOS information recorded in a file, boot the system from a floppy disk and use the CMOS backup/restore utility to restore the file. You should then be able to restart the system as if nothing had ever happened.

> Some CMOS RAM ICs can retain their contents for hours on a "latent" charge and may not have to be reprogrammed after replacing the battery. However, there is no guarantee of just how long CMOS contents will remain intact. Always be prepared to restore CMOS settings.

If you're going to be storing old (replaced) motherboards for any period of time, make it a point to remove the CMOS backup battery FIRST. Batteries tend to be very safe and reliable, but there are many instances where they can and **do** leak. Since batteries use an acid-based electrolyte, battery leakage can easily damage battery contacts, or spill over onto the motherboard itself—damaging circuit traces and ruining the motherboard beyond repair.

Further Study

American Megatrends: **http://www.megatrends.com**

Award BIOS: **http://www.award.com**

Dallas Semicon.: **http://www.dalsemi.com/DocControl/Overviews.web/PnP_RTC/overview.html**

IBM SurePath BIOS page: **http://www.surepath.ibm.com/**

MicroFirmware: **http://www.firmware.com/catalog2.htm**

Mr. BIOS: **http://www.mrbios.com/**

Unicore: **http://www.unicore.com/**

Wim's BIOS Page: **http://www.ping.be/bios/**

12

CONFLICT TROUBLESHOOTING

CHAPTER AT A GLANCE

The incredible acceptance and popularity of the PC is largely due to the use of an *open architecture*. An open architecture allows any manufacturer to develop new devices (video cards, modems, sound cards, etc.) that will work in conjunction with the PC. When a new expansion card is added to the PC, the device makes use of various system resources in order to obtain CPU time and transfer data across the expansion bus. Ultimately, each device that is added to the system requires unique resources. No two devices can use the same resources—otherwise, a hardware conflict will result. Low-level software (such as device drivers and TSRs) that use system resources can also conflict with one another during normal operation. This chapter explains the concept of *system resources*, then shows you how to detect and correct conflicts that can arise in both hardware and software.

Understanding System Resources

The key to mastering and eliminating conflicts is to understand the importance of each system resource that is available to you. PCs provide three typical types of resources: interrupts (or IRQs), DMA channels, and I/O areas. Many controllers and network devices also utilize BIOS, which requires memory space. Do not underestimate the importance of these resource areas—conflicts can occur anywhere, and they carry dire consequences for a system.

INTERRUPTS

An *interrupt* is probably the most well known and understood type of resource. Interrupts are used to demand attention from the CPU. This allows a device or subsystem to work in the background until a particular event occurs that requires system processing. Such an event may include receiving a character at the serial port, striking a key on the keyboard, or any number of other real-world situations. An interrupt is invoked by asserting a logic level on one of the physical *interrupt request* (or IRQ) lines accessible through any of the motherboard's expansion bus slots. AT-compatible PCs provide 16 IRQ lines (noted IRQ 0 to IRQ 15). Table 12-1 illustrates the IRQ assignments for classic XT and current AT systems. These signal lines run from pins on the expansion bus connector or key ICs on the motherboard to Programmable Interrupt Controllers (PICs) on the motherboard. The output signals generated by a PIC trigger the CPU interrupt. Keep in mind that Table 12-1 covers hardware interrupts only. There are also a proliferation of processor and software-generated interrupts.

The use of IRQ 2 in an AT system deserves a bit of explanation. An AT uses IRQ 2 right on the motherboard, which means the expansion bus pin for IRQ 2 is now empty. Instead of leaving this pin unused, IRQ 9 from the AT extended slot is wired to the pin previously occupied by IRQ 2. In other words, IRQ 9 is being *redirected* to IRQ 2. Any AT expansion device set to use IRQ 2 is actually using IRQ 9. Of course, the vector interrupt table is adjusted to compensate for this sleight of hand.

After an interrupt is triggered, an *interrupt handling routine* saves the current CPU register states to a small area of memory (called the *stack*), then directs the CPU to the *interrupt vector table*. The interrupt vector table is a list of program locations that correspond to each interrupt. When an interrupt occurs, the CPU will jump to the interrupt handler routine at the location specified in the interrupt vector table and execute the routine. In most cases, the interrupt handler is a device driver associated with the board generating the interrupt. For example, an IRQ from a network card will likely call a network device driver to operate the card. For a hard disk controller, an IRQ calls the BIOS ROM code that operates the drive. When the handling routine is finished, the CPU's original register contents are "popped" from the stack, and the CPU picks up from where it left off without interruption.

As a technician, it is not vital that you understand precisely how interrupts are initialized and enabled, but you should know the basic terminology. The term *assigned* simply means that a device is set to produce a particular IRQ signal. For example, a typical hard drive controller board is assigned to IRQ 14 (primary controller) and IRQ 15 (secondary controller). Assignments are usually made with one or more jumpers or DIP switches, or are configured automatically through the use of plug-and-play (PnP). Next, interrupts can be selectively enabled or disabled under software control. An *enabled* interrupt is an interrupt where the PIC has been programmed to pass an IRQ to the CPU. Just because an interrupt is enabled does not mean that there are any devices assigned to it. Finally, an *active* interrupt is a line where real IRQs are being generated. Note that active does not mean assigned or enabled.

TABLE 12-1 XT AND AT INTERRUPT ASSIGNMENTS

IBM PC/XT

IRQ	FUNCTION
0	System Timer IC
1	Keyboard Controller IC
2	Unused
3	Serial Port 2 (COM2: 2F8h-2FFh and COM4: 2E8h-2EFh)
4	Serial Port 1 (COM1: 3F8h-3FFh and COM3: 3E8h-3EFh)
5	XT Hard Disk Controller Board
6	Floppy Disk Controller Board
7	Parallel Port 1 (LPT1: 3BCh [mono] or 378h [color])

IBM PC/AT

IRQ	FUNCTION
0	System Timer IC
1	Keyboard Controller IC
2	Second IRQ Controller IC
3	Serial Port 2 (COM2: 2F8h-2FFh and COM4: 2E8h-2EFh)
4	Serial Port 1 (COM1: 3F8h-3FFh and COM3: 3E8h-3EFh)
5	Parallel Port 2 (LPT2: 378h or 278h)
6	Floppy Disk Controller
7	Parallel Port 1 (LPT1: 3BCh [mono] or 378h [color])
8	Real-Time Clock (RTC)
9	Unused (redirected to IRQ 2)
10	USB (on systems so equipped—can be disabled)
11	Windows sound system (on systems so equipped—can be disabled)
12	Motherboard Mouse Port (PS/2 port)
13	Math Coprocessor
14	Primary AT/IDE Hard Disk Controller
15	Secondary AT/IDE Hard Disk Controller (on systems so equipped—can be disabled)

Interrupts are an effective and reliable means of signaling the CPU, but the conventional ISA bus architecture—used in virtually all PCs—does not provide a means of determining which slot contains the board that called the interrupt. As a result, interrupts cannot be shared by multiple devices. In other words, no two devices can be actively generating interrupt requests on the same IRQ line at the same time. If more than one device is assigned to the same interrupt line, a hardware conflict can occur. In most circumstances, a conflict may prevent the newly installed board (or other previously installed boards) from working. In some cases, a hardware conflict can hang up the entire system.

The MCA (MicroChannel Architecture) and EISA (Extended ISA) busses overcome this IRQ sharing limitation, but MCA was never widely accepted in the PC industry because the slots are not backward compatible with the well-established base of ISA boards. EISA bus slots are backward compatible with ISA boards, but an ISA board in an EISA slot is still faced with the same IRQ limitations.

DMA CHANNELS

The CPU is very adept at moving data. It can transfer data between memory locations, I/O locations, or from memory to I/O and back with equal ease. However, PC designers realized that transferring large amounts of data (one word at a time) through the CPU is a hideous waste of CPU time. After all, the CPU really isn't *processing* anything during a data move—it's just shuttling data from one place to another. If there were a way to "off-load" such redundant tasks from the CPU, data could be moved faster than would be possible with CPU intervention. *Direct Memory Access* (DMA) is a technique designed to move large amounts of data from memory to an I/O location, or vice versa, without direct intervention by the CPU. In theory, the DMA controller chip acts as a stand-alone "data processor," leaving the CPU free to handle other tasks.

A DMA transfer starts with a DMA Request (DRQ) signal generated by the requesting device (such as the floppy disk controller board). If the channel has been previously enabled through software drivers or BIOS routines, the request will reach the corresponding DMA controller chip on the motherboard. The DMA controller will then send a HOLD request to the CPU, which responds with a Hold Acknowledge (HLDA) signal. When the DMA controller receives the HLDA signal, it instructs the bus controller to effectively disconnect the CPU from the expansion bus and allow the DMA controller IC to take control of the bus itself. The DMA controller sends a DMA Acknowledge (DACK) signal to the requesting device, and the transfer process may begin. Up to 64KB can be moved during a single DMA transfer. After the transfer is done, the DMA controller will reconnect the CPU and drop its HOLD request—the CPU then continues with whatever it was doing without interruption.

Table 12-2 illustrates the use of DMA channels for both classic XT and current AT systems. There are twice as many DMA channels available in an AT than an XT, but you may wonder why the AT commits fewer channels. The issue is DMA performance. DMA was developed when CPUs ran at 4.77MHz and is artificially limited to 4MHz operation. When CPUs began to work at 8MHz and higher, CPU transfers

12

TABLE 12-2 XT AND AT DMA ASSIGNMENTS

IBM PC/XT DMA	FUNCTION
0	Dynamic RAM refresh
1	Unused
2	Floppy disk controller board
3	XT hard disk controller board

IBM PC/AT DMA	TRADITIONAL FUNCTION	CURRENT FUNCTION(S)
0	Dynamic RAM refresh	Audio system
1	Unused	Audio system or parallel port
2	Floppy disk controller	Floppy disk controller
3	Unused	ECP parallel port or audio system
4	Reserved (used internally)	Reserved (used internally)
5	Unused	Unused
6	Unused	Unused
7	Unused	Unused

(redundant as they are) actually became *faster* than a DMA channel. As a result, the AT has many channels available, but only the floppy drive controller and other limited-performance devices (such as sound cards) continue to use DMA. In an AT system, DMA channel 4 serves as a cascade line linking DMA controller ICs.

As with interrupts, a DMA channel is selected by setting a physical jumper or DIP switch on the particular expansion board (or through plug-and-play). When the board is installed in an expansion slot, the channel setting establishes a connection between the board and DMA controller chip. Often, accompanying software drivers must use a command-line switch that points to the corresponding hardware DMA assignment. Also, DMA channels cannot be shared between two or more devices. Although DMA sharing is possible in theory, it is extremely difficult to implement in actual practice. If more than one device attempts to use the same DMA channel at the same time, a conflict will result.

I/O AREAS

Both XT and AT computers provide space for I/O (input/output) ports. An *I/O port* acts very much like a memory address, but it's not for storage. Instead, an I/O port provides the means for a PC to communicate directly with a device—allowing the PC to efficiently pass commands and data between the system and various expansion devices. Each device must be assigned to a unique address (or address range). Table 12-3 lists the typical I/O port assignments for classic XT and classic AT systems. PS/2 systems use many of the same address assignments, but also add some wrinkles of their own (as shown in Table 12-4). Finally, the I/O scheme for a recent Pentium-based system is listed in Table 12-5.

TABLE 12-3 XT/AT I/O PORT ADDRESSES

CLASSIC IBM PC/XT SYSTEMS

ADDRESS	RESERVED FOR
000h-00Fh	8237 DMA IC—channels 0-3
020h-021h	8259 Programmable Interrupt Controller IC
040h-043h	8253 System Timer IC
060h-063h	8255 Programmable Peripheral Interface IC
070h,071h	Real-Time Clock/CMOS, NMI mask
080h	POST code port
081h-083h, 087h	DMA Page Registers (0-3)
0A0h	NMI mask register
0C0h-0CFh	Reserved
0E0h-0EFh	Reserved
0F0h-0FFh	Math coprocessor
108h-12Fh	Reserved
130h-13Fh	Available
140h-14Fh	Available
150h-1EFh	Reserved
200h-207h	Game ports
208h-20Bh	Available
20Ch-20Dh	Reserved

TABLE 12-3 XT/AT I/O PORT ADDRESSES *(CONTINUED)*

CLASSIC IBM PC/XT SYSTEMS

ADDRESS	RESERVED FOR
20Eh-21Eh	Available
21Fh	Reserved
220h-22Fh	Available
230h-23Fh	Available
240h-247h	Available
250h-277h	Available
278h-27Fh	Parallel Port 2 or 3 (LPT2 or LPT3)
280h-2AFh	Available
2B0h-2DFh	Alternate EGA ports
2E1h	GPIB port 0 (Adapter 0)
2E2h-2E3h	Data Acquisition port 0 (Adapter 0)
2E4h-2E7h	Available
2E8h-2EFh	Serial port 4 (COM4)
2F8h-2FFh	Serial port 2 (COM2)
300h-31Fh	IBM prototype card
320h-323h	Primary XT HDD controller
324h-327h	Secondary XT HDD controller
328h-32Fh	Available
330h	Available
340h	Available
350h-35Fh	Available
360h-363h	Network card ports (low I/O)
364h-367h	Reserved
368h-36Ah	Network Card Ports (high I/O)
36Ch-36Fh	Reserved
370h-377h	Secondary FDD controller
378h-37Fh	Parallel Port 1 or 2 (LPT1 or LPT2)
380h-38Ch	SDLC 2 (or Bisync 1) ports
390h-393h	Cluster ports (Adapter 0)
394h-3A9h	Available
3A0h-3ACh	SDLC 1 (or Bisync 2) ports
3B0h-3BFh	MDA (monochrome video) port
3BCh-3BFh	First LPT port of monochrome video board
3C0h-3CFh	EGA port
3D0h-3DFh	CGA port
3E0h-3E7h	Available
3E8h-3EFh	Serial Port 3 (COM3)
3F0h-3F7h	Primary FDD controller
3F8h-3FFh	Serial Port 1 (COM1)

TABLE 12-3 XT/AT I/O PORT ADDRESSES *(CONTINUED)*

CLASSIC IBM PC/AT SYSTEMS

ADDRESS	RESERVED FOR
000h-00Fh	DMA Controller IC #1 (channels 0-3)
020h-03Fh	Programmable Interrupt Controller (PIC) IC #1
040h-05Fh	System Timer IC
060h	Keyboard/Mouse controller
061h	System Board I/O port
064h	Keyboard/Mouse controller IC
070h-07Fh	RTC port and NMI mask port
080h	POST code port
081h-08Fh	DMA Page Registers
0A0h-0BFh	Programmable Interrupt Controller IC #2
0C0h-0DEh	DMA Controller IC #2 (channels 4-7)
0F0h-0F8h	Math Coprocessor ports
1F0h-1F8h	Hard Disk Controller Ports
108h-12Fh	Available
130h-13Fh	Available
140h-14Fh	Available
150h-15Fh	Available
170h-177h	Secondary HDD controller
1F0h-1F7h	Primary HDD controller
200h-207h	Game port
208h-20Bh	Available
20Ch-20Dh	Reserved
20Eh-21Eh	Available
21Fh	Reserved
220h-2FFh	Available
230h-23Fh	Available
240h-247h	Available
250h-277h	Available
278h-27Fh	Parallel Printer 2 (LPT2)
280h-2AFh	Available
2B0h-2DFh	Alternate EGA ports
2E0h-2E7h	GPIB (Adapter 0)
2E8h-2EFh	Serial Port 4 (COM4)
2F8h-2FFh	Serial Port 2 (COM2)
300h-31Fh	Available
320h-32Fh	Available
330h	Available
340h	Available
350h-35Fh	Available

TABLE 12-3 XT/AT I/O PORT ADDRESSES *(CONTINUED)*

CLASSIC IBM PC/AT SYSTEMS

ADDRESS	RESERVED FOR
360h-363h	Network card port (low I/O)
364h-367h	Reserved
368h-36Ah	Network card port (high I/O)
36Ch-36Fh	Reserved
370h-377h	Secondary FDD controller
378h-37Fh	Parallel Printer 1 (LPT1)
380h-38Ch	SDLC 2 (or Bisync 1) port
390h-393h	Cluster ports
394h-3A9h	Available
3A0h-3ACh	SDLC 1 (or Bisync 2) port
3B0h-3BFh	Monochrome Display Adapter (MDA) port
3BCh-3BFh	Parallel Printer 3 (LPT3)
3C0h-3CFh	Enhanced Graphics Adapter (EGA) port
3D0h-3DFh	Color Graphics Adapter (CGA) port
3E0h-3E7h	Available
3E8h-3EFh	Serial Port 3 (COM3)
3F0h-3F7h	Primary FDD controller
3F8h-3FFh	Serial Port 1 (COM1)

TABLE 12-4 I/O PORT VARIATIONS FOR PS/2 SYSTEMS

ADDRESS	RESERVED FOR
061h-06Fh	System control port B
090h	Central arbitration control port
091h	Card select feedback
092h	System control port A
094h	System board enable/setup register
096h	Adapter enable/setup register
100h-107h	PS/2 programmable option select
3220h-3227h	COM2
3228h-322Fh	COM3
4220h-3227h	COM4
4228h-322Fh	COM5
5220h-3227h	COM6
5228h-322Fh	COM7

TABLE 12-5 MODERN AT I/O ASSIGNMENTS

ADDRESS	RESERVED FOR
0000h-000Fh	PIIX4—DMA 1
0020h-0021h	PIIX4—Interrupt Controller 1
002Eh-002Fh	Super I/O Controller configuration registers
0040h-0043h	PIIX4—Counter/Timer 1
0048h-004Bh	PIIX4—Counter/Timer 2
0060h	Keyboard Controller byte—Reset IRQ
0061h	PIIX4—NMI, speaker control
0064h	Keyboard Controller, CMD/STAT byte
0070h	(Bit 7) PIIX4—Enable NMI
0070h	(Bits 6-0) PIIX4—Real-Time Clock, address
0071h	PIIX4—Real-Time Clock, data
0078h	Reserved—board configuration
0079h	Reserved—board configuration
0081h-008Fh	PIIX4—DMA Page Registers
00A0h-00A1h	PIIX4—Interrupt Controller 2
00B2h-00B3h	APM Control
00C0h-00DEh	PIIX4—DMA 2
00F0h	Reset Numeric Error
0170h-0177h	Secondary IDE Controller channel
01F0h-01F7h	Primary IDE Controller channel
0200h-0207h	Audio/Game Port
0220h-022Fh	Audio (Sound Blaster compatible)
0240h-024Fh	Audio (Sound Blaster compatible)
0278h-027Fh	LPT2
0290h-0297h	Management extension hardware
02E8h-02EFh	COM4/Video (8514A)
02F8h-02FFh	COM2
0300h-0301h	MPU-401 (MIDI)
0330h-0331h	MPU-401 (MIDI)
0332h-0333h	MPU-401 (MIDI)
0334h-0335h	MPU-401 (MIDI)
0376h	Secondary IDE Channel command port
0377h	Secondary Floppy Channel command port
0378h-037Fh	LPT1
0388h-038Dh	AdLib (FM synthesizer)
03B4h-03B5h	Video (VGA)
03BAh	Video (VGA)
03BCh-03BFh	LPT3
03C0h-03CAh	Video (VGA)
03CCh	Video (VGA)

TABLE 12-5 MODERN AT I/O ASSIGNMENTS *(CONTINUED)*

ADDRESS	RESERVED FOR
03CEh-03CFh	Video (VGA)
03D4h-03D5h	Video (VGA)
03DAh	Video (VGA)
03E8h-03EFh	COM3
03F0h-03F5h	Primary Floppy Channel
03F6h	Primary IDE Channel command port
03F7h	Primary Floppy Channel command port
03F8h-03FFh	COM1
04D0h-04D1h	Edge/level triggered PIC
0530h-0537h	Windows Sound System
0604h-060Bh	Windows Sound System
LPT n + 400h	ECP port, LPT n base address + 400h
0CF8h-0CFBh	PCI Configuration Address Register
0CF9h	Turbo and Reset Control Register
0CFCh-0CFFh	PCI Configuration Data Register
0E80h-0E87h	Windows Sound System
0F40h-0F47h	Windows Sound System
0F86h-0F87h	Yamaha OPL3-SA Configuration
FF00h-FF07h	IDE Bus Master Register
FFA0h-FFA7	Primary Bus Master IDE Registers
FFA8h-FFAFh	Secondary Bus Master IDE Registers

I/O assignments are generally made manually by setting jumpers or DIP switches on the expansion device itself (or automatically through the use of plug-and-play). As with other system resources, it is vitally important that no two devices use the same I/O port(s) at the same time. If one or more I/O addresses overlap, a hardware conflict will result. Commands meant for one device may be erroneously interpreted by another. Keep in mind that while many expansion devices can be set at a variety of addresses, some devices cannot.

MEMORY ASSIGNMENTS

Memory is another vital resource for the PC. While early devices relied on the assignment of IRQ, DMA channels, and I/O ports, most current devices (SCSI controllers, network cards, video boards, modems, etc.) are demanding memory space for the support of each device's onboard BIOS ROM (their firmware). No two ROMs can overlap in their addresses—otherwise, a conflict will occur. Table 12-6 lists a memory map for a modern PC.

INDEX OF TYPICAL ASSIGNMENTS

Now that you've got a handle on the way resources are allocated, it's time to put some of that information to work. Table 12-7 presents a cross-section of typical devices and ports found in today's PCs, and lists the

TABLE 12-6 PENTIUM PC MEMORY MAP

ADDRESS RANGE (DECIMAL)	ADDRESS RANGE (HEX)	SIZE	DESCRIPTION
1024K-262144K	100000-10000000	255MB	Extended Memory
960K-1024K	F0000-FFFFF	64KB	BIOS
944K-960K	EC000-EFFFF	16KB	Boot Block (available as UMB)
936K-944K	EA000-EBFFF	8KB	ESCD (PnP/DMI configuration)
932K-936K	E9000-E9FFF	4KB	Reserved for BIOS
928K-932K	E8000-E8FFF	4KB	OEM Logo or Scan User Flash
896K-928K	E0000-E7FFF	32KB	POST BIOS (available as UMB)
800K-896K	C8000-DFFFF	96KB	Available High DOS memory
640K-800K	A0000-C7FFF	160KB	Video memory and BIOS
639K-640K	9FC00-9FFFF	1KB	Extended BIOS data
512K-639K	80000-9FBFF	127KB	Extended conventional memory
0K-512K	00000-7FFFF	512KB	Conventional memory

standard resource assignments most often associated with them. This may assist you in spotting potential conflicts before installing new devices. Note that you may encounter any combination of resources listed in the table for a given device.

TABLE 12-7 TYPICAL DEVICE ASSIGNMENTS

DEVICE	IRQS	DMA CHANNELS	I/O ADDRESSES
AdLib Sound Device			228h 238h 239h 289h 388h 389h
Aria Synthesizers			280h-288h 290h-298h 2A0h-2A8h 2B0h-2B8h
Drive Controllers FDD1	6	2	03F0h-03F5h
FDD2	6	2	370h-377h
HDD1	14		01F0h-01F7h
HDD2	15		0170h-0177h
Game Port Adapters			201-211h

TABLE 12-8 TYPICAL DEVICE ASSIGNMENTS *(CONTINUED)*

DEVICE	IRQS	DMA CHANNELS	I/O ADDRESSES
Internal Ports COM1	4		03F8h-03FFh
COM2	3		02F8h-02FFh
COM3	4		03E8h-03Efh
COM4	3		02E8h-02Efh
LPT1	7		0378h-037Fh
LPT2	5		0278h-027Fh
LPT3	5		03BCh-03BFh
PS/2 Mouse	12		064h
MPU-401 (MIDI)			300h
(IRQ shared with Sound Blaster)			320h
			330h
Network Interface Cards (NICs)	2	1	280h-283h
	3	3	280h-2FFh
	4	5	2A0h-2A3h
	5	7	2A0h-2BFh
	7		300h-303h
	10		300h-31Fh
	11		320h-323h
			320h-33Fh
			340h-343h
			340h-35Fh
			360h-363h
			360h-37Fh
Reserved System Resources	0	0	
	1	2	
	4		
SCSI host adapters	10	3	130h-14Fh
	11	5	140h-15Fh
	14		220h-23Fh
	15		330h-34Fh
			340h-35Fh
Sound Blaster	5	1	220h-22Eh
(DMA playback)	7	3	240h-24Eh
	9	5	
	10	7	
	11		
Windows Sound System	5	0	530h
(DMA playback)	7	1	E80h
	9	3	530h-F48h
	10		
	11		

12

Recognizing and Dealing with Conflicts

Fortunately, conflicts are almost always the result of a PC upgrade gone awry. Thus, a technician can be alerted to the possibility of a system conflict by applying the Last Upgrade rule. The rule consists of three parts:

1. A piece of hardware and/or software has been added to the system very recently.
2. The trouble occurred *after* a piece of hardware and/or software was added to the system.
3. The system was working fine *before* the hardware and/or software was added.

If all three of these common-sense factors are true, chances are very good that you are faced with a hardware or software conflict (rather than a defective device). Unlike most other types of PC problems, which tend to be specific to the faulty subassembly, conflicts usually manifest themselves as much more general and perplexing problems. The following symptoms are typical of serious hardware or software conflicts:

- The system locks up during the POST or operating system initialization.
- The system locks up during a particular application.
- The system locks up when a particular device (such as a TWAIN scanner) is used.
- The system locks up randomly or without warning regardless of the application.
- The system may not crash, but the device that was added may not function (even though it seems properly configured). Devices that were in the system previously may still work correctly.
- The system may not crash, but a device or application that was working previously no longer seems to function. The newly added device (and accompanying software) may or may not work properly.

What makes these problems so generic is that the severity and frequency of a fault, as well as the point at which the fault occurs, depends on such factors as the particular *devices* that are conflicting, the *resource(s)* that are conflicting among the devices (IRQs, DMAs, or I/O addresses), and the *function* being performed by the PC when the conflict manifests itself. Since every PC is equipped and configured a bit differently, it is virtually impossible to predict a conflict's symptoms more precisely.

CONFIRMING AND RESOLVING CONFLICTS

Recognizing the possibility of a conflict is one thing; proving and correcting it is another issue entirely. However, there are some very effective tactics at your disposal. The first rule of conflict resolution is *Last In First Out* (or LIFO). The LIFO principle basically says that *the fastest means of overcoming a conflict problem is to remove the hardware or software that resulted in the conflict.* In other words, if you install board X and board Y ceases to function, board X is probably conflicting with the system, so removing board X should restore board Y to normal operation. The same concept holds true for software. If you add a new application to your system, then find that an existing application fails to work properly, the new application is likely at fault. Unfortunately, removing the offending element is not enough. You still have to install the new device or software in such a way that it will no longer conflict with the system.

DEALING WITH SOFTWARE CONFLICTS

There are two types of software that can cause conflicts in a typical PC: TSRs and device drivers. *TSRs* (sometimes called *popup utilities*) load into memory, usually during initialization, and wait for a system event (such as a modem ring or a keyboard "hot key" combination). There are no DOS or system rules that define how such utilities should be written. As a result, many tend to conflict with application programs (and even DOS itself). If you suspect that such a popup utility is causing the problem, find its reference in the AUTOEXEC.BAT file and disable it by placing the command REM in front of its command line (for example, REM C:\UTILS\NEWMENU.EXE /A:360 /D:3). The REM command turns the line into a "REMark," which can easily be removed later if you choose to restore the line. Remember to reboot the computer so that your changes will take effect.

Device drivers present another potential problem. Most hardware upgrades require the addition of one or more device drivers. Such drivers are called from the CONFIG.SYS file during system initialization (or are loaded with Windows), and they use a series of command-line parameters to specify the system resources that are being used. This is often necessary to ensure that the driver operates its associated hardware properly. If the command-line options used for the device driver do not match the hardware settings (or overlap the settings of another device driver), system problems can result. If you suspect that a device driver is causing the problem, find its reference in the CONFIG.SYS file and disable it by placing the command REM in front of its command line such as:

```
REM DEVICE = C:\DRIVERS\NEWDRIVE.SYS /A360 /I:5
```

The REM command turns the line into a REMark, which can easily be removed later if you choose to restore the line. Remember that disabling the device driver in this way will prevent the associated hardware from working, but if the problem clears, you can work with the driver settings until the problem is resolved. Remember to reboot the computer so that your changes will take effect.

Finally, consider the possibility that the offending software is buggy or defective. Try contacting the software manufacturer. There may be a fix or undocumented feature that you are unaware of. There may also be a patch or update that will solve the problem.

12

DEALING WITH HARDWARE CONFLICTS

Consider an example: a PC user recently added a CD-ROM and adapter board to her system. The installation went flawlessly using the defaults—a ten-minute job. Several days later when attempting to back up the system, the user noticed that the parallel port tape backup did not respond (although the printer that had been connected to the parallel port was working fine). The user tried booting the system from a clean bootable floppy disk (no CONFIG.SYS or AUTOEXEC.BAT files to eliminate the device drivers), but the problem remained. After a bit of consideration, the user powered down the system, removed the CD-ROM adapter board, and booted the system from a clean bootable floppy disk. Sure enough, the parallel port tape backup started working again.

Stories such as this remind technicians that hardware conflicts are not always the monstrous, system-smashing mistakes that they are made out to be. In many cases, conflicts have subtle, noncatastrophic consequences. Since the CD-ROM was the last device to be added, it was the first to be removed. It took about five minutes to realize and remove the problem. However, removing the problem is only part of conflict troubleshooting—reinstalling the device without a conflict is the real challenge.

Ideally, the way to correct a conflict would be to alter the conflicting setting. That's dynamite in theory, but another thing in practice. The trick is that you need to know what resources are in use and which ones are free. Unfortunately, there are only two ways to find out under DOS. On one hand, you can track down the user manual for every board in the system, then inspect each board individually to find their settings, then work accordingly. This will work (assuming you have the documentation), but it is cumbersome and time consuming.

As an alternative, you can use a resource testing tool such as the Discovery Card (by ForeFront Group). The Discovery Card plugs into a 16-bit ISA slot and uses a series of LEDs to display each IRQ and DMA channel in use. Any LED not illuminated is an available resource. It is then simply a matter of setting your expansion hardware to an IRQ and DMA channel that is not illuminated. Remember that you may have to alter the command-line switches of any device drivers. The only resources *not* illustrated by the Discovery Card are I/O addresses, but since most I/O ports are reserved for particular functions (as you saw in Tables 12-3 to 12-5), you can typically locate an unused I/O port with a minimum of effort.

Determining resources is a bit easier under Windows 95/98 using the Device Manager. When you open the Device Manager, double-click the Computer entry at the top of the device list. The Computer Properties dialog will open. Select the View Resources tab, and you can check the assignments for IRQs, DMA, I/O, or memory. By reviewing these entries, you can quickly determine which resources are assigned and which are free.

Device Manager Error Codes

The Windows 95/98 Device Manager is a powerful resource that's designed to help you inspect the configuration and settings of almost every device in your system. When a problem occurs, the Device Manager can often identify the problem and provide valuable clues that will help you resolve the trouble. Before we start working through the "conflict resolution" process, let's take some time to study the typical Device Manager errors. Check your Device Manager for error codes:

1. Click Start, highlight Settings, and click Control Panel.
2. In the Control Panel, double-click the System icon.
3. Click the Device Manager tab.
4. Double-click a device type (for example, Mouse) to see the devices in that category.
5. Double-click a device to view its Properties dialog.
6. If an error code has been generated, the code appears in the Device Status box on the General tab. In some cases, there will be a Solution button (Windows 98 only).

The codes are listed as follows:

Code 1 "This device is not configured correctly. To update the drivers for this device, click Update Driver." This code means the system has not had a chance to configure the offending device. To resolve the problem, follow the instructions in the Device Status box (usually update the driver). You may also be able to resolve this issue by removing the device in Device Manager and then running the Add New Hardware wizard from Control Panel.

Code 2 You may see either of two different messages (depending on which device is failing). This code means that the device loader (DevLoader) did not load a device. When this device is a Root Bus DevLoader (for example, ISAPNP, PCI, or BIOS), the following message is displayed: "Windows could not load the driver for this device because the computer is reporting two <type> bus types. Contact your computer manufacturer to get an updated BIOS for your computer." The <type> entry designates ISAPNP, PCI, BIOS, EISA, or ACPI. In this case, you should check for an updated BIOS for your system.

When the device is not a root bus DevLoader, the following message is displayed: "The <type> device loader(s) for this device could not load the device driver." The <type> designation is the DevLoader such as FLOP, ESDI, SCSI, and so on. To fix this trouble, click the Update Driver button to update the device driver. In addition, try removing the device from Device Manager, and then run the Add New Hardware wizard to redetect the offending device.

Code 3 "The driver for this device may be bad, or your system may be running low on memory or other resources." Make sure you have sufficient memory and drive space for the devices and software on your system. To check your system's memory and system resources, right-click My Computer on your desktop, click Properties, and then click the Performance tab. If there are adequate resources, try clicking the Update Driver button and update the offending device's driver(s). As an alternative, try using Device Manager to remove the device; then run the Add New Hardware tool in Control Panel.

Code 4 "This device is not working properly because one of its drivers may be bad, or your registry may be bad." This code indicates that the INF file for this device may be incorrect, or the registry may be damaged. This error code is displayed if the INF file specifies a field that should be text, but is binary instead. To update the drivers for this device, click the Update Driver button. If the problem persists, run SCANREGW.EXE to check your registry. Alternately, you can use Device Manager to remove the device, and then run the Add New Hardware wizard to reinstall the device. If you continue to receive this error, contact the hardware manufacturer for an updated INF file.

Code 5 "The driver for this device requested a resource that Windows does not know how to handle." This code indicates that there was a device failure due to the lack of an "arbitrator." If a device requests a resource type for which there is no arbitrator, you'll receive this error code. To resolve this problem, update the device driver, or use Device Manager to remove the device, and then run the Add New Hardware wizard in Control Panel.

Code 6 "Another device is using the resources this device needs." This code means that there's a conflict between this device and another device. To fix this problem, shut down your computer, turn it off, and then change the resources for this device. When you've finished, start Device Manager and change the resource settings for this device.

Code 7 "The drivers for this device need to be reinstalled." This code means that no configuration can be performed on the given device. The message text that is displayed for this error is specific to the driver or enumerator. To reinstall the drivers for this device, click Reinstall Driver and install the latest versions of the device drivers. If the device does not work correctly, use Device Manager to remove the device, and then run the Add New Hardware wizard in Control Panel. If you continue to receive this error code (and the device does not function properly), check with the hardware manufacturer for an updated driver.

Code 8 Several different error messages can be displayed for this error code. If the device loader (DevLoader) for a device cannot be found, you should reinstall or update the driver. As an alternative, use Device Manager to remove the device, and then run the Add New Hardware wizard in Control Panel. If you continue to receive this error code, contact the hardware manufacturer for updated drivers. When the problem DevLoader is a system DevLoader, Windows should be reinstalled because this driver is built into the VMM32.VXD file.

Code 9 The information in the registry for this device is invalid. If this is a BIOS or ACPI enumerated device, the following text is displayed: "This device is not working properly because the BIOS in your computer is reporting the resources for the device incorrectly." Contact your computer manufacturer to get an updated BIOS for your motherboard. If this is not a BIOS or ACPI enumerated device (that is, an add-in adapter or a device that was plugged into the computer), the following text is displayed: "This device is not working properly because the BIOS in the device is reporting the resources for the device incorrectly." Contact the device manufacturer to get an updated firmware version for your offending device.

Code 10 "This device is either not present, not working properly, or does not have all the drivers installed." To resolve this error, make sure the device is connected to the computer correctly. For example, make sure all cables are plugged in fully and that all adapter cards are properly seated. Try upgrading the driver(s) for this device.

Code 11 "Windows stopped responding while attempting to start this device, and therefore will never attempt to start this device again." To work around this error, run the Automatic Skip Driver utility from the System Information tool. If the problem persists, contact the hardware manufacturer for updated drivers.

Code 12 "This device cannot find any free <type> resources to use." This code means that one of the resource arbitrators failed. This can occur if the device is software configurable, and it does not currently have an available resource (that is, all the interrupts are in use, or the device requests a resource that is currently in use by another device that will not release the resource). If you want to use this device, you must disable another device that is using the resources this device needs. To do this, click the Hardware Troubleshooter and follow the instructions in the wizard.

Code 13 "This device is either not present, not working properly, or does not have all the drivers installed." This code indicates that the device driver did not find its related hardware. To have Windows detect whether the device is present, click Detect Hardware. As an alternative, use Device Manager to remove the device, and then run the Add New Hardware wizard in Control Panel.

Code 14 "This device cannot work properly until you restart your computer." To resolve this error, shut down Windows, shut down your computer, and then turn the system back on.

Code 15 "This device is causing a resource conflict." This code means that the device's resources are conflicting with another device's resources—likely caused by reenumeration. To resolve the conflict, use the process outlined in this chapter, or click Hardware Troubleshooter and follow the instructions in the wizard.

Code 16 "Windows could not identify all the resources this device uses." This code means that the device was not fully detected—when a device is not fully detected, all of its resources may not be recorded. To resolve this error code, click the Resources tab in Device Manager to manually enter the resource settings.

Code 17 "The driver information file <name> is telling this child device to use a resource that the parent device does not have or recognize." This code means that the hardware is a multiple-function device, and the INF file for that device is providing invalid information on how to split the device's resources to the child devices. To resolve this error, use the Device Manager to remove the device, and then run the Add New Hardware wizard in Control Panel. If you continue to receive this error code, contact the hardware's manufacturer about an updated INF file.

Code 18 "The drivers for this device need to be reinstalled." This code means that an error has occurred, and the device (and its drivers) needs to be reinstalled. To resolve this issue, reinstall the latest drivers for this device. If you cannot use the Windows 98 Update Drivers button, try removing the device from Device Manager, then running the Add New Hardware wizard in Control Panel.

Code 19 "Your registry may be bad." This code means that your registry returned an unknown result. To resolve this problem, click Check Registry (which will run SCANREG.EXE). If this does not correct the issue, type **scanreg /restore** from a command prompt. Finally, remove the device from Device Manager; then redetect it using the Add New Hardware wizard in Control Panel.

Code 20 "Windows could not load one of the drivers for this device." This code means that the VxD Loader (Vxdldr) returned an unknown result—for example, there might be a version mismatch between the device driver and the operating system. To resolve this issue, download the latest drivers and click Update Driver to update the drivers for this device. If that doesn't work, try removing the device from Device Manager; then redetect it by running the Add New Hardware wizard in Control Panel.

Code 21 "Windows is removing this device." This code means that the device has a problem (usually with initialization) that may be resolved by restarting your computer. To resolve this error, shut down Windows, turn off your computer, wait several seconds, and then turn the system back on.

Code 22 There are several possible errors that may be displayed depending on your particular system configuration and operating circumstances. If the device is disabled because you disabled it using Device Manager, the following text is displayed: "This device is disabled." This code means that the device is either disabled or has not started. Simply click Enable Device to reenable this device. If you cannot reenable the device, it may be damaged. If the device is not started, the following text is displayed: "This device is not started." Just click Start Device to activate this device. If the device is disabled by a driver or program, the following text is displayed: "This device is disabled." However, you can't enable this device here because it's been disabled by a Windows driver. Try removing the device in Device Manager; then redetect it using the Add New Hardware wizard. If the problem persists, try a clean boot to rule out software interference.

Code 23 There are several possible error codes that may appear depending on your particular situation. If the offending device is a secondary display adapter, the following text appears: "This display adapter is functioning correctly. The problem is with the main display adapter." This message means that the device loader delayed the start of a device and then did not inform Windows when it was ready to start the device. Verify the settings for the primary display adapter in Display properties. Try removing the primary and secondary display adapters from Device Manager; then reboot to allow Windows to reenumerate these devices. Verify that the drivers are current and installed correctly.

If the offending device is not a display adapter, the following text appears: "The loaders for this device cannot load the required drivers." To update the device drivers, download the latest drivers, and then click Update Driver. If that does not work, try removing the device from Device Manager, and redetect the device using the Add New Hardware wizard.

Code 24 "This device is either not present, not working properly, or does not have all the drivers installed." Make sure the device is connected to your computer correctly. For example, make sure all cables are correctly installed, or that the adapter cards are properly seated in their slots. To have Windows detect this device, simply click Detect Hardware. If the device is plug-and-play, you may also try upgrading the drivers for this device.

Code 25 "Windows is in the process of setting up this device." This problem typically exists only during the first and second boots after Windows setup copies all the files. So if this code is identified, it is likely to be caused by an incomplete installation. To complete the setup, click Restart Computer to reboot the system. Reinstalling Windows *may* be required if the reboot does not resolve the issue.

Code 26 "Windows is in the process of setting up this device." This error means that a device did not load. There may be a problem in the device driver, or not all of the drivers were installed. Click Restart Computer to reboot the system. Windows should detect the device upon restart. If this does not work, use Device Manager to remove the device; then run the Add New Hardware wizard in Control Panel. If problems persist, check with the hardware's manufacturer for an updated driver.

Code 27 "Windows can't specify the resources for this device." This error indicates that a portion of the registry describing possible resources for a device does not contain valid entries (the device is marked as "configurable," but the configuration information in the INF file is set to "hardwired"). Click the Resources tab, and then select the basic configuration for the resources this device uses. You might also use Device Manager to remove the device, and then run the Add New Hardware wizard in Control Panel. If the device still does not work, consult the hardware's manufacturer for updated drivers or other assistance.

Code 28 "The drivers for this device are not installed." This message means that the device was not installed completely. To reinstall the drivers for this device, click Reinstall Driver. You may need to obtain updated drivers if the error persists.

Code 29 "This device is disabled because the BIOS for the device did not give it any resources." This error means that the device has been disabled because it does not work properly, and cannot be made to work properly with Windows. This code may also be present if the device is intentionally disabled in the BIOS. You may be able to resolve this problem by enabling or disabling the device in the computer's CMOS settings—Windows *cannot* override this setting. Otherwise, the offending device may be defective and needs to be replaced.

Code 30 "This device is using an Interrupt Request (IRQ) resource that is in use by another device and cannot be shared. You must change the conflicting setting or remove the real-mode driver causing the conflict." This message indicates that an IRQ cannot be shared. This may occur when a PCI/EISA SCSI controller is sharing an IRQ that is also in use by a real-mode device driver that Windows cannot change. To resolve this problem, remove the real-mode driver that is using the same IRQ as this device. (The real-mode driver may be loading in your CONFIG.SYS or AUTOEXEC.BAT file.)

Code 31 "This device is not working properly because <device> is not working properly." This code appears when one device is dependent upon another device to be functioning correctly. (This does not include devices that are enumerated by the parent device.) The <device> is the dependent device that must be fixed in order for this device to work properly. The Properties button displays the properties for the other device. More than likely, the other device will also have one of these Device Manager error codes. Follow all the recommended solutions offered by the error dialog. If the devices still do not work, remove them both from the Device Manager, and then use the Add New Hardware wizard to redetect them. Finally, consult with the hardware manufacturer(s) for updated drivers.

Code 32 "Windows cannot install the drivers for this device because it cannot access the drive or network location that has the setup files on it." This code indicates that the installation disk or CD was not available to install the drivers (that is, the CD-ROM drive or network connection is not available). This error typically occurs during the first or second reboot after all the files are copied during setup. To correct this problem, click Restart Computer to reboot the system. If that doesn't help, copy all the setup files onto your local hard disk, and run setup from there. If the problem persists, determine why the installation disk or CD is not available. Typically, these devices will also have Device Manager codes (such as the CD-ROM controller or network adapter).

Code 33 The message text that is displayed for this error is specific to the driver or enumerator. If the driver does not provide information as to why it did not work, the following message is displayed: "This device isn't responding to its driver." This code typically is displayed when the hardware has failed. Recheck the hardware installation, and replace the defective device if necessary.

CONFLICT TROUBLESHOOTING WITH WINDOWS 95/98

One of the biggest problems with conflict troubleshooting is that every conflict situation is a bit different. Variations in PC equipment and available resources often reduce conflict troubleshooting to a hit-or-miss process. Fortunately, conflict troubleshooting can be accomplished quickly and easily using the tools provided by Windows 95/98 (namely, the Device Manager). This part of the chapter provides a step-by-step process that you can use for conflict resolution under Windows 95/98.

> The steps described below should be read like a flow chart, and you'll find many references that will take you back and forth to various steps throughout this section.

Step 1: Getting started Start the Device Manager in Windows 95/98:

1. Click the Start button, click Settings, and then select Control Panel.
2. Double-click the System icon, and then click on the Device Manager tab (Figure 12-1).
3. Make sure "View devices by type" is selected.

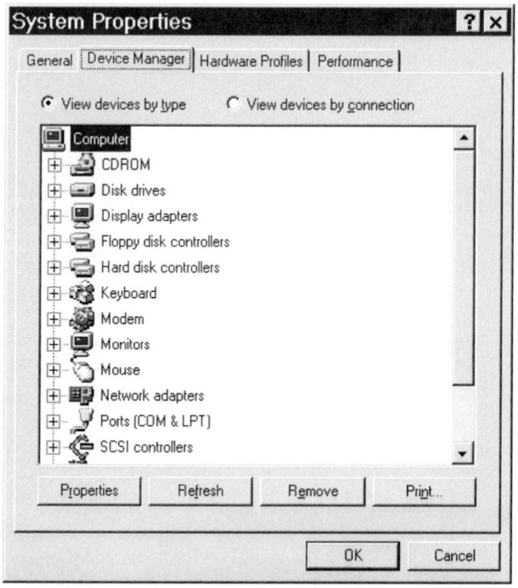

FIGURE 12-1 The Device Manager dialog

The hardware suffering from a conflict should be shown in the device list. If the hardware that has the conflict isn't visible in the list, click the plus sign (+) next to the type of hardware.

Check to see if the device was installed twice. Is the device you were installing (or that suffers from the conflict) listed twice in Device Manager?

- If the device is listed only once, go to Step 2.
- If the device is listed twice, and there's only supposed to be one such device in the system, go to Step 3.
- If the device is listed twice, but there are supposed to be two such devices in the system, go to Step 2.

Step 2: Device listed only once View the resource settings for the conflicting device:

1. Double-click on the hardware that shows a conflict. Its Properties dialog should open with the General tab selected.
2. In the Device Usage area, make sure there is a check in the box next to the configuration marked "Current." If the box isn't checked, check the box now. Under Windows 98, the "Disable in this hardware profile" box should be unchecked (Figure 12-2).
3. Click the Resources tab.

Do you see a box with resource settings (as in Figure 12-3)? Check to see if the "Conflicting device list" has any entries that indicate a problem.

- If the box with resource settings appears, go to Step 4.
- If the Set Configuration Manually button appears instead, go to Step 5.
- If the device doesn't have a Resources tab, go to Step 6.

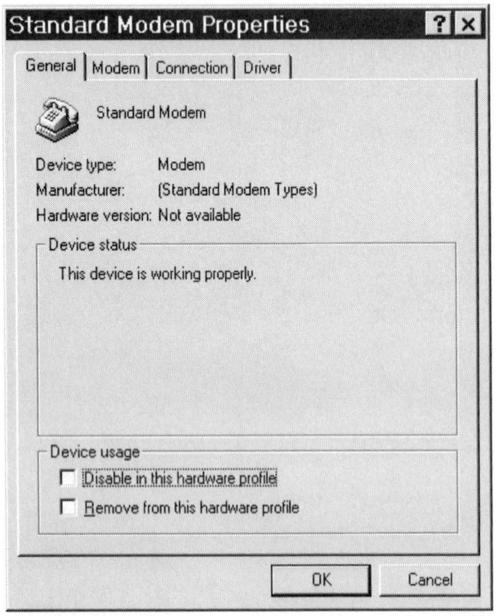

FIGURE 12-2 Checking the usage of a typical device

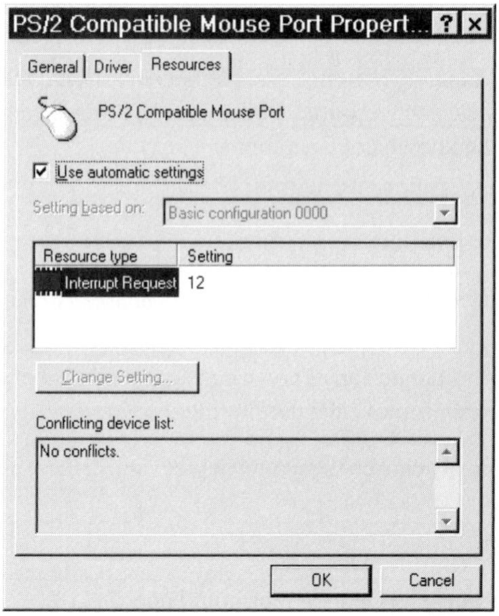

FIGURE 12-3 Checking for conflicting devices

Step 3: Device listed twice Remove all instances of the duplicated device(s), and install the device again:

1. Remove each duplicate item from the hardware list. Click its name, and then click Remove. When you are finished, no instances of the conflicting hardware should be listed.
2. Click OK.
3. Now (while still within the Control Panel), double-click on the Add New Hardware icon. If you see a message that you already have a wizard open, click Finish in that wizard, and then click the button in this step to start a new wizard.
4. Click Next.
5. Click the option to automatically detect your hardware, and then click Next. Continue until you finish with the wizard.

Did this fix the problem?

- If the conflict no longer appears, this should correct the problem, and you should be done. Exit the Control Panel and restart Windows 95/98.
- If the conflict still appears, go to Step 2.

Step 4: Resource settings appear You'll need to identify exactly *which* resources are causing the conflict. In the Conflicting Device List box, identify the hardware that is using conflicting resources. Determine whether more than one resource conflict is listed.

- If more than one resource conflict is listed, go to Step 7.
- If only one conflict is listed, go to Step 8.
- If no conflicts are listed, or if one or more indications show System Reserved as the conflict, go to Step 9.

Step 5: Manual button appears Determine why the resources are not displayed:

1. When the Resources tab shows a Set Configuration Manually button, it is either because the device has a conflict or other problem and is disabled, or because the resource settings used by this device are working properly but they don't match any of the known configurations.
2. You can tell which situation applies by reading the text above the button.

Which text message do you see?

- If you see a message that reads "The device is conflicting, or the device is not currently enabled or has a problem," go to Step 10.
- If you see a message that reads "The resource settings don't match any known configurations," there is no further solution to the problem. You should probably remove the conflicting device.

Step 6: There is no Resources tab You have probably chosen the wrong device. Select the correct device:

1. Click Cancel to return to the hardware list.
2. Carefully double-click the hardware that has a conflict. The General tab should appear.
3. In the Device Usage area, make sure there is a check in the box next to the configuration marked "Current." If the box isn't checked, check it now. Under Windows 98, the "Disable in this hardware profile" box should be unchecked (Figure 12-2).
4. Click the Resources tab.

Do you see a box with resource settings now?

- If the box with resource settings now appears, go to Step 4.
- If you see a Set Configuration Manually button, go to Step 5.
- If the resource settings still do not appear, there is no further solution to the problem. You should probably remove the conflicting device.

Step 7: More than one conflict is listed At this point, you should determine just how many devices are listed as being conflicting.

- If you only see one device causing all the conflicts, go to Step 11.
- If more than one device is causing the conflicts, go to Step 12.

Step 8: Only one conflict is listed Look for a resource setting that doesn't conflict:

1. In the Resource Settings box, double-click the icon next to the resource setting that is *conflicting*. If you see a message that reads "you must clear the Use Automatic Settings box before you can change a resource setting," click OK to close the message, and then clear the Use Automatic Settings box.
2. Scroll through the available resource settings.
3. For each setting, look at the Conflicting Device List box to see if it conflicts with any other hardware.
4. If you find a free setting, click OK.

Did you find a setting that doesn't conflict with any other hardware?

- If you can find a setting that does not conflict, go to Step 13.
- If you cannot find a setting that does not conflict, go to Step 14.
- If you see a message stating that the resource setting cannot be modified, go to Step 15.

Step 9: No conflicts are listed If there are no conflicts listed in the Conflicting Device List box, either you are not viewing resources for the correct device, or the conflict has already been resolved. (You need to restart your computer to allow Windows 95/98 to configure the hardware.) Look at the top of the dialog box to see if you're viewing resources for the correct device.

There is no further solution to this problem. If restarting Windows 95/98 does not clear the problem, you may simply need to remove the conflicting device.

Step 10: The device is conflicting Now you need to identify which hardware is conflicting:

1. Click Set Configuration Manually. In Windows 98, clear the "Use automatic settings" box.
2. In the Conflicting Device List box, identify the other hardware that is using the conflicting resources.

Is more than one resource conflict listed?

- If more than one resource conflict is listed, go to Step 16.
- If only one resource conflict is listed, go to Step 17.
- If no conflicts are listed, go to Step 9.

Step 11: Only one device is conflicting Do you want to disable the device that is causing all the conflicts?

- If you wish to disable the conflicting device, go to Step 18.
- If you must use the hardware that is causing the conflicts, go to Step 17.

Step 12: More than one device is conflicting Look for resource settings that don't conflict:

1. In the Resource Settings box, double-click the icon next to a resource setting that is conflicting. If you see a message that reads "you must clear the Use Automatic Settings box before you can change a resource setting," click OK to close the message, and then clear the Use Automatic Settings box.
2. Scroll through the available resource setting(s).
3. For each setting, look in the Conflicting Device List box to see if it conflicts with any other hardware.
4. When you find a free setting, click OK.
5. Repeat steps 1 through 4 for each conflicting resource.

Did you find a free setting for each conflicting resource?

- If you do find free settings for each conflicting resource, go to Step 19.
- If some (or all) resources are still conflicting, go to Step 20.
- If you see a message indicating that the resource setting cannot be modified, go to Step 15.

Step 13: There is a free setting When a free setting is available, change the configuration:

1. Enter the new setting value.
2. Make a note of the old and new settings to refer to later.
3. Click OK. If you see a message prompting you to restart your computer, click No.

> Depending on the type of hardware you have, you may have to change the jumpers on your hardware card to match the new setting(s), or you may have to run a configuration utility provided by your hardware manufacturer. If the jumper settings on your card aren't set properly, your hardware will not work, even if you resolved the conflict correctly. Refer to your hardware documentation for instructions on changing jumpers.

Restart your computer:

1. Click OK.
2. You may see a message prompting you to restart your computer. Click No.
3. Click the Start button, click Shut Down, and then click Yes.
4. When Windows says it is safe to do so, turn off your computer so you can configure the hardware devices that you've changed.

This should correct the problem, and the hardware conflict should now be resolved once the PC is restarted.

Step 14: All other settings conflict Identify hardware you no longer need:

1. Scroll through the available resource settings.
2. When a conflict appears in the Conflicting Device List box, determine whether you still need to use the device that is causing the conflict.

Can you identify a hardware device that you no longer need to use?

- If you can disable the conflicting device, go to Step 21.
- If you cannot disable the conflicting device, go to Step 22.

Step 15: Resource settings cannot be modified View the resources for the other device:

1. In the Conflicting Device List box, make a note of which device is using the resource that cannot be modified.
2. Click Cancel.
3. In the hardware list, find and double-click the device that is using the resource.

Does this device have a Resources tab?

- If a Resources tab is available, go to Step 23.
- If a Resources tab is not available, go to Step 24.

Step 16: There is more than one conflict How many devices are listed as *conflicting*?

- If only one device is causing the conflicts, go to Step 11.
- If more than one device is causing the conflicts, go to Step 12.

Step 17: There is only one conflict Look for a resource setting that doesn't conflict:

1. In the Resource Settings box, double-click the icon next to the resource setting that is conflicting. If you see a message that reads "you must clear the Use Automatic Settings box before you can change a resource setting," click OK to close the message, and then clear the Use Automatic Settings box.
2. Scroll through the available resource settings.
3. For each setting, look in the Conflicting Device List box to see if it conflicts with any other hardware.
4. If you find a free setting, click OK.

Did you find a setting that doesn't conflict with any other hardware?

- If you manage to find a setting that does not conflict, go to Step 13.
- If you see a message indicating that the resource setting cannot be modified, go to Step 15.
- If all other settings conflict with other hardware, there is no further solution to the problem, and you should probably remove the conflicting device.

Step 18: Disable conflicting hardware Determine how to best disable the conflicting hardware:

1. On the hardware list, double-click the hardware that you want to disable. If you do not see the hardware list, click Cancel until you return to it.
2. In the Device Usage area, click the box next to the configuration marked "Current" to remove the check mark. Under Windows 98, the "Disable in this hardware profile" box should be unchecked (Figure 12-2).
3. Click the Resources tab. If there is a Set Configuration Manually button, Windows 95/98 can disable and free up resources used by this hardware *without* your removing its card from your computer.

Do you see a Set Configuration Manually button?

- If the button exists, you can effectively disable the device, so go to Step 19.
- If the button is not available, go to Step 25.

Step 19: Resources now set without conflicts Print out a report for each device you changed:

1. In the hardware list, click a device whose resource settings you changed while resolving the conflict. If you do not see the hardware list, click OK until you return to it.
2. Click Print.
3. Click the second option to print the selected class or device.
4. Click OK.
5. Repeat steps 1 through 4 for each device that you changed during this troubleshooting process.

This should correct the problem, and you should be done.

Step 20: Some resources are still conflicting Set resources to conflict with only one device:

1 Double-click a resource that is still conflicting. If you see a message that reads "you must clear the Use Automatic Settings box before you can change a resource setting," click OK to close the message, and then clear the Use Automatic Settings box.
2 Scroll through the available resource settings. For each value, write down the setting and the name of the hardware it conflicts with. Then click Cancel.
3 Repeat steps 1 and 2 for each conflicting resource.
4 Looking at the list, see if you can change the resource settings so they conflict with only one device—*preferably* one you could disable.

Are all conflicts with one device?

- If all the conflicts are with only one device, go to Step 21.
- If resources still conflict with more than one device, there is no further solution to the problem, and you should probably remove the conflicting device.

Step 21: Disable the unneeded device Determine whether the hardware you want to disable is plug-and-play:

1 Select each resource setting that conflicts with the hardware you will disable, and then click OK.
2 When the message appears saying the setting conflicts with another device, click Yes to continue.
3 Click OK until you return to the hardware list.
4 Click the plus sign (+) next to the type of hardware that you want to disable.
5 Double-click the hardware that you want to disable.
6 In the Device Usage area, click the box next to the configuration marked "Current" to remove the check mark. Under Windows 98, the "Disable in this hardware profile" box should be unchecked (Figure 12-2).
7 Click the Resources tab.
8 If there is a Set Configuration Manually button, Windows 95 can disable and free up resources used by this hardware *without* your removing its card from your computer.

Do you see a Set Configuration Manually button?

- If the button exists, you can effectively disable the device, so go to Step 19.
- If the button is not available, go to Step 25.

Step 22: All devices are in use Write down a list of all devices using resources:

1 Scroll through the resource settings. On a piece of paper, write down the name of each piece of conflicting hardware and its setting.
2 Click Cancel until you return to the hardware list.

Rearrange resource settings for conflicting hardware:

1. On the hardware list, click the plus sign (+) next to the hardware type for the first item on your written list.
2. Double-click the hardware.
3. Click the Resources tab.
4. Double-click the resource setting that you wrote down. If you see a message that reads "you must clear the Use Automatic Settings box before you can change a resource setting," click OK to close the message, and then clear the Use Automatic Settings box.
5. Scroll through the available resource settings. For each setting, look in the Conflicting Device List box to see if it conflicts with any other hardware.
6. If you find a free setting other than the one you wrote down, write down the new values, and continue.
7. If you do not find a free setting, repeat steps 1 through 5 until you run out of hardware to try or you find a free setting.

Did you find a free resource setting?

- If you found free resources, go to Step 26.
- If you could not locate free resources, go to Step 27.

Step 23: Resource information is available Check to see if the device can use a different resource:

1. Click the Resources tab.
2. In the Resource Settings box, double-click the resource setting that you need to free for the other device. If you see a message that reads "you must clear the Use Automatic Settings box before you can change a resource setting," click OK to close the message, and then clear the Use Automatic Settings box.
3. Scroll through the available resource settings.
4. For each setting, look in the Conflicting Device List box to see if it conflicts with any other hardware.
5. If you find a free setting, click OK. If you see a message prompting you to restart your computer, click No.

Did you find a free resource setting?

- If yes, go to Step 28.
- If no (or the settings cannot be modified), go to Step 29.

Step 24: Resource information is not available Decide which device you should disable. Because both devices need to use the same resource setting, you must decide which device you want to use. You must disable and/or remove the other device. It probably is easier to remove the device that had the original conflict. If you choose to remove the *other* device, you may see a message telling you that you still have a conflict after completing the procedure. Just restart the procedure and continue resolving the conflict.

Which device would you like to disable?

- If you'd rather disable the original device, go to Step 30.
- If you'd rather disable the other conflicting device, go to Step 31.

Step 25: Manual button not available Disable the conflicting hardware by removing it:

1. On the hardware list, click the plus sign (+) next to the type of hardware that you want to disable. If you do not see the hardware list, click Cancel until you return to it.
2. Click the hardware you want to disable.
3. Click Remove.

Go to Step 19.

Step 26: Free resources found Change the resource settings to utilize the free resources:

1. Save the new setting by clicking OK and then clicking OK again.
2. If you see a message about restarting your computer, click No.
3. Double-click the hardware that first had the conflict.
4. Click the Resources tab.
5. Double-click the resource that is conflicting. If you see a message that reads "you must clear the Use Automatic Settings box before you can change a resource setting," click OK to close the message, and then clear the Use Automatic Settings box.
6. Change the resource setting to the value you just freed. The Conflicting Device List box may show a conflict with the other hardware that you just changed.
7. Click OK. If you see a message, click Yes to continue.

Go to Step 19.

Step 27: No free resources available You must disable some hardware to relieve the conflict. Do you want to disable the hardware that caused the original conflict?

- If you want to disable the hardware that originally caused the conflict, go to Step 18.
- If you must use all of the hardware in the system, there is no further solution to the problem since the conflict cannot be resolved.

Step 28: Free setting found Determine whether there are any remaining conflicts:

1. Click OK to return to the hardware list.
2. Double-click the device that had the original conflict.
3. Click the Resources tab.
4. See if there are any remaining conflicts listed in the Conflicting Device List box.

> If the conflict you just resolved is listed, you can ignore it. It will no longer conflict after you restart your computer later.

Are there still conflicts listed?

- If all the resources are now set without any conflicts, go to Step 19.
- If some or all of the resources are still conflicting, go to Step 20.

Step 29: No free setting found You must decide which device to disable. Because both devices need to use the same resource setting, you must decide which device you want to use. You must disable and remove the other device. It probably is easier to remove the device that had the original conflict at this point. If you choose to remove the other device, you may see a message telling you that you still have a conflict after you finish and restart your computer. Just restart this procedure and continue resolving the conflict.

Which device would you like to disable?

- If you choose to disable the device with the original conflict, go to Step 30.
- If you choose to disable the other device that it is conflicting with, go to Step 31.

Step 30: Disable original conflicting device Determine whether you have to remove the card to disable the hardware:

1. On the hardware list, double-click the hardware that you want to disable. If you do not see the hardware list, click Cancel until you return to it.
2. In the Device Usage area, make sure there is a check in the box next to the configuration marked "Current." If the box isn't checked, check it now. Under Windows 98, the "Disable in this hardware profile" box should be unchecked (Figure 12-2).
3. Click the Resources tab. If there is a Set Configuration Manually button, Windows 95 can free up resources for this hardware without your removing its card from your computer.

When you see a Set Configuration Manually button: if you do see that button, and there are no resource settings listed in the box, you'll need to restart your computer.

1. Click OK, and then click OK again.
2. You may be prompted to restart your computer. Click Yes.

When you don't see a Set Configuration Manually button: if no button is available, you'll need to disable the physical hardware by removing it from the system.

1. On the hardware list, click the plus sign (+) next to the type of hardware that you want to disable. If you do not see the hardware list, click Cancel until you return to it.
2. Click the hardware you want to disable.
3. Click Remove, and then click OK.
4. You may be prompted to restart your computer. You will have to remove the card for this hardware from your computer, so you need to shut down instead of restarting. Click No.

5. Click the Start button, click Shut Down, and then click Yes. When the message says it is safe to do so, turn off your computer and remove the card from your computer.
6. Restart your PC and check to see if your problem has been resolved.

This should correct the conflict and complete your troubleshooting procedure.

Step 31: Disable other conflicting device Determine whether you have to remove the card to disable the hardware:

1. On the hardware list, double-click the hardware that you want to disable. If you do not see the hardware list, click Cancel until you return to it.
2. In the Device Usage area, click the box next to the configuration marked "Current" to remove the check mark. Under Windows 98, the "Disable in this hardware profile" box should be checked (Figure 12-2).
3. Click the Resources tab. If there is a Set Configuration Manually button, Windows 95 can free up resources for this hardware without your removing its card from your computer.

Do you see a Set Configuration Manually button?

- If you see the button, go to Step 32.
- If you don't see the button, go to Step 33.

Step 32: Disable the other device Determine whether there are any remaining conflicts:

1. Click OK to return to the hardware list.
2. Double-click the device that had the original conflict.
3. Click the Resources tab.
4. See if there are any remaining conflicts listed in the Conflicting Device List box. If the conflict you just resolved is listed, you can ignore it. It will no longer conflict after you restart your computer later.

Are there still conflicts listed?

- If there are no further conflicts, go to Step 19.
- If one or more conflicts are still listed, go to Step 34.

Step 33: Remove the other device Disable hardware by removing it:

1. On the hardware list, click the plus sign (+) next to the type of hardware that you want to disable. If you do not see the hardware list, click Cancel until you return to it.
2. Click the hardware you want to disable.
3. Click Remove.

Go to Step 19.

Step 34: There are still some conflicts Try setting resources to conflict with only one device:

1. Double-click a resource that is still conflicting. If you see a message that reads "you must clear the Use Automatic Settings box before you can change a resource setting," click OK to close the message, and then clear the Use Automatic Settings box.
2. Scroll through the available resource settings. For each value, write down the setting and the name of the hardware it conflicts with; then click Cancel.
3. Repeat steps 1 and 2 for each conflicting resource.
4. Looking at the list, see if you can change the resource settings so they conflict with only one device—preferably one you could disable.

Are all conflicts now with one device?

- When all the conflicts are with only one device, go to Step 11.
- If the resources still conflict with more than one device (or cannot be changed), there is no further solution to this problem, and you should probably remove the conflicting device.

THE ROLE OF PLUG-AND-PLAY (PNP)

Traditional PCs used devices that required manual configuration—each IRQ, DMA, I/O port, and memory address space had to be specifically set through jumpers on the particular device. If you accidentally configured two or more devices to use the same resource, a conflict would result. This would require you to isolate the offending device(s), identify available resources, and reconfigure the offending device(s) manually. Taken together, this was often a cumbersome and time-consuming process.

In the early 1990s, PC designers realized that it was possible to automate the process of resource allocation each time the system initializes. This way, a device need only be installed, and the system would handle its configuration and assign available resources without the assistance or intervention of the installer. This concept became known as *plug-and-play* (PnP) and has long been standard in the PC arena. PnP systems require three elements in order to function:

- PnP-compliant devices (such as video boards, modems, and drive controllers)
- PnP-compliant BIOS (now used in all Pentium-class systems)
- PnP-compliant operating systems (such as Windows 95/98)

When the PnP system works properly, a PnP device can be installed in an available expansion slot on a PnP-supported motherboard (with a PnP BIOS). When Windows 95/98 starts, it recognizes the new PnP device, assigns resources, and then attempts to install the proper protected-mode driver (which could be installed from a manufacturer's floppy disk or a Windows 95/98 installation CD). Thereafter, the system "remembers" the new device and reconfigures it each time the system starts. Ideally, if the PnP device is ever removed, Windows 95/98 would automatically clear the device from its "system," and free the resources for other devices.

However, if any of these elements is missing, devices will not be autoconfigured. For example, PnP won't work under DOS (though there are DOS PnP drivers that can be used to initialize PnP devices). Older, jumper-configured devices (called *legacy devices*) also won't support PnP, and resources need to be reserved for legacy devices in order to prevent the PnP system from ignoring them entirely.

PnP autoconfiguration information is stored in the Extended System Configuration Data (ESCD) area and is cleared when the CMOS RAM is cleared or lost.

KEEP YOUR NOTES

Having determined the IRQ, DMA, and I/O settings that are in use, a thorough technician will note each setting on paper, then tape the notes inside the system's enclosure. This extra step will greatly ease future expansion and troubleshooting.

Further Study

Data Depot: **http://www.datadepo.com/datadepo.htm**

Download MSD 2.11: **http://support.microsoft.com/download/support/mslfiles/GA0363.EXE**

The Discovery Card: **http://www.ffg.com/pcproducts/discover.html**

Windsor Technologies: **http://www.windsortech.com/**

13

CPU IDENTIFICATION AND TROUBLESHOOTING

CHAPTER AT A GLANCE

The *central processing unit* (also called a *CPU*, *microprocessor*, or simply a *processor*) has become one of the most important developments ever realized in integrated circuit technology (Figure 13-1). On the surface, a CPU is a rather boring device. In spite of its relative complexity, a typical CPU only performs three general functions: mathematical calculations, logical comparisons, and data manipulation. This isn't a very big repertoire for a device carrying well over 20 million transistors. When you look deeper, however, you realize that it is not the *number* of functions that makes a CPU so remarkable, but that each function is carried out as part of a program that the CPU reads and follows. By changing the program, the activities of a CPU could be completely rearranged without modifying the computer's circuitry.

Once the concept of a generic central processing function was born, designers realized that the same system could be used to solve an incredibly diverse array of problems (given the right set of instructions). This was the quantum leap in thinking that gave birth to the modern computer and created the two domains that we know today as *hardware* and *software*. As you might have guessed, the idea of central processing is hardly new. The very earliest computers of the late 1940s and 1950s applied this concept to simple programs stored on punched cards or paper tape. The mainframe and minicomputers of the 1960s and 1970s also followed the central processing concept. However, it was the integration of central processing functions onto a *single* IC (the *microprocessor chip*) in the mid-1970s that made the first "personal" computers possible and spawned the explosive developments in CPU speed and performance that we have seen ever since.

Although a CPU can handle mathematical calculations, the CPU itself was not (until recently) designed to handle floating-point math as an internal function. Of course, floating-point math was possible through software emulation, but the performance of such an approach was unacceptable for math-intensive applications (such as CAD, scientific programs, and 3D graphic calculations). In order to deal with high-performance floating-point math in hardware, a *math coprocessor* (MCP) or *numerical processing unit* (NPU) was developed to work in conjunction with the CPU. Although the classical MCP

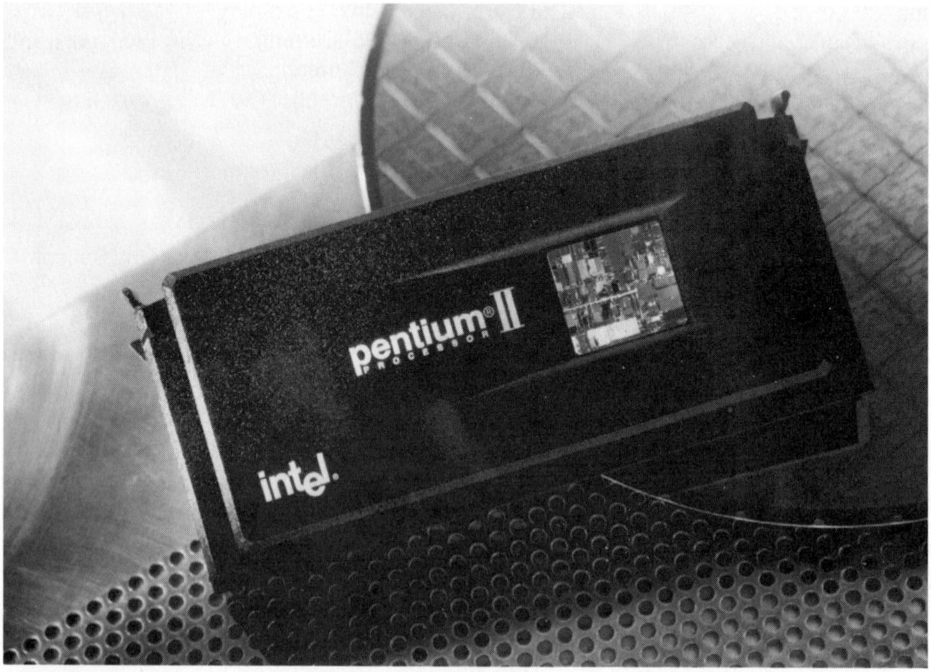

FIGURE 13-1 An Intel Pentium II processor

was implemented as a stand-alone device (such as the Intel 8087, 80287, and 80387), newer generations of CPU incorporate the MCP's functions right into the CPU itself. You'll find that all current processors incorporate MCP features.

The CPU is closely related to the overall speed and performance of personal computers. As a technician, you should understand the essential specifications and characteristics of CPUs. This chapter is intended to provide some insights into CPU evolution and capabilities, and to illustrate some of the problems that can manifest themselves in microprocessor operation.

The Basic CPU

A generic microprocessor can be represented by a block diagram such as the one in Figure 13-2. As you can see, there are several sets of signals (or *busses*) that you should be familiar with: the *data bus*, the *address bus*, and the *control bus*. It is these three busses that allow the CPU to communicate with the other elements of the PC and control its operations.

THE BUSSES

The data bus carries information to and from the CPU, and it is perhaps the most familiar yardstick of CPU performance. The number of wires in the bus represents the number of bits (or data volume) that can be carried at any point in time. Data lines are typically labeled with a *D* prefix (D0, D1, D2, D*n*, etc.). The size of a data bus is typically 8, 16, 32, or 64 bits. As you might expect, larger data busses are preferred because they allow more data to be transferred faster.

In order for the CPU to read or write data, it must be able to specify the precise I/O port or location in system memory. "Locations" are defined through the use of an address bus. The number of bits in the address bus represent the number of physical locations that the CPU can access. For example, a CPU with 20 address lines can address 2^{20} (1,048,576) bytes. A CPU with 25 address lines can address 2^{24} (16,777,216) bytes, and so on. Address lines are generally represented with an *A* prefix (A0, A1, A19, etc.).

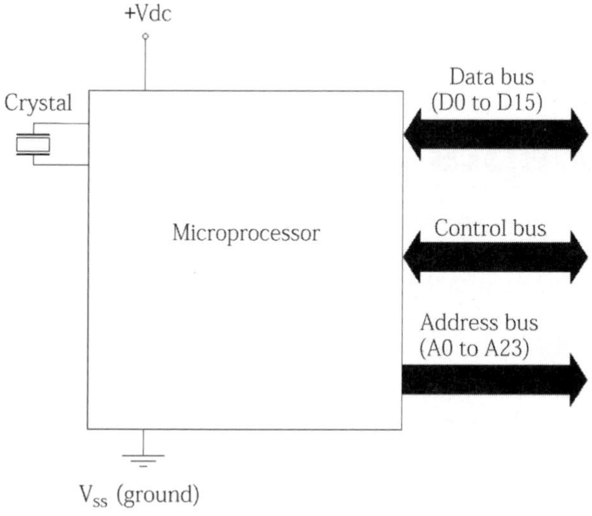

FIGURE 13-2 Diagram of a generic CPU

Control signals are used to synchronize and coordinate the operation of a CPU with other devices in the computer. Although the number and use of each control signal varies a bit from generation to generation, most control signals fall into several categories:

- Reading or writing functions (to memory or I/O locations)
- Interrupt channels
- CPU test and reset
- Bus arbitration and control
- DMA control
- CPU status
- Parity checking
- Cache operation

ADDRESSING MODES

When you consider a microprocessor, you must also consider the means it uses to address its memory. As you will see later in this chapter, the original Intel CPUs (such as the 8088 and 8086) used only 20 address lines (labeled A0 to A19). With 20 address lines, the CPU can access only one million addresses (actually, 1,048,576 addresses). Technically, this was not a problem, and DOS was written to work within this 1MB of space. Unfortunately, when newer CPUs were designed to break the 1MB memory barrier, DOS was stuck with this 1MB limitation (although more sophisticated software such as DOS extenders and extended memory managers allow DOS programs to access memory areas above 1MB).

To maintain backward compatibility with older CPUs, newer CPUs can operate in one of two modes. In the *real mode*, a CPU behaves like an 8088/8086, and will only access up to 1MB. DOS and DOS programs operate in the real mode exclusively. Newer operating systems (such as Windows 95/98 and OS/2) allow a CPU to utilize *all* of its address lines when accessing memory. This is known as *protected-mode* operation. Protected-mode operation not only supports *much* greater amounts of physical memory, but it also supports *virtual memory*. When a program calls for more memory than actually exists in a system, the CPU is able to swap code between memory and the hard drive—in effect, your hard drive space can be used to simulate extra RAM. The software running on a CPU in protected mode can be far more sophisticated than real-mode programs.

Modern CPU Concepts

There is a lot more to CPU technology than just busses and addressing modes—in fact, there are entire books written on CPUs. We won't get into many of those concepts in this book, but there are a wide range of concepts that you *should* understand when working with today's PCs.

THE P-RATING (PR) SYSTEM

CPUs are traditionally classified by their clock speed. For example, a 650MHz Pentium III is generally regarded as a better-performing CPU than a 550MHz Pentium III. However, this presents unique and perplexing marketing problems for competing CPU manufacturers. Even though Intel continues to lead CPU development, other CPU makers like AMD and Cyrix are keeping the pressure on by packing more performance into fewer clock cycles. Unfortunately, it is difficult for an everyday user to understand that a non-Intel CPU at a given clock speed can perform as well as an Intel processor at another clock speed. In early 1996, Cyrix, IBM Microelectronics, and SGS Thomson (all Intel competitors) gathered to create the P-rating (or PR) system for describing their CPUs. By using a "PR" designation, a CPU can be equated to an Intel Pentium. As an example, the AMD 133MHz Am5x86 processor is marked PR75, and performs comparably to an Intel 75MHz Pentium. When the rating includes a "+" or "++" suffix (as in PR75++), it means that the CPU is delivering *better* performance than the corresponding Intel part. P-ratings are determined through a method of direct comparison:

- The Winstone benchmark is run on a specifically configured PC system powered by an Intel processor of a given clock speed.
- The Intel processor is removed from the system and replaced with a competing processor. The Winstone benchmark is run again and a second Winstone score is obtained from the same system now running the competing processor. The system configuration remains identical, and all peripherals are carefully documented.
- The competing processor is assigned the highest P-rating at which it delivers Winstone scores equal to or greater than a given Pentium. For example, if an AMD K5 processor delivers performance equal to or better than a 90MHz Pentium, it receives a P-rating of 90 (or PR90).

CPU SOCKETS

Another important idea in CPU development and upgradability is the concept of *sockets*. Each generation of CPU uses a different number of pins (and pin assignments), so a different physical socket must be used on the motherboard to accommodate each new generation of processor. Early CPUs were not readily interchangeable, and upgrading a CPU typically meant upgrading the motherboard. With the introduction of the i486 CPUs, the notion of "OverDrive" processors became popular—replacing an existing CPU with a pin-compatible replacement processor that operated at higher internal clock speeds to enhance system performance. Table 13-1 shows that the earliest sockets were designated Socket 1 for early 486SX and DX processors. (You can see the corresponding sockets illustrated in Figure 13-3.) As CPUs advanced, socket types proliferated to support an ever-growing selection of compatible processors.

Today, the most common type of socket is Socket 7. Socket 7 motherboards support most Pentium-type processors (Intel Pentium, Intel Pentium MMX, AMD K5, AMD K6, AMD K6-2, Cyrix 6x86, Cyrix 6x86MX, and Cyrix MX II). By setting the proper clock speed and multiplier, a Socket 7 motherboard can support a wide variety of Pentium-class CPUs without making any other hardware changes. It is this kind of versatility that has made sockets so important, and extended the working life of current PCs by providing an upgrade path for CPUs. Although high-performance processors from Intel and AMD use proprietary slots and sockets, the Socket 7 scheme remains popular and available because of its versatility.

Many leading-edge processors (such as the Intel Pentium II/III and the AMD Athlon) have shifted to a slot-based connector rather than a socket. Remember that slot-based processors are not compatible with socket-based motherboards and vice versa.

TABLE 13-1 COMPATIBILITY DETAILS FOR MAJOR CPU SOCKETS

SOCKET	PINS	VOLTS	CPU	COMPATIBLE OVERDRIVE PROCESSOR(S)	
Socket 1	169	5v	486 SX 486 DX	BOXDX4ODP75 BOXDX4ODPR75	BOXDX4ODP100 BOXDX4ODPR100
Socket 2	238	5v	486 SX 486 DX 486 DX2	BOXDX4ODP75 BOXDX4ODPR75 BOXPODP5V63	BOXDX4ODP100 BOXDX4ODPR100 BOXPODP5V83
Socket 3	237	3v/5v	486 SX 486 DX 486 DX2 486 DX4	BOXDX4ODP75 BOXDX4ODP100 BOXPODP5V63 N/A	BOXDX4ODPR75 BOXDX4ODPR100 BOXPODP5V83
Socket 4	273	5v	60/66MHz Pentium	BOXPODP5V133	
Socket 5	320	3v	75/90/100MHz Pentium	BOXPODP3V125 BOXPODP3V150 BOXPODP3V166	
Socket 6	235	3v	486 DX4	N/A	
Socket 7	321	2.5v/3.3v	75/90/100MHz Pentium	BOXPODP3V125 BOXPODP3V150 BOXPODP3V166	
Socket 8	387	2.5v	Pentium Pro	N/A	
Slot 1	242	N/A	Pentium II/III	N/A	
Slot 2		N/A	Pentium II/III Xeon	N/A	
Slot A		N/A	AMD Athlon	N/A	

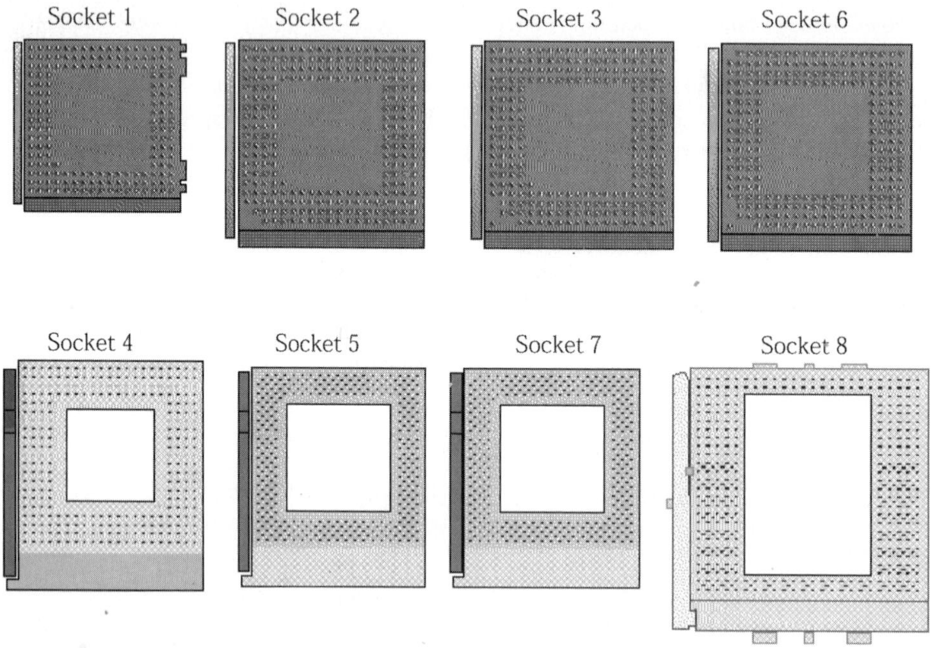

FIGURE 13-3 Comparison of major CPU socket configurations

CISC VS. RISC CPUS

You may sometimes see processors referred to as "CISC" or "RISC" processors. Traditional CPUs are based on a CISC (Complex Instruction Set Computing) architecture. This approach allows any number of instructions to be used in the CPU, and the CPU must provide all of the internal circuitry needed to process each instruction. Since each new instruction requires many new transistors for processing, CISC offers versatility at the expense of CPU performance. CISC CPUs (such as Intel Pentium II/III or AMD Athlon devices) are typically found in general-purpose desktop and mobile computers. By comparison, a RISC (Reduced Instruction Set Computing) architecture uses a limited number of very powerful instructions. This requires fewer transistors in the CPU for processing, and generally results in faster CPU performance with far lower power consumption. However, RISC processors are often less versatile than their CISC counterparts. CISC CPUs appear in dedicated peripheral devices such as laser printers. Designers are still trying to develop processors that combine CISC versatility with RISC performance, though a number of RISC-type CPUs (like the DEC Alpha or MIPS Orion 4600 devices) appear in high-end workstations.

PIPELINING

CPUs process instructions and generate results through a complex series of transistor switches inside the CPU die itself (just like any other logic chip). Early CPUs processed *one* instruction at a time—that is, an instruction was fetched and processed *completely*, and then a new instruction was fetched. Processing could be accomplished in several clock cycles. (The exact number of clock cycles depended on the particular instruction.) Simple instructions could be processed in two or three clocks, while complex instructions might demand as much as seven or eight clocks.

The *pipelining* technique (also called *instruction pipelining*) allows a new instruction to start processing while a current instruction is still being processed. This way, a CPU can actually work on several instructions during the same clock cycle. In other words, for any given clock cycle, there may be several instructions "in the pipeline." Pipelining lets the CPU make use of execution resources that would otherwise sit idle while an instruction is being completed. Still, the CPU can only finish (generate results for) one instruction per clock cycle.

13

BRANCH PREDICTION

Since pipelined CPUs must fetch the next instruction before they have completely executed the previous instruction, this presents a processing dilemma. If the previous instruction was a *branch* (an if-then statement), the next instruction fetch could have been from the wrong place. *Branch prediction* is a technique that attempts to infer the proper address of the next instruction while knowing only the current one. If the improper branch is predicted (called a *mispredict*), the proper branch must be determined, and this can cause delays that impair processing performance. As a consequence, the branch prediction feature of a modern CPU must be extremely powerful.

SUPERSCALAR EXECUTION

Traditional CPUs used a single *execution engine* to process instructions. Even if the CPU supports instruction pipelining, the CPU can only generate results for one instruction for any given clock cycle. By adding more than one execution engine to the CPU, designers have provided the CPU with an ability to process more than one instruction per clock. These are known as *superscalar* processors. For example, the Pentium Pro processor uses two execution "pipes" (dubbed *U* and *V*). By combining pipelining with the multiple execution engines of a superscalar architecture, CPUs are making extremely efficient use of every clock cycle.

DYNAMIC EXECUTION

Even the fastest CPU executes instructions in the order in which they are written within the particular program. This means an improperly or inefficiently written program can reduce the processing efficiency of the CPU. In many cases, even well-written code can become impaired during the software assembly and linking process. The *dynamic execution* technique allows the processor to evaluate the program's flow and "choose" the best order in which to process instructions. When implemented properly, this selective reordering of instructions allows the CPU to make even better use of its processing resources—and aids overall CPU performance.

MULTIMEDIA EXTENSIONS

With the growth in graphics and presentation software, processor throughput often bogged down with the intensive calculations that were required. It became necessary to speed up certain computer-intensive processing/calculation procedures related to multimedia and communications applications. While those processes typically occupy 10 percent or less of the overall application code, they can account for up to 90 percent of the program's execution time. Intel and AMD have been locked in a bitter rivalry to provide the best multimedia extensions to their processors.

- **MMX** By 1996, Intel had introduced its MMX extensions into the Pentium processor family (dubbed Pentium MMX) with 57 powerful new instructions. MMX instructions process multiple data elements in parallel using a technique called Single Instruction Multiple Data (SIMD). This technique allows processes to be performed on large amounts of data simultaneously and reduces the overall processing required to handle the large amounts of video and audio information typically associated with multimedia. Subsequent Intel processors (such as the Pentium II/III and Celeron) are compatible with the MMX instruction set. MMX provides most of its support for 2D images and audio.
- **3DNow** AMD also saw the need to optimize a processor's multimedia capability. But rather than focus on 2D instructions, as Intel did with MMX, AMD chose to focus 21 new instructions on 3D-related features that significantly enhanced the processing of 3D graphics images (as well as MPEG decoding). AMD released its 3DNow technology in 1998 (nine months ahead of Intel's SSE technology). Since 3DNow offered enhanced 3D processing well ahead of Intel, AMD's K6, K6-2, and Athlon processor lines presented an appealing alternative for 3D games and visualization programs. You can learn more about 3DNow at **http://www.amd.com/products/cpg/k623d/inside3d.html**.
- **SSE** By 1999, Intel had updated its multimedia extensions by introducing SSE (Streaming SIMD Extensions) for the Pentium III processor. SSE builds on MMX by adding 70 new instructions that enable advanced imaging, powerful 3D graphics (floating-point) processing, streaming video and audio, speech recognition, and added Internet features. SSE features are intended for the standard end-user family of Pentium III processors.

The Intel CPUs

There is little doubt that Intel Corporation has been a driving force behind the personal computer revolution. Each new generation of microprocessor represents not just mediocre improvements in processing speed, but technological leaps in execution efficiency, raw speed, data throughput, and design enhancements (such as dynamic execution and SIMD). This part of the chapter provides a historical overview of Intel microprocessors and compares their current characteristics.

8086/8088 (1978/1979)

The 29,000-transistor 8086 marked the *first* 16-bit microprocessor—that is, there are 16 data bits available from the CPU itself. This immediately offered twice the data throughput of earlier 8-bit CPUs. Each of the 24 registers in the 8086/8088 is expanded to 16 bits rather than just 8. Twenty address lines allow direct access to 1,048,576 bytes (1MB) of external system memory. Although 1MB of RAM is considered almost negligible today, IC designers at the time never suspected that more than 1MB would ever be needed. Both the 8086 and 8088 (as well as many subsequent Intel CPUs) can address 64KB of I/O space (as opposed to RAM space). The 8086 was available for four clock speeds: 5MHz, 6MHz, 8MHz, and 10MHz. Three clock speeds allowed the 8086 to process 0.33, 0.66, and 0.75 MIPS (millions of instructions per second), respectively. The 8088 was only available in 5MHz and 8MHz versions (for 0.33 and 0.75 MIPS, respectively), but its rather unique multiplexing nature reduces its data bandwidth to only 2MB/s.

For all intents and purposes, the 8088 is identical to the 8086. They are the same microprocessor, with one exception: the 8088 multiplexes (time-shares) 8 of the 16 address lines between the address bus and the data bus. If you look at a pinout of an 8088, you will see only 8 data lines available to the outside world (D8 to D15). During one part of a bus cycle, the lower 8 address lines serve as the lower 8 data bits (D0 to D7). During another part of the bus cycle, those 8 shared bits are used as the lower 8 bits of the address bus (A0 to A7). Both CPUs are designed to work with the 8087 MCP.

80186 (1980)

The 16-bit 80186 was built on the x86 foundation to offer additional features such as an internal clock generator, system controller, interrupt controller, DMA (Direct Memory Access) controller, and timer/counter circuitry right on the CPU itself. No Intel CPU before or since has offered so much integration in a single CPU. The x186 was also first to abandon 5MHz clock speeds in favor of 8MHz, 10MHz, and 12.5MHz. Aside from these advances, however, the x186 remained similar to the 8086/8088, with 24 registers and 20 address lines to access up to 1MB of RAM. The x186s were used as CPUs in embedded applications and never saw service in personal computers. The limitations of the early x86 architecture in the PC demanded a much faster CPU capable of accessing far more than 1MB of RAM.

80286 (1982)

The 24-register, 134,000-transistor 80286 CPU (first used in the IBM PC/AT and compatibles) offered some substantial advantages over older CPUs. Design advances allow the i286 to operate at 1.2 MIPS, 1.5 MIPS, and 2.66 MIPS (for 8, 10, and 12.5MHz, respectively). The i286 also breaks the 1MB RAM barrier by offering 24 address lines instead of 20, which allow it to directly address 16MB of RAM. In addition to 16MB of directly accessible RAM, the i286 can handle up to 1GB of *virtual memory*, which allows blocks of program code and data to be swapped between the i286's real memory (up to 16MB) and a secondary (or "virtual") storage location such as a hard disk. To maintain backward compatibility with the 8086/8088 (which can only address 1MB of RAM), the i286 can operate in a real mode. One of the great failings of the i286 is that it can switch from real mode to protected mode, but it cannot switch *back* to real mode without a warm reboot of the system. The i286 uses a stand-alone math coprocessor, the 80287.

80386 (1985–1990)

The next major microprocessor released by Intel was the 275,000-transistor, 32-register, 80386DX CPU in 1985. With a full 32-bit data bus, data throughput is immediately double that of the 80286. The 16, 20, 25, and 33MHz versions allow data throughput up to 50MB/s and processing power up to 11.4 MIPS at 33MHz.

A full 32-bit address bus allows direct access to an unprecedented 4GB of RAM in addition to a staggering 64TB (terabytes) of virtual memory capacity. The i386 was the first Intel CPU to enhance processing through the use of instruction pipelining, which allows the CPU to start working on a new instruction while waiting for the current instruction to finish. A new operating mode (called the *virtual real mode*) enables the CPU to run several real-mode sessions simultaneously under operating systems such as Windows.

Intel took a small step backward in 1988 to produce the 80386SX CPU. The i386SX uses 24 address lines for 16MB of addressable RAM and an external data bus of 16 bits instead of a full 32 bits from the DX. Correspondingly, the processing power for the i386SX is only 3.6 MIPS at 33MHz. In spite of these compromises, this offered a significantly less expensive CPU, which helped to propagate the i386 family into desktop and portable computers. Aside from changes to the address and bus width, the i386 architecture is virtually unchanged from that of the i386DX.

By 1990, Intel integrated the i386 into an 855,000-transistor, low-power version called the 80386SL. The i386SL incorporated a chipset compatible with the Industry Standard Architecture (ISA) along with power management circuitry that optimized the i386 for use in mobile computers. The i386SL resembled the i386SX version in its 24 address lines and 16-bit external data bus.

Each member of the i386 family uses stand-alone math coprocessors (80387DX, 80387SX, and 80387SL, respectively). All versions of the 80386 can switch between real mode and protected mode as needed, so they are backward compatible and will run the same software as the 80286 and the 8086/8088.

80486 (1989–1994)

The consistent push for higher speed and performance resulted in the development of Intel's 1.2 million-transistor, 29-register, 32-bit microprocessor called the 80486DX in 1989. The i486DX provides full 32-bit addressing for access to 4GB of physical RAM and up to 64TB (terabytes) of virtual memory. The i486DX offers twice the performance of the i386DX with 26.9 MIPS at 33MHz. Two initial versions (25MHz, 33MHz) were available.

As with the i386 family, the i486 series uses pipelining to improve instruction execution, but the i486 series also adds 8KB of *cache memory* right on the IC. Cache saves memory access time by predicting the next instructions that will be needed by the CPU and loading them into the cache memory *before* the CPU actually needs them. If the needed instruction is indeed in cache, the CPU can access the information from cache without wasting time waiting for memory access. Another improvement of the i486DX is the inclusion of a *floating-point unit* (an MCP) in the CPU itself rather than requiring a separate coprocessor IC. This is not true of all members of the i486 family, however. A third departure for the i486DX is that it is offered in 5-volt and 3-volt versions. The 3-volt version is intended for laptop, notebook, and other low-power mobile computing applications.

Finally, the i486DX is upgradable. Up to 1989/1990, personal computers were limited by their CPU—when the CPU became obsolete, so did the computer (more specifically, the *motherboard*). This traditionally forced the computer user to purchase new computers (or upgrade the motherboard) every few years in order to utilize current technology. The architecture of the i486 is intended to support CPU upgrades, where a future CPU using a faster internal clock can be inserted into the existing system. Intel has dubbed this as "OverDrive" technology. While OverDrive performance is not as high as a newer PC would be, it is much less expensive, and allows computer users to protect their computer investments for a longer period of time. It is vital to note that not all i486 versions are upgradable, and the CPU socket on the motherboard itself must be designed specifically to accept an OverDrive CPU. (See the "CPU Sockets" section above.)

The i486DX was only the first in a long line of variations from Intel. In 1991, Intel released the 80486SX and the 80486DX/50. Both the i486SX and i486DX/50 offer 32-bit addressing, a 32-bit data path, and 8KB of on-chip cache memory. The i486SX takes a small step backward from the i486DX by removing the math coprocessor and offering slower versions at 16, 20, 25, and 33MHz. At 33MHz, the i486SX is rated at 20.2 MIPS. Such design compromises reduced the cost and power dissipation of the i486SX, which accelerated its acceptance into desktop and portable computers. The i486SX is upgradable with an OverDrive CPU (if the computer's motherboard is designed to accept an OverDrive CPU), it is compatible with an 80487 CPU/MCP, and it is available in 5-volt and 3-volt versions. The i486DX/50 operates at a clock speed of 50MHz, where it performs at 41.1 MIPS. The i486DX/50 does integrate an onboard math coprocessor, but it is not OverDrive upgradable, and it is not available in a 3-volt version.

The first wave of OverDrive CPUs arrived in 1992 with the introduction of the 80486DX2/50 and the 80486DX2/66. The "2" along with the "DX" indicates that the IC is using an internal clock that is double the frequency of the system. The i486DX2/50 actually runs in a 25MHz system, yet the CPU performs at 40.5 MIPS. The i486DX2/66 runs in a 33MHz system, but it runs internally at 54.5 MIPS. The slower system speed allowed the CPU to work directly with existing PC motherboard designs. Both OverDrive CPUs offer onboard math coprocessors, and are themselves upgradable to even faster OverDrive versions. The i486DX2/50 is available in 5-volt and 3-volt versions, while the i486DX2/66 is only available in the 5-volt version.

In 1992, Intel produced a highly integrated, low-power version of the 80486 called the 80486SL. Its 32-bit data bus, 32-bit address bus, 8KB of onboard cache, and integrated math coprocessor make it virtually identical to other i486 CPUs, but the SL uses 1.4 million transistors. The extra circuitry provides a low-power management capability that optimizes the SL for mobile computers. The i486SL is available in 25MHz and 33MHz versions, as well as 3-volt and 5-volt designs. At 33MHz, the i486SL operates at 26.9 MIPS.

Intel rounded out its i486 family in 1993 with the introduction of three other CPU models: the 80486DX2/40, the 80486SX/SL-enhanced, and the 80486DX/SL-enhanced. The i486DX2/40 is the third OverDrive CPU intended to run in 20MHz PCs, while the CPU's internal clock runs at 40MHz and performs at 21.1 MIPS. The i486SX/SL (26.9 MIPS at 33MHz) and i486DX/SL (26.9 MIPS at 33MHz) are identical to their original SX and DX versions, but the SL enhancement provides power management capability intended to support portable computers such as notebook and sub-notebook computers.

By 1994, Intel was finishing its work with the i486 series with the DX4 OverDrive processors. Contrary to the "DX4" designation, these 3.3V OverDrive devices are clock *triplers*—so an i486DX4/100 actually runs at a motherboard clock speed of 33MHz. It is important to note that all versions of the 80486 will run the same software and are backward compatible with all CPUs back to the 8086/8088.

PENTIUM (1993–1998)

By 1992, the i486 series had become well entrenched in everyday desktop computing, and Intel was already laying the groundwork for its next generation of CPU. While most users expected Intel to continue with its traditional numbering scheme and dub its next CPU the 80586, legal conflicts regarding trademarking forced Intel to use a name that it could trademark and call its own. In 1993, the 3.21 million-transistor Pentium microprocessor (dubbed "P5" or "P54" series) was introduced to eager PC manufacturers. The Pentium retains the 32-bit address bus width of the i486 family. With 32 address bits, the Pentium can directly address 4GB of RAM, and can access up to 64TB of virtual memory. The 64-bit external data bus width can handle twice the data throughput of the i486s. At 60MHz, the Pentium performs at 100 MIPS, and 66MHz yields 111.6 MIPS (twice the processing power of the i486DX2/66). Table 13-2 shows a comparison of Pentium performance ratings in versions from 60MHz to 200MHz. All versions of the Pentium include an onboard math coprocessor, and are intended to be compatible with future OverDrive designs.

TABLE 13-2 PENTIUM FAMILY COMPARISON

CHIP	MHZ SPEED	BUS CACHE	L1 CACHE	L2 FACTOR	FABRIC. SPECFP	TRANS.	FORM	VOLTS	WATTS	SPECINT	AVAIL-ABILITY
Pentium											
	60	60	16KB	—	0.8	3.1 mil	Socket 4	N/A	N/A	N/A	Obsolete
	66	66	16KB	—	0.8	3.1 mil	Socket 4	N/A	N/A	N/A	Obsolete
	75	50	16KB	—	0.6	3.3 mil	Socket 5/7	N/A	N/A	N/A	Obsolete
	90	60	16KB	—	0.6	3.3 mil	Socket 5/7	N/A	N/A	N/A	Obsolete
	100	66	16KB	—	0.6	3.3 mil	Socket 5/7	N/A	N/A	N/A	Obsolete
	120	60	16KB	—	0.6	3.3 mil	Socket 5/7	N/A	N/A	N/A	Obsolete
	133	66	16KB	—	0.35	3.3 mil	Socket 5/7	N/A	N/A	N/A	Available
	150	60	16KB	—	0.35	3.3 mil	Socket 7	N/A	N/A	N/A	Available
	166	66	16KB	—	0.35	3.3 mil	Socket 7	N/A	N/A	N/A	Available
	200	66	16KB	—	0.35	3.3 mil	Socket 7	N/A	N/A	N/A	Available
Pentium MMX											
	133	66	32KB	off chip	0.35	4.5 mil	Socket 7	N/A	N/A	N/A	Obsolete
	150	66	32KB	off chip	0.35	4.5 mil	Socket 7	N/A	N/A	N/A	Obsolete
	166	66	32KB	off chip	0.35	4.5 mil	Socket 7	N/A	N/A	N/A	Available
	200	66	32KB	off chip	0.35	4.5 mil	Socket 7	N/A	N/A	N/A	Available
	233	66	32KB	off chip	0.35	4.5 mil	Socket 7	N/A	N/A	N/A	Available
Mobile Pentium MMX (*Tillamook*)											
	166	66	32KB	off chip	0.25	4.5 mil	MMO	N/A	N/A	N/A	Obsolete
	200	66	32KB	off chip	0.25	4.5 mil	MMO	N/A	N/A	N/A	Obsolete
	233	66	32KB	off chip	0.25	4.5 mil	MMO	N/A	N/A	N/A	Obsolete
	266	66	32KB	off chip	0.25	4.5 mil	MMO	N/A	N/A	N/A	Available
	300	66	32KB	off chip	0.25	4.5 mil	MMO	N/A	N/A	N/A	Available
Pentium Pro											
	150	60	16KB	256KB	0.35	5.5 mil	Socket 8	N/A	N/A	N/A	Obsolete
	166	66	16KB	256KB	0.35	5.5 mil	Socket 8	N/A	N/A	N/A	Obsolete
	166	66	16KB	512KB	0.35	5.5 mil	Socket 8	N/A	N/A	N/A	Obsolete
	180	60	16KB	256KB	0.35	5.5 mil	Socket 8	N/A	N/A	N/A	Available
	200	66	16KB	256KB	0.35	5.5 mil	Socket 8	N/A	N/A	N/A	Available
	200	66	16KB	512KB	0.35	5.5 mil	Socket 8	N/A	N/A	N/A	Available
	200	66	16KB	1MB	0.35	5.5 mil	Socket 8	N/A	N/A	N/A	Available
Pentium II (*Klamath*)											
	233	66	32KB	512KB	0.35	7.5 mil	Slot 1	N/A	N/A	9.4/6.7	Available
	266	66	32KB	512KB	0.35	7.5 mil	Slot 1	N/A	N/A	10.7/7.5	Available
	300	66	32KB	512KB	0.35	7.5 mil	Slot 1	2.8	43	13.0/8.3	Available

TABLE 13-2 PENTIUM FAMILY COMPARISON *(CONTINUED)*

CHIP	MHZ SPEED	BUS CACHE	L1 CACHE	L2 FACTOR	FABRIC. SPECFP	TRANS.	FORM	VOLTS	WATTS	SPECINT	AVAIL-ABILITY
Pentium II (*Deschutes*)											
	333	66	32KB	128KB	0.25	7.5 mil	Slot 1/Soc 370	2.0	26	N/A	Available
	333	66	32KB	512KB	0.25	7.5 mil	Slot 1	N/A	N/A	14.0/9.1	Available
	350	100		512KB	0.25	7.5 mil	Slot 1	N/A	N/A	14.9/10.3	Available
	366	66	32KB	128KB	0.25	7.5 mil	Slot 1/Soc 370	2.0	26	N/A	Available
	400	66	32KB	128KB	0.25	7.5 mil	Slot 1/Soc 370	2.0	26	N/A	Available
	400	100	32KB	128KB	N/A	7.5 mil	Socket 370	2.0	26	N/A	Available
	400	100	32KB	512KB	0.25	7.5 mil	Slot 1	2.0	36	16.9/11.5	Available
	433	66	32KB	128KB	0.25	7.5 mil	Slot 1/Soc 370	2.0	26	N/A	Available
	450	100	32KB	128KB	N/A	7.5 mil	Slot 1/Soc 370	2.0	26	N/A	Available
	450	100	32KB	512KB	0.25	7.5 mil	Slot 1	2.0	36	18.5/11.9	Available
	466	66	32KB	128KB	0.25	7.5 mil	Socket 370	2.0	N/A	N/A	Available
	500	66	32KB	128KB	0.25	7.5 mil	Socket 370	N/A	30	N/A	Available
	500	100	32KB	128KB	N/A	7.5 mil	Socket 370	N/A	30	N/A	Available
	533	66	32KB	128KB	0.25	7.5 mil	Socket 370	N/A	N/A	N/A	Available
	566	66	32KB	128KB	N/A	7.5 mil	Socket 370	N/A	N/A	N/A	Q2 2000
	600	66	32KB	128KB	N/A	7.5 mil	Socket 370	N/A	N/A	N/A	Q4 2000
	633	66	32KB	128KB	N/A	7.5 mil	Socket 370	N/A	N/A	N/A	Q4 2000
Pentium II (*Timna*)											
	N/A	100	32KB	128KB	0.18	22 mil	Slot 1	N/A	N/A	N/A	Q4 2000
Mobile Pentium II (*Deschutes*)											
	233	66	32KB	512KB	0.25	7.5 mil	MMO	1.7	N/A	N/A	Available
	266	66	32KB	512KB	0.25	7.5 mil	MMO	1.7	N/A	N/A	Available
	300	66	32KB	512KB	0.25	7.5 mil	MMO	1.6	N/A	N/A	Available
Mobile Pentium II—PE (*Dixon*)											
	333	66	32KB	256KB	0.25	37 mil	MMO mini-cart	N/A	N/A	N.A	Available
	366	66	32KB	256KB	0.25	37 mil	MMO mini-cart	N/A	N/A	N/A	Available
	400	66	32KB	256KB	0.18	37 mil	MMO mini-cart	N/A	N/A	N/A	Available

TABLE 13-2 PENTIUM FAMILY COMPARISON *(CONTINUED)*

CHIP	MHZ SPEED	BUS CACHE	L1 CACHE	L2 FACTOR	FABRIC. SPECFP	TRANS.	FORM	VOLTS	WATTS	SPECINT	AVAIL-ABILITY
Pentium II Celeron (*Covington*)											
	266	66	32KB	none	0.25	7.5 mil	Slot 1	N/A	N/A	N/A	Available
	300	66	32KB	none	0.25	7.5 mil	Slot 1	N/A	N/A	N/A	Available
Pentium II Celeron (*Mendocino/300A*)											
	300	66	32KB	128KB	0.25	7.5 mil	Slot 1/Soc 370	2.0	26	N/A	Available
	266	66	32KB	128KB	0.25	22 mil	N/A	N/A	N/A	N/A	Available
	300	66	32KB	128KB	0.25	22 mil	N/A	N/A	N/A	N/A	Available
	333	66	32KB	128KB	0.25	22 mil	N/A	1.6	6	N/A	Available
	366	66	32KB	128KB	0.25	22 mil	N/A	N/A	N/A	N/A	Available
	400	66	32KB	128KB	0.18	22 mil	N/A	N/A	N/A	N/A	Available
	433	66	32KB	128KB	0.18	22 mil	N/A	N/A	N/A	N/A	Available
	466	66	32KB	128KB	0.18	22 mil	N/A	N/A	N/A	N/A	Available
Pentium II Xeon											
	400	100	32KB	512KB-1MB	0.25	7.5 mil	Slot 2	N/A	N/A	N/A	Available
	450	100	32KB	512KB-2MB	0.25	7.5 mil	Slot 2	N/A	N/A	N/A	Available
Pentium III (*Katmai*)											
	450	100	32KB	512KB	0.25	9.5 mil	Slot 1	2.0	25	18.7/13.7	Available
	500	100	32KB	512KB	0.25	9.5 mil	Slot 1	2.0	28	20.6/14.7	Available
	533B	133	32KB	512KB	0.18	9.5 mil	Slot 1	1.6	N/A	N/A	Available
	550	100	32KB	512KB	0.25	9.5 mil	Slot 1	2.0	31	22.2/15.0	Available
	600	100	32KB	512KB	0.25	9.5 mil	Slot 1	2.05	34	24.0/15.9	Available
	600B	133	32KB	512KB	0.18/0.25	9.5 mil	Slot 1	1.6/2.05	N/A	N/A	Available
Pentium III (*Coppermine*)											
	500E	100	32KB	256KB	0.18	28 mil	Soc 370/FC	1.6	N/A	N/A	Available
	533EB	133	32KB	256KB	0.18	28 mil	Slot 1	1.6	N/A	N/A	Available
	550E	100	32KB	256KB	0.18	28 mil	Soc 370/FC	1.6	N/A	N/A	Available
	600E	100	32KB	256KB	0.18	28 mil	Slot 1	1.6	N/A	N/A	Available
	600EB	133	32KB	256KB	0.18	28 mil	Slot 1	1.6	N/A	N/A	Available

TABLE 13-2 PENTIUM FAMILY COMPARISON *(CONTINUED)*

CHIP	MHZ SPEED	BUS CACHE	L1 CACHE	L2 FACTOR	FABRIC. SPECFP	TRANS.	FORM	VOLTS	WATTS	SPECINT	AVAIL-ABILITY
Pentium III (*Coppermine*) *(continued)*											
	650E	100	32KB	256KB	0.18	28 mil	Slot 1	1.6	N/A	N/A	Available
	667EB	133	32KB	256KB	0.18	28 mil	Slot 1	1.6	N/A	N/A	Available
	700E	100	32KB	256KB	0.18	28 mil	Slot 1	1.6	N/A	N/A	Available
	733EB	133	32KB	256KB	0.18	28 mil	Slot 1	1.6	N/A	32.8/19.5	Available
	750E	100	32KB	256KB	0.18	28 mil	Slot 1	N/A	N/A	N/A	Available
	800E	100	32KB	256KB	0.18	28 mil	Slot 1	N/A	N/A	38.4/28.9	Available
	800EB	133	32KB	256KB	0.18	28 mil	Slot 1	N/A	N/A	N/A	Available
	850E	100	32KB	256KB	0.18	28 mil	Slot 1	N/A	N/A	N/A	Q2 2000
	866EB	133	32KB	256KB	0.18	28 mil	Slot 1	N/A	N/A	N/A	Q2 2000
	933EB	133	32KB	256KB	0.18	28 mil	Slot 1	N/A	N/A	N/A	Q3 2000
	1000EB	133	32KB	256KB	0.18	28 mil	Slot 1	N/A	N/A	N/A	Q4 2000
Mobile Pentium III (*Coppermine*)											
	400	100	32KB	256KB	0.18	28 mil	N/A	N/A	N/A	N/A	Available
	450	100	32KB	256KB	0.18	28 mil	N/A	N/A	N/A	N/A	Available
	500	100	32KB	256KB	0.18	28 mil	N/A	N/A	N/A	N/A	Available
(Speedstep)	600/500	100	32KB	256KB	0.18	28 mil	N/A	N/A	N/A	N/A	Available
	650/500	100	32KB	256KB	0.18	28 mil	N/A	N/A	N/A	N/A	Available
	700	100	32KB	256KB	0.18	28 mil	N/A	N/A	N/A	N/A	mid 2000
Pentium III Celeron											
	533	66	32KB	128KB	0.25	N/A	Soc 370	N/A	N/A	N/A	Available
	550	100	32KB	128KB	0.18	N/A	Soc 370	N/A	N/A	N/A	Q2 2000
Pentium III Xeon (*Tanner*)											
	500	100	32KB	512KB-2MB	0.25	9.5 mil	Slot 2	N/A	36	N/A	Available
	550	100	32KB	512KB-2MB	0.25	9.5 mil	Slot 2	N/A	34	N/A	Available
	600	133	32KB	256KB	0.18	28 mil	Slot 2	N/A	N/A	N/A	Available
Pentium III Xeon (*Cascades*)											
	667	133	32KB	256KB	0.18	28 mil	Slot 2	N/A	N/A	N/A	Available
	733	133	32KB	256KB	0.18	28 mil	Slot 2	N/A	N/A	N/A	Available
	800	133	32KB	256KB	0.18	28 mil	Slot 2	N/A	N/A	N/A	Available

13

TABLE 13-3 DETAILED CPU MANUALS AND TECHNICAL INFORMATION

MANUAL	WEB SITE
Pentium Processor Manuals	http://developer.intel.com/design/pentium/manuals/
Pentium MMX Manuals	http://developer.intel.com/design/mmx/manuals/
Pentium Pro Processor Manuals	http://developer.intel.com/design/pro/manuals/
Pentium II Manuals	http://developer.intel.com/design/PentiumII/manuals/
Am486DX2 Manual	http://www.amd.com/products/cpg/techdocs/datasheets/19200d.pdf
Am486DX4 Manual	http://www.amd.com/products/cpg/techdocs/datasheets/19160d.pdf
5x85 Manual	http://www.amd.com/products/cpg/techdocs/datasheets/19751c.pdf
K5 Manual	http://www.amd.com/products/cpg/techdocs/appnotes/18524c.pdf
K6 Manual	http://www.amd.com/K6/k6docs/pdf/20695e.pdf
6x86 Processor Manuals	http://www.cyrix.com/process/hardwrdc/6x-dbk1.htm
Cyrix MediaGX	No technical manuals available, check www.cyrix.com
6x86MX Manuals	http://www.cyrix.com/process/hardwrdc/6xMX-dbk.htm

The Pentium uses two 8KB caches—one for instructions and another for data (16KB total). A dual pipelining technique allows the Pentium to work on more than one instruction per clock cycle. Another substantial improvement in the Pentium's design is onboard power management features (similar to the i486SL line), allowing it to be used effectively in portable computers. Early Pentium models started at 5 volts, but all models starting at about 100MHz (P54C) use 3.3 volts or less. Finally, the Pentium is fully backward compatible with all software written for the 8086/8088 and later CPUs. As of this writing, Intel has released various versions of the Pentium up to 200MHz. Faster versions are unlikely because of more powerful processors such as the Pentium MMX, Pentium Pro, and Pentium II/III. For technicians who want the nitty-gritty details on Pentium operation, you can download the Pentium-family processor manuals from the Internet, as listed in Table 13-3.

The number of Pentium versions and features has simply proliferated over the last few years—so much so that it is *extremely* difficult to tell whether a motherboard is configured properly for a given CPU. However, you can use the "S-spec" rating marked on each Pentium or Pentium MMX processor to reveal key operating characteristics of the particular CPU. Table 13-4 presents the S-specs for Pentium and Pentium MMX processors.

TABLE 13-4 S-SPEC REFERENCE FOR PENTIUM AND PENTIUM MMX PROCESSORS

S-SPEC	STEP	SPEED (MHZ) CORE/BUS	COMMENTS
Q016	mxA3	150/60	ES, TCP
Q017	mxA3	166/66	ES, TCP
Q018	xA3	200/66	ES, PPGA
Q019	xA3	166/66	ES, PPGA
Q020	xA3	150/60	ES, PPGA
Q024	mcC0	150/60	TCP, VRT
Q040	mcC0	150/60	SPGA, VRT

TABLE 13-4 S-SPEC REFERENCE FOR PENTIUM AND PENTIUM MMX PROCESSORS (CONTINUED)

S-SPEC	STEP	SPEED (MHZ) CORE/BUS	COMMENTS
Q0540	B1	75/50	ES
Q0541	B1	75/50	ES
Q0542	B1	90/60	STD
Q0543	B1	90/60	DP
Q0563	B1	100/66	STD
Q0587	B1	100/66	VR
Q0601	B1	75/50	TCP, Mobile
Q0606	B3	75/50	TCP, Mobile
Q061	mxA3	150/60	ES, PPGA
Q0611	B3	90/60	STD
Q0612	B3	90/60	VR
Q0613	B1	90/60	VR
Q0614	B1	100/66	VR
Q062	mxA3	166/66	ES, PPGA
Q0628	B3	90/60	STD
Q0653	B5	90/60	STD
Q0654	B5	90/60	VR
Q0655	B5	90/60	MD
Q0656	B5	100/66	MD
Q0657	B5	100/66	VR, MD
Q0658	B5	100/66	VRE, MD
Q0666	B5	75/50	STD
Q0677	B3	100/66	VRE, MD
Q0686	mA14	75/50	VRT2, TCP
Q0689	mA14	75/50	VRT2, SPGA
Q0694	mA14	90/60	VRT2, TCP
Q0695	mA14	90/60	VRT2, SPGA
Q0697	C2	100/50 or 66	STD
Q0698	C2	100/50 or 66	VRE, MD
Q0699	C2	90/60	STD
Q0700	C2	75/50	STD
Q0704	B5	75/50	TCP, Mobile
Q0707	B5	120/60	VRE, MD1
Q0708	B5	120/60	STD1
Q0711	C2	120/60	VRE, MD
Q0725	C2	75/50	TCP, Mobile
Q0732	C2	120/60	VRE/MD
Q0733	C2	133/66	MD
Q0749	C2	75/50	MD
Q0751	C2	133/66	MD
Q0772	cB1	133/66	STD/No Kit

TABLE 13-4 S-SPEC REFERENCE FOR PENTIUM AND PENTIUM MMX PROCESSORS *(CONTINUED)*

S-SPEC	STEP	SPEED (MHZ) CORE/BUS	COMMENTS
Q0773	cB1	133/66	STD
Q0774	cB1	133/66	VRE, MD (No Kit)
Q0775	C2	133/66	VRE, MD
Q0776	cB1	120/60	STD/No Kit
Q0779	mcB1	120/60	VRT2, TCP
Q0783	E0	90/60	STD
Q0784	E0	100/50 or 66	STD
Q0785	E0	120/60	VRE
Q0808	mcB1	120/60	3.3V, SPGA
Q0835	cC0	150/60	STD
Q0836	cC0	166/66	VRE/No Kit
Q0837	E0	75/50	STD
Q0841	cC0	166/66	VRE
Q0843	cC0	133/66	STD/No Kit
Q0844	cC0	133/66	STD
Q0846	E0	75/50	TCP, Mobile
Q0848	mA4	75/50	VRT, TCP
Q0849	mA4	90/60	VRT, TCP
Q0850	mA4	100/66	VRT, TCP
Q0851	mA4	75/50	VRT, SPGA
Q0852	mA4	90/60	VRT, SPGA
Q0853	mA4	100/66	VRT, SPGA
Q0878	cC0	150/60	STD, PPGA9
Q0879	mcC0	120/60	TCP, VRT
Q0880	mcC0	120/60	SPGA, 3.1V
Q0881	mcC0	133/66	TCP, VRT
Q0882	mcC0	133/66	SPGA, 3.1V
Q0884	mcB1	100/66	VRT2, TCP
Q0886	cC0	166/66	VRE, PPGA9
Q0887	mcC0	100/66	TCP, VRT
Q0890	cC0	166/66	VRE, PPGA9
Q0906	mcC0	150/60	TCP, 3.1V
Q09498	cC0	166/66	VRE, PPGA9
Q0951	cC0	200/66	VRE, PPGA
Q0951F	cC0	200/6610	VRE, PPGA9
Q115	mxB1	166/66	ES, TCP
Q116	mxB1	150/60	ES, TCP
Q124	xB1	200/66	ES, PPGA
Q125	xB1	166/66	ES, PPGA
Q126	xB1	166/66	ES, SPGA

TABLE 13-4 S-SPEC REFERENCE FOR PENTIUM AND PENTIUM MMX PROCESSORS *(CONTINUED)*

S-SPEC	STEP	SPEED (MHZ) CORE/BUS	COMMENTS
Q127	mxB1	166/66	ES, PPGA
Q128	mxB1	150/60	ES, PPGA
Q129	mxB1	133/66	ES, PPGA
Q130	mxB1	133/66	ES, TCP
Q146	myA0	200/66	TCP
Q147	myA0	233/66	TCP
Q230	mxB1	120/60	ES, TCP
Q250	myA0	266/66	TCP
Q251	myA0	266/66	TCP
Q252	myA0	166/66	TCP
Q255	myA0	166/66	TCP
Q430	xB1	200/66	SPGA
Q586	mxB1	200/66	PPGA
Q695	myA0	266/66	TCP
Q766	myB2	266/66	TCP
Q767	myB2	266/66	TCP
Q768	myB2	300/60	TCP
S106J7	cB1	133/66	STD/No Kit
SK079	C2	75/50	TCP Mobile
SK086	C2	120/60	VRE, MD
SK089	mA14	75/50	VRT2, TCP
SK090	mA14	90/60	VRT2, TCP
SK091	mA14	75/50	VRT2, SPGA
SK092	mA14	90/60	VRT2, SPGA
SK098	C2	133/66	MD
SK106	cB1	133/66	STD/No Kit
SK107	cB1	133/66	STD
SK110	cB1	120/60	STD/No Kit
SK113	mcB1	120/60	VRT, TCP
SK1187	mcB1	120/60	VRT, TCP
SK119	mA4	75/50	VRT, TCP
SK120	mA4	90/60	VRT, TCP
SK121	mA4	100/66	VRT, TCP
SK122	mA4	75/50	VRT, SPGA
SK123	mA4	90/60	VRT, SPGA
SK124	mA4	100/66	VRT, SPGA
SL22F	mxA3	166/66	TCP
SL22G	mxA3	150/60	TCP
SL22M	cC0	120/60	STD
SL22Q	cC0	133/66	STD
SL239	xA3	166/66	SPGA

TABLE 13-4 S-SPEC REFERENCE FOR PENTIUM AND PENTIUM MMX PROCESSORS *(CONTINUED)*

S-SPEC	STEP	SPEED (MHZ) CORE/BUS	COMMENTS
SL23M	myB2	266/66	TCP
SL23P	myB2	266/66	TCP
SL23R	xA3	166/66	PPGA
SL23S	xA3	200/66	PPGA
SL23T	xA3	166/66	SPGA
SL23V	xB1	166/66	PPGA
SL23W	xB1	200/66	PPGA
SL23X	xB1	166/66	SPGA
SL23Z	mxA3	166/66	PPGA
SL246	mxA3	150/60	PPGA
SL24Q	cC0	200/66	VRE, PPGA, No Kit
SL24R	cC0	166/66	VRE, No Kit
SL25H	cC0	200/66	VRE, PPGA
SL25J	cC0	120/60	STD
SL25L	cC0	133/66	STD
SL25M	xA3	166/66	PPGA
SL25N	xA3	200/66	PPGA
SL26H	xA3	166/66	PPGA
SL26J	xA3	200/66	PPGA
SL26Q	xA3	200/66	PPGA
SL26T	mxB1	166/66	TCP
SL26U	mxB1	150/60	TCP
SL26V	xA3	166/66	SPGA
SL274	xA3	200/66	PPGA
SL27A	mxB1	166/66	PPGA
SL27B	mxB1	150/60	PPGA
SL27C	mxB1	133/66	PPGA
SL27D	mxB1	133/66	TCP
SL27H	xB1	166/66	PPGA
SL27J	xB1	200/66	PPGA
SL27K	xB1	166/66	SPGA
SL27S	xB1	233/66	PPGA
SL28P	myA0	200/66	TCP
SL28Q	myA0	233/66	TCP
SL293	xB1	233/66	PPGA
SL2BM	xB1	233/66	PPGA
SL2FP	xB1	166/66	PPGA
SL2FQ	xB1	200/66	PPGA
SL2HU	xA3	166/66	SPGA

TABLE 13-4 S-SPEC REFERENCE FOR PENTIUM AND PENTIUM MMX PROCESSORS *(CONTINUED)*

S-SPEC	STEP	SPEED (MHZ) CORE/BUS	COMMENTS
SL2HX	xB1	166/66	SPGA
SL2N5	myA0	266/66	TCP
SL2N6	myA0	166/66	TCP
SL2RY	xB1	200/66	SPGA
SL2S9	xB1	200/66	SPGA
SL2WK	mxB1	200/66	PPGA
SL2WW	E0	90/60	STD
SL2ZH	myA0	266/66	TCP
SL34N	myB2	300/66	TCP
SU0316	C2	90/60	STD
SU0326	C2	100/50 or 66	STD
SU0336	C2	120/60	VRE, MD
SU038	cB1	133/66	STD/No Kit
SU0706	C2	75/50	STD
SU071	cC0	150/60	STD
SU072	cC0	166/66	VRE, No Kit
SU073	cC0	133/66	STD/ No Kit
SU097	E0	75/50	STD
SU098	E0	75/50	STD
SU099	E0	100/50 or 66	STD
SU100	E0	120/60	STD
SU110	E0	100/50 or 66	STD
SU114	cC0	200/66	VRE, PPGA
SU1226	cC0	150/60	STD
SX874	B1	90/60	DP, STD
SX879	B1	90/60	STD
SX885	B1	90/60	MD
SX886	B1	100/66	MD
SX909	B1	90/60	VR
SX910	B1	100/66	VR, MD
SX921	B3	90/60	MD
SX922	B3	90/60	VR
SX923	B3	90/60	STD
SX942	B3	90/60	DP, STD
SX943	B3	90/60	DP, VR
SX944	B3	90/60	DP, MD
SX951	B3	75/50	TCP, Mobile
SX957	B5	90/60	STD
SX958	B5	90/60	VR
SX959	B5	90/60	MD
SX960	B3	100/66	VRE, MD

13

TABLE 13-4 S-SPEC REFERENCE FOR PENTIUM AND PENTIUM MMX PROCESSORS *(CONTINUED)*

S-SPEC	STEP	SPEED (MHZ) CORE/BUS	COMMENTS
SX961	B5	75/50	STD
SX962	B5	100/66	VRE, MD
SX963	C2	100/50 or 66	STD
SX968	C2	90/60	STD
SX969	C2	75/50	STD
SX970	C2	100/50 or 66	VRE, MD
SX975	B5	75/50	TCP, Mobile
SX994	C2	120/60	VRE, MD
SX998	C2	75/50	MD
SX999	mcB1	120/60	3.3V, SPGA
SY005	E0	75/50	STD
SY006	E0	90/60	STD
SY007	E0	100/50 or 66	STD
SY009	E0	75/50	TCP, Mobile
SY015	cC0	150/60	STD
SY016	cC0	166/66	VRE, No Kit
SY017	cC0	166/66	VRE
SY019	mcC0	133/66	TCP, VRT
SY020	mcC0	100/66	TCP, VRT
SY021	mcC0	120/60	TCP, VRT
SY022	cC0	133/66	STD
SY023	cC0	133/66	STD/ No Kit
SY027	mcC0	120/60	SPGA, 3.1V
SY028	mcC0	133/66	SPGA, 3.1V
SY029	mcB1	100/66	VRT2, TCP
SY030	mcC0	120/60	SPGA, 3.3V
SY033	E0	120/60	STD
SY037	cC0	166/66	VRE, PPGA
SY043	mcC0	150/60	TCP, 3.1V
SY044	cC0	200/66	VRE, PPGA
SY045	cC0	200/66	VRE, PPGA
SY046	mcC0	100/66	SPGA, 3.1V
SY055	cC0	166/66	VRE/No Kit
SY056	mcC0	75/50	TCP, VRT
SY058	mcC0	150/60	SPGA, VRT
SY059	xA3	166/66	PPGA
SY060	xA3	200/66	PPGA
SY061	mcC0	150/60	TCP, VRT
SY062	cC0	120/60	STD
SZ951	B3	90/60	STD
SZ977	B5	75/50	STD

TABLE 13-4 S-SPEC REFERENCE FOR PENTIUM AND PENTIUM MMX PROCESSORS *(CONTINUED)*

S-SPEC	STEP	SPEED (MHZ) CORE/BUS	COMMENTS
SZ9785	B5	90/60	STD
SZ994	C2	75/505	STD
SZ9955	C2	90/60	STD
SZ9965	C2	100/50 or 66	STD

NOTES:

- PPGA, TCP, and SPGA are all case styles.
- ES means "engineering sample."
- DP means for use in a "dual processor" configuration only.
- Mobile means the CPU was developed for mobile operation.
- MD means designed to accommodate "minimum timing."
- VR means "voltage reduced" (3.3–3.465 volts).
- VRE means the CPU uses 3.4–3.6 volts.
- VRT means the CPU uses "split voltage" (2.8V/3.3V).
- STD means "standard part" using normal timing and 3.135–3.6 volts.

1. T_{CASE} = 60°C.
2. VRT (Voltage Reduction Technology): The V_{CC} for I/O is 3.3V, but the core V_{CC} (accounting for about 90% of power usage) is reduced to 2.9V to reduce power consumption and heating.
3. No Kit means that part meets the specifications (but is not tested) to support 82498/82493 and 82497/82492 cache timings.
4. The cB1 step is logically equivalent to the C2 step, but on a different manufacturing process. The mcB1 step is logically equivalent to the cB1 step (except it does not support DP, APIC, or FRC). The mcB1, mA1, mA4, and mcC0 steps also use VRT (see note 2) and are available in the TCP and/or SPGA package, primarily to support mobile applications. The mxA3 is logically equivalent to the xA3 step (except it does not support DP or APIC). All mobile steps are distinguished by an additional *m* prefix, for "mobile." All steps of the Pentium MMX are distinguished by an additional *x* prefix.
5. This is a boxed Pentium processor *without* an attached fan heat sink.
6. This is a boxed Pentium processor *with* an attached fan heat sink.
7. These parts do not support boundary scan testing. S106J was previously marked (and is the same as) SK106J.
8. DP, FRC, and APIC features are not supported on these parts.
9. These parts are packaged in the Plastic Pin Grid Array (PPGA) package.
10. Some Q0951F units are marked on the bottom with spec number Q0951 and with an additional line immediately underneath spelling out "Full Feature" to properly identify the unit.
11. This is a mobile Pentium MMX with a core operating voltage of 2.285V–2.665V.
12. This is a desktop Pentium MMX with a core operating voltage of 2.7V–2.9V.
13. The part may run only at the maximum specified frequency. A 200MHz unit may be run at 200MHz +0/–5MHz (195–200MHz) and a 166MHz may be run at 166 MHz +0/–5MHz (161–166MHz).
14. SU114 units are marked on the bottom with a VMU code of "VSS." This is incorrect—the proper code should read "VSU," since the units do not support DP, FRC, or APIC features. This spec number has been discontinued and is replaced by spec number SY045.
15. This part ships as a boxed processor with an unattached fan heat sink.

13

PENTIUM PRO (1995–1999)

Even though the Pentium has proven adept at handling 16- and 32-bit operating systems, designers continued to seek ways to optimize the Pentium for 32-bit performance—especially for operating systems like Windows NT, and the then-emerging Windows 95. The Pentium Pro (dubbed "P6" or "PPro") evolved as an optimized Pentium intended to support business systems such as high-end desktop workstations and network servers. The P6 processors range from 150MHz to 200MHz, and can handle multiprocessing in systems with up to four CPUs.

The Pentium Pro uses dynamic execution to improve its performance and employs two separate 8KB L1 caches—one for data and one for instructions. Another major improvement in the Pentium Pro is its use of up to 1MB of onboard L2 cache. This maximizes the P6's performance without relying on the motherboard to supply L2 cache. You can see the use of L1 and L2 cache and Pentium Pro family performance in Table 13-2.

While not as prolific as the "classic" Pentium and Pentium MMX, there are still a number of Pentium Pro versions and features to contend with. This can make it difficult to determine the proper motherboard configuration for a given P6. However, you can use the S-spec rating marked on each Pentium Pro processor to reveal key operating characteristics of the particular CPU. Table 13-5 presents the S-specs for Pentium Pro processors.

TABLE 13-5 S-SPEC NUMBERS FOR PENTIUM PRO PROCESSORS

S-SPEC	MANUFACTURER'S STEP	L2 SIZE (KB)	SPEED (MHZ) CORE/BUS	COMMENTS
Q008	sB1	512	166/66	Note 4
Q009	sB1	512	166/66	Note 4
Q010	sB1	512	200/66	Note 4
Q011	sB1	512	200/66	Note 4
Q033	sB1	256	180/60	Note 4
Q034	sB1	256	200/66	Note 4
Q035	sB1	256	180/60	Note 4
Q036	sB1	256	200/66	Note 4
Q076	sA1	256	200/66	Note 7
Q0812	B0	256	133/66	Notes 3, 4
Q0813	B0	256	150/60	Notes 3, 4
Q0815	B0	256	133/66	Notes 3, 4
Q0816	B0	256	150/60	Notes 3, 4
Q0822	C0	256	150/60	Notes 3, 4
Q0825	C0	256	150/60	Note 4
Q0826	C0	256	150/60	Note 4
Q083	sB1	256	200/66	Note 7
Q084	sB1	256	200/66	Note 7
Q0858	sA0	256	180/60	Notes 2, 4
Q0859	sA0	256	200/66	Notes 2, 4
Q0860	sA0	256	180/60	Notes 2, 4, 5
Q0861	sA0	256	200/66	Notes 2, 4, 5

TABLE 13-5 S-SPEC NUMBERS FOR PENTIUM PRO PROCESSORS *(CONTINUED)*

S-SPEC	MANUFACTURER'S STEP	L2 SIZE (KB)	SPEED (MHZ) CORE/BUS	COMMENTS
Q0864	sA0	512	166/66	Notes 2, 4, 6
Q0865	sA0	512	200/66	Notes 2, 4, 6
Q0871	sA1	256	180/60	Note 4
Q0872	sA1	256	200/66	Note 4
Q0873	sA0	256	180/60	Notes 2, 4
Q0874	sA0	256	200/66	Notes 2, 4
Q0907	sA1	256	180/60	Note 4
Q0908	sA1	256	200/66	Note 4
Q0909	sA1	256	200/66	Note 4
Q0910	sA0	256	180/60	Note 2
Q0918	sA1	512	166/66	Notes 4, 6
Q0920	sA1	512	200/66	Notes 4, 6
Q0924	sA1	512	200/66	Notes 4, 6
Q0929	sA1	512	166/66	Note 4
Q932	sA1	512	200/66	Note 4
Q935	sA1	512	166/66	Note 4
Q936	sA1	512	200/66	Note 4
SL22S	sB1	256	180/60	
SL22T	sB1	256	200/66	
SL22U	sB1	256	180/60	
SL22V	sB1	256	200/66	
SL22X	sB1	512	166/66	
SL22Z	sB1	512	200/66	
SL23L	sB1	256	180/60	
SL23M	sB1	256	200/66	
SL245	sA1	256	200/66	Note 7
SL247	sA1	256	200/66	Note 7
SL254	sB1	256	200/66	Note 7
SL255	sB1	256	200/66	Note 7
SU103	sA1	256	180/60	
SU104	sA1	256	200/66	
SY002	B0	256	150/60	Note 3
SY010	C0	256	150/60	
SY011	B0	256	150/60	
SY012	sA0	256	180/60	Note 2
SY013	sA0	256	200/66	Note 2
SY014	B0	256	150/60	
SY031	sA1	256	180/60	
SY032	sA1	256	200/66	
SY034	sA1	512	166/66	

TABLE 13-5 S-SPEC NUMBERS FOR PENTIUM PRO PROCESSORS *(CONTINUED)*

S-SPEC	MANUFACTURER'S STEP	L2 SIZE (KB)	SPEED (MHZ) CORE/BUS	COMMENTS
SY039	sA1	256	180/60	
SY040	sA1	256	200/66	
SY047	sA1	512	166/66	
SY048	sA1	512	200/66	

NOTES:

1. L2 Size refers to the silicon revision of the 256KB or 512KB on-chip L2 cache.
2. The sA0 step is logically equivalent to the C0 step, but on a different manufacturing process.
3. The VID pins are not supported on these parts.
4. These are engineering samples only.
5. The VID pins are functional but not tested on these parts.
6. These sample parts are equipped with a preproduction 512KB L2 cache.
7. These components have additional specification changes associated with them:
   a) Primary voltage = 3.5V ± 5%
   b) Max. Thermal Design Power = 39.4W @ 200MHz, 256K L2
   c) Current = 11.9A
   d) The VID pins are not supported on these parts.
   e) T9 = Minimum GTL + Input Hold Time = 0.9ns
   f) Minimum Non-GTL + Input High Voltage = 2.2V

PENTIUM MMX (1997–CURRENT)

The data processing demands imposed by multimedia applications continue to be a burden to most PCs, especially for graphics-intensive games and other video applications. In 1997, Intel released an important enhancement to the Pentium known as multimedia extensions (or MMX). By streamlining and improving the existing Pentium architecture, and adding 57 new MMX instructions, the Pentium MMX was poised as the premier midrange CPU into the late 1990s. With current speeds from 133MHz to 233MHz, the Pentium MMX can typically execute existing software 10 percent to 20 percent faster than classic Pentium processors at the same clock speed. When using software written specifically for MMX instructions, the PC can deliver higher color depths and higher resolutions while maintaining high frame rates for rendering and video.

The Pentium MMX has doubled code and data caches to 16KB each. Larger separate internal caches improve performance by reducing the average memory access time and providing fast access to recently used instructions and data. The data cache supports a write-back (or write-through on a line-by-line basis) policy for memory updates. Pentium MMX processors also employ improved dynamic branch prediction to boost performance by predicting the *most likely* set of instructions to be executed.

The Pentium MMX line includes many other features. The superscalar architecture is capable of executing two integer instructions in parallel in a single clock cycle for improved integer processing performance. A pipelined floating-point unit (FPU) supporting 32-bit, 64-bit, and 80-bit formats is capable of executing two floating-point instructions in a single clock. An additional instruction pipe has been added to further improve instruction processing. A pool of four write buffers is now shared between the dual pipelines to improve memory write performance. There is also a multiprocessor interrupt controller on the chip, which allows low-cost symmetric multiprocessing (SMP) and SL technology power management features for efficient power control. Table 13-4 lists the S-spec numbers for Pentium MMX processors.

PENTIUM II (1997–CURRENT)

With the Pentium MMX and Pentium Pro processors firmly entrenched in the PC community, Intel sought to combine the best features of both—the software performance of the Pentium Pro and the multimedia performance of the Pentium MMX. The result appeared in 1997 as the Pentium II (or "P II," previously dubbed the "Klamath"). As with the Pentium Pro, the Pentium II is optimized for use with 32-bit operating systems and software (such as Windows 98 or Windows NT). Yet the P II also includes the architecture and 57 new instructions needed to handle MMX applications. At 266MHz, the Pentium II processor can provide from 1.6 to over 2 times the performance of a 200MHz Pentium processor.

The Pentium II also employs the dynamic execution technology used in the Pentium Pro. Dynamic execution uses multiple branch prediction to predict the flow of the program through several branches (accelerating the flow of work to the processor). A data flow analysis then creates an optimized (reordered) schedule of instructions by analyzing the relationships between instructions. And speculative execution finally carries out the instructions "speculatively" (believing the execution order to be correct) based on this optimized schedule. Dynamic execution keeps the processor's superscalar execution engines busy and boosts overall performance.

The Pentium II uses a 32KB L1 cache, which allows a 16KB cache for data and a 16KB cache for instructions. It also provides 512KB of L2 cache right in the CPU package to maximize the processor's performance without relying on the motherboard for cache. The P II supports up to 64GB of physical RAM and allows dual processors; so motherboards can be designed for basic symmetric multiprocessing (SMP). A pipelined floating-point unit (FPU) supporting 32-bit, 64-bit, and 80-bit formats is capable of executing two floating-point instructions in a single clock and sustaining over 300 million floating-point instructions per second at 300MHz. Table 13-2 outlines the performance comparison for Pentium II processors from 233MHz to 633MHz.

One of the most noticeable departures from previous CPUs is the package style. Intel has abandoned the use of Socket 7 (Pentium) and Socket 8 (Pentium Pro) packages, and adopted a cartridge-style package known as the Single Edge Contact (or SEC) cartridge. We generally know this as the "Slot 1" style of connector.

While not quite as prolific as the classic Pentium and Pentium MMX (or even as prolific as the Pentium Pro), there are still a large number of Pentium II versions and features to contend with. This can make it difficult to determine the proper motherboard configuration for a given P II. However, you can use the S-spec rating marked on each Pentium II processor to reveal key operating characteristics of the particular CPU. Table 13-6 presents the S-specs for Pentium II and Celeron processors.

PENTIUM II OVERDRIVE (1998–CURRENT)

Two Pentium II OverDrive processors have been produced for upgrading Pentium Pro (Socket 8) processors. One OverDrive replaces the 150–180MHz Pentium Pros (60MHz bus speed) and provides a performance increase to 300MHz. The other OverDrive replaces the 166–200MHz (66MHz bus speed) Pentium Pro processors and increases performance to 333MHz. The integrated on-die L2 cache design of the Socket 8 package style also provides a performance increase by allowing the L2 cache to operate at full core speed.

TABLE 13-6 S-SPEC NUMBERS FOR PENTIUM II AND CELERON PROCESSORS

PENTIUM II PROCESSORS

S-SPEC	MANUFACTURER'S STEP	L2 SIZE (KB)	TAG RAM STEP	MEMORY SUPPORT	SPEED (MHZ) CORE/BUS
SL264	C0	512	T6/B0	non-ECC	233/66
SL265	C0	512	T6/B0	non-ECC	266/66
SL268	C0	512	T6/B0	ECC	233/66
SL269	C0	512	T6/B0	ECC	266/66
SL28K	C0	512	T6/B0	non-ECC	233/66
SL28L	C0	512	T6/B0	non-ECC	266/66
SL28R	C0	512	T6/B0	ECC	300/66
SL2HA	C1	512	T6/B0	ECC	300/66
SL2HC	C1	512	T6/B0	non-ECC	266/66
SL2HD	C1	512	T6/B0	non-ECC	233/66
SL2HE	C1	512	T6/B0	ECC	266/66
SL2HF	C1	512	T6/B0	ECC	233/66
SL2K9	dA0	512	T6P/A3	ECC	266/66
SL2KA	dA0	512	T6P/A3	ECC	333/66
SL2KE	TdB0	512	C6C/A3	ECC	333/66
SL2MZ	C0	512	T6/B0	ECC	300/66
SL2QA	C1	512	T6/B0	non-ECC	233/66
SL2QB	C1	512	T6/B0	non-ECC	266/66
SL2QC	C1	512	T6/B0	ECC	300/66
SL2QF	dA0	512	T6P/A3	ECC	333/66
SL2QH	dA1	512	T6P-e/A0	ECC	333/66
SL2S5	dA1	512	T6P-e/A0	ECC	333/66
SL2S6	dA1	512	T6P-e/A0	ECC	350/100
SL2S7	dA1	512	T6P-e/A0	ECC	400/100
SL2SF	dA1	512	T6P-e/A0	ECC	350/100
SL2SH	dA1	512	T6P-e/A0	ECC	400/100
SL2TV	dB0	512	T6P-e/A0	ECC	333/66
SL2U3	dB0	512	T6P-e/A0	ECC	350/100
SL2U4	dB0	512	T6P-e/A0	ECC	350/100
SL2U5	dB0	512	T6P-e/A0	ECC	400/100
SL2U6	dB0	512	T6P-e/A0	ECC	400/100
SL2U7	dB0	512	T6P-e/A0	ECC	450/100
SL2VY	dA1	512	T6P-e/A0	ECC	300/66
SL2W7	dB0	512	T6P-e/A0	ECC	266/66
SL2W8	dB0	512	T6P-e/A0	ECC	300/66
SL2WB	dB0	512	T6P-e/A0	ECC	450/100
SL2WZ	dB0	512	T6P-e/A0	ECC	350/100
SL2YK	dB0	512	T6P-e/A0	ECC	300/66
SL2YM	dB0	512	T6P-e/A0	ECC	400/100

TABLE 13-6 S-SPEC NUMBERS FOR PENTIUM II AND CELERON PROCESSORS *(CONTINUED)*

PENTIUM II PROCESSORS

S-SPEC	MANUFACTURER'S STEP	L2 SIZE (KB)	TAG RAM STEP	MEMORY SUPPORT	SPEED (MHZ) CORE/BUS
SL2ZP	dA1	512	T6P-e/A0	ECC	333/66
SL2ZQ	dA1	512	T6P-e/A0	ECC	350/100
SL33D	dB0	512	T6P-e/A0	ECC	266/66
SL356	dB0	512	T6P-e/A0	ECC	350/100
SL357	dB0	512	T6P-e/A0	ECC	400/100
SL358	dB0	512	T6P-e/A0	ECC	450/100
SL35V	dA1	512	T6P-e/A0	ECC	300/66
SL36U	dB1	512	T6P-e/A0	ECC	350/100
SL37F	dB0	512	T6P-e/A0	ECC	350/100
SL37G	dB0	512	T6P-e/A0	ECC	400/100
SL37H	dB0	512	T6P-e/A0	ECC	450/100
SL38M	dB1	512	T6P-e/A0	ECC	350/100
SL38N	dB1	512	T6P-e/A0	ECC	400/100
SL38Z	dB1	512	T6P-e/A0	ECC	400/100
SL3D5	dB1	512	T6P-e/A0	ECC	400/100
SL3EE	dB0	512	T6P-e/0	ECC	400/100
SL3F9	dB0	512	T6Pe/A0	ECC	400/100
SL3FN	dB0	512	T6P-e/0	ECC	350/100
SL3J2	dB1	512	T6P-e/A0	ECC	350/100

PENTIUM II CELERON PROCESSORS

S-SPEC	MANUFACTURER'S STEP	SPEED (MHZ) CORE/BUS	NOTES
SL2QG	dA1		SEPP (Single Edge Processor Package) Rev. 1
SL2SY	dA0	266/66	SEPP Rev. 1
SL2TR	dA1	266/66	SEPP Rev. 1
SL2WM	mA0	300A/66	SEPP Rev. 1
SL2WN	mA0	333/66	SEPP Rev. 1
SL2X8	dA1	300/66	SEPP Rev. 1
SL2Y2	dA1	300/66	SEPP Rev. 1
SL2Y3	dB0	266/66	SEPP Rev. 1
SL2Y4	dB0	300/66	SEPP Rev. 1
SL2YN	dA0	266/66	SEPP Rev. 1
SL2YP	dA0	300/66	SEPP Rev. 1
SL2Z7	dA0	300/66	SEPP Rev. 1
SL32A	mA0	300A/66	SEPP Rev. 1
SL32B	mA0	333/66	SEPP Rev. 1

TABLE 13-6 S-SPEC NUMBERS FOR PENTIUM II AND CELERON PROCESSORS *(CONTINUED)*

PENTIUM II CELERON PROCESSORS

S-SPEC	MANUFACTURER'S STEP	SPEED (MHZ) CORE/BUS	NOTES
SL35Q	mB0	300A/66	PPGA
SL35R	mB0	333/66	PPGA
SL35S	mB0	366/66	PPGA
SL36A	mB0	300A/66	PPGA
SL36B	mB0	333/66	PPGA
SL36C	mB0	366/66	PPGA
SL376	mA0	366/66	SEPP Rev. 1
SL37Q	mA0	366/66	SEPP Rev. 1
SL37V	mA0	400/66	SEPP Rev. 1
SL37X	mB0	400/66	PPGA
SL39Z	mA0	400/66	SEPP Rev. 1
SL3A2	mB0	400/66	PPGA
SL3BA	mB0	433/66	PPGA
SL3BC	mA0	433/66	SEPP Rev. 1
SL3BS	mB0	433/66	PPGA
SL3EH	mB0	466/66	PPGA
SL3FL	mB0	466/66	PPGA
SL3FY	MB0	500/66	PPGA
SL3FZ	MB0	533/66	PPGA
SL3LQ	MB0	500/66	PPGA
SL3PZ	MB0	533/66	PPGA

PENTIUM II CELERON (1998–CURRENT)

Better known as just the Celeron, Intel introduced this CPU in April 1998. It was originally manufactured as a stripped-down version of the Pentium II. Most noticeably *missing* from the first Celerons was the presence of an L2 cache. This cost-cutting maneuver was intended to compete against the low-cost CPUs being produced by AMD and Cyrix, while continuing to trade on the selling power of the "Intel Inside" mystique. Additional cost reductions are achieved by eliminating the fancy Pentium II plastic cover, creating the Single Edge Processor Package (SEPP or Slot 1-style) Celeron, and adding a PPGA (Plastic Pin Grid Array) case for use in Socket 370 connectors.

The lack of built-in L2 cache severely limited the performance of Intel's early Celerons. Less expensive competing processors *included* L2 cache and outperformed Celerons of the same or similar clock speeds. Beginning with the Celeron 300A model, Intel returned 128KB of built-in cache to the Celeron processors. For the Celeron PPGA, Intel integrated the L2 cache directly on the processor die. This allows the L2 cache speed to scale (or match) processor speed, and improves performance even further. In fact, 128KB of integrated L2 Celeron cache running at the processor speed is said to match the performance of the Pentium II 512KB off-die L2 cache running at half the processor speed.

The Intel Celeron uses the same Pentium Pro and Pentium II "P6" core, providing the same features. It has 32KB L1 cache, 16KB for data, and 16KB for instructions. It includes MMX features, pipelined floating-point unit, dynamic execution architecture, and is constructed with the same 0.25 micron process to reduce heat production.

The Pentium II features that are missing in the Celeron include no support for dual processors and a lower Front Side Bus (FSB) speed—66MHz compared to 100MHz. This allows computer manufacturers to use lower-cost, lower-performance parts and reduce overall system cost. The Celeron also lacks the Pentium III's streaming SIMD extensions, limiting the Celeron's versatility in multimedia applications.

Intel has settled on the PPGA package for the Celeron processor. This provides for lower cost, better cooling, integrated L2 cache, and less expensive motherboard redesign costs (due to the Socket 370-style attachment). The changes required to go from a Socket 7 to a Socket 370 are fewer and less expensive than redesigning for a Slot 1 connector. Third parties make an adapter (referred to as a "Slot-Ket") that allows Socket 370 Celerons to be used in Slot 1 motherboards. Celerons from 266MHz to 433MHz are available in the Single Edge Processor Package (SEPP) style, while Celerons from 300MHz and up are available in the Plastic Pin Grid Array (PPGA) style. The different cache and package style make for an interesting variety, as you can see in Table 13-2. In addition, you can use the S-spec rating marked on each Pentium II Celeron processor to reveal key operating characteristics of the particular CPU. Table 13-6 presents the S-specs for Pentium II and Celeron processors.

PENTIUM III (1999–CURRENT)

First made available in February 1999, the Intel Pentium III may be the last major addition to the Pentium family before the release of Intel's planned 64-bit processor chip. The Pentium III continues to use the same basic P6 core as the Pentium Pro and the Pentium II (so the main issues of the Pentium III remain unchanged). Later Pentium III implementations use a 0.18 micron manufacturing process (compared to the standard 0.25 micron process), which helps lower processor operating temperatures. Processor heat is also addressed with the use of a new SECC 2 (Single Edge Contact Cartridge) package that covers only one side of the chip. This approach decreases weight, lowers cost, and allows for a more efficient attachment of the heat sink assembly. Realizing the advantages of a socket connector with the Pentium III (as well as the Celeron), Intel began to produce the Pentium III in an FC-PGA (Flip Chip–Pin Grid Array) package. Some public statements suggest that Intel will gradually move all processors to the socket style and end their development of edge-connected processors.

The overall performance of the Pentium III continues to improve, with the introduction of higher processor speeds and the ability to utilize a 133MHz Front Side Bus (FSB). You can see the proliferation of Pentium III models in Table 13-2. Intel's Streaming SIMD Extensions (SSE) technology (introduced in the Pentium III) added new registers and instructions to the processor chip—bringing the total number of transistors in the core logic to over 9.5 million. As with MMX extensions, applications must be specifically written to take advantage of these SSE instructions and produce any increase in 3D/graphics performance. Other performance features include a 32KB L1 cache, 512KB L2 cache (operating at half the core processor speed), 4GB addressable memory with ECC, and dual processor support.

Intel introduced the integrated "processor serial number" (or PSN) with the Pentium III. This would allow individual processors (and possibly systems), to be identified remotely over a network. Identification could even take place over the Internet. Seen by Intel as a security enhancement for online transactions, it was viewed as an invasion of privacy by a large segment of users. Public pressure first forced Intel to make it possible to disable this feature, and finally to ship Pentium IIIs with this feature disabled by default. End users can still enable processor serial number identification if they wish.

13

There are a large number of Pentium III versions and features to contend with, and this can make it difficult to determine the proper motherboard configuration for a given P III. However, you can use the S-spec rating marked on each Pentium III processor to reveal key operating characteristics of the particular CPU. Table 13-7 presents the S-specs for the Pentium III processor family.

PENTIUM II/III XEON (1999–CURRENT)

The Xeon processor is the high-performance model of the Pentium II/III family. It is intended for demanding workstation and server environments. The Pentium Xeon's expanded features include support for up to eight processors, L2 cache speed *equal* to core processor speed, and an increased choice of L2 cache size. The Xeon processor is available with L2 cache amounts of 512KB, 1MB, and 2MB. The physical size of the larger cache amounts prohibits placing the cache directly on the processor die—it must be in a separate package next to the core processor. Intel has overcome the cache speed problems associated with

TABLE 13-7 S-SPEC NUMBERS FOR PENTIUM III PROCESSORS

S-SPEC	MANUFACTURER'S STEP	L2 SIZE (KB)	TAG RAM STEP	MEMORY SUPPORT	SPEED (MHZ) CORE/BUS
SL35D	kC0	512	T6P-e/A0	ECC	450/100
SL35E	kC0	512	T6P-e/A0	ECC	500/100
SL364	kB0	512	T6P-e/A0	ECC	450/100
SL365	kB0	512	T6P-e/A0	ECC	500/100
SL37C	kC0	512	T6P-e/A0	ECC	450/100
SL37D	kC0	512	T6P-e/A0	ECC	500/100
SL38E	kB0	512	T6P-e/A0	ECC	450/100
SL38F	kB0	512	T6P-e/A0	ECC	500/100
SL3BN	kC0	512	T6P-e/A0	ECC	533B/133
SL3CC	kB0	512	T6P-e/A0	ECC	450/100
SL3CD	kB0	512	T6P-e/A0	ECC	500/100
SL3E9	kC0	512	T6P-e/A0	ECC	533B/133
SL3F7	kC0	512	T6P-e/A0	ECC	550/100
SL3FJ	kC0	512	T6P-e/A0	ECC	550/100
SL3H6	cA2	256	N/A	ECC	600E/100
SL3H7	cA2	256	N/A	ECC	600EB/133
SL3JM	kC0	512	T6P-e/A0	ECC	600/100
SL3JP	kC0	512	T6p-e/A0	ECC	600B/133
SL3JT	kC0	512	T6P-e/A0	ECC	600/100
SL3JU	kC0	512	T6P-e/A0	ECC	600B/133
SL3KV	cA2	256	N/A	ECC	650/100
SL3KW	cA2	256	N/A	ECC	667/133
SL3N6	cA2	256	N/A	ECC	533EB/133
SL3NA	cA2	256	N/A	ECC	600E/100
SL3NB	cA2	256	N/A	ECC	600EB/133

TABLE 13-7 S-SPEC NUMBERS FOR PENTIUM III PROCESSORS *(CONTINUED)*

S-SPEC	MANUFACTURER'S STEP	L2 SIZE (KB)	TAG RAM STEP	MEMORY SUPPORT	SPEED (MHZ) CORE/BUS
SL3ND	cA2	256	N/A	ECC	667/133
SL3NR	cA2	256	N/A	ECC	650/100
SL3Q9	cA2	256	N/A	ECC	500E/100
SL3QA	cA2	256	N/A	ECC	550E/100
SL3R2	cA2	256	N/A	ECC	500E/100
SL3R3	cA2	256	N/A	ECC	550E/100
SL3S9	cA2	256	N/A	ECC	700/100
SL3SB	cA2	256	N/A	ECC	733/133
SL3SX	cA2	256	N/A	ECC	533EB/133
SL3SY	cA2	256	N/A	ECC	700/100
SL3SZ	cA2	256	N/A	ECC	733/133
SL3VF	cA2	256	N/A	ECC	533EB/133
SL3VH	cA2	256	N/A	ECC	600E/100
SL3VJ	cA2	256	N/A	ECC	650/100
SL3VK	cA2	256	N/A	ECC	667/133
SL3VL	cA2	256	N/A	ECC	700/100
SL3VM	cA2	256	N/A	ECC	733/133
SL3VN	cA2	256	N/A	ECC	750/100
SL3WA	cA2	256	N/A	ECC	800EB/133
SL3WC	cA2	256	N/A	ECC	750/100
SL3Z6	cA2	256	N/A	ECC	800/100
SLVG	cA2	256	N/A	ECC	600EB/133

the separate core—cache location—thus enabling the Xeon cache to run at core processor speeds. The increased physical size created by this arrangement also means the Pentium Xeon cannot use the Slot 1 motherboard connector. The Slot 2 connector was developed to accommodate the Xeon's increased size.

ITANIUM (MID-2000–FUTURE)

Scheduled for release in mid-2000, the Intel Itanium will be the first 64-bit processor. Intel's IA-64 architecture is a combination of innovative features, which addresses the performance limitations of traditional processor types. The Itanium architecture is based on next-generation performance features such as "Explicit Parallelism" and "Predication and Speculation," resulting in superior processing efficiency and increased instructions per cycle (IPC). This added processing power can help to address the future requirements of demanding Internet, high-end server, and workstation applications. In addition, the IA-64 architecture provides headroom and scalability for continued future growth.

The first engineering samples of Intel's Itanium processor have already been delivered to Intel motherboard developers. With the processor on schedule for production in mid-2000, the Itanium processor-based servers and workstations should be available in the second half of the year.

The AMD CPUs

Advanced Micro Devices (AMD), once Intel's ally, has become its single biggest competitor. AMD is known for providing well-designed and highly compatible alternative processors to the PC industry, and has been active in processor manufacturing and marketing since the days of the 386 (with its Am386). Although AMD tends to lag just a little behind the release of new Intel CPUs, that gap is closing fast. With the release of AMD's newest processors (such as the Athlon), AMD is actually pushing a bit ahead in terms of processor performance and operating speeds.

AM486DX SERIES (1994–1995)

The Am486 series was AMD's answer to Intel's i486 clock-doubling and -tripling OverDrive processors of the early 1990s. They incorporate write-back cache and enhanced power management features, including 3-volt operation, SMM (system management mode), and clock control (appealing for Energy Star–compliant "green" desktop systems and portable PCs). Available as Am486DX4/75, Am486DX4/100, and Am486DX4/120, the AMD 486 line saw service in many late-model, low-cost 486-compatible platforms. These processors are totally obsolete today, and chances are that you will not see such processors in service unless you're retrofitting an older system.

AM5X86 (1995–CURRENT)

The Am5x86 is the processor that put AMD on the map. With the appearance of Intel's Pentium line, PC users were faced with the choice of upgrading their motherboard to accommodate a true Pentium CPU, or using an expensive Pentium OverDrive processor in a 486 system. AMD rose to the challenge by developing the Am5x86 (or simply the "5x86") as an alternative to Intel's Pentium OverDrive processors. The Am5x86 achieves Pentium-level performance by running "clock quadrupled" at 133MHz (using the 33MHz bus speed of a 486 motherboard). This native 33MHz speed also supported the then-emerging 33MHz PCI bus perfectly. Additional features such as a unified 16KB cache using write-back technology further improved the 5x86's performance. In actual practice, Am5x86 microprocessors provide greater performance than a Pentium 75MHz while costing far less than a Pentium at the time. The 5x85 became the standard CPU upgrade for 486 owners who wanted to utilize Pentium-class software without a major hardware upgrade.

The 5x86 also offered integrated power management features, including 3-volt operation, SMM, and clock control. This allowed the 5x86 to consume less power and run cooler than Pentium 75MHz or i486DX4/100 processors. Both desktop and mobile PCs benefited from these features. The 5x86 is totally obsolete today, though you may encounter them when retrofitting older 486-based systems.

K5 SERIES (1996–CURRENT)

Although the Am5x86 proved to be an extremely popular processor, it was not a true Pentium alternative. It was not until 1996 that AMD released its K5 series to the PC industry. As a true Pentium alternative, it is fully compatible with Socket 7 (Pentium) motherboards—a drop-in replacement. At most, the K5 might require a motherboard BIOS upgrade for proper identification and support with the motherboard's chipset. But the K5 is fully compatible with all x86 operating systems and software.

The K5 series is rated using the P-rating (or PR) system. (See the "The P-Rating (PR) System" section earlier in the chapter.) Rather than using iCOMP or SPEC benchmarks to categorize the processor's performance, each K5 is assigned a PR number that corresponds to an Intel Pentium operating at the given

TABLE 13-8 AMD FAMILY COMPARISON

CHIP	MHZ	BUS SPEED	L1 CACHE	L2 CACHE	FABRIC. FACTOR	TRANS. SPECFP	FORM	VOLTS	WATTS	SPECINT	AVAIL-ABILITY
AMD K5.x											
K5.0—P75 (no MMX)	75	50	24KB	—	0.35	4.3 mil	Socket 7	N/A	N/A	N/A	Obsolete
K5.0—P90	90	60	24KB	—	0.35	4.3 mil	Socket 7	N/A	N/A	N/A	Obsolete
K5.0—P100	100	66	24KB	—	0.35	4.3 mil	Socket 7	N/A	N/A	N/A	Obsolete
K5.1—P120	90	60	24KB	—	0.35	4.3 mil	Socket 7	N/A	N/A	N/A	Obsolete
K5.1—P133	100	66	24KB	—	0.35	4.3 mil	Socket 7	N/A	N/A	N/A	Obsolete
K5.2—P166	116	66	24KB	—	0.35	4.3 mil	Socket 7	N/A	N/A	N/A	Available
AMD K6 (Classic with MMX)											
	166	66	64KB	—	0.35	8.8 mil	Socket 7	N/A	N/A	N/A	Obsolete
	200	66	64KB	—	0.35	8.8 mil	Socket 7	N/A	N/A	N/A	Obsolete
	233	66	64KB	—	0.35/0.25	8.8 mil	Socket 7	3.2	28	N/A	Available
	266	66	64KB	—	0.25	8.8 mil	Socket 7	2.2	15	N/A	Available
	300	66/100	64KB	—	0.25	8.8 mil	Super 7	2.2	N/A	N/A	Available
AMD K6 Mobile											
	233	66	64KB	—	0.25	9.3 mil	Socket 7	2.1	N/A	N/A	Obsolete
	266	66	64KB	—	0.25	9.3 mil	Socket 7	2.1	N/A	N/A	Available
	300	66	64KB	—	0.25	9.3 mil	Socket 7	2.2	N/A	N/A	Available
AMD K6-2 (*Chompers* or K6 3D MMX)											
	266	66	64KB	—	0.25	9.3 mil	Socket 7	2.2	N/A	N/A	Obsolete
	300	66/100	64KB	—	0.25	9.3 mil	Soc 7/Sup 7	2.2	N/A	N/A	Available
	333	95	64KB	—	0.25	9.3 mil	Super 7	2.2	N/A	N/A	Available
	350	100	64KB	—	0.25	9.3 mil	Super 7	2.2	N/A	N/A	Available
	366	66	64KB	—	0.25	9.3 mil	Socket 7	2.2	N/A	N/A	Available
	380	95	64KB	—	0.25	9.3 mil	Super 7	2.2	N/A	N/A	Available
	400	100/66	64KB	—	0.25	9.3 mil	Super 7	2.2	N/A	N/A	Available

13

TABLE 13-8 AMD FAMILY COMPARISON *(CONTINUED)*

CHIP	MHZ	BUS SPEED	L1 CACHE	L2 CACHE	FABRIC. FACTOR	TRANS. SPECFP	FORM	VOLTS	WATTS	SPECINT	AVAIL-ABILITY
AMD K6-2 (*Chompers* or K6 3D MMX) *(Continued)*											
	450	100	64KB	—	0.25	9.3 mil	Super 7	2.4	28	N/A	Available
	475	95	64KB	—	0.25	9.3 mil	Super 7	2.4	30	N/A	Available
	500	100	64KB	—	0.25	9.3 mil	Super 7	N/A	N/A	N/A	Available
	533	133	64KB	—	0.18	9.3 mil	Super 7	N/A	N/A	N/A	Available
AMD K6-2/P (Mobile K6-2)											
	266	66	64KB	—	0.25	9.3 mil	Socket 7	N/A	N/A	N/A	Obsolete
	300	100	64KB	—	0.25	9.3 mil	Super 7	N/A	N/A	N/A	Available
	333	66	64KB	—	0.25	9.3 mil	Socket 7	1.8	11	N/A	Available
	350	100	64KB	—	0.25	9.3 mil	Super 7	N/A	N/A	N/A	Available
	366	66	64KB	—	0.25	9.3 mil	Super 7	N/A	N/A	N/A	Available
	380	95	64KB	—	0.25	9.3 mil	Super 7	N/A	N/A	N/A	Available
	400	100	64KB	—	0.25	9.3 mil	Super 7	N/A	N/A	N/A	Available
	433	66	64KB	—	0.25	9.3 mil	Super 7	N/A	N/A	N/A	Available
	450	100	64KB	—	0.25	9.3 mil	Super 7	N/A	N/A	N/A	Available
	475	95	64KB	—	0.25	9.3 mil	Super 7	N/A	N/A	N/A	Available
AMD K6-2+											
	500	100	64KB	—	0.18	N/A	Super 7	N/A	N/A	N/A	Available
	533	133	64KB	128KB	0.18	N/A	Super 7	N/A	N/A	N/A	Available
AMD K6-3 (*Sharptooth* or K6+ 3D MMX)											
	400	100/66	64KB	256KB	0.25	21.3 mil	Super 7	2.4	N/A	N/A	Available
	450	100	64KB	256KB	0.25	21.3 mil	Super 7	2.4	30	N/A	Available
	475	95	64KB	256KB	0.25	21.3 mil	Super 7	N/A	N/A	N/A	mid-2000
	500	100	64KB	256KB	0.25	21.3 mil	Super 7	N/A	N/A	N/A	mid-2000
	550	100	64KB	256KB	0.18	21.3 mil	Super 7	N/A	N/A	N/A	mid-2000
	600	100	64KB	256KB	0.18	21.3 mil	Super 7	N/A	N/A	N/A	mid-2000

TABLE 13-8 AMD FAMILY COMPARISON *(CONTINUED)*

CHIP	MHZ	BUS SPEED	L1 CACHE	L2 CACHE	FABRIC. FACTOR	TRANS. SPECFP	FORM	VOLTS	WATTS	SPECINT	AVAIL-ABILITY
AMD K6-3/P (Mobile K6-3)											
	350	100	64KB	256KB	0.25	21.3 mil	N/A	2.2	12	N/A	Available
	366	66	64KB	256KB	0.25	21.3 mil	N/A	2.2	12	N/A	Available
	380	95	64KB	256KB	0.25	21.3 mil	N/A	2.2	12	N/A	Available
	400	100	64KB	256KB	0.25	21.3 mil	N/A	N/A	N/A	N/A	Available
	433	N/A	64KB	256KB	0.25	21.3 mil	N/A	N/A	N/A	N/A	Available
	450	N/A	64KB	256KB	0.25	21.3 mil	N/A	N/A	N/A	N/A	Available
AMD Athlon (K7)											
	500	200	128KB	512KB	0.25	22 mil	Slot A	1.6	42	N/A	Available
	550	200	128KB	512KB	0.25	22 mil	Slot A	1.6	46	N/A	Available
	600	200	128KB	512KB	0.25	22 mil	Slot A	1.6	50	28/22	Available
	650	200	128KB	512KB	0.25	22 mil	Slot A	1.6	54	30/23	Available
	700	200	128KB	512KB	0.25	22 mil	Slot A	N/A	50	32/24	Available
	750	200	128KB	512KB	0.18	22 mil	Slot A	N/A	N/A	N/A	Available
	800	200	128KB	512KB	0.18	22 mil	Slot A	N/A	N/A	N/A	Available
	900	200	128KB	512KB	0.18	22 mil	Slot A	N/A	N/A	N/A	Q1 2000
(Copper)	1000	200	128KB	512KB	0.18	22 mil	Slot A	N/A	N/A	N/A	Q2 2000
AMD Athlon "Ultra" (*Thunderbird*)											
	1000	266	128KB	256KB	0.18	22 mil	Slot A	N/A	60	N/A	Q2 2000
AMD Athlon "Select" (*Spitfire*)											
	600+	200	128KB	512KB	0.18	22 mil	Socket A	N/A	N/A	N/A	Q2 2000
AMD Mobile K7											
	500+	N/A	128KB	multi-MB	0.18	N/A	N/A	N/A	N/A	N/A	2000
AMD Athlon 2 (*Mustang*)											
	N/A	200	128KB	up to 2MB	0.18	N/A	Soc A/Slot A ?		N/A	N/A	Q2 2000

13

clock speed. For example, a K5 PR120 performs equivalently to a true Pentium at 120MHz. Table 13-8 lists a comparison of K5 performance figures.

K6 SERIES (1997–CURRENT)

The K6 processor closed much of the performance gap between AMD and Intel processors. Based on AMD's RISC86 superscalar microarchitecture, the K6 was touted as being competitive with Intel's Pentium II processor in terms of performance. The K6 also incorporates a full suite of support for MMX instructions, and should be fully compatible with all x86 operating systems and software (as well as software designed for MMX enhancements). Since the K6 continues to use the well-established Socket 7 architecture, it should serve as a drop-in replacement for K5 and Pentium CPUs to provide MMX capability. At most, the K6 may require an upgrade to the motherboard BIOS for proper identification and support with the motherboard chipset. Table 13-8 lists the major K6 variations.

The K6 incorporates seven parallel execution engines and employs two-level branch prediction. When coupled with speculative and full-out-of-order execution techniques, the 166–300MHz K6 family presented a serious challenge to Intel's Pentium MMX and early Pentium II processors. A large 64KB L1 cache provides 32KB for data and 32KB for instructions. The IEEE 754-compatible floating-point unit (FPU) provides performance at least equivalent to the Pentium MMX, and full support for SMM (system management mode) ensures excellent power control. Mobile versions of the K6 have been optimized for use in laptop PC systems.

K6-2 AND K6-3 (1998–CURRENT)

AMD introduced an improved K6 processor in 1998. The "2" in K6-2 is earned with the addition of higher clock speeds and higher bus speeds with the K6 core. Bus speeds up to 100MHz are supported on Super 7 (Socket 7 with AGP support) motherboards. A significant addition to the K6-2 was the introduction of AMD's 3DNow technology. 3DNow is a set of 21 multimedia instructions increasing performance in 3D, multimedia, and floating-point-intensive applications. It is an extension to MMX using SIMD (Single Instruction Multiple Data) technology. The 3DNow technology is also employed by IDT/Centaur and Cyrix in their newer processors. The use of 3DNow, a large L1 cache, integrated "core speed" L2 cache, and Socket 7 compatibility are a few of the features that contribute to the K6-2's continued popularity and performance. The K6-3 is merely a K6-2 with 256KB of full core speed, on-die L2 cache. The K6-2 and K6-3 are AMD's answer to Intel's Pentium II/III. (Competing with the Pentium name is as important as competing with Pentium performance.) Table 13-8 lists the available K6-2 and K6-3 processors.

To compete in the performance arena, AMD runs the K6 family of processors as close to their upper limits as possible. Compatible motherboards must be capable of supplying the required split voltages at *very* close tolerances. A list of truly compatible and tested motherboards is kept at the AMD Web site (**www.amd.com**). The upper-limit operation of the K6 processors requires that close attention be paid to heat dissipation. Heat sinks and fans must be securely attached, and thermal grease must be used. System airflow should provide for maximum CPU cooling. When working on an AMD system exhibiting erratic behavior, both these areas should be examined closely.

> If you plan to upgrade your system from a K6-2 to a K6-3 processor, you may need a BIOS upgrade to fully support the K6-3.

ATHLON (1999–CURRENT)

With the introduction of the AMD Athlon, competition in the high-performance processor market reached a whole new level. First produced at 500MHz, the Athlon's current speeds are over 850MHz (with AMD promising 1GHz sometime in the year 2000). The AMD Athlon and Intel's Itanium basically eliminate any other manufacturer's ability to compete in this market. AMD's constantly improving ability to compete head-to-head with Intel in the Socket 7–style processors is thought to be part of the reason Intel changed to a slot-style connector. Rather than developing a compatible Slot 1 processor, AMD decided it was time to implement their own ideas on how a processor should be integrated in a system. They accepted the slot form factor so that motherboard manufacturers would not have to completely redesign the layout of their motherboards to accept the AMD Athlon, but shape and pin count are the only similarities. AMD's slot connector is named Slot A. Although both the AMD and Intel processors utilize a 242-pin interface, Slot A and Slot 1 processors are not interchangeable.

The Athlon is optimized for high clock frequencies featuring a super-pipelined, superscalar microarchitecture. It contains a total of nine execution pipelines: three for address calculations, three for integer calculations, and three for executing x87 (floating-point), 3DNow, and MMX instructions. AMD specifically addressed its floating point and gaming image problem with the first fully pipelined superscalar floating-point engine and enhanced 3DNow technology. According to some tests, the floating-point performance of the AMD Athlon is more than 35 percent higher than an equally clocked Pentium III Xeon processor.

Enhanced 3DNow adds 24 new instructions—19 instructions to improve MMX integer math calculations and enhance data movement for Internet streaming applications, and 5 DSP extensions for soft modem, soft ADSL, Dolby Digital, and MP3 applications. This new DSP functionality of the AMD Athlon is *not* supported by the Pentium III. L1 cache on the Athlon is 128KB, and the 64-bit backside L2 cache controller supports L2 cache sizes from 512KB to 8MB. The cache design utilizes the processor's high-performance system bus and minimizes bottlenecks caused by bus bandwidth limitations.

AMD supports its claim that the Athlon is a seventh generation (7x86) processor with the implementation of an entirely different system bus architecture than that utilized by the Intel Pentium family of CPUs. AMD licensed the Alpha EV-6 bus technology from Digital Equipment Corporation. The Athlon system bus operates at 200MHz with a bandwidth capable of 1.6GB/second data transfer speeds. With multiple processors, the system bus can scale up to 3.2GB/sec at 400MHz. It includes advanced technology such as point-to-point topology, source-synchronous packet-based transfers, and low-voltage signaling. You can compare the 500–800MHz Athlon models in Table 13-8.

The AMD Athlon processor bus architecture is designed to support scalable multiprocessing. The number of AMD Athlon processors in a multiprocessor system is a function of chipset implementation, and not the AMD Athlon processor design. Forthcoming optimized chipsets are planned to enable multiprocessor system designs based on 2, 4, 8, or more AMD Athlon processors. Although supporting chipsets were scarce at first, all major motherboard manufacturers are now producing models supporting the AMD Athlon with a choice of chipsets from AMD, VIA, or ALi.

The Cyrix CPUs

Cyrix emerged as a major alternative processor manufacturer in 1992 with their release of the Cyrix 486SLC, and later in 1993 with their 486DX4. By 1995, the Cyrix 5x86 (the "M1sc") had presented the only serious competition to the AMD 5x86. Based in no small part on their relationship with IBM, Cyrix has established itself in the PC industry behind Intel and AMD, but they have been working very hard to close the technology and performance gap, which seems to have plagued some of their more recent Cyrix offerings.

6X86 SERIES (1995–CURRENT)

Cyrix introduced their 6x86 (dubbed the "M1"—later versions were called "M1R") in 1995 as an answer to the Intel Pentium optimized for both 16-bit and 32-bit software. The 6x86 Socket 7 processor achieves its performance through the use of two optimized super-pipelined integer units and an on-chip FPU. The integer and floating-point units are tailored for maximum instruction throughput by using techniques the include register renaming, out-of-order completion, data dependency removal, branch prediction, and speculative execution. The processor includes a 16KB unified write-back cache. In most respects, the 6x86 uses many of the same techniques found in other Pentium-class processors.

The 6x86 series uses P-rating (or PR) figures instead of iCOMP or SPEC numbers to indicate relative performance. For example, a Cyrix PR150+ processor will perform as well as a Pentium processor running at 150MHz. You'll find PR120+, PR133+, PR150+, PR166+, and PR200+ versions of the 6x86 available (the "+" indicates performance better than the corresponding Pentium). Table 13-9 outlines the various clock settings for each version.

There are two drawbacks to the Cyrix 6x86. First, the floating-point unit (FPU) does not perform as well as those of similar Intel and AMD processors. Although this does not really affect most basic software and operating systems, math-intensive programs (especially 3D computer games) can suffer reduced performance. There is little that can be done with this issue in the 6x86 family, though subsequent processor versions (like the M2) do provide a better FPU. The second drawback to the 6x86 has been excessive heating. In practice, 6x86 processors produce more heat than their AMD or Intel counterparts. Cyrix has addressed this issue by releasing the 6x86L (or M1R) series in 1996. The *L* designation means "low power." More specifically, the 6x86L uses a split voltage of 3.3 volts to handle I/O operations with other chips, and 2.8 volts to run the core of the CPU itself. Traditional 6x86 processors use 3.3 volts or 3.52 volts only. In order to support a 6x86L, a motherboard must provide split voltages, or a voltage regulator module must be added between the CPU socket and processor.

> The split voltage operation of a 6x86L uses the same voltage levels as an MMX processor. However, the 6x86L is not an MMX processor. These split voltages were chosen so that the 6x86L would be compatible with split voltage motherboards, and could be later replaced with an MMX-compatible device such as the 6x86MX (or M2).

MEDIAGX (1996–CURRENT)

Traditional PCs use stand-alone media-related devices such as a video card and a sound card. This increases the overall cost of a PC and opens the opportunity for hardware conflicts. The Cyrix MediaGX processor incorporates the features of audio and video, along with many other conventional motherboard components. This high level of integration provides the basis for low-cost entry-level systems that still offer good performance. The 3.3–3.6-volt MediaGX system actually consists of two chips—the MediaGX processor itself and the MediaGX Cx5510 companion chip.

The MediaGX processor is a 64-bit device with a proven x86-compatible processor core. The CPU directly interfaces to a PCI bus and DRAM memory. High-quality SVGA graphics are provided by an advanced graphics accelerator right on the MediaGX processor. The graphics frame buffer is stored in main memory without the performance degradation associated with traditional Unified Memory Archi-

TABLE 13-9 CYRIX FAMILY COMPARISON

CHIP	MHZ	BUS SPEED	L1 CACHE	L2 CACHE	FABRIC. FACTOR	TRANS. SPECFP	FORM	VOLTS	WATTS	SPECINT	AVAIL-ABILITY
Cyrix 6x86 (M1)											
6x86-P120	100	50	16KB	—	0.6	3 mil	Socket 7	N/A	N/A	N/A	Obsolete
6x86-P133	110	55	16KB	—	0.6	3 mil	Socket 7	N/A	N/A	N/A	Obsolete
6x86-P150	120	60	16KB	—	0.6	3 mil	Socket 7	N/A	N/A	N/A	Obsolete
6x86-P166	133	66	16KB	—	0.6	3 mil	Socket 7	N/A	N/A	N/A	Obsolete
6x86-P200	150	75	16KB	—	0.6	3 mil	Socket 7	N/A	N/A	N/A	Obsolete
Cyrix MediaGX/MediaPC											
	120	60	16KB	—	0.45	N/A	N/A	N/A	N/A	N/A	Obsolete
	133	66	16KB	—	0.45	N/A	N/A	N/A	N/A	N/A	Obsolete
	150	60	16KB	—	0.45	N/A	N/A	N/A	N/A	N/A	Obsolete
	166	66	16KB	—	0.35	N/A	N/A	N/A	N/A	N/A	Obsolete
	180	60	16KB	—	0.35	N/A	N/A	N/A	N/A	N/A	Obsolete
	200	60	16KB	—	N/A	N/A	N/A	N/A	N/A	N/A	Obsolete
	233	66	16KB	—	N/A	N/A	N/A	N/A	N/A	N/A	Available
	266	66	16KB	—	N/A	N/A	N/A	N/A	N/A	N/A	Available
	300	66	16KB	—	N/A	N/A	N/A	N/A	N/A	N/A	Available

13

TABLE 13-9 CYRIX FAMILY COMPARISON *(CONTINUED)*

CHIP	MHZ	BUS SPEED	L1 CACHE	L2 CACHE	FABRIC. FACTOR	TRANS. SPECFP	FORM	VOLTS	WATTS	SPECINT	AVAIL-ABILITY
Via/Cyrix 6x86MX (M2)											
166-PR	150/133	60/66	64KB	—	0.35	N/A	Socket 7	N/A	N/A	N/A	Obsolete
200-PR	160/150	66/75	64KB	—	0.35	N/A	Socket 7	N/A	N/A	N/A	Obsolete
233-PR	188/166	75/83	64KB	—	0.35	N/A	Socket 7	N/A	N/A	N/A	Available
266-PR	208	83	64KB	—	0.30	N/A	Socket 7	N/A	N/A	N/A	Available
300-PR	233	66	64KB	—	0.30	N/A	Socket 7	N/A	N/A	N/A	Available
333-PR	250	83	64KB	—	0.30	N/A	Socket 7	N/A	N/A	N/A	Available
366-PR	250	100	64KB	—	0.25	N/A	Super 7	N/A	N/A	N/A	Available
400-PR	266	100	64KB	—	0.18	N/A	Super 7	N/A	N/A	N/A	Q1 2000
433-PR	300	100	64KB	—	0.18	N/A	Super 7	N/A	N/A	N/A	Q1 2000
466-PR	333	100	64KB	—	0.18	N/A	Super 7	N/A	N/A	N/A	Q1 2000
Via "Joshua" (a.k.a. *Gobi/Jedi*/MII+)											
PR400	N/A	133	64KB	256KB	0.18	N/A	Soc 370	N/A	N/A	N/A	Q1 2000
PR450	N/A	133	64KB	256KB	0.18	N/A	Soc 370	N/A	N/A	N/A	Q1 2000
PR500	N/A	133	64KB	256KB	0.18	N/A	Soc 370	N/A	N/A	N/A	Q2 2000
Cyrix Mojave (*Jalapeno*/MIII)											
	1200	N/A	N/A	256KB	0.18	N/A	Soc 370	N/A	N/A	N/A	Q4 2000
Cyrix MXi											
	466	N/A	64KB	N/A	0.18	N/A	N/A	N/A	N/A	N/A	Available
	500	N/A	64KB	N/A	0.18	N/A	N/A	N/A	N/A	N/A	Available

tecture (UMA) system designs due to Cyrix's Display Compression Technology (DCT) approach. The processor is available from 120MHz to 300MHz (Table 13-9). It includes a 16KB unified L1 cache, a floating-point unit, and enhanced system management mode (SMM) features. The PCI controller handles fixed, rotating, hybrid, or ping-pong bus arbitration. It supports four masters (three on PCI bus). It uses a synchronous CPU/PCI bus frequency, and supports concurrent CPU and PCI operations. The video system supports up to 1280×1024×8, and 1024×768×16 display modes. The MediaGX also works with EDO RAM and supports up to 128MB of RAM in four banks.

The MediaGX Cx5510 companion chip represents a new generation of integrated, single-chip controllers for Cyrix's line of MediaGX-compatible processors. The Cx5510 bridges the MediaGX processor over the PCI bus to the ISA bus, performs traditional chipset functions, and supports a sound interface compatible with industry-standard sound cards such as the Creative Labs Sound Blaster.

The key issue to keep in mind with the MediaGX series is that it is not Socket 7 compatible. The MediaGX and companion chip are a surface-mounted solution designed for dedicated motherboards. This means that MediaGX motherboards are not upgradable to other Socket 7 processors.

6X86MX (1997–CURRENT)

The 6x86MX (referred to as the "M2") is the Cyrix response to MMX processors like the AMD K6 and Intel Pentium MMX. The 6x86MX design quadruples the original 6x86 internal cache size to 64KB, and increases the operating frequency to 200MHz and beyond. Additionally, it features the 57 new MMX instructions that speed up the processing of certain computing-intensive loops found in multimedia and communication applications. The 6x86MX processor also contains a scratch-pad RAM feature, and supports performance monitoring. It delivers optimum 16-bit and 32-bit performance while running Windows 95/98, Windows NT, OS/2, DOS, UNIX, and other x86 operating systems. The 6x86MX processor features a super-pipelined architecture and advanced techniques including register renaming, out-of-order completion, data dependency removal, branch prediction, and speculative execution.

You'll find 6x86MX processors available in 150MHz (PR166), 166MHz (PR200), 188MHz (PR233), 225MHz (PR266), and 250MHz (PR300) versions. Current Cyrix M2 processors are produced at speeds up to 333MHZ (PR466). As with other Cyrix processors, performance is rated using the P-rating (or PR) nomenclature. For example, a Cyrix 6x86MX at 160MHz performs equally to an Intel Pentium processor at 200MHz (Table 13-9).

Cyrix was purchased by VIA Technologies—better known for their chipsets. VIA also purchased IDT's Centaur design subsidiary, including intellectual property related to WinChip microprocessor technology and the x86 microprocessor design team located in Austin, Texas. VIA has announced plans to produce a Socket 370–compatible processor code-named "Joshua." It will feature an integrated 64KB L1 cache, 256KB L2 cache, 133MHz FSB, 3DNow compatibility, and enhanced dual pipelined MMX and FPU. It will be manufactured using 0.18 micron technology. VIA has announced it will target the lower-priced, entry-level PC market.

CPU Overclocking

PC evolution is often a race for performance, and designers are constantly struggling to make the most of every last clock tick. Many factors are involved in computer performance, but CPU speed is one of the most important. Faster and better CPUs have been a driving force in computer development, and older CPUs are frequently upgraded with new ones in order to wring ever-more performance from current systems. While outright CPU replacements are common, they can also be expensive. As an alternative to

CPU replacement, PC users and technicians alike are turning to *overclocking* as a means of maximizing the performance of an existing CPU. This part of the chapter offers a comprehensive set of guidelines and procedures that can help you make informed overclocking decisions.

Overclocking is basically the practice of reconfiguring a PC to operate a CPU at a higher clock speed (or *bus speed*) than the particular CPU has been specified for. A system can be reconfigured to overclock a CPU in a matter of minutes simply by changing one or two jumpers on the motherboard. Ideally, this higher clock speed should increase the CPU's performance without damaging the CPU or reducing its working life. The economics of overclocking can be compelling. In most cases, overclocking can be accomplished with most modern CPUs for less than $30 for a new cooling unit—as opposed to $300 to $800 or more for a new CPU.

Overclocking carries inherent risks to the CPU, including permanent damage to the CPU itself, and should never be undertaken without careful consideration of the consequences. CPU overclocking is not encouraged as a regular practice, and can be illegal if an overclocked system is sold without informing the buyer!

REQUIREMENTS FOR OVERCLOCKING

The most important factor to grasp about CPU overclocking is that it is not a *universally* successful technique. In many cases, your efforts to overclock a PC will fail. There are four critical elements of any PC that influence overclocking: the CPU, the motherboard, system RAM, and CPU cooling. Trouble in any one of those elements will result in overclocking problems.

CPU Issues CPUs manufactured by Intel (especially the Celerons) seem to be the most successful at overclocking—usually because AMD and Cyrix/IBM CPUs are often running very close to their rated limits already, to compete with their Intel counterparts. However, not all Intel CPUs are suitable for overclocking. CPUs marked with the SY022 and SU073 S-spec numbers are often limited to clock multipliers of more than x2. Also check for "faked" CPUs (which have been remarked and resold at higher clock speeds already). Remarked CPUs are a frequent practice in Europe, but it's always worth a check of the CPU first before proceeding. As a rule, if you can peel off any stickers underneath the CPU, it is remarked, and most likely running over its originally rated speed anyway.

Most current CPUs have locked clock multipliers. The manufacturers claim that this is to protect the end user from remarked CPUs and to assure the integrity of performance claims. The overclocking community thinks that locked multipliers are implemented in order to force the purchase of a new CPU to improve performance.

Motherboard Issues Even if your CPU seems perfect for overclocking, the motherboard may not be. Signal reflections and other electrical limitations with its bus signals can cause the system to crash or hang. Overclocked CPUs are also more sensitive to unstable signals from the bus and will crash if the motherboard can't deliver "clean" signals. Brand-name motherboards such as Tyan (**www.tyan com**) or Supermicro (**www.supermicro.com**) will *tend* to support CPU overclocking better than cut-priced no-name motherboards. As a result, you may find that some PCs can be overclocked easily, while others suffer severe performance problems (or will not operate at all after overclocking).

Motherboard bus speeds can present another wrinkle. Most traditional motherboards only support bus speeds up to 66MHz or 100MHz, but more recent motherboard designs can operate at 112MHz or 143MHz. These higher bus speeds will greatly affect the clock multiplier ratio when configuring your overclocking strategy, so be sure to understand the clock speed limits and multipliers for your particular motherboard.

The motherboard should also support a wide range of CPU supply voltages. For example, a "STD" voltage of 3.3V and a "VRE" voltage of 3.45V are common with Pentium-class systems. If you use an MMX-type CPU (such as the P55C, the 6x86MX, or the K6), you'll need access to "split voltage" support (2.8V and 3.3V are typical). This may not sound so important because you're not "changing" the CPU. But in some cases, you may need to boost the CPU supply voltage just a bit to support overclocking. Today, you'll find that Slot1/Slot A motherboards set their CPU voltages automatically when the CPU is installed, so don't panic if you have trouble locating CPU voltage jumpers.

RAM Issues System RAM can also be a problem in overclocked systems when the bus speed exceeds 66MHz—you'll require high-end EDO RAM or SDRAM. As a rule, EDO RAM works best with 66MHz motherboards, while low-end SDRAM tends to be best with 75MHz and 83MHz motherboards. Current bus speeds of 100MHz and 133MHz require high-end SDRAM memory certified for PC100 (100MHz) and PC133 (133MHz) bus speeds, respectively.

Cooling Issues Perhaps the most overlooked problem with CPU overclocking is insufficient cooling. CPUs draw current with each clock tick. The more clock cycles in a given period, the more current is required, and the more heat is generated. Most current CPUs run hot to begin with, but when overclocked, a CPU can easily overheat and crash (or perhaps suffer permanent damage). As a consequence, you should never attempt to overclock a CPU without making accommodations for better cooling. Consider a high-capacity, top-quality heat sink/fan assembly with a reliable ball-bearing fan offering a K/W (kelvin per watt) value of 1K/W or less. You may need to go to a hobby electronics store or full-featured computer store to find a good-quality heat sink/fan. When installing the cooling unit, make sure it fits to the CPU tightly without any air gaps, and use a thin layer of thermal grease between the CPU and heat sink.

POTENTIAL PITFALLS

Before we actually get into the techniques of CPU overclocking, there are some potential faults that you should be aware of. There are three typical failures associated with CPU overclocking: intermittent operation, shortened life span, and outright failure. All three faults are heat related.

- *Intermittent operation* The added heat produced in the CPU can result in internal signal errors (a lost bit or shift of signal timing) that can easily cause the PC to crash—forcing you to power-down the system until the CPU cools.
- *Shortened life span* This is another heat-related problem. Rather than an immediate failure, excessive heat can shorten a CPU's life through a process called *electromigration*. Rather than a CPU working for 10 years, it may only work for 2 years or 5 years (it's impossible to say for certain).
- *Outright failure* A CPU is designed to operate from –25 to 80 degrees C. If the CPU is not cooled properly, the CPU die can exceed its maximum working temperature, and the CPU can fail. Though there are millions of transistors on a modern CPU, it only takes the failure of one or two to destroy a CPU.

OVERCLOCKING THE SYSTEM

At this point, you're ready to try some overclocking yourself. Generally speaking, overclocking requires three basic steps: change the bus speed, change the multiplier, and change the supply voltage. Note that you do not always have to change all three settings in order to successfully overclock a CPU. The general steps to overclock a CPU are outlined below. To give you an idea of what may change, Tables 13-10 and 13-11 list some generic overclocking suggestions for older 486 and Pentium-class systems.

1. Turn off the computer. Open it up and get your motherboard manual.
2. Check the markings on the top and bottom of your CPU, write them down, and reinstall the CPU. (This helps to ensure that the CPU is "real" and not remarked.)
3. Check the current clock speed and multiplier jumper settings on your motherboard, compare them with your manual, and write them down.
4. Check the supply voltage jumper settings on your motherboard, compare them with the manual and your CPU marking, and write them down.
5. Inspect the cooling unit on your CPU, and upgrade the cooling unit (if necessary).
6. Change the jumper settings for clock speed and/or multiplier according to your target overclocked level.
7. Double-check that the jumpers are set as expected.
8. Start the computer and allow it to boot.
9. Does it boot or reach the CMOS setup? If yes, go to step 12; if no, go to step 10.
10. Turn off the computer and change CPU voltage jumper to a *slightly* higher voltage (if possible).
11. If you still can't boot or reach the CMOS setup, return the voltage setting to its original value. You cannot overclock at this desired speed. Return the clock speed and multiplier settings to their original values and quit, or repeat step 6 with a lower bus/multiplier combination.
12. Tweak your CMOS setup settings to optimum performance values as required. (This may not be necessary.)
13. Does the system boot to a full working operation system? If no, go to step 15; if yes, go to step 14.
14. Start testing with a utility like Winstone 97 and allow the system to "burn in" thoroughly. Check for any crashes or other intermittent system operation. If the system proves unstable, you cannot overclock at this level. Return the clock speed and multiplier settings to their original values and quit, or repeat step 6 with a lower bus/multiplier combination.
15. Check your cooling unit and repeat step 11.
16. If everything works well—congratulations. If not, check your cooling unit and repeat step 11.

TABLE 13-10 GENERIC 486 OVERCLOCKING SUGGESTIONS

CLOCK RATE (MHZ)	PROBABLE SUCCESS AT: (MHZ)	POSSIBLE SUCCESS AT: (MHZ)
16	20	—
20	25	33
25	33	40 or even 50
33	40	50
40	50	—
66	80	—
100	120	—

TABLE 13-11 GENERIC PENTIUM/6X86 OVERCLOCKING SUGGESTIONS

CLOCK RATE (MHZ)	PROBABLE SUCCESS AT: (MHZ)	POSSIBLE SUCCESS AT: (MHZ)
60	66	—
75	90	100-133
90	100	120-133
100	120	133
120	133	—
133	150	166-180
150	166	—
166	180	187.5
200	225	—

Windows 95/98 is very sensitive to overclocking. You may not be able to overclock a system with Windows 95/98, even though the system may overclock fine under DOS or Windows 3.1x.

Change the Bus Speed The *internal* clock of a CPU runs at a different speed than the *external* clock (or bus speed). The external clock is the speed at which the cache and the main memory run—and when divided by two, yields the speed of the PCI bus. There are only three different "official" bus speeds used by the Pentium, Pentium Pro, and the AMD K5: 50, 60, and 66MHz. The Cyrix/IBM 6x86 uses five bus speeds: 50, 55, 60, 66, and 75MHz. There are also new motherboards available that support the unofficial bus speeds of 83MHz to 148MHz. Typical Pentium II/III motherboards run at speeds between 66MHz and 100MHz (with a few reaching 133MHz).

To change the bus speed, look in your motherboard manual for something like "Clock Speed," "CPU External (BUS) Frequency Selection," or "Front Side Bus (FSB)"—these are the jumpers you will have to change. You will probably have to change several different jumpers to establish each new bus speed. If you are lucky and happen to have a motherboard with SoftMenu technology, you can change the bus speed settings in the CMOS setup menu without even opening the case.

Only increase the bus speed one step at a time (for example, go from 60MHz to 66MHz, not 60MHz to 75MHz or 66MHz to 133MHz). This is usually the most successful way to overclock. Using this method, almost every P150 CPU runs at 166MHz, and most 6x86 P150+ CPUs run at a P166+ level.

Change the Multiplier The CPU's internal clock is controlled by an internal clock multiplier in each CPU that is programmed via CPU pins. Intel Pentium CPUs support the following multipliers: x1.5, x2, x2.5, and x3. Intel Pentium Pro CPUs support x2.5, x3, x3.5, and x4. The 6x86 CPUs only support x2 and x3, but the upcoming M2 will support x2, x2.5, x3, x3.5. Current Pentium II/IIIs support multipliers from x3.5 up to x7 or more.

To change the multiplier setting, find a set of jumpers marked something like "Clock Multiplier" or "CPU to BUS Frequency Ratio Selection" in your motherboard manual. There are usually two jumpers used to change these settings. Again, you can do all of this in the CMOS setup menu if you have a SoftMenu motherboard, such as the newer Abit motherboards (**www.abit.com.tw**).

Change the Supply Voltage There are some circumstances when boosting the CPU supply voltage (for example, from 3.3V STD to 3.45V VRE) may be necessary to make the CPU run reliably at a higher bus speed. This is due to a bigger voltage difference between the digital "high" and "low" conditions, which results in cleaner signals for the CPU and other motherboard devices. If you can't run your CPU reliably at one particular clock speed, it's always worth considering jumping to the higher supply voltage. However, more voltage will produce more heat, so you must be very careful about cooling.

SPECIAL NOTES FOR 75MHZ AND 83MHZ BUS SPEEDS

Many traditional Pentium-class motherboards handle clock speeds up to 66MHz, but later-model Pentium/MMX motherboards operate up to 75MHz, and even 83MHz. There are some precautions to keep in mind when using these older motherboards:

- *PCI bus issues* The PCI bus is taken from the clock speed. At 60 or 66MHz, the PCI bus speed is 30 or 33MHz (the recommended speed for PCI). However, at 75 or 83 MHz, the PCI bus runs at 37.5 or 41.6MHz, respectively. This can lead to problems with some PCI devices such as SCSI controllers, video cards, and network cards. Often, SCSI controllers and network cards refuse to work at the faster speed, but some video boards just get much hotter than usual (though some video cards like the Diamond Stealth 64 aren't affected at all by higher bus speeds).
- *EIDE bus issues* The speed of an EIDE interface is not only determined by the PIO or DMA modes, but is also highly dependent on the PCI clock. This is one reason why an EIDE interface is always slower in systems with 60MHz bus speeds or less. However, the EIDE interface will be faster when you are running at 75 or 83MHz bus speeds. This sounds fine at first, but either the interface or the hard disk is often not up to the faster bus speeds. For example, I've seen HDDs work fine at 75MHz bus speeds, but at 83MHz, I've had to scale back to PIO mode 2. This is also true for EIDE CD-ROM drives, and could very well be the culprit if you're running into strange lockups under Windows.
- *ISA bus issues* In some cases, the ISA bus speed is divided directly from the PCI bus. If the PCI bus is running faster, the ISA bus may also be running faster. This can cause some serious problems for ISA boards (especially older ISA boards). For example, I've heard AWE32 sound boards make strange whistling sounds when being run at a fast bus speed. You can sometimes correct for ISA speed problems by introducing ISA wait states in the CMOS setup.

These issues generally do not relate to today's Pentium II/III motherboards, which reach 100MHz to 133MHz.

OVERCLOCKING NOTES FOR THE INTEL PENTIUM

Intel's Pentium and Pentium MMX processors are generally regarded as some of the easiest CPUs to overclock. This can be attributed to Intel's increased quality demands put in place after their early floating-point flaw disaster with the 60 and 66MHz Pentiums. For example, a Pentium MMX 200 seems to run fine with 2.8V at 208/83MHz and 225/75MHz. For 250/83MHz, you may need to increase the voltage to 2.9V. Table 13-12 lists some typical options for Pentium overclocking.

TABLE 13-12 PENTIUM OVERCLOCKING OPTIONS

CLOCK SPEED	FIRST CHOICE	SECOND CHOICE	THIRD CHOICE	FOURTH CHOICE
75MHz	112.5MHz (1.5 x 75MHz)	100MHz (1.5 x 66MHz)	90MHz (1.5 x 60MHz)	83MHz (1.5 x 55MHz)
90MHz	125MHz (1.5 x 83MHz)	112.5MHz (1.5 x 75MHz)	100MHz (1.5 x 66MHz)	—
100MHz	125MHz (1.5 x 83 MHz)	112.5MHz (1.5 x 75MHz)	—	—
120MHz	125MHz (1.5 x 83 MHz)	133MHz (2 x 66MHz)	112.5MHz (1.5 x 75MHz)	—
133MHz	166MHz (2 x 83 MHz)	150MHz (2 x 75MHz)	166MHz (2.5 x 66MHz)	—
150MHz	166MHz (2 x 83 MHz)	187.5MHz (2.5 x 75MHz)	200MHz (3 x 66MHz)	150MHz (2 x 75MHz)
166MHz	208MHz (2.5 x 83MHz)	166MHz (2 x 83MHz)	187.5MHz (2.5 x 75MHz)	200MHz (3 x 66MHz)
200MHz	250MHz (3 x 83MHz)	225MHz (3 x 75MHz)	208 MHz (2.5 x 83Mhz)	—

OVERCLOCKING NOTES FOR THE INTEL PENTIUM PRO

Since reliability is a key attribute for server-type platforms, the Pentium Pro is typically not overclocked. But according to the information that's available, you *should* be able to overclock a Pentium Pro the same as you would a classic Pentium or Pentium MMX. The main problem seems to be that there are few (if any) motherboards that operate at 75 or 83MHz (leaving only 50, 60, and 66MHz). Table 13-13 lists some overclocking options for the Pentium Pro.

OVERCLOCKING NOTES FOR THE INTEL CELERON

With the addition of L2 cache, the Intel Pentium II Celeron has become an overclocker's favorite. The Pentium core, lower price, and production quality combined to attract users looking for performance gains through overclocking. Intel sought to limit the Celeron's use in overclocking with a locked multiplier and a locked bus speed of 66MHz. Some motherboard makers have not complied with the locked bus speed implementation, providing an avenue to overclock Celerons through higher bus speeds. Common motherboard bus speeds higher than 66MHZ are 75MHz, 83MHz, and 100MHz. Table 13-14 lists some of the popular Celeron models and their general success rates at various overclocked levels.

TABLE 13-13 PENTIUM PRO OVERCLOCKING OPTIONS

CLOCK SPEED	FIRST CHOICE	SECOND CHOICE
150MHz	166MHz (2.5 x 66MHz)	
180MHz	233MHz (3.5 x 66 MHz)	200MHz (3 x 66MHz)
200MHz	266MHz (4 x 66MHz)	233MHz (3.5 x 66MHz)

TABLE 13-14 PENTIUM II CELERON OVERCLOCKING OPTIONS

	SPEED	SUCCESS RATE
Intel Celeron Processor 300MHz (300A)		
	4.5 x 75MHz = 338MHz	100%
	4.5 x 83MHz = 374MHz	100%
	4.5 x 100MHz = 450MHz	75%
	4.5 x 103MHz = 464MHz	45%
	4.5 x 112MHz = 504MHz	15%
	4.5 x 117MHz = 527MHz	0.5%
Intel Celeron Processor 333MHz		
	5.0 x 75MHz = 375MHz	100%
	5.0 x 83MHz = 415MHz	75%
	5.0 x 100MHz = 500MHz	10%
	5.0 x 103MHz = 515MHz	1%
	5.0 x 112MHz = 560MHz	0.1%
	5.0 x 117MHz = 585MHz	Unknown
Intel Celeron Processor 366MHz		
	5.5 x 75MHz = 413MHz	100%
	5.5 x 83MHz = 457MHz	90%
	5.5 x 100MHz = 550MHz	10%
	5.5 x 103MHz = 567MHz	5%
	5.5 x 112MHz = 616MHz	Unknown
	5.5 x 117MHz = 644MHz	Unknown
Intel Celeron Processor 400MHz		
	6.0 x 75MHz = 450MHz	100%
	6.0 x 83MHz = 498MHz	85%
	6.0 x 100MHz = 600MHz	2%
	6.0 x 103MHz = 618MHz	Unknown
	6.0 x 112MHz = 672MHz	Unknown
	6.0 x 117MHz = 702MHz	Unknown
Intel Celeron Processor 433MHz		
	6.5 x 75MHz = 488MHz	100%
	6.5 x 83MHz = 541MHz	20%
	6.5 x 100MHz = 650MHz	Unknown
	6.5 x 103MHz = 670MHz	Unknown
	6.5 x 112MHz = 628MHz	Unknown
	6.5 x 117MHz = 761MHz	Unknown
Intel Celeron Processor 466MHz (PPGA package only)		
	7.0 x 75MHz = 525MHz	75%
	7.0 x 83MHz = 581MHz	15%
	7.0 x 100MHz = 700MHz	Unknown
	7.0 x 103MHz = 721MHz	Unknown
	7.0 x 112MHz = 784MHz	Unknown
	7.0 x 117MHz = 819MHz	Unknown

TABLE 13-14 PENTIUM II CELERON OVERCLOCKING OPTIONS *(CONTINUED)*

	SPEED	SUCCESS RATE
Intel Celeron Processor 500MHz (PPGA package only)		
	7.5 x 75MHz = 563MHz	80%
	7.5 x 83MHz = 623MHz	10%
	7.5 x 100MHz = 750MHz	Unknown
	7.5 x 103MHz = 772MHz	Unknown
	7.5 x 112MHz = 840MHz	Unknown
	7.5 x 117MHz = 878MHz	Unknown

OVERCLOCKING NOTES FOR THE PENTIUM II/III

Early Pentium II (Klamath) processors were manufactured using a 0.35 micron process and were available in speeds from 233MHz to 300MHz using a 66MHz Front Side Bus (FSB). Intel then moved to a 0.25 micron process for Pentium II (Deschutes) processors at speeds of 333MHz to 450MHz. The 333MHz Pentium II still used the 66MHz FSB, but from 350MHz up, the FSB was increased to 100MHz.

Since August 1998, Intel has been locking the clock multiplier on its CPUs, so it probably will not be possible to change the multiplier when overclocking a 350MHz, 400MHz, or 450MHz Pentium II. If you try, the CPU will either refuse to boot the machine, or it will boot it up at one third of its proper speed. To get around this limitation, a Pentium II overclocker's primary option is to increase the speed of the Front Side Bus. Increasing the speed of the FSB also increases the speed of the PCI and AGP buses, so errors might result from some older components refusing to run properly at the higher bus speeds. For instance, overclocking a 100MHz FSB to 112MHz results in the PCI bus being overclocked to 37MHz (instead of 33 MHz), and the AGP bus being overclocked to 74MHz (instead of 66MHz). Since newer PCI and AGP cards are being designed with greater tolerances, however, this is becoming less of a problem.

Depending on the model of Pentium II that you're attempting to overclock, you'll need to be able to adjust the clock multiplier, Front Side Bus speed, and/or core voltage. You will also need to examine the effectiveness of your CPU cooling arrangement and improve the cooling if possible. Installing some kind of CPU temperature monitor is highly recommended. Many of the most current motherboards have a wide range of settings for multipliers, FSB speeds, and voltages—some even include integrated temperature monitors. Table 13-15 lists some popular options for Pentium II overclocking—the rules should also hold true for Pentium III overclocking (the main difference being the Pentium III's use of SSE).

> To run reliably with a 100MHz FSB, you need to have 100MHz SDRAM (PC100 RAM) installed in your system. In many of the cases listed above, increasing the FSB speed requires you to lower the clock multiplier on your system.

OVERCLOCKING NOTES FOR THE CYRIX/IBM 6X86

The Cyrix/IBM 6x86 CPUs are much more difficult to overclock than comparable Intel CPUs. There are two reasons for this. First, Cyrix CPUs (even the later production steps) produce tremendous amounts of heat. Overclocking them would produce so much heat that it would be difficult to remove it all without huge heat sink/fans or powered Peltier coolers. Second, 6x86 CPUs only support two multiplier settings (x2 and x3), so there are far fewer overclocking options available. Try a Cyrix P120+ (100MHz) as a

TABLE 13-15 PENTIUM II/III OVERCLOCKING OPTIONS

OVERCLOCKED SPEED	CLOCK MULTIPLIER	FSB SPEED	CHIPSET
233MHz and 266MHz Pentium II (66MHz FSB)			
300MHz	4.0	75MHz	440LX
300MHz	3.0	100MHz	440BX
336MHz	3.0	112MHz	440BX
300MHz Pentium II (66MHz FSB)			
338MHz	4.5	75MHz	440LX
350MHz	3.5	100MHz	440BX
392MHz	3.5	112MHz	440BX
400MHz	4.0	100MHz	440BX
333MHz Pentium II (66MHz FSB)			
350MHz	3.5	100MHz	440BX
375MHz	5.0	75MHz	440BX
392MHz	3.5	112MHz	440BX
400MHz	4.0	100MHz	440BX
350MHz to 450MHz Pentium II (100MHz FSB)			
392MHz	3.5	112MHz	—
448MHz	4.0	112MHz	—
504MHz	4.5	112MHz	—

P133+ (110MHz). Try a P133+ (110MHz) as a P150+ (120MHz). Finally, try a P150+ (120MHz) as a P166+ (133MHz).

You'll generally achieve the best success with 2.7 or 3.7 stepped 6x86 CPUs—they are more stable and produce less heat.

Cooling is *critical* for overclocked 6x86 CPUs, so don't even consider overclocking a 6x86 without a very capable heat sink/fan or a powered Peltier cooler.

OVERCLOCKING THE AMD K5

AMD has put itself on the map with its 5x86/133MHz CPU, and earned a lot of respect with the K5. However, the older PR75, PR90, and PR100 versions of the K5 do not seem to tolerate overclocking very well—probably because those CPUs were running at their performance limits already. By comparison, the later K5 versions (such as the PR120, PR133, PR150, and PR166) and the newer K6 and K6-2 seem to be much more tolerant of overclocking. When selecting an overclocking level, choose the next level up. For example, if you have a K5 PR120, try configuring it as a PR133, and so on.

TIPS FOR CONTROLLING HEAT

Heat remains the greatest enemy of overclocking, so managing that heat is an important priority. Try some of the following suggestions to help overcome CPU heating issues:

- Use a good-quality heat sink/fan that is more than adequately rated for your particular CPU.
- Use a thin layer of heat-sink compound to improve heat transfer between the CPU case and heat sink (available at RadioShack: Cat. No. 276-1372).
- For extremely hot CPUs, try a Peltier cooler or similar refrigeration unit. (Contact information is listed at the end of this chapter.)
- Select reliable ball-bearing type fans with extended service lifetimes.
- Fold and tie cables away from areas requiring free air circulation (such as the vicinity of the CPU fan). Keep any obstructions clear.
- Make sure the CPU heat sink/fan is in close thermal contact with the processor surface (using heat-sink compound if needed). It should attach securely to the CPU, or CPU and socket. If not, get a new heat sink/fan.
- Use a CPU cooler with an audio alarm system that will alert you in case of either fan malfunction or excessive CPU temperature.
- If you are overclocking your CPU, compensate for the increased heat generated by using an "upsized" heat sink/fan or Peltier active cooler.
- Clean fan blades, fan support struts, and power supply louvers of accumulated dirt at least annually. Canned compressed air and vacuum sweeper brushes work well.
- Increase air circulation in and out of your computer case by using an auxiliary fan.

Troubleshooting CPU Problems

The term *microprocessor troubleshooting* is not the misnomer it once was. Early CPUs such as the 8088 carried only 29,000 transistors. When one of those transistors failed, it would usually result in a complete system failure—the PC would crash or freeze entirely. Further, the system would subsequently fail to boot at all. However, CPUs have become far more complex in the last 20 years or so, and new generations such as the Pentium III are exceeding *21 million* transistors. With so many more transistors, the probability of an immediate *catastrophic* fault is far less. Of course, any CPU fault is very serious, but there are now many cases when a system may boot, but crash when certain *specific* CPU functions are attempted (for example, trying to execute protected-mode instructions). These kinds of errors may give the impression that a piece of software is corrupt, or that one or more expansion devices may be faulty. This part of the chapter looks at a selection of CPU failure modes and offers some tactics to help resolve the problem.

> Your Companion CD offers several utilities that can help you identify and quantify your CPU. Use CLIBENCH.ZIP to test the clock speed of a system. You can identify processors with general system inspection tools like DRHW25E.ZIP and COLINF.ZIP.

GENERAL SYMPTOMS

SYMPTOM 13-1 The system is completely dead (the system power LED lights properly) CPU faults are never subtle. When a CPU problem manifests itself, the system will invariably crash. Consequently, systems that do not boot (or freeze without warning during the boot process) stand an excellent chance of suffering from a CPU fault. The frustration with this kind of symptom is that the PC typically does not run long enough to execute its POST diagnostics, nor does the system boot to run any third-party DOS diagnostics. As a result, such "dead" systems require a bit of blind faith on the part of a technician.

Before considering a CPU replacement, you should use a multimeter and check the power supply outputs very carefully. Even though the power LED is lit, one or more outputs may be low or absent. Excessively low outputs can easily result in logic errors that will freeze the system. If this problem occurred *after* adding an upgrade, the supply may be overloaded. Try removing the upgrade. If system operation returns, consider upgrading the power supply. If an output is low or absent and there has been no upgrade (or the problem continues after removing the upgrade), try replacing the power supply.

Next, strip the system of its peripherals and expansion boards, and then try the system again. If operation returns, one of the expansion devices is interrupting system operation. Reinstall one device at a time and check the system. The last expansion device to be installed when the PC fails is the culprit. Replace the defective device. If the failure persists, try a new CPU.

Remember to shut down and unplug the PC before continuing. When removing the original CPU, be extremely careful to avoid bending any of the pins. (You may want to reinstall the CPU later.) Use care when installing the new CPU as well. Bent pins will almost always ruin the IC. If a new CPU fails to correct the problem, replace the motherboard outright.

SYMPTOM 13-2 You get a beep code or I/O POST code indicating a possible CPU fault The system will almost always fail to boot. When the POST starts, it will test each of the PC's key motherboard components (including the CPU). If a CPU fault is indicated during the POST (usually a single-byte hexadecimal code written to port 80h and read with a POST card), check each output from the system power supply. If one or more outputs is low or absent, there may be a problem in the supply. Try a new supply. If all supply outputs measure properly, try a new CPU. If a new CPU does not resolve the problem, replace the motherboard. Refer to Chapter 19 for beep codes and POST code messages.

SYMPTOM 13-3 The system boots with no problem, but crashes or freezes when certain applications are run It may seem as if the application is corrupt, but try a diagnostic such as AMIDIAG from AMI or The Troubleshooter by AllMicro. Run repetitive tests on the CPU. Although the CPU may work in real mode, diagnostics can detect errors running protected-mode instructions and perform thorough register checking. AMIDIAG stands out here because of the very specific error codes that are returned. Not only will it tell you if the CPU checks bad, but you will also know the specific reason *why*. When an error code is returned suggesting a CPU fault, try another CPU. If a CPU fault is not detected, expand the diagnostic to test other portions of the motherboard. If the entire system checks properly, you may indeed have a corrupt file in your application.

SYMPTOM 13-4 The system boots with no problem, but crashes or freezes after several minutes of operation (regardless of the application being run) Also, you will probably note that no diagnostic indicates a CPU problem. If you shut the system off and wait several minutes, the system will probably boot fine and run for several more minutes before stopping again. This is typical of thermal failure. When the system halts, check the CPU for heat. *Use extreme caution when checking for heat—you can be easily burned.* Your CPU may not be fitted with a heat sink, or its cooling fan may be disconnected (or failed). As a rule, all Pentium, Pentium MMX, Pentium II, and Pentium III processors require a heat sink/fan assembly for adequate cooling. Replace any defective cooling fan.

Make sure that the system cooling fan is working and that there is an unobstructed path over the CPU. If not, consider applying a heat sink with a generous helping of thermal compound. If the CPU is already fitted with a heat sink, make sure there is an ample layer of thermal compound between the CPU case and heat sink base. In many cases, the compound is omitted. This ruins the transfer of heat and allows the CPU to run much hotter. If you find that there is no thermal compound, allow the PC to cool; then add thermal compound between the CPU case and heat sink.

SYMPTOM 13-5 An older system refuses to run properly when the CPU's internal (L1) cache is enabled This type of symptom occurred frequently with older processors (such as the AMD Am486) and can almost always be traced to a configuration issue. The processor may fail if run at an incorrect bus speed (as in overclocking), so check and correct the motherboard bus speed to accommodate the CPU. This symptom can also occur when running the CPU at an incorrect operating voltage. Check the voltage level and reconfigure the motherboard for the correct voltage (if necessary). Finally, the motherboard must be compatible with the L1 cache type on the CPU. For example, installing a CPU with a write-back cache on a motherboard that doesn't support write-back cache can cause problems.

SYMPTOM 13-6 You cannot run a 3.45V CPU in a 5V motherboard, even though an appropriate voltage regulator module is being used Double-check the voltage regulator module (VRM). The VRM must have adequate current-handling capacity to support the CPU's power demands. Otherwise, the VRM will be overloaded and fail to provide adequate power. Check with the CPU manufacturer for their VRM recommendations. You might also try the CPU/VRM in another 5V motherboard. If the CPU/VRM fails in another 5V motherboard, chances are that the VRM is underrated or has failed. If the CPU/VRM does work on another 5V motherboard, it is possible that the original motherboard's BIOS could not support the particular requirements of the new CPU. Check with the motherboard manufacturer to see if there is an updated BIOS (either flash or ROM IC) available for the system.

SYMPTOM 13-7 A system malfunctions under HIMEM.SYS or DOS4GW.EXE after installing a new CPU This type of symptom occurred frequently with older CPUs and could generally be traced to errors in the motherboard CPU voltage and type settings (opposed to the newer bus speed/multiplier configurations). Check the motherboard's CPU configuration jumpers. Also, running a 3.45V CPU at 5V, or running a non-SL-enhanced CPU as an SL-enhanced part can cause these types of problems to occur. So make sure that the correct part is being used, and see that the CPU voltage is correct. (Use a voltage regulator module if necessary.)

SYMPTOM 13-8 The system runs fine, but reports the wrong type of CPU In virtually all cases, the motherboard BIOS was not written to support the particular CPU directly. Start by checking the motherboard's CPU configuration jumpers to see that the motherboard is set properly for the particular CPU. If the problem persists, you'll probably need a BIOS upgrade (either a flash file or ROM IC) to accommodate the processor. Check with the motherboard or system maker to determine whether an appropriate BIOS upgrade is available.

SYMPTOM 13-9 After reconfiguring a VL motherboard for a faster CPU, the VESA VL video card no longer functions Other VL cards may also malfunction. This frequently occurs on older VL motherboards with support for 40MHz bus speeds. Since the VL bus speed is tied to the motherboard bus speed, setting the motherboard to 40MHz can cause some VL cards to malfunction. Try running the motherboard at 33MHz (the native frequency for VL cards), and set the Local Bus Clock Rate jumper for <=33MHz. If the problem disappears, you have an issue with one or more VL cards. Try altering the number of VL bus wait-states until the VL devices will support 40MHz. (This will compromise system performance.) If you cannot resolve the issue, you may not be able to use the motherboard at 40MHz. You may also try finding a VL board that *will* operate properly at 40MHz.

SYMPTOM 13-10 **Some software locks up on systems running 5x86 processors** This is a frequent problem with high-end software such as AutoDesk's 3D Studio. Often, programs like 3D Studio use software timing loops in the code. The 5x86 processor executes these loop instructions faster than previous x86 CPUs, and this interferes with timing-dependent code inside the program. In most cases, the software manufacturer will offer a patch for the offending program. For 3D Studio, you can download the FSTCPUFX.EXE file from Kinetix (**ftp://ftp.fh-merseburg.de/pub/hardware/mainboard/asus/fstcpufx.exe**). Run the executable patch file and follow the instructions. The patch alters the 3D Studio executable file.

Another prime example of software-related problems is with Clipper applications. Clipper inserts software timing loops into the applications when the code is compiled, and this also interferes with timing-dependent code in the program. For Clipper, you can download the PIPELOOP.EXE file (**ftp://ftp.ascod.ru/SOFT/Cyrix/pipeloop.exe**) and put it in your AUTOEXEC.BAT file.

SYMPTOM 13-11 **The Windows 95 Device Manager identifies the CPU incorrectly** In many cases, the CPU is misidentified as a 486 or other older CPU. This is due to an issue with Windows 95. The algorithm used in Windows 95 to detect the CPU was likely completed before the particular CPU was released, and therefore the CPU responds to the algorithm just as a 486 does. Use a diagnostic that will identify your particular CPU correctly, or check with the CPU maker for a Windows 95 patch that will support proper identification. This problem happens often with Cyrix 6x86 CPUs and can be corrected by downloading a patch such as 6XOPT074.ZIP. (See the "Performance enhancement software" bullet under the "Cyrix 6x86 Symptoms" section below.)

SYMPTOM 13-12 **The heat sink/fan will not secure properly** It is not tight against the surface of the CPU. This can be a serious problem for the system because a loose heat sink/fan will not cool the processor correctly. There are three classical solutions to this issue. First, make sure you have the heat sink/fan model that is recommended for your particular CPU (a common error when building a new PC). Second, make sure the heat sink attaches to either the CPU chip itself or the ZIF socket that the CPU mounts in. Third, verify that the CPU has not been altered or faked. Faked CPUs are often ground down to remove their original markings, and then new markings are placed on the CPU. The grinding process reduces the package thickness and can prevent the heat sink/fan from being secure. (Faked CPUs are a common occurrence in Europe.)

CYRIX 6X86 SYMPTOMS

From a technological standpoint, the Cyrix 6x86 (or M1, as it used to be called) is a strong competitor to the Intel Pentium. In a properly configured system, the 6x86 can actually outclass the Pentium in some areas. In addition, the 200MHz version of the 6x86 uses a bus speed of 75MHz (replacing the established 66MHz bus speed). However, there are some special circumstances and symptoms to keep in mind when working on Cyrix-based platforms:

- *Bus speed* This is where Cyrix's problems start, since the higher bus speeds demand very fast memory technologies and advanced motherboard chipsets. You can't run the P200 chip in a Triton FX or HX motherboard because those chipsets don't support a bus speed of 75MHz. In practice, the 6x86 P200 runs at a clock speed of 150MHz by multiplying the 75MHz motherboard bus speed by 2. If you were to try running the P200 at a bus speed of 50MHz and a multiplier of 3, you would lose any performance benefit due to the slow bus speed. For the P166, P150, and P120 versions, motherboard compatibility is much better.

- *Excess heating* Heat is an important issue with every leading-edge CPU, but the 6x86 runs *extremely* hot compared to similar Intel and AMD processors. Excess heat can cause data corruption and system crashes, and even shorten the working life of the CPU. In the worst cases, excess heat can destroy the CPU. Such reliability issues force the use of good-quality heat sink/fan assemblies with all 6x86 models. The recent release of the 6x86L (low-voltage) versions promises to help combat the issues of heating by using a "split voltage" architecture of 2.8 volts and 3.3 volts—the same voltages used by new MMX processors. Cyrix expects that the "L" series will reduce power demands by more than 25 percent. If you must replace a 6x86, go for a version 2.7 of the 6x86, or a 6x86L version (with proper voltage regulation) if you can.
- *FPU issues* Another point of contention among 6x86 users is that the floating-point capability of a 6x86 is measurably below that of similar Pentiums. For example, the FPU performance of a 6x86 P166 is only rated equivalent to a Pentium 90MHz unit. There is no real solution for the current 6x86 versions, but the forthcoming M2 from Cyrix is expected to correct these problems.
- *Performance under Windows NT* Here's another serious problem that plagued earlier 6x86 versions. The CPU is *so* sensitive to signal reflections from the CPU busses, that NT would switch off the L1 cache in the 6x86. This, in turn, causes a performance degradation. Cyrix has resolved many of these issues in the version 2.7 releases, as well as the new 6x86L CPUs, but you may continue to see NT performance problems in systems with older 6x86 versions.
- *Performance enhancement software* Given the various limitations of the Cyrix 6x86, there are a number of utilities available to enhance the 6x86. You can obtain each utility from the Web resources listed below:

  6XOPT074.ZIP A 6x86 optimizer written by Mikael Johansson. It configures 6x86 CPU registers to increase performance, and it allows Windows 95 to "see" the 6x86 CPU in the Device Manager (**ftp://ftp.cyberway.com.sg/pub/coast/msdos/sysutil/6xopt074.zip**).

  DIRECTNT.ZIP This utility enables the 6x86 cache under Windows NT 4 (**ftp://ftp.westend.com/pub/magazine/ct/ctsi/directnt.zip**).

SYMPTOM 13-13 The Cyrix 6x86 system is crashing or freezing after some period of operation This is almost always a heat-related problem caused by inadequate cooling of the 6x86. If you're not using a heat sink/fan, install one before continuing. (Be sure to use a thin layer of thermal grease to improve heat transfer between the CPU and heat sink.) Make sure you are using a good-quality heat sink/fan with plenty of capacity, and see that it is securely attached to the CPU. Also see that the CPU itself is securely seated in its socket.

You might also consider installing a different 6x86 model. The Type C028 version uses 3.52 volts, and the Type C016 uses 3.3 volts, so just changing models can reduce power demands. You might also try installing a version 2.7 or later 6x86, which is better able to deal with heat. Best yet, install a 6x86L CPU (and regulator). A third possible cause of intermittent system operation is a poorly compatible BIOS. Check with the motherboard maker or system manufacturer, and see if there is a BIOS upgrade to better support Cyrix CPUs.

SYMPTOM 13-14 The Cyrix 6x86 system crashes and refuses to restart This is another classic heat-related problem and may often indicate that the CPU or its associated voltage regulator has failed. Check the voltage regulator. Regulators are more susceptible to failure with Cyrix 6x86 CPUs because of the higher current demands. If the voltage regulator checks out, replace the CPU itself (perhaps with a lower-power model, as mentioned in Symptom 13-13).

SYMPTOM 13-15 **You notice poor Cyrix 6x86 performance under Windows NT 4.0** In virtually all cases, NT has detected the 6x86 and has elected to shut down the write-back L1 cache completely. This results in the performance hit. Fortunately, there are several ways to address this problem. First, you can download a patch from the Cyrix Web site (**www.cyrix.com**), which reenables the L1 cache under NT 4.0. This brings performance back up, but it also can cause instability for NT. A more practical resolution is to replace the CPU with a 6x86 version 2.7 or higher, or a 6x86L (and suitable voltage regulator), as mentioned in Symptom 13-13.

SYMPTOM 13-16 **You can't get Quake (or other graphics-intensive program) to run nearly as well on a Cyrix 6x86 system as it does with a similar Pentium system** This is due to the issues with Cyrix FPU performance. There is no real resolution for the problem at this time—later 6x86 versions do not correct the FPU. You may replace the CPU with an AMD or Intel model, or wait to see the performance offered by the Cyrix 6x86MX (M2).

SYMPTOM 13-17 **A Cyrix 6x86 CPU won't work on your motherboard** There are several possible problems when upgrading to any non-Intel CPU. First, check the motherboard's chipset and make sure the chipset (and other attributes such as bus speed) are compatible with the 6x86. As you saw earlier, some 6x86 iterations require unusual bus speeds in order to function.

Motherboard settings are always important when installing a CPU. You will probably need to set a new clock speed to accommodate the 6x86. In some cases, you may also need to specify a CPU type. Finally, you'll need to set the CPU voltage (if your motherboard provides a "switchable" voltage regulator). Otherwise, you'll need to install a voltage regulator with enough power capacity to handle a 6x86 adequately. If you select an underrated regulator, the regulator can overheat and burn out.

The last issue to consider is your BIOS. Often the BIOS must detect a CPU correctly and make slight variations in BIOS routines to use the new CPU most effectively. If the BIOS does not support your 6x86, you'll need to get a BIOS upgrade from the motherboard maker or system manufacturer.

If all else fails, try slowing down the clock speed to the next slower level. If the CPU runs properly then, there is probably an incompatibility between your motherboard and the 6x86. Check with the motherboard manufacturer (or system maker), and see if any compatibility issues have been identified (and if there is a fix available).

SYMPTOM 13-18 **You notice performance degradation when using a Cyrix 6x86 under Windows 3.1x or Windows 95** In many cases, performance problems when using non-Intel CPUs is related to BIOS support. Often the BIOS must identify a CPU and adjust to accommodate any particular nuances. If the BIOS is not supporting the CPU correctly, it can result in overall performance problems. Check with the motherboard maker or system manufacturer for any BIOS upgrades that will better support your new CPU.

Clock speed and cache are two other issues that can affect system performance. Check the motherboard jumpers and verify that the clock speed is set correctly for your Cyrix CPU. Also check for cache jumpers, and see that any cache settings are correct. You may also verify that internal (L1) and external (L2) caching are enabled in BIOS.

OVERCLOCKING SYMPTOMS

The process of CPU overclocking is hardly a perfect one. Many variables are involved, such as the CPU type, motherboard quality, and available clock speed and multiplier settings. There are many cases when overclocking results in system problems. Some of the more common problems are identified in this section.

SYMPTOM 13-19 The system does not boot up at all after reconfiguring the system for overclocking This is a common problem that almost always means you cannot overclock the CPU at the level you have chosen. Scale back the clock speed or the multiplier until the system starts up, or return the clock and multiplier to their original values.

SYMPTOM 13-20 The system starts after overclocking, but locks up or crashes after some short period of time Overclocking causes substantial heat dissipation from the CPU, and cooling must be improved to compensate for this additional heat. Otherwise, the overheated CPU can lock up and crash the system. Check the heat sink/fan, and see that it is attached correctly with a thin layer of thermal grease between the CPU and heat sink. It may be necessary to "up-size" the heat sink/fan, or use a Peltier cooler.

SYMPTOM 13-21 You see memory errors after increasing the bus speed for overclocking Memory performance is tightly coupled to bus speed (or clock speed). Most 60ns RAM types will work fine up to 66MHz, but you may need high-end 50ns EDO RAM or 50ns SDRAM when pushing the bus speed to 75MHz or 83MHz. Try some faster memory in the PC, or do not attempt to overclock the system.

SYMPTOM 13-22 After reconfiguring for overclocking, the system works, but you see a rash of CPU failures Chances are that the CPU is running far too hot, resulting in premature CPU failures. Check the cooling unit, and see that it is securely attached with a thin layer of thermal grease between the CPU and heat sink. It may be necessary to "up-size" the heat sink/fan, or use a Peltier cooler.

SYMPTOM 13-23 After reconfiguring for overclocking, you find that some expansion board or other hardware is no longer recognized or working Since PCI and ISA clocks are typically tied to the system clock speed, increasing the clock speed will also increase the PCI and ISA clocks. This can upset the operation of some sensitive adapter boards. You may be able to replace the suspect hardware with a more tolerant adapter, but it is often safer to return the clock speed and multiplier settings to their original values.

SYMPTOM 13-24 After reconfiguring for overclocking, you notice that a number of recent files are corrupt, inaccessible, or missing In effect, the system is not stable. Check for excessive heat first (as in Symptom 13-4). Otherwise, you should not overclock this particular system. Try scaling back the overclocking configuration, or return the clock speed and multiplier settings to their original values.

Further Study

AMD: **http://www.amd.com**

AMI: **http://www.megatrends.com** (AMIDIAG)

ARM: **http://www.arm.com/**

Cyrix: **http://www.cyrix.com** (purchased by VIA Technologies)

Compaq: **http://www.compaq.com/**

DEC Alpha: **http://www.digital.com/info/semiconductor/alpha.htm** (purchased by Compaq)

IBM PowerPC: **http://www.chips.ibm.com/products/ppc/**

Intel: **http://www.intel.com**

MIPS: **http://www.mips.com/**

TI: **ftp.ti.com**

VIA Technologies: **http://www.viatech.com/**

NEWSGROUPS

comp.sys.arm

comp.sys.dec

comp.sys.hp.hardware

comp.sys.intel

comp.sys.mips

comp.sys.sun.hardware

14

DATA RECOVERY TECHNIQUES

CHAPTER AT A GLANCE

It's almost ironic that the value of a PC's hardware is often insignificant when considered against the data that PC contains. Recent history is replete with examples of businesses that have suffered terrible financial hardship—even gone out of business—after losing vital data files. While the consequences are not nearly as severe for home offices or casual PC users, damaged files, accidental deletions, and hard drive failures are always difficult. This chapter is intended to provide some guidance that will help to protect your drive from failure, and offer some procedures that will help you recover lost or damaged data. The one thing to keep in mind here is that the drive hardware must be working—if the drive should fail outright, you may not be able to recover anything.

If you must recover data from a damaged hard drive, there are numerous "data recovery" businesses (listed at the end of this chapter) that might be able to help. Recovering data from a damaged drive is expensive and is usually only worthwhile for corporations and government organizations.

Causes of Data Loss

The first step in understanding data loss is to know the causes behind data loss. Data is extremely vulnerable and may be damaged by many different factors. This part of the chapter explains the major causes of data loss and offers some suggestions to minimize the dangers.

HARDWARE AND SYSTEM FAILURES

By far, hardware faults are the leading cause of data failure—accounting for at least 44 percent of all data loss. Hardware failures can occur from such events as an electrical failure (or shutting down the PC improperly), a disk drive head crash, or an outright failure of the drive circuitry or electromechanical mechanisms. You'll see hardware problems indicated by error messages (for example, an error message stating that the device is "not recognized" or "not available"). You may also notice that previously accessible data is suddenly gone. In many cases, the hard drive may not even spin, or you may hear a scraping or rattling sound coming from the hard drive.

You can usually work to prevent hardware and system failures by keeping the system in a clean, temperature- and humidity-controlled environment. Protect against power surges and other types of electrical failures by employing an Uninterruptible Power Supply (or UPS). For mission-critical data—such as an important network server—use a RAID (Redundant Array of Independent Disks) system to mirror your main data drive(s).

As a rule, never open a hard drive in other than a Class 100 (or better) clean-room environment—otherwise the accumulation of dust and debris in everyday air can render the drive unusable. If you must reclaim data from a failed drive, send it to a company that has the specialized clean-room facilities to attempt a hard drive repair (such as those listed at the end of this chapter). Do not attempt to operate a hard drive that you suspect may have hardware or system failure—the failure may continue to corrupt data on the drive and exacerbate the data loss. Finally, never use software recovery utilities (such as Norton Disk Doctor) to recover data in a hardware failure situation. These utilities assume that the hardware is functional, and they can cause further damage to the data.

HUMAN ERROR

Contrary to popular belief, human error ranks second (about 32 percent) as the cause of all data loss. In most cases when the system seems to work properly, but previously accessible data is suddenly gone, chances are that human error is responsible at some level. It may be as simple as an accidental deletion of a file, or as serious as impact damage caused by accidentally dropping a drive or tape.

Human error can be prevented by keeping regular and up-to-date data backups of your current work. Also, you should avoid attempting any installations, repairs, or system operations with which you do not have previous experience. Fortunately, files and folders that are accidentally deleted can usually be recovered with the "undelete" feature included with most operating systems such as DOS (or the Recycle Bin of Windows 95/98). If you must bring in another individual to help recover your data, make sure the individual has the experience needed to recover files successfully.

SOFTWARE BUGS

Improper software design accounts for roughly 14 percent of all data loss. We typically refer to these as bugs in the software, and they are usually caused by improper software design and testing on the part of the software maker. Even when software is working perfectly, the software may have unforeseen effects on particular system platforms or combinations of hardware. In many cases, you'll notice software bugs as error messages stating that the data is inaccessible or corrupted. You may also see memory errors or other PC errors. You'll need to identify the software responsible for your data loss, and contact the software maker for the appropriate patches or upgrades.

COMPUTER VIRUSES

Although the popular media seems to focus on computer viruses as a primary cause of data loss, viruses really only account for about 7 percent of all data loss (though that percentage is growing a bit with the popularity of Internet downloads). Thousands of computer viruses are currently known to exist, and that number grows daily, but viruses have still had a limited impact on data. In most cases, you'll see a virus infection broadcast with a message on the display (for example, "Your computer is now stoned"), though there may be many other strange or unpredictable behaviors that accompany the data loss. (See Chapter 48 for a more comprehensive discussion of viruses.)

Your best defenses against computer viruses are to use a *current* antivirus tool, and to scan all incoming floppy disks for viruses (this includes packaged software, software carried on-site by users, and software downloaded from the Internet via modem). Also, do not accept e-mail file attachments from people you do not know, and virus check any attachments that you do receive before opening them. Data is usually accessible after the virus has been removed, but be sure to remove the virus first. Finally, avoid reformatting your hard drive or floppy disk as a means of eliminating viruses—this doesn't always work.

NATURAL DISASTERS

Fire, flood, earthquake, lightning strikes—all the forces of nature account for just 3 percent of all data loss. While there is little you can do to prevent the physical destruction of your system in the face of a natural disaster, your best protection is to keep a current backup of your data stored off-site in another protected water/fire-proof location.

Protecting the Drive and Data

Sooner or later, your hard drive is going to fail. It is not a question of whether, it is a question of when. Although this may sound gloomy, there is absolutely no reason why a hard drive should not perform perfectly through its entire normal working life. Just as people can improve the quality of their life by eating right and exercising regularly, *drive life* can be lengthened by taking some fairly common-sense precautions. The pointers below can reduce downtime and are sure ways to win a customer's loyalty:

- *Listen for drive noise.* Hard drives often make a little bit of whirring noise when spinning up, and subtle clicking as the heads move from track to track—this is perfectly normal. However, drives that make loud clacking or grinding noises may be close to failure. You should back up and replace such suspect drives at your earliest opportunity before they fail. If such a noisy drive cannot be accessed, it may have already failed.
- *Check the power quality.* Hard drives tend to be quite sensitive to variations in AC power—*especially* voltage spikes caused by lightning or inductive equipment (such as motors) sharing the same AC cir-

cuit in your home or office. If there is a lot of motorized equipment or high-energy equipment in the same area as the PC, consider having a new AC line installed exclusively for the computer, or consider investing in an Uninterruptible Power Supply (UPS).

- *Be careful about smoke.* Cigar and cigarette smoke can be detrimental to a hard drive. Although the air drawn into a hard drive is passed through an extremely fine filter, any smoke particles that do manage to penetrate the drive housing are much larger than the spacing between a R/W head and platter. A single smoke particle caught between the head and platter can be dragged along the disk, eventually resulting in media damage.
- *Be careful about mounting.* In spite of their rigid enclosure, hard drives can be warped just slightly when tightly secured by four mounting screws. In some cases, this effect is just enough to throw out a drive's alignment and cause data problems. If you encounter drive problems after moving or remounting the drive, try loosening one or more of the screws (you need not remove them). Just taking the pressure off will usually eliminate the problem.
- *Be careful about handling.* If you must remove the drive for any reason (for example, during an upgrade), be very careful to handle the drive gently and rest it on a soft, antistatic foam surface. You should avoid any impacts or hard surfaces. When reinstalling the drive, be certain to use only the correct screws—otherwise, screws that are too long will warp the drive. Worse, excessive force can crack the cast enclosure, allowing dust and smoke to enter the drive freely, and precipitate a rapid drive failure. Also be sure to use an antistatic wrist strap whenever working inside a PC or handling a drive outside of the system.
- *Be careful about vibration.* Hard drives are very sensitive to physical vibration. Shocks and impacts can cause R/W heads to mark platter surfaces. If the drive is not secured properly, a pattern of regular vibrations may set up in the mechanical assemblies. While such subtle vibrations will rarely damage the drive outright, they can certainly shorten the drive's working life. Be sure to mount the drive evenly with four screws—do not leave screws out.
- *Format in the proper environment.* Since the drive works in terms of microscopic dimensions, the effects of gravity and thermal expansion play a role in the accuracy of head positioning. Make sure the drive is at a running temperature (perhaps 15 minutes or more) before partitioning and formatting it. Also see that the drive is oriented correctly (horizontally or vertically) prior to partitioning and formatting. If you've moved a drive from one place to another, be sure to let the drive adjust to its new environment (temperature and humidity) for at least 24 hours before using it.
- *Keep the disk defragmented.* The FAT16 and FAT32 file systems have the ability to divide a file into clusters (groups of sectors) that can be spread all over the drive. Ideally, clusters should be contiguous along adjacent tracks of the disk. This reduces the amount of seek time required to position R/W heads. As files grow beyond their original cluster size, the OS will assign other (sometimes distant) clusters to hold part of the file. It is this scattering of clusters that *fragments* files. By itself, fragmentation is a normal part of the "FAT" approach, but excessive fragmentation forces the drive to rush all over the disk. Over time, a large number of fragmented files can cause enough wear to shorten the drive's life. Use a DOS or Windows 95/98 disk defragmenter regularly (such as the Defrag utility) to keep the disk file clusters contiguous.
- *Avoid manual head parking.* In the early days of hard drives, designers realized that head impact could damage the media. Drive designers allowed for a *landing zone*—an unused track where heads could be positioned before power-down. With a landing zone, it did not matter if heads contacted the platter since there was no data there to lose. A utility could "park" the heads over the landing zone. However, virtually all drives are now designed to be "autoparking"—before the drive spins down,

heads are automatically positioned over the landing zone based on CMOS setup data. Parking programs are no longer needed, and they can even position the heads *incorrectly* before power-down (a common problem with older IDE drives that operate in translation mode). Also, most drives are dynamically loaded, so R/W heads are removed from the platters once power is removed. Avoid using parking utilities unless the utility is intended specifically for the drive.

- *Keep the drive backed up*. Regular, complete system backups are generally regarded to be the best, most reliable protection against drive failures. No matter what happens to the drive, you can't really lose anything as long as you have a copy of it. In addition to applications and data files, however, you should also make it a point to back up the partition table, autoconfigure record, file allocation table, and root directory. Utilities such as DrivePro from MicroHouse can create backup copies of these critical areas. If you have a proper low-level formatter utility for your particular drive, you might try backing up the drive completely, performing a fresh low-level format to rewrite track and sector IDs, then repartitioning, reformatting, and restoring data to the drive.
- *Keep viruses in check*. You should also protect against the possible infection of a drive by using a *current* antivirus program. Run the virus checker regularly, and be sure to check new software, file attachments, and file downloads before executing them.

Recovering Files and Folders

Sooner or later, you're going to delete a file (or folder) that you need. Although this is frustrating, it's almost always possible to recover your deleted file(s). In most cases, you can recover files and folders using the Windows 95/98 Recycle Bin:

1. On the desktop, double-click the Recycle Bin icon.
2. The Recycle Bin dialog will open (Figure 14-1).
3. Scroll through the list of files in the Recycle Bin.
4. Highlight the file(s) or shortcut(s) to retrieve, click File, and then click Restore.
5. If you wish to restore several files at once, hold down the CTRL key and click each desired file; then click File and Restore.

The file should be returned to its original location on the drive. If you restore a file that was originally located in a deleted folder, the folder is re-created, and that file is restored in the folder. If you're working under DOS 6.2x, you can use the UNDELETE command (derived from the old Central Point PC Tools package) to recover your deleted file(s):

1. From a command prompt, switch to the directory that contained your deleted file(s).
2. Type **undelete** to start the Undelete utility. Table 14-1 lists the command-line switches for Undelete.
3. DOS will list the deleted file(s) that it finds and prompt you for which ones you want to recover.
4. When you see the file(s) you want, simply answer yes.

You must remember here that Windows 95/98 uses the Recycle Bin as its Undelete function, and there is no real-mode Undelete feature under Windows 9x. This means if you empty the Recycle Bin or delete files under DOS, you *cannot* restore those files without a third-party data recovery tool such as Ontrack's

14

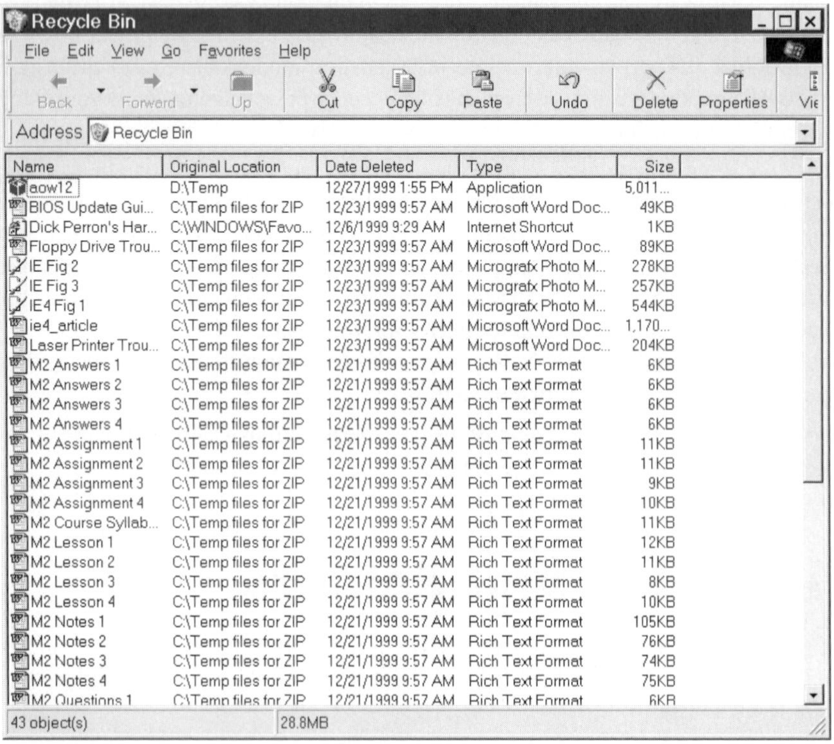
Recycle Bin
File Edit View Go Favorites Help
Back Forward Up Cut Copy Paste Undo Delete Properties Vie
Address Recycle Bin
Name Original Location Date Deleted Type Size
aow12 D:\Temp 12/27/1999 1:55 PM Application 5,011...
BIOS Update Gui... C:\Temp files for ZIP 12/23/1999 9:57 AM Microsoft Word Doc... 49KB
Dick Perron's Har... C:\WINDOWS\Favo... 12/6/1999 9:29 AM Internet Shortcut 1KB
Floppy Drive Trou... C:\Temp files for ZIP 12/23/1999 9:57 AM Microsoft Word Doc... 89KB
IE Fig 2 C:\Temp files for ZIP 12/23/1999 9:57 AM Micrografx Photo M... 278KB
IE Fig 3 C:\Temp files for ZIP 12/23/1999 9:57 AM Micrografx Photo M... 257KB
IE4 Fig 1 C:\Temp files for ZIP 12/23/1999 9:57 AM Micrografx Photo M... 544KB
ie4_article C:\Temp files for ZIP 12/23/1999 9:57 AM Microsoft Word Doc... 1,170...
Laser Printer Trou... C:\Temp files for ZIP 12/23/1999 9:57 AM Microsoft Word Doc... 204KB
M2 Answers 1 C:\Temp files for ZIP 12/21/1999 9:57 AM Rich Text Format 6KB
M2 Answers 2 C:\Temp files for ZIP 12/21/1999 9:57 AM Rich Text Format 6KB
M2 Answers 3 C:\Temp files for ZIP 12/21/1999 9:57 AM Rich Text Format 6KB
M2 Answers 4 C:\Temp files for ZIP 12/21/1999 9:57 AM Rich Text Format 6KB
M2 Assignment 1 C:\Temp files for ZIP 12/21/1999 9:57 AM Rich Text Format 11KB
M2 Assignment 2 C:\Temp files for ZIP 12/21/1999 9:57 AM Rich Text Format 11KB
M2 Assignment 3 C:\Temp files for ZIP 12/21/1999 9:57 AM Rich Text Format 9KB
M2 Assignment 4 C:\Temp files for ZIP 12/21/1999 9:57 AM Rich Text Format 10KB
M2 Course Syllab... C:\Temp files for ZIP 12/21/1999 9:57 AM Rich Text Format 11KB
M2 Lesson 1 C:\Temp files for ZIP 12/21/1999 9:57 AM Rich Text Format 12KB
M2 Lesson 2 C:\Temp files for ZIP 12/21/1999 9:57 AM Rich Text Format 11KB
M2 Lesson 3 C:\Temp files for ZIP 12/21/1999 9:57 AM Rich Text Format 8KB
M2 Lesson 4 C:\Temp files for ZIP 12/21/1999 9:57 AM Rich Text Format 10KB
M2 Notes 1 C:\Temp files for ZIP 12/21/1999 9:57 AM Rich Text Format 105KB
M2 Notes 2 C:\Temp files for ZIP 12/21/1999 9:57 AM Rich Text Format 76KB
M2 Notes 3 C:\Temp files for ZIP 12/21/1999 9:57 AM Rich Text Format 74KB
M2 Notes 4 C:\Temp files for ZIP 12/21/1999 9:57 AM Rich Text Format 75KB
43 object(s)
28.8MB

FIGURE 14-1 The Recycle Bin dialog

TABLE 14-1 COMMAND-LINE SWITCHES FOR DOS 6.2X UNDELETE

SWITCH	DESCRIPTION
/ALL	Causes Undelete to recover everything possible using the best possible recovery method.
/DS	Uses Undelete Sentry mode for recovery.
/DT	Uses Undelete Tracking mode for recovery.
/LIST	Lists the deleted files in the current directory, but does not recover them.
/LOAD	Loads Undelete into memory (making Undelete a TSR).
/PURGE[drive]	Cleans the contents of your Undelete Sentry directory. You can no longer recover those files, but you'll protect yourself from anyone who might try to recover your private erased file(s).
/S[drive]	Enables Undelete Sentry mode to protect the drive indicated. For example, **undelete /SC** enables the Undelete Sentry for drive C:.
/STATUS	Shows the current status of Undelete.
/T[drive][-entries]	Enables Undelete Tracking mode to protect the drive indicated, and defines the number of files that will be tracked (1 to 999 files). For example, to track 50 file deletions on drive C: you'd use **undelete /TC-50**.
/U	Unloads Undelete from memory (if it's been placed in memory).

EasyRecovery. If you have access to an older DOS 6.2x system with Undelete on it (and your current system is using FAT16), you *may* be able to use Undelete copied onto your boot disk.

> The most important issue in file recovery is to restore your file(s) *as soon as possible* after deletion. Remember that "deleted" files are not wiped out—their clusters are simply marked as "free." If you go on and save new files, you may overwrite some or all of the clusters containing your deleted file(s), and this may render them unrecoverable.

Recovering FAT and Directory Damage

Many drives eventually develop file structure problems because of viruses, age, and even normal everyday operation. DOS and Windows 95/98 provide tools that allow you to check the disk's condition and (to some extent) define and repair problems with the directory structure and File Allocation Table (FAT). The CHKDSK utility is a basic DOS disk "fix" utility that you can use, and ScanDisk is a somewhat more powerful tool that you should be familiar with.

UNDERSTANDING CHKDSK

Although it's rather crude compared to ScanDisk or third-party software tools, CHKDSK allows you to perform several important disk operations. First, CHKDSK processes the disk to provide a detailed report on disk space and available memory. The disk report is what most users think of when they consider CHKDSK, but its real function is to inspect directories and FATs for any discrepancies. Keep in mind that CHKDSK does not actually check *individual* files. CHKDSK can also check files for contiguity. Contiguous files occupy adjacent clusters on a disk, which makes the files much faster to load and save. When files become noncontiguous (fragmented), not only does disk access take longer, but portions of the fragmented file may become lost or disassociated. CHKDSK can identify and recover such "lost" clusters (also known as *allocation units*).

Running CHKDSK

The generic DOS command line for CHKDSK is **CHKDSK *drive:\path filename* /F /V**. The *drive* parameter specifies which logical drive is to be analyzed. By default, the current drive will be examined, but if you boot from the A: drive, you should specify C:\ as the drive and path. If you wish to check specific files for fragmentation (in addition to the full drive analysis), you should include the appropriate entries for the *path* and *filename* parameters. The /F switch allows CHKDSK to fix any problems that it finds with directories or FATs. Keep in mind that if the /F switch is removed, CHKDSK is prohibited from writing to the disk. This allows you to run CHKDSK at your discretion without the danger of accidental file corruption. You are advised to always run CHKDSK in this read-only mode until you understand the nature and extent of any problems. The /V switch forces CHKDSK to display the results of its testing "verbatim," which will list all files in a disk's directories and (in some cases) provide details of any errors encountered.

> Before initiating CHKDSK, you should exit Windows to the native DOS mode. It is also wise to boot the system with an absolute minimum of device drivers and TSRs. As a general rule, CHKDSK should only be run with all other files closed and unchanging. If you're using a FAT32 OS (such as Windows 98) be sure to use the version of CHKDSK offered in the \Windows\Command directory.

```
129652736   bytes total disk space

   282624   bytes in 3 hidden files

   409600   bytes in 156 directories

126298112   bytes in 3930 user files

  2662400   bytes available on disk


     2048   bytes in each allocation unit

    63307   total allocation units on disk

     1300   available allocation units on disk


   655360   total bytes memory

   517088   bytes free
```

FIGURE 14-2 A typical report generated by CHKDSK

Interpreting a CHKDSK Report

By itself, the CHKDSK report (such as the one shown in Figure 14-2) is straightforward. The first five lines indicate the overall drive size, how much of that space is consumed by files, and how much space is left. If there were bad sectors on the disk, a sixth report line would be added to show the number of bytes in bad sectors. Keep in mind that a bad sector report poses no danger and does not reflect a faulty drive. Virtually all drives have some bad sectors that are marked in the FAT so that DOS will never attempt to use those bad areas. Most IDE-type drives can map out such elements entirely so that DOS does not even have to deal with such problems—you may not see a bad sector report, but even the best drives have bad sectors.

The next three lines indicate the size of each cluster (or allocation unit), the total number of clusters, and the remaining clusters. For this particular drive, you see that each cluster is 2KB. You also see that there are 63307 available allocation units on the disk (63307×2048 = 129652736, which is the total disk space shown in line 1). The last two lines indicate the total amount of DOS memory available and the amount of free DOS memory.

If you were to add a path and file name to the CHKDSK command line, one or more lines would be added to the report indicating the file's contiguity. If the file was contiguous, you would see "All specified file(s) are contiguous." If there was one or more noncontiguous file blocks, you would see a report similar to "*filename* Contains *xxx* non-contiguous blocks," where the *filename* is the name of the file being tested, and *xxx* corresponds to the number of noncontiguous blocks found. If disk errors are detected, one or more error messages will be produced.

Using CHKDSK

Simply stated, CHKDSK is a directory checker and patcher. CHKDSK compares the drive's directory tree with the FAT to ensure that there is a match between the two. When a discrepancy is detected between the FAT and directory structure, a corresponding error message is generated. As a result of this operation, most problems that CHKDSK reports are software related rather than a drive hardware fault. Four types of errors are reported most commonly: lost allocation units, allocation errors, cross-linked files, and invalid allocation units. Of these four categories, CHKDSK will only help you resolve lost allocation units and cross-linked files.

Recovering Lost Allocation Units

Lost allocation units are usually generated when a program stops running unexpectedly without saving or deleting temporary files. Over time, lost allocation units can accumulate and take up valuable file space. When lost allocation units are detected, CHKDSK will alert you with an error message such as:

```
10 lost allocation units found in 3 chains.
Convert lost chains to files?
```

If you answer yes, lost allocation units will be converted to files with file names such as FILE0000.CHK. You can then delete these files to free the recovered space for reuse. It's a great idea to use CHKDSK to recover lost allocation units before running a defragmenter or compression utility such as DoubleSpace.

> It's important for you to realize that this is the only type of problem that CHKDSK can actually "fix" effectively. Any other errors reported by CHKDSK cannot be fixed with CHKDSK. This is why it is so important that CHKDSK be run without the /F switch until you are aware of any particular problems. Allowing CHKDSK to fix a disk indiscriminately can do more harm than good.

Freeing Cross-Linked Files

Cross-linked files are generated when two or more files or directories are listed in the FAT as using the same disk space (one or more allocation units are overlapping). When cross-linked files are detected, you will see an error message similar to this:

```
JOHNSON.TXT is cross linked on allocation unit 11234
```

CHKDSK cannot fix a cross-linked file—it has no way to separate the overlap in allocation units. You should copy the file(s) specified in the error message somewhere else on the drive (so it will use different allocation units), and then erase the original file(s). Keep in mind that some information in the cross-linked files may be corrupt, and you may have to restore any such damaged files from a backup.

Limitations of CHKDSK

There are a number of instances where CHKDSK may not operate properly (if at all). CHKDSK will not process drives—or portions of drives—that have been created using SUBST, ASSIGN, or JOIN commands. CHKDSK also does not work on network drives. SUBST creates a "virtual" volume, which is little more than a subdirectory under the original volume that uses a different logical drive name. To use CHKDSK in a subdirectory created using SUBST, you must use the TRUENAME function to specify the actual path to the desired files. Note that TRUENAME is only available in DOS 4.0 and later. Suppose you used the SUBST function to create a virtual volume such as:

```
C:\> subst e: c:\tests\diagnostics
```

When you switch to the E: drive, you are actually switching to the C:\TESTS\DIAGNOSTICS subdirectory. If you do not know what the actual subdirectory is, use the TRUENAME function:

```
E:\> truename e:
```

The system would respond with:

```
C:\TESTS\DIAGNOSTICS
```

You can then use the CHKDSK function on the true directory listing:

```
E:\> chkdsk c:\tests\diagnostics\*.*
```

To use CHKDSK on an ASSIGNed drive, you must first "unassign" the drive. For example, if you assign a drive, such as ASSIGN A=B, you will have to unassign the drive, such as ASSIGN A=A. You can then run CHKDSK. After CHKDSK is complete, you can reassign the drive. There is no known way to use CHKDSK on a JOINed drive, which is basically a directory tree created by the JOIN command. JOIN adds one disk volume to another disk volume as a subdirectory. Only the portion that is JOINed is skipped—all other portions of the drive are checked. In order to run CHKDSK on a network drive, you must reach the desired PC with the drive to be tested and suspend or disable any sharing of the drive while CHKDSK is executed.

UNDERSTANDING SCANDISK

More recent versions of DOS and Windows 95/98 have basically paired the older CHKDSK utility with ScanDisk. In most respects, ScanDisk performs all of the same functions found in CHKDSK, such as checking the directory structure, locating and recovering lost allocation units, and identifying cross-linked files. However, ScanDisk also provides additional checking and media surface scan features that can not only help to identify a wider array of problems, but also mark out sectors on the drive that may be failing. Today, you can use ScanDisk for all the features found in older versions of CHKDSK.

Running ScanDisk

ScanDisk is primarily a protected-mode (Windows 95/98) tool that you launch by clicking Start, highlighting Programs, selecting Accessories, highlighting System Tools, and then clicking ScanDisk. The main ScanDisk dialog will appear, as in Figure 14-3. From this dialog, you can select the partition to be tested and invoke a thorough surface scan of the media. If you wish ScanDisk to fix any errors that it finds, simply select the "Automatically fix errors" check box.

> Performing a surface scan of the drive may take a considerable amount of time, especially for large drives partitioned and formatted under FAT32.

Clicking the Advanced button opens the ScanDisk Advanced Options dialog (Figure 14-4), where you can tailor the behavior of ScanDisk—especially the way it deals with lost file fragments and cross-linked files. When you allow ScanDisk to run a complete cycle, it generates a report remarkably similar to CHKDSK (Figure 14-5), including any errors that may have been detected on the disk. If ScanDisk does detect lost file fragments or cross-linked files on the disk, you may need to erase the files involved, defragment the disk, and then recopy the offending file(s) to their proper directory from your most current backup.

Please return the items by the
due date(s) listed below, to
any Memphis Public Library
location: For renewals:
Automated line: 452-2047
Levi Branch: 415-2773
Online: www.memphislibrary.org

Date due: 12/31/2012,23:59
Item ID: 0115234775829
Title: Troubleshooting, maintaining, & rep
airing PCs
Author: Bigelow, Stephen J.

NO RENEWALS FOR:
Audio-visual material or
7-day Popular Library books
****
In the interest of providing
our customers with the best
library experience possible,
please take a few minutes to
complete a brief, confidential
survey, which can be accessed
at:
http://tinyurl.com/mplsurvey
Thank you!

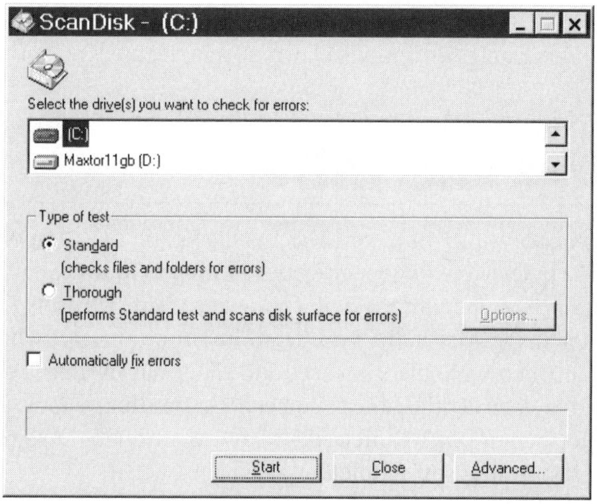

FIGURE 14-3 The main ScanDisk dialog

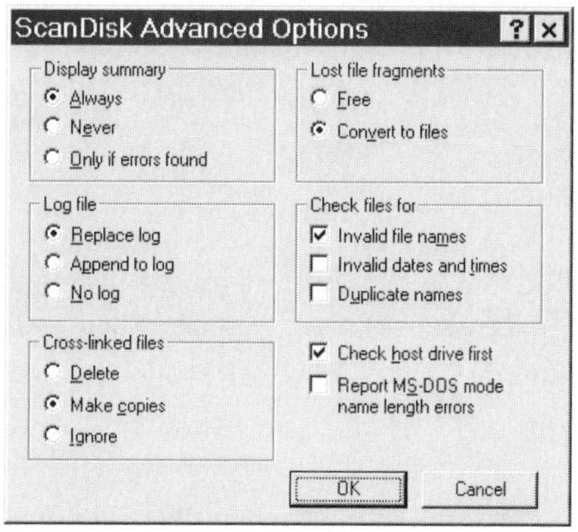

FIGURE 14-4 The ScanDisk Advanced Options dialog

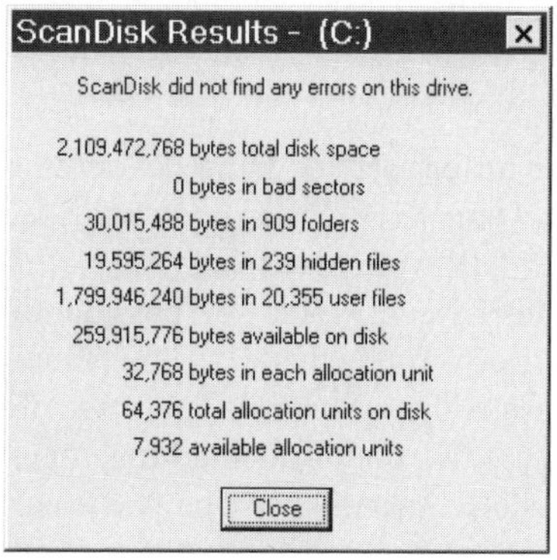

FIGURE 14-5 A typical ScanDisk report

14

Do not use an older version of ScanDisk (FAT16) on a newer FAT32 partition. Older versions of ScanDisk can report a great deal of erroneous information and can even cause extensive file corruption if left to "fix errors" automatically.

Recovering the MBR

The partition table (the *master boot record* or MBR) is the single most important sector on your hard drive. This one sector (512 bytes) contains specifications for up to four logical partitions, but it also provides instructions for starting the operating system. Without a viable MBR, the system will not even recognize the presence of the drive—let alone boot from it. Unfortunately, when the MBR is lost, it is *extremely difficult* to reconstruct (without losing access to all the data on the hard drive). There are several tools available for rebuilding these critical files. You can use third-party tools (such as Norton Utilities) under Windows 95/98, you can use MIRROR and UNFORMAT under DOS 6.2x (and FAT16), or you can use FDISK as a last-resort means of rebuilding a damaged MBR.

USING MIRROR AND UNFORMAT

Prevention is always faster and easier than a cure—the same is true of data recovery. If you are using DOS 5.0 or later, you have access to two DOS utilities that allow you to back up and restore the MBR: MIRROR.EXE and UNFORMAT.COM. Before the hard drive fails, type

```
MIRROR /PARTN
```

MIRROR will start and prompt you for a drive. Place a bootable floppy disk in A: (or B:), and let MIRROR copy the partition table to the floppy drive. If you do this regularly (say, twice a year), you will have a good emergency backup in the event of drive trouble. When trouble occurs, simply boot from the floppy disk (which should contain a copy of UNFORMAT and the partition backup file); then type

```
UNFORMAT /PARTN
```

UNFORMAT will ask for the location of the backup file (usually named PARTNSAV.FIL). Reference drive A: or B: (whichever drive contains the file) and continue. If the partition information looks appropriate, you can confirm the restoration, and then reboot the system from the hard drive. Assuming a faulty MBR was the only problem, the hard drive should now work properly.

USING FDISK /MBR

Earlier, you read that FDISK should not be used for data recovery since it makes changes that render your data inaccessible—that is not *entirely* true. There is an undocumented feature of FDISK that restores the startup code at the beginning of the MBR without touching the partition table itself. When the MBR cannot be rebuilt or restored by any other means, it may be possible to use **FDISK /MBR** and attempt to rebuild part of the MBR. When FDISK is run in this way, it is virtually automatic. You will not even see the FDISK menu—it will simply restore the startup code and return to the DOS prompt. Given the touchy nature of FDISK, you should attempt this undocumented function *only* as a last resort. FDISK /MBR should not render your data inaccessible, but it might, so be sure to back up as much of your drive as possible before proceeding.

When using FDISK, be sure to use the version that corresponds to your operating system. For example, if you're using Windows 98, use the version of FDISK that's placed on a Windows 98 startup disk.

USING "RESCUE PROFESSIONAL"

So what happens when you need the data on a hard drive, but the partition data is lost and unrecoverable, or you see an error such as "Track 0 bad, disk unusable"? Rescue Professional by AllMicro is a self-booting data recovery tool that is designed to interact directly with drive hardware and recover individual files or entire subdirectories. Unlike other procedures covered in this chapter, which attempt to restore some sort of functionality to the drive, Rescue Professional makes no attempt to correct lost partition tables or DOS boot records—its sole job is to operate the hard drive (if physically possible) and recover as many files as it can locate.

Recovering an Accidental Reformat

A high-level format process is invoked with the FORMAT command, and this rewrites the boot sector, FAT, and root directory of your disk. Formatting also checks each cluster to map out any damaged or unreadable clusters in the FAT. Normally, formatting is destructive to your data—the data itself is not overwritten, but formatting renders it inaccessible. This means if you accidentally format the wrong partition on your drive, the data on it can be lost.

Windows 95/98 offers no native tools for recovering from an accidental format, but there are third-party tools that will save a copy of the critical data and use it to reconstruct the partition lost during an accidental format. If you're working under DOS 6.2x, you can use the Unformat command (also a relative of the old Unformat tool with Central Point's PC Tools package) to recover your disk. For example:


```
unformat c:
```

The important thing to remember here is that you must use Unformat immediately after formatting. Once the format process is finished, the FAT is cleared; so writing new files to the disk may upset the Unformat process and prevent some (or all) of your files from being recovered.

Using EasyRecovery

When a hard drive physically fails, you'll need to send the disk to a professional data recovery house and let them try to resurrect the unit just long enough to wring your data from it. If the drive hardware is still working, however, you can often use software tools such as Ontrack's EasyRecovery utility to search out and rescue inaccessible data. EasyRecovery is a do-it-yourself data recovery tool that is capable of capturing lost or inaccessible data from your drive and reconstructing the file system (including partitions larger than 8.4GB). EasyRecovery does not attempt to repair corruption on the drive itself and never writes to the suspect drive. Instead, it rebuilds the file table in memory to allow safe transfer of data to another device (such as another hard drive). This part of the chapter offers some practical data recovery tips by examining some of the features and attributes of EasyRecovery.

OBTAINING EASYRECOVERY

EasyRecovery is not located on the companion CD. A free demo version of the software (which will identify all recoverable files and recover up to five files) can be downloaded from Ontrack at

http://www.ontrack.com/re/do/do.asp. If you find the software useful, you can purchase it online directly from Ontrack.

ABOUT EASYRECOVERY

The interesting thing about EasyRecovery is that it's a nondestructive and read-only tool that does not place any data onto the suspect (crashed) drive. Instead, data that's read from the drive is placed in memory and written to another drive (another hard drive, floppy disk, or network). EasyRecovery can recover data from drives without readable boot sectors, readable FATs, or readable directories. It can also handle drives that are no longer recognized by the operating system. This type of operation makes EasyRecovery particularly handy for disks that have been formatted, partitioned, crashed with a power failure, damaged by a computer virus, or damaged by rogue software (bugs).

EasyRecovery automatically creates a "virtual drive" in memory and offers access to the files through an ordinary-looking file manager applet. You can see the lost directories and files from your crashed drive. Files and directories can be viewed and copied to a safe medium (another drive) where the software's pattern recognition technology allows the various pieces of a recovered file to be assembled properly.

> Like virtually all software data recovery tools, EasyRecovery is not intended to operate a defective drive unit. If you experience drive damage (for example, you hear strange grinding noises), turn off the PC immediately—you may require the services of a data recovery house.

EasyRecovery works from a DOS command line to recover files from DOS, Windows 3.x, Windows 95/98, Windows NT, or Novell. It is not recommended that EasyRecovery be used in a DOS window within Windows 95/98. Several different versions of EasyRecovery can be downloaded based on your particular system requirements:

- *EasyRecovery for FAT16* Use on DOS and Windows 3.x and Windows 95, 98, and NT partitions that use FAT16. All files can be recovered, but long file names will be truncated to DOS 8.3 characters.
- *EasyRecovery for FAT32* Use on Windows 95 OSR2 or Windows 98/SE platforms with FAT32. EasyRecovery for FAT32 only works on FAT32 partitions. In order to copy files to a FAT32 partition, EasyRecovery must be booted to DOS 7 for Windows 95 OSR2 or Windows 98/SE. EasyRecovery for FAT32 does support the recovery of long file names.
- *EasyRecovery for NTFS* Use on any Windows NT system with NTFS partitions (workstation or server). EasyRecovery will copy files compressed with native NTFS compression. However, EasyRecovery is a DOS program and cannot copy files to an NTFS destination.
- *EasyRecovery for Novell* Use on Novell 3.XX and 4.XX only (with or without file compression). However, EasyRecovery is a DOS program and cannot copy to a Novell volume.
- *EasyRecovery for Zip drives* This is similar to EasyRecovery for FAT16, but only works with Iomega Zip or Jaz drives.

USING EASYRECOVERY

In most cases, data recovery consists of booting the system with EasyRecovery on a bootable disk, selecting the drive to be recovered, then allowing EasyRecovery to process the selected drive. When EasyRecovery finishes its analysis, you'll see a listing of the virtual drive, and you can select and copy desired files/folders to the recovery drive. Of course, there are numerous features and options that can be selected within the EasyRecovery program, but you'll need to refer to the documentation files for complete explanations.

Depending on your system's speed, the size of your drive, and the number of files on the drive, EasyRecovery can take from 15 minutes to several hours to complete its task. EasyRecovery may require up to 24 hours to analyze the partition of an NTFS or Novell drive.

Tips for Successful Data Recovery

Data recovery can be much easier if you follow a few simple rules:

- The most important data recovery tip is to always keep a current backup of your work in progress. Even if you have to reinstall an operating system and applications from scratch, you can easily restore the backup of your work and keep going. If you have no backup, and you're unable to recover the data, you may need to start from scratch.
- Always make sure that the suspect drive is specified correctly in the CMOS setup. Changing a drive's geometry can render the drive inaccessible (until the original drive geometry settings are restored).
- Don't mix and match data recovery tools. For example, don't use CHKDSK before running EasyRecovery. Advanced tools may misinterpret the disk recovery efforts of basic tools like CHKDSK.
- Select a recovery drive in advance (such as another hard drive, network drive, Jaz drive, or Zip drive). This is where the recovery program will place your recovered data, so make sure that there is ample space on the recovery drive, or see that you have ample Zip/Jaz media available.
- Select as much RAM as possible for your swap area (where recovered data is held before writing to the recovery drive). If you can create swap space on a drive, make sure there is ample space available on that drive, and never swap to the suspect drive.
- Data recovery routines can take quite some time to run, so be sure to allow plenty of time to run your data recovery software.
- Before using any data recovery software, verify that it's compatible with your partition type (FAT16 or FAT32 or NTFS) and partition size (25GB vs. 8GB). If the software cannot handle your partition type or size, running the software will probably destroy any chance of ever recovering your lost data—in fact, the software may make things worse. Make sure that you obtain the latest updates and patches for your data recovery software before running it.
- Use a UPS to prevent the system from crashing during data analysis and recovery.

Data Recovery Troubleshooting

Whether you use EasyRecovery or some other data recovery tool, you may encounter errors and problems during the process of your recovery. This part of the chapter examines a few typical troubles that often plague data recovery efforts.

SYMPTOM 14-1 **The system stops responding, and the data recovery software seems to have crashed** If there is no error message, it may simply be that the data recovery process is still running. It can take many hours to fully analyze a disk. Be patient and allow up to 24 hours for a data recovery cycle to run.

Data recovery software often performs analysis in conventional memory, then swaps the results out to extended memory (or a disk file). If there is severe data corruption, or a large number of small files, there may not be enough conventional or extended memory (or disk space) available. There are a few tricks that might help (depending on your software's particular options):

- Try recovering only a part of the drive at a time. This can be accomplished by selecting a range of sectors on the drive to be analyzed.
- Try lowering the threshold where a file is considered "bad" (sometimes called a "Bad File Acceptance Setting").
- Try swapping the analysis out to a disk file (on a known-good drive) rather than extended memory.

If the problem persists, you may need to try another data recovery tool, or send the drive out for professional data recovery techniques.

SYMPTOM 14-2 **The data recovery software reports the wrong drive size** Check the drive size as reported by the data recovery software and verify that it accurately reflects the size of the drive you're trying to recover. If the software takes an incorrect drive size from your system BIOS, you will not get reliable data recovery results. Check the following issues:

- Check the CMOS setup and verify that the drive geometry is accurate for your drive. If not, enter the correct values. If you've entered exact values, try to let the BIOS autodetect the drive. Check with the drive's manufacturer and see if there's an acceptable "translation geometry" that you can use instead.
- If the drive has "disk overlay" software installed (such as Disk Manager or MaxBlast), the CMOS setup may not contain the appropriate drive values. You may need to use a boot disk that enables the DDO first, before booting and launching the data recovery software.
- Check the LBA mode—drives bigger than 528MB should have the LBA mode enabled in the CMOS setup.
- Check the drive's reported values. Some huge drives report their geometry as 16383x16x63 regardless of their actual size. This may mean you'll need a BIOS upgrade or new drive controller to adequately support the suspect drive.

SYMPTOM 14-3 **Your data recovery software returns invalid results because it could not recognize the correct drive structure** If your data recovery software supports automatic drive structure recognition, you should try turning that feature off, then running the recover operation again. Without automatic identification, the software should present its interpretation of the drive structure for your approval (for example, cluster size (number of sectors in a cluster), data start cluster, and data end cluster). Since the size of your partition (in KB) is roughly defined by

```
([data end cluster-data start cluster] * [cluster size * 512]) / 2
```

if the result is equal to the partition size that you're trying to recover, you can try proceeding with the recovery. If you're not satisfied with the results, you can search again and look for the correct structure.

If you simply cannot find an appropriate structure, make sure you're using the data recovery software that's right for your file system (for example, using software for FAT32 may show structure errors if you're using a FAT16 drive).

SYMPTOM 14-4 **The data recovery software does not recover all missing files or directories** This may often occur if the software's recognition routine is too loose. Try tightening the recognition routine. The recovery process may take longer, but a stronger setting may catch more directories and files.

SYMPTOM 14-5 **The hard drive is making loud scraping noises, or there is clanking during disk access** All disks make a little bit of noise as the platters spin and the disk is accessed—this is perfectly normal. But when a drive makes loud or "damaged-sounding" noises, it probably is damaged. If the drive is accessible, back up as much data as possible and replace the drive before it fails. If the drive has already failed, do not attempt to use data recovery software. Instead, send the drive out for professional data recovery, or replace the drive outright and restore your most recent backup.

Further Study

CBL Data Recovery: **http://www.cbltech.com**

Data Recovery Group: **http://www.datarecoverygroup.com**

Data Recovery Labs: **http://www.datarec.com**

Data Recovery Software: **http://www.istonline.com/recovery.htm**

IBM: **http://ppdbooks.pok.ibm.com/cgi-bin/bookmgr/bookmgr.cmd/BOOKS/GG243994/TITLE**

Imation Data Recovery: **http://www.imation.com/solutions/datarecovery/**

Norton Utilities: **http://www.symantec.com/sabu/n2000r/index.html**

Ontrack Data Advisor: **http://www.ontrack.com/op/op_1.asp**

Ontrack: **http://www.ontrack.com**

Reynolds Utilities: **http://www.data-recovery.com/reynolds/**

TechParts: **http://www.recoverdata.com**

Uptime: **http://felix.scvnet.com/~uptime/index.html**

15

DISK COMPRESSION TROUBLESHOOTING

CHAPTER AT A GLANCE

Isn't it weird that we never seem to have enough storage space? No matter how large our hard drive is, or how many hard drives may be in the system, just about all PC users find themselves removing files and applications at one time or another in order to make room for new software. Looking back, it is hard to imagine that 10MB and 20MB hard drives were once considered spacious. Today, ordinary Windows games and applications can span several hundred megabytes. For many years, overcoming storage limitations has meant replacing the hard drive with a larger model. Given the rate at which hard drive technology is moving, a new drive generally doubles or triples a system's available space. While new drive hardware is remarkably inexpensive (typically around $16 per GB, or $0.016 per MB), the total bill for a 25GB to 35GB drive is a serious expense for everyday PC owners.

In the late 1980s and early 1990s, companies such as Stac Electronics and Microsoft had developed a reliable and efficient means of packing more data onto an existing disk—known as *disk compression.* Instead of an invasive procedure to upgrade and reconfigure a PC's hardware, a software utility reorganizes the drive using compression techniques that can allow a drive to safely store up to 100 percent (or more) than its rated capacity. For example, a properly compressed 100MB hard drive would typically be able to offer around 180MB or more of effective storage space. Since the initial introduction of disk compression, its acceptance and popularity has soared, and compression is now quite commonplace on DOS and Windows platforms. As you can imagine, however, disk compression is not always flawless—the vast differences between PC designs and the software used on them virtually guarantee problems at some point. This chapter is intended to illustrate the factors that affect disk compression and show you the symptoms and solutions for a wide variety of compression problems.

Although disk compression remains widely used in today's DOS and Windows 95 platforms, it seems to be slowly losing popularity because of the huge capacities and low costs of today's hard drives. Disk compression is also generally incompatible with FAT32 file systems, so compression is often abandoned when moving to FAT32 partitions on Windows 98 systems.

Concepts of Compression

In order to understand some of the problems associated with disk compression, it is important that you be familiar with the basic concepts of compression and how those concepts are implemented on a typical drive. Disk compression generally achieves its goals through two means: superior disk space allocation and an effective data compression algorithm.

DISK SPACE ALLOCATION

The traditional DOS system of file allocation assigns disk space in terms of clusters (where a *cluster* can be 4, 8, 16, or more *sectors*—where each *sector* is 512 bytes long). The larger a drive is, the more sectors are used in each cluster. For example, a 2GB drive typically consumes 64 sectors in each cluster. When you consider it, each cluster commits (512 x 64) 32,768 bytes per cluster. Since the drive's File Allocation Table (FAT) works in terms of clusters, a file that only takes 20 bytes, or 1000 bytes, or 20KB will still be given the *entire* cluster, even though *much* less than the full cluster may be needed. This can be phenomenally wasteful of disk space. (The total amount of waste on a disk is referred to as *slack space.*) Disk compression forms a barrier between the DOS file system and the drive. This "compression interface" simulates a FAT for the compressed drive, so the compressed drive also allocates space in terms of clusters, but now a compressed cluster can have a variable number of sectors rather than a fixed number. That way, a file that only needs three sectors has three sectors assigned to the cluster. A file that needs eight sectors has eight sectors assigned to its cluster, and so on.

DATA COMPRESSION

Now that the DOS limitations of file allocation have been overcome, the data that is stored in each sector is compressed as it is written to disk, then decompressed as it is read from the disk into memory. This is known as *on-the-fly* compression. That way, the program that might ordinarily need 20 sectors on a disk may be compressed to only 10 sectors. You can start to see that this combination of "cluster packing" and compression offers some powerful tools for optimizing drive space.

Data compression basically works by locating repetitive data in some given length of data and replacing the repetitive data with a short representative data fragment (called a *token*). For example, consider any ordinary sentence. In an uncompressed form, each text character would require 1 byte of disk space. On closer inspection, however, you can detect a surprising amount of repetition. In the last sentence alone, the letters *er* are used twice, the letters *on* are used three times, and the letters *tion* are used twice. You can probably find other repetitions as well. If each repetition were replaced by a 1 byte token, the overall volume of data could be reduced—sometimes significantly. The key to data compression is the ability to search sequences of data and replace repeated sequences with shorter tokens.

The *amount* of compression then depends on the power of the search-and-replace algorithm. A more powerful algorithm may be able to search larger amounts of data for larger repeating sequences, and replacing larger sequences results in better compression. Unfortunately, more powerful compression algorithms usually require larger commitments of CPU time, and this in turn slows down a disk's operations. Of course, any token must be shorter than the sequence it is replacing; otherwise, there would be no point to compression in the first place. Microsoft's DoubleSpace looks at data in 8KB blocks, so the chances of finding repetitive data sequences are much higher than that of a single sentence.

The importance of repeating data sequences raises an important question. What happens when a data sequence does not repeat? This is a very real and common possibility in everyday operation. If a data stream has few repeating elements, it cannot be compressed very well (if at all). For example, a graphic image (such as a screen shot) undergoes a certain amount of compression when the screen pixels are saved to a file. The PCX file format uses an early form of compression called *run-length encoding*, which finds and removes repeating pixels (a much faster and simpler process than looking for repeating pixel sequences). When a compression utility tries to compress that PCX file, there may be little or no effect on the file because many of the repeating sections have already been replaced with tokens of their own. As a rule, remember that *compression is only as effective as the data it is compressing*. Highly repetitive data will be compressed much better than data with few or no repetitions. Table 15-1 illustrates some typical compression ratios for various file types.

THE COMPRESSION SYSTEM

At this point, you can see how compression is implemented on the system. Traditionally, DOS assigns a logical drive letter to each drive (such as drive C: for the first hard drive). When a compression system is installed on a PC, a portion of your drive is compressed into what is known as the *compressed volume file* (or CVF). The CVF effectively becomes the *compressed* drive. It contains all compressed files, and it is treated by DOS as if it were a separate logical drive. The drive that holds the CVF (such as your original C: drive) is known as the *host drive*. Since the majority of the drive will be compressed into the CVF, there

TABLE 15-1 TYPICAL COMPRESSION RATIOS

TYPE OF FILE	EXTENSION	RATIO
Executable Programs	(EXE and COM files)	1.4:1
Word Processor Documents	(DOC files)	2.8:1
Spreadsheet Files	(XLS files)	3.3:1
Raw Graphic Bitmaps	(BMP files)	4.0:1
Conventional ASCII Text	(TXT or BAT files)	2.0:1
Sound Files	(WAV files)	1.1:1
Already Compressed Files	(ZIP files)	1.0:1 (no subsequent compression)

will be little space left on the host drive. In actual practice, some files (such as the Windows permanent swap file) *must* be left uncompressed, so you will normally leave anywhere from 20MB to 50MB uncompressed—the remainder of the drive can be compressed.

Figure 15-1 illustrates the process for a small 70MB drive. Suppose your uncompressed drive C: contains 60MB in files throughout various directories. On a 70MB drive, this leaves only 10MB free for your use. When a compression system is installed, the host drive is renamed to another drive letter (in this case, drive H:), and some small amount of space is kept aside as uncompressed space (say, 2MB). The remaining 68MB of the 70MB drive undergoes compression and becomes the CVF. Even though the CVF is physically located on the same hard drive, the CVF is assigned its own drive letter. (In this case the CVF is "mounted as drive C:.") If we assume an average compression ratio of 2.0:1, our compressed drive C: should now have about (68MB x 2.0) 136MB available. Since the original drive C: had 60MB in files, those same files are now available in compressed form. Instead of only 10MB free, the compressed volume now has about 76MB free. As far as the operating system is concerned, any access to drive C: will affect the CVF. Any access to drive H: will affect the uncompressed area. The system boot drive is now drive H:.

If you list the directory for a host drive (using the /ah switch to include archive and hidden files), you will see the three DOS files: IO.SYS, MSDOS.SYS, and COMMAND.COM. If you use Windows, you may also find a fairly large file with a .PAR extension (such as 386SPART.PAR). This is the Windows permanent swap file. There are also several files that are critical for compression. For DoubleSpace, three files are needed. DBLSPACE.000 is the CVF file itself—the heart and soul of compression. Microsoft's more recent DriveSpace uses the file DRVSPACE.000. Stacker uses the file name STACVOL.DSK. If you were to erase this file, your compressed drive C: would be gone. DBLSPACE.BIN is the DoubleSpace driver that allows DOS access to the CVF (DRVSPACE.BIN for DriveSpace). DBLSPACE.INI is the DoubleSpace initialization file containing all of the information needed to configure DoubleSpace (DRVSPACE.INI for DriveSpace).

FACTORS THAT AFFECT COMPRESSION

As a technician, you should understand the factors that influence compression performance: the extra *space* created, the *speed* of compression/decompression, and the amount of *memory* needed to support

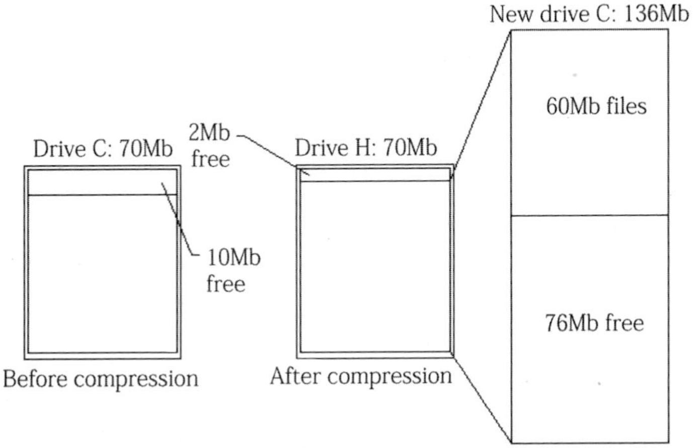

FIGURE 15-1 A hard disk before and after compression

compression/decompression. Of course, the primary purpose of compression is to provide additional disk space, so that is the principal measure of compression performance. Since compression products add a layer of processing between DOS and the disk, reads and writes will take a bit longer. These delays work to slow down the system—hardly crippling—but it can be annoying. Finally, compression needs memory-resident software to handle compression. Since software consumes conventional memory (often more than 35KB), this puts a serious strain on precious system resources (especially with DOS applications). If possible, you should load compressor software into the upper memory area (UMA) rather than conventional memory. If not, there may not be enough conventional memory left to run the applications you need. Under Windows 95/98, memory management is not such a serious concern.

Before and After Compression

Whether you're installing a compression system for yourself or a customer, there are some steps and precautions that should be taken in advance of the actual installation. A few minutes of advance planning can make the process much less painful. First, you must realize that the compression process requires about 1 minute per MB of space. If you are compressing 60MB, the process will take about 60 minutes, so even though the process is automated, the system is going to be on your bench for a while. Do yourself a favor and start the installation in the morning. You will also need to decide in advance how you want to arrange the compressed and uncompressed drives on the system. Do you want a single compressed volume? Do you want two or more compressed volumes? How much uncompressed space is required? Hammer this out with your customer if you can. Finally, back up, back up, back up! Don't even consider installing a compression system unless a complete system backup is performed.

SCAN THE DISK FOR PHYSICAL DEFECTS

Compression problems can arise if the CVF tries to use sectors on the physical drive that are defective. If this occurs, you will not be able to access the file written in the damaged sector. To ensure that there are no undetected defects in the drive, run a disk scanning utility such as ScanDisk (included with DOS 6.2x, Windows 95, and Windows 98), or use the scanning functions included with third-party diagnostics like PC Tools or Norton Utilities. Any sectors that check bad will be marked in the FAT and avoided in the compression process.

DEFRAGMENT THE DISK AND CHECK FREE SPACE

Fragmentation is a common and undesirable by-product of DOS file allocation. The clusters that are used to hold a file become scattered around a disk rather than positioned contiguously. When clusters become scattered, the drive has to work much harder to locate and reach each part of the file. Defragmentation rearranges the files on your disk so that the clusters associated with each file are contiguous. You should thoroughly defragment your disk *prior* to compression. Use DEFRAG (included with DOS 6.x, Windows 95, and Windows 98) or a third-party defragmentation utility such as PC Tools or Norton Utilities. After compressing the disk, check that there is at least 1.5MB of free space on the disk—some free workspace is needed in order to perform the compression process.

CHECK THE DISK FOR FILE DEFECTS

It is important to detect any lost clusters or cross-linked files before installing a compression product. ScanDisk will generally perform this checking for you, or you may use the DOS CHKDSK utility to find any disk errors. If lost clusters are reported, rerun CHKDSK with the /f (fix) switch to recover the lost clusters. Each lost cluster is recovered as a root directory file with a .CHK extension. You can then simply delete all CHK files before continuing. If cross-linked files are indicated, note the names of those cross-linked files. Copy those files to new files and delete the originals. This should clear the cross-link conditions, but one or both of those files are now likely to be defective, so restore all cross-linked files from the system backup or original installation disks. If you have DOS 6.2x available (or a Windows 95/98 startup disk), you can fix disk errors using ScanDisk instead of CHKDSK.

CHECK THE MEMORY

Keep in mind that a compression package will need to run a TSR or device driver to achieve on-the-fly operation. This compression utility should be loaded into the upper memory area (if possible). Otherwise, it will consume precious conventional memory, which may prevent other memory-hungry DOS applications from running. Use the MEM function and look at the report for the "largest free upper memory block." If that number is larger than 45KB, chances are good that you can load the utility into the UMA during system initialization. If there is little or no upper memory free, you will have to free sufficient memory by removing other drivers or TSRs, or *seriously* consider the impact of leaving the compression utility in conventional memory (this is highly undesirable).

INSTALL THE COMPRESSION UTILITY

If everything looks good up to now, you can go ahead and begin installation of the compression product. Both DoubleSpace/DriveSpace and Stacker can be started very simply, and the installation process for each is automated. For specific installation and operation information, refer to the detailed instructions that accompany each product.

CREATE A BOOTABLE DISK

You will find that hard disks *do* fail for a wide variety of reasons. Now that your drive is compressed, you will need to create bootable disks that are "compression aware." You could certainly boot the system from a conventional boot disk, but you would be unable to access your compressed drive(s). Fortunately, creating a compression-compatible boot disk is a simple matter.

For DoubleSpace/DriveSpace, follow these steps:

1. Format a blank floppy disk using the /s switch (FORMAT /s). For DOS 6.0 and later, DBLSPACE.BIN (or DRVSPACE.BIN) will be copied along with IO.SYS, MSDOS.SYS, and COMMAND.COM.
2. Copy CONFIG.SYS to the floppy (COPY CONFIG.SYS A:).
3. Copy AUTOEXEC.BAT to the floppy (COPY AUTOEXEC.BAT A:).
4. Copy needed files referenced by CONFIG.SYS and AUTOEXEC.BAT, such as HIMEM.SYS, EMM386.EXE, MOUSE.COM, MSCDEX.EXE, and so on. Check the startup files to find exactly what files are needed. You may have to edit CONFIG.SYS and AUTOEXEC.BAT to change the file paths to the floppy disk.
5. Copy other important DOS utilities such as FDISK.EXE, FORMAT.COM, CHKDSK.EXE, DBLSPACE.EXE (or DRVSPACE.EXE), SYS.COM, and MEM.EXE.

For Stacker, follow these steps:

1. Format a blank floppy disk using the /s switch (FORMAT /s).
2. Copy CONFIG.SYS to the floppy (COPY CONFIG.SYS A:).
3. Copy AUTOEXEC.BAT to the floppy (COPY AUTOEXEC.BAT A:).
4. Copy needed files referenced by CONFIG.SYS and AUTOEXEC.BAT, such as HIMEM.SYS, EMM386.EXE, MOUSE.COM, MSCDEX.EXE, and so on. Check the startup files to find exactly what files are needed. You may have to edit CONFIG.SYS and AUTOEXEC.BAT to change the file paths to the floppy disk.
5. Copy other important DOS utilities such as FDISK.EXE, FORMAT.COM, CHKDSK.EXE, STACKER.EXE, SYS.COM, and MEM.EXE.

Test the boot disk and see that there are no errors during initialization. You should also have access to the compressed drive(s) after booting from the compression-aware disk.

DBLSPACE.INI and DRVSPACE.INI File Settings

Whether operating under DOS or Windows 95/98, DoubleSpace and DriveSpace disk compression tools record their operating parameters in a file called DBLSPACE.INI (or DRVSPACE.INI). In order to successfully troubleshoot these utilities, you'll need to understand the contents of these INI files and adjust them if necessary. The DBLSPACE.INI (or DRVSPACE.INI) file may contain any of the following variables:

- MaxRemovableDrives=
- FirstDrive=
- LastDrive=
- MaxFileFragments=
- ActivateDrive=
- Automount= (MS-DOS 6.2 and Windows 95)
- DoubleGuard= (MS-DOS 6.2 Only)
- RomServer= (MS-DOS 6.2 Only)
- Switches= (MS-DOS 6.2 Only)

DBLSPACE.INI and DRVSPACE.INI are text files with Read-Only, Hidden, and System attributes. These files are stored in the root directory of your startup drive (either C: or the host drive for C:). Always make a backup copy of the INI file before you modify it! To uncover the file, use the ATTRIB command to remove the Read-Only, System, and Hidden attributes on the DBLSPACE.INI or DRVSPACE.INI file, for example: attrib -s -h -r h:\dblspace.ini.

Although you can change these variables yourself, you should avoid changing settings unless *absolutely* necessary. When possible, you should let DoubleSpace change the DBLSPACE.INI file for you (or allow DriveSpace to modify DRVSPACE.INI).

MaxRemovableDrives=n

The entry for this variable specifies how many additional drives DoubleSpace (or DriveSpace) should allocate memory for when your computer starts. The compression utility allocates a small amount of memory for each additional drive, and this variable determines how many additional compressed drives you can create or mount without restarting your computer.

To change this setting in DoubleSpace versions up to DOS 6.2, start DBLSPACE and choose Options from the Tools menu. The MaxRemovableDrives setting corresponds to the "Number of removable media drives" option. To change this setting in later versions of DoubleSpace or DriveSpace, edit the DBLSPACE.INI or DRVSPACE.INI file with a text editor.

FirstDrive=x

The entry for this variable specifies the *lowest* drive letter available for use by DoubleSpace. FirstDrive is set by DBLSPACE.EXE each time it modifies the DBLSPACE.INI file, so do *not* attempt to change the FirstDrive variable yourself.

LastDrive=y

The entry for this variable specifies the *highest* drive letter available for use by DoubleSpace or DriveSpace. The compression utility assigns drive letters starting at LastDrive and works back to FirstDrive. If another program uses one of the drive letters specified for DoubleSpace or DriveSpace, the highest drive letter available to the compression tool will be *higher* than LastDrive.

To change this entry in versions up to DOS 6.2, run DBLSPACE and choose Options from the Tools menu. The LastDrive setting corresponds to the "Last drive reserved for DoubleSpace's use" option. To change this setting in later versions of DoubleSpace or DriveSpace, edit the DBLSPACE.INI or DRVSPACE.INI file with a text editor.

> If you change the DBLSPACE.INI file, do not set FirstDrive to a letter used by a physical or logical drive (such as drive C:). Also, do not set LastDrive and FirstDrive more than 13 letters apart.

MaxFileFragments=n

The value for this variable is set by DoubleSpace or DriveSpace to specify the degree of fragmentation to allow in all mounted compressed volume files (CVFs). After the compression tool is installed, the MaxFileFragments setting is changed to reflect the new number of file fragments in all CVFs each time a CVF is changed (deleted, mounted, or resized). The new value is the sum of file fragments in all mounted CVFs plus 110. For example, if the CVF on drive C: has six fragments, and the CVF on drive D: has three fragments, then MaxFileFragments=119 (110 + 6 + 3). The new value is used to allocate memory the next time a CVF is mounted. Changes to DBLSPACE.INI that affect memory allocation take effect after you restart your computer.

To change this setting, you must edit the DBLSPACE.INI or DRVSPACE.INI file. However, with MS-DOS 6.2 (DoubleSpace), you can use the DBLSPACE /MAXFILEFRAGMENTS= command. The initial MaxFileFragments setting (2600 for MS-DOS 6.0, or 10000 for MS-DOS 6.2) and the number added when a CVF is changed (110) are both read from the DBLSPACE.INF file. (This is not the case with Windows 95/98.)

> If you decrease the MaxFileFragments setting below the necessary value, DoubleSpace or DriveSpace may not be able to mount your compressed drives.

ActivateDrive=X,Yn

This variable specifies a CVF that DoubleSpace or DriveSpace should mount automatically when your computer starts. The DBLSPACE.INI and DRVSPACE.INI files can contain as many ActivateDrive= lines as there are CVFs, but only the first 15 ActivateDrive= lines are processed by the compression utilities. DoubleSpace and DriveSpace use the "X", "Y", and "n" parameters to determine which CVF to mount and how to assign drive letters. The way these parameters are used depends on whether the specified CVF was created by compressing existing files, or by using free space on a drive, or if *both* types of CVFs exist on the same drive. The three options are explained below:

- *CVF created by compressing existing files* If the specified CVF was created by compressing existing files, the CVF name is DBLSPACE.000 (or DRVSPACE.000). In this case, "X" specifies the drive letter assigned to the uncompressed (host) drive where the CVF is stored after it is mounted—this is the newly created drive letter. "Y" specifies the drive letter assigned to the compressed drive, and "n" specifies the file name extension of the DBLSPACE.00n/DRVSPACE.00n CVF file (which is 0 in most cases). For example, "ActivateDrive=H,C0" indicates that the CVF file name is DBLSPACE.000. When mounted, the CVF is assigned drive letter C:, and the uncompressed (host) drive (which contains the CVF after startup) is assigned drive letter H:. If the CVF is unmounted, the CVF exists on drive C:, and drive H: does not exist.
- *CVF created by compressing free space* If the specified CVF was created by compressing free space on an existing drive, the CVF file name is DBLSPACE.001 for the first drive created, DBLSPACE.002 for the second drive created, and so on (substitute DRVSPACE if using DriveSpace). In this case, "X" specifies the drive letter assigned to the compressed drive—this is the newly created drive letter. "Y" specifies the drive letter assigned to the uncompressed (host) drive. "n" specifies the file name extension of the DBLSPACE.00n/DRVSPACE.00n CVF file, which is set to 1 for the first new CVF, 2 for the second new CVF, and so on. For example, "ActivateDrive=G,D2" indicates that the CVF file name is DBLSPACE.002 (the second CVF created by compressing free space). When mounted, the CVF is assigned drive letter G:, and the uncompressed (host) drive which contains the CVF before and after startup is assigned drive letter D:. If not mounted, the CVF exists on drive D:, and drive G: does not exist.
- *Both types of CVF on the same drive* If the specified CVF was created by compressing free space on an MS-DOS drive that also contains a DBLSPACE.000 or DRVSPACE.000 CVF (created by compressing existing files), the CVF file name is the same as noted above (DBLSPACE.001, DBLSPACE.002, and so on), but it now doesn't matter which CVF was created first. "X" specifies the drive letter assigned to the compressed drive—this is the newly created drive letter. "Y" specifies the drive letter of the DBLSPACE.000 or DRVSPACE.000 CVF when mounted on the same MS-DOS drive. If DBLSPACE.000 is not mounted, this is the drive letter where both the existing CVF and new CVF are stored. The "n" parameter specifies the file name extension of the DBLSPACE.00n or DRVSPACE.00n CVF file.

To change the ActivateDrive= line, edit the DBLSPACE.INI or DRVSPACE.INI file with a text editor. However, with MS-DOS 6.2, you can use the DBLSPACE /HOST command.

AutoMount=0, 1, A...Z (MS-DOS 6.2 and Windows 95 only)

This feature enables or disables the automatic mounting of removable drives (including floppy disk drives). By default, DoubleSpace automatically mounts all removable drives (AutoMount=1), and no entries are required in the DBLSPACE.INI file. DoubleSpace consumes 4KB of additional memory with this setting enabled. To disable this setting, you must edit the DBLSPACE.INI file in a text editor. However, in MS-DOS versions you can use the DBLSPACE /AUTOMOUNT=0 command.

DoubleGuard=0, 1 (MS-DOS 6.2 only)

This feature enables or disables DoubleGuard safety checking for older versions of DoubleSpace. When DoubleGuard is enabled, DoubleSpace will constantly check its memory for damage by some other program. DoubleGuard safety checking detects when another program has violated DoubleSpace's memory and immediately shuts down your computer to minimize the chance of data loss. If further disk activity were to occur, you could lose some or all of the data on your drive since the data DoubleSpace has in memory is probably invalid due to damage by the other program. By default, DoubleGuard is enabled (DoubleGuard=1), and no entries are required in the DBLSPACE.INI file. To disable this setting, type DBLSPACE/DOUBLEGUARD=0 at the MS-DOS command prompt. As a rule, do not disable DoubleGuard.

RomServer=0, 1 (MS-DOS 6.2 only)

This feature enables or disables the check for a ROM BIOS Microsoft Real-time Compression Interface (MRCI) server under older versions of DoubleSpace. By default, the ROM MRCI check is disabled (RomServer=0), and no entries are required in the DBLSPACE.INI file. To enable this setting, type **DBLSPACE /ROMSERVER=1** at the command prompt.

> You should not enable the ROM MRCI check unless you are certain that your hardware supports this feature.

Switches=/F, /N, /FN (MS-DOS 6.2 only)

This feature controls the way the CTRL+F5 and CTRL+F8 keys work. Normally, you can press CTRL+F5 or CTRL+F8 to bypass older versions of DoubleSpace when your computer starts, and no entries are required in the DBLSPACE.INI file.

Making the Most of Compression

Compression is a demanding process that has a profound impact on the way your valuable data is stored on a drive or other media. It's important that you understand the major techniques for installing, configuring, optimizing, and removing/upgrading compression systems on your computer. This part of the chapter highlights a series of procedures that you can use to manage disk compression most effectively.

CHECKING FOR DISK COMPRESSION

During your troubleshooting efforts, you'll probably need to determine whether or not a given drive is compressed. Even if you're running Windows 95/98, you should restart your PC to the command prompt and follow the steps below:

- *Run ScanDisk from the command prompt.* When you run ScanDisk from a prompt, it asks you to check the host drive *first* if the hard drive is compressed. If you receive this prompt, the disk you're attempting to scan is compressed. You can then try ScanDisk on each of the other hard drives in your system to determine whether those hard drives are also compressed. To run ScanDisk, try the following command line,

  ```
  scandisk &lt;drive&gt;:
  ```

  where "drive" is the drive letter of the hard disk you need to check.
- *Bypass the compression driver.* If you do not load the compression driver when Windows starts, and you do have a compressed drive, you will not have access to any compressed drives, and one or more

compressed volume files (CVFs) will appear in the root directory of your hard drive. To bypass the compression driver, select the Start menu and choose Step-by-Step Confirmation; then answer no to each question until the command prompt appears. Once you see a command prompt, try the following command line:

```
dir d*.* /a /p
```

If you see any files named DBLSPACE.<NNN> or DRVSPACE.<NNN> (where "NNN" is a number from 000 to 254), the drive is compressed—otherwise, it is not.

COMPRESSING A DRIVE

1. Start DriveSpace (Figure 15-2), and click the drive you want to compress.
2. On the Drive menu, click Compress, and then click Start.
3. If you're prompted to update your startup disk, click Yes, insert your floppy disk in drive A:, and then click Create Disk.
4. If you wish to back up your files before upgrading the compression system, click Back Up Files, follow the instructions on your screen, and then click Upgrade Now.
5. Click Compress Now.
6. If prompted to restart your computer, click Yes.

UPGRADING A COMPRESSED DRIVE TO DRIVESPACE 3

1. Start DriveSpace and select the compressed hard disk you want to upgrade.
2. On the Drive menu, click Upgrade, and then click Start.
3. If you're prompted to update your startup disk, click Yes, insert your floppy disk in drive A:, and then click Create Disk.
4. If you wish to back up your files before upgrading the compression system, click Back Up Files, follow the instructions on your screen, and then click Upgrade Now.
5. If prompted to restart your computer, click Yes.

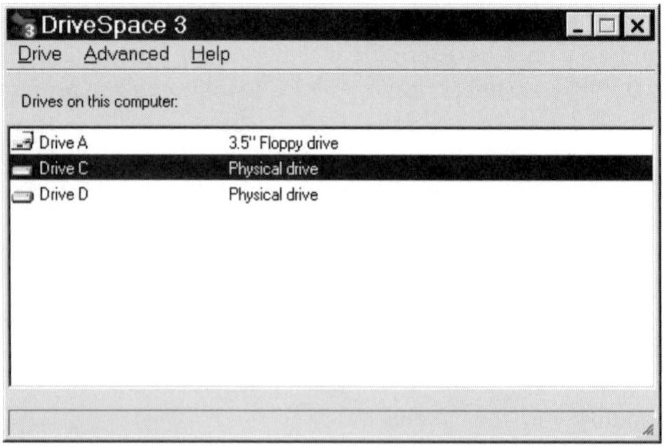

FIGURE 15-2 The DriveSpace 3 dialog

> Always back up your important data before attempting to make any changes or upgrades involving your compression system. Remember that you can only upgrade hard drives that have been compressed by DoubleSpace, DriveSpace for MS-DOS, or DriveSpace for Windows 95.

UPGRADING A COMPRESSED FLOPPY DISK

1. Create a new folder on your hard disk, and then copy the contents of your compressed floppy disk to it.
2. Start DriveSpace 3 and click the letter of the floppy drive.
3. On the Advanced menu, click Delete to delete the compressed data on the floppy disk.
4. On the Drive menu, click Compress to recompress the floppy disk using DriveSpace 3.
5. In Windows Explorer, copy the contents from the new folder on your hard disk to the newly compressed floppy disk (and delete the new folder from your hard disk if you wish).

MOUNTING/UNMOUNTING A CVF

1. Start DriveSpace 3 and click the drive that contains the CVF you need to mount.
2. On the Advanced menu, click Mount.
3. Click the compressed volume file (CVF) that you wish to mount.
4. If prompted to restart your computer, click Yes.

> To unmount a drive, simply start DriveSpace 3 and click the compressed drive you want to unmount. Open the Advanced menu and click Unmount.

CHECKING A DRIVE IN THE EVENT OF AN ERROR

If DriveSpace 3 detects an error on the disk, you can use ScanDisk to test and repair errors.

1. Start ScanDisk.
2. Once ScanDisk starts, click the drive you were compressing in DriveSpace 3.
3. Make sure the Automatically Fix Errors check box is unchecked.
4. Under Type of test, click Thorough, and then click Options.
5. Under "Areas of the disk to scan," make sure "System and data areas" is selected. The two check boxes at the bottom of this dialog box should not be selected.
6. Click Advanced, make sure the "Invalid file names, check host drive first" and "Report MS-DOS mode name length errors" check boxes are selected, and then click Start.

ADJUSTING FREE SPACE ON THE COMPRESSED/HOST DRIVE

1. Start DriveSpace 3 and click the compressed drive where you want to reallocate free space.
2. On the Drive menu, click Adjust Free Space.
3. Move the slider to adjust the space on the compressed drive and the host drive.
4. If prompted to restart your computer, click Yes.

CHANGING THE ESTIMATED COMPRESSION RATIO

1. Start Drive Space 3 and click the compressed drive whose ratio you need to change.
2. On the Advanced menu, click Change Ratio.
3. Move the slider to the left or right to change the compression ratio.
4. If prompted to restart your computer, click Yes.

> Remember that Windows uses the "estimated compression ratio" to report how much free space is available on the selected drive. You should keep this value set as close as possible to the "actual compression ratio."

CHANGING THE COMPRESSION METHOD

1. Start DriveSpace 3.
2. On the Advanced menu, click Settings (Figure 15-3).
3. In the Compression Method entry, click the method you want. Try using the "No compression, unless drive is at least 90% full…" option. Windows saves your files *uncompressed* if you have enough hard disk space. If your hard disk becomes full, Windows saves your files by using standard compression. If you use the "No compression" option for optimum speed, the free space reported by Windows will drop significantly. To regain the extra free space, use Compression Agent to compress your files while you're not using the computer.

> You can change the point at which Windows starts compressing your files by changing the disk-space percentage.

OPTIMIZING YOUR FILE COMPRESSION

DriveSpace allows you to fine-tune your compression system in order to achieve maximum disk space, maximum speed, or your most comfortable balance between these two characteristics.

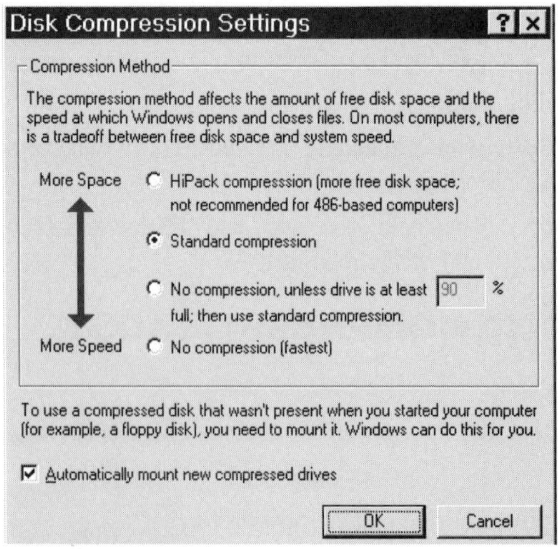

FIGURE 15-3 The Disk Compression Settings dialog

Optimum Speed

To achieve optimum speed, you should save your files uncompressed.

1. Start DriveSpace 3.
2. On the Advanced menu, click Settings.
3. Select No compression. You may want to compress files only if you're running low on free disk space. In that case, click "No compression, unless the drive is at least 90% full...." You can change the disk-space percentage as needed.

Maximum Drive Space

Configure DriveSpace 3 to compress files as you save them.

1. Start DriveSpace 3.
2. On the Advanced menu, click Settings.
3. Click Standard compression. Standard compression provides good compression without much loss in speed. If you're low on hard disk space and have a fast processor, try using HiPack compression to free up even more drive space.

A Balance of Speed and Space

Use Compression Agent to achieve this balance of speed and space.

1. Click Start, highlight Programs, point to Accessories, select System Tools, and then click Compression Agent.
2. Click the drive you want to change compression settings for (if you have more than one DriveSpace 3 compressed drive), and then click Settings.
3. Click "Do not UltraPack any files (maximum performance)," and then click Yes to use HiPack compression on the rest of your files.

> For maximum speed, select "No, store them uncompressed" to uncompress all of your files. Your files will take up considerably more disk space.

USING DRIVESPACE WITH UNMOUNTED DRIVES

If you remove the DriveSpace compression driver, and then discover later that you need it to use unmounted compressed drives (or compressed removable media), you can use the following steps:

1. Start DriveSpace.
2. On the Advanced menu, click Settings.
3. Make sure that the Automatically Mount New Compressed Drives option is selected.
4. Reboot the computer if you're prompted to do so.

UNCOMPRESSING A DRIVE

1. Start DriveSpace and click the drive you want to uncompress.
2. On the Drive menu, click Uncompress, and then click Start.
3. If you wish to back up your files before upgrading the compression system, click Back Up Files, follow the instructions on your screen, and then click Upgrade Now.

4 Click Uncompress Now.

5 If you're prompted to restart your computer, click Yes.

DELETING A COMPRESSED DRIVE

1 Start DriveSpace 3 and click the compressed drive you want to delete.

2 On the Advanced menu, click Delete.

> Deleting a compressed drive unmounts the drive and deletes the compressed volume file (CVF) from the boot drive. This offers a quick and easy way to delete all information on a compressed drive.

REMOVING DOS DOUBLESPACE OR DRIVESPACE MANUALLY

Ideally, the process of removing disk compression should be automatic. The maintenance program for DoubleSpace and DriveSpace should allow you to remove compression by choosing the Uncompress feature in the Tools menu. Still, there may be some situations in which automatic decompression will not work, and it may be necessary to remove a compression package manually. The following procedure outlines a method of removing compression while preserving files. If you do not need to preserve your files, DoubleSpace provides a way to delete a compressed drive without manual intervention. You can delete a compressed volume file (CVF) using the DoubleSpace maintenance program interface or the command-line interface. To delete DoubleSpace using the DoubleSpace maintenance program, choose Delete from the Drive menu.

> The following procedure assumes that you have compressed your boot drive (C:) and that your compressed host partition is H:.

> The following procedure refers to DOS 6.2 and DoubleSpace. However, if you're using MS-DOS 6.22, the procedure will work just as well. Just substitute DRVSPACE for DBLSPACE commands, DRVSPACE.* for DBLSPACE.*, and DRVSPACE.SYS for DBLSPACE.SYS.

1 Back up all the files you want to preserve from your compressed drive (C:). You can use any suitable backup technique for this.

2 When you finally remove DoubleSpace, what is now drive H: will become drive C:, which means you'll boot from drive H:. To boot from drive H: and restore your backup files, the DoubleSpace host partition must contain the necessary MS-DOS system files and utilities. Also, if you stored your backup files on a network drive, network redirectors must be available.

3 Use the DIR command to determine how much free space you'll need to copy the MS-DOS files (and network redirectors) on the DoubleSpace host partition (drive H:). For example, to see how much space is needed for your MS-DOS files, type

```
dir c:\dos
```

You'll see a list of files, then a set of statistics like this:

```
194 file(s)     7003143 bytes
12959744 bytes free
```

The next-to-last line shows the number of bytes used by the files in the DOS directory. This is the amount of free disk space needed to store the necessary files and utilities after DoubleSpace is removed.

4 To free unused disk space from the DoubleSpace compressed volume, use the /SIZE switch like this:

```
dblspace /size
```

5 Determine how much free space there is on the DoubleSpace host partition (drive H:). Change to drive H: and use the DIR /A command. The last line of the report shows the number of bytes free on drive H:. If this number is *greater* than the number you found in Step 3, there is enough space to copy the necessary files and utilities, and you can proceed.

6 If there is not enough space on the DoubleSpace host partition, delete enough files on drive C: to create the needed space. (*Do not delete any MS-DOS or network files; those files must be present during this procedure.*) You can use the DELTREE command to do this. For example, to remove the WORD directory and all the files and subdirectories it contains, type

```
deltree /y c:\word
```

After you delete some files, shrink the DoubleSpace volume file again by typing the following:

```
dblspace /size
```

To find out if you've created enough free disk space, change to drive H: and use the DIR command. The *bytes in use* and *bytes free* are displayed. If the bytes free line shows enough free disk space, continue. Otherwise, clear additional space.

7 Copy all the MS-DOS and network files that you need to the DoubleSpace host partition (drive H:). To preserve the file and directory structure, you can use the XCOPY command with the /S switch. For example, to copy all the MS-DOS files into a DOS directory on H:, type

```
md h:\dos xcopy c:\dos\*.* h:\dos /s
```

Make sure there is a copy of COMMAND.COM in the root of the DoubleSpace host partition (H:):

```
dir h:\command.com
```

If COMMAND.COM is not present, copy it from the boot drive (C:) with the following command:

```
copy c:\command.com h:\
```

Repeat this step for AUTOEXEC.BAT and CONFIG.SYS files. These files need to be in the root of the DoubleSpace host partition as well. You now have all the files you need in order to boot from the uncompressed drive and restore your backup files. You can begin removing the DoubleSpace volume.

8 Switch to the root of the DoubleSpace host partition by typing

```
h: cd\
```

9 Delete the DoubleSpace files by using the command

```
deltree /y dblspace.*
```

10 If you are removing DoubleSpace from your boot drive, open the CONFIG.SYS file from the DoubleSpace host partition (H:) in a text editor, such as EDIT. If you are not removing DoubleSpace from your boot drive, open the CONFIG.SYS file for drive C:. Remove any reference to DBLSPACE.SYS. For example, change your DBLSPACE.SYS DEVICE command to appear as follows:

```
rem device=c:\dos\dblspace.sys
```

11 You can now restart your computer by pressing CTRL+ALT+DEL. Once the system reboots in the uncompressed form, you can restore your backup files.

Troubleshooting Compressed Drives

Disk compression products are some of the most thoroughly tested and robust computer programs ever released. They *have* to be—programs that trash a customer's vital data don't last long in the marketplace. However, the bewildering assortment of PC setups and utilities now in service will result in incompatibilities or disk errors somewhere along the line. This part of the chapter takes you through a selection of symptoms and solutions for DriveSpace, DoubleSpace, and Stacker. Keep in mind that a complete system backup should be made (if possible) before attempting to deal with compression problems.

TROUBLESHOOTING WINDOWS 95/98 DRIVESPACE

Windows 95 also offers disk compression in the form of DriveSpace 3, which is included in the MS Plus! pack (sold separately), and Windows 98 incorporates DriveSpace 3 natively. With DriveSpace 3, you can access drives that were compressed using DoubleSpace (included with MS-DOS versions 6.0 and 6.2) as well as DriveSpace for MS-DOS (included in MS-DOS version 6.22). In addition, DriveSpace 3 allows higher compression ratios on drives up to 2GB. (Earlier versions only support drives up to 512MB.)

> DriveSpace 3 only works on FAT16 partitions. Drives that are partitioned as FAT32 (Windows 95 OSR2 or Windows 98) cannot be compressed. Microsoft is considering a FAT32-compatible compression tool, but for now, do not use DriveSpace with OSR2 or Windows 98.

SYMPTOM 15-1 **DriveSpace cannot mount two CVFs with the same extension** If you have two or more compressed drives, one of the compressed drives may not be mounted because DriveSpace reports that it has *already* been mounted. This problem occurs when the two compressed volume files (CVFs) have the same extension. For example, this problem creeps up when one CVF is named Drvspace.002 and another CVF is named Dblspace.002. You'll need to rename *one* of the CVFs so that it does not have the same extension as the other(s). Use a number between 001 and 255 for the extension.

Reboot the system directly to a DOS prompt, change to the drive and directory containing the CVF file to be renamed, and then type the following command to "unhide" the CVF (where <filename> is the original name of the CVF to be renamed):

```
attrib -s -h -r <filename>
```

Now type the following command:

```
ren <filename> <new filename>
```

Here, <filename> is the original name of the CVF, and <new filename> is the new name for that CVF. Now "rehide" the CVF with the following command (<new filename> is the new name of the CVF):

```
attrib +s +h +r <new filename>
```

Finally, reboot the system.

SYMPTOM 15-2 DriveSpace 3 reports much less free space than the amount you specified If you manually adjust the free space on a compressed drive using DriveSpace 3, the amount of free space reported by the system may then be only *half* the amount you specified in your adjustment. This problem occurs when you're using the No Compression option in DriveSpace 3. To avoid this problem, readjust your free space using the Adjust Free Space slider in DriveSpace 3, or avoid the No Compression option—instead, use the HiPack or Standard compression method.

SYMPTOM 15-3 You cannot create a DriveSpace 3 startup disk under Windows 95 If you install Microsoft Plus! for Windows 95 and DriveSpace 3, and then reinstall Windows 95, you cannot create a startup disk that is compatible with DriveSpace 3. This is because the original Windows 95 setup replaces the MSDOS.INF and LAYOUT.INF files used to create the startup disk with the original versions of the files—those original files are not DriveSpace 3 compliant. You'll need to update those required files:

1. Click Start, select Programs, highlight Accessories, point to System Tools, and then click DriveSpace.
2. Click an uncompressed drive, and then click Create Empty on the Advanced menu.
3. In the Using box, enter **1**, and then click Start. The 1 indicates the size for the new compressed drive (in MB).
4. When you're prompted to update the current startup disk, click Yes.

Now you'll need to delete that new compressed drive:

1. Click the new compressed drive in DriveSpace, and then click Delete on the Advanced menu.
2. To confirm that you want to delete the drive, click Yes, and then click OK.
3. Close DriveSpace.

SYMPTOM 15-4 Windows 95 setup's version of ScanDisk does not scan a compressed drive's MDFAT When you install Windows 95 over an existing installation of Windows 95 that's on a hard disk compressed with DriveSpace 3, the version of ScanDisk run by setup only checks the FAT for potential errors. This version of ScanDisk cannot check the Microsoft DoubleSpace FAT (MDFAT). This version of ScanDisk run by setup is not designed to work with DriveSpace 3. Before you run setup again, run ScanDisk with the Thorough option on all drives, including the compressed drive and its host drive. Run ScanDisk from the System Tools menu.

SYMPTOM 15-5 The system halts when accessing bad clusters on a compressed drive When you're using a real-mode driver (DRVSPACE.BIN or DBLSPACE.BIN) and you try to access a file on a DriveSpace or DoubleSpace compressed drive, the computer crashes. If you're using a protected-mode driver (DRVSPACX.VXD), you may receive a "Read Fault" error message. This occurs when the file being accessed is stored in one or more bad clusters. A bad cluster on a compressed drive is a cluster that cannot be read successfully. (An unreadable cluster on a compressed drive does not always represent a media defect on the physical surface of the disk.) With the protected-mode DriveSpace driver loaded, run ScanDisk for Windows and use the Thorough option in the Type Of Test box. Test the system and data areas on the compressed drive, as well as on the host drive. This should identify and correct cluster errors.

SYMPTOM 15-6 DriveSpace 3 cannot compress a drive on a system with 22 "local drives" When you try to use DriveSpace 3 to compress a drive on a Windows 95/98 computer with 22 local drives, you receive an error message such as:

```
Drive letters C through Z are in use. You need a free drive letter to mount
a compressed drive.
```

To free a drive letter, disconnect a network drive or unmount a compressed drive that you aren't using. To compress a drive on this type of system configuration, add the line **firstdrive=Y** to the DRVSPACE.INI file. The DRVSPACE.INI file should be located in the root directory of your compressed drive, and should have its Hidden, Read-Only, and System attributes set. To edit the file, remove those attributes at the DOS prompt:

```
attrib -r -h -s drvspace.ini
```

Now add the line **firstdrive=Y** to the beginning of the file, save and close the file, and then restart Windows 95/98.

SYMPTOM 15-7 You cannot uncompress DriveSpace after using the PartitionMagic utility When you try to uncompress a drive that's been compressed with DriveSpace 3, the process may stop at about 24 percent finished, and indicate that it needs to restart Windows 95/98 in a "special mode." When your computer reboots, it restarts Windows 95/98, and the uncompress operation is not completed. This problem is known to occur if you use PartitionMagic to create additional partitions on the drive. When you do, PartitionMagic may change the drive letter assignment for the host drive from its default letter (usually drive H:). You'll need to reconfigure the DriveSpace INI file in order to correct this problem:

1. Restart your computer to the "Safe Mode Command Prompt" using the Windows Startup menu.
2. Change the attributes of the DRVSPACE.INI or DBLSPACE.INI file in the root directory of your boot drive. Change to the root directory of your boot drive, and type the following command (where <filename> is either DBLSPACE.INI or DRVSPACE.INI):

   ```
   attrib -s -h -r <filename>
   ```

3. Open the DRVSPACE.INI or DBLSPACE.INI file using any text editor, and then locate the line that reads

   ```
   ActivateDrive=H,C0
   ```

4. Change the *H* in this line to the drive letter that is assigned to the host drive. For example, if the host drive is actually drive I:, change the line to read

   ```
   ActivateDrive=I,C0
   ```

5. Save your changes and close the file. Then restart your computer.
6. Run the uncompress operation again.

SYMPTOM 15-8 When DriveSpace is removed under Windows 95/98, its command line isn't removed from CONFIG.SYS After you remove your last compressed drive from the system, DriveSpace asks whether you want to remove the compression driver from memory, and generally fails to remove the compression device statement in your CONFIG.SYS file. When the last compressed drive is removed (either uncompressed or deleted), DriveSpace asks if the compression driver (DRVSPACX.VXD) should be removed from memory. After you restart the computer, DRVSPACX.VXD is successfully removed from memory, but the following command line may remain in CONFIG.SYS:

```
device=<path>\DRVSPACE.SYS /move
```

Here, <path> is the Windows 95/98 "command" subdirectory (such as C:\Windows\Command). It is safe to manually remove or REMark out this line from your CONFIG.SYS file.

SYMPTOM 15-9 DriveSpace 3 changes file names when compression is invoked When you use DriveSpace 3 to compress a drive on a computer that had a beta version of Windows 95 installed, DriveSpace 3 may change short file names (that is, the 8.3 file name format) to the Windows 95 format. The Windows 95 format omits spaces and places "~1" at the end of the file name. This is a normal process that happens because DriveSpace renames files to adhere to the default naming conventions of Windows 95. You can leave the files as they are named, or you can manually rename them to the original file names.

SYMPTOM 15-10 Large files are left on the host drive after compressing a drive with DriveSpace 3 When you use DriveSpace 3 (DRVSPACE.EXE) to compress a drive under Windows 95, you may receive an error message such as:

```
There was not enough free space on drive C: to complete this task. Some files
have been left uncompressed on drive h: If you want to compress these files,
you must delete unwanted files from drive C: and then try again.
```

When DriveSpace compresses files, it makes a second copy of each file on the compressed drive *before* it deletes the duplicated file on your host drive. If the compressed drive does not have enough free space to store a copy of the larger file, it leaves the larger file(s) uncompressed on the host drive. This is a normal safety mechanism of DriveSpace 3 that is designed to protect your data as the drive becomes full. When you use DriveSpace in Windows 95, free some additional space on the compressed drive first, and *then* copy the files from your host drive to the compressed drive.

SYMPTOM 15-11 You cannot install CorelDraw 3.0 (rev B) with DriveSpace 3 on the system When you try to install CorelDraw 3.0 "B" on a Windows 95 platform running DriveSpace 3, your computer may crash after you receive a message from CorelDraw setup, such as:

```
CorelDraw is checking for space available on your drives
```

To escape the setup program, press CTRL+ALT+DEL and use the Close Program dialog box. This problem occurs because DriveSpace 3 uses 32KB clusters on the hard disk, but CorelDraw 3.0 "B" cannot be installed on drives with 32KB clusters. This problem does not plague earlier versions of DoubleSpace and DriveSpace since they do not use 32KB clusters for disk compression. Corel Corporation has since released a patch (named INSTFX.EXE) that resolves this problem. You can download this patch from the Corel Web site.

SYMPTOM 15-12 DriveSpace reports that it cannot work with a removable-media drive under Windows 95/98 When you try to compress a removable-media drive, you may receive an error message such as:

```
DriveSpace cannot work with <drive letter> because the drive was formatted
using a non-standard sector length.
```

This problem happens because DriveSpace and DriveSpace 3 do not compress drives with a nonstandard sector size. For example, a 640MB magneto-optical disk can use a nonstandard sector size of 2KB. You'll need to use drives with standard sector sizes—otherwise, leave the removable-media drive uncompressed.

SYMPTOM 15-13 You receive a "write protection" error when using DriveSpace 3 under Windows 95 This may occur on any computer with a write-protected, mounted, and compressed removable drive. You will probably receive a write error message on a "blue screen" originating from the compression driver. The compression driver does not have write access to the host drive. You'll need to remove the write protection from your removable drive and retry the operation.

SYMPTOM 15-14 You cannot add or remove compression tools from the Windows 98 Setup tab After you install Windows 98, you cannot uninstall DriveSpace and its associated components. If you do not yet have DriveSpace installed (and you want to install it), the option to install this feature may no longer appear. This was done intentionally to help protect and ensure access to any compressed media that you have. You'll need to make some changes to your system configuration in order to restore the compression tools option on your system. Start by backing up and editing your APPLETS1.INF file:

1. Back up the APPLETS1.INF file located in your \WINDOWS\INF folder. You should make a copy of this file to another folder or floppy disk.
2. Open your APPLETS1.INF file into a text editor (for example, Notepad). If you're using Notepad, do not enable the Word Wrap feature.
3. Under the Disk Compression Install Sections entry, add the following line to the [dxxspace] area:

   ```
   Uninstall=dxxspace_remove
   ```

4. Also add the following section headers and information. Note that the "DelFiles" and "StubPath" entries (below) must all be on a single line.

```
[dxxspace_remove]
DelFiles=dxxspace.sys.files,dxxspace.ios.files,dxxspace.cmd.files,dxxspace.win.files
```

> The DelFiles and StubPath (below) entries must all be on single line.

```
DelReg=dxxspace.addreg
Addreg=dxxspace.remove.reg
UpdateInis=dxxspace_remove.links
PerUserInstall=dxxspace_remove.links.pui
Reboot=1

[dxxspace_remove.links]
STOOLS_DESC%"
setup.ini,group11,,"""%DrvSpace_Desc%"""
setup.ini,group11,,"""%CmpAgent_Desc%"""

[dxxspace_remove.links.pui]
GUID="PerUser_dxxspace_Links"
DisplayName=%PUI_DESC_DXXSPACE_LINKS%
Version=%PUI_VERSION%
```

```
IsInstalled=0
StubPath="rundll.exe%11%\setupx.dll,InstallHinfSectionPerUser_dxxspace_remove_Links
64 %17%\applets1.inf"

[dxxspace.remove.reg]
HKLM,%KEY_OPTIONAL%\Dxxspace,Installed,,"0"
```

5. Now save this updated file in the \WINDOWS\INF folder. If you get in trouble, you can always restore the original APPLETS1.INF file from your backup.
6. Use your text editor to create a file named Drvspace.reg, and enter the following lines into the file. Note that all of the HKEY_LOCAL_MACHINE entries must be on one continuous line. And for the "Installed" entry (about four lines down), set the value to 1 if DriveSpace is currently installed, or 0 if DriveSpace is not installed.

```
[HKEY_LOCAL_MACHINE\Software\Microsoft\Windows\CurrentVersion\Setup\OptionalComponents\
Dxxspace]
```

> All of the HKEY_LOCAL_MACHINE entries must be on one continuous line.

```
"INF"="applets1.inf"
"Section"="dxxspace"
"Installed"="1"
```

> For the "Installed" entry, set the value to "1" if DriveSpace is currently installed, or "0" if DriveSpace is not installed.

```
[HKEY_LOCAL_MACHINE\Software\Microsoft\Windows\CurrentVersion\Setup\OptionalComponents]
"Dxxspace"="Dxxspace"
```

7. Add a few line breaks at the bottom of this file, and then save it to your desktop as DRVSPACE.REG.
8. Right-click this file, click Merge, and then click OK.
9. Now try removing or reinstalling DriveSpace as needed.

15

SYMPTOM 15-15 You receive a Windows 95/98 error message such as "The Decompression of %s failed" You notice that when you try to install a program that uses InstallShield, you receive the following error message (even if you have sufficient free disk space on the destination drive):

```
The Decompression of %s failed. There may not be enough free disk space.
```

In most cases, this problem occurs when the \Windows\TEMP folder is damaged. Rename the \Windows\TEMP folder to OLDTEMP, and then create a new \Windows\TEMP folder. Alternately, if a TEMP folder exists in the root directory of drive C:, rename it to OLDTEMP. (If a TEMP folder does not exist in the root directory of drive C:, create a new TEMP folder in the root directory.)

SYMPTOM 15-16 The "Mace Utilities Sector Editor" corrupts a DriveSpace compressed volume file (CVF) This is known to happen under DOS 6.22. When Mace Utilities indicates that the "in memory" copy of your File Allocation Table (FAT) should be written to the disk, if you select Yes, the CVF can be corrupted. To avoid this problem and prevent possible CVF corruption, use ScanDisk rather than third-party tools such as Mace Utilities to analyze your DriveSpace-compressed drives. There is no way to recover the corrupted CVF, and the drive must be partitioned and reformatted from scratch.

SYMPTOM 15-17 **DriveSpace will not compress your existing drive under Windows 95/98** When you're using DriveSpace to compress an existing drive, the mini-Windows portion of DriveSpace does not load correctly (if at all). This problem is known to happen if you're using a Diamond SpeedStar Pro VL Bus video adapter, and the following line has been disabled or removed from the AUTOEXEC.BAT file:

```
C:\UTIL1\SPEED\PROMODE MONITOR
```

This line is needed in order for the video adapter to support VGA in the mini-Windows mode. Some older Diamond video adapters need the PROMODE.EXE driver for VGA support. When you try to compress an existing drive, the computer restarts and cannot load the mini-Windows mode—so no compression takes place. There are three possible ways to reenable the driver:

- Add PROMODE.EXE to the [FAILSAFE] section of the DRVSPACE.INF file.
- Copy the PROMODE.EXE file to the fail-safe directory on the host drive.
- Add a line in the AUTOEXEC.BAT file to load PROMODE.EXE, and then restart the computer.

SYMPTOM 15-18 **You cannot upgrade a drive to DriveSpace 3 under Windows 95/98** You may receive the following error message when you try to upgrade to DriveSpace 3:

```
Not enough free space on H (Host_For_C) to complete the task
```

You are then prompted to resize drive C: in order to increase the free space on drive H:. If you click Yes, you'll see an error message indicating that Windows could not resize the drive, and you're told to increase the free space on drive H: to at least 4MB. Note that you'll continue to receive this error message regardless of how much free space there is on drive H:. This problem occurs when drive C: is compressed with DriveSpace, the CVF for drive C: is smaller than 67MB, and the host drive for drive C: has less than 2.2MB of free space. You should correct the problem by removing files on the host drive so that there is at least 2.2MB of free space.

SYMPTOM 15-19 **You cannot use DriveSpace to compress an incorrectly configured drive under Windows 95/98** You'll find that when you try to compress a drive with DriveSpace, you receive an error message such as:

```
DriveSpace cannot write to the C:\DRVSPACE.000 file. Drive C is probably
full, or it might be write-protected or damaged. Move or delete unwanted
files, remove any write-protection, or try running ScanDisk.
```

You may also receive subsequent errors (and error ID numbers) when clicking OK to close the error dialog(s). If you then run ScanDisk, you cannot find any errors on the drive. In virtually all cases, the problem is caused when the drive is configured incorrectly in the computer's CMOS settings. To correct this problem, you must configure the drive correctly in the computer's CMOS settings. Pay particular attention to the following issues:

- Change the "hard disk type" to the correct value below 1024.
- Enable logical block addressing (LBA).
- Try autodetecting the drive.

> Altering the drive's entry in the CMOS setup may render the drive unreadable, so be sure to perform a full drive backup before making any changes to the CMOS setup.

SYMPTOM 15-20 **You find that automatic drive mounting is disabled in the real mode for DriveSpace 3** When you boot your computer to a command prompt (DOS), you notice that compressed, removable-media drives are not mounted. You may also notice that the physical boot drive is not mounted when you boot your previous operating system. Finally, when you change the Automatically Mount New Compressed Drives setting in DriveSpace, the DRVSPACE.INI file is not updated, but the registry *is* updated. This is a DriveSpace 3 issue. By default, it does not support automatic drive mounting in real mode. You can mount compressed drive(s) manually. The example below illustrates how to use ScanDisk in real mode to mount a compressed volume on the A: drive:

1. At the command prompt, type the following command (where <compressed_volume_name> is the name of the compressed volume file (CVF) on drive A:):

   ```
   c:\windows\command\scandisk.exe a:\<compressed_volume_name>
   ```

   If the name of the CVF on drive A: were DBLSPACE.000, you would type the following line:

   ```
   c:\windows\command\scandisk.exe a:\dblspace.000
   ```

2. ScanDisk detects that the CVF has not been mounted and offers to check the host drive. Choose not to check the host drive by clicking No.
3. When you're prompted to mount drive A:, click Yes.
4. Quit ScanDisk. The volume on drive A: is mounted for the duration of the session.

You can also enable automatic mounting in the real mode using this procedure:

1. Open Windows Explorer and right-click the DRVSPACE.INI or DBLSPACE.INI file in the root folder of your physical boot disk. Then click Properties on the menu.
2. Click the Read-Only check box to clear it, and then click OK.
3. Double-click the DRVSPACE.INI or DBLSPACE.INI file to open it.
4. Change the line that reads AutoMount=0 to read AutoMount=1.
5. Save your changes and close the file. Then restart your computer.

> Incorrectly modifying the DBLSPACE.INI or DRVSPACE.INI file can cause serious problems that may require you to reinstall Windows 95/98. Use extreme caution when editing these files at any time.

SYMPTOM 15-21 **The DriveSpace reboot fails when compressing a large hard drive** When you're trying to compress a large hard drive with DriveSpace, Windows 95/98 may not restart successfully in the mini-Windows mode. Some large hard drives demand that drivers be loaded from the

CONFIG.SYS file. These drivers may call overlay (OVL) files, but since the OVL files are not directly called by the CONFIG.SYS file, they are not copied into the FAILSAFE.DRV folder on the host drive. You'll need to copy any necessary OVL files to the FAILSAFE.DRV folder on the host drive. Run DriveSpace, and then try the compression process again.

SYMPTOM 15-22 **You receive a DriveSpace alarm "11" during the Windows 98 setup** You may see an additional error indicating that "a program has corrupted memory belonging to DriveSpace." After the message appears, the computer may halt. To resolve this issue, follow these steps to verify that the DriveSpace command line has been disabled:

1. Restart your computer to the safe mode command prompt.
2. Start a text editor and load the CONFIG.SYS file.
3. Check the CONFIG.SYS file to verify that it contains the following lines:

   ```
   device=c:\windows\himem.sys
   device=c:\windows\emm386.exe x=A000-F7FF noems
   dos=high, umb
   rem DeviceHigh=c:\windows\command\drvspace.sys /move
   ```

4. If your CONFIG.SYS file contains the line

   ```
   devicehigh=c:\windows\command\drvspace.sys /move
   ```

   place a REM statement at the beginning of the line to disable it.
5. Now restart the computer and try your Windows 98 setup again.

SYMPTOM 15-23 **You encounter a DoubleGuard error code** This can occur under any version of DoubleSpace or DriveSpace. DoubleGuard has detected that an application (usually a device driver or TSR) has corrupted memory that DoubleSpace or DriveSpace was using. DoubleGuard halts your computer to prevent any further damage to your data. A typical DoubleGuard alarm message reads

```
DoubleGuard Alarm #<nn>
```

where <nn> is 13 (BitFAT buffer), 14 (MDFAT buffer), 15 (File Fragment List), or 16 (DBLSPACE.BIN Code Block).

DoubleGuard errors are frequently caused by QEMM operating in the "stealth" mode, and Vertisoft SpaceManager 1.53 operating on a 286 machine running MS-DOS 6.2. Restart your computer by turning the power switch off and then on again. Boot to the DOS prompt. (Do not allow Windows 95/98 to start.) At the DOS command prompt, type

```
SCANDISK /ALL
```

This runs ScanDisk on all your drives to detect and correct any problems that might have been caused by the program that violated the memory used by DoubleSpace. Make a note of which program(s) you were running (if any) when the DoubleGuard alarm occurred. That program is probably (but not necessarily) the program that caused the DoubleGuard alarm.

If you receive additional DoubleGuard alarms, take notes about what you were doing and see if you can detect a pattern. You'll probably notice that a particular program, or combination of programs, is causing the alarm.

SYMPTOM 15-24 **You cannot compress a FAT 32 drive** This error is almost always encountered with DriveSpace and DriveSpace 3. The error reads something like:

```
Drive C cannot be compressed because it is a FAT32 drive.
ID Number: DRVSPACE378
```

This is because DriveSpace and DriveSpace 3 were both designed to work with the FAT12 and FAT16 file systems. They *cannot* be used with drives using the FAT32 file system implemented with Windows 95 OSR2 and Windows 98. There is no resolution for this problem except to abandon DriveSpace and use a FAT32-compatible disk compression tool.

SYMPTOM 15-25 **Your system is caught in a reboot loop after installing DriveSpace** If you press the F8 key when your computer restarts and then choose Command Prompt Only, your computer reboots again. If you choose Step-By-Step Confirmation, you can start Windows 95/98. But when you run DriveSpace, your computer reboots again. Windows 95/98 must load the real-mode compression drivers into memory. As Windows 95/98 starts, RESTART.DRV tests for the existence of the real-mode compression drivers. If the real-mode compression drivers have not been loaded, the computer is restarted until the compression drivers have been loaded. If the real-mode compression drivers cannot be loaded, the computer restarts indefinitely. There are three potential causes for this problem:

- A DRVSpace=0 or DBLSpace=0 setting is present in the MSDOS.SYS file.
- The DRVSPACE.BIN or DBLSPACE.BIN file is damaged and was not loaded at startup.
- The EMM386 memory manager is using the lower E000h memory range. (This is a known problem on Compaq Deskpro 386/20e computers, and may occur elsewhere.)

Load the MSDOS.SYS file into a text editor and check for DRVSpace=0 or DBLSpace=0 settings. Disable the setting(s) by placing a semicolon at the beginning of the line, such as:

```
;DRVSpace=0
```

If there are no DRVSpace=0 or DBLSpace=0 settings in the MSDOS.SYS file (or the problem persists), rename the existing DRVSPACE.BIN and DBLSPACE.BIN files, and then extract new copies of the files from your original Windows disks or CD:

1. Restart the computer to the Safe Mode Command Prompt Only from the Startup menu.
2. Delete the RESTART.DRV file from the hidden FAILSAFE.DRV folder on the physical boot drive (usually either drive C: or the host for drive C: if drive C: is compressed). In this example, <drive> is the physical boot drive:

   ```
   deltree <drive>:\failsafe.drv\restart.drv
   ```

3. Copy the AUTOEXEC.BAT and CONFIG.SYS files from the hidden FAILSAFE.DRV folder on the physical boot to the root folder of drive C:, replacing the files that are already there, such as:

   ```
   copy <drive>:\failsafe.drv\autoexec.bat c:\ /y
   copy <drive>:\failsafe.drv\config.sys c:\ /y
   ```

   Again, <drive> is the physical boot drive.
4. Remove the read-only, system, and hidden attributes from the DRVSPACE.BIN and DBLSPACE.BIN files in the root folder of the physical boot drive, such as:

   ```
   attrib -r -s -h *.bin
   ```

15

5. Rename the DRVSPACE.BIN and DBLSPACE.BIN files in the root folder of the physical boot drive, such as:

   ```
   ren *.bin *.bix
   ```

6. If you use the Microsoft Plus! pack (Windows 95), extract the DRVSPACE.BIN file from your original Microsoft Plus! disks or CD to the root folder of the physical boot drive. If you're using the retail version of Windows 95, extract the DRVSPACE.BIN file from your original Windows 95 disks or CD to the root folder of the physical boot drive. If you use OEM Service Release 2 (OSR2), extract the DRVSPACE.BIN file from your original OEM Service Release 2 disks or CD to the root folder of the physical boot drive.
7. Copy the DRVSPACE.BIN file in the root folder of the physical boot drive to a file named DBLSPACE.BIN in the root folder of the physical boot drive, such as:

   ```
   copy <drive>:\drvspace.bin c:\dblspace.bin
   ```

Again, <drive> is the physical boot drive. If drive C: is compressed, copy the DRVSPACE.BIN file to the root folder of the host drive, such as:

```
copy <drive>:\drvspace.bin <x>:\dblspace.bin
```

Here, <drive> is the physical boot drive, and <x> is the host drive for drive C.

You can now restart your computer normally. If this *still* does not resolve the problem, you may need to prevent EMM386 from loading. Simply restart your computer to use Step-By-Step Confirmation from the Startup menu. When you're prompted to start EMM386, select No. If the problem disappears, you may need to reconfigure EMM386 to use (or exclude) a different memory range.

SYMPTOM 15-26 The DriveSpace real-mode driver is not properly removed from memory The real-mode memory (conventional or upper) used by DriveSpace (DRVSPACE.BIN or DBLSPACE.BIN) should normally be reclaimed when you start Windows 95/98 (when the 32-bit DriveSpace driver DRVSPACX.VXD is initialized while Windows loads). However, you may notice that this real-mode memory is not made available again, which may cause problems if you subsequently try to run DOS-based programs that require more conventional memory than is available. There are several possible issues that can cause this problem:

- You booted to a command prompt, then started Windows again by typing **win**. The real-mode memory used by your compression driver cannot be reclaimed if you interrupt the normal Windows boot process.
- The real-mode memory used by your compression driver cannot be reclaimed if it is loaded into an upper memory block (UMB)—for example, if you used a command line such as:

  ```
  devicehigh=<path>\drvspace.sys /move
  ```

- You added the LoadTop=0 line in your MSDOS.SYS file. A setting of 0 does not let Windows load compression drivers at the top of conventional memory (just below 640K), and this can prevent unloading the compression drivers.
- Memory will also not be reclaimed if the 32-bit DriveSpace driver (DRVSPACX.VXD) is not loaded. Run DriveSpace, and then click About DriveSpace on the Help menu. Table 15-2 lists the compression driver file names, sizes, and versions for DriveSpace. You can use this table to help you determine which compression driver is at work on your system.

TABLE 15-2 COMPARISON OF COMPRESSION DRIVER VERSIONS

FILE NAME	PRODUCT	FILE SIZE	ABOUT DRIVESPACE
Drvspace.bin	Windows 95	71,287	Real-mode driver version 2
Drvspace.bin	MS Plus!	64,135	Real-mode driver version 3
Drvspacx.vxd	Windows 95	54,207	32-bit driver version 2
Drvspacx.vxd	MS Plus!	61,719	32-bit driver version 3
Drvspace.bin	Windows 98	68,871	Real-mode driver
Drvspacx.vxd	Windows 98	57,642	32-bit driver

To correct this problem, use the steps below:

1. Start Windows normally. (Do not boot to a command prompt first, then start Windows by typing **win**.)
2. Change the compression command line in your CONFIG.SYS file from

```
devicehigh=<path>\drvspace.sys /move
```

   to

```
device=<path>\drvspace.sys /move
```

3. Remove LoadTop=0 from the MSDOS.SYS file.
4. Rename the DRVSPACX.VXD file in the Windows\System\Iosubsys folder, and then use the procedure below that applies to your configuration:

   Run Windows 95/98 setup again.

   Choose "Restore Windows files that are changed or corrupted" when you are prompted.

   Manually extract the DRVSPACX.VXD file from the original Windows or Plus! CD. If Plus! is installed, extract the file from the Plus! CD-ROM, not from the Windows 95/98 CD.

> The DRVSPACX.VXD file for Windows 95 is located in the WIN95_09.CAB file on the CD. The DRVSPACE.BIN file for Windows 98 is located in the PRECOPY1.CAB file. The DRVSPACX.VXD file for Windows 98 is located in the WIN98_47.CAB file. The DRVSPACX.VXD file for Plus! is located in the PLUS_1.CAB file on the CD.

SYMPTOM 15-27 **DriveSpace does not restart in mini-Windows mode** When you perform a DriveSpace operation that requires Windows 95/98 to restart, you find that Windows is unable to restart in mini-Windows mode, so the operation fails. This problem generally occurs if the files in the hidden FAILSAFE.DRV folder or the MINI.CAB file in the \Windows\System folder are damaged. These files are *required* for Windows to restart in mini-Windows mode. The computer may lock up, or generate an error message such as:

```
DrvSpace caused a General Protection Fault in module W31SPACE.EXE
DrvSpace caused a Page Fault in module W31SPACE.EXE
Error Loading PROGMAN.EXE
```

```
Error Loading GDI.EXE
Error Loading USER.EXE
Error loading VGA.DRV
Cannot start Windows in standard mode
Segment load failure in W31space.exe
Standard Mode: Bad fault in MSDos Extender
```

Restart your computer and boot to the DOS command prompt. (Press the F8 key when you see the "Starting Windows" message, and then choose Command Prompt Only from the Startup menu.) Next, copy the AUTOEXEC.BAT and CONFIG.SYS files from the hidden FAILSAFE.DRV folder on the physical boot drive (usually either drive C: or the host for drive C: if drive C: is compressed) to the root directory of drive C:, replacing the files that are already there:

```
copy <drive>:\failsafe.drv\autoexec.bat c:\ /y
copy <drive>:\failsafe.drv\config.sys c:\ /y
```

Here, <drive> is the physical boot drive. Now remove the FAILSAFE.DRV folder from the physical boot drive, such as:

```
deltree <drive>:\failsafe.drv
```

Again, <drive> is the physical boot drive.

Copy the MINI.CAB file from your original Windows 95 disks or ROM to the \Windows\System folder. The MINI.CAB file is located on disk 1 of the standard 3.5-inch Windows 95 disks, or in the Win95 folder on the Windows 95 CD. You can copy this file using Windows Explorer or the COPY command. If you are using Microsoft Plus! for Windows 95 and you do not have access to your original Windows 95 disks or CD, you can extract the MINI.CAB file from the Microsoft Plus! disks or CD. The MINI.CAB file is located in the PLUS_2.CAB file on the CD, or in the PLUS_1.CAB file on the disks. Finally, restart Windows normally and run DriveSpace to repeat your operation.

> The FAILSAFE.DRV folder may contain drivers necessary for troubleshooting if you cannot correct the problem. Copy the FAILSAFE.DRV folder and all its contents to another drive or folder *before* deleting it.

SYMPTOM 15-28 **The MINI.CAB file is missing or corrupt** When you are compressing a drive using DriveSpace or DriveSpace 3, you receive one of the following error messages when the operation is about 25 percent complete:

```
The MINI.CAB file is missing or damaged—ID Number: DRVSPACE331

Windows cannot create the C:\FAILSAFE\FAILSAFE.DRV\W31SPACE.EXE file—ID
Number: DRVSPACE125
```

Either of these error messages may be followed by the error message "ID Number: DRVSPACE311." These error messages can occur if you are running IBM AntiVirus for Windows 95/98 with certain virus protection features enabled. Run the IBM AntiVirus program and *disable* the Warn When Viral Activity Occurs and Check Files When Opened options in System Shield (located under the Setup menu item).

> When the two options listed above are enabled, IBM AntiVirus also impairs your ability to create a startup disk from the Add/Remove Programs tool in Control Panel, and may cause problems with some self-extracting installation programs. When these problems occur, you may receive an error message such as "File Copying Problem."

SYMPTOM 15-29 **You encounter a DRVSPACE 125 error when using DriveSpace 3** When you try to compress drive C: with DriveSpace 3, you may receive the following error message when the compression process is 25 percent finished:

```
Windows cannot create the C:\Msdossys.tmp file. There might not be enough
free space on the drive C, the root directory of drive C may be full, or the
disk may be write-protected—ID Number: DRVSPACE125.
```

In almost all cases, this error occurs if the root folder on drive C: already contains the maximum allowable number of files (512). When this happens, DriveSpace 3 cannot create the temporary files it needs to finish the compression process. You'll need to move or delete unnecessary files in the root folder on drive C: and then continue the compression process.

This error may also occur when the compression process is 100 percent finished if you are compressing a drive that is not the boot drive. The actual file name referenced in the error message can also vary. For example, the error message "Cannot create the file DRVSPACE.000" is generated when the root folder of the drive being compressed is full. A similar error message may occur if there is a file named FAILSAFE.DRV in the root folder of drive C: (or the host for drive C:). If you find this to be the case, remove the FAILSAFE.DRV file and continue the compression operation.

SYMPTOM 15-30 **The DriveSpace VxD and real-mode driver are mismatched** If you install, remove, and then reinstall Windows 95/98, you may receive the following error message when you start Windows:

```
DriveSpace Warning—The DriveSpace VxD and the DriveSpace real-mode driver
are mismatched. You may need to reinstall them. Press any key to continue.
```

When you press a key, Windows 95/98 will probably start, but it will likely be unstable. You may see unusual characters on the screen, and you may receive "fatal exception" error messages. This is because DriveSpace 3 places real-mode drivers on the hard disk that are not removed when you delete the Windows folder. When you reinstall Windows, setup places a DriveSpace VxD in the \Iosubsys folder that is incompatible with the DriveSpace 3 drivers. You'll need to replace the DRVSPACX.VXD file in the \Iosubsys folder with the correct version from the original Microsoft CD(s).

Restart your computer normally. When you see the "Starting Windows" message, press the F8 key and choose Command Prompt Only from the Startup menu. Change to the \Windows\System\Iosubsys folder and rename the DRVSPACX.VXD file to DRVSPACX.OLD. Extract the DRVSPACX.VXD file from the Microsoft Plus! CD or original disks to the \Iosubsys folder. (The DRVSPACX.VXD file is located in the PLUS_1.CAB file on *both* the Microsoft Plus! disks and CD.) In this example, <destination> is the Windows\System\Iosubsys folder, and <drive> is the drive containing the Microsoft Plus! disk or CD:

```
extract <drive>:\plus_1.cab drvspacx.vxd /L <destination>
```

Now restart your computer normally.

If you still receive a "mismatch" error message when the computer starts (and the DRVSPACE.BIN file is the correct version), check for a DBLSPACE.BIN file dated 7/11/95 or earlier (Table 15-3). This file is a hidden file in the root folder of the boot drive. If this file *exists*, rename it to DBLSPACE.OLD, and then restart your computer. DriveSpace 3 does not require DBLSPACE.BIN in order to mount compressed volumes. This problem can also occur if you reinstall Windows 95/98 to a different folder than its original folder. If you reinstalled Windows 95/98 in a different folder, edit the MSDOS.SYS file on both the host drive and the compressed drive. Make sure the PATH statement points to the correct folder. After you edit the MSDOS.SYS file(s), save the file(s) and then restart your computer.

SYMPTOM 15-31 **Windows 95/98 detects a compressed drive access error** This error typically crops up when the system first starts. Windows cannot mount the compressed drive used during startup because the names of the BIN and the INI files used for compression do not match. Verify that the versions of the BIN files match the compression version in use. DriveSpace for Windows 95 has file dates of 7/11/95. DriveSpace 3 (included with Microsoft Plus!) has file dates of 7/14/95. If the BIN files do not have the correct date, update the files on the hard disk and the startup disk. (If you do not have a startup disk yet, you should create one.)

If the DRVSPACE.BIN file is present and the DBLSPACE.BIN file is not (and there is a DBLSPACE.INI file), create a DBLSPACE.BIN file. Restart your computer. When you see the "Starting Windows" message, press the F8 key, and then choose Safe Mode Command Prompt Only from the Startup menu. At the command prompt, type the following line, and then press ENTER:

```
copy drvspace.bin dblspace.bin
```

Restart your computer normally. If the problem persists, rename the DBLSPACE.INI file to DRVSPACE.INI by rebooting to the Safe Mode Command Prompt Only and typing

```
ren dblspace.ini drvspace.ini
```

TABLE 15-3 DOUBLESPACE FILE VERSIONS WITH AND WITHOUT MICROSOFT PLUS!

WINDOWS 95 WITHOUT MICROSOFT PLUS!			
FILE NAME	**DATE/TIME**	**SIZE**	**LOCATION**
Drvspace.bin	07-11-95 9:50am	71,287	C:\ and root of compressed drive
Dblspace.bin	07-11-95 9:50am	71,287	C:\ and root of compressed drive
Drvspacx.vxd	07-11-95 9:50am	54,207	C:\windows\system\iosubsys
WINDOWS 95 WITH MICROSOFT PLUS!			
FILE NAME	**DATE/TIME**	**SIZE**	**LOCATION**
Drvspace.bin	07-14-95 12:00am		C:\ and root of compressed drive
Dblspace.bin	07-14-95 12:00am	64,135	C:\ and root of compressed drive
Drvspacx.vxd	07-14-95 12:00am	61,719	C:\windows\system\iosubsys
WINDOWS 95 OEM SERVICE RELEASE 2			
FILE NAME	**DATE/TIME**	**SIZE**	**LOCATION**
Drvspace.bin	08-24-96 12:00am	65,271	C:\ and root of compressed drive
Dblspace.bin	08-24-96 12:00am	65,271	C:\ and root of compressed drive
Drvspacx.vxd	07-14-95 12:00am	57,466	C:\windows\system\iosubsys

Restart your computer normally. If the problem persists, use ScanDisk to check the compressed volume. Reboot to the Save Mode Command Prompt Only and start ScanDisk:

```
scandisk /mount=<yyy> <x>:
```

Here, <yyy> is the file name extension of the compressed volume file (CVF), and <x> is the drive containing the CVF. ScanDisk creates a DBLSPACE.BIN file and mounts the CFV. For example, to mount a CVF named DRVSPACE.000 on drive C, type the following line:

```
scandisk /mount=000 c:
```

SYMPTOM 15-32 **Windows 95/98 cannot delete a compressed drive** When you attempt to delete a compressed drive under Windows 95/98, an error message appears, such as:

```
Windows cannot perform this operation because the enhanced mode disk
compression driver could not be loaded. You may need to run setup again to
install additional disk components. DRVSPACE 545.
```

This problem occurs if the Windows 95/98 protected-mode DriveSpace driver (DRVSPACX.VXD) is missing or corrupted. In these cases, Windows 95/98 loads the real-mode DriveSpace driver for minimum support, but deletion operations are not possible with the real-mode driver. You'll need to reinstall the protected-mode compression driver DRVSPACX.VXD from the original Windows disks or CD.

Rename the DRVSPACX.VXD file on your hard disk. This file should be located in the \Windows\System\Iosubsys subdirectory. Click the Start button on the task bar, and click Files Or Folders on the Find menu. In the Find: All Files dialog box, type **DRVSPACX.VXD** in the Named box. Click the Find Now button. In the file listing box, use the right mouse button to click the file DRVSPACX.VXD, and then click Rename. Rename the file DRVSPACX.OLD, and then press ENTER.

If the DRVSPACX.VXD file is missing (not found on the hard disk that contains Windows 95/98), you'll need to extract DRVSPACX.VXD from the original Windows disk(s) to the \Windows\System\Iosubsys subdirectory. Insert Disk 11 in the floppy disk drive, or insert the Windows 95 setup CD in the CD-ROM drive. On the task bar, click Start, then Programs, and then click MS-DOS Prompt. At the command line, type

```
extract /l <drive>:\windows\system\iosubsys <drive>:\A drvspacx.vxd
```

where <drive> indicates the letter designating the drive containing the floppy disk or CD-ROM. Now restart the system.

SYMPTOM 15-33 **DriveSpace for Windows 95/98 reports that drive C: contains errors that must be corrected** Such problems may occur when upgrading from DriveSpace to DriveSpace 3, when you compress an existing uncompressed drive, when you uncompress a compressed drive, or when you create a new empty compressed drive. You may encounter any of the following error messages:

```
You cannot upgrade drive X because it contains errors. To upgrade this
drive, first run ScanDisk on it, and then try again to upgrade it. ID
Number: DRVSPACE 424.
```

Drive X contains errors that must be corrected before the drive can be compressed. To correct them run ScanDisk. ID Number: DRVSPACE 306.

Drive X contains errors that must be corrected before the drive can be uncompressed. To correct them, run ScanDisk. ID Number: DRVSPACE 307.

Drive C contains errors that must be corrected before the drive can be used to create a new compressed drive. To correct them run ScanDisk. ID Number: DRVSPACE 308.

In virtually all cases, these errors occur if the drive contains a folder with a path that contains more than 66 characters. Fortunately, you can work around the problem. Start the ScanDisk utility. Click the Automatically Fix Errors check box to clear it, and then begin checking the drive. When you receive the following error message,

```
The <path> folder could not be opened in MS-DOS mode because its complete
short name was longer than 66 characters.
```

make a note of the path that is longer than 66 characters, and then click Ignore. If you receive more than one such message, note each path. After ScanDisk is finished, move each folder whose path contains more than 66 characters to another location with a shorter path. Now proceed to perform the desired DriveSpace operation. After DriveSpace has finished, move each folder that you moved back to its *original* location (path).

SYMPTOM 15-34 You encounter "Out of memory" errors on systems with compressed hard drives When starting a program on a Windows 95/98 system using disk compression, you get either of the following errors:

```
Out of memory
```

or

```
There is not enough memory to perform this operation. Close unneeded
applications and then try the operation again.
```

This happens most frequently when Windows 95/98 is installed on the compressed drive. The setup program may place the swap file on the host drive of the compressed drive. If the host drive does not have enough free space, the swap file may not have the space to accommodate large programs. If you're using a Microsoft-based compression program (such as DriveSpace or DoubleSpace), the swap file can safely be moved to the compressed drive. (Make sure there is enough free space on the compressed drive first.) If you're using a non-Microsoft compression program, you must enlarge the host drive to accommodate the swap file, or move the swap file to another uncompressed drive.

SYMPTOM 15-35 DriveSpace 3 indicates that you only have 2GB of drive space Your actual drive may be much larger. This is a limitation of DriveSpace 3. DriveSpace 3 was designed to work with the FAT12 and FAT16 file systems, and cannot be used on hard drives with FAT32 partitions. When you try to compress a drive with DriveSpace 3, you may receive the following error message:

```
Drive C cannot be compressed because it is a FAT32 drive
```

You can verify your hard drive's file system using the steps below:

1. Double-click the My Computer icon on your Windows desktop.
2. Right-click the Drive you're interested in (normally the C: drive).
3. Left-click the Properties entry on the drop-down menu.

4 On the General tab, you will receive a suite of information about the drive, including the volume label, hard drive type, file system, used space, free space, and drive capacity. The "file system" entry will tell you whether you're using FAT16 or FAT32.

SYMPTOM 15-36 **Windows 95/98 hangs up when loading POPDOS.EXE** If you load the POPDOS.EXE TSR program in your AUTOEXEC.BAT file, the computer may stall when you start Windows 95/98. This is because of a memory conflict between POPDOS and your compression driver (such as DBLSPACE.BIN). POPDOS functions properly only if it's loaded at the top of conventional memory, but other programs (such as the compression driver) typically load ahead of POPDOS.EXE at the top of conventional memory, and this causes POPDOS to crash. There are several ways to work around this problem. You can run POPDOS from a DOS prompt within Windows, or run POPDOS in the native DOS mode. Alternately, you can prevent files like COMMAND.COM or DBLSPACE.BIN from loading at the top of conventional memory:

1 Use Windows Explorer to locate the MSDOS.SYS file in the boot drive's root directory.
2 Right-click the MSDOS.SYS file, and then click Properties from the drop-down menu.
3 Click the Read-Only and Hidden check boxes to clear them; then click OK.
4 Load the MSDOS.SYS file into Notepad or Wordpad.
5 Add the following line to the [options] section of the file:

```
LoadTop=0
```

6 Save your changes to the file, and then quit your text editor.
7 Once again, locate the MSDOS.SYS file, right-click the file, and click Properties.
8 Click the Read-Only and Hidden check boxes to select them; then click OK.
9 Reboot Windows 95/98.

Using the LoadTop=0 entry reduces the amount of memory available in DOS sessions because Windows cannot recover the memory used by the real-mode DoubleSpace driver. This may be important when running complex DOS applications.

SYMPTOM 15-37 **When starting the Windows 98 system, you receive a compression driver error** After you start a computer with a Windows 98 startup disk, you may not be able to gain access to a hard disk compressed with DriveSpace. In other cases, when you boot with a Windows 98 startup disk (or when you restart your computer after upgrading to Windows 98), you may receive a message such as:

```
The compression driver cannot be set up correctly. Get a version from your
vendor that is compatible with this version of Windows.
```

In virtually every case, Windows 98 does not update the DriveSpace compression files (DRVSPACE.BIN and DBLSPACE.BIN) in the root folder of your compressed drive C:. When you created the Windows 98 startup disk, the older compression files from compressed drive C: were probably copied to the startup disk. To correct this problem, copy the updated compression files to drive C:, and then create a new startup disk:

1 Click Start, select Programs, and then click MS-DOS Prompt.

2. At the DOS prompt, check the date of your DBLSPACE.BIN and/or DRVSPACE.BIN files in the root folder of drive C: by typing

```
dir /a c:\d??space.bin        <Enter>
```

3. If the files are not dated 5/11/98, type the following commands (followed by ENTER):

```
c:
cd\
attrib -s -h -r c:\d??space.bin
ren c:\d??space.bin *.old
copy windows\command\drvspace.bin c:\
copy windows\command\drvspace.bin c:\dblspace.bin
attrib +r +s +h c:\d??space.bin
exit
```

4. Restart your computer, and follow steps 5, 6, and 7 to create a new startup disk.
5. Click Start, select Settings, and then click Control Panel.
6. Double-click Add/Remove Programs.
7. On the Startup Disk tab, click Create Disk.

SYMPTOM 15-38 After compressing an IBM system, the computer will not start

You cannot load Windows 95/98. This is a known issue if you use DriveSpace to compress a drive on an IBM Aptiva or PS/1 computer. You may receive the following error when you start your computer after the compression process is finished, or when DriveSpace restarts your computer during the compression process:

```
Windows has disabled direct disk access to protect your long filenames. To
override this protection, see the LOCK /? command for more information. The
system has been halted. Press CTRL+ALT+DEL to restart your computer.
```

This problem generally occurs when you run PS1PFILE.EXE from the AUTOEXEC.BAT file. This program tries to bypass the operating system and system BIOS and write directly to the hard disk. When programs try to access a hard disk in this way, Windows prevents the program from doing so, and displays the message.

If the message appears when you attempt to start your computer *after* the compression process is finished, configure your computer so that PS1PFILE.EXE is allowed to write to all hard disks on your computer directly:

1. Start Windows in the Safe Mode, and then use any text editor (such as Notepad) to open the AUTOEXEC.BAT file.
2. Before the line that contains PS1PFILE.EXE, insert a line for each hard disk, such as,

```
echo y | lock <drive>:\ > nul
```

where <drive> is the hard disk letter. For example, if your computer contains drive C: and drive H:, insert the following lines *before* the command line that contains PS1PFILE.EXE:

```
echo y | lock c:\ > nul
echo y | lock h:\ > nul
```

3 After the line that contains PS1PFILE.EXE, insert a line for each hard disk, such as,

```
unlock <drive>: > nul
```

where <drive> is the hard disk letter. For our example of a drive with C: and H:, the lines might appear as

```
unlock c: > nul
unlock h: > nul
```

4 Save and then close the AUTOEXEC.BAT file.

5 Restart your computer.

If the message is displayed when DriveSpace restarts your computer during the compression process, you'll need to remove or disable the line in the AUTOEXEC.BAT file that contains the PS1PFILE.EXE command line. The steps are given below.

> The PS1PFILE.EXE file may be necessary to use some of the Advanced Power Management (APM) features of Windows 95/98 and your IBM computer. If you cannot use APM features reliably after removing the PS1PFILE.EXE command line, replace the line immediately. If the error is returned again after you replace the line, perform the first series of steps to work around the problem.

1 Start your system directly to the DOS command prompt, and then use any text editor (such as EDIT) to open the AUTOEXEC.BAT file.

2 Remove or disable the command line that contains PS1PFILE.EXE. You should also remove or disable any lines around PS1PFILE that contain the LOCK or UNLOCK command. A typical example would be

```
REM echo y | REM lock c:\ nul
REM c:\ps1tools\ps1pfile.exe
REM unlock c: nul
```

3 Save and then close the AUTOEXEC.BAT file.

4 Restart your computer.

When you restart your computer, DriveSpace should automatically continue the operation that it was performing when the error message first appeared.

SYMPTOM 15-39 You notice that the Disk Compression Tools check box may be missing from the System Tools dialog box You'll probably notice this when you try to use the Add/Remove Programs wizard in the Windows 98 Control Panel. This issue can occur if your disk compression tools are *already* installed. When the disk compression tools are installed, Windows 98 removes this check box to prevent the accidental removal of DriveSpace. To overcome this issue (if you want to reinstall your disk compression tools), manually create an INF file to restore the Disk Compression Tools check box:

1 Use any text editor within Windows 98 (such as Notepad) to create a new file with the following lines:

```
[version]
signature="$CHICAGO$"
[DefaultInstall]
```

```
AddReg=Enable.Drvspace
[Enable.Drvspace]
HKLM,%KEY_OPTIONAL%,"Dxxspace",,"dxxspace"
HKLM,%KEY_OPTIONAL%\dxxspace,INF,,"applets1.inf"
HKLM,%KEY_OPTIONAL%\dxxspace,Section,,"dxxspace"
HKLM,%KEY_OPTIONAL%\dxxspace,Installed,,"0"
[Strings]
KEY_OPTIONAL="SOFTWARE\Microsoft\Windows\CurrentVersion\Setup\OptionalComponents"
```

2. Save the new file, and then rename it to DXXSPACE.INF.
3. Right-click the file, and then click Install.
4. Restart your computer.

SYMPTOM 15-40 You receive a "Not enough disk space" error when installing Windows 98 on a drive compressed with DriveSpace The complete error usually reads something like this:

```
Not Enough Disk Space—There is not enough space on one or more of your
drives to set up Windows 98. Setup may need to copy some files to your
compressed drive's host drive or to your startup drive.
```

This behavior is typically caused by insufficient free disk space on the DriveSpace host drive. The default amount of free disk space that DriveSpace allocates on the host drive is 2MB, but keep in mind that setup may require as much as 7MB of free space on your host drive. To correct this fault, increase the amount of free disk space on the host drive, or resize the host drive using DriveSpace.

SYMPTOM 15-41 You find that some Windows 98 System Configuration utilities will not work This is a problem with Windows 98. When you run the System Configuration utility, the following items may not work properly (if at all):

- Diagnostic Startup—Interactively Load Device Drivers And Software
- Enable Startup Menu
- Disable Scandisk After bad shutdown
- Disable SCSI Double-Buffering

This fault can occur if you use any version of the DriveSpace software to compress your hard drive "in place" (in other words, you compressed the *entire* hard drive). When you compress a hard drive in place, DriveSpace swaps hard drive letters after the initialization of the compressed volume file (CVF). Since the System Configuration utility is not aware of the drive letter swap, it edits the MSDOS.SYS file on the CVF instead of the MSDOS.SYS file on the host drive.

To correct this fault, you must edit the MSDOS.SYS file on the host drive (usually drive H:) after DriveSpace is loaded. Note that DriveSpace hides the host drive by default, so you will have to make the host drive "visible":

1. Click Start, select Programs, point to Accessories, select System Tools, and then click DriveSpace.
2. Click the compressed drive where the hidden drive is a host drive, and then click Properties on the Drive menu.

3 Click the Hide Host Drive check box to clear it.
4 Click OK.

Now you can load the host drive's version of the MSDOS.SYS file into your text editor and enable or disable the options that you need. If the appropriate line does not exist, create it in the [Options] section of your MSDOS.SYS file:

- To enable Diagnostic Startup, edit or add the line **orig_diag_BootMenu=1**. To disable the option, remove the line, or change the value from 1 to 0.
- To enable the Startup menu, edit or add the line **BootMenu=1**. To disable the option, change the value from 1 to 0.
- To disable Automatic ScanDisk after an incorrect shutdown, edit or add the line **AutoScan=0**. To enable the option, change the value from 0 to 1.
- To enable SCSI double-buffering, edit or add the line DoubleBuffer=1. To disable SCSI double-buffering, change the value from 1 to 0.

TROUBLESHOOTING DOS DOUBLESPACE AND DRIVESPACE

DoubleSpace emerged in the early 1990s with MS-DOS 6.0 as a means of maximizing available drive space. Although early implementations of DoubleSpace suffered from questionable reliability, subsequent patches and releases proved to be adequate. DoubleSpace then came under attack from Stac Electronics (makers of Stacker), who claimed that Microsoft absconded with key DoubleSpace code. In the ensuing litigation, Microsoft dropped DoubleSpace and replaced it with their own DOS product called DriveSpace. Both DoubleSpace and DriveSpace support DOS and Windows 3.1x. The latest version of DriveSpace supports Windows 95 natively.

15

SYMPTOM 15-42 DriveSpace indicates that there are too many files in the root directory This happens if you have more than 500 files in the root directory of your startup drive. If you run DoubleSpace or DriveSpace, you may receive one of the following error messages:

```
Too many files in the root directory, remove some files from the root and
try this operation again.
```

or

```
Error Copying <filename>
```

Here, the <filename> is DRVSPACE.BIN, DRVSPACE.EXE, DEFRAG.EXE, DRVSPACE.HLP, or DRVSPACE.INF. If you try to convert a DoubleSpace compressed drive to a DriveSpace compressed drive, you may face the following error message:

```
There is not enough free space on your original startup drive, which is now
drive C. DriveSpace will need at least 0.58 MB of free space on that drive.
Delete some files from that drive, and try this operation again.
```

In all cases, these error messages are displayed when there are too many files in the root directory of your compressed drive or host drive. You can work around these errors simply by deleting several unneeded files from the root directory, or moving them to a subdirectory.

SYMPTOM 15-43 **You receive a DriveSpace error message after installing MS-DOS over PC-DOS 6.1 or 6.3** When you try to run the DriveSpace utility from MS-DOS 6.22 (after upgrading from PC-DOS version 6.1 or 6.3), the following error message is displayed:

```
Your computer is running an incompatible version of the DRVSPACE.BIN file.
You must update DRVSPACE.BIN on the root directory of your drive.
```

This error occurs because the compression driver that IBM ships with PC-DOS versions 6.1 and 6.3 is incompatible with DriveSpace. The MS-DOS 6.22 setup runs correctly since compression is not on the boot drive. Setup finishes with no data loss, but if you try to run DriveSpace to convert the compressed drive, the error message occurs. You must copy the original PC-DOS DoubleSpace files back to the host drive, back up the data, reformat the host drive to remove compression, and then restore your data.

> As a rule, PC-DOS users should remove disk compression before upgrading.

SYMPTOM 15-44 **Some applications do not run properly on a DoubleSpace compressed drive** There are a number of DOS games and utilities that do not run well (if at all) from a drive compressed with DoubleSpace. The following list highlights some of the more notable products:

- Argus Financial Software
- Complete PC software that uses voice files
- Empire Deluxe
- Epic Megagames' Zone66 and Ken's Labyrinth
- Informix relational database
- Links and Links 386 from Access Software
- Lotus 1-2-3 version 2.01
- Movie Master version 4.0
- MultiMate versions 3.3 and 4.0
- Quicken (MS-DOS-based version)
- Tony LaRussa Baseball II
- Zsoft PhotoFinish

Most DOS and Windows applications should work just fine with DoubleSpace, but with the proliferation of complex software in the marketplace today, there may be some applications that are copy protected, or do not perform well from the compressed state. If such a situation occurs, try moving the application to the uncompressed host drive (or reinstalling it to the uncompressed drive outright). To fit your application into uncompressed space, you may have to resize the CVF to free additional space on the host drive. You can resize the CVF through the DBLSPACE control panel, or directly from the DOS command line. For example,

```
C:\> dblspace /size /reserve=3
```

will change the CVF size so that there are 3MB free on the host drive. It may also be that the application needs an unusually large amount of conventional memory. Since DBLSPACE.BIN needs about 33KB of memory, try loading DBLSPACE.BIN into upper memory by changing the command line in CONFIG.SYS to

```
devicehigh=c:\dos\dblspace.bin /move
```

SYMPTOM 15-45 **You see an "A CVF is damaged" error message when the system starts** The compressed volume file (or CVF) is a single file that contains all of the compressed drive's data and is accessed as a unique logical drive. In effect, the CVF *is* the compressed drive. The physical hard drive that contains the CVF is the host drive. Under most circumstances, the CVF occupies most of the host drive except for some areas that should not be compressed (such as a Windows permanent swap file).

When DoubleSpace activates on system startup, it performs a check on the CVF's internal data structures that is equivalent to a DOS CHKDSK. If DoubleSpace detects an error such as lost allocation units or cross-linked files, the "CVF is damaged" error message appears. The way to correct this type of problem is to run a correction utility. DOS 6.2 offers the ScanDisk utility, but DOS 6.0 and earlier versions of DOS provide you with CHKDSK. Once the disk is corrected, DoubleSpace should work correctly.

SYMPTOM 15-46 **You see a DoubleGuard alert in DOS** DoubleGuard is a DOS 6.2 utility that helps protect DoubleSpace and DriveSpace from memory conflicts that otherwise might corrupt data on the CVF. If DoubleGuard detects a checksum error in the memory used by disk compression, a rogue program or device driver has probably written in the DoubleSpace memory area. When an error is detected by DoubleGuard, the system simply halts before damage can occur. (You'll have to reboot the computer to continue.)

Boot the system clean (with no device drivers), and then use ScanDisk or CHKDSK to deal with any potential errors on the hard disk. Reactivate one device driver at a time until you can re-create the error. When you find the offending device driver, you can keep it unloaded, or find a way to load it without conflict.

SYMPTOM 15-47 **Free space is exhausted on a compressed drive** One of the problems with DoubleSpace and DriveSpace is that it is difficult to know how much space is available. Since different files compress differently, there is no way to be *absolutely* sure just how much space you have to work with. Available disk space must be "predicted" using a compression ratio that you set. By adjusting the predicted compression ratio, you can adjust the amount of reported free space. As a result, MS-DOS can "lie." If you seem to be running low on space, try changing the compression ratio from the DOS command line, such as:

```
C:\> dblspace /ratio=2.5
```

Ideally, you want to set the compression ratio as close as possible to the *actual* compression ratio. This will yield the most accurate prediction of available space. If you are unable to change your drive's compression ratio, it may be time to defragment the drive. Disk compression tools have trouble making use of highly fragmented drives for file storage. If you are having trouble with drive space, try defragmenting the drive with DOS DEFRAG or another defragmentation utility. If the drive really *is* out of space, you can increase the size of the CVF by taking space from the uncompressed host (if there is any more uncompressed space available). From the DOS command line, start DBLSPACE and use the Change Size function to alter the compressed volume size. You can also adjust the volume size directly from the command line. For example:

```
C:\> dblspace /size /reserve=1.5
```

This command will change the compressed drive size, leaving 1.5MB of uncompressed space on the host drive. If you need to free space on the host drive so that you can increase the size of the CVF, try deleting unneeded files from the uncompressed host drive.

SYMPTOM 15-48 **Free space is exhausted on the host drive** Under normal use, there will be little free space reserved for the host drive anyway. The greatest space advantage with DoubleSpace will be realized when the maximum amount of host drive space is compressed. Only Windows swap files and noncompressible applications normally reside outside the CVF. However, there will be occasions when it becomes necessary to place data on the uncompressed drive. Eventually, the host may run out of space. If the files listed in the host directory do not seem large enough to exhaust the space, there may be some hidden files on the host drive. Perform a DIR /AH to list all files, including archive and hidden files. The easiest way to correct this problem is to resize the CVF to reserve more free space for the host drive. This can be done from the DBLSPACE control panel or directly from the DOS command line with a command such as

```
C:\> dblspace /size /reserve=4
```

This would resize the CVF to keep 4MB of uncompressed space on the host drive. Of course, there must be enough free space on the CVF to be freed to the host drive. If the CVF is very full, or is highly fragmented, it may not be possible to resize the CVF.

SYMPTOM 15-49 **Estimated compression ratio cannot be changed** You may be setting the estimated compression ratio too high. Keep in mind that the amount of free space reported for the CVF is only an estimate based on the compression ratio that you set in DoubleSpace or DriveSpace. If you make the estimated compression ratio larger, more free space is reported, and vice versa. However, DoubleSpace can only work with compressed drive sizes up to 512MB. (DriveSpace 3 for Windows 95/98 can handle up to 2GB.) An example will make this clearer.

Assume you have a compressed drive with 300MB of files and 100MB of true (uncompressed) free space. A compression ratio of 2:1 would cause this 100MB to be reported as 200MB. The 200MB estimated free space plus the 300MB of used space results in total CVF drive space of (300MB + 200MB) 500MB. If you try adjusting the estimated compression ratio to 2.5:1, that 100MB of true free drive space would be reported as 250MB. Since 300MB and 250MB add up to more than 512MB, an error will be produced. Keep the compression ratio down so that the total CVF drive space does not exceed 512MB.

SYMPTOM 15-50 **Compressed drive size cannot be reduced** DoubleSpace and DriveSpace are extremely sensitive to file fragmentation because of the way disk space is assigned. As a result, it is important to defragment the CVF regularly in order to keep your compressed drive's performance at an optimum level. You can use DEFRAG or other defragmentation utilities to defragment the drive.

Other factors may contribute to fragmentation warnings that prevent reducing the CVF size. A delete-tracking program such as MIRROR may be saving its MIRORSAV.FIL file at the end of the drive volume. This creates immediate fragmentation of the drive since the file skips all free space to the very end of the volume. The Norton Utilities delete-tracking program IMAGE creates the same problem by saving its IMAGE.IDX file at the end of the CVF. Thus, DoubleSpace cannot reduce the size of the CVF since the tracking file now occupies the highest sectors. Your best tactic here is to disable the delete-tracking utility in CONFIG.SYS or AUTOEXEC.BAT, change the tracking file's attributes with the DOS ATTRIB function, erase the tracking file, and defragment the drive.

For files created by MIRROR:

```
C:\> attrib mirorsav.fil -s -h -r
```

For files created by IMAGE:

```
C:\> attrib image.idx -s -h -r
```

You should then be able to resize the CVF without problems. It may also be impossible to reduce the size of your CVF because a FAT entry for the CVF indicates that an allocation unit is unreadable (including a "bad allocation unit" entry). The CVF can only be reduced to the point at which the bad entry occurs. If you suspect a problem with a bad cluster, it is possible to use a disk editor such as Norton Utilities or PC Tools to change the FAT entry from bad (FFF7h) to unused (0h). Be sure to use extreme caution if you choose to use a disk editor. *You can corrupt the entire disk by making erroneous changes to the FAT.*

SYMPTOM 15-51 **DEFRAG fails to fully defragment the drive** DoubleSpace reports that the drive is still fragmented even after performing a full defragmentation procedure. This type of symptom is another manifestation of hidden system delete-tracking files generated by utilities such as IMAGE or MIRROR. You can see the file by performing a DIR /AH. Since both utilities place hidden system files at the end of the drive volume, DEFRAG cannot move the file. You can delete the offending file.

For files created by MIRROR:

```
C:\> deltree mirorsav.fil
```

For files created by IMAGE:

```
C:\> deltree image.idx
```

Then disable the delete-tracking utility from your AUTOEXEC.BAT or CONFIG.SYS files. You can also change the attributes of the offending file, which will allow DEFRAG to move the file appropriately during the defragmentation process.

For files created by MIRROR:

```
C:\> attrib mirorsav.fil -s -h -r
```

For files created by IMAGE:

```
C:\> attrib image.idx -s -h -r
```

SYMPTOM 15-52 **You see a "Swap File is Corrupt" error message when starting Windows 3.1x** Unless your PC carries more than 16MB of RAM, Windows 3.1x will need supplemental storage space to support the various applications that are loaded and run during normal operation. The hard drive is used to provide this supplemental space in the form of *virtual memory*—that is, an area of the hard drive is used to hold the contents of RAM. This virtual area is known as the *swap file*. Although you have the choice between a permanent and temporary swap file, most installations of Windows use a permanent swap file (or PSF). Unfortunately, Windows does not support a *compressed* permanent swap file under DoubleSpace or DriveSpace. If you compress your drive and include the Windows PSF, the swap file will be reported as corrupt when you try to start Windows. You will need to re-create a PSF on the host (uncompressed) drive.

Start the Control Panel from the Program Manager's Main group. Double-click on the 386 Enhanced icon to open the 386 Enhanced dialog box; then click on the Virtual Memory button to access the Virtual Memory dialog box. Click on the Change button. Choose an uncompressed drive (usually the host drive) by selecting the drive from the Drive pull-down list. Choose the Permanent file type from the Type pull-down list. Enter the desired size for the new PSF in the New Size box. (Windows will suggest a default size based on the amount of memory and disk space available.) You can select the default or enter a new value. Select OK to initiate the new PSF.

SYMPTOM 15-53 You cannot access compressed drive(s) after booting from a system disk created by Windows 3.1x The DoubleSpace or DriveSpace utility has not been copied to the floppy. The Windows 3.1x File Manager allows you to create bootable floppy disks. However, Windows will not copy the vital DBLSPACE.BIN file (or DRVSPACE.BIN) to the floppy, although the FORMAT /s command under DOS 6.0 and 6.2 *will*. If you make a bootable disk from Windows 3.1x, you'll have to complete the process in DOS by manually copying the DBLSPACE.BIN (or DRVSPACE.BIN) file to the floppy, using a command such as:

```
C:\> copy \dos\dblspace.bin a:\
```

SYMPTOM 15-54 The compressed drive is too fragmented to resize When you try to resize a DoubleSpace or DriveSpace drive, you receive an error message such as:

```
Drive <X> is too fragmented to resize. Before resizing drive <X>, defragment
it by typing DEFRAG.EXE /H /Q <X>: at the DOS command prompt.
```

Here, <X> is the drive letter of the compressed drive. Try running Defrag as suggested. If DEFRAG /H /Q <X>: does not correct the problem, you have a system file located at the end of your DoubleSpace or DriveSpace drive (possibly IO.SYS, MSDOS.SYS, or a system file created by delete-tracking, disk image, erase-protect, or format-protection software).

You might have a bad sector on your host drive near the end of the compressed volume file (CVF). Also, there may be software installed on your system that uses a copy-protection scheme that uses clusters marked as "bad" to store data. The programs in Table 15-4 write system files at the end of a drive and commonly cause the error message noted above.

TABLE 15-4 PROGRAMS KNOWN TO INTERFERE WITH CVF OPERATION

PROGRAM NAME	PROGRAM FILE NAME	SYSTEM FILE CREATED
Microsoft MS-DOS Mirror	MIRROR.COM	MIRORSAV.FIL
Central Point Mirror	MIRROR.COM	MIRORSAV.FIL
Symantec Norton Image	IMAGE.EXE	IMAGE.IDX
Symantec Norton Format Recover	FR.EXE	FRECOVER.IDX
Microsoft MS-DOS 5.0 Undelete	MIRROR.COM	PCTRACKR.DEL
MS-DOS 6.0/6.2 Delete Tracker	UNDELETE.EXE	PCTRACKR.DEL
MS-DOS 6.0/6.2 Delete Sentry	UNDELETE.EXE	CONTROL.FIL
Central Point Delete Tracker	UNDELETE.EXE	PCTRACKR.DEL
Central Point Delete Sentry	UNDELETE.EXE	CONTROL.FIL

If you are running MS-DOS 6.2 (and there is no copy-protected software on the system), run ScanDisk to perform a surface scan on your host drive. For example, type the following command at the MS-DOS prompt, and press ENTER:

```
scandisk <host drive>: /surface
```

If you are running MS-DOS 6.0, unmount the compressed drive and run a third-party surface scan product, such as Symantec's Norton Utilities Norton Disk Doctor (NDD.EXE) or Central Point Software's DiskFix. If the surface scan program detects and corrects a bad cluster, you should now be able to resize your drive. If you still cannot resize the drive, use the DIR command to search for hidden system files on the compressed drive. For example, if your compressed drive is drive C:, type this command at the MS-DOS prompt, and press ENTER:

```
dir c: /s /as /p
```

Use ATTRIB to remove the file attributes on the system files you found above. For example, if you have a Mirror file on drive C:, type the following at the DOS prompt, and press ENTER:

```
attrib -r -s -h c:\mirorsav.fil
```

> If the system files you detect are used by a delete-tracking program, you need to reboot your computer *without* loading the corresponding program file before you change the file attributes on the system file.

You should now be able to resize the compressed drive with Defrag. If you can successfully resize the compressed drive, reset the file attributes on the system files you found above. For example, type the following at the DOS prompt, and press ENTER:


```
attrib +r +s +h c:\mirorsav.fil
```

If you were not able to resize the compressed drive, edit the DBLSPACE.INI file and increase the MaxFileFragments entry. Start by removing the read-only, system, and hidden file attributes on the DBLSPACE.INI file. For example, if drive H: is your host drive, type the following at the command prompt, and press ENTER:

```
attrib -r -s -h h:\dblspace.ini
```

Using a text editor such as EDIT, alter the DBLSPACE.INI file and increase the value for MaxFileFragments (2000 is a good number to try). Save the DBLSPACE.INI file and exit the text editor. Restart your computer and try to resize the drive now.

If you are using copy-protected software, you may be able to work around this problem by using a third-party disk-edit program, such as Symantec's Norton Utilities or Central Point Software's PC Tools, to change the cluster's status from "bad" to "unused." (Change the status from FFF7 to 0.) However, this usually leaves the copy-protected software unusable. Uninstall the copy-protected software (if possible), resize the compressed drive, and then reinstall the copy-protected software.

SYMPTOM 15-55 There is an error writing to the CVF during defragmenting If you run Defrag and the compressed volume file (CVF) is full or nearly full, Defrag may report

```
Error writing cluster nnn,nnn
Use a disk repair program to fix, and then run DEFRAG again.
```

If CHKDSK shows no problems, and a surface scan utility (such as Symantec's Norton Disk Doctor [NDD.EXE]) shows no problems, the error message is occurring because Defrag is unable to write the information that it has read.

Defrag is trying to copy a cluster before moving it, but since the compressed drive is too fragmented or full, there is no space large enough to write the cluster. Chances are that the CVF itself is OK. You can work around this issue by increasing the size of your compressed drive and then running Defrag, or simply deleting enough files to allow Defrag to run.

SYMPTOM 15-56 DoubleSpace or DriveSpace does not work properly on systems with Promise Technologies VL IDE controller cards The Promise Technologies (**www.promise.com**) model 4030VL VESA local-bus cached IDE controller card and the model DC200 ISA-cached IDE controller card both need a firmware update to run properly with the DoubleSpace and DriveSpace disk compression programs. There are three EPROMs for the model 4030VL controller card. Check the last four digits of the EPROM number. If the last four digits are 203E, 203O, or 203X, the card is compatible with DoubleSpace and DriveSpace. The compatible revisions as of 6/20/93 are P43204-E, P43204-O, and P43204-X. The model DC200 controller card also has three EPROMs. If the number on the EPROMs is P20103E, P20103O, or P20103X, the card is compatible with DoubleSpace and DriveSpace.

SYMPTOM 15-57 The disk compression program has used all reserved memory
When you try to create or mount a DoubleSpace or DriveSpace drive, you may receive an error message such as:

```
DoubleSpace has used all the memory reserved by the settings in the Options
dialog box. To enable DoubleSpace to allocate more memory, you should
restart your computer now. Do you want to restart your computer now?
```

Under MS-DOS 6.22, you may see a DriveSpace error message like this:

```
Not enough MEMORY to allocate more drives for DBLSPACE or DRVSPACE. Reboot
and quit other applications?
```

Chances are that restarting the computer does not help—you still cannot mount the drive. This error occurs if you try to compress or mount more drives than are specified by the Number of Removable-Media Drives setting in the DoubleSpace Options dialog box, or if the total number of mounted drives is greater than 15. The Number of Removable-Media Drives setting specifies how much memory the compression software reserves for mounting additional compressed drives after startup. If you try to mount or create more compressed drives than DoubleSpace has reserved memory for, you receive an error.

You can adjust the Number of Removable-Media Drives setting by running DoubleSpace or DriveSpace, choosing Options from the Tools menu, and changing the setting. This modifies the MaxRemovableDrives setting in the DBLSPACE.INI file. If restarting the computer still does not correct this error, you may *already* have 15 compressed drives mounted. Restarting does not allow you to mount or create any more compressed drives using DoubleSpace or DriveSpace until you have fewer than 15 compressed drives mounted. To mount another compressed drive, you must first unmount one or more of the currently mounted drives. To unmount a compressed drive, start DoubleSpace or DriveSpace and select the drive to unmount; then choose Unmount from the Drive menu.

> You can create more than 15 compressed drives, but only a maximum of 15 can be mounted at the same time.

SYMPTOM 15-58 **A compression error indicates that drive <X> is not available** When you use the DBLSPACE /HOST command to change your compression host drive letter, you may receive a message like this, where <X> is the drive letter you specified:

```
The drive letter <X> is not available for DoubleSpace's use.
```

This error may occur when the letter you specify for the new host drive is in use by an existing physical drive (or compressed drive). Also, the drive letter you specified is greater than the LastDrive= entry in the DBLSPACE.INI file. Use the DBLSPACE /LASTDRIVE command to increase the LastDrive= entry in the DBLSPACE.INI file. For example, type

```
dblspace /lastdrive=j
```

Restart your computer.

You can also use the DBLSPACE /HOST command to change your compressed host drive letter. For example, if your compressed drive is drive C:, and you want to change your host drive to drive I:, type the following:

```
dblspace c: /host=i:
```

Now restart your computer.

SYMPTOM 15-59 **DIR /C fails to report the file compression ratio** DIR /C won't report a compression ratio if the DoubleSpace FAT (MDFAT) is damaged, if the file is open in another Windows virtual machine (VM) and the MDFAT has not been updated, or if the file was created by Microsoft Backup (or Microsoft Backup for Windows). To work around the problem, check the file compression ratio in File Manager, or run ScanDisk.

SYMPTOM 15-60 **FORMAT overwrites the CVF on a floppy disk** You may actually see an error message such as:

```
You must use "DBLSPACE /FORMAT <drive>:" to format that drive
```

As a result, you have a freshly formatted uncompressed floppy disk. This problem occurs if you access an uncompressed floppy disk (for example, DIR A:), remove the uncompressed floppy, insert a compressed floppy, and attempt to format it. When this happens, the DoubleSpace Automount code is never called, and the DoubleSpace-compressed floppy disk is not mounted.

This problem may also occur if the Automount feature has been disabled. If you have already formatted over a DoubleSpace-compressed floppy disk, recompress the disk with the DBLSPACE /COMPRESS command. To prevent this problem, access the compressed floppy disks *before* formatting them. For example, type the following at the command prompt:

```
a:
format a:
```

SYMPTOM 15-61 **The system hangs when a SCSI driver is loaded after DBLSPACE.SYS** SCSI device drivers loaded "high," or loaded *after* MS-DOS 6.2 DBLSPACE.SYS in the CONFIG.SYS file, may cause the system to hang. To correct this problem, load your SCSI device driver *before* DBLSPACE.SYS. If your system still hangs, load the device driver "low": change DEVICEHIGH= to DEVICE=, and remove the /L parameter. For example, change

```
devicehigh /L:1,1234 =c:\scsi.sys
```

to

```
device=c:\scsi.sys
```

SYMPTOM 15-62 **You cannot mount a compressed disk in a BackPack drive** DoubleSpace and DriveSpace may fail to automatically mount compressed disks in BackPack drives (from Micro Solutions—**www.micro-solutions.com**). This problem occurs when the BACKPACK.SYS device driver is loaded *after* the DBLSPACE.SYS driver in a CONFIG.SYS file. Since the Automount code works on block device drivers only when they are loaded *before* DBLSPACE.SYS, load BACKPACK.SYS before DBLSPACE.SYS in the CONFIG.SYS file.

SYMPTOM 15-63 **DOS compression restarts the computer and loops endlessly** When DoubleSpace or DriveSpace restarts your computer to increase the DBLSPACE.INI MaxFileFragments setting (because your DoubleSpace-compressed drive is too fragmented to mount), your computer becomes trapped in an endless loop. This occurs when a compressed drive on your hard disk drive is too fragmented to mount, and you are booting your computer from a floppy disk (typically in drive A:). The compression software modifies the DBLSPACE.INI file on the host drive for the overly fragmented compressed drive, but does not consider which drive is the boot drive. Ensure that the floppy disk drives are empty, and reboot your computer. Press F5 when the "Starting MS-DOS" prompt appears. Run Defrag to defragment the drive; then restart the system.

SYMPTOM 15-64 **You cannot use compression on a drive partitioned with Disk Manager** If the DMDRVR.BIN command is loaded after SMARTDRV /DOUBLE_BUFFER in your CONFIG.SYS file (and your hard disk drive has more than 1024 cylinders), it may appear that your compressed data is lost after you create a new compressed drive. This happens when you have other compressed drives and you try to create a new compressed drive using the Disk Manager partitioned drive as the host. DMDRVR.BIN should be the first device loaded in the CONFIG.SYS file.

Restart the computer and press CTRL+F5 when the "Starting MS-DOS" message appears. Delete the C:\DBLSPACE.BIN and C:\DBLSPACE.INI files. (You'll probably have to unhide the files first.) Restart the computer and edit your CONFIG.SYS file with a text editor. Move the DMDRVR.BIN command to the top of your CONFIG.SYS file. Save the CONFIG.SYS file and exit the text editor; then restart the computer. Run the compression software and create the new compressed drive again.

SYMPTOM 15-65 **Compression software mounts a Bernoulli disk as nonremovable** If you are using Bernoulli Iomega OAD version 1.21 device drivers with MS-DOS 6.2, DoubleSpace creates a permanently mounted drive when you compress existing data on a Bernoulli drive. When you restart your computer, DoubleSpace attempts to mount the newly created compressed disk, even if the Bernoulli drive is empty. To work around this problem, unmount the compressed Bernoulli disk, and then reboot your computer. After rebooting your computer, the disk should mount automatically when you access it.

SYMPTOM 15-66 **DriveSpace reports an "incompatible version" error** DriveSpace may indicate that an incompatible version of DRVSPACE.BIN is running, and that the BIN file in the root directory must be updated. This error is also displayed if you try to run DoubleSpace. (However, the <drive letter> is replaced by an @ symbol rather than the actual drive letter.) At this point, your compressed volumes are probably inaccessible.

This error occurs after you install MS-DOS 6.22 to a directory *other* than the one that contains your MS-DOS 6.0 DoubleSpace files (typically C:\DOS). In this situation, the DBLSPACE.BIN file has not been properly updated. To correct the problem, uninstall MS-DOS 6.22, and then reinstall MS-DOS 6.22 into the directory that contains your MS-DOS files.

SYMPTOM 15-67 **DRIVER.SYS causes an "insert diskette" error when compression software is running** When you try to create a compressed drive using DoubleSpace or DriveSpace, you may encounter an error like this:

```
Please insert a diskette for drive <x>: and press any key when ready
```

Here, <x> is a second logical drive associated with a single physical floppy disk drive. This message occurs when DRIVER.SYS is loading in the CONFIG.SYS file.

DRIVER.SYS is a device driver that can be used to create a logical drive that refers to a physical floppy disk drive. When an attempt is made to access the drive through this second logical drive letter, DRIVER.SYS prompts you to insert a disk and press any key before attempting to read the drive. To correct this problem, start MS-DOS by pressing F8 as soon as the "Starting MS-DOS" message appears. When prompted to load DRIVER.SYS, choose No. You can then safely restart DoubleSpace or DriveSpace.

SYMPTOM 15-68 **A compressed drive refuses to mount after installing RAMDrive** If you use compression software with a removable hard drive (such as Syquest, Bernoulli, or Quatam Passport XL), and later install RAMDrive, DoubleSpace may refuse to mount its compressed drive(s). This is because the RAMDrive DEVICE command in the CONFIG.SYS file precedes the removable hard drive DEVICE command line. Since RAMDrive may inadvertently use the drive letter of the removable drive, DoubleSpace or DriveSpace may not find the compressed volume on the expected drive. The same problem may occur if you remove RAMDrive *after* compressing your removable hard drive.

If this problem was caused by installing RAMDrive, you can simply move the RAMDrive DEVICE command past the removable drive's DEVICE command in the CONFIG.SYS file. The advantage of this solution is that the drive letter assignments stay the same. If this problem occurs after removing RAMDrive, run DBLSPACE. From the Drive menu, choose Mount. DoubleSpace scans all your drives for compressed volumes and reassigns drive letters appropriately. However, this may cause problems for programs configured to *specific* drive letters.

15

SYMPTOM 15-69 **A compressed SCSI drive doesn't mount at startup** DoubleSpace or DriveSpace may not be able to mount the CVF on your SCSI drive when you start your computer if you load SSTOR.SYS into upper memory *after* DBLSPACE.SYS. Load SSTOR.SYS into upper memory *before* DBLSPACE.SYS. For example:

```
devicehigh=c:\sstor.sys
devicehigh=c:\dos\dblspace.sys /move
```

SYMPTOM 15-70 **DoubleSpace cannot copy the DBLSPACE.INF file** This happens because the root directory of the drive contains an excessive number of entries. The root directory of a hard disk can contain up to 512 entries, including both files and directories. You'll need to reduce the number of entries in the root directory.

SYMPTOM 15-71 EZTape hangs or produces an error with a compressed drive When you run Irwin Magnetic Systems' EZTape for MS-DOS (version 2.22 or version 3.1) on a DoubleSpace-compressed drive, EZTape may hang when performing a backup or restore on the DoubleSpace-compressed drive. Or EZTape may display one of the following error messages when performing a backup or restore on a compressed drive:

```
Run-time error R6001 null pointer assignment
EMM386 exception error #12, enter to reboot computer
```

EZTape for MS-DOS version 2.22 or 3.1 may identify a DoubleSpace-compressed drive as a nonstandard drive and may require that the DOSONLY environment variable is set before you can begin an action on a compressed drive. Set the MS-DOS environment variable to DOSONLY=1 before you use EZTape for MS-DOS. Use a text editor to insert the following statement in the AUTOEXEC.BAT file:

```
SET DOSONLY=1
```

Setting the DOSONLY environment variable forces EZTape for MS-DOS to use standard MS-DOS system calls to access the drive. You must reboot your computer for this change to take effect.

SYMPTOM 15-72 Compression software hangs the system with a DTC 3280 SCSI drive If you install DoubleSpace or DriveSpace on a DTC 3280 SCSI removable drive, your system may hang. This problem is almost always caused by the DTC device driver, ASCSI.EXE. You'll need to upgrade the SCSI driver to a newer version that will coexist with disk compression. The GSCSI4 driver in your AUTOEXEC.BAT file will also need to be upgraded. You can download the latest drivers from the DTC Web site (**www.datatechnology.com**).

SYMPTOM 15-73 A compression error indicates cross-linked files between C: and C: This kind of error suggests a file problem (cross-linked files) on the drive. The reason drive letters are displayed instead of file names, and the two drive letters shown are the same, is because there are cross-linked entries in the MDFAT. Because these entries (or clusters) are marked as allocated in the MDFAT (but free in the FAT), they are not considered to be parts of any file or files. To correct the cross-linked entries in the MDFAT, run CHKDSK /F. If CHKDSK does not correct the problem, either run ScanDisk (from DOS 6.22 or Windows 95/98 startup disk) on the compressed drive, or obtain a third-party compression-aware surface scan program.

SYMPTOM 15-74 Compression software indicates an "R6003—Integer Divide by Zero" error This error is typically caused by corrupted DoubleSpace or DriveSpace files, or incompatible TSR programs. Copy the DBLSPACE.BIN (or DRVSPACE.BIN) file from Disk 1 of the original MS-DOS upgrade disk set to the root directory for your host drive. For example, if your compressed drive is C:, and your host drive is H:, type the following at the DOS command prompt and then press ENTER:

```
copy a:\dblspace.bin h:\
```

If there is already an existing BIN file on the host drive, but it is corrupted, remove the attributes from the file *before* copying a new one to the drive. For example, type **attrib h:\dblspace.bin -r -s -h**.

DBLSPACE.EX_ is located on Disk 3 of the 1.44MB 3.5-inch disk set, and on Disk 4 of the 1.2MB 5.25-inch disk set. Expand the DBLSPACE.EXE files from the original DOS installation disks, such as:

```
expand a:\dblspace.ex_ c:\dblspace.exe
```

Now restart the computer by pressing the reset button, or by turning the machine off and then on again.

TROUBLESHOOTING DOS STACKER

Stac Inc. was once considered to be the leading disk compression company, and led the early development of disk compression technology. However, with the entry of Microsoft into the compression arena, the ensuing litigation over the use of DoubleSpace, and Microsoft's subsequent release and support of DriveSpace with DOS 6.2x and DriveSpace 3 for Windows 95/98, Stac is no longer a major force in disk compression. Their Stacker 4.1 for Windows 95 (their last release of disk compression software) uses the real-mode code of their 4.0 version, and does not provide the compression performance demanded by users. No additional compression products are listed or announced on the Stac Web site. Still, there is a broad base of installed Stacker systems, and this part of the chapter outlines many of the important Stacker problems that you may encounter.

SYMPTOM 15-75 **You see an error message indicating "Lost Sector Groups"** You will typically see this error when running the Stacker CHECK utility. This is not nearly as ominous as it may sound—data has not yet been lost or corrupted. A lost sector group can occur on a Stacker drive when data is written to a cluster, but the cluster has not been allocated to a file. Once the operating system does allocate the cluster to a file, the error goes away. In most cases, CHECK will report a lost sector group when a file is extended and truncated without the operating system updating the FAT. For the most part, you can leave lost sector groups alone. If you want to clear any such groups, however, run SDEFRAG or select the Stacker Optimizer in the Stacker Toolbox. You can select Full Optimize, Quick Optimize, or Restack, and any of these choices will completely clear lost sector groups.

15

SYMPTOM 15-76 **You see the error message "SIZE MISMATCH, EXISTING INSTALLATION"** This kind of error can result if the STACKVOL.DSK file is corrupted or destroyed (either by a hardware disk fault or software error). When Stacker initializes, it verifies the STACVOL.DSK (the CVF) file before mounting a compressed drive. If the size of the STACVOL.DSK file is incorrect, Stacker pauses the normal startup of your computer with this message until the problem is corrected:

```
E: = C:STACVOL.DSK (Size mismatch) (Write protected)
Press any key to continue...
```

The solution for this type of fault is rather involved, and you will require the REPAIR.EXE utility included with your Stacker disks (or available from the Stac Web site). Note the compressed and uncompressed volume letters. For this example, the compressed volume is C:, while the host drive (containing STACVOL.DSK) is E:. Next, *unmount* the Stacker drive by typing **STACKER -*d***, where *d* is the compressed drive (C:). Run a disk repair utility such as CHKDSK or ScanDisk on the host drive (E:). As the disk utility runs, it will ask if you want to save lost chains as files—do not! *Remember, you should not save new files to the disk while this recovery procedure is in progress.* If the disk utility indicates that STACVOL is cross-linked with other files, delete the other files and run the disk utility again until the STACVOL file checks clean.

At this point, insert the floppy disk containing REPAIR.EXE and switch to the floppy drive. (If REPAIR.EXE is in a floppy subdirectory, switch to that subdirectory as well.) Run the REPAIR utility using the syntax

```
REPAIR /=U <d:\STACVOL.XXX>
```

where <d:\STACVOL.XXX> is the uncompressed drive letter and STACVOL file name you determined in a previous step. For example:

```
REPAIR /=U E:\STACVOL.DSK
```

You will see a series of messages as the REPAIR.EXE executes. If the repair process is successful, you will have to remove the REPAIR floppy and reboot the machine for changes to take effect. You should now have access to the compressed volume again.

SYMPTOM 15-77 You see an error message such as "The drive is too fragmented"
You may encounter this kind of message when attempting to upgrade Stacker from a previous version. Abort the upgrade procedure and use the Stacker Optimizer to defragment the drive. You can then rerun the upgrade installation. If the upgrade process introduces additional fragmentation, the upgrade process may fail again. In that event, you can update the Stacker drive manually. Perform a quick optimization by typing **SDEFRAG /Q**, and continue with the procedure even if the drive reports zero percent fragmentation. After optimization, type **STACKER** and locate the line referring to the drive that failed to update. For example, you may see a line such as:

```
Drive C was drive C at boot time [D:\STACVOL.DSK = 115.3MB]
```

Take note of the drive letter inside the brackets (D:). Next, start the manual conversion,

```
HCONVERT <drive:>\STACVOL.DSK /C
```

where <drive:> is the host drive letter (D:). Once the drive is updated, run the Stacker Optimizer again to take full advantage of Stacker 4.0 compression.

SYMPTOM 15-78 The Stacker drive does not update, or HCONVERT hangs up
The upgrade to Stacker 4.0 should yield a noticeable gain in drive space over previous versions. If you do not notice an improvement, the update process may not have been successful. There may be situations where you do not receive warnings about excessive fragmentation, yet the disk may be too fragmented to sustain an update. The first step here is to determine whether the drive has indeed been updated. Switch to the Stacker directory and type **SYSINFO** to find information concerning your system. Find the area detailing the system's physical drives—the second column of information is labeled "version." Stacker drives will have a version number listed in this column.

A version of 3.0 (or earlier) indicates that the Stacker drive has not been updated. A version of 5.0 indicates that the Stacker drive has been updated, but not recompressed to gain additional space. If this is the case, leave the system information screen and start the Stacker Toolbox. Select Optimize, then Full-MaxSpace. This should recompress the drive to provide additional space. A version of 5.01 indicates that the drive has been updated and recompressed. When the disk has *not* been updated, switch to the Stacker directory and type **STACKER**. You will see a profile of your Stacker drive(s). For example:

```
Drive C was drive C at boot time [D:\STACVOL.DSK = 112.3MB]
```

This shows drive C: is the Stacker drive, and drive D: is the uncompressed drive. Run CHKDSK against the host drive. If errors are reported, run CHKDSK /f to correct the errors.

Now, defragment the drive using SDEFRAG /Q <drive:>, where <drive:> is the Stacker drive (C:). Once the drive is defragmented, update the drive immediately. (Do not perform any other write operations.) Unmount the Stacker drive by typing **STACKER -<drive:>** where <drive:> is the Stacker drive (C:). Next, type

```
HCONVERT /C <drive:>\STACVOL.XXX
```

where <drive:> is the host drive (D:), and *.XXX* is the STACVOL extension (for example, .DSK). Remove any floppy disks and reboot the PC for changes to take effect. Finally, recompress the drive by entering the Stacker Toolbox, selecting Optimize and then Full-MaxSpace.

SYMPTOM 15-79 You see a "Setup Error #2002" This error occurs when a floppy drive writes information to the Stacker installation disk improperly. This may be due to improper floppy drive alignment or floppy drive damage, but chances are that the vital Stacker files on the floppy disk(s) are already corrupted. This is why software manufacturers tell you to make a backup copy of the product and to install from the *backup* copy. By formatting and copying backup disks on your PC, you compensate for any mild alignment problems. It might not be a bad idea to clean the floppy drive heads. When alignment problems persist, replace the floppy drive. If you have not made a backup copy of your Stacker installation disks, contact Stac for a new set of disks. When the new disks arrive, create a backup set and write-protect the master disks.

SYMPTOM 15-80 After converting a DoubleSpace or SuperStor /DS drive to Stacker, there is no additional space detected In some cases, drive space will not increase after moving to Stacker 4.0—usually when you are near the DOS limit for a drive. DOS limits refer to the size of clusters on a drive. For example, a 512MB drive uses 8KB clusters, a 1GB drive usually employs 16KB clusters, and a 2GB drive offers 32KB clusters. However, the following techniques may draw additional space from a converted drive.

Start by recompressing the drive after Stacker is installed. Open the Stacker Toolbox, select Optimize, and select Full-MaxSpace. When the drive is recompressed, check the space available on the drive and write it down. Next, uncompress the drive and rerun Stacker setup. This step allows Stacker to select the optimum cluster size for the drive. As an alternative to removing and reinstalling Stacker, try to *shrink*—then *grow*—the Stacker drive size. This will not set a new cluster size, but may gain additional space. Keep in mind that you may not have much latitude to change the STACVOL file size if the compressed drive is quite full already.

SYMPTOM 15-81 When using the Stacker CHECK utility, you see an error message indicating that the File Allocation Tables are not identical Normally, a hard drive maintains two copies of the File Allocation Table (FAT) in the event of just such an emergency. This is a potentially disastrous fault for your hard drive, and you must carefully choose which copy of the FAT to use when repairing the problem. After this initial warning, CHECK will run a second integrity check using the alternate copy of the FAT. After CHECK completes its second examination, you will be presented with three choices: (1) exit and try using the first FAT, (2) exit and try using the second FAT, or (3) copy the first FAT over the second FAT and let CHECK repair any errors. *Keep in mind that the FAT currently being tested is considered the first FAT.* The objective here is to make sure that the first (the currently tested) FAT is the error-free version. You can then copy that error-free FAT to the second FAT and repair the damage. Here is procedure that will help you.

Select option 1—this will return you to DOS (if you started CHECK from DOS). If you started CHECK from the Stacker Toolbox in Windows, leave Windows and return to the DOS prompt. Run CHECK again, and pay close attention to whether the errors are reported running the first FAT or the second FAT. If the errors are on the first FAT, end CHECK using menu option 2 (exit and try using the second FAT). If the errors are on the second FAT, end CHECK using menu option 1 (exit and try using the first FAT). At the DOS command line, run CHECK /f to fix the disk. When presented with the menu options again, select option 3 (copy the first FAT over the second FAT and let CHECK repair the drive).

SYMPTOM 15-82 You encounter SDEFRAG errors 109/110, 120, or 170 A media error has been detected on the disk during the defragmentation process. The 109/110 or 170 errors indicate that SDEFRAG is unable to read, write, or verify a physical cluster on the disk—often the result of a media problem. The 120 error indicates that SDEFRAG is unable to decompress a physical cluster. Either the media is damaged, or the cluster is corrupted. In either case, you are faced with a serious defect. If a physical disk flaw is crippling your Stacker drive, a disk repair utility can be used to detect and repair the fault. Physical disk utilities can be found in packages such as Norton Utilities, PC Tools, or SpinRite. Start by locating a file attribute utility such as ATTRIB. Type **STACKER** and locate the drive reference line. It should look something like this:

```
Drive C was drive C at boot time [ E:\STACVOL.DSK = 173.5MB]
```

The drive letter in brackets is the host drive. The drive outside of brackets is the compressed drive. Go to the DOS subdirectory on your uncompressed drive (or wherever ATTRIB is located). Next, reboot the system with a clean boot disk—*do not load any device drivers at all.* At the A: prompt, switch to the DOS subdirectory on the host drive and use ATTRIB to unhide STACVOL.DSK, such as:

```
attrib -s -h -r <drive:>\STACVOL.*
```

Here, <drive:> is the drive letter you are repairing (for example, E:). Now that STACVOL is readily available as an ordinary file, run the surface scan on the drive. Be sure to run the surface scan utility from a *floppy* drive. Use the most rigorous test pattern available, and allow the utility to repair any defective areas. Keep in mind that such a thorough scan may take up to several hours depending on the size and speed of the drive. After repairs are complete, remove the floppy disk and reboot the PC.

Now, run CHECK /f and allow it to perform a surface check. If CHECK detects any errors and asks you to delete damaged files, respond Yes, and be sure to follow any on-screen instructions that CHECK provides. You are now ready to run SDEFRAG again. If the error code(s) persist, you will need to invoke the special diagnostic mode in CHECK /f as shown below.

For this procedure, you will need to modify your floppy boot disk to disable all device drivers except STACKER.COM and SWAP.COM. Use REM statements to remark out all other device drivers in the CONFIG.SYS file, as shown in Table 15-5. After you complete these modifications, reboot the computer and run CHECK /f. When asked to perform a surface scan test, answer Yes. If CHECK detects errors and prompts you to delete damaged files, answer Yes, and follow any further instructions provided by CHECK. After CHECK is complete, run SDEFRAG /r again. If SDEFRAG executes without errors, the system is fully optimized, and you can reboot the system from its original configuration files. Otherwise, switch the PC to a slower speed and try running SDEFRAG again.

TABLE 15-5 DISABLING ALL DEVICE DRIVERS EXCEPT STACKER.COM AND SWAP.COM

```
REM device=c:\dos\himem.sys
REM device=c:\dos\emm386.exe noems
REM dos=high,umb
buffers=20
files=30
lastdrive=e
REM devicehigh=c:\mouse\mouse.sys /c1
REM devicehigh=c:\dos\smartdrv.sys 1024
devicehigh=c:\stacker\stacker.com
device=c:\stacker\sswap.com
```

SYMPTOM 15-83 **You encounter an SDEFRAG/OPTIMIZER error 101** This error indicates that your system does not have enough memory to run the SDEFRAG utility. Increase the conventional memory available to your system (or reduce SDEFRAG's memory requirements). Typical memory requirements depend on cluster size:

- 4KB clusters = 503KB SDEFRAG
- 8KB clusters = 534KB SDEFRAG
- 16KB clusters = 560KB SDEFRAG
- 32KB clusters = 642KB SDEFRAG

To run SDEFRAG, you must increase the amount of conventional memory available, or reduce the memory requirement. If you have access to a memory management tool such as QEMM, 386MAX, NETROOM, or MemMaker, running such a manager will often increase the available conventional memory and allow SDEFRAG to run successfully. If you cannot use any of these tools, use a boot disk and edit its CONFIG.SYS or AUTOEXEC.BAT file to disable various device drivers and TSRs. This will leave more conventional memory space. Remember, do not disable your memory managers or Stacker command lines. If problems persist, try running SDEFRAG with its /buffer=# switch, where # is a value between 256 and 4096. Larger numbers save more memory:

- SDEFRAG /buffer=3072 = 21KB of conventional memory saved
- SDEFRAG /buffer=2048 = 42KB of conventional memory saved
- SDEFRAG /buffer=256 = 78KB of conventional memory saved

Some final notes: If you receive these error messages while trying to grow or shrink the Stacker drive, run the Optimizer as SDEFRAG /buffer=*nnn* /GP, where *nnn* is the memory number. If the errors occur when trying to change the Expected Compression Ratio (ECR), run the Optimizer as SDEFRAG /buffer=*nnn* /GL, where *nnn* is the memory number.

SYMPTOM 15-84 **While running the Stacker CHECK utility, you see an error indicating "not enough disk space to save header"** The header of a STACVOL file contains control information about how and where data is stored, and information relating to the data area in which all of the drive's compressed data is stored. A copy of the STACVOL header is saved every time CHECK is run. If the STACVOL header is damaged, it can be repaired by using the saved copy. CHECK runs automatically each time the system is started. If there is not enough space on the host drive to save the header, you will see an error message similar to "not enough disk space to save header." Start by determining the host drive letter. Type **STACKER** and find the information line similar to the one below:

```
Drive D was drive D at boot time [F:\STACVOL.DSK = 123.4MB]
```

The drive letter within brackets (F:) is the host drive, and the drive outside of the bracket (D:) is the compressed drive. Also, take note of the STACVOL file extension.

Next, find the space needed to store the STACVOL file by switching to the host drive. Take a directory of the drive and note the free space available. Type **DIR /AH** to display all hidden or archive files on the drive; then note the size of the STACVOL file. You should expect the header size to approximate the sizes shown in Table 15-6.

Now that you know approximately the amount of space needed for the header, you can make extra uncompressed space available. Type **SDEFRAG /GP**, select the host drive, and then select the More Uncompressed Space Available option. After the drive is defragmented, you will be allowed to enter the desired amount of uncompressed space in KB. Add 50KB to the anticipated amount of space needed for a header, and enter that value. Select the "Perform changes on Stacker drive" option, and restart the system to allow your changes to take effect. You should now have enough space to store the STACVOL header.

SYMPTOM 15-85 The uncompress process fails UNCOMP.EXE is used to uncompress a Stacker drive. Before uncompressing the drive, SDEFRAG is invoked to defragment the drive. If UNCOMP fails, you will have to determine where the fault occurred, find the specific error message (if possible), and correct the error. First, find where the error occurred. When UNCOMP is running, "UNCOMP" is shown in a title bar at the top of the screen. When SDEFRAG is running, "Stacker Optimizer" is shown in the title bar. Note which title is shown when the error occurs. Next, note any SDEFRAG error message. If the process fails without any error message (for example, the system freezes or drops back to DOS unexpectedly), note what was happening before the fault. Read the following procedures carefully before proceeding:

For UNCOMP problems: If UNCOMP drops back to DOS without uncompressing the Stacker drive, download an updated UNCOMP tool, UNCMP4.EXE, from the Stac Web site. Place the file in a temporary subdirectory and run it. UNCMP4.EXE is a self-extracting file that will make other files available in your subdirectory. Copy the newly generated files UNCOMP2.EXE and SDEFRAG2.EXE to the STACKER subdirectory, and then run UNCOMP again.

If UNCOMP hangs up while uncompressing files, you will probably have to reboot your system to get control. On reboot, you will likely see the error "Size Mismatch—Write Protected." The Stacker drive is

TABLE 15-6 TYPICAL STACVOL HEADER SIZES

COMPRESSED DRIVE	HEADER SIZE
50MB	94KB
120MB	108KB
200MB	171KB
500MB	207KB
1000MB	396KB

partially uncompressed and is no longer the size indicated by the header. A write-protect function prevents any further damage. Try running UNCOMP again. In some cases, UNCOMP may start where it left off and begin uncompressing the drive normally. If problems continue, locate and unhide the STACVOL file, unfragment the drive, and run UNCOMP again. This can be accomplished by typing **STACKER** and noting the drive letter and file name in brackets (for example, D:\STACVOL.DSK). Use the DOS ATTRIB utility to unhide the STACVOL file (for example, **ATTRIB -S -H -R D:\STACVOL.DSK**). From a floppy disk, defragment the host drive (such as D:) using a defragmenter such as Norton Speedisk or MS-DOS DEFRAG. Be sure to do a full optimization. Then, run UNCOMP from a floppy disk.

If UNCOMP still fails, check the available (uncompressed) space on the host drive. If there is sufficient uncompressed space to hold the remaining Stacker files, copy (or XCOPY) the files from the Stacker drive to the uncompressed drive, or floppy disks; then remove the Stacker drive using the REMOVDRV function. Note that REMOVDRV deletes all data on the Stacker drive, so make sure you recover any necessary files before deleting the Stacker drive. One way or another, you should be able to recover your vital files before deleting the Stacker drive. If you see an error message indicating "Drive x: is not a Stacker Drive," type **STACKER** to find the drive descriptions (Stac calls this a *drive map*), and it appears similar to

```
Drive C was drive C at boot time [D:\STACVOL.DSK=123.4MB]
```

Remember that the drive letter within the brackets is the host drive, and the drive letter outside of the brackets is the Stacker drive. If you inadvertently tried to UNCOMP the host drive, the process certainly will not work.

If you see a message indicating "The Stacker drive x: contains more data than will fit on the host drive. You must delete about nnn Kbytes before uncompressing," there is more data on the compressed drive than will fit on the physical drive when it is uncompressed. Your only real option here is to back up and delete enough files so that the remainder will fit on the drive when uncompressed. After you off-load or back up a sufficient number of files, run UNCOMP again.

15

If you see an error message such as "There is insufficient free space on the uncompressed drive x: to uncompress the drive. You must free up at least nnn Kbytes on the uncompressed drive, or about twice that amount on the Stacker drive, and re-run UNCOMP," there is not enough working space on the host drive to uncompress the Stacker drive. Try backing up and deleting the prescribed amount of space—that may clear the problem. Otherwise, type **SDEFRAG /GP** at the DOS prompt, and select the "More uncompressed Space Available" option. This will defragment the drive and ask how much space you wish to uncompress. Enter a number larger than the prescribed amount, and allow the changes to be made. Restart the system and run UNCOMP.

If you see an error message such as "There are errors on the Stacker Drive. Please run CHKDSK or another disk repair utility before uncompressing," there are lost clusters or cross-linked files on the Stacker drive. Run CHKDSK to determine the nature of any errors. Run CHKDSK /f to fix lost clusters. You may also run disk repair utilities such as Norton Disk Doctor or PC Tools DiskFix. When the disk errors are corrected, try running UNCOMP again.

For SDEFRAG problems: If you see "SDEFRAG Error 101," refer to Symptom 15-51. If you see "SDEFRAG Error 109/110, 120, or 170," refer to Symptom 15-50. If you see "SDEFRAG Error 157; Internal Error," you may need updated files from the Stac Web site. Download UNCMP4.EXE into a temporary subdirectory and run it. It will self-extract into several new files. Copy the new files UNCOMP2.EXE and SDEFRAG2.EXE into the Stacker subdirectory, and run UNCOMP again.

SYMPTOM 15-86 **You see the error message "Not a Stacker STACVOL file—NOT MOUNTED" or "Invalid # reserved sectors—NOT MOUNTED"** Each Stacker drive is a STACVOL file stored on the uncompressed drive. Each STACVOL file includes a header that contains information on how and where data is stored, as well as the actual compressed data. Either of the error messages listed above indicate that the STACVOL header is damaged or corrupt. Fortunately, a copy of the header is saved for each Stacker drive and can be used to restore a damaged header. Each time the PC starts, CHECK /WP saves the header as STACSAVQ.*nnn*. When you start Windows or use the CHECK utility yourself, the header is saved as STACSAVE.*nnn*. Start by determining which of these saved headers is newest. *Warning: Do not follow this procedure if you have just run SDEFRAG without running CHECK or restarting your PC.*

Start your PC (from a bootable floppy if necessary), switch to the root directory of the uncompressed drive, and type **DIR STACSAV*.* /AH** to see the hidden header file(s). Note the saved file with the latest date and time. Now, restore the header. Type **DIR /AH** to see a directory, including all hidden files, and note the STACVOL extension (such as .DSK). Use the ATTRIB function to unhide the STACVOL file. Type **ATTRIB -S -H -R <drive:>\STACVOL.*xxx***, where <drive:> is the drive letter containing STACVOL, and *.xxx* is the STACVOL extension. Insert a disk containing the REPAIR.EXE utility. If the newest backup header is a STACSAVE file, type **REPAIR /F <drive:>\STACVOL.*xxx***, where <drive:> is the drive containing STACVOL, and *.xxx* is the proper STACVOL extension. If the newest backup header is a STACSAVQ file, type **REPAIR /F <drive:>\STACVOL.*xxx* /Q**, where <drive:> is the drive containing STACVOL, and *.xxx* is the proper STACVOL extension. Then, remove all disks from the system and restart the computer.

SYMPTOM 15-87 **You see an error message similar to "CHECK I/O Access Denied; Error 27"** You have corrupt data in the drive's FAT. Such errors may be due to bad sectors on the physical drive itself, a faulty program or virus that overwrote the FAT, or a program that incorrectly uses EMS (expanded memory). You will have to determine which areas of the hard drive have been damaged, then correct the damaged areas. Boot the system from a clean floppy drive to disable all device drivers and unhide the STACVOL file using the ATTRIB function. Look at the CONFIG.SYS file. If you see a command line that appears similar to

```
DEVICE=C:\STACKER\STACKER.COM
```

then Stacker does not preload. Otherwise, you have a preloading version of Stacker.

For preloading versions of Stacker, type **STACKER** and note the drive map (for example, "Drive C was drive C at boot time [D:\STACVOL.DSK = 123.4MB]"). You need to know the drive letter and STACVOL extension in the brackets. Restart the PC and press F8 when MS-DOS starts. When presented with a command-line prompt, unhide the STACVOL file (for example, **ATTRIB -S -H -R <drive:>\STACVOL.*xxx***, where <drive:> is the drive letter containing STACVOL, and *.xxx* is the STACVOL extension). Change to the Stacker subdirectory and type **STACKER -<drive:>** (where <drive:> is the letter of the compressed drive).

If Stacker does not preload, type **STACKER** and note the drive map (for example, "Drive C was drive C at boot time [D:\STACVOL.DSK = 123.4MB]"). You need to know the drive letter and STACVOL extension in the brackets. Change to the DOS subdirectory and copy ATTRIB to an uncompressed directory. Clean-boot the system to disable all device drivers, switch to the host drive and subdirectory containing

ATTRIB, and then unhide the STACVOL file (for example, **ATTRIB -S -H -R <drive:>\STACVOL.*xxx***, where <drive:> is the drive letter containing STACVOL, and *.xxx* is the STACVOL extension).

Now that the disk and STACVOL file have been prepared, run a disk repair utility such as Norton Utilities, PC Tools DiskFix, or Gibson Research SpinRite to detect and correct damaged disk areas. *Be sure to run any such utility from a floppy disk.* Run a vigorous test (which may take a few hours), and allow the utility to fix any defective areas. When the test is complete, remove any floppy disks and restart the computer. Run CHECK /f to perform a Stacker check of the drive. When no errors are reported, the drive is fixed, and normal use may resume. If problems persist, there are three procedures that may allow you to access the damaged drive before having to start from scratch.

First, try removing write protection on the drive by typing **CHECK /=W *x:***, where *x:* is the compressed drive. *Warning: You must complete this entire procedure before resuming use of the drive.* Now, run CHECK /f again, and follow the instructions to repair the drive. When asked to perform a surface test, answer Yes and delete any damaged files. When CHECK reports no more errors, the drive should be repaired.

If problems persist, the drive's FAT may be damaged, so try removing the /EMS parameter in the STACKER.INI file. Some programs that use EMS do so improperly, and this can damage a FAT. Further corruption can be prevented by disabling Stacker's use of EMS. Type **ED /I** and look for an entry similar to /EMS. Delete the line and press CTRL+Z to save the file and exit. Then restart the system and run CHECK /f to finish the repairs.

If errors continue, try restoring a backup copy of the STACVOL header. If the STACVOL header is error free, restoring it to the STACVOL file may correct a FAT error. Unhide the STACVOL file as you saw earlier in this procedure. Insert a floppy disk containing REPAIR.EXE, switch to that drive, and type **REPAIR /F <drive:>\STACVOL.*xxx***, where <drive:> and *.xxx* are the drive and extension you used when unhiding STACVOL. Allow REPAIR to replace the STACVOL file header. Restart the system and run CHECK /f to see if the damage was repaired. If the problem persists, the FAT may be damaged beyond repair. You may have to repartition and reformat the drive, then reinstall the compression package and restore the most recent system backup.

Further Study

Microsoft Windows 98: **http://www.microsoft.com/windows98/**

Stacker support: **http://support.stac.com/technote/Stacker/default.shtm**

16

DRIVE ADAPTERS AND RAID BASICS

CHAPTER AT A GLANCE

Drives are generally considered to be peripheral devices. This means they must be interfaced to the host system so that the drive and system may communicate with one another. IDE (Integrated Drive Electronics) has proven to be an extremely versatile and cost-effective interface scheme that can support hard drives, CD-ROM drives, DVD-ROM drives, and almost any other drive device. IDE has also proven its longevity by enduring numerous upgrades and improvements through the years. The latest iteration of IDE (referred to as Ultra-DMA/66) offers burst data transfer rates of up to 66MB/sec, and this puts IDE data transfers on par with many basic SCSI implementations. In addition, RAID (Redundant Array of Independent Disks) technology is growing in popularity as users seek more powerful and inexpensive ways to protect their valuable data. This chapter outlines the important issues of IDE and RAID, discusses controller installation issues, and offers a suite of controller troubleshooting procedures.

Understanding the IDE Family

The Integrated Drive Electronics interface developed in 1988 in response to an industry push to create a standard software interface for SCSI peripherals. The industry consortium, known as the Common Access Method Committee (or CAMC), attempted to originate an AT Attachment (ATA) interface that could be incorporated into low-cost AT-compatible motherboards. The CAMC completed its specification, which was later approved by ANSI. The term *ATA interface* generally refers to the controller interface, while IDE refers to the drive. Today, IDE simply refers to an interface type and can be applied to either the drive or controller. For example, an IDE drive will require an IDE controller.

Even though there are numerous iterations of the IDE family today (such as EIDE, UDMA/33, and UDMA/66), the family is still commonly referred to as "IDE type."

IDE/ATA

IDE and ATA are basically one and the same thing—a scheme designed to integrate the controller onto the drive itself instead of relying on a stand-alone controller board as older MFM and RLL drives did. This approach reduces interface costs and makes drive firmware implementations easier. IDE proved to be a low-cost, easily configured system—so much so that it created a boom in the disk drive industry. Although the terms IDE and ATA are sometimes used interchangeably, ATA is the formal standard that defines the drive and how it operates, while IDE is really the "trade name" that refers to the 40-pin interface and drive controller architecture designed to implement the ATA standard.

Classic IDE Features and Architecture

IDE drives are typically intelligent—that is, almost all functions relegated to a controller board in older drives are now integrated onto the drive itself. Data is transferred through a single cable attached to a relatively straightforward *adapter board* (a simple controller board that is often little more than a buffer) attached to the system's ISA or PCI expansion bus. Exterior circuitry is so limited that virtually all motherboard chipsets provide a dual-channel IDE controller, eliminating the need for an expansion card controller. Today, classical IDE drives are fairly slow, offering data transfer rates rarely exceeding 10Mbits/s. "Classic" IDE is also limited to supporting drives up to 528MB. (EIDE and later iterations of the IDE interface break the traditional 528MB barrier and can support drives larger than 32GB at this time.) IDE lacks the flexibility and expandability of SCSI, but IDE is relatively inexpensive to implement. Thus, it is often the choice for simple, inexpensive, low-to-midrange PCs that are not expected to expand much. More recently, the use of an IDE interface has extended beyond only hard drives to include such devices as CD-ROMs and tape drives through the use of the AT Attachment Packet Interface (ATAPI) protocol (more on ATAPI a little later in the chapter).

A great deal of discussion has concentrated on IDE intelligence. The *intelligence* of an IDE system is determined by the capabilities of the onboard controller. For the purposes of this book, intelligent IDE drives are capable of the following functions. First, intelligent IDE drives support *drive translation*—the feature that allows CMOS drive parameters to be entered in any combination of cylinders, heads, and sectors that add up to equal or less than the true number of sectors on the drive. This is particularly handy when the actual number of cylinders exceeds 1024 (as all modern IDE-type drives do). Nonintelligent IDE drives were limited to physical mode, where CMOS parameters were entered to match physical parameters. Intelligent drives also support a number of enhanced commands that are an optional part of the original ATA specification.

Another advancement of intelligent IDE technology is *zoned recording*, which allows a variable number of sectors per track. This allows an overall increase in the number of sectors—and the drive's overall capacity. However, BIOS can only deal with a fixed number of sectors per track, so the zoned IDE drive must always run in translation mode. When running IDE drives in translation mode, you cannot alter interleave or sector skew factors. You also cannot change factory defect information.

A typical IDE-type controller layout is shown in Figure 16-1. The physical interface for a standard IDE device consists of a 40-pin data/control cable. (Old IBM implementations used either a 44-pin or 72-pin cable.) This *signal cable* is responsible for carrying data and control signals between the drive and controller board. IDE-type drives also use terminating resistors to ensure reliable signal characteristics, but IDE/EIDE terminating resistors are usually fixed and cannot be removed. In most cases, two IDE/EIDE drives can work together with terminating resistors in place. While there will be several jumpers on the drive, a set of *drive select* jumpers allow the drive to be set as the primary (master) or secondary (slave) drive.

The signal cable for an IDE-type drive is typically a 40-pin insulation displacement connector (IDC) cable, as shown in Table 16-1. Unlike the obsolete ST506/412 or ESDI interfaces, the IDE family uses both the even- and odd-numbered wires as signal-carrying lines. Also note that most of the signal labels have dashes beside their names. The dash indicates that the particular signal is *active low*—that is, the signal is *true* in the logic 0 state instead of being true in the logic 1 state. All signal lines on the IDE interface are fully TTL compatible where a logic 0 is 0.0 to +0.8 Vdc, and a logic 1 is +2.0 to Vcc.

Data points and registers in the IDE-type drive are addressed using the Drive Address Bus lines DA0 to DA2 (pins 35, 33, and 36, respectively) in conjunction with the -Chip Select Drive inputs -CS1FX and -CS3FX (pins 37 and 38). When a true signal is sent along the -Drive I/O Read (-DIOR, pin 25) line, the drive executes a read cycle, while a true on the -Drive I/O Write (-DIOW, pin 23) line initiates a write cycle. The IDE interface provides TTL-level input and output signals. Where older interfaces were serial, the IDE interface provides 16 bidirectional data lines (DD0 to DD15, pins 3 to 18) to carry data bits into or out of the drive. Once a data transfer is completed, a -DMA Acknowledge (-DMACK, pin 29) signal is provided to the drive from the hard disk controller IC. Finally, a true signal on the drive's Reset line (pin 1) will restore the drive to its original condition at power-on. A Reset is sent when the computer is first powered on or rebooted.

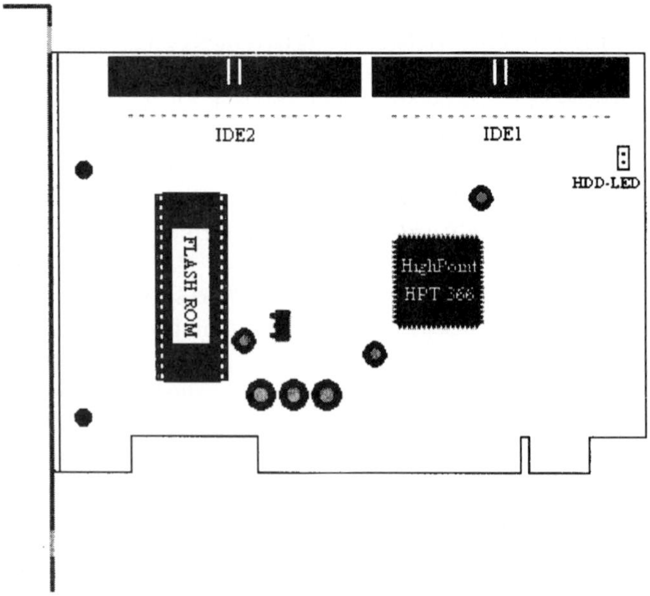

FIGURE 16-1 A typical dual-port Ultra-DMA/66 controller card

TABLE 16-1 PINOUT FOR AN IDE-TYPE SIGNAL CABLE

PIN	NAME	PIN	NAME
1	Reset	2	Ground
3	DD7	4	DD8
5	DD6	6	DD9
7	DD5	8	DD10
9	DD4	10	DD11
11	DD3	12	DD12
13	DD2	14	DD13
15	DD1	16	DD14
17	DD0	18	DD15
19	Ground	20	Key (slot only)
21	DMARQ	22	Ground
23	-I/O Write Data (-DIOW)	24	Ground
25	-I/O Read Data (-DIOR)	26	Ground
27	-I/O Channel Ready (-IORDY)	28	Unused
29	-DMA Acknowledge (-DMACK)	30	Ground
31	Interrupt Request (INTRQ)	32	-Host 16-bit I/O (-IOCS16)
33	DA1	34	-Passed Diagnostics (-PDIAG)
35	DA0	36	DA2
37	-Host Chip Sel 0 (-CS1FX)	38	-Host Chip Sel 1 (-CS3FX)
39	-Drive Active (-DASP)	40	Ground

An IDE-type physical interface also provides a number of outputs back to the motherboard. A Direct Memory Access Request (DMARQ, pin 21) is used to initiate the transfer of data to or from the drive. The direction of data transfer is dependent on the condition of the -DIOR and -DIOW inputs. A -DMACK signal is generated in response when the DMARQ line is asserted (made true). -IORDY (pin 27) is an -I/O Channel Ready signal that keeps a system's attention if the drive is not quite ready to respond to a data transfer request. A drive Interrupt Request (INTRQ, pin 31) is asserted by a drive when there is a drive interrupt pending (the drive is about to transfer information to or from the motherboard). The -Drive Active line (DASP, pin 39) becomes logic 0 when there is any hard drive activity occurring. A -Passed Diagnostic (PDIAG, pin 34) line provides the results of any diagnostic command or reset action. When PDIAG is logic 0, the system knows that the drive is ready to use. Finally, the 16-bit -I/O Control line (IOCS16, pin 32) tells the motherboard that the drive is ready to send or receive data. Notice that there are several return (ground) lines (pins 2, 19, 22, 24, 26, 30, and 40) and a key pin (20), which is removed from the male connector.

Cabling the IDE/EIDE Interface

The ATA IDE interface is intended to support up to two drives on the same cable (or channel) in a daisy-chain fashion. A typical IDE controller cable is illustrated in Figure 16-2. Although tradition dictates that drive 0 be attached to the end connector (as the primary or master drive) and a second drive be attached to the middle connector (as a secondary or slave drive), it is important to note that IDE supports either drive in either location. For the purposes of IDE, you need only set the proper drive jumpers to select

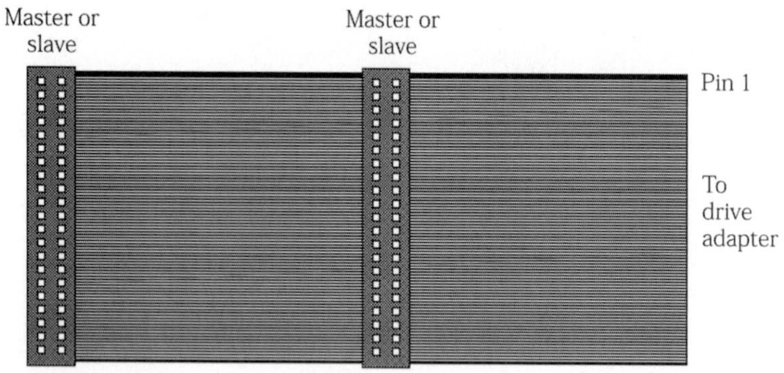

FIGURE 16-2 Data and control cabling for an IDE/EIDE drive

a drive as a master or slave. The 40-pin ribbon cable (IBM uses 44-pin or 72-pin cables) should not exceed 61 cm (24 inches) in length. Since IDE-type drives rely on *distributed termination* as a means of signal conditioning, it is not necessary to install or remove terminating resistors.

However, you may encounter problems when running two IDE drives together. Older IDE drives did not fully adhere to the CAMC ATA IDE specification. When trying to run older drives together (especially drives from different manufacturers), they may not respond to their master/slave relationship properly, and conflicts will result—in many cases, such problems will disable both drives. When planning a dual-IDE installation, try to use newer drives that are both from the same manufacturer.

BIOS Support of the IDE Family

Unlike SCSI controllers, which use an expansion ROM to provide supplemental BIOS, the firmware needed to provide IDE support is written into the motherboard's BIOS. Although systems manufactured since about 1990 are fully compatible with ATA IDE drives, adding an IDE drive to an older PC often resulted in problems. After the broad introduction of IDE, it was discovered that IDE drive operations placed different timing demands on the PC, which frequently caused disk errors such as data corruption and failure to boot. BIOS makers quickly found a solution to this timing problem, and it was incorporated into BIOS that appeared after early 1990. If you encounter a PC with pre-1990 BIOS, you should consider upgrading it before adding an IDE drive, or if the current IDE drive is exhibiting problems. Today, you may also need to upgrade a motherboard's BIOS if the drive controller cannot support the full size of a given drive (32GB).

ATAPI

One of the major disadvantages of ATA is that it was designed for hard drives only. With the broad introduction of CD-ROM drives in the late 1980s, designers needed a means of attaching CD-ROMs (and other devices such as tape drives) to the existing ATA (IDE) interface—rather than employing a stand-alone (proprietary) controller card. The ATA Packet Interface (ATAPI) is an extension of the ATA (IDE) interface designed to allow devices other than hard drives to plug into an ordinary ATA (IDE) port. While hard drives enjoy ATA (IDE) support through BIOS, ATAPI devices require a device driver to support them. Booting from an ATAPI CD-ROM is only possible with an El Torito CD-ROM and the latest motherboard BIOS versions.

ATA-2, FAST-ATA, AND EIDE

By the early 1990s, it became clear that ATA architecture would soon be overwhelmed by advances in hard drive technology. The hard drive industry responded by developing the ATA-2 standard as an extension of ATA. ATA-2 is largely regarded as a significant improvement to ATA. It defines faster PIO (Programmed I/O) and DMA (Direct Memory Access) data transfer modes, adds more powerful drive commands (such as the "Identify Drive" command to support autoidentification in CMOS), adds support for a second drive channel, handles block data transfers (Block Transfer Mode), and defines a new means of addressing sectors on the hard drive using Logical Block Addressing (LBA). LBA has proven to be a very effective vehicle for overcoming the traditional 528MB hard drive size limit. Yet ATA-2 continues to use the same 40-pin physical interface used by ATA, and the interface scheme is backward compatible with ATA (IDE) drives.

Along with ATA-2, you'll probably find two additional terms: EIDE (Enhanced IDE) and Fast-ATA. These are not standards—merely different implementations of the ATA-2 standard. EIDE represents the Western Digital implementation of ATA-2 that builds upon both the ATA-2 and ATAPI standards. This has been so effective that EIDE has become the generic term. Seagate and Quantum have thrown their support behind the Fast-ATA implementation of the ATA-2 standard. However, Fast-ATA builds on ATA-2 only. For all practical purposes, there is no significant difference between ATA-2, EIDE, and Fast-ATA, and you'll probably see these three terms used interchangeably (though this is not technically correct).

Understanding the Classic 528MB IDE Limit

The 528MB limit, probably the most important and compelling limitation to IDE architecture, is the result of a simple lack of planning between the developers of BIOS and the developers of the WD1003 drive controller architecture. To understand the limitations of drive size, you must understand how IDE drives are addressed. The classic addressing scheme is known as Cylinder Head Sector (or CHS) addressing. Simply stated, you place the cylinder number, head number, and sector number you need to get to into the WD1003 controller registers, then call the Int 13 routine in BIOS, which runs the drive to the desired location for reading or writing.

This works just fine in theory, but there is a problem. You see, the limiting values for cylinders, heads, and sectors are not the same in both the BIOS and the WD1003 architecture. Table 16-2 illustrates these values, and you can see their impact on drive size. BIOS specifies a maximum of 1024 cylinders, 255 heads, and 63 sectors per track. If you multiply these together, then multiply 512 bytes/sector, you get 8422686720 bytes (or 8.4GB) of theoretical capacity. For the WD1003 controller, you should be able to have 65536 cylinders, 16 heads, and 255 sectors per track. When this is multiplied by 512 bytes per sector, you get a whopping 1.36899_{10}^{11} bytes (or 136.9GB) of theoretical capacity.

The problem is that you can only use the lowest common number for each approach. Therefore, the maximum number of cylinders you can use is 1024, the maximum number of heads is 16, and the maxi-

TABLE 16-2 CHS VALUES VS. DRIVE SIZE

	BIOS	WD1003	RESULTING LIMIT
Cylinders	1024	65536	1024
Heads	255	16	16
Sectors	63	255	63
Max. Capacity	8.4GB	136.9GB	528MB

mum number of sectors of 63. When you multiply these out, then multiply times 512 bytes/sector, you get 528MB. The real tragedy here is that if BIOS designers and WD1003 designers had sat down and come up with the *same* numbers, we could easily have had IDE drives with capacities up to 136.9GB, and this entire issue would be moot. But instead, an IDE hard drive can only address up to 528MB.

This explains why IDE worked so well with drives up to 528MB—but not more. Of course, there are ways to work around this limitation. Since BIOS is essentially software, the easiest and most economical way to overcome the 528MB barrier is to "augment" the BIOS Int 13 routine by introducing a driver when the PC is initialized. Int 13 enhancements allow the support of drive sizes up to 8.4GB and more. The Drive Rocket and Disk Manager by Ontrack are two of the most popular drivers available. They allow the PC to access the entire space of a large IDE drive—not just 528MB.

EIDE and UDMA modes can work with such "overlay" drivers, and Disk Manager (or one of its similar cousins) is frequently bundled with today's huge hard drives. However, there are some compelling reasons why overlay drivers are not desirable. First, drivers take memory space—typically precious space within the first 640KB of RAM. Few systems have space remaining in the upper memory area for an overlay driver. Second, older overlay drivers don't always accommodate Windows 95/98 very well at all, so using large hard drives under Windows has traditionally been a problem. Third, the overlay driver may conflict with other device drivers and TSRs that may be on your PC.

Ultimately, the preferred method of large drive support for EIDE and UDMA modes is to update the BIOS itself with a version that contains the necessary Int 13 enhancements. AMI and Micro Firmware are early entrants into the EIDE-compatible BIOS arena, but EIDE support quickly became standard in all BIOS and drive controller versions. Today, UDMA/66 support is common, but this is fully backward compatible with EIDE and IDE. Although upgrading a BIOS is a bit more involved than adding a driver, the rewards (more free memory and better OS compatibility) are almost always worth it. As an effective alternative to the trials of a motherboard BIOS upgrade, you can choose to upgrade your current drive controller with a new drive adapter containing *onboard* BIOS extensions for Int 13.

Understanding LBA

Another great source of confusion in the use of EIDE and UDMA modes is the need for Logical Block Addressing (or LBA). Where CHS addressing requires the specification of a discrete cylinder, head, and sector, an LBA address simply requires the specification of a sector (for example, "go to sector 324534"). The LBA algorithm (implemented in BIOS) will translate the sector to the appropriate CHS equivalent. FAT-based operating systems such as DOS and Windows *require* the use of LBA addressing. As a consequence, you'll need to update your motherboard BIOS, or use an EIDE/UDMA controller with onboard BIOS. On the other hand, non-FAT operating systems (such as OS/2 and Novell NetWare) do *not* require LBA addressing. When you actually have an EIDE controller in hand, you may note that the controller provides a jumper allowing you to enable or disable LBA addressing. If you are using DOS (or Windows), keep this jumper *enabled*.

> Current UDMA-compliant controllers will forgo a physical jumper for an entry in the CMOS setup. Locate the "LBA" entry and verify that it's enabled.

An important consideration in choosing CHS or LBA addressing is the format of your hard drive(s). If you choose to invoke LBA addressing, you'll need to repartition and reformat your hard drive(s). You must also remember that once a hard drive is formatted for LBA, the drive will *only* be recognized by PCs that support LBA. As a result, if you take an LBA-formatted drive (EIDE) and install it into a PC whose BIOS does not support LBA (such as an older IDE-supported system), the drive will simply not be recognized, and you will have to repartition and reformat the drive again. In all cases, remember to perform a *complete* backup of your hard drive(s) before implementing EIDE on your system.

Drive Support

One of the main advantages of SCSI has traditionally been its ability to support up to seven varied devices on the same bus (hard drives, CD-ROMs, tape drives, etc.). This approach went a long way toward eliminating the proliferation of proprietary controllers and system configuration problems that remain prevalent in non-SCSI systems. While a classic IDE controller allows two drives (master and slave) to reside on the same controller port (1F0h) and interrupt (IRQ 14), it does not support any other devices. EIDE and UDMA modes seek to overcome this limitation by adding a second "channel" to the EIDE/UDMA controller.

Be careful when evaluating a controller with two channels. While the primary channel will normally support the fastest devices, the secondary channel may not. For example, it was common for EIDE controllers to fully support EIDE on the primary channel, but only support ATAPI IDE on the secondary channel. Today, it's not uncommon for a UDMA/66 controller to support up to two UDMA/66 devices on the primary channel, but only support UDMA/33 or EIDE on the secondary channel. Check the specifications before you start attaching devices.

In theory, an older IDE drive will work on an EIDE channel, but you may run into trouble when mixing an EIDE and IDE device on the same EIDE channel. A classic example of this is on systems that use a new fast EIDE hard drive, then add an IDE ATAPI CD-ROM as the slave device. In many cases, the slower CD-ROM interferes with the EIDE drive, reducing the drive's maximum data transfer rates and slowing drive performance. In more pronounced cases, the CD-ROM may not be recognized. In extreme cases, the hard drive (and perhaps the CD-ROM also) may not be recognized, and the system won't even boot. Reconfiguring the hardware to make the CD-ROM a master device on the IDE (secondary) controller channel will almost always correct the problem.

Today's UDMA/33 and UDMA/66 drive controllers are somewhat more intelligent and are better able to adjust the data transfer speeds to accommodate devices of differing speeds on the same channel. Still, speed compatibility issues can come into play. For example, you may find that using a UDMA/66 hard drive and non-UDMA/66 device together on the same channel may cause the maximum data transfer to fall to UDMA/33 levels.

> As a rule, keep the faster devices on the primary controller channel, and use the slower devices on the secondary controller channel.

ATA-3

A more recent implementation of the ATA standard is ATA-3. It does not define any new data transfer modes, but it does improve the reliability of PIO mode 4. It also offers a simple password-based security scheme, more sophisticated power management features, and Self-Monitoring Analysis and Reporting Technology (or SMART). ATA-3 is also backward compatible with ATA-2, ATAPI, and ATA devices. Since no new data transfer modes are defined by ATA-3, you may also see the generic term "EIDE" used interchangeably (though this is also not technically correct).

ULTRA-ATA/33

The push for ever-faster data transfer rates is a never-ending one, and the Ultra-ATA standard represents an implementation of ATA/ATAPI-4 by providing a high-performance bus mastering at burst data rates up to 33MB/s using DMA data transfers. The implementation of Ultra-ATA is usually called Ultra-DMA/33 (or UDMA/33). You'll need an Ultra-ATA drive, controller, and BIOS to support an Ultra-ATA drive system, but it is fully backward compatible with previous ATA standards. You can use ordinary 40-pin IDE-type cables for UDMA/33 unless any of the following issues occur:

- The standard cable is low quality, damaged, or weakened by many installs/removals.
- The system suffers from excessive signal noise—these systems may have multiple drives, dual power supplies, or an integrated CRT.
- The system is overclocked (or otherwise configured beyond the manufacturer's supported specifications).

ULTRA-ATA/66

The Ultra-ATA standard for ATA/ATAPI-4 was upgraded to support an even faster high-performance bus mastering with burst data rates up to 66MB/sec using DMA data transfers. This more recent implementation of Ultra-ATA is usually called Ultra-DMA/66 (or UDMA/66). You'll need an Ultra-ATA/66 drive, controller, cable, and BIOS to support an Ultra-ATA/66 drive system, but it is fully backward compatible with previous ATA standards. Unlike the Ultra-ATA/33 approach, you cannot use ordinary 40-pin IDE-type cables to connect drives and controllers. Instead, you'll need a specially designed 40-pin/80-conductor cable (typically provided with UDMA/66 drives). Also keep in mind that the operating system (such as Windows 98) must be enabled for DMA transfers.

Common UDMA/66 Issues

- Make sure the signal cable is Ultra-ATA/66 capable. An Ultra-ATA/66-compliant cable is a 40-pin, 80-conductor cable with a black connector on one end, a blue connector on the other end, and a gray connector in the middle. In addition, pin 34 on the cable should be notched or cut (though this may be difficult to see with the human eye).
- Make sure the system board (motherboard) controller is capable of supporting Ultra-ATA/66. An Ultra-ATA/66-capable controller has a detect circuit which can detect that line 34 is missing on the cable. If there is no detect circuit, the system can wrongly detect the presence of an Ultra-ATA/66 cable and try to configure the device for a higher transfer rate.
- Some system board (motherboard) controllers may not successfully handle Ultra-ATA/66 on both the primary and secondary channels. If you have difficulty with a UDMA/66 device on the secondary controller channel, consider troubleshooting with the device in the primary master position.
- If you have trouble getting a UDMA/66 system configured properly, contact the system board (motherboard) or controller card manufacturer for the latest BIOS upgrade (and any Ultra-ATA/66 device drivers or patches).
- Make sure the operating system is DMA capable, and verify that the DMA mode is activated. For Windows 95/98, check the drive's Properties dialog in the Device Manager.
- Make sure the Ultra-ATA/66-capable drive has been configured to run at Ultra-ATA/66 transfer rates. Some drives ship with the UDMA/66 mode disabled by default and require a jumper change and/or software utility in order to activate the UDMA/66 mode.

DATA TRANSFER RATES

Data transfer rates play a major role in drive performance. In practice, there are two measures of data transfer: the rate at which data is taken from the platters and the rate at which data is passed between the drive and controller. The internal data transfer between the platters and drive buffer is typically the slower rate. Older drives could run around 5MB/sec, but newer Ultra-ATA drives like the Maxtor DiamondMax 2160 runs at 14MB/s. The external data transfer between the drive and controller (the *interface rate*) is often the *faster* rate. Older drives provided between 5 and 8MB/sec, but ATA-2 (EIDE) drives can operate up to 16MB/sec. Ultra-DMA/33 drives can run at 33MB/sec, and Ultra-DMA/66 drives can handle burst data transfers of 66MB/sec. The modern standards of IDE/EIDE external data transfer are listed as PIO (or Programmed I/O) and DMA (Direct Memory Access) modes. The PIO mode specifies how fast the data is transferred to and from the drive, as shown in Table 16-3.

You may notice that the EIDE-specific modes (PIO-3 and PIO-4) use the IORDY hardware flow control line. This means that the drive can use the IORDY line to slow down the interface when necessary. Interfaces without proper IORDY support may cause data corruption in the fast PIO modes (so you'd be stuck with the slower modes). When choosing an EIDE drive and controller, always be sure to check that the IORDY line is being used.

By comparison, DMA data transfers mean that the data is transferred *directly* between the drive and memory without using the CPU as an intermediary (as is the case with PIO). In true multitasking operating systems like OS/2, Windows NT, or Linux, DMA transfers leave the CPU free to do something useful during disk transfers. In a DOS or Windows environment, the CPU will have to wait for the transfer to finish anyway, so in these cases DMA transfers don't offer that much of a multitasking advantage. There are two distinct types of Direct Memory Access: ordinary DMA and bus mastering DMA. Ordinary DMA uses the DMA controller on the system's motherboard to perform the complex task of arbitration, grabbing the system bus, and transferring the data. With bus mastering DMA, all this is done by logic in the drive controller itself.

TABLE 16-3 COMPARISON OF DATA TRANSFER SPEEDS

PIO MODE	CYCLE TIME (NS)	TRANSFER RATE (MB/S)	NOTES
0	600	3.3	The old ATA (IDE) modes
1	383	5.2	
2	240	8.3	
3	180 IORDY		Newer ATA-2 (EIDE) modes
4	120 IORDY	16.6	
DMA MODE	**CYCLE TIME (NS)**	**TRANSFER RATE (MB/S)**	**NOTES**
Single Word	0 960	2.1	Also in ATA
	1 480	4.2	
	2 240	8.3	
Multiword	0 480	4.2	Also in ATA
	1 150	13.3	
	2 120	16.6	
	3 —	33.0	Ultra-DMA/33
	4 —	66.0	Ultra-DMA/66

Unfortunately, the DMA controller on traditional ISA bus systems is slow—out of the question for use with a modern hard disk. VL bus controller cards cannot be used as DMA targets at all and can only handle bus mastering DMA. Only EISA and PCI-based interfaces make non–bus mastering DMA viable: EISA type "B" DMA will transfer 4MB/s, and PCI type "F" DMA will transfer between 6 and 8MB/s. Today, the proper software support for DMA is relatively rare (as well as the interfaces supporting it). Still, the DMA data transfer modes are listed in Table 16-3.

Controller Installation

In many cases, you'll find that the motherboard will provide a primary and secondary drive controller channel that will suit a wide variety of drives in the market at the time the system was manufactured. Over time, new drive types, larger drive capacities, and enhanced data transfer modes may require you to upgrade the motherboard's controller feature. It may also be necessary to install a new controller in the event that an existing controller fails. This part of the chapter highlights the major points involved in controller installation.

PREPARING FOR A NEW CONTROLLER

Although a new drive controller should work with your existing drives, there may be some circumstances in which a new controller may cause problems. This happens most frequently when the old controller is not removed or disabled properly, or the new controller uses an addressing scheme that does not comply with the drive's current setup. Before you start unwrapping that new controller, take some time to prepare your system:

- *Back up the drive(s).* Before performing any type of drive-related work, protect your valuable data by creating a complete backup of the drive(s) on your system to tape, CD-R, Iomega Jaz, or other suitable media. Boot to the CMOS setup and record the geometry settings for each drive. (You may need to reenter them later.)
- *Ready your software.* You should have your Windows 98 CD handy in the event you need to reinstall the operating system or load new drivers when the controller is installed. If there are drivers with the new controller, you should also have that disc on hand (or download the newest driver versions from the controller's manufacturer).
- *Review your current controller.* Eventually, you'll need to remove or disable the current controller, so take a moment to review the documentation for your system and understand the required methods for disabling the current controller. If the controller is currently integrated into your motherboard, it can typically be disabled through the CMOS setup. (Older motherboards may use a jumper instead.) Controllers that are implemented on stand-alone expansion cards can usually just be removed.
- *Preconfigure your new controller.* Study the documentation that comes with your new controller card. If the controller offers a number of controller features (a floppy controller, game port, COM ports, or other features), you should make it a point to disable any features that are not going to be used. Remember that each feature will demand system resources, so don't allow those extra features to remain enabled and conflict with similar features still operating on the motherboard.
- *Check the BIOS version.* It's not uncommon for firmware updates to change frequently. Check with the new controller's manufacturer to see if there's a new firmware version that should be updated after you've installed the new controller.

INSTALLING THE NEW CONTROLLER

There's certainly no magic to successfully installing a new controller card, but there are a few tricks that you should be aware of.

- Turn off and unplug the system; then unbolt the outer housing and remove it. Set the housing and screws aside in a safe place.
- Locate the old drive controller and gently disconnect the 40-pin cables from the controller end, but leave them connected to the drive(s). You may choose to label the signal cables so that you can easily locate the primary and secondary channels.
- Remove the old controller card (if there is one), and insert the new controller card into its expansion slot. Otherwise, unbolt the bracket from another appropriate expansion slot and insert the new controller there (use the bracket to cover the unused slot). Bolt the new controller card to the chassis. If the original controller is integrated onto the motherboard, there is nothing to remove, but you will need to disable the controller through a motherboard jumper or the system's CMOS setup once you reboot the system again.
- If your computer case offers a "hard drive activity" LED, you can generally connect this cable to the small "activity" header on the new controller card. However, this is generally optional, and you may leave the activity LED connected to a drive if you wish.
- Locate the new drive controller headers. The primary channel may be labeled "Pri-IDE" or "IDE 0." The secondary channel may be labeled "Sec-IDE" or "IDE 1." Connect the primary and secondary drive cables to their corresponding headers on the controller.

> Remember that UDMA/66 drives and controllers must be connected via a 40-pin/80-conductor cable specially intended for UDMA/66 use. If you're upgrading drives along with the controller, be sure to use this cable.

CONFIGURING THE NEW CONTROLLER

Once the new controller is secure and connected, it's time to start the computer and make any necessary configuration changes to use the new controller and avoid system conflicts. Leave the computer's housing off for the time being and follow the tips below:

- Adjust the motherboard's CMOS setup. Boot the system directly to the CMOS setup. If your old controller was integrated into the motherboard, you may need to disable the controller(s). However, since we're not changing drives in this exercise, you should verify the drive geometry settings, or reenter them if necessary. No changes are needed for CD-ROM (or other ATAPI) drives that are attached to the controller. The motherboard will automatically assign the IRQ and I/O resources to the new controller. Save your changes and reboot the system.
- Access the new controller's BIOS. Since virtually all drive controller cards use their own onboard BIOS chip, chances are that you'll see a BIOS banner for the controller's BIOS. If you press the key listed in the controller's BIOS banner while rebooting the system, you can access the BIOS and configure specific attributes of the controller's operation. Refer to the controller's manual for specific options and suggested settings. Most installations work just fine with default settings, and you never need to change the controller's internal configuration.

SOFTWARE INSTALLATION

The new controller's onboard BIOS should fully support normal system operation in the real mode (DOS). However, Windows 95/98 will probably require the installation of numerous drivers to support the controller (especially the UDMA/66 DMA drivers). The steps below highlight a general installation scenario:

- Try booting the system to DOS, and then check each drive letter. Try taking a directory of each drive. If you can access all of the drives that you could before installing the new controller, you can be confident that the hardware portion of your installation was successful. If you cannot access one or more drives, recheck the motherboard's CMOS setup and verify that all of the drive-related settings are identical to those used for the old controller. If you cannot emulate the LBA translation characteristics of the original controller, you may need to repartition and reformat the drive(s).
- Reboot the system and allow Windows 95/98 to boot normally. Chances are that you'll see "New Hardware Detected" as a "PCI Mass Storage Controller." (The exact hardware found will depend on your version of Windows.)
- In most cases, the Add New Hardware wizard will appear, informing you that the new device has been found. Click Next.
- Select "Search for a better driver than the one your device is using now," and then click Next.
- Click Browse, insert the floppy or CD with the controller's device drivers, and then browse to the folder containing the drivers. Click Next.
- When the driver location is found, click Next.
- When the installation is complete, click Finished.
- It is common for modern controllers to install twice—once for the primary channel and once for the secondary channel. Do *not* reboot the computer after installing the primary channel. Finish the secondary channel (generally, repeat these steps for the second "PCI Mass Storage Device"), and then reboot the PC.
- When the new controller is installed properly, you'll see the entries listed under Hard Disk Controllers or SCSI Controllers in your Device Manager.

UPGRADING THE CONTROLLER'S BIOS

From time to time, you may need to upgrade the drive controller's firmware in order to correct bugs, streamline features, or improve compatibility with various systems and devices. When you see that a suitable BIOS update is available, download the update and then follow these guidelines:

1. Create a bootable floppy disk, and then copy the flash utility (for example, PTIFLASH.EXE) and the new BIOS file (for example, ULBIOS.BIN) to the disk.
2. Reboot the system from the floppy disk. (You'll see the A: command prompt.)
3. Launch the flash loader program (for example, type **ptiflash** and press ENTER). A main menu should appear.
4. Select the option to save a backup copy of the controller's firmware to the floppy disk.
5. Once the firmware backup is finished, select the option to update the BIOS from a file.
6. A dialog will appear. Enter the path and name of the new BIOS file (for example, **a:\ulbios.bin**). If you see an error indicating that the file was not found, double-check your path and file name.

7 The utility will update the controller's firmware, and you will see a message when the process is complete.

8 Remove the disk and reboot the system.

9 When the controller's BIOS banner appears, make sure that the BIOS version is in fact the new version.

RAID Primer

Traditionally, the most common means of protecting valuable data has been to perform routine and consistent backups to tape or other media. While this has proven to be a tried-and-true method, it is often not implemented properly. Backups are frequently forgotten or performed inconsistently. Even automated backup schemes require human interaction at some level. All too often, some data is lost during a disk failure. Designers realized that if a controller could write data to *one* drive, then the data could be written to *two* drives just as easily. One or more drives can be made to "mirror" a master drive in real time—if the master drive were to fail, the data would be accessed from a secondary drive. This is the basic premise behind a Redundant Array of Independent Disks (or RAID).

The problem with RAID is that it costs money to implement. You'll need a drive controller that supports RAID (such as the Promise FastTrack66 for UDMA/66 drives) and an additional drive for each drive that you need to mirror. The extra drives don't give you more storage space, they simply mimic the original drive(s), and you need additional power and drive space for the RAID drives. End users don't often choose to spend their money on such protection, but it's common on servers and busy workstations. This part of the chapter highlights several basic RAID concepts and explains some setup options that you may encounter.

DISK ARRAY

A *disk array* is formed from a group of two or more disk drives that appear to the system as a single drive. The advantage of an array is to provide better performance and data fault tolerance. Better performance is accomplished by sharing the data transfer workload in parallel among multiple physical drives. *Fault tolerance* is achieved through data redundant operation, where if one (or more) drives should fail (or suffer a sector failure), a mirrored copy of the data can be found on another drive(s). For optimal results, select identical drives for installation in disk arrays. The drives' matched performance allows the array to function better as a single drive. The individual disk drives in an array are called *members*. Each member of a specific disk array is coded in its reserved sector with configuration information that identifies the drive as a member of the given array.

DISK ARRAY ADAPTER (DAA)

The generic term used for the RAID controller is the *disk array adapter*—the device that supports your mirrored drive(s), which are generally termed the disk array. Most RAID controllers are implemented using the SCSI interface, but Promise Technologies offers the FastTrack66, which supports RAID functions for UDMA/66 hard drives. The controller will virtually always incorporate a BIOS that fully supports the drive operations (such as UDMA/66) and provide a setup feature (similar to the CMOS setup) that will allow you to configure the RAID controller's features.

RESERVED SECTOR

Vital information is saved in a special location on each disk member called the *reserved sector*. This area contains array configuration data about the drive and other members in the disk array. If reserved data on any member of the array becomes corrupt or lost, the redundant configuration data on the other members can be used for rebuilds. As a rule, disk array members do not have specific drive positions. This allows drives to be placed on different RAID controller connectors or cards within the system without reconfiguring or rebuilding the array.

DISK ARRAY TYPES

A typical RAID controller will support four general operating modes: striping, mirroring, stripe/mirror, and spanning. The choice of RAID mode will affect your drive capacity, drive performance, or fault tolerance. To appreciate the versatility of RAID, you should understand a little more about each of these RAID modes.

> Remember that all disk members in a formed disk array are recognized as a single physical drive to the host system.

Striping (RAID 0)

In the striping mode, sectors of data are interleaved between multiple drives, effectively forming one large drive from two or more smaller ones. Striping is regarded as a performance enhancement rather than fault tolerance. Performance is better than a single drive because the read/write workload is duplicated between the array members, and this array type is encountered in high-performance systems. Identical drives are recommended for performance (as well as data storage efficiency). The disk array data capacity is equal to the number of drive members times the smallest member capacity. For example, one 1GB and three 1.2GB drives will form a 4GB (4 x 1GB) disk array. The weakness with RAID 0 is that there is no redundancy—when any disk member fails, it affects the entire array because some portion of the overall "drive" is lost.

Mirroring (RAID 1)

The mirroring approach writes duplicate data onto a pair of drives, while reads are performed in parallel (improving read performance). IDE-type RAID 1 is fault tolerant because data is duplicated, and each drive of a mirrored pair is installed on separate connectors. The RAID controller (such as FastTrack66) performs reads using data handling techniques that distribute the workload in a more efficient manner than using a single drive. When a read request is made, the controller selects the drive positioned closest to the requested data, then looks to the *idle* drive to perform the next read access.

If one of the mirrored drives suffers a mechanical failure (such as a spindle failure) or does not respond, the remaining drive will continue to function. (This is called fault tolerance.) If one drive has a physical sector error, the mirrored drive will also continue to function. On the next reboot, the RAID software utility will display an error in the array and recommend replacing the failed drive. Users may choose to continue using their PC; however, it's often best to replace the failed drive as soon as possible.

Due to redundancy, the drive capacity of the array is half the total drive capacity. For example, two 1GB drives that have a combined capacity of 2GB would have 1GB of usable storage. With drives of different capacities, there may be unused capacity on the larger drive.

Spare Drive

Under a RAID 1 configuration, an extra *hot spare* drive can be attached to the RAID controller, but not assigned to the array. In this case, the spare drive will be put on standby. This drive will be activated to replace a failed drive that is part of the mirrored array. In most cases, a rebuild is performed automatically in the background to mirror the good drive onto the spare. At a later time, the system can be powered off, and the failed drive can be physically removed and replaced. Spare drives must be the same or larger capacity than the smallest array member.

Striping/Mirror (RAID 0+1)

As its name suggests, striping/mirror mode is a combination of the array types detailed above. It can increase performance by reading and writing data in parallel while protecting data with duplication. A minimum of four drives must be installed. With a four-drive disk array, two pairs of drives are striped, and each pair mirrors the data on the other pair of striped drives. The data capacity is similar to a standard mirroring array with half of the total capacity dedicated for redundancy.

Spanning (JBOD)

A spanning disk array (also aptly named "JBOD" for "just a bunch of drives") is equal to the sum of all drives when the drives used are of different capacities. Spanning stores data onto a drive until it is full, then proceeds to store files onto the next drive in the array. There are no major performance or fault tolerance array features in this mode. When any disk member fails, the failure affects the entire array.

Spanning may be considered for performance in certain instances. With striping, array performance is affected directly by the stripe block size. Block size should be tailored to the typical I/O on the drive, whether it is generally more random or sequential. However, if there is no predictability of the type of I/O access, and both random and sequential I/Os occur unpredictably, the performance of a striped array will fluctuate. In the end, this may result in no overall performance gain. With spanning, the performance factor simply reflects a single drive's performance level. This offers a more predictable transfer rate and allows the use of mismatched drives.

Troubleshooting a Drive Adapter

A properly configured drive adapter will rarely cause problems in a PC because BIOS, IRQ, and I/O assignments are very strongly established in the PC industry. Nevertheless, a variety of problems can plague drive adapter replacements and upgrades. This part of the chapter looks at troubleshooting IDE-type drive systems.

SYMPTOM 16-1 You cannot get the drive adapter software to install properly

When installing or upgrading drive controller software, it is not uncommon to encounter problems, usually due to the many advanced features of the drive controller itself. If you cannot get new software installed, try the following steps to overcome the problem. First, start the CMOS setup and disable the high-performance features usually related to drive controllers, such as IDE Block Mode, Multi-Sector Transfer, and 32-bit Disk Access. If there are other options for the secondary drive controller channel, try disabling them as well. You might also try moving the controller BIOS address range (for example, change the address range from C800h to CF00h).

If you still cannot get the controller software installed, there may also be trouble with "overlay software" (such as Ontrack's Disk Manager or EZ-Drive software) used to partition and format a drive. You may need to uninstall the overlay software and update the CMOS setup by enabling LBA support for the drive. If you can't uninstall the overlay software, you can run FDISK /MBR to overwrite the overlay software. Once the overlay software is removed, repartition and reformat the drive. If you cannot wipe the drive clean, check with the drive manufacturer for such a utility. You should now be able to install the new drive software.

> The above step is destructive to any data on the drive. Be sure to make a complete system backup (and have a bootable disk on hand) before removing the overlay software.

SYMPTOM 16-2 **The controller will not support a drive with more than 1024 cylinders** This often happens when building a new system or piecing together a system from used parts. In order to support a drive with more than 1024 cylinders, the controller must support a feature called LBA (Logical Block Addressing), and the feature must be enabled. The controller's onboard BIOS should support LBA, but you may need to install a driver for the controller in order to support LBA. (For example, a Promise Technologies controller needs the DOSEIDE.SYS driver to support LBA.) If the controller is integrated onto the motherboard, the motherboard BIOS must support LBA. If not, you'll need to upgrade the motherboard BIOS or install a drive adapter with an LBA-aware BIOS. Second, the hard drive itself must support LBA. Make sure the drive is an EIDE hard drive. Finally, check the CMOS setup and verify that the drive is using the LBA mode rather than the older CHS mode. You may need to repartition and reformat the hard drive.

SYMPTOM 16-3 **Loading a disk driver causes the system to hang or generate a "Bad or missing COMMAND.COM" error** This is a known problem with some versions of the DTC DTC22XX.SYS or DOSEIDE.SYS drivers, but frequently occurs with other controller makers that use disk drivers. The controller is probably transferring data *too fast* to the drive. When the disk driver loads, it obtains information from the drive, including drive speed. Sometimes the drive reports that it can support PIO mode 4 or PIO mode 3 when in actuality it cannot. In many cases, the original drivers are outdated, and the immediate solution is to slow down the data transfer rate manually. Download and install the newest drivers—until then, you may be able to add a command-line switch to the disk driver. For example, DTC recommends adding a switch to their DOSEIDE.SYS driver as in the following (where *x* is the drive designation):

```
DOSEIDE.SYS /v /dx:m0 /dx:p0
```

If your problems started after loading the disk drivers "high" (into the upper memory area), adjust CONFIG.SYS to load the drivers into conventional memory. Some drive adapters have reported better success with driver software when the "Hidden Refresh" feature is enabled in CMOS setup (in the Advanced CMOS setup area). This alters the way the system timing refreshes RAM and may better support the disk drivers. Also try disabling advanced controller options such as IDE Block Mode, Multi-Sector Transfer, and 32-bit Disk Access. Finally, if you're using overlay software (such as Disk Manager), the disk driver may not work with the overlay software. You'll then need to remove the overlay software and repartition and reformat the drive before the disk driver will work.

SYMPTOM 16-4 **Drive performance is poor—data transfer rates are slow** This often happens when installing a replacement drive controller. First, make sure you're not running any antivirus software. Antivirus utilities that load at boot time can degrade drive performance. If the controller uses a "speed" jumper, make sure you have properly configured the jumper settings on the card to match the speed of the IDE drive and processor. (This is a known issue with DTC's 2278VL and 2270 controllers.) Also make sure that the highest possible data transfer rate is selected in the CMOS setup (PIO mode 4 for older setups, or UDMA/33 or UDMA/66 in newer systems). If the drive adapter uses a disk driver for optimum performance, make sure the correct disk driver software is loaded, and see that any necessary command-line switches are entered. Finally, remove any third-party software (such as Disk Manager or EZ-Drive) that may have shipped with the drive itself.

SYMPTOM 16-5 **The PC refuses to boot after a drive adapter is installed** There are many possible reasons for this kind of problem. First make sure the drive adapter is installed properly and completely into its bus slot, and then verify that the drive signal cables are oriented and attached properly. If the drive adapter uses jumpers to match the drive and processor speeds (such as the DTC 2278VL or 2270), make sure the adapter is configured correctly. Verify that the drive itself is properly jumpered as a master or slave. Finally, check the CMOS setup and confirm that the proper drive parameters are being used. Try disabling advanced features like IDE Block Mode and 32-bit Disk Access. If the problem persists, try repartitioning and reformatting the drive.

SYMPTOM 16-6 **Windows generates a "Validation Failed 03,3F" error** This type of problem most frequently occurs after loading the Windows disk driver and is almost always due to a 1024-cylinder limit in the drive system. Make sure the drive and drive controller are able to support more than 1024 cylinders (both EIDE). Check the CMOS setup and verify that the LBA mode is selected. Once the proper hardware is configured correctly, try reinstalling the disk driver.

SYMPTOM 16-7 **Windows hangs or fails to load files after loading the controller's driver** In most cases, Windows hangs, or every file after the offending driver is unable to load. In some cases, you may see an error message such as "Cannot find KRN.386." Load SYSTEM.INI into a text editor and move the controller's driver (such as WINEIDE.386) to the last line in the [386enh] section. Also make sure the classic WDCTRL driver is commented out as in:

```
;device=*WDCTRL
```

If problems persist, the controller's driver may be old or buggy. Download and install the newest disk driver version from the controller maker. If all else fails, disable the block mode and mode speed using the driver's internal switches or setup routine. For example, the WINEIDE.386 driver provides the switch WINEIDESWITCH that you can use as shown here:

```
device=wineide.386
wineideswitch= /dx:m0 /dx:p0
```

16

SYMPTOM 16-8 **After replacing a drive adapter with a different model, the hard drive is no longer recognized** This can happen frequently with all types of IDE drives and controllers. You will find that the new controller is probably not using the same translation geometry used when the drive was originally partitioned. Verify that the drive geometry and LBA settings are as close as possible to the settings used on the older controller. You may need to use "user-defined" settings rather than "autodetect" to ensure that the geometry settings are identical. In order for the new drive adapter card to recognize an existing drive, you'll have to repartition and reformat the drive with FDISK and FORMAT. Reinstall the original controller and perform a complete system backup before continuing.

SYMPTOM 16-9 **System problems occur after installing a VL drive adapter** It is quite common for a combination of components on VL bus systems to exceed the tolerance limits for that specific motherboard. VL bus noise generated by the motherboard chipset can easily contribute to floppy disk, floppy tape, and other drive failures. This may cause the system to hang on boot-up and render it unable to access the hard drive. VESA video and controller cards also contribute to the load on the VL bus. If the load on the VL bus for a given motherboard is too high, you will see compatibility problems with VESA video cards, intermittent system crashes, and HDD controller failures. System problems can manifest themselves in a wide variety of ways, such as:

- Incompatibility with some VESA video cards (for example, devices with S3 chipsets)
- Incompatibility with Colorado floppy tape

- Floppy disk failures
- System hangs on boot or when trying to access IDE hard drive
- Drive won't hold a partition
- Performance not improved with new drive adapter
- Intermittent system crash in Windows or other graphics program
- Modem status failures

In some cases, upgrading the disk controller to a later revision VL board that causes less loading and signal issues may provide a proper solution. For an immediate solution, try rearranging the VL devices or slowing the VL bus speed to stabilize VL bus operation.

SYMPTOM 16-10 **You cannot enable 32-bit Disk Access under Windows** In most cases, you're using the wrong protected-mode driver, or the driver should be upgraded with a newer version. Download and install the latest disk drivers for your drive adapter. Before installing the new driver(s), be sure to disable advanced data transfer features such as IDE Block Mode and 32-bit Disk Access (if enabled). Load SYSTEM.INI into a text editor. Make sure the protected-mode disk driver is installed under the [386enh] section, and verify that the WDCTRL driver is remarked out. Note that many Windows drivers will not support an IBMSLC2 processor or Ontrack's Disk Manager, and will *not* work with 32-bit disk access.

SYMPTOM 16-11 **The IDE-type drive adapter's secondary port refuses to work** If the drive adapter has a secondary drive channel, that secondary channel is not working. In many cases, this type of problem occurs when the drive adapter relies on a disk driver for proper operation. Often the secondary channel must be enabled specifically through the disk driver's command line in CONFIG.SYS such as:

```
DEVICE=DOSEIDE.SYS /V /2
```

Make sure the drive attached to the secondary channel is jumpered as the master drive, and verify that the signal cable between the drive and controller is oriented properly. Also remember that a secondary drive channel requires a unique interrupt (usually IRQ 15). Make sure there is no hardware conflict between the secondary port's IRQ and other devices in the system. Try disabling advanced data transfer features in the CMOS setup like IDE Block Mode and 32-bit Disk Access. If your hard drive is an older IDE drive, it may not support Multi-Sector Transfer. Try disabling this feature in the CMOS setup, or add the necessary command-line switch to the disk driver command line in CONFIG.SYS such as:

```
DEVICE=DOSEIDE.SYS /V /2 /D0:M0
```

SYMPTOM 16-12 **The drive adapter's BIOS doesn't load** First, make sure the BIOS is enabled (usually through a jumper on the drive adapter), and see that the BIOS IC is seated correctly and completely in its socket on the drive adapter. If problems persist, try changing the BIOS address—it's probably conflicting with another BIOS in the system. Also check the IRQ and I/O port assignments for the drive adapter for possible conflicts. If all else fails, try another drive controller.

SYMPTOM 16-13 **The drive adapter BIOS loads, but the system hangs up** First make sure the drive parameters are set properly in the CMOS setup. Inexperienced users frequently mistake the parameters for a second drive in CMOS with a drive on the secondary channel. When there is no drive in the primary slave position, the second drive should be "none" or "not installed." If you have an onboard drive controller, make sure to disable it—otherwise, you'll have a hardware conflict between the two drive controllers. Check the individual drives attached to the controller and verify that each drive is jumpered as a unique master or slave device. (Try reversing the drive order or working with only one drive.) Finally, try disabling some of the advanced drive performance parameters in CMOS, such as IDE Block Mode.

SYMPTOM 16-14 **The ATAPI CD-ROM is not recognized as the slave device vs. an IDE master** First, verify that the CD-ROM is in fact ATAPI compatible and suitable for use on an IDE-type interface. Second, make sure the proper low-level ATAPI driver for the CD-ROM drive is in use. If the driver is old, try downloading and installing the newest version of the driver. If problems persist, the trouble is probably due to a fast IDE-type device coexisting with a slower IDE ATAPI device. Reconfigure the CD-ROM as the master device on the secondary drive controller channel. You may need to update the ATAPI driver command line in CONFIG.SYS.

SYMPTOM 16-15 **Hard drives are not recognized on the secondary drive controller channel** Make sure all the hard drives are jumpered correctly. If only one drive is on the secondary channel, it should be configured as the single or master drive. If there are two drives on the secondary channel, verify that the drives are jumpered as master and slave. If the drive adapter uses a disk driver to support EIDE or secondary channel operation, make sure the command line in CONFIG.SYS uses the correct switch(es) to enable the secondary drive channel. For example, the Promise Technologies 2300 would add an /S switch to the command line such as:

```
device=c:\eide2300\eide2300.sys /S
```

Check that your system's power management features are not enabled on IRQ 15 (and confirm that there are no other devices conflicting with IRQ 15). If the drive is set to "autoconfigure" in the CMOS setup, try entering the drive's parameters specifically. (The drive may be too old to understand the IDC (Identify Drive Command) needed for autoconfiguration.) Finally, try booting the system clean (with just disk driver software if necessary) to see if there are any other driver or TSR conflicts.

SYMPTOM 16-16 **The drive adapter can only support 528MB per disk** First make sure that the LBA mode is enabled. This is often accomplished through the CMOS setup, but it may also be necessary to enable an LBA support jumper on some older EIDE drive adapters. If problems persist, the drive adapter's BIOS is probably too old and should be upgraded to a new version. If you cannot upgrade the drive adapter BIOS, install a new drive adapter outright.

SYMPTOM 16-17 **You get a "code 10" error relative to the drive adapter** You notice that Windows 95/98 is running in MS-DOS Compatibility Mode, and the system only boots in Safe Mode. You'll probably find one or more devices (including the drive adapter) marked with a yellow exclamation point. Disk overlay software (such as Disk Manager, EZ-Drive, or MaxBlast) will often cause problems when used in conjunction with drive adapters that use their own disk driver software. The disk overlay must be removed *before* installing the adapter's disk drivers. Remove the overlay software, or simply repartition and reformat the drive. (Remember to do a complete backup before repartitioning.) Next, remove or disable any 32-bit disk drivers previously installed under Windows. With Promise Technologies drive adapters, you'll probably see the following under SYSTEM.INI:

```
[386enh]
device=*int13
;device=*wdctrl
```

```
;device=c:\windows\system\eide2300.386 (for eide2300plus)
;device=ontrackw.386
;device=c:\windows\system\pti13.386 (for the 4030)
;device=c:\windows\system\ptictrl.386 (for the 4030)
;device=wdcdrv.386
;device=c:\windows\system\maxi13.386 (for the eidemax)
;device=c:\windows\system\maxctrl.386 (for the eidemax)
32bitdiskaccess=off
```

When first installing the disk driver (such as the Promise Windows 95 driver), follow the steps below. (Note that some EIDE drive adapters—especially new ones—do not require special drivers.)

1. Open the Control Panel and double-click the System icon.
2. Choose Device Manager, and double-click on Hard Disk Controller.
3. Click once on the driver (standard IDE/ESDI driver), and click on Remove.
4. Reboot the computer.
5. Reopen the Control Panel and start the Add New Hardware wizard.
6. Answer No when prompted for Windows 95 to autodetect the device(s).
7. Select Hard Disk Controller, and click on Have Disk.
8. Either insert the floppy disk, or choose Browse and move to the subdirectory where the disk drivers are located.
9. Follow the prompts and choose Finish, but do not reboot the computer yet.
10. Open the Control Panel and double-click the System icon.
11. Choose Device Manager and double-click on Hard Disk Controller. Click once on the installed driver and choose Properties. Select the Resource tab. If you see Basic Configuration of 1, IRQ 15, change this to Basic Configuration of 0, IRQ 14.
12. *Now* reboot the computer so that your changes can take effect.

There may also be a DMA conflict. Some drive adapters take advantage of DMA when the parallel port is in the ECP mode. (The conflict occurs most often with the sound board.) In order to find out which devices use DMA, open the Control Panel, double-click on the System icon, select Device Manager, and double-click on Computer. Choose Direct Memory Access. You can then either switch the controller's use of DMA or disable it altogether. You may need to alter the DMA setting on the drive controller itself, then switch the parallel port's mode to EPP.

SYMPTOM 16-18 You encounter mouse problems after changing the drive adapter

This is a known problem with Logitech pointing devices or standard pointing devices using Logitech drivers. In most cases, you can correct the problem by downloading and installing version 7.0 or later Logitech drivers, or switch to the Windows 95 serial mouse driver:

1. Open the Control Panel and double-click on the System icon.
2. Select Device Manager and double-click on the Mouse.
3. Click once on Logitech and choose Remove.

4 Start the Add New Hardware wizard in the Control Panel.
5 Choose No when Windows prompts to autodetect the device.
6 Select Mouse. Click on Standard Serial Mouse. Click on Finish.
7 Reboot the computer.

Another solution may be to disable the COM port's FIFO buffer. Open the Control Panel and choose the System icon. Click on Device Manager. Double-click on Ports [COM & LPT]. Choose the communications port that the mouse uses (such as COM 1) by clicking on it once; then click on Properties. Select Port Settings and choose Advanced. Uncheck the box next to "Use FIFO buffers"; then click OK.

SYMPTOM 16-19 **You cannot run Norton Anti-Virus 95 with Promise drive adapters** This appears to be an issue with the Norton Anti-Virus (NAV) software itself. According to Symantec (**www.symantec.com**), a patch has been released that corrects this problem.

SYMPTOM 16-20 **The system hangs after counting through system memory** You may also receive error messages such as "Get Configuration Failed!" or "HDD Controller Failure." First make sure you have at least one hard drive attached to the controller, and see that the signal cable is oriented properly at both ends. It is also possible that you may have a problem when more than one drive is connected. See that the drives are jumpered in the desired master and slave relationship. Try working with only one drive, or reverse the drive relationship. In all cases, verify that the CMOS setup entries accurately reflect the drives that are connected. If your drive adapter uses onboard RAM, the RAM may be bad. Try replacing the controller's onboard RAM.

SYMPTOM 16-21 **After replacing/upgrading a VL drive adapter, the system hangs intermittently during use** This is a somewhat common complaint with VL motherboards and drive adapters, and it is often due to bad memory on the drive controller or a bad VL bus slot. Try replacing the RAM on the drive adapter. If the problem persists, try putting the drive controller in a different VL bus slot. If you have a VESA VL video card also, try swapping in a 16-bit (ISA) video card. Some motherboards may become unstable with two VL cards in the system, especially when the VL bus is being run over 33MHz. (There is a great likelihood of this happening at 50MHz.)

SYMPTOM 16-22 **There are errors reading or writing to floppies after replacing/upgrading a drive adapter** This is almost always due to a hardware conflict between the floppy adapter on the new controller and another floppy adapter elsewhere in the system. Disable the floppy adapter port on the new drive controller card. If you're using the new floppy port, disable the floppy port already in the system.

> If you cannot successfully disable a current or preexisting floppy controller, you'll need to remove the new drive controller and install a controller without a floppy port (or one that can be disabled properly).

SYMPTOM 16-23 **Your drive controller won't function with a 75MHz bus speed** This occurs because the odd bus speed results in a PCI speed of about 37.5MHz (which is higher than the 33MHz that the PCI bus is designed for). This effectively "overclocks" the PCI bus and can often result in unstable or erratic operation for sensitive PCI devices such as the drive controller. The best solution here is to drop the bus speed to 66MHz so that the clock can be divided down to 33MHz for the PCI bus.

SYMPTOM 16-24 **You cannot use APM with hard drives operated from a new drive controller** This is a known issue with high-end controllers such as the Promise FastTrack66. In most cases, this is because the system sees the new controller card as a SCSI controller. Using IDE commands for APM will not work because the card is seen as a SCSI card. SCSI commands for APM will not work because the drives are IDE.

SYMPTOM 16-25 **You can't boot from a new IDE controller if you have a SCSI card in the system already** Chances are that you'll need to tweak the setup of your new IDE controller (such as Ultra66) and existing SCSI card. If you have an actual SCSI controller in the system, the computer will attempt to boot from whichever controller is seen first. To get one controller to be seen before another, you must get its BIOS to load first. Manipulating the BIOS address that the card is set to use normally takes care of this.

However, virtually all IDE controllers are fully PnP, which means that only the PnP BIOS on the motherboard can control which resources the card uses. Generally, the PCI slot with the highest priority will be assigned the lowest BIOS address. On most motherboards, the PCI slot with the highest priority is PCI slot 1. If you cannot assign a specific memory address or loading order to your PCI devices through the CMOS setup, try inserting the IDE drive controller so that it's in PCI slot 1.

SYMPTOM 16-26 **EMM386 fails to load after installing a new IDE controller** This is a known issue with some Promise IDE controllers (such as the FastTrack66) and is caused by the way the motherboard handles memory. There is no work-around for this problem at the moment, but check for an updated controller BIOS from the manufacturer. If there is no update available, you'll need to disable the use of EMM386.

SYMPTOM 16-27 **You cannot get QuickBooks 5.0 to start with an IDE controller in the system** This is a known issue with some Promise controllers such as the Ultra33 and is caused by the controller's driver. I have found that if you use the Ultra33 driver version 1.33 and set it to Business mode with the UltraTune utility, QuickBooks will start. You can download this driver version from **ftp://ftp.promise.com/Controllers/IDE/U33_133.zip**.

SYMPTOM 16-28 **You find that your IDE controller is conflicting with the USB controller** This is a BIOS problem with the IDE controller itself. Check to see if a new BIOS version is available for your controller. For a Promise Ultra66, a new BIOS has been released to fix the conflict. You can download the BIOS from **ftp://ftp.promise.com/Controllers/IDE/Ultra66/U66_0628.zip**.

Further Study

DTC: **http://www.datatechnology.com**

Adaptec: **http://www.adaptec.com**

Advansys: **http://www.advansys.com**

Promise Technologies: **http://www.promise.com**

17

DVD DRIVES

CHAPTER AT A GLANCE

The *compact disc* opened up a whole new world of possibilities for the PC. These simple, mass-produced plastic discs could hold up to an hour of stereo music, or as much as 650MB of computer programs and data. Software makers quickly found the CD-ROM to be an outstanding medium for all types of multimedia applications, large databases, and interactive games. But today, the CD-ROM is showing its age, and a single CD no longer provides enough storage for the increasing demands of data-intensive applications. A new generation of high-density optical storage called *DVD* is now widely available for the desktop PC (Figure 17-1). DVD stands for "digital versatile disc" (because it can hold programs and data as

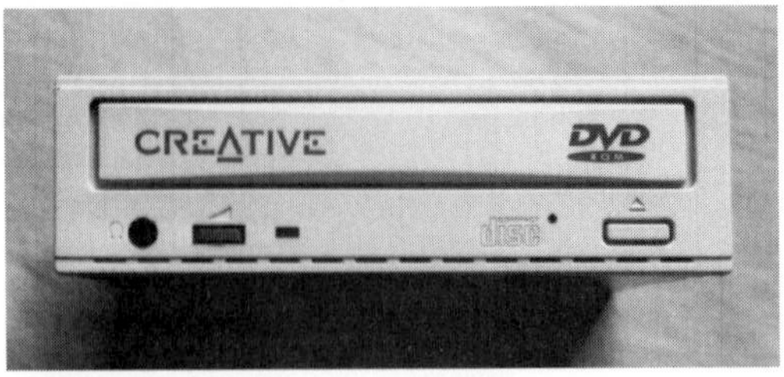

FIGURE 17-1 A DVD-ROM drive

well as video and sound). But whatever you call it, DVD technology promises to supply up to 17GB of removable storage on your desktop PC. This chapter covers the background and workings of a DVD package, shows you the steps for DVD installation, and offers a series of basic troubleshooting solutions.

The Potential of DVD

The argument for DVD is a compelling one because having gigabytes of removable storage to work with opens up some exciting possibilities for entertainment and software development. As DVD works its way into the marketplace, you're going to see two designations: DVD-Video and DVD-ROM. DVD-Video is the approach used to store movies on the disc (analogous to the way audio is placed on CDs). Eventually, DVD-Video is expected to replace videotape players in home entertainment. DVD-ROM refers to computer-based software and data recorded on the disc. Where audio CDs can be played on CD-ROM drives, DVD-Video discs will be playable on DVD-ROM drives in your PC. Understandably, there are a lot of players interested in making the most of what DVD has to offer:

- Hollywood has been a major factor in the development of DVD-Video, placing full-length movies, sound tracks, and even multilingual subtitling on a single disc. Since all DVD discs are read by laser, there is no physical contact between the disc and its player. The result is that the disc won't wear out like VHS videotapes.
- Business presentations, education, and professional training will also benefit from DVD technology. Animations, charts, and interactive applets can be integrated with real-time video. This offers a truly immersive training experience that has never been fully realized by CD-ROM technology.
- Applications for archiving are limitless. Mapping programs, telephone directories, encyclopedias—any software that now spans several CDs—can be concentrated on one DVD disc and expanded to offer unprecedented detail.
- Any data-intensive computer software (especially 3D and other interactive games) will get a real boost from the sheer storage volume offered by DVD-ROM.

Specifications and Standards

The next step in exploring DVD is to understand the various specifications "on the box" and to become familiar with the specifications that make DVD work and what a DVD will support. You don't need a lot of technical details, but you should recognize the most important points that you'll probably run across while reading documentation.

ACCESS TIME

The *access time* is the time required for the drive to locate the required information on a disc. Optical drives like CD and DVD drives are relatively slow, and can demand up to several hundred milliseconds to access information. For a DVD drive like the Creative Labs (Matsushita) DVD drive, access time is 470ms (almost half a second), while access time for an ordinary CD is 180ms. The reason DVDs require so much more time is because of the greater density of data. However, not all drives are as slow. The Toshiba DVD drive bundled with Diamond Multimedia's Maximum DVD Kit quotes a DVD access time of only 200ms (130ms for CDs).

DATA TRANSFER RATES

Once data has been accessed, it must be transferred off the disc to the system. The *data transfer rate* measures how fast data can be read from the disc. There are two typical means of measuring the data rate: the speed at which data is read into the drive's onboard buffer (the *sequential* data transfer rate), and the speed at which data is transferred across the interface to the drive controller (the *buffered* data transfer rate). The Creative Labs (Matsushita) DVD drive offers a sequential data transfer rate of 1.35MB/s, and 900KB/s for an ordinary CD (about equal to a 6X CD-ROM drive). By comparison the drive can support buffered data transfer rates of 8.3MB/s (DMA mode 2), 13.3MB/s (DMA mode 1), or 11.1MB/s (PIO mode 3). As a result, the DVD-ROM drive is compatible with most EIDE (and later) drive controllers in the marketplace today.

BOOKS AND STANDARDS

CD technology is defined by a set of accepted standards, which we have come to know as "books." Since each CD book was bound in a different colored jacket, each standard is named by color. For example, the standard that defines CD audio is called Red Book. Similarly, DVD technology is defined by a set of books. There are five books (labeled A through E) that relate to different DVD technology applications:

- *Book A* defines the format and approach used for DVD-ROM (programs and data).
- *Book B* defines DVD-Video.
- *Book C* defines DVD-Audio (this specification is still under development).
- *Book D* defines DVD-WO (write once).
- *Book E* defines DVD-E (erasable or rewritable) and DVD-RAM.

DATA FORMATS

All DVD discs must use a data format that describes how data is laid out. Data formats are critical because they outline data structures on the disc such as volumes, files, blocks, sectors, CRCs, paths, records, File Allocation Tables, partitions, character sets, time stamps, as well as methods for reading and writing. The format used by books A, B, and C is called the *UDF Bridge*. The UDF Bridge is a combination of the UDF (Universal Disk Format created by OSTA—the Optical Storage Technology Association) and the established ISO 9660 format used for CDs. You may see the UDF referred to as standard ISO/IEC 13346. The UDF is a very flexible format that has been adapted to DVD, and made backward compatible to existing ISO 9660 operating system software (such as Windows 95/98). Actual utilization of this disk system on DVD discs will depend in large part on what Microsoft dictates as the future operating system standard. Stand-alone DVD movie players are supposed to use UDF. With the release of Windows 98, the UDF Bridge has been abandoned in favor of full UDF support.

AUDIO AND VIDEO STANDARDS

Even with the huge data capacities offered by DVD, an entire movie's worth of real-time audio and video would never fit on a DVD without some form of compression. Both audio and video must be extensively compressed, and MPEG (Motion Pictures Experts Group) compression has been the scheme of choice. Video compression uses fixed data rate MPEG-1 (ISO/IEC 1117-2) at 30 frames per second with resolutions of 352 x 240, or variable data rate MPEG-2 (ISO/IEC 13818-2) at 60 frames per second with resolutions of 720 x 480. Audio compression uses MPEG-1 (ISO/IEC 1117-3) stereo, MPEG-2 (ISO/IEC 13818-3) 5.1 and 7.1 surround sound, or Dolby AC-3 5.1 surround and stereo. MPEG-2 and AC-3 audio compression allow 48 thousand samples per second, whereas MPEG-1 allows only 44.1 thousand samples per second. MPEG-2 compression is typically regarded as the preferred scheme for DVD.

> The audio designations "5.1" and "7.1" indicate five (or seven) signal channels, plus one subwoofer channel.

Content Protection

One of the problems with electronic media is that it's easy to transfer and manipulate. Copyright laws prohibit the unauthorized use of electronic media, but with the ease of electronic data transfers, companies are constantly devising new ways to protect and control the distribution of their intellectual property. There are several approaches in place to manage content protection.

Region Code Control Motion picture studios want to control the home release of movies in different countries because theater releases are not simultaneous. Therefore, they have required that the DVD standard include codes that can be used to prevent playback of certain discs in certain geographical regions. Each player is given a code for the region in which it's sold. The player won't play discs that are not allowed in that region. This means that discs bought in one country may not play on players bought in another country. Table 17-1 lists the code numbers and the regions each number covers. Keep in mind that region codes are entirely optional, and discs without codes will play on any player in any country.

Macrovision 7 Macrovision 7 is a proprietary piracy protection scheme that utilizes the signal in the nondisplayed region of a video signal to prevent copying. Macrovision varies the signal that controls the automatic gain control (AGC) of a recording deck, thereby washing out and darkening the recording signal of a tape or DVD disc being recorded.

Copy Generation Management System (CGMS) DVD-Video discs may contain information that can be used to prevent copying of the disc on equipment (such as a VCR) if the VCR is equipped with

TABLE 17-1 DVD REGION CODES

CODE	REGION
1	Canada, U.S., and U.S. territories
2	Japan, Europe, South Africa, Middle East (including Egypt)
3	Southeast Asia, East Asia (including Hong Kong)
4	Australia, New Zealand, Pacific Islands, Central America, South America, Caribbean
5	Former Soviet Union, Indian Subcontinent, Africa (also North Korea, Mongolia)
6	China

a Copy Generation Management System (CGMS). Several video recorder manufacturers have adopted CGMS, which works by embedding a signal in the video image in an area of the screen. (This area is not normally seen by viewers.) CGMS does not work unless both the player and recorder allow the signal to be present during playback.

> The importance of CGMS is expected to increase as Universal Serial Bus (USB) and Firewire (IEEE 1394) become widespread with newer computers. Both technologies will support a digital form of the CGMS standard to prevent digital copying of movies.

Content Scrambling System (CSS) To protect its movie titles from being copied in perfect digital fidelity, the motion picture industry endorses a key-based data encryption system called Content Scrambling System (or CSS). Operation involves authentication of the device, the exchange of keys, and decryption of the DVD content. Some PC-DVD solutions include hardware decryption integrated within the decoder board.

Digital Video Express (Divx) Digital Video Express (or Divx) is a proprietary encoding scheme principally sponsored by consumer electronics retailer Circuit City and the law firm of Ziffren, Brittenham, Branca, and Fischer. This requires users to have a Divx player for playback and a dial-up connection. Divx players are more expensive than DVD players (costing nearly $100 more than a standard DVD player) and did not reach the market until February of 1998.

After purchasing a Divx DVD disc—a suggested retail price of $4.99—the disc will play back for a 48-hour period starting when the disc is inserted in the drive. Once the 48 hours have passed, the player will no longer play the disc. Not only will the disc be unplayable, the player automatically registers the disc online when it's inserted in the player. Disconnecting the Divx player from the phone line renders the player unusable until it's reconnected to the Divx online service. The disc also may not be played in any other player unless the user chooses to connect and buy more time (a.k.a. "pay for view"), or the user pays to completely unlock the disc.

Regular DVD players are unable to access a Divx disc because the access coding method directs playback *first* to an embedded instruction that is not recognized by normal DVD players. The normal DVD player will display an error indicating that there are no playable files on the disc.

> The Divx scheme has largely fallen into disuse today because of lingering problems involving Divx disc and player compatibility.

CD COMPATIBILITY

One of the most important aspects of any technology is backward compatibility—how well the new device will support existing media. The same issue is true for DVD drives. Since DVD technology is designed as an improvement over existing CD-ROMs, the DVD was designed to *replace* the CD-ROM rather than coexist with it. Ideally, you'd remove your CD-ROM and replace it with a DVD-ROM drive. This means the DVD must be compatible with as many existing CD-ROM standards as possible. A typical DVD-ROM drive will support CD audio, CD-ROM, CD-I, CD Extra, CD-ROM/XA, and Video CD formats. Multisession formats such as Photo CD are not yet supported on all DVD drives (especially older DVD drive models).

> One notable format that may not be supported by older DVD drives is the CD-R (recordable CD) format. The laser used in older DVD drives could not read the CD-R, and in some cases, may even damage the CD-R disc. However, developments in CD-R discs and DVD drive design have largely overcome this problem.

Aspect Ratios

Aspect ratio refers to the width-to-height ratio of a television image. Traditional television sets have always conformed to the 4:3 ratio (roughly square in appearance). Wide-screen displays with a 16:9 or 20:9 ratio appear more rectangular. DVD technology brings more versatility to on-screen viewing by incorporating four different display capabilities. Video can be stored on a DVD disc in a standard TV 4:3 format or 16:9 wide screen. DVD players can output video in the following four ways:

- Full frame 4:3 video (for 4:3 display)
- Letterbox 16:9 video (for 4:3 display)
- Pan and scan 16:9 video (for 4:3 display)
- Wide screen 16:9 video (for 16:9 display)

Full-frame video is generally normal television footage converted for storage on DVD disc. This would include most television shows on the market today and movies that have been converted for television viewing.

When viewing a movie in letterbox mode, the player adds black bars to the top and bottom of the image. The image is then filtered so that the remaining area of the screen is filled in, allowing the viewer to see the movie in the same aspect as it appeared in the theater. With NTSC titles, this results in an image consisting of 360 lines—the image still contains a third more viewable lines than VHS tape, which consists of 242 viewable lines.

Pan and scan can either be automatic or manual sideways panning in a movie. Automatic pan and scan will change the camera view based upon a prerecorded selection made by the producer of the DVD disc. Manual pan and scan allows viewers to choose between different camera viewpoints at their leisure. Like other features (such as language selection), the publisher of the disc must incorporate the feature for it to be available to the viewer.

With zooming (often confused with pan and scan), the hardware will store a portion of the screen in memory and then allow a user to dynamically enlarge that portion of the screen. Usually, the zoomed image will be enhanced so that it does not appear grainy when enlarged. Zooming is *not* a feature supported by the DVD standard.

The wide-screen mode is often compared to letterbox mode when viewed on a computer monitor or television, but it's not the same thing. TVs and monitors are designed to a standard 4:3 ratio, and the displayed image will be put into a letterbox when displayed on the screen. Look carefully at the top and bottom of a wide-screen image—there will be a few extra black lines added. The black lines were added when the movie was mastered to DVD because movie film does not exactly match the 16:9 screen ration of wide screen. (Movies are slightly wider.)

Unlike letterbox images, wide-screen movies do not sacrifice vertical resolution to fill the display area. On a high-resolution computer monitor, it would be easy to see the crispness of the image compared to a letterboxed image. If the player did not letterbox the image (and the image were allowed to fill the whole screen), the characters in the movie would seem stretched to appear very tall and skinny. As wide-screen digital television becomes more available, wide-screen movies will be able to play back to their full height and width without the letterbox.

TABLE 17-2 SPECIFICATIONS OF DVD AND CD MEDIA

SPECIFICATION	DVD	CD-ROM
Diameter (mm)	120	120
Disc Thickness (mm)	1.2	1.2
Substrate Thickness (mm)	0.6	1.2
Track Pitch (μm)	0.74	1.6
Minimum Pit Size (μm)	0.4	0.83
Wavelength (nm)	635/650	780
Single Layer Capacity (GB)	4.7	0.65

DVD Media

At its core, DVD technology is identical to classical CD-ROMs—data is recorded in a spiral pattern as a series of pits and lands pressed into a plastic substrate. The actual size and dimensions of a DVD are identical to our current compact discs. However, there are some key differences that give DVD its advantages. First, data is highly concentrated on the disc. Where classical CDs use spiral tracks that are 1.6μm apart, DVD tracks are only 0.74μm apart. A typical pit on a classic CD is 0.83μm, but DVD pits are just 0.4μm. Table 17-2 compares the specifications for DVD and CD media. In short, the data on a DVD is *much* denser than on a regular CD. (Figure 17-2 illustrates the differences between DVDs and CDs.) In order to

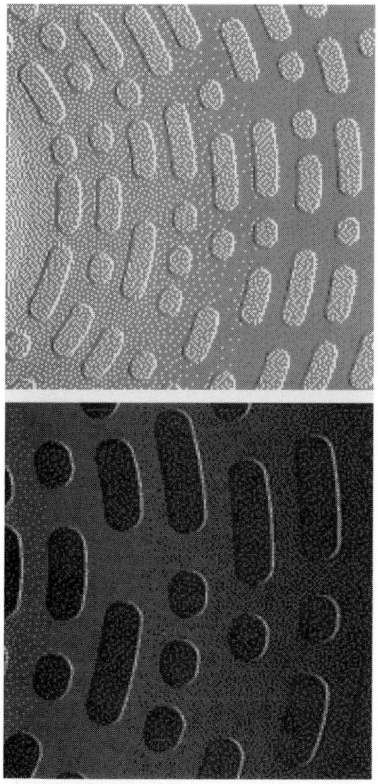

An example of DVD pits and lands

An example of ordinary CD pits and lands

FIGURE 17-2 Comparison of DVD and CD data density

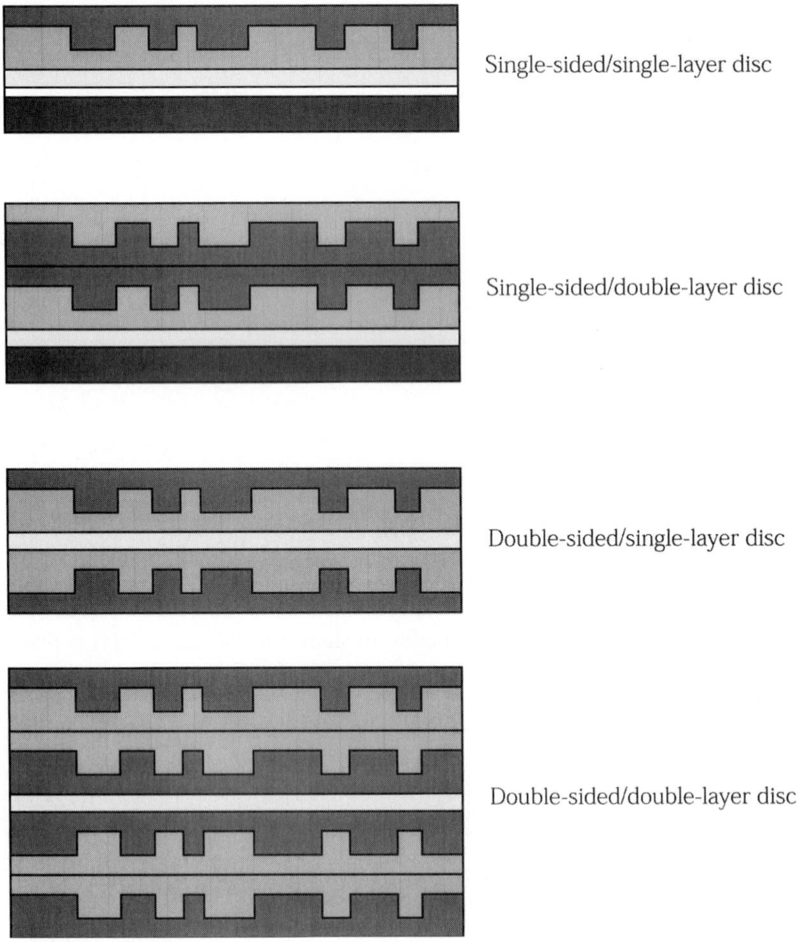

FIGURE 17-3 Layers and sides in DVD discs

detect these smaller geometries, the laser used in a DVD operates at a much shorter wavelength (a short-wavelength red laser).

Second, DVD can employ multiple layers of pits and lands (each in its own reflective layer), so one physical disk can hold several layers worth of data. The DVD drive's laser focus control can select which layer to read. Finally, a regular CD only uses one side of the disc, but both sides of the DVD can be used. Combined with this multilayer technique, the DVD can supply up to four layers of data to a DVD drive (Figure 17-3). In practice, DVD-ROM discs will likely only use one side of the disc—at least for a while. What all this means is that a DVD disc can offer up to 8.5GB of storage for a single-sided double-layer disc, or up to 17GB of storage for a double-sided double-layer disc.

CARING FOR A DVD DISC

As with CDs, a DVD disc is a remarkably reliable long-term storage medium. (Conservative estimates of the life of a DVD disc are about 100 years.) However, the longevity of an optical disc is affected by its storage and handling. A faulty CD can cause file and data errors that you might otherwise interpret as a defect in the drive itself. You can get the most life out of your optical disc by obeying the following rules:

- *Don't bend the disc.* Polycarbonate is a forgiving material, but you risk cracking or snapping (and thus ruining) the disc.
- *Don't heat the disk.* Remember, the disc is plastic. Leaving it by a heater or on the dashboard of your car will cause melting.
- *Don't scratch the disc.* Laser wavelengths have a tendency to "look past" minor scratches, but a major scratch can cause problems. Be especially careful of circular scratches (one that follows the spiral track). A circular scratch can easily wipe out entire segments of data, which would be unrecoverable.
- *Don't use chemicals on the disc.* Chemicals containing solvents such as ammonia, benzene, acetone, carbon tetrachloride, or chlorinated cleaning solvents can easily damage the plastic surface.

Eventually, a buildup of excessive dust or fingerprints can interfere with the laser beam enough to cause disc errors. When this happens, the disc can be cleaned easily using a dry, soft, lint-free cloth. Hold the disc from its edges and wipe radially (from hub to edge). *Do not wipe in a circular motion.* For stubborn stains, moisten the cloth in a bit of fresh isopropyl alcohol. (*Do not use water.*) Place the cleaned disc in a caddie or jewel case for transport and storage.

Contrary to popular belief, DVD discs are not more sensitive to scratches or dust than ordinary CDs.

DVD Drives

A DVD drive looks almost identical to a CD-ROM drive in size, shape, and layout. In fact, if not for the "DVD" logo on the tray, you'll probably mistake a DVD-ROM drive for a CD-ROM drive. The front of a DVD drive (Figure 17-4) carries all of the standard features that you'd find on any CD-ROM. A motorized *disc tray* loads and unloads the disc. You can close or open the tray by toggling the Eject button. It's interesting to note that the Creative Labs DVD-ROM won't eject a disc that is "locked" by a software application (such as a running movie). You will need to close your DVD application before ejecting the locked disc. The

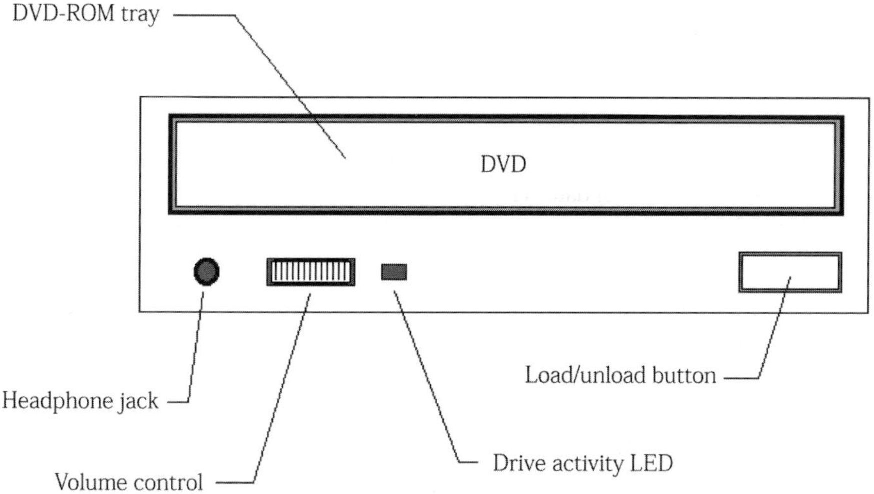

FIGURE 17-4 Front view of a DVD-ROM drive

Busy indicator lights whenever data is being read from the drive. Since the DVD drive also supports CD audio, you can connect headphones to the headphone jack and adjust volume right from the front panel.

Much of the rear of a DVD-ROM will also probably look familiar (Figure 17-5). Power is connected through a 4-pin Molex connector, so you can use any suitable power connector from your power supply. The signal connector, which is typically either EIDE/UDMA (40-pin) or SCSI (50-pin), connects the drive directly to your existing drive adapter. Unlike early CD-ROM drives, DVD-ROM drives do not use proprietary drive controllers. A series of small jumpers allows you to set the drive's identity. For SCSI-type drives, you can set the SCSI ID (usually ID2 through ID6). For EIDE or UDMA-type drives, you will set the drive as either a primary (master) or secondary (slave) drive. If you're running an EIDE/UDMA DVD-ROM along with a hard drive, the hard drive would typically be the master device, and the DVD-ROM drive would be the slave device. If you're running the DVD-ROM drive alone, set it as the master device. Finally, there are two audio output connectors: a 4-pin CD audio connector that attaches to a sound board, and a 2-pin digital audio connector that supplies sound to a digital audio tape (DAT) or other digital recording system.

Since DVD drives almost always use EIDE/UDMA interfaces rather than older IDE interfaces, they may be used along with fast EIDE hard drives on the same EIDE controller channel with no (or negligible) degradation in drive performance.

INSIDE THE DRIVE

Things get a little more interesting when you look inside the DVD-ROM drive (Figure 17-6). Looking in from the top of the drive, you'll see the major subassemblies needed to operate the drive. That black circular wheel near the tray is the *spindle motor* that turns the disc. You can also see the laser assembly and the *laser sled* that the laser rides back and forth on. A small motor drives a screw that runs the sled. The load/unload mechanics run the disc tray in and out (though the mechanical parts are obscured below the

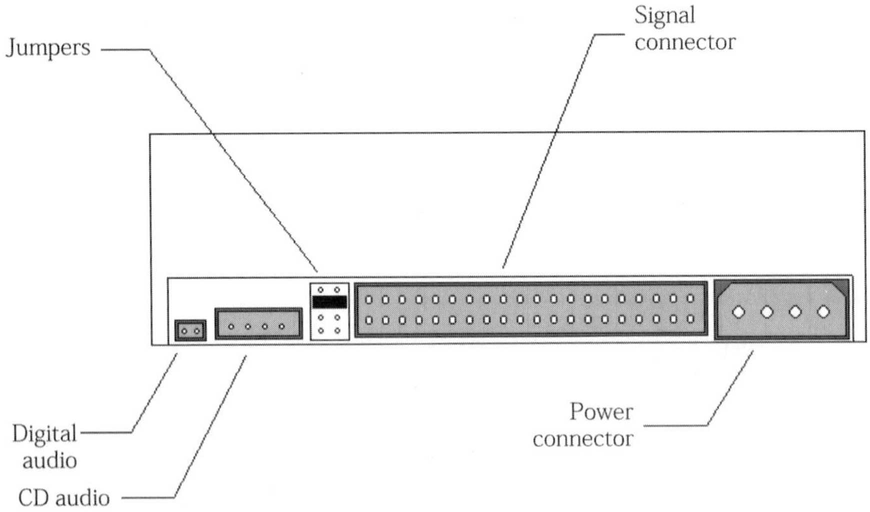

FIGURE 17-5 Rear view of a DVD-ROM drive

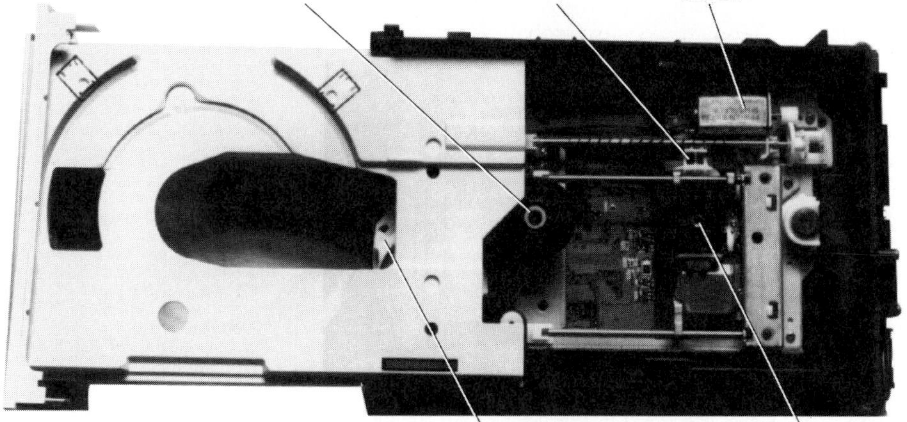

FIGURE 17-6 Looking into the top of a DVD-ROM drive

plastic tray). The main electronics deck is mounted on the underside of the drive (Figure 17-7). This is a single printed circuit board that contains all of the circuitry needed to run the drive interface, load/unload motor, audio amplifiers, spindle motor, laser, and laser sled.

REGION CODE CONTROL

One item of particular interest in Figure 17-7 is the removable chip. This chip contains firmware for the drive, as well as the *region codes* for the drive. As mentioned earlier, motion picture studios want to control the home release of movies in different countries because theater releases are not simultaneous. Therefore, they have required that the DVD standard include codes that can be used to prevent playback of certain discs in certain geographical regions. Each player is given a code for the region in which it's sold. The player won't play discs that are not allowed in that region. This means that discs bought in one country may not play on players bought in another country. Table 17-1 earlier in the chapter lists the code numbers and the regions each number covers. Keep in mind that region codes are entirely optional, and discs without codes will play on any player in any country.

The MPEG-2 Decoder Board

Although the DVD drive requires a SCSI or EIDE/UDMA drive controller for normal program data, DVD video and audio do *not* use this data path. There are two reasons for this. First, the data required to reproduce real-time video and audio would bog down even the fastest PC. Second, video and audio data are highly compressed using MPEG standards, so even if the PC bus isn't bogged down by the compressed data, the decompression process would load down the system with processing overhead. In order to play DVD audio and video (DVD-Video), DVD-ROM drives require a stand-alone, hardware-based

FIGURE 17-7 Looking at the bottom of a DVD-ROM drive

PCI bus MPEG-2 decoder board, such as the one in Figure 17-8. This MPEG-2 decoder board works *independently* of the drive controller system, video system, and sound system.

A LOOK AT MPEG-2

When the original video source is recorded for DVD, MPEG-2 analyzes the video picture for redundant data. In fact, over 95 percent of the digital data that represents a video signal is redundant and can be compressed without visibly harming the picture quality (also referred to as *loss-less compression*). By eliminating redundant data, MPEG-2 achieves excellent video quality at far lower bit rates.

MPEG-2 encoding for DVD is a two-stage process. The original signal is first evaluated for complexity; then higher bit rates are assigned to complex pictures, and lower bit rates are assigned to simple pictures. This allows for an "adaptive" variable bit-rate process. The DVD-Video format uses compressed bit rates with a range of up to 10Mbits/s. Although the average bit rate for digital video is often quoted as

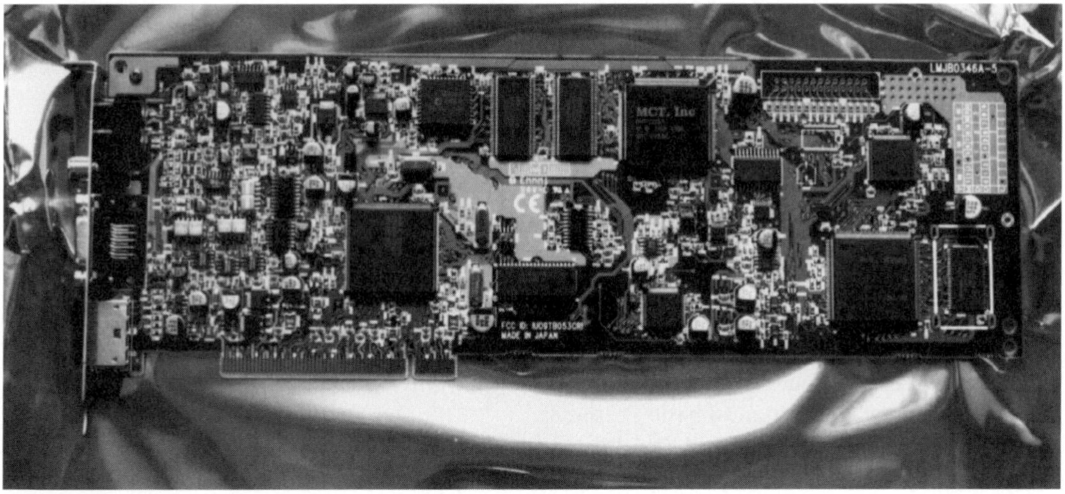

FIGURE 17-8 An MPEG-2 board for DVD video and audio playback

3.5Mbits/s, the actual figure will vary according to movie length, picture complexity, and the number of audio channels required. With MPEG-2 compression, a single-layer, single-sided DVD disc has enough capacity to hold 2 hours and 13 minutes of video and audio on a 12 cm disc. At the nominal average data rate of 3.5Mbits/s, this still leaves enough capacity for discrete 5.1 channel digital sound in three languages, plus subtitles in four additional languages.

SOFTWARE DVD DECODERS

Although a hardware decoder card is highly recommended, it is not always required—decoding can be accomplished using software applications. The advantage of software decoding is simplicity. DVD upgrades are easier since you don't need the hardware decoder card. However, considering the amount of processing power required for real-time MPEG-2 decoding, you will need a very fast Pentium II/III platform in order to sustain an adequate DVD-Video frame rate. Slower PCs (or other processing overhead such as running background applications) may not be able to support software-only decoding. This may manifest itself as choppy video, lost frames, and/or distorted audio. Make certain that your PC meets the minimum system requirements (preferably the recommended system configuration) for DVD decoding software.

If your PC does not meet the minimum requirements for decoding software, you may wish to update your video card to a model that offers motion compensation, or other types of DVD playback assistance. For example, various ATI graphics chips (including the Rage 128, Rage PRO, and Rage LT PRO) contain DVD-processing hardware that can assist in decoding DVD without the need for a full-blown hardware decoder card. Still, if you need to consider a video card upgrade, it is often more efficient to leave the video device in place and add a full hardware decoder card instead.

NOTES ON DOLBY AC-3

Dolby AC-3 (also called Dolby Surround AC-3 or Dolby Digital) is another method of encoding DVD audio besides MPEG-2 audio. With five channels and a common subwoofer channel (known as "5.1"), you get the effects of 3D surround sound with right, left, center, left ear, right ear, and common subwoofer speakers. AC-3 runs at 384Kbits/s. In actual practice, DVD products sold in North America and Japan will include Dolby AC-3 sound on the accompanying MPEG-2 board, while DVD products sold in Europe will likely use the MPEG-2 audio standard.

DECODER BOARD CONNECTIONS

There are five major connections on the MPEG-2 decoder board, as shown in Figure 17-9: an analog input jack, an analog output jack, a digital output jack, a monitor connector, and a video input connector. The analog input is rarely (if ever) used in normal operations, but it may be handy for mixing in an auxiliary audio signal to the decoder board. The analog output signal provides the master audio signal that is fed to the line input of your existing sound board. The advantage of using a line input is that you don't need a volume control on the decoder board. Instead, you can set the line input volume through your sound board's mixer applet. When you play a DVD video, any audio will continue to play through your sound board and speakers. The digital output is intended to drive an external Dolby Digital device, so you will probably not be using the digital output in most basic PC setups.

The MPEG-2 decoder board will now drive your VGA/SVGA monitor through the monitor connector. This is important because the decoded video stream is converted to RGB information and fed to the monitor directly. This avoids having to pass the video data across the PCI bus to your video card. The normal output from your video card is looped from your video board to the decoder card; so while the decoder board is idle, your normal video signal is just "passed through" the MPEG-2 board to the monitor.

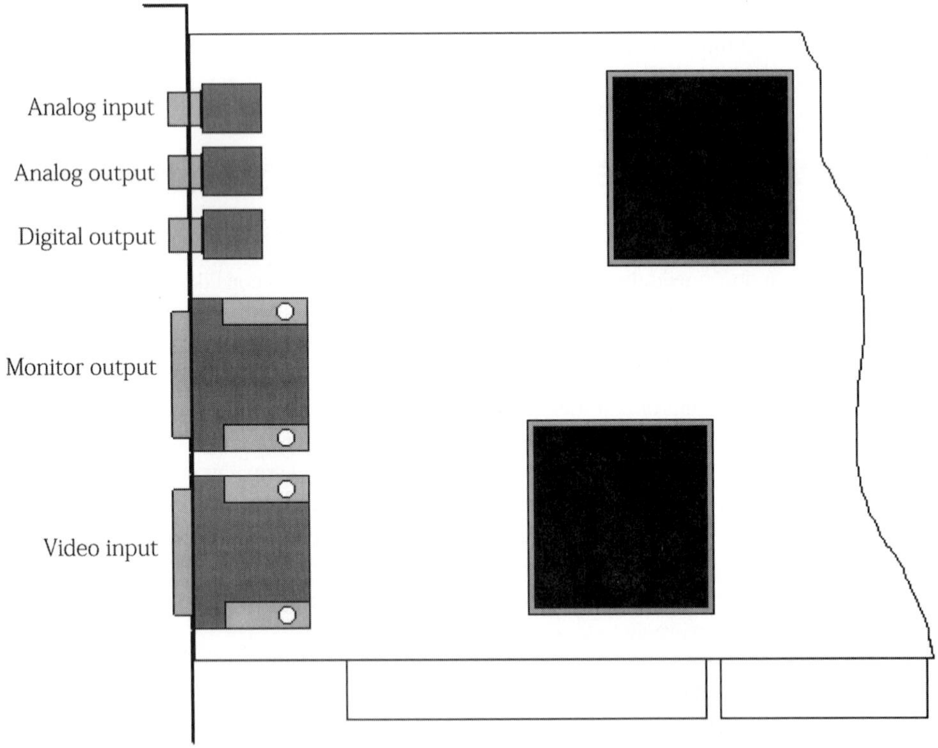

FIGURE 17-9 Decoder board connections

DVD-ROM Installation and Replacement

DVD-ROM drives are generally easy devices to install or replace. Most are installed as master devices located on the secondary EIDE/UDMA drive controller channel, though a few will coexist as slave devices alongside a hard drive or other drive device. The most important issue to remember is that the BIOS will not support the DVD-ROM directly (even if the BIOS identifies the DVD-ROM at boot time). You'll need real-mode drivers for the DVD-ROM under DOS, or protected-mode drivers for the DVD-ROM under Windows 95/98. Keep in mind that real-mode (DOS) drivers for DVD-ROM drives are extremely rare, so be sure that your particular DVD offers real-mode drivers before making a purchase. This part of the chapter covers the guidelines needed to install a basic internal ATAPI IDE-type DVD-ROM.

> Before beginning the installation, be sure to set the display mode to 640 x 480 x 16 (60Hz refresh rate) or other default video mode as suggested by the DVD maker's installation instructions. Once the DVD drive is installed and running, you can readjust the video mode to an appropriate resolution, color depth, and vertical refresh rate.

SELECT JUMPER CONFIGURATIONS

An IDE-type DVD-ROM drive may be installed as a master or slave device on any hard drive controller channel. These master/slave settings are handled through one or two jumpers located on the rear of the drive (right next to the 40-pin signal cable connector). One of your first decisions when planning an installation should be to decide the drive's configuration:

- If you're installing the DVD-ROM as the first drive on the secondary drive controller channel, it must be jumpered as the master device.
- If you're installing the DVD-ROM drive alongside another drive (on either the primary or secondary drive controller channel), the DVD-ROM must be jumpered as the slave device.

> Refer to the documentation that accompanies your particular DVD-ROM drive to determine the exact master/slave jumper settings. If you do not have the drive documentation handy, check the drive manufacturer's Web site for online information.

ATTACH CABLES AND MOUNT THE DRIVE

1. Turn off and unplug the PC; then remove the outer cover to expose the computer's drive bays.
2. Attach one end of the 40-pin drive interface cable to the drive controller connector on your motherboard (or drive controller card). Remember to align pin 1 on the cable (the side of the cable with the blue or red stripe) with pin 1 on the drive controller connector.
3. Locate an available drive bay for the DVD-ROM drive. Remove the plastic housing covering the drive bay, and slide the drive inside. Locate the four screw holes needed to mount the drive. In some cases, you may need to attach mounting rails to the drive so that the drive will be wide enough to fit in the drive bay. In virtually all cases, you should mount a tray-driven DVD-ROM drive horizontally (though caddy-loaded DVD-ROM drives may be mounted vertically).

4 Attach the 40-pin signal cable and the 4-pin power connector to the new drive, and then bolt the drive securely into place. Do not overtighten the screws since this may damage the drive. If you do not have an available 4-pin power connector, you may use an appropriate Y-splitter if necessary to "split" power from another drive (preferably the floppy drive).

5 Attach the small 4-pin digital audio (a.k.a. CD audio) signal cable from the DVD-ROM to the CD audio input connector on your sound card. This connection allows you to play music CDs directly from the DVD-ROM through your sound card. Verify that the CD audio cable is compatible with your sound card. (Otherwise, you may need a specialized cable from the sound card's manufacturer.)

> If you already have a CD-ROM drive in the system providing CD audio to the sound card, you may choose to use the DVD-ROM instead, or leave the CD-ROM's audio cable alone. If your sound card has a second CD audio connector, you may be able to wire the DVD-ROM's audio to your sound card also.

INSTALLING THE DECODER CARD

Locate an open PCI card slot, and install the PnP MPEG-2 decoder card into the slot. In most cases, you simply need to disconnect the monitor from the video output, attach the monitor to the decoder card's monitor output port, and then use a short pass-through cable to connect the video output to the decoder card's video input connector. This ties in the decoder card with the video system.

> If you'll be using a software decoder, you may not need to install a hardware decoder card, and this part of the installation may be omitted.

CONFIGURING THE CMOS SETUP

Although the DVD-ROM does require driver support, recent motherboard designs can identify the ATAPI IDE DVD-ROM drive in BIOS, so you should configure your computer's BIOS to accept the drive if possible (through the CMOS setup).

1 Turn the computer on. As your computer starts, watch for a message that describes how to run the CMOS setup (for example, "Press F1 for Setup"). Press the appropriate key to start the CMOS setup program.

2 Select the "hard drive settings" menu, and choose the drive location occupied by the DVD-ROM drive (for example, "primary slave," "secondary slave," or "secondary master" depending on how you've physically jumpered and installed the drive).

3 Select "automatic drive detection" if available. This option will automatically identify the new drive. If your BIOS does not provide automatic drive detection, select NONE or NOT INSTALLED for the DVD-ROM, and rely on drivers only.

4 Save the settings and exit the CMOS setup program. Your computer will automatically reboot.

REASSEMBLE THE COMPUTER

Double-check all of your signal and power cables to verify that they are secure; then tuck the cables gently into the computer's chassis. Check that there are no loose tools, screws, or cables inside the chassis. Now reattach the computer's outer housing(s).

INSTALL THE SOFTWARE

To complete your DVD-ROM installation, you'll need to install the software drivers that accompanied the drive on floppy disk or CD. Windows 95 OSR2 and Windows 98 systems will generally detect the presence of the new DVD-ROM (and hardware decoder if appropriate) and prompt you for the protected-mode drivers automatically. After you install the drivers and reboot the system, the DVD-ROM should be ready for use. Before you can play DVD movie discs, you'll also need to install the DVD player software (such as Zoran SoftDVD) and other utilities from the drive's installation disc.

> Many DVD-ROM drives will not support real-mode (DOS) drivers, so they will only work under Windows 95/98.

UPGRADING DVD-ROM FIRMWARE

You may be able to update the firmware used in your DVD-ROM drive. This may be necessary to correct bugs or fix drive compatibility problems with the system. The steps below offer a guideline that you can refer to when upgrading DVD-ROM firmware.

> You should always refer to the Web page or README file that accompanies the new firmware download. Be sure to download the correct firmware version for your drive. Installing the wrong firmware can permanently disable the drive.

1. Power-off your system completely.
2. Locate the DVD-ROM drive and place its "flash" jumper in the flash upgrade position. If there is no flash jumper, it may not be possible to upgrade the drive's firmware.
3. Make sure the power cable and the signal cable (SCSI or IDE) are still connected.
4. Power-on your system and boot clean to a command-line prompt.
5. Make sure that the DVD-ROM appears in program mode. You'll need to refer to the documentation for your particular drive in order to identify the correct program mode.
6. When the system comes up, execute the new firmware program (such as FIRM412.EXE), which you may receive or download from the manufacturer, and use the new firmware (*.BIN) file.
7. When the EXE application starts, specify the location of the BIN file.
8. Click the Update button to begin the flash process.
9. When the Update button becomes highlighted again, the flash process is complete.
10. Power-off the system and reset the DVD-ROM drive's flash jumper to its original position.
11. Power-on the system normally.

Troubleshooting DVD-ROM Drives

Even though a DVD-ROM package should install with an absolute minimum of muss and fuss, and run with all the reliability of a CD-ROM, there are times when things just don't go according to plan. Both software and hardware problems can interrupt your DVD-ROM system. The following symptoms cover some of the most common troubleshooting issues.

DVD drives use lasers in normal operation. Although these are very low power semiconductor lasers, and the chances of injury to your eyes is extremely slight, you should still take the proper precautions and not operate a DVD drive with the protective covers open. Turn off and unplug the PC before opening a DVD drive.

INITIAL SETUP AND TIPS

When installing or correcting problems on a DVD-ROM system, it may help to set the DVD system configuration to a default state using the criteria outlined below:

- *Video configuration* Regardless of the amount of video RAM provided by your video adapter, try setting the display to 640 x 480 using 16-bit color (the high-color mode). You might also try setting the monitor type to standard VGA.
- *DirectX installation* If you're not yet using Windows 95 OSR2 (4.00.950 B), or do not have any Windows 95 games installed, chances are that you don't have DirectX installed (or you're using a very old version). Though DirectX versions 2.0 and higher should support DVD, using the latest version may increase your system's video performance (since it also includes newer DirectDraw drivers for your video card). Check for the latest version of DirectX (at this time, DirectX7a) at **http://www.microsoft.com/directx**.
- *DVD drivers* Drivers are being updated regularly to provide better hardware compatibility, so you should check for the latest Cinemaster drivers and the latest release of DVD Player from Quadrant International: **http://www.qi.com/**.
- *Video drivers* Many video drivers are also updated regularly for better video performance and compatibility. Check the Web page of your video card vendor for updated video card drivers. This may be especially important if you're using a video card with motion compensation or other DVD video decoding features instead of a full hardware decoder card.
- *IDE controller compatibility* There is also a lingering issue with the IDE controllers on some motherboards (depending on which version of Windows 95/98 you're using). If you have trouble with your IDE controllers, check the Intel Developer's Page for more details and fixes at **http://developer.intel.com/design/motherbd/IDEINFUP.HTM.** Late versions of Windows 95 and Windows 98 should have no problems with IDE controller identification and setup.

DVD SOFTWARE AND WINDOWS 98

Although Windows 98 is supposed to offer full support for DVD systems, you may find that DVD systems don't install properly (or cease working) once Windows 98 is installed. If this is the case, check the DVD manufacturer's Web site for updated DVD-ROM drivers and software applets. Microsoft supports DVD discs within Windows 98 using SCSI and ATAPI-compliant DVD-ROM drives. Playing movies (DVD-Video) is supported only with the following decoder adapters:

- Toshiba DVD decoder adapters used with Toshiba Infinia DVD systems with either S3 or ATI display adapters.
- Quadrant Cinemaster C rev. 1.2 decoder adapters included with Dell XPS series computers. Note that updated Quadrant Cinemaster decoder drivers are available on the Windows 98 CD-ROM in the drivers\dvd\quadrant folder.
- Windows 98 DVD player is designed to work with the Windows 98 decoder drivers, so the option to add or remove DVD player is not available until a supported DVD decoder adapter is installed and detected.

- Once a DVD decoder adapter is detected and the Windows 98 drivers are installed, a shortcut for DVD player is added to the Entertainment menu. The option to add or remove DVD player becomes available under Multimedia on the Windows Setup tab (in the Add/Remove Programs tool). After being installed, the DVD player software can be removed and reinstalled without having to reinstall the decoder drivers.

If an appropriate DVD decoder card is used, but has third-party drivers installed, Windows 98 will not install the Windows 98 drivers or DVD player software until the third-party drivers are removed using Device Manager.

Other DVD playback software and decoder cards (including other Cinemaster DVD decoder adapters like the Cinemaster S) are not supported, and require the drivers and software provided by the manufacturer in order to function properly.

INSTALLATION AND STARTUP SYMPTOMS

SYMPTOM 17-1 The DVD drivers refuse to install This is almost always because Windows 95/98 is having a problem with one or more INF files on your driver installation disk(s). Check with your DVD vendor to confirm whether you need to delete one or more entries in your OEM*xx*.INF file(s) (where *xx* is any suffix). If you're using an MKE DVD kit, you may also need to delete one or more entries from an MKEDVD.INF file. The INF files are typically contained in the C:\WINDOWS\INF\OTHER directory. Once you've corrected the appropriate INF file(s), you can reinstall the DVD drivers:

1. Click Start, select Settings, and then click on Control Panel. Double-click the System icon.
2. Click on the Device Manager tab, and then select Sound, Video, and Game Controllers or CD-ROM.
3. Select the DVD driver(s); then click Remove.
4. Exit the Device Manager and reinstall the drivers.

SYMPTOM 17-2 The DVD drive isn't detected There are several possible reasons why the DVD drive would not be detected. Check the power connector attached to the drive, and make sure that the drive isn't being powered from a Y-splitter power cable. Check the signal cable next. Both SCSI and EIDE signal cables must be attached securely to the drive. SCSI interfaces are complicated a bit by termination, so verify that any SCSI bus is properly terminated. Make sure that the drive is jumpered properly for its SCSI ID or EIDE master or slave relationship. Finally, make sure that the DVD drivers are installed and running. Check the drivers under the Sound, Video, and Game Controllers (or CD-ROM) entry of your Device Manager.

SYMPTOM 17-3 You see an error message that the drive is not fully compatible with the software You may also see this as a message that no DVD drive is found. This frequently occurs when installing a DVD-ROM drive in conjunction with Zip, Jaz, tape, or CD-ROM drives. The DVD drive will need to be the next available drive letter after any IDE or SCSI hard drives. Alphabetically, there should be no other drives (such as Zip, Jaz, tape, or CD-ROM drives) with drive letters *before* that of the DVD drive.

To change the drive letter assignment in your system, power-down and disconnect all the affected drives *except* the DVD drive; then boot to Windows 95/98 Safe Mode and remove the drives (including the DVD drive) from Device Manager. Restart to normal mode, and the DVD drive will be reassigned the lowest available drive letter. Next, power-down again and reconnect the other drives. Restart the system, and they will be automatically redetected and assigned drive letters higher than the DVD drive.

You should also check the version of three Windows 95 files: WINASPI.DLL, WNASPI32.DLL, and APIX.VXD. Click on Start, then Find, and select Files or Folders. This will open the Find: All Files dialog box. Type one of the file names in the Named box (make sure the Look In box is referring to the C:\ drive), and press ENTER. If no files are found, go to Windows Explorer, click on View, and select Options. Click on the radio button next to Show All Files, and finally, click on the Apply button. Now try to find the files again. Once you've located these files, you should see that each of the files has a time stamp of either 9:50 (for Windows 95 versions 0 or A) or 11:11 (for Windows 95 version B).

> To check your version of Windows 95, open the System applet from Control Panel. Below "Microsoft Windows 95," you should see 4.00.950 followed by 0 or A, denoting your version.

If the time stamps are incorrect, you'll need to restore the original versions of WINASPI.DLL, WNASPI32.DLL, and APIX.VXD. First, rename the current versions of the files using an extension of .OEM. For example, APIX.VXD should be renamed APIX.OEM. Next, extract the original files directly from the Windows 95 CD (or copy the files from another system where the files are of the proper time stamp). You may also wish to update the system to Windows 98.

SYMPTOM 17-4 You see an error indicating the DVD device driver could not be loaded You'll need to check the DVD driver installation, or manually install the drivers. To do this, you will need to open the Control Panel, open System Properties, and then select the Device Manager tab. In the category of Other Devices, select PCI Multimedia Device and click on Properties. In the Properties dialog, select the Driver tab and click on Change Driver. Browse to the DVD Drivers Installation Disk and click on OK. Click on OK again, select the proper MPEG board (such as MKE DVD-AV Decoder Board), and click on OK again. Exit the PCI Multimedia Device Properties by clicking on OK again, and Windows 95/98 will copy over the proper drivers. You will then need to restart the machine.

SYMPTOM 17-5 You see an error such as "Cannot open <filename>, video and audio glitches may occur" This type of error almost always indicates a fault with the driver installation, and you should rerun the setup utility that accompanies your the DVD drive product. You may also wish to check for driver bug fixes or patches from the drive maker.

SYMPTOM 17-6 There is no audio when playing an audio CD This is a common problem, especially during new DVD-ROM drive installations. Chances are that you did not connect the four-wire CD audio cable between the DVD-ROM drive and the sound board. If so, the cable may be reversed (or defective). Of course, if you're still using your original CD-ROM drive, and the CD-ROM is connected to the sound board, there will be no CD audio from the DVD-ROM drive—there is no way to "parallel" or "gang" the sound cable. If the DVD-ROM audio cable is connected to the sound board, make sure the CD audio input of your sound board's mixer applet is turned up to a reasonable level.

If you wish to continue using an existing CD-ROM drive as the CD audio drive, you can still use audio from the DVD-ROM drive by using a patch cable to feed the headphone output signal from the drive to the sound card's line in jack. Then adjust the sound card's line in mixer so that you can hear audio from the DVD-ROM headphone.

SYMPTOM 17-7 The system will not restart to normal mode after DVD-ROM drive installation This problem sometimes occurs when installing the DVD on a system with the USB Supplement for Windows 95 (OSR2). You may need to uninstall the USR Supplement.

- *Remove the USR Supplement.* Boot into Windows 95 Safe Mode and open the Add/Remove Programs applet from Control Panel. If the Universal Serial Bus Supplement is listed, highlight it and click on the Add/Remove button. This will uninstall the supplement, and you will be prompted to restart the system.
- *Check the decoder IRQ.* The DVD system's MPEG-2 decoder card should be assigned a unique interrupt request (IRQ). Open the System applet from Control Panel, click on the Device Manager tab, and double-click on Computer. Here you'll see a list of IRQs and the name of the device using each IRQ. If the decoder card is not listed (or its IRQ is being shared with any device other than the IRQ holder for PCI steering), assign a unique IRQ to the card. This can usually be accomplished through the BIOS of your computer, or possibly by moving the decoder card to another PCI slot.
- *Check the decoder memory range.* You may need to change the memory range used by the MPEG-2 decoder card. Open the System applet from Control Panel, click on the Device Manager tab, and then double-click on Sound, Video and Game Controllers. Finally, double-click on the MPEG-2 decoder card. Click on the Resources tab and remove the check mark next to "Use automatic settings." Finally, double-click on the Memory Range entry and enter **D1000000-D10FFFFF**. Click on OK and restart the PC for your changes to take effect.

SYMPTOM 17-8 You experience error messages or system lockups during DVD software installation Movies play, but white lines appear randomly on the screen. In virtually all cases, the problem is being caused by an IRQ or memory range conflict.

- *Check the decoder IRQ.* Open the System applet from Control Panel, click on the Device Manager tab, and double-click on Computer. Here you'll see a list of IRQs and the name of the device using each IRQ. If the decoder card is not listed (or its IRQ is being shared with any device other than the IRQ holder for PCI steering), assign a unique IRQ to the card. This can usually be accomplished through the BIOS of your computer, or possibly by moving the decoder card to another PCI slot.
- *Check the decoder memory range.* You may need to change the memory range used by the MPEG-2 decoder card. Open the System applet from Control Panel, click on the Device Manager tab, and then double-click on Sound, Video and Game Controllers. Finally, double-click on the MPEG-2 decoder card. Click on the Resources tab and remove the check mark next to "Use automatic settings." Finally, double-click on the Memory Range entry and enter **D1000000-D10FFFFF**. Click on OK and restart for the changes to take effect.

SYMPTOM 17-9 Your DVD-ROM will not autoconfigure using the automatic configuration utility provided with the drive In many cases, this is a problem caused by an unusually high video refresh rate. DVD systems seem to operate best at video refresh rates of 60Hz or so. Try lowering your video refresh rate to 75Hz, or lower, through the video card's Properties dialog or Display control settings.

SYMPTOM 17-10 You can play DVD-based games (such as Wing Commander 4 or Silent Steel), but the system hangs up when inserting a DVD-Video When the system hangs, the video window either stays black, or the DVD logo comes up, and then the machine freezes. This is often a surprisingly simple issue. Setting the video adapter's settings to the default values (a.k.a. "Initial Setup Recommendations") will frequently correct the problem. Although your current video settings may work wonderfully with static images (even through other player software), the unique demands of your DVD decoder board may cause too much information to be directed at your video card at once. Start with your basic video default settings, and then systematically increase resolution and color depth to an acceptable quality level.

As an alternative, you might try setting the drive letter for the DVD-ROM drive to be the first "CD-ROM" in the system. This is a particularly useful tactic when playing back CD-I and VideoCD movies with software (such as Xing), but it also helps the DVD player software utilize the DVD-ROM drive.

SYMPTOM 17-11 Movies appear bright (then dim) when watching a DVD-Video from the video card's TV output This problem only occurs when a VCR is connected between the "TV output" of the video adapter and the TV set. Video display adapters with TV output capability will enable MACROVISION copy protection during DVD movie playback. The MACROVISION-encoded video signal will effectively prevent a VCR from recording a watchable movie.

If you videotape a MACROVISION-encoded movie, and then play it back, you'll typically see occasional glimpses of the movie interspersed with 20 to 30 seconds of no picture (or possibly just a blue screen). Even if you're not actually recording, the VCR attempts to compensate for the MACROVISION-encoded signal, and this generally leads to the symptom described. To resolve this symptom, simply connect the video card's TV output directly to the TV set using either the "composite" or "S-Video" connections.

> Remember that sound connections are completely independent of video connections, and if you wish to hear the DVD movie through the TV set, you will also need to connect the audio output of the PC to the TV set.

SYMPTOM 17-12 When playing DVD-Video, the image appears distorted (often described as a "spaghetti western") This type of issue is often associated with Matrox Millennium or Mystique video cards, but can also occur with other types of video cards. In virtually all cases, the trouble is with your video drivers. They may be old or buggy or incompatible with the DVD drivers and video player software at work on your system. Download and install the latest video drivers, and try flashing the video card's BIOS (if possible). If the problem persists, disable DirectDraw for Overlays, and resize the screen to the default sizes recommended.

SYMPTOM 17-13 You cannot resize the movie display to full screen (or select any display size other than the default) This is particularly associated with Matrox video cards, but may occur with other video cards. These video cards probably don't support the hardware-based video scaling required for DVD. Try upgrading the video drivers, and flash the video card's BIOS (if possible). Otherwise, you have little alternative except to upgrade the video card, or continue using the smaller screen size.

SYMPTOM 17-14 You receive a "display overlay not available" error message when launching the DVD player software This is a known issue with the ATI DVD player 1.2 software, but similar problems can occur with other players. Chances are that the DVD player software requires additional display adapter memory (beyond what is used by the current display mode). If the current display mode uses most of the display adapter's memory, there's no memory left over for the DVD player, and the error message will occur.

This message is most likely to occur when the display adapter has only 4MB of display memory, and 1152 x 864 at 32 bits per pixel (bpp) is selected as the display mode. This display mode consumes almost 4MB of display memory just to paint the Windows desktop. To resolve this problem, simply select a lower color depth or (lower resolution). For example, if you're running at 32bpp, try 16bpp. This will consume only half as much display memory, and should leave an adequate amount for the display overlay and other DVD functions.

If the error message persists after reducing the display resolution (and/or color depth), it may be the result of interference by other video-related processes. Check for "WebTV" or "WaveTop" background tasks—these are normally visible in the task bar. Right-click the icons for these tasks and select Pause, Suspend, Quit, or Exit to disable them; then try the DVD player software again.

SYMPTOM 17-15 You encounter a "card required" error when installing SoftDVD player software This is a known problem with ATI video cards and Zoran SoftDVD player software (you may see "ATI AGP card required"), and it is almost always due to inadequate system requirements. The SoftDVD player has several major system requirements:

- An appropriate video card must be present.
- AGP support must be enabled at the operating system level.
- An Intel Pentium II processor is required.
- Only a 16bpp color depth (65K colors) is supported.
- The sound drivers must be DirectX compliant.

To resolve this problem, ensure that all requirements of the SoftDVD player are met:

- *Check the video card.* A PCI video card may not be supported. If you are uncertain which video card is installed, use Device Manager to examine the Display Adapter. Click the Status button on the diagnostics page—the ASIC Type entry should include the AGP designation.
- *Check the operating system.* AGP support must be enabled. The following components must be installed on the system to properly enable AGP:

Windows 95 OSR 2 (950b or 950c) Right-click My Computer and select Properties. You should see "Microsoft Windows 95 4.00.950 B or 4.00.950 C."

USB supplement This is available from Microsoft's Web site and on some later Windows 95 CDs. Windows 95 (950C) normally has the USB patch preinstalled. For 950B, check the Add/Remove Programs list in Control Panel to determine whether the "USB Supplement to OSR2" has been installed.

AGP-to-PCI bridge drivers This is also known as a "chipset patch" or "PIIX4 patch" and usually comes on a floppy disk or CD from the motherboard manufacturer. Examine the Device Manager and look for "Unknown" or "Other" entries related to the PCI bridge. If any such entries are present, this is an indication that the proper chipset patch is not installed. You may need to install such a patch before proceeding.

DirectX5 (or later) This is available from Microsoft's Web site and may also be included with your video card's driver CD. From the Control Panel, open Add/Remove Programs, and double-click on the DirectX entry. (If there isn't one, then DirectX is not installed at all.) The DirectDraw component should show a version number of 4.05.00.0155 (or later). If not, your system is using an earlier version of DirectX, and this will need to be updated to DirectX5.0 or later (for example, DirectX6 or DirectX6.1).

- *Check your processor.* The software may demand an Intel Pentium II/III processor. Even if your motherboard uses a compatible Socket 7 processor (such as an AMD K6-2), the software may not operate without a Pentium II/III. Other DVD player software may not be so stringent. Otherwise, you may need to upgrade the motherboard and CPU.
- *Check the video color depth.* The software may only support limited color depths. Right-click on the desktop, select Properties, and then select the Settings tab. The Color Palette entry should read "High Color (16 bit)." Change the setting to this value if necessary.
- *Check the sound drivers.* In most cases, sound drivers must be DirectX compliant. From Control Panel, open Add/Remove Programs, and double-click on DirectX. Check the listing for "Primary Sound

Driver"—it should indicate "Certified." If the sound driver is not certified, or indicates "no hardware support," check with the sound card manufacturer (or system maker) for updated sound drivers.

PERFORMANCE/OPERATING SYMPTOMS

SYMPTOM 17-16 **The DVD motorized tray won't open or close** The most common issue here is the DVD application itself. Some DVD applications (such as DVD-Video player applications) will lock the disc tray closed while a video DVD disc is playing. Try closing all open applications. If the tray still won't open, try restarting the PC. This should clear any software lock. If the tray still refuses to open or close, the drive itself may be defective. You can force the tray open using a straightened paper clip in the emergency eject hole in the front of the drive.

SYMPTOM 17-17 **There is no DVD audio while playing a movie or other multimedia presentation** Here's another common oversight during new DVD installations. Check the external audio cable attached between the MPEG-2 decoder board and the line in jack of your sound board. The cable may be plugged into the wrong jack(s), or the cable may simply be defective. Also check the sound board's mixer applet and see that the line in volume control setting is turned up to an acceptable level. If you're connecting the DVD-ROM's CD audio cable to the sound card, verify that the cable is attached securely, and see that the cable is compatible with the drive and the sound card.

SYMPTOM 17-18 **Video quality is poor** MPEG-2 compression is well respected for its ability to reproduce high-quality images. The problem of poor image quality is almost always caused by your video configuration—your color depth or resolution are too low. DVD-Video playback is best at resolutions of 800 x 600 or higher and color depths of 16 bits (high color) or higher (for example, 24-bit true color). In most cases, 256 colors will result in a dithered image.

SYMPTOM 17-19 **The video image is distorted when trying to play an MPEG file** Other video operations probably seem fine. A distorted MPEG image can be the result of two problems. First, the video connections on the back of the card could be loose. Verify that all connections to the MPEG-2 decoder card are secure. Another common cause of distorted playbacks is that the refresh rate on your video card is set too high. It is recommended that the video refresh rate be kept *below* 85Hz when running MPEG files. Try adjusting the vertical refresh rate to 72Hz, or even 60Hz.

SYMPTOM 17-20 **The picture is beginning to occasionally pixelize or "break apart"** The audio may also seem periodically distorted. It is highly likely that the DVD disc needs to be cleaned. Clean the DVD disc properly and try it again, or try another disc. Also try closing any unused applications running in the background. If the problem persists with another DVD disc as well (and both discs are in good condition), try reinitializing the drive by powering down and rebooting the system. If the problem persists, the internal optics of the DVD-ROM drive may need to be cleaned with a bit of photography-grade compressed air. Otherwise, try replacing the DVD-ROM drive.

SYMPTOM 17-21 **You notice the DVD-ROM light flashing regularly without a disc inserted** System performance may be reduced. This is often because the DVD-ROM drive's properties are set for "Auto insert notification" under Windows 95/98. Start the Device Manager, highlight the DVD-ROM drive, and click the Properties button. You'll see the DVD-ROM Properties dialog. In the Options area of the Properties dialog, locate the check box for "Auto insert notification," and uncheck it. Save your changes. (You might need to reboot the system). This should stop the drive's constant checking for a disc.

SYMPTOM 17-22 The DVD drive's "busy" indicator flashes slowly once a disc is inserted The drive is not recognizing the disc. In most cases, the disc is simply dirty. Try cleaning the disc in a radial motion (from the hub to the edge like the spokes of a wheel). Try another disc. If the drive cannot recognize other discs, the drive's optical reader may be dirty. Try using a can of photography-grade compressed air to clean any accumulations of dust from the drive. If the drive's "busy" indicator is on all the time (and doesn't recognize any discs), the drive may be defective.

SYMPTOM 17-23 You see an error message that reads "Disk playback unauthorized" The region code on the DVD disc does not match the code embedded into the drive. There isn't much that can be done when this error occurs. Note that region code limitations are only applied to DVD-Video movie releases—programs and data discs are generally not marked with region codes.

SYMPTOM 17-24 You receive an "authentication error" when playing DVD movies with a Zoran SoftDVD player The error suggests that the region code for the DVD disc is not supported by the player software. This problem normally occurs when the DVD disc is designed for a region that is different from the one for the player. For example, the error message would appear when attempting to play a "region 2" DVD disc on a "region 1" version of SoftDVD software. However, there are rare reports of this error occurring in situations where the DVD region codes are correct. The following suggestions may help to correct region problems with the Zoran SoftDVD player:

- Ensure that the DVD title being played is designed for the appropriate region. Today, the SoftDVD player is designed for the playback of region 1 DVD titles. You may need to upgrade the player software.
- If you're using SoftDVD with a SCSI DVD drive, ensure that the most recent ASPI driver is installed for the SCSI controller.
- Panasonic A01 F/W 1.12 DVD drives will yield authentication errors when attempting to play DVDs with Zoran SoftDVD software. This appears to be an issue with the DVD drive itself, and no solution exists with that specific drive.
- Toshiba SM-M1002 DVD drives using a firmware version prior to 3426 should be updated to the current firmware revision.
- For Matsushita SR-852 DVD drives, the following DVD-ROM driver files should be used:

  MKEATAPI.MPD and MKEVSD.VXD (on the SR-8582 installation disc)
  MKEUPD.VXD (on the SR-8581 installation disc)

SYMPTOM 17-25 The display turns magenta (red) when attempting to adjust the DVD video overlay feature When adjusting the video overlay, you may have some trouble finding the video window. It often helps to change your background to magenta so you can see where the video window is. To do this, right-click on your background, and select Properties. Select the Background tab and select "none" as both the Pattern and the Wallpaper. Then select the Appearance tab, and select Magenta as the color of the desktop. Click on OK to finish changing your background color to magenta. It should now be easier to locate the video window while adjusting the overlay.

SYMPTOM 17-26 The DVD drive cannot read CD-R or Photo CD discs This is not an error. Most first-generation DVD drives will not read CD recordable or Photo CD (Kodak) discs. In some cases, it is even possible to damage CD recordable disks due to the laser wavelength and energy used in the

DVD drive. Do not attempt to read CD-R or Photo CD discs in the DVD unless the drive specifications specifically state that the drive is compatible with those types of discs. Chances are that you'll need to update the older DVD drive's firmware (or replace the DVD drive completely) in order to correct the problem.

SYMPTOM 17-27 **You experience difficulties with a particular DVD movie title, even though others play normally** If most movies play normally, chances are that the problem movie is an older edition (version). Some older DVD-ROM movie releases contain mastering problems that cause playback errors. Try exchanging the movie for a later edition. If the problem persists (or you cannot play most movies properly), you may need updated DVD-ROM drivers. Download the latest drivers from the DVD manufacturer's Web site and install them. The following instructions explain a driver upgrade for a Creative Labs DVD-ROM drive:

1. Create a directory called DVDNEW in the root directory of the boot drive.
2. Download the file DVDEW95.EXE into this directory.
3. Click on Start, then Programs, and select MS-DOS Prompt.
4. Change to the DVDNEW directory you created (for example, C:\DVDNEW); then type **DVDEW95 -D** and press ENTER.
5. The file will extract and create a SETUP subdirectory within C:\DVDNEW.
6. Now follow the instructions in the README.1ST file to install the new drivers and programs.

SYMPTOM 17-28 **You experience difficulties with the DVD software's Parental Control feature** The Parental Control feature is not working properly, or is causing user problems. This is often because the feature is not working properly in the DVD software, and you'll need to uninstall and reinstall the DVD software to disable Parental Control.

First, uninstall the DVD software. To do this, open the Add/Remove Programs applet from Control Panel. Highlight the particular DVD software (such as Encore software), and click on Add/Remove. After the uninstall is complete, reinstall the software, choosing the option for a custom install. Make sure there is no check mark next to "Parental Control" in the select list. This will reinstall the software without this feature. A later release of the DVD software (or a patch) may address this problem and allow you to resume using the Parental Control feature.

SYMPTOM 17-29 **When playing some DVD-Video titles, you encounter a "blue screen" error that mentions Parental Control** You notice the Parental Control feature is set to "kids" and will not retain any other settings. The problem is outdated Quadrant driver/player software. This issue has been corrected in the Quadrant software released after December 23, 1997. You must go to Quadrant International's Web site (**http://www.qi.com/**). Then download the latest player and the drivers from the "S Series 2.x" Cinemaster section.

> The drivers mentioned above are only for the S Series 2.3 version of the card. If you have the 2.2 version of the card, use the links that point to the last updates for the 2.2 cards.

SYMPTOM 17-30 **Your screen saver turns on while playing a DVD title** Since a screen saver is activated after some period of inactivity, leaving the keyboard/mouse untouched while watching a DVD movie can allow the screen saver to activate. Screen savers do not check for the presence of DVD activity, so you'll need to disable the screen saver (through the Display icon in the Control Panel) before using the DVD-ROM drive to watch movies.

SYMPTOM 17-31 You notice a reddish tint when playing movies with the DVD-ROM drive This is typically an end-user issue that can easily be corrected by reducing contrast, or adjusting the tint setting through the DVD player application software.

SYMPTOM 17-32 You find that MPEG-1 files play back fine on your DVD player software, but there is no sound However, MPEG-2 files and DVD-Video (movies) play back correctly with sound. This is generally a problem with the DVD player software that may require a patch or upgrade. (Check with the player software's manufacturer.) As a temporary work-around, use a generic MPEG file player (such as Windows Media Player) to run MPEG-1 files until the DVD player can be upgraded or replaced.

SYMPTOM 17-33 You cannot play a DVD or CD in the DVD drive, or certain types of discs cannot be read in the drive There are many possible (often simple) issues that can prevent a disc from playing in an optical drive:

- *Check the disc.* The disc may be placed upside down in the disc tray, or the disc may be dirty. Recheck the disc orientation, and clean the disc if necessary. If the disc is warped or seriously damaged, it may need to be replaced.
- *Check the drive.* The drive's optical reader may be dirty. This can happen on older drives or on drives that are operated in dusty/dirty environments. Use a can of photography-grade compressed air to gently blow dust out of the drive.
- *Check the region code.* DVD movie discs are released with a region code that must correspond to the code contained in the drive. If the codes are different, the DVD disc will not play. You may need to obtain a disc with the correct region code.

17

SYMPTOM 17-34 When attempting to play a disc, you receive a message such as "Disc does not contain DVD Video data" DVD player software cannot find the title track and/or information files on the disc. If you're trying to use a DVD disc, the disc may be scratched or damaged. Clean the disc if possible, or replace the damaged disc. If you're simply trying to play MPEG video from an ordinary CD, click OK to close the error dialog—the disc may still play.

SYMPTOM 17-35 You receive an error message such as "Unable to locate DVD-ROM drive—assume drive D:—Error1" The DVD drive may not have been properly configured by Windows 95/98 or may be disconnected.

- *Check the cables.* Verify that the DVD drive is jumpered properly, and see that its power and signal cables are oriented and secured. Try another signal cable if necessary, or try the DVD drive as the only device on the drive controller.
- *Try a manual installation.* Reboot the PC from a cold start and see if Windows will redetect the DVD drive. If not, run the Windows 95/98 Add New Hardware wizard to "force" Windows to detect the hardware. If the Add New Hardware wizard fails to detect the DVD drive, you may need to specify the drive make and model manually. In all cases, be sure to have the latest DVD drivers on hand.

SYMPTOM 17-36 During the DVD video configuration process, you receive an error such as "Auto Alignment failed" This error almost always suggests that the hardware MPEG-2 decoder card cable may not be properly connected. Check the cable connection on the hardware decoder card (particularly "VGA In" and "VGA Out"), and see that the cable is secure. Try another cable if possible. Start the DVD player software, press the Settings button, and select Video Configuration. Press the Auto button to have the video automatically configured.

SYMPTOM 17-37 After connecting an MPEG-2 decoder card, the video image seems blue (or contains a blue tint) This is generally due to the improper connection or setup of the MPEG-2 card:

- *Check the loopback cable.* VGA loopback cable between the video card and the MPEG-2 decoder card is not connected correctly. Check the loopback cable, and try reseating the connector if possible.
- *Check the video alignment.* DVD video alignment is not set correctly. Open the Video Configuration utility and set the video alignment. Try using the Auto button to automatically configure the video. If automatic configuration does not work, try making minor adjustments manually.
- *Check the "color key" setting.* Your color key value is not set correctly. Change the color scheme of your Windows 95/98 desktop. Right-click on the Windows 95/98 desktop and click Properties. In the Display Properties dialog, click the Appearance tab. Then select Desktop in the Item list, and select a different color scheme from the list. Click OK to accept the changes.

SYMPTOM 17-38 The DVD-ROM drive cannot play a DVD disc or certain other types of disc media (such as CD-plus) There are several possible issues that might cause this type of problem:

- *Check the drivers.* Make sure the entire suite of drivers has been installed for your drive. Check for the latest drivers and download any available patches or updates.
- *Check the player software.* You may not have the correct player software for your drive. Make sure to download and install the latest version of your player software.
- *Check the format.* Verify that the DVD disc is the correct format for the type of system that you're using. For example, a PC should use an ISO 9660–compatible format, rather than an Apple/Mac HFS disc or UNIX disc format.
- *Check for viruses.* Your DVD drivers/software may have been corrupted by a virus. Run a virus scan program, and then remove/reinstall any damaged software.

Windows-Related Symptoms

SYMPTOM 17-39 After upgrading the video card, DVD movies will not play Chances are that your new video card is neither defective nor incompatible—instead, the problem is that the link(s) between your video and DVD drivers have been broken. When new video cards are installed, they change entries in the registry that associate MPEG playback with video card drivers. The new video card's MPEG drivers are probably not DVD compliant, but since they took precedence over the MPEG drivers of the older DVD system, this is likely to be the problem. Try reinstalling the video card from scratch, and then reinstall the DVD drivers and software. This should reinstall the proper DVD MPEG-ready drivers and correct the problem.

SYMPTOM 17-40 DVD-Video movies will only play on the primary monitor When DVD player software is installed in a multimonitor Windows 98 system, DVD movies will only play on the primary monitor. If the DVD player window is moved to the secondary monitor, no picture appears.

This is a limitation of secondary displays under Windows 98. The primary display has a full complement of 3D and video acceleration features, but a secondary display does not. To correct this problem, move the DVD player window back to the primary monitor.

SYMPTOM 17-41 Windows 98 halts or reboots when running a software DVD player designed for Windows 95 This is an issue most frequently associated with the Zoran SoftDVD player, but may occur with other software products. In most cases, the system halts immediately after the Play button is clicked, but this may also occur at other points within the player software. In some instances, the system may reboot or report an "Unrecoverable Application Error." Generally, the SoftDVD player may successfully play a single DVD movie or file and then report an error (such as "your computer is not configured to start DVD") when attempting to play a second movie. Chances are that the subtle design changes between Windows 95 and Windows 98 are causing a problem with the player software (tailored for Windows 95). Try the following:

- Remove and reinstall the DVD player application.
- Check to see if a patch or update is available for your DVD player.
- Experiment with different video resolutions, color depths, and refresh rates.
- Try an alternate or updated video driver.

SYMPTOM 17-42 Even when a DVD system is properly configured under Windows 95, you get no sound from the speakers This is almost always due to an old (original) release of Windows 95. The use of old Windows 95 drivers was corrected in Windows 95 OSR2 and is not an issue with Windows 98. If you cannot upgrade your operating system to Windows 95 OSR2 or Windows 95, check with the DVD package manufacturer for updated drivers and patches that might correct the problem. Keep in mind that the DVD drive will still read data DVD discs and other CDs properly.

17

SYMPTOM 17-43 Creative and MKE DVD drives may not work with Windows 98 If you're using a first-generation Creative Labs DVD kit or an MKE DVD kit, the kit may not work properly with Windows 98. (Note that newer kits should operate properly.) For example, you may no longer be able to read from the drive. These older DVD kits rely on the Compact Disc File System (CDFS), but Windows 98 loads the Universal Disk Format (UDF) file system by default for DVD drives. To work around this incompatibility, disable UDF support for the DVD drives:

1. Click Start, click Run, type **msconfig** in the Open box, and then click OK.
2. Click the Advanced option.
3. Click to select (check) the Disable UDF File System check box, and then click OK.
4. Click OK again. When you're prompted to restart your computer, click Yes.

When your computer restarts, UDF support is disabled, and the DVD kit should work.

SYMPTOM 17-44 You receive a "media error" when using Windows Explorer to eject a DVD movie This issue has been reported with Toshiba DVD players. When you use Windows Explorer to eject a DVD movie that is currently being played by a Toshiba DVD player, you receive the following "blue screen" error message:

```
Re-insert the media and press any key to continue.
```

When you insert the DVD movie back into the player and press a key, you may receive the same error message (and the movie may be automatically ejected). This problem may occur if you press a key before the DVD movie is fully spun up. To resolve the problem, insert the DVD movie into the player, but wait to press a key until the light on the Toshiba DVD player is turned off. This indicates that the DVD movie is fully spun up.

SYMPTOM 17-45 **You cannot capture a DVD video image with the PRINT SCREEN key under Windows 98** If you try to capture a still image of a DVD movie with the PRINT SCREEN key, then paste the image into a program, only a blue or black box may be pasted into the program. This is the normal design of your DVD system. The DVD data stream is decoded by the DVD decoder card and then redirected back to the video adapter. When the computer uses an external patch cable, the video stream is sent from the video adapter to the DVD decoder card and then directly to the monitor as an "overlay." This is done to improve the playback performance of DVD video by bypassing slower portions of the computer. Since the DVD data stream does not pass through the Windows API layer, the video output cannot be captured, and you only capture the playback area in which the movie is displayed.

SYMPTOM 17-46 **You encounter problems when using a SoftDVD player in Windows 98** When you view a DVD movie using the SoftDVD player program included with some computers, you may experience various playback problems. In most cases, you can correct these types of problems by modifying the player's INI file:

1. Click Start, select Find, and then click Files or Folders.
2. In the Named box, type **SOFTDVD.INI**, and then click Find Now.
3. In the list of "found files," double-click the SOFTDVD.INI file.
4. Type the following lines in the SOFTDVD.INI file:

```
 [dvdfs]
AlignedAccess=0
```

> Be sure to insert a blank line above and below these two lines.

5. In the File menu, click Save, then Exit.
6. Restart your computer when prompted to do so.

SYMPTOM 17-47 **The screen appears clipped when playing a DVD movie** This is a known issue when using Cinemaster 1.2 drivers under Windows 98—both sides of the screen may appear "clipped." This is caused by an aspect ratio bug in the DVD player software. You'll need to contact Microsoft or the maker of your DVD player software in order to obtain the correct patch or software update for your DVD player. For example, Microsoft offers an update for the DVDPLAY.EXE file (09/29/98, 9:43a, 125,440 bytes), which should correct this aspect ratio problem. Keep in mind that you may also need to update your DirectX components (you may need the Microsoft DirectX Media 6.0 Run Time module) before updating the DVD player software.

SYMPTOM 17-48 **You encounter problems with the DVD/TV tuner unit after upgrading Windows** After you upgrade a Toshiba Infinia 72xx laptop PC to Windows 98, a yellow exclamation point may be displayed next to the DVD/TV Tuner device in the Device Manager, and your

DVD/TV Tuner device may not work correctly (if at all). This problem can occur if your computer is configured to use the Toshiba TV/FM version 2.13B2 device driver. This driver is not totally compatible with Windows 98. Contact Toshiba to obtain an upgraded driver for your PC.

SYMPTOM 17-49 **A Creative Labs DXR2 DVD drive will not work under Windows 98** After upgrading your computer to Windows 98, your Creative Labs Encore DXR2 DVD drive may no longer work correctly. This problem occurs because the Windows 98 setup process updates the DLL files used by the DVD drive. Those new files may not be compatible with the Creative Labs DXR2. There are two methods of correcting the problem:

- *Update your drivers.* Contact Creative Labs to obtain updated drivers designed specifically for Windows 98. You can download drivers from Creative Labs at **http://www.soundblaster.com/wwwnew/tech/ftp/ftp-cd.html**.
- *Replace older DLL files.* You can try renaming WINASPI.DLL, WNASPI32.DLL, and APIX.VXD. Then extract new copies of WINASPI.DLL, WNASPI32.DLL, and APIX.VXD from your original Windows 98 CD-ROM. (The WINASPI.DLL and WNASPI32.DLL files are in the WIN98_40.CAB file, and the APIX.VXD file is in the WIN98_47.CAB file.

SYMPTOM 17-50 **Windows 98 may lock up if the DVD drive tray is left open at boot time** If your portable computer includes a DVD drive, and the nonmotorized drive tray is left open during and after the Windows 98 startup, you may find that Windows 98 locks up several minutes after Windows is started. This is a known problem with the Toshiba Tecra 8000 DVD under Windows 98, and usually occurs because the DVD drive or CD-ROM drive supports Media Event Status Notification (MESN) according to the PC98 specification. Since those portable drives have nonmotorized trays, the trays are not closed automatically when Windows boots, so Windows fails because of false reporting from the MESN feature.

First, close the drive tray while Windows is starting (or within one minute after it starts). You should generally keep the DVD drive or CD-ROM drive tray closed except when you're inserting or removing discs. This policy also reduces the risk of drive problems due to dust buildup (or damage from striking the open tray). Another option is to disable DMA support for the DVD drive or CD-ROM drive:

1. Click Start, highlight Settings, and then click Control Panel.
2. Double-click the System icon; then click the Device Manager tab.
3. Click the CD-ROM branch to expand it, click your CD-ROM drive or DVD drive, and then click Properties.
4. Click the Settings tab.
5. Click the DMA check box to clear it, and then click OK.
6. Click OK, and then restart your computer when prompted to do so.

Finally, you can try disabling the auto-insert notification feature for the DVD drive or CD-ROM drive:

1. Click Start, highlight Settings, and then click Control Panel.
2. Double-click the System icon; then click the Device Manager tab.
3. Click the CD-ROM branch to expand it, click your CD-ROM drive or DVD drive, and then click Properties.

4 Click the Settings tab.
5 Click the Auto Insert Notification check box to clear it, and then click OK.
6 Click OK, and then restart your computer when prompted to do so.

For more information on Media Event Status Notification (MESN), review the SFF8090 (a.k.a. Mt. Fuji) specification available from ftp://fission.dt.wdc.com/pub/standards/SFF/ specs/.

SYMPTOM 17-51 **You receive a "fatal exception in CDVSD" when starting Windows 98** When starting the computer, you encounter the following "blue screen" error message:

```
An exception 0E has occurred at 0028:C143EADA in VXD CDVSD(01) + 00001CFA.
This was called from 0028:C18413E8 in VXD voltrack(04)+ 00000A18. It may be
possible to continue normally.
```

This problem is reported to occur with the Agate Technologies AGAATAPI.MPD and Intel IDEATAPI.MPD miniport drivers, and can generally occur if a disc is not in the DVD drive (or when a disc is ejected from the DVD drive) while you're using a third-party SCSI miniport driver. An incorrect communication method is used when an IOS "VSD" is installed between the CDVSD and SCSIPORT layers, *and* the DVD drive supports Group 2 timeout commands. Check with Microsoft (or your DVD drive maker) to see if an updated version of CDVSD.VXD is available.

Further Study

ATI: **http://support.atitech.ca/**

Creative Labs: **http://www-nt-ok.creaf.com/mmuk/pcdvd/**

Diamond Multimedia: **http://www.diamondmm.com**

DVD Forum: **http://www.dvdforum.org/**

Hitachi: **http://www.hitachi.com/**

Matsushita: **http://www.panasonic.com/PCEC/dvd/index-dvd.html**

Panasonic: **http://www.panasonic.com/**

Toshiba: **http://www.toshiba.com/taisdpd/dvdrom.htm**

18

ENHANCING SYSTEM PERFORMANCE

CHAPTER AT A GLANCE

PC users receive the best return on their system investment when it's operating at peak efficiency. However, new hardware isn't always the answer. Even with state-of-the-art hardware, many important operating system and setup factors affect the performance of your system. Swap file problems, inadequate memory, and poor system settings are just a few of the issues that can reduce your system's effectiveness. This chapter is intended to help you identify the key performance areas of a typical Windows 95/98 PC and offer a set of handy guidelines that will help you get the most from your system.

Checking Performance Under Windows 95/98

The first step in improving your system's performance is to investigate the current performance level of your system. If you're using Windows 95/98, you can get an overview of the system's performance through the System Properties dialog. This will give you a picture of the system's key resources and the way in which Windows perceives them. You can access this dialog through the System icon:

1. Click Start, highlight Settings, and then click Control Panel.
2. Once the Control Panel opens, double-click the System icon.
3. Click the Performance tab (Figure 18-1).

The Performance tab lists six major parameters that affect your system performance. You should understand how to interpret each of these settings.

- *Memory* Specifies the amount of physical memory (RAM) in your computer that's recognized by Windows 95/98. If this value is less than the amount reported by BIOS during the POST memory count, you may have a problem with the way Windows recognizes or handles your RAM. This is also a quick way to tell how much RAM is in your customer's system.

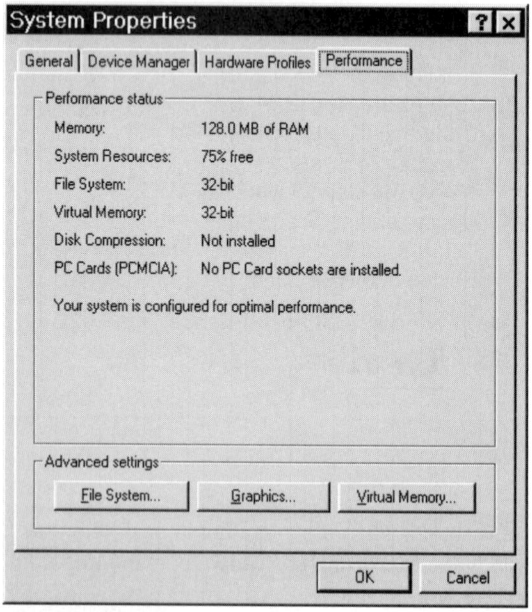

FIGURE 18-1 The System Properties Performance tab

- *System Resources* Indicates the percentage of "free system resources" (generally taken to mean "free RAM"). If this number is too low, your computer may perform slowly due to excessive use of virtual memory. You can correct this by closing unused background applications or by adding more RAM to the system.
- *File System* Specifies the type of file system that you're using (such as MS-DOS or 32-bit). This will affect the efficiency with which files are read from or written to your system drives. Your disk's performance will be slower if you're using the DOS Compatibility Mode, and this may mean that one or more drives in the system are using the incorrect drivers or are configured improperly. Windows will perform best using the 32-bit file system.
- *Virtual Memory* Virtual memory is hard disk space that is used as extra RAM. This entry indicates whether virtual memory is enabled (using 32-bit or DOS Compatibility Mode) or disabled. If virtual memory is enabled in the DOS Compatibility Mode, the disk being used for virtual memory is also using that mode. The same is true for the 32-bit virtual memory mode. A disk using DOS Compatibility Mode is slower than a disk using 32-bit mode, and system performance will suffer accordingly.
- *Disk Compression* Specifies whether you've installed any disk compression software on your computer (such as DriveSpace 3). If not, the entry will read "Not installed." If you do use compression software, the 32-bit version will yield optimal performance. Real-mode (DOS Compatibility Mode) compression software will run more slowly and impair overall system performance.
- *PC Cards (PCMCIA)* Indicates whether you have a PC (a.k.a. PCMCIA) card slot enabled. This is most commonly used with laptop systems. If there are no socket services installed, the entry will note "No PC Card sockets are installed." Otherwise, the entry will list either 32-bit software (for optimum performance) or DOS Compatibility Mode (real-mode) software. With 32-bit Windows PC card support, you can insert and remove PC cards while your computer is running.

Ideally, your system should offer ample memory and utilize 32-bit protected-mode drivers for all of the features installed on your system. This will generally offer the best overall performance, and the system will typically display a message such as "Your system is configured for optimal performance" below the PC Cards entry. If you're missing a protected-mode driver, or there's a device installed in the system that Windows doesn't recognize, it will almost always "fall back" to suitable real-mode (DOS Compatibility Mode) drivers instead. If your computer's performance status is not optimal, a description of the performance problem(s) will appear below the PC Cards line. For more information on a given problem, click an item, and then click Details.

System Monitor and Performance

System Monitor is a Windows 95/98 tool that measures the performance of hardware, software services, and applications. (The version included with Windows 98 will also log performance over time.) When you make changes to the system configuration, System Monitor shows the effect of your changes on overall system performance. This offers you a powerful tool that can help determine the effect of system upgrades or help find the cause of problems on a local or remote computer. For example, logging memory allocation while using a specific application could be helpful in identifying programs with "memory leaks" or unexpected processing overhead. As another example, you could measure system performance before making a configuration change, and changes in performance may help you identify performance bottlenecks.

USING SYSTEM MONITOR

System Monitor is normally not installed under Windows 98. Before attempting to install it, check to see if it's already on your system:

1. Click Start, highlight Programs, and click Accessories.
2. Select System Tools.
3. If System Monitor is installed, it will appear near the bottom of the System Tools menu. If it's present, you can start System Monitor simply by clicking on the menu entry.
4. By default, the System Monitor display appears as shown in Figure 18-2, and the charting will start automatically.

INSTALLING SYSTEM MONITOR

If System Monitor is not currently installed on your system, you may install System Monitor using the Add/Remove Programs wizard, as shown below:

1. Click Start, highlight Settings, and then click Control Panel.
2. Once the Control Panel is open, select the Add/Remove Programs icon.
3. Click the Windows Setup tab.
4. Select System Tools, and then click Details.
5. Click System Monitor, and then click OK. This will install System Monitor on your system.

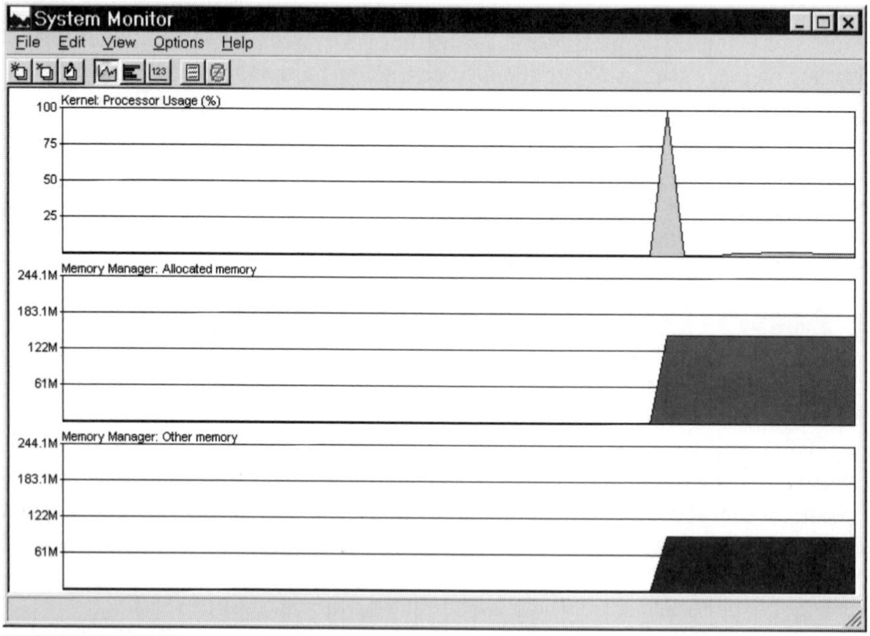

FIGURE 18-2 The default System Monitor dialog

ADJUSTING THE CHART FORMAT

By default, System Monitor uses a "strip-chart" format, but it also offers bar charts or numeric charts, depending on how you prefer to view the information. Once System Monitor is running, you can click View, then select the desired chart format. There are also shortcut buttons below the main menu.

ADJUSTING THE CHART APPEARANCE

You can control the color and update frequency under System Monitor. To adjust a color, click Edit, and then select Edit Item. Choose the item you want to adjust, and the Chart Options dialog will appear. If you need to adjust the update frequency, click the Options menu, click Chart, and adjust the update slider accordingly.

LOGGING SYSTEM PERFORMANCE

System Monitor offers the ability to log the parameters that it's measuring. To begin a logging session:

1. Start System Monitor (if it's not already running).
2. Click File, and then select Start Logging.
3. Enter a file name for the log file, and then click Save.
4. On the File menu, click Stop Logging to halt the log process.

CONFIGURING SYSTEM MONITOR

System Monitor uses the dynamic data information in the registry to report on the state of many different processes. You can select exactly which of those processes must be displayed in System Monitor:

1. With System Monitor running, click the Edit menu, and then click Add Item.
2. In the Category list, click the resource that you want to monitor. System Monitor will work with seven major categories, which are outlined in Table 18-1.
3. In the Item list, select one or more resources that you want to monitor.

> To select more than one item, press CTRL while clicking the items that you want to select. To select several items in a row, click the first item, and then hold down SHIFT while clicking the last item.

4. When you've selected an item, you may click Explain for more information about a selected resource.
5. Click OK. You'll see the performance chart of that resource added to System Monitor.
6. If you wish to remove an item later, simply click Edit, select Remove Item, highlight the item to be removed, and then click OK.

TROUBLESHOOTING WITH SYSTEM MONITOR

System Monitor is a versatile program that can measure a variety of important system parameters, but you'll need to have some idea of just what you're looking for in order to interpret the data that's displayed. Here are some guidelines for performance troubleshooting:

Memory Leaks If you suspect that an application might not be freeing memory when it finishes using it (sometimes called memory leaks), you should monitor the value of Kernel/Threads over time.

TABLE 18-1 SYSTEM MONITOR PARAMETERS

DIAL-UP ADAPTER SETTINGS

SETTING	MEASUREMENT
Alignment errors	Serial port alignment errors.
Buffer overruns	Serial port buffer overrun errors.
Bytes received/second	Number of bytes received per second.
Bytes transmitted/second	Number of bytes transmitted per second.
Connection speed	Connection speed in bits per second.
CRC errors	Number of frames with CRC errors.
Frames received/second	Number of good frames received per second.
Frames transmitted/second	Number of frames transmitted per second.
Framing errors	Serial port framing errors.
Incomplete frames	Number of incomplete frames received.
Overrun errors	Serial port overrun errors.
Timeout errors	Serial port timeout errors.
Total bytes received	Total number of bytes received.
Total bytes transmitted	Total number of bytes transmitted.

DISK CACHE SETTINGS

SETTING	MEASUREMENT
Cache buffers	Number of active buffers in a cache, including any and all compressed buffers.
Cache hits	Number of times data found in the cache, resulting in I/O requests.
Cache misses	Number of times data not found in the cache, resulting in I/O requests.
Cache pages	Current number of disk cache pages.
Failed cache recycles	Number of times a recycling request (either least recently used (LRU) or random) has failed. This can happen in low memory situations or when all cache buffers are currently in use.
LRU cache recycles	Number of times the cache is sequentially searched for a buffer to recycle, beginning with the oldest data. This happens when new data needs to be added to the cache, or when Memory Manager needs to borrow memory from the cache.
Maximum cache pages	Maximum number of disk cache pages.
Minimum cache pages	Minimum number of disk cache pages.
Random cache recycles	Number of times the cache is randomly searched for a buffer to recycle. This can happen whenever the cache becomes filled with data not used lately.

FILE SYSTEM SETTINGS

SETTING	MEASUREMENT
Bytes read/second	The number of bytes read from the file system each second.
Bytes written/second	The number of bytes written by the file system each second.
Dirty data	The number of bytes waiting to be written to the disk. Dirty data is stored in cache blocks, so the number reported might be larger than the actual number of bytes waiting.
Reads/second	The number of read operations delivered to the file system each second.

TABLE 18-1 SYSTEM MONITOR PARAMETERS *(CONTINUED)*

FILE SYSTEM SETTINGS *(CONTINUED)*	
SETTING	**MEASUREMENT**
Writes/second	The number of write operations delivered to the file system each second.
KERNEL SETTINGS	
SETTING	**MEASUREMENT**
Processor usage (%)	The approximate percentage of time the processor is busy.
Threads	The current number of threads present in the system.
Virtual machines	The current number of virtual machines present in the system.
MEMORY MANAGER VMM32 SETTINGS	
SETTING	**MEASUREMENT**
Allocated memory	The total amount in bytes of Other memory and Swappable memory. If this value is changing when there is no activity on the computer, it indicates that the disk cache is resizing itself.
Discards	The number of pages discarded from memory each second. (The pages are not swapped to the disk because the information is already on the disk.)
Disk cache size	The current size, in bytes, of the disk cache.
Instance faults	The number of instance faults each second.
Locked memory	The amount of allocated memory that is locked.
Locked noncache pages	Number of noncache locked pages.
Maximum disk cache size	The largest size possible for a disk cache. This is a fixed value loaded at system startup.
Mid-disk cache size	The mid-disk cache size. This is a fixed value loaded at system startup.
Minimum disk cache size	The smallest size possible for a disk cache. This is a fixed value loaded at system startup.
Other memory	The amount of allocated memory not stored in the swap file—for example, code from Win32 dynamic link libraries (DLLs) and executable files, memory-mapped files, nonpageable memory, and disk cache pages.
Page faults	The number of page faults each second.
Page-ins	The number of pages swapped into memory each second, including pages loaded from a Win32-based executable file or memory-mapped files. Consequently, this value does not necessarily indicate low memory.
Page-outs	The number of pages swapped out of memory and written to disk each second.
Pages mapped from cache	Used to monitor MapCache/WinAlign changes. The swap file size in use at the same time as this setting should be monitored for differences after running the WinAlign tool.
Swap file defective	The number of bytes in the swap file that are found to be physically defective on the swap medium. Because swap file frames are allocated in 4096-byte blocks, a single damaged sector causes the whole block to be marked as defective.
Swap file in use	The number of bytes being used in the current swap file.
Swap file size	The size, in bytes, of the current swap file.

TABLE 18-1 SYSTEM MONITOR PARAMETERS *(CONTINUED)*

MEMORY MANAGER VMM32 SETTINGS *(CONTINUED)*	
SETTING	**MEASUREMENT**
Swappable memory	The number of bytes allocated from the swap file. Locked pages still count for the purpose of this metric. This includes code from 16-bit applications and DLLs, but not code from Win32 DLLs and executable files.
Unused physical memory	Amount of physical memory (RAM) not currently in use.
MICROSOFT NETWORK CLIENT SETTINGS	
SETTING	**MEASUREMENT**
Bytes read/second	The number of bytes read from the redirector each second.
Bytes written/second	The number of bytes written to the redirector each second.
Number of nets	Number of networks currently running.
Open files	Number of open files on the network.
Resources	Number of resources.
Sessions	Number of sessions.
Transactions/second	The number of server message block (SMB) transactions managed by the redirector each second.
MICROSOFT NETWORK SERVER/NETWARE SETTINGS	
SETTING	**MEASUREMENT**
Buffers	The number of buffers used by the server.
Bytes read/sec	The total number of bytes read from a disk.
Bytes written/sec	The total number of bytes written to a disk.
Bytes/sec	The total number of bytes read from and written to a disk.
Memory	The total memory used by the server.
NBs	Server network buffers.
Server threads	The current number of threads used by the server.

This will indicate whether the application is starting threads and not reclaiming them later. Windows 98 should automatically remove such threads when the application closes, but if you identify a leak while the application is running, you may decide to restart the application periodically.

Insufficient Memory If the values for Memory Manager/Discards and Memory Manager/Page-outs indicate a great deal of activity, performance problems might be related to system memory "stress." These values might indicate a need for more physical memory (RAM) in the system.

Poor Overall Performance If a computer seems slow, check the values reported by Kernel/Processor Usage (%), by Memory Manager/Page Faults, and by Memory Manager/Locked Memory. Then interpret them using the following guide:

- If values for Kernel/Processor Usage (%) are high even when the user is not working, check to see which application(s) might be keeping it busy. To do this, press CTRL+ALT+DEL to see the list of tasks running in the Close Program dialog box.
- If the values for Memory Manager/Page Faults are high, the application(s) being used might have memory needs beyond the computer's capabilities, so you may need to add more RAM to the system.

- If the Memory Manager/Locked Memory statistics continually assume a large portion of the Memory Manager/Allocated Memory value, inadequate free memory might be affecting performance. Also, you might be running an application that locks memory unnecessarily. ("Locked memory" indicates the portion of memory used that cannot be paged out.) Check your application(s) first to verify they're not locking memory; then try adding more RAM to the system.

Graphics Performance

Graphics adapter technology is advancing in leaps and bounds, especially in the area of graphics acceleration. Power 2D and 3D acceleration schemes speed the opening of screens and dialog boxes, or vastly increase the frame rate in your favorite 3D "shooter." Unfortunately, graphics acceleration techniques are not always standard, and Windows 95/98 may sometimes assume that a particular accelerator feature is present when in fact it is not. You might see such problems ranging anywhere from small display irregularities to random system crashes. Windows 95/98 allows control over your graphics accelerator in order to isolate possible accelerator-related problems. This allows you to continue using Windows until the driver can be updated (or the adapter can be replaced).

ADJUSTING GRAPHICS ACCELERATION

You can manage the level of graphics acceleration used on your system through the Advanced Graphics Settings dialog and slider:

1. Click Start, highlight Settings, and then select Control Panel.
2. When the Control Panel opens, click the Performance tab.
3. Click the Graphics button in the Advanced Settings area.
4. The Advanced Graphics Settings dialog will appear (Figure 18-3).

You can alter the level of hardware acceleration by moving the slider left or right:

- The default setting is Full. This turns on *all* graphics hardware acceleration features available in the display driver.
- The first notch from the right (75%) can often be set to correct mouse pointer display problems. This setting disables hardware cursor support in the display driver by adding the SwCursor=1 entry to the [Display] section of SYSTEM.INI.

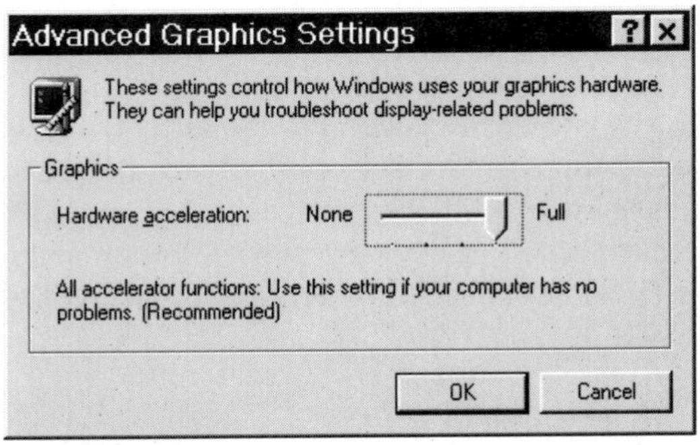

FIGURE 18-3 The Advanced Graphics Settings dialog

18

- The second notch from the right (50%) can be set to correct certain display errors. This setting prevents some bit block transfers from being performed on the display card and disables memory-mapped I/O for some display drivers. This setting adds the SwCursor=1 and Mmio=0 entries to the [Display] section of SYSTEM.INI, and the SafeMode=1 setting to the [Windows] section of WIN.INI.
- The last notch from the right (None) can be selected to correct problems if your computer frequently stops responding to input or suffers other severe problems. This setting adds the SafeMode=2 entry to the [Windows] section of WIN.INI, which removes *all* driver acceleration support and causes Windows 98 to use only the device-independent bitmap (DIB) engine rather than bit block transfers for displaying images.

As an example, an error message at system startup stating that an application caused "an invalid page fault in module <unknown>" might indicate a problem between the display driver and the Windows 98 DIB engine. In such cases, the None setting should correct the problem until you can update the display driver or replace the video card.

Memory Performance

Memory interacts closely with the CPU and can have a profound impact on overall system performance. You must install an adequate amount of memory with the right characteristics and configure the system to utilize that memory in the best possible way. You should also be concerned with system cache and verify that it's properly enabled. This section covers memory issues that you should be aware of.

- *Memory amount* You should install enough physical memory to adequately support your operating system and the application(s) that you intend to run. Generally, 32MB is considered to be the minimum amount of memory for Windows 98 and most general applications, but most systems today are fitted with 128MB of RAM. More memory is helpful for graphics, multimedia, and other memory-intensive applications (such as 3D computer action games). If there is not enough memory to support your system, you'll see a great deal of hard drive activity as data is passed back and forth to the swap file, and overall system performance will suffer.

Cache and memory are related. Since cache can only support a limited amount of RAM, any memory access that takes place outside of the cached memory range will be slowed. This will also impair overall system performance. When selecting RAM for your system, be sure that you do not exceed the "Maximum Cacheable RAM" specification listed for your motherboard. If you must add more RAM, check to see if you must add more cache to support the additional RAM.

- *Memory characteristics* When selecting RAM for your system, choose RAM with the optimum characteristics for your particular motherboard. Consider the "memory type" first. SDRAM is generally considered to be the fastest memory type and is supported by virtually all current Pentium II/III motherboards. Although the motherboard may be able to support older memory types such as EDO or FPM RAM, those older memory types will slow your system's overall performance. Also consider the "memory speed," since faster memory will respond better than slower memory. For example, SDRAM uses 12ns, 10ns, or 8ns "Cycle Time." The 8ns SDRAM will be faster. Also select SDRAM with a "CAS Latency" of 2 rather than 3 (if possible).

Error checking features such as parity or ECC generally do not affect memory performance, so you may select RAM with or without such features.

- *Avoid "SIMM stackers"* As DIMM slots became commonplace on motherboards, some manufacturers developed adapters that allowed you to "stack" several SIMMs into a single device that would fit in a DIMM slot. This technology worked fine, but the added distance between the RAM and the motherboard (introduced by the SIMM adapter) can degrade the RAM's performance. You may need to add a wait-state in the system's CMOS setup in order to compensate for this added delay.
- *Optimize the CMOS setup* You can often wring a bit more performance from your memory by optimizing the memory settings in your CMOS setup (usually under the Advanced Chipset Setup menu). The trick is to keep wait-states and latencies as low as possible, while keeping memory access techniques at a level that is appropriate with the memory type that you're using. You should refer to the manual that accompanies your motherboard for detailed information regarding your CMOS setup (or see Chapter 11).

OPTIMIZING CACHE

Cache serves a vital role in the PC by holding frequently used program code and data in memory, rather than having to constantly refer to the disk. This can substantially speed your "apparent" drive performance on the system. In Windows 98, the disk cache system is dynamic, so you do not need to configure its size as part of your normal system configuration. This means certain settings used for Windows 3.x are not required in Windows 98 and should be removed from your startup files:

- Share and SmartDrive entries should be removed from AUTOEXEC.BAT.
- SmartDrive double-buffer entries should be removed from CONFIG.SYS.

Windows 98 aggressively writes the contents of "dirty" memory pages (pages that contain changes) during system idle time, even if it does not need the memory at that point. This activity causes more disk action during idle times, but speeds up future memory allocations by doing some of the work while the system is idle.

Drive Performance

To improve the performance of a hard drive, you must first understand the factors that influence drive performance. The two most important factors are time related: the amount of time it takes to locate a file, and the rate at which data can be passed back and forth between the drive and system. Every other concern is intimately related to those two issues.

SEEK TIME

Since read/write heads are mechanical devices, it takes a finite amount of time to move them across a disk platter. The amount of time required to accomplish this move depends on two things: the size of the drive and the type of mechanism moving the heads. Newer drives are typically quite small, so the distances that must be traversed are short. Smooth and efficient voice-coil actuators are the head drive mechanism of choice, so movement is also enhanced. The combination of these factors has drastically reduced seek time over the last 15 years, but seek time is still a major part of overall drive delays.

Unfortunately, *seek time* is a rather generic term—different manufacturers each measure seek time as a slightly different parameter. The best-case seek time is referred to as *track-to-track seek time*, where the R/W heads only need to step in or out to the next adjacent track (or cylinder). This time is typically only a few hundred microseconds. If the best-case seek time is the time required to step between two adjacent tracks, the worst-case seek time is the time needed to step from the outermost track to the innermost track (or vice versa). Few manufacturers actually use this time since it seems so large. Instead, most drive manufacturers use an *average seek time*, which is the time needed to step halfway across the disk surface. Today, most drives offer average seek times between 6ms and 12ms. There is no way to accelerate seek times other than to simply upgrade the drive to a newer model.

DATA TRANSFER RATE

Once the R/W heads have moved into position (during the seek time), data can flow to or from the drive. The rate at which data can flow is known as the *data transfer rate*. Data transfer is generally given in Mbits/s. If you divide this figure by 8, you will get MB/s. A more practical measure of data transfer is the data rate between the hard drive and the drive controller (across the interface). EIDE hard drives can support burst data transfer rates up to 16MB/s, though Ultra-ATA hard drives can reach 33MB/s (or 66MB/s for Ultra-DMA/66 devices). This is comparable with fast SCSI-2 drive configurations, as shown in Table 18-2. In virtually all cases, you can speed the performance of your hard drive system by upgrading the drive and controller to newer models (such as an Ultra-DMA/66 drive and compatible PCI-based controller card).

Data transfer rates are a key part of drive delay. Most of the hesitation and pauses you see in the everyday operation of DOS or Windows 95/98 are largely because the operating system is waiting for the drive to catch up. The operating system typically must wait for a file to be loaded or saved before any other operations can continue. The faster a file's data can be transferred to or from the drive, the shorter those delays

TABLE 18-2 COMPARISON OF HARD DRIVE DATA TRANSFER RATES

DATA TRANSFER MODE	BURST DATA RATE	NOTES
Single Word DMA 0	2.1MB/s	Old ATA (IDE) drives
PIO Mode 0	3.3MB/s	IDE drives
Single Word DMA 1	4.2MB/s	IDE drives
Multi Word DMA 0	4.2MB/s	IDE drives
SCSI-1	5.0MB/s	8-bit SCSI
PIO Mode 1	5.2MB/s	IDE drives
PIO Mode 2	8.3MB/s	IDE drives
Single Word DMA 2	8.3MB/s	IDE drives
Fast SCSI-2	10.0MB/s	16-bit SCSI
Wide SCSI-2	10.0MB/s	16-bit SCSI
PIO Mode 3	11.1MB/s	Newer ATA-2 (EIDE) drives
Multi Word DMA 1	13.3MB/s	EIDE drives
PIO Mode 4	16.6MB/s	EIDE drives
Multi Word DMA 2	16.6MB/s	EIDE drives
Fast/Wide SCSI-2	20.0MB/s	16-bit SCSI
Fast-20 SCSI-3	20.0MB/s	8-bit SCSI
Multi Word DMA 3	33.0MB/s	Ultra-ATA (Ultra-DMA/33) drives
Wide/Fast-20 SCSI-3	40.0MB/s	16-bit SCSI
Fast-40 SCSI-3	40.0MB/s	8-bit SCSI
Multi Word DMA 4	66.0MB/s	Ultra-ATA (Ultra-DMA/66) drives
Wide/Fast-40 SCSI-3	80.0MB/s	16-bit SCSI

will be. Today, "apparent" drive performance is enhanced through the aggressive use of caching—where drive data is cached to RAM so the system may continue, then written to the drive as time allows.

FILE FRAGMENTATION

The interaction of operating systems also affects drive performance. When a drive is high-level formatted with an operating system, the drive's space is segregated into sets of adjacent sectors (called *clusters*). The size of a cluster depends on the size of the drive, but today's large, multigigabyte drives usually use 32KB to 64KB clusters under FAT16, or 4KB to 8KB clusters under FAT32. The cluster approach was designed to simplify file "housekeeping"—easing file storage tracking requirements while keeping wasted space acceptable. Although the system is less than ideal, it works, and has been in use since DOS was able to support hard drives. The problem with cluster-based file storage is that files are stored *wherever* clusters are available. Ideally, all of the clusters that compose a file should be contiguous, but that is a rare occurrence in practice. As a drive fills and old files are erased, clusters are filled and reclaimed throughout the drive.

As a result, changing files gradually become scattered across the drive as DOS searches frantically for any available clusters. This scattering behavior is called *file fragmentation*, and it is a natural side effect of DOS. The problem with file fragmentation is that each time the continuity of a file is broken, the R/W heads have to be repositioned before another cluster can be read. If a file uses four clusters, and each cluster is several tracks apart, the heads will have to be repositioned four times to read or write that file. These additional seek times all add up to prolong the loading or saving of a file. In addition to these delays, the extra mechanical demands of R/W head positioning can eventually lead to premature drive failure.

MANAGING FILE FRAGMENTATION

DOS and Windows 95/98 offer the Disk Defragmenter tool (a.k.a. Defrag), which should be used periodically to reorganize the disk clusters so that all clusters related to a particular file are made contiguous. Once your related clusters are relocated together, the drive doesn't have to work as hard to load or save files, and this often makes your drive access *seem* faster. You can find Defrag in your Windows 98 System Tools menu:

18

1. Click Start, highlight Programs, choose Accessories, and select System Tools.
2. Click on Disk Defragmenter. The Defrag window will open (Figure 18-4).
3. You can select the drive(s) to be defragmented; then start the process by clicking OK.

It may take a while for Defrag to finish depending on the size of the drive, the number of files it contains, and the extent of fragmentation. FAT32 drives can take much longer to finish because there are many more clusters for Defrag to work with.

If you're using Windows 98, you can also configure Defrag to help your applications start faster. Select the Settings option in your Defrag dialog. The Disk Defragmenter Settings dialog will appear (Figure 18-5). Check the "Rearrange program files so my programs start faster" box so that Defrag will rearrange your applications for faster boot-up. If you do not select this option, Defrag will simply group your file clusters without any consideration of startup speed.

USING FAT32

Windows 98 offers full support for FAT32 partitions. FAT32 uses smaller clusters than FAT16 and allows drives over 2GB to be partitioned as a single logical volume. Windows 98 provides a Drive

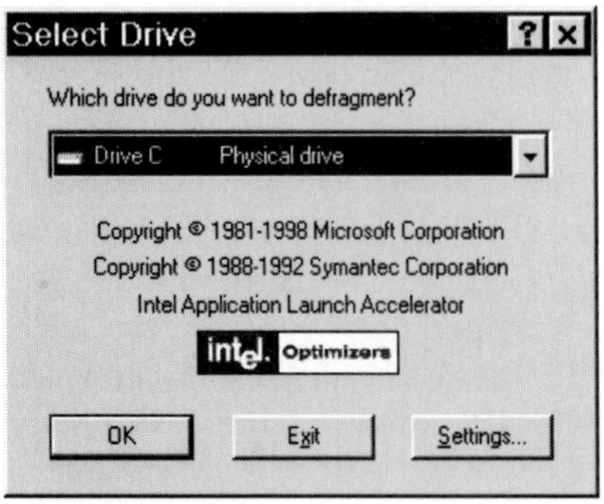

FIGURE 18-4 The Disk Defragmenter dialog

Converter (FAT32) utility that can convert your existing FAT16 partition(s) to FAT32. Since clusters are smaller, “slack space” can be reduced dramatically—freeing up as much as several hundred megabytes on your drive. Windows 98 also uses FAT32 partitions far more efficiently, which allows fast disk access (and fast application loading in conjunction with Disk Defragmenter). You can start Drive Converter by clicking Start, highlighting Programs, pointing to Accessories, selecting System Tools, and then clicking Drive Converter. The converter will start and allow you to convert your selected drive(s). However, there are some important tips to remember before you use the converter:

- Once you convert a partition to FAT32 format using Drive Converter, you cannot return to the FAT16 format unless you repartition and reformat the FAT32 drive. If you converted the drive where Windows 98 is installed, you must reinstall Windows 98 after repartitioning the drive as FAT16.
- Older disk compression software (including DriveSpace 3) is not compatible with FAT32. If your drive is already compressed, you may not be able to convert to FAT32.
- If you convert a removable disk to FAT32 and use that disk with an operating system that is not FAT32 compatible, you cannot access the disk when running the other operating system.
- If your computer has a “hibernate” feature, the conversion process may turn this feature off. You may need to reenable this feature manually.
- Because previous versions of Windows are not compatible with FAT32, you cannot uninstall Windows 98 after converting.

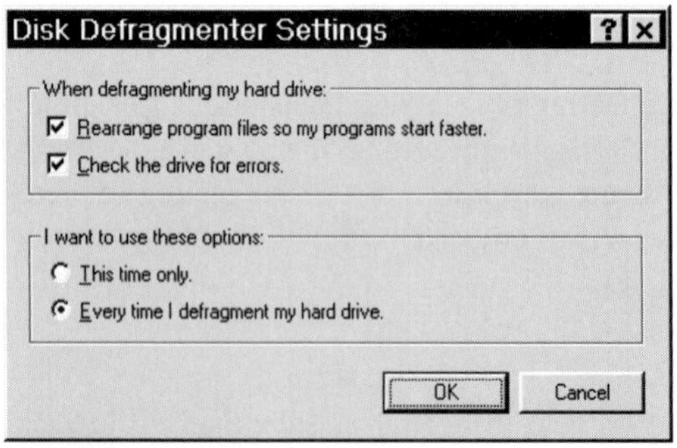

FIGURE 18-5 The Disk Defragmenter Settings dialog

- Some disk utilities that depend on FAT16 may not work with FAT32 drives. You will be prompted if you're running one of these utilities. Contact your disk utility manufacturer to see if there is an updated version that is compatible with FAT32.
- If you convert your hard drive to FAT32 using Drive Converter, you can no longer use dual boot to run earlier versions of Windows (including Windows 95, Version 4.00.950, Windows NT 3.x, Windows NT 4.0, or Windows 3.x).

> FAT32 drives may perform significantly slower on disk-intensive operations when your computer is running in DOS mode, or when you're running Windows 98 in Safe Mode. If you use the DOS mode with FAT32 drives, you may find that performance is improved significantly if you load the SmartDrive disk-caching program.

CHECKING FOR DISK ERRORS

You can use the ScanDisk utility to check the disk for file problems such as lost allocation units and cross-linked files. Such file problems are quite common with FAT-based operating systems, and file damage can corrupt an application, driver, or data file. You should run ScanDisk periodically and allow it to correct any problems that it finds. If you detect damaged file(s), be sure to defragment the drive and reinstall the damaged file(s) from a backup or the original installation disks. You can run ScanDisk from DOS by simply exiting Windows to DOS, switching to the drive that you need to test, then typing:

```
C:> SCANDISK
```

You can then follow the on-screen directions to correct any error that's encountered. For a deeper test, select Yes to perform a surface test on the drive. (This may take anywhere from several minutes to several hours.) Finally, select View Log to review any actions and results taken by ScanDisk. If you're having trouble starting Windows, use the DOS version of ScanDisk. Otherwise, use ScanDisk through Windows:

1. Click Start, select Programs, select Accessories, and click System Tools.
2. Click ScanDisk. The ScanDisk dialog will open.
3. You can select the drive to be tested along with a surface scan or other advanced options.

In most cases, you should run ScanDisk to test for errors first, but do not allow ScanDisk to fix errors automatically until you've identified the errors.

> Be very careful with ScanDisk versions. If you're using a FAT32 partition, be sure to use the Windows 98 version of ScanDisk. Using an older version of ScanDisk on a FAT32 partition may cause file damage.

32-BIT DRIVERS

Ideally, Windows 98 will apply a 32-bit protected-mode driver to every drive in the system, which ensures optimum performance. You can verify the use of 32-bit drivers by reviewing the File System entry in your Performance tab under the System icon. By default, 32-bit disk access is always enabled unless Windows 98 detects a real-mode disk driver that does not have a protected-mode replacement. This could be an older Stacker driver, a hard-disk security or encryption driver, or other legacy driver for a hard drive. To prevent the performance loss that occurs when Windows 98 is forced to use a real-mode disk driver, upgrade to a protected-mode replacement for the offending driver.

If you need to determine why a Windows 98 real-mode disk driver was installed, check the IOS.LOG file.

BUS MASTERING

Traditionally, a *bus* is simply a means of allowing devices access to system resources, and this was almost always accomplished under the direction of a master device—the system CPU. This meant that most data transfers between the drive controller and host system were accomplished through Programmed I/O (or PIO) modes (see Table 18-2). With the introduction of "intelligent" bus architectures such as PCI, it became possible for individual devices on the bus to assume control and initiate data transfers *without* the direct intervention of the CPU. This technique is generally called Direct Memory Access (or DMA). There's nothing really new about DMA, and PCs have offered DMA channels since the early IBM PCs. The difference is that today's busses allow high-performance DMA transfers by devices that temporarily assume control of that bus. Such *bus mastering* requires the use of bus master drivers.

If your system has bus mastering drivers installed (and devices that support DMA data transfers), you'll see a DMA check box in the Options area of the Properties dialog for that device, as shown in Figure 18-6. By default, the DMA check box is usually unselected. If you select the DMA check box, the drive will attempt to use DMA data transfers. Be extremely careful when enabling DMA data transfers. If your system hardware does not fully support bus mastering (or the bus master drivers are old or corrupt), you may find that drive performance actually decreases, or the system may even become unstable. Try installing the latest bus master drivers for your chipset before enabling DMA data transfers.

OPTIMIZING THE SWAP FILE

Windows 98 uses a special file on your hard disk called a *virtual memory swap file* (also called a *paging file*). When using virtual memory under Windows 98, some of your program code and data are kept in

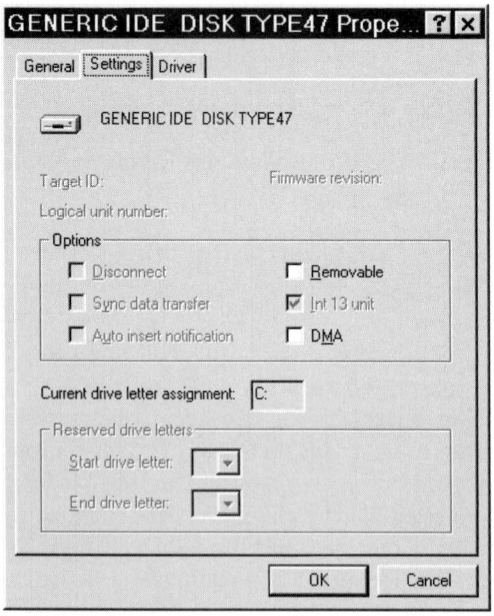

FIGURE 18-6 Identifying a bus master–compliant drive

memory (system RAM), while other information is swapped temporarily to virtual memory. When that information is required again, Windows 98 pulls it back into RAM (and swaps other information to virtual memory if necessary). This activity is transparent to the end user, though you might notice that your hard disk is working. Virtual memory allows you to run more programs at one time than the computer's existing RAM would normally allow. The Windows 98 swap file is dynamic, so it can shrink or grow as needed based on the tasks at hand and available disk space. It can also occupy a fragmented region of the hard disk with no substantial performance penalty.

The best way to ensure good swap file performance is to ensure that the drive containing your swap file has ample free space. This way, the swap file size can shrink and grow as needed.

Although the system default settings usually provide good overall swap file performance, you can adjust the parameters used to define the swap file. For example, to optimize swap file performance on a computer with multiple hard drives, you can override the default location of the Windows 98 swap file. As a rule, the swap file should be placed on the drive with the fastest performance. If you've placed the swap file on a drive that's extremely busy, performance might be boosted by relocating the swap file to another one of the drives that's not as busy. To adjust your virtual memory swap file size:

1. Open the Control Panel, double-click the System icon, click the Performance tab, and then click Virtual Memory. The Virtual Memory dialog appears, as in Figure 18-7.
2. By default, the "Let Windows manage my virtual memory settings" option is selected.
3. To specify a different hard disk, click the "Let me specify my own virtual memory settings" option, and then specify the new disk in the "Hard disk" box. As an alternative, type values (in KB) in the Minimum or Maximum box, and then click OK.

If you set the maximum swap file size in the Virtual Memory dialog to use the amount of free space currently on a drive, Windows 98 assumes that it can increase the swap file *beyond* that size if more free disk space becomes available. If you want to impose a fixed limit on the swap file size, make sure the limit you choose is less than the current maximum drive space.

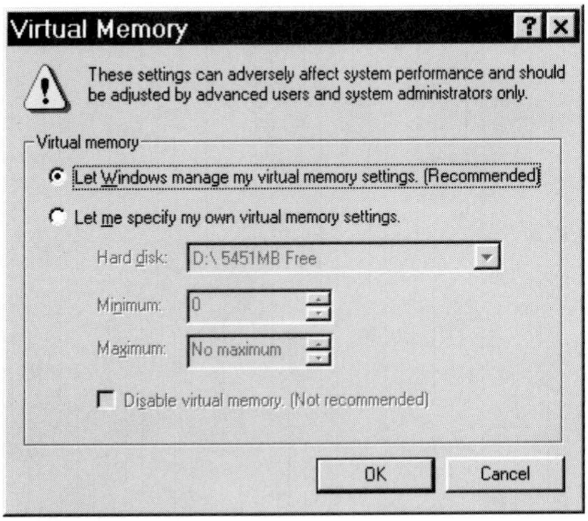

FIGURE 18-7 The Virtual Memory dialog box

OPTIMIZING THE HARD DRIVE FILE SYSTEM

In Windows 98, file system and drive performance can be controlled based on how the computer is used in most situations. The option for configuring file system performance is controlled only by the user. None of these settings are affected by other configuration changes that might be made in Windows 98 (such as installing file and printer sharing services). To optimize file system performance, open the Control Panel, double-click the System icon, click the Performance tab, and then click File System. In the "Typical role of this computer" entry on your Hard Disk tab (Figure 18-8), select the most common role for this computer, and then click OK. Each role is outlined below:

- *Desktop computer* This is a normal computer acting primarily as a network client, or an individual computer with no networking. This configuration assumes that there is more than the minimum required RAM and that the computer is running on AC power (rather than the battery).
- *Mobile or docking system* This is usually any computer with limited memory. This configuration assumes that RAM is limited, and the computer is commonly running on battery power, so the disk cache should be flushed frequently.
- *Network server* This is a computer used primarily as a peer server for file or printer sharing. This configuration assumes that the computer has adequate RAM and frequent disk activity, so the system is optimized for a large amount of disk access.

The time it takes to launch an application often depends on cluster size (therefore, the particular file system). Smaller cluster sizes allow applications to launch faster—a 4KB cluster size (FAT32) is best, but larger cluster sizes (such as FAT16) give less of a performance boost.

Each disk performance profile adjusts the values of the following file system settings in the registry:

- PathCache specifies the size of the cache that the Virtual File Allocation Table (VFAT) can use to save the locations of the most recently used directory paths. This cache improves performance by reducing the number of times the file system must seek paths by searching the File Allocation Table. There are 32 paths for the Desktop profile, 16 paths for Mobile or docking system, and 64 paths for Network server.

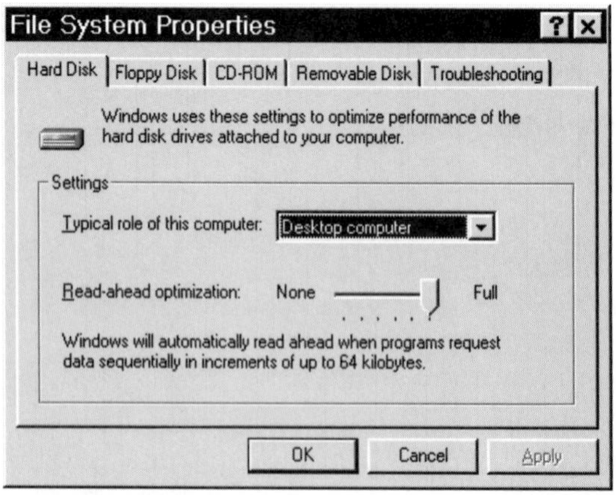

FIGURE 18-8 The hard disk File System Properties dialog

- NameCache stores the locations of the most recently accessed file names. The use of PathCache and NameCache together means that VFAT never searches the disk for the location of cached file names. Both PathCache and NameCache use memory out of the general system heap. There are about 677 file names (8KB) for the Desktop computer profile, 337 file names (4KB) for Mobile or docking system, and 2729 file names (16KB) for Network server.
- The BufferIdleTimeout, BufferAgeTimeout, and VolumeIdleTimeout settings control the time between changes being placed in the buffer and when they are written to the hard disk.

The values assigned to each disk performance profile are stored in the following registry key:

```
HKEY_LOCAL_MACHINE \Software \Microsoft \Windows \CurrentVersion \FS
Templates
```

The following subkey contains the actual settings for the profile currently used:

```
HKEY_LOCAL_MACHINE \System \CurrentControlSet \Control \FileSystem
```

An additional performance setting in the FileSystem subkey can be used to change the size of the contiguous space that VFAT searches for when allocating disk space. Under DOS, the file system begins allocating the first available space found on the disk. This causes a great deal of disk fragmentation and related performance problems. Under Windows 98, VFAT first tries to allocate space in the first contiguous 0.5MB of free space and then returns to the DOS method if it cannot find at least this much contiguous free space. This optimizes performance for both the swap file and multimedia applications.

In some cases, you might choose to set a smaller value in the registry (for example, when you're not running demanding applications). A smaller value for ContigFileAllocSize can lead to more fragmentation on the disk and more disk access for the swap file.

OPTIMIZING THE CD-ROM FILE SYSTEM

The CD-ROM cache is separate from the cache used for disk file and network access because the performance characteristics of the CD-ROM are different. This cache can be paged to disk (the file and network cache cannot), and this reduces the work for Windows 98, but still allows better CD-ROM performance. When Windows 98 is retrieving data from a compact disc, it's still faster to read a record from the cache—even if it's been paged to disk—since the disk access time is much faster than the CD-ROM access time.

> A small CD-ROM cache makes a big difference in streaming performance, but a much larger cache does not pay off as significantly unless the cache is large enough to contain entire multimedia streams.

To set the supplemental cache size for your CD file system:

1. Open the Control Panel, double-click the System icon, click the Performance tab, and then click File System.
2. Click the CD-ROM tab, and then drag the slider to set the "Supplemental cache size" (Figure 18-9).
3. Move the "Supplemental cache size" slider to the right to allocate more RAM for caching data from the CD-ROM drive, or to the left to allocate less RAM for caching data. Note that many multimedia programs perform better with a smaller cache because they tend not to reuse data.

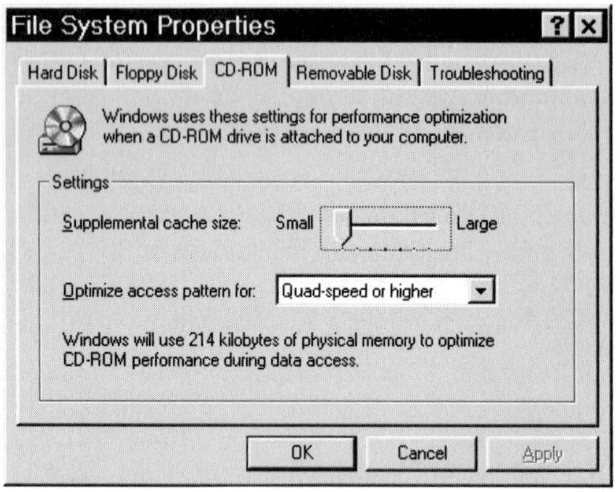

FIGURE 18-9 The CD-ROM File System Properties dialog

4. In the "Optimize access pattern for" box, select a setting based on your computer's CD-ROM drive speed.
5. Click OK; then shut down and restart the computer.

OPTIMIZING REMOVABLE DISK PERFORMANCE

Windows 98 gives you the option to use write-behind caching to improve the performance of removable disk drives, such as the Zip or Jaz drives. To set write-behind caching for removable disk drives:

1. Open the Control Panel, double-click the System icon, click the Performance tab, click File System, and then click the Removable Disk tab.
2. Select the "Enable write-behind caching on all removable disk drives" check box, and then click OK.
3. If this causes a problem with disk operations, repeat the first step, and then clear the "Enable write-behind caching on all removable disk drives" check box, and click OK.

File System Troubleshooting Tips

The System option in Control Panel presents a set of options for changing file system performance. You can use these options when you experience rare hardware or software compatibility problems. To display the file system troubleshooting options:

1. Open the Control Panel, double-click the System icon, and then click the Performance tab.
2. Click File System, and then click the Troubleshooting tab.

> Enabling any of these file system troubleshooting options will seriously degrade system performance. Enable these options only if necessary, and disable them as soon as possible.

You can the select one or more troubleshooting options. Each option is described here:

- *Disable new file sharing and locking semantics* This option alters the internal rules for file sharing and locking on hard disks (governing whether some processes can access open files in certain share modes). This option should be selected if a DOS-based application has problems with sharing under Windows 98. (This sets SoftCompatMode=0 in the registry.)
- *Disable long name preservation for old programs* This option turns off the "tunneling" feature, which preserves long file names when files are opened and saved by applications that do not recognize long file names. This option should be checked when an important legacy program is not compatible with long file names. (This sets PreserveLongNames=0 in the registry.)
- *Disable protected-mode hard disk interrupt handling* This option prevents Windows 98 from terminating interrupts from the hard disk controller and bypassing the BIOS routine that handles these interrupts. Some hard disk drives might require this option to be checked in order for interrupts to be processed correctly. If this option is checked, the BIOS routine handles the interrupts, slowing system performance. (This sets VirtualHDIRQ=1 in the registry, but this setting is off by default in Windows 98.)
- *Disable synchronous buffer commits* The "file commit" function is used to guarantee the integrity of user data being written to a disk. Normally, the function is used by applications to ensure that critical data is written to the disk before returning from a call made to the file commit function. Choosing this option disables this feature. Data is still written to disk, but it is written to disk in the background—at the discretion of the file system. Keep in mind that choosing this option can compromise data written to disk by an application should the system crash before the data is actually written.
- *Disable all 32-bit protected-mode disk drivers* This option ensures that no 32-bit disk drivers are loaded in the system (except the floppy driver). Typically, you'd check this option if the computer does not start because of disk peripheral I/O problems. If this option is enabled, all I/O will go through real-mode drivers or the BIOS. In this case, all disk drives that are visible only in protected mode will no longer be visible. (This sets ForceRMIO=1 in the registry.)
- *Disable write-behind caching for all drives* This option ensures that all data is flushed continually to the hard disk, removing any performance benefits gained from disk caching. This option should be checked if you're performing risky operations and must ensure prevention of data loss. (This sets DriveWriteBehind=0 in the registry.)

Managing the Registry

The Windows 95/98 registry is a critical part of your Windows platform that maintains a great deal of information about your system. When problems occur with the registry, your system may become unstable or even fail to start in extreme circumstances. Windows 98 offers several tools that allow you to manage and maintain your registry. This part of the chapter offers a series of handy tips for RegClean (Registry Clean), and ScanReg (Registry Checker).

UNDERSTANDING REGCLEAN 4.1A

When you install, uninstall, and reinstall programs on your computer, you'll find that registry entries (or *keys*) are created, modified, and deleted. Over time, your computer's registry may begin to contain corrupted, unused, and unnecessary keys, especially if unneeded keys are not removed when you uninstall a program. As a result, you may eventually experience problems when using important Windows features (such as OLE to embed objects, or automation to control other programs). The RegClean utility is designed to clean up unnecessary entries in your registry.

RUNNING REGCLEAN

If you do not have RegClean installed on your system, download it from the Microsoft Web site and install it. Double-click the RegClean icon to start the utility. RegClean displays a progress dialog. While the progress dialog box is displayed, RegClean loads a copy of the parts of the registry that it's going to check and then performs the actual scanning. Depending on how much information is in your registry (and the speed of your CPU), the scanning process takes from about 30 seconds to as much as 30 minutes.

> If you have many entries in your registry, RegClean might sometimes appear to have stopped working. RegClean might appear completely halted whenever it is checking remote or removable drives. Don't worry about this; simply allow RegClean to finish its cycle.

Once these progress meters have disappeared, you will be prompted for the next action. You can do two things at this point:

- *Exit RegClean.* If RegClean did not find any errors in your registry (or if you don't want RegClean to fix the errors that it may have found), click Cancel.
- *Allow RegClean to fix the errors that it found.* Click Fix Errors to prompt RegClean to remove any entries containing errors that may have been found in the registry. A progress meter is displayed while RegClean does this. When the progress meter disappears, RegClean is done. Click Exit to close RegClean.

Clicking Fix Errors also creates an UNDO.REG file in the folder where you ran RegClean. The file will have the following title,

```
UNDO <computer> yyyymmddhhmmss.REG
```

where <computer> is the name of your computer, yyyymmdd is the date, and hhmmss is the time. If you'd like to "undo" or replace what RegClean removed from your registry at any point, double-click the UNDO.REG file.

> RegClean does not fix every known problem with the registry. It does not fix a "corrupt" registry. It is limited to fixing problems with normal registry entries located in HKEY_CLASSES_ROOT. RegClean will generally leave any entries in the registry that it does not understand or that could possibly be correct. Consequently, it is very possible that RegClean will not correct a problem that you have encountered.

WHEN YOU CANNOT UNDO

Normally, you should be able to undo changes made by RegClean simply by double-clicking on the UNDO.REG file. If Windows displays several error message boxes when you try to double-click the UNDO.REG file, chances are that you have a problem with the associated program(s) or REG files (rather than the UNDO file itself). Try correcting the problem by following these steps:

1. Open an Explorer window, click the View menu, and select Options.

2 In the Options dialog box, select the File Types tab.

3 Scroll down in the "Registered file types" list until you find the entry "Registration Entries."

4 Double-click this item, or click the Edit button.

5 In the Edit File Type dialog box, select the "Merge" entry, and either double-click this item or click the Edit button.

6 In the "Editing action for type: Registration Entries" dialog box, make sure that the text in the "Application used to perform action" field has the following entry (including the double quotes):

```
regedit.exe "%1"
```

7 Click the OK buttons to close all three dialog boxes.

8 You should be able to double-click on the UNDO.REG file.

UNDERSTANDING SCANREG

When you start your computer successfully, the Registry Checker (SCANREG.EXE) automatically creates a backup of system files and registry configuration information (including user account information, protocol bindings, software program settings, and user preferences) once daily. Files that the Registry Checker backs up include SYSTEM.DAT, USER.DAT, SYSTEM.INI, and WIN.INI. ScanReg automatically scans the system registry for invalid entries and empty data blocks each time it's started. If invalid registry entries are detected, it will restore the previous day's backup. If no backups are available, ScanReg tries to make repairs to the registry. If the registry contains more than 500KB of empty data blocks, ScanReg automatically optimizes it. Finally, Windows 98 setup runs ScanReg to verify the integrity of the existing registry before it performs an upgrade. (If it detects registry damage, ScanReg tries to fix the damage automatically.) This part of the chapter describes how to run ScanReg and customize ScanReg by manually editing the SCANREG.INI file.

USING SCANREG

You can start ScanReg through the Windows 95 System Information utility. Simply click Start, highlight Programs, point to Accessories, select System Tools, and then click System Information. On the Tools menu, click Registry Checker. You can also start ScanReg from the Windows 95/98 "Run" command line. Simply click Start, click Run, type **SCANREGW.EXE** (or **SCANREG.EXE** for the real-mode version) in the Open box, and then click OK. To restore individual files, follow the steps below:

1 Click Start, select Find, and click Files or Folders.

2 In the Named box, type **rb0*.cab**, and then click Find Now.

3 Double-click on the "cabinet file" that has the correct registry file to be restored.

4 Right-click the file you want to restore, click Extract, and then choose the folder where the new file is to be placed.

To use ScanReg with the /restore parameter, it *must* be run from a command prompt running outside of Windows (that is, from a command prompt booted from your emergency startup disk). You can choose up to five registry backup files listed for you to restore.

EDITING SCANREG.INI

The SCANREG.INI file contains all of the settings used to run SCANREG.EXE (or the protected-mode version of ScanReg called SCANREGW.EXE). You can edit SCANREG.INI by loading it into any text editor such as Notepad. The typical entries for SCANREG.INI (and their meanings) are outlined below:

- *Backup* A value of 1 (default) causes a backup copy of your registry to be made the first time you start your computer on any given day (determined by the system clock). A value of 0 disables this automatic registry backup. Note that disabling the registry backup is not recommended.
- *Optimize* A value of 1 (default) automatically optimizes your current registry if it contains 500KB of unused space. A value of 0 disables this automatic optimization process.
- *MaxBackupCopies* A value of 5 (default) saves the last 5 registry backups in the \Windows\Sysbckup folder. In practice, you can set this value between 0 and 99. Note that when you restore a registry backup using ScanReg for DOS, only the five earliest backups are displayed.
- *BackupDirectory* By default, this entry does not contain a value, and registry backups are automatically saved in the \Windows\Sysbckup folder. To change the location where registry backups are saved, type the full path to the folder. For example, if you want to save registry backups in the c:\registry\backups folder, change the BackupDirectory line to read

```
BackupDirectory=c:\registry\backups
```

More Windows 98 Performance Tips

Following are some more ways to get Windows 98 to perform as well as possible on your computer. Not all of them will create noticeable performance boosts for every computer, but they are ways to get the best performance for your PC.

Use Windows Update It's hard to know when you need to update important Windows files on your computer. Windows 98 provides a resource site on the Web (called "Windows Update") that you can use to identify new updates and patches that might help your computer run better. Windows Update can automatically review the system software on your computer and then recommend when you need to install updates specific to your computer. To use Windows Update while you're online, click Start, and then click Windows Update.

Check Your Registry Since the registry often loads drivers and other programs at start time, you should periodically run ScanReg or RegClean to inspect the registry for unused or faulty entries that can waste time and valuable RAM loading unneeded elements on your Windows platform. Use the steps below to launch Registry Checker:

1. Click Start, highlight Programs, select Accessories, and then highlight System Tools.
2. Click System Information.
3. Click Tools from the menu bar, and then click Registry Checker.

Remove Unwanted Files If you're running short of drive space, but don't want to take the chance of installing DriveSpace 3, you can periodically use the Disk Cleanup utility included with Windows 98. This utility helps you free disk space by searching the drive and listing files that you can remove safely:

1 Click Start, highlight Programs, select Accessories, point to System Tools, and then click Disk Cleanup.
2 Select the drive you want to clean up.
3 On the Disk Cleanup tab (Figure 18-10), select the files you want to delete.
4 To free even more space, click the More Options tab. (Here you can remove Windows components or other programs or files that you don't use.)

Turn Off Desktop Animations Animations may seem pretty and interesting, but they can demand a surprising amount of memory and processing power. You can free these resources by turning off your desktop animations:

1 Right-click your desktop, select Active Desktop, and click Customize My Desktop.
2 Click the Effects tab.
3 Clear the "Animate windows, menus, and lists" and "Show window contents while dragging" options.
4 Save your changes.

Turn Off Power Conservation Power-saving techniques often spin down the hard drive and power-off the monitor during periods of inactivity. Make sure that your idle periods are suitable for the way you use the system. If your idle periods are too short, you may find yourself waiting for the display to reappear or the drive to spin up for disk access. If you cannot determine more suitable idle time settings, disable your power-saving modes.

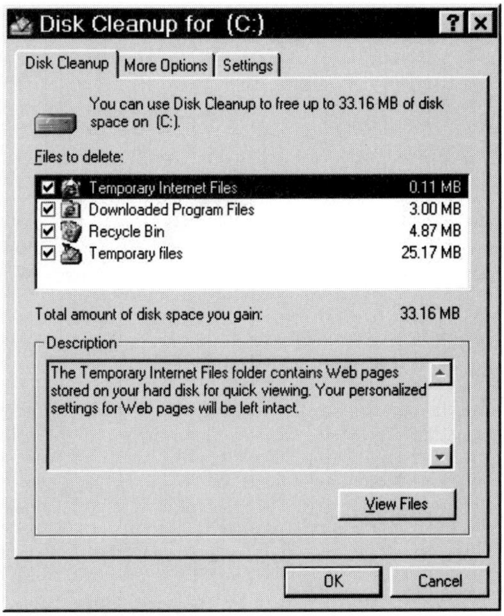

FIGURE 18-10 The Disk Cleanup tab

Remove Disk Compression Disk compression utilities (such as DriveSpace 3) slow the drive performance a bit due to their use of on-the-fly compression. You can reconfigure DriveSpace to compress files only if drive space drops below some preset amount, or disable/remove the compression utility outright. This will reduce your free drive space, but speed the drive's performance.

Further Study

Maxtor: **http://www.maxtor.com**

Microsoft: **http://www.microsoft.com** (SmartDrive and DriveSpace 3)

Quantum: **http://www.quantum.com**

Seagate: **http://www.seagate.com**

Western Digital: **http://www.wdc.com**

19

ERROR CODES

CHAPTER AT A GLANCE

Even with the proliferation of diagnostics and test equipment in the PC industry, most computers are remarkably adept at testing their own hardware and reporting serious errors during start time. This is accomplished through the Power-On Self-Test (POST) routine written into BIOS. Since BIOS is written expressly for a particular processor, chipset, and other motherboard hardware, it is an ideal choice for startup diagnostics. However, startup diagnostics pose a unique problem: it's hard to report an error when the system isn't fully functional. BIOS reports POST errors through the use of audible signals (called *beep codes*) as well as through hexadecimal codes (called *POST codes*) that are written to established I/O addresses. IBM has also established a standardized set of diagnostic codes for indicating system problems. This chapter explores the IBM diagnostic codes, then presents a compilation of beep and POST codes tracked down from just about every BIOS maker.

IBM Diagnostic Codes

IBM has taken an unusually thorough approach to diagnosing and reporting system errors through the use of their *Advanced Diagnostics* program (which can be purchased directly from IBM, but is available on many PS/2 reference disks). When the diagnostic is run, it will test and report on every possible subsystem—new or old—that may be in the PC. Unfortunately, IBM has never really done a very good job of documenting their vast array of codes. This section of the chapter is intended as a reference to assist you in interpreting these codes, and to help you select some repair alternatives.

READING THE CODES

IBM-type diagnostic codes are split into two sections: the test code and the fault code. The *test code* is simply the number that corresponds to the particular test being run. The *fault code* is a two-digit decimal number that corresponds to the specific type of error that is identified. A fault code of 00 indicates that no problem was found. For example, the message "100" means that the motherboard was tested (01) and that no errors were detected (00)—thus "0100" or just "100." If a fault code appears *other* than 00, a problem has been detected that a technician will have to address. System initialization may or may not continue depending on the location and severity of the error. Table 19-1 provides a relatively comprehensive list of diagnostic codes for XT, AT, and PS/2 systems.

TABLE 19-1 IBM-TYPE DIAGNOSTIC CODES

SYSTEM BOARD (01xx)	
101	Interrupt failure (unexpected interrupt)
102	BIOS ROM checksum error (PC, XT); timer error (AT, MCA)
103	BASIC ROM checksum error (PC, XT); timer interrupt error (AT, MCA)
104	Interrupt controller error (PC, XT); protected mode error (AT, MCA)
105	Timer failure (PC, XT); keyboard controller failure (MCA)
106	System board converting logic test failure
107	System board adapter card or math coprocessor fault; Hot NMI test failed (MCA)
108	System board timer bus failure
109	DMA test memory select failure
110	PS/2 system board memory problem (ISA); system board parity check error (MCA)
111	PS/2 adapter memory problem (ISA); memory adapter parity check error (MCA)
112	PS/2 watchdog time-out error
113	PS/2 DMA arbitration time-out error
114	PS/2 external ROM checksum error
115	Cache parity error, BIOS ROM checksum error, or DMA error
116	System board port R/W error
118	System board L2 cache error
119	2.88MB floppy drive installed but not supported by floppy disk controller
120	CPU self-test error
121	Unexpected hardware interrupt occurred
131	Cassette wrap test (PC)
132	DMA extended registers error
133	DMA verify logic error
134	DMA arbitration logic error
151	Battery, real-time clock, or CMOS RAM failure
152	Real-time clock or CMOS RAM failure
158	Command password not set, but supervisor password is
159	Command password set but not the same as supervisor password
160	PS/2 system board ID not recognized
161	CMOS chip lost power—battery dead
162	CMOS checksum or CRC error
163	CMOS error—time and date not set (the clock not updating)
164	Memory size error—CMOS data does not match system memory found
165	PS/2 adapter ID mismatch

TABLE 19-1 IBM-TYPE DIAGNOSTIC CODES *(CONTINUED)*

166	PS/2 adapter time-out—card busy
167	PS/2 system clock not updating
168	Math coprocessor error in the CMOS configuration
169	System board and processor card configuration mismatch
170	ASCII setup conflict error
171	Rolling bit test failure on CMOS shutdown byte
172	Rolling bit test failure on NVRAM diagnostic byte
173	Bad CMOS/NVRAM checksum
174	Bad system configuration
175	Bad EEPROM CRC
177	Bad password CRC
178	Bad EEPROM
179	NVRAM error log full
180x	Subaddress data error in slot x
181	Unsupported configuration
182	Password switch is not in the writing position
183	System halted—password required
184	Bad power-on password
185	Bad startup sequence
186	Password protection hardware error
187	Serial number error
188	Bad EEPROM checksum
189	Too many incorrect password attempts
191	Cache controller test failure (82385)
194	System board memory error
195	Configuration read from hibernation area of HDD doesn't match actual configuration
196	Read error occurred in hibernation area of HDD
199	User-indicated device list not correct
SYSTEM MEMORY (02xx)	
201	Memory error (physical location will likely be displayed)
202	Memory address line 0–15 error
203	Memory address line 16–23 error; line 16–31 error (MCA)
204	Memory remapped to compensate for error (PS/2)
205	Error in first 128K (PS/2 ISA) of RAM
207	BIOS ROM failure
210	System board memory parity error
211	Error in first 64K of RAM (MCA)
212	Watchdog timer error
213	DMA bus arbitration time-out
215	Memory address error; 64K on daughter/SIP 2 failed (70)
216	Memory address error; 64K on daughter/SIP 1 failed (70)
221	ROM to RAM copy (shadowing) failed (MCA)
225	Wrong speed memory on system board (MCA)
230	Memory on motherboard and adapter board overlaps
231	Noncontiguous adapter memory installed
235	Stuck data line on memory module
241	Memory module 2 failed
251	Memory module 3 failed

19

TABLE 19-1 IBM-TYPE DIAGNOSTIC CODES *(CONTINUED)*

KEYBOARD (03xx)	
301	Keyboard did not respond correctly (stuck key detected)
302	Keyboard locked (AT, models 25, 30)
303	Keyboard/system board interface error—keyboard controller fault
304	Keyboard or system unit error (keyboard clock stuck high)
305	Keyboard fuse failed on system board (PS/2 50, 60, 80) or +5V error (PS/2 70)
306	Unsupported keyboard attached
341	Keyboard error
342	Keyboard cable error
343	Enhancement card or cable error
365	Keyboard failure
366	Interface cable failure
367	Enhancement card or cable failure
MONOCHROME DISPLAY ADAPTER (04xx)	
401	Memory, horizontal sync frequency, or vertical sync test failure
408	User-indicated display attribute failure
416	User-indicated character set failure
424	User-indicated 80x25 mode failure
432	MDA card parallel port test failure
COLOR GRAPHICS ADAPTER (05xx)	
501	Memory, horizontal sync frequency, or vertical sync test failure
503	CGA adapter controller failure
508	User-indicated display attribute failure
516	User-indicated character set failure
524	User-indicated 80x25 mode failure
532	User-indicated 40x25 mode failure
540	User-indicated 320x200 graphics mode failure
548	User-indicated 640x200 graphics mode failure
556	Light pen test failed
564	User-indicated screen paging test failed
FLOPPY DRIVES AND ADAPTERS (06xx)	
601	General disk or adapter test failure
602	Disk boot sector is not valid
603	Disk size error
604	Media sense error
605	Disk drive locked
606	Disk verify test failure
607	Write protect error
608	Drive command error
610	Disk initialization failure
611	Drive time-out error
612	NEC drive controller IC error
613	Floppy system DMA error
614	Floppy system DMA boundary overrun error
615	Drive index timing error
616	Drive speed error
621	Drive seek error
622	Drive CRC error
623	Sector not found error

TABLE 19-1 IBM-TYPE DIAGNOSTIC CODES *(CONTINUED)*

624	Disk address mark error
625	NEC drive controller IC seek error
626	Disk data compare error
627	Disk change line error
628	Disk removed from drive
630	Drive A index stuck high
631	Drive A index stuck low
632	Drive A track 0 stuck off
633	Drive A track 0 stuck on
640	Drive B index stuck high
641	Drive B index stuck low
642	Drive B track 0 stuck off
643	Drive B track 0 stuck on
645	No index pulse
646	Drive track 00 detection failed
647	No transitions on Read Data line
648	Format test failed
649	Incorrect media type in drive
650	Drive speed incorrect
651	Format failure
652	Verify failure
653	Read failure
654	Write failure
655	Drive controller error
656	Drive mechanism failure
657	Write protect stuck in protected state
658	Change line stuck in changed state
659	Write protect stuck in unprotected state
660	Change line stuck in unchanged state
MATH COPROCESSOR (07xx)	
701	MCP presence or initialization error
702	Exception errors test failure
703	Rounding test failure
704	Arithmetic test 1 failure
705	Arithmetic test 2 failure
706	Arithmetic test 3 (80387 only)
707	Combination test failure
708	Integer load/store test failure
709	Equivalent expressions errors
710	Exception (interrupt) errors
711	Save state errors
712	Protected mode test failure
713	Voltage/temperature sensitivity test failure
PARALLEL PRINTER ADAPTER (09xx)	
901	Data register latch error
902	Control register latch error
903	Register address decode error
904	Address decode error

19

TABLE 19-1	IBM-TYPE DIAGNOSTIC CODES *(CONTINUED)*
PARALLEL PRINTER ADAPTER (09xx) *(Continued)*	
910	Status line wrap connector error
911	Status line bit 8 wrap error
912	Status line bit 7 wrap error
913	Status line bit 6 wrap error
914	Status line bit 5 wrap error
915	Status line bit 4 wrap error
916	Printer adapter interrupt wrap error
917	Unexpected printer adapter interrupt
92x	Feature register error
ALTERNATE PRINTER ADAPTER (10xx)	
1001	Data register latch error
1002	Control register latch error
1003	Register address decode error
1004	Address decode error
1010	Status line wrap connector error
1011	Status line bit 8 wrap error
1012	Status line bit 7 wrap error
1013	Status line bit 6 wrap error
1014	Status line bit 5 wrap error
1015	Status line bit 4 wrap error
1016	Printer adapter interrupt wrap error
1017	Unexpected printer adapter interrupt
102x	Feature register error
COMMUNICATION DEVICES (11xx)	
1101	16450/16550 UART error
1102	Card-selected feedback error
1103	Port 102h register test failure
1106	Serial option cannot be shut down
1107	Communications cable or system board error
1108	IRQ 3 error
1109	IRQ 4 error
1110	16450/16550 chip register failure
1111	UART control line internal wrap test failure
1112	UART control line external wrap test failure
1113	UART transmit error
1114	UART receive error
1115	UART transmit and receive data unequal—receive error
1116	UART interrupt function error
1117	UART baud rate test failure
1118	UART interrupt-driven receive external data wrap test error
1119	UART FIFO buffer failure
1120	UART interrupt enable register failure: all bits cannot be set
1121	UART interrupt enable register failure: all bits cannot be reset
1122	Interrupt pending—stuck on
1123	Interrupt ID register stuck on
1124	Modem control register failure: all bits cannot be set
1125	Modem control register failure: all bits cannot be reset
1126	Modem status register failure: all bits cannot be set

TABLE 19-1 IBM-TYPE DIAGNOSTIC CODES *(CONTINUED)*

1127	Modem status register failure: all bits cannot be reset
1128	Interrupt ID error
1129	Cannot force overrun error
1130	No modem status interrupt
1131	Invalid interrupt pending
1132	No data ready
1133	No data available at interrupt
1134	No transmit holding at interrupt
1135	No interrupts
1136	No received line status interrupt
1137	No receive data available
1138	Transmit holding register not empty
1139	No modem status interrupt
1140	Transmit holding register not empty
1141	No interrupts
1142	No IRQ4 interrupt
1143	No IRQ3 interrupt
1144	No data transferred
1145	Maximum baud rate error
1146	Minimum baud rate error
1148	Time-out error
1149	Invalid data returned
1150	Modem status register error
1151	No DSR and delta DSR
1152	No DSR
1153	No delta DSR
1154	Modem status register not clear
1155	No CTS and delta CTS
1156	No CTS
1157	No delta CTS
ALTERNATE COMMUNICATIONS DEVICES (12xx)	
1201	16450/16550 UART error
1202	Card-selected feedback error
1203	Port 102h register test failure
1206	Serial option cannot be shut down
1207	Communications cable or system board error
1208	IRQ 3 error
1209	IRQ 4 error
1210	16450/16550 chip register failure
1211	UART control line internal wrap test failure
1212	UART control line external wrap test failure
1213	UART transmit error
1214	UART receive error
1215	UART transmit and receive data unequal—receive error
1216	UART interrupt function error
1217	UART baud rate test failure
1218	UART interrupt-driven receive external data wrap test error
1219	UART FIFO buffer failure

TABLE 19-1 IBM-TYPE DIAGNOSTIC CODES *(CONTINUED)*

ALTERNATE COMMUNICATIONS DEVICES (12xx) *(Continued)*	
1220	UART interrupt enable register failure: all bits cannot be set
1221	UART interrupt enable register failure: all bits cannot be reset
1222	Interrupt pending—stuck on
1223	Interrupt ID register stuck on
1224	Modem control register failure: all bits cannot be set
1225	Modem control register failure: all bits cannot be reset
1226	Modem status register failure: all bits cannot be set
1227	Modem status register failure: all bits cannot be reset
1228	Interrupt ID error
1229	Cannot force overrun error
1230	No modem status interrupt
1231	Invalid interrupt pending
1232	No data ready
1233	No data available at interrupt
1234	No transmit holding at interrupt
1235	No interrupts
1236	No received line status interrupt
1237	No receive data available
1238	Transmit holding register not empty
1239	No modem status interrupt
1240	Transmit holding register not empty
1241	No interrupts
1242	No IRQ4 interrupt
1243	No IRQ3 interrupt
1244	No data transferred
1245	Maximum baud rate error
1246	Minimum baud rate error
1248	Time-out error
1249	Invalid data returned
1250	Modem status register error
1251	No DSR and delta DSR
1252	No DSR
1253	No delta DSR
1254	Modem status register not clear
1255	No CTS and delta CTS
1256	No CTS
1257	No delta CTS
GAME PORT ADAPTERS (13xx)	
1301	Game port adapter test failure
1302	Joystick test failure
MATRIX PRINTERS (14xx)	
1401	Printer test failure
1402	Printer not ready, not online, or out of paper
1403	Printer "no paper" error
1404	Matrix printer test failure; system board time-out
1405	Parallel adapter failure
1406	Printer presence test failed

TABLE 19-1 IBM-TYPE DIAGNOSTIC CODES *(CONTINUED)*

SDLC COMMUNICATIONS ADAPTER (15xx)	
1501	SDLC adapter test failure
1510	8255 port B failure
1511	8255 port A failure
1512	8255 port C failure
1513	8253 timer 1 did not reach terminal count
1514	8253 timer 1 output stuck on
1515	8253 timer 0 did not reach terminal count
1516	8253 timer 0 output stuck on
1517	8253 timer 2 did not reach terminal count
1518	8253 timer 2 output stuck on
1519	8273 port B error
1520	8273 port A error
1521	8273 command/read time-out error
1522	Interrupt level 4 error
1523	Ring indicator stuck on
1524	Receive clock stuck on
1525	Transmit clock stuck on
1526	Test Indicate stuck on
1527	Ring Indicate not on
1528	Receive clock not on
1529	Transmit clock not on
1530	Test Indicate not on
1531	Data Set Ready not on
1532	Carrier Detect not on
1533	Clear To Send not on
1534	Data Set Ready stuck on
1535	Carrier Detect stuck on
1536	Clear To Send stuck on
1537	Interrupt level 3 failure
1538	Receive interrupt results error
1539	Wrap data compare error
1540	DMA channel 1 transmit error
1541	DMA channel 1 receive error
1542	8273 error-checking or status-reporting error
1547	Stray interrupt level 4 error
1548	Stray interrupt level 3 error
1549	Interrupt presentation sequence time-out
DSEA UNITS (16xx)	
1604	DSEA or Twinaxial network adapter
1608	DSEA or Twinaxial network adapter
1624–1658	DSEA system error
1662	DSEA interrupt level error
1664	DSEA system error
1668	DSEA interrupt level error
1669	DSEA diagnostics error
1674	DSEA diagnostics error
1684	DSEA device address error
1688	DSEA device address error

TABLE 19-1 IBM-TYPE DIAGNOSTIC CODES *(CONTINUED)*

HARD DRIVES AND ADAPTERS (17xx)	
1701	Fixed disk or adapter general error
1702	Drive and controller time-out error
1703	Drive seek error
1704	Drive controller failed
1705	Drive sector not found error
1706	Write fault error
1707	Drive track 00 error
1708	Head select error
1709	Bad ECC returned
1710	Sector buffer overrun
1711	Bad address mark
1712	Internal controller diagnostics failure
1713	Data compare error
1714	Drive not ready
1715	Track 00 indicator failure
1716	Diagnostics cylinder errors
1717	Surface read errors
1718	Hard drive type error
1720	Bad diagnostics cylinder
1726	Data compare error
1730	Drive controller error
1731	Drive controller error
1732	Drive controller error
1733	BIOS undefined error return
1735	Bad command error
1736	Data corrected error
1737	Bad drive track error
1738	Bad sector error
1739	Bad initialization error
1740	Bad sense error
1750	Drive verify error
1751	Drive read error
1752	Drive write error
1753	Drive random read test failure
1754	Drive seek test failure
1755	Drive controller failure
1756	Controller ECC test failure
1757	Controller head select failure
1780	Drive seek failure (drive 0)
1781	Drive seek failure (drive 1)
1782	Hard disk controller failure
1790	Diagnostic cylinder read error (drive 0)
1791	Diagnostic cylinder read error (drive 1)
I/O EXPANSION UNIT (18xx)	
1801	Expansion unit POST error
1810	Enable/disable failure
1811	Extender card wrap test failure while disabled
1812	High-order address lines failure while disabled

TABLE 19-1 IBM-TYPE DIAGNOSTIC CODES *(CONTINUED)*

1813	Wait state failure while disabled
1814	Enable/disable could not be set on
1815	Wait state failure while enabled
1816	Extender card wrap test failure while enabled
1817	High-order address lines failure while enabled
1818	Disable not functioning
1819	Wait request switch not set correctly
1820	Receiver card wrap test failed
1821	Receiver high-order address lines failure
BISYNCHRONOUS COMMUNICATIONS ADAPTERS (20xx)	
2001	BSC adapter test failure
2010	8255 port A failure
2011	8255 port B failure
2012	8255 port C failure
2013	8253 timer 1 did not reach terminal count
2014	8253 timer 1 output stuck on
2015	8253 timer 2 did not reach terminal count
2016	8253 timer 2 output stuck on
2017	8251 Data Set Ready failed to come on
2018	8251 Clear To Send not sensed
2019	8251 Data Set Ready stuck on
2020	8251 Clear To Send stuck on
2021	8251 hardware reset failure
2022	8251 software reset command failure
2023	8251 software error-reset command failure
2024	8251 Transmit Ready did not come on
2025	8251 Receive Ready did not come on
2026	8251 could not force overrun error status
2027	Interrupt failure—no timer interrupt
2028	Interrupt failure—replace card or planar board
2029	Interrupt failure—replace card only
2030	Interrupt failure—replace card or planar board
2031	Interrupt failure—replace card only
2033	Ring Indicate signal stuck on
2034	Receive clock stuck on
2035	Transmit clock stuck on
2036	Test Indicate stuck on
2037	Ring Indicate not on
2038	Receive clock not on
2039	Transmit clock not on
2040	Test Indicate not on
2041	Data Set Ready stuck on
2042	Carrier Detect not on
2043	Clear To Send not on
2044	Data Set Ready stuck on
2045	Carrier Detect stuck on
2046	Clear To Send stuck on
2047	Unexpected transmit interrupt
2048	Unexpected receive interrupt

TABLE 19-1 IBM-TYPE DIAGNOSTIC CODES *(CONTINUED)*

BISYNCHRONOUS COMMUNICATIONS ADAPTERS (20xx)	
2049	Transmit data did not equal receive data
2050	8251 detected overrun error
2051	Lost Data Set Ready signal during data wrap
2052	Receive time-out during data wrap
ALTERNATE BISYNCHRONOUS COMMUNICATIONS ADAPTERS (21xx)	
2101	BSC adapter test failure
2110	8255 port A failure
2111	8255 port B failure
2112	8255 port C failure
2113	8253 timer 1 did not reach terminal count
2114	8253 timer 1 output stuck on
2115	8253 timer 2 did not reach terminal count
2116	8253 timer 2 output stuck on
2117	8251 Data Set Ready failed to come on
2118	8251 Clear To Send not sensed
2119	8251 Data Set Ready stuck on
2120	8251 Clear To Send stuck on
2121	8251 hardware reset failure
2122	8251 software reset command failure
2123	8251 software error-reset command failure
2124	8251 Transmit Ready did not come on
2125	8251 Receive Ready did not come on
2126	8251 could not force overrun error status
2127	Interrupt failure—no timer interrupt
2128	Interrupt failure—replace card or planar board
2129	Interrupt failure—replace card only
2130	Interrupt failure—replace card or planar board
2131	Interrupt failure—replace card only
2133	Ring Indicate signal stuck on
2134	Receive clock stuck on
2135	Transmit clock stuck on
2136	Test Indicate stuck on
2137	Ring Indicate not on
2138	Receive clock not on
2139	Transmit clock not on
2140	Test Indicate not on
2141	Data Set Ready stuck on
2142	Carrier Detect not on
2143	Clear To Send not on
2144	Data Set Ready stuck on
2145	Carrier Detect stuck on
2146	Clear To Send stuck on
2147	Unexpected transmit interrupt
2148	Unexpected receive interrupt
2149	Transmit data did not equal receive data
2150	8251 detected overrun error
2151	Lost Data Set Ready signal during data wrap
2152	Receive time-out during data wrap

TABLE 19-1 IBM-TYPE DIAGNOSTIC CODES *(CONTINUED)*

CLUSTER ADAPTERS (22xx)	
22xx	Cluster adapter error encountered—replace the cluster adapter
PLASMA MONITOR ADAPTER (23xx)	
23xx	Plasma display fault detected—replace the plasma monitor assembly
ENHANCED GRAPHICS ADAPTER (24xx)	
2401	Video adapter test failure
2402	Video display (monitor) error
2408	User-indicated display attribute test failed
2409	Video display (monitor) error
2410	Video adapter error
2416	User-indicated character set test failed
2424	User-indicated 80x25 mode failure
2432	User-indicated 40x25 mode failure
2440	User-indicated 320x200 graphics mode failure
2448	User-indicated 640x200 graphics mode failure
2456	User-indicated light pen test failure
2464	User-indicated screen paging test failure
ALTERNATE ENHANCED GRAPHICS ADAPTER (25xx)	
2501	Video adapter test failure
2502	Video display (monitor) error
2508	User-indicated display attribute test failed
2509	Video display (monitor) error
2510	Video adapter error
2516	User-indicated character set test failed
2524	User-indicated 80x25 mode failure
2532	User-indicated 40x25 mode failure
2540	User-indicated 320x200 graphics mode failure
2548	User-indicated 640x200 graphics mode failure
2556	User-indicated light pen test failure
2564	User-indicated screen paging test failure
PC/370-M ADAPTER (26xx)	
2601–2672	370-M (memory) adapter error
2673– 2680	370-P (processor) adapter error
2681	370-M (memory) adapter error
2682–2697	370-P (processor) adapter error
2698	XT or AT/370 diagnostic disk error
PC3277 EMULATION ADAPTER (27xx)	
2701	3277-EM adapter error
2702	3277-EM adapter error
2703	3277-EM adapter error
3278/3279 EMULATION ADAPTER (28xx)	
28xx	Emulation adapter fault detected—replace the adapter
COLOR/GRAPHICS PRINTERS (29xx)	
29xx	General fault detected with the printer or its printer port—replace the printer or adapter port
PRIMARY PC NETWORK ADAPTER (30xx)	
3001	Network adapter test failure
3002	ROM checksum test failure
3003	Unit ID PROM test failure

19

TABLE 19-1 IBM-TYPE DIAGNOSTIC CODES *(CONTINUED)*

PRIMARY PC NETWORK ADAPTER (30xx) *(Continued)*	
3004	RAM test failure
3005	Host Interface Controller (HIC) test failure
3006	+/–12Vdc test failure
3007	Digital loopback test failure
3008	Host-detected HIC failure
3009	Sync signal failure and no-go bit
3010	HIC test OK and no-go bit
3011	Go bit OK but no command 41
3012	Card not present
3013	Digital failure—fall-through
3015	Analog failure
3041	Hot carrier—on other card
3042	Hot carrier—on this card
SECONDARY PC NETWORK ADAPTER (31xx)	
3101	Network adapter test failure
3102	ROM checksum test failure
3103	Unit ID PROM test failure
3104	RAM test failure
3105	Host interface controller (HIC) test failure
3106	+/–12Vdc test failure
3107	Digital loopback test failure
3108	Host-detected HIC failure
3109	Sync signal failure and no-go bit
3110	HIC test OK and no-go bit
3111	Go bit OK but no command 41
3112	Card not present
3113	Digital failure: fall-through
3115	Analog failure
3141	Hot carrier on other card
3142	Hot carrier on this card
3270 PC/AT DISPLAY (32xx)	
32xx	Fault detected in the display system—replace the display system
COMPACT PRINTER ERRORS (33xx)	
33xx	Fault detected in the printer or printer adapter—replace the printer or adapter
ENHANCED DSEA UNITS (35xx)	
3504	Adapter connected to twinaxial cable during offline test
3508	Workstation address error
3509	Diagnostic program failure; retry on new disk
3540	Workstation address invalid
3588	Adapter address switch error
3599	Diagnostic program failure; retry on new disk
IEEE 488 (GPIB) ADAPTER (36xx)	
3601	Adapter test failure
3602	Write error at Serial Poll Mode Register (SPMR)
3603	Adapter addressing problems
3610	Adapter cannot be programmed to listen
3611	Adapter cannot be programmed to talk
3612	Adapter control error

TABLE 19-1 IBM-TYPE DIAGNOSTIC CODES *(CONTINUED)*

3613	Adapter cannot switch to standby mode
3614	Adapter cannot take control asynchronously
3615	Adapter cannot take control asynchronously
3616	Adapter cannot pass control
3617	Adapter cannot be addressed to listen
3618	Adapter cannot be unaddressed to listen
3619	Adapter cannot be addressed to talk
3620	Adapter cannot be unaddressed to talk
3621	Adapter cannot be addressed to listen with extended addressing
3622	Adapter cannot be unaddressed to listen with extended addressing
3623	Adapter cannot be addressed to talk with extended addressing
3624	Adapter cannot be unaddressed to talk with extended addressing
3625	Adapter cannot write to self
3626	Adapter error—cannot generate handshake signal
3627	Adapter error—cannot detect Device Clear (DCL) message
3628	Adapter error—cannot detect Selected Device Clear (SDC) message
3629	Adapter error—cannot detect end of transfer with EOI signal
3630	Adapter error—cannot detect end of transmission with EOI signal
3631	Adapter cannot detect END with 0-bit EOS
3632	Adapter cannot detect END with 7-bit EOS
3633	Adapter cannot detect Group Execute Trigger (GET)
3634	Mode 3 addressing not functioning
3635	Adapter cannot recognize undefined command
3636	Adapter error—cannot detect REM, REMC, LOK, or LOKC signals
3637	Adapter error—cannot clear REM or LOK signals
3638	Adapter cannot detect Service Request (SRQ)
3639	Adapter cannot conduct serial poll
3640	Adapter cannot conduct parallel poll
3650	Adapter error: cannot DMA to 7210
3651	Data error on DMA to 7210
3652	Adapter error: cannot DMA from 7210
3653	Data error on DMA from 7210
3658	Uninvoked interrupt received
3659	Adapter cannot interrupt on ADSC signal
3660	Adapter cannot interrupt on ADSC signal
3661	Adapter cannot interrupt on CO
3662	Adapter cannot interrupt on DO
3663	Adapter cannot interrupt on DI
3664	Adapter cannot interrupt on ERR
3665	Adapter cannot interrupt on DEC
3666	Adapter cannot interrupt on END
3667	Adapter cannot interrupt on DET
3668	Adapter cannot interrupt on APT
3669	Adapter cannot interrupt on CPT
3670	Adapter cannot interrupt on REMC
3671	Adapter cannot interrupt on LOKC
3672	Adapter cannot interrupt on SRQI
3673	Adapter cannot interrupt on terminal count on DMA to 7210
3674	Adapter cannot interrupt on terminal count on DMA from 7210

TABLE 19-1 IBM-TYPE DIAGNOSTIC CODES *(CONTINUED)*

IEEE 488 (GPIB) ADAPTER (36xx) *(Continued)*	
3675	Spurious DMA terminal count interrupt
3697	Illegal DMA configuration setting detected
3698	Illegal interrupt level configuration setting detected
SYSTEM BOARD SCSI CONTROLLER (37xx)	
37xx	System board SCSI controller has failed—replace motherboard
DATA ACQUISITION ADAPTER (38xx)	
3801	Adapter test failure
3810	Timer read test failure
3811	Timer interrupt test failure
3812	Binary input 13 test failure
3813	Binary input 13 test failure
3814	Binary output 14: interrupt request test failure
3815	Binary output 0, count-in test failure
3816	Binary input strobe (STB), count-out test failure
3817	Binary output 0, Clear To Send (CTS) test failure
3818	Binary output 1, binary input 0 test failure
3819	Binary output 2, binary input 1 test failure
3820	Binary output 3, binary input 2 test failure
3821	Binary output 4, binary input 3 test failure
3822	Binary output 5, binary input 4 test failure
3823	Binary output 6, binary input 5 test failure
3824	Binary output 7, binary input 6 test failure
3825	Binary output 8, binary input 7 test failure
3826	Binary output 9, binary input 8 test failure
3827	Binary output 10, binary input 9 test failure
3828	Binary output 11, binary input 10 test failure
3829	Binary output 12, binary input 11 test failure
3830	Binary output 13, binary input 12 test failure
3831	Binary output 15, analog input CE test failure
3832	Binary output Strobe (STB), binary output GATE test failure
3833	Binary input Clear To Send (CTS), binary input HOLD test failure
3834	Analog input Command Output (CO), binary input 15 test failure
3835	Counter interrupt test failure
3836	Counter read test failure
3837	Analog output 0 ranges test failure
3838	Analog output 1 ranges test failure
3839	Analog input 0 values test failure
3840	Analog input 1 values test failure
3841	Analog input 2 values test failure
3842	Analog input 3 values test failure
3843	Analog input interrupt test failure
3844	Analog input 23 address or value test failure
PROFESSIONAL GRAPHICS ADAPTER (PGA) (39xx)	
3901	PGA test failure
3902	ROM1 self-test failure
3903	ROM2 self-test failure
3904	RAM self-test failure
3905	Cold start cycle power error

TABLE 19-1 IBM-TYPE DIAGNOSTIC CODES *(CONTINUED)*

3906	Data error in communications RAM
3907	Address error in communications RAM
3908	Bad data detected while read/write to 6845 register
3909	Bad data detected in lower E0h bytes while read/writing 6845 registers
3910	Display bank output latch error
3911	Basic clock error
3912	Command control error
3913	Vertical sync scanner error
3914	Horizontal sync scanner error
3915	Intech error
3916	Lookup table (LUT) address error
3917	LUT "red" RAM chip error
3918	LUT "green" RAM chip error
3919	LUT "blue" RAM chip error
3920	LUT data latch error
3921	Horizontal display error
3922	Vertical display error
3923	Light pen error
3924	Unexpected error
3925	Emulator addressing error
3926	Emulator data latch error
3927–3930	Emulator RAM error
3931	Emulator horizontal/vertical display problem
3932	Emulator cursor position error
3933	Emulator attribute display problem
3934	Emulator cursor display error
3935	Fundamental emulation RAM problem
3936	Emulation character set problem
3937	Emulation graphics display error
3938	Emulation character display problem
3939	Emulation bank select error
3940	Display RAM U2 error
3941	Display RAM U4 error
3942	Display RAM U6 error
3943	Display RAM U8 error
3944	Display RAM U10 error
3945	Display RAM U1 error
3946	Display RAM U3 error
3947	Display RAM U5 error
3948	Display RAM U7 error
3949	Display RAM U9 error
3950	Display RAM U12 error
3951	Display RAM U14 error
3952	Display RAM U16 error
3953	Display RAM U18 error
3954	Display RAM U20 error
3955	Display RAM U11 error
3956	Display RAM U13 error
3957	Display RAM U15 error

TABLE 19-1 IBM-TYPE DIAGNOSTIC CODES *(CONTINUED)*

PROFESSIONAL GRAPHICS ADAPTER (PGA) (39xx) *(Continued)*	
3958	Display RAM U17 error
3959	Display RAM U19 error
3960	Display RAM U22 error
3961	Display RAM U24 error
3962	Display RAM U26 error
3963	Display RAM U28 error
3964	Display RAM U30 error
3965	Display RAM U21 error
3966	Display RAM U23 error
3967	Display RAM U25 error
3968	Display RAM U27 error
3969	Display RAM U29 error
3970	Display RAM U32 error
3971	Display RAM U34 error
3972	Display RAM U36 error
3973	Display RAM U38 error
3974	Display RAM U40 error
3975	Display RAM U31 error
3976	Display RAM U33 error
3977	Display RAM U35 error
3978	Display RAM U37 error
3979	Display RAM U39 error
3980	Graphics controller RAM timing error
3981	Graphics controller read/write latch error
3982	Shift register bus output latch error
3983	Addressing error (vertical column of memory; U2 at top)
3984	Addressing error (vertical column of memory; U4 at top)
3985	Addressing error (vertical column of memory; U6 at top)
3986	Addressing error (vertical column of memory; U8 at top)
3987	Addressing error (vertical column of memory; U10 at top)
3988–3991	Horizontal bank latch errors
3992	RAG/CAG graphics controller error
3993	Multiple write modes, nibble mask errors
3994	Row nibble (display RAM) error
3995	Graphics controller addressing error
5278 DISPLAY ATTACHMENT UNIT AND 5279 DISPLAY (44xx)	
44xx	Fault detected with display system—replace display system
IEEE 488 (GPIB) INTERFACE ADAPTER (45xx)	
45xx	A fault has been detected with GPIB—replace adapter
ARTIC MULTIPORT/2 INTERFACE ADAPTER (46xx)	
4611	ARTIC adapter error
4612 or 4613	Memory module error
4630	ARTIC adapter error
4640 or 4641	Memory module error
4650	ARTIC interface cable error
INTERNAL MODEM (48xx)	
48xx	Internal modem has failed—replace internal modem
ALTERNATE INTERNAL MODEM (49xx)	
49xx	Alternate internal modem has failed—replace the alternate internal modem

TABLE 19-1 IBM-TYPE DIAGNOSTIC CODES *(CONTINUED)*

PC CONVERTIBLE LCD (50xx)	
5001	LCD buffer failure
5002	LCD font buffer failure
5003	LCD controller failure
5004	User-indicated PEL/drive test failed
5008	User-indicated display attribute test failed
5016	User-indicated character set test failed
5020	User-indicated alternate character set test failure
5024	User-indicated 80x25 mode test failure
5032	User-indicated 40x25 mode test failure
5040	User-indicated 320x200 graphics test failure
5048	User-indicated 640x200 graphics test failure
5064	User-indicated paging test failure
PC CONVERTIBLE PORTABLE PRINTER (51xx)	
5101	Portable printer interface failure
5102	Portable printer busy error
5103	Portable printer paper or ribbon error
5104	Portable printer time-out
5105	User-indicated print pattern test error
FINANCIAL COMMUNICATION SYSTEM (56xx)	
56xx	Fault detected in the financial communication system—replace the financial communication system
PHOENIX BIOS/CHIPSET SPECIFIC ERROR CODES (70xx)	
7000	Chipset CMOS failure
7001	Shadow RAM failure (ROM not shadowed to RAM)
7002	Chipset CMOS configuration data error
VOICE COMMUNICATIONS ADAPTER (VCA) (71xx)	
7101	Adapter test failure
7102	Instruction or external data memory error
7103	PC to VCA interrupt error
7104	Internal data memory error
7105	DMA error
7106	Internal registers error
7107	Interactive shared memory error
7108	VCA to PC interrupt error
7109	DC wrap error
7111	External analog wrap and tone output error
7114	Telephone attachment test failure
3.5" FLOPPY DISK DRIVE (73xx)	
7301	Disk drive/adapter test failure
7306	Disk change line error
7307	Write-protected disk
7308	Drive command error
7310	Disk initialization failure—track 00 error
7311	Drive time-out error
7312	NEC drive controller IC error
7313	DMA error
7314	DMA boundary overrun error
7315	Drive index timing error

19

TABLE 19-1 IBM-TYPE DIAGNOSTIC CODES *(CONTINUED)*

3.5" FLOPPY DISK DRIVE (73xx) *(Continued)*	
7316	Drive speed error
7321	Drive seek error
7322	Drive CRC check error
7323	Sector not found error
7324	Address mark error
7325	NEC controller IC seek error
8514/A DISPLAY ADAPTER (74xx)	
7426	8514 display error
7440–7475	8514/A memory module error
4216 PAGE PRINTER ADAPTER (76xx)	
7601	Adapter test failure
7602	Adapter card error
7603	Printer error
7604	Printer cable error
PCMCIA ADAPTER	
8081	Presence test failure (PCMCIA revision number also checked)
8082	PCMCIA register test failure
PS/2 SPEECH ADAPTER (84xx)	
84xx	Fault detected in the speech adapter—replace the speech adapter
2MB XMA MEMORY ADAPTER (85xx)	
85xx	Fault detected in the memory adapter—replace the memory adapter
PS/2 POINTING DEVICE (86xx)	
8601	Pointing device; mouse time-out error
8602	Pointing device; mouse interface error
8603	System board; mouse interrupt failure
8604	Pointing device or system board error
8611	System bus error
8612	TrackPoint II error
8613	System bus or TrackPoint II error
MIDI INTERFACE (89xx)	
89xx	Fault detected in the MIDI adapter—replace the MIDI adapter
3363 WORM OPTICAL DRIVE/ADAPTERS (91xx)	
91xx	Fault detected in the drive or adapter—replace the adapter and the drive
SCSI ADAPTER (W/32-BIT CACHE) (96xx)	
96xx	Fault detected in the SCSI adapter—replace the adapter board
MULTIPROTOCOL ADAPTERS (100xx)	
10001	Presence test failure
10002	Card selected feedback error
10003	Port 102h register rest failure
10004	Port 103h register rest failure
10006	Serial option cannot be disabled
10007	Cable error
10008	IRQ3 error
10009	IRQ4 error
10010	UART register failure
10011	Internal wrap test of UART control line failed
10012	External wrap test of UART control line failed
10013	UART transmit error

TABLE 19-1 IBM-TYPE DIAGNOSTIC CODES *(CONTINUED)*

10014	UART receive error
10015	UART receive error—data not equal to transmit data
10016	UART interrupt error
10017	UART baud rate test failure
10018	UART receive external wrap test failure
10019	UART FIFO buffer failure
10026	8255 port A error
10027	8255 port B error
10028	8255 port C error
10029	8254 timer 0 error
10030	8254 timer 1 error
10031	8254 timer 2 error
10032	Bisync Data Set Ready (DSR) response error
10033	Bisync Clear To Send (CTS) error
10034	8251 hardware reset test failed
10035	8251 function generator
10036	8251 status error
10037	Bisync timer interrupt error
10038	Bisync transmit interrupt error
10039	Bisync receive interrupt error
10040	Stray IRQ3 error
10041	Stray IRQ4 error
10042	Bisync external wrap error
10044	Bisync data wrap error
10045	Bisync line status error
10046	Bisync time-out error during wrap test
10050	8273 command acceptance or time-out error
10051	8273 port A error
10052	8273 port B error
10053	SDLC modem status logic error
10054	SDLC timer IRQ4 error
10055	SDLC IRQ4 error
10056	SDLC external wrap error
10057	SDLC interrupt results error
10058	SDLC data wrap error
10059	SDLC transmit interrupt error
10060	SDLC receive interrupt error
10061	DMA channel 1 transmit error
10062	DMA channel 1 receive error
10063	8273 status detect failure
10064	8273 error detect failure
INTERNAL 300/1200BPS MODEM (101xx)	
10101	Presence test failure
10102	Card-selected feedback error
10103	Port 102h register test error
10106	Serial option cannot be disabled
10108	IRQ3 error
10109	IRQ4 error
10110	UART chip register failure

19

TABLE 19-1 IBM-TYPE DIAGNOSTIC CODES *(CONTINUED)*

INTERNAL 300/1200BPS MODEM (101xx)	
10111	UART control line internal wrap test failure
10113	UART transmit error
10114	UART receive error
10115	UART error—transmit and receive data not equal
10116	UART interrupt function error
10117	UART baud rate test failure
10118	UART interrupt driven receive external data wrap test failure
10125	Modem reset result code error
10126	Modem general result code error
10127	Modem S registers write/read error
10128	Modem echo on/off error
10129	Modem enable/disable result codes error
10130	Modem enable number/word result codes error
10133	Connect results for 300 baud not received
10134	Connect results for 1200 baud not received
10135	Modem fails local analog loopback 300 baud test
10136	Modem fails local analog loopback 1200 baud test
10137	Modem does not respond to Escape/reset sequence
10138	S register 13 shows incorrect parity or number of data bits
10139	S register 15 shows incorrect bit rate
ESDI OR MCA IDE DRIVE/ADAPTERS (104xx)	
10450	Write/read test failed
10451	Read verify test failed
10452	Seek test failed
10453	Wrong drive type indicated
10454	Controller failed sector buffer test
10455	Controller failed—invalid
10456	Controller diagnostic command failure
10461	Drive format error
10462	Controller head select error
10463	Drive write/read sector error
10464	Drive primary defect map unreadable
10465	Controller ECC 8-bit error
10466	Controller ECC 9-bit error
10467	Drive soft seek error
10468	Drive hard seek error
10469	Drive soft seek error count exceeded
10470	Controller attachment diagnostic error
10471	Controller wrap mode interface error
10472	Controller wrap mode drive select error
10473	Error during ESDI read verify test
10480	Seek failure on drive 0
10481	Seek failure on drive 1
10482	Controller transfer acknowledge error
10483	Controller reset error
10484	Controller head select 3 selected bad

TABLE 19-1 IBM-TYPE DIAGNOSTIC CODES *(CONTINUED)*

10485	Controller head select 2 selected bad
10486	Controller head select 1 selected bad
10487	Controller head select 0 selected bad
10488	Read gate command error
10489	Read gate command error
10490	Diagnostic read error on drive 0
10491	Diagnostic read error on drive 1
10492	Drive 1 controller error
10493	Drive 1 reset error
10499	Controller failure
5.25" EXTERNAL DISK DRIVE/ADAPTER (107xx)	
107xx	Fault detected in the drive or adapter—replace the adapter and drive
SCSI ADAPTER (16-BIT W/O CACHE) (112xx)	
112xx	Fault detected in the SCSI adapter—replace the SCSI adapter
SYSTEM BOARD SCSI ADAPTER (113xx)	
113xx	Fault detected in the SCSI adapter—replace the motherboard
CPU BOARD (129xx)	
12901	Processor test failed
12902	CPU board cache test failed
12904	Second-level (L2) cache failure
12905	Cache enable/disable errors
12907	Cache fatal error
12908	Cache POST program error
12912	Hardware failure
12913	MCA bus time-out
12914	Software failure
12915	CPU board error
12916	CPU board error
12917	CPU board error
12918	CPU board error
12919	CPU board error
12940	CPU board error
12950	CPU board error
12990	CPU serial number mismatch
P70/P75 PLASMA DISPLAY/ADAPTER (149xx)	
14901	Plasma display adapter failure
14902	Plasma display adapter failure
14922	Plasma display failure
14932	External display device failure
XGA DISPLAY ADAPTER (152xx)	
152xx	Fault detected in the XGA adapter—replace the adapter
120MB INTERNAL TAPE DRIVE (164xx)	
164xx	Fault detected in the tape drive—replace the tape drive
6157 STREAMING TAPE DRIVE (165xx)	
16520	Streaming tape drive failure
16540	Tape attachment adapter failure
PRIMARY TOKEN RING NETWORK ADAPTERS (166xx)	
166xx	Fault detected with the network adapter—replace the network adapter

19

TABLE 19-1 IBM-TYPE DIAGNOSTIC CODES *(CONTINUED)*

SECONDARY TOKEN RING NETWORK ADAPTERS (167xx)	
167xx	Fault detected with the network adapter—replace the network adapter
PS/2 WIZARD ADAPTER (180xx)	
18001	Interrupt controller failure
18002	Incorrect timer count
18003	Timer interrupt failure
18004	Sync check interrupt failure
18005	Parity check interrupt failure
18006	Access error interrupt failure
18012	Bad checksum
18013	MCA bus interface error
18021	Wizard memory compare or parity error
18022	Wizard memory address line error
18023	Dynamic RAM controller failure
18029	Wizard memory byte enable error
18031	Wizard memory expansion module compare or parity error
18032	Wizard memory expansion module address line error
18039	Wizard memory expansion module byte enable error
DBCS JAPANESE DISPLAY ADAPTER (185xx)	
185xx	Fault detected in the display adapter—replace the adapter
80286 MEMORY EXPANSION OPTION MODULE (194xx)	
194xx	Fault detected in the memory module—replace the memory module
IMAGE ADAPTER (200xx)	
200xx	Fault detected in the image adapter—replace the image adapter
UNKNOWN SCSI DEVICES (208xx)	
208xx	Fault detected in an unknown SCSI device—systematically isolate and replace the defective SCSI device
SCSI REMOVABLE DISK (209xx)	
209xx	Fault detected in the SCSI removable disk—replace the removable disk
SCSI FIXED DISK (210xx)	
210xx	Fault detected in the SCSI fixed disk—replace the fixed disk
210PLSC	"PLSC" codes offer detailed SCSI drive error reporting: P = SCSI ID number (physical unit number or PUN) L = Logical unit number (LUN, usually 0) S = Host adapter slot number C = SCSI drive capacity: A = 60MB, B = 80MB, C = 120MB, D = 160MB, E = 320MB, F = 400MB, H = 1,024MB (1GB), I = 104MB, J = 212MB, U = undetermined or non–IBM OEM drive
SCSI TAPE DRIVE (211xx)	
211xx	Fault detected in the SCSI tape drive—replace the tape drive
SCSI PRINTER (212xx)	
212xx	Fault detected with the SCSI printer—check the printer and replace if necessary
SCSI PROCESSOR (213xx)	
213xx	SCSI processor has failed or is not responding—replace the SCSI processor
SCSI WORM DRIVE (214xx)	
214xx	Problems with the SCSI Write-Once/Read Multiple (WORM) drive—check and replace the drive as required.
SCSI CD-ROM (215xx)	
215xx	Fault detected with the SCSI CD-ROM drive—replace the drive

TABLE 19-1 IBM-TYPE DIAGNOSTIC CODES *(CONTINUED)*

SCSI SCANNER (216xx)	
216xx	SCSI scanner has failed or is not responding—check the scanner and replace if necessary
SCSI MO DRIVE (217xx)	
217xx	Fault detected with the SCSI Magneto-Optical (MO) drive—replace the drive
SCSI CD JUKEBOX (218xx)	
218xx	SCSI jukebox changer has failed or is not responding—check the jukebox and replace if necessary
SCSI COMMUNICATION (219xx)	
219xx	SCSI system has encountered communications errors—check the SCSI communication devices and replace them if necessary
ISDN ADAPTERS (242xxYx)	
24201Y0 or 24210Y0	ISDN/2 adapter
XGA ADAPTER (243xxxx)	
243xxxx	XGA-2 adapter/A errors
IR LAN ADAPTER (273xx)	
273XX	1 Mbps Micro Channel Infrared LAN adapter
SERVER-RELATED ERRORS (275xx)	
27501	ServerGuard adapter, system board
27503	ServerGuard adapter, system board
27506	ServerGuard adapter, system board
27507	ServerGuard adapter, system board
27537	ServerGuard adapter
27509	Remove redundant adapters, run Auto Configuration program, then retest
27512	WMSELF.DGS diagnostics file missing, incorrect
27535	3V lithium backup battery
27554	Internal temperature out of range
27557	7.2V NiCad main battery pack
27562	External power control not connected
275XX	Update diagnostic software
PERSONAL DICTATION SYSTEM (PDS) ERRORS (278xx)	
27801–27879	Personal dictation system (PDS) adapter or system board
27880–27889	External unit (such as speaker or microphone)
DYNAMIC CONFIGURATION SELECT (DCS) INFORMATION CODES (I998xxxx)	
I998001x	Bad integrity of DCS master boot record
I988002x	Read failure of DCS master boot record
I988003x	DCS master boot record is not compatible with the planar ID
I988004x	DCS master boot record is not compatible with the model/submodel byte
I988005x	Bad integrity of CMOS/NVRAM (or internal process error)
I988006x	Read failure of header/mask/configuration record
I988007x	Bad integrity of header/mask/configuration record
I988008x	Hard disk does not support the command to set the maximum RBA
I988009x	DCS master boot record is older than system ROM
I9880402	Copyright notice in E000 segment does not match the one in DCS MBR
I9880403	DCS MBR is not compatible with the system board ID or model/submodel byte
INITIAL MICROCODE LOAD (IML) ERROR (I99900xx)	
I999001x	Invalid disk IML record
I999002x	Disk IML record load error

19

TABLE 19-1 IBM-TYPE DIAGNOSTIC CODES *(CONTINUED)*

INITIAL MICROCODE LOAD (IML) ERROR (I99900xx) *(Continued)*	
I999003x	Disk IML record incompatible with system board
I999004x	Disk IML record incompatible with processor/processor card
I999005x	Disk IML not attempted
I999006x	Disk stage II system image load error
I999007x	Disk stage II image checksum error
I999008x	IML not supported on primary disk drive
I999009x	Disk IML record is older than ROM
I99900x1	Invalid disk IML record
I99900x2	Disk IML record load error
I99900x3	Disk IML record incompatible with system board
I99900x4	Disk IML record incompatible with processor card
I99900x5	Disk IML recovery prevented (valid password and CE override not set)
I99900x6	Disk stage II image load error
I99900x7	Disk stage II image checksum error
I99900x9	Disk IML record older than ROM
NO BOOTABLE DEVICE, INITIAL PROGRAM LOAD (IPL) ERRORS (I9990xxx)	
I9990301	Hard disk error
I9990302	Invalid hard disk boot record
I9990305	No bootable device
I9990303	Bank-2 flash ROM checksum error
I9990303	IML system partition boot failure
I9990304	No bootable device with ASCII console
I9990306	Invalid SCSI device boot record
I99904xx	IML-to-system mismatch
I9990401	Unauthorized access (manufacturing boot request with valid password)
I9990402	Missing ROM IBM copyright notice
I9990403	IML boot record incompatible with system board/processor card
I99906xx	IML (boot) errors

TROUBLESHOOTING WITH DIAGNOSTIC CODES

Now that you have an idea of the diagnostic areas that are covered and the error codes you can expect to see, you should have an understanding of how to deal with those errors when they occur. Generally speaking, a PC can be divided into a motherboard, expansion boards, drives, and a power supply—each area can be considered as a replaceable module. When an error code is generated, you can match the code to its description in Table 19-1. The rule of thumb here is that you should replace the failed module. For example, if a video adapter fails, it should be replaced; if a motherboard fails, it should be replaced; if a hard drive fails, it should be replaced; and so on. The following notes explain some of the finer points.

Motherboard The motherboard manages virtually all of the PC's processing resources (that is, DMAs, IRQs, memory, and so on). As a consequence, the motherboard is perhaps the most difficult and time-consuming module to replace due to the the labor required. Before electing to replace the motherboard, be certain that the faulty component(s) cannot be swapped out. For example, the CPU, BIOS ROM, math coprocessor, expansion memory (SIMMs), RTC/CMOS IC, and CMOS backup battery are almost always socket mounted. (In fact, when you purchase a new motherboard, it typically comes without those socket-mounted elements.) Therefore, if an error message indicates that the CPU has failed, try another CPU. Of course, if the defective element is hard-soldered to the motherboard, you should probably go ahead and order another motherboard, then simply transfer any of the socket-mounted devices from the old motherboard.

Memory Memory plays a vital role in every PC—the CPU is useless unless there is memory to hold data and program instructions. Since even one bad bit can cause an error that may crash a system, memory is perhaps the most thoroughly tested area of a computer. From a troubleshooting standpoint, memory can often be divided into two areas: the memory located on the motherboard (often called "base memory") and the memory added in the form of SIMMs, DIMMs, or RIMMs. When a failure occurs in a SIMM, DIMM, or RIMM module, it's a simple matter to locate and replace the suspect module. If the fault is on the motherboard, you are often faced with the prospect of replacing the defective RAM chip(s), or (more frequently) replacing the entire motherboard.

> Today's motherboards typically do *not* include base memory on the motherboard, so all RAM is added in the form of SIMMs, DIMMs, or RIMMs.

Keyboard Not only is the keyboard the most popular and reliable input device for the PC, the keyboard controller chip is also in control of the A20 gate, which allows the CPU to enter its "protected mode" (while in protected mode, a CPU can address memory above 1MB). When a problem is detected in the keyboard assembly itself, it is usually a quick and easy process to replace the keyboard assembly. When a problem is located outside of the keyboard itself (or a protected-mode fault is found), the keyboard controller chip on the motherboard has probably failed. On some motherboards, the keyboard controller is mounted in an socket and can be replaced easily. Where the keyboard controller is hard-soldered to the motherboard, it will probably be easiest to simply replace the motherboard outright.

Video You may have noticed that among the error codes in Table 19-1, there are sections dedicated to older video standards such as MDA and CGA. If you encounter a system with older video adapters that prove to be defective, it will be extremely difficult (if not impossible) to locate new replacement boards. As a result, you should expect to replace an older video board with one of the newer video adapters, such as VGA or SVGA, that offer backward compatibility to the older standards. Unfortunately, older video used TTL monitors, where VGA and SVGA adapters are designed for analog monitors. Keep in mind that it may be necessary to upgrade your customer's monitor as well as their video adapter.

Serial/Parallel Ports Diagnostics typically attempt to test any serial or parallel ports that can be identified. In the early days of PCs, serial and parallel ports were typically added as expansion boards. When such add-on ports fail, it is a simple matter to replace the defective board. With most of today's systems, however, at least one serial and parallel port are integrated right on the motherboard. When these built-in ports check bad, there is often little that can be done other than replace the motherboard outright. Also, if an error code indicates a fault outside of the port circuit (for example, the modem or printer), always try a new cable between the port and peripheral first. If a new cable does not correct the problem, try replacing the suspect peripheral. Also keep in mind that some test procedures require you to attach a loopback plug (rather than connect a live peripheral).

Drives Diagnostics typically check the complete suite of floppy drives, hard drives, and even CD-ROM drives. However, you must realize that a drive system includes not only the drive itself but also its controller board. When a drive problem is indicated, you should automatically inspect the signal and power cables at the drive. A loose power connector or frayed signal cable can easily disable the drive. If in doubt, try a new signal cable (which is much less expensive than replacing a drive).

Of course, if a new cable fails to correct the fault, you must decide whether the drive or controller has failed. Often, the diagnostic error code will pinpoint the fault to either the drive or controller circuit for you. If the drive has failed, replace the drive. If the controller has failed, things can get a bit more complicated. If the controller is implemented as an expansion board, it is easy enough to replace, but make sure that the new controller has any jumpers and DIP switches set similarly to the defective controller. If the controller is incorporated on the motherboard, you may find yourself replacing the entire motherboard.

Beep Codes

When a fault is detected *before* the video system is initialized, errors are indicated with a series of beeps (or *beep codes*). Since each BIOS is a bit different, the accuracy, precision, and quality of error detection and reporting varies from BIOS to BIOS. While most POST routines today follow a remarkably similar pattern, the reporting style can vary greatly. Some routines (such as AMI) generate a continuous string of beeps, while other routines (such as Phoenix) create short beep sequences. This part of the chapter is intended to help you understand and interpret the beep codes produced by major BIOS makers. The following list will help you locate the appropriate table:

AMI (American Megatrends)	Table 19-2	IBM ThinkPad	Table 19-8
AST	Table 19-3	Mylex	Table 19-9
Dell (PowerEdge)	Table 19-4	Mylex 386	Table 19-10
Compaq (AlphaServer)	Table 19-5	Phoenix Technologies	Table 19-11
IBM desktop (classic)	Table 19-6	Quadtel	Table 19-12
IBM desktop (Aptiva)	Table 19-7		

TABLE 19-2 AMI BEEP CODES

BEEPS	ERROR
1s	System RAM refresh failure. The programmable interrupt timer (PIT) or programmable interrupt controller (PIC) has probably failed. Replace the motherboard.
2s	Memory parity error. A parity error has been detected in the first 64KB of RAM. The RAM IC is probably defective. Replace the memory or motherboard.
3s	Base 64KB memory failure. A memory failure has been detected in the first 64KB of RAM. The RAM IC is probably defective. Replace the memory or motherboard.
4s	System timer failure. The system clock/timer IC has failed.
5s	CPU failure. The system CPU has failed. Try replacing the CPU or motherboard.
6s	Gate A20 failure. The keyboard controller IC has failed, so gate A20 is no longer available to switch the CPU into protected mode. Replace the keyboard controller or motherboard.
7s	Exception error. The CPU has generated an exception error due to a fault in the CPU or some combination of motherboard conditions. Try replacing the motherboard.
8s	Video memory read/write error. The system video adapter is missing or defective. Try replacing the video adapter.
9s	ROM checksum error. The content of the system BIOS ROM does not match the expected checksum value. The BIOS ROM is probably defective and should be replaced.
10s	Shutdown register read/write error. The shutdown register for the CMOS memory has failed. Try replacing the RTC/CMOS IC.
11s	Cache error/L2 cache bad. The L2 cache is faulty. Replace the L2 cache or integrated L2 cache hardware device.
1l-3s	Memory test failure. A fault has been detected in memory over 64K. Replace the memory or the motherboard.
1l-8s	Display test failure. The display adapter is missing or defective. Replace the video adapter board. If the video adapter is on the motherboard, try replacing the motherboard.

l=long s=short

TABLE 19-3 AST BEEP CODES

BEEPS	ERROR
1s	CPU register test failure. The CPU has failed. Try replacing the CPU or replace the motherboard.
2s	Keyboard controller buffer failure. The keyboard controller IC has failed.
3s	Keyboard controller reset failure. The keyboard controller IC or its associated circuitry has failed.
4s	Keyboard communication failure. The keyboard controller IC or its associated circuitry has failed. Try replacing the keyboard assembly. Try replacing the motherboard.
5s	Keyboard input port failure. The keyboard controller IC has failed.
6s	System board chipset initialization failure. The chipset(s) used on the motherboard cannot be initialized. Either an element of the chipset(s) or the motherboard has failed.
9s	BIOS ROM checksum error. The BIOS ROM has failed. Try replacing the BIOS ROM or replace the motherboard.
10s	System timer test failure. The master system clock IC has failed.
11s	ASIC register test failure. Motherboard circuitry has failed. Replace the motherboard.
12s	CMOS RAM shutdown register failure. The RTC/CMOS IC has failed. Try replacing the RTC/CMOS IC or replace the motherboard.
1l	DMA controller 0 failure. The DMA controller IC for channel 0 has failed.
1l-1s	DMA controller 1 failure. The DMA controller IC for channel 1 has failed.
1l-2s	Video vertical retrace failure. The video adapter has failed. Replace the video adapter board.
1l-3s	Video memory test failure. A fault has occurred in video memory. Replace the video adapter.
1l-4s	Video adapter test failure. The video adapter has failed. Replace the video adapter board.
1l-5s	64K base memory failure. A failure has occurred in the low 64K of system RAM. Replace memory or replace the motherboard.
1l-6s	Unable to load interrupt vectors. BIOS was unable to load interrupt vectors into low memory. Replace the motherboard.
1l-7s	Unable to initialize video system. There is a defect in the video system. Replace the video adapter board. Replace the motherboard.
1l-8s	Video memory failure. There is a defect in video memory. Replace the video adapter or replace the motherboard.

l=long s=short

TABLE 19-4 DELL (POWEREDGE 6350) BEEP CODES

BEEPS	ERROR
1-1-3	NVRAM write/read failure. The CMOS RAM has probably failed. Replace the main board.
1-1-4	BIOS checksum failure. The BIOS chip has probably failed. Replace the main board.
1-2-1	Programmable interval timer failure. Replace the main board.
1-2-2	DMA initialization failure. Replace the main board.
1-2-3	DMA page register write/read failure. Replace the main board.
1-3-1	Main memory refresh verification failure. Remove and reseat the DIMMs. If the problem persists, replace the memory module(s).
1-3-2	No memory installed. Remove and reseat the DIMMs and reboot the system. If the problem persists, replace the memory module(s).
1-3-3	Chip or data line failure in the first 64K of main memory. Remove and reseat the DIMMs and reboot the system. If the problem persists, replace the memory module(s).
1-3-4	Odd/even logic failure in the first 64K of main memory. Remove and reseat the DIMMs and reboot the system. If the problem persists, replace the memory module(s).

TABLE 19-4 DELL (POWEREDGE 6350) BEEP CODES *(CONTINUED)*

BEEPS	ERROR
1-4-1	Address line failure in the first 64K of main memory. Remove and reseat the DIMMs and reboot the system. If the problem persists, replace the memory module(s).
1-4-2	Parity failure in the first 64K of main memory. Remove and reseat the DIMMs and reboot the system. If the problem persists, replace the memory module(s).
2-1-1 to 2-4-4	Bit failure in the first 64K of main memory. Remove and reseat the DIMMs and reboot the system. If the problem persists, replace the memory module(s).
3-1-1	Slave DMA register failure. Replace the main board.
3-1-2	Master DMA register failure. Replace the main board.
3-1-3	Master interrupt-mask register failure. Replace the main board.
3-1-4	Slave interrupt-mask register failure. Replace the main board.
3-2-4	Keyboard-controller test failure. Check the keyboard cable and connector for proper connection. If the problem persists, replace the main board.
3-3-1	CMOS RAM failure. Replace CMOS/RTC chip or the main board.
3-3-2	System configuration check failure. Replace the main board.
3-3-3	Keyboard controller not detected.
3-3-4	Screen initialization failure. Verify that the monitor cable is correctly connected. If the problem persists, replace the main board.
3-4-1	Screen retrace test failure. Ensure that the monitor cable is correctly connected. If the problem persists, replace the main board.
3-4-2	Video ROM detection failure. Replace the main board or install another video card.
4-2-1	No timer tick. Replace the main board.
4-2-2	Shutdown failure. Replace the main board.
4-2-3	Gate A20 failure. Replace the main board.
4-2-4	Unexpected interrupt in protected mode. Verify that all expansion cards are properly seated, and then reboot the system.
4-3-1	Improperly seated or faulty DIMM, DIMMs not installed in sets of four, or a faulty or improperly seated memory module. Be sure that the DIMMs are installed in sets of four and in the proper sockets for each memory bank in use. If this does not resolve the problem, remove and reseat the DIMMs. If the problem persists, replace the DIMMs or the memory module(s).
4-3-3	Defective system board. Replace the main board.
4-3-4	Time-of-day clock stopped. Replace the battery. If the problem persists, replace the main board.
4-4-1	Faulty I/O chip or Super I/O controller failure. The system board is defective, so replace the system board.
4-4-2	Parallel port test failure. The system board is defective, so replace the system board.
4-4-3	Math coprocessor failure. This means a defective microprocessor, so replace the microprocessor.
4-4-4	Cache test failure. This means a defective microprocessor, so replace the microprocessor.

TABLE 19-5 COMPAQ (ALPHASERVER) BEEP CODES

BEEPS	ERROR
1	No error.
1-3	VGA monitor not plugged in. Graphics option card different from the one shipped with the system.
1-1-2	A ROM data path error was detected while loading SRM/AlphaBIOS console code.
1-1-4	The SROM code is unable to load the console code, or FROM header area or checksum error detected.

TABLE 19-5 COMPAQ (ALPHASERVER) BEEP CODES *(CONTINUED)*

BEEPS	ERROR
1-1-7	No boot block on floppy device.
1-2-1	TOY NVRAM failure.
1-2-4	B-cache error.
1-3-3	No usable memory detected.
3-3-1	Generic system failure.
3-3-3	Failure of onboard SCSI controller.

TABLE 19-6 IBM DESKTOP BEEP CODES (CLASSIC)

BEEPS	ERROR
1s	Start of test
2s	Initialization error
1l-1s	System board error
1l-2s	Video adapter error
1l-3s	EGA/VGA adapter error
3l	Keyboard adapter error
999s	Power supply error

l=long s=short

TABLE 19-7 IBM DESKTOP BEEP CODES (APTIVA 2173)

BEEPS	ERROR
1-1-3	CMOS read/write error. The system may be configured improperly. Run the system setup routine.
1-1-4	ROM BIOS checksum error. Replace the main board.
1-2-X	DMA controller error. Replace the main board.
1-3-X	Memory module error. Check, reinstall, or replace the memory module(s) or replace the main board.
1-4-4	Keyboard error. Check the keyboard and its installation. Replace the keyboard, or replace the main board.
1-4-X	Error detected in first 64K of RAM. One or more memory modules may have failed. First try reseating the memory module(s); if necessary, replace the memory module(s) or the main board.
2-1-1	System board fault. Run the system setup routine, or replace the main board.
2-1-2	System board fault. Run the system setup routine, or replace the main board.
2-1-X	Error detected in first 64K of RAM. One or more memory modules may have failed. Try reseating the memory module(s), replace the memory module(s), then replace the main board.
2-2-2	Video adapter fault. The onboard video system has failed. Install a standalone video card, or replace the main board.
2-2-X	Error detected in first 64K of RAM. One or more memory modules may have failed. Try reseating the memory module(s); if necessary, replace the memory module(s), then replace the main board.
2-3-X	Memory module error. Check, reinstall, or replace the memory module(s) or replace the main board.
2-4-X	Memory module error. Check, reinstall, or replace the memory module(s) or replace the main board.

19

TABLE 19-7 IBM DESKTOP BEEP CODES (APTIVA 2173) *(CONTINUED)*

BEEPS	ERROR
3-1-X	DMA register failed. Replace the main board.
3-2-4	Keyboard controller chip failed. Replace the main board.
3-3-4	Screen initialization failed. The video system has failed. Replace the video adapter, or replace the main board if the video system is integrated into the main board.
3-4-1	Screen retrace test error. The video system has failed. Replace the video adapter, or replace the main board if the video system is integrated into the main board.
3-4-2	Cannot locate video ROM. The video system has failed. Replace the video adapter, or replace the main board if the video system is integrated into the main board.
4	Video adapter fault. The onboard video system has failed. Install a standalone video card, or replace the main board.
1l-1s	Base 640K memory error or shadow RAM error. Replace the defective memory module(s) or replace the motherboard.
1l-2s	Video adapter fault. The onboard video system has failed. Install a standalone video card, or replace the main board.
1l-3s	Video adapter fault. The onboard video system has failed. Install a standalone video card, or replace the main board.
3s	Memory failure. Check, reinstall, or replace the memory module(s) or replace the main board.
Continuous beep.	System board failure. Replace the motherboard.
Repeating beeps.	Stuck key on the keyboard, keyboard cable detached or damaged, or main board failure. Clean or replace the keyboard, or replace the motherboard.

l=long s=short

All other beep code sequences indicate a motherboard fault, so try replacing the motherboard.

TABLE 19-8 IBM THINKPAD BEEP CODES

BEEPS	ERROR
Continuous beeps	System board failure.
One beep and a blank, unreadable, or flashing LCD	LCD connector problem. LCD backlight inverter problem. Video adapter problem. LCD assembly failure. System board failure. Power supply (DC/DC) failure.
One beep and message "Unable to access boot source"	Boot device (drive) failure. System board failure.
One long and two short beeps and a blank or unreadable LCD	System board failure. Video adapter problem. LCD assembly failure.
One long beep followed by four short beeps each time the power switch is operated	Low battery voltage. Connect the AC adapter or install a fully charged laptop battery.
One beep every second	Low battery voltage. Connect the AC adapter or install a fully charged battery.

TABLE 19-8 IBM THINKPAD BEEP CODES *(CONTINUED)*

BEEPS	ERROR
No beeps, but the system is shutting down due to low battery voltage	Allow the system to completely shut down before changing the battery.
Two short beeps with error codes	POST error (refer to Table 19-1 for error code explanations).
Two short beeps with blank screen	System board failure.

TABLE 19-9 MYLEX BEEP CODES

BEEPS	ERROR
1	Start of test
2	Video adapter error
3	Keyboard controller error
4	Keyboard error
5	PIC 0 error
6	PIC 1 error
7	DMA page register error
8	RAM refresh error
9	RAM data error
10	RAM parity error
11	DMA controller 0 error
12	CMOS RAM error
13	DMA controller 1 error
14	CMOS RAM battery error
15	CMOS RAM checksum error
16	BIOS ROM checksum error

TABLE 19-10 MYLEX 386 BEEP CODES

BEEPS	ERROR
1l	Start of test
2l	Video adapter fault (or adapter missing)
1l-1s-1l	Keyboard controller error
1l-2s-1l	Keyboard error
1l-3s-1l	PIC 0 error
1l-4s-1l	PIC 1 error
1l-5s-1l	DMA page register error
1l-6s-1l	RAM refresh error
1l-7s-1l	RAM data test error
1l-8s-1l	RAM parity error
1l-9s-1l	DMA controller 1 error
1l-10s-1l	CMOS RAM failure
1l-11s-1l	DMA controller 2 error
1l-12s-1l	CMOS RAM battery failure
1l-13s-1l	CMOS checksum failure
1l-14s-1l	BIOS ROM checksum failure
>1l	Multiple faults detected.

l=long s=short

TABLE 19-11 PHOENIX BEEP CODES FOR ISA/MCA/EISA POST)

BEEPS	ERROR
1-1-2	CPU register test failure. The CPU has likely failed. Replace the CPU.
Low 1-1-2	System board select failure. The motherboard is suffering from an undetermined fault. Try replacing the motherboard.
1-1-3	CMOS read/write failure. The RTC/CMOS IC has probably failed. Try replacing the RTC/CMOS IC.
Low 1-1-3	Extended CMOS RAM failure. The extended portion of the RTC/CMOS IC has failed. Try replacing the RTC/CMOS IC.
1-1-4	BIOS ROM Checksum error. The BIOS ROM has probably failed.
1-2-1	Programmable interval timer (PIT) failure. The PIT has probably failed.
1-2-2	DMA initialization failure. The DMA controller has probably failed.
1-2-3	DMA page register read/write failure. The DMA controller has probably failed.
1-3-1	RAM refresh failure. The refresh controller has failed.
1-3-2	64K RAM test disabled. The test of the first 64K of system RAM could not begin. Try replacing the motherboard.
1-3-3	First 64K RAM IC or data line failure. The first RAM IC has failed.
1-3-4	First 64K odd/even logic failure. The first RAM control logic has failed.
1-4-1	Address line failure 64K of RAM.
1-4-2	Parity failure first 64K of RAM. The first RAM IC has failed.
1-4-3	EISA failsafe timer test fault. Replace the motherboard.
1-4-4	EISA NMI port 462 test failure. Replace the motherboard.
2-1-1	Bit 0 first 64K RAM failure. This data bit in the first RAM IC has failed.
2-1-2	Bit 1 first 64K RAM failure.
2-1-3	Bit 2 first 64K RAM failure.
2-1-4	Bit 3 first 64K RAM failure.
2-2-1	Bit 4 first 64K RAM failure.
2-2-2	Bit 5 first 64K RAM failure.
2-2-3	Bit 6 first 64K RAM failure.
2-2-4	Bit 7 first 64K RAM failure.
2-3-1	Bit 8 first 64K RAM failure.
2-3-2	Bit 9 first 64K RAM failure.
2-3-3	Bit 10 first 64K RAM failure.
2-3-4	Bit 11 first 64K RAM failure.
2-4-1	Bit 12 first 64K RAM failure.
2-4-2	Bit 13 first 64K RAM failure.
2-4-3	Bit 14 first 64K RAM failure.
2-4-4	Bit 15 first 64K RAM failure.
3-1-1	Slave DMA register failure. The DMA controller has probably failed.
3-1-2	Master DMA register failure. The DMA controller has probably failed.
3-1-3	Master interrupt mask register failure. The interrupt controller has probably failed.
3-1-4	Slave interrupt mask register failure. The interrupt controller has probably failed.
3-2-2	Interrupt vector loading error. BIOS is unable to load the interrupt vectors into low RAM. Replace the motherboard.
3-2-3	Reserved
3-2-4	Keyboard controller test failure. The keyboard controller has failed.
3-3-1	CMOS RAM power bad. Try replacing the CMOS backup battery. Try replacing the RTC/CMOS IC. Replace the motherboard.
3-3-2	CMOS Configuration error. The CMOS configuration has failed. Restore the configuration. Replace the CMOS backup battery. Replace the RTC/CMOS IC. Replace the motherboard.

TABLE 19-11 PHOENIX BEEP CODES FOR ISA/MCA/EISA POST *(CONTINUED)*

BEEPS	ERROR
3-3-3	Reserved
3-3-4	Video memory test failed. There is a problem with the video memory. Replace video memory or replace the video adapter board.
3-4-1	Video initialization test failure. There is a problem with the video system. Replace the video adapter.
4-2-1	Timer tick failure. The system timer IC has failed.
4-2-2	Shutdown test failure. The CMOS IC has failed.
4-2-3	Gate A20 failure. The keyboard controller has probably failed.
4-2-4	Unexpected interrupt in protected mode. There is a problem with the CPU.
4-3-1	RAM test address failure. System RAM addressing circuitry has failed.
4-3-3	Interval timer channel 2 failure. The system timer IC has probably failed.
4-3-4	Time-of-day clock failure. The RTC/CMOS IC has failed.
4-4-1	Serial port test failure. A fault has developed in the serial port circuit.
4-4-2	Parallel port test failure. A fault has developed in the parallel port circuit.
4-4-3	Math coprocessor failure. Try replacing the math coprocessor.

TABLE 19-12 QUADTEL BEEP CODES

BEEPS	ERROR
1s	Start of test
2s	CMOS IC error
1l-2s	Video controller error
1l>2s	Peripheral controller error

l=long s=short

19

POST Codes

During initialization, the POST performs a self-diagnostic routine designed to check key areas of the motherboard (and common peripherals) for major faults. When an error is detected early in the test cycle, you'll probably hear a series of one or more beep codes as described in the previous section. However, BIOS makers soon realized that most beep code sequences are not terribly specific, and a beep code can often represent any one of a number of possible failures. In order to make more specific information available to technicians, POST procedures are designed to output a single hexadecimal byte to I/O port 80h (or other suitable I/O address) as each step in the initialization is started or completed. If the PC should fail at any point during startup, the code at port 80h represents the *last* step to be successfully completed. By knowing the full sequence of I/O POST codes generated by a BIOS, a technician can quickly determine the test step that failed—and thus pinpoint the fault with reasonable confidence. This part of the chapter presents the POST sequences for popular PC BIOS versions.

INTERPRETING THE POST CODES

When working with POST codes, it is important to understand that not all codes are the direct result of a test. Many codes simply indicate that a CPU is attempting to initialize various areas of the PC. These types of codes are known as *checkpoints*, which simply show that certain initialization steps are being completed. Just because you see a hexadecimal code does not *necessarily* mean that anything has failed.

Also, remember that few listings of BIOS codes are actually complete. With the exception of publicly available code lists (for the IBM PC, XT, and AT), most BIOS manufacturers are generally unwilling to release the full context of their POST codes. As a result, POST code indexes such as those in this book are often compilations of data extracted from a number of different sources. If you encounter a POST code that is not covered in this book, your best course is usually to contact the BIOS manufacturer directly for specific details (and let Dynamic Learning Systems know so that we can get it into the next update for this book).

Another area of confusion can arise when the POST process starts and ends. This can be especially confusing to a novice technician. When a system is first started with a POST board installed, the POST display is typically blank—this is *normal* for the initial moments after PC power is applied. After that, codes should begin flashing across the seven-segment LEDs. If the LEDs remain blank, you can assume that no data is reaching the card. In that event, make sure that your system produces POST codes (a few systems do *not*), and see that the POST board's I/O address is set properly (some systems use I/O ports other than 80h). After the POST is complete, the system will attempt to boot an operating system. Ordinarily, the last code on the display is 00h or FFh, so don't worry if either of these codes remain on the seven-segment display. In some cases—depending on the particular BIOS—some *other* code may be left in the display. If the system appears to boot normally, you rarely need to worry about this. Also keep in mind that not all tests are performed in numerical order. You will find that the POST code sequences in many of the following tables are a bit mixed, so look over each table carefully. The following list points you toward the appropriate table:

> Remember that all of the POST codes presented in the following tables are hexadecimal (or "h") numbers. For example, a POST code of 13 would be 13h or 13 hex.

ACER	Table 19-13
ALR	Table 19-14 (see Phoenix codes also)
Ambra	n/a (see Phoenix codes)
AMI (prior to 04/1990)	Table 19-15
AMI (04/1990–02/1991)	Table 19-16
AMI (02/1991–12/1991)	Table 19-17
AMI (06/1992–08/1993)	Table 19-18
AMI WinBIOS (12/1993+)	Table 19-19
AMI version 2.2x	Table 19-20
AMI Plus BIOS	Table 19-21
AMI Color BIOS	Table 19-22
AMI EZ-Flex BIOS	Table 19-23
Arche Legacy	Table 19-24
AST BIOS	Table 19-25 (see Phoenix and Award codes also)
AT&T BIOS	Table 19-26 (see Phoenix, Olivetti, and NCR codes also)
Award XT BIOS	Table 19-27
Award XT BIOS v.3.1	Table 19-28
Award AT BIOS v.3.0	Table 19-29
Award AT BIOS v.3.0-3.03	Table 19-30
Award AT BIOS v.3.1	Table 19-31
Award AT BIOS 3.3	Table 19-32
Award AT ISA/EISA BIOS 4.0	Table 19-33
Award EISA BIOS	Table 19-34
Award PnP BIOS (4-5.x)	Table 19-35
Award non-PnP BIOS (4-5x)	Table 19-36
Chips & Technologies BIOS	Table 19-37
Compaq BIOS (general)	Table 19-38
Compaq i286 Deskpro BIOS	Table 19-39
Compaq i386 Deskpro BIOS	Table 19-40
Compaq i486 Deskpro BIOS	Table 19-41
Compaq Video BIOS	Table 19-42
Dell BIOS	Table 19-43
DTK BIOS	Table 19-44
Eurosoft/Mylex BIOS	Table 19-45
Eurosoft 4.71 BIOS	Table 19-46
Faraday A-Tease BIOS	Table 19-47
Headstart	n/a (see Philips codes)
Hewlett-Packard Vectra	Table 19-48
IBM PC/XT BIOS	Table 19-49
IBM PC/AT BIOS	Table 19-50
IBM PS/2 BIOS	Table 19-51

TABLE 19-13 POST CODES FOR ACER BIOS

CODE	DESCRIPTION
04	POST start
08	Shutdown condition 0
0C	Test the BIOS ROM checksum
10	Test the CMOS RAM shutdown byte
14	Test the DMA controller
18	Initialize the system timer
1C	Test the memory refresh system
1E	Determine the memory type
20	Test the low 128K of memory
24	Test the 8042 keyboard controller IC
28	Test the CPU descriptor instruction
2C	Test the 8259 interrupt controller IC
30	Set up a temporary interrupt
34	Configure the BIOS interrupt vectors and routines
38	Test the CMOS RAM
3C	Determine the memory size
40	Shutdown condition 1
44	Initialize the video BIOS ROM
45	Set up and testing RAM
46	Test cache memory and controller
48	Test memory
4C	Shutdown condition 3
50	Shutdown condition 2
54	Shutdown condition 7

TABLE 19-13 POST CODES FOR ACER BIOS *(CONTINUED)*

CODE	DESCRIPTION
58	Shutdown condition 6
5C	Test the keyboard and auxiliary I/O
60	Set up BIOS interrupt routines
64	Test the real-time clock
68	Test the disk
6C	Test the hard drive
70	Test the parallel port
74	Test the serial port
78	Set the time of day
7C	Detect and invoke any optional ROMs
80	Check for the math coprocessor
84	Initialize the keyboard
88	Initialize the system (step 1)
8C	Initialize the system (step 2)
90	Boot the operating system
94	Shutdown condition 5
98	Shutdown condition A
9C	Shutdown condition B

TABLE 19-14 POST CODES FOR ALR BIOS

CODE	DESCRIPTION
01	CPU register test in progress
02	Real-time clock write/read failure
03	ROM BIOS checksum failure
04	Programmable internal timer failure (or no video card)
05	DMA initialization failure
06	DMA page register write/read failure
08	RAM refresh verification failure
09	First 64K RAM test in progress
0A	First 64K RAM chip or data line multibit failure
0B	First 64K RAM odd/even logic failure
0C	Address line failure first 64K RAM
0D	Parity failure first 64K RAM
10–1F	Bit 0–15 64K RAM failure
20	Slave DMA register failure
21	Master DMA register failure
22	Master interrupt mask register failure
23	Slave interrupt mask register failure
25	Interrupt vector loading in progress
27	Keyboard controller test failure
28	RTC power failure and checksum calculation in progress
29	Real-time clock configuration validation in progress
2B	Screen memory test failure
2C	Screen initialization failure
2D	Screen retrace test failure

TABLE 19-14 POST CODES FOR ALR BIOS *(CONTINUED)*

CODE	DESCRIPTION
2E	Search for video ROM in progress
30	Screen believed operational or screen believed running with video ROM
31	Monochrome display believed operable
32	Color display (40 column) believed operable
33	Color display (80 column) believed operable
34	Timer tick interrupt test in progress or failed (nonfatal)
35	Shutdown failure (nonfatal)
36	Gate A20 failure (nonfatal)
37	Unexpected interrupt in protected mode (nonfatal)
38	Memory high address line failure at 01000–0A000 (nonfatal)
39	Memory high address line failure at 100000–FFFFFF (nonfatal)
3A	Timer chip counter 2 failed (nonfatal)
3B	Time-of-day clock stopped
3C	Serial port test
3D	Parallel port test
3E	Math coprocessor test
41	System board select bad
42	Extended CMOS RAM bad

TABLE 19-15 POST CODES FOR AMI BIOS (PRIOR TO APRIL 1990)

CODE	DESCRIPTION
01	NMI disabled and i286 register test about to start
02	i286 register test passed
03	ROM BIOS checksum test (32KB from F8000h) passed OK
04	8259 PIC initialized OK
05	CMOS interrupt disabled
06	Video system disabled and the system timer checks OK
07	8253/4 programmable interval timer test OK
08	Delta counter channel 2 OK
09	Delta counter channel 1 OK
0A	Delta counter channel 0 OK
0B	Parity status cleared
0C	Refresh and system timer check OK
0D	Refresh check OK
0E	Refresh period checks OK
10	Ready to start 64K base memory test
11	Address line test OK
12	64K base memory test OK
13	System interrupt vectors initialized
14	8042 keyboard controller checks OK
15	CMOS read/write test OK
16	CMOS checksum and battery OK
17	Monochrome video mode OK
18	CGA color mode set OK
19	Attempting to pass control to video ROM at C0000h
1A	Returned from video ROM

TABLE 19-15 POST CODES FOR AMI BIOS (PRIOR TO APRIL 1990) *(CONTINUED)*

CODE	DESCRIPTION
1B	Display memory R/W test OK
1C	Display memory R/W alternative test OK
1D	Video retrace test OK
1E	Global equipment byte set for proper video operation
1F	Ready to initialize video system
20	Video test OK
21	Video display OK
22	Power-on message displayed
30	Ready to start virtual mode memory test
31	Virtual memory mode test started
32	CPU switched to virtual mode
33	Testing memory address lines
34	Testing memory address lines
35	Lower 1MB of RAM found
36	Memory size computation checks OK
37	Memory test in progress
38	Memory below 1MB is initialized
39	Memory above 1MB is initialized
3A	Memory size is displayed
3B	Ready to test the lower 1MB of RAM
3C	Memory test of lower 1MB OK
3D	Memory test above 1MB OK
3E	Ready to shut down for real-mode testing
3F	Shutdown OK—now in real-mode
40	Ready to disable gate A20
41	A20 line disabled successfully
42	Ready to start DMA controller test
4E	Address line test OK
4F	System still in real mode
50	DMA page register test OK
51	Starting DMA controller 1 register test
52	DMA controller 1 test passed, starting DMA controller 2 register test
53	DMA controller 2 test passed
54	Ready to test latch on DMA controller 1 and 2
55	DMA controller 1 and 2 latch test OK
56	DMA controller 1 and 2 configured OK
57	8259 PIC initialized OK
58	8259 PIC mask register check OK
59	Master 8259 PIC mask register OK
5A	Ready to check timer interrupts
5B	Timer interrupt check OK
5C	Ready to test keyboard interrupt
5D	Error detected in timer or keyboard interrupt
5E	8259 PIC controller error
5F	8259 PIC controller OK
70	Start of keyboard test
71	Keyboard controller OK
72	Keyboard test OK

TABLE 19-15 POST CODES FOR AMI BIOS (PRIOR TO APRIL 1990) *(CONTINUED)*

CODE	DESCRIPTION
73	Keyboard global initialization OK
74	Floppy setup ready to start
75	Floppy controller setup OK
76	Hard disk setup ready to start
77	Hard disk controller setup OK
79	Ready to initialize timer data
7A	Verifying CMOS battery power
7B	CMOS battery verified OK
7D	Analyzing CMOS RAM size
7E	CMOS memory size updated
7F	Send control to adapter ROM
80	Enable Setup routine if Delete pressed
81	Return from adapter ROM
82	Printer data initialization is OK
83	RS-232 data initialization is OK
84	80x87 check and test OK
85	Display any soft-error message
86	Give control to ROM at E0000h
87	Return from system ROM
00	Call the INT19 boot loader

TABLE 19-16 POST CODES FOR AMI BIOS (APRIL 1990 TO FEBRUARY 1991)

CODE	DESCRIPTION
01	NMI disabled and 286 register test about to start
02	286 register test passed
03	ROM BIOS checksum (32K at F800:0) passed
04	Keyboard controller test with and without mouse passed
05	Chipset initialization over; DMA and interrupt controller disabled
06	Video disabled and system timer test begin
07	CH-2 of 8254 initialization half-way through
08	CH-2 of timer initialization over
09	CH-1 of timer initialization over
0A	CH-0 of timer initialization over
0B	Refresh started
0C	System timer started
0D	Refresh link toggling passed
10	Refresh on and about to start 64K base memory test
11	Address line test passed
12	64K base memory test passed
15	Interrupt vectors initialized
17	Monochrome mode set
18	Color mode set
19	About to look for optional video ROM at C000 and give control to ROM if present
1A	Return from optional video ROM
1B	Shadow RAM enable/disable completed
1C	Display memory read/write test for main display type as set in the CMOS setup program over

19

TABLE 19-16 POST CODES FOR AMI BIOS (APRIL 1990 TO FEBRUARY 1991) *(CONTINUED)*

CODE	DESCRIPTION
1D	Display memory read/write test for alternate display type complete if main display memory read/write test returns error
1E	Global equipment byte set for proper display type
1F	Video mode set call for mono/color begins
20	Video mode set completed
21	ROM type 27256 verified
23	Power on message displayed
30	Virtual mode memory test about to begin
31	Virtual mode memory test started
32	Processor executing in virtual mode
33	Memory address line test in progress
34	Memory address line test in progress
35	Memory below 1MB calculated
36	Memory above 1MB calculated
37	Memory test about to start
38	Memory below 1MB initialized
39	Memory above 1MB initialized
3A	Memory size display initiated; will be updated when BIOS goes through memory test
3B	About to start below 1MB memory test
3C	Memory test below 1MB completed; about to start above 1MB test
3D	Memory test above 1MB completed
3E	About to go to real mode (shutdown)
3F	Shutdown successful and processor in real mode
40	Cache memory on and about to disable A20 address line
41	A20 address line disable successful
42	486 internal cache turned on
43	About to start DMA controller test
50	DMA page register test complete
51	DMA unit 1 base register test about to start
52	DMA unit 1 base register test complete
53	DMA unit 2 base register test complete
54	About to check F/F latch for unit 1 and unit 2
55	F/F latch for both units checked
56	DMA unit 1 and 2 programming over; about to initialize 8259 interrupt controller
57	8259 initialization over
70	About to start keyboard test
71	Keyboard controller BAT test over
72	Keyboard interface test over; mouse interface test started
73	Global data initialization for keyboard/mouse over
74	Display Setup prompt and about to start floppy setup
75	Floppy setup over
76	Hard disk setup about to start
77	Hard disk setup over
79	About to initialize timer data area
7A	Timer data initialized and about to verify CMOS battery power
7B	CMOS battery verification over
7D	About to analyze POST results
7E	CMOS memory size updated

TABLE 19-16 POST CODES FOR AMI BIOS (APRIL 1990 TO FEBRUARY 1991) *(CONTINUED)*

CODE	DESCRIPTION
7F	Look for Delete key and get into CMOS setup if found
80	About to give control to optional ROM in segment C800 to DE00
81	Optional ROM control over
82	Check for printer ports and put the addresses in global data area
83	Check for RS232 ports and put the addresses in global data area
84	Coprocessor detection over
85	About to display soft error messages
86	About to give control to system ROM at segment E000
00	System ROM control at E000 over now give control to Int 19h boot loader

TABLE 19-17 POST CODES FOR AMI BIOS (FEBRUARY 1991 TO DECEMBER 1991)

CODE	DESCRIPTION
01	Processor register test about to start and NMI to be disabled
02	NMI is disabled; power on delay starting
03	Power on delay complete; any initialization before keyboard BAT is in progress
04	Initialization before keyboard BAT complete; reading keyboard SYS bit to check soft reset/power-on
05	Soft reset/ power-on determined; going to enable ROM (disable shadow RAM/cache)
06	ROM enabled; calculating ROM BIOS checksum, waiting for K controller input buffer to be free
07	ROM BIOS checksum passed; K controller I/B free; going to issue BAT command to keyboard controller
08	BAT command to keyboard controller issued; going to verify BAT command
09	Keyboard controller BAT result verified; keyboard command byte to be written next
0A	Keyboard command byte code issued; going to write command byte data
0B	Keyboard controller command byte written; going to issue Pin 23 and 24 blocking/unblocking command
0C	Pin 23 and 24 of keyboard controller is blocked/unblocked; NOP command of keyboard controller to be issued next
0D	NOP command processing done; CMOS shutdown register test to be done next
0E	CMOS shutdown register R/W test passed; going to calculate CMOS checksum and update DIAG byte
0F	CMOS checksum calculation is done DIAG byte written; CMOS initialization to begin (If INIT CMOS IN EVERY BOOT is set)
10	CMOS initialization done (if any; CMOS status register about to initialize for date and time
11	CMOS status register initialized; going to disable DMA and interrupt controllers
12	DMA controllers 1 and 2, interrupt controllers 1 and 2 disabled; about to disable video display and initialize port B
13	Video display disabled and port B initialized; chipset initialization/auto memory detection about to begin
14	Chipset initialization/auto memory detection over; 8254 timer test about to start
15	Channel 2 timer test halfway through; 8254 Channel 2 timer test to be completed

19

TABLE 19-17 POST CODES FOR AMI BIOS (FEBRUARY 1991 TO DECEMBER 1991) *(CONTINUED)*

CODE	DESCRIPTION
16	Channel 2 timer test over; 8254 Channel 1 timer test to be completed
17	Channel 1 timer test over; 8254 Channel 0 timer test to be completed
18	Channel 0 timer test over; about to start memory refresh
19	Memory refresh started; memory refresh test to be done next
1A	Memory refresh line is toggling; going to check 15 microsecond on/off time
1B	Memory refresh period 30 microsecond test complete; base 64K memory test about to start
20	Base 64K memory test started; address line test to be done next
21	Address line test passed; going to do toggle parity
22	Toggle parity over; going for sequential data R/W test
23	Base 64K sequential data R/W test passed; setup before interrupt vector initialization about to start
24	Setup before vector initialization complete; interrupt vector initialization about to begin
25	Interrupt vector initialization done; going to read I/O port of 8042 for turbo switch (if any)
26	I/O port of 8042 is read; going to initialize global data for turbo switch
27	Global data initialization is over; any initialization after interrupt vector to be done next
28	Initialization after interrupt vector is complete; going for monochrome mode setting
29	Monochrome mode setting is done; going for color mode setting
2A	Color mode setting is done; about to go for toggle parity before optional ROM test
2B	Toggle parity over; about to give control for any setup before optional video ROM check
2C	Processing before video ROM control done; about to look for optional video ROM and give control
2D	Optional video ROM control done; about to give control to do any processing after video ROM returns control
2E	Return from processing after the video ROM control; if EGA/VGA not found, then do display memory R/W test
2F	EGA/VGA not found; display memory R/W test about to begin
30	Display memory R/W test passed; about to look for retrace checking
31	Display memory R/W test/retrace check failed; about to do alternate display memory R/W test
32	Alternate display memory R/W test passed; about to look for alternate display retrace checking
33	Video display checking over; verification of display with switch setting and card to begin
34	Verification of display adapter done; display mode to be set next
35	Display mode set complete; BIOS ROM data area about to be checked
36	BIOS ROM data area check over; going to set cursor for power-on message
37	Cursor setting for power on message ID complete; going to display the power-on message
38	Power-on message display complete; going to read new cursor position
39	New cursor position read and saved; going to display the reference string
3A	Reference string display is over; going to display the Hit Esc message
3B	Hit Esc message displayed; virtual mode memory test about to start
40	Preparation for virtual mode test started; going to verify from video memory
41	Returned after verifying from display memory; going to prepare the descriptor tables
42	Descriptor tables prepared; going to enter in virtual mode for memory test
43	Entered in the virtual mode; going to enable interrupts for diagnostics mode
44	Interrupts enabled (if diagnostics switch is on); going to initialize data to check memory wrap around at 0:0

TABLE 19-17 POST CODES FOR AMI BIOS (FEBRUARY 1991 TO DECEMBER 1991) *(CONTINUED)*

CODE	DESCRIPTION
45	Data initialized; going to check for memory wrap around at 0:0 and find the total system memory size
46	Memory wrap around test done; memory size calculation over; about to go for writing patterns to test memory
47	Pattern to be tested written in extended memory; going to write patterns in base 640K
48	Patterns written in base memory; going to determine amount of memory below 1MB
49	Amount of memory below 1MB found and verified; going to determine amount of memory above 1MB
4A	Amount of memory above 1MB found and verified; going for BIOS ROM data area check
4B	BIOS ROM data area check over; going to check Esc and clear memory below 1MB for soft reset
4C	Memory below 1MB cleared (soft reset); going to clear memory above 1MB
4D	Memory above 1MB cleared (soft reset); going to save the memory size
4E	Memory test started (no soft reset); about to display the first 64K memory test
4F	Memory size display started; this will be updated during memory test; going for sequential and random memory test
50	Memory test below 1MB complete; going to adjust memory size for relocation/shadow
51	Memory size adjusted due to relocation/shadow; memory test above 1MB to follow
52	Memory test above 1MB complete; preparing to go back to real mode
53	CPU registers are saved, including memory size; going to enter real mode
54	Shutdown successful; CPU in real mode; going to restore registers saved during preparation for shutdown
55	Registers restored; going to disable gate A20 address line
56	A20 address line disable successful; BIOS ROM data area about to be checked
57	BIOS ROM data area check halfway; BIOS ROM data area check to be complete
58	BIOS ROM data area check over; going to clear Hit Esc message
59	Hit Esc message cleared and Wait message displayed; about to start DMA and interrupt controller test
60	DMA page register test passed; about to verify from display memory
61	Display memory verification over; about to go for DMA 1 base register test
62	DMA 1 base register test passed; about to go for DMA 2 base register test
63	DMA 2 base register test passed; about to go for BIOS ROM data area check
64	BIOS ROM data area check halfway through; BIOS ROM data area check to be completed
65	BIOS ROM data area check over; about to program DMA units 1 and 2
66	DMA units 1 and 2 programming over; about to initialize 8259 interrupt controller
67	8259 initialization over; about to start keyboard test
80	Keyboard test started; clearing output buffer, checking for stuck key; about to issue keyboard reset
81	Keyboard reset error/stuck key found; about to issue keyboard controller test command
82	Keyboard controller interface test over; about to write command byte and initialize circular buffer
83	Command byte written; global data initialization done; about to check for lock-key
84	Lock-key checking over; about to check for memory size mismatch with CMOS
85	Memory size check done; about to display soft error; check for password or bypass setup
86	Password checked; about to do programming before setup

19

TABLE 19-17 POST CODES FOR AMI BIOS (FEBRUARY 1991 TO DECEMBER 1991) *(CONTINUED)*

CODE	DESCRIPTION
87	Programming before setup complete; going to CMOS setup program
88	Returned from CMOS setup and screen cleared; about to do programming after setup
89	Programming after setup is complete; going to display power-on screen message
8A	First screen message displayed; about to display Wait message
8B	Wait message displayed; about to perform main and video BIOS shadow
8C	Main/video BIOS shadow successful; setup options programming after CMOS setup about to start
8D	Setup options are programmed; mouse check and initialization to be done next
8E	Mouse check and initialization complete; going for hard disk floppy reset
8F	Floppy check returns that floppy is to be initialized; floppy setup to follow
90	Floppy setup is over; test for hard disk presence
91	Hard disk presence test over; hard disk setup to follow
92	Hard disk setup complete; about to go for BIOS ROM data area check
93	BIOS ROM data area check halfway through; BIOS ROM data area check to be completed
94	BIOS ROM data area check over; going to set base and extended memory size
95	Memory size adjusted due to mouse support hdisk type 47; going to verify from display memory
96	Returned after verifying from display memory; going to do any initialization before C800 option ROM control
97	Any initialization before C800 option ROM control is over; option ROM check and control next
98	Option ROM control is done; about to give control to do any required processing after option ROM returns control
99	Any initialization required after option ROM test over; going to set up timer data area and printer base address
9A	Return after setting timer and printer base address; going to set the RS-232 base address
9B	Return after RS-232 base address; going to do any initialization before coprocessor test
9C	Required initialization before coprocessor is over; going to initialize the coprocessor next
9D	Coprocessor initialized; going to do any initialization after coprocessor test
9E	Initialization after coprocessor test complete; going to check extended keyboard and ID and Num Lock
9F	Extended keyboard check done, ID flag set, Num Lock on/off; keyboard ID command to be issued
A0	Keyboard ID command issued; keyboard ID flag to be reset
A1	Keyboard ID flag reset; cache memory test to follow
A2	Cache memory test over; going to display any soft errors
A3	Soft error display complete; going to set the keyboard typematic rate
A4	Keyboard typematic rate set; going to program memory wait states
A5	Memory wait states programming over; screen to be cleared next
A6	Screen cleared; going to enable parity and NMI
A7	NMI and parity enabled; going to do any initialization required before giving control to optional ROM at E000
A8	Initialization before E000 ROM control over; E000 ROM to get control next
A9	Returned from E000 ROM control; going to do any initialization required after E000 optional ROM control
AA	Initialization after E000 optional ROM control is over; going to display system configuration
00	System configuration is displayed; giving control to INT 19h boot loader

TABLE 19-18 POST CODES FOR AMI BIOS (JUNE 1992 TO AUGUST 1993)

CODE	DESCRIPTION
01	Processor register test about to start and NMI to be disabled
02	NMI is disabled; power-on delay starting
03	Power-on delay complete; any initialization before keyboard BAT is in progress next
04	Any initialization before keyboard BAT is complete; reading keyboard SYS bit to check soft reset/power-on
05	Soft reset/power-on determined; going to enable ROM (disable shadow RAM/cache) if any
06	ROM is enabled; calculating ROM BIOS checksum and waiting for 8042 keyboard controller input buffer to be free
07	ROM BIOS checksum passed; keyboard controller input buffer free; going to issue BAT command to the keyboard controller
08	BAT command to keyboard controller is issued; going to verify the BAT command
09	Keyboard controller BAT result verified; keyboard command byte to be written next
0A	Keyboard command byte code is issued; going to write command byte data
0B	Keyboard controller command byte is written; going to issue Pin 23 and 24 blocking/unblocking command
0C	Pin 23 and 24 of keyboard controller is blocked/unblocked; NOP command of keyboard controller to be issued next
0D	NOP command processing is done; CMOS shutdown register test to be done next
0E	CMOS shutdown register R/W test passed; going to calculate CMOS checksum and update DIAG byte
0F	CMOS checksum calculation is done and DIAG byte written; CMOS initialization to begin (if INIT CMOS IN EVERY BOOT is set)
10	CMOS initialization done (if any); CMOS status register about to initialize for date and time
11	CMOS status register initialized; going to disable DMA and interrupt controllers
12	DMA controllers 1 and 2, interrupt controllers 1 and 2 disabled; about to disable video display and initialize port B
13	Disable video display and initialize port B; chipset initialize/auto memory detection about to begin
14	Chipset initialization/auto memory detection complete; 8254 timer test about to start
15	Channel 2 timer test halfway through; 8254 Channel 2 timer test to be completed
16	Channel 2 timer test over; 8254 Channel 1 timer test to be completed
17	Channel 1 timer test over; 8254 Channel 0 timer test to be completed
18	Channel 0 timer test over; about to start memory refresh
19	Memory refresh started; memory refresh test to be done next
1A	Memory refresh line is toggling; going to check 15 microsecond on/off time
1B	Memory refresh period 30 microsecond test complete; base 64K memory test about to start
20	Base 64K memory test started; address line test to be done next
21	Address line test passed; going to do toggle parity
22	Toggle parity over; going for sequential data R/W test
23	Base 64K sequential data R/W test passed; any setup before interrupt vector initialization about to start
24	Setup required before vector initialization complete; interrupt vector initialization about to begin
25	Interrupt vector initialization done; going to read I/O port of 8042 for turbo switch (if any)
26	I/O port of 8042 is read; going to initialize global data for turbo switch
27	Global data initialization is over; any initialization after interrupt vector to be done next
28	Initialization after interrupt vector is complete; going for monochrome mode setting
29	Monochrome mode setting is done; going for color mode setting

TABLE 19-18 POST CODES FOR AMI BIOS (JUNE 1992 TO AUGUST 1993) *(CONTINUED)*

CODE	DESCRIPTION
2A	Color mode setting is done; about to try toggle parity before option ROM test
2B	Toggle parity over; about to give control for any setup required before option video ROM check
2C	Processing before video ROM control is done; about to look for optional video ROM and give control
2D	Option video ROM control done; about to give control for processing after video ROM returns control
2E	Return from processing after video ROM control; if EGA/VGA not found, do display memory R/W test
2F	EGA/VGA not found; display memory R/W test about to begin
30	Display memory R/W test passed; about to look for the retrace checking
31	Display memory R/W test or retrace checking failed; about to do alternate display memory R/W test
32	Alternate display memory R/W test passed; about to look for the alternate display retrace checking
33	Video display checking over; verification of display type with switch setting and actual card to begin
34	Verification of display adapter done; display mode to be set next
35	Display mode set complete; BIOS ROM data area about to be checked
36	BIOS ROM data area check over; going to set cursor for power-on message
37	Cursor setting for power-on message complete; going to display power-on message
38	Power-on message display complete; going to read new cursor position
39	New cursor position read and saved; going to display the reference string
3A	Reference string display over; going to display the Hit Esc message
3B	Hit Esc message displayed; virtual mode memory test about to start
40	Preparation for virtual mode test started; going to verify from video memory
41	Returned after verifying from display memory; going to prepare descriptor tables
42	Descriptor tables prepared; going to enter in virtual mode for memory test
43	Entered in virtual mode; going to enable interrupts for diagnostics mode
44	Interrupts enabled (if “diags” switch on); going to initialize data to check memory wrap around at 0:0
45	Data initialized; going to check for memory wrap around at 0:0 and find total memory size
46	Memory wrap around test done; size calculation finished; about to go for writing patterns to test memory
47	Pattern to be tested written in extended memory; going to write patterns in base 640K memory
48	Patterns written in base memory; going to find amount of memory below 1MB
49	Amount of memory below 1MB found and verified; going to find amount of memory above 1MB
4A	Amount of memory above 1MB found and verified; going for BIOS ROM data area check
4B	BIOS ROM data area check over; going to check Esc and clear memory below 1MB for soft reset
4C	Memory below 1MB cleared (soft reset); going to clear memory above 1MB
4D	Memory above 1MB cleared (soft reset); going to save memory size
4E	Memory test started (no soft reset); about to display first 64K memory test
4F	Memory size display started (will be updated during memory test); going for sequential and random memory test
50	Memory test below 1MB complete; going to adjust memory size for relocation/shadow
51	Memory size adjusted due to relocation/shadow; memory test above 1MB to follow

TABLE 19-18 POST CODES FOR AMI BIOS (JUNE 1992 TO AUGUST 1993) *(CONTINUED)*

CODE	DESCRIPTION
52	Memory test above 1MB complete; preparing to go back to real mode
53	CPU registers saved, including memory size; going to enter real mode
54	Shutdown successful (CPU in real mode); going to restore registers saved during prep for shutdown
55	Registers restored; going to disable gate A20 address line
56	A20 address line disable successful; BIOS ROM data area about to be checked
57	BIOS ROM data area check halfway through; BIOS ROM data area check to be completed
58	BIOS ROM data area check over; going to clear Hit Esc message
59	Hit Esc message cleared and Wait message displayed; about to start DMA and PIC test
60	DMA page register test passed; about to verify from display memory
61	Display memory verification over; about to go for DMA 1 base register test
62	DMA 1 base register test passed; about to go for DMA 2 base register test
63	DMA 2 base register test passed; about to go for BIOS ROM data area check
64	BIOS ROM data area check halfway through; BIOS ROM data area check to be completed
65	BIOS ROM data area check over; about to program DMA units 1 and 2
66	DMA units 1 and 2 programming over; about to initialize 8259 interrupt controller
67	8259 initialization over; about to start keyboard test
80	Keyboard test started; clearing output buffer and checking for stuck key; about to issue keyboard reset
81	Keyboard reset error/stuck key found; about to issue keyboard controller interface command
82	Keyboard controller interface test over; about to write command byte and initialize circular buffer
83	Command byte written and global data initialization done; about to check for lock-key
84	Lock-key checking over; about to check for memory size mismatch with CMOS
85	Memory size check done; about to display soft error and check for password or bypass setup
86	Password checked; about to do programming before setup
87	Programming before setup complete; going to CMOS setup program
88	Returned from CMOS setup program, screen cleared; about to do programming after setup
89	Programming after setup complete; going to display power-on screen message
8A	First screen message displayed; about to display Wait message
8B	Wait message displayed; about to do main and video BIOS shadow
8C	Main/video BIOS shadow successful; setup options programming after CMOS setup about to start
8D	Setup options programmed; mouse check and initialization to be performed next
8E	Mouse check and initialization complete; going for hard disk and floppy reset
8F	Floppy check indicates that floppy is to be initialized; floppy setup to follow
90	Floppy setup is over; test for hard disk presence to be performed
91	Hard disk presence test over; hard disk setup to follow
92	Hard disk setup complete; about to go for BIOS ROM data area check
93	BIOS ROM data area check halfway through; BIOS ROM data area check to be completed
94	BIOS ROM data area check over; going to set base and extended memory size
95	Memory size adjusted due to mouse support and hard disk type 47; going to verify from display memory
96	Returned after verifying from display memory; going to do any initialization before C800 option ROM control
97	Any initialization before C800 option ROM control over; option ROM check and control will be done next

19

TABLE 19-18 POST CODES FOR AMI BIOS (JUNE 1992 TO AUGUST 1993) *(CONTINUED)*

CODE	DESCRIPTION
98	Option ROM control done; about to give control to do any required processing after option ROM returns control
99	Any initialization required after option ROM test over; going to set up timer data area and printer base address
9A	Return after setting timer and printer base address; going to set the RS-232 base address
9B	Return after RS-232 base address; going to do any initialization before coprocessor test
9C	Required initialization before coprocessor over; going to initialize coprocessor next
9D	Coprocessor initialized; going to do any initialization after coprocessor test
9E	Initialization after coprocessor test complete; going to check extended keyboard and keyboard ID and NUM LOCK
9F	Extended keyboard check is done, ID flag set, NUM LOCK on/off; keyboard ID command to be issued
A0	Keyboard ID command issued; keyboard ID flag to be reset
A1	Keyboard ID flag reset; cache memory test to follow
A2	Cache memory test over; going to display soft errors
A3	Soft error display complete; going to set keyboard typematic rate
A4	Keyboard typematic rate set; going to program memory wait states
A5	Memory wait states programming over; screen to be cleared next
A6	Screen cleared; going to enable parity and NMI
A7	NMI and parity enabled; going to do any initialization before giving control to option ROM at E000
A8	Initialization before E000 ROM control over; E000 ROM to get control next
A9	Returned from E000 ROM control; going to do any initialization after E000 option ROM control
AA	Initialization after E000 option ROM control is over; going to display the system configuration
00	System configuration is displayed; giving control to INT 19h boot loader

TABLE 19-19 POST CODES FOR AMI WINBIOS (DECEMBER 1993 AND LATER)

CODE	DESCRIPTION
01	Processor register test about to start; disable NMI next
02	NMI is disabled; power-on delay starting
03	Power-on delay complete (to check soft reset/power-on)
05	Soft reset/power-on determined; going to enable ROM (disable shadow RAM cache if any)
06	ROM is enabled; calculating ROM BIOS checksum
07	ROM BIOS checksum passed; CMOS shutdown register test to be done next
08	CMOS shutdown register test done; CMOS checksum calculation next
09	CMOS checksum calculation done; CMOS diagnostic byte written; and CMOS initialization to begin
0A	CMOS initialization done (if needed); CMOS status register about to initialize date and time
0B	CMOS status register initialization done; any initialization before keyboard BAT to be done next
0C	Keyboard controller I/B free; going to issue the BAT command to keyboard controller
0D	BAT command to keyboard controller is issued; going to verify the BAT command

TABLE 19-19 POST CODES FOR AMI WINBIOS (DECEMBER 1993 AND LATER) *(CONTINUED)*

CODE	DESCRIPTION
0E	Keyboard controller BAT result verified; any initialization after keyboard controller BAT next
0F	Initialization after keyboard controller BAT done; keyboard command byte to be written next
10	Keyboard controller command byte is written; going to issue Pin 23 and 24 blocking/unblocking command
11	Keyboard controller Pin 23 and 24 blocked/unblocked; check for Ins key during power-on
12	Checking for Ins key during power-on finished; going to disable DMA/IRQ controllers
13	DMA controllers 1 and 2 and IRQ controllers 1 and 2 disabled; video display disabled and port B initialized; chipset initialization/auto memory detection about to begin
14	Chipset initialization/auto memory detection over; uncompress the POST code if using a compressed BIOS
15	POST code is uncompressed; 8254 timer test about to start
19	8254 timer test over; about to start memory refresh test
1A	Memory refresh line is toggling; going to check 15 microsecond on/off time
20	Memory refresh 30 microsecond test complete; base 64K memory/address line test about to start
21	Address line test passed; going to try toggle parity
22	Toggle parity finished; going for sequential data R/W test on base 64K memory
23	Base 64K sequential data R/W test passed; going to set BIOS stack and do any setup before interrupt
24	Setup required before vector initialization complete; interrupt vector initialization about to begin
25	Interrupt vector initialization done; going to read input port of 8042 for turbo switch (if any) and clear password if POST diagnostic switch is on
26	Input port of 8042 is read; going to initialize global data for turbo switch
27	Global data initialization for turbo switch is over; any initialization before setting video mode to be done next
28	Initialization before setting video mode is complete; testing mono mode and color mode setting
2A	Monochrome and color mode settings done; about to toggle parity before option ROM test
2B	Toggle parity is finished; about to give control for any setup required before option video ROM check
2C	Processing before video ROM control is finished; about to look for option video ROM and give system control
2D	Option video ROM control is finished; about to give control for any processing after video ROM returns control
2E	Return from processing after video ROM control; if EGA/VGA not found, do display memory R/W test
2F	EGA/VGA not found; display memory R/W test about to begin
30	Display memory R/W test passed; about to look for the retrace checking
31	Display memory R/W test or retrace checking failed; about to do alternate display memory R/W test
32	Alternate display memory R/W test passed; about to look for the alternate display retrace checking
34	Video display checking over; display mode to be set next
37	Display mode set; going to display the power on message
39	New cursor position read and saved; going to display the Hit Del message
3B	Hit Del message displayed; virtual mode memory test about to start
40	Going to prepare the descriptor tables

TABLE 19-19 POST CODES FOR AMI WINBIOS (DECEMBER 1993 AND LATER) (CONTINUED)

CODE	DESCRIPTION
42	Descriptor tables prepared; going to enter in virtual mode for memory test
43	Entered in virtual mode; going to enable interrupts for diagnostics mode
44	Interrupts enabled (if diagnostic switch is on); going to initialize data to check memory wrap around at 0:0
45	Data initialized; going to check for memory wrap around at 0:0 and find total system memory size
46	Memory wrap around test done; memory size calculation over; about to write patterns to test memory
47	Pattern to be tested written to extended memory; going to write patterns in base 640K memory
48	Patterns written to base memory; going to find amount of memory below 1MB
49	Amount of memory below 1MB found and verified; going to find amount of memory above 1MB
4B	Amount of memory above 1MB found and verified; check for soft reset; going to clear memory below 1MB for soft reset next (if power-on, go to POST step 4Eh)
4C	Memory below 1MB cleared (soft reset)
4D	Memory above 1MB cleared (soft reset); save memory size next (go to POST step 52h)
4E	Memory test started (not soft reset); display first 64K memory size next
4F	Memory size display started (this will be updated during memory test); sequential and random memory test next
50	Memory testing/initialization below 1MB complete; going to adjust displayed memory size for relocation/shadow
51	Memory size display adjusted due to relocation/shadow; memory test above 1MB to follow
52	Memory testing/initialization above 1MB complete; going to save memory size information
53	Memory size information saved and CPU registers saved; going to enter real mode
54	Shutdown successful (CPU in real mode); disable gate A20 line next
57	A20 address line disable successful; going to adjust memory size depending on relocation/shadow
58	Memory size adjusted for relocation/shadow; going to clear Hit Del message
59	Hit Del message cleared, and Wait message displayed; about to start DMA and interrupt controller test
60	DMA page register test passed; about to go for DMA 1 base register test
62	DMA 1 base register test passed; about to go for DMA 2 base register test
65	DMA 2 base register test passed; about to program DMA units 1 and 2
66	DMA units 1 and 2 programming over; about to initialize 8259 interrupt controller
67	8259 initialization finished; about to start keyboard test
F4	Extended NMI sources enabling is in progress (EISA BIOS)
80	Keyboard test started; clear output buffer, check for stuck key, and issue reset keyboard command next
81	Keyboard reset error/stuck key found; about to issue keyboard controller interface test command
82	Keyboard controller interface test over; about to write command byte and initialize circular buffer
83	Command byte written and global data initialization done; check for lock-key next
84	Lock-key checking finished; about to check for memory size mismatch with CMOS
85	Memory size check done; about to display soft error and check for password or bypass setup
86	Password checked; about to do programming before setup
87	Programming before setup complete; uncompress Setup code and execute CMOS setup

TABLE 19-19 POST CODES FOR AMI WINBIOS (DECEMBER 1993 AND LATER) *(CONTINUED)*

CODE	DESCRIPTION
88	Returned from CMOS setup and screen is cleared; about to do programming after setup
89	Programming after setup complete; going to display power-on screen message
8B	First screen message displayed, and Wait message displayed; about to do main/video BIOS shadow
8C	Main and video BIOS shadow successful; setup options programming after CMOS setup about to start
8D	Setup options are programmed; mouse check and initialization next
8E	Mouse check and initialization complete; going for hard disk controller reset
8F	Hard disk controller reset done; floppy setup to be done next
91	Floppy setup is complete; hard disk setup to be done next
94	Hard disk setup is complete; going to set base and extended memory sizes
96	Memory size adjusted due to mouse support and hard disk type 47; any initialization before C800 done; option ROM control next
97	Initialization before C800 option ROM control is finished; option ROM check and control next
98	Option ROM control finished; about to give control for any required processing after option ROM returns control next
99	Any initialization required after option ROM test over; going to set up timer data area and printer base address
9A	Return after setting timer and printer base address; going to set the RS-232 base address
9B	Returned after RS-232 base address; going to do any initialization before coprocessor test
9C	Required initialization before coprocessor is finished; going to initialize the coprocessor next
9D	Coprocessor initialized; going to do any initialization after coprocessor test
9E	Initialization after coprocessor test complete; going to check extended keyboard and test keyboard ID and NUM LOCK
9F	Extended keyboard check is done and ID flag is set; NUM LOCK on/off; issue keyboard ID command next
A0	Keyboard ID command issued; keyboard ID flag to be reset
A1	Keyboard ID flag reset; cache memory test to follow
A2	Cache memory test over; going to display any soft errors
A3	Soft error display complete; going to set the keyboard typematic rate
A4	Keyboard typematic rate set; going to program memory wait states
A5	Memory wait state programming over; going to clear the screen and enable parity/NMI
A7	NMI and parity enabled; going to do any initialization required before giving control to option ROM at E000
A8	Initialization before E000 ROM control over; E000 ROM to get control next
A9	Returned from E000 ROM control; going to do required initialization
AA	Initialization after E000 option ROM control is finished; going to display the system configuration
B0	System configuration is displayed; going to uncompress Setup code for hot-key setup
B1	Uncompressing of Setup code is complete; going to copy any code to specific area
00	Copying of code to specific area done; giving control to INT 19h boot loader
EISA Extensions	
F0	Initialization of I/O cards in slots is in progress (EISA)
F1	Extended NMI sources enabling is in progress (EISA)
F2	Extended NMI test is in progress (EISA)
F3	Display any slot initialization messages
F4	Extended NMI sources enabling in progress

TABLE 19-20 POST CODES FOR AMI BIOS VERSION 2.2X

CODE	DESCRIPTION
00	Flag test (the CPU is being tested)
03	Register test
06	System hardware initialization
09	Test BIOS ROM checksum
0C	Page register test
0F	8254 timer test
12	Memory refresh initialization
15	8237 DMA controller test
18	8237 DMA controller initialization
1B	8259 PIC initialization
1E	8259 PIC test
21	Memory refresh test
24	Base 64K address test
27	Base 64K memory test
2A	8742 keyboard test
2D	MC146818 CMOS IC test
30	Start the protected-mode test
33	Start the memory sizing test
36	First protected-mode test passed
39	First protected-mode test failed
3C	CPU speed calculation
3F	Reading the 8742 hardware switches
42	Initializing the interrupt vector area
45	Verifying the CMOS configuration
48	Testing and initializing the video system
4B	Testing unexpected interrupts
4E	Starting second protected-mode test
51	Verifying the LDT instruction
54	Verifying the TR instruction
57	Verifying the LSL instruction
5A	Verifying the LAR instruction
5D	Verifying the VERR instruction
60	Address line A20 test
63	Testing unexpected exceptions
66	Starting the third protected-mode test
69	Address line test
6A	Scan DDNIL bits for null pattern
6C	System memory test
6F	Shadow memory test
72	Extended memory test
75	Verify the memory configuration
78	Display configuration error messages
7B	Copy system BIOS to shadow memory
7E	8254 clock test
81	MC46818 real-time clock test
84	Keyboard test
87	Determining the keyboard type
8A	Stuck key test

TABLE 19-20 POST CODES FOR AMI BIOS VERSION 2.2X *(CONTINUED)*

CODE	DESCRIPTION
8D	Initializing hardware interrupt vectors
90	Testing the math coprocessor
93	Finding available COM ports
96	Finding available LPT ports
99	Initializing the BIOS data area
9C	Fixed/floppy disk controller test
9F	Floppy disk test
A2	Fixed disk test
A5	Check for external ROMs
A8	System key lock test
AE	F1 error message test
AE	System boot initialization
B1	Call INT 19 boot loader

TABLE 19-21 POST CODES FOR AMI PLUS BIOS

CODE	DESCRIPTION
01	NMI disabled
02	CPU register test complete
03	ROM checksum tests OK
04	8259 PIC initialization OK
05	CMOS interrupt disabled
06	System timer (PIT) OK
07	PIC channel 0 test OK
08	Delta count channel (DMA) 2 test OK
09	Delta count channel (DMA) 1 test OK
0A	Delta count channel (DMA) 0 test OK
0B	Parity status cleared (DMA/PIT)
0C	Refresh and system time check OK (DMA/PIT)
0D	Refresh link toggling OK (DMA/PIT)
0E	Refresh period on/off 50% OK (RAM IC or address line)
10	Ready to start 64K base memory test
11	Address line test OK
12	64K base memory test OK
13	Interrupt vectors initialized
14	8042 keyboard controller test
15	CMOS read/write test OK
16	CMOS checksum and battery test
17	Monochrome mode set OK (6845 IC)
18	CGA mode set OK (6845 IC)
19	Checking video ROM
1A	Optional video ROM checks OK
1B	Display memory R/W test OK
1C	Alternate display memory checks OK
1D	Video retrace check OK

TABLE 19-21 POST CODES FOR AMI PLUS BIOS *(CONTINUED)*

CODE	DESCRIPTION
1E	Global byte set for video OK (video adapter)
1F	Mode set for mono/color OK (video adapter)
20	Video test OK
21	Video display OK
22	Power-on message display OK
30	Ready for virtual mode memory test
31	Starting virtual mode memory test
32	CPU now in virtual mode
33	Memory address line test
34	Memory address line test
35	Memory below 1MB calculated
36	Memory size computation OK
37	Memory test in progress
38	Memory initialization below 1MB complete
39	Memory initialization above 1MB complete
3A	Display memory size
3B	Ready to start memory below 1MB
3C	Memory test below 1MB OK
3D	Memory test above 1MB OK
3E	Ready to switch to real mode
3F	Shutdown successful
40	Ready to disable A20 gate (8042 IC)
41	A20 gate disabled (8042 IC)
42	Ready to test DMA controller (8237 DMA IC)
4E	Address line test OK
4F	CPU now in real mode
50	DMA page register test OK
51	DMA unit 1 base register OK
52	DMA unit 1 channel OK
53	DMA unit 2 base register OK
54	DMA unit 2 channel OK
55	Latch test for both DMA units OK
56	DMA units 1 and 2 initialized OK
57	8259 PIC initialization complete
58	8259 PIC mask register OK
59	Master 8259 PIC mask register OK
5A	Check timer and keyboard interrupt
5B	PIT timer interrupt OK
5C	Ready to test keyboard interrupt
5D	Error: timer/keyboard interrupt
5E	8259 PIC error
5F	8259 PIC test OK
70	Start the keyboard test
71	Keyboard test OK
72	Keyboard test OK
73	Keyboard global data initialized (8042 IC)
74	Ready to start floppy controller setup

TABLE 19-21 POST CODES FOR AMI PLUS BIOS *(CONTINUED)*

CODE	DESCRIPTION
75	Floppy controller setup OK
76	Ready to start hard drive controller setup
77	Hard drive controller setup OK
79	Ready to initialize timer data
7A	Verifying CMOS battery power
7B	CMOS battery verification complete
7D	Analyze test results for memory
7E	CMOS memory size update OK
7F	Check for optional ROM at C0000h
80	Keyboard checked for Setup keystroke
81	Optional ROM control OK
82	Printer ports initialized OK
83	Serial ports initialized OK
84	80x87 test OK
85	Ready to display any soft errors
86	Send control to system ROM E0000h
87	System ROM E0000h check complete
00	Call INT 19 boot loader

TABLE 19-22 POST CODES FOR AMI COLOR BIOS

CODE	DESCRIPTION
01	CPU flag test
02	Power-on delay
03	Chipset initialization
04	Hard/soft reset
05	ROM enable
06	ROM BIOS checksum
07	8042 keyboard controller test
08	8042 keyboard controller test
09	8042 keyboard controller test
0A	8042 keyboard controller test
0B	8042 protected-mode test
0C	8042 keyboard controller test
0D	8042 keyboard controller test
0E	CMOS checksum test
0F	CMOS initialization
10	CMOS/RTC status OK
11	DMA/PIC disabled
12	DMA/PIC initialization
13	Chipset and memory initialization
14	8254 PIT test
15	PIT channel 2 test
16	PIT channel 1 test
17	PIT channel 0 test
18	Memory refresh test (PIT IC)

TABLE 19-22 POST CODES FOR AMI COLOR BIOS *(CONTINUED)*

CODE	DESCRIPTION
19	Memory refresh test (PIT IC)
1A	Check 15µS refresh (PIT IC)
1B	Check 30µS refresh (PIT IC)
20	Base 64K memory test
21	Base 64K memory parity test
22	Memory read/write test
23	BIOS vector table initialization
24	BIOS vector table initialization
25	Check of 8042 keyboard controller
26	Global data for keyboard controller set
27	Video mode test
28	Monochrome mode test
29	CGA mode test
2A	Parity enable test
2B	Check for optional ROMs in the system
2C	Check video ROM
2D	Reinitialize the main chipset
2E	Test video memory
2F	Test video memory
30	Test video adapter
31	Test alternate video memory
32	Test alternate video adapter
33	Video mode test
34	Video mode set
35	Initialize the BIOS ROM data area
36	Power-on message display
37	Power-on message display
38	Read cursor position
39	Display cursor reference
3A	Display Setup start message
40	Start protected-mode test
41	Build descriptor tables
42	CPU enters protected mode
43	Protected-mode interrupt enable
44	Check descriptor tables
45	Check memory size
46	Memory read/write test
47	Base 640K memory test
48	Check 640K memory size
49	Check extended memory size
4A	Verify CMOS extended memory
4B	Check for soft/hard reset
4C	Clear extended memory locations
4D	Update CMOS memory size
4E	Display base RAM size
4F	Perform memory test on base 640K
50	Update CMOS RAM size
51	Perform extended memory test

TABLE 19-22 POST CODES FOR AMI COLOR BIOS *(CONTINUED)*

CODE	DESCRIPTION
52	Resize extended memory
53	Return CPU to real mode
54	Restore CPU registers for real mode
55	Disable the A20 gate
56	Recheck the BIOS vectors
57	BIOS vector check complete
58	Display the Setup start message
59	Perform DMA and PIT test
60	Perform DMA page register test
61	Perform DMA 1 test
62	Perform DMA 2 test
63	Check BIOS data area
64	BIOS data area checked
65	Initialize DMA ICs
66	Perform 8259 PIC initialization
67	Perform keyboard test
80	Keyboard reset
81	Perform stuck key and batch test (keyboard)
82	Run 8042 keyboard controller test
83	Perform lock-key check
84	Compare memory size with CMOS
85	Perform password/soft-error check
86	Run CMOS equipment check
87	CMOS setup test
88	Reinitialize the main chipset
89	Display the power-on message
8A	Display the wait and mouse check
8B	Attempt to shadow any option ROMs
8C	Initialize XCMOS settings
8D	Rest hard/floppy disks
8E	Compare floppy setup to CMOS
8F	Initialize the floppy disk controller
90	Compare hard disk setup to CMOS
91	Initialize the hard disk controller
92	Check the BIOS data table
93	BIOS data table check complete
94	Set memory size
95	Verify the display memory
96	Clear all interrupts
97	Check any optional ROMs
98	Clear all interrupts
99	Set up timer data
9A	Locate and check serial ports
9B	Clear all interrupts
9C	Perform the math coprocessor test
9D	Clear all interrupts
9E	Perform an extended keyboard check
9F	Set the NUM LOCK on the keyboard

TABLE 19-22 POST CODES FOR AMI COLOR BIOS *(CONTINUED)*

CODE	DESCRIPTION
A0	Keyboard reset
A1	Cache memory test
A2	Display any soft errors
A3	Set typematic rate
A4	Set memory wait states
A5	Clear the display
A6	Enable parity and NMI
A7	Clear all interrupts
A8	Turn over system control to the ROM at E0000
A9	Clear all interrupts
AA	Display configuration
00	Call INT 19 boot loader

TABLE 19-23 POST CODES FOR AMI EZ-FLEX BIOS

CODE	DESCRIPTION
01	NMI disabled; starting CPU flag test
02	Power-on delay
03	Chipset initialization
04	Check keyboard for hard/soft reset
05	ROM enable
06	ROM BIOS checksum
07	8042 keyboard controller test
08	8042 keyboard controller test
09	8042 keyboard controller test
0A	8042 keyboard controller test
0B	8042 protected-mode test
0C	8042 keyboard controller test
0D	Test CMOS RAM shutdown register
0E	CMOS checksum test
0F	CMOS initialization
10	CMOS/RTC status OK
11	DMA/PIC disable
12	Disable video display
13	Chipset and memory initialization
14	8254 PIT test
15	PIT channel 2 test
16	PIT channel 1 test
17	PIT channel 0 test
18	Memory refresh test (PIT IC)
19	Memory refresh test (PIT IC)
1A	Check 15μS refresh (PIT IC)
1B	Test 64K base memory
20	Test address lines
21	Base 64K memory parity test
22	Memory read/write test

TABLE 19-23 POST CODES FOR AMI EZ-FLEX BIOS *(CONTINUED)*

CODE	DESCRIPTION
23	Perform any setups needed prior to vector table initialization
24	BIOS vector table initialization in lower 1KB of system RAM
25	Check of 8042 keyboard controller
26	Global data for keyboard controller set
27	Perform any setups needed after vector table initialization
28	Monochrome mode test
29	CGA mode test
2A	Parity enable test
2B	Check for optional ROMs in the system
2C	Check video ROM
2D	Determine if EGA/VGA is installed
2E	Test video memory (EGA/VGA not installed)
2F	Test video memory
30	Test video adapter
31	Test alternate video memory
32	Test alternate video adapter
33	Video mode test
34	Video mode set
35	Initialize the BIOS ROM data area
36	Set cursor for power-on message display
37	Display power-on message
38	Read cursor position
39	Display cursor reference
3A	Display Setup start message
40	Start protected-mode test
41	Build descriptor tables
42	CPU enters protected mode
43	Protected-mode interrupt enabled
44	Check descriptor tables
45	Check memory size
46	Memory read/write test
47	Base 640K memory test
48	Find amount of memory below 1MB
49	Find amount of memory above 1MB
4A	Check ROM BIOS data area
4B	Clear memory below 1MB for soft reset
4C	Clear memory above 1MB for soft reset
4D	Update CMOS memory size
4E	Display base 64K memory test
4F	Perform memory test on base 640K
50	Update RAM size for shadow operation
51	Perform extended memory test
52	Ready to return to real mode
53	Return CPU to real mode
54	Restore CPU registers for real mode
55	Disable the A20 gate
56	Recheck the BIOS data area

TABLE 19-23 POST CODES FOR AMI EZ-FLEX BIOS *(CONTINUED)*

CODE	DESCRIPTION
57	BIOS data area check complete
58	Display the Setup start message
59	Perform DMA page register test
60	Verify display memory
61	Perform DMA 1 test
62	Perform DMA 2 test
63	Check BIOS data area
64	BIOS data area checked
65	Initialize DMA ICs
66	Perform 8259 PIC initialization
67	Perform keyboard test
80	Keyboard reset
81	Perform stuck key and batch test (keyboard)
82	Run 8042 keyboard controller test
83	Perform lock key check
84	Compare memory size with CMOS
85	Perform password/soft-error check
86	Run CMOS equipment check
87	Run CMOS setup if selected
88	Reinitialize the main chipset after setup
89	Display the power-on message
8A	Display the wait and mouse check
8B	Attempt to shadow any option ROMs
8C	Initialize system per CMOS settings
8D	Rest hard/floppy disks
8E	Compare floppy setup to CMOS
8F	Initialize the floppy disk controller
90	Compare hard disk setup to CMOS
91	Initialize the hard disk controller
92	Check the BIOS data table
93	BIOS data table check complete
94	Set memory size
95	Verify the display memory
96	Clear all interrupts
97	Check any optional ROMs
98	Clear all interrupts
99	Set up timer data
9A	Locate and check serial ports
9B	Clear all interrupts
9C	Perform the math coprocessor test
9D	Clear all interrupts
9E	Perform an extended keyboard check
9F	Set the NUM LOCK on the keyboard
A0	Keyboard reset
A1	Cache memory test
A2	Display any soft errors
A3	Set typematic rate

TABLE 19-23 POST CODES FOR AMI EZ-FLEX BIOS *(CONTINUED)*

CODE	DESCRIPTION
A4	Set memory wait states
A5	Clear the display
A6	Enable parity and NMI
A7	Clear all interrupts
A8	Turn over system control to the ROM at E0000
A9	Clear all interrupts
AA	Display configuration
00	Call INT 19 boot loader

TABLE 19-24 POST CODES FOR ARCHE LEGACY BIOS

CODE	DESCRIPTION
01	Disable the NMI and test CPU registers
02	Verify the BIOS ROM checksum (32K at F8000h)
03	Initialize the keyboard controller and CMOS RAM
04	Disable the DMA and PIC; test the CMOS RAM interrupt
05	Reset the video controller
06	Test the 8254 PIT
07	Test delta count timer channel 2
08	Test delta count timer channel 1
09	Test delta count timer channel 0
0A	Test parity circuit and turn on refresh
0B	Enable parity check and test system timer
0C	Test refresh trace link toggle
0D	Test refresh timing synchronization
10	Disable cache and shadow memory; test 64K base memory
11	Perform 64K memory R/W test
12	Initialize interrupt vector table in lower 1K of RAM
14	Test CMOS RAM shutdown register; disable DMA and interrupt controllers
15	Test CMOS RAM battery and checksum
16	Test for floppy drive based on CMOS setup; initialize monochrome video
17	Initialize CGA video
18	Clear the parity status (if any)
19	Test for EGA/VGA video BIOS at C0000h and pass control
1A	Return from video ROM
1B	Test primary video adapter; test video memory
1C	Test secondary video adapter; test video memory
1D	Compare CMOS settings to video adapter
1E	Set video mode according to CMOS settings
20	Display CMOS RAM R/W errors and halt
21	Set cursor and call INT 10 to display status message
22	Display power-on message
23	Read new cursor position
24	Display AMI copyright message at the bottom of the screen
25	Test shadow RAM
F0	Shadow RAM test failed

19

TABLE 19-24 POST CODES FOR ARCHE LEGACY BIOS *(CONTINUED)*

CODE	DESCRIPTION
30	Ready to enter protected mode
31	Enter protected mode (A20 gate) and enable timer interrupt (IRQ0)
32	Get memory size above 1MB
33	Get memory size below 640K
34	Test memory above 1MB
35	Test memory below 1MB
37	Clear memory below 1MB
38	Clear memory above 1MB
39	Use CMOS shutdown byte and return to real mode
3A	Test 64K R/W
3B	Test RAM below 1MB and show the area being tested
3C	Test RAM above 1MB and show the area being tested
3D	RAM test completed OK
3E	Ready to return to real mode
3F	Back in real mode
40	Disable A20 gate
41	Check for AMI copyright message in ROM
42	Display the AMI copyright message if found
43	Test cache memory
4E	Process shutdown 1
4F	Restore interrupt vectors and data in BIOS RAM area
50	Test DMA controller
51	Initialize DMA controller
52	Test the DMA controller with patterns
54	Test DMA controller latches
55	Initialize and enable DMA controllers 1 and 2
56	Initialize 8259 PICs
57	Test 8259 PICs and set up interrupt mask registers
61	Check DDNIL status bit and display message
70	Perform keyboard basic assurance test
71	Program keyboard to AT type
72	Disable keyboard and initialize keyboard circular buffer
73	Display message and initialize floppy controller and drive
74	Attempt to access the floppy drive
75	If CMOS RAM good, check and initialize hard disk controller and drive
76	Attempt to access the hard disk drive
77	Shuffle any internal error codes
79	Check CMOS RAM battery and checksum; clear parity status
7A	Compare size of base/extended memory to CMOS information
7C	Display AMI copyright
7D	Set AT memory expansion bit
7E	Verify the ROM contains an AMI copyright
7F	Clear the Del message from the display; check if Del was pressed
80	Locate option ROM at C800h to DE00h and pass control to any found
81	Return from option ROM and initialize timer and data area
82	Setup parallel and serial ports
83	Test for math coprocessor
84	Check if keyboard locked

TABLE 19-24 POST CODES FOR ARCHE LEGACY BIOS *(CONTINUED)*

CODE	DESCRIPTION
85	Display any soft error messages
86	Test for option ROM at E0000h
A0	Error found in 256KB or 1MB RAM IC in lower 640K
A1	Base 64K random access and data pattern test
A9	Initialize on-board VGA controller
B0	Error in 256K RAM IC in lower 640K
B1	Base 64K random access and data pattern test
E0	Return to real mode and initialize base 64K RAM
E1	Initialize 640K RAM
EF	Configuration memory error: can't find memory
F0	Test shadow RAM from 04000h
00	Call the INT 19 boot loader

TABLE 19-25 POST CODES FOR AST BIOS

CODE	DESCRIPTION
01	Test CPU registers
02	Test the 8042 keyboard controller buffer
03	Test the 8042 keyboard controller reset
04	Verify presence of keyboard and check communication
05	Read keyboard input port
06	Initialize system board support chipset
09	Test BIOS ROM checksum
0D	Test 8254 PIT registers
0E	Test ASIC registers
0F	Test CMOS RAM shutdown byte
10	Test DMA controller 0 registers
11	Test DMA controller 1 registers
12	Test DMA page registers (EGA/VGA vertical retrace failed)
13	EGA/VGA RAM test failed
14	Test memory refresh toggle (EGA/VGA CRT registers failed)
15	Test base 64K memory
16	Set interrupt vectors in base memory
17	Initialize video
18	Test display memory
20	EISA bus board power on
30	Test PIC 1 mask register
31	Test PIC 2 mask register
32	Test PICs for stuck interrupts
33	Test for stuck NMI
34	Test for stuck DDINIL status
40	Test CMOS RAM backup battery
41	Calculate and verify CMOS checksum
42	Set up CMOS RAM options
50	Test protected mode
51	Test protected mode exceptions

TABLE 19-25 POST CODES FOR AST BIOS *(CONTINUED)*

CODE	DESCRIPTION
60	Calculate RAM size
61	Test RAM
62	Test shadow RAM
63	Test cache memory
64	Copy system BIOS to shadow RAM
65	Copy video BIOS to shadow RAM
66	Test 8254 PIT channel 2
67	Initialize memory

TABLE 19-26 POST CODES FOR AT&T BIOS

CODE	DESCRIPTION
01	CPU test
02	System I/O port test
03	ROM checksum test
05	DMA page register test
06	Timer 1 test
07	Timer 2 test
08	RAM refresh test
09	8/19-Bit bus conversion check
0A	Interrupt controller 1 test
0B	Interrupt controller 2 test
0C	Keyboard controller test
0D	CMOS RAM/RTC test
0E	Battery power lost
0F	CMOS RAM checksum test
10	CPU protected mode test
11	Display configuration test
12	Display controller test
13	Primary display error
14	Extended CMOS test
15	AT-Bus reset
16	Initialize chipset registers
17	Check for extension ROMs
18	Internal memory address test
19	Remap memory
1A	Memory interleave mode test
1B	Remap shadow memory
1C	Set up MRAM
1D	Expanded memory test
1E	AT memory error
1F	Internal memory error
20	Minimum POST tests complete
21	DMA controller 1 test
22	DMA controller 2 test
23	Timer 0 test
24	Initialize internal controllers

TABLE 19-26 POST CODES FOR AT&T BIOS *(CONTINUED)*

CODE	DESCRIPTION
25	Unexpected interrupt
26	Expected interrupt
30	Switch to protected mode
31	Size AT-Bus memory or size external memory
32	Address lines A16 to A23 test
33	Internal memory test or conventional memory test
34	AT-Bus memory test or external memory test
38	Shadow ROM BIOS to RAM
39	Shadow extension BIOS to RAM
40	Enable/disable keyboard
41	Keyboard clock and data test
42	Keyboard reset
43	Keyboard controller test
44	A20 gate test
50	Initialize interrupt table
51	Enable timer interrupt
60	Floppy controller/drive test
61	Hard disk controller test
62	Initialize floppy drives
63	Initialize hard drives
70	Real-time clock (RTC) test
71	Set real-time clock
72	Test parallel interfaces
73	Test serial interfaces
74	Check external ROMs
75	Numeric coprocessor test
76	Enable keyboard and RTC interrupts (IRQ9)
F0	Display system startup message
F1	Check for ROM at E000H
F2	Boot from floppy or hard disk
F3	Run setup program
F4	Run password program
FC	DRAM type detection
FD	CPU register test

TABLE 19-27 POST CODES FOR EARLY AWARD XT BIOS

CODE	DESCRIPTION
03	Test CPU flag registers
06	Test CPU registers
09	System chipset initialization
0C	Test BIOS checksum
0F	DMA page register initialization
12	Test DMA address and count registers
15	DMA initialization
18	8253 PIT test
1B	8253 PIT initialization

TABLE 19-27 POST CODES FOR EARLY AWARD XT BIOS *(CONTINUED)*

CODE	DESCRIPTION
1E	Start RAM refresh
21	Test base 64K RAM
24	Set up interrupt vectors and stack
27	Initialize the 8259 PIC
2A	Test PIT interrupt mask register
2D	Test PIC hot interrupt test
30	Run V40 DMA test if present
33	Initialize the system clock
36	Run the keyboard test
39	Set up interrupt vector table
3C	Read system configuration switches
3F	Run video test
42	Locate and initialize serial ports
45	Locate and initialize parallel ports
48	Locate game port
4B	Display copyright message
4E	Calculation of CPU speed
54	Test of system memory
55	Test floppy drive
57	Finish system initialization before boot
5A	Call INT 19 boot loader

TABLE 19-28 POST CODES FOR AWARD XT BIOS VERSION 3.1

CODE	DESCRIPTION
01	Test CPU flag registers
02	Determine type of POST and check keyboard buffer
06	Initialize the PIT, PIC, DMA, and 6845
07	Check processor registers
09	ROM checksum
0A	Initialize the video system
15	Test the first 64K RAM
16	Set up interrupt tables
17	Set up video system
18	Test video memory
19	Test 8259 PIC mask bits channel 1
1A	Test 8259 PIC mask bits channel 2
1E	Check memory size
1F	Test base memory above 64K
20	Test stuck interrupts
21	Test stuck NMI
22	Initialize the floppy drive controller
2C	Locate and initialize COM ports
2D	Locate and initialize LPT ports
2F	Initialize the math coprocessor
31	Locate and initialize option ROMs
FF	Call the INT 19 boot loader

TABLE 19-29 POST CODES FOR AWARD AT BIOS VERSION 3.0

CODE	DESCRIPTION
01	Test CPU flag registers
02	Power-up check; initialize motherboard chipset
03	Clear the 8042 keyboard controller
04	Reset the 8042 keyboard controller
05	Test the keyboard
06	Disable video system, parity, and DMA controller
07	Test CPU registers
08	Initialize CMOS/RTC IC
09	Perform BIOS ROM checksum
0A	Initialize the video interface
0B	Test the 8254 timer channel 0
0C	Test the 8254 timer channel 1
0D	Test the 8254 timer channel 2
0E	Test CMOS RAM shutdown byte
0F	Test extended CMOS RAM (if present)
10	Test the 8237 DMA controller channel 0
11	Test the 8237 DMA controller channel 1
12	Test the 8237 DMA controller page registers
13	Test the 8741 keyboard controller interface
14	Test the memory refresh and toggle circuits
15	Test the first 64K of system memory
16	Set up the interrupt vector tables in low memory
17	Set up video I/O operations
18	Test MDA/CGA video memory unless an EGA/VGA adapter is found
19	Test the 8259 PIC mask bits channel 1
1A	Test the 8259 PIC mask bits channel 2
1B	Test the CMOS RAM battery level
1C	Test the CMOS RAM checksum
1D	Set system memory size from CMOS information
1E	Check base memory size 64K at a time
1F	Test base memory from 64K to 640K
20	Test stuck interrupt lines
21	Test for stuck NMI
22	Test the 8259 PIC
23	Test protected mode and A20 gate
24	Check the size of extended memory above 1MB
25	Test all base and extended memory found up to 16MB
26	Test protected-mode exceptions
27	Initialize shadow RAM and move system BIOS (and video BIOS) into shadow RAM
28	Detect and initialize 8242 or 8248 IC
2A	Initialize the keyboard
2B	Detect and initialize the floppy drive
2C	Detect and initialize serial ports
2D	Detect and initialize parallel ports
2E	Detect and initialize the hard drive
2F	Detect and initialize the math coprocessor
31	Detect and initialize any adapter ROMs

TABLE 19-29 POST CODES FOR AWARD AT BIOS VERSION 3.0 *(CONTINUED)*

CODE	DESCRIPTION
BD	Initialize the cache controller if present
CA	Initialize cache memory
CC	Shutdown the NMI handler
EE	Test for unexpected processor exception
FF	Call the INT 19 boot loader

TABLE 19-30 POST CODES FOR AWARD BIOS 3.0-3.03 (AUGUST 1987)

CODE	DESCRIPTION
01	Processor test part 1: processor status verification; tests following CPU status flags: set/clear carry zero sign and overflow (fatal); infinite loop if failed or continue test if OK
02	Determine type of POST test; fails if keyboard interface buffer filled with data; infinite loop if failed or continue test if OK
03	Clear 8042 keyboard interface; send verify TEST_KBRD command (AAh); continue test if OK
04	Reset 8042 keyboard controller; verify AAh return from 03
05	Get 8042 keyboard controller manufacturing status; read input port via keyboard controller to determine manufacturing or normal mode operation
06	Initialization chips on board LSI chips; disable color/mono video, parity, and DMA (8237A); reset coprocessor, initialize (8254) timer 1, clear DMA page registers and CMOS shutdown byte
07	Processor test part 2: read/write verify SS/SP/BP registers with FFh and 00h data pattern
08	Initialize CMOS chip
09	EPROM checksum for 32 K
0A	Initialize video interface
0B	Test 8254 channel 0
0C	Test 8254 channel 1
0D	Test 8254 channel 2
0E	Test CMOS date and timer
0F	Test CMOS shutdown byte
10	Test DMA channel 0
11	Test DMA channel 1
12	Test DMA page registers
13	Test 8741 keyboard controller
14	Test memory refresh toggle circuits
15	Test first 64K of system memory
16	Set up interrupt vector table
17	Set up video I/O operations
18	Test video memory
19	Test 8259 channel 1 mask bits
1A	Test 8259 channel 2 mask bits
1B	Test CMOS battery level
1C	Test CMOS checksum
1D	Set up configuration byte from CMOS
1E	Size system memory and compare to CMOS
1F	Test found system memory
20	Test stuck 8259 interrupt bits
21	Test stuck NMI (parity or I/O check) bits

TABLE 19-30 POST CODES FOR AWARD BIOS 3.0-3.03 (AUGUST 1987) *(CONTINUED)*

CODE	DESCRIPTION
22	Test 8259 interrupt functionality
23	Test protected mode and A20 gate
24	Sizing extended memory above 1MB
25	Test found system/extended memory
26	Test exceptions in protected mode
27	Reserved
286 N3.03 Extensions	
2A	POST_KEYBOARD present during reset keyboard before boot has no relationship to POST 19
2B	POST_FLOPPY present during initialization of floppy controller and drive(s)
2C	POST_COMM present during initialization of serial cards
2D	POST_PRN present during initialization of parallel cards
2E	POST_DISK present during initialization of hard disk controller and drive(s)
2F	POST_MATH present during initialization of math coprocessor; result remains after DOS boot; left on the port 80 display
30	POST_EXCEPTION present during protected-mode access or when processor exceptions occur—a failure indicates that protected-mode return was not possible
CC	POST_NMI present when selecting the F2 system halt option

TABLE 19-31 POST CODES FOR AWARD AT BIOS VERSION 3.1

CODE	DESCRIPTION
01	Test CPU flag registers
02	Power-up check; initialize motherboard chipset
03	Clear the 8042 keyboard controller
04	Reset the 8042 keyboard controller
05	Test the keyboard
06	Disable video system, parity, and DMA controller
07	Test CPU registers
08	Initialize CMOS/RTC IC
09	Perform BIOS ROM checksum
0A	Initialize the video interface
0B	Test the 8254 timer channel 0
0C	Test the 8254 timer channel 1
0D	Test the 8254 timer channel 2
0E	Test CMOS RAM shutdown byte
0F	Test extended CMOS RAM (if present)
10	Test the 8237 DMA controller channel 0
11	Test the 8237 DMA controller channel 1
12	Test the 8237 DMA controller page registers
13	Test the 8741 keyboard controller interface
14	Test the memory refresh and toggle circuits
15	Test the first 64K of system memory
16	Set up the interrupt vector tables in low memory
17	Set up video I/O operations
18	Test MDA/CGA video memory unless an EGA/VGA adapter is found
19	Test the 8259 PIC mask bits channel 1
1A	Test the 8259 PIC mask bits channel 2

TABLE 19-31 POST CODES FOR AWARD AT BIOS VERSION 3.1 *(CONTINUED)*

CODE	DESCRIPTION
1B	Test the CMOS RAM battery level
1C	Test the CMOS RAM checksum
1D	Set system memory size from CMOS information
1E	Check base memory size 64K at a time
1F	Test base memory
20	Test stuck interrupt lines
21	Test for stuck NMI
22	Test the 8259 PIC
23	Test the protected mode and A20 gate
24	Check the size of extended memory above 1MB
25	Test all base and extended memory found up to 16MB
26	Test protected mode exceptions
27	Initialize shadow RAM and move system BIOS (and video BIOS) into shadow RAM
28	Detect and initialize 8242 or 8248 IC
2A	Initialize the keyboard
2B	Detect and initialize the floppy drive
2C	Detect and initialize serial ports
2D	Detect and initialize parallel ports
2E	Detect and initialize the hard drive
2F	Detect and initialize the math coprocessor
31	Detect and initialize any adapter ROMs at C8000h to EFFFFh (and F0000h to F7FFFh)
39	Initialize the cache controller if present
3B	Initialize cache memory
CA	Detect and initialize alternate cache controller
CC	Shut down the NMI handler
EE	Test for unexpected processor exception
FF	Call the INT 19 boot loader

TABLE 19-32 POST CODES FOR AWARD AT BIOS VERSION 3.3

CODE	DESCRIPTION
01	Test 8042 keyboard controller
02	Test 8042 keyboard controller
03	Test 8042 keyboard controller
04	Test 8042 keyboard controller
05	Test 8042 keyboard controller
06	Initialize any system chipsets
07	Test the CPU flags
08	Calculate the CMOS checksum
09	Initialize the 8254 PIT
0A	Test the 8254 PIT
0B	Test the DMA controller
0C	Initialize the 8259 PIC
0D	Test the 8259 PIC
0E	Test ROM BIOS checksum
0F	Test extended CMOS
10	Test the 8259 PIT IC
11	Test the 8259 PIT IC
12	Test the 8259 PIT IC

TABLE 19-32 POST CODES FOR AWARD AT BIOS VERSION 3.3 *(CONTINUED)*

CODE	DESCRIPTION
13	Test the 8259 PIT IC
14	Test the 8259 PIT IC
15	Test the first 64K of RAM
16	Initialize the BIOS interrupt vector tables
17	Initialize the video system
18	Check video memory
19	Test 8259 PIC 1 mask
1A	Test 8259 PIC 2 mask
1B	Check CMOS battery level
1C	Verify the CMOS checksum
1D	Verify the CMOS/RTC IC
1E	Check memory size
1F	Verify memory in the system
20	Initialize DMA ICs
21	Initialize PIC ICs
22	Initialize PIT ICs
24	Check extended memory size
25	Test all extended memory detected
26	Enter the protected mode
27	Initialize the shadow RAM and cache controller
28	Test shadow RAM and the cache controller
2A	Initialize the keyboard
2B	Initialize the floppy drive controller
2C	Check and initialize serial ports
2D	Check and initialize parallel ports
2E	Initialize the hard drive controller
2F	Initialize the math coprocessor
31	Check for any option ROMs in the system
FF	Call the INT 19 boot loader

EISA codes may be sent to I/O port 300h. Be sure to set your POST reader card to the address that's appropriate for your system.

TABLE 19-33 POST CODES FOR AWARD AT ISA/EISA BIOS VERSION 4.0

CODE	DESCRIPTION
01	Processor test part 1: verify CPU status flags; set, test, clear, and test the carry, zero, sign, overflow flags (fatal)
02	Processor test part 2: write/read/verify all CPU registers, except SS, SP and BP with data patterns FF and 00
03	Calculate BIOS EPROM and sign-on message checksum; fail if not 0
04	Test CMOS RAM interface and verify battery power is available
05	Initialize chips: disable NMI, PIE, AIE, UEI, SQWV; disable video, parity checking, and DMA; reset math coprocessor; clear all page registers and CMOS RAM shutdown byte:
	Initialize timers 0, 1 and 2; set EISA timer to a known state; initialize DMA controllers 0 and 1; initialize interrupt controllers 0 and 1; initialize EISA registers
06	Test memory refresh toggle to ensure memory chips can retain data

TABLE 19-33 POST CODES FOR AWARD AT ISA/EISA BIOS VERSION 4.0 *(CONTINUED)*

CODE	DESCRIPTION
07	Set up low memory; initialize chipset early; test presence of memory; run OEM chipset initialization routines; clear lower 256K of memory; enable parity checking and test parity in lower 256K; test lower 256K of memory
08	Set up interrupt vector table and initialize first 120 interrupt vectors with SPURIOUS_INT_HDLR and initialize INT 00-1F according to INT_TBL
09	Test CMOS RAM checksum and load default if checksum is bad
0A	Initialize keyboard; detect type of keyboard controller (optional); set Num Lock status
0B	Initialize video interface; read CMOS RAM location 14 to find out type of video in use; detect and initialize the video adapter
0C	Test video memory and write sign-on message to screen
0D	OEM specific
0E	Reserved
0F	Test DMA controller 0 with AA, 55, FF, 00 pattern
10	Test DMA controller 1 with AA, 55, FF, 00 pattern
11	DMA page registers; use I/O ports to test address circuits
12–13	Reserved
14	Test 3254 timer 0 counter 2
15	Verify 8259 interrupt controller channel 1 by toggling interrupt lines off/on
16	Verify 8259 interrupt controller channel 2 by toggling interrupt lines off/on
17	Test stuck 8259 interrupt bits; turn interrupt bits off and verify no interrupt mask register is on
18	Test 8259 functionality; force an interrupt and verify the interrupt occurred
19	Test stuck NMI bits (parity I/O check); verify NMI can be cleared
1A–1E	Reserved
1F	Set EISA mode; if EISA nonvolatile memory checksum is good, execute EISA initialization; if not, execute ISA tests and clear EISA mode; test EISA configuration, memory checksum, and communication ability
20	Initialize and enable EISA slot 0 (system board)
21–2F	Initialize and enable EISA slots 1–15
30	Size base memory from 256–640K and test with various patterns
31	Test extended memory above 1MB using various patterns; press Esc to skip
32	If EISA mode flag set, test EISA memory found during slot initialization; press Esc to skip
33–3B	Reserved
3C	Verify CPU can switch in/out of protected, virtual 86, and 8086 page modes
3D	Detect if mouse is present, initialize it, and install interrupt vectors
3E	Initialize cache controller according to CMOS RAM setup
3F	Enable shadow RAM according to CMOS RAM setup or if MEM TYPE is SYS in the EISA configuration information
40	Reserved
41	Initialize floppy disk drive controller and any drives
42	Initialize hard disk drive controller and any drives
43	Detect and initialize serial ports
44	Detect and initialize parallel ports
45	Detect and initialize math coprocessor
46	Print Setup message (such as "Press Ctrl-Alt-Esc to enter Setup" at bottom of the screen) and enable setup
47	Set speed for boot
48–4D	Reserved

TABLE 19-33 POST CODES FOR AWARD AT ISA/EISA BIOS VERSION 4.0 *(CONTINUED)*

CODE	DESCRIPTION
4E	Reboot if manufacturing POST loop pin is set; otherwise, display any messages for nonfatal POST errors; enter setup if user pressed CTRL-ALT-ESC
4F	Security check (optional); ask for password
50	Write all CMOS RAM values back to CMOS RAM; clear the screen
51	Preboot enable; enable parity, NMI, cache before boot
52	Initialize ROMs between C80000-EFFFF; when FSCAN enabled, initialize from C80000 to F7FFF
53	Initialize time value at address 40 of BIOS RAM area
55	Initialize DDNIL counter to NULLs
63	Boot attempt; set low stack and boot by calling INT 19
B0	Spurious interrupt occurred in protected mode
B1	Unclaimed NMI; if unmasked NMI occurs, display "Press F1 to disable NMI, F2 to boot"
BF	Program chipset; called by POST 7 to program chipset from CT table
C0	OEM specific; turn on/off cache
C1	OEM specific; test for memory presence and size on-board memory
C2	OEM specific; initialize board and turn on shadow and cache for fast boot
C3	OEM specific; turn on extended memory DRAM select and initialize RAM
C4	OEM specific; handle display/video switch to prevent display switch errors
C5	OEM specific; fast gate A20 handling
C6	OEM specific; cache routine for setting regions that are cacheable
C7	OEM specific; shadow video/system BIOS after memory proven good
C8	OEM specific; handle special speed switching
C9	OEM specific; handle normal shadow RAM operations
D0–DF	Debug; available POST codes for use during development
E0	Reserved
E1–EF	Setup pages: E1 = page 1, E2 = page 2, and so on
FF	If no error flags such as memory size are set, boot via INT 19; load system from drive A or C; display error message if boot device not found

19

TABLE 19-34 POST CODES FOR AWARD EISA BIOS

CODE	DESCRIPTION
01	Test the CPU flags
02	Test the CPU registers
03	Initialize the DMA controller, PIC, and PIT
04	Initialize memory refresh
05	Initialize the keyboard
06	Test BIOS ROM checksum
07	Check CMOS battery level
08	Test lower 256K or RAM
09	Test cache memory
0A	Configure the BIOS interrupt table
0B	Test the CMOS RAM checksum
0C	Initialize the keyboard
0D	Initialize the video adapter

TABLE 19-34 POST CODES FOR AWARD EISA BIOS *(CONTINUED)*

CODE	DESCRIPTION
0E	Test video memory
0F	Test DMA controller 0
10	Test DMA controller 1
11	Test page registers
14	Test the 8254 PIT IC
15	Verify 8259 PIC channel 1
16	Verify 8259 PIC channel 2
17	Test for stuck interrupts
18	Test 8259 functions
19	Test for stuck NMI
1F	Check extended CMOS RAM (if available)
20	Initialize and enable EISA slot 0
21-2F	Initialize and enable EISA slots 1–15
30	Check memory size below 256K
31	Check memory size above 256K
32	Test any EISA memory found during slot initialization
3C	Enter protected mode
3D	Detect and initialize mouse
3E	Initialize the cache controller
3F	Enable and test shadow RAM
41	Initialize floppy disk drive controller
42	Initialize hard disk drive controller
43	Detect and initialize serial ports
45	Detect and initialize math coprocessor
47	Set speed for boot
4E	Display any soft errors
4F	Ask for password (if feature is enabled)
50	Check all CMOS RAM values and clear the display
51	Enable parity, NMI, and cache memory
52	Initialize any option ROMs present from C8000h to EFFFFh or F7FFFh
53	Initialize time value at address 40 of BIOS RAM area
63	Call INT 19 for boot loader
B0	NMI still in protected mode (protected mode failed)
B1	Disable NMI
BF	Initialize any system-specific chipsets
C0	Cache memory on/off
C1	Check memory size
C2	Test base 256K RAM
C3	Test DRAM page select
C4	Check video modes
C5	Test shadow RAM
C6	Configure cache memory
C8	Check system speed switch
C9	Test shadow RAM
CA	Initialize OEM chipset
FF	Call INT 19 boot loader

TABLE 19-35 POST CODES FOR AWARD PNP BIOS VERSION 4-5.X

CODE	DESCRIPTION
C0	Turn off OEM-specific cache, shadow RAM; initialize all the standard devices with default values
C1	Auto detection of onboard DRAM and cache
C3	Test the first 256K DRAM; expand compressed codes into temporary DRAM area including the compressed system BIOS and Option ROMs
C5	Copy BIOS from ROM into E000-FFFF shadow RAM so that POST will go faster
01–02	Reserved
03	Initialize EISA registers (EISA BIOS only)
04	Reserved
05	Keyboard controller self-test; enable keyboard interface
06	Reserved
07	Verifies CMOS's basic R/W functionality
BE	Program defaults values into chipset
09	Program configuration register of Cyrix CPU; OEM-specific cache initialization
0A	Initialize first 32 interrupt vectors; initialize INTs 33 to 120; issue CPUID instruction to identify CPU type; early power management initialization
0B	Verify RTC time; detect bad battery; read CMOS data into BIOS stack area; perform PnP initializations (PnP BIOS only); assign IO and memory for PCI devices (PCI BIOS only)
0C	Initialization of the BIOS data area (40:00–40:FF)
0D	Program some of chipset's value; measure CPU speed for display; video initialization including MDA, CGA, EGA/VGA.
0E	Initialize APIC (multiprocessor BIOS only); test video RAM (if monochrome display device found); show startup screen message
0F	DMA channel 0 test
10	DMA channel 1 test
11	DMA page registers test
12–13	Reserved
14	Test 8254 timer 0 counter 2
15	Test 8259 interrupt mask bits for channel 1
16	Test 8259 interrupt mask bits for channel 2
17	Reserved
19	Test 8259 functionality
1A–1D	Reserved
1E	If EISA NVM checksum is good, execute EISA initialization (EISA BIOS only)
1F–29	Reserved
30	Get base memory and extended memory size
31	Test base memory from 256K to 640K. Test extended memory from 1MB to the top of memory
32	Display Award Plug-and-Play BIOS extension message (PnP BIOS only); program all onboard super I/O chips (if any) including COM ports, LPT ports, FDD port, and so on
33–3B	Reserved
3C	Set flag to allow users to enter CMOS setup utility
3D	Initialize keyboard; install PS/2 mouse
3E	Try to turn on level 2 cache
3F–40	Reserved
BF	Program rest of the chipset
41	Initialize floppy disk drive controller
42	Initialize hard drive controller
43	If it is a PnP BIOS, initialize serial and parallel ports
44	Reserved
45	Initialize math coprocessor
46-4D	Reserved

TABLE 19-35 POST CODES FOR AWARD PNP BIOS VERSION 4-5.X *(CONTINUED)*

CODE	DESCRIPTION
4E	If any error, show all error messages on the screen; wait for user to press F1
4F	If password is needed, ask for password; clear the Energy Star logo (Green BIOS only)
50	Write all CMOS values currently in the BIOS stack areas back into CMOS
51	Reserved
52	Initialize all ISA ROMs; later PCI initializations (PCI BIOS only); PnP initializations (PnP BIOS only); program shadow RAM according to setup settings; program parity according to setup setting; power management initialization
53	If not a PnP BIOS, initialize serial and parallel ports; initialize time in BIOS data area
54–5F	Reserved
60	Set up virus protection (boot sector protection)
61	Try to turn on level 2 cache; set the boot-up speed according to setup setting; last chance for chipset initialization; last chance for power management initialization; show the system configuration table
62	Set up daylight saving according to setup values; program the Num Lock, type rate, and type speed according to setup setting
63	If any changes in the hardware configuration, update the ESCD information (PnP BIOS only); clear used memory; boot system via INT 19h
FF	System booting: BIOS already passed control to the operating system

TABLE 19-36 POST CODES FOR AWARD NON-PNP BIOS 4-5.X

CODE	DESCRIPTION
C0	Turn off chipset, OEM-specific cache control
01	Processor test part 1: processor status (1FLAGS) verification
02	Processor test part 2: read/write/verify all CPU registers
03	Initialize chipset; disable NMI, PIE, AIE, UEI, SQWV; disable video, parity checking, DMA; reset math coprocessor; clear all page registers and CMOS shutdown byte; initialize DMA controllers 0 and 1; initialize interrupt controllers 0 and 1
04	Test memory refresh toggle: RAM must be periodically refreshed to keep memory from decaying
05	Blank video and initialize keyboard; keyboard controller initialization
06	Reserved
07	Test CMOS interface and verify battery status: CMOS is working correctly, detects bad battery
BE	Chipset default initialization: program chipset registers with power-on BIOS defaults
C1	Memory presence test: OEM-specific test to size on-board memory
C5	Early shadow: OEM-specific early shadow enable for fast boot
C6	Cache presence: external cache size detection test
08	Set up low memory; early chipset initialization; memory presence test; OEM chipset routines; clear low 64K of memory; test first 64K memory.
09	Early cache initialization: Cyrix CPU initialization and cache initialization
0A	Set up interrupt vector table; initialize first 120 interrupt vectors
0B	Test CMOS RAM checksum; test checksum; if bad or INS key pressed, load defaults
0C	Initialize keyboard; detect type of keyboard controller
0D	Initialize video interface; detect CPU clock; read CMOS location 14h to find type of video in use; detect and initialize video adapter
0E	Test video memory; write sign-on message to screen; set up shadow RAM
0F	Test DMA controller 0; BIOS checksum test; keyboard detect and initialization
10	Test DMA controller 1
11	Test DMA page registers

TABLE 19-36 POST CODES FOR AWARD NON-PNP BIOS 4-5.X *(CONTINUED)*

CODE	DESCRIPTION
12–13	Reserved
14	Test timer counter 2
15	Test 8259-1 mask
16	Test 8259-2 mask
17	Test stuck keys
18	Test 8259 interrupt functionality
19	Test stuck NMI bits
1A	Display CPU clock
1B–1E	Reserved
1F	Set EISA mode; if EISA nonvolatile memory checksum is good, execute EISA initialization; if not, execute ISA tests and clear EISA mode flag
20	Enable slot 0; initialize slot 0 (system board)
21–2F	Enable slots 1–15; initialize slots 1–15
30	Size base and extended memory: size base memory from 256K to 640K and extended memory above 1MB
31	Test base and extended memory: test base memory from 256K to 640K and extended memory above 1MB using various bit patterns
32	Test EISA extended memory; if EISA flag is set, then test EISA memory found in slots
33–3B	Reserved
3C	Setup enabled
3D	Initialize and install mouse; detect if mouse is present, initialize and install interrupt vectors
3E	Set up cache controller
3F	Reserved
BF	Chipset initialization: program chipset registers with Setup values
40	Display "virus protect" disable or enable
41	Initialize floppy drive and controller
42	Initialize hard drive and controller
43	Detect and initialize serial/parallel ports
44	Reserved
45	Detect and initialize math coprocessor
46	Reserved
47	Reserved
48–4D	Reserved
4E	Manufacturing POST loop or display messages
4F	Security password
50	Write CMOS: write all CMOS values back to RAM and clear screen
51	Preboot enable; enable parity checker; enable NMI; enable cache before boot
52	Initialize option ROMs: initialize any option ROMs present from C8000h–EFFFFh
53	Initialize time value
60	Set up virus protect
61	Set boot speed
62	Set up Num Lock.
63	Boot attempt
B0	Spurious: if interrupt occurs in protected mode
B1	Unclaimed NMI: if unmasked NMI occurs, display "Press F1 to disable NMI, F1 reboot"
E1–EF	Set up pages
FF	Call boot loader

You'll find that these codes generally apply with NEAT, PEAK/DM, OC8291, and ELEAT BIOS versions.

TABLE 19-37 POST CODES FOR CHIPS AND TECHNOLOGIES BIOS

CODE	DESCRIPTION
00h	Error in POS register
01h	Flag register failed
02h	CPU register failed
03h	System ROM did not checksum
04h	DMA controller failed
05h	System timer failed
06h	Base 64K RAM failed address test: not installed, misconfigured, or bad addressing
07h	Base 64K RAM failed data test
08h	Interrupt controller failed
09h	Hot (unexpected) interrupt occurred
0Ah	System timer does not interrupt
0Bh	CPU still in protected mode
0Ch	DMA page registers failed
0Dh	Refresh not occurring
0Eh	Keyboard controller not responding
0Fh	Could not enter protected mode
10h	GDT or IDT failed
11h	LDT register failed
12h	Task register failed
13h	LSL instruction failed
14h	LAR instruction failed
15h	VERR/VERW failed
16h	Keyboard controller gate A20 failed
17h	Exception failed/unexpected exception
18h	Shutdown during memory test
19h	Last used error code
1Ah	Copyright checksum error
1Bh	Shutdown during memory sizing
1Ch	Chipset initialization
50h	Initialize hardware
51h	Initialize timer
52h	Initialize DMA controller
53h	Initialize interrupt controller
54h	Initialize Chipset
55h	Set up EMS configuration
56h	Entering protected mode for first time
57h	Size memory chips
58h	Configure memory chip interleave
59h	Exiting protected mode for first time
5Ah	Determine system board memory size
5Bh	Relocate shadow RAM
5Ch	Configure EMS
5Dh	Set up wait state configuration
5Eh	Retest 64K RAM
5Fh	Test shadow RAM
60h	Test CMOS RAM

TABLE 19-37 POST CODES FOR CHIPS AND TECHNOLOGIES BIOS *(CONTINUED)*

CODE	DESCRIPTION
61h	Test video
62h	Test and initialize DDNIL bits
63h	Test protected mode interrupt
64h	Test address line A20
65h	Test memory address lines
66h	Test memory
67h	Test extended memory
68h	Test timer interrupt
69h	Test real time clock (RTC)
6Ah	Test keyboard
6Bh	Test 80x87 math chip
6Ch	Test RS232 serial ports
6Dh	Test parallel ports
6Eh	Test dual card
6Fh	Test floppy drive controller
70h	Test hard drive controller
71h	Test key-lock
72h	Test pointing device
90h	Set up RAM
91h	Calculate CPU speed
92h	Check configuration
93h	Initialize BIOS
94h	POST Bootstrap
95h	Reset ICs
96h	PEAK: system board POS; NEAT/OC8291 ELEAT: test/initialize cache RAM and controller
97h	VGA power-on diagnostics and setup
98h	Adapter POS
99h	Reinitialize DDNIL bits
A0h	Exception 0
A1h	Exception 1
A2h	Exception 2
A3h	Exception 3
A4h	Exception 4
A5h	Exception 5
A6h	Exception 6
A7h	Exception 7
A8h	Exception 8
A9h	Exception 9
AAh	Exception A
ABh	Exception B
ACh	Exception C
ADh	Exception D
C0h	System board memory failure
C1h	I/O channel check activated
C2h	Watchdog timer timeout
C3h	Bus timer timeout

19

TABLE 19-38 POST CODES FOR GENERAL COMPAQ BIOS

CODE	DESCRIPTION
General	
00	Initialize flags
01	Read manufacturing jumper
02	8042 Received Read command
03	No response from 8042
04	Look for ROM at E000
05	Look for ROM at C800
06	Normal CMOS reset code
08	Initialize 8259
09	Reset code in CMOS byte
0A	Vector via 40:67 reset function
0B	Vector via 40:67 with E01 function
0C	Boot reset function
0D	Test 2 8254 counter 0
0E	Test 2 8254 counter 2
0F	Warm boot
Power-up Sequence	
10	PPI disabled
11	Initialize VDU controller
12	Clear screen; turn on video
13	Test time 0
14	Disable RTC interrupts
15	Check battery power
16	Battery has lost power
17	Clear CMOS diagnostics
18	Test base memory (first 128K)
19	Initialize base memory
1A	Initialize VDU adapters
1B	System ROM
1C	CMOS checksum
1D	DMA controller/page registers
1E	Test keyboard controller
1F	Test 286 protected mode
20	Test real and extended memory
21	Initialize time-of-day
22	Initialize 287 coprocessor
23	Test keyboard and 8042
24	Reset A20
25	Test disk subsystem
26	Test fixed disk subsystem
27	Initialize parallel printer
28	Perform search for optional ROMs
29	Test valid system configuration
2A	Clear screen
2B	Check for invalid time and date
2C	Optional ROM search
2D	Test timer 2
2F	Write to diagnostic byte

TABLE 19-38 POST CODES FOR GENERAL COMPAQ BIOS *(CONTINUED)*

CODE	DESCRIPTION
Base RAM Initialization	
30	Clear first 128K bytes of RAM
31	Load interrupt vectors 70–77
32	Load interrupt vectors 00–1F
33	Initialize MEMSIZE and RESETWD
34	Verify CMOS checksum
35	CMOS checksum not valid
36	Check battery power
37	Check for game adapters
38	Check for serial ports
39	Check for parallel printer ports
3A	Initialize port and communication timeouts
3B	Flush keyboard buffer
Base RAM Test	
40	Save RESETWD value
41	Check RAM refresh
42	Start write of 128K RAM test
43	Rest parity checks
44	Start verify of 128K RAM test
45	Check for parity errors
46	No RAM errors
47	RAM error detected
VDU Initialization and Test	
50	Check for dual frequency in CMOS
51	Check CMOS VDU configuration
52	Start VDU ROM search
53	Vector to VDU option ROMs
54	Initialize first display adapter
55	Initialize second display adapter
56	No display adapters installed
57	Initialize primary VDU mode
58	Start of VDU test (each adapter)
59	Check existence of adapter
5A	Check VDU registers
5B	Start screen memory test
5C	End test of adapter
5D	Error detected on an adapter
5E	Test next adapter
5F	All adapters successfully tested
Memory Test	
60	Start memory tests
61	Enter protected mode
62	Start memory sizing
63	Get CMOS size
64	Start test of real memory
65	Start test of extended memory
66	Save size memory (base)
67	128K option installed CMOS bit

19

TABLE 19-38 POST CODES FOR GENERAL COMPAQ BIOS *(CONTINUED)*

CODE	DESCRIPTION
Memory Test *(Continued)*	
68	Prepare to return to real mode
69	Back in real mode attempt successful
6A	Protected mode error during test
6B	Display error message
6C	End of memory test
6D	Initialize keyboard "OK" string
6E	Determine size to test
6F	Start MEMTEST
70	Display XXXXXKB "OK"
71	Test each RAM segment
72	High order address test
73	Exit MEMTEST
74	Parity error on bus
80286 Protected Mode	
75	Start protected mode test
76	Prepare to enter protected mode
77	Test software exceptions
78	Prepare to return to real mode
79	Back in real mode successful
7A	Back in real mode not successful
7B	Exit protected test
7C	High-order address test failure
7D	Entered cache controller test
7E	Programming memory cache
7F	Copy system ROM to high RAM
8042 and Keyboard	
80	Start of 8042 test
81	Do 8042 self-test
82	Check result received
83	Error result
84	OK 8042
86	Start test
87	Got acknowledgement
88	Got result
89	Test for stuck keys
8A	Key seems to be stuck
8B	Test keyboard interface
8C	Got result
8D	End of test
System Board Test	
90	Start of CMOS test
92	CMOS seems to be OK
92	Error on CMOS read/write test
93	Start of DMA controller test
94	Page registers seem OK
95	DMA controller is OK
96	8237 initialization is complete
97	Start of NCA RAM test

TABLE 19-38 POST CODES FOR GENERAL COMPAQ BIOS *(CONTINUED)*

CODE	DESCRIPTION
Disk Test	
A0	Start of disk tests
A1	FDC reset active (3F2h bit 2)
A2	FDC reset inactive (3F2h bit 2)
A3	FDC motor on
A4	FDC timeout error
A5	FDC failed reset
A6	FDC passed reset
A8	Start to determine drive type
A9	Seek operation initiated
AA	Waiting for FDC seek status
AF	Disk tests completed
B0	Start of fixed disk drive tests
B1	Combo board not found; exit
B2	Combo controller failed; exit
B3	Testing drive 1
B4	Testing drive 2
B5	Drive error (error condition)
B6	Drive failed (failed to respond)
B7	No fixed drives; exit
B8	Fixed drive tests complete
B9	Attempt to boot disk
BA	Attempt to boot fixed drive
BB	Boot attempt failed FD/HD
BC	Boot record read, jump to boot record
BD	Drive error, retry booting
BE	Weitek coprocessor test (386, 386/xxe, 386 & 486/33L, P486c)
EISA Tests (Deskpro/M, /LT, /33L, P486c, and so on)	
C0	EISA nonvolatile memory checksum
C1	EISA DDF map initialization
C2	EISA IRQ initialization
C3	EISA DMA initialization
C4	EISA slot initialization
C5	EISA display configuration error messages
C6	EISA PZ initialization begun
C7	EISA PZ initialization done
C8	System manager board self-test
LT, SLT, LTE	
C0	Disable NMI
C1	Turn off hard disk subsystem
C2	Turn off video subsystem
C3	Turn off floppy disk subsystem
C4	Turn off hard disk/modem subsystems
C5	Go to standby
C6	Update BIOS time of day
C7	Turn on hard disk/modem subsystems
C8	Turn on floppy disk subsystem
C9	Turn on video subsystem

19

TABLE 19-38 POST CODES FOR GENERAL COMPAQ BIOS *(CONTINUED)*

CODE	DESCRIPTION
LT, SLT, LTE *(Continued)*	
CB	Flush keyboard input buffer
CC	Re-enable MNI
Standard POST Functions	
D0	Entry to clear memory routine
D1	Ready to go to protected mode
D2	Ready to clear extended memory
D3	Ready to reset back to real mode
D4	Back in real mode, ready to clear
D5	Clear base memory, CLIM register initialization failure (SLT/286)
D7	Scan and clear DDNIL bits
D9	Four-way cache detect
DD	Built-in self-test failed
Option ROM Shadow	
E0	Ready to replace E000h ROM
E1	Completed E000h ROM replacement
E2	Ready to replace EGA ROM
E3	Completed EGA ROM replacement
E8	Looking for serial external boot ID (Deskpro 2/386N, 386s/20)
E9	Receiving for serial external boot sector (2/386N, 386s/20)
EA	Looking for parallel external boot ID (2/386N, 386s/20)
EB	Receiving parallel external boot sector (2/386N, 386s/20)
EC	Boot record read, jump to boot record (2/386N, 386s/20)

TABLE 19-39 POST CODES FOR COMPAQ i286 DESKPRO BIOS

CODE	DESCRIPTION
01	Test the CPU
02	Test the math coprocessor
03	Testing 8237 DMA controller
04	Testing 8259 PIC
05	Testing KBC port 61h
06	Testing 8042 keyboard controller
07	CMOS test
08	CMOS test
09	CMOS test
10	Testing 8254 PIT
11	Testing 8254 PIT refresh detect
12	System speed test
14	Speaker test
21	Memory R/W test
24	Memory address test
25	Memory walking I/O test
31	Keyboard short test
32	Keyboard long test
33	Keyboard LED test
35	Keyboard lock test

TABLE 19-39 POST CODES FOR COMPAQ i286 DESKPRO BIOS *(CONTINUED)*

CODE	DESCRIPTION
41	Printer test failed
42	Testing printer port
43	Testing printer port
48	Parallel port failure
51	Video controller test
52	Video controller test
53	Video attribute test
54	Video character set test
55	Video 80x25 mode test
56	Video 80x25 mode test
57	Video 40x25 mode test
60	Floppy disk ID test
61	Floppy disk format test
62	Floppy disk read test
63	Floppy disk R/W compare test
64	Floppy disk random seek test
65	Floppy disk media ID test
66	Floppy disk speed test
67	Floppy disk wrap test
68	Floppy disk write protect test
69	Floppy disk reset controller test

TABLE 19-40 POST CODES FOR COMPAQ i386 DESKPRO BIOS

CODE	DESCRIPTION
01	I/O ROM checksum error
02	System memory board failure
12	System option error
13	Time and date not set (not expected from CMOS)
14	Memory size error (not what was expected from CMOS settings)
21	System memory error
23	Memory address line error
25	Memory test error
26	Keyboard error
33	Keyboard controller error
34	Keyboard or keyboard controller error
41	Parallel port error
42	Monochrome video adapter failure
51	Display adapter failure
61	Floppy disk controller error
62	Floppy disk boot error
65	Floppy drive error
67	Floppy disk controller failed
6A	Floppy port address conflict
6B	Floppy port address conflict
72	Math coprocessor detected

TABLE 19-41 POST CODES FOR COMPAQ i486 DESKPRO BIOS

CODE	DESCRIPTION
01	CPU test failed
02	Math coprocessor test failed
03	Testing 8237 DMA page registers
04	Testing 8259 PIC
05	8042 keyboard controller port 61 error
06	8042 keyboard controller self-test error
07	CMOS RAM test failed
08	CMOS interrupt test failed
09	CMOS clock load data test failed
10	8254 PIT test failed
11	8254 PIT refresh detect test failed
12	System speed test mode too slow
13	Protected-mode test failed
14	Speaker test failed
16	Cache memory configuration failed
19	Testing installed devices
21	Memory configuration test failed
22	BIOS ROM checksum failed
23	Memory R/W test failed
24	Memory address line test failed
25	Walking I/O test failed
26	Memory increment pattern test failed
31	Keyboard short test
32	Keyboard long test
33	Keyboard LED test
34	Keyboard typematic test failed
41	Printer test failed or not connected (parallel port circuits)
42	Printer data register failed (parallel port circuits)
43	Printer pattern test (parallel port circuits)
48	Printer not connected (parallel port circuits)
51	Video controller test failed
52	Video memory test failed
53	Video attribute test failed
54	Video character set test failed
55	Video 80x25 mode test failed
56	Video 80x25 mode test failed
57	Video 40x25 mode test failed
58	Video 320x200 mode color set 1 test
59	Video 320x200 mode color set 1 test
60	Floppy disk ID drive types test failed
61	Floppy disk format failed
62	Floppy disk read test failed
63	Floppy disk write, read, seek test failed
65	Floppy disk ID media failed
66	Floppy disk speed test failed
67	Floppy disk wrap test failed
68	Floppy disk write protect failed
69	Floppy disk reset controller test failed
82	Video memory test failed
84	Video adapter test failed

TABLE 19-42 POST CODES FOR COMPAQ VIDEO BIOS

CODE	DESCRIPTION
00	Entry into video option ROM
01	Alternate adapter tests
02	Vertical sync tests
03	Horizontal sync tests
04	Static tests
05	Bus tests
06	Configuration tests
07	Alternate ROM tests
08	Color gun off tests
09	Color gun on tests
0A	Video memory tests
0B	Board present tests
10	Illegal configuration error
20	No vertical sync present
21	Vertical sync out of range
30	No horizontal sync present
40	Color register failure
50	Slot type conflict error
51	Video memory conflict error
52	ROM conflict error
60	Red DAC stuck low error
61	Green DAC stuck low error
62	Blue DAC stuck low error
63	DAC stuck high error
64	Red DAC fault error
65	Green DAC fault error
66	Blue DAC fault error
70	Bad alternate ROM version
80	Color gun stuck on base code
90	Color gun stuck off base code
A0	Video memory failure base code
F0	Equipment failure base code
00	Video POST over (also send 00– 85)

NOTE: Video BIOS codes written to I/O port 85h

TABLE 19-43 POST CODES FOR DELL BIOS

CODE	DESCRIPTION
01	CPU register test in progress
02	CMOS R/W test failed
03	BIOS ROM checksum bad
04	8254 PIT test failed
05	DMA controller initialization failed
06	DMA page register test failed
08	RAM refresh verification failed

TABLE 19-43 POST CODES FOR DELL BIOS *(CONTINUED)*

CODE	DESCRIPTION
09	Starting first 64K RAM test
0A	First 64K RAM IC or data line bad
0B	First 64K RAM odd/even logic bad
0C	First 64K address line bad
0D	First 64K parity error
10	Bit 0 bad in first 64K
11	Bit 1 bad in first 64K
12	Bit 2 bad in first 64K
13	Bit 3 bad in first 64K
14	Bit 4 bad in first 64K
15	Bit 5 bad in first 64K
16	Bit 6 bad in first 64K
17	Bit 7 bad in first 64K
18	Bit 8 bad in first 64K
19	Bit 9 bad in first 64K
1A	Bit 10 bad in first 64K
1B	Bit 11 bad in first 64K
1C	Bit 12 bad in first 64K
1D	Bit 13 bad in first 64K
1E	Bit 14 bad in first 64K
1F	Bit 15 bad in first 64K
20	Slave DMA register bad
21	Master DMA register bad
22	Master interrupt mask register bad
23	Slave interrupt mask register bad
25	Loading interrupt vectors
27	Keyboard controller test failed
28	CMOS RAM battery bad
29	CMOS configuration validation in progress
2B	Video memory test failed
2C	Video initialization failed
2D	Video retrace failure
2E	Searching for a video ROM
30	Switching to video ROM
31	Monochrome operation OK
32	Color (CGA) operation OK
33	Color operation OK
34	Timer tick interrupt in progress (or bad)
35	CMOS shutdown test in progress (or bad)
36	Gate A20 bad
37	Unexpected interrupt in protected mode
38	RAM test in progress or high address line is bad
3A	Interval timer channel 2 bad
3B	Time-of-day test bad
3C	Serial port test bad
3D	Parallel port test bad
3E	Math coprocessor test bad
3F	Cache memory test bad

TABLE 19-44 POST CODES FOR DTK BIOS

CODE	DESCRIPTION
01	Test the CPU
03	Initialize the 8258 interrupt controller
05	Initialize the video board
0D	Initialize the DMA controller
0E	Initialize the DMA page register
12	Test the 8042 keyboard controller
16	Test the DMA controller and timer
22	Test DRAM refresh circuitry
25	Base 64K memory test
30	Set up system stack
33	Read system configuration through keyboard controller
37	Test keyboard clock and data line
40	Determine video type
44	Locating and testing MDA and CGA video
48	Initialize video 80x25 mode
4D	Display DTK BIOS copyright message
4F	Check serial and parallel ports
50	Check floppy disk controller
55	Check shadow RAM
58	Display total memory and switch to real mode
5A	Successful switch back to real mode
60	Check hard disk drive controller
62	Initialize floppy drive
65	Initialize hard drive
67	Initialize the drives
6A	Disable gate A20 and test math coprocessor
70	Set system date and time
77	Call Int 19 boot loader

TABLE 19-45 POST CODES FOR EUROSOFT/MYLEX BIOS

CODE	DESCRIPTION
01	CPU test failed
02	DMA page register test failed
03	Keyboard controller test failed
04	BIOS ROM checksum error
05	Keyboard command test failed
06	CMOS RAM test failed
07	RAM refresh test failed
08	First 64K memory test failed
09	DMA controller test failed
0A	Initialize DMA controller
0B	Interrupt test failed
0C	Checking RAM size
0D	Initializing video system
0E	Video BIOS checksum failed

19

TABLE 19-45 POST CODES FOR EUROSOFT/MYLEX BIOS *(CONTINUED)*

CODE	DESCRIPTION
10	Search for monochrome video adapter
11	Search for color video adapter
12	Word splitter and byte shift test failed (keyboard controller)
13	Keyboard test failed
14	RAM test failed
15	System timer test failed
16	Initialize keyboard controller output port
17	Keyboard interrupt test failed
18	Initialize keyboard
19	Real-time clock test failed
1A	Math coprocessor test failed
1B	Reset floppy and hard drive controllers
1C	Initialize the floppy drive
1D	Initialize the hard drive
1E	Locate adapter ROMs from C800h–DFFFh
1F	Locate and initialize serial and parallel ports
20	Initialize time-of-day in RTC
21	Locate adapter ROMs from E000h– EFFFh
22	Search for boot device
23	Boot from floppy disk
24	Boot from hard disk
25	Gate A20 enable/disable failure
26	Parity error
30	DDNIL bit scan failure
FF	Fatal error: system halted

TABLE 19-46 POST CODES FOR EUROSOFT 4.71 BIOS

PASS CODE	FAIL CODE	DESCRIPTION
03	04	DMA page register test
05	06	Keyboard test
07	08	Keyboard self-test
09	0A	8042 keyboard controller checking links
0B	—	RATMOD/DIAG link
0C	0D	Keyboard port 60h test
0E	0F	Keyboard parameter test
10	11	Keyboard command byte
12	13	Keyboard command byte return
14	15	RAM refresh toggle test
16	17	RAM bit test
18	19	RAM parity test
1A	1B	CMOS RAM test
1C	1D	CMOS RAM battery test
1E	1F	CMOS RAM checksum test
—	20	CMOS RAM battery fault bit set
21	22	Master DMA controller 1 test
21	23	Slave DMA controller 2 test

TABLE 19-46 POST CODES FOR EUROSOFT 4.71 BIOS *(CONTINUED)*

PASS CODE	FAIL CODE	DESCRIPTION
24	—	Protected mode entered successfully
25	—	RAM test completed
26	27	BIOS RAM checksum test
28	—	Exiting protected mode
29	2A	Keyboard power-up reply received test
2B	2C	Keyboard disable command test
—	2D	Checking for video system
—	2E	POST errors have been reported
—	2F	About to halt
30	—	Protected mode entered safely
31	—	RAM test complete
32	33	Master interrupt controller test
34	35	Slave interrupt controller test
36	37	Chipset initialization
38	39	Shadowing system BIOS
3A	3B	Shadowing video BIOS

TABLE 19-47 POST CODES FOR FARADAY A-TEASE BIOS

CODE	DESCRIPTION
01	CPU test failed
02	BIOS ROM checksum test failed
03	CMOS shutdown byte failed
04	Testing DMA page register
05	Testing system timer (PIT)
06	Testing system refresh
07	Testing 8042 keyboard controller
08	Testing lower 128K of RAM
09	Testing video controller
0A	Testing RAM 128K to 640K
0B	Testing DMA controller 1
0C	Testing DMA controller 2
0D	Testing interrupt controller 1
0E	Testing interrupt controller 2
0F	Testing control port
10	Testing parity
11	Testing CMOS RAM checksum
12	Testing for manufacturing mode jumper
13	Configure interrupt vectors
14	Testing the keyboard
15	Configuring parallel ports
16	Configuring serial ports
17	Configuring lower 640K RAM
18	Configuring RAM above 1MB
19	Configuring keyboard
1A	Configuring floppy drive
1B	Configuring hard disk drive

TABLE 19-47 POST CODES FOR FARADAY A-TEASE BIOS *(CONTINUED)*

CODE	DESCRIPTION
1C	Configuring game port adapter
1D	Testing and initializing math coprocessor
1E	Checking CMOS real-time clock
1F	Calculate and verify CMOS RAM checksum
21	Initialize PROM drivers
22	Test parallel port loopback
23	Test serial port loopback
24	Test CMOS RTC
25	Test the CMOS shutdown
26	Test memory over 1MB
80	Error: divide overflow
81	Error: single-step fault
82	Error: NMI stuck or error
83	Error: breakpoint fault
84	Error: INT 0 detect fault
85	Error: bound error
86	Error: invalid opcode (BIOS or CPU fault)
87	Error: processor extension not available
88	Error: double exception error
89	Error: processor extended segment error
8A	Error: invalid task state segment
8B	Error: needed segment not present
8C	Error: stack segment not present
8D	Error: general protection error
8E	Error: general protection error
8F	Error: general protection error
90	Error: processor extension error
91-FF	Error: spurious interrupts
F3	Error: CPU protected mode fault
F9	Error: virtual block move error

TABLE 19-48 POST CODES FOR HEWLETT-PACKARD VECTRA

CODE	DESCRIPTION
01	LED test
02	Processor test
03	System (BIOS) ROM test
04	RAM refresh timer test
05	Interrupt RAM test
06	Shadow the system ROM BIOS
07	CMOS RAM test
08	Internal cache memory test
09	Initialize the video card
10	Test external cache
11	Shadow option ROMs
12	Memory subsystem test
13	Initialize EISA/ISA hardware

TABLE 19-48 POST CODES FOR HEWLETT-PACKARD VECTRA *(CONTINUED)*

CODE	DESCRIPTION
14	8042 self-test
15	Timer 0/Timer 2 test
16	DMA subsystem test
17	Interrupt controller test
18	RAM address line independence test
19	Size the extended memory
20	Real-mode memory test (first 640K)
21	Shadow RAM test
22	Protect mode RAM test (extended RAM)
23	Real-time clock (RTC) test
24	Keyboard test
25	Mouse test
26	Hard disk test
27	LAN test
28	Flexible disk controller subsystem test
29	Internal numeric coprocessor test
30	Weitek coprocessor test
31	Clock speed switching test
32	Serial port test
33	Parallel port test

TABLE 19-49 POST CODES FOR IBM XT BIOS

CODE	DESCRIPTION
00 or FF	CPU register test failed
01	BIOS ROM checksum failed
02	System timer 1 failed
03	8237 DMA register R/W failed
04	Base 32K RAM failed

TABLE 19-50 POST CODES FOR IBM AT BIOS

CODE	DESCRIPTION
01	CPU flag and register test
02	BIOS ROM checksum test
03	CMOS shutdown byte test
04	8254 PIT test; bits on
05	8254 PIT test; bits on
06	8237 DMA initialize registers test 0
07	8237 DMA initialize registers test 1
08	DMA page register test
09	Memory refresh test
0A	Soft reset test
0B	Reset 8042 keyboard controller
0C	Keyboard controller reset OK
0D	Initialize the 8042 keyboard controller

TABLE 19-50 POST CODES FOR IBM AT BIOS *(CONTINUED)*

CODE	DESCRIPTION
0E	Test memory
0F	Get I/P buffer switch settings
DD	RAM error
11	Initialize protected mode
12	Test protected mode registers
13	Initialize 8259 PIC 2
14	Set up temporary interrupt vectors
15	Establish BIOS interrupt vectors
16	Verify CMOS checksum and battery OK
17	Set the defective CMOS battery flag
18	Ensure CMOS set
19	Set return address byte in CMOS
1A	Set temporary stack
1B	Test segment address 01-0000 (second 64K)
1C	Decide if 512K or 640K installed
1D	Test segment address 10-0000 (over 640K)
1E	Set expansion memory as contained in CMOS
1F	Test address lines 19–23
20	Ready to return from protected mode
21	Successful return from protected mode
22	Test video controller
23	Check for EGA/VGA BIOS
24	Test 8259 PIC R/W mask register
25	Test interrupt mask registers
26	Check for hot (unexpected) interrupts
05	Display 101 error (system board error)
27	Check the POST logic (system board error)
28	Check unexpected NMI interrupts (system board error)
29	Test timer 2 (system board error)
2A	Test 8254 timer
2B	System board error
2C	System board error
2D	Check 8042 keyboard controller for last command
2F	Go to next area during a warm boot
30	Set shutdown return 2
31	Switch to protected mode
33	Test next block of 64K
34	Switch back to real mode
F0	Set data segment
F1	Test interrupts
F2	Test exception interrupts
F3	Verify protected mode instructions
F4	Verify protected mode instructions
F5	Verify protected mode instructions
F6	Verify protected mode instructions
F7	Verify protected mode instructions
F8	Verify protected mode instructions
F9	Verify protected mode instructions

TABLE 19-50 POST CODES FOR IBM AT BIOS *(CONTINUED)*

CODE	DESCRIPTION
FA	Verify protected mode instructions
34	Test keyboard
35	Test keyboard type
36	Check for AA scan code
38	Check for stuck key
39	8042 keyboard controller error
3A	Initialize the 8042
3B	Check for expansion ROM in 2K blocks
40	Enable hardware interrupts
41	Check system code at segment E0000h
42	Exit to system code
43	Call boot loader
3C	Check for initial program load
3D	Initialize floppy for drive type
3E	Initialize hard drive
81	Build descriptor table
82	Switch to virtual mode
90–B6	Memory and bootstrap tests
32	Test address lines 0–15
44	Attempt to boot from fixed disk
45	Unable to boot: go to BASIC

TABLE 19-51 POST CODES FOR IBM PS/2 BIOS

CODE	DESCRIPTION
00	CPU flag test
01	32-bit CPU register test
02	Test BIOS ROM checksum
03	Test system enable
04	Test system POS register
05	Test adapter setup port
06	Test RTC/CMOS RAM shutdown byte
07	Test extended CMOS RAM
08	Test DMA and page register channels
09	Initialize DMA command and mode registers
0A	Test memory refresh toggle
0B	Test keyboard controller buffers
0C	Keyboard controller self-test
0D	Continue keyboard controller self-test
0E	Keyboard self-test error
0F	Set up system memory configuration
10	Test first 512K RAM
11	Halt system if memory test occurs
12	Test protected mode instructions
13	Initialize interrupt controller 1
14	Initialize interrupt controller 2
15	Initialize 120 interrupt vectors

TABLE 19-51 POST CODES FOR IBM PS/2 BIOS *(CONTINUED)*

CODE	DESCRIPTION
16	Initialize 16 interrupt vectors
17	Check CMOS/RTC battery
18	Check CMOS/RTC checksum
19	CMOS/RTC battery bad
1A	Skip memory test in protected mode
1B	Prepare for CMOS shutdown
1C	Set up stack pointer to end of first 64K
1D	Calculate low memory size in protected mode
1E	Save the memory size detected
1F	Set up system memory split address
20	Check for extended memory beyond 64MB
21	Test memory address bus lines
22	Clear parity error and channel lock
23	Initialize interrupt 0
24	Check CMOS RAM validity
25	Write keyboard controller command byte
40	Check valid CMOS RAM and video system
41	Display error code 160
42	Test registers in both interrupt controllers
43	Test interrupt controller registers
44	Test interrupt mask registers
45	Test NMI
46	NMI error has been detected
47	Test system timer 0
48	Check stuck speaker clock
49	Test system timer 0 count
4A	Test system timer 2 count
4B	Check if timer interrupt occurred
4C	Test timer 0 for improper operation (too fast or too slow)
4D	Verify timer interrupt 0
4E	Check 8042 keyboard controller
4F	Check for soft reset
50	Prepare for shutdown
51	Start protected-mode test
52	Test memory in 64K increments
53	Check if memory test done
54	Return to real mode
55	Test for regular or manufacturing mode
56	Disable the keyboard
57	Check for keyboard self-test
58	Keyboard test passed
59	Test the keyboard controller
5A	Configure the mouse
5B	Disable the mouse
5C	Initialize interrupt vectors
5D	Initialize interrupt vectors
5E	Initialize interrupt vectors
60	Save DDNIL status

TABLE 19-51 POST CODES FOR IBM PS/2 BIOS *(CONTINUED)*

CODE	DESCRIPTION
61	Reset floppy drive
62	Test floppy drive
63	Turn floppy drive motor off
64	Set up serial ports
65	Enable real-time clock interrupt
66	Configure floppy drives
67	Configure hard drives
68	Enable system CPU arbitration
69	Scan for adapter ROMs
6A	Verify serial and parallel ports
6B	Set up equipment byte
6C	Set up configuration
6D	Set keyboard typematic rate
6E	Call INT 19 boot loader

TABLE 19-52 POST CODES FOR LANDMARK JUMPSTART XT BIOS

CODE	DESCRIPTION
01	Jump to reset area in BIOS ROM
02	Initialize DMA page register
03	Initialize DMA refresh register
04	Clear all RAM
05	Perform RAM test on first 64K
06	Clear first 64K
07	Initialize BIOS stack to 0FC0h
08	Set the equipment flag based on XT switches
09	Initialize default interrupt vectors
0A	Initialize the 8255 if it exists
0B	Initialize the 8259 PIT and enable interrupts
0C	Set up adapters and peripherals
0D	Set up video system
0E	Initialize the video system
0F	Initialize the equipment
10	Initialize memory configuration
11	Set up system timer function
12	Initialize system timer
13	Set up time-of-day function
14	Initialize time of day from real-time clock data
15	Set up and initialize print-screen function
16	Set up and initialize cassette interface if available
17	Set up and initialize bootstrap function
18	Set up and initialize keyboard function
19	Enable speaker
1A	Set up system timer
1B	Enable the real-time clock
1C	Set up timer 2
1D	Determine memory size

19

TABLE 19-52 POST CODES FOR LANDMARK JUMPSTART XT BIOS *(CONTINUED)*

CODE	DESCRIPTION
1E	Read first and last word of segment
1F	Compare first and last words
20	Report found memory size to display
21	Perform BIOS ROM checksum test
22	Perform complete RAM testing on cold boot
23	Move system stack to bottom of memory and save pointer
24	Reset parity after RAM sizing
25	Enable timer and keyboard interrupts
26	Set up the serial and parallel ports
27	Set up the game port
28	Set up the floppy disk controller
29	Scan for optional ROMs in 2K chunks from C8000h
2A	Call the boot loader

TABLE 19-53 POST CODES FOR LANDMARK JUMPSTART AT BIOS

CODE	DESCRIPTION
03	Sound one short beep
04	Initialize the bell tone
05	Enable CMOS RAM
06	Reset video controller
07	Disable parity checking
08	Start memory refresh
09	Clear the reset flag in RAM
0A	Test DMA page registers
10	Use CMOS to determine if a soft reset has occurred
11	Check BIOS ROM checksum
12	Test system timer A
13	Test DMA channel 0
14	Test DMA channel 1
15	Test memory refresh
16	Flush 8042 keyboard controller input buffer
17	Reset the 8042
18	Get keyboard type
19	Initialize the keyboard
1A	Clear any existing parity
1B	Enable on-board parity
1C	Test base 64K memory
1D	Test base 64K parity
1E	Initialize POST stack
20	Check keyboard type
65	Set video speed
21	Test protected mode CPU registers
22	Initialize 8259 PIC
23	Initialize all interrupts
24	Test all interrupts
25	Perform DRAM checksum

TABLE 19-53 POST CODES FOR LANDMARK JUMPSTART AT BIOS *(CONTINUED)*

CODE	DESCRIPTION
26	Adjust configuration based on hardware found and CMOS settings
27	Check for presence of manufacturing switch
28	Initialize video controller
2A	Test video memory
2B	Test video sync
2C	Check for auxiliary video controller
2D	Change video configuration
2F	Initialize the video system
30	Change video interrupt
31	Display any POST messages
32	Test memory and calculate size
33	Adjust memory configuration
34	Enable I/O parity
35	Test 8259 PIC
36	Perform byte swap test
37	Test NMI
38	Perform timer test
39	Initialize system timer A
3A	Protected mode memory test
3B	Test keyboard
3C	Test keyboard interrupt
3D	Enable A20
3E	Reset hard disk controller
3F	Set up floppy disk controller
40	Test floppy drive system
41	Set up keyboard
42	Enable interrupt timer
43	Check for dual floppy disk/hard drive controller
44	Locate floppy drive A
45	Locate floppy drive B
46	Reset hard disk controller
47	Enable slave DMA
48	Locate any external ROMs
49	Initialize the parallel port(s)
4A	Initialize the serial port(s)
4B	Initialize the math coprocessor
4C	Read CMOS RAM status
4D	Check CMOS configuration against detected hardware
4E	Initialize timer ticks
4F	Enable IRQ9
50	Enable on-board parity
51	Run any add-on ROMs
52	Enable keyboard interrupt
53	Reset the parallel port
60	Check for any errors
61	Sound one short beep
62	Print sign-on message
64	Call INT 19 boot loader

TABLE 19-54 POST CODES FOR LANDMARK SUPERSOFT AT BIOS

CODE	DESCRIPTION
11	CPU register or logic error
12	ROMPOST A checksum error
13	ROMPOST B checksum error
14	8253 timer channel 0
15	8253 timer channel 1
16	8253 timer channel 2
17	8237 DMA controller 1 error
18	8237 DMA controller 2 error
19	DMA page register error
1A	8042 keyboard controller parity error
21	Scan 16K critical RAM error
22	Memory refresh error
23	CPU protected mode error
24	8259 interrupt controller 1 error
25	8259 interrupt controller 2 error
26	Unexpected interrupt detected
27	Interrupt 0 (system timer) error
28	CMOS RTC error
29	NMI error
2A	Locate and test math coprocessor
31	Keyboard controller error
32	Stuck key detected or CMOS RAM error
33	Floppy controller error
34	Floppy disk read error
35	MDA video memory error
36	Color video memory error
37	EGA/VGA RAM error
38	BIOS ROM checksum error
41	Memory error
42	Refresh fault
43-45	Display problem
59	No monitor detected

TABLE 19-55 POST CODES FOR MICROID RESEARCH BIOS 1.0A

CODE	DESCRIPTION
01	Chipset problem
02	Disable NMI and DMA
03	Check BIOS ROM checksum
04	Test DMA page register
05	Keyboard controller test
06	Initialize the RTC, 8237, 8254, and 8259

TABLE 19-55 POST CODES FOR MICROID RESEARCH BIOS 1.0A *(CONTINUED)*

CODE	DESCRIPTION
07	Check memory refresh
08	DMA master test
09	OEM-specific test
0A	Test memory bank 0
0B	Test PIC units
0C	Test PIC controllers
0D	Initialize PIT channel 0
0E	Initialize PIT channel 2
0F	Test CMOS RAM battery
10	Check video ROM
11	Test real-time clock
12	Test keyboard controller
13	OEM-specific test
14	Run memory test
15	Keyboard controller
16	OEM-specific test
17	Test keyboard controller
18	Run memory test
19	Execute OEM memory test
1A	Update real-time clock contents
1B	Initialize serial ports
1C	Initialize parallel ports
1D	Test math coprocessor
1E	Test floppy disk
1F	Test hard disk
20	Validate CMOS contents
21	Check keyboard lock
22	Set Num Lock on keyboard
23	OEM-specific test
29	Test adapter ROMs
2F	Call INT 19 boot loader

TABLE 19-56 POST AND BEEP CODES FOR CONTEMPORARY MICROID RESEARCH BIOS

BEEP CODE*	POST CODE	DESCRIPTION
LH-LLL	03	ROM BIOS checksum failure
LH-HLL	04	DMA page register failure
LH-LHL	05	Keyboard controller self-test failure
LH-HHL	08	Memory refresh circuitry failure
LH-LLH	09	Master (16-bit) DMA controller failure
LH-HLH	09	Slave (8-bit) DMA controller failure
LH-LLLL	0A	Base 64K pattern test failure
LH-HLLL	0A	Base 64K parity circuitry failure
LH-LHLL	0A	Base 64K parity error

TABLE 19-56 POST AND BEEP CODES FOR CONTEMPORARY MICROID RESEARCH BIOS *(CONTINUED)*

BEEP CODE*	POST CODE	DESCRIPTION
LH-HHLL	0A	Base 64K data bus failure
LH-LLHL	0A	Base 64K address bus failure
LH-HLHL	0A	Base 64K block access read failure
LH-LHHL	0A	Base 64K block access write failure
LH-HHHL	0B	Master 8259 failure
LH-LLLH	0B	Slave 8259 failure
LH-HLLH	0C	Master 8259 interrupt address failure
LH-LHLH	0C	Slave 8259 interrupt address failure
LH-HHLH	0C	8259 interrupt address error
LH-LLHH	0C	Master 8259 stuck interrupt error
LH-HLHH	0C	Slave 8259 stuck interrupt error
LH-LHHH	0C	System timer 8254 CH0/IRQ0 failure
LH-HHHH	0D	8254 channel 0 (system timer) failure
LH-LLLLH	0E	8254 channel 2 (speaker) failure
LH-HLLLH	0E	8254 OUT2 (speaker detect) failure
LH-LHLLH	0F	CMOS RAM read/write test failure
LH-HHLLH	0F	Real-time clock periodic interrupt/IRQ8 failure
LH-LLHLH	10	Video ROM checksum failure
None	11	Real-time clock battery discharged or CMOS contents corrupt
LH-HLHLH	12	Keyboard controller failure
None	12	Keyboard error: stuck key
LH-LHHLH	14	Memory parity error
LH-HHHLH	14	I/O channel error
None	14	RAM pattern test failed
None	15	Keyboard failure or no keyboard present
LH-LLLHH	17	A20 test failure due to 8042 timeout
LH-HLLHH	17	A20 gate stuck in disabled state
None	17	A20 gate stuck in asserted state
None	18	Parity circuit failure
None	19	Data bus test failed or address line test failed or block access read failure or block access read/write failure or banks decode to same location
LH-LHLHH	1A	Real-time clock is not updating
None	1A	Real-time clock settings are invalid
None	1E	Disk CMOS configuration invalid or disk controller failure or disk drive A failure or disk drive B failure
None	1F	FDD CMOS configuration invalid or fixed disk C failure or fixed disk D failure
None	20	Fixed disk configuration change or disk configuration change or serial port configuration change or parallel port configuration change or video configuration change or memory configuration change or coprocessor configuration change
None	21	System key in locked position
None	29	Adapter ROM checksum failure

*L=low tone and H=high tone

TABLE 19-57 POST CODES FOR MICROID RESEARCH 3.4X BIOS

CODE	DESCRIPTION
00	Cold start; output EDX register to I/O ports 85h, 86h, 8Dh, 8Eh for later use
01	Initialize any custom keyboard controller; disable CPU cache; cold initialize onboard I/O chipset; size and test RAM; size cache
02	Disable critical IO (monitor, DMA, FDC, I/O ports, speaker, NMI)
03	Checksum the BIOS ROM
04	Test page registers
05	Enable A20 gate; issue 8042 self-test
06	Initialize ISA I/O
07	Warm initialize custom keyboard controller; warm initialize onboard I/O chipset
08	Refresh toggle test
09	Test DMA master registers; test DMA slave registers
0A	Test first 64K of base memory
0B	Test master 8259 mask; test slave 8259 mask
0C	Test 8259 slave; test 8259 slave's interrupt range; initialize interrupt vectors 00, 77h; initialize keyboard buffer variables
0D	Test timer 0, 8254 channel 0
0E	Test 8254 Channel 2, speaker channel
0F	Test real-time clock; CMOS RAM read/write test
10	Turn on monitor; show any possible error messages
11	Read and checksum the CMOS
12	Call video ROM initialization routines; show display sign-on message; show Esc delay message
13	Set 8MHz AT-Bus
14	Size and test the base memory; stuck NMI check
15	No keyboard and power-on: retry keyboard initialization
16	Size and test CPU cache
17	Test A20 off and on states
18	Size and test external memory; stuck NMI check
19	Size and test system memory; stuck NMI check
1A	Test real-time clock time
1B	Determine serial ports
1C	Determine parallel ports
1D	Initialize numeric coprocessor
1E	Determine floppy diskette controllers
1F	Determine IDE controllers
20	Display CMOS configuration changes
21	Clear screens
22	Set/reset Num Lock LED; perform security functions
23	Final determination of on-board serial/parallel ports
24	Set keyboard typematic rate
25	Initialize floppy controller
26	Initialize ATA discs
27	Set the video mode for primary adapter
28	Cyrix WB-CPU support, Green PC: purge 8259 slave; relieve any trapped IRRs before enabling power management; set 8042 pins; CTRL-ALT-DEL possible now; enable CPU features
29	Reset A20 to off; install adapter ROMs
2A	Clear primary screen; convert real-time clock to system ticks; set final DOS timer variables
2B	Enable NMI and latch

19

TABLE 19-57 POST CODES FOR MICROID RESEARCH 3.4X BIOS *(CONTINUED)*

CODE	DESCRIPTION
2C	Reserved
2D	Reserved
2E	Fast A20: fix A20
2F	Purge 8259 slave; relieve any trapped IRRs before enabling Green-PC; pass control to INT 19 boot
32	Test CPU burst
33	Reserved
34	Determine 8042; set 8042 warm-boot flag STS.2
35	Test HMA wrap; verify A20 enabled via F000:10 HMA
36	Reserved
37	Validate CPU: CPU step NZ, CPUID check; disable CPU features
38	Set 8042 pins (hi-speed, cache off)
39	PCI Bus: load PCI; processor vector initialized; BIOS vector initialized; OEM vector initialized
3A	Scan PCI Bus
3B	Initialize PCI Bus with intermediate defaults
3C	Initialize PCI OEM with intermediate defaults, OEM bridge
3D	PCI Bus or plug-and-play: initialize AT slotmap from AT-Bus CDE usage
3E	Find phantom CDE ROM PCI cards
3F	PCI Bus: final fast back-to-back state
40	OEM POST initialization, hook audio
41	Allocate I/O on PCI Bus; log in PCI IDE
42	Hook PCI-ATA chips
43	Allocate IRQs on the PCI Bus
44	Allocate/enable PCI memory/ROM space
45	Determine PS/2 mouse
46	Map IRQs to PCI Bus per user CMOS; enable ATA IRQs
47	PCI ROM install; note user CMOS
48	If setup conditions: execute setup utility
49	Test F000 shadow integrity; transfer EPROM to shadow RAM
4A	Hook VL ATA chip
4B	Identify and spin up all drives
4C	Detect secondary IRQ, if VL/AT-Bus IDE exists but its IRQ not known yet, then auto-detect it
4D	Detect/log 32-bit I/O ATA devices
4E	ATAPI drive M/S bitmap to shadow RAM; set INT13 vector
4F	Finalize shadow RAM variables
50	Chain INT 13
51	Load PnP; processor vector initialized; BIOS vector initialized; OEM vector initialized
52	Scan plug-and-play; update PnP device count
53	Supplement IRQ usage; AT IRQs
54	Conditionally assign everything PnP wants
58	Perform OEM custom boot sequence just prior to INT 19 boot
59	Return from OEM custom boot sequence; pass control to INT 19 boot
5A	Display MR BIOS logo
88	Dead motherboard and/or CPU and/or BIOS ROM
FF	BIOS POST finished

TABLE 19-58 POST CODES FOR MYLEX BIOS

CODE	DESCRIPTION
01	CPU test
02	DMA page register test
03	Keyboard controller test
04	ROM BIOS checksum
05	Send keyboard command test
06	CMOS RAM test
08	RAM refresh test
09	First 64K memory test
0A	DMA controller test
0B	Initialize DMA
0C	Interrupt test
0D	Determine RAM size
0E	Initialize video and verify EGA or VGA checksum
10	Search for monochrome card
11	Search for color card
12	Word splitter and byte shifter test
13	Keyboard test
14	RAM test
15	System timer test
16	Initialize keyboard controller output port
17	Keyboard interrupt test

TABLE 19-59 POST CODES FOR NCR PC6 (XT) BIOS

CODE	DESCRIPTION
AA	8088 CPU failure
B1	2764 EPROM checksum failure
B2	8237 DMA controller failure
B3	8253 PIT failure
B4	RAM failure
B5	8259 PIC failure
B6	RAM parity error
BB	All tests passed: ready to boot

TABLE 19-60 POST CODES FOR NCR AT BIOS

CODE	DESCRIPTION
01	Test CPU registers
02	Test system support I/O
03	Test BIOS ROM checksum
04	Test DMA page registers
05	Test timer channel 1
06	Test timer channel 2

TABLE 19-60 POST CODES FOR NCR AT BIOS *(CONTINUED)*

CODE	DESCRIPTION
07	Test RAM refresh logic
08	Test base 64K
09	Test 8/16-bit bus conversion
0A	Test interrupt controller 1
0B	Test interrupt controller 2
0C	Test I/O controller
0D	Test CMOS RAM R/W operation
0E	Test battery power
0F	Test CMOS RAM checksum
10	Test CPU protected mode
11	Test video configuration
12	Test primary video controller
13	Test secondary video controller
20	Display results of tests to this point
21	Test DMA controller 1
22	Test DMA controller 2
23	Test system timer channel 0
24	Initialize interrupt controllers
25	Test interrupts
26	Test interrupts
30	Check base 640K memory
31	Check extended memory size
32	Test higher 8 address lines
33	Test base memory
34	Test extended memory
40	Test keyboard
41	Test keyboard
42	Test keyboard
43	Test keyboard
44	Test A20 gate
50	Set up hardware interrupt vectors
51	Enable interrupt timer channel 0
52	Check BIOS ROM
60	Test floppy disk controller and drive
61	Test hard drive controller
62	Initialize floppy drives
63	Initialize hard drives
70	Test real-time clock
71	Set time-of-day in real-time clock
72	Check parallel interface port(s)
73	Check serial interface port(s)
74	Check for any option ROMs
75	Check math coprocessors
76	Enable keyboard and real-time clock interrupts
F0	System not configured properly (or hardware defect)
F1	Scan and execute any option ROMs
F2	Call INT 19 boot loader

TABLE 19-61 POST CODES FOR NCR PC916 BIOS

CODE	DESCRIPTION
01	Test CPU registers
03	Test BIOS ROM checksum
04	Test DMA page registers
05	Test timer channel 1
06	Test timer channel 2
0C	Test 8042 keyboard controller
14	Test disabling speed stretch at port 69h
15	Start refresh timer 1
16	Enable speed stretch at port 69h
17	Clear write protect bit
1B	Test 64K shadow RAM
18	Write and test interrupt descriptor table
19	Verify RAM
02	Verify port 61h
07	Test refresh logic
08	Test base 64K RAM
09	Test 8/16-bit bus conversion logic
0A	Test interrupt mask register A
0B	Test interrupt mask register B
1A	Check 8042 keyboard controller
0D	Test CMOS RAM shutdown byte
0E	Test CMOS RAM battery power
0F	Test CMOS RAM checksum
10	Test CPU protected mode
11	Test video configuration
12	Initialize and test primary video controller
13	Primary video error
20	Display results of tests to this point
21	Test DMA controller 1
22	Test DMA controller 2
23	Test timer 1 counter 0 840nS clock timer
27	Test timer 2 counter 0 for NMI
28	Test timer 2 counter 1
24	Initialize both interrupt controllers
25	Check for unexpected interrupts
26	Wait for interrupt
30	Check base 640K memory
31	Check extended memory size
32	Test higher 8 address lines
33	Test base memory
34	Test extended memory (up to 256MB)
35	Test RAM in segment E000h
40	Test keyboard enable/disable
41	Test keyboard reset command
42	Test keyboard
43	Test keyboard
F4	Display speed setting
45	Initialize the mouse and enable IRQ1

TABLE 19-61 POST CODES FOR NCR PC916 BIOS *(CONTINUED)*

CODE	DESCRIPTION
44	Test address overrun capability
50	Set up hardware interrupt vectors
51	Enable IRQ0 interval interrupt from timer 0
60	Test for floppy and hard disk controllers and drives
61	Test disk controller
62	Initialize floppy drives
63	Initialize hard drives
74	Check and execute option ROMs from C8000h to DFFFFh
70	Test real-time clock
71	Set interval timer
72	Configure and test parallel interface
73	Configure and test serial interface
75	Test math coprocessor if installed
76	Enable keyboard and real-time clock
F0	Display any logged errors
F6	Test base memory
F7	Run comprehensive base memory test
F3	Go to setup if F1 was pressed
F4	Display speed setting
F5	Initialize counter 2 for speed testing
F1	Test system code at E0000h and copy video ROM to shadow memory
F2	Call INT 19 boot loader
F6	Test base memory
F7	Test extended memory

TABLE 19-62 POST CODES FOR OLIVETTI 1076/AT&T BIOS

PASS CODE	FAIL CODE	DESCRIPTION
41	7F	CPU flag and register test
42	7E	Check and verify CMOS shutdown code
43	7D	BIOS ROM checksum test
44	7C	Test the 8253 timer
45	7B	Start memory refresh
46	7A	Test the 8041 keyboard controller
47	79	Test the first 8K of RAM
48	78	Test protected mode operation
49	77	Test CMOS RAM shutdown byte
4A	76	Test protected mode operation
4B	75	Test RAM from 8K–640K
4C	74	Test all RAM above 1MB
4D	73	Test NMI
4E	72	Test RAM parity system
50	71	Test 8259 PIC 1
51	6F	Test 8259 PIC 2

TABLE 19-62 POST CODES FOR OLIVETTI 1076/AT&T BIOS *(CONTINUED)*

PASS CODE	FAIL CODE	DESCRIPTION
52	6E	Test DMA page register
53	6D	Test 8237 DMA controller 1
54	6C	Test 8237 DMA controller 2
55	6B	Test PIO port 61h
56	6A	Test keyboard controller
57	69	Test CMOS clock/calendar IC
59	68	Test CPU protected mode
5A	66	Test CMOS RAM battery
5B	65	Test CMOS RAM
5C	64	Verify CMOS RAM checksum
5D	63	Test parallel port configuration
5E	62	Test serial port configuration
5F	61	Test memory configuration below 640K
60	60	Test memory configuration above 1MB
61	5F	Detect and test math coprocessor
62	5E	Test configuration of game port adapter
62	5D	Test key-lock switch
63	5D	Test hard drive configuration
64	5C	Configure floppy drives
66	5B	Test option ROMs
—	—	Call INT 19 boot loader

19

TABLE 19-63 POST CODES FOR OLIVETTI M20 BIOS

CODE	DESCRIPTION
Triangle	Test CPU registers and instructions
Triangle	Test system RAM
Four vertical lines	Test CPU call and trap instructions
Diamond	Initialize screen and printer drivers
EC0	8255 parallel interface IC test failed
EC1	6845 CRT controller IC test failed
EC2	1797 floppy disk controller chip failed
EC3	8253 timer IC failed
EC4	8251 keyboard interface failed
EC5	8251 keyboard test failed
EC6	8259 PIC IC test failed
EK0	Keyboard did not respond
EK1	Keyboard responds but self-test failed
ED1	Disk drive 1 test failed
ED0	Disk drive 0 test failed
EI0	Nonvectored interrupt error
E11	Vectored interrupt error

NOTE: M20 codes are displayed on the monitor and sent to printer port.

TABLE 19-64 POST CODES FOR OLIVETTI M21/M24 (AT&T) BIOS

CODE	DESCRIPTION
40	CPU flags and register test failed
41	BIOS ROM checksum test failed
42	Disable 8253 timer channel 1
43	8237 DMA controller test failed
44	8259 PIC test failed
45	Install the real interrupt vectors
48	Send beep and initialize all basic hardware

TABLE 19-65 POST CODES FOR OLIVETTI EISA 2.01 BIOS

CODE	DESCRIPTION
01	Test CPU flags, registers; initialize interrupt controller
02	Test memory refresh
03	Test CMOS RTC periodic interrupt
04	Test gate A20 line
05	Test mapping memory SRAM
06	Test first 128K RAM; stack has now been established
07	Test for console presence and initialize
08	Verify system BIOS ROM checksum
09	Test 8042 keyboard controller; normal burn-in/manufacturing mode established
0A	Test timer ratio
0B	Test CMOS RAM battery
0C	Verify CMOS RAM checksum
0D	Test for unexpected NMI
0E	Test interrupt controller 1
0F	Test interrupt controller 2
10	Test timer 1 counter 0
11	Test system control port B
12	Test system control port A
13	Verify checksum of NVRAM configuration memory
14	Initialize system board
15	Initialize adapter
16	Initialize ESC SCSI adapter
17	Initialize system video
18	Test and copy shadow RAM; video is initialized (display banner and nonfatal errors)
19	Test DMA page registers
1A	Test DMA address registers
1B	Test DMA count registers
1C	Test DMA mask registers
1D	Test DMA stop registers; initialize DMA controllers
1E	Test IDTR and GDTR
1F	Test CMOS shutdown byte
20	Test real/protected mode
21	Check system memory configuration
22	Size memory
23	Test 640K base memory
24	Verify base memory configuration
25	Test extended memory (above 1MB)

TABLE 19-65 POST CODES FOR OLIVETTI EISA 2.01 BIOS *(CONTINUED)*

CODE	DESCRIPTION
26	Verify extended memory configuration
27	Check for contiguous extended memory
28	Test cache memory; extended BIOS data area created and POST errors logged
29	Test protected mode instructions
2A	Test CMOS RAM
2B	Test real-time clock
2C	Check calendar values
2D	Test keyboard/AUX device fuse
2E	Test keyboard
2F	Initialize keyboard typematic rate and delay
30	Test auxiliary device
31	Test 80x87 math coprocessor
32	Test and initialize Weitek math coprocessor
33	Run 1860 CPU basic and advanced diagnostics
34	Test and configure serial ports
35	Test and configure parallel ports
36	Detect game port
37	Test and initialize hard drives
38	Test and initialize floppy drives
39	Scan for and pass control to adapter ROMs
3A	INT 19 boot; load operating system

These codes are delivered to ports 278h, 378h, or 3BCh (printer ports) rather than port 80h.

TABLE 19-66 POST CODES FOR OLIVETTI PS/2 BIOS

CODE	DESCRIPTION
01	Test CPU
02	Check CMOS shutdown byte
03	Initialize the PIC
04	Test refresh
05	Test CMOS/RTC periodic interrupt
06	Test timer ratio
07	Test first 64K of RAM
08	Test 8042 keyboard controller
09	Test NMI
0A	Test 8254 PIT
0B	Test port 94h
0C	Test port 103h
0D	Test port 102h
0E	Test port 96h
0F	Test port 107h
10	Blank the display
11	Check the keyboard
12	Test CMOS RAM battery
13	Verify CMOS RAM checksum
14	Verify extended CMOS RAM checksum

TABLE 19-66 POST CODES FOR OLIVETTI PS/2 BIOS *(CONTINUED)*

CODE	DESCRIPTION
15	Initialize system board and adapter
16	Initialize and test RAM
17	Test protected mode registers
18	Test CMOS RAM shutdown byte
19	Test CMOS protected mode
1A	Initiate video adapter ROM scan
1B	Test BIOS ROM checksum
1C	Test PIC 1
1D	Test PIC 2
1E	Initialize interrupt vectors
1F	Test CMOS RAM
20	Test extended CMOS RAM
21	Test CMOS real-time clock
22	Test clock calendar
23	Dummy checkpoint
24	Test watchdog timer
25	Test 64K–640K RAM
26	Configure lower 640K RAM
27	Test extended memory
28	Initialize extended BIOS data segment and log POST errors
29	Configure memory above 1MB
2A	Dummy checkpoint
2B	Test RAM parity
2C	Test DMA page registers
2D	Test DMA controller registers
2E	Test DMA transfer count register
2F	Initialize DMA controller
30	Test PIO 61
31	Test the keyboard
32	Initialize keyboard typematic rate and delay
33	Test auxiliary device
34	Test advanced protected mode
35	Configure parallel ports
36	Configure 8250 serial ports
37	Test and configure math coprocessor
38	Test and configure game port adapter
39	Configure and initialize hard disk
3A	Floppy disk configuration
3B	Initialize ROM drivers
3C	Display total memory and hard drives
3D	Final initialization
3E	Detect and initialize parallel ports
3F	Initialize hard drive and controller
40	Initialize math coprocessor
42	Initiate adapter ROM scan
CC	Unexpected processor exception occurred
DD	Save DDNIL status
EE	NMI handler shutdown
FF	Call INT 19 boot loader

TABLE 19-67 POST CODES FOR PHILIPS BIOS

CODE	DESCRIPTION
0A	DMA page register R/W bad
10	CMOS RAM R/W error
11	System BIOS ROM checksum error
12	Timer A error
13	DMA controller A error
14	DMA controller B error
15	Memory refresh error
16	Keyboard controller error
17	Keyboard controller error
19	Keyboard controller error
1C	Base 64K RAM error
1D	Base 64K RAM parity error
1F	LSI sync missing
21	PVAM register error
25	System options error
2B	Video sync error
2C	Video BIOS ROM error
2D	Monochrome/color configuration error
2E	No video memory detected
35	Interrupt controller error
36	Byte swapper error
37	NMI error
38	Timer interrupt fault
39	LSI timer halted
3A	Main memory test error
3B	Keyboard error
3C	Keyboard interrupt error
3D	DDNIL scan halted and cache disabled
40	Disk error
48	Adapter card error
4C	CMOS battery/checksum error
4D	System options error
52	Keyboard controller error
6A	Failure shadowing BIOS ROM
70	Memory size configuration error

TABLE 19-68 POST CODES FOR PHOENIX TECHNOLOGIES XT 2.52 BIOS

CODE	DESCRIPTION
01	Test 8253 system timer
02	First 64K RAM failure
03	First 1K parity check failed
04	Initialize the 8259 PIC IC
05	Second 1K RAM (BIOS data area) failed
—	Initialize the display

19

TABLE 19-69 POST CODES FOR PHOENIX TECHNOLOGIES ISA/EISA/MCA BIOS

CODE	DESCRIPTION
01	CPU register test
02	CMOS R/W test
03	Testing BIOS ROM checksum
04	Testing 8253 PIT IC
05	Initializing the 8237 DMA controller
06	Testing the 8237 DMA page register
08	RAM refresh circuit test
09	Test first 64K of RAM
0A	Test first 64K RAM data lines
0B	Test first 64K RAM parity
0C	Test first 64K RAM address lines
0D	Parity failure detected for first 64K RAM
10-1F	Data bit (0–15) bad in first 64K RAM
20	Slave DMA register faulty
21	Master DMA register faulty
22	Master PIC register faulty
23	Slave PIC register faulty
25	Initializing interrupt vectors
27	Keyboard controller test
28	Testing CMOS checksum and battery power
29	Validate CMOS contents
2B	Video initialization faulty
2C	Video retrace test failed
2D	Search for video ROM
2E	Test video ROM
30	Video system checks OK
31	Monochrome video mode detected
32	Color (40-column) mode detected
33	Color (80-column) mode detected
34	Timer tick interrupt test
35	CMOS shutdown byte test
36	Gate A20 failure (8042 keyboard controller)
37	Unexpected interrupt
38	Extended RAM test
3A	Interval timer channel 2
3B	Test time-of-day clock
3C	Locate and test serial ports
3D	Locate and test parallel ports
3E	Locate and test math coprocessor
41	System board select bad
42	Extended CMOS RAM bad

TABLE 19-70 POST CODES FOR PHOENIX BIOS PLUS (V.1.0)

CODE	BEEP CODE	DESCRIPTION
01	none	CPU register test in progress
02	1-1-3	CMOS write/read failure
03	1-1-4	ROM BIOS checksum failure

TABLE 19-70 POST CODES FOR PHOENIX BIOS PLUS (V.1.0) *(CONTINUED)*

CODE	BEEP CODE	DESCRIPTION
04	1-2-1	Programmable interval timer failure
05	1-2-2	DMA initialization failure
06	1-2-3	DMA page register write/read failure
08	1-3-1	RAM refresh verification failure
09	none	First 64K RAM test in progress
0A	1-3-3	First 64K RAM chip or data line failure multibit
0B	1-3-4	First RAM odd/even logic failure
0C	1-4-1	Address line failure first 64K RAM
0D	1-4-2	Parity failure first 64K RAM
10	2-1-1	Bit 0 first 64K RAM failure
11	2-1-2	Bit 1 first 64K RAM failure
12	2-1-3	Bit 2 first 64K RAM failure
13	2-1-4	Bit 3 first 64K RAM failure
14	2-2-1	Bit 4 first 64K RAM failure
15	2-2-2	Bit 5 first 64K RAM failure
16	2-2-3	Bit 6 first 64K RAM failure
17	2-2-4	Bit 7 first 64K RAM failure
18	2-3-1	Bit 8 first 64K RAM failure
19	2-3-2	Bit 9 first 64K RAM failure
1A	2-3-3	Bit A(10) first 64K RAM failure
1B	2-3-2	Bit B(11) first 64K RAM failure
1C	2-4-2	Bit C(12) first 64K RAM failure
1D	2-4-2	Bit D(13) first 64K RAM failure
1E	2-4-3	Bit E(14) first 64K RAM failure
1F	2-4-4	Bit F(15) first 64K RAM failure
20	3-1-1	Slave DMA register failure
21	3-1-2	Master DMA register failure
22	3-1-3	Master interrupt mask register failure
23	3-1-4	Slave interrupt mask register failure
25	none	Interrupt vector loading in progress
27	3-2-4	8042 keyboard controller test failure
28	none	CMOS power failure/checksum calculation in progress
29	none	CMOS configuration validation in progress
2B	3-3-4	Screen memory test failure
2C	3-4-1	Screen initialization failure
2D	3-4-2	Screen retrace test failure
2E	none	Search for video ROM in progress
30	none	Screen believed running with video ROM
31	none	Mono monitor believed operable
32	none	Color monitor (40-column) believed operable
33	none	Color monitor (80-column) believed operable
34	4-2-1	Timer tick interrupt test in progress or failed (nonfatal)
35	4-2-2	Shutdown failure (nonfatal)
36	4-2-3	Gate A20 failure (nonfatal)
37	4-2-4	Unexpected interrupt in protected mode (nonfatal)
38	4-3-1	Memory high address line fail at 01000–0A000 (nonfatal)
39	4-3-2	Memory high address line fail at 100000–FFFFFF (nonfatal)
3A	4-3-3	Timer chip counter 2 failed (nonfatal)
3B	4-3-4	Time-of-day clock stopped
3C	4-4-1	Serial port test

TABLE 19-70 POST CODES FOR PHOENIX BIOS PLUS (V.1.0) *(CONTINUED)*

CODE	BEEP CODE	DESCRIPTION
3D	4-4-2	Parallel port test
3E	4-4-3	Math coprocessor test
41	low 1-1-2	System board select bad
42	low 1-1-3	Extended CMOS RAM bad

TABLE 19-71 POST CODES FOR PHOENIX UMC CHIPSET PCI BIOS

CODE	DESCRIPTION
02	Verify real mode
04	Get CPU type
06	Initialize system hardware
08	Initialize chipset registers with initial POST values
09	Set in POST flag
0A	Initialize CPU registers
0C	Initialize cache to initial POST values
0E	Initialize I/O
10	Initialize power management
11	Load alternate registers with initial POST values
12	Jump to User Patch 0
14	Initialize keyboard controller
16	BIOS ROM checksum
18	8254 timer initialization
1A	8237 DMA controller initialization
1C	Reset PIC
20	Test DRAM refresh
22	Test 8742 keyboard controller
24	Set ES segment register to 4GB
26	Enable address line A20
28	Autosize DRAM
2A	Clear 512K base RAM
2C	Test 512K base address lines
2E	Test 512K base memory
30	Test base address memory
32	Test CPU bus clock frequency
34	Test CMOS RAM
35	Test chipset register initialize
36	Test check resume
37	Reinitialize the chipset
38	Shadow system BIOS ROM
39	Reinitialize the cache
3A	Autosize the cache
3C	Configure advanced chipset registers
3D	Load alternate registers with CMOS values
3E	Read hardware configuration from keyboard controller
40	Set initial CPU speed
42	Initialize interrupt vectors
44	Initialize BIOS interrupts
46	Check ROM copyright notice

TABLE 19-71 POST CODES FOR PHOENIX UMC CHIPSET PCI BIOS *(CONTINUED)*

CODE	DESCRIPTION
47	Initialize manager for PCI option ROMs
48	Check video configuration against CMOS
49	Initialize PCI bus and devices
4A	Initialize all video adapters
4C	Shadow video BIOS ROM
4E	Display copyright notice
50	Display CPU type and speed
52	Test keyboard
54	Set key click if enabled
56	Enable keyboard
58	Test for unexpected interrupts
5A	Display prompt "Press F2 to Enter Setup"
5C	Test RAM between 512K and 640K
5E	Test base memory
60	Test expanded memory
62	Test extended memory address lines
64	Jump to User Patch 1
66	Configure advanced cache registers
68	Enable external and CPU caches
69	Set up power management
6A	Display external cache size
6C	Display shadow message
6E	Display nondisposable segments
70	Display error messages
72	Check for configuration errors
74	Test real-time clock
76	Check for keyboard errors
7A	Enable key-lock
7C	Set up hardware interrupt vectors
7E	Test coprocessor if present
80	Disable onboard I/O ports
82	Detect and install external RS232 ports
84	Detect and install external parallel ports
86	Reinitialize onboard I/O ports
88	Initialize BIOS data area
8A	Initialize extended BIOS data area
8C	Initialize floppy controller
8E	Hard disk "auto-type" configuration
90	Initialize hard disk controller
91	Initialize local bus hard disk controller
92	Jump to User Patch 2
94	Disable A20 address line
96	Clear huge ES segment register
98	Search for option ROMs
9A	Shadow option ROMs
9C	Set up power management
9E	Enable hardware interrupts
A0	Set time of day
A2	Check key-lock
A4	Initialize typematic rate

19

TABLE 19-71 POST CODES FOR PHOENIX UMC CHIPSET PCI BIOS *(CONTINUED)*

CODE	DESCRIPTION
A8	Erase F2 prompt
AA	Scan for F2 key stroke
AC	Enter Setup
AE	Clear in-POST flag
B0	Check for errors
B2	POST done
B4	One beep
B6	Check password (optional)
B8	Clear global descriptor table
BC	Clear parity checkers
BE	Clear screen (optional)
BF	Check virus and backup reminders
C0	Try to boot with INT 19
D0	Interrupt handler error
D2	Unknown interrupt error
D4	Pending interrupt error
D6	Initialize option ROM error
D8	Shutdown error
DA	Extended block move
DC	Shutdown 10 error
E2	Initialize the chipset
E3	Check for forced flash
E5	Check HW status of ROM
E6	BIOS ROM is OK
E7	Do a complete RAM test
E8	Do OEM initialization
E9	Initialize interrupt controller
EA	Read in the bootstrap code
EB	Initialize all vectors
EC	Boot the flash program
ED	Initialize the boot device
EE	Boot code was read OK

TABLE 19-72 POST CODES FOR PHOENIX PCI BIOS

CODE	DESCRIPTION
02	If CPU in protected mode, turn on A20 and pulse reset line to force shutdown
04	On cold boot, save CPU type information value in CMOS
06	Reset DMA controllers; disable videos; clear pending interrupts from real-time clock; set up port B register
08	Initialize chipset control registers to power-on defaults
0A	Set bit in CMOS that indicates POST to determine if current configuration causes BIOS to hang
0C	Initialize I/O module control registers
0E	External CPU caches initialized and cache registers set to default
10/12/14	Verify response of 8742
16	Verify BIOS ROM checksums to zero
18	Initialize all three 8254 timers
1A	Initialize DMA command register and initialize eight DMA channels

TABLE 19-72 POST CODES FOR PHOENIX PCI BIOS *(CONTINUED)*

CODE	DESCRIPTION
1C	Initialize 8259 interrupt controller and cascade and edge-triggered mode
20	Test DRAM refresh by polling refresh bit in port B
22	Test 8742 keyboard controller; send self-test command to 8742; read switch inputs from 8742; write keyboard controller command byte
24	Set ES segment register to 4GB
26	Enable address line A20
28	Autosize DRAM
2A	Clear first 64K of RAM
2C	Test RAM address lines
2E	Test first 64K bank of memory consisting of chip address line test and RAM test
30/32	Find true MHz value
34	Clear CMOS diagnostic byte; check real-time clock and verify battery has not lost power; checksum the CMOS and verify it has not been corrupted
36/38/3A	External cache auto-sized and configuration saved for enabling later in POST
3C	Configure advanced cache features; configure external cache's configurable parameters
3E	Read hardware configuration from keyboard controller
40	Set system power-on speed to rate determined by CMOS; if CMOS is invalid use conservative speed
42	Initialize interrupt vectors 0–77h to BIOS general interrupt handler
44	Initialize interrupt vectors 0–20h to proper values from BIOS interrupt table
46	Check copyright message checksum
48	Check video configuration
4A	Initialize both monochrome and color graphics video adapters
4C/4E	Display copyright message
50	Display CPU type and speed
52	Test for self-test code if cold start; when powered the keyboard performs self-test and sends AA if successful
54	Initialize keystroke clicker during POST
56	Enable keyboard
58	Test for unexpected interrupts
5A	Display prompt "Press F2 to Enter Setup"
5C	Determine and test amount of memory available
5E	Perform address test on base memory
60	Determine and test amount of extended memory available
62	Perform address line test on A0 to amount of memory available
68	External and CPU caches are enabled (if present) and noncacheable regions are configured if necessary
6A	Display cache size on screen if nonzero
6C	Display BIOS shadow status
6E	Display starting offset of the nondisposable section of the BIOS
70	Check flags in CMOS and in BIOS data area to see if any errors have been detected during POST; if so, display error messages on screen
72	Check status bits for configuration errors; if so, display error messages on screen
74	Test real-time clock if the battery has not lost power
76	Check status bits for keyboard errors; if so, display error messages on screen
78	Check for stuck keys on keyboard; if so, display error messages on screen
7A	Enable key-lock
7C	Set up hardware interrupt vectors
7E	Test coprocessor if present
80-82	Detect and install RS232 ports

TABLE 19-72 POST CODES FOR PHOENIX PCI BIOS *(CONTINUED)*

CODE	DESCRIPTION
84	Detect and install parallel ports
86-88	Initialize timeouts/key buffer/soft reset flag
8A	Initialize extended BIOS data area and initialize the mouse
8C	Initialize both floppy disks and display an error message if failure was detected
8E	Hard disk autotype configuration
90	If CMOS RAM is valid and intact and fixed disks are defined, call fixed disk routine to initialize fixed disk system and take over appropriate interrupt vectors
92-94	Disable A20 address line
96-98	Scan for ROM BIOS extensions
9E	Enable hardware interrupts
A0	Set time of day
A2	Set up Num Lock indication and display message if key switch locked
A4	Initialize typematic rate
A6	Initialize hard disk autoparking
A8	Erase F2 prompt
AA	Scan for F2 key strokes
AC	Check if Setup should be executed
AE	Clear ConfigFailedBit and InPostBit in CMOS
B0	Check for POST errors
B2	Set/clear status bits to reflect POST complete
B4	One beep
B6	Check for password before boot
B8	Clear global descriptor table (GDT)
BA	Initialize screen saver
BC	Clear parity error latch
BE	Clear screen
C0	Try to boot with INT 19
D0-D2	If interrupt occurs before interrupt vectors have been initialized, this interrupt handler will try to see if interrupt caused was 8259 interrupt; if interrupt is unknown, InterruptFlag will be FF; otherwise it will contain IRQ number that occurred
D4	Clear pending timer and keyboard interrupts; transfer control to the double-word address located at RomCheck
D6-D8-DA	Return from extended block move

TABLE 19-73 POST CODES FOR PHOENIX BIOS 4.0

BEEP CODE	POST CODE	DESCRIPTION
1-1-1-3	02	Verify real mode operation
1-1-2-1	04	Get the CPU type
1-1-2-3	06	Initialize system hardware
1-1-3-1	08	Initialize chipset registers with POST values
1-1-3-2	09	Set POST flag
1-1-3-3	0A	Initialize CPU registers
1-1-4-1	0C	Initialize cache to initial POST values
1-1-4-3	0E	Initialize I/O
1-2-1-1	10	Initialize power management
1-2-1-2	11	Load alternate registers with POST values
1-2-1-3	12	Jump to User Patch 0
1-2-2-1	14	Initialize keyboard controller

TABLE 19-73 POST CODES FOR PHOENIX BIOS 4.0 *(CONTINUED)*

BEEP CODE	POST CODE	DESCRIPTION
1-2-2-3	16	BIOS ROM checksum
1-2-3-1	18	8254 timer initialization
1-2-3-3	1A	8237 DMA controller initialization
1-2-4-1	1C	Reset programmable interrupt controller
1-3-1-1	20	Test DRAM refresh
1-3-1-3	22	Test 8742 keyboard controller
1-3-2-1	24	Set ES segment to register to 4GB
1-3-3-1	28	Autosize DRAM
1-3-3-3	2A	Clear 512K base RAM
1-3-4-1	2C	Test 512K base address lines
1-3-4-3	2E	Test 512K base memory
1-4-1-3	32	Test CPU bus-clock frequency
1-4-2-4	37	Reinitialize the motherboard chipset
1-4-3-1	38	Shadow system BIOS ROM
1-4-3-2	39	Reinitialize the cache
1-4-3-3	3A	Autosize cache
1-4-4-1	3C	Configure advanced chipset registers
1-4-4-2	3D	Load alternate registers with CMOS values
2-1-1-1	40	Set initial CPU speed
2-1-1-3	42	Initialize interrupt vectors
2-1-2-1	44	Initialize BIOS interrupts
2-1-2-3	46	Check ROM copyright notice
2-1-2-4	47	Initialize manager for PCI Options ROMs
2-1-3-1	48	Check video configuration against CMOS
2-1-3-2	49	Initialize PCI bus and devices
2-1-3-3	4A	Initialize all video adapters in system
2-1-4-1	4C	Shadow video BIOS ROM
2-1-4-3	4E	Display copyright notice
2-2-1-1	50	Display CPU type and speed
2-2-1-3	52	Test keyboard
2-2-2-1	54	Set key click if enabled
2-2-2-3	56	Enable keyboard
2-2-3-1	58	Test for unexpected interrupts
2-2-3-3	5A	Display prompt "Press F2 to Enter Setup"
2-2-4-1	5C	Test RAM between 512K and 640K
2-3-1-1	60	Test expanded memory
2-3-1-3	62	Test extended memory address lines
2-3-2-1	64	Jump to User Patch 1
2-3-2-3	66	Configure advanced cache registers
2-3-3-1	68	Enable external and CPU caches
2-3-3-3	6A	Display external cache size
2-3-4-1	6C	Display shadow message
2-3-4-3	6E	Display nondisposable segments
2-4-1-1	70	Display error messages
2-4-1-3	72	Check for configuration errors
2-4-2-1	74	Test real-time clock
2-4-2-3	76	Check for keyboard errors
2-4-4-1	7C	Set up hardware interrupts vectors
2-4-4-3	7E	Test coprocessor if present
3-1-1-1	80	Disable onboard I/O ports

TABLE 19-73 POST CODES FOR PHOENIX BIOS 4.0 *(CONTINUED)*

BEEP CODE	POST CODE	DESCRIPTION
3-1-1-3	82	Detect and install external RS232 ports
3-1-2-1	84	Detect and install external parallel ports
3-1-2-3	86	Reinitialize onboard I/O ports
3-1-3-1	88	Initialize BIOS data area
3-1-3-3	8A	Initialize Extended BIOS data area
3-1-4-1	8C	Initialize floppy controller
3-2-1-1	90	Initialize hard disk controller
3-2-1-2	91	Initialize local-bus hard disk controller
3-2-1-3	92	Jump to User Patch 2
3-2-2-1	94	Disable A20 address line
3-2-2-3	96	Clear huge ES segment register
3-2-3-1	98	Search for option ROMs
3-2-3-3	9A	Shadow option ROMs
3-2-4-1	9C	Set up power management
3-2-4-3	9E	Enable hardware interrupts
3-3-1-1	A0	Set time of day
3-3-1-3	A2	Check key-lock
3-3-3-1	A8	Erase F2 prompt
3-3-3-3	AA	Scan for F2 key stroke
3-3-4-1	AC	Enter Setup
3-3-4-3	AE	Clear in-POST flag
3-4-1-1	B0	Check for errors
3-4-1-3	B2	POST done; prepare to boot operating system
3-4-2-1	B4	One beep
3-4-2-3	B6	Check password (optional)
3-4-3-1	B8	Clear global descriptor table
3-4-4-1	BC	Clear parity checkers
3-4-4-3	BE	Clear screen (optional)
3-4-4-4	BF	Check virus and backup reminders
4-1-1-1	C0	Try to boot with INT 19
4-2-1-1	D0	Interrupt handler error
4-2-1-3	D2	Unknown interrupt error
4-2-2-1	D4	Pending interrupt error
4-2-2-3	D6	Initialize option ROM error
4-2-3-1	D8	Shutdown error
4-2-3-3	DA	Extended block move
4-2-4-1	DC	Shutdown 10 error
4-3-1-3	E2	Initialize the motherboard chipset
4-3-1-4	E3	Initialize refresh counter
4-3-2-1	E4	Check for forced flash
4-3-2-2	E5	Check HW status of ROM
4-3-2-3	E6	BIOS ROM is OK
4-3-2-4	E7	Do a complete RAM test
4-3-3-1	E8	Do OEM initialization
4-3-3-2	E9	Initialize interrupt controller
4-3-3-3	EA	Read in bootstrap code
4-3-3-4	EB	Initialize all vectors
4-3-4-1	EC	Boot the flash program
4-3-4-2	ED	Initialize the boot device
4-3-4-3	EE	Boot code was read OK

TABLE 19-74 POST CODES FOR QUADTEL XT BIOS

CODE	DESCRIPTION
03	Test CPU flags
06	Test CPU registers
09	Initialize any system-specific chipsets
0C	Test BIOS ROM checksum
0F	Initialize 8237 DMA page registers
12	Test 8237 DMA address and count registers
15	Initialize 8237 DMA
18	Test 8253 system timer IC (PIT)
1B	Initialize the 8253 PIT
1E	Start memory refresh test
21	Test the base 64K RAM
24	Set up interrupt vectors
27	Initialize 8259 PIC
2A	Test interrupt mask register
2D	Test for unexpected interrupt
30	Test V40 DMA if present
31	Test for DDNIL bits
33	Verify system clock interrupt
36	Test the keyboard
39	Set up interrupt table
3C	Read system configuration switches
3F	Test and initialize video
42	Locate and test COM ports
45	Locate and test LPT ports
48	Locate and test game adapter port
4B	Display BIOS copyright message on screen
4E	Calculate CPU speed
54	Test system memory
55	Test floppy drive
57	Initialize system before boot
5A	Call INT 19 boot loader

TABLE 19-75 POST CODES FOR QUADTEL AT 3.00/3.07 BIOS

CODE	DESCRIPTION
02	Test CPU flags
04	Test CPU registers
06	Perform system hardware initialization
08	Initialize specific chipset registers
0A	Test BIOS ROM checksum
0C	Test 8237 DMA page registers
0E	Test 8254 PIT
10	Initialize the 8254 PIT
12	Test 8237 DMA controller
14	Initialize 8237 DMA controller
16	Initialize 8259 PIC
18	Test and set the 8259 PIC
1A	Test memory refresh
1C	Test base 64K memory
1E	Test base 64K memory

TABLE 19-75 POST CODES FOR QUADTEL AT 3.00/3.07 BIOS *(CONTINUED)*

CODE	DESCRIPTION
20	Test base 64K memory
22	Test keyboard and keyboard controller
24	Test CMOS checksum and battery
26	Start first protected mode test
28	Check memory size
2A	Autosize memory
2C	Set memory IC interleave
2E	Exit first protected mode test
30	Unexpected shutdown
32	System board memory size
34	Relocate shadow RAM if available
36	Configure extended memory
38	Configure wait states
3A	Retest 64K base RAM
3C	Calculate CPU speed
3E	Get configuration from 8042 keyboard controller
40	Configure CPU speed
42	Initialize interrupt vectors
44	Verify video configuration
46	Initialize the video system
48	Test unexpected interrupts
4A	Start second protected mode test
4B	Verify protected mode instruction
4D	Verify protected mode instruction
50	Verify protected mode instruction
52	Verify protected mode instruction
54	Verify protected mode instruction
56	Unexpected exception
58	Test address line A20
5A	Test keyboard
5C	Determine AT or XT keyboard
5E	Start third protected mode test
60	Test base memory
62	Test base memory address
64	Test shadow memory
66	Test extended memory
68	Test extended memory addresses
6A	Determine memory size
6C	Display error messages
6E	Copy BIOS to shadow memory
70	Test 8254 PIT
72	Test real-time clock
74	Test keyboard for stuck keys
76	Initialize system hardware
78	Locate and test the math coprocessor
7A	Determine COM ports
7C	Determine LPT ports
7E	Initialize the BIOS data area
80	Check for a floppy/hard drive controller
82	Test floppy disk
84	Test fixed disk

TABLE 19-75 POST CODES FOR QUADTEL AT 3.00/3.07 BIOS *(CONTINUED)*

CODE	DESCRIPTION
86	Check for option ROMs
88	Check for keyboard lock
8A	Wait for F1 key pressed
8C	Final system initialization
8E	Call INT 19 boot loader

TABLE 19-76 POST CODES FOR SUPERSOFT XT/AT BIOS

CODE	DESCRIPTION: XT	DESCRIPTION: AT
11	CPU register or logic error	CPU register or logic error
12	ROM POST checksum error	ROM POST A checksum error
13	8253 timer channel 0 error	ROM POST B checksum error
14	8253 timer channel 1 error	8254 timer channel 0 error
15	8253 timer channel 2 error	8254 timer channel 1 error
16	8237A DMA controller error	8254 timer channel 2 error
17	8255 parity error detected	8237A DMA controller 1 error
18	16K critical RAM region error	8237A DMA controller 2 error
19	Memory refresh error	DMA page registers error
1A	—	8042 parity error detected
21	8259 interrupt controller error	16K critical RAM region
22	Unexpected interrupt detected	Memory refresh error
23	Interrupt 0 (timer) error	CPU protected mode error
24	Nonmaskable interrupt error	8259 interrupt controller 1 error
25	MDA video memory error	8259 interrupt controller 2 error
26	CGA video memory error	Unexpected interrupt detected
27	EGA/VGA memory error	Interrupt 0 (timer) error
28	8087 math chip error	CMOS real-time clock error
29	Keyboard controller error	Nonmaskable interrupt error
2A	—	80x87 math chip error
31	Keyboard scan lines/stuck key	Keyboard controller error
32	Floppy controller error	Stuck key or CMOS RAM error
33	Floppy disk read error	Floppy controller error
34	Memory error at address x	Floppy disk read error
35	Slow refresh, address x	MDA video memory error
36, 37	—	CGA, EGA/VGA RAM error
38	—	BIOS checksum error
41	BIOS checksum error	Memory error at address x
42	BASIC ROM 1 checksum	Slow refresh, address x
43-45	BASIC ROM 2, 3, 4	Display pass count
59	No monitor	No monitor

TABLE 19-77 POST CODES FOR TANDON TYPE A BIOS

CODE	DESCRIPTION
01	Test CPU flags and registers
02	Test BIOS ROM checksum
03	Test CMOS RAM battery

19

TABLE 19-77 POST CODES FOR TANDON TYPE A BIOS *(CONTINUED)*

CODE	DESCRIPTION
04	Test 8254 timer
05	8254 timer test failed
06	Test RAM refresh
07	Test first 16K RAM
08	Initialize interrupt vectors
09	Test 8259 PIC
0A	Configure temporary interrupt vectors
0B	Initialize interrupt vector table 1
0C	Initialize interrupt vector table 2
0D	Initialize fixed disk vector
0E	Interrupt vector test failed
0F	Clear keyboard controller
10	Keyboard controller test failed
11	Run keyboard controller self-test
12	Initialize equipment check data area
13	Check and initialize math coprocessor
14	Test CMOS RAM contents
15	Test and configure parallel ports
16	Test and configure serial ports
17	Call INT 19 boot loader

TABLE 19-78 POST CODES FOR TANDON TYPE B BIOS

CODE	DESCRIPTION
01	Cold boot initialization started
06	Initialize any specialized chipsets
07	Warm reboot starts here
08	Keyboard initialization passed
09	Keyboard self-test finished
0A	Test CMOS RAM battery
0B	Save CMOS RAM battery level in CMOS diagnostic register
0C	Finished saving CMOS battery condition
0D	Test 8254 PIT and disable RAM parity check
0E	8254 PIT test failed
0F	Initialize 8254 PIT channels and start memory refresh test
10	Refresh test failed
11	Test base 64K RAM
12	Base 64K RAM test failed
13	Base 64K RAM test passed
14	Perform R/W test of CMOS RAM
15	CMOS RAM R/W test complete
16	Calculating CPU speed
18	Test and initialize 8259 PICs
1A	8259 PIC initialization complete
1B	Spurious interrupt detected
1C	Spurious interrupt did not occur
1D	Error: timer 0 interrupt failed
1E	8259 PIC tests passed
20	Set up interrupt vectors 02–1F

TABLE 19-78 POST CODES FOR TANDON TYPE B BIOS *(CONTINUED)*

CODE	DESCRIPTION
21	Set up interrupt vectors 70–77
22	Clear interrupt vectors 41–46
23	Read 8042 self-test result
24	Test for proper 8042 keyboard controller self-test
25	Error: keyboard controller self-test failed
26	8042 keyboard controller self-test passed
27	Confirm DMA working
28	Initialize video system
29	Set video with cursor off
2A	Video parameters are initialized
2B	Enable NMI and I/O channel check
2C	Run RAM test to check RAM size
2D	RAM sizing complete
2E	Reset keyboard controller
2F	Initialize the CMOS real-time clock
30	Initialize floppy drive controller
31	Initialize hard disk controller
32	Disk controller has been initialized
33	Perform equipment check and initialize math coprocessor
34	Initialize serial and parallel ports
35	Test CMOS RAM battery level
36	Check for keystroke
37	Enable 8254 PIT channel 0
38	Configure cache memory
39	Enable keyboard interface and interrupts
3A	Setup finished; clear display
3B	Test the floppy and hard disk drives
3C	Scan and run any option BIOS ROMs between C800h and E000h
3D	Disable gate A20
3E	Gate A20 is disabled
3F	Call INT 19 boot loader

TABLE 19-79 POST CODES FOR TANDON i486 EISA BIOS

CODE	DESCRIPTION
01	Disable cache and EISA NMIs; enable BIOS ROM
05	Initialize address decoder and 640K RAM
06	Clear CMOS RAM shutdown flag
07	Test 8042 keyboard controller
08	Run 8042 keyboard controller self-test
AA	8042 keyboard controller self-test result
09	Test BIOS ROM checksum
0A	Read CMOS registers three times
0B	Bad CMOS RAM battery
0C	Send command to port 61 to disable speaker
0D	Test 8254 PIT
0E	8254 PIT is faulty
0F	Enable and test memory refresh

TABLE 19-79 POST CODES FOR TANDON i486 EISA BIOS *(CONTINUED)*

CODE	DESCRIPTION
10	Memory refresh failed
11	Check and clear first 64K of RAM
12	First 64K RAM failed
13	First 64K memory test passed
14	Test CMOS RAM
15	Shadow BIOS and set system speed high
16	Check CMOS shutdown flag
17	Reset was cold boot
18	Prepare 8259 PICs
19	8259 PIC initialization failed
1A	Test 8259 PIC
1B	Check for spurious interrupts
1C	Check system timer IC
1D	PIT failure
1E	Initialize interrupt vectors
1F	Initialize interrupt vectors 00–6F
20	Set vectors for interrupt 02–1F
21	Set interrupt vectors for 70–77
22	Clear interrupt vectors for 41 and 46
23	Read 8042 self-test results from DMA page register
24	Test for proper 8042 self-test result
25	8042 self-test failed
26	Initialize the 8042 keyboard controller
27	Check shutdown flag
28	Install video ROM and initialize video
29	Install video ROM, set for mono/color operation, and initialize video
2A	Check for bad CMOS RAM
2B	Check shutdown flag
2C	Test memory for proper size
2D	Display any error messages
2E	Initialize 8042 keyboard controller
2F	Initialize time-of-day in the real-time clock
30	Test for and initialize floppy disk controller
31	Enable C&T IDE interface and test for hard drive
32	Test and initialize 8259 DMA registers
33	Test and initialize math coprocessor
34	Test and initialize parallel and serial ports
35	Check CMOS RAM
36	Check for keyboard lock
37	Enable system clock tick, keyboard, and interrupt controller interrupts
38	Initialize RAM variables
39	Enter CMOS setup mode if proper keystroke pressed
3A	Clear display
3B	Initialize floppy and fixed disk drives
3C	Scan and run option ROMs
3D	Clear CMOS shutdown flag and turn off gate A20
3E	Set interrupt vectors
3F	Call INT 19 boot loader

TABLE 19-80 POST CODES FOR ZENITH ORION 4.1E BIOS

CODE	DESCRIPTION
02	Enter protected mode
03	Perform main board initialization
F0	Start basic hardware initialization
F1	Clear CMOS status locations
F2	Starting CLIO initialization
F3	Initialize SYSCFG register
F4	DXPI initialization for boot block
F5	Turning cache off
F6	Configure CPU socket
F7	Checking for math coprocessor
F8	82C206 default initialization
F9	Chipset default initialization
FF	End of machine-specific boot block
04	Check the flash ROM checksum
05	Flash ROM OK
06	Reset or power-up
07	CLIO default initialization
08	SYSCFG registers initialized
09	CMOS RAM initialization
10	SCP initialized
11	DRAM autosize detection complete
12	Parity checking enabled
18	Video ROM test at C0000h
19	Internal video ROM checked
1A	Returning to real mode
1B	Internal video hardware enabled
1D	CPU clock frequency detected
1E	BIOS data area cleared
20	Reset
21	Continue after setting memory size
22	Continue after memory test
23	Continue after memory error
24	Continue with boot loader request
25	Jump to user code
26	Continue after protected mode passed
27	Continue after protected mode failed
28	Continue after extended protected mode test
29	Continue after block move
2A	Jump to user code
30	Exit from protected-mode
31	Test/reset passed
32	Check the ROM checksum
33	Clear the video screen
34	Check system DRAM configuration
35	Check CMOS contents
36	Turn off the UMB RAM
37	Test parity generation
38	Initialize system variables
39	Check for power errors
3A	Initialize SCP mode

19

TABLE 19-80 POST CODES FOR ZENITH ORION 4.1E BIOS *(CONTINUED)*

CODE	DESCRIPTION
3B	Test CMOS diagnostic power reset
3C	Test CPU reset
3D	Save CPU ID
3E	Initialize the video system
3F	Initialize the DMA controllers
40	System speed error detected
41	Test EEPROM checksum
42	Configure parallel ports, floppy disks, and hard disks
43	Test extended video BIOS
44	Turn cache off
45	Test extended RAM
46	Test base RAM
47	Determine the amount of memory in the system
48	Set warm boot flag
49	Clear 16K of base RAM
4A	Install BIOS interrupt vector
4B	Test system timer
4C	Initialize interrupt
4D	Enable default hardware initialization
4E	Determine global I/O configuration
4F	Initialize video
50	Initialize WD90C30 scratchpad
51	Check for errors before boot
53	Test system and initialize
55	Initialize the keyboard processor
56	Initialize the PS/2 mouse
57	Configure CLIO for mouse
58	Configure CLIO for LAN
59	Configure CLIO for SCSI
5A	Configure CLIO for WAM
5B	Wait for user to enter password
5C	Initialize and enable system clock
5D	Test and initialize the floppy drive
5E	Check for Z150-type disk
5F	Initialize hard drive subsystem
60	Set default I/O device parameters
61	Get LAN ID from LAN
62	Install option ROM(s) at C8000h
63	Install option ROM(s) at E0000h
64	Initialize the SCSI interface
65	Run with A20 line off
66	Turn off the SCP
67	Set machine speed based on CMOS contents
68	Turn on cache
69	Calibrate 1-ms constants
6A	Enable NMI
6C	Clear warm boot flag
6D	Check for errors before boot
6E	Call INT 19 boot loader

TABLE 19-81 POST CODES FOR ZENITH 191 BIOS (1992)

CODE	DESCRIPTION
0	Start of slush test
1	Processor test
2	CACHE and CLIO
3	ISP defaults set
4	Into protected mode
5	Memory SIMMs count
6	Memory controller
7	Prep to test block
8	First 1MB of RAM
9	Checksum OEM ROM
10	Low flash ROM checks
11	F000h ROM checks
12	Aurora video ROM
13	F000h ROM slushed
14	Sep initialized
15	Language slushed
16	Do video-specific tests
17	Done slushing
32	Point interrupt vectors
33	Turn on parity generation
34	Initialize system variables
35	Initialize interrupt controllers
36	Check error that occurred
37	Reinitialize SCP warm boot
38	Test CMOS diag, power, reset
39	Reserved, or DDNIL status flag check
3A	Test CPU reset (80386)
3B	Save the CPU ID in GS
3C	Slush video ROM to C0000h
3D	Initialize the video and timers
3E	Initialize CMA ports, clear page
3F	Set speed too fast for now
40	Checksum the nonvolatile RAM
41	Initialize configuration
42	Initialize expansion boards from VRAM
43	Turn cache off for memory test
44	Initialize memory controller, test extended memory
45	Test base RAM
46	Determine amount of system RAM
47	Test and initialize cache if installed
48	Test system timer tick
49	Initialize the write queues
4A	Initialize monitor RAM
4B	Clear 16K of base RAM
4C	Install BIOS interrupt vectors
4D	Enable default hardware initialization
4E	Determine global I/O configuration
4F	Reserved
50	Initialize video

19

TABLE 19-81 POST CODES FOR ZENITH 191 BIOS (1992) *(CONTINUED)*

CODE	DESCRIPTION
51	Initialize WD90C30 scratchpad register
52	Initialize the keyboard processor
53	Turn off IRQ12 if mouse is off
54	Wait for user to enter correct password
55	Initialize system clock time of day
56	Test, initialize floppy system; track seeks
57	Initialize Winchester subsystem
58	Install ROMs starting at C80000h
59	Install ROM starting at E0000h
5A	Initialize SCSI interface
5B	Set default I/O device parameters
5C	Initialize the cache speed and clock
5D	Always tell system ROM
5E	Run with A20 off in PC mode
5F	Really turn off the SCP
60	Set machine speed using CFG
61	Turn on cache if machine halt
62	Calibrate 1-ms constants
63	Enable NMI
64	Test for errors before boot
65	Boot

The POST Reader Card

Although virtually all current PC BIOS versions make use of port 80h, the port itself is merely a repository for that information. In order for you to read the contents of port 80h, you will need a POST board (such as the Micro2000 Post-Probe shown in Figure 19-1) that should be installed in an open slot prior to troubleshooting and then removed once troubleshooting is completed. *Remember to turn the PC off before*

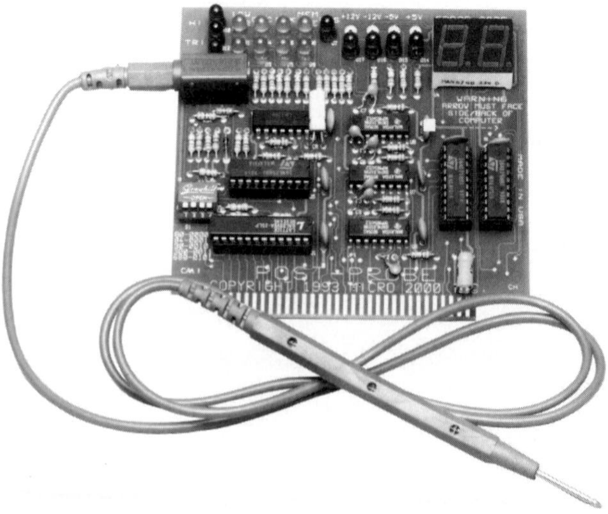

FIGURE 19-1 The PostProbe from Micro2000. Micro2000, Inc.

installing or removing a POST card. Essentially, the design of a POST board is quite simple. It reads the byte at the POST I/O port, and displays the hexadecimal code in the two seven-segment displays. However, many POST boards today provide a technician with a much more powerful troubleshooting tool. As an example, the Post-Probe supplies a series of LEDs which checks for main voltages (+12Vdc, -12Vdc, +5Vdc, and -5Vdc), and the presence of key signals on the expansion bus (such as address latch, I/O read, I/O write, memory read, memory write, system clock, and so on). Even an on-board logic probe attachment is provided.

I/O PORTS

While most traditional ISA-based PCs make use of port 80h, not all PCs follow this rule. The Compaq PC outputs codes to port 84h, and PS/2 models 25 and 30 send codes to port 90h. PS/2 model 20-286 sends codes to port 190h. Even most EISA-based PCs use port 80h, but Compaq PCs continue to use port 84h. EISA machines with Award BIOS use port 300h. Systems with a microchannel bus architecture (MCA) use port 680h. Take note that some PS/2 models, Olivetti, early AT&T, some NCR, and a few AT clones will send POST codes to a printer port at 3BCh, 278h, or 378h. The current generation of POST boards typically provides a DIP switch or jumper array for selecting the active port location. Before choosing a POST board, make sure that it can read the *proper* port address for your system.

Another issue to keep in mind is that not *all* PCs produce POST codes. The original IBM PC, the AMI XT, and some systems using HP, DTK, and ERSO BIOS do not send out POST codes during initialization. If you are testing such a system, you will be unable to see hexadecimal codes using the POST card (but power and signal indicators should still work).

INTERPRETING THE LEDS

Before working with the various POST codes in detail, you should have an understanding of the many discrete signal LEDs that accompany current POST boards. These individual signals can be a great asset when interpreted in conjunction with the POST code. Keep in mind that each POST card will offer a different selection of LEDs, so your own POST card *may not* have all of the indicators shown here.

- ***Power LEDs*** The PC will not work correctly (if at all) if one or more power supply voltages is low or absent. Typical POST cards provide four LEDs that light when +5Vdc, +12Vdc, -5Vdc, and -12Vdc are available. If any of those LEDs are dim or out, there may be a problem with the power supply or its connection to the motherboard. If problems occur after upgrading the system, the power supply may be overloaded. In any case, power LEDs help you to identify power problems quickly and effectively.
- ***ALE*** The *Address Latch Enable* signal is generated by the CPU and is used by virtually all devices in the PC that must capture address signals (such as BIOS). When this LED is on, address generation by the CPU is probably working fine. If this LED is out, there is a problem manipulating addresses in the system. You should then suspect the CPU, DMA controller, bus buffer/controller, or clock generator/system controller IC. This can be very helpful for technicians who choose to troubleshoot to the component level.
- ***I/OW*** An *I/O Write* LED will generally light whenever BIOS attempts to write data to an I/O device such as a floppy disk. The BIOS will then attempt to read what was written to confirm that portion of the system is working as expected. If the I/OW LED stays out, you should suspect a fault in either the BIOS or the system's DMA controller IC.

19

- ***I/OR*** An *I/O Read* LED will generally light whenever BIOS attempts to read data back from an I/O device after data has been written. If this LED remains out, you should suspect a fault in either the BIOS or the system's DMA controller IC.
- ***MR/W*** During POST, the BIOS will attempt to write various data patterns into memory, then read those patterns back to verify memory integrity. The *Memory R/W* LED will light during both the read and write operations (it will flicker a bit). If the MR/W LED does not light, there is likely to be a problem with the BIOS, DMA controller, memory controller, or system controller IC.
- ***Reset*** When the system is first turned on, the reset line will be asserted. This keeps the CPU neutralized until the Power Good signal is received from the power supply. At this point, the reset line should be released, and the Reset LED should go out; the initialization process will begin. The reset line should not light again unless the PC's reset button is pressed. If the Reset LED stays lit, it could indicate a problem with the Power Good signal at the supply or motherboard. The reset line may also be shorted, in which case you may have to replace the motherboard.
- ***CLK*** The *clock* LED(s) lights to indicate the presence of synchronizing signals generated by the PC's clock generator IC. If these signals are not being generated, the CPU simply will not function. If the clock indicator(s) do not light, you should suspect a fault in the system time base crystal or the clock generator IC. Keep in mind that microchannel systems do not supply clock signals to the bus.
- ***OSC*** The oscillator LEDs indicate the presence of a 14.138MHz signal. XT systems used this signal for all internal timing, but AT systems only use the oscillator as a color burst signal for the video adapter. If the oscillator indicator(s) do not light, you should suspect a fault in the color burst crystal or the clock generating circuitry.

Beep/POST Troubleshooting

Generally speaking, a POST board is one of the best all-around PC hardware troubleshooting tools available. They are quick and easy to use, compatible across ISA, EISA, and MCA platforms, and even the simplest POST board can provide you with a remarkable insight into a troubled system's operation. The problem with POST boards is that every BIOS—although testing virtually the same functions—uses varying codes that are often cryptic and poorly documented. (This chapter takes great pains to provide you with fairly comprehensive index of POST codes.) Armed with the proper code list, a POST board can often pinpoint a fault to the exact IC—and if not to the exact IC, then certainly to the major subassembly.

SYMPTOM 19-1 **The power and cooling fan(s) are on, but nothing else happens.** You should first suspect that incoming AC power is very low, or that the power connector between the supply and motherboard has become loose or disconnected. Start by using a multimeter to check AC power available at the wall outlet. *Use extreme caution to protect yourself from accidental electrocution.* If the AC level is unusually low, try the PC in an outlet with an adequate voltage level. If the AC level is acceptable, check the power connector at the motherboard. Observe the power LEDs on the POST board. If one or more power LEDs is dim or absent, there may be a fault in the power supply. Troubleshoot or replace the supply.

SYMPTOM 19-2 **After power-up, you hear the fan change pitch noticeably (there may also be a chirping sound coming from the supply).** First, be aware that some PCs use a variable-speed fan to optimize cooling. If you hear the fan pitch vary, you should confirm that this behavior is abnormal for your particular system before pursuing a repair. If varying fan pitch is *not* correct for your system, the AC power level reaching the PC is probably low and allowing the power supply to drop out of regulation. Use a multimeter and check the AC level at the wall outlet. *Use extreme caution to protect yourself from accidental electrocution.* If the AC level is too low of unsteady, try the PC in a functional AC outlet. If AC levels measure correctly, check the power LEDs on your POST board. If one or more LEDs is dim or out (or if the supply is producing a "chirping" sound), the supply is probably defective. Troubleshoot or repair the power supply.

SYMPTOM 19-3 You see one or more POST board power LEDs off, very dim, or flickering. Before suspecting a problem with the supply, try the POST board in a different socket; the expansion bus connector at that location may be bad. If the symptom persists (and the PC is behaving strangely), check the power connector between the supply and motherboard. If the connector is intact, the supply may be defective. Troubleshoot or replace the power supply.

SYMPTOM 19-4 The Reset LED remains on (the POST display will probably remain blank). In most PC designs, the CPU is held in the reset state until a "power good" signal is received from the power supply. This typically requires no more than a few milliseconds. If the reset LED remains on longer than that, it may be held up by a problem with the "power good" signal. Use a logic probe (or the probe that comes with the POST board) to check the "power good" signal. If the signal changes state as expected, the reset line may be shorted somewhere on the motherboard; try replacing the motherboard. If the signal does not change as expected, there may be a problem in the power supply. Try replacing the power supply.

SYMPTOM 19-5 One or more activity LEDs is out (the POST display will probably remain blank). Most POST boards provide a selection of LEDs that are used to indicate signal activity on major bus lines. If one or more of these LEDs is out, there is probably a motherboard fault in the corresponding circuit:

19

- *ALE* The clock generator, CPU, DMA controller, or bus controller may have failed. Try replacing the motherboard.
- *OSC* The clock generator IC or time-base crystal may have failed. Replace those components, or replace the motherboard.
- *CLK* Check for excessive ripple in the AC source. Try a clean AC source. There may also be a problem with the clock generator or time-base crystal. Replace those components or replace the motherboard.
- *I/OR, I/OW* Check for excessive ripple or inadequate ground in the system power lines. Try a new power supply if necessary. There may also be a fault in the DMA controller, CPU, PIT, or PIC devices. Try another motherboard.
- *MR/W* There may be a fault in the DMA controller, bus controller, BIOS ROM, PIT, or PIC devices. Try another motherboard.

SYMPTOM 19-6 You hear a beep code pattern from the system speaker, but no POST code is displayed. Any beep pattern other than a single short beep indicates a serious system problem; however, there may be several reasons why the POST board is not displaying POST codes. First, make sure that the BIOS for your system actually generates POST codes; most do, but a few do not. Also be sure that your POST board is set to read the proper I/O address that the codes are being written to. Many systems send codes to port 80h, but other ports such as 1080h, 680h, and 378h may be used. Configure the POST board to use the proper address. If problems persist, the BIOS itself may be defective. Try a different BIOS, or refer to Chapter 15 to troubleshoot the beep code.

SYMPTOM 19-7 The POST display stops at some code (the system probably hangs up). The CPU and clock systems are probably working to fetch instructions from BIOS, but POST has detected a fault in the system. Locate the table for your appropriate manufacturer in this chapter, and find the POST code's meaning. If the code refers to a fault on the motherboard, you can either attempt to replace the defective component, or replace the motherboard outright. If the code refers to an expansion device such as a drive or video adapter, take steps to replace the defective device.

SYMPTOM 19-8 A POST or beep code indicates a video problem (there is no monitor display). Chances are that the system was unable to detect video ROM instructions or locate video memory. As a result, no display is available. Try a new video adapter board in the system. If the video adapter is located on the motherboard, try a new motherboard, or disable the motherboard video (usually with a jumper) and install an expansion video adapter.

SYMPTOM 19-9 A POST or beep code indicates a drive or controller problem. Chances are that the video system is working. If possible, load the CMOS setup program and make sure that the drive selections entered are accurate for your system. An incorrect set of entries can disable your drives. Make sure that the drive being used is properly formatted and partitioned for your system. If the problem persists, either the drive or drive controller has failed. Start by trying an alternative drive controller. If the problem remains, try a new drive.

Further Study

American Megatrends (AMI): **http://www.megatrends.com/**

Data Depot: **http://www.datadepo.com**

ForeFront: **http://www.ffg.com**

Micro2000: **http://www.micro2000.com**

Phoenix Technologies: **http://www.phoenix.com/**

TriniTech Omni Analyzer: **http://www.pcanalyzer.com/Eng_omni.htm**

Ultra X Post Cards: **http://www.uxd.com/products.html**

20

FANS AND COOLING DEVICES

CHAPTER AT A GLANCE

When electrical power is applied to a circuit, the circuit uses that power to perform work. In the case of a PC, *work* would be the myriad of processing operations that go on throughout the computer every moment. For computers (as with all machines), the conversion of power into work is not a perfect one—a portion of power is dissipated in the form of *heat*. Over time, an excessive buildup of heat will cause a chip (and thus the PC) to fail prematurely. As a result, it is very important that a computer system be properly outfitted to deal with heat.

You might wonder why heat is taken so seriously—after all, the majority of chips and passive components found in a PC dissipate very little heat at all. Unfortunately, it is the few components that do produce heat that cause most problems: drive motors, power supply regulating circuits, and the CPU. When taken together with the lower heat output from other devices, the temperature inside a PC cabinet can easily exceed 80°C. You see, heat has dramatic effects on materials and semiconductors. Heat accelerates the breakdown of insulating enamel on transformer and motor windings. Excessive heat also causes semiconductor junctions to change characteristics and eventually break down. Thus, proper cooling is vital to a computer's overall processing stability and long-term reliability. This chapter is intended to illustrate the various methods used to cool a PC, explain the effects that inhibit cooling, and show you how to deal with cooling problems.

Understanding Cooling Methodologies

In order to understand how various cooling devices work, you must understand some basic principles about heat transfer. First, heat tends to travel from places of *more* heat to places of *less* heat. If you don't believe this, apply a hot soldering iron to one end of a wire, and see how long it takes for other end to get warm. While this is a tremendous oversimplification, you get the basic idea. There are three general modes of heat transfer: convection, conduction, and radiation.

Convection is the transfer of heat through air currents. A heat source warms nearby air, which rises. The warmer rising air is replaced by cooler air, which is then heated. Eventually, a circulating airflow develops. This is the basic principle behind the radiators that heat your home in the winter. It is also an essential element of PC cooling. You might ask how heating and cooling can be the same thing. Well, as heat is transferred to the air, the device providing the heat is cooled. When a CPU heats up, it tends to heat the surrounding air. Unfortunately, such *static convection* has limited effect in a PC. Static convection does not remove enough heat to cool a very hot device (such as a CPU). Static convection also relies on circulating flows of air, which are difficult to establish in the close quarters of a highly obstructed PC. A way to multiply the effect of convection is to force an airflow across the heated device. Fans are used to force air through the PC. This *forced convection* provides much more effective cooling and can be directed to specific areas around the PC. Most of the cooling methods covered in this chapter rely on forced convection.

Conduction is the transfer of heat through physical contact. The radiator system in your car works this way. By circulating cooler liquid around a warmer surface, the cooler liquid picks up the surface heat—thus cooling the surface. The liquid, now warmed, is circulated to a chilling assembly, which is intended to take away any heat picked up by the liquid, so the liquid is kept cooled. In a car, this is the front radiator, which is cooled by the forced air of a large fan. Although conduction is a much more effective means of cooling than convection, conduction can only cool the areas of contact, while convection can cool large areas. Some CPU cooling devices use circulating liquid, but these are rare and expensive. As a consequence, you will rarely find conductive cooling techniques in PCs.

Finally, *radiation* is the transfer of heat through infrared emission. For example, the warmth you feel from sunlight or a sun lamp is due to the effects of infrared radiation. Since there are no significant infrared emission sources in a PC, radiation will not be discussed further. At this point, you can see how these heat transfer principles are employed in a PC environment.

NATURAL CONVECTION

Natural (or static) convection is the cooling technique employed in most computer monitors. Take a look at the rear enclosure on your monitor, and notice that there are open slots along the top and bottom of the enclosure. The openings beneath the monitor are for air intake, and the upper slots allow air to escape. These slots provide a free flow of air through the monitor. Yet, this process works without the benefit of a fan. You can easily see how this process works. Let the monitor run for a while, and place your hand over the upper slots—you can feel hot air rising. The warm circuitry inside the running monitor heats the surrounding air, which rises up and out. As warm air is displaced, new cooler air is drawn in from the bottom slots. Although monitor circuits will heat up (especially the power supply), none of the components become hot enough to require forced convection.

As you might expect, the success of this method depends on an unobstructed air path. If "Fluffy" the cat curls up on top of the monitor, the exhaust vents will be blocked. This interrupts the flow of air, and temperatures inside the monitor will increase. Eventually, you may notice the display rolling or shifting position—initial warnings that the monitor circuits are overheating. If the blockage continues for an extended period, the monitor may fail prematurely. Besides monitors, dot matrix and ink-jet printers typically rely on convection to cool their circuits.

HEAT SINKS

Another rule of heat transfer is that the effectiveness with which heat is transferred depends on the amount of surface area that is exposed. Check out the radiator in your car—each of those tiny fins adds a small amount of surface area to the overall radiating surface. This is the principle behind *heat sinks* (Figure 20-1). By adding a heat sink to a heated component, you increase the effective surface area that is open to the air. Since more air can flow over a larger surface (through natural or forced convection), the component stays cooler. For components that become inordinately hot during normal operation (such as regulator ICs or CPUs), a heat sink is a very simple and inexpensive way to enhance cooling (Figure 20-2). Of course, heat sinks are not just for chips. Take a look at the print head of a dot matrix printer. You'll find a set of cast aluminum fins set right into the head assembly.

CHASSIS FANS

20

Natural convection is fine for cooling monitors and printers, but PCs are too cramped and obstructed to establish a consistent airflow. As a result, air must be forced through the enclosure. This is usually accomplished with one or more fans positioned in the rear chassis. By positioning the fans blowing out of the enclosure, cooler air can be vacuumed into the system through strategically located intake slots in the housing. Some systems use a second fan blowing into the enclosure from the front chassis. This kind of push-pull cooling develops a very strong airflow.

FIGURE 20-1 IERC self-adhesive heat sinks (International Electronics Research Corporation)

FIGURE 20-2 An IERC CPU fan and heat sink (International Electronics Research Corporation)

FAN CARDS

Even with good-quality, chassis-mounted fans, some high-performance systems require an extra measure of cooling, especially in the CPU area. An ongoing trend in PC cooling is the use of a *fan card*—a standard-sized ISA expansion board with one or two +12 Vdc fans mounted to it. This allows you to place the fan card in the immediate vicinity of a CPU or drive to improve the local airflow. However, there are some limitations to fan cards that you should be aware of. First, many expansion boards are full-sized boards, so the chances are very good that at least one side of the fan card will be somewhat obstructed by another full-slot expansion board. As long as the fan card is blowing *away* from the adjacent expansion board, this should not present a problem. If the fan card is blowing *toward* the adjacent expansion board, a region of turbulent air will be produced, which reduces the fan card's overall effectiveness.

Another concern is EMI produced by the fan motors. As inductive devices, fans are notorious for producing unwanted electromagnetic interference. If the fan card is placed in close proximity of a sensitive device such as a drive controller or video capture board, the electrical noise produced by the fans can degrade the other device's performance or cause operating errors. There is also the possibility that electrical noise from the fans may travel back along the +12 Vdc voltage line and interfere with other devices in the system that are using +12 Vdc. It is always wise to approach fan cards with a certain amount of suspicion, especially if you have problems with a device once the fan card is installed.

> The vibrations produced by fan cards are also notorious for rocking the fan card right out of its slot, so be sure to bolt the fan card into its slot using the expansion card bracket.

CPU FANS

CPUs have always run hot, and the reason is readily understandable—a single microscopic transistor dissipates virtually no heat, but the combined heat from over 15 million transistors crammed into a wafer the size of a fingernail becomes *extreme*. The surface temperature of a Pentium processor can easily exceed 100°C. (Pentium II/III processors can run even higher.) With such a strong concentration of heat, even forced air through a heat sink can leave a CPU running hot. To manage heat in the latest Athlon and Pentium III processors, a CPU fan can be employed. Basically, a CPU fan mounts a small, high-speed fan that blows down into a heat sink assembly. The in-rushing air cools the heat sink (and thus the CPU) very effectively.

Unfortunately, there are some disadvantages to the CPU fan. First, the added height of a heat sink/fan combination can obstruct full-length expansion boards. This is typical of poorly designed AT-style motherboards (though ATX and NLX motherboards position the CPU well away from expansion slots). Similarly, if your particular motherboard places the CPU under a low-hanging drive or other chassis obstruction, a CPU fan may not fit. Before using a CPU fan, make sure you have several cubic inches of available space *over* the CPU.

The CPU fan also requires power. Check that you have a power connector available from the power supply, or make sure the CPU fan assembly comes with a built-in Y-connector. Today, the power management and cooling features provided by most motherboards allow you to plug the fan(s) directly into connectors on the motherboard.

Another possible problem involves vibration. Since the fan is now physically coupled to the CPU, there is a bit of debate over what (if any) damage is done to the CPU by fan vibrations over the long term. The best defense against vibration and premature failure is to use a good-quality ball bearing fan unit. There are three attributes to consider when selecting a processor cooling unit:

- Large heat sink area for extra heat dissipation area
- Long-life and low-noise ball bearing fan
- Convenient and well-designed clips to ease installation

> If you must use a Y-splitter cable to power a CPU heat sink/fan, never split power from a hard drive or other critical drive. Split power from a floppy drive instead.

LIQUID COOLING (THE "HEAT PIPE")

CPU cooling can also be accomplished through conductive devices generally known as heat pipes. There are a small number of liquid cooling devices available for CPUs, most of which are used in Pentium II/III notebook systems that do not have the space for heat sinks or CPU fans. The drawback to a liquid-cooled system is clear enough—a breach in the cooling loop can deposit liquid onto the motherboard and result in real damage. Extra expense is another consideration.

The basic principles behind the heat pipe are well known among refrigeration professionals, but are not all that intuitive to computer technicians. Basically, a vacuum-tight tube is filled with a *low* boiling point fluid. The tube is run through a small heat sink fitted over the CPU. The advantage here is that since heat does not have to dissipate to the air, the heat sink can be quite thin, as shown in Figure 20-3.

This CPU heat sink is known as the *evaporator*, since the fluid running through it is evaporated ("flashed" to vapor) by the CPU's heat. Since the process of evaporation is a cooling process, heat is transferred from the CPU to the evaporated fluid, which then travels back up through the tube where it runs through a somewhat larger metal plate known as the *condenser*. The condenser is usually located under the

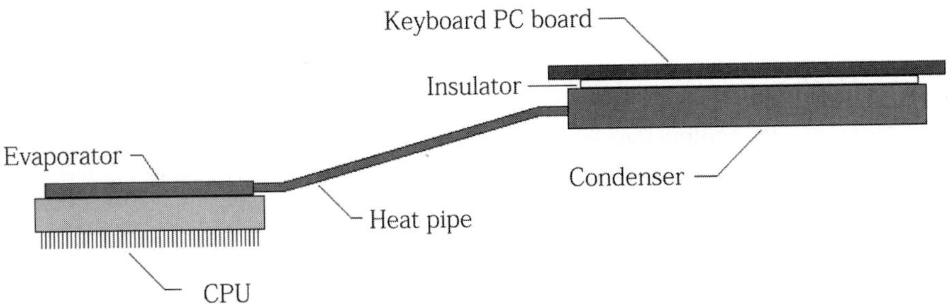

FIGURE 20-3 Basic diagram of a CPU heat pipe

notebook's keyboard assembly where there is enough empty space for the heat to dissipate and allow the fluid to return to its liquid state. Once the liquid returns to its liquid state, it is free to recirculate back to the heat sink. Two of the most interesting elements of the heat pipe are that it requires absolutely no electricity and has no moving parts. So long as the evaporator remains in good contact with the CPU, the heat pipe should continue operating indefinitely. Circulation is driven by the natural phase changes of the liquid.

Although the heat pipe is a relatively simple and reliable mechanism, it poses some unique problems for small computer assemblies. If you upgrade or repair mobile computers at all, you will need to know the important issues for heat pipe assembly and installation:

- *Be careful of liquid.* Remember that you are basically dealing with a delicate liquid vessel mounted in the bowels of your mobile computer. As a result, you must be extremely careful during disassembly and reassembly procedures. Crimping the tube at any point will reduce the pipe's effectiveness. Breaking the heat pipe can result in chemicals being spilled into the main board.
- *Be careful of dust and debris.* As you saw, the evaporated liquid sheds its heat in the condenser, which is located under the keyboard. But just like convection heating in the home, heat will have trouble leaving the condenser if it is "insulated"—covered with dust and debris accumulated from long periods of use. If you find yourself working on a mobile PC using a heat pipe, be sure that the condenser is clean and free of dust. You may choose to blow away any dust and debris with compressed air.
- *Be careful of contact.* As far as the CPU is concerned, the heat pipe's evaporator is just another heat sink. Like any heat sink, there must be good physical contact between the CPU and the evaporator in order for proper cooling to occur. If the evaporator is left loose (or otherwise mounted incorrectly), the heat pipe will be ineffective.

PIEZOELECTRIC COOLERS

Piezoelectric devices (called "Peltier coolers") mount a layer of piezoelectric material over the CPU. As the crystal layer vibrates, a temperature differential develops through it, which actually results in a cooler surface (applied against the CPU). The problem with piezoelectric "chillers" is their expense, as well as the yet-unclear potential for CPU damage from long-term exposure to vibration.

Cooling Problems

Cooling is often the most overlooked and neglected feature of a PC. In many off-the-shelf systems, cooling is sufficient. But as time, constant use, environmental factors, and upgrades take their toll, the cooling plan may need to be reviewed or revised. As with so many other elements of PC service, successful troubleshooting means knowing where to look. This part of the chapter shows you the factors to consider when evaluating PC cooling and cooling problems.

FAN WEAR

Fans don't last forever. They are electromechanical devices, and eventually the motor or rotating shaft will wear out and fail. Normally, PC cooling fans are very quiet devices—they have to be, since loud operation in a home or office environment would quickly become maddening. The first sign of fan failure is excessive *noise*. A persistent buzz or grinding sound immediately points to a fan problem. The fan motor may also be unusually hot. In extreme cases, the fan will hang up and stop altogether (it may start again if you nudge it gently). The best way to deal with a cranky fan is to replace it outright. A new fan must have the same three major characteristics of the original fan: (1) physical mounting dimensions, (2) operating voltage—usually +12 Vdc, and (3) airflow rate.

BAD HEAT SINK CONTACT

In order for a heat sink to be effective, it must have a strong physical connection to the host chip that it's cooling. This ensures that the maximum amount of heat is transferred from the chip to the heat sink/fan. The better that contact is, the more efficiently that heat is transferred into the heat sink—and the cooler the chip runs. There are a variety of ways to secure a heat sink/fan, but clipping the chip and heat sink together has been easiest and most popular. However, not all heat sink clips are tight, and even a tight clip does not guarantee good contact. Check to see that the heat sink is attached securely, and be sure to add a layer of thermally conductive compound (typically a thick white acrid cream) between the chip and heat sink. Thermal grease fills in any air space between the IC and heat sink, so heat transfer is enhanced. Suspect heat sink problems when the system locks up randomly for no apparent reason or the CPU suffers chronic failures.

> Thermal grease is toxic and can stain clothing. When using thermal grease, be sure to work carefully, and avoid getting it on hands and clothing.

One of the more recent trends in heat sink marketing is the use of stick-on heat sinks—just peel off an adhesive backing and stick the heat sink in place. It sounds terrific in principle, but adhesive is often more of a thermal insulator than a thermal conductor. As a general rule, go with the clip-on heat sinks wherever possible.

CPU VIBRATION FAILURE

CPU heat sink/fans are generally regarded as one of the most effective CPU cooling devices available, but there is a certain amount of debate over the effect of long-term fan vibration on the CPU. Some manufacturers argue that since the fan is physically attached to the heat sink (and CPU), the fan's vibrations will be carried directly into the CPU, which will shorten the CPU's working life. However, there are no studies available to prove or disprove that possibility. As a result, you should rely on your own experience when checking or recommending CPU heat sinks. Normally, it is reasonable to expect that the cooler CPU should run longer and more reliably. So if you find that the CPU fails frequently when fitted with a CPU fan, try a large heat sink or high-quality heat sink/fan instead.

SUNLIGHT

Anyone who has ever been in the sunlight understands how warming it can be. This natural warming can be magnified through glass, so sunlight indoors can feel even warmer. When a PC sits exposed to sunlight for prolonged periods, the metal enclosures tend to pick up much of that heat (and heat the air inside). While sunlight alone rarely provides enough heating to endanger the system, it can intensify the cooling demands while the system is operating. As a general rule, do not expose the PC and its peripherals to direct sunlight for extended periods of time.

THERMAL CYCLING

Turn it off or leave it on? This is the perennial PC question and one that continues to be a hotbed of debate among technicians. The best way to answer this question is to approach it both theoretically and practically. Theoretically, each time material heats up, it expands. When the material cools down again, it contracts. Thus, every time a PC is turned on, the chips, solder joints, and wiring tend to expand until the system reaches a stable operating temperature. When the PC is turned off, it gradually cools down, and its components contract until the PC returns to room temperature. Over time, this "accordion effect" of expansion and contraction (referred to as *thermal cycling*) is known to cause material to fatigue and fracture—a chip breaks down, or a solder joint becomes intermittent—you get the idea. As a consequence of this effect, long-time PC veterans argue that the PC should be left on constantly. This allows the system to achieve a stable temperature, so thermal cycling is eliminated.

From a practical standpoint, however, the view is a bit different. First, the damaging effect of thermal cycling is dependent on the *amount of temperature difference*. Frankly, today's PCs just don't get that hot (although the CPUs can blaze if not properly cooled). Cooler PCs are affected less by thermal damage. Drive wear is another nonissue, with current, cool-running designs exhibiting MTBFs of over 300,000 hours. The other consideration is the rising cost of power, which is wasted by simply leaving the PC on overnight. On the other hand, there is no reason to power-down the PC each time you get up for coffee. Ultimately, the current thinking is to go ahead and turn the PC off overnight, or whenever you must leave the system for more than a few hours. If your system offers power conservation support (such as "standby" and "hibernation" modes), you should employ those techniques to lower the system's total power demands.

EXCESSIVE DEVICES

Many PCs are eventually upgraded with more RAM, more drives, new CPUs, and so on. Each new device added to the system contributes to its overall heat production. For heavily expanded systems, it may be necessary to augment cooling with a supplemental exhaust fan or inlet fan at the chassis. The general yardstick for judging the need for extra cooling is to feel the air exhausting from the system. If the air feels comfortable or somewhat warm, chances are that cooling is adequate. If the air feels hot, it's time to add a new fan. True, this is a rather subjective means of measurement, but it is accurate enough for most situations.

DUST

Perhaps the most significant problem of reliable, long-term PC cooling is *dust*, which is always present in everyday air. For the purposes of this book, dust includes other contaminants such as pet hair and cigarette smoke. Dust has two effects on the PC. First, dust collects on the fan blades and intake vents or filters. This interrupts and limits airflow into and out of the system. Second, dust can collect on a printed circuit board where airflow is limited. The dust acts as a *thermal blanket*, which prevents normal convective cooling. When upgrading or servicing a PC, make it a point to vacuum any accumulations of dust in or around the system.

AC POWER PROBLEMS

Power supplies can be serious sources of heat, especially in the regulator portion of the supply, which is designed to maintain a stable voltage output as AC input levels and load demands change. If AC climbs over its nominal value, the regulator must work harder to maintain a constant output. This results in excessive power supply heating. Lagging AC levels result in larger amounts of current being drawn to keep the power output steady, which also causes extra heating. Persistent power supply failures or unusually hot operation may suggest problems with AC (or an overloaded system power supply).

BLOCKED VENTS

Air needs a clear path into and out of the system, which is usually accommodated through vent slots located around the enclosure. If the vent slots are obstructed or blocked, airflow may be interrupted. (This is especially detrimental to devices relying on natural convection for cooling.) You can see the importance of proper ventilation by reviewing the installation guidelines for almost any piece of consumer electronics. Most guidelines recommend that you leave several inches of free space on each side of the enclosure. Make sure that vent slots are unobstructed and clear of dust or debris.

EXCESSIVE CPU VOLTAGE

Not all CPUs use the same voltage. Intel, AMD, and Cyrix CPUs use slightly different voltage levels for proper operation (usually between +2.4 Vdc and +3.6 Vdc). If the CPU voltage is tweaked a bit too high for the particular CPU, it will generate excessive heat. Another typical oversight comes with the use of Pentium MMX (or compatible) processors that use dual voltages (approximately +2.8 Vdc and +3.3 Vdc) for reduced power and lower heating. Again, if the CPU voltage is set too high, excessive heating will result, which can shorten the CPU's working life. Devices like Autotime's Processor Protector (Figure 20-4) are tools that you can use to quickly and efficiently verify the CPU voltage(s).

FIGURE 20-4 The Processor Protector CPU voltage measurement tool from AutoTime

20

Troubleshooting Cooling Problems

Cooling problems manifest themselves in a variety of ways—usually through intermittent system operation and frequent failures. This part of the chapter is intended to illustrate some of the more perplexing cooling problems that you should be aware of.

HEAT DETECTORS

In order to deal with system heat problems, you should know when excessive heating occurs. Today, the power management and cooling systems of most motherboards incorporate hardware monitoring that will report cooling fan speeds and (if properly equipped) indicate the CPU temperature. You can then set alarm points that will alert you if a cooling fan stops or CPU temperature exceeds your preset value. If you're working with older systems (or systems that do not incorporate such hardware monitoring features), you can use after-market heat detectors (such as the 110 Alert unit from PC Power & Cooling) to alert you to excess heat.

Devices like the 110 Alert monitor the interior case temperature and processor cooler fan rotation inside any computer. At 110°F (40°C) a loud alarm will sound. The 110 Alert also monitors electrical current to the processor's cooling fan, so the audible alarm will sound when the cooling fan slows by 30 percent or more. To install a device such as the 110 Alert, connect a spare power lead to the connector labeled "110 Alert," and then connect the opposite end directly to the processor's cooling fan power connector. (Power for the processor cooling fan must be supplied by the 110 Alert; otherwise the alarm may sound continuously.) Remove the protective backing from the mounting tape, and mount the unit on a smooth, clean surface in a convenient location within the top third of the computer. A note of caution: do not locate the heat detector near the CPU or other high heat source since this may result in a nuisance alarm.

> Do not connect a Y-splitter between a 110 Alert and the processor cooling fan. You cannot split the power to the processor cooling fan and another device such as a hard disk drive. This will cause intermittent nuisance alarms because the 110 Alert is sensing the current of both devices

GENERAL SYMPTOMS

SYMPTOM 20-1 **The fan is producing an unusual amount of noise, but it seems to be working properly** This can often happen after replacing a fan and is typically the result of fan vibrations being introduced to the PC chassis. While this is rarely harmful to the system, it can become quite annoying. Check the way the new fan is mounted, and be sure that any damping material is in place. Otherwise, you may try adding small standoffs of foam around each mounting screw to damp vibration. Of course, if the fan is original equipment, it may be wearing out and need to be replaced. Try a new fan.

SYMPTOM 20-2 **The fan has stopped turning** First, check to see if the fan is the type that works intermittently by means of a small internal thermostat. If so, it may simply be that the fan has stopped normally. You should see it start and stop as required. However, most fans turn continuously, so if the fan has stopped, it may have become disconnected, or it may have failed. Check the fan's power connection. If the problem persists, try a new fan.

SYMPTOM 20-3 **The CPU freezes intermittently** This is a classic sign of CPU overheating. While overheating will not necessarily destroy a CPU immediately, prolonged or repeated overheating can precipitate a permanent failure. Check the heat sink or CPU fan attached to the CPU. **Warning:** Be sure to let the system cool before touching the heat sink. If the cooling device is loose, reattach it securely. (Be sure to use thermal compound.) If the heat sink is secure, but overheating continues, try a more aggressive device such as a CPU fan.

SYMPTOM 20-4 **You are experiencing frequent CPU failures** Chronic CPU failures are rare occurrences and can often be traced to insufficient cooling. If the CPU does not have a heat sink, try adding one. If a heat sink is already attached, try a larger heat sink or CPU fan. However, if a CPU fan is already in use, there may be a vibration problem, which shortens the CPU's working life. Try "downgrading" to a regular heat sink, or use an alternative cooling device such as a Peltier cooler.

SYMPTOM 20-5 **You are experiencing frequent drive failures** This is typical of the hard drive in an overloaded system. When replacing the hard drive, take careful note of the exhaust heat and the overall number of devices in the system. If the exhaust is unusually warm, or there are many adjacent drives in the system, try mounting the replacement drive by itself, away from other drives—maybe in a rear drive bay. If possible, try mounting the drive vertically. If it is impossible to relocate the offending drive, try adding a supplemental fan, or a fan card, to improve airflow over the drive.

Further Study

Autotime: **http://www.autotime.com**

PC Power and Cooling: **http://www.pcpowercooling.com**

21

FLOPPY AND LS-120 DRIVES

CHAPTER AT A GLANCE

The ability to interchange programs and data between various compatible computers is a fundamental requirement of almost every computer system. It is just this kind of file exchange compatibility that helped rocket IBM PC/XTs into everyday use and spur the personal computer industry into the early 1980s. A standardized operating system, file structure, and recording media also breathed life into the fledgling software industry. With the floppy disk, early software developers could finally distribute programs and data to a mass market of compatible computer users. The mechanism that allowed this quantum leap in compatibility is the floppy disk drive (Figure 21-1). Although floppy drives are quite inexpensive and reliable, they are also very limited in their storage space—allowing up to 1.44MB on a disk. The LS-120 is an ultra-high-density floppy system (compatible with all 3.5-inch disks) that can support up to 120MB on a single LS-120 disk. This chapter examines the operating concepts, installation guidelines, and troubleshooting issues for both conventional floppy drives and LS-120 devices.

The Floppy Drive

A venerable floppy disk drive (or FDD) is one of the least expensive and most reliable forms of mass storage ever used in computer systems. Virtually every one of the millions of personal computers sold each year incorporates at least one floppy drive. Most notebook and laptop computers also offer a single floppy drive.

FIGURE 21-1 NEC FD1138H floppy drive (NEC Technologies, Inc.)

Not only are floppy drives useful for transferring files and data between various systems, but the advantage of removable media—the floppy disk itself—makes floppy drives an almost intuitive backup for your important data files. Although floppy drives have evolved through a number of iterations, from 8 inches to 5.25 inches to 3.5 inches, their basic components and operating principles have changed very little.

MAGNETIC STORAGE CONCEPTS

Magnetic storage media have been attractive to computer designers for many years—long before the personal computer had established itself in homes and offices. This popularity is primarily due to the fact that magnetic media is *nonvolatile*. Unlike system RAM, no electrical energy is needed to maintain the information once it is stored on magnetic media. Although electrical energy is used to read and write magnetic data, magnetic fields do not change on their own, so data remains intact until other forces (such as another floppy drive) act upon it. It is this smooth, straightforward translation from electricity to magnetism and back again that has made magnetic storage such a natural choice. To understand how a floppy drive works and why it fails, you should have an understanding of magnetic storage. This part of the chapter describes the basic storage concepts used for floppy drives.

Media

For the purposes of this book, *media* is the physical material that actually holds recorded information. In a floppy disk, the media is a small mylar disk coated on both sides with a precisely formulated magnetic material often referred to as the *oxide* layer. Every disk manufacturer uses their own particular formula for magnetic coatings, but most coatings are based on a naturally magnetic element (such as iron, nickel, or cobalt) that has been alloyed with nonmagnetic materials or rare earth. This magnetic material is then compounded with plastic, bonding chemicals, and lubricant to form the actual disk media coating.

The fascinating aspect of these magnetic layers is that each and every particle of the media acts as a microscopic magnet. Each magnetic particle can be aligned in one orientation or another under the influence of an external magnetic field. If you have ever magnetized a screwdriver's steel shaft by running a permanent magnet along its length, you have already seen this magnetizing process in action. For a floppy disk, microscopic points along the disk's surfaces are magnetized in one alignment or another by the precise forces applied by read/write (R/W) heads. The shifting of alignment polarities would indicate a logic

1, while no change in polarity would indicate a logic 0. (You will read more about data recording and organization later in this chapter.)

In analog recording (such as audiotapes), the magnetic field generated by read/write heads varies in direct proportion to the signal being recorded. Such linear variations in field strength cause varying amounts of magnetic particles to align as the media moves. On the other hand, digital recordings such as floppy disks save binary 1's and 0's by applying an overwhelming amount of field strength. Very strong magnetic fields *saturate* the media—that is, *so much* field strength is applied that any further increase in field strength will not cause a better alignment of magnetic particles at that point on the media. The advantage to operating in saturation is that 1's and 0's are remarkably resistant to the degrading effects of noise that eventually appear in analog magnetic recordings.

Although the orientation of magnetic particles on a disk's media can be reversed by using an external magnetic field, particles tend to resist the reversal of polarity. *Coercitivity* is the strength with which magnetic particles resist change. Higher coercitivity material has a greater resistance to change, so a stronger external field will be needed to cause changes. High coercitivity is generally considered to be desirable (up to a point) because signals stand out much better against background noise, and signals will resist natural degradation because of age, temperature, and random magnetic influences. As you might expect, a highly coercive media requires a more powerful field to record new information.

Another advantage of increased coercitivity is greater "information density" for media. The greater strength of each media particle allows more bits to be packed into less area. The move from 5.25-inch to 3.5-inch floppy disks was possible due largely to a superior (more coercitive) magnetic layer. This coercitivity principle also holds true for hard drives. In order to pack more information onto ever-smaller platters, the media must be more coercive. Coercitivity is a common magnetic measurement with units in *oersteds* (pronounced "or-steds"). The coercitivity of a typical floppy disk can range anywhere from 300 oersteds to 750 oersteds. By comparison, hard drive and magneto-optical (MO) drive media usually offer coercitivities up to 6000 oersteds or higher.

The main premise of magnetic storage is that it is *static* (once recorded, information is retained without any electrical energy). Such stored information is presumed to last forever, but in actual practice, magnetic information begins to degrade as soon as it is recorded. A good magnetic media will reliably "remember" (or retain) the alignment of its particles over a long period of time. The ability of a media to retain its magnetic information is known as *retentivity*. Even the finest, best-formulated floppy disks degrade eventually (although it could take many years before an actual data error materializes).

Ultimately, the ideal answer to media degradation is to refresh (or write over) the data and sector ID information. Data is rewritten normally each time a file is saved, but sector IDs are only written once when the disk is formatted. If a sector ID should fail, you will see the dreaded "Sector Not Found" disk error, and any data stored in the sector cannot be accessed. This failure mode also occurs in hard drives. There is little that can be done to ensure the integrity of floppy disks other than maintaining one or more backups on freshly formatted disks. However, some commercial software is available for restoring disk data (especially hard drives).

Magnetic Recording Principles

The first step in understanding digital recording is to see how binary data is stored on a disk. Binary 1's and 0's are not represented by discrete polarities of magnetic field orientations as you may have thought. Instead, binary digits are represented by the presence or absence of flux *transitions*, as illustrated in Figure 21-2. By detecting the *change* from one polarity to another instead of simply detecting a discrete polarity itself, maximum sensitivity can be achieved with very simple circuitry.

In its simplest form, a logic 1 is indicated by the presence of a flux reversal within a fixed time frame, while a logic 0 is indicated by the absence of a flux reversal. Most floppy drive systems insert artificial flux reversals between consecutive 0's to prevent reversals from occurring at great intervals. You can see some example magnetic states recorded on the media of Figure 21-2. Notice that the direction of reversal does not matter at all—it is the reversal event that defines a 1 or 0. For example, the first 0 uses left-to-right orientation, while the second 0 uses a right-to-left orientation, but both can represent 0's.

The second trace in Figure 21-2 represents an amplified output signal from a typical read/write head. Notice that the analog signal peaks wherever there is a flux transition—long slopes indicate a 0, and short slopes indicate a 1. When such peaks are encountered, peak detection circuits in the floppy drive cause marking pulses in the ultimate data signal. Each bit is usually encoded in about 4 µS.

Often, the most confusing aspect of flux transitions is the artificial reversals. Why reverse the polarities for consecutive 0's? Artificial reversals are added to guarantee synchronization in the floppy disk circuitry. Remember that data read or written to a floppy disk is serial, and without any clock signal, such serial data is *asynchronous* of the drive's circuitry. Regular flux reversals (even if added artificially) create reference pulses that help to synchronize the drive and data without use of clocks or other timing signals. This approach is loosely referred to as the *modified frequency modulation* (MFM) recording technique. Early hard drives (such as ST506/412 drives) also employed MFM recording.

The ability of floppy disks to store information depends upon being able to write new magnetic field polarities on top of old or existing orientations. A drive must also be able to sense the existing polarities on a disk during read operations. The mechanism responsible for translating electrical signals into magnetic signals (and vice versa) is the read/write head (R/W head). In principle, a *head* is little more than a coil of very fine wire wrapped around a soft, highly permeable core material, as illustrated in Figure 21-3.

When the head is energized with current flow from a driver IC, a path of magnetic flux is established in the head core. The direction (or orientation) of flux depends on the direction of energizing current. To reverse a head's magnetic orientation, the direction of energizing current must be reversed. The small head size and low current levels needed to energize a head allow very high frequency flux reversals. As

21

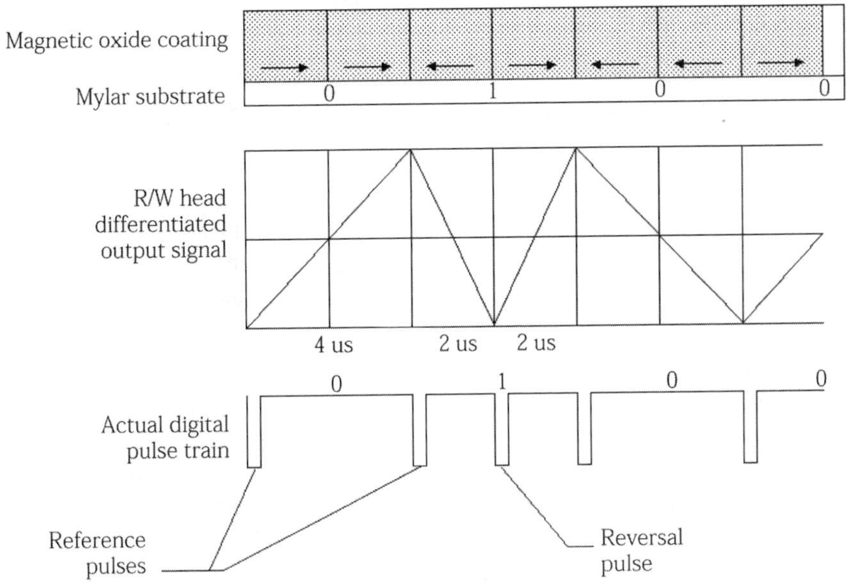

FIGURE 21-2 Flux transitions in floppy disks

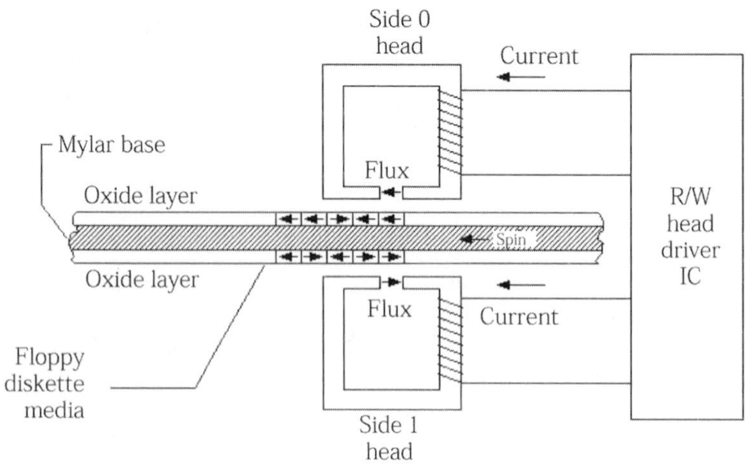

FIGURE 21-3 Floppy drive recording principles

magnetic flux is generated in a head, the resulting tightly focused magnetic field aligns the floppy disk's particles at that point. In general practice, the current signal magnetizes an almost microscopic area on the media. R/W heads actually contact the media while a disk is inserted into a drive.

During a read operation, the heads are left unenergized while the disk spins. Just as varying current produces magnetism in a head, the reverse is also true—varying magnetic influences cause currents to be developed in the head(s). As the spinning media moves across a R/W head, a current is produced in the head coil. The direction of induced current depends on the polarity of each flux orientation. Induced current is proportional to the flux density (how closely each flux transition is placed) and the velocity of the media across each head. In other words, signal strength depends on the rate of change of flux versus time.

Data and Disk Organization

Another important aspect of drive troubleshooting is to understand how data is arranged on the disk. You cannot place data just *anywhere*. The drive would have no idea where to look for the data later on, or would not even know if the data was valid. In order for a disk to be of use, information must be sorted and organized into known, standard locations. Standardized organization ensures that a disk written by one drive will be readable by another drive in a different machine. Table 21-1 compares the major specifications of today's popular drive types.

It is important to note that a floppy disk is a two-dimensional entity possessing both height and width (depth is irrelevant here). This two-dimensional characteristic allows disk information to be recorded in concentric circles, which creates a random-access type of media. *Random access* means that it is possible to move around the disk almost instantly to obtain a desired piece of information. This is a much faster and more convenient approach than a sequential recording medium such as magnetic tape.

Floppy disk organization is not terribly complicated, but there are several important concepts that you must be familiar with. The disk itself is rotated in one direction (usually clockwise) under read/write heads that are perpendicular (at right angles) to the disk's plane. The path of the disk beneath a head describes a circle. As a head steps in and out along a disk's radius, each step describes a circle with a different circumference—rather like lanes on a roadway. Each of these concentric "lanes" is known as a *track*. A typical

TABLE 21-1 COMPARISON OF FLOPPY DISK DRIVE SPECIFICATIONS

SPEC.	5.25 INCH (360KB)	5.25 INCH (1.2MB)	3.5 INCH (720KB)	3.5 INCH (1.44MB)	3.5 INCH (2.88MB)
Bytes per Sector	512	512	512	512	512
Sectors per Track	9	15	9	18	36
Tracks per Side	40	80	80	80	80
Sectors per Cluster	2	1	2	1	2
FAT Length (sectors)	2	7	3	9	9
Number of FATs	2	2	2	2	2
Root Dir Length	7 sectors	14 sectors	7 sectors	14 sectors	15 sectors
Max. Root Entries	112	224	112	224	240
Total Sectors on Disk	708	2371	1426	2847	5726
Media Base	Ferrite	Ferrite	Cobalt	Cobalt	Cobalt
Coercitivity (oersteds)	300	300	600	600	720
Media Descriptor Byte	FDh	F9h	F9h	F0h	F0h
Encoding Format	MFM or FM	MFM or FM	MFM	MFM	MFM
Data Rate (KB/sec)	250 or 125	500 or 250	500	500	500

3.5-inch disk offers 160 tracks—80 tracks on each side of the media. Tracks have a finite width that is defined largely by the drive size, head size, and media. When a R/W head jumps from track to track, it must jump precisely the correct distance to position itself in the middle of another track. If positioning is not correct, the head may encounter data signals from two adjacent tracks. Faulty positioning almost invariably results in disk errors. Also notice that the circumference of each track drops as the head moves toward the disk's center. With less space and a constant rate of spin, data is densest on the innermost tracks (79 or 159 depending on the disk side) and least dense on the outermost tracks (0 or 80). A track is also known as a *cylinder*.

Every cylinder is divided into smaller units called *sectors*. There are 18 sectors on every track of a 3.5-inch disk. Sectors serve two purposes. First, a sector stores 512 bytes of data. With 18 sectors per track and 160 tracks per disk, an 8.89 cm disk holds 2880 sectors (18 x 160). At 512 bytes per sector, a formatted disk can handle about (2880 x 512) 1,474,560 bytes of data. In actual practice, this amount is often slightly less, to allow for boot sector and file allocation information. Sectors are referenced in groups called *clusters* or *allocation units*. While hard drives can group 16 or more sectors into a cluster, floppy drives only use 1 or 2 sectors in a cluster.

Second, and perhaps more important, a sector provides housekeeping data that identifies the sector, the track, and error-checking results from cyclical redundancy check (CRC) calculations. The location of each sector and housekeeping information is set down during the format process. Once formatted, only the sector data and CRC results are updated when a disk is written. Sector ID and synchronization data is never rewritten unless the disk is reformatted. This extra information means that each sector actually holds more than 512 bytes, but you only have access to the 512 data bytes in a sector during normal disk read/write operations. If sector ID data is accidentally overwritten or corrupted, the user data in the afflicted sector becomes unreadable.

The format process also writes a bit of other important information to the disk. The boot record is the first sector on a disk (sector 0). It contains several key parameters that describe the characteristics of the disk. If the disk is bootable, the boot sector will also run the files (IO.SYS and MSDOS.SYS) that load DOS. In addition to the boot record, a File Allocation Table (FAT) is placed on track 00. The FAT acts as a table of contents for the disk. As files are added and erased, the FAT is updated to reflect the contents of each cluster. As you might imagine, a working FAT is critical to the proper operation of a disk. If the FAT is accidentally overwritten or corrupted, the entire disk can become useless. Without a viable FAT, the computer has no other way to determine what files are available or where they are spread throughout the disk. The very first byte in a FAT is the *media descriptor* byte, which allows the drive to recognize the type of disk that is inserted.

Media Problems

Magnetic media has come a long way in the last decade or so. Today's high-quality magnetic materials, combined with the benefits of precise, high-volume production equipment, produce disks that are exceptionally reliable over normal long-term use in a floppy disk drive. However, floppy disks are removable items. The care they receive in physical handling and the storage environment where they are kept will greatly impact a disk's life span.

The most troubling and insidious problem plaguing floppy disk media is the accidental influence of magnetic fields. Any magnetized item in close proximity to a floppy disk poses a potential threat. Permanent magnets such as refrigerator magnets or magnetic paper clips are prime sources of stray fields. Electromagnetic sources like telephone ringers, monitor or TV degaussing coils, and all types of motors will corrupt data if the media is close enough. The best policy is to keep all floppy disks in a dedicated container placed well away from stray magnetic fields.

Disks and magnetic media are also subject to a wide variety of physical damage. Substrates and media are manufactured to very tight tolerances, so anything at all that alters the precise surface features of a floppy disk can cause problems. The introduction of hair, dirt, or dust through the disk's head access aperture, wild temperature variations, fingerprints on the media, or any substantial impact or flexing of the media can cause temporary loss of contact between media and head. When loss of contact occurs, data is lost and a number of disk errors can occur. Head wear and the accumulation of worn oxides also affect head contact. Once again, storing disks in a dedicated container located well out of harm's way is often the best means of protection.

DRIVE CONSTRUCTION

At the core of a floppy drive (Figure 21-4) is a frame assembly (15). It is the single, main structure for mounting the drive's mechanisms and electronics. Frames are typically made from die-cast aluminum to provide a strong, rigid foundation for the drive. The front bezel (18) attaches to the frame to provide a clean, cosmetic appearance and to offer a fixed slot for disk insertion or removal. For 3.5-inch drives, bezels often include a small colored lens, a disk ejection button hole, and a flap to cover the disk slot when the drive is empty. A spindle motor assembly (17) uses an outer-rotor DC motor fabricated onto a small PC board. The motor's shaft is inserted into that large hole in the frame. A disk's metal drive hub automatically interlocks to the spindle. For 5.25-inch disks, the center hole is clamped between two halves of a spindle assembly. The halves clamp the disk when the drive lever is locked down. The disk activity LED (20) illuminates through the bezel's colored lens whenever spindle motor activity is in progress. Figure 21-5 shows the spindle motor assembly from the underside of the drive.

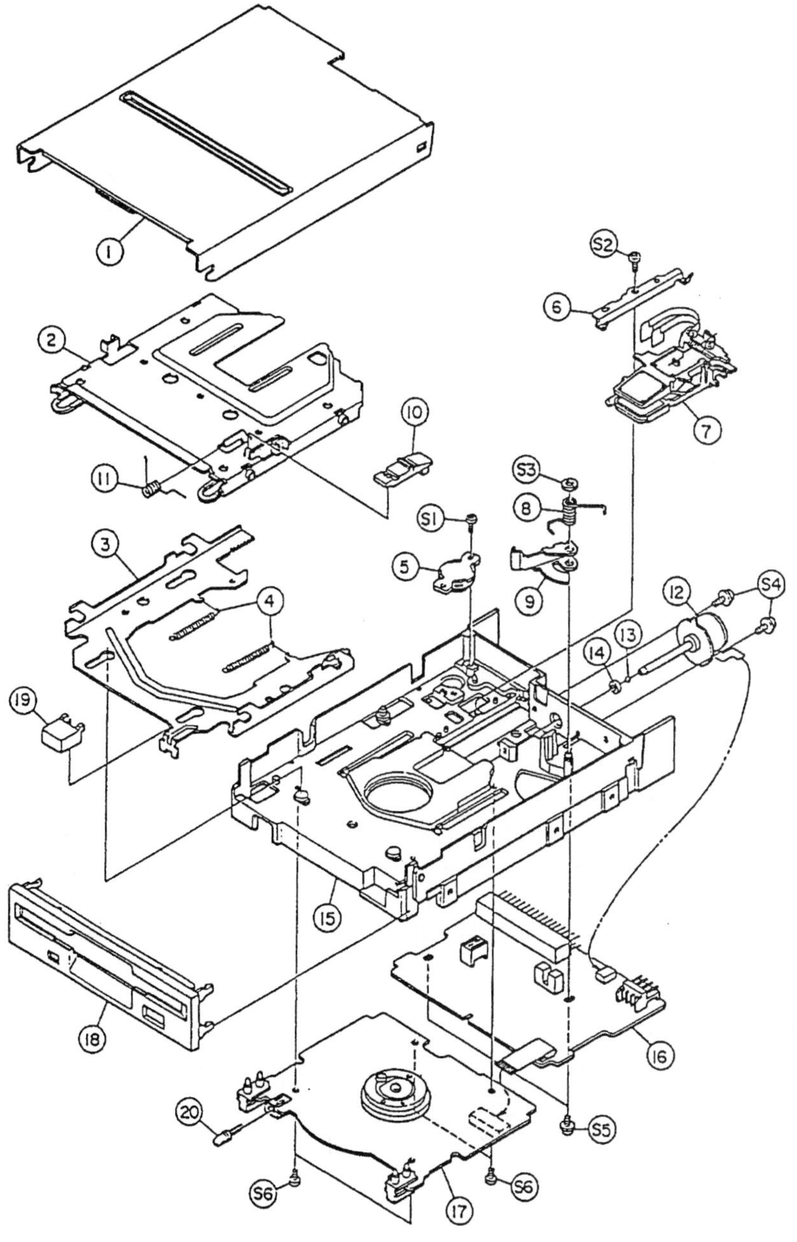

FIGURE 21-4 Exploded diagram of a floppy disk drive assembly (Teac America, Inc.)

Just behind the spindle motor is the drive's control electronics (16 on Figure 21-4). It contains the circuitry needed to operate the drive's motors, R/W heads, and sensors. A standardized interface is used to connect the drive to a floppy drive controller. Figure 21-6 shows a close-up of a drive's control board

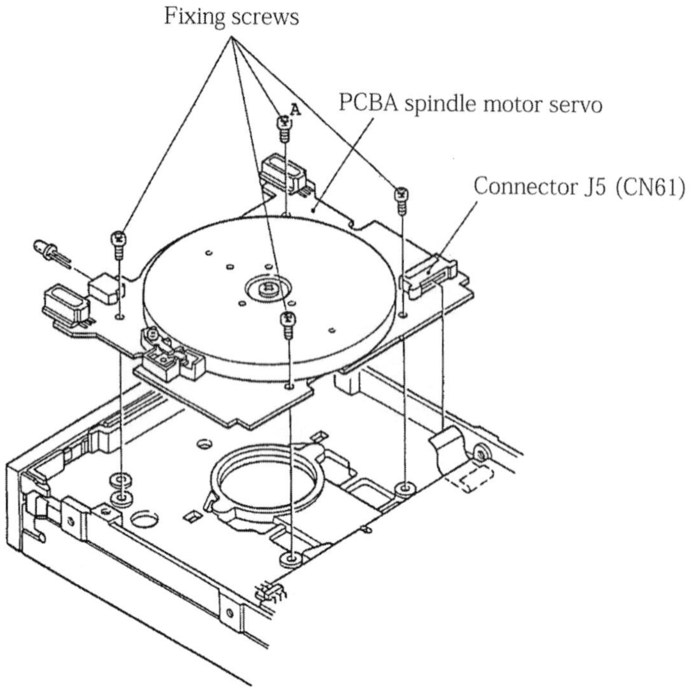

FIGURE 21-5 Underside view of a floppy drive spindle motor assembly (Teac America, Inc.)

(note the optoisolator just below U1). The read/write head assembly (7 on Figure 21-4), also sometimes called a head carriage assembly, holds a set of two R/W heads. Head 0 is the lower head (underside of the disk), and head 1 is on top. A head stepping motor (12) is added to ensure even and consistent movement between tracks. A threaded rod at the motor end is what actually moves the heads. A mechanical damper (5) helps to smooth the disk's travel into or out of the drive. Figure 21-7 shows a close-up of the R/W heads and stepping motor.

When a disk is inserted through the bezel, the disk is restrained by a diskette clamp assembly (2 on Figure 21-4). To eject the disk, you would press the ejector button (19), which pushes a slider mechanism (3). When the ejector button is fully depressed, the disk will disengage from the spindle and pop out of the drive. For 5.25-inch drives, the disk is released whenever the drive door is opened. Your particular drive may contain other miscellaneous components. Finally, the entire upper portion of a drive can be covered by a metal shield (1).

Drive Electronics

Proper drive operation depends on the intimate cooperation between magnetic media, electromechanical devices, and dedicated electronics. Floppy drive electronics is responsible for two major tasks: controlling the drive's physical operations and managing the flow of data in or out of the drive. These tasks are not nearly as simple as they sound, but the sleek, low-profile drives in today's computer systems are a far cry from the clunky, full-height drives found in early systems. Older drives needed a large number of ICs spanning several boards that had to be fitted to the chassis. However, the drive in your computer right now

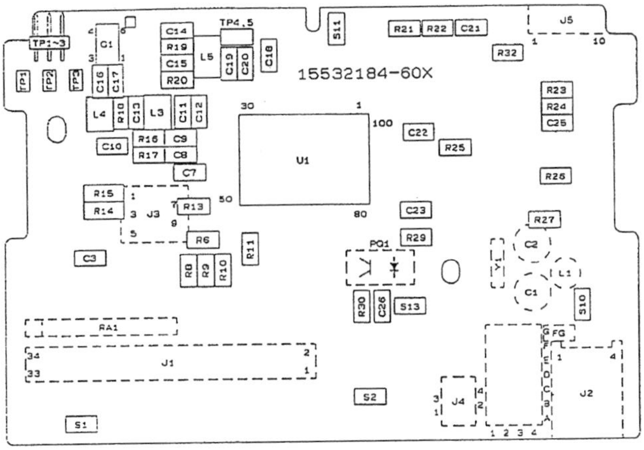

FIGURE 21-6 Typical floppy drive main logic/interface board (Teac America, Inc.)

is probably implemented with only a few highly integrated ICs that are neatly surface mounted on two small, opposing PC boards. This part of the chapter discusses the drive's operating circuits. A complete block diagram for a Teac 3.5-inch floppy drive is illustrated in Figure 21-8. (The figure is shown with a floppy disk *inserted.*)

Write-protect sensors are used to detect the position of a disk's file-protect tab. For 3.5-inch disks, the write-protect notch must be covered to allow both read and write operations. If the notch is open, the disk can only be read. Optoisolators are commonly used as write-protect sensors since an open notch will easily allow light through, while a closed notch will cut off the light path.

21

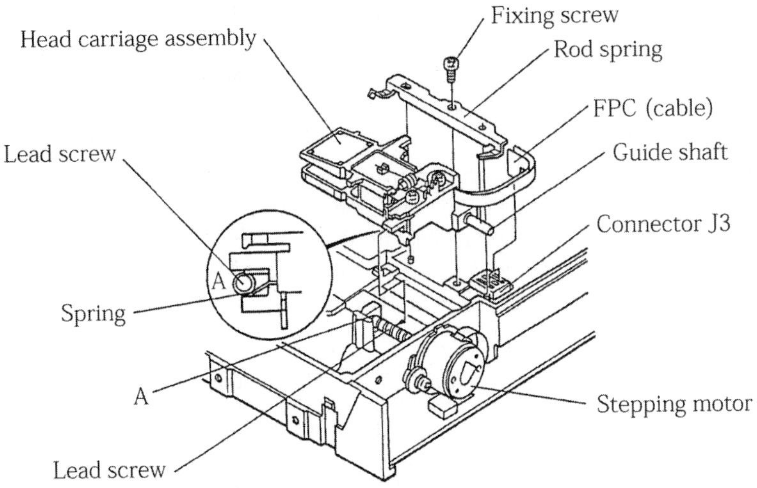

FIGURE 21-7 Detailed view of a R/W head and stepping motor (Teac America, Inc.)

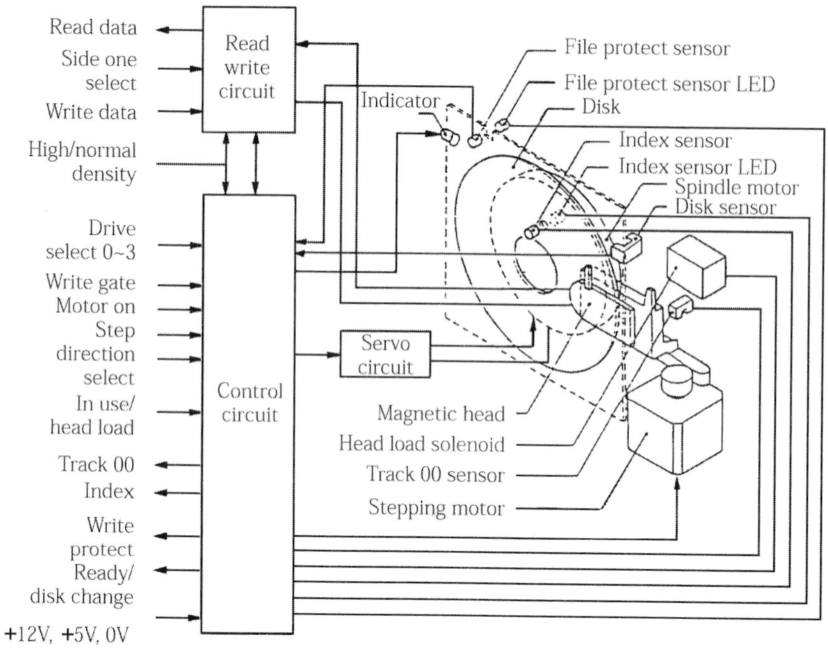

FIGURE 21-8 Block diagram of a floppy drive

Before the drive is allowed to operate at all, a disk must be inserted properly and interlocked with the spindle. A disk-in-place sensor detects the presence or absence of a disk. Like the write-protect sensor, disk sensors are often mechanical switches that are activated by disk contact. If drive access is attempted without a disk in place, the sensor causes the drive's logic to induce a DOS "Disk Not Ready" error code. It is not unusual to find an optoisolator acting as a disk-in-place sensor.

The electronics of a 3.5-inch drive must be able to detect whether the disk contains normal (double) density or high-density media. A high-density sensor looks for the hole that is found near the top of all high-density disk bodies. A mechanical switch is typically used to detect the high-density hole, but a separate LED/detector pair may also be used. When the hole is absent (a double-density disk), the switch is activated upon disk insertion. If the hole is present (a high-density disk), the switch is not actuated. All switch conditions are translated into logic signals used by the drive electronics.

Before disk data can be read or written, the system must read the disk's boot sector information and FAT. Programs and data can be broken up and scattered all over a disk, but the FAT must always be located at a known location so that the drive knows where to look for it. The FAT is always located on track 00—the first track of disk side 0. A track 00 sensor provides a logic signal when the heads are positioned over track 00. Each time a read or write is ordered, the head assembly is stepped to track 00. Although a drive "remembers" how many steps should be needed to position the heads precisely over track 00, an optoisolator or switch senses the head carriage assembly position. At track 00, the head carriage should interrupt the optoisolator or actuate the switch. If the drive supposedly steps to track 00 and there is no sensor signal to confirm the position (or the signal occurs *before* the drive has finished stepping), the drive assumes that a head-positioning error has occurred. Head step counts and sensor outputs virtually always agree unless the sensor has failed or the drive has been physically damaged.

Spindle speed is a critically important drive parameter. Once the disk has reached its running velocity (300 or 360 RPM), the drive must maintain that velocity for the duration of the disk access process. Unfortunately, simply telling the spindle motor to move is no guarantee that the motor is turning—a sensor is required to measure the motor's speed. This is the *index sensor*. Signals from an index sensor are fed back to the drive electronics, and spindle speed is adjusted in order to maintain a constant rotation. Most drives use optoisolators as index sensors. They work by detecting the motion of small slots cut in a template or the spindle rotor itself. When a disk is spinning, the output from an index sensor is a fast logic pulse sent along to the drive electronics. Keep in mind that some index sensors are magnetic. A magnetic sensor typically operates by detecting the proximity of small slots in a template or the spindle rotor, but the pulse output is essentially identical to that of the optoisolator.

Physical Interface

The drive must receive control and data signals from the computer and deliver status and data signals back to the computer as required. The series of connections between a floppy disk PC board and the floppy disk controller circuit is known as the *physical interface*. The advantage to using a standard interface is that various drives made by different manufacturers can be "mixed and matched" by computer designers. A floppy drive working in one computer will operate properly in another computer regardless of the manufacturer as long as the same physical interface scheme is being used.

Floppy drives use a physical interface that includes two cables: a power cable and a signal cable. Both cable pinouts are illustrated in Figure 21-9. The classical power connector is a 4-pin Molex connector, although many low-profile drives used in mobile computers (laptops or notebooks) may use much smaller

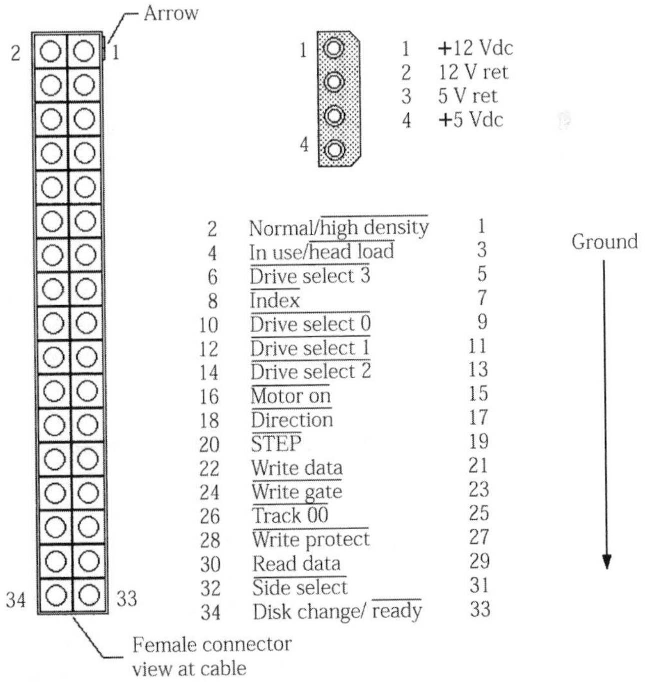

FIGURE 21-9 Diagram of a standard 34-pin floppy drive interface

connector designs. Floppy drives require two voltage levels: +5.0 Vdc for logic and +12.0 Vdc for motors. The return (ground) for each supply is also provided at the connector. The signal connector is typically a 34-pin *insulation displacement connector* (IDC) cable. Notice that all odd-numbered pins are ground lines, while the even-numbered pins carry active signals. Logic signals are all TTL-level signals.

In a system with more than one floppy drive, the particular destination drive must be selected before any read or write is attempted. A drive is selected using the appropriate "drive select" line (drive select 0 to 3) on pins 10, 12, 14, and 6, respectively. For notebook or sub-notebook systems where only one floppy drive is used, only drive select 0 is used. The remaining select inputs may simply be disconnected. The spindle motor servo circuit is controlled through the "motor on" signal (pin 16). When pin 16 is logic 0, the spindle motor should *spin up* (approach a stable operating speed). The media must be spinning at the proper rate before reading or writing can take place.

To move the R/W heads, the host computer must specify the number of steps a head carriage assembly must move and the direction in which steps must occur. A "direction select" signal (pin 18) tells the coil driver circuit whether the heads should be moved inward (toward the spindle) or outward (away from the spindle). The "step" signal (pin 20) provides the pulse sequence that actually steps the head motor in the desired direction. The combination of step and direction select controls can position the R/W heads over the disk very precisely. The "side select" control pin (pin 32) determines whether head 0 or head 1 is active for reading or writing—only one side of the disk can be manipulated at a time.

Two signals are needed to write data to a disk. The "write gate" signal (pin 24) is logic 0 when writing is to occur, and logic 1 when writing is inhibited (or reading). After the write gate is asserted, data can be written to the disk over the "write data" line (pin 22). When reading, the data that is extracted from the disk is delivered from the "read data" line (pin 30).

Each of the drive's sensor conditions is sent over the physical interface. The "track 00" signal (pin 26) is logic 0 whenever the head carriage assembly is positioned over track 00. The "write protect" line (pin 28) is logic 0 whenever the disk's write-protect notch is in place. Writing is inhibited whenever the write protect signal is asserted. The "index" signal (pin 8) supplies a chain of pulses from the index sensor. Media type is indicated by the "normal/high-density" sensor (pin 2). The status of the disk-in-place sensor is indicated over the "disk change ready" line (pin 34).

FLOPPY DRIVE INSTALLATION AND REPLACEMENT

Unlike many of the various peripherals and drives that are now available for a PC, floppy drives are almost universal in their design and features. There is usually very little to consider since the drives are all the same. However, there are three issues that you must concern yourself with: available drive bay space, BIOS compatibility, and power connections. After you've selected the drive, installation should be straightforward.

- *Drive bay space* The trend toward smaller, low-profile enclosures has put a lot of pressure on available drive space. Given that many systems are already fitted with a floppy drive, hard drive, and CD-ROM drive, there is rarely a fourth bay available for even a second hard drive. One of the first problems when planning for a new floppy drive is to locate an external drive bay. If you do not have an external drive bay available, you may be able to move a hard drive to an internal drive bay. This relocates the hard drive and frees an external drive bay for another floppy drive. If you cannot free a drive bay for another floppy drive, you may need to consider a larger case (one with more external drive bays), use an external "parallel port" floppy drive, or remove another unneeded drive to make space for the floppy.

- *BIOS compatibility* One problem with the PC/AT (i286) and early i386 systems was that their BIOS often did not support the high-density 3.5-inch drive format. The drive could be read from and written to properly, but the BIOS would only allow disks to be formatted to 720KB (instead of 1.44MB). The solution to this incompatibility has been either to upgrade the BIOS (to a version later than 11/85) or use the DRIVER.SYS utility in DOS to explicitly specify the physical drive as a high-density device. If you suspect that DRIVER.SYS is needed to support a 3.5-inch high-density floppy drive on an older PC, open your CONFIG.SYS file and try a command line such as:

  ```
  device=c:\dos\driver.sys /D:1 /F:7
  ```

  This command line creates a new "logical" floppy drive that is actually the same physical floppy drive specified by the /D switch (0=A:, 1=B:). The /F switch determines the type of drive to be created. In this case, a value of 7 indicates a 3.5-inch 1.44MB drive. Check your DOS manual for additional parameters. This problem has been completely eliminated in virtually all subsequent BIOS releases after late 1985 and early 1986, but it can cause some confusion when dealing with very old PCs.
- *Power connections* A power supply only offers a limited number of drive power connectors. In small systems, there may not be a free drive power connector for another floppy drive. When this occurs, you may use a Y-splitter cable to add another power connector. However, place the Y cable in with the existing floppy drive. (Never split power from critical drives such as the hard drive.) If you're simply replacing a defective floppy, just reuse the existing power connector.

Typical Installation

In most cases, installing a second floppy drive is a three-step process: configure the drive jumper(s), mount and cable the drive, and configure the new drive in CMOS. Although a floppy drive installation is often a quick and painless procedure—even for a novice—there are a few nuances that you should be aware of. When followed carefully, this process can typically be completed in under 30 minutes. If you're simply replacing an old or defective floppy drive, remove the old drive first, then follow the procedures below.

> It's normally a good idea to perform a complete system backup of your hard drives before attempting any kind of drive work. Although drive installation should not affect your hard drives in any way, backups will protect your data and system configuration from accidental data loss.

> Turn the system off and unplug it from the AC receptacle before proceeding. This protects the new device and your personal safety.

Prepare the System Remove the screws holding down the outer cover, and place those screws aside in a safe place. Gently remove the PC's outer cover and set it aside (out of the path of normal floor traffic). You should now be able to look into the PC and observe the open drive bay, the motherboard, and any expansion boards and drives that are installed.

> Remember to use an antistatic wrist strap whenever working inside a PC. This will prevent accidental static discharge, which can damage the computer's delicate electronics.

Prepare the Drive Bay Now that the outer cover is removed, open the desired drive bay. In many cases, this is as simple as removing the plastic bezel that covers an empty bay. (The bezel will usually pop right out.) If you must relocate an existing drive, things get a bit more complicated. First, decide where the drive (almost always a hard drive) will be located—often an internal bay in the rear of the PC. You can then remove the mounting screws, disconnect the power and signal cables from the hard drive, and slide the hard drive out of the bay. Remount the hard drive in the internal bay, and gently secure each screw into place. (Be careful not to overtighten the screws.) Reattach the power and signal cables to the hard drive. Pay particular attention when connecting the signal cable. If the cable is installed backward, the hard drive will not function. The red or blue stripe along one side of the ribbon cable always marks pin 1.

The procedure is a bit different when replacing an existing floppy drive. Unbolt the existing drive, and then disconnect the power and signal cables. Slide the old drive out of the bay and set it aside carefully. If you have a good-quality antistatic bag available, seal the old drive in the antistatic bag. At this point, you should have an open drive bay. Take a quick inventory and make sure that you have a floppy signal cable and power connector available. You may need a Y-splitter connector in order to tap power from another drive.

> When using a Y-splitter to tap power from another drive, never split power from a hard drive. This can cause erratic drive (and system) operation.

Set the Floppy Jumpers Before installing the new drive, remove it from any protective packaging and locate any jumpers or DIP switches on the drive. A manual will be important here. It will be necessary to set at least four conditions: the drive select jumper, the disk change jumper, the media sensor jumper, and the terminating resistors.

The drive select (or DS) jumper allows the drive to be set as drive 0, 1, 2, or 3. Although most XT and AT controllers support four floppy drives, each cable supports only two. As a general rule, you will set both the drives as B:. (You'll see why below.) However, interpreting the jumper selections is not always intuitive, because different manufacturers mark the jumpers differently. For example, instead of 0, 1, 2, and 3, a drive may be labeled 1, 2, 3, and 4. Other variations include DS0 and DS1, or DS1 and DS2. As a rule of thumb, the lowest designation is generally considered to be drive A:, the next highest digit is considered drive B:, and so on. Since just about all floppy drive cables use a twist between the two floppy drive connectors, both floppy drives can be set to the second jumper position (drive B:). As a consequence, the twist will automatically swap the *endmost* drive to A:. If in doubt, and there's a twist in the cable, set the drive select jumpers to B:. Now, if there is no twist in the floppy cable (a very rare occurrence), be sure to set the endmost drive to A:, and set the middle drive to B:. (Since this is a daisy-chain configuration, you could actually reverse this order, but it is not traditional.)

Terminating resistors add another wrinkle to the drive setup. As with many other daisy-chain cable applications, terminating resistors are used at both ends of the signal cable to establish ideal signal characteristics. Normally, floppy drives come equipped with terminating resistors installed. Since most systems use a single drive installed at the end of the cable (as drive A:), this is generally a good default. When installing a single drive, be sure that the drive has terminating resistors installed. When installing a second floppy drive as drive A:, be sure it has terminating resistors in place, and check that the second drive (in the middle cable position) has no terminating resistors. When installing a second floppy drive as drive B:, be sure that the terminating resistors are removed.

> Although the "middle" (B:) floppy drive should have its terminating resistors removed or disabled, this is not always necessary because of the low-frequency signals on the floppy drive cable. In most cases, you could leave the middle (B:) floppy drive with its terminating resistors in place.

The disk change jumper is a vital part of almost all contemporary drives. This signal tells the PC when a disk is removed so that when a new disk is inserted and read, the directory information will be cached in the system. The disk change signal should be enabled on all drives except for old 5.25-inch 360KB drives. Finally, the media sensor (on 1.44MB and 2.88MB drives) jumper should be enabled wherever possible. The sensor allows the drive to detect whether a 760KB, 1.44MB, or 2.88MB disk is installed.

> Today, virtually all commercial floppy drives are configured to serve as the A: drive (jumpered as B: but connected after the floppy cable twist) in a single-floppy system.

Mount the New Floppy Drive Now that the floppy drive is configured, slide it gently into the open drive bay. Line up the four mounting holes, and screw the drive in carefully. Be sure not to tighten the mounting screws excessively. This can warp the drive's frame and cause R/W problems or premature drive failure. Make it a point to use screws of the proper size and length to do the job.

Connect Power and Signal Cables Once the drive is installed and mounted securely, connect the power and signal cables as required. The four-pin power cable is relatively foolproof because of its keyed shape. For the signal cable, however, take care to install the card edge or IDC-type connector in the correct orientation. If the signal cable is installed backward, the drive will not work. (The system may not even boot.) The red or blue stripe along one side of the ribbon cable always represents pin 1.

Update CMOS Settings If the steps are performed correctly, the new floppy drive should now be fully installed. Before you can actually use the drive, you must update the system CMOS entries to accommodate the new drive. Make sure that any tools or extra hardware are removed from the system, reattach the AC cord to the power supply, and then reboot the computer. As the system boots, start the CMOS setup routine and adjust the configuration as needed for your new floppy drive. You'll need to specify whether a 5.25-inch 360KB, 5.25-inch 1.2MB, 3.5-inch 720KB, 3.5-inch 1.44MB, or 3.5-inch 2.88MB floppy drive is installed. If you have updated or replaced an old drive, make sure that the drive parameters reflect the *new* device. If you have added a second drive, enter the appropriate parameters for that new drive. When the settings are correct, save the system CMOS and reboot the system so that your changes can take effect.

Test the Drive Insert a known-good floppy disk in the drive. If the installation is correct, you should see the new drive designator under DOS, as an available option under the Windows File Manager, or as a new drive entry when double-clicking on My Computer on the Windows 95/98 desktop. Try writing and reading a few files from the drive. You might also try formatting a blank disk in the new drive. If these tests are successful, you can be confident that the new drive is working properly. Be sure to remove any tools or hardware from the system, and then reinstall the system's outer housings. Do not use excessive pressure to tighten the screws. Try the drive one more time, and return the system to service.

Reversing Floppy Drive Assignments

Sometimes it may be necessary to reverse the letter assignments of your floppy drives. This often happens when you wish to boot from a floppy drive that is not in a boot order supported by the BIOS. For example, you may want to change the boot order if you have a 5.25-inch drive as A: and a 3.5-inch drive as B:, and the boot order doesn't support booting from the B: drive. Fortunately, you can easily reverse the drive order by reversing the drives physically and logically. Remember to power-down and unplug the computer before beginning.

Leave the Drive Jumpers in Place Remember that for most PCs, both floppy drives are jumpered as B:. (It is the "flip" in the floppy drive cable that turns the endmost drive to A:.) If your floppy drive cable does indeed have a flip, you can leave the floppy drives jumpered the way they are. The only time you'll need to reverse the drive's ID jumpers is when there is no flip in the cable, and each drive must be jumpered with a unique ID.

Exchange the Floppy Cable Connections Now reconnect the floppy drive cable, placing the middle drive at the end, and the endmost drive at the middle. Depending on the way each drive is arranged in your system's case (and the amount of slack in the floppy cable), it may be necessary to actually exchange the floppy drives in the drive bays also. If this is the case, you should disconnect the power cables from the floppy drives, unbolt each drive, reinstall each drive in the opposite drive bay, and then reattach the power and signal cables.

> Now is a good time to check the floppy signal cable. If the cable is loose or appears damaged, it should be replaced.

> If the middle drive had terminating resistors disabled, you may need to enable those terminating resistors when you place that drive at the end of the cable (A:), and disable the terminating resistors in the drive that you swapped to the middle (B:).

Reverse the Drive Assignments in CMOS When you first reapply power to the PC, you will probably receive an error message indicating that the equipment detected does not match the equipment specified in the CMOS setup. This is because the physical drives are now reversed, but the CMOS still "expects" to find the floppy drives in their original positions. You'll need to start the CMOS setup and reverse the floppy drive assignments. For example, if you had a 5.25-inch 1.2MB floppy as A: and a 3.5-inch 1.44MB floppy as B:, you'll need to assign a 3.5-inch 1.44MB floppy as A: and a 5.25-inch 1.2MB floppy as B: after you make the physical drive swap. Save your changes and reboot the computer so that your changes can take effect. Test both drives to verify that each is working.

TROUBLESHOOTING FLOPPY DISK SYSTEMS

This part of the chapter is concerned with drive problems that cannot be corrected with cleaning or mechanical adjustments. To perform some of the following tests, you should have a known-good floppy disk that has been properly formatted. The disk can contain files, but be certain that any such files are backed up properly on a hard drive or another floppy disk. *If you can't afford to lose the files on a disk, don't use the disk.*

Repair vs. Replace

As with so many other PC assemblies, the price of floppy drives has dropped tremendously over the last few years. Now that the price of a standard 3.5-inch drive is roughly equal to one hour of labor, most technicians ask whether it is better to simply replace a floppy drive outright rather than attempt a repair. Ultimately, the decision should depend on volume. Clearly, it makes little sense for a anyone to invest valuable time in repairing a single drive. When there are a large number of drives to be repaired, however, enterprising technicians who choose to deal in floppy drive service can effectively provide rebuilt or refurbished drives to their customers. (See Chapter 22 for floppy drive testing and alignment information.)

Preliminary Testing

Proper testing is essential for any type of drive repair. Most drive alignment packages, such as DriveProbe by Accurite Technologies or DriveProbe by DataDepot, measure and display a drive's parameters (Figure 21-10). When floppy drive trouble occurs, running a diagnostic can help determine whether the drive mechanics or electronics are at fault. Although you can swap a drive symptomatically, thorough testing is an inexpensive means to verify your suspicions before spending money to replace subassemblies.

Guidelines for Troubleshooting Floppy Disks Under Windows 95/98

Today, a great deal of everyday work takes place under Windows 95/98. As a result, floppy drive problems are often first noticed under Windows. When Windows reports trouble reading a floppy drive, try the steps below to identify and resolve the issue through Windows.

AUTOMATIC Drive Test 'Esc'- For Previous Menu

Test	Track	Head 0 Data	Head 1 Data	Test Limits	Results	
Speed	NA	300 RPM / 199.7 mS		300 ± 6 RPM	Pass	NA
Eccentricity	44	100 uI	NA	0 ± 300 uI	Pass	NA
Radial	0	96% 50 uI	100% 0 uI	60 - 100 %	Pass	Pass
Radial	40	93% -100 uI	90% -150 uI	60 - 100 %	Pass	Pass
Radial	79	96% 50 uI	90% -150 uI	60 - 100 %	Pass	Pass
Azimuth	76	6 Min	4 Min	0 ± 30 Min	Pass	Pass
Index	0	414 uS	407 uS	400 ± 600 uS	Pass	Pass
Index	79	397 uS	380 uS	400 ± 600 uS	Pass	Pass
Hysteresis	40	100 uI	NA	0 ± 250 uI	Pass	NA

uI = Micro-inches uS = Microsecond mS = Millisecond
Min = Minutes NA = Not Applicable NT = Not Tested

Note: Radial is expressed as LOBE RATIO and OFFSET from track center line.
Auto Test Completed 'Esc' For Previous Menu

FIGURE 21-10 A DriveProbe screen display for automatic drive testing (Accurite Technologies, Inc.)

Check the Floppy Controller Using the Safe Mode Start Windows in Safe Mode and try to access the floppy drive. To start Windows 95 in Safe Mode, restart the computer, and then press F8 when you see the message "Starting Windows 95." Then choose Safe Mode from the Startup menu. To start Windows 98 in Safe Mode, restart your computer, press and hold down the CTRL key after your computer completes the power-on self-test (POST), and then choose Safe Mode from the Startup menu. If you can access the floppy drive in Safe Mode, follow these steps:

1. Right-click the My Computer icon from your desktop, and then click Properties on the menu that appears.
2. Click the Device Manager tab, and then double-click the Floppy Disk Controllers entry.
3. Highlight the floppy disk controller for the drive you are having problems with, and then click Properties.
4. In Windows 95, click the Original Configuration (Current) check box to clear it. In Windows 98, click the Disable In This Hardware Profile check box to select it. This disables the Windows protected-mode driver for the floppy disk drive controller.
5. Click OK and restart Windows normally.

If you can now access the floppy disk drive successfully after following the procedure above, you may be faced with one or more of the following conditions:

- The floppy disk drive controller may not be supported in protected mode.
- There are drivers loading in the CONFIG.SYS or AUTOEXEC.BAT file that may be necessary for protected-mode access.
- There are drivers loading in the CONFIG.SYS or AUTOEXEC.BAT file that may be causing conflicts in Windows and need to be disabled.

21

If you still cannot access the floppy disk drive, follow these steps to redetect the floppy drive controller:

1. Right-click the My Computer icon from your desktop, and then click Properties on the menu that appears.
2. Click the Device Manager tab, and then double-click the Floppy Disk Controllers entry.
3. Highlight the floppy disk controller, click Remove to remove the controller, and then click OK.
4. Open your Control Panel, and then double-click the Add New Hardware icon.
5. Click Next, and then click Yes to allow Windows to detect the hardware in your computer.
6. When the Add New Hardware wizard is finished, restart the computer and try the floppy drive again.

Redetecting the floppy disk controller should correct addressing problems with the controller by detecting the correct address range. If the floppy disk controller is not detected correctly, there may be a problem with the floppy disk controller. If the floppy disk controller is redetected, but you still cannot access the floppy drive, there may be a problem with the disk itself.

Suspect Your Disk(s) One or more of your disks may be damaged. Use a disk utility (such as ScanDisk) to test the disk for damage, or try a known-good, high-quality disk.

> Never use a disk utility that is not compliant with Windows 95 or Windows 98. Noncompliant disk utilities can damage DMF (compressed) disks. The Windows ScanDisk tool recognizes DMF disks and does not damage them.

You may also try the following command from a DOS command prompt:

```
C:\> copy a:\*.* nul
```

For example, if you are having problems with drive A:, insert a disk you are having problems with in drive A:, and type the command. This command copies the files on the disk to a null device. If there is a problem copying the files, error messages appear on the screen, and that disk is probably defective.

Suspect Your Tape Backup Floppy problems are known to occur under Windows when using an Irwin tape backup unit under Windows 95/98. Windows 95/98 setup should remove the following statement from the [386Enh] section of the SYSTEM.INI file:

```
device=<path>\VIRWT.386
```

If you reinstall the Irwin tape backup software after you install Windows 95/98, this statement is placed in the SYSTEM.INI file again, and can cause conflicts with floppy disk access in Windows. When this occurs, you must comment-out that line in SYSTEM.INI.

Check the CMOS Setup Reboot your computer and verify that the floppy drive entries in your CMOS setup are correct. If not, Windows will not be able to recognize your floppy drive hardware. If you must make changes to your CMOS setup, remember to save your changes as you exit.

Check for Device Conflicts Device conflicts (reported by the Device Manager) can cause problems reading from and writing to floppy disks. You can generally resolve device conflict problems by changing or removing the resources from Device Manager that are causing the conflict. Typical conflicts occur with hard drive controller cards, video cards, or COM ports.

Symptoms

SYMPTOM 21-1 **The floppy drive is completely dead** The system boots, but the disk does not even initialize when inserted. This behavior can be caused by a number of important problems, so consider each possibility carefully before acting.

- *Check the floppy disk.* Make sure the disk is properly inserted into the floppy drive assembly. If the disk does not enter and seat just right within the drive, disk access will be impossible. Try several different disks to ensure that the test disk is not defective. It may be necessary to partially disassemble the computer to access the drive and see the overall assembly. Free or adjust any jammed assemblies or linkages to correct disk insertion. If you can not get disks to insert properly, replace the floppy drive.
- *Check the drive power.* Loose connectors or faulty cable wiring can easily disable a floppy drive. Use your multimeter to measure DC voltages at the power connector. Place your meter's ground lead on pin 2 and measure +12 Vdc at pin 1. Ground your meter on pin 3 and measure +5 Vdc at pin 4. If either or both of these voltages is low or missing, troubleshoot your computer power supply or replace the supply outright.
- *Check the signal cable.* Verify that the drive's 34-pin ribbon cable is attached securely at the drive(s) and at the drive controller. Reattach the signal cable if it's loose, and try another signal cable if necessary.
- *Replace the floppy drive.* If the problem persists, chances are that the floppy drive is defective. (Perhaps the disk-in-place sensor has failed.) Try replacing the floppy drive with a known-good drive from another system.
- *Replace the floppy drive controller.* If a new floppy drive still does not resolve the problem, you may have a defective floppy drive controller circuit. If so, you may also receive a floppy drive or controller error from the system BIOS at boot time. Try disabling the existing floppy controller and install an expansion card controller (with only the floppy controller portion enabled).

21

SYMPTOM 21-2 **The floppy drive rotates a disk, but will not seek to the desired track** This type of symptom generally suggests that the head-positioning stepping motor is inhibited or defective, but all other floppy drive functions are working properly.

- *Check the drive for obstructions.* Carefully inspect the head-positioning assembly to be certain that there are no broken parts or obstructions that could jam the read/write heads. You may wish to examine the mechanical system with a disk inserted to be certain that the trouble is not a disk alignment problem, which may be interfering with head movement. Gently remove any obstructions that you may find. Be careful not to accidentally misalign any linkages or mechanical components in the process of clearing an obstruction.
- *Check the drive power.* Remove any disk from the drive and reconnect the drive's signal and power cables. Apply power to the computer and measure drive voltages with your multimeter. Ground your multimeter on pin 2 of the power connector and measure +12 Vdc at pin 1. Move the meter ground to pin 3 and measure +5 Vdc on pin 4. If either voltage is low or absent, troubleshoot your computer power supply or replace the supply outright.
- *Check the signal cable.* Verify that the drive's 34-pin ribbon cable is attached securely at the drive(s) and at the drive controller. Reattach the signal cable if it's loose, and try another signal cable if necessary.
- *Replace the floppy drive.* If the problem persists, chances are that the floppy drive is defective. (Perhaps the head-positioning system has failed.) Try replacing the floppy drive with a known-good drive from another system.

- *Replace the floppy drive controller.* If a new floppy drive still does not resolve the problem, you may have a defective floppy drive controller circuit. If so, you may also receive a floppy drive or controller error from the system BIOS at boot time. Try disabling the existing floppy controller and install an expansion card controller (with only the floppy controller portion enabled).

SYMPTOM 21-3 **The floppy drive heads seek properly, but the spindle does not turn**
This symptom suggests that the spindle motor is inhibited or defective, but all other floppy drive functions are working properly.

- *Check the drive for obstructions.* Power-down the computer and remove the floppy drive. Carefully inspect the spindle motor, drive belt (if used), and spindle assembly. Make certain that there are no broken parts or obstructions that could jam the spindle. If there is a belt between the motor and spindle, make sure the belt is reasonably tight—it should not slip. You should also examine the floppy drive with a disk inserted to be certain that the disk's insertion or alignment is not causing the problem. Double-check your observations using several different disks. Gently remove any obstruction(s) that you may find. Be careful not to cause any accidental damage in the process of clearing an obstruction. Do not add any lubricating agents to the assembly, but gently vacuum or wipe away any significant accumulations of dust or dirt.
- *Check the drive power.* Remove any disk from the drive and reconnect the drive's signal and power cables. Apply power to the computer and measure drive voltages with your multimeter. Ground your multimeter on pin 2 of the power connector and measure +12 Vdc at pin 1. Move the meter ground to pin 3 and measure +5 Vdc on pin 4. If either voltage is low or absent, troubleshoot your computer power supply or replace the supply outright.
- *Check the signal cable.* Verify that the drive's 34-pin ribbon cable is attached securely at the drive(s) and at the drive controller. Reattach the signal cable if it's loose, and try another signal cable if necessary.
- *Replace the floppy drive.* If the problem persists, chances are that the floppy drive is defective. (Perhaps the spindle motor control system has failed.) Try replacing the floppy drive with a known-good drive from another system.
- *Replace the floppy drive controller.* If a new floppy drive still does not resolve the problem, you may have a defective floppy drive controller circuit. If so, you may also receive a floppy drive or controller error from the system BIOS at boot time. Try disabling the existing floppy controller and install an expansion card controller (with only the floppy controller portion enabled).

SYMPTOM 21-4 **The floppy drive will not read from/write to the disk** All other operations appear normal. This type of problem can manifest itself in several ways, but your computer's operating system will usually inform you when a disk read or write error has occurred.

- *Check the disk.* Begin by trying a known-good, properly formatted disk in your suspect drive. A faulty disk can generate some very perplexing read/write problems.
- *Clean the floppy drive.* If a known-good disk does not resolve the problem, try cleaning the read/write heads thoroughly. Do not run the drive with a head-cleaning disk inserted for more than 30 seconds at a time, or you risk damaging the heads with excessive friction.
- *Check the signal cable.* Verify that the drive's 34-pin ribbon cable is attached securely at the drive(s) and at the drive controller. Reattach the signal cable if it's loose, and try another signal cable if necessary.

- *Replace the floppy drive.* If the problem persists, chances are that the floppy drive is defective. (Perhaps the head read/write system has failed.) Try replacing the floppy drive with a known-good drive from another system.
- *Replace the floppy drive controller.* If a new floppy drive still does not resolve the problem, you may have a defective floppy drive controller circuit. If so, you may also receive a floppy drive or controller error from the system BIOS at boot time. Try disabling the existing floppy controller and install an expansion card controller (with only the floppy controller portion enabled).

SYMPTOM 21-5 **The drive is able to write to a write-protected disk** When this kind of problem occurs, it is almost always the drive itself that is defective.

- *Check the disk.* Remove and examine the disk itself to verify that it is actually write protected. If the disk is not write protected, write-protect it appropriately, and try the disk again. You might also try a different disk.
- *Clean the floppy drive.* Try cleaning the drive by blowing clean compressed air into the drive. (Pay particular attention to cleaning off the write-protect sensor.)
- *Replace the floppy drive.* If the problem persists, chances are that the floppy drive is defective—perhaps the write-protect sensor or onboard drive electronics has failed. Try replacing the floppy drive with a known-good drive from another system.

SYMPTOM 21-6 **The drive can only recognize either high- or double-density media, but not both** This type of problem usually appears in 3.5-inch drives during the disk format process when the drive must check the media type.

- *Check the disk.* Verify that you're using the correct disk type. (This is actually a common oversight since many generic disks are unmarked.)
- *Clean the floppy drive.* Try cleaning the drive by blowing clean compressed air into the drive. (Pay particular attention to cleaning off the "media type" sensor.)
- *Check the signal cable.* Verify that the drive's 34-pin ribbon cable is attached securely at the drive(s) and at the drive controller. Reattach the signal cable if it's loose, and try another signal cable if necessary.
- *Replace the floppy drive.* If the problem persists, chances are that the floppy drive is defective—perhaps the "media type" sensor or onboard drive electronics has failed. Try replacing the floppy drive with a known-good drive from another system.

SYMPTOM 21-7 **When a new disk is inserted in the drive, a directory from a previous disk appears** You may have to reset the system in order to get the new disk to be recognized. This is the classic "phantom directory" problem and is usually due to a drive or cable fault.

- *Check the signal cable.* Verify that the drive's 34-pin ribbon cable is attached securely at the drive(s) and at the drive controller. Reattach the signal cable if it's loose, and try another signal cable if necessary.
- *Check the drive's jumpers.* If this is a *new* drive installation, check the floppy drive's jumpers. Some floppy drives allow the DISK CHANGE signal to be enabled or disabled. Make sure the DISK CHANGE signal is enabled.
- *Replace the floppy drive.* If the problem persists, chances are that the floppy drive is defective—perhaps the disk change logic has failed in the drive's electronics. Try replacing the floppy drive with a known-good drive from another system.

> If you suspect a phantom directory, do not initiate any writing to the disk. Its FAT table and directories could be overwritten, rendering the disk's contents inaccessible without careful data recovery procedures.

SYMPTOM 21-8 Double-density (720KB) 3.5-inch disks are not working properly when formatted as high-density (1.44MB) disks This is a common problem when double-density disks are pressed into service as high-density disks. In actual practice, double-density disks use a lower-grade media than high-density disks, which makes double-density disks unreliable when used in high-density mode. Some good-quality disks will tolerate this misuse better than other lower-quality disks. As a general rule, do not use double-density disks as high-density disks.

SYMPTOM 21-9 Your 3.5-inch high-density floppy disk cannot format high-density disks You can read and write to them just fine. This is a problem that plagues older computers (i286 and i386 systems) with after-market high-density drives added. The problem is a lack of BIOS support for high-density formatting—the system is just too old. In such a case, you have a choice. First, you can upgrade your motherboard BIOS to a version that directly supports 3.5-inch high-density disks. You could also use the DRIVER.SYS utility—a DOS driver that allows an existing 3.5-inch drive to be "redefined" as a new logical drive providing high-density support. A typical DRIVER.SYS command line would appear in CONFIG.SYS such as:

```
device = c:\dos\driver.sys /D:1
```

SYMPTOM 21-10 There are no jumpers available on the floppy disk, so it is impossible to change settings This is not a problem as much as it is an inconvenience. Typically, you can expect "unjumpered" floppy disks to be set to the following specifications:

- Drive select: 1 (B: drive)
- Disk change (pin 34): enabled
- Frame ground: enabled

This configuration supports traditional single and dual (1.44MB) floppy drive systems using twisted floppy cables.

SYMPTOM 21-11 When using a combination floppy drive (called a "combo drive"), one of the drives does not work, but the other works fine This problem is often caused by a drive fault. First, check the power connector. Make sure that both +5 volts and +12 volts are adequately provided to the drive through the 4-pin "mate-n-lock" connector. If the drive is receiving the proper power, the drive itself has almost certainly failed—try a new drive.

SYMPTOM 21-12 DOS reports an error such as "Cannot read from drive A:" A disk is fully inserted in the drive, and the drive LED indicates that access is being attempted.

- *Check the disk.* Begin by trying a known-good, properly formatted disk in your suspect drive. A faulty disk can generate some very perplexing read/write problems.
- *Check the drive for obstructions.* Carefully inspect the spindle motor, drive belt (if used), and read/write head assembly. Make certain that there are no broken parts or obstructions that could jam

the heads. You should also examine the floppy drive with a disk inserted to be certain that the disk's insertion or alignment is not causing the problem. Double-check your observations using several different disks. Gently remove any obstruction(s) that you may find. Be careful not to cause any accidental damage in the process of clearing an obstruction.

- *Clean the floppy drive.* If a known-good disk does not resolve the problem, try cleaning the read/write heads thoroughly. Do not run the drive with a head-cleaning disk inserted for more than 30 seconds at a time, or you risk damaging the heads with excessive friction.
- *Check the signal cable.* Verify that the drive's 34-pin ribbon cable is attached securely at the drive(s) and at the drive controller. Reattach the signal cable if it's loose, and try another signal cable if necessary.
- *Replace the floppy drive.* If the problem persists, chances are that the floppy drive is defective. (Perhaps the head read/write system has failed.) Try replacing the floppy drive with a known-good drive from another system.
- *Replace the floppy drive controller.* If a new floppy drive still does not resolve the problem, you may have a defective floppy drive controller circuit. If so, you may also receive a floppy drive or controller error from the system BIOS at boot time. Try disabling the existing floppy controller and install an expansion card controller (with only the floppy controller portion enabled).

SYMPTOM 21-13 You cannot upgrade an XT-class PC with a 3.5-inch floppy disk
XT systems support up to four double-density 5.25-inch floppy disk drives. They will not support 3.5-inch floppy disks at all. To install 3.5-inch floppy disks, you should check your DOS version. (You need to have DOS 3.3 or later installed.) Next, you'll need to install an 8-bit floppy drive controller board. (Remember to disable any existing floppy controller in the system first.) The floppy controller will have its own onboard BIOS to support floppy disk operations. Finally, take a look at the XT configuration switches and see that any entries for your floppy drives are set correctly. If you're using a stand-alone floppy controller, you may need to set the motherboard jumpers to "no floppy drives."

SYMPTOM 21-14 The floppy drive activity LED stays on as soon as the computer is powered up This is a classic signaling problem that occurs after changing or upgrading a drive system. In virtually all cases, one end of the drive cable has been inserted backwards. Make sure that pin 1 on the 34-pin cable is aligned properly with the connector on both the drive and controller. If problems remain, the drive controller may have failed. This is rare, but try a new drive controller.

SYMPTOM 21-15 You are unable to swap floppy drives so that A: becomes B:, and B: becomes A: This often happens on older systems when users want to make their 3.5-inch after-market B: drive into their A: drive, and relegate their aging 5.25-inch drive to B: instead.

- *Check the signal cable.* For floppy cables with a wire twist, the endmost connector is A:, and the connector prior to the twist is B:. Reverse the connectors at each floppy drive to reverse their identities.
- *Check the drive jumpers.* If the cable has no twist (this is rare), reset the jumper ID on each drive so that your desired A: drive is set to DS0 (Drive Select 0), and your desired B: drive is jumpered to DS1. If you accomplish this exchange, but one drive is not recognized, try a new floppy signal cable.
- *Check the CMOS settings.* You'll need to reverse the floppy drive entries for your A: and B: drives, then reboot the system.

21

SYMPTOM 21-16 **The new drive does not work, or the system does not recognize the new drive** This classic problem of the system not recognizing the newly installed drive is typically the result of incorrect or overlooked CMOS settings.

- *Check the CMOS settings.* Reboot the system and start the CMOS setup routine. Verify the floppy drive parameters against the actual physical drives in the system, and then make sure the correct data is entered in CMOS. You may have forgotten to save the data initially. Save the new data correctly and try the system again.
- *Check the signal cables.* Inspect the power and signal cables at the drive. Loose or incorrectly attached cables can effectively disable the drive. Install each cable carefully and try the system again.
- *Replace the floppy drive.* If the problem persists, chances are that the new floppy drive is defective. Try replacing the floppy drive with a known-good drive from another system.

SYMPTOM 21-17 **You cannot boot the system from the new floppy drive** If the drive is recognized properly and operates as expected, the failure to boot actually may not be a failure— rather, the boot order established in your CMOS setup may not be set to include the new drive. Often, the boot order is A: then C:, or C: then A:. If you installed a new floppy as B:, the system will not attempt to boot because it is not included in the boot order. Restart the CMOS setup routine, and adjust the boot order to address your new floppy drive first (for example, B:/C:, or A:/B:/C:).

SYMPTOM 21-18 **After the second floppy is installed, there are a lot of signal problems, such as read or write errors** Chances are that you left the terminating resistors in place on the second (middle) floppy drive, resulting in signal errors. You should have a terminating resistor pack on the drive at the *end* of the daisy-chain cable. Check that the terminating resistors are in place on drive A:, and remove the terminating resistors from the middle drive (B:). Also check that the signal cables are installed securely on both drives. Loose or damaged cables can cause signal problems.

SYMPTOM 21-19 **The floppy drive light comes on even when there is no disk in the drive** This may happen at any time, or particularly during shutdown or reboot of the system. One of the most common causes of excessive floppy drive activity is a Windows PIF (Program Information File) shortcut pointing to the floppy drive. A PIF shortcut is one that points to a DOS program, while a LNK shortcut points to a Windows program. You should check for PIF shortcuts to your floppy drive. Windows Explorer doesn't normally show the PIF or LNK extensions for shortcuts, but you can find them manually using the Windows 95/98 Find feature:

1. Click Start, highlight Find, and then click on Files or Folders.
2. Enter ***.PIF** in the Named field.
3. Use the Browse button to select your \Windows directory.
4. Check "Include subdirectories."
5. Click the Advanced tab and enter either **A:** or **B:** in the "Containing text" field.
6. Click the Find Now button.

If "Find" locates any shortcuts in the \Windows\Desktop or any folder in the \Windows\Start Menu structure, that shortcut is probably causing the problem. The solution is to delete the reference or move the shortcut(s) to a directory other than the \Desktop or \Start Menu folder(s).

When floppy drive access seems to occur during shutdown or reboot, it may be that you have antivirus software (such as McAfee's VShield or Norton Anti-Virus Auto-Protect) set to check the floppy drive automatically. You'll need to disable autochecking of the floppy drive. For McAfee's Vshield, right-click its icon from the task bar and select Properties. Under the Scan Floppies On entry in the Detection tab, uncheck the Shutdown box. Remember to save your changes. For Norton AntiVirus Auto-Protect, right-click its icon from the task bar and select Options. Click the Advanced button, and under the "Check floppies" entry, uncheck the "Check floppies when reboot computer" box. Remember to save your changes.

SYMPTOM 21-20 **You cannot create a Windows 95/98 startup disk** There are many possible problems that may prevent Windows from properly creating a startup disk, but the points below outline the most common issues.

- *Check the disk.* The disk itself may have ten or more bad sectors, or the first sector may be damaged. Try a known-good disk (preferably a high-quality or premium-grade disk). Also, Windows 95/98 generally requires a high-density (1.44MB) floppy disk in order to create a startup disk.
- *Check your antivirus software.* Many antivirus tools can interfere with floppy disk operations. Disable or uninstall your antivirus software according to the manufacturer's instructions.
- *Check the CMOS settings.* Reboot the system and start the CMOS setup routine. Verify the floppy drive parameters against the actual physical drives in the system; then make sure the correct data is entered in CMOS. You may have forgotten to save the data initially. Save the new data correctly and try the system again.
- *Disable/remove floppy tape devices.* Some older tape backup devices utilizing the floppy controller may prevent you from gaining access to the floppy drive. To work around this behavior, disconnect the tape backup device from the floppy controller before you attempt to create a Windows 95/98 startup disk, or disable the tape backup driver.
- *Replace the floppy drive.* If the problem persists, chances are that the new floppy drive is defective. Try replacing the floppy drive with a known-good drive from another system.

21

The LS-120 Drive

With multimegabyte text, image, multimedia, and CAD files now commonplace, the traditional 1.44MB disk is falling into disuse because it's hard to fit today's huge files on it. The LS-120 drive is intended to offer higher storage capacities (up to 120MB) on magneto-optical disks, while providing full backward compatibility with existing floppy disks. The LS-120 also employs an ATAPI IDE interface (the same class of interface used by CD-ROMs and hard drives), so its performance is far better than the traditional 300KB/s found with floppy drives. This part of the chapter explains the LS-120 capabilities, highlights a typical LS-120 installation, and covers many of the most persistent troubleshooting problems.

LS-120 DRIVE LAYOUT AND CHARACTERISTICS

The LS-120 drive uses both magnetic and optical reading/writing techniques. This makes an LS-120 something of a cross between a floppy drive and a CD-ROM. Using these "hybrid" technologies, the LS-120 can offer storage capacities of 120MB (equivalent to about 83 floppy disks) on specially designed and formatted "SuperDisks." (SuperDisk LS-120 disks by Imation are usually recommended.) At the same time, it is fully backward compatible with existing 1.44MB disks. (So any existing floppy disks are still usable.) The LS-120 also provides much faster data transfers at up to 750KB/s (five times the rate of a standard floppy). Unlike ordinary floppy drives, the LS-120 uses an ATAPI IDE interface, so the drive can be installed alongside existing hard drives and CD-ROM drives. The standard 3.5-inch form factor means that the LS-120 can be installed in any existing drive bay as a floppy disk replacement. In fact, you might not even notice the difference between a floppy and LS-120 drive at first glance.

Disk Compatibility and Cleaning

Since the LS-120 is designed to work with 120MB and 1.44MB disks, there is often some confusion as to how disks may be interchanged. Here are the basic rules for disks:

- The LS-120 can read and write 120MB, 1.44MB, and 720KB disks. You can even format 1.44MB and 720KB disks on the LS-120 (though you may need the latest LS-120 driver to ensure compatibility).
- Disks of 1.44MB and 720KB cannot be formatted to 120MB in the LS-120. (Only specially designed magneto-optical disk can work at 120MB.)
- LS-120 disks cannot be read on 1.44MB floppy drives. You must have an LS-120 drive in the system.

Imation (and other LS-120 clone makers) generally recommends that the drive heads be cleaned after 40 to 80 hours of operation depending on the cleanliness of the operating environment. As with floppy drive head cleaning, this regular maintenance offers an easy, practical, and thorough method for safely removing error-causing dust and debris from magnetic recording heads. As a rule, you should use a head-cleaning kit designed specifically for an LS-120 drive. Ordinary floppy head-cleaning disks can be too abrasive for an LS-120.

LS-120 DRIVE INSTALLATION AND REPLACEMENT

The LS-120 drive offers higher storage capacities and faster performance, as well as bootable operation. However, you'll need to verify several important elements of your PC before installation can begin. As a minimum, you should check the following points.

- *Computing power* The LS-120 drive typically requires a *minimum* of a 486DX2/66MHz processor, 8MB of RAM, and 5MB of free hard drive space. While modern PCs easily meet these requirements, older systems should be evaluated carefully before planning an LS-120 installation.
- *Power connections* A power supply offers a limited number of drive power connectors. In small systems, there may not be a free drive power connector for another drive device. When this occurs, you may use a Y-splitter cable to add another power connector. However, place the Y cable in with the existing floppy drive. (Never split power from critical drives such as the hard drive.) If you're using the LS-120 to replace an existing floppy, just reuse the existing power connector.
- *Drive bay space* The trend toward smaller, low-profile enclosures has put a lot of pressure on available drive space, so one of the first problems when planning for a new LS-120 drive is locating an external drive bay. If you do not have an external drive bay available, you may be able to move a hard drive to an internal drive bay. This relocates the hard drive and frees an external drive bay for the LS-120 drive. If you're using the LS-120 as a replacement for your existing floppy drive, it's a matter of removing the existing floppy drive, then installing the LS-120 in that drive space.

> If you're planning to replace a floppy with the LS-120, be sure to copy the LS-120 driver disk to your hard drive before removing the floppy drive.

- *Drive controller space* Remember that the LS-120 drive uses your hard drive controller rather than the floppy drive controller. This means that you'll need an open connector on either your primary or secondary drive controller channels. If you do not have an available signal connector (for example, your system has two HDDs, a CD-ROM, and a DVD-ROM drive), you may not be able to install the LS-120 drive without removing one of those existing drives first. Also, the LS-120 requires the LBA (Logical Block Addressing) mode for proper operation, so your drive controller should be an EIDE or Ultra-DMA type. Also keep in mind that the LS-120 will not operate from a tertiary IDE controller such as the IDE controller integrated onto a sound card.
- *BIOS compatibility* If you plan to use the LS-120 as a secondary storage device and not as a bootable drive, you'll probably continue to use your existing floppy drive, and no BIOS adjustments are needed. The LS-120 will be enabled *solely* by device drivers. If you plan to use the LS-120 as a bootable drive, remember that you'll need to check the system BIOS for compatibility. The boot order in your CMOS setup should include the option for an LS-120 drive. (Your BIOS may use another designator, such as UHD Floppy, Floptical, or Removable Drive.) If your BIOS does not provide such support, you may need to upgrade the BIOS before installing the LS-120 drive. Once the drive is installed, and the old floppy drive is removed, remember to disable the floppy controller and change the boot order so that the system will boot from the LS-120.

> IBM MicroChannel PCs do not support bootable LS-120 drives.

Typical Installation of the LS-120

Installing an LS-120 drive is often a three-step process: configure the drive jumper(s), mount and cable the drive, and configure the new drive in CMOS. Although most LS-120 installations are quick and painless procedures—even for a novice—there are a few nuances that you should be aware of. When followed carefully, this process can typically be completed in under 30 minutes. If you're replacing an existing floppy drive, remove the floppy drive and its cable first, and then follow the procedures below.

> It's normally a good idea to perform a complete system backup of your hard drives before attempting any kind of drive work. Although LS-120 installation should not affect your hard drives in any way, backups will protect your data and system configuration from accidental data loss.

> Turn the system off and unplug it from the AC receptacle before proceeding. This protects the new device and your personal safety.

Prepare the System Remove the screws holding down the outer cover, and place those screws aside in a safe place. Gently remove the PC's outer cover and set it aside (out of the path of normal floor traffic). You should now be able to look into the PC and observe the open drive bay, the motherboard, and any expansion boards and drives that are installed.

> Remember to use an antistatic wrist strap whenever working inside a PC. This will prevent accidental static discharge, which can damage the computer's delicate electronics.

Prepare the Drive Bay Now that the outer cover is removed, you should open the desired drive bay. This is as simple as removing the plastic bezel covering an empty bay. (The bezel will usually pop right out.) If you must relocate an existing drive, things get a bit more complicated. First, decide where the drive (almost always a hard drive) will be located—often an internal bay in the rear of the PC. You can then remove the mounting screws, disconnect the power and signal cables from the hard drive, and slide the hard drive out of the bay. Remount the hard drive in the internal bay, and gently secure each screw into place. (Be careful not to overtighten the screws.) Reattach the power and signal cables to the hard drive. Pay particular attention when connecting the signal cable. If the cable is installed backward, the hard drive will not function. The red or blue stripe along one side of the ribbon cable always marks pin 1.

The procedure is a bit easier when replacing an existing floppy drive. Unbolt the existing drive, and then disconnect the power and signal cables. Slide the old drive out of the bay and set it aside carefully. If you have a good-quality antistatic bag available, seal the old drive in the antistatic bag. Also remove the floppy drive cable from the system. At this point, you should now have an open drive bay. Take a quick inventory and make sure that you have an available IDE signal cable and power connector available.

> When using a Y-splitter to tap power from another drive, never split power from a hard drive. This can cause erratic drive (and system) operation.

Set the LS-120 Jumpers In almost all cases, the LS-120 drive will be connected as the slave device to an existing master device (such as a CD-ROM drive) on the secondary drive controller channel. Check the LS-120 jumpers and verify that it is configured as a slave device. If there are currently no devices on the secondary channel (for example, the system has only one HDD and CD-ROM—both on the primary channel), you may need to use the LS-120 jumpers to reconfigure the drive as a master device. This allows the LS-120 to exist by itself on the secondary channel. Of course, you should refer to the documentation enclosed with your LS-120 drive for specific jumper arrangements and cautions.

Mount the LS-120 Drive Now that the LS-120 drive is configured, slide it gently into the open drive bay. Line up the four mounting holes, and screw the drive in carefully. Be sure not to tighten the mounting screws excessively—this can warp the drive's frame and cause R/W problems or premature drive failure. Make it a point to use screws of the proper size and length to do the job. If you're placing the LS-120 into a larger 5.25-inch drive bay, be sure to premount the drive into its extended frame before sliding the complete assembly into the drive bay.

Connect Power and Signal Cables Once the drive is installed and mounted securely, connect the power and signal cables as required. The 4-pin power cable is relatively foolproof because of its keyed shape. For the signal cable, however, take care to install the 40-pin signal cable connector in the correct orientation. If the signal cable is installed backward, the drive will not work. (The system may not even boot.) The red or blue stripe along one side of the ribbon cable always represents pin 1. As long as the drive is jumpered properly, you may place the LS-120 in either the middle or endmost IDE connector. *Do not use the floppy drive signal cable.*

Update CMOS Settings If you're using the LS-120 as a supplemental drive rather than a bootable drive (and the old floppy is still in place), skip this step. Otherwise, you must update the system CMOS entries to accommodate the new drive. Make sure that any tools or extra hardware are removed from the system, reattach the AC cord to the power supply, and then reboot the computer. As the system boots, start the CMOS setup routine and adjust the configuration as needed to disable the old floppy drive and floppy controller. Check to make sure that the LS-120 drive is identified properly along with your other IDE drive devices. Also configure the boot order to select the LS-120 as the first boot device. With the floppy removed and the LS-120 set as a boot device, the LS-120 should become the new A: drive. When the settings are correct, save the system CMOS and reboot the system so that your changes can take effect.

Test the Drive To test for bootability, insert a blank disk into the LS-120 and restart the PC. If you get a "non-system disk" error, the system has tried to boot from the LS-120. Now try booting the system from a known-good bootable disk. You should wind up at the A: command prompt. Try writing and reading a few files from the drive. You might also try formatting a blank disk in the new drive. If these tests are successful, you can be confident that the new drive is working properly. Be sure to remove any tools or hardware from the system, and then reinstall the system's outer housings. Do not use excessive pressure to tighten the screws.

Driver Installation

You do not need separate drivers when using the LS-120 under Windows 98, Windows 95 (OSR2), Windows NT 4.0, or Windows NT 3.51 with Service Pack 5. These operating systems should automatically detect your LS-120 drive. The drive shows up as the logical A: drive (3.5-inch floppy) under My Computer. If you have other peripheral devices such as hard drives or CD-ROMs, they are automatically assigned the next available drive letter. If your operating system is Windows NT 4.0 or NT 3.51 (with SP5), you do not need to change your system settings. However, you will need drivers under DOS, Windows 3.1/3.11, Windows NT 3.51 (without SP5), and Windows 95/95A.

> Since it's normal for LS-120 installation to shift your CD-ROM (and other drive) letters, you may have trouble running certain applications that expect to see the original drive letter. You may need to reinstall those applications.

For a DOS/Windows 3.1x driver installation, follow these steps:

1. For Windows 3.1x, select the Run option. Enter the path to the LS-120 drivers (for example, **a:\install** or **c:\temp\install**) and press ENTER.
2. After the installer starts, select Express Install for the quickest install process, and then press ENTER.
3. Remove the driver disk (if you used one) and reboot the PC.
4. The system modifies your CONFIG.SYS file and saves a backup of the original file. Your system displays this message to verify the installation:

```
ID 2: LS- 120 Ver 4 420 Direct Access Device (removable)
ID 2 Drive Letter is D LS- 120
LS-120 driver(s) connected
LS-120 driver installed
```

5. If these messages do not appear, check your operating system type and version, and then reinstall the device driver.

For a Windows 95/95A/NT 3.51 (without SP5) driver installation, follow these steps:

1. Click Start and select Run. Enter the path to the LS-120 drivers (for example, **a:\setup** or **c:\temp\setup**) and press ENTER.
2. A menu-driven installation program guides you through the installation process. This process automatically updates the system's registry with the appropriate drivers.
3. When the installation process is complete, remove the driver disk (if you used one) and reboot the PC.

For a Windows NT 4.0/NT 3.51 (with SP5) driver installation, follow these steps:

1. From the Control Panel, double-click the System icon, and then click Device Manager. A list of all the drivers used by the system appears.
2. Select the ATAPI device driver and change its setting to "Started at boot."

3 Restart your computer. The LS-120 drive is now recognized as the logical A: or B: drive within My Computer.

For new NT installations, install the LS-120 drive before installing Windows NT. As you install Windows NT, your system automatically identifies the LS-120 drive and loads the appropriate drivers. After you restart your computer, the system recognizes the LS-120 drive as the logical A: or B: drive.

Uninstalling the Device Driver

When you remove the LS-120 drive, you'll also need to remove the drivers that accompany it. This is not a problem under Windows 98 and other newer operating systems, but you'll need to address the issue manually under Windows 95 and DOS.

- Under Windows 95, restart the SETUP.EXE install program and check the Uninstall SuperDisk Device Driver & Utility button. Run the deinstallation process as you would an installation, as described above.
- Under DOS or Windows 3.1x, search for these lines in the CONFIG.SYS file: c:\atlas\atapimgr.sys and c:\atlas\mkels120.sys. REMark out these lines everywhere they occur. Then reboot the system.

Changing the LS-120 Drive Letter

There may be times when it's necessary for you to change the LS-120 drive letter from its default setting. Follow the steps below to adjust the drive letter:

1. Click Start, select Settings, and then click Control Panel.
2. In the Control Panel, double-click the System icon.
3. Click on the Device Manager tab.
4. Click on Disk Drives, and then double-click on the LS-120 drive.
5. Click on Settings, and set the desired drive letter.
6. Restart your computer when prompted.

LS-120 CONSIDERATIONS AND ISSUES

Ideally, you should be able to install and boot from an LS-120 drive with an absolute minimum of fuss. But the LS-120 is a relatively new class of bootable drive, and a system must meet several minimum requirements in order to support the drive. There are also several potential system compatibility problems that you should be aware of.

Booting and System BIOS

Perhaps the most interesting aspect of the LS-120 is that it's bootable in both 120MB and 1.44MB modes, so you boot from either size of disk. However, you'll need a motherboard or drive controller BIOS that is designed to accommodate the LS-120. (You'll see "LS-120" as a boot option in the CMOS setup "Boot Order" entry.) If your BIOS does not recognize the LS-120, you may need to upgrade the BIOS. The following three BIOS versions are known to support LS-120 technology:

- Award BIOS version 4.51PG or later
- AMI BIOS version 6.26.02 or later
- Phoenix BIOS version 6.0 or later

Booting and Operating Systems

Although the LS-120 will work in DOS, and in all versions of Windows, only Windows 95 release B (4.00.950B) and *later* will treat the LS-120 as bootable. All older versions of Windows only support the drive as a removable and nonbootable disk, which will not be assigned to drive letter A: or B:. Make sure the LS-120 disk has been formatted to be bootable. This will be available as a check box item when formatting in Windows, or as a command-line switch when formatting from a DOS prompt (adding the traditional /S switch to the Format command line). As an example, if formatting the A: drive (which is your LS-120) to be bootable, type

```
FORMAT A: /S
```

Also, the LS-120 does work under Windows NT, but there are several things you must pay particular attention to during installation. NT 4.0 and NT 3.51 (Service Pack 5) have built-in support for the LS-120 and require no special drivers. Other versions of NT require running the SETUP.EXE utility from the Windows directory on the LS-120 driver disk. Remember to have the ATAPI service set to "ENABLED AT BOOT."

Compatibility with System Manufacturers

You may encounter problems installing the retail version of an LS-120 drive on some systems built by major system houses such as Packard Bell or Compaq. Many major system houses use their own OEM version of the LS-120, which must be installed instead of the retail version. If you encounter such difficulties, check with technical support for the system manufacturer, and see if there are any known problems with retail LS-120 compatibility, or driver updates/patches that may be necessary.

Compatibility with System Utilities

The LS-120 is not fully compatible with all system utilities—most notably antivirus programs, some backup software, and drive utilities such as Norton Utilities. When the LS-120 is installed with such software, the drive (or the software) may fail to function normally. If you encounter read/write difficulties while using any such system utilities, try disabling or temporarily uninstalling them to see if the problem goes away.

LS-120 Device Conflicts

Although the LS-120 is an IDE device, it is known to have problems when installed in conjunction with certain other device configurations. In most cases, the LS-120 (or the other IDE device on the ribbon cable) may not be detected. This type of problem is usually fixed by reversing the drive positions on the ribbon cable, or reversing the master/slave jumper relationship of the two devices.

For example, if your LS-120 is connected to the secondary IDE port and jumpered as the master device, and an IDE CD-ROM is also connected to the secondary IDE port as a slave device, and now the CD-ROM is not functioning properly, change the jumpering on the two devices so that the LS-120 is now the slave and the CD-ROM is the master.

In other cases, the LS-120 drive is not seen on the secondary IDE port regardless of the jumper settings. This is often because the motherboard chipset is not recognized properly by Windows 95, and the secondary IDE port is left disabled. If the IDE port you are connecting to is listed in the Device Manager as a "Standard ESDI/IDE PORT," you'll need to contact your motherboard maker for the updated INF file for Windows 95. If your motherboard uses an Intel chipset, you can go to Intel's Developer page, and search for the INF file to update Windows 95. The URL for the Intel Developers site is **http://developer.intel.com/design/motherbd/ideinfup.htm**.

Finally, the LS-120 may be misidentified as a CD-ROM by the BIOS during system boot. If this occurs, you'll need to update your system BIOS from the system maker or motherboard manufacturer. Ideally, the drive should be identified as an "LS-120" or "UHD Floppy" (Ultra High Density).

Drive Overlay Software

There are numerous types of drive overlay software in use today, such as Disk Manager, EZ-Drive, MaxBlast, and more. This overlay software is used to partition and prepare hard drives when the system BIOS will not support the drive's full size. In practice, overlay software can also affect other IDE drives (such as the LS-120) and result in performance problems.

If you're having trouble using the LS-120 and drive overlay software is installed on the hard drive, you may need to remove the overlay software from the hard drive. If your system hardware will not support the full size of a given hard drive, you may need to upgrade the system BIOS or drive controller BIOS first in order to accommodate the drive. Then you can remove the overlay software.

> Removing the overlay software will normally require you to change the drive geometry in the CMOS setup, then repartition and reformat the drive completely using FDISK and FORMAT. Be sure to perform a complete system backup before attempting to remove the overlay software.

Driver Support Under Windows 95 "A"

There have been reports that the "A" version of Windows 95 indicates driver support for the LS-120 is already available when in fact it is not. This is almost always because some utility program(s) installed *after* Windows 95 has changed the dates of certain files from your original Windows 95 install, or has changed the generic IDE driver for Windows 95 to a newer one in order to support another piece of hardware you have installed. To fix this, you will need to use the RegEdit utility located in your Windows directory.

> Improper editing of your registry can make your system fail to boot, or result in a loss of data, or force you to reinstall Windows 95. Changes should only be made under the direction of an experienced technician, or someone experienced in editing the registry. Be sure to make a backup copy of your registry files before proceeding.

Find the following section in your registry:

```
HKey_Local_Machine\System\CurrentControlSet\Services\Class\HDC
```

Find the entries under this section that refer to ATAPI.MPD. Change all ATAPI.MPD entries to ESDI_506.PDR. Exit your registry editor and save your changes. If you have problems restarting Windows 95 after editing the registry, you can always reboot from a rescue disk and reload your backup copy of the registry.

TROUBLESHOOTING LS-120 DISK SYSTEMS

SYMPTOM 21-21 After installing a parallel port LS-120 drive, you cannot access programs protected by a parallel port hardware key (a "dongle") This is almost always a limitation of the "dongle" itself. Those hardware keys must generally be connected to the parallel port first (then other parallel port devices can be added). If the LS-120 drive is installed before the dongle, the dongle may not respond properly, and software that uses it may refuse to work. Try connecting the dongle first.

SYMPTOM 21-22 You cannot boot from the LS-120 drive using a DOS 6.22, Windows 95, or Windows 95A (OSR1) boot disk In order to boot from an LS-120 device, both your operating system and motherboard BIOS must support the LS-120.

- *Check your operating system.* Only Windows 98, Windows 95 (OSR2), and Windows NT 4.0 allow you to boot from either a 1.44MB or 120MB disk. If your operating system is too old to support the LS-120 as a boot device, you'll need to upgrade your operating system.
- *Check the CMOS settings.* Examine the available options under your boot order. If you see an option such as SuperDisk, Floptical, LS-120, UHD Floppy, Removable Device, or Removable Drive, be sure to select that device as the first drive in your boot order. If there are no such entries to choose from, your BIOS may not fully support the LS-120 drive as a boot device, and a BIOS upgrade may be in order. If you cannot obtain a BIOS upgrade from the original system or motherboard maker, you can probably obtain a suitable upgrade from Unicore at **http://www.unicore.com** or 800-800-BIOS.

SYMPTOM 21-23 After you install an LS-120 drive, your CD-ROM (or other IDE-type device) does not work properly A number of typical installation issues may cause the new LS-120 drive to interfere with your existing drive(s).

- *Check your drive jumpers.* One drive must be set as the master device, and the other must be set as the slave device. Make sure that the drives are not both set the same way, or try reversing the master/slave relationship.
- *Check the signal cable.* Verify that the LS-120 is cabled properly. The signal cable should be secure and inserted in the proper orientation.
- *Try a different channel.* In a few cases, the LS-120 drive may not be compatible with the other drive on that same channel. You might try moving the drive to a different IDE channel, or disconnect the other drive from that channel and see if the LS-120 drive will operate normally by itself. If so, you might like to replace that drive with one from another manufacturer.

21

SYMPTOM 21-24 After installing the LS-120 device drivers, you can no longer play music CDs This is a problem that sometimes occurs when the LS-120 drivers do not interact properly with the CD-ROM drivers. In many cases, this type of issue can be corrected by updating both the LS-120 and CD-ROM drives to their very latest protected-mode (Windows 95/98) drivers.

SYMPTOM 21-25 The install program aborts after stating your system already has support for the LS-120 When running a SETUP.EXE program to install the LS-120 device drivers, you find an error message stating that your system already has support for the drive. The install program then aborts without finishing the install, but your LS-120 drive does not work. This can occur because the last step performed by the install program is to look at the date stamp of the ESDI_506.PDR file. If the file is *newer* than July 1995, the install program aborts. Edit the registry to change that entry from ESDI_506.PDR to ATAPI.MPD. Once you've renamed that entry, the setup program should operate normally and complete your installation.

SYMPTOM 21-26 The CD-ROM drive letter shifts after installing the LS-120 drive For example, the CD-ROM was D:, but after installing the LS-120, the LS-120 is now D:, and the CD-ROM is now E:. This is normal if the LS-120 drive is not made bootable (A:) in the CMOS setup. When the LS-120 is not bootable, the LS-120 drivers are typically loaded first, and they take precedence over the CD-ROM when drive letters are assigned.

This condition is normal. Do not try to reverse the CD-ROM and LS-120 drive letters (although you can do this through the drive's Properties dialogs under Windows). Doing so may cause one or both of the drives to be unreadable. If you have installed something from CD-ROM and it will not run now, try reinstalling the application on top of the older installation, so it updates the drive letter for the new configuration.

SYMPTOM 21-27 The LS-120 drive letter is greater than C:, but you cannot boot from the LS-120 because the floppy drive (that you removed from the system) still appears as A: There are several important oversights that may account for this type of problem.

- *Check the CMOS settings.* Make sure you have altered the boot order in your CMOS setup such that the LS-120 drive is selected as the first boot device.
- *Upgrade the BIOS.* If you find that the LS-120 (or other similar entry such as UHD Floppy or Floptical) drive is not listed in your available boot options, you may need to update your motherboard's BIOS and then adjust the boot order as outlined above.
- *Replace the floppy drive.* As an interim measure, you can replace the floppy drive A: so that you can boot from a floppy disk.

SYMPTOM 21-28 After physically installing the LS-120 drive, it is not detected as an ATAPI IDE device This problem frequently occurs when trying to install the LS-120 with an older drive controller. The LS-120 requires LBA (Logical Block Addressing)—the same mode used for newer hard drives. This requires an EIDE or newer Ultra-DMA drive controller. In some cases, you may be able to upgrade the system BIOS in order for the existing drive controller to support the LBA mode. If this is not possible, you may need to replace the existing drive controller with a newer drive controller card (incorporating its own onboard BIOS).

SYMPTOM 21-29 After plugging in the USB LS-120 drive, you don't see an icon appear on the desktop There are several possible reasons why the LS-120 drive might not appear after making the USB connection:

- Make sure a properly formatted LS-120 disk is in the drive.
- Make sure you are using the cables that came with the drive, and see that all cables are securely connected.
- Make sure the computer and drive both have power (or that the USB hub controlling the drive is powered).

If problems persist, eject the disk and power-down the drive. Unplug and reseat the USB connection on the drive end. Plug the drive back into the power source (or hub), reconnect the USB cable at the computer end, and reinsert the disk into the drive. If you still cannot get the USB LS-120 drive to work, try another drive.

SYMPTOM 21-30 You disconnected the LS-120 drive while the PC was in suspend ("sleep") mode, but now it doesn't work right after connecting it to another PC In virtually all cases, the LS-120 disk may be corrupted. You cannot disconnect the drive or eject the disk while files are open on the LS-120 disk. If there were files open when you disconnected the drive, the file (and perhaps the entire disk) may be corrupted. Try rebooting the PC, and see if you can access any of the files on the disk.

SYMPTOM 21-31 When copying files to/from a USB LS-120 drive, the computer froze when you disconnected the cable Even though USB devices are physically "hot pluggable," they cannot be connected or disconnected while data transfer is taking place. The USB device must be idle before it's disconnected. In the future, be sure that the LS-120 drive's activity LED is out before disconnecting the USB cable.

SYMPTOM 21-32 You cannot format a 1.44MB disk in an LS-120 drive Virtually all LS-120 drives should be able to format older 720KB and 1.44MB disks. If you cannot get the disk to format properly, chances are that you're using an older SuperDisk driver. For the Imation SuperDisk LS-120, you need driver version 1.2.5 or later. Check with the LS-120 drive maker to see if there's a driver patch or update available for download.

SYMPTOM 21-33 You cannot format a 1.44MB disk in an LS-120 drive on a Windows NT platform This is almost always caused by a problem with NT 4.0 using Service Pack 3. There are several possible solutions to this problem:

- Replace the ATAPI.SYS driver from Service Pack 2. (Follow the procedure outlined in Microsoft's Knowledge Base article Q170572.)
- Install Microsoft Post SP3 hot fixes (ATA-FIXI.EXE and IDE-FIXI.EXE) available from **ftp://ftp.microsoft.com/bussys/winnt/winnt-public/fixes/usa/nt40/hotfixes-postSP3/**.
- Upgrade your version of Windows NT to Service Pack 4.

SYMPTOM 21-34 You find one or more phantom drives with the LS-120 A *phantom drive* is a condition in which an extra drive designation appears, but neither the drive you are accessing, nor the "extra" drive are readable.

- *Check your drivers.* You may be loading the driver for the LS-120 in DOS, as well as a DOS CD-ROM driver. If this is the case, REM out the line loading MSCDEX in your AUTOEXEC.BAT file. You may also need to manually set the drive letter for the CD-ROM in the Device Manager.
- *Check the CMOS settings.* If you removed your A: drive (intending to use your LS-120 as your boot drive), but now you have a "removable disk" and a floppy drive that doesn't display in My Computer (or the Device Manager), it is likely that your CMOS setup still has a drive type set for drive A:. If the LS-120 is replacing your old A: drive, set the DRIVE TYPE for drive A: to "none" or "not installed." If the phantom drive still appears, make sure you have enabled the option to boot from the LS-120 drive.

SYMPTOM 21-35 You cannot read or format LS-120 media This happens most frequently under Windows 3.1x and the initial release (the "A" version) of Windows 95. In this case, you probably need to have the DOS version of the LS-120 driver installed. Run the LS-120 setup disk from a DOS window and install the DOS driver support.

> If you are using the "B" version of Windows 95, do not load the DOS driver support for the LS-120 (LS120.SYS). When active in the background, this DOS driver can cause data corruption.

This is also a known problem on some platforms that use the FMTLS120.EXE utility included with the Imation LS-120 SuperDisk drive. Do not use this utility. Remove it from the system. Use the standard DOS or Windows FORMAT function. The media formatted with the FMTLS120 utility may now be corrupt and unrecoverable.

SYMPTOM 21-36 **You find that the LS-120 drive is running very slowly when using Windows 98** The LS-120 is supported natively under Windows 98, but you may need to make some changes to the disk setup. Right-click on My Computer, then select Control Panel, then System. The System Properties dialog will appear. Select the Performance tab, and click on the File System button. You should then see a Removable Disk tab. Select that tab, and then enable "Write-Behind caching on all removable drives." Restart the PC if necessary. Intermittent slowdowns may indicate a dirty drive. Use a disk cleaning kit certified for LS-120 drives to clean your LS-120 read/write heads.

SYMPTOM 21-37 **The LS-120 drive is running in the "DOS Compatibility Mode"** You'll need some new drivers to overcome this problem. Go to Microsoft's Web site at **http://support.microsoft.com/support/downloads** and download the files REMIDEUP.EXE and IOSUPD.EXE. After you install these new files, the LS-120 drive should be able to run in protected mode.

SYMPTOM 21-38 **The LS-120 drive's LED is constantly on after inserting a new disk in the drive** This almost always means that the LS-120 disk is damaged. Carefully eject the disk and insert a new LS-120 disk into the drive. If the new disk works properly, the disk that you removed should be reformatted or discarded.

SYMPTOM 21-39 **The LS-120's drive power indicator never flashes, or it remains lit continuously** This is almost always a problem with the drive's connections to your system. If the power LED *never* comes on at all, chances are that the drive is not receiving power. Check the 4-pin power connector to the LS-120 drive. Reseat the power connector securely if necessary. If the power LED remains on *continuously*, it probably means that there's a problem with the signal cable—one end of the cable may be reversed or loose. Verify that the IDE cable is oriented properly, and see that it's secure. Reseat the signal cable (or try a new signal cable) if necessary.

SYMPTOM 21-40 **After installing the LS-120 drive, you find that the drive isn't responding and has no icon under Windows** There are several possible issues for you to consider:

- *Check the desktop.* The icon may simply be hidden—this is a common oversight. Autoarranging the icons on your desktop should reveal any icons that may have been hidden under one another.
- *Check the physical installation.* The drive may not be installed properly. Recheck the power and signal cables attached to the drive. See that they're secure and oriented properly. Also verify that the IDE port you've installed the LS-120 drive on is enabled. (You can usually enable an IDE port through the CMOS setup.) If there is another device on the same IDE channel, you may wish to temporarily disconnect that device and try the LS-120 drive by itself, or move the LS-120 drive to another IDE channel.
- *Update your bus mastering drivers.* Bus mastering can adversely affect the LS-120 drive. If you're using bus mastering, obtain and install the updated drivers for your system. If you cannot locate updated bus mastering drivers, use Microsoft's default drivers. Get the READIMDE.EXE file from **ftp://ftp.microsoft.com/bussys/winnt/winnnt-public/fixes/usa/hotfixes-postSP3**.

SYMPTOM 21-41 **The system crashes with "blue screen" errors each time the LS-120 drive is accessed** This is a known problem when using antivirus software. If you're running McAfee's VirusScan software (or other antivirus software), disable the "Scan Floppies on Access" option, or any "removable disk" option that scans the LS-120 drive. This scanning process takes a great deal of time and can seriously bog down the drive's performance.

SYMPTOM 21-42 When copying large files, the copy process is eventually interrupted with a "blue screen error" In virtually all cases, this indicates a defective disk. The error occurs when the copy process encounters bad sectors on the 120MB disk. Try a new or known-good disk to see if the problem goes away. If you find that the 120MB disk is bad, you may be able to run ScanDisk (in the media test mode) in an effort to map out the bad sectors. This may make the bad disk usable again, though its reliability cannot be guaranteed.

This may also be an operating system problem. If you're using an older version of Windows 95 (the original release or OSR1 version), you'll need to install the latest device drivers for the LS-120 drive so that Windows 95 will support the LS-120 properly.

SYMPTOM 21-43 A disk is stuck in the LS-120 drive This can happen on rare occasions when a poorly made disk fails, or when foreign matter interferes with the disk eject mechanism. Carefully insert a pin or paper clip into the emergency eject hole located on the Eject button. Press the pin or clip in the hole gently until the disk ejects from the slot. You can then replace the disk or clean the drive as necessary.

SYMPTOM 21-44 You encounter "insufficient disk space" messages when using an LS-120 disk You may also see this kind of problem with an error such as "cannot create file or folder." An LS-120 disk will hold up to 120MB of files, so "disk space" warnings often mean that the disk is either full, or there are too many files in the disk's directory.

- *Check the free space.* The first thing to do is to verify that there is adequate free space left on the LS-120 media. If the disk has been used previously, it may already contain files that take up a considerable amount of space. If there are already files on the disk, use a fresh disk, or delete unneeded files from the disk.
- *Check the file count.* Note the number of files listed in the root directory. FAT-based file systems impose a limit of 253 files in the root directory. If there are already 253+ files in the root directory, try creating subdirectories on the disk and storing additional files there, or use a fresh LS-120 disk.

21

SYMPTOM 21-45 You find that you cannot "quick format" an LS-120 disk under Windows 95/98 This is a common problem when using an LS-120 drive under Windows. Windows 95 and Windows 98 do not natively support the LS-120's "quick format" option. Right-click on your LS-120 drive icon and select the "format" option to perform a full format. After the first disk has been fully formatted, subsequent quick formats should work fine.

SYMPTOM 21-46 You cannot use the DiskCopy command with an LS-120 drive This is a known limitation of the DOS DiskCopy command. It will not support disks larger than 32MB. If you need to copy 120MB disks, use the utility suite that accompanies your LS-120 drive.

SYMPTOM 21-47 Microsoft Backup does not eject the first LS-120 disk when asking for the second disk This is a known issue with older versions of Microsoft Backup under Windows 95. You should upgrade to Windows 98 (or switch to a new third-party backup utility), which will properly support the LS-120 as a removable media drive.

SYMPTOM 21-48 You cannot use Microsoft Backup to back up to an LS-120 drive Although Microsoft Backup will work with an LS-120 drive, the software does not support disks larger than 32MB. Microsoft will likely address the Backup issue in their next release of the utility. In the meantime, Imation has a software toolkit for the LS-120 drive. The SuperDisk Tools Kit is available from **http://store.imation.com** and includes the following utilities:

- CA Backup for fast and easy data protection
- CA InnocuLAN Anti-Virus to protect your files with virus detection
- Disk Consolidator, which combines multiple 3.5-inch disks on a single 120MB disk
- Copy Disk to duplicate LS-120 disks

NovaStor offers a downloadable trial version of their NovaDisk backup program that works flawlessly with the LS-120MB disks. You can obtain the program directly from their Internet site at **http://www.novastor.com**.

Further Study

Imation: **http://www.imation.com**

Mitsumi: **http://www.mitsumi.com**

Sony: **http://www.ita.sel.sony.com/products/storage/**

Teac: **http://www.teac.com**

22

FLOPPY DRIVE TESTING AND ALIGNMENT

CHAPTER AT A GLANCE

Floppy disk drives (Figure 22-1) are basically electromechanical devices. Their motors, lead screws, sliders, levers, and linkages are all subject to eventual wear and tear. As a result, a drive can develop problems that are due to mechanical defects instead of electronic problems. Fortunately, few mechanical problems are fatal to a drive. With adequate routine cleaning and the proper software tools, you can test a troublesome drive and often correct problems simply through careful inspection and alignment. This chapter explains the concepts and procedures for floppy drive testing and alignment.

Understanding Alignment Problems

The causes behind floppy drive alignment problems will vary somewhat depending on the design of the drive itself, but there are some common causes that crop up time after time:

- Wear in the drive's head-positioning mechanism can eventually cause the radial alignment to drift out of specification.
- Various forms of debris often find their way into the drive's mechanical parts. This will accelerate wear in the drive and, in some cases, affect alignment directly by changing the way the drive's sensors and mechanisms respond.

FIGURE 22-1 Teac FD-235 3.5-inch floppy drive (Teac America, Inc.)

- Dirt and normal wear may cause the head mechanism to bind up (not slide as easily as it should). This puts an excessive load on the small stepper motor used to position the heads.
- The read/write head assembly itself can become bent or otherwise damaged from accidental abuse—often not enough to cause a complete failure, but enough to significantly affect the alignment and cause problems when reading a floppy disk recorded by another drive.
- Drive alignment problems may also be revealed by marginal disks. If a drive is slightly out of alignment, it may work with a good data disk, but not with a marginal, cut-priced one.

RECOGNIZING THE PROBLEMS

As a technician, you'll need to understand when a floppy drive is showing signs that may be related to alignment errors. In general, you should always respond to a chronic drive error by examining the disk media itself. Slowly spin the disk and observe both sides of the oxide layer. The layer should be smooth and even throughout—like the smooth surface of a quiet pond. If you see any marks or scratches on the disk, you should suspect that either the R/W heads are misaligned, or that there is a significant buildup of oxides on the R/W head(s). If you have not already cleaned the R/W heads as part of your regular repair practices, clean them now. If the problem persists, the head assembly is probably severely misaligned, and you should replace the drive or realign it as you see fit. Try another disk.

Other classical indicators of alignment trouble are reading and writing errors. You see, data is checked when it's read from or written to a drive. When you encounter a drive that has difficulty reading disks that were written on another PC (or one that writes disks that other PCs have difficulty reading), the drive's alignment is in serious doubt. Fortunately, alignment software can test the drive and report on its specifications, allowing you to see any unacceptable performance characteristics. If you find that the drive is faulty, you can then decide to replace or realign the drive at your discretion.

REPAIR VS. REPLACE

Floppy drive alignment continues to be a matter of debate. The cost of a floppy drive alignment package is significantly higher than the cost of a new drive. When compared with the rising costs of labor and alignment packages, many technicians question the practice of drive alignment when new drives are readily available for less than $40. Clearly, most casual PC enthusiasts would not choose to try realigning a misbehaving drive, but floppy testing software has an important place in any professional's toolbox. At the very least, test software can confirm the faulty alignment of a drive and eliminate the guesswork involved in drive replacement. For enthusiasts and technicians who have a volume of drives to service, alignment tools offer a relatively efficient means of recovering drives that might otherwise be discarded. Ultimately, one of a technician's most vital tools is an open mind—you can repair or replace the drive depending on what makes the most economic sense in your particular situation.

TIPS TO REDUCE FLOPPY DRIVE PROBLEMS

Now that you've seen the most common causes of floppy drive problems, you can recommend some proactive steps to avoid or reduce problems in the future:

- *Keep the floppy drives clean.* Not only is it important to keep the drive's R/W heads clean, but it is also important to keep dust and debris from accumulating inside the drive's mechanisms. A static-safe vacuum cleaner can usually remove unwanted dust, or the debris can be removed by "blowing down" the drive with a can of electronics-grade compressed air and a long, thin nozzle.
- *Do not force disks in or out.* This is a classic cause of drive problems. Disks that become stuck in the floppy drive (usually because the drive does not release the 3.5-inch disk's protective shroud properly) should be removed with the utmost care.
- *Keep air from circulating through the drive.* Floppy drives should generally be installed outside of the normal air flow in a PC. This will reduce the amount of dust and debris that flows around and through the drive.
- *Use good-quality disks.* "Bargain" disks often use inferior oxides that tend to rub off and accumulate on the R/W heads. If you encounter an unusual number of failures with bargain disks, clean the R/W heads, and switch to a better brand of disks.

Using Alignment Tools

Drive alignment is not a new concept. Technicians have tested and aligned floppy drives for years using oscilloscopes and test disks containing precise, specially recorded data patterns. You may already be familiar with the classic "cat's eye" or "index burst" alignment patterns seen on oscilloscopes. This kind of manual alignment required you to find the right test point on your particular drive's PC board, locate the proper adjustment in the drive assembly, and interpret complex (sometimes rather confusing) oscilloscope displays. Traditionally, manual alignment required a substantial investment in an oscilloscope, test disk, and stand-alone drive exerciser equipment to run a drive outside of the computer.

Although manual drive alignment techniques are still used today, they are being largely replaced by *automatic* alignment techniques. Software developers have created interactive control programs to operate with their specially recorded data disks. These software tool kits provide all the features necessary to operate a suspect drive through a wide variety of tests while displaying the results numerically or graphically on a computer monitor (Figure 22-2). As you make adjustments, you can see real-time results displayed on the monitor. Software-based testing eliminates the need for an oscilloscope and ancillary test equipment. You also do not need to know the specific signal test points for every possible drive. There are several popular tool kits on the market, including FloppyTune, by Data Depot, or DriveProbe (shown in Figure 22-3), by Accurite Technologies. The contact information for both manufacturers is listed at the end of the chapter.

AUTOMATIC Drive Test 'Esc'- For Previous Menu

Test	Track	Head 0 Data	Head 1 Data	Test Limits	Results	
Speed	NA	300 RPM / 199.7 mS		300 ± 6 RPM	Pass	NA
Eccentricity	44	100 uI	NA	0 ± 300 uI	Pass	NA
Radial	0	96% 50 uI	100% 0 uI	60 - 100 %	Pass	Pass
Radial	40	93% -100 uI	90% -150 uI	60 - 100 %	Pass	Pass
Radial	79	96% 50 uI	90% -150 uI	60 - 100 %	Pass	Pass
Azimuth	76	6 Min	4 Min	0 ± 30 Min	Pass	Pass
Index	0	414 uS	407 uS	400 ± 600 uS	Pass	Pass
Index	79	397 uS	380 uS	400 ± 600 uS	Pass	Pass
Hysteresis	40	100 uI	NA	0 ± 250 uI	Pass	NA

uI = Micro-inches   uS = Microsecond   mS = Millisecond
Min = Minutes   NA = Not Applicable   NT = Not Tested

Note: Radial is expressed as LOBE RATIO and OFFSET from track center line.
Auto Test Completed 'Esc' For Previous Menu

FIGURE 22-2 DriveProbe automatic drive-test display (Accurite Technologies, Inc.)

ADVANCED TOOLS

Although software tools make up a majority of the typical floppy drive service options, the tools available to serious floppy drive service technicians do not stop at software. With the proper supplemental test hardware (such as the DriveProbe Advanced Edition from Accurite Technologies, shown in Figure 22-3), a PC can be turned into a comprehensive floppy drive test bed that supports all types of standard PC drives, as well as Macintosh drives and many types of floppy disk duplicator drives.

FIGURE 22-3 DriveProbe: the Advanced Edition (Accurite Technologies, Inc.)

Aligning the Drive

At this point in the chapter, you are ready to start the testing/alignment software and go to work. Before starting your software, however, you should disable any caching software (such as SmartDrive) that will cache your floppy drive(s). Since caching software affects the way data is read or written to the floppy disk, caching will adversely affect the measurements produced by the alignment software. To ensure the truest transfer of data to or from the floppy disk, boot the PC from a clean boot disk to disable all TSRs or device drivers in the system. Once the alignment software is started, there are eight major tests to gauge the performance of a floppy drive: clamping, spindle speed, track 00, radial alignment, azimuth alignment, head step, hysteresis, and head width. Keep in mind that not *all* tests have adjustments that can correct the corresponding fault.

DRIVE CLEANING

Floppy drive R/W heads are not terribly complex devices, but they do require precision positioning. Heads must contact the disk media in order to read or write information reliably. As the disk spins, particles from the disk's magnetic coating eventually wear off and form a deposit on the heads. Accumulations of everyday contaminants such as dust and cigarette smoke also contribute to deposits on the heads. Head deposits present several serious problems. First, deposits act as a wedge—forcing heads away from the disk surface, resulting in lost data and read/write errors, and generally unreliable and intermittent operation. Deposits tend to be more abrasive than the head itself, so dirty heads can generally reduce a disk's working life. Finally, dirty heads can cause erroneous readings during testing and alignment. Since alignment disks are specially recorded in a very precise fashion, faulty readings will yield erroneous information that might actually cause you to improperly adjust the drive. As a general procedure, clean the drive thoroughly before you test or align it.

R/W heads can also be cleaned manually or automatically. The manual method is just as the name implies. Use a high-quality electronic head cleaner on a soft, lint-free, antistatic swab, and scrub both head surfaces by hand. *Wet the swab, but do not soak it.* You may need to repeat the cleaning with fresh swabs to ensure that all residual deposits are removed. Be certain that all computer power is off before manual cleaning, and allow a few minutes for the cleaner to dry completely before restoring power. If you do not have head-cleaning chemicals on hand, you can use fresh ethyl or isopropyl alcohol. The advantage to manual cleaning is thoroughness—heads can be cleaned very well with no chance of damage due to excessive friction.

Most software tool kits provide a cleaning disk and software option that allows you to clean the disk automatically. With computer power on and the software tool kit loaded and running, insert the cleaning disk and choose the cleaning option from your software menu. Software will then spin the drive for some period of time—10 to 30 seconds should be adequate, but do not exceed 60 seconds of continuous cleaning. Choose high-quality cleaning disks that are impregnated with a lubricant. Avoid "bargain" off-the-shelf cleaning disks that force you to wet the disk. Wetted cleaning disks are often harsh, and prolonged use can actually damage the heads from excessive friction. Once the drive is clean, it can be tested and aligned.

CLAMPING

A floppy disk is formatted into individual tracks laid down in concentric circles along the media. Since each track is ideally a perfect circle, it is critical that the disk rotate evenly in a drive. If the disk is not on center for any reason, it will not spin evenly. If a disk is not clamped evenly, the eccentricity introduced into the spin may be enough to allow heads to read or write data to adjoining tracks. A clamping test should be the first test performed after the drive is cleaned, because high eccentricity can adversely affect other disk tests. Clamping problems are more pronounced on 5.25-inch drives where the soft Mylar hub ring is vulnerable to damage from the clamping mechanism.

Start your software tool kit from your computer's hard drive, and then insert the alignment disk containing test patterns into the questionable drive. Select a clamping or eccentricity test, and allow the test to run a bit. You will probably see a display similar to the one shown in Figure 22-4. Typical software tool kits can measure eccentricity in terms of microinches from true center. If clamping is off by more than a few hundred microinches, the spindle or clamping mechanisms should be replaced. (Make sure the disk itself is not damaged.) You can also simply replace the floppy drive. Try reinserting and retesting the disk several times (or try a different disk) to confirm your results. Repeated failures confirm a faulty spindle system.

SPINDLE SPEED

Media must be rotated at a fixed rate in order for data to be read or written properly. A drive that is too fast or too slow may be able to read files that it has written at that wrong speed without error, but that disk may not be readable in other drives operating at a normal speed. Files recorded at a normal speed also may not be readable in drives that are too fast or too slow. Such transfer problems between drives are a classic sign of speed trouble (usually signaled as "general disk read/write errors"). Drive speeds should be accurate to within +/-1.5 percent, so a drive running at 300 RPM should be accurate to +/-4.5 RPM (295.5 RPM to 304.5 RPM), and a drive running at 360 RPM should be accurate to within +/-5.4 RPM (354.6 RPM to 365.4 RPM).

After cleaning the R/W heads and testing disk eccentricity, select the spindle speed test from your software menu. The display will probably appear much like the one in Figure 22-5. Today's floppy drives rarely drift out of alignment here because rotational speed is regulated by feedback from the spindle's index sensor. The servo circuit is constantly adjusting motor torque to achieve optimal spindle speed. If a self-compensating drive is out of tolerance, excess motor wear, mechanical obstructions, or index sensor failure is indicated. Check and replace the index sensor or the entire spindle motor assembly. You can also replace the entire floppy drive outright.

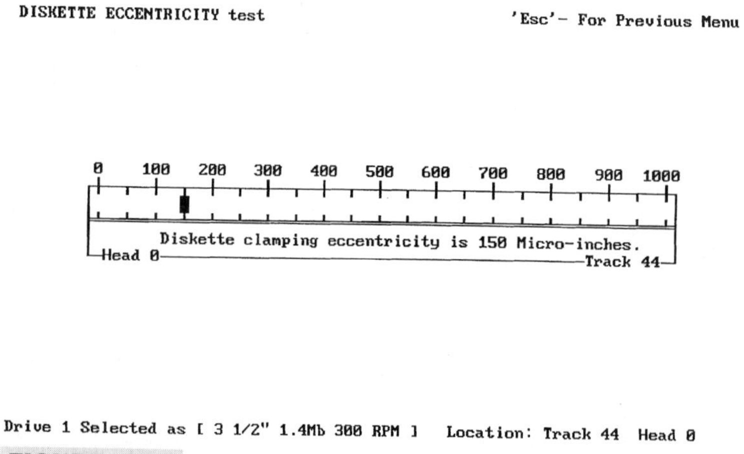

FIGURE 22-4 Screen display from a DriveProbe eccentricity test (Accurite Technologies, Inc.)

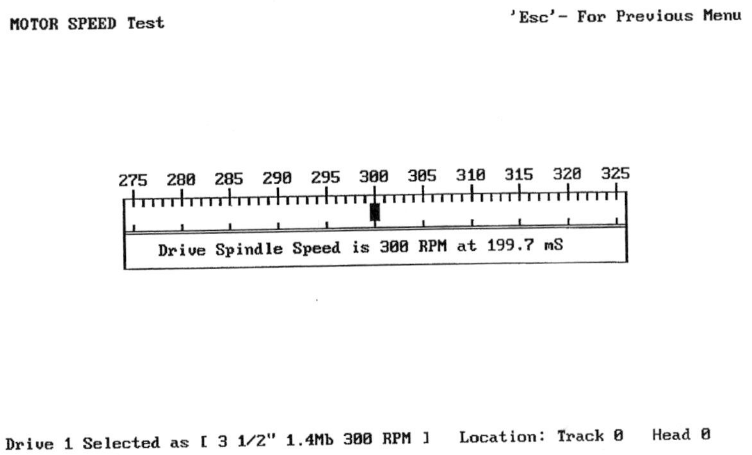

FIGURE 22-5 Screen display from a DriveProbe motor speed test (Accurite Technologies, Inc.)

TRACK 00 TEST

The first track on any floppy disk is the outermost track of side 0, which is track 00. Track 00 is important because it contains the boot record and file allocation information vital for finding disk files. The particular files saved on a disk can be broken up and spread out all over the disk, but the FAT data must always be in a *known* location. If the drive cannot find track 00 reliably, the system may not be able to boot from the floppy drive (or even use disks). Floppy drives utilize a sensor such as an optoisolator to physically determine when the R/W heads are over the outermost track.

Select the track 00 test from your software menu, and allow the test to run. A track 00 test measures the difference between the actual location of track 00 versus the point at which the track 00 sensor indicates that track 00 is reached. The difference should be less than +/-1.5 mils (one-thousandths of an inch). A larger error may cause the drive to encounter problems reading or writing to the disk. The easiest and quickest fix is to alter the track 00 sensor position. This adjustment usually involves loosening the sensor and moving it until the monitor display indicates an acceptable reading. Remember that you only need to move the sensor a small fraction—a patient and steady hand is required. The track 00 sensor is almost always located along the head carriage lead screw. Mark the original position of the sensor with indelible ink so that you can return it to its original position if you get in trouble.

RADIAL ALIGNMENT

The alignment of a drive's R/W heads versus the disk is critical to reliable drive operation because this alignment directly affects contact between heads and media. If head contact is not precise, data read or written to the disk may be vulnerable. The radial alignment test measures the head's actual position versus the precise center of the outer, middle, and inner tracks (as established by ANSI standards). Ideally, R/W heads should be centered perfectly when positioned over any track, but any differences are measured in microinches. A radial alignment error more than several hundred microinches may suggest a head alignment error.

Select the radial alignment test from your software tool kit, and allow the test to run. A typical radial alignment test display is illustrated in Figure 22-6. If you must perform an adjustment, you can start by loos-

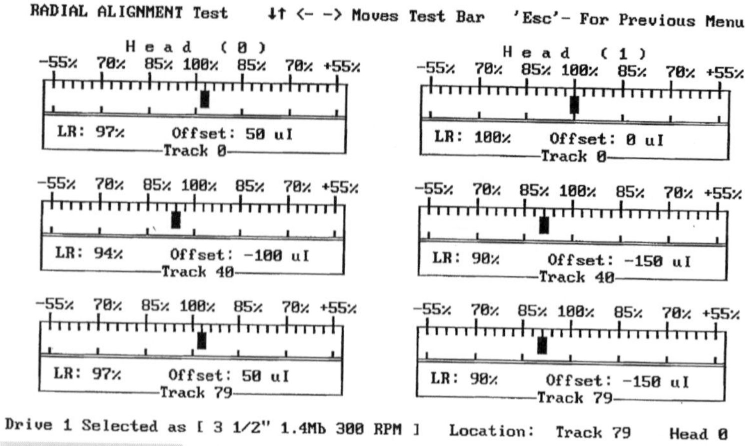

FIGURE 22-6 Screen display from a DriveProbe radial alignment test (Accurite Technologies, Inc.)

ening the slotted screws that secure the stepping motor, and gently rotate the motor to alter lead screw position. As you make adjustments with the test in progress, watch the display for the middle track. When error is minimized on the inner track, secure the stepping motor carefully to keep the assembly from shifting position. Use extreme caution when adjusting radial head position. You only need to move the head a fraction, so a very steady hand is needed. You should also recheck the track 00 sensor to make sure the sensor position is acceptable. If you are unable to adjust radial head alignment, the drive should be replaced.

AZIMUTH ALIGNMENT

Not only must the heads be centered perfectly along a disk's radius, but the heads must also be perfectly perpendicular (at a right angle) to the disk plane. If the head azimuth is off by more than a few minutes (1/60th of a degree), data integrity can be compromised, and interchanging disks between drives—especially high-density drives—may become unreliable. When the heads are perfectly perpendicular to the disk (at 90 degrees), the azimuth should be 0 minutes.

Select the azimuth test from your software tool kit, and allow the test to run. Figure 22-7 shows an azimuth alignment test display. An azimuth alignment test measures the rotation (or *twist*) of R/W heads in terms of plus (+) or minus (-) minutes. A clockwise twist is expressed as a plus (+) number, while a counterclockwise twist is expressed as a negative (-) number. Heads should be perpendicular to within about +/-10 minutes. It is important to note that most floppy drives do not allow azimuth adjustments easily. Unless you want to experiment with the adjustment, it is often easiest to replace a severely misaligned drive.

HEAD STEP

The head step (or *index step*) test measures the amount of time between a step pulse from the coil driver circuits and a set of timing mark data recorded on the test disk. In manual oscilloscope adjustments, this would be seen as the "index burst." Average index time is typically 200μS for 5.25-inch drives and 400μS

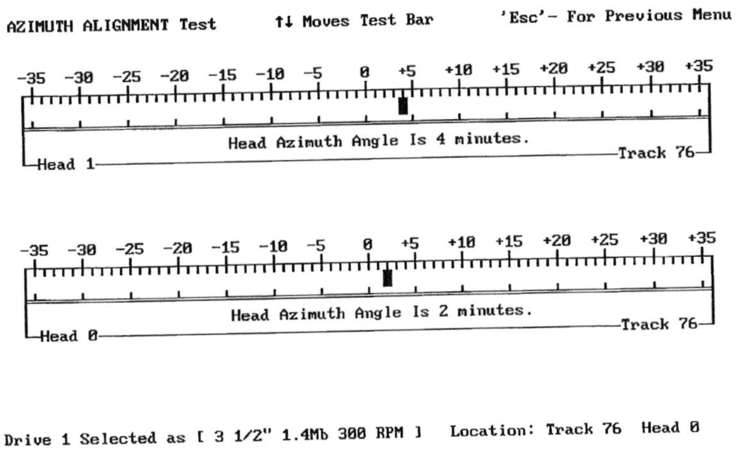

FIGURE 22-7 Screen display from a DriveProbe azimuth alignment test (Accurite Technologies, Inc.)

for 3.5-inch drives. In automatic testing with your software tool kit, you will see time measurements for both heads on the inner and outer tracks, as shown in Figure 22-8. The actual range of acceptable time depends on your particular drive, but variations of +/-100µS or more are not unusual.

If the head step timing is off too far, you can adjust timing by moving the index sensor. As with all other drive adjustments, you need only move the sensor a small fraction, so be extremely careful about moving the sensor. A steady hand is very important here. Make sure to secure the sensor when you're done with your timing adjustments.

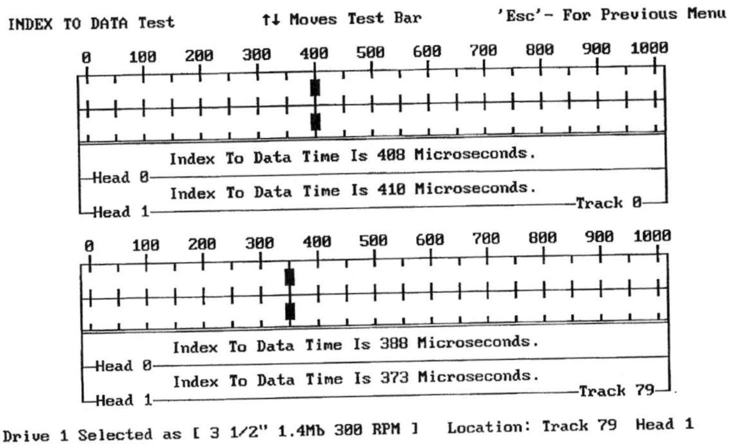

FIGURE 22-8 Screen display from a DriveProbe index-to-data test (Accurite Technologies, Inc.)

HYSTERESIS

It is natural for wear and debris in the mechanical head-positioning system to result in some "play"—that is, the head will not wind up in the exact position moving from outside in, as moving from the inside out. Excessive play, however, will make it difficult to find the correct track reliably. Testing is accomplished by starting the heads at a known track, stepping the heads out to track 00, then stepping back to the starting track. Head position is then measured and recorded. The heads are then stepped in to the innermost track, then back to the starting track. Head position is measured and recorded again. Under ideal conditions, the head carriage should wind up in precisely the same place (zero hysteresis), but natural play almost guarantees some minor difference. You can see a typical hysteresis test measurement display in Figure 22-9. If excessive hysteresis is encountered, the drive should be replaced since it is difficult to determine exactly where the excess play is caused in the drive.

HEAD WIDTH

Another test of a drive's R/W heads is the measurement of their effective width. Effective head widths are 12 or 13 mils for 5.25-inch double-density drives, 5 or 6 mils for 5.25-inch high-density drives, and 4 or 5 mils for all 3.5-inch drives. As you run the head-width test with your software tool kit, you will see effective width displayed on the monitor, as shown in Figure 22-10. As R/W heads wear down, their effective width increases. If the effective width is too low, the heads may be contaminated with oxide buildup. When small head widths are detected, try cleaning the drive again to remove any remaining contaminants. If the width reading remains too small (or measures too large), the heads or head carriage may be damaged. You can replace the R/W head assembly, but often the best course is simply to replace the drive outright.

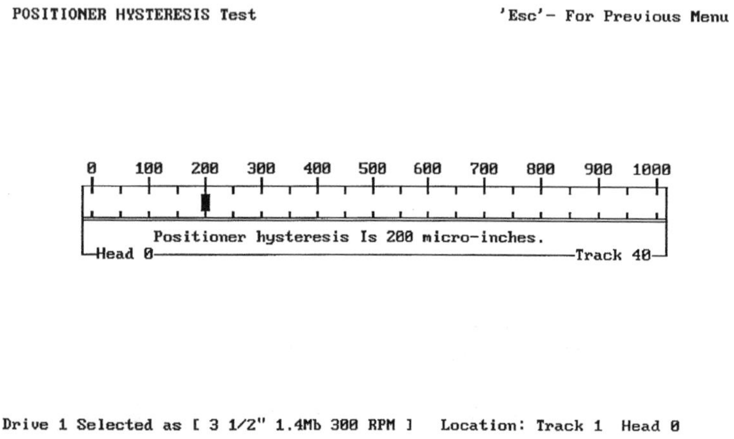

FIGURE 22-9 Screen display from a DriveProbe hysteresis test (Accurite Technologies, Inc.)

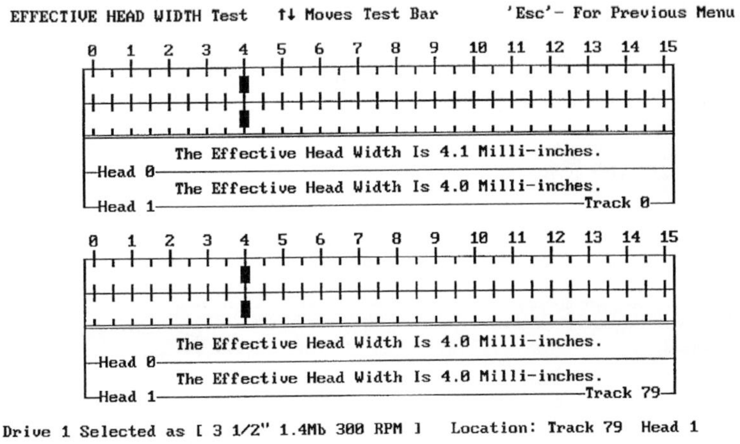

FIGURE 22-10 Screen display from a DriveProbe head width test (Accurite Technologies, Inc.)

Further Study

Accurite Technologies: **http://www.accurite.com**

Data Depot: **http://www.datadepo.com**

NEC: **http://www.nec.com**

22

23

HARD DRIVES

CHAPTER AT A GLANCE

The hard disk drive (or HDD) evolved to answer the incessant demands for permanent, high-volume, high-speed file and data storage in the PC (Figure 23-1). Early floppy disks provided simple and inexpensive storage, but they are slow, and programs quickly became far too large to store adequately on floppy disks. Switching between multiple disks also proved to be a cumbersome proposition. By the early 1980s, hard drives had become an important part of PC architecture and helped to fuel further OS and applications development. Today, the hard drive is an absolutely indispensable element of the modern PC. The hard drive holds the operating system that boots the system, stores the multimegabyte applications and files we rely on, and even provides virtual memory for systems that are lean on RAM. Hard drive performance also has a profound effect on overall system performance. As you might imagine, hard drive problems can easily cripple a system. This chapter presents some essential principles of hard disk drives and provides you with some solutions for drive testing and troubleshooting.

Basic Drive Concepts

The first step in understanding hard drives is to learn the basic concepts involved. Many of the terms covered for floppy drives also apply to hard drives, but the additional performance requirements and operating demands placed on hard drives have resulted in an array of important new ideas. In principle, a hard disk drive is very similar to a floppy drive—a magnetic recording media is applied to a substrate material that is then spun at a high rate of speed. Magnetic read/write heads in close proximity to the media can step rapidly across the spinning media to detect or create flux transitions as required. When you look closely, however, you can see that there are some major physical differences between floppy and hard drives.

PLATTERS AND MEDIA

23

Where floppy disks use magnetic material applied over a thin, flexible substrate of Mylar (or some other plastic), hard drives use rugged, solid substrates called *platters*. You can clearly view the platters of a hard drive in Figure 23-2. A platter is traditionally made of aluminum because aluminum is a light material, it is easy to machine to desired tolerances, and it holds its shape under the high centrifugal forces that occur at high rotation rates. But today, most platters are made from materials like glass or ceramic composite. These light, strong materials have a *very* low thermal expansion (so there are fewer media problems), and

FIGURE 23-1 Contemporary hard drive unit (NEC Technologies, Inc.)

compared to aluminum, they can withstand higher centrifugal forces. Since a major advantage of a hard drive is speed, platters are rotated at about 7600 RPM to as much as 10,000 RPM (compared to older hard drives that ran at 3600 to 5200 RPM). A hard drive generally uses two or more platters, though extremely small drive assemblies may use only one platter.

Hard drives must be capable of tremendous recording densities—well over 10,000 bits per inch (BPI). To achieve such substantial recording densities, platter media is far superior to the oxide media used for floppy disks. First, the media must possess a high coercitivity so that each flux transition is well defined and easily discernible from every other flux transition. Coercitivity of hard drive media typically exceeds 1400 oersteds. Second, the media must be extremely flat across the entire platter surface, to within microscopic tolerances. Hard drive R/W heads do not actually contact the media as floppy drives do, but ride within a microscopic flow of air over the platter surfaces. A miniscule surface defect or foreign matter (such as a dust particle) can collide with a head and destroy it. Such a *head crash* is often a catastrophic defect that requires hard drive replacement. You'll see more about head flight and surface defects later in this chapter.

Today, *thin-film media* has long since replaced magnetic oxides. Thin-film media is a microscopic layer of pure metal (or a metal compound) bonded to the substrate surface through an interim layer. The media is then coated with a protective layer to help survive head crashing. Thin-film media also tends to be very flat, so R/W heads can be run at microscopic distances from the platter surfaces.

AIRFLOW AND HEAD FLIGHT

Read/write heads in a hard disk drive must travel extremely close to the surface of each platter, but can never actually contact the media while the drive is running. The heads could be mechanically fixed, but fixed-altitude flight does not allow for shock or natural vibration that is always present in a drive assembly. Instead, R/W heads are made to float above a platter surface by suspending the heads on a layer of moving air. Figure 23-3 illustrates the typical airflow in a hard drive. Disk (platter) rotation creates a slight cushion that elevates the heads. You may also notice that some air is channeled through a fine filter that helps to remove any particles from the drive's enclosure.

It is important to note that all hard drives seal their platter assemblies into an airtight chamber. The reason for such a seal is to prevent contamination from dust, dirt, spills, or strands of hair. Contamination that lands on a platter's surface can easily result in a head crash. A head crash can damage the head, the media, or both, and any physical damage can result in an unusable drive. Consider the comparison shown

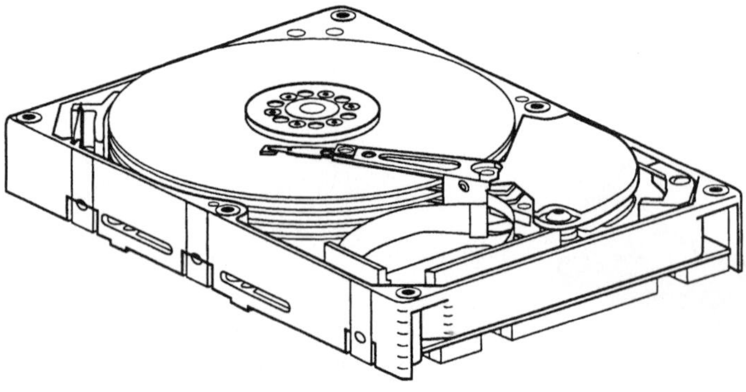

FIGURE 23-2 Maxtor hard drive (Maxtor Corporation)

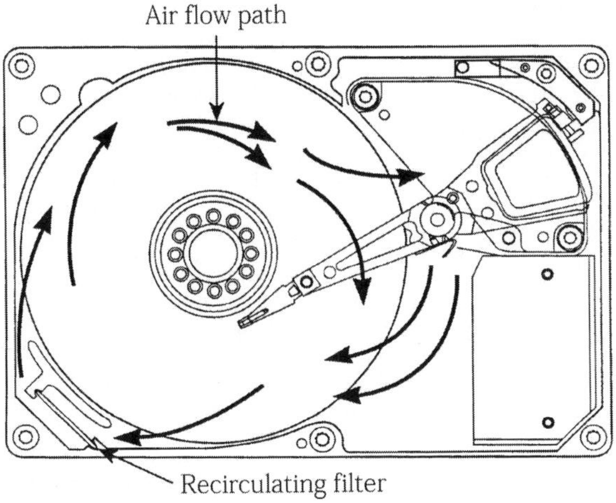

FIGURE 23-3 Airflow patterns in a hard drive (Maxtor Corporation)

in Figure 23-4. During normal operation, a hard drive's R/W head flies above the media at microscopic distances. Many technical professionals relate this to a jumbo jet flying 30 feet above the ground at 600 miles per hour. It follows then that any variation in surface flatness due to platter defects or contaminants can have catastrophic effects on head height. Even an average particle of smoke is ten times *wider* than this flying height. With such proportions, you can understand why it's critically important that the platter compartment remain sealed at all times. The platter compartment can only be opened in a *cleanroom* environment (a small, enclosed room where the air is filtered to remove any contaminants larger than 3 microns). Hard drive assemblers wear gloves and cleanroom suits that cover all but their faces. Masks cover their mouth and nose to prevent breath vapor from contaminating the platters.

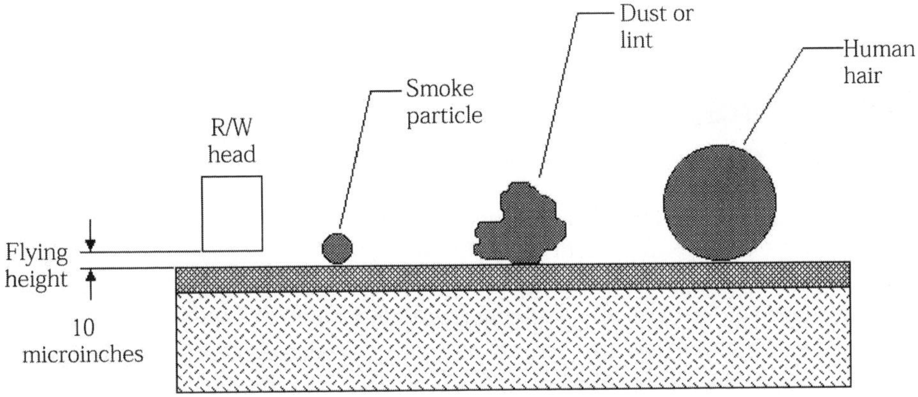

FIGURE 23-4 Comparison of foreign objects on a hard drive platter

DATA DENSITY CHARACTERISTICS

It is desirable to pack as much information as possible in the media of hard drive platters. The *areal density* of a media describes this maximum amount of capacity in terms of megabytes per square inch (sometimes noted as MBSI or MB/in^2). Today's hard drives used in most computers use media supporting 2500 MBSI or more. (Years ago, this figure was more like 400 to 800 MBSI.) As you might imagine, physically smaller platters must hold media with a higher areal density to offer storage capacities similar to larger drives.

Several major factors affect areal density. First, the actual size of magnetic particles in the media places an upper barrier on areal density—smaller particles allow higher areal densities. Larger coercitivity of the media and smaller R/W heads with tighter magnetization fields allow higher areal densities. Finally, head height—the "altitude" of a R/W head over the platter surface—controls density. The closer a R/W head passes to its media, the higher areal densities can be. As heads fly farther away, magnetic fields spread out, resulting in lower densities. Surface smoothness is then another major limiting factor in areal density since smoother surfaces allow R/W heads to fly closer to the media.

There are other factors that define the way data can be packed onto a drive, most of which are related to areal density. Track density indicates the number of tracks per inch (or TPI). The track density is also influenced by the precision of the R/W head-positioning system—finer precision allows more tracks to be defined. Flux density highlights the number of individual magnetic flux transitions per linear inch of track space rated as flux changes per inch (termed FCI, or KFCI for "thousands of FCI"). Finally, you'll probably see references to recording density, which is basically the number of bits per linear inch of track space listed as bits per inch (called BPI, or KBPI for "thousands of BPI").

LATENCY

As fast as a hard drive is, it cannot work instantaneously. There is a finite period of delay between the moment that a read or write command is initiated over the drive's physical interface, and the moment that desired information is available (or placed). This delay is known as *latency*. More specifically, latency refers to the time it takes for needed bytes to pass under a R/W head. If the head has not quite reached the desired location yet, latency can be quite short. If the head has just missed the desired location, the head must wait almost a full rotation before the needed bits are available again, so latency can be rather long. In general, a disk drive is specified with average latency that (statistically) is time for the spindle to make half of a full rotation. For a disk rotating at 3600 RPM (or 60 rotations per second), a full rotation is completed in (1/60) 16.7mS. Average latency would then be (16.7/2) 8.3mS. Disks spinning at 5200 RPM offer an average latency of 5.8mS, and so on. As a rule, the faster a disk spins, the lower its latency will be. Ultimately, disk speed is limited by centrifugal forces acting on the platters.

TRACKS, SECTORS, AND CYLINDERS

As with floppy drives, you cannot simply place data anywhere on a hard drive platter—the drive would have no idea where to look for data or whether the data was even valid. The information on each platter must be sorted and organized into a series of known, standard locations. Each platter side can be considered as a two-dimensional field possessing length and width. With this sort of geometry, data is recorded in sets of concentric circles running from the disk spindle to the platter edge. A drive can move its R/W heads over the spinning media to locate needed data or programs in a matter of milliseconds. Every concentric circle on a platter is known as a *track*. A modern platter generally contains 2048 to more than 16,278 tracks. You can see a comparison of tracks versus drive capacity for several current Maxtor hard drives outlined in Table 23-1. Figure 23-5 shows data organization on a simple platter assembly. Note that only one side of the three platters is shown.

TABLE 23-1 COMPARISON OF MAXTOR DRIVE PARAMETERS VS. CAPACITY

MODEL	TRACKS (CYLINDERS)	HEADS	SECTORS	CAPACITY
88400D8	16278	16	63	8400MB
86480D6	13395	15	63	6480MB
84320D4	8930	15	63	4320MB
83240D3	6697	15	63	3240MB
82160D2	4465	15	63	2160MB

Although each surface of a platter is a two-dimensional area, the number of platter surfaces involved in a hard drive (4, 6, 8, or more) bring a third dimension (height) into play. Since each track is located directly over the same tracks on subsequent platters, each track in a platter assembly can be visualized as a "cylinder" that passes through every platter. The number of cylinders is equal to the number of tracks on one side of a platter.

Once a R/W head finishes reading one track, the head must be stepped to another (usually adjacent) track. This stepping process, no matter how rapid, does require some finite amount of time. This is called *seek time*, and is often under 1ms for track-to-track seeks. When the head tries to step directly from the end of one track to the beginning of another, the head will arrive too late to catch the new track's index pulse(s), so the drive will have to wait almost an entire rotation to synchronize with the track index pulse. By offsetting the start points of each track, as in Figure 23-6, head travel time can be compensated for. This *cylinder skewing* technique is intended to improve hard drive performance by reducing the disk time lost during normal head steps. A head should be able to identify and read the desired information from a track within one disk rotation.

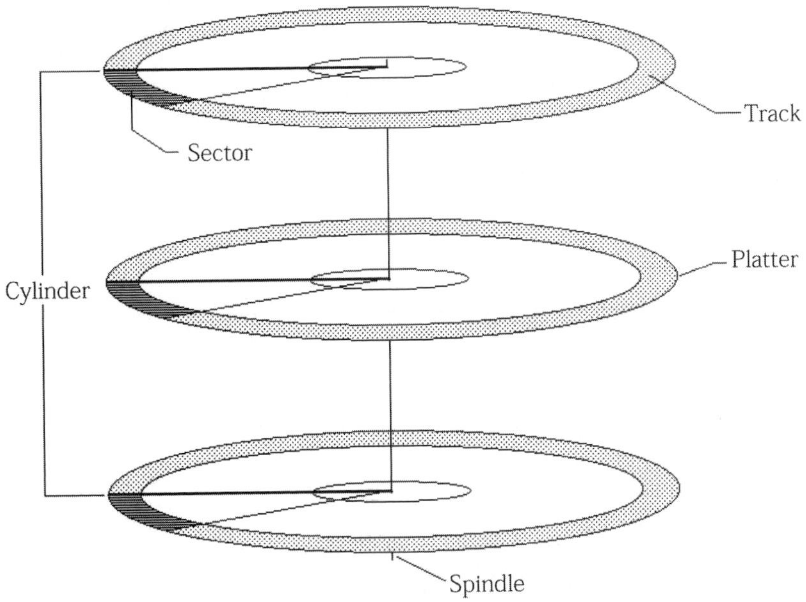

FIGURE 23-5 Data organization on a hard drive

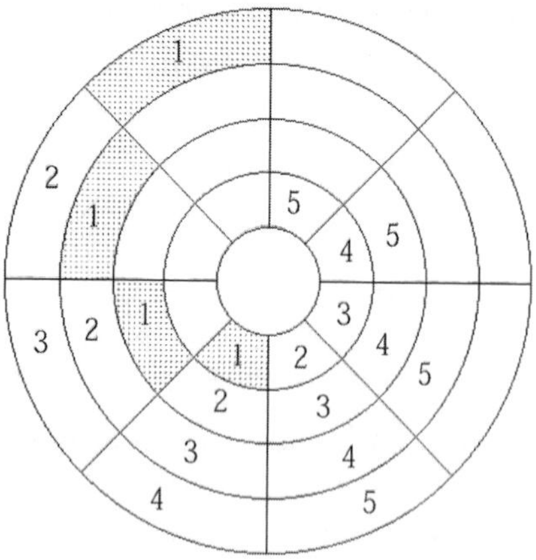

FIGURE 23-6 An example of cylinder skewing

Tracks are broken down even further into small segments called *sectors*. As with DOS floppy disks, a sector holds 512 bytes of data, along with error checking and housekeeping data that identifies the sector, track, and results calculated by cyclical redundancy checking (CRC). The location and ID information for each sector is developed when the drive is low-level formatted at the factory. After formatting, only sector data and CRC bytes are updated during writing. If sector ID information is accidentally overwritten or corrupted, the data recorded in the afflicted sector becomes unreadable.

Figure 23-7 shows the layout for a typical sector on a Maxtor SCSI drive. As you can see, there is much more than just 512 bytes of data. The start of every sector is marked with a pulse. The pulse signaling the first sector of a track is called the *index pulse*. There are two portions to every sector: an address area and data area. The address area is used to identify the sector. This is critically important because the drive must be able to identify precisely which cylinder, head, and sector is about to be read or written. This location information is recorded in the address field, and is followed by two bytes of cyclical redundancy check (CRC) data. When a drive identifies a location, it generates a CRC code that it compares to the CRC code recorded on the disk. If the two CRC codes match, the address is assumed to be valid, and disk operation can continue. Otherwise, an error has occurred and the entire sector is considered invalid. This failure usually precipitates a catastrophic DOS error message.

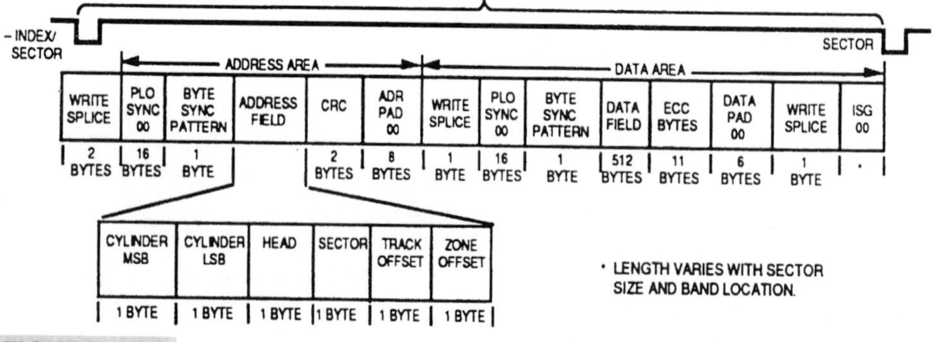

FIGURE 23-7 A typical hard drive sector layout (Maxtor Corporation)

After a number of bytes are encountered for drive timing and synchronization, up to 512 bytes can be read or written to the data field. The data is processed to derive 11 bytes of ECC error checking code using Reed Solomon encoding. If data is being read, the derived ECC is compared to the recorded ECC. When the codes match, data is assumed to be valid and drive operation continues. Otherwise, a data read error is assumed. During writing, the old ECC data is replaced with the new ECC data derived for the current data. It is interesting to note that only the data and ECC fields of a sector are written after formatting. All other sector data remains untouched until the drive is reformatted. If a retentivity problem should eventually allow one or more bits to become corrupt in the address area, the sector will fail.

ZONED RECORDING

In the early days of hard drives, every track had the same number of sectors (64, or 0 through 63). This worked well, but designers realized that for a constant angular velocity (CAV) drive, the data was recorded more densely on the inner tracks where the circumference is lower, and less densely on the outer tracks where the circumference is higher. A feature known as *zoned recording* was added to the drive, which allows a variable number of tracks. The total number of tracks is divided into a number of areas, or zones (16 zones). All of the tracks within a zone use the same number of sectors, but inner zones use fewer sectors, while outer zones use more sectors. Zoned recording lets hard drives make the most efficient use of their storage space. Zoned recording is managed by the drive itself, so you may still be able to enter a fixed number in the "Sectors per Track" entry under the CMOS setup. Current hard drives can run from 195 to 312 physical sectors per track.

SECTOR SPARING (DEFECT MANAGEMENT)

Not all sectors on a hard drive are usable. When a drive is formatted, bad sectors must be removed from normal use. The *sparing process* works to ensure that each track has access to the appropriate number of working sectors. When sparing is performed in-line (as a drive is being formatted), faulty sectors cause all subsequent sectors to be shifted up one sector. In-line sparing is not widely used. Field defect sparing (after the format process is complete) assigns (or remaps) faulty sectors to other working sectors located in spare disk tracks that are reserved for that purpose. For example, EIDE/UDMA hard drives use field defect sparing. It reserves a full 16 tracks for spare sectors (often referred to as the *defect management zone*). Faulty sectors are typically marked for reallocation when the disk is formatted.

The only place where faulty sectors are *absolutely* not permitted is on track 00. Track 00 is used to hold a hard drive's partition and FAT information. If a drive cannot read or write to track 00, the entire drive is rendered unusable. If a sector in track 00 should fail during operation, reformatting the drive to lock out the bad sector will not necessarily recover the drive's operation. Track 00 failures usually necessitate reformatting the drive from scratch, or replacing it entirely.

LANDING ZONE

The R/W heads of a hard drive fly only a microscopic distance from their respective platter surfaces. They are held aloft with air currents produced by the spinning platters. When the drive is turned off, however, the platters slow to a halt. During this spindown period, airflow falls rapidly, and heads can literally "crash" into the platter surfaces. Whenever a head touches a platter surface, data can be irretrievably destroyed. Even during normal operation, a sudden shock or bump can cause one or more heads to skid across their surfaces. Although a drive can usually be reformatted after a head crash, data and programs would have to be reloaded from scratch.

In order to avoid a head crash during normal spindown, a cylinder is reserved (either the innermost or outermost cylinder) as a *landing zone* (or LZ). No data is stored on the landing zone, so any surface problems caused by head landings are harmless. All hard drives today will automatically move the head assembly over the landing zone before spindown, then gently lock the heads into place until power is restored. Locking helps to ensure that random shocks and vibrations do not shake the heads onto adjacent data-carrying tracks and cause damage while power is off. Older hard drives required a specific "landing zone" entry in the CMOS setup. But today, the process is automatic, so you can usually just enter **0** for the LZ, or allow the system to autodetect the LZ.

INTERLEAVE

The *interleave* of a hard drive refers to the order in which sectors are numbered on a platter. Interleave was a critical factor in older desktop computer systems where the core logic (the CPU and memory) was relatively slow compared to drive performance. It was necessary to create artificial delays in the drive to allow core logic to catch up. Delays were accomplished by physically separating the sectors (numbering contiguous sectors out of order). This ordering forced the drive to read a sector, then skip one or more sectors (1, 2, 3 or more) to reach the next subsequent sector. Effectively, the "interleaved" drive would have to make several rotations before all sectors on a track could be read.

The ratio of a sector's length versus the distance between two subsequent sectors is known as the *interleave factor*. For example, if a drive reads a sector and skips a sector to reach the next sequential sector, the interleave factor would be 1:3, and so on. The greater the interleave, the more rotations needed to read all the sectors on a track, and the slower the drive. To achieve the highest disk performance, interleave should be eliminated. Since drive and interface logic today is so much faster than even the fastest hard drive, the issue of interleave is largely irrelevant now. Drives no longer interleave their sectors, so all sectors are in sequential order around the track, and the interleave factor is 1:1—all data on a track can be read in one disk rotation (minus latency). An interleave factor of 1:1 yields optimal drive performance.

> As a rule, do not allow any drive utility to adjust or "optimize" the drive interleave. Changing the interleave not only destroys existing data, but it can also seriously impair drive performance.

WRITE PRECOMPENSATION

As you have already seen, a hard drive spins its platter(s) at a constant rate. This is known as *constant angular velocity* (or CAV). Although constant rotation requires only a very simple motor circuit, extra demands are placed on the media. Tracks closer to the spindle are physically shorter than tracks toward the platter's outer edge. Shorter tracks result in shorter sectors. For inner sectors to hold the same amount of data as outer sectors, data must be packed more densely on the inner sectors—each magnetic flux reversal is actually closer together. Unfortunately, smaller flux reversals produce weaker magnetic fields in the R/W heads during reading.

If the inner sectors are written with a stronger magnetic field, flux transitions stored in the media will be stronger. When the inner sectors are then read, a clearer, more well-defined signal will result. The use of increased writing current to compensate for diminished disk response is known as *write precompensation* (or WP). The track where write precompensation is expected to begin is specified in the drive's parameter table in CMOS setup. Write precompensation filled an important role in early drives that used older, oxide-based media. Today's thin-film media and very small drive geometries (combined with zoned recording techniques) result in low signal differences across the platter area, so write precompensation (although still specified) is rarely meaningful anymore. In most cases, you can enter **0** for WP, or allow the system to autodetect the WP.

DRIVE PARAMETERS AND TRANSLATION

A host computer must know the key parameters of its installed hard drive before the drive can be used. There are six parameters that a system must know: the number of cylinders, heads, and sectors, as well as the track where write precompensation begins, what track the landing zone is on, and the drive's total formatted capacity. These parameters are stored in the computer's CMOS RAM and configured with the CMOS setup utility. If a new drive is installed, the CMOS setup can easily be updated to show the changes. You can tell a lot about a drive by reviewing its parameters. Consider the Maxtor 88400D8 shown in Table 23-1. With 16 heads, 63 sectors per track, and 16,278 tracks (cylinders), the capacity works out as (16278 x 16 x 63 x 512) 8,401,010,688 bytes (or 8.4GB).

There are two interesting things to note about the drives of Table 23-1. First, the write precompensation and landing zone entries are essentially unused. In most cases, the landing zone is now an automated feature of the particular drive. The second issue to consider is that these numbers are logical, *not* physical. Just imagine that with two heads per platter, you'd need 8 platters to support 16 heads—not too likely in today's small form-factor drives. Also, in practice, the number of sectors per track can differ because of zoned recording techniques. What this means is that the drive parameters you are entering into CMOS are translation parameters. The electronics on the drive itself converts (or *translates*) those parameters into actual physical drive locations.

START TIME

Booting a computer can take up to 30 seconds—often more. Some of this time is an artificial delay needed to initialize the hard drive. From the moment power is applied to the hard drive, it can take anywhere from 7 to 10 seconds for the drive's onboard controller to start and initialize the drive where it can be recognized by the system POST. This is known as the drive's *start time*. Boot problems with a new hard drive are frequently caused by an insufficient delay at boot time. The BIOS attempts to check for the presence of a hard drive that has not yet had time to initialize.

POWER MODE DEFINITIONS

Modern hard drives are not simply "on" or "off." They operate in any one of several modes, and each mode makes different power demands on the host system. This is particularly important because today's PCs are becoming ever-more power conscious, so the ability to control drive power is an integral part of PC power conservation systems. Typical hard drives operate in any of five different power modes:

- *Spin-up* The drive is spinning up following initial application of power and has not yet reached full speed. This demands about 14W and is particularly demanding of the power supply. (If the supply is marginal or overloaded, the hard drive may not spin up properly.)
- *Seek* This is a random access operation by the disk drive as it tries to locate the required track for reading or writing. This demands about 8.5–9.0W.
- *Read/Write* A seek has been completed, and data is being read from or written to the drive. This uses about 5W.
- *Idle* This is a basic power conservation mode where the drive is spinning and all other circuitry is powered on, but the head actuator is parked and powered off. This drops power demands to about 4W, yet the drive is capable of responding to read commands within 40ms.
- *Standby* The spindle motor is not running (the drive spins down). This is the main power conservation mode, which requires just 1W. It may take up to several seconds for the drive to leave this mode (or spin up) upon receipt of a command that requires disk access.

IDE/EIDE HARD DRIVE CONCEPTS

IDE hard drives have come a long way since their introduction in the late 1980s. In fact, IDE technology has come so far that it's difficult to keep all of the concepts straight. Let's start by examining the important concepts and attributes of IDE and its successors.

Binary Megabytes vs. Decimal Megabytes

Most folks know that hard drive sizes are measured in megabytes (or MB) and gigabytes (or GB). However, beginners and experienced technicians alike are often confused by the difference between "binary megabytes" and "decimal megabytes" (as well as for gigabytes). For example, you'll notice that when you install a new 4GB hard drive, utilities like the CMOS setup, FDISK, and Windows Explorer will report only about 3.72GB, but other utilities like CHKDSK report about 4GB. This difference is often confusing, but it's due to the way manufacturers and software makers calculate drive capacity. Technically, hard drive capacity is calculated by multiplying the number of cylinders, sectors, and heads times 512 such as this:

Capacity = Cylinders x Heads xSectors x 512 (bytes per sector)

So if you're using an AC2850 drive with 1654 cylinders, 16 heads, and 63 sectors, you'd wind up with:

1654 x 16 x 63 x 512 = 853,622,784 bytes

By comparison, an AC34000 drive with 7752 cylinders, 16 heads, and 63 sectors would yield

7752 x 16 x 63 x512 = 4,000,776,192 bytes

The problem is that hard drive manufacturers use the notion of decimal megabytes (or decimal gigabytes) to determine the size of their hard drives. To calculate drive sizes in decimal megabytes, just divide the drive size by 1,000,000 (or 1,000,000,000 for GB). For the AC2850, you'd get

853,622,784 / 1,000,000 = 853.6MB

For the AC34000, you'd get

4,000,776,192 / 1,000,000,000 = 4.0GB

Makes sense right? The problem is that many software makers will use binary megabytes (or binary gigabytes) to calculate drive sizes. A binary megabyte is 1,048,576 bytes, and a binary gigabyte is 1,073,741,824 bytes; so here's how a lot of software will report the AC2850:

853,622,784 bytes / 1,048,576 = 814MB

And here's the calculation for the AC34000:

4,000,776,192 bytes / 1,073,741,824 = 3.72GB

These are simply two slightly different ways of representing the same drives, so both methods are correct. The important issue here is that you recognize the difference and do not mistake that difference as being a problem with the drive.

IDE/ATA

IDE (Integrated Drive Electronics) and ATA (AT Attachment) are basically one and the same thing—a disk drive scheme designed to integrate the controller onto the drive itself instead of relying on a stand-alone controller board as older MFM and RLL drives did. This approach reduces interface costs and makes drive firmware implementations easier. IDE proved to be a low-cost, easily configured system—so much so that it created a boom in the disk drive industry. Although the terms IDE and ATA are sometimes used interchangeably, ATA is the formal standard that defines the drive and how it operates, while IDE is really the trade name that refers to the 40-pin interface and drive controller architecture designed to implement the ATA standard.

ATAPI

One of the major disadvantages of ATA is that it was designed for hard drives only. With the broad introduction of CD-ROM drives in the late 1980s, designers needed a means of attaching CD-ROMs (and other devices such as tape drives) to the existing ATA (IDE) interface—rather than employing a stand-alone (proprietary) controller card. The ATA Packet Interface (or ATAPI) is an extension of the ATA (IDE) interface designed to allow non-hard-drive devices to plug into an ordinary ATA (IDE) port. While hard drives enjoy ATA (IDE) support through BIOS, ATAPI devices require a device driver to support them. Booting from an ATAPI CD-ROM is only possible with an El Torito CD-ROM and the latest BIOS.

ATA-2, Fast-ATA, and EIDE

By the early 1990s, it became clear that ATA architecture would soon be overwhelmed by advances in hard drive technology. The hard drive industry responded by developing the ATA-2 standard as an extension of ATA. ATA-2 is largely regarded as a significant improvement to ATA. It defines faster PIO (Programmed I/O) and DMA (Direct Memory Access) data transfer modes, adds more powerful drive commands (such as the "Identify Drive" command to support auto-identification in CMOS), adds support for a second drive channel, handles block data transfers (Block Transfer Mode), and defines a new means of addressing sectors on the hard drive using Logical Block Addressing (LBA). LBA has proven to be a very effective vehicle for overcoming the traditional 528MB hard drive size limit. Yet ATA-2 continues to use the same 40-pin physical interface used by ATA and is backward compatible with ATA (IDE) drives.

Along with ATA-2, you'll probably find two additional terms: EIDE (Enhanced IDE) and Fast-ATA. These are not standards—merely different implementations of the ATA-2 standard. EIDE represents the Western Digital implementation of ATA-2 that builds upon both the ATA-2 and ATAPI standards. This has been so effective that EIDE has become the "generic" term. Seagate and Quantum have thrown their support behind the Fast-ATA implementation of the ATA-2 standard. However, Fast-ATA builds on ATA-2 only. For all practical purposes, there is no significant difference between ATA-2, EIDE, and Fast-ATA, and you'll probably see these three terms used interchangeably (though this is not *technically* correct).

ATA-3

A more recent implementation of the ATA standard is ATA-3. It does not define any new data transfer modes, but it does improve the reliability of PIO mode 4. It also offers a simple password-based security scheme, more sophisticated power management features, and Self-Monitoring Analysis and Reporting Technology (SMART). ATA-3 is also backward compatible with ATA-2, ATAPI, and ATA devices. Since no new data transfer modes are defined by ATA-3, you may also see the generic term EIDE used interchangeably (though this is also not technically correct).

Ultra-ATA/33

The push for ever-faster data transfer rates is a never-ending one, and the Ultra-ATA standard represents an implementation of ATA/ATAPI-4 by providing a high-performance bus mastering 33MB/s DMA data transfer rate. The implementation of Ultra-ATA is usually called Ultra-DMA/33 (or UDMA/33). You'll need an Ultra-ATA drive, controller, and BIOS to support an Ultra-ATA drive system, but it is fully backward compatible with previous ATA standards. You can use ordinary 40-pin IDE-type cables for UDMA/33 unless any of the following issues occurs:

- The standard cable is low-quality, damaged, or weakened by many installs.
- The system suffers from excessive signal noise. These systems may have multiple drives, dual power supplies, or an integrated CRT.
- The system is overclocked (or otherwise configured beyond the manufacturer's supported specifications).

Ultra-ATA/66

The Ultra-ATA standard for ATA/ATAPI-4 was upgraded to support an even faster high-performance bus mastering 66MB/s DMA data transfer rate. This more recent implementation of Ultra-ATA is usually called Ultra-DMA/66 (or UDMA/66). You'll need an Ultra-ATA/66 drive, controller, and BIOS to support an Ultra-ATA/66 drive system, but it is fully backward compatible with previous ATA standards. Unlike the Ultra-ATA/33 approach, you cannot use ordinary 40-pin IDE-type cables to connect drives and controllers. Instead, you'll need a specially designed 40-pin/80-conductor cable (typically provided with UDMA/66 drives). Also keep in mind that the operating system must be enabled for DMA transfers.

The following are some common UDMA/66 issues you should be aware of.

- Make sure the signal cable is Ultra-ATA/66 capable. An Ultra-ATA/66-compliant cable is a 40-pin, 80-conductor cable with a black connector on one end, a blue connector on the other end, and a gray connector in the middle. In addition, pin 34 on the cable should be notched or cut (though this may be difficult to see with the human eye).
- Make sure the system board (motherboard) controller is capable of supporting Ultra-ATA/66. An Ultra-ATA/66-capable controller has a detect circuit that can detect line 34 missing on the cable. If there is no detect circuit, the system can wrongly detect the presence of an Ultra-ATA/66 cable and try to configure the device for a higher transfer rate.
- Some system board (motherboard) controllers may not successfully handle Ultra-ATA/66 on both the primary and secondary channels. If you have difficulty with a UDMA/66 device on the secondary controller channel, consider troubleshooting with the device in the primary master position.
- If you have trouble getting a UDMA/66 system configured properly, contact the system board (motherboard) or controller card manufacturer for the latest BIOS upgrade (and any Ultra-ATA/66 device drivers or patches).
- Make sure the operating system is DMA capable, and verify that the DMA mode is activated. For Windows 95/98, check the drive's Properties dialog in the Device Manager.
- Make sure the Ultra-ATA/66-capable drive has been configured to run at Ultra-ATA/66 transfer rates. Some drives ship with the UDMA/66 mode disabled by default and require a jumper change and/or software utility in order to activate the UDMA/66 mode.

DATA TRANSFER RATES

Data transfer rates play a major role in drive performance. In practice, there are two measures of data transfer: the rate at which data is taken from the platters and the rate at which data is passed between the drive and controller. The internal data transfer between the platters and drive buffer is typically the slower rate. Older drives could run around 5MB/sec, but newer Ultra-ATA drives like the Maxtor DiamondMax 2160 run at 14MB/s. The external data transfer between the drive and controller (the "interface rate") is often the *faster* rate. Older drives provided between 5 and 8MB/sec, but ATA-2 (EIDE) drives can operate up to 16MB/sec. Ultra-DMA/33 drives can run at 33MB/s, and Ultra-DMA/66 drives can handle burst data transfers of 66MB/s. The modern standards of IDE/EIDE external data transfer are listed as PIO (or Programmed I/O) and DMA (Direct Memory Access) modes. The PIO mode specifies how fast data is transferred to and from the drive, as shown in Table 23-2.

You may notice that the EIDE-specific modes (PIO-3 and PIO-4) use the IORDY hardware flow control line. This means that the drive can use the IORDY line to slow down the interface when necessary. Interfaces without proper IORDY support may cause data corruption in the fast PIO modes (so you'd be stuck with the slower modes). When choosing an EIDE drive and controller, always be sure to check that the IORDY line is being used.

By comparison, DMA data transfers mean that the data is transferred *directly* between the drive and memory without using the CPU as an intermediary (as is the case with PIO). In true multitasking operating systems like OS/2, Windows NT, or Linux, DMA transfers leave the CPU free to do something useful during disk transfers. In a DOS or Windows environment, the CPU will have to wait for the transfer to finish anyway, so in these cases DMA transfers don't offer that much of a multitasking advantage. There are two distinct types of Direct Memory Access: ordinary DMA and bus mastering DMA. Ordinary DMA uses the DMA controller on the system's motherboard to perform the complex task of arbitration, grabbing the system bus, and transferring the data. With bus mastering DMA, all this is done by logic in the drive controller itself.

Unfortunately, the DMA controller on traditional ISA bus systems is slow—and out of the question for use with a modern hard disk. VL bus controller cards cannot be used as DMA targets at all, and can only handle bus mastering DMA. Only EISA and PCI-based interfaces make non-bus-mastering DMA viable: EISA type "B" DMA will transfer 4MB/s, and PCI type "F" DMA will transfer between 6 and 8MB/s. Today, the proper software support for DMA is relatively rare (as well as the interfaces supporting it). Still, the DMA data transfer modes are listed in Table 23-3.

TABLE 23-2 DATA TRANSFER SPEEDS VS. PIO MODES

PIO MODE	CYCLE TIME (NS)	TRANSFER RATE (MB/S)	NOTES
0	600		These are the old ATA (IDE) modes.
1	383	5.2	
2	240	8.3	
3	180 IORDY	11.1	These are the newer ATA-2 (EIDE) modes.
4	120 IORDY	16.6	

TABLE 23-3 DATA TRANSFER SPEEDS VS. DMA MODES

DMA MODE		CYCLE TIME (NS)	TRANSFER RATE (MB/S)	NOTES
Single Word	0	960	2.1	Also in ATA
	1	480	4.2	
	2	240	8.3	
Multiword	0	480	4.2	Also in ATA
	1	150	13.3	
	2	120	16.6	
	3	—	33.0	Ultra-DMA/33
	4	—	66.0	Ultra-DMA/66

BLOCK MODE TRANSFERS

Traditionally, an interrupt (IRQ) is generated each time a read or write command is passed to the drive. This causes a certain amount of overhead work for the host system and CPU. If it were possible to transfer *multiple* sectors of data between the drive and host without generating an IRQ, data transfer could be accomplished much more efficiently. Block mode transfers allow up to 128 sectors of data to be transferred at a single time, and can improve transfers as much as 30 percent. However, block mode transfers are not terribly effective on single-tasking operating systems like DOS—any improvement over a few percent usually indicates bad buffer cache management on the part of the drive. Finally, the block size that is optimal for drive throughput isn't always the best for system performance. For example, the DOS FAT file system tends to favor a block size equal to the cluster size.

IDEAS OF BUS MASTERING

Bus mastering is a high-performance enhancement to the drive controller interface on your system. (You may see some motherboards or chipsets mention bus master support as "BM-IDE.") When configured properly, bus mastering uses Direct Memory Access (DMA) data transfers to reduce the CPU's workload when it comes to saving or recalling data from the EIDE/IDE drive (such as a hard drive or ATAPI CD-ROM). By comparison, Programmed I/O (PIO) data transfer modes are very CPU intensive. Bus mastering is particularly useful if you have multiple disk-intensive applications running simultaneously. Many modern PCs support bus mastering, but to make the most of bus master performance, your system must have all of the following elements:

- The motherboard (drive controller) must be bus master IDE compliant.
- The motherboard BIOS must support bus mastering.
- You need a multitasking operating system such as Windows 95/98/2000.
- A bus mastering device driver is needed for the operating system.
- You need a bus-mastering-compatible EIDE/IDE device (disk drive, CD-ROM) that supports "DMA multiword" modes.

You can use bus master IDE and non-bus-master IDE devices in the same system, but the non-bus-master IDE devices will reduce the overall performance of the bus mastering devices. However, bus mastering IDE is not a cure-all for system performance problems. In fact, bus mastering will probably not benefit the system significantly if you run DOS applications, work with only single applications at a time, or use multiple applications that are not disk intensive.

Windows 95/98 IDE Bus Master Drivers

As you noticed above, you'll need a bus master driver to support your operating system (namely, Windows 95/98). The commercial release of Windows 95 offered only a generic solution (ESDI_506.PDR), and the version released with OSR2 is still quite basic. The bus master drivers shipped with Windows 98 will generally offer better performance. For top performance, you should use the bus master driver that accompanies your motherboard or other bus-master-compliant drive controller. You can check some of the following sources for current bus master drivers:

- Drivers Headquarters: **http://www.drivershq.com/**
- Intel Bus Master Driver 3.0: **http://web2.iadfw.net/ksm/drivers/bmide_95.exe**
- Intel Bus Master Driver 2.85: **http://web2.iadfw.net/ksm/drivers/bmide285.exe**
- ASUS Bus Master Driver: **ftp://ftp1.asus.com.tw/pub/ASUS/Drivers/bmide_95.exe**
- Elitegroup (ECS) Bus Master Driver: **ftp://ftp.ecs.com.tw/pub/ide/triton/430v17.exe**
- Tyan Bus Master Driver 2.0: **ftp://204.156.147.247:21/pub/motherboard/tynbm20.zip**

Bus Master Driver Problems Under Windows 95/98

While bus mastering can clearly enhance the drive performance of a busy multitasking system, it is not without its problems. As it turns out, bus master driver issues are the most prevalent problems. The two most common issues are (1) the CD-ROM or IDE-type HDD on the secondary drive channel disappears after installing bus master driver, and (2) Windows 95/98 takes a long time to boot after bus master drivers are installed.

In both cases, you'll notice that the secondary controller channel (IDE) no longer appears in the Device Manager. This is because bus master drivers do not support ATA (IDE) controllers correctly. You'll need to install the bus master driver for the primary (EIDE) drive channel and leave the PIO driver in place to support the secondary (IDE) drive channel. Install the bus master driver, and then alter the registry to manually redirect the secondary IDE drive channel to use a standard IDE driver again:

> Altering the Windows 95/98 registry can have a profound effect on your system, or even prevent the system from booting. Always make a backup copy of the original registry files (SYSTEM.DAT and USER.DAT) before attempting to edit them.

1. Start RegEdit, load the Registry file, and find the entry HKEY_LOCAL_MACHINE/System/CurrentControlSet/control/Services/Class/hdc.
2. There should be four subdirectories: 0000–0003.
3. Find the one where DriverDesc reads something like "Primary Bus Master IDE controller" or "Secondary Bus Master IDE controller," according to the port you want to change (should be 0002 or 0003). You'd most likely want to change the secondary entry.
4. In this subdirectory, change PortDriver from ESDI_506.PDR (or whatever bus master driver you're using) to IDEATAPI.MPD.
5. You can also change the DriverDesc to something like "Standard IDE/ESDI controller," which will produce a more familiar entry when viewed in the System Manager.
6. Save your changes and reboot the computer.

Your secondary (IDE) drive controller channel should now be using a standard IDE driver, and the IDE devices on that channel (such as the CD-ROM) should now appear normally. Here's another trick that may shorten the startup time: start Windows 95/98 in Safe Mode and delete all drives in System Manager. Then reboot the PC and allow Windows 95/98 to redetect all the drives automatically.

Some technicians have suggested that configuring an ATAPI CD-ROM as the slave device when it's the only device on the secondary (IDE) drive channel might work when using bus master drivers. Normally, the only IDE device would be jumpered as the master. Please note that this suggestion won't damage the CD-ROM or drive controller, but it has not been tested to verify whether it actually works. Given the proliferation of bus master hardware and software, this suggestion may or may not work. Consider this suggestion as a last resort.

UNDERSTANDING SMART TECHNOLOGY

SMART (Self-Monitoring Analysis and Reporting Technology) is a self-diagnostic system that enables the PC to predict the impending failures of devices such as disk drives. With a given failure prediction, the user or system manager can back up key data, replace a suspect device *before* data loss, and avoid undesired downtime. SMART is a key for improving data integrity and data availability of the PC.

SMART goes by a variety of names in the computer industry. The term "Predictive Failure Analysis" (PFA) was given to SMART technology by its inventor, IBM. PFA is implemented in all of IBM's mainframe computer systems. Compaq was one of the first companies to implement SMART in their hard drives, and this was dubbed "Drive Failure Prediction" (DFP). The initial Compaq Computer SMART specification was modified and submitted for general industry consideration by the Small Form Factor Committee. SMART is now being standardized by ANSI in the ATA-4 (ANSI X3T13 ATA\ATAPI-4) specification.

To implement SMART, the host computer must have BIOS or device driver support that is capable of sending SMART commands to and from the ATA interface registers. SMART technology is growing in popularity, and all current Maxtor drives are SMART ready. You can learn more about SMART from Maxtor at **http://www.maxtor.com/technology/whitepapers/smart0.html**. You can also check with StorageSoft at **http://www.storagesoft.com/** for detailed information on their SMART utility.

UNDERSTANDING DRIVE CACHING

Ideally, a drive should respond instantaneously—data should be available the moment it's requested. Unfortunately, the instant access and transfer of data is impossible even with today's magnetic (and optical) storage technologies. The inescapable laws of physics govern the limitations of mechanical systems such as spindles and head stepping, and mechanical delays will always be present (to some extent) in drive systems. The problem now facing computer designers is that mechanical drive systems—as fast and precise as they are—still lag far behind the computer circuitry handling the information. In the world of personal computers, a millisecond is a very long time. For DOS-based systems, you often must wait for disk access to be completed before DOS allows another operation to begin. Such delays can be quite irritating when the drive is accessing huge programs and data files typical of current software packages. Drives use a technique called *drive caching* to increase the apparent speed of drive systems.

Caching basically allocates a small amount of solid-state memory that acts as an interim storage area (or *buffer*) located right on the drive. A cache is typically loaded with information that is *anticipated* to be required by the system. When a disk read is initiated, the cache is checked for desired information. If the desired information is actually in the cache (a *cache hit*), that information is transferred from the cache buffer to the core logic at electronic rates. No disk access occurs, and very fast data transfer is achieved. If the desired information is not in the cache (a *cache miss*), the data is taken from the hard disk at normal drive speeds with no improvement in performance. Today's hard drives use as much as 256KB of modern high-performance memory such as EDO RAM (the same type of RAM used on many Pentium motherboards) for onboard drive cache. A variety of complex software algorithms are used to predict what disk information to load and save in a cache. Figure 23-8 illustrates the caching algorithm used by Maxtor Corporation for some of their ProDrive hard drives.

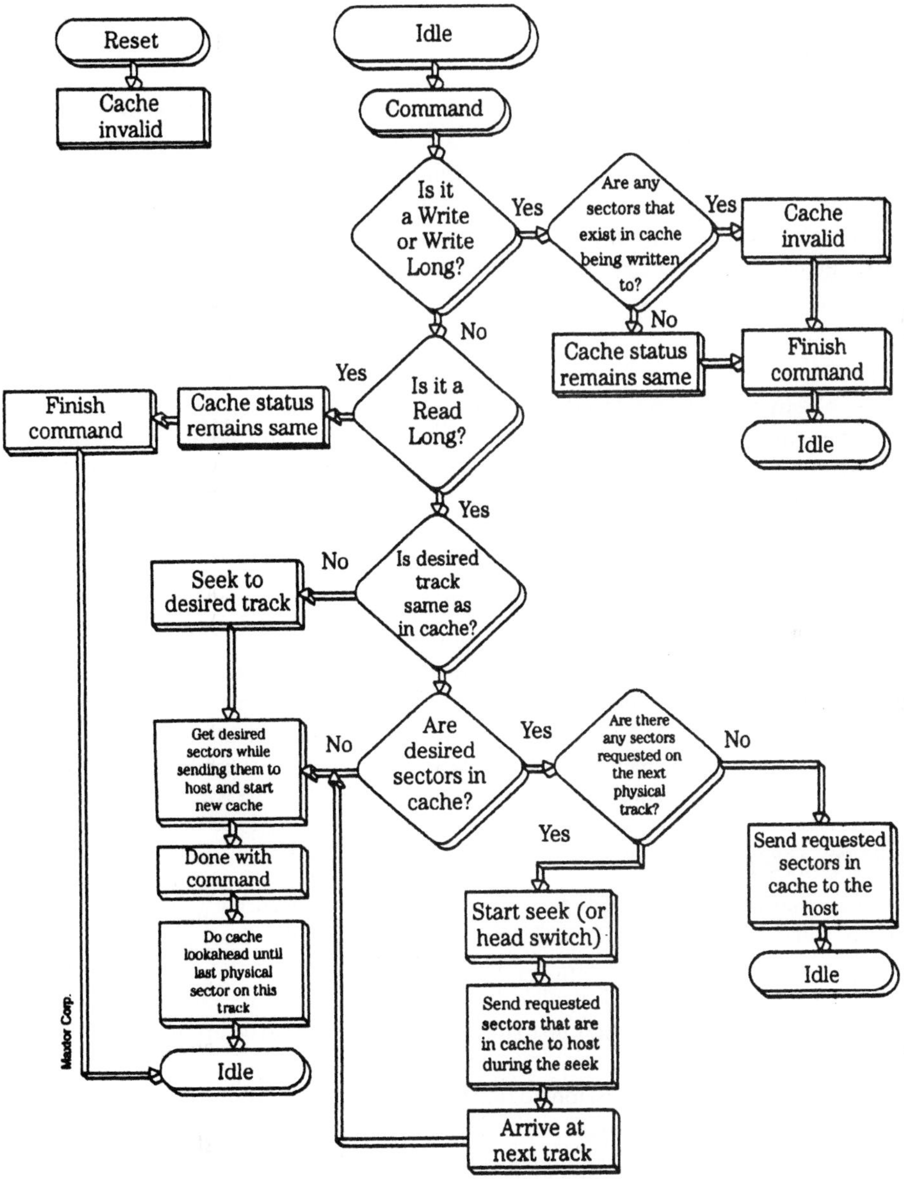

FIGURE 23-8 A cache control algorithm (Maxtor Corporation)

Although the majority of caches are intended to buffer read operations, some caches also buffer write operations. A write cache accepts the data to be saved from core logic, then returns system control while the drive works separately to save the information. Keep in mind that a cache does not accelerate the drive itself. A cache merely helps to move your system along so that you need not wait for drive delays. In terms of general implementation, a cache can be located on the hard drive itself, or on the drive controller board. For most computers using system-level hard drive interfaces (UDMA or SCSI), any cache is usually located on the drive itself.

Drive Construction

Now that you have a background in major hard drive concepts and operations, it is time to take a drive apart and show you how all the key pieces fit together. While it's extremely rare that you should ever need to disassemble a hard drive, the understanding of each part and its placement will help you to appreciate drive testing and the various hard drive failure modes. An exploded diagram for a Quantum hard drive is illustrated in Figure 23-9. This book concentrates on six areas: the frame, platters, R/W heads, head actuators, spindle motor, and electronics package. Let's look at each area in turn.

FRAME

The mechanical frame is remarkably important to the successful operation of a hard drive. The frame (or *chassis*) affects a drive's structural, thermal, and electrical integrity. A frame must be rigid, and provide a steady platform for mounting the working components. Larger drives typically use a chassis of cast aluminum, but the small drive in your notebook or sub-notebook computer may use a plastic frame. The particular frame material really depends on the *form factor* (dimensions) of your drive.

PLATTERS

As you probably read early in this chapter, platters are relatively heavy-duty disks of aluminum, glass, or ceramic composite material. Platters are then coated on both sides with a layer of magnetic material (the actual media) and covered with a protective layer. Finished and polished platters are then stacked and coupled to the spindle motor. Note that some drives may only use one platter. Before the platter stack is fixed to the chassis, the R/W head assembly is fitted in between each disk. There is usually one head per platter side, so a drive with two platters should have three or four heads. During drive operation, the platter stack spins at 5200 RPM or higher (up to 10,000 RPM).

READ/WRITE HEADS

As with floppy drives, read/write (R/W) heads form the interface between a drive's electronic circuitry and magnetic media. During writing, a head translates electronic signals into magnetic flux transitions that saturate points on the media where those transitions take place. A read operation works roughly in reverse. Flux transitions along the disk induce electrical signals in the head that are amplified, filtered, and translated into corresponding logic signals. It is up to the drive's electronics to determine whether a head is reading or writing.

Early hard drive R/W heads generally resembled floppy drive heads—soft iron cores with a core of 8 to 34 turns of fine copper wire. Such heads were physically large and relatively heavy, which limited the number of tracks available on a platter surface and presented more inertia to be overcome by the head-positioning system. Virtually all current hard drive designs have abandoned classical "wound coil"

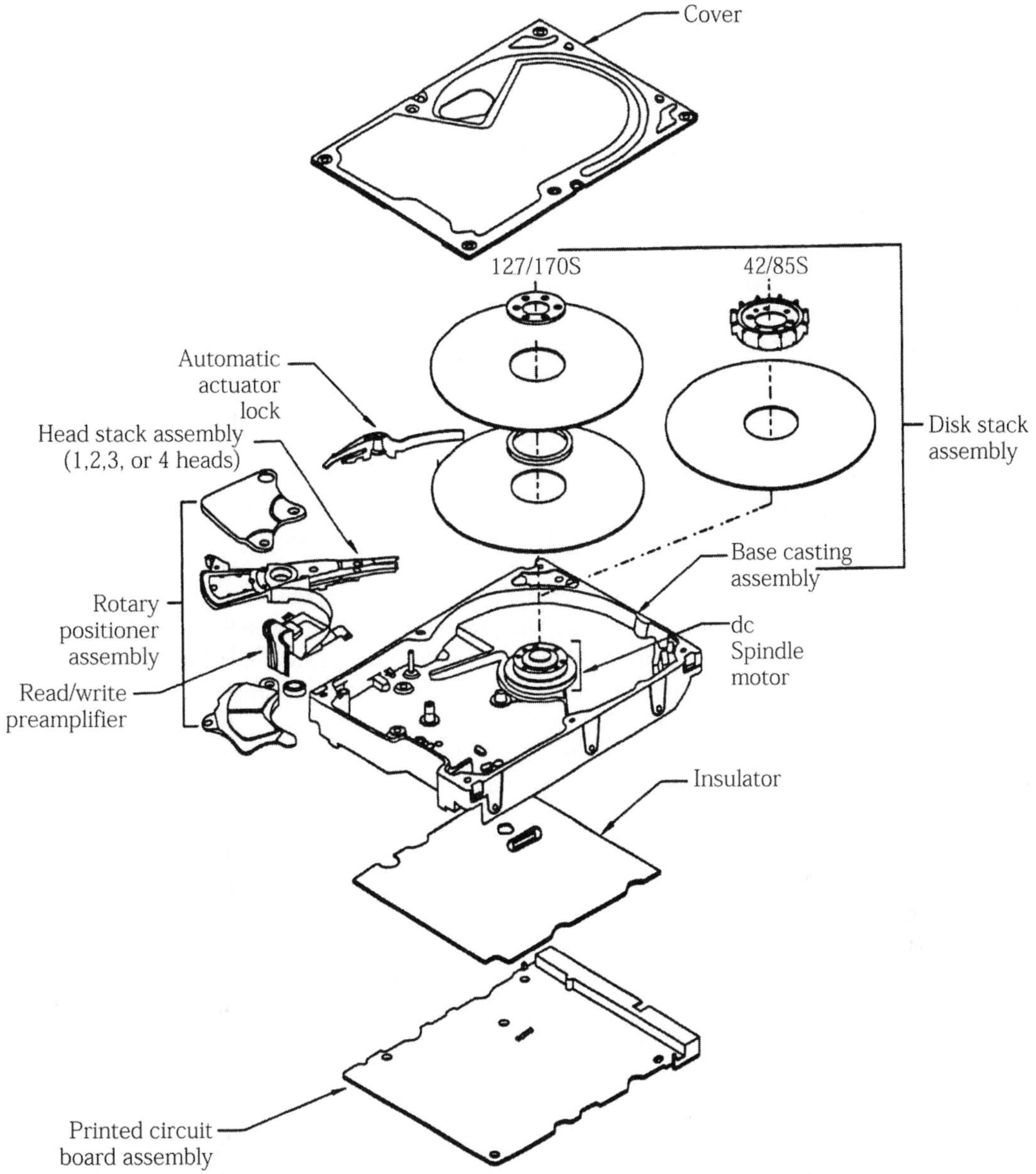

FIGURE 23-9 An exploded diagram of a Quantum hard drive (Quantum Corporation)

heads in favor of thin-film R/W heads. Thin-film heads are fabricated in much the same way as ICs or platter media, using photochemical processes. The result is a very flat, sensitive, small, and durable R/W head, but even thin-film heads use an air gap and 8 to 34 turns of copper wire. Small size and light weight allow for smaller track widths (large drives today can use over 16,000 tracks) and faster head travel time. The inherent flatness of thin-film heads helps to reduce flying height to only 5 microns or so.

In assemblies, the heads themselves are attached to long metal arms that are moved by the head actuator motor(s), as shown in Figure 23-10. Read/write preamp chips are typically mounted on a small PC board that is attached to the head/actuator assembly. The entire subassembly is sealed in the platter compartment, and is generally inaccessible unless opened in a cleanroom environment. The compartment is sealed with a metal lid/gasket assembly.

HEAD ACTUATORS

Unlike floppy motors that step their R/W heads in and out, hard drives *swing* the heads along a slight arc to achieve radial travel from edge to spindle. Many hard drives use *voice coil motors* (also called *rotary coil motors* or *servos*) to actuate head movement. Voice coil motors work using the same principle as analog meter movements: a permanent magnet is enclosed within two opposing coils. As current flows through the coils, a magnetic field is produced that opposes the permanent magnet. Head arms are attached to the rotating magnet, so the force of opposition causes a deflection that is directly proportional to the amount of driving current. Greater current signals result in greater opposition and greater deflection. Cylinders are selected by incrementing the servo signal and maintaining the signal at the desired level. Voice coil motors are very small and light assemblies that are well suited to fast access times and small hard drive assemblies.

The greatest challenge to head movement is to keep the heads centered on the desired track. Otherwise, aerodynamic disturbances, thermal effects in the platters, and variations in voice coil driver signals can cause head positioning error. Head position must be constantly checked and adjusted in real time to ensure that desired tracks are followed exactly. The process of track following is called *servoing* the heads. Information is required to compare the head's expected position to its actual position. Any resulting difference can then be corrected by adjusting the voice coil signal. Servo information is located somewhere on the platters using a variety of techniques.

Dedicated servo information is recorded on a reserved platter side. For example, a two-platter drive using dedicated servo tracking may use three sides for data, but use a fourth surface exclusively for track

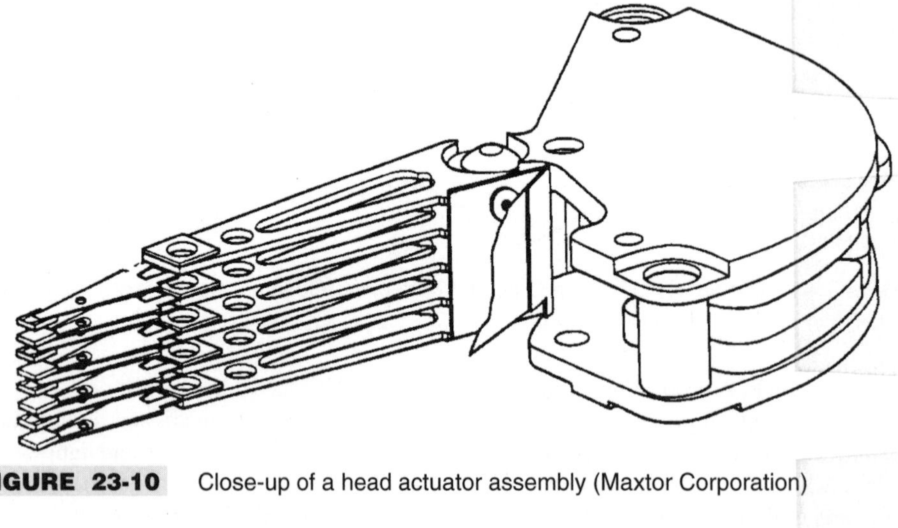

FIGURE 23-10 Close-up of a head actuator assembly (Maxtor Corporation)

locating information. Since all heads are positioned along the same track (a cylinder), a single surface can provide data that is needed to correct all heads simultaneously. *Embedded servo* information, however, is encoded as short bursts of data placed between every sector. All surfaces then can hold data and provide tracking information. The servo system uses the phase shift of pulses between adjacent tracks to determine whether heads are centered on the desired track, or drifting to one side or another. For the purposes of this book, you are not concerned with the particular tracking techniques—only that tracking information must be provided to keep the heads in proper alignment.

SPINDLE MOTOR

One of the major factors contributing to hard drive performance is the speed at which the media passes under the R/W heads. Media is passed under the R/W heads by spinning the platter(s) at a high rate of speed (at least 3600 RPM, to as high as 10,000 RPM). The *spindle motor* is responsible for spinning the platter(s). A spindle motor is typically a brushless, low-profile DC motor (similar in principle to the spindle motors used in floppy disk drives).

An index sensor provides a feedback pulse signal that detects the spindle as it rotates. The drive's control electronics uses the index signal to regulate spindle speed as precisely as possible. Today's drives typically use magnetic sensors that detect iron tabs on the spindle shaft, or optoisolators that monitor holes or tabs rotating along the spindle. The spindle motor and index sensor are also sealed in the platter compartment.

Older hard drives used a rubber or cork pad to slow the spindle to a stop after drive power is removed, but virtually all IDE drives use a technique called *dynamic braking*. When power is applied to a spindle motor, a magnetic field is developed in the motor coils. When power is removed, the magnetic energy stored in the coils is released as a reverse voltage pulse. Dynamic braking channels the energy of that reverse voltage to stop the drive faster and more reliably than physical braking.

DRIVE ELECTRONICS

Hard drives are controlled by a suite of remarkably sophisticated circuitry. The drive electronics board mounted below the chassis contains all of the circuitry necessary to communicate control and data signals with the particular physical interface, maneuver the R/W heads, read or write as required, and spin the platter(s). Each of these functions must be accomplished to high levels of precision. In spite of the demands and complexity involved in drive electronics, the entire circuit can be fabricated on a single PC board.

A practical hard disk is illustrated in the block diagram of Figure 23-11. You should understand the purpose of each part. The heart of this drive is a microcontroller (μC). A μC is basically a customized version of a microprocessor that can process program instructions as well as provide a selection of specialized control signals that are not available from ordinary microprocessors. A μC can be considered an application-specific IC (ASIC). The program that operates this drive is stored in a small, programmable read-only memory (PROM). The microcontroller provides enable signals to the voice coil driver IC, read/write preamplifier IC, read/write ASIC, and disk controller/interface ASIC. A controller/interface ASIC works in conjunction with the μC by managing data and control signals on the physical interface. For the drive shown, the ASIC is designed to support a SCSI interface, but variations of this model can use interface ASICs that support IDE interfaces.

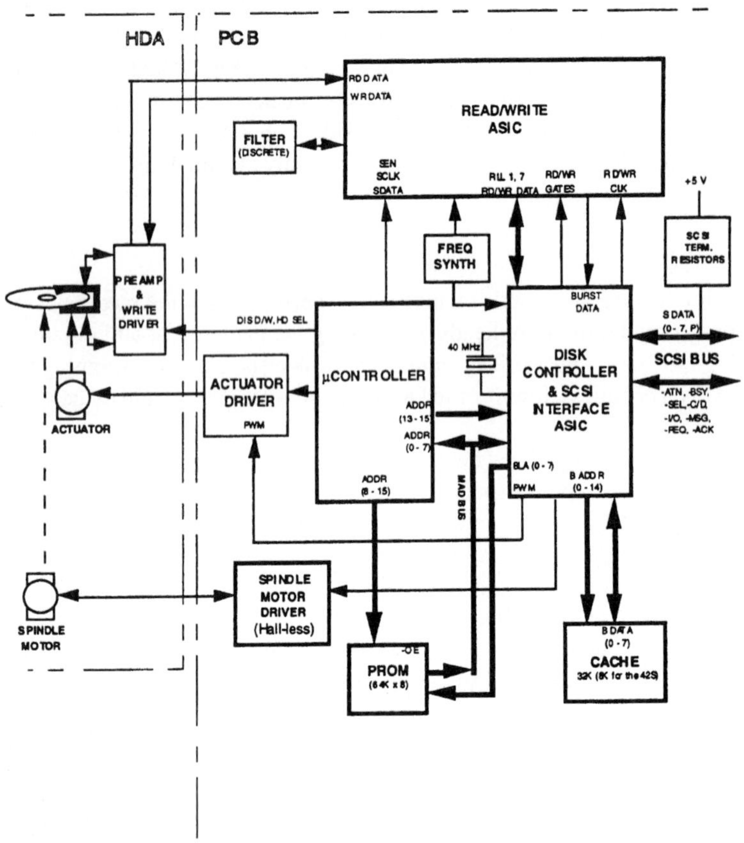

FIGURE 23-11 Block diagram of a high-performance Quantum drive system (Quantum Corporation)

The primary activity of the controller/interface ASIC is to coordinate the flow of data into or out of the drive. The controller determines read or write operations, handles clock synchronization, and organizes data flow to the read/write ASIC. The controller also manages the local cache memory (located on the drive itself). Commands received over the physical interface are passed on to the µC for processing and response. The frequency synthesizer helps to synchronize the controller and read/write ASIC. Finally, the disk controller ASIC is responsible for selecting the head position and controlling the spindle and motor driver.

The read/write ASIC is another major IC on the drive's PC board. A R/W ASIC accepts data from the controller IC and translates data into serial signals that are sent to the write driver for writing. The R/W ASIC also receives signals amplified by the read preamp, and translates serial signals into parallel digital information available to the controller ASIC. A discrete filter affects the way analog signals are handled. R/W heads are connected directly to the read preamplifier/write driver IC, which is little more than a bidirectional amplifier IC.

The actuator driver accepts a logic enable signal from the μC and a proportional logic signal from the controller ASIC. The actuator driver then produces an analog output current that positions the R/W heads by driving a voice coil motor. The spindle motor driver is turned on and off by a logic enable signal from the controller ASIC. Once the spindle motor driver is enabled, it will self-regulate its own speed using feedback from an index sensor. All components within the dotted area marked "HDA" are located within the sealed platter compartment, while other components in the area marked "PCB" are located on the drive PC board. Most of the drive's intelligence is contained in the μC, controller ASIC, and R/W ASIC.

Concepts of Drive Formatting

You can think of a disk drive as a big file cabinet. When the drive is first installed, the "file cabinet" is completely empty—there are no dividers or folders or labels of any kind to organize information. In order to make the drive useful, it must be formatted and partitioned. There are basically three steps to the format process: a low-level format, partitioning, and a high-level format. Each of these steps is critically important for the proper operation of a drive.

LOW-LEVEL FORMATTING

The *low-level format* is perhaps the most important step (and is responsible for most of a drive's long-term problems). Sector header and trailer information is written—along with dummy data. Intersector and intertrack gaps are also created. As you might imagine, the low-level format forms the foundation of a hard drive's organization. Since this information is only written once, age and wear can allow sector information eventually to fail. When this happens, the failed sector(s) are unreadable. Advanced drive features like translation, defect management, and zoned recording also complicate a proper low-level format.

This problem is further compounded by the fact that low-level formatting is hardware specific, and most current drive makers perform the low-level format at the factory. Those routines are rarely made available to technicians and end users. If you determine that an IDE or SCSI drive must be low-level formatted, make it a point to contact the drive manufacturer and obtain a proper low-level format utility written expressly for that particular drive model. Even leading professional utilities such as DrivePro strongly urge *against* low-level formats for IDE/EIDE drives except as a measure of last resort. If you attempt to invoke low-level IDE/EIDE formatting with a DOS DEBUG sequence or software utility, one of four things may happen:

- The drive will ignore the low-level formatter entirely.
- The drive will accept the formatter, but only erase areas containing data (and fail to rewrite sector ID information).
- The drive will accept the formatter and erase vital servo information and other sector information. (Thus, the drive will be rendered completely unusable.)
- The drive will accept the formatter and perform a correct low-level format—this is highly unlikely.

Any low-level format process will completely destroy all data on a drive. Back up as much of the drive as possible before attempting a low-level format. Do not attempt to low-level format a hard drive unless you have an appropriate utility from the drive maker—and then only as a procedure of last resort.

There are three compelling reasons to try low-level formatting a hard drive:

- The drive has contracted a virus that cannot be removed without destroying the boot sector.
- The drive is developing bad sectors at an increasing rate (usually due to age or failure).
- You are changing from one operating system to another and wish to remove *everything* from the drive.

If you determine that low-level formatting is necessary, two courses are open to you: you can use a low-level formatter tool included in the BIOS (such as an AMI BIOS), or you can use a software tool provided by your drive's manufacturer.

Low-Level Formatting Through BIOS

Some BIOS versions have a built-in ATA-compatible "low-level format" utility. (AMI is known for this, but other BIOS makers may incorporate that type of feature.) Before using the AMI BIOS formatting utility, make sure the AMI BIOS is dated after April 9, 1990. From the CMOS setup, select Hard Disk Utilities, and then select Hard Disk Format. The formatting utility will automatically take the hard drive parameters from the CMOS setup so that you can verify them. The only major issue is the Interleave setting. The BIOS defaults to 3, but change it to 1. The other issue is Mark Bad Tracks. Answer no to that question and proceed. This process may take anywhere from 15 minutes to an hour or more. When the process is complete, reboot the system to a DOS boot disk. Run FDISK to partition the drive, and then use FORMAT to format the drive.

> The AMI BIOS may offer two other options: Auto Interleave and Media Analysis. There is no need to run either of these utilities. If you do run the Auto Interleave utility, keep in mind that it may give inaccurate readings. Remember that the Interleave setting should always be 1.

Low-Level Formatting Through Software

A somewhat safer and more versatile approach is to use low-level-formatting software provided by your hard drive's manufacturer. Such software would be ideally suited to your particular drive, and reduces the possibility of accidental drive damage. For example, if you need to low-level format a Seagate drive, you could probably use the SGATFMT4.ZIP (Seagate Format) tool available from the Seagate Web site at **http://www.seagate.com/support/disc/drivers/discfile.shtml**. (Detailed instructions will be included in the self-extracting file.)

PARTITIONING

While low-level formatting is a hardware-specific process, *partitioning* is an operating system–specific process. After low-level formatting is complete, the drive must be partitioned before an OS file system or boot information is written to the drive. Also, partitioning allows a large physical drive to be divided into several smaller *logical* drives. There are several file systems in service today, but DOS and Windows 95/98 continue to use the File Allocation Table (FAT) system. The main criticism of the FAT is that sectors are grouped and assigned as clusters, which wastes drive space (especially for large drives where up to 64 sectors—32KB—may be in a single cluster). One of the newly created partitions will be assigned as the boot partition, and a *master boot sector* (MBS), containing a special boot program and partition table, will be written to the first sector. The MBS is often referred to as the *master boot record* (MBR). FDISK is the DOS utility used for drive partitioning. Different operating systems carry their own partitioning limitations:

- Versions of MS-DOS and PC-DOS after 3.30 (but before 4.0) have a 32MB per partition limit.
- All versions of DOS have a 1024 cylinder limitation. To access more cylinders, you'll need a device driver or a controller card that offers a "translate mode" (for example, LBA).

- DOS and Windows 95 are limited to 2.1GB per partition.
- Versions of Windows NT 4.0 and earlier are limited to a 4.2GB boot partition.
- Windows 95 OSR2 and Windows 98 use FAT32 partitions that can support up to 2TB partitions.

HIGH-LEVEL (DOS) FORMATTING

Even after partitioning, an operating system cannot store files on a drive. A series of data structures must be written to the drive. A volume boot sector (VBS), two copies of the File Allocation Table (FAT), and a root directory are written to each logical partition. High-level formatting also checks and locks out bad sectors so that they will not be used during normal operation. FORMAT is the DOS utility used for high-level formatting. It is interesting to note that the FORMAT utility will perform both low-level and high-level formatting for a floppy disk, but *not* for a hard drive.

File Systems and Tips

When you purchase a UDMA or SCSI hard drive today, it's already low-level formatted—that is, the cylinder, track, and sector information is already written onto the drive. This means you can partition the drive with FDISK and format the drive with FORMAT right out of the box. FDISK and FORMAT prepare the drive for a particular file system. I won't talk much about the complexities of file systems in detail, but you should understand the basic FAT system and know some implications of FAT16 and FAT32.

FAT BASICS

Microsoft DOS and Windows 95/98 use a File Allocation Table to organize files on the drive. Sectors are organized into groups called *clusters*, and each cluster is assigned a number. Early drives (floppy drives) used a 12-bit number (known as FAT12), but hard drives typically used a 16-bit number (called FAT16). The newest releases of Windows 95 (OSR2) and Windows 98 assign a 32-bit number to each cluster (called FAT32). By assigning each cluster its own number, it is possible to store files in any available (unused) clusters throughout the drive without worrying about the file's size. As files are erased, those clusters become available for reuse. Overall, the FAT system has proven to be a versatile and reliable file management system.

The problem with the FAT system is that you can only have as many clusters as can be specified by the number of bits available. For a 12-bit FAT, you can only have 4096 (2^{12}) clusters. For a 16-bit FAT, you can have 65,536 (2^{16}) clusters. If the drive is 120MB, each cluster must then be about (120MB / 65,536) 1.8KB (2KB in actual practice). If the drive were 500MB, each cluster must be about (540MB / 65,536) 7.6KB (8KB in actual practice). Since only *one* file can be assigned to any given cluster, the entire space for that cluster is assigned (even if the file is very small). So if you were to store a 2KB file in an 8KB cluster, you'd waste (8KB – 2KB) 6KB! This wasted space is known as *slack space*. Of course, the FAT12 system was long since abandoned while hard drives were still about 32MB, but you get the idea that very large drives can waste a serious amount of space when using a FAT system.

Another frequent complaint about the FAT file system is the phenomenon of file fragmentation. Since clusters are all independent, and clusters are assigned wherever they can be found, a file requiring more than one cluster can be scattered anywhere on the disk. For example, suppose you're editing a large image (it can take several MB). The file may use the 20 available clusters on track 345, two more available clusters on track 1012, 50 available clusters on track 2011, and so on. In theory, fragmentation is simply a harmless side effect of the FAT system. But in practice, badly fragmented files can force the hard drive to work unusually hard chasing down the various clusters associated with the file. Not only does this slow the drive's effective performance, but the extra work required of the drive may ultimately shorten its working life. The best way to correct this issue is to periodically defragment the disk with a utility like Defrag. Defragmenting the disk will rearrange all the clusters so that all of the clusters for any given file will be contiguous.

FAT16

DOS (including the DOS under Windows 95/98) uses the FAT16 file system to store data. The FAT16 system uses 16-bit-cluster address numbers that allow up to 65,536 clusters. Under FAT16, a cluster can be as big as 32KB, which translates into a maximum partition size of (65,536 x 32768) 2,147,483,648 bytes (2.1GB). While a 16-bit cluster number is much more efficient than a 12-bit cluster number, every file must take up at least one cluster—even if the file size is much smaller than the cluster. For the very large drives we have today, the correspondingly large clusters can result in a significant amount of slack space. If the physical drive is larger than 2.1GB, you must create subsequent logical partitions to utilize the additional space. For example, if you have a 3.1GB drive, you can create one 2.1GB partition, then create a second 1.0GB partition. One way to reduce slack space is to create a larger number of smaller logical partitions. This results in smaller clusters.

PARTITIONING LARGE HARD DRIVES

Chances are that you're already familiar with the DOS FDISK partitioning utility and have used it at one time or another to partition older hard drives. However, large hard drives (over 2GB) present an unusual wrinkle for technicians because DOS and Windows 95 only support partitions up to 2GB. When you install a hard drive that's larger than 2GB, you need to create multiple partitions on the drive—otherwise, you won't be able to take advantage of the full drive capacity. The procedure below offers a step-by-step guide for partitioning a large hard drive with FAT16 FDISK:

1. At the FDISK Options menu, select "4. Display partition information" and press ENTER. If the partition information display indicates that there are existing partition(s) on the drive, these partitions must be deleted before proceeding. (Select "3. Delete partition information" on the FDISK Options menu to remove any existing partitions.)
2. At the FDISK Options menu, select "1. Create DOS partition or Logical DOS drive" and press ENTER. The "Create DOS partition or Logical DOS Drive" menu is displayed. Select "1. Create Primary DOS partition" and press ENTER.
3. The message "Do you wish to use the maximum available size for a Primary DOS Partition and make the Partition active(Y/N)" is displayed. Press N and then ENTER

> When the message in step 3 is displayed, you *must* respond with no. If you reply yes, a primary partition of 2.048GB will be created, and the system will not be able to access the remainder of the drive's capacity unless the partition is deleted.

4. Type in the size of the Primary Partition (in MB). This value can be anywhere from 1MB to 2048MB (default). Then press ENTER. The message "Primary DOS Partition created" is displayed. Press ESC to continue.
5. At the FDISK Options menu, select "1. Create DOS partition or Logical DOS drive" and press ENTER. The "Create DOS partition or Logical DOS Drive" menu is displayed. Select "2. Create Extended DOS partition" and press ENTER.

6 The Create Extended DOS Partition screen is displayed. Press ENTER to place the remaining available space on the drive into the Extended DOS partition.

If all of the remaining drive space is not placed into the Extended DOS partition, the total capacity of the hard drive will not be available to the system.

7 Press ESC to continue when the FDISK message "Extended DOS Partition created" appears on the monitor. FDISK will now prompt you to create logical drives for the Extended DOS partition. The message "Enter logical drive size in megabytes or percent of disk space (%)..." is displayed.

8 Type the value desired for the capacity value of the logical drive size (up to 2048MB) and press ENTER. If you choose a value less than the displayed total size, you must continue entering drive sizes until all of the available space has been assigned logical drive letters.

Remember that each logical DOS drive created represents a drive letter (C:, D:, E:, or F:).

9 Press ESC to continue when the FDISK message "All available space in the Extended DOS Partition is assigned to logical drives" appears.

10 If the drive is going to be the primary boot drive, select "2. Set active partition" and press ENTER at the FDISK Options menu. The Set Active Partition screen is displayed, and the message "Enter the number of the partition you want to make active" is displayed. Press 1, then ENTER. The message "Partition 1 made active" is displayed. Press ESC.

11 Press ESC to exit FDISK. Exiting FDISK under DOS will cause the system to reboot. Under Windows 95 the system will return to the C:\WINDOWS\COMMAND> prompt, and the user will have to manually reboot the system.

12 After the system reboots, each drive letter assigned to the partitioned hard drive must be formatted with FORMAT. You should now be able to use the drive.

There have been a number of problems reported with the Windows 95 version of FDISK. As a rule, use the DOS 6.22 version of FDISK, or the 16-bit version of FDISK included with OSR2.

FAT32

Obviously, the limitations of FAT16 are presenting a serious issue with hard drives over 6GB and beyond. Microsoft has responded by developing a 32-bit FAT system to implement in a service release of Windows 95 (called OSR2)—and now in Windows 98. The upper 4 bits are reserved, so the system will actually access (2^{28}) 268,435,456 clusters (over 256 million clusters). This allows single partitions of 8GB with clusters only 4KB in size. The maximum size of any given partition is 2TB (yes, *terabytes*—thousands of gigabytes). FAT32 also eliminates the fixed size for a root directory, so you can have as many files and directories in the root as you want.

On the surface, this probably sounds like a great deal, but there are some major problems that you'll need to consider before updating to FAT32. First, DOS applications (without being rewritten) can only access files up to 2GB, and Win32 applications can work with files up to 4GB. By itself, that's not so bad, but FAT32 partitions are *only* accessible through the OSR2-enhanced Windows 95, Windows 98, and the corresponding DOS 7.X. No other operating system can read the partitions (including Windows NT). Also, any disk utilities written for FAT16 won't work for FAT32 (and can seriously damage your data).

Even though the OSR2 release ships with FAT32 versions of FDISK, FORMAT, ScanDisk, and Defrag, the version of DriveSpace 3 will not support FAT32. So if you're using drive compression, you're out of luck. Further, there are older APIs (application programming interfaces) in service that simply won't support FAT32; so some programs may refuse to work outright until the software is recompiled with FAT32-compliant APIs. DOS device drivers (such as those needed to support SCSI devices) will also have to be updated for FAT32. In other words, you'll lose your SCSI drives until suitable drivers become available. Finally, the OSR2 version of Windows 95 appears to *decrease* FAT32 drive performance (though that's not really an issue under Windows 98).

PARTITIONING AND FORMATTING FOR FAT32

Before you make the decision to use FAT32, you'll need to be familiar with the issues involved in partitioning and formatting. The basic steps in drive preparation are the same as FAT16, but FAT32 introduces a few wrinkles that you should understand. This part of the chapter describes the general process used to partition and format the drive under FAT32. First, a FAT32 partition can only be created (with Windows 95 OSR2 or Windows 98) under the following circumstances:

- The hard drive must be greater than 528MB in *total* capacity.
- The partition size must be greater than 528MB.
- You need an OSR2 setup disk or OSR2 startup disk made from another OSR2-configured PC (or a suitable Windows 98 startup disk).
- When the OSR2/98 FDISK prompts "Do you wish to enable large disk support? Y or N," you'll need to answer yes. If you answer no, a FAT16 partition will be created.

Partitioning a Large Hard Drive with FAT32 (OSR2/98) FDISK

1. Boot the PC with the Windows 95 OSR2 (or Windows 98) startup disk.
2. At the Welcome to Setup screen, press the F3 key twice. This will terminate the execution of the Setup program and take you to the A: prompt.

> If you have an OSR2 startup disk from another PC, you can boot from that disk instead and avoid the hassle of exiting the OSR2 setup routine.

3. Type **FDISK** and press ENTER. You'll be prompted with "Do you wish to enable large disk support? Y or N."
4. Press Y to create a FAT32 partition, and press ENTER. At this point, the FDISK Options menu will appear on the screen. If there is more than one hard drive in the system, use option 5 ("Change current fixed drive") to select the desired drive to partition. Careful—partitioning the wrong drive will render any existing data on that drive inaccessible.
5. Select option 4 for Display Partition Information, and press ENTER. For a brand-new hard drive, FDISK should respond "No Partitions Defined." Any preexisting partitions (such as FAT16 partitions) must be deleted before continuing. Remember, this will delete all existing data on the hard drive.
6. Press ESC to return to the FDISK Options menu, select option 1 for "Create DOS partition or Logical DOS drive," and press ENTER. Next, select option 1 for "Create Primary DOS Partition," and press ENTER.

7 After FDISK verifies the drive integrity, it will prompt you with "Do you wish to use the maximum available size for a Primary DOS Partition and make the Partition active (Y/N)?" Press Y, and press ENTER.

8 Exit FDISK by press the ESC key until you see the message; "You must restart the system for changes to take effect". Press the ESC key to exit FDISK, and remove the floppy diskette in drive A:. Reboot the computer using CTRL+ALT+DEL.

Formatting a Large Hard Drive with FAT32 (OSR2/98) FORMAT

1 Boot the PC with the Windows 95 OSR2 (or Windows 98) startup disk.

2 At the Welcome to Setup screen, press the F3 key twice. This will terminate the execution of the Setup program and take you to the A: prompt.

> If you have an OSR2 startup disk from another PC, you can boot from that disk instead and avoid the hassle of exiting the OSR2 setup routine.

3 Type **FORMAT** and your drive letter, and press ENTER to start formatting (for example, **FORMAT D:**). After FORMAT starts, you'll see the message "WARNING all data on non-removable disk drive <letter:> will be lost proceed with format? Y/N."

4 Press Y and then ENTER. The OSR2 FORMAT utility will then prepare the hard drive for use with FAT32.

USING THE FAT32 DRIVE CONVERTER

Windows 98 provides a drive converter that allows you to convert FAT16 partitions to FAT32 format. The simplest method is to type **cvt <drive>: /cvt32**, and then press ENTER. Remember that <drive> is the drive that you want to convert to the FAT32 file system. Another step-by-step approach is listed below:

1 Click Start, select Programs, highlight Accessories, choose System Tools, click Drive Converter (FAT32), and then click Next.

2 In the Drives box, click the drive that you want to convert to the FAT32 file system.

3 Click Next, and then click OK.

4 Click Next, click Next, and then click Next again.

5 Allow the conversion process to complete.

6 When the conversion is complete, click Finish and reboot the PC if necessary.

> After you convert your hard disk to FAT32, you cannot convert back to the original FAT system. Before you convert to the FAT32 file system, uninstall any utilities or tools that protect or encrypt the MBR or partition table (for example, uninstall Bootlock, included with Symantec Norton Your Eyes Only).

> The FAT32 converter may fail if your hard drive is less than 512MB or has bad sectors (often resulting in data corruption).

CREATING A FAT32 STARTUP DISK FOR WINDOWS 98

When booting from a floppy disk, it is often difficult for you to access FAT32 partitions because the operating system version on the floppy disk is not FAT32 aware. The Windows 98 CD-ROM contains a program you can use to create a startup disk that is capable of creating and reading FAT32 partitions. Once you create the new disk, you can simply leave the disk in the drive and reboot the PC. Note that this boot disk does not contain all the programs included on the Windows 98 startup disk.

To create a FAT32-aware Windows 98 startup disk within Windows 98:

1. Place the Windows 98 CD in your CD-ROM drive, and have a floppy disk handy.
2. Click Start, highlight Programs, and then click Windows Explorer.
3. Open the following folder on the Windows 98 CD: \Tools\Mtsutil\Fat32ebd.
4. Double-click the Fat32ebd.exe file, and then follow the instructions to finish creating the disk.
5. Write-protect the floppy disk.

If you want to create a FAT32-aware boot disk from DOS:

1. Place the Windows 98 CD-ROM in your CD-ROM drive, and have a floppy disk handy.
2. Type each of the following lines (where <drive> is the drive letter of your CD-ROM drive):

```
windows\smartdrv.exe <drive>:
cd\tools\mtsutil\fat32ebd
fat32ebd.exe
```

3. Now follow the instructions to create the disk.
4. Write-protect the floppy disk.

The SMARTDRV.EXE utility is not required to create a Windows 98 startup disk—it simply helps speed up the creation process.

UNDERSTANDING THE MASTER BOOT RECORD

The master boot record (or MBR) is information that is normally stored in the first sector of the hard drive. This information is simply a small data structure that identifies where an operating system (OS) is located on the drive so that the OS can be loaded into the system's memory (RAM) at boot time. The MBR contains two elements: executable code (a.k.a. a program) and a *partition table* that identifies each partition residing on the hard drive.

The executable code (or MBR program) begins the boot process by looking up the partition table to determine what partition holds the operating system. It then loads the boot sector of the partition containing the OS into RAM, and transfers execution of the "program" to the partition boot sector. The partition boot sector then finishes loading the operating system files into RAM.

Creating/Restoring the MBR

The MBR is created during the partition process (using FDISK). If the MBR is corrupted or damaged, you can often restore the MBR using FDISK with the /MBR switch, such as:

```
C:\> FDISK /MBR
```

Remember to back up the drive before attempting this command. It should not corrupt the drive partitions or its data, but it *could*.

The MBR and "Drive Overlay" Software

When a system BIOS or drive controller will not support the full size of a drive, you typically have the option of upgrading the BIOS (and/or drive controller) or using "drive overlay" software such as EZ-Drive, MaxBlast, or other products. The use of overlay software will affect the way an MBR is configured. When drive overlay software (such as EZ-Drive) controls a hard drive, the MBR is stored on the *second* sector of the hard drive—the first sector contains EZ-Drive code (also known as EZ-BIOS). Sectors 3 through 17 also contain EZ-Drive code that is referred to as the "INT13 Handler." (INT13 deals with hard disk services.) When the system is powered on, it looks at the first sector of the hard drive for boot instructions. In this case, the boot sequence is as follows:

- EZ-Drive code loads from sector 1 on the drive.
- EZ-Drive loads the INT13 Handler located in sectors 3 through 17 and uses this information to set up the hard drive for proper access at its full capacity.
- EZ-Drive loads the regular master boot record found on sector 2, which in turn loads the operating system.

Viruses and the MBR

A common type of virus is one that replaces the MBR with its own code. Each time a computer is started, the code in the MBR is loaded into memory. If the MBR contains a virus, the virus code is loaded every time a system starts up, making this type of virus *very* dangerous. Some MBR viruses do little more than display a message on your screen, while others can destroy your data. An MBR virus usually enters a system through a floppy disk that the system accessed either at startup or while the system was on. If your BIOS supports an "MBR protection" feature, this prevents new information from being written to the MBR; so make sure this feature is enabled in the CMOS setup.

23

Understanding Drive Capacity Limits

Capacity limitations are encountered whenever a computer system BIOS (and operating system) is unable to identify (or *address*) physical locations on a hard drive. This is not a problem with the design or structure of the hard drive itself, but rather a limitation of the system's BIOS or operating system. For the BIOS, it is not capable of translating the addresses of the sectors beyond a certain number of cylinders—thus limiting the capacity of the hard drive to less than its full amount. For the operating system, the file structure (FAT) is limited in the number of physical locations (or addresses) that can be entered in the FAT. Drive manufacturers first encountered BIOS limitations in 1994 with the release of 540MB (ATA-2/EIDE) hard drives. Operating system limitations were discovered with the release of hard drives larger than 2.1GB. Your exact limitations vary depending on your BIOS version and the operating system. Today, you'll probably encounter BIOS with limitations at 2.1GB, 4.2GB, and 8.4GB levels. Operating systems like DOS and Windows 95 have a 2.1GB partition size limitation, and Windows NT has a 4.2GB partition size limit, but Windows 95 OSR2 and Windows 98 can access much larger drives using the FAT32 file system. This part of the chapter is intended to help you understand and correct these drive size limitations.

CYLINDER LIMITS IN BIOS

BIOS is the key to hard drive addressing through the use of Int. 13 services. Today, you'll find that there are three major BIOS limitations:

- BIOS versions dated before July 1994 will typically experience a 528MB drive size limit. BIOS cannot support more than 1024 cylinders. Logical Block Addressing (LBA) mode capability did not become widely accepted until after this point.
- BIOS versions dated after July 1994 will typically experience a 2.1GB drive size limit. BIOS cannot support more than 4093–4096 cylinders. Even though LBA is being used correctly, the BIOS makers simply imposed an artificial limit on the number of addressable cylinders.
- BIOS versions dated after 1996 can support drives over 528MB and drives over 2.1GB, but may experience a 4.2GB or 8.4GB drive size limit. Once again, the BIOS cannot support the number of cylinders (around 8190) needed to handle these larger drives, even though LBA is being used correctly.

  There are some more specifics:

- Phoenix Technologies (**http://www.ptltd.com/**) version 4 revision 6 or greater can support capacities greater than 8.4GB. If the BIOS is revision 5.12, it does not support extended INT 13. All Phoenix BIOS are version 4, so 5.12 is an older release than 6. Phoenix recommends MicroFirmware (**http://max.firmware.com/**) for BIOS upgrades.
- Award (**http://www.award.com/**) BIOS dated after November 1997 will support drives greater than 8.4GB. Award recommends Unicore (**http://www.unicore.com/**) for BIOS upgrades.
- American Megatrends (AMI) (**http://www.megatrends.com/**) BIOS versions with a date of January 1, 1998, or later support drives greater than 8.4GB.

PARTITION LIMITS IN THE OPERATING SYSTEM

File systems used by various operating systems are also subject to drive size limits. FAT16-type operating systems (DOS, the commercial release of Windows 95, Windows NT with FAT16, and OS/2 with FAT16) are typically limited to 2.1GB drive sizes. Windows NT using NTFS suffers a 4GB drive size limit. When using a physical hard drive that is larger than these limits, you'll need to create multiple partitions on the drive in order to access all of the available space. With the introduction of FAT32 with Windows 95 OSR2 and Windows 98, drives up to 2TB (terabytes) can be accessed as a single partition.

OVERCOMING CAPACITY LIMITS

Since 1994, the PC industry has been working hard to overcome the drive size limits imposed by BIOS and operating systems. Unfortunately, drive size limits still plague older systems. This is particularly prevalent because many systems a few years old are now being upgraded with the huge hard drives that are on the market. As a result, drive size support problems are the most frequent issues encountered during drive upgrades. Still, there are several tactics that have become available for technicians.

The 528MB Limit

Supporting large (EIDE) hard drives over 528MB will clearly require a system upgrade. There are three possible solutions to the problem: upgrade the motherboard BIOS to support LBA, upgrade the drive controller with one that uses an onboard BIOS supporting LBA, or partition the drive with a drive overlay utility like Disk Manager or EZ-Drive. If the system is older than 1994, a new drive controller and onboard

BIOS will probably yield a noticeable drive system performance improvement. If price is the primary concern, drive overlay software is free (included with most new hard drives) and requires no invasive hardware upgrade.

Limits of 2.1GB, 4.2GB, 8.4GB, and 32GB

The difficulty with these limits is that there are several possible symptoms that can crop up:

- *Truncation of cylinders* Cylinder truncation is when the BIOS limits the number of cylinders reported to the operating system to 4095. The BIOS may display the drive as having more than 4095 cylinders, but it still only reports a total of 4095.
- *System hang-up at POST* A system hang-up occurs when the BIOS has a problem truncating the cylinders and locks the system during power-on self-test (POST). This is most frequently caused by the autodetect feature that some BIOS versions have implemented.
- *Cylinder wrap* Cylinder wrapping is when the BIOS takes the remaining number of cylinders from the maximum allowed (4095) and reports it to the operating system. For example, if the drive listed 4096 cylinders, the BIOS would report only 1 cylinder to the operating system.
- *System hangs at boot time* This usually occurs for drives larger than 4.2GB (8.4GB or 32GB drives). A system hang is when the operating system hangs up during initial loading (either from floppy disk or existing hard drives). This can be caused by the BIOS reporting the number of heads to the operating system as 256 (100h). The register size used by DOS and Windows 95/98 for the head count has a capacity of two hex digits (equivalent to decimal values 255).

In virtually all cases, these symptoms represent a BIOS compatibility problem and can be corrected by a BIOS upgrade. You should contact the system or motherboard maker to inquire whether a BIOS update is available. If you cannot upgrade the motherboard BIOS directly, you can install a new drive controller with an LBA-compatible BIOS that will support additional cylinders.

You may also be able to adjust the drive's "translation" to overcome BIOS cylinder limits. You may find that these huge hard drives seem to auto-detect correctly in BIOS, and the problem crops up when trying to partition the drive. The partition may seem to be created properly through FDISK, but the system hangs when rebooting. Although this is an operating system limitation, it appears that the appropriate way to deal with this problem is to account for it in the system BIOS. Fortunately, there is a temporary work-around to the problem (until you get the BIOS upgraded).

> You should first verify that you have a new enough BIOS to handle drives *over* 2GB, 4GB, 8.1GB, or 32GB correctly.

To set up a drive over 4GB (under an older BIOS):

1. Autodetect the drive in CMOS setup.
2. Manually adjust the number of heads from 16 to 15.
3. Multiply the number of cylinders by 16/15 (rounded down to whole number). Since 16/15 is 1.06667, the simplest way to multiply by 16/15 would be to multiply by 1.06667 (and then round down to a whole number).
4. Adjust the number of cylinders to this larger amount.
5. Write down these adjusted values for cylinders, heads, and sectors.
6. Save changes to CMOS, and then partition and format the drive.

TABLE 23-4 POSSIBLE CMOS WORK-AROUNDS FOR HUGE HARD DRIVES

MODEL	FACTORY CHS VALUES	WORK-AROUND CHS VALUES
Maxtor 85120A	9924 x 16 x 63	10585 x 15 x 63
Micropolis 4550A	9692 x 16 x 63	10338 x 15 x 63

As an example, Table 23-4 illustrates some work-around parameters that can be used with popular models of hard drives over 4GB. Although this can be considered a temporary work-around, there should be no problem with continuing to use a hard drive set up this way. If the computer receives an updated BIOS version at a later date, it should not be necessary to repartition and reformat the drive.

The important thing to keep in mind in using the above work-around is that you must keep a record of the translation values used so that they can be reentered if the contents of CMOS RAM are lost, or if the drive is moved to another system. Write the values on masking tape, and stick the tape on the drive itself.

Operating System Limits

You basically have two solutions for overcoming drive size limits through an operating system. If you continue to use FAT16, you'll need to create partitions equal to or smaller than 2GB. If the drive is larger than 2GB, you can make multiple partitions on the drive. This makes more than one "logical drive" for the system to deal with, but it will allow you to use the entire drive capacity. As an alternative, you can upgrade to a FAT32 system, such as the OSR2 version of Windows 95 (or Windows 98), that should easily handle partitions over 32GB.

But there are some other issues. For example, hard disks and other media that are larger than 32GB in size are not supported in any version of Windows 95. Media at this capacity were not available at the time Windows 95 and OSR versions were developed. If you want to use media larger than 32GB in size, you should upgrade to Windows 98 or Microsoft Windows NT. Note that you must use Windows NT 4.0, Service Pack 4 (or newer) to address this capacity limitation.

Also, the protected-mode (Windows) version of ScanDisk may misreport cluster sizes on IDE hard drives whose capacity exceeds 32GB. The resulting symptoms may also include an inability to access areas of the hard drive beyond the first 32GB. You can correct this problem by downloading the file 243450US8.EXE (release date 12/10/99) from the Microsoft Web site. (See Microsoft Knowledge Base article Q243450 for more information.) Note this problem does not occur if the BIOS uses true Logical Block Addressing (LBA) "assist translation" instead of "BitShift" translation.

Hard Drive Installation/Replacement Guidelines

Hard drives must be installed when building new PCs, adding supplemental drives to an existing system, or replacing outdated or failed drives. The installation process is not terribly complicated, but it can be confusing to the novice. This part of the chapter offers some basic guidelines for IDE-type drive installation.

SELECT JUMPER CONFIGURATIONS

An IDE-type drive may be installed as a master or slave device on any hard drive controller channel. These master/slave settings are handled through one or two jumpers located on the rear of the drive (right next to the 40-pin signal cable connector). One of your first decisions when planning an installation should be to decide the drive's configuration:

- If you're installing only one hard drive in the system, it must be jumpered as the master device. Note that the master drive on the primary drive controller channel will be the boot drive (drive C:).
- If you're installing a second hard drive alongside the first, that second drive must be jumpered as the slave device.
- If you're installing a second hard drive on the second drive controller channel, it should be jumpered as the master device. (Any other device should be reconfigured as a slave device.)

> Refer to the documentation that accompanies your particular hard drive in order to determine the exact master/slave jumper settings. If you do not have the drive documentation handy, check the drive manufacturer's Web site for online information.

ATTACH CABLES AND MOUNT THE DRIVE

- Turn off and unplug the PC. Then remove the outer cover to expose the computer's drive bays.
- Attach one end of the 40-pin drive interface cable to the drive controller connector on your motherboard (or drive controller card). Remember to align pin 1 on the cable (the side of the cable with the blue or red stripe) with pin 1 on the drive controller connector.

> A 40-pin/80-conductor cable is required to run in Ultra-DMA/66 mode. Attach the blue end of the connector to the drive controller end, the black connector to the master (or single) drive, and the gray connector (if there is one) to the slave drive.

- Locate an available drive bay for the hard drive. Remove the plastic housing covering the drive bay, and then slide the drive inside. Locate the four screw holes needed to mount the drive. In some cases, you may need to attach mounting rails to the drive so that the drive will be wide enough to fit in the drive bay. You may mount the drive horizontally (usually with the circuit board down) or vertically.
- Attach the 40-pin signal cable and the 4-pin power connector to the new drive, and then bolt the drive securely into place. Do not overtighten the screws since this may damage the drive. If you do not have an available 4-pin power connector, you may use an appropriate Y-splitter if necessary to split power from another drive (preferably the floppy drive).

CONFIGURING THE CMOS SETUP

Before you attempt to partition or format your new drive, you must configure your computer's BIOS to accept the drive (through the CMOS setup).

- Turn the computer on. As your computer starts, watch for a message that describes how to run the CMOS setup (for example, "Press F1 for Setup"). Press the appropriate key to start the CMOS setup program.
- Select the "hard drive settings" menu. To set the drive parameters, choose the "primary master" or "primary slave" (or "secondary master/slave" depending on how you've physically installed the drive).
- Select "automatic drive detection" if available. This option automatically configures the computer for your new drive. If your BIOS does not provide automatic drive detection, select "user-defined" drive settings and enter the appropriate geometry values from the drive documentation. As a rule, "Write Precomp" and "Landing Zone" parameters are set to zero.

- Verify that the "LBA mode" is enabled for your drive. Many BIOS versions use the Logical Block Addressing mode to access drives with capacities greater than 528MB. Most BIOS will automatically set this mode during the autodetection process.
- Enable the Ultra-DMA mode if it is available (and both the drive and controller support it).
- Save the settings and exit the CMOS setup program. Your computer will automatically reboot.

FINISH THE DRIVE PREPARATION

Boot the system with a Windows 95/98 startup disk containing FDISK and FORMAT. You will use these utilities to partition and format the drive, respectively. Partition the disk with FDISK. If you use a FAT16 version of FDISK, you cannot create partitions greater than 2.1GB. If you use the FAT32 version of FDISK, you can create extremely large partitions. Now use FORMAT to prepare the drive for your operating system. Again, use the proper version of the FORMAT utility depending on which FAT system you plan on using. You can find detailed instructions in the "File Systems and Tips" section earlier in the chapter.

REASSEMBLE THE COMPUTER

Double-check all of your signal and power cables to verify that they are secure, and then tuck the cables gently into the computer's chassis. Check that there are no loose tools, screws, or cables inside the chassis. Now reattach the computer's outer housing(s).

Drive Testing and Troubleshooting

Fortunately, not all hard drive problems are necessarily fatal. True, you may lose some programs and data (back up your hard drive frequently), but many drive problems are recoverable without resorting to drive replacement. Instead of focusing on repairing a hard drive's electronics or mechanics, today's repair tactics focus on repairing a drive's *data*. By reconstructing or relocating faulty drive information, it is often possible to recover from a wide variety of drive problems. If that fails, the drive (and/or its controller) must be replaced. Before you begin any sort of drive troubleshooting, you should take the following steps:

- Gather a DOS boot disk or Windows 95/98 startup disk. If you don't have a boot disk on hand, you should make one now *before* continuing.
- Gather your DOS installation disk(s) or Windows 95/98 Installation CD-ROM. If you need to reinstall the operating system or any of its components at some point, these will be invaluable.
- Gather any hard drive/controller diagnostics that you'll need.
- Back up as much as you can from your hard drive(s) before attempting any sort of drive service.

GENERAL TROUBLESHOOTING GUIDELINES

Although most drive installations and replacements will proceed flawlessly, there are many times when problems will crop up. If you've installed a hard drive and it does not function properly, perform the following basic checks before examining specific symptoms:

- *Be careful with power and static.* Always turn off the computer before changing jumpers or unplugging cables and cards. Wear an antistatic wrist strap (or use other antistatic precautions) while working on your computer or handling a drive.

- *Verify compatibility.* Verify that the drive controller and drive are appropriately matched to each other (and to your computer). For example, an Ultra-DMA/66 drive will not run at top speed on an Ultra-DMA/33 controller.
- *Check all cards.* Verify that all expansion cards (including the drive controller card) are seated in their slots on the motherboard and are secured with mounting screws. Often one or more cards may be displaced when a PC is opened for service.
- *Check all connectors and cables.* Make sure that all ribbon and power cables are securely connected. Ribbon cables are easily damaged (especially at the connectors). Try a new cable that you know is good. Make sure no connector pins are bent. Verify that pin 1 on the interface cable is aligned with pin 1 on the drive and the controller.
- *Verify drive jumper settings.* Review the instructions in your drive's manual (and in your host adapter installation guide), and see that all appropriate jumpers are installed—or removed—as necessary. Incorrect or duplicated jumper settings (such as two master drives on the same channel) can easily interfere with drive operation.
- *Check your power supply capacity.* Each time you add a new device to your computer, make sure your computer's power supply can support the total power demand. Install a larger (higher wattage) power supply if necessary.
- *Verify the drive settings in your CMOS setup.* The drive settings in the CMOS setup must not exceed the physical specifications of your drive. Also, the settings must not exceed the limitations set by the operating system and BIOS. Try the CMOS setup's autodetect feature to identify the drive, or consider upgrading the BIOS and/or drive controller.
- *Check for viruses.* Before you use an unknown disk in your system for the first time, scan it for viruses. Also scan the system for viruses periodically.

POTENTIAL PROBLEMS WITH Y-SPLITTERS

On rare occasions, you may find that a drive will not function—or is damaged outright—when using a Y power adapter (or Y-splitter). This can happen because a number of Y-splitters on the market are incorrectly wired. Y-splitters consist of a clear plastic plug with four metal prongs on one end (which attach to an existing power connector from the power supply) and two sets of wires leading to two plugs with female connections on the other ends (which are attached to internal devices such as hard drives, CD-ROM drives, etc.). The problem with some of these newer connectors is that the wires are attached incorrectly on one of the female connectors.

Examine both female connectors. Make certain that both of the female connectors are lined up with the two rounded corners facing up and both of the squared corners facing down. The four wires attached to the female connectors should now be in the following order (from left to right): Yellow (+12 Vdc), Black (ground), Black (ground), and Red (+5 Vdc)

If this order is reversed on one of the connectors, your Y-splitter is faulty and should not be used. As a rule, you should never split power from the hard drive under any circumstances.

POTENTIAL PROBLEMS WITH BUS SPEEDS ABOVE 66MHZ

Many Pentium and later motherboards offer an adjustable system bus clock that may be set by either the system BIOS or with jumpers. This "bus speed" setting allows you to increase the system bus clock above 66MHz—usually to 75MHz or 83MHz. Most drives have no problem with the higher bus clock speeds, but some problems may result because of the way some motherboards handle the interaction between the higher bus speeds (above 66MHz) and the IDE-type interface.

On some motherboards, when the system clock is increased above 66MHz, the PCI bus (ideally 33MHz) is also increased. This higher speed reduces the PCI bus "I/O Cycle Time." This change in the I/O Cycle Time violates the IDE specification and may cause disruptions in the communications between the hard drive and the PCI bus. This is not a faulty hard drive or drive design. When the PCI bus speed is forced over 33MHz because of higher bus speed settings, you may see problems such as data loss, data corruption, and failure of the system to recognize the hard drive on boot-up. Higher bus speeds will not cause any kind of permanent hard drive failure, and returning the system bus speed to 66MHz can usually eliminate the problem(s). The best solution to this problem is either to return the motherboard to a 66MHz bus speed, or upgrade the motherboard with a model where the PCI bus speed is "asynchronous" with the bus speed. This allows you to increase the bus speed, but the PCI clock will remain fixed at 33MHz.

> Due to the differences between drive designs, it is possible that some drives may not have any problems responding at higher bus speeds, while other drive models may produce serious problems. It's virtually impossible to determine which drives will or won't be affected.

> Current Pentium II and Pentium III motherboards designed to operate up to 100MHz or higher are almost all asynchronous and should not pose a problem. But this issue may crop up when working with slightly older motherboards or systems.

TROUBLESHOOTING "DOS COMPATIBILITY MODE" PROBLEMS

One of the great advantages of Windows 95/98 is that it operates in the protected mode: drivers and software can be executed beyond the traditional real-mode RAM limit of 1MB. By comparison, DOS is a real-mode environment. DOS programs and drivers can only be executed within the first 640KB of RAM (the "conventional memory" area). If Windows 95/98 cannot establish protected-mode operation for a drive, it will fall back to real-mode driver support. This is known as *DOS compatibility mode*. Unfortunately, real-mode support often impairs system performance. If you notice that one or more of the hard drives in a system is using DOS compatibility mode (there may be an error message such as "Compatibility Mode Paging reduces overall system performance"), you'll need to track down and correct the cause. In general, Windows 95/98 may invoke the DOS compatibility mode for any of the following reasons:

- A questionable device driver, TSR, or computer virus has hooked the INT 21h or INT 13h chain before Windows 95/98 loaded.
- The hard disk controller in your computer was not detected by Windows 95/98.
- The hard disk controller was removed from the current configuration in Device Manager.
- There is a resource conflict between the hard disk controller and another hardware device.
- The Windows 95/98 protected-mode driver is missing or damaged.
- The Windows 95/98 protected-mode driver detected incompatible or unsupportable hardware.

You can use the following procedure to isolate and correct the cause of DOS compatibility mode problems:

1. Open the Control Panel, double-click the System icon, and then choose the Performance tab in the System Properties dialog. You can identify which drive is using DOS compatibility mode and why.

2 If the driver name listed as causing the DOS compatibility mode is MBRINT13.SYS, your computer may be infected with a boot-sector virus, or you are running real-mode disk overlay software (for an IDE hard disk with more than 1024 cylinders) that is *not* compatible with Windows 95/98 protected-mode disk drivers.

- Run a current antivirus program to detect and remove boot sector viruses (such as Norton Anti-Virus). You may need to rewrite your boot sector using a DOS command such as FDISK /MBR.
- If you cannot detect any virus activity, check any drive overlay software. For example, if you're using Disk Manager, make sure you're using version 7.0 or later. (Use Disk Manager 7.04 if you're running DriveSpace 3 included with the Microsoft Plus! pack.) You may need to make similar updates if you're running other drive overlay software.

3 If the driver name that is listed in step 2 is also in the CONFIG.SYS file, contact the driver's manufacturer to determine whether there is a more recent version of the driver that allows protected-mode operation in Windows 95/98. You may be able to download and install the latest driver version from the driver manufacturer's Web site.

4 If no driver is listed on the Performance tab, check to make sure that the hard disk controller is listed in the Device Manager. If not, install it through the Add New Hardware wizard. If the wizard cannot detect the controller automatically, run the wizard again but do not let it attempt to detect the hardware in your computer. Instead, select the controller specifically from the hardware list. If your particular controller is not listed, contact the manufacturer of the disk controller to obtain a Windows 95/98 protected-mode disk driver (or a Windows 3.1x 32-bit disk access "FastDisk" driver if available).

If the hard disk controller is listed in Device Manager, but has a red *X* over it, it has been removed from the current hardware profile. Click Properties for the controller in Device Manager, and then click the check box corresponding to the current hardware profile under Device Usage.

5 If the hard disk controller is listed in the Device Manager, but has a yellow ! over it, there is a resource conflict (IRQ, I/O, DMA, or BIOS address range) with another device, the protected-mode driver is missing or damaged, or the "Disable all 32-bit protected-mode disk drivers" check box has been selected in File System properties.

- Double-click the System icon in the Control Panel, click the Performance tab, and then click File System. Select the Troubleshooting tab and see that the "Disable all 32-bit protected-mode disk drivers" check box has not been selected.
- Resolve any resource conflicts with other devices in the system.
- Check to make sure that the protected-mode driver is in the \Windows\SYSTEM\ IOSUBSYS directory and is loading properly. To find which driver is providing 32-bit disk access, click Properties for the disk controller in Device Manager, and click the Driver tab to see which driver files are associated with the controller. For most IDE, EIDE, and ESDI disk controllers, 32-bit disk access is provided by the ESDI_506.PDR driver. For SCSI controllers, Windows 95 often uses SCSIPORT.PDR and a "miniport" (or MPD) driver. Restart Windows 95/98, press F8 when the "Starting Windows 95/98" message appears, and then select a "Logged" (BOOTLOG.TXT) start. If the 32-bit driver is listed as loading properly, you're all set. Otherwise, the driver may be missing or damaged. Try reinstalling the respective 32-bit drivers.

6 Load SYSTEM.INI into a text editor and check to see if the MH32BIT.386 driver is being loaded. (Check for a line that reads device=mh32bit.386.) This driver is installed by MicroHouse EZ-Drive software and is not compatible with the Windows 95/98 protected-mode disk drivers. Unfortunately, this driver is not removed by Windows 95/98 setup, so you'll need to disable the line manually, save your changes, and reboot the PC.

7 If all else fails, you may be able to achieve protected-mode support from the disk controller by disabling any of the controller's advanced features (such as caching, fast or "turbo" modes) or by reducing data transfer rates. You may also try systematically disabling advanced IDE controller features in the CMOS setup.

8 If problems persist, you may have to replace the drive controller with a model that better supports protected-mode operation.

DETECTING A DDO

A Dynamic Drive Overlay (or DDO) is used to support access to a large hard drive when the system BIOS or drive controller is unable to. Since the DDO can sometimes cause problems with drive access and system performance, it must be detected before removal. You can use the tell-tale signs below to identify the presence of a DDO on a Windows 95/98 system:

- *DDO startup message* When you boot your computer, a message may be displayed on the screen that shows the DDO manufacturer's name (or prompts you to press a key to boot to a floppy disk). Current versions of drive overlay software may not display this message by default.
- *BIOS revision date* Computers made before 1994 generally do not support LBA. If your BIOS shows an early revision date, it will probably need a DDO in order to support hard drives over 528MB.
- *FDISK /status switch* Boot your computer with a Windows 95/98 startup disk and type **fdisk /status** from the command prompt. Verify that the sum of the existing partitions is larger than the total hard disk space. If so, a DDO is at work.
- *Windows 95/98 startup disk* Reboot your computer with the Windows 95/98 startup disk. (This prevents the DDO program from loading.) Then boot to a command prompt. Check to see if files on the C: drive are accessible. If not, the drive is inaccessible because a DDO has not been loaded for the hard drive.
- *File name extensions* Some drive overlay files use an .OVL or a .BIN extension. At the command prompt, type **dir /a *.bin** or **dir /a *.ovl** to check for the existence of files other than DRVSPACE.BIN and DBLSPACE.BIN. If there are other such files, a DDO is probably installed.
- *CONFIG.SYS files* Drive overlay software may be loaded from the CONFIG.SYS file in order to access drives *other* than the active boot partition of the master drive on the primary IDE controller. If there is DDO software called in CONFIG.SYS, you'd disable it there if necessary.

REMOVING A DDO

When you install a drive overlay utility like EZ-Drive or MaxBlast (or other similar software), there may be a point when it's necessary to remove it. You may need to do this when upgrading the BIOS and/or drive controller, and the Dynamic Drive Overlay software is no longer required. In most cases, you can remove your DDO without losing any data—as long as you have an alternative means of accessing the drive (such as an updated BIOS or drive controller). The example below illustrates the use of Disk Manager, but other utilities will follow a similar process.

Before you remove a DDO from a drive, make a complete backup copy of all the data on your hard drive. Also run CHKDSK or ScanDisk (or a third-party equivalent) to detect and repair any damaged files. If the DDO removal program encounters a serious file problem (or is interrupted by a power loss or hardware failure), the removal will fail and your data can be lost.

1. Boot the computer to drive C:, and then insert your DiscWizard disk (or CD).
2. Type **DM** to start Disk Manager, and choose the Select Installation Options menu.
3. Select the Maintenance Menu.
4. Select Migrate Dynamic Drive. This option moves the data on your drive so that it can be accessed *without* the DDO. Remember that this conversion may take up to an hour to complete (depending on the size of your drive).
5. When the conversion has finished, exit Disk Manager, remove the disk, and reboot the computer.
6. Enter your CMOS setup program, and configure the hard drive with the appropriate number of cylinders, heads, and sectors as specified for your drive model.
7. Save your changes in the CMOS setup and reboot again.
8. When your computer has rebooted, insert the DiscWizard disk into drive A:.
9. Type **A:\DM** to start Disk Manager, and choose the Maintenance menu.
10. Select Uninstall Disk Manager.
11. Select the correct drive to uninstall from, and allow the process to complete.
12. When the uninstall is complete, exit Disk Manager and reboot the system.

Disk Manager can also remove a drive overlay placed by the EZ-Drive program. Simply select Convert Drive Format from the Maintenance menu.

DRIVE NOT RECOGNIZED BY THE OPERATING SYSTEM

There are some circumstances when a hard drive is recognized correctly by the BIOS (the drive is properly autodetected), but it is not properly identified by the operating system. In virtually all cases, the problem can be traced to installation issues or drive software (code-related) issues. Check the essential installation points first:

- Check the parameters in the CMOS setup and verify that the drive parameters *and* translation mode are set correctly.
- Contact the system or motherboard manufacturer to verify potential BIOS capacity limitations. For example, you may need a BIOS upgrade to accommodate the drive sizes that you're using.
- Ensure that newly installed EIDE or UDMA controller cards do not conflict with the existing system BIOS. You may need to disable the motherboard's existing drive controller channel(s) through the CMOS setup before the new controller card will be recognized by the OS.
- Systematically "step down" the enhanced features of your BIOS (block mode, multisector transfers, 32-bit transfers, PIO mode settings, and so on) to their minimum values, or disable the features entirely. You may also try the "BIOS Default" settings in your CMOS setup.
- If your motherboard uses ISA bus slots, check "AT BUS Clock" speed in your CMOS setup and verify that it's set between 8MHz and 10MHz (ideally, 8.33MHz).

- Increase the boot process time in your CMOS setup. You can enable "Floppy Seek At Boot," "Test Memory Above 1MB," and/or set the "Boot Sequence" to "A: then C:."
- Set "Boot Speed" to its lowest value in the CMOS setup, and set the "Boot Pre-delay" entry (if present) to its highest value.
- Use FDISK to double-check your partitions. If the drive was not previously partitioned, create a primary DOS partition on the drive. Use option 2 to set the partition "active." Exit FDISK and reboot. Format the new partition and install the system files. If the drive was previously partitioned, make sure the first partition is "PRI DOS" and its Status is "A." Compare the sum of all partition sizes to the "Total Disk Space"—this should be the same within about 1MB. If the total is different, correct the drive parameters or translation mode in CMOS setup and repartition the drive.

> If the drive was previously partitioned, but no partitions are currently seen in FDISK, do not attempt to create new partitions if data on the drive is to be saved.

- Double-check the master/slave jumpers on all drives using the primary controller.
- Install (set) the jumper for "I/O Channel Ready" on the drive (if that option is present).
- If you're using a SCSI drive, verify that the "Parity" jumper is installed.
- Check all of your cable connections, and try a shorter replacement cable (or connect the drive to the middle cable connector).
- Replace the drive controller card.
- Remove the slave drive (if present) to determine the presence of any compatibility issues.

You may also need to check for data corruption or errors on the drive:

- Clean boot the system to a boot disk and execute FDISK /MBR and SYS C:. Make sure the DOS version on the floppy disk is the *same* version as on the hard drive before using the SYS command.
- Bypass CONFIG.SYS and AUTOEXEC.BAT to check for problems in your startup files. If this works, use the "step-by-step" boot mode in the Windows Startup menu to walk through each step of these files until the problem is found. Then edit both the CONFIG.SYS and AUTOEXEC.BAT files and comment out the statement(s) causing the problem.
- Check for drive compression, and try removing the compression drivers if there is no important data on the drive.
- Use FDISK to delete the partition; then repartition and reformat the drive.
- Replace the hard drive.

CHECKING FOR FAT16 AND FAT32

It may be necessary for you to identify the presence of a FAT16 or FAT32 partition before using disk utilities, backup software, or other applications. This will prevent accidental data loss caused by using an incompatible software version (for example, using a FAT16 version of ScanDisk on a FAT32 partition).

- Under Windows 98, double-click the My Computer icon on your desktop, and then right-click the drive you're interested in. Click Properties from the drop-down menu. Look at the General tab on the line marked "File system." A FAT16 partition will simply say "FAT," while a FAT32 partition will specify "FAT32."

- Try the "ver" (version) command from a DOS prompt:

```
Windows 95A. [Version 4.00.950]
Windows 95B. [Version 4.00.1111]
Windows 98. [Version 4.10.1998]
```

- If you need a FAT32 version of FDISK, check to see that FDISK asks, "Do you wish to enable large disk support (Y/N)." If it does *not* ask this question, it's probably a FAT16 version.
- You can also check the partition type using a FAT32 version of FDISK. Select option 4 to display the partition information. The System field will read "FAT32" or "FAT16," or if the partition has not been formatted, it will read "Unknown."

DEALING WITH DRIVE NOISE

All hard drives make a certain amount of noise during normal operation, and the noise level will vary depending on whether the drive is spinning or accessing. However, when the drive makes substantial or abnormal noises, this may indicate an impending failure. The trick here is to distinguish the "normal" noises from the "abnormal" noises. A drive makes three basic sounds:

- A whining noise during the drive spinup (and a mild "whir" while the system is on).
- Regular clicking or tapping sounds during drive access (the R/W heads stepping across the platters).
- Hard clicks when the drive heads park before power-off.

You should develop a keen ear for abnormal drive sounds:

- A high-pitched whining sound (such as a screech or squeal) can be an indication of problems.
- Noises (vibrations) caused by mounting issues. This is due to either a high-frequency vibration in the mounting hardware or a potential drive failure.
- Repeated, regular tapping, grinding, or beeping. When the hard drive is suspect, it is always important to make an immediate backup of your data.

> To isolate the drive further, try disconnecting the drive's signal cable, and power-up the system. If the noise persists, the drive should be backed up and replaced at your earliest convenience. If the noise stops, there may be an issue with the cable or controller that you should investigate further.

DEALING WITH SPIN PROBLEMS

All hard drives must spin their platters at a constant rate of speed, so any spin problems can render the drive inaccessible. Spin problems can usually be broken down into three types:

- *Drive does not spin at all* When a system is turned on, the characteristic hard drive wind-up sounds are not present. This can also occur if the hard drive spins down (without cause) after working for a period of time.
- *Drive spins up and spins down again* This normally occurs during the initial power-up. The hard drive will start spinning and then slow down again (or it cycles up to a point and ceases to spin).
- *Drive spins down following period of inactivity* The hard drive fails to spin up when access is attempted.

The first thing to check for are installation errors:

- Check the jumper settings on all hard drives attached to the same interface cable. For example, check the master/slave jumpers on each drive, and then check for "energy management" or "deferred spinup" jumpers. Most SCSI (and a few IDE) hard drives contain one or both jumper options.
- Check all of the power supply cable connections.
- Check the interface (ribbon) cable connections.
- Check for any system software for power management, and disable or uninstall that software if necessary.
- Next, check for "green" or power management features that might be set improperly:
- Disable your drive-related power management features in the CMOS setup.
- Disable the power management jumper on your hard drive (if present).
- Some overlay software can set power management features. For example, you can disable power management under Maxtor's MaxBlast software (versions 7.04–7.12) by removing the /E switch. Clean boot the system if other power management software is the suspected culprit.
- Windows 95 and Windows 98 can enable power management. This feature will need to be disabled through the operating system's Power Management icon in the Control Panel.

Finally, check for hardware failures with the drive and/or its controller:

- Try installing the drive in another system. This will verify that the problem is with the drive, not the system.
- Use a different power supply plug.
- Use a different interface (ribbon) cable.
- Use a different drive controller (for example, try a PCI drive controller card).
- Disconnect the ribbon cable from the drive.
- Replace the drive outright.

HARDWARE SYMPTOMS

Now it's time to review some problems and solutions. The important concept here is that a hard drive *problem* does not necessarily mean a hard drive *failure*. The failure of a sector or track does not automatically indicate physical head or platter damage—that is why software tools have been so successful at restoring operation (and even recovering data).

> Drive troubleshooting has the potential of destroying any data on the drive(s). Before attempting to troubleshoot hard disk drive problems, be sure to back up as much of the drive as possible. If there is no backup available, do not repartition or reformat the drive unless absolutely necessary and all other possible alternatives have been exhausted.

> The term "IDE-type" drive is taken to mean any drive using a 40-pin IDE-style interface: IDE, EIDE, ATAPI IDE, Ultra-DMA/33, and Ultra-DMA/66 (using the 40-pin/80-conductor cable). Specific drive types or exceptions will be noted.

SYMPTOM 23-1 **The hard drive is completely dead** The drive does not spin up, the drive light doesn't illuminate during power-up, or you see an error message indicating that the drive is not found or ready.

- *Check the drive power.* Make sure the 4-pin power connector is inserted properly and completely. If the drive is being powered by a Y-connector, make sure any interim connections are secure. Use a voltmeter and measure the +5 volt (pin 4) and +12 volt (pin 1) levels. If either voltage (especially the +12 volt supply) is unusually low or absent, replace the power supply.
- *Check the signal cable.* Also check your signal cable. See that the drive's signal interface cable is connected securely at both the drive and controller ends. For IDE-type drives, this is the 40-pin ribbon cable. If the cable is visibly worn or damaged, try a new cable.
- *Check the CMOS setup.* The PC cannot use a hard drive that it can't recognize, so enter the CMOS setup routine and see that all of the parameters entered for the drive are correct. Heads, cylinders, sectors per track, landing zone, and write precompensation must all be correct—otherwise, POST will not recognize the drive. If you have an autodetect option available, try that also. Remember to save your changes in CMOS and reboot the system.
- *Replace the drive or controller.* If problems continue, the hard drive itself may be defective. Try a known-good hard drive. If a known-good drive works as expected, your original drive is probably defective and should be replaced. If a known-good hard drive fails to operate, replace the drive controller board.

SYMPTOM 23-2 **You see drive activity, but the computer will not boot from the hard drive** In most cases, there is a drive failure, boot sector failure, or DOS/Windows file corruption.

- *Check the signal cable.* Make sure the drive's signal cable is connected securely at both the drive and controller. If the cable is visibly worn or damaged, try a new one.
- *Check the CMOS setup.* Verify that all of the parameters entered for the drive are correct. Heads, cylinders, sectors per track, landing zone, and write precompensation must all be correct—otherwise, POST will not recognize the drive. If the BIOS provides an option to autodetect the drive, try that as well.
- *Check the boot sector.* Boot from a floppy disk and try accessing the hard drive. If the hard drive is accessible, chances are that the boot files are missing or corrupt. Try a utility such as DrivePro's Drive Boot Fixer. You might also try running FDISK /MBR, which will rebuild the drive's master boot record. *Be careful: the FDISK /MBR command may render the files on your drive inaccessible.*
- *Check the drive and controller.* You may have a problem with your drive system hardware. If you cannot access the hard drive, run a diagnostic such as Windsor Technologies' PC Technician. Test the drive and drive controller. If the controller responds but the drive does not, try repartitioning and reformatting the hard drive. If the drive still doesn't respond, replace the hard drive outright. If the controller doesn't respond, replace the hard drive controller.

SYMPTOM 23-3 **There are errors during drive reads or writes** Magnetic information does not last forever, and sector ID information can gradually degrade to a point where you encounter file errors.

- *Check for file problems.* Start by checking for any file structure problems on the drive. Use a utility such as ScanDisk to examine the drive and search for bad sectors. If a failed sector involves part of an EXE or COM file, that file is now corrupt and should be restored from a backup.
- *Try a low-level format.* If you cannot isolate file problems, you may need to consider a low-level (LL) format. Low-level formatting rewrites sector ID information, but the sophistication of today's drives makes LL formatting almost impossible. If the drive manufacturer provides a "drive preparation" utility, you should back up the drive, run the utility, then run FDISK, FORMAT, and restore the drive from its backup.

SYMPTOM 23-4 **Hard drive performance appears to be slowing down over time** In virtually all cases, diminishing drive performance can be caused by file fragmentation. To a far lesser extent, you may be faced with a computer virus.

- *Boot the system clean.* Start the PC with a clean boot disk and make sure there are no TSRs or drivers being loaded.
- *Check for viruses.* After a clean boot, run your antivirus checker and make sure there are no memory-resident or file-based viruses.
- *Check for file fragmentation.* If the system checks clean for computer viruses, you should check for file fragmentation next. Start your defragmentation utility (such as Defrag) and check to see the percentage of file fragmentation. If there is more than 10 percent fragmentation, consider running the defragmentation utility after preparing Windows. Before defragmenting a drive, reboot the system normally, start Windows, access the Virtual Memory controls for your version of Windows, and shut down virtual memory. Leave Windows and boot the system clean again. Restart your defragmentation utility and proceed to defragment the disk. This process may take several minutes depending on the size of your drive. Once defragmentation is complete, reboot the system normally, start Windows, access the Virtual Memory controls for your version of Windows, and re-create a permanent swap file to support virtual memory. You should now notice a performance improvement.

SYMPTOM 23-5 **You can access the hard drive correctly, but the drive light stays on continuously** A continuous LED indication is not *necessarily* a problem as long as the drive seems to be operating properly. Check the drive and drive controller for drive "light jumpers." Examine the drive itself for any jumper that might select "latched" mode versus "activity" mode. If there are no such jumpers on the drive, check the drive controller or motherboard. Set the jumper to "activity" mode to see the drive light during access only. Next, consider the possibility of drive light *error messages*. Some drive types (especially SCSI drives) use the drive activity light to signal drive and controller errors. Check the drive and controller documents to determine whether there is any error indicated by the light remaining on.

SYMPTOM 23-6 **You cannot access the hard drive, and the drive light stays on continuously** This usually indicates a reversed signal cable and is most common when upgrading or replacing a drive system.

- *Check the signal cable.* In virtually all cases, one end of the signal cable is reversed. Make sure that both ends of the cable are installed properly. (Remember that the red or blue stripe on one side of the cable represents pin 1.)

- *Replace the drive controller.* If problems persist, replace the drive controller. It is rare for a fault in the drive controller to cause this type of problem, but if trouble persists, try a known-good drive controller board.

SYMPTOM 23-7 **You see a "No Fixed Disk Present" error message on the monitor**

This kind of problem can occur during installation, or at any point in the PC's working life.

- *Check the power connector.* Make sure the 4-pin power connector is inserted properly and completely. If the drive is being powered by a Y-connector, make sure any interim connections are secure. Use a voltmeter and measure the +5 volt (pin 4) and +12 volt (pin 1) levels. If either voltage (especially the +12 volt supply) is unusually low or absent, replace the power supply.
- *Check the signal connector.* Make sure the drive's signal cable is connected securely at both the drive and controller. If the cable is visibly worn or damaged, try a new one.
- *Check the CMOS setup.* Enter the CMOS setup routine and see that all of the parameters entered for the drive are correct. Heads, cylinders, sectors per track, landing zone, and write precompensation must all be correct—otherwise, POST will not recognize the drive. You might also try autodetecting the drive.
- *Check for hardware conflicts.* Make sure there are no other expansion devices in the system using the same IRQs or I/O addresses used by your drive controller. If so, change the resources used by the conflicting device. If your drive system uses a SCSI interface, make sure the SCSI cable is terminated properly.
- *Replace the hard drive or controller.* If problems continue, try a known-good hard drive. If a known-good drive works as expected, your original drive is probably defective. If problems persist with a known-good hard drive, replace the drive controller board.

SYMPTOM 23-8 **Your drive spins up, but the system fails to recognize the drive**

Your computer may flag this as a "Hard-disk error" or "Hard-disk controller failure" during system initialization.

- *Check the signal connector.* Make sure the interface signal cable is inserted properly and completely at the drive and controller. Try a new signal cable.
- *Check the drive jumpers.* See that a primary (master) drive is configured as primary, and a secondary (slave) drive is configured as secondary. For SCSI drives, see that each drive has a unique ID setting, and check that the SCSI bus is terminated properly.
- *Check the CMOS setup.* Enter the CMOS setup routine and see that all of the parameters entered for the drive are correct. Heads, cylinders, sectors per track, landing zone, and write precompensation must all be correct—otherwise, POST will not recognize the drive. Try using the autodetect feature if it is available.
- *Check the partition.* If the CMOS is configured properly, you should suspect a problem with the partition. Boot from a floppy disk and run FDISK to check the partitions on your hard drive. Make sure there is at least one DOS partition. If the drive is to be your boot drive, the primary partition must be active and bootable. Repartition and reformat the drive if necessary.
- *Try another hard drive or controller.* If a known-good drive works as expected, your original drive is probably defective. If a known-good hard drive fails to work as expected, replace the drive controller. If problems persist with a known-good floppy drive, replace the drive controller board.

SYMPTOM 23-9 **Your IDE drive spins up when power is applied, then rapidly spins down again** The drive is defective, or it is not communicating properly with its host system.

- *Check the power connector.* Make sure the 4-pin power connector is inserted properly and completely into the drive.
- *Check the signal connector next.* See that the interface signal cable is inserted properly and completely at the drive and controller. Try a new signal cable.
- *Check the drive jumpers.* The primary (master) drive should be configured as primary, and a secondary (slave) drive should be configured as secondary. For SCSI drives, see that each drive has a unique ID setting, and check that the SCSI bus is terminated properly.
- *Replace the drive.* If problems persist, try a known-good hard drive. If a known-good drive works as expected, your original drive is probably defective.

SYMPTOM 23-10 **You see a "Sector not found" error message** This problem usually occurs after the drive has been in operation for quite some time, and is typically the result of a media failure. Fortunately, a bad sector will only affect one file.

- *Try recovering the file.* Use a utility such as SpinRite from Gibson Research (or another data recovery utility), and attempt to recover the damaged file. Note that you may be unsuccessful and have to restore the file from a backup later.
- *Check the disk media.* Use a disk utility (such as ScanDisk) to evaluate the drive; then locate and map out any bad sectors that are located on the drive.
- *Try a low-level format.* If problems persist, perform a low-level format (if possible). Lost sectors often occur as drives age and sector ID information degrades. Low-level formatting restores the sector IDs, but LL formatting is performed at the factory for IDE/EIDE and SCSI drives. If there is a LL formatting utility for your particular drive (available from the drive manufacturer), and ScanDisk reveals a large number of bad sectors, you may consider backing up the drive completely, running the LL utility, repartitioning, reformatting, and then restoring the drive. If ScanDisk maps out bad sectors, you may need to restore those files from a backup.

SYMPTOM 23-11 **You see a "1780 or 1781 ERROR" on the system** The classical 1780 error code indicates a "Hard Disk 0 Failure," while the 1781 error code marks a "Hard Disk 1 Failure."

- *Boot the system clean.* Start the PC with a clean boot disk, and make sure there are no TSRs or drivers being loaded.
- *Check for viruses.* If you haven't done so already, run your antivirus checker and make sure there are no memory-resident or file-based viruses.
- *Check the boot files.* If you can access the hard drive once your system is booted, chances are that the boot files are missing or corrupt. Try a utility such as DrivePro's Drive Boot Fixer to recover the boot files, or recopy the boot files with SYS, and re-create the master boot record with FDISK /MBR. Otherwise, you will need to repartition and reformat the disk, then restore disk files from a backup.
- *Replace the hard drive or controller.* If you cannot access the hard drive, run a diagnostic such as Windsor Technologies' PC Technician. Test the drive and drive controller. If the controller responds but the drive does not, try repartitioning and reformatting the hard drive. If the drive still doesn't respond, replace the hard drive outright. If the controller doesn't respond, replace the hard drive controller.

SYMPTOM 23-12 **You see a "1790 or 1791 ERROR" on the system** The classical 1790 error code indicates a "Hard Disk 0 Error," while the 1791 error code marks a "Hard Disk 1 Error."

- *Check the signal connector.* Make sure the interface signal cable is inserted properly and completely at the drive and controller. Try a new signal cable.
- *Check the partition.* Boot from a floppy disk and run FDISK to check the partitions on your hard drive. Make sure there is at least one DOS partition. If the drive is to be your boot drive, the primary partition must be active and bootable. Repartition and reformat the drive if necessary.
- *Replace the hard drive or controller.* If a known-good drive works as expected, your original drive is probably defective. If problems persist with a known-good floppy drive, replace the drive controller board.

SYMPTOM 23-13 **You see a "1701 ERROR" on the system** The 1701 error code indicates a hard drive POST error—the drive did not pass its power-on self-test.

- *Check the power connector.* Make sure the 4-pin power connector is inserted properly and completely. If the drive is being powered by a Y-connector, make sure any interim connections are secure. Use a voltmeter and measure the +5 volt (pin 4) and +12 volt (pin 1) levels. If either voltage (especially the +12 volt supply) is unusually low or absent, replace the power supply.
- *Check the CMOS setup.* Enter the CMOS setup routine and see that all of the parameters entered for the drive are correct. Heads, cylinders, sectors per track, landing zone, and write precompensation must all be correct—otherwise, POST will not recognize the drive. Try autodetecting the drive.
- *Try a low-level format.* If problems persist, perform a low-level format (if possible). If there is a LL formatting utility for your particular drive (available from the drive manufacturer), you may consider backing up the drive completely, running the LL utility, repartitioning, reformatting, then restoring the drive.

SYMPTOM 23-14 **The system reports random data, seek, or format errors** Random errors rarely indicate a permanent problem, but identifying the problem source can be a time-consuming task.

- *Check the power connector.* Make sure the 4-pin power connector is inserted properly and completely. If the drive is being powered by a Y-connector, make sure any interim connections are secure. Use a voltmeter and measure the +5 volt (pin 4) and +12 volt (pin 1) levels. If either voltage (especially the +12 volt supply) is unusually low, replace the power supply.
- *Check the signal connector.* Make sure the interface signal cable is inserted properly and completely at the drive and controller. Try a new signal cable. Also try rerouting the signal cable away from the power supply or "noisy" expansion devices.
- *Check the drive orientation.* If problems occur after remounting the drive in a different orientation, you may need to repartition and reformat the drive, or return it to its original orientation. Try relocating the drive controller away from cables and "noisy" expansion devices.
- *Check the "turbo mode."* If your system has a turbo mode, your ISA drive controller may have trouble operating while the system is in this mode. Take the system out of turbo mode.
- *Replace the drive controller.* If the problem disappears, try a new drive controller.

- *Check the media.* The disk media may also be defective. Use a utility such as ScanDisk to check for and map out any bad sectors. Once bad sectors are mapped out, you may need to restore some files from your backup.
- *Try the hard drive and controller in another system.* If the drive and controller work in another system, there is probably excessive noise or grounding problems in the original system. Reinstall the drive and controller in the original system and remove all extra expansion boards. If the problem goes away, replace one board at a time and retest the system until the problem returns. The last board you inserted when the problem returned is probably the culprit. If the problem persists, there may be a ground problem on the motherboard. Try replacing the motherboard as an absolute last effort.

SYMPTOM 23-15 **You see an "Error reading drive C:" error message** Read errors in a hard drive typically indicate problems with the disk media, but may also indicate viruses or signaling problems.

- *Check the signal connector.* Make sure the interface signal cable is inserted properly and completely at the drive and controller. Try a new signal cable.
- *Boot the PC clean.* Start the PC with a clean boot disk, and make sure there are no TSRs or drivers being loaded.
- *Check for viruses.* If you haven't done so already, run your antivirus checker and make sure there are no memory-resident or file-based viruses.
- *Consider the drive's orientation.* If problems occur after remounting the drive in a different orientation, you may need to repartition and reformat the drive, or return it to its original orientation.
- *Check the disk media.* Use a utility such as ScanDisk to check for and map out any bad sectors. Once bad sectors are mapped out, you may need to restore some files from your backup.
- *Try another hard drive.* If a known-good drive works as expected, your original drive is probably defective and should be replaced.

SYMPTOM 23-16 **You see a "Track 0 not found" error message** A fault on track 00 can disable the entire drive since track 00 contains the drive's File Allocation Table (FAT). This can be a serious error that may require you to replace the drive.

- *Check the signal connector.* Examine the drive signal connector, and verify that the interface signal cable is inserted properly and completely at the drive and controller. Try a new signal cable.
- *Check your partitions.* Boot from a floppy disk and run FDISK to check the partitions on your hard drive. Make sure there is at least one DOS partition. If the drive is to be your boot drive, the primary partition must be "active" and bootable. Repartition and reformat the drive if necessary.
- *Replace the hard drive.* Try a known-good hard drive. If a known-good drive works as expected, your original drive is probably defective.

SYMPTOM 23-17 **You see a "Hard Disk Controller Failure" or a large number of defects in the last logical partition** This is typically a CMOS setup or drive controller problem. Enter the CMOS setup routine and see that all of the parameters entered for the drive are correct. If the geometry specifies a larger drive, the system will attempt to format areas of the drive that don't exist, resulting in a large number of errors. If CMOS is configured correctly, there may be a problem with the hard drive controller. Try a new hard drive controller. If a new drive controller does not correct the problem, the drive itself is probably defective, and should be replaced.

SYMPTOM 23-18 **The IDE drive (<528MB) does not partition or format to full capacity** When relatively small hard drives do not realize their full capacity, the CMOS setup is usually at fault. The drive parameters entered into CMOS must specify the full capacity of the drive, using a geometry setup that is acceptable. If you use parameters that specify a smaller drive, any extra capacity will be ignored. If there are over 1024 cylinders, you must use an alternate "translation geometry" to realize the drive's full potential. The drive maker can provide you with the correct translation geometry. Also check your DOS version—older versions of DOS use a partition limit of 32MB. Upgrade your older version of DOS to 6.22 (or MS-DOS 7.0 with Windows 95).

SYMPTOM 23-19 **The EIDE drive (>528MB) does not partition or format to full capacity** This type of problem may also be due to a CMOS setup error, but is almost always due to poor system configuration.

- *Check the CMOS setup.* The drive parameters entered into CMOS must specify the full capacity of the drive. If you use parameters that specify a smaller drive, any extra capacity will be ignored. If there are over 1024 cylinders, you must use an alternate "translation geometry" to realize the drive's full potential. The drive maker can provide you with the correct translation geometry. Also check the CMOS setup for LBA. EIDE drives need Logical Block Addressing to access more than 528MB. Make sure that there is an entry such as "LBA Mode" in CMOS. Otherwise, you may need to upgrade your motherboard BIOS to have full drive capacity.
- *Check the drive controller.* If you cannot upgrade an older motherboard BIOS, install an EIDE drive controller with its own controller BIOS. This will supplement the motherboard BIOS.
- *Check the drive overlay software.* If neither your motherboard nor controller BIOS will support LBA mode, you will need to install drive overlay software (such as EZ-Drive or Drive Manager).

SYMPTOM 23-20 **You see "Disk Boot Failure," "non system disk," or "No ROM Basic—SYSTEM HALTED" error messages** There are several possible reasons for these errors.

- *Check the signal connector.* Make sure the interface signal cables are inserted properly and completely at the drive and controller. Try some new signal cables.
- *Boot the PC clean.* Start the PC with a clean boot disk and make sure there are no TSRs or drivers being loaded that might interfere with drive operation. If you haven't done so already, run your antivirus checker and make sure there are no memory-resident or file-based viruses.
- *Check the CMOS setup.* Enter the CMOS setup routine and see that all of the parameters entered for the drive are correct. Heads, cylinders, sectors per track, landing zone, and write precompensation must all be entered accurately.
- *Check your partitions.* Boot from a floppy disk and run FDISK to check the partitions on your hard drive. Make sure there is at least one DOS partition. If the drive is to be your boot drive, the primary partition must be active and bootable.
- *Replace the drive or controller.* It is also possible that the hard drive itself is defective. Try a known-good hard drive. If a known-good drive works as expected, your original drive is probably defective. If problems persist with a known-good floppy drive, replace the drive controller.

SYMPTOM 23-21 **The hard drive in a PC is suffering frequent breakdowns (between 6 to 12 months)** When drives tend to fail within a few months, these are some factors to consider:

- *Check the PC power.* If the AC power supplying your PC is "dirty" (has lots of spikes and surges), power anomalies can often make it through the power supply and damage other components. Remove any high-load devices such as air conditioners, motors, or coffee makers from the same AC circuit used by the PC, or try the PC on a known-good AC circuit. You might also consider a good UPS to power your PC.
- *Consider drive utilization.* Excessive drive use may be another factor. If the drive is being worked hard by applications and swap files, consider upgrading RAM, adding cache, or disabling virtual memory to reduce dependency on the drive.
- *Defragment the drive.* Periodically run a utility like Defrag to reorganize the files. This reduces the amount of "drive thrashing" that occurs when loading and saving files.
- *Consider the environment.* Constant, low-level vibrations, such as those in an industrial environment, can kill a hard drive. Smoke (even cigarette smoke), high humidity, very low humidity, and caustic vapors can ruin drives. Make sure the system is used in a stable office-type environment.

SYMPTOM 23-22 **A hard drive controller is replaced, but during initialization, the system displays error messages such as "Hard Disk Failure" or "Not a recognized drive type"** The PC may also lock up. Some drive controllers may be incompatible in some systems. Check with the controller manufacturer and see if there have been any reports of incompatibilities with your PC. If so, try a different drive controller board.

SYMPTOM 23-23 **A new hard drive is installed, but it will not boot, or a message appears such as "HDD controller failure"** The new drive has probably not been installed or prepared properly.

- *Check the power connector.* Make sure the 4-pin power connector is inserted properly and completely. If the drive is being powered by a Y-connector, make sure any interim connections are secure. Use a voltmeter and measure the +5 volt (pin 4) and +12 volt (pin 1) levels. If either voltage (especially the +12 volt supply) is unusually low or absent, replace the power supply.
- *Check the signal cable.* Make sure the drive's signal interface cable is connected securely at both the drive and controller. If the cable is visibly worn or damaged, try a new one.
- *Check the CMOS setup.* Enter the CMOS setup routine and see that all of the parameters entered for the drive are correct. Heads, cylinders, sectors per track, landing zone, and write precompensation must all be correct—otherwise, POST will not recognize the drive.
- *Check the drive's preparation.* The drive may not be prepared properly. Run FDISK from a bootable disk to partition the drive; then run FORMAT to initialize the drive. Then run SYS C: to make the drive bootable.

SYMPTOM 23-24 **The drive will work as a primary drive, but not as a secondary (or vice versa)** In most cases, the drive is simply jumpered incorrectly, but there may also be timing problems. Check the drive jumpers first. Make sure that the drive is jumpered properly as a primary (single drive), primary (dual drive), or secondary drive. The drive signal timing may also be off. Some

IDE/EIDE drives do not work as primary or secondary drives with certain other drives in the system. Reverse the primary/secondary relationship. If the problem persists, try the drives separately. If the drives work individually, there is probably a timing problem, so try a different drive as the primary or secondary.

SYMPTOM 23-25 **You install a Y-adapter that fails to work** Some Y-adapters are incorrectly wired and can cause severe damage to any device attached to them. Examine the power connector first. Make certain that both of the female connectors are lined up with the two chamfered (rounded) corners facing up and both of the squared corners facing down. The four wires attached to the female connectors should now be in the following order from left to right: Yellow (+12 Vdc), Black (ground), Black (ground), Red (+5 Vdc). If this order is reversed on one of the connectors, your Y power adapter is faulty and should not be used.

SYMPTOM 23-26 **During the POST, you hear a drive begin to spin up and produce a sharp noise** This problem can be encountered with some combinations of drives, motherboards, and motherboard BIOS. This type of problem can easily result in data loss (and media damage). Check the motherboard BIOS version first; then contact the PC system manufacturer and see if a BIOS upgrade is necessary. Try a BIOS upgrade. Otherwise, replace the drive controller. Often a new drive controller may resolve the problem if the motherboard BIOS cannot be replaced.

SYMPTOM 23-27 **You're using an Ultra-DMA hard drive, but there is no "DMA" check box available in the drive's Properties dialog** If the DMA check box is unavailable, this may suggest that Windows does not view the drive as Ultra-DMA capable. This could be a driver issue, or your hard drive (or motherboard drive controller) does not support Ultra-DMA. Assuming the drive and motherboard both support Ultra-DMA operation, make sure you are running the latest bus mastering drivers. (These are installed by default if your motherboard supports them.) You may need to download the latest bus master drivers from the drive controller maker or motherboard manufacturer. Once the proper drivers are installed, Windows 98 will automatically handle all transfer rates that the drive and motherboard support.

SYMPTOM 23-28 **After installing a large HDD (unpartitioned), you cannot access the floppy drive** This will effectively hang the system and prevent you from completing the hard drive's installation. In most cases, this is due to an issue with the drive size. Some BIOS versions cannot perform the proper translation on an 8.4GB (or larger) drive and will hang the system as a result. Try setting up the drive using the following parameters:

Cylinders: 1023
Heads: 16
Sectors: 63

Of course, this represents a small IDE drive, and the system will tell you that this is a 504MB or 528MB drive. If you are then able to boot to a floppy disk, you may either upgrade the BIOS or drive controller to support the large hard drive natively, or install drive overlay software such as Disk Manager or MaxBlast.

SYMPTOM 23-29 **After configuring a drive with the correct parameters (16383 x 16 x 63), the system still indicates that the drive is only 504MB or 528MB** Keep in mind that 528MB (or 504MB) is the limitation of the original Cylinder/Head/Sector translation method used on IDE drives. This problem was resolved with LBA translation techniques. Make sure the CMOS setup is configured to use Logical Block Addressing if it is available. If not, you may need to upgrade the BIOS (or drive controller), or install drive overlay software such as Disk Manager or MaxBlast.

23

SYMPTOM 23-30 When replacing or repartitioning certain Compaq systems, you can no longer access the system's setup This occurs because you removed the "diagnostic partition." Some Compaq computers store the system BIOS information in a non-DOS or diagnostic partition on the hard drive, instead of storing it on a chip on the motherboard as most other systems do. If you have such a Compaq model and you install the new drive as a master, you will need to copy or reinstall the diagnostic partition onto the new drive. If you don't, you will not be able to access your CMOS setup upon boot-up. If you install the new drive as a slave or non-boot drive, you do not need to reinstall this partition. In addition, if you're planning to install the drive with an older version of Western Digital's EZ-Drive, you must use version 9.06w or later.

If you install the new drive as a master, you can use drive overlay software to copy the diagnostic partition and your data from the old drive to the new one. If you're only concerned about the diagnostic partition, you can use the drive overlay software to transfer the data, then reformat the drive. As long as you do this under the DDO's control (assuming EZ-BIOS installed itself), it will not affect the diagnostic partition. Just boot to C:, insert the startup disk, and start formatting. If you have more than one partition, make sure you format the correct drive letters corresponding to the other partitions.

> When trying to access the diagnostic partition, you may encounter an error message that refers to a memory conflict. This is a known issue, and you will need to contact Compaq directly for detailed instructions should this occur.

SYMPTOM 23-31 You detect hard drive errors caused by damaged data or physical damage You may receive one of the following error messages when you are starting or using your computer:

- `Serious Disk Error Writing Drive <X>`
- `Data Error Reading Drive <X>`
- `Error Reading Drive <X>`
- `I/O Error`
- `Seek Error—Sector not found`

These error messages indicate either damaged data or physical damage on the hard disk. Run ScanDisk to examine the hard drive. Running ScanDisk with the "Thorough" option selected examines the drive for physical damage. If damaged data is detected, ScanDisk allows you to save the damaged data to a file (or discard the data). Keep in mind that ScanDisk's "surface scan" may take a considerable amount of time on large hard disks. If ScanDisk is unable to repair damaged data (or indicates that the drive suffers from physical damage), you'll need to replace the drive.

SYMPTOM 23-32 You find that a PC using an Ultra-DMA controller/drive may lock up when running Windows 95 (OSR2) The lockup occurs when the drive is being accessed. This problem occurs when there's a hardware error while data is being read from the hard drive. When the error happens during an Ultra-DMA data transfer, the Windows device driver does not successfully recover from the error and retry the operation—so the system halts. This is a known issue with Windows 95 OSR2, and an update file (REMIDEUP.EXE) is available for download from the Microsoft Web site. The updated file ESDI_506.PDR version 4.00.1116 (dated 8/25/97 or later) should fix the problem under Windows 95 OSR2.

SYMPTOM 23-33 You encounter errors accessing a hard drive with its "spin-down" feature enabled This frequently occurs under Windows 95 (and OSR2), and you may find that incorrect data is read or written to the drive, or you may encounter GPFs. This type of problem is known to occur under Windows 95 (and OSR2) if the drive requires more than 7.5 seconds to spin up. An error is then generated in the Windows 95 driver, resulting in incorrect data being read from the drive (which can result in GPFs).

You can work around this problem by disabling hard disk spindown on the Disk Drives tab using the Power tool in Control Panel. An update file (REMIDEUP.EXE) is available for download from the Microsoft Web site. The updated file ESDI_506.PDR version 4.00.1113 (dated 12/6/96 or later) should fix the problem under Windows 95 (and OSR2). For Windows 95, the VOLTRACK.VXD version 4.00.954 (dated 3/6/96 or later) file is also installed.

File System Symptoms

SYMPTOM 23-34 One or more subdirectories appear lost or damaged Both the root directory of a drive and its FAT contain references to subdirectories. If data in either the root directory or File Allocation Table is corrupt, one or more subdirectories may be inaccessible by the drive. Try repairing the drive's directory structure. Use ScanDisk (with DOS 6.2 or later) to check the disk's directory structure for problems. Then correct any problems that are reported.

SYMPTOM 23-35 The hard drive was formatted accidentally A high-level format (using the FORMAT utility) does not actually "destroy" data, but rather, it clears the file names and locations kept in the root directory and FAT. This prevents DOS from finding those files. You will need to recover those files. Use a utility such as UNFORMAT (or other file recovery utilities), which can reconstruct root directory and FAT data. This is not always a perfect process, and you may not be able to recover all files. If that's the case, you can restore the missing files from a backup.

23

SYMPTOM 23-36 A file has been deleted accidentally Mistyping a file name (or forgetting to add the proper drive specification) can accidentally erase files from places you did not intend to erase. You can often recover those files if you act quickly. Use a utility such as UNDELETE (or other file recovery utilities) to restore the deleted file(s). This is not always a perfect process, and you may not be able to recover every file.

SYMPTOM 23-37 The hard drive's root directory is damaged A faulty root directory can cripple the entire disk, rendering *all* subdirectories inaccessible. You may be able to recover the root directory structure. Use a utility like DISKFIX (with PC Tools) to reconstruct the damaged FATs and directories. If you have been running MIRROR, DISKFIX should be able to perform a very reliable recovery. You may also try other recovery/corrective utilities such as DrivePro or ScanDisk. However, if you cannot recover the root directory reliably, you'll need to reformat the drive, then restore its contents from a backup.

SYMPTOM 23-38 You see a "Bad or Missing Command Interpreter" error message This is a typical error that appears when a drive is formatted in one DOS version but loaded with another. Compatibility problems occur when you mix DOS versions. Start by booting the PC with a clean boot disk, and make sure there are no TSRs or drivers being loaded. If you haven't done so already, run your antivirus checker and make sure there are no memory-resident or file-based viruses. Finally, make sure that the drive is partitioned and formatted with the version of DOS you intend to use. Also be sure to use FORMAT with the /S switch, or SYS C: in order to transfer system files to the drive.

SYMPTOM 23-39 You see an "Incorrect DOS version" error You attempted to execute an external DOS command (such as FORMAT) using a version of the utility that is not from the same DOS version as the COMMAND.COM file that is currently running. Reboot with a corresponding version of COMMAND.COM, or get a version of the utility that matches the current version of COMMAND.COM.

SYMPTOM 23-40 The hard drive is infected by a bootblock virus You may detect the presence of a bootblock virus (a virus that infects the MBR) by running an antivirus utility or receiving a warning from the BIOS bootblock protection feature. In every case, you should attempt to use the antivirus utility to eradicate the virus. You may also remove a bootblock virus by using FDISK /MBR (though that could render the contents of your disk inaccessible). If you're using drive overlay software such as Disk Manager, you can usually rewrite the code through the Maintenance menu within the Disk Manager utility itself.

SYMPTOM 23-41 You see a "File Allocation Table Bad" error The operating system has encountered a problem with the FAT. Normally, there are two copies of the FAT on a drive—chances are that one of the copies has become damaged. It may also be possible that there is no partition on the drive to begin with. Run ScanDisk. This may be able to correct the problem by allowing you to select which copy of the FAT you wish to use. If the problem continues, you'll need to back up as many files as possible and reformat the drive.

SYMPTOM 23-42 DOS requires you to "Enter Volume Label," but the label is corrupt Some versions of DOS (such as DOS 3.x) require you to enter the volume label when formatting a hard drive or deleting a logical drive partition using the FDISK command. However, if the volume label is corrupted (or was changed by a third-party utility to contain lowercase letters), this is impossible. To correct this problem, use the LABEL command to delete the volume label, and then use FORMAT or FDISK. When you are prompted for the volume label, press ENTER (which indicates no volume label). If LABEL doesn't successfully delete the volume label, you can use the following debug script to erase the first sector of the drive and make it appear unformatted, then repartition and reformat the drive. Start DEBUG, and then type the following:

```
-  F 100 L 200 0  ;Create a sector of zeros at address 100
-  W 100 2 0 1    ;Write information at address 100 to sector 0 of drive 2
-  Q              ;Quit DEBUG
```

For DOS versions 5.x and later, you can use the following command to handle the problem (where <VOLUME> is the new volume name you want to assign to the hard disk drive, and <x:> is the drive letter you want to format):

```
format /q /v:<VOLUME> <x:>
```

SYMPTOM 23-43 You cannot empty the Recycle Bin under Windows 95/98 There are several possible issues. When you right-click the Recycle Bin, the Empty Recycle Bin command may be unavailable (or the Properties command may be unavailable). You may also find that files you delete are permanently deleted, rather than simply moved to the Recycle Bin. In virtually all cases this problem is caused when your fixed hard disk is marked as a removable drive. You'll have to "unmark" the hard drive:

1. Click Start, select Settings, and then double-click Control Panel.
2. Double-click the System icon.
3. Click the Device Manager tab.
4. Double-click the Disk Drives branch to expand it.
5. Click your hard disk, and then click Properties.
6. On the Settings tab, click the Removable check box to clear it.
7. Click OK, and then click OK again.
8. Restart your computer.

You cannot use this procedure on a "true" removable drive. If the drive is removable, the Removable option is reset when you restart the computer.

Software-Oriented Symptoms

Following are some of the more common symptoms that your diagnostic software may report.

SYMPTOM 23-44 Software diagnostics indicate an average access time that is longer than specified for the drive The average access time is the average amount of time needed for a drive to reach the track and sector where a needed file begins.

- *Check your timing.* Review your drive specifications and verify the timing specifications for your particular drive—its timing may be correct.
- *Defragment the drive.* Start your defragmentation utility (such as Defrag), and check to see the percentage of file fragmentation. If there is more than 10 percent fragmentation, you should consider running the defragmentation utility.
- *Check your software.* Also keep in mind that different software packages measure access time differently. Make sure that the diagnostic subtracts system overhead processing from the access time calculation. Try one or two other diagnostics to confirm the measurement.
- *Check similar drives.* Before you panic and replace a drive, try testing several similar drives for comparison. If only the suspect drive measures incorrectly, you may not need to replace the drive itself just yet, but you should at least maintain frequent backups in case the drive is near failure.

SYMPTOM 23-45 Software diagnostics indicate a slower data transfer rate than specified This is often due to less-than-ideal data transfer rates rather than an actual hardware failure.

- *Check your timing.* Review your drive specifications and verify the timing specifications for your particular drive—its timing may be correct.
- *Check your data transfer modes.* Enter the CMOS setup routine and verify that any enhanced data transfer modes are enabled (such as PIO mode 4). This can increase the data transfer rate substantially.

- *Defragment the drive.* Start your defragmentation utility (such as Defrag), and check to see the percentage of file fragmentation. If there is more than 10 percent fragmentation, you should consider running the defragmentation utility.
- *Check your software.* Also keep in mind that different software packages measure access time differently. Make sure that the diagnostic subtracts system overhead processing from the access time calculation. Try one or two other diagnostics to confirm the measurement.
- *Check for low-level formatting.* If the drive is an IDE/EIDE type, make sure no one performed a low-level format—this may remove head and cylinder skewing optimization and result in a degradation of data transfer. This error generally cannot be corrected by end-user software.
- *Check termination.* If the drive is a SCSI type, make sure the SCSI bus is terminated properly. Poor termination can cause data errors and result in retransmissions that degrade overall data transfer rates.

SYMPTOM 23-46 The FDISK procedure hangs up or fails to create or save a partition record for the drive(s) You may also see an error message such as "Runtime error." This type of problem often indicates a problem with track 00 on the drive.

- *Check the signal connector.* Make sure the interface signal cables are inserted properly and completely at the drive and controller. Try some new signal cables.
- *Check the drive setup.* Enter the CMOS setup routine and see that all of the parameters entered for the drive are correct. Heads, cylinders, sectors per track, landing zone, and write precompensation must all be appropriate. Check with the drive maker and see if there is an alternate "translation geometry" that you can enter instead. If the BIOS supports autodetection, try autodetecting the drive.
- *Check your version of FDISK.* The version of FDISK you are using must be the same as the DOS version on your boot disk. Older versions may not work.
- *Check your partition(s).* Run FDISK and see if there are any partitions already on the drive. If so, you may need to erase any existing partitions, then create your new partition from scratch. Remember that erasing a partition will destroy any data already on the drive.
- *Check for media defects.* Use a utility such as ScanDisk to check the media for physical defects, especially at track 00. If there is physical damage in the boot sector, you should replace the drive.
- *Check for emergency drive utilities.* Some drive makers provide low-level preparation utilities that can rewrite track 00. For example, Western Digital provides the WD_CLEAR.EXE utility.
- *Replace the hard drive.* If problems still persist, replace the defective hard drive.

SYMPTOM 23-47 After using FDISK to partition a large hard drive, the system hangs when booting from a floppy disk This is almost always an issue with the system BIOS (or drive controller), which cannot properly support a large (8.4GB+) drive. Some BIOS versions are confused when they encounter an 8.4GB or larger hard drive, and they assign it 0 heads by mistake. Under these conditions, you'll be able to partition the drive with FDISK, but the partition table that it creates will contain invalid information. When you boot to a floppy disk, the operating system on that floppy disk attempts to access the partition table on the hard drive. The invalid information created by FDISK causes the OS to hang. The solution is to upgrade the system BIOS (or the drive controller) to support the large drive natively, or install drive overlay software such as Disk Manager or MaxBlast.

SYMPTOM 23-48 **FDISK reports an error such as "no space to create partition" or "disk is write protected"** There are several possible issues that may cause this type of behavior.

- *Check the CMOS setup.* Chances are that your BIOS has enabled virus protection for the master boot record (also referred to as "Boot Sector Write Protect"). You must go into the system's CMOS setup and disable that feature before partitioning a drive (or installing/upgrading an operating system).
- *Check the drive jumpers.* Some hard drives require the use of two jumpers rather than one. Verify that your drive is jumpered properly for its place in your particular drive configuration (for example, "single master," "master with slave," or "slave").
- *Upgrade the BIOS or drive controller.* If the problem persists, the BIOS may not be able to support your drive properly. Check for a BIOS upgrade (or upgrade the drive controller), or install drive overlay software such as Disk Manager or MaxBlast.

SYMPTOM 23-49 **FDISK refuses to partition the drive and hangs the system or returns a "runtime error"** In many cases, track 00 on the drive has been corrupted. If you can perform a low-level format of the drive, try using the disk manufacturer's LL formatting (or "drive preparation") utility to reconstruct track 00. For example, Western Digital's Data Lifeguard Tools utility (**http://www.wdc.com/service/ftp/drives.html#dlgtools**) can be used to perform a "pseudo" LL format on Western Digital drives. From the main menu, choose Diagnostics, select the correct drive, and choose Write Zeros. After the operation completes, run FDISK again. Your particular drive manufacturer may offer other similar utilities. If this does not resolve the problem, the drive itself may need to be replaced.

SYMPTOM 23-50 **The high-level (DOS) format process takes too long** In almost all cases, long formats are the result of older DOS versions. Check your DOS version. MS-DOS version 4.x tries to recover hard errors, which can consume quite a bit of extra time. You will probably see a number of "Attempting to recover allocation units" messages. Your best course is to upgrade the MS-DOS version to 6.22 (or MS-DOS 7.x with Windows 95/98). Later versions of DOS abandon hard error retries.

23

SYMPTOM 23-51 **You install Disk Manager to a hard drive, then install DOS, but DOS formats the drive back to 528MB** After Disk Manager is installed, you must create a "rescue disk" to use in conjunction with your DOS installation. There are two means of accomplishing this. First:

1. Create a clean DOS bootable disk.
2. Copy two files from the original Disk Manager disk to your bootable disk: XBIOS.OVL and DMDRVR.BIN.
3. Create a CONFIG.SYS file on this bootable disk with these three lines:

```
DEVICE=DMDRVR.BIN
FILES=35
BUFFERS=35
```

4. Remove the bootable disk and reboot the system.
5. When you see "Press space bar to boot from diskette," do so. The system will halt.
6. Insert the rescue disk in drive A:, and press any key to resume the boot process.
7. At the A: prompt, remove your rescue disk, insert the DOS installation disk, and type **SETUP**.

You will now install DOS files without overwriting the Disk Manager files. Or use an alternative approach:

1. Create a clean DOS bootable disk.
2. Insert the original Disk Manager disk in the A: drive and type

   ```
   DMCFIG/D=A:
   ```

   You will be prompted to insert a bootable floppy in drive A:.
3. You will need to remove and insert the bootable disk a few times as Drive Manager files are copied.
4. Remove the floppy and reboot the system.
5. When you see "Press space bar to boot from diskette," do so. The system will halt.
6. Insert the rescue disk in drive A:, and press any key to resume the boot process.
7. At the A: prompt, remove your rescue disk, insert the DOS installation disk, and type **SETUP**.

You will now install DOS files without overwriting the Disk Manager files.

SYMPTOM 23-52 ScanDisk reports some bad sectors, but cannot map them out during a surface analysis You may need a surface analysis utility for your particular drive that is provided by the drive maker. For example, Western Digital provides the WDATIDE.EXE utility for its Caviar series of drives. It will mark all "grown" defects and compensate for lost capacity by utilizing spare tracks.

> These types of surface analysis utilities are typically destructive. Make sure to have a complete backup of the drive before proceeding. Also, the utility may take a very long time to run depending on your drive's capacity.

SYMPTOM 23-53 ScanDisk reports an "Out of Memory" error after copying data from a smaller drive to a larger one The data seems to copy successfully, but when you run ScanDisk, you get an "Out of Memory" error (or you have a problem using Defrag). Chances are that you've copied data from a smaller drive to a larger drive that uses FAT32 (you're running Windows 95 OSR2 or Windows 98) using some utility that can copy the contents of one hard drive to another. The utility may have created an image of the drive that was copied to the other, or it copied data sector by sector from one drive to the other.

If you used an older utility (or version of EZ-Drive) to copy the data, the clusters were probably not correctly resized for the new FAT32 partition. When a partition becomes formatted, it is divided into clusters—or small blocks. These clusters are used to store data, and the size of a cluster is determined by the size of the partition. Older copy utilities often do not support FAT32 properly and will incorrectly size the cluster on the new FAT32 partition when they transfer data from the old drive to the new one. You can verify whether this has occurred by running CHKDSK from a DOS prompt. The correct cluster sizes for FAT32 partitions are listed here:

512MB to 8.2GB = 4KB cluster size
8.2GB to 16.4GB = 8KB cluster size
16.4GB to 32.8GB = 16KB cluster size
32.8GB and higher = 32KB cluster size

If CHKDSK reports an incorrect cluster size for your partition, you need to erase the data and copy it using an updated utility.

SYMPTOM 23-54 **You cannot get 32-bit access to work under Windows 3.1x** You are probably not using the correct hard drive driver. Check your EIDE BIOS. If your motherboard (or drive controller) BIOS supports LBA, obtaining a driver should be easy. The drive maker either provides a 32-bit driver on a disk accompanying the drive, or a driver can be downloaded from the drive maker's BBS or Internet Web site. If the motherboard (or drive controller) does not support LBA directly, you can install drive overlay software such as Ontrack's Disk Manager (7.0 or later), and run DMCFIG to install the 32-bit driver software.

SYMPTOM 23-55 **Drive diagnostics reveal a great deal of wasted space on the drive** You probably have a large drive partitioned as one or more FAT16 logical volumes. If you deal with large numbers of small files, it may be more efficient to create multiple smaller partitions utilizing smaller clusters. As an alternative, you may choose to repartition the drive using FAT32, which supports much larger partitions (while allowing for smaller clusters).

SYMPTOM 23-56 **After installing a new hard drive, Windows 98 only detects the drive if it's noted as "removable" in the Device Manager** Chances are that you missed one or two steps and neglected to partition and format the drive. All hard disk drives must be partitioned before they can be formatted, even if the drive is only going to have a single partition. Windows 98 incorrectly allows you to format an unpartitioned drive if you designate the drive as "removable." Using a drive this way will almost certainly result in data loss. The solution is to back up any data on the drive, then remove the checkmark from the "removable" box in the Windows 98 Device Manager. Next, use FDISK to create at least one primary and active partition. Reboot the system, and then format the partition(s) with FORMAT. This process will destroy any data on the drive, but should correct the recognition issue.

23

SYMPTOM 23-57 **When upgrading Windows 95 OSR2 to Windows 98, you see an "SU0013" error** When drive C: is configured as a "removable media" device and uses the FAT32 file system, you may see an error such as "SU0013—Setup cannot create files on your startup drive and cannot set up Windows 98." To circumvent this issue, you'll need to run setup from DOS:

1. Boot your computer with a Windows 98 startup disk.
2. On the Startup menu, choose Start Computer with CD-ROM Support, and then press ENTER.
3. At the A: prompt, type **<drive>:\win98\setup**, where <drive> is the drive letter assigned to your CD-ROM drive, and then press ENTER.
4. Follow the instructions shown to complete the setup process and complete the upgrade.

SYMPTOM 23-58 **You find that the System Configuration utility will not work under Windows 98** When you run the System Configuration utility, the following items may not work:

- Diagnostic Startup—Interactive Load
- Enable Startup Menu
- Disable Scandisk After bad shutdown
- Disable SCSI Double-Buffering

This problem occurs if you use any version of the DriveSpace disk compression software to compress your hard disk in place (that is, you compressed the entire hard disk). When you compress a hard disk in place, DriveSpace swaps hard disk letters after the initialization of the compressed volume file (CVF). Because the System Configuration utility is not aware of the drive letter swap, it edits the MSDOS.SYS file on the CVF instead of the MSDOS.SYS file on the host drive. This is a problem with Windows 98.

To correct this problem, edit the MSDOS.SYS file on the host drive (usually drive H:) after DriveSpace is loaded. Note that DriveSpace hides the host drive by default. To make the host drive visible, follow these steps:

1. Click Start, highlight Programs, select Accessories, select System Tools, and then click DriveSpace.
2. Click the compressed drive (where the hidden drive is a host drive), and then click Properties on the Drive menu.
3. Click the Hide Host Drive check box to clear it.
4. Click OK.

Now start a word processor such as EDIT and load the MSDOS.SYS file for the host drive. Then adjust the MSDOS.SYS file as follows. (If the appropriate line does not exist, create it in the [Options] section.)

- To enable "diagnostic startup," edit or add the line **orig_diag_BootMenu=1**. To disable the option, remove the line or change the value from 1 to 0.
- To enable the Startup menu, edit or add the line **BootMenu=1**. To disable the option, change the value from 1 to 0.
- To disable "automatic ScanDisk after an incorrect shutdown," edit or add the line **AutoScan=0**. To enable the option, change the value from 0 to 1.
- To enable "SCSI double-buffering," edit or add the line **DoubleBuffer=1**. To disable SCSI double-buffering, change the value from 1 to 0.

SYMPTOM 23-59 You encounter an "invalid command line" error when using NAI Nuts & Bolts DiskMinder This problem occurs when recovering after an improper shutdown under Windows 98. This problem occurs if you're using the NAI Nuts & Bolts DiskMinder program instead of ScanDisk as your disk repair program. NAI Nuts & Bolts DiskMinder is unable to correctly interpret the /simpleui switch used with ScanDisk in the WIN.COM file. To work around this problem, simply ignore the error message, and DiskMinder can continue normally. Check with the program maker to see if a patch or update is available.

SYMPTOM 23-60 Norton DiskDoctor refuses to run after an improper shutdown under Windows 95/98. After you upgrade Windows 95 to Windows 98 (or reinstall Windows 95/98), the Norton DiskDoctor utility (included with Symantec Norton Utilities 2.0s or 3.0x) doesn't run automatically after an improper shutdown of Windows—ScanDisk for DOS is used instead. Norton Utilities updates the WIN.COM file to run the Norton DiskDoctor utility (NDD.EXE) when Windows 95/98 is shut down incorrectly. When you upgrade Windows 95 to Windows 98 (or reinstall Windows 95/98), the WIN.COM file is replaced, and ScanDisk is then used as the default disk utility. You can correct this problem simply by reinstalling Norton Utilities. You could also create an alternative utility file for DiskDoctor. At a command prompt (within Windows 95/98), enter the following commands:

```
cd\windows\command
copy ndd.exe scandisk.alt
```

This creates a copy of the Norton DiskDoctor utility named SCANDISK.ALT. When Windows 95/98 is shut down improperly, the SCANDISK.ALT file (now the Norton DiskDoctor utility) is run automatically.

SYMPTOM 23-61 ScanDisk incorrectly reports hard drive problems under Windows 98 When you upgrade from Windows 3.x to Windows 98, setup may quit and recommend you run ScanDisk to repair your hard disk, but no errors are found after you run ScanDisk. This is a known problem with Windows 98 and occurs when your Windows 3.x-based computer is configured to use a network server for virtual memory. To work around this issue, run Windows 98 setup with the /is parameter. (Setup runs normally, but skips ScanDisk.) For example:

```
setup /is
```

SYMPTOM 23-62 When running CHKDSK.EXE from a command prompt, you receive an "F parameter not specified" error This issue may occur under Windows 95/98, and the entire error message usually appears, such as:

```
Errors found, F parameter not specified. Corrections will not be written to
disk. CHKDSK cannot check the validity of this drive because the following
path is too long:

<Path>
```

This problem typically occurs when the command line you type contains more than 67 characters. To get around this issue, use ScanDisk instead of CHKDSK to check your hard disk for errors.

SYMPTOM 23-63 While using APC PowerChute, Defrag locks up the system after selecting a disk to defragment This problem occurs when you're using APC PowerChute Plus 5.0 or 5.0.1 under Windows 98. These versions of PowerChute Plus are designed for Windows 95 only. To work around this problem, quit PowerChute Plus before using Defrag:

1. Press CTRL+ALT+DEL to open the Close Program dialog box.
2. Click PowerChute Plus, and then click End Task.
3. Do the same thing for Iconclnt.
4. Now run Defrag normally.

To restart PowerChute Plus after Defrag is completed, simply reboot the computer. For a more permanent fix to this problem, obtain updated software from APC.

SYMPTOM 23-64 Defrag causes a GPF in USER.EXE under Windows 95/98 When you try to run Defrag from System Agent or Task Scheduler, you may receive a General Protection Fault (or GPF) in USER.EXE. This may occur if the task information for Defrag has become damaged. Delete the Defrag task from System Agent or Task Scheduler, and then create a new task.

23

FAT32 Symptoms

There are a number of symptoms that are unique to FAT32. The most common of these are detailed below.

SYMPTOM 23-65 You cannot place a FAT32 partition on a drive The trick to establishing a FAT32 partition on a drive is to partition the drive correctly. Try the following steps to partition a drive:

1. In the Windows 95/98 Device Manager, select the drive, and then click on Properties.
2. Click Settings, and then click the Int13 Unit check box to select it.
3. Quit the Device Manager and restart Windows 95/98.
4. Once Windows 95/98 is restarted, open an MS-DOS session and use the FDISK command to partition the drive. (Be careful not to partition an existing drive accidentally.)
5. Restart Windows 95/98. You should be able to format the drive and use the FAT32 file system.

SYMPTOM 23-66 After moving a FAT32 SCSI hard drive from one controller to another, you cannot read or write reliably to the SCSI drive This is because SCSI drives are highly controller dependent to begin with, and you should be prepared to repartition and reformat SCSI drives *whenever* changing the SCSI host controller. This behavior is particularly evident when you partition and format a hard disk using a SCSI controller that fully supports Int 13 extensions, and you then move the hard disk to a controller that does not fully support Int 13 extensions. To move a drive using the FAT32 file system to a different controller, you must verify that both controllers fully support Int 13 extensions in the same manner. If they do not, data loss will most likely occur.

SYMPTOM 23-67 When you try to compress a drive with DriveSpace or DriveSpace 3, you receive the following error message: "Drive C cannot be compressed because it is a FAT32 drive" This is because DriveSpace was designed to work with the FAT12 and FAT16 file systems, and cannot be used on drives with the FAT32 file system. Unfortunately, there is no correction for this problem, and Microsoft is considering an update for a future release. In the meantime, your only options are to avoid using drive compression, or use a third-party drive compression tool that is FAT32 compatible. Check out the Stacker site (**www.stac.com**).

SYMPTOM 23-68 When booting from a floppy disk, you cannot access your FAT32 hard drive partition(s) The system boots fine from the hard drive. This is an issue with the boot disk. Boot disks made with older versions of DOS or Windows are not "FAT32 aware" and cannot support access to your FAT32 hard drive partition(s). For example, you cannot access your Windows 98 FAT32 drive when booting from a Windows 95a startup disk. Create a Windows 98 startup disk in order to boot your FAT32 system.

SYMPTOM 23-69 You encounter an error message such as "Setup found a compressed volume or a disk cache utility" This can occur if you try to install a retail version of Windows 95 over an OSR2 version of Windows 95. There are actually a number of problems that can crop up when installing an older version of Windows 95. The initial error usually reads

```
Setup found a compressed volume or a disk-cache utility on your computer.
Quit setup and check your compressed volume with your disk-compression
software or remove the disk-cache utility. Then run Setup again.
```

If you continue trying to install Windows 95 on a hard disk using the FAT32 file system, you may receive the following error message:

```
SU-0013
```

If you are installing the retail version of Windows 95 over OSR2 on a hard disk using the FAT16 file system, setup continues, but experiences numerous file version conflicts that generate the following message:

```
A file being copied is older than the file currently on your computer. It is
recommended that you keep your existing file.
```

If you click Yes to keep the newer files, setup finishes, but when you restart the computer you may experience any of the following symptoms:

- The computer stops responding (hangs) at the logo screen.
- You receive the error message "Fatal Exception 0D has occurred at 0117:00007E1F."

Starting Windows 95 in Safe Mode may generate the following error message:

```
Fatal Exception 0D has occurred at 0117:00007E1F
```

To verify the version you are installing, type **ver** at a command prompt. Version 4.00.950 (files dated 7-11-95) is the retail version and OEM (non-OSR2) version. Version 4.00.1111 (files dated 8-24-96) indicates the Windows 95 OEM Service Release 2 (OSR2). Do not install the retail or OEM (non-OSR2) version of Windows 95 into an existing Windows 95 OSR2 folder. If you are installing to a hard disk using the FAT16 file system, install to a *different* folder.

> Do not install the retail or OEM version of Windows 95 on a hard disk using the FAT32 file system.

You should reinstall OSR2 using the OSR2 CD provided by your OEM. If an OSR2 CD-ROM was not provided to you by your OEM, the OSR2 files may have been provided in a folder on your hard disk. To locate this folder, type the following command at a command prompt:

```
dir *.cab /s
```

To reinstall OSR2, run SETUP.EXE from the folder containing the OSR2 cabinet (.cab) files. If you cannot reinstall OSR2, contact your the company that sold the system for assistance.

SYMPTOM 23-70 **You cannot use SHARE.EXE in Windows 95** The SHARE.EXE utility is not supported in the OSR2 release of Windows 95. In order to support the FAT32 file system, SHARE.EXE support has been disabled in the real-mode MS-DOS kernel regardless of whether you have any drives using the FAT32 file system. Instead, file sharing and locking capabilities are provided by VSHARE.VXD in OSR2 and are not supported in MS-DOS mode.

> You may not be able to install or run some MS-DOS-based programs or 16-bit Windows-based programs that require SHARE.EXE.

Some programs (such as Microsoft Word version 6.0 for Windows and Quattro Pro version 6.0 for Windows) do not require SHARE.EXE to be loaded in order to start. Instead, some programs simply look for a file named SHARE.EXE in either the root folder or the DOS folder. This file can be a zero-byte file created with a text editor like EDIT or Notepad. Other programs may simply look for the string "share" in the AUTOEXEC.BAT file.

SYMPTOM 23-71 **The system may hang up when certain drive software is used under FAT32** After installing the drive software (such as PC Tools Pro 9.0), the computer will probably hang up during startup after you see the following message:

```
Analyzing drive C:
Reading system areas
```

In virtually all cases, this occurs because your drive software is not compatible with the FAT32 file system in Windows 95 OSR2 (or Windows 98). You can contact the software maker (such as Symantec for PC Tools Pro 9.0 at **www.symantec.com**) for a FAT32-aware version of the software. As a work-around, you can use a text editor (EDIT or Notepad) to edit the AUTOEXEC.BAT file and disable the command line that starts the software. For PC Tools Pro 9.0, you'd REM out its line, such as:

```
REM call pctools.bat
```

SYMPTOM 23-72 **You encounter errors using IBM antivirus utilities on a FAT32 file system** In actual practice, you'll probably encounter either of the following symptoms:

- When you are installing IBM Anti-Virus, the setup program offers to scan for viruses. If you choose to scan, you may receive an error message stating that the master boot record could not be read.
- When you are scanning for viruses on a drive using the FAT32 file system, IBM Anti-Virus may report that errors occurred while it was checking for viruses. The error log may contain the following information: "Errors during virus checking: unexpected error code 18."

Older versions of IBM Anti-Virus are not written to work with the new FAT32 file system included with OSR2 and Windows 98. There is no work-around for this, and you'll need to obtain an updated version of IBM software, or use a different antivirus tool that is FAT32 aware.

SYMPTOM 23-73 **When using Defrag on a FAT32 system, you encounter an error message such as "DEFRAG0026 Make sure disk is formatted"** You may also see an error such as:

```
Windows cannot defragment this drive. Make sure the disk is formatted and
free of errors. Then try defragmenting the drive again.
```

This error can be caused when running a version of DEFRAG.EXE that is earlier than the version included with Windows 95 OSR2 (or Windows 98). To resolve this problem, extract a new copy of the DEFRAG.EXE file from your original Windows 95 OSR2 (or Windows 98) CD:

1. Open an MS-DOS prompt in Windows 95/98.
2. Change to the Windows folder, and then type the following line:

   ```
   ren defrag.exe defrag.xxx
   ```

3 Insert the OSR2 CD, OSR2 disk 6, or Windows 98 CD in the appropriate drive. If you are using the CD-ROM, type the following line (where <x> is the CD-ROM drive letter and <z> is the drive containing the Windows folder):

```
extract <x>:\win95\win95_05.cab defrag.exe /l <z>:\windows
```

If you are using disk 6, type the following line (where <x> is the drive containing disk 6 and <z> is the drive containing the Windows folder):

```
extract <x>:\win95_06.cab defrag.exe /l <z>:\windows
```

SYMPTOM 23-74 **You see an "Invalid Media" error message when formatting a FAT32 partition** When you try to format a FAT32 file system partition larger than 8025MB (8GB) from Windows 95/98, you may receive the following error message (where <xxx.xx> is the size of the partition):

```
Verifying <xxx.xx>M
Invalid media or track 0 bad-disk unusable
Format terminated
```

This error occurs if there is a non-DOS partition preceding the extended DOS partition, and the primary DOS partition has been formatted using the real-mode FORMAT.EXE command. To correct this problem, you'll need to reformat the volume using the following steps:

1 Click the Start button, click Shut Down, click Restart The Computer In MS-DOS Mode, and then click Yes.

2 Type the following command (where <drive> is the drive letter for the partition you want to format), and then press Enter:

```
format <drive>:
```

3 When the partition is formatted, type **exit** to restart Windows 95/98.

SYMPTOM 23-75 **Opening a folder seems to take a very long time** When you open a folder in Microsoft Explorer on a drive using the FAT32 file system, one or both of the following problems may occur:

- It may seem to take an unusually long time before the window is accessible.
- The Working in Background pointer may appear for a long time.

This problem occurs because the total space used by all directory entries in the folder exceeds 32KB. To resolve this issue, move some files to a different folder.

SYMPTOM 23-76 **You find that your FAT32 system works in "Compatibility Mode" when using Ontrack Disk Manager** After you install FAT32 on a drive that uses Ontrack Disk Manager (version 6.03 or 7.04), one or both of the following problems may occur:

- All drives use MS-DOS compatibility mode.
- The computer seems to take an unusually long time to boot.

23

This happens because the Dynamic Drive Overlay (or DDO) is unable to find files in the root folder that it needs in order to start correctly.

A Dynamic Drive Overlay makes calculations for the starting root folder cluster based on FAT12 and FAT16 volumes and returns a value of zero for FAT32 volumes. (This is due to changes made in the root directory structure.) The overlay software searches all possible clusters in the root folder for its overlay files. You'll need to configure Disk Manager to avoid searching the root folder for overlay files.

> Configuring Disk Manager software to avoid searching the root folder causes Disk Manager not to hook the DOS area chain—forcing Disk Manager to load low in conventional memory.

SYMPTOM 23-77 **The OSR2 version of Windows 95 will not allow dual booting with Windows 3.1x** If you try to dual-boot Windows version 3.x on a computer running Windows 95 OSR2, you'll receive one of the following error messages:

- This version of Windows does not run on MS-DOS 6.x or earlier.
- You started your computer with a version of MS-DOS incompatible with this version of Windows. Insert a Startup diskette matching this version of Windows and then restart.
- The system has been halted. Press CTRL+ALT+DELETE to restart your computer.
- This version of Windows cannot be run on this version of DOS.

Beginning with OSR2, dual booting with Windows 3.x is not supported in Windows 95. To dual-boot between Windows 3.x and Windows 95, you'll need to install the retail version of Windows 95. If you have FAT32 drives, you need to remove the FAT32 partitions and create FAT16 partitions with the Windows 95 or MS-DOS 6.x version of FDISK.EXE.

> Neither MS-DOS 6.x or the early retail version of Windows 95 will recognize a FAT32 volume.

> Windows 3.x was designed to use the FAT12 and FAT16 file system and could potentially damage a FAT32 volume.

SYMPTOM 23-78 **After you install Windows 98 (or convert a partition to FAT32), Windows 98 reports "DOS Compatibility Mode"** This can occur when the drive controller has not been detected properly under Windows 98. Try rebooting the PC and see if Windows 98 will redetect the drive controller. (You may need to remove the drive controller entry from the Device Manager before rebooting the system.) For specific details about resolving compatibility mode problems, refer to the earlier section "Troubleshooting DOS Compatibility Mode Problems."

SYMPTOM 23-79 **After converting a drive to FAT32, you notice that tools like ScanDisk and Defrag take much longer to run** This is an undesired side effect of the FAT32 file system. It takes Defrag and ScanDisk the same amount of time to examine a single cluster, regardless of that cluster's size. Since FAT32 uses smaller clusters, there are many times more clusters, and such utilities take considerably longer than they used to. Microsoft compensates for this by including the Tune Up wizard, which allows you to schedule such tasks to take place when you're away from the computer.

SYMPTOM 23-80 The FAT32 conversion utility crashed after reporting that it found bad sectors This is a side effect of ScanDisk. If ScanDisk has marked any sectors as bad, the FAT32 converter will refuse to run, even if the sectors are fixed by third-party disk utilities (such as Data Lifeguard Tools). ScanDisk uses the FAT table to keep track of bad sectors. But even if third-party utilities remap bad sectors at the hardware level, ScanDisk is not aware of those changes. One solution is to wipe the hard drive clean and start over (in which case you'd just partition the drive using FAT32 to begin with). Here's an easier work-around when there are only a few bad sectors:

1. Before using the FAT32 conversion utility, perform a complete backup of your hard drive.
2. Run your third-party disk utility software (for example, Data Lifeguard Tools) to make sure that any bad sectors have been remapped.
3. Open a DOS window and type the following line (where <x:> is the drive letter you wish to convert):

```
cvt <x:> /cvt32
```

The converter will then run, disregarding any sectors that have previously been marked bad by ScanDisk.

SYMPTOM 23-81 The FAT32 converter under Windows 98 cannot locate the drive partition to be converted When using the Windows 98 "drive converter" tool to convert a drive from FAT16 to FAT32, you may receive an error message such as "Drive converter unable to find the drive partition." This problem can occur if you try to convert a FAT16 logical drive that begins above the 8.0GB mark. For example, if you have a 10GB hard disk with five 2.0GB FAT16 partitions, you may have trouble converting the fifth drive (drive G:) to FAT32. To work around this problem, delete all of your partitions above the 8.0GB mark, and then re-create your partitions.

> All data on the specific partition or drive will be deleted, so back up your data before you perform the following steps.

1. Click Start, select Programs, and then click MS-DOS Prompt.
2. At the command prompt, type **FDISK**, press Y when you're prompted to "enable large disk support," and then press ENTER.
3. Press 4, and then press ENTER.
4. Press Y, and then press ENTER. Observe the partition information for all of the drives listed on this screen, and then press ESC.
5. Press 3, press ENTER, press 3, and then press ENTER again.
6. Press the letter that corresponds with the last drive listed in the extended partition, and then press ENTER. For a 10.0GB drive with five 2.0GB partitions, the fifth "drive" would be G: (the only one remaining in FAT16 format).
7. Type the "volume label" displayed to the left of the drive letter exactly as it is displayed, and then press ENTER.
8. Press Y, press ENTER, press ESC, and then press ESC again.
9. Press 1, press ENTER, press 3, and then press ENTER again.
10. You're prompted to use all of the remaining available drive space—press Y, and then press ENTER.
11. Press ESC to exit FDISK, type **EXIT**, and then press ENTER.

12 Restart your computer so that your changes will take effect

13 Double-click My Computer, right-click drive G:, and then click Format.

14 Click Full, click Start, and then click OK.

UPGRADE/INSTALLATION SYMPTOMS

SYMPTOM 23-82 **The screen goes blank when the system is powered up** This is a problem frequently encountered during new drive installation. If the display does not appear immediately after power-up (you should initially see a BIOS ROM Copyright notice and the memory test), there is likely to be a hardware conflict between the drive controller board and your system. Make a quick check of the monitor to be sure its power cord or video cable has not worked loose during the hard drive installation process. Power-down the computer, remove the new controller board, and check the I/O address, DMA, and IRQ settings on the drive controller board. If you're replacing controllers on the motherboard, verify that the motherboard controller(s) are properly disabled.

However, if the controller board settings check properly, reinstall the drive and controller board, power-up the system again, and measure each output from your power supply. If one or more supply outputs becomes low or absent, the supply may be undersized, or there may be a serious short circuit somewhere in the controller or drive. Try a new or similar controller. If the problem persists, try a larger power supply, or remove other expansion boards from the system to reduce loading on the supply.

SYMPTOM 23-83 **Your drive fails to spin up properly after power is applied** This problem usually occurs when a new drive or controller board is installed or upgraded. A signal cable between the drive and controller board is probably flipped on one side. Check the signal cable alignments and ensure that both ends of the cable(s) are inserted properly. Also verify that the drive is properly identified in the CMOS setup.

SYMPTOM 23-84 **You see a "Drive not ready" error or similar message displayed on the monitor** This problem is typically encountered during installations and upgrades. The system is not recognizing your drive. Begin your inspection by checking the signal cable between the controller and drive. One end of the cable may be reversed. Inspect outputs from the power supply next. Power is typically through a 4-pin mate-n-lock connector. The middle two pins are ground. One end provides +5 Vdc, and the other end provides +12 Vdc. If one or both of the supply voltages is low or absent, the supply may be undersized for the power load demanded by the system. You could try a larger supply. If power is adequate, make sure that the drive spins up.

Inspect any jumpers or dip switches, and make sure the drive is set properly for the type of controller being used. An ESDI drive must be set to drive 0 or drive 1, an EIDE/UDMA drive must be set as either a master or slave, and a SCSI drive must have a valid, unique ID (usually ID0 or ID1). If the drive is not configured properly, your system will not recognize the drive. For ESDI or SCSI drives, you should also check for the proper positions of terminating resistors. An ESDI drive may be low-level formatted improperly. Check the low-level drive parameters used in low-level formatting. If any of the parameters are incorrect, correct the parameters and try reformatting the drive.

SYMPTOM 23-85 **You install a drive that has been formatted by a dealer, but it does not operate after installation** Start by checking the controller and cable installation. Also check the system CMOS to be sure that the proper parameters are entered for the drive being used. This is especially important when using an IDE/EIDE/Ultra-ATA drive in "translation mode." Find out if the DOS version used to partition and high-level format the drive is compatible with your current system. A hard drive with an incompatible format or partition table will not function in your system. Make sure you are using the same drive controller board used by the dealer who prepared the drive. Also check that you are using the same type of cables. It may be necessary to repartition the hard drive from scratch to ensure compatibility.

SYMPTOM 23-86 **You see a "No SCSI device found" or similar error** Check the installation of any SCSI adapter software. If you booted from a clean floppy, the SCSI drivers probably did not load, so the SCSI host adapter may not be available. If the host adapter is running properly, check that the SCSI cables are attached to each device. No cables should be pinched, scraped, or cut. Next, check the SCSI adapter to see that all jumper or DIP switch settings are configured properly—a hardware conflict can easily cause problems with the adapter. If problems persist, try a new SCSI adapter. On the other hand, if the drive shows a series of LED flashes when powered up, it may be the SCSI hard drive that is defective.

SYMPTOM 23-87 **While using FDISK, you see an error such as "Error reading fixed disk" or "No fixed disk present"** Double-check the signal cable(s) connected to the drive, and make sure the drive select jumper is set properly. Try a different signal cable. Also check the drive adapter's installation. Next, try a fresh version of FDISK—the version you are using may be old or corrupted. If you are using a dual-drive system, try swapping the drive 0/drive 1 (master/slave) relationship. If the problem persists, remove one of the two drives—they may simply be incompatible. Try a drive from another manufacturer.

SYMPTOM 23-88 **After running FDISK, you receive an error message indicating an "Invalid drive specification" or similar problem** FDISK failed to create a proper partition on your hard drive. Try running FDISK again, and be sure to save the partition configurations. Try shutting down the system before attempting a DOS format. Try a fresh version of FDISK. The version you are using may be corrupted. In a dual-drive configuration, try reversing the drive 0/drive 1 (master/slave) relationship—the drives may be incompatible. Try each drive individually. If problems continue on the offending drive when used alone, the drive's partition table may be damaged. Try a new drive.

SYMPTOM 23-89 **You see an error such as "Track 0 bad, disk unusable"** This is perhaps the most serious indication of a drive failure. With track 0 damaged, there is no partition or boot sector information available to the drive, so the system cannot use it. Check the CMOS setup to verify the drive parameters. If the drive is an ESDI type, check the DEBUG command used for low-level formatting, and try the LL format again. For IDE and SCSI drives, the drive is probably defective. If you have an LL format routing for the IDE drive, you might give that a try. Otherwise, replace the defective drive.

SYMPTOM 23-90 **You are unable to access the second physical hard drive** This is a classic sign of configuration problems. Check the drive jumper settings and see that the drive 0/drive 1 (master/slave) assignments are correct. Also check that any terminating resistors are inserted or removed as required. Try reversing the drive assignments—the drives may be incompatible. Try each drive separately. If the offending hard drive fails to work alone, it is probably defective and should be replaced. If both hard drives work individually, the drives are incompatible. Try a new drive from a different manufacturer.

Further Study

Maxtor: **http://www.maxtor.com**

MicroHouse: **http://www.microhouse.com**

PowerQuest: **http://www.powerquest.com**

Quantum: **http://www.quantum.com**

Seagate: **http://www.seagate.com**

StorageSoft, Inc.: **http://www.storagesoft.com/**

Symantec: **http://www.symantec.com**

Western Digital: **http://www.wdc.com**

Windows 95 Emergency Recover Utility: **http://www.microsoft.com/windows/download/eruzip.exe**

USENET FAQ: **http://www.cis.ohio-state.edu/hypertext/faq/bngusenet/comp/ sys/ibm/pc/ hardware/storage/top.html**

24

JOYSTICKS AND GAME PORTS

Few peripheral devices have come to represent PC entertainment like the *joystick* (Figure 24-1). Although it is one of the simplest peripherals available for a PC, the joystick allows a user to bring an element of hand-eye coordination to interactive programs (such as flight simulators and 3D "walk-through" games) that would simply be impossible with a keyboard or mouse. The joystick interfaces to the host PC through a board called the *game port adapter* (or simply the game port). This chapter discusses the joystick and game port, then covers a selection of troubleshooting issues.

Understanding the Game Port System

The typical game port uses a relatively simple interface to the PC. Only the lower 8 data bits are used (which explains why so many older game ports used the older 8-bit XT card style rather than switching to

FIGURE 24-1 A general-purpose analog joystick (Suncom Technologies)

a 16-bit AT ISA card type). Also, only the lower 10 address bits are needed. Since the game port is an I/O device, the card uses I/OR and I/OW control signals. On virtually all PCs, port 201h is reserved for the game port. Figure 24-2 illustrates a typical game port system.

INSIDE THE JOYSTICK

Each analog joystick is assembled with two separate potentiometers. These are "adjustable resistors," which are typically 100 kOhms arranged perpendicularly to one another. One potentiometer represents the X axis, and the other potentiometer represents the Y axis. Both potentiometers are linked together mechanically and attached to a movable stick. As the stick is moved left or right, one potentiometer is moved. As the stick moves up or down, the other potentiometer is moved. Of course, the stick can be moved in both the X and Y axis simultaneously, with the proportions of resistance reflecting the stick's

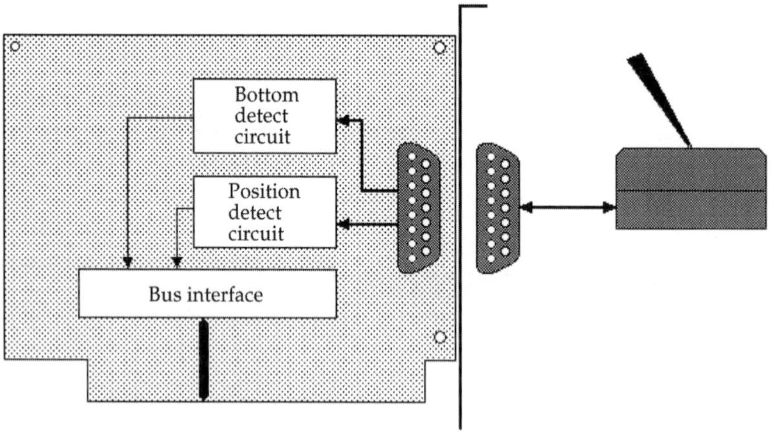

FIGURE 24-2 Simplified diagram of a game port system

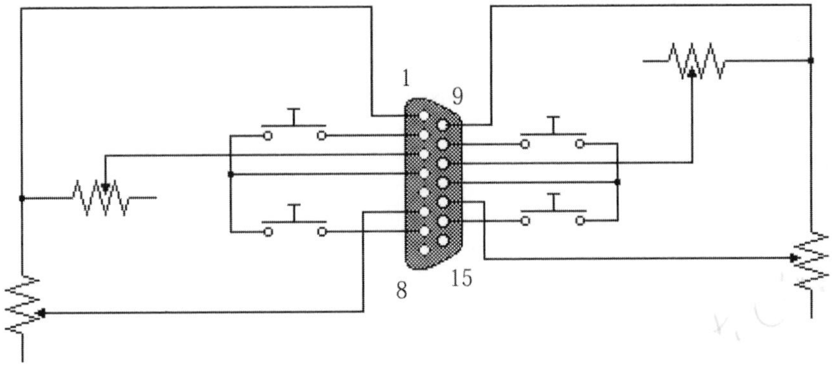

FIGURE 24-3 Wiring diagram for a dual joystick port

position. You can see the wiring scheme for a standard 15-pin dual joystick port in Figure 24-3. The pinout for a standard joystick port is listed in Table 24-1.

Detecting the stick's X and Y position is not an intuitively obvious process. Ultimately, the analog value of each potentiometer must be converted to a digital value that is read by the application software. This is an important wrinkle—since the game port does not generate an interrupt, it is up to the particular *application* to interrogate the joystick port regularly. You might imagine that such a conversion would use an analog-to-digital converter (ADC). However, an ADC provides much greater resolution than is needed, and its conversions require a relatively long time. Current game port conversion circuits use a "multivibrator" element.

TABLE 24-1 PINOUT FOR A STANDARD JOYSTICK PORT

PIN	JOYSTICK
1	XY1 (Joystick 1 +5V supply)
2	Switch 1
3	Potentiometer X1 signal
4	Ground (for switch 1 & 2)
5	Ground (for switch 2)
6	Potentiometer Y1 signal
7	Switch 2
8	N.C. (or +5V)
9	XY2 (Joystick 2 +5V supply)
10	Switch 3
11	Potentiometer X2 signal
12	Ground (for switch 3 & 4)
13	Potentiometer Y2 signal
14	Switch 4
15	N.C. (or +5V)

*The standard game port uses a DB-15 female connector.

Ultimately, the resistance of each potentiometer is determined indirectly by measuring the amount of time required for a charged capacitor to discharge through the particular potentiometer. If a certain axis is at 0 ohms, the multivibrator's internal capacitor will discharge in about 24.2µS, while at 100 kOhms, the multivibrator's capacitor will discharge in about 1124µS. Since this is a relatively linear relationship, the discharge time can easily be equated to potentiometer position. (An actual routine to accomplish this requires only about 16 lines of assembler code.) The multivibrator technique also simplifies the circuitry needed on the game port adapter—it is really the *application* that is doing the work.

A joystick also has one or two buttons. As you see from Figure 24-3, the buttons are typically open, and their closed state can be detected by reading the byte at 201h. Since the game port is capable of supporting two joysticks simultaneously (each with two buttons), the upper 4 bits of 201h indicate the on/off status of all four buttons.

> Windows 95/98 supports a joystick as a game controller through an icon in the Control Panel. You can access, add, delete, and modify your joysticks through that properties dialog (Figure 24-4). Unlike DOS applications, Windows 95/98 provides joystick support to all applications, so you need only identify and calibrate the joystick once.

ADAPTING A SECOND JOYSTICK

Although the typical game port is capable of supporting two joysticks, most joystick products only connect a single joystick. This means only "half" the game port is being utilized. You can purchase a joystick Y-adapter from any computer store, or construct a Y-adapter using the pinout in Table 24-2. You'll need a DB-15 male connector to attach to the game port and two DB-15 female connectors to attach to each of the two joysticks.

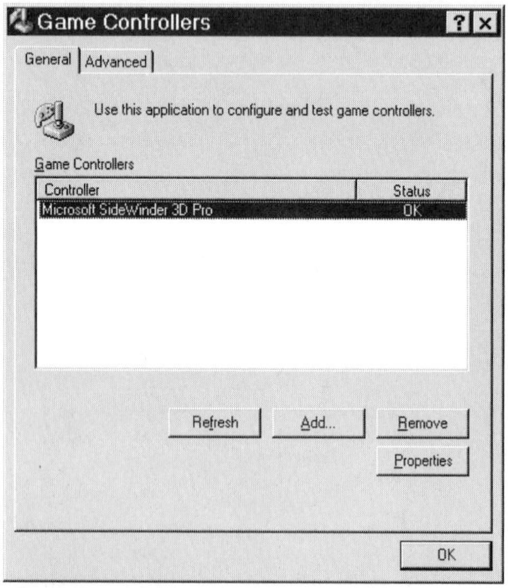

FIGURE 24-4 The Game Controllers properties dialog

TABLE 24-2 PINOUT FOR A JOYSTICK Y-ADAPTER

GAME PORT DB-15 MALE		JOYSTICK 1 DB-15 FEMALE	JOYSTICK 2 DB-15 FEMALE
1	XY1 (Joystick 1 +5V supply)	1	
2	Switch 1	2	
3	Potentiometer X1 signal	3	
4	Ground (for switch 1 & 2)	4	
5	Ground (for switch 2)	5	
6	Potentiometer Y1 signal	6	
7	Switch 2	7	
8	N.C. (or +5V)	8	
9	XY2 (Joystick 2 +5V supply)		1
10	Switch 3		2
11	Potentiometer X2 signal		3
12	Ground (for switch 3 & 4)		4 and 5
13	Potentiometer Y2 signal		6
14	Switch 4		7
15	N.C. (or +5V)		8

Some types of game port boards provide a separate 15-pin connector for each joystick. Some cut-price game port boards only provide one connector and the circuitry for one joystick. Verify the capabilities of your game port before using or replacing a joystick Y-adapter.

DIGITAL JOYSTICKS (GAME PADS)

Where an analog joystick uses two potentiometers to provide linear information about the joystick's relative position, a digital joystick (also called a *game pad*) simply uses an array of switches to indicate abso-

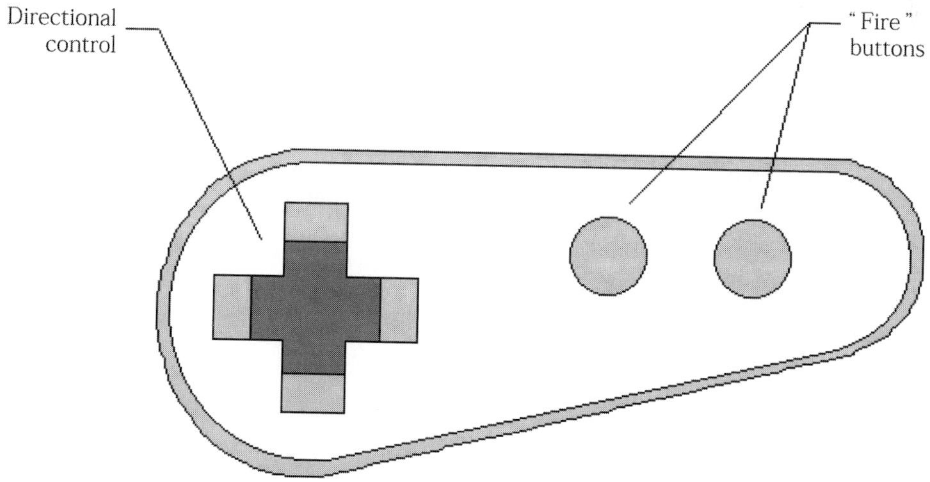

FIGURE 24-5 Typical Nintendo-style digital joystick

TABLE 24-3 PINOUT FOR AN AMIGA-TYPE GAME PAD

PIN	GAME PAD
1	Forward
2	Back
3	Left
4	Right
5	n/c
6	Button (fire) 1
7	+5V
8	Gnd
9	Button (fire) 2

*Game pads often use a DB-9 female connector.

lute direction—usually up, down, left, right, and fire (Figure 24-5). The game pad actually predates the analog joystick a bit, and uses a 9-pin TTL interface, as in the Amiga-style game pad shown in Table 24-3. Current versions of the digital joystick (such as the Gravis GamePad Pro) use a 15-pin PC game port interface. This book will not go further with game pad control devices, but you should at least understand how they compare to analog joysticks.

Nine-pin "game pad" joysticks are not directly compatible with the PC analog game port, and you should not attempt to adapt a 9-pin game pad to a 15-pin PC game port without some appropriate interface circuitry. Game pads specifically marked as PC joystick compatible (using 15-pin connectors) can usually be attached to ordinary game ports without problems.

JOYSTICK CALIBRATION

Unfortunately, the values of time versus resistance that you saw above are not the same for every system. Variations in joystick potentiometers, game port adapter circuits, and computer speed will all affect the relationship of time versus resistance value. Even variations in component temperature as the PC warms up can cause changes in resistance interpretation. This is why each application program that uses a joystick comes with a calibration routine. *Calibration* allows the given application to measure values for center and corner positions. With this data as a base, the application can extrapolate all other joystick positions.

Take it slow when calibrating. This is most important when you're setting up the controller in a game. The game will ask you to supply it with specific information about your controller. If you do not provide the correct information, or do not follow the calibration process, it cannot correctly interpret the controller signals during game play. There are several types of calibration that you should be familiar with: corner-to-corner calibration, low and high axis value calibration, full circle calibration, and invisible calibration.

Corner-to-Corner Calibration

Some games ask you to move your controller like this:

- Move the controller to the upper-left corner and press a button.
- Move the controller to the lower-right corner and press a button.
- Center the controller and press a button.

This type of software calibration teaches the software what values your controller uses for these three requested locations. The software can then make calculations based on these positions to determine where the joystick is located at any time. The main difficulty with this type of calibration is that many joysticks don't have "corners" that a game player can feel. (Many joysticks use circular openings rather than square ones.) To position the joystick in a corner, you'd need to know where the electrical corners are located, or make your best guess.

> Make sure you hold the joystick handle in position until after you have pressed the button. If you release the handle *before* you press the button, it will self-center and the game will read the wrong values.

Low and High Axis Value Calibration

Other games ask you to perform controller movements like these:

- Move the controller to the left and press a button.
- Move the controller to the right and press a button.
- Move the controller forward and press a button.
- Move the controller back and press a button.
- Center the controller and press a button.

This type of software calibration teaches the software the extreme positions of each axis for your joystick. The software can then make calculations based on these positions to determine where the joystick is located at any time. This is often a more comprehensive and reliable means of calibration.

Full-Circle Calibration

Other calibration programs ask you to move the controller around in a full circle. After you have completed the requested movements, a button press or keystroke allows the software to determine the minimum and maximum values for the horizontal and vertical axes of the controller. Software calibration programs like this sometimes display a graph of the controller axes. This is a particularly useful approach when you're using a joystick with a circular housing opening.

Invisible Calibration

There could be several reasons why you may not notice any kind of calibration program when you begin some games. Some games "remember" the calibration from a previous session, so if you're having problems controlling a craft or character, look at the manual (or the game's online help) for a keystroke that will allow you to recalibrate the joystick. Some games "assume" that the readings from a controller at game startup represent the joystick's *center* position. If your controller was not centered at game startup, you may experience problems. Once again, it may be necessary to recalibrate the joystick manually.

Another reason you may not see any prompt to calibrate a joystick at the beginning of a game is because the game is defaulting to the mouse or keyboard. You will need to locate an option in the game that lets you select the correct input device. Look for a "configure" menu, or an installation or setup program. Choosing "joystick or game pad" as an input device should activate the calibration program.

JOYSTICK DRIFT

The term *drift* (or rolling) is used to indicate a loss of control by the joystick. There are several possible reasons for this. As a technician, you should understand the reasons why drift occurs, and how to correct such problems. First, drift may be the result of a system conflict. Since the game port does not generate an interrupt, conflicts rarely result in system crashes or lockups, but another device feeding data to port 201h can easily upset joystick operation. If you have sound boards or multiport I/O boards in your system that are equipped with game ports, be sure to disable any unused ports. (Check with the user instructions for individual boards to disable extra game ports.)

Another possible cause of drift is heat. Once PCs are started, it is natural for the power used by most components to be dissipated as heat. Unfortunately, heating tends to change the value of components. For logic circuits, this is typically not a problem, but for analog circuits, the consequences can be much more pronounced. As heat changes the values of a multivibrator circuit, timing (and thus positional values) will shift. As the circuit warms up, an error creeps into the joystick. Well-designed game port adapters will use high-quality, low-drift components that minimize the effects of heat-related drift. It is interesting to note that the joystick itself is rarely the cause of drift. If you can't compensate for drift by periodically recalibrating the joystick, try a better-quality game port adapter board.

Finally, the quality of calibration is only as good as the calibration routine itself. A poor or inaccurate routine will tend to calibrate the joystick incorrectly. Try another application. If another application can calibrate and use the joystick properly, you should suspect a bug in the particular application. Try contacting the application manufacturer to find out if there is a patch or fix available.

Cleaning Joysticks

Ordinarily, the typical joystick should not require routine cleaning or maintenance. Most joysticks use reasonably reliable potentiometers that should last for the life of the joystick. The two major enemies of a joystick are wear and dust. Wear occurs during normal use as potentiometer sliders move across the resistive surface—it can't be avoided. Over time, wear will affect the contact resistance values of both potentiometers. Uneven wear will result in uneven performance. When this becomes noticeable, it is time to buy a new joystick. The violent movements also endured by joysticks during game play can shorten their working life.

Dust presents another problem. The open aperture at the top of a joystick is an invitation for dust and other debris. Since dust is conductive, it can adversely affect potentiometer values and interfere with slider contacts. If the joystick seems to produce a jumpy or nonlinear response to the application, it might be worth trying to clean the joystick rather than scrapping it. Turn off the computer and disconnect the joystick. Open the joystick, which is usually held together by two screws in the bottom housing. Remove the bottom housing and locate the two potentiometers. Most potentiometers have small openings somewhere around their circumference. Dust out the joystick area with compressed air, and spray a small quantity of good-quality electrical contact cleaner into each potentiometer. Move the potentiometer through its complete range of motion a few times, and allow several minutes for the cleaner to dry. Reassemble the housing and try the joystick again. If problems persist, replace the joystick.

Joysticks and Windows 95/98

Games have traditionally been a domain of DOS, so there has been little support for joysticks under older Windows versions. However, now that games are routinely using Windows 95/98 (taking advantage of features like DirectX and Direct3D), you can install and calibrate a variety of joysticks under Windows 95/98. Open your Control Panel and look for the joystick icon labeled Game Controllers. If a joystick icon appears in your Control Panel, joystick support is already installed, and you can skip to the Game Controller setup. If you have not yet added your PC game port as "New Hardware" in the Windows 95/98 Control Panel, you should do this first:

1 Click the Start button.
2 Select Settings, then Control Panel.
3 In the Control Panel, look for a Joystick icon. If it's there, skip to the Game Controller setup. If not, double-click the Add New Hardware icon to start the Add New Hardware wizard.
4 When prompted to have Windows search for new hardware, select No. Click Next to continue.
5 Select Sound, Video and Game Controllers, and then click Next.
6 Select the manufacturer and game port joystick (or other appropriate model). This will add the game port as a device. Click Next.
7 If resource settings are given as 0201-0201, click Next. Windows will look for the required files. If it can't find these files, it will ask you to insert your Windows 95/98 CD.
8 When the files have been installed, click Finished.
9 Shut down your computer and restart Windows 95/98 to enable your game port support.

Once your game port driver has been added, a joystick icon appears in your Control Panel. Use this to set up and calibrate your joystick:

1 Double-click the Game Controllers icon in the Control Panel.
2 In the Game Controllers section, choose the appropriate joystick type from the list, and then click Properties.
3 The Game Controller Properties dialog will appear (Figure 24-6). Test the joystick's range of motion and buttons, and then save your calibration.

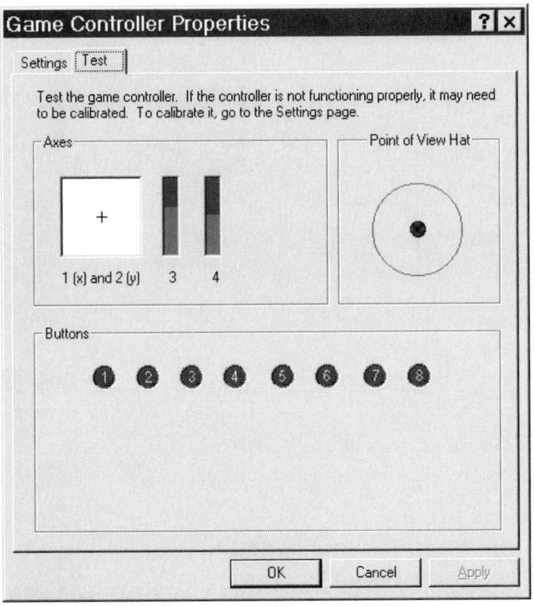

FIGURE 24-6 Calibrating the game controller device

4 You should now be able to use the joystick under any Windows 95/98 game or other joystick-aware application.

Troubleshooting Joysticks and Game Ports

The unique advantage to troubleshooting this area of a PC is that there is surprisingly little to actually go *wrong*. In virtually all cases, problems reside in either the joystick, the game port adapter, or the application software. This part of the chapter provides you with some handy troubleshooting issues and examines a suite of perplexing joystick problems.

JOYSTICK ELIMINATOR PLUG

From time to time, you may find yourself testing a game port, but have no joystick handy (or it might be too much of a hassle to "borrow" a joystick already connected to a working PC). You can construct a very simple circuit with two resistors (Figure 24-7) that can "fool" the game port into thinking that a real joystick is attached. This "joystick eliminator" plug simply places the cursor in a far corner of the display.

ADAPTING "HEADER" CONNECTIONS

Some multi-I/O boards implement the game port as a 16-pin "header" (ribbon cable) connector—assuming that you'll use a DB-15 connector "plate" in another open card slot and simply connect the DB-15 plate to the multi-I/O card using a 16-pin ribbon cable. The pin assignments are all identical (pin 16 of the IDC connector is unused), but remember that the pin *order* is different between "header" and DB-style connectors. For example, the top row of a DB-15 connector runs pins 9 through 15, but the top row of a ribbon cable uses pins 2, 4, 5, 6, 10, 12, 14, and 16.

SOUND CARDS AND Y-ADAPTER PROBLEMS

You will probably encounter difficulties when connecting commercial joystick Y-adapters to the game port on a sound board. This is because many sound card manufacturers (such as Creative Labs) have replaced pin 12 (ground for joystick 2 switches 3 and 4) and pin 15 (N.C. or +5V) with specialized MIDI interface pins. The problem doesn't surface using a single joystick because pins 12 and 15 are normally unused. But when a second joystick is added through a Y-adapter, the second joystick will probably fail to function. Table 24-4 illustrates a simple correction to enable a commercial Y-adapter. Essentially, you

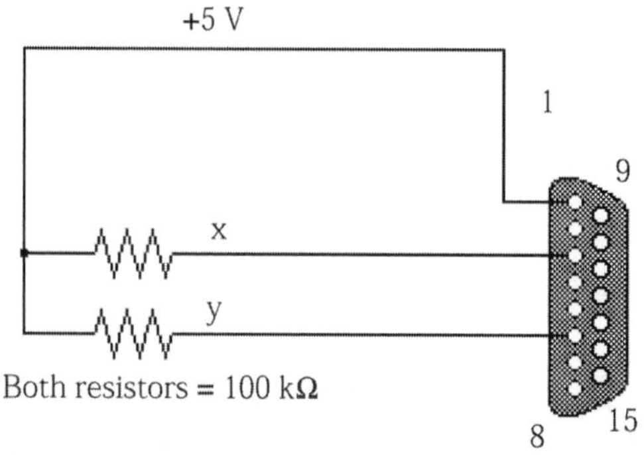

FIGURE 24-7 A simple "joystick eliminator" plug for game port testing

TABLE 24-4 PINOUT FOR A SOUND BOARD JOYSTICK CABLE ADAPTER

DB-15 MALE (TO GAME PORT)	DB-15 FEMALE (TO JOYSTICK Y-ADAPTER)
Wire pin…	To pin(s)…
1	1
2	2
3	3
4	4
5	5 and 12
6	6
7	7
8	8
9	9 and 15
10	10
11	11
12 unused	To pin 5
13	13
14	14
15 unused	To pin 9

TABLE 24-5 PINOUT FOR A SOUND BOARD–COMPATIBLE JOYSTICK Y-ADAPTER

GAME PORT DB-15 MALE		JOYSTICK 1 DB-15 FEMALE	JOYSTICK 2 DB-15 FEMALE
Wire pin…		To pin…	And to pin…
1	XY1 (Joystick 1 +5V supply)	1	1
2	Switch 1	2	
3	Potentiometer X1 signal	3	
4	Ground (for switch 1 & 2)	4	4
5	Ground (for switch 2)	5	5
6	Potentiometer Y1 signal	6	
7	Switch 2	7	
8	N.C. (or +5V)	8	
9	XY2 (Joystick 2 +5V supply)		8
10	Switch 3		2
11	Potentiometer X2 signal		3
12	MIDI		Unused
13	Potentiometer Y2 signal		6
14	Switch 4		7
15	MIDI		Unused

must disconnect pins 12 and 15 at the game port (sound board) end, then cross-wire pin 12 to pin 5 (ground), and cross-wire pin 15 to pin 9 (+5V). If you want to make your own sound board–compatible Y-adapter, follow the pinout in Table 24-5.

> Do not attempt to connect a MIDI device to the sound card while this modified Y-adapter is in place. Doing so can easily damage the MIDI device or the sound card's MIDI/game port.

BASIC JOYSTICK/CONTROLLER TROUBLESHOOTING GUIDELINES

There may be instances when your new game port or joystick is not detected or fails to respond. When this happens, you should try the guidelines below before attempting to research specific symptoms. The guidelines below can help you isolate problems with analog, USB, and serial device detection.

It is important to discern whether the issue is a *detection* issue or a *game setup* issue. Click Start, highlight Settings, click Control Panel, and then click the Game Controllers icon. If the manufacturer's gaming device is listed under Game Controllers, and its status is listed as OK, you'll know that the hardware is being detected properly by the system, and the device *should* work in the Control Panel if you try to calibrate it. (Go ahead and test this.) If it *does* work properly, the issue lies within the setup of the game, and not in your hardware. However, if the gaming device is not listed under Game Controllers (or shows that the status is "Not Connected"), you should follow the troubleshooting steps below.

Troubleshooting an Analog Device

If you're using an analog device, follow the guidelines given here.

Check Hardware Connections Visually examine the connectors on both the joystick cable and ports on the computer, and look for bent pins or other damage. Insure that the connector on the joystick's cable is completely seated in the game port on the computer. If the device is attached through a switch box or Y-adapter, try connecting *directly* to the computer.

> Also verify that you've connected the 15-pin connector to a game port rather than a MIDI port. If your 15-pin port can serve as either a game port or MIDI port, see that the port is configured as a game port.

Check Game Port Verify that the game port is enabled and that it is the only game port enabled on the system—two active ports can cause an address conflict. In some cases, a game port is integrated into the motherboard of the computer, and when a game card is installed in the system, it conflicts with the pre-existing port. Disable or remove any conflicting game port hardware.

Check Joystick Properties Make sure the proper device has been activated in the Windows 95/98 Joystick Properties tab—it should be set as Joystick 1. This will also reinitialize the device driver:

1. Click Start, highlight Settings, and then click Control Panel.
2. Double-click the Game Controllers icon.
3. For the Joystick Configuration entry, select None and click Apply.
4. Now reselect your particular gaming device and click Apply.

Change Game Port Address Verify that the game port is using the correct resources and that they do not conflict with other devices in the system:

1. Click Start, highlight Settings, and then click Control Panel.
2. Double-click the System icon, and then click the Device Manager tab.
3. Click the plus (+) next to "Sound, video and game controllers."
4. Double-click on the game port entry to bring up its Properties dialog.
5. Click the Resources tab and uncheck the Use Automatic Settings box.
6. Select Input/Output Range under Resource Type, click on Change Setting (if the game port allows you to), and select either 0200-0207 or 0201-0201.
7. Click OK until the system asks to restart the computer, and answer Yes or OK.

> If the problem persists, skip down to the "Check for Software Problems" section below.

Troubleshooting a Digital (USB) Device

If you're using a digital (USB) device, follow the guidelines given here.

Check Hardware Connections Connect the gaming device directly to the computer's USB port. If a USB port hub is being used, try connecting the device directly to the USB port on the computer. If the device works correctly when *directly* connected to the computer, please contact the manufacturer of the USB hub for assistance. For some advanced joysticks (such as the Logitech WingMan Force or the WingMan Formula Force), make sure the power adapter is plugged in and connected to the gaming device. Many early USB systems (with motherboards using the PIX 3 chip) shipped with the USB ports disabled. These systems must have their USB ports enabled through the CMOS setup before a USB device will be detected and function properly.

> Do not connect a gaming device to the serial and USB ports at the same time. Connecting a gaming device to both ports simultaneously can cause detection problems or erratic joystick behavior.

Check USB Port Configuration Use the Device Manager to verify that the USB port is correctly configured:

1. Click Start, highlight Settings, and then click Control Panel.
2. Double-click the System icon, and then click the Device Manager tab.
3. Verify that you have an entry called "Universal serial bus controller." If this entry does not exist, you'll need to contact your USB hardware vendor to correctly configure the USB controller.
4. Open the "Universal serial bus controller" entry by clicking on its plus (+) sign. Verify that there is a "USB Root Hub" entry and an entry for the "USB Port." If either of these icons is missing (or has an exclamation point or red *X* on it), contact your USB hardware vendor to correctly configure the USB controller.

Check Game Port Driver Most USB gaming devices will function on computers without game ports or sound cards. However, DirectX requires a game port entry in the "Sound, video and game controllers" section of the Device Manager in order for gaming devices to be added in the Control Panel. Check for the presence of a game port driver:

1. Click Start, highlight Settings, and then click Control Panel.
2. Double-click the System icon, and then click the Device Manager tab.

3. Click the plus (+) sign next to "Sound, video and game controllers" and verify there is a listing for "Game port joystick." If there is no listing, you'll need to add a game port driver.

If the problem persists, skip down to the "Check for Software Problems" section below.

Troubleshooting a Serial Device

If you're using a serial device, follow the guidelines given here.

Check Hardware Connections Visually examine the connectors on both the joystick cable and serial ports on the computer, and look for bent pins or other damage. Ensure that the connector on the joystick is completely seated in the serial port on the computer. If the gaming device came with a power supply (such as a Logitech WingMan Force), see that the AC adapter is connected to the gaming device. If the device is attached to the serial port through a switch box or Y-adapter, try connecting it *directly* to the computer.

Check Game Port Driver Most serial gaming devices will function on computers without game ports or sound cards. However, DirectX requires a game port entry in the "Sound, video and game controllers" section of the Device Manager in order for gaming devices to be added in the Control Panel. Check for the presence of a game port driver:

1. Click Start, highlight Settings, and then click Control Panel.
2. Double-click the System icon, and then click the Device Manager tab.
3. Click the plus (+) sign next to "Sound, video and game controllers" and verify there is a listing for "Game port joystick." If there is no listing, you'll need to add a game port driver.

Check Serial Port Configuration Ensure that the serial port is correctly configured. Most serial gaming devices do not have a preset address or IRQ. They will assume the settings of the port they are connected to, such as:

- COM1: IRQ4 Address 03F8h
- COM2: IRQ3 Address 02F8h
- COM3: IRQ4 Address 03E8h
- COM4: IRQ3 Address 02E8h

For example, if you attach the joystick to COM 3 and another device in the system is using COM 1, then an IRQ conflict will arise between these two devices. To correct this, connect the joystick to another serial port (if available). Also, verify that Windows 95/98 has the correct settings for the serial ports:

1. Click Start, highlight Settings, and then click Control Panel.
2. Double-click the System icon, and then click the Device Manager tab.
3. Double-click on the Ports, COM and LPT entry.
4. Select the COM port where the gaming device is attached, and then click the Properties button.
5. Click on the Resources tab and verify the "I/O Address" and "IRQ" entries are set to the proper settings.
6. Disable Use Automatic Settings.

7 Check the conflicting device list for possible conflicts if everything appears to be OK.

> If the serial ports appear to be configured correctly, it's possible that a modem or other internal card in the system is interfering with the serial port that the joystick is attached to. Try removing these cards to see if the conflict is eliminated.

Check for Software Problems

Software conflicts can interfere with the communications between the computer and the gaming device. If the hardware seems to be working properly, try eliminating any programs running in the background temporarily and retest the gaming device.

Clear the Startup Folder Programs in the Startup folder load and stay in memory, and may interfere with the detection of the gaming device. To determine whether there is a conflicting application in the Startup group, remove the icons from the Startup folder and restart Windows. To do this, click on Start, Settings, then Taskbar. Click on the Start Menu Programs button, and then click on Advanced. Click the plus (+) sign next to Programs, and then click on the Startup folder. Drag all the program icons onto the desktop area. This will prevent them from loading automatically when the computer boots. Restart the system and see if the issue has been resolved. If so, drag the program icons back into the Startup group, one by one, and see where the problem returns.

Clear the Registry Run Folder The Run folder of your registry is another place where programs are automatically executed when the system is started. Programs starting from this area may also interfere with the detection of your gaming device. Launch the Registry Editor by clicking Start, and then select Run. In the Open line, type **C:\WINDOWS\REGEDIT.EXE** and click the OK button. The Run folder is located in the following key:


```
HKEY_LOCAL_MACHINE\Software\Microsoft\Windows\CurrentVersion\Run
```

Once Run is highlighted, click on Registry and choose Export. Give the file a name and save it to the desktop. This procedure makes a backup of the Run folder, which can be restored by double-clicking on the REG file you saved to the desktop. When Run is highlighted, the contents of the Run folder will be displayed. Check this folder to see what else may be launched during the boot process—only Explorer and Systray are necessary to the system. Start removing other programs, one by one, rebooting between each removal. If the problem goes away, the last program removed from the Run folder may be the conflicting software.

> Editing the registry incorrectly may stop Windows from booting. Be sure to make complete backups of the registry to your startup disk before proceeding.

Clear the WIN.INI File Software programs may also be loaded from the "Load=" and "Run=" lines of your WIN.INI file, and may also interfere with the detection of your gaming device. To check for these programs, click Start and select Run. In the Open line, type **WIN.INI**, and then click the OK button. The WIN.INI file should be opened in Notepad. Place a semicolon (;) in front the following two lines (if present) as shown below:

```
[Windows]
;Load=
;Run=
```

Putting a semicolon at the beginning of these lines will prevent any programs listed in these lines from being loaded. Save the changes and restart Windows. If this resolves the conflict, remove the semicolons, one by one, from the "Run=" and "Load=" lines, and restart Windows each time to see if the symptom is corrected.

Reinstall/Update DirectX Most Windows 95/98 software today requires the latest version of DirectX in order to operate pointing and gaming devices properly. If an earlier version of DirectX is installed (or if the installed version is damaged), the gaming device properties will show the device as "Not Connected" under the Game Controllers icon in your Control Panel. Try reinstalling DirectX, or download and install the latest version from Microsoft at **http://www.microsoft.com/directx**.

Install a New Game Controller Driver In some cases, installing an HID-compliant game controller driver will resolve some detection issues:

1. Click Start, highlight Settings, and click Control Panel.
2. Double-click the Game Controllers icon.
3. Click Add, and then click Add Other.
4. On the left side of the window, select "standard game device."
5. On the right side of the window, select "HID-compliant game controller."
6. Click Next, and then click Finish.
7. Close the Game Controllers properties and restart the system.

"FORCE FEEDBACK" TROUBLESHOOTING GUIDELINES

The idea of "force feedback" adds yet another level of realism to computer gaming. Imagine feeling the rat-tat-tat of a submachine gun, or the tremor when your fighter takes a direct hit. Computer games written to take advantage of the force feedback protocols in DirectX will be able to transfer such real-world signals to your force feedback–compliant joystick, such as Microsoft's SideWinder Force Feedback Pro. This type of joystick uses MIDI signals to transmit force feedback effects. If the MIDI features of your sound card are not functioning properly, the force feedback effects will not be felt. If your game supports force feedback, but you do not feel those effects through the joystick, you can use this guide to help you isolate the problem.

Testing the Force Feedback System

The Windows Control Panel allows you to check the force feedback operation of your joystick and determine whether it and the MIDI port on your sound card are operating correctly:

1. Click Start, highlight Settings, and then click Control Panel.
2. Double-click the Game Controllers icon.
3. In the list of game devices, select your joystick (for example, SideWinder Force Feedback Pro), and click Properties.
4. If your joystick is not listed in the Controller column, click Add, select the joystick, and then click OK.
5. Click the Test Forces tab.
6. Grasp the joystick handle and press several buttons on the joystick that correspond to the types of forces you want to feel.

If the forces work correctly in this test mode, chances are that it's the game configuration that's not set properly, so see the "Checking the Game Configuration" section below. If the test mode does not work, see the "Checking the Force Feedback LED" section.

Checking the Game Configuration

If force feedback effects are working in test mode, the joystick and MIDI/game port are working. Since your joystick and software are working correctly, the lack of force feedback effects in your game is most likely caused by one (or more) of the following:

- Your game is not force feedback enabled.
- An incorrect setting or option was chosen in your force feedback game (forces were disabled).

To resolve these problems, review the manual that came with your game and take note of any special instructions that refer to enabling force feedback. Also, you may need to reinstall your game (paying particular attention to any selections that have to do with the type of sound card in your computer).

Checking the Force Feedback LED

The LED on the front of the joystick must remain lit. If it's blinking, it indicates that the joystick is not properly connected to its AC adapter (there's no power for forces), and no force feedback effects will be felt. Connect the AC adapter. The LED should be lit and not blinking. Also make sure that the joystick is connected *directly* to the game port on the computer (rather than a Y-adapter or switch box) before you continue.

If the LED is now on continuously, test the forces again. If the LED was on, and it's still not responding to force signals, you should remove the device from your Device Manager, download the latest version of the joystick's force feedback drivers from the manufacturer, and then reinstall the joystick drivers from scratch.

Checking the MIDI Port

Make sure the MIDI port is enabled on the sound card, and verify that it's using a valid MIDI address. The MIDI port supplied on your sound card must be enabled in order for force feedback to work with your joystick.

1. Click Start, highlight Settings, and then click Control Panel.
2. Double-click the Multimedia icon, and then click the Advanced tab.
3. In the Multimedia Devices area, double-click MIDI Devices and Instruments to display the list of MIDI ports installed on your computer.
4. Click the entry in the list that identifies your MIDI port (such as MIDI for External MIDI Port, MIDI for MPU-401, MIDI for SoundBlaster, or MPU-401 Compatible).
5. Click Properties and click the General tab. Make sure that Use MIDI Features On This Device is selected.

If the forces on your joystick still seem sluggish or intermittent, try selecting the MIDI for FM Synthesis option. If you have two external MIDI ports listed (you have both MIDI for External MIDI Port and MIDI for MPU-401), your computer has two external MIDI ports. If you enable one of the external MIDI ports and your joystick doesn't provide force feedback, enable the other external MIDI port and try the joystick again.

When There's No MIDI Port If there is no MIDI port listed, your MIDI port is not enabled. There are two possible reasons for this:

- Your sound card driver is installed, but the MIDI port is not configured properly. (Use the Windows Device Manager to check the configuration of your external MIDI port.)
- The incorrect driver is installed (or not set up properly) for your external MIDI port. (Install the correct driver for your sound card, and then test the forces again.)

You can usually install the correct driver either by reinstalling the sound card software from your original CD or disks, or by downloading the latest driver from your sound card manufacturer's Web site. After reinstalling the sound card software (or installing new sound card drivers), check the sound card manual (or any instructions that accompanied the new drivers) to learn how to enable the external MIDI/game port.

Configure the MIDI Port You'll need to configure your computer's external MIDI port:

1. Click Start, highlight Settings, and then click Control Panel.
2. Double-click the System icon, and then click the Device Manager tab.
3. Make sure the View Devices By Type option is selected.
4. Scroll down the list and double-click "Sound, video and game controllers."
5. Click the MIDI entry in the list that corresponds to your exact sound card.
6. Click Properties, and then click the Resources tab.
7. Scroll down the Resource Settings list until you see a listing for Input/Output Range. There may be more than one entry. In order for the external MIDI port to operate, there must be one Resource Type entry in the list with one of the following Setting values:

    0300-0301
    0310-0311
    0320-0321
    0330-0331

Enable Your MIDI Port Find a configuration from the listing above that enables the MIDI port. If the Use Automatic Settings box is not checked, select it, and then click OK. Windows will attempt to configure your sound card for all available resources. It may be necessary to restart Windows in order to complete the process. Check new configuration settings as shown in the previous section.

Try a "Basic Configuration" If you still have trouble getting the MIDI port to respond, try a new "basic configuration" for the sound card:

1. Clear the Use Automatic Settings check box.
2. Select Basic Configuration 0000 from the Setting Based On list box.
3. Check the Resource Settings list again to see if the necessary Resource Type and Setting are listed. Look for one of the following four values:

    0300-0301
    0310-0311
    0320-0321
    0330-0331

4 If none of the values match, select the next configuration setting in the Setting Based On list (such as Basic Configuration 1, Basic Configuration 2, etc.). Repeat this process until you find a Resource Type and Setting that contains one of the four required values.

5 If you find the proper Resource Type and Setting, but a device conflict message appears in the Conflicting Device list, resolve the problem with the Windows Hardware Conflict Troubleshooter.

If none of the basic configurations have the necessary Resource Type and Setting, your sound card is not set up properly (its external MIDI port is not installed). In this case you should run the installation/setup procedure that came with your sound card again. If your computer came with the sound card already installed, look for the installation disk or CD for the sound card that came with your computer.

It's also possible that you do not have an external MIDI port that is compatible with the joystick. In this case, you'll need to purchase a compatible sound card, equipped with an "MPU-401 compatible port," before you can use the joystick.

Checking for "Unknown Devices"

Check for your sound card in the "Unknown Devices" section of Device Manager. If your sound or MIDI device is listed here, it may not operate properly. If your sound card is listed here, you may need to remove it and reinstall it following the directions provided by the sound card's manufacturer. You may also need to obtain an updated sound card driver from the manufacturer.

Checking for Multiple Game Ports and Unnecessary Connections

It's possible that your computer is equipped with more than one game port—check for this. Examine the back of your computer for an adapter that has 15-pin game ports mounted on it. If you have an adapter that contains two 15-pin game ports, you'll probably need to remove this adapter from your computer for the game port on your sound card to work properly.

Also see that the joystick is connected *directly* to the sound card's MIDI port. Verify that there is not an extension cable or Y-adapter connected to the joystick—this is very important. Some extension cables do not transmit MIDI, and some are too long to support the MIDI signal. For best joystick communications, you should have the joystick directly connected to the computer.

Checking for "Single Mode DMA"

If the joystick seems sluggish or intermittent (or even stops responding) while playing your game—especially when music is playing—you may have a sound card that requires "single mode DMA":

1 Click Start, highlight Settings, and then click Control Panel.

2 Double-click the Multimedia icon, and then click the Advanced tab.

3 In the Multimedia Devices area, double-click Audio Devices.

4 Select the listed audio device, click Properties, and then click Settings.

5 If the Settings button is unavailable (shaded), there is no Use Single-Mode DMA option on your computer. If there is a Use Single-Mode DMA check box, select it and reboot the system if necessary.

Closing Background Software

If problems persist, try closing other programs that might be running in the background. Use the Task Manager (CTRL+ALT+DEL) to systematically shut down everything but Explorer and Systray.

SYMPTOMS

SYMPTOM 24-1 **The joystick does not respond** Make sure the joystick is plugged into the game port correctly. When the game port has more than one connector, be sure that the joystick is plugged into the *correct* connector (joystick 1 or joystick 2). If the game port is running through a sound board, make sure the sound board is configured to use the port as a game port instead of a MIDI port, and see that any joystick Y-adapter is wired properly. Refer to the application and see that it is configured to run from the joystick. (If mouse or keyboard control is selected, the joystick will not function.) Now that many new joysticks are appearing with supplemental functions (hat switches, throttle controls, etc.), make sure that the application is written to take advantage of the particular joystick. If problems persist, make sure that the game port is set for the proper I/O address. (Most are fixed at 201h, but check the user documentation to be sure.) Try a known-good joystick with the game port. If a known-good joystick works, the original joystick is defective and should be replaced. If another joystick is not the problem, try a different game port board.

SYMPTOM 24-2 **Joystick performance is erratic or choppy** Start by checking the joystick to be sure that it is connected properly. Try another joystick. When a new joystick works properly, the original joystick is probably damaged and should be replaced. If a new joystick fails to solve the problem, the game port board may be too slow for the system. Remember that many game ports still use XT board types. An older board design may not be able to process joystick signals fast enough to provide adequate signaling to the system. Not only should you try another game port adapter, but you should use a speed-adjusting game port.

SYMPTOM 24-3 **The joystick is sending incorrect information to the system—the joystick appears to be drifting** First, check the application to be sure that the joystick is calibrated correctly. If you cannot calibrate the joystick, the application may not support the joystick properly—try another application. Make sure there are no other active devices in the system (such as other game ports) using I/O port 201h. If this happens, data produced on those other boards will adversely affect the game port you are using. If all unused game ports are disabled, check the active game port. Poor-quality game ports can drift. Try a newer, low-drift or speed-adjusting game port board.

SYMPTOM 24-4 **The basic X/Y, two-button features of the joystick work, but the hat switch, throttle controls, and supplemental buttons do not seem to respond** In virtually all cases, the joystick is configured wrong. Check the application first. Many new applications provide several different joystick options and even allow you to define the particular use of each feature within the application itself.

Check the joystick definition files next. Your joystick probably requires a supplemental definition file (such as an FCS file) in order to use all of the joystick's particular features. Finally, check the game port type. You may need a dual-port game port adapter rather than an inexpensive single-port game port adapter. Some enhanced joysticks use both joystick positions (the X/Y axis and fire buttons make up one joystick, while the throttle and other buttons take up the other position). You may need to install a dual-port game port card.

SYMPTOM 24-5 **You see an error such as "Joystick not connected" under Windows 95/98** Windows 95/98 doesn't recognize the game port hardware. Check the game port driver first. Use the Device Manager under Windows 95/98 to examine the resources assigned to the game port driver. Typically, the resource range should be set to 201h through 201h (only one address location). If the game port entry has a yellow icon next to it, there is a hardware conflict in the system, and other hardware is also trying to use the same I/O location.

Next, check the game port hardware for proper configuration. The game port card should be installed properly into its bus slot. Make sure the game port is enabled (this is typical of game ports integrated onto sound cards or multi-I/O cards). If a sound card enables you to switch a 15-pin port between MIDI and joystick, see that the jumper is set to the "joystick" position. Make sure the joystick cable is not cut or damaged anywhere, and see that it is attached securely to the game port. Finally, test a known-good joystick on the system. If a new joystick works as expected, the original joystick is probably suffering from internal wiring damage.

SYMPTOM 24-6 **The joystick drifts frequently and requires recalibration** This type of symptom is usually the result of problems with the game port adapter. Try a different game port adapter and see if the problem persists. If problems disappear, you simply need a better-quality or speed-adjusting game port. Otherwise, test a known-good joystick on the system. If a new joystick works as expected, the original joystick is probably suffering from internal wiring damage, and should be replaced.

SYMPTOM 24-7 **The joystick handle has lost tension—it no longer "snaps" back to the center** This problem may be accompanied by a rattling sound within the joystick. In most cases, a spring has popped out of place inside the joystick. Check the joystick for internal damage. Open the joystick and see if any springs or clips have slipped out of place. Replace any springs or clips (if possible). Some joysticks also employ mechanical latches that can enable or disable the "spring action" of the X and Y axis. Check to see that any such latches are enabled. If you cannot locate or correct the problem, simply replace the joystick outright.

SYMPTOM 24-8 **The joystick responds, but refuses to accept a calibration** In virtually all cases, the problem is with your game port adapter. Check the hardware setup. Make sure there are no other devices in the system using the I/O address assigned to your game port (201h). If more than one adapter in your system has game port capability, see that only one game port is enabled. Replace the game port, or enable a different game port in the system. If drift issues continue with different applications, you may need to replace the game port adapter with a low-drift or speed-adjusting model.

24

SYMPTOM 24-9 **The hat switch and buttons on a joystick work only intermittently (if at all)** This problem also applies to stand-alone pedals. In most cases, erratic behavior of a joystick's "enhanced features" is a symptom of game port speed problems. Check the joystick first. Try a known-good joystick. If the problems disappear, the original joystick may in fact be defective. If the problems persist, you have a game port problem. Make sure there are no other devices in the system using the I/O address assigned to your game port (201h). If more than one adapter in your system has game port capability, see that only one game port is enabled. If drift issues continue with different applications, you may need to replace the game port adapter with a low-drift or speed-adjusting model.

SYMPTOM 24-10 **When downloading FCS (or "calibration") files to a joystick, the line "put switch into calibrate" doesn't change when the download switch is moved** This is a typical problem with advanced joysticks. In most cases, the joystick needs to be "cleared." To clear the joystick, rock the download switch back to "analog," and then to "calibrate." This should clear the joystick for a new calibration download. Try downloading the FCS file again. If problems persist, the actual switch may be defective. Try a known-good joystick instead.

SYMPTOM 24-11 To download a calibration file, you need to rock the red switch back and forth a number of times (or press *ENTER* a number of times) to get it to 100 percent This is virtually always the result of a keyboard controller (keyboard BIOS) compatibility problem. Upgrade the keyboard controller (keyboard BIOS). Some advanced joystick products do not interact well with the host computer's keyboard controller. For example, Thrustmaster's Mark II experiences known microcode problems with a few of the keyboard controller chips on the market. These include AMI versions (D, B, 8, 0), Acer, and Phoenix. You may need to replace the keyboard controller or system BIOS with a later version.

SYMPTOM 24-12 You cannot use a joystick on a PC using a sound card with an ESS or OPTi chipset The joystick may stop responding while using an application, or report a "not connected" status in the Game Controllers area of the Control Panel. This is a known problem with the ESS and OPTi sound chipsets. You'll need to set Single Mode DMA to use the joystick:

1. Click Start, select Settings, and then click Control Panel.
2. Double-click Multimedia.
3. On the Advanced tab, double-click the Audio Devices entry to expand it.
4. Click the "Audio for..." entry that corresponds to your particular sound card, and then click Properties.
5. Click Settings.
6. Click the Use Single Mode DMA check box to select it.
7. Click OK until you return to Windows, and then restart the PC.

SYMPTOM 24-13 The joystick port is not removed when the sound card is removed The entry for your game port will still be visible in the Windows 95/98 Device Manager. This is not really a problem. Windows 95/98 does not recognize the game port as being part of the sound card, so removing the sound card doesn't automatically disable the game port. Also, the virtual joystick device driver (VJOYD.VXD) cannot detect whether the game port or joystick is installed or not, so the driver is always active. You'll need to manually remove the game port in Device Manager:

1. Use the right mouse button to click My Computer, and then click Properties on the menu.
2. Click the Device Manager tab.
3. Double-click the "Sound, video, and game controllers" entry to expand it.
4. Click the joystick port, and then click Remove.
5. Return to Windows 95/98 and restart the system.

SYMPTOM 24-14 You cannot disable a "jumperless" joystick port This is an issue that frequently crops up with newer sound boards like the Ensoniq VIVO and jumperless boards that are controlled exclusively through drivers. The VIVO also uses drivers to disable certain functions like the joystick port. Use the following steps to disable the VIVO's joystick port. (The specific command lines for your own sound board may be different, but the idea is very similar.)

1. Leave Windows 95/98 and enter DOS mode.
2. Edit the SNDSCAPE.INI file in the \Windows directory. Change the line JSEnable=true to JSEnable=false. (Check your particular sound board's documentation for the correct command line.)
3. Save the file and reboot the system. The joystick will now be disabled.

SYMPTOM 24-15 **Your joystick doesn't work with a SoundBlaster Live card** This is an issue with the SoundBlaster Live card. It's an excellent sound card, but the game port on the card is very slow. This means any fast analog device that is used with the SoundBlaster Live card will have trouble being "seen" by Windows. In this instance, your best solution is to disable the sound card's game port, and install a fast game port card instead.

SYMPTOM 24-16 **The cross-hair on your axis is off center** This is a frequent issue with digital joysticks such as the Gravis Blackhawk Digital. Chances are that you're dealing with a Windows 95/98 "shadow driver" problem. You'll need to restart your system in the Safe Mode:

1. Open your Control Panel, double-click the System icon, and then choose the Device Manager tab.
2. Click on the (+) in front of the "Sound, video and game controllers" entry to expand the list. You can only have one driver that contains "game port" or "joystick" in its name.
3. Make sure you have the Windows 95/98 CD or the disc containing your game port driver; then remove all listings that refer to your game port or joystick.
4. When you restart the computer, it should detect new hardware, and may ask for the installation CD. If it tells you that it is recommended to keep your newer driver, select No and install the drivers from your disc(s).
5. Save the changes and reboot the system if necessary. Your joystick should now be on center.

SYMPTOM 24-17 **You get a "fatal exception" error when you open the Gaming Devices wizard in the Control Panel** For example, you may see an error such as:

```
A Fatal Exception Error 0E occurred at 0028:58C10F3F
```

This error can usually occur if the game port is conflicting with another device. Use the Device Manager to see whether another device is conflicting with the game port. If Device Manager reports that there's a problem with the configuration of the game port, reconfigure the game port so that it uses resources that are not already in use by another device. If the game port is a PnP device, and is conflicting with another device, you must disable the device *before* attempting to change the resource settings. Use the steps below under Windows 95:

1. Open the Control Panel and double-click the System icon.
2. Click the Device Manager tab and double-click "Sound, video and game controllers."
3. Double-click the Gameport Joystick entry.
4. In the Gameport Joystick Properties dialog, click the General tab, click the Original Configuration check box to clear it, and then click OK. Under Windows 98, check the box "Disable in this hardware configuration."

SYMPTOM 24-18 **The joystick's throttle or slider control does not work in certain games** For example, when you use the SideWinder 3D Pro joystick, the throttle or slider control may not work in one or more of your games. This is because the throttle works only while the joystick is emulating a more basic model. For the SideWinder 3D Pro, the mode switch should be in position one. This position causes the SideWinder 3D Pro to emulate a CH Flightstick Pro. Make sure the switch is set in this position, and calibrate the SideWinder as a CH Flightstick Pro joystick. This should correct the problem.

You may also be able to correct the problem by patching or upgrading your offending game(s) to a version that supports your specific joystick type directly.

SYMPTOM 24-19 The Game Controllers tool switches between "OK" and "Not Connected" When you use the Game Controllers tool in Control Panel to check the status of a USB game controller, the game controller status may toggle between OK and Not Connected. In addition, you may see random buttons light up on the screen when you use the Game Controllers tool to test a USB game controller. This problem occurs when the USB game controller is connected to the game port on your computer, and the game port on your computer is not working correctly. To correct this problem, connect the USB game controller to the USB port on your computer, or install a working game port in your computer. If there is no USB port on your computer, you may be able to resolve this problem by contacting the manufacturer of your sound card to obtain updated drivers. This may correct problems or incompatibilities with the sound card's game port controller, and allow the joystick to function properly.

Further Study

Advanced Gravis: **http://www.gravis.com**

Logitech: **http://www.logitech.com**

Thrustmaster: **http://www.thrustmaster.com**

CH Products: **http://www.chproducts.com/**

25

KEYBOARDS

CHAPTER AT A GLANCE

Keyboards are the classical input device (Figure 25-1). By manipulating a matrix of individual electrical switches, commands and instructions can be entered into the computer one character at a time. If you've used computers or typewriters to any extent, you already have an excellent grasp of keyboard handling. However, keyboards are not without their share of drawbacks and limitations. Although today's keyboard switches are not mechanically complex, there are a number of important moving parts. When you multiply this number of moving parts by the 80 to 100+ keys on a typical keyboard, you are faced with a substantial number of moving parts. A jam or failure in any one of these many mechanical parts results in a keyboard problem. Most keyboard failures are hardly catastrophic, but they can certainly be inconvenient. This chapter gives you the information needed to understand and repair computer keyboards.

Keyboard Construction

To understand a keyboard, you must first understand the kinds of switches that are used. In general, there are two types of switches that you should be concerned with: mechanical switches and membrane switches. Both switches are used extensively throughout the computer industry, but any single keyboard will use only one type of switch.

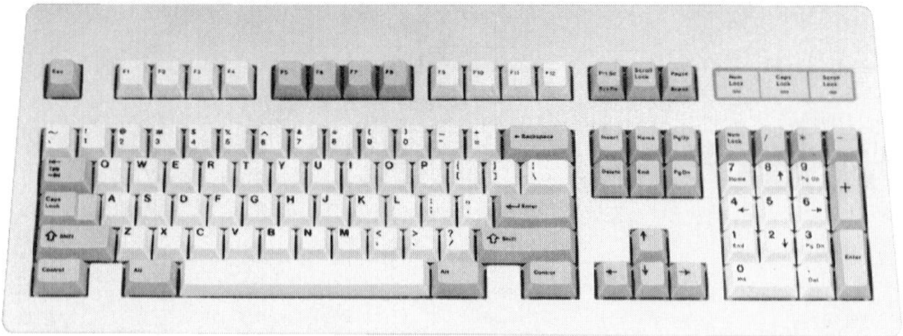

FIGURE 25-1 A Cherry G83-3000 keyboard (Cherry Electrical Products)

A *mechanical key switch* is shown in Figure 25-2. Two tempered bronze contacts are separated by a plastic actuator bar. The bar is pushed up by a spring in the switch base. When the key cap is pressed, the actuator bar slides down. This action compresses the spring and allows the gold-plated contacts to touch. Since gold is a soft metal and an excellent conductor, a good, low-resistance electrical contact is developed. When the key cap is released, the compressed spring expands and drives the plastic actuator bar between the contacts once again. The entire stroke of travel on a mechanical switch is little more than 3.56mm (0.140 inch), but an electrical contact (a *make* condition) can be established in as little as 1.78mm (0.070 inch). Mechanical switches are typically quite rugged—many are rated for 100 million cycles or more.

A *membrane key switch* is illustrated in Figure 25-3. A plastic actuator rests on top of a soft rubber boot. Inside, the rubber boot is coated with a conductive silver-carbon compound. Beneath the rubber boot are two open PC board contacts. When the key cap is pressed, the plastic actuator collapses the rubber boot. Collapse forces the conductive material across both PC board contacts to complete the switch. When the key cap is released, the compressed rubber boot breaks its contact on the PC board and returns to its original shape. The full travel stroke of a membrane key switch is about 3.56mm (0.140 inch)—roughly the same as a mechanical switch. An electrical contact is established in about 2.29mm (0.090 inch). Membrane switches are not quite as durable as mechanical switches. Most switches are rated for 20 million cycles or less.

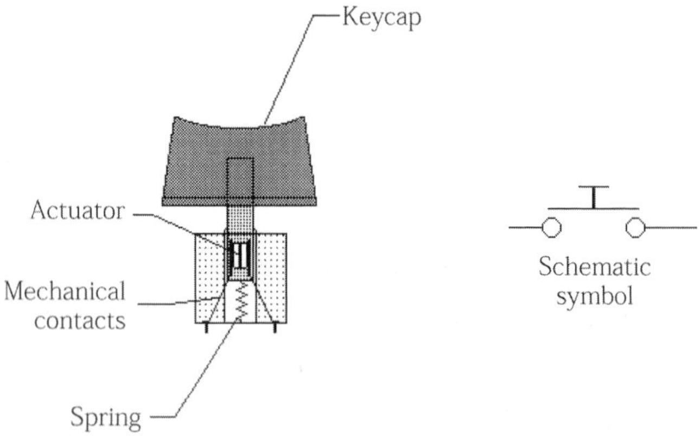

FIGURE 25-2 Mechanical switch assembly

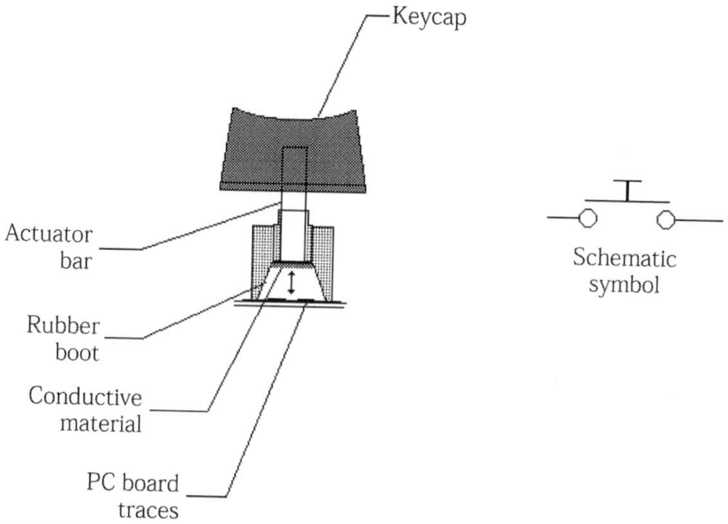

FIGURE 25-3 Membrane switch assembly

Mechanical and membrane switches offer a number of unique advantages and disadvantages. Mechanical switches tend to be highly reliable and provide a good tactile feedback when typing (that clicking noise we usually associate with offices). On the other hand, mechanical keyboards are more expensive to manufacture and can be extremely sensitive to spills and foreign matter. Membrane switches are not quite as reliable and tend to offer a softer, "mushier" feel when typing. (Some people prefer this feel.) Due to the membrane cover used in the keyboard, membrane switches seem to withstand spills and foreign matter better than mechanical switches.

25

The next step in understanding a keyboard is to learn about the *key matrix*. Keys are not interpreted individually—that is, each switch is not wired directly to the motherboard. Instead, keys are arranged in a matrix of rows and columns, as shown in Figure 25-4. When a key is pressed, a unique row (top to bottom) and column (left to right) signal is generated to represent the corresponding key. The great advantage of a matrix approach is that a huge array of keys can be identified using only a few row and column signals. Wiring from the keyboard is vastly simplified. An 84-key keyboard can be identified using only 12 column signals and 8 row signals.

KEY CODES

When a key is pressed, the row and column signals that are generated are interpreted by a *keyboard interface* IC (typically located on the keyboard assembly itself). The keyboard interface converts the row and column signals into a single-byte code (called a *key code* or *scan code*). Two unique scan codes are produced during a key stroke cycle. When the key is pressed, a *make code* byte is sent along to the system. When the key is released, a *break code* byte is generated. Both codes are transmitted to the host computer in a serial fashion. For example, a make code of 1Eh is sent when the *A* key is pressed. A 9Eh code is sent when the *A* key is subsequently released. By using two individual codes, the computer can determine when a key is held down, or when keys are held in combinations. Just about every key on a keyboard is *typematic*—that is, it will repeat automatically if it is held down for more than 500mS or so. Typematic settings can usually be adjusted in the CMOS advanced settings for your system.

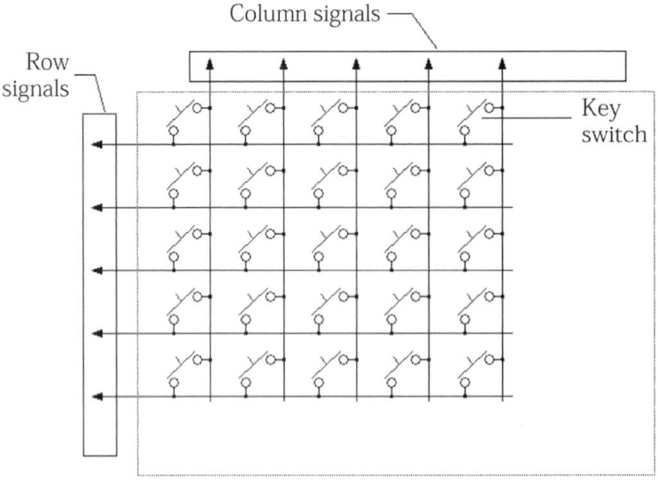

FIGURE 25-4 Simplified diagram of a keyboard matrix

Most computers today are prepared for multinational operation. To accommodate the special characters and punctuation used in various different countries, keyboard controllers (KBCs) can be configured to provide scan codes for different languages. Table 25-1 illustrates the make and break codes for conventional keyboards used in the domestic United States.

TABLE 25-1 STANDARD SCAN CODES FOR U.S. KEYBOARDS

KEY	MAKE CODE	BREAK CODE	I	KEY	MAKE CODE	BREAK CODE
A	1E	9E	I	B	30	B0
C	2E	AE	I	D	20	A0
E	12	92	I	F	21	A1
G	22	A2	I	H	23	A3
I	17	97	I	J	24	A4
K	25	A5	I	L	26	A6
M	32	B2	I	N	31	B1
O	18	98	I	P	19	99
Q	10	90	I	R	13	93
S	1F	9F	I	T	14	94
U	16	96	I	V	2F	AF
W	11	91	I	X	2D	AD
Y	15	95	I	Z	2C	AC
0 /)	0B	8B	I	1 / !	02	82
2 / @	03	83	I	3 / #	04	84
4 / $	05	85	I	5 / %	06	86

TABLE 25-1 STANDARD SCAN CODES FOR U.S. KEYBOARDS *(CONTINUED)*

KEY	MAKE CODE	BREAK CODE		KEY	MAKE CODE	BREAK CODE
6 / ^	07	87	|	7 / &	08	88
8 / *	09	89	|	9 / (	0A	8A
. / >	29	A9	|	- / _	0C	8C
= / +	0D	8D	|	[	1A	9A
]	1B	9B	|	; / :	27	A7
' / "	28	A8	|	, / <	33	B3
/ / ?	35	B5	|	L Sh	2A	AA
L Ctrl	1D	9D	|	L Alt	38	B8
R Sh	36	B6	|	R Alt	E0 38	E0 B8
R Ctrl	E0 1D	E0 9D	|	Caps	3A	BA
BK SP	0E	8E	|	Tab	0F	8F
Space	39	B9	|	Enter	1C	9C
ESC	01	81	|	F1	3B	BB
F2	3C	BC	|	F3	3D	BD
F4	3E	BE	|	F5	3F	BF
F6	40	C0	|	F7	41	C1
F8	42	C2	|	F9	43	C3
F10	44	C4	|	F11	57	D7
F12	58	D8	|	Up Ar	E0 48	E0 C8
Dn Ar	E0 50	E0 D0	|	Lt Ar	E0 4B	E0 CB
Rt Ar	E0 4D	E0 CD	|	Ins	E0 52	E0 D2
Home	E0 47	E0 C7	|	Pg Up	E0 49	E0 C9
Del	E0 53	E0 D3	|	End	E0 4F	E0 CF
Pg Dn	E0 51	E0 D1	|	ScrLk	46	C6

* All make and break codes are given in hexadecimal (hex) values.
* Alphabetic characters represent both upper- and lowercase.

KEYBOARD INTERFACES

Once a key is pressed and the keyboard interface converts the key matrix signals into a suitable scan code, that code must be transmitted to the keyboard controller (KBC) on the host computer motherboard. Once key data reaches the keyboard controller, it is converted to parallel data by the KBC, which in turn generates an interrupt that forces the system to handle the key. The actual transfer of scan codes between the keyboard and PC is accomplished *serially* using one of the interfaces shown in Figure 25-5.

Note that there are really three important signals in a keyboard interface: the keyboard clock (KBCLOCK), the keyboard data (KBDATA), and the signal ground. Unlike most serial communication, which is asynchronous, the transfer of data from keyboard to controller is accomplished *synchronously*—data bits are returned in sync with the clock signals. As you might expect, the signal ground provides a common reference for the keyboard and system. The keyboard is powered by +5 Vdc, which is also provided through the keyboard interface. It is also important for you to note that most XT-style

IBM PC/XT/AT configuration — 6 pin mini-DIN connector

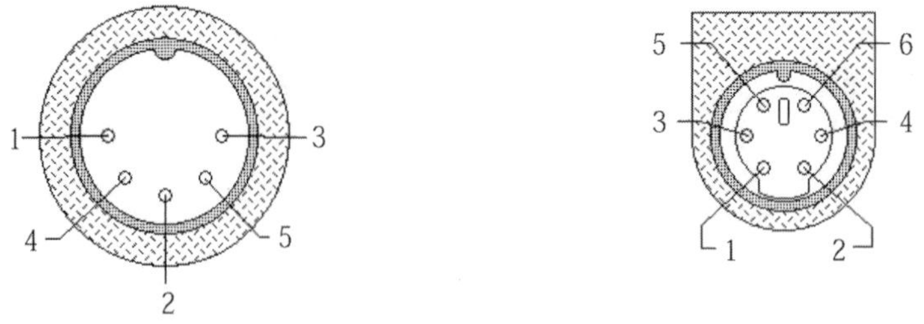

IBM PC/XT/AT configuration

1 KBCLOCK
2 KBDATA
3 nc
4 Ground
5 +5 Vdc (or +3.0 or +3.3 Vdc)

6 pin mini-DIN connector

1 KBDATA
2 nc
3 Ground
4 +5 Vdc (or +3.0 or +3.3 Vdc)
5 KBCLOCK
6 nc

FIGURE 25-5 Keyboard interface connectors

systems are designed with a unidirectional data path (from keyboard to system). AT-style keyboard interfaces are bidirectional. This feature allows AT keyboards to be controlled and programmed from the PC.

Dvorak Keyboards

Most technicians are familiar with QWERTY-style keyboards, the standard format for typewriters that was adopted in the late 1800s. A popular alternative to the QWERTY keyboard is the *Dvorak keyboard.* Mechanically and electronically, the Dvorak keyboard is identical to conventional keyboards. Only the key order is different. All of the vowels are located on the left side of your *home row* (the middle row of letters) in the pattern AOEUIDHTNS.

Dvorak keyboards claim several advantages over QWERTY models. Most letters typed (about 70 percent) are on the home row, so finger (and wrist strain) can be reduced. With less reach to deal with, typing can be accomplished faster and with fewer errors. On a Dvorak keyboard, the majority of words use both hands for typing, whereas there are thousands of words that demand one-handed typing on QWERTY keyboards. The Dvorak spreads out the strain on your hands more evenly.

CONVERTING TO DVORAK KEYBOARDS

There are two classical methods of implementing Dvorak keyboards: dedicated keyboards and keyboard conversions. Dedicated keyboards are just as the name implies—you buy a ready-made Dvorak keyboard and plug it in. Although the keys are located in different places, the key codes are the same, so your PC doesn't know the difference. As a result, you can interchange QWERTY and Dvorak keyboards at will without any changes to the PC or operating system. You can also convert your existing QWERTY keyboard to Dvorak under Windows 95/98:

1 Open the Control Panel and double-click on the Keyboard icon.

2 Select the Language page and double-click on the English (United States) entry (or your own default entry for a different country).

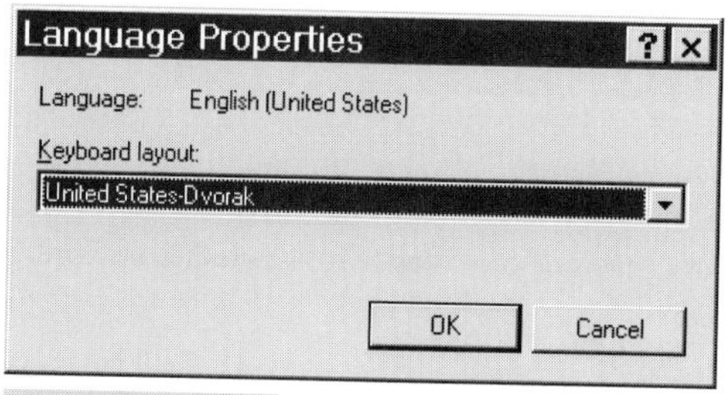

FIGURE 25-6 The keyboard Language Properties dialog

3. Select United States-Dvorak from the list that appears (Figure 25-6).
4. Save your changes. You may need to install a floppy disk with the proper drivers.
5. It may be necessary to reboot the system.

Under DOS, you will need a DOS TSR to handle the conversion. For MS-DOS 5.0 through 6.22, you can find the Dvorak TSR on the MS-DOS Supplemental Disk. You can obtain the driver files from Microsoft's FTP or Web site (**www.microsoft.com**), or from the Microsoft forum on CompuServe (GO MSDOS). Download the file DOS62S.EXE.

> If you do download and extract these supplemental DOS files, make very sure to extract them to a new or temporary directory. Under no circumstances should you allow DOS files to overwrite files in the DOS directory or in any of your Windows directories.

Once the software conversion is made, you will need to exchange the keys on your QWERTY keyboard. Figure 25-7 illustrates the difference between a QWERTY key layout and a Dvorak key layout. You can use a key-pulling tool to physically exchange the key caps, or use key stickers or overlays from Hooleon Corporation at (602)-634-7515 or Keytime at (206)-522-8973. You can also obtain more detailed information directly from Dvorak International at (802)-287-2434.

```
QWERTY
------------
Q W E R T Y U I O P
A S D F G H J K L ; '
Z X C V B N M , . /
Dvorak
---------
" , . P Y F G C R L /
A O E U I D H T N S -
; Q J K X B M W V Z
```

FIGURE 25-7 QWERTY vs. Dvorak keyboards

Keyboard Cleaning and Maintenance

Keyboards are perhaps the most abused part of any computer, yet they are often ignored until serious problems develop. With some regular cleaning and maintenance, however, a keyboard can easily last for the lifetime of a computer. This part of the chapter shows you some practical techniques for keyboard service.

CORRECTING PROBLEM KEYBOARDS

Virtually all computer keyboards are open to the air. Over time, everyday dust, pet hair, air vapor, cigar/cigarette smoke, and debris from hands and ordinary use will settle into the keyboard. Eventually, accumulations of this foreign matter will cause keys to stick, or will prevent keys from making proper contact (for example, a key may not work every time it is pressed). In either case, keyboard problems will develop. Fortunately, correcting a finicky keyboard is a relatively straightforward process. First, remove the key caps of the offending keys. Be sure to note where each key is placed before starting your disassembly—especially if the keyboard is a Dvorak-type or unusual ergonomic design. To remove a key cap, bend an ordinary paper clip into the shape of a narrow U, and bend in small tabs at the ends of the U shape. Slip the small tabs under the key cap and pull up gently. Do not struggle with the key cap. If a cap will not come off, remove one or more adjacent caps. If there is a substantial accumulation of foreign matter in the keyboard, you should consider removing all of the key caps for a thorough cleaning, but this requires more time.

Avoid removing the SPACEBAR unless it is absolutely necessary, since the SPACEBAR is often much more difficult to replace than ordinary keys.

Flip the keyboard upside down and rap gently on the case. This will loosen and dislodge any larger, heavier foreign matter, and allow it to fall out of the keyboard. A soft-bristled brush will help loosen the debris. Return the keyboard to an upright position. Use a can of compressed air (available from almost any electronics or photography store) to blow out the remainder of foreign matter. Since this tends to blow dust and debris in all directions, you may wish to use the compressed air outside or in an area away from your workbench. A medium or firm-bristled brush will help loosen any stubborn debris.

Now that the keyboard is cleaned out, squirt a small amount of good-quality electronics-grade contact cleaner (also available from almost any electronics store) into each key contact, and work the key to distribute the cleaner evenly. Allow a few minutes for the contact cleaner to dry completely, and test the keyboard again before reinstalling the key caps. If the problems persist, the keyboard may be damaged, or the individual key(s) may simply be worn out beyond recovery. In such an event, replace the keyboard outright.

VACUUM CLEANERS AND KEYBOARDS

There is an ongoing debate as to the safety of vacuum cleaners with computer equipment. The problem is static discharge. Many vacuum cleaners—especially small, inexpensive models—use cheap plastic and synthetic fabrics in their construction. When a fast airflow passes over those materials, a static charge is developed (just like combing your hair with a plastic comb). If the charged vacuum touches the keyboard, a static discharge may have enough potential to damage the keyboard controller IC, or even travel back into the motherboard for more serious damage.

If you do choose to use a vacuum for keyboard cleaning, take these two steps to prevent damage. First, make sure that the computer is powered down, and disconnect the keyboard from the computer before starting service. If a static discharge does occur, the most that would be damaged is the keyboard itself. Second, use a vacuum cleaner that is made for electronics work and certified as "static safe." Third, try

FIGURE 25-8 A Curtis antistatic keyboard mat (Curtis, a division of Rolodex, Secaucus, NJ 07094)

working on an antistatic mat (such as the mat in Figure 25-8) that is properly grounded. This will tend to "bleed off" static charges before they can enter the keyboard or PC.

REPLACING THE SPACEBAR

Of all the keys on the keyboard, replacing the SPACEBAR is probably the most difficult. The SPACEBAR is kept even by a metal wire that is inserted into slots on each leg of the plastic bar key. However, you have to get the wire into the slots *without pressing the wire*. If you push the wire down, you compress the wire, and installation becomes impossible. As a general rule, do not remove the SPACEBAR unless absolutely necessary. If you must remove the SPACEBAR, remove several surrounding key caps also. This will let you get some tools under the SPACEBAR wire later on. Once the SPACEBAR is reinserted, you can easily replace any of the other key caps.

PREVENTING THE PROBLEMS

Keyboard problems do not happen suddenly (unless the keyboard is dropped or physically abused). The accumulation of dust and debris is a slow process that can take months (sometimes years) to produce serious, repetitive keyboard problems. By following a regimen of regular cleaning, you can stop problems before they manifest themselves in your keyboard. In normal office environments, keyboards should be cleaned once every four months. Keyboards in home environments should be cleaned every two months. Keyboards in harsh or industrial environments should be cleaned even more frequently.

Turn your keyboard upside down and use a soft-bristled brush to clean between the keys. This prevents debris that may already be on the keys from entering the keyboard. Next, run the long, thin nozzle of your compressed air can between the key spaces to blow out any accumulations of dust. Since compressed air will tend to blow dust in all directions, you may consider doing this outside, or in an area away from your workbench. Instead of compressed air, you may use a static-safe vacuum cleaner to remove dust and debris.

DEALING WITH LARGE OBJECTS

Staples and paper clips pose a clear and present danger to keyboards. Although the odds of a staple or paper clip finding its way into a keyboard are generally slight, foreign objects can jam the key, or short it out. If the keyboard is moved, the object can wind up in the keyboard's circuitry where serious damage can occur. When a foreign object falls into the keyboard, do not move the keyboard. Power-down the PC, locate the object, and find the nearest key. Use a paper clip bent in a U shape with the ends of the U angled inward to remove the nearest key cap. Use a pair of nonconductive tweezers or needle-nose pliers to remove the object. Replace the key cap.

DEALING WITH SPILLS

Accidental spills are probably the most serious and dangerous keyboard problem. Coffee, soda, and even tap water are highly conductive (even corrosive). Your keyboard will almost certainly short circuit. Immediately shut down your computer (you may be able to exit your application using a mouse), and disconnect the keyboard. The popular tactic is simply to let the liquid dry. The problem with this tactic is that most liquids contain minerals and materials that are corrosive to metals. Your keyboard will never be the same unless the offending liquid is *removed* before it dries. Also, liquids tend to turn any dust and smoke film into a sticky glue that will jam the keys when dry (not even considering the sticky sugar in most sodas).

Disassemble the keyboard's main housings and remove the keyboard printed circuit assembly. As quickly as you can after the incident, rinse the assembly thoroughly in clean, room-temperature, demineralized water (available from any pharmacy for contact lens maintenance). You can clean the plastic housings separately. *Do not use tap water.* Let the assembly drip dry in air. Do not attempt to accelerate the drying process with a hair dryer or other such heat source. The demineralized water should dry clean without mineral deposits or any sticky, conductive residue. Once the assembly is dry, you may wish to squirt a small amount of good-quality, electronics-grade contact cleaner into each key switch to ensure no residue is left on the contacts. Assuming that the keyboard's circuitry was not damaged by the initial spill, you should be able to reassemble the keyboard and continue using it without problems. If the keyboard behaves erratically (or not at all), replace the keyboard outright.

DISABLING A KEYBOARD

Keyboards are an essential peripheral for all computers except servers. There are many cases where network administrators would prefer to restrict direct access to the server, and prevent potential tampering. Traditional PCs did not allow you to disable the keyboard, but newer systems do offer a CMOS setup entry that can enable or disable the keyboard. When the keyboard is disabled through CMOS, the PC will boot without suffering "Keyboard not found" errors. Before starting service on a server, it may be necessary to reattach and reenable the keyboard.

Keyboard Troubleshooting

Although their appearance may seem daunting at first glance, keyboard systems are not terribly difficult to troubleshoot. This ease is primarily due to the keyboard's modularity—if all else fails, it's a simple matter to replace a keyboard outright. The keyboard's great weakness, however, is its vulnerability to the elements. Spills, dust, and any other foreign matter that finds its way between the key caps can easily ruin a keyboard. The keyboard's PC board is also a likely candidate to be damaged by impacts or other physical abuse. The following procedures address many of the most troublesome keyboard problems.

SYMPTOM 25-1 During initialization, you see an error message indicating that there is no keyboard connected Check your keyboard cable and see that it is inserted properly and completely into the PC connector. Remember that you will have to reboot your system to clear this error message. Try another compatible keyboard. If a new keyboard assembly works properly, there is probably a wiring fault in the original keyboard. Given the very low price of new keyboards, it is usually most economical to simply replace a defective keyboard. If you're working on a file or network server, see that the CMOS setup has enabled the keyboard.

If a known-good keyboard fails to function, try the original keyboard on a known-good PC to verify that the keyboard itself is indeed operational. If so, your trouble now lies in the PC. Check the wiring between the PC keyboard connector and the motherboard. Check the connector pins to make sure that none of them have bent or pushed in (resulting in a bad connection). You might also want to check the soldering connections where the keyboard connector attaches to the motherboard. Repeated removals and insertions of the keyboard may have fatigued the solder joints. Reheat any defective solder joints. If the keyboard connector is intact, it is likely that the keyboard controller IC (KBC) has failed. Try booting the PC with a POST board installed (as discussed in Chapter 19). A KBC failure will usually be indicated by the system stopping on the appropriate POST code. You can attempt to replace the KBC, or replace the motherboard outright. If a POST board indicates a fault other than a KBC (such as the programmable interrupt controller that manages the KBC's interrupt), you can attempt to replace that component, or simply exchange the motherboard anyway.

SYMPTOM 25-2 **During initialization, you see an error message indicating that the keyboard lock is on** In many cases, the detection of a "locked" keyboard will halt system initialization. Make sure the keyboard lock switch is set completely to the "unlocked" position. If the switch is unlocked, but the system detects it as locked, the switch may be defective. Turn off and unplug the system; then use a multimeter to measure continuity across the lock switch. (You may need to disconnect the lock switch cable from the motherboard.) In one position, the switch should measure as an open circuit. In the opposing position, the switch should measure as a short circuit. If this is not the case, the lock switch is probably bad and should be replaced. If the switch measures properly, there is probably a logic fault on the motherboard (perhaps the keyboard controller). Your best course is to try another motherboard.

25

SYMPTOM 25-3 **The keyboard is completely dead—no keys appear to function at all** All other computer operations are normal. This symptom assumes that your computer initializes and boots to its DOS prompt or other operating system as expected, but the keyboard does not respond when touched. Keyboard status LEDs may or may not be working properly. Your first step in such a situation is to try a known-good keyboard in the system. *Note that you should reboot the system when a keyboard is replaced.* If a known-good keyboard works, the fault is probably on the keyboard interface IC. You can attempt to replace this IC if you wish, but it is often most economical to simply replace the keyboard outright.

If another keyboard fails to correct the problem, use a multimeter and check the +5V supply at the keyboard connector (refer to Figure 25-5). If the +5V signal is missing, the female connector may be broken. Check the connector's soldering junctions on the motherboard. Reheat any connectors that appear fatigued or intermittent. Many motherboards also use a "pico-fuse" to protect the +5V supply feeding the keyboard connector. If your +5V is lost, locate and check the keyboard connector fuse. If problems continue, replace the motherboard.

SYMPTOM 25-4 **The keyboard is acting erratically. One or more keys appear to work intermittently, or are inoperative** The computer operates normally and most keys work just fine, but there seems to be one or more keys that do not respond when pressed. Extra force or repeated strikes may be needed to operate the key. This type of problem can usually range from a minor nuisance to a major headache. Chances are that your key contacts are dirty. Sooner or later, dust and debris works into all key switches. Electrical contacts eventually become coated and fail to make contact reliably. This symptom is typical of older keyboards, or keyboards that have been in service for prolonged periods of time. In many cases, you need only vacuum the keyboard and clean the suspect contacts with a good-quality electronic contact cleaner.

Begin by disconnecting the keyboard. Use a static-safe, fine-tipped vacuum to remove any accumulations of dust or debris that may have accumulated on the keyboard's PC board. You may wish to vacuum your keyboard regularly as preventive maintenance. Once the keyboard is clean, gently remove the plastic key cap from the offending key(s). The use of a key cap removal tool is highly recommended, but you may also use a modified set of blunt-ended tweezers with their flat ends (just the tips) bent inward. Grasp the key cap and pull up evenly. You can expect the cap to slide off with little resistance. Do not *rip* the key cap off—you stand a good chance of marring the cap and causing permanent key switch damage.

Use a can of good-quality electronics-grade contact cleaner, and spray a little bit of cleaner into the switch assembly. When spraying, attach the long narrow tube to the spray nozzle—this directs cleaner into the switch. Work the switch in and out to distribute the cleaner. Repeat once or twice to clean the switch thoroughly. Allow residual cleaner to dry thoroughly before retesting the keyboard. *Never use harsh cleaners or solvents.* Industrial-strength chemicals can easily ruin plastic components and housings. Reapply power and retest the system. If the suspect key(s) respond normally again, install the removed key caps and return the system to service. As a preventive measure, you might wish to go through the process of cleaning every key.

Membrane keys must be cleaned somewhat differently from mechanical keys. It is necessary for you to remove the rubber or plastic boot to clean the PC board contacts. Depending on the design of your particular membrane switch, this may not be an easy task. If you are able to see the contact boot, use a pick or tweezers to gently lift the boot. Spray a bit of cleaner under the boot, and then work the key to distribute the cleaner. If the boot is confined within the individual key, you may have to remove the suspect key before applying cleaner.

If cleaning does not work, your next step should be to disassemble the keyboard and replace the defective key switch(es). Observe the board closely for cracks or fractures. Many key switch designs still utilize through-hole technology, but you should exercise extreme care when desoldering and resoldering. Extra care helps prevent accidental damage to the PC keyboard. You also have the more economical option of replacing the entire keyboard assembly outright.

SYMPTOM 25-5 The keyboard is acting erratically. One or more keys may be stuck or repeating Suspect a shorted or jammed key. Short circuits can be caused by conductive foreign objects (such as staples, paper clips) falling into the keyboard and landing across PC board contacts. Remove all power and disassemble the keyboard housing assembly. Once the keyboard is exposed, shake out the foreign object or remove it with a pair of needle-nose pliers or sharp tweezers.

Accumulations of dirt or debris can work into the key actuator shaft and restrict its movement. Apply good-quality electronics-grade cleaners to the key, and work the key in and out to distribute cleaner evenly. If the key returns to normal, you may reassemble the computer and return it to service. Keys that remain jammed should be replaced. If you cannot clear the jammed key, simply replace the entire keyboard assembly outright. If you elect to replace the keyboard assembly, retain the old assembly for parts. Key caps, good switches, and cable assemblies can be scavenged for use in future repairs.

SYMPTOM 25-6 You see "KBC Error" (or a similar message) displayed during system startup When your computer initializes (either from a warm or cold start) it executes a comprehensive self-test routine that checks the key ICs in the system (the CPU, memory, drive controllers, etc.). As part of this power-on self-test (POST) routine, the computer looks for the KBCLK signal, along with a series of test scan codes generated by the KB controller IC. You can see the keyboard LEDs flash as the controller sequences through its codes. If either the keyboard clock or keyboard data signals are missing, the POST knows that either the keyboard is disconnected, or the keyboard controller has failed. If you are using a POST board, it will probably be displaying a code corresponding to a KBC error. Unless you have the tools and inclination to replace a KBC controller IC, your best course is simply to replace the motherboard outright.

SYMPTOM 25-7 **You cannot clear macros from a programmable keyboard** In most cases, you need to use the correct key combination in order to clear the macros. If the keyboard has a REMAP key, press that first (a Program light or other LED will start blinking). Press the CTRL key twice to map the key to itself. Press ALT twice to map the key to itself. Press the SUSPEND MACRO key (the Program light should stop blinking). Press the CTRL and ALT keys while pressing SUSPEND MACRO. This will clear all of the keyboard's programming. The key sequence used for your keyboard may be different, so be sure to check the procedure for your own keyboard. If problems persist, replace the keyboard.

SYMPTOM 25-8 **The keyboard keys are not functioning as expected** Pressing a key causes unexpected results, or a series of operations that would ordinarily not be attributed to that key. Chances are that the keyboard has been programmed with macros, and you'll need to clear those macros to restore normal keyboard operation. If the keyboard has a REMAP key, press that first (a Program light or other LED will start blinking). Press the CTRL key twice to map the key to itself. Press ALT twice to map the key to itself. Press the SUSPEND MACRO key (the Program light should stop blinking). Press the CTRL and ALT keys while pressing SUSPEND MACRO. This will clear all of the keyboard's programming. The key sequence used for your keyboard may be different, so be sure to check the procedure for your own keyboard. If problems persist, replace the keyboard.

SYMPTOM 25-9 **Some keys on a programmable keyboard will not remap to their default state** This can happen with some Gateway 2000 (AnyKey) keyboards—as well as other programmable keyboards—and you may have to "force clear" the keyboard at boot time. Power-down the system. While holding down the SUSPEND MACRO key, turn the system power back on. Continue booting with the SUSPEND MACRO key pressed until the Program light (or similar LED) quits flashing. This light will stay lit until you press and release it.

For Gateway 2000 AnyKey keyboards, if there is an "AnykeyXX T" line in the AUTOEXEC.BAT file, this will terminate any programming function of the keyboard. If there is an "AnykeyXX A" line in the AUTOEXEC.BAT file, this will activate the programming function.

SYMPTOM 25-10 **A wireless keyboard types random characters** You'll need to reset both ends of the wireless system. First, take a look at the DIP switch settings controlling the RF channel for the wireless transmitter and receiver (usually under the battery cover at the keyboard). Make sure that the transmitter and receiver are both set for the same channel. Find the "reset" button on both the transmitter and receiver. Press the RF receiver reset button first, and then press the RF transmitter button immediately after (usually within 15 seconds of one another). If the problem persists, reboot the system and try the reset process again.

SYMPTOM 25-11 **The wireless keyboard beeps while typing** In virtually all cases, the batteries in the wireless keyboard are running low. Replace the batteries and try the wireless keyboard again—the beeping should stop.

SYMPTOM 25-12 **Typed characters do not appear, but the cursor moves** This issue is a result of the color scheme being used. Some of the applications reported as suffering this problem are MSWORKS 4.0, CASHGRAF, MSBOB (address book and letter writer), and MSPUBLISHER. Check the color scheme selected by right-clicking on the desktop. Click on Properties and then the Appearance tab. Set the scheme to Windows Standard. Click on OK to return to the desktop. The text should now appear normal. This solution can generally be attempted with any application.

SYMPTOM 25-13 **Some function keys and Windows keys may not work on some PC configurations** For example, this is a known problem with Toshiba 8500 desktop systems and the Microsoft Natural Keyboard. In virtually all cases (including the Toshiba 8500), the PC keyboard controller BIOS recognizes the keyboard during the power-on self-test (POST), but it does not recognize some of the keys—including certain function keys and Windows-specific keys. You'll need to try a generic keyboard, or upgrade the system's keyboard controller BIOS.

SYMPTOM 25-14 **One or more Windows-specific keys don't work** This is almost always a limitation of the keyboard controller BIOS. For example, a Jetkey keyboard controller BIOS (v.3.0) will not recognize the right Windows key on a Microsoft Natural Keyboard. You'll need to try a generic keyboard, or upgrade the system's keyboard controller BIOS.

SYMPTOM 25-15 **Remote control programs don't work after installing keyboard drivers** Many PC "remote control" programs (such as PC Anywhere, ReachOut, and Carbon Copy) use keyboard and mouse drivers that are simply not compatible with the keyboard's specific drivers. For example, the remote control programs listed above will not work when IntelliType software is installed for the Microsoft Natural Keyboard. You'll need to disable the remote control software, install patches for the remote control software that will properly support the keyboard, or replace the keyboard with a more generic model.

SYMPTOM 25-16 **On a PS/2 system, you encounter keyboard errors, even though the keyboard driver loads successfully** Often, you'll see an error like "Keyboard error: keyboard not found," and you cannot access the keyboard. This type of problem is known to occur on PS/2 systems when the IBM ROM BIOS patch file (DASDDRVR.SYS) is loaded *after* the keyboard driver in CONFIG.SYS. Rearrange the CONFIG.SYS file to load the DASDDRVR.SYS file before the keyboard driver. Make sure you are loading the patch driver (DASDDRVR.SYS) that is designed for your *specific* computer (for example, you cannot use the DASDDRVR.SYS file that ships with an IBM PS/2 Model 80 on a PS/2 Model 70 computer). This device driver can normally be found on the setup disk that you received with your IBM PS/2. Otherwise, you can obtain it from IBM (**www.ibm.com**).

SYMPTOM 25-17 **Assigned key sounds do not work** When you assign sounds to keystrokes (under the Options tab in the Keyboard tool in your Control Panel), the sounds may play when you press the assigned keys. This problem is known to occur with some programmable keyboards when HiJaak Pro or HiJaak 95 Graphics Suite is installed on your computer. These products may load a device driver named "Runner" that disables programmable keyboard sounds. You may be able to work around the problem by closing the "Runner" task:

1. Press CTRL+ALT+DEL to open the Close Program dialog box.
2. If "Runner" is listed, click Runner, and then click End Task.

SYMPTOM 25-18 You cannot use Windows-specific keys to start task-switching software other than TASKSW16.EXE You *can* start the desired task-switching software using CTRL+ESC, or by double-clicking the desktop. Chances are that your Windows-specific key will not start any other task-switching utility if TASKSW16.EXE can be found on the path. You'll need to update the task-switching program reference in SYSTEM.INI. Load SYSTEM.INI into any text editor, and modify the line that reads

```
TASKMAN=TASKSW16.EXE
```

to read

```
TASKMAN=<task manager>
```

where <task manager> is the name of the executable file you want to start when you press the Windows key. Rename the TASKSW16.EXE file (for example, to TASKSW16.OLD), or move it to a directory that is not in the path. Save and close the SYSTEM.INI file, and then restart the computer.

SYMPTOM 25-19 The NumLock feature may not activate when the NUMLOCK key is pressed This can happen with some programmable keyboards when pen software is installed on the system. You should be able to correct the problem by disabling the pen device:

1. Click Start, select Settings, and then click Control Panel.
2. Double-click the System icon and select the Device Manager tab.
3. Double-click the Ports entry to expand it.
4. Double-click the port to which the pen (or touch-screen) device is connected.
5. In the Device Usage area on the General tab, click the Original Configuration (Current) check box to clear it. (If you're using OSR2, click the Disable In This Hardware Profile check box to select it.)
6. Click OK, and then restart the system when prompted.

> To enable your pen device again, repeat the steps above, but reselect (or re-clear) the check box in step 5.

SYMPTOM 25-20 The "Language" section of the Keyboard tool is disabled under Windows 95/98 When you're using the Keyboard tool in Control Panel, you may encounter the following symptom(s): a message may say "Old-Style Keyboard detected, pane disabled," or the language list may be blank (and you may not be able to change any language settings). This problem can occur if the keyboard registry key is damaged or missing:

```
HKEY_LOCAL_MACHINE\System\CurrentControlSet\control\keyboard layouts
```

To resolve this problem, reinstall Windows 95 or Windows 98 into the same folder as the original installation.

SYMPTOM 25-21 You encounter keyboard problems when using IE 4.0x/5 and an Adobe Acrobat (PDF) file under Windows 98 If you have an Adobe Acrobat (PDF) file open in Internet Explorer, you may lose some keyboard functionality. Keys that may not work may include the

PAGE UP, PAGE DOWN, and arrow keys. To work around this problem, minimize and restore the IE window, use the Zoom buttons on the Adobe Acrobat toolbar, or use the mouse to scroll through the file.

SYMPTOM 25-22 You have problems using a real-mode keyboard driver with an international code page If an "international code page" is installed in conjunction with a real-mode keyboard driver (such as KEYBOARD.SYS), you may find that console programs cannot detect extended character keystrokes (such as INSERT, DELETE, HOME, etc.). Console programs that don't work directly with the console API may not recognize extended keystrokes. When a real-mode keyboard driver is installed, the current character in the keyboard buffer is sent to the console program. With an international code page loaded, the data returned through the console API is slightly different from that in Windows 95/98. This problem has been corrected in Windows 98 SE, but for older versions of Windows, you can download the patch (a new version of CONAGENT.EXE) from: **http://www.microsoft.com/support/supportnet/overview/overview.asp**.

SYMPTOM 25-23 You find two keyboards listed in the Windows 98 Device Manager When you restart your computer after installing a USB keyboard, both the USB keyboard device and the "Standard 101/102-Key" or "Microsoft Natural Keyboard" device are listed in the Keyboard branch of your Device Manager. This occurs because USB keyboards may still require the Standard 101/102-Key or Natural Keyboard driver to work properly (if your BIOS does not fully support USB in the real mode). This may seem awkward, but it's perfectly normal. If you disable the Standard 101/102-Key or Microsoft Natural Keyboard device in Device Manager and restart your computer, the USB keyboard will not work—Windows 98 automatically installs the device again. You might try a system BIOS upgrade to better support the USB ports on your motherboard.

SYMPTOM 25-24 The new USB keyboard does not operate properly under Windows 98 after installation You know that your system should fully support USB devices. This problem can occur when you install a new USB keyboard while your system is off, and your computer is set up to have you log on when you start it. USB keyboards are not enumerated until *after* you log on to your computer. To correct this problem, click Cancel when you're prompted to log on, click Start, click Log Off <user name>, click Yes, and *then* log on to your computer.

SYMPTOM 25-25 You notice that the keyboard language unexpectedly changes to a "default" language When you start a program under Windows 95/98 (or when a program is started using OLE), your keyboard may revert to the "default" language—regardless of the language you're currently using. For example, when you start a program, you'll see the language icon on the task bar change to indicate that the default language is being used (but when a program is started using OLE, the language icon may not change). To work around this problem, simply change the keyboard driver to the desired language after you start the program. Click the Language icon on the task bar, and then click the language that you want. Now press the appropriate shortcut key combination for switching keyboard layouts (by default, this is LEFT ARROW+ALT+SHIFT).

SYMPTOM 25-26 The "automatic repeat" feature doesn't work for USB keyboards after returning from suspend mode under Windows 98 SE This is a known problem with Windows 98 SE, but a patch is available from Microsoft at **http://www.microsoft.com/support/supportnet/overview/overview.asp**. The English version of this patch should have the following file attributes (or later):

```
KBDHID.VXD  10/04/99  05:32p    4.10.2223    16,666KB
```

SYMPTOM 25-27 After upgrading to Windows 98, your custom keyboard layout may be lost This problem occurs when "user profiles" are enabled in Windows 95 and a custom keyboard layout option is selected in a user profile (rather than the "default" profile). Since Windows 98 setup only parses the settings for a default user during the upgrade to Windows 98, the keyboard setting changes to the default user profile during the upgrade. To correct this problem, log on to the computer using a user profile *other* than the default, and then modify the keyboard layout in Windows 98:

1. Click Start, highlight Settings, and then click Control Panel.
2. Click Keyboard, click Language, click Properties, and then click the layout you want to use in the Keyboard Layout box.
3. Click OK, click OK again, and then restart the computer.

SYMPTOM 25-28 Your laptop does not detect a PS/2 keyboard This is a known problem with configurations such as the IBM ThinkPad and a Natural Keyboard Elite. For example, when you connect the Natural Keyboard Elite to the PS/2 port on an IBM ThinkPad laptop, the keyboard may not be detected. This problem generally occurs because the PS/2 port on the IBM ThinkPad does not detect any PS/2 keyboard without the correct adapter cable or docking station. To correct this problem, you must connect the keyboard to an appropriate docking station.

SYMPTOM 25-29 Your particular keyboard doesn't work with a Compaq DeskPro 4000 system For example, the Natural Keyboard Elite is known to have trouble with the Compaq DeskPro 4000. When you connect the keyboard to your computer, the keyboard may be detected the first time you start the system, but the keyboard may not be detected during subsequent starts. In virtually all cases, the keyboard device you're using will not operate on systems using the VIA UHCI chipset. Try a different (basic model) keyboard.

25

SYMPTOM 25-30 You find that you cannot use the USB Natural Keyboard Elite in the DOS mode For example, when you start the computer (or restart your computer) in DOS mode, the Natural Keyboard Elite may not function properly. You may also receive either of the following error messages:

```
Keyboard Error
```

or

```
Keyboard Not Present
```

This problem can occur if you connect the Natural Keyboard Elite to your computer using a USB adapter, but your computer's BIOS doesn't fully support USB keyboards. Your system BIOS must support USB devices in order for any type of USB keyboard to work in DOS. You should upgrade the system BIOS with a version that supports USB devices. To work around this issue temporarily, shut down Windows and turn off the computer. Disconnect the keyboard from the USB port, and then remove the USB adapter. Connect another keyboard to a PS/2 port on the computer, and then restart the system normally.

SYMPTOM 25-31 Keyboard lights do not illuminate in the DOS mode This is a known problem when using the Natural Keyboard Elite with a Compaq Presario system under DOS. The LED lights on the keyboard may remain unlit in DOS, but may work properly under Windows. This is an issue with the Compaq system (rather than the keyboard), but no features are lost in the DOS mode.

SYMPTOM 25-32 **Your keyboard does not work properly on an IBM Aptiva system** For example, when you connect a Natural Keyboard or Natural Keyboard Elite to an IBM Aptiva computer, the keyboard may not work properly. This problem may occur if you have "IBM Rapid Access Keyboard" software running on the Aptiva system. To correct this issue, remove the IBM Rapid Access Keyboard software. (This software is not needed if you use another keyboard, such as the Natural Keyboard family.)

1. Click Start, highlight Settings, and then click Control Panel.
2. Double-click the Add/Remove Programs icon.
3. In the list of installed programs, click IBM Rapid Access Keyboard, and then click Add/Remove.
4. Follow the instructions on the screen to remove the IBM Rapid Access Keyboard software.

> The EZ-Button program is a component of the IBM Rapid Access Keyboard software, so this program is also removed when you remove the IBM Rapid Access Keyboard software.

SYMPTOM 25-33 **Your Natural Keyboard does not work properly on certain Toshiba laptops** For example, when you use a Natural Keyboard Elite attached to the PS/2 port on one of the following Toshiba laptops, the keyboard may not function properly:

- Satellite 110C
- Satellite Pro 400C
- Tecra 720CDT
- Tecra 500CDT

This problem can occur because plug-and-play hardware detection on the PS/2 port times out *before* the computer enumerates the keyboard—this is a problem with the keyboard. To get around this issue, use the USB adapter included with the keyboard to connect the keyboard to the USB port on the laptop (if one is available). If a USB port is not available on your computer, you'll need to return the keyboard for an updated model that will operate properly on the Toshiba family of laptops.

Further Study

NMB Technologies: **http://www.nmbtech.com/**

Keytronic: **http://www.keytronic.com**

Mitsumi: **http://www.mitsumi.com**

Microsoft: **http://www.microsoft.com/products/prodref/310_ov.htm (Natural Keyboard)**

Chicony: http://**www.chicony.com/**

26

MEMORY TROUBLESHOOTING

CHAPTER AT A GLANCE

Memory holds the program code and data that is processed by the CPU—and it is this intimate relationship between memory and the CPU that forms the basis of computer performance. Larger and faster CPUs are constantly being introduced, and more complex software is regularly developed to take advantage of the processing power. In turn, more complex software demands larger amounts of faster memory. With the explosive growth of Windows (and more recently Windows 98/SE), the demands made on memory performance are more acute than ever. These demands have resulted in a proliferation of memory types that go far beyond the simple, traditional DRAM. Pipeline-burst cache, video memory (VRAM), fast synchronous DRAM (SDRAM), flash BIOS, and other exotic memory types (such as RAMBUS) now compete for the attention of PC technicians. These new forms of memory also present some new problems. This chapter will give you an understanding of memory types, configurations, installation concerns, and troubleshooting solutions.

Essential Memory Concepts

The first step in any discussion of memory is to understand basically how memory works. If you already have a good grasp of memory basics, feel free to skip this beginning part of the chapter.

MEMORY ORGANIZATION

All memory is basically an *array* organized as rows and columns, as shown in Figure 26-1. Each row is known as an *address*—there may be 1 million, 2 million, or 4 million or more addresses on a single memory IC. The columns represent *data bits*—a typical high-density memory chip has 1 bit, but may have 2 or 4 bits depending on the overall amount of memory required.

As you can see in Figure 26-1, the intersection of each column and row is an individual memory bit (known as a *cell*). The cell is important because the number of its components—and the way those compo-

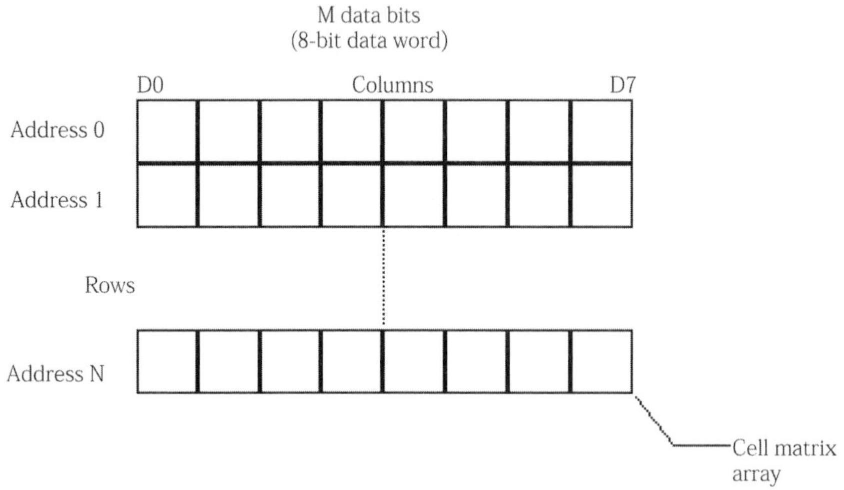

FIGURE 26-1 Simplified Diagram of a Memory Array

nents are fabricated onto the memory chip—will have a profound impact on memory performance. For example, a classic DRAM cell is a single MOS transistor, while static RAM (or SRAM) cells often pack several transistors and other components onto the chip's die. Although you don't have to be an expert on chip design, you should realize that the *internal fabrication* of a memory chip has more to do with its performance than just the way it is soldered into your computer.

MEMORY SIGNALS

A memory chip communicates with the "outside world" through three sets of signals: address lines, data lines, and control lines. Figure 26-2 illustrates these signal types. *Address lines* define which row of the memory array will be active. In actual practice, the address is specified as a binary number, and conversion circuitry inside the memory chip translates the binary number into a specific row signal. *Data lines* pass binary values back and forth to the defined address. *Control lines* are used to operate the memory chip. A Read/-Write (R/-W) line defines whether data is being read from the specified address or is written to it. A -Chip Select (-CS) signal makes a memory chip active or inactive (this ability to "disconnect" from a circuit is what allows a myriad of memory chips to all share common address and data signals in the computer). Some memory types require additional signals, such as row address-select (RAS) and column address-select (CAS) for refresh operations. More exotic memory types may require additional control signals.

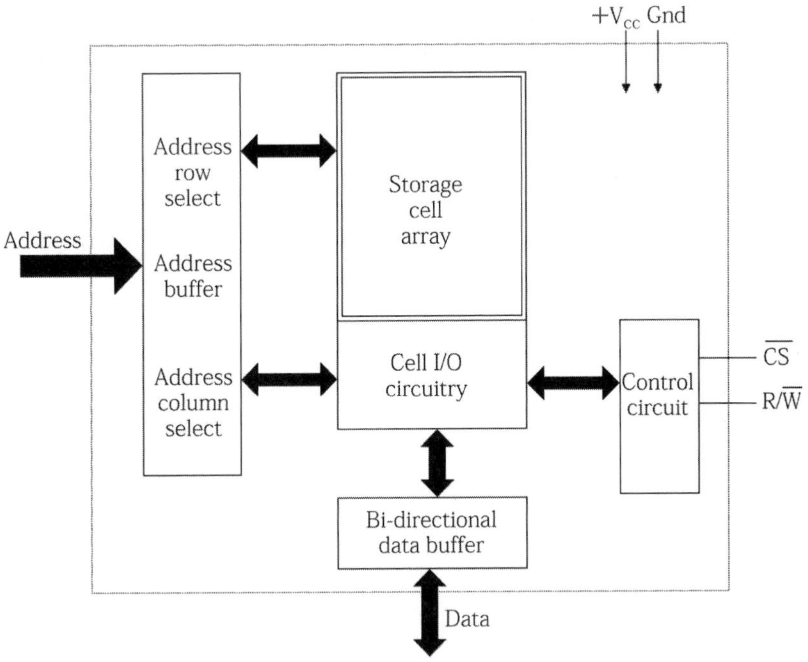

FIGURE 26-2 Diagram of a Typical Memory IC

Memory Package Styles and Structures

Ultimately, the memory die is mounted in a package just like any other chip. The completed memory packages can then be soldered to the motherboard or attached to plug-in structures such as SIMMs, DIMMs, and memory cards. There are really only four package styles normally used for memory devices:

- *DIP (Dual In-line Package)* This is the classic "chip" package used for through-hole mounting (prior to surface-mount technology). The advantage of DIP packages is their compatibility with sockets, which allows chips to be inserted or removed as required. Unfortunately, the long metal pins can bend and break if the chip is inserted or removed incorrectly. Also, the overall size of the package demands extra space. DIP chips can be found in older PCs (such as 286 and earlier systems) and older VGA/SVGA video boards. DIPs are still sometimes used on motherboards to provide cache RAM.
- *SIP (Single In-line Package)* This type of package is rarely used today—there are simply not enough pins. However, they did make a short appearance with memory devices in late-model 286 and early 386 systems that flirted with proprietary memory expansions. I remember NEC using such devices in a 2MB add-on module for its 386SX/20—and you needed to add that module *before* you added even more memory in the form of proprietary SIMMs. SIPs can be troublesome because they are difficult to find replacements for, so expect replacement memory modules using them to cost a premium.
- *SOJ (Small-Outline "J" Lead)* This is the contemporary package style for surface-mount circuits. The leads protrude from the package like a DIP, but are bent around just under the package in the form of a "j." There are sockets for SOJ packages, which are often employed for replaceable memory chips like the BIOS ROM, but most RAM devices are soldered directly to the motherboard as system memory (or a video board as video RAM). SIMMs often use SOJ-type memory components.
- *TSOP (Thin, Small-Outline Package)* Like the SOJ, a TSOP is also a surface-mount package style. However, its small, thin body makes TSOP memory ideal for narrow spaces. Expect to find such devices serving as memory in notebook/sub-notebook systems, or PCMCIA cards (a.k.a. PC Cards).

ADD-ON MEMORY DEVICES

Memory has always pushed the envelope of integrated circuit design. This trend has given us tremendous amounts of memory in very small packages, but it also has kept memory relatively expensive. Manufacturers responded by providing a minimum amount of memory with the system, then selling more memory as an add-on option—doing this keeps the cost of a basic machine down and increases profit through add-on sales. As a technician, you should understand the three basic types of add-on memory:

Proprietary Add-on Modules Once the Intel i286 opened the door for more than 1MB of memory, PC makers scrambled to fill the void. However, the rush to more memory resulted in a proliferation of nonstandard (and incompatible) memory modules. Each new motherboard came with a new add-on memory scheme—this development invariably led to a great deal of confusion among PC users and makers alike. You will likely find proprietary memory modules in 286 and early 386 systems.

SIMMs and DIMMs By the time 386 systems took hold in the PC industry, proprietary memory modules had been largely abandoned in favor of the "standard" 30-pin memory module (Figure 26-3). A

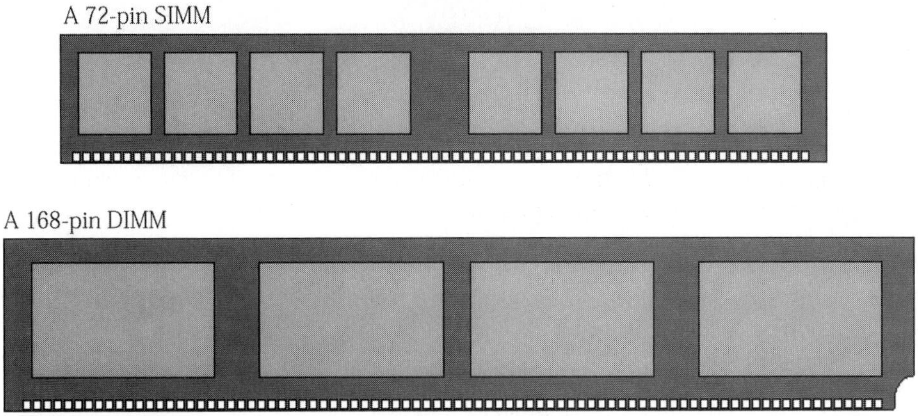

FIGURE 26-3 Comparison of SIMMs and DIMMs

SIMM (Single In-line Memory Module) is light, small, and contains a relatively large block of memory, but perhaps the greatest advantage of a SIMM is *standardization*—using a *standard* pin layout, a SIMM from one PC can be installed into almost any other PC. The 30-pin SIMM (Table 26-1) provides 8 data bits and generally holds up to 4MB of RAM. The 30-pin SIMM proved its worth in 386 and early 486 systems, but it fell short in later-model PCs. The 72-pin SIMM (Table 26-2), which replaced the 30-pin SIMM version, provides 32 data bits and may hold up to 32MB (or more). Table 26-3 outlines a variation of the standard 72-pin SIMM, highlighting the use of Error Correction Code (ECC) instead of parity.

TABLE 26-1 PINOUT OF A STANDARD 30-PIN SIMM

PIN	NAME	DESCRIPTION
1	VCC	+5 VDC
2	-CAS	-Column Address Strobe
3	DQ0	Data 0
4	A0	Address 0
5	A1	Address 1
6	DQ1	Data 1
7	A2	Address 2
8	A3	Address 3
9	GND	Ground
10	DQ2	Data 2
11	A4	Address 4
12	A5	Address 5
13	DQ3	Data 3
14	A6	Address 6
15	A7	Address 7
16	DQ4	Data 4
17	A8	Address 8

TABLE 26-1 PINOUT OF A STANDARD 30-PIN SIMM *(CONTINUED)*

PIN	NAME	DESCRIPTION
18	A9	Address 9
19	A10	Address 10
20	DQ5	Data 5
21	-WE	-Write Enable
22	GND	Ground
23	DQ6	Data 6
24	n/c	Not connected
25	DQ7	Data 7
26	QP	Data Parity Out
27	-RAS	-Row Address Strobe
28	-CASP	-Parity Control
29	DP	Data Parity In
30	VCC	+5 VDC

TABLE 26-2 PINOUT OF A STANDARD 72-PIN SIMM

PIN	NON-PARITY	PARITY	DESCRIPTION
1	VSS	VSS	Ground
2	DQ0	DQ0	Data 0
3	DQ18	DQ18	Data 18
4	DQ1	DQ1	Data 1
5	DQ19	DQ19	Data 19
6	DQ2	DQ2	Data 2
7	DQ20	DQ20	Data 20
8	DQ3	DQ3	Data 3
9	DQ21	DQ21	Data 21
10	VCC	VCC	+5 VDC
11	n/c	n/c	Not connected
12	A0	A0	Address 0
13	A1	A1	Address 1
14	A2	A2	Address 2
15	A3	A3	Address 3
16	A4	A4	Address 4
17	A5	A5	Address 5
18	A6	A6	Address 6
19	A10	A10	Address 10
20	DQ4	DQ4	Data 4
21	DQ22	DQ22	Data 22
22	DQ5	DQ5	Data 5
23	DQ23	DQ23	Data 23
24	DQ6	DQ6	Data 6

TABLE 26-2 PINOUT OF A STANDARD 72-PIN SIMM *(CONTINUED)*

PIN	NON-PARITY	PARITY	DESCRIPTION
25	DQ24	DQ24	Data 24
26	DQ7	DQ7	Data 7
27	DQ25	DQ25	Data 25
28	A7	A7	Address 7
29	A11	A11	Address 11
30	VCC	VCC	+5 VDC
31	A8	A8	Address 8
32	A9	A9	Address 9
33	-RAS3	-RAS3	-Row Address Strobe 3
34	-RAS2	-RAS2	-Row Address Strobe 2
35	n/c	PQ26	Parity 26 (3rd)
36	n/c	PQ8	Parity 8 (1st)
37	n/c	PQ17	Parity 17 (3rd)
38	n/c	PQ35	Parity 35 (4th)
39	VSS	VSS	Ground
40	-CAS0	-CAS0	-Column Address Strobe 0
41	-CAS2	-CAS2	-Column Address Strobe 2
42	-CAS3	-CAS3	-Column Address Strobe 3
43	-CAS1	-CAS1	-Column Address Strobe 1
44	-RAS0	-RAS0	-Row Address Strobe 0
45	-RAS1	-RAS1	-Row Address Strobe 1
46	n/c	n/c	Not connected
47	-WE	-WE	Read/-Write
48	n/c	n/c	Not connected
49	DQ9	DQ9	Data 9
50	DQ27	DQ27	Data 27
51	DQ10	DQ10	Data 10
52	DQ28	DQ28	Data 28
53	DQ11	DQ11	Data 11
54	DQ29	DQ29	Data 29
55	DQ12	DQ12	Data 12
56	DQ30	DQ30	Data 30
57	DQ13	DQ13	Data 13
58	DQ31	DQ31	Data 31
59	VCC	VCC	+5 VDC
60	DQ32	DQ32	Data 32
61	DQ14	DQ14	Data 14
62	DQ33	DQ33	Data 33
63	DQ15	DQ15	Data 15
64	DQ34	DQ34	Data 34
65	DQ16	DQ16	Data 16
66	n/c	n/c	Not connected

TABLE 26-2 PINOUT OF A STANDARD 72-PIN SIMM *(CONTINUED)*

PIN	NON-PARITY	PARITY	DESCRIPTION
67	PD1	PD1	Presence Detect 1
68	PD2	PD2	Presence Detect 2
69	PD3	PD3	Presence Detect 3
70	PD4	PD4	Presence Detect 4
71	n/c	n/c	Not connected
72	VSS	VSS	Ground
Size: (presence detect lines)			
PD2	**PD1**	**Size**	
GND	GND	4 or 64MB	
GND	NC	2 or 32MB	
NC	GND	1 or 16MB	
NC	NC	8MB	
AccessTime: (presence detect lines)			
PD4	**PD3**	**Accesstime**	
GND	GND	50ns, 100ns	
GND	NC	80ns	
NC	GND	70ns	
NC	NC	60ns	

TABLE 26-3 PINOUT OF A 72-PIN ECC SIMM

PIN	ECC	OPTIMIZED	DESCRIPTION
1	VSS	VSS	Ground
2	DQ0	DQ0	Data 0
3	DQ1	DQ1	Data 1
4	DQ2	DQ2	Data 2
5	DQ3	DQ3	Data 3
6	DQ4	DQ4	Data 4
7	DQ5	DQ5	Data 5
8	DQ6	DQ6	Data 6
9	DQ7	DQ7	Data 7
10	VCC	VCC	+5 VDC
11	PD5	PD5	Presence Detect 5
12	A0	A0	Address 0
13	A1	A1	Address 1
14	A2	A2	Address 2
15	A3	A3	Address 3
16	A4	A4	Address 4
17	A5	A5	Address 5

TABLE 26-3 PINOUT OF A 72-PIN ECC SIMM *(CONTINUED)*

PIN	ECC	OPTIMIZED	DESCRIPTION
18	A6	A6	Address 6
19	n/c	n/c	Not connected
20	DQ8	DQ8	Data 8
21	DQ9	DQ9	Data 9
22	DQ10	DQ10	Data 10
23	DQ11	DQ11	Data 11
24	DQ12	DQ12	Data 12
25	DQ13	DQ13	Data 13
26	DQ14	DQ14	Data 14
27	DQ15	DQ15	Data 15
28	A7	A7	Address 7
29	DQ16	DQ16	Data 16
30	VCC	VCC	+5 VDC
31	A8	A8	Address 8
32	A9	A9	Address 9
33	n/c	n/c	Not connected
34	-RAS1	-RAS1	-Row Address Strobe 1
35	DQ17	DQ17	Data 17
36	DQ18	DQ18	Data 18
37	DQ19	DQ19	Data 19
38	DQ20	DQ20	Data 20
39	VSS	VSS	Ground
40	-CAS0	-CAS0	-Column Address Strobe 0
41	A10	A10	Address 10
42	A11	A11	Address 11
43	-CAS1	-CAS1	-Column Address Strobe 1
44	-RAS0	-RAS0	-Row Address Strobe 0
45	-RAS1	-RAS1	-Row Address Strobe 1
46	DQ21	DQ21	Data 21
47	-WE	-WE	Read/-Write
48	-ECC	-ECC	-Error correction control
49	DQ22	DQ22	Data 22
50	DQ23	DQ23	Data 23
51	DQ24	DQ24	Data 24
52	DQ25	DQ25	Data 25
53	DQ26	DQ26	Data 26
54	DQ27	DQ27	Data 27
55	DQ28	DQ28	Data 28
56	DQ29	DQ29	Data 29
57	DQ30	DQ30	Data 30
58	DQ31	DQ31	Data 31

TABLE 26-3 PINOUT OF A 72-PIN ECC SIMM *(CONTINUED)*

PIN	ECC	OPTIMIZED	DESCRIPTION
59	VCC	VCC	+5 VDC
60	DQ32	DQ32	Data 32
61	DQ33	DQ33	Data 33
62	DQ34	DQ34	Data 34
63	DQ35	DQ35	Data 35
64	n/c	DQ36	Data 36
65	n/c	DQ37	Data 37
66	n/c	DQ38	Data 38
67	PD1	PD1	Presence Detect 1
68	PD2	PD2	Presence Detect 2
69	PD3	PD3	Presence Detect 3
70	PD4	PD4	Presence Detect 4
71	n/c	DQ39	Data 39
72	VSS	VSS	Ground

You'll also find such structures referred to as DIMMs (or Dual In-Line Memory Modules). DIMMs appear to be virtually identical to SIMMs, but they are physically *larger*. And where each electrical contact on the SIMM is tied together between the front and back, the DIMM keeps front and back contacts separate—effectively doubling the number of contacts available on the device. For example, if you look at a 72-pin SIMM, you will see 72 electrical contacts on both sides of the device (144 contacts total)—but these are tied together, so there are only 72 signals (even with 144 contacts). On the other hand, a DIMM keeps the front and back contacts electrically *separate* (and usually adds some additional pins to keep SIMMs and DIMMs from accidentally being mixed). Table 26-4 outlines a 144-pin DIMM. Today, virtually all DIMM versions provide 168-pins (84-pins on each side). DIMMs first appeared in high-end 64-bit data bus PCs (such as Pentium, PentiumPro, and PowerPC RISC workstations). As PCs have continued to advance, DIMMs have almost completely replaced SIMMs as the preferred memory expansion device. Table 26-5 lists the pinout for an unbuffered DRAM DIMM, while Table 26-6 presents the pinout for an unbuffered SDRAM DIMM.

TABLE 26-4 PINOUT FOR AN OLDER 144-PIN SMALL-OUTLINE (SO) DIMM

PIN	NORMAL	ECC	DESCRIPTION
1	VSS	VSS	Ground
2	VSS	VSS	Ground
3	DQ0	DQ0	Data 0
4	DQ32	DQ32	Data 32
5	DQ1	DQ1	Data 1
6	DQ33	DQ33	Data 33
7	DQ2	DQ2	Data 2
8	DQ34	DQ34	Data 34

TABLE 26-4 PINOUT FOR AN OLDER 144-PIN SMALL-OUTLINE (SO) DIMM *(CONTINUED)*

PIN	NORMAL	ECC	DESCRIPTION
9	DQ3	DQ3	Data 3
10	DQ35	DQ35	Data 35
11	VCC	VCC	+5 VDC
12	VCC	VCC	+5 VDC
13	DQ4	DQ4	Data 4
14	DQ36	DQ36	Data 36
15	DQ5	DQ5	Data 5
16	DQ37	DQ37	Data 37
17	DQ6	DQ6	Data 6
18	DQ38	DQ38	Data 38
19	DQ7	DQ7	Data 7
20	DQ39	DQ39	Data 39
21	VSS	VSS	Ground
22	VSS	VSS	Ground
23	-CAS0	-CAS0	-Column Address Strobe 0
24	-CAS4	-CAS4	-Column Address Strobe 4
25	-CAS1	-CAS1	-Column Address Strobe 1
26	-CAS5	-CAS5	-Column Address Strobe 5
27	VCC	VCC	+5 VDC
28	VCC	VCC	+5 VDC
29	A0	A0	Address 0
30	A3	A3	Address 3
31	A1	A1	Address 1
32	A4	A4	Address 4
33	A2	A2	Address 2
34	A5	A5	Address 5
35	VSS	VSS	Ground
36	VSS	VSS	Ground
37	DQ8	DQ8	Data 8
38	DQ40	DQ40	Data 40
39	DQ9	DQ9	Data 9
40	DQ41	DQ41	Data 41
41	DQ10	DQ10	Data 10
42	DQ42	DQ42	Data 42
43	DQ11	DQ11	Data 11
44	DQ43	DQ43	Data 43
45	VCC	VCC	+5 VDC
46	VCC	VCC	+5 VDC
47	DQ12	DQ12	Data 12
48	DQ44	DQ44	Data 44
49	DQ13	DQ13	Data 13
50	DQ45	DQ45	Data 45

TABLE 26-4 PINOUT FOR AN OLDER 144-PIN SMALL-OUTLINE (SO) DIMM *(CONTINUED)*

PIN	NORMAL	ECC	DESCRIPTION
51	DQ14	DQ14	Data 14
52	DQ46	DQ46	Data 46
53	DQ15	DQ15	Data 15
54	DQ47	DQ47	Data 47
55	VSS	VSS	Ground
56	VSS	VSS	Ground
57	n/c	CB0	
58	n/c	CB4	
59	n/c	CB1	
60	n/c	CB5	
61	DU	DU	Don't use
62	DU	DU	Don't use
63	VCC	VCC	+5 VDC
64	VCC	VCC	+5 VDC
65	DU	DU	Don't use
66	DU	DU	Don't use
67	-WE	-WE	Read/-Write
68	n/c	n/c	Not connected
69	-RAS0	-RAS0	-Row Address Strobe 0
70	n/c	n/c	Not connected
71	-RAS1	-RAS1	-Row Address Strobe 1
72	n/c	n/c	Not connected
73	-OE	-OE	-Output Enable
74	n/c	n/c	Not connected
75	VSS	VSS	Ground
76	VSS	VSS	Ground
77	n/c	CB2	
78	n/c	CB6	
79	n/c	CB3	
80	n/c	CB7	
81	VCC	VCC	+5 VDC
82	VCC	VCC	+5 VDC
83	DQ16	DQ16	Data 16
84	DQ48	DQ48	Data 48
85	DQ17	DQ17	Data 17
86	DQ49	DQ49	Data 49
87	DQ18	DQ18	Data 18
88	DQ50	DQ50	Data 50
89	DQ19	DQ19	Data 19
90	DQ51	DQ51	Data 51
91	VSS	VSS	Ground
92	VSS	VSS	Ground

TABLE 26-4 PINOUT FOR AN OLDER 144-PIN SMALL-OUTLINE (SO) DIMM *(CONTINUED)*

PIN	NORMAL	ECC	DESCRIPTION
93	DQ20	DQ20	Data 20
94	DQ52	DQ52	Data 52
95	DQ21	DQ21	Data 21
96	DQ53	DQ53	Data 53
97	DQ22	DQ22	Data 22
98	DQ54	DQ54	Data 54
99	DQ23	DQ23	Data 23
100	DQ55	DQ55	Data 55
101	VCC	VCC	+5 VDC
102	VCC	VCC	+5 VDC
103	A6	A6	Address 6
104	A7	A7	Address 7
105	A8	A8	Address 8
106	A11	A11	Address 11
107	VSS	VSS	Ground
108	VSS	VSS	Ground
109	A9	A9	Address 9
110	A12	A12	Address 12
111	A10	A10	Address 10
112	A13	A13	Address 13
113	VCC	VCC	+5 VDC
114	VCC	VCC	+5 VDC
115	-CAS2	-CAS2	-Column Address Strobe 2
116	-CAS6	-CAS6	-Column Address Strobe 6
117	-CAS3	-CAS3	-Column Address Strobe 3
118	-CAS7	-CAS7	-Column Address Strobe 7
119	VSS	VSS	Ground
120	VSS	VSS	Ground
121	DQ24	DQ24	Data 24
122	DQ56	DQ56	Data 56
123	DQ25	DQ25	Data 25
124	DQ57	DQ57	Data 57
125	DQ26	DQ26	Data 26
126	DQ58	DQ58	Data 58
127	DQ27	DQ27	Data 27
128	DQ59	DQ59	Data 59
129	VCC	VCC	+5 VDC
130	VCC	VCC	+5 VDC
131	DQ28	DQ28	Data 28
132	DQ60	DQ60	Data 60
133	DQ29	DQ29	Data 29
134	DQ61	DQ61	Data 61

TABLE 26-4 PINOUT FOR AN OLDER 144-PIN SMALL-OUTLINE (SO) DIMM *(CONTINUED)*

PIN	NORMAL	ECC	DESCRIPTION
135	DQ30	DQ30	Data 30
136	DQ62	DQ62	Data 62
137	DQ31	DQ31	Data 31
138	DQ63	DQ63	Data 63
139	VSS	VSS	Ground
140	VSS	VSS	Ground
141	SDA	SDA	
142	SCL	SCL	
143	VCC	VCC	+5 VDC
144	VCC	VCC	+5 VDC

TABLE 26-5 PINOUT OF A 168-PIN UNBUFFERED DRAM DIMM

PIN	NON-PARITY	PARITY	72 ECC	80 ECC	DESCRIPTION
1	VSS	VSS	VSS	VSS	Ground
2	DQ0	DQ0	DQ0	DQ0	Data 0
3	DQ1	DQ1	DQ1	DQ1	Data 1
4	DQ2	DQ2	DQ2	DQ2	Data 2
5	DQ3	DQ3	DQ3	DQ3	Data 3
6	VCC	VCC	VCC	VCC	+5 VDC or +3.3 VDC
7	DQ4	DQ4	DQ4	DQ4	Data 4
8	DQ5	DQ5	DQ5	DQ5	Data 5
9	DQ6	DQ6	DQ6	DQ6	Data 6
10	DQ7	DQ7	DQ7	DQ7	Data 7
11	DQ8	DQ8	DQ8	DQ8	Data 8
12	VSS	VSS	VSS	VSS	Ground
13	DQ9	DQ9	DQ9	DQ9	Data 9
14	DQ10	DQ10	DQ10	DQ10	Data 10
15	DQ11	DQ11	DQ11	DQ11	Data 11
16	DQ12	DQ12	DQ12	DQ12	Data 12
17	DQ13	DQ13	DQ13	DQ13	Data 13
18	VCC	VCC	VCC	VCC	+5 VDC or +3.3 VDC
19	DQ14	DQ14	DQ14	DQ14	Data 14
20	DQ15	DQ15	DQ15	DQ15	Data 15
21	n/c	CB0	CB0	CB0	Parity/Check Bit Input/Output 0
22	n/c	CB1	CB1	CB1	Parity/Check Bit Input/Output 1
23	VSS	VSS	VSS	VSS	Ground
24	n/c	n/c	n/c	CB8	Parity/Check Bit Input/Output 8
25	n/c	n/c	n/c	CB9	Parity/Check Bit Input/Output 9
26	VCC	VCC	VCC	VCC	+5 VDC or +3.3 VDC
27	-WE0	-WE0	-WE0	-WE0	Read/-Write Input

TABLE 26-5 PINOUT OF A 168-PIN UNBUFFERED DRAM DIMM *(CONTINUED)*

PIN	NON-PARITY	PARITY	72 ECC	80 ECC	DESCRIPTION
28	-CAS0	-CAS0	-CAS0	-CAS0	-Column Address Strobe 0
29	-CAS1	-CAS1	-CAS1	-CAS1	-Column Address Strobe 1
30	-RAS0	-RAS0	-RAS0	-RAS0	-Row Address Strobe 0
31	-OE0	-OE0	-OE0	-OE0	-Output Enable
32	VSS	VSS	VSS	VSS	Ground
33	A0	A0	A0	A0	Address 0
34	A2	A2	A2	A2	Address 2
35	A4	A4	A4	A4	Address 4
36	A6	A6	A6	A6	Address 6
37	A8	A8	A8	A8	Address 8
38	A10	A10	A10	A10	Address 10
39	A12	A12	A12	A12	Address 12
40	VCC	VCC	VCC	VCC	+5 VDC or +3.3 VDC
41	VCC	VCC	VCC	VCC	+5 VDC or +3.3 VDC
42	DU	DU	DU	DU	Don't Use
43	VSS	VSS	VSS	VSS	Ground
44	-OE2	-OE2	-OE2	-OE2	-Output Enable 2
45	-RAS2	-RAS2	-RAS2	-RAS2	-Row Address Strobe 2
46	-CAS2	-CAS2	-CAS2	-CAS2	-Column Address Strobe 2
47	-CAS3	-CAS3	-CAS3	-CAS3	-Column Address Strobe 3
48	-WE2	-WE2	-WE2	-WE2	Read/-Write Input 2
49	VCC	VCC	VCC	VCC	+5 VDC or +3.3 VDC
50	n/c	n/c	n/c	CB10	Parity/Check Bit Input/Output 10
51	n/c	n/c	n/c	CB11	Parity/Check Bit Input/Output 11
52	n/c	CB2	CB2	CB2	Parity/Check Bit Input/Output 2
53	n/c	CB3	CB3	CB3	Parity/Check Bit Input/Output 3
54	VSS	VSS	VSS	VSS	Ground
55	DQ16	DQ16	DQ16	DQ16	Data 16
56	DQ17	DQ17	DQ17	DQ17	Data 17
57	DQ18	DQ18	DQ18	DQ18	Data 18
58	DQ19	DQ19	DQ19	DQ19	Data 19
59	VCC	VCC	VCC	VCC	+5 VDC or +3.3 VDC
60	DQ20	DQ20	DQ20	DQ20	Data 20
61	n/c	n/c	n/c	n/c	Not connected
62	DU	DU	DU	DU	Don't Use
63	n/c	n/c	n/c	n/c	Not connected
64	VSS	VSS	VSS	VSS	Ground
65	DQ21	DQ21	DQ21	DQ21	Data 21
66	DQ22	DQ22	DQ22	DQ22	Data 22
67	DQ23	DQ23	DQ23	DQ23	Data 23
68	VSS	VSS	VSS	VSS	Ground
69	DQ24	DQ24	DQ24	DQ24	Data 24

TABLE 26-5 PINOUT OF A 168-PIN UNBUFFERED DRAM DIMM *(CONTINUED)*

PIN	NON-PARITY	PARITY	72 ECC	80 ECC	DESCRIPTION
70	DQ25	DQ25	DQ25	DQ25	Data 25
71	DQ26	DQ26	DQ26	DQ26	Data 26
72	DQ27	DQ27	DQ27	DQ27	Data 27
73	VCC	VCC	VCC	VCC	+5 VDC or +3.3 VDC
74	DQ28	DQ28	DQ28	DQ28	Data 28
75	DQ29	DQ29	DQ29	DQ29	Data 29
76	DQ30	DQ30	DQ30	DQ30	Data 30
77	DQ31	DQ31	DQ31	DQ31	Data 31
78	VSS	VSS	VSS	VSS	Ground
79	n/c	n/c	n/c	n/c	Not connected
80	n/c	n/c	n/c	n/c	Not connected
81	n/c	n/c	n/c	n/c	Not connected
82	SDA	SDA	SDA	SDA	Serial Data
83	SCL	SCL	SCL	SCL	Serial Clock
84	VCC	VCC	VCC	VCC	+5 VDC or +3.3 VDC
85	VSS	VSS	VSS	VSS	Ground
86	DQ32	DQ32	DQ32	DQ32	Data 32
87	DQ33	DQ33	DQ33	DQ33	Data 33
88	DQ34	DQ34	DQ34	DQ34	Data 34
89	DQ35	DQ35	DQ35	DQ35	Data 35
90	VCC	VCC	VCC	VCC	+5 VDC or +3.3 VDC
91	DQ36	DQ36	DQ36	DQ36	Data 36
92	DQ37	DQ37	DQ37	DQ37	Data 37
93	DQ38	DQ38	DQ38	DQ38	Data 38
94	DQ39	DQ39	DQ39	DQ39	Data 39
95	DQ40	DQ40	DQ40	DQ40	Data 40
96	VSS	VSS	VSS	VSS	Ground
97	DQ41	DQ41	DQ41	DQ41	Data 41
98	DQ42	DQ42	DQ42	DQ42	Data 42
99	DQ43	DQ43	DQ43	DQ43	Data 43
100	DQ44	DQ44	DQ44	DQ44	Data 44
101	DQ45	DQ45	DQ45	DQ45	Data 45
102	VCC	VCC	VCC	VCC	+5 VDC or +3.3 VDC
103	DQ46	DQ46	DQ46	DQ46	Data 46
104	DQ47	DQ47	DQ47	DQ47	Data 47
105	n/c	CB4	CB4	CB4	Parity/Check Bit Input/Output 4
106	n/c	CB5	CB5	CB5	Parity/Check Bit Input/Output 5
107	VSS	VSS	VSS	VSS	Ground
108	n/c	n/c	n/c	CB12	Parity/Check Bit Input/Output 12
109	n/c	n/c	n/c	CB13	Parity/Check Bit Input/Output 13
110	VCC	VCC	VCC	VCC	+5 VDC or +3.3 VDC
111	DU	DU	DU	DU	Don't Use

TABLE 26-5 PINOUT OF A 168-PIN UNBUFFERED DRAM DIMM *(CONTINUED)*

PIN	NON-PARITY	PARITY	72 ECC	80 ECC	DESCRIPTION
112	-CAS4	-CAS4	-CAS4	-CAS4	-Column Address Strobe 4
113	-CAS5	-CAS5	-CAS5	-CAS5	-Column Address Strobe 5
114	-RAS1	-RAS1	-RAS1	-RAS1	-Row Address Strobe 1
115	DU	DU	DU	DU	Don't Use
116	VSS	VSS	VSS	VSS	Ground
117	A1	A1	A1	A1	Address 1
118	A3	A3	A3	A3	Address 3
119	A5	A5	A5	A5	Address 5
120	A7	A7	A7	A7	Address 7
121	A9	A9	A9	A9	Address 9
122	A11	A11	A11	A11	Address 11
123	A13	A13	A13	A13	Address 13
124	VCC	VCC	VCC	VCC	+5 VDC or +3.3 VDC
125	DU	DU	DU	DU	Don't Use
126	DU	DU	DU	DU	Don't Use
127	VSS	VSS	VSS	VSS	Ground
128	DU	DU	DU	DU	Don't Use
129	-RAS3	-RAS3	-RAS3	-RAS3	-Column Address Strobe 3
130	-CAS6	-CAS6	-CAS6	-CAS6	-Column Address Strobe 6
131	-CAS7	-CAS7	. -CAS7	-CAS7	-Column Address Strobe 7
132	DU	DU	DU	DU	Don't Use
133	VCC	VCC	VCC	VCC	+5 VDC or +3.3 VDC
134	n/c	n/c	n/c	CB14	Parity/Check Bit Input/Output 14
135	n/c	n/c	n/c	CB15	Parity/Check Bit Input/Output 15
136	n/c	CB6	CB6	CB6	Parity/Check Bit Input/Output 6
137	n/c	CB7	CB7	CB7	Parity/Check Bit Input/Output 7
138	VSS	VSS	VSS	VSS	Ground
139	DQ48	DQ48	DQ48	DQ48	Data 48
140	DQ49	DQ49	DQ49	DQ49	Data 49
141	DQ50	DQ50	DQ50	DQ50	Data 50
142	DQ51	DQ51	DQ51	DQ51	Data 51
143	VCC	VCC	VCC	VCC	+5 VDC or +3.3 VDC
144	DQ52	DQ52	DQ52	DQ52	Data 52
145	n/c	n/c	n/c	n/c	Not connected
146	DU	DU	DU	DU	Don't Use
147	n/c	n/c	n/c	n/c	Not connected
148	VSS	VSS	VSS	VSS	Ground
149	DQ53	DQ53	DQ53	DQ53	Data 53
150	DQ54	DQ54	DQ54	DQ54	Data 54
151	DQ55	DQ55	DQ55	DQ55	Data 55
152	VSS	VSS	VSS	VSS	Ground
153	DQ56	DQ56	DQ56	DQ56	Data 56

TABLE 26-5 PINOUT OF A 168-PIN UNBUFFERED DRAM DIMM *(CONTINUED)*

PIN	NON-PARITY	PARITY	72 ECC	80 ECC	DESCRIPTION
154	DQ57	DQ57	DQ57	DQ57	Data 57
155	DQ58	DQ58	DQ58	DQ58	Data 58
156	DQ59	DQ59	DQ59	DQ59	Data 59
157	VCC	VCC	VCC	VCC	+5 VDC or +3.3 VDC
158	DQ60	DQ60	DQ60	DQ60	Data 60
159	DQ61	DQ61	DQ61	DQ61	Data 61
160	DQ62	DQ62	DQ62	DQ62	Data 62
161	DQ63	DQ63	DQ63	DQ63	Data 63
162	VSS	VSS	VSS	VSS	Ground
163	CK3	CK3	CK3	CK3	
164	n/c	n/c	n/c	n/c	Not connected
165	SA0	SA0	SA0	SA0	Serial Address 0
166	SA1	SA1	SA1	SA1	Serial Address 1
167	SA2	SA2	SA2	SA2	Serial Address 2
168	VCC	VCC	VCC	VCC	+5 VDC or +3.3 VDC

TABLE 26-6 PINOUT OF A 168-PIN UNBUFFERED SDRAM DIMM

PIN	NON-PARITY	72 ECC	80 ECC	DESCRIPTION
1	VSS	VSS	VSS	Ground
2	DQ0	DQ0	DQ0	Data 0
3	DQ1	DQ1	DQ1	Data 1
4	DQ2	DQ2	DQ2	Data 2
5	DQ3	DQ3	DQ3	Data 3
6	VDD	VDD	VDD	+5 VDC or +3.3 VDC
7	DQ4	DQ4	DQ4	Data 4
8	DQ5	DQ5	DQ5	Data 5
9	DQ6	DQ6	DQ6	Data 6
10	DQ7	DQ7	DQ7	Data 7
11	DQ8	DQ8	DQ8	Data 8
12	VSS	VSS	VSS	Ground
13	DQ9	DQ9	DQ9	Data 9
14	DQ10	DQ10	DQ10	Data 10
15	DQ11	DQ11	DQ11	Data 11
16	DQ12	DQ12	DQ12	Data 12
17	DQ13	DQ13	DQ13	Data 13
18	VDD	VDD	VDD	+5 VDC or +3.3 VDC
19	DQ14	DQ14	DQ14	Data 14
20	DQ15	DQ15	DQ15	Data 15
21	n/c	CB0	CB0	Parity/Check Bit Input/Output 0

TABLE 26-6 PINOUT OF A 168-PIN UNBUFFERED SDRAM DIMM *(CONTINUED)*

PIN	NON-PARITY	72 ECC	80 ECC	DESCRIPTION
22	n/c	CB1	CB1	Parity/Check Bit Input/Output 1
23	VSS	VSS	VSS	Ground
24	n/c	n/c	CB8	Parity/Check Bit Input/Output 8
25	n/c	n/c	CB9	Parity/Check Bit Input/Output 9
26	VDD	VDD	VDD	+5 VDC or +3.3 VDC
27	-WE	-WE	-WE	Read/-Write
28	DQMB0	DQMB0	DQMB0	Byte Mask signal 0
29	DQMB1	DQMB1	DQMB1	Byte Mask signal 1
30	-S0	-S0	-S0	-Chip Select 0
31	DU	DU	DU	Don't Use
32	VSS	VSS	VSS	Ground
33	A0	A0	A0	Address 0
34	A2	A2	A2	Address 2
35	A4	A4	A4	Address 4
36	A6	A6	A6	Address 6
37	A8	A8	A8	Address 8
38	A10/AP	A10/AP	A10/AP	Address 10
39	BA1	BA1	BA1	Bank Address 1
40	VDD	VDD	VDD	+5 VDC or +3.3 VDC
41	VDD	VDD	VDD	+5 VDC or +3.3 VDC
42	CK0	CK0	CK0	Clock signal 0
43	VSS	VSS	VSS	Ground
44	DU	DU	DU	Don't Use
45	-S2	-S2	-S2	-Chip Select 2
46	DQMB2	DQMB2	DQMB2	Byte Mask signal 2
47	DQMB3	DQMB3	DQMB3	Byte Mask signal 3
48	DU	DU	DU	Don't Use
49	VDD	VDD	VDD	+5 VDC or +3.3 VDC
50	n/c	n/c	CB10	Parity/Check Bit Input/Output 10
51	n/c	n/c	CB11	Parity/Check Bit Input/Output 11
52	n/c	CB2	CB2	Parity/Check Bit Input/Output 2
53	n/c	CB3	CB3	Parity/Check Bit Input/Output 3
54	VSS	VSS	VSS	Ground
55	DQ16	DQ16	DQ16	Data 16
56	DQ17	DQ17	DQ17	Data 17
57	DQ18	DQ18	DQ18	Data 18
58	DQ19	DQ19	DQ19	Data 19
59	VDD	VDD	VDD	+5 VDC or +3.3 VDC
60	DQ20	DQ20	DQ20	Data 20
61	n/c	n/c	n/c	Not connected
62	Vref,NC	Vref,NC	Vref,NC	
63	CKE1	CKE1	CKE1	Clock Enable Signal 1

TABLE 26-6 PINOUT OF A 168-PIN UNBUFFERED SDRAM DIMM *(CONTINUED)*

PIN	NON-PARITY	72 ECC	80 ECC	DESCRIPTION
64	VSS	VSS	VSS	Ground
65	DQ21	DQ21	DQ21	Data 21
66	DQ22	DQ22	DQ22	Data 22
67	DQ23	DQ23	DQ23	Data 23
68	VSS	VSS	VSS	Ground
69	DQ24	DQ24	DQ24	Data 24
70	DQ25	DQ25	DQ25	Data 25
71	DQ26	DQ26	DQ26	Data 26
72	DQ27	DQ27	DQ27	Data 27
73	VDD	VDD	VDD	+5 VDC or +3.3 VDC
74	DQ28	DQ28	DQ28	Data 28
75	DQ29	DQ29	DQ29	Data 29
76	DQ30	DQ30	DQ30	Data 30
77	DQ31	DQ31	DQ31	Data 31
78	VSS	VSS	VSS	Ground
79	CK2	CK2	CK2	Clock signal 2
80	n/c	n/c	n/c	Not connected
81	n/c	n/c	n/c	Not connected
82S	DAS	DAS	DAS	Serial Data
83S	CLS	CLS	CLS	Serial Clock
84	VDD	VDD	VDD	+5 VDC or +3.3 VDC
85	VSS	VSS	VSS	Ground
86	DQ32	DQ32	DQ32	Data 32
87	DQ33	DQ33	DQ33	Data 33
88	DQ34	DQ34	DQ34	Data 34
89	DQ35	DQ35	DQ35	Data 35
90	VDD	VDD	VDD	+5 VDC or +3.3 VDC
91	DQ36	DQ36	DQ36	Data 36
92	DQ37	DQ37	DQ37	Data 37
93	DQ38	DQ38	DQ38	Data 38
94	DQ39	DQ39	DQ39	Data 39
95	DQ40	DQ40	DQ40	Data 40
96	VSS	VSS	VSS	Ground
97	DQ41	DQ41	DQ41	Data 41
98	DQ42	DQ42	DQ42	Data 42
99	DQ43	DQ43	DQ43	Data 43
100	DQ44	DQ44	DQ44	Data 44
101	DQ45	DQ45	DQ45	Data 45
102	VDD	VDD	VDD	+5 VDC or +3.3 VDC
103	DQ46	DQ46	DQ46	Data 46
104	DQ47	DQ47	DQ47	Data 47
105	n/c	CB4	CB4	Parity/Check Bit Input/Output 4

TABLE 26-6 PINOUT OF A 168-PIN UNBUFFERED SDRAM DIMM *(CONTINUED)*

PIN	NON-PARITY	72 ECC	80 ECC	DESCRIPTION
106	n/c	CB5	CB5	Parity/Check Bit Input/Output 5
107	VSS	VSS	VSS	Ground
108	n/c	n/c	CB12	Parity/Check Bit Input/Output 12
109	n/c	n/c	CB13	Parity/Check Bit Input/Output 13
110	VDD	VDD	VDD	+5 VDC or +3.3 VDC
111	-CAS	-CAS	-CAS	-Column Address Strobe
112	DQMB4	DQMB4	DQMB4	Byte Mask signal 4
113	DQMB5	DQMB5	DQMB5	Byte Mask signal 5
114	-S1	-S1	-S1	-Chip Select 1
115	-RAS	-RAS	-RAS	-Row Address Strobe
116	VSS	VSS	VSS	Ground
117	A1	A1	A1	Address 1
118	A3	A3	A3	Address 3
119	A5	A5	A5	Address 5
120	A7	A7	A7	Address 7
121	A9	A9	A9	Address 9
122	BA0	BA0	BA0	Bank Address 0
123	A11	A11	A11	Address 11
124	VDD	VDD	VDD	+5 VDC or +3.3 VDC
125	CK1	CK1	CK1	Clock signal 1
126	A12	A12	A12	Address 12
127	VSS	VSS	VSS	Ground
128	CKE0	CKE0	CKE0	Clock Enable Signal 0
129	-S3	-S3	-S3	-Chip Select 3
130	DQMB6	DQMB6	DQMB6	Byte Mask signal 6
131	DQMB7	DQMB7	DQMB7	Byte Mask signal 7
132	A13	A13	A13	Address 13
133	VDD	VDD	VDD	+5 VDC or +3.3 VDC
134	n/c	n/c	CB14	Parity/Check Bit Input/Output 14
135	n/c	n/c	CB15	Parity/Check Bit Input/Output 15
136	n/c	CB6	CB6	Parity/Check Bit Input/Output 6
137	n/c	CB7	CB7	Parity/Check Bit Input/Output 7
138	VSS	VSS	VSS	Ground
139	DQ48	DQ48	DQ48	Data 48
140	DQ49	DQ49	DQ49	Data 49
141	DQ50	DQ50	DQ50	Data 50
142	DQ51	DQ51	DQ51	Data 51
143	VDD	VDD	VDD	+5 VDC or +3.3 VDC
144	DQ52	DQ52	DQ52	Data 52
145	n/c	n/c	n/c	Not connected
146	Vref,NC	Vref,NC	Vref,NC	
147	n/c	n/c	n/c	Not connected

TABLE 26-6 PINOUT OF A 168-PIN UNBUFFERED SDRAM DIMM *(CONTINUED)*

PIN	NON-PARITY	72 ECC	80 ECC	DESCRIPTION
148	VSS	VSS	VSS	Ground
149	DQ53	DQ53	DQ53	Data 53
150	DQ54	DQ54	DQ54	Data 54
151	DQ55	DQ55	DQ55	Data 55
152	VSS	VSS	VSS	Ground
153	DQ56	DQ56	DQ56	Data 56
154	DQ57	DQ57	DQ57	Data 57
155	DQ58	DQ58	DQ58	Data 58
156	DQ59	DQ59	DQ59	Data 59
157	VDD	VDD	VDD	+5 VDC or +3.3 VDC
158	DQ60	DQ60	DQ60	Data 60
159	DQ61	DQ61	DQ61	Data 61
160	DQ62	DQ62	DQ62	Data 62
161	DQ63	DQ63	DQ63	Data 63
162	VSS	VSS	VSS	Ground
163	CK3	CK3	CK3	Clock signal 3
164	n/c	n/c	n/c	Not connected
165	SA0	SA0	SA0	Serial address 0
166	SA1	SA1	SA1	Serial address 1
167	SA2	SA2	SA2	Serial address 2
168	VDD	VDD	VDD	+5 VDC or +3.3 VDC

Finally, you may see SIMMs and DIMMs referred to as "composite" or "non-composite" modules. These terms are used infrequently to describe the technology level of the memory module. For example, a *composite* module uses older, lower-density memory, so more ICs are needed to achieve the required storage capacity. Conversely, a *non-composite* module uses newer memory technology, so fewer ICs are needed to reach the same storage capacity. In other words, if you encounter a high-density SIMM with only a few ICs on it, chances are that the SIMM is non-composite.

Memory Organization

The memory in your computer represents the result of evolution over several computer generations. Memory access and timing support is taken care of by your system's microprocessor and chipset. So as CPUs and chipsets have improved, so also have memory handling capabilities. Today's microprocessors (such as the Intel Pentium Pro, Pentium II, and Pentium III) are capable of addressing more than 4GB of system memory—well beyond the levels of contemporary software applications. Unfortunately, the early PCs were not nearly so powerful. Older PCs could only address 1MB of memory because of limitations of the 8088 microprocessor.

Since backward compatibility is so important to computer users, the drawbacks and limitations of older systems had to be carried *forward* into newer computers instead of being eliminated. Newer systems overcome their inherent limitations by adding different "types" of memory, along with the hardware and software needed to access the memory. The next part of the chapter describes the typical classifications of computer memory: conventional, extended, and expanded memory. There will also be a description of high memory. Note that these memory types do not refer to the actual memory chips in your system, but to the way in which system software *uses* the memory.

CONVENTIONAL MEMORY

Conventional memory is the traditional 640KB assigned to the DOS Memory Area (10000h to 9FFFFh, as shown in Figure 26-4). The original PCs used microprocessors that could address only 1MB of memory (called *real-mode memory* or *base memory*). Out of that 1MB, portions of the memory must be set aside for basic system functions. BIOS code, video memory, interrupt vectors, and BIOS data are only some of the areas that require reserved memory. The remaining 640KB became available to load and run your applications, which can be any combination of executable code and data. The original PCs provided only 512KB for the DOS program area, but computer designers quickly learned that another 128KB could be added to the DOS area while still retaining enough memory for overhead functions, so 512KB became 640KB.

Every IBM-compatible PC still provides a 640KB "base memory" range, and most DOS application programs continue to fit within that limit to ensure backward compatibility to older systems. However, the drawbacks to the 8088 CPU were readily apparent: more memory *had* to be added to the computer for its evolution to continue. Yet, memory had to be added in a way that did not interfere with the conventional memory area. Table 26-7 illustrates a comprehensive memory map for a typical PC.

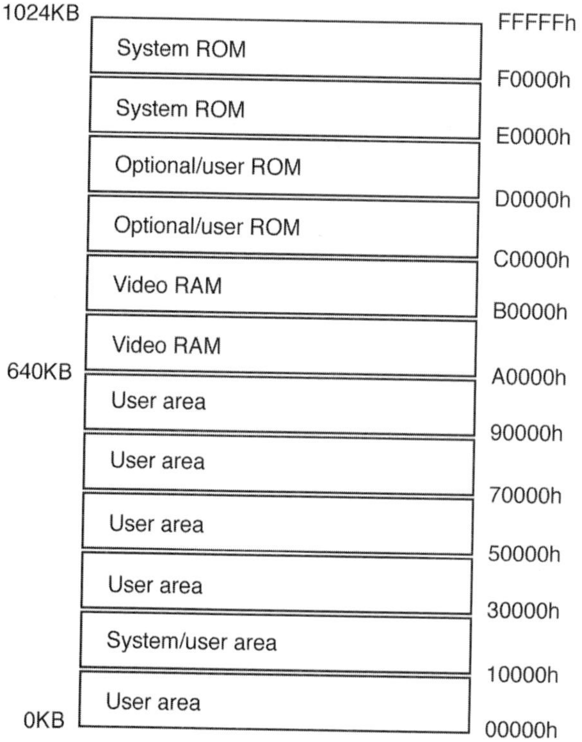

FIGURE 26-4 Conventional and Upper Memory in a Typical PC

TABLE 26-7 REAL-MODE MEMORY MAP OF A TYPICAL PC

ADDRESS RANGE (H)	DESCRIPTION
00000-003FF	**Interrupt Vector Table (256 double words):**
00000	INT 00H Divide by Zero interrupt handler
00004	INT 01H Single Step interrupt handler
00008	INT 02H Non-Maskable Interrupt (memory parity or I/O error)
0000C	INT 03H Breakpoint
00010	INT 04H Arithmetic Overflow interrupt handler
00014	INT 05H Print Screen
00018	INT 06H Reserved
0001C	INT 07H Reserved
00020	INT 08H Timer Interrupt Routine (18.21590 /sec) IRQ0
00024	INT 09H Keyboard Service Routine IRQ1
00028	INT 0AH VGA Retrace (and AT Slave Interrupts) IRQ2
0002C	INT 0BH Serial Device 2 Service Routine IRQ3
00030	INT 0CH Serial Device 1 Service Routine IRQ4
00034	INT 0DH Hard Disk Interrupt Routine IRQ5
00038	INT 0EH Diskette Interrupt Routine IRQ6
0003C	INT 0FH Parallel Port Service Routine IRQ7
00040	INT 10H Video Services
00044	INT 11H Equipment Check
00048	INT 12H Memory Size Check
0004C	INT 13H Diskette and Hard Disk I/O
00050	INT 14H RS-232 Service Call
00054	INT 15H System Services Calls
00058	INT 16H Keyboard Call
0005C	INT 17H Printer I/O Call
00060	INT 18H Basic ROM Entry (startup)
00064	INT 19H Boot Loader: Implement System (IPL) from disk
00068	INT 1AH Time of Day Call
0006C	INT 1BH Keyboard Break Address
00070	INT 1CH User Timer Interrupt
00074	INT 1DH Monitor ROM—for 6845 Video Initialization
00078	INT 1EH Disk Control Table Pointer
0007C	INT 1FH Alphanumeric Character Pattern Table Pointer
00080	INT 20H DOS Terminate Program
00084	INT 21H Microsoft DOS Function Calls
00088	INT 22H DOS Terminate Address (not a callable function)
0008C	INT 23H DOS Ctrl-break Exit Address (not a callable function)
00090	INT 24H DOS Fatal Error Exit Address (not a callable function)
00094	INT 25H DOS Absolute Disk Read
00098	INT 26H DOS Absolute Disk Write
0009C	INT 27H Terminate and Stay Resident (control passes to COMMAND.COM)
000A0	INT 28H Idle Loop, spooler waiting; issued by DOS when waiting
000A4	INT 29H CON Device Raw Output Handler
000A8	INT 2AH 3.x Network Communications
000AC	INT 2BH-2DH Reserved for DOS
000B8	INT 2EH Execute DOS Command (undocumented)

TABLE 26-7 REAL-MODE MEMORY MAP OF A TYPICAL PC *(CONTINUED)*

ADDRESS RANGE (H)	DESCRIPTION
000BC	INT 2FH Print Spool Control (Multiplex Interrupt)
000C0	INT 30H-31H Internal Use
000C8	INT 32H Reserved for DOS
000CC	INT 33H Microsoft Mouse Driver Calls
000D0	INT 34H-3EH Reserved for DOS
000FC	INT 3FH Used by LINK to manage overlay segments
00100	INT 40H Fixed disk/Floppy Disk Handler
00104	INT 41H ROM pointer; Fixed Disk Parameters
00108	INT 42H EGA: Video Vector Screen BIOS Entry
0010C	INT 43H EGA: Initialization Parameters
00100	INT 44H EGA: Graphics Character Patterns
00114	INT 45H Reserved
00118	INT 46H AT: Pointer to Second Fixed Disk Parameters
0011C	INT 47H Reserved
00120	INT 48H PCjr Cordless Keyboard Xlat Routine
00124	INT 49H PCjr Non-Keyboard Scan Code Xlat Table
00128	INT 4AH AT, PS/2 User Alarm Routine
0012C	INT 4BH-4FH Reserved
00140	INT 50H Periodic Alarm Interrupt from Timer
00144	INT 51H-59H Reserved
00168	INT 5AH Cluster Adapter BIOS-entry Address
0016C	INT 5BH Cluster Boot
00170	INT 5CH NETBIOS Entry Point
00174	INT 5DH-5FH Reserved
00180	INT 60H-66H Reserved for user program interrupts
0019C	INT 67H EMM: Expanded Memory Manager Routines
001A0	INT 68H-6BH Unused
001B0	INT 6CH System Resume Vector
001B4	INT 6DH-6FH Unused
001C0	INT 70H Real Time Clock IRQ8
001C4	INT 71H LAN Adapter IRQ9
001C8	INT 72H Reserved IRQ10
001CC	INT 73H Reserved IRQ11
001D0	INT 74H Mouse Interrupt IRQ12
001D4	INT 75H 80287 NMI Error IRQ13
001D8	INT 76H Fixed disk controller IRQ14
001DC	INT 77H Reserved IRQ15
001E0	INT 78H-7FH Unused
00200	INT 80H-85H Reserved for BASIC
00218	INT 86H AT: NetBIOS relocated INT 18H
0021C	INT 87H-F0H Reserved for BASIC Interpreter
003C4	INT F1H-FFH Reserved for User Program Interrupts
003FF	Used for power-on and initial boot stack
00400-004FF	**BIOS Data Area:**
00400	COM1: to COM4: port addresses
00408	LPT1: to LPT3: port addresses
0040E	LPT4: address except PS/2 Reserved

TABLE 26-7 REAL-MODE MEMORY MAP OF A TYPICAL PC *(CONTINUED)*

ADDRESS RANGE (H)	DESCRIPTION
00410	Equipment flag bits: 15-14 number of LPTs attached 13 internal modem (CVT) or reserved 12 joystick 11-9 number of COMs 8 unused (jr: DMS chip present) 7-6 number of disk drives 5 1=80x25 0=40x25 screen 4 1=color 0=monochrome 3-2 00=64K chips; 11=256K chips (PC,XT,AT) 1 math coprocessor installed 0 IPL disk installed
00412	Init Flag; Reserved (CVT self-test status)
00413	Memory size in K bytes
00415	Reserved
00416	Reserved
00417	Keyboard monitor flag bytes 0 and 1: bit: 7 ins lock 7 ins pressed 6 caps lock 6 caps pressed 5 num lock 5 num lock pressed 4 scroll lock 4 scroll pressed 3 alt pressed 3 pause locked 2 crtl pressed 2 sysreq pressed 1 <shift press 1 <alt pressed 0 >shift press 0 >alt pressed
00419	Alternate keypad entry
0041A	Keyboard buffer head pointer
0041C	Keyboard buffer tail pointer
0041E	Keyboard buffer
0043E	Drive recalibration status bit: 7 Interrupt flag 6-4 reserved 3 recalibrate drive 3 2 recalibrate drive 2 1 recalibrate drive 1 0 recalibrate drive 0
0043F	Motor Status bit: 7 Currently reading or writing 6 reserved 5-4 00 drive 0 selected 01 drive 1 selected 10 drive 2 selected 11 drive 3 selected 3-0 Drive 3-0 Motor On status
00440	Motor Control time-out counter

TABLE 26-7 REAL-MODE MEMORY MAP OF A TYPICAL PC *(CONTINUED)*

ADDRESS RANGE (H)	DESCRIPTION
00441	Diskette Status Return Code 00H—No error 01H—Invalid diskette drive parameter 02H—Address Mark not found 03H—Write-protect error 04H—Requested Sector not found 05H—reserved 06H—Diskette Change Line active 07H—reserved 08H—DMA overrun on operation 09H—Attempt to DMA Across a 64K boundary 0AH—reserved 0BH—reserved 0CH—Media Type not found 0DH—reserved 0EH—reserved 0FH—reserved 10H—CRC error on diskette read 20H—General Controller failure 40H—Seek operation failed 80H—Diskette drive not ready
00442	Diskette Drive Controller Status Bytes (NEC)
00449	CRT_MODE bit: 7 text 80x25 mono on mono card 6 graphics 640x200 mono on color card 5 graphics 320x200 mono on color card 4 graphics 320x200 on color card 3 text 80x25 color 2 text 80x25 mono on color 1 text 40x25 color 0 text 40x25 mono on color card
0044A	CRT_COLS Number of columns (80)
0044C	CRT_LEN Length of Regen Buffer in bytes
0044E	CRT_START Starting Address in Regen Buffer
00450	Cursor Position on each of eight pages
00460	CURSOR_MODE top-bottom line of cursor (Cursor Type)
00462	ACTIVE_PAGE index
00463	ADDR_6845 Base Address for 6845 Display Chip 3B4H for monochrome 3D4H for color
00465	CRT_MODE_SETTING for 3x8 Register 3B8H for MDA 3D8H for CGA
00466	CRT_PALLETTE Setting Register (3D9H) on Color Card

26

TABLE 26-7 REAL-MODE MEMORY MAP OF A TYPICAL PC *(CONTINUED)*

ADDRESS RANGE (H)	DESCRIPTION
00467	Temporary storage for SS:SP during shutdown
0046B	Flag to indicate interrupt
0046C	Timer counter (Timer Low, Timer High words)
00470	Timer overflow (24 hour roll over flag byte)
00471	Break key state (bit 7=1 if break key pressed)
00472	Reset flag word: 1234 bypass memory test 4321 preserve memory 5678 system suspend 9ABC manufacturing test ABCD system POST loop (CVT)
00474	Hard Disk status or Reserved for ESDI Adapter/A 00H—No error 01H—Invalid Function Request 02H—Address Mark not found 03H—Write Protect error 04H—Requested Sector not found 05H—Reset Failed 06H—Reserved 07H—Drive Parameter Activity Failed 08H—DMA overrun on operation 09H—Data boundary error 0AH—Bad Sector Flag detected 0BH—Bad Track detected 0CH—Reserved 0DH—Invalid number of sectors on format 0EH—Control Data Address Mark detected 0FH—DMA Arbitration Level out of range 10H—Uncorrectable ECC or CRC error 20H—General Controller failure 40H—Seek operation failed 80H—Time out AAH—Drive not ready BBH—Undefined error occurred CCH—Write fault on selected drive E0H—Status error/Error Register 0 FFH—Sense operation failed
00475	Number of hard disk drives
00476	Fixed Disk Drive Control byte (PC XT)
00477	Fixed Disk Drive Controller Port (PC XT)
00478	LPT1: to LPT4: time-out byte values (PS/2 has no LPT4:)
0047C	COM1: to COM4: timeout byte values
00480	Keyboard buffer start pointer (word)
00482	Keyboard buffer end pointer (word)
00484	ROWS Video Character Rows—1
00485	POINTS Height of character matrix-bytes per character

TABLE 26-7 REAL-MODE MEMORY MAP OF A TYPICAL PC *(CONTINUED)*

ADDRESS RANGE (H)	DESCRIPTION
00487	INFO byte: bit: 7 Video mode number (of INT 10H funct.0) 6-5 Size of video RAM 00-64K 10-192K 01-128K 11-256K 4 reserved 3 (1) video subsystem is inactive 2 reserved 1 (1) video subsystem on monochrome 0 (1) alphanumeric cursor emulation enabled
00488	INFO_3 byte: bit: 7 Input FEAT1 (bit 6 of ISR0 (Input Status Reg.) 6 Input FEAT1 (bit 5 of ISR0) 5 Input FEAT0 (bit 6 of ISR0) 4 Input FEAT0 (bit 5 of ISR0) 3 EGA Config. switch 4 (1=off) 2 EGA Config. switch 3 1 EGA Config. switch 2 0 EGA Config. switch 1
00489	Flags bit: 7 bit 4 Alphanumeric scan lines: 00 350 line mode 01 400 10 200 11 reserved 6 (1) display switching enabled 5 reserved 3 (1) default palette loading is disabled 2 (1) using monochrome monitor 1 (1) gray scale is enabled 0 (1) VGA is active
0048A	DCC Display Combination Code table index (VGA)
0048B	Media Control bit: 7-6 Last diskette drive data rate selected 00—500Kb per second 01—300Kb per second 10—250Kb per second 11—reserved 5-4 Last diskette drive step rate selected 3-0 reserved
0048C	Hard Disk Status Register
0048D	Hard Disk Error Register
0048E	Hard Disk Interrupt Control Flag
0048F	Combination Hard Disk/Floppy Card (bit 0=1)
00490	Drive 0 media state byte
00491	Drive 1 media state byte

26

TABLE 26-7 REAL-MODE MEMORY MAP OF A TYPICAL PC *(CONTINUED)*

ADDRESS RANGE (H)	DESCRIPTION
00492	Drive 2 media state byte
00493	Drive 3 media state byte bit: 7-6 Diskette drive date rate 00–500Kb per second 01–300Kb per second 10–250Kb per second 11–reserved 5 Double stepping required 4 Media established 3 Reserved 2-0 Drive/Media State 000–360Kb diskette/360Kb drive not established 001–360Kb diskette/1.2Mb drive not established 010–1.2Mb diskette/1.2Mb drive not established 011–360Kb diskette/360Kb drive established 100–360Kb diskette/1.2Mb drive established 101–1.2Mb diskette/1.2Mb drive established 110–Reserved 111–None of the above
00494	Drive 0 track currently selected
00495	Drive 1 track currently selected
00496	Keyboard mode state and type flags bit: 7 Read ID in progress 6 Last character was first ID character 5 Force Num Lock if read ID and KBX 4 101/102 keyboard installed 3 Right Alt key pressed 2 Right Ctrl key pressed 1 Last code was E0 hidden code 0 Last code was E1 hidden code
00497	Keyboard LED flags bit: 7 Keyboard transmit error flag 6 Mode indicator update 5 Cancel receive flag 4 Acknowledgment received 3 = 0 reserved 2-0 Keyboard LED state bits
00498	Offset address to user wait complete flag
0049A	Segment to user wait complete flag
0049C	User wait count, microseconds low word
0049E	User wait count, microseconds high word
004A0	Wait active flag bit: 7 wait-time elapse and post flag 6-1 reserved
004A1	LANA DMA channel flags
004A2	LANA 0 status
004A3	LANA 1 status

TABLE 26-7 REAL-MODE MEMORY MAP OF A TYPICAL PC *(CONTINUED)*

ADDRESS RANGE (H)	DESCRIPTION
004A4	Saved hardfile interrupt vector
004A8	BIOS Video Save Table and overrides
004AC	Reserved
004B4	Keyboard NMI control flags (CVT)
004B5	Keyboard break pending flags (CVT)
004B9	Port 60 single byte queue (CVT)
004BA	Scan code of last key (CVT)
004BB	Pointer to NMI buffer head (CVT)
004BC	Pointer to NMI buffer tail (CVT)
004BD	NMI scan code buffer (CVT)
004CE	Day counter (CVT and after)
004D0	Reserved
004F0	Application program communication area
00500-005FF	**DOS Data Area:**
00500	Print screen status flag 1 = printer active 0FFH = printer fault
00501	Reserved for BASIC and POST work area
00504	Single-drive mode status byte 0=drive A 1=drive B
00505	Reserved POST work area
00510	Reserved for BASIC
0050F	BASIC Shell Flag =2 if current shell
00510	BASIC segment address storage set with DEF SEG
00512	BASIC int 1Ch clock interrupt vector
00516	BASIC int 23h ctrl-break interrupt vector
0051A	BASIC int 24h disk error interrupt vector
0051B	BASIC dynamic storage
00520	DOS dynamic storage
00522	Used by DOS for diskette initialization
00530	Used by MODE command
00534	Reserved for DOS data
00600	Reserved for DOS
00700	I/O drivers from xIO.SYS
00847-0FFFF	xIO.SYS IRET for interrupts 1, 3, and 0FH during POST MS-DOS kernel from xDOS.SYS: Interrupt handlers and routines MS-DOS disk buffer cache, FCBs and installable device drivers MCB (Memory control block, 16 bytes, paragraph aligned) Start of Transient Program
10000-9FFFF	**User Data Area (programs and data)**
A0000-AFFFF	Start of EGA and VGA graphics display RAM Modes 0Dh and above
B0000-B3FFF	Start of MDPA and Hercules graphics display RAM
B4000-B7FFF	Reserved for Graphics display RAM
B8000-BBFFF	Start of CGA Color graphics display RAM
BC000-BFFFF	Reserved for Graphics display RAM

26

TABLE 26-7 REAL-MODE MEMORY MAP OF A TYPICAL PC *(CONTINUED)*

ADDRESS RANGE (H)	DESCRIPTION
C0000-C3FFF	EGA BIOS ROM
C4000-C5FFF	Video adapter ROM space
C6000-C63FF	256 bytes of PGA communication area
C6400-C7FFF	Last 7Kb of video adapter ROM space
C8000-CBFFF	16K of hard disk BIOS adapter ROM space
CC000-CFFFF	
D0000-D7FFF	32K cluster adapter BIOS ROM
D8000-DBFFF	
DC000-DFFFF	Last 16Kb of adapter ROM space
E0000-EFFFF	64K expansion ROM space (AT, PS/2)
F0000-F3FFF	System Monitor ROM
F4000-F7FFF	System Expansion ROMs
F8000-FBFFF	
FC000-FEFFF	BIOS ROM, BASIC, and simple BIOS
FF000-FFFEF	System ROM
FFFF0-FFFF3	Hardware boot far jump vector

EXTENDED MEMORY

The 80286 processor introduced in IBM's PC/AT was envisioned to overcome the 640KB barrier by incorporating a *protected-mode* of addressing. The 80286 can address up to 16MB of memory in protected-mode, while its successors (the 80386 and later) can handle 4GB of protected-mode memory. Today, virtually all computer systems provide several MB of *extended memory* (called XMS). Besides an advanced microprocessor, another key element for extended memory is *software*. Memory management software *must* be loaded in advance for the computer to access its extended memory. Microsoft's later DOS versions (up to MS-DOS 6.22) provide an extended memory manager utility (HIMEM.SYS), but there are other off-the-shelf utilities as well—Windows 95/98 supplies its own memory manager tools.

Unfortunately, DOS itself cannot make use of extended memory. You may fill the extended memory area with data, but the executable code comprising the program remains limited to the original 640KB of base memory. Some programs written with DOS extenders can overcome the 640KB limit, but the additional code needed for these DOS extenders can make such programs a bit clunky.

A *DOS extender* is basically a software module containing its own memory management code that is compiled into the final application program. The DOS extender loads a program in real-mode memory. After the program is loaded, it switches program control to the protected-mode memory. When the program in protected mode needs to execute a DOS (real-mode) function, the DOS extender converts protected-mode addresses into real-mode addresses, copies any necessary program data from protected to real-mode locations, switches the CPU to real-mode addressing, and carries out the function. The DOS extender then copies any results (if necessary) back to protected-mode addresses, switches the system to protected mode once again, and the program continues to run. This back-and-forth conversion overhead results in less than optimum performance compared to strictly real-mode programs, or *true* protected-mode programs.

With multiple megabytes of extended memory typically available, it is possible (but unlikely) that any one program will utilize all of the extended memory. Multiple programs that use extended memory must NOT attempt to utilize the same memory locations. If conflicts occur, a catastrophic system crash is almost inevitable. To prevent conflicts in extended memory, memory manager software can make use of three major industry standards: the *Extended Memory Specification* (XMS), the *Virtual Control Program Interface* (VCPI), and the *DOS Protected-Mode Interface* (DPMI). This chapter will not describe these standards, but you should know that they're used.

EXPANDED MEMORY

Expanded memory (or EMS) is another popular technique used to overcome the traditional 640KB limit of real-mode addressing. Expanded memory uses the same "physical" RAM chips, but differs from extended memory in the way that physical memory is used. Instead of trying to address physical memory locations outside of the conventional memory range as extended memory does, expanded memory blocks are switched into the base memory range where the CPU can access it in real-mode. The original expanded memory specification (called the Lotus-Intel-Microsoft: *LIM*, or *EMS* specification) used 16KB blocks of memory that were mapped into a 64KB range of real-mode memory existing just above the video memory range. Thus, four "blocks" of expanded memory could be dealt with simultaneously in the real mode.

Early implementations of expanded memory utilized special expansion boards that switched blocks of memory, but later CPUs that support memory mapping allowed expanded memory managers (EMMs or LIMs) to supply software-only solutions for i386, i486, Pentium, and later machines. EMS/LIM 4.0 is the latest version of the expanded memory standard that handles up to 32MB of memory. An expanded memory manager (such as the DOS utility EMM386.EXE) allows the extended memory sitting in your computer to emulate expanded memory. For most practical purposes, expanded memory is more useful than extended memory because its ability to map directly to the real mode allows support for program multitasking. To use expanded memory, programs must be written specifically to take advantage of the function calls and subroutines needed to switch memory blocks. Functions are completely specified in the LIM/EMS 4.0 standard.

UPPER MEMORY AREA (UMA)

The upper 384KB of real-mode memory is not available to DOS because it is dedicated to handling memory requirements of the physical computer system. This is called the *High DOS Memory Range* or *Upper Memory Area* (UMA). However, even the most advanced PCs do not use the *entire* 384KB, so there is often a substantial amount of unused memory existing in your system's real-mode range. Late model CPUs like the i386 and i486 can remap extended memory into the range unused by your system. Since this "found" memory space is not contiguous with the 640KB DOS space, DOS application programs cannot use the space, but small independent drivers and TSRs *can* be loaded and run from this UMA. The advantage of using this high DOS memory is that more of the 640KB DOS range remains available for your application program. Memory management programs (such as the utilities found with DOS 5.0 and higher) are needed to locate and remap these memory "blocks."

HIGH MEMORY

There is a peculiar anomaly that occurs with CPUs supporting extended memory—they can access one *segment* (about 64KB) of extended memory *beyond* the real-mode area. This capability arises because of the address line layout on late model CPUs. As a result, the real-mode operation can access roughly 64KB *above* the 1MB limit. Like high DOS memory, this "found" 64KB is not contiguous with the normal 640KB DOS memory range, so DOS cannot use this high memory to load a DOS application, but device drivers and TSRs can be placed in high memory. DOS 5.0 is intentionally designed so that its 40-50KB of code can be easily moved into this high memory area. With DOS loaded into high memory, an extra 40-50KB or so will be available within the 640KB DOS range.

Memory Considerations

Memory has become far more important than just a place to store bits for the microprocessor. It has proliferated and specialized to the point where it is difficult to keep track of all the memory options and architectures that are available. This part of the chapter reviews established memory types and explains some of the current memory architectures.

MEMORY SPEED AND WAIT STATES

The PC industry is constantly struggling with the balance between price and performance. Higher prices usually bring higher performance, but low cost makes the PC appealing to more people. In terms of memory, cost-cutting typically involves using cheaper (slower) memory devices. Unfortunately, when slower memory is used, the CPU must be made to wait until memory can catch up. All memory is rated in terms of speed—specifically access time. Access time is the delay from the time data in memory is successfully addressed to the point at which the data has been successfully delivered to the data bus. For PC memory, access time is measured in nanoseconds (ns), and current memory offers access times of 50-60ns. 70ns memory is very common in older i486 systems.

SDRAM is an exception to this rule and is typically rated in terms of cycle time rather than access time. "Cycle time" is the minimum amount of time needed between accesses. Cycle time for SDRAM averages around 12ns, with 10ns, 8ns (and faster) SDRAM devices available.

It is almost always *possible* to use faster memory than the manufacturer recommends. The system should continue to operate normally, but there's rarely ever a performance benefit. As you'll see in the following sections, memory and architectures are typically tailored for specific performance. Using memory that is faster should not hurt the memory or impair system performance, but it costs more and will not produce a noticeable performance improvement—the system is simply not equipped to employ the faster memory to its best advantage. The only time such a tactic would be advised is when your current system is almost obsolete and you would want the new memory to be useable on a new, faster motherboard if you choose to upgrade the motherboard later on.

A *wait state* orders the CPU to pause for one clock cycle in order to give memory additional time to operate. Typical PCs use one wait state, though very old systems may require two or three. The latest PC designs with high-end memory or aggressive caching may be able to operate with no (zero) wait states. As you might imagine, a wait state is basically a waste of time, so more wait states result in lower system performance. Zero wait states allow optimum system performance. Wait states let the system support old, slow memory, but the resulting system performance would be so poor that there would be little point in using the system in the first place.

There are three classic means of selecting wait states. First, the number of wait states may be fixed (common in old XT systems). Second, wait states may be selected with one or more jumpers on the motherboard (typical of i286 and early i386 systems). Third, mid-range and later systems (such as i486, Pentium, and Pentium II/III computers) place the wait state or "memory speed" control in the CMOS

Setup routine. You may have to look in an "advanced settings" area to find the appropriate entry. When optimizing a computer, you should be sure to set the *minimum* number of wait states.

Setting **too few** wait states can cause the PC to behave erratically, or even prevent the system from starting.

DETERMINING MEMORY SPEED

It's often necessary to check SIMMs or DIMMs for proper memory speed (a.k.a. "access time," or "cycle time" for SDRAM) during troubleshooting or when selecting replacement parts. Unfortunately, it can be very difficult to determine memory speed accurately on the basis of part markings. Speeds are normally marked cryptically by adding a number to the end of the part number. For example, a part number ending in -6 often means 60ns, a -7 is usually 70ns, and -8 can be 80ns. SDRAM often uses markings such as -12 for 12ns cycle time, or -10 for 10ns cycle time. Still, the only means of being absolutely certain of the memory speed is to cross-reference the memory part number with a manufacturer's catalog, and then determine the speed from the catalog's description (for example, 4Mx32 50ns EDO).

MEGABYTES AND MEMORY LAYOUT

Now is a good time to explain the idea of "bytes" and "megabytes." Very simply, a *byte* is 8 bits (binary 1s and 0s), and a *megabyte* is one million of those bytes (1,048,576 bytes to be exact—but manufacturers often round down to the nearest million or so). The idea of megabytes (MB) is important when measuring memory in your PC. For example, if a SIMM is laid out as 1M by 8 bits, it has 1MB. If the SIMM is laid out as 4M by 8 bits, it has 4MB. Unfortunately, memory has not been laid out as 8 bits since the IBM XT.

More practical memory layouts involve 32-bit memory (for 486 and OverDrive processors) or 64-bit memory (for Pentium II/III processors). When memory is "wider" than one byte, it is still measured in MB. For example, a 1M x 32-bit (4 bytes) SIMM would be 4MB (that is, the *capacity* of the device is 4MB), while a 4M x 32-bit SIMM would be 16MB. So when you go shopping for an 8MB 72-pin SIMM, chances are you're getting a 2M x 32-bit memory module. Table 26-8 provides an index to help in identifying common 72-pin SIMMs and 168-pin DIMMs based on the number and type of RAM chips on board. You can see the relationship between memory layout and overall capacity. Table 26-9 outlines standard part numbers for common memory modules.

TABLE 26-8 SIMM/DIMM IDENTIFICATION GUIDELINES

168-PIN SYNCHRONOUS DIMMS

TYPE OF COMPONENT	# CHIPS ON BOARD	MODULE TYPE	DIMM CAPACITY
2x8 TSOP SDRAM	8	2MBx64	16MB
2x8 TSOP SDRAM	16	4MBx64	32MB
4x4 TSOP SDRAM	32	8MBx64	64MB
8x8 TSOP SDRAM	8	8MBx64 (Non-composite)	64MB
8x8 TSOP SDRAM	9	8MBx72 (Non-composite)	64MB
8x8 TSOP SDRAM	16	16MBx64 (Non-composite)	128MB
8x8 TSOP SDRAM	18	16MBx72 (Non-composite)	128MB

TABLE 26-8 SIMM/DIMM IDENTIFICATION GUIDELINES *(CONTINUED)*

168-PIN PC DIMMS

TYPE OF COMPONENT	# CHIPS ON BOARD	MODULE TYPE	DIMM CAPACITY
4x4 SOJ/TSOP DRAM	16	4MBx64	32MB
4x4 SOJ/TSOP DRAM	18	4MBx72 ECC	32MB
4x4 SOJ/TSOP DRAM	32	8MBx64	64MB
4x4 SOJ/TSOP DRAM	36	8MBx72 ECC	64MB
8x8 SOJ/TSOP DRAM	16	16MBx64	128MB

72-PIN SIMM MODULES

TYPE OF COMPONENT	# CHIPS ON BOARD	MODULE TYPE	SIMM CAPACITY
1x4 SOJ	8	1MBx32	4MB
1x16 SOJ	2	1MBx32	4MB
1x4 / 1x1 SOJ	8 / 4	1MBx36	4MB
1x4 SOJ	16	2MBx32	8MB
1x16 SOJ	4	2MBx32	8MB
1x4 / 1x1 SOJ	16 / 8	2MBx36	8MB
4x4 SOJ/TSOP	8	4MBx32	16MB
4x4 / 4x1 SOJ/TSOP	8 / 4	4MBx36	16MB
4x4 SOJ	16	8MBx32	32MB
4x4 / 4x1 SOJ	16 / 8	8MBx36	32MB
16x1 SOJ	32	16MBx32	64MB
16x1 SOJ	36	16MBx36	64MB

Legend:
TSOP—Thin Small-Outline Package
SOJ—Small-Outline "J"-lead package
ECC—Error Correction Code (a more powerful form of parity)
x8, x32, x64—non-parity RAM
x9, x36, x72—parity or ECC RAM

TABLE 26-9 TYPICAL PART NUMBERS FOR COMMON MEMORY MODULES

168-PIN STANDARD DIMMS

EDO	ECC BUFFERED	NON-BUFFERED	NON-ECC BUFFERED	NON-BUFFERED
16MB	KTM2x72VN82-60EG	KTM2x72VN44-60EG	----	KTM2x64VN61-60EG
32MB	KTM4x72V82-60EG	KTM4x72VN44-60EG	----	KTM4x64VN42-60EG
64MB	KTM8x72V84-64EG	KTM8x72VN84-60EG	----	KTM8x64VN84-60EG
128MB	KTM16x72V44-60EG	KTM16x72VN84-60EG	----	KTM16x64VN84-60EG
256MB	KTM32x72V44-60EG	----	----	----

TABLE 26-9 TYPICAL PART NUMBERS FOR COMMON MEMORY MODULES *(CONTINUED)*

FPM	ECC BUFFERED	NON-BUFFERED	NON-ECC BUFFERED	NON-BUFFERED
16MB	KTM2x72V82-60G	----	----	----
32MB	KTM4x72V44-60G	----	----	----
64MB	KTM8x72V84-60G	----	----	----
128MB	KTM16x72V48-60G	----	----	----

SDRAM	ECC 66MHZ	100MHZ	NON-ECC 66MHZ	100MHZ
16MB	KTM66x72/16	----	KTM66x64/16	----
32MB	KTM66x72/32	KGM100x72C#/32	KTM66x64/32	KGM100x64C#/32
64MB	KTM66x72/64	KGM100x72C#/64	KTM66x64/64	KGM100x64C#/64
128MB	KTM66x72/128	KGM100x72C#/128	KTM66x64/128	KGM100x64C#/128

NOTE: *FOR 100MHz SDRAM DIMMs, substitute either a 2 or 3 for the # to indicate CAS latency speed. The modules are interchangeable and can be mixed, but the system will run at the slower CAS Latency 3 speed.*

72-PIN STANDARD SIMMS

EDO	60 NANO-SECONDS NON-PARITY	PARITY	NON-PARITY	70 NANO-SECONDS PARITY	
8MB	Tin leads	KTM2x32L-60ET	KTM2x36L-60ET	KTM2x32L-70ET	----
	Gold leads	KTM2x32L-60EG	KTM2x36L-60EG	KTM2x32L-70EG	----
16MB	Tin leads	KTM4x32L-60ET	KTM4x36L-60ET	KTM4x32L-70ET	----
	Gold leads	KTM4x32L-60EG	KTM4x36L-60EG	KTM4x32L-70EG	----
32MB	Tin leads	KTM8x32L-60ET	KTM8x36L-60ET	KTM8x32L-70ET	----
	Gold leads	KTM8x32L-60EG	KTM8x36L-60EG	KTM8x32L-70EG	----
64MB	Tin leads	KTM16x32LA-60ET	-----	----	----
	Gold leads	KTM16x32LA-60EG	----	----	----
128MB	Tin leads	KTM32x32LA-60ET	-----	----	----
	Gold leads	KTM32x32LA-60EG	----	----	----

FPM	60 NANO-SECONDS NON-PARITY	PARITY	NON-PARITY	70 NANO-SECONDS PARITY	
8MB	Tin leads	KTM2x32L-60T	KTM2x36L-60T	KTM2x32L-70T	KTM2x36L-70T
	Gold leads	KTM2x32L-60G	KTM2x36L-60G	KTM2x32L-70G	KTM2x36L-70G
16MB	Tin leads	KTM4x32L-60T	KTM4x36L-60T	KTM4x32L-70T	KTM4x36L-70T
	Gold leads	KTM4x32L-60G	KTM4x36L-60G	KTM4x32L-70G	KTM4x36L-70G
32MB	Tin leads	KTM8x32L-60T	KTM8x36L-60T	KTM8x32L-70T	KTM8x36L-70T
	Gold leads	KTM8x32L-60G	KTM8x36L-60G	KTM8x32L-70G	KTM8x36L-70G
64MB	Tin leads	KTM16x32L-60T	KTM16x36L-60T	KTM16x32L-70T	KTM16x36L-70T
	Gold leads	KTM16x32L-60G	KTM16x36L-60G	KTM16x32L-70G	KTM16x36L-70G
128MB	Tin leads	KTM32x32L-60T	KTM32x36L-60T	----	----
	Gold leads	KTM32x32L-60G	KTM32x36L-60G	----	----

26

PRESENCE DETECT (PD)

Another feature of modern memory devices is a series of physical signals known as the *Presence Detect* lines. By setting the appropriate conditions of the PD signals, it is possible for a computer to immediately recognize the characteristics of the installed memory devices and configure itself accordingly. Presence Detect lines typically specify three operating characteristics of memory: size, device layout, and speed. Table 26-10 highlights many of the most commonly used signal combinations.

UNDERSTANDING MEMORY "REFRESH"

The electrical signals placed in each DRAM storage cell must be replenished (or *refreshed*) every few milliseconds. Without this refresh, DRAM data will be lost. In principle, refresh requires that each storage cell be read and rewritten to the memory array. This is typically accomplished by reading and rewriting an entire row of the array at one time. Each row of bits is sequentially read into a sense/refresh amplifier (part of the DRAM chip), which basically recharges the appropriate storage capacitors, then rewrites each row bit to the array. In actual operation, a row of bits is automatically refreshed whenever an array row is selected—the entire memory array can be refreshed by reading each row in the array every few milliseconds.

The key to refresh is in the *way* DRAM is addressed. Unlike other memory chips that supply all address signals to the IC simultaneously, a DRAM is addressed in a two-step sequence. The overall address is separated into a row (low) address and a column (high) address. Row address bits are placed on the DRAM address bus first, and the -Row Address Select (-RAS) line is pulsed logic 0 to multiplex the bits into the chip's address decoding circuitry. The low portion of the address activates an entire array row and causes each bit in the row to be sensed and refreshed. Logic 0s remain logic 0s, and logic 1s are recharged to their full value.

TABLE 26-10 INDEX OF PRESENCE DETECT (PD) SIGNALS

	72-PIN SIMM	PIN 67 (PD1)	PIN 68 (PD2)	PIN 69 (PD3)	PIN 70 (PD4)	PIN 71 (PD5)
SIZE (parity pinout)	256K x 32/36	GND	N/C	--	--	--
	512K x 32/36	N/C	GND	--	--	--
	1M x 32/36	GND	GND	--	--	--
	2M x 32/36	N/C	N/C	--	--	--
	4M x 32/36	GND	N/C	--	--	N/C
	8M x 32/36	N/C	GND	--	--	N/C
SIZE (ECC pinout)	256K x 32/36	GND	N/C	--	--	N/C
	512K x 32/36	N/C	GND	--	--	N/C
	1M x 32/36	GND	GND	--	--	N/C
	2M x 32/36	N/C	N/C	--	--	N/C
	4M x 32/36	GND	N/C	--	--	GND
	8M x 32/36	N/C	GND	--	--	GND
SPEED (parity/ECC pinout)	60ns	--	--	N/C	N/C	--
	70ns	--	--	GND	N/C	--
	80ns	--	--	N/C	GND	--
	100ns	--	--	GND	GND	--
	120ns	--	--	N/C	N/C	--

GND = Jumper Installed
N/C = No Jumper Installed

Column address bits are then placed on the DRAM address bus, and the -Column Address Select (-CAS) is pulsed to logic 0. The column portion of the address selects the appropriate bits within the chosen row. If a read operation is taking place, the selected bits pass through the data buffer to the data bus. During a write operation, the read/write line must be logic 0, and valid data must be available to the chip before -CAS is strobed. New data bits are then placed in their corresponding locations in the memory array.

Even if the chip is not being accessed for reading or writing, the memory must still be refreshed to ensure data integrity. Fortunately, refresh can be accomplished by interrupting the microprocessor to run a refresh routine that simply steps through every row address in sequence (column addresses need not be selected for simple refresh). This row-only (or –RAS-only) refresh technique speeds the refresh process. Although refreshing DRAM every few milliseconds may seem like a constant aggravation, the computer can execute quite a few instructions before being interrupted for refresh. Refresh operations are generally handled by the chipset on your motherboard. Often, memory problems (especially "parity errors") that cannot be resolved by replacing a SIMM can be traced to a refresh fault on the motherboard.

MEMORY TYPES

In order for a computer to work, the CPU must take program instructions and exchange data directly with memory. As a consequence, memory must keep pace with the CPU (or make the CPU wait for it to catch up). Now that processors are so incredibly fast (and getting faster every few months), traditional memory architectures are being replaced by specialized memory devices that have been tailored to serve specific functions in the PC. As you upgrade and repair various systems, you will undoubtedly encounter some of the memory designations explained in the following sections (listed alphabetically).

BEDO (Burst Extended Data Output RAM) This powerful variation of EDO RAM reads data in a burst, meaning that after a valid address has been provided, subsequent data addresses can be read in only one clock cycle each. The CPU can read BEDO data in a 5-1-1-1 pattern (5 clock cycles for the first address, then one clock cycle for subsequent addresses). While BEDO offers an advantage over EDO, it is supported currently only by the VIA chipsets: 580VP, 590VP, 680VP. Also, BEDO seems to have difficulty supporting motherboards over 66MHz.

CDRAM (Cached DRAM) As with EDRAM, the CDRAM from Mitsubishi incorporates cache and DRAM on the same IC. This arrangement eliminates the need for an external (or L2) cache and has the extra benefit of adding cache whenever RAM is added to the system. The difference is that CDRAM uses a "set-associative" cache approach that can be 15 to 20 percent more efficient than the EDRAM cache scheme. On the other hand, EDRAM appears to offer better overall performance.

DDR SDRAM One limitation of SDRAM is that the theoretical limitation of the design is 125MHz (though technology advances may allow up to 133MHz and 150MHz operation), but bus speeds will need to increase well beyond that in order for memory bandwidth to keep up with future processors. There are several competing standards on the horizon; however, most of them require special pinouts, smaller bus widths, or other design features. In the meantime, Double Data Rate SDRAM (DDR SDRAM) allows output operations to occur on both the rising and falling edge of the clock. Currently, only the rising edge signals an event to occur, so the DDR SDRAM design can effectively double the speed of operation up to at least 200MHz (a prime candidate for AMD Athlon motherboards). There is already one Socket 7 chipset that has support for DDR SDRAM, and more will certainly follow if manufacturers decide to make this memory available.

DRAM (Dynamic Random Access Memory) DRAM was first utilized in early personal computers. It achieves a good mix of speed and density, while being relatively simple and inexpensive to produce—only a single transistor and capacitor is needed to hold a bit. Unfortunately, DRAM contents must be refreshed every few milliseconds, or the contents of each bit location will decay. DRAM performance is also limited because of relatively long access times. Today, a few low-end video boards continue to use DRAM SIMMs to supply video memory. DRAM remains the most recognized and common form of computer memory, and we often use the term "DRAM" to refer, inaccurately, to other types of RAM.

A typical DRAM memory access would occur as follows: the row address bits are placed onto the address pins. After a period of time, the RAS signal falls, which activates sense amps and causes the row address to be latched into the row address buffer. When the RAS signal stabilizes, the selected row is transferred onto the sense amps. Next, the column address bits are set up and then latched into the column address buffer when CAS falls. At that point, the output buffer is also turned on. When CAS stabilizes, the selected sense amp feeds its data to the output buffer.

EDO RAM (Extended Data Out RAM) EDO RAM is a well-established variation of DRAM that extends the time which output data is valid—thus the data's presence on the data bus is "extended." This effect is accomplished by modifying the DRAM's output buffer to prolong the time where *read data* is valid. The data will remain valid until a motherboard signal is received to release it. This eases timing constraints on the memory and allows a 15 to 30 percent improvement in memory performance with little real increase in cost. Because a new external signal is needed to operate EDO RAM, the motherboard must use a chipset designed to accommodate EDO. Intel's Triton chipset was one of the first to support EDO, and now most current chipsets (and motherboards) support EDO. You should realize that EDO RAM can be used in non-EDO motherboards, but there will be no performance improvement.

EDRAM (Enhanced DRAM) This is another, lesser-known variation of the classic DRAM developed by Ramtron International and United Memories. First demonstrated in August 1994, the EDRAM eliminates an external cache by placing a small amount of static RAM (cache) into each EDRAM device itself. In essence, the cache is distributed *within* the system RAM, and as more memory is added to the PC, more cache is effectively added as well. The internal construction of an EDRAM allows it to act like page-mode memory—if a subsequent read requests data that is in the EDRAM's cache (known as a *hit*), the data is made available in about 15ns—roughly equal to the speed of a fair external cache. If the subsequent read requests data that is not in the cache (called a *miss*), the data is accessed from the DRAM portion of memory in about 35ns—which is still much faster than ordinary DRAM.

FPM DRAM (Fast-Page Mode DRAM) This is a popular twist on conventional DRAM. Typical DRAM access is accomplished in a fashion similar to reading from a book—a memory "page" is accessed first, then the contents of that page can be located. The problem is that every access requires the DRAM to re-locate the "page." The *fast-page mode* overcomes this delay by allowing the CPU to access multiple pieces of data on the same page without having to "re-locate" the page every time. As long as the subsequent read or write cycle is on the previously located "page," the FPDRAM can access the specific location on that page directly.

For a time, FPM became the most widely used access method for DRAMs, and it is still used on many older systems. The general benefit of FPM memory is reduced power consumption (since sense and restore current is not necessary during page mode access). Though FPM was a major innovation, there are still some drawbacks. The most significant limitation is that the output buffers turn off when CAS goes high. Also, the minimum cycle time is 5ns before the output buffers turn off, essentially adding at least 5ns to the cycle time.

Today, FPM memory is one of the least desirable forms of memory. You should consider using FPM only if your system does not support any of the later memory types (such as a 486 based system). Typical timings are 6-3-3-3 (initial latency of 3 clocks, with a 3-clock page access). Due to the limited demand, you may find that FPM is actually more expensive now than most of the faster memories now available.

PC100 SDRAM When Intel decided to officially implement a 100MHz system bus speed, it understood that most of the SDRAM modules available at that time would not operate properly above 83MHz. In order to support 100MHz bus speeds, Intel introduced the PC100 specification as a guideline to manufacturers for building modules that would function properly on its 100MHz chipsets (for example, the 440BX). With the PC100 specification, Intel laid out a number of guidelines for trace lengths, trace widths and spacing, the number of printed circuit layers, EEPROM programming specs, and so on.

There is still quite a bit of confusion regarding what a "true" PC100 module actually consists of. Unfortunately, there are quite a few modules being sold today as PC100 that do not operate reliably at 100MHz. While the chip speed rating is used most often to determine the overall performance of the chip, a number of other timings are very important: *tRCD* (RAS to CAS Delay), *tRP* (RAS precharge time), and *CAS Latency* all play a role in determining the fastest bus speed the module will operate on and still achieve a 4-1-1-1 timing.

PC100 SDRAM on a 100MHz (or faster) system bus will provide a significant performance boost for Socket 7 systems—between 10 and 15 percent—since the L2 cache is running at system bus speed. Pentium II/III systems will not see as big a boost because the L2 cache is running at half the processor speed (with the exception of the cacheless Celeron chips, of course).

> You may encounter even faster types of "certified" RAM, including PC133 (133MHz) and even PC150 (150MHz) SDRAM.

RDRAM (Rambus DRAM) Most of the memory alternatives so far have been variations of the same basic architecture. Rambus, Inc. (joint developers of EDRAM) has created a new memory architecture called the RAMBUS Channel. A CPU or specialized IC is used as the "master" device, and the RDRAMs are used as "slave" devices. Data is then sent back and forth across the RAMBUS channel in 256 byte blocks. With a dual 250MHz clock, the RAMBUS channel can transfer data based on the timing of both clocks—this process results in data transfer rates approaching 500MB/s (roughly equivalent to 2ns access time). The problem with RDRAM is that a RAMBUS channel would require an extensive redesign of the current PC memory architecture. PC makers have generally resisted this move, but as Intel embraces RAMBUS for use with the Pentium III, you will begin to see RDRAM in high-end systems.

SDRAM (Synchronous or Synchronized DRAM) Typical memory can only transfer data during certain portions of a clock cycle. The SDRAM modifies memory operation so that outputs can be valid at *any* point in the clock cycle. By itself, this fact is not really significant, but SDRAM also provides a "pipeline burst" mode that allows a second access to begin before the current access is complete. This "continuous" memory access offers effective access speeds as fast as 10ns and allows transfers of data at up to 100MB/s. SDRAM is now quite popular on current motherboard designs, and it is supported by the Intel VX (and later) chipsets as well as by VIA 580VP, 590VP, and 680VP (and later) chipsets. Like BEDO, SDRAM can transfer data in a 5-1-1-1 pattern, but it can also support motherboard speeds up to 100MHz, making it ideal for the 75MHz and 82MHz motherboards as well as the 100MHz motherboards that are now so vital for Pentium II/III systems. Check out the references below for more information on SDRAM:

- **http://www.chips.ibm.com/products/memory/sdramart/sdramart.html**
- **http://www.fujitsu-ede.com/sdram/index.html**
- **http://www.ti.com/sc/docs/memory/brief.htm**

SRAM (Static Random Access Memory) The SRAM is also a "classical" memory design—it is even older than DRAM. SRAM does not require regular refresh operations and can be made to operate at access speeds that are much faster than DRAM speeds. However, SRAM uses six transistors or more to hold a single bit. This feature reduces the density of SRAM and increases its power demands (which is why SRAM was never adopted for general PC use in the first place). Still, the high speed of SRAM has earned it a place as the PC's L2 (or external) cache. You'll probably encounter three types of SRAM cache schemes; Asynchronous, Synchronous Burst, and Pipeline Burst.

- *Asynchronous Static RAM (Async SRAM or ASRAM)* This is the "traditional" form of L2 cache introduced with i386 systems. There's really nothing too special about ASRAM except that its contents can be accessed much faster (20ns, 15ns, or 12ns) than DRAM. ASRAM does not have enough performance to be accessed synchronously and has long since been replaced by better types of cache.
- *Synchronous Burst Static RAM (Sync SRAM or SBSRAM)* This is largely regarded as the best type of L2 cache for intermediate speed motherboards (~60-66MHz). With access times of 8.5ns and 12ns, the SBSRAM can provide synchronous bursts of cache information in 2-1-1-1 cycles (that is, 2 clock cycles for the first access, then 1 cycle per access—in time with the CPU clock). However, as motherboards pass 66MHz (for example, 75MHz and 83MHz designs), SBSRAM looses its advantage to Pipelined Burst SRAM.
- *Pipelined Burst Static RAM (PB SRAM)* At 4.5ns to 8ns, this is the fastest form of high-performance cache now available for 75MHz+ motherboards. PBSRAM requires an extra clock cycle for "lead off," but then can sync with the motherboard clock (with timing such as 3-1-1-1) across a wide range of motherboard frequencies. If you're interested in more technical details about PBSRAM, check out the ASUS site at: **http://asustek.asus.com.tw/Products/TB/mem-0001.html**.
- *VRAM (Video Random Access Memory)* DRAM has been the traditional choice for video memory, but the ever-increasing demand for fast video information (for example, high-resolution SVGA displays) requires a more efficient means of transferring data to and from video memory. Originally developed by Samsung Electronics, video RAM achieves speed improvements by using a "dual data bus" scheme. Ordinary RAM uses a single data bus—data enters or leaves the RAM through a single set of signals. Video RAM provides an "input" data bus and an "output" data bus. This arrangement allows data to be read from video RAM at the same time new information is being written to it. You should realize that the advantages of VRAM will be achieved only on high-end video systems, such as 1024x768x256 (or higher), where you can get up to a 40 percent performance gain over a DRAM video adapter. Below that, you will see no perceivable improvement with a VRAM video adapter.
- *WRAM (Windows RAM)* Samsung Electronics has introduced WRAM as a new video-specific memory device. WRAM uses multiple bit arrays connected with an extensive internal bus and high-speed registers that can transfer data almost continuously. Other specialized registers support attributes such as foreground color, background color, write-block control bits, and true-byte masking. Samsung claims data transfer rates of up to 640MB/s—about 50 percent faster than VRAM—yet WRAM devices are cheaper than their VRAM counterparts. While WRAM has received some serious consideration in the last few years, it has been largely ignored in favor of SDRAM for video systems.

MEMORY TECHNIQUES

Rather than incur the added expense of specialized memory devices, PC makers often use inexpensive, well-established memory types in unique architectures designed to make the most of low-end memory.

There are three popular architectures that you will probably encounter in almost all systems: paged memory, interleaved memory, and memory caching.

Paged Memory This approach basically divides system RAM into small groups (or "pages") from 512 bytes to several KB long. Memory management circuitry on the motherboard allows subsequent memory accesses on the same page to be accomplished with zero wait states. If the subsequent access takes place outside of the current page, one or more wait states may be added while the new page is found. This is identical in principle to fast-page mode DRAM explained above. You will find page mode architectures implemented on high-end i286, PS/2 (models 70 and 80), and many i386 systems.

Interleaved Memory This is a technique that provides better performance than paged memory. Simply put, interleaved memory combines two banks of memory into one. The first portion is "even," while the second portion is "odd"—so memory contents are alternated between these two areas. This process allows a memory access in the second portion to begin before the memory access in the first portion has finished. In effect, interleaving can double memory performance. The problem with interleaving is that you must provide twice the amount of memory as matched pairs. Most PCs that employ interleaving will allow you to add memory one bank at a time, but interleaving will be disabled and system performance will suffer.

Memory Caching This is perhaps the most recognized form of memory enhancement architecture (Figure 26-5). Cache is a small amount (anywhere from 8KB to 1MB) of very fast SRAM that forms an interface between the CPU and ordinary DRAM. The SRAM typically operates on the order of 5ns to 15ns, which is fast enough to keep pace with a CPU using zero wait states. A *cache controller* IC on the motherboard keeps track of frequently accessed memory locations (as well as predicted memory locations) and copies those contents into cache. When a CPU reads from memory, it checks the cache first. If the needed contents are present in cache (called a *cache hit*), the data is read at zero wait states. If the needed contents are not present in the cache (known as a *cache miss*), the data must be read directly from DRAM at a penalty of one or more wait states. A small quantity of very fast cache (called *Tag RAM*) acts as an index, recording the various locations of data stored in cache. A well-designed caching system can achieve a hit ratio of 95 percent or more—in other words, memory can run *without* wait states 95 percent of the time.

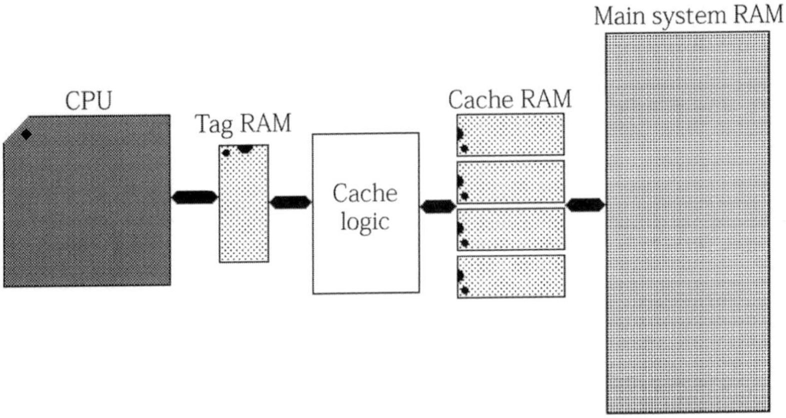

FIGURE 26-5 Major Cache System Components

26

There are two levels of cache in the contemporary PC. CPUs from the i486 onward have a small "internal cache" that is known as *L1 cache*, while "external cache" (SRAM installed as DIPs or COAST modules on the motherboard) is referred to as *L2 cache*. The i386 CPUs have no internal cache (though IBM's 386SLC offers 8KB of L1 cache). Most i486 CPUs provide an 8KB internal cache. Early Pentium processors are fitted with two 8KB internal caches—one for data and one for instructions. Today's Pentium II/III Slot 1 CPU incorporates 256KB to 512KB of L2 cache into the processor cartridge itself.

Shadow Memory ROM devices (whether the BIOS ROM on your motherboard or a ROM IC on an expansion board) are frustratingly slow, with access times often exceeding several hundred nanoseconds. ROM access then requires a large number of wait states, slowing down the system's performance. This problem is compounded because the routines stored in BIOS (especially the video BIOS ROM on the video board) are some of the most frequently accessed memory in your computer.

Beginning with the i386-class computers, some designs employed a memory technique called *shadowing*. ROM contents are loaded into an area of fast RAM during system initialization, then the computer maps the fast RAM into memory locations used by the ROM devices. Whenever ROM routines must be accessed during run time, information is taken from the "shadowed ROM" instead of the actual ROM IC. The ROM performance can be improved by at least 300 percent.

Shadow memory is also useful for ROM devices that do not use the full available data bus width. For example, a 16-bit computer system may hold an expansion board containing an 8-bit ROM IC. The system would have to access the ROM not once, but *twice,* to extract a single 16-bit word. If the computer is a 32-bit machine, that 8-bit ROM would have to be addressed four times to make a complete 32-bit word. You can imagine the hideous system delays that would be encountered. Loading the ROM to shadow memory in advance virtually eliminates such delays. Shadowing can usually be turned on or off through the system's CMOS Setup routines.

The Issue of Parity

As you might imagine, it is *vital* that data and program instructions remain error-free. Even one incorrect bit due to electrical noise or a component failure can crash the PC, corrupt drive information, cause video problems, or result in myriad other faults. PC designers approached the issue of memory integrity by employing a technique known as *parity* (the same technique used to check serial data integrity).

THE PARITY PRINCIPLE

The basic idea behind parity is simple—each byte written to memory is checked, and a 9th bit is added to the byte as a checking (or "parity") bit. When a memory address is later read by the CPU, memory checking circuitry on the motherboard will calculate the *expected* parity bit, and compare it to the bit actually *read* from memory. In this fashion, the PC can continuously diagnose system memory by checking the integrity of its data. If the read parity bit *matches* the expected parity bit, the data (and indirectly the RAM) is assumed to be valid, and the CPU can go on its way. If the read and expected parity bits *do not* match, the system registers an error and halts. Every *byte* is given a parity bit, so for a 32-bit PC there are 4 parity bits for every address, for a 64-bit PC there are 8 parity bits, and so on.

EVEN VERSUS ODD

There are two types of parity—even and odd. With *even parity*, the parity bit is set to 0 if there are an even number of 1s already in the corresponding byte (keeping the number of 1s even). If there is not an even number of 1s in the byte, the even parity bit will be 1 (making the number of 1s even).

With *odd parity*, the parity bit is set to 0 if there is an odd number of 1s already in the corresponding byte (keeping the number of 1s odd). If there is not an odd number of 1s in the byte, the odd parity bit will be 1 (making the number of 1s odd).

Although even and odd parity work opposite of one another, both schemes serve exactly the same purpose and have the same probability of catching a bad bit. The memory device itself does not care at all about what type of parity is being used—it just needs to have the parity bits available. The use of parity (and the choice of even or odd) is left up to the motherboard's memory control circuit.

THE PROBLEMS WITH PARITY

While parity has proven to be a simple and cost-effective means of continuously checking memory, there are two significant limitations. First, though parity can detect an error, it cannot correct the error because there is no way to tell *which* bit has gone bad—this is why a system simply halts when a parity error is detected. Second, parity is unable to detect multi-bit errors. For example, if a 1 accidentally becomes a 0 and a 0 accidentally becomes a 1 within the same byte, parity conditions will still be satisfied. Fortunately, the probability of a multi-bit error in the same byte is extremely remote.

CIRCUMVENTING PARITY

Over the last few years, parity has come under fire from PC makers and memory manufacturers alike. Opponents claim that the rate of parity errors due to hardware (RAM) faults is very small, and that the expense of providing parity bits in a memory-hungry marketplace just isn't justified anymore. There is some truth to this argument, considering that the parity technique is over 15 years old and has serious limitations.

As a consequence, some motherboard makers have begun removing parity support from their low-end motherboards, and others are providing motherboards that will function with or without parity (usually set in CMOS or with a motherboard jumper). Similarly, some memory makers are now providing nonparity and "fake" parity memory as cheaper alternatives to conventional parity memory. *Nonparity* memory simply foregoes the 9th bit. For example, a nonparity SIMM would be designated x8 or x32 (that is, 4Mx8 or 4Mx32). If the SIMM supports parity, it will be designated x9 or x36 (that is, 4Mx9 or 4Mx36). *Fake parity* is a bit more devious—the 9th bit is replaced by a simple (and dirt cheap) parity generator chip that "looks" like a normal DRAM IC. When a read cycle occurs, the parity chip on the SIMM provides the proper parity bit to the motherboard *all the time*. In effect, your memory is "lying" to the motherboard.

While there's a cost savings, your memory is left with no means of error checking at all. It's a little like driving a car without a speedometer—you could go for miles without a problem, but sooner or later you'll cross a speed trap. In actual practice, you can go indefinitely without parity, but when an error *does* occur, having parity in place can save you immeasurable frustration. Unless the "lowest cost" is your absolute highest priority, it is recommended that you spend the extra few dollars for parity RAM.

> Most motherboards can be operated with nonparity RAM. It is also usually possible to mix parity and nonparity memory in the same system. But in either case, you will need to disable ALL parity checking features for the RAM.

ABUSE AND DETECTION OF FAKE MEMORY

Another potential problem with "fake" parity memory is fraud. There have been numerous instances where memory was purchased as "parity" at full price—only to find that the parity ICs were actually parity generators. This was determined by dissecting the IC packages and finding that the IC die in the parity position did not match the IC dies in the other bit positions. The buyer doesn't know because parity generators are packaged to look just like DRAM ICs, and there's no other obvious way to tell just by looking at the SIMM or other memory device. System diagnostic software also cannot detect the presence of parity memory versus fake memory.

There are really only two ways to protect yourself from fake memory fraud. First, industry experts indicate that many fake parity ICs (the parity generators) are marked with designations such as "BP," "VT," "GSM," or "MPEC." If you find that 1 out of every 9 ICs on your SIMM carries such a designation (or any other designation *not* matching the first 8), you may have a fraud situation. Of course, the prudent first step is to give "benefit of the doubt," so contact the organization you purchased the memory from—it may simply have sent the wrong SIMMs.

Second, you can check the IC dies themselves. Unfortunately, this requires you to carefully dissect several IC packages on the SIMM and compare the IC dies under a microscope—resulting in the destruction of the memory device(s). If the 9th die looks radically different (usually much simpler) than the other 8, you've likely got fake parity. A non-destructive way to check the SIMM is to use a SIMM checker (if you have access to one) with a testing routine specially written to test parity memory. If the SIMM works but the parity IC test fails (that is, the tester cannot *write* to the parity memory), chances are you've got fake parity.

If you determine that you have been sold fake parity memory in place of real parity memory and you cannot get any satisfaction from the seller, you are encouraged to convey your information to the Attorney General in the seller's state. After all, if you're being stiffed, chances are a lot of other people are too—and they probably don't even know it.

ALTERNATIVE ERROR CORRECTION

Although this book supports the use of parity, it is also quick to recognize its old age. In the world of personal computing, parity is an *ancient* technique. Frankly, it could easily be replaced by more sophisticated techniques, such as *Error Correction Code* (ECC) or *ECC-on-SIMM* (EOS). ECC (which is already being employed in high-end PCs and file servers) uses a mathematical process in conjunction with the motherboard's memory controller and appends a number of ECC bits to the data bits. When data is read back from memory, the ECC memory controller checks the ECC data read back as well.

ECC has two important advantages over parity. It can actually *correct* single-bit errors "on-the-fly" without the user ever knowing there's been a problem. In addition, ECC can successfully detect 2-bit, 3-bit, and 4-bit errors, making it an incredibly powerful error detection tool. If a rare multi-bit error is detected, ECC will not be able to correct it, but it will be reported and the system will halt.

It takes 7 or 8 bits at each address to successfully implement ECC. For a 32-bit system, you'll need to use x39 or x40 SIMMs (that is, 8Mx39 or 8Mx40). These are relatively new designations, so you should at least recognize them as ECC SIMMs if you encounter them. As an alternative, some 64-bit systems use two 36-bit SIMMs for a total of 72 bits—64 bits for data and 8 bits (which would otherwise be for parity) for ECC information.

EOS is a relatively new (and rather expensive) technology that places ECC functions on the memory module itself, but provides ECC results as parity—so while the memory module runs ECC, the motherboard continues to see parity. This is an interesting experiment, but it is unlikely that EOS will gain significant market share. Systems that use parity can be fitted with parity memory much more cheaply than EOS memory.

Selecting and Installing Memory in PCs

Installing memory is not nearly as easy as it used to be. Certainly, today's memory modules just plug right in, but deciding which memory to buy, how much (or how little) to buy, and how to use existing memory in new systems presents technicians with a bewildering variety of choices. This part of the chapter illustrates the important ideas behind choosing and using memory.

GETTING THE RIGHT AMOUNT

"How much memory do I need?" This is an old question that has plagued the PC industry ever since Intel's 80286 CPU broke the 1MB memory barrier. With more memory, additional programs and data can be run by the CPU at any given time—which indirectly helps to improve the productivity of the particular PC. The problem is cost. Today's SDRAM is running around $2/MB (U.S.), compared with about $1.25/MB (about $12.50/GB) for hard drive space. Consequently, memory is far more expensive then hard drive space, so the goal of good system configuration is to install *enough* memory to support the PC's routine tasks. Installing *too much* memory means that you've spent money for PC resources that just remain idle. Installing *too little* memory results in programs that will not run (typical under DOS), or diminished system performance because of extensive swap file use (typical under Windows).

So how much memory *is* enough? The fact of the matter is that "enough" is an ever-changing figure. DOS systems of the early 1980s (8088/8086) worked just fine with 1MB. By the mid-1980s (80286), DOS systems with 2MB were adequate. Into the late 1980s (80386), Windows 3.0 and 3.1 needed 4MB. As the 1990s got underway (80486), Windows systems with 8MB were common (even DOS applications were using 4 to 6MB of EMS). Today, with Pentium II/III systems and Windows 98, 32MB is considered to be a minimum requirement, and 64MB-128MB systems are readily available. For today, 32MB is the minimum benchmark that you should use for general-purpose home and office systems. But by the end of the decade, 128MB systems will probably be the norm. And this is not to say that 128MB systems are the pinnacle of performance. Today's file servers and industrial-strength design packages are employing 256MB to 512MB of RAM—motherboard chipsets can often support up to 768MB of RAM or more.

FILLING BANKS

Another point of confusion is the idea of a "memory bank." Most memory devices are installed in sets (or banks). The amount of memory in the bank can vary depending on how much you wish to add, but there must always be enough data bits in the bank to *fill* each bit position. Table 26-11 illustrates a relationship between data bits and banks for the range of typical CPUs. For example, the 8086 is a 16-bit microprocessor (2 bytes). This means that 2 extra bits are required for parity giving a total of 18 bits. Thus, one bank is 18 bits wide. You may fill the bank by adding eighteen 1-bit DIPs, or two 30-pin SIMMs. As another example, an 80486DX is a 32-bit CPU, so 36 bits are needed to fill a bank (32 bits plus 4 parity bits). If you use 30-pin SIMMs, you will need four to fill a bank. If you use 72-pin SIMMs, only one is needed. For a newer Pentium II or III CPU, you can fill a "bank" with *only one* 168-pin DIMM. Note that the size of the memory in MB does not really matter, so long as the *entire* bank is filled.

TABLE 26-11 CPUs VERSUS MEMORY BANK SIZE

CPU	DATA WIDTH (W/PARITY)	xMB BY 1 DIPs	30-PIN SIMMS	72-PIN SIMMS	168-PIN DIMMS
8088	9 bits	9	1	-	-
8086	18 bits	18	2	-	-
80286	18 bits	-	2	1 (2 banks)	-
80386SX, SL, SLC	18 bits	-	2	1 (2 banks)	-
80386DX	36 bits	-	4	1	-
80486SLC, SLC2	18 bits	-	2	1 (2 banks)	-
80486DX, SX, DX2, DX4	36 bits	-	4	1	-
Pentium (Socket 7)	64 bits	-	8	2	1
Pentium II/III (Slot 1)	64 bits	-	-	-	1

BANK REQUIREMENTS

There is more to filling a memory bank than just installing the right number of bits. Memory amount, memory matching, and bank order are three additional considerations. First, you must use the proper *memory amount* that will bring you to the expected volume of total memory. Suppose a Pentium system has 8MB already installed in Bank 0, and you need to put another 8MB into the system in Bank 1. Table 26-11 shows that two 72-pin SIMMs are needed to fill a bank, but each SIMM need only be 1M. Remember from the discussion of megabytes that a 1Mx36-bit (w/parity) device is 4MB. Since 2 such SIMMs are needed to fill a bank, the total would be 8MB. When added to the 8MB already in the system, the total would be 16MB.

How about another example? Suppose the same 8MB is already installed in your Pentium system, and you want to add 16MB to Bank 1 rather than 8MB (bringing the total system memory to 24MB). In that case, you could use two 2M 72-pin SIMMs where 2Mx36 is 8MB (w/parity) per SIMM. Two 8MB SIMMs yield 16MB, bringing the system total to (16MB+8MB) or 24MB.

Now for a curve. Suppose you want to outfit that Pentium as a network server with 128MB of RAM. Remember that there's already 8MB in Bank 0, which means there's only Bank 1 available. Since the largest commercially available SIMMs are 8Mx36 (32MB w/parity), you can add only up to 64MB to Bank 1 (for a system total of 72MB). To get around this, you should *remove* the existing 1Mx36 SIMMs in Bank 0 and fill both Bank 0 and Bank 1 with 8Mx36 SIMMs, putting 64MB in Bank 0 and 64MB in Bank 1 and yielding 128MB in total. You can review many of the recommended SIMM/DIMM combinations for a typical Pentium motherboard in Table 26-12.

Another bank requirement demands *memory matching*—using SIMMs of the same size and speed within a bank. For example, when adding multiple SIMMs to a bank, each SIMM must be rated for the same access speed and share the same memory configuration (e.g., 2Mx36). This issue is not quite so

TABLE 26-12 MEMORY COMBINATIONS FOR A TYPICAL MOTHERBOARD

MEMORY SIZE	SIMM 1	SIMM 2	SIMM 3	SIMM 4	SIMM 5	SIMM 6	DIMM 1	DIMM 2
8MB	1Mx32	1Mx32	-	-	-	-	-	-
8MB	-	-	-	-	-	-	1Mx64	-
16MB	2Mx32	2Mx32	-	-	-	-	-	-
16MB	1Mx32	1Mx32	1Mx32	1Mx32	-	-	-	-
16MB	-	-	-	-	-	-	2Mx64	-
16MB	-	-	-	-	-	-	1Mx64	1Mx64
24MB	1Mx32	1Mx32	2Mx32	2Mx32	-	-	-	-
24MB	1Mx32	1Mx32	1Mx32	1Mx32	1Mx32	1Mx32	-	-
24MB	-	-	-	-	-	-	1Mx64	2Mx64
32MB	4Mx32	4Mx32	-	-	-	-	-	-
32MB	2Mx32	2Mx32	2Mx32	2Mx32	-	-	-	-
32MB	1Mx32	1Mx32	1Mx32	1Mx32	2Mx32	2Mx32	-	-
32MB	-	-	-	-	-	-	4Mx64	-
32MB	-	-	-	-	-	-	2Mx64	2Mx64
40MB	1Mx32	1Mx32	4Mx32	4Mx32	-	-	-	-
40MB	-	-	-	-	-	-	1Mx64	4Mx64
48MB	2Mx32	2Mx32	4Mx32	4Mx32	-	-	-	-
48MB	1Mx32	1Mx32	1Mx32	1Mx32	4Mx32	4Mx32	-	-
48MB	2Mx32	2Mx32	2Mx32	2Mx32	2Mx32	2Mx32	-	-
48MB	-	-	-	-	-	-	2Mx64	4Mx64
64MB	8Mx32	8Mx32	-	-	-	-	-	-
64MB	4Mx32	4Mx32	4Mx32	4Mx32	-	-	-	-
64MB	2Mx32	2Mx32	2Mx32	2Mx32	4Mx32	4Mx32	-	-
64MB	-	-	-	-	-	-	8Mx64	-
64MB	-	-	-	-	-	-	4Mx64	4Mx64
72MB	1Mx32	1Mx32	8Mx32	8Mx32	-	-	-	-
72MB	-	-	-	-	-	-	1Mx64	8Mx64
80MB	2Mx32	2Mx32	8Mx32	8Mx32	-	-	-	-
80MB	1Mx32	1Mx32	1Mx32	1Mx32	8Mx32	8Mx32	-	-
80MB	-	-	-	-	-	-	2Mx64	8Mx64
96MB	4Mx32	4Mx32	8Mx32	8Mx32	-	-	-	-
96MB	2Mx32	2Mx32	2Mx32	2Mx32	8Mx32	8Mx32	-	-
96MB	4Mx32	4Mx32	4Mx32	4Mx32	4Mx32	4Mx32	-	-
96MB	-	-	-	-	-	-	4Mx64	8Mx64
128MB	16Mx32	16Mx32	-	-	-	-	-	-
128MB	8Mx32	8Mx32	8Mx32	8Mx32	-	-	-	-
128MB	4Mx32	4Mx32	4Mx32	4Mx32	8Mx32	8Mx32	-	-

TABLE 26-12 MEMORY COMBINATIONS FOR A TYPICAL MOTHERBOARD *(CONTINUED)*

MEMORY SIZE	SIMM 1	SIMM 2	SIMM 3	SIMM 4	SIMM 5	SIMM 6	DIMM 1	DIMM 2
128MB	-	-	-	-	-	-	8Mx64	8Mx64
136MB	1Mx32	1Mx32	16Mx32	16Mx32	-	-	-	-
144MB	2Mx32	2Mx32	16Mx32	16Mx32	-	-	-	-
144MB	1Mx32	1Mx32	1Mx32	1Mx32	16Mx32	16Mx32	-	-
160MB	4Mx32	4Mx32	16Mx32	16Mx32	-	-	-	-
160MB	2Mx32	2Mx32	2Mx32	2Mx32	16Mx32	16Mx32	-	-
192MB	8Mx32	8Mx32	16Mx32	16Mx32	-	-	-	-
192MB	4Mx32	4Mx32	4Mx32	4Mx32	16Mx32	16Mx32	-	-
192MB	8Mx32	8Mx32	8Mx32	8Mx32	8Mx32	8Mx32	-	-
256MB	32Mx32	32Mx32	-	-	-	-	-	-
256MB	16Mx32	16Mx32	16Mx32	16Mx32	-	-	-	-
256MB	8Mx32	8Mx32	8Mx32	8Mx32	16Mx32	16Mx32	-	-
256MB	-	-	-	-	-	-	16Mx64	16Mx64

critical with DIMMs, where only one device is needed to constitute a "bank." Still, most DIMM-based systems are not without their own special requirements:

- DIMMs must meet the required guidelines for your motherboard (that is, 100MHz SDRAM in 32MB, 64MB, or 128MB modules using 64Mbit or 128Mbit technology). If the DIMM does not use the correct speed, memory type, memory size, or RAM chip technology, the system may act erratically or fail to recognize the DIMM.
- If you have two identical DIMMs—that is, DIMMs of the same speed, type, size, and chip technology—and both are single-sided (or both double-sided), then you may install them in *either* bank 0 or bank 1.
- If you have two DIMMs of different sizes (for example, a 64MB and 128MB DIMM), install the *larger* DIMM in Bank 0 and the smaller DIMM in Bank 1.
- If you have two DIMMs of the same size, and one is single-sided and one is double-sided, install the *single-sided* DIMM in Bank 0 and the *double-sided* DIMM in bank 1.

Finally, you should generally follow the *bank order*. The rule is that you'd fill Bank 0 first, then Bank 1, then Bank 2, and so on. Otherwise, memory will not be contiguous within the PC, and CMOS will not recognize the additional RAM. Keep in mind that most current motherboards will support DIMMs in almost any bank (following the DIMM guidelines above), so you may not *need* to fill DIMM banks in a given order.

Recycling Older Memory Devices

Given the relatively high cost of PC memory, it is only natural that users and technicians alike would choose to reuse memory as much as possible when systems are upgraded or replaced. It is a simple matter to reuse memory—just as you would reuse hard drives or video boards. But there are some special issues to consider before you make plans to transfer memory from one system to another.

MEMORY SPEED

The goal of memory is to keep pace with the microprocessor using a minimum of wait states. It is *possible* to place a 100ns SIMM in a Pentium system, but the wait states required to allow this awful mismatch would negate any benefits from the advanced microprocessor. As a consequence, it is most effective to use memory that is fast enough to handle the CPU in the system that will be *receiving* the memory. Table 26-10 shows typical memory speeds for various microprocessors. It is possible to use memory if the speed is *faster* than the minimum requirement, but all the memory in the bank should be the same speed. Ordinarily, there is no reason to buy memory that is faster than necessary—no additional benefit is realized by the system. The only time it might be advisable to invest in faster memory is if you know in advance that the memory will eventually be transferred to another system.

MEMORY TYPE

You should also be sure to use the same type of memory (EDO, FPM, SDRAM, and so on). For example, if your motherboard is designed to use EDO RAM, and you have EDO RAM already installed, you should be sure to install more EDO RAM. Some motherboard designs allow you to mix memory types, but mixing memory types on other (especially older) motherboards may cause the system to malfunction.

SIMM STACKERS

Although your memory type should be able to fit into the new computer, if it doesn't there are ways to *make it fit*. One of the most popular memory adapters is the "SIMM Stacker." The devices are actually known by a variety of trade names, but all allow you to convert four 30-pin SIMMs into a 72-pin SIMM frame. However, there are two drawbacks with SIMM Stackers:

- *Cramped Quarters* SIMM adapter products take up significant amounts of space. Remember that the adapter snaps into the SIMM socket, and SIMMs attach to the adapter. As a result, the filled SIMM adapter looks a bit like a tree with branches. This is rarely a problem when SIMM sockets are placed side-to-side, but with several banks close together, multiple SIMM sockets may interfere with one another.
- *Timing Penalty* Timing is everything for memory, and with signals traveling on the order of nanoseconds, the very length of a printed signal run can adversely impact system performance. Generally speaking, you can expect access times to be increased by 10ns or so when using a SIMM adapter. This is not a problem when the memory is measurably faster than needed. But if your memory speed is on the border, a SIMM adapter may necessitate an additional wait state.

MIXING "COMPOSITE" AND "NON-COMPOSITE" SIMMS

Most ordinary 30-pin SIMMs use 9 ICs (8 for data and 1 for parity). From time to time, you may encounter SIMMs with just a few ICs (usually three). The composite SIMM (with 9 ICs) is older—using less-dense memory. The non-composite SIMM (with 3 or so ICs) generally uses newer memory devices. In theory, it should be possible to mix composite and non-composite SIMMs together in the same bank or in the same system. However, there have been system problems reported when this happens. As a rule, you can try mixing these two generations of memory, but if you encounter memory problems with the system, remove either memory type and see if the problem goes away.

REMOUNTING AND REBUILDING MEMORY

Memory "recycling" has taken another more unexpected turn—some small companies are actually taking older memory devices and remounting them on SIMMs and other memory structures. In this way, you can use DIPs that are remounted on a SIMM. For example, a company called Autotime (**www.autotime.com**) in Portland, Oregon will remove memory devices from one SIMM and install them on a SIMM that you need (for example, remove the ICs from four 1MB 30-pin SIMMs and install and test them on one 4MB 72-pin SIMM).

Memory Troubleshooting

Unfortunately, even the best memory devices fail from time to time. An accidental static discharge during installation, incorrect installation, a poor system configuration, operating system problems, and even outright failures due to old age or poor manufacture can cause memory problems. This part of the chapter looks at some of the troubles that plague memory systems, and offers advise on how to deal with them.

> There are several tools on the Companion CD that can aid you in testing and troubleshooting PC memory. Check out FreeMem Pro 4.1 (FMEMPRO.ZIP) and Graphical Memory 1.1 (MEMSTAT.ZIP) for RAM performance testing.

MEMORY TEST EQUIPMENT

If you're working in a repair-shop environment or planning to test a substantial number of memory devices, you should consider acquiring some specialized test equipment. A memory tester, such as the SIMCHECK (Figure 26-6) from Innoventions, Inc. is a modular microprocessor-based system that can perform a thorough, comprehensive test of various SIMMs and indicate the specific IC that has failed (if any). The system can be configured to work with specific SIMMs by installing an appropriate adapter module, like the one shown in Figure 26-7. Intelligent testers work automatically and show the progress and results of their examinations on a multiline LCD—guesswork is totally eliminated from memory testing.

Single ICs such as DIPs and SIPs can be tested using a single chip plug-in module. The static RAM checker illustrated in Figure 26-8 is another test bed for checking high-performance static RAM components in a DIP package. Both Innoventions test devices work together to provide a full-featured test system.

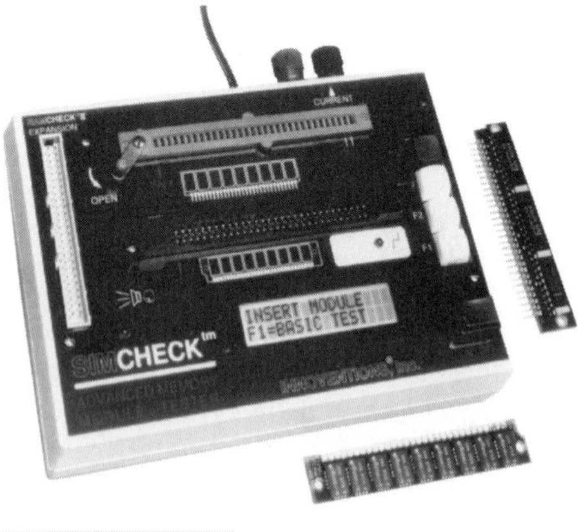

FIGURE 26-6 The SIMCHECK Main Unit. Innoventions, Inc.

FIGURE 26-7 The SIMCHECK PS/2 SIMM Adapter. Innoventions, Inc.

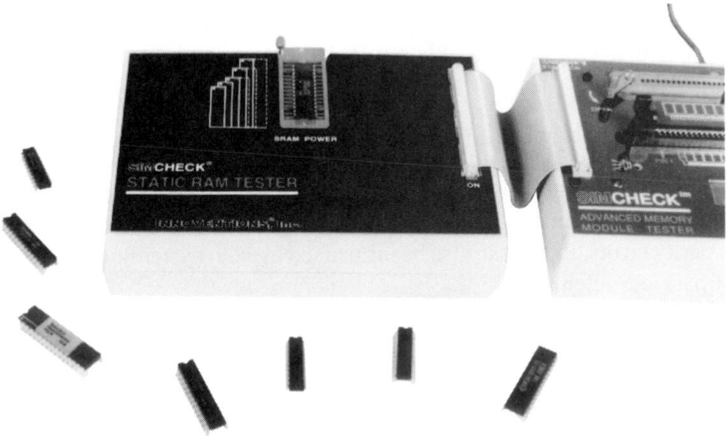

FIGURE 26-8 The SIMCHECK Static RAM Unit. Innoventions, Inc.

Specialized tools can be an added expense—but no more so than an oscilloscope or other piece of useful test equipment. The returns on your investment are less time wasted in the repair and fewer parts to replace.

REPAIRING SIMM/DIMM SOCKETS

If there is one weak link in the architecture of a SIMM or DIMM, it is the *socket* that connects it to the motherboard. Ideally, the SIMM or DIMM should sit comfortably in the socket, then gently snap back—held in place by two clips on either side of the socket. In actual practice, you really have to push that SIMM or DIMM to get it into place. Taking it out again is just as tricky. As a result, it is not uncommon for a socket to break and render your extra memory unusable.

The best (a.k.a. "textbook") solution is to remove the damaged socket and install a new one. Clearly there are some problems with this tactic. First, removing the old socket will require you to remove the motherboard, desolder the broken socket, and then solder in a new socket (which you can buy from a full-feature electronics store such as DigiKey). In the hands of a skilled technician with the right tools, doing this is not so hard. But the printed circuit runs of a computer motherboard are *extremely* delicate, and the slightest amount of excess heat can easily destroy the sensitive, multilayer connections, ruining the motherboard entirely.

Fortunately, there are some tricks that might help you. If either of the SIMM/DIMM clips have bent or broken, you can usually make use of a medium-weight rubber band that is about one inch shorter than the socket. Wrap the rubber band around the SIMM/DIMM and socket, and the rubber band should do a fair job holding the memory module in place. If any part of the socket should crack or break, it can be repaired (or at least reinforced) with a good-quality epoxy. If you choose to use epoxy, be sure to work in a ventilated area and allow plenty of time for the epoxy to dry. This does not "fix" the problem, but it does contain the damage and may allow the motherboard to serve a long and reliable working life.

CONTACT CORROSION

Corrosion can occur on SIMM/DIMM contacts if the module's contact metal is *not* the same as the socket's contact metal—this will eventually cause contact (and memory) problems. As a rule, check that the metal on the socket contact is the same as the SIMM/DIMM contacts (usually tin or gold). You may be able get around the problem in the short term by cleaning corrosion off the contacts manually with a cotton swab and good electronics-grade contact cleaner. In the meantime, if you discover that your memory and connectors have dissimilar metals, you may be able to get the memory seller to exchange your memory modules.

PARITY ERRORS

Parity errors constitute many of the memory faults that you will see as a technician. As you saw earlier in this chapter, *parity* is an important part of a computer's self-checking capability. Errors in memory will cause the system to halt, rather than to continue blindly along with a potentially catastrophic error. But it is not just faulty memory that causes parity errors. Parity can also be influenced by your system's configuration. Here are the major causes of parity problems:

- One or more memory bits is intermittent or has failed entirely.
- Poor connections between the SIMM/DIMM and socket.
- Too few wait states entered in BIOS (memory is too slow for the CPU).
- An intermittent failure or other fault has occurred in the power supply.
- A bug, computer virus, or other rogue software is operating.
- A fault has occurred in the memory controller IC or BIOS.

When you're faced with a parity error after a memory upgrade, you should suspect a problem with wait states or memory type settings in the CMOS Setup routine, so check them first. If the wait states or other memory settings are correct, systematically remove each SIMM/DIMM, clean the contacts, and reseat each SIMM/DIMM. If the errors continue, try removing one bank of memory modules at a time (chances are that the memory is bad). You may have to relocate memory so that Bank 0 remains filled. When the error disappears, the memory you removed is likely to be defective.

Some "full-service" PC shops may have a SIMM/DIMM memory tester unit available. If so, they may be persuaded to test your suspect memory module(s) for a nominal cost (perhaps even for free).

When parity errors occur spontaneously (with no apparent cause), you should clean and reinstall each SIMM/DIMM *first* to eliminate the possibility of bad contacts. Next, check the power supply outputs—low or electrically "noisy" outputs may allow random bit errors. You may have to upgrade the supply if it is overloaded. Try booting the system "clean" from a write-protected floppy disk to eliminate the possibility of buggy software or computer viruses. If the problem persists, suspect a memory defect in the memory module.

TROUBLESHOOTING CLASSIC XT MEMORY

It seems only fitting to start an examination of memory problems with a brief overview of the original IBM PC/XT computer. In the "good old days" of personal computing when there were only one or two commercial computers in the market, there were few memory arrangements. POST could be written very specifically, and errors could be correlated directly to memory IC location. The POST routine in an XT's BIOS ROM is designed to identify the exact bank and bit where a memory error is detected and to display that information on the computer's monitor.

IBM PC/XT computers classify a memory (RAM) failure as error code 201. In actual operation, a RAM error would appear as "XXYY 201," where "XX" is the bank, and "YY" is the bit where the fault is detected. As a result, it was often a simple matter to locate and replace a defective RAM IC. An XT is built with four RAM banks—each with 9 bits (parity plus 8 bits). Table 26-13 shows some bank and bit error

TABLE 26-13 INDEX OF IBM PC/XT ERROR CODES

"XXYY 201": MEMORY FAILURE

XX	BANK	YY	BIT
00	0	00	parity bit
04	1	01	D0
08	2	02	D1
0C	3	04	D2
		08	D3
		10	D4
		20	D5
		40	D6
		80	D7

codes for XT-class computers. As an example, suppose an XT system displayed **0002 201**. This would indicate a memory failure in bank 0 at data bit D1. You need only replace the DIP memory IC residing at that location.

SYMPTOM 26-1 **You see 1055 201 or 2055 201 error message** Both of these error codes indicate a problem with the system's DIP switch settings. Remember that XTs do not use CMOS RAM to contain a system setup configuration, so DIP switches are used to tell the system how much memory should be present. If memory is added or removed, the appropriate switches in switch bank 2 (bits 1 to 8) and switch bank 1 (bits 3 and 4) must be set properly. Turn off the computer, check your switch settings, and reboot the computer.

SYMPTOM 26-2 **You see a "PARITY CHECK 1" error message** This error typically suggests a power supply problem—RAM ICs are not receiving the proper voltage levels, so their contents are being lost or corrupted. When this happens, parity errors will be produced. Remove all power from the computer and repair or replace the power supply.

SYMPTOM 26-3 **You see a "XXYY 201" error message** This is a general RAM failure format for XT computers indicating the *bank* and *bit* where the fault is located. XX is the faulty bank, and YY is the faulty bit. See Table 26-13 to decipher the specific bank and bit in an XT. For example, an error code of 0004 201 indicates a memory fault in bank 0 (00) and bit D2 (04). Replace the defective IC, or bank of ICs.

SYMPTOM 26-4 **You see a "PARITY ERROR 1" error message** Multiple addresses or multiple data bits are detected as faulty in the XT. In some cases, one or more ICs may be loose or inserted incorrectly in their sockets. Remove power from the system and reseat all RAM ICs. If all RAM ICs are inserted correctly, rotate a new DRAM IC through each occupied IC location until the defective IC is located.

TROUBLESHOOTING CLASSIC AT MEMORY

IBM's PC/AT was the leader of the 80286 generation. Since there was only one model (at the time), ATs use some specific error messages to pinpoint memory (RAM or ROM) problems on the motherboard as

TABLE 26-14 200-SERIES ERROR CODES

201	Memory error (physical location will likely be displayed)
202	Memory address line 0-15 error
203	Memory address line 16-23 error; line 16-31 error (MCA)
204	Memory remapped to compensate for error (PS/2)
205	Error in first 128K (PS/2 ISA) of RAM
207	BIOS ROM failure
210	System board memory parity error
211	Error in first 64K of RAM (MCA)
212	Watchdog timer error
213	DMA bus arbitration time-out
215	Memory address error; 64K on daughter/SIP 2 failed (70)
216	Memory address error; 64K on daughter/SIP 1 failed (70)
221	ROM to RAM copy (shadowing) failed (MCA)
225	Wrong speed memory on system board (MCA)
230	Memory on motherboard and adapter board overlaps
231	Non-contiguous adapter memory installed
235	Stuck data line on memory module
241	Memory module 2 failed
251	Memory module 3 failed

well as in its standard memory expansion devices. The 200 series error codes represent system memory errors (Table 26-14). ATs present memory failures in this format: AAXXXX YYYY 20x. The ten-digit code can be broken down to indicate the specific system bank and chip number, although the particular bit failure is not indicated. The first two digits ("AA") represent the defective *bank*, while the last four digits ("YYYY") show the defective *IC number*. It is then a matter or finding and replacing the faulty DIP IC. Table 26-15 shows a set of error codes for early AT-class computers. For example, suppose an IBM PC/AT displayed this error message: 05xxxxxx 0001 201 (we don't care about the x's). That message would place the error in IC 0 of bank 1 on the AT's system memory.

CONTEMPORARY MEMORY SYMPTOMS

With the rapid advances in computer technology, specific numerical (or "bank and bit") error codes have long-since been rendered impractical in newer systems where megabytes can be stored in just a few ICs. The i486, Pentium, Pentium II, and today's Pentium III computers use a series of generic error codes. The *address* of a fault is always presented, but there is no attempt made to correlate the fault's address to a physical IC. Fortunately, today's memory systems are so small and modular that trial-and-error isolation can often be performed rapidly on just a few SIMMs or DIMMs. The symptoms below highlight many of the most common memory problems encountered in "contemporary" systems.

SYMPTOM 26-5 **You see the number "164" displayed on the monitor** This is a generic "memory size error"—the amount of memory found during the POST does not match the amount of memory listed in the system's CMOS Setup. Run the CMOS Setup routine, and make sure that the

TABLE 26-15 CLASSIC AT ERROR CODES

"AAXXXXYYYY 20X": MEMORY FAILURE

AA	BOARD	BANK
00 01 02 03	Motherboard	0
04 05 06 07	Motherboard	1
08 09	128KB memory expansion	n/a
10 11 12 13	1st 512KB memory adapter	0
14 15 16 17	1st 512KB memory adapter	1
18 19 1A 1B	2nd 512KB memory adapter	0
1C 1D 1E 1F	2nd 512KB memory adapter	1
20 21 22 23	3rd 512KB memory adapter	0
24 25 26 27	3rd 512KB memory adapter	1
28 29 2A 2B	4th 512KB memory adapter	0
2C 2D 2E 2F	4th 512KB memory adapter	1
30 31 32 33	5th 512KB memory adapter	0
34 35 36 37	5th 512KB memory adapter	1

YYYY	FAILED IC	YYYY	FAILED IC
0000	parity IC	0100	8
0001	0	0200	9
0002	1	0400	10
0004	2	0800	11
0008	3	1000	12
0010	4	2000	13
0020	5	4000	14
0040	6	8000	15
0080	7		

listed memory amount matches the actual memory amount. If memory has been added to or removed from the system, you will have to adjust the figure in the CMOS Setup to reflect that configuration change. If CMOS Setup parameters do not remain in the system after power is removed, try replacing the CMOS backup battery or CMOS/RTC IC.

The latest CMOS Setup routines do not actually *list* the amount of RAM—it is detected automatically. However, you may simply have to enter the CMOS Setup, then immediately "save changes and exit" to reset the amount of detected RAM in your system.

SYMPTOM 26-6 **You see an "Incorrect Memory Size" error message** This message can be displayed if the CMOS system setup is incorrect or if there is an actual memory failure that is not caught with a numerical 200-series or "164" codes.

- ***Check the CMOS settings.*** If the CMOS Setup is not updated to reflect memory additions (or removals), or the overall memory size changes because of a memory failure, you may need to adjust or resave your CMOS Setup. If the error persists, there is probably a failure in some portion of RAM.

- ***Isolate your memory.*** Remove all expansion memory from the system, alter the CMOS Setup to reflect base memory (system board) only, and retest the system. If the problem disappears, the fault is in some portion of expansion memory.
- ***Check the base memory.*** If the problem still persists, you know the trouble is likely to be in your base (system board) memory. Take a known-good SIMM or DIMM and systematically swap devices until you locate the defective device. If you have access to a repair shop with a memory tester, the process will be much faster.
- ***Check the expansion memory.*** If you successfully isolate the problem to a memory expansion board (often found in older proprietary PCs), you can adopt the same strategy for the board(s). Return one board at a time to the system (and update the CMOS setup to keep track of available memory). When the error message reappears, you will have found the defective board. Use a known-good RAM IC, SIMM, or DIMM and begin a systematic swapping process until you have found the defective memory device.

SYMPTOM 26-7 **You see a "ROM Error" message displayed on the monitor** This may also appear as a "207" error on some systems. To guarantee the integrity of system ROM, a checksum error test is performed as part of the POST. If this error occurs, one or more ROM locations may be faulty. Your only alternative here is to replace the system BIOS ROM(s) and retest the system (you cannot flash older AT-class ROM).

SYMPTOM 26-8 **New memory is installed, but the system refuses to recognize it** New memory installation has always presented some unique problems since different generations of PC deal with new memory differently.

- ***Verify RAM identification.*** The oldest PCs require you to set jumpers or DIP switches in order to recognize new blocks of memory. The vintage i286 and i386 systems (for example, a PS/2) use a setup disk to tell CMOS about the PC's configuration (including new memory). More recent i386 and i486 systems incorporate an "installed memory" setting into a CMOS Setup utility in BIOS that must be updated after the memory is installed or removed. Late-model i486, Pentium, and Pentium II/III systems actually "autodetect" installed memory each time the system is booted (so it need not be entered in the CMOS Setup, though setup may need to "auto detect" the new RAM amount on first boot).
- ***Verify bank assignments.*** Also check that a correct bank has been filled properly. The PC may not recognize any additional memory unless an entire bank has been filled and the bank is next in order (that is, Bank 0, then Bank 1, and so on). You may wish to check the PC's user manual for any unique rules or limitations in the particular motherboard.

> Many late-model Pentium II/III motherboards do NOT need banks filled in order, though that's usually the safest policy to follow when upgrading or troubleshooting any PC.

SYMPTOM 26-9 **New memory has been installed or replaced, and the system refuses to boot** Memory installations often proceed flawlessly, but when boot problems occur, you can usually narrow the problem down to several key areas.

- ***Check the power.*** Always start by checking AC power, the system power switch, and power connections to the motherboard. Check that none of the system cabling was dislodged during the memory installation.

- ***Check the expansion devices.*** See that all expansion boards are inserted evenly and completely in their expansion slots. Flexing the motherboard during memory installation may have pried one or more boards slightly out of their slots.
- ***Recheck the memory installation.*** Your memory modules might not be inserted correctly. Take the modules out and seat them again, making sure the locking arm is holding the module securely in place.
- ***Check the module type.*** If the problem continues, you probably do not have the right memory module for that particular computer. Make sure that the memory module (SIMM or DIMM) is the correct part that is compatible with your PC.
- ***Check the installation order.*** Finally, check for any particular "device order" that may be required by the motherboard. Certain systems require that memory be installed in pairs or in descending order by size. Refer to the system or motherboard manual for specific details on your exact system.

SYMPTOM 26-10 You see an "XXXX Optional ROM Bad, Checksum = YYYY" error message Part of the POST sequence checks for the presence of any other ROMs in the system. When another ROM is located, a checksum test is performed to check its integrity. This error message indicates that an external BIOS ROM (such as a SCSI adapter BIOS or video card BIOS) has checked *bad,* or its address conflicts with another device in the system. In either case, system initialization cannot continue.

- ***Check the ROM address setting.*** If you have just installed a new peripheral device when this error occurs (for example, a SCSI controller board), try changing the new device's ROM address jumpers to resolve the conflict.
- ***Check the new device.*** Remove the peripheral board—the fault should disappear. Try the board on another PC. If the problem continues on another PC, the adapter (or its ROM) may be defective. If this error has occurred spontaneously, remove one peripheral board at a time and retest the system until you isolate the faulty board, then replace the faulty board (or just replace its ROM if possible).

SYMPTOM 26-11 You see a general RAM error with fault addresses listed In actual practice, the error message may appear as any of the examples below depending on the specific fault, where the fault was detected, and the BIOS version reporting the error:

```
Memory address line failure at <XXXX>, read <YYYY>, expecting <ZZZZ>
Memory data line failure at <XXXX>, read <YYYY>, expecting <ZZZZ>
Memory high address failure at <XXXX>, read <YYYY>, expecting <ZZZZ>
Memory logic failure at <XXXX>, read <YYYY>, expecting <ZZZZ>
Memory odd/even logic failure at <XXXX>, read <YYYY>, expecting <ZZZZ>
Memory parity failure at <XXXX>, read <YYYY>, expecting <ZZZZ>
Memory read/write failure at <XXXX>, read <YYYY>, expecting <ZZZZ>
```

Each of the errors shown above are general RAM error messages indicating a problem in base or extended/expanded RAM. The code "XXXX" is the failure segment address—an offset address may be included. The word "YYYY" is what was read back from the address, and "ZZZZ" is the word that was expected. The difference between these read and expected words is what precipitated the error. In general, these errors indicate that at least one base RAM IC (if you have RAM soldered to the motherboard) or at least one SIMM/DIMM has failed. A trial-and-error approach is usually the least expensive route in finding the problem. First, reseat each SIMM or DIMM and retest the system to be sure that each SIMM/DIMM is inserted and secured properly. Rotate a known-good SIMM/DIMM through each occupied SIMM/DIMM socket in sequence. If the error disappears when the known-good SIMM or DIMM is in a slot, the old device that had been displaced is probably the faulty one. You can go on to use specialized SIMM troubleshooting equipment to identify the defective IC, but such equipment is rather expensive unless you intend to repair a large volume of SIMMs/DIMMs to the IC level.

If the problem remains unchanged even though every SIMM has been checked, the error is probably in the motherboard RAM or RAM support circuitry. Run a thorough system diagnostic, if possible, and check for failures in other areas of the motherboard that effect memory (such as the interrupt controller, cache controller, DMA controller, or memory management chips). If the problem prohibits a software diagnostic, use a POST board and try identifying any hexadecimal error code. If a support chip is identified, you can replace the defective chip or replace the motherboard outright. If RAM continues to be the problem, try replacing the motherboard RAM (or replace the entire motherboard) and retest the system.

SYMPTOM 26-12 **You see a "Cache Memory Failure—Disabling Cache" error** The cache system has failed. The tag RAM, cache logic (motherboard chipset), or cache memory on your motherboard is defective. Your best course is to replace the cache RAM IC(s) or COAST (Cache-on-a-Stick) module. If the problem persists, try replacing the cache logic or tag RAM (or replace the entire motherboard). You will probably need a schematic diagram or a detailed block diagram of your system in order to locate the cache memory chip(s), so refer to the system or motherboard manual for detailed information.

SYMPTOM 26-13 **You see a "Decreasing Available Memory" error message** This is basically a confirmation message that indicates that a failure has been detected in extended or expanded memory and that all memory *after* the failure has been disabled to allow the system to continue operating (although at a substantially reduced level). Your first step should be to reseat each SIMM/DIMM and ensure that they are properly inserted and secured. Next, take a known-good SIMM or DIMM and step through each occupied SIMM/DIMM slot until the problem disappears—the device that had been removed is probably the faulty one. Keep in mind that you may have to alter the system's CMOS Setup parameters as you move memory around the machine (an incorrect setup can cause problems during system initialization).

SYMPTOM 26-14 **You are encountering a memory error with HIMEM.SYS under DOS** In many cases, this is a compatibility problem with system memory. For example, the Intel Advanced/AS motherboard is incompatible with two specific Texas Instruments EDO SIMMs (part numbers TM124FBK32S-60 and TM248GBK32S-60). Other EDO SIMMs from TI and other vendors will not cause this error. Try a SIMM from a different manufacturer. Also make sure that you're using the latest version of HIMEM.SYS.

SYMPTOM 26-15 **Memory devices from various vendors refuse to work together** The system experiences a "memory failure" during the memory count at start time. This is a very "machine-specific" problem. For example, Gateway Solo PCs can suffer this problem when customers use the same size memory modules (4MB, 8MB, or 16MB) made from *different* vendors. Try matching the memory modules from the same manufacturer (including part number and speed).

WINDOWS-RELATED MEMORY ERRORS

SYMPTOM 26-16 **Windows 95/98 "Protection" errors occur after adding SIMMs/DIMMs** Windows 95/98 stalls with "Windows Protection Errors" during boot, or randomly crashes with "Fatal Exception Errors" when opening applications. This is a known problem with the Intel

Thor motherboard using the 1.00.01.CNOT BIOS after installing 32MB of RAM. This issue is usually due to certain third-party SIMMs operating at speeds faster or slower than 60ns. The motherboard probably has tight memory specifications, and SIMMs that operate at *correct* speed are required (not faster or slower—even though the SIMMs are "marked" properly). Some SIMM manufacturers mark the SIMMs at 60ns, but the SIMMs actually run at 45ns. Try some SIMMs from a different manufacturer. It is also possible that a BIOS upgrade may loosen timing enough to make the SIMMs usable.

SYMPTOM 26-17 **Windows returns a fault in the MS-DOS extender** This kind or error can occur in Windows 3.1, 3.11, 95, or 98 and usually happens in one of two formats: "Bad fault in MS-DOS extender" or "Fault outside of MS-DOS extender." You may also see a "stack dump" with a format such as:

```
Raw fault frame:
EC=0344 CS=031F IP=85E2 AX=001D BX=0005 CX=1800 DX=155F
SI=0178 DI=0178 BP=016E DS=027F ES=027F SS=027F SP=0166
```

An error such as: *"Bad fault in MS-DOS extender"* generally occurs when the fault handler in DOSX.EXE (the DOS extender) generates another cascaded fault while trying to handle a protected-mode exception. This error is usually caused by one of the following factors:

- HIMEM.SYS is unable to control the A20 line (which may indicate a motherboard problem).
- DOS=HIGH is not functioning properly (perhaps HIMEM.SYS is not loaded or is corrupt).
- Your RAM may be defective. You might try a RAM diagnostic to isolate any memory problems.
- You are not running MS-DOS (e.g., your system is running DR DOS).
- The third-party memory manager (for example, 386MAX) is not configured correctly.
- A "EMM386.EXE NOEMS x=A000-EFFF" command line is missing from the CONFIG.SYS file.
- You have an old, out-of-date BIOS ROM that isn't supporting the DOS extender properly.
- Your memory-related CMOS Setup configuration is incorrect.
- Your Windows files are old or corrupted. Run ScanDisk to test for file problems, then reinstall Windows if necessary.
- Your system is infected with a computer virus (for example, Form, Forms, Noint, or Yankee Doodle are known to cause this type of problem). Check the system with a current antivirus utility.

If you see an error such as *"Standard mode fault outside MS-DOS extender,"* the Windows kernel may be generating a processor exception during initialization (before it has installed its own exception handlers) or when the kernel determines that it cannot handle an exception. The underlying causes are almost always the same as outlined above. The portion of the error display labeled "Raw fault frame" contains information generated by the 80286 or 80386 processor in response to the original fault. The meaning of these entries is outlined in Table 26-16.

SYMPTOM 26-18 **Windows returns a "General Protection Fault" (or GPF)** There are several possible causes of general protection faults under Windows 3.1*x*, 95, or 98. An x86-type CPU (from 80286 to Pentium III processors) can detect when a program encounters a problem. The most common problems include "stack faults," "invalid instructions" (a.k.a. software bugs), "divide errors" (divide

TABLE 26-16 DOS EXTENDER MESSAGE CODES

SETTING	MEANING
EC=xxxx	An exception code produced by the processor in response to the original fault.
*IP=xxxx	The program counter of the faulting instruction (8086 register "IP").
*CS=xxxx	The code segment of the fault instruction. If this is "0053" or "005B," the original fault was in DOSX.EXE.
FL=xxxx	The flag's image at the time of the original fault.
SP=xxxx	The stack pointer at the time of the original fault.
SS=xxxx	The stack segment at the time of the original fault. If this is "004B," the fault occurred on a stack belonging to DOSX.EXE.

* The CS and IP sections indicate the point in the program where the original problem was detected.

by zero or "math" errors), and "general protection faults." These problems generally indicate nonstandard code in a Windows application, in Windows itself, or in a Windows device driver:

Stack Fault (a.k.a. Interrupt 12) There are several possible reasons for a "stack fault." An instruction may try to access memory beyond the limits of the current Stack segment or load the "SS" register with invalid information (though that shouldn't happen under Windows 95/98). Stack faults are always fatal to the current application in Windows, but Windows may not crash completely.

Invalid Instruction (a.k.a. Interrupt 6) The CPU detects most invalid instructions and generates a software interrupt to report them. Invalid instructions are always fatal to the application. This should never happen, but it is usually caused by coding errors that accidentally execute data instead of code.

Divide Error (a.k.a. Interrupt 0) This error is caused when the CPU's intended destination register cannot hold the result of a divide operation—it could be divide by zero or divide overflow. In either case, the problem is almost always due to a problem with the program.

General Protection Fault (a.k.a. Interrupt 13) Any protection violations that do not cause another exception cause a "general" protection exception because one of the following conditions are true:

- Exceeding a segment limit when using the CS, DS, ES, FS, GS memory segments. This is a very common bug in programs—usually caused by miscalculating how much memory is required in an allocation.
- Transferring program execution to a segment of memory that is not executable (for example, jumping to a location that contains garbage).
- Writing to a read-only or a code segment of memory.
- Loading a bad value into a segment register.
- Using a NULL pointer. A value of 0 is defined as a NULL pointer. In protected mode, it is always invalid to use a segment register that contains 0.

In virtually all cases, the solution to a "protection fault" is to try reloading the suspect program, driver, or Windows module (run ScanDisk to check the disk file system for errors). If the suspect program or driver is buggy, it may be necessary to download and install a patch file to correct potential programming errors.

SYMPTOM 26-19 **You see a memory error such as: "Unable to control A20 line"** This error is almost always related to the HIMEM.SYS driver. The A20 line controls access to the first 64KB of extended memory (known as the *high memory area*, or "HMA"). The HIMEM.SYS device driver must control the A20 line in order to manage extended memory. The error message is reported by HIMEM.SYS if it *incorrectly* identifies the extended memory handling mechanism of the computer or if the handling method in your PC's BIOS is unknown. There are two workarounds for this problem:

- ***Set the "Machine" switch.*** Add the "/M:x" (the "machine type") switch to the HIMEM.SYS command line in your CONFIG.SYS file (where "x" is the "machine number" between 1-14 or 16). Shut down and then restart your computer. For example:

```
DEVICE=C:\DOS\HIMEM.SYS /M:1
```

> An incorrect A20 machine handler may hang the system at boot up. You should have an MS-DOS version 5.0 (or Windows 95/98) bootable floppy disk available to boot from before you experiment with different machine switches.

- ***Check the BIOS version.*** It may be necessary to upgrade your machine's BIOS or to contact your system vendor for assistance in modifying your CMOS settings—you may need to disable a FastGate (or similar) option.

SYMPTOM 26-20 **You see a memory error such as: "Cannot setup EMS buffer," or "Unable to set page frame base address"** This is a known problem with many Dell Inspiron 7000 computers under Windows 98, and appears when starting a DOS-based program that requires Expanded Memory (EMS) page frames. EMS page frames normally require 64KB of upper memory; however, Dell Inspiron 7000-series computers can provide only 54K of upper memory. This problem is an issue with the Dell system design and generally cannot be corrected unless you turn off the program's use of EMS page frames (or run the program on another system).

SYMPTOM 26-21 **Memory contents are corrupted (or the PC halts) when entering a CPU power-down state under Windows 98** If your system's power management settings are configured to allow the processor to enter a "C3" power state on a computer supporting the "Advanced Configuration and Power Interface" (ACPI) standard, you may encounter symptoms such as corrupted memory after several minutes of inactivity, or the computer may stop responding after several minutes of inactivity.

This problem is due to an issue with the Intel 440BX chipset under Windows 98 (caused by Windows 98), which may allow memory contents to be corrupted when a CPU enters or leaves its power-down state. If that motherboard uses the Intel PIIX4-E IDE controller chipset, the computer might hang (known to occur if a bus mastering operation occurs while in the power-down state).

Until a patch is available for Windows 98, you can work around this issue by preventing the CPU from entering the C3 power state. To accomplish this, exit Windows and reboot the computer. Enter your CMOS Setup and set the "lvl3_latency" entry to a value greater than 0x3E8h (1000 decimal)—if "lvl3_latency" is greater than 0x3E8h, the Windows 98 ACPI driver does not enter the C3 state. You'll need to save your changes and reboot the PC for those changes to take effect.

SYMPTOM 26-22 **Windows 98 appears unstable after disabling virtual memory (the "swap file")** There is not enough RAM in the system. This condition can occur if you disable virtual memory with only 16MB of RAM. Windows 98 has higher memory requirements than Windows 95, so while 16MB may be the "theoretical" minimum for Windows 98, 32MB of RAM or more would result in better system performance and stability. To resolve this problem, install more RAM in your computer, enable virtual memory, or both. To enable virtual memory:

- Restart your computer and hold down the CTRL key until the Windows 98 Startup Menu appears.
- Choose Safe Mode from the Startup Menu.
- Click Start, highlight Settings, and then click Control Panel.
- Double-click System, click the Performance tab, and then click Virtual Memory.
- Click the option labeled: "Let Windows manage my virtual memory settings."
- Click OK, click Close, and then click Yes when you are prompted to restart your computer.

SYMPTOM 26-23 **You encounter a Windows 98 "protection error" involving NTKERN**
This problem occurs when installing Windows 98 and restarting for the first time. You may see an error message such as:

```
While initializing device NTKERN: Windows Protection Error. You need to
restart your computer.
```

or you may receive an error message after the Windows 98 Setup is completed such as:

```
Invalid VxD Dynamic Link Call to Device 3 Service B
```

or:

```
While Initialing Device <filename> Windows Protection Error. You need to
restart your computer.
```

If you try to start in the Safe Mode, you may receive a message like:

```
HIMEM.SYS Has Detected Unreliable XMS Memory at <address>.
```

In virtually every case, there is defective memory (RAM) in your computer. You'll need to systematically remove or replace the SIMM(s) or DIMM(s) (or memory chips) in your computer to eliminate any bad memory. You can use any of the techniques below to try working around the memory problem until you can identify and replace the defective memory.

Limit RAM through SYSTEM.INI If your computer has over 16MB of memory, it may be possible to configure your computer to only use 16MB of memory (factoring out any RAM above 16MB):

- Use Notepad to open the SYSTEM.INI file in the \Windows folder.
- Add the following line to the [386enh] section of the SYSTEM.INI file:

```
MaxPhysPage=01000
```

- Save this file and quit Notepad.
- Restart the computer and then restart the Windows 98 Setup utility.

> If you can't start in the Safe Mode, restart your computer and hold down the CTRL key until the Windows 98 Startup Menu appears—then choose Command Prompt Only. Use a DOS text editor like EDIT to update the \Windows\System.ini file as shown above.

Limit RAM through System Configuration Use the System Configuration tool to limit the amount of memory (RAM) available to Windows 98:

- Restart your computer, hold the CTRL key until the Windows 98 Startup Menu appears, and choose the Safe Mode.
- Click Start, highlight Programs, select *Accessories*, select System Tools, and then click System Information.
- On the Tools menu, click the *System Configuration* utility.
- On the General tab, click *Advanced*.
- Click the *Limit Memory To <n> MB* check box (where <n> is a number) to select it, and then set the memory limit value to **16MB**.
- Click *OK*, click *OK* again, and then restart your computer.

SYMPTOM 26-24 The Windows 95/98 system slows or locks up when playing MIDI files continuously When a MIDI (*Musical Instrument Device Interface* or .MID) file is played repeatedly or continuously, your computer may lock up, or the computer may seem sluggish for a short time after you stop playing the MIDI file. Screen savers and games that use repeated MIDI playback are typically susceptible to this problem. The problem is caused by the Windows MIDI sequencer (MCISEQ.DRV), which loses a small amount of memory for each successive playback of a MIDI file.

This is a known problem with the MIDI sequencer in Windows 95 and Windows 98, so until a suitable update or patch file becomes available to correct the MIDI sequencer, you should avoid using the screen saver or game or disable MIDI playback. Note that closing and then reloading a MIDI file releases the lost memory.

SYMPTOM 26-25 After installing Windows 98, the Device Manager may show a yellow exclamation mark next to the PC Card (PCMCIA) network adapter You may also see a status message such as "Error Code 10" in the adapter's Properties. This is known to occur on laptops such as the DEC HiNote Ultra II when the PC Card network adapter uses memory that the computer's BIOS has reserved. Windows 98 determines a free range of memory and then assigns that range to the network adapter for use—but the network adapter driver may not be able to use the assigned range if it is reserved by the BIOS. To get around this problem, try excluding the memory range that is being reserved by the BIOS so that Windows 98 will not use it:

- Click Start, highlight Settings, and click Control Panel.
- Double-click the System icon.
- Double-click Computer on the Device Manager tab.
- Click the Reserve Resources tab, and then click Memory.
- Click Add, type **CA000** in the Start Value box, then type **CB000** in the End Value box.
- Click OK, and click OK again.
- Click the PC Card network adapter to highlight it, and then click Remove.
- Click OK, and then click Close.
- Restart your computer. The network adapter will be redetected and reinstalled by Windows 98.

SYMPTOM 26-26 **You notice that Windows 98 system resources remain lower after quitting a program** This condition is often referred to as "memory leakage," when memory is not freed by a program after it quits.

- *Restart the PC.* Rebooting the PC from scratch should return any "leaked" memory. You can use this trick as a temporary workaround.
- *Use Care when exiting programs.* Memory leakage can occur if you start a program and then quit before it has completely started. Do not quit a program before it has completely started.
- *Patch the offending program(s).* Memory leakage is often caused by poorly coded or buggy software rather than Windows itself. If you notice "leakage" with a particular program, check with the software maker's Web site to see if there is a downloadable patch or update that will correct the memory leakage.

SYMPTOM 26-27 **You see an error message such as "Insufficient memory to initialize Windows" even though there is plenty of RAM** This problem may be "too much" RAM. When attempting to install or start Windows 95/98 with over 768MB of RAM (perhaps 1GB or more), the system may return an erroneous "insufficient memory" message. This is generally regarded as a problem with Windows 95/98, and you can work around the problem by limiting the amount of RAM that Windows can use to 768MB:

- Use Notepad to edit the SYSTEM.INI file.
- Add the following line in the [386Enh] section of the SYSTEM.INI file:

```
MaxPhysPage=30000
```

- Save the SYSTEM.INI file and then restart your computer.

If this problem occurs during Windows Setup, start the system to the command prompt (a.k.a. DOS) mode and use the DOS-based EDIT utility to modify the SYSTEM.INI file. When you save the edited SYSTEM.INI file and reboot the PC, the Windows Setup should continue.

SYMPTOM 26-28 **When trying to format a hard drive under Windows 98, you see an error message such as: "Insufficient memory to load system files."** The format process will terminate. This error occurs if you attempt to format your hard disk using the **format c: /q /u /s /v** command at a command prompt, and there is not enough free conventional memory to use the **/s** switch. This error may also occur if you start your computer using the Windows 98 Startup Disk and then attempt to format your hard disk. This is a problem with Windows 98, but there are ways to work around it. First, do not use the **/s** switch with the **format** command—after the format process is finished, transfer the system files to the hard disk using the **SYS C:** command. If you're restarting your computer using the Windows 98 Startup Disk, choose "Start Computer With CD-ROM Support" on the Windows 98 Startup Menu, and then use the **format** command to format your hard disk.

SYMPTOM 26-29 **Your Windows 95/98 system returns an "internal stack overflow" error** "Stacks" are small sections of reserved memory that programs use for processing hardware events. A "stack overflow" occurs when there is not enough space in memory to run the hardware interrupt routines. When Windows shows an "internal stack overflow" error, there is not enough space in memory (either set aside or available to handle the calls being made to the system hardware).

- *Check Stacks in CONFIG.SYS.* The CONFIG.SYS file may not be properly configured for the Windows installation. Try the following values: STACKS=64,512 (this is the maximum allowed), FILES=60, and BUFFERS=40.
- *Check for old memory managers.* Examine the CONFIG.SYS file to determine if files such as HIMEM.SYS or EMM386.EXE are being loaded from a folder other than the Windows folder. If so, boot Windows using the Safe Mode Command Prompt Only (DOS) option. Rename the CONFIG.SYS file to CONFIG.DOS, and the AUTOEXEC.BAT file to AUTOEXEC.DOS, and then restart the computer.
- *Eliminate TSRs.* Some TSRs may be interfering with Windows. Disable any non-boot device drivers in the CONFIG.SYS and AUTOEXEC.BAT files. If you are installing from Windows 3.*x* and getting a stack overflow error, check the WIN.INI and SYSTEM.INI files for non-Windows-based programs or drivers that may be loading.
- *Check for resource conflicts.* There may be an incompatible hardware configuration. Check the port and IRQ settings of any network card, sound card, and/or modem. Make sure that there are no COM2/COM4 or COM1/COM3 conflicts and that no devices are sharing IRQs. Disable or remove conflicting devices.
- *Upgrade the BIOS.* The computer may need a BIOS upgrade. Check the BIOS version and contact the manufacturer of your computer for information about a BIOS upgrade.

SYMPTOM 26-30 You encounter random "fatal exception" errors under Windows 95/98 You may also notice that there are more "fatal exception" errors under Windows 95/98 than under Windows 3.1*x*. The most common cause for these error messages is faulty physical memory (RAM) on the computer.

- *Check for drivers.* Try starting the system in Safe Mode. If the "fatal exception" errors disappear, the problem may be with one or more buggy or corrupted drivers loading in the normal mode. You may then need to systematically disable background software and drivers in order to isolate the offending software.
- *Check the CMOS Setup.* In some circumstances it may be possible to adjust the CMOS settings (such as changing memory wait states or disabling the motherboard's L2 cache) to stabilize Windows 95/98 successfully.
- *Check/replace the RAM.* To resolve "fatal exception" errors, it is often necessary to isolate and replace the defective RAM. In rare cases, the problem may be on the motherboard.

SYMPTOM 26-31 An error indicates that there is not enough memory to start Windows 95/98 (or an application) This problem can occur if there is not enough real and virtual memory to start the Windows shell (or the particular program). Start your computer to the DOS prompt and free some space on the hard disk containing your swap file (virtual memory). Once you free some space on your hard disk, restart Windows normally and try to run the program again. If the problem persists (or you cannot free more space on the drive), try adding RAM to the system.

> If you try to start a program on a PC with only 4MB of free RAM, and less than 8MB of free space on the hard disk with a swap file, you may *not* be able to shutdown and restart your computer normally. You must press CTRL+ALT+DEL to open the Close Program dialog box, and then click Shut Down to shut down Windows.

SYMPTOM 26-32 **EMM386 refuses to load after installing Windows 98** This issue can occur if you load EMM386.EXE using the /Highscan switch. The /Highscan switch can interfere with hardware detection during Setup, so it is disabled by Windows 98 Setup. You can re-enable EMM386 using the following steps:

- Use Notepad to open the CONFIG.SYS file.
- Locate the line that loads EMM386.EXE, and remove the following text from the beginning of the line:

```
rem -- by Windows 98 setup -
```

- Save and close the CONFIG.SYS file.
- Restart the computer.

SYMPTOM 26-33 **General protection faults are generated after restarting a program in Windows 95/98** If you close a 16-bit program that is marked as "not responding" in the *Close Program* dialog box, and then restart the program, you may receive a general protection fault (GPF) error. This happens because of the way the offending program was originally closed. When a program is closed normally, its dynamic link libraries (DLLs) are unloaded from memory. When you use the Close Program dialog to close a program that is not responding, the program's DLLs are *not* unloaded (and are not reinitialized when you restart the program later). The only real solution here is to shut down the computer, and then restart it from scratch.

SYMPTOM 26-34 **You find that you cannot use 256MB DIMMs that contain 64Mbit RAM components** You should double-check the manufacturer's recommendations for your motherboard and verify the type of DIMM sizes and technologies best suited to the particular motherboard. Some motherboard models (such as Intel's JN440BX motherboard) cannot use such sophisticated RAM components on a DIMM of that capacity. This can cause the motherboard to produce invalid timing signals and cause unpredictable system behavior. Try smaller DIMMs, or use DIMMs with less dense memory components on board.

Further Study

Autotime: **http://www.autotime.com**

Cameleon Technology: **http://www.camusa.com/**

CST, Inc: **http://www.simmtester.com/**

Innoventions: **http://www.simcheck.com/**

Jaguar Marketing Group: **http://www2.inow.com/~degeorge/jaguar.htm**

Kingston: **http://www.kingston.com**

PNY: **http://www.pny.com**

Simmsaver Technology, Inc.: **http://www.simmsaver.com/**

27

MEMORY MANAGERS

CHAPTER AT A GLANCE

As personal computers broke the 1MB mark, there has been a problem utilizing memory over 640KB (conventional memory). In order for application programs to utilize memory beyond 640KB, a *memory manager* is required to support the physical RAM present in the system and configure the RAM as *extended* (XMS) or *expanded* (EMS) memory. In general, memory managers provide a series of critical services to a modern PC:

- They allow the operating system and applications to access extended memory (XMS) over 1MB.
- They allow extended memory (XMS) to simulate expanded memory (EMS), which otherwise would require specialized hardware support.
- They locate and free unused memory in the upper memory area (UMA) to make it available for use.
- They utilize the high memory area (HMA)—that 64KB segment just above the 1MB mark.
- They support the use of shadow RAM, where slower ROM contents are copied to faster RAM in order to provide faster system performance.

- They can rearrange the address order of physical memory in the PC so that faster memory appears in the lower addresses—a technique known as *memory sorting*.
- They can fill in empty addresses below 640KB with memory contents from extended memory (XMS) to utilize the entire 640KB at all times—a technique called *backfilling*.

Because of these features, use of memory managers offers some significant advantages for a computer. Larger applications (or applications with huge volumes of data) and more sophisticated operating systems can be created. Extended memory supports the execution of code beyond 1MB, so programs can be run outside of conventional memory. Multiple programs can be loaded into the available RAM space for more effective multitasking. Unused space in the UMA and HMA can be loaded with DOS or real-mode device drivers—freeing more conventional memory for DOS applications. The most recent generations of memory managers also offer a suite of advanced features and conveniences such as accelerating software loading and execution times, better memory utilization and performance reporting, and more aggressive location of unused memory.

Though most recent memory managers are generally compatible with Windows 95 and Windows 98, memory managers are not as vital as they once were. Windows 95/98 and later operating systems now incorporate many of the memory management functions needed by the PC—relegating DOS and third-party memory manager utilities to DOS platforms or "game machines," as well as DOS applications running in a Windows 95/98 "window." Although memory managers are well-developed pieces of software, they are not always as well-behaved as they should be. This chapter presents some tips for optimizing your use of memory and examines a selection of symptoms and solutions for the three major memory manager families: Quarterdeck (QEMM), Microsoft (HIMEM/EMM386), and Qualitas (386MAX).

> If you are using a Windows 95/98 computer with no DOS or real-mode drivers or applications, you generally will not require a separate memory manager—such software can typically be disabled or removed without penalty to the system. This chapter is intended to support systems using stand-alone memory manager products for "legacy" DOS software.

Making the Most of "Conventional" Memory

Even under the DOS shells of Windows 95/98, DOS applications are still dependent on an ample amount of conventional memory for proper operation. Freeing conventional memory, and loading real-mode drivers and DOS into upper memory, are still two key objectives of memory management. The memory management process usually consists of enabling the memory managers, then rearranging real-mode software in an optimum fashion to free the maximum amount of conventional memory. Since every PC configuration is different, and can use an incredibly diverse array of software, there is no single set of rules that can ensure optimum memory utilization (even memory optimizers like DOS MEMMAKER are known to fail under some circumstances). As a consequence, optimizing a PC's memory is sometimes more of an art than a science. This part of the chapter outlines the essential concepts of using memory managers and offers some tips to help you utilize memory better.

PROTECT THE CONFIGURATION

Optimizing memory is largely a matter of tweaking a system's CONFIG.SYS and AUTOEXEC.BAT files. Though Windows 95/98 tries to eliminate them, these startup files are still the only way to configure a PC for real-mode (DOS) operation. Before you attempt to modify the startup files, you should always make it a point to back up the startup files by copying CONFIG.SYS and AUTOEXEC.BAT to different file names, such as:

```
C:\> copy config.sys config.bak
C:\> copy autoexec.bat autoexec.bak
```

This creates two backup files and allows you to modify the original startup files. If you make a mistake modifying the startup files, you can always restore the original CONFIG.SYS and AUTOEXEC.BAT files by recopying the backup files to the original file names, such as:

```
C:\> copy config.bak config.sys
C:\> copy autoexec.bak autoexec.bat
```

Once the files have been restored, you can resume modifying them. If you have a boot disk, you should also consider placing a copy of the original startup files on the boot disk.

Also make it a point to use the Startup menu with the F8 key. When you see the message "Starting Windows 95," press F8 to load a Startup menu. From here, you can control the ways in which your system starts. This can be a valuable tool when checking to see just which drivers or utilities load (or not). If you're working on an older DOS/Windows 3.1x platform, use the F5 key to bypass CONFIG.SYS when the "Starting MS-DOS" message appears, or use F8 to step through each line in the startup files.

OPTIMIZATIONS FOR CONFIG.SYS

The first step in optimizing your system's memory is to enable your high memory area (or HMA). To do this, you will need to place HIMEM.SYS and EMM386.EXE into your CONFIG.SYS startup file. From the DOS prompt, start a text editor such as EDIT and load your CONFIG.SYS file. One of the first things that CONFIG.SYS should do is load HIMEM and EMM386, as shown in Figure 27-1. (This is shown as an example only—your CONFIG.SYS file may be radically different.) Remember that there are a number of command-line switches for both HIMEM and EMM386. Depending on the vintage and particular configuration of your PC, you may need to add one or more switches to achieve proper driver operation. Table 27-1 lists the syntax and command-line switches for HIMEM, and Table 27-2 lists the syntax and command-line switches for EMM386. If you intend to make use of both high memory and any available UMAs, you should use the RAM switch with EMM386.

When MEM /C is run with the CONFIG.SYS file shown in Figure 27-1, only 441KB of the total 640KB conventional memory space is available. Large DOS applications may fail to function with so little conventional memory. Now that we know the high memory is active (thanks to HIMEM and EMM386), we can optimize CONFIG.SYS to free as much conventional memory as possible.

```
device = c:\dos\himem.sys
device = c:\dos\setver.exe
device = c:\dos\emm386.exe
stacks = 9,256
files = 80
buffers = 50
lastdrive = Z
device = c:\sb16\drv\sbcd.sys /D:mscd001 /P:220
device = c:\rodent\oldmouse.exe
```

FIGURE 27-1 A simple but inefficient CONFIG.SYS file

27

TABLE 27-1 SYNTAX AND COMMAND-LINE SWITCHES FOR HIMEM

SYNTAX

device=[drive:][path]himem.sys [/hmamin=m] [/numhandles=n] [/int15=xxxx] [/machine:g] [/a2Ocontrol:onloff] [/shadowram:onloff] [/cpuclock:onloff]

PARAMETERS

[drive:][path]	Specifies the location of the HIMEM.SYS file.
/hmamin=m	Specifies the amount of memory (in kilobytes) that a program must use before HIMEM.SYS permits the program to use the high memory area. Valid values for *m* are 0-63. The default value is 0.
/numhandles=n	Specifies the maximum number of extended memory block (EMB) handles that can be used simultaneously. Valid values for *n* are 1-128. The default value is 32. Each additional handle requires an additional 6 bytes of resident memory.
/int15=xxxx	Allocates the specified amount of extended memory (in kilobytes) for the Interrupt 15h interface. Some older programs use a conflicting extended memory scheme. To use memory allocated by this switch, programs must recognize VDisk headers. To ensure enough memory is available, add 64 to the value you want to specify for xxxx. Valid values for xxxx are 64-65535. If you specify a value less than 64, the value becomes 0. The default value is 0.
/machine:xxxx	Specifies the A20 handler to be used. An A20 handler is a part of your computer that gives it access to the high memory area. The xxxx value can be any of the following codes or their equivalent numbers:

CODE	NUMBER	A20 HANDLER
at	1	IBM PC/AT or COMPUADD 386 or JDR 386/33
ps2	2	IBM PS/2 or Datamedia 386/486 or UNISYS PowerPort
ptlcascade	3	Phoenix Cascade BIOS
hpvectra	4	HP Vectra (A and A+)
att6300plus	5	AT&T 6300 Plus
acer1100	6	Acer 1100
toshiba	7	Toshiba 1600 and 1200XE or Toshiba 5100
wyse	8	Wyse 12.5MHz i286 or COMPUADD 386 or Hitachi HL500C or Intel 301z or 302
tulip	9	Tulip SX
zenith	10	Zenith ZBIOS
at	11	IBM PC/AT
at2	12	IBM PC/AT (alternative delay)
css	12	CSS Labs
at3	13	IBM PC/AT (alternative delay)
philips	13	Philips
fasthp	14	HP Vectra
ibm7552	15	IBM 7552 Industrial Computer
bullmicral	16	Bull Micral 60
dell	17	Dell XBIOS

TABLE 27-1 SYNTAX AND COMMAND-LINE SWITCHES FOR HIMEM *(CONTINUED)*

PARAMETERS

/a20control:on|off	Specifies whether HIMEM.SYS is to take control of the A20 line, even if A20 was on when HIMEM.SYS was loaded. If you specify /a20control:off, HIMEM.SYS takes control of the A20 line only if A20 was off when HIMEM.SYS was loaded. The default setting is /a20control:on.
/shadowram:on|off	Specifies whether HIMEM.SYS is to switch off shadow RAM used for read-only memory, and add that RAM to its memory pool. If your computer has less than 2MB of RAM, the default setting is /shadowram:off. This parameter is supported only on some computers.
/cpuclock:on|off	Specifies whether HIMEM.SYS is to affect the clock speed of your computer. If your computer's speed changes when you install HIMEM.SYS, specifying /cpuclock:on might correct the problem. Enabling this switch slows down HIMEM.SYS.

TABLE 27-2 SYNTAX AND COMMAND-LINE SWITCHES FOR EMM386

SYNTAX

```
device=[drive:][path]emm386.exe [on|off|auto] [memory] [w=on|w=off]
[mx|frame=address|/pmmmm] [pn=address] [x=mmmm-nnnn] [i=mmmm-nnnn]
[b=address] [L=minXMS] [a=altregs] [h=handles] [d=nnn] [ram] [noems]
```

PARAMETERS

[drive:][path]	Specifies the location of the EMM386.EXE file.
[on|off|auto]	Activates the EMM386.EXE device driver (if set to on), or suspends the EMM386.EXE device driver (if set to off), or places the EMM386.EXE device driver in auto mode (if set to auto). Auto mode enables expanded memory support only when a program calls for it. The default value is on. Use the emm386 command to change this value after EMM386 has started.
memory	Specifies the amount of memory (in kilobytes) that you want to allocate to EMM386.EXE. Values for memory are 16-32768. The default value is 256. EMM386.EXE rounds the value down to the nearest multiple of 16. If you are using expanded memory, this value is in addition to the memory used for low-memory backfilling.
w=on|w=off	Enables or disables support for the Weitek coprocessor. The default setting is w=off.
mx	Specifies the address of the page frame. Valid values for x are 1-14. The following list shows each value and its associated base address in hexadecimal format. (Values 10-14 should be used only on old computers with 512KB of memory.) 1 = C000h 8 = DC00h 2 = C400h 9 = E000h 3 = C800h 10 = 8000h 4 = CC00h 11 = 8400h 5 = D000h 12 = 8800h 6 = D400h 13 = 8C00h 7 = D800h 14 = 9000h

27

TABLE 27-2 SYNTAX AND COMMAND-LINE SWITCHES FOR EMM386 *(CONTINUED)*

SYNTAX	
frame=address	Specifies the page-frame segment base directly. To specify a specific segment-base address for the page frame, use the frame switch and specify the address you want. Valid values for addresses are 8000h-9000h and C000h-E000h, in increments of 400h.
/pmmmm	Specifies the address of the page frame. Valid values for mmmm are 8000h 9000h and C000h-E000h, in increments of 400h.
pn=address	Specifies the segment address of a specific page, where *n* is the number of the page you are specifying and *address* is the segment address you want. Valid values for *n* are 0-255. Valid values for *address* are 8000h-9C00h and C000h-EC00h, in increments of 400h. The addresses for pages 0 through 3 must be contiguous in order to maintain compatibility with version 3.2 of the Lotus/Intel/Microsoft Expanded Memory Specification (LIM EMS). If you use the mx switch, the frame switch, or the /pmmmm switch, you cannot specify the addresses for pages 0 through 3 for the /pmmmm switch.
x=mmmm-nnnn	Prevents EMM386.EXE from using a particular range of segment addresses for an EMS page. Valid values for mmmm and nnnn are A000h-FFFFh and are rounded down to the nearest 4KB boundary. The x switch takes precedence over the i switch if the two ranges overlap.
i=mmmm-nnnn	Specifies a range of segment addresses to be used (included) for an EMS page or for RAM. Valid values for mmmm and nnnn are A000h-FFFFh and are rounded down to the nearest 4KB boundary. The x switch takes precedence over the i switch if the two ranges overlap.
b=address	Specifies the lowest segment address available for EMS "banking" (swapping of 16KB pages). Valid values are 1000h-4000h. The default value is 4000h.
L=minXMS	Ensures that the specified amount (in kilobytes) of extended memory will still be available after you load EMM386.EXE. The default value is 0.
a=altregs	Specifies how many fast alternate register sets (used for multitasking) you want to allocate to EMM386.EXE. Valid values are 0-254. The default value is 7. Every alternate register set adds about 200 bytes to the size in memory of EMM386.EXE.
h=handles	Specifies how many handles EMM386.EXE can use. Valid values are 2-255. The default value is 64.
d=nnn	Specifies how many kilobytes of memory should be reserved for buffered Direct Memory Access (DMA). Discounting floppy-disk DMA, this value should reflect the largest DMA transfer that will occur while EMM386.EXE is active. Valid values for nnn are 16-256. The default value is 16.
ram	Provides access to both expanded memory and the upper memory area.
noems	Provides access to upper memory area but prevents access to expanded memory.

Eliminate or Disable Unnecessary Entries The first and simplest step in freeing conventional memory is to remove any entries that are no longer being used. For example, when old peripherals are upgraded, the old device driver should be removed and the new one loaded. Look through the CONFIG.SYS file and erase any obsolete entries. Suppose for Figure 27-1 that the file OLDMOUSE.EXE was an old mouse driver that was no longer needed. You can simply erase the entry. If you are not certain whether the entry is needed or not, you can disable the entry rather than remove it by adding the term REM before the entry, such as:

```
REM device = c:\rodent\oldmouse.exe
```

This effectively "REMarks out" the entry. If you find that you need the entry after all, you can remove the REM statement later to reenable the entry without having to type it in again from scratch. (This feature goes a long way toward minimizing typing errors.)

Allocate Files and Buffers Sparingly The FILES entry defines how many files MS-DOS can have open at one time. The BUFFERS entry sets the number of 500-byte buffers that MS-DOS reserves for data transfer to and from disk. Large numbers of FILES and BUFFERS waste conventional memory. Make sure that the number of FILES and BUFFERS allocated for your system are sufficient without being excessive. For example, if you have been using a complex application that required 80 files and 50 buffers, but the application has been removed from your system, you can return the number of FILES and buffers to a lower level (60 FILES and 40 BUFFERS are usually typical for most systems), like this:

```
files = 60
buffers = 40
```

Tighten the "LASTDRIVE=" Entry DOS allows up to 26 letters to be used as logical drive references. In many cases, the "LASTDRIVE=" function is set to Z: (as in Figure 27-1), but the *actual* last drive to be enabled on your system may only be E:, H:, or K:. Each letter requires about 100 bytes of conventional memory, so use a lower letter that more closely reflects the true last drive. For this example, we might change the LASTDRIVE reference to M:, such as:

```
lastdrive = M
```

27

Set the Stacks Properly If you are running DOS only, you can usually remove the interrupt stack reference entirely, or set it to 0,0. For Windows and Windows 95/98 systems, however, the setting of 9256 is adequate for most systems.

Relocate DOS MS-DOS is one of the largest files to occupy conventional memory. One of your priorities in optimizing conventional memory should be to move DOS to either an available part of the upper memory area (UMA), or to the high memory area (HMA) using the "dos=" command in CONFIG.SYS. Remember that you'll need to load HIMEM first in order to load DOS into high memory, and use the RAM switch with EMM386 if you plan to try DOS in the UMA. Make sure the following line is added *after* the EMM386.EXE entry in CONFIG.SYS:

```
dos=umb,high
```

If you do not wish to try putting DOS in the UMA, you can omit the "umb" portion of the line above. Figure 27-2 shows our refined CONFIG.SYS file beginning to take shape.

Make Use of DEVICEHIGH The "DEVICEHIGH=" function allows you to place most device drivers into the UMA; otherwise, they would be loaded into conventional memory. There are only a few rules to keep in mind when using DEVICEHIGH. First, you must add the "umb" reference to the "dos=" function in order to use DEVICEHIGH at all. Second, you cannot use DEVICEHIGH until your memory managers are loaded, so HIMEM and EMM386 must always be loaded in conventional memory with the ordinary DEVICE function, as shown in Figure 27-2. Third, if you have any DEVICE references placed

```
device = c:\dos\himem.sys
device = c:\dos\emm386.exe ram
dos = umb,high
stacks = 9,256
files = 60
buffers = 40
lastdrive = M
devicehigh = c:\sb16\drv\sbcd.sys /D:mscd001 /P:220
devicehigh = c:\dos\setver.exe
```

FIGURE 27-2 A reasonably optimized CONFIG.SYS file

before your memory managers (such as the SETVER.EXE reference placed before EMM386.EXE in Figure 27-1), relocate the statement(s) *after* the memory managers, as shown in Figure 27-2.

You can then use the DOS MEM function to check the new amount of free conventional memory. After booting a system using the CONFIG.SYS file of Figure 27-2, free conventional memory reported by MEM (the "Largest executable program size" entry) rose to 555KB. For only a few minutes worth of work, the system picked up over 114KB of conventional memory.

OPTIMIZATIONS FOR AUTOEXEC.BAT

Working with the AUTOEXEC.BAT system startup file is a bit easier than dealing with CONFIG.SYS. AUTOEXEC.BAT is used to set system variables and to start any noncritical device drivers or TSRs (such as mouse drivers and caching programs) that may be needed to streamline the system. Before you attempt to work with the AUTOEXEC.BAT file, remember to make a backup of the original file just in case you get into trouble. If you need guidance making a backup of AUTOEXEC.BAT, see the section above entitled "Protect the Configuration." Start a text editor and load the AUTOEXEC.BAT file.

Eliminate Unnecessary Entries This is the most common method of streamlining an AUTOEXEC file. As applications come and go on your system, you will likely be left with a number of system variables that are no longer used, as well as very long PATH statements that you probably do not need. You may also find obsolete or unused drivers and TSRs in AUTOEXEC.BAT that can be removed without problems. If you're not sure whether an entry can be removed safely, place a REM statement in front of the entry. This effectively REMarks out (disables) the entry without removing it. If you find that you need the entry after all, you can simply remove the REM statement later to reenable the entry.

Make Use of LOADHIGH The "LOADHIGH=" function is used to load a program into the UMA; otherwise, it would be loaded into conventional memory. As with DEVICEHIGH, there are some rules that must be followed in order to use LOADHIGH successfully. The "umb" reference must be added to the "dos=" statement in CONFIG.SYS, and the LOADHIGH function cannot be used until the memory managers are loaded in CONFIG.SYS. A typical application of LOADHIGH is shown in the sample AUTOEXEC.BAT file of Figure 27-3. It is important to note that DOS does not report whether a LOADHIGH was successful or not. If a file cannot be loaded into upper memory, it will be loaded into conventional memory. Keep in mind that you can use the letters *lh* instead of LOADHIGH.

REVIEWING YOUR RESULTS WITH MEM

DOS offers the MEM function, which provides a comprehensive breakdown of memory in the system and how it is used. You can use the MEM function before and after an optimization to see the results of your work. Figure 27-4 illustrates a typical memory report using the /C switch. Since this chapter is primarily

```
set blaster = A220 I5 D1 H5 P330 T6
set sound = c:\sb16
prompt $p$g
loadhigh c:\sb16\sb16set /M:220 /VOC:220 /CD:220 /MIDI:220 /LINE:220 /TREBLE:0
loadhigh c:\sb16\sbconfig.exe /S
loadhigh c:\sb16\drv\mscdex.exe /D:MSCD001 /V /M:15
loadhigh c:\dos\smartdrv.exe
loadhigh c:\mouse\mouse.com
loadhigh c:\dos\share.exe /L:100
```

FIGURE 27-3 A typical AUTOEXEC.BAT file using the LOADHIGH command

concerned with freeing as much conventional memory as possible, you should be most concerned with the third line from the bottom: "Largest executable program size." The objective is to make this number as large (as close to 640KB) as possible.

```
Modules using memory below 1MB:

Name        Total       =    Conventional     +     Upper Memory
-------  -------------     ----------------       ----------------
MSDOS      17149   (17K)      17149   (17K)            0    (0K)
HIMEM       1168    (1K)       1168    (1K)            0    (0K)
EMM386      4144    (4K)       4144    (4K)            0    (0K)
COMMAND     2912    (2K)       2912    (2K)            0    (0K)
SMARTDRV   28816   (28K)      28816   (28K)            0    (0K)
MOUSE      24560   (24K)      24560   (24K)            0    (0K)
SHARE       7648    (7K)       7648    (7K)            0    (0K)
SBCD       11584   (11K)          0    (0K)        11584   (11K)
SETVER       640    (1K)          0    (0K)          640    (1K)
MSCDEX     46576   (45K)          0    (0K)        46576   (45K)
Free      570432  (557K)     568688  (555K)         1744    (2K)

Memory Summary:

Type of Memory        Total       =      Used        +     Free
---------------   --------------    --------------    ---------------
Conventional        655360    (640K)     86672    (85K)    568688   (555K)
Upper                60544     (59K)     58800    (57K)      1744     (2K)
Adapter RAM/ROM     393216    (384K)    393216   (384K)         0     (0K)
Extended (XMS)*   15668096  (15310K)   2610048  (2549K)  13058048(12752K)
---------------   --------------    --------------    ---------------
Total Memory      16777216  (1638K)    3148736  (3075K)  13628480(13309K)

Total under 1MB     715904    (699K)    145472   (142K)    570432   (557K)

Total Expanded (EMS)              16056320 (15680K)
Free Expanded (EMS)*              13303808 (12992K)

* EMM386 is using XMS memory to simulate EMS memory as needed.
  Free EMS memory may change as free XMS memory changes.

Largest executable program size      568592   (555K)
Largest free upper memory block        1296     (1K)
MS-DOS is resident in the high memory area.
```

FIGURE 27-4 A breakdown of memory utilization using the DOS MEM /C function

27

MIX AND MATCH

Chances are that not all of the drivers or TSRs you've attempted to load high (with DEVICEHIGH or LOADHIGH) will actually fit into the available space in the UMA. The trick to "optimizing" memory is to fit as much as possible into the UMA. Once you review the status of your memory with MEM (as in Figure 27-4), you can then return to your text editor and continue tweaking the CONFIG.SYS and AUTOEXEC.BAT files to load other drivers high. For Figure 27-4, the MEM report indicates that there is a total of 59KB of upper memory available. It also reports that 57KB of that space has been utilized by DOS and other drivers—specifically SBDC (a Sound Blaster CD driver), SETVER, and MSCDEX. This leaves only 2KB (1744 bytes) available. If you find a utility in the MEM report that uses less than 1744 bytes, you may also be able to load that driver high, and use the remainder of free upper memory.

ADJUSTING THE DOS ENVIRONMENT UNDER WINDOWS 95/98

Windows 95/98 provides the ability to run MS-DOS programs in a "DOS window." This requires you to configure a suitable environment for the DOS program. You can modify the DOS environment using the following steps under Windows:

1. On the desktop, right-click the MS-DOS icon, and then select Properties.
2. Click the Program tab, and then click the Advanced button.
3. The Advanced Program Settings dialog appears (Figure 27-5).
4. Now you can adjust the CONFIG.SYS and AUTOEXEC.BAT attributes you want to use when running the MS-DOS window.

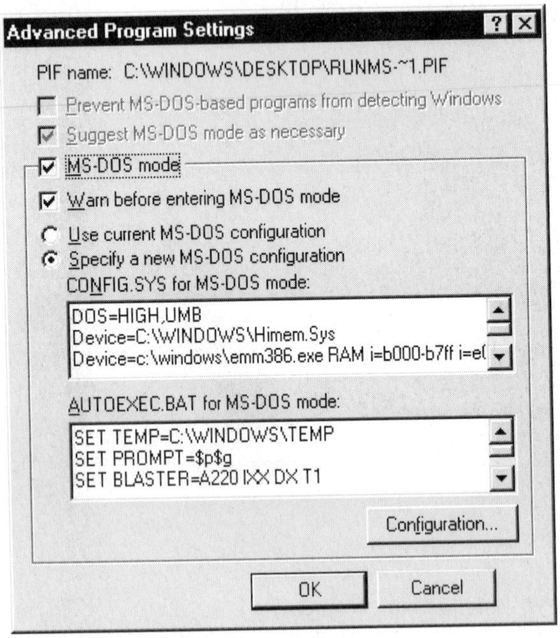

FIGURE 27-5 The Advanced Program Settings dialog

TROUBLESHOOTING TYPICAL OPTIMIZATION PROBLEMS

In an ideal world, you should be able to load DOS, TSRs, and real-mode device drivers into the UMA and high memory without any difficulty. But in the practical PC world, there are many situations that can prevent a program from being relocated out of conventional memory. In many cases, the result is harmless—the program will simply load into conventional memory as it did before. In other cases, however, system operation can be adversely affected when programs are relocated. The following symptoms explain a number of common problems related to memory optimization.

SYMPTOM 27-1 **You see an error message from a driver or TSR when attempting to relocate it** This is not necessarily a problem. It may simply be that there is not enough memory available in the UMA to handle the program you are trying to relocate. Try rearranging the order in which the drivers or TSRs are loaded. Also, the available space in the upper memory area will vary depending on how the PC is configured. A PC with a great many expansion boards and expansion BIOS ROMs may not leave enough upper memory to hold more than a couple of drivers or TSRs. There is little else to be done with such a problem except to leave the uncooperative code in conventional memory.

SYMPTOM 27-2 **The system locks up when a program is relocated** Not all software is suitable for operation within the UMA. Check the screen messages carefully as the PC initializes and attempt to determine the *last* program to load successfully before a fault occurs. If you can find the fault, it is a simple matter to remove the DEVICEHIGH= statement and replace it with the DEVICE statement. This will load the uncooperative program in conventional memory. Keep in mind that it may be necessary to boot the system from a backup or alternate boot disk so that you are able to use a text editor to make and save such a correction.

If you're unable to determine the point at which the system locks up, start with the last DEVICEHIGH statement in the CONFIG.SYS file and change each one to DEVICE. Reboot the PC after each change is made. The *last* line to be changed before system operation returns is likely to be the problem. You can then leave that line (to load into conventional memory) and return all subsequent lines to the DEVICEHIGH function.

27

SYMPTOM 27-3 **A device driver small enough for the available UMA fails to load there** Some device drivers "expand" when they are loaded into memory. In most cases, the program will be loaded into conventional memory. You can find the actual amount of space a driver needs by allowing the driver to load into conventional memory, then using the MEM /C command to see the file and its corresponding file size. This will be the true amount of memory needed by the driver. You can then try loading the driver with DEVICEHIGH using its "size=" switch.

SYMPTOM 27-4 **A program works erratically or improperly when loaded into the UMA** Some device drivers simply do not work well (or at all) from within the UMA. It could be that the program needs a certain amount of memory above it, or the driver does not recognize addresses in the UMA. In either case, the offending program should be loaded into conventional memory. If the offending program is being loaded from CONFIG.SYS, change its DEVICEHIGH statement to DEVICE. If the problem is occurring in AUTOEXEC.BAT, remove the LOADHIGH (or "lh") statement.

SYMPTOM 27-5 **Nothing is being loaded into the UMA** You can see this by looking at the MEM report. Chances are that you have missed a configuration step that is preventing your system from using the UMA. Check the following items. First, check CONFIG.SYS to see that the "dos=umb" or "dos=umb,high" statement is included after the memory managers are loaded. Second, check that

HIMEM and EMM386 are loaded using the DEVICE statement rather than the DEVICEHIGH statement. HIMEM should be loaded *before* EMM386. Also see that the EMM386 entry is using the "noems" or "ram" switch. This configuration should enable use of the UMA. At this point, simply make sure that you are using DEVICEHIGH statements for any CONFIG.SYS device drivers to be loaded in the UMA, and LOADHIGH statements for any AUTOEXEC.BAT device drivers.

Troubleshooting QEMM

QEMM was developed by Quarterdeck as a more powerful and aggressive answer to Microsoft's "canned" memory manager utilities. Although QEMM enjoyed a long lineage of successful versions, it also became known for serious system conflicts and problems. Not all software and hardware dealt with QEMM's aggressive detection and use of high memory areas. This section highlights some techniques to help you manage QEMM most effectively and resolve system errors as you find them.

INSTALLING QEMM UNDER DOS ONLY

When you install QEMM, it normally installs itself under Windows as well as DOS. This is not always desirable, and you can force QEMM to install in DOS only. If your computer automatically starts in Windows, you will need to temporarily disable Windows so that it does not start (that is, boot to the command prompt only). Run QEMM's DOS installation and allow it to finish. After installation is complete, edit the WIN.INI file (located in your Windows directory) and find the reference to INSTGRP.EXE (it will be on either the Load= or Run= line). Remove or disable this reference, and save the changes to your WIN.INI file. You may then reboot the system and allow Windows to start normally.

INSTALLING QEMM 97 UNDER WINDOWS 98

Although Windows 98 offers its own memory management capability for protected-mode operation, you can install QEMM under Windows 98 so that DOS programs (run through a DOS window) will have the appropriate memory management. The following steps will help to ensure that you obtain the maximum amount of conventional memory:

1. Before installing QEMM, check the \WINDOWS folder for the existence of a DOSSTART.BAT file. If the DOSSTART.BAT file is present, use a text editor to add the following line to the end of AUTOEXEC.BAT:

   ```
   CALL DOSSTART.BAT
   ```

2. Save the AUTOEXEC.BAT file after making the change.
3. Now use your text editor to open your CONFIG.SYS file, and add the following line(s) if they're not present already:

   ```
   DEVICE=C:\WINDOWS\IFSHLP.SYS
   DEVICE=C:\WINDOWS\SETVER.EXE
   FILES=60
   LASTDRIVE=Z
   BUFFERS=30
   FCBS=4,0
   STACKS=9,256
   SHELL=C:\COMMAND.COM /P
   DOS=HIGH,NOUMB
   ```

These are the default settings that are loaded from IO.SYS when your computer is booted.

4 To maximize the amount of conventional memory that QEMM makes available, you may also want to:

Reduce the number of buffers allocated by changing to BUFFERS=15. (Some programs may require the default value or higher.)

Reduce the amount of memory required by the drive table by changing the LASTDRIVE statement to LASTDRIVE=E (or whatever is the highest drive letter you use).

Reduce the number of stacks to STACKS=0,0. (Some programs may require the default value or higher.)

5 Save your changes to CONFIG.SYS and exit the text editor.

6 Install QEMM, and choose Custom Installation.

7 At the end of the installation, you will be presented with the QEMM Setup screen. Select DOS-Up, and disable the DOS-Up features. If you're using DriveSpace, select Stealth D*Space and disable this feature as well.

8 Save the configuration and exit. Then run Optimize.

9 After Optimize has finished, edit the AUTOEXEC.BAT file again and remove the CALL DOSSTART.BAT line (if you added it in step 1) from the end of the file. You need this line in your AUTOEXEC.BAT only when you run Optimize.

TEMPORARILY DISABLING QEMM

When you suspect system problems related to QEMM, you can disable QEMM temporarily in order to determine whether QEMM is the problem. This allows you to troubleshoot without the hassle of removing and reinstalling QEMM each time. To boot without QEMM:

1 Shut down Windows and cold boot your system. (Use the power switch to turn it off and back on.)

2 Wait until you hear a beep, and then hold down the ALT key until the boot sequence stops.

If you're using QEMM's DOS-Up feature, you'll see a message asking if you want to unload DOSDATA (one of the DOS-Up drivers). In this case, press ESC to unload DOSDATA, and then immediately press and hold down the ALT key again. You'll be prompted to press ESC to unload QEMM.

If you're using DOS with multiple configurations, you'll be prompted to press ESC to unload QEMM.

In all of these cases, your system will proceed with the boot sequence. QEMM will not load, and no programs will be loaded into upper memory. You may see messages about programs loading low—this is normal when you boot without QEMM.

UNINSTALLING QEMM 97

QEMM is known to conflict with certain drivers and devices, and Windows 95/98 does offer its own memory management tools. These and other reasons may cause you to uninstall QEMM at some point. In many cases, the automated uninstallation tool included with QEMM does not remove all traces from the system, so this part of the chapter explains how to remove QEMM completely.

Specifically, the QEMM 97 uninstaller does not remove QEMM from the PATH statement in the AUTOEXEC.BAT file. Uninstalling QEMM on Windows 95/98 systems will also leave optimized MS-DOS program PIFs in an optimized state (which may prevent your real-mode programs from running

27

without QEMM). If you want to remove QEMM from your system and you have optimized DOS PIFs, you must restore the unoptimized backup of each PIF, or edit each PIF:

1. Right-click the PIF shortcut, and click Properties.
2. Click the Program tab, and click Advanced.
3. Edit the CONFIG.SYS and AUTOEXEC.BAT files manually.

> Uninstallation may not remove QEMM-related statements from "CALLed" batch files that are not in the DOS path (unless you have supplied a full path to the CALLed batch file).

MANUALLY UNINSTALLING QEMM 8.0X AND QEMM 97

In most cases, the automatic removal of QEMM is satisfactory (though certain traces may be left behind). If you're unable to complete a standard removal of QEMM, you can use the steps below to completely uninstall the product without requiring the Uninstall or Optimize programs.

1. Restart the computer, and then boot directly to the command prompt (using F8 and the Windows Startup menu).
2. At the DOS prompt, type **EDIT CONFIG.SYS** and press ENTER. This will load CONFIG.SYS into your text editor.
3. Find and delete all lines containing the following QEMM drivers:
   - DOSDATA.SYS
   - HOOKROM.SYS
   - QEMM386.SYS
   - DOS-UP.SYS
   - QDPMI.SYS
   - ST-DSPC.SYS
4. Look for the command line beginning with SHELL=. If this line also contains LOADHI.COM, you will need to remove the reference to this QEMM driver. A typical SHELL line containing LOADHI.COM reads as follows:

   ```
   SHELL=C:\QEMM\LOADHI.COM /r:2 /size=xxxxx C:\COMMAND.COM /E:1024 /P
   ```
5. In this case, simply remove everything between the = sign and C:\COMMAND.COM. Using the example above, your line after editing would become

   ```
   SHELL=C:\COMMAND.COM /E:1024 /P
   ```
6. Find any command lines containing LOADHI.SYS. These lines will need to be edited so that the QEMM driver (LOADHI.SYS) does not load. However, the driver at the end of the line should remain. It may be required for your system to operate properly. A typical device line containing LOADHI.SYS may appear such as:

   ```
   DEVICE=C:\QEMM\LOADHI.SYS /r:3 /size=4000 C:\WINDOWS\IFSHLP.SYS
   ```
7. Simply remove everything between the = sign and the driver at the end of the line. Using the example above, your line after editing would become

```
DEVICE=C:\WINDOWS\IFSHLP.SYS
```

8. You may have device lines where the driver at the end of the line has extra parameters (such as a CD-ROM driver), for example:

```
C:\SCSI\ASPI2DOS.SYS /D /Z /Q9
```

9. If so, be sure to leave the extra parameters at the end of the line. They may be required for your system to operate properly.
10. Return to the top of the CONFIG.SYS file and enter the following:

```
DEVICE=C:\WINDOWS\HIMEM.SYS
DEVICE=C:\WINDOWS\EMM386.EXE ON RAM 1024
```

11. Save your changes to CONFIG.SYS and exit the text editor.
12. At the DOS prompt, type **EDIT AUTOEXEC.BAT** and press ENTER. This will load AUTOEXEC.BAT into your text editor.
13. Look for lines containing LOADHI. These lines will need to be edited so that the QEMM driver (LOADHI.COM) does not load. However, the TSR or program at the end of the line should remain. It may be required for your system. A typical line in the AUTOEXEC.BAT file containing a LOADHI statement might read

```
C:\QEMM\LOADHI /r:3 /size=3238 C:\MY_TSR\MY_TSR /1 /2 /3
```

14. This time, remove everything *before* the actual program. Using the example above, your line would become something like:

```
C:\MY_TSR\MY_TSR /1 /2 /3
```

15. Save your changes to AUTOEXEC.BAT and exit the text editor.
16. Delete the QEMM directory. For example, assuming QEMM was installed to its default location, type

```
DELTREE /Y C:\QEMM
```

> If you installed QEMM to a location other than the default directory, substitute the correct directory for C:\QEMM.

Additional Steps for Windows Users

If you have Windows 95/98 installed, restart the computer. You'll receive warnings that several files that may be needed to run Windows are missing. Bypass these errors for now. (We'll correct them shortly.) After the desktop loads, you may be told that "QLOGO" cannot be found, and you may be prompted to browse for it. Simply cancel the error message at this time, and follow the steps below.

> Some of the following steps will depend on the version of QEMM that you are using. If you cannot find an item that corresponds to the step below, assume that it is not a required step for your computer.

1. Click Start, point to Settings, and then click Taskbar & Start Menu.
2. Click the Start Menu Programs tab, and then click Remove.
3. Click the plus (+) sign beside the Startup group.

4. Click the item labeled "Qlogo" so that it is selected, and then click Remove.
5. Find the group labeled "Quarterdeck QEMM" or "Quarterdeck QEMM 97," and click so that it is selected; then click Remove.
6. Click Close.

   The remaining steps require editing the Windows registry.

> It is strongly recommend that you back up your system registry before making any changes. Incorrect changes to your registry could result in permanent data loss or corrupted files.

7. Click Start, then Run.
8. In the Open box, type **REGEDIT** and click OK.
9. Click the plus (+) sign beside HKEY_LOCAL_MACHINE to expand that level.
10. Expand the System level of the tree.
11. Expand the CurrentControlSet level of the tree.
12. Expand the Services level of the tree.
13. Expand the VxD level of the tree.
14. Carefully delete the following registry keys:
    - Quarterdeck_CacheBack
    - Quarterdeck_Magnaram
    - Quarterdeck_MemLink
    - Quarterdeck_TurboLoad
15. If you're using QEMM 8.0x, collapse all open trees, and then locate and expand the following key:

    `HKEY_LOCAL_MACHINE\Software\Microsoft\Windows\CurrentVersion\Run`
16. In the right pane, you should see an item that contains the value C:\QEMM\LOGO95.EXE. Select *only* this item (*not* the entire key) and press Delete.
17. Exit the registry editor.
18. Shut down and restart the system.
19. QEMM is now completely uninstalled and will not attempt to load when you start your computer.

QEMM CONFIGURATION SUGGESTIONS

QEMM can generally be used with most hardware and software without any special consideration. Still, QEMM is an aggressive memory manager, and there are numerous devices and programs that require particular attention in order to be compatible with QEMM and/or the Stealth ROM feature. Table 27-3 outlines the considerations for many hardware devices, and Table 27-4 lists the special settings for a variety of software products.

> Keep in mind that you should use QEMM's Analysis feature to determine the exact areas involved in memory exclusions.

TABLE 27-3 QEMM SETTINGS FOR HARDWARE

DEVICE	DESCRIPTION
Miscellaneous laptop systems	The QuickBoot feature can interfere with a laptop's Advanced Power Management (APM). After a QuickBoot, laptops with APM will restart at their default power-on speed. If you notice that your laptop is running faster (or slower) than you expect after a QuickBoot, check the default power-on configuration settings for your system, and adjust them accordingly.
Acer 1120SX	This older system may need exclusions in the F000h-FFFFh region if you're using the Stealth ROM feature. Typical exclusion ranges include X=F300-F3FF and X=FA00-FAFF with Stealth ROM. Acer 1120SX systems may also need a X=C600-C7FF exclusion in the QEMM command line even *without* Stealth ROM.
Adaptec ASPI drivers	If the ASPI4DOS.SYS or ASPI2DOS.SYS driver is loaded *before* QEMM386.SYS, you may need to exclude up to 12KB of the F000h-FFFFh memory range when using the Stealth ROM function. This problem does not occur if ASPI4DOS is loaded *after* QEMM, but QEMM will then use 2KB of conventional memory for a disk buffer to prevent bus mastering problems when ASPI4DOS loads high.
AT&T Globalyst systems	The AT&T Globalyst 360 Pentium systems (and possibly other systems with recent Award BIOS versions) have large ROMs in the E000h region. The Optimize Stealth Testing process will finish without problems, but will not "Stealth" all of the ROMs on the machine. Much of this ROM can be included through QEMM's Analysis procedure if you add the parameter S=EF00:4K to the end of the QEMM386.SYS command line in CONFIG.SYS.
Compaq (and other) systems with PCMSMIX.EXE	Some Compaq laptop/notebook systems come with PCMSMIX.EXE, which allows the machine to receive incoming faxes while in a power-saving mode. Since this program conflicts with QEMM's QuickBoot feature, Optimize disables the QuickBoot feature whenever PCMSMIX is loaded in CONFIG.SYS.
Compaq systems (general)	If your Compaq system with QEMM does not recognize memory above the 16MB line, add the parameter USERAM=1M:xxM, where xx is the amount of memory that you have in your system.
Compaq XL systems with PCNTNW.COM	Compaq XL desktop systems come with PCNTNW.COM, which is a driver for the built-in network interface hardware on XL systems. PCNTNW seems to make VDS calls to eliminate potential conflicts between the network hardware and memory managers (like QEMM). This means that it may be necessary to force PCNTNW to load low. This can be accomplished by adding the term PCNTNW to the OPTIMIZE.NOT file in your QEMM directory. If no such file exists, create one that contains the single line PCNTNW. There are also reports that the QEMM parameter EXCLUDE=F600-FFFF is needed on some Compaq XL systems.
DEC Celebris and Venturis systems	See the issues with plug-and-play BIOS systems below.
Gateway 2000 systems	See the issues with Phoenix Green BIOS systems below. Also see the STB PowerGraph 64 PCI video card issues below.

27

TABLE 27-3 QEMM SETTINGS FOR HARDWARE *(CONTINUED)*

DEVICE	DESCRIPTION
Gravis Ultrasound card	When your system is using a Gravis Ultrasound device, the MegaEM emulator for the Gravis Ultrasound may require the P:VME:N parameter to be added to the QEMM386.SYS command line in CONFIG.SYS.
Hewlett-Packard OmniBook 600 systems	This system will report an Exception #414 at startup. This occurs because QEMM will detect that the B000h-B7FFh and C000h-EBFFh regions contain Adapter RAM, and thus will not create high RAM in these areas by default. However, you may include these regions by adding I= parameters to the QEMM386.SYS command line in CONFIG.SYS. Keep in mind that power management routines exist in the EE00h-EEFFh region, so this area must be excluded. Also, the address range used by any PCMCIA hardware on the system must be excluded. The range depends on your PCMCIA configuration, but a typical QEMM386.SYS command line for an OmniBook will look like this: `I=B000:32K I=C000:176K X=EE00:4K X=D000:8K`
Hewlett-Packard Vectra systems	Some models of the Vectra may require the QEMM386.SYS parameter S=F400:4K in order to properly support graphics modes when QEMM's Stealth feature is active. Some models may also require the parameter X=F000:8K for the system's "sleep mode" to work properly.
IBM PS/2 Model L40SX systems	These laptop models may need the following exclusions in order to work with ST:M, such as: `X=E000-E0FF X=E200-E3FF X=E600-E6FF` By comparison, the ST:F option requires no exclusions, and the suspend/resume feature works on this system automatically.
IBM Token Ring cards	PS/2 users with Token Ring cards and QEMM may find that conventional memory ends at 576KB rather than 640KB. A Token Ring card has both an adapter RAM and ROM in upper memory (either 8KB or 16KB). The default addresses for the RAM and ROM are D800h and CC00h, respectively. This default configuration may not allow room in upper memory for the EMS page frame, especially on PS/2 systems. If the page frame does not fit in upper memory, QEMM will place the page frame in the last 64KB of conventional memory, decreasing the memory available for programs. A message will appear at boot-up if the page frame has been placed in conventional memory. You can resolve this problem by using your PS/2 reference disk to move the Token Ring adapter RAM and ROM to one end or the other of upper memory. Moving both RAM and ROM as low as possible in the C000h area is usually a good choice. On non-PS/2 systems, if the address ranges of the card are movable, contiguous address ranges starting at D000h are often a good choice.

TABLE 27-3 QEMM SETTINGS FOR HARDWARE *(CONTINUED)*

DEVICE	DESCRIPTION
Invisible network cards	If you use the boot ROM on an invisible network card, it loads 32KB of code at the top of conventional memory and grabs interrupt 13. Rather than using XSTI=13 and a corresponding exclude statement, disable the ROM on the network card and load IS2BIOS instead. This will give you an additional 32KB of conventional memory (since IS2BIOS can be loaded high), and the network card's ROM will not break up your upper memory address space.
Micro Electronics WinBook systems	With QEMM installed on the Micro Electronics WinBook XPS, a certain call to the APM (Advanced Power Management) BIOS routines may cause the keyboard controller to emit an escape key code. This will cause the exit screen to appear, or may cause the keyboard to lock. You may need to uninstall QEMM until a BIOS update becomes available.
NEC Versa systems	See the issues with plug-and-play BIOS systems below.
Orchid Technology Kelvin 64 video cards	The Kelvin EZ Setup utility that comes with this card permits video resolution switching while inside Microsoft Windows. When the Stealth ROM feature is active, this utility requires the EMS page frame to be placed at C000h, or requires the SVGA:256 parameter in the QEMM command line if the page frame is not at C000h.
Phoenix PCMCIA card manager drivers	The Phoenix PCMCIA Card Manager software includes a driver called CNFIGNAM.EXE. In version 3.0 of the Card Manager (and perhaps in other versions, depending on your system configuration), this will generate an error message and refuse to load if Optimize attempts to load it high. To prevent this problem, add a new line containing only the term CNFIGNAM to the OPTIMIZE.NOT file in your QEMM directory. If no such file exists, create one that contains the single line CNFIGNAM.
Plug-and-play BIOS systems	QEMM searches aggressively for address ranges that are used by the plug-and-play BIOS extensions used on many recent systems. When QEMM finds this BIOS code, it does not map High RAM over the associated address ranges. This avoids conflicts with installed plug-and-play hardware. The plug-and-play configuration driver DWCFGMG.SYS conflicts with Optimize (and often with DOS memory management utilities as well). The best course is to REMark out this driver from CONFIG.SYS while you're running Optimize. Unless you're using plug-and-play-compatible hardware under DOS, you may consider removing this driver altogether.
Plus Impulse/HardCard II drives	These hard drives may need the XST parameter applied to their ROM addresses when using the QEMM Stealth feature. For example, the default location for a Hardcard II ROM is C800h. In this case adding XST=C800 to the QEMM386.SYS command line may be adequate.
PSI HyperStor 816/1600 disk controllers	When QEMM is installed, some versions of this controller may require that the page frame be located at the beginning of the controller's ROM (which is often at C800h). A small exclusion in the F000h-FFFFh range may also be necessary. As a rule, QEMM's Analysis procedure should make the appropriate corrections.

TABLE 27-3 QEMM SETTINGS FOR HARDWARE *(CONTINUED)*

DEVICE	DESCRIPTION
QLogic Fast SCSI controllers	When QEMM is installed, certain models of this controller may require the XBDA:N parameter to be added to the QEMM command line, and may also require the parameter XST=nnnn, where nnnn is the address of the ROM on the controller (typically C800h by default).
Setup programs and hot keys	Some systems allow you to access the CMOS setup at any time by pressing a hot key. On many of these systems, you must exclude some portion of the F000h-FFFFh address range in order to use these setup programs when QEMM's Stealth ROM feature is enabled. As an alternative, you can fix the entry point to these programs with an S= parameter. Optimize may be able to help you find an appropriate S= parameter to permit running the CMOS setup (at a lower cost in high RAM). Hot-key-based setups usually work without exclusions if you're using the ST:F feature. The best way to deal with this problem is to avoid exclusions and to prevent QEMM from loading on the rare occasions when you need to access your CMOS setup program.
STB 800/16 VGA video cards	These graphics cards work well with the page frame at C000h when the Stealth ROM mapping method (ST:M) is being used. QEMM places the page frame at C000h by default when ST:M is enabled. If ST:M is enabled and the page frame is not at C000h, it is likely that some address range conflict is preventing QEMM from putting the page frame there. In this case, you may need to exclude a portion of the C000h-C7FFh area.
STB PowerGraph video cards	There may be a conflict between the video card and the system's hardware ROM shadowing. Though QEMM is not the root of this problem, this conflict causes QEMM to report that it cannot find the ROM handler for INT 10, and it disables the Stealth ROM feature. The best work-around is to disable hardware video ROM shadowing on the motherboard, and to use QEMM's ROM parameter instead. An alternative is to disable QEMM's use of Shadow RAM with its SH:N parameter. In addition, the STB PowerGraph 64 PCI video card (included on some Gateway 2000 machines) requires a 4KB exclusion at C500h to work properly with the QEMM Stealth ROM feature, such as: `DEVICE=C:\QEMM\QEMM386.SYS RAM ST:M X=C500:4K`
Toshiba laptop systems (pop-up menus)	Many Toshiba laptop computers use a pop-up menu that displays information on the status of the computer's battery. In order for the pop-up menu to work when the computer is in Virtual 8086 mode (when QEMM is providing expanded memory or high RAM), a TSR called T386.EXE must be run. This tiny program is included on the QEMM disks.
Toshiba 4400SXC laptop systems	If you use the battery pop-up feature of this laptop, you may need the QEMM exclusion parameters X=F400-F7FF and X=FC00-FFFF. You may be able to narrow these exclusions a bit if you wish to tinker.
Toshiba 5100 systems	This computer is generally incompatible with the Stealth ROM mapping method (ST:M) of QEMM. The Optimize feature should automatically detect and work around any such incompatibility.

TABLE 27-3 QEMM SETTINGS FOR HARDWARE *(CONTINUED)*

DEVICE	DESCRIPTION

UltraStor Disk controller	When using an UltraStor SCSI disk controller (or other SCSI disk controller) and QEMM's DOS-Up feature, you see a "Device not found" message during boot time. You may be able to fix this problem with the FIXINT13.SYS driver that accompanies QEMM. Load the driver in a command line immediately *before* QEMM386.SYS in CONFIG.SYS, and then add the /STACKSIZE parameter, such as:
	`DEVICE=C:\QEMM\FIXINT13.SYS`
	`DEVICE=C:\QEMM\QEMM386.SYS RAM <your other parameters>`

WD90C11-based video cards	If you're using a video card based on the Western Digital WD90C11 chipset, some versions of the Windows Super VGA driver may not work properly. You may need to use a different video driver, or exclude the B000h-B7FFh range from QEMM386.SYS, such as: `DEVICE=C:\QEMM\QEMM386.SYS ST:M RAM X=B000-B7FF`
Zenith systems	Zenith systems with some versions of DOS may need the parameter XSTI=18 in order to print on a Zenith system when Stealth ROM is enabled. You will also need a small 4K exclusion somewhere in the F000h-FFFFh range. The exclusion X=F500-F5FF is reported to work on many systems.

TABLE 27-4 QEMM SETTINGS FOR SOFTWARE

Program	Description
1DIR Plus	Some versions of this program need the QEMM parameter UFP:N when Stealth mode is in effect if 1DIR Plus is using EMS. Another solution might be to configure 1DIR Plus so that it does not put its stacks in the EMS page frame.
AllClear	This charting software may need an exclusion in the C000h-C7FFh region if you use its View Chart or Print Preview option with QEMM's Stealth ROM enabled.
Avery Label Pro	Some versions of this software may put display characters incorrectly on the screen when the Stealth ROM feature is enabled unless you use the X=F000-F0FF exclusion parameter on the QEMM command line.
BootCon	BootCon (version 2.02) is a utility that allows you to boot different configurations without having to constantly edit the CONFIG.SYS files. BootCon is compatible with QEMM's Optimize program, but you must run BootCon in STANDALONE mode to achieve this. This mode disables the MENU mode and boots the system with a single (or "flat") configuration. Each configuration that is to be Optimized has to be booted as a STANDALONE. To change the BootCon program from MENU to STANDALONE, run the BCSETUP program, go to the main menu, and select SET MODE from the menu. After all setups have been Optimized, you may go back to the MENU mode so that each time the system boots, you may select a configuration from the menu.
Btrieve	Btrieve is a database record manager sold by Novell and used by many applications to perform database activities. Btrieve is usually run before these applications as a TSR. It uses expanded memory, unless you prevent it from doing so by giving it the /E parameter. Quarterdeck reports many cases where systems did not function properly unless Btrieve was stopped from using expanded memory with the /E parameter.

TABLE 27-4 QEMM SETTINGS FOR SOFTWARE *(CONTINUED)*

Program	Description
Clarion	This is an application that uses Btrieve. Clarion 3 (and perhaps other versions) loads Btrieve from a batch file called CDD.BAT. If this batch file does not already specify the /E parameter on its Btrieve command line, you should place it there to prevent failures when using Clarion with one of QEMM's Stealth features.

CACHE86	When using the Cache86 expanded memory cache with Stealth DoubleSpace, you must specify the EXPCACHE parameter to the ST-DSPC driver in CONFIG.SYS, such as:
	`DEVICE=C:\QEMM\ST-DSPC.SYS /EXPCACHE:4`
	When using EMS, Cache86 is also incompatible with the Optimize SqueezeTemp feature. The alternatives are to see that Cache86 is not using expanded memory, or to start Optimize with the /NT parameter, such as:
	`OPTIMIZE /NT`

DAC Easy	This is an application that uses Btrieve. There are reports that DAC Easy (versions 4 and 5) will fail when used with QEMM's D*Space feature unless Btrieve is using the /E parameter. In DAC Easy 5, the symptom is often a DoubleGuard alarm error when DAC Easy starts. DAC Easy loads Btrieve from a batch file called DEA4.BAT or DEA5.BAT. If this batch file does not already specify the /E parameter on its Btrieve command line, you should place it there.
Delrina DOSFax	Delrina's DOSFax program requires that you place the exclusion X=B000-B0FF on the QEMM386.SYS command line in your CONFIG.SYS file. Without this parameter, DOSFax may fail after it captures a document to print.
GeoWorks Ensemble	As of version 1.2, GeoWorks is incompatible with QEMM's Stealth ROM feature if GeoWorks is configured to use expanded (EMS) memory. If you set up GeoWorks to use extended (XMS) and conventional memory, it will work with Stealth ROM.
Glyphix	Some versions of the font program Glyphix need the QEMM parameter UFP:N when Stealth is in effect and Glyphix is using EMS.
IBM PC-DOS	A quirk in the way PC-DOS 6.1 handles "CALLed" batch files can cause problems for Optimize. With a CALLed batch file in most versions of DOS, a GOTO <label> statement for which there is no valid destination <label> will cause the current batch file to terminate and return control to the batch file that CALLed it. In PC-DOS 6.1, a GOTO <label> statement will cause all batch files to terminate if there is no valid <label>, and this will cause the Optimize process to terminate abnormally. There are two work-arounds. One is to ensure that all GOTO statements point to valid destinations. The alternative is to upgrade your version of PC-DOS to any later version (such as 6.3 and 7.0). It is also possible that installing QEMM from inside Microsoft Windows (and then choosing to run Optimize from QSetup in Windows) may cause the message "Invalid COMMAND.COM, System halted." In this case, reboot your system, verify that all GOTO entries have valid destinations, and run Optimize from DOS.
Infinite Disk	The QEMM directory (and especially any DOS device drivers or Windows VxD files within it) should not be compressed by Infinite Disk. The drivers might be required at boot time or during the Optimize process before the Infinite Disk software loads. Make sure that the files in your QEMM directory are uncompressed, and then type the command `C:\INFINITE\PROTECT C:\QEMM\*.* /P` This will protect the files from being compressed.

TABLE 27-4 QEMM SETTINGS FOR SOFTWARE *(CONTINUED)*

Program	Description
LANtastic 6.0	Two of the network drivers that ship with LANtastic 6.0 (SERVER.EXE and REDIR.EXE) load into memory in such a way that QEMM's Optimize program assumes they are larger than they really are. As a result, Optimize usually loads these programs low. If your copy of LANtastic 6.0 contains versions of SERVER and REDIR that accept the /LOAD_HIGH parameter, you should specify this parameter to both LANtastic drivers. You should also make sure that the DOS=UMB or DOS=HIGH,UMB statement is in your CONFIG.SYS file. (LANtastic requires the DOS=UMB interface in order to use upper memory.) The /LOAD_HIGH parameter and DOS=UMB will allow Optimize to load SERVER and REDIR high if there is enough room for them in upper memory.
Lotus 1-2-3	If you're using QEMM's VIDRAM feature, Lotus 1-2-3 may report that "123 cannot start because the driver set is invalid." VIDRAM works with DOS text-based programs, but does not allow EGA or VGA graphics. 1-2-3 is checking your graphics card's capabilities, but VIDRAM is telling it that no graphics are allowed. The solution is to run 1-2-3's INSTALL program and make a driver set with no graphics entry. Use 1-2-3 INSTALL's Advanced Options and Modify Current Driver Set selections. Select the Graph Display item. Press the DEL key on the driver that is currently selected. Press the ESC key and use Save Changes to save the driver set with a different name. When you want to use 1-2-3 with VIDRAM, type **123 123VID** at the DOS prompt, and the correct video driver will be used.
Logitech Mouse drivers	Some versions of Logitech MOUSE.COM drivers load an overlay file (LVESA.OVL) that Optimize does not detect. Consequently, the mouse driver does not load high. A message appears saying "Insufficient Memory To Load Video Module" when LOADHI attempts to load the mouse driver high. Updated mouse drivers that do not exhibit this problem are available from Logitech. Alternatively, you may choose to remove the line from the LMOUSE.INI file, `VideoModule=LVESA.OVL` or use the NOVCI switch to the Logitech mouse driver.
MIRROR	MIRROR (written by Central Point Software) is packaged with MS/IBM DOS version 5 and 6. MIRROR is used to recover deleted files. MIRROR first makes a backup copy of your FATs, then loads a resident portion of itself that tracks files as they are deleted in order to expedite their recovery. The file tracking feature is enabled by using the /Tx switch (where x is the letter of the drive to be monitored) on the MIRROR command line. The copy of the FAT(s) that MIRROR makes may be too large to load into available high RAM. If this happens when MIRROR loads, it will report that it has failed to perform this function. However, the Undelete Tracking feature may have installed successfully. Type **LOADHI** at the DOS prompt to make sure that MIRROR loaded successfully. You may load MIRROR low once without the /Tx switch (to perform MIRROR's first function), and then load MIRROR high with the /Tx switch in order to load its resident portion above 640K and make a successful copy of the FAT.
Miscellaneous drivers	The QEMM 7.5 installation program adds several drivers (by default) to the OPTIMIZE.NOT file. This is because such drivers may not be loaded high, or may interfere with the Optimize process. If you feel that your version of a particular driver may load high successfully (even though it's listed in OPTIMIZE.NOT), edit the file to remove the line referring to that driver. Use an ASCII text editor such as EDIT. The following programs are typically added to OPTIMIZE.NOT: CNFIGNAM, DPMS, MTDDRV, MINI406A, CASCMOD1, PCNTNW, MEMDRV, and AUTODRV.

27

TABLE 27-4 QEMM SETTINGS FOR SOFTWARE *(CONTINUED)*

Program	Description
Norton Anti-Virus	Norton Anti-Virus (version 2.00) is known to interfere with the ability of LOADHI.COM to load the command processor. Upgrade your software to NAV 2.1 or later. In the meantime, use QSETUP to load the command processor low by choosing DOS-Up Options from the main menu, and then select Partial. On the following screen, set COMMAND.COM to No.
Norton Backup	If you frequently change your configuration from Stealth ROM enabled to Stealth ROM disabled, some versions of Norton Backup may require that you exclude the range X=FE00-FFFF and that you reconfigure the backup program.
pcANYWHERE	This is an application that uses Btrieve. pcANYWHERE (and perhaps other versions) loads Btrieve automatically with its AWHOST program. To verify that Btrieve does not use expanded memory, you must load Btrieve with the /E parameter—either manually or from a batch file—before loading AWHOST. AWHOST will see that Btrieve is already loaded, and will use the already active copy in memory.
PCSA	PCSA's EMS loaders (DMNETHLD and EMSLOAD) do not work if Stealth ROM is enabled. The QEMM386.SYS parameter XST=F000 may resolve the problem when this occurs. Some DEPCA cards may fail with the PCSA software and ST:M switch unless you place the page frame at the starting address of the DEPCA card's 16KB ROM.
PrintQ	You should use this print spooler's /LSX parameter to ensure that it uses extended memory rather than expanded memory if you are using the QEMM Stealth ROM feature.
Repeat Performance	Like other keyboard-enhancement programs that create a new type-ahead buffer, the Repeat Performance keyboard-enhancing program will malfunction if it is loaded above 63KB. As a result, it cannot be loaded high with all of its features enabled. However, RP.SYS will load high if you use its BUFFERS=OFF parameter (which disables Repeat Performance's type-ahead buffer).
Space-Manager	If you're using SpaceManager's SuperMount feature (as well as DOS 6.0 and QEMM's Stealth ROM feature), your PC may hang at boot time. To fix the boot problem, add the following parameter to the QEMM386.SYS device line in your CONFIG.SYS file: **DBF=n** (where *n* is a number—1 and 2 are commonly used values).
SideKick Plus	SideKick Plus will not work with Stealth ROM unless it is prevented from using EMS. One work-around is to use QEMM's EMS.COM program to temporarily allocate all EMS *before* SKPLUS is loaded, then use EMS.COM again to free your machine's EMS memory after loading SKPLUS.
Super PC-Kwik	When Super PC-Kwik is using expanded memory, you're using Stealth D*Space, and you do not have StealthROM enabled, you must use the Super PC-Kwik parameter, EMSMapSaves=Always. This forces Super PC-Kwik to make the necessary EMS calls to be compatible with Stealth D*Space.
Talking Icons	Aristosoft's Talking Icons FX function can cause video display refresh problems when used with QEMM and Windows. It is recommended that the FX function not be used while QEMM is in service.

TABLE 27-4 QEMM SETTINGS FOR SOFTWARE *(CONTINUED)*

Program	Description
Ventura Publisher (Professional)	When QEMM's Stealth ROM feature is enabled, and you have the line STACKS=0,0 in your CONFIG.SYS file, Ventura Professional (Version 2) will not operate properly. Removing the STACKS=0,0 statement should solve the problem. DR DOS 6 does not use hardware interrupt stacks. As a result, you cannot use DR DOS 6 with Ventura Professional 2 if you're using Stealth ROM. Ventura Professional (Version 3) does not put its stacks in the EMS page frame, and does work properly with Stealth ROM. Ventura Publisher 2 will not work properly if the EMS page frame is located at an address higher than E000h. To find out where your page frame is located, type **QEMM** at the DOS prompt. If you're using a page frame, you'll see its address listed. If the address is higher than E000h, type **QEMM** again and look at the list of areas and sizes. Find the first high RAM area below E000h that is at least 64KB in size and jot down its starting address. Then add the FRAME=xxxx parameter to the QEMM line, replacing xxxx with the address you wrote down (such as **FRAME=D000**).
Video accelerator drivers	Several video cards come with programs such as SPEED_UP.SYS, RAMBIOS.SYS, or FASTBIOS.SYS. These programs make a copy of the video ROM in RAM in order to speed up your video. If loaded after QEMM on a system with Stealth ROM enabled, they may refuse to load (generating an error that something else has taken Interrupt 10). If loaded *before* QEMM on the same system, Stealth ROM will be disabled because QEMM cannot find the ROM handler for Interrupt 10. You can solve both of these problems with the XSTI=10 parameter. No exclusion is necessary because the video ROM is no longer being used. SPEED_UP.SYS can then be loaded after QEMM (and can be loaded into upper memory). However, you should remember that SPEED_UP.SYS, RAMBIOS.SYS, FASTBIOS.SYS, or any similar driver uses as much as 36KB of memory. Instead, use QEMM's ROM parameter. It does the same job, but uses no address space between 0-1024KB.
VP Planner	Some versions of the VP Planner spreadsheet need the parameter UFP:N when Stealth is in effect if VP Planner is using EMS.
XtraDrive	IIT's XtraDrive disk compression utility ships with a disk cache that is not compatible with QEMM's Stealth ROM feature. Disable QEMM or remove XtraDrive.

27

QEMM SYMPTOMS

SYMPTOM 27-6 The QEMM Optimize process will not finish on a computer with a Zip drive installed Either add "GUEST" (not "GUEST.EXE") to the OPTIMIZE.NOT file, or obtain version 3.1 (or later) of this driver from Iomega (**www.iomega.com**). The most recent GUEST.EXE drivers (version 4.12 and later) will load high with QEMM. However, when run while loaded high, these drivers will return a run-time error such as "R6003 Integer divide by 0." When loaded low or run off a floppy disk, the drivers work fine. The older version 3.1 of this driver (which comes with version 3.03 of Iomega's installation software, dated Nov. 3, 1995) seems to work fine loaded high (at least with QEMM versions 8.01, 8.03, and 97). You may consider "downgrading" the Iomega driver if necessary.

SYMPTOM 27-7 With QEMM and an S3 video adapter, Windows 95/98 may hang at start time You'll notice that this problem occurs only when you're using a 640 x 480 x 256 screen mode with an older S3 video adapter. The trouble does not seem to occur in 16-color mode, or with newer S3 video adapters. This problem occurs because of a conflict between the QEMM file called QDPMI.SYS and the S3 video adapter. There are three possible work-arounds to this problem:

- Remove or disable the following LOADHI.SYS command line in the CONFIG.SYS file, and then restart your computer:

  ```
  device=c:\qemm\loadhi.sys /r:1 c:\qemm\qdpmi.sys swapfile=dpmi.swp
  ```

- Uninstall QEMM and use the standard DOS memory managers (HIMEM and EMM386).
- Use a higher resolution and/or color depth (such as 16-color mode).

SYMPTOM 27-8 The MEM function displays inaccurate information with QEMM 7.01 When you're using Quarterdeck's QEMM (version 7.01), you may find that the "Upper" and "Total under 1MB" values are displayed incorrectly under the MEM function (as in Figure 27-6). The "Upper" value should read 4,193,6nn,nnn (where *n* is an unknown number), but MEM does not correctly handle the large values for upper memory returned by QEMM. The use of commas makes the problem appear worse. The best solution is to upgrade QEMM to a later version that is more compatible with the DOS MEM feature, or uninstall QEMM in favor of HIMEM and EMM386 or another memory manager.

SYMPTOM 27-9 The QEMM optimize process will not finish on an HP Vectra system This is known to happen on a Hewlett-Packard Vectra system running DOS 6.2x. While trying to optimize with QEMM, your computer stops responding during the final phase—requiring a restart. When the optimize process continues, it starts the exclusion/detection phase and hangs again. After restarting, Optimize reports the optimize process did not finish, and your previous configuration has been restored. You can often use the steps below to resolve this problem:

1. Load the CONFIG.SYS file into your text editor, and locate the QEMM386.SYS command line.
2. At the end of the QEMM386.SYS command line, add a space and the following parameters: RH:N SH:N XBDA:N, such as:

   ```
   DEVICE=C:\QEMM\QEMM386.SYS RAM RH:N SH:N XBDA:N
   ```

3. Save your changes to CONFIG.SYS and exit the text editor.
4. Restart the computer and rerun Optimize.

```
Memory Type            Total  =    Used   +   Free
................     .......   ........   .......
Conventional           640K        19K      621K
Upper                4,193,6    4,193,6      12K  <== Incorrect Display
Reserved               384K       384K        0K
Extended (XMS)       15,998K     3,102K   12,896K
................     .......   ........   .......
Total memory         16,386K     2,854K   13,530K

Total under 1 MB          2K    4,193,6     634K  <== Incorrect Display
```

FIGURE 27-6 Incorrect MEM display under QEMM 7.01

SYMPTOM 27-10 **After uninstalling QEMM97, Windows 95/98 produces one or more VxD error messages** The error messages may appear such as

```
"Cannot find a device file that may be needed to run Windows or a Windows
application."
```

or

```
"The windows registry or SYSTEM.INI file refers to this device file, but the
device file no longer exists."
```

or

```
"If you deleted this file on purpose, try uninstalling the associated
application using its uninstall or setup program."
```

or

```
"If you still want to use the application associated with this device file
try reinstalling that application to replace the missing file."
```

In virtually all cases, the files referred to are to QEMM's MagnaRAM, TurboLoad, Memlink, and CacheBack VxD files. Unfortunately, the uninstall process was unable to modify the registry in order to remove the entries QEMM placed there. This can happen if the original optimize process did not finish. Under Windows 95/98, use the registry editor (REGEDIT.EXE) to remove the reference to these files by following these steps:

1. Click Start and click Run. The Run dialog box appears.
2. Type **REGEDIT**, and then click OK. The registry editor opens.
3. Press CTRL+F. The Find dialog box appears.
4. Type **QEMM** and click Find Next.
5. When the search stops, press DEL on your keyboard, and click OK at the confirmation.
6. Press F3 to search for the next reference.
7. Repeat these steps until the "Finished searching the registry" message appears.
8. Exit the registry editor and restart the computer.

SYMPTOM 27-11 **The QEMM optimize process will not finish on a Toshiba 750 laptop** This is known to occur with certain Toshiba models because additional parameters are needed on the QEMM command line:

1. Start your computer to the Windows 95/98 Safe Mode.
2. Click Start, click Run, type **SYSEDIT**, and press ENTER. The system configuration editor starts.
3. Select the CONFIG.SYS window, and locate the QEMM386.SYS command line.
4. At the end of the QEMM386.SYS command line, add a space and the following parameters: XBDA:N RH:N SH:N TM:N FILL:N BE:N MR:N, such as:

   ```
   DEVICE=C:\QEMM\QEMM386.SYS RAM XBDA:N RH:N SH:N TM:N FILL:N BE:N MR:N
   ```

5 Save your changes to CONFIG.SYS and exit the system configuration editor.

6 Restart your computer, and then rerun the optimize process.

SYMPTOM 27-12 Systems with an Adaptec SCSI controller and QEMM have trouble running Optimize When you're using an Adaptec SCSI controller and loading ASPIxDOS.SYS (where x is usually an even number) along with the parameter ST:x, there are often problems during the Optimize detection phase under QEMM. The problem will manifest itself with messages like "Bad command or filename, error in CONFIG.SYS line xx." Load the CONFIG.SYS file into a text editor, move the ASPIxDOS.SYS line so that it loads *before* the QEMM386.SYS line, and then add the following line before the ASPIxDOS.SYS line:

```
DEVICE=C:\QEMM\HOOKROM.SYS
```

SYMPTOM 27-13 The QEMM optimize process won't run when using a SoundBlaster or Vibra16 card You're trying to run the optimize process, but it fails to finish. Both of these cards use a driver called "Diagnose" to test their current settings, but this tool can interfere with QEMM. This driver is generally not required for your sound card to work properly. Work around this problem using the steps below:

1 Load the AUTOEXEC.BAT file into your text editor.

2 Look for the command line containing the Diagnose tool.

3 When you locate the line, REMark out the command line, such as:

```
REM DIAGNOSE
```

4 Save your changes to AUTOEXEC.BAT and exit the text editor.

5 Type **C:\QEMM\OPTIMIZE /Q** and press ENTER to try the optimize process again.

SYMPTOM 27-14 The QEMM optimize process will not finish on a Compaq system In most cases, you have installed QEMM and run Optimize for the first time. Your computer restarts three times. On the fourth restart, the Windows 95/98 desktop loads. You never get a message saying that Optimize has finished. Chances are that Optimize did not finish—a conflict with the Compaq shell kept Optimize from receiving its completion signal. You can probably work around the problem using the steps below:

1 Click Start, click Shut Down, click Restart in MS-DOS Mode, and then click OK.

2 If Optimize continues at this time, keep "restarting to DOS" until it is finished.

3 If Optimize no longer starts when you exit to DOS, enter the following:

```
UNOPT
EDIT SYSTEM.INI
```

4 In the SYSTEM.INI file, find the line that reads SHELL=C:\CPQWIN\CPQSHELL.EXE.

5 Type a semicolon (;) at the beginning of that line.

6 Create a blank line directly above the ;SHELL=C:\CPQWIN\CPQSHELL.EXE line, and on that blank line, type **SHELL=EXPLORER.EXE**.

7 Save your changes and exit the text editor.

8 Restart your computer.

You may receive a message such as "Your Compaq software will work with your new shell, but your new shell will not work with your Compaq software. Do you wish to continue using your Compaq software?" Answer no to this message and continue with the steps below:

9 After Windows 95/98 loads, click Start, click Run, enter **OPTIMIZE**, and click OK.

10 Click Optimize. Optimize will reboot your computer several times during its process.

11 When Optimize is complete, Windows 95 will load and inform you that Optimize has finished.

12 After you accept or reject the configuration, restart your computer in MS-DOS mode.

13 At the command prompt, type **EDIT SYSTEM.INI** and press ENTER.

14 Find the line you just added, SHELL=EXPLORER.EXE, and delete it.

15 Find the line right below that, ;SHELL=C:\CPQWIN\CPQSHELL.EXE, and remove the semicolon from the front of the line, so that it reads

```
SHELL=C:\CPQWIN\CPQSHELL.EXE
```

16 Save your changes and exit the text editor.

17 Restart the computer normally.

SYMPTOM 27-15 You have trouble printing from Windows applications after installing QEMM For example, after installing QEMM and running the initial optimize, you have difficulty printing from Windows applications such as Microsoft Word. The problem is that some printer drivers are not able to utilize DOS resources that QEMM has moved into high memory. You can use the steps below to rearrange resources:

1 Click Start, and then click Run.

2 Type **QSETUP** and click OK. (You may need to type **C:\QEMM\QSETUP** instead.)

3 Click the DOS-Up tab.

4 Click the option "Use the specified features of DOS-Up" (partial).

5 Check only the "Move COMMAND.COM" and "Set DOS=HIGH" entries, and click Save.

6 You'll be prompted to optimize, restart, or exit. Choose Optimize.

Your computer will restart several times. When it has finished, you should receive the message saying "Optimize is complete." Now try printing again.

SYMPTOM 27-16 QEMM does not "see" all of the memory on your system
Chances are that QEMM is installed on a PCI-based system. When QEMM starts, you notice that it only recognizes 15MB or 16MB of RAM when you actually have more. If you add the UR=1M:xxM parameter to your QEMM386.SYS line, it will cause a Windows Protection Error, and you cannot boot the computer. PCI motherboards have the ability to create a 1MB "hole" in memory at the 15MB point. The system uses this hole to speed up certain operations. However, this hole also makes it difficult for QEMM to see all the memory. Forcing QEMM to scan the area disturbs the data your motherboard has placed there. To work around this problem, you'll have to tweak the QEMM command line in CONFIG.SYS:

1 Quit Windows 95/98 to the DOS prompt.

2 Open the CONFIG.SYS file into your text editor.

27

3. Locate the device line containing QEMM386.SYS.
4. At the end of this line, add the following parameters: UR=1M:xxM NUR=15M:1M (where xx is the amount of physical memory in megabytes). For example:

   ```
   DEVICE=C:\QEMM\QEMM386.SYS RAM UR=1M:xxM NUR=15M:1M
   ```
5. Save your changes to CONFIG.SYS and exit the text editor.
6. Restart the computer normally. All the system RAM should now be "visible."

SYMPTOM 27-17 **The QEMM QuickBoot option resets the system's APM features** This generally occurs after you have turned off the Advanced Power Management (APM) features in BIOS. On a cold boot, it does not affect APM. But on a warm boot with QuickBoot enabled, the settings for your APM features are reset to a default setting of On, which activates the system's power-saving modes after a certain amount of idle time. There are two methods of resolving the problem:

- First, try adding the APM:N and SUS parameters to your QEMM386.SYS command line in the CONFIG.SYS file, such as:

  ```
  DEVICE=C:\QEMM\QEMM386.SYS RAM APM:N SUS
  ```
- If this does not resolve the problem, you can disable QuickBoot by placing the BE:N parameter on your QEMM386.SYS command line in the CONFIG.SYS file, such as:

  ```
  DEVICE=C:\QEMM\QEMM386.SYS RAM BE:N
  ```

SYMPTOM 27-18 **The QEMM QuickBoot feature stops working after loading Windows 98** You notice that after installing Windows 98, the QuickBoot feature no longer seems to be active. When you have Windows restart the computer, you must sit through the full power-up routine instead of the shortened QuickBoot. If you restart the computer after loading the DOS mode, this behavior does not occur.

The problem is that Windows 98 includes a new feature called "Fast Shutdown," which takes advantage of a certain system call in very advanced BIOS versions in order to shut down quickly. Fast Shutdown monitors a system interrupt—the same interrupt that QEMM's QuickBoot monitors in order to predict a reboot and restart the machine. If your BIOS supports the Fast Shutdown feature, it may be preferable to QEMM's QuickBoot. In this case, you may need to disable QuickBoot. However, if your BIOS does *not* support Fast Shutdown, you can tell Windows 98 to disable Fast Shutdown and stick with QuickBoot instead:

1. Click Start, and then click Run.
2. Type **MSCONFIG** and click OK.
3. Click Advanced, and then check "Disable fast shutdown."
4. Click OK, and then click OK again.
5. You'll be asked to restart your computer. *Do not do so at this time.*
6. Click Start, click Shut Down, then click Shut Down, and click OK.
7. Once the computer has stopped at the "It is now safe to turn off your computer" message, restart your computer by pressing CTRL+ALT+DEL (or simply pressing the reset button or power switch).

QEMM's QuickBoot will be working again the next time you attempt to restart your computer.

SYMPTOM 27-19 There are serious video problems with QEMM under Windows 95/98 You may have recently installed a new video card (or installed QEMM to a system with an advanced video accelerator). When the computer tries to display graphics (such as the Windows desktop), the screen becomes highly distorted and unreadable. In virtually all cases, the video card's ROM size was not properly detected, and some of the area reserved for graphics routines has been used to load programs instead. You will need to exclude a portion of memory that is needed by the video card (often A000h-CFFFh).

1. Turn the computer off, wait ten seconds or more, and then restart the computer to the Safe Mode Command Prompt Only using the Windows Startup menu.
2. Load the CONFIG.SYS file into your text editor (such as EDIT).
3. Locate the command line containing QEMM386.SYS.
4. At the end of this line, add the following exclusion: **X=A000-CFFF**.
5. Save your changes to the CONFIG.SYS file, and then exit the text editor.
6. Restart the computer normally. The display should appear normal. You may now rerun Optimize.

SYMPTOM 27-20 Your sound card fails after installing QEMM In most cases, the problem involves tweaking the DMA setting on the QEMM command line. For example, you may need to add DMA=64 to the QEMM command line. For a SoundBlaster or SoundBlaster Pro, you may need to add DMA=128 to the QEMM command line. You may also need to change the DMA channel that the sound card is using. This is usually accomplished by changing a jumper on the card itself, or through the device's Properties dialog.

SYMPTOM 27-21 The system no longer boots properly after changing the command-line order in CONFIG.SYS Chances are that you were recently making changes to the CONFIG.SYS file. When you reboot now, you may receive various error messages. Some errors may refer to the QEMM386.SYS driver not being loaded and then may indicate that other drivers are "loading low." In virtually every case, you have placed a device driver line *ahead* of the QEMM386.SYS command line. Make sure that the DEVICE= lines for DOSDATA (if enabled), QEMM386.SYS, and DOS-Up (if enabled) are the first three lines in your CONFIG.SYS file. If they are not, edit the CONFIG.SYS file to move any other entries down below these three critical command lines. That should resolve the problem.

SYMPTOM 27-22 Windows 95/98 becomes unstable after installing QEMM After installing QEMM you receive several errors such as "General Protection Faults" and "Invalid Page Faults." Sometimes Windows may not start (or it locks up while shutting down). In general, the system's behavior seems unstable. This is due to a memory conflict between QEMM and Windows. QEMM is noted for finding unused areas of memory that many applications cannot. It then uses these areas to store information in high memory. However, Windows also detects these unused areas and assumes that they are not in use. When Windows tries to use one of these areas for program information, conflicts occur, and your system will suffer from errors. You can fix this error by tweaking the QEMM command line in CONFIG.SYS:

1. Exit Windows to the DOS prompt.
2. Load the CONFIG.SYS file into your text editor.
3. Locate the QEMM386 command line.
4. On the QEMM386.SYS command line, add the following parameters: **RH:N SH:N**.

5. Save your changes to the CONFIG.SYS file, and then exit the text editor.
6. Restart the computer normally. The conflict should be resolved.

SYMPTOM 27-23 **Windows 95/98 refuses to shut down after installing QEMM** After installing QEMM on your system, you're no longer able to shut down your computer. The computer hangs at the message "Please wait while your computer shuts down." In most circumstances, the problem is due to a conflict with Update-It. The solution is to remove Update-It from your Startup folder:

1. With Windows running, press CTRL+ALT+DEL. The Close Program dialog box appears.
2. Select Update-it and click End Task.
3. Click Start, point to Settings, and then click Taskbar & Start Menu.
4. Click the Start Menu Programs tab.
5. Click Remove.
6. Click the plus (+) next to the Startup folder.
7. Select Update-It and click Remove.
8. Click Close, and then click OK.
9. Restart the computer. You should now be able to shut down correctly.

To use Update-It in the future, launch it manually from the QEMM Control Panel.

SYMPTOM 27-24 **You notice that QEMM's DOS drivers keep loading into CONFIG.SYS** The DOS-Up drivers (DOS-UP, DOSDATA, and LOADHI.COM) load into the CONFIG.SYS file—even though you removed the lines—and COMMAND.COM is loading high. The problem is that DOS-Up is listed in OPTIMIZE.INI, so removing the lines from your CONFIG.SYS file is not enough. As long as the OPTIMIZE.INI file exists (and informs Optimize that the drivers should be used), Optimize will continue to add them to CONFIG.SYS. You must run QSETUP and turn the drivers off, or edit the OPTIMIZE.INI file and change all the driver settings to 0 (instead of 1). If you attempt to merely delete the files, existing DOS-Up drivers will remain and Optimize will decide whether the COMMAND.COM file can be loaded high or not.

> If you have no DOS-Up drivers loaded, Optimize will still attempt to load the command processor high. To prevent Optimize from doing this, you must either put COMMAND.COM in the OPTIMIZE.EXC file, or have an OPTIMIZE.INI file with a ShellCOMMAND=0 line in it.

SYMPTOM 27-25 **You see the message "Address wrap at xxxx"** This message is not really an error, but it means that QEMM's SCANMEM feature has detected that your PC's address space is smaller than the 4GB that the processor can address. In most cases, you can continue to use QEMM normally.

SYMPTOM 27-26 **You see the error "NOUSERAM=xxxxx-yyyyy"** This error indicates that QEMM's SCANMEM feature does not detect physical memory in the address range "xxxxx-yyyyy," even though your system's BIOS has reported enough extended memory (XMS) to fill these addresses. If you see this message, use your PC's CMOS setup to reconfigure the machine so that the BIOS reports extended memory properly. Otherwise, there may be a problem with the RAM that went undetected by the BIOS during its POST. Try running a memory diagnostic for possible RAM problems, or simply try replacing the suspect RAM.

SYMPTOM 27-27 **You see the error "Invalid USERAM due to memory cache"** This error means that QEMM's SCANMEM feature has detected that the "USERAM=xxxxx-yyyyy" parameter that it last printed to the display is invalid and should not be used. You should ignore only the last USERAM message printed to the screen—previous USERAM messages are valid. This error may occur when an unusual memory cache architecture makes the contents of memory appear to be variable to SCANMEM.

SYMPTOM 27-28 **QEMM 8.0x refuses to function properly under Windows 95 on an IBM ThinkPad** There is a problem with the BIOS on IBM ThinkPads running Windows 95. Call the IBM BBS at 919-517-0001 to download TPWIN95.EXE. This file explains the solution and provides a patch for the IBM BIOS problem. You may also be able to download the appropriate files from the IBM Web site.

SYMPTOM 27-29 **You see the error "QEMM386: Cannot load because there is not enough memory"** This error message can appear for several different reasons, but often occurs on machines with a total of 1MB of RAM (640K conventional + 384K extended). When QEMM386 starts, it finds all of the memory in your system and puts it into one big pool. Then it checks the parameters that were specified in the QEMM386 command line in the CONFIG.SYS file. If there's not enough memory available to provide all of the services requested by the user (as well as those that QEMM386 performs by default), QEMM386 will terminate with this error message.

Remove any EXTMEM (EXT) or MEMORY (MEM) parameters that may exist on the QEMM386.SYS command line. (These parameters can easily prevent QEMM from loading when set incorrectly.) Supply QEMM386 with parameters that will cause it to use less memory. These include NOFILL (NO), NOROM (NR), and MAPS=0. If you have specified the ROM parameter, remove it. Also, you may need to exclude some of your usable high RAM areas. On an EGA/VGA system, try X=B000-B7FF. On a Hercules system, the NV parameter should be sufficient. If your system uses shadow RAM, QEMM386 can usually use it also, so enabling the shadow RAM is a good idea when this message appears.

Of course, the preferable solution to this problem is to install more memory in the computer. This allows QEMM386 to perform all of its requested functions, while also providing more expanded memory for applications that need it.

SYMPTOM 27-30 **You see the error "QEMM386: Cannot load because the processor is already in Virtual 86 mode"** The Intel i386 and later processors can run in one of three different modes: real mode, protected mode, and virtual 8086 mode. When QEMM386 starts, its default settings tell it to place the processor in Virtual 86 mode. However, QEMM386 will not load if some other program (for example, some other memory manager) has already done this.

Check to make sure that QEMM386 is the *first* line in your CONFIG.SYS file. If not, move the QEMM386 command line to the beginning of the CONFIG.SYS file, and see if QEMM386 will load. If QEMM386 still refuses to load (or it was already the first program to load in CONFIG.SYS), then you should check your machine's BIOS settings for integrated memory management features that might have to be disabled.

SYMPTOM 27-31 **You see the error "QEMM386: Cannot load because an expanded memory manager is already loaded"** Only one expanded memory manager can be running on the computer at any given time. When QEMM386 initializes, it checks to see if another expanded memory manager has already been loaded into the system. If it detects the presence of such a memory manager, it

27

will abort with this error message rather than attempt to install itself. Since QEMM386 is designed to provide all of the features you need in an expanded memory manager, the old expanded memory manager is no longer needed. Check your CONFIG.SYS for another expanded memory manager, or place QEMM386 on the first line of CONFIG.SYS. (Expanded memory managers tend to have the letters "EMM" or "EMS" in their names.) If you see a line that looks like any one of these,

```
DEVICE=C:\DOS\EMM386.EXE
DEVICE=C:\REMM.SYS
DEVICE=C:\EMM.SYS
DEVICE=C:\EMS.SYS
DEVICE=C:\CEMM.EXE
```

remove or REMark out the appropriate line(s) from the CONFIG.SYS file.

SYMPTOM 27-32 You see the error "QEMM386: Unknown Microchannel Adapter ID: XXXX" On MicroChannel (MCA) computers, each installed adapter has its own ID number. This number is a four-digit alphanumeric code. When QEMM386 initializes during boot-up, it notes the names of all of the adapters that are present, and compares them to a list of adapters contained in its MCA.ADL file. If an adapter is present that is not listed in the MCA.ADL file, QEMM386 will display the error message. You'll need to add the adapter ID information to your existing ADL file, or update the ADL file by downloading the latest version from Quarterdeck's Web site (**www.quarterdeck.com**). Note that Quarterdeck is now owned by Symantec.

SYMPTOM 27-33 You see the error "QEMM386: Cannot find file MCA.ADL" TheQEMM386.SYS device driver is reporting that it cannot find the MCA.ADL file that it uses to determine memory locations used by adapter cards in MicroChannel (MCA) machines. QEMM386.SYS looks for MCA.ADL in the directory from which it was loaded in the CONFIG.SYS file. For example, if your CONFIG.SYS contains a line that reads

```
device=c:\qemm\qemm386.sys
```

QEMM will look in the C:\QEMM directory for the MCA.ADL file. Ensure that the MCA.ADL file is located in the directory that is specified on the QEMM386.SYS device line in your CONFIG.SYS file.

SYMPTOM 27-34 You see the error "QEMM38452 Cannot load because this is not an 80386" When QEMM386 initializes, it checks the machine to ensure that a 386/486 processor is present. QEMM386 cannot run on 80286, 8088, or 8086 machines. If QEMM386 displays this error on a 386/486 machine, you should reinstall QEMM386. If the message still appears, you should obtain a new copy of QEMM386 and try again. If you have a 386 add-in board, this error message may appear if QEMM386.SYS appears in the CONFIG.SYS file before the driver for your particular 386 add-in board. Put the add-in board's driver *before* QEMM386.SYS in the CONFIG.SYS, and the problem should go away.

SYMPTOM 27-35 You see the error "QEMM386: Cannot load because there is no room for a page frame" In order to create and utilize expanded memory, QEMM386 must create a page frame that is 64KB in size. By default, QEMM386 attempts to put the page frame between A000h (640KB) and F000h (960KB). However, some system configurations prevent QEMM386 from placing a page frame above A000h by splitting or fragmenting the unused areas above A000h into chunks that are less than 64KB in size. If QEMM386 cannot place the page frame above A000h, it will attempt to place it in conventional memory. When it cannot create a page frame at all, QEMM386 will display the above error message.

Try rearranging any adapter cards in the system so that a 64KB area above A000h is unused. This may involve changing physical switch settings on the adapters (reconfiguring the adapter ROMs). On PS/2 and other MicroChannel (MCA) machines, this will entail using the reference disk. If rearranging the adapter locations above A000h is not possible, remove any exclusion (X=xxxx-xxxx) statements that reference areas between 0000h and 9FFFh.

SYMPTOM 27-36 **You see the error "QEMM386: Cannot load because QEMM is already loaded"** QEMM386 is a "control program"—that is, software that oversees virtually all aspects of the computer's operation. By definition, there can only be one control program in charge of the system at any given time. As a result, QEMM386 *cannot* be loaded on top of itself. QEMM386 is intelligent enough to detect its own presence while loading. If it sees that it has already been loaded, it will abort with this error message. This error will only result if you have multiple lines in your CONFIG.SYS file that load the QEMM386.SYS device file. By removing all but one of these lines, you should correct the problem.

SYMPTOM 27-37 **You see the error "QEMM386: Disabling StealthROM:F because the page frame does not overlap any ROM"** QEMM's Stealth technology (introduced with QEMM386 version 6.0) effectively "hides" ROM areas above 640KB and allows them to be used as either high RAM, or part of the EMS page frame. In order to use the STEALTHROM:F feature, the page frame must be located atop a "stealthed" ROM area. By default, QEMM will do its best to place the page frame properly. However, if the page frame has been explicitly set (by using QEMM's FRAME= parameter) at an address that is not occupied by a ROM (or if all ROMS have been excluded with the X= parameter), QEMM will disable ST:F and continue. This may result in an overall reduction of the amount of high RAM created by QEMM386. Remove the FRAME= parameter from your QEMM386.SYS command line in your CONFIG.SYS file. If there are no FRAME= parameters on the command line, check for exclusions (EXCLUDE= or X= parameters) that may be "covering" ROM areas. Remove the exclusions and try again.

SYMPTOM 27-38 **You see the error "QEMM386: Disabling StealthROM:M because there is no page frame"** A "page frame" is required in order to use the ST:M parameter and take full advantage of QEMM's Stealth feature. Check your QEMM386.SYS device line in your CONFIG.SYS file for the following parameters

```
FRAME=NONE (or FR=NONE)
NOEMS
FRAMELENGTH=x (or FL=x)
```

where x is a value less than 4. If your QEMM386.SYS device line contains any of the above parameters, Stealth will be automatically disabled. To use Stealth, remove the appropriate parameters, save your changes to CONFIG.SYS, and try again.

SYMPTOM 27-39 **You see the error "QEMM386: Disabling stealth because QEMM could not locate the ROM handler for INT xx"** When using Stealth features, QEMM386 must monitor some interrupts at all times. When these interrupts have been diverted by another program, QEMM386 will disable Stealth features. As a result, QEMM386 should usually be loaded on the *first* line of your machine's CONFIG.SYS file. This is practical in the majority of system configurations. However, there are times when it is desirable to load other device drivers *before* QEMM386.SYS. When doing this, some device drivers may make it impossible for Stealth to "see" all of the activity in the machine, and problems can result.

If possible, place the QEMM386.SYS device line at the beginning of your CONFIG.SYS file. If this is not possible, use HOOKROM.SYS (included with QEMM386 version 6.0 and later). This device driver must be placed at the beginning of the CONFIG.SYS file. HOOKROM.SYS acts as a secretary for QEMM386—noting the state of the machine as CONFIG.SYS is processed and then passing these notes to QEMM386 so that it can operate properly with Stealth features active.

SYMPTOM 27-40 You see the error "Cannot load because QEMM is not registered. Run the INSTALL program to register" The files on the QEMM386 product disk must be installed by running the INSTALL program. They will not function properly when copied over by the DOS COPY command. Run the INSTALL program from the original QEMM386 product distribution disk.

SYMPTOM 27-41 You see the errors "CONTEXTS is no longer a QEMM parameter!" or "NAMES is no longer a QEMM parameter!" QEMM386 versions 4.23 and earlier featured a CONTEXTS parameter that allows users to specify the maximum number of mapping contexts that QEMM386 could save at one time. Mapping contexts are now determined by the number of HANDLES provided by QEMM386 (ranging from 16 to 255—64 by default). Similarly, it was determined that the function of the NAMES parameter (also from QEMM386 versions 4.23 and earlier), which specified the maximum number of named handles, could be included in the HANDLES parameter. As a result, the CONTEXTS and NAMES parameters were abandoned in QEMM386 version 5.0 and later. Remove the CONTEXTS=xxx and NAMES=xxx parameters from your QEMM386.SYS command line in the CONFIG.SYS file.

SYMPTOM 27-42 You see the error "LOADHI: The high memory chain is corrupted" QEMM386 uses a collection of high memory areas called a *memory chain* to keep track of the TSRs and device drivers that are loaded high by the LOADHI programs. If there is a conflict in high memory, this chain can become corrupted. This error message is usually accompanied by an address (such as C800h). You can frequently resolve the conflict with a memory exclusion on the QEMM386 command line in the CONFIG.SYS file. It is also possible that other drivers or programs that are being loaded in CONFIG.SYS or AUTOEXEC.BAT may be corrupting the high memory chain. In this case you should disable all device drivers or TSRs that aren't absolutely vital to your machine's operation, then reenable each line—one at a time—rebooting each time you make a change, until the conflicting driver or TSR is discovered.

SYMPTOM 27-43 You see the error "LOADHI: Cannot write to log file" This error usually appears when there is a copy of the QEMM386.SYS device driver in the root directory of the hard drive, as well as in the \QEMM subdirectory. This can cause confusion when loading high. Make sure that QEMM386.SYS is only found in the \QEMM subdirectory and that the QEMM386 device line in the CONFIG.SYS file specifically points to that subdirectory, such as:

```
device=c:\qemm\qemm386.sys
```

SYMPTOM 27-44 You see the error "Stealth ROM is being disabled because it cannot find ROM handler 05 76" This error indicates a Stealth compatibility problem with QEMM 8.0x. To work around this problem, exclude Stealth features from the indicated memory area, or turn off Stealth features entirely. If you must continue using QEMM, consider upgrading your version of QEMM.

SYMPTOM 27-45 The system will hang when attempting to use Colorado Tape Backup Some system implementations of shadow RAM do not allow QEMM to reclaim them properly. This can manifest itself in a number of ways, including the tape backup working perfectly with QEMM 7.0x, but failing with QEMM 7.5x. Add the SH:N switch to the QEMM386.SYS command line in the CONFIG.SYS.

SYMPTOM 27-46 There is no specific error message, but Optimize won't complete You are probably running Ontrack's Disk Manager overlay program in conjunction with QEMM 8.0x. To work around this problem, move the DMDRVR.BIN file in CONFIG.SYS so it directly precedes the QEMM386.SYS command line. Optimize should now complete normally.

SYMPTOM 27-47 After Optimize is complete, you see the error "Fixed disk parameter error or BIOS error" This type of problem often occurs when using QEMM 8.0x on Compaq Prolinea 5120 systems. You can usually work around this problem by adding the CF:N and BE:N switches to the QEMM386.SYS command line in your CONFIG.SYS. (You can do this using QSETUP.) Then rerun Optimize. Another option is to update your version of QEMM.

SYMPTOM 27-48 Optimize won't complete on a PC with a Plextor 6X CD-ROM and Adaptec 1515 SCSI controller This is a known problem with QEMM 8.0x and the ASPI2DOS.SYS SCSI driver. This adapter's drivers will only work with the following configurations:

- With the ST:M switch, load the ASPI driver *after* QEMM. In this configuration, QEMM will optimize and load the driver high.
- With the ST:F switch, load the ASPI driver *before* QEMM with the /u and /p140 switches added to the ASPI2DOS.SYS driver line.

SYMPTOM 27-49 An NEC UltraLite Versa PC suffers Exception 13 errors in the Exxxh range You may also find that Windows 3.1x loads PROGMAN, then drops back to the C:\WINDOWS prompt and hangs up. The problem is due to a memory conflict and can usually be corrected by adding an exclusion (such as X=E000-EFFF) on the QEMM 7.0 command line.

The NEC UltraLite Versa has the video ROM in E000h-E7FFh. It has additional ROM in E800h-EFFFh (power management code). QEMM detects the video ROM properly and requires no exclusion for it, but QEMM maps over E800h-EFFFh. So this does require an exclusion if you wish to use the power management features of the system.

SYMPTOM 27-50 A Phillips CD Recorder (such as CDD200) fails to function if you put the USERAM=1M:32M parameter on the QEMM386.SYS line in CONFIG.SYS A Phillips CD Recorder (CDD200) fails to function if you put the USERAM=1M:32M parameter on the QEMM386.SYS line in CONFIG.SYS. You find this problem most readily with Compaq systems. Apparently, the Corel "CD Creator" software (provided by Adaptec) is not compatible with Compaq's CPQCFG plug-and-play (PnP) configuration manager. You need to turn off the PnP switch on the Adaptec SCSI (AHA1535) board, and run the CMOS configuration editor. Keep in mind that you'll need to specify the exact parameters (addresses) for your Adaptec SCSI board if you're not using PnP features.

SYMPTOM 27-51 **QEMM 8.0x refuses to complete an optimization on a Compaq computer** You are possibly having a conflict with some of the built-in Compaq BIOS features. Use the following switches in the QEMM command line in CONFIG.SYS to get around the problems:

- *CF:Y or :N* This enables or disables all three Compaq features: Compaq EGA ROM, Compaq Half ROM, and Compaq ROM Memory. By default, all are enabled. CF:Y enables all features, and CF:N disables all features.
- *CER:Y or :N* This enables or disables Compaq EGA ROM. Disabling this can require 32KB of upper memory addresses on some Compaq computers. However, QEMM cannot be turned off if this feature is enabled.
- *CHR:Y or :N* This enables or disables Compaq Half ROM. Disabling this can require 32KB of upper memory addresses on some Compaq computers.
- *CRM:Y or :N* This enables or disables the Compaq Memory ROM. QEMM cannot be turned off if this feature is enabled.

SYMPTOM 27-52 **You cannot install XtraDrive on the desired drive** You see the error "Drive 1 is being controlled by a program that appropriates INT13." This often occurs when using QEMM386 in the Stealth mode. Try removing the ST:M or ST:F parameters from the QEMM386 command line, and try to install again. (This only needs to be removed during the installation of XtraDrive.) Otherwise, you may need to disable QEMM before attempting to install XtraDrive, then reenable QEMM later.

SYMPTOM 27-53 **You cannot install QEMM on a system with XtraDrive** When you install QEMM386 on a system that has XtraDrive already installed, you get a system lockup or "Exception 13" error when you reboot the machine (and the QEMM386 loading process starts). You need to add a memory exception to the QEMM command line. Simply reboot without QEMM, edit the CONFIG.SYS file, and add X=9000-9FFF to the QEMM command line. Save your changes, and restart the system.

SYMPTOM 27-54 **You cannot load the XtraDrive device driver into high RAM** This is a known problem with SCSI bus mastering controllers and XtraDrive. Even with double buffering, you will not be able to load XtraDrive into high RAM when using a SCSI bus mastering device. This is not really a QEMM memory manager issue, but a problem with XtraDrive. Try loading XtraDrive in conventional memory.

SYMPTOM 27-55 **You see the error "This program is attempting to access the disk via the page frame"** This is often a problem with the EMS XtraDrive disk cache when using QEMM in the Stealth mode. You cannot use the XtraDrive EMS cache with QEMM. You must disable the XtraDrive cache. (A DBF=2 parameter will not work on the QEMM command line.)

SYMPTOM 27-56 **Windows 95 hangs on the opening logo screen, or your video display appears distorted** This usually happens after installing QEMM 8.0x. In virtually all cases, this type of problem is caused by QEMM mapping program memory across some portion of the video memory area. A memory exclusion is required to correct the issue. Start by excluding the address range A000-C7FF. If the problem is solved, you can try reducing the exclude statement range to further pinpoint the exact video range involved in the conflict.

SYMPTOM 27-57 **After accepting the Optimize results, the system gets caught in a loop and eventually stops in a Windows protection fault 14** This kind of problem can occur with QEMM 8.0x, which is Windows 95 compliant. To work around this problem, add SH:N and RH:N switches to the QEMM386.SYS command line in CONFIG.SYS, and reboot the system. After rebooting, check the Startup folder and remove all programs from the Startup folder. Rebooting the system again should now take care of the looping and protection fault.

SYMPTOM 27-58 **You see an error "Configuration Too Large for Memory" while running Optimize under Windows 95** This also typically occurs with a standard QEMM installation. You'll need to modify the configuration of your CONFIG.SYS file. Open the CONFIG.SYS file in a text editor and add the following lines to the end of the file:

```
device=c:\windows\setver.exe
device=c:\windows\ifshlp.sys
dos=noumb
```

If you're loading any ASPI drivers (ASPI2DOS.SYS or ASPI4DOS.SYS), or have a SCSI CD-ROM or SCSI hard disk, add this line also:

```
device=c:\windows\aspi2hlp.sys
```

Save this modified file, and then run the QEMM Optimize feature. If the problem continues, open a DOS prompt, and switch to your QEMM directory. Type **OPTIMIZE /NH**, and then select the OPTIMIZE Custom feature (Option F3). At the beginning of the "software detection" phase (when it says "Starting Windows 95"), press SHIFT+F8. You'll be prompted to load each driver. Respond yes to each line, and watch what is loading. Look for any line that begins with the command "DEVICEHIGH=." If you find one, write this line down, and then reboot the system. When you see "Starting Windows 95" again, press SHIFT+F5. Switch to your QEMM directory, type **UNOPT**, and press ENTER. Now edit your CONFIG.SYS file and replace the "DEVICEHIGH=" line with "DEVICE=.". Run Optimize again and repeat your search-and-replace of DEVICEHIGH= lines.

SYMPTOM 27-59 **You encounter floppy drive problems after installing QEMM** QEMM is generally regarded as an aggressive memory manager because it seeks out areas of memory that can be utilized—rather than simply use the memory that is readily available. As a result, it is possible that QEMM can impair some system functions under the right conditions (usually from using the Stealth or ROM hole-detection features). Start by editing the CONFIG.SYS file, and add the XST=F000 switch to the QEMM386.SYS command line. The new command line will appear like this:

```
device=c:\qemm\qemm386.sys ram st:m xst=f000
```

Save your changes, and then reboot the system and test your floppy drive(s). If the problem persists, you'll need to troubleshoot the "ROM hole." Reopen the CONFIG.SYS file in a text editor and remove the "XST" switch you added above; then add the exclusion "X=F400-FFFF," such as:

```
device=c:\qemm\qemm386.sys ram x=f400-ffff
```

Save your changes, reboot the system, and test your floppy drive(s). Once the problem is fixed, Quarterdeck suggests that you reoptimize QEMM by typing **C:\QEMM\OPTIMIZE /Q** at the DOS prompt.

If the problem persists, chances are that the floppy problem is not due to QEMM. You can test this by rebooting the machine. After the machine beeps, press and hold the ALT key. You should see a message telling you to press ESC to unload DOSDATA.SYS. Press ESC, and then immediately press and hold ALT again. You will see a message telling you to press ESC to unload QEMM. Press ESC. If QDPMI is normally loaded after QEMM, a message will indicate that it cannot load without a memory manager. Press any key to bypass this message. LOADHI entries will warn about drivers not loading high. (This is normal when testing.) Once the system finishes booting, try the floppy drive(s) again. If the problem continues, it is caused by something other than QEMM. If the problem disappears, you may need to remove QEMM from the system.

SYMPTOM 27-60 **You cannot format a floppy disk with QEMM installed** After installing QEMM on a Windows 95/98 machine, you're no longer able to format floppy disks from Windows or DOS. The floppy drive seems to work fine otherwise. In almost every case, QEMM is loading a TSR or device driver in the location that normally controls your floppy drive. Try excluding a range of memory from QEMM:

1. Quit Windows to a DOS prompt.
2. Type **CD** and press ENTER.
3. Type **EDIT CONFIG.SYS** and press ENTER.
4. Find the command line containing QEMM386.SYS.
5. At the end of this line, press the SPACEBAR and type **X=F000-FFFF**.
6. Save your changes and exit the text editor; then reboot the PC normally.
7. Try the floppy drive again.

SYMPTOM 27-61 **Using the RAM parameter with QEMM causes an IBM ThinkPad to hang** In most cases, the ThinkPad will hang after 10 to 15 seconds. The extended BIOS Data Area (XBDA) is a data area normally located at the top of conventional memory—just below 640KB. This memory is used to hold BIOS-specific information. By default, QEMM will relocate this XBDA, reclaiming the conventional memory it uses and allowing programs such as VIDRAM to extend conventional memory past 640K. On the IBM ThinkPad, this relocation can result in a crash when the ThinkPad operating system writes data intended for the XBDA into the wrong place (usually around 10 to 15 seconds after loading QEMM). Add the XBDA:L switch to the QEMM386.SYS command line. This will tell QEMM to move the XBDA to low conventional memory (but demands 1KB of conventional memory).

SYMPTOM 27-62 **You have trouble loading programs high, or the system hangs, or there is other odd behavior from TSRs, device drivers, or PC cards** This often happens when QEMM is loaded onto an IBM ThinkPad and cannot determine which addresses the ThinkPad's PC card(s) are using. Each PC card will demand from 0KB to 64KB of upper memory addressing space that must be excluded from QEMM, and there is no guarantee that QEMM can autodetect the region. You'll need to specifically exclude the upper memory range where the PCMCIA card is mapped.

If your PCMCIA card is properly configured, there should be a line in your CONFIG.SYS that loads a driver called DICRMU01.SYS. This driver is the PC card resource map utility that tells the card what area of memory it is supposed to use. Check that command line for an /MA= parameter. This parameter will be followed by the ranges of memory to exclude with the X= parameter on the QEMM386.SYS line. For example, if your CONFIG.SYS file has a DICRMU01.SYS line with /MA=D000-D3FF, you would need to add X=D000-D3FF to the end of your QEMM386.SYS command line in the CONFIG.SYS file.

SYMPTOM 27-63 **QEMM generates an Exception 6, 12, or 13 error** Generally speaking, an "exception error" indicates a programming fault that the CPU cannot deal with. An exception error can be caused by a problem with QEMM itself (corruption in the QEMM files) or an application (due to a software bug or simple incompatibility running under QEMM). Run a virus checker to scan for any possible virus activity on disk or in memory. Run ScanDisk to check and correct any file problems on the disk. Check with the application's maker to see if there are known incompatibilities with QEMM and if there are any work-arounds or patches to the application. Finally, try booting without QEMM or using another memory manager to correct the problem.

SYMPTOM 27-64 **Systems with Disk Manager fail to optimize properly** This often happens with Disk Manager and QEMM 8.00 (dated 11/4/95). Optimize hangs during the software detection phase. With QEMM 8.00, the XBIOS.OVL overlay file could not be loaded high successfully during the optimize process. This file does not appear in CONFIG.SYS or AUTOEXEC.BAT—it is loaded automatically and invisibly by Disk Manager at start time. Contact Quarterdeck and obtain the patch for QEMM 8.01. Until you can obtain QEMM 8.01, you may work around the problem using a text editor to add the line XBIOS to the end of the OPTIMIZE.NOT file in your QEMM directory.

SYMPTOM 27-65 **QEMM 97 halts with an Adaptec 2940 card in the system** This is a known problem when you try to install QEMM 97 on a computer using an ATC5000 BIOS (v1.1), including an AMD K6/200 processor, and fitted with an Adaptec 2940 SCSI card. When the computer tries to process the QEMM command line, it hangs after the "memory available to QEMM" line. This problem is due to a conflict between the system BIOS, QEMM 97, and the Adaptec 2940 board. In virtually all instances, you can correct this problem by upgrading the system BIOS or removing the Adaptec SCSI controller. After upgrading the BIOS, you should be able to install and run QEMM 97 without difficulty.

27

SYMPTOM 27-66 **Windows 98 will not load after installing QEMM** This kind of problem generally occurs after you install Windows 98 and then reinstall QEMM. After starting the optimize process, the computer refuses to load Windows. In short, the only change that has been made to the system is the installation of Windows 98. In almost every case, a third-party driver is conflicting with QEMM or Windows 98. To locate the offending driver, follow these steps:

1. Restart the computer, and then press F8 when you see the "Starting Windows 98" message.
2. At the Startup menu, choose Step-by-Step Confirmation.
3. Load all of the drivers until you see "Load all Windows Drivers?" Answer no to this question.
4. If Windows 98 starts in the Safe Mode, continue with the steps below. If not, you may need to remove QEMM from the system.
5. Restart the computer, and then press F8 when you see the "Starting Windows 98" message.
6. At the Startup menu, choose Step-by-Step Confirmation.
7. Load all of the drivers until you see "Load all Windows Drivers?" Answer yes to this question.
8. Answer yes to load the first driver, but answer no to avoid loading the rest of the drivers.
9. Let Windows try to load.

If Windows 98 loads successfully, repeat this process and allow another driver to load in each cycle until the problem reoccurs. Note the name of the last driver that was loaded before the problem recurred (the last driver you answered yes to); then restart the system and allow all drivers to load except for the driver you noted previously. You will be loading all drivers but the one that caused the error. Once you determine the offending driver, contact the manufacturer of that driver for an upgrade. (You can usually determine the manufacturer by viewing the properties of the driver.)

SYMPTOM 27-67 **The Compaq Presario 4000 or DeskPro locks up after installing QEMM** You've installed QEMM on a Compaq Presario or DeskPro (4000 series). Optimize didn't finish, and the system locks up during restart. Presarios and DeskPros in the 4000 series require additional QEMM parameters because of the way they use the high memory region. Follow these steps to add the necessary parameters:

1. Restart your computer. As soon as you see the "Starting Windows 95/98" message (or the Compaq startup logo), press the F8 key on the keyboard.
2. Once the Startup menu appears, choose the Safe Mode Command Prompt Only option and press ENTER.
3. At the DOS prompt, enter the following:

   ```
   CD\QEMM
   UNOPT
   ```
4. After the UNOPT routine finishes, your machine will reboot.
5. If your computer locks up again, repeat the first step. At the DOS prompt, type the following two commands:

   ```
   COPY C:\QEMM\Q_BACKUP\CONF0000.000 C:\CONFIG.SYS
   COPY C:\QEMM\Q_BACKUP\AUTO0001.000 C:\AUTOEXEC.BAT
   ```
6. If your computer reboots correctly, click the Start button and click Run.
7. Type **SYSEDIT** and press ENTER; then open the CONFIG.SYS file.
8. REMark out the DEVICE= lines for HIMEM.SYS and EMM386.EXE.
9. Enter the following line:

   ```
   DEVICE=C:\QEMM\QEMM386.SYS RAM APM:N SUS RH:N SH:N BE:N CF:N X=E800-EFFF
   ```
10. Choose File, click Exit, and allow the changes to be saved.
11. Restart your computer and type the following Optimize command:

    ```
    OPTIMIZE /NOSQF /NOSQT /NOSTEALTH /Q
    ```
12. When Optimize finishes, accept its results and allow the computer to restart normally.

SYMPTOM 27-68 **QEMM fails (or Windows fails to start) on a Compaq Contura** The Optimize feature fails during Stealth testing, or Windows refuses to boot. This is a known problem with QEMM on the Compaq Contura systems, but the underlying cause is still under investigation. You can typically work around this problem by adding MEMDRV to the OPTIMIZE.NOT file and adding the BE:N X=FE00:4k switches to the end of the QEMM command line in your CONFIG.SYS file.

SYMPTOM 27-69 **Your Dell laptop locks up when starting Windows 95/98** This is a known problem with Dell Inspiron 3000 series laptops when attempting to install QEMM 97. The optimization process does not finish, and Windows 95/98 stops responding at the banner screen. Your computer will only restart if you press F8 and boot up into the Safe Mode. Laptops like the Dell Inspiron 3000 require additional parameters and a memory exclusion. Follow these steps to resolve the issue:

1 Restart your computer in Safe Mode.
2 Click Start, and then click Run. Type **SYSEDIT** and press ENTER. (The system configuration editor starts.)
3 Select the C:\CONFIG.SYS window.
4 Locate the QEMM386.SYS command line, type a space at the end of the line, and then add the parameters X=E800-EFFF APM:N SUS DB:2, such as:

```
DEVICE=C:\QEMM\QEMM386.SYS RAM X=E800-EFFF APM:N SUS DB:2
```

5 Exit the system configuration editor, and save your changes.
6 Restart your computer and try the optimization process again.

SYMPTOM 27-70 **After installing QEMM 97, you find that DriveSpace is using a large portion of conventional memory** QEMM supports all versions of DoubleSpace or DriveSpace that accompany MS-DOS version 6.00 through 6.22. However, QEMM does not currently support the version of DriveSpace that comes with Windows 95/98—or the version of DriveSpace that comes with the "Microsoft Plus Pack." The only way to get more conventional memory in this situation is to use DoubleSpace (or earlier versions of DriveSpace). As an alternative, try uninstalling QEMM 97.

SYMPTOM 27-71 **After uninstalling QEMM 97 from DOS, you get errors in CONFIG.SYS** When you reboot the system after uninstalling, you get messages about errors in the CONFIG.SYS file. If you look at the CONFIG.SYS file, you'll notice two lines of characters that don't make sense in the context of the CONFIG.SYS file. You can work around this problem by taking the following steps:

27

1 Restart your computer in the DOS mode and load CONFIG.SYS into a text editor.
2 Use the REM statement to REMark out each line of gibberish text.
3 Save your changes and exit the text editor.
4 Reboot your computer. The errors should be corrected.

SYMPTOM 27-72 **When QEMM is installed, you may find that your SCSI device(s) no longer function** This may result in erratic behavior or data corruption on the drive. In its default configuration, QEMM is unable to provide data to the SCSI device at the rate that is being requested. QEMM is designed to create a "double buffer" in these situations, but it was unable to determine that the buffer was required. To work around this problem:

1 Quit Windows to the DOS prompt and load CONFIG.SYS into a text editor.
2 Locate the QEMM command line.
3 At the end of the command line line, type **DB:2**.
4 Save your changes and exit the text editor.
5 Reboot your computer. Your SCSI device(s) should work more reliably.

SYMPTOM 27-73 **You notice graphics resolution errors after running Optimize** After running QEMM's Optimize, things appeared to finish fine, but when the Windows desktop loaded, the image appeared much larger and had lost most of its color. A warning appeared that said your graphics card was not capable of this resolution, but you have not changed anything other than running Optimize. QEMM is not interacting properly with your video card. Some graphics cards use a small region of memory directly above the area normally reserved for graphics operations. QEMM does not recognize this nonstandard behavior and loads programs into the region. When your graphics card tries to initialize, it cannot use that area and is forced into a lower resolution. Try excluding the video card's address range from QEMM's use:

1. Quit Windows to DOS and load CONFIG.SYS into a text editor.
2. Locate the QEMM386.SYS command line.
3. At the end of the command line, exclude the range X=B000-B3FF X=C000-C7FF.
4. Save your changes and exit the text editor.
5. Restart your computer.

You may get warning messages about programs loading "low" or invalid regions being specified. When Windows finishes loading, you'll need to rerun Optimize.

SYMPTOM 27-74 **When booting with QEMM, you get the message "Parity Check 1 0000"** This occurs most frequently with versions of Phoenix BIOS, but you can generally work around this kind of problem using the TM:N parameter and USERAM= entry at an appropriate size. For example, on an 8MB system, the QEMM line would look something like:

```
DEVICE=C:\QEMM\QEMM386.SYS RAM TM:N UR=1M:8M
```

SYMPTOM 27-75 **After running Optimize, you receive an error "Cannot find device file that may be needed to run Windows"** After installing QEMM 97 and running the initial Optimize, Windows 95/98 tries to load, but you get an error message. This error refers to the VxD files IFSMGR.VxD and IOS.VxD, and the computer boots to a DOS prompt. An error occurred during the QEMM installation process (probably due to a conflict between one or more programs). To work around this problem, follow these steps:

1. Determine whether you can access your CD-ROM drive. (If you cannot, type **DOSSTART**.)
2. Reinstall Windows95/98. This will replace the missing files.
3. After Windows boots up, press CTRL+ALT+DELETE. The Close Programs dialog box appears.
4. Choose to "End Task" on everything *except* Explorer and Systray. Do this by clicking on one of the items in the list and then clicking End Task.
5. After everything *except* Explorer and Systray has been closed, reinstall QEMM 97.

SYMPTOM 27-76 **You receive "Out of memory" errors when installing QEMM 97 in place of MagnaRAM under Windows 95/98** This type of error generally occurs if you recently installed QEMM 97 in place of your previous version of MagnaRAM. In Windows, you now receive "Out of memory" errors that you never received before. This is often caused by leftover settings from MagnaRAM interfering with the settings for QEMM 97. You can reconfigure the setup of QEMM to work around this problem:

1. Go to the QEMM 97 Control Panel, choose Options, and click Setup.
2. Click the Windows tab and uncheck Auto.
3. Specify a buffer size equal to 25 percent of the physical RAM present on the machine.
4. Save your changes and exit.
5. Review your virtual memory settings. Specify the *maximum* swap file size as roughly three times the physical RAM. (Windows 98 can manage virtual memory automatically, so you may not need to take this step unless problems persist.)
6. Save your virtual memory changes and exit.
7. Restart the computer.

SYMPTOM 27-77 **When running Optimize, you receive an "Unable to find COMMAND.COM" error** This error typically occurs with older versions of QEMM (7.0–7.52). You'll often find that Optimize fails during the software detection phase, generating an "Unable to find COMMAND.COM" message. Optimize may recover, but at the end there is an error while gathering LOADHI information. Normally, COMMAND.COM should not be hidden. Check to see if COMMAND.COM is in the DOS (or root) directory using the following command:

```
DIR COMMAND.COM /AH
```

If COMMAND.COM appears, use the ATTRIB command to "unhide" COMMAND.COM:

```
ATTRIB -H COMMAND.COM
```

Now rerun Optimize—it should finish normally.

In QEMM 7.0x, 7.50, 7.51, and 7.52, the LOADHI command could not see hidden files. The QEMM 7.53 (and later) LOADHI command now supports hidden files. This problem has been most prevalent on Packard Bell computers, which seem to ship with COMMAND.COM hidden.

SYMPTOM 27-78 **QEMM produces a "Windows Protection Error #0" after installing a SoundBlaster card** After installing a SoundBlaster 32 PnP sound card, you encounter "Windows Protection Error #0" after choosing any of the Windows 95/98 shutdown options. When you remove the SoundBlaster drivers (or QEMM), the error does not appear. To correct this situation, add a switch to the QEMM386.SYS line in the CONFIG.SYS file that will exclude the memory area used by the plug-and-play BIOS extensions (often the E000h area of high memory).

1. Quit Windows to the DOS prompt.
2. Open the CONFIG.SYS file in a text editor, such as EDIT.
3. Locate the QEMM386.SYS command line, and then add the X=E000-EFFF parameter to the end of the QEMM line, such as:

   ```
   DEVICE=C:\QEMM\QEMM386.SYS X=E000-EFFF
   ```

4. Save the changes to CONFIG.SYS and exit the editor.
5. Restart the computer.

> The E000h-EFFFh area is the most common area used by plug-and-play extensions. If you continue to have problems after making this change, you may need to exclude a different area. See your hardware manual or consult the computer manufacturer for information.

SYMPTOM 27-79 After installing QEMM under Windows 95/98, you receive a "Windows Protection Error" whenever shutting down or restarting a computer In virtually all situations, the problem is due to a video driver conflict with QEMM. Try switching to the Standard VGA video driver. If the Standard VGA driver resolves the situation, then you have confirmed the presence of a driver conflict. Contact the technical support Web site for your video card and obtain the latest driver version.

SYMPTOM 27-80 With QEMM 7.0 installed, you're prompted for "SWITCHES" at start time This often occurs under DOS (version 6.0 or 6.2) when you're performing an interactive boot. If QEMM 7.0 is installed, you'll receive the following request before the usual "PROCESS AUTOEXEC.BAT [Y/N]" prompt:

```
SWITCHES /N /F [Y/N]
```

If you're running DOS 6.2 and you choose Y, the AUTOEXEC.BAT file is processed, but you're not given the option to step through it line by line. The "SWITCHES" prompt appears after the QEMM LOADHI.COM command is added to the Shell= statement in your CONFIG.SYS file, such as:

```
shell=c:\qemm loadhi.com /r:2 c:\dos\command.com c:\dos\ /p
```

Remove the QEMM LOADHI.COM reference from the Shell= line, and remove or disable the QEMM device driver called DOSUP.SYS, which is often added to the CONFIG.SYS file, such as:

```
device=c:\qemm\dosup.sys
```

> In the CONFIG.SYS file, the /N switch normally prevents you from using the F5 and F8 keyboard options. The /F switch normally skips the two-second delay before starting the operating system.

SYMPTOM 27-81 You encounter errors in CONFIG.SYS after running MemMaker under QEMM 7.02 and DOS-Up The DOS-Up feature provided by Quarterdeck's QEMM (version 7.02) is designed to put some DOS data structures into the upper memory blocks (UMBs). If you use MemMaker to try and optimize your memory, it fails to remove the following two lines from CONFIG.SYS:

```
device=c:\qemm\dosdata.sys
device=c:\qemm\dos-up.sys
```

Consequently, both file entries cause error messages when you start your system. To get around this problem, edit your CONFIG.SYS file and manually remove or disable the two lines shown above. Save your changes and restart the system. The error messages should be gone.

SYMPTOM 27-82 After restarting Windows 95 from the DOS mode, you notice as much as 2MB of extended memory is "missing" This is a known problem that can occur if you're using QEMM version 7.50 with Windows 95 OSR2. With OSR2, loading WIN.COM automatically starts SmartDrive. This is normally not a problem because SmartDrive is released by WIN.COM in the transition from real mode to protected mode. Unfortunately, QEMM allocates extended memory that Windows 95 *cannot* reclaim when WIN.COM unloads SmartDrive. This is the memory that was used by SmartDrive. There are three methods of resolving this problem:

- Type **exit** instead of **win** to return to Windows 95 from the DOS mode.
- Upgrade to QEMM version 8.0 or later.
- After you type **win** to restart Windows 95, shut down and restart the computer.

SYMPTOM 27-83 **You receive a GPF from QEMM 97 under Windows 98** This typically occurs when you're running QEMM 97. If you click Details on the File menu in the QEMM Control Panel, and then click Help, you may get an error such as

```
QEMMDETA caused a general protection fault in module DETAILS.EXE at 0003:000070ce
```

or

```
Program Error. Integer Divide by 0
```

This is a known problem with Windows 98 and QEMM 97. You should check the Quarterdeck Web site (**www.quarterdeck.com**), and see if there are any patches or updates that can correct this error.

SYMPTOM 27-84 **MemMaker generates "Bad command or filename" errors when under QEMM** If you're using QEMM to load files into upper memory, and the FILES command has a plus sign (+) for a delimiter (such as C:\QEMM\LOADHI /R:1 FILES+30), you will receive an error such as:

```
Bad Command or Filename
```

This problem occurs because the plus sign is not a valid delimiter for DOS. If your QEMM command contains an entry such as "FILES+nn," MemMaker will return the error. Remove the QEMM "FILES+nn" command from your AUTOEXEC.BAT file, and then use the "files=" setting in CONFIG.SYS to specify the number of open files. After you correct this problem, run MemMaker again to ensure that you have an optimal memory configuration.

SYMPTOM 27-85 **You find that MemMaker doesn't remove all references to QEMM** Chances are that you've had QEMM previously installed on your system. After running MemMaker, you receive an error message stating that another expanded memory manager (EMM) is already running. MemMaker tries to remove all references to QEMM. However, if one of your QEMM statements in the CONFIG.SYS file does not have an equal sign (=), MemMaker ignores it. This means the driver is not loaded by MemMaker, and it is not removed from the CONFIG.SYS file. MemMaker also fails to remove DEVICE=QDPMI statements in your CONFIG.SYS file if you're using QEMM version 7.01. In order to correct this problem, edit your CONFIG.SYS file with a text editor such as EDIT, and put equal signs in your DEVICE commands. You may also wish to remove the DEVICE=QDPMI reference.

Troubleshooting HIMEM/EMM386

The following systems deal with problems found with high memory managers, particularly with HIMEM and EMM386.

SYMPTOM 27-86 You receive memory manager errors when upgrading DOS versions on a Compaq system The DOS upgrade setup routine does not recognize the Compaq extended memory services (XMS) device driver (named EXMEM.EXE). As a result, setup adds a new command line for HIMEM.SYS at the end of your CONFIG.SYS file. When the second XMS driver tries to load at start time, you receive an error such as:

```
ERROR: An Extended Memory Manager is already installed.
```

This occurs because setup does not recognize EXMEM.SYS. To the system, it looks like the DOS HIMEM.SYS driver. Since setup finds what appears to be HIMEM already in memory, it determines that it must update the existing HIMEM.SYS line in the CONFIG.SYS file. But since the HIMEM command line isn't there, setup adds a command for it. When the system restarts, this conflict causes the error. Edit your CONFIG.SYS file with EDIT and remove the command line for one of the XMS managers (usually the new HIMEM line).

SYMPTOM 27-87 The system doesn't operate properly if you have a SCSI controller installed, but you have no SCSI drivers loaded in CONFIG.SYS This type of problem is common under various DOS versions where you may forget to add vital device drivers for the SCSI adapter and devices. If your SCSI device driver is not loaded, you may experience problems ranging from occasional system hang-ups to extensive data loss. These symptoms are usually worse if you're using an upper memory block (UMB) utility (such as EMM386.EXE). Any device (SCSI being the most common) that uses direct memory access (DMA) controller hardware to transfer data to and from system memory can encounter problems if it's used in conjunction with a memory manager (such as EMM386.EXE, QEMM.EXE, or 386MAX.EXE).

If you don't have the correct driver for your SCSI controller, contact your SCSI hardware vendor for the latest driver version(s). In the meantime, try adding the following command line to your CONFIG.SYS file:

```
DEVICE=C:\DOS\SMARTDRV.EXE /DOUBLE_BUFFER
```

SYMPTOM 27-88 You encounter a Windows 95/98 setup error "G1" After you type **setup** to start the Windows 95/98 setup program, you may receive the following error message:

```
Setup Warning G1: Setup cannot run from MS-DOS with EMM386.EXE or other memory
managers (such as QEMM or 386Max) running on your computer. If Windows is on
your computer, run Setup from Windows. Otherwise, remove the memory manager from
your CONFIG.SYS file, and then restart your computer before running Setup. After
Windows 95 is installed, you can safely add the memory manager back to your
CONFIG.SYS file.
```

This error is often generated on older Gateway 2000 computers. Such systems use BIOS versions that cause this error message when you run setup from DOS and you're loading EMM386.EXE (or a similar memory manager) in the CONFIG.SYS file. Two BIOS versions reported to cause this problem are the Phoenix 486 ROM BIOS Plus, dated 1/15/88, and the Phoenix ROM BIOS version 0.10, copyright 1990. There are three ways to work around the problem:

- Remove EMM386.EXE (or the similar memory manager) *before* you run setup.

- Run setup from Windows (that is, perform an upgrade over a previous version of Windows).
- Upgrade the BIOS in your computer.

SYMPTOM 27-89 **You cannot disable the "backfill" feature for EMM386** You'll generally find this kind of error on older 386 systems with less than 640KB of conventional memory and an expansion memory card configured for extended memory. Normally, this configuration will "backfill" the conventional memory to 640KB under EMM386. However, when the system starts, you may see an error such as:

```
Unable to start enhanced mode windows due to base memory backfill
```

Unfortunately, there is no way to disable the backfill that EMM386 performs. Since the /X switch excludes memory only from 640KB to 1024KB, and the /B switch raises the base for backfilling only up to 256KB, there is no effective way to change the way EMM386 handles memory between 256KB and 640KB.

This is a known problem with EMM386 version 4.20 (provided with MS-DOS 5.0) and version 4.33 (provided with MS-DOS 5.00a). This problem does not appear in later versions of EMM386.EXE. You may be using a very old version of EMM386. To correct this issue, use EMM386 version 4.44 or later. Later versions do not backfill as do the previous two versions. As an alternative, you can disable EMM386 in favor of another memory manager, or add memory to the system in order to provide up to 640KB without backfilling.

SYMPTOM 27-90 **Memory diagnostic tests hang up the system** In many cases, you may have to cold boot to restart the system. You may have a conflict between the system's memory manager software and the memory diagnostic utility. This is a fairly rare problem that may occur on some Leading Edge systems. For example, to run the Leading Edge memory test successfully, HIMEM.SYS, EMM386.EXE, and any other memory managers must be disabled, and DOS must not be loaded into the high memory area (HMA). Remove all references to the memory manager software (such as HIMEM.SYS and EMM386.EXE) from your CONFIG.SYS file, and reboot the computer. Once the diagnostics have been completed, return the CONFIG.SYS file to its original state.

SYMPTOM 27-91 **The system hangs up when using AboveDisc with HIMEM** The AboveDisc utility uses a driver (ABOVE.EXE) to emulate expanded memory within extended memory (or on a hard disk). A conflict occurs when ABOVE.EXE is used with HIMEM.SYS and the DOS=HIGH command. The computer may hang up at start time, beep uncontrollably, or continually reboot. ABOVE.EXE may also cause problems with caching utilities (such as SMARTDRV.SYS) and other memory managers (such as EMM386 and QEMM). If you cannot upgrade your AboveDisc installation to a later version, you may be able to work around the problem with the steps below:

1. Run the install program for AboveDisc from inside the ABOVE subdirectory.
2. Set hardware to normal I/O 286/386.
3. Under Change Feature, make sure EMS 4.0 is selected with a check mark.

> This procedure may not work on all systems. Some systems still will not work with the DOS=HIGH setting.

SYMPTOM 27-92 **System hangs using HIMEM /TESTMEM** The memory test performed by HIMEM.SYS (version 3.10) may fail—possibly causing your system to hang up—if your machine uses a hardware cache controller. This is because some hardware cache controllers do not handle 16MB and 32MB memory boundaries well. As a result, the HIMEM.SYS memory test fails. To work around this problem, disable the hardware cache controller in your system, or remove the /TESTMEM switch from the HIMEM command line.

SYMPTOM 27-93 **You encounter A20 gate problems when installing HIMEM** The selection of A20 gate handlers is accomplished automatically. HIMEM runs through a series of autodetection schemes trying to find a match. When a match is found, the particular A20 handler is installed. If no match is found, the default A20 handler is installed. Due to the diverse and nonstandard nature of today's PCs, HIMEM autodetection fails and the default handler is installed. Unfortunately, the default handler may not work too well. In this case, you should use the /a20 switch, along with the corresponding machine designation number (Table 27-1), to select the proper A20 handler for your particular PC.

SYMPTOM 27-94 **You encounter a general error or system problem with EMM386** In most cases, you'll notice that the system or an application will lock up when using EMM386. Table 27-5 lists the version designations for EMM386. Fully reinitialize the system by turning your machine off, then turning it back on (a.k.a. cold boot). When the message "Starting MS-DOS" appears, press F8 and elect to start the system interactively. When prompted to load EMM386.EXE, choose N for no. If the problem persists when EMM386.EXE is not loaded, something other than EMM386.EXE is causing the problem. If the problem disappears when EMM386.EXE is not loaded, edit the CONFIG.SYS file as follows using an ASCII text editor:

```
device=c:\dos\emm386.exe x=a000-f7ff nohi noems novcpi nomovexbda notr
```

Cold boot the system again. If the problem persists, the system may have faulty RAM or may require a special machine switch for HIMEM.SYS. Also, advanced memory-related CMOS settings (such as shadow RAM) may need to be disabled. The system BIOS may also need to be upgraded. If the problem

TABLE 27-5 VERSION DESIGNATIONS FOR EMM386

MS-DOS VERSION	EMM386 VERSION
MS-DOS 5.0	4.20
MS-DOS 5.00a	4.33
MS-DOS 6.0	4.45
MS-DOS 6.2	4.48
MS-DOS 6.21	4.48
MS-DOS 6.22	4.49
Windows 3.1	4.44
Windows 3.11	4.44
Windows for Workgroups 3.1	4.44
Windows for Workgroups 3.11	4.48
Windows 95	4.95

disappears after loading the modified EMM386 command line, the problem is probably related to some service that EMM386 provides.

Try removing the X=A000-F7FF switch. If the problem reappears, EMM386.EXE may be scanning memory too aggressively and configuring upper memory blocks on top of some adapter ROM or RAM. Restore the exclusion, but try narrowing the exclusion range. Try removing the NOHI switch. If the problem reappears, EMM386.EXE may be loading into an occupied UMB. If all such regions are excluded, EMM386.EXE cannot be loaded high on the system, and NOHI must be used. Try removing the NOEMS switch. If the problem reappears, EMM386.EXE may be conflicting with some hardware ROM or RAM address in the UMA when attempting to establish an expanded memory (EMS) page frame. If EMS is required to run MS-DOS-based applications, use the parameter FRAME= or Mx (where x is the defined hexadecimal address) to explicitly specify placement of the EMS page frame in a nonconflicting region. If no applications require EMS, simply continue to use the NOEMS parameter.

Next, try removing the NOVCPI switch. The NOVCPI switch disables Virtual Control Program Interface (VCPI) support and can be used only in conjunction with the NOEMS parameter. If the problem reappears, the application may not be fully compatible with the EMM386.EXE VCPI allocation scheme. Either continue using the NOVCPI parameter, or do not load EMM386.EXE when using the application. Remove the NOMOVEXBDA switch. Some machines use the last 1KB of conventional memory for an extended BIOS Data Area (or XBDA). By default, EMM386.EXE remaps this memory area into the UMA instead of conventional memory. If this causes unexpected system behavior, the NOMOVEXBDA parameter must be used. Finally, try removing the NOTR switch. EMM386.EXE has a detection code to search for the presence of a Token Ring network adapter—this detection code may cause some computers to hang. The NOTR switch can be used to disable this search.

SYMPTOM 27-95 You see an error "Unable to set page frame base address—EMS unavailable" This error is displayed if EMM386 cannot locate a 64KB contiguous "hole" in the UMA for the EMS page frame. According to the LIM 3.2 specification, a "page frame" consists of four contiguous 16KB pages, and a LIM provider (EMM386) must set the page frame. According to the LIM 4.0 specification, an EMS provider need not set a 64KB page frame, but it should set a 16KB page at the minimum.

Although EMM386 conforms to the LIM 4.0 specification, it does not load as an EMS provider if it cannot find a 64KB contiguous hole that can be used for the page frame. This is because the majority of LIM 3.2 applications assume the existence of a page frame. EMM386 can be forced to load without a LIM 3.2 (64KB) page frame by using the Pn parameters (see Table 27-2). If you force EMM386 to load as a LIM 4.0 provider, do not attempt to run LIM 3.2 applications. The best solution is to free a 64KB block of memory in the UMA so that EMM386 can support LIM 3.2 and higher.

SYMPTOM 27-96 You see the error "Size of expanded memory pool adjusted" This message is displayed if EMM386 cannot provide all the EMS memory requested on the command line. For example, if you use the command line

```
device=emm386.exe 2048
```

and your computer only has 1024KB of XMS memory, EMM386 displays this error message and provides as much EMS as possible. (Note that EMM386 uses some XMS memory for its own code and data, and this reduces the amount of XMS memory available for EMS simulation.) There is little that can be done to correct this error except to reduce the EMS called for on the EMM386 command line, or add more physical memory to the PC.

SYMPTOM 27-97 **Windows cannot provide EMS when using the NOEMS switch** According to the LIM 4.0 specification, an EMS page can also reside in conventional memory (0–640KB). The EMM386 EMS line starts at 256KB by default. If the NOEMS switch is added to the command line, all the holes in the adapter region A000h–FFFFh are used for UMBs, and EMM386 cannot provide any EMS. If Windows and an MS-DOS session are started, EMM386 may or may not be able to provide EMS. If Windows 3.0 is running in 386 Enhanced mode, EMM386 can provide EMS within an MS-DOS session. However, the EMS pages are in conventional memory. This can cause problems because of the behavior of LIM 3.2 applications. In a Windows 3.1 386 Enhanced mode MS-DOS session, EMS is not provided. Your best course here is to remove the NOEMS switch from the EMM386 command line.

SYMPTOM 27-98 **You find that EMM386 locks up the computer** Although EMM386 is generally considered to be a basic and robust memory manager, under some conditions, its use may result in a system crash. The /HIGHSCAN feature cannot be used on some computers. If the EMM386 command line in the CONFIG.SYS file contains the /HIGHSCAN parameter, remove /HIGHSCAN from the command line, save the CONFIG.SYS file, and restart your computer.

Next, use excludes to isolate potential EMM386 memory conflicts. EMM386 may have incorrectly identified an area being used by the system as a *hole* (a region that can be used as a UMB or an EMS page frame). As a result, EMM386 accidentally overwrites a portion of memory that is used by a hardware adapter in your computer. Start by excluding addresses in the range A000h–EFFFh. EMM386 does not use any part of the excluded region for a UMB or EMS page frame. If the problem disappears, you may be able to identify the correct region(s) with some experimentation. Start by excluding a large region and then reducing the size of the region. For example, start with

```
device=emm386.exe noems x=a000-efff
```

If that works, try narrowing the range to

```
device=emm386.exe noems x=c000-dfff
```

If that works too, try narrowing the range further to

```
device=emm386.exe noems x=c800-cfff
```

Remember that you can use multiple exclusions on the same EMM386 command line, such as:

```
device=emm386.exe noems x=c000-c7ff x=e000-efff
```

If the computer has a SCSI disk controller and requires a device driver to operate the SCSI adapter, be sure the DEVICE= line for the SCSI driver appears *before* the EMM386 command line. Examples of SCSI device drivers include ASPI4DOS.SYS and USPI14.SYS.

If problems continue, try loading the SmartDrive double buffer driver. The driver should appear before the EMM386 command line in CONFIG.SYS. If you're using DOS 6.0 or later, Windows 3.1 or later, or Windows for Workgroups, the SmartDrive double buffer driver is loaded from the CONFIG.SYS file, such as:

```
device=c:\windows\smartdrv.exe /double_buffer
```

In the AUTOEXEC.BAT file, add a /L to the end of the SMARTDRV.EXE line, such as:

```
c:\windows\smartdrv.exe /L
```

If the problems persist, add a plus sign (+) to the end of the double buffer device line as follows:

```
device=c:\windows\smartdrv.exe /double_buffer+
```

If you use the SMARTDRV.SYS driver included with MS-DOS 5.x, the SmartDrive double buffer driver is loaded in the CONFIG.SYS, such as:

```
device=c:\dos\smartdrv.sys /b+
```

If the problem with EMM386 continues, experiment with different HIMEM.SYS A20 handlers. This is done using the /MACHINE: switch on the HIMEM.SYS device line (see Table 27-1).

SYMPTOM 27-99 **You see an error "Insufficient memory for UMBs or virtual HMA"** This can often happen when using an AMI or Phoenix BIOS. EMM386 may provide this message even though there is more than 384KB of extended memory. To work around this problem, modify your CMOS RAM settings to disable the "Fast A20 Gating" feature. You may also be able to update your motherboard's BIOS. This message may also appear on systems with only 384K of extended memory if MS-DOS is loaded high. The solution is to exclude 64KB from EMM386 in order to accommodate loading MS-DOS high.

SYMPTOM 27-100 **You see an error "Unable to create page frame"** If EMM386 is unable to find 64KB of contiguous memory in the upper memory area, it cannot create an expanded memory page frame. If you don't want expanded memory for your system, you can substitute the NOEMS switch for the RAM switch in your EMM386 command line in CONFIG.SYS. If you do want expanded memory, you can try establishing a page frame in a portion of the upper memory area not normally used by EMM386. You can try putting the page frame in the E000h memory block by modifying the EMM386 command line such as:


```
device=c:\dos\emm386 m9 ram
```

> Do not try this procedure on an IBM model PS/2 computer. Always remember to back up your existing copy of CONFIG.SYS and AUTOEXEC.BAT (preferably to a bootable floppy disk) before attempting any modifications to your startup file.

SYMPTOM 27-101 **You see an error "EMM386 Privileged Operation Error #01"** There is a problem with EMM386 and the AST 386 FastBoard. AST Research has confirmed that loading EMM386 (MS-DOS 5.0 and later versions) on an AST Premium 286 computer with an AST 386 FastBoard upgrade may cause the error. The AST 386 FastBoard is an 80386 upgrade for AST 80286 motherboards. This error may occur if the 386 FastBoard driver (FB386.SYS) is not loaded before EMM386 in the CONFIG.SYS file. Load the 386 FastBoard device driver (FB386.SYS) before EMM386, such as:

```
device=c:\fb386.sys
device=c:\dos\himem.sys
device=c:\dos\emm386.exe
```

SYMPTOM 27-102 **You see an error "EMM386 Not Installed—Unable to set page frame base address"** This message indicates that EMM386 was unable to find 64KB of contiguous space needed for the expanded memory page frame. When you specify the RAM switch (or no switch at all),

EMM386 attempts to create a 64KB page frame in the upper memory area (UMA). The actual amount of extended memory used will be 108KB (64KB + 44KB = 108KB). The extra 44KB is used for tables that EMM386 sets up to emulate expanded memory. This 64KB of space acts as a window into expanded memory, allowing programs to see all the available expanded memory, 64KB at a time. Try using the NOEMS switch if expanded memory is not needed. Next, make sure HIMEM is installed above EMM386 in the CONFIG.SYS file. (Other devices should be loaded *after* EMM386, except drivers like DMDRVR.BIN, EMM.SYS, or ADAPTEC.SYS.) If you're not working on an IBM machine, add the following switches to the EMM386 command line in the CONFIG.SYS file:

```
device=c:\dos\emm386.exe i=e000-efff (m9 or frame=e000) ram
```

The "included" E000h-EFFFh memory range is generally not used by non-IBM machines, and including this range can allow you to find 64KB of free contiguous memory. The mx switch also allows you to specify different locations for the page frame to begin (see Table 27-2). For m9, the page frame will attempt to begin at E000h.

If the program requiring expanded memory can use the LIM 4.0 specification, then the 64KB page frame can be set noncontiguously. Add the "Pn=address" parameter to the EMM386 command line in CONFIG.SYS, such as:

```
device=c:\dos\emm386.exe p0=c800 p1=d400 p2=e000 p3=d000 ram
```

SYMPTOM 27-103 **An AT&T 6386E system hangs with a RAM option in EMM386**
An expanded memory page frame set to DC00h or higher on an AT&T 6386E causes the system to hang up. For example, the following DEVICE= statement hangs the system:

```
device=emm386.exe m8 ram
```

The AT&T 6386E has a ROM option at address E800h that is used during system operations. Setting a page frame to DC00h or higher overlaps with the ROM option, resulting in a system lockup. Alter the mx switch to start the page frame at an address that avoids the conflict.

SYMPTOM 27-104 **A Plus Hardcard II is very slow with EMM386** You may need to exclude the Hardcard XL BIOS from the EMM386 command line, such as:

```
device=c:\dos\emm386.exe x=c000-c800
```

Note that the exclusion range is only an example—the exact addresses to exclude will depend on your configuration. If you are not using UMBs, use the frame= parameter to set the address of the page frame such that the page frame will not conflict with the addresses being used by the Hardcard. For example, if the Hardcard is using addresses C000h–C800h, you might use

```
device=c:\dos\emm386.exe frame=d000
```

This sets the page frame for the D000h–DFFFh range of memory.

SYMPTOM 27-105 **You encounter exception errors with EMM386** This kind of error means that the CPU has encountered a general protection violation. Because the EMM386 driver operates the CPU in virtual real mode, the CPU checks for valid memory accesses. If a program tries to access memory that it is not allowed to access, the CPU generates an exception fault error that is detected by

EMM386. In effect, EMM386 is reporting a program error detected by the CPU. In general, this error should not occur on PCs that are strictly 100 percent IBM compatible. Incompatible machines may require an OEM version of EMM386. Table 27-6 lists protected-mode exception errors and their names.

Troubleshooting 386MAX

Qualitas's 386MAX is another high memory manager that may cause difficulties. A list of symptoms and solutions can be found below.

SYMPTOM 27-106 When clicking the toolbox icon in the Qualitas MAX group, you set the toolbox for PC-Kwik's WinMaster instead (or vice versa) Both MAX 8 from Qualitas and PC-Kwik's WinMaster ship a program named TOOLBOX.EXE. The first program to be run is kept in a cache, causing that program to run the next time the program name is invoked. To avoid this conflict, rename one of the files, and change the icon properties to match the name. For example, rename the TOOLBOX.EXE file in the Qualitas MAX directory to QTOOLBOX.EXE. If you're using Windows 95/98, right-click on the icon and choose Properties to change the command line.

SYMPTOM 27-107 The 386MAX ASQ utility hangs the system when the EMS=0 parameter is used When you use the EMS=0 parameter with third-party memory managers, ASQ (the 386MAX system analyzer program) hangs up the system. This only seems to occur when ASQ is running from the DOS prompt in full-screen mode from Windows. To work around this trouble, you should use the NOFRAME parameter with 386MAX *instead* of EMS=0. This provides the same performance with 386MAX. Another alternative is to use the ASQ utility outside of Windows rather than through a DOS window.

TABLE 27-6 PROTECTED MODE EXCEPTION ERRORS FOR EMM386

CODE	MEANING
0	Divide error
1	Debugger interrupt
2	Nonmaskable interrupt
3	Breakpoint
4	Overflow interrupt
5	Array boundary violation
6	Invalid opcode
7	Coprocessor not available
8	Double fault
9	Coprocessor segment overrun
10	Invalid task state segment
11	Segment not present
12	Stack exception
13	General protection violation
14	Page fault
16	Coprocessor error

Third-party memory managers that have the EMS parameter include 386MAX version 6.0, 386MAX version 6.1, and BlueMAX—all from Qualitas.

SYMPTOM 27-108 **You cannot boot when 386MAX is using 2 or 3 handles** If the 386MAX program from Qualitas is using the XMSHNDL parameter (extend memory handles), which is set to 2 or 3, Windows may not load. Other extended memory managers may have similar parameters that might prevent Windows from loading. 386MAX is a memory manager that effectively replaces HIMEM.SYS. By using a *low* number of extended memory handles, 386MAX is limited to the number of requests it can make for extended memory. Windows may not run if it cannot allocate enough blocks of extended memory. To correct the number of extended memory handles, increase the number of available handles on the command line, or remove the parameter and accept the default.

You might encounter the same problem with HIMEM.SYS if you limit the number of handles using the NUMHANDLES switch on the HIMEM.SYS command line in CONFIG.SYS.

SYMPTOM 27-109 **The Qualitas DOSMAX utility doesn't function as expected** DOSMAX for Windows won't work if there is software loaded at the top of conventional memory (near 640KB). Most resident programs load into the lowest address memory available. If the software loads into the top of low DOS memory, DOSMAX for Windows won't work. Disk controller software is the most common software that uses memory at the top of low DOS, but CD-ROM device drivers sometimes configure a buffer in this area as well. Certain viruses have also been known to attach themselves to this area of memory.

DOSMAX also won't work if the system's Qualitas MAX profile includes the option "NOXBIOS" (Qualitas MAX is not relocating the extended BIOS into high DOS)—DOSMAX is disabled. The extended BIOS normally resides at the top of conventional memory. There can also be a problem if you have a system with less than 640KB base memory. Qualitas MAX backfills this memory to 640KB, but these systems aren't compatible with Windows 3.x.

If you're still having problems with DOSMAX, exit Windows and add the "DOSMAXMono=OFF" switch to the [Qualitas] section of SYSTEM.INI. Add the line (and the section if it doesn't already exist). Restart Windows and retry DOSMAX. You might also try exiting Windows and editing your 386MAX.PRO file. Using a semicolon, comment out the "VGASWAP" and "USE=B000-B800" options. Rerun Maximize and see if DOSMAX works properly. If problems persist, check to see that you have the most current version of your video drivers. (Try the standard VGA drivers that come with Windows.)

SYMPTOM 27-110 **You see the message "ERROR 1014: Disk cache or other file I/O software using EMS memory"** Qualitas MAX has detected EMS memory in use by a disk cache or other resident file I/O software. (The other software may be a disk compression utility or a network.) It is recommended that these programs use extended (XMS) memory when operating in a Windows environment. Check EMS memory usage by typing **386util /e** in the Qualitas MAX directory to determine which programs are using EMS memory. If you must run Windows with this type of software, you may override the error message by editing your AUTOEXEC.BAT file and adding the DOS command SET EMSCACHE=OK.

SYMPTOM 27-111 **The system may hang up after installing BlueMAX** After you install BlueMAX from Qualitas, your system may halt, or you may experience data corruption. In addition, you may encounter error message(s) such as "Divide overflow," "Memory allocation error," or

"Cannot load COMMAND, System halted." These problems are almost always caused by changes to the CONFIG.SYS file that were made by the BlueMAX installer. BlueMAX does not detect the presence of SMARTDRV.EXE (versions prior to 4.0) and installs its own disk cache (Qcache). After that, the BlueMAX installer tries to load the double-buffering option of SMARTDRV.EXE high if a device line for SMARTDRV.EXE exists in CONFIG.SYS, such as:

```
DEVICE=C:\WINDOWS\SMARTDRV.EXE /DOUBLE_BUFFER
```

You can resolve this problem by upgrading SmartDrive to version 4.0 or later (if you're not using Windows 95 or Windows 98). You can also try removing the double-buffering option from the SmartDrive command line in CONFIG.SYS. If all else fails, try using HIMEM and/or EMM386 rather than BlueMAX for memory management.

SYMPTOM 27-112 You see the message "VxD ERROR: Unable to provide DOSMAX features" DOSMAX has detected that your system has less than 640KB of conventional memory. Because the top of conventional memory does not correspond to the bottom of graphics memory (as it does on a system with 640KB), DOSMAX features are unavailable. Most resident programs load into the lowest address memory available. If the software loads into the top of low DOS memory, DOSMAX for Windows won't work. The most common software that loads in this manner is software that is necessary for certain hard disk controllers, as well as some CD-ROM buffers. The best way to overcome this kind of problem is to bring conventional memory to 640KB or disable software that loads at the top of DOS memory.

SYMPTOM 27-113 You see the message "VxD ERROR: Qpopup is not running" The Qualitas MAX device driver will not be able to protect this DOSMAX window from programs attempting to enter graphics mode. QPOPUP.EXE is not loading from the WIN.INI file or the Startup group. Without this file, Qualitas MAX can't protect DOSMAX windows from programs that attempt to enter graphics mode. Check the "LOAD=" line in the WIN.INI file. You can also try to reinstall DOSMAX by using the DOSMAX entry on the Startup tab of the Toolbox (Windows 95/98).

SYMPTOM 27-114 You see the message "ERROR 1021: Qualitas MAX stacks required for DOSMAX support" There is a problem with the assignment of stacks in MAX. Qualitas MAX stacks must be enabled in order to use the DOSMAX feature. Click "Load DOS Stacks high" on the Startup tab of Toolbox (Windows 95/98), or remove the STACKS=0 option from the 386MAX.PRO file and reboot your system.

SYMPTOM 27-115 You see the message "ERROR 1011: Bus master disk subsystem detected that requires Qcache or other compliant disk cache to be loaded" Qualitas MAX detected a bus mastering hard disk controller that does not support VDS. Also, your 386MAX.PRO file may contain the NOSCSI option. In either case, 386MAX.VXD expects to find a VDS-compliant disk cache program in memory. You'll need to update the bus mastering driver.

SYMPTOM 27-116 You see the message "ERROR 2035: V86 RAM page(s) in use" The error message may also ask you to modify RAM= statement(s) in the 386MAX.PRO file to remove one or more memory regions. Windows 95/98 is attempting to use RAM pages that are already in use by Qualitas MAX. Remove the overlapping portion of the RAM= statement from the 386MAX.PRO file and reboot the system.

SYMPTOM 27-117 **You see the message "ERROR 1020: 386MAX.SYS version mismatch"** The versions of 386MAX.SYS and 386MAX.VXD that are in use do not match. Check that the current version of each file is in the Qualitas MAX subdirectory. You may need to reinstall MAX from scratch.

SYMPTOM 27-118 **You encounter video problems or conflicts using MAX** Common video symptoms include a blank screen on entering or exiting a program, spontaneous system reboots, strange graphics or characters appearing on the screen, or a system hang-up after the Qualitas MAX initialization screen. Several regions in the high DOS area have predetermined uses. The first 128KB (between addresses A000h and C000h) is for memory on video boards. Each kind of video display uses a different amount of address space. Just above the video RAM area is a 32KB area (C000h–C800h) for the ROM on many VGA video adapters. In most cases, 386MAX automatically identifies used memory and does not map into the appropriate video regions of most systems. However, there are some circumstances under which video cannot be accurately identified.

If you experience any odd video symptoms, Qualitas MAX may have remapped high DOS memory into a region that the video adapter needs, or it may have unsuccessfully relocated the video ROMs via the VGASWAP option. To correct this conflict, disable VGASWAP and "USE=B000-B800" in the 386MAX.PRO file. You may do this in Windows 95/98 by using the UMB/Adapters tab in Toolbox to deactivate use of the MDA (Monochrome Display Area) and VGASWAP. When you make these changes, Toolbox displays a message suggesting that you run Maximize. Choose Exit, and then reboot the system to activate your changes, which result in a change to the configuration of high DOS memory. If the problem is resolved, it is important to rerun Maximize at this time to reoptimize your memory configuration.

In a DOS environment, edit the 386MAX.PRO file to make the changes. Use any text editor to look at the profile located in the Qualitas MAX directory (QMAX is the default directory). If there is a "USE=B000-B800" or any "USE=" statement in the B000h range, comment that line out of the profile by placing a semicolon (;) in front of the line. Repeat the process for the keyword VGASWAP. Reboot the system to activate the changes. Again, if the problem is resolved, it is important to rerun Maximize at this time to reoptimize your memory configuration.

Further Study

Microsoft (HIMEM and EMM386): **http://www.microsoft.com**

Qualitas (386MAX and BlueMAX): **http://www.qualitas.com**

Quarterdeck (QEMM): **http://www.quarterdeck.com**

28

MICE AND TRACKBALLS

CHAPTER AT A GLANCE

As software packages evolved beyond simple menus and began to make use of the powerful graphics systems coming into popular use during the mid-1980s (such as EGA and VGA graphics), ever-larger amounts of information were presented in the display. Simple, multilayered text menus were aggressively replaced with striking graphical user interfaces (GUIs). System options and selections were soon represented with symbols (graphic "buttons" or "icons") instead of plain text. Using a keyboard to maneuver through such visual software soon became a cumbersome (if not impossible) chore.

Peripherals designers responded to this situation by developing a family of *pointing devices* (Figure 28-1). Pointing devices use a combination of hardware and software to produce and control a graphical screen *cursor*. A software *device driver* generates the cursor and reports its position. As the pointing device is moved around, hardware signals from the pointing device are interpreted by the device driver, which moves the cursor in a like manner. By positioning the cursor over a graphic symbol and activating one, two, or three of the buttons on the pointing device, it is now possible to select ("click" or "double-click") and manipulate ("drag") options in the application program instead of using a keyboard.

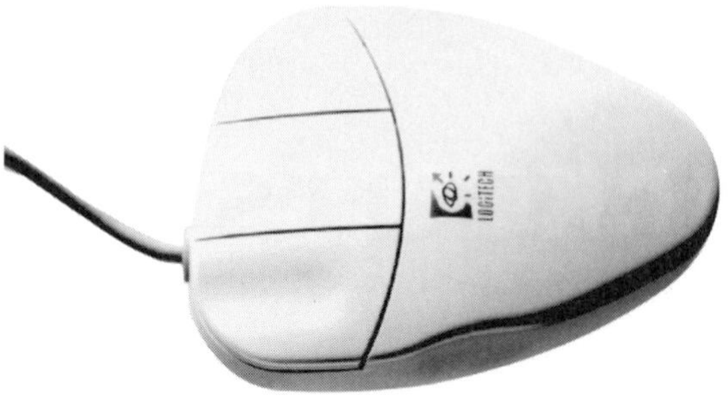

FIGURE 28-1 A Logitech MouseMan (Logitech, Inc.)

There are three factors needed to make pointing devices work: the physical signal-generating hardware itself, a software driver (the device driver), and the application program, which must be written to make use of the device driver. If any of these three items is missing, the pointing device will not work. This chapter looks at the technology, maintenance, and troubleshooting of two popular pointing devices: the mouse and the trackball.

The Mouse

Although the development of computer pointing devices has been ongoing since the early 1970s, the first commercial pointing device for IBM-compatible systems was widely introduced in the early 1980s. The device was small enough to be held under your palm, and your fingertips rested on its button(s). A small, thin cord connects the device to its host computer. The device's small size, long tail-like cord, and quick scurrying movements around the desk immediately earned it the label of *mouse*.

Every mouse needs at least one button. By pressing the button, you indicate that a *selection* is being made at the current cursor location. Many mouse-compatible software packages only make use of a single mouse button even to this day. A two-button mouse is more popular (reflecting the endurance of the mouse design) because a second button can add more flexibility to the mouse. For example, one button can work to select an item, while the second button can be used to deselect that item, or activate other menus and options. A few mouse designs use three buttons, but the third button is rarely supported by application programs other than CAD or high-end art applications.

MOUSE GESTURES

The first mouse "gesture" is called *clicking*, which is little more than a single momentary press of the left mouse button (on a two-button mouse). Clicking is the primary means of making a selection in the particular application program. The second common gesture is *double-clicking*, which is simply two single clicks in immediate succession. A double-click also represents selection, but its exact use depends upon the application program—under Windows 95/98, a double-click will launch a selected application or open a desired data file. The third type of mouse gesture is the *drag*, where a graphical item can literally be moved around the display. Dragging is almost always accomplished by pressing and holding the left mouse button over the desired item, then (without releasing the button) moving the item to its new location. When the item is moved to its new position, releasing the left mouse button will "drop" the item in that location.

It is interesting to note that pen gestures are interpreted by the computer's operating system, but mouse movements and button conditions are handled by the actual application program (such as a word processor or game). Thus, the same mouse gestures can be made to represent different actions depending on which program is executing.

MOUSE CONSTRUCTION

A mouse is a relatively straightforward device consisting of four major parts: the plastic housing, the mouse ball, the electronics PC board, and the signal cable. Figure 28-2 illustrates a typical mouse assembly. The housing assembly will vary a little depending on the manufacturer and vintage of your particular mouse (just walk through a computer store and look at the variety of mouse styles available on the shelf), but the overall scheme is almost always identical. The mouse ball is a hard rubber ball situated inside the mouse body just below a small PC board. When the mouse is positioned on a desktop, the ball contacts two actuators that register the mouse ball's movement in the X (left-to-right) and Y (up-to-down) directions. Both sensors generate a series of pulses that represent movement in both axis. Pulses equate to mouse movement—more pulses mean more movement. The pulses from both axis are amplified by the PC board and sent back to the computer along with information on the condition of each mouse button. Figure 28-3 shows an older Suncom Crystal mouse that allows you to see the internal mouse construction.

The mouse device driver must be loaded before the mouse will work. Under DOS, the real-mode driver is loaded in CONFIG.SYS or AUTOEXEC.BAT. Under Windows 95/98, the protected-mode mouse driver is loaded as Windows boots. Once the driver is loaded, it interprets the pulses generated by

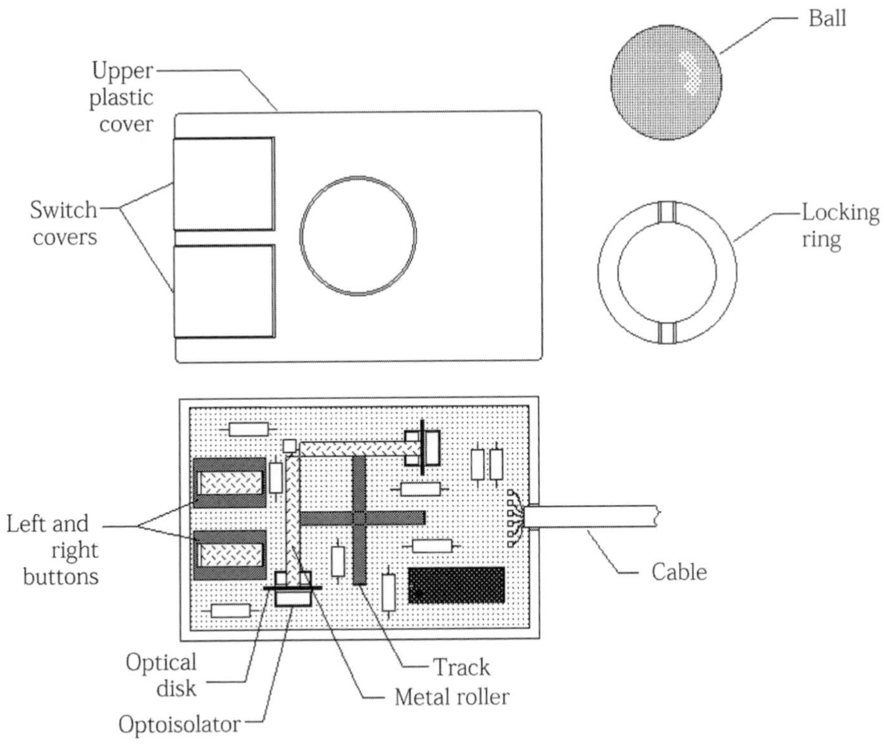

FIGURE 28-2 Internal construction of a basic mouse

28

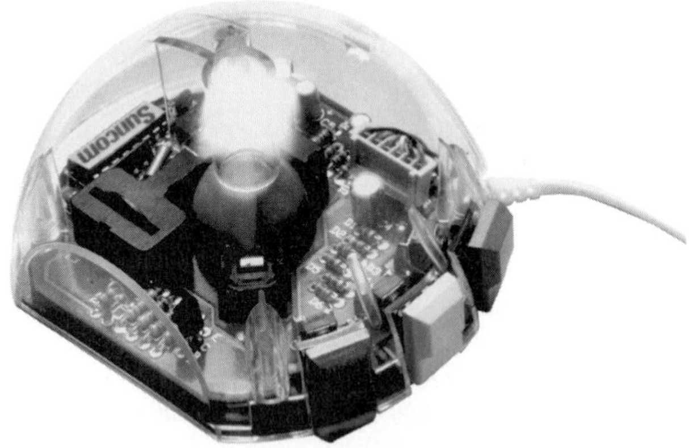

FIGURE 28-3 The CrystalMouse from Suncom Technologies (Suncom Technologies)

the mouse and translates them into X and Y screen locations where the visible mouse cursor is positioned. As the mouse moves left and right or up and down, pulses are added or subtracted from the cursor's X and Y screen coordinates by the device driver. The application program can then call for the X and Y coordinates, as well as button states. The key to a working mouse is its sensor devices. Sensors (or actuators) must be responsive enough to detect minute shifts in mouse position and generate pulses accordingly, yet be reliable enough to withstand wear, abuse, and environmental effects. There are two general types of sensors: mechanical and optomechanical.

MECHANICAL SENSORS

The greatest challenge in mouse design (and the largest cause of failures) is the reliable and repeatable conversion of mouse movement into serial electrical pulses. Early mouse versions used purely *mechanical* sensors to encode the mouse ball's movements. As the mouse ball turned against a roller (or shaft), copper contacts on the shaft would sweep across contacts on the mouse PC board—much like commutating rings and brushes on a DC motor. Each time a roller contact touches a corresponding contact in the mouse, an electrical pulse is generated. Since a mouse must typically generate hundreds of pulses for every linear inch of mouse movement, there are several sets of contacts for each axis.

It is important to note that mouse pulses can be positive or negative depending on the relative direction of the mouse in an axis. For example, moving the mouse right may produce positive pulses, while moving the mouse left may produce negative pulses. Similarly, moving the mouse down along its Y axis may produce positive pulses, while moving the mouse up may produce negative pulses. All pulses are then interpreted and tracked by the host computer.

Although mechanical sensors are simple, straightforward, and very inexpensive to produce, there are some significant problems that can plague the mechanical mouse. Mechanical mouse designs are not terribly reliable. The metal-on-metal contact sets used to generate pulses are prone to wear and breakage. Dust, dirt, hair, and any other foreign matter carried into the mouse by the ball can also interfere with contacts. Any contact interference prevents pulses from being generated. This condition results in a frustratingly intermittent "skip" or "stall" of the cursor while you move the mouse. Fortunately, it is often a simple matter to disassemble and clean the contacts.

OPTOMECHANICAL SENSORS

The next generation of mouse designs replaced the mechanical contacts with an *optoisolator* arrangement, as illustrated in Figure 28-4. A hard rubber mouse ball still rests against two perpendicularly opposed metal or plastic actuator rollers, but instead of each roller driving an array of contacts, the rollers rotate slotted wheels that are inserted into optoisolators. An optoisolator shines LED light across an air gap where it is detected by a photodiode or phototransistor. When a roller (and slotted wheel) spins, the light path between LED and detector is alternated or "chopped." This causes the detector's output signal to oscillate—thus, pulses are generated. The pulse frequency is dependent upon mouse speed. As with the mechanical mouse, the *optomechanical* mouse produces both positive and negative serial pulses depending on the direction of mouse movement.

The optomechanical mouse is a great improvement over the plain mechanical approach. By eliminating mechanical contacts, wear and tear on the mouse is significantly reduced, resulting in much longer life and higher reliability. However, the mouse is still subject to the interference of dust and other foreign matter that invariably finds its way into the mouse housing. Regular cleaning and internal dusting can prevent or correct instances of cursor skip or stall. Most mouse models in production today use optomechanical sensors.

The Trackball

The *trackball* is basically an inverted mouse. Instead of using your hand to move a mouse body around on a desk surface, a trackball remains stationary. Your hand or fingertips move the ball itself, which is mounted through the top of the device. The advantage to a trackball is that it does not move. As a result, trackballs can be incorporated into desktop keyboards, or added to your work area with a minimum of required space. Such characteristics have made trackballs extremely popular with laptop and notebook computers. Today, most notebook computers incorporate pointing devices directly.

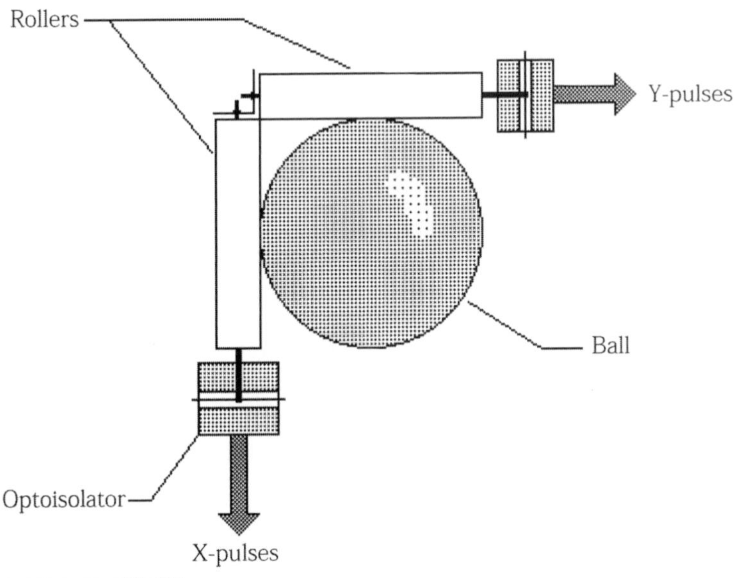

FIGURE 28-4 Sensor layout for an optomechanical mouse or trackball

In spite of their advantages, however, a trackball is not quite as easy to use as a mouse. The successful use of a mouse is largely a matter of hand-eye coordination—a flick of the wrist and a click or two can maneuver you through a program at an impressive rate. Since you can move the mouse and manipulate its buttons simultaneously, dragging is a very intuitive gesture. Trackballs are usually turned with only your thumb. This positions the rest of your hand such that you can only reach one trackball button. That is a fine arrangement as long as you're only clicking a single button, but you often have to move your hand around completely to get to the second button (or you must at least let go of the ball). Dragging is also typically a cumbersome effort. Even a clumsy trackball is better than none at all, so you should be as familiar with trackballs as with a mouse.

TRACKBALL CONSTRUCTION

Virtually all trackballs use the same optomechanical sensor technology that is used with mice. Instead of the mouse PC board resting over the ball, a trackball sits on top of a PC board. The hard rubber ball sits at the intersection of a set of small plastic rails (or *tracks*)—thus, the term trackball. This positions the ball between two perpendicularly oriented metal or plastic rollers. Each roller drives a slotted wheel, which, in turn, runs between the LED and detector of an optoisolator. As the ball and rollers are made to turn, the slotted wheels cause the respective optoisolator's light path to alternate and generate signal pulses. Pulse frequency is dependent on the relative movements of each roller. Pulses are read and interpreted just like a mouse.

During initialization, your computer must load a device driver designed to read the proper port, interpret any signals generated by the trackball, and make switch and roller information available to whatever program calls for it. Given the similarities of mice and trackballs, many mouse-compatible applications are capable of accessing trackball data and responding just like a mouse—even the trackball device driver is virtually identical to a mouse driver. (Trackball drivers are usually "adopted" mouse drivers that simply compensate for the inversion of the ball.) Since the technologies and construction techniques of mice and trackballs are essentially the same, the remainder of this chapter will treat a mouse and trackball as interchangeable devices.

Cleaning a Pointing Device

Pointing devices are perhaps the simplest peripheral available for your computer. While they are reasonably forgiving to wear and tear, trackballs and mice can easily be fouled by dust, debris, and foreign matter introduced from the ball. Contamination of this sort is almost never damaging, but it can cause some maddening problems when using the pointing device. A regimen of routine cleaning will help to prevent contamination problems. You can use prefabricated mouse cleaning kits (Figure 28-5) to speed the cleaning process. Turn your computer off and disconnect the mouse from the system before performing any cleaning procedures:

- *Remove the ball.* A ball is held in place by a retaining ring. For a mouse, the retaining ring is on the bottom. For a trackball, the ring is in the top. Rotate the ring (usually counterclockwise) and remove it gently—the ball will fall out. Place the retaining ring in a safe place.
- *Clean the ball.* Wash the ball in warm, soapy water, and then dry it thoroughly with a clean, lint-free towel. Place the ball in a safe place with the retaining ring.
- *Blow out the dust.* Use a can of photography-grade compressed air to blow out any dust or debris that has accumulated inside the pointing device. You may want to do this in an open or outdoor area.

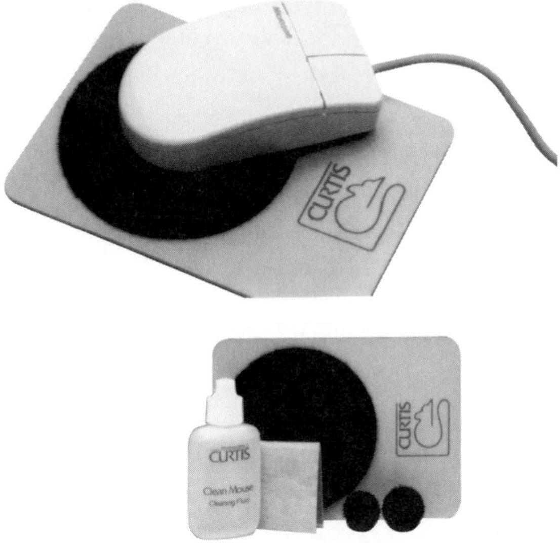

FIGURE 28-5 A Curtis mouse cleaning kit (Curtis, a division of Rolodex, Secaucus, NJ 07094)

- *Clean the rollers.* Notice that there are three rollers in the mouse/trackball: an X roller, a Y roller, and a small pressure roller that keeps the ball pressed against the X and Y rollers. Use a cotton swab dipped in isopropyl alcohol to clean off any layer of gunk that may have accumulated on the rollers. If any gunk falls off the rollers, you'll need to remove it.
- *Reassemble and test.* Allow everything to dry completely, and then replace the ball and secure the retaining ring (usually by turning it clockwise again). You should then reconnect and test the pointing device to be sure that it is performing as expected.

Do not use harsh solvents, wood alcohol, or chemicals inside the pointing device or on the ball. Chemicals can easily melt the plastic and result in permanent damage to the pointing device.

Troubleshooting a Pointing Device

The weakest link in a pointing system is the peripheral pointing device itself. Few peripheral devices are subjected to the wear and general abuse seen by trackballs or mice. They are dropped, yanked, and moved constantly from place to place. Damage to the device's PC board, cabling, and connector is extremely common due to abuse. Accumulations of dust and debris can easily work into the housing and create havoc with the rubber ball, tracks, and rollers. Hardware conflicts and driver configuration issues can also result in frequent problems. This part of the chapter guides you through some simple troubleshooting techniques for your trackball and mouse.

MOUSE/TRACKBALL INTERFACES

From time to time, you may need to check the physical interface on a mouse or trackball. At its core, the mouse is a simple serial device—that is, it can pass serial data back and forth with the host computer using communication protocols managed by the mouse driver. There are four types of mouse interfaces commonly found in the field: serial mice, bus mice, PS/2 mice, and USB mice. This part of the chapter highlights the pinouts for each interface type.

- *Serial mice* A serial mouse connects to an existing RS-232 serial port at the PC (usually COM1 or COM2) using a standard DB-9F (9-pin female) or DB-25F (25-pin female) connector. Table 28-1 lists the pinout for a Logitech Type M, V, or W serial mouse connector.
- *Bus mice* There are many circumstances when it is not possible to use a serial mouse on an open COM port, and the older PC is not fitted with a PS/2 port. In this case, it may be necessary to use a bus mouse, which basically involves using a stand-alone mouse controller board (a bus mouse controller) and mouse fitted with a bus mouse connector—usually a male subminiature D-type connector or a miniature male DIN (circular) connector. Be careful not to mistake the 9-pin DIN connector of a bus mouse for the 6-pin circular connector of a PS/2 mouse. Table 28-2 lists the pinout for a Logitech bus mouse.

TABLE 28-1 PINOUT OF A SERIAL MOUSE PORT (LOGITECH)

DB-9F 9 PIN	DB-25F 25 PIN	WIRE NAME	COMMENTS
shell	1	Protective Ground	
3	2	Receive Data	Serial data from host to mouse
2	3	Transmit Data	Serial data from mouse to host (for power only)
7	4	RTS	Request to Send
8	5	CTS	Clear to Send
6	6	DSR	Data Set Ready
5	7	Signal Ground	
4	20	DTR	Data Terminal Ready

TABLE 28-2 PINOUT OF A BUS MOUSE PORT (LOGITECH)

WIRE COLOR	MINI-DIN PIN	LOGITECH P-SERIES SIGNAL	MICROSOFT INPORT SIGNAL
Black	1	+5V	+5V
Brown	2	X2	XA
Red	3	X1	XB
Orange	4	Y1	YA
Yellow	5	Y2	YB
Green	6	Left	SW1
Violet	7	Middle	SW2
Gray	8	Right	SW3
White	9	GND	Logic GND
SHIELD	shell	Chassis	Chassis

- *PS/2 mice* Most current computers are fitted with one or two PS/2 ports. (These are often called PIX ports because the motherboard's PIX controller(s) can manage the ports directly.) PS/2 ports are basic serial interfaces that are ideal for keyboards and mice. PS/2 mice use a 6-pin DIN (barrel) connector, as shown in Table 28-3. Bidirectional data transmission is controlled by the CLK and DATA lines—both are fed by an "open collector" device that lets either the host or mouse control the lines. During nontransmission, CLK is at logic "1," and DATA is at logic "0" or "1." The PC can inhibit mouse transmission by forcing CLK to logic "0."
- *USB mice* Most current computers are fitted with one or two USB (Universal Serial Bus) connections and can accommodate a USB mouse/trackball. The advantage of USB ports is their convenience—you can connect and disconnect USB devices with the system running, and the device will automatically be identified and enumerated under Windows 95/98. USB also allows you to "mix-and-match" many different types of USB devices on the same port, so you can connect a USB mouse directly to the computer's main USB port, or to a connector on any USB hub attached to the system. The simple 4-pin USB connection follows the layout below:
    - Pin 1: Power
    - Pin 2: Data –
    - Pin 3: Data +
    - Pin 4: Ground

MOUSE DRIVER SOFTWARE ISSUES

Device drivers are often underrated when it comes to mouse/trackball troubleshooting. The driver plays a vital role in mouse performance, and any driver bugs or incompatibilities will have direct consequences on mouse operation. Mouse drivers are also surprisingly versatile programs that can be extensively configured through the use of command-line switches. Table 28-4 lists the command-line switches for Microsoft's real-mode mouse driver 9.0x. When dealing with any kind of mouse issue, always start by checking that the correct driver is installed, that the driver is the latest version, and that it is using any necessary command-line switches to adapt itself to the particular PC. (Default settings are not always adequate.)

The /E and /F switches are new in version 9.0; /Q is new in 9.01.

TABLE 28-3 PINOUT OF A PS/2 MOUSE PORT (LOGITECH)

PIN	WIRE NAME
1	DATA
2	Reserved
3	Ground
4	+5V Supply
5	CLK
6	Reserved
Shield	Chassis

28

TABLE 28-4 COMMAND-LINE SWITCHES FOR MICROSOFT MOUSE DRIVER 9.0X

SWITCH	EXPLANATION
ON	Enable mouse
OFF	Disable mouse
/B	Bus mouse type
/C<n>	Serial mouse on COM1 or COM2
/E	Load mouse in low memory
/F	Find pointing device
/H<n>	Horizontal sensitivity (5-100)
/I<n>	InPort mouse type (1 or 2)
/KP<n>	Small button selection (P = Primary, S = Secondary)
/K<n>	ClickLock (/KC = ON, /K = OFF)
/M<n>	Enable default cursor (/M1 = ON, /M = OFF)
/N<n>	Cursor delay (0-10)
/O<n>	Rotation angle (0-359)
/P<n>	Active acceleration profile
/Q	Load mouse quietly (no startup messages; only in 9.01)
/R<n>	Interrupt rate
/S<n>	Horizontal and vertical sensitivity (5-100)
/V<n>	Vertical sensitivity (5-100)
/Y	Disables hardware cursor
/Z	PS/2 mouse type

MOUSEKEYS UNDER WINDOWS 9X

Windows 95/98 traditionally relies on a mouse for clicking and dragging, but there is a little-known feature of Windows 95/98 called "MouseKeys," which allows you to use the numeric keypad to move the mouse around the screen, click, double-click, and drag. MouseKeys can be helpful if you're caught without a mouse (or troubleshooting a defective mouse system), and you need to navigate the Windows 95/98 environment.

The MouseKeys feature is activated through the Accessibility properties under the Control Panel. Click on Start, select Settings, and then open the Control Panel. Double-click on the Accessibility icon and select the Mouse tab (Figure 28-6). You can enable or disable MouseKeys by checking or clearing the check box. Once MouseKeys is enabled, you can further optimize its settings by clicking the Settings button (Figure 28-7). If you check the Use shortcut box, you can turn MouseKeys on and off by toggling the LEFT ALT+LEFT SHIFT+NUM LOCK keys.

Once the MouseKeys feature is turned on, move the cursor by pressing the arrow keys on the numeric keypad. Use the HOME, END, PAGE UP, and PAGE DOWN keys to move the mouse cursor diagonally.

You can left-click by pressing the 5 key on the numeric keypad. To left-double-click, press the + key on the numeric keypad. To right-click, press the – button on the numeric keypad first, then press 5 to click or + to double-click. To click as if you were using both mouse buttons at once, press the * key on your numeric keypad, and then press 5 to click or + to double-click. If you want to switch back to *standard* clicking, press / on your numeric keypad.

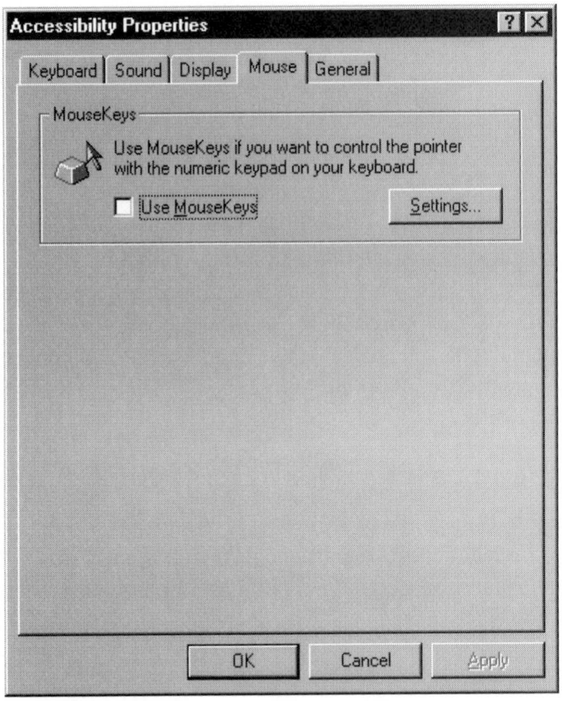

FIGURE 28-6 Controlling the Windows 95 MouseKeys feature

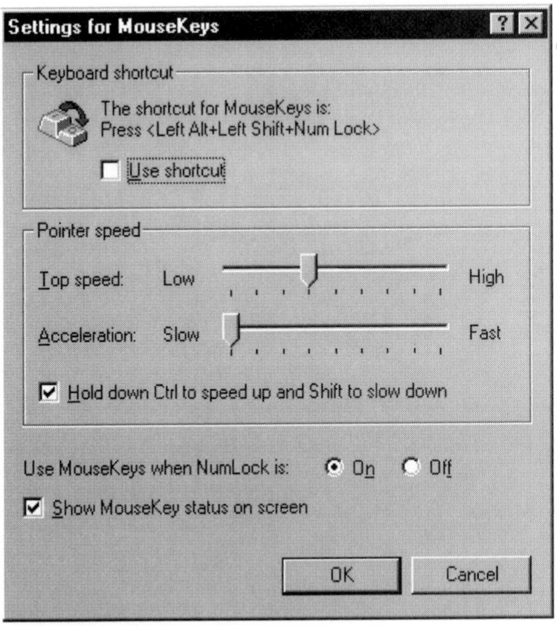

FIGURE 28-7 Configuring MouseKeys operation

You'll also need to be able to drag using MouseKeys. Make sure that the MouseKeys feature is turned on, and then move the mouse pointer over the desired object. Press INS on the numeric keypad to hold down the mouse button and grab the object. Move the mouse pointer over the new desired area, and then press DEL on the numeric keypad to drop the object.

ADJUSTING MOUSE PROPERTIES

In order to use a mouse comfortably and successfully, the mouse must be adjusted for your personal preferences. You'd be surprised at how many people get frustrated because they can't double-click, only to find that the "Double-click speed" property for the mouse is set too high. You can tailor the mouse to your own tastes through the Mouse Properties dialog (Figure 28-8). Click Start, highlight Settings, and then click Control Panel. When the Control Panel is open, double-click the Mouse icon. You can select the "handedness" of the mouse, its double-click speed (sensitivity), its pointer format, movement sensitivity, and cursor "trails" (very handy in older LCD laptop displays).

COMMON MOUSE DETECTION ISSUES

When installing, replacing, or upgrading a pointing device, you may encounter a Windows 95/98 error such as "Mouse Not Detected." If Windows starts, you will be forced to use keyboard shortcuts (Appendix G) to navigate around and exit Windows again. If you're faced with a mouse detection problem, use the checklist below to isolate the most common hardware issues:

- A port-specific pointing device has been connected to the wrong port (for example, a serial-only mouse has been connected to a PS/2 mouse port using an adapter).
- The port being used by the mouse/trackball is disabled, defective, or incorrectly configured.

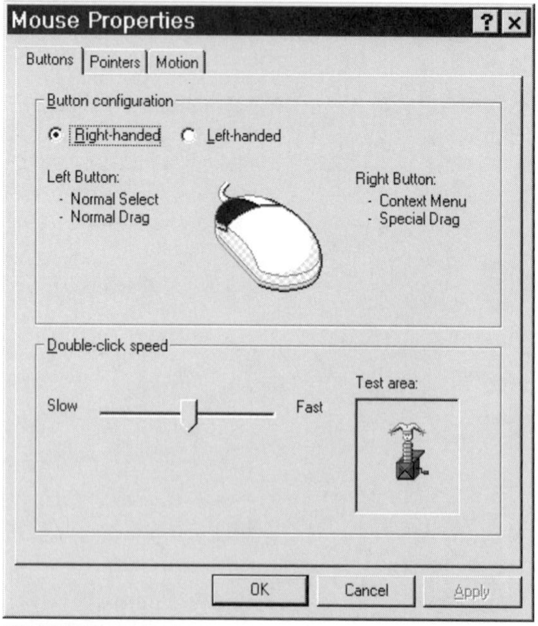

FIGURE 28-8 The Mouse Properties dialog

- You're using an incompatible bus mouse adapter card. For example, when using a Logitech bus mouse, Logitech bus adapters must be used. Verify that any third-party bus mouse adapters have been removed from the system.
- The port being used by the mouse/trackball is experiencing a hardware conflict with another device in the system (for example, an IRQ or I/O address conflict).
- You're inserting an extension cable or switch box between the pointing device and the system. Most pointing devices do not support the use of extension cables or switch boxes. If a switch box or extension cable is being used, remove it and connect the pointing device *directly* to the system.
- The pointing device is defective—verify this by trying the device on another system. Replace the defective pointing device if necessary.
- The pointing device is incompatible with your system—verify this by trying another pointing device connected to the same system and port. If another pointing device fails on the same port, the problem may be with that system or port. Otherwise, try a different pointing device.

MOUSE ISSUES WITH VIDEO DRIVERS

Installing some third-party video drivers can cause the Windows 98 mouse pointer to behave erratically (or not move at all). It may also cause odd types of "video corruption" (for example, the mouse pointer destroys screen elements). Since the mouse driver uses video driver information to generate the screen cursor, some video drivers may not operate properly with your particular mouse driver. Try changing the video mode to a lower resolution or color depth (such as the "standard VGA" mode), and see if the problem disappears. If it does, you should try updating the video driver or the mouse driver. Otherwise, you may need to update the video card's firmware, or use a different pointing device.

USB MOUSE TROUBLESHOOTING TIPS

Check the OS Versions Generally speaking, USB mice require Windows 98 and Windows 98/SE. Windows 95 OSR2.x with the USB supplement is not supported.

Check the Driver Versions Connecting a USB pointing device to a USB port on your system should result in the device being detected by the system (and the default USB drivers being installed). This may require the Windows 98 CD, so please insert the CD when prompted by Windows. You may use the default USB drivers that ship with Windows 98. But in order to utilize the enhanced features of your mouse, the very latest mouse driver versions for your mouse are needed. In most cases, you can obtain the latest mouse drivers directly from the manufacturer's Web site. Please uninstall any older version(s) of the pointing device software from your system before installing the version that shipped with your current device.

Check the Product Version Verify that your USB mouse/trackball is using the latest firmware. Initial product releases or prerelease (evaluation) units may not function reliably.

Enable the USB Controller Many early USB (PIX3) systems shipped with the USB ports disabled. These systems must have their USB ports enabled before the mouse will be detected and function properly. These USB ports are generally enabled through the CMOS setup. If a USB add-on card is being used, please be sure that it is a *retail* version. Prerelease versions of USB cards may not function correctly with current USB hardware. Check with the USB card's manufacturer for new drivers or firmware updates.

Check the USB Host Controller In order for a USB pointing device to function properly on the USB port, the USB Host Controller must be identified correctly by Windows 98. Click Start, highlight

Settings, and then click Control Panel. Double-click the System icon and select the Device Manager tab. Verify that there is an entry called "Universal Serial Bus Controller." If this entry is missing, the controller may not be enabled or detected properly.

Check the Mouse Entry in Device Manager Click Start, highlight Settings, and then click Control Panel. Double-click the System icon, select the Device Manager tab, and then click the Mouse entry. Verify that there is a mouse entry that reads "HID-compliant mouse" and another entry that states the name of your USB device. If any errors are reported on these icons (by exclamation points or red *X*s), highlight these icons and click the Remove button. Once these icons have been removed, click the Refresh button and allow Windows 98 to redetect the pointing device. Open the Mouse entry again and verify that there are no errors reported. Power-down the computer and restart Windows. Then test the USB device to see if it's working.

Check Your External Hubs If two external hubs are daisy-chained together, at least one must be powered (connected to AC). If you're using two or more unpowered hubs, there may not be enough current in the second hub to properly power the USB devices connected to it. If this occurs, connect the pointing device to the first hub and test it (or try connecting the mouse directly to the USB port instead of a hub).

Check Your USB Hardware Detection If the USB pointing device is not detected by Windows 98 after plugging in the device and installing the drivers, try the following:

1. Shut down the system, allow it to power-off, and then restart it.
2. Try connecting the pointing device to a second USB port (if your system has one).
3. Try connecting the mouse to a second system with a working USB port to verify the USB mouse hardware is working. Any Windows 98 system equipped with a USB port should detect the mouse.
4. Try connecting another USB device to the same USB port. If the second device is detected correctly, the mouse may be defective. If the second device is also not detected correctly, the USB port may be disabled or malfunctioning.
5. If you're using a USB hub to connect the mouse, try connecting the mouse directly to the USB port on your system.

Check for Software Issues Windows 98 includes a system configuration utility that can boot your system without resident programs loading from the Windows registry, the Startup folder, and system files. Use this tool to isolate possible software conflicts:

1. Click Start and select Run. In the Open command line, type **MSCONFIG** and click OK. The system configuration utility should appear.
2. On the General tab, click Selective . Click on the tab labeled WIN.INI, and then click on the plus (+) sign next to the [windows] section. Check for the presence of the LOAD= and RUN= lines. If programs are loading from either of these lines, remove the check marks from those entries. This will prevent anything in those lines from loading upon startup.
3. Next, click on the tab labeled Startup, and remove the check mark from every box, except the entry for "System Tray (SysTray.Exe)." This will prevent memory resident programs from loading from the Run folder and other startup folders of the registry.
4. When finished, click the OK button, and Windows should prompt you to reboot. After rebooting, test the device to see if the problem has disappeared. If it has, one of the programs loading at startup

is causing the issue. Re-add each item systematically (one at time, rebooting between each addition). When you find the problem application, contact that program's manufacturer for more information or a possible work-around.

SYMPTOMS

SYMPTOM 28-1 The mouse cursor appears, but it only moves erratically as the ball moves (if at all) This symptom may occur in either the horizontal or vertical axis. This symptom suggests that an intermittent condition is occurring somewhere in the pointing device. You should not have to disassemble your computer at all during this procedure. Start your investigation by powering down the computer. Check the device's cable connector at the computer. Make sure the connector is tight and inserted properly. If you are in the habit of continually plugging and unplugging the mouse/trackball, excessive wear can develop in the connector pins over time. If the connector does not seem to fit tightly in the computer, try a new pointing device.

A more likely problem is that the device's rollers are not turning, or turning only intermittently. In most cases, roller stall is due to a dirty or damaged ball, or an accumulation of dirt blocking one or both sensors. Clean the ball and blow out any dust or debris that may have settled into the mouse/trackball housing. Refer to the earlier section on cleaning, and attempt to clean the device thoroughly. *Never use harsh solvents or chemicals to clean the housings or ball.*

If you have the mouse connected to a standard serial communication port (a COM port), you should check that no other devices are using the same interrupt (IRQ). For example, COM1 and COM3 use the same IRQ, while COM2 and COM4 share another IRQ. If you have a mouse on COM1 and a modem on COM3, there will almost invariably be a hardware conflict. If possible, switch the mouse (or conflicting device) to another port and try the system again.

28

If there is no hardware conflict, and cleaning does not correct an intermittent condition, remove the device's upper housing to expose the PC board, and use your multimeter to check continuity across each wire in the connecting cable. Since you probably will not know which connector pins correspond to which wires at the sensor PC board, place one meter probe on a device's wire and "ring-out" each connector pin until you find continuity. Make a wiring chart as you go. Each time you find a wire path, wiggle the cable to stimulate any possible intermittent wiring. Repair any intermittent wiring if possible. If you cannot find continuity or repair faulty wiring, simply replace the pointing device.

SYMPTOM 28-2 One or both buttons function erratically (if at all) Buttons are prone to problems from dust accumulation and general contact corrosion. Your first step should be to power-down your computer and disconnect the pointing device. Remove the ball and upper housing to expose the PC board and switches. Spray a small amount of electronics-grade contact cleaner into each switch, and then work each switch to circulate the cleaner.

If cleaning does not improve intermittent switch contacts, you may wish to check continuity across the connecting cable. With the ball and housing cover removed, use your multimeter to check continuity across each wire in the connecting cable. Since you probably do not know which connector pins correspond to which wires at the device, place one meter lead on a device wire and "ring-out" each connector pin until you find continuity. Once you find continuity, wiggle the cable to stimulate any possible intermittent wiring. Repair any intermittent wiring if you can, or simply replace the pointing device.

SYMPTOM 28-3 The screen cursor appears on the display, but it does not move If the cursor appears, the device driver has loaded correctly and the application program is communicating with the driver. Your first step should be to suspect the serial connection. If there is no serial connection, however, there will be no pulses to modify the cursor's position. If you find a bad connection, power-down your computer before reattaching the device's serial connector, and then restore power and allow the system to reinitialize.

If the device is attached correctly to its proper serial port, the problem probably exists in the pointing device's wiring. Remove the ball and upper housing to expose the PC board; then use your multimeter to check continuity across each wire in the connecting cable. Since you probably do not know which connector pins correspond to which wires in the device, place one meter lead on a device wire and "ring out" each connector pin until you find continuity. Once you find continuity, wiggle the cable to stimulate any possible intermittent wiring. Repair any intermittent or open wiring if you can, or simply replace the pointing device.

SYMPTOM 28-4 **The mouse/trackball device driver fails to load** The device driver is a short program that allows an application program to access information from a pointing device. Most computer users prefer to load their device drivers during system initialization by invoking the drivers in the CONFIG.SYS or AUTOEXEC.BAT file. Most drivers are written to check for the presence of their respective device first—if the expected device does not respond, the driver will not be loaded into memory. Other drivers load blindly regardless of whether the expected device is present or not.

If the device driver fails to load during initialization, your pointing device may not have been detected. Power-down your computer and check the connection of your pointing device. Ensure the device is securely plugged into the proper serial port (or other mouse port). If the device is missing or incorrectly inserted, install or resecure the pointing device and allow the system to reinitialize. If you see a "File Not Found" error message displayed at the point your device driver was supposed to load, the driver may have been accidentally erased, may be corrupted, or may be located in a subdirectory where the CONFIG.SYS or AUTOEXEC.BAT files are not looking. Try reinstalling a valid copy of your mouse device driver and ensure that the driver is located where your calling batch file can access it. Reboot your system.

Most well-designed application programs check for the presence of a pointing device through the device driver during initial program execution. If the application program aborts or fails to execute because of a "No Mouse Found" or "No Mouse Driver" error, return to the paragraphs above and recheck the device and driver installation.

SYMPTOM 28-5 **You see a "General Protection Fault" after installing a new mouse and driver under Windows.** First, this is probably not a hardware fault (although it would be helpful to check any mouse driver command-line switches in CONFIG.SYS or AUTOEXEC.BAT). It is more likely that the new mouse driver is conflicting with one or more applications. Try several different applications—most will probably work just fine. Check with the mouse manufacturer to see if there are any other reported problems, and find out if any patches are planned. If you have an older version of the mouse driver available, try replacing that one. An older driver may not work as well as a newer one, but it may not suffer from this kind of compatibility problem. If there are no older drivers available, and no patches that you can use, you may be forced to change the mouse and mouse driver to something completely different in order to eliminate the problem.

SYMPTOM 28-6 **You see an error "This pointer device requires a newer version"** In virtually all cases, you have the wrong driver installed on the system for your driver. Check the driver and make sure that the driver you are using is appropriate for the particular mouse. For example, a Logitech or Genius mouse selected in Windows setup can cause this kind of problem if you have a Microsoft mouse on the system. Change the mouse type under Windows. Under Windows 95, you'll need to remove the old mouse reference from the Device Manager, and then use the Add New Hardware wizard to install the new mouse manually.

SYMPTOM 28-7 You see an error "Mouse port disabled or mouse not present" This is almost always a connection problem or a setup problem. Check the signal connector first. Make sure the mouse cable is not cut or damaged anywhere, and see that it is attached securely to the serial or PS/2 port. Many newer system BIOS versions now provide an option in the CMOS setup for a mouse port. Check the CMOS setup and see that any entries for your mouse are enabled properly.

SYMPTOM 28-8 The mouse works for a few minutes, then stops When the computer is rebooted, the mouse starts working again. This is a problem that often plagues cut-price mice, and is almost always due to buildups of static in the mouse. The static charges are interfering with the mouse circuitry and causing the mouse to stop responding (though charges are not enough to actually damage the mouse). There are generally three ways to resolve the problem: (1) spray the surrounding carpet and upholstery with very dilute fabric softener to dissipate static buildup; (2) hire an electrician to ensure that the computer and house wiring are grounded properly; or (3) replace the mouse with a more static-resistant model.

SYMPTOM 28-9 You attempt a double-click but get quadruple-click, or you attempt a single-click and get a double-click This is a phenomenon called "button bounce" and is the result of a hardware defect (broken or poorly buffered mouse buttons). You may be able to clean the mouse buttons by spraying in some good-quality electronics-grade contact cleaner. Otherwise, you'll need to replace the mouse outright.

SYMPTOM 28-10 A single mouse click works, but double-click doesn't When this problem occurs, it is almost always because the double-click speed is set too high in the Windows 95 mouse control panel. Try setting it lower. Click Start, select Settings, and then open the Control Panel. Double-click the Mouse icon and adjust the "Double-click speed" slider under the Buttons tab.

28

SYMPTOM 28-11 A PS/2 mouse is not detected by a notebook PC under Windows 95 There is a known problem with PS/2 mouse detection on a Toshiba portable computer under Windows 95. You can usually correct the problem by taking the following steps:

1. Shut down the computer entirely, and physically disconnect the PS/2 mouse from the PS/2 port.
2. Restart the PC to the DOS mode and create backup copies of your CONFIG.SYS and AUTOEXEC.BAT files.
3. Restart Windows 95 (reboot the PC if necessary).
4. Click Start, select Settings, open the Control Panel, and double-click on the System icon.
5. Select the Device Manager tab and double-click the Mouse entry.
6. Select the mouse entry that is not being detected (for example, "Toshiba AccuPoint"), and click Remove.
7. Select and remove any other mouse entries.
8. Shut down the computer and reconnect the mouse; then turn the PC back on.
9. When the system reboots, it should detect the mouse and attempt to reinstall the appropriate drivers.

If this doesn't fix the problem, a hardware issue could exist. Try a different PS/2 mouse (preferably from a manufacturer different from the current one). If a different make and model PS/2 mouse does not work, the PS/2 port may require service.

SYMPTOM 28-12 **Mouse pointer options are not saved** This is a known problem when you use the "extra points" features in the Mouse Manager program included with the Microsoft mouse driver. The pointer options are not saved or written to the MOUSE.INI file when you are running a virus-protection program such as Microsoft Anti-Virus (MSAV) or Norton Anti-Virus (NAV). To correct this problem, remove the CHKLIST.MS or CHKLIST.CPS file in the directory that contains the mouse files. To determine the location of that directory, type **set** at the MS-DOS command prompt—it will return a list of locations of various files and memory strings. Look for the MOUSE= line, and then go to that directory and delete the CHKLIST.MS or CHKLIST.CPS file. Reboot the system and try saving options again.

SYMPTOM 28-13 **Clicking the right mouse button doesn't start the default context menus of Windows 95** If the mouse manager software you're running is using an assignment set for the right button, this assignment will override the Windows 95 default setting of "context menus." Open the mouse management software utility and change the assignment for the right button to "Unassigned." Save your changes. The right mouse button will now access the default context menus.

SYMPTOM 28-14 **The Packard Bell "Fast Media" device no longer functions after installing a pointing device under Windows 95/98** The Fast Media device is an infrared remote control device that allows you to control the mouse pointer as well as a CD player, TV tuner, modem, radio card, and other items. This device only works with native Microsoft drivers. When you install pointing device drivers, the Fast Media device no longer functions. This happens because the Fast Media software installs some virtual drivers that only communicate with the native Microsoft drivers.

Unfortunately, you may need to choose the Fast Media system (and forgo the advanced features of your new pointing device), or disable the Fast Media system in order to use all the features of your pointing device. You may also check with Packard Bell to see if there is an update to the Fast Media drivers that is more compliant with other device drivers.

SYMPTOM 28-15 **Your Packard Bell only detects a basic 2-button mouse after plugging it into a "Media Select" unit** The Packard Bell Media Select is a box that fits underneath the monitor and plugs into the PS/2 port of the computer system. This Media Select device also has a PS/2 port for a PS/2-style mouse. It seems that the Media Select unit uses a pass-through PS/2 port connection that causes detection problems for some pointing devices. In most cases, cleaning up the registry and removing unneeded entries can clear this problem:

> Do not attempt to edit your registry without first creating a complete registry backup on your boot disk. Incorrectly editing the registry may prevent the system from booting.

1. Click Start and select Run.
2. On the Open line, type **C:\WINDOWS\REGEDIT.EXE** and press ENTER.
3. Open the following key:

   `Hkey_Local_Machine\System\CurrentControlSet\Services\Class\Mouse\xxxx`

   where xxxx is an incremental 4-digit number starting at 0000.
4. Click on each folder under the Mouse folder and delete them until there are no 000X folders remaining.
5. Save your changes and exit the registry editor.
6. Remove the FMEDIA reference from the Windows Startup group or WIN.INI file as necessary.

7 Save any changes, shut down, and then restart the system normally.

8 Open the Properties dialog or applet for your pointing device to verify the correct detection.

If this does not correct the detection issue, you'll need to connect the pointing device directly to the computer system's PS/2 port (bypassing the Media Select box). You may also use the serial port if the pointing device is a PS/2-serial combination unit—this will allow you to keep the Media Select and achieve correct detection if the serial port is working properly.

SYMPTOM 28-16 The mouse pointer does not move after installing a Logitech "First Mouse" on a Packard Bell system Windows will generally not indicate any problems with mouse detection. There is a known compatibility problem with some Packard Bell computers and Logitech's two-button First Mouse (version M/N:M34). You can use the keyboard to invoke a basic work-around:

1 Press CTRL+ESC to open the Start menu.

2 Use the arrow keys to highlight Settings, then Control Panel, and press ENTER.

3 Move the arrow key over to the Mouse icon and press ENTER. This will open the Mouse Properties dialog box.

4 Using the TAB key, tab over to the Quick Setup tab, and then use the RIGHT ARROW key to open the Devices tab.

5 Once on the Devices tab, tab over to the Add Mouse button and press ENTER.

The pointing device applet should now detect the two-button serial mouse, and the pointer should now move properly. However, you'll need to perform this procedure each time you start the system. If your Packard Bell system has a dedicated PS/2 mouse port, another option is to contact the pointing device maker to see if you can exchange the serial version for a PS/2 version.

SYMPTOM 28-17 After installing a three-button mouse, you receive an error such as "pointing device on unknown port" You may also find that the device is only shown as a two-button mouse. In most cases, there are older mouse traces in the registry that must be removed before the new pointing device can be properly detected:

> Do not attempt to edit your registry without first creating a complete registry backup on your boot disk. Incorrectly editing the registry may prevent the system from booting.

1 Click Start and select Run.

2 On the Open line, type **C:\WINDOWS\REGEDIT.EXE** and press ENTER.

3 Open the following key:

```
Hkey_Local_Machine\System\CurrentControlSet\Services\Class\Mouse\xxxx
```

where xxxx is an incremental 4-digit number starting at 0000.

4 Click on each folder under the Mouse folder and delete them until there are no 000X folders remaining.

5 Save your changes and exit the registry editor.

6 Open the Properties dialog or applet for your pointing device to verify the correct detection.

SYMPTOM 28-18 When installing a three- or four-button PS/2 pointing device on a laptop with its own pointing device, the new device only shows up as a two-button mouse. There are several possible solutions to this issue depending on what laptop and pointing device you're using. Try disabling the internal pointing device. Some systems may require that you disable the internal pointing device *first* (usually through the CMOS setup) in order to detect a new pointing device on the external mouse port. You may also wish to contact the system manufacturer to see if there is a BIOS update available, or any further information related to using external pointing devices on the system.

SYMPTOM 28-19 You receive a "KBC error" when connecting a pointing device to certain laptop PS/2 ports For example, this is a known compatibility issue between the Toshiba 400 series notebook and Logitech PS/2 "combo" pointing devices. These Toshiba systems have a single PS/2 connector on the back that may accept either a mouse or keyboard, and the problem is caused by a BIOS oversight. Toshiba has a BIOS upgrade that resolves this issue. (Version v.5.40 or later can be obtained by contacting Toshiba America.) If a BIOS upgrade is not available, you may connect the Logitech "combo" pointing device to the serial port instead (use only Logitech adapters).

SYMPTOM 28-20 After installing the applets for your pointing device, you receive an "0E Exception" error on a blue screen You may also find that you can press ENTER and still access Windows, but this error appears on each boot. This problem is often encountered on IBM systems. IBM has found a problem with version 1.10 of their "TrackPoint" drivers. This error produces a blue screen on boot-up if the mouse drivers are changed. The work-around for this trouble is to uninstall the IBM TrackPoint software through the Add/Remove Programs icon in the Windows Control Panel.

SYMPTOM 28-21 The pointing device (or system) freezes when the system wakes from its suspend mode Many current mouse drivers can perform a search for mice when a system wakes from its suspend mode. (For Windows 95/98, this is defined by a key in the Windows registry.) This registry setting defines the action that the driver will perform upon power management suspend/resume commands. If the mouse stops working after a resume, this parameter should be set to Off, as described below:

1. Click Start and select Run.
2. On the Open line, type **REGEDIT.EXE** and press ENTER.
3. Click the plus (+) sign next to HKEY_LOCAL_MACHINE.
4. Click the plus sign next to SOFTWARE.
5. Click the plus sign next to your pointing device maker (for example, Logitech).
6. Click the plus sign next to the software name (for example, MouseWare).
7. Click the plus sign next to CurrentVersion.
8. Single-click on Technical folder, and information should be displayed on the right side of the registry editor screen.
9. Under the Name column, double-click on the APMMode entry, and an Edit String dialog box should appear.
10. Modify the Value Data line to read Off, and click the OK button. The full line should now read

```
HKEY_LOCAL_MACHINE\SOFTWARE\Logitech\MouseWare\CurrentVersion\Technical\APMMode=Off
```

11 Exit the registry editor and restart your system. Then test the computer again to see if it resumes without freezing.

If you still experience APM issues, try uninstalling the mouse applet(s) using the Add/Remove Programs icon in the Control Panel. This will restore the system to the native drivers supplied by Windows. Now test your system again to see if it resumes correctly. If it still fails, try another mouse in the same port.

SYMPTOM 28-22 When running a DOS program from Windows 95/98, the mouse cursor moves very slowly compared to native Windows applications There are several possible issues to consider here. If the problem only occurs under one DOS application (and not in others), the problem may be with the particular application. You may need a patch or update for that application, or you may want to try installing the very latest mouse driver. Also try shutting down to DOS and running the program from the native DOS mode (rather than through a DOS window).

SYMPTOM 28-23 The modem won't start after installing new mouse management software For example, this is a known problem when installing Logitech's MouseWare 6.60 or later under Windows 95. Sometimes the mouse drivers may detect the modem as a second mouse and try to initialize it. This can cause the modem to go into a busy state. However, you can prevent the mouse drivers from searching the serial port that the modem is using:

1 Download the current mouse driver for Windows 95.

2 Edit the Windows 95 registry by clicking on the Start menu and selecting Run.

3 Type **C:\WINDOWS\REGEDIT.EXE** on the Open line.

4 Click OK. The registry editor will start.

5 Double-click on the HKEY_LOCAL_MACHINE folder.

6 Double-click on the SOFTWARE folder.

7 Double-click on the manufacturer's folder (for example, Logitech).

8 Double-click on the manufacturer's driver folder (for example, MouseWare).

9 Double-click on the CurrentVersion folder.

10 Click on the Global folder.

11 Let's assume the mouse is on COM1 and the modem is on COM2. On the right side of the screen, there will be a list of value data strings. Double-click on the "PortSearchOrder" string. An Edit String dialog box will appear. The Value Data line will read

```
COM1, COM2
```

12 Remove the space, the comma and "COM2" so the line reads

```
COM1
```

13 If you only plan to use one mouse on the system, change the "MaximumDevices" value data line to 1 using the same steps as above. This will tell the driver to stop searching for additional mice after the primary mouse has been found.

If you are not using a serial mouse, remove "Serial" from the "SearchOrder" value data line so that no serial devices are searched for at all. In general, remove any reference to the port the modem is using.

14 Now click OK, and the values under the data value section on the right side of the screen should change. Exit the registry editor (saving is automatic). Shut down the computer and reboot from a cold start so that your changes can take effect.

SYMPTOM 28-24 **The mouse pointer moves only vertically** The mouse is connected to a PS/2 port under Windows 95. If the mouse works along one axis but not the other, it's usually due to a hardware problem—either the mouse needs cleaning or repair. However, in some cases a software configuration problem can occur when the mouse driver (for example, Mouse Power v9.5) is installed on a system with plug-and-play BIOS running Windows 95, and the mouse is connected to the PS/2-style mouse port. As soon as you touch the mouse, the pointer darts over the right edge of the screen, and then will move only up and down.

1. To regain control over your computer, reboot in Safe Mode.
2. Click Start, then Run, and then type **REGEDIT** and press ENTER.
3. Open the HKEY_LOCAL_MACHINE\Enum folder and see if "BIOS" is listed under Enum. If it is, then you know the software configuration problem is causing the issue.
4. Open HKEY_LOCAL_MACHINE\Enum\BIOS*PNP0F13, and look for a key (usually "05" or "07") under "*PNP0F13." Click on this key to highlight it. The key under "*PNP0F13" should now be highlighted, and the corresponding values should be displayed on the right side of the window. Note that there are "string values" with an "ab" icon next to them, and "binary values" with a "011" icon next to them.
5. Compare your values to those shown below. Edit your entries until all your values shown on the screen match the values shown below:

```
ab  Class     "Mouse"
011 ConfigFlags 00 00 00 00
ab  DeviceDesc  "Mouse Systems v2.18"
ab  Driver     "Mouse\0000"
ab  HardwareID  "*PNP0F0C"
ab  Mfg      "Mouse Systems"
```

6. Open HKEY_LOCAL_MACHINE\System\CurrentControlSet\Services\Class\Mouse. There should be multiple keys under Mouse (such as "0000" and "0001"). All but one are to be deleted. Carefully determine which one pertains to your current mouse (by looking at the values associated with each key), and delete all keys under Mouse except the related one.
7. Make sure the one remaining key under Mouse is labeled "0000" (rename it if necessary).
8. Click on the X box in the upper-right corner of the registry editor to close it.
9. Reboot the computer from a cold start. The computer should reboot in normal mode, and the problem with the mouse and keyboard should be gone.

Further Study

Microsoft: **http://www.microsoft.com**

Logitech: **http://www.logitech.com**

Genius: **http://www.genius-kye.com/**

Mitsumi: **http://www.mitsumi.com**

Mouse Systems: **http://www.mousesystems.com/**

Mouse Trak: **http://www.mousetrak.com/**

No Hands Mouse: **http://www.footmouse.com/**

29

MODEMS AND FAX CARDS

CHAPTER AT A GLANCE

Long before computers ever became "personal," the mainframe and mini computers of the 1960s and 1970s needed to communicate over large geographic distances that could sometimes stretch across town, and sometimes around the world. Designers faced the problem of wiring the computers together—stringing a cable across even a few miles represents a serious logistical challenge. Instead of installing a network of *new* cabling, computer designers realized that they already had a sophisticated worldwide wiring system in place: the *public switched telephone network* (PSTN). For computers to "call" one another and exchange data, they could use telephone lines and be able to communicate anywhere a telephone jack is available (even using cellular facilities).

Of course, computers cannot work *directly* on your telephone line. The digital information processed by computers must be translated (or *modulated*) into audible sounds that are carried across telephone lines. Sound signals from the telephone lines must be converted back into digital information (or *demodulated*) for the computer. This continuous process of modulation and demodulation between a computer and telephone line is performed by a device called a MOdulator/DEModulator—or *modem*. As the number of personal computers has grown into the millions, the increased demand for faster and more reliable modem communication has resulted in impressive speed and performance. Today's modems have also enabled entirely new developments, such as "fax" and "voice over data" capabilities. This chapter is intended to explain the operations, standards, and connections of today's modems, as well as provide you with a compendium of modem symptoms and solutions.

Basic Modem Construction and Operation

To understand how a modem works and how to react when things go wrong, you should be familiar with the typical sections of a modem circuit. Although most modems today can be fabricated with only a few specialized chips and discrete parts, virtually all computer communication systems contain the same essential parts. First, data must be translated from parallel into serial form and back again. Serial data being transmitted must be converted into an audio signal, and then placed on an ordinary telephone circuit. Audio signals received from the telephone line must be separated from transmitted signals, then converted back into serial data. All of these activities must take place under the direction of a controller circuit. Finally, a modem uses non-volatile RAM (NVRAM) to maintain a lengthy list of setup parameters (or *S registers*). For the purposes of this book, there are two types of modems: internal and external.

THE INTERNAL MODEM

The *internal* modem is fabricated as a stand-alone board that plugs directly into the PC expansion bus. You can see each major modem function detailed in the block diagram of Figure 29-1. The internal modem contains its own *universal asynchronous receiver/transmitter* (UART)—it is the UART that is responsible for manipulating data into and out of serial form. A UART forms the foundation of a serial port, potentially presenting a serious hardware conflict for your PC—when installing an internal modem,

29

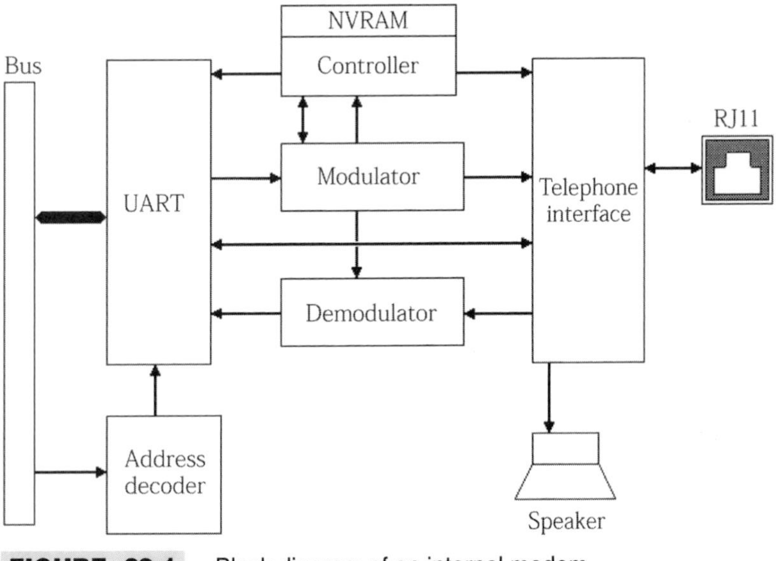

FIGURE 29-1 Block diagram of an internal modem

be sure that the IRQ line and I/O address chosen for the UART "serial port" does not conflict with other serial ports (a.k.a. COM ports) already in the system. It may be necessary to disable conflicting ports.

Before being transmitted over telephone lines, serial data must be converted into audio signals. This process is carried out by a *modulator* circuit. The modulated audio is then coupled to the telephone line using a circuit very similar to that used by ordinary telephones to couple voice signals. Audio signals are made available to a single RJ11-type ("telephone" line) connector at the rear of the modem. Many modems provide a second RJ11 jack for a telephone, which allows you to check the line and make calls while the modem is idle. Signals received from the telephone line must be translated back into serial data. The telephone interface separates received signals and passes them to the *demodulator*. After demodulation, the resulting serial data is passed to the UART, which in turn converts the serial bits into parallel words that are placed on the system's data bus.

Besides combining and separating modulated audio data, the *telephone interface* generates the dual-tone multi-frequency (DTMF) dialing signals needed to reach a remote modem—a process that is much the same as a touch-tone telephone uses. When a remote modem dials in, the telephone interface detects the incoming ring and alerts the UART to begin negotiating a connection. Finally, the telephone interface drives a small speaker. During the first stages of modem operation, the speaker is used to hear a dial tone, dialing signals, and audio negotiation between the two modems. Once a connection is established, the speaker is usually disabled.

A *controller* circuit manages the overall operation of the modem, and, in a more general sense, it switches the modem between its "control" and "data" operating modes. The controller accepts commands from the modulator that allow modem characteristics and operating parameters to be changed. In the event of power loss or reset conditions, default modem parameters can be loaded from NVRAM. Permanent changes to modem parameters are stored in NVRAM.

THE EXTERNAL MODEM

For all practical intents and purposes, the *external* modem provides virtually all of the essential functions offered by an internal modem. As you can see by the block diagram of Figure 29-2, many of the external

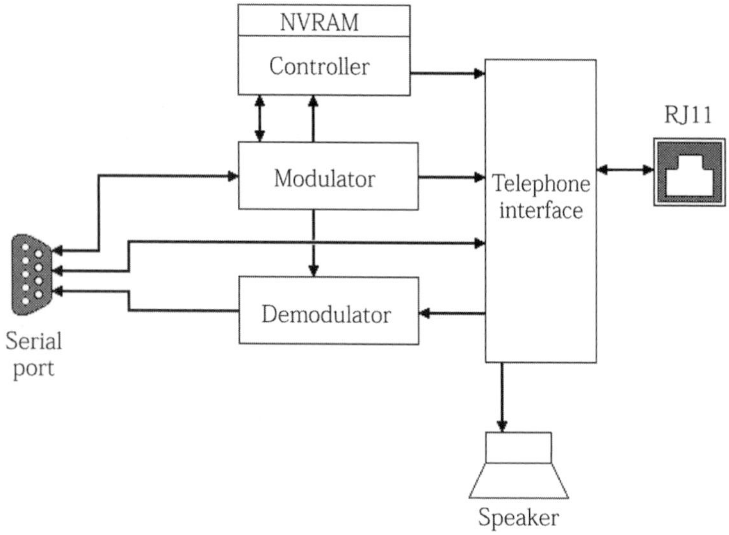

FIGURE 29-2 Block diagram of an external modem

functions are *identical* to those of an internal modem. The major difference between modems is that the external modem does *not* include a built-in UART to provide a serial port. Instead, the external modem relies on an existing serial port (or COM port) already configured in the PC. A 9-pin or 25-pin serial cable connects the PC serial port to the modem. It is often faster and easier to set up external modems because you need not worry about interrupt lines and I/O address settings—hardware conflicts are rare with external modems.

The other practical difference in an external modem is the way it is powered. Where internal modems are powered directly from the expansion bus, external modems must be powered from a small AC adapter. In locations where AC outlets are scarce, this requirement may be a problem. On the plus side, external modems provide a series of signal status LEDs. The LEDs allow you to easily check the state of serial communications.

ADVANCED MODEM FEATURES

Today's modems do far more than just exchange data between computers. There are myriad advanced features built into current modems that you should be aware of—a few of the more notable advancements are listed below:

x2 Technology Although the designation "x2" is generally trademarked by US Robotics, x2 is often used generically to refer to high-speed modem technology employed for 56Kbps modems. The x2 technology is a new method developed for 56Kbps downloads from the Internet, corporate networks, and online services over regular phone lines. While x2 doesn't support 56Kbps uploads or 56Kbps transfers between modems, it does offer a powerful enhancement for PC users seeking more speed from the Internet or other online services. You need three elements to support x2 at 56Kbps downloads: an ISP or other remote *x2 compatible server*, an *analog loop* between your home/office and the local central office, and an *x2 modem* (such as a US Robotics Sportster). However, x2 technology is very sensitive to telephone line issues, and there must be close to ideal conditions to achieve top speed downloads. When uploading or communicating with other modems, an x2 modem typically runs at 28.8Kbps.

29

K56flex Lucent Technologies and Rockwell Semiconductor Systems coauthored the K56flex protocol, which allows Lucent's and Rockwell's modem chipsets to interoperate. Lucent and Rockwell had to introduce their own version of 56Kbps-capable technology in order to remain competitive. Their version was named "K56flex" and was *not* compatible with x2 modems at speeds over 33.6Kbps. Internet Service Providers wanting to provide 56Kbps support had to choose between these two competing technologies. Users desiring high-speed access had to first check with their ISP to determine which version was implemented at the provider's end, and then purchase a compatible modem. All this was happening even while the ITU (International Telecommunications Union) was in the process of finalizing a universal standard for 56Kbps (now dubbed V.90).

K56flex technology uses a pure digital "downstream" connection to achieve its high-speed data transfer to your computer. The K56flex technology is different from other modem technologies in that the downstream data is digitally encoded instead of modulated. This method of data transfer eliminates one analog loop, lowers noise levels, and allows the higher transmission rates. This is an *asymmetrical* technique, so "upstream" transmissions (mostly keystroke and mouse commands from your computer, which require less bandwidth) continue to flow at the slower V.34 rate. The upstream direction remains slower because an analog to digital conversion must still be made at the client end.

In order to maintain sales (and alleviate customers' fears of buying a modem that will shortly become obsolete), all modem manufacturers try to guarantee that their modems will be upgradable through a software patch (a "firmware" upgrade) to meet almost any universal standard. If it turns out that the modem can *not* be upgraded through software, the modem would have to be replaced. Both the firmware and replacement options are provided at no cost to the consumer.

V.90 The finalized ITU standard for 56Kbps modem transmission speeds was introduced in February of 1998. The working name of this standard was *V.pcm* (pulse code modulation), with a final release name of *V.90*. This standard continues to enable high-speed downstream data transfers by digitally encoding all downstream data. Upstream transmissions continue to run at the conventional rates of up to 33.6Kbps (that is, upstream data—data sent from your modem—is sent as an analog signal that mirrors the V.34 standard).

Since the existing telephone network infrastructure cannot support data speeds faster than 56Kbps, V.90 will almost certainly be the *final* analog modem speed standard. Analysts predict that modem sales will grow to about 75 million modems sold per year in 2000, and almost all of these will be V.90. In order to support higher data transfer speeds, computer users will need to move to more performance-oriented communication technologies, such as *cable modem* and *digital subscriber line* (DSL) services. A complete V.90 overview is available in PDF Adobe Acrobat format at **http://www.3com.com/technology/tech_net/white_papers/pdf/50065901.pdf**.

DSVD In addition to simply sending and receiving data, some modern modems incorporate a feature called *Dual Simultaneous Voice and Data* (DSVD). The modem can carry your analog voice as well as computer data. In effect, the modem becomes a speakerphone able to transfer real-time voice and data at the same time (though the bandwidth needed to transfer voice information reduces the available bandwidth for data transfers). Note that the DSVD feature can only be used between two DSVD modems. To use DSVD, you need a sound board with a microphone (to digitize your voice), as well as a set of speakers (to play the voice from the other end). DSVD has found a small but powerful niche among online computer gamers who wish to communicate in real-time as they play.

Voice Mail Some modern modems are providing advanced voice mail features that essentially allow the modem (and PC) to serve as an intelligent answering machine or digital information system. When installed and configured properly, voice mail allows you to create mailboxes, record voice greetings/announcements for each mailbox, record messages to each mailbox, access each mailbox remotely, and even support "fax-on-demand." Voice mail features are particularly popular with small businesses or small-office home-office (SOHO) environments looking to automate messaging and information distribution.

Autodetection/Autoswitching Virtually all current modems can detect the difference between a voice call, a modem call, and an incoming fax and can automatically employ the proper software tools to record the voice message (used with voice mail systems), start BBS or other electronic messaging software to communicate with the calling modem (ideal for remote access software), or record the fax image to the hard drive.

Distinctive Ring Many local phone service areas now support the *distinctive ring* feature that allows several phone numbers to be assigned to the same *physical* telephone line—each assigned number rings with a different ringing pattern. Modems that are compatible with distinctive ring can be placed on the same physical phone line with other devices, but will only answer when a certain ringing pattern is detected.

Caller ID Modern modems are also able to detect the caller's originating telephone number, which is transmitted to the receiving end of the communications link. In its simplest form, Caller ID simply provides an "on-screen" display of the caller's telephone number (used most often when you're receiving calls with the modem in speakerphone mode. In its most enhanced form, database software can trap the Caller ID number and then automatically pull up contact information, notes of past phone conversations, or a wide range of other caller-related information. This is an ideal feature for sales or help desk services.

ISDN Integrated Services Digital Network (or ISDN) technology is a system of digital phone connections that has been available for over a decade. This system allows data to be transmitted in purely digital form. Since ISDN is completely digital, data transfers can be extremely fast—up to 128Kbps. There are two basic types of ISDN service: the *Basic Rate Interface* (BRI) and the *Primary Rate Interface* (PRI). BRI consists of two 64Kbps "B" channels and one 16Kbps "D" channel for a total of 144Kbps. This basic service is intended to meet the needs of most individual users.

For a Basic Rate Interface ISDN line equipped with two "B" channels, one or both of the 64Kbs "B" channels are connected in a virtual permanent circuit. Home and business users who install ISDN adapters in place of their modems can see complex graphic Web pages arriving very quickly (up to 128Kbps). ISDN requires adapters at *both* ends of the transmission, so your Internet service provider also needs an ISDN adapter. To access BRI service, it's necessary to subscribe to an ISDN phone line. The customer must also be within 18,000 feet (about 3.4 miles or 5.5 km) of the telephone company's central office for BRI service—beyond that, expensive repeater devices are required, or ISDN service may not be available at all. Customers will also need special equipment to communicate with the phone company switch and with other ISDN devices. These devices include ISDN Terminal Adapters (sometimes called "ISDN Modems," though that term is technically incorrect) and ISDN Routers. ISDN is generally available from your phone company in most urban areas in the United States and Europe.

xDSL The *Digital Subscriber Line* (or xDSL) is the next generation of PC communication technology that allows for the transmission of voice, video, and data over existing copper telephone lines at very high speeds. xDSL provides dedicated bandwidth that can be up to 143 times *faster* than a 56Kbps modem, and 62 times faster than ISDN. xDSL uses your ordinary phone line, but doesn't tie it up—you can access the Internet while you're using the same phone line for a conversation (or faxing) in addition to the permanent Internet connection.

> The copper telephone lines are often referred to as the "local loop"—or the last mile from the telephone company's central office (CO) to the end-user's home or business.

There are several variations of xDSL technologies; the best known of these technologies are ADSL (*Asymmetric Digital Subscriber Line*) and ADSL Lite (*Splitterless ADSL*, *Universal ADSL*, or *G.lite*). Standard ADSL service is often referred to as *Full Rate ADSL* or *G.dmt*, and is now also known by the ITU standard G.992.1. This technology supports up to 8Mbps bandwidth downstream, and up to 1Mbps upstream. The asymmetrical aspect of ADSL technology makes it ideal for Internet/intranet surfing, video-on-demand, and remote local area network (LAN) access, since these users typically download more information than they send. ADSL requires a voice/data splitter—commonly called a POTS Splitter (for "Plain Old Telephone Service") to be installed at the consumer's home or business location. This device separates voice from data transmissions. For simultaneous use of the telephone and data access, additional phone wires may need to be installed at the location. Full Rate ADSL supports service up to a maximum range of 18,000 feet (about 3.4 miles or 5.5 km) from the telephone company's central office to the end-user.

ADSL Lite technology does *not* require a POTS splitter to be installed at the consumer's home or business, but its performance is slower. ADSL Lite provides a downstream bandwidth up to 1.5Mbps, and an upstream bandwidth up to 512Kbps. It also supports service up to a maximum range of 18,000 feet (about 3.4 miles or 5.5 km) from the central office. ADSL Lite has also been approved as a separate standard by ITU.

With xDSL, telephone companies are competing with cable companies and their cable modem services, and it is thought that quite a few telephone companies will replace their ISDN services with xDSL in most areas. Consequently, ADSL services (and other forms of xDSL) are expected to become more widely available in 2000 and beyond.

WinModems Over the last few years, the PC industry has seen a trend away from conventional hardware "fax/modem" devices and toward simpler, less expensive *software modems* (dubbed "Windows Modems" or "WinModems"). A *hardware modem* (or fax/modem) contains a controller, data pump, and phone network circuit—all integrated into the hardware of the modem device itself. The host computer simply sends data to the modem, and the modem does the rest. By comparison, a software modem eliminates both the controller and data pump portions of a modem, and relies on the host computer's CPU to handle these functions instead. As a result, WinModems are the simplest and least expensive modem type (generally found in low-end PCs), but they make the greatest demands on system processing power.

It is important for you to realize that most modern WinModem designs are quite reliable, but they will *only* work under Windows 95/98. If you use DOS programs that require modem access, you'll need to replace the WinModem with a conventional fax/modem device.

MODEM COMMANDS

Modems used to be "dumb" devices. It was almost impossible for them to do things like answer the ringing telephone line, dial a number, set speaker volume, and so on. Hayes Microcomputer Products developed a product called a "Smartmodem," which accepted high-level commands in the form of ASCII text strings. This technology was dubbed the *Hayes AT command set* (now simply the *AT command set*) and has been the de-facto standard for modem commands ever since. As a consequence, virtually every modem that is *Hayes-compatible* is capable of using the AT command set. Ultimately, the AT commands go a long way to simplify the interface between a modem and communication software. Table 29-1 provides an extensive index of the AT commands—this reference can be particularly helpful when trying to interpret command strings.

TABLE 29-1 INDEX OF THE AT COMMAND SET

Basic AT commands
Note: Settings with an underline (for example, F0) are the default settings for an entry.

(A/) *Repeat Last Command*

(A) *Answer*

(Bx) *CCITT or Bell Modulation*

- **B0** CCITT operation at 300 or 1200bps.
- **B1** BELL operation at 300 or 1200bps.
- **B2** V.23 originate mode: receive 1200bps, transmit 75bps; answer mode: receive 75bps, transmit 1200bps.
- **B3** V.23 originate mode: receive 75bps, transmit 1200bps; answer mode: receive 1200bps, transmit 75bps.
- **B15** Selects V.21 when the modem is at 300 bits/s.
- **B16** Selects Bell 103J when the modem is at 300 bits/s (default).

TABLE 29-1 INDEX OF THE AT COMMAND SET *(CONTINUED)*

(Cx) Carrier Control The modem will accept the C1 command without error in order to assure backward compatibility with communications software that issues the C1 command. The C0 command may instruct some modems not to send carrier (that is, it puts them in a receive-only mode).

- **C0** Transmit carrier always off.
- **C1** Normal transmit carrier switching.

(Dx) *Dial* The valid dial string parameters are described below. Punctuation characters may be used for clarity, with parentheses, hyphen, and spaces being ignored:

0-9 *DTMF digits:* the numbers 0 to 9.

*** *The "star" digit:*** (tone dialing only).

 # *The "pound" digit:* (tone dialing only).

! *Flash:* The modem will go on-hook for a time defined by the value of S29.

, *Dial pause:* The modem will pause for a time specified by S8 before dialing the digits following ",".

; *Return to command state:* Added to the end of a dial string, this causes the modem to return to the command state after it processes the portion of the dial string preceding the ";". This allows the user to issue additional AT commands while remaining off-hook. The additional AT commands may be placed in the original command line following the ";" or may be entered on subsequent command lines. The modem will enter call progress only after an additional dial command is issued without the ";" terminator. Use "H" to abort the dial in progress and go back on-hook.

^ *Enable calling tone:* Applicable to current dial attempt only. The calling tone is an 1800 Hz tone every 3 to 4 seconds that alerts recipient of automatic calling equipment (as defined in CCITT V.25).

> *Ground pulse:* If enabled by country-specific parameter, the modem will generate a grounding pulse on the EARTH relay output.

@ *Wait for silence:* The modem will wait for at least 5 seconds of silence in the call progress frequency band before continuing with the next dial string parameter. If the modem does not detect these 5 seconds of silence before the expiration of the call abort timer (S7), the modem will terminate the call attempt with a NO ANSWER message. If busy detection is enabled, the modem may terminate the call with the BUSY result code. If answer tone arrives during execution of this parameter, the modem handshakes.

$ *List:* Displays a list of dial commands or "Bong Tone" detection.

A-D *DTMF letters:* A, B, C, and D.

J *Fastest speed:* Perform MNP 10 link negotiation at the highest supported speed for this call only.

K *Power adjustment:* Enable power level adjustment during MNP 10 link negotiation for this call only.

L *Redial last number:* The modem will redial the last valid telephone number. This command must be immediately after the "D" with all the following characters ignored.

P *Select pulse dialing:* Pulse dial the numbers that follow until a "T" is encountered. Affects current and subsequent dialing.

R *Delay:* This command will cause the modem to wait 10 seconds after dialing then go into answer mode. This command must be placed at the end of the dial string.

T *Select tone dialing:* Tone dial the numbers that follow until a "P" is encountered. Affects current and subsequent dialing.

W *Wait for dial tone:* The modem will wait for a dial tone before dialing the digits following "W." If no dial tone is detected within the time specified by S6, the modem will abort the rest of the sequence, return on-hook, and generate an error message.

TABLE 29-1 INDEX OF THE AT COMMAND SET *(CONTINUED)*

(Ex) ***Command Echo***

- **E0** Disables command echo.
- **E1** Enables command echo.

(Fx) ***Select Line Modulation***

- **F0** Selects autodetect mode—all connect speeds are possible.
- **F1** Selects V.21 or Bell 103 according to the "B" setting.
- **F2** *Not supported* (some modems use this setting for 600bps).
- **F3** Originator is at 75bps and answerer is at 1200bps.
- **F4** Selects V.22 1200bps or Bell 212A according to the "B" setting.
- **F5** Selects V.22bis as the only acceptable line modulation.
- **F6** Select V.32bis 4800bps or V.32 4800bps as the only acceptable line modulation.
- **F7** Selects V.32bis 7200bps as the only acceptable line modulation.
- **F8** Selects V.32bis 9600bps or V.32 9600bps as the only acceptable line modulation.
- **F9** Selects V.32bis 12000bps as the only acceptable line modulation.
- **F10** Selects V.32bis 14,000bps as the only acceptable line modulation.

(Hx) ***Disconnect [Hangup]***

- **H0** The modem will release the line if the modem is currently online and will terminate any test (AT&T) that is in progress.
- **H1** If on-hook, the modem will go off-hook and enter command mode. The modem will return on-hook after a period of time determined by S7.

(Ix) ***Identification***

- **I0** Reports product code.
- **I1** Reports pre-computed checksum from ROM.
- **I2** The modem will respond OK.
- **I3** Reports firmware revision.
- **I4** Reports modem identifier string.
- **I5** Reports Country Code parameter (for example, "022").
- **I6** Reports modem data pump model and internal code revision.

(Lx) ***Speaker Volume***

- **L0** Low speaker volume.
- **L1** Low speaker volume.
- **L2** Medium speaker volume.
- **L3** High speaker volume.

(Mx) ***Speaker Control***

- **M0** Speaker is always off.
- **M1** Speaker is on during call establishment, but off when receiving carrier.
- **M2** Speaker is always on.
- **M3** Speaker is off when receiving carrier and during dialing, but on during answering.

TABLE 29-1 INDEX OF THE AT COMMAND SET *(CONTINUED)*

(Nx) ***Automode Enable***

- **N0** Automode detection is disabled.
- **N1** Automode detection is enabled.

(Ox) ***Return to On-Line Data Mode***

- **O0** Enters on-line data mode without a retrain.
- **O1** Enters on-line data mode with a retrain before returning to on-line data mode.
- **O3-14** Forces the modem to a new rate that is User Defined (defined in S62).

(P) ***Set Pulse Dial Default***

(Qx) ***Quiet Results Codes***

- **Q0** Enables result codes to the DTE.
- **Q1** Disables result codes to the DTE.

(Sn) ***Read/Write S-Registers***

- **n=v** Sets S-register "n" to the value "v."
- **n?** Reports the value of S-register "n."

(T) ***Set Tone Dial Default***

(Vx) ***Result Code Form***

- **V0** Enables short-form (terse) result codes.
- **V1** Enables long-form (verbose) result codes.

(Wx) ***Error Correction Message Control***

- **W0** Upon connection, the modem reports only the DTE speed.
- **W1** Upon connection, the modem reports the line speed, the error correction protocol, and the DTE speed respectively.
- **W2** Upon connection, the modem reports the DCE speed.

(Xx) ***Extended Result Codes***

- **X0** Sends only OK, CONNECT, RING, NO CARRIER, ERROR, and NO ANSWER result codes.
- **X1** Sends only OK, CONNECT, RING, NO CARRIER, ERROR, NO ANSWER, and CONNECT XXXX.
- **X2** Sends only OK, CONNECT, RING, NO CARRIER, ERROR, NO DIAL TONE, NO ANSWER, and CONNECT XXXX.
- **X3** Sends only OK, CONNECT, RING, NO CARRIER, ERROR, NO ANSWER, CONNECT XXXX and BUSY.
- **X4** Enables monitoring of busy tones; sends all messages.

(Yx) ***Long Space Disconnect***

- **Y0** Disables long space disconnect.
- **Y1** Enables long space disconnect.

(Zx) ***Soft Reset and Restore Profile***

- **Z0** Soft reset and restore stored profile 0.
- **Z1** Soft reset and restore stored profile 1.

TABLE 29-1 INDEX OF THE AT COMMAND SET *(CONTINUED)*

AT "&" commands

(&Bx) ***Autoretrain***

- **&B0** Hang up on a poor received signal.
- **&B1** Retrain on a poor received signal. Hang up if the condition persists.
- **&B2** Do not hang up; do not retrain (i.e., tolerate any line).

(&Cx) ***RLSD (DCD) Option***

- **&C0** RLSD remains ON at all times.
- **&C1** RLSD follows the state of the carrier.

(&Dx) ***DTR Option***

- **&D0** DTR drop is interpreted according to the current &Q setting as follows:
  (&Q0, 5, 6) DTR is ignored (assumed ON). Allows operation with DTE's, which don't provide DTR.
  (&Q1, 4) DTR drop causes the modem to hang up. Auto-answer is not affected.
  (&Q2, 3) DTR drop causes the modem to hang up. Auto-answer is inhibited.
- **&D1** DTR drop is interpreted according to the current &Q setting as follows:
  (&Q0, 1, 4, 5, 6) DTR drop is interpreted by the modem as if the asynchronous escape sequence had been entered. The modem returns to asynchronous command state without disconnecting.
  (&Q2, 3) DTR drop causes the modem to hang up. Auto-answer is inhibited.
- **&D2** DTR drop is interpreted according to the current &Q setting as follows:
  (&Q0-6) DTR drop causes the modem to hang up. Auto-answer is inhibited.
- **&D3** DTR drop is interpreted according to the current &Q setting as follows:
  (&Q0, 1, 4, 5, 6) DTR drop causes the modem to perform a soft reset as if the "Z" command were received. The &Y setting determines which profile is loaded.
  (&Q2, 3) DTR drop causes the modem to hang up. Auto-answer is inhibited.

(&Fx) ***Restore Factory Configuration***

- **&F0** Restore factory configuration 0.
- **&F1** Restore factory configuration 1.

(&Gx) ***Select Guard Tone***

- **&G0** Disables Guard Tone.
- **&G1** Disables Guard Tone.
- **&G2** Selects 1800 Hz guard tone.

(&Hn) ***Sets Transmit Data (TD) flow control (see also &Rn)***

- **&H0** Flow control disabled.
- **&H1** Hardware flow control, Clear to Send (CTS) (default).
- **&H2** Software flow control, XON/XOFF.
- **&H3** Hardware and software flow control.

(&In) ***Sets Receive Data (RD) software flow control (see also &Rn)***

- **&I0** Software flow control disabled (default).
- **&I1** XON/XOFF signals to your modem and remote system.
- **&I2** XON/XOFF signals to your modem only.

(&Jx) ***Telephone Jack Type***

- **&J0** RJ11 telephone jack.
- **&J1** RJ12 or RJ13 telephone jack.

(&Kx) ***Flow Control***

- **&K0** Disables flow control.
- **&K3** Enables RTS/CTS flow control.
- **&K4** Enables XON/XOFF flow control.
- **&K5** Enables transparent XON/XOFF flow control.
- **&K6** Enables both RTS/CTS and XON/XOFF flow control.

TABLE 29-1 INDEX OF THE AT COMMAND SET *(CONTINUED)*

(&Lx) ***Dial Up/Lease Line Option***

- **&L0** Dial line.
- **&L1** Leased line.

(&Mx) ***Asynchronous/Synchronous Mode Selection***

- **&M0** Selects direct asynchronous operation.
- **&M1** Selects synchronous connect mode with asynchronous off-line command mode.
- **&M2** Selects synchronous connect mode with asynchronous off-line command mode.
- **&M3** Selects synchronous connect mode.
- **&M4** Hayes AutoSync mode.

(&Nn) ***Sets connect speed***

- **&N0** Variable rate (default).
- **&N1** 300bps.
- **&N2** 1200bps.
- **&N3** 2400bps.
- **&N4** 4800bps.
- **&N5** 7200bps.
- **&N6** 9600bps.
- **&N7** 12,000bps.
- **&N8** 14,400bps.
- **&N9** 16,800bps.
- **&N10** 19,200bps.
- **&N11** 21,600bps.
- **&N12** 24,000bps.
- **&N13** 26,400bps.
- **&N14** 28,800bps.
- **&N15** 31,200bps.
- **&N16** 33,600bps.
- **&N17** 33,333bps.
- **&N18** 37,333bps.
- **&N19** 41,333bps.
- **&N20** 42,666bps.
- **&N21** 44,000bps.
- **&N22** 45,333bps.
- **&N23** 46,666bps.
- **&N24** 48,000bps.
- **&N25** 49,333bps.
- **&N26** 50,666bps.
- **&N27** 52,000bps.
- **&N28** 53,333bps.
- **&N29** 54,666bps.
- **&N30** 56,000bps.
- **&N31** 57,333bps.

29

TABLE 29-1 INDEX OF THE AT COMMAND SET *(CONTINUED)*

(&Px) ***Dial Pulse Ratio***

- **&P0** Make=39%, break=61% (at 10pps for the US).
- **&P1** Make=33%, break=67% (at 10pps for Europe).
- **&P2** Make=33%, break=67% (at 20pps for Japan).

(&Qx) ***Sync/Async Mode***

- **&Q0** Selects direct asynchronous operation.
- **&Q1** Selects synchronous connect mode with async off-line command mode.
- **&Q2** Selects synchronous connect mode with async off-line command mode.
- **&Q3** Selects synchronous connect mode.
- **&Q4** Select AutoSync operation.
- **&Q5** The modem will try to negotiate an error-corrected link.
- **&Q6** Selects asynchronous operation in normal mode (speed buffering).
- **&Q8** MNP error control mode. If an MNP error control protocol is not established, the modem will fallback according to the current user setting in S36.
- **&Q9** V.42 or MNP error control mode. If neither error control protocol is established, the modem will fallback according to the current user setting in S36.

Starting AutoSync. Set registers S19, S20, and S25 to the desired values before selecting AutoSync operation with &Q4. After the CONNECT message is issued, the modem waits the period of time specified by S25 before examining DTR. If DTR is on, the modem enters the synchronous operating state; if DTR is off, the modem terminates the line connection and returns to the asynchronous command state.

Stopping AutoSync. AutoSync operation is stopped upon loss of carrier or the ON-to-OFF transition of DTR. Loss of carrier will cause the modem to return to the asynchronous command state. An ON-to-OFF transition of DTR will cause the modem to return to the asynchronous command state and either not terminate the line connection (&D1 active) or terminate the line connection (any other &Dn command active).

(&Rx) ***RTS/CTS Option***

- **&R0** In Sync mode, CTS tracks the state of RTS; the RTS-to-CTS delay is defined by S26. In Async mode, CTS acts according to V.25bis handshake.
- **&R1** In Sync mode, CTS is always ON (RTS transitions are ignored). In Async, CTS will drop only if required by flow control.
- **&R2** Received Data to computer only on RTS.

(&Sx) ***DSR Override***

- **&S0** DSR will remain ON at all times.
- **&S1** DSR will become active after answer tone has been detected and inactive after the carrier has been lost.

(&Tx) ***Test and Diagnostics***

- **&T0** Terminates the test in progress. Clears S16.
- **&T1** Initiates local analog loopback, V.54 Loop 3.
- **&T2** Returns an ERROR message.
- **&T3** Initiates local digital loopback, V.54 Loop 2.
- **&T4** Enables digital loopback acknowledgment for remote request.
- **&T5** Disables digital loopback acknowledgement for remote request.
- **&T6** Initiates remote digital loopback.
- **&T7** Remote digital with self-test and error detector.
- **&T8** Initiates local analog loopback, V.54 Loop 3, with self test.

TABLE 29-1 INDEX OF THE AT COMMAND SET *(CONTINUED)*

(&Un) ***Sets floor connect speed***

- **&U0** Disabled (the default).
- **&U1** 300bps.
- **&U2** 1200bps.
- **&U3** 2400bps.
- **&U4** 4800bps.
- **&U5** 7200bps.
- **&U6** 9600bps.
- **&U7** 12,000bps.
- **&U8** 14,400bps.
- **&U9** 16,800bps.
- **&U10** 19,200bps.
- **&U11** 21,600bps.
- **&U12** 24,000bps.
- **&U13** 26,400bps.
- **&U14** 28,800bps.
- **&U15** 31,200bps.
- **&U16** 33,600bps.
- **&U17** 33,333bps.
- **&U18** 37,333bps.
- **&U19** 41,333bps.
- **&U20** 42,666bps.
- **&U21** 44,000bps.
- **&U22** 45,333bps.
- **&U23** 46,666bps.
- **&U24** 48,000bps.
- **&U25** 49,333bps.
- **&U26** 50,666bps.
- **&U27** 52,000bps.
- **&U28** 53,333bps.
- **&U29** 54,666bps.
- **&U30** 56,000bps.
- **&U31** 57,333bps.

(&Vx) ***Display Current Configuration and Stored Profiles***

- **&V0** View active file, stored profile 0, and stored phone numbers.
- **&V1** View active file, stored profile 1, and stored phone numbers.

(&Wx) ***Store Current Configuration***

- **&W0** Store the current configuration as profile 0.
- **&W1** Store the current configuration as profile 1.

(&Xx) ***Sync Transmit Clock Source Option***

- **&X0** The modem generates the transmit clock.
- **&X1** The DTE generates the transmit clock.
- **&X2** The modem derives the transmit clock.

29

TABLE 29-1 INDEX OF THE AT COMMAND SET *(CONTINUED)*

(&Yx) ***Designate a Default Reset Profile***

- **&Y0** The modem will use profile 0.
- **&Y1** The modem will use profile 1.

(&ZL?) ***Displays the last executed dial string***

(&Zn?) ***Displays the phone number stored at position "n" (n = 0-3)***

(&Zn=x) ***Store Telephone Number***

- **&Zn=x** (n = 0 to 3, and x = dial string)

AT "%" commands

(%BAUD) ***Bit Rate Multiplier***

(%Cx) ***Enable/Disable Data Compression***

- **%C0** Disables data compression. Resets S46 bit 1.
- **%C1** Enables MNP 5 data compression negotiation. Resets S46 bit 1.
- **%C2** Enables V.42bis data compression. Sets S46 bit 1.
- **%C3** Enables both V.42bis and MNP 5 data compression. Sets S46 bit 1.

(%CCID) ***Enable Caller ID***

(%CD) ***Carrier Detect Lamp***

(%CDIA) ***Display last DIAG***

(%CIDS) ***Store ID Numbers***

(%CRID) ***Repeat Last ID***

(%CSIG) ***Store SIG Numbers***

(%CXID) ***XID Enable***

(%Dx) ***V.42bis Dictionary Size***

- **%D0** Dictionary set to 512.
- **%D1** Dictionary set to 1024.
- **%D2** Dictionary set to 2048.
- **%D3** Dictionary set to 4096.

(%Ex) ***Enable/Disable Line Quality Monitor and Auto-Retrain Fallback/Fall Forward***

- **%E0** Disable line quality monitor and auto-retrain.
- **%E1** Enable line quality monitor and auto-retrain.
- **%E2** Enable line quality monitor and fallback/fall forward.
- **%E3** Enable line quality monitor and auto-retrain, but hang-up when EQM reaches threshold.

(%Gx) ***Auto Fall Forward/Fallback Enable***

- **%G0** Disabled.
- **%G1** Enabled.

(%L) ***Line Signal Level***

(%Mx) ***Compression Type***

- **%M0** Compression disabled.
- **%M1** Transmit compression only.
- **%M2** Receive compression only.
- **%M3** Two-way compression.

(%P) ***Clear Encoder Dictionary***

(%Q) ***Line Signal Quality***

(%Sx) ***Set Maximum String Length in V.42bis***

(%SCBR) ***Call Back Reference Outgoing Calls***

(%SKEY) ***Store Authentication Key Outgoing Call***

(%SPRT) ***Security Mode—Outgoing Calls***

(%SPNP) ***Serial Plug and Play Control***

TABLE 29-1 INDEX OF THE AT COMMAND SET *(CONTINUED)*

(%SPWD) ***Password Outgoing Calls***

(%SSPW) ***Supervisor Password Outgoing Calls***

(%SUID) ***User ID Outgoing Calls***

(%TTx) ***PTT Testing Utilities***

- **%TT00-%TT09** DTMF tone dial digits 0 to 9.
- **%TT0A** DTMF digit *.
- **%TT0B** DTMF digit A.
- **%TT0C** DTMF digit B.
- **%TT0D** DTMF digit C.
- **%TT0E** DTMF digit #.
- **%TT0F** DTMF digit D.
- **%TT10** V.21 channel no. 1 mark (originate) symbol.
- **%TT11** V.21 channel no. 2 mark symbol.
- **%TT12** V.23 backward channel mark symbol.
- **%TT13** V.23 forward channel mark symbol.
- **%TT14** V.22 originate (call mark) signaling at 600bps (NOT SUPPORTED).
- **%TT15** V.22 originate (call mark) signaling at 1200bps.
- **%TT16** V.22bis originate (call mark) signaling at 2400bps.
- **%TT17** V.22 answer signaling (guard tone if PTT required).
- **%TT18** V.22bis answer signaling (guard tone if required).
- **%TT19** V.21 channel no. 1 space symbol.
- **%TT20** V.32 9600bps.
- **%TT21** V.32bis 14,000bps.
- **%TT1A** V.21 channel no. 2 space symbol.
- **%TT1B** V.23 backward channel space symbol.
- **%TT1C** V.23 forward channel space symbol.
- **%TT30** Silence (on-line), that is, go off-hook.
- **%TT31** V.25 answer tone.
- **%TT32** 1800 Hz guard tone.
- **%TT33** V.25 calling tone (1300 Hz).
- **%TT34** Fax calling tone (1100 Hz).
- **%TT40** V.21 channel 2.
- **%TT41** V.27ter 2400bps.
- **%TT42** V.27ter 4800bps.
- **%TT43** V.29 7200bps.
- **%TT44** V.29 9600bps.
- **%TT45** V.17 7200bps long train.
- **%TT46** V.17 7200bps short train.
- **%TT47** V.17 9600bps long train.
- **%TT48** V.17 9600bps short train.
- **%TT49** V.17 12,000bps long train.
- **%TT4A** V.17 12,000bps short train.
- **%TT4B** V.17 14,000bps long train.
- **%TT4C** V.17 14,000bps short train.

TABLE 29-1 INDEX OF THE AT COMMAND SET *(CONTINUED)*

AT "/" commands

(\Ax) ***Select Maximum MNP Block Size***

- **\A0** 64 characters.
- **\A1** 128 characters.
- **\A2** 192 characters.
- **\A3** 256 characters.
- **\A4** Max 32 characters (for ETC enhanced throughput cellular).

(\Bx) ***Transmit Break to Remote***

- **\B1–\B9** Break length in 100mS units (default = 3—non-error corrected mode only).

(\Cx) ***Set Autoreliable Buffer***

- **\C0** Does not buffer data.
- **\C1** Buffers data on the answering modem for 4 seconds.
- **\C2** Does not buffer data on the answering modem.

(\Ex) ***Optimize Local Echo***

(\Gx) ***Modem-to-Modem Flow Control (XON/XOFF)***

- **\G0** Disables modem-to-modem XON/XOFF flow control.
- **\G1** Enables modem-to-modem XON/XOFF flow control.

(\Jx) ***Constant DTE Speed Option***

- **\J0** DCE and DTE rates are independent.
- **\J1** DTE rate adjusts to DCE connection rate after on-line.

(\Kx) ***Break Control.*** If the modem receives a break from the DTE when the modem is operating in data transfer mode:

- **\K0** Enter on-line command mode, no break sent to the remote modem.
- **\K1** Clear data buffers and send break to remote modem.
- **\K2** Same as \K0.
- **\K3** Send break to remote modem immediately.
- **\K4** Same as \K0.
- **\K5** Send break to remote modem in sequence with transmitted data.

If the modem is in the on-line command state (waiting for AT commands) during a data connection, and the \B command is received in order to send a break to the remote modem:

- **\K0** Clear data buffers and send break to remote modem.
- **\K1** Clear data buffers and send break to remote modem (same as \K0).
- **\K2** Send break to remote modem immediately.
- **\K3** Send break to remote modem immediately (same as \K2).
- **\K4** Send break to remote modem in sequence with data.
- **\K5** Send break to remote modem in sequence with data (same as \K4).

If there is a break received from a remote modem during a non-error corrected connection:

- **\K0** Clears data buffers and sends break to the DTE.
- **\K1** Clears data buffers and sends break to the DTE (same as \K0).
- **\K2** Send a break immediately to DTE.
- **\K3** Send a break immediately to DTE (same as \K2).
- **\K4** Send a break in sequence with received data to DTE.
- **\K5** Send a break in sequence with received data to DTE (same as \K4).

(\Lx) ***MNP Block/Stream Mode Select***

- **\L0** Use stream mode for MNP connection.
- **\L1** Use interactive block mode for MNP connection.

TABLE 29-1 INDEX OF THE AT COMMAND SET *(CONTINUED)*

(\Nx) ***Operating Mode***

- **\N0** Selects normal speed buffered mode.
- **\N1** Selects direct mode.
- **\N2** Selects reliable (error correction) mode.
- **\N3** Selects auto reliable mode.
- **\N4** Selects LAPM error correction mode.
- **\N5** Selects MNP error correction mode.

(\O) ***Originate Reliable Link Control***

(\Qx) ***DTE Flow Control Options***

- **\Q0** Disables flow control.
- **\Q1** XON/XOFF software flow control.
- **\Q2** CTS flow control to the DTE.
- **\Q3** RTS/CTS hardware flow control.

(\S) ***Report Active Configuration***

(\Tx) ***Set Inactivity Timer***

- **n=0** Disable the inactivity timer.
- **n=1-90** Length in minutes.

(\U) ***Accept Reliable Link Control***

(\Vx) ***Protocol Result Code***

- **\V0** Disable protocol result code (i.e. CONNECT 9600).
- **\V1** Enable protocol result code (i.e. CONNECT 9600/LAPM).

(\Xx) ***Set XON/XOFF Pass-through Option***

- **\X0** If XON/XOFF flow control enabled, do not pass XON/XOFF to remote modem or local DTE.
- **\X1** Always pass XON/XOFF to the remote modem or local DTE.

(\Y) ***Switch to Reliable Operation***

(\Z) ***Switch to Normal Operation***

AT "-" commands

(-Jx) ***Set V.42 Detection Phase***

- **-J0** Disables the V.42 detection phase.
- **-J1** Enables the V.42 detection phase.

(-Kx) ***MNP Extended Services***

- **-K0** Disables V.42 LAPM to MNP 10 conversion.
- **-K1** Enables V.42 LAPM to MNP 10 conversion.
- **-K2** Enables V.42 LAPM to MNP 10 conversion; inhibits MNP Extended Services.

(-Qx) ***Enable Fallback to V.22 bis/V.22***

- **-Q0** Disables fallback to 2400bps (V.22bis) and 1200bps (V.22). Fallback only to 4800bps.
- **-Q1** Enables fallback to 2400bps (V.22bis) and 1200bps (V.22).

(-SDR=n) ***Distinctive Ring Reporting***

- **-SDR=1** Type 1 Distinctive Ring Detect.
- **-SDR=2** Type 2 Distinctive Ring Detect.
- **-SDR=3** Type 1 and Type 2 Distinctive Ring Detect.
- **-SDR=4** Type 3 Distinctive Ring Detect.
- **-SDR=5** Type 1 and Type 3 Distinctive Ring Detect.
- **-SDR=6** Type 2 and Type 3 Distinctive Ring Detect.
- **-SDR=7** Types 1, 2, and 3 Distinctive Ring Detect.

TABLE 29-1 INDEX OF THE AT COMMAND SET *(CONTINUED)*

Distinctive Ring Types

TYPE	ON	OFF	ON	OFF	ON	OFF	SOUND
1	2.0	4.0					Rinnnnnnnnnng
2	0.8	0.4	0.8	4.0			Ring Ring
3	0.4	0.2	0.4	0.2	0.8	4.0	Ring Ring Rinnng

(-SEC=n) ***LAPM and MNP Link Control***

- **-SEC=0** Disable LAPM or MNP10. EC transmit level set in register S91.
- **-SEC=1, 0-30** Enable LAPM or MNP10. EC transmit level set to value after comma (0 to 30).

(-SKEY) ***Program Key***

(-SPRT) ***Remote Security Mode***

(-SPWD) ***Program Password***

(-SSE) ***Simultaneous Voice Data***

(-SSG) ***Set DSVD Receive Gain***

(-SSKY) ***Program Supervisor Key***

(-SSP) ***Select DVSD Port***

(-SSPW) ***Supervisor Password***

(-SUID) ***Program User ID***

(-V) ***Display Root Firmware Version Number***

AT " commands

("Hx) ***V.42bis Compression Control***

- **"H0** Disable V.42bis.
- **"H1** Enable V.42bis only when transmitting data.
- **"H2** Enable V.42bis only when receiving data.
- **"H3** Enable V.42bis for both directions.

("Nx) ***V.42bis Dictionary Size***

- **"N0** 512 bytes.
- **"N1** 1024 bytes.
- **"N2** 1536 bytes.

("Ox) ***Select V.42bis Maximum String Length***

- **n=6-64**
- **n=32**

AT "~" commands

(~Dx) ***Factory Configured Operating Profile***

- **~D0** Disable (No Error Correction, No Data Compression).
- **~D1** MNP4.
- **~D2** MNP5.
- **~D3** V.42.
- **~D4** V.42bis.

AT "~~" commands

(~~Lx) ***Digital Line Current Sensing On/Off***

- **~~L0** Turn off digital line current sensing.
- **~~L1** Turn on digital line current sensing.

TABLE 29-1 INDEX OF THE AT COMMAND SET *(CONTINUED)*

(~~S=m) *Digital Line Over-Current Sense Time Set.*

- m=0 through 9
- m=4

(~~S?) *Display Line Over-Current Sense Time Display*

AT "+" fax commands

Some modems support fax commands conforming to EIA standard 578. These commands are given here with short descriptions—they also typically support error correction and V.17terbo at 19.2KB.

(+FAA) *Auto Answer Mode Parameter*

(+FAXERR=x) *Fax Error Value Parameter*

(+FBOR=x) *Phase C Data Bit Order Parameter*

(+FBUF?) *Read the Buffer Size*

(+FCLASS?) *Service Class Indication*

- **+FCLASS?** 000 if in data mode; 001 if in fax class 1.

(+FCLASS=x) *Service Class Capabilities*

- **+FCLASS=?.**
- 0—modem is set up for data mode.
- 0,1—modem is capable of data and fax class I services.

(+FCLASS=n) *Service Class Selection*

- **+FCLASS=0** Select data mode.
- **+FCLASS=1** Select fax class 1.

(+FCR) *Capability to Receive*

(+FDCC=x) *Modem Capabilities Parameter*

(+FDCS=x) *Current Session Results*

(+FDIS=x) *Current Session Negotiation Parameters*

(+FDR) *Begin or Continue Phase C Receive Data*

(+FDT=x) *Data Transmission*

(+FET=x) *Transmit Page Punctuation*

(+FK) *Terminate Session*

(+FLID=x) *Local ID String Parameter*

(+FMDL?) *Request Modem Model*

(+FMFR?) *Request Modem IC Manufacturer*

(+FPHCTO) *Phase C Time Out*

(+FPTS=x) *Page Transfer Status*

(+FREV?) *Request Modem Revision*

(+FRH=?) *FAX SDLC Receive Capabilities*

(+FRH=n) *Modem Accept Training (SDLC)*

(+FRM=?) *FAX Normal Mode Receive Capabilities*

(+FRM=n) *Modem Accept Training*

(+FRS=?) *FRS Range Capabilities*

(+FRS=n) *Receive Silence*

- **+FRS=4** That is, wait 40mS for silence.

(+FTH=?) *FAX SDLC Mode Transmit Capabilities*

(+FTH=n) *Modem Initiate Training (SDLC)*

(+FTM=?) *FAX Normal Mode Transmit Capabilities*

(+FTM=n) *Modem Initiate Training*

TABLE 29-1 INDEX OF THE AT COMMAND SET *(CONTINUED)*

(+FTS=?) ***FTS Range Capabilities***

(+FTS=n) ***Transmission Silence***

- **+FTS=5** That is, fax transmission silence for 50mS.

(+VCID) ***Caller ID Service***

Other AT commands

(_+BRC+_) ***Remote Escape into BRC State (from Host Online Data Mode)***

($BRC) ***Enable/Disable Host***

(#CID) ***Enable Caller ID Detection***

(:E) ***Compromise Equalizer Enable***

- **:E0** Disables the equalizer.
- **:E1** Enables the equalizer.

($GIVEBRC) ***Enter BRC State (from Target Online Command State)***

(*Hx) ***Link Negotiation Speed***

- ***H0** Link negotiation occurs at the highest supported speed.
- ***H1** Link negotiation occurs at 1200bps.
- ***H2** Link negotiation occurs at 4800bps.

()Mx) ***Enable Cellular Power Level Adjustment***

- **)M0** Disables power level adjustment during MNP 10 link negotiation.
- **)M1** Enables power level adjustment during MNP 10 link negotiation.

(@Mx) ***Initial Cellular Power Level Setting***

- **@M0** -26 dBm.
- **@M1** -30 dBm.
- **@M2** -10 dBm.
- **@M26** 26 dBm.

Virtually all AT command strings start with the prefix "AT" (Attention). For example, the command string: "ATZE1Q0V1" contains five separate commands: Attention (AT), Reset the modem to its power-up defaults (Z), Enable the command echo to send command characters back to the sender (E1), Send command result codes back to the PC (Q0), and Select text result codes, which causes words to be used as result codes (V1). While this may seem like a mouthful, a typical modem can accept command strings up to 40 characters long. The term *result codes* refers to the messages that the modem generates when a command string is processed. Table 29-2 outlines a series of typical result codes. Either numbers (default) or words (using the V1 command) can be returned. When a command is processed correctly, a result code OK is produced, or CONNECT when a successful connection is established.

Many attributes of the Hayes-compatible modem are programmable. To accommodate this feature, each parameter must be held in a series of memory locations (called *S-registers*). Each S-register is described in Table 29-3. For example, the default escape sequence for the AT command set is a series of three plusses: "+++". You could change this character by writing a new ASCII character to register S2. For the most part, default S-register values are fine for most work, but you can often optimize the modem's operation by experimenting with the register values. Since S-register contents must be maintained after power is removed from the modem, the registers are stored in nonvolatile RAM (NVRAM).

TABLE 29-2 LIST OF TYPICAL MODEM RESULT CODES

RESPONSE CODE #	VERBOSE	DEFINITION
0	OK	The OK code is returned by the modem to acknowledge execution of a command line.
1	CONNECT	Sent alone when speed is 300bps.
2	RING	The modem sends this result code when incoming ringing is detected on the line.
3	NO CARRIER	No modem carrier signal is detected.
4	ERROR	Generated from AT command string errors, if a command cannot be executed, or if a parameter is outside of range.
5	CONNECT 1200	Connection at 1200bps.
6	NO DIAL TONE	No dial tone was received from the local line.
7	BUSY	A busy tone has been detected.
8	NO ANSWER	The remote modem does not answer properly.
9	CONNECT 600	Connection at 600bps.
10	CONNECT 2400	Connection at 2400bps.
11	CONNECT 4800	Connection at 4800bps.
12	CONNECT 9600	Connection at 9600bps.
13	CONNECT 14400	Connection at 14,400bps.
14	CONNECT 19200	Connection at 19,200bps.
15	CONNECT 16800	Connection at 16,800bps.
16	CONNECT 19200	Connection at 19,200bps.
17	CONNECT 38400	Connection at 38,400bps.
18	CONNECT 57600	Connection at 57,600bps.
22	CONNECT 1200TX/75RX	Connection at 1200bps/75bps.
23	CONNECT 75TX/1200RX	Connection at 75bps/1200bps.
24	CONNECT 7200	Connection at 7200bps.
25	CONNECT 12000	Connection at 12,000bps.
26	CONNECT 1200/75	Connection at 1200bps/75bps (V.23).
27	CONNECT 75/1200	Connection at 75bps/1200bps (V.23).
28	CONNECT 38400	Connection at 38,400bps.
29	CONNECT 21600	Connection at 21,600bps.
30	CONNECT 24000	Connection at 24,000bps.
31	CONNECT 26400	Connection at 26,400bps.
32	CONNECT 28800	Connection at 28,800bps.
33	CONNECT 115200	Connection at 115.2Kbps.
35	DATA	Modem data is present.
40	CARRIER 300	A V.21 or Bell 103 carrier has been detected on the line.
42	CARRIER 75/1200	A V.23 backward channel carrier has been detected on the line.
43	CARRIER 1200/75	A V.23 forward channel carrier has been detected on the line.
44	CARRIER 1200/75	A V.23 forward channel carrier has been detected on the line.
45	CARRIER 75/1200	A V.23 backward channel carrier has been detected on the line.
46	CARRIER 1200	The high or low channel carrier in either V.22 or Bell 212 mode has been detected on the line.

29

TABLE 29-2 LIST OF TYPICAL MODEM RESULT CODES *(CONTINUED)*

RESPONSE CODE #	VERBOSE	DEFINITION
47	CARRIER 2400	The high or low channel carrier in V.22bis or V.34 mode has been detected on the line.
48	CARRIER 4800	The channel carrier in V.32, V.32bis, or V.34 has been detected on the line.
49	CARRIER 7200	The channel carrier in V.32bis or V.34 has been detected.
50	CARRIER 9600	The channel carrier in V.32, V.32bis, or V.34 mode has been detected on the line.
51	CARRIER 12000	The channel carrier in V.32bis or V.34 mode has been detected.
52	CARRIER 14400	The channel carrier in V.32bis or V.34 mode has been detected.
53	CARRIER 16800	The channel carrier in V.32terbo or V.34 mode has been detected on the line.
54	CARRIER 19200	The channel carrier in V.32terbo or V.34 mode has been detected on the line.
55	CARRIER 21600	The channel carrier in V.34 mode has been detected on the line.
56	CARRIER 24000	The channel carrier in V.34 mode has been detected on the line.
57	CARRIER 26400	The channel carrier in V.34 mode has been detected on the line.
58	CARRIER 28800	The channel carrier in V.34 mode has been detected on the line.
66	COMPRESSION: CLASS 5	The modem has connected with MNP class 5 data compression.
67	COMPRESSION: V.42bis	The modem has connected with V.42bis data compression.
69	COMPRESSION: NONE	The modem has connected without data compression.
70	PROTOCOL: NONE	The modem has connected without any form of error correction.
76	PROTOCOL: NONE	The modem has connected without any form of error correction.
77	PROTOCOL: LAP-M	The modem has connected with V.42 LAPM error correction.
80	PROTOCOL: MNP	The modem has connected with MNP error correction.
81	PROTOCOL: MNP 2	The modem has connected with MNP error correction.
82	PROTOCOL: MNP 3	The modem has connected with MNP error correction.
83	PROTOCOL: MNP 2, 4	The modem has connected with MNP error correction.
84	PROTOCOL: MNP 3, 4	The modem has connected with MNP error correction.
100	CONNECT 28000 EC*	Connection at 28,000 bit/s (V.90 mode), (Lucent Technologies).
101	CONNECT 29333 EC*	Connection at 29,333 bit/s (V.90 mode), (Lucent Technologies).
102	CONNECT 30666 EC*	Connection at 30,666 bit/s (V.90 mode), (Lucent Technologies).
103	CONNECT 33333 EC*	Connection at 33,333 bit/s (V.90 mode), (Lucent Technologies).
104	CONNECT 34666 EC*	Connection at 34,666 bit/s (V.90 mode) (Lucent Technologies)
105	CONNECT 37333 EC*	Connection at 37,333 bit/s (V.90 mode) (Lucent Technologies)
106	CONNECT 38666 EC*	Connection at 38,666 bit/s (V.90 mode) (Lucent Technologies)
107	CONNECT 41333 EC*	Connection at 41,333 bit/s (V.90 mode) (Lucent Technologies)
108	CONNECT 42666 EC*	Connection at 42,666 bit/s (V.90 mode), (Lucent Technologies).
109	CONNECT 45333 EC*	Connection at 45,333 bit/s (V.90 mode), (Lucent Technologies).
110	CONNECT 46666 EC*	Connection at 46,666 bit/s (V.90 mode), (Lucent Technologies).
111	CONNECT 49333 EC*	Connection at 49,333 bit/s (V.90 mode), (Lucent Technologies).
112	CONNECT 50666 EC*	Connection at 50,666 bit/s (V.90 mode), (Lucent Technologies).
113	CONNECT 53333 EC*	Connection at 53,333 bit/s (V.90 mode), (Lucent Technologies).
114	CONNECT 54666 EC*	Connection at 54,666 bit/s (V.90 mode), (Lucent Technologies).
151	CONNECT 31200	Connection at 31,200bps.

TABLE 29-2 LIST OF TYPICAL MODEM RESULT CODES *(CONTINUED)*

RESPONSE CODE #	VERBOSE	DEFINITION
152	CONNECT 31200/ARQ	Connection at 31,200bps with Automatic Repeat Request.
153	CONNECT 31200/V34	Connection at 31,200bps with fallback to 28.8KB (V.34).
154	CONNECT 31200/ARQ/V34	Connection at 31,200bps with ARQ and fallback to 28.8KB.
155	CONNECT 33600	Connection at 33,600bps.
156	CONNECT 33600/ARQ	Connection at 33,600bps with Automatic Repeat Request.
157	CONNECT 33600/V34	Connection at 33,600bps with fallback to 28.8KB (V.34).
158	CONNECT 33600/ARQ/V34	Connection at 33,600bps with ARQ and fallback to 28.8KB.
180	CONNECT 33333	(3COM—USR Modem).
184	CONNECT 37333	(3COM—USR Modem).
188	CONNECT 41333	(3COM—USR Modem).
192	CONNECT 42666	(3COM—USR Modem).
196	CONNECT 44000	(3COM—USR Modem).
200	CONNECT 45333	(3COM—USR Modem).
204	CONNECT 46666	(3COM—USR Modem).
208	CONNECT 48000	(3COM—USR Modem).
212	CONNECT 49333	(3COM—USR Modem).
216	CONNECT 50666	(3COM—USR Modem).
220	CONNECT 52000	(3COM—USR Modem).
224	CONNECT 53333	(3COM—USR Modem).
228	CONNECT 54666	(3COM—USR Modem).
232	CONNECT 56000	(3COM—USR Modem).
236	CONNECT 57333	(3COM—USR Modem).

* EC appears only when the extended result codes configuration option is enabled. EC is replaced by one of the following symbols, depending upon the error control method used:

- V42bis—V.42 error control and V.42bis data compression.
- V42—V.42 error control only.
- MNP 5—MNP class 4 error control and MNP class 5 data compression.
- MNP 4—MNP class 4 error control only.

TABLE 29-3 INDEX OF S-REGISTER ASSIGNMENTS

REGISTER	FUNCTION	RANGE	UNITS	DEFAULT
S0	Rings to Auto-Answer	0-255	Rings	0
S1	Ring Counter	0-255	Rings	0
S2	Escape Character	0-255	ASCII	43
S3	Carriage Return Character	0-127	ASCII	13
S4	Line Feed Character	0-127	ASCII	10
S5	Backspace Character	0-255	ASCII	8
S6	Wait Time for Dial Tone	2-255	Seconds	4
S7	Wait for Carrier	1-255	Seconds	50
S8	Pause Time for (,) Comma	0-255	Seconds	2

TABLE 29-3 INDEX OF S-REGISTER ASSIGNMENTS *(CONTINUED)*

REGISTER	FUNCTION	RANGE	UNITS	DEFAULT
S9	Carrier Detect Response Time	1-255	1/10 sec	6
S10	Carrier Loss Disconnect Time	1-255	1/10 sec	14
S11	Touch Tone (DTMF) Duration	50-255	1/1000 sec	95
S12	Escape Code Guard Time	0-255	2/100 sec	50
S13	*Reserved*	---	---	---
S14	General Bit Mapped Options	---	---	138 (8Ah)
S15	*Reserved*	---	---	---
S16	Test Mode Bit Map Options (&T)	---	---	0
S17	*Reserved*	---	---	---
S18	Test Timer	0-255	Seconds	0
S19	Auto-Sync Bit Map Register	---	---	0
S20	AutoSync HDLC Address or BSC Sync Character	0-255	---	0
S21	V.24/General Bit Map Options	---	---	4 (04h)
S22	Speaker/Results Bit Map Options	---	---	118 (76h)
S23	General Bit Map Options	---	---	55 (37h)
S24	Sleep Inactivity Timer	0-255	Seconds	1
S25	Delay to DTR Off	0-255	1/100 sec	5
S26	RTS-to-CTS Delay	0-255	1/100 sec	1
S27	General Bit Map Options	---	---	73 (49h) with ECC 74 (4Ah) without ECC
S28	General Bit Map Options	---	---	0
S29	Flash Dial Modifier Time	0-255	10 ms	70
S30	Disconnect Activity Timer	0-255	10 sec	0
S31	General Bit Map Options	---	---	194 (C2h)
S32	XON Character	0-255	ASCII	17 (11h)
S33	XOFF Character	0-255	ASCII	19 (13h)
S34	*Reserved*	---	---	---
S35	*Reserved*	---	---	---
S36	LAPM Failure Control	---	---	7
S37	Line Connection Speed	---	---	0
S38	Delay Before Forced Hangup	0-255	Seconds	20
S39	Flow Control	---	---	3
S40	General Bit Map Options	---	---	105 (69h) No MNP 10 107 (6Bh) MNP 10
S41	General Bit Mapped Options	---	---	131 (83h)
S43	Auto Fallback Character for MNP Negotiation	0-255	---	13
S44	Data Framing	---	---	---
S46	Data Compression Control	---	---	136 (no compression) 138 (with compression)
S46*	Automatic Sleep Timer	0-255	100 mS	100
S47	Forced Sleep Timer with Powerdown Mode in PCMCIA	0-255	100 mS	10
S48	V.42 Negotiation Control	---	---	7

TABLE 29-3 INDEX OF S-REGISTER ASSIGNMENTS *(CONTINUED)*

REGISTER	FUNCTION	RANGE	UNITS	DEFAULT
S49	Buffer Low Limit	---	---	---
S50	Buffer High Limit	---	---	---
S50*	FAX/Data Mode Selection	---	---	0 (data mode) 1 (fax mode)
S53	Global PAD Configuration	---	---	---
S55	AutoStream Protocol Request	---	---	---
S56	AutoStream Protocol Status	---	---	---
S57	Network Options Register	---	---	---
S58	BTLZ String Length	6-64	bytes	32
S59	Leased Line Failure Alarm	---	---	---
S60	Leased Line Failure Action	---	---	---
S61	Leased Line Retry Number	---	---	---
S62	Leased Line Restoral Options	---	---	---
S62*	DTE Rate Status	0-17	---	16 (57,600bps)
S63	Leased Line Transmit Level	---	---	---
S64	Leased Line Receive Level	---	---	---
S69	Link Layer k Protocol	---	---	---
S70	Max Number of Retransmissions	---	---	---
S71	Link Layer Timeout	---	---	---
S72	Loss of Flag Idle Timeout	---	---	---
S72*	DTE Speed Select	0-18	---	0 (last autobaud)
S73	No Activity Timeout	---	---	---
S74	Minimum Incoming LCN	---	---	---
S75	Minimum Incoming LCN	---	---	---
S76	Maximum Incoming LCN	---	---	---
S77	Maximum Incoming LCN	---	---	---
S78	Outgoing LCN	---	---	---
S79	Outgoing LCN	---	---	---
S80	X.25 Packet Level N20 Parameter	---	---	---
S80*	Soft Switch Functions	---	---	1
S81	X.25 Packet Level T20 Parameter	---	---	---
S82	LAPM Break Control	---	---	128 (40h)
S84	ASU Negotiation	---	---	---
S85	ASU Negotiation Status	---	---	---
S86	Call Failure Reason Code	0-255	---	---
S87	Fixed Speed DTE Interface	---	---	---
S91	PSTN Xmit Attenuation Level	0-15	-dBm	10
S92	Fax Xmit Attenuation Level	0-15	-dBm	10
S92*	MI/MIC Options	---	---	---
S93	V.25bis Async Interface Speed	---	---	---
S94	V.25bis Mode Control	---	---	---
S95	Result Code Messages Control	---	---	0
S97	V.32 Late Connecting Handshake Timing	---	---	---

TABLE 29-3 INDEX OF S-REGISTER ASSIGNMENTS *(CONTINUED)*

REGISTER	FUNCTION	RANGE	UNITS	DEFAULT
S99	Leased Line Transmit Level	0-15	-dBm	10
S101	Distinctive Ring Reporting	0-63	---	0
S105	Frame Size	---	---	---
S108	Signal Quality Selector	---	---	---
S109	Carrier Speed Selector	---	---	---
S110	V.32/V.32bis Selector	---	---	---
S113	Calling Tone Control	---	---	---
S116	Connection Timeout	---	---	---
S121	Use of DTR	---	---	---
S122	V.13 Selection	---	---	---
S141	Detection Phase Timer	---	---	---
S142	Online Character Format	---	---	---
S143	KDS Handshake Mode	---	---	---
S144	Autobaud Group Selection	---	---	---
S150	V.42 Options	---	---	---
S151	Simultaneous Voice Data Control	---	---	---
S154	Force Port Speed	---	---	---
S157	Timeout Result Code	---	---	---
S201	Cellular Transmit Level (MNP 10)	10-63	---	58 (3Ah)
S202	Remote Access Escape Character	0-255	ASCII	170

* The register may be used for different purposes by some modems.

MODEM MODES

The modem is always in one of two primary modes: the *command mode* or the *data mode*. When first switched on (or reset), the modem starts up in command mode. In this mode, the controller circuit (sometimes called a *command processor*) is constantly checking to see if you have typed a valid AT command. When the modem receives a valid command, it executes that command for you. While your modem is in the command mode, you can instruct it to answer the telephone, change an S-Register value, hang up or dial the telephone, and perform any number of other command functions.

In the other mode, the data mode, your modem is transmitting all of the data it receives from your computer or terminal along the telephone line to the remote modem. Your modem is constantly checking the state of the *Data Carrier Detect* (DCD) and *Data Terminal Ready* (DTR) signals (depending on the system configuration). It is also watching the local data stream for a command mode escape sequence. The default escape sequence of the AT command set is "+++". When the proper escape sequence (or a change in the state of the DCD or DTR signal) occurs, the modem returns to a command mode where it waits for the next AT command.

MODEM NEGOTIATION

Now that you have seen the essential elements of a modem and learned about modem signaling, you can use that background to form a picture of how the modem works in actual practice. You see, modem communication is not an event—it is a *process* whose success depends on not only on your modem, but on the modem and PC you are trying to communicate with. This part of the chapter is intended to familiarize you with an operating session for a typical modem.

Communication begins when you instruct the communication software to establish a connection. Control signals sent to the selected serial port causes the UART to assert the Data Terminal Ready (DTR) signal. This tells the attached modem that the PC is turned on and ready to transmit. The modem responds by asserting the Data Set Ready (DSR) line. The serial port receives this signal and tells the software that the modem is ready—both DTR and DSR must be present for communication to take place.

The communication software then sends an AT initialization string to the COM port, which forwards the string to the modem. In the command mode, the controller circuit interprets the initialization string, which tells the modem to go off hook (get dial tone) and then dial the telephone number of the destination modem. Dialing may take place in pulse (rotary) or tone (DTMF) mode depending on the initialization string. The modem transmits an acknowledgment back to the COM port—this acknowledgment is often displayed right on the communication software window. The line at the destination end begins to ring. If configured properly and running communication software of its own, the remote modem will pick up the ringing line, and a complete wiring path will be established between the two modems.

When the destination modem picks up the line, your local modem sends out a standard tone (a *carrier* tone)—this tone lets the remote modem know it's being called by another modem. If the remote modem recognizes the carrier, it sends out en even higher pitched tone. You can often hear these tones when your modem is equipped with a speaker. Once your modem recognizes the remote modem, it sends a Carrier Detect (CD) signal to the serial port. These mutual carriers will be modulated to exchange data.

OK, both modems know they are talking to other modems, but now there has to be a mutual agreement on *how* they'll exchange data. They must agree on transmission speed, the proper size of a data packet, the signaling bits on each end of the data packet, whether or not parity will be used, and whether the modems will operate in half- or full-duplex mode—*both* modems must settle on these parameters, or the data exchanged between them will make no sense. This process is known as *negotiation*. Assuming that the negotiation process is successful, both modems can now exchange data.

When the communication software attempts to send data, it tells the serial port to assert the Request to Send (RTS) signal. This signal checks to see if your modem is free to receive data. If the PC is busy doing something else (such as disk access), it will disable the RTS signal until it is ready to resume sending. When the modem is ready for data, it will return a Clear to Send (CTS) signal to the serial port. The PC can then begin sending data to the modem, and receiving data returned from the remote end. If the modem gets backed up with work, it will drop the CTS line until it is ready to resume communication. Since a standard system of tones is used, both modems can exchange data simultaneously. Data can now be exchanged between the two systems simultaneously.

When the time comes to terminate the connection, the communication software will send another AT command string to the serial port that causes it to break the connection. If the connection is broken by the remote modem, the local modem will drop the Carrier Detect line and the communication software will interpret this as a Dropped Carrier condition. That is basically all the phases involved in modem communication. If you're looking for more details on modem connections, Table 29-4 highlights the specific connect-sequences for V.22bis and V.32 modems.

READING THE LIGHTS

One of the appealing attributes of external modems is the series of lights that typically adorns the front face. By observing each light and the sequence in which they light, you can often follow the progress of a communication—or quickly discern the cause of a communication failure. The following markings are

TABLE 29-4 CONNECT SEQUENCES FOR V.22BIS AND V.32 MODEMS

V.22bis

- **Step 1:** *Pickup.* The receiving modem picks up the ringing line (goes "off-hook"). It then waits at least two seconds. This is known as a *billing delay* and is required by the telephone company to ensure that the connection has been properly established. No data transfer is allowed during the billing delay.
- **Step 2:** *Answer Tone.* The receiving modem transmits an answer tone back to the network. A 2100Hz tone lasts for about 3.3 seconds. An answer tone serves two purposes. First, you can hear this tone in the receiving modem's speaker, so manual modem users know when to place their modem into data mode. Even more important, the answer tone is used by the telephone network to disable echo suppressers in the connection in order to allow optimum data throughput. If echo suppressers remain active, data transfer will be half-duplex (one direction at a time). The answering modem then goes silent for about 75ms to separate the answer tone from data.
- **Step 3:** *The USB1 Signal.* The receiving modem then transmits alternating binary 1s at 1200bps (the USB1 signal). This signal results in the static sound you hear just after the answer tone. The s*ending mode*m detects the USB1 signal in about 155ms, and then falls silent for about 456ms.
- **Step 4:** *The S1 Signal.* After the 456ms silence, the sending modem transmits double digits (that is, 00 and 11) at 1200bps for 100ms (the *S1* signal). An older Bell 212 or V.22 modem does not send the S1 signal, so if the S1 signal is absent, the receiving V.22bis modem will fall back to 1200bps. The receiving modem (still generating a USB1 signal) receives the S1 signal. It responds by sending a 100ms burst of S1 signal so that the sending modem knows the receiving modem can handle 2400bps operation. At this point, both modems know whether they will be operating in 1200bps or 2400bps mode.
- **Step 5:** *The SB1 Signal.* At this point, the sending modem sends scrambled 1s at 1200bps (the SB1 signal). The "scrambling" creates white noise that checks power across the whole audio bandwidth. The receiving modem then replies with the SB1 signal for 500ms.
- **Step 6:** *Ready to Answer.* After 500ms, the receiving modem starts sending scrambled 1s at 2400bps for 200ms. A full 600ms after getting the SB1 signal from the receiving modem, the sending modem also sends scrambled 1s at 2400bps for 200ms. After both modems have finished their final 200ms transmissions, they are ready to pass data.

V.32

- **Step 1:** *Pickup.* The receiving modem picks up the ringing line (goes "off-hook"). It then waits at least two seconds. This is known as a *billing delay* and is required by the telephone company to ensure that the connection has been properly established. As with the V.22bis modem, no data transfer is allowed during the billing delay.
- **Step 2:** *Answer Tone.* The receiving modem transmits an answer tone back to the network. A V.25 answer tone (a 2100Hz tone with a duration of about 3.3 seconds) is returned to the calling modem. However, the V.32 modem uses a modified answer tone where the signal phase is reversed every 450ms—this tone sounds like little "clicks" in the signal. An answer tone serves two purposes. First, you can *hear* this tone in the receiving modem's speaker, so manual modem users know when to place their modem into "data mode." Even more important, the answer tone is used by the telephone network to disable echo suppressers in the connection in order to allow optimum data throughput. The modems themselves will handle echo suppression.
- **Step 3:** *Signal AA.* The sending modem waits about 1 second after receiving the answer tone; it then generates an 1800Hz tone (known as Signal AA). When the receiving modem interprets this signal, it knows (quite early on) that it is communicating with another V.32 modem.
- **Step 4:** *The USB1 Fall Back.* If the answering modem heard Signal AA, it will immediately try establishing a connection; otherwise, it will reply to the sending modem with a USB1 signal (alternating binary 1s at 1200bps). This signal causes the connection to "fall back" to a V.22bis connection. This fall back attempt will continue for three seconds. If the sending modem does not respond to the USB1 signal within three seconds, the receiving modem will continue trying the connection as a V.32.

TABLE 29-4 CONNECT SEQUENCES FOR V.22BIS AND V.32 MODEMS *(CONTINUED)*

- **Step 5:** *Signal AC and CA.* During a V.32 connection, the receiving modem sends Signal AC (a mixed 600Hz and 3000Hz tone signal) for at least 1/2400th of a second, and then it reverses the signal phase—creating Signal CA.
- **Step 6:** *Signal CC.* When the sending modem detects the phase change in Signal AC/CA, it reverses the phase of its own Signal AA—creating a new signal (called Signal CC).
- **Step 7:** *Echo Canceller Configuration.* Once the answering modem receives the phase-changed signal CC, it again changes the phase of CA—returning it to signal AC. This multitude of phase changes may seem like a ridiculous waste of time, but this exchange between the two modems is vital for approximating the round-trip (propagation) delay of the communication circuit so that the modem's echo canceller circuitry may be set properly.
- **Step 8:** *Agreeing on Specifics.* Once the exchange of phase changes sets the echo cancellers, both modems exchange data in half-duplex mode in order to set up adaptive equalizers, test the phone line quality, and agree on an acceptable data rate. In actual practice, the answering modem sends first (from 650ms to 3525ms). The sending modem responds, but leaves the signal on while the answering modem sends another burst of signals (this is when the final data rate is established).
- **Step 9:** *Passing Data.* Once the data rate is established, both modems proceed to send scrambled binary 1s for at least 1/1200th of a second (a brief white-noise sound); then they are ready to pass data.

typical of many modems, but keep in mind that your particular modem may use fewer indicators (or be marked differently):

- **HS** *(High Speed)* When this indicator is lit, the modem is operating at its very highest transfer rate.
- **AA** *(Auto Answer)* When illuminated, your modem will answer any incoming calls automatically. This feature is vital for unattended systems such as bulletin boards.
- **CD** *(Carrier Detect)* This lights whenever the modem detects a carrier signal, indicating it has successfully connected to a remote computer. This LED will go out when either one of the modems drops the line.
- **OH** *(Off Hook)* This LED lights any time the modem takes control of the telephone line—equivalent to taking the telephone off-hook.
- **RD** *(Receive Data)* This LED flickers as data is received by the modem from a remote modem. (Also marked Rx.)
- **SD** *(Send Data)* This LED flickers as data is sent from your modem to the remote modem. (Also marked Tx.)
- **TR** *(Terminal Ready)* This light illuminates when the modem detects a DTR signal from the communication software.
- **MR** *(Modem Ready)* A simple power-on light that indicates the modem is turned on and ready to operate.

Understanding Signal Modulation

Once the modem accepts a bipolar signal from an RS-232 port, the carrier signal being generated on the telephone line must be modulated to reflect the logic levels being transmitted. Several different means of signal modulation have been developed through the years to improve the efficiency of data transfers. This part of the chapter gives you a brief explanation of each scheme. As you would expect, both modems must be capable of the same modulation scheme.

BPS VERSUS BAUD RATE

In the early days of modem communication, each audio signal *transition* represented a single bit. Each audio signal is known as a *baud*, and the *baud rate* naturally equaled the transmission rate in bits-per-second (bps). Unlike those early modems, newer modem schemes can encode 2, 3, 4, or more bits into every audio signal transition (or baud). This capability means that modem throughput now equals 2x, 3x, or 4x the baud rate being carried across the telephone line.

For example, a modem operating at 2400 baud (2400 audio signal transitions per second) can carry 4800bps if 2 bits are encoded onto every baud. The same 2400 baud modem could also carry 9600bps if 4 bits are encoded onto every baud. Today, the modem's baud rate *rarely* matches the modem's throughput in bps unless a very old signaling standard is being used. If the modem were operating at 4800 baud and used 3 bit encoding, the modem would be handling 14,400bps (14.4Kbps), and so on. The concept of *encoding* is different from *data compression* since encoding transfers *all* original data bits from system to system, while data compression replaces repeating sequences of bits with much shorter bit sequences (known as *symbols* or *tokens*). You will see much more about encoding schemes and data compression later in this section.

MODULATION SCHEMES

To discuss modulation, you must first understand a sinusoidal waveform. There are basically three physical characteristics to any waveform: amplitude, frequency, and phase. Each of these characteristics can be adjusted to represent a bit. *Amplitude* is simply the magnitude of the wave (usually measured in volts peak-to-peak or volts RMS). Amplitude represents how far above and below the zero axis that waveform travels. *Frequency* indicates the number of times that a single wave will repeat over any period of time (measured as cycles-per-second, Hertz, or Hz). An 1800Hz signal repeats 1800 times per second. The signal also has a time reference known as *phase*. Phase is measured in degrees where 90 degrees is the time to travel 25 percent of a wave, 180 degrees is the time to travel 50 percent of the wave, 270 degrees is the time to travel 75 percent of a wave, and so on. Since phase can take on any one of four states (degrees), phase shifts can be made to represent two bits simultaneously. Data between modems is commonly modulated by altering the amplitude, frequency, and phase of a carrier signal.

Frequency Shift Keying (FSK) is very similar to frequency modulation (FM) where only the frequency of a carrier is changed, and is one of the oldest modulation schemes still in service. FSK sends a logic 1 as one particular frequency, usually 1750Hz, and a logic 0 is sent as another discrete frequency, often 1080Hz. Frequencies are typically sent at 300 baud and each baud can carry 1 bit, so FSK can send 300bps. This early technique resulted in the classical "baud=bps" confusion that is still prevalent today.

Phase Shift Keying (PSK) is a close cousin of FSK, but the phase timing of a carrier wave is altered while the carrier's frequency stays the same. By altering the carrier's phase, a logic 1 or 0 is represented. Since phase can be shifted in several precise increments (for example, 0, 90, 180, or 270 degrees), PSK can encode 1, 2, 3, or more bits bit per baud. For example, a 1200 baud modem using PSK can transmit 2400bps over an 1800Hz carrier. PSK can also be used in conjunction with FSK to encode even more bits per baud.

Quadrature Amplitude Modulation (QAM) uses both phase and amplitude modulation to encode up to 6 bits onto every baud, although 4 bits are usually reserved for data. Not only can four phase states represent 2 bits, but four levels of amplitude can represent another 2 bits. Most QAM modems use a 1700 Hz or 1800Hz carrier and a base rate of 2400 baud, so they carry up to 9600bps.

Trellis Coded Quadrature Amplitude Modulation (TCQAM or TCM) also uses an 1800Hz carrier at a 2400 baud base rate, but uses the full 6 bit encoding capability of QAM to handle 14,000bps. Most newer modems using TCM offer high speed and excellent echo cancellation circuitry. TCM is currently the most popular modulation scheme for high-performance modems since data can be checked on-the-fly with much better reliability than using a parity bit.

Pulse Code Modulation (PCM) a sampling technique for digitizing analog signals, especially audio signals. PCM samples the signal 8000 times a second: each sample is represented by 8 bits for a total of 64Kbps. There are two standards for coding the sample level: Mu-Law and A-Law. The Mu-Law standard is used in North America and Japan, while the A-Law standard is used in most other countries.

PCM is used with high-performance T-1 and T-3 carrier systems. These carrier systems combine the PCM signals from many lines and transmit them over a single cable or other medium.

Signaling Standards

Now that you have covered serial concepts and modulation techniques, you can see how modulation is used in conjunction with the many communications standards (or *protocols*) that have appeared. This part of the chapter details each of the major standards for modems, data compression, and error correction that are now in force today. In addition to the simple transfer of data, however, current modem standards embrace two other facets of data communication: data compression and error correction.

Most data sent between modems contains some amount of repetitive or redundant information. If the redundant information is located and replaced by a small token during transmission—the data is *compressed*. A token could be passed much faster than the redundant data, with the receiving modem accurately re-creating the original data based on the token. *Data compression* has become an important technique that allows modems to increase their data throughput without increasing the baud rate or bps. Data compression can occur only when the two communicating modems support the same compression protocol. If modems support more than one type of compression, the communicating modems will use the most powerful technique common to both.

Modem *error correction* is the ability of some modems to detect data errors that may have occurred in transit between modems and then automatically to re-send the data until a correct copy is received. As with modulation standards, both modems must be using the same error correction standard in order to operate together. However, there are few error correction standards, and most modem manufacturers adhere closely to the few that are available.

BELL STANDARDS

The old Bell System largely dictated North American telecommunications standards before it was broken up into AT&T and seven regional operating companies in 1984. Before that time, two major standards were developed that set the stage for future modem development:

- *BELL103* Was the first widely accepted modem standard using simple FSK modulation at 300 baud. This is the *only* standard where the data rate matches the baud rate. It is interesting to note that some modems today *still* support BELL103 as a lowest common denominator when all other modulation techniques fail.

- *BELL212A* Represents a second widely accepted modem standard in North America using PSK modulation at 600 baud to transmit 1200bps. Many European countries ignored BELL212A in favor of the similar (but not entirely identical) European standard called V.22.

ITU (CCITT) STANDARDS

After the Bell System breakup, AT&T no longer wielded enough clout to dictate standards in North America—and certainly not to the international community that had developed serious computing interest. It was at that time that the ITU (International Telecommunications Union, formally the CCITT) gained prominence and acceptance in the U.S, and all U.S. modems have been built to ITU standards ever since. ITU specifications are characterized by the letter *V* (for example, V.17). The *V* simply means *standard* (rather like the "RS" in RS-232). The subsequent number simply denotes the particular standard. Some standards also add the term *bis*, which means the *second version* of a particular standard. You may also soon see the terms *ter* or *terbo*, which refer to the *third version* of a standard. The list below provides a comprehensive look at ITU standards. Only the **bolded** standards relate to modems in particular, but *all* are related to communications. This index may aid you in understanding the broad specifications that are required to fully characterize the computer communications environment:

- *V.1* A very early standard that defines binary 0/1 bits as space/mark line conditions and voltage levels.
- *V.2* Limits the power levels (in decibels or dB) of modems used on phone lines.
- *V.4* Describes the sequence of bits within a character as transmitted (the data frame).
- *V.5* Describes the standard synchronous signaling rates for dialup lines.
- *V.6* Describes the standard synchronous signaling rates for leased lines.
- *V.7* Provides a list of modem terms in English, Spanish, French.
- *V.8* Describes the initial handshaking (negotiation) process between modems, and forms the basis for call autodetection or autoswitching (voice/fax/modem).
- *V.10* Describes unbalanced high-speed electrical interface characteristics (RS-423).
- *V.11* Describes balanced high-speed electrical characteristics (RS-422).
- *V.13* Explains simulated carrier control (with a full-duplex modem used as half-duplex modem).
- *V.14* Explains the procedure for asynchronous to synchronous conversion.
- *V.15* Describes the requirements and designs for telephone acoustic couplers. This is largely unused today, since most telephone equipment is modular and can be plugged into telephone adapters directly rather than loosely attached to the telephone handset.
- ***V.17*** Describes an application-specific modulation scheme for Group 3 fax that provides 2-wire half-duplex trellis-coded transmission at 7200, 9600, 12,000, and 14,000bps. In spite of the low number, this is a fairly recent standard.
- *V.19* Describes early DTMF modems using low-speed parallel transmission. This standard is largely obsolete.
- *V.20* Explains modems with parallel data transmission. This standard is largely obsolete.
- ***V.21*** Provides the specifications for 300bps FSK serial modems (based upon BELL103).
- ***V.22*** Provides the specifications for 1200bps (600 baud) PSK modems (similar to BELL212A).

- ***V.22bis*** Describes 2400bps modems operating at 600 baud using QAM.
- *V.23* Describes the operation of a rather unusual type of FM modem working at 1200/75bps. That is, the host transmits at 1200bps and receives at 75bps. The remote modem transmits at 75bps and receives at 1200bps. V.23 is used in Europe to support some videotext applications.
- *V.24* This is known as EIA RS-232 in the US. V.24 defines *only* the functions of the serial port circuits. EIA-232-E (the current version of the standard) also defines electrical characteristics and connectors.
- *V.25* Defines automatic answering equipment and parallel automatic dialing. It also defines the answer tone that modems send.
- *V.25bis* Defines serial automatic calling and answering, which is the ITU (CCITT) equivalent of AT commands. This is the current ITU standard for modem control by computers via serial interface. The Hayes AT command set is used primarily in the U.S.
- ***V.26*** Defines a 2400bps PSK full-duplex modem operating at 1200 baud.
- ***V.26bis*** Defines a 2400bps PSK half-duplex modem operating at 1200 baud.
- ***V.26terbo*** Defines a 2400/1200bps switchable PSK full-duplex modem operating at 1200 baud.
- ***V.27*** Defines a 4800bps PSK modem operating at 1600 baud.
- ***V.27bis*** Defines a more advanced 4800/2400bps switchable PSK modem operating at 1600/1200 baud.
- ***V.27terbo*** Defines a 4800/2400bps switchable PSK modem commonly used in half-duplex mode at 1600/1200 baud to handle Group 3 fax rather than computer modems.
- *V.28* Defines the electrical characteristics and connections for V.24 (RS-232). Where the RS-232 specification defines all necessary parameters, the ITU (CCITT) breaks the specifications down into two separate documents.
- ***V.29*** Defines a 9600/7200/4800bps switchable PSK/QAM modem operating at 2400 baud. This type of modem is often used to implement Group 3 fax rather than computer modems.
- ***V.32*** Defines the first of the truly modern modems as a 9600/4800bps switchable QAM full-duplex modem operating at 2400 baud. This standard also incorporates trellis coding and echo cancellation to produce a stable, reliable, high-speed modem.
- ***V.32bis*** A fairly new standard extending the V.32 specification to define a 4800/7200/9600/12,000/14,000bps switchable TCQAM full-duplex modem operating at 2400 baud. Trellis coding, automatic transfer rate negotiation, and echo cancellation make this type of modem one of the most popular and least expensive for everyday PC communication.
- ***V.32terbo*** Continues to extend the V.32 specification by using advanced techniques to implement a 14,000/16,800/19,200bps switchable TCQAM full-duplex modem operating at 2400 baud. Unlike V.32bis, V.32terbo is not widely used due to the rather high cost of components.
- ***V.32fast*** This is the informal name to a standard that the ITU (CCITT) has not yet completed. When finished, a V.32fast modem will likely replace V.32bis with speeds up to 28,800bps. It is anticipated that this will be the last *analog* protocol—eventually giving way to all-digital protocols as local telephone services become entirely digital. V.32fast will probably be renamed V.34 on completion and acceptance.
- ***V.33*** Defines a specialized 14,000bps TCQAM full-duplex modem operating at 2400 baud.

- ***V.34*** Defines the standard for modem communication at 2400 through 28,800bps.
- ***V.34+*** An update to V.34 outlining the enhancements needed for modem communication at 33,600bps.
- ***V.36*** Defines a specialized 48,000bps "group" modem, which is rarely if ever used commercially. This type of modem uses several conventional telephone lines.
- ***V.37*** Defines a specialized 72,000bps "group" modem that combines several telephone channels.
- ***V.42*** Is the only ITU error correcting procedure for modems using V.22, V.22bis, V.26ter, V.32, and V.32bis protocols. The standard is also defined as a *Link Access Procedure for Modems* (LAPM) protocol. ITU V.42 is considered very efficient, and is about 20 percent faster than MNP4. If a V.42 connection can not be established between modems, V.42 automatically provides fallback to the MNP4 error correction standard.
- ***V.42bis*** Uses a Lempel-Ziv-based data compression scheme for use in conjunction with V.42 LAPM (error correction). V.42bis is a data compression standard for high-speed modems that can compress data by as much as 4:1 (depending on the type of file you send). Thus, a 9600 baud modem can transmit data at up to 38,400bps using V.42bis. A 14.4Kbps modem can transmit up to a startling 57,600bps.
- *V.50* Sets standard telephony limits for modem transmission quality.
- *V.51* Outlines required maintenance of international data circuits.
- *V.52* Describes apparatus for measuring data transmission distortion and error rates.
- *V.53* Outlines impairment limits for data circuits.
- *V.54* Describes loop test devices for modem testing.
- *V.55* Describes impulse noise measuring equipment for line testing.
- *V.56* Outlines the comparative testing of modems.
- *V.57* Describes comprehensive test equipment for high-speed data transmission.
- ***V.90*** A standard for 56Kbps modems approved by the International Telecommunication Union (ITU) in February 1998.
- *V.100* Describes the interconnection techniques between PDNs (Public Data Networks) and PSTNs (Public Switched Telephone Networks).

MNP STANDARDS

The *Microcom Networking Protocol* (MNP) is a complete hierarchy of standards developed during the mid-1980s that are designed to work with other modem technologies for error correction and data compression. While most ITU standards refer to modem data transfer, MNP standards concentrate on providing error correction and data compression when your modem is communicating with another modem that supports MNP. For example, MNP class 4 is specified by ITU V.42 as a backup error control scheme for LAPM in the event that V.24 cannot be invoked. Out of nine recognized MNP levels, your modem probably supports the first five. Each MNP class has all the features of the previous class plus its own:

- *MNP class 1 (block mode)* An old data transfer mode that sends data in only one direction at a time—about 70 percent as fast as data transmissions using no error correction. This level is now virtually obsolete.

- *MNP class 2 (stream mode)* An older data transfer mode that sends data in both directions at the same time—about 84 percent as fast as data transmissions using no error correction.
- *MNP class 3* The sending modem strips start and stop bits from data block before sending it, while the receiving modem adds start and stop bits before passing the data to the receiving computer. About eight percent faster than data transmissions using no error correction. The increased throughput is realized only if modems on both ends of the connection are operating in a *split speed* (or *locked COM port*) fashion—that is, the rate of data transfer from computer to modem is *higher* than the data transfer rate from modem to modem. Also, data is being transferred in big blocks (that is, 1KB) or continuously (using, for example, the Zmodem file transfer protocol).
- *MNP class 4* A protocol (with limited data compression) that checks telephone connection quality and uses a transfer technique called *Adaptive Packet Assembly*. On a noise-free line, the modem sends larger blocks of data. If the line is noisy, the modem sends smaller blocks of data (less data will have to be resent). This means more successful transmissions on the first try. About 20 percent faster than data transmissions using no error correction at all, so most current modems are MNP4 compatible.
- *MNP class 5* Classic MNP data compression. MNP5 provides data compression by detecting redundant data and recoding it to fewer bits, thus increasing effective data throughput. A receiving modem decompresses the data before passing it to the receiving computer. MNP5 can speed data transmissions up to 2x over using no data compression or error correction (depending on the kind of data transmitted). In effect, MNP5 gives a 2400bps modem and effective data throughput of as much as 4800bps, and a 9600bps system as much as 19,200bps.
- *MNP class 6* Uses *Universal Link Negotiation* to let modems get maximum performance out of a line. Modems start at low speeds, and then move to higher speeds until the best speed is found. MNP6 also provides *Statistical Duplexing* to help half-duplex modems simulate full-duplex modems.
- *MNP class 7* Offers a much more powerful data compression process (Huffman encoding) than MNP5. MNP7 modems can increase the data throughput by as much as 3x in some cases. Although it is more efficient than MNP5, not all modems are designed to handle the MNP7 protocol. Also, MNP7 is faster than MNP5, but MNP7 is still generally considered slower than the ITU's V.42bis.
- *MNP class 9* Reduces the data overhead (the "housekeeping bits") encountered with each data packet. MNP9 also improves error correction performance because only the data that was in error has to be resent instead of resending the entire data packet.
- *MNP class 10* Uses a set of protocols known as *Adverse Channel Enhancements* to help modems overcome poor telephone connections by adjusting data packet size and transmission speed until the most reliable transmission is established. This is a more powerful version of MNP4.

29

FILE TRANSFER PROTOCOLS

Even with powerful data transfer, compression, and correction protocols, the way in which data is packaged and exchanged is still largely undefined by ITU and MNP standards. You see, a typical modem has no way of knowing the difference between a keyboard stroke or data being downloaded from a hard drive—the modem does not understand a file. Instead, it only works with bytes, bits, timing, and tones. As a consequence, the modem relies on communications software to manage file characteristics such as filename, file size, and content. The software routines that bundle and organize data between modems are called *file transfer protocols*. Errors that occur during file transfer are automatically detected and corrected by file transfer protocols. If a block of data is received incorrectly, the receiving system sends a message to the sending system and requests the retransmission. This process is automatic and essentially transparent to the computer users (except perhaps for a display in the communication software's file transfer status window). The following are some of the more common transfer protocols:

- *ASCII* This protocol is designed to work with ASCII text files only. You do *not* have to use this protocol when transferring text files. The ASCII protocol is useful for uploading a text file when you are composing e-mail on-line.
- *Xmodem* This is one of the most widely used file transfer protocols. Introduced in 1977 by Ward Christensen, this protocol is slow, but reliable. The original Xmodem protocol used 128-byte packets and a simple *checksum* method of error detection. A later enhancement, Xmodem-CRC, uses a more secure *Cyclic Redundancy Check* (CRC) method for error detection. Xmodem protocols always attempt to use CRC first. If the sender does not acknowledge the requests for CRC, the receiver shifts to the checksum mode and continues its request for transmission. Mismatching the two variants of Xmodem during file transfers is usually the reason for transfer problems, although many communication systems can now detect the differences automatically.
- *Xmodem-1K* The Xmodem-1K protocol is essentially Xmodem CRC with 1KB (1024 bytes) packets. On some systems and bulletin boards, it may also be referred to as Ymodem. Some communication software programs, most notably Procomm Plus 1.x, also list Xmodem-1K as Ymodem. Procomm Plus 2.0 no longer refers to Xmodem-1K as Ymodem.
- *Ymodem* A Ymodem protocol is little more than a version of Xmodem-1K that allows multiple batch file transfer (sending/receiving several files one after another unattended). On some systems it is listed as Ymodem Batch (and is sometimes called "true Ymodem"). Ymodem offers a faster transmission rate than Xmodem as well as better data security through a refined CRC checksum method.
- *Ymodem-g* The Ymodem-g protocol is a variant of basic Ymodem. It is designed to be used with modems that support error correction. This protocol does not provide software error correction or recovery itself, but expects the *modem* to provide the service. It is a streaming protocol that sends and receives 1K packets in a continuous stream until instructed to stop. It does not wait for positive acknowledgment after each block is sent, but rather sends blocks in rapid succession. If any block is unsuccessfully transferred, the entire transfer is canceled.
- *Zmodem* This is generally the best protocol to use if the electronic service you are calling supports it. Zmodem has two significant features: it is extremely efficient, and it provides automatic "crash" recovery. Like Ymodem-g, Zmodem does not wait for positive acknowledgment after each block is sent, but rather sends blocks in rapid succession. If a Zmodem transfer "crashes" (canceled or interrupted for any reason), the transfer can be resurrected later and the previously transferred information need *not* be resent. Zmodem can detect excessive line noise and can automatically drop to a shorter, more reliable data packet size when necessary. Data integrity and accuracy is assured by the use of a 16 bit CRC (cyclic redundancy check) method that is more reliable than the CRC checking of Ymodem and Xmodem.
- *Kermit* The Kermit protocol was developed at Columbia University. It was designed to facilitate the exchange of data among very different types of computers (mainly minicomputers and mainframes). You probably will not need to use Kermit unless you are calling a minicomputer or mainframe at an educational institution.
- *Sealink* The Sealink protocol is a variant of Xmodem. It was developed to overcome the transmission delays caused by satellite relays or packet-switching networks.

Installing an "Analog" Modem

Both internal and external modem devices are typically PnP devices that are designed for automatic detection and resource assignments. Still, most modem, especially WinModem, problems *start* when the card is first installed in the system—usually problems due to inadequate or incorrect installation of the hardware and software. This part of the chapter offers an overview of the installation process so that you can check for missing steps.

> Always use proper static precautions (such as wearing an anti-static wrist strap) when working inside a system with sensitive devices—such as the modem card.

INTERNAL HARDWARE INSTALLATION

Installing a new modem or upgrading an existing one begins the hardware modifications outlined next.

1. Shut down Windows 98/SE, and then turn off and unplug the computer.
2. Unbolt the outer case, and then remove the housing and set it (and the screws) aside in a safe place.
3. If you're replacing an existing modem with a newer, faster model, you'll need to remove the old modem first. Disconnect the telephone line cord (and other telephone cords) from the modem. Unbolt the old modem card bracket from the chassis and remove the old modem from its expansion slot. Be sure to set the old modem aside on a static-safe surface or in an antistatic bag.
4. Locate a slot for the new modem card. Many modem card devices will require an ISA slot, though most "newer" modem cards (V.90 56Kbps and later) will need a PCI slot. Find an available slot that's appropriate for your modem card. Remove the cover for the slot you intend to use (if it's not already removed) and save the screw for the mounting bracket.
5. Insert the modem card. Push the card in firmly and evenly until it's fully seated in the slot. Replace the screw to secure the bracket of your modem card to the computer's chassis.
6. Reconnect the modem to the telephone wall jack using the modem's LINE or TELCO jack.

> The phone jack you use must be for an *analog* phone line (the type found in most homes). Many office buildings have digital phone lines. Be sure you know which type of line you have. The modem may be damaged if you use a digital phone line.

- If you wish to use a phone on the same line that the modem is using (when the modem is not in use), plug your phone's line cord into the modem's PHONE jack.
- If your modem model supports "simultaneous voice and data," you may need a microphone to support that feature. If so, plug the microphone into the MIC jack on the modem.
- If your modem offers full-duplex speakerphone capabilities, plug a set of powered external speakers (not included) into the SPEAKER jack on the modem.

SOFTWARE INSTALLATION

Now that the physical hardware for your new modem card has been installed, it's time to install the modem drivers and application software that you'll need to identify the device under Windows 98/SE and to use advanced features (such as a voice mail system). Leave the computer's housing off for now, but reconnect the AC cord to the computer and prepare to start the system again.

Always refer to the README file on the modem card's driver disc to obtain the very latest feature descriptions and software installation guidelines for your particular card.

1. When Windows restarts, it should detect the modem automatically.
2. Click "Driver from disk provided by hardware manufacturer." Then click OK.
3. Insert the driver CD into the CD-ROM, and then select the CD-ROM drive letter.
4. Click OK. Windows will load the modem's drivers.
5. Once Windows finishes loading the information from the driver CD, you should verify that the modem installation was a success. When your desktop returns, click Start, highlight Settings, and then click Control Panel.
6. Double-click the Modems icon.
7. In the Modems Properties dialog, you should see a suitable description for your modem (Figure 29-3). If so, your modem installed properly.

Next you should test your modem:

1. Click the Diagnostics tab. Select the modem (or the COM port that your modem is on), and then click the More Info button.
2. After a few moments, you should see the More Info dialog (Figure 29-4), which lists the modem's Port Information as well as a series of standard modem commands.
3. If the modem responds to each of the commands, it should be working, and you're ready to try the modem online. You can reattach the computer's outer housing and return the system to normal ser-

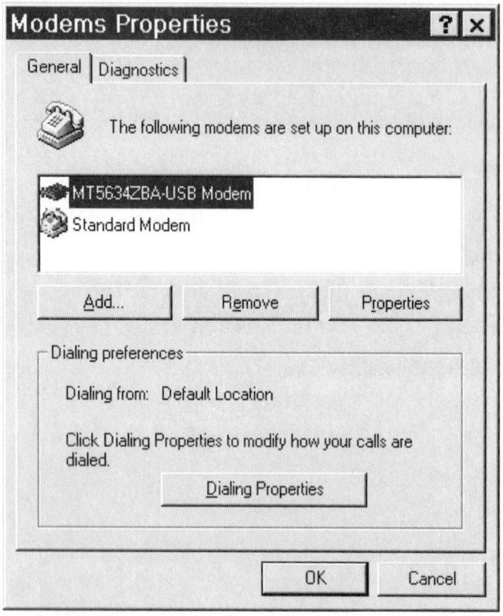

FIGURE 29-3 Checking the new modem installation

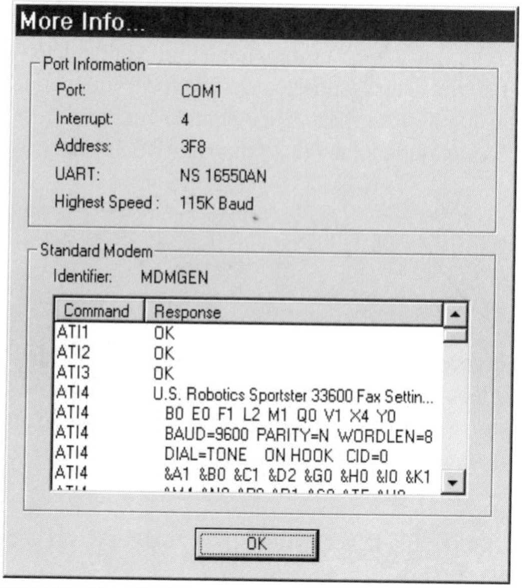

FIGURE 29-4 Running basic diagnostics on your modem

vice. If the modem does *not* respond or an error is generated, you should double-check the modem's installation and verify that it has been properly identified.

4 Once the modem is working, you can install any other applications or support software (for example, voice mail or fax software) that accompany your modem.

29

Installing a "Cable" Modem

Over the last few years, the Internet has exploded with content. Not only can you view text and images, but you can now access real-time audio and video broadcasting, Java applets, ShockWave multimedia presentations, and so much more. The intense growth in Internet use and the increasing complexity of Internet media have placed a strain on the "bandwidth" offered by Internet Service Providers (ISPs). There are simply too many users trying to access gobs of data-intensive information. Most Internet connections are "dial-up," and conventional computer modems have improved in order to pass more data across the existing global telephone network—but that is no longer enough. With 56Kbps modems pushing the capabilities of today's phone network, another large network is positioning for the Internet—the cable television system. This part of the chapter presents the essential requirements and installation steps for typical cable modems.

UNDERSTANDING THE "CABLE" MODEM

In most regions of the United States (and other areas of the world offering cable television access), Cable Television (or CATV) systems are being adapted to deliver Internet access. Local cable companies offering

Internet access can serve as ISPs—incorporating Internet charges with your existing cable television bill. Typically, cable modems are "one way" devices. This means you'll wind up supplementing your conventional analog modem with a high-speed "cable modem." Internet data is requested upstream via your phone line (using your existing modem in much the way that you do now), and that data is sent downstream from the Internet via the CATV network to your computer's "cable modem" at burst rates of up to 38Mbps.

The cable industry is working feverishly to establish "two way" cable Internet access, which should render your existing modem unnecessary, so be sure to understand the requirements of your local cable provider.

Preparing for a Cable Modem

Commercial cable modems are not much different than your current analog modem—except that they connect to a CATV jack rather than a telephone jack. You can find both internal and external cable modems, so you can either install the modem internally or use an external modem to take advantage of an external COM port if your system is short on resources. In order to use a cable modem at all, you'll need to meet *all* of the following requirements:

- ***Computer.*** As a minimum, you'll need a 486/33 PC (preferably faster) with at least 8MB of RAM and 5MB of hard drive space.
- ***Operating system.*** Plan on using Windows 95 or later and be sure to have the Windows installation CD handy during the cable modem's installation process.

If you don't have your Windows installation CD, you may be able to find any required files on your hard drive. Use the path c:\windows\options\cabs (where C: is the letter for your hard drive) instead of the CD-ROM path referred to in most installation instructions.

- ***Analog modem.*** Since you typically cannot transmit data upstream to the CATV network, you *will* require an analog modem—your system's current modem (28.8KB or faster) should do fine. However, this requirement is changing, and "two-way" cable modem access may now be available in your service area.
- ***POTS service.*** You'll need regular telephone service so that you can transmit data with your analog modem. As with all analog modem installations, the line quality from your local telephone company should be as good as possible. *Do not* attempt to use an analog modem through a digital telephone line (such as a PBX switching system). If your cable modem service is "two-way," you will *not* need a phone line or analog modem.
- ***Cable service wiring.*** You should have at least one CATV jack on the premises. If you do not have cable service, you will need to have cable service installed. Virtually all homes built in the last 10 years will have CATV jacks in at least one room.
- ***Cable modem service.*** You should check with your local cable provider to verify that it *does* offer Internet access at your particular location. *Confirm it!* Just because your local cable provider offers Internet service does *not* mean the service is enabled or working properly at your physical location.
- ***Cable modem.*** Finally, you'll need a suitable internal or external cable modem. Be sure to have the modem's latest drivers and communications software on CD (or disk). You might also wish to use your current Internet provider to download the modem's latest drivers and software before beginning your cable modem installation. In many cases, your local cable company may supply you with the cable modem and software as part of the monthly service fee.

Getting Connected

Before you install the cable modem, you'll need to contact your local cable company to establish your Internet access account. Once you verify that the cable company can provide Internet access at your location, you'll need to provide the modem's *Media Access Control* (MAC) address, which is usually located on a bar code sticker on the modem itself. The MAC address is a 12-character number typically beginning with 00C049. Be sure to write the complete MAC address in the modem's manual or somewhere in your PC's documentation—once the modem is installed, you may not be able to get at the MAC number.

Once you've established the account, your cable company will probably provide you with a user name and password (which you can change later once you're online). Be sure to write your user name and password in the modem's manual or somewhere in your PC's documentation.

INSTALLING A CABLE MODEM

The actual installation of a cable modem is not terribly complicated, but there are some stringent operating system and support software requirements that must be dealt with both before and after the physical modem is installed. Successful installation requires that you prepare the system, install the hardware, install the software, and then test the connection. This part of the chapter offers you a set of basic guidelines that can help you identify possible problem areas.

Prepare the System

Before you even open the cover to install a cable modem, you should take the proper steps to verify that your PC is ready for a cable modem. As a rule, a cable modem requires Dial-Up Networking (DUN), TCP/IP, and an SNMP agent. If your system isn't ready for the cable modem, you can install the required features.

> Some versions of Windows 95 will not support *both* the cable modem and a network interface card (such as Ethernet cards). You may need to uninstall or disable any existing network interface cards in your computer before installing the cable modem card.

Dial-Up Networking (DUN) allows the modem to access the Internet. You should verify that DUN is installed on your PC, and install DUN if necessary:

1. Click Start, select Settings, and then click Control Panel.
2. Double-click the Add/Remove Programs icon.
3. Click the Windows Setup tab.
4. In the Components list, click Communications, and then click Details.
5. If the Dial-Up Networking box *is* checked, DUN is installed, so close all open windows and go on to check TCP/IP.
6. If the Dial-Up Networking box is *not* checked, DUN is not installed. Click the box so that a check appears. Click OK, and then click OK again. Windows will ask for the Windows Installation CD. Follow the on-screen instructions to install Dial-Up Networking. When you are finished, close all open windows and go on to check TCP/IP.

TCP/IP is the communications protocol required by the cable modem to access the Internet. You should verify that a TCP/IP stack is installed on your PC, and install a TCP/IP stack if necessary:

1. Click Start, select Settings, and then click Control Panel.
2. Double-click the Network icon.

3. A list of installed network components appears. Look for "TCP/IP -> Dial-Up Adapter" in the list.
4. If this entry *is* present, TCP/IP is installed, so close all open windows and go to check the SNMP agent.
5. If this entry is *not* present, TCP/IP is not installed. Click Add.
6. Click Protocol, and then click Add.
7. Click Microsoft in the Manufacturers list, click TCP/IP in the Network Protocols list, and then click OK.
8. "TCP/IP" will appear in the list of installed network components. Click OK.
9. Windows will now ask you if you would like to restart your computer. Click No for now.
10. Close all open windows and go on to check the SNMP agent.

Finally, check the SNMP agent. This is not a vital component, but it will help with remote diagnostics, if necessary. You should verify that the SNMP agent is installed on your PC; if it is not, install it as follows:

1. Click Start, select Settings, and then click Control Panel.
2. Double-click the Network icon.
3. A list of installed network components appears. Look for "Microsoft SNMP Agent" in the list.
4. If it *is* listed, the agent is installed; close all open windows and install the cable modem hardware.
5. If it is *not* listed, the agent is not installed. Click Add.
6. Click Service, and then click Add.
7. Click Have Disk. Next, while holding down the SHIFT key on your keyboard, insert the Windows CD into your CD-ROM drive. When the CD is completely inserted into your CD-ROM drive, you can release the SHIFT key.
8. Type **d:\admin\nettools\snmp** and then press ENTER.

> If you do not have a Windows installation CD, you will need to obtain the SNMP Agent from Microsoft's Web site (**www.microsoft.com/windows95/info/admintools.htm**).

When SNMP agent installation is complete, "Microsoft SNMP Agent" will be added to the list of installed network components on the Network dialog. Windows will ask you if you would like to restart your computer. Click Yes to reboot the system, and then you can install the modem hardware.

Hardware Installation

Turn off and unplug the computer. You can now install your cable modem using the specific instructions accompanying the particular device. Pay particular attention to any jumper or switch settings on the cable modem. Once the modem is physically installed, you can reboot the PC and begin the software installation process. Be particularly careful to follow any special instructions provided by your local cable company.

Software Installation

In virtually all cases, PCs will automatically detect the presence of a PnP device such as the cable modem, but you will need to install the cable modem drivers and other software in order to complete the modem's setup. There may be slight differences in driver installation depending on whether you're running Windows 95 versions 950 and 950a (OSR1), or version 950b (OSR2), or Windows 98.

Windows 95 Versions 950 and 950a

1. Insert the first driver disk, select "Driver from disk provided by hardware manufacturer," and click OK.
2. You will see an Install From Disk dialog box. Click OK.
3. After copying files from the disk(s), Windows may ask for the Windows installation CD. While holding down the SHIFT key on your keyboard, insert the Windows installation CD into your CD-ROM drive. When the CD is completely inserted into your CD-ROM drive, you can release the SHIFT key. Click OK.
4. In the dialog box that appears next, type **d:** and click OK.

Go on to install the cable modem's dial-up protocol.

Windows 95 Version "950b"/Windows 98

1. Insert the first driver disk into your floppy drive.
2. Click Next, and then click Finish.
3. Windows 95/98 may ask for the file NETUSR.INF. If so, type **a:** and then press ENTER.

Cable Modem Dial-Up Protocol

1. Insert the first driver disk into the floppy drive.
2. Click Start, select Settings, and click Control Panel.
3. Double-click the Network icon in the Control Panel.
4. Click Add and double-click Protocol.
5. When the Select Network Protocol dialog appears, click Have Disk. You'll see an Install From Disk dialog. Make sure "a:" appears in the text box, and then click OK.
6. A second Select Network Protocol dialog will appear. In the Models column, you should see the reference to your modem (for example, "3Com CM Dial Up Protocol"). Double-click that entry, and Windows will start copying files from the disk.
7. During the file copying process, Windows will ask for the Windows installation CD. Insert the CD into your CD-ROM drive and click OK. A Copying Files dialog will appear. Make sure the path in the "Copy files from" field matches the letter for your CD-ROM drive. Then click OK.
8. When Windows finishes copying files, it will ask if you wish to restart your computer. Remove the Windows installation CD from your CD-ROM drive, remove the driver diskette from your floppy drive, and then click No.

Cable Modem Communication Software

1. Insert the disk (or CD) containing the cable modem's communications control (CMCC) software into the computer.
2. Click Start, and then click Run.
3. At the Run dialog box, type **a:\setup.exe** and then press ENTER. If you're installing from a CD, type **d:\setup.exe** and press ENTER.

4 Now follow the on-screen instructions to install the CMCC.

5 At the end of the installation, you will be asked if you wish to restart your computer. Click the Yes radio button, eject the diskette (or CD) from your drive, and then click Finish.

6 When Windows restarts, the CMCC software will initiate a channel scan and lock on to the first active downstream channel it detects. This automatic scan occurs only upon your first restart after installing the CMCC software (if the CMCC fails to lock onto a channel, you may need to troubleshoot the modem). The cable modem will use this channel until you scan for a different channel or your cable company supplies you with new channel information. Click OK.

7 The CMCC software will then run a diagnostic test of your cable modem system. Errors indicated by this diagnostic may mean you'll need to troubleshoot the modem:

- Problems "checking required system components" mean that you overlooked one or more of the network components needed by the cable modem. You may need to install DUN, TCP/IP, or the SNMP agent.
- Problems "searching for a cable modem driver" mean that the cable modem is not properly installed and the driver(s) have not loaded. Uninstall the modem and reinstall it from scratch.
- Problems "searching for a cable signal" means the cable modem isn't receiving a signal from the cable company. Check the cable connection, and then try rebooting the PC. Otherwise, you'll need to have your cable company check the line.

8 When you see the Cable Modem Diagnostic Summary dialog, click OK.

> If you see a dialog indicating that your IP lease will expire and that you need to dial in to obtain a new one, you have not yet connected to obtain an IP address. Click Cancel to ignore this message.

Testing Your Connection

At this point, the cable modem should be installed properly, but you'll need to do a bit of configuring in the CMCC software while you start your first cable modem session:

1 Start the CMCC software (double-click the CMCC icon in the system tray). The main CMCC screen will appear.

2 To begin the session, click the Connect button.

3 When the "Enroll" dialog appears, there should be at least two options in the Service Provider field. One should be Manual Enrollment, and another should correspond to your cable company's particular Internet service.

Highlight the entry in the Service Provider field that corresponds to your cable company (for example, "ACME Cable Co."). If your cable company's Internet service does not appear in the Service Provider field, call your cable company for assistance. If your cable company *has* provided you with a login name and password, do the following:

4 Click Copy to Manual Enrollment. The Manual Enrollment option should now be highlighted in the Service Provider field, and the fields will show the information for your cable company's Internet service.

5 Enter your Login name and Password in the appropriate fields. Click Enroll Now.

6 Your analog modem should dial the cable company's Internet server and make your connection.

If your cable company *has not* provided you with a login name and password:

7 Click Enroll Now.

8 Your analog modem should dial the cable company's Internet server and make your connection.

When the enrollment process is completed, you can launch your browser or e-mail software and begin using the Internet. After this initial connection, you can simply click the Connect button to initiate future cable modem sessions.

> These steps outline only one method of making your first cable modem connection. If you have trouble connecting using these instructions (or your cable company has provided you with different instructions), follow your cable company's specific instructions, or contact them for assistance.

UNINSTALLING A CABLE MODEM

There are times when it may be necessary to uninstall a cable modem system. You may need to correct a hardware conflict, upgrade an older cable modem unit, replace a defective cable modem, or move an existing cable modem to another PC. In each case, you'll need to reverse the installation process in order to uninstall the cable modem properly.

Remove the Cable Modem's Software

1. Stop the CMCC software. Right-click the CMCC icon in your system tray, and then click Exit. A dialog box will ask if you are sure you wish to exit. Click Yes.
2. Click Start, select Settings, and click Control Panel.
3. Double-click the Add/Remove Programs icon.
4. Double-click the entry for your CMCC software.
5. Windows asks if you are sure you want to remove the cable modem and all of its components. Click OK, and then follow the on-screen instructions to completely remove the software from your system.

29

Remove the Cable Modem's Dial-up Protocol

1. Click Start, select Settings, and click Control Panel.
2. Double-click Network.
3. Click the DUN entry for your cable modem (for example, "3Com CM Dial Up Protocol") in the list that appears. This highlights the entry.
4. Click Remove, and then click OK.
5. Windows will tell you that you must restart your computer before these changes will take effect. When asked to restart now, click No (we'll restart the system after the drivers and modem are removed).

Remove the Cable Modem's Drivers

1. Click Start, select Settings, and click Control Panel.
2. Double-click the System icon, and click the Device Manager tab.
3. Double-click Network Adapters.
4. Select your cable modem (for example, "3Com U.S. Robotics Cable Modem") and click Remove.

5 Windows displays the message; "Warning, you are about to remove this device from your system." Click OK—the modem is now uninstalled from your system.

Remove the Cable Modem

Now it's time to remove the physical modem:

1. Shut down and unplug your computer.
2. Disconnect your cable line from the modem's CABLE jack.
3. Remove the computer's cover.
4. Remove the screw that holds the cable modem in its slot, and then pull the cable modem out of the slot. Place the modem card back into an antistatic bag.
5. Cover the slot with the original bracket you removed during installation and screw it into place.
6. Replace the computer's cover, plug it back into the electrical outlet, and turn the computer back on.

When the PC boots, all traces of the cable modem should be completely removed.

Modem Troubleshooting

Okay, the modem is installed (or replaced), the drivers are installed, the communication software is loaded, the telephone line is connected—and nothing happens. This is an all too common theme for today's technicians and computer enthusiasts. Although the actual failure rate among ordinary modems is quite small, it turns out that modems (and serial ports, as you will see later in the book) are some of the difficult and time-consuming devices to set up and configure. As a consequence, proper setup from the start can simplify troubleshooting significantly. When a modem fails to work properly, there are a number of conditions to explore:

- *Incorrect hardware resources* An internal modem must be set with a unique IRQ line and I/O port. If the assigned resources are also used by another serial device in the system (such as a mouse), the modem or the conflicting device (or perhaps both) will not function properly. Remove the modem and use a diagnostic to check available resources. Under Windows 95/98, you can use the Device Manager to investigate devices and examine their configurations. Reconfigure the internal modem to clear the conflict. External modems make use of existing COM ports.
- *Defective telecommunication resources* All modems need access to a telephone line in order to establish connections with other modems. If the telephone jack is defective or hooked up improperly, the modem may work fine but no connection is possible. Remove the telephone line cord from the modem and try the line cord on an ordinary telephone. When you lift the receiver, you should draw dial tone. Try dialing a local number—if the line rings, chances are good that the telephone line is working. Check the RJ11 jack on the modem. One or more bent connector pins can break the line even though the line cord is inserted properly.
- *Improper cabling* An external modem must be connected to the PC serial port with a cable. Traditional serial cables were 25-pin assemblies. Later, 9-pin serial connectors and cables became common—out of those 9 wires, only three are really vital. As a result, quite a few cable assemblies may be incorrect or otherwise specialized. Make sure that the serial cable between the PC and modem is a "straight-through" type cable. Also check that both ends of the cable are intact that is, installed evenly, no bent pins, and so on). Try a new cable if necessary.

- *Improper power* External modems must receive power from batteries or from an AC eliminator. Make sure that any batteries are fresh and installed completely. If an AC adapter is used, see that it is connected to the modem properly.
- *Incorrect software settings* Both internal and external modems must be initialized with an AT ASCII command string before a connection is established. If these settings are absent or incorrect, the modem will not respond as expected (if at all). Check the communication software and make sure that the AT command strings are appropriate for the modem being used—different modems often require slightly different command strings.
- *Suspect the modem itself* Modems are typically quite reliable in everyday use. If there are jumpers or DIP switches on the modem, check that each setting is placed correctly. Perhaps their most vulnerable point is the telephone interface, which is particularly susceptible to high-voltage spikes that might enter through the telephone line. If all else fails, try another modem.

CHECKING THE COMMAND PROCESSOR

The *command processor* is the controller that manages the modem's operation in the command mode, and it is the command processor that interprets AT command strings. When the new modem installation fails to behave as it should, you should first check the modem command processor using the procedure outlined below. Before going too far with this, make sure you have the modem's user guide on hand (if possible). When the command processor checks out, but the modem refuses to work under normal communication software operations, the software may be refusing to save settings such as COM port selection, speed, and character format:

1. Make sure the modem is installed properly and connected to the desired PC serial port. Of course, if the modem is internal, you will only need to worry about IRQ and I/O port settings. Check the Device Manager to see that the internal modem's COM port setting is not conflicting with an existing COM port on the PC.
2. Start the communication software and select a "direct connection" to establish a path from your keyboard to the modem (this is sometimes referred to as "terminal mode"). You will probably see a dialog box appear with a blinking cursor. If the modem is working and installed properly, you should now be able to send commands directly to the modem.
3. Type the command **AT** and then press the ENTER key. The modem should return an OK result code. When an OK is returned, chances are that the modem is working correctly. If you see double characters being displayed, try the command **ATE0** to disable the command mode echo. If you do not see an OK, try issuing an **ATE1** command to enable the command mode echo. If there is still no response, commands are not reaching the modem, or the modem is defective. Check the connections between the modem and serial port. If the modem is internal, check that it is installed correctly and that all jumpers are placed properly.
4. Try *resetting* the modem with the **ATZ** command and the ENTER key. This should reset the modem. If the modem now responds with OK, you may have to adjust the initialization command string in the communication software, the Registry, or the "Extra settings" line in your modem's properties.
5. Try factory default settings by typing the command **AT&F** then pressing the ENTER key. Doing this should restore the factory default values for each S-register. You may also try the command **AT&Q0** and ENTER to deliberately place the modem into asynchronous mode. You should see OK

responses to each attempt, which indicate the modem is responding as expected—it may be necessary to update the modem's initialization command string. If the modem still does not respond, the communication software may be incompatible or the modem may be defective.

CHECKING THE DIALER AND TELEPHONE LINE

After you've demonstrated that the modem's command processor is responding properly, you can also check the "telephone interface" by attempting a call—doing this also can verify an active telephone line. When the telephone interface checks out, but the modem refuses to work under normal communication software operations, the software may be refusing to save settings such as COM port selection, speed, and character format:

1. Make sure the modem is installed properly and connected to the desired PC serial port. Of course, if the modem is internal, you will only need to worry about IRQ and I/O port settings. Check that there is no conflict between the modem's COM port and the system's COM port(s).
2. Start the communication software and select a "direct connection" to establish a path from your keyboard to the modem (this is sometimes referred to as "terminal mode"). You will probably see a dialog box appear with a blinking cursor. If the modem is working and installed properly, you should now be able to send commands directly to the modem. See the HyperTerminal example above.
3. Dial a number by using the **DT** (dial using tones) command followed by the full number being called—for example, **ATDT15083667683** followed by pressing the ENTER key. If your local telephone line only supports rotary dialing, use the modifier **R** after the **D**. If calling from a PBX, be sure to dial 9 or other outside-access codes. Listen for a dial tone, followed by the tone dialing beeps. You should also hear the destination phone ringing. When these occur, they ensure that your telephone interface dials correctly, and the local phone line is responding properly.
4. If there is no dial tone, check the phone line by dialing with an ordinary phone. Note that some PBX systems must be modified to produce at least 48 volts DC for the modem to work. If there is no dial tone, but the modem attempts to dial, the telephone interface is not grabbing the telephone line correctly (the dialer is working). If the modem draws dial tone, but no digits are generated, the dialer may be defective. In either case, try another modem.

TYPICAL COMMUNICATION PROBLEMS

Even when the modem hardware is working perfectly, the serial communication process is *anything* but flawless. Problems ranging from accidental loss of carrier to a catastrophic loss of data regularly plague computer communication. To make your on-line time as foolproof as possible, this section of the chapter shows you how to deal with some of the most pernicious communication problems.

Modem Settings Modem settings are critically important to inter-modem communication. The number of data bits, use of parity, number of stop bits, and data transfer speed must be set *precisely* the same way on both modems. Otherwise, the valid data leaving one modem will be interpreted as complete "junk" at the receiving end. Normally, this should not happen when modems are set to auto-answer—negotiation should allow both modems to settle at the same parameters. The time that incompatible settings really become a factor is when negotiation is unsuccessful, or when communication is being established manually. A typical example is an avid BBS user with communication software set to 8 data bits, no parity bit, and 1 stop bit trying to use a network that runs at 7 data bits, even parity, and 2 stop bits. The aspect that stands out with incompatible settings is that virtually nothing is intelligible—and the connection is typically lost.

Modems and UART Types The UART is clearly the heart of a modem system. It is the modem that converts bus data into serial data (and vice versa). However, the UART must be able to keep pace with the modem's data transfer rate. As modem speeds have increased, UARTs have become faster also. When installing a new external modem on an older PC, an older PC's serial port may simply not be fast enough to deal with the modem. The result is often limited modem performance (if the modem works at all). Today, the 16550A UART is the device of choice. Table 29-5 compares the major UART types. When faced with an older UART, it may be possible to replace the UART chip outright—otherwise, it is a simple matter to *disable* the existing serial port and install a newer serial adapter card incorporating a new UART.

Line Noise Where faulty settings can load a transmission with trash, even a properly established connection can lose integrity periodically. Remember that serial communication is made possible by a global network of switched telephone wiring. Each time you dial the same number, you typically get a different set of "wiring." Faulty wiring at any point along the network, electrical storms, wet or snowy weather, and other natural or man-made disasters can interrupt the network momentarily or cut communication entirely. Most of the time, brief interruptions can result in small patches of garbled text. This type of behavior is most prominent in real-time on-line sessions (such as typing in a "chat" message). When uploading or downloading files, file transfer protocols can usually catch such anomalies and correct errors or request new data packets to overcome the errors. When you have trouble moving files or notice a high level of "junk" on-line, try calling back—when a new telephone line is established, the connection might be better.

Transmit and Receive Levels Other factors that affect both leased and dial-up telephone lines are the transmit and receive levels. These settings determine the signal levels used by the modem in each direction. Some Hayes-compatible modems permit these levels to be adjusted. The range and availability

29

TABLE 29-5 COMPARISON OF POPULAR UARTS

UART	DESCRIPTION
8250	This is the original PC/XT serial port UART. There are several minor bugs in the UART, but the original PC/XT BIOS corrected for them. The 8250 was replaced by the 8250B.
8250A	This slightly updated UART fixed many of the problems in the 8250 but would not work in PC/XT systems because the BIOS was written to circumvent the 8250's problems. In any case, the 8250A will not work adequately over 9600bps.
8250B	The last of the 8250 series re-inserted the bugs that existed in the original 8250 so that PC/XT BIOS would function properly. The 8250B also does not run above 9600bps.
16450	This higher-speed UART was the desired choice for AT (i286) systems. Stable at 9600bps, the 16450 laid the groundwork for the first "high-speed" modems. However, the 16450 will not work in PC/XT systems. This IC should be replaced by the 16550A.
16550	The 16550 was faster than the 16450, allowing operation above 9600bps, but its performance was still limited by internal design problems. This IC should be replaced by the 16550A.
16550A	The fastest of the UARTs, a 16550A eliminates many of the serial port problems countered when using a fast modem.

of these adjustments is in large part controlled by the local telephone system. For example, the recommended settings and ranges are different for modems sold in the UK than for those sold in the U.S. See the documentation accompanying the modem to determine whether this capability is supported.

System Processor Limitations Some multitasking operating systems can occasionally lose small amounts of data if the computer is heavily loaded and cannot allocate processing time to the communications task frequently enough. In such cases, the data is corrupted by the host computer itself. There may also be incomplete data transmission to the remote system. Host processor capabilities should be a concern when choosing software for data communications when the line speed is greater than 9600bps and the modem-to-DTE connection is 19,200bps or higher (for example, when data compression is used). The modem will provide exact transmission of the data it receives, but if the host PC cannot "keep up" with the modem because of other tasks or speed restrictions, precautions should be taken when writing software or when adding modems with extra high-speed capabilities. One way to avoid the problem of data loss caused by the host PC is the use of an upgraded serial port, such as a Hayes Enhanced Serial Port card, or a newer modem with a 16550 UART. Such advanced modems are powerful enough to take some of the load off of the PC processor. When processor time is stretched to the limit, try shutting down any unnecessary applications to reduce load on the system. Processor loading can become a notable issue with today's WinModem devices.

Call Waiting The call waiting feature now available on most dial-up lines momentarily interrupts a call. This interruption causes a click that informs voice call users that another call is coming through. While this technique is dynamite for voice communication, it is also quite effective at interrupting a modem's carrier signal—and may cause some modems to drop the connection. One way around this is to set S-register S10 to a higher value so the modem tolerates a fairly long loss of carrier signal. Data loss may still occur, but the connection will not drop. Of course, the remote modem must be similarly configured. When originating the call, a special prefix (usually *70) can be issued as part of the dialing string to disable call waiting for the duration of the call. The exact procedure varies from area to area, so contact your local telephone system for details.

Automatic Timeout Some Hayes-compatible modems offer an automatic *timeout* feature. Automatic timeout prevents an inactive connection from being maintained. This "watchdog" feature prevents undesired long-distance charges for a connection that was maintained for too long. This inactivity delay can be set or disabled with S-register S30.

System Lock Up There are situations where host systems *do* lock up, but in many cases it is simply that one or the other of the computers has been *flowed off*—that is, the character that stops data transfer has been inadvertently sent. This can happen during error-control connections if the wrong kind of local flow control has been selected. In addition, the problem could be the result of incompatible EIA 232-D/ITU V.24 signaling. When systems seem to cease transmitting or receiving without warning, but do not disconnect, perform a thorough examination of flow control and, if possible, try a different flow control method.

Modem Initialization Strings As you saw earlier in this chapter, modems rely on initialization strings for proper configuration at start time or when new communication software is initialized. The initialization string *must* be correct for your particular modem in order to utilize all of the modem's features and achieve optimum performance. You may be able to use "generic" initialization strings but may not be able to get full functionality from the modem (for example, you may be able to use a Hayes-compatible initialization string, but Caller ID may not work). Check the modem's initialization string, try a new driver, or enter the preferred string in the "Extra settings" line of the modem's properties dialog.

MODEM TROUBLESHOOTING IN WINDOWS 98

Even with the versatility and support provided by Plug-and-Play, many modem setups are still plagued by installation, configuration, and performance problems—especially when used under a Windows platform such as Windows 98. This part of the chapter is intended to offer a basic troubleshooting guide for when your modem fails to dial out under Windows 98.

Verifying Your Modem

Begin by checking the modem's status in your Windows 98 system. It should be identified correctly and installed with the proper device drivers:

1. Click Start, highlight Settings, and then click Control Panel.
2. Double-click the Modems icon.
3. Select the General tab, and then verify that the modem listed in that entry is correct.

If there is no modem listed or an incorrect modem is listed (even though Windows 98 reported that a modem was detected), you should download the very latest driver for your modem, *remove* the current modem reference(s), and then update the modem drivers:

1. Click Start, highlight Settings, and then click Control Panel.
2. Double-click the System icon.
3. Select the Device Manager tab.
4. If a Modem entry exists, double-click the Modem branch to expand it. If the entry does not exist, look for an Other Devices branch, and then double-click to expand that branch.
5. Double-click your modem entry, click the Driver tab, and then click the Update Driver button.

Your Windows 98 *Update Device Driver* wizard will then search for the best driver (or display a list from which you can select the appropriate driver). If you use the Update Device Driver wizard to search for a driver, you can also specify a location for the driver. Drivers for some additional modems are included in the \Drivers\Modem folder on the Windows 98 CD, but if you've downloaded a new set of modem drivers from the manufacturer's Web site, you may need to look for the new drivers in your Temp or Download directories. After the modem drivers are updated, reboot the system and verify that the correct drivers are listed and then try using your modem again.

If the correct driver appears in your Device Manager, but the modem still refuses to operate properly, you may need to troubleshoot further. Follow the appropriate steps below, depending on whether your modem is a "WinModem" or "Standard Modem."

WinModem Issues A "WinModem" (also called a "Windows-only modem" or "software modem") depends on drivers that are *specific* to the operating system in order to function. This means that your modem *must* be recognized by the operating system *before* any troubleshooting can be performed. Windows 98 should normally detect the presence of a WinModem and add it to the Device Manager properly. If a WinModem is *not* detected, you should expect one of three possible causes:

- The WinModem has previously been detected (even though the correct drivers may not have been installed for it). In this case, the WinModem should be listed in your Device Manager, and the driver can be updated using the "Verifying Your Modem" procedure above.

- The WinModem drivers were installed and then removed, but some Registry entries remain. The Registry entries need to be removed before the WinModem can be detected again. For 3Com/US Robotics modems, use the WMREGDEL.EXE tool included on your Windows 98 CD to clear all WinModem-related Registry entries and then restart your computer. The WMREGDEL.EXE tool is located in the \Drivers\Modem\3com-usr\Winmodem folder. If Windows 98 still does not detect your WinModem, the WMREGDEL.EXE tool may not have removed all the necessary Registry entries. If this occurs, you may need to contact the particular modem maker in order to obtain a specific fix or workaround instructions (for example, there may be a specific Registry entry that needs to be deleted manually).
- The last option is to consider an actual WinModem defect—something may be wrong with the actual WinModem device. Try another WinModem (perhaps one from a different manufacturer), or check with your WinModem maker for specific testing instructions.

WinModem Driver Notes If there are no default Windows 98 drivers for your WinModem, Windows 98 prompts you to search for drivers. Suitable drivers may exist in the \Drivers\Modem folder on your Windows 98 CD. If no drivers are located for your particular WinModem, Windows 98 adds the device under the Other Devices branch of your Device Manager. You can then use the Device Manager to update the existing drivers with new drivers provided by your WinModem manufacturer.

If your WinModem still does not work after installing and/or updating the drivers, there may be a resource conflict or an issue specific to your particular WinModem. Use the following sections of this discussion to troubleshoot further.

> Given the dependence of a WinModem on operating system drivers, you *cannot* perform any troubleshooting outside of the operating system. For example, you *cannot* test a Windows 98 WinModem at a command prompt in the DOS mode.

FAX/MODEM ISSUES

A standard fax/modem does not offload important tasks to the host system or rely on the operating system for direct support. This means you may test the modem in DOS—even if it isn't detected by Windows. One of the easiest means of modem testing is to check direct communications with the modem port (COM port). Open a DOS windows under Windows 98, type the following command, and then press ENTER:

```
echo ATM1L3X0DT12345 > COM1
```

or replace "COM1" with the serial port number to which the modem is connected (for example, COM2 or COM3). The first command, **AT** (attention), signals that the modem is about to receive information. **M1** is a universal command to turn the modem's speaker on (if it is off by default). **L3** is a universal command to raise the modem's speaker volume to the maximum level (if it is at the lowest by default). **X0** signals the modem to run the command without waiting for a dial tone—this is useful if modem and voice calls use the same phone line. Finally, the **DT12345** command instructs the modem to dial the digits "12345." To hang up the modem again, simply type

```
echo ATH0 > COM1
```

and then press ENTER. If your modem is on a port other than COM1, replace COM1 with the serial port number to which the modem is connected (for example,. COM2 or COM3).

> To place your computer in DOS mode, click Start, click Shut Down, click "Restart In MS-DOS Mode," and then click OK. To quit MS-DOS mode, type **exit** at the command prompt, and then press ENTER.

If the modem does not respond with a dial tone or communication signal in DOS mode, there may be something physically wrong with either the modem or the COM port. Verify that the modem's COM port is configured as expected, or reconfigure the modem manually. If there is a resource conflict between the COM port and another device in the system, you may need to resolve the conflict in order to enable the modem. Otherwise, try a new modem.

If the modem does *not* respond with a dial tone or communication signal in Windows 98, but *does* respond in DOS mode, Windows 98 itself may not be communicating correctly with your COM port. This trouble can occur for several reasons:

- The COM port has not been detected. Click Start, highlight Settings, click Control Panel, double-click Add New Hardware, and then follow the instructions on your screen to detect and install the COM port.
- The serial port device drivers are corrupt. Use the System File Checker (or SFC) tool to verify the integrity of the SERIAL.VXD, VCOMM.VXD, and SERIALUI.DLL serial port drivers. To access the System File Checker (Figure 29-5), click Start, highlight Programs, highlight Accessories, point to System Tools, and then choose the System Information utility. Once the System Information utility starts, click Tools on the main menu, and then select the System File Checker. You may need to reinstall or update any damaged files.
- There is a resource conflict between your COM port and another device in the system. You'll need to resolve the conflict using the Device Manager as shown in the next section of this chapter.

RESOLVING RESOURCE CONFLICTS

A COM port requires the use of an interrupt (or IRQ) signal and an I/O port address. If you're using a WinModem, you should also plan on using a direct memory access (or DMA) channel. Normally, devices should use unique resources, with no two devices in the system can sharing the same resources. When the same resources are used by two or more devices, a *resource conflict* is said to occur. Conflicts may prevent

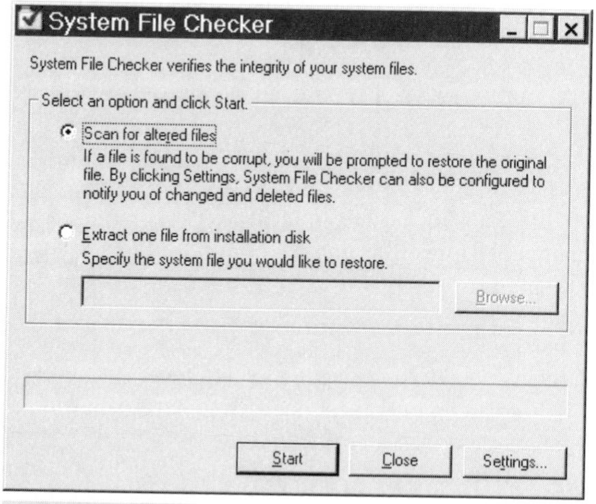

FIGURE 29-5 Using the System File Checker (SFC)

one or both conflicting devices from functioning until the conflict is identified and resolved. In virtually all cases, you can manage resources and resolve conflicts using the Device Manager:

1. Click Start, highlight Settings, and then click Control Panel.
2. Double-click the System icon, and then select the Device Manager tab.

   If a resource conflict prevents one device from working, an exclamation point in a yellow circle is displayed for the device. However, a WinModem that conflicts with another device *may not* have an exclamation point in a yellow circle—in this case, you must determine if there is a conflict yourself. Follow these steps to view the resource settings used by your modem:
3. On the Device Manager tab, double-click the Modem branch to expand it.
4. Double-click your modem, and then click the Resources tab.

> If a Resources tab does not exist, your modem's resources cannot be configured by Windows 98—to determine the resources your modem is using, consult the documentation included with your modem.

5. Write down the resource settings used by your modem, and then click OK.
6. Double-click Computer (at the top of your Device Manager hardware list) to view all the resource settings in use on your computer. Click each resource setting to determine if there is another device using any of the same settings your modem is using.

> Any hardware using the "IRQ Holder For PCI Steering" setting can be disregarded—this does *not* cause a resource conflict.

If another device is using any of the settings in use by your modem, you'll need to change the setting for that device (or your modem). If the device is Plug-and-Play compliant, you may be able to do this through the Resources tab in Device Manager (although some devices may require you to change jumper pins or dip switches on the device itself). Since WinModems are invariably Plug-and-Play devices, you should be able to change the settings for the modem through your Device Manager:

1. Double-click the Modem branch to expand it, and then double-click your WinModem entry.
2. On the Resources tab, click the Use Automatic Settings check box to clear it.
3. In the Setting Based On box, click a basic configuration with settings that do *not* conflict with any other device.

If *none* of the available basic configurations have settings that do not conflict with any other device, you may need to change some resource settings manually. Click the last available basic configuration and then double-click the resource setting you need to change. If you still cannot clear the conflict, you may need to remove the other conflicting device (at least temporarily).

Dealing with Other Issues

The general instructions covered in this discussion are designed to provide the essential troubleshooting guidelines for most common modem problems. Still, there are many other specific modem issues under Windows 98 that a technician should be aware of.

US Robotics WinModems Some US Robotics WinModems may *not* be detected properly during the Windows 98 upgrade process—this may occur even if the WinModem was working perfectly under

Windows 95. If your US Robotics WinModem is not detected when Windows 98 starts and is not listed in the Device Manager (under either the Modem or Other Devices branch), use the WMREGDEL.EXE tool included on the Windows 98 CD-ROM to clear all WinModem-related Registry entries, and then restart your computer. The WMREGDEL.EXE tool is located in the \Drivers\Modem\3com-usr\Winmodem folder on the Windows 98 CD.

If Windows 98 still does not detect your US Robotics WinModem, the WMREGDEL.EXE tool may not have removed all the necessary Registry entries—try an updated version of the WMREGDEL.EXE tool from the 3Com/US Robotics FTP site.

Sound4 WinModems Packard Bell systems typically incorporate the Sound4 WinModems, and these modems may *not* be detected properly during the Windows 98 upgrade process. If the WinModem stops working properly after upgrading to Windows 98, you'll need to contact Packard Bell technical support for a suitable workaround (depending on your system model).

WinModem Not Found After you upgrade to Windows 98 and then double-click the WinModem icon in your Control Panel, you may receive an error such as:

```
Error: There is no WinModem found in your computer, but some corrupted files
were found and they have been cleaned.
```

If you view your WinModem in Device Manager, you may also notice multiple WinModem entries. This problem will typically occur if your WinModem is not using the most current setup information (INF) file or device driver. You'll need to delete all of your WinModem entries, erase any WinModem references from the Registry, and then redetect/reinstall the WinModem using the very latest INF and driver files available from the modem maker.

29

Port Errors When you try to use your modem, you may receive an error message such as this:

```
Could not open port
```

This type of "hardware" error message is generally the result of a resource conflict between the modem and another device (or a program is loading in the Startup folder that opens a COM port for some other use other than the modem. If you'd like to weed out any possible resource conflicts, refer to the guidelines at the beginning of the "Resolving Resource Conflicts" section above. If you'd like to check for possible Startup folder issues, you can use the steps below to temporarily disable programs in the Startup folder:

1. Click Start, highlight Programs, select Accessories, highlight System Tools, and then click System Information.
2. On the Tools menu, select the System Configuration Utility.
3. Click the Startup tab.

   Identify any program that may control your modem, and then click that program's check box to clear it. If you're unsure whether or not a specific program should be disabled, clear *all* of the check boxes *except* for the following utilities:

   - ScanRegistry
   - SystemTray
   - LoadPowerProfile
   - TaskMonitor

4 Save your changes. Then reboot the system and see if your changes have cleared the problem. If they haven't, try disabling other nonessential files in the Startup folder.

DUN Error 630 When you attempt to use Dial-Up Networking (or DUN) services, you may receive an error message such as:

```
Error 630: The computer is not receiving a response from the modem. Check
that the modem is plugged in. Turn the modem off, and then turn it back on.
```

This error message will occur if the modem is using an adjusted serial port assignment caused when new devices are installed by Windows 98 hardware detection. In these cases, change the properties of your Dial-Up Networking (DUN) connection to use the new modem settings (rather than wrestle with tweaking the modem's settings).

> Certain programs in the Startup folder can also cause this error message. Systematically disable programs in the Startup folder as outlined in the "Port Errors" section above.

DUN Error 633 When you attempt to use Dial-Up Networking (or DUN) services, you may receive an error message such as:

```
Error 633: The modem is not installed or configured for Dial-Up Networking. To
check your modem configuration, double-click the Modems icon in Control Panel.
```

In many cases, you may need to delete and reconfigure the DUN settings for your modem. In other cases, this error message can occur if the TELEPHON.INI file is missing or damaged.

DUN Error 745 When you attempt to use Dial-Up Networking (or DUN) services, you may receive an error message such as:

```
Error 745: An essential file is missing. Re-install Dial-Up Networking.
```

This error message typically occurs when a Dial-Up Networking dynamic-link library (DLL) file is missing or damaged. You may need to remove DUN support from Windows 98 Setup, and then reinstall the support from the Windows 98 CD.

TAPI Issues Check the modem's diagnostics by clicking Start, highlighting Settings, and then clicking Control Panel. Double-click the Modems icon, and then select the Diagnostics tab. Click the More Info button to test the modem. When the modem passes its diagnostic tests, but is not available in HyperTerminal, Phone Dialer, or Dial-Up Networking (DUN), there may be a problem with the computer's Telephony Application Programming Interface (TAPI) setup, or the TELEPHON.INI file may be missing or damaged. You may need to reinstall TAPI support, or remove and reinstall the damaged TELEPHON.INI file.

CHECKING MODEM FIRMWARE

Today, it is common for modems to sport a "flash" BIOS ("firmware") that can be updated as new firmware versions are made available. Many late-model 33.6Kbps, x2 56Kbps, and K56flex 56Kbps modems offered such upgradable firmware in preparation for the V.90 standard. If you're considering a modem firmware upgrade, you'll need to check the current firmware version on your modem. You can use HyperTerminal to interrogate the firmware version of your modem:

1. Click Start, highlight Programs, select Accessories, and choose HyperTerminal.
2. Double-click the Hyperterm icon.
3. When the program starts, type **TEST** for a name, and proceed.
4. When you're asked for a telephone number, just type **1234**, and make sure that the correct modem device is selected from the Connect Using drop down menu. Click OK to proceed.
5. Now click Cancel (don't actually try connecting)—this will bring you to the terminal window.
6. Type in **ATE1** (even if you don't see it appear on the screen) and press ENTER. The modem should respond with "OK."
7. Now you can type any AT commands you wish. Try typing **ATi3** or **ATi92**—these two AT commands will tell you the exact firmware version and type of modem that you're using. For example, my modem responds:

```
U.S. Robotics Sportster 33600 Fax V4.3.185
```

Once you find the firmware version, you can compare it with the new version available for download, and upgrade your firmware if the online version is newer. To determine if your modem supports the V.90 standard, follow these steps:

1. Click Start, select Settings, click Control Panel, and then double-click the Modems icon.
2. On the Diagnostics tab, click the correct modem, and then click More Info.
3. After a few moments, a series of AT commands and responses will appear in the information box.
4. Locate the line that begins with "ATI7." If your modem supports the V.90 standard, "V.90" should be listed beside that command.
5. Click OK.

GENERAL SYMPTOMS

Many of the problems that you will encounter with modems/fax boards are related to their physical and software configuration. The host PC also plays an important role in the modem's overall performance and reliability. Modems themselves are rarely at fault—although they are hardly invulnerable. This part of the chapter presents you with an index of potential troubleshooting problems and solutions. When you determine that the modem itself is at fault, you should replace the modem outright. When replacing the modem, remember that the initialization and operating strings often vary slightly between modem manufacturers—be sure to alter any AT command strings in the communication software to accommodate the new modem.

SYMPTOM 29-1 The PC (or communication software) refuses to recognize the modem First, verify that the modem is turned on (external modems only)—for internal modems, see that the modem is installed correctly and completely in its expansion slot. Check your CMOS settings and verify that the COM port for your external modem is even enabled. There may be a COM port (IRQ) conflict in the system. Check the configuration of your internal modem (try the Windows 95 Device Manager) and verify that there are no hardware conflicts. If you have trouble running the modem in terminal mode (the modem doesn't respond to AT commands), make sure that you're entering everything in either upper-case (AT) or lower-case (at) format—mixing cases can sometimes confuse a modem.

SYMPTOM 29-2 Your 33.6Kbps modem is detected as a 28.8Kbps modem This can happen if your version of Windows 95/98 doesn't supply hardware information about the faster modem that you're trying to use. In virtually every case, you'll need to supply a suitable Windows 95/98 driver for the modem in the form of an INF file that accompanied the modem device or is available for download from the modem manufacturer's Web site.

SYMPTOM 29-3 The modem appears to be functioning properly, but you can't see what you are typing There are two types of duplex, *full* and *half*. Half-duplex systems simply transmit to and receive from each other. Full-duplex systems also do that, plus they "receive" what they transmit—echoing the data back to the sender. Since half-duplex systems do not echo, what is being sent is typically not shown on the screen. Most terminal programs have an option to enable LOCAL ECHO, so that what is transmitted is also displayed. You can often enable the modem's local echo by typing the **ATE1** command during a direct connection, or add the **E1** entry to the modem's initialization string. When local echo is not an option, switching to full-duplex mode will often do the same thing. Customer complaints that they can't see what they are typing are solved by turning on local echo or switching to full-duplex.

SYMPTOM 29-4 The modem appears to be functioning properly, but you see double characters while typing By their nature, full-duplex modem connections produce an echo. If local echo is enabled in addition, you'll see not only what you are transmitting but also that character being echoed, creating a double display—for example, when you hit "A," you'll see "AA." This can be annoying, but is totally harmless. Customer complaints of double letters are solved by turning off local echo by entering the **ATE0** command during direct connection, or adding the **E0** command to the modem's initialization string.

SYMPTOM 29-5 Your 32-bit TAPI-compliant programs cannot detect your modem Even though you have a modem installed under Windows 95/98/SE, a 32-bit TAPI program may not be able to access the modem. The TAPI program may even start the Install New Modem wizard. For example, the Install New Modem wizard may start when you launch the Make New Connection wizard in Dial-Up Networking—even though a modem is already installed. The following error message may appear after you attempt to dial a connection:

```
Error 633 The modem is not installed or configured for dial up networking.
To check your modem configuration, double click on the modems icon in the
Control Panel.
```

In virtually all cases, this fault will occur if the "Unimodem TAPI Service Provider" file (UNIMDM.TSP) is missing or damaged. To correct the fault, extract a new copy of the UNIMDM.TSP file from your original Windows disks or CD to the \Windows\System folder. For Windows 95, the UNIMDM.TSP file is located in the WIN95_03.CAB cabinet file. For Windows 98, the UNIMDM.TSP file is located in the WIN98_63.CAB cabinet file. For Windows 98 Second Edition, the UNIMDM.TSP file is located in the WIN98_69.CAB cabinet file.

SYMPTOM 29-6 Your modem diagnostics feature cannot access the modem under Windows 98 When you attempt to run modem diagnostics on the modem (for example, a 3Com Megahertz 10/100 LAN+56K Modem PC Card) after "resuming" your laptop from standby mode, you may receive the following error message:

```
Couldn't open port.
```

This problem can occur if you try running the modem diagnostics before the computer goes into standby mode. Modem diagnostics leaves the modem's communication port open. If the port is open when your computer goes into standby mode, it remains open after you "resume" your computer. This is a problem with Windows 98, and a patch is now available from Microsoft. The English version of this patch contains the following attributes:

```
VCOMM.VXD   6/25/99   12:51:29P   4.10.2017   WINDOWS 98
```

SYMPTOM 29-7 **You have trouble with a Sierra Semiconductor 33.6Kbps modem** When you try to use a Sierra Semiconductor 33.6Kbps modem under Windows 98, you may encounter an "Error 630" message, and your modem may not connect successfully. This problem may not occur with every program that uses your modem. This trouble can occur because the Sierra Semiconductor 33.6 modem driver is *not* fully compatible with Windows 98. To correct this issue, update the modem driver to a version that's fully compliant with Windows 98. To work around this issue, you can configure your modem to use the "Sierra 28800 PnP SQ3456" modem driver (though this will operate the modem at a slower speed than normal):

1 Click Start, highlight Settings, click Control Panel, and then double-click the System icon.
2 Click the Device Manager tab, double-click the Modem entry, click your Sierra modem, and then click Properties.
3 Click the Driver tab, click Update Driver, and then click "Display a list of all the drivers in a specific location, so you can select the driver you want."
4 In the Manufacturer's box, click Sierra Semiconductor.
5 In the Models box, click Sierra 28800 PnP SQ3456.
6 Click Next, and then follow the instructions on the screen to finish installing the driver.

29

SYMPTOM 29-8 **When creating a connection, your modem is missing from the Select A Device box** If you try to use an existing connection under Windows 98, you may receive an error such as:

```
Error 633: The modem is not installed or configured for Dial-Up Networking.
To check your modem configuration, double-click the Modems icon in Control Panel
```

If you test your modem by clicking More Info on the Diagnostics tab under the Modems icon in your Control Panel, your modem may respond normally—and appear to be working correctly. This problem can occur if the "TAPI service provider" entry in your Registry is missing (or corrupted), or if the TELEPHON.INI file is missing or damaged. Access the system Registry and use REGEDIT to view the following key:

```
HKEY_LOCAL_MACHINE\Software\Microsoft\Windows\Current Version\
Telephony\Providers
```

Set the value of the ProviderFilename0 value to **TSP3216L.TSP**. Save the changes, quit the Registry Editor, and then restart your computer. If the TELEPHON.INI file is missing or damaged, you'll need to recreate it:

1 Click Start, highlight Find, and then click Files Or Folders.

2. In the Named box, type **telephon.ini**, and then click Find Now.
3. If you do *not* find the TELEPHON.INI file, skip the next step. If you *do* find the TELEPHON.INI file, right-click the file, click Rename, type **telephon.old**, and then press ENTER.
4. Quit the Find tool, click Start, click Run, type **tapiini.exe**, and then press ENTER.
5. Restart your computer.

SYMPTOM 29-9 You encounter trouble with a PhoebeMicro 56Kbps modem under Windows 98/SE The modem may refuse to dial out. It may also hang up and crash the communication software with an error such as:

```
The modem failed to respond. Make sure it is properly connected and turned
on. If it is an internal modem or is connected, verify that the interrupt
for the port is properly set.
```

In virtually every case, the problem is due to faulty or outdated modem drivers accompanying the device. Contact the modem manufacturer to obtain the very latest drivers, or try default drivers on the Windows 98/SE CD.

SYMPTOM 29-10 Your modem refuses to dial out when using a TAPI program When you use a TAPI program under Windows 95/98 (such as Dial-Up Networking, Phone Dialer, or HyperTerminal), you may receive an error message such as:

```
There is no dialtone. Make sure your modem is connected to the phone line.
```

In most cases, this error occurs when you're trying to dial using a calling card, and you have enabled *the* "Wait for dial tone before dialing" option. You must disable the "Wait for dial tone before dialing" option:

1. Click Start, highlight Settings, and then click Control Panel.
2. Double-click the Modems icon.
3. Select your modem, and then click Properties.
4. On the Connection tab, click the "Wait for dial tone before dialing" check box to *clear* it.
5. Click OK, and then click OK again.
6. It may be necessary to restart the computer.

SYMPTOM 29-11 Your modem properties are not available through the modems icon in the Control Panel When you modify your modem's properties under Windows 95/98, the Configure button may be unavailable in HyperTerminal or Dial-Up Networking. Also, when you click your modem and then click Properties in the Modems tool under the Control Panel, you may receive an error message such as:

```
The modem properties cannot be displayed because the modem information is
corrupt. Remove this modem by clicking Remove and add it again.
```

However, you find that removing and reinstalling the modem does *not* correct the problem. In a few cases, this problem can occur if an incorrect version of the UMDM16.DLL file is installed in the \Windows\System folder. If this occurs, rename the UMDM16.DLL file and extract a new copy of the file from your original Windows CD. In the vast majority of cases, this problem will occur if the MODEMUI.DLL file is damaged. To correct this problem, use Windows Explorer or My Computer to rename the MODEMUI.DLL file in the \Windows\System folder to MODEMUI.OLD, and then extract a new copy of the MODEMUI.DLL file from your Windows CD to your \Windows\System folder.

SYMPTOM 29-12 **Your faxes are garbled when using a class 2 fax/modem** When you open the fax in a Windows 95/98 application such as Fax Viewer, the output may resemble a bar code, or contain blank pages. This is almost always a problem with the fax/modem, since some class 2 fax/modems reverse the bit order of incoming faxes. To correct this problem, switch the bit order of incoming faxes for each of your affected fax/modems by editing the Registry:

1 Exit your fax/modem software, and then launch your Registry Editor (REGEDIT).
2 Locate the following Registry key:

```
Hkey_Local_Machine\Software\Microsoft\At Work Fax\Local Modems\TAPI0001<xxxx>
```

where <xxxx> is a unique TAPI identifier for the fax/modem), and then add the string value **CL2SWBOR** to that Registry key.

3 Set the string value for CL2SWBOR to **1**.
4 Save your changes, quit the Registry Editor, and then restart your computer.

SYMPTOM 29-13 **Your V.34 internal 28.8Kbps modem is not detected properly** When you run the Add New Hardware wizard under Windows 95/98, the V.34 modem may be detected as a "standard modem," even though the modem is included in the hardware list. This problem occurs since the V.34 modem included in the hardware list is not a 28.8Kbps modem, but the actual installed modem *is* a 28.8Kbps modem. To install the modem correctly, you'll need to provide the manufacturer's drivers:

1 Click Start, highlight Settings, and then click Control Panel.
2 Double-click the Modems icon.
3 Click Add.
4 Click the "Don't detect my modem; I will select it from a list" check box to select it, and then click Next.
5 Click Have Disk.
6 In the Copy Manufacturer's File From box, type the path to the disk containing the manufacturer's driver files, and then click OK.
7 Follow the instructions on the screen to complete the installation.

SYMPTOM 29-14 **You cannot dial phone numbers of more than 32 characters** When you try to dial a long phone number (over 32 characters) under Windows 98, your modem may not respond or dial out. This is typically a driver issue and usually occurs when using a "controller-less" modem with a "standard" (or generic) modem driver instead of the driver that is specifically designed for your particular modem. To resolve this issue, you should obtain and install the most current modem driver for your particular modem.

SYMPTOM 29-15 **You cannot initialize your modem properly when using pcANYWHERE under Windows 98** When you use Symantec's pcANYWHERE 7.0 to dial out by modem and establish a connection, you may receive an *"Error initializing modem"* error message. The modem then continues to dial out, and the connection *is* established. The performance of pcANYWHERE is not affected, but the error message may appear every time you dial out with a modem to establish a pcANYWHERE connection. This problem is known to occur with version 7.0 of this software, and you will need to upgrade to pcANYWHERE 7.5 or later in order to correct the problem.

SYMPTOM 29-16 **The modem is detected on the wrong COM port on your PC** The modem may not respond or work correctly, and the modem may appear to be using COM3 even if you've configured your modem to use COM1. This is a known issue with systems such as the Acer Aspire and is caused by an issue with the system's BIOS. For example, this problem can occur if COM1 is disabled in your computer's BIOS, but the system incorrectly reports the disabled status of COM1—Windows 95/98 still detects COM1, and may assign your modem to COM3 to avoid resource conflicts. The proper long-term fix is to upgrade the system BIOS. But you may work around the issue by disabling COM1 in the Device Manager:

1. Right-click My Computer, click Properties, and then click the Device Manager tab.
2. Double-click the Ports (COM & LPT) branch to expand it, click Communications Port (COM1), and then click Properties.
3. Click to select the "Disable in this hardware profile" check box, and then click OK.
4. Double-click the Modems branch to expand it, click your modem, click Remove, click OK, and then restart your computer.
5. When your computer restarts, follow the instructions on the screen to reinstall your modem.

SYMPTOM 29-17 **You encounter an "Error 630" when dialing out with your modem** When you attempt to dial out under Windows 98, you may receive an error message such as:

```
Error 630: The computer is not receiving a response from the modem. Check
that the modem is plugged in, and if necessary, turn the modem off, and then
turn it back on.
```

You may also see an error indicating that the communication port is invalid or busy. This fault can occur if you have the "Support SerialKey devices" accessibility option configured to use the same COM port where your modem is connected. You'll need to disable or reconfigure the "Support SerialKey devices" option:

1. Click Start, highlight Settings, click Control Panel, and then double-click Accessibility Options.
2. On the General tab, either click to *clear* the "Support SerialKey devices" check box, or click Settings, click a different COM port in the Serial port box, and then click OK.
3. Click OK.

SYMPTOM 29-18 **You cannot get CU-SeeMe Videoconferencing to work with ADSL under Windows 98/SE** When you try to establish a CU-SeeMe video conference with an Internet Connection Sharing (or "ICS") host over an Asymmetric Digital Subscriber Line (ADSL) connection, you may be unable to connect to any Internet conference site. If you *are* able to initialize a conference, it may time out. You should disable ICS on the host computer:

1. Click Start, highlight Settings, click Control Panel, and then double-click Internet Options.
2. Click the Connections tab, and then click Sharing.

3 Click to *clear* the Enable Internet Connection Sharing check box, and then click OK.

4 Use CU-SeeMe on the ICS host.

SYMPTOM 29-19 The modem will not answer at the customer's site, but it works fine in the shop Since deregulation of the original Bell Telephone company, customers have been allowed to attach devices to phone lines with the proviso that they notify the phone company of each device's FCC registration and ringer equivalence number (REN). While few customers make it a point of informing their local telephone company how many phones and gadgets are connected to the telephone line, there is a good reason for having this information—you see, the amount of *ringing voltage* supplied to a site is fixed. If you load down the line beyond its maximum rating, not enough voltage will be available to ring all of the bells. The *ringer equivalence* is the amount of load that the device will place on the line. Modems have to be able to detect a ring signal before they know to pick up. If the ringing signal is too weak, the modem will not detect it properly and initiate an answer sequence.

Have the customer remove some other equipment from their phone lines and see if the problem disappears. With today's fax machines, modems, multiple extension phones and answering machines all plugged into the same line, it would be easy to overload the ringing voltage. The customer should also take a listing of the registration numbers and ringer equivalence numbers on *all* devices connected to phone lines and notify the local phone company of them. The phone company can then boost the ringer voltage to compensate for the added loads.

As a precaution, make sure that your customer is starting the communication software properly before attempting to receive a modem call—the modem will not pick up a ringing line unless the proper software is running and the modem is in an auto-answer mode.

SYMPTOM 29-20 Your modem is receiving or transmitting garbage or is having great difficulty displaying anything at all Serial communication is totally dependent on the data frame settings and transfer rate of the receiver and the transmitter being an exact match. The baud rate, word bits, stop bits, and parity must all match exactly or errors will show up. These errors can show as either *no* data or as *incorrect* data (garbage) on screen. You'll see this one crop up a lot when customers switch from calling a local BBS to CompuServe. Local BBS's are usually set for 8 bit words, no parity, and one stop bit. CompuServe, on the other hand, uses 7 bit words, even parity and 2 stop bits. The terminal software must be reconfigured to match the settings of each service being called. Most programs allow for these differences by letting you specify a configuration for each entry in the dialing directory. Also check the method of flow control being used (for example, XOFF/XON, DTR/DSR, CTS/RTS) and make sure that it is set properly.

Baud rate mismatches most often result in what looks like a dead modem—often, nothing is displayed on either end. Modems will automatically negotiate a common baud rate to connect at without regard to the terminal settings. The modems will normally connect at the highest baud rate available to the SLOWEST modem, so if a 14,000bps modem connects to a 2400bps modem, both will set themselves to 2400bps. If the software on the higher speed modem is still set for the higher speed, you'll typically get large amounts of garbage, or nothing at all.

If the problem is a result of being connected to a service such as a BBS, call the SYSOP and find out the settings. You can also let the modem tell you what transfer rate it connects at. Before dialing, set a direct connection and send the command **ATQ0V1** to the modem. This command tells the modem to send result codes in plain English. When connected, you'll see a message similar to "CONNECT 2400." The actual number you see is the bps rate, and you can reconfigure your software accordingly. Working out the word, stop, and parity bits may be a process of trial and error, but almost all BBS installations use 8 data

29

bits, no parity, and 1 stop bit. If you are forced to attempt trial and error, target one item to get right at a time. First get the baud rates to match. Next get word bits settled down, and then go for parity and stop bits. If you make more than one change you'll never know which change made the difference. It may *seem* slower, but your overall service time will be cut.

SYMPTOM 29-21 The modem is connected and turned on, but there is no response from the modem The communication software's configuration must match the port settings of the modem. Check to make sure that any modem parameters are entered and saved properly. Establish a direct connection with the modem and enter the **ATZ** command. Doing this will reset the modem. The modem should respond "OK" or "0" (the numerical equivalent of OK). If that doesn't work, change to COM2 and try again, and then COM3 and COM4. If none of the combinations work, check the DIP switches or jumpers on the modem for the correct configuration. Finally, try the modem on another PC, or replace the suspect modem outright.

SYMPTOM 29-22 The modem will not pick up phone line The modem is not able to initiate a call or answer an incoming call. Most modems today come with two RJ11 telephone line connectors for the phone lines: one labeled "LINE" (where the outside line enters the modem) and the other labeled "PHONE" (where an extension telephone can be plugged in). Check that the outgoing telephone line is plugged into the LINE jack. Leave the PHONE connector disconnected while the modem is in use.

Test the modem manually by establishing a direct connection and typing a dial command such as **ATDT15083667683**. When you enter this command string, the modem should go off hook, draw a dial tone, and dial the numbers. If this happens as expected, you can be reasonably sure that the modem is working properly—and the communication software is at fault. Check the modem initialization strings, or try a new communication package. If the modem does not respond during a direct connection, check that the modem is installed and configured properly. You may need to try a new modem.

SYMPTOM 29-23 The modem appears to work fine, but prints garbage whenever it's supposed to show IBM text graphics such as boxes or ANSI graphics Your terminal emulation mode is wrong. The communication software is probably set for 7-bit words. The IBM text graphic character set starts at ASCII 128 and has to have the eighth bit. Adjust the communication software configuration to handle 8 bit words. You may also be using an unusual ASCII character set during the connection—try setting the character set emulation to ANSI BBS or TTY.

SYMPTOM 29-24 Strange character groups like "[0m" frequently appear in the text These are ANSI control codes attempting to control your display. Popular among BBS software, ANSI codes can be used to set colors, draw ASCII boxes, clear the screen, move the cursor, and so on. DOS provides an ANSI screen driver called ANSI.SYS that can be loaded into the CONFIG.SYS when the computer is rebooted. Most of today's terminal software offer a setting for this as well. If you are able to select character set emulation in your communication software, try setting to ANSI BBS.

SYMPTOM 29-25 The modem makes audible "clicking" noises when connected to phone line There is probably a short in the phone line. The clicking is the noise of the modem trying to pick up when it sees the short and hang up when the short clears. Try replacing the line cord going from the modem to the telephone wall jack—line cords don't last very long under constant use and abuse. If problems continue, try using a different telephone line—the physical wiring may be defective between the wall jack and telephone pole. Contact your local telephone company if you suspect this to be the case.

Next, try establishing a direct connection to the modem and enter an **AT&F** command, which will restore the modem's factory default settings. If that clears the problem, the modem's initialized state may not be fully compatible with the current telephone line characteristics. Check each modem setting carefully and adjust parameters to try and settle its operation down. If factory default settings do not help and the telephone line seems reliable, there may be a problem with the modem's telephone interface circuit—try replacing the modem.

SYMPTOM 29-26 **The modem is having difficulty connecting to another modem** The modem is powered and connected properly. It dials the desired number and you can hear the modems negotiating, but they never quite seem to make a connection. This is a classic software configuration problem. You may often see a NO CARRIER message associated with this problem. Check each parameter in your communication software—especially the modem's AT initialization string. Make sure that each entry in the string is appropriate for your modem. If the string looks correct, try disabling the modem's MNP5 protocol. You will have to refer to the modem's manual to find the exact command, but many modems use **AT\N0**. If your modem is using MNP5 and the destination modem does not support it, the negotiation can hang up. If problems persist, try lowering the modem's data transfer rate. While most modems can set the proper transfer rate automatically, some modems that do not support it may also cause the negotiation to freeze.

Another problem may be that your modem is not configured to wait long enough for carrier from the remote modem. You can adjust this delay by entering a larger number for S-register S7. Start the communication software, establish a direct connection (terminal mode), and type **ATS7?** followed by the ENTER key. Doing this will return the current value of register S7. You can then use the command **ATS7=10** to enter a larger delay (in this case, 10 seconds). That should give the destination modem more time to respond. If all else fails, try a modem from a different manufacturer.

29

SYMPTOM 29-27 **The modem starts dialing before it draws dialtone** As a result one or more of the numbers are lost during dialing making it difficult to establish a connection. Chances are that the modem is working just fine, but the modem does not wait long enough for dial tone to be present once it goes off hook. The solution is to increase the time delay *before* the modem starts dialing. This can be done by changing the value in S-register S6. To find the current value, start the communication software and establish a direct connection (terminal mode), and then type **ATS6?** followed by pressing the ENTER key. This queries the S-register. You can then enter a new value such as **ATS6=10** to provide a 10 second delay.

SYMPTOM 29-28 **The modem has trouble sending or receiving when the system's power-saving features are turned on** This type of problem is most prevalent with PCMCIA modems running on a notebook PC. The power conservation features found on many notebook systems often interferes with the modem's operation—proper modem operation typically relies on full processing speed, which is often scaled back when power conservation is turned on. Ultimately, the most effective resolution to this problem is simply to turn the power conservation features off while you use the modem (you can reset the power features later). However, it may be possible to correct these types of problems using a BIOS upgrade for the mobile PC or an updated modem driver.

SYMPTOM 29-29 **You see an error such as "Already on line" or "Carrier already established"** These types of errors often arise when you start a communications package while the modem is already online. You might also find this problem when the Carrier Detect (CD) signal is set to "always on" (using a command string such as **AT&C0**). To make sure that the CD signal is on only when the modem makes a connection, use a command string such as **AT&C1&D2&W**. The **&W** suffix loads the settings into non-volatile RAM. If this problem arises when you hang up the connection without signing off the modem, you will have to reboot the system to clear CD—**AT&F** and **ATZ** will *not* clear the signal.

SYMPTOM 29-30 The modem refuses to answer the incoming line First, make sure to set the communication software to answer the calling modem—or set the modem to auto-answer mode (set S-register S0 to 1 or more). On external modems, you will see the AA LED lit when the auto-answer mode is active. Problems can also occur if your external modem does not recognize the DTR signal generated by the host PC. The command **AT&D** controls how the modem responds to the computer's DTR signal. An external modem turns on the TR light when it is set to see the DTR signal. If the TR light is out, the modem will not answer (regardless of whether the auto-answer mode is enabled or not). Use the **AT&D0** command if your serial port does not support the DTR signal, or if your modem cable does not connect to it. Otherwise, you should use the **AT&D2** command.

SYMPTOM 29-31 The modem switches into the command mode intermittently When this problem develops, you may have to tweak the DTR arrangement. To correct this fault, try changing the modem's DTR setting using the command **AT&D2&W**.

SYMPTOM 29-32 Your current modem won't connect at 2400bps with a 2400bps modem This is a compatibility issue between vastly different generations of hardware. The modem you're trying to connect with is almost certainly an older model that doesn't support error control (that is, MNP protocols). You can disable error control on your modem with the command **AT&M0** and ENTER; after doing so, try placing the call to the modem again. When you're finished, reset your modem with **ATZ** to re-enable the error control features.

SYMPTOM 29-33 The communications software is reporting many cyclic redundancy check (CRC) errors and low characters per second (CPS) transfers This may simply be a matter of a poor phone connection established through the telephone network. Try making the call again—chances are that the call will be routed differently and result in a more reliable connection. Next, check the flow control scheme (XOFF/XON, CTS/RTS, and so on) to verify that it is optimum, or type **AT&F1** from the terminal mode to load the optimum flow control setting. The serial port rate in your communications software may be set too high for your modem's UART or your area's phone lines. Try lowering the serial port rate in your communications software to 38,400bps or 19,200bps (or lower for slower modems). The remote site you are dialing into may have trouble with the file transfer protocol you've selected. Try using a different file transfer protocol (such as Ymodem-g rather than Zmodem). Do not use Xmodem if other protocols are available. Finally, there may be a TSR program running in the background and interfering with data communications. Disable any TSR programs running in the background, and try the communication again.

SYMPTOM 29-34 Errors are constantly occurring in your v.17 fax transmissions As a rule, sending fax transmissions over a modem should present no special problems for a PC, but there are some issues to keep in mind. First, your modem initialization string could be insufficient or incomplete for fax transmissions. Enter the correct initialization string for fax support (for example, **AT&H3&I2&R2S7=90**). You could also have a disruptive TSR program running in the background. Disable any TSR programs and try the communication again. There could be an outdated communications driver on your system. Load the communications driver that came with your fax software (doing this may require that you reinstall your internal modem). Finally your baud rate may be set too high. Try a lower baud rate of 9600bps.

SYMPTOM 29-35 **Your 32-bit communications programs may report a slower speed than your 16-bit communications programs** For example, if your 16-bit programs report that they are communicating at 38400 bits per second (bps), your 32-bit Windows 95/98 programs may report that they are communicating at 14000bps. The problem here is a difference in the way 16-bit and 32-bit programs report communication speeds.

A 32-bit communication program designed for Windows 95/98/NT reports the modem *line speed* when reporting the speed at which the program is communicating. The modem line speed is the speed between your modem and the modem you're connected to (the speed at which data is transmitted over the telephone line). By comparison, most 16-bit communications programs that are designed for DOS/Windows 3.x report the *port speed* when reporting the speed at which the program is communicating. The port speed is the speed between your modem and your computer (the speed between the serial port that your modem is connected to and your computer). Since port speed is typically faster than modem line speed, 16-bit programs generally report a faster speed than 32-bit programs. You can use the following workaround to correct the issue:

1. Click Start, highlight Settings, and then click Control Panel.
2. Double-click Modems.
3. Click your modem and then click Properties.
4. On the Connection tab, click Advanced.
5. In the Extra Settings box, type **S95=0** and then click OK.
6. Click OK and then click Close.

SYMPTOM 29-36 **During installation, a modem setup program cannot find the internal modem** In virtually all cases, this is a hardware conflict between the modem and another device in the system. Check the hardware installation first. For internal modems, make sure the IRQ and I/O address are set correctly and see that there are no other devices using the same IRQ or I/O space as your modem. Under Windows 95/98, the Device Manager can usually display any conflicting devices with yellow icons (exclamation marks). Next, make sure that the modem is inserted properly into its bus slot. If any of the card's gold "fingers" appear corroded or soiled, clean the fingers gently with a pencil eraser. Try the modem in another bus slot. Finally, check the modem switches. Most external modems use a series of DIP switches to configure their various features. Refer to the modem's documentation and see that any modem switches are set properly.

SYMPTOM 29-37 **After installing a new internal modem, the system mouse driver no longer loads or the mouse behaves erratically** In virtually all cases, there is a hardware conflict between the new modem and the existing mouse port. Check the hardware installation. If the mouse is connected to a COM port, make sure that your internal modem is set to use a different COM port. You may need to disable COM2 on the motherboard or I/O controller and set up the modem as COM2. Under Windows 95/98, the Device Manager can usually display any conflicting devices with a yellow icon (exclamation mark).

SYMPTOM 29-38 After installing modem driver software, Windows locks up or crashes This is almost always the result of a defective or outdated modem driver. Check the software installation. Make sure that the modem driver software you have installed is the proper version for the particular modem, *and* your version of Windows (that is, 3.1, 3.11, 95, or 98). You can usually check the driver version on the modem's manufacturer's BBS, CompuServe forum, or Internet web site. If you do find that the modem driver is incorrect, run any "uninstall" utility that accompanied the software in order to remove the driver cleanly—otherwise, you'll have to remove the modem driver references from SYSTEM.INI manually. Under Windows 95/98, you can often *Remove* a device from the Device Manager, and then allow Windows to re-detect the modem during the next boot (and reinstall the new drivers at that point).

SYMPTOM 29-39 DOS communication software works fine, but Windows communication software does not You may also see Windows error messages suggesting that certain files are missing. In most cases, the modem drivers (and any required parameters) have not been loaded properly. Check the software installation and make sure that the modem driver software you have installed is the proper version for the particular modem *and* your version of Windows (that is, 3.1, 3.11, 95, or 98). Try uninstalling the modem drivers (if possible), and then reload the drivers from scratch, making sure that they are set up properly for your system configuration. Next, check the manufacturer's BBS, CompuServe forum, or Internet web site for any adjustments or workarounds that may be required for your particular modem and drivers. You may need to make manual adjustments to SYSTEM.INI and WIN.INI files, as well as to the Windows 95/98 Registry files.

SYMPTOM 29-40 You cannot get the modem's "distinctive ring" feature to work Some new modems support the "distinctive ring" service provided by many telephone companies. This allows the modem to reside on the same physical telephone line as other devices, but only answer when the proper ringing pattern is received. Improper modem configuration is the most common problem. Try calling the distinctive ring numbers associated to your telephone line and see that each number rings with the required pattern. Note that the distinctive ring service is not available from all telephone companies and service areas. Next, check the initialization string for S101. Modems supporting distinctive ring usually control the feature through register S101. A typical AT command string may appear such as **AT&FS101=60**. A typical setting list is shown below:

- **S101=0** Detects all ringing cadences and report them with RING result code.
- **S101=1** Enables the RING result codes; all ringing types will be reported.
- **S101=30** Reports only unidentified ring types.
- **S101=46** Reports only ring type D.
- **S101=54** Reports only ring type C.
- **S101=58** Reports only ring type B.
- **S101=60** Reports only ring type A.
- **S101=62** Disables *all* ringing detection—the modem will not answer any ring.

> To specify a particular ring type, you must DISABLE the other ring types with this register.

Next, check the initialization string for -SDR. Rather than using S-register 101, some modems use the -SDR command to configure distinctive ring operation. A typical AT command string may appear as **AT&F-SDR=1**. A setting list is shown below:

- **-SDR=0** Disables the distinctive ring function.
- **-SDR=1** Enables distinctive ring type 1.
- **-SDR=2** Enables distinctive ring type 2.
- **-SDR=3** Enables distinctive ring types 1 and 2.
- **-SDR=4** Enables distinctive ring type 3.
- **-SDR=5** Enables distinctive ring types 1 and 3.
- **-SDR=6** Enables distinctive ring types 2 and 3.
- **-SDR=7** Enables distinctive ring types 1, 2, and 3.

SYMPTOM 29-41 **You cannot get the modem's caller ID Feature to Work** Some new modems support the Caller ID service provided by many telephone companies. This feature allows the modem to identify the telephone number and caller to the computer's communication software when the ringing line is answered. Improper modem configuration is the most common problem. Before you do anything else, check the Caller ID service. Connect any Caller ID-compatible telephone or phone box to the telephone line and make sure that the ID service is working properly. Note that the Caller ID service is not available from all telephone companies and service areas. Also, remove other Caller ID devices. It is possible that other Caller ID-compatible telephones or phone boxes may be interfering with the modem. Try removing any other devices from the phone line. Check the initialization string for %CCID. Modems supporting Caller ID usually control the feature through a %CCID command. A typical AT command string may appear such as **AT&F%CCID=1**. A setting list is shown below:

- **%CCID=0** Turns Caller ID off.
- **%CCID=1** Gives Caller ID data using a formatted output.
- **%CCID=2** Gives Caller ID data using an unformatted output.

Finally, check the initialization string for #CID. Rather than using the %CCID command, some modems support Caller ID using the #CID command. A typical command string may appear such as **AT&F#CID=1**. A setting list is shown below:

- **AT#CID=0** Turns Caller ID off.
- **AT#CID=1** Gives Caller ID data using a formatted output.
- **AT#CID=2** Gives Caller ID data using an unformatted output.

> There are two special messages that may be sent instead of Caller ID information. "O" means that the caller is *Out* of the Caller ID service area—usually a long-distance call. "P" is for *Private* and will be displayed for callers who have made arrangements with their phone company to have their numbers blocked.

SYMPTOM 29-42 **You cannot recall previous Caller ID data** This assumes that normal Caller ID features are proven to be working correctly. In most cases, your communication software is not sending the correct AT command to your modem. Check the Caller ID feature and make sure that Caller

ID is enabled using the %CCID or #CID commands as in the previous symptom. Caller ID *must* be enabled first before data can be recalled. Check the initialization string for %CRID. Caller ID data can typically be recalled using the %CRID command, such as **AT%CRID=0** (recall formatted data) or "**AT%CRID=1**" (recall unformatted data).

SYMPTOM 29-43 The modem will not provide synchronous communication

Modems are typically asynchronous devices, but most can be configured for synchronous communication with host systems such as mainframe computers. If your modem will not work in synchronous mode, chances are that the modem is not configured properly. You *must* configure *both* the originating modem and the answering modem. The originating modem will be configured for *synchronous originate* mode and will dial a stored number when a connection is attempted. You will need a dumb terminal or terminal emulation software to configure the modem:

1. Attach the modem to a serial port on a PC or dumb terminal using a standard RS-232 cable.
2. Configure the *port speed* setting in the dumb terminal or the terminal emulation software to match the speed that will be used on the synchronous port.
3. Configure the software for *direct connect* or *terminal mode* and open the connection to the port.
4. Type **AT&F&W** and press ENTER. The modem should respond with "OK." If double characters appear, type **ATE0** and press ENTER to disable local character echo.
5. Type **AT&Q2&S2&W** and press ENTER. The modem should respond with "OK."
6. Type **AT&Z0=T[*phone number to store*]** and press ENTER. The modem should respond with "OK."
7. Type **AT&D2&W** and press ENTER. The modem should respond with "OK."
8. Type **AT&C1E0Q1&W** and press ENTER. The modem should *not* respond with "OK" because character echo and result code reporting have been disabled.

Next, configure the answering modem. The answering modem must be configured for *synchronous answer* mode. Although the answering modem is usually attached to the mainframe host system, you will first need to connect it to a dumb terminal for configuration. To configure the answering modem:

1. Attach the modem to a serial port on a PC or dumb terminal using a standard RS-232 cable.
2. Configure the *port speed* setting in the dumb terminal or the terminal emulation software to match the speed that will be used on the synchronous port.
3. Type **AT** and press ENTER. The modem should respond with "OK." If double characters appear, type **ATE0** and press ENTER to disable local character echo.
4. Type **AT&F&W** and press ENTER. The modem should respond with "OK."
5. Type **AT&Q1&S2&W** and press ENTER. The modem should respond with "OK."
6. Type **ATS0=1** (or the number of rings you want the modem to answer on) and press ENTER. The modem should respond with "OK."
7. Type **AT&D2&W** and press ENTER. The modem should respond with "OK."
8. Type **AT&C1E0Q1&W** and press ENTER. The modem should *not* respond with "OK" because character echo and result code reporting have been disabled.

Now, disable command recognition. After each modem has been configured properly, the command recognition should be disabled as follows:

1. Turn the modems off.
2. Locate the DIP switches that define modem operations.
3. Move the proper DIP switch to turn *command recognition* off. If the modem is internal, move the appropriate jumper. The particular DIP switch or jumper will depend on your specific modem, so check with the modem's documentation.
4. Turn the modems on.

Finally, establish a synchronous connection. Attach the originating modem to the SDLC or synchronous port and turn the power on. When a connection is attempted, the modem will automatically dial the stored number and attempt to connect to the other modem. Attach the answering modem to the synchronous port on the host system. The modem will answer incoming calls in "&Q1" synchronous mode.

SYMPTOM 29-44 The modem appears to be set up and configured properly, but it is experiencing data loss Such symptoms may appear as excessive file transfer errors, missing text or characters, and jumbled ASCII text. Though modern modems are capable of data rates up to 230400bps, data rates over 19200bps can cause problems for older PCs due to inadequate serial port hardware. Check the UART first—your serial ports should be using 16550A UARTs for optimum performance. If the UART is older, data throughput will be limited. If you cannot upgrade the UART chip directly, you can often disable the existing serial port and install an upgraded I/O board. Any diagnostic program such as MSD can identify the UARTs in your system. Check your modem drivers and make sure that the modem driver software is up-to-date and optimized for your particular version of Windows (that is, 3.1, 3.11, 95, or 98). Finally, reduce your data rates. If you cannot resolve the problem through a driver or new UART, try reducing the modem's data rate in your communication software.

29

SYMPTOM 29-45 When running modem software, you see an error such as "Can't run on a Plug and Play ready system" In most cases, the PCMCIA modem is incompatible with a PC's PnP architecture. Check your PnP driver. You may need to load an alternative PnP driver for your modem. Check with the modem manufacturer's BBS, CompuServe forum, or Internet web site to obtain any updated driver software. You may need to disable the existing DOS PnP driver in CONFIG.SYS.

SYMPTOM 29-46 The modem appears to be set up and configured properly, but it regularly connects at slower speeds than it is capable of There are several different factors that can account for such a problem. First, modems can connect only at the maximum speed of the slowest modem. If the remote modem is slower than yours, your connection speed will be limited. Try connecting to a faster BBS or other online connection. Check the modem initialization string next—there may be one or more important commands missing from the command string. Look for the recommended initialization string in the modem's documentation. Also see that the correct modem is selected in the communication software. Check the modem's firmware version. Use the **ATI3** command to check the modem's ID information (including the firmware revision). If the firmware is old, it may need to be updated. If the firmware is very new, it may contain a bug that the manufacturer should be made aware of. Finally, try a different phone line. Faulty or noisy telephone connections can reduce effective communication speed. Try the call at an off time, or try calling on a different phone line.

SYMPTOM 29-47 **Windows 95/98 insists on assigning the modem to COM5** You will need to reconfigure the modem's port assignment through the Control Panel. First, you'll need to remove any unused modem entries. Software that has been loaded for previous modems may interfere with the current modem's software. Remove unused modem hardware references through the Device Manager:

1. Select My Computer, double-click on Control Panel, and then choose Modems.
2. Highlight any modems that are no longer in the system and click on the Remove button.
3. If there are multiple entries for the same modem, remove all entries for the modem, restart the system, and then reinstall the software.

   Next, verify the modem on COM5. Check to see that the modem is identified and checks properly before continuing:

4. Select My Computer, double-click on Control Panel, and then choose Modems.
5. Select the Diagnostics tab.
6. Highlight COM5 and press the More Info... button.
7. Verify that the modem responds to the **ATI3** command with its proper ID information.
8. Click OK.

Now find an unused COM port. Check the Diagnostics screen and examine the COM ports in use—any ports not in use are available. Next, use REGEDIT.EXE to edit the Windows 95/98 Registry. You can change the COM port assignment by adjusting the Registry:

1. Click on the Start button, and then select Run.
2. Type **regedit** and click OK.
3. Select the Edit/Find option, and then type **COM5**.
4. Click Find Next—this should highlight PORTNAME under a Registry key.
5. Double-click on PORTNAME.
6. Enter the new COM port, such as **COM2**.
7. Click OK, and then close REGEDIT.
8. Shut down and restart Windows 95/98.

> Before attempting to edit a Windows 95 Registry file, make sure to have a complete backup of the registry files SYSTEM.DAT and USER.DAT.

Finally, check the updated configuration and verify that modem now works on new COM port:

1. Select My Computer, double-click on Control Panel, and then choose Modems.
2. Select the Diagnostics tab.
3. Select the new COM port that you selected for the modem.
4. Click the More Info... button.
5. Verify that the modem responds to the **ATI3** command with its proper ID information.
6. Click OK.

SYMPTOM 29-48 You cannot get the modem to work with a Winsock, but conventional bbs or Compuserve connections work fine In almost all cases, one or more command strings in your Internet connection configuration files is causing an error with the modem. First, make sure that you are using the Winsock version that is appropriate for your particular Internet connection software. Next, check the configuration file. Contact your modem manufacturer to check on any fixes or workarounds (some modems may not work with the default command strings provided with their Internet software). For example, the Motorola Power 14.4 PCMCIA modem will not work with Trumpet Winsock because of an error in the LOGIN.CMD file—the $modemsetup= string is wrong.

SYMPTOM 29-49 You are having trouble configuring the modem for hardware and software flow control This problem is usually due to invalid command strings. Try some generic command strings. The following two AT command strings can configure most Hayes-compatible modems for hardware or software flow control. Keep in mind that you may need to add additional commands in order to configure the modem completely:

- Software flow control (XON/XOFF) **AT&F1&C1&D2**
- Hardware flow control (CTS/RTS) **AT&F1&C1&D2\Q3**

SYMPTOM 29-50 The modem will not establish a connection through a cellular telephone In most cases, the modem is not configured properly. Check the SCM setting first—make sure that the *Station Class Mark* (SCM) level is set correctly. Try resetting the modem with an **AT&F1** command. Check the phone type. Make sure that the telephone is set to *analog* mode—the digital mode may interfere with modem operation.

SYMPTOM 29-51 The modem will not fax properly through a cellular telephone In most cases, the modem is not configured properly. Check the modem's initialization string first and make sure that it's set correctly. A basic command string may be **AT&F1E1V1&C1&D2\Q3S7=90S10=60** (though this may not work on all modems). Check the *data rate* next. For faxing, see that the data rate is set to 4800. You may use the command **AT%B4800**.

29

SYMPTOM 29-52 Windows 95/98 recognizes the modem, but 16-bit communications software will not see it Windows 95/98 may not have updated the SYSTEM.INI file to reflect changes to the COM port settings. Check the SYSTEM.INI file. Your COM port base address and IRQs are defined in the [386Enh] section of your SYSTEM.INI file. Check these settings to make sure that they match your modem's settings. The following lines need to be added to your SYSTEM.INI file in the [386enh] section:

```
com1irq=4
com1base=03f8
com2irq=3
com2base=02f8
com3irq=4
com3base=03e8
com4irq=3
com4base=02e8
```

SYMPTOM 29-53 DOS ICU software is installed, but it will not allow configuring the modem on COM1 or COM2 The ICU software may be inappropriate for your particular modem and system configuration. Check with the modem manufacturer and see if there is a replacement DOS PnP driver or other workaround. If there is alternate PnP software available, you may need to remove the installation of ICU before proceeding:

1 Delete the ESCD.RF file from the root directory of c:\.
2 In the CONFIG.SYS file, delete the line that says: "device=c:\plugplay\..." then save your changes.
3 In the [386Enh] section of SYSTEM.INI, delete the lines that start with "device=c:\plugplay..." then save your changes.
4 In the [windows] section of WIN.INI, the RUN= entry should have no reference to ICU or PLUGPLAY after the equal sign. Save your changes if any were made.
5 Delete the c:\plugplay directory.
6 Exit Windows and reboot your system.

SYMPTOM 29-54 The modem's flash ROM update will not install because it cannot recognize the modem's current firmware version This is invariably a problem with the flash ROM update software itself. Check the software source. Contact the manufacturer to see if there is a corrected update available or see if there is a workaround to the problem. There may be one or more command line switches that can override the update's firmware autodetection.

SYMPTOM 29-55 The modem establishes connections properly, but it frequently drops connections Both hardware and software issues can cause this kind of trouble. Problems with the telephone connection itself can cause connection problems. Try connecting to various different places. If problems seem to occur more frequently in one connection over another, the remote location may be suffering from communications problems. Also try using a different local telephone line. Next, check the modem's initialization string and make sure that the modem is set up properly for data compression and error correction. Finally, check the Windows driver. If you are using Windows-based communications software, it must be able to support high speed. The standard Windows drivers will not support 28.8KB operation unless third-party communications software modifies it (though Windows 98 drivers are more current). To find out what communications driver you are currently using, review the [Boot] section of your SYSTEM.INI file.

SYMPTOM 29-56 When selecting a modem in your communication software, your particular modem is not listed You will need to obtain the proper driver supplements from the modem manufacturer (or software maker). Try running the modem as a Hayes-compatible—virtually all modems will function as generic Hayes-compatible modems "AT&F&C1&D2."

SYMPTOM 29-57 The modem seems to take a long time to hang up The carrier delay time is probably set too long. Check the carrier delay time. Modems can be set to wait (often for as long as 25 seconds) after a carrier is lost to see whether it comes back—if you frequently encounter poor signal quality, this feature can be quite convenient. After a legitimate hang-up, however, the modem may continue to wait. In this case, you may want to set the value of the S10 register to a low number—10 or less.

SYMPTOM 29-58 The modem is configured as COM4 (IRQ3) under Windows 95/98, but the modem refuses to work There may be a hardware acceleration issue. Go into the Windows 95/98 Control Panel, double-click the System icon, select Performance, and then click Graphics. Set Hardware Acceleration to "None" and try the modem again. Some advanced modem manufacturers have found an addressing conflict with certain graphic accelerator cards. If you configure your Windows 95 graphic driver to basic VGA and find the modem now works at that setting, and then the problem is probably an addressing conflict with your graphics card. You may want to try using one of the more commonly used COM port and IRQ settings. such as:

■ COM 1	IRQ 4
■ COM 2	IRQ 3
■ COM 3	IRQ 5 (if not used by your sound card)

SYMPTOM 29-59 When autodetect tries to add a new modem at COM2, Windows 95/98 locks up Open the Control Panel (System Settings) and deselect COM2. This can be accomplished by selecting COM2 under System Settings and then choosing Properties. There should be a red *X* in a box down towards the bottom of the Properties screen. Click once on the red *X* and it should clear. This disables the COM port in Windows 95. Click OK, and then restart the machine. When Windows 95/98 restarts, it should now find the COM port. This technique can apply to all available COM ports.

SYMPTOM 29-60 HyperTerminal works using PCMCIA support under Windows 95/98, but no 16-bit communication programs work Using a text editor, edit the SYSTEM.INI file in your Windows directory. Under the [386Enh] section of your SYSTEM.INI file, change the COMM.DRV line back to its original COMM.DRV. This line should read "comm.drv=comm.drv." Also check that there is a line that states "device=*vcd." If your SYSTEM.INI has a line that reads "device=*vrdd," place a semicolon (;) in front of it. Your 16-bit applications should now work.

SYMPTOM 29-61 A WinModem installed correctly and responds to AT commands fine, but whenever you call out, the modem makes a 9600 V.34 connection This is typically due to a problem with the current communications driver. Adding the following line:

```
ForceBridgeOrRouter=TRUE
```

to the SYSTEM.INI file may correct this problem by bypassing the current communications driver and going directly to the WinModem driver. You should also make sure that your Port Rate is set to 19200 in your Control Panel (Port Settings) in Windows 3.1*x*, and that it is set to 38400 or higher under Windows 95/98.

WINMODEM SYMPTOMS

Following are symptoms related to using a WinModem.

SYMPTOM 29-62 Windows 95/98 doesn't detect the WinModem First, make sure that the system has a free COM port or IRQ to use. If the WinModem was previously installed on the system with Windows 3.1*x* running, you'll need to search the SYSTEM.INI and WIN.INI files and remove all WinModem settings so that Windows 95/98 can detect the WinModem properly. Under Windows 95/98, make sure that the modem is not listed in the Device Manager under Other Devices. If it is, delete the reference and reinstall. Next, make sure the WinModem's key (for example, "USR1001" for the USR WinModem) is not in the Registry—if it is, remove the reference(s) from the Registry.

SYMPTOM 29-63 **You have difficulty using a WinModem after upgrading to Windows 98** If you double-click the WinModem icon in Control Panel, you may receive the following error message:

```
Error: There is no WinModem found in your computer, but some corrupted files
were found and they have been cleaned.
```

If you view your modem in the Device Manager, you may also notice more than one WinModem entry. This problem generally occurs because your WinModem is *not* using the most current INF file or device driver. To correct this problem, uninstall the WinModem drivers, remove the multiple WinModem entries in Device Manager, and then reinstall the most current WinModem drivers:

1. Click Start, highlight Settings, click Control Panel, double-click the WinModem icon, and then click Uninstall. This should uninstall the WinModem drivers.
2. See if the WinModem icon is still in the Control Panel. If the WinModem icon is gone, the uninstall process was successful. If the WinModem icon is still available, the uninstall process was not successful, and you will need to contact the modem manufacturer for detailed removal instructions.
3. Now remove the WinModem entries in Device Manager. Right-click My Computer, click Properties, and then click the Device Manager tab.
4. Double-click the Modem branch to expand it, click a WinModem entry, and then click Remove. Repeat this until *all* WinModem entries are removed, and then click OK.
5. Reinstall the most current WinModem drivers.

SYMPTOM 29-64 **The WinModem is repeatedly detected when you start Windows 98** For example, after you uninstall a WinModem and restart your computer, Windows 98 may try to install the modem and prompt you to restart your computer. After you restart your computer, Windows may prompt you to restart your computer again, and this behavior may continue indefinitely. This problem can occur if you uninstall the WinModem by using Device Manager (or the Modems tool in your Control Panel) instead of using the WinModem utility provided by the modem's manufacturer. To fix this problem, use the WinModem utility to uninstall your WinModem *instead* of using the Device Manager or the Modems tool:

1. Restart your computer and start Windows 98 in the Safe Mode.
2. Click Start, highlight Settings, and then click Control Panel.
3. Use the WinModem utility to uninstall your WinModem. For detailed information about how to use the WinModem utility to uninstall your WinModem, review the documentation included with your particular modem.
4. Restart your computer normally.
5. If you're prompted to install your WinModem again, use the software included with your modem to do so.

CABLE MODEM SYMPTOMS

Following are symptoms related to using a cable modem.

SYMPTOM 29-65 **The cable modem is installed, but it doesn't work** Your cable modem may have been installed with an IRQ conflict. Right-click the My Computer icon on your desktop, and then click Properties. Click the Device Manager tab at the top of the System Properties dialog, and look for a yellow exclamation point over the cable modem's entry (for example, "3Com U.S. Robotics Cable Modem") in the Network Adapters section. If the modem has a yellow exclamation point, it suffers from a resource conflict. Uninstall the modem by highlighting it and then clicking the Remove button. You will be asked if you wish to uninstall the device. Click OK. Next, you need to free an IRQ for the modem.

Double-click the Computer icon at the top of the Device Manager screen. In the Setting column, look for numbers between 3 and 15 that *are not* listed—these are IRQs available for use by the cable modem. If none are available, choose an unneeded device to be removed or disabled (you might consider disabling any serial or COM ports that are not in use). Once you have freed the necessary IRQ, restart your computer and try reinstalling the cable modem again.

Some versions of Windows 95 will not support *both* the cable modem *and* a network interface card (such as an Ethernet card) at the same time. You may need to uninstall or disable any existing network interface cards in your computer before installing the cable modem card.

SYMPTOM 29-66 When the PC comes out of "power save" mode, your system is frozen If the upstream (analog modem) connection is active when a computer goes into its power save mode, the computer may freeze when coming out of power save mode again. Either hang up the analog modem *before* your computer goes into power save mode or disable the power save features on your PC. If you choose to disable the power save mode, disable it in *both* the Windows 95/98 Control Panel and the system's CMOS Setup. To disable power save in Windows, click Start, select Settings, and click Control Panel. Double-click the Power icon, and select OFF in the Power Management box. Now click Apply. You may need to reboot the PC for your changes to take effect.

SYMPTOM 29-67 The cable modem scans for an active channel, pauses on an active channel, but instead of locking onto it, continues to scan for active channels Your cable modem may be assigned to IRQ 12, which is often a problem—though Windows 95/98 will not report it as a problem. IRQ 12 is normally reserved as the interrupt for a system's PS/2 (mouse) port. Right-click the My Computer icon on your desktop and then click Properties. Click Device Manager and then click Network Adapters. Double-click the entry for your cable modem (for example, "3Com Cable Modem") and then click Resources. Look for "Interrupt Request" in the Resource Type column. If the number listed to the right is 12, you will need to move the cable modem to a different IRQ.

SYMPTOM 29-68 The cable modem scans for an active channel but never locks onto one Check the cable and connections between your cable modem and the CATV jack at the wall—make sure the connections are reasonably tight. Try rebooting the PC and see if the cable modem will rescan and achieve a good channel lock. If the problem persists, the signal from your cable company's equipment may be too weak. Call your cable company to verify whether or not this is the problem.

SYMPTOM 29-69 During registration, you receive a "DHCP offer receive" error This type of error generally means that the cable modem is encountering difficulties obtaining an IP address. Click on the Register again button—registration may proceed in spite of this error.

Check the network adapter. Click Start, select Settings, and click Control Panel. Double-click the Network icon. In the list of installed network components that appears, highlight the "TCP/IP -> Dial-Up Adapter" entry and then click Properties. In the TCP/IP Properties dialog that appears, click the IP Address tab. Make sure the "Obtain an IP address automatically" option is checked. Click OK and close all open windows. Reboot the PC and try the cable modem again.

Check the IP configuration. Click Start and then click Run. Type **WINIPCFG.EXE** and press ENTER. When the IP Configuration dialog appears, make sure the values in the IP Address and Default Gateway fields are identical and do *not* equal zero. If they are *not* identical or *are* equal to zero, contact the cable modem manufacturer for technical support.

Check the CMCC software. In your CMCC application, click Options, click Preferences, and then click DHCP IP Address. Make sure Auto Detect is enabled unless your cable company recommends against it. If problems persist, check with the cable company for additional support or suggestions.

SYMPTOM 29-70 **During registration, you receive a "TFTP Error code=4 (timeout)"** This type of error generally means that the cable modem is having troubles with the system's TCP/IP stack. Click on the "Register again" button—registration may proceed in spite of this error. Check the TCP/IP stack next. Click Start, select Settings, and click Control Panel. Double-click the Network icon. In the list of installed network components, highlight the "TCP/IP -> Dial-Up Adapter" entry and then click Properties. In the "TCP/IP Properties" dialog that appears, click the IP Address tab. Make sure the "Obtain an IP address automatically" option is checked. Click OK and close all open windows. Reboot your computer and try again. If registration fails again after rebooting the system, contact your cable company for additional support or suggestions.

SYMPTOM 29-71 **Your cable modem setup does not use the analog modem to dial the cable company's server** This condition generally indicates an issue with the analog modem or your telephone line. Check for dial tone at the telephone line (no dial tone may mean the line is dead). Also double-check the access number for your cable company's server. You will not be able to access the Internet with your cable modem until your analog modem connects properly. If the problem persists, you may need to troubleshoot or replace the analog modem.

Further Study

You can find out more by checking out these Web sites:

Boca Research: **http://www.bocaresearch.com**

Diamond Multimedia: **http://www.diamondmm.com**

ITU: **http://www.itu.int/**

Lucent Technologies: **http://www.lucent.com/micro/**

Motorola: **http://www.mot.com**

US Robotics: **http://www.3com.com/56k/index.html**

Zoom Telephonics: **http://www.zoomtel.com/**

ModemHelp: **http://www.modemhelp.com/index3.html**

news:comp.dcom.modems

news:comp.sys.ibm.pc.hardware.comm

news:misc.forsale.computers.modems

30

MONITOR TROUBLESHOOTING

CHAPTER AT A GLANCE

From their humble beginnings as basic monochrome text displays, monitors (Figure 30-1) have grown to provide real-time photo-realistic images of unprecedented quality and color. Monitors have allowed real-time video playback, stunning graphics, and information-filled illustrations to replace the generic "command-line" user interface of just a few years ago. In effect, monitors have become our virtual window into the modern computer. With many millions of computers now in service, the economical maintenance and repair of computer monitors represents a serious challenge to technicians and hobbyists alike. Fortunately, the basic principles and operations of a computer monitor have changed very little since the days of terminal displays. This chapter explains the basic concepts behind today's computer monitors and provides a cross-section of handy troubleshooting procedures.

FIGURE 30-1 A CTX EX910 color monitor (CTX International, Inc.)

Monitor Specifications and Characteristics

While PCs are defined by a set of fairly well-understood specifications such as RAM size, hard drive space, and clock speed, monitor specifications describe a whole series of physical properties that PCs never deal with. With this in mind, perhaps the best introduction to monitor troubleshooting is to discuss each specification in detail and show you how each specification and characteristic affects a monitor's performance.

CRT

The *cathode ray tube* (or CRT) is essentially a large vacuum tube. One end of the CRT is formed as a long, narrow neck, while the other end is a broad, almost-flat surface. A coating of colored phosphors is applied inside the CRT along the front face. The neck end of the CRT contains an element (called the *cathode*) that is energized and heated to very high temperatures (much like an incandescent lamp). At high temperatures, the cathode liberates electrons. When a very high positive voltage potential is applied at the front face of the CRT, electrons liberated by the cathode (which are negatively charged) are accelerated toward the front face. When the electrons strike the phosphor on the front face, light is produced. By directing the stream of electrons across the front face, a visible image is produced. Of course, other elements are needed to control and direct the electron stream, but this is CRT operation in a nutshell. CRT face size (or *screen size*) is generally measured as a *diagonal* dimension—that is, a 43.2cm (17-inch) CRT is 43.2cm (17 inches) between opposing corners. Larger CRTs are more expensive, but produce larger images that are usually easier on the eyes.

PIXELS AND RESOLUTION

The picture element (or *pixel*) is the smallest point that can be controlled on a CRT. For monochrome displays, a pixel may simply be turned on or off. For a color display, a pixel may assume any of a number of different colors. Pixels are combined in the form of an array (rows and columns). It is the size of that overall pixel array that defines the display's *resolution*. Thus, resolution is the total number of pixels in *width* by the total number of pixels in *height*. For example, a typical VGA resolution is 640 pixels wide by 480 pixels high (a total of 307,200 pixels). Typical Super VGA (SVGA) resolution is 800 pixels wide by 600 pixels high (a total of 480,000 pixels). Today's monitors can easily support a resolution 1280 pixels wide by 1024 pixels high (a whopping 1,310,720 pixels). Resolution is important for computer monitors since higher resolutions allow finer image detail.

TRIADS AND DOT PITCH

While monochrome CRTs use a single, uniform phosphor coating (usually white, amber, or green), color CRTs use three color phosphors (red, green, and blue) arranged as triangles (or *triads*). Figure 30-2 illustrates a simple series of color phosphor triads. On a color monitor, each triad represents *one* pixel (even though there are three *dots* in the pixel). By using the electron streams from three electron guns—one gun for red, one for blue, and another for green—to excite each dot, a broad spectrum of colors can be produced. The three dots are placed so close together that they appear as a single point to the unaided eye.

> It's important to remember here that electrons themselves are invisible—they have no color. Color is produced when the invisible electron strikes a colored phosphor.

30

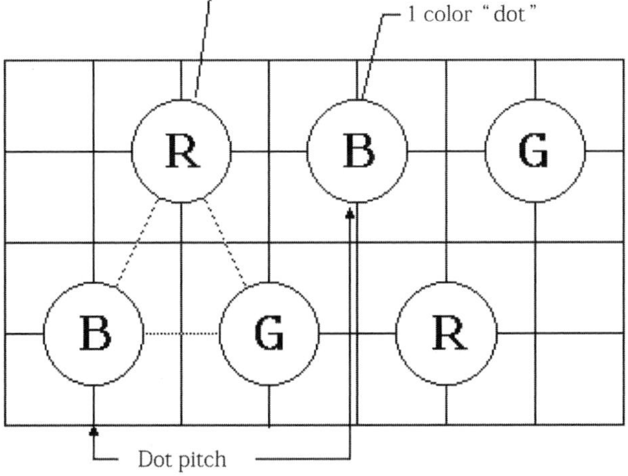

FIGURE 30-2 Arranging color phosphors in a triad

The quality of a color image is related to just how close each of the three dots are to one another. The closer together they are, the purer the image appears. As the dots are spaced farther apart, the image quality degrades because the eye can begin to discern the individual dots in each pixel. This results in lines that no longer appear straight and colors that are no longer pure. *Dot pitch* is a measure of the distance between two adjacent phosphor dots on the display. This is also the same dimension for the distance between openings in a shadow mask. Displays with a dot pitch of 0.30mm or less generally provide adequate image quality, though a dot pitch of 0.28mm or less is preferred.

SHADOW AND SLOT MASKS

The *shadow mask* is a thin sheet of perforated metal that is placed in the color CRT just behind the phosphor coating. Electron beams from each of the three electron guns are focused to converge at each hole in the mask—*not* at the phosphor screen (Figure 30-3). The microscopic holes act as apertures that let the electron beams through *only* to their corresponding color phosphors. In this way, any stray electrons are masked, and color is kept pure. Some CRT designs substitute a shadow mask with a *slot mask* (also called an *aperture grille*) that is made up of vertical wires behind the phosphor screen. The dot pitch for CRTs with slot masks is defined as the distance between each slot. Keep in mind that monochrome CRTs do not need a shadow mask at all since the entire phosphor surface is the same color.

CONVERGENCE

Remember that three electron guns are used in a color monitor—the electrons themselves are invisible, but each gun excites a particular color phosphor. All three electron beams are tracking around the screen simultaneously, and the beams converge at holes in the shadow mask. This *convergence* of electron beams is closely related to color purity in the screen image. Ideally, the three beams converge perfectly at all points on the display, and the resulting color is perfectly pure throughout (pure white). If one or more beams do not converge properly, the image color will not be pure. In most cases, poor convergence will result in colored shadows. For example, you may see a red, green, or blue shadow when looking at a white line. Serious convergence problems can result in a blurred or distorted image. Monitor specifications usually list typical convergence error as *misconvergence* at both the display center and the overall display

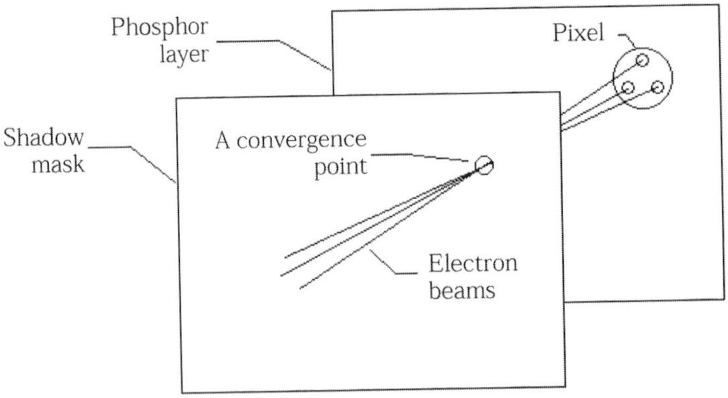

FIGURE 30-3 The importance of convergence in a color monitor

area. Typical center misconvergence runs approximately 0.45mm, while overall display area misconvergence is about 0.65mm. Larger numbers result in poorer convergence. Fortunately, monitor convergence can be calibrated (see Chapter 31).

PINCUSHION AND BARREL DISTORTION

The front face of most CRTs is slightly convex (bulging outward). However, digital images are perfectly square (that is, two dimensional). When a flat (2D) image is projected onto a curved (3D) surface, distortion results. Ideally, a monitor's raster circuits will compensate for this screen shape so that the image appears flat when viewed at normal distances. In actual practice, however, the image is rarely flat. The sides of the image (top to bottom) and (left to right) may be bent slightly inward or slightly outward. Figure 30-4 illustrates an exaggerated view of these effects. *Pincushioning* occurs when sides are bent inward, making the image's border appear concave. *Barreling* occurs when the sides are bent outward, making the image's border appear convex. In most cases, these distortions should be just barely noticeable (no more than 2.0mm or 3.0mm). Keep in mind that many technicians refer to barrel distortion as pincushioning, though this is not technically correct.

HORIZONTAL SCANNING, VERTICAL SCANNING, RASTER, AND RETRACE

To understand what *scanning* is, you must first understand how a monitor's image is formed. A monitor's image is generated one horizontal line of pixels at a time starting from the upper-left corner of the display (Figure 30-5). As the beams travel horizontally across the line, each pixel in the line is excited based on the video data contained in the corresponding location of video RAM on the video adapter board. When a line is complete, the beam turns off (known as *horizontal blanking*). The beam is then directed horizontally (and slightly lower vertically) to the beginning of the next subsequent line. A new horizontal line can then be drawn. This process continues until all horizontal lines are drawn and the beam is in the lower-right

30

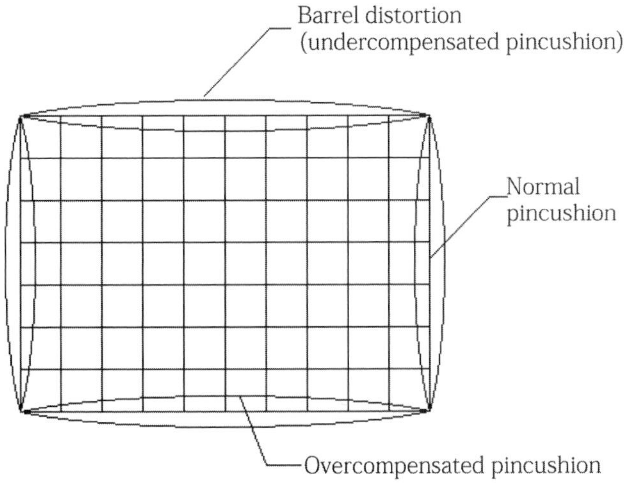

FIGURE 30-4 The effects of pincushion and barrel distortion

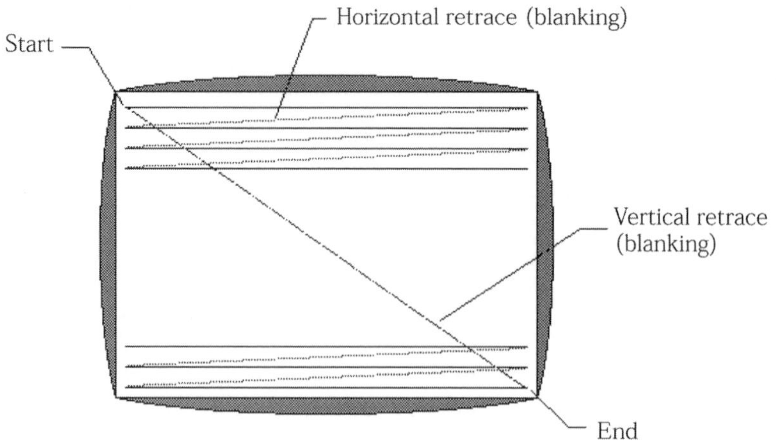

FIGURE 30-5 Forming a screen image on a CRT

corner of the display. When this image "page" is complete, the beam turns off (called *vertical blanking*) and is redirected back to the upper-left corner of the display to start all over again.

The rate at which horizontal lines are drawn is known as the *horizontal scanning rate* (sometimes called *horizontal sync rate*). The rate at which a complete page of horizontal lines is generated is known as the *vertical scanning rate* (or *vertical sync rate*). Both the horizontal and vertical blanking times are known as *retrace times* since the deactivated beams are "retracing" their path before starting a new trace. A typical horizontal retrace time is 5μS, while the typical vertical retrace time is 700SμS. This continuous horizontal and vertical scanning action is generally referred to as the *raster*.

We can easily apply numbers to scanning rates to give you an even better idea of their relationship. A typical VGA monitor with a resolution of 640x480 pixels uses a horizontal scanning rate of 30.5kHz. This means that 30,500 lines can be drawn in one second, or a single line of 640 pixels can be drawn in 30.7μS. Since there are 480 horizontal lines to be drawn in one page, a complete page can be drawn in (480x30.7μS) 15.2mS. If a single page can be drawn in 15.2mS, the screen can be refreshed 65.7 times per second (65.7Hz). This is roughly the vertical rate that will be set for VGA operation at 640x480 resolution. In actual practice, the vertical scanning rate will be set to a whole number, such as 60Hz, which leaves a lot of spare time for blanking and synchronization. It was discovered early in TV design that vertical scanning rates *under* 60Hz resulted in perceivable flicker that causes eye strain and fatigue. You can start to see now that horizontal scanning rates are not chosen arbitrarily. The objective is to select a horizontal frequency that will cover a page's worth of horizontal pixel lines for any given resolution at *about* 60 times per second (or even higher for reduced flicker). Table 30-1 compares typical monitor resolutions and scan rates.

INTERLACING

Images are "painted" onto a display one horizontal row at a time, but the sequence in which those lines are drawn can be *noninterlaced* or *interlaced*. As you see in Figure 30-6, a noninterlaced monitor draws all of the lines that compose an image in *one* pass. This is preferable since a noninterlaced image is easier on your eyes—the entire image is refreshed at the vertical scanning frequency—so a 60Hz vertical scanning rate will update the entire image 60 times in one second. A noninterlaced display draws an image as *two*

TABLE 30-1 SCAN RATES VS. MONITOR RESOLUTION

RESOLUTION	HORIZONTAL SCAN	VERTICAL SCAN	MONITOR
720x348	18.43kHz	50Hz	MDA
320x200	15.85kHz	60.5Hz	CGA
640x350	21.8kHz	60Hz	EGA
640x350	30.5kHz	70Hz	MCGA
640x480	30.5kHz	60Hz	VGA-G
640x480	37.5kHz	75Hz	EVGA
640x480	43.3kHz	85Hz	VESA
720x400	30.5kHz	70Hz	VGA-Text
720x400	37.9kHz	85Hz	VESA
800x600	37.9kHz	60Hz	SVGA
800x600	46.9kHz	75Hz	ESVGA
800x600	53.7kHz	85Hz	VESA
832x624	49.7kHz	75Hz	Macintosh 16-inch Color
1024x768	48.4kHz	60Hz	VESA
1024x768	56.5kHz	70Hz	VESA
1024x768	60.0kHz	75Hz	EUVGA
1024x768	60.2kHz	75Hz	Macintosh 19-inch Color
1024x768	68.7kHz	85Hz	VESA
1152x864	67.5kHz	75Hz	VESA
1152x870	68.7kHz	75Hz	Macintosh 21-inch Color
1280x960	60.0kHz	60 Hz	VESA
1280x960	85.9kHz	85Hz	VESA
1280x1024	64.0kHz	60Hz	VESA
1280x1024	80.0kHz	75Hz	VESA
1280x1024	91.1kHz	85Hz	VESA
1600x1200	75.0kHz	60Hz	VESA
1600x1200	81.3kHz	65Hz	VESA
1600x1200	87.5kHz	70Hz	VESA
1600x1200	93.8kHz	75Hz	VESA

passes. Once the first pass is complete, a second pass fills in the rest of the image. The effective image refresh rate is only half the stated vertical scanning rate. The typical 1024x768 SVGA monitor offers a vertical scanning rate of 87Hz, but since the monitor is interlaced, effective refresh is only 43.5Hz, and screen flicker is much more noticeable.

BANDWIDTH

In the simplest terms, the *bandwidth* of a monitor is the absolute maximum rate at which pixels can be sent to the monitor. Typical VGA displays offer a bandwidth of 30MHz. That is, the monitor could generate up to 30 million pixels per second on the display. Consider that each scan line of a VGA display uses 640 pixels, and the horizontal scan rate of 30.45kHz allows 30,450 scan lines per second to be written. At that rate, the monitor is processing (640 pixels/scan line x 30,450 scan lines/second) 20,128,000 pixels/sec-

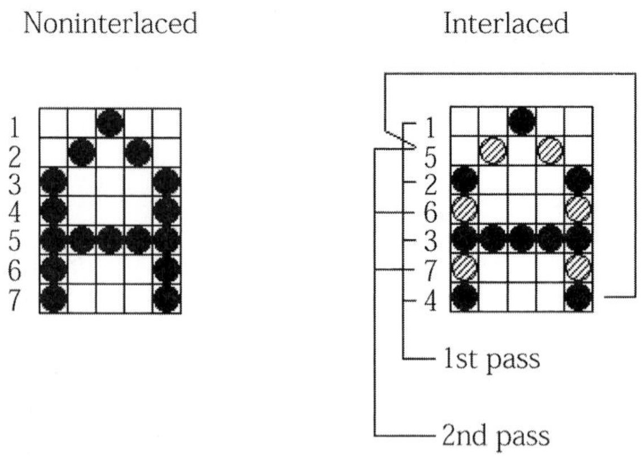

FIGURE 30-6 Interlaced vs. noninterlaced scanning

ond—well within the monitor's 30MHz bandwidth. The newest color monitors offer bandwidths of 135MHz. Such high-resolution 1280x1024 monitors with scanning rates of 79kHz would need to process at least (1280 pixels/scan line x 79,000 scan lines/second) 101,120,000 pixels/second (101.12MHz), so enhanced bandwidth is truly a *necessity* for high resolutions.

SWIM, JITTER, AND DRIFT

The electron beam(s) that form an image are directed around a display using variable magnetic fields generated by separate vertical and horizontal *deflection coils* mounted around the CRT's neck. The analog signals that drive each deflection coil are produced by horizontal and vertical deflection circuitry. Ideally, deflection circuitry should steer the electron beam(s) precisely the same way in each pass. This would result in an absolutely rock-solid image on the display. In the real world, however, there are minute variations in the placement of images over any given period of time. *Jitter* is a term used to measure such variation over a 15 second period. *Swim* (sometimes called *wave*) is a measure of position variation over a 30 second period. *Drift* is a measure of position variation over a 1 minute period. Note that all three terms represent essentially the same problem over different amounts of time. Swim, jitter, and drift may be expressed as fractions of a pixel or as physical measurements such as millimeters.

VIDEO SIGNAL

This specification lists signal levels and characteristics of the analog video input channel(s). In most cases, a video signal in the 0.7 Vpp (peak to peak) range is used. Circuitry inside the monitor amplifies and manipulates these relatively small signals. A related specification is input impedance, which is often at 75 ohms. Older monitors using digital (on-off) video signals typically operate with signals up to 1.5 volts.

SYNCHRONIZATION AND POLARITY

After a line is drawn on the display, the electron beams are turned off (blanked) and repositioned to start the next horizontal line. However, no data is contained in the retrace line. In order for the new line to be "in sync" with the data for that line, a *synchronization pulse* is sent from the video adapter to the monitor. There is a separate pulse for horizontal synchronization and vertical synchronization. In most current monitors, synchronization signals are edge triggered TTL (transistor-transistor logic) signals. *Polarity* refers to the edge that triggers the synchronization. A falling trigger (marked "-" or "positive/negative") indicates that synchronization takes place at the high-to-low transition of the sync signal. A leading trigger (marked "+" or "negative/positive") indicates that synchronization takes place on the low-to-high transition of the sync signal.

The Color Circuits

In order to have a full understanding of color monitors, it is best to start with a block diagram. The block diagram for a VGA monitor is shown in Figure 30-7. Three complete video drive circuits are needed (one for each primary color—red, green, and blue). While early color monitors used logic levels to represent video signals, current monitors use *analog* signals that allow the intensity of each color to be varied. The CRT is designed to provide three electron beams that are directed at corresponding color phosphors. By varying the intensity of each electron beam, virtually any color can be produced. For all practical purposes, the color monitor can be considered in three subsections: the video drive circuits, the vertical drive circuit, and the horizontal drive circuit (including the high-voltage system).

VIDEO DRIVE CIRCUITS

The schematic diagram for a typical RGB (red, green, and blue) drive circuit is shown in Figure 30-8. This schematic is actually part of a Tandy VGM-220 analog color monitor. You will see that there are three separate video drive circuits. Components with a 5xx designation (such as IC501) are part of the *red* video drive circuit. The 6xx designation (such as Q602) shows a part in the *green* video drive circuit. A 7xx

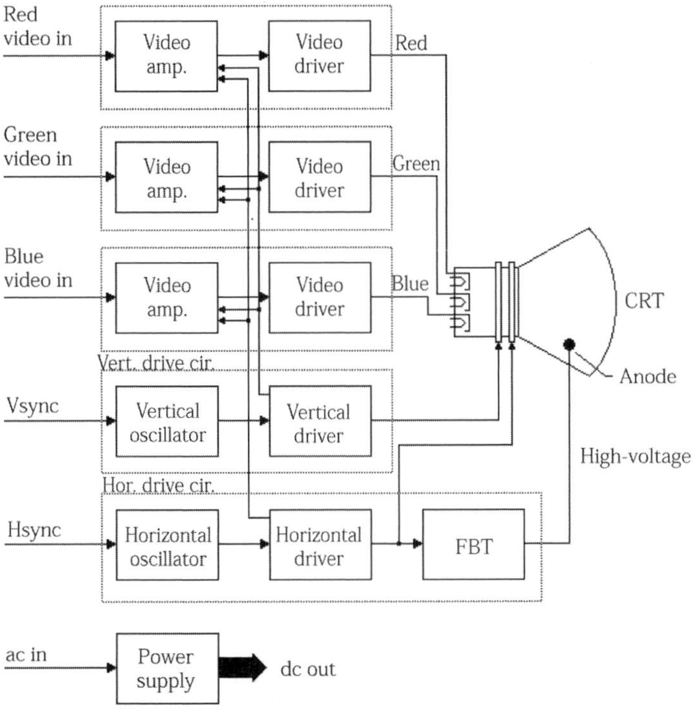

FIGURE 30-7 Block diagram of a color (VGA) monitor

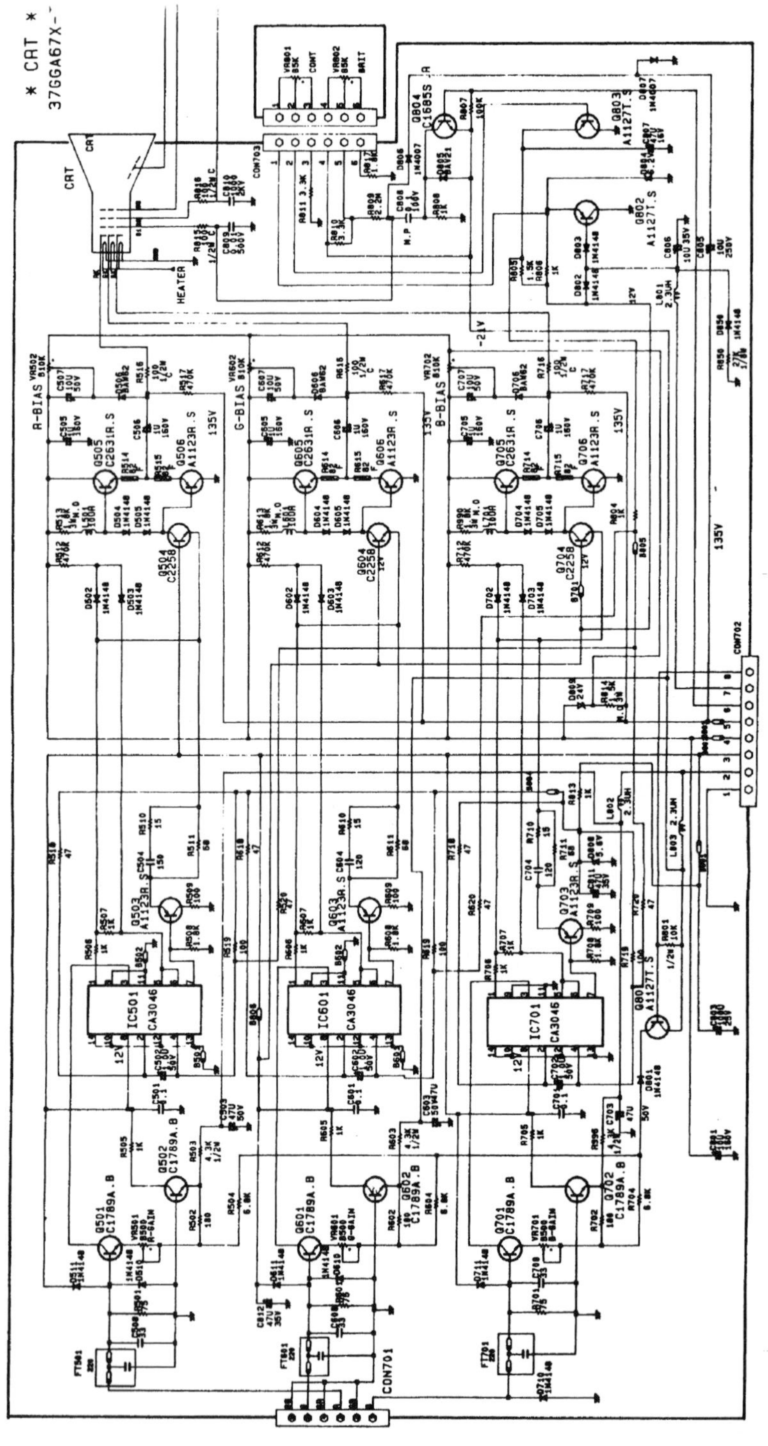

FIGURE 30-8 Schematic of a VGM-220 video circuit (Tandy Corporation)

marking (such as C704) indicates a component in the *blue* video drive circuit. Other components marked with 8xx designations (such as Q803) are included to operate the CRT control grid. Let's walk through the operation of one of these video circuits.

The red analog signal is filtered by the small array of F501. The ferrite beads on either side of the small filter capacitor serve to reduce noise that may otherwise interfere with the weak analog signal. The video signal is amplified by transistor Q501. Potentiometer VR501 adjusts the signal *gain* (the amount of amplification applied to the video signal). Collector signals are then passed to the differential amplifier circuit in IC501. Once again, noise is a major concern in color signals, and differential amplifiers help to improve signal strength while eliminating noise. The resulting video signal is applied to a "push-pull" amplifier circuit consisting of Q503 and Q504, then fed to a subsequent "push-pull" amplifier pair of Q505 and Q506. Potentiometer VR502 controls the amount of DC bias used to generate the final output signal. The output from this final amplifier stage is coupled directly to the corresponding CRT video control grid. The remaining two drive circuits both work the same way.

Problems with the video circuits in color monitors rarely disable the image entirely. Even if one video drive circuit should fail, there are still two others to drive the CRT. Of course, the loss of one primary color will severely distort the image colors, but the image should still be visible. You can tell when one of the video drive circuits fails: the faulty circuit will either saturate the display with that color or cut that color out completely. For example, if the red video drive circuit should fail, the resulting screen image will either be saturated with red, or red will be absent (leaving a greenish-blue or cyan image).

VERTICAL DRIVE CIRCUIT

The vertical drive circuit is designed to operate the monitor's vertical deflection yoke (dubbed V-DY). To give you a broad perspective of vertical drive operation and its inter-relation to other important monitor circuits, Figure 30-9 illustrates the vertical drive, horizontal drive, high-voltage, and power supply circuits all combined in the same schematic. This schematic is essentially the main PC board for the Tandy VGM-220 monitor. Components marked with 4xx numbers (such as IC401) are part of the vertical drive system.

The vertical sync pulses enter the monitor at connector CH202 (the line marked "V"). A simple exclusive-OR gate (IC201) is used to condition the sync pulses and select the video mode being used. Since the polarity of horizontal and vertical sync pulses will be different for each video mode, IC201 detects those polarities and causes the digitally controlled analog switch (IC401) to select one of three vertical size (V-SIZE) control sets, which is connected to the vertical sawtooth oscillator (IC402). This mode-switching circuit allows the monitor to autosize the display.

The vertical sync pulse fires the vertical sawtooth oscillator on pin 2 of IC402. The frequency of the vertical sweep is set to 60Hz, but can be optimized by adjusting the vertical frequency control (V-FREQ) VR404. It is highly recommended that you do not attempt to adjust the vertical frequency unless you have an oscilloscope available. Vertical linearity (V-LIN) is adjusted through potentiometer VR405. Vertical centering (V-CENTER) is controlled through VR406. Linearity and centering adjustments should only be made while displaying an appropriate test pattern. It is interesting to note that there are no discrete power amplifiers needed to drive the vertical deflection yoke—IC402 pin 6 drives the deflection yoke directly through an internal power amplifier.

The pincushion circuit forms a link between the vertical and horizontal deflection systems through the pincushion transformer (T304). Transistors Q401 and Q402 form a compensator circuit that slightly modulates horizontal deflection. This prevents distortion in the image when projecting a flat, two-dimensional image onto a curved surface (the CRT). Potentiometer VR407 provides the pincushion control (PCC). As with other alignments, you should not attempt to adjust the pincushion unless an appropriate test pattern is displayed.

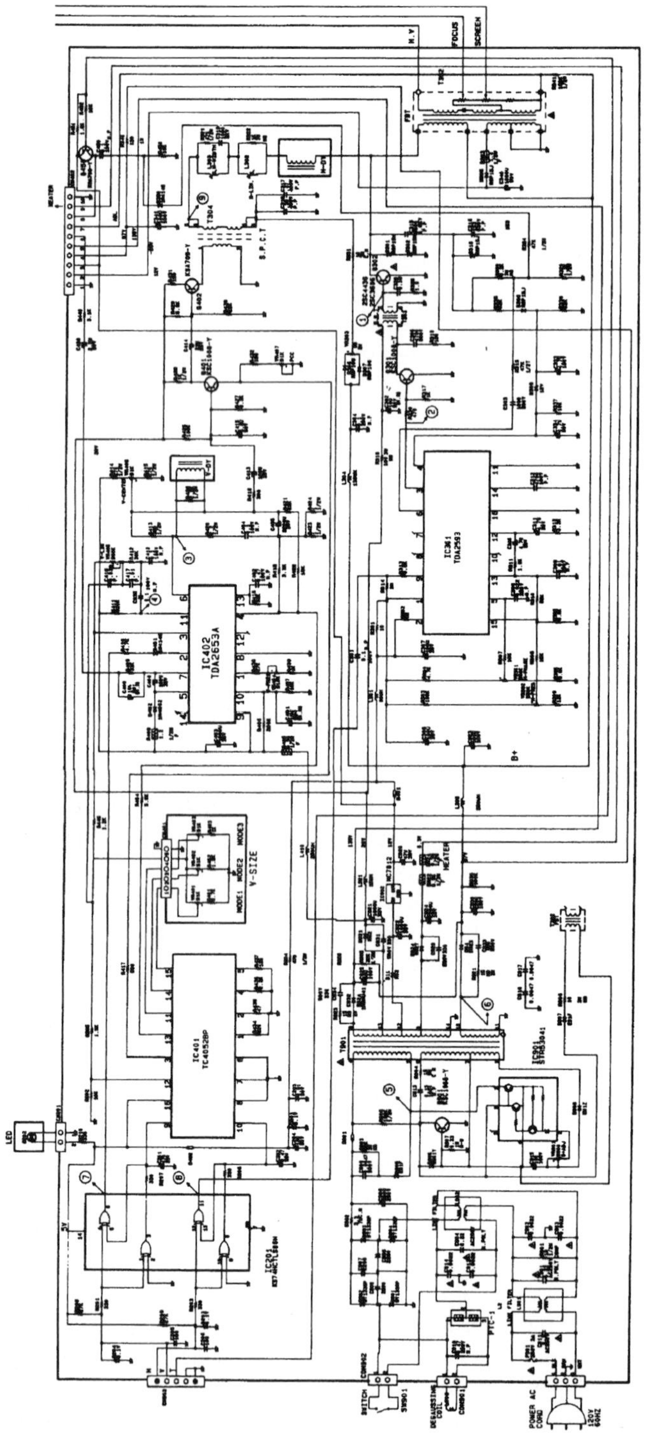

FIGURE 30-9 Schematic of a VGM-220 main (raster) circuit (Tandy Corporation)

Problems that develop in the vertical amplifier will invariably affect the appearance of the CRT image. A catastrophic fault in the vertical oscillator or amplifier will leave a narrow horizontal line in the display. The likeliest cause is the vertical drive IC (IC402) since that component handles both sawtooth generation and amplification. If only the upper or lower half of an image disappears, only one part of the vertical amplifier in IC402 may have failed. However, any fault on the PC board that interrupts the vertical sawtooth will disable vertical deflection entirely. When the vertical deflection is marginal (too expanded or too compressed), suspect a fault in IC402, but its related components may also be breaking down. An image that is overexpanded will usually appear "folded over," with a whitish haze along the bottom. It may also be interesting to note that vertical drive problems do not affect display colors.

HORIZONTAL DRIVE CIRCUIT

The horizontal drive circuit is responsible for operating the horizontal deflection yoke (H-DY). It is this circuit that sweeps the electron beams left and right across the display. To understand how the horizontal drive works, you should again refer to the schematic of Figure 30-9. All components marked 3xx numbers (such as IC301) relate to the horizontal drive circuit. Horizontal sync signals enter the monitor at connector CH202 (the line marked "H") and are conditioned by the executive-OR gates of IC201. Conditioned sync pulses fire the horizontal oscillator (IC301). Horizontal frequency should be locked at 30.5kHz, but potentiometer VR302 can be used to optimize the frequency. Do not attempt to adjust horizontal frequency unless you have an oscilloscope available. Horizontal phase can be adjusted with VR301. You should avoid altering any alignments until a suitable test pattern is displayed.

IC301 is a highly integrated device designed to provide precision horizontal square wave pulses to the driver transistors Q301 and Q302. IC301 pin 3 provides the horizontal pulses to Q301. Transistor Q301 switches on and off, causing current pulses in the horizontal output transformer (T303). Current pulses produced by the secondary winding of T303 fire the horizontal output transistor (Q302). Output from the HOT (High-voltage Output Transistor circuit) drives the horizontal deflection yoke (H-DY). The deflection circuit includes two adjustable coils to control horizontal linearity (H-LIN; L302) and horizontal width (H-WIDTH; L303). You will also notice that the collector signal from Q302 is directly connected to the flyback transformer (FBT). Operation of the high-voltage system is covered in the next section.

Problems in the horizontal drive circuit can take several forms. One common manifestation is the loss of horizontal sweep, leaving a vertical line in the center of the display. This is generally due to a fault in the horizontal oscillator (IC301) rather than the horizontal driver transistors. The second common symptom is a loss of image (including raster), and is almost always the result of a failure in the HOT. Since the HOT also operates the flyback transformer, a loss of horizontal output will disrupt high-voltage generation, and the image will disappear.

THE FLYBACK CIRCUIT

The presence of a large positive potential on the CRT's anode is needed in order to accelerate an electron beam across the distance between the cathode and CRT phosphor. Electrons must strike the phosphor hard enough to liberate visible light. Under normal circumstances, this requires a potential of 15,000 to 30,000 volts. Larger CRTs need higher voltages because there is a greater physical distance to overcome. Monitors generate high-voltage through the *flyback circuit.*

The heart of the high-voltage circuit is the *flyback transformer* (FBT), as shown in Figure 30-9. The FBT's primary winding is directly coupled to the horizontal output transistor (Q302). Another primary winding is used to compensate the high-voltage level for changes in brightness and contrast. Flyback voltage is generated during the horizontal *retrace* (the time between the end of one scan line and the beginning

30

of another) when the sudden drop in deflection signal causes a strong voltage spike on the FBT secondary windings. You will notice that the FBT in Figure 30-9 provides one multitapped secondary winding. The topmost tap from the FBT secondary provides high-voltage to the CRT anode. A high-voltage rectifier diode added to the FBT assembly forms a half-wave rectifier—only positive voltages reach the CRT anode. The effective capacitance of the CRT anode will act to filter the high-voltage spikes into DC. You can read the high-voltage level with a high-voltage probe. The CRT needs additional voltages in order to function. The lower tap from the FBT secondary supplies voltage to the focus and screen grid adjustments. These adjustments, in turn, drive the CRT directly.

Trouble in the high-voltage circuit can render the monitor inoperative. Typically, a high-voltage fault manifests itself as a loss of image and raster. In many cases where the HOT and deflection signals prove to be intact, the flyback transformer has probably failed, causing a loss of output in one or more of the three FBT secondary windings. The troubleshooting procedures coming up in this chapter will cover high-voltage symptoms and solutions in more detail.

CONSTRUCTION

Before jumping right into troubleshooting, it would be helpful to understand how the circuits shown in Figure 30-9 are assembled. A wiring diagram for the Tandy VGM-220 is shown in Figure 30-10. There are two PC boards: the video drive PC board and the main PC board. The main PC board contains the raster circuits, power supply, and high-voltage circuitry. The video drive PC board contains red, green, and blue video circuits. Video signals, focus grid voltage, screen grid voltage, and brightness and contrast controls connect to the video drive board. The video PC board plugs into the CRT at its neck (although the diagram of Figure 30-10 may not show this clearly). A power switch, power LED, and CRT degaussing coil plug into the main PC board. There are also connections at the main PC board for the AC line cord and video sync signals.

Troubleshooting a CRT

In spite of its age, the cathode ray tube (CRT) continues to play an important role in modern computer monitors. There are some very important reasons for this longevity. First, the CRT is relatively inexpensive to make, and it needs only simple circuitry in order to operate. Second, the CRT is extremely rugged and reliable. Typical working lives can extend to ten years or more. It is this combination of low cost, ease of operation, and long-term reliability that has allowed the CRT to keep pace with today's personal computers. However, CRTs are certainly not perfect devices—the delicate assemblies within the CRT used to generate and direct electron beams can eventually open, short-circuit, or wear out. And like most classical vacuum tubes, CRT failures often occur slowly over a period of weeks or months. This part of the chapter shows you the assemblies in a typical color CRT, explains the faults that often occur, and offers some alternatives for dealing with CRT problems.

INSIDE THE CRT

Before we discuss CRT problems, you should have an understanding of the color CRT itself. Figure 30-11 shows a cross-section of a typical color CRT. To produce an image, electron beams are generated, concentrated, and directed across a phosphor-coated face. When electron beams (which are invisible) strike phosphor, light is liberated. This is the light you see from the CRT. The color of light is determined by the particular phosphor chemistry. You will note that there are three electron guns in the color CRT: a beam for red, a beam for green, and a beam for blue.

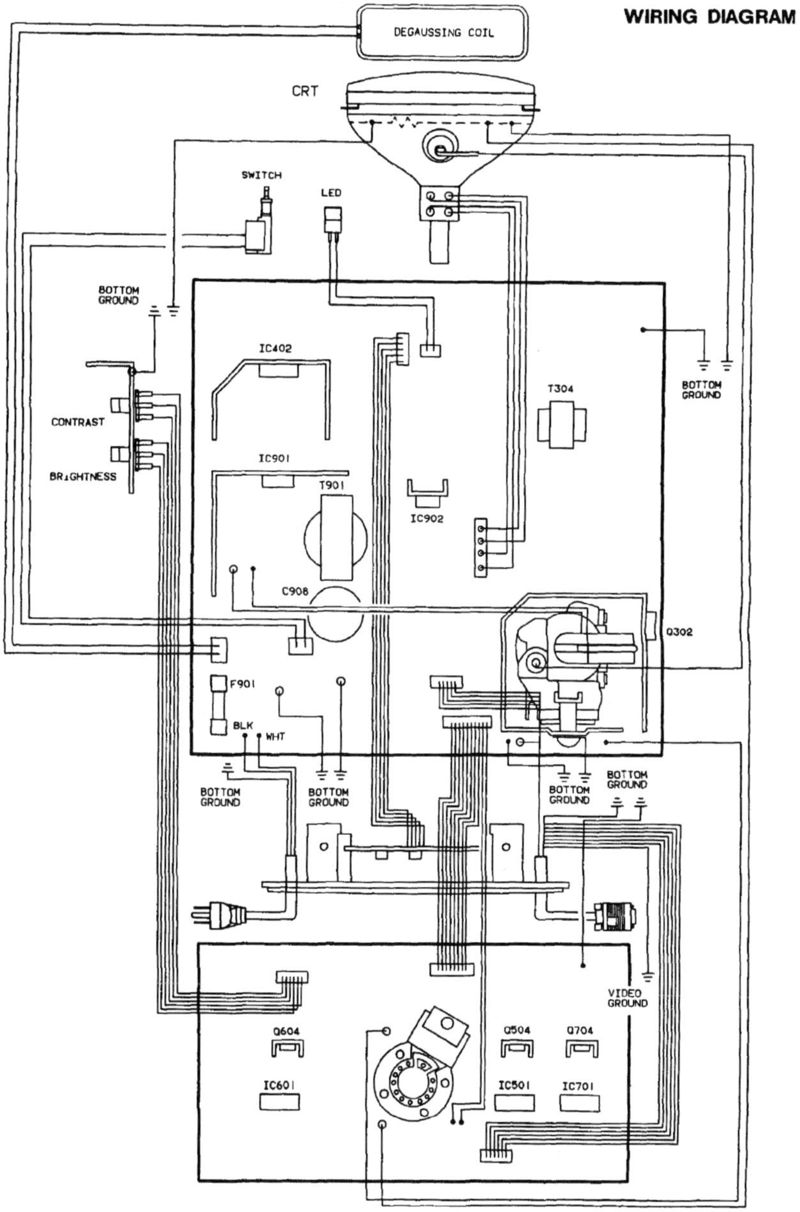

FIGURE 30-10 A wiring diagram for the VGM-220 (Tandy Corporation)

Electron beams start with a heater wire. When energized, the heater becomes extremely hot. (This is the glow you see in the CRT neck.) The heat from a heater warms its corresponding cathode, and a barium tip on the cathode begins "boiling off" electrons. Ordinarily, electrons would simply boil off into a big, clumsy cloud. But since electrons are negatively charged, they will be attracted to any large positive potential. A moderate positive potential (+500 volts or so) on the screen grid starts accelerating the electrons down the CRT's neck, while the control grid voltage limits the electrons—effectively forcing the unruly cloud into a beam. Once electrons pass the screen grid, a high positive potential on the CRT anode (anywhere from 15 to 30 kV) rockets the electrons toward the CRT face. The beam is still rather wide, so a focus grid applies another potential that works to concentrate the beam.

All this is very effective at generating narrow, high-velocity electron beams. But unless you want to watch a big, bright spot in the middle of the CRT, there has to be some method of tracing the beams around the CRT face. Beam tracing is accomplished through the use of deflection magnets placed around the CRT neck—you will see these magnets (actually electromagnets) as heavy coils of wire where the CRT funnel meets the neck. There are actually four electromagnets in this deflection assembly: two opposing electromagnets direct the beam in the vertical direction, while another set of opposing magnets direct the beam in the horizontal direction. Using electrical signals from the monitor's raster circuits, an electron beam can trace across the entire CRT face.

Another element of the CRT that you should understand is called the shadow mask. A shadow mask is basically a thin metal sheet with a series of small holes punched in it. Some CRTs use a mask of rectangular openings referred to as an aperture grille or slot mask. Both types of mask perform the same purpose—to ensure that electron beams strike *only* the color phosphors of the intended pixel. This is a vital element of a color monitor. In a monochrome monitor, the CRT is coated with a single homogenous layer of phosphor—if stray electrons strike nearby phosphor particles, a letter or line may simply appear to be a bit out of focus. For a color CRT, however, stray electrons can cause incorrect colors to appear on nearby pixels. Masks help to preserve color purity. Color purity is also aided by a purity magnet, which helps correct fine beam positioning. A convergence magnet helps ensure that all three electron beams meet (or converge) at the shadow mask.

Of course, grids, heaters, and cathodes are all located inside the glass CRT vessel. Electrical connections are made through a circular arrangement of sealed pins in the neck. Table 30-2 explains the designa-

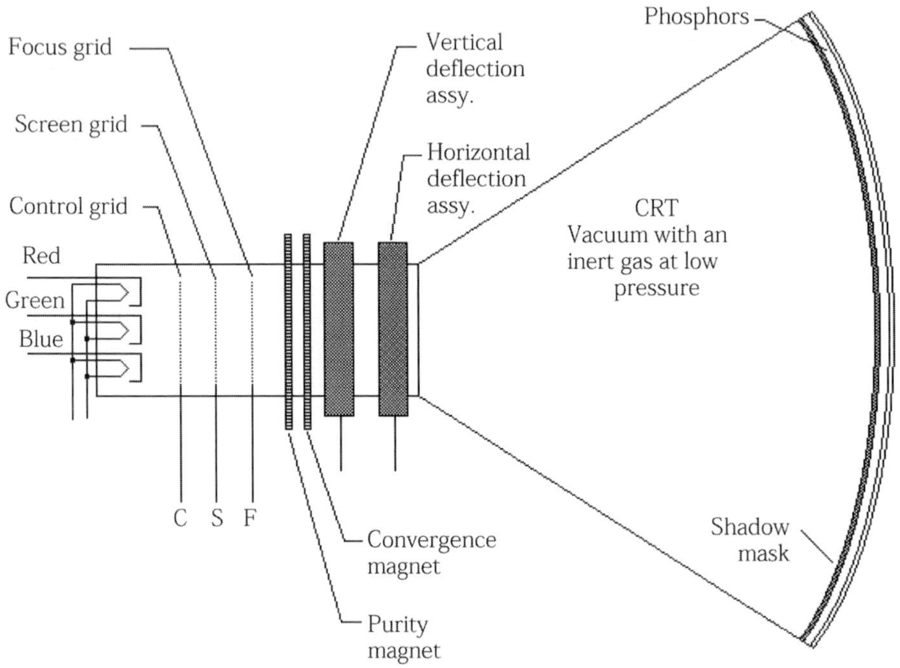

FIGURE 30-11 Cross-section of a color CRT

tions for each pin. Keep in mind that the high-voltage anode is attached directly to the CRT in the upper-right part of the glass funnel. Also remember that some CRT designs may use additional pins.

IDENTIFYING CRT PROBLEMS

CRTs enjoy a long, reliable working life because there are really no moving parts—merely a set of stationary metal elements. However, the grids and cathodes are arranged in very close proximity to one another. Physical shocks can dislodge elements and cause sudden short circuits. Eventually, regular use will alter the physical dimensions of cathodes and grids (resulting in the development of a slower, more gradual short circuit). The stress of regular wear can also cause open circuits in the heater, cathode, or grid. Let's take a look at some of the typical problems that manifest themselves in a CRT.

When considering a CRT replacement, you should remember that the CRT is typically the most expensive part of the monitor. For larger monitors, the CRT becomes an even larger percentage of the monitor's overall cost. In many cases, the cost for a replacement CRT approaches the original cost of the entire monitor. As a consequence, you should carefully evaluate the economics of replacing the CRT versus buying a new monitor outright.

SYMPTOM 30-1 **Heater opens in the CRT** Each time the heater runs, it expands. When the CRT turns off, the heater cools and contracts again. This regular thermal expansion and contraction may eventually fatigue the heater and cause it to open. You will see this as a complete loss of the corresponding color. Since heaters are all tied together electrically, there is no way to measure a particular heater directly, but you may see only two glowing heaters in the CRT neck instead of three. An open heater cannot be recovered, and the only available alternative is to replace the CRT itself.

SYMPTOM 30-2 **Heater shorts to a cathode in the CRT** This is not as strange as it might seem at first. In order to heat a cathode effectively, the heater must be in *extremely* close proximity to the cathode—especially to the barium element that actually liberates the electrons. Over time, the heater may develop accumulations of corrosion that might eventually cause the heater to contact the cathode. In theory, this should never happen because the inert low-pressure gasses inside the CRT should prevent this. But in actual practice, some small amount of oxygen will still be present in the CRT, and oxidation may occur. A shorted heater will cause the electron gun to fire at full power—in effect, the electron gun will be stuck "on." The image will appear saturated with the color of the defective electron gun. For example, if

TABLE 30-2 TYPICAL CRT PIN DESIGNATIONS

DESIGNATION	DESCRIPTION
G1	Control grid voltage
G2	Screen grid voltage
G3 or F	Focus grid voltage
KG	Green video signal
KR	Red video signal
KB	Blue video signal
H1	Heater voltage in
H2	Heater voltage out

the blue heater shorts to the cathode, the image will appear saturated with blue. You will also likely see visible retrace lines in the image.

You can verify this problem by removing all power from the monitor, removing the video drive board from the CRT's neck, and measuring the resistance between a heater wire and the suspect cathode. For the CRT pinout listed in Table 30-2, you could check the blue cathode by measuring resistance between the KB and H1 (or H2) pins. Ideally, there should be *infinite* resistance between the heaters and cathodes. If there is measurable resistance (or a direct short circuit), you have found the problem. If the resistance measures infinity as expected, you may have a defect on the video drive board.

SYMPTOM 30-3 **Cathode shorts to the control grid in the CRT** A cathode can also short-circuit to the control grid. Often, corrosion flakes off the cathode and comes in contact with the control grid. When this happens, the control grid loses its effectiveness, and the corresponding color will appear saturated. In practice, this symptom will appear very much like a heater short. Fortunately, you should be able to verify this problem with your meter by measuring resistance between the control grid and the suspect cathode. Ideally, there should be infinite resistance between the control grid and all cathodes. If you read a measurable resistance (or a direct short circuit), chances are good that you're facing a cathode-to-control grid short.

SYMPTOM 30-4 **One or more colors appear weak** This is a common symptom in many older CRTs. Over time, the barium emitter in your cathodes will wear out, or develop a layer of ions (referred to as *cathode poisoning*) that inhibit the release of electrons. In either case, the afflicted cathode will lose efficiency, resulting in weakened screen colors. Typically, you might expect all three cathodes to degrade evenly over time—and they will. But by the time the problem becomes serious enough for service, you will usually notice one color weaker than the others. Try increasing the gain of the afflicted signal on the video drive board. If the cathode is indeed afflicted, increasing signal gain should *not* have a substantial effect on the color brightness, and you should consider replacing the CRT.

SYMPTOM 30-5 **CRT phosphors appear aged or worn** Phosphors are specially formulated chemicals that glow in a particular color when excited by a high-energy electron beam. Typically, phosphors will last for the lifetime of the monitor, but age and normal use will eventually reduce the sensitivity of the phosphors. For old CRTs, you may see this as dull, low-contrast colors. Perhaps a more dramatic problem occurs with "phosphor burn," which occurs when a monitor is left on, displaying the same image for a very long period of time. If you turn the monitor off, you can see the latent image burned onto the CRT as a dark shadow. In both cases, there is no way to rejuvenate phosphors, so the CRT will have to be replaced. You can advise customers to prolong the life of their CRT by keeping the brightness at a minimum and using a screen saver utility if an image will sit unchanging for a long time.

SYMPTOM 30-6 **The CRT suffers from bad cutoff (a.k.a. bad gamma)** On a CRT, color linearity is a function of the cathode's ability to adjust the level of electron emission—in other words, beam intensity must be linear across the entire range of the video signal (0 to 20 volts or 0 to 50 volts). As cathodes age, however, they tend to become nonlinear. When this happens, images tend to be too "black and white" rather than display a smooth transition of colors. Technicians often refer to this as a "gassy" CRT, which is actually a CRT gamma problem. In addition to cathode wear, control grid failure can adversely affect beam intensity.

SYMPTOM 30-7 **Open control grid in the CRT** The control grid is used to limit the beam intensity produced by a cathode by applying a potential on the grid. Occasionally, you will find that a control grid might open. In that case, there is no longer a potential available to control the beam intensity, and the beam will fire at full intensity. At first glance, you might think this is a cathode-to-control grid short or a heater-to-cathode short. But if you can't find a short with your multimeter, the control grid is probably open, and the CRT will have to be replaced.

SYMPTOM 30-8 **Open screen grid in the CRT** The screen grid plays an important role in image brightness by accelerating the electron beam toward the CRT phosphors. If the screen grid opens, there will be no potential available to begin accelerating the beam. This will result in a very dark image—even with the screen voltage at maximum. You might think this is a control-to-screen grid short, but if you can't find the short with your multimeter, the screen grid is probably open, and the CRT will have to be replaced.

SYMPTOM 30-9 **Open focus grid in the CRT** A focus grid assembly serves to concentrate electron beams into narrow pinpoints by the time the beam reaches the shadow mask. There is typically a focus control located around the flyback transformer. If the focus grid fails, the image will appear highly distorted, and the focus adjustment will have no effect. When a focus grid fails, the entire CRT will have to be replaced.

SYMPTOM 30-10 **Control grid shorts to screen grid in the CRT** The same flakes of oxidation that can short a cathode to the control grid can also short the control grid to the screen grid. The screen grid starts accelerating the electrons toward the CRT face. If the screen grid is shorted, it will reduce the energy imparted to the electrons. In effect, a shorted screen grid will significantly reduce the overall image brightness (even with the brightness at maximum). In extreme cases, the image may disappear entirely. You can measure the screen grid voltage at G2, which typically runs from 250 volts to 750 volts in normal operation. If the voltage is low (even with the screen grid control at maximum), power-down the monitor, remove the video drive board from the monitor's neck, restart the monitor, and measure the screen voltage again. If the screen voltage returns to normal, you can be confident that the screen grid is shorted. If screen voltage remains low, you may have a fault in the screen voltage circuit. You can also verify a short between the control and screen grids by powering down the monitor and measuring resistance between the G1 and G2 pins on the CRT neck. Ideally, there should be infinite resistance.

30

CORRECTING SHORTS

You can probably guess that short circuits within a CRT can be maddening—there is just no way to get to them. However, most shorts are not held in place by anything more than gravity, or a slight arc during contact. As a result, it may be possible to dislodge the short by turning the monitor over and gently rapping on the CRT neck with the plastic end of a screwdriver. Obviously, this is also a prime way to shatter the CRT, so be *very* careful if you attempt to dislodge a suspected short. If a few light taps don't do the job, quit while the CRT is still in one piece.

CRT TESTERS/REJUVENATORS

Since shorts are small fragments of conductive material, they can be "burned" away using a surge of electricity. This is much safer than the "tap-and-pray" method mentioned above. Devices such as Sencore's CR70 Universal CRT Restorer/Analyzer can help check the CRT for shorts and opens, and can also burn out a wide variety of shorts, and (in many cases) rejuvenate weak elements. As another advantage, a tester can usually check and rejuvenate a CRT without having the whole monitor available. Most CRT test equipment can perform four major operations: color balance testing, emission testing, removing shorts, and beam rejuvenation:

- *Color balance testing* In order to produce pure white (and all other *true* colors), all three electron guns must be able to run at the same intensity. A color balance test can compare the strongest gun to the weakest gun. If there is a variation of more than 55 percent, the weakest gun will be displayed as "bad." But it is possible to recover a portion of the weaker beam's operation through a "Beam Builder" or "Beam Rejuvenator" function on the tester.
- *Emission testing* A cathode must be able to "emit" electrons—that is the basis of all vacuum tubes. As the cathode ages, ions generated from air in the CRT gradually block the cathode's ability to produce electrons. This is *ion poisoning*, which results in weakened electron beams. A rejuvenator function can usually overcome low-emission problems.
- *Removing shorts* Generally speaking, a decent CRT tester/rejuvenator can remove shorts between the control grid and the cathode or the screen grid. In practice, you may see such a function marked "Remove G1 Short" or some similar nomenclature. However, few testers attempt to remove heater-to-cathode shorts because the energy needed to clear a short there would usually burn out the heater element entirely.
- *Beam rejuvenation* The purpose of rejuvenation is basically to restore the emission of weak electron guns. This is usually accomplished by boosting the heater voltage (making the cathode extremely hot), then passing a 100 mA to 150 mA current through the cathode. The effect of rejuvenation exposes fresh emitting material, which in turn adds new life to weakened guns. A current meter measures beam current. When beam current reaches its nominal range during rejuvenation, the electron gun is restored.

Troubleshooting a Color Monitor

Any discussion of monitor troubleshooting must start with a reminder of the dangers involved. Computer monitors use very high voltages for proper operation. *Potentially lethal shock hazards exist within the monitor assembly—both from ordinary AC line voltage and from the CRT anode voltage developed by the flyback transformer. You must exercise extreme caution whenever a monitor's outer housings are removed.* If you are uncomfortable with the idea of working around high voltages, defer your troubleshooting to an experienced technician.

WRAPPING IT UP

When you finally get your monitor working again and are ready to reassemble it, be very careful to see that all wiring and connectors are routed properly. No wires should be pinched or lodged between the chassis or other metal parts (especially sharp edges). After the wiring is secure, make sure that any insulators, shielding, or protective enclosures are installed. This is even more important for larger monitors with supplemental X-ray shielding. Replace all plastic enclosures and secure them with their full complement of screws.

POSTREPAIR TESTING AND ALIGNMENT

Regardless of the problem with your monitor or how you go about repairing it, a check of the monitor's alignment is always worthwhile before returning the unit to service. Your first procedure after a repair is complete should be to ensure that the high-voltage level does not exceed the maximum specified value. Excessive high-voltage can liberate x-radiation from the CRT. Over prolonged exposure, X rays can present a serious biohazard. The high-voltage value is usually marked on the specification plate glued to the outer housing, or recorded on a sticker placed somewhere inside the housing. If you cannot find the high-voltage level, refer to service data from the monitor's manufacturer. Once high-voltage is correct, you can proceed with other alignment tests. Refer to Chapter 31 for testing and alignment procedures. When testing (and realignment) is complete, it is wise to let the monitor run for 24 hours or so (called a *burn-in test*) before returning it to service. Running the monitor for a prolonged period helps ensure that the original problem has indeed been resolved. This is a form of quality control. If the problem resurfaces, there may be another more serious problem elsewhere in the monitor.

SYMPTOMS

SYMPTOM 30-11 **The image is saturated with red, or appears greenish-blue (cyan)** If there are any user color controls available from the front or rear housings, make sure those controls have not been accidentally adjusted. If color controls are set properly (or are not available externally), the red video drive circuit has probably failed. Refer to the example circuit of Figure 30-8. Use your oscilloscope to trace the video signal from its initial input to the final output. If there is no red video signal at the amplifier input (the base of Q501), check the connection between the monitor and the video adapter board. If the connection is intact, try a known-good monitor. If the problem persists on a known-good monitor, replace the video adapter board. As you trace the video signal, you can compare the signal to characteristics at the corresponding points in the green or blue video circuits. The point at which the signal disappears is probably the point of failure, and the offending component should be replaced. If you do not have the tools or inclination to perform component-level troubleshooting, try replacing the video drive PC board entirely.

If the video signal measures properly all the way to the CRT (or a new video drive PC board does not correct the problem), suspect a fault in the CRT itself—the corresponding cathode or video control grid may have failed. If you have access to a CRT tester/rejuvenator, test the CRT. If the CRT measures bad (and cannot be recovered through any available rejuvenation procedure), it should be replaced. Keep in mind that a color CRT is usually the most expensive component in the monitor. As with any CRT replacement, you should carefully consider the economics of the repair versus buying a new or rebuilt monitor.

SYMPTOM 30-12 **The image is saturated with blue, or appears yellow** If there are any user color controls available from the front or rear housings, make sure those controls have not been accidentally adjusted. If color controls are set properly (or are not available externally), the blue video drive circuit has probably failed. Refer to the example circuit of Figure 30-8. Use your oscilloscope to trace the video signal from its initial input to the final output. If there is no blue video signal at the amplifier input (the base of Q701), check the connection between the monitor and the video adapter board. If the connection is intact, try a known-good monitor. If the problem persists on a known-good monitor, replace the video adapter board. As you trace the video signal, you can compare the signal to characteristics at the corresponding points in the green or red video circuits. The point at which the signal disappears is probably the point of failure, and the offending component should be replaced. If you do not have the tools or inclination to perform component-level troubleshooting, try replacing the video drive PC board entirely.

If the video signal measures properly all the way to the CRT (or a new video drive PC board does not correct the problem), suspect a fault in the CRT itself—the corresponding cathode or video control grid may have failed. If you have access to a CRT tester/rejuvenator, test the CRT. If the CRT measures bad (and cannot be recovered through any available rejuvenation procedure), it should be replaced. Keep in mind that a color CRT is usually the most expensive component in the monitor. As with any CRT replacement, you should carefully consider the economics of the repair versus buying a new or rebuilt monitor.

SYMPTOM 30-13 **The image is saturated with green, or appears bluish-red (magenta)** If there are any user color controls available from the front or rear housings, make sure those controls have not been accidentally adjusted. If color controls are set properly (or are not available externally), the green video drive circuit has probably failed. Refer to the example circuit of Figure 30-8. Use your oscilloscope to trace the video signal from its initial input to the final output. If there is no green video signal at the amplifier input (the base of Q601), check the connection between the monitor and the video adapter board. If the connection is intact, try a known-good monitor. If the problem persists on a known-good monitor, replace the video adapter board. As you trace the video signal, you can compare the signal to characteristics at the corresponding points in the red or blue video circuits. The point at which the signal disappears is probably the point of failure, and the offending component should be replaced. If you do not have the tools or inclination to perform component-level troubleshooting, try replacing the video drive PC board entirely.

If the video signal measures properly all the way to the CRT (or a new video drive PC board does not correct the problem), suspect a fault in the CRT itself—the corresponding cathode or video control grid may have failed. If you have access to a CRT tester/rejuvenator, test the CRT. If the CRT measures bad (and cannot be recovered through any available rejuvenation procedure), it should be replaced. Keep in mind that a color CRT is usually the most expensive component in the monitor. As with any CRT replacement, you should carefully consider the economics of the repair versus buying a new or rebuilt monitor.

SYMPTOM 30-14 **Raster is present, but there is no image** When the monitor is properly connected to a PC, a series of text information should appear as the PC initializes. We can use this as our baseline image. Isolate the monitor by trying a known-good monitor on your host PC. If the known-good monitor works, you prove that the PC and video adapter are working properly. Reconnect the suspect monitor to the PC and turn up the brightness (and contrast if necessary). You should see a faint white haze covering the display. This is the raster generated by the normal sweep of an electron beam. Remember that the PC *must* be on and running. Without the horizontal and vertical retrace signals provided by the video adapter, there will be no raster.

For a color image to fail completely, all three video drive circuits will have to be disabled. You should check all connectors between the video adapter board and the monitor's main PC board. A loose or severed wire can interrupt the voltage(s) powering the board. You should also check each output from your power supply. A low or missing voltage can disable your video circuits as effectively as a loose connector. If you find a faulty supply output, you can attempt to troubleshoot the supply, or you can replace the power supply outright. For monitors that incorporate the power supply onto the main PC board, the entire main PC board would have to be replaced.

If supply voltage levels and connections are intact, use an oscilloscope to trace the video signals through their respective amplifier circuits. Chances are that you will see all three video signals fail at the same location of each circuit. This is usually due to a problem in common parts of the video circuits. In the example video drive board of Figure 30-8, such common circuitry involves the components marked with 8xx numbers (such as Q801). If you do not have the tools or inclination to perform such component-level troubleshooting, replace the video drive PC board.

You should also suspect a problem with the raster blanking circuits. During horizontal and vertical retrace periods, video signals are cut off. If visible raster lines appear in your image, check the blanking signals. If you are unable to check the blanking signals, try replacing the video drive PC board. If a new video drive board fails to correct the problem, replace the main PC board.

If you should find that all three video signals check correctly all the way to the CRT (or replacing the video drive circuit does not restore the image), you should suspect a major fault in the CRT itself—there is little else that can fail. If you have a CRT tester/rejuvenator available, you should test the CRT thoroughly for shorted grids or a weak cathode. If the problem cannot be rectified through rejuvenation (or you do not have access to a CRT tester), try replacing the CRT. Keep in mind, however, that a CRT is usually the most expensive part of the monochrome monitor. If each step up to now has not restored your image, you should weigh the economics of replacing the CRT versus scrapping it in favor of a new or rebuilt unit.

SYMPTOM 30-15 **A single horizontal line appears in the middle of the display** The horizontal sweep is working properly, but there is no vertical deflection. A fault has almost certainly developed in the vertical drive circuit (refer to Figure 30-9). Use your oscilloscope to check the sawtooth wave being generated by the vertical oscillator/amplifier chip (pin 6 of IC402). If the sawtooth wave is missing, the fault is almost certainly in the chip. For the circuit of Figure 30-9, try replacing IC402. If the sawtooth wave is available on IC402 pin 6, you should suspect a defect in the horizontal deflection yoke itself, or one of its related components. If you are not able to check signals to the component level, simply replace the monitor's main PC board.

SYMPTOM 30-16 **Only the upper or lower half of an image appears** In most cases, there is a problem in the vertical amplifier. For the example circuit of Figure 30-9, the trouble is likely located in the vertical oscillator/amplifier (IC402). Use your oscilloscope to check the sawtooth waveform leaving IC402 pin 6. If the sawtooth is distorted, replace IC402. If the sawtooth signal reads properly, check for other faulty components in the vertical deflection yoke circuit. If you do not have the tools or inclination to check and replace devices at the component level, replace the monitor's main PC board. When the image is restored, be sure to check vertical linearity, as described in Chapter 32.

SYMPTOM 30-17 **A single vertical line appears along the middle of the display** The vertical sweep is working properly, but there is no horizontal deflection. However, in order to even see the display at normal brightness, there must be high voltage present in the monitor—the horizontal drive circuit must be working (refer to Figure 30-9). The fault probably lies in the horizontal deflection yoke. Check the yoke and all wiring connected to it. It may be necessary to replace the horizontal deflection yoke, or the entire yoke assembly.

If horizontal deflection is lost as well as substantial screen brightness, there may be a marginal fault in the horizontal drive circuit. If there is a problem with the horizontal oscillator pulses, the switching characteristics of the horizontal amplifier will change. In turn, this affects high-voltage development and horizontal deflection. Use your oscilloscope to check the square wave generated by the horizontal oscillator IC301 pin 3, as shown in Figure 30-9. You should see a square wave. If the square wave is distorted, replace the oscillator chip (IC301). If the horizontal pulse is correct, check the horizontal switching transistors (Q301 and Q302). Replace any transistor that appears defective. If the collector signal at the HOT is low or distorted, there may be a short circuit in the flyback transformer's primary winding. Try replacing the FBT. If you do not have the tools or inclination to check components to the component level (or the problem persists), replace the monitor's main PC board. When the repair is complete, check the horizontal linearity and size.

SYMPTOM 30-18 **There is no image and no raster** When the monitor is properly connected to a PC, a series of text information should appear as the PC initializes. We can use this as our baseline image. Isolate the monitor by trying a known-good monitor on your host PC. If the known-good monitor works, you prove that the PC and video adapter are working properly. Reconnect the suspect monitor to the PC and turn up the brightness (and contrast if necessary). Start by checking for the presence of horizontal and vertical synchronization pulses. If pulses are absent, no raster will be generated. If sync pulses are present, there is likely a problem somewhere in the horizontal drive or high-voltage circuits.

Always suspect a power supply problem, so check every output from the supply (especially the 20 Vdc and 135 Vdc outputs, as shown in Figure 30-9). A low or absent supply voltage will disable the horizontal deflection and high-voltage circuits. If one or more supply outputs are low or absent, you can troubleshoot the power supply circuit, or replace the power supply outright. (When the power circuit is combined on the monitor's main PC board, the entire main PC board would have to be replaced.)

If the supply outputs read correctly, suspect your horizontal drive circuit. Use your oscilloscope to check the horizontal oscillator output at the base of Q301, as shown in Figure 30-9. You should see a square wave. If the square wave is low, distorted, or absent, replace the horizontal oscillator IC (IC301). If a regular pulse is present, the horizontal oscillator is working. Since Q301 is intended to act as a switch, you should also find a pulse at the collector of Q301. If the pulse output is severely distorted or absent, Q301 is probably damaged (remove Q301 and test it). If Q301 reads as faulty, it should be replaced. If Q301 reads good, check the horizontal coupling transformer (T303) for shorted or open windings. Try replacing T303. (There is little else that can go wrong in this part of the circuit.)

Check the HOT (Q302) next by removing it from the circuit and testing it. If Q302 reads faulty, it should be replaced with an exact replacement part. If Q302 reads good, the fault probably lies in the flyback transformer. Try replacing the FBT. If you do not have the tools or inclination to perform these component-level checks, simply replace the monitor's main PC board outright.

In the event that these steps fail to restore the image, the CRT has probably failed. If you have access to a CRT tester/rejuvenator, you can test the CRT. When the CRT measures as bad (and cannot be restored through rejuvenation), it should be replaced. If you do not have a CRT test instrument, you can simply replace the CRT. Keep in mind, however, that a CRT is usually the most expensive part of a color monitor. If each step up to now has not restored your image, you should weigh the economics of replacing the CRT versus scrapping it in favor of a new or rebuilt unit. If you choose to replace the CRT, you should perform a full set of alignments, as described in Chapter 31.

SYMPTOM 30-19 **The image is too compressed or too expanded** A whitish haze may appear along the bottom of the image. Start by checking your vertical size control to be sure that it was not adjusted accidentally. Since vertical size is a function of the vertical sawtooth oscillator, you should suspect the vertical oscillator circuit. A sawtooth signal that is too large will result in an overexpanded image, while a signal that is too small will appear to compress the image. Use your oscilloscope to check the vertical sawtooth signal. For the vertical drive circuit of Figure 30-9, you should find a sawtooth signal on IC402 pin 6. If the signal is incorrect, try replacing IC 402. You may also wish to check the PC board for any cracks or faulty soldering connections around the vertical oscillator circuit. If the problem persists, or you do not have the tools or inclination to perform component-level troubleshooting, simply replace the monitor's main PC board outright.

SYMPTOM 30-20 **The displayed characters appear to be distorted** The term "distortion" can be interpreted in many different ways. For our purposes, we will simply say that the image (usually text) is difficult to read. Before even opening your toolbox, check the monitor's location. The presence of stray magnetic fields in close proximity to the monitor can cause bizarre forms of distortion. Try moving the monitor to another location. Remove any electromagnetic or magnetic objects (such as motors or refrigerator magnets) from the area. If the problem persists, it is likely that the monitor is at fault.

If only certain areas of the display appear affected (or affected worse than other areas), the trouble is probably due to poor linearity (either horizontal, vertical, or both). If raster speed varies across the display, the pixels in some areas of the image may appear too close together, while the pixels in other areas of the image may appear too far apart. You can check and correct horizontal and vertical linearity using a test pattern. If alignment fails to correct poor linearity, your best course is often simply to replace the monitor's main PC board. If the image is difficult to read because it is out of focus, you should check the focus alignment. If you can not achieve a sharp focus using controls either on the front panel of the monitor or on the flyback transformer assembly, there is probably a fault in the flyback transformer. Try replacing the FBT. If the problem persists, your best course is often simply to replace the monitor's main PC board.

SYMPTOM 30-21 **The display appears wavy** There are visible waves appearing along the edges of the display as the image sways back and forth. This is almost always the result of a power supply problem—one or more outputs is failing. Use your multimeter and check each supply output. If you find a low or absent output, you can proceed to troubleshoot the supply, or you can simply replace the supply outright. If the power supply is integrated onto the main PC board, you will have to replace the entire main PC board.

SYMPTOM 30-22 **The display is too bright or too dim** Before opening the monitor, be sure to check the brightness and contrast controls. If the controls have been accidentally adjusted, set contrast to maximum, and adjust the brightness level until a clear, crisp display is produced. When front panel controls fail to provide the proper display (but focus seems steady), suspect a fault in the monitor's power supply. Refer to the example schematic of Figure 30-9. If the 135 Vdc supply is too low or too high, brightness levels controlling the CRT screen grid will shift. If you find one or more incorrect outputs from the power supply, you can troubleshoot the supply or replace the supply outright. For those monitors that incorporate the power supply on the main PC board, the entire main PC board will have to be replaced.

SYMPTOM 30-23 **You see visible raster scan lines in the display** The very first thing you should do is check the front panel brightness and contrast controls. If contrast is set too low and/or brightness is set too high, raster will be visible on top of the image. This will tend to make the image appear a bit fuzzy. If the front panel controls cannot eliminate visible raster from the image, chances are that you have a problem with the power supply. Use your multimeter and check each output from the supply. If one or more outputs appear too high (or too low), you can troubleshoot the supply or replace the supply outright. If the supply is integrated with the monitor's main PC board, the entire PC board will have to be replaced.

If the power supply is intact, you should suspect a problem with the raster blanking circuits. During horizontal and vertical retrace periods, video signals are cut off. If visible raster lines appear in your image, check the blanking signals. If you are unable to check the blanking signals, try replacing the video drive PC board. If a new video drive board fails to correct the problem, replace the main PC board.

SYMPTOM 30-24 **Colors bleed or smear** Ultimately, this symptom occurs when unwanted pixels are excited in the CRT. However, this can be caused by several different problems. Perhaps the most common problem is a fault in the video cable between the video board and the monitor. Electrical noise (sometimes called *crosstalk*) in the cable may allow signals representing one color to accidentally be picked up in another color signal wire. This can easily cause unwanted colors to appear in the display. Although the video cable is designed to be shielded and carefully filtered, age or poor installation can precipitate this type of problem. Try wiggling the cable. If the problem stops, appears intermittent, or shifts around, you have likely found the source of the problem—replace the cable with a proper replacement assembly.

If the video cable appears intact, suspect failing capacitors in the video amplifier circuits. You can see these capacitors in the schematic of Figure 30-8. Capacitors such as C505 and C506 are typically low-value, high-voltage components, so they tend to degrade rather quickly. Fortunately, such capacitors are easy to spot on the video amplifier board. If the color problem appears intermittent (or occurs when the monitor warms up), try a bit of liquid refrigerant on each capacitor. If the problem disappears, the one you froze is probably defective. Otherwise, you can turn off and unplug the monitor, then check each capacitor individually. When replacing capacitors in the video amplifier circuit, be sure to replace them with the same type and voltage rating.

If capacitors are not at fault, suspect the amplifier transistors on the video amplifier board (Q504, Q505, or Q506). Turn off and unplug the monitor, and then try checking each of the transistors. Chances are that your readings will be inconclusive, so try comparing readings from each transistor to find a device that gives the most unusual readings. Try replacing any defective or questionable amplifier transistors. If you do not have the time or inclination to troubleshoot the video amplifier board, try replacing the board outright.

SYMPTOM 30-25 Colors appear to change when the monitor is warm Either colors will appear correctly when the monitor is cold, then change as the monitor warms up, or vice versa. In both cases, there is likely to be some kind of thermal problem in the video amplifier circuits. Turn off and unplug the monitor, and then start by checking the video cable—especially its connection to the raster board inside the monitor. If this connection is loose, it may be intermittent or unreliable. Tighten any loose connections and try the monitor again. Also check the cable that connects the video amplifier board to the raster board.

If the connections appear tight, your best course of action is often to remove the video amplifier board and try resoldering each of the junctions. Chances are that age or thermal stress has fatigued one or more connections. By resoldering the connections, you should be able to correct any potential connection problems. You might also try resoldering the connector that passes video data from the raster board to the video amplifier board. If your problems persist, try replacing the video amplifier board.

SYMPTOM 30-26 An image appears distorted in 350 or 400 line mode In most cases, the "distortion" is an image that appears excessively compressed. As you probably read earlier in this book, different screen modes have a different number of horizontal lines (for example, a 640x480 display offers 480 horizontal traces of 640 pixels each). When the screen mode changes, the number of lines changes as well (for example, to a 320x200 mode). As you might expect, in order to keep the image roughly square, the "size" of each pixel has to be adjusted when the screen mode changes—otherwise the image simply "shrinks." Monitors detect the screen mode by checking the polarity of the sync signals. You can see this function in the schematic of Figure 30-9.

Typically, each screen mode size can be optimized by an adjustment on the raster board. However, if a mode adjustment is thrown off (or the sync sensing circuit fails), an image can easily appear with an incorrect size. If you notice this kind of distortion without warning, suspect a problem with the sync sensing circuit. If the sync sensing circuit is incorporated into a single chip (such as IC201), replace the chip outright. If you notice a size problem after aligning the monitor, you may have accidentally upset a size adjustment. Readjust the size controls to restore proper image dimensions.

SYMPTOM 30-27 The fine detail of high-resolution graphic images appears a bit fuzzy At best, this kind of symptom may not be noticeable without careful inspection, but it may signal a serious problem in the video amplifier circuit. High resolutions demand high bandwidth—a video amplifier must respond quickly to the rapid variations between pixels. If a weakness in the video amplifier(s) occurs, it can limit bandwidth and degrade video performance at high resolutions. The problem will likely disappear at lower resolutions. The particular problem with this symptom is that it is almost impossible to isolate a defective component—the video amplifier board *is* working. As a result, your best course of action is to check all connectors for secure installation first. Nicked or frayed video cables can also contribute to the problem. If the problem remains, replace the video amplifier board.

SYMPTOM 30-28 **The display changes color, flickers, or cuts out when the video cable is moved** Check the video cable's connection to the video adapter at the PC. A loose connection will almost certainly result in such intermittent problems. If the connection is secure, there is an intermittent connection in the video cable. Before replacing the cable, check its connections within the monitor itself. When connections are intact, replace the intermittent video cable outright. Do not bother cutting or splicing the cable—any breaks in the signal shielding will cause crosstalk, which will result in color bleeding.

SYMPTOM 30-29 **The image expands in the horizontal direction when the monitor gets warm** One or more components in the horizontal retrace circuit are weak—and changing value a bit once the monitor gets warm. Turn off and unplug the monitor. You should inspect any capacitors located around the "horizontal output transistor" (or HOT). The problem is that thermal problems such as this can be extremely difficult to isolate because you can't measure capacitor values while the monitor is running, and after the monitor is turned off, the parts will cool too quickly to catch a thermal problem. It is often most effective to simply replace several of the key capacitors around the HOT outright. If you don't want to bother with individual components, replace the raster board.

SYMPTOM 30-30 **The image shrinks in the horizontal direction when the monitor gets warm** This is another thermal-related problem that indicates either a weakness in one or more components, or a mild soldering-related problem. Turn off and unplug the monitor. Start by checking for a poor solder connection—especially around the horizontal deflection yoke wiring, the horizontal output transistor (HOT), and the flyback transformer. If nothing appears obvious, you might consider resoldering all of the components in the HOT area of the raster board. If problems continue, suspect a failure in the HOT itself. Semiconductors rarely become marginal—they either work or they don't. Still, semiconductor junctions can become unstable when temperatures change, which can result in circuit characteristic changes. You could also try replacing the HOT outright.

It is also possible that one or more midrange power supply outputs (such as 12 or 20 volts) are sagging when the monitor warms up. Use a voltmeter and measure the outputs from your power supply. If the 12 volt or 20 volt outputs appear to drop once the monitor has been running for a bit, you should troubleshoot the power supply.

30

SYMPTOM 30-31 **High-voltage fails after the monitor is warm** There are a large number of possible causes behind this problem, but no matter what permutation you find, you will likely be dealing with soldering problems, or thermal-related failures. Turn off and unplug the monitor. Inspect the HOT's heat sink assembly. There may be a bad solder connection on the heat sink ground. There may also be an open solder connection on one or more of the flyback transformer pins. If you cannot locate a faulty soldering connection, you may simply choose to resolder all of the connections in the flyback area.

If the problem persists, you should suspect that either your HOT or flyback transformer is failing under load (after the monitor warms up). One possible means of isolating the problem is to measure pulses from the HOT output with your oscilloscope. If the pulses stop at the same time your high voltage fails, you can suspect a problem with your HOT or other horizontal components. Try replacing the HOT. If high voltage fails but the HOT pulses remain, your flyback transformer has likely failed. Replace the flyback transformer. If you do not have an oscilloscope, try replacing the HOT first since that is the least-expensive part, and then replace the flyback transformer if necessary.

In the unlikely event that both a new HOT and flyback transformer do not correct the problem, you should carefully inspect the capacitors in the HOT circuit. One or more might be failing. Unfortunately, it is very difficult to identify a marginal capacitor (especially one that is suffering from a thermal failure). You may try replacing the major capacitors in the HOT circuit, or replace the raster board entirely.

SYMPTOM 30-32 **The image blooms intermittently** The amount of high voltage driving the CRT is varying intermittently. Since high voltage is related to the HOT circuit and flyback transformer, you should concentrate your search in those two areas of the raster board. Examine the soldering of your HOT and FBT connections—especially the ground connections if you can identify them. You may try resoldering all of the connections in those areas (remember to turn off and unplug the monitor before soldering). There may also be a ground problem on the video amplifier board that allows all three color signals to vary in amplitude. When this happens, the overall brightness of the image changes, and the image may grow or shrink a bit in response. Try resoldering connections on the video amplifier board.

If the problem remains (even after soldering), your FBT may be failing—probably due to an age-related internal short. High-end test equipment such as Sencore's monitor test station provides the instrumentation to test a flyback transformer. If you do not have access to such dedicated test equipment, however, try replacing the FBT assembly. If you do not have the time or inclination to deal with component replacement, go ahead and replace the raster board outright. In the unlikely event that your problem persists, suspect a fault in the CRT itself. If you have access to a CRT tester/rejuvenator, you can check the CRT's operation. Some weaknesses in the CRT may be corrected (at least temporarily) by rejuvenation. If the fault cannot be corrected, you may have to replace the CRT.

SYMPTOM 30-33 **The image appears out of focus** Before suspecting a component failure, try adjusting the focus control. In most cases, the focus control is located adjacent to the flyback transformer. Keep in mind that the focus control should be adjusted with brightness and contrast set to optimum values. Excessively bright images may lose focus naturally. If the focus control is unable to restore a proper image, check the CRT focus voltage. In Figure 30-9, you can find the focus voltage off a flyback transformer tap. If the focus voltage is low (often combined with a dim image), you may have a failing FBT. It is possible to test the FBT if you have the specialized test instrumentation—otherwise, you should just replace the FBT outright. If you lack the time or inclination to replace the FBT, you can simply replace the raster board.

If a new FBT does not resolve your focus problem, suspect a fault in the CRT—probably in the focus grid. You can use a CRT tester/rejuvenator to examine the CRT, and it may be possible to restore normal operation (at least temporarily). If you do not have such equipment, you will simply have to try a new CRT.

SYMPTOM 30-34 **The image appears to flip or scroll horizontally** There is a synchronization problem in your horizontal raster circuit. Begin by checking the video cable to be sure that it is installed and connected securely. Cables that behave intermittently (or that appear frayed or nicked) should be replaced. If the cable is intact, suspect a problem in your horizontal circuit. If there is a horizontal sync (or "horizontal hold") adjustment on the raster board, adjust it in small increments until the image snaps back into sync. If there is no such adjustment on your particular monitor, try resoldering all of the connections in the horizontal processing circuit. If the problem persists, replace the horizontal oscillator chip, or replace the entire raster board.

SYMPTOM 30-35 **The image appears to flip or scroll vertically** There is a synchronization problem in your vertical raster circuit. Begin by checking the video cable to be sure that it is installed and connected securely. Cables that behave intermittently (or that appear frayed or nicked) should be replaced. If the cable is intact, suspect a problem in your vertical circuit. If there is a vertical sync (or "vertical hold") adjustment on the raster board, adjust it in small increments until the image snaps back into sync. If there is no such adjustment on your particular monitor, try resoldering all of the connections in the vertical processing circuit. If the problem persists, replace the vertical oscillator chip, or replace the entire raster board.

SYMPTOM 30-36 **The image appears to shake or oscillate in size** This may occur in bursts, but it typically occurs constantly. In most cases, this is due to a fault in the power supply—usually the 135 volt (B+) output. Try measuring your power supply outputs with an oscilloscope and see if an output is varying along with the screen size changes. If you locate such an output, the filtering portion of that output may be malfunctioning. Track the output back into the supply and replace any defective components. If you are unable to isolate a faulty component, replace the power supply. When the power supply is integrated onto the raster board, you may have to replace the raster board entirely.

If the outputs from your power supply appear stable, you should suspect a weak capacitor in your horizontal circuit. Try resoldering the FBT, HOT, and other horizontal circuit components to eliminate the possibility of a soldering problem. If the problem remains, you will have to systematically replace the capacitors in the horizontal circuit. If you do not have the time or inclination to replace individual components, replace the raster board outright.

Here's an unusual problem. The shaking you see may be related to a problem in the degaussing coil located around the CRT funnel. Ordinarily, the degaussing coil should unleash most of its energy in the initial moments after monitor power is turned on. Thermistors (or posistors) in the power supply quickly diminish coil voltage—effectively cutting off the degaussing coil's operation. A fault in the degaussing coil circuit (in the power supply) may continue to allow enough power to the coil to affect the image's stability. Try disconnecting the degaussing coil. If the problem remains, the degaussing coil is likely operating properly. If the problem disappears, you have a fault in the degaussing coil circuit.

Further Study

Acer: **http://www.aci.acer.com.tw**

CTX: **http://www.ctxintl.com**

Hitachi: **http://www.hitachi.com**

Magnavox: **http://www.magnavox.com**

Nanao: **http://www.traveller.com/nanao/**

NEC: **http://webserver.nectech.com/textgraph/tocmon.htm**

Sony: **http://www.sel.sony.com/SEL/ccpg/index.html**

Viewsonic: **http://www.viewsonic.com**

31

MONITOR TESTING AND ALIGNMENT

CHAPTER AT A GLANCE

When set up and ventilated properly, computer monitors are notoriously rugged devices. The CRT itself enjoys a reasonably long life span. By their very nature, CRTs are remarkably tolerant to physical abuse and can withstand wide variations in power and signal voltages. However, even the best CRT and its associated circuitry suffers eventual degradation with age and use. Monitor operation can also be upset when major subassemblies are replaced, such as circuit boards or deflection assemblies. Maintenance and alignment procedures are available to evaluate a monitor's performance and allow you to keep it working within its specifications. This chapter illustrates a comprehensive set of procedures that can be performed to test and adjust the monitor's performance. Keep in mind that this chapter uses test patterns generated with the commercial utility MONITORS, available on the companion CD.

> The MONITORS utility is commercial software that is included on the Companion CD in encrypted format. To use MONITORS, you'll need to purchase the unlock code. See the order form at the back of this book for more ordering information.

Before You Begin

Adjusting a monitor is a serious matter and should not be undertaken without careful consideration. There are a myriad of adjustments found on the main circuit board—any of which can render a screen image unviewable if adjusted improperly. The delicate magnets and deflection assemblies around the CRT's neck can easily be damaged or knocked out of alignment by careless handling. In short, *aligning a monitor can do more harm than good unless you have the patience to understand the purpose of each procedure.* You also need to have a calm, methodical approach. The following points may help to keep you out of trouble.

TESTING VS. ALIGNMENT

There is a distinct difference between monitor testing and monitor alignment. *Testing* is a low-level operation. Testing is also unobtrusive, so you can test a monitor at any point in the repair process. By using the MONITORS companion software with your PC, you can test any monitor that is compatible with your video adapter. Testing is accomplished by displaying one or more test pattern(s) on the monitor. After observing the condition of each pattern, you can usually deduce the monitor's fault area very quickly. Once the monitor is working (able to display a steady, full-screen image), you can also use test patterns to evaluate the monitor's current state of alignment.

Alignment is a high-level operation—a task that is performed only *after* the monitor has been completely repaired. Since alignment requires you to make adjustments to the monitor circuits, the monitor circuits *must* be working properly. *After all, alignment does no good if a fault is preventing the monitor from displaying an image in the first place.* Proper alignment is important to ensure that the monitor is displaying images as crisply and cleanly as possible.

KNOW THE WARRANTY

A warranty is a written promise made by a manufacturer that their product will be free of most problems for some period of time. For monitors, typical warranties cover parts and labor for a period of one year from the date of purchase. The CRT itself is often covered for up to three years. Before even touching the monitor, you should check to see if the warranty is still in force. Monitors that are still under warranty should be sent back to the *manufacturer* for repair. This book does *not* advocate voiding any warranty, and the reasoning is very simple—*why spend your time and effort to do a job that the manufacturer will do for free?* You (or your customer) paid for that warranty when the monitor was purchased. Of course, most monitors in need of service are already out of warranty.

There are only three exceptions that might prompt you to ignore a warranty. First, the warranty may already be void if you purchased the monitor used. Manufacturers typically support the warranty only for the original purchaser (the individual that returns the warranty card). Third-party claims are often refused, but it may still be worth a call to the manufacturer's service manager just to be sure. Second, any warranty is only as good as the manufacturer. A manufacturer that goes out of business is not concerned with supporting your monitor, although reputable manufacturers that close their doors will turn over their service operations to an independent repair house. Again, a bit of detective work may be required to find out if the ultimate service provider will honor the unit's warranty. Finally, you may choose to ignore a warranty for organizations with poor or unclear service performance. Call the service provider and ask about the turn-around time and return procedures. If they "don't know," or you can't get a straight answer, chances are that your monitor is going to sit untouched for quite a while.

GETTING FROM HERE TO THERE

Monitors require special care in moving and handling. A monitor is typically a heavy device (most of the weight being contributed by the CRT and chassis). Back injury is a serious concern. If you *must* move the monitor between locations, remember to lift from the knees and *not* from the back—it's hard to fix a monitor while you're in traction. When carrying the monitor, keep the CRT screen toward your chest with your arms wrapped carefully around the enclosure to support the weight. Large monitors (17 inches to 20 inches and bigger) are particularly unwieldy. You are wise to get another person's help when moving such bulky, expensive devices. If the monitor is to be used in-house, keep it on a roll-around cart so that you will not have to carry it.

When transporting a monitor from place to place in an automobile, the monitor should be sealed in a well-cushioned box. If an appropriate box is not available, place the monitor on a car seat that is well-cushioned with soft foam or blankets—even an old pillow or two will do. Sit the monitor on its cushioning *face down*, since that will lower the monitor's center of gravity and make it as stable as possible. Use twine or thin rope to secure the monitor so it will not shift in transit.

When shipping the monitor to a distant location, the monitor should be shipped in its original container and packing materials. If the original shipping material has been discarded, purchase a heavy-gauge cardboard box. The box dimensions should be at least four to six inches bigger in every dimension than the monitor. Fill the empty space with plenty of foam padding or bubble wrap that can be obtained from any full-service stationary store. The box should be sealed and reinforced with heavy-gauge box tape. It does not pay to skimp here—a monitor's weight demands a serious level of protection.

HIGH-VOLTAGE CAUTIONS

It is also important to remind you that a computer monitor uses very high voltages for proper operation. Potentially *lethal* shock hazards exist within the monitor assembly—both from ordinary AC line voltage and from the CRT anode voltage developed by the flyback transformer. You must exercise extreme caution whenever the monitor's outer housings are removed.

THE MIRROR TRICK

Monitor alignment poses a special problem for technicians. You must watch the adjustment that you are moving while also watching the display to see what effect the adjustment is having. Sure, you could watch the display and reach around the back of the monitor, but given the serious shock hazards that exist with exposed monitor circuitry, that is a very unwise tactic. (You would place your personal safety at risk.) Monitor technicians use an ordinary mirror placed several feet in front of the CRT. That way, you can watch inside the monitor as you make an adjustment, then glance up to see the display reflected in the mirror. If a suitable mirror is not to be found, ask someone to watch the display for you and relate what is happening. Ultimately, the idea is that you should *never take your eyes off of your hand(s)* while making an adjustment.

MAKING AN ADJUSTMENT

Monitor adjustments are not difficult to make, but each adjustment should be the result of careful consideration rather than a random, haphazard "shot-in-the-dark." The reason for this concern is simple—it's just as easy to make the display *worse*. Changing adjustments indiscriminately can quickly ruin display quality beyond your ability to correct it. The following three guidelines will help you make the most effective adjustments with the greatest probability of improving image quality.

First, *mark* your adjustment, as shown in Figure 31-1. Use a narrow-tip indelible marker to make a reference mark along the body of the adjustment. It does not have to be anything fancy. By making a reference mark, you can quickly return the adjustment to the exact place it started. A reference mark can really save the day if you get lost or move the wrong adjustment.

Second, concentrate on only *one* adjustment for any one alignment procedure. For example, if you're trying to optimize horizontal linearity, you should only be concerned with the horizontal linearity adjustment. If you do not have documentation that describes the location of each control, check the silk-screen labels on the PC board. If you absolutely cannot locate the needed adjustment point, skip the alignment and move on to the next test. When you do move an adjustment, move it slowly and in *very* small increments (perhaps 1/8 to 1/4 turn). Check the display after each step. If the display fails to improve, return the control to its original location (a snap to do if you've made a reference mark) and try it in the opposite direction.

Finally, avoid using metal tools (such as screwdrivers) to make your adjustments. Some of the controls in a monitor are based on coils with permeable cores. Inserting steel tools to make an adjustment will throw the setting off. The display may look fine with the tool inserted but degrade when the tool is removed. As a general rule, use plastic tools (such as TV alignment tools) that are available from almost any electronics store.

Tests and Procedures

Testing a computer monitor is easy and can be accomplished through the use of relatively standard test patterns. Once the MONITORS alignment software is started, you can select the test pattern for the specific test you wish to run. Each of the following procedures discusses how to interpret the pattern and provides a step-by-step procedure for making adjustments. For the purposes of this discussion, you should refer to the sample main board shown in Figure 31-2. Remember that the PC board(s) used in your particular monitor may be quite different, so examine your own PC board closely before attempting an adjustment.

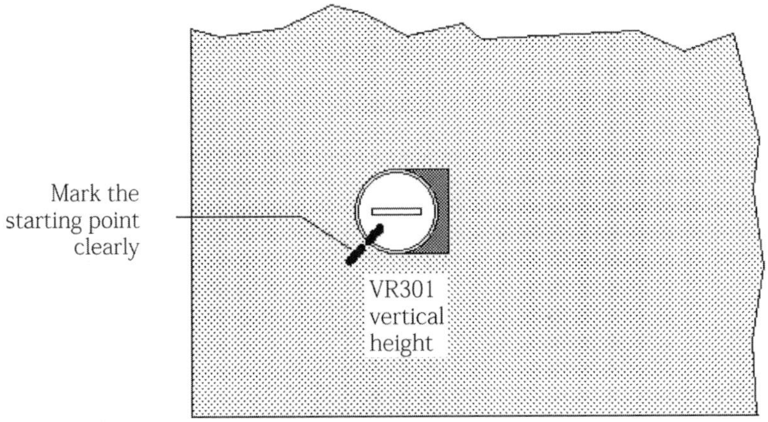

FIGURE 31-1 Mark a starting point before making an adjustment

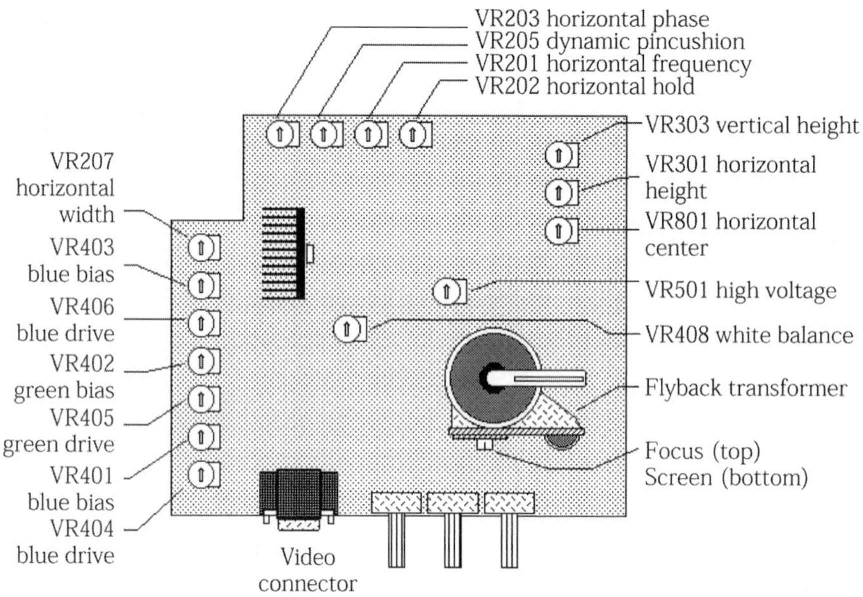

FIGURE 31-2 A typical main PC board for a monitor

Many newer monitors forgo the use of discrete adjustments in favor of electronic on-screen controls. Before opening a monitor for alignment, check for on-screen controls.

HIGH-VOLTAGE TEST AND REGULATION

The high-voltage test is one of the more important tests that you will perform on computer monitors. Excessive high-voltage levels can allow x-radiation to escape the CRT. Over long-term exposure, X rays pose a serious biohazard. Your first check should be to use a high-voltage probe. Ground the probe appropriately and insert the metal test tip under the rubber CRT anode cap. You can then read the high-voltage level directly from the probe's meter. *Be certain to refer to any particular operating and safety instructions that accompany your high-voltage probe.* If the high-voltage level is unusually high or unusually low, carefully adjust the level using a high-voltage control, which is usually located near the flyback transformer. (Figure 31-2 shows VR501 as the high-voltage control.)

Regulation is the ability of a power supply to provide a constant output as the load's demands change. The high-voltage supply must also provide regulation within specified limits. As the display image changes, high-voltage levels should remain relatively steady. If not, the display image will "flinch" as image brightness changes. Select the High-Voltage Test pattern (Figure 31-3) from the alignment software main menu. This is a narrow white double border with a solid white center. Watch the border as the center switches on and off at two-second intervals. A well-regulated high-voltage system set at the correct level will keep the white border reasonably steady—there should be very little variation in image height or width. If the image flinches significantly, the high-voltage system may be damaged or failing.

SCREEN CONTROL

The CRT screen grid provides a form of "master control" over the electron beam(s) that affects the display's overall brightness. A proper screen grid setting is important so that the brightness and contrast con-

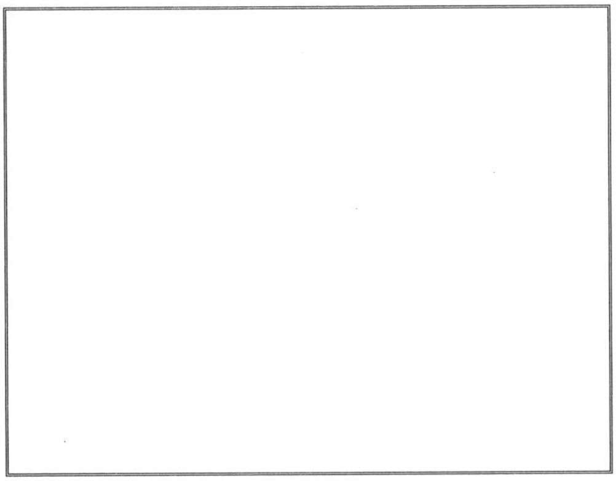

FIGURE 31-3 High-voltage regulation test pattern

trols work within an appropriate range. Select the Blank Raster test from the alignment software main menu. Adjust the monitor's brightness and contrast controls to their maximum levels—the background raster should be plainly visible.

Locate the screen voltage control. In the example of Figure 31-2, the screen voltage control is located just below the focus control on the flyback transformer assembly. Slowly adjust the screen voltage control until the background raster is just *barely* visible. Set the monitor's brightness control to its middle (detent) position. The background raster should now be invisible. Press any key to return to the main menu. You may reduce the monitor's contrast control to achieve a clear image, and it should not be too bright.

FOCUS

When an electron beam is first generated in a CRT, electrons are not directed very well. A "focus electrode" in the CRT's neck acts to narrow the electron stream. An improperly focused image is difficult to see and can lead to excessive eyestrain, resulting in headaches, fatigue, and so on. The Focus test pattern allows you to check the image clarity and optimize the focus if necessary. Keep in mind that focus is a subjective measurement—it depends on your perception. You would be wise to confer with another person while making focus adjustments since someone else's perception of the display may be different from yours.

Since focus is indirectly related to screen brightness and contrast, you should set the screen controls for an optimum display. An image that is too bright or has poor contrast may adversely affect your perception of focus. Start the MONITORS software if it is not running already. Select the Blank Raster test from the alignment software main menu. Adjust screen brightness to its middle (detent) position, or until the display's background raster disappears (the screen should be perfectly dark). Press any key to return to the main menu, and then select the White Purity test. The display should be filled with a solid white box. Adjust screen contrast to its maximum position, or until a good white image is achieved. Once the display conditions are set properly, press any key to return to the main menu.

Now, select the Focus Test pattern (Figure 31-4) from the main menu. You'll see a screen filled with the letter *m*. Review the entire screen carefully to determine whether the image is out of focus. Again, it is wise to get a second opinion before altering the focus. If the image requires a focus adjustment, gently and slowly alter the focus control. For the sample main board shown in Figure 31-2, the focus control is located on the flyback transformer assembly. Once you are satisfied with the focus, press any key to return to the main menu.

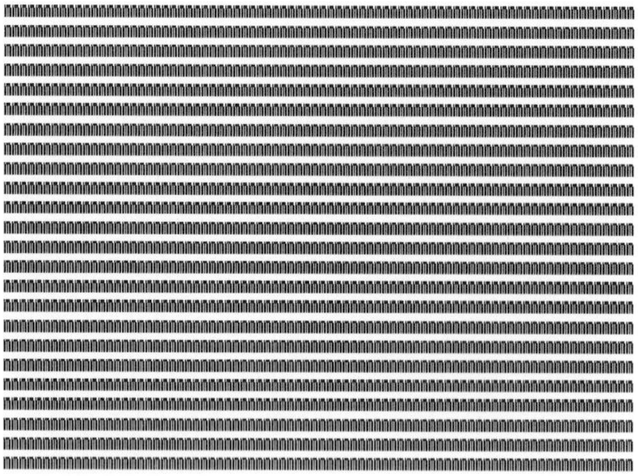

FIGURE 31-4 Screen focus test pattern

DYNAMIC PINCUSHION

A computer-generated image is produced in two dimensions—it is essentially flat. Unfortunately, the traditional CRT face is *not* flat (although some new CRT designs use an extremely flat face). When a flat image is projected onto a curved surface, the image becomes distorted. Typically, the edges of the image bow outward, making straight lines appear convex (known as barrel distortion). Monitor raster circuitry is designed to compensate for this distortion and allows the image to appear flat, even though it is being projected onto a slightly curved surface. This is known as the *dynamic pincushion* circuit (or just the pincushion). However, if the pincushion circuit overcompensates for curvature, the edges of an image will appear to bow inward, making straight lines appear concave.

It is a simple matter to check the dynamic pincushion. Select the Convergence Test (Crosshatch) pattern from the main menu. A white grid will appear in the display. Inspect the outer border of the grid pattern. If the edges of the border appear straight and true, the dynamic pincushion is set properly, and no further action is needed. If the edges appear to bow outward, the pincushion is undercompensated. If the edges appear to bow inward, the pincushion is overcompensated. In either case, you will need to make a minor adjustment to the dynamic pincushion control. Figure 31-2 lists VR205 as the dynamic pincushion control, but your monitor probably uses different nomenclature. Before making such an adjustment, you may wish to confer with another individual since someone else's perception of the display may be different from yours. If you cannot locate the dynamic pincushion control, simply move on to the next test.

HORIZONTAL PHASE

When brightness and contrast are set to their maximum levels, you will see a dim, dark gray rectangle formed around the screen image. This border is part of the *raster*—the overall area of the screen that is hit by the electron beam(s). Ideally, the raster is just slightly larger than the typical image. You can control the position of an image within this raster area. This is known as horizontal *phase*. The image should be horizontally centered within the raster area. The term "phase" is used since phase refers to the amount of delay between the time that horizontal scan (raster) starts and pixel data starts. By adjusting this delay, you effectively shift the image left or right in the raster area (which should remain perfectly still).

Select the Phase Test pattern from the alignment software main menu. A phase pattern will appear as shown in Figure 31-5. Set the monitor's brightness and contrast controls to their maximum values—raster should now be visible around the image. Locate the horizontal phase control. The sample main board shown

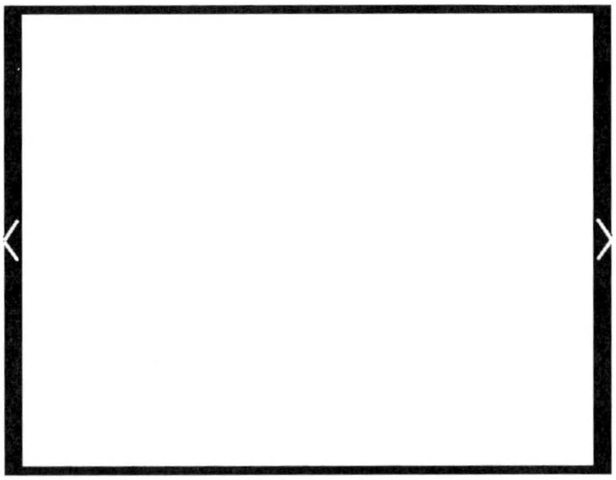

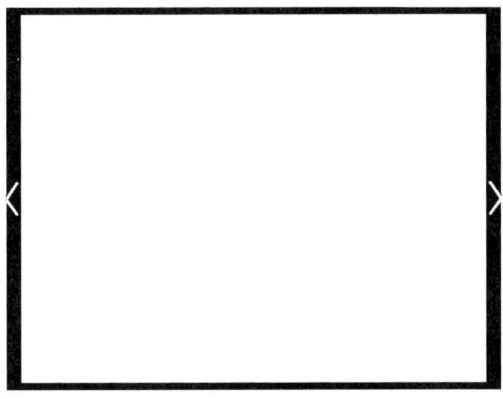

FIGURE 31-5 Phase test pattern

in Figure 31-2 indicates VR203 as the horizontal phase control. Carefully adjust the horizontal phase control until the image is approximately centered in the raster. This need not be a precise adjustment, but a bit of raster should be visible all around the image. Return the monitor brightness control to its middle (detent) position, and reduce the monitor contrast control if necessary to achieve a crisp, clear image.

HORIZONTAL AND VERTICAL CENTERING

Now that the image has been centered in the raster, it is time to center the image in the display. Centering ensures that the image is shown evenly so that you can check and adjust linearity later without the added distortion of an off-center image. Select the Convergence Test (Crosshatch) pattern from the alignment software main menu. If the image appears well centered, no further action is required.

The sample main PC board shown in Figure 31-2 indicates VR801 as the horizontal centering control. Adjust the centering control so that the image is centered horizontally in the display. Figure 31-2 also shows VR303 as the vertical centering control. Adjust this centering control so that the image is centered vertically in the display. These need not be precise adjustments. Keep in mind that many monitors make their centering controls user accessible from the front or rear housings (along with brightness and contrast).

HORIZONTAL AND VERTICAL SIZE (HEIGHT AND WIDTH)

Many monitors are capable of displaying more than one video mode. Unless the monitor offers an autosizing feature, however, the image will shift in size (especially vertical height) for each different video mode. Now that you have a focused, centered image, it should be set to the proper width and height. Remember that image size depends on the CRT size, so you will have to check the specifications for your particular monitor. If you do not have specifications available (or they do not specify image dimensions), you can at least approach a properly proportioned image using alignment software.

Select the Convergence Test (Crosshatch) pattern from the main menu. This pattern produces a grid, and each square of the grid should be roughly square. If the image is proportioned correctly, no further action is needed. Figure 31-2 uses VR301 to control vertical height. Slowly adjust vertical height until the grid squares are actually about *square*. The entire grid will be a rectangle that is wider than it is high. If the overall image is too small, you can adjust the horizontal width (VR207 is shown in Figure 31-2) to make the grid wider, and then adjust the vertical height again to keep the grid squares in a square shape. Of course, if the image is too large, you can reverse this procedure to shrink the image.

If your monitor is a multimode design and able to display images in several different graphics modes, there may be several independent vertical height adjustments—one for each available mode. You will have to check the test mode you have selected against the vertical control to be sure that the vertical height control you are changing is appropriate for the test mode being used. If you are using a 640x480 graphics mode, for example, you should be adjusting the vertical height control for the monitor's 640x480 mode. If the monitor offers an autosizing feature that automatically compensates image size for changes in screen mode, there may not be a vertical height adjustment available on the main PC board.

HORIZONTAL AND VERTICAL LINEARITY

The concept of *linearity* is often a difficult one to grasp because there are so few real-life examples for us to draw from. Linearity is best related to consistency—everything should be the same as everything else. For a computer monitor, there must be both horizontal and vertical linearity for an image to appear properly. An image is formed as a series of horizontally scanned lines. Each line should be scanned at the same speed from start to finish. If horizontal scanning speed fluctuates, vertical lines will appear closer together (or farther apart) than they actually are. Circles will appear compressed (or elongated) in the horizontal direction. Each horizontal line should be spaced exactly the same vertical distance apart. If the spacing between scanned lines varies, horizontal lines will appear closer together (or farther apart) than they actually are. Circles will appear compressed (or elongated) in the vertical direction. Any "nonlinearity" will result in distortion to the image.

Before testing, you should understand that the screen mode will have an effect on the test pattern. When screen modes change, the vertical height of the image will also change. This is especially prevalent in multifrequency and multimode monitor designs that can display images in more than one graphics mode. Before testing for linearity, the height and width of the image should be set properly for the selected screen mode, as described in the previous procedures. Otherwise, the image may appear compressed or elongated and result in a false diagnosis.

Select the Linearity Test (Lines & Circles Test) from the alignment software main menu. A grid will appear with an array of five circles, as shown in Figure 31-6. Observe the test pattern carefully. The spacing between each horizontal line should be equal. The spacing between each vertical line should be equal. Assuming the vertical height and horizontal width are set properly, each of the five circles should appear round and even. Each grid square should appear square. If the image looks correct, no further action is needed.

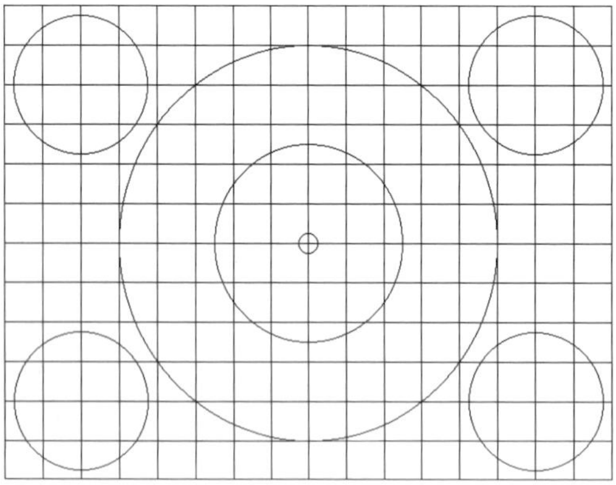

FIGURE 31-6 Linearity test pattern

If the vertical lines are not spaced evenly apart, there may be a horizontal linearity problem. Find the horizontal linearity adjustment (Figure 31-2 shows VR202). Be sure to mark the starting point, and then slowly adjust the control until the horizontal linearity improves. If there is no improvement in one direction (or linearity worsens), return to the starting point and try the adjustment in the opposite direction. If there is still no improvement (or linearity worsens again), *return the control to its starting position and take no further action*—there may be a fault in the horizontal drive circuit.

If the horizontal lines are not spaced evenly apart, there may be a vertical linearity problem. Find the vertical linearity adjustment (Figure 31-2 shows VR201). Mark the starting point, and then slowly adjust the control until the vertical linearity improves. If there is no improvement in one direction (or linearity worsens), return to the starting point and try the adjustment in the opposite direction. If there is still no improvement (or linearity worsens again), *return the control to its starting position and take no further action*—there may be a fault in the vertical drive circuit.

STATIC CONVERGENCE

Convergence is a concept that relates expressly to color CRTs. A color CRT produces three electron beams—one for each of the primary colors (red, green, and blue). These electron beams strike color phosphors on the CRT face. By adjusting the intensity of each electron beam, any color can be produced, including white. The three electron beams must converge at the shadow mask, which is mounted just behind the phosphor layer. The shadow mask maintains color purity by allowing the beams to impinge only where needed. (Any stray or misdirected electrons are physically blocked.) Without the shadow mask, stray electrons could excite adjacent color phosphors and result in strange or unsteady colors. If the beams are not aligned properly, a beam may pass through an adjacent mask aperture and excite an undesired color dot. Proper convergence is important for a quality color display.

It is a simple matter to check convergence. Be certain to allow at least 15 minutes for the monitor to warm up. Select the Convergence Test (Dots) from the alignment software main menu. An array of white dots should appear on the display. Observe the dots carefully. If you can see any shadows of red, green, or blue around the dots, convergence alignment may be necessary. If the dot pattern looks good, select the Convergence Test (Crosshatch) pattern from the main menu. A white grid should appear. Once again, observe the display carefully to locate any primary color shadows that may appear around the white lines. If the crosshatch pattern looks good, no further action is necessary, so press any key to return to the main menu.

When you determine that a convergence alignment is necessary, be sure to select the Convergence Test (Crosshatch) from the main menu. Locate the *convergence rings* on the CRT's neck just behind the deflection yokes, as shown in Figure 31-7. Using a fine-tip black marker, mark the starting position of each convergence ring relative to the glass CRT neck. This is a vital step since it will allow you to quickly return the rings to their original positions if you run into trouble. Convergence alignment is delicate, so it is easy to make the display *much* worse if you are not very careful. Also, this alignment must be performed with monitor power applied, so be *extremely* careful to protect yourself from shock hazards. The alignment process is not difficult, but requires a bit of practice and patience to become proficient. As the following procedure shows, you will align the red and blue electron beams to make magenta, and then you will align the green electron beam over the magenta pattern to make white. Keep in mind that this procedure uses the monitor alignment software (MONITORS) included on the companion CD.

While the crosshatch pattern is displayed, press M on the keyboard, which will switch the crosshatch pattern to a magenta color. Magenta is a combination of blue and red. (By choosing magenta, the green electron beam is effectively shut down, so there is less clutter in the display.) Loosen the metal band holding the rings in place. *Do not remove the band.* You may also have to loosen a locking ring before moving

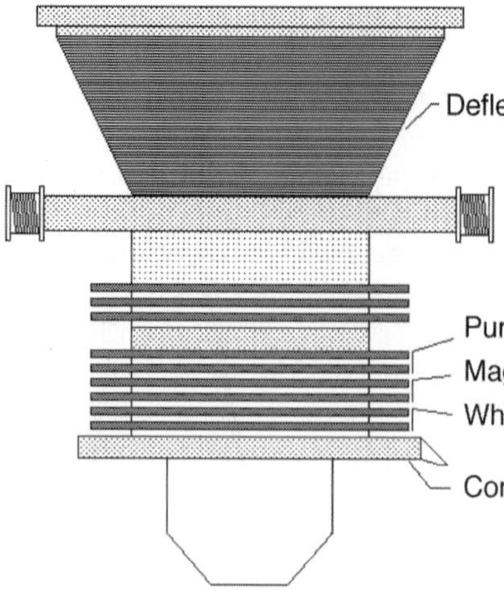

FIGURE 31-7 A typical convergence ring assembly

the convergence rings. Move the magenta convergence rings together or separately until the blue and red shadows overlap to form a uniform magenta crosshatch pattern. Be sure to move these rings only in small, careful steps. By moving the rings *together*, you adjust red and blue overlap in the vertical lines. By moving the rings *separately*, you adjust red and blue overlap in the horizontal lines. If you get into trouble, use the starting marks to return the rings to their original locations and start again.

Once the magenta pattern is aligned, press W on the keyboard, which will switch the crosshatch pattern to its original white color (thus activating the green electron beam). Adjust the white convergence rings until any green shadows overlap the crosshatch to form a uniform white grid as desired. As with the magenta rings, moving the white convergence rings *together* will adjust green overlap in the vertical lines. Moving the white convergence rings *separately* will adjust green overlap in the horizontal lines. When the image appears white, carefully secure the locking ring and setup band. Recheck the convergence as you tighten the assembly to be sure nothing has shifted. *Do not over-tighten the setup band*—you stand a good chance of damaging the CRT.

DYNAMIC CONVERGENCE

You will probably hear convergence referred to as "static" and "dynamic." These terms refer to the convergence in different areas of the display. Static refers to the convergence in the center area of the display. Dynamic refers to the convergence around the perimeter of the display. While static convergence provides a good overall alignment with a minimum of fuss, dynamic convergence is a more difficult alignment since it requires inserting rubber wedges between the edge of the deflection yoke(s) and the CRT funnel—touchy procedures even for a practiced hand. If there is visible misconvergence around the display perimeter even after a careful static convergence alignment, you will have to consider a dynamic convergence procedure.

As you might expect, dynamic convergence is perhaps the most unforgiving alignment procedure. Once you remove the wedges or alter their positions, it is extremely difficult to restore them (even with alignment marks). Unfortunately, there are no formal procedures for positioning the wedges, so you are often left to your own trial-and-error calls. In the end, you should avoid dynamic convergence adjustments if possible.

Dynamic convergence alignment requires several important steps. First, start the white convergence (crosshatch) pattern and allow the monitor to warm up for at least 15 minutes. Then mark and remove all three wedges (make sure they are free to move). When you tilt the deflection yoke up and down, you will see distortion, as illustrated in the "A" portion of Figure 31-8. As you see, misconvergence increases near the screen edge. Use the first two wedges to align the up/down positioning of the deflection yoke. The distortion shown in Figure 31-8 should disappear. Next, when you tilt the deflection yoke right and left, you will see distortion as illustrated in the "B" portion of Figure 31-8. Use the third wedge to eliminate that distortion. You may have to tweak the three wedges to optimize the dynamic convergence. Finally, you should secure the wedges in place with a dab of high-temperature/high-voltage epoxy.

The problem with dynamic convergence is that you often make the display worse when removing the wedges (even with installation marks) because you typically have to break the hold of any epoxy and wrench the wedges free. As a consequence, it is extremely difficult to tweak an existing dynamic convergence calibration—in virtually all cases, it is an all-or-nothing proposition. With this in mind, you should evaluate the need for dynamic convergence very carefully before proceeding, and if you do choose to proceed, make sure to leave yourself plenty of time.

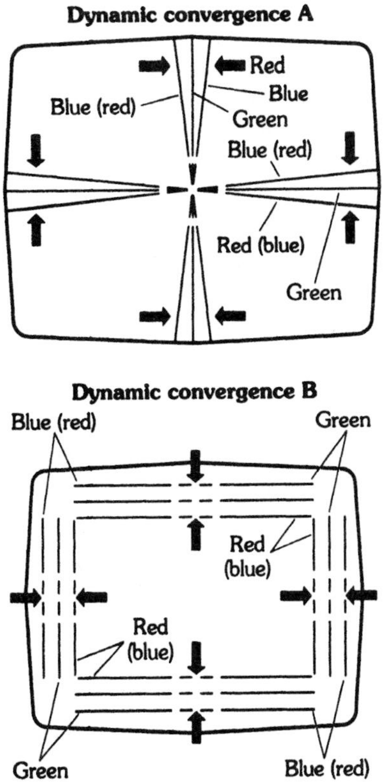

FIGURE 31-8 Calibrating dynamic convergence

COLOR PURITY

Another concern is color *purity*—that is, a solid color should have the same hue across the entire display. If discoloration develops in the display, purity may need to be restored by degaussing (demagnetizing) the monitor. Typically, the discoloration follows a semicircular pattern around one side or corner with several bands of different color—the color banding appears almost like a rainbow. Sometimes the discoloration involves the entire screen, but that is rare.

Such discoloration may be caused by an externally induced magnetic field that has permanently magnetized some material in the monitor. The three CRT electron beams are guided to their appropriate phosphor dots by a magnetic deflection system. The beams converge and pass through a shadow mask near the phosphor surface, assuring that the red beam hits the red phosphor, the blue beam hits the blue phosphor, and the green beam hits the green phosphor. If some component within the CRT (frequently it is the shadow mask itself) has become sufficiently magnetized, the beams receive an undesired deflection and will not land on the appropriate phosphor (or will land partly on one color and partly on another). The result is an impure color that arcs around the magnetized area.

Location is an important clue to this problem. If the discoloration moves or disappears when the monitor is moved, it is not being caused by a permanent magnetization, but by some magnetic interference in or near the monitor. Placing a highly magnetic or electromagnetic source (such as a strong industrial magnet or power supply) on or near the monitor can cause such discoloration. If the discoloration does not move when the monitor is moved, it may be caused by permanent magnetization in the shadow mask. In that case, degaussing is necessary.

Checking color purity is a straightforward procedure. Select the White Purity test from the main menu. A white box will fill the entire screen. If there are any areas of discoloration, degaussing is probably necessary. Degaussing removes permanent magnetization by introducing an alternating magnetic field that is stronger than the offending permanent magnetization. This field will energize the magnetic domains of the material and induce an alternating magnetic field. Then if the amplitude of the alternating magnetic field is gradually reduced to zero, the magnetic domains in the material will be left disorganized and scrambled. This effectively demagnetizes the monitor.

The easiest way to degauss a monitor is often to let the *monitor* do it. All modern color monitors have built-in degaussing coils and circuits. There will be a thick, black coil of wire wrapped in tape or other insulation surrounding the CRT face plate. Usually, it is coiled around the CRT behind its mounting ears. That is the internal degaussing coil. The coil is connected to the AC supply through a thermistor current-limiting circuit. The thermistor has a low resistance when cold and a higher resistance when warm (typically a 10:1 ratio). It is in series with the degaussing coil so that when started cold, a large current will flow through the coil and then will decrease to a low value. The internal degaussing coil thus automatically degausses the monitor every time it is turned on. This degaussing takes place while the monitor screen is blank (the video system has not yet initialized) so that the resulting discoloration during autodegaussing is not visible. Unfortunately, design limitations reduce the magnetic field strength available from internal degaussing coils. That limits the amount of permanent magnetization that can be neutralized by internal degaussing. If a monitor has been strongly magnetized, internal degaussing may not be enough, and discoloration eventually results.

Manual degaussing requires a handheld degaussing coil. You may have to search a bit to find one, but they are available. The basic principle involved in operating a manual degaussing coil is the same as the autodegaussing assemblies already in place on color monitors: introduce a strong alternating magnetic field, and then slowly reduce its amplitude to zero. Start the companion software (if it is not already running) and select the White Purity test from the main menu. A white rectangle should fill the entire image. Discoloration should be visible. Hold the degaussing coil near the monitor, flip the degaussing coil switch on, and slowly move the coil away from the monitor as smoothly as you can. The image will discolor drastically when the degaussing coil is activated. When the coil is at arm's length from the monitor, flip the degaussing switch off. You may need to repeat this procedure several times. When the monitor is degaussed properly, the white image should be consistent at all points on the display.

Excessive degaussing can damage the monitor. Wait between 15 and 30 minutes before repeating a degaussing procedure.

COLOR DRIVE

Once color convergence and purity are set correctly, you should turn your attention to the color drive levels (also known as *white balance*). Select the White Purity test from the alignment software main menu. A white box will fill the entire screen. Set screen contrast to its highest level and reduce brightness to its middle (detent) position. The background raster should disappear. Ideally, all three color signal levels should be equal, and the resulting image should be a pure white—rather like a blank piece of white photocopier paper. However, judging the quality of a display color is largely a subjective evaluation. You will need an oscilloscope to measure the actual voltage level of each color signal in order to set them equally. If you do not have an oscilloscope (or do not have access to one), do not attempt to adjust the color drive settings by eye.

Use your oscilloscope to measure the signal levels being generated by the red, green, and blue video drivers. These are the three color signals that are actually driving the CRT. With the full white pattern being displayed, all three color signals should be equal (probably around 30 volts, although your own monitor may use slightly different signal levels). Even if you are not quite sure what the level should be, all three signals must be set to the *same* level to ensure a white image. If you do not know what the level should be, find the highest of the three color signals and use that as a reference. Adjust the gain levels of the other two colors until both levels match the reference. Reduce contrast and inspect the image again. It should remain white (and all three signals should be equal). Disconnect your oscilloscope and press any key to return to the main menu.

CLEANING AND VACUUMING

Once the monitor is checked and aligned, your final step before returning the unit to service should be to inspect the housings and PC boards for accumulations of dust and debris. Look for dust accumulating in the housing vents. A monitor is typically cooled by convection. (Hot air rises—drawing in cooler air from the lower vents.) If these vents become clogged, heat will build up inside the monitor and lead to operational problems and perhaps even cause a premature breakdown. Dust is also conductive. If enough dust builds up within the monitor, the dust may short-circuit two or more components and cause operational problems. Vacuum away any dust or debris that may have accumulated in the outer housing. When you see dust buildup around the monitor PC boards and CRT, turn off and unplug the monitor, then vacuum away any buildups. Carefully reassemble the monitor's housing(s) and return it to service.

Further Study

AnaTek: **http://www.anatekcorp.com**

Repair World: **http://www.repairworld.com**

MonitorWorld: **http://www.monitorworld.com/monitors_home.html**

Monitor schematics: **http://www.mitechnologies.com/schematics.html**

Monitor schematics: **http://www.electronix.com/schematics/**

32

MOTHERBOARD TROUBLESHOOTING

CHAPTER AT A GLANCE

The *motherboard* is the heart of any personal computer (see Figure 32-1). The motherboard provides system resources (such as IRQ lines, DMA channels, and I/O locations) and supports the "core" components such as the CPU, chipset(s), real-time clock, and all system memory, including SDRAM, BIOS ROM, and CMOS RAM. Indeed, most of a PC's capabilities are defined by motherboard components. This chapter is intended to provide a guided tour of contemporary motherboards and show you how to translate error information and symptoms into motherboard repairs.

Active, Passive, and Modular

Before going any further, you should understand the difference between a "motherboard" and a "backplane." For the purposes of this book, a *motherboard* is a printed circuit board containing most of the processing components required by the computer. This style is certainly the most common form of motherboard that you will encounter as a technician. PC purists often refer to a motherboard as an *active backplane*. The term "active" is used because there are sophisticated chips running on the board. The

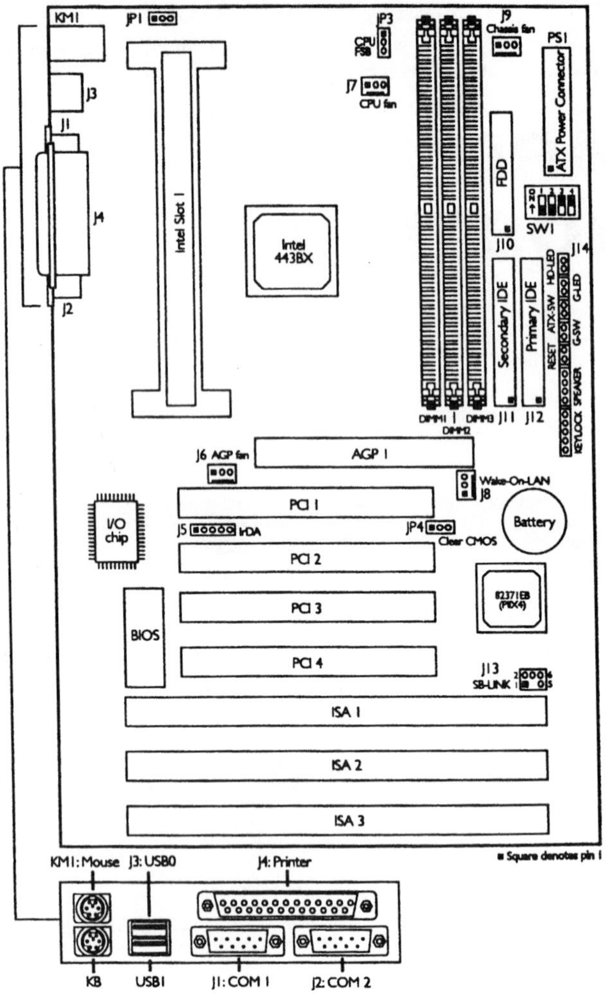

FIGURE 32-1 A contemporary motherboard design

advantage of a motherboard is its comprehensive nature—the motherboard virtually *is* the PC. Unfortunately, the motherboard has disadvantages. Namely, it is difficult to upgrade. Aside from plugging in an upgraded CPU or adding RAM, the only real way to upgrade a motherboard is to replace it outright with a newer one. For example, the only way to add PCI bus slots to an all-ISA motherboard is to replace the motherboard with one containing PCI slots.

On the other hand, a *backplane* (also referred to as a *passive backplane*) is little more than a board containing interconnecting slots—there are no major chips on the backplane (except perhaps some power supply regulating circuitry). The CPU, system RAM, BIOS ROM, and other central processing components are fabricated onto a board that simply plugs into one of the backplane slots. Other expansion devices (such as a video board, drive controller, sound board, and so on) just plug into adjacent slots. The PS/2 was one of the first PCs to use a backplane design. Backplane systems range from easy to somewhat easier to troubleshoot: unlike traditional motherboards, which require the entire system to be disassembled, a processor board can be removed and replaced as easily as any other board, so it is also a simple matter to upgrade the PC by installing a new processor board. The great limitation to backplane-based systems is the bus. Where traditional motherboards can optimize a system with different busses, the backplane is limited to a single bus style that interconnects the various cards (usually ISA or MCA). High-performance bus architectures like VL or PCI are not readily available.

In an effort to provide a motherboard that is more upgradeable and serviceable, manufacturers often experiment with *modular* motherboards. The modular motherboard places the CPU, math coprocessor, and key support chips on a replaceable card that plugs into a motherboard that in turn holds the BIOS ROM, CMOS RAM, system RAM, other system controllers, and bus interfaces. The modular approach allows this type of motherboard to be upgraded far more than a traditional motherboard without having to replace it outright—the replacement processing card is then much cheaper than a new motherboard. However, today's PC architectures can usually support a variety of CPU versions and an extensive amount of RAM on the original motherboard, so "modular" motherboards have never become a very popular approach.

Contrary to popular belief, expansion bus connectors are *not* needed to make a motherboard. You can see this in any laptop or notebook computer motherboard. The devices that traditionally demanded expansion slots (such as video and drive controllers) are easily fabricated directly onto the motherboard. Even the motherboards used in most desktop and tower PCs over the last few years integrate video and drive controller circuits. If upgrades are needed in the future, the motherboard-based circuits can be disabled with jumpers, and replacement subsystems are plugged into expansion slots.

Understanding an "Active" Motherboard

Before you can troubleshoot a motherboard effectively, it's important that you know your way around and be able to identify at least most of the available components. Although each motherboard is designed differently, this process of identification is not nearly as difficult as it might sound. This part of the chapter will familiarize you with the essential functions and components that you'll find on a modern motherboard.

SOCKETS AND SLOTS

When examining a motherboard, you'll probably find it designated as "Socket 7," "Socket 8," "Slot 1," "Slot 2," or "Slot A." These classifications refer to the type of CPU that the motherboard will support. *Socket 7* (also called Super 7) motherboards are generally designed for Pentium and Pentium MMX CPUs, as well as AMD K6-2, K6-3, or Cyrix MIII processors. *Socket 8* motherboards are made for PentiumPro CPUs. You won't find many Socket 8 motherboards still in use, and those that you do encounter will mainly be in older network servers or workstations. *Slot 1* motherboards use a single-edge cartridge (or SEC) processor "box" rather than a pin grid array IC (a conventional chip) and are slated for Pentium II and Pentium III systems. *Slot 2* motherboards are also intended for SEC processors, but they accommodate the slightly advanced Pentium II/III Xeon processors. In virtually all cases, Slot 2 motherboards are used in high-end network server and workstation systems, so you'll rarely (if ever) find Slot 2 motherboards in the hands of home or small-business users. Finally, *Slot A* motherboards are intended for the AMD Athlon processor—AMD's answer to the Intel Pentium III. While Slot 1 and Slot A connectors may appear identical at first glance, they are incompatible, so you *must* use a Slot A motherboard when building or working on an Athlon-based system.

The important thing to remember here is that motherboard sockets/slots have distinct limitations. A given socket or slot type is not only limited in the "type" of processors that it can accept, it is also limited in the processor speeds that can be used. For example, a DFI "P2XBL" (440BX chipset-based) motherboard can support Slot 1 (Pentium II) processors from 233MHz to 500MHz. By comparison, the newer Intel "VC820" (i820 chipset-based) motherboard can support Slot 1 (Pentium III) processors from 450MHz to 733MHz. Both motherboards use the Slot 1 processor connector but a different range of processors. Just because a motherboard offers a particular slot or socket, don't just assume that a corresponding processor type will work: *it may not*, so always check the system or motherboard documentation to verify the compatible processors for a given motherboard model.

THE POWER OF CHIPSETS

The next thing you'll notice about most modern motherboards is the general absence of chips—there are perhaps two or three large chips on the whole motherboard. That's because virtually *all* of the motherboard's many functions are handled by a suite of powerful interrelated chips (known as the *chipset*). The chipset forms the glue that connects your processor and memory with your drive controllers (the FDD and HDD controllers), expansion busses (ISA, PCI, and AGP), I/O ports (serial, parallel, PS/2, USB), and sometimes even a video controller and sound controller. Figure 32-2 illustrates the importance of chipsets on the Intel VC820 motherboard.

This block diagram places the 820 chipset squarely at the center of the motherboard's functionality. There's an *82820 Memory Controller Hub* (MCH), which is responsible for interfacing to the processor, system memory, and AGP bus (this is not a mistake, since AGP makes use of system RAM, so a direct connection is needed through the chipset). The *82801 I/O Controller Hub* (ICH) manages the UDMA/66 drive controllers, USB ports, hardware monitor, PCI bus, and a sound subsystem (eliminating the need for a separate sound card). There is also an *82802 Firmware Hub* (FWH), which basically manages the system firmware (the BIOS) and CMOS RAM/RTC functions. A powerful *I/O Controller* chip provides the floppy drive interface and all of your I/O ports. Other than a few other buffer and voltage regulator chips, that's it—that's your computer.

> The block diagram of Figure 32-2 is intended to serve as an example for this discussion. Your own motherboard may use a very different selection of chips and features.

EXPANSION SLOTS

Of course, our motherboard is rather incomplete by itself. There are numerous other features and functions (such as a video adapter, SCSI host controller, network card, or other devices) that may be added to

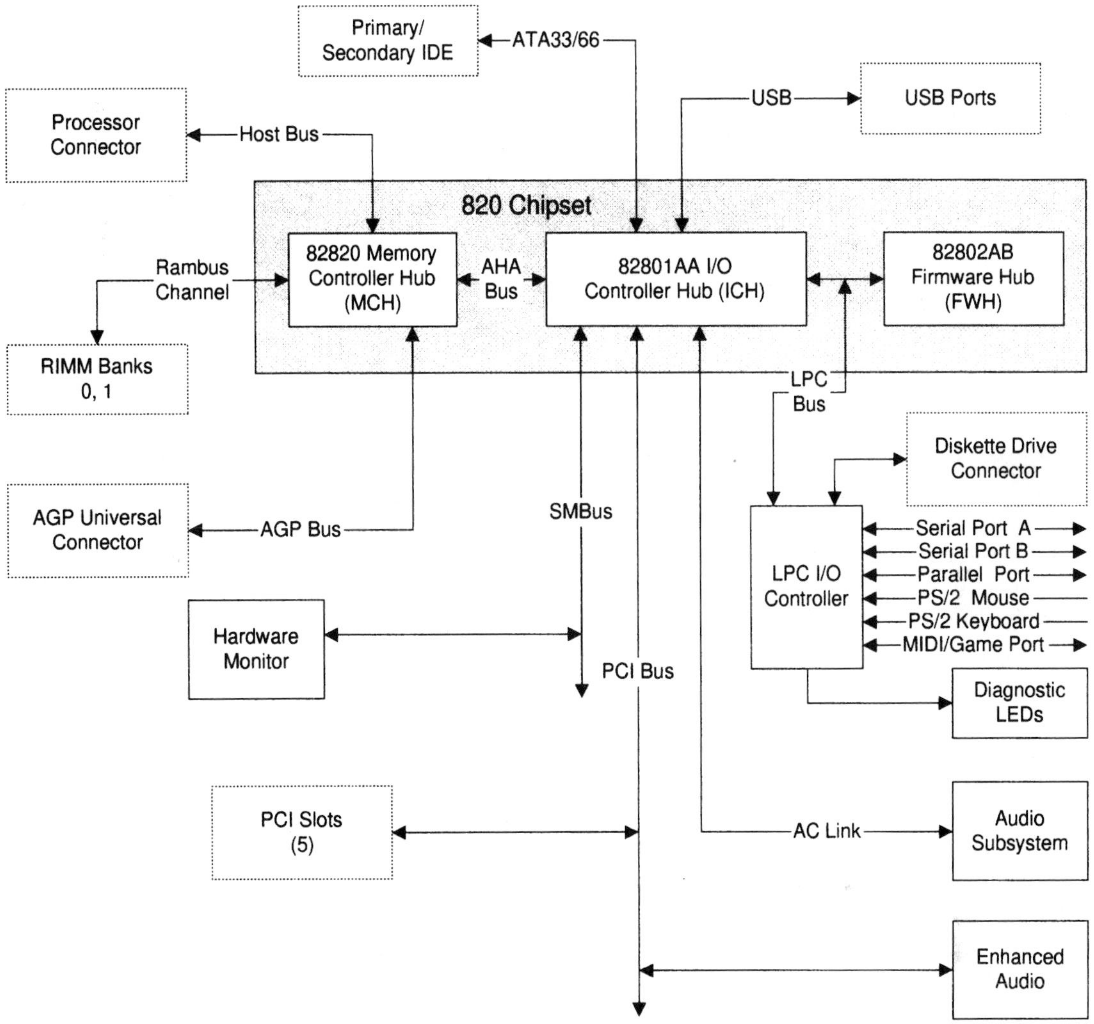

FIGURE 32-2 A block diagram of the Intel VC820 motherboard. (Courtesy of Intel Corporation)

the system—depending on your particular needs. These expansion devices are added through the use of expansion slots on the motherboard. There are three general types of expansion slots: ISA, PCI, and AGP.

- ***ISA*** The *Industry Standard Architecture* bus is the granddaddy of expansion slots, and it is rapidly falling into disuse (you'll note that there are *none* on the VC820 motherboard). You might use an ISA slot to accommodate a low-bandwidth device such as a legacy modem or sound card, but most contemporary data-intensive devices are better served by the newer expansion slots.
- ***PCI*** The *Peripheral Component Interconnect* scheme is a versatile, high-speed, "intelligent" bus. It is the preferred bus architecture for today's demanding devices such as SCSI host adapters, video cap-

ture cards, and network interface cards. The VC820 offers five PCI slots that are all handled by the ICH component of the chipset.

- *AGP* Although you can use PCI video adapters, the *Accelerated Graphics Port* is intended to provide a high-speed data path directly between the graphics card and system memory—allowing improved frame rates for 3D games, visualization programs, and other "calculation intensive" graphics work. There is only one AGP slot on the motherboard.

> Expansion slots are a vital consideration during a motherboard upgrade because existing expansion cards must typically be added to the new motherboard. If the new motherboard doesn't offer a suitable number of appropriate slots, you may have to select alternate expansion devices.

MEMORY SLOTS

Today, motherboards generally do *not* include "base RAM," so all memory in the system must be added through DIMM/SIMM slots. The Intel VC820 motherboard is one of the first to offer the new generation of RIMM (Rambus Inline Memory Module) slots for high-speed memory access. The problem with DIMM/RIMM slots is that there are only a few of them—perhaps two or three. Now DIMM/RIMM units can supply *lots* of memory, so it's easy to stuff a motherboard with RAM, but it's harder to upgrade your RAM. With one or two memory slots, you may find yourself replacing existing DIMMs/RIMMs with larger ones (rather then just adding more modules like you could in the "good old days" of SIMM modules). With memory prices on the rise, replacing a DIMM/RIMM with a larger model may add an unforeseen expense to the system. It's important for you to familiarize yourself with the location of the DIMM/RIMM slots on your motherboard. Understand the memory characteristics that are required, and learn just what size combinations are acceptable.

THE CMOS BATTERY

Your CMOS RAM contents are maintained through a small coin cell on the motherboard. Normally you don't need to mess with the battery, but when you're upgrading or replacing the motherboard, you may need to install the battery (or remove protective material between the battery and holder). The battery should sit properly and securely in its holder.

THE FORM FACTOR (AT, ATX, AND NLX)

Another important classification that you must be familiar with is the motherboard's form factor. In simplest terms, the *form factor* is little more than the dimensions of the board and its mounting hole positions, as well as the general layout and placement of key components such as the CPU, SIMMs/DIMMs, expansion slots, and I/O ports. Today, there are three major form factors to consider: AT, ATX, and NLX. It is important for you to understand that form factors do not directly influence performance—a "baby AT" motherboard and an NLX motherboard can offer exactly the same performance characteristics. Form factor is most important in system assembly and access for service or upgrading.

AT-style Motherboards The AT-style motherboards really represent the classic approach to component placement, as shown in the Tyan S1590 Trinity 100 AT motherboard of Figure 32-3. AT-style motherboards are typically available in two variations, the "baby AT" and the "full AT". Both variations simply refer to the overall dimensions of the motherboard (full AT motherboards are larger). You can usually identify an AT-style motherboard based upon three distinctions. First, look at the power connectors where the power supply attaches. An AT-style motherboard uses two sets of 6-pin inline connectors usu-

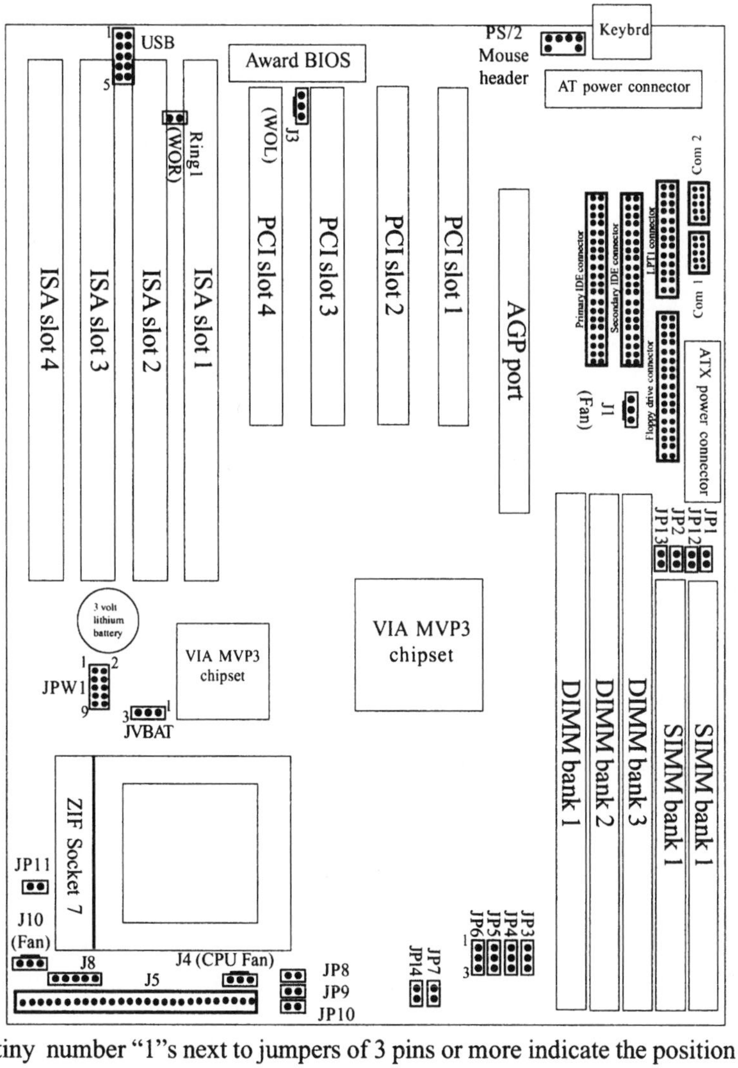

The tiny number "1"s next to jumpers of 3 pins or more indicate the position of pin 1 for that jumper.

FIGURE 32-3 The Tyan S1590 Trinity 100 AT-style motherboard layout. (Courtesy of Tyan Computer Corporation)

ally designated P8 and P9. Second, the CPU is usually positioned inline with one or more of the ISA bus slots (almost always obstructing full-length ISA cards). Third, the I/O ports of an AT motherboard (for example, COM ports, LPT ports, PS/2 ports, USB ports, and so on) are often spread out along the back panel of the chassis.

ATX-style Motherboards The ATX-style motherboards are the result of the first serious industry push to standardize the dimensions, device layouts, and connection schemes of a PC motherboard, such as the Intel VC820 ATX Slot 1 motherboard shown in Figure 32-4. As with an AT layout, an ATX mother-

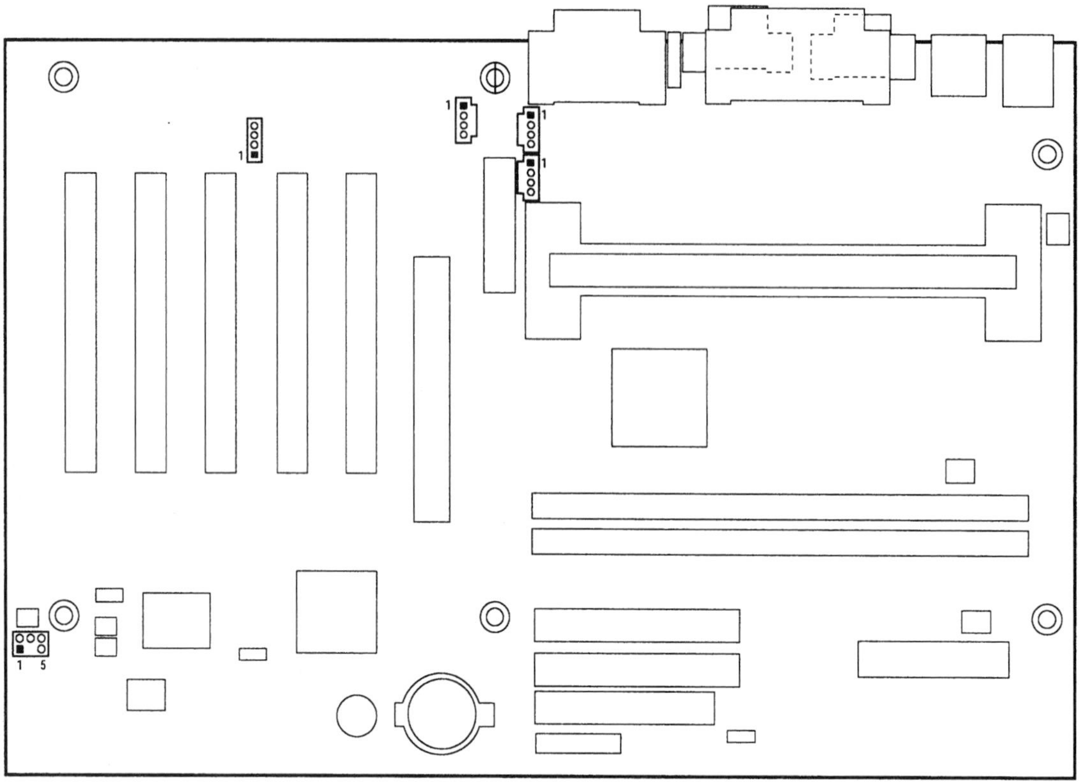

FIGURE 32-4 The Intel VC820 ATX-style motherboard layout. (Courtesy of Intel Corporation)

board is distinguished by three points. First, all I/O port connectors (such as COM ports, LPT ports, USB ports, PS/2 ports, and so on) are concentrated into a single I/O panel located at the rear of the motherboard. Second, the ATX motherboard uses a 20-pin power connection from the power supply (and perhaps a supplemental 8-pin connection). Third, the CPU is located clear and away from all expansion bus slots—eliminating any interference with full-slot expansion cards. ATX motherboards can be found supporting all current CPU types (Socket/Super 7, Slot 1, Slot 2, and Slot A CPUs).

NLX-style Motherboards While ATX motherboards represented a good effort at standardization, they still retain all the assembly problems of AT-style motherboards—namely that the motherboard is cumbersome to install and time-consuming to upgrade or replace. The NLX-style motherboards (such as the Intel JN440BX NLX motherboard of Figure 32-5) overcome this disadvantage by making the motherboard a replaceable (also referred to as a *dockable*) device and moving all expansion slots and connection

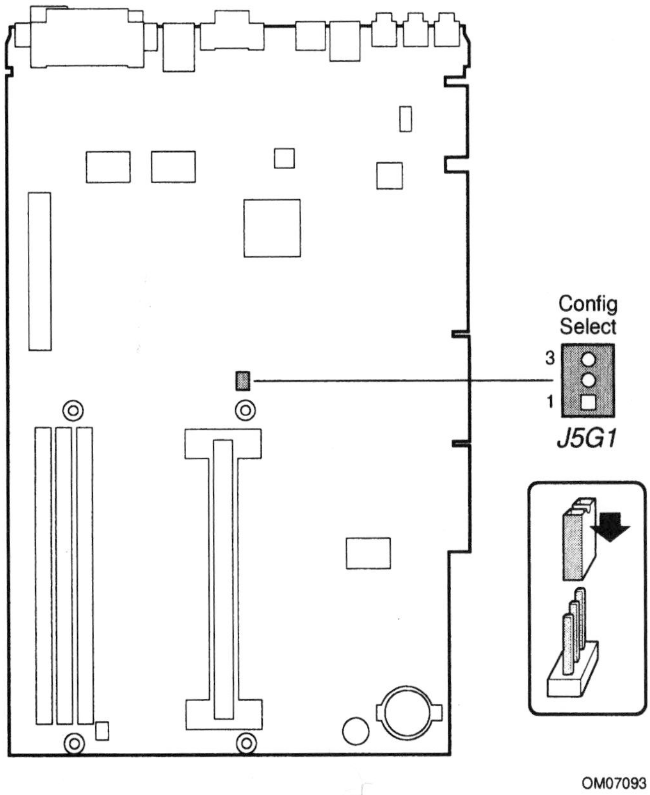

FIGURE 32-5 Simplified view of the Intel JN440BX NLX-style motherboard layout. (Courtesy of Intel Corporation)

headers (such as speaker connector, power switch connector, and so on) to a *riser card*. The NLX motherboard itself then plugs into the riser card. Note the long "card edge" connector along the right side of the board, which interfaces with the riser. In this fashion, the motherboard can quickly and easily be removed from the system to change jumpers, add memory, or install a replacement motherboard.

LEARNING YOUR WAY AROUND

Now that you've seen some essential motherboard attributes, it's time to actually look up close at a current motherboard and identify the critical parts that you should expect to find. For the purposes of this book, we'll use the Intel VC820 ATX Slot 1 motherboard shown again in Figure 32-6. Other motherboards and form factors will appear a bit different, but the basic parts are all the same.

These chipset components are presented for example purposes only. Your motherboard will undoubtedly use different chips (and chipsets)—each offering their own set of characteristics.

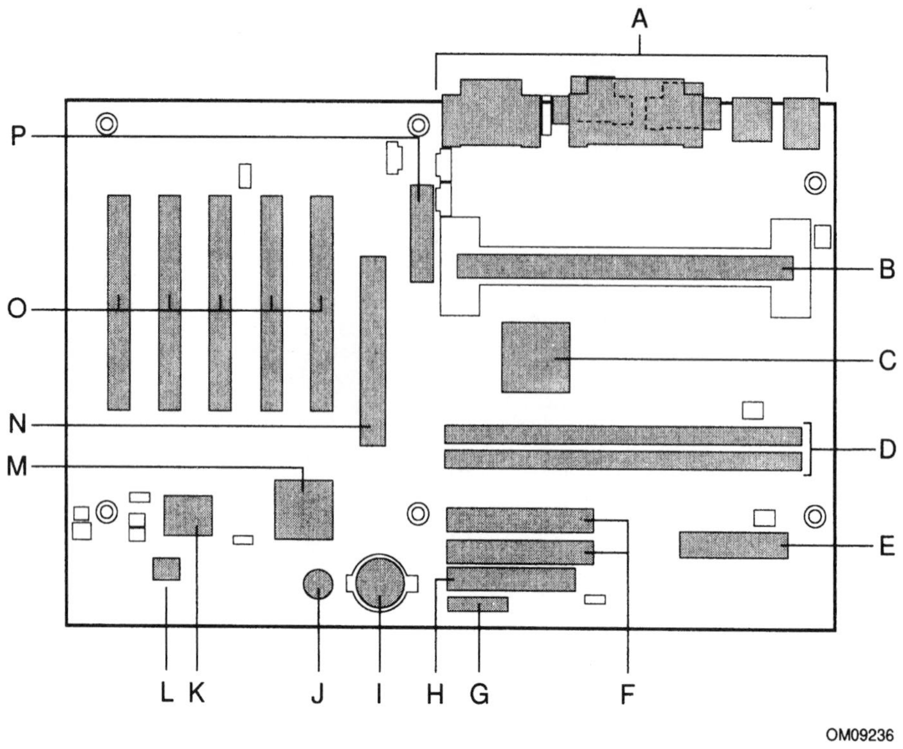

A	Back panel connectors	I	Battery
B	242-contact slot connector	J	Speaker
C	Intel 82820 Memory Controller Hub (MCH)	K	SMSC LPC47M102 I/O Controller
D	RIMM sockets	L	Intel 82802AB 4 Mbit Firmware Hub (FWH)
E	Power connector	M	Intel 82801AA I/O Controller Hub (ICH)
F	IDE connectors	N	AGP universal connector
G	Front panel connector	O	PCI bus add-in board connectors
H	Diskette drive connector	P	Audio/Modem Riser (AMR) connector

FIGURE 32-6 Identifying the major elements of a motherboard. (Courtesy of Intel Corporation)

A ***I/O panel connections.*** These are the serial, parallel, USB, and PS/2 ports that you'll use to connect peripheral devices to the system. Figure 32-7 illustrates the port layout for a VC820. The number of ports and their relative location may vary from model to model, but this figure is a good overall example:

B ***Slot 1 connector.*** This is the 242-pin connector for your Pentium II/III processor. Be sure that the retention mechanism is secure and attaches properly to the CPU cartridge.

C ***82820 Memory Controller Hub chip.*** This is the core processing chip that interfaces the CPU, memory, and AGP bus.

D ***RIMM sockets.*** These sockets support up to two Rambus memory modules (RIMMs). If these were DIMM sockets, you'd probably be using SDRAM DIMMs.

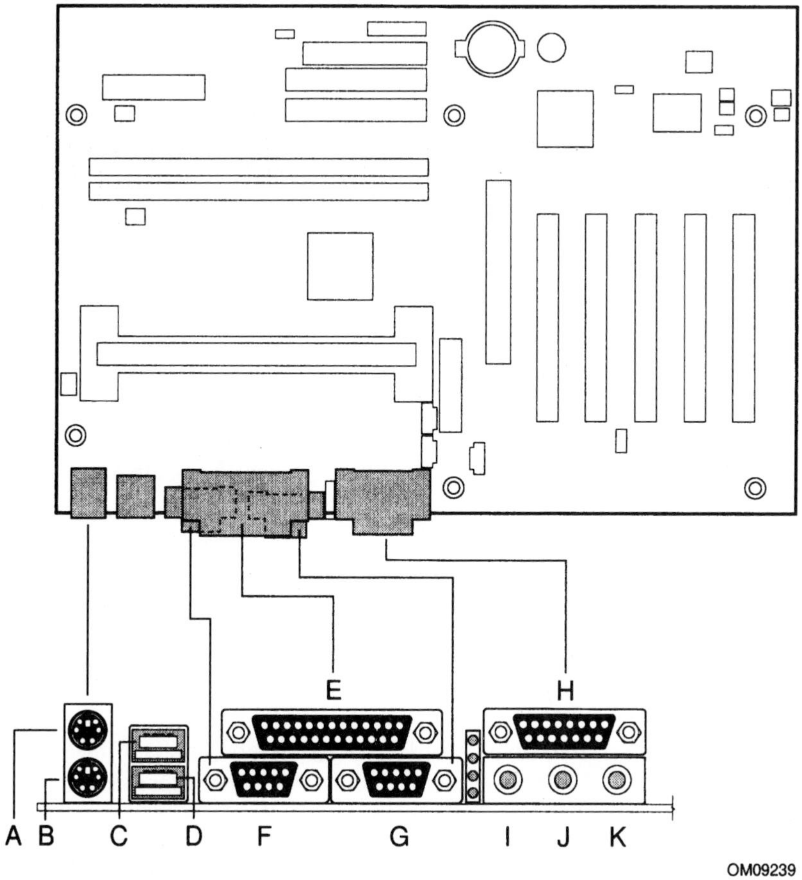

Item	Description	Color
A	PS/2 mouse port	Green
B	PS/2 keyboard port	Purple
C	USB port 0	Black
D	USB port 1	Black
E	Parallel port	Burgundy
F	Serial port A	Teal
G	Serial port B	Teal
H	MIDI/Game port	Gold
I	Audio line out	Lime green
J	Audio line in	Light blue
K	Mic in	Pink

FIGURE 32-7 View of ATX back-panel connectors. (Courtesy of Intel Corporation)

E ***ATX power connector.*** This is the standard 20-pin ATX power connector provided by the power supply.

F ***IDE connectors.*** These are the primary and secondary 40-pin IDE controller ports for your hard drives and other ATAPI devices like CD-ROM or DVD-ROM drives. This system supports Ultra-DMA/66.

G ***Front panel connector.*** This header provides the pins that connect to the case wires (such as the power LED, power switch, key lock, and so on).

H ***Floppy connector.*** This is the standard 34-pin floppy controller port.

I ***CMOS battery.*** This is the coin cell that maintains your CMOS RAM contents. Be sure to replace the battery with an identical type.

J ***Speaker.*** Normally the speaker serves little purpose except to handle beep codes generated by the BIOS POST.

K ***LPC47M102 I/O Controller chip.*** This chip handles all of the I/O ports in the system, as well as the floppy controller function.

L ***82802 Firmware Hub chip.*** This is the 4Mbit controller that handles your BIOS and CMOS RAM.

M ***82081 I/O Controller Hub chip.*** This is a highly integrated controller that supports your HDD controller channels, USB ports, PCI bus, and audio system.

N ***AGP bus connector.*** This is your AGP bus slot for the connection of your video adapter.

O ***PCI bus connectors.*** These are your main expansion slots for other devices in the system.

P ***Audio/Modem Riser (AMR) connector.*** This connector supports the relatively new Intel standard interface for audio/modem devices.

There are also numerous smaller connectors on the motherboard that you should be familiar with, and you can see several of them illustrated in Figure 32-8. Your particular motherboard may offer more or different connectors, but the VC820 supplies the following:

A ***"Legacy" CD audio connector.*** This is the conventional "audio connector" found on most sound cards. Since the VC820 offers on-board sound support, you can feed the audio from a CD to this connector. The Legacy pinout is as follows:

PIN	SIGNAL NAME
Pin 1	CD ground
Pin 2	Audio left channel
Pin 3	CD ground
Pin 4	Audio right channel

B ***ATAPI CD audio connector.*** This is a slightly different CD audio connector scheme using differential signaling. The presence of this second connector also lets you mix audio from a second compliant CD-ROM drive. The pinout is as follows:

PIN	SIGNAL NAME
Pin 1	Left audio signal
Pin 2	Differential ground
Pin 3	Differential ground
Pin 4	Right audio signal

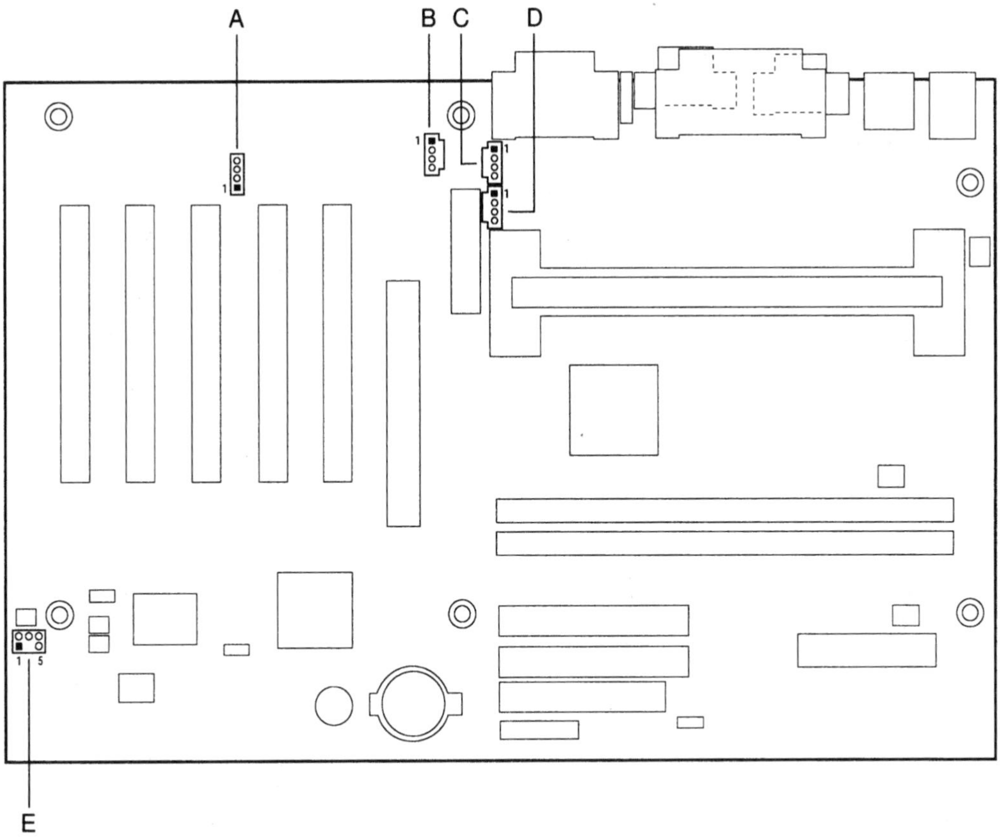

Item	Description	Color	Style	Reference Designator
A	CD-ROM	N/A	Legacy-style, 2 mm	J2C1
B	CD-ROM	Black	ATAPI	J1F1
C	Telephony	Green	ATAPI	J2F1
D	Auxiliary line in	Tan	ATAPI	J2F2
E	PC/PCI	N/A	2x3	J7A2

FIGURE 32-8 Identifying audio-based motherboard connectors. (Courtesy of Intel Corporation)

C ***Telephony connector.*** This is the connector that you would use to attach telephony devices to the system. The telephony connector pinout is

PIN	SIGNAL NAME
Pin 1	Analog audio mono input
Pin 2	Ground
Pin 3	Ground
Pin 4	Analog audio mono input

D ***Auxiliary line input.*** This is a sound channel, which allows you to mix in an auxiliary audio signal. The pinout is as follows:

PIN	SIGNAL NAME
Pin 1	Left auxiliary signal
Pin 2	Ground
Pin 3	Ground
Pin 4	Right auxiliary signal

E ***PC/PCI connector.*** This is a serial interface to the PCI bus that can be used with several PCI-based devices that do not necessarily use a PCI bus. The pinout for this connector follows:

PIN	SIGNAL NAME
Pin 1	PCI data in
Pin 2	Ground
Pin 3	No connection
Pin 4	PCI request out
Pin 5	Ground
Pin 6	Serial IRQ out

There are numerous hardware control and power connections on the motherboard as shown in Figure 32-9. These connectors are used to attach the power supply, operate fans, and manage "wake" devices. These features are vital for proper cooling and effective power management. The VC820 offers the following connections:

F ***Power supply fan.*** This is a three-wire fan cable that provides power to the +12Vdc supply fan. The third wire provides a tachometer signal to the motherboard, which the motherboard can use to monitor the fan's performance.

G ***Processor cooling fan.*** This is a three-wire fan cable that powers the processor's +12Vdc cooling fan. The third wire provides a tachometer signal to the motherboard, which the motherboard can use to monitor the fan's performance.

H ***Power connector.*** This is the 20-pin ATX cable that powers the motherboard. It is vital that this cable be securely attached to the motherboard connector. Otherwise, power may cut out erratically—data loss and damage to the motherboard may result. Here is the pinout for the ATX power cable:

CONNECTOR	SIGNAL NAME	CONNECTOR	SIGNAL NAME
Pin 1	+3.3Vdc	Pin 11	+3.3Vdc
Pin 2	+3.3Vdc	Pin 12	-12Vdc
Pin 3	Ground	Pin 13	Ground
Pin 4	+5Vdc	Pin 14	PS-ON ("soft" power control signal)
Pin 5	Ground	Pin 15	Ground
Pin 6	+5Vdc	Pin 16	Ground
Pin 7	Ground	Pin 17	Ground
Pin 8	Power Good	Pin 18	-5Vdc
Pin 9	+5Vdc (standby)	Pin 19	+5dc
Pin 10	+12Vdc	Pin 20	+5dc

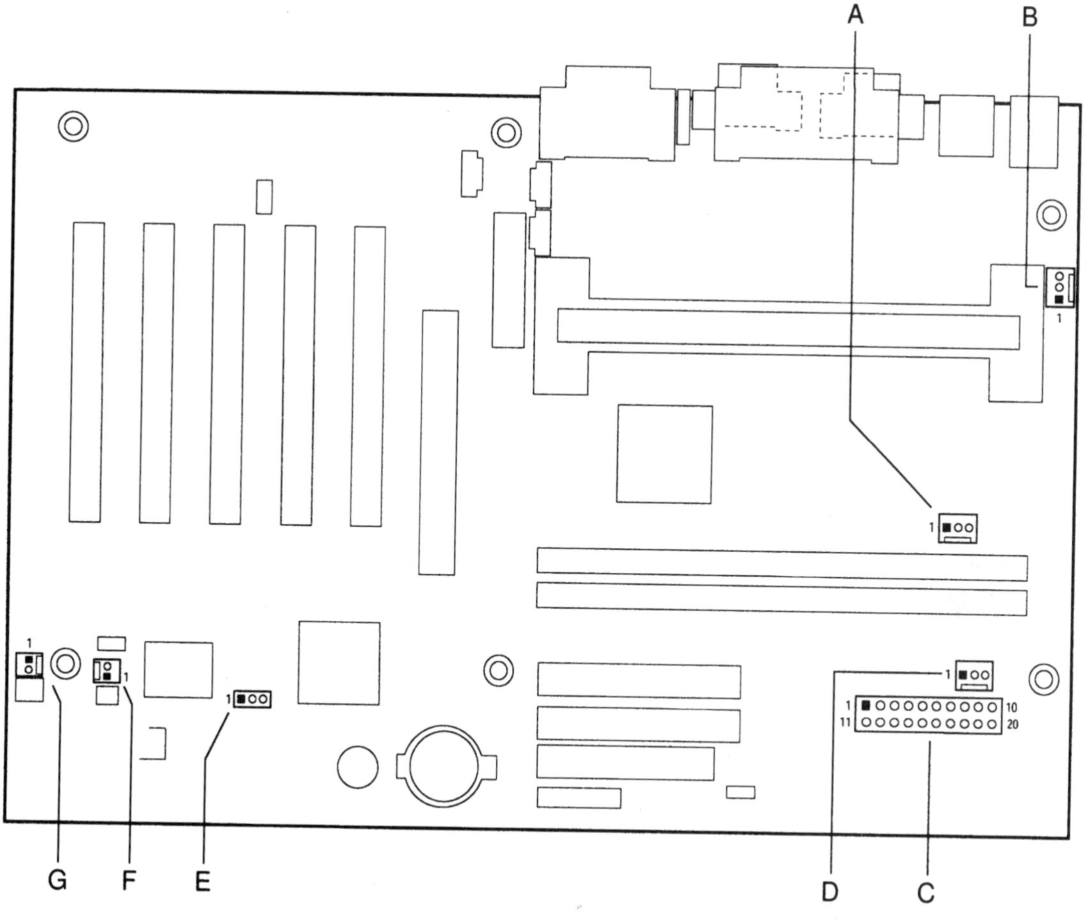

Item	Description	Reference Designator
A	Power supply fan control (Fan 2)	J5L1
B	Processor fan (Fan 3)	J2M1
C	Power	J7L2
D	System fan (Fan 1)	J7L1
E	Wake on LAN technology	J7C1
F	Wake on Ring	J7B2
G	Chassis intrusion	J7A1

FIGURE 32-9 Identifying power and power management connections. (Courtesy of Intel Corporation)

- ***System fan.*** This is a three-wire fan cable that powers the system's +12Vdc chassis cooling fan. The third wire provides a tachometer signal to the motherboard, which the motherboard can use to monitor the fan's performance.

J ***Wake On LAN connector.*** This connector allows you to attach a device that will "wake" the system from a LAN when a system is in the power-down state. The three pins are:

PIN	SIGNAL NAME
Pin 1	+5Vdc (standby)
Pin 2	Ground
Pin 3	Wake On LAN signal

K ***Wake On Ring connector.*** This two-pin connector allows you to attach a device that will "wake" the system from a modem when an incoming ring is detected. The two signals are Ground and Ring.

L ***Chassis Intrusion connector.*** This two-pin connector is usually wired to a switch on the chassis that will alert the system when the cover is opened. This is often done as a safety interlock to prevent users from opening the system and interrupting mission-critical processes. The two signals are Ground and Open.

Ultimately, you'll need to connect "front panel" cables to the motherboard to control power, reset, and so on. Figure 32-10 highlights the front panel connector used on the VC820 motherboard, and the following table lists the pin assignments for the front panel connector.

PIN	SIGNAL NAME	PIN	SIGNAL NAME
Pin 1	HDD Power	Pin 2	Front panel LED (green)
Pin 3	HDD Active LED	Pin 4	Front panel LED (yellow)
Pin 5	Ground	Pin 6	Power switch
Pin 7	Reset switch	Pin 8	Ground
Pin 9	+5Vdc (IR power)	Pin 10	no connection
Pin 11	IR serial input	Pin 12	Ground
Pin 13	Ground	Pin 14	no connection
Pin 15	IR serial output	Pin 16	+5Vdc

MAKING SOME COMPARISONS

If you'd like to see how easily motherboards can vary from model to model, let's take another look at the Tyan motherboard in Figure 32-3. There are some striking similarities, but here are a few of the differences that should stand out against a motherboard like the VC820:

- The CPU connector is different. The Tyan Super 7 motherboard accommodates a Socket 7 processor rather than a Slot 1 processor; you'd need to stick with an AMD or Cyrix Socket 7 processor rather than a Pentium II or III slot-based processor.
- The expansion slot layout is different. There are four ISA slots, four PCI slots, and an AGP slot. This should not pose a problem unless you have no ISA cards and need more than four PCI slots.
- The chipset is different. The Tyan uses a VIA MVP3 chipset (see Chapter 10 for details of the MVP3) rather than Intel's i820 chipset.
- I/O ports are almost nonexistent. Look closely at Figure 32-3, and you'll find connections for USB, PS/2 mouse, COM ports, and printer (LPT) ports. The problem is that these are "headers" rather than actual connectors. This means you'll need to purchase the port connectors on expansion card brackets using small ribbon cables that plug into those headers—an inconvenient and error-prone approach, especially when you're shuffling expansion cards around.

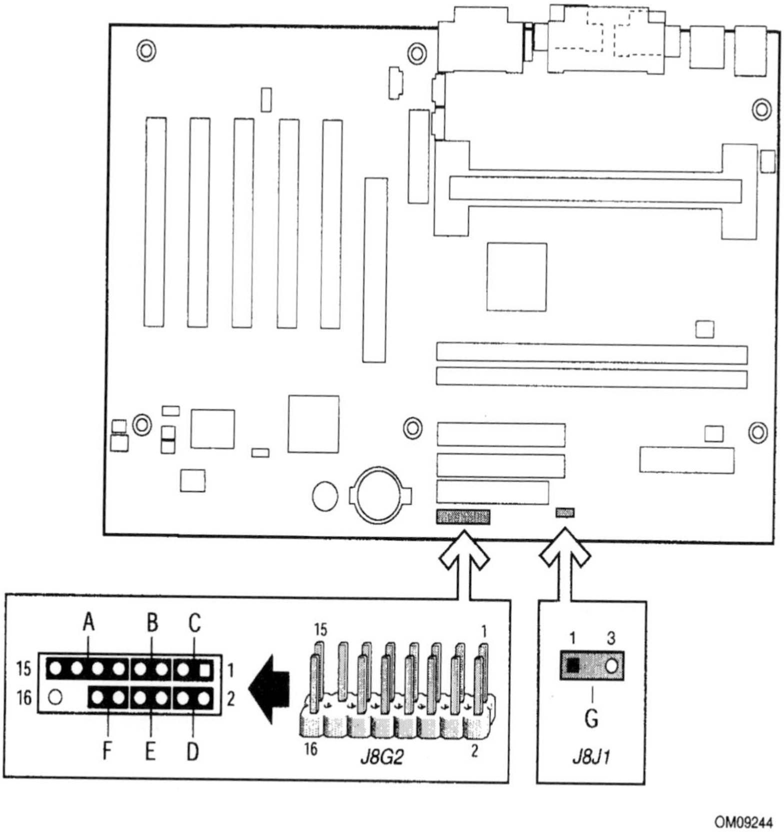

	Item	Pins	Description
Front Panel Connector (see Table 43)	A	9, 11, 13, and 15	Infrared port
	B	5 and 7	Reset switch
	C	1 and 3	Hard drive activity LED
	D	2 and 4	Power / Sleep / Message waiting LED
	E	6 and 8	Power switch
	F	10 and 12	No connect
Auxiliary Front Panel Power LED Connector (see Table 46)	G	1 and 3	Auxiliary Power LED connector (Pin 2 keyed)

FIGURE 32-10 Identifying front panel connections. (Courtesy of Intel Corporation)

- The memory configuration is different. Where the VC820 uses new Rambus memory, the Tyan motherboard offers both 72-pin SIMM and 168-pin DIMM slots for memory modules. Immediately, this means the memory used for the VC820 is *not* compatible with the Tyan motherboard.

Upgrading a Motherboard

As a PC ages, it is the motherboard that limits the system's upgradability. True, you can add RAM and upgrade a CPU, and while these tactics can prolong the working life of older systems, they have a limited impact on the overall performance of a motherboard (especially older i486 and Pentium/MMX motherboards). As PC technology surges ahead and the price of advanced motherboards continues to drop, replacing an outdated motherboard outright is becoming an ever-more cost-effective upgrade option. This part of the chapter illustrates the most important concerns when planning a motherboard upgrade, walks you through an upgrade process, and shows you how to deal with typical upgrade problems.

CONSIDERING THE UPGRADE

Upgrading a motherboard is not particularly difficult, but it *is* a time-consuming, detail-oriented process. As a result, advance planning can be of substantial benefit. The next few tips cover some important points to keep in mind when planning a motherboard upgrade. As with any upgrade, make it a point to call around and find the best price and delivery terms. Given the added expense of a motherboard, you should find a vendor with a liberal return policy just in case you accidentally obtain an incorrect or defective ("dead-out-of-the-box") replacement.

- ***Compare features.*** All motherboards are not created equal, so check the specifications closely before making a choice. BIOS plays a vital role in such advanced features as Plug and Play, APM, Ultra-ATA/66 support, USB support, boot sector virus protection, and so much more. The move toward PC power conservation (referred to as *green* PCs) is resulting in features like ACPI. The amount of cache has a great impact on CPU performance. The number and type of I/O slots defines system expandability. Most modern motherboards provide on-board features like drive controllers, video adapters, and COM/LPT ports. If your major interest is enhanced video/multimedia performance, a Pentium II/III motherboard with a single AGP bus slot will probably do the trick.
- ***Check the motherboard dimensions and mounting points.*** You cannot overlook the nuts and bolts involved in a motherboard upgrade. Unfortunately, this is often the most difficult (and neglected) consideration. First, the physical dimensions of the motherboard must fit within the space currently available in your PC. A smaller motherboard is generally not a problem, but a larger (or oddly shaped) motherboard will invariably encounter interference from drives and the power supply. The other issue is mounting holes: chances are very good that mounting holes on the new motherboard will not match the original mounting holes. The use of ATX and NLX motherboards and cases goes a long way to easing the problems of dimensioning. Since ATX and NLX form-factor motherboards, cases, and power supplies are all designed to be interchangeable, moving to these form factors can greatly ease the upgrade problems associated with physical motherboard mounting.

> If you elect to replace a full AT or baby AT motherboard with an ATX or NLX motherboard, you *must* also upgrade the case and power supply as well.

- ***Check the CPU location relative to your expansion slots.*** Check the sales literature or online product documentation for the new motherboard and find the location of the new CPU relative to the expansion slots. Since it is assumed that you will be upgrading your system to a Pentium MMX, Pentium II, or Pentium III motherboard, the use of a CPU heat sink will be mandatory. As a result, the CPU/heat sink combination could easily interfere with the installation of one or more expansion boards—a real problem if your current system is heavily loaded. (You can see how the CPU socket would interfere with full-length ISA cards in Figure 32-3.) Try to pick a motherboard that places the CPU out of the way of expansion boards. For ATX and NLX motherboards, the CPU's placement normally does *not* interfere with the expansion slots.

- ***Consider collateral upgrades.*** Before finally committing to a new motherboard, take a moment to evaluate the other subassemblies found in the PC, and anticipate any other immediate upgrade needs. Will your old EIDE hard drive really take advantage of the new motherboard's Ultra-DMA/66 drive controller? Do you need a new memory type (for example, SDRAM DIMMs rather than EDO SIMMs)? Will your old PCI video accelerator be retired in favor of a high-performance AGP 3D graphics card? Each of these "added extras" will boost the ultimate cost of the upgrade that much higher, so it is always worthwhile to compare this adjusted cost against the purchase price of a similar PC available off the shelf. In some cases, it may be in your customer's best interest to simply buy or build a new PC outright.
- ***Check the costs.*** Choose your new motherboard carefully, using a balance between price and cutting-edge features. New motherboards are expensive, and top-of-the-line motherboards will always be pricey, but you can usually find a great deal if you look 6 to 12 months back. For example, a new Pentium III motherboard (with the Pentium III installed) can easily run over $800, while a recent Pentium II motherboard (plus CPU) can be had for well under $400. The idea is that you can save a bundle of money if you can make due with upgrades that are just slightly off the cutting edge.

Perhaps even more important, make sure you are aware of any hidden costs with the motherboard. For example, make sure that you know whether the new motherboard comes with current BIOS, a CPU, and CMOS backup battery. If you plan to be running software that demands MMX capability, see that the CPU is MMX compliant. Also find out how much RAM is on the motherboard, and see if your current RAM is compatible—you might find yourself buying 32MB to 64MB of new SDRAM DIMMs because you can't transfer the EDO SIMMs from the old motherboard to the new one. This will bump up the cost of the upgrade by at least several hundred dollars.

32

Pros and Cons of Traditional Upgrades

Motherboard upgrades provide a much more sweeping and comprehensive improvement in system performance than changing any one element on the original motherboard itself. A new motherboard not only supports better and faster processors, it provides better caching, space and support for larger amounts of faster RAM (such as SDRAM or Rambus DRAM), advanced bus slots for added system performance, and superior data handling through the use of current BIOS and streamlined, highly-integrated chipsets.

Such upgrades, however, can also consume a fair amount of time (sometimes an hour or more), depending on the amount of mechanical disassembly that is required. The other disadvantage is that of physical incompatibility. If the mounting holes on a new motherboard do not align with the original mounting standoffs, for example, new mounting holes will have to be created (or the case will have to be replaced).

Pros and Cons of Proprietary Daughtercard Upgrades

The two great drawbacks to motherboard replacement are price and time. Some companies like Compaq addressed these disadvantages by designing a *modular motherboard*—a unit that mounts the CPU, cache, and often the system RAM, on a readily accessible module referred to as a *daughtercard*. The daughtercard can be replaced in a matter of only a few minutes, with no real disassembly required. Since the daughtercard is specifically designed to carry the core processing components, an upgrade can easily yield a 100% to 600% performance improvement.

These are compelling advantages, especially when there are a large number of systems that need to be upgraded. The problem with daughtercards is that they are proprietary devices that must be designed to mate with a specific motherboard. As a result, a daughtercard is generally quite expensive—sometimes costing more than a conventional motherboard. Daughterboard upgrades also prevent new bus architectures from being introduced to the system.

Pros and Cons of Processor Card Upgrades

Older bus-mastering systems (such as the PS/2) have found another alternative to motherboard upgrades. Instead of taking the time to replace the main motherboard assembly, MicroChannel systems allow a supplemental CPU board (called a *processor card*) to be installed in any available expansion slot. Since the MicroChannel architecture allows bus-mastering, the processor card can take over system control from the CPU resident on the motherboard—effectively shutting down the original CPU—and provide a CPU enhancement of 200% or more. As with any expansion board, the processor card can be configured and installed in a matter of minutes.

On the down side, a processor card is still rather pricey when compared to another CPU itself, and more expensive than a conventional motherboard. Although processor cards are more standardized than daughtercards, they are generally limited to MCA systems. ISA and PCI systems typically do not incorporate this design philosophy. Processor cards also do not support the introduction of new bus architectures into a system.

PERFORMING THE UPGRADE

Unlike CPU or expansion card upgrades, replacing an entire motherboard is a rather involved process that requires a substantial amount of care to be accomplished successfully. This part of the chapter covers the essential steps and precautions that you will need to remember during the upgrade. Before starting the upgrade, it is a good idea to run a benchmarking program and note the system performance benchmark figure—it gives you something to measure the system against once the upgrade is finished. You are also strongly urged to perform a complete system backup before proceeding—*collateral system damage during an upgrade is a serious possibility.*

Static Precautions

Virtually all of the chips used in today's computers are fabricated with technologies that make them *extremely* sensitive to electrostatic discharge (ESD). To ensure the safe handling of motherboards and other system components during the upgrade, make it a point to take the following precautions:

- First, invest in an antistatic mat that is large enough to cover a majority of your work area. See that the antistatic mat is properly cabled and attached to a reliable earth ground. Under no circumstances should you allow a motherboard to rest on a synthetic or static-prone surface.
- Second, use an antistatic wrist strap whenever handling components or tools inside the PC. Cable the wrist strap to the antistatic mat or to another reliable earth ground.
- Third, always try to handle printed circuit boards by their edges—avoid touching the individual IC pins or printed wiring.
- Fourth, have a supply of good-quality antistatic bags on hand to hold the system's expansion boards as they are temporarily removed.
- Finally, excessively dry environments tend to allow substantial buildups of static charges in objects, clothing, and bodies. If it is possible, try to work in an environment with at least 40 percent humidity.

Save Your CMOS

Before starting your upgrade, make it a point to obtain a current record of your CMOS settings. You can do this by pressing Print Screen to take shots of each CMOS setup page. You should be particularly interested in the hard drive setup information, since you will certainly need to load that data into the new motherboard's CMOS before the system will recognize your boot drive and other devices. Once you have the CMOS information, set it aside in a safe place.

Prepare the System

At this point, you can prepare the system for its upgrade. A word of caution is in order here: *be especially careful of screwdriver blades when working inside the PC.* If you should slip, the blade can easily gouge the motherboard and result in broken traces. It pays to be careful and gentle when upgrading a motherboard. *Before you even consider opening the PC cover, turn the system off, and unplug it from the AC receptacle.* This helps to ensure your safety by preventing the PC from being powered accidentally while you are working on it.

Remove the screws holding down the outer cover, and place those screws aside in a safe place. Gently remove the PC's outer cover and set it aside (out of the path of normal floor traffic). You should now be able to look into the PC and observe the motherboard, along with any expansion boards and drives that are installed. Now that you are looking at the complete PC, this is the time for you to *label* things. Clearly marked labels will help you remember the purpose of each cable (such as power, drives, key lock, speaker, drive light, and so on), and show you where each item went on the original motherboard or on various expansion boards. *Don't be afraid to label things.* Labels need not be fancy—a roll of masking tape and an indelible marker are all you need. Remember that you'll have to take this all apart, so anything that will help you remember where things go will be of help.

Remove the Original Motherboard

At this point, you should begin clearing the obstructions to the motherboard. Start by removing each expansion board. Place each board into an antistatic bag, and set each bag aside on the antistatic mat. Next, remove any cables that are attached to the motherboard (such as the key-lock or speaker cables). If there are floppy drive and hard drive cables connected to the motherboard, remove them as well. Finally, disconnect the power cable(s). For AT-style motherboards, you'll find two 6-pin power connectors from the power supply. For ATX motherboards, you'll find a single 20-pin power connector. If there are any drives or chassis assemblies interfering with the motherboard, remove them now, and set them aside carefully.

> NLX motherboards do not carry any of the burden found in AT-style or ATX motherboards—all peripheral equipment is attached to the NLX riser card. You need only detach and unplug the NLX motherboard from its riser card.

You should now have an unobstructed view of the motherboard. Locate and remove each of the screws holding the motherboard in place. In many cases, there may be at least six (sometimes eight or more). Once each of the screws have been removed, gently lift out the motherboard and lay it aside onto the antistatic mat—preferably in its own antistatic bag (the whole board should fit on the mat). Frankly, the motherboard should lift out without difficulty. If the motherboard does not budge or lift out easily, you may have overlooked a screw, nylon standoff, or cable. *DO NOT FORCE THE MOTHERBOARD!* Often, there may be one or more white nylon standoffs that are still clipping the motherboard in place. Patiently locate the obstruction(s) and clear each one carefully.

After you remove the original motherboard, you should also remove the CMOS backup battery and place it into a heavy gauge plastic bag before storing the original motherboard. This will prevent an aging CMOS backup battery from rupturing and damaging the original motherboard with leaking electrolyte.

Install the New Motherboard

You can now place the new motherboard into the chassis and see that each I/O port and mounting hole line up properly. Secure it into place. Do not use excessive force when tightening the screws—excessive force can cause the motherboard to warp and result in failure. When securing the board, check that there are no metal brackets or standoffs that might touch the new motherboard and cause a short circuit. It is usually recommended that you to use a thin, nonconductive washer between each standoff and the motherboard. Once the new motherboard is installed mechanically, you can start reassembling the other devices that you stripped from the system.

Refer to the user's guide that accompanies the new motherboard, and check each jumper or DIP switch. This is a *particularly* important step because many contemporary motherboards provide services right on-board that have traditionally been assigned to expansion boards (such as video adapters and drive controllers). For example, if you used a dual serial port board with your original motherboard, but your new motherboard provides two serial ports, you won't need the dual serial port board. If you need to use that board, you will have to set motherboard jumpers to disable the on-board serial ports. The same thing is true of video adapters. If a video port is available on the new motherboard, but you have a 3D graphics accelerator board on hand, you will have to disable the on-board video port to prevent a hardware conflict. If the new motherboard provides a floppy and IDE controller, you can abandon that drive controller board and plug the drives right into the appropriate connectors on the motherboard. In that case, check the drive control jumpers to be sure they are enabled. Be sure to review each available jumper carefully. Also verify that the motherboard's bus speed, clock multiplier, and CPU voltage settings are all configured properly for the CPU.

Reassemble the System

Once the motherboard jumpers are set, you can install the CPU, system RAM, and power/case cables. CPU installation should go easily, but be aware that a Socket 7 CPU must be oriented properly in the socket relative to pin 1. Slot 1/Slot A processors will generally only insert in one orientation. Chances are that the CPU will require a heat sink/fan, so be sure to install it securely if needed (along with thermal compound to improve heat transfer between the CPU and heat sink/fan assembly). If you need to install the BIOS chip(s), you may do that next. Be careful to orient each BIOS ROM properly relative to pin 1. If there is more than one BIOS ROM, be sure to install the chips in their proper places. Reversing the BIOS ROM locations should not damage them, but the system will probably not boot. The new motherboard will need a backup battery to support the CMOS/RTC chip. If there is not a battery already on the new motherboard, install a new battery (or reconnect the original battery pack).

Make sure that each SIMM, DIMM, or RIMM snaps gently into place—if it does not, it may be inserted backward. When inserting cables, note that the red strip on each ribbon cable is pin 1. Make sure that pin 1 on the cable is matched to pin 1 on the corresponding connector. Inserting a ribbon cable backward is rarely damaging, but it may prevent the system from booting. Reconnect the power cables. Finally, install the expansion boards that you will need in the system. Remember that you may not need *all* of the adapter boards you started with if the motherboard will be taking over particular functions. If you had disassembled any drives or chassis subassemblies before removing the original motherboard, be sure to reassemble any of those items now, and check that their power and signal cabling are secure. Reconnect any ancillary devices such as the mouse, keyboard, and monitor.

Testing the System

At last, you will face the moment of truth. If things have gone well, this procedure should have taken no more than an hour. Once the components and cabling are all secure, it will be time to reconnect the AC line cord and try applying power to the system. Make sure that your hands and any tools are clear of the PC. Turn on the monitor, double-check your power cable installation one more time, then go ahead and hit the power switch.

After a moment or two, you should see a BIOS message appear on the monitor—*this is a good sign.* When the POST displays its message asking to start the SETUP procedure (usually by pressing the F1 key), go ahead and start it. Review each screen in the SETUP routine, and restore as many CMOS settings as possible (especially the memory amount, floppy drive types, and hard drive configuration). Chances are that there will be several SETUP variables that were not in the original system. Just leave them in their default states for now—you can always optimize them later. Save the CMOS Setup and reboot the computer. Your upgraded system should now complete its POST successfully, and boot to the operating system.

When booting to Windows 95/98, the Windows platform will automatically identify the new device(s) and try installing the appropriate drivers for them. You may need to have your Windows installation CD handy. Once Windows has reconfigured itself for the new hardware, install any patches from the motherboard's installation CD (if needed). Finally, check the Device Manager for any hardware problems or conflicts.

Congratulations, you have completed your motherboard upgrade.

> If you cannot adequately reconfigure the CMOS Setup, select the BIOS Defaults option, which should apply the variables necessary to get the PC working. You can then tweak the CMOS values later to improve system performance.

When the system boots as expected, the last step should be to power-down the computer and reassemble the outer housing. You can then run your benchmarking program again to determine the new benchmarks for your PC. You can see the relative improvement in performance over that of the original system.

Troubleshooting a Motherboard

Since motherboards contain the majority of system processing components, it is likely that you will encounter a faulty motherboard sooner or later. The BIOS POST is written to test each subsection of the motherboard each time the PC is powered up, so most problems are detected well before you ever see the DOS prompt. Errors are reported in a myriad of ways. Beep codes and POST codes (Chapter 19) provide indications of fatal errors that occur before the video system is initialized. Still, there are plenty of symptoms that can elude the initial testing at start time. This part of the chapter digs in and presents a lengthy selection of motherboard symptoms for you to reference.

REPAIR VS. REPLACE

This is the perennial troubleshooting dilemma. The problem with motherboard repair is not so much the availability of replacement parts (although that *can* be a challenge) as it is the use of surface-mount soldering (SMT). You see, a surface-mounted chip cannot be desoldered with conventional tools. To successfully desolder a surface-mounted chip, you need to heat each of the chip's pins (often in excess of 100) simultaneously, then lift the IC off the board. It's then a simple matter to clean up any residual solder. Unfortunately, specialized surface-mount soldering equipment is required to do this. The equipment is readily available commercially, so it's easy to buy—but you can invest $1,000 to $2,000 to equip your workbench properly.

As you can imagine, the "repair vs. replace" decision is an economic one. It makes little sense for the part-time PC enthusiast to make such a substantial investment to exchange a defective chip (which usually cost under $20). It is generally better to replace the motherboard outright, which is only a fraction of the cost of such SMT equipment. On the other hand, professionals who intend to pursue PC repair as a living are well served with surface-mount equipment. The customer's cost for labor, the part(s), and markup is typically much less than purchasing a new motherboard (especially the high-end boards such as Pentium II/III motherboards).

START WITH THE BASICS

Since motherboard troubleshooting does represent a significant expense, you should be sure to start any motherboard repair by inspecting the following points in the PC. *Remember to turn all power off before performing these inspections.*

- ***Check all connectors.*** Connector problems can happen easily when the PC is serviced or upgraded, and you accidentally forget to replace every cable (or the cable is installed incorrectly). Start with the power connector, and inspect each cable and connector attached to the motherboard. Frayed cables should be replaced. Loose or detached cables should be reattached properly.
- ***Check all socket-mounted ICs.*** Some ICs in the computer (especially the CPU) get hot during normal operation. It is not unheard of for the repetitive expansion and contraction encountered with everyday use to eventually "rock" an IC out of its socket. The CPU, BIOS ROM, and often the CMOS/RTC module are socket mounted, so check them carefully.
- ***Check power levels.*** Low or erratic AC power levels can cause problems in the PC. Use a multimeter and check AC at the wall outlet. Be very careful whenever dealing with AC. Take all precautions to protect yourself from injury. If the AC is low or is heavily loaded by motors, coffee pots, or other highly inductive loads, try the PC in another outlet running from a different circuit. If AC checks properly, use your multimeter (or a measurement tool such as PC Power Check from Data Depot) to check the power supply outputs. If one or more outputs is low or absent, you should repair or replace the supply.
- ***Check the motherboard for foreign objects.*** A screw, paper clip, or free strand of wire can cause a short circuit that may disable the motherboard. Examine the motherboard carefully, and use ample lighting.
- ***Check that all motherboard DIP switches and jumpers are correct.*** For example, if the motherboard provides a video port, and you have a video board plugged into the expansion bus, the motherboard's video circuit will have to be disabled through a switch or jumper—otherwise, a hardware conflict can result that may interfere with motherboard operation. You will need the user manual for the PC in order to identify and check each jumper or switch. Today, virtually all motherboard configuration issues (including clock speeds and multipliers) are handled through the system's CMOS Setup, so jumper settings are no longer as critical as they used to be.
- ***Check for intermittent connections and accidental grounding.*** Inspect each of the motherboard's mounting screws, and see that they are not touching nearby printed traces. Also check the space under the motherboard and see that there is nothing that might be grounding the motherboard and chassis. As an experiment, you may try loosening the motherboard mounting screws. If the fault goes away, the motherboard may be suffering from an intermittent connection—when all screws are tight, the board is bent just enough to let the intermittent appear. Unfortunately, intermittent connections are almost impossible to find.

GENERAL MOTHERBOARD SYMPTOMS

SYMPTOM 32-1 The slot 1 retention mechanism is not holding the slot 1 processor securely in place. You find that there is "play" that allows the processor to move (and possibly fall out of its slot). In virtually all cases, this means the retention mechanism is not mounted securely on the motherboard. It's probably sitting too high and allowing the CPU to float. You'll need to check the installation of that retention mechanism. Support the motherboard so that it will not bend while the retention mechanism is being pressed into the mounting holes (but do not place the motherboard on a hard surface to install the retention mechanism). If the retention mechanism push pins are not secured properly, the retention mechanism can become loose, causing the processor to fall out of the motherboard.

To install a retention mechanism with captive brass fasteners, simply use a medium Phillips screwdriver to screw the fasteners into the preinstalled brass Pemstuds. To install the retention mechanism with plastic fasteners,

1. Leave space below each mounting hole so that the fastener can protrude through the hole.
2. Find the slot 1 connector on the motherboard.
3. Position the retention mechanism on the motherboard next to the slot 1 connector.
4. Push down on the retention bracket until the black plastic fasteners are correctly seated, and the retention mechanism fits *snugly* against the board.
5. Push each white retainer pin into its respective black fastener until the head of each pin is seated onto the head of each fastener. This should keep the retention mechanism securely in place.

SYMPTOM 32-2 After removing a hard drive or other IDE device, the system seems to boot slowly but seems fine otherwise. Chances are that the BIOS still expects an IDE device to respond, and it is waiting for the device that you removed—this is where the delay is coming from. If you remove a secondary drive on the primary channel, or any drive on the secondary channel, you should check the CMOS Setup and set that corresponding drive position to "none" or "not installed." Save your changes and reboot the system. You should see that the BIOS is no longer waiting for devices that you marked out in the CMOS Setup.

SYMPTOM 32-3 You notice that your system automatically powers back on after a power failure. This is probably the result of a CMOS Setup configuration rather than a hardware fault, and it occurs on standard Intel-manufactured motherboard products that use a Phoenix BIOS and use either the Intel 430TX PCIset or the Intel 440LX PCIset (or later chipset). You'll probably find a feature in the BIOS setup utility (usually under Boot Menu) that controls the action of the computer following a power failure: Stay Off, Last State (to restore the previous power state before AC power was lost—either on or off), or Power On (so the system will always power back on). If you check this setting in the CMOS Setup, you'll probably notice that it's set to Power On or Last State. If you'd prefer the system to remain off after a power failure, set this entry to Stay Off.

> In all cases, the computer powers up for 300mS when AC power is restored, reads the current setup boot values, and goes to the appropriate state (on or off).

SYMPTOM 32-4 You receive a static device resource conflict error message. A static device resource conflict warning message while booting Windows 95/98 may be generated from numerous (and often unrelated) situations. The majority of technicians reporting this problem have a Pro Audio Spectrum 16 card installed. The Windows 95/98 registration for this card includes both 10-bit I/O addresses (201H and 388H) and 16-bit aliases to these addresses (A201H and F388H). The BIOS detects that the 10-bit address will also overlap with the 16-bit address and flags this as a resource conflict. Since it is a single card requesting both these resources, the warning can be ignored if that is the case. There are also reports of other configurations causing "static resource conflict" warnings. Some of these instances appear to be corrected by clearing the ESCD area in NVRAM—this can be accomplished by performing a CMOS clear:

1. Note your current settings.
2. Turn power off.
3. Set the CMOS Clear jumper or switch to the Clear position (see the product documentation).
4. Turn power on.
5. After approximately 30 seconds, turn the power off.
6. Set the CMOS Clear jumper or switch to the Off or Normal position.
7. Turn your system on and enter the CMOS Setup to change settings as you require (hard drive, and so on).

SYMPTOM 32-5 **You cannot operate or boot from an LS-120 "floptical" drive.** In virtually all cases, this is a limitation of the motherboard's BIOS. For example, Intel motherboards that have a Phoenix BIOS and use either the Intel 430TX, 440LX, 440BX, 440EX chipsets support booting from an LS-120 floppy drive. Most other motherboards with a Pentium MMX-compliant (or later) chipset will support LS-120 drives. If you have trouble recognizing or booting from the LS-120, check with the motherboard or system maker for a BIOS upgrade.

SYMPTOM 32-6 **When upgrading the motherboard, the system won't boot when using an older CPU, but it boots fine with a newer CPU.** You find that the older CPU runs fine on another system. This generally means that the newer motherboard contains a "lockout" that prevents 66MHz bus speeds. This forces the motherboard to use 100MHz or 133MHz bus speeds. If a 66MHz host bus processor is installed, the motherboard will not boot. If this is the case, there is no way around the problem except to use an appropriate processor model.

SYMPTOM 32-7 **The system displays PC100 memory even though PC133 memory is installed.** First verify that your system bus is actually set to 133MHz—if the bus is set to 100MHz, the memory speed may be reported incorrectly. This error may also sometimes occur when the *DRAM Clock* entry in your CMOS Setup is set incorrectly. Try setting the DRAM Clock to *Host CLK* in the Chipset features section of your CMOS Setup.

SYMPTOM 32-8 **The motherboard's COM port(s) won't work.** In almost every case that I've ever heard of, an inability to use a COM port is the result of *not* using the supplied header cables, or the COM ports are disabled in the CMOS Setup. To ensure that the motherboard is recognizing and initializing the COM ports correctly, boot the system and check the CMOS Setup. Locate the settings that control your COM ports. Verify that the COM ports are enabled. You should also see that the IRQs and I/O addresses are configured properly for each port.

Now examine your COM port header cables closely. See that the header is fit over every pin and is oriented properly (look for "pin 1"). Since many motherboard makers use different pin assignments for COM port headers, make sure that you're using the header cable that's specifically intended for your particular motherboard model.

One other point. If your system has internal modems or other serial devices (such as a multi-I/O card with one or more COM ports), see that those other serial devices are *not* conflicting with the motherboard's COM port(s). You may need to reconfigure or remove the conflicting device(s).

SYMPTOM 32-9 The system halts during boot and displays an "Incompatible ATAPI Device" error. This problem may occur after installing a new ATAPI device or upgrading the motherboard with existing ATAPI device(s). It is a known issue with the Pioneer 32X CD-ROM and an AMI BIOS, and it can also occur with other incompatible BIOS versions and ATAPI devices. In almost every case, the solution is to upgrade the motherboard's BIOS to a newer version. Of course, you could also try a different ATAPI device, instead.

SYMPTOM 32-10 The system will not turn off when you press the power button. This is an issue with the motherboard's power management settings. In many cases, the power button is designed to turn off the system *only* when you press and hold the power button for more than 5 seconds. You may be able to reconfigure the power button for "instant off" through the CMOS Setup. If you cannot reconfigure the power button for "instant off," you may need a BIOS upgrade.

SYMPTOM 32-11 You discover the "Wake On LAN" device has damaged your power supply. This is probably because your power supply did not provide adequate standby current. You need to use a power supply with 800mA provided through the +5Vsb (standby) power line. This is required by most "Wake On LAN" network cards, which require +5V@750mA in sleep mode. Try an ATX power supply with minimum 800mA at the +5Vsb output to avoid over-current damage to the power supply.

SYMPTOM 32-12 You encounter a "Serial Presence Detect" error at boot time. This is a problem with the system RAM being properly identified to the BIOS. If "non-SPD" memory is detected during the POST, or if the BIOS cannot determine that the memory installed meets SPD 100MHz requirements, the BIOS will display this error message:

```
SERIAL PRESENCE DETECT (SPD) device data missing or inconclusive
Properly programmed SPD device data is required for reliable operation
Do you wish to continue?
Y/N Type [Y] to continue, [N] to shut down
```

While non-SPD memory remains present on the system, subsequent boots will display the following message:

```
SERIAL PRESENCE DETECT (SPD) device data missing or inconclusive
100MHz memory assumed
```

If SPD 100MHz memory cannot be confirmed during POST, the BIOS will provide this information to the user and offer the option to run the system with memory that may *not* meet the full 100MHz operating requirements. If the system will be used in a mission-critical application where data integrity is vital, the system should be shut down, and SPD 100MHz memory should be installed prior to operation.

SYMPTOM 32-13 After installing one or more RIMM modules in the system, you get a repeating beep code and no video. This is often a problem with the way you installed your new Rambus DRAM. Chances are that the beep code indicates a problem during detection of the RIMM modules. If a RIMM socket is not populated with memory, ensure it is populated with a "Continuity RIMM."

32

Also check that system memory is securely installed and that any RIMMs in use have been specifically recommended by the motherboard manufacturer.

SYMPTOM 32-14 You find that IRQ9 is not available to assign an ISA device. Chances are that this is an issue related to your particular motherboard's power management system. For example, IRQ9 is not available to ISA devices on the Intel JN440BX motherboard because it is dedicated to the power management function on the motherboard's PIIX4 controller—this is also true for other motherboards that utilize the PIIX4 controller. You may free the IRQ by disabling the motherboard's power management features, or select another available IRQ for the device.

SYMPTOM 32-15 Windows 98 reports insufficient memory with 32MB installed. This is a known issue on motherboards that use the VIA MVP4 chipset (such as the AOpen MX59 Pro motherboard). The MVP4 chipset supports shared memory between system RAM and the video system; 8MB of system RAM is assigned to the onboard graphics controller by default. If this is the case, you may actually have only 24MB RAM for Windows 98, and this may *not* be enough. You can add more RAM to the system. You may also enter the CMOS Setup and reduce the Frame Buffer Size value from 8MB to 2MB in order to keep more of the 32MB available for Windows 98. If you do reduce the Frame Buffer Size, be sure to also reduce the color depth and resolution under Windows 98.

SYMPTOM 32-16 The system runs fine with Setup Defaults but is unstable with Turbo Defaults. This problem occurs because the Turbo defaults generally use more aggressive settings that wring more performance out of the motherboard. In some cases, certain hardware combinations may not respond well to Turbo settings and result in system instability. Check your hardware list against the requirements for the Turbo default settings. If you identify an item that is not appropriate (for example, slow RAM), you can upgrade that hardware. Otherwise, you may simply need to select the Setup defaults and stick with an acceptable level of system performance.

SYMPTOM 32-17 A motherboard failure is reported, but it goes away when the PC's outer cover is removed. There is likely to be an intermittent connection on the motherboard. When the housing is secured, the PC chassis warps just slightly—this may be enough to precipitate an intermittent contact. When the housing is removed, the chassis relaxes and hides the intermittent connection. Replace the outer cover and gently retighten each screw with the system running. Chances are that you will find one screw that triggers the problem. You can leave that screw out, but it is advisable to replace the motherboard as a long-term fix.

SYMPTOM 32-18 The POST (or your software diagnostic) reports a CPU fault. This is a fatal error, and chances are that system initialization has halted. CPU problems are generally reported when one or more CPU registers do not respond as expected, or when the CPU has trouble switching to protected mode. In either case, the CPU is probably at fault. Fortunately, the CPU is socket/slot mounted, and it should be very straightforward to replace. Be sure to disconnect all power to the PC, and make careful use of static controls when replacing a CPU. Mark the questionable CPU with indelible ink *before* replacing it.

Zero-insertion force (ZIF) sockets are easiest, since the IC will be released simply by lifting the metal lever at the socket's side. Slide out the original CPU and insert a new one. Secure the metal lever, and try the PC again. However, many CPUs are mounted in *pin grid array* (PGA) sockets, and a specialized PGA removal tool is strongly suggested for proper removal. You should also be able to use a small, regular screwdriver to gently pry up each of the four sides of the CPU, but be very careful to avoid cracking the IC, the socket, or the motherboard—never use excessive force. When the IC is free, install the new CPU with close attention to pin alignment, then gently press the new CPU into place. If you're working with Slot 1/Slot A processors, you'll need to release the processor's retention mechanism before removing the processor from its slot.

A word about heat sink/fans. Most Pentium MMX and later CPUs are equipped with a metal heat sink (or heat sink/fan) assembly. It is vital to the proper operation of your system that the heat sink be reinstalled correctly—otherwise, the new CPU will eventually overheat and lock up or fail. Be sure to use good-quality thermal compound to ensure proper heat transfer to the heat sink (remember that a sound *mechanical* connection does not guarantee a good *thermal* connection).

SYMPTOM 32-19 The POST (or your software diagnostic) reports a problem with the floating point unit. Math coprocessor (MCP, also called the Floating Point Unit or FPU) problems are generally reported when one or more MCP registers do not respond as expected. Fortunately, MCP faults are not always fatal. It is often possible to remove the MCP or disable the MCP availability through the CMOS Setup. Of course, programs that depend on the MCP will no longer run, but at least the system can be used until a new one is installed. On older systems that use separate MCPs, the device is socket mounted and should be very straightforward to replace. Be sure to remove all power to the PC, and make careful use of static controls when replacing an MCP. Mark the questionable MCP with indelible ink *before* replacing it. When the MCP function is integrated into the CPU (such as i486DX, Pentium, Pentium II/III, and later CPUs), the process is a bit more expensive because you'll need to replace the entire CPU, but the replacement process is no more difficult (remember to remount any heat sink/fan assembly properly).

SYMPTOM 32-20 The POST (or your software diagnostic) reports a BIOS ROM checksum error. The integrity of your system BIOS ROM is verified after the CPU is tested. This is necessary to ensure that there are no unwanted instructions or data that might easily crash the system during POST or normal operation. A checksum is performed on the ROM contents, and that value is compared with the value stored in the ROM itself. If the two values are equal, the ROM is considered good and initialization continues—otherwise, the BIOS is considered defective and should be replaced.

Traditionally, BIOS ROM is implemented as one or two ICs that are plugged into DIP or PLCC sockets. They can be removed easily with the blade of a regular screwdriver, as long as you pry the chip up slowly and gently (be sure to pry the chip evenly from both ends). When installing new DIP ICs, you may have to straighten their pins against the surface of a table, or use a DIP pin straightening tool. Ultimately, the IC pins will fit nicely into each receptacle in the DIP socket. You can then ease the IC evenly down into the socket. Alignment is critical to ensure that all pins are inserted. If not, one or more pins may be bent under the IC and ruin the new ROM. Also, be sure to insert the new IC(s) in the proper orientation. If they are accidentally installed backward, they may be damaged.

Newer BIOS chips use flash ROM technology, which allows the device to be erased and reprogrammed in the field without having to replace the entire BIOS ROM chip outright. When a flash BIOS fails its checksum test, it also has probably failed. Since flash BIOS devices are often fabricated as PLCC ICs, it is a bit easier to replace them, but you will need a PLCC removal tool to take the original IC out of its socket—there simply is not enough room for a screwdriver.

SYMPTOM 32-21 The POST (or software diagnostic) reports a timer (PIT) failure, a real-time clock update problem, or a refresh failure. The PIT is often an 8254 or compatible device. Ultimately, one or more of the its three channels may have failed, and the PIT should be replaced. It is important to realize that many modern motherboards incorporate the PIT functions into a system controller or other chipset device (refer to Chapter 10 for a listing of chipsets and functions). Since the PIT is typically surface mounted, you can attempt to replace the device or replace the motherboard entirely.

SYMPTOM 32-22 The POST (or software diagnostic) reports an interrupt controller (PIC) failure. The PIC is often an 8259 or compatible device, and there are two PICs on the typical AT motherboard (PIC 1 handles IRQ0 through IRQ7, and PIC 2 handles IRQ8 through IRQ15). Of the two, PIC 1 is more important since the lower interrupts have a higher priority, and the lowest channels handle critical low-level functions such as the system timer and keyboard interface. Generally, a diagnostic will reveal which of the two PICs have failed. Make sure that there are no interrupt conflicts between two or more system devices. You can then replace the defective PIC. In virtually all current systems, both PICs are integrated into a system controller chip or chipset device. You can replace the defective chip if you have the appropriate surface-mount equipment available, or replace the motherboard entirely.

SYMPTOM 32-23 The POST (or software diagnostic) reports a DMA controller (DMAC) failure. The DMAC is often an 8237 or compatible device, and there are two DMACs on the typical AT motherboard (DMAC 1 handles channel 0 through channel 3, and DMAC 2 handles channel 4 through channel 7). Of the two, DMAC 1 is more important since channel 2 runs the floppy disk controller. Generally, a diagnostic will reveal which of the two DMACs have failed. Make sure that there are no DMA conflicts between two or more system devices. You can then replace the defective DMAC. In many current systems, both DMACs are integrated into a system controller chip or chipset device. You can replace the defective chip if you have the appropriate surface-mount equipment available, or replace the motherboard entirely.

SYMPTOM 32-24 The POST (or software diagnostic) reports a keyboard controller fault. The keyboard controller (KBC) is often either an 8042 or an 8742. Since the KBC is a microcontroller in its own right, diagnostics can usually detect a KBC fault with great accuracy. The KBC may either be a socket-mounted PLCC device, or (in rare cases) a surface-mounted chip. Remember to remove all power and mark the old KBC before you remove it from the PC. You'll probably need a PLCC removal tool to take out the old KBC. If you cannot exchange a defective KBC, you'll need to replace the motherboard.

SYMPTOM 32-25 A keyboard error is reported, but a new keyboard has no effect. The keyboard fuse on the motherboard may have failed. Many motherboard designs incorporate a small fuse (called a *pico-fuse*) in the +5Vdc line that drives the keyboard. If this fuse fails, the keyboard will be dead. Use your multimeter and measure the +5Vdc line at the keyboard connector. If this reads 0Vdc, locate the keyboard fuse on the motherboard and replace it (you may have to trace the line back to the fuse, which looks *almost exactly* like a resistor).

SYMPTOM 32-26 The POST (or software diagnostic) reports a CMOS or real-time clock fault. With either error, it is the same device that is usually at fault. The CMOS RAM and real-time clock (RTC) are generally fabricated onto the same device. RTC problems indicate that the RTC portion of the chip has failed or is not being updated. CMOS RAM failure can be due to a dead backup battery or a failure of the chip itself. When dealing with a CMOS or Setup problem, try the following protocol. First, try a new backup battery and reload the CMOS Setup variables. If a new battery does not resolve the problem, the CMOS/RTC IC should be replaced. Often, the CMOS/RTC chip is surface mounted and will have to be replaced (or the motherboard will have to be replaced). However, there is a growing trend toward making the chip socket mounted and including the battery in a single replaceable module (such as the Dallas Semiconductor-type devices). Modules are typically replaceable DIP devices.

SYMPTOM 32-27 **The POST (or software diagnostic) reports a fault in the first 64K of RAM.** The first RAM page is important since it holds the BIOS data area (BDA) and interrupt vectors—the system will *not* work without it. When a RAM error is indicated, your only real recourse is to replace the motherboard RAM. On older motherboards, if the diagnostic indicates which bit has failed, and you can correlate the bit to a specific memory chip, you can sometimes replace the defective chip (typically surface mounted). Otherwise, you'll need to systematically locate and replace all of the motherboard RAM, or replace the motherboard entirely. Newer motherboards utilize DIMMs (and sometimes RIMMs) for *all* system memory, so it should be a relatively simple matter to cycle through each memory module with a known good unit to isolate the defective memory.

SYMPTOM 32-28 **The math coprocessor does not work properly when installed on a motherboard when external caching is enabled.** This is an issue that you might encounter when resurrecting older motherboards. Some non-Intel math coprocessors (MCPs, or floating point units) work in areas that must be noncached. For example, a Cyrix EMC87 MCP with an AMI Mark IV i386 motherboard has been known to cause these types of problems. When MCP problems arise (especially during upgrades), try disabling the external cache through CMOS Setup. As another alternative, try a different MCP.

SYMPTOM 32-29 **A "jumperless motherboard" receives incorrect CPU Soft Menu settings and now refuses to boot.** This problem may occur on a motherboard such as the Abit IT5V, and it is usually due to accidental settings made during system configuration. Fortunately, this type of problem can be corrected by removing power from the motherboard—try turning off the system and unplugging it for several minutes. When you restore power to the system, the CPU Soft Menu will automatically reset the CPU frequency for the lowest setting and allow the motherboard to boot. You can then go back into the CPU Soft Menu and correct any speed setting errors. If this were a jumpered motherboard, you would need to find the CPU speed jumper and set it correctly.

32

SYMPTOM 32-30 **When you install two 64MB SIMMs, only 32MB of RAM are displayed when you turn on the computer.** This tends to be a chipset-related problem—the motherboard is probably using a 430VX chipset that (though supporting 128MB of RAM) will not support 64MB memory devices. The 430VX supports only the following memory devices:

- 512Kx32-bit (2MB)
- 1Mx32-bit (4MB)
- 2Mx32-bit (8MB)
- 4Mx32-bit (16MB)

The layout for a 64MB SIMM is 16Mx32-bit, which isn't in the list shown above. When you install two 64MB SIMMs, the system will use the 4Mx32-bit specification to calculate the memory, thus displaying 32MB. Unfortunately, this is a limitation of the motherboard, and it cannot be corrected without upgrading the motherboard (or using smaller memory modules).

SYMPTOM 32-31 **A Creative Labs Plug and Play sound board refuses to work on one motherboard, but the board works just fine on another motherboard.** This usually is an issue where the Plug and Play (PnP) BIOS is at fault. Check with the motherboard manufacturer to see if there is a BIOS update to correct PnP problems. If not, you may need to disable the sound card's PnP compatibility and configure the card manually. If that's not possible, you may need to select another sound card for the system.

SYMPTOM 32-32 The system CD-ROM drive refuses to work once an IDE bus master driver is installed. This problem is almost always due to a driver not interacting properly with the IDE/EIDE bus controller on the motherboard. In almost all cases, you should contact the motherboard or system manufacturer and update the IDE bus master driver(s), or disable bus mastering completely.

SYMPTOM 32-33 You cannot get an AMD 5x86 133MHz CPU to run on your motherboard. Check your voltage first. The AMD 5x86 runs on 3.3V, so you may need a voltage regulator in the CPU socket (the AMD CPU may already be damaged). Also check your BIOS version—you may need an updated BIOS to support the AMD CPU properly. Check your jumper settings next—the speed or CPU type selection is almost always set wrong. If you cannot jumper the motherboard correctly (for example, 33MHz bus speed), then the motherboard itself is limited—it cannot enable the 4x internal CPU clock for the AMD 5x86. In this case, you will need to use a different CPU or replace the motherboard outright.

SYMPTOM 32-34 You cannot get a Cyrix 5x86 CPU to run on your motherboard. Check your voltage first. The Cyrix 5x86 uses 3.3V, so you may need a voltage regulator in the CPU socket (the Cyrix CPU may already be damaged). Also check your BIOS version—you may need an updated BIOS to support the Cyrix CPU properly. Check your jumper settings next—the speed (33MHz) or CPU type selection is almost always set wrong. If problems persist, you may need a different CPU or motherboard.

SYMPTOM 32-35 You see the error message "System Resource Conflict" on the AMI BIOS POST display. This error is generated by AMI PnP BIOS (though other Plug and Play BIOS may produce similar errors), and is generated when the BIOS detects a resource conflict during initialization. You may try to force the BIOS to reconfigure the conflicting resource by pressing the INS key during POST. If problems continue, you may need a BIOS update that may be able to resolve assignment conflicts more intelligently. Otherwise, you may need to try reconfigure the conflicting resource manually (disabling its Plug and Play support) or remove the offending device entirely.

SYMPTOM 32-36 The system hangs after using MEMMAKER under DOS. This is most prevalent with AMI's WinBIOS, which cannot support the "highscan" option used with EMM386.EXE. Make sure to disable the highscan option from EMM386 *before* running MEMMAKER. You may also choose to upgrade the system BIOS to a more recent version that may be more robust when testing memory.

SYMPTOM 32-37 Your Power Management icon does not appear in the Windows 95/98 Control Panel. This occurs even though the APM parameter under the BIOS Power Management Setup is *enabled*. This problem occurs if you do not enable the APM function *before* you install Windows 95/98. If you have already installed Windows 95/98, you should reinstall it. Before doing so, however, make sure that the APM function is enabled.

SYMPTOM 32-38 Systems with a Western Digital 1.6GB hard drives fail to boot even though BIOS recognizes the presence of HDD. This is a typical problem with large hard drives, which often need additional time to start up after powering the system. Check your BIOS Advanced Setup and increase the power-on delay time. This should correct the problem. This problem may reoccur if CMOS default values are reloaded or CMOS contents are lost.

SYMPTOM 32-39 After installing Windows 95, the system can no longer find the CD-ROM drive on the secondary IDE channel. You may also find that the IDE drives are running in MS-DOS compatibility mode. This problem occurs often with motherboards using the Intel 430HX chipset: Windows 95 is not recognizing the Intel 82371SB drive controller on the motherboard, which causes BIOS to disable the secondary IDE channel—devices on the secondary channel are not being detected after the system is rebooted. In most cases, you can upgrade the BIOS to correct this problem or move the IDE devices to a separate IDE controller. You may also be able to download a patch to update the MSHDC.INF file that will force Windows 95 to recognize the 82371SB controller.

SYMPTOM 32-40 The system hangs or crashes when the chipset-specific PCI-IDE DOS driver is loaded. This is a known problem with Micro-Star motherboards using a VIA VP1 chipset and Award BIOS 4.50PG. The problem is with the BIOS version and its interaction with the PCI controller portion of the VIA chipset. Upgrading the BIOS version should resolve the problem.

SYMPTOM 32-41 You notice that your Pentium motherboard is unusually picky about which SIMMs it will accept. This occurs even though the SIMMs are all within the proper type and rating. There are several possible problems to consider. First, Intel chipsets are very discriminating when it comes to memory speed, so make sure that the memory speed is well *within* the required range (usually 70nS or faster). Second, try changing the wait states in the CMOS Setup to a lower speed (such as 4-4-4-4). If your system works under this low speed, then increase the speed (for example to 3-3-3-3, 3-2-2-2, 3-1-1-1, and so on) and keep trying till the best number has been reached. Finally, the memory itself may be of questionable quality—try good-quality memory bought from a reputable vendor. Make sure the vendor offers a liberal return policy so that you can return questionable memory easily.

SYMPTOM 32-42 You experience a problem with pipeline burst cache. This is a recognized problem with UMC pipeline burst cache (especially on an Amptron motherboard). The problem can usually be solved by adjusting the cache control to 4-4-4-4 (the default in CMOS is typically 2-3-3-3). This will reduce performance, but it should stabilize cache operations.

32

SYMPTOM 32-43 You get no display, or the system refuses to boot because of the keyboard controller. Note that the video adapter proves to be fine in another system. This is a problem with the VIA 82C41 24-pin keyboard controller (especially on the Amptron PM-7600 motherboard). A fault with the keyboard controller may cause a "no display" or "fail to boot" condition. The VIA 82C41 is extremely sensitive to damage from power supply surges/spikes and ESD damage. Replace the keyboard controller, or replace the motherboard with a more robust model.

SYMPTOM 32-44 Your customer forgets their password. The PC password is stored in the CMOS RAM, which is located in either the motherboard chipset or the real-time clock (RTC) chip. If it is stored in the chipset, the CMOS memory is backed up by a coin-shaped lithium battery (or other battery). If it is stored in the RTC chip, it has an internal battery to back up the CMOS RAM. For the external battery, follow these steps: First, make a complete backup of the CMOS settings. Turn off the system, and then remove the battery for a period of at least two hours. This should clear the CMOS setting and erase the password. For the RTC battery, follow these steps: Determine which RTC chip you have—there are five different kinds of RTC CMOS chips:

- Dallas DS 12887 Real Time
- Benchmarc

- Dallas DS 12B887
- Dallas DS 12887A
- BQ3287A

For the Dallas DS 12887 and Benchmarc RTC chips, if you can boot to the A: prompt, then flash the BIOS chip with the same boot block record, but different BIOS revision. For example, if you have a P/I P55TP4XE motherboard with BIOS revision 0202, flash the BIOS chip to BIOS revision 0115. A BIOS checksum error will be generated. Enter the CMOS Setup screen, reload setup defaults, then save and exit. At this point, the password has been cleared. You can flash the BIOS back to the original revision. If you can't boot to the A: prompt, turn off the system, remove the BIOS chip, and insert another with the same boot block record but different BIOS revision. Power-on the system. A BIOS checksum error will be generated. Turn off the system. Reinstall the original BIOS. Power-on the system again, and hit Del to enter the BIOS setup screen. Reload the setup defaults, then save and exit.

For the Dallas DS 12887A, there is a jumper on the motherboard that clears the CMOS. Please check your manual for the location of this jumper (it will vary between motherboards). Shorting this jumper should erase the system configuration information (including password) stored in the CMOS. To clear the CMOS, make sure the system is off. Short the jumper for a moment and then remove it. *Do not leave this jumper shorted.* After clearing the CMOS, the password should be erased.

For the BQ3287A and Dallas DS12B887 RTC chips, short the same jumper as in the previous section, but make sure to power the system on and off *before* removing the jumper.

SYMPTOM 32-45 You encounter problems with Western Digital hard drives (but the drives work on other systems). This type of problem has been identified with Asus motherboards using Award BIOS with older Western Digital (~1.6GB) drives. Note that problems do not appear in newer Western Digital drives. There are several means of addressing the problems: First, disable Quick Power-on Self Test in your CMOS Setup, and enable the Floppy Seek option. This will increase the time that the drive gets to spin-up. If your CMOS offers a Power-on Delay Time instead, try increasing that time. Also avoid using Defrag or the disk surface scan feature of ScanDisk with Western Digital drives—both have been reported to increase the number of bad blocks on the disk.

Next, consider a BIOS upgrade (especially if you're using a motherboard with the Intel 430FX chipset). Some BIOS versions use a "park head" command that can cause problems with Western Digital hard drives. Finally, check the Western Digital web site (**www.wdc.com**) for any drive patches that might be currently available. If all else fails, you might replace the drive outright.

SYMPTOM 32-46 You encounter memory parity errors at boot-up. If you're using nonparity memory devices (such as a 32-bit device instead of a 36-bit device), you will need to disable DRAM ECC or parity checking through the CMOS Chipset Features settings. This problem can occur if you reload default CMOS settings, which restores parity/ECC on a system with nonparity memory. Also keep in mind that the Triton chipset does not support parity, so even if you use parity RAM, you should try disabling parity checking. If the system is configured properly, you may actually have a memory failure, and you'll need to isolate the memory fault.

SYMPTOM 32-47 You flash a BIOS, but now you get no video. When you flash a BIOS, the old CMOS settings are usually left useless. This means you'll have to restore the proper CMOS settings before the system may run properly. Clear your CMOS RAM and reload the proper settings (or choose the BIOS Defaults for a good system baseline). The BIOS chip itself may also be troublesome. There are some problems when flashing an Intel flash ROM chip. Make sure that there are no warnings or cautions in the system documentation or from the manufacturer's Web site before flashing a particular BIOS chip. Try restoring the original BIOS if possible, or contact the manufacturer for a replacement BIOS.

SYMPTOM 32-48 **You are trying to use a Plug and Play sound card and Plug and Play modem together on the same system, but you're getting hardware conflicts.** This is an all-too-common problem with PnP systems. In general, the modem should take COM2 (2F8h and IRQ3), and the sound card should take 220h, IRQ5, and DMA 1. Try adding the cards one at a time—install the sound card first and let Windows 95/98 detect it. Add the modem next. If problems persist, configure the cards manually (disable their PnP support) if possible, or try alternative cards.

SYMPTOM 32-49 **After setting the DRAM speed to 70nS in the Advanced Chipset Setup, the system crashes or refuses to boot.** Chances are that you have the incorrect number of wait states set for your memory configuration—70nS RAM typically requires at least one wait state. Disable any Auto Configure DRAM Timing feature, then set the number of wait states to 1. That should clear up the problem.

SYMPTOM 32-50 **There are 32MB (or more) of memory, and the BIOS counts it all during POST, but you see only 16MB in the CMOS Setup screen.** This is a problem that has been identified with some Award BIOS versions. To correct the problem, make sure that the "memory hole" option in the Advanced Chipset Setup area is *disabled*. The memory hole option assumes a maximum of 16MB of physical RAM in the system. You may also try disabling the system's shadow RAM or BIOS shadow option.

32

SYMPTOM 32-51 **You move a working IDE drive from an older 386/486 system to your new Pentium system, and the system no longer works.** In most cases, the data transfer mode is set improperly for the old IDE hard drive (for example, using LBA mode when the IDE drive requires CHS mode). Find the Peripheral Setup screen in your CMOS Setup and make sure to change all the PIO mode settings to *Mode 0* (chances are the settings are currently at *Automatic* and are configuring the data transfer incorrectly). The idea is to ensure that the drive is configured exactly the same way as it was on its original system. If you cannot duplicate the original BIOS configuration, get the settings as close as you can, then repartition and reformat the drive in order to use it on a different (older) controller.

SYMPTOM 32-52 **Windows 95 locks up when you install a Diamond Stealth Video 3200 board and an Intel EtherExpress Pro 10/100 network card.** First you verify that both cards work fine on other systems. Problems begin when you load the Intel network driver. This is a problem that has been identified with Premio motherboards and is due to a problem in the system BIOS. Upgrade the Premio BIOS to the latest version.

SYMPTOM 32-53 **You install an Intel Pentium P55C (MMX) 200MHz CPU, and you set the CPU speed jumper(s) for 200MHz, but the system still reports 166MHz.** In virtually all cases, you have set the speed jumper(s) incorrectly. Take another look at the documentation for your motherboard, and see that the speed is indeed set correctly. If problems persist, the BIOS may not recognize the higher CPU speed correctly, so try upgrading the motherboard BIOS. As an additional check, verify that the CPU is not fake or mismarked.

SYMPTOM 32-54 **The system frequently locks up or crashes after installing a Cyrix 6x86 CPU.** In most cases, the Cyrix 6x86 is not being cooled properly and is overheating. Make sure that you have a heat sink/fan assembly attached properly to the Cyrix, and see that the fan is running. Also, the Cyrix 6x86 P166+ is a 3.52V CPU. Check your voltage regulator and see that it is set to provide 3.45 to 3.6 volts.

SYMPTOM 32-55 **After installing a Pentium 120MHz motherboard, you get registry corruption or "out of memory" errors from Windows 95.** This happens most often with slightly older Pentium motherboards (~100–120MHz), and is almost always a BIOS version problem that causes the motherboard to misbehave under Windows 95. You will need to update the BIOS version for your particular motherboard.

SYMPTOM 32-56 **The motherboard fails to auto-detect the hard drive parameters.** This is a known problem on Dataexpert EXP8551S motherboards and is due to a problem with Windows 95 in recognizing the PCI/ISA/I/O controller portion of the chipset. You can use the following procedure to force Windows 95 to recognize the chipset properly:

1. Boot up the Windows 95 system normally.
2. Change the directory to /WINDOWS/INF.
3. Edit the hidden file MSHDC.INF.
4. Search for all lines with the 1230 device ID. Copy the lines and replace 1230 with 7010 (the correct device ID).
5. Save the file MSHDC.INF.
6. Remove the Standard IDE/ESDI Hard Disk Controller entry from the Device Manager.
7. Restart the computer, then choose the Windows default driver, following the instructions shown on the screen.

> You should make a backup copy of the MSHDC.INF file before editing the file. That way, you can easily restore the original file if necessary.

If the problem persists, you should try entering the specific hard drive parameters for your particular drive into the CMOS Setup.

SYMPTOM 32-57 **The motherboard refuses to detect the SCSI controller during boot-up.** This problem has been identified with the Dataexpert EXP8551 motherboard, but it may occur on many different types of PCI motherboards. In most cases, you will have to change the configuration of your PCI slots on the motherboard. For example, if the SCSI controller is installed on slot 2, you will need to configure the PCI slot 2 in CMOS Setup.

SYMPTOM 32-58 **You find that you cannot run a Cyrix 6x86 CPU on a particular motherboard.** This is a problem that has been identified on Eurone/Matsonic motherboards, and it is usually the result of an incompatible motherboard clock generator. Some clock generators support the Cyrix 120, 133, and 166MHz models but exempt the 200MHz model; other clock generators support the 120, 150, 166, and 200MHz models but exempt the 133MHz model. So if you're using a 133MHz or 200MHz Cyrix CPU, you may be using the wrong clock generator. You will have to replace the CPU with a speed suitable to the particular clock generator, or change the motherboard to one that will accommodate the particular CPU speed.

SYMPTOM 32-59 The system can only count up to and recognize 8MB of RAM though the system can accommodate even more. This is often a problem identified with Freetech 586F61x motherboards using Award BIOS version D or earlier. You can duplicate the problem by initiating a software reset with CTRL+ALT+DEL, then hitting the hardware reset—BIOS will only count memory up to 8MB. You will need to update the Award BIOS to version E or later. Freetech provides the BIOS patch on their Web site.

SYMPTOM 32-60 When four 8MB SIMMs are installed in the system (32MB), the system only counts up to 24MB. This is a known problem with gigabyte motherboards (typically the GA-586ATE, ATM, and AP ver 1.x). The motherboard does not support double-sided SIMMs (for example, 2MB, 8MB, 32MB, or 128MB) in the center bank. Install the SIMMs in bank 0 and bank 2—leaving bank 1 empty.

Some motherboards require the banks to be filled in sequential order or allow you to change the bank order with jumpers.

SYMPTOM 32-61 Gold-plated SIMMs do not work properly in tin-plated sockets. As a general rule, you should avoid mixing metal types when choosing SIMMs—the metal in the SIMM socket must be the same as the metal on the SIMM itself. Otherwise, tin debris will transfer to the gold surface and oxidize. This will eventually result in memory failures that suggest faulty SIMMs.

SYMPTOM 32-62 Even though all peripherals in the system are SCSI, Windows 95 continues to detect the PCI IDE controller. You notice that this problem occurs even though the controller was disabled in CMOS. This is a known problem with the Iwill P54TS motherboard. Normally, Windows 95 will try to recognize and try to enable I/O devices, but it should not enable devices that are deliberately disabled in CMOS. This is typically a BIOS problem (the onboard IDE controllers were not properly disabled), so try upgrading your BIOS to the latest version.

SYMPTOM 32-63 You get an "EISA CMOS Configuration Error" when the system starts up. For EISA systems, you *must* run the EISA configuration utility in order to properly set up the system. Without this step, the system will not be able to detect any possible resource conflicts. This type of problem is most common when installing a new EISA motherboard, when CMOS contents are lost, or when devices (such as memory) are added or removed.

SYMPTOM 32-64 The SMP (dual processor) mode refuses to run in Windows NT. The most common problem is an incompatibility with the SMP HAL shipped with Windows NT (versions prior to 3.51) and the motherboard's chipset. If you are upgrading from an older version of NT (prior to 3.51), first install NT as a standard PC (single processor kernel), then install NT with the default multiprocessor kernel it provides. (NT will not recognize your dual CPUs if you upgrade straight to a multiprocessor configuration.)

SYMPTOM 32-65 When attempting to upgrade your flash BIOS, you encounter an insufficient memory error. In most cases, you simply don't have enough conventional memory available to execute the flash program. Most flash programs require about 560K of conventional RAM. Try booting clean with a DOS disk, then run the flash upgrade.

SYMPTOM 32-66 You see a prolonged system message saying "Updating ESCD..." each time the system boots. The Extended System Configuration Data (ESCD) area is part of a Plug and Play system. One or more PnP devices are attempting to update your BIOS settings. To stop this from occurring, set the BIOS to program mode.

SYMPTOM 32-67 You notice a yellow (!) sign over your USB port in the Device Manager. Windows 95/98 indicates that it has detected an unknown PCI device. In virtually all cases, the proper driver for the USB on your system has not been installed, and Windows 95/98 cannot recognize the USB hardware. You can usually correct this problem by updating your system BIOS to a newer version that supports the USB hardware better under Windows 95/98.

SYMPTOM 32-68 The Device Manager under Windows 95 indicates four COM ports (at unusual IRQs and I/O addresses), but there are only two physical ports on the motherboard. This problem has been identified with the Ocean Rhino motherboard, which is running a very old Award BIOS. The Award BIOS has since been upgraded to provide full support for Windows 95, so download the newest BIOS version from the motherboard manufacturer.

SYMPTOM 32-69 The performance of a motherboard with an AMD K5 CPU seems extremely poor. This is almost always because of the motherboard BIOS. Chances are the BIOS was released before the AMD K5 was widely introduced, so there may be problems providing proper AMD support. Make sure that you are using the very latest BIOS, which supplies adequate AMD support.

SYMPTOM 32-70 The system hangs after installing a Cyrix 6x86 CPU. There is probably a problem with the utilization of system cache, which is causing the system to hang. Try disabling the internal (L1) and external (L2) cache.

SYMPTOM 32-71 When attempting to upgrade the BIOS version, you cannot use a key sequence such as Ctrl+Home to reboot the PC in order to start the flash process. The current BIOS version does not support such key sequences. To flash the BIOS, start the flash program manually from the DOS prompt. For example:

```
A:\> AMIFL PAIV17.ROM <Enter>
```

SYMPTOM 32-72 You find that a particular SVGA board refuses to work on a particular motherboard. However, the video board proves out fine on other systems. In most cases, this is a compatibility problem between the video chipset and the motherboard. There may be a BIOS upgrade for the motherboard or video board that can overcome the problem. You may simply have to use a different video board.

SYMPTOM 32-73 When the on-board printer port is set to 3BCh (and EPP/SPP mode) and another parallel port add-on card is set to 378h or 278h, the BIOS recognizes only the add-on card. Port 3BCh seems to disappear. This may be a configuration problem with the Winbond chipset which specifies that LPT1 on the motherboard should be set at 378h (EPP or SPP), while add-on parallel ports should be set at 278h or 3BCh. The Winbond chip was designed this way for Windows 95. Check with the motherboard manufacturer for any available BIOS upgrades that can correct this issue.

SYMPTOM 32-74 **With 32MB of RAM on the motherboard, Checkit 3.0 causes the system to reboot when performing DRAM tests.** This is because Checkit 3.0 will not perform memory testing over 16MB. This is an issue with Checkit, not the motherboard. Upgrade to a later version of Checkit.

SYMPTOM 32-75 **The IBM Blue Lighting CPU will not run on a motherboard that should support it.** In most cases, the problem is an older BIOS version. Make sure that you are running the latest version of BIOS before installing the IBM Blue Lightning (basically this is a Cyrix processor). Also check to make sure that any CPU type and speed jumpers are set properly for the CPU.

SYMPTOM 32-76 **When using a benchmark program such as SYSINFO, the overall performance rating of a Pentium 100 system marks better than a Pentium 120 system.** This result is because of the PCI bus speed. For a 100MHz system, the PCI bus speed is 33MHz. For a 120MHz system, the bus speed is 30MHz. The slightly faster PCI system will register a bit better performance.

> Always make sure that your benchmark and diagnostic programs are updated for the CPUs and other hardware that you are testing.

SYMPTOM 32-77 **You cannot get parallel port devices to work on your motherboard.** In most cases, you must set the proper parallel port mode (such as SPP/ECP/EPP) for the particular device you plan to use. Often, setting the port to Compatibility Mode will work for many common peripherals. Parallel port modes are selected through the CMOS Setup—usually under Integrated Peripherals or some similar heading.

SYMPTOM 32-78 **You notice that some configurations of memory provide less performance than others.** This type of problem is most noted on motherboards with 440FX chipsets, and it is usually the result of a BIOS problem. Try updating your BIOS to the latest available version.

SYMPTOM 32-79 **You see no performance improvement when enabling PCI/IDE bus mastering.** The problem is often that you are using an older (or buggy) driver. Make sure that you have installed the most recent bus mastering driver file. (Triton I, Triton II and Natoma chipsets may use the same driver.)

SYMPTOM 32-80 **The BIOS banner displayed on power-on is showing the wrong motherboard model.** In virtually all cases, this problem is due to the BIOS version being unable to identify the correct hardware platform. Get the latest update for your motherboard BIOS.

SYMPTOM 32-81 **The Pentium P55CM BIOS shows a 150MHz CPU even though the CPU is a 166MHz model.** This is almost always due to a BIOS fault. You should upgrade to the very latest BIOS version for your particular motherboard. If you cannot flash the BIOS, replace the BIOS chip outright.

SYMPTOM 32-82 **You see "Static Device Resource Conflict" error message after the system memory count when using the P55CM CPU.** This is usually a problem with the PCI bus system. Press and hold the INSERT key before turning on the computer. Release the INSERT key when the video comes up. This forces the system to reassign PCI resources. If the error message still appears, remove all PCI cards (except for the video card) and try again. Reinsert one PCI card at a time until the problem returns—*that* is where the problem is.

MOTHERBOARD UPGRADE SYMPTOMS

SYMPTOM 32-83 **The motherboard is installed, but the system won't boot.** This is a classic sign of installation problems. Start with the basics. Check all of the cables and connectors—especially the power connectors. Also, make sure that there are no metal standoffs or brackets shorting the motherboard from underneath. Next, check for any wiring or cables that may be installed backward. While this will rarely keep a PC from booting, it is possible. Be sure that pin 1 on each cable aligns with pin 1 of each connector. Finally, double-check the socket-mounted ICs, such as the CPU, BIOS ROM(s), and SIMMs. They should all be aligned properly and inserted evenly and completely. If you locate an incorrectly installed IC, it may or may not be damaged. Remove it from the motherboard, check it for bent or broken pins, reinsert it correctly, and try the motherboard again. If the IC is damaged, it should be replaced.

SYMPTOM 32-84 **The motherboard starts, but it will not boot from the hard drive or recognize the correct amount of RAM in the system.** You may see an error message such as "CMOS Error; press F1 to run SETUP." This error generally indicates that the motherboard is working, but the system CMOS contains incorrect information. Either you forgot to enter the new CMOS variables; you forgot to save the settings when you updated them; or the backup battery is not installed and CMOS contents were lost after the system was powered down. Check the backup battery first. If the battery is a coin cell, see that it is inserted properly and completely into its holder. If the battery is a pack-type, check to see that it is plugged into the proper motherboard connector in the right polarity. If the battery is installed correctly, try a new one. Run the Setup program and check each drive and memory setting. If you entered a drive parameter or RAM amount improperly, correct the settings and save CMOS again. Reboot the PC. If new CMOS settings are lost after the PC is powered down, the backup battery has failed—try a new battery.

SYMPTOM 32-85 **You cannot use one or more drives in the PC.** Either the drive(s) have been entered improperly in the CMOS Setup routine, or the drive(s) are cabled improperly. Start by checking the CMOS Setup. Make sure that there are proper references for the floppy drives and hard drives in the system. Fill in any missing information, and reboot the computer. If the CMOS settings are all correct, check the data cables and power cables at each drive—loose power or signal cables can easily disable a drive.

SYMPTOM 32-86 **The system boots and runs, but it locks up unpredictably.** Make sure that the CPU and all system RAM is installed correctly and securely. Try reseating the RAM. Check the system CPU for excessive heat. An overheated CPU can lock up without warning. If the CPU is fitted with a heat sink, make sure that the heat sink is securely attached, and that you have used ample amounts of thermal compound to aid heat transfer. If the CPU runs hot and there is no heat sink, try adding one.

Another factor to consider is the possibility of controller conflicts. For example, if there is a video port on the new motherboard, but you also have a video board installed in an expansion slot, you will have to set jumpers to disable the motherboard's video port. The same thing is true for drive controller conflicts, as well as serial or parallel port conflicts. Take another close look at the expansion boards in your system, and make sure that the board functions do not conflict with the functions provided on the motherboard.

SYMPTOM 32-87 **There is system activity, but the video is erratic or absent.** Check that there is no video conflict between the motherboard and a video expansion board. If there is a video port on the motherboard, it probably should be disabled when an expansion video board is used in the system. Also check that the monitor is turned on and that the video cable is securely connected to the video port. If problems persist, check that the video board is installed correctly and that, if extra memory must be excluded from the upper memory area, the proper command-line switches are included with EMM386 in the CONFIG.SYS file.

Further Study

Abit Computer Corp.: **http://www.abit.com.tw/html/emain.htm**

Acer America Corp.: **http://www.acer.com**

American Megatrends (AMI): **http://www.megatrends.com**

American Predator Corp.: **http://www.americanpredator.com**

ASUS: **http://www.asus.com**

Biostar Microtech Intl.: **http://www.biostar.net**

CompuTrend Systems, Inc. (Premio): **http://www.premiopc.com**

Data Expert Corp.: **http://www.dataexpert.com**

Diamond Flower, Inc. (DFI): **http://www.dfiusa.com**

Elitegroup Computers, Ltd. (ECS): **http://www.ecs.com.tw**

Famous Technology Co., Ltd.: **http://www1.magic-pro.com.hk/famous/index.html**

First International Computer, Inc. (FIC): **http://www.fica.com**

Fong Kai Industrial Co. (FKI): **http://www.fkusa.com**

Gemlight Computer Ltd.: **http://www.gemlight.com.hk**

Genoa Systems Corp.: **http://www.genoasys.com**

Giga-Byte Technology Co., Ltd.: **http://www.giga-byte.com**

Intel Corp.: **http://www.intel.com**

Iwill Computer: **http://www.iwill.com.tw**

Jbond: **http://www.jbond.com**

J-Mark Computer Corp.: **http://www.j-mark.com**

Kam-Tronic Computer Co., Ltd.: **http://megastar.kamtronic.com**

Micronics Computers, Inc.: **http://www.micronics.com**

Microway: **http://www.microway.com**

Micro Star International Co., Ltd. (MSI): **http://www.msi.com.tw**

PC Chips Manufacturing Ltd.: **http://www.pcchips.com**

Pine Technology Ltd.: **http://www.pinegroup.com**

Shuttle Computer International: **http://www.shuttlegroup.com**

Soyo Computer Inc.: **http://www.soyo.com.tw**

Supermicro Computer Inc.: **http://www.supermicro.com**

Tekram Technology: **http://www.tekram.com**

Tyan Computer: **http://www.tyan.com**

33

OVERLAY SOFTWARE TROUBLESHOOTING

CHAPTER AT A GLANCE

Hard drives have undergone phenomenal growth. Drives of 500MB to 800MB that were considered spacious just a few years ago are now considered insignificant against the 25GB to 32GB+ drives that are now on store shelves. While the battle for ever-larger drives has been waged relentlessly by drive manufacturers, the struggle to actually *use* those massive drives has rested squarely on the shoulders of computer users. Since traditional BIOS calls for IDE drives that limit drive sizes to 528MB, making use of space *beyond* the 528MB mark has required PC users to employ several different tactics. Updated motherboard BIOS and enhanced controllers (such as EIDE and Ultra-DMA controllers) have been two popular solutions, but drive overlay software (from manufacturers like Ontrack, Western Digital, and Maxtor) has proven to be particularly useful.

Software solutions like Disk Manager, MaxBlast, Data Lifeguard Tools, or EZ-Drive allow older systems to access the full capacity of a drive without ever touching the PC's hardware. Still, software solutions are not always as elegant and reliable as we would like to believe, and overlay software is certainly subject to a range of performance and compatibility problems under the right combinations of BIOS, operating systems, and drivers. This chapter provides symptoms and solutions for several premier drive overlay software products: MaxBlast, Data Lifeguard Tools, Disk Manager, EZ-Drive, and Drive Rocket.

MaxBlast Troubleshooting

MaxBlast is a one-step IDE hard drive installation utility (a version of EZ-Drive) that's been prepared for Maxtor Corporation. It automatically identifies, partitions, and formats any IDE-type hard drive, making it fully accessible in about one minute. It supports Maxtor drives with capacities greater than 32GB, includes a diagnostic utility, and now uses DR-DOS as its operating system to launch the EZ-Drive software. This part of the chapter outlines the major tips and troubleshooting that can help you get the most from MaxBlast.

CREATING A MAXBLAST BOOT DISK

Chances are that you may need to create a MaxBlast-compatible boot disk. This may be necessary if you need to boot the system from a disk yet still access the hard drive. Use the steps below to create a boot disk with MaxBlast:

1 Download the MAXBLAST.EXE file to your hard drive. This file can be run from a DOS prompt or in a window (from Windows 95/98). Keep in mind that you cannot make a MaxBlast boot disk from a floppy disk, nor under Windows NT or OS/2.

2 Under Windows, just double-click on the MAXBLAST.EXE file. Under DOS, type the file name **maxblast** and press ENTER.

3 The program will prompt you to insert a 1.44MB 3.5-inch floppy disk into your A: drive. Any files on the floppy will be erased during the MaxBlast disk creation procedure.

4 Once the program is complete, exit Windows (if applicable), reboot the system to the MaxBlast disk that you just created, and the installation process will begin. Make sure that you label this disk as "MaxBlast 9.10M."

33

INSTALLING MAXBLAST 9.XXM

When you install a drive that cannot be fully translated by your BIOS or drive controller hardware, it may be necessary for you to install drive overlay software in order to access the entire drive capacity. In most cases, MaxBlast comes on a disk that accompanies the new hard drive (and you can use that disk directly). If you need to download MaxBlast first, you'll need to create a MaxBlast bootable disk before proceeding (see "Creating a MaxBlast Boot Disk" above). Once you have MaxBlast 9.xxM (or later) on a bootable floppy disk, simply follow the steps below to install the software:

1 Before proceeding, you should verify that the drive has been correctly installed and configured in the CMOS setup.

2 Boot the system using the MaxBlast disk (received with the hard drive or the bootable disk created with the downloaded software). You'll see the Maxtor logo screen while the MaxBlast program is loading, and then you'll see the following message:

```
Please write the following information down on your drive information sheet.
Press <Enter> to continue.
```

3 The "drive information sheet" is inside the drive's static bag. Locate the sheet, and then press ENTER to continue.

4 The System Configuration information is displayed. The information contained here will vary depending on the number and type of devices attached to the system. Please enter this drive information into the drive information sheet, and then press ENTER to continue.

5 The System Notes screen now appears, providing general information for setting the system BIOS and accessing different BIOS versions. Press ENTER to continue.

6 The Maxtor logo screen is displayed while the MaxBlast program is loading. The message "Loading EZ-Drive, please wait..." is displayed as well.

7 The License Screen appears and provides a summary of the license agreement. To view the complete license agreement, press F1. Pressing ESC will terminate the installation program. Press ENTER to continue with the installation.

8 The main menu is displayed, and you're ready to install MaxBlast.

> The "system information" and "system notes" displays are generally not shown on subsequent executions of the MaxBlast software.

9 If the hard drive does not contain data, a screen with the option "Setup drive (0,1,2,3) now" will be displayed. Simply press Y to continue with the installation.

10 If the main menu is displayed, highlight Setup Hard Drive. A list of found devices is displayed.

11 A partial file list is displayed if data exists on the hard drive. Type the complete word **YES** to continue with the installation. All data on this drive will be lost.

12 System files are required to make the hard drive bootable. If this is the primary drive, a screen appears asking for a system disk to be placed in the A: drive. Once the system disk is inserted, press Y.

13 A menu with partition options is displayed. The partition sizes shown are the minimum default sizes for the operating system. If these are acceptable, highlight "Use these partition sizes" and press ENTER. If you wish to change the sizes of one or more partitions, highlight "Enter new partition sizes" and press ENTER. Enter the size of each partition (in megabytes) until all available drive space is used.

14 You have one last chance to cancel the setup. If you wish to proceed, highlight Continue Setup and press ENTER. MaxBlast will display its status during the installation process. You'll be notified once the process is complete.

15 Remove the floppy disk from the A: drive, and press ESC to reboot the system. MaxBlast should be installed.

> If this is the primary system hard drive, an operating system needs to be installed now.

BOOTING A MAXBLAST DRIVE FROM FLOPPY

There are many occasions when it may be necessary to boot the system from a floppy disk. However, you may not be able to switch to your hard drive or access its contents because the overlay software has not loaded. You can use the steps below to boot safely from a floppy disk, yet still access the hard drive without corrupting data.

1 Reboot the system with no floppy disk in the floppy drive.

2 Press the CTRL key when the "EZ-BIOS Initializing" message appears. Watch carefully, as this banner only appears for a moment or two.

3 A status screen will appear, showing some important information about EZ-BIOS. At the bottom of the screen, there will be two options: "Press A to boot from Drive A" or "Press C to Boot from Drive C:."

4 Now you may insert a bootable floppy disk and press A to boot from drive A: as instructed. The system will now continue to boot from the disk, and you will wind up at the A: prompt.

CONVERTING DISK MANAGER TO EZ-DRIVE

In some cases, it may be necessary for you to convert existing overlay software to new or alternate versions. The steps below explain the procedure for converting Ontrack's Disk Manager (MaxBlast 6.x or 7.x) to Storage Soft's EZ-Drive (MaxBlast 9.02M or later). This conversion is designed for drives that are currently set up and functioning correctly using Ontrack's Disk Manager (version 6.x and 7.x). If you're experiencing problems with your current overlay software, making this conversion will probably not help.

> Be sure to perform a complete drive backup before attempting this procedure.

1 Verify that the drive is correctly mounted, cabled, connected, jumpered, and configured in the system's CMOS setup. Correct any problems with the drive's physical installation *before* continuing.

2 Boot the computer with your MaxBlast (version 9.02M or newer) bootable disk.

3 Press ENTER when you see the System Configuration screen.

4 Users must either select F1 to view general information about accessing the system BIOS, or press ENTER to continue installing MaxBlast.

5 Press ENTER to accept the terms of the license agreement.

6 Select Advanced Options and press ENTER. If this is a dual-drive system, the message "Select a drive for EZ-BIOS setup" will appear. If this message appears, select the hard drive that was previously installed using Disk Manager, and then press ENTER.

7 From the Advanced Options submenu, select the EZ-BIOS Setup option and press ENTER. Press Y to install EZ-BIOS.

8 From the next menu, press Y to replace Disk Manager with EZ-BIOS and continue.

9 Press ESC to return to the main menu. Select Exit EZ-Drive, press ENTER, and reboot the system.

10 Reboot the computer once again with the MaxBlast (version 9.02M or newer) bootable disk.

11 Press ENTER twice to continue installing and to accept the license terms.

12 Select Advanced Options from the main menu and press ENTER.

13 Select the Remove 63 Sector Offset option and press ENTER. Highlight Yes and press ENTER to continue.

14 Press any key to continue after the 63 sector offset is converted.

15 Press ESC to return to the main menu.

16 Select Exit EZ Drive, press ENTER, remove the MaxBlast disk, and reboot the system normally. The hard drive is now controlled by the EZ-BIOS.

RESTORING AN MBR USING MAXBLAST

If you work with hard drives for any length of time, you'll discover that the master boot record can become corrupted. This can stem from an operating system installation error, boot sector viruses, and anything in between. In most cases, a simple DOS command line, such as **FDISK/MBR**, can refresh a damaged

MBR, but this doesn't work when drive overlay software is installed (data corruption can result). You can use the procedures below to restore an MBR when you're using MaxBlast 9.xxM or MaxBlast Plus 1.xx.

Using MaxBlast 9.xxM (or later)

1. Clean boot the PC with a DOS system disk or Windows 95/98 startup disk. This will take you to the A: prompt.
2. At the A: prompt, insert the MaxBlast 9.xxM disk.
3. Type **EZDRIVE/MBR** and press ENTER. MaxBlast will confirm reinstallation on all affected hard drives.
4. When complete, remove the MaxBlast 9.xxM disk and reboot the system. The computer should then boot normally to its operating system.

If you cannot restore the MBR using the steps above, try the supplemental steps below:

1. Boot the PC with the bootable MaxBlast disk.
2. Press ENTER until you reach the main menu.
3. Select Advanced Options and press ENTER. The Advanced Options submenu will appear.
4. Select Backup/Restore Track 0 and press ENTER.
5. Select the primary master hard drive from the drive list and press ENTER (if there is more than one drive in the system).
6. A screen will appear showing all saved backup tracks. (Tracks range from 0 to 9, with 0 being the oldest.) Select the most recent backup track and press ENTER. MaxBlast will verify restoration of the boot track.
7. After restoration, remove all floppies and reboot the computer normally.
8. The system should boot normally to its operating system. If the PC does not boot correctly, reboot the system with MaxBlast and repeat the same steps, selecting the *next* subsequent backup track(s) until the system boots normally.

Using MaxBlast Plus 1.xx (or later)

1. Clean boot the PC with a DOS system or Windows 95/98 startup disk. This will take you to the A: prompt.
2. At the A: prompt, insert the MaxBlast Plus 1.xx disk.
3. Type **DG MBR** and press ENTER. Table 33-1 illustrates the various command-line switches available for MaxBlast Plus 1.xx. MaxBlast Plus will confirm reinstallation on all affected hard drives.
4. When complete, remove the MaxBlast Plus 1.xx disk and reboot the system. The computer should then boot normally to its operating system.

If you cannot restore the MBR using the steps above, try the supplemental steps below:

1. Clean boot the PC with a DOS system or Windows 95/98 startup disk. This will take you to the A: prompt.
2. At the A: prompt, insert the MaxBlast Plus 1.xx disk.
3. Type **DG MBR** and press ENTER. Follow the on-screen prompts until the main menu is displayed.

TABLE 33-1 MAXBLAST PLUS 1.XX COMMAND-LINE SWITCHES

SWITCH	DESCRIPTION
DG /CLRCONFIG	The configuration file contains the location of drives installed in the system. This switch allows you to clear the configuration file in the event that you want to start fresh with a new installation. This command-line switch should be used if the drive has been installed in another position in the PC (changed from a primary slave to a primary master).
DG /TEXT	This switch allows you to access MaxBlast Plus in the text mode. You should use this switch if there are problems loading MaxBlast Plus in the GUI (Graphical User Interface) mode (that is, if you have video problems). The new drive must be physically installed before running MaxBlast Plus in text mode.
DG /VER	This switch allows you to see what driver version is being used. This should only be used by technicians to verify a revision.
DG /CORE	This switch will display the available core memory and open pointers to allocated memory while in the graphics mode. This should only be used by programmers to debug memory problems while executing the overlay software, and is not intended for casual use.
DG /MBR	This switch is similar to EZDRIVE /MBR—it's designed to refresh the EZ-BIOS driver on systems where the overlay MBR has been corrupted. This reinstalls EZ-BIOS in the master boot record of any drive that requires EZ-BIOS (MaxBlast).

4. From the main menu, select Advanced Options and press ENTER. At this point the Advanced Options submenu will appear.
5. Select Backup/Restore Track 0 and press ENTER.
6. Select the primary master hard drive from the drive list and press ENTER (if there is more than one drive in the system).
7. A screen will appear showing all saved backup tracks. (Tracks range from 0 to 9, with 0 being the oldest.) Select the most recent backup track and press ENTER. MaxBlast Plus will verify restoration of the boot track.
8. After restoration, remove all floppies and reboot the computer normally.
9. The system should boot normally to its operating system. If the PC does not boot correctly, reboot the system with MaxBlast and repeat the same steps, selecting the *next* subsequent backup track(s) until the system boots normally.

UNINSTALLING MAXBLAST 9.XXM

When you upgrade a system's BIOS or drive controller in order to support the drive's entire capacity, you may need to uninstall the drive overlay software. This improves drive performance slightly and reduces the potential for system conflicts with the overlay driver. Follow the steps below to remove MaxBlast 9.xxM. We will start by disabling the EZ-BIOS control.

> Before attempting this procedure, be sure to perform a complete backup of your data, and verify that your BIOS can now translate the drive's full capacity. This protects you from data loss and ensures that your drive will run at its full capacity after MaxBlast is removed.

1. Insert the MaxBlast 9.xxM bootable disk into drive A: and turn the system on.
2. During boot, the EZ-MAX window will appear on the screen. Press ENTER to continue executing MaxBlast.
3. Press ENTER twice to continue loading MaxBlast.
4. Press ENTER to accept the terms of the license agreement.
5. From the main menu, select Advanced Options and press ENTER.
6. Select EZ-BIOS Setup and press ENTER. If necessary, select the appropriate hard drive.
7. Highlight the Controlled by EZ-BIOS option and press ENTER.
8. Press the Y key and press ENTER to disable EZ-BIOS control.
9. Highlight the Exit—Save Changes option and press ENTER.

Remember that the LBA translation provided by EZ-BIOS is not always compatible with the hardware controller/BIOS IDE translation ("LBA Mode"). This means that the new hardware may be able to handle the hard drive just fine. But since the hard drive was formatted using MaxBlast 9.xxM, the LBA Mode may be slightly different—possibly enough to render the data inaccessible on the drive. The following will test whether the EZ-BIOS LBA Mode is compatible with the new hardware's LBA Mode. It's time to uninstall the EZ-BIOS software:

1. Boot the system from the MaxBlast 9.xxM bootable disk and run EZ-DRIVE.
2. From the main menu, select Advanced Options and press ENTER.
3. Select EZ-BIOS Setup and press ENTER. Select the appropriate hard drive from the displayed drive list if necessary.
4. Highlight Uninstall EZ-BIOS and press ENTER.
5. Type Y and press ENTER to uninstall the EZ-BIOS.
6. Press ESC to return to the Advanced Options menu.
7. Highlight Exit This Menu and press ENTER.
8. Remove the MaxBlast disk and reboot the system normally. The system is now under control of the new hardware controller/BIOS.

You must repeat this process on the primary master device (Drive 0) if MaxBlast was initially removed from Drive 1 (primary slave), Drive 2 (secondary master), or Drive 3 (secondary slave).

MAXBLAST SYMPTOMS

SYMPTOM 33-1 **You find that MaxBlast produces a "Config Error"** This error is known to occur in some system configurations with MaxBlast Plus (versions 1.0 and 1.1) and is generally caused by compatibility issues between the system and the MaxBlast graphics mode. You can try either of the solutions outlined below:

- *Use the text mode.* Clean boot the PC with a DOS, Windows 95, or Windows 98 system disk. At the A: prompt, type **DG TEXT** and press ENTER. This will allow you to install MaxBlast Plus in nongraphical mode.
- *Update your version of MaxBlast.* A newer version of MaxBlast may overcome some compatibility issues, so download the latest version of MaxBlast from the Maxtor Web site (**www.maxtor.com**).

SYMPTOM 33-2 When booting, you see a "NO PT" or "PT Error" generated by MaxBlast In virtually all cases, this error is caused by a fault in the partition table (or MBR). To correct this problem, you'll need to use the procedures in the "Restoring an MBR Using MaxBlast" section earlier in the chapter to restore the MaxBlast or MaxBlast Plus boot record.

SYMPTOM 33-3 You receive an error indicating an "unknown partition type on drive 1" This may happen on systems that use a diagnostic partition on the primary master drive. (Compaq PCs are notorious for this.) The installation of EZ-BIOS on the master drive when the system's BIOS does not support the new hard drive's capacity can conflict with the diagnostic partition. There are two solutions for this issue:

- Upgrade the system's BIOS to support the full capacity of the new drive so that EZ-BIOS is not needed.
- Obtain MaxBlast version 9.06M or newer. This (and newer) versions will recognize diagnostic partitions.

You may also wish to reference the section "Configuring Disk Manager with a 'Diagnostic Partition'," later in the chapter.

SYMPTOM 33-4 During installation, MaxBlast indicates that the system BIOS is not capable of handling the capacity of the new drive However, the system is brand new, and the BIOS *should* handle the full capacity of that drive. Chances are that the problem is related to your BIOS. For example, newer versions of American Megatrends (AMI) and Award BIOS use an LBA translation scheme that's slightly different from the one in MaxBlast. MaxBlast thinks the BIOS cannot handle the full capacity of the drive and wants to load EZ-BIOS. MaxBlast versions 9.00M through 9.04M exhibited this issue. To install the drive correctly there are two options: obtain MaxBlast version 9.06M (or later), or use the operating system's utilities for partitioning and formatting the hard drive.

SYMPTOM 33-5 The drive was prepared with MaxBlast, but you don't see the "EZ-BIOS Initializing" message You also cannot access the drive. If the master drive was recently formatted, or a utility was used that changes the master boot record on the master drive, EZ-BIOS *can* be restored, usually without data loss. In the MaxBlast Advanced Options menu, choose the "Backup/restore track zero" option. (See the section "Restoring an MBR Using MaxBlast" above.) In most cases, the most recently dated backup should be chosen. This should restore EZ-BIOS to the master hard drive (and, hopefully, restore access to your data).

Data Lifeguard Tools Troubleshooting

Data Lifeguard Tools is a variation of EZ-Drive that is typically distributed with Western Digital hard drives. As with most drive overlay software tools, you can use Data Lifeguard Tools to overcome BIOS limitations for your drive. For example:

- BIOS dates prior to August 1994 may not support hard drives larger than 528MB.
- BIOS dates prior to February 1996 may not support hard drives larger than 2.1GB.

33

- BIOS dates prior to January 1998 may not support hard drives larger than 8.4GB.
- Current BIOS may have trouble supporting 32GB hard drives or larger.

TIPS TO CONFIGURE THE CMOS SETUP

Before you attempt to install Data Lifeguard Tools, you should configure the drive entry(s) in your CMOS setup such that the EZ-BIOS software will interact with the drive in an optimum fashion. When you're preparing a new drive to accept Data Lifeguard Tools, the following tips may help to keep things moving smoothly:

- Enable the "LBA" or "translation" modes for your drive(s). If you do not have either option, you must either use Data Lifeguard EZ-Install to install your new hard drive, upgrade the system BIOS, or install an EIDE controller card with onboard BIOS that supports the full drive capacity.
- Select "autoconfig" or "autodetect" as the drive type. The full capacity of your drive should appear. If your system BIOS does *not* support the autoconfig or autodetect drive type, disable LBA, select "user defined," and enter 1023 cylinders, 16 heads, and 63 sectors for the drive parameters. Selecting "user defined" ensures that EZ-Install will install on your system.
- If your system BIOS does not offer support for autoconfig or "user defined," select Type 9. Selecting Type 9 ensures that EZ-BIOS will install on your system.

INSTALLING DATA LIFEGUARD TOOLS

You can use the following steps as a guideline for installing Western Digital's Data Lifeguard Tools utility:

1. Insert the Data Lifeguard Tools disk into drive A: and reboot the system.
2. The Data Lifeguard introduction screen appears. Press any key to continue.
3. From the Data Lifeguard Tools main menu, select EZ-Install, and then press ENTER.
4. The Data Lifeguard EZ-Install software Welcome screen appears. Press any key to continue.
5. The Data Lifeguard EZ-Install software license agreement appears. Press ENTER to begin installation.
6. From the Data Lifeguard EZ-Install main menu, select Fully Automatic Install to set up the hard drive.
7. In *second* hard drive installations, Data Lifeguard EZ-Install detects and displays the new Western Digital hard drive. If the selected drive is the one you want to partition and format, select Yes to set up your hard drive.
8. If appears, type Y to install EZ-BIOS and access the full capacity of the hard drive.

> The "EZ-BIOS Required" message only appears if your system BIOS does not support the full capacity of your new hard drive. If your system does support the full capacity of that new drive, verify that your settings in CMOS setup are correct.

9. Now copy your system files. If the hard drive is the only drive in the system, locate the Copy System Files screen, and then insert a DOS system disk or a Windows 95/98 startup disk. It's important to use the same version of the operating system that you're planning to install after using Data Lifeguard EZ-Install. Press ENTER to continue the setup. When the hard drive is the second drive in the system, select Copy System Files to make the hard drive bootable.

10 For FAT32 partitions, select Yes to accept the FAT32 partition, or select No to use multiple FAT16 partitions, and then press ENTER. Select Use This Partition Size to accept the default partition sizes, or select Enter New Partition Sizes to create custom partitions.

11 For FAT16 partitions, locate the Partition and Format display. Select Use These Partition Sizes to accept the default partition sizes, or select Enter New Partition Sizes to create custom partitions (up to 2GB each).

12 Select Continue Setup to have EZ-Install set up the hard drive.

13 When the installation process concludes, your hard drive should now be partitioned, formatted, and ready for use. When the Hard Drive Setup Complete screen appears, remove the disk from the floppy drive and press ESC to reboot the system. If this was a single hard drive installation, you're now ready to install the operating system.

CONVERTING DISK MANAGER PARTITIONS TO EZ-BIOS PARTITIONS

If you have a version of Ontrack's Disk Manager installed on your system, you can convert your existing Disk Manager partitions into EZ-BIOS partitions that are compatible with Data Lifeguard Tools without the need to repartition or reformat your drive.

> Even though EZ-BIOS should convert Ontrack's Disk Manager partitions to EZ-BIOS partitions without data loss, be sure to back up your existing hard drive(s) before beginning the conversion process.

1 Place the Data Lifeguard Tools disk in drive A: and reboot the computer.

2 After Data Lifeguard Tools loads, choose the **EZ-Install** option.

3 From the next menu, select **Advanced Options**, and then select **EZ-BIOS Setup**.

4 EZ-BIOS displays the following message:

```
This drive does not have EZ-BIOS installed
Press Y to install EZ-BIOS now
```

5 Press Y. Then EZ-BIOS displays the following message:

```
EZ-BIOS has detected a drive with Disk Manager installed
Since Disk Manager is not compatible with EZ-BIOS, you may not setup
any drive
until Disk Manager is removed
Press Y to replace Disk Manager with EZ-BIOS
```

6 Press Y, and EZ-BIOS displays the following message:

```
Disk Manager replaced with EZ-BIOS
```

7 Exit EZ-BIOS, and then remove the Data Lifeguard Tools disk from the floppy drive. (The system will reboot.) EZ-BIOS will now load instead of Disk Manager.

USING DATA LIFEGUARD TOOLS WITH COMPAQ "DIAGNOSTIC PARTITIONS"

The Data Lifeguard Tools version of EZ-BIOS now supports Compaq systems that have the personal diagnostic software preinstalled onto the hard drive (this diagnostic software is used for diagnostic testing and system setup). The software resides in a special partition on the Compaq's hard drive and is accessed by pressing a key during the computer's boot sequence. Current versions of EZ-BIOS can coexist with these diagnostic partitions *only* when installed in a two-drive system (master/slave). This will also work when Data Lifeguard Tools is used to transfer data from an existing hard drive with the diagnostic partition to another hard drive. (The existing hard drive can then be removed without affecting access to the diagnostic partition on the new hard drive.) If EZ-BIOS is installed in a single-drive system, it will overwrite Compaq's code, preventing access to the diagnostic partition. If you'd like to read more about installing a drive in a Compaq system, check the Western Digital Web site at **http://www.westerndigital.com/service/tip_dir/tip0399.html**.

REMOVING DATA LIFEGUARD TOOLS (EZ-BIOS)

You may need to remove Data Lifeguard Tools when upgrading the system's support for large hard drives. If your BIOS can translate your HDD(s) the same way EZ-BIOS does, then you can remove Data Lifeguard Tools without losing any of your data.

1. Insert the Data Lifeguard Tools disk in drive A:, and then reboot the system.
2. Once you've booted to the disk, choose EZ-Install from the menu.
3. From the next menu, select Advanced Options, and then select the EZ-BIOS Setup option.
4. Highlight Controlled by EZ-BIOS and press ENTER to toggle the selection to Disabled. (If EZ-BIOS displays the message "Your ROM BIOS is not set up to correctly handle this drive," see the note below.)
5. Select Exit—Save Changes and exit EZ-BIOS. Your system will now reboot.
6. Verify that the hard drive boots properly and that your data is accessible.
7. If so, reboot the system again with the Data Lifeguard Tools disk in drive A:, and again choose EZ-Install.
8. From the next menu, select Advanced Options, and then select EZ-BIOS Setup.
9. Select Uninstall EZ-BIOS and press ENTER. EZ-BIOS will display the following message:

```
Be absolutely sure that your BIOS can access all of the drives
correctly before uninstalling EZ-BIOS

Press Y if you really want to uninstall EZ-BIOS
Press ESC to cancel uninstalling EZ-BIOS
```

10. Press Y to uninstall EZ-BIOS. EZ-BIOS will display the message:

```
EZ-BIOS has been removed from drive 1
```

11. Press any key to continue, and then exit Data Lifeguard Tools. EZ-BIOS has now been uninstalled.

If your drive/directories are not accessible after EZ-BIOS is removed from the drive, the BIOS translation is different from the translation EZ-BIOS used. In this case, enter your BIOS setup and disable LBA translation. Leave the drive parameters as they are. Boot to the Data Lifeguard Tools disk, go to the EZ-Install menu, and have EZ-BIOS regain control of the drive. Back up your data, reboot to a floppy, and run FDISK /MBR. Repartition and format the drive using FDISK and FORMAT, and then restore your data.

DATA LIFEGUARD TOOLS SYMPTOMS

SYMPTOM 33-6 You cannot use Data Lifeguard Tools version of EZ-BIOS with System Commander In virtually all cases, the problem is an incompatibility between Data Lifeguard Tools and an older version of System Commander. You must use System Commander Deluxe version 4.01 (or higher), which has support for EZ-BIOS. (Version 4.0 will overwrite the EZ-BIOS code on the hard drive.) A patch that updates 4.0 to 4.01 can be downloaded from the V Communications Web site.

SYMPTOM 33-7 The Data Lifeguard Tools disk doesn't boot You see a message such as "Non-system disk or disk error." Reboot your computer to a DOS system disk or a Windows 95/98 startup disk. When the DOS prompt appears, insert your Data Lifeguard Tools disk into drive A:, type DLG**,** and press ENTER. This will start Data Lifeguard Tools manually.

SYMPTOM 33-8 When installing Data Lifeguard Tools, you see a message such as "No IDE drives identified" First, turn off your system power, and then check the IDE interface cable(s) and power supply cable(s). Next, verify that the hard drive is configured properly in the CMOS setup. Normally, Data Lifeguard Tools can still identify an IDE drive with nothing set in the BIOS (CMOS setup), but occasionally Data Lifeguard Tools will report "No IDE hard drives identified," even though a drive is present. If the CMOS setup has no values for the drive, it may inhibit the setup process. If this is the case, select an "autoconfig" or "autodetect" drive type. (The full capacity of your drive should display.)

Otherwise, select a "user defined" drive type and enter 1023 cylinders, 16 heads, and 63 sectors for the drive parameters. If your system BIOS does not have a "user defined" drive type, select Type 9. Even though these are not the actual parameters of the hard drive, Data Lifeguard Tools will be able to detect the drive and configure it correctly.

SYMPTOM 33-9 You cannot create partitions larger than 2.1GB with Data Lifeguard Tools Data Lifeguard Tools will allow you to partition huge HDDs as a single partition, but *only* if the software detects system files that support the FAT32 file system (Windows 95 OSR2 or Windows 98). If system files that do not support FAT32 are detected, partitioning will be restricted to the FAT16 limitation of 2.1GB per partition. This means you'll need to create more than one partition on drives larger than 2.1GB.

SYMPTOM 33-10 After creating custom partition sizes, the primary partition is slightly smaller than you expected This is a Data Lifeguard Tools issue—partitions must begin on a cylinder boundary. To start a partition on a cylinder boundary, utilities such as Data Lifeguard Tools and FDISK create a primary partition that may be a few MB *smaller* than the size you entered. Both Data Lifeguard Tools and FDISK add these megabytes to your next partition, so you don't lose any space.

SYMPTOM 33-11 EZ-BIOS doesn't load after booting from a nonsystem floppy disk If you turn on the machine with a disk (that does not contain bootable system files) in the floppy drive, the message "Non-system disk or disk error" appears on the display. If you remove the floppy disk and reboot the system, EZ-BIOS will no longer load, and the computer hangs. In all cases, this error has been linked to a virus on the floppy disk that infects the hard drive and overwrites EZ-BIOS. The following procedure will restore EZ-BIOS to the drive:

1. Boot directly from a write-protected bootable floppy disk to the DOS prompt.
2. Insert the write-protected Data Lifeguard Tools disk.

3. Type **DLGEZ /MBR** and press ENTER.
4. Remove the Data Lifeguard Tools floppy disk and reboot the computer. EZ-BIOS should load normally.
5. Run a current version of virus-scan software on your hard drive and floppy disks.

SYMPTOM 33-12 **You ran a program that hung the PC, and now the system hangs at "EZ-BIOS Initializing"** In almost every case, the program that originally crashed your system has damaged the EZ-BIOS master boot record (MBR). You should be able to restore the MBR without losing any data. Boot the system to DOS from a bootable floppy disk, and then insert the Data Lifeguard Tools program disk in drive A:. Type **DLGEZ /MBR** at the A: prompt and press ENTER. This will rewrite the EZ-BIOS MBR code and keep your data intact.

SYMPTOM 33-13 **Your antivirus program detects a virus in the EZ-BIOS master boot record (MBR), but the drive seems to run fine** Chances are that your antivirus program has mistakenly identified your EZ-BIOS code as a virus. Do not allow the antivirus program to remove or clean the "virus" in the MBR. If EZ-BIOS is removed, you will lose large hard drive support (and lose access to your data). Your best solution is to update your antivirus tool to a version that recognizes EZ-BIOS, or ignore the virus warning.

Disk Manager Troubleshooting

Ontrack's Disk Manager is a utility that partitions and formats a hard drive, and allows you to access the full capacity of the drive (even when your system BIOS is unable to do so). Current versions of Disk Manager are fully compatible with 32-bit disk and file access under Windows 95/98. The Disk Manager driver is loaded from the master boot record (MBR) when the drive is set up as a primary (master) drive. When the drive is set up as a secondary (slave) drive, Disk Manager is called by the CONFIG.SYS file.

UNINSTALLING DISK MANAGER 9.X, 7.X, AND 6.X

When a system BIOS is replaced or a drive controller is updated to support the full capacity of a drive, it may be necessary to uninstall Disk Manager. Normally, you cannot remove Disk Manager by repartitioning and reformatting the drive, so you'll need to remove the software using a step-by-step procedure. Remember to back up your data before attempting this procedure, because removing the partition information will render your drive inaccessible. Disk Manager 9.x is one of the latest versions of the software that can be uninstalled using the following steps.

> The uninstall process with Disk Manager 9.x can often be conducted without the loss of data. Older versions of Disk Manager will not preserve your data.

1. First, you *must* have a BIOS that can translate the drive's full capacity.
2. You must have a "clean," write-protected DOS bootable disk containing FDISK.EXE, SYS.COM, and FORMAT.COM.
3. You must also have your version of Disk Manager on a disk.
4. Remember to back up all of the data on your drive.

5 Boot the system to your CMOS setup, set the Type to Auto, and set the Mode to LBA.
6 Boot the clean DOS disk to the A: prompt.
7 Insert the Disk Manager disk and type **DM**.
8 Choose Advanced Options, choose Maintenance Options, and then choose the Dynamic Drive Overlay option.
9 Choose the Remove Dynamic Drive Overlay option.
10 At this point, Disk Manager will inform you whether this process will be data destructive. If you receive a large red box informing you that you'll lose access to the data, cancel the operation. This means your BIOS is not translating the drive the same as Disk Manager is.
11 If your BIOS *can* translate the drive, choose the Quick Uninstall feature.
12 The BIOS Standard Uninstall will finish its process.

You can remove Disk Manager 7.x with the following process:

1 Remember to back up all of the data on your drive.
2 Insert a clean bootable DOS disk (without AUTOEXEC.BAT or CONFIG.SYS files) in drive A:.
3 Turn on your computer and allow it to boot from the floppy.
4 At the A: prompt, switch to the Disk Manager software disk and type **DM**.
5 From the Select An Installation Option menu, select Maintenance Menu.
6 Select Uninstall Disk Manager and allow the process to finish.

33

The procedure for removing Disk Manager 6.x is a little more involved, but you can use the steps below:

1 Remember to back up all of the data on your drive.
2 Insert a clean bootable DOS disk (without AUTOEXEC.BAT or CONFIG.SYS files), which contains FDISK.
3 Turn on your computer and boot to the CMOS setup.
4 Check the CMOS settings and make sure the boot order is set to "A: then C:." Then set up the drive entries to "autodetect," and select Logical Block Addressing (LBA) or "translation" mode (if available).
5 Reboot and allow the system to boot to the A: drive.
6 After booting to an A: prompt, type **fdisk /mbr** and press ENTER.
7 You'll return to the A: prompt.
8 Type **fdisk** and press ENTER.
9 Select the "Delete partitions" option.
10 Select the "Delete non-DOS partition" option.
11 Create a new Primary DOS or Extended DOS partition.
12 You may then format the new partition(s) and reinstall your data.

UNIVERSALLY DELETING DISK MANAGER

To remove Disk Manager from your drive, boot from a clean floppy (no AUTOEXEC.BAT or CONFIG.SYS). Run the FDISK command, delete the non-DOS partition, and then run the DOS FORMAT command. The Dynamic Drive Overlay (DDO) will be completely removed. Remember that removing the DDO is data destructive, so you must back up your data before commencing.

CONFIGURING DISK MANAGER WITH A "DIAGNOSTIC PARTITION"

Installing Disk Manager can get a little tricky when you're dealing with a diagnostic partition. Compaq (and other) systems are typical candidates that place system setup information on a small diagnostic partition. If this partition is lost, it may not be possible to reconfigure the system.

1. You must have a clean, write-protected DOS bootable disk containing FDISK.EXE, SYS.COM, and FORMAT.COM.
2. You must also have your version of Disk Manager on a disk.
3. Run the Compaq Diagnostic and Setup software.
4. Boot to the A: prompt.
5. Run Disk Manager, such as A:\dm.exe/m.
6. Choose Edit/View Partitions and press ENTER.
7. Choose your hard drive and press ENTER.
8. In the lower-left box (on either line 1 or line 3), you should see this:

   ```
   18 (12H) 0 0 3.8
   ```

   This is the diagnostic partition.
9. Move the highlighted bar to either line 1 or 2 and press INSERT.
10. Select the DOS-FAT12/16 or DOS-FAT32 partition type and press ENTER.
11. Select Mbytes and press ENTER.
12. Press ENTER to accept the leftover space available on the drive.
13. Move the highlighted bar to "Save and Continue" and press ENTER.
14. At the Select a Disk box, press ESC.
15. Choose Format/Check Partitions and press ENTER.
16. Choose your hard drive and press ENTER.
17. Choose Format a Single Partition and press ENTER.
18. Choose the "DOS/FAT partition" and press ENTER.
19. Use the Fast Format feature.
20. Enter the desired label for the partition or press ENTER. Proceed with the format.

DISK MANAGER SYMPTOMS

SYMPTOM 33-14 You cannot boot Disk Manager from a Windows 95/98 startup disk
If you're unable to boot from a Windows 95/98 startup disk and your drive is installed using a Dynamic Drive Overlay (DDO), try making your Windows 95/98 startup disk an overlay boot disk:

1. Run Disk Manager, and then select Advanced Options, Maintenance Options, and Create Boot Diskette.
2. Choose "Make existing boot diskette an <Ontrack> Boot Diskette" to add the Dynamic Drive Overlay software (DDLOADER.BIN) to an existing Windows 95/98 startup disk.
3. As an alternative, make a copy of your Windows 95/98 startup disk by selecting "Copy bootable diskette to create an <Ontrack> Boot Diskette." The original will remain intact, and the Dynamic Drive Overlay will be added to the copied disk.
4. Reboot directly from the new Windows 95/98 startup disk (not from the hard disk) to continue the installation.

SYMPTOM 33-15 You are having difficulty installing Ontrack's Disk Manager software from the B: drive Ontrack software must be installed from the A: drive. If your A: drive is the wrong size for your Ontrack distribution disk, copy the disk to a floppy disk sized properly for drive A:, and then try reinstalling Disk Manager.

SYMPTOM 33-16 Windows 95/98 reports that the system is operating in "DOS Compatibility Mode" This type of problem is not necessarily related to Disk Manager (though older versions or poorly configured installations can cause the problem). The DOS Compatibility Mode is invoked by Windows 95/98 whenever the system loads a real-mode driver. This would happen when Windows 95/98 doesn't have an equivalent 32-bit protected-mode driver to replace a real-mode driver. Click on the Performance page under the System icon for details on what devices are causing the problem. Often, this problem is triggered when real-mode drivers for a device are loaded in CONFIG.SYS and AUTOEXEC.BAT. Try disabling any such real-mode entries, and then restart the system. If the problem persists, make sure you are using the latest protected-mode driver version for each device.

SYMPTOM 33-17 Disk Manager does not appear to function properly with Windows 95/98 In virtually all cases, you are using an older version of Disk Manager. Version 6.0 or higher is known to work with Windows 95/98. It may be necessary to download the patch file (DMPATCH.EXE) from the Ontrack Internet Web site (**www.ontrack.com**), which will update the Dynamic Drive Overlay (DDO) to 6.03d (or later).

SYMPTOM 33-18 When using Disk Manager 6.0x, Windows 95/98 reports operating in the "DOS Compatibility Mode" Although Disk Manager version 6.0x is supported by Windows 95/98, there are some factors that can keep the utility from running properly with Windows 95/98. First, be sure that the number of cylinders set for the drive under CMOS setup is 1024 or less. There are often "translation geometries" available from the drive maker that provide alternate entries for heads, sectors, cylinders, and so on.

Next, be sure that any 32-bit disk access drivers (such as WDCDRV.386) loaded in the Windows 3.1x SYSTEM.INI file are disabled prior to installing Windows 95/98 in the first place. Otherwise, you will need to edit the [386Enh] portion of your SYSTEM.INI file and disable 32-bit disk access by inserting a semicolon before the driver entry, such as:

```
;32Bit DiskAccess=On
```

You could also simply change On to Off on this line. Windows 95/98 provides its own 32-bit protected-mode drivers for support of your IDE drives. Finally, check once again to be sure that you are in fact using the latest version of Disk Manager. If not, you can download the 6.03 patch file (DMPATCH.EXE), or later version, from the Ontrack Internet Web site.

SYMPTOM 33-19 You encounter trouble with the disk driver (such as WDCDRV.386) for 32-bit disk access in Windows 95/98 Don't use any third-party disk drivers under Windows 95/98, which provides its own native IDE protected-mode drivers. If there are still references to third-party disk drivers in SYSTEM.INI, you will need to edit out those references manually.

SYMPTOM 33-20 When installing a new, large drive (and reinstalling Disk Manager to the new drive), you encounter errors with cluster sizes In virtually all cases, you are using an older version of Disk Manager that does not support cluster sizes over 8KB. Be sure to obtain the very latest version of Disk Manager, which will support larger cluster sizes.

SYMPTOM 33-21 Disk Manager fails to identify the hard drive correctly Some OEM versions of Disk Manager (such as the version distributed by Western Digital) check for the presence of a particular hard drive. Disk Manager starts by sending a query to the drive. If the response is anything other than the expected ID, Disk Manager will produce an error message. Some sophisticated IDE cards will intercept queries and commands sent to the drive. This will cause Disk Manager to believe there is no expected drive, even if there is. To avoid this problem, you should try to disable the BIOS on your controller, or format the drive using another controller card (or use a generic commercial version of Disk Manager).

SYMPTOM 33-22 You have problems removing Disk Manager Disk Manager installs itself in the master boot record (MBR) of your primary (master) hard drive. To eliminate Disk Manager, you simply need to boot from a bootable disk, repartition the hard drive with FDISK, and then reformat the drive. Keep in mind that this process is destructive to your data. Be sure to perform a complete backup of the drive before proceeding.

SYMPTOM 33-23 You find "Out of disk space" errors after loading as little as 800MB of data onto a 1GB drive This is not a direct effect of Disk Manager (though it may appear so). In reality, you are seeing a limitation of the FAT 16 (DOS) file allocation system that is based in clusters. In DOS, every file that is stored gets at least one cluster (or "allocation unit") no matter what the size of the file is. The size of the cluster grows incrementally with the size of the partition. For example, if you have a 1.08GB partition, the cluster size will be 32KB. This means that even a 62-byte batch file is going to consume 32KB of storage space. (The difference between the 32KB cluster size and the 62 bytes that the file really needs is called *slack space*.) The only feasible way to reduce the cluster size is to reduce the partition size. To utilize drives larger than 2.1GB under FAT 16, you need to create additional partitions.

SYMPTOM 33-24 Disk Manager appears to conflict with other programs in conventional memory The Dynamic Drive Overlay (DDO) used by Disk Manager first loads into conventional memory, where it takes 6KB. It then moves into 4KB of upper memory. When the program code leaves conventional memory, it leaves a 62-byte "footprint" at the top of conventional memory. This footprint can sometimes conflict with other programs. You may have to change the way Disk Manager loads. During the boot process, when you see the message that tells you to press the SPACEBAR to boot from a floppy disk, press the S key instead, and then press Y in answer to the next question. This will cause Disk Manager to stay in conventional memory rather than moving to high memory, and may resolve the conflict you are experiencing.

If this does resolve the problem, there is a special version of Disk Manager (LOADLOW.ZIP) that you can use to avoid having to press the S key every time you boot. You can obtain the file from the Ontrack BBS at (612)-937-0860, or from the Ontrack Internet Web site (**www.ontrack.com**).

SYMPTOM 33-25 Disk Manager installed properly and responded as expected, but after installing DOS 6.2, the drive ended up at 504MB To install DOS properly, you must load the Dynamic Drive Overlay (DDO) before running the DOS installation floppy. Start by booting from the hard drive. When you see the message "Press spacebar to boot from diskette," press the SPACEBAR, insert the DOS startup disk, and press any key to continue. The boot process will proceed from the floppy, but the DDO will have had a chance to load into memory first. The partitions will now make sense, so the DOS installation will not overwrite the partition information.

SYMPTOM 33-26 Disk Manager installed and ran properly, but now you get a "DDO Integrity Error" and cannot access the hard drive This is a very serious error that indicates the hard drive sector containing the DDO (Dynamic Drive Overlay) information has become corrupted. Such problems can be caused by:

- Infection by a boot or partition sector virus. (Boot from a clean DOS disk and run virus-scan software.)
- A power surge.
- A hardware failure (usually the controller card).
- Shutting the computer down in the middle of a write process.

Unfortunately, there is little that can be done to correct the problem. If a virus is found and eliminated, you can reinstall Disk Manager. If hardware is at fault, you will have to replace the hardware. In either case, any data on the drive that is not backed up will be lost.

SYMPTOM 33-27 You can only get 16-bit file access on the secondary (slave) drive formatted with Disk Manager When Disk Manager is used to format the primary (master) drive, the DDO is loaded during the boot process. In this situation, there is no "device=dmdrvr.bin" line in the CONFIG.SYS file. When Disk Manager is used to prepare the secondary (slave) drive and the primary drive was prepared without Disk Manager, there will be a driver loaded in the CONFIG.SYS file, and the DDO is loaded differently. It is this difference in how the DDO is loaded that is causing the 16-bit file access on the secondary drive. The only solution here is to back up all the data on the primary drive and prepare it with Disk Manager. This causes the DDO to be loaded during the boot process and allows 32-bit file access on both drives.

33

SYMPTOM 33-28 Drive letters are all switched around when booting from a bootable disk DOS allocates drive letters every time you boot. It starts on cylinder 1, then goes on to subsequent cylinders, looking first for primary DOS partitions and then for DOS extended partitions. When this allocation is complete, DOS then proceeds to allocate drive letters as requested by drivers loaded in CONFIG.SYS (CD-ROMs, hardcards, etc.).

When you boot from a hard drive, the DDO is loaded before DOS. This means that when DOS looks at cylinder 1, it can identify that primary DOS partition and assigns it to C:. It then goes to the second drive and allocates D:. When you boot from a floppy, the driver line in CONFIG.SYS (the DMDRVR.BIN file) starts the DDO—but not until after DOS has already assigned drive letters. Because the DDO wasn't in memory when it looked at cylinder 1, it did not see that partition. It did see the partition on the non-Disk Manager cylinder, and that became C:. When CONFIG.SYS loaded the driver that started the DDO and asked for drive letters, DOS saw the partition on cylinder 1 and gave it the next drive letter—D:.

An easy way to avoid this problem is to start the boot from the hard drive. When you see the "Press spacebar to boot from diskette" message, press the SPACEBAR to halt the boot process and insert your boot floppy. The boot will continue on the floppy, but DDO will have loaded and the drive letters will be allocated as usual.

SYMPTOM 33-29 You have trouble creating a floppy so that you can boot from a disk and still have the DDO load You should insert a floppy disk and use the DMCFIG utility, such as:

```
DMCFIG /d=a:
```

You will need to answer a series of questions as DMCFIG runs.

SYMPTOM 33-30 You encounter problems using certain utilities on your hard drive Generally speaking, utilities that use interrupt 13 for communicating with drive hardware will be compatible with Disk Manager. Utilities that attempt to communicate with drive hardware directly may encounter some problems and data corruption. Be suspicious of any disk utility that claims high performance by communicating directly with drive hardware.

EZ-Drive Troubleshooting

EZ-Drive is very similar in nature to Disk Manager. It provides large-drive support for older BIOS. It also works around problems with BIOS versions that hang on drives larger than 2.1GB. As with Disk Manager, however, EZ-Drive also suffers from its share of problems under the right conditions.

SYMPTOM 33-31 EZ-Drive refuses to work properly with the system's VLB IDE controller EZ-Drive has a number of compatibility problems with some VL bus drive controllers. Fortunately, there is a work-around in most cases:

- **Appian ADI2** This is fully compatible. The HVLIDE.SYS driver is fully compatible with EZ-Drive. The ADI2C143.SYS driver is also fully compatible with EZ-Drive. Install EZ-Drive, and then install one of these drivers in your CONFIG.SYS file.
- **CMD640x** This is fully compatible. The CMD640X.SYS driver is fully compatible with EZ-Drive. Install EZ-Drive, and then install the driver in your CONFIG.SYS file.

- **PC Tech RZ1000** This is not supported. The ZEOS/Phoenix BIOS does not need EZ-Drive, as it natively supports large drives. If EZ-Drive sets up a large drive, it will take over from the BIOS, and the drive will be slower than with native BIOS support. Set up the drive through BIOS and not EZ-Drive.
- **Opti 611A and 621A** This is not supported by any product or hardware. The OPTIVIC.SYS driver (dated 5-11-94) is incompatible with large drives—with and without EZ-Drive. An updated driver is under development by Opti.

SYMPTOM 33-32 The keyboard or mouse does not function normally after exiting Windows on an EZ-Drive system This is almost always due to a problem with the mouse driver installation. Some mouse drivers change a line in the SYSTEM.INI file to

```
Keyboard=C:\MOUSE\mousevkd.386
```

To correct the problem, change that line in the SYSTEM.INI file back to

```
Keyboard=*vkd
```

SYMPTOM 33-33 With EZ-Drive installed on the system, QEMM 7.5 will not load in Stealth mode This is often a problem with QEMM related to the way in which QEMM processes software interrupt 76. Add the following switch to the QEMM command line in CONFIG.SYS, which will force QEMM to ignore software interrupt 76:

```
XSTI=76
```

SYMPTOM 33-34 Windows crashes with EZ-Drive installed on your drive This problem has been reported on systems using Award BIOS version 4.50G. A patch file is available from MicroHouse (EZPCH502.EXE) that can update the EZ-Drive MBR. You can download the patch file from the MicroHouse BBS at (303)-443-9957 or from the Web (**www.microhouse.com**).

SYMPTOM 33-35 You have trouble removing EZ-Drive from the system You will need to rewrite the drive's master boot record (MBR). Disable any BIOS MBR virus protection that may be enabled through the CMOS setup. Boot the system from a floppy disk containing FDISK, and then run FDISK /MBR. This will overwrite the MBR and effectively remove EZ-Drive.

> The FDISK /MBR command is very powerful, and data on the drive may be lost. Be sure to make a complete backup of the drive's contents before performing this procedure.

SYMPTOM 33-36 You see an error message such as "No IDE Drive Installed" EZ-Drive may not be reading the particular drive properly. Normally, EZ-Drive identifies an IDE drive, even though the CMOS setup may have no drive geometry information entered (or set to autodetect). Occasionally, EZ-Drive reports that no IDE drive is installed, even when a drive is present. If CMOS has no values for the drive, it may inhibit the EZ-Drive setup. You should simply run the autodetect feature of the BIOS before running EZ-Drive. A more reliable solution is to insert the proper drive parameters into the CMOS setup (heads, cylinders, sectors, etc.).

SYMPTOM 33-37 **You have trouble removing EZ-Drive from a system with available LBA support** There are actually two methods you can use to eliminate EZ-Drive from an LBA-compatible system. Before attempting either of these methods, make sure you are using EZ-Drive 5.00 or later. Here is the first method:

1. Insert the EZ-Drive disk.
2. Run EZ.
3. Pick Change Installed features.
4. Enable Windows NT Compatibility Mode for 5.00.

The second method is as follows:

1. Disable Floppy Boot Protection for EZ 5.02 and later.
2. Pick Save Changes.
3. Exit EZ-Drive.
4. Boot the system and enter CMOS setup.
5. Autodetect the hard drive or enter cylinders, sector, and heads under User Definable Type.
6. Enable LBA mode.
7. Save your changes and exit CMOS setup.
8. Boot the system from a bootable floppy disk (bypassing EZ-Drive).
9. If all drives/directories are accessible, run the command FDISK /MBR to remove the EZ-Drive MBR.
10. If all drives/directories are not accessible, the BIOS LBA translation is different from the translation EZ-Drive used. (In this case, the data must be backed up before proceeding.)
11. Boot directly from a floppy disk, run FDISK /MBR, and then repartition the drive with FDISK. Format the drive using FORMAT, and then restore your data.

> The FDISK /MBR command is very powerful, and data on the drive may be lost. Be sure to make a complete backup of the drive's contents before performing this procedure.

SYMPTOM 33-38 **You keep getting the message "Hold down the CTRL key..."** In virtually all cases, the system has been infected with the "Ripper" virus. To correct the problem, try the procedures below. (You will need EZ-Drive 5.00 or later.)

1. Boot directly from a floppy disk.
2. Insert the EZ-Drive disk.
3. Type **EZ /MBR** and press ENTER.
4. Run EZ.
5. Pick Change Installed features.
6. Enable Windows NT Compatibility Mode for 5.00.

Or you can follow these steps:

1. Disable Floppy Boot Protection for EZ 5.02 and later.
2. Pick Save Changes.
3. Run virus scan software.

SYMPTOM 33-39 **The system hangs after booting directly from a nonsystem disk** A user turns on the machine with a disk in the floppy drive that does not contain bootable system files. The message "Non System Disk or Disk Error" is displayed on the screen. After the user removes the floppy and reboots the system, it hangs and will not boot. All cases of this error have been linked to the "Antiexe" virus. To correct the problem, try the procedures below. (You will need EZ-Drive 5.00 or later.)

1. Boot directly from a floppy disk.
2. Insert the EZ-Drive disk.
3. Type **EZ/MBR** and press ENTER.
4. Run EZ.
5. Pick Change Installed features.
6. Enable Windows NT Compatibility Mode for 5.00.

Or you can follow these steps:

1. Disable Floppy Boot Protection for EZ 5.02 and later.
2. Pick Save Changes.
3. Run virus scan software.

33

SYMPTOM 33-40 **You encounter an "Unrecognized DBR" message from EZ-Drive** An unrecognized Disk Boot Record (DBR) message may mean that the DBR on the floppy disk has been corrupted or simply is not one that is easily recognized by the program (for example, a language-specific version of DOS). If the DBR is on a bootable floppy someone else has created, the first recommendation is to abort the boot process and SYS the disk again, such as:

```
C:\> SYS a:
```

If the DBR is on a DOS disk like DOS Disk1, answer yes to complete the system transfer. If the hard drive refuses to boot with a "Non-System Disk Error," reset the system and hold down the SPACEBAR. Insert a bootable floppy when prompted and press a key to get to an A: prompt. Then SYS the hard drive to transfer the bootable files. At that point, the hard drive should be able to boot without any problems.

SYMPTOM 33-41 **You cannot get EZ-Drive to work on some PS/1 and PS/2 systems** EZ-Drive will not work on microchannel PCs.

SYMPTOM 33-42 **Windows 95 reports a problem with the MH32BIT.386 driver** The MH32BIT.386 driver should not be used with Windows 95, which already has all the support needed for EZ-Drive. Open the SYSTEM.INI file and comment out any references to the MH32BIT.386 driver.

SYMPTOM 33-43 **After removing EZ-Drive, the data on a hard drive is inaccessible** That is because (1) the drive controller does not support large hard drives, or (2) the drive geometry entered into CMOS setup is different from the configuration EZ-Drive had used. If the drive system does not support large hard drives, you must upgrade the drive controller or motherboard BIOS to support EIDE drives. If the drive system already supports EIDE, check the drive parameters entered in CMOS setup, or try using the autodetect feature in CMOS. If both of these options fail, you will need to repartition and reformat the drive, then restore the drive files from a backup.

SYMPTOM 33-44 **The ALT+T function was accidentally invoked under Disk Manager, and the DDO could not be recovered through EZ-Drive** Unfortunately, once the partition data on the first cylinder is wiped out, it cannot be recovered. You will have to reinstall the Dynamic Drive Overlay (DDO) and restore the drive files from a backup.

Drive Rocket Troubleshooting

Unlike Disk Manager or EZ-Drive, which allow a system to use EIDE/UDMA hard drives, Ontrack's Drive Rocket is disk enhancement software that allows an IDE drive to transfer data in large "chunks." This speeds the transfer of data and improves drive performance. Today's hard drives allow for very fast and efficient data transfer, so Drive Rocket is no longer in popular use, but older systems and drives may still utilize Drive Rocket.

SYMPTOM 33-45 **When running Drive Rocket, the QEMM Stealth ROM feature indicates "Disabling Stealth ROM" and then reports a reference to INT 76** The Stealth ROM feature is monitoring interrupts and is disabling itself when Drive Rocket uses INT 13. You can disable the interrupt detection by adding the XSTI switch to the QEMM386 command line, such as:

```
XSTI=76
```

This switch forces QEMM's Stealth mode to ignore INT 76.

SYMPTOM 33-46 **During installation, Drive Rocket produces an error that says it can't recognize the driver** There are some machines that simply will not support the Drive Rocket software because of the way Drive Rocket interacts with PC hardware. Do not manually override a failed installation. Specific areas where Drive Rocket might fail are on machines that already have a number of performance enhancements in place (such as a Pentium with PCI, LBA, or some other technology that is translating the drive parameters). When you see such an error, do not proceed with the Drive Rocket installation.

SYMPTOM 33-47 **You cannot remove Drive Rocket** Drive Rocket is called as a command line in CONFIG.SYS, such as:

```
device=rocket.bin
```

To remove Drive Rocket, simply disable the command line. You should also delete the ROCKET.BIN file from the hard drive's root directory.

SYMPTOM 33-48 **Drive Rocket refuses to identify the hard drive correctly** Some OEM versions of Drive Rocket (such as the version distributed by Western Digital) check for the presence of a particular hard drive. Drive Rocket starts by sending a query to the drive. If the response is anything other than the expected ID, Drive Rocket will produce an error message. Some sophisticated IDE cards will intercept queries and commands sent to the drive. This will cause Drive Rocket to believe there is no expected drive, even if there is. You should try to disable the BIOS on your controller, or format the drive using another controller card to avoid this problem. You could also install a non-OEM version of Drive Rocket.

SYMPTOM 33-49 **You have trouble loading Drive Rocket into high memory** Ideally, Drive Rocket can be loaded into the upper memory area (UMA). However, there are reports of problems with the QEMM LOADHI statement loading Drive Rocket. Try using a different memory manager, such as EMM386, or try loading other drivers into the UMA to free space in conventional memory for Drive Rocket.

SYMPTOM 33-50 **Drive Rocket reports a –35 percent increase** This typically occurs in contemporary, high-performance systems. It means that Drive Rocket is conflicting with some other driver or device and is probably not a good choice for that particular computer. Remove the Drive Rocket command line from CONFIG.SYS, and delete ROCKET.BIN from the root directory.

SYMPTOM 33-51 **You encounter a GPF when working with the Control Panel in Windows 3.1x** You need to define the drives that contain Drive Rocket. Add a command-line switch to the end of the line in CONFIG.SYS that calls the Drive Rocket driver. Add the following switch if Drive Rocket is on a primary and secondary drive:

```
/w=1,1
```

If Drive Rocket is only on the primary drive, use the command

```
/w=1,
```

If Drive Rocket is only on the secondary drive, use the command

```
/w=,1
```

Further Study

MicroHouse: **http://www.microhouse.com**

Ontrack: **http://www.ontrack.com**

Download MaxBlast: **ftp://ftp.maxtor.com/pub/main/MAXBLAST.EXE**

Download WD Data Lifeguard Tools: **http://www.wdc.com/service/ftp/dlgtools/dlgt22.exe**

33

34

PARALLEL PORT TROUBLESHOOTING

CHAPTER AT A GLANCE

Even after more than a decade of intense computer development, the *parallel port* (also called the *LPT port*, *Centronics port*, or *printer port*) remains one of the fastest and most reliable printer connection techniques in the computer industry. By sending an entire byte of data from computer to printer port simultaneously, and managing the flow of data with discrete handshaking signals, the circuitry required to bundle and decode data and control signals (such as that needed by serial ports) is virtually eliminated. The longevity of parallel ports has been due largely to the their simplicity and good overall performance, but today's parallel ports are not invulnerable to failure. Cable problems, static discharge damage, and spontaneous IC faults can easily disable printer communication. Additional parallel port problems can arise from the new generation of high-performance printers and other parallel port devices. This chapter explains the pinout and operation of conventional parallel ports, explains the advances that have taken place, and presents a series of troubleshooting procedures intended to help you isolate and correct port problems.

Understanding the Parallel Port

The parallel port interface is one of the simplest and most straightforward circuits that you will encounter in a PC. Figure 34-1 illustrates a typical bi-directional port. A parallel port is composed of three separate

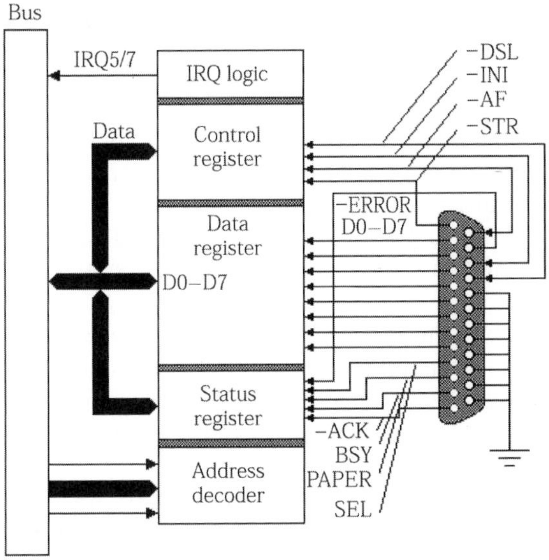

FIGURE 34-1 Block diagram of a bi-directional parallel port

registers: the data register, the status register, and the control register. Address bits A0 to A9 are decoded to determine which of the three registers are active. The use of -I/OR (-I/O Read) and -I/OW (-I/O Write) lines determine whether signals on the data bus (D0 to D7) are being read from or written to the respective register. When the port is ready to accept another character, handshaking line conditions will trigger an interrupt to request a new character.

The heart of a parallel port is the *data register*. In older PCs, the data register could only be written to (which renders the port unidirectional). But virtually all PCs since the release of i386 systems provide data registers that can be read *and* written to (which makes the port bi-directional). To access a printer, the system CPU simply loads the port data register with the value to be passed. The bi-directional *control register* manages the behavior of the port and sets the conditions under which new characters are requested from the CPU. For example, the control register is typically set up to generate an interrupt whenever the printer is ready to accept another character (for instance, IRQ7 for LPT1 and IRQ5 for LPT2). Finally, the *status register* is read to determine the printer's status (extracted from the logic conditions of several printer handshaking lines). All that remains is the port connector itself, which is a female 25-pin sub-miniature D-type connector.

ADDRESSES AND INTERRUPTS

As previously mentioned, the conventional parallel port in a PC is implemented through a series of three registers—one register simply buffers the 8 data bits while the other two registers handle the port's handshaking lines. While older BIOS versions supported only two or three parallel ports, today's PCs use BIOS written to support up to four complete parallel ports, designated LPT1, LPT2, LPT3, and LPT4. The base addresses allocated for each port are 0378h (LPT1), 0278h (LPT2), 03BCh (LPT3), and 02BCh (LPT4). The base address of each port corresponds to the data register. The status register of a respective port is accessed from the base address with an offset of 01h (that is, 0379h, 0279h, 03BDh, and 02BDh), and the control register is accessed with an offset of 02h (that is, 037Ah, 027Ah, 03BEh, and 02BEh).

Although a typical PC can theoretically support four LPT ports, it is extremely rare for a PC to offer more than two ports. Even then, the IRQ for LPT2 (IRQ5) often conflicts with the IRQ assigned to Sound Blaster-type sound boards.

During initialization, ports are checked in the following order: 03BCh, 0378h, 0278h, and 02BCh, and LPT designations are assigned depending on what ports are found, so keep in mind that LPT addresses may be exchanged in a manner depending on your particular system. The specific I/O addresses for each port are kept in the BIOS data area of RAM starting at 0408h. As you might expect, only one LPT port can be assigned to a base address. If more than one parallel port is assigned to the same address, system problems will almost certainly occur.

The use of interrupts gets a bit complicated. There are basically two modes of requesting new characters for the printer: polling and interrupt-driven. *Polling,* the most popular method, occurs when the BIOS "polls" (or checks) a port's status register to see if it is ready to accept another character—no interrupts are generated. An *interrupt-driven* interface is much more efficient, but it can bog down other important operations during printing.

For technicians who work on older machines, it is important to keep in mind that address 03BCh was originally reserved for a parallel port located on the IBM Monochrome Display Adapter (MDA). If you are servicing an older system with *no* video support on the motherboard, the address 03BCh may be reserved in the event that you, for some reason, want to install an IBM MDA card. For newer systems with video support located on the motherboard, address 03BCh may be the first parallel port address.

Always begin your service examination by checking the number of parallel ports in your system. Parallel ports are so simple and easy to add to various expansion cards, you can exceed the limit of four parallel ports without even knowing it. If more than four ports are active, a hardware conflict can result and crash the system—you will have to remove or disable the extra ports.

PARALLEL PORT SIGNALS

IBM and compatible PCs implement a parallel port as a 25-pin sub-miniature D-type female connector similar to the one shown in Figure 34-2. The parallel connection at the printer uses a 36-pin Centronics-type connector (Amphenol type 57-30360). The exact reasoning for this rather specialized connector is not clear, since 11 pins of the Centronics connector will remain unused. There are three types of signals to be concerned with in parallel connections: data lines, control (or *handshaking*) lines, and ground lines. Table 34-1 identifies the name and description of each pin. The following section describes each signal. The pin num-

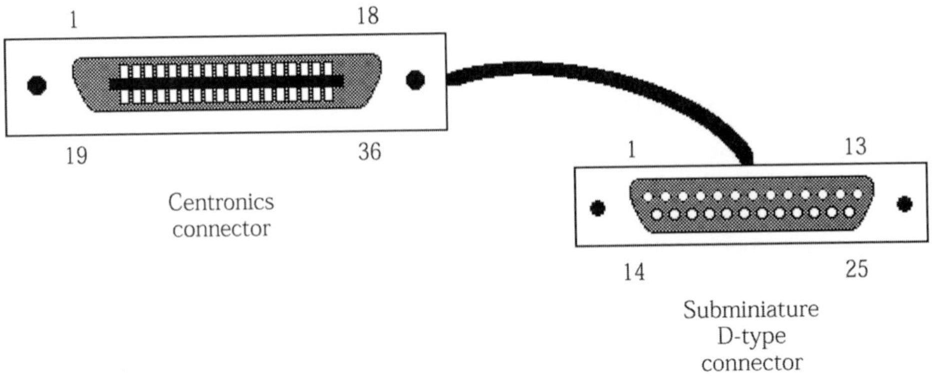

FIGURE 34-2 A typical parallel (printer) cable assembly.

TABLE 34-1 THE PARALLEL PORT INTERFACE ASSIGNMENTS

SIGNAL NAME	LABEL	SIGNAL PIN			GROUND RETURN PIN		
		D-SUB	CENTRONICS		D-SUB	CENTRONICS	
		IEEE 1284A	IEEE 1284B	IEEE 1284C	IEEE 1284A	IEEE 1284B	IEEE 1284C
Data bit 0	*D0*	2	2	6	19	20	24
Data bit 1	*D1*	3	3	7	19	21	25
Data bit 2	*D2*	4	4	8	20	22	26
Data bit 3	*D3*	5	5	9	20	23	27
Data bit 4	*D4*	6	6	10	21	24	28
Data bit 5	*D5*	7	7	11	21	25	29
Data bit 6	*D6*	8	8	12	22	26	30
Data bit 7	*D7*	9	9	13	22	27	31
Error (Fault)	*S3*	15	32	4	23	29	22
Select	*S4*	13	13	2	24	28	20
PaperEnd	*S5*	12	12	5	24	28	23
Acknowledge	*S6*	10	10	3	24	28	21
Busy	*S7*	11	11	1	23	29	19
Strobe	*-C0*	1	1	15	18	19	33
AutoLF	*-C1*	14	14	17	25	30	35
Init	*C2*	16	31	14	25	30	32
SelectIn	*-C3*	17	36	16	25	30	34
HostLogicHigh				18			18
PeriphLogicHigh				36			36

bers at both the PC and printer ends are listed for your reference. Also remember that all signals on the parallel port are compatible with TTL signal levels.

Data lines The *data lines* are the actual data-carrying conductors that convey information from the parallel port to or from the printer or other peripheral. There are eight data lines (D0 to D7), located on pins 2 through 9. To reduce the effects of signal noise on parallel cables, each data line is given a corresponding *data ground* line (pins 20 to 27). Ground lines also provide a common electrical reference between the computer and peripheral. The remainder of a parallel port is devoted to handshaking.

Initialize and select To ensure that the printer starts in a known initialized state, an *-Initialize* signal (-INI on pin 16) sent from the computer is used to reset a printer to the state it powered up in. Initializing the peripheral has the same effect as turning it off, then turning it on again. The initialize line is "active-low," so the printer must apply a logic 0 to trigger an initialization.

The *Select line* (SEL on pin 13) tells the waiting computer that the peripheral is "online" and ready to receive data. Select is an "active-high" logic signal, so a logic 1 indicates that a device is online and ready, while a logic 0 indicates that the printer is not ready to receive data. The computer will not send data when the select line is logic 0. You can usually determine the Select line's general condition from the printer's front panel "online" light.

Strobe, busy, and acknowledge Once a computer has placed eight valid bits on the parallel data lines, the peripheral must be told that the data is ready. A *-Strobe* signal (-STR on pin 1) is applied to the peripheral from the computer just after data is valid. The brief -Strobe signal causes the peripheral to accept the byte and store it in the printer's internal buffer for processing.

Under ideal circumstances, parallel printer ports can achieve data rates of up to 500,000 characters per second. With such a tremendous throughput, the printer needs some method of coordinating data transfer—the computer must wait between characters until the printer is ready to resume accepting new characters. Printers use the *Busy* signal (BSY on pin 11) to delay the computer until the printer is ready. Peripherals drive the busy line to logic 1 anytime a -Strobe signal is received. The Busy signal remains logic 1 for as long as it takes the peripheral to prepare for the next byte. It is important to note that a Busy signal can delay the computer indefinitely if a serious peripheral error has occurred (for instance, paper exhausted or ribbon jammed).

When the peripheral has received a byte and dealt with it, the peripheral must then request another character from the waiting computer. The printer drops the busy line and initiates a brief *-Acknowledge* pulse (-ACK on pin 10). -Acknowledge signals are always active-low logic signals, and a typical acknowledge pulse lasts about 8μS. It is this interaction of data, -Strobe, Busy, and -Acknowledge signals that handles the bulk of data transfer in a parallel port.

Auto feed Some printers make the assumption that a "carriage return" signal (or <CR>) will automatically advance the paper to the next line, while other printers simply return the carriage to the beginning of the existing line without advancing the paper. Many printers make this feature selectable through the use of a DIP switch in the printer, but an *-Auto Feed* signal (-AF on pin 14) from the computer can control that feature. A TTL logic 0 from the computer causes the printer to feed one line of paper automatically when a carriage return command is detected. A TTL logic 1 from the computer allows only a carriage return (paper would have to be fed manually). Most computer parallel ports keep this line at logic 0.

Device select The *-Device Select* line (-DSL on pin 17) allows the computer to bring the peripheral on and off-line remotely. Many parallel ports leave this signal as a logic 0 so that peripherals will automatically accept data. A logic 1 on this line would inhibit printer operation.

Error The *-Error* signal (-ERROR on pin 15) generated by a printer (or other peripheral) tells the computer that trouble has occurred, but it is not specific about the exact problem. A variety of problems can cause an error—it depends on your particular peripheral and what it is capable of detecting. The error line uses active-low logic, so it is normally logic 1 until an error has occurred. An -Error signal can typically indicate an "Out of Paper," "Printer Offline," or "General Printer Fault" error condition.

PORT OPERATION

This part of the chapter describes a standard sequence of events in a basic parallel port. The parallel data transfer begins by placing the printer online. -Strobe and -Acknowledge must be TTL logic 1, while Busy must be logic 0. In this state, the peripheral can now accept a byte of data. When printing is attempted, the CPU polls the desired LPT port and checks its status register. If the post is ready, a byte is written to the data register and passed to the peripheral.

Data must be valid for at least 0.5μS *before* the computer initiates a logic 0 -Strobe. The printer responds by returning a logic 1 Busy signal, which changes the port's status. Subsequent polling of the status register will indicate that the port is unavailable. The -Strobe pulse must last at least 1.0μS. Data must be held valid at least 0.5μS *after* the -Strobe pulse passes. This timing ensures that the peripheral has enough time to receive the data. Since Busy is now logic 1, communication stops until the data byte has been processed. Processing can take 1mS if the printer's buffer is not full. If the printer's buffer is full, communication may be halted for a second or more. After the data byte has been processed, Busy is dropped to logic 0 and the printer sends a 5.0μS logic 0 -Acknowledge pulse to request another data byte from the waiting computer. Once the -Acknowledge line returns to a TTL logic 1 condition, the interface

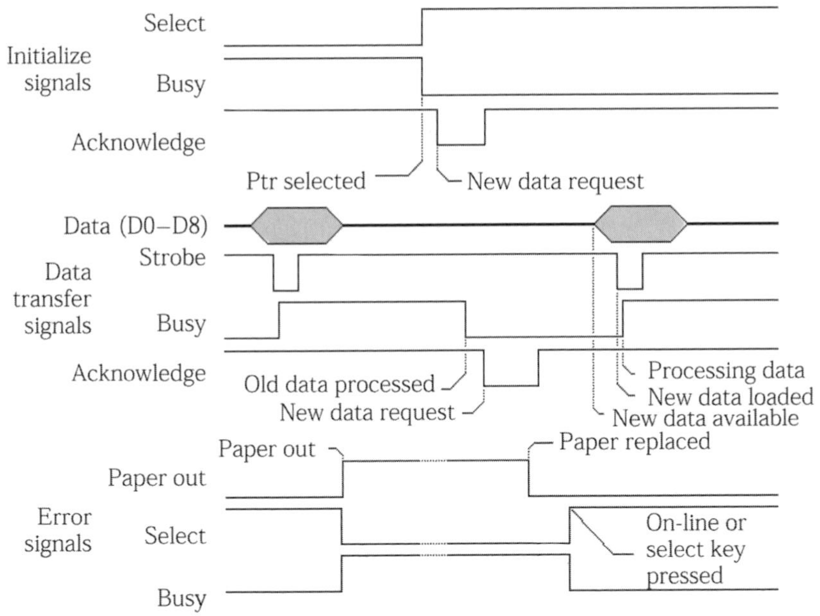

FIGURE 34-3 Typical parallel port timing diagram.

is ready to begin a new transfer. The status register then indicates the port is ready, and when the port is next polled, a new byte can be written. Figure 34-3 illustrates this relationship—one complete cycle can take a bit over 1mS.

34

ADVANCED PARALLEL PORTS

The appeal of a parallel port is easy to understand—it is *simple*. While serial devices struggle with baud rates, stop bits, and parity (problems that continue to this day), parallel devices just plug into the 25-pin D-type connector, and away you go. The parallel port offered "plug-and-play" convenience long before the term ever came in vogue. Although the parallel port has been a staple of PC communication, it certainly has not gone unchanged over the last 15 years. If you've been shopping for new computers or I/O boards over the last year or two, you've probably noticed the terms "Enhanced Parallel Port" (EPP) or "Enhanced Capabilities Port" (ECP) associated with the parallel port. With a recent parallel port standard (IEEE 1284) developed by the Institute of Electrical and Electronic Engineers (IEEE), the PC industry has *finally* moved past the "classic" parallel port architecture and embraced a truly improved parallel port. This part of the chapter compares the various parallel port "modes."

Unidirectional ports The original PC utilized a unidirectional parallel port. That is, the port sent data only one way (from the PC to the peripheral device, which was almost always a printer). For the time, unidirectional communication was adequate for general-purpose PCs, and the parallel port became synonymous with "printer port." Unidirectional ports reigned supreme in the PC market until 1987 (around the time of the i386).

"Type 1" bi-directional ports By 1987, IBM had launched its PS/2 line. Among the other technological advances in the PS/2, IBM incorporated a *bi-directional* parallel port. Now, bi-directional ports were hardly a breakthrough (older hobby-type PCs had used similar ports), but IBM was really the first to use a bi-directional port in a commercial PC. The bi-directional port was really not any faster or better than a unidirectional port, but the ability to send data back to the PC opened up the parallel port to other devices besides printers. Clone PC manufacturers jumped on the improvement, and bi-directional ports became common in almost all subsequent clones.

"Type 3" bi-directional ports One of the problems with bi-directional parallel ports is that they are CPU-intensive, requiring relatively large amounts of CPU attention in order to manage the transfer of data. Later models of the PS/2 (the 57, 90, and 95) made an attempt to increase the throughput of a parallel port by using direct memory access (DMA) techniques. The DMA approach allows the CPU to define a block of memory (for instance, printer ASCII characters) to be sent. A DMA controller takes over control from the CPU and transfers the data without CPU intervention—generally resulting in faster data transfer. This approach also worked when receiving data. In current practice, Type 3 bi-directional ports are rarely used because today's high-performance CPUs can transfer data much faster than a DMA process.

IEEE 1284 MODES

By the end of the 1980s, it was becoming clear that conventional bi-directional parallel ports were simply not adequate to handle the new generations of faster peripherals that were appearing for the parallel port (particularly CD-ROMs, tape drives, and laser printers). The 150KB/s parallel transfer rates that were once considered speedy were now severely limiting the performance of the new peripherals. In 1991, a group of major PC manufacturers—including IBM, Lexmark, and Texas Instruments—formed the Network Printing Alliance (NPA) in an attempt to develop a new parallel port architecture. In 1994, the IEEE (in conjunction with the NPA) released the *Standard Signaling Method for a Bi-Directional Parallel Peripheral Interface*, also known as IEEE standard 1284.

The IEEE 1284 does not define a single parallel approach, but instead outlines *five* different operational modes for the parallel port: compatibility mode, nibble mode, byte mode, ECP mode, and EPP mode. All five modes offer some amount of bi-directional capability (known under IEEE 1284 as *back channel communication*). When the 1284-compliant parallel port is initialized, it checks to see which operating mode is most appropriate.

Currently, the only operating systems that have built-in support for IEEE 1284 are Windows 95 and Windows 98. They have support for IEEE 1284 negotiation (a.k.a. "parallel port plug-and-play") and fast printing in ECP mode. In order to take advantage of this capability, you must have a printer and a parallel port with ECP capability. In addition, the parallel port must be configured in the Windows 95/98 Device Manager as an "ECP Printer Port" with an IRQ and DMA channel configured. You can determine your parallel port's configuration in the Device Manager (Figure 34-4). If you don't have these settings configured (but *do* have an ECP-capable printer), the driver will "fall back" to the fast Centronics mode. If neither of these conditions is met, the driver stays in the old "slow" mode.

Compatibility mode This mode defines the basic protocol used by most PCs to transfer data to a simple printer. It's commonly called the "Centronics" mode and is the method commonly associated with the standard parallel port. In this mode, data is placed on the port's data lines, the printer status is checked for errors and busy conditions, then a data strobe is generated by the software that clocks the data to the printer. In order to output one byte of data, this port requires four I/O instructions (and at least as many additional instructions). This type of operation limits the bandwidth capabilities at the port to about 150KB per second. This bandwidth is sufficient for communicating with dot matrix, ink jet, and many older laser printers, but it's a serious limitation when communicating with LAN adapters, removable disk drives, and the newest generation of laser printers.

Many of the integrated IEEE 1284 I/O controller chips have implemented a mode that uses a FIFO (First In/First Out) buffer to transfer data with the Compatibility mode protocol—this mode is referred to

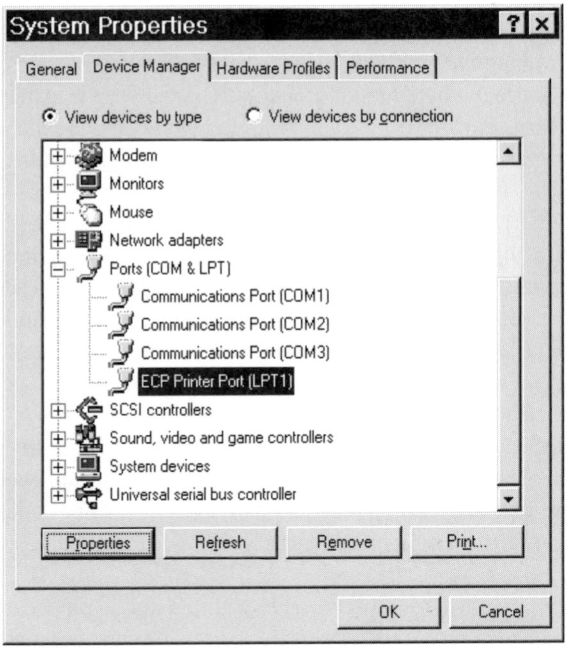

FIGURE 34-4 Checking the parallel port mode in Device Manager

as Fast Centronics (or Parallel Port FIFO) mode. When this mode is enabled, data written to the FIFO port will be transferred to the printer using hardware-generated strobes for the handshaking. Since there is very little latency between transfers, and the software does not have to do any of the strobing or handshake checking, data rates over 500KB per second are achievable with some systems. Remember that this mode is *not* an IEEE 1284-defined mode.

Whenever problems are encountered operating parallel port devices, try setting the parallel port to compatibility mode in the system's CMOS setup. You may lose data transfer speed, but you should gain compatibility with older devices.

Nibble mode The nibble mode is the most common way to get "reverse" channel data back from a printer or other peripheral. This mode is usually combined with the compatibility mode (or a proprietary forward channel mode) to create a complete *bi-directional* data channel. All standard parallel ports provide five lines from the peripheral to the PC that can be used for external status indications. Using these lines, a peripheral can send a byte of data (8 bits) by sending 2 "nibbles" (4 bits per "nibble") of information to the PC in two data transfer cycles.

Nibble mode (like compatibility mode) requires that the software drive the protocol by setting and reading lines on the parallel port. Nibble mode is the most software-intensive mode for reverse channel data communication—for this reason, there's a *severe* bandwidth limitation of approximately 50KB per second for this type of data transfer. The major advantage of this approach is the ability to operate on *all* PCs that have a parallel port. The performance limitations don't have much effect on "low bandwidth" peripherals such, as printers, but can be intolerable when used with other bi-directional devices.

Byte mode With later implementations of the parallel port interface, some manufacturers (led by IBM on its PS/2 parallel port) added the capability to disable the drivers used for driving the data lines and allowed the data port to become an "input" data port. This change enables a peripheral to send an entire byte of data to the PC in one data transfer cycle by using the eight data lines (rather than the two cycles required using the nibble mode). This approach enables the byte mode for reverse channel data transfer that can be used to provide data rates *into* the PC approaching that of the compatibility mode (which sends data *from* the PC). This type of port is sometimes referred to as an "enhanced bi-directional" port and is often mistaken for an Enhanced Parallel Port (EPP)—the two port types are *not* the same thing.

ECP mode The Extended Capability Port (ECP) protocol was proposed by Hewlett-Packard and Microsoft as an advanced mode for communication with printer and scanner-type peripherals. Like the EPP protocol below, ECP provides a high-performance bi-directional communication path between the host system and the peripheral. When the ECP protocol was proposed, a standard register implementation was also proposed (this can be found in *The IEEE 1284 Extended Capabilities Port Protocol and ISA Interface Standard,* available from Microsoft).

The many features of ECP include Run Length Encoding (RLE) data compression for the host system's LPT port, FIFO buffers for both the forward and reverse channels, DMA channel use, and programmed I/O (or "PIO"). The RLE feature enables real-time data compression that can achieve compression ratios up to 64:1—particularly useful for printers and scanners that are transferring huge amounts of data that have large strings of repetitive information. In order for the RLE mode to be enabled, both the host *and* the peripheral must support it.

Channel addressing is a scheme used to address multiple logical devices within a single physical device. For example, in a multi-function device such as a FAX/printer/modem, there's a single parallel port attached to a printer, fax, and modem. Using ECP channel addressing to access each of these devices, you could receive data from the modem device while the printer data channel is busy processing a print image. With the compatibility mode protocol, if the printer gets too busy, no more communication can occur until the printer data channel is free—but with ECP the software driver simply addresses another channel, and communication can continue.

With the EPP scheme described below, a software driver may intermix read and write operations without any overhead or protocol handshaking. With the ECP protocol, however, changes in the data direction *must* be negotiated—the host must request a "reverse channel transfer" by asserting a request, and then wait for the peripheral to acknowledge the request by asserting an acknowledge signal—only then can a reverse channel data transfer take place. Since the previous transfer may have been DMA-driven, the host software must either wait for the DMA transfer to complete or interrupt the DMA, "backflush" the FIFO (to determine the exact transferred byte count), then request the reverse channel.

EPP mode The Enhanced Parallel Port (EPP) protocol was originally developed by Intel, Xircom, and Zenith Data Systems as a means of providing a high-performance parallel port link that would still be compatible with the standard parallel port. This protocol was originally implemented by Intel in its 386SL chipset (the 82360 I/O chip). This was done prior to the establishment of the IEEE 1284 committee and the associated standards work. The EPP protocol offered many advantages to parallel port peripheral manufacturers, and it was quickly adopted by many manufacturers as an optional data transfer method. A loose association of around 80 interested manufacturers was formed to develop and promote the EPP protocol. This association became the EPP Committee, which was instrumental in helping to get this protocol adopted as an IEEE 1284 advanced mode. Since EPP-capable parallel ports were available *prior* to the release of the IEEE 1284 standard, there is a minor difference between the pre-1284 EPP ports and established 1284 EPP protocol.

One of the most important features to note here is that the entire data transfer occurs within one ISA I/O cycle. The effect is that, by using the EPP protocol for data transfer, a system can achieve transfer rates between 500KB and 2MB per second. This performance level means that parallel port peripherals can operate at *close* to the same performance levels as an equivalent ISA plug-in card (the performance level from a parallel port device is one of the major features of the EPP protocol). Data transfer will take place at the speed of the *slowest* part of the interface (the host adapter or the peripheral device), but this "speed adaptive" property is transparent to both the host and peripheral. The EPP controller will generate the necessary handshake signals and strobes to transfer the data, using an EPP Data Write cycle, and will run exactly like a standard parallel port.

The ability to transfer data to or from the PC by the use of a single instruction is what enables EPP mode parallel ports to transfer data at ISA-type bus speeds. Rather than having the software implement an I/O intensive software loop, a block of data can be transferred with a single instruction. Depending upon the host adapter port implementation and the capability of the peripheral, an EPP port can transfer data from 500KB to nearly 2MB per second. This data transfer rate is more than enough to enable data-intensive devices such as network adapters, CD-ROM drives, tape backups, and other peripherals. The EPP protocol provides a high degree of coupling between the peripheral driver and the peripheral, meaning that the software driver is always able to determine and control the state of communication to the peripheral at any given time. Mixing the read and write operations (as well as block transfers) can be accomplished easily.

ECP/EPP CABLE QUALITY

Conventional parallel ports are limited to cable lengths of about 10 feet (about 3 meters). Beyond that, cross-talk in the parallel cable can result in data errors. Ideally, high-quality, well-shielded cable assemblies can extend that range even more, but the cheap, mass-produced cable assemblies that you often find in stores are rarely suited to support communication over more than 6 feet (about 2 meters). To support the high-speed communication promised by IEEE 1284, a new cable specification also had to be devised. This is hardly a trivial concern—especially considering that IEEE 1284 seeks to extend parallel port operation to as much as 30 feet (about 10 meters). Be sure to use an appropriate high-quality cable when configuring a parallel port in ECP or EPP modes.

34

IEEE 1284 ISSUES

Unfortunately, while the potential and promise of IEEE 1284 offers a lot of appeal, there are some serious considerations involved in configuring an enhanced port arrangement. Specifically, you will require an IEEE 1284-compliant parallel port, cable, and peripheral (printer, tape drive, hard drive, and so on) to take full advantage of enhanced capabilities.

Installing an IEEE 1284 parallel port is certainly not a problem—virtually all current multi-I/O boards and motherboards are now providing IEEE 1284-compliant ports. The trouble is that using a $5 printer cable with your old Panasonic KX-P1124 dot-matrix printer will just *not* provide any advantage. To start benefiting from an IEEE 1284 port, you'll need at least an IEEE 1284 cable and a device with significant memory capacity (such as a laser printer). At that point, you may start to see some speed improvements, but the additional speed will still fall far short of the projected figures. Ultimately, you will need to install IEEE 1284-compliant peripherals, which will provide ID information to the port and allow optimum performance.

Troubleshooting the Parallel Port

While the typical parallel port is a rather simple I/O device, it presents some special challenges for the technician. Older PCs provided their parallel ports in the form of 8-bit expansion boards—when a port failed, it was a simple matter to replace the board outright. Today, however, virtually all PCs provide at least one parallel port directly on the motherboard—the feature usually supported by an I/O Controller component of the motherboard's main chipset. When a problem is detected with a motherboard parallel port, a technician often has three choices:

- Replace the chipset IC that supports the parallel port(s). Doing this requires access to surface-mount soldering tools and replacement ICs and can be quite economical in volume. But this is a totally impractical solution for end-user troubleshooting.
- Set the motherboard jumpers (if possible) to *disable* the defective parallel port, and install an expansion "multi-I/O" board to take the place of the defective port. This fix assumes there is an available expansion slot. This solution uses an expansion slot, but offers a cheap, fast fix for a defective parallel port. Remember to disable all other unused ports of the multi-I/O board.
- Replace the motherboard outright. This is a simple tactic that requires little overhead equipment, but can be rather expensive—a general solution of last resort if you can confirm the parallel port to be defective.

> If a diagnostic cannot identify the presence of a physical parallel port (a loopback plug may need to be attached), chances are that the port is confirmed defective.

TIPS FOR FIXING PARALLEL PORTS

Parallel ports are generally not complex devices, but there are some common issues that show up regularly. Before you check out the symptoms described later in this chapter, take a look at some of the points below:

- ***Check the cable.*** You'd be surprised how many LPT problems are caused by loose, cheap, or damaged printer cables. Make sure the cable is 6 feet or less in length, see that it is secure at *both* ends, and try a different cable (or try the cable in place of a known-good one).
- ***Beware of the port mode.*** Remember that modern parallel ports can operate in several different modes such as compatibility, ECP, or EPP. Not all parallel port devices work properly with ECP or EPP modes. If you have trouble with a printer or other parallel port device, try setting the parallel port to compatibility mode or standard mode in the system's CMOS setup.
- ***Hardware conflicts.*** LPT ports use IRQ7 and IRQ5. For systems with a second LPT port (LPT2), it is common for IRQ5 to have a conflict, because it is almost always used by sound boards. If you must use two or more LPT ports on your system, it may be necessary to reconfigure the sound board to use another IRQ or to remove the sound board entirely.
- ***Printer driver conflicts.*** This is a problem that often arises with parallel port devices such as Iomega Zip drives or SyQuest SyJet drives. The drive software sends special reserved nonprintable characters to the parallel port; this process signals the drive that the next data being placed on the parallel port cable is for that drive (not the printer). Color printers and multiple font printers can also be using some of these special characters for their printer setups. This situation can cause conflicts between the two drivers and make each unit (the printer and the parallel port drive) look defective to the system. Many printer companies, such as Hewlett Packard, are in the process of rewriting printer drivers to stay clear of these reserved nonprintable characters, but some drivers still use these characters and will cause conflicts that cannot be resolved. The only way to correct this problem is to use one LPT port for the parallel port drive and another LPT port for the printer. You should contact the printer manufacture to see if it has updated drivers that will not interfere with the parallel port device.
- ***Problems with printer monitoring software.*** Another form of driver conflicts happens with printer monitoring software. Some companies such as Hewlett Packard have status drivers that monitor the printer's status. If you have these printers connected to the pass-through port of a parallel port drive,

these printer monitoring drivers should be disabled. These drivers can also cause data corruption and system problems. Disabling status communications does not affect the printing.

SYMPTOMS

SYMPTOM 34-1 You hear a beep code or see a POST error indicating a parallel port error The system initialization may or may not halt depending on how the BIOS is written. Low-level initialization problems generally indicate trouble in the computer's hardware. If the computer's beep code sequence is indistinct, you could try rebooting the computer with a POST analyzer card installed. The BIOS POST code displayed on the card can be matched to a specific error explanation in the POST card's documentation. Once you have clearly identified the error as a parallel port fault, you can proceed with troubleshooting.

Start with the system as a whole and remove any expansion boards that have parallel ports available. Retest the computer after removing each board. If the error disappears after removing a particular card, then that card is likely at fault. You can simply replace the card with a new one or attempt to repair the card to the component level. If there is only one parallel port in the system, it is most likely built into the motherboard.

For older systems, the fault is probably in one or more of the discrete I/O chips or latches directing the port's operation. You will need to refer to the schematic(s) for your particular system motherboard to determine exact signal flows and component locations. Newer system motherboards enjoy a far lower component count, so all parallel port circuitry is usually integrated onto the same application-specific IC (ASIC). A schematic would still be valuable to determine signal paths, but you could probably trace the parallel port connector directly to its controlling chip. Replace any defective components or replace the motherboard outright.

SYMPTOM 34-2 You see a 9xx parallel adapter displayed on your XT or early AT system BIOS has not located any parallel circuit defects on initialization but has been unable to map LPT labels to the appropriate hardware-level ports. As in Symptom 34-1, the 9xx series error codes usually indicate a hardware fault in the computer. Follow the procedures in Symptom 34-1 to isolate and resolve the problem.

SYMPTOM 34-3 The computer initializes properly, but the peripheral (printer) does not work Your applications software may indicate a "printer timeout" or "general printer" error. Before you even open your toolkit, you must determine whether the trouble lies in your computer or your peripheral. When your printer stops working, run a self-test to ensure the device is at least operational. Check all cables and connectors (perhaps try a different cable). If the peripheral offers multiple interfaces, such as serial and parallel, make sure the parallel interface is activated in the peripheral. Also be sure to check the software package being used (word processor, painting package, system diagnostic, and so on) to operate the printer. Ensure that the software is configured properly to use the appropriate LPT port and that any necessary printer driver is selected. If no software is available, you can try printing from the DOS command line using the SHIFT and PRINT SCREEN keys. This key sequence will dump the screen contents to a printer.

Disconnect the printer at the computer and install a parallel loopback plug. Run a diagnostic to inspect each available parallel port. Take note of any port that registers as defective. Locate the corresponding parallel port. If the port is installed as an expansion board, replace the defective expansion board. If the port is on the motherboard, you can replace the defective port controller chip, install an alternate expansion board, or replace the motherboard outright.

SYMPTOM 34-4 The peripheral (printer) will not go online Before data can be transferred across a parallel port, proper handshaking conditions must exist: the Busy (pin 11) and Paper Out (pin 12) lines must be TTL logic 0, and the Select (pin 13) and -Error (pin 15) lines must be TTL logic 1. All four signals are outputs from the peripheral. You can examine these levels with an ordinary logic probe. If any of these signals is incorrect, the peripheral will not be online. First, try a new communication cable. An old or worn cable may have developed a fault in one or more of its connections. Next, try the computer with a different peripheral. If a new peripheral *does* come online, the error exists in the original peripheral's parallel port circuitry.

If a different peripheral does not operate properly, there is a problem with the computer's parallel port. Examine and alter the computer configuration to ensure that there is no conflict between multiple parallel ports. Disconnect the printer at the computer and install a parallel loopback plug. Run a diagnostic to inspect each available parallel port. Take note of any port that registers as defective. Locate the corresponding parallel port. If the port is installed as an expansion board, replace the defective expansion board. If the port is on the motherboard, you can replace the defective port controller chip, install an alternate expansion board, or replace the motherboard outright.

SYMPTOM 34-5 **Data is randomly lost or garbled** Your first step should be to check the communication cable. Make sure the cable is intact and properly secured at both ends. The cable should also be less than 2 meters (about 6 feet) long. Very long cables can allow crosstalk to generate erroneous signals. If the cable checks properly, either the port or peripheral is at fault. Start by suspecting the parallel port. Disconnect the printer at the computer and install a parallel loopback plug. Run a diagnostic to inspect each available parallel port. Take note of any port that registers as defective. Locate the corresponding parallel port. If the port is installed as an expansion board, replace the defective expansion board. If the port is on the motherboard, you can replace the defective port controller chip, install an alternate expansion board, or replace the motherboard outright.

If you cannot test the computer's parallel port directly, test the port indirectly by trying the peripheral on another known-good computer. If the peripheral works properly on another computer, the trouble is probably in the original computer's parallel port circuitry. Replace any defective circuitry or replace the motherboard. If the peripheral remains defective on another computer, the peripheral itself is probably faulty.

SYMPTOM 34-6 **You see a continuous "paper out" error even though paper is available and the printer's paper sensor works properly** Try another printer. If another printer works, the problem is in your original printer and not in the parallel port. Use a logic probe and check the Paper Out signal at the computer. Try removing and re-inserting paper while the printer is running. You should see the Paper Out signal vary between a TTL logic 0 (paper available) and a TTL logic 1 (paper missing). If the signal remains TTL logic 1 regardless of paper availability, the printer's sensor or communication circuits are probably defective. If the Paper Out signal correctly follows the paper availability, the trouble is probably in your computer's communication circuitry.

When you suspect that the problem is in the parallel port, disconnect the printer at the computer and install a parallel loopback plug. Run a diagnostic to inspect each available parallel port. Take note of any port that registers as defective. Locate the corresponding parallel port. If the port is installed as an expansion board, replace the defective expansion board. If the port is on the motherboard, you can replace the defective port controller chip, install an alternate expansion board, or replace the motherboard outright.

Further Study

LPT Ports and Parallel Drives: **http://syquest.com/support/papers.html**

HP: **http://www.hp.com**

IEEE 1284: **http://www.fapo.com/ieee1284.htm**

ECP Technical Document: **http://www.fapo.com/files/ecp_reg.pdf**

35

PLUG-AND-PLAY CONFIGURATION AND TROUBLESHOOTING

CHAPTER AT A GLANCE

One of the key assets of the IBM-type personal computer architecture is its functional modularity—its ability to accept a variety of expansion devices such as modems, video controllers, drive adapters, video capture/TV boards, and so on. Each device that is added to a system needs to be configured in order to utilize unique IRQ, DMA, and I/O resources. Traditionally, devices were configured manually using a series of jumpers on the device. Although this proved to be a straightforward approach, it also opened the way for many configuration conflicts (devices accidentally configured to use overlapping resources). Reporting utilities are also imprecise, making conflict resolution somewhat of a tedious, hit-and-miss process. Current operating systems typically provide better tools for conflict resolution (see Chapter 12), but resolving conflicts still demands a certain amount of patience and expertise.

Designers have long sought to automate this device configuration process, removing the error-prone task of device configuration from the hands of end users and busy technicians. The result of this automatic configuration technology has become known as *plug-and-play* (or PnP). First introduced with late-model i486 systems, PnP is now a standard technology implemented in all current PCs. Although PnP simplifies much of the configuration problems with new systems, there are still many situations where PnP doesn't work perfectly (especially when running devices under DOS, or using pre-PnP devices in a PnP system). This chapter describes the requirements for PnP, outlines the special requirements for implementing PnP under DOS, and provides a series of troubleshooting points.

Understanding PnP Under Windows 95/98

The first step in troubleshooting plug-and-play is to understand the issues involved in making it run. PnP is not one particular technology, but rather it is a combination of features brought together in a single approach. There are three components involved in a PnP system: PnP devices, PnP BIOS, and a PnP-compliant operating system. Each part must be PnP compatible.

PNP DEVICES

A PnP system requires one or more devices—the modems, video adapters, chipsets, drive adapters, and myriad other hardware elements in the PC. Ideally, every device in the PC will be PnP compatible, and today's systems do contain virtually all PnP devices. PnP devices are capable of identifying themselves and their resource requirements to the rest of the system. The only wrinkles occur when non-PnP (or "legacy") devices are mixed into the system hardware.

35

PNP BIOS

A PnP system requires a PnP BIOS, especially at boot time. Since PnP devices initialize in the inactive state by default, the PnP BIOS is needed to initialize the core PnP devices (the video adapter and boot drive) in order to complete the POST and launch the operating system. You should also note that the original version of PnP BIOS (version 1.0) was finalized in May 1994. By October 1994 (version 1.0a), additional clarifications were added. As a consequence, older PnP systems are not fully compliant with the current specification. PnP support problems on older systems can usually be corrected with a BIOS upgrade. System PnP support can typically be enabled or disabled through the CMOS setup routine.

PNP OPERATING SYSTEM

The PnP OS takes over where the PnP BIOS leaves off by identifying and configuring the remaining PnP devices in the system, then loading the appropriate drivers needed to initialize and operate each respective device. The OS also must keep resources aside for non-PnP (legacy) devices, and report any changes to the hardware complement in the system. Windows 95 and Windows 98 are generally regarded as the premier PnP operating systems for end users and general-purpose PCs, while Windows NT provides PnP support for networked and business systems.

OVERVIEW OF PNP BEHAVIOR

Now that you've seen the essential elements of PnP, it's time to look at how it all works. A PnP system must be robust enough to handle several important functions. The major functions that must be handled by these three PnP components can be summarized as follows:

- *Identification of installed devices* The PnP system must be able to identify each installed device. This requires the device to have a certain amount of onboard intelligence.
- *Determination of device resource requirements* Based on the device identification, the PnP system must be able to determine the kinds of resources (IRQ, DMA, I/O addresses, or BIOS space) required to support the device.
- *Creation of a complete system configuration, eliminating all resource conflicts* After all devices have been identified, and their resource needs evaluated, the PnP system must then allocate the required resources to each device every time the system initializes (without causing a resource conflict).
- *Loading of device drivers* After the operating system starts, it then must load the appropriate device drivers needed to support every device in the system.
- *Notification of configuration changes* Each time a PnP device is added or removed from the PC, the PnP system reports the configuration change. When a device is added, the PnP system attempts to identify it and install the appropriate device drivers. When a device is removed, the PnP system attempts to remove all traces of the device and its drivers.

The PnP system starts with the BIOS at boot time. A certain amount of configuration must first be performed by the system BIOS during system initialization. In order for the system to boot, the PnP BIOS must configure a display device, input device, and initial boot device (for example, video adapter, keyboard, and floppy/hard drives). Then, the PnP BIOS must pass the information about each of these devices to the operating system (for example, Windows 95/98) for additional configuration of the remaining system devices.

The operating system then continues the configuration process by identifying every device in the system and gathering their respective resource requirements. Each nonboot device (such as modems and video capture devices) must be inactive upon power-up so that the operating system can identify any conflicts between the resource requirements of different devices before configuring them. When different devices require the same resources, the devices must be able to provide information to the operating system about alternative resource requirements. The operating system then uses initial or alternative requirements to assemble a working system configuration. Once any resource conflicts have been resolved, the operating system automatically programs each hardware device with its working configuration and then stores all configuration information in the central database contained in ESCD (Extended System Configuration Data) memory, which is part of the CMOS RAM space. Finally, the operating system loads the device drivers for each device and notifies these drivers of each resource assignment.

If a change occurs to the system configuration during operation (for example, a device is installed or removed), the hardware must be able to notify the operating system of the event so that the operating system can configure the new device. Additionally, applications must be able to respond to configuration changes to take advantage of new devices and to cease calling devices that have been removed. Such dynamic configuration events might include the insertion of a PC Card, the addition or removal of a peripheral such as a mouse, CD-ROM drive, printer, or a docking/undocking event for a notebook computer.

In most cases, configuration changes are made before boot time while system power is off. Only PC Card and laptop designs support "hot" insertion and removal.

DEVICE TYPES AND IDENTIFICATION

The PnP system is designed to support a wide variety of devices across a number of different bus architectures. In general, there are nine classifications of PnP devices:

- ISA bus cards
- PCI bus cards
- MicroChannel (MCA) bus cards
- VESA local bus (VLB) cards
- IDE devices (for hard drives and CD-ROM drives)
- SCSI controllers and devices
- PC Card devices
- Serial port devices (such as modems)
- Parallel port devices (such as printers and parallel port drives)

In order for the PC to recognize and configure a PnP device, each and every device must be able to identify itself and its resource requirements to the system—even motherboard busses and devices must be able to identify themselves. Identification is accomplished through a seven-character code. Each manufacturer is assigned a three-character prefix, the following character identifies the device type, and the remaining three characters identify the particular device. For example, the PnP code PNP0907 identifies a "Western Digital VGA" device adapter. Microsoft reserves the code "PNP" for itself, but other manufacturers are assigned their own codes (for example, Creative Labs uses the "CTL" prefix). The advantage of Microsoft's prefixes is that they are generic, and you can usually identify a device adequately by utilizing the Microsoft generic equivalent. Table 35-1 lists the generic PnP identification categories and codes used by Microsoft.

TABLE 35-1 MICROSOFT GENERIC PNP DEVICE IDENTIFICATION CODES

CODES	DEVICE CATEGORIES
PNP0xxx	System devices
PNP8xxx	Network adapters
PNPAxxx	SCSI, proprietary CD adapters
PNPBxxx	Sound, video capture, multimedia
PNPCxxx—Dxxx	Modems
Device ID Codes	
DEVICE ID	**DESCRIPTION**
System Devices—PNP0xxx—Interrupt Controllers	
PNP0000	AT interrupt controller
PNP0001	EISA interrupt controller
PNP0002	MCA interrupt controller
PNP0003	APIC
PNP0004	Cyrix SLiC MP interrupt controller

TABLE 35-1 MICROSOFT GENERIC PNP DEVICE IDENTIFICATION CODES *(CONTINUED)*

DEVICE ID	DESCRIPTION
System Devices—PNP0xxx—Timers	
PNP0100	AT timer
PNP0101	EISA timer
PNP0102	MCA timer
System Devices—PNP0xxx—DMA	
PNP0200	AT DMA controller
PNP0201	EISA DMA controller
PNP0202	MCA DMA controller
System Devices—PNP0xxx—Keyboards	
PNP0300	IBM PC/XT keyboard controller (83-key)
PNP0301	IBM PC/AT keyboard controller (86-key)
PNP0302	IBM PC/XT keyboard controller (84-key)
PNP0303	IBM Enhanced (101/102-key, PS/2 mouse support)
PNP0304	Olivetti keyboard (83-key)
PNP0305	Olivetti keyboard (102-key)
PNP0306	Olivetti keyboard (86-key)
PNP0307	Microsoft Windows keyboard
PNP0308	General Input Device Emulation Interface (GIDEI) legacy
PNP0309	Olivetti keyboard (A101/102 key)
PNP030A	AT&T 302 keyboard
PNP030B	Reserved (by Microsoft)
PNP0320	Japanese 106-key keyboard A01
PNP0321	Japanese 101-key keyboard
PNP0322	Japanese AX keyboard
PNP0323	Japanese 106-key keyboard 002/003
PNP0324	Japanese 106-key keyboard 001
PNP0325	Japanese Toshiba desktop keyboard
PNP0326	Japanese Toshiba laptop keyboard
PNP0327	Japanese Toshiba notebook keyboard
PNP0340	Korean 84-key keyboard
PNP0340	Korean 86-key keyboard
PNP0342	Korean enhanced keyboard
PNP0343	Korean enhanced keyboard 101b
PNP0343	Korean enhanced keyboard 101c
PNP0344	Korean enhanced keyboard 103
System Devices—PNP0xxx—Parallel Devices	
PNP0400	Standard LPT printer port
PNP0401	ECP printer port

TABLE 35-1 MICROSOFT GENERIC PNP DEVICE IDENTIFICATION CODES *(CONTINUED)*

DEVICE ID	DESCRIPTION
System Devices—PNP0xxx—Serial Devices	
PNP0500	Standard PC COM port
PNP0501	16550A-compatible COM port
PNP0502	Multiport serial device (non-intelligent 16550)
PNP0510	Generic IRDA-compatible device
System Devices—PNP0xxx—Disk Controllers	
PNP0600	Generic ESDI/IDE/ATA compatible hard disk controller
PNP0601	Plus Hardcard II
PNP0602	Plus Hardcard IIXL/EZ
PNP0603	Generic IDE supporting Microsoft Device Bay Specification
PNP0700	PC standard floppy disk controller
PNP0701	Standard floppy controller supporting MS Device Bay Spec.
System Devices—PNP0xxx—Early Sound Systems	
PNP0802	Microsoft Sound System device (now obsolete—use PNPB0xx instead)
System Devices—PNP0xxx—Display Adapters	
PNP0900	VGA Compatible
PNP0901	Video Seven VRAM/VRAM II/1024i
PNP0902	8514/A Compatible
PNP0903	Trident VGA
PNP0904	Cirrus Logic Laptop VGA
PNP0905	Cirrus Logic VGA
PNP0906	Tseng ET4000
PNP0907	Western Digital VGA
PNP0908	Western Digital Laptop VGA
PNP0909	S3 Inc. 911/924
PNP090A	ATI Ultra Pro/Plus (Mach 32)
PNP090B	ATI Ultra (Mach 8)
PNP090C	XGA Compatible
PNP090D	ATI VGA Wonder
PNP090E	Weitek P9000 Graphics Adapter
PNP090F	Oak Technology VGA
PNP0910	Compaq QVision
PNP0911	XGA/2
PNP0912	Tseng Labs W32/W32i/W32p
PNP0913	S3 Inc. 801/928/964
PNP0914	Cirrus Logic 5429/5434 (memory mapped)
PNP0915	Compaq Advanced VGA (AVGA)
PNP0916	ATI Ultra Pro Turbo (Mach64)
PNP0917	Reserved (by Microsoft)
PNP0918	Matrox MGA
PNP0919	Compaq QVision 2000

TABLE 35-1 MICROSOFT GENERIC PNP DEVICE IDENTIFICATION CODES *(CONTINUED)*

DEVICE ID	DESCRIPTION
PNP091A	Tseng W128
PNP0930	Chips & Technologies Super VGA
PNP0931	Chips & Technologies Accelerator
PNP0940	NCR 77c22e Super VGA
PNP0940	NCR 77c32blt
PNP09FF	Plug and Play Monitors (VESA DDC)
System Devices—PNP0xxx—Peripheral Buses	
PNP0A00	ISA Bus
PNP0A01	EISA Bus
PNP0A02	MCA Bus
PNP0A03	PCI Bus
PNP0A04	VESA/VL Bus
PNP0A05	Generic ACPI Bus
PNP0A06	Generic ACPI Extended-IO Bus (EIO bus)
System Devices—PNP0xxx—Real-Time Clock, BIOS, Motherboard Devices	
PNP0800	AT-style speaker sound
PNP0B00	AT Real-Time Clock
PNP0C00	Plug-and-Play BIOS
PNP0C01	System Board
PNP0C02	General ID for reserving resources required by plug-and-play motherboard registers.
PNP0C03	Plug-and-play BIOS Event Notification Interrupt
PNP0C04	Math Coprocessor
PNP0C05	APM BIOS (Version independent)
PNP0C06	Reserved for identification of early plug-and-play BIOS implementation.
PNP0C07	Reserved for identification of early plug-and-play BIOS implementation.
PNP0C08	ACPI system board hardware
PNP0C09	ACPI Embedded Controller
PNP0C0A	ACPI Control Method Battery
PNP0C0B	ACPI Fan
PNP0C0C	ACPI power button device
PNP0C0D	ACPI lid device
PNP0C0E	ACPI sleep button device
PNP0C0F	PCI interrupt link device
PNP0C10	ACPI system indicator device
PNP0C11	ACPI thermal zone
PNP0C12	Device Bay Controller
System Devices—PNP0xxx—PCMCIA Controller Chipsets	
PNP0E00	Intel 82365-Compatible PCMCIA Controller
PNP0E01	Cirrus Logic CL-PD6720 PCMCIA Controller
PNP0E02	VLSI VL82C146 PCMCIA Controller
PNP0E03	Intel 82365-compatible CardBus controller

TABLE 35-1 MICROSOFT GENERIC PNP DEVICE IDENTIFICATION CODES *(CONTINUED)*

System Devices—PNP0xxx—Mice	
PNP0F00	Microsoft Bus Mouse
PNP0F01	Microsoft Serial Mouse
PNP0F02	Microsoft InPort Mouse
PNP0F03	Microsoft PS/2-style Mouse
PNP0F04	Mouse Systems Mouse
PNP0F05	Mouse Systems 3-Button Mouse (COM2)
PNP0F06	Genius Mouse (COM1)
PNP0F07	Genius Mouse (COM2)
PNP0F08	Logitech Serial Mouse
PNP0F09	Microsoft BallPoint Serial Mouse
PNP0F0A	Microsoft Plug-and-Play Mouse
PNP0F0B	Microsoft Plug-and-Play BallPoint Mouse
PNP0F0C	Microsoft-compatible Serial Mouse
PNP0F0D	Microsoft-compatible InPort-compatible Mouse
PNP0F0E	Microsoft-compatible PS/2-style Mouse
PNP0F0F	Microsoft-compatible Serial BallPoint-compatible Mouse
PNP0F10	Texas Instruments QuickPort Mouse
PNP0F11	Microsoft-compatible Bus Mouse
PNP0F12	Logitech PS/2-style Mouse
PNP0F13	PS/2 Port for PS/2-style Mice
PNP0F14	Microsoft Kids Mouse
PNP0F15	Logitech bus mouse
PNP0F16	Logitech SWIFT device
PNP0F17	Logitech-compatible serial mouse
PNP0F18	Logitech-compatible bus mouse
PNP0F19	Logitech-compatible PS/2-style Mouse
PNP0F1A	Logitech-compatible SWIFT Device
PNP0F1B	HP Omnibook Mouse
PNP0F1C	Compaq LTE Trackball PS/2-style Mouse
PNP0F1D	Compaq LTE Trackball Serial Mouse
PNP0F1E	Microsoft Kids Trackball Mouse
PNP0F1F	Reserved (by Microsoft Input Device Group)
PNP0F20	Reserved (by Microsoft Input Device Group)
PNP0F21	Reserved (by Microsoft Input Device Group)
PNP0F22	Reserved (by Microsoft Input Device Group)
PNP0F23	Reserved (by Microsoft Input Device Group)
PNP0FFF	Reserved (by Microsoft Systems)
System Devices—PNP8xxx—Network Adapters	
PNP8001	Novell/Anthem NE3200
PNP8004	Compaq NE3200
PNP8006	Intel EtherExpress/32

35

TABLE 35-1 MICROSOFT GENERIC PNP DEVICE IDENTIFICATION CODES *(CONTINUED)*

DEVICE ID	DESCRIPTION
PNP8008	HP EtherTwist EISA LAN Adapter/32 (HP27248A)
PNP8065	Ungermann-Bass NIUps or NIUps/EOTP
PNP8072	DEC (DE211) EtherWorks MC/TP
PNP8073	DEC (DE212) EtherWorks MC/TP_BNC
PNP8078	DCA 10Mb MCA
PNP8074	HP MC LAN Adapter/16 TP (PC27246)
PNP80C9	IBM Token Ring
PNP80CA	IBM Token Ring II
PNP80CB	IBM Token Ring II/Short
PNP80CC	IBM Token Ring 4/16Mbs
PNP80D3	Novell/Anthem NE1000
PNP80D4	Novell/Anthem NE2000
PNP80D5	NE1000 Compatible
PNP80D6	NE2000 Compatible
PNP80D7	Novell/Anthem NE1500T
PNP80D8	Novell/Anthem NE2100
PNP80DD	SMC ARCNETPC
PNP80DE	SMC ARCNET PC100, PC200
PNP80DF	SMC ARCNET PC110, PC210, PC250
PNP80E0	SMC ARCNET PC130/E
PNP80E1	SMC ARCNET PC120, PC220, PC260
PNP80E2	SMC ARCNET PC270/E
PNP80E5	SMC ARCNET PC600W, PC650W
PNP80E7	DEC DEPCA
PNP80E8	DEC (DE100) EtherWorks LC
PNP80E9	DEC (DE200) EtherWorks Turbo
PNP80EA	DEC (DE101) EtherWorks LC/TP
PNP80EB	DEC (DE201) EtherWorks Turbo/TP
PNP80EC	DEC (DE202) EtherWorks Turbo/TP_BNC
PNP80ED	DEC (DE102) EtherWorks LC/TP_BNC
PNP80EE	DEC EE101 (Built-In)
PNP80EF	DECpc 433 WS (Built-In)
PNP80F1	3Com EtherLink Plus
PNP80F3	3Com EtherLink II or IITP (8 or 16-bit)
PNP80F4	3Com TokenLink
PNP80F6	3Com EtherLink 16
PNP80F7	3Com EtherLink III
PNP80F8	3Com Generic Etherlink Plug-and-Play Device
PNP80FB	Thomas Conrad TC6045
PNP80FC	Thomas Conrad TC6042
PNP80FD	Thomas Conrad TC6142
PNP80FE	Thomas Conrad TC6145

TABLE 35-1 MICROSOFT GENERIC PNP DEVICE IDENTIFICATION CODES *(CONTINUED)*

DEVICE ID	DESCRIPTION
PNP80FF	Thomas Conrad TC6242
PNP8100	Thomas Conrad TC6245
PNP8105	DCA 10MB
PNP8106	DCA 10MB Fiber Optic
PNP8107	DCA 10MB Twisted Pair
PNP8113	Racal NI6510
PNP811C	Ungermann-Bass NIUpc
PNP8120	Ungermann-Bass NIUpc/EOTP
PNP8123	SMC StarCard PLUS (WD/8003S)
PNP8124	SMC StarCard PLUS With On Board Hub (WD/8003SH)
PNP8125	SMC EtherCard PLUS (WD/8003E)
PNP8126	SMC EtherCard PLUS With Boot ROM Socket (WD/8003EBT)
PNP8127	SMC EtherCard PLUS With Boot ROM Socket (WD/8003EB)
PNP8128	SMC EtherCard PLUS TP (WD/8003WT)
PNP812A	SMC EtherCard PLUS 16 With Boot ROM Socket (WD/8013EBT)
PNP812D	Intel EtherExpress 16 or 16TP
PNP812F	Intel TokenExpress 16/4
PNP8130	Intel TokenExpress MCA 16/4
PNP8132	Intel EtherExpress 16 (MCA)
PNP8137	Artisoft AE-1
PNP8138	Artisoft AE-2 or AE-3
PNP8140	Amplicard AC 210/XT
PNP8142	Amplicard AC 210/AT
PNP814B	Everex SpeedLink /PC16 (EV2027)
PNP8155	HP PC LAN Adapter/8 TP (HP27245)
PNP8156	HP PC LAN Adapter/16 TP (HP27247A)
PNP8157	HP PC LAN Adapter/8 TL (HP27250)
PNP8158	HP PC LAN Adapter/16 TP Plus (HP27247B)
PNP8159	HP PC LAN Adapter/16 TL Plus (HP27252)
PNP815F	National Semiconductor Ethernode *16AT
PNP8160	National Semiconductor AT/LANTIC EtherNODE 16-AT3
PNP816A	NCR Token-Ring 4Mbs ISA
PNP816D	NCR Token-Ring 16/4Mbs ISA
PNP8191	Olicom 16/4 Token-Ring Adapter
PNP81C3	SMC EtherCard PLUS Elite (WD/8003EP)
PNP81C4	SMC EtherCard PLUS 10T (WD/8003W)
PNP81C5	SMC EtherCard PLUS Elite 16 (WD/8013EP)
PNP81C6	SMC EtherCard PLUS Elite 16T (WD/8013W)
PNP81C7	SMC EtherCard PLUS Elite 16 Combo (WD/8013EW or 8013EWC)
PNP81C8	SMC EtherElite Ultra 16
PNP81E4	Pure Data PDI9025-32 (Token Ring)
PNP81E6	Pure Data PDI508+ (ArcNet)

TABLE 35-1 MICROSOFT GENERIC PNP DEVICE IDENTIFICATION CODES *(CONTINUED)*

DEVICE ID	DESCRIPTION
PNP81E7	Pure Data PDI516+ (ArcNet)
PNP81EB	Proteon Token Ring (P1390)
PNP81EC	Proteon Token Ring (P1392)
PNP81ED	Proteon ISA Token Ring (1340)
PNP81EE	Proteon ISA Token Ring (1342)
PNP81EF	Proteon ISA Token Ring (1346)
PNP81F0	Proteon ISA Token Ring (1347)
PNP81FF	Cabletron E2000 Series DNI
PNP8200	Cabletron E2100 Series DNI
PNP8209	Zenith Data Systems Z-Note
PNP820A	Zenith Data Systems NE2000-Compatible
PNP8213	Xircom Pocket Ethernet II
PNP8214	Xircom Pocket Ethernet I
PNP821D	RadiSys EXM-10
PNP8227	SMC 3000 Series
PNP8228	SMC 91C2 controller
PNP8231	Advanced Micro Devices AM2100/AM1500T
PNP8263	Tulip NCC-16
PNP8277	Exos 105
PNP828A	Intel '595 based Ethernet
PNP828B	TI2000-style Token Ring
PNP828C	AMD PCNet Family cards
PNP828D	AMD PCNet32 (VL version)
PNP8294	IrDA Infrared NDIS driver (Microsoft-supplied)
PNP82BD	IBM PCMCIA-NIC
PNP82C2	Xircom CE10
PNP82C3	Xircom CEM2
PNP8321	DEC Ethernet (All Types)
PNP8323	SMC EtherCard (All Types except 8013/A)
PNP8324	ARCNET Compatible
PNP8326	Thomas Conrad (All Arcnet Types)
PNP8327	IBM Token Ring (All Types)
PNP8385	Remote Network Access Driver
PNP8387	RNA Point-to-point Protocol Driver
PNP8388	Reserved (for Microsoft Networking components)
PNP8389	Peer IrLAN infrared driver (Microsoft-supplied)
PNP8390	Generic network adapter
System Devices—PNPAxxx—SCSI and Proprietary CD Adapters	
PNPA002	Future Domain 16-700 compatible controller
PNPA003	Panasonic proprietary CD-ROM adapter (SBPro/SB16)

TABLE 35-1 MICROSOFT GENERIC PNP DEVICE IDENTIFICATION CODES *(CONTINUED)*

DEVICE ID	DESCRIPTION
PNPA01B	Trantor 128 SCSI Controller
PNPA01D	Trantor T160 SCSI Controller
PNPA01E	Trantor T338 Parallel SCSI controller
PNPA01F	Trantor T348 Parallel SCSI controller
PNPA020	Trantor Media Vision SCSI controller
PNPA022	Always IN-2000 SCSI controller
PNPA02B	Sony proprietary CD-ROM controller
PNPA02D	Trantor T13b 8-bit SCSI controller
PNPA02F	Trantor T358 Parallel SCSI controller
PNPA030	Mitsumi LU-005 Single Speed CD-ROM controller + drive
PNPA031	Mitsumi FX-001 Single Speed CD-ROM controller + drive
PNPA032	Mitsumi FX-001 Double Speed CD-ROM controller + drive
System Devices—PNPBxxx—Sound, Video Capture, and Multimedia	
PNPB000	Sound Blaster 1.5-compatible sound device
PNPB001	Sound Blaster 2.0-compatible sound device
PNPB002	Sound Blaster Pro-compatible sound device
PNPB003	Sound Blaster 16-compatible sound device
PNPB004	Thunderboard-compatible sound device
PNPB005	Adlib-compatible FM synthesizer device
PNPB006	MPU401 compatible
PNPB007	Microsoft Windows Sound System-compatible sound device
PNPB008	Compaq Business Audio
PNPB009	Plug-and-Play Microsoft Windows Sound System Device
PNPB00A	MediaVision Pro Audio Spectrum (Trantor SCSI enabled, Thunder Chip Disabled)
PNPB00B	MediaVision Pro Audio 3D
PNPB00C	MusicQuest MQX-32M
PNPB00D	MediaVision Pro Audio Spectrum Basic (No Trantor SCSI, Thunder Chip Enabled)
PNPB00E	MediaVision Pro Audio Spectrum (Trantor SCSI enabled, Thunder Chip Enabled)
PNPB00F	MediaVision Jazz-16 chipset (OEM Versions)
PNPB010	Auravision VxP500 chipset—Orchid Videola
PNPB018	MediaVision Pro Audio Spectrum 8-bit
PNPB019	MediaVision Pro Audio Spectrum Basic (no Trantor SCSI, Thunder chip Disabled)
PNPB020	Yamaha OPL3-compatible FM synthesizer device
PNPB02F	Joystick/Game port
System Devices—PNPCxxx-Dxxx—Modems	
PNPC000	Compaq 14400 Modem
PNPC001	Compaq 2400/9600 Modem

DETECTION VS. ENUMERATION

Detection is the process that Windows 95/98 uses during its search for legacy (or non-plug-and-play) devices on a computer. Detection is used during Windows 95/98 setup and any time that you use the Add New Hardware wizard to search for new hardware installed in your computer. Detection does not take place each time you start Windows 95/98. During the detection process, Windows 95/98 creates a file called DETLOG.TXT in the root directory of the boot drive. You can use this file as a basic troubleshooting tool in order to determine which devices were detected, or any errors that are encountered.

By comparison, *enumeration* is the process that Windows 95/98 uses to identify the plug-and-play devices in your computer—including those devices on plug-and-play busses such as ISAPNP, PCI, and PCMCIA (PC card) devices. Enumeration occurs each time Windows 95/98 starts and whenever Windows 95/98 receives notification that a change has occurred in the computer's hardware configuration (for example, when you remove a PCMCIA card).

LEGACY DEVICES

Another issue to consider when working with PnP systems is the support of non-PnP devices (called legacy devices). These are the traditional "jumpered" devices that need to be configured manually. Under DOS, legacy devices run just fine and require no special support, but they can cause a problem under Windows 95/98. Remember that a PnP system relies on the ability to *automatically* identify each and every device in the system. Since legacy devices are not designed to communicate their configuration to the operating system, there is no way for Windows 95/98 to detect the device, much less assign resources for it. This means Windows 95/98 can assign resources to a PnP device that is already in use by a legacy device. Windows 95/98 circumvents this problem by requiring you to register legacy devices using the Add New Hardware wizard under the Control Panel. Once a legacy device is installed and the system is rebooted, use the Add New Hardware wizard to "tell" Windows 95/98 about the new device and install the proper drivers for it.

Enabling PnP Under DOS

Now that PnP devices are virtually standard, a new problem has developed for technicians—PnP support under DOS. Although Windows 95/98 was designed to be a platform for PnP devices, DOS cannot automatically identify and configure PnP devices without additional real-mode software drivers. This makes it difficult to use many PnP devices under DOS, but with a proliferation of DOS games and other applications still in service, PnP support is often a necessity. In other cases, older hardware platforms may lack the support to fully implement a PnP system (such as older BIOS). This part of the chapter examines the techniques used to implement PnP support under DOS and Windows 3.1x.

If you do not have access to a PnP operating system (you're using DOS or Windows 3.1x), you will need to install a PnP configuration driver in CONFIG.SYS that will perform resource allocation and configuration for a PnP device. A PnP *configuration driver* determines the resource settings of all your system devices and legacy cards, configures PnP cards, and provides relevant configuration information to other drivers or applications that access your PnP cards. By contrast, a PnP *configuration utility* allows you to view, enter, or change the resource settings of the PnP and legacy cards in your system. The new or changed settings are then used by the PnP configuration driver to configure new PnP cards. For example, the PnP driver for an Ensonique SoundScape board is DWCFGMG.SYS entered into a CONFIG.SYS command line. The corresponding PnP utility for that Ensonique board is SSINIT.EXE, which is entered into an AUTOEXEC.BAT command line.

THE PNP CONFIGURATION DRIVER

A PnP driver is loaded in the CONFIG.SYS file. For example, the Creative Labs PnP Configuration Manager (for Creative Labs PnP devices) would load the driver CTCM.EXE in a command line such as:

```
device=c:\ctcmdir\ctcm.exe
```

where c:\ctcmdir is the directory where you have installed CTCM. This CTCM statement will be placed before all the statements that load other low-level device drivers (such as CTSB16.SYS and SBIDE.SYS) so that your Creative PnP cards will be configured before these device drivers try to use them. For an Ensonique SoundScape sound board, the PnP driver would be installed such as:

```
device=c:\plugplay\drivers\dos\dwcfgmg.sys
```

In most cases, an automated installation routine will copy the PnP files to your hard drive and make any necessary changes to your CONFIG.SYS file. But if you have to install the software manually, make sure to place the driver command lines for each PnP device *after* the PnP configuration manager.

THE PNP CONFIGURATION UTILITY

A PnP utility is loaded in the AUTOEXEC.BAT file. It is this utility that actually configures and initializes the PnP device. For Creative Labs PnP devices, the utility CTCU is entered in an AUTOEXEC.BAT command line(s) such as these:

```
set CTCM=C:\ctcmdir
C:\ctcmdir\CTCU /S /W=C:\windows
```

where C:\ctcmdir and C:\windows are the directories where your CTCM, CTCU, and Windows 3.x files are installed, respectively. For an Ensonique SoundScape sound board, a typical entry would appear similar to this:

```
set sndscape=c:\sndscape
lh c:\sndscape\ssinit /I
```

Once again, most PnP products will come with an automated installation routine on disk. But when you are troubleshooting a defective installation or performing a manual installation, the format shown above can help you avoid problems.

BLASTER VARIABLES

When configuring a PnP sound board, you will usually have to deal with a BLASTER variable in the AUTOEXEC.BAT file. For legacy sound cards, the BLASTER variable includes fixed settings for address, interrupt, and DMA information, such as:

```
set BLASTER=A220 I5 D1 T1
```

With a PnP installation, however, the BLASTER variable is redefined to "X out" the interrupt and DMA entries as illustrated below:

```
set BLASTER=A220 IXX DX T1
```

The actual values for interrupt and DMA will be entered when the PnP configuration utility runs.

POTENTIAL PROBLEMS WITH GENERIC PNP CONFIGURATION SOFTWARE

There are a number of generic PnP driver/utility sets designed to support a wide range of PnP devices under DOS or Windows 3.1x. One of the most popular is the Intel Configuration Manager (ICM) and ISA Configuration Utility (ICU)—both developed by Intel Corporation. In fact, this software may already be installed on your PC (or bundled with PnP cards). Although the idea of generic PnP software is an appealing one, such generic software is not necessarily compatible with all types of PnP boards. When the software and hardware are incompatible, you will see one of the following error messages:

- Failed NVS write
- Failure to detect PnP BIOS machine
- Failure to assign new configuration to PnP card
- ICM may not be able to configure your PnP card properly

As a general rule, you should use the manufacturer-specific software that accompanies a PnP device rather than generic PnP software.

POTENTIAL PROBLEMS WITH MANUFACTURERS' PNP SOFTWARE

Although manufacturer-specific PnP software will generally provide excellent service, there are some potential limitations to keep in mind. When you use a non-PnP operating system like DOS or Windows 3.1x (and you do not have a PnP BIOS), your PnP card works like a software-configurable card. In such a situation, the PnP driver needs to know which resources have been reserved by each legacy card, PnP card, and system device in your system before it can allocate conflict-free resources to your new PnP card. Normally, the PnP driver can "see" all the resource settings, but you may need to use the PnP utility to enter the resource settings of all the legacy cards in your PC.

You may still encounter hardware conflicts if the resource settings specified through a PnP utility are incomplete or wrong. If this happens, use the configuration utility to select a different group of resources for the PnP card that caused the conflict. You may need to try a few combinations until you find one that works. This can be tedious, but it is easier than the traditional method of changing DIP switches or jumpers.

HANDLING PNP CONFIGURATION ISSUES UNDER DOS

DOS PnP software allows you to use PnP devices in the DOS environment. In many cases, DOS support for PnP works adequately, but there are several issues that can arise which you should know how to deal with:

- *Choosing between the PnP BIOS, PnP software, or PnP OS* There are a number of PC setups that allow you to configure a PnP device based on the PnP BIOS, the PnP driver/utility software, or the PnP operating system. When you are faced with such a choice, it is often better to use the PnP software or operating system *rather* than the BIOS. Set the BIOS so that it will not configure PnP devices. The reason is that a BIOS does not have any way of knowing how legacy devices are configured, so allowing the BIOS to configure a mixed system (with legacy and PnP devices) introduces an excellent chance for hardware conflicts.

> For "pure" system configurations (containing all PnP devices), you can choose to let the PnP BIOS configure PnP devices.

- *Upgrading a PnP system to Windows 95/98* You may have a system with PnP devices that is running with PnP driver and utility software under DOS or Windows 3.1x. When Windows 95/98 is installed, it should recognize the PnP device(s) during the hardware detection phase of the installation, then install the proper software for dealing with the device(s) under Windows 95/98. At the same time, Windows 95/98 should REMark out the real-mode driver and utility software entries under CONFIG.SYS and AUTOEXEC.BAT. This loss of real-mode drivers can cause a problem when returning to the DOS mode later.
- *Replacing generic PnP software with manufacturer-specific software* If generic software is already being used to initialize and run your PnP device(s), that software should be disabled *before* installing manufacturer-specific software. You can do this by placing the REM statement before the generic software's command lines in CONFIG.SYS and AUTOEXEC.BAT. It is not necessary to remove generic PnP software files from the system.
- *The system hangs or reboots whenever the driver software loads* The upper memory area of your PnP BIOS machine is probably mapped by EMM386 using the HIGHSCAN option (and thus can get corrupted easily). When it does, CTCM (or other DOS PnP software) will not work properly. Your system may then hang or reboot whenever you load CTCM. To resolve this problem, remove the HIGHSCAN option in the EMM386 statement in the CONFIG.SYS file. For example, change the statement

  ```
  device=c:\dir\emm386.exe highscan
  ```

  to

  ```
  device=c:\dir\emm386.exe
  ```

  where C:\dir is the directory in which your EMM386 utility is installed.

35

Managing and Troubleshooting PnP Devices

Plug-and-play technology provides technicians and end users with a powerful configuration tool that takes much of the guesswork and trial and error out of hardware installations and upgrades. Still, PnP platforms are far from perfect, and managing the mix of PnP and legacy devices in many of today's systems takes a bit of care. This part of the chapter provides some tips for working with PnP and legacy devices under Windows 95/98, then examines a series of PnP troubleshooting procedures.

INSTALLING PNP DEVICES

Ideally, you simply need to install the physical device in the system. When Windows 95/98 starts, it should recognize the new device automatically and install the appropriate drivers for it. If Windows 95/98 cannot locate an appropriate driver already onboard, it will prompt you to provide a disk, CD, or path containing the correct driver.

INSTALLING LEGACY DEVICES

Remember that legacy devices are configured manually and cannot report their configuration to Windows 95/98 automatically. When installing new legacy hardware in the system, you must run the Add New Hardware wizard to register the device with Windows 95/98 and add the appropriate driver:

1 In the Control Panel, double-click the Add New Hardware icon.

2 In the Add New Hardware wizard, click Next, and then select Automatically Detect Installed Hardware.

3 Allow Windows 95/98 to detect the new device, and then follow the instructions to configure the driver.

> There are some cases where the Add New Hardware wizard cannot detect the new device. When this occurs, select Install Specific Hardware, and you'll need to specify the new device type, manufacturer, and model. Then install the driver.

UPDATING DEVICE DRIVERS

All devices installed under Windows 95/98 (both PnP and legacy) are heavily dependent on drivers. Over time, drivers often need to be updated in order to resolve bugs with the driver, streamline the performance of the particular device, or overcome incompatibilities with other devices or drivers. An important part of device management under Windows 95/98 involves driver updates. In some cases, new drivers are provided on a "maintenance disk" sent by the manufacturer. In other cases, the new driver is downloaded from the manufacturer's tech support Web site. But in either case, all drivers must be properly installed—usually through the Add New Hardware wizard. The following steps outline the process for installing a new driver:

1 In the Control Panel, double-click the Add New Hardware icon.

2 Click Next, click No, and then click Next. (Do not let the wizard autodetect devices.)

3 Click the type of hardware for which you are installing the driver, and then click Next.

4 Click Have Disk.

5 Type the path for the driver you are installing and click OK, or click Browse and locate the driver manually. You must type the path for or locate the OEMSETUP.INF file from the manufacturer.

6 In the dialog box listing the INF file, click OK. Click OK to continue.

7 Click the correct driver, and then click OK.

8 Click Finish.

For Windows 98 systems, drivers can typically be updated just by clicking the Update Driver button on the Driver tab in the device's Properties dialog (Figure 35-1). That will start the Update Driver wizard (Figure 35-2), which will automatically walk you through the driver update process. However, you can still use the Add New Hardware wizard to update device drivers if necessary.

INSTALLING MODEMS MANUALLY

With the popularity of online resources such as AOL and the Internet, most current PCs are equipped with a modem. Modem installation is very similar to other device installations, but modems offer some peculiar wrinkles that often demand a slightly different installation approach. (They are also not always detected with 100 percent reliability.) The steps below outline a modem installation:

1 In the Control Panel, double-click the Modems icon.

2 If this is to be the first modem installed in the computer, the Install New Modem wizard starts automatically (Figure 35-3). If not, click Add on the General tab.

3 If you want Windows 95/98 to autodetect your modem, click Next. If not, click the "Don't detect my modem..." check box to select it, and then click Next.

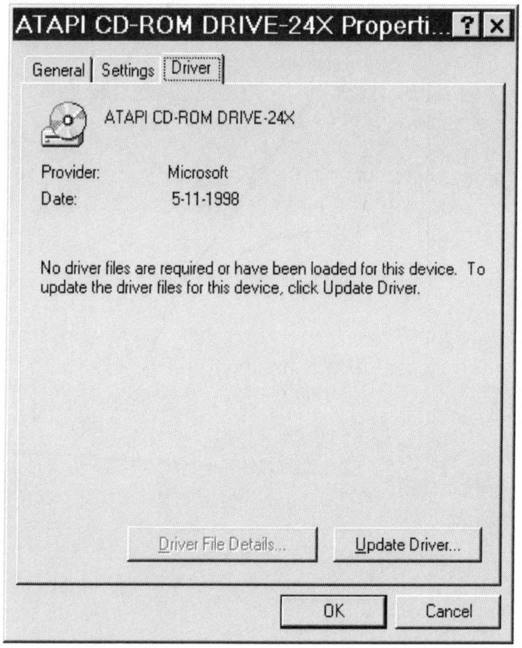

FIGURE 35-1 Using the Update Driver button under Windows 98

4 If you chose to have Windows 95/98 detect your modem, Windows 95/98 queries the serial ports on your computer, looking for a modem. If Windows detects an incorrect modem, click Change, and select the appropriate manufacturer and model. Click Next, and then continue with step 7.

5 If you chose to select your modem manually, click the appropriate manufacturer and model, and then click Next.

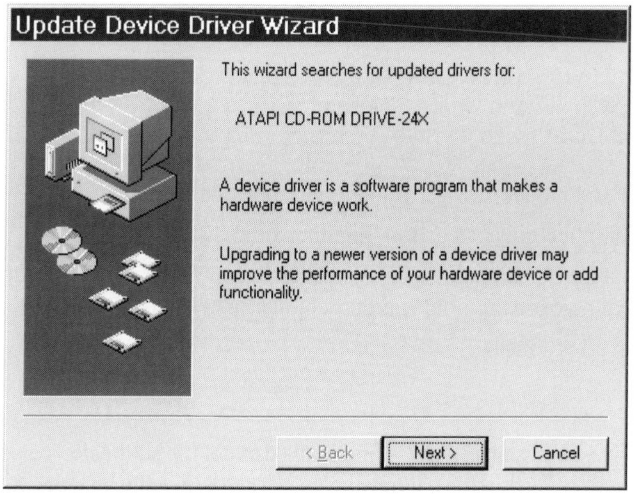

FIGURE 35-2 Starting the Update Device Driver wizard

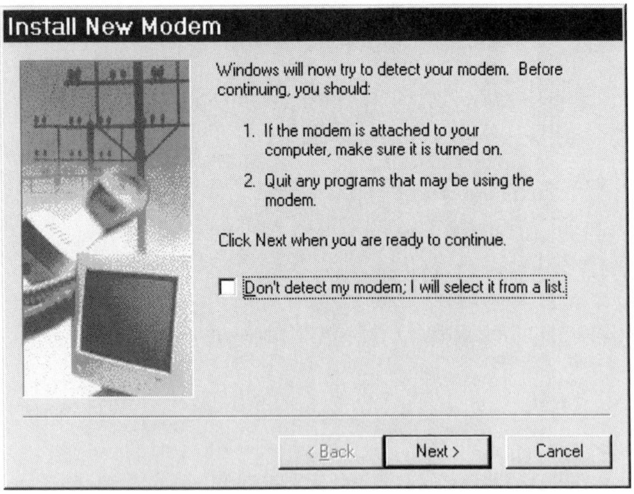

FIGURE 35-3 Starting the Install New Modem wizard

6 Click the appropriate communications port, and then click Next.

7 Click Finish.

INSTALLING PRINTERS MANUALLY

Although the newest generation of printers are PnP compatible and can be identified automatically, most traditional printers must be specified under Windows 95/98 manually. This is accomplished through the Printers icon as specified below:

1 Click the Start button, point to Settings, and then click Printers.

2 Double-click Add Printer, and then click Next.

3 Click Local Printer or Network Printer as appropriate, and then click Next.

> If you click Network Printer, you are prompted for the network path for the printer. If you do not know the correct path, click Browse, or check with your network administrator. Click either Yes or No as appropriate in the "Do you print from MS-DOS-based programs?" area, and then click Next.

4 Click the appropriate manufacturer and model for your printer, and then click Next.

5 If you chose to install a local printer, click the correct port, and then click Next.

6 Type a name for the printer (or accept the default name), and then click either Yes or No in the "Do you want your Windows-based programs to use this printer as the default printer?" area. Click Next.

7 To print a test page, click Yes; then click Finish.

DISABLING A DEVICE

Ordinarily, Windows 95/98 identifies devices, assigns resources, and loads drivers for all the devices it finds. From time to time (especially during troubleshooting), it may be necessary to disable a device. In effect, disabling a device prevents Windows 95/98 from loading drivers or allocating resources associated with the device, but does not remove the device from the system. This is a particularly handy trick when checking for resource assignment problems.

1 Click the Start button, point to Settings, and then click Control Panel.
2 Double-click the System icon.
3 On the Device Manager tab, click the device you want, and then click Properties.
4 On the General tab, click the Original Configuration (Current) check box to clear it, and then click OK. Under Windows 98, you should check the box marked "Disable in this hardware profile"; and then click OK.

You may need to reboot the system in order to free the resources, but the neutralized device should no longer be available.

REMOVING A DEVICE

There will be times (especially during troubleshooting) when it may be necessary to remove a device entirely from the Windows 95/98 platform in order to free resources otherwise assigned to the device. Normally, Windows 95/98 should free the resources of a PnP device simply by disabling it (see "Disabling a Device" above), or when the device is physically removed. But legacy cards may need to be removed manually before their assigned resources can be freed. To free resource settings used by disabled hardware:

1 Click Start, Settings, and Control Panel. Click the System icon and select the Device Manager tab.
2 In the hardware list, click the plus sign next to the type of hardware, and then click the device that is disabled.
3 Click Remove, and then click OK.
4 Click the Start button, and then click Shut Down. Click OK. When the message appears saying it is safe to do so, turn off and unplug your computer, and then remove the physical hardware device from inside the computer.

> PnP device resources are freed automatically when you disable or remove a device. To see if resources are free after the device is disabled but *before* removing the device, double-click the device in the hardware list in Device Manager, and then click the Resources tab.

SYMPTOMS

SYMPTOM 35-1 **Windows setup crashes on first boot after configuring PnP devices**
This problem can occur if all the following conditions exist: (1) your computer has a PCI bus with PCI adapters, (2) there is an ISA adapter (such as a sound card) in your computer, (3) the ISA adapter was not configured (or was not running in real mode) before you ran setup, and (4) you have not changed any of your computer's CMOS settings. If all of these conditions are true, chances are that one hardware device in the computer is conflicting with another. When this occurs, Windows may hang up or crash.

For example, if you have a PCI-based computer with a PCI video card, PCI SCSI adapter, and ISA sound card, setup runs its hardware detection and finds the ISA device. When setup is finished, your computer is restarted and the sound card driver is loaded. When Windows enumerates the PCI bus and its adapters, it finds that the BIOS has set the IRQ for one of the PCI devices to the same IRQ as the sound card—causing the conflict.

There are several possible techniques to correct this problem. First, try reserving the IRQ for your ISA devices in the CMOS setup. This prevents the BIOS from assigning the IRQ to another device such as the PCI system. You can try removing the ISA device(s) until the computer is completely configured to run Windows 95/98, then reinstall the device(s). After you reinstall each ISA adapter, run the Add New Hardware wizard to configure the device. Third, if the ISA device is software configurable, you may be able to assign nonconflicting resources using your Device Manager:

1. Reboot your computer. When you see the "Starting Windows" message, press F8, and then choose Safe Mode from the Startup menu.
2. Click Start, highlight Settings, and then click Control Panel.
3. Double-click the System icon, and then click the Device Manager tab.
4. Click the offending ISA device, and then click Properties.
5. Click the Original Configuration (Current) check box to clear it, and then click OK. Under Windows 98, select the "Disable in this hardware profile" check box. Now restart Windows 95/98.
6. If Windows 95/98 starts and finishes the setup configuration, click Start, highlight Settings, and then click Control Panel.
7. Double-click the System icon, and then click the Device Manager tab.
8. Click the offending ISA device, and then click Properties.
9. Click the Resources tab. On the Resources tab, select a nonconflicting resource for the ISA device (if one is available). If you do not have a suitable resource available, you may need to reconfigure another device to free the appropriate resources (or remove the offending ISA device outright).
10. Restart the system if necessary.

SYMPTOM 35-2 Selecting a "None of the above" hardware profile under Windows 95/98 may reset your device configurations When you have multiple hardware profiles configured on your system, an option labeled "None of the above" is included in the list of available hardware profiles when you start the computer. If you select "None of the above," plug-and-play enumeration occurs, and *some* devices may be reset to configurations that the drivers cannot support. When this occurs, you may have to manually reload the original device drivers. This problem is corrected in the following updated file(s):

- For Windows 95 version 4.00.950 (retail release) and 4.00.950 A (Service Pack 1), use the update:

```
IO.SYS   dated 12/22/97  5:53pm     223,230 bytes
```

- For Windows 95 version 4.00.950 B (OSR 2 and 2.1) and 4.00.950 C (OSR 2.5), use the update:

```
IO.SYS   dated 12/22/97  6:10pm     214,918 bytes
```

- For Windows 98 version 4.10.1998 (retail release), use the update:

```
IO.SYS   dated 05/21/99  05:13p     222,456 bytes
```

SYMPTOM 35-3 The Energy Star check box is not available for your monitor When you check the Monitor tab in the Display Properties dialog box under Windows 98, the Monitor Is Energy Star Compliant check box may not be available. This trouble can occur if Windows 98 is configured to automatically detect plug-and-play monitors. You must disable the automatic detection of any plug-and-play monitor(s):

1. Click Start, highlight Settings, click Control Panel, and then double-click Display.
2. Click the Settings tab, and then click Advanced.
3. Click the Monitor tab, click the "Automatically detect plug-and-play monitors" check box to clear it, click OK, and click OK again.
4. Restart the computer.

SYMPTOM 35-4 After upgrading to Windows 98 SE, the ES1869 sound device is disabled When you review the ES1869 Plug-and-Play Audio Drive sound card in Device Manager, you'll notice a yellow exclamation point and a status of "Code 10" for the sound card. This problem occurs after you upgrade your Windows 95/98 system to Windows 98 Second Edition (SE). To fix this problem, you'll need to remove and reinstall the ES1869 plug-and-play sound card:

1. Click Start, highlight Settings, click Control Panel, and then double-click the System icon.
2. Click the Device Manager tab, click the "ES1869 Plug and Play AudioDrive" sound card, click Remove, click OK, and then click OK again.
3. Click Yes when you're prompted to restart your computer.

After your computer restarts, the ES1869 Plug-and-Play AudioDrive sound card should be detected and installed properly.

35

SYMPTOM 35-5 The system crashes when you run the Add New Hardware wizard under Windows 98 This issue may be caused by the incorrect interpretation of data stored in the computer's CMOS RAM (set up by the BIOS). On certain motherboards, Windows 98 may not be able to successfully complete the plug-and-play detection process. You can probably resolve this issue by upgrading the system BIOS.

SYMPTOM 35-6 You encounter an error when updating the Crystal PnP Audio Codec driver under Windows 98 After you update the Crystal Plug and Play Audio Codec driver in your Device Manager, you may receive an error message such as:

```
Crystal PnP Audio CODEC
Setup cannot upgrade the existing driver for this device. Press OK to continue.
```

This problem can occur if Windows 98 cannot safely upgrade the driver that's already installed. The problem might also occur if such an upgrade might disable a feature that the current driver provides, or if the information (or INF) file for the driver is missing.

SYMPTOM 35-7 You find that a joystick port is not removed when you remove the sound card When you remove a sound card from your computer, and remove the sound card in the Windows 95/98 Device Manager, the joystick (game port) on the sound card continues to appear in Device Manager. This trouble occurs because there is no parent-child relationship between the sound card and the joystick port. The virtual joystick device driver (VJOYD.VXD) is unable to detect whether the joystick port has been removed (or the joystick port is present but has no joystick attached), so the driver is always active. When you remove the sound card in Device Manager, the joystick port is not automatically removed. You'll need to remove the game port device manually:

1. Right-click the My Computer icon on your desktop, and then click Properties.
2. Click the Device Manager tab.
3. Click the plus (+) next to "Sound, video, and game controllers" to expand the branch.
4. Click the Gameport Joystick device to highlight it, and then click Remove.

SYMPTOM 35-8 **You notice more than one instance of the same port in the Windows 95/98 Add New Hardware wizard** When you're manually installing new hardware (such as a modem) using the Add New Hardware wizard, multiple instances of COM or LPT ports may appear as options in the port selection dialog. This trouble can occur when there are duplicate entries for a COM or LPT port in the registry. (Duplicate entries can occur if the computer does not contain a plug-and-play BIOS.) You can generally correct this problem by editing the redundant registry entries manually.

> Editing the registry incorrectly may prevent the system from booting. Before you edit the registry, you should first make a backup copy of the registry files (SYSTEM.DAT and USER.DAT) to your boot disk. Both are hidden files in the \Windows folder.

1. In the registry editor (RegEdit), export the appropriate registry keys (for backup purposes):

   HKEY_LOCAL_Machine\Enum\Bios*PNP0400 (or *PNP0401) for duplicate LPT ports
   HKEY_LOCAL_Machine\Enum\Bios*PNP0500 (or *PNP0501) for duplicate COM ports
2. Now delete the appropriate registry keys.
3. Quit RegEdit, and then shut down and restart your computer normally.
4. Click Start, highlight Settings, click Control Panel, and then double-click Add New Hardware.
5. Click Next, click Yes, and then click Next again. Windows automatically locates the installed ports and re-creates the correct entries in the registry without duplicates.

SYMPTOM 35-9 **You cannot select a higher display resolution in the Windows 98 Display Properties dialog** When you try to increase the screen resolution in the Display Properties dialog, you may be unable to choose a higher resolution than the video system is capable of. For example, your monitor may support a maximum resolution of 1600×1200 pixels, but this setting may be missing from the Screen Area box. In virtually all cases, the system's ESCD contains incorrect information about your particular monitor. You'll need to install your monitor manually:

1. Click Start, highlight Settings, click Control Panel, and then double-click Display.
2. Click the Settings tab, and then click Advanced.
3. Click the Monitor tab, click the "Automatically detect Plug & Play monitors" check box to clear it, and then click Apply.
4. Click Change, click Next, click "Display a list of all the drivers in a specific location, so you can select the driver you want," and then click Next.
5. Click Show All Hardware, and then follow the instructions on the screen to finish installing your specific monitor.

SYMPTOM 35-10 You see wavy lines when using a MAG DX-1795 monitor under Windows 98 This problem may occur if your video adapter is configured for 1600×1200 resolution, and the "Automatically detect Plug & Play monitors" check box is selected on the Monitor tab in the Display Properties dialog. To correct this problem, you'll need to reinstall your monitor manually:

1 Click Start, highlight Settings, click Control Panel, and then double-click Display.
2 Click the Settings tab, and then click Advanced.
3 On the Monitor tab, click the "Automatically detect Plug & Play monitors" check box to clear it, and then click Change.
4 Click Next, click "Display a list of all the drivers in a specific location, so you can select the driver you want," and then click Next.
5 Click Show All Hardware.
6 In the Manufacturers box, click "MAG Technology Co., Ltd.," and then click MAG DX-1795 in the Models box.
7 Click Next, and then follow the instructions on your screen to finish installing the monitor.

SYMPTOM 35-11 The PC powers down when you shut down Windows 95/98 When you use the Shut Down command on the Start menu to shut down Windows, your computer may automatically power down after displaying the message "Please wait while your computer shuts down." This behavior is a normal Advanced Power Management (APM) feature. There is no way to change this action—the hardware powers down in response to a software request. However, this occurs only on computers with a PnP BIOS that supports APM features.

35

SYMPTOM 35-12 You have trouble restarting the PC when a device uses IRQ 12 When you try to restart your computer under Windows 95/98 using the Restart option in your Shut Down dialog box, your computer may hang up. This is often a problem on computers with a BIOS that "expects" IRQ 12 to be used by a PS/2-style mouse port, but instead it is used by a software-configurable hardware device such as a PnP expansion card. To work around this problem, reserve IRQ 12 in Device Manager (or change the IRQ for the software-configurable device in Device Manager). You may also consider upgrading the BIOS in your computer to a later version. To reserve an IRQ with Device Manager:

1 Open the Control Panel, and then double-click the System icon.
2 On the Device Manager tab, double-click the Computer entry.
3 Click the Reserve Resources tab, click the Interrupt Request (IRQ) option, and then click Add.
4 In the Value box, click the IRQ you want to reserve (IRQ 12).
5 Click OK until you return to the Control Panel.
6 Reboot the PC if necessary.

SYMPTOM 35-13 The "volume control" tool may not be installed with some sound cards under Windows 95/98 Tools such as Volume Control are installed based on the hardware detected during the installation of Windows 95/98. If the computer contains an ISA PnP device that is not enabled by the BIOS, the device is not detected until after Windows is installed. There are two ways around this. If you're just installing Windows 95/98 now, use the Custom Setup option. When you're prompted to select the components you want, select Volume Control in the Multimedia section. If Windows 95/98 is already installed, follow these steps to install Volume Control:

1. Open the Control Panel, and then double-click the Add/Remove Programs icon.
2. Click the Windows Setup tab, click Multimedia, and then click Details.
3. Click the Volume Control check box to select it.
4. Click OK; then click OK again.
5. Reboot the PC if necessary.

SYMPTOM 35-14 The ES1788 or ES688 sound device is not detected when it's installed under Windows 98 This happens because the device is not fully PnP compliant. You'll need to install the device manually using the Add New Hardware wizard:

1. Click Start, highlight Settings, and then click Control Panel.
2. Double-click the Add New Hardware icon, click Next, and then click Next again.
3. Click "No, I want to select the hardware from a list," and then click Next.
4. In the Manufacturers box, click ESS Technology, Inc.
5. In the Models box, click ESS AudioDrive, click Next, and then click Next again.
6. Restart Windows when you're prompted to do so.

SYMPTOM 35-15 After reinstalling Windows 98 on a multimonitor system, you have to reconfigure some monitors after setup is completed This is a known problem with some ATI video adapters. Windows 98 disables PnP functionality for ATI video adapters because they do not handle plug-and-play correctly. To work around this problem, manually configure each monitor connected to an ATI video adapter:

1. Click Start, highlight Settings, and then click Control Panel.
2. Double-click the Display icon, and then click the Settings tab.
3. In the Display box, click the adapter you want, and then click Advanced.
4. On the Monitor tab, click Change.
5. Click Next, click "Display a list of all the drivers in a specific location, so you can select the driver you want," and then click Next.
6. Click Show All Hardware.
7. Click the appropriate manufacturer and model of your monitor, click Next, and then click Finish.
8. Click Close, click OK, and then reboot the system if necessary.

SYMPTOM 35-16 After upgrading Windows 95 to Windows 98, the Display Adapters entry is missing in the Device Manager This problem is known to occur when your video adapter uses the Nvidia Riva 128 chipset and is unable to secure an IRQ during the PnP detection portion of Windows 98 setup. One solution is to assign an IRQ to the video system using the "Assign IRQ to VGA" option in your CMOS setup (if available). Another option is to disable PCI bus IRQ steering in the Device Manager.

SYMPTOM 35-17 You see an error such as "CTSOUND1008: Invalid /BLASTER=A:xxxx argument" When you upgrade Windows 3.x to Windows 98 on a computer with a Creative Labs Sound Blaster 16 sound card installed, you may receive the following error when your computer restarts:

```
Error CTSOUND1008: Invalid "/BLASTER=A:xxx" argument
```

Or the error may look like this:

```
Error: DIGN8002 The BLASTER environment settings are invalid
```

This problem will generally occur if the plug-and-play configuration drivers for your Sound Blaster 16 sound card are being loaded from the AUTOEXEC.BAT and CONFIG.SYS files. To correct this problem, you'll need to open your startup files in a text editor and REMark out the command lines related to your sound card. For example, in AUTOEXEC.BAT the line might read

```
REM c:\vibra16\diagnose /s /w=c:\windows
```

And under CONFIG.SYS the line might read

```
REM device=c:\vibra16\drv\vibra16.sys /unit=0 /blaster=a:220 i:10 d:3 h:7
```

Save your changes and reboot the system.

SYMPTOM 35-18 Windows 98 locks up when using a Diamond Stealth II S220 video adapter This problem occurs most frequently when you start the Add New Hardware wizard while the Windows 98 default drivers for the Diamond Multimedia Stealth II S220 are installed—your computer may crash. If the "standard VGA" video driver is installed, the Add New Hardware wizard runs successfully. This is almost always due to a driver problem, so be sure to obtain and install the most current version of driver for this display adapter.

35

SYMPTOM 35-19 You find a "Code 8" is shown for a PnP BIOS device after upgrading to Windows 98 After upgrading, a yellow exclamation point may be displayed next to the "Plug-and-Play BIOS" device in Device Manager. If you view the Properties for the "Plug-and-Play BIOS" device, the following message may appear:

```
This device is not working properly because the file (BIOS.VXD) that loads
the drivers for this device is bad (Code 8). To fix this problem, click
Update Driver to update the driver for this device.
```

If you then click the Update Driver button and attempt to search for a better driver, you may receive a message saying that the best driver is already installed. In virtually all cases, the Windows 95 version of the BIOS.VXD file is in the \Windows folder, and you'll need to correct this:

1. Click Start, select Find, and then click Files Or Folders.
2. In the Named box, type **bios.vxd**, and then click Find Now.
3. In the Look In box, click the drive on which the \Windows folder is located.

4. In the list of found files, right-click the BIOS.VXD file located in the \Windows folder, click Delete, and then click Yes.
5. Quit the Find tool, and restart your computer.

SYMPTOM 35-20 Windows 95 fails to recognize the computer as plug-and-play
This type of problem often occurs with Intel OEM motherboards. Windows 95 does not recognize the computer as a plug-and-play platform, even though you receive a message during startup such as "Intel PnP BIOS Extensions Installed." Intel has developed some OEM motherboards that are equipped with a plug-and-play BIOS that does not contain the run-time services necessary to configure motherboard devices. An example of such a motherboard is the Intel P5/90. Gateway 2000 (and possibly other OEMs) ship computers with the P5/90 motherboard. You'll need to upgrade the system BIOS to comply with the plug-and-play BIOS version 1.0a specification or later.

SYMPTOM 35-21 You notice IRQ conflicts with PCI display adapters When you install a PCI video adapter that is configured to use a particular interrupt (IRQ), Windows 95/98 may configure it to use another IRQ that is already in use by another device. While PCI devices can share PCI IRQs, Windows 95/98 does not support sharing PCI IRQs with other non-PCI devices (such as an IDE controller). Use the Device Manager to resolve the conflict by assigning a different IRQ to one of the conflicting devices (usually the new PCI video adapter).

> This kind of behavior does not occur with ISA or VESA Local Bus VLB display adapters.

SYMPTOM 35-22 The resources for disabled devices are not freed Even though you disable a device in your computer's CMOS setup, Windows 95/98 reenables the device and allocates its resources. Windows 95/98 may also reinstall a device that is removed from Device Manager. This happens because Windows 95/98 detects plug-and-play devices regardless of the CMOS setup. To prevent Windows 95/98 from reactivating disabled hardware, you must disable the hardware in the computer's CMOS setup and remove it from the current configuration in Windows 95/98. This frees the device's resources for other devices to use.

1. Click the Start button, point to Settings, and then click Control Panel.
2. Double-click the System icon.
3. Click the Device Manager tab, and then double-click the device you want to disable.
4. Click the General tab, and then click the Original Configuration (Current) check box to clear it. Under Windows 98, check the box marked "Disable in this hardware profile."
5. Click the OK button.
6. Restart Windows 95/98 when prompted.
7. Immediately start the CMOS setup routine and disable the device in the CMOS setup.
8. Save the changes to CMOS, and allow the system to boot normally.

> When you disable a device in Device Manager, you must restart your computer before you can reassign the device's resources to another device.

SYMPTOM 35-23 An AST PnP BIOS is not registered as PnP The AST plug-and-play BIOS is not registered as plug-and-play capable under Windows 95/98. This is usually because the AST PnP BIOS contains incorrect information in its 16-bit protected-mode entry point. When Windows 95/98 detects this incorrect code in the AST BIOS it will not recognize the BIOS as plug-and-play capable. You'll need to contact AST for a BIOS upgrade.

SYMPTOM 35-24 **A PnP ISA adapter is not recognized automatically** If you insert a PnP ISA adapter in a computer whose motherboard does not contain PCI slots, Windows 95/98 may not recognize the new ISA adapter automatically. The Device Manager may also display a "PCI bus" entry with an exclamation point in a yellow circle, with the status "No Plug and Play ISA bus was found. (Code 29)." This problem is typically caused by a PnP BIOS that is not supported by Windows 95/98 on computers that have a PCI BIOS, but not a PCI bus. On PCI computers, it is usually the PCI driver that starts the PnP ISA driver. If the PCI driver fails, the ISA driver is not loaded, and therefore PnP ISA adapters are not automatically recognized or configured. To add a PnP adapter so that Windows 95/98 automatically recognizes it, enable the ISA PnP bus manually:

1. In the Control Panel, double-click the Add New Hardware icon, and then click Next.
2. Click No, and then click Next.
3. Click System Devices, and then click Next.
4. Click ISA Plug And Play Bus, and then click Next.
5. Click Finish.
6. Restart your computer when you are prompted to do so.

You may also want to contact your computer manufacturer to see about obtaining an updated PnP BIOS that is better supported by Windows 95/98.

35

SYMPTOM 35-25 **The computer no longer operates properly after docking or undocking** As an example, the keyboard or mouse may stop working. "Hot docking" and "hot undocking" refer to inserting the computer in a docking station or removing it from the docking station while the computer is running at full power. By contrast, "warm docking" refers to docking or undocking the computer while it is in suspend mode. Laptop or portable computers with a PnP BIOS can be hot or warm docked or undocked. In virtually all cases, the computer does not have a suitable PnP BIOS. (This is mandatory for hot or warm docking and undocking.) To correct this problem on a permanent basis, you'll need to upgrade the laptop's BIOS to a version that better supports PnP. In the meantime, you can work around this problem by turning the computer off before you dock or undock it.

SYMPTOM 35-26 **Serial PnP devices are not recognized when an adapter is used to connect them** For example, when you use a 9-pin to 25-pin serial adapter with a serial PnP device, the device may not be enumerated by the configuration manager at startup. This is caused by the adapter. Some 9-pin to 25-pin serial adapters do not connect the lines that pass the PnP initialization string (including adapters made by Microsoft before the release of Windows 95). Try another (more current) serial adapter. If the problem persists, add the device manually using the Add New Hardware wizard in the Control Panel.

SYMPTOM 35-27 **Windows 95/98 setup hangs up when detecting SCSI controllers** This often happens with Adaptec SCSI controllers on the first reboot while PnP devices are being detected, and is known to happen when a SCSI hard disk is supported by an Adaptec AHA 2940, Adaptec 2940AU, or Adaptec 2940W controller. You can work around this problem by disabling the SCSI controller and allowing setup to finish the PnP device detection:

1. Enable PnP SCAM support in the Adaptec SCSI controller BIOS setup.

2. Disable BIOS Support For Int13 Extension in the Adaptec SCSI controller BIOS setup.
3. Restart Windows 95/98, press the F8 key when you see the "Starting Windows" message, and then choose Safe Mode from the Startup menu.
4. In Control Panel, double-click the System icon, click the Performance tab, click File System, and then click the Troubleshooting tab.
5. Enable the following two options: "Disable protect-mode hard disk interrupt handling" and "Disable all 32 bit protect-mode disk drivers."
6. Click OK, and then click OK again.
7. When you are prompted to restart your computer, click Yes to continue with setup.
8. After Windows 95 is installed, disable the options you enabled in step 5.

SYMPTOM 35-28 **After installing an HP OfficeJet 300 printer, you encounter a "Fatal Exception Error" each time you run the Add New Hardware wizard** You'll typically see Exception Errors 06, 0E, 0C, or 0D. This is because the HP OfficeJet Series 300 Device Manager contends with Windows 95/98 for control of the PnP system. The HP installation process sets up a shortcut in the Startup folder that runs HPOJDMAN.EXE /AUTOPROMPT. This causes HPOJDMAN.EXE to run in the background. Start the Close Program dialog box by pressing CTRL-ALT-DELETE. Click HPOJDMAN in the list of tasks, and then click End Task. Check with HP (**www.hp.com**) for updated printer software utilities.

SYMPTOM 35-29 **The PS/2 mouse is disabled after installing an ISA PnP device** For example, installing a SoundBlaster 16 "value" sound card disables the PS/2 mouse. This problem can occur on computers where the PnP BIOS (rather than Windows 95/98) assigns resources to ISA PnP devices. The PnP BIOS may assign IRQ 12 to the IDE drive and disable the mouse port. To correct this problem, disable the BIOS PnP support in the computer's CMOS setup to allow Windows 95/98 to configure the hardware instead.

SYMPTOM 35-30 **When running the Add New Hardware wizard, it doesn't detect a device that has been removed in Device Manager on a multiple-profile system** This is because removing a PnP device from one profile and leaving it in another causes a flag to be set in the registry to prevent the device from being enumerated on the next startup. This may also cause the Add New Hardware wizard to bypass the device. The flag exists only in the profile in which the device was removed. To prevent this type of problem from occurring, disable the device in Device Manager instead of removing it. To disable a device, click the Disable In This Hardware Profile check box for the device in Device Manager. To restore (or redetect) the device, remove it from all profiles, and then run the Add New Hardware wizard.

SYMPTOM 35-31 **An extra serial port is displayed in the Device Manager** When you are using Windows 95 OSR 2 or 2.1, you may see an extra communications port in Device Manager. There is an exclamation point in a yellow circle next to the port. If you remove the port, it is redetected the next time you restart your computer. The computer's PnP BIOS is probably reporting (incorrectly) that the COM ports are not using resources, though they were detected during setup. This is a problem with Windows 95. Check with Microsoft (**www.microsoft.com**) for any available upgrades or patches.

SYMPTOM 35-32 **You cannot set up Windows 95/98 while a PnP program is active** When you try to install Windows 95/98, you may receive the following error message:

```
A fatal exception OE has occurred at 0028:xxxxxxxx in VxD VMM(06) + xxxxxxxx
```

Or, you may receive a Vwin32 error message displayed on a blue screen, a registry error message, or a general protection (GP) fault error message. This problem can occur if you have a PnP program active in memory when you try to install Windows 95/98. To work around this issue, install Windows 95/98 from a command prompt. Restart the computer. When you see the "Starting Windows" message, press the F8 key, and then choose Command Prompt Only from the Startup menu. At the command prompt, type

```
<drive>:\setup.exe
```

where <drive> is the drive containing your original Windows 95/98 setup disk or CD-ROM.

SYMPTOM 35-33 **An IBM ThinkPad doesn't support PnP under Windows 95/98** Chances are that the ThinkPad requires a BIOS update. The following IBM ThinkPad models are known to need specific BIOS versions:

- ThinkPad 750 family: 750/360/755 System Program Service Diskette version 1.20 or later
- ThinkPad 755C/Cs and 360/355 family: 750/360/755 System Program Service Diskette version 1.20 or later
- ThinkPad 755CE/CD, ThinkPad 755CX/CV, ThinkPad 755CDV: 755 System Program Service Diskette version 1.30 or later
- ThinkPad 701C: 701C System Program Service Diskette version 3H or later
- ThinkPad 340CSE and 370C: 340 System Program Service Diskette version 1.10 or later

The following ThinkPad models require APM BIOS 1.1 or later and PnP BIOS 1.0a or later in order for these features to work correctly with Windows 95/98:

- ThinkPad 755C/Cs
- ThinkPad 360/355 family
- ThinkPad 755CE/CD/CX/CV/CDV
- ThinkPad 340CSE
- ThinkPad 370C
- ThinkPad 701C
- ThinkPad 530CS

The following ThinkPad models require APM BIOS version 1.0 to work correctly with Windows 95/98. There is no PnP BIOS support for these models:

- ThinkPad 750 family
- ThinkPad 340 monochrome display system
- ThinkPad 230Cs

To obtain an updated BIOS or System Program Service Diskette for an IBM ThinkPad computer, please contact IBM (**www.ibm.com**).

SYMPTOM 35-34 **A PnP pointing device is not detected** When you connect a PnP pointing device (such as Microsoft PnP serial mouse, Microsoft EasyBall, or Microsoft IntelliMouse), the new device may not be detected by Windows 95/98. Running the Add New Hardware wizard does not correct the problem. This is almost always because the registry entries for your *previous* pointing device were not properly removed from the registry. This problem is known to occur when your previous pointing device was a Microsoft, Microsoft-compatible, or Logitech mouse. To work around this problem, use the registry editor (RegEdit) to remove the registry entries for your previous pointing device. Remove the following registry keys:

```
Hkey_Local_Machine\System\CurrentControlSet\Services\Class\Mouse\<nnnn>
```

where <nnnn> is an incremental four-digit number starting at 0000. Also remove the following registry keys (if they exist):

```
Hkey_Local_Machine\Enum\Root\Mouse\<nnnn>
```

where <nnnn> is an incremental four-digit number starting at 0000. Remove all registry keys under the following registry keys (if they exist):

```
Hkey_Local_Machine\Enum\Serenum
```

Remove the following registry key (if it exists):

```
Hkey_Local_Machine\Software\Logitech\Mouseware
```

Use the right mouse button to click My Computer, and then click Properties on the menu that appears. Click the Device Manager tab. Click each serial pointing device, and then click Remove. Click OK, and then restart Windows 95/98. When you restart Windows, the attached pointing device will be detected, and the appropriate drivers will be installed.

Editing the registry incorrectly may prevent the system from booting. Before you edit the registry, you should first make a backup copy of the registry files (SYSTEM.DAT and USER.DAT) to your boot disk. Both are hidden files in the \Windows folder.

SYMPTOM 35-35 The PnP printer is redetected every time Windows 95/98 starts This occurs even when the printer is already installed. When you start Windows 95/98, the following message may be displayed:

```
New Hardware Found
<device>
Windows has found new hardware and is installing the software for it
```

This problem is known to occur with Hewlett-Packard 4L and Hewlett-Packard DeskJet 660C PnP printers, and is usually caused by damage to the following registry key:

```
Hkey_Local_Machine\Enum\Lptenum
```

Remove the registry key, and then restart your computer. When Windows restarts, it will detect the printer and install support for it. Once the printer is installed, it will no longer be detected each time you start Windows 95/98.

Editing the registry incorrectly may prevent the system from booting. Before you edit the registry, you should first make a backup copy of the registry files (SYSTEM.DAT and USER.DAT). Both are hidden files in the \Windows folder.

SYMPTOM 35-36 **After installing Windows 95/98, none of the APM features were installed** You may also note that there is no "battery meter" for laptops. Some computers and BIOS revisions are known to be incompatible with the APM 1.1 specification. You are probably running Windows 95/98 on such a computer. As a result, the hardware "suspend" functions of your computer should still function correctly, but you cannot use the Windows 95/98 APM features. Windows 95 turns off APM support completely on the following computers:

- AMIBIOS 07/08/1994
- Any Gateway ColorBook later than 1.0 with SystemSoft BIOS or ColorBook with APM 1.0
- AST Ascentia 900N
- Canon Innova 150C
- DECpc LPv+ 1.00, 1.01, 1.02
- NCR/AT&T 3150
- Ultra laptop 486sx33
- Wyse Forte GSV 486/66
- Zenon P5/90

Windows 95 turns off power status polling (so you do not see a battery meter) on the following computers:

- IBM ThinkPad 500
- LexBook
- WinBook

35

Windows 95 uses APM 1.0 mode on NEC Versa and AT&T Globalyst systems with APM 1.1 BIOS and no plug-and-play BIOS. The following IBM ThinkPad computers support APM 1.1:

- ThinkPad 755C
- ThinkPad 360/355 Family
- ThinkPad 755CE/CD/CX/CV/CDV
- ThinkPad 340CSE
- ThinkPad 370C
- ThinkPad 701C
- ThinkPad 530CS

The following IBM ThinkPad computers work with Windows 95, but only APM BIOS 1.0 is supported:

- ThinkPad 750 family
- ThinkPad 340 (monochrome)
- ThinkPad 230Cs

The ASUS PCI/I P55SP4 motherboard with a SiS 5511/5512/5513 chipset and an Award BIOS has been known to exhibit similar problems. (The battery meter may appear on the task bar when it should not.) This problem should be fixed with PnP BIOS version 0110 (11/21/95) for revision 1.2 and 1.3 motherboards. Revision 1.4 motherboards have this fix using PnP BIOS version 0303 (11/21/95).

SYMPTOM 35-37 **The Device Manager reports a "PCI-to-ISA Bridge Conflict"** The Device Manager displays a PCI-to-ISA bridge entry with an exclamation point in a yellow circle, indicating that there is a resource conflict. This problem is typically caused by a PnP BIOS that reports both a PCI and an ISA bus, but only an ISA bus is present, so there is no actual conflict. You'll need to update the PnP BIOS to a version with better detection and reporting capability.

SYMPTOM 35-38 **The PnP BIOS is disabled on a laptop or notebook computer** When you install Windows 95/98 on a dockable notebook computer with a PnP BIOS, you see no "Eject PC" command on the Start menu when the notebook computer is docked in a docking station. Also, no PnP BIOS node is displayed in System Devices under the Device Manager. This problem was known to occur on IBM ThinkPad (360/750/755 series) dockable notebook computers with a PnP BIOS, and occurs because early versions of dockable notebook computers with PnP BIOS are not fully compatible with Windows 95/98. When a PnP BIOS is disabled in Windows 95/98, certain features (such as warm docking) no longer work. To make your dockable notebook computer compatible with Windows 95/98, contact the manufacturer of your notebook computer and obtain the most recent PnP BIOS.

> In general, a PnP BIOS dated after 7/1/95 is compatible with Windows 95/98.

SYMPTOM 35-39 **The sound device on a DEC HiNote Ultra isn't working** When you install Windows 95/98 over an existing Windows for Workgroups 3.1x or Windows 3.1x installation on a DEC HiNote Ultra computer with a PnP BIOS, the sound device no longer works properly. Also, the wrong sound device is installed in Windows 95/98. This is a PnP BIOS problem. Early versions of the DEC HiNote Ultra shipped with a PnP BIOS are not compatible with Windows 95/98. Contact DEC and obtain the most recent PnP BIOS for the DEC HiNote Ultra.

SYMPTOM 35-40 **Device resources are not updated in a "forced" configuration** You'll notice that an exclamation point appears over a resource icon in Computer properties in Device Manager, or that changes you make to the resources assigned to a PnP device in the computer's CMOS setup are not reflected in the "Settings" column in Computer properties under Device Manager. This is because the device is using a "forced" configuration instead of an automatic configuration. To remove a forced configuration and allow the PnP device to be fully configurable by the computer's BIOS and Windows 95/98, set the device to use automatic settings:

1. Double-click the System icon in Control Panel.
2. Click the Device Manager tab.
3. Double-click the device, and then click the Resources tab.
4. Click the Use Automatic Settings check box to select it.
5. Click OK.

> A "forced" configuration overrides any BIOS or ROM settings (even if Windows 95/98 knows the device is currently consuming a different set of resources). If you move a device to a different set of resources, you must update the forced configuration manually. When you are diagnosing hardware problems, it is a good idea to look for forced configurations and remove them.

SYMPTOM 35-41 **Restarting the computer causes the PC to hang** This often happens when you try to restart your computer using the "Restart the computer" option in the Shut Down Windows dialog box. This problem can occur on computers with a BIOS that expects IRQ 12 to be used by a PS/2-style mouse port, but instead have a software-configurable hardware device (such as a PnP adapter) using IRQ 12. To work around this problem, reserve IRQ 12 in Device Manager, or change the IRQ for the software-configurable device in Device Manager. You may also want to consider upgrading the BIOS in the computer to a later version. To reserve an IRQ with Device Manager:

1. In the Control Panel, double-click the System icon.
2. On the Device Manager tab, double-click Computer.
3. On the Reserve Resources tab, click the Interrupt Request (IRQ) option, and then click Add.
4. In the Value box, click the IRQ you want to reserve.
5. Click OK until you return to Control Panel.

SYMPTOM 35-42 **Adding a PCI device to a Dell Dimension causes the system to hang in Windows 95/98** The BIOS in the Dell computer has probably configured the new PCI device to use IRQ 10, but another legacy device installed in the system is already configured to use IRQ 10. Although Windows 95/98 is designed to recognize resource conflicts such as this, this particular conflict causes the computer to hang before the Windows Configuration Manager recognizes that the conflict exists. Although the PCI bus is normally a PnP-compatible bus, the BIOS in Dell Dimension computers statically allocates IRQ 10 to a new PCI device. There is no way disable this behavior. To work around this problem, configure the existing legacy device to use an IRQ *other* than IRQ 10.

SYMPTOM 35-43 **You cannot configure disabled devices in the Device Manager** When you're using a PnP BIOS, you may not be able to configure (through Device Manager) a device that has been disabled in the BIOS, even though the BIOS supports configuring devices for the next time the computer starts. When you click the device in Device Manager and then click Properties, you see a message such as:

```
The device has been disabled in the hardware. In order to use this device,
you must re-enable the hardware. See your hardware documentation for details
(Code 29).
```

This is a problem with Windows 95. You'll need to enable the device in the BIOS *before* you try to configure it in Device Manager.

SYMPTOM 35-44 **A Toshiba T4900 laptop doesn't switch from LCD to external monitor** If you place a Toshiba T4900 computer into its docking station while Windows 95/98 is running (a "warm dock" operation), the display may not switch from the LCD screen to the external monitor. Toshiba's PnP BIOS does not switch the display properly between the LCD screen and an external monitor. For a short-term work-around, press the F5 key to manually toggle the display between the LCD screen and the external monitor. In the meantime, contact Toshiba for a PnP BIOS upgrade.

SYMPTOM 35-45 **A third port is detected with a CMD PCI dual-port IDE controller** When using a CMD PCI Dual Port IDE controller (with at least *one* device on both the primary and secondary port), the Device Manager displays a third port. This "false" third port is displayed with an exclamation point inside a yellow circle. This happens because the PnP BIOS in your computer is erroneously reporting that a third port is present. Windows 95/98 does not allocate any resources to the third port, and the existence of the third port in Device Manager should not cause any problems. However, if you want to disable the third port, follow these steps:

1. Use the right mouse button to click My Computer, and then click Properties on the menu that appears.
2. Click the Device Manager tab.
3. Click the third port, and then click Properties. Note that you may need to expand a branch of the hardware tree by double-clicking the branch, or by clicking the plus sign (+) to the left of the branch, before you can click the port.
4. Click the Original Configuration (Current) check box to clear it, and then click OK. With Windows 98, click the "Disable in this hardware profile" box to select it, and then click OK.

Further Study

Microsoft's plug-and-play page: **http://www.microsoft.com/hwdev/specs/pnpspecs.htm**

Microsoft PnP technology: **http://www.microsoft.com/win32dev/base/pnp.htm**

Intel's plug-and-play page: **http://www.intel.com/IAL/plugplay/index.htm**

36

POWER PROTECTION

CHAPTER AT A GLANCE

Power is one of those issues that's often taken for granted (or at least treated as an afterthought). Surges, spikes, and other power anomalies that occur in commercial power systems every day can damage the PC's power supply, and they can often adversely affect the drives and motherboard circuitry as well. Even when no serious damage occurs to the system, a loss of power can result in a loss of time and vital data—a serious consequence for any office or organization. This chapter is intended to explain the concept of power protection and show you the four major types of power protection devices that are available. As a PC technician, you can make use of this information in assisting your customers in developing adequate and reliable power protection plans that will suit their needs and budget. Proper power protection improves system reliability and reduces down-time.

Understanding Power Problems

Generally speaking, we have all come to take power for granted. In most cases, we simply tend to plug a device in the nearest available outlet and turn it on, *assuming* that an appropriate amount of voltage and current is available. If the device fails to function as expected, the natural assumption is that the *device* is at fault. In truth, this is not always the case. Computers and peripherals need certain minimum amounts of current and voltage at the AC line. If either value is too high or too low, the computer may behave erratically (or not work at all).

Commercial power is generated as a sinusoidal (AC) wave similar to the one shown in Figure 36-1. The amplitude of the wave represents *voltage*, and the rate at which the wave repeats represents *frequency*. Voltage and frequency characteristics vary in different regions of the world. Regardless of region, however, the AC signal should be perfectly smooth and regular. In actual practice, AC can suffer from a variety of ills: blackouts, brownouts, surges, and spikes.

BLACKOUTS

A *blackout* is a complete loss of electrical power where voltage and current drop to a very low value (typically zero). Blackouts are usually caused by a physical interruption in the local power network due to accidental damage by a person or act of nature. The interruption may affect an area as small as a street or as large as an entire region, depending on the point in the power distribution network where damage occurs.

Unless backup power is available, the loss of AC will invariably shut down the computer in a matter of milliseconds. In most cases, simply losing power does not damage a PC—memory is simply lost (along with any unsaved information), often just an inconvenience for casual home users. For business users, however, losing power can mean the loss of valuable data, representing hours of lost productivity. In extremely rare cases, a sudden and complete power loss can corrupt a hard drive's file structure and possibly damage files. The best and least expensive means of protection against a rare blackout is to save work

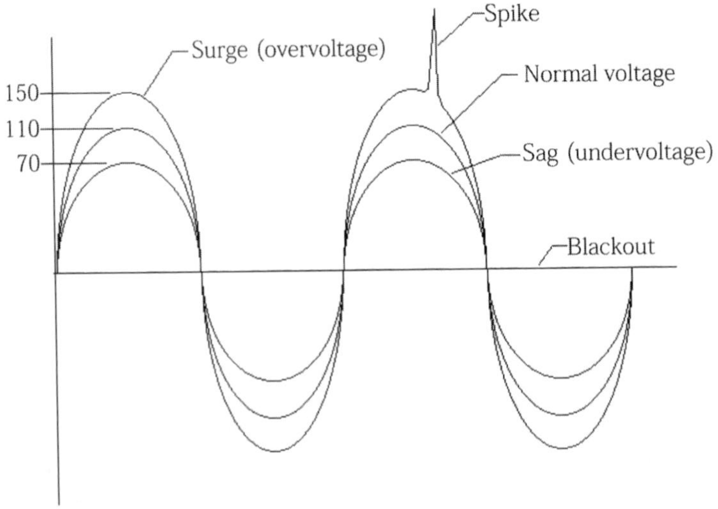

FIGURE 36-1 A comparison of AC sine waves during typical power problems

regularly—every 30 minutes to an hour. By taking this precaution, no more than an hour of work could be lost if power fails. For remote areas or regions that are subject to frequent power outages, a fast-switching backup power supply (BPS) or a reliable uninterruptible power supply (UPS) is highly recommended.

BROWNOUTS

Perhaps more dangerous than a sudden, complete power loss is the *brownout* (also called *sags*), an undervoltage condition caused by questionable electrical wiring or excessive electrical load on an AC circuit. High-load items (like air conditioners, coffee pots, fan motors, overhead projectors, photocopiers, and so on) draw so much current that the AC voltage level drops. PC supplies are *regulated,* which means the DC output provided to the computer circuitry will be constant over a range of AC input conditions. However, when AC conditions fall outside of that tolerable range, the supply will fall out of regulation, resulting in intermittent system operation (the system mysteriously "freezes," random memory errors occur, files may be lost or corrupted on the hard drive, and so on).

Undervoltage conditions can also damage the power supply. Since the PC's power supply responds to low AC voltages by drawing excessive current, serious undervoltage conditions can cause unusual heating that will eventually damage a PC power supply. If your customers complain of unusual system problems such as those described above, ask them to try their system on another circuit. Although one circuit may be loaded down, other circuits are probably not. If your customer cannot find a lightly-used circuit (or does not have access to one), ask him or her to try disconnecting high-load devices in their area, such as air conditioners, fans, and heaters. If the problems disappear, advise your customer to have a new AC circuit installed from the circuit breaker (make it very clear that the new AC circuit should be from another line phase). Urban areas suffer from summer brownouts that effect entire areas. Such regional brownouts are usually due to massive air conditioner load in the summertime.

It is difficult to overcome brownout conditions since most backup power supplies do not engage until voltage levels drop below brownout levels (usually 85 to 95 Vac). However, an uninterruptible power supply will prevent unpleasant surprises since the computer runs from the UPS normally anyway. Brownouts and blackouts do not interrupt UPS operation.

SURGES AND SPIKES

Basically, spikes and surges are the same villain—they just take different forms. *Surges* are small overvoltage conditions (140 Vac or more) that take place over relatively long periods (usually more than 1 second). In order to regulate power to a desired level, excess energy must be switched (in switching power supplies) or thrown away (in linear power supplies). In either case, excessive voltage creates overheating in the supply and will eventually destroy it. Some power supplies are designed to shut down in the event of voltage or thermal overloads, but you cannot always count on this feature in today's proliferation of inexpensive clone PCs.

A *spike* is a large overvoltage condition (perhaps as much as 2,500 volts) that occurs in the space of milliseconds. Lightning strikes and high-energy switching can cause spikes on the AC line. Heavy equipment like drill presses, welders, grinders, and other highly motorized devices can produce tremendous power spikes during normal operation or when switched on and off. If your PC is on the same AC circuit as that heavy equipment, the spikes can damage the power supply. While some supplies are designed with surge suppression components (transformers, capacitors, gas discharge tubes, and metal oxide varistors or "MOVs"), spikes that pass through surge suppression can damage the supply regulator or pass through the supply to damage many portions of the motherboard. Also bear in mind that spikes can also pass along the everyday telephone line and damage your modem.

SYMPTOMS OF POWER PROBLEMS

Before you run right out and invest hard-earned money in power protection equipment, you should have some indication of power problems in the first place. Power problems are often difficult to measure because the power "event" occurs too quickly to measure without very specialized power monitoring equipment. Still, there are some situations that may suggest chronic power problems:

- The lights tend to flicker or periodically vary in intensity.
- There are frequent or regular errors in data transmission between network nodes.
- The PC stalls, crashes, or reboots for no apparent reason.
- You suffer chronic or frequent component failures (for example, modems don't seem to last long).
- You suffer chronic or frequent hard drive failures or file problems.
- The CMOS RAM or Modem NVRAM periodically lose their contents or become corrupted.
- The PC behaves erratically when other high-energy devices are turned on.
- The modem regularly loses its connection, or fails data transfers.
- The monitor display flickers of waves.
- You encounter frequent or chronic write errors to disks.

These symptoms do not establish the existence of a power problem, but they should alert you to their possibility.

Protection Devices

A well-designed power supply is built to withstand many of the perils of urban and suburban AC power distribution. Unfortunately, the never-ending push to reduce component count and cost in clone systems has meant that compromises have been made in the PC supply. You cannot always count on the presence of effective spike or overvoltage protection in original or replacement supplies. Therefore, you should understand the various options that are available to you and your customer.

SURGE AND SPIKE SUPPRESSERS

Surge suppressers, such as the Best SpikeFree in Figure 36-2, are simple and relatively inexpensive devices ($20 to $200) that are designed to absorb high-voltage transients produced by lightning and other high-energy equipment. Protection is accomplished by clamping (or shunting) voltages above a certain level (usually above 200 volts). MOVs are often included that can respond quickly and clamp voltages as high as 6000 volts. However, powerful surges such as direct lightning strikes can blow right through an MOV. Also, MOVs degrade with each spike. Once they have passed a number of surges, they are destroyed and must be replaced. There is no way to know whether the MOV is working or not, so there is no way to really tell if a surge suppresser is actually protecting the system.

Many protectors show a neon lamp or LED that goes out when the MOV has blown or when the protector is no longer active. Good suppressers also incorporate a circuit breaker rather than a fuse. This feature is a great convenience since a circuit breaker can be reset, while many fused units must be disassembled to replace the fuse. If possible, select a surge suppresser approved under UL1449 (or an international equivalent). Remember that, as a rule, surge/spike protectors are the simplest and least expensive power protection devices—they are also the most limited.

FIGURE 36-2 The SpikeFree product line from Best Power. (Best Power Technology, Inc.)

Modems and fax boards are also susceptible to damage from spikes present on everyday telephone lines. When recommending protection schemes, do not forget to include telephone line spike protection as well. Several of the Best SpikeFree devices shown in Figure 36-2 also provide data line protection along with AC line protection.

LINE POWER CONDITIONERS

Line conditioners perform all of the functions that a surge suppresser does, but they also provide some additional power protection. Whereas surge suppressers are passive devices (functioning only when a surge is present), line conditioners (such as the Best Citadel line conditioners shown in Figure 36-3) use transformers and capacitors for power isolation and high-frequency RF noise filtering. This approach results in a larger and more expensive—but more effective—power protection scheme. Another advantage of line conditioners is their tolerance to brief brownout conditions. Since transformers and capacitors are energy storage components, those components will continue to provide energy to the power supply during short brownouts (on the order of several milliseconds).

BACKUP POWER

Surge suppressers and line conditioners will take your customers only just so far. Those devices can protect a computer from brief power anomalies and keep their systems off your workbench until it is time to upgrade. Sooner or later, though, power *will* fail. When your customer cannot afford to be in the dark (literally), you should recommend a supplemental power system. A *backup power system* (BPS) is an off-line power system that provides power to your computer *only* when main AC power fails. Power is supplied from a series of batteries that are kept charged while AC power is available. When AC fails, the DC battery power is modulated into AC and switched in-line to provide power to the system. Any decent BPS (like the Best Patriot backup supply in Figure 36-4) can provide power for 15 to 60 minutes, depend-

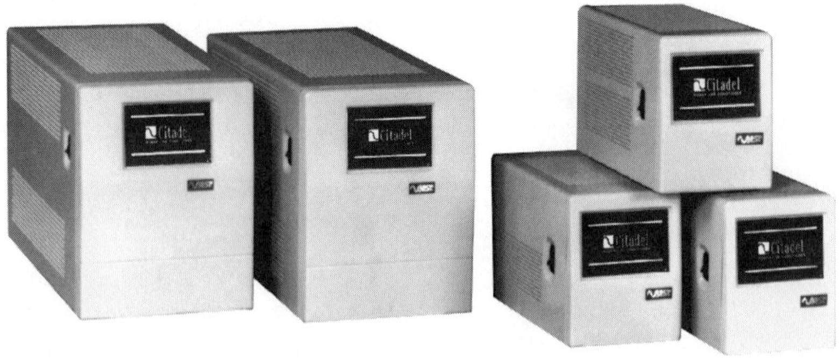

FIGURE 36-3 The Citadel product line from Best Power. (Best Power Technology, Inc.)

ing on the amount of load attached to it—plenty of time to save any work in progress and shut down in an orderly fashion.

The problem with some bargain-priced BPS units is their *switching time*. It many take several milliseconds to detect the loss of power and actually initiate the switch-over to battery power. In that few milliseconds, a PC may brownout or reboot anyway and defeat the point of having backup power in the first place. If customers are having problems with power switch-over, ask them to lighten the load on the BPS. Instead of trying to back up four machines with a BPS, try one or two and experiment a bit. A lighter load may allow the BPS to switch faster and preserve the PC's operation. If operation is acceptable with a lighter load, the prescription might be more BPS installations. If problems persist, find a better BPS for your customer. A BPS that offers a *ferroresonant transformer* (FRT) is often a good bet, since an FRT can provide energy for several milliseconds to smooth the transfer to battery power.

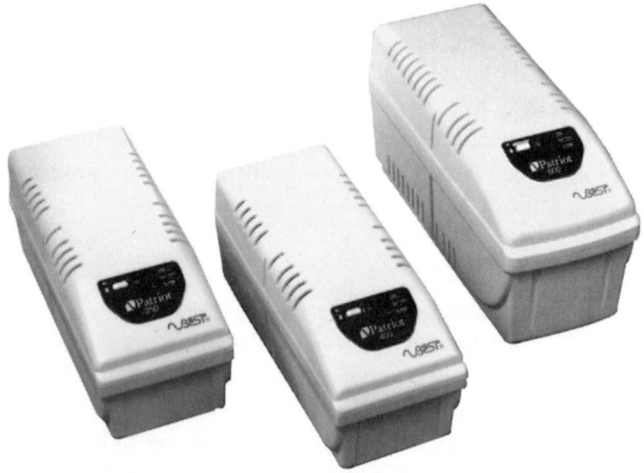

FIGURE 36-4 The Patriot BPS power line from Best Power. (Best Power Technology, Inc.)

Another problem to be aware of is that a backup power system may not offer any significant level of power protection. Since battery power is free of AC anomalies, inexpensive BPS designs may omit surge suppression or line conditioning features for the direct AC circuit. If power protection devices are already available, the problem is moot. However, if your customer is not yet using power protection devices, recommend a BPS (such as the Best Patriot) that incorporates surge/spike protection.

UNINTERRUPTIBLE POWER SUPPLIES

The uninterruptible power supply (UPS) is probably the best all-around form of power protection available. It is also the most expensive. While a BPS provides modulated power only when AC fails, a UPS is designed to provide modulated DC continuously—the PC runs from battery power *all the time*. AC keeps the batteries charged, but line AC does not power the PC directly. As a result, the PC is isolated from even the worse line power anomalies. Like a BPS, a UPS will provide power only for a limited time (the duration depending on the attached load) after AC fails, allowing the user to save data and shut down. However, there are no switching problems to contend with. High-end UPS systems, such as the Best Fortress UPS in Figure 36-5, provide an excellent combination of uninterruptible power, brownout correction, and surge and spike protection.

One thing to consider when recommending a UPS is the type of modulation provided by the modulator. Inexpensive UPS devices modulate DC battery power into an AC square wave. This is "technically" AC, but remember that some PCs and peripherals do not work well with square waves. It is preferable to recommend a UPS with a power *inverter* circuit. The inverter produces a precise sine wave (rather than a square wave), which is compatible with all PCs and peripherals.

SIZING A BPS/UPS

Selecting a BPS or UPS is somewhat of an imprecise science, because it involves determining both the load required for backup and the amount of time needed to operate that load once power fails. The rule for BPS and UPS systems is that backup power is provided *only* long enough to save work and shut down the PC or network in an orderly fashion—anywhere from 5 to 15 minutes. With this in mind, Table 36-1 offers

FIGURE 36-5 The Fortress UPS product line from Best Power. (Best Power Technology, Inc.)

TABLE 36-1 TYPICAL BACKUP POWER CAPACITIES

COMPUTER	BPS/UPS FOR SINGLE PCS	BPS/UPS FOR NETWORKED PCS
Pentium PC with 15 in. monitor	325VA	450VA
MMX PC with 15 in. monitor	325VA	450VA
386/486 PC with 15 in. monitor	325VA	280VA
Pentium PC with 17 in. monitor	450VA	450VA
MMX PC with 17 in. monitor	450VA	450VA
386/486 PC with 17 in. monitor	325VA	280VA
Pentium PC with 21 in. monitor	450VA	450VA
MMX PC with 21 in. monitor	450VA	450VA
386/486 PC with 21 in. monitor	450VA	450VA

some examples of typical backup power capacities. Note that backup power capacity is rated in Volt-Amperes (or "VA") rather than Watts (W).

> The computers include external accessories such as modem, speakers, scanner, CD-ROM, and Zip drives.

Backup, Backup, Backup

It is a strange fact of today's society that the *information* contained in computers is often more valuable than the computer system itself. Serious power interruptions can damage a computer, but even more important is the loss of vital data from memory or the hard drive. Power protection devices are intended to protect the PC from damage and to keep the system operating in the face of poor or absent AC—at least until the system can be shut down safely. However, power protection devices are not foolproof. Regular backups of memory and disk files are vital to any protection plan.

Advise your customers to save their work religiously. Saving every 30 to 60 minutes is usually prudent (more often in a busy office environment)—it is also *free*. If your customers do not have a tape backup to support their hard drive files, strongly recommend a tape drive. System backups once a day (even once a week) can preserve vital data in the rare event that a hard drive is damaged by a spike or brownout.

Troubleshooting Power Protection Devices

Power protection devices (especially BPS and UPS systems) are often ignored once they are installed. In fact, power systems require a certain level of regular attention and are themselves subject to a wide array of problems that can affect the reliability of your PC or network. This part of the chapter examines many of the common problems that can affect BPS/UPS systems and offers some suggestions for corrective action.

VERIFYING ELECTRICAL SAFETY

Before we discuss troubleshooting specifically, it would be wise to review the overall electrical power and interconnection scheme used by the PC. Electrical power "events" can be conducted by any long cable connected to your computer, LAN, or modem. The tips listed below can help you protect your equipment from potential damage:

- Use a UPS or surge suppresser to protect all AC operated PC equipment—especially the main system (desktop or tower) and monitor.
- Verify that your AC power receptacles are properly wired (you may need the services of a licensed electrician for this). Even though PC equipment may appear to operate properly under normal conditions, operating computer equipment from improperly wired outlets can pose a shock hazard.
- Plug in all power protection and/or PC equipment line cords to the same AC circuit wherever possible. This basically means that power to all the PC equipment is controlled by the same building fuse or circuit breaker.
- RS-232 serial interface ports on computers, terminals, printers, plotters, and modems are especially sensitive to damage from electrical transients because they use the computer chassis ground as a signal common. Protect both ends of an RS-232 serial interface cable longer than 5 feet (1.5 meters) with good quality serial port protection devices specifically designed for that purpose. Do not attempt to run RS-232 links between equipment in separate buildings—use good quality short-haul modems instead.
- Use good quality network protection devices to protect your Ethernet network interface cards (NICs) and other LAN equipment at each end of a network's 10Base-T UTP or coaxial Thinnet cable. Thinnet (10Base2) networks are especially susceptible to intersystem ground noise when the cable shields are inadvertently grounded at more than one location. Verify your system's true single ground point and check to be sure that "T" connectors or any exposed connector barrels are not touching the metal chassis of your computer.
- Use good quality network protection devices to protect your 4 and 16 Mbps Token Ring network interface cards (NICs) and other LAN equipment at each end of a network's UTP cable.
- Protect the telephone port of your telecommunications equipment (modem, fax, telex, answering machine, and so on) from damage due to nearby lightning activity with a good quality lightning or surge arrestor designed specifically for telecommunications equipment.

ROUTINE UPS BATTERY REPLACEMENT

Batteries are electrochemical devices. This characteristically means batteries will eventually wear out after an ample number of charge and discharge cycles, and you'll need to replace them. As a rule of thumb, you can expect to change your batteries every three to five years under normal use. Other circumstances such as bad commercial power sources, elevated temperatures where the batteries are stored, and improper maintenance procedures can all reduce the working life of a battery. You should suspect battery problems when they cannot hold a charge (short run times and "low battery" alarms even after ample charging time).

TESTING BATTERY BACKUP/UPS BATTERIES

Another result of batteries being electrochemical devices is that they all will fail eventually. BPS/UPS backup batteries are certainly no exception. If there is trouble with your BPS/UPS system (or as part of regular maintenance on the power system), you should test the batteries in a BPS or UPS for integrity. The following steps outline testing for +12Vdc batteries:

1. Make sure that your BPS or UPS is connected correctly and has at least 50 percent of its total load devices plugged in (desktop unit, monitor, scanner, and so on).
2. Turn the system and attached peripherals on, and allow the PC to boot normally.
3. Simulate a power outage by disconnecting the BPS or UPS line cord.
4. Use a standard digital voltmeter and measure each individual battery voltage.
5. Each +12Vdc battery should read between +11.5Vdc and +12.5Vdc. Any battery measuring outside of that range should be considered defective and should be replaced.
6. All batteries should measure about the same. Any battery that differs more than 0.4 volts from the rest of the batteries should be considered bad and replaced.
7. Wait about 5 minutes and repeat the test (looking for one weak battery to discharge faster than the others). If any battery appears to be discharging faster than the others, it should be considered bad and replaced.

UPS LOCATION TIPS

While the physical location of a UPS may not be critical, there are some tips that may help prevent backup power problems:

- Install the UPS as close as possible to the equipment that it will protect. If this distance is more than 25 feet (7.6 meters), transient noise can appear in the electrical distribution system.
- If the UPS batteries are in a separate cabinet, the battery cabinet should be as close to the UPS as possible. If the batteries will be farther away from the unit than the standard cables allow, you may need to replace the battery cables with a larger gauge wire to reduce voltage losses across the line.
- The UPS should be in a flat location in a controlled, indoor environment. Do not install the UPS next to open windows.
- Keep the UPS away from heat sources, direct sunshine, moisture, or corrosive gas.
- Do not place any objects on top of the UPS and do not install it in any type of enclosure. Do not operate the UPS or batteries in a sealed room or container.

UNDERSTANDING "LINE LOAD" INDICATORS

During normal operation, a UPS rectifies the AC input, then uses it to charge the batteries and feed the inverter circuit. If your UPS provides a "Line load" indicator, this will show the amount (percentage) of UPS power that your system is actually using. Remember that a UPS can provide only a limited amount of power, so you should verify that the line load power being provided to your PC equipment is *less than* 100 percent of the total UPS capacity—otherwise you'll overload the UPS. A line load indicator that's approaching 100 percent is in danger of overloading, and you'll need to reduce the number of devices demanding power from the UPS (or replace the UPS with a larger model).

> If the line load indicator flashes and the UPS cuts out the AC source power, chances are that the AC feeding the UPS is too high or too low. You'll need a licensed electrician to "buck" or "boost" the AC power within a range that's appropriate for the UPS.

UNDERSTANDING BATTERY POWER INDICATORS

When the UPS runs on battery backup power (the *inverter*), the "Battery" and "Inverter" indicators are typically illuminated—this commonly happens during a power outage or when AC input power is not acceptable to the UPS (too high or too low). If your UPS provides a "Battery charge" indicator, this will show the amount of battery charge that's left in the UPS. As the UPS runs on battery power, the amount of charge (and the amount of time the UPS can continue running on battery) will decrease, and the display will generally show this decrease in operating time. It's important that main AC power be restored (or the system be shut down) before the battery charge drops out. If the Battery indicator starts flashing, the battery voltage is low and shutdown of the UPS is imminent.

UNDERSTANDING THE "BYPASS" INDICATOR

Ideally, the UPS is providing power through its inverter, so AC is never *directly* connected to the system. However, if your UPS is equipped with a "Bypass" button and indicator, you can sometimes bypass the UPS and run the system from AC power—this happens if there is a UPS overload, if the UPS cannot run on battery power (for example, because of an inverter failure), or if you press the Bypass button. If the cause of the bypass was an overload, the UPS can automatically transfer back to normal operation after the overload has been removed.

UNDERSTANDING THE "ALARM" INDICATOR

When the UPS detects a problem, you'll generally see a flashing "Alarm" indicator (often in conjunction with an alarm beep or tone). You can typically silence the audible alarm by pressing an Alarm button, but the flashing indicator will still display a problem until it's corrected. If you don't see a solution listed in the following sections, refer to the UPS manual or manufacturer's technical support.

36

UPS QUICK CHECKLIST

- ***The UPS is on but is not supplying power to the equipment.*** The output circuit breaker on the back of the UPS may have been tripped. Reset the breaker.
- ***No UPS indicators are on, and no alarm is sounding.*** The UPS is not operating. Input power might not be available to the UPS (for example, an extended power outage may have occurred) or the input circuit breaker on the back of the UPS may have been tripped. Check the AC input power supply, then reset the breaker and restart the UPS.
- ***The green "Line" indicator is not on even though AC line input seems to be available. The UPS beeps every few seconds.*** Input power might not be available to the UPS. The output circuit breaker on the back of the UPS may have been tripped. Check the AC input power supply, then reset the breaker and restart the UPS.
- ***The amount of UPS battery run time is less than the rating.*** The battery may not be fully charged, or it may be bad, or the charger may have failed. Recharge the battery for at least 10 hours by connecting the UPS to a source of AC line input, then retest the battery backup time. If the problem persists, the batteries may need to be replaced, or the charger may need repair or replacement.
- ***The yellow "Battery" indicator is flashing.*** The battery voltage is low. Recharge the battery for at least 10 hours by connecting the UPS to a source of AC line input. If the problem persists, the batteries may need to be replaced, or the charger may need repair or replacement.

TIPS FOR DEALING WITH COMMON "ALARM" CONDITIONS

Many of the current generation of BPS and UPS systems incorporate a certain amount of "intelligence" that oversees features such as battery charging and self-diagnostics. When important conditions are not met or errors are detected, the BPS/UPS will produce an "alarm." While the actual means used to present the alarm (for example, beeps, 7-segment codes, or alphanumeric LCD readouts) can vary quite a bit, you should understand the essential alarm meanings and know how to respond quickly.

- ***Batteries Disconnected*** The BPS/UPS batteries are not properly connected. Verify the connection of all batteries in the BPS/UPS. The UPS will *not* protect your system until this fault is corrected.
- ***Batteries Undercharged*** The PC is receiving power, but the batteries have an insufficient charge and will not protect your system for long. See that the batteries are allowed ample time to charge. If this is a persistent problem, you may wish to inspect each of the batteries.
- ***Check Battery*** The BPS/UPS has detected a possible problem with its batteries. Verify that all of your batteries are properly connected in the BPS/UPS. You should test and replace any defective batteries.
- ***Check Fan*** The cooling fan inside the BPS/UPS is not functioning properly. The fan may need to be replaced, or the BPS/UPS may require factory service or replacement.
- ***Check Fuse Board*** The BPS/UPS has detected a possible problem with an internal fuse board. It may be possible to check/replace the fuse board, but doing this usually means that the BPS/UPS has failed and is in need of factory service or replacement.
- ***Check Inverter*** The BPS/UPS has detected a possible problem with its inverter circuit (the circuit that actually turns battery DC back into AC for the computer). This usually means that the BPS/UPS has failed and is in need of factory service or replacement.
- ***Check MOVs*** The BPS/UPS has detected a problem with an MOV (Metal Oxide Varistor) inside the unit. This type of problem usually means that the BPS/UPS has failed and is in need of factory service or replacement.
- ***Check Power Supply*** The unit has detected a possible problem with its internal power supply (which powers the BPS/UPS microprocessor controls). This type of problem usually means that the BPS/UPS has failed and is in need of factory service or replacement.
- ***Circuit Breaker Warning/Shutdown*** There is high output current being provided by the BPS/UPS. This usually occurs because excessive PC equipment is overloading the BPS/UPS. Shut down all of the PC equipment and reset the BPS/UPS. Then disconnect the extra PC equipment that is overloading the BPS/UPS.
- ***High AC Out/Shutdown*** The BPS/UPS is generating an unusually high AC output voltage, and will shutdown to prevent damaging the PC equipment. This condition usually means that the BPS/UPS has failed and is in need of factory service or replacement.
- ***High Ambient Temperature*** The temperature inside the BPS/UPS is too high. Make sure that the BPS/UPS is placed where room temperature is within the system's recommended range (high-temperature industrial environments are typically bad). Also, see that there is nothing blocking the cooling vents in the BPS/UPS.

- *High Battery* The battery voltage in the BPS/UPS is high. There may be a problem with the battery charger settings, the charging circuit itself, or one or more batteries. This condition usually means that the BPS/UPS has failed and is in need of factory service or replacement.
- *Low AC Out/Shutdown* The BPS/UPS is generating an unusually low AC output voltage, and will shutdown to prevent damaging the PC equipment. This condition usually means that the BPS/UPS has failed and is in need of factory service or replacement.
- *Low Battery* Battery voltage is too low for the BPS/UPS to operate on battery power, and the unit will subsequently shut down. In most cases, you should see a low runtime error first. If the batteries are too low even while the BPS/UPS is operating from AC, there may be a problem with the charging circuit or batteries in the unit.
- *Low Runtime* The PC is running on battery power, and the amount of battery time remaining is low (usually two minutes or less). Do an orderly shutdown of your PC equipment *immediately*. In most cases, you do not need to shut off the BPS/UPS (when AC power returns, the BPS/UPS can automatically restart and begin to recharge its batteries).
- *Memory Error* On startup, the BPS/UPS unit has failed its automatic memory validity test (usually in "intelligent" microprocessor-based BPS/UPS units). This usually means that the BPS/UPS has failed, and is in need of factory service or replacement.
- *Output Short Circuit* This problem is usually signaled by a continuous error tone, and typically indicates an overload condition when the UPS unit is turned on. Check the wiring and verify that you're not loading down the UPS with excessive equipment. (Similar to "Overload" below.)
- *Overload* The PC equipment is drawing more power than the BPS/UPS is designed to provide. This condition can seriously reduce battery runtime. You'll need to shut down extra PC equipment (for instance, scanners, printers, and so on) until the error stops.
- *Replace Batteries* This error is typically generated as one or more beep patterns from the UPS and suggests that one or more batteries in the unit will not hold a proper charge. You should check each battery in the UPS and replace any questionable batteries at your earliest convenience.
- *UPS Fault* This indicates that a serious error has occurred in the UPS. The UPS will probably not protect your system during this error condition until the fault is cleared or the UPS is replaced.

SYMPTOMS AND SOLUTIONS

SYMPTOM 36-1 **The BPS/UPS will not turn on** This is usually indicated when the power light doesn't come on, or the unit doesn't beep. Check that the AC power is available at the outlet and see that the AC line cord is connected to the BPS/UPS properly. If the unit has a circuit breaker or fuse, check to see if it has tripped. Reset the circuit breaker or replace the fuse as necessary. Also make sure that the unit is not overloaded with excessive PC equipment (which can draw excess current and pop the fuse or circuit breaker).

SYMPTOM 36-2 **A "site wiring fault" is indicated (usually while the BPS/UPS is powering loads)** This condition is most likely due to a building wiring error (such as a missing ground), an overload on the neutral wiring, or polarity reversal between the hot and the neutral wires. There may be a "cheater" plug or adapter installed onto the unit's line cord plug—resulting in no connection to ground. You'll need a licensed electrician to check and correct the building wiring as needed.

SYMPTOM 36-3 The BPS/UPS is on, but the PC equipment is not receiving power The unit's circuit breaker may or may not be tripped. In most cases, this condition is accompanied by a loud tone or error message indicating an overload. The problem is that the BPS/UPS has shut down because there is too much PC equipment plugged in (such as a laser printer). Shut off the PC equipment and disconnect any "excess" devices—you may place them on a simple surge suppresser on a different AC outlet. Then reset the BPS/UPS (reset the circuit breaker if necessary).

SYMPTOM 36-4 The BPS/UPS indicates a power failure, even though AC power has not failed This often happens if the unit's AC line cord has become loose. Make sure the line cord is installed properly. If the unit's circuit breaker has tripped, there may be an excessive load on the BPS/UPS by too much PS equipment. Disconnect excessive devices and plug them into ordinary surge suppressers instead.

SYMPTOM 36-5 The BPS/UPS beeps (kicks in) occasionally The PC equipment operates normally. This symptom typically indicates that the BPS/UPS is noting brief lapses in AC or other power anomalies. In most cases, this kind of operation is perfectly normal and indicates that the BPS/UPS is busy protecting the PC equipment from power problems. If there is an audible tone that is distracting, you can often disable the audible alarm on most BPS/UPS systems.

SYMPTOM 36-6 The BPS/UPS beeps (kicks in) frequently (often several times each hour) The PC equipment operates normally. This almost always indicates that the AC line voltage powering the BPS/UPS is low to begin with or heavily loaded by other devices drawing current elsewhere. First, have the line voltage checked by a licensed electrician and corrected, if necessary. You might also reduce the sensitivity of the BPS/UPS by reducing the "transfer voltage" (the voltage at which the unit "kicks in") by several volts—not all BPS/UPS systems provide this capability. Finally, try removing any unnecessary devices that may be "loading down" the AC line voltage (for instance, coffee pots or air conditioners).

SYMPTOM 36-7 The BPS/UPS does not provide the expected runtime First, check to see if there is an excessive load on the BPS/UPS (such as a laser printer). Disconnect any excess devices and plug them into ordinary surge suppressers elsewhere. If the problem persists, the batteries in the BPS/UPS itself may be weak from age or abuse or from not having been charged completely after a prior use. Make sure that the BPS/UPS is given ample time to charge. Otherwise, test and replace weak batteries as needed.

SYMPTOM 36-8 The computer reboots when the BPS/UPS "kicks in" This conditions occurs because the PC equipment does not have enough "ride-through time" until the BPS/UPS can react. In most cases, there is an excessive load on the BPS/UPS. Remove excessive PC equipment from the BPS/UPS and try the system again. If the problem persists, you may need to replace the BPS/UPS with one offering a faster "switch-over" time.

Further Study

APC: **http://www.apcc.com**

Best Power: **http://www.bestpower.com/**

TrippLite: **http://www.tripplite.com**

37

POWER SUPPLIES AND POWER MANAGEMENT

CHAPTER AT A GLANCE

Power supplies play a vital role in the operation of PCs and their peripherals. A power supply converts commercial AC into one or more various levels of DC that can be used by electronic and electromechanical devices. This may not sound like a very glamorous function, but a faulty or low-quality supply can cause serious system problems, stability issues, data loss, and in extreme cases even damage to your motherboard or drives. Every technician should understand the operation of a *switching power supply* and know the important characteristics to look for when replacing or upgrading a supply.

But during the last few years, "power" has become more important than just plugging in a little silver box. Global concerns about limited natural resources and "greenhouse" gasses have focused attention on the tens of millions of PCs that consume power around the world. Not only must a power supply operate correctly, but a computer's power must be *managed* to reduce its power consumption significantly during idle periods. This chapter will explain the operation of a typical switching power supply, offer reliable guidelines for selecting and upgrading a supply, and cover solutions for the most common power supply problems. You'll also review the major power management schemes for desktop and mobile PCs, see how to use those schemes, and learn how to troubleshoot many of the more troublesome power management problems.

Understanding Switching Supplies

The great disadvantage to ordinary *linear* power supplies is their tremendous *waste*. At least half of all power provided to a linear supply is literally thrown away as heat—most of this waste occurs in the *regulator* portion of the supply. Ideally, if there were just enough energy supplied to the regulator to achieve and maintain a stable output voltage, regulator waste could be reduced almost entirely, and supply efficiency would be vastly improved. This goal is the underlying basis for a switching power supply.

CONCEPTS OF SWITCHING REGULATION

Instead of throwing away extra input energy, a switching power supply creates a feedback loop. Feedback senses the output voltage provided to a load, and then switches the AC primary (or secondary) voltage on or off as needed to maintain steady levels at the output. In effect, a switching power supply is constantly turning on and off in order to keep the output voltage(s) steady. A block diagram of a typical switching power supply is shown in Figure 37-1. There are a variety of possible configurations, but Figure 37-1 illustrates one classic design approach.

Raw AC line voltage entering the supply is immediately converted to pulsating DC, and then filtered to provide a *primary DC* voltage. Notice that, unlike a linear supply, AC is *not* transformed before rectification, so primary DC can easily reach levels exceeding 170 volts. Remember that AC is 120 volts RMS. Since capacitors charge to the peak voltage (peak = RMS x 1.414), DC levels can be higher than your AC voltmeter readings.

Keep in mind that high-voltage pulsating DC can be as dangerous as AC line voltage and should be treated with extreme caution.

On start-up, the switching transistor is turned on and off at a high frequency (usually 20kHz to 40kHz) and a long duty cycle. The switching transistor acts as a *chopper*, breaking up this primary DC to form *chopped DC,* which can then be used as the primary signal for a step-down transformer. The duty cycle of chopped DC will affect the AC voltage level generated on the transformer's secondary. A long duty cycle means a larger output voltage (for heavy loads) and a short duty cycle means lower output voltage (for

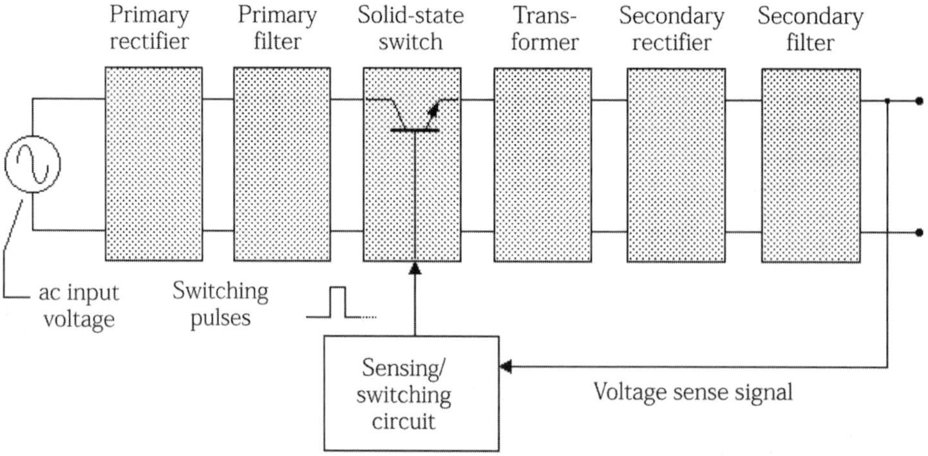

FIGURE 37-1 Block diagram of a switching power supply

light loads). *Duty cycle* itself refers to the amount of time that a signal is "on" compared to its overall cycle. The duty cycle is continuously adjusted by the sensing/switching circuit. You can use an oscilloscope to view switching and chopped DC signals. Figure 37-2 illustrates a more practical representation for a switching supply.

AC voltage produced on the transformer's secondary winding (typically a step-down transformer) is *not* a pure sine wave, but it alternates regularly enough to be treated as AC by the remainder of the supply. Secondary voltage is re-rectified and refiltered to form a *secondary DC* voltage that is actually applied to the load. Output voltage is sensed by the sensing/switching circuit, which constantly adjusts the chopped DC duty cycle. As load increases on the secondary circuit (more current is drawn by the load), output voltage tends to drop. This is a perfectly normal result, and the same thing happens in every unregulated supply. However, a sensing circuit detects this voltage drop and increases the switching duty cycle. In turn, the duty cycle for chopped DC increases, which increases the voltage produced by the secondary winding. Output voltage climbs back up again to its desired value—output voltage is regulated.

The reverse will happen as load decreases on the secondary circuit (less current is drawn by the load). A smaller load will tend to make output voltage climb. Again, the same actions happen in an unregulated supply. The sensing/switching circuit detects this increase in voltage and reduces the switching duty cycle. As a result, the duty cycle for chopped DC decreases, and transformer secondary voltage decreases. Output voltage drops back to its desired value—output voltage remains regulated.

Consider the advantages of a switching power circuit. Current is drawn only in the primary circuit when its switching transistor is on, so very little power is wasted in the primary circuit. The secondary circuit will supply just enough power to keep load voltage constant (regulated), but very little power is wasted by the secondary rectifier, filter, or switching circuit. Switching power supplies can reach efficiencies higher than 85 percent (35 percent *more* efficient than most comparable linear supplies). More efficiency means less heat is generated by the supply, so components can be smaller and packaged more tightly.

Unfortunately, there are several disadvantages to switching supplies. First, switching supplies tend to act as radio transmitters. Their 20kHz to 40kHz operating frequencies can wreak havoc to radio and television reception, not to mention the circuitry within the PC or peripheral itself. This is why you will see most switching supplies covered or shielded in a metal casing. It is critically important that you replace any shielding removed during your repair. Strong electromagnetic interference (EMI) can easily disturb the operation of a logic circuit.

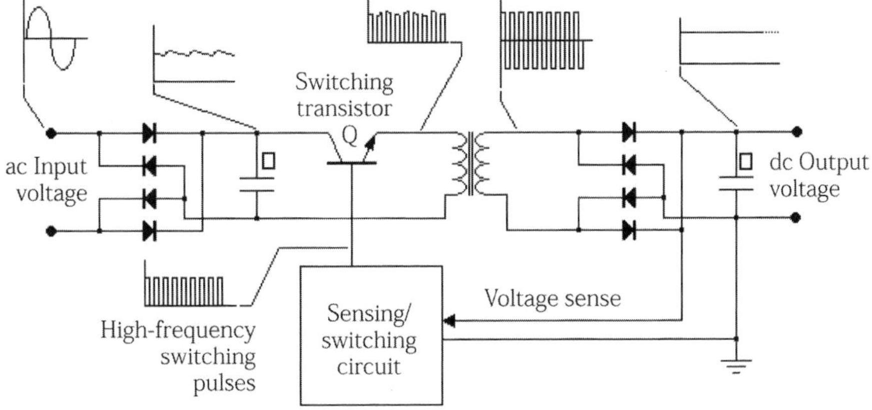

FIGURE 37-2 Simplified diagram of a switching power supply

37

Second, the output voltage will always contain some amount of high-frequency ripple. In many applications, this is not enough noise to present interference to the load. In fact, most of the noise is filtered out in a carefully designed supply. Finally, a switching supply often contains more components, and is more difficult to troubleshoot, than a linear supply. This is often outweighed by the smaller, lighter packaging of switching supplies. In virtually all cases today, a defective power supply unit is simply replaced.

In actual practice, sensing and switching functions can be fabricated right onto an integrated circuit. IC-based switching circuits allow simple, inexpensive circuits to be built as shown in Figure 37-3. Notice how similar this looks versus a linear supply. AC line voltage is transformed (usually stepped down) and then rectified and filtered before reaching a switch-regulating IC. The IC chops DC voltage at a duty cycle that will provide adequate power to the load. Chopped DC from the switching regulator is filtered by the combination of choke and output filter capacitor to reform a steady DC signal at the output. The output voltage is sampled back at the IC, which constantly adjusts the chopped DC duty cycle.

CONNECTING A POWER SUPPLY

PC power supplies operate the motherboard directly as well as a number of internal drives. This part of the chapter presents the typical connection schemes for AT, ATX, and NLX power supplies and highlights the major signals that you should be familiar with.

AT-style Power Connections

The AT-style power supply is largely considered to be the classic connection scheme for IBM-compatible PCs. An AT-style supply provides four voltages to the motherboard (+5Vdc, -5Vdc, +12Vdc, and -12Vdc) through a series of two heavy 6-pin connectors, as shown in Figure 37-4. You may notice that there are several wires for Ground and other voltage signals such as +5Vdc. There is no difference between these like-colored wires—the extra wires are provided simply because the additional wire is needed to help carry the required current.

> If you can't remember the orientation of P8 and P9 connectors, just remember that the black ends of each connector go together.

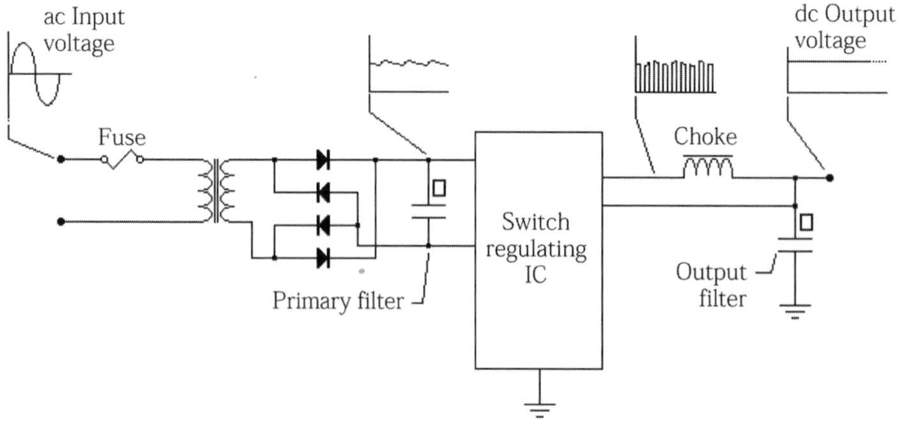

FIGURE 37-3 Simplified schematic of a chip-based switching power supply

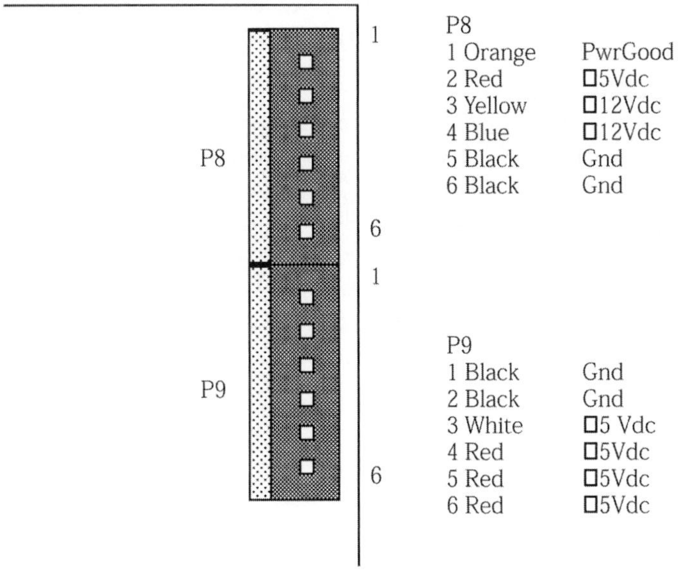

FIGURE 37-4 AT-style motherboard power connections

The only discrete "signal" in the AT-style power connector is the Power Good (or PwrGood or PG) signal. This signal is typically tied to the CPU's Reset pin. When the PC is first powered up, this signal is logic 0, and the CPU is forced into a continuous Reset mode. After the power supply is stable (usually about 0.5 seconds from the time you flip the power switch), the signal rises to a logic 1 and releases the Reset—the CPU can begin processing, starting the POST and boot process.

Drive Power Connections

The internal drives of a PC (floppy drives, hard drives, CD-ROM drives, and so on) must also be powered. Since drives are electromechanical devices, which typically demand a substantial amount of current, they are powered directly from the power supply rather than from their respective interfaces. Drives traditionally use a heavy-duty 4-wire connector to provide +12Vdc and +5Vdc to each drive. The +12Vdc signal powers the drive's motor(s), while the +5Vdc signal operates the drive's logic circuits. The wire colors are identified as follows:

- Yellow: +12Vdc
- Black: Ground
- Black: Ground
- Red: +5Vdc

As a rule, there should be one drive power connector for *each* drive in the system. Higher-capacity power supplies typically offer more drive power connectors. If you do not have enough drive power connectors to power all of the drives in your system, you may be able to use a Y splitter to transform one power connector into two. However, you should be *extremely* judicious in the use of Y splitters. Inadequate power connectors may suggest that you're pushing the power supply beyond its capacity, and erratic system behavior can result (if the system boots at all). Also, *never* split the power connector operating a hard drive—the power diverted from a hard drive may result in erratic HDD performance and data corruption.

ATX/NLX-style Power Connections

ATX and NLX form-factor systems now constitute virtually all new systems entering service, and their power requirements are remarkably similar. The ATX/NLX power supply provides five voltages to the motherboard (+5Vdc, -5Vdc, +12Vdc, -12Vdc, and +3.3Vdc) through a 20-pin connector, as shown in Figure 37-5. The +3.3Vdc supply is added to support the broad use of "low-voltage logic" that is now standard in the PC. Older AT-style motherboards also incorporated low-voltage logic but required an on-board voltage regulator to supply the +3.3Vdc rather than the power supply. The ATX/NLX signals can be identified by their unique wire colors:

- Black: Ground
- Blue: -12Vdc
- Brown: 3.3V sense
- Gray: Power OK
- Green: PS-ON (the "soft power" control signal)
- Orange: +3.3Vdc
- Purple: 5Vsb ("standby" voltage for power-managed devices)
- Red: +5Vdc
- White: -5Vdc
- Yellow: +12Vdc

In addition to the actual DC voltages feeding the motherboard, there are also several important logic signals used to control the power system:

PS-ON PS-ON is an active-low signal received from the motherboard that turns on all of the main power outputs (+3.3Vdc, +5Vdc, -5Vdc, +12Vdc, and -12Vdc). When this signal is held high (logic 1) or left open-circuited, the power supply outputs should be *off*. In effect, this is the signal that allows "soft control" of the system power (that is, automatic power-down when shutting down Windows 95/98).

5VSB 5VSB is a "standby voltage" source that may be used to "tickle" power-managed devices that require power input during the powered-down state. The 5VSB pin should deliver 5Vdc (+/- 5%) at a minimum of 10mA for devices to operate.

PW-OK PW-OK (or Power OK) is a Power Good signal and should be set at logic 1 by the power supply to indicate that the +5Vdc and +3.3Vdc outputs are above the undervoltage thresholds of the power supply. Once this signal is received from the supply, the motherboard can begin its POST and boot process.

Optional ATX/NLX Power Connector

The ATX and NLX form-factor specifications also provide for an *optional* 6-pin power connector such as the one illustrated in Figure 37-6. Each signal adds a certain amount of versatility to the ATX/NLX system. You can identify the optional power connector signals by their wire colors:

- White: FanM
- White/Blue stripe: FanC

- White/Brown stripe: 3.3V Sense
- White/Red stripe: 1394V
- White/Black stripe: 1394R

FanM Signal The FanM (*Fan Monitor*) signal is an open-collector, 2 pulse per revolution tachometer signal from the power supply fan. This signal allows the system to monitor the power supply for fan speed or failures. If this signal is not implemented on the motherboard, it should not impact the power supply function.

FanC Signal The FanC (*Fan Control*) signal is an optional fan speed and shutdown control signal. The fan speed and shutdown are controlled by a *variable* voltage on this pin. This signal allows the system to request control of the power supply fan from full speed to off. The control circuit on the motherboard should supply voltage to this pin from +12Vdc to 0Vdc for the fan control request.

3.3V Sense Line A remote 3.3V sense line can be added to the optional connector to allow for accurate control of the 3.3VDC line directly at motherboard loads.

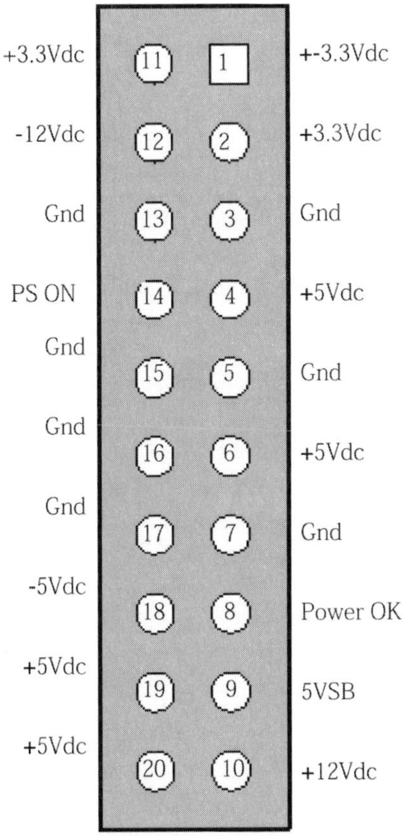

FIGURE 37-5 ATX/NLX-style motherboard power connections

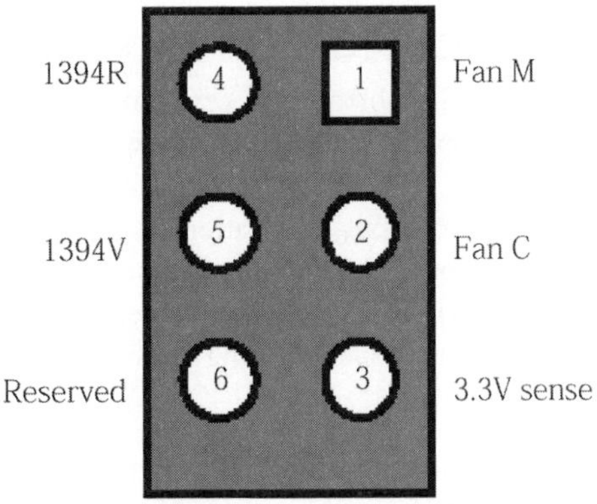

FIGURE 37-6 Optional ATX/NLX-style motherboard power connector

1394V Pin This pin on the optional connector allows for implementation of a segregated voltage supply rail for use with unpowered IEEE-1394 ("fire wire") solutions. The power derived from this pin should be used to power *only* 1394 connectors (unregulated anywhere from 8 to 40 volts).

1394R Pin The 1394R pin provides an isolated ground path for unpowered IEEE-1394 ("fire wire") implementations. This ground should be used *only* for 1394 connections and should be fully isolated from other ground planes in the system.

VOLTAGE TOLERANCES

If you pursue power supply testing or troubleshooting at any level, you're going to need to test the output voltages. One important aspect of voltage measurements often overlooked by novice technicians is the idea of *voltage tolerance*. Voltage outputs are rarely *exact* and may vary from their rated value by as much as 5% (often 3 to 4% for the +3.3Vdc output). For example, a +5Vdc output may actually read from +4.75Vdc to +5.25Vdc, while a +12Vdc output may read from +11.4Vdc to +12.6Vdc. As long as the measured voltage is within a *reasonable* tolerance, the output should be considered *good*. If the measured voltage strays *outside* of this reasonable tolerance (usually to the low side), chances are that the output is being overloaded by excessive devices. If the output measures extremely low—or is absent—chances are that the output (and the power supply) is defective. You can then choose to repair or replace the power supply as you see fit.

Upgrading a Power Supply

Power is the lifeblood of every PC. Each element of a PC—from hard drives and memory to video boards, motherboards, and modems—demands energy from the power supply. Many of today's IBM-compatible clones cut costs by using power supplies that provide enough power to run the basic system—but not much else. When you upgrade or refit such a PC, you can often run into system problems such as random lockups, error messages, and a variety of other strange behaviors. This part of the chapter shows you how to recognize potential power problems and upgrade the supply if needed. *Use extreme caution whenever working with power systems.* AC at the wall outlet (and inside the power supply itself) can be very dangerous in the hands of untrained personnel. If you're uncomfortable dealing with the hazards of AC, refer the actual testing and upgrade procedures shown here to more experienced individuals.

RECOGNIZING POTENTIAL POWER PROBLEMS

As with most PC problems, the key to recognizing power problems is proper diagnosis. Diagnosing a failed power supply is a relatively simple process. First, a supply malfunction will typically prevent a PC from booting—a fairly obvious symptom. A low or absent power output registered on a multimeter or POST board offers a direct indication of the problem. After you identify a failed supply, it becomes a matter of troubleshooting the supply or replacing it outright. Unfortunately, a great many power problems are intermittent. The power supply has not necessarily failed, but it is not able to supply enough power to keep the system running properly. Being aware of the following chronic problems can often help you navigate this gray area:

- ***Computer freezes intermittently.*** Just because your system locks up does not necessarily mean that you should call the power company. Most computers are prone to freeze due to software application and configuration errors (which are never due to power problems), especially after you install a new application. The time you should suspect power problems is when your system that has been working fine for some time suddenly starts freezing for no reason at all (and regardless of the operating system or applications being used). Not just once, but several times a day, and maybe even several times an hour. If the system tends to freeze when it is moved to a new location, power problems may also be to blame.

- ***Random memory errors.*** As with system lockups, an occasional memory error message does not necessarily indicate a power problem, especially if you have just added a new application or device driver. If you suddenly see a rash of memory errors (or have just finished upgrading the system), it's time to check your power. When memory errors occur after moving the PC to a new location, power problems are likely at fault.
- ***Data is lost or corrupted on the hard drive.*** Hard drive problems can be the result of several factors—everything from a loose data cable to operator error. Check the drive carefully to be sure that it is connected securely. If the drive seems to be having difficulty reading or writing to the disk, check power *first* before attempting to back up the disk or run any disk-based diagnostics. If you attempt to defragment or test the disk with power problems present, subsequent problems can do even more damage. This symptom also suggests that the supply may be overloaded. This condition may be the case if problems developed after you installed another drive or a power-hungry expansion board into your system. If power checks correctly, you can proceed with disk diagnostics.
- ***Trouble communicating with modems or peripherals.*** You may see a rash of communication errors when trying to use a modem or mouse (you may see other communication driver error messages). Make sure that the peripherals connected to your system are installed and configured properly. Established systems that suddenly have trouble staying online or interacting with the printer may be suffering from a power problem. In some cases, the loss of -5V from the power supply can disable the modem (and cause odd connection sounds) without causing any other system problems.
- ***Chronic hardware failures.*** These problems are characterized by a fault that seems to recur after a few days or a week. For example, you saw a memory error, replaced the memory, and the fault went away, but the same fault returned a few days later. This type of problem suggests that power spikes (brief, high-voltage surges of electricity) are entering the system from the AC line. Many economy power supplies omit even the most rudimentary spike and surge suppression circuitry, so power anomalies often pass through the supply to the motherboard and drives with little if any protection at all. In most cases, a power anomaly will crash the system but not result in any real damage. In extreme cases, a strong power anomaly can actually damage one or more ICs on the motherboard, expansion board(s), or drive(s).

DEALING WITH POWER PROBLEMS

Now that you have an idea of how power problems tend to manifest themselves in the PC, you can take some decisive steps to isolate and rectify the problem. Regardless of what symptoms your particular system may be exhibiting, you should not automatically assume that your system (or power supply) is at fault. Before you even think about opening the PC, you should check the AC line voltage.

Checking the AC

Even the most forgiving power supply needs a stable source of AC in order to function correctly. Industrial devices such as motors and heaters can draw so much power that there is insufficient AC voltage remaining to power the computer. Commercial and domestic appliances such as air conditioners, stoves, coffee makers, and refrigerators can also result in low or unsteady AC levels. Appliances are also notorious for their introduction of voltage spikes, which can easily result in circuit damage.

For the most part, it is rather pointless to look for power problems with ordinary test instruments. Multimeters are good for testing overall AC levels, but they are usually too slow to catch rapidly changing power levels such as spikes. Even most surges will go undetected. Oscilloscopes are too expensive for casual 50/60Hz measurements, and they rarely save information on any anomalies that are detected—once the problem is displayed, it is gone. As a result, you are forced to sit and watch the oscilloscope until a problem occurs. *Serious* power observations require a dedicated power test instrument with data logging or long-term chart recording capabilities. Such equipment is available, but is far too expensive for ordinary users (though technicians may consider the "PC Power Check" board from Data Depot). Fortunately, there *are* some trial-and-error steps that can be taken to test the problem.

First, you need to make sure that your AC outlet is providing the right amount of voltage. Use a multimeter and measure the output at your wall outlet. Domestic US voltage levels should be between 110 and 130 Vac. If voltage is too low (or too high), the objective is to find out if there is anything on the line that might be causing the voltage problem. Check to see if there are any high-energy devices on the same circuit (such as coffee makers or air conditioners). If so, try turning those devices off. If the AC at your computer's outlet returns to a normal value, try your system *now*—that may have been the problem. Eventually, you will need to turn your air conditioner or coffee maker back on, so be sure to shut down your system until you can have a new line installed or find another line for the computer.

If there are no other devices on the line (or the line voltage fails to return to a normal level), your next step should immediately be to find an outlet with the proper voltage level. If an outlet with a proper voltage cannot be found, an electrician should be consulted to install a proper AC line. An electrician should also be able to ensure that the AC line is properly grounded. When the AC line voltage seems correct, suspect the computer supply itself.

Suspect the Supply

When the AC input seems correct, you should suspect the computer supply. If the system is suffering from chronic hardware problems, try putting a good quality surge protector between the AC wall outlet and computer AC cord. It also would be acceptable to try the system on another AC line that may be free of surges or spikes. Open the computer and use a multimeter to check the voltage level at each supply output against the pinout shown in Table 37-1. The +12 Vdc and +5 Vdc levels should be correct. The power

TABLE 37-1 INDEX OF POWER SUPPLY OUTPUTS

WIRE COLOR	VOLTAGE OR DESIGNATION
Black	Ground
Blue	-12Vdc
Brown	+3.3V Sense (ATX and NLX supplies)
Gray	Power OK (~ +5Vdc in ATX and NLX supplies)
Green	Power Supply ON ("soft control signal" for ATX and NLX supplies)
Orange	+3.3Vdc (ATX and NLX supplies)
Orange	Power Good (~ +5Vdc in AT-style supplies)
Purple	+5Vdc Standby (ATX and NLX supplies)
Red	+5Vdc
White	-5Vdc
Yellow	+12Vdc

LEDs on a PC Power Check (or suitably equipped POST board) will also give you an approximation of supply output levels.

If any supply output level is low, the supply may be overloaded by too many devices in the system. If you have just upgraded the system with a new drive or expansion board, try removing or disabling the upgrade and see if DC voltages climb to their normal levels. If they do, the supply is overloaded and should be upgraded as shown below. If levels do not return to normal (or either or both of the voltages are high), the supply may be defective. If you determine the supply to be defective, you may troubleshoot or replace the supply at your discretion.

UPGRADING THE POWER SUPPLY

It is not uncommon for power supplies to become overloaded by upgrades and peripherals or to fail after prolonged use or repeated voltage spikes. When most consumers go out to buy a PC, the power supply capacity is often the *last* specification on their minds. It is the more exciting specifications such as CPU speed and hard drive capacity that get all the attention—few people worry about the effects of future upgrades when buying a brand new system. As a technical professional, the best advice you can give consumers is very simple: *"don't skimp on power."* If you buy a new system, get one with a supply capacity that will be big enough to support a few typical upgrades like a video capture board, an additional hard drive, a CD-ROM, an internal modem, and at least double the amount of memory currently fitted into the system. You need not invest in the biggest and best supply (unless you're building a network server, or you have a lot of expansion devices from a previous system), but don't trap yourself by getting the smallest (cheapest) one either.

Choosing a Supply

When you determine that your supply has failed or needs to be upgraded, there are two important factors that you need to consider: the power capacity of the new supply and its physical dimensions. The *capacity* of a power supply is measured in *watts* (W). This is the maximum amount of power that can be supplied to a load (the computer) safely. Today's PC power supplies range from about 50W to 300W. Choosing the proper power rating for an upgraded supply is often a matter of approximation—you can usually calculate a safe upgrade by adding 50W to the original supply rating. For example, a fair upgrade for an IBM AT supply (usually 192W) would be the next closest rating to (192 +50) 242W. The actual supply might be 230W or 260W or something in that range, but at least you're in an acceptable range of ratings.

Before you finally choose a replacement supply, you will need to consider its physical *dimensions*. The new supply must be able to fit within the space allotted inside the PC. The new supply must be bolted into place, so its mounting holes should align properly with the holes in the original supply. This problem is largely taken care of with the new generation of ATX and NLX form-factor power supplies, which are specifically designed to be readily interchangeable with ATX/NLX cases and motherboards. A new supply must also have a *connector* scheme that is compatible with the motherboard. The 4-pin mate-n-lock connectors are standard for powering the drives in a PC (the hard drives and CD-ROM drives), but motherboard power connectors can vary a bit from model to model. Figure 37-4 illustrates a typical "AT-style" motherboard power connector set, while Figure 37-5 shows an ATX/NLX motherboard power connector. Be sure to get a supply with the correct connector configuration for your motherboard. If you cannot find a compatible third-party supply, contact the PC's manufacturer. Some computer enthusiasts might be tempted to splice a power supply into the old motherboard connector. Doing this should be avoided at all costs—a new power supply is typically warranted for 90 days to 1 year. Splicing its wiring immediately voids any warranty.

Test the Upgrade Carefully

When installing a new supply, be sure that it is unplugged and turned off. Locate the line voltage selector switch (110/220) and verify that it is set appropriately for your region of the world. Before firing up the supply for the first time, remove any optional or noncritical expansion boards until you can verify that the PC is working correctly. You can then power-down the PC again, re-install any additional boards or peripherals, and then burn-in the system for at least 48 hours before returning it to service.

Troubleshooting Switching Power Supplies

Troubleshooting a switching power supply can be a complex and time-consuming task. Although the operation of rectifier and filter sections are reasonably straightforward, sensing/switching circuits can be complex oscillators that are difficult to follow without a schematic. Sub-assembly replacement of DC switching supplies is quite common.

TIPS FOR POWER SUPPLY SERVICE

Power and power supply problems can manifest themselves in a stunning variety of ways, but the tips below should help you to stay out of trouble:

- Power supply cooling is important—keep the vent openings and cooling fan blades clean.
- Make sure that the *line voltage switch* (120/220Vac) is set correctly for your region.
- Verify that the power supply connectors are attached to the motherboard and drives securely.
- Remember that, for AT-style power connections: *the black wires go together*.
- Do not use a Y splitter to split power from a HDD (avoid Y splitters entirely if possible).
- Some Y splitters are wired improperly. If you have trouble with a device after installing a Y splitter, check the splitter or try powering the device directly.
- Voltage tolerances are usually +/- 5% (+/- 3% for 3.3Vdc), so be sure each output is within tolerance.
- Erratic system behavior after adding a new device can be the result of an overload. Try removing the device. If the system stabilizes, consider a power supply upgrade.

AN EXAMPLE POWER SUPPLY

For the purposes of this troubleshooting discussion, consider the IC-based switching supply of Figure 37-7. The STK7554 is a switching regulator IC manufactured as a 16 pin SIP (single in-line package). It offers a dual output of 24Vdc and 5Vdc. Notice that *both* output waveforms from the STK7554 are 38 volt square waves, but it is the *duty cycle* of those square waves that sets the desired output levels. The square wave's amplitude simply provides energy to the filter circuits. Filters made from coils (or "chokes") and high-value polarized capacitors smooth the square wave input (actually a form of pulsating DC) into a steady source of DC. There will be some small amount of high-frequency ripple on each DC output. Smaller, nonpolarized capacitors on each output act to filter out high-frequency components of the DC output. Finally, note the resistor-capacitor-diode combinations on each output. These form a surge and flyback protector that prevents energy stored in the choke from reentering the IC and damaging it. Refer to Figure 37-7 for the following symptoms.

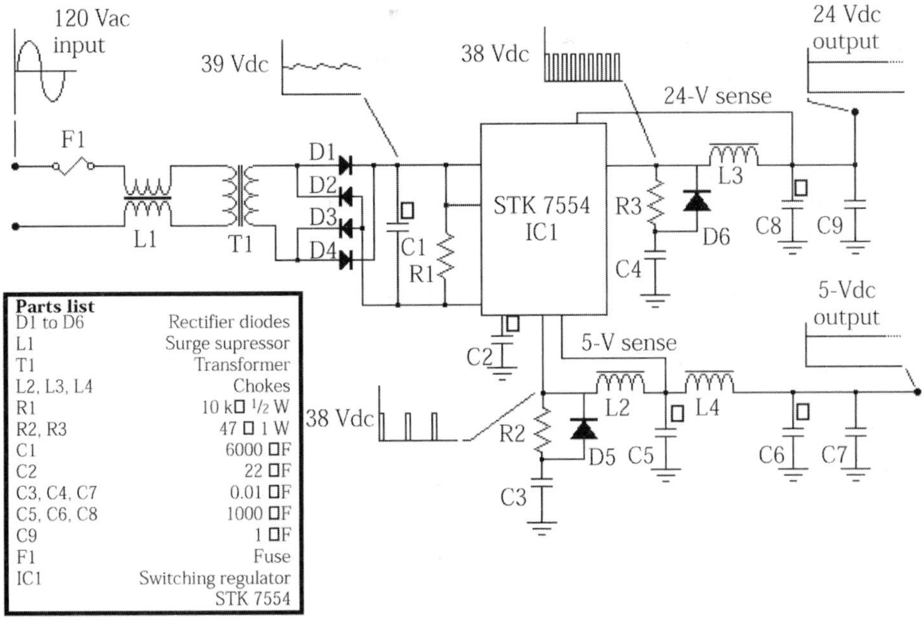

FIGURE 37-7 A complete chip-based switching power supply.

SYMPTOMS

SYMPTOM 37-1 The PC or peripheral is completely dead—no power indicators are lit As with linear supplies, check the AC line voltage entering the PC before beginning any major repair work. Use your multimeter to measure the AC line voltage available at the wall outlet powering your computer or peripheral. *Use extreme caution whenever measuring AC line voltage levels.* Normally, you should read between 105 and 130Vac to ensure proper supply operation. If you find either very high or low AC voltage, try the device in an outlet that provides the correct amount of AC voltage. Unusual line voltage levels may damage your power supply, so proceed cautiously.

If AC line voltage is normal, suspect the main power fuse in the supply. Most power fuses are accessible from the rear of the computer near the AC line cord, but some fuses may be accessible only by disassembling the device and opening the supply. Unplug the device and remove the fuse from its holder. You should find the fusible link intact, but use your multimeter to measure continuity across the fuse. A good fuse should measure as a short circuit (0 ohms), while a failed fuse will measure as an open circuit (infinity). Replace any failed fuse and re-test the PC. If the fuse continually fails, there is a serious defect elsewhere within the power supply or other computer/peripheral circuits. If your supply has an AC selector switch that sets the supply for 120Vac or 240Vac operation, be sure that switch is in the proper position for your region of the world (an improperly set AC switch can disable the entire system).

Unplug the computer and disassemble it enough to expose the power supply clearly. Restore power to the PC and measure each DC output with your multimeter or oscilloscope (you can usually find a power connector at the motherboard or other main board). Make sure that any power cables are securely attached. If each output measures correctly, and then your trouble lies *outside* of the supply—a key circuit has failed elsewhere in the device. You can try a POST board or diagnostic to trace the specific problem further. A low output voltage suggests a problem within the supply itself. Check each connector and all interconnecting wiring leading to or from the supply. Remember that many switching supplies *must* be attached to a load for proper switching to occur. If the load circuit is disconnected from its supply, the voltage signal could shut down or oscillate wildly.

When supply outputs continue to measure incorrectly with all connectors and wiring intact, chances are that your problem is inside the supply. With a linear supply, you begin testing at the output, and then work back toward the AC input. For a switching supply, you should begin testing at the AC input, and then work toward the defective output.

Measure the primary AC voltage applied across the transformer (T1). Use extreme caution when measuring high-voltage AC. You should read approximately 120Vac for Figure 37-7. If voltage has been interrupted in that primary circuit, you will read 0Vac. Check the primary circuit for any fault that might interrupt power. Measure secondary AC voltage supplying the rectifier stage. It should read higher than the highest output voltage that you expect. For the example of Figure 37-7, the highest expected DC output is 24 volts, so AC secondary voltage should be several volts higher than this. The example shows this as 28Vac. If primary voltage reads correctly and secondary voltage does not, you may have an open circuit in the primary or secondary transformer winding—try replacing the transformer.

Next, check the preswitched DC voltage supplying the switching IC. Use your multimeter or oscilloscope to measure this DC level. You should read approximately the peak value of whatever secondary AC voltage you just measured. For Figure 37-7, a secondary voltage of 28Vac should yield a DC voltage of about 39Vdc (28Vac RMS x 1.414). If this voltage is low or nonexistent, unplug the AC from the supply and check each rectifier diode and then inspect the filter capacitor.

Use your oscilloscope to measure each chopped DC output signal. You should find a high-frequency square wave at each output (20kHz to 40kHz) with an amplitude approximately equal to the pre-switched DC level (38 to 39 volts in this case). Set your oscilloscope to a time base of 5 or 10 μS/DIV and start your VOLTS/DIV setting at 10 VOLTS/DIV. Once you have established a clear trace, adjust the time base and vertical sensitivity to optimize the display.

If you do not read a chopped DC output from the switching IC, either the IC is defective or one (or more) of the polarized output filter capacitors may be shorted. Unplug the PC and inspect each questionable filter capacitor. Replace any capacitors that appear shorted. As a general rule, filter capacitors tend to fail more readily in switching supplies than in linear supplies because of high-frequency electrical stress and the smaller physical size of most switching supply components. If all filter capacitors check out correctly, replace the switching chip. Use care when desoldering the old regulator. Install an IC socket (if possible) to avoid repeat soldering work, and then just plug in the new IC. If you do not have the tools to perform the work outlined above (or the problem persists), replace the power supply outright.

SYMPTOM 37-2 Supply operation is intermittent—device operation cuts in and out with the supply Begin by inspecting the AC line voltage into your printer. Be sure that the AC line cord is secured properly at the wall outlet and printer. Make sure that the power fuse is installed securely. If the PC/peripheral comes on at all, the fuse *has* to be intact. Unplug the device and expose your power supply. Inspect every connector or interconnecting wire leading into or out of the supply. A loose or improperly installed connector can play havoc with the system's operation. Pay particular attention to any output connections. In almost all cases, a switching power supply *must* be connected to its load circuit in order to operate. Without a load, the supply may cut out or oscillate wildly.

In many cases, intermittent operation may be the result of a PC board problem. PC board problems are often the result of physical abuse or impact, but they can also be caused by accidental damage during a repair. *Lead pull-through* occurs when a wire or component lead is pulled away from its solder joint, usually through its hole in the PC board. This type of defect can easily be repaired by re-inserting the pulled lead and properly resoldering the defective joint. *Trace breaks* are hairline fractures between a solder pad and its printed trace. Such breaks can usually render a circuit inoperative, and they are almost impossible to spot without a careful visual inspection. *Board cracks* can sever any number of printed traces, but they are often very easy to spot. The best method for repairing trace breaks and board cracks is to solder jumper wires across the damage between two adjacent solder pads. You may also simply replace the power supply outright.

Some forms of intermittent failures are time or temperature related. If your system works just fine when first turned on, but fails only after a period of use, and then spontaneously returns to operation later on (or after it has been off for a while), you may be faced with a thermally intermittent component—a component may work when cool but fail later on after reaching or exceeding its working temperature. After a system quits under such circumstances, check for any unusually hot components. *Never touch an operating circuit with your fingers—injury is almost certain.* Instead, smell around the circuit for any trace of burning semiconductor or unusually heated air. If you detect an overheated component, spray it with a liquid refrigerant. Spray in short bursts for the best cooling. If normal operation returns, you have isolated the defective component. Replace any components that behave intermittently. If operation does not return, test any other unusually warm components. If problems persist, replace the entire power supply outright.

Understanding Power Management

As millions of new PCs enter service each year, *power conservation* has become a matter of increasing importance. By designing PCs that use less power and employ comprehensive power-down techniques during periods of non-use, a computer can actually be left on all the time yet use only about 5W of power in its "deepest" power-saving state (less than most nightlights)—this strategy also reduces electric bills and lowers the cost of running your PC(s). Power conservation is also important for mobile PCs in order to get the longest possible working time from each battery charge. For the purposes of this book, *power management* is the result of a system's BIOS, chipset, operating system, and devices all cooperating together to reduce the power demands of an idle computer. This part of the chapter explains the basic concepts of popular power management techniques and covers a number of power management problems for desktop and mobile systems.

POWER MANAGEMENT AND WINDOWS 98

There are several important elements required to support power management: the BIOS, chipset, devices, and operating system. The operating system provides the controls and dialogs needed for selecting your power management strategy, and it runs the various drivers needed to control each piece of "power managed" hardware. Windows 98 is largely considered to be the premier operating system for power management, and you can configure just about any "power managed" part of the PC through Windows 98 Power Management Properties dialog (Figure 37-8).

Power management under Windows 98 begins by selecting a "power scheme"—this basic categorization uses a collection of predefined settings that control the power-down timing of your hardware devices. However, you can also tailor the settings of a given scheme to suit your particular tastes. There are three classic power-saving modes that you should be familiar with:

- ***Basic conservation*** You can turn off your monitor (LCD backlight) and hard drive(s) automatically after a given period of inactivity (conserving a great deal of power while the rest of the system may be running normally).
- ***Standby*** You can put the computer into a *standby* mode when it's idle. While in standby mode, your monitor and hard drive(s) turn off, and some computer devices are powered down. When you want to

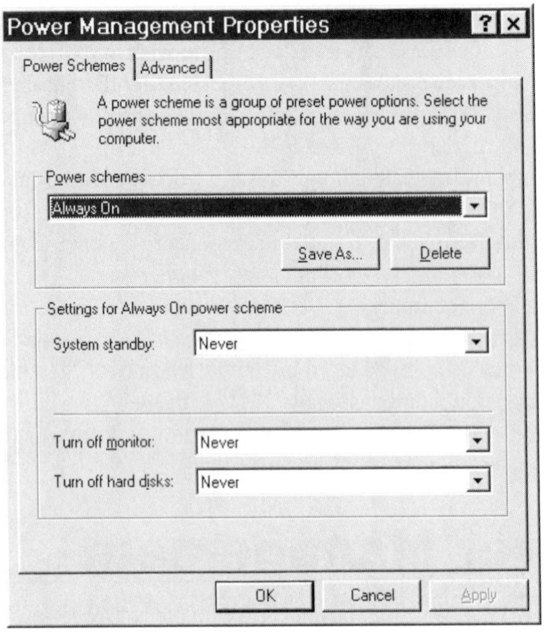

FIGURE 37-8 The Power Management Properties dialog

use the computer again, it comes out of "standby" mode quickly, and your desktop (along with your important work) is restored exactly as you left it. Standby is particularly handy for saving battery power in laptop computers.

- ***Hibernation*** You can put your computer into *hibernate mode* after longer periods of inactivity (for instance, you leave your office for the day). Power management's hibernate feature turns off your monitor and hard drive(s) first (that is, it enters the standby mode first). If idle time continues, the system will save everything in memory on disk and then turn off your computer. When you restart your computer, your computer's last state is restored to memory from the disk, and your desktop is restored exactly as you left it.

The following sections outline a number of techniques that you can use to control power management under Windows 98.

Selecting a Power Scheme

To enable the system's standby mode and take advantage of your computer's power management features, you first need to select a *power scheme*. Click Start, highlight Settings, click Control Panel, and then double-click the Power Management icon. The Power Management Properties dialog will appear (Figure 37-8). Click the Power Schemes drop-down menu and select from the available choices, which loosely define how the PC is used:

- Always on
- Home/Office Desk
- Portable/Laptop

When you select a scheme, you'll notice that the settings for that power scheme (System standby, Turn off monitor, and Turn off hard disks) will be updated to their default values. If you wish to tweak the default timer values (for example, you want to add more time before the system drops into standby mode), you can simply click on the respective timer and select the desired time value from the drop-down list. Using these timer entries, you can configure the monitor, hard drive, and standby delays according to your own personal preferences. Be sure to Apply your changes before clicking OK.

> If you're using a laptop computer, you can specify a different standby delay for battery power, and a different setting for AC power.

Saving/Deleting a Power Scheme

If you've made changes to your power scheme's timer value(s), you can save all of those settings as a unique power scheme. Once you have your timer settings the way you want them, simply click Save As, and then enter the name for your new scheme—the new scheme is added to the Power Schemes drop-down list. If you no longer wish to save a particular power scheme on your system, simply select the scheme from the Power Schemes drop-down list, and click Delete.

Manually Invoking the Standby Mode

The easiest way to place your PC in the standby mode is to use the Shut Down Windows dialog (Figure 37-9). You can also configure the system to let you use the standby mode whenever you press the Power button on your system (or whenever you close the lid on your laptop). Click Start, highlight Settings, click Control Panel, and then double-click the Power Management icon. The Power Management Properties dialog will appear (Figure 37-8). Click the Advanced tab. Locate the entry "When I press the power button on my computer," then click Standby. If you're using a laptop, locate the entry "When I close the lid of my portable computer," then click Standby. Click Apply (or OK), and then turn off the power or close the laptop's lid.

> It's a good idea to save your work before putting a computer into standby mode. While the computer is in standby, information in RAM is not saved to your hard drive—if there's an interruption in power, the information in memory can easily be lost.

Manually Invoking the Hibernate Mode

When you put your computer in hibernation, *everything* in the computer's memory is saved on your hard disk. When you turn the computer back on, all programs and documents that were open when you put the PC into hibernation are restored on the desktop. Click Start, highlight Settings, click Control Panel, and then double-click the Power Management icon. The Power Management Properties dialog will appear. Click the Hibernate tab and select the check box (*not* shown in Figure 37-8). Click the Advanced tab. Locate the entry "When I press the power button on my computer," then click Hibernate. If you're using a laptop, locate the entry "When I close the lid of my portable computer," and then click Standby. Click Apply (or OK), and then turn off the power or close the laptop's lid.

> If the Hibernate tab is not displayed, your computer does not support this feature. Your system will also *not* support hibernation if you're using FAT32 drives. If your system currently supports the hibernate feature, using the FAT32 Converter (under Windows 98) should disable the hibernate feature.

Receiving Phone Calls in Standby Mode

Normally, a PC in standby mode will wake when the modem answers an incoming call. You must start the program that you use to answer the telephone (that is, your modem's communication software) and make

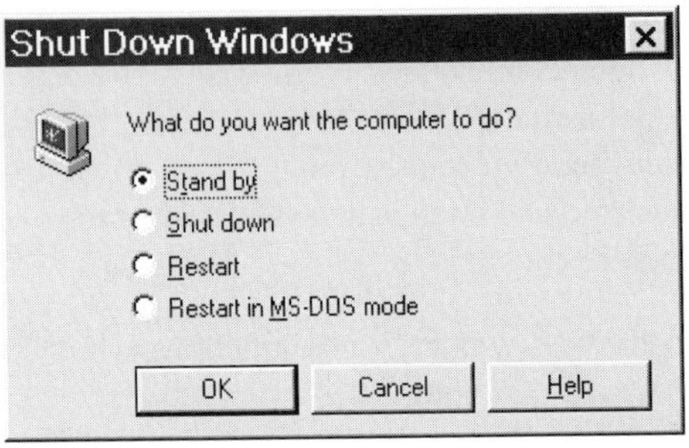

FIGURE 37-9 Using the Stand by feature of the Shut Down Windows dialog

sure that your external modem is turned on. After the PC enters its standby mode, it should come out of standby for the duration of the call, and then return to standby automatically.

Configuring Battery Warnings

You can configure your laptop system to produce warnings for "low" and "critical" battery conditions and instruct the PC how to respond to such alarms. Click Start, highlight Settings, click Control Panel, and then double-click the Power Management icon. The Power Management Properties dialog will appear. Click the Alarms tab (*not* shown in Figure 37-8). For both the "Low battery alarm" and "Critical battery alarm" entries, you can specify the settings you want by dragging the slider to the appropriate level. Click the Alarm Actions entry to select the *type* of alarm notification and power level you want. For example, if you want your computer to shut down when an alarm occurs, click "When the alarm goes off, the computer will" in the Alarm Actions dialog box.

Using Passwords in Standby or Hibernation

In order to prevent anyone from moving a mouse or pressing a key to bring your system out of standby or hibernation, you can use passwords to protect your system on waking. Click Start, highlight Settings, click Control Panel, and then double-click the Power Management icon. The Power Management Properties dialog will appear. Click the Advanced tab, and then click "Prompt for password when computer goes off standby." You use your Windows password for both standby and hibernation

ADVANCED POWER MANAGEMENT (APM)

APM represents the first major industry effort to establish a standardized power conservation method on the PC. Although APM concepts were in place with later versions of DOS and Windows 3.1x, APM was really first embraced as a "systemwide" standard with the introduction of Windows 95. Today, APM support is now implemented in virtually every BIOS, chipset, and device in production and is carried through into Windows 98/SE. Stated simply, APM provides you with a mechanism for shutting down major power-consuming devices such as the monitor (or laptop's LCD backlight), spinning down the system hard drive(s), and "throttling back" the CPU during idle periods. APM can also query the battery to obtain its current charge information and report remaining battery life with great accuracy.

You can check for the presence of APM support by opening your Control Panel and double-clicking the System icon, and then selecting the Device Manager tab. Double-click the System devices entry and look for the "Advanced Power Management support" line, as shown in Figure 37-10. If your system has not installed APM, you may install it manually:

1. Open the Control Panel and double-click the Add New Hardware wizard.
2. Click Next.
3. Click Yes (recommended) and then click Next.
4. Click Next.

Now verify that APM support has been enabled as explained in the paragraph above.

Today there are several different versions of APM, but version 1.2 is current. Some computers conform to the APM specification 1.0—others use APM 1.1 or 1.2. Although Windows 95/98 works with all of these specifications, there are advantages to using APM 1.2. Version 1.1 is designed to give the operating system more control over power management than APM 1.0 permitted. For example, if a computer is using APM 1.2, the operating system can force the BIOS to wait until it has prepared the running programs and drivers for suspend mode. Also, a computer using APM 1.2 allows the operating system to reject the request for suspend mode. However, there may be instances where your system does not fully support APM 1.1 or 1.2, and you may need to "force" Windows to use the initial APM 1.0 system. You can do this by double-clicking the "Advanced Power Management support" entry in your Device Manager, and then clicking the Settings tab (Figure 37-11). Simply click the "Force APM 1.0 mode" check box. If the system stabilizes, you'll know that one or more devices (or drivers) are having trouble with APM 1.1 or 1.2 on your system, and you can isolate and update the offending device(s) accordingly.

ADVANCED CONFIGURATION AND POWER INTERFACE (ACPI)

ACPI has largely been introduced under Windows 98/SE, and builds on the basics of APM by allowing much more comprehensive control of each device in the power-managed state. For example, an ACPI system can turn off (or "throttle back") a wider range of devices such as CD-ROMs, DVD-ROMs, modems,

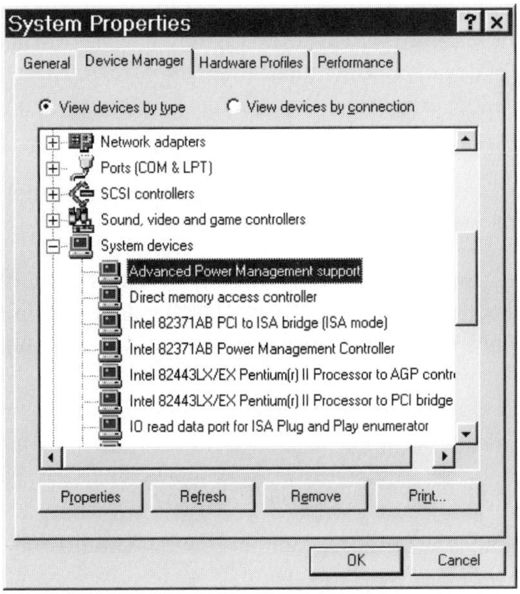

FIGURE 37-10 Checking the Device Manager for APM support

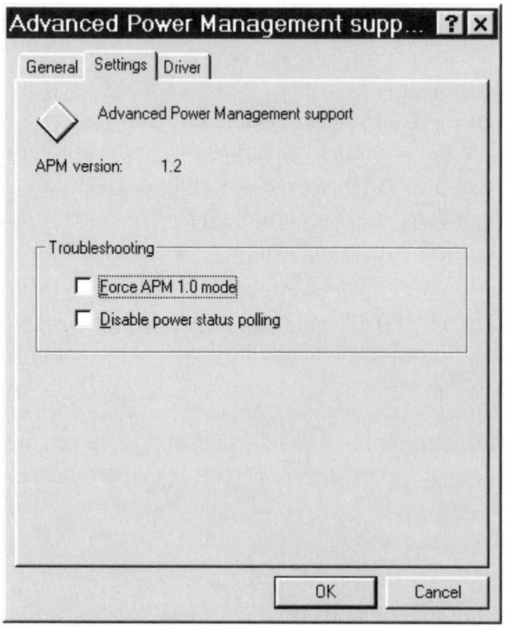

FIGURE 37-11 Forcing the APM 1.0 mode

and network devices. ACPI also allows the system to "wake" and perform predetermined tasks based upon real-world events. For example, an ACPI system may "wake" when the modem receives a call, connect and exchange data, and then return to a standby or hibernate state after the call is completed.

In addition to enabling OS-controlled power management, ACPI provides a generic system event mechanism for Plug-and-Play, and an OS-independent interface for device configuration control. This capability means your ACPI system can actually manage device configuration as well as power. In effect, ACPI is a "marriage" of PnP and APM that offers much more precise and versatile control over a system's devices.

> Hibernate modes are known to have trouble on FAT32 systems. If you use the hibernate mode, be sure that you're using a FAT16 disk. Newer systems are overcoming this limitation.

If you do not have ACPI support already in place when you install Windows 98, you can add ACPI support by reinstalling Windows 98 with the **/p j** command line switches. This adds the **ACPIOption** string value with a value data of 1 to the Registry. To run Windows 98 Setup using the **/p j** switches, click Start, click Run, type the following command in the Open box, and then click OK:

```
setup /p j
```

Reinstalling Windows 98 is the best way to ensure that all devices are configured correctly.

> To enable ACPI support in Windows 98, you must first have an ACPI-compatible motherboard and an ACPI 1.0-compliant BIOS.

POWER MANAGEMENT TROUBLESHOOTING

Power management offers some compelling advantages for the PC: systems can be extremely responsive, yet use little real power while idle. Ideally, the BIOS, chipset, devices, and operating system work together seamlessly in order to avoid system crashes and data corruption. Unfortunately, this ideal isn't always met (especially with older systems). BIOS incompatibilities, buggy drivers, and noncompliant hardware devices are just some of the issues that can result in power management problems. This part of the chapter explores a range of power management symptoms and solutions.

ACPI Symptoms

SYMPTOM 37-3 **The Windows 98 system with ACPI BIOS and UDMA-compliant device(s) will crash when resuming from suspend mode** If an ATAPI storage device requires the use of a Get Task File (or _GTF) method to resume from the suspend mode on a computer with an ACPI BIOS, the computer may crash during the resume process. Most Ultra-DMA (UDMA) CD-ROM and optical drives cause this problem on computers that attempt to suspend and then resume. This error occurs because Windows 98 (Second Edition) supports *only* the optional ACPI _GTF technique for IDE hard disks—ATAPI devices are not well-supported.

The best solution to this problem is to update your BIOS to a version that supports the _GTF technique for ATAPI IDE devices. Until you do update, try changing the ACPI Sleep state to S1 instead of S3 (if your computer's BIOS allows you to do so). Otherwise, you can work around this problem by disabling the DMA support (disable the UDMA mode) on your ATAPI device(s). This will reduce the performance of such device(s), but allow for better power management operation until you can update the BIOS.

SYMPTOM 37-4 **When starting Windows 98, you see ACPI errors against a red screen** ACPI error messages on a red screen are generated by the computer's BIOS, so this problem occurs most frequently if your computer has a hardware or BIOS problem. To correct this problem, contact your system or BIOS manufacturer to download a BIOS upgrade (which may be all you need). If a hardware device is mentioned in the error, check for updated drivers or firmware for the suspect hardware device. You can usually determine the precise error using the guidelines below:

- A *1xxx* error code on a red (or blue) background indicates an error during initialization phase of the ACPI driver, and usually means the driver cannot read one or more of the ACPI devices.
- A *2xxx* error code usually indicates an ACPI machine language (or "AML") interpreter error.
- A *3xxx* error code indicates an error within the ACPI driver event handler—usually when the event handler is running as the result of a general-purpose event (GPE).
- A *4xxx* error code indicates a thermal management error.
- A *5xxx* error code typically suggests an error with a particular piece of ACPI-compliant hardware.

SYMPTOM 37-5 **The Windows 98 low battery alarm does not play the alarm sound or display the low battery message** There are two possible variations of this problem corresponding to how you've configured your laptop:

- If you've set up a low (or critical) battery alarm to play a sound and display a warning message, you may find that the message is displayed, but the sound may not be played. Instead, the sound may be played when you click OK to close the message window, or when the window closes automatically after a five-minute delay.

37

- If you've set up the battery alarm to perform an *action* (such as enter the standby mode) in addition to playing a sound or displaying a warning message, you may notice that the standby/shutdown action is performed, but the sound might not be played and the warning message might not be displayed.

In virtually all cases, this fault occurs on computers that fully conform to the ACPI specification *if* any action is configured for the battery alarm *in addition to* notification through a sound. This is a known problem with Windows 98, and may have a patch or update available at the Microsoft "Update Windows" site. You can work around this problem in the mean time. In order to receive audible notification for a low or critical battery alarm, simply do *not* configure any other type of notification or action in addition to the sound alarm.

SYMPTOM 37-6 **When a standby mode is invoked under Windows 98, the ACPI computer enters the hibernate mode instead** This problem may take three different forms—depending on how you try to enter the standby mode:

- If you select the Standby action for the Power button on the Advanced tab of the Power Management tool in your Control Panel, and you press the Power button, the computer may hibernate instead of entering the standby mode.
- If you select the standby mode when the laptop computer lid is closed, the computer may also hibernate instead of standing by when the lid is closed.
- If you click Start, select Shut down, and then click Stand by, the computer may hibernate instead of standing by.

This problem is common on ACPI systems when the Enable Hibernation Support option is enabled on the Hibernate tab in your Power Management Properties dialog. With this setup, Windows 98 causes the computer to hibernate instead of entering standby mode. This is a problem with Windows 98 (corrected in Windows 98 SE), and Microsoft has developed a patch that should correct the issue. The English patch should have the following file attributes or later:

```
6/29/98 9:01pm 4.10.2101 115,665 CONFIGMG.VXD
6/29/98 9:01pm 4.10.2101 37,523 VPOWERD.VXD
7/21/98 9:02pm 4.10.2102 194,494 NTKERN.VXD
```

> The Hibernate tab appears in Power Management Properties *only* if the computer is configured to support hibernation.

SYMPTOM 37-7 **When resuming from suspend or standby mode and running a Windows 98 DirectX6 program, the PC may crash** This is a known problem with Windows 98 (reported to be fixed in Windows 98 SE), and is known to occur on Compaq Presario 5720 systems). This problem can occur if *all* of the following conditions exist on your system:

- Your computer uses ACPI for power management.
- Your computer contains an AGP-based video adapter.
- You run a program that uses DirectX6 (or later) after you resume your computer.

Microsoft has developed a patch that should correct the problem. You should contact Microsoft for the patch or download it from the Microsoft Web site. The patch should have the following file attributes or later:

```
Pci.vxd 4.10.2017 11/6/98 6:28pm 65,919 bytes
Pcimp.pci 4.10.2017 11/6/98 6:33pm 16,240 bytes
```

SYMPTOM 37-8 One or more ACPI devices report Device Manager problems under Windows 98 After you start Windows 98 on an ACPI-compliant computer, one or more hardware devices may not function properly (if at all)—they may have the following problems in *Device Manager*:

```
This device is not working properly because the BIOS in your computer is
reporting the resources for the device incorrectly (Code 9).

This device is either not present, not working properly, or does not have
all the drivers installed (Code 10).

The drivers for this device are not installed (Code 28).

This device is causing a resource conflict (Code 15).
```

In virtually all cases, the Windows 98 ACPI driver (ACPI.SYS) does not properly release the ACPI GlobalLock feature, even though it's been explicitly released by ACPI Source Language (or ASL) code. This is a problem with Windows 98. GlobalLock is a feature of ACPI that allows the protection of resources between ASL code executed by the operating system and the legacy BIOS/SMI environment. The original release of Windows 98 does not release this feature. This problem has a number of ramifications—including exclamation points on all the devices that requires access to a resource that's "jammed" by GlobalLock. You can download and install a new version of ACPI.SYS from Microsoft.

```
ACPI.SYS 4.10.2000 11/23/98 7:51pm 80,256 bytes
```

37

SYMPTOM 37-9 You find the Sleep button disabled after waking an ACPI computer under Windows 98 This often happens when you press the Sleep button *while* the system is waking. This is a known problem with Windows 98, and there's a patch available from Microsoft. The English version of this fix should have the following file attributes (or later):

```
12/13/99 11:32p 4.10.2103 194,518 NTKERN.VXD
```

SYMPTOM 37-10 A Packard Bell system restarts continuously under Windows 98/SE After you enable ACPI support on a Packard Bell Multimedia 4350 computer, the system may restart continuously. This fault can occur if you have a Yamaha DS-XG sound card installed in your computer, and both the sound card and the ACPI system attempt to use interrupt IRQ9. To resolve this issue, modify the IRQ used for your sound card:

1. Start your system in the Safe Mode.
2. Click Start, highlight Settings, and then click Control Panel.
3. Double-click the System icon, and then click the Device Manager tab.
4. Double-click the entry for "Sound, video and game controllers," then double-click the "Legacy sound controller."
5. On the Resources tab, clear the "Use Automatic Settings" check box and click Interrupt Request.

6 In the Resource Type column, click Change Setting.
7 In the Value box, click or type a number of an available IRQ that does *not* conflict with any other device in your computer, and then click OK until you return to the Control Panel.
8 Close the Control Panel and reboot the computer if prompted to do so.

SYMPTOM 37-11 You cannot use ACPI properly under Windows 98 with Asus P2B-type motherboards After you install Windows 98/SE on a computer with an Asus P2B-type motherboard, the computer may *not* wake up after it has been suspended. This is a known problem with P2B-series motherboards using BIOS version 1008—this version may not function properly with ACPI. You'll need to use a BIOS version that corrects the problem. You can fall back to version 1007 or try upgrading to a later version.

SYMPTOM 37-12 Your system prompts you twice for a hardware profile when ACPI is enabled under Windows 98/SE This is a known issue with certain laptop models. When you start a system that uses ACPI power management, you may be prompted for a hardware profile *twice*. If you create more than one hardware profile and restart your computer, you may receive a message such as: *"Windows cannot determine what configuration your computer is in."* This problem occurs when the computer's BIOS supports both ACPI and Plug-and-Play. The real-mode boot process detects the PnP BIOS and prompts for the profile, and then the protected-mode boot process detects ACPI support, but a blue screen error requests the profile again.

To work around this problem temporarily, read each prompt carefully, and then select the same hardware profile during the first and second prompt. Microsoft has a patch available for Windows 98/SE that should address this problem. The English version of the Windows 98 patch should have the following file attributes (or later):

```
08/18/99 12:30p 4.10.2103 222,670 WINBOOT.SYS
12/13/99 11:01p 115,689 CONFIGMG.VXD
```

The English version of the Windows 98 SE patch should have the following attributes (or later):

```
09/13/99 05:45p 4.10.2223 222,670 WINBOOT.SYS
08/18/99 11:51a 125,081 CONFIGMG.VXD
```

SYMPTOM 37-13 A system entering the ACPI S4 mode locks up when a USB device is attached This is a problem with Windows 98 SE. When the computer tries to enter the ACPI S4 (suspend to disk) mode, the USB Host controller is removed. When in the S4 mode, Windows is unable to cancel requests previously made to the USB devices. This problem occurs with Windows 98/SE, and Microsoft has a fix that should correct the trouble. The English version of this patch should have the following file attributes (or later):

```
09/08/99 03:46p 4.10.2224 18,928 USBD.SYS
```

SYMPTOM 37-14 You notice that some legacy devices may not respond after resuming from a power-saving state under Windows 98/SE This can happen when you resume an ACPI system, and legacy (non-PnP) devices stop functioning. The Virtual Communications Device (VCOMM) doesn't attempt to put LPT ports into the D0 power state (full power) when the port is opened—it is assumed to always be powered on. The problem is that VCOMM puts the LPT port into the D3 power state (powered off) when you suspend your computer but does not return it to the D0 state after you resume your computer. This issue can be traced to Windows 98/SE, and Microsoft has a patch that can be installed. The English version of this patch should have the following file attributes (or later):

```
9/27/99 11:06pm 4.10.2018 33,107 VCOMM.VXD
```

> PnP printers that do not turn on before the computer starts may also stop working. This problem affects any device that's connected to a parallel (LPT) port on a computer running Windows 98 and Windows 98 SE.

SYMPTOM 37-15 **Windows 98 does not support the "passive cooling" mode in ACPI** The ACPI specification defines two categories of cooling: active and passive. *Active cooling* methods may include running one or more fans to provide increased airflow and improve the dissipation of heat from active components. *Passive cooling* methods may include slowing down (throttling) the computer's CPU so that it generates less heat. The problem is that Windows 98 supports only the "active cooling" mode.

In active cooling mode, the computer first uses active cooling methods to control the temperature of the computer. If the system's temperature continues to rise when the active cooling methods are in use, the computer uses passive cooling methods to cool overheated components. In passive cooling mode, the computer first uses passive cooling methods to control the temperature of the computer. If the computer's temperature continues to rise when the passive cooling methods are in use, the computer uses active cooling methods to cool overheated components. In either cooling mode, if the temperature continues to rise to critical levels, the computer may shut down or go to some other nonoperating, lower-power state—doing so helps prevent thermal damage to components.

The computer's cooling mode is controlled by a temperature *set point*—this is the temperature at which each cooling method is activated. For example, if the set point for the active cooling method is lower than the set point for the passive cooling method, the active method is employed first, and the computer goes to active cooling mode. If the set point for the passive cooling method is lower than the set point for the active cooling method, the passive method is employed first, and the computer goes to passive cooling mode.

Windows 98 configures the computer to operate *only* in active cooling mode and does not provide an interface for changing the active and passive cooling set points to operate in passive cooling mode.

SYMPTOM 37-16 **The Windows 98 system may hang up when you connect and disconnect a laptop's AC power cord** If you connect and then disconnect the power cord on a battery-powered ACPI-compliant computer, one of two symptoms may occur: either the computer will hang up or you will receive a Fatal Exception 0E error. This problem occurs with Windows 98 and has been reported with IBM ThinkPad 600 systems.

Your computer may seem to retain some amount of functionality, including the ability to shut down or restart the system, but certain ACPI functions (such as thermal management) may be disabled—in some circumstances, the computer's internal temperature may reach dangerously high levels without Windows 98 activating the appropriate cooling methods to reduce the temperature.

To get around this problem temporarily, shut down and restart your computer normally. If you're unable to shut down Windows properly, you may have to turn your computer off and then back on. To prevent this problem from occurring again, *do not* connect and disconnect the power cord repeatedly (in rapid succession).

SYMPTOM 37-17 **The system is slow to resume from the hibernate mode on certain systems** This is a known problem on systems such as the Toshiba Tecra 8000 or Protege 7020 and generally appears as a slow boot when the system resumes. This problem typically occurs when the Battery Mode setting in the computer's CMOS Setup is set to Full Power. This setting is incorrect in the BIOS—this setting actually enables the PCI Clock Run power-saving feature, which causes all PCI peripherals not to run at full capacity until an ACPI-aware operating system is booted. When the computer resumes from its hibernate mode, the slow boot takes place because the boot loader is not ACPI-aware. If you cannot update the BIOS to correct this misrepresentation, you can generally work around it by setting the following CMOS Setup options:

1. Set the Battery Mode or BIOS Power Management option to User Setting *instead* of Full Power.
2. Change the CPU Sleep Mode option to Disable.
3. Change the Processing Speed option to High.
4. Change the Cooling Method option to Performance.

> The CPU speed may *still* be slower than expected, even if you change all of the settings listed above. For example, the Protege 7020 has a built-in power-saving feature that slows down the CPU when the remaining battery power is less than 50 percent (until an ACPI-aware operating system overrides the setting).

APM Symptoms

SYMPTOM 37-18 **Your computer hangs while you try to shut it down** After you click the Shut Down The Computer option in the Shut Down Windows dialog, the computer may halt (or display a black screen) after you see the "Please wait while your computer shuts down" message. In many cases, this problem is caused by an incompatibility between the Windows APM system and the APM BIOS in your computer—if the BIOS in your computer instructs the system to *suspend* (rather than shut down), Windows cannot shut down correctly. As a temporary fix, disable your APM support by double-clicking the Power icon in your Control Panel, and then setting the Power Management option to Off. To correct the problem on a more permanent basis, you'll probably need to upgrade the system BIOS.

SYMPTOM 37-19 **You receive errors when using EMM386 under DOS on laptops with "suspend/resume" features** If you're using EMM386 v.4.45, you may receive an error such as: "Serious disk error has occurred" or "Segment Load Failure" (in Windows-based applications). In virtually all cases, this error is caused by a faulty interaction between the laptop power manager feature and EMM386.EXE. To work around this problem, try the following:

- First, try removing EMM386.EXE to see if the problem is related to using EMM386.EXE. If the problem remains after disabling EMM386, you may need to update the system BIOS.
- Try to determine if there is a region that needs to be *excluded* from the system's upper memory area (UMA) to allow the laptop's power management to work with EMM386.EXE (4.45). This information may be available in your laptop manual. As an alternative, you can try excluding the A000h-EFFFh memory range to test for a UMA conflict, as in:

  ```
  device=c:\dos\emm386.exe noems x=a000-efff
  ```

- If the problem occurs only with EMM386.EXE version 4.45, and cannot be corrected with the previous tips, use the version of EMM386.EXE that came with the laptop. Remember that using a different (OEM) version of EMM386 may prevent you from using MemMaker.

SYMPTOM 37-20 You find that a laptop PC in a docking station may not offer APM support under Windows 95 When you use Windows 95 on a mobile computer with APM, you see that the Suspend command does not appear on the Start menu (and the APM icon does not appear in Control Panel). You may also find that the Windows 95 Setup program does not correctly detect APM support on an APM-capable computer; however, the DOS real-mode APM support (POWER.EXE) should not be affected and should continue to function properly. This problem occurs if your computer disables APM functionality while it is in a docking station.

Some systems (such as the Zenith 420s and 425s) will disable APM when in a docking station, preventing access to the APM features in Windows 95. This condition is simply part of the individual system's design, and APM support on these computers is not available while they're docked. You may be able to upgrade the system's BIOS to correct this issue, but, in the meantime, you'll simply need to add APM support back into Windows 95 *after* you remove the machine from its docking station.

SYMPTOM 37-21 You cannot use APM 1.1 on certain systems under Windows 95/98 This is a known problem with the AST Ascentia 900N laptop—you cannot use APM features with this system. In virtually all cases, this is a BIOS problem. For example, the Ascentia 900N computer *supports* APM version 1.1, but the BIOS installed in this system returns an unexpected value when Windows 95/98 makes function calls. Therefore, the Windows protected-mode APM driver (VPOWERD.VXD) is unable to load, and APM support is not provided. A BIOS upgrade should correct the problem. In the meantime, you may be able to use APM 1.0 instead of 1.1:

1. Right-click My Computer, and then click Properties on the menu that appears.
2. Click the Device Manager tab.
3. Click Advanced Power Management Support, and then click Properties. You may need to expand the System Devices branch of the hardware tree by double-clicking the branch before you can select APM Support.
4. Click the Settings tab.
5. Click the Force APM 1.0 Mode check box to select it.
6. Click OK and reboot the system if necessary.

SYMPTOM 37-22 Your system reboots shortly after resuming to Windows 95/98 This is a known problem with certain laptops such as the Toshiba 4500. If you shut down Windows in suspend mode (or close the lid), Windows appears to shut down successfully. But when you resume Windows, the computer reboots after a short time. This condition occurs because those systems (for example, the Toshiba 4500) require an additional driver file to successfully implement APM features. The APM features do not function correctly without that driver. For the Toshiba 4500, that driver is WRESUME.386. You'll need to obtain that additional driver file, and then add it to the SYSTEM.INI file. Let's use the Toshiba 4500 as an example:

1. Open a text editor (such as Notepad or WordPad) and load the SYSTEM.INI file into the editor.
2. In the [386Enh] section of the file, add the following line:

   ```
   device=<path>\wresume.386
   ```

   where <path> is the path to the WRESUME.386 file. For example, if the WRESUME.386 file is located in the \Windows folder on drive C:, add the following line:

   ```
   device=c:\windows\wresume.386
   ```

3. Save your changes to the SYSTEM.INI file and exit the text editor.
4. Shut down Windows and restart your computer normally. The system should wake properly without rebooting.

SYMPTOM 37-23 **The suspend option appears on the Windows 95/98 Start menu, but it doesn't work** When you're using Windows 95/98 on a computer that supports APM, you may find that nothing happens when you click the suspend option on the Start menu. This trouble is known to occur on numerous systems, including the Compaq Summit 60 system. In virtually all cases, the system simply doesn't support the suspend feature (though it *does* support APM). Windows cannot detect whether or not a particular computer supports the suspend feature, so the suspend command is always on the Start menu when APM is enabled.

To correct this problem, you should consider a BIOS upgrade to a newer version that *will* properly support the suspend function under APM. In the meantime, you can disable the suspend feature on the Start menu:

1. Click Start, highlight Settings, and then click Control Panel.
2. Double-click the Power icon.
3. In the "Show Suspend Command On Start Menu" box, click the Never option.
4. Apply or save your changes, and then reboot the system if necessary.

SYMPTOM 37-24 **You find that your system is constantly suspending and resuming** If you click Suspend on the Start menu, and then press the Suspend button on your system before it goes completely to sleep, the computer continually suspends and resumes. You need to reboot the PC in order to stop the loop. This is a known issue on systems such as the Compaq Elite under Windows 95 and occurs because the APM BIOS in the Compaq Elite computer has trouble processing a software suspend request *and* a hardware suspend request at the same time. You may be able to correct this problem by upgrading the system's BIOS. When you need to suspend your Compaq Elite system in the meantime, use *either* the Suspend command on the Start menu, or the Suspend button on the computer itself. Wait for the suspend procedure to finish *before* you perform any other operation.

SYMPTOM 37-25 **Your system does not shut down after periods of inactivity (even though you've configured the APM features properly)** This is a known problem on systems such as the Compaq Contura Aero under Windows 95—the computer's hard disk may stop spinning to save power during periods of inactivity and then start spinning again two seconds later. In virtually all cases, this is a problem with the system's BIOS when running under Windows 95, and it can be corrected by updating the system's BIOS.

SYMPTOM 37-26 **Your laptop may not suspend automatically under Windows 95/98** This problem often occurs on certain Toshiba laptops under Windows—the computer may not *automatically* go into its low-power suspend mode. This problem happens because some laptop computers (such as the Toshiba T1910, T2100, T2400, and T4850) monitor the system IRQ lines to determine if the system is busy. Any hardware interrupt (other than IRQ0) resets the auto-suspend timer. Windows generates interrupts that prevent these computers from going into their low-power suspended mode. A BIOS upgrade may correct this problem. In the meantime, you can suspend the computer manually by clicking Start and then clicking Suspend or by using the hardware Suspend switch.

SYMPTOM 37-27 **Your display (monitor) does not wake after an EnergyStar shutdown under Windows 95** When you try to wake your computer after APM has shut down the display, the monitor may remain in its sleep mode. To reactivate the monitor, you must turn the computer off and back on. This problem is known to occur with several different Compaq computers (and other systems) using the Cirrus Logic 54xxx video chipset—there is a conflict between the Windows APM and the computer's BIOS. The Compaq Presario 520, 522, 524, 526, 528, and Prolinea 466 are known to exhibit this problem. There are generally four options for dealing with this type of problem:

- Do *not* enable APM in the computer's CMOS Setup.
- Do *not* inform Windows 95/98 that the monitor is EnergyStar compliant.
- Disable APM in the *Device Manager* under Windows 95/98.
- Obtain a BIOS upgrade for the system.

SYMPTOM 37-28 **You cannot install APM on a system under Windows 95/98** When you install Windows 95/98 on some systems (such as the Midwest Micro Elite Soundbook), the APM features are *not* installed, and you cannot add Windows 95/98 APM support using the Add/Remove Programs wizard. In virtually all such cases, the Windows 95/98 APM drivers do *not* work correctly with the system's BIOS, so APM support cannot be installed. To use APM features in Windows 95/98, you must install the OEM-version APM drivers that came with the particular computer. If you don't have such drivers handy, check with the system manufacturer for driver patches or updates.

SYMPTOM 37-29 **You encounter a system error when trying to suspend a computer under Windows 95** Some systems (such as the Global Dynamic 466 computer) will produce a system error message on a blue screen when you select the Suspend command on the Start menu under Windows 95. This is almost always a BIOS problem. For example, the APM BIOS in the Global Dynamic 466 computer is defective and does not support the suspend process correctly. The best solution is to upgrade the system BIOS to a version that provides better APM support. In the meantime, do not use the Suspend command. You should remove the Suspend command from your Start menu:

1. Click Start, highlight Settings, and then click Control Panel.
2. In Control Panel, double-click the Power icon.
3. In the Power Properties dialog, click the "Never Show Suspend Command in Start Menu" option.

SYMPTOM 37-30 **The display flashes when the system tries to use APM features under Windows 95** This type of problem is reported to occur with some AMI BIOS versions. A number of "green" computer systems that have built-in power management support may experience a constant flashing of the display—the display may start flashing as soon as Windows 95 starts, after a long period of inactivity on the computer, or after you attempt to suspend the computer. Also, the mouse cursor may jump to the center of the screen, and the system may respond so slowly that you're unable to use it.

This problem happens when Windows 95 APM polls the BIOS for APM events, and the BIOS returns a Resume From Suspend command. This causes Windows 95 to reinitialize some software and hardware (such as the display and the mouse), resulting in the display flashing, the mouse centering, and the system delays. You must disable power management support under Windows 95:

1. Click Start, highlight Settings, and then click Control Panel.

2. In Control Panel, double-click the System icon.
3. In the System Properties dialog box, click the Device Manager tab, and then double-click System Devices.
4. Double-click Advanced Power Management Support.
5. Click the Settings tab.
6. Make sure that the "Enable Power Management Support" box is *not* checked.
7. Click the OK button, shut down the computer, and then restart Windows 95 normally.

SYMPTOM 37-31 Systems using APM 1.0 may not restore all necessary hardware states under Windows 95 If you're faced with one or more of the following conditions, your system may lose certain functions when returning from the suspend mode:

- A DOS session was active when you suspended the system.
- You activated the suspend mode with a hardware switch (such as a Suspend button on the computer).
- The computer contains an APM 1.0-compliant BIOS version.

For example, if you're playing a DOS-based game with sound when you suspend the system, sound support may not function when the system resumes. In most cases, the problem is related to the hardware switch. When you suspend the system using a hardware switch, your APM 1.0 BIOS may process the suspend request too *quickly* for Windows 95 to save the current hardware settings. As a result, Windows 95 may not be able to reinitialize all the hardware devices properly when the system resumes. To work around this problem, use the Suspend feature on the Start menu to suspend the system *instead* of using a hardware switch.

> APM 1.1 (and later) systems do not have this problem because Windows 95 can request that the hardware wait until the operating system is ready to be suspended.

SYMPTOM 37-32 Using the hardware suspend button crashes your computer under Windows 95 As an example of this problem, when Windows 95 APM features are enabled, the PC will halt when you press the Suspend button. Turning the computer off and then back on does *not* correct the problem. In most situations, there is a mismatch between the system BIOS and the Windows APM version. For example, this problem is known to occur on systems such as the AcerNote 782 laptop—Windows 95 uses APM version 1.1, but the AcerNote 782 does *not* reliably support APM 1.1. To circumvent this problem, configure Windows 95 to use APM version 1.0:

1. Open your Control Panel and double-click the System icon.
2. On the Device Manager tab, double-click the System branch, and then double-click Advanced Power Management Support.
3. On the Settings tab, click the "Force APM 1.0 Mode" check box to *select* it.
4. Click OK until you return to the Control Panel.
5. Restart your computer when prompted to do so.

SYMPTOM 37-33 You cannot suspend a Canon NoteJet II 486C computer under Windows 95 When you click the Suspend command on the Start menu of a Canon NoteJet II 486C computer, the computer does not suspend. When you use the computer's Suspend button to suspend the computer, the system suspends, but it will not resume. This problem happens because the APM BIOS on the Canon NoteJet II 486C does *not* support the Suspend option in Windows 95. Do *not* suspend the Canon NoteJet II 486C when you're running Windows 95. Try removing the Suspend command from the Start menu:

1. Click Start, highlight Settings, and then click Control Panel.
2. In Control Panel, double-click the Power icon.
3. In the Power Properties dialog box, click the "Never Show Suspend Command In Start Menu" option.
4. Apply the changes and reboot the system if necessary.

SYMPTOM 37-34 You cannot use APM with an NEC Image P90 system and Matrox MGA PCI video adapter under Windows 95 With this combination of hardware and operating system, the system may crash when you try the Suspend command on the Start menu. There is currently no way to use APM features reliably on a NEC Image P90 computer with a Matrox MGA PCI display adapter. You'll need to *disable* APM on the system:

1. Open the Control Panel and double-click the System icon.
2. On the Device Manager tab, double-click the System Devices entry to expand it.
3. Double-click Advanced Power Management Support.
4. On the Settings tab, click the Enable Power Management Support check box to *clear* it.
5. Click OK until you return to Control Panel and reboot the system, if necessary.

37

SYMPTOM 37-35 The computer will not suspend when a DOS session is running under Windows 95 You find that an APM-compliant computer is not suspended when a DOS session (or virtual machine) is active. When no screen saver is selected *and* the Shut Off Monitor option is enabled, the monitor is not shut off when a DOS session is running. To get around this problem, simply enable a screen saver:

1. Open the Control Panel, and then double-click the Display icon.
2. Click the Screen Saver tab.
3. Click a screen saver in the Screen Saver box, and then click OK.

SYMPTOM 37-36 When installing Windows, you receive an "Exception 0E in VPOWERD" message when the system first boots The VPOWERD driver may cause a page fault ("Fatal Exception error 0E") on the first reboot during Windows Setup on certain computer models that support APM. The best fix for this problem is to upgrade the system's BIOS version to one that offers better APM/ACPI support. Otherwise, you can circumvent this problem by disabling APM during the Windows Setup process:

- If you're *not* using Automated Setup, click the Custom button in the Setup Options screen, and then click the Advanced Power Management check box to *clear* it.
- If you *are* using Automated Setup, add the following line to the [System] section of the Msbatch.inf file such as:

```
"Power"="No APM"
```

You *must* include the quotation marks. Remember that this method disables all APM functions in Windows.

As an alternative, Microsoft reports that they have a Windows fix for this problem. Check with Microsoft at **www.microsoft.com** for an appropriate patch file.

SYMPTOM 37-37 Your laptop system continues to drain power even when in the suspend mode under Windows 95/98 This type of problem is known to occur on a number of Gateway 2000 laptop systems (such as the ColorBook 4SX25, 4SX33, 4DX33, Liberty, and Solo), and is always caused by a BIOS problem. You should contact the system manufacturer for a current BIOS upgrade.

SYMPTOM 37-38 You encounter a "Fatal Exception 0E" error when the system is performing a suspend process On an APM-compliant system under Windows 95/OSR1, a "Fatal Exception 0E" error may occur in VPOWERD module if a "critical suspend" event takes place while the computer is already in the process of suspending normally. This problem happens because your Windows 95 power management driver does *not* properly handle the new "critical suspend" request while it is processing a normal suspend request.

For example, this error may crop up if you manually suspend the computer when the computer's battery is critically low. The low-battery condition could cause a "critical suspend" request to be issued by the system BIOS. The "critical suspend" request is issued while Windows 95 is *already* processing the normal suspend request—and then the problem occurs. This trouble (which does not occur under Windows 98) is corrected by the following update for Windows 95:

```
VPOWERD.VXD     4.00.952     11/13/96     19,693 bytes
```

This patch does *not* work properly with Windows 95 OSR 2 or later.

SYMPTOM 37-39 You notice that the Windows 95 clock loses time when APM is enabled When you enable APM on a computer running Windows 95, the clock may slow down or stop when the computer switches to suspend mode. However, the system clock continues to keep the correct time—and you can reset the clock to the correct time by restarting the computer. This problem can occur if you enabled APM in the computer's CMOS settings *after* Windows 95 was installed, or if your computer's BIOS supports an older version of APM. If APM was enabled in CMOS *after* installing Windows 95, it may be that the Windows APM features have not been installed. Reinstall Windows 95 to install APM support. To verify that APM support is enabled:

1. Open the Control Panel and double-click the System icon.
2. Click the Device Manager tab, and then double-click the System Devices branch to expand it.
3. Double-click Advanced Power Management Support.
4. On the Settings tab, verify that the Enable Power Management Support check box is *selected.*

If APM support is installed, you can "suspend" the system by clicking the Start button, and then clicking Suspend before the computer switches into its suspend mode. If the trouble is that your system's BIOS supports older version(s) of APM, you may be able to correct the problem by upgrading the computer's BIOS.

SYMPTOM 37-40 **You see that the Windows 98 shutdown display appears before the system powers off** If your system is configured to automatically power off when you shut down Windows 98, the message: "It's now safe to turn off your computer" may be displayed briefly on your monitor *before* your computer powers off. When you shut down Windows 98 on a computer that supports APM, the Windows 98 shutdown display (LOGO.SYS) is displayed at the same time APM procedures are being processed. This behavior is a normal result of the new "Fast Shutdown" functionality in Windows 98.

SYMPTOM 37-41 **You receive an error indicating that your system cannot enter standby mode** When your attempt to put Windows 98/SE in standby mode, you may see an error message such as:

```
Your computer cannot go on standby because a device driver or program won't
allow it. Close all programs and try again.
```

However, if you close all programs and attempt to put Windows 98 into standby mode again, you'll receive the same error message. This error can occur if a program, driver, or other hardware device is preventing Windows 98 from going into standby mode (this is sometimes referred to as a *veto* of the suspend command). To isolate this problem, use the "Power Management Troubleshooter" (PMTSHOOT.EXE) tool to determine just where the trouble is.

SYMPTOM 37-42 **Your system will not suspend if the Deluxe CD Player utility is running under Windows 98** With Deluxe CD Player running on a laptop, the computer's APM software may not activate the suspend mode. To work around this issue, quit the Deluxe CD Player before trying to suspend the system. This is a known problem with the Windows 98 Plus pack, so check with Microsoft for a patch or update for the CD player utility.

SYMPTOM 37-43 **Your Windows 98 system does not wake to run the task you asked it to** When you use the "Wake the computer to run this task" option for a given task in the Task Scheduler, your computer may *not* resume from its suspend state to run the scheduled task at the required time. This problem can occur if your computer's BIOS does *not* support APM version 1.2 or later. Unfortunately, the "Wake the computer to run this task" check box is available on any computer—even though this feature works only on computers that support APM 1.2 or later. To fix this problem, upgrade your computer's BIOS to a version that supports APM version 1.2 (or later).

SYMPTOM 37-44 **When your display is turned off by APM under Windows 98, you cannot resume the display** This is a known problem with Windows 98, and trouble can crop up if any of the following situations are true:

- The 3D Maze screen saver is currently running. Shut down and restart the system, and then disable the screen saver (or select another one).
- Your display resolution is set to 800x600 or higher. Shut down and restart the system, open the Control Panel, select the Display icon, and choose a lower (or higher) display resolution.
- You're using a Matrox MGA Impression Lite, Plus, Plus 220, or Ultima video adapter and driver. Check with Matrox for an updated driver or firmware, or remove the Matrox card and install another display adapter.

SYMPTOM 37-45 **You find that the APM device in the Windows 98 Device Manager shows a code of 10** When you view the Advanced Power Management Support device in your Device Manager, you see a yellow exclamation point displayed on the device, along with the following status message:

```
This device is not present, not working properly, or does not have all the
drivers installed (Code 10).
```

This problem can occur if APM support is disabled in the computer's BIOS (or if your computer does not support Microsoft's implementation of APM). Enable APM support in the computer's CMOS Setup. If APM is enabled but the status remains unchanged, it may be necessary to upgrade the system's BIOS to a later version that offers better APM support. In extreme cases, you may need to upgrade the system's motherboard.

SYMPTOM 37-46 **The computer cannot enter its suspend mode in Windows 98** When your computer has been inactive long enough for it to go to standby mode, it may not enter the standby mode properly. You may also receive a message saying that your computer will stand by in 15 seconds, but the standby mode is not invoked. This problem is known to occur if a Windows 98 screen saver is currently active, such as *3D Flower Box*, *3D Flying Objects*, *3D Maze*, *3D Text*, or *Channel Screen Saver*. This problem applies only to computers that support APM or the ACPI specification, and it is a known problem in Microsoft Windows 98, There are several ways to work around the problem:

- Use a different screen saver.
- Disable the screen saver outright.
- Reduce the screen saver's complexity.

SYMPTOM 37-47 **You find that the Windows 95/98/SE taskbar clock seems to be losing time** There are several ways that this problem may manifest itself. First, when you use the Date/Time tool to select a different year, the clock may stop until you click Apply or OK, and the clock does *not* compensate for the length of time it was stopped. When you use the Date/Time tool to select a different month or date, the time may be decreased by 5 to10 seconds. Finally, when you leave your computer on for an extended amount of time, the time may lose from two minutes up to an hour per day.

- Check your APM settings. Disable APM in the CMOS Setup and configure Windows to manage APM.
- Disable third-party programs and utilities such as antivirus, screen saver, and system utilities.
- Use a clean boot to isolate possible driver or software issues.
- Check for a weak CMOS backup battery. Open a DOS window and use the TIME function to check time under DOS. Compare the DOS and Windows time entries. If the times are the same, try a new battery. If the times are *not* the same, there may be a hardware or configuration problem under Windows that is unsetting the time under Windows.

> The CMOS *does* keep the correct time, and if you restart the computer, the Windows clock is updated. Also, if you start your computer in Safe Mode, Windows *does not* lose time.

SYMPTOM 37-48 **The hard drive appears to remain active even after Windows 98 shuts down** You may notice that the system's hard drive appears to be active even after you see the message: "It's now safe to turn off your computer." On newer computers that use ACPI features, APM makes it possible for you to put your computer in standby or hibernate mode to save power resources. The OnNow feature allows only the devices that need to be active to "wake up." In certain situations, the OnNow feature may continue to activate the hard disk even though the computer has shut down. This problem may be caused by the APM features in Windows 98, and does *not* cause any problem or loss of features.

SYMPTOM 37-49 When Windows 95/98 resumes from suspend mode, one or more hard drives seem to be missing This is a known issue with some Toshiba laptops. After you resume your laptop computer from suspend mode, hard drives attached to the AMD SCSI controller may be missing in My Computer and Windows Explorer. This problem occurs when you suspend and resume your computer while it's in its docking station, though the APM BIOS used by Toshiba laptop computers *does* support suspending and resuming while the computer is docked. To prevent this problem from occurring, you'll need a patch for the laptop. For the Toshiba systems, obtain the TAP utility from Toshiba's Web site (the TAP utility prevents the computer from going into suspend mode while it is docked).

SYMPTOM 37-50 You encounter a write data error when using a CD-RW under Windows 98 When you try to format a blank disc with a CD-RW drive, you may receive the following error message:

```
Error: Write Data
Illegal Start Block Address (0x4000004b)
```

You will *not* be able to read or write to the disc. In virtually all cases, this problem can occur if APM is enabled on your computer. You can try disabling the APM permanently:

1. Click Start, highlight Settings, click Control Panel, and then double-click the Power Management icon.
2. In the System Standby box, click Never, click Never in the Turn Off Monitor box, and then click Never in the Turn Off Hard Drive box.
3. Click Apply, click OK, and then restart your computer.

If you don't want to permanently disable APM, you can temporarily disable it, use your CD-RW drive, and then re-enable APM:

1. Click Start, highlight Settings, click Control Panel, and then double-click the Power Management icon.
2. In the System Standby box, click Never, click Never in the Turn Off Monitor box, and then click Never in the Turn Off Hard Drive box.
3. Click Apply, click OK, and then restart your computer.
4. Use your CD-RW drive, and then restart your computer normally.
5. Click Start, highlight Settings, click Control Panel, and then double-click the Power Management icon.
6. In the System Standby, Turn Off Monitor, and Turn Off Hard Drive boxes, click the appropriate time settings that you want to use.
7. Click Apply, click OK, and then restart your computer.

SYMPTOM 37-51 **The computer halts when you try to shut down Windows 98 (not SE)** This problem can occur if your computer uses ACPI and the Fast Shutdown feature is *disabled*. This issue is a problem with Windows 98 that is known to affect the following computers:

- Compaq Deskpro EN Series 6350
- Compaq Presario 7234 5680, 5670, 5690, 5686, 5695, 5680
- Toshiba Tecra 750
- Generic computer with AMD P233 K6 CPU and Award BIOS version 4.51PG (1995)
- IBM Aptiva 2137

You can install a patch from Microsoft that should address this problem. The English version of this fix should have the following file attributes (or later):

```
ACPI.SYS 4.10.2000 11/23/98 7:51pm 80,256 bytes
```

To work around this problem temporarily, enable the Fast Shutdown feature:

1. Click Start, highlight Programs, point to Accessories, select System Tools, and then click System Information.
2. On the Tools menu, click the System Configuration Utility.
3. On the General tab, click Advanced.
4. Click the Disable Fast Shutdown check box to clear it, click OK, and then click OK again.
5. Click Yes when you're prompted to restart your computer.

SYMPTOM 37-52 **The monitor turns off while your DVD movie is playing under Windows 98/SE** This problem can crop up if you're using APM, and the DVD player program you're using is not designed to work with APM. To resolve this problem, contact the manufacturer to see if there's an APM-aware version of your DVD player program. If there is no player update, you should try disabling APM:

1. Click Start, point to Settings, click Control Panel, and then double-click the Power Management icon.
2. On the Power Schemes tab, click Never in the "Turn off monitor" box.
3. Click OK and reboot the PC if necessary.

SYMPTOM 37-53 **Windows 98/SE doesn't shut down or restart properly in the DOS mode** After you install Windows 98/SE, you may not be able to use the "Shut down" or "Restart in MS-DOS mode" options successfully. This problem can occur if your video adapter requires an IRQ in the DOS mode, but your computer's BIOS doesn't assign one to it. Windows 98/SE includes updates for ACPI, OnNow, and APM and may require the latest BIOS upgrade. To resolve this problem:

- Check your computer's BIOS for a setting to assign an IRQ to the video adapter.
- Check for an updated video adapter BIOS (firmware).
- Check for an updated system BIOS.

SYMPTOM 37-54 **Your Windows 98/SE system reports low drive space after the system exits its standby mode** This issue can occur if CyberWarner software is running when the computer enters its standby or suspend modes. CyberWarner is a program designed to protect system files from replacement or damage by backing up the files. On computers that support APM, CyberWarner may make multiple backups of the same files when the computer is in standby or suspend mode. To work around this problem, quit the CyberWarner software before the computer enters standby or suspend mode.

SYMPTOM 37-55 **You notice that the laptop's battery may drain faster when a USB device is attached** This may happen under both Windows 95/98/SE. Battery-powered computers that use APM or ACPI may experience increased power consumption leading to an increased drain of battery power when a USB device is attached. This condition happens because the bus activity required to maintain communications with the USB device prevents the CPU from switching to a "C3" (Clock-Stopped) power state. When a USB device is not connected, the CPU can spend a significant amount of time in the "C3" state—which reduces power consumption and extends battery life significantly. Try to conserve battery power—disconnect all USB devices if you're not using them. As an alternative, use the Power Management tool in the Control Panel to adjust the power scheme settings. Doing this allows you to use shorter time-out values for turning off the monitor and hard drives and placing the computer in a system standby state.

Further Study

ACPI Specification: **http://www.teleport.com/~acpi/spec.htm**

ACPI web site: **http://www.teleport.com/%7Eacpi/**

Amtrade: **http://www.amtrade.com**

Astec: **http://www.astec.com/**

ATX: **http://www.teleport.com/~atx/**

Data Depot: **http://www.datadepo.com**

Intel's Instantly Available PC site: **http://developer.intel.com/technology/iapc/**

Microsoft's ACPI and OnNow site: **http://www.microsoft.com/hwdev/onnow.htm**

NLX: **http://www.teleport.com/~nlx/**

PC Power and Cooling: **http://www.pcpowercooling.com**

TUV (German Standards): **http://www.tuv.com/**

UL (Underwriter's Laboratories): **http://www.ul.com/**

38

PREVENTIVE MAINTENANCE

CHAPTER AT A GLANCE

For most end-users, the purchase of a PC is a substantial investment of both time and money. For corporations and organizations with hundreds (even thousands) of PCs, this investment is that much higher. But after the money is spent and the PC is in our home or office, few PC users ever take the time to *maintain* their PC. Routine maintenance is an *important* part of PC ownership and can go a long way toward keeping your computer's hardware *and* software error-free. Proper routine maintenance can also help to avoid costly visits to the repair shop (U.S. rates are $50 to $70 per hour). Businesses can save a substantial amount of money by assigning technicians to perform regular maintenance. If you're in business for yourself, offering "preventive maintenance" services as part of a normal repair, or as seasonal "specials," can provide you with an added income stream. This chapter provides you with a comprehensive, step-by-step procedure for protecting and maintaining a personal computer investment.

This chapter is geared primarily for novices, though experienced technicians may also get some helpful tips and pointers. If you're comfortable with practical routine maintenance procedures, feel free to skip this chapter.

Protecting Your Data

It's interesting to note that the data recorded on our computer is often far more valuable than the actual cost of a new drive. But if the drive fails, that precious data is usually lost along with the hardware. Months (perhaps years) of records and data could be irretrievably lost. One of the first steps in any routine maintenance plan is to make regular *backups* of the system's contents—as well as the system's configuration. Backups ensure that you can recover from any hardware glitch, accidental file erasure, or virus attack.

STEP 1: FILE BACKUPS

File backups are important for all types of PC users, from major corporations to occasional home users. By creating a copy of your system files (or even just a portion of them), you can restore the copy and continue working in the event of a disaster. Before you proceed with any type of system checks, consider performing a file backup.

What you need You're going to need two items in order to back up your files; a backup drive and backup software. The actual choice of backup drive is really quite open. Tape drives, such as the Iomega Ditto drive (**www.iomega.com**) or the MicroSolutions 8000t 8GB Backpack drive (**www.micro-solutions.com**), are the traditional choice, but other high-volume removable media drives like Iomega's 100MB Zip drive, its 1GB Jaz drive, or the SyQuest 1.5GB SyJet drive (**www.syquest.com**) are very popular. You may choose an internal or external version of a drive, but you might consider an *external* parallel port drive because it is portable—it can be shared among any PCs.

You'll also need some backup software to format the media and handle your backup and restore operations. If you're using Windows 95/98, try the native Backup applet (click on Start, Programs, Accessories, System Tools, and Backup). If Backup doesn't suit your needs (or doesn't support your choice for a backup drive), many drives ship with a backup utility on disk. Just make sure that the backup drive and backup software are compatible with one another.

Types of backups Backups generally fall into two categories: incremental and complete. Both types of backups offer unique advantages and disadvantages. An *incremental* backup records only the differences from the last backup. This process usually results in a faster backup and uses less tape (or other media), but restores take longer because you need to walk through each "increment" in order. A *complete* backup records the drive's full contents. This process takes much longer and uses a lot more media, but restores are easier. Many PC users employ a combination of complete and incremental backups. For example, you might start with a complete backup on January 1, then make incremental backups each week until the end of February. By March 1, you'd make another complete backup, and start the incremental backup process again.

Backup frequency Perhaps the most overlooked issue with backups is the "frequency"—how often should backups be performed? The answer to that question is not always a simple one because everyone's needs are different. Major corporations with busy order entry systems may back up several times each day, while individual home users may not even consider backups to be necessary. The standard that I use is this: "can you afford to lose the data on this drive?" If the answer is "no," it's time to back up. Table 38-1 summarizes the recommended periods for preventive maintenance procedures.

TABLE 38-1 SUMMARY OF PC PREVENTIVE MAINTENANCE PERIODS

PROCEDURE	FREQUENCY
File Backup	Whenever important data cannot be recreated: Order Entry—daily Business/Art/Multimedia—weekly SOHO/Accounting—biweekly or monthly Home Use—every several months
CMOS Backup	As required, whenever changes are made to the system's configuration
Cleaning	Every four months, or as required Vacuum—clear accumulations of dust and debris as required
External Check	Every four months CRT Degauss—only if necessary
Internal Check	Every six months
Drive Check	Monthly, or when major files are added/deleted from the system Boot Disk—update disk whenever hardware changes are made to the system

File backup tips Regardless of how you choose to handle file backups, there are some tips that will help you get the most from your backup efforts:

- Keep the backup(s) in a secure location (such as a fire-proof safe or cabinet).
- Keep the backup(s) in a different physical location away from the original PC.
- Back up consistently—backups are useless if they are out of date.
- If time is a factor, start with a complete backup, then use incremental backups.
- Use a parallel port tape drive (or other "backup" drive) for maximum portability between PCs.

STEP 2: CMOS BACKUPS

All PCs use a sophisticated set of configuration settings (everything from "Date" and "Time" to "Video Palette Snoop" and "Memory Hole") that define how the system should be operated. These settings are stored in a small amount of very low power memory called CMOS RAM. Each time the PC starts, motherboard BIOS reads the CMOS RAM and copies the contents into low system memory (the BIOS Data Area or BDA). While system power is off, CMOS RAM contents are maintained with a small battery. If this battery goes dead, CMOS contents can be lost. In most cases, this will prevent the system from even starting until you reconfigure the CMOS setup from scratch. By making a backup of the CMOS setup, you can restore lost settings in a matter of minutes. CMOS backups are simply printed screens of your CMOS setup pages.

What you need The one item that you'll need to perform a CMOS backup is a *printer*—it really doesn't matter what kind of printer (that is, dot-matrix, ink jet, or laser). The printer should be attached to the PC's parallel port. After starting the CMOS setup routine, visit each page of the setup and use the PRINT SCREEN key to "capture" each page to the printer. Since every BIOS is written differently, be sure to check for sub-menus that might be buried under each main menu option.

CMOS backup tips CMOS backups are quick and simple, but you'll get the most benefit from a CMOS backup by following the pointers below:

- Make it a point to print out *every* CMOS setup page.
- Keep the printed pages taped to the PC's housing, or with the system's original documentation.
- You should back up the CMOS setup whenever you make a change to the system's configuration.

Cleaning

Now that you've backed up the system's vital information, you can proceed with the actual maintenance procedures. The first set of procedures involve exterior cleaning. This may hardly sound like a glamorous process, but you'd be surprised how quickly dust, pet hair, and other debris can accumulate around a computer. You'll need four items for cleaning: a supply of Windex or other mild ammonia-based cleaner (a little ordinary ammonia in demineralized water will work just as well), a supply of paper towels or clean lint-free cloths, a canister of electronics-grade compressed air (which can be obtained from any electronics store), and a small static-safe vacuum cleaner.

Avoid the use of ordinary household vacuum cleaners. The rush of air tends to generate significant amounts of static electricity along plastic hoses and tubes that can accidentally damage the sensitive electronics in a PC.

Never use harsh or industrial-grade cleaners around a PC. Harsh cleaners often contain chemicals that can damage the finish of (or even melt) the plastics used in PC housings. Use a highly diluted ammonia solution only.

As a rule, exterior cleaning can be performed every four months (three times per year) or as required. If the PC is operating in dusty, industrial, or other adverse environments, you many need to clean the system more frequently. Systems operating in clean office environments may need to be cleaned only once or twice each year. Always remember to turn off the computer and unplug the AC cord from the wall outlet before cleaning.

STEP 3: CLEAN THE CASE

Use a clean cloth lightly dampened with ammonia cleaner to remove dust, dirt, or stains from the exterior of the PC. Start at the top and work down. Add a little bit of extra cleaner to remove stubborn stains. You'll find that the housing base is typically the dirtiest (especially for tower systems). When cleaning, be careful not to accidentally alter the CD-ROM volume or sound card master volume controls. Also do not dislodge any cables or connectors behind the PC.

Always dampen a clean towel with cleaner—*never* spray cleaner directly onto any part of the computer.

STEP 4: CLEAN THE AIR INTAKE

While cleaning the case, pay particular attention to the air intakes which are usually located in the front (or front sides) of the housing. Check for accumulations of dust or debris around the intakes, or caught in an intake filter. Clean away any accumulations from the intake area, then use your static-safe vacuum to clean the intake filter, if possible—you may need to remove the intake filter for better access. If the intake filter is washable, you may choose to rinse the filter in simple soap and water for best cleaning (remember to dry the filter *thoroughly* before putting it back). Of course, if there is no intake filter, simply clean around the intake area.

STEP 5: CLEAN THE SPEAKERS

Multimedia speakers offer a countless number of ridges and openings that are just perfect for accumulating dust and debris. Use your can of compressed air to gently dust-out the speaker's openings. Do not insert the long, thin air nozzle into the speaker—you can easily puncture the speaker cone and ruin it. Instead, remove the long nozzle and spray air directly from the can. Afterward, use a clean cloth lightly dampened with ammonia solution to remove any dirt or stains from the speaker housings.

STEP 6: CLEAN THE KEYBOARD

Keyboards are open to the environment, so dust and debris readily settle between the keys. Over time, these accumulations can jam keys or cause repeated keystrokes. Attach the long thin nozzle to your can of compressed air and use the air to blow through the horizontal gaps between key rows. *Careful!* Doing this will kick up a lot of dust—so keep the keyboard away from your face. Afterward, use a clean cloth lightly dampened with ammonia solution to remove dirt or stains from the keys and keyboard housing. If any keys seem unresponsive or "sticky," you can remove the corresponding keycap and spray a bit of good-quality electronic contact cleaner into the key assembly, then gently replace the keycap.

> Do not remove the ENTER key or SPACEBAR. These keys are held in place by metal brackets that are *extremely* difficult to reattach once the key is removed. Only the most experienced technicians should work with these keys.

STEP 7: CLEAN THE MONITOR

There are several important issues when cleaning a monitor: ventilation, case, and CRT. Monitors rely on vent openings for proper cooling. Use your vacuum cleaner and carefully remove any accumulations of dust and debris from the vents underneath the case, as well as those on top of the case. Make sure that none of the vent openings are blocked by paper or other objects (this can restrict ventilation and force the monitor to run hot).

Next, use a clean cloth lightly dampened with ammonia solution to clean the monitor's plastic case. There is active circuitry directly under the top vents, so under no circumstances should you spray cleaner directly onto the monitor housings. Do *not* use ammonia or *any* chemicals to clean the CRT face. The CRT is often treated with anti-glare and other coatings, and even mild chemicals can react with some coatings. Instead, use clean tap water *only* to clean the CRT face. Be sure to dry the CRT face completely.

STEP 8: CLEAN THE MOUSE

Like the keyboard, a mouse is particularly susceptible to dust and debris, which are carried from the mouse pad up into the mouse ball and rollers. When enough foreign matter has accumulated, you'll find that the mouse cursor hesitates or refuses to move completely. Loosen the retaining ring and remove the mouse ball. Clean the mouse ball using a clean cloth and an ammonia solution. Dry the mouse ball thoroughly and set it aside with the retaining ring. Next, locate three rollers inside the mouse (an "X" roller, a "Y" roller, and a small "pressure" roller). Use a clean cloth dampened with ammonia solution to clean all of the rollers completely. Use your can of compressed air to blow out any remaining dust or debris that may still be inside the mouse. Finally, replace the mouse ball and secure it in place with its retaining ring.

External Check

Now that the system is clean, it's time to perform a few practical checks of the system interconnections and take care of some basic drive maintenance. Gather a small regular screwdriver (a "jeweler's" screwdriver), along with a commercial floppy drive cleaning kit. If your system uses a tape drive, arrange to have a tape drive cleaning kit on-hand also. If you cannot locate the appropriate cleaning kits, you can use isopropyl alcohol and long electronics-grade swabs. A hand-held degaussing coil is recommended, but may not be necessary. For this part of the chapter, you'll need to power up the PC.

These checks should be performed every four months (three times per year) or as required. If the PC is operating in dusty, industrial, or other adverse environments, you many need to check the system more frequently. Systems operating in clean office environments may need to be checked only once or twice each year.

STEP 9: CHECK EXTERNAL CABLES

There are myriad external cables interconnecting the computer to its peripheral devices. You should examine each cable and verify that it is securely connected. If the cable can be secured to its connector with screws, make sure that the cable is secured properly. As a minimum, check the following cables:

- AC power cable for the PC
- AC power cable for the monitor
- AC power cable for the printer
- AC/DC power pack for an external modem (if used)
- Keyboard cable
- Mouse cable
- Joystick cable (if used)
- Video cable to the monitor
- Speaker cable(s) from the sound board
- Microphone cable to the sound board (if used)
- Serial port cable to external modem (if used)
- Parallel port cable to printer
- RJ11 telephone line cable to internal or external modem (if used)

38

STEP 10: CLEAN THE FLOPPY DRIVE

Although they've been around for many generations of PCs, floppy disks remain a reliable and highly standardized media, and every new PC sold today still carries a 3.5" 1.44MB floppy drive. However, floppy disks are a "contact" media—the read/write heads of the floppy drive actually come into contact with the floppy disk. This contact transfers some of the magnetic oxides from the floppy disk to the drive's read write heads. Eventually, enough oxides can accumulate on the read/write heads to cause reading or writing problems with the floppy drive. You should periodically clean the floppy drive to remove any excess oxides.

Cleaning can be accomplished in several ways—you can use a pre-packaged "cleaning kit," or you can swab the read/write heads with fresh isopropyl alcohol. You can obtain cleaning kits from almost any store with a computer or consumer electronics department. With a cleaning kit, you simply dampen a mildly abrasive "cleaning disk" with cleaning solution (typically alcohol-based), then run the cleaning disk in the drive for 15 to 30 seconds. You can often get 10 to 20 cleanings from a cleaning disk before discarding it.

If you don't have a cleaning kit handy, you can use a thin fabric swab dampened in fresh isopropyl alcohol to gently scrub between the read/write heads (Figure 38-1). Remember to turn off and unplug the PC before attempting a manual cleaning. Repeat the scrubbing with several fresh swabs, then use a dry swab to gently dry the heads. Allow several minutes for any residual alcohol to dry before turning the PC back on.

STEP 11: CLEAN THE TAPE DRIVE

As with floppy drives, tape drives are also a "contact" media, and the tape head is in constant contact with the moving tape. This contact causes oxides from the tape to transfer to the tape head and capstans and can ultimately result in reading or writing errors from the tape drive. If a tape drive is present with your system, you should periodically clean the tape head(s) and capstans to remove any dust and excess oxides. You may be able to find a pre-packaged drive cleaning kit for your particular tape drive. Otherwise, you'll need to clean the tape drive manually.

Turn off and unplug the PC. Use a thin fabric swab dampened in fresh isopropyl alcohol to gently scrub the tape head(s) and capstan. Repeat the scrubbing with several fresh swabs, then use a dry swab to gently dry the tape head(s). Allow several minutes for any residual alcohol to dry before turning the computer back on.

This step is *only* needed if you have an internal or external tape drive with your system. If not, you can omit this step.

STEP 12: CHECK THE CD TRAY

Most CD-ROM drives operate using a tray to hold the CD. Try ejecting and closing the tray several times—make sure that the motion is smooth and that there is no hesitation or grinding that might suggest a problem with the drive mechanism (you do *not* need a CD in the drive for this). While the tray is open, check for any accumulations of dust, pet hair, or other debris in the tray that might interfere with a CD. Clean the tray with a cloth lightly dampened in water *only*. Be sure the tray is completely dry before closing it again. Do not use ammonia or ammonia-based cleaners around the CD-ROM—prolonged exposure to ammonia vapors can damage a CD.

STEP 13: CHECK THE SOUND SYSTEM

Next, you should make sure that your sound system is set properly. Begin playing an ordinary audio CD in the CD-ROM drive. Check the sound board itself and locate the master volume control (not all sound

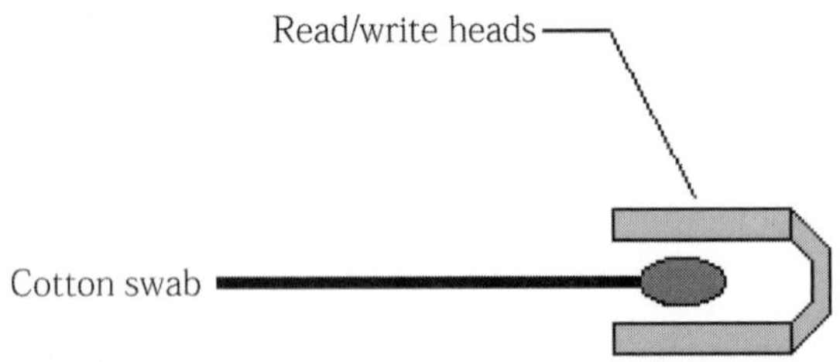

FIGURE 38-1 Manually cleaning a floppy drive.

boards have a physical volume knob). Make sure that the master volume is set at 75 percent or higher. If it is not, you may need to keep the speaker volume abnormally high, and this can result in a hum or other noise in the speakers. If the sound board does not have a master volume control, check the board's "mixer" applet and see that the master volume is set properly. Once the sound board is set, you can adjust the speaker volume to achieve the best sound quality.

> Speakers are magnetic devices that can interfere with the color purity of a monitor. Keep unshielded speakers at least six inches away from your monitor.

STEP 14: CHECK COLOR PURITY

Color monitors use a fine metal screen located just behind the CRT face in order to isolate the individual color pixels in the display. This screen ensures that stray electrons don't strike adjacent phosphors and cause incorrect colors. If part (or all) of this metal screen becomes magnetized, it will deflect the electron beams and cause color distortion. Normally, a color CRT is demagnetized (or "degaussed") each time the monitor is turned on. This is accomplished through a "degaussing coil" located around the perimeter of the CRT face. However, if the CRT is subjected to external magnetic fields (such as unshielded speakers, motors, or other strong magnets), color problems may occur across the entire CRT or in small localized areas.

Check the CRT for color purity by displaying an image of a known color (preferably white). Examine the image for discoloration or discolored areas. For example, if you display an image that you know is white and it appears bluish (or there are bluish patches), chances are that you've got color purity problems.

There are three means of correcting color purity problems. First, try moving anything that might be magnetic (such as speakers) *away* from the monitor. Second, try degaussing the monitor by turning it off, waiting 30 seconds, then turning it on again. This process allows the monitor's built-in degaussing coil to cycle. If the problem persists, wait 20 to 30 minutes and try cycling the monitor again. Finally, if the image is still discolored, you should use a hand-held degaussing coil to demagnetize the CRT.

> When degaussing "by hand," remember to wait 20 to 30 minutes before repeating the degaussing procedure. Excessive degaussing can damage the CRT.

Internal Check

At this point, we can move into the PC and perform some internal checks to verify that critical parts and cables are secure and that all cooling systems are working. Internal checks can usually be performed every six months (twice per year). Gather a small Phillips screwdriver and an antistatic wrist strap. Use your screwdriver to unbolt the outer cover. Remove the outer cover and set it aside (be careful of sharp edges on the cover and in the case). Attach the wrist strap from your wrist to a good earth ground—doing this allows you to work safely inside the PC without the risk of accidental damage from electrostatic discharge (or ESD).

STEP 15: CHECK THE FANS

PCs tend to generate a substantial amount of heat during normal operation, and this heat must be ventilated with fans. If one or more fans fail, excess heat can build up in the PC enclosure and result in system crashes or premature system failures. Now that the cover is off, your first check should be to see that *all* the fans are running. As a minimum, check the power supply fan, the case exhaust fan (both usually located at the rear of the enclosure), and the CPU heat sink/fan. Other PCs such as tower systems may sport even more fans. If any fans are not running, they should be replaced—or the power supply driving the fans should be checked.

Pay particular attention to the CPU heat sink/fan. Virtually all Intel Pentium/Pentium MMX, AMD K5/K6, and Cyrix 6x86/M2 CPUs are fitted with a heat sink/fan (Pentium II CPU assemblies use their own internal fan). This fan *must* be running, or the CPU runs a very real risk of overheating and failing. If you notice that the fan has stopped, you should replace the heat sink/fan assembly *as soon as possible*.

STEP 16: CLEAN FANS AND FILTERS

Turn off and unplug the PC, then examine the fans and exhaust filters for accumulations of dust or other debris. Use your static-safe vacuum to clean the fan blades. Clean away any accumulations from the exhaust area, then clean the exhaust filter if possible—you may need to remove the exhaust filter for better access. If the exhaust filter is washable, you may choose to rinse the filter in simple soap and water for best cleaning (remember to dry the filter *thoroughly* before putting it back). Of course, if there is no exhaust filter, simply clean around the exhaust area. Also vacuum away any other accumulations of dust that you may find on the motherboard or around the drives, but *be very careful to avoid vacuuming up the little jumpers on the motherboard.*

> Remember that PC electronics are *extremely* sensitive to ESD, so make sure to use a static-safe vacuum inside the PC.

STEP 17: CHECK EXPANSION BOARDS

Most PCs use several expansion boards that are plugged into expansion slots on the motherboard. Internal modems, video boards, SCSI adapters, and network cards are just a few types of expansion boards that you may encounter. Each expansion board must be inserted completely into its corresponding slot, and the metal mounting bracket on the board should be secured to the chassis with a single screw. Make sure that every board is installed evenly and completely and see that the mounting bolts are snugged down. Pay particular attention to any expansion board that may be inserted unevenly or incompletely.

STEP 18: CHECK INTERNAL CABLES

You'll notice that there are a large number of cables inside the PC. Each cable must be installed securely—especially the wide ribbon cable connectors that can easily be tugged off. Take a moment to check any wiring between the case and the motherboard, such as the keyboard connector, power LED, on/off switch, drive activity LED, turbo switch, turbo LED, and so on. Next, check the following cables:

- Motherboard power connector(s)
- All 4-pin drive power cables
- Floppy drive ribbon cable
- Hard drive ribbon cable
- CD-ROM ribbon cable (usually separate from the hard drive cable)
- CD 4 wire audio cable (between the CD-ROM and sound board)
- SCSI ribbon cable (if used)
- SCSI terminating resistors (if used)

STEP 19: CHECK MEMORY

Most modern PC memory is provided in the form of SIMMs (single in-line memory modules) or DIMMs (dual in-line memory modules), which simply clip into sockets on the motherboard. Loose SIMMs or DIMMs can cause serious startup problems for the PC. Examine each SIMM/DIMM—verify that they are inserted properly into each socket and that both ends of each SIMM/DIMM are clipped into place.

STEP 20: CHECK THE CPU

The CPU is the single largest IC on the motherboard and is installed into a ZIF (zero insertion force) socket for easy replacement or upgrade. Examine the CPU and see that it is inserted evenly into its socket. The ZIF socket lever should be in the closed position and locked down at the socket itself. Check the CPU's heat sink/fan next—it should sit flush against the top of the CPU. It should not slide around or be loose. If it is, the heat sink/fan should be secured or replaced.

> Slot 1 CPUs, such as the Pentium II/III, or Slot A CPUs, such as the AMD Athlon, are installed into a slot on the motherboard and are held in place by a retaining clip. When working with a Pentium II/III system, see that the CPU is installed evenly and completely and that the retaining clip is secure.

STEP 21: CHECK DRIVE MOUNTING

The final step in your internal check should be to inspect the drive mountings. Each drive should be mounted in place with four screws—fewer screws may allow excessive vibration in the drive, which can lead to vibration noise from the chassis or premature failure of the drive itself. Make sure that each drive has four mounting bolts and use your Phillips screwdriver to snug down each bolt.

> Do not overtighten the bolts. Doing so can actually warp the drive frame and cause errors or drive failure.

Drive Check

After the PC has been cleaned and checked inside and out, it's time to check the hard drive for potential problems. This step involves checking the drive's file system, reorganizing files, and creating an updated boot disk. To perform a drive check, you'll need a copy of ScanDisk and Defrag. Since these utilities are already built into Windows 95/98, you can reboot the system and use those utilities directly. If you're more comfortable with running these utilities from DOS, create a startup disk from within Windows 95/98 and boot from that disk—then run ScanDisk and Defrag right from the startup disk. As a rule, you should perform the drive check regularly—once a month is usually recommended, or whenever you make major additions or deletions of files from your system.

STEP 22: UPDATE THE BOOT DISK

Your PC should always have a boot disk that can start the system from a floppy drive in the event of an emergency. Windows 95/98 has the ability to create a startup disk automatically. If you have access to a Windows 95/98 system, use the following procedure to create a DOS 7.x startup disk:

1. Label a blank preformatted disk and insert it into your floppy drive.
2. Click on Start, Settings, and Control Panel.

3. Double-click on the Add/Remove Programs icon.
4. Select the Startup Disk tab.
5. Click on Create Disk (Figure 38-2)
6. The utility will remind you to insert a disk, then prepare the disk automatically. When the preparation is complete, test the disk.

The preparation process takes several minutes and will copy the following files to your disk: ATTRIB, CHKDSK, COMMAND, DEBUG, DRVSPACE.BIN, EDIT, FDISK, FORMAT, REGEDIT, SCANDISK, SYS, and UNINSTAL. All of these files are DOS 7.x-based files, so you can run them from the A: prompt. If these files are not copied automatically, you can copy many of them manually.

STEP 23: RUN SCANDISK

The ScanDisk utility is designed to check your drive for file problems (such as lost or cross-linked clusters) and then correct those problems. ScanDisk is also particularly useful in testing for potential media (surface) errors on a disk. If you're running from the startup disk, start ScanDisk by typing:

```
A:\> scandisk     <Enter>
```

If you're running from Windows 95/98, click Start, Programs, Accessories, System Tools, and ScanDisk. Select the drive to be tested and start the test cycle. ScanDisk will report any problems and give you the option of repairing the problems.

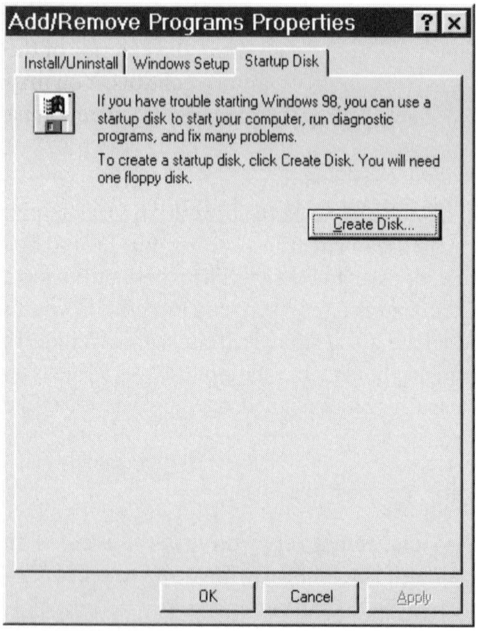

FIGURE 38-2 Making a startup disk

STEP 24: RUN DEFRAG

Operating systems like DOS and Windows 95/98 segregate drive space into groups of sectors called *clusters*. Clusters are used on an "as found" basis, so it is possible for the clusters that compose a file to be scattered across a drive. This forces the drive to work harder (and take longer) to read or write the complete file because a lot of time is wasted moving around the drive. The Defrag utility allows related file clusters to be relocated together. If you're running from the startup disk, start Defrag by typing:

```
A:\> defrag     <Enter>
```

If you're running from Windows 95/98, click Start, Programs, Accessories, System Tools, and Disk Defragmenter. Select the drive to be tested and start the cycle. Defrag will relocate every file on the disk so that all their clusters are positioned together (contiguous).

> You can run Defrag any time, but you do not *need* to run Defrag until your disk is more than 10 percent fragmented.

Preventive Maintenance Problems

Ideally, the preventive maintenance process is designed to *prevent* problems—not cause them. However, there are times that an accidental oversight or careless effort can result in problems. Fortunately, most maintenance-related issues are easy to spot and resolve.

SYMPTOM 38-1 You can no longer hear CD audio through the CD-ROM headphone jack, or there is no sound from the system speakers The sound may also be too high now. In virtually all cases, you accidentally changed a volume control when wiping-down the exterior of the PC. Your cloth may have rubbed across the CD-ROM or sound board master volume controls. You may also have changed the speaker volume control. Recheck all of your system volume controls and re-adjust the sound volume.

SYMPTOM 38-2 The system no longer boots correctly, or key feature(s) no longer work correctly This is typical after an internal check, and is almost always because of an oversight in checking or seating a cable or expansion board inside the PC. Recheck the seating of all power and signal cables, recheck the seating of all expansion devices, and recheck the CPU and SIMM/DIMM seating on the motherboard.

SYMPTOM 38-3 The system seems to boot, but there is no display on the monitor Chances are that you dislodged or loosened the monitor cable during your inspection. Power down the PC. Check to see that the video card is seated properly and verify that the monitor cable is attached securely.

SYMPTOM 38-4 The keyboard/mouse isn't responding when you test the system In most cases, the keyboard and/or mouse cable were probably dislodged during your cleaning process, or you did not reattach them correctly. Double-check each of those cables, and see that they're secure.

Further Study

CompUSA: **http://www.compusa.com** (cleaning kits and supplies)

Iomega: **http://www.iomega.com**

MicroSolutions: **http://www.micro-solutions.com**

SyQuest: **http://www.syquest.com**

39

SCSI SYSTEMS AND TROUBLESHOOTING

CHAPTER AT A GLANCE

PC designers have always sought ways to connect more devices to fewer cables. Doing this reduces the amount of adapter card hardware in the system, so that lower costs as well as lower demands on power, space, cost, and maintenance are achieved. In the early 1980s, it became clear that a more versatile and intelligent interface would be needed to overcome the myriad proprietary interfaces appearing at the time. By 1986, PC designers responded with the introduction of the *Small Computer System Interface* (*SCSI*, pronounced *"scuzzy"*). SCSI proved to be a revolution for PC "power-users"—a single adapter could operate a number of unique devices simultaneously—all "daisy-chained" to the same cable. Where other "low-end" PCs needed one adapter for hard drives, one adapter for the CD-ROM, another adapter for a tape drive, and so on, a system fitted with a SCSI adapter could handle all of these devices (and more) and achieve data throughputs that other interfaces of the day couldn't begin to approach.

Today's PC industry has changed. Proprietary interfaces have largely been abandoned in favor of the "standardized" interfaces (such as UDMA/33 and UDMA/66), and these standard interface schemes now support a variety of devices while offering low cost and performance levels rivaling SCSI. Yet, SCSI has endured and evolved, and it remains the interface of choice for multitasking, servers, and other high-end systems. This chapter will provide an overview of the SCSI interface, cover the essential installation and setup of a SCSI host adapter, and show you how to deal with the most important troubleshooting problems.

Understanding SCSI Concepts

Ideally, peripheral devices should be *independent* of the microprocessor's operation. The computer should only have to send commands and data to the peripheral and then wait for the peripheral to respond. Printers work this way. The parallel and serial ports are actually *device-level* interfaces. The computer is unconcerned with "what" device is attached to the port. In other words, you can take a printer built twelve years ago and connect it to a new Pentium-based system—and the printer will work just fine because only data and commands are being sent across the interface. This is a simple example of the concept behind SCSI. Computers and peripherals can be designed, developed, and integrated without worrying about hardware compatibility—such compatibility is established entirely by the SCSI interface.

DEVICE INDEPENDENCE

From a practical standpoint, SCSI is a *bus*—an organization of physical wires and terminations where each wire has its own name and purpose. SCSI also consists of a *command set*—a limited set of instructions that allows the computer and peripherals to communicate over that physical bus. The SCSI bus is used in systems that want to achieve device independence. For example, all hard disk drives look alike to the SCSI interface (except for their total capacity), all optical drives look alike, all printers look alike, and so on. For any particular type of SCSI device, you should be able to replace an existing device with another device without any system modifications, and new SCSI devices can often be added to the bus with little more than a driver upgrade. Since the intelligence of SCSI resides in the peripheral device itself and *not* in the computer, the computer is able to employ a small set of standard commands to accomplish data transfer back and forth to the peripheral.

Now that you understand a bit about the nature of the SCSI interface, the following sections explain some of the important terms and concepts you'll need to know.

SCSI VARIATIONS

At this point, let's take a look at the evolution of the SCSI interface and examine the ways in which it has evolved and proliferated. SCSI began life in 1979 when Shugart Associates (PC "old-timers" might remember them as one of the first PC hard drive makers) released their "Shugart Associates Systems Interface" (or SASI) standard. The X3T9.2 committee was formed by ANSI in 1982 to develop the SASI standard, which was renamed SCSI. SCSI drives and interfaces that were developed under the evolving X3T9.2 SCSI standard were known as SCSI-1, though the actual SCSI-1 standard (ANSI X3.131-1986) didn't become official until 1986. SCSI-1 provided a system-level 8-bit bus (referred to as *narrow*), which could operate up to 8 devices and transfer data at up to 5MB/s. However, the delay in standardization lead to a lot of configuration and compatibility problems with SCSI-1 setups. Table 39-1 compares the specifications of each SCSI standard.

TABLE 39-1 COMPARISON OF SCSI CONVENTIONS

TERMS	NAME	MHZ	BUS WIDTH	MB/S	MBIT/S
SCSI-1	SCSI-1	5	8	5	40
Fast SCSI	SCSI-2	10	8	10	80
Fast-Wide SCSI	SCSI-2/SCSI-3	10	16	20	160
Ultra SCSI	SCSI-3	20	8	20	160
Ultra-Wide SCSI	SCSI-3	20	16	40	320
Ultra2 SCSI	SCSI-4	40	8	40	320
Ultra2-Wide SCSI	SCSI-4	40	16	80	640
Ultra3 SCSI	Ultra160/m	40*2[1]	8	80	640
Ultra3-Wide SCSI	Ultra160/m	40*2[1]	16	160	1280
Ultra4 SCSI	not yet defined				
Ultra4-Wide SCSI	not yet defined				

NOTES: NOTE[1] Ultra3 features the same base frequency as Ultra2 (40MHz), but transmits 2 bytes per data clock—thus doubling the total throughput.

Fast-Wide SCSI is actually SCSI-2, however, many cable manufacturers refer to the 68-pin plugs as "SCSI-3." This is incorrect, according to the definition of **http://www.scsita.org**.

Most SCSI 1-4 and 160/m devices can be mixed on the same bus; however, the *slowest* device/controller determines the bus speed during negotiating and, in some cases, during data transfers.

You cannot mix "single ended" and "differential" (or "low-voltage differential" (LVD)) devices/controllers on the same SCSI bus.

Fast-Wide SCSI-2 is also sometimes called *SCSI-3* (especially when referring to the 68 HP connector).

You can mix Wide and Narrow, Fast-SCSI2, and Ultra SCSI Compaq Pluggable drives. However, you cannot plug in a Wide SCSI drive into an old Narrow SCSI server, since the connectors are too wide.

Although SCSI-1 was supposed to support all SCSI devices, manufacturers took liberties with the evolving standard. This trend frequently led to installation and compatibility problems between SCSI-1 devices that should "theoretically" have worked together perfectly. Today, all existing SCSI-1 adapters should be upgraded to SCSI-2 installations.

Earlier in 1986 (even before the SCSI-1 standard was ratified), work started on the SCSI-2 standard, which was intended to overcome many of the speed and compatibility problems encountered with SCSI-1. By 1994, ANSI blessed the SCSI-2 standard (X3.131-1994). SCSI-2 was designed to be backwardly compatible with SCSI-1, but SCSI-2 also provided for several variations. Fast SCSI-2 (or Fast SCSI) doubles the SCSI bus clock speed and allows 10MB/s data transfers across the 8-bit SCSI data bus. Wide SCSI-2 (or Wide SCSI), which also doubles the original data transfer rate to 10MB/s, uses a 16-bit data bus instead of the original 8-bit data bus (the SCSI clock is left unchanged). To support the larger data bus, Wide SCSI uses a 68-pin cable instead of the traditional 50-pin cable. Wide SCSI can also support up to 16 SCSI devices. Designers then combined the attributes of fast and wide operation to create Fast Wide SCSI-2 (or Fast Wide SCSI"), which supports 20MB/s data transfers across a 16-bit data bus. Whenever you see references to "Fast SCSI," "Wide SCSI," or "Fast Wide SCSI," you're *always* dealing with a SCSI-2 implementation.

But SCSI advancement didn't stopped there. ANSI began development of the SCSI-3 standard in 1993 (even before SCSI-2 was adopted). SCSI-3 is intended to be backward compatible with SCSI-2 and SCSI-1 devices, and there are many SCSI devices and controllers that are making use of the advances offered by SCSI-3 development. These typical SCSI-3 devices are generally known as Fast-20 SCSI (or Ultra SCSI-3, also termed Ultra SCSI). Ultra SCSI uses a 20MHz SCSI bus clock with an 8-bit data bus to achieve 20MB/s data transfers. By using a 16-bit data bus, SCSI-3 offers Wide Fast-20 SCSI (or Ultra Wide SCSI-3, also termed Ultra Wide SCSI), which handles 40MB/s data transfers.

SCSI development continued with the SCSI-4 implementations. The SCSI-4 standard covers Fast-40 SCSI (called Ultra2 SCSI-4 and Ultra2 SCSI) using a 40MHz bus clock to provide 40MB/s data transfers with an 8-bit data bus. The 16-bit data bus version is known as Wide Fast-40 SCSI (also called Ultra2 Wide SCSI-4 or Ultra2 Wide SCSI), which is supposed to support 80MB/s data transfers. Whenever you see references to "Ultra2" or "Fast-40," you're almost certain to be faced with a SCSI-4 setup.

But SCSI advances have not stopped there. The Ultra3 SCSI standard (a.k.a. Ultra160) employs a 40MHz bus clock, which is "double-transitioned." This feature allows twice the effective data transfer on the same 40MHz clock, yielding data transfers up to 80MB/s. The Ultra3 Wide SCSI standard offers 16 data bits rather than 8. On the same "double-transitioned 40MHz clock, Ultra3 Wide SCSI can achieve data transfers up to 160MB/s. While Ultra4 SCSI standards have not yet been fully defined, you can be sure that even faster SCSI implementations are on the horizon.

Also keep in mind that SCSI has traditionally been a "parallel" bus—that is, 8 or 16 bits of data are transferred at a time across parallel data lines. SCSI-3 is proposing three new *serial* connection schemes. You'll see these referred to as Serial Storage Architecture (SSA), Fibre Channel, and IEEE P1394 (a.k.a. Fire Wire). These serial schemes will offer faster data transfers than their parallel bus cousins, but they are not backward compatible with SCSI-2 or SCSI-1.

BUS LENGTH

As you're already aware, SCSI devices are daisy-chained together with a 50-pin or 68-pin cable. The total length of this cable makes up the overall SCSI "bus." When there are only *internal* SCSI devices, the bus length is measured from the SCSI host adapter to the last internal SCSI device on the chain (the terminated device). When there are only *external* SCSI devices, the bus length is measured from the SCSI host adapter to the last external SCSI device on the chain (it should also be terminated). When there are *both* internal and external SCSI devices, the bus length is measured from the last external device to the last internal device. There are finite limits on the length of your SCSI bus. As SCSI implementations have become faster over the years, that effective bus length has shortened. Table 39-2 illustrates the maximum SCSI bus lengths for single-ended, differential, and low-voltage differential (or LVD) signaling approaches.

INITIATORS AND TARGETS

There are basically two types of devices on the SCSI bus: initiators and targets. An *initiator* starts communication when something has to be done, and a *target* responds to the initiator's commands. The important thing for you to understand here is that this "master/slave" relationship is not a one-way arrangement—an initiator may become a target at some points in the data transfer cycle, and the target may become the initiator at other points. You will see more about this role duality later in this chapter. A SCSI bus can support up to 8 devices simultaneously, but there *must* be at least one initiator and one target in the system. A SCSI *host adapter* (the expansion card installed in one of the computer's expansion slots) is typically the initiator, and all other devices for instance, the hard drives or CD-ROMs) are usually targets, but that arrangement is not necessarily the only possible one.

TABLE 39-2 MAXIMUM SCSI BUS LENGTHS

TERMS	SINGLE-ENDED	DIFFERENTIAL	LVD
SCSI-1	6m	25m	12m [2]
Fast SCSI	3m	25m	12m [2]
Fast Wide SCSI	3m	25m	12m [2]
Ultra SCSI	1.5m-3m	Up to 25m	Up to 12m
Wide Ultra SCSI	Up to 3m	Up to 25m	Up to 12m
Ultra2 SCSI	[1]	25m	12m
Wide Ultra2 SCSI	[1]	25m	12m
Ultra3 SCSI	[1]	25m	12m
Wide Ultra3 SCSI	[1]	25m	12m

NOTE[1] Single-ended and high-powered differential are not defined at Ultra2 and Ultra3 speeds.

NOTE[2] Only if all devices on the bus support LVD.

Many kinds of computer peripherals are candidates for the SCSI bus. Each peripheral offers unique characteristics and applications, but each also requires different methods of control. By adding SCSI "intelligence" to these devices, they can all be made to share the same bus together. The SCSI nomenclature groups similar devices together into specific "device types." The original SCSI standard defines six devices:

- Random access devices (for example, hard drives)
- Sequential access (for example, tape drives)
- Printers
- Processors
- WORM (write once read many) drives
- Read-only random access devices

The SCSI-2 interface adds five more devices to the specification:

- CD-ROM drives
- Scanners
- Magneto-optical drives
- Media changer (jukebox)
- Communication devices

39

SYNCHRONOUS AND ASYNCHRONOUS

As a system-level interface, SCSI requires an operating *handshaking protocol* that organizes the transfer of data from a sending point to a requesting point. There are typically three handshaking protocols for SCSI: asynchronous, synchronous, and fast synchronous. The *asynchronous* protocol works rather like a parallel port. Each byte must be requested and acknowledged before the next byte can be sent. Asynchronous operation generally results in very reliable (but slow) performance. *Synchronous* and *fast synchro-*

nous operation both ignore the request/acknowledge handshake for data transfer only. Doing this allows slightly faster operation than an asynchronous protocol, but a certain fixed amount of time delay (sometimes called an *offset*) must be allowed for request and acknowledge effects. The fast synchronous protocol uses slightly shorter signals, resulting in even faster speed. An important point to remember is that SCSI systems can typically use any of these three protocols as desired. The actual protocol that is used must be mutually agreed to by the initiator and the target through their communications. SCSI systems normally initialize in an asynchronous protocol.

DISCONNECT AND RECONNECT

There are a number of instances when it would be desirable to allow a target to operate offline while the initiator is occupied elsewhere—tape rewind time is just one example. An important feature of SCSI is the ability to *disconnect* two communicating devices, then *reconnect* them again later. Disconnect and reconnect operations allow several different operations to occur simultaneously in the system—the main reason why SCSI architecture is so desirable in a multitasking environment. It is up to the initiator to grant a disconnect privilege to a target.

SINGLE-ENDED AND DIFFERENTIAL

The signal wiring used in an SCSI bus has a definite impact on bus performance. There are two generally used wiring techniques for SCSI: single-ended and differential. Both wiring schemes have advantages and disadvantages.

The *single-ended* (SE) wiring technique is, just as the name implies, a single wire carrying a particular signal from initiator to target. Each signal requires only one wire. Terminating resistors at each end of the cable help to maintain acceptable signal levels. A common ground (return) provides the reference for all single-ended signals. Unfortunately, single-ended circuitry is not very noise resistant, so single-ended cabling is generally limited to about 6 meters at data transfer speeds of 5MHz or less. At higher data transfer speeds, cable length may be as short as 1.5 meters. In spite of the disadvantages, single-ended operation is popular because of its simplicity.

The *differential* (DIF) wiring approach uses *two* wires for each signal (instead of one wire referenced to a common ground). A differential signal offers excellent noise resistance because it does not rely on a common ground. This approach allows much longer cables (up to 25 meters) and higher-speed operation (10 MHz). An array of pull-up resistors at each end of the cable help to ensure signal integrity. The drawback of differential wiring is that it is more complicated than single-ended interfaces.

Low-voltage differential (or LVD) SCSI is an emerging standard defined in the SPI-2 document of SCSI-3 that runs on 3.3 VDC rather than 5 VDC. The goal of LVD is to allow higher data rates while combining the benefits of single-ended and differential SCSI bus schemes. LVD is less sensitive to electromagnetic noise and allows high data rates at greater cable lengths than a single-ended bus. LVD is the interface specified for use with Ultra-2 SCSI and Ultra160/m specifications.

While LVD is not directly compatible with single-ended, the devices will use multimode driver circuits that automatically detect the type of bus used and switch to the appropriate mode of operation. This capability allows you to use an LVD/SE device on a single-ended bus without having to set any switches or jumpers. Therefore, LVD has been introduced gradually without the loss of the current investment in single-ended devices. Still, the advantages of LVD are lost when an LVD/SE device is used in a single-ended bus—as soon as one single-ended device is connected to LVD/SE bus, the whole bus switches to single-ended mode (with all its limitations).

TERMINATORS

When high-frequency signals are transmitted over adjacent wires, signals tend to degrade and interfere with one another over the length of the cable. This process is a very natural and relatively well understood electrical phenomenon. In the PC, SCSI signal integrity is enhanced by using powered resistors at each end of the data cable to "pull up" active signals. Most high-frequency signal cables in the PC are *already* terminated by pull-up resistors at drives and controller cards. The small resistor array is known as a *terminator*. Since there is a distinct limit to the number of devices that can be added to a floppy drive or IDE cable, designers have never made a big deal about termination—they just added the resistors, and that was it. With SCSI, however, up to eight devices can be added to the bus cable. The SCSI cable also must be terminated, but the location of terminating resistors depends on which devices are added to the bus and *where* they are placed. As a result, termination is a much more vital element of SCSI setup and troubleshooting. As you will see later in this chapter, poor or incorrect termination can cause intermittent signal problems. Later on. you will see how to determine the proper placement of terminating resistors.

Termination is typically either active or passive. Basically, *passive* termination is simply plugging a resistor pack into a SCSI device. Passive resistors are powered by the TERMPWR line. Passive termination is simple and effective over short distances (up to about 1 meter) and usually works just fine for the cable lengths inside a PC, but it can be a drawback over longer distances. *Active* terminators provide their own regulated power sources which makes them most effective for longer cables (such as those found in external SCSI devices like page scanners) or Wide SCSI systems. Most SCSI-2 and later implementations use active terminators. A variation on active termination is *forced perfect termination* (or FPT). FPT includes diode clamps that prevent signal overshoot and undershoot. This makes FPT effective for long SCSI cable lengths.

39

SCSI IDS

A typical SCSI bus will support up to eight devices, so each device on the bus must have its own unique ID number (0 to 7). If two devices use the same ID, there will be a conflict. IDs are typically set for the SCSI adapter and each SCSI device using jumpers or DIP switches. Typically, the SCSI adapter is set to ID 7, the primary SCSI hard drive to ID 0, and a second SCSI hard drive to ID 1. Other devices can usually be placed anywhere from ID 2 to ID 6.

BUS CONFIGURATIONS

Most of the SCSI implementations currently available use single-ended cabling that supports an 8-bit data bus (known as an *A-cable*). An A-cable is a 50-pin assembly outlined in Table 39-3. There are three major sections to the 50-pin single-ended SCSI cable: ground wires, data signals, and control signals. You will notice that at least half of the single-ended interface carries ground lines. There are eight data lines (D0 to D7) and a data parity bit (DPAR). Note that SCSI parity is always *odd*. There are four terminator power lines (TERMPWR) and nine control signal wires. Each signal is explained below:

- **-C/D**—Control/Data (driven by target): allows the target device to select whether it will be returning a command or data to the initiator.
- **-I/O**—Input/Output (driven by target): allows the target device to determine whether it will be receiving or sending information along the data bus.
- **-MSG**—Message (driven by target): allows the target device to send coded status or error messages back to the initiator during the "message" portion of the SCSI bus cycle.

- **-REQ**—Request (driven by target): a data strobe signal that allows a potential target device to obtain data on the bus.
- **-ACK**—Acknowledge (driven by initiator): a data strobe signal sent in response to the target's REQ signal that informs the target device that it has gained use of the bus.
- **-BSY**—Busy (driven by initiator or target): allows a device to inform the bus that the device is currently busy.
- **-SEL**—Select (driven by initiator or target): a signal used by an initiator in order to select a target device.
- **-ATN**—Attention (driven by initiator): a signal produced by the initiator that informs the target that the initiator has a message ready. The target should switch to the "message" phase.
- **-RST**—Reset (driven by initiator or target): a strobe signal that triggers a bus-wide reset of all devices. Usually, only one device produces a Reset signal.

TABLE 39-3 PINOUT OF A STANDARD SINGLE-ENDED A-CABLE

SIGNAL	PIN	PIN	SIGNAL
Ground	1	2	Data 0
Ground	3	4	Data 1
Ground	5	6	Data 2
Ground	7	8	Data 3
Ground	9	10	Data 4
Ground	11	12	Data 5
Ground	13	14	Data 6
Ground	15	16	Data 7
Ground	17	18	Data Parity
Ground	19	20	Ground
Ground	21	22	Ground
Reserved	23	24	Reserved
Open	25	26	TERMPWR
Reserved	27	28	Reserved
Ground	29	30	Ground
Ground	31	32	-ATN (-Attention)
Ground	33	34	Ground
Ground	35	36	-BSY (-Busy)
Ground	37	38	-ACK (-Acknowledge)
Ground	39	40	-RST (-Reset)
Ground	41	42	-MSG (-Message)
Ground	43	44	-SEL (-Select)
Ground	45	46	-C/D (-Control/Data)
Ground	47	48	-REQ (-Request)
Ground	49	50	-I/O (-Input/Output)

The differential SCSI interface replaces most of the ground wires with "+ signal" leads. For example, pin 2 represents +D0, while pin 27 is -D0. These + and - signal pairs are the differential signals. Note that there are still a few ground wires, but the grounds are not related to differential signals as they are to single-ended signals. Just about all of the data and control signals in the differential interface serve an identical purpose in the single-ended interface, but you will notice that the signal locations have been rearranged as shown in Table 39-4. There is one additional differential signal: the DIFFSENS (Differential Sense) line, which provides an active high-enable for differential drivers. Keep in mind that plugging a differential cable into a single-ended interface (or vice versa) can damage the device, the SCSI adapter, or both.

As you might imagine, wide SCSI implementations will not work with A-cables. A 16-bit cable is needed. Early implementations of wide SCSI used a second cable to provide the extra signal lines, but this approach was quickly abandoned for a single cable assembly (called a P-cable). The single-ended P-cable is shown in Table 39-5. While many of the signals may look familiar, you will notice that there are 68 pins instead of 50—primarily to support the eight additional data lines (D8 to D15). Control lines are identical to those in the A-cable. Table 39-6 shows the pinout for a differential 68-pin P-cable. The 80-pin implementation for a SCSI cable is listed in Table 39-7.

TABLE 39-4 PINOUT OF A STANDARD DIFFERENTIAL A-CABLE

SIGNAL	PIN	PIN	SIGNAL	
Ground	1	2	Ground	
+Data 0	3	4	-Data 0	
+Data 1	5	6	-Data 1	
+Data 2	7	8	-Data 2	
+Data 3	9	10	-Data 3	
+Data 4	11	12	-Data 4	
+Data 5	13	14	-Data 5	
+Data 6	15	16	-Data 6	
+Data 7	17	18	-Data 7	
+Data Parity	19	20	-Data Parity	
DIFFSENS	21	22	Ground	
reserved	23	24	reserved	
TERMPWR	25	26	TERMPWR	
Reserved	27	28	Reserved	
+ATN	29	30	-ATN	(Attention)
Ground	31	32	Ground	
+BSY	33	34	-BSY	(Busy)
+ACK	35	36	-ACK	(Acknowledge)
+RST	37	38	-RST	(Reset)
+MSG	39	40	-MSG	(Message)
+SEL	41	42	-SEL	(Select)
+C/D	43	44	-C/D)	(Control/Data
+REQ	45	46	-REQ	(Request)
+I/O	47	48	-I/O	(Input/Output)
Ground	49	50	Ground	

TABLE 39-5 PINOUT OF A STANDARD SINGLE-ENDED P-CABLE

SIGNAL	PIN	PIN	SIGNAL	
Ground	1	35	Data 12	
Ground	2	36	Data 13	
Ground	3	37	Data 14	
Ground	4	38	Data 15	
Ground	5	39	Data Parity 1	
Ground	6	40	Data 0	
Ground	7	41	Data 1	
Ground	8	42	Data 2	
Ground	9	43	Data 3	
Ground	10	44	Data 4	
Ground	11	45	Data 5	
Ground	12	46	Data 6	
Ground	13	47	Data 7	
Ground	14	48	Data Parity 0	
Ground	15	49	Ground	
Ground	16	50	Ground	
TERMPWR	17	51	TERMPWR	
TERMPWR	18	52	TERMPWR	
Reserved	19	53	Reserved	
Ground	20	54	Ground	
Ground	21	55	-ATN	(-Attention)
Ground	22	56	Ground	
Ground	23	57	-BSY	(-Busy)
Ground	24	58	-ACK	(-Acknowledge)
Ground	25	59	-RST	(-Reset)
Ground	26	60	-MSG	(-Message)
Ground	27	61	-SEL	(-Select)
Ground	28	62	-C/D	(-Control/Data)
Ground	29	63	-REQ	(-Request)
Ground	30	64	-I/O	(-Input/Output)
Ground	31	65	Data 8	
Ground	32	66	Data 9	
Ground	33	67	Data 10	
Ground	34	68	Data 11	

TABLE 39-6 PINOUT OF A STANDARD DIFFERENTIAL P-CABLE

SIGNAL	PIN	PIN	SIGNAL	
+Data 12	1	35	-Data 12	
+Data 13	2	36	-Data 13	
+Data 14	3	37	-Data 14	
+Data 15	4	38	-Data 15	
+Data Parity 1	5	39	-Data Parity 1	
Ground	6	40	Ground	
+Data 0	7	41	-Data 0	
+Data 1	8	42	-Data 1	
+Data 2	9	43	-Data 2	
+Data 3	10	44	-Data 3	
+Data 4	11	45	-Data 4	
+Data 5	12	46	-Data 5	
+Data 6	13	47	-Data 6	
+Data 7	14	48	-Data 7	
+Data Parity 0	15	49	-Data Parity 0	
DIFFSENS	16	50	Ground	
TERMPWR	17	51	TERMPWR	
TERMPWR	18	52	TERMPWR	
Reserved	19	53	Reserved	
+ATN	20	54	-ATN	(Attention)
Ground	21	55	Ground	
+BSY	22	56	+BSY	(Busy)
+ACK	23	57	-ACK	(Acknowledge)
+RST	24	58	-RST	(Reset)
+MSG	25	59	-MSG	(Message)
+SEL	26	60	-SEL	(Select)
+C/D	27	61	-C/D	(Control/Data)
+REQ	28	62	-REQ	(Request)
+I/O	29	63	-I/O	(Input/Output)
Ground	30	64	Ground	
+Data 8	31	65	-Data 8	
+Data 9	32	66	-Data 9	
+Data 10	33	67	-Data 10	
+Data 11	34	68	-Data 11	

TABLE 39-7 80-PIN SINGLE-ENDED SCSI CABLE PINOUT

SIGNAL	PIN	PIN	SIGNAL
12 VOLT	1	41	12 volt GROUND
12 VOLT	2	42	12 volt GROUND
12 VOLT	3	43	12 volt GROUND
12 VOLT	4	44	12 volt GROUND
Reserved/NC	5	45	Reserved/NC
Reserved/NC	6	46	Reserved/NC
DB (11)	7	47	GROUND
DB (10)	8	48	GROUND
DB (9)	9	49	GROUND
DB (8)	10	50	GROUND
I/O	11	51	GROUND
REQ	12	52	GROUND
C/D	13	53	GROUND
SEL	14	54	GROUND
MSG	15	55	GROUND
RST	16	56	GROUND
ACK	17	57	GROUND
BSY	18	58	GROUND
ATN	19	59	GROUND
DB (PO)	20	60	GROUND
DB (7)	21	61	GROUND
DB (6)	22	62	GROUND
DB (5)	23	63	GROUND
DB (4)	24	64	GROUND
DB (3)	25	65	GROUND
DB (2)	26	66	GROUND
DB (1)	27	67	GROUND
DB (0)	28	68	GROUND
DB (P1)	29	69	GROUND
DB (15)	30	70	GROUND
DB (14)	31	71	GROUND
DB (13)	32	72	GROUND
DB (12)	33	73	GROUND
5 volt	34	74	5 volt GROUND
5 volt	35	75	5 volt GROUND
5 volt	36	76	5 volt GROUND
SYNC	37	77	ACTIVE LED OUT
RMT START	38	78	DLYD START
SCSI ID (0)	39	79	SCSI ID (1)
SCSI ID (2)	40	80	SCSI ID (3)

Understanding SCSI Bus Operation

Now that you have learned about SCSI bus concepts and structure, you can see how the interface behaves during normal operation. Since bus wires are common to every device attached to the bus, a device must obtain permission from all other devices before it can take control of the bus. This attempt to access the bus is called the *arbitration phase*. Once a device (such as the SCSI controller) has won the bus arbitration, it must then make contact with the device to be communicated with. This device selection is known as the *selection phase*. When this contact is established, data transfer can take place. This part of the chapter will detail negotiation and information transfer over the SCSI bus.

NEGOTIATION

Devices must *negotiate* to access and use an SCSI bus. Negotiation begins when the bus is free (BSY and SEL lines are idle). A device begins arbitration by activating the BSY line and its own data ID line (data bit D0 to D7, depending on the device). If more than one device tries to control the bus simultaneously, the device with the higher ID line wins. The winning device (an initiator) attempts to acquire a target device by asserting the SEL line and the data ID line (data bit D0 to D7) of the desired device. The BSY line is then released by the initiator, and the desired target device asserts the BSY line to confirm it has been selected. The initiator then releases the SEL and data bus lines. Information transfer can now take place.

INFORMATION

The selected target controls the data being transferred and the direction of transfer. Information transfer lasts until the target device releases the BSY line, thus returning the bus to the idle state. If a piece of information will take a long time to prepare for, the target can end the connection by issuing a *disconnect* message. It will try to reestablish the connection later with a new arbitration and selection procedure.

39

During information transfer, the initiator tells its target how to act on a command and establishes the mode of data transfer during the *message out phase*. A specific SCSI command follows the message during the *command phase*. After a command is sent, data transfer takes place during the *data in* and/or *data out* phases. The target relinquishes control to the initiator during the *command phase*. For example, the command itself may ask that more information be transferred. The target then tells the initiator whether the command was successfully completed or not by returning status information during a *status phase*. Finally, the command is finished when the target sends a progress report to the initiator during the *message in* phase. Consider the simple SCSI communication example below:

1	*Bus free phase*	*(system is idle)*
2	*Arbitration phase*	*(a device takes control of the bus)*
3	*Select phase*	*(the desired device is selected)*
4	*Message-out phase*	*(target sets up data transfer)*
5	*Command phase*	*(send command)*
6	*Data-in phase*	*(exchange data)*
7	*Status phase*	*(indicate the results of the exchange)*
8	*Message-in phase*	*(indicate exchange is complete)*
9	*Bus free phase*	*(system is idle)*

Installing a SCSI System

Today, virtually all SCSI host adapters are PnP devices that are designed for automatic detection and resource assignments. Still, most SCSI host adapter problems *start* when the card is first installed in the system; problems are usually due to inadequate or incorrect installation of the hardware and software. This part of the chapter offers an overview of the SCSI adapter installation process and SCSI BIOS setup so that you can check your own installation for missing steps.

> Always use proper static precautions (such as an antistatic wrist strap) when working inside a system with sensitive devices—such as the SCSI host adapter card.

INTERNAL HARDWARE INSTALLATION

Follow the steps below when installing or replacing a SCSI adapter card:

1. Shut down Windows 98/SE, then turn off and unplug the computer.
2. Unbolt the outer case, then remove the housing and set it (and the screws) aside in a safe place.
3. If you're replacing an existing SCSI host adapter with a newer, faster model, you'll need to remove the old SCSI adapter first. Disconnect the internal and external SCSI cable(s) from the SCSI adapter. Unbolt the old SCSI card bracket from the chassis and remove the old SCSI adapter from its expansion slot. Be sure to set the old SCSI adapter aside on a static-safe surface or in an antistatic bag.
4. Locate a slot for the new SCSI host adapter card. Most current SCSI host adapter devices will require a PCI slot, though some older SCSI cards will use an ISA slot. Find an available bus-mastering PCI slot that's appropriate for your SCSI adapter card. Remove the cover for the slot you intend to use (if it's not already removed) and save the screw for the mounting bracket.
5. Insert the SCSI host adapter card. Push the card in firmly and evenly until it's fully seated in the slot. Replace the screw to secure the bracket of your SCSI card to the computer's chassis.
6. If you're connecting any internal SCSI devices, plug the 50-pin or 68-pin SCSI connector on the end of the internal SCSI ribbon cable into the SCSI card's header. Make sure to align pin-1 on both connectors.
7. Connect your computer's "drive activity" LED cable to the appropriate connector on the SCSI card (if desired). This connection is intended to operate the front panel LED found on most PC cabinets to indicate activity on the SCSI bus.
8. Make any external SCSI bus connections (for instance, from your SCSI scanner or external SCSI drives).

> The SCSI bus requires proper termination and no duplicate SCSI IDs. Before you attempt to reboot the computer, verify the SCSI IDs for each SCSI device, and double-check the SCSI termination at the end(s) of your SCSI chain.

SOFTWARE INSTALLATION

Now that the physical hardware for your new SCSI host adapter card has been installed, it's time to install the SCSI adapter drivers and application software that you'll need to identify the device under Windows

98/SE. Leave the computer's housing off for now, but reconnect the AC cord to the computer and prepare to start the system again.

> Always refer to the README file on the SCSI adapter card's driver disc to obtain the very latest feature descriptions and software installation guidelines for your particular card.

1. When Windows restarts, it should detect the SCSI host adapter automatically.
2. Click "Driver from disk provided by hardware manufacturer." Then click OK.
3. Insert the driver CD into the CD-ROM, then select the CD-ROM drive letter.
4. Click OK. Windows will load the SCSI adapter's drivers.
5. Once Windows finishes loading the information from the driver CD, you should verify that the SCSI adapter's installation was a success. When your desktop returns, click Start, highlight Settings, then click Control Panel.
6. Double-click the System icon, then click the Device Manager tab.
7. Double-click on the "SCSI controllers" branch to expand it.
8. See that your new SCSI host adapter is listed (Figure 39-1). If it is, your new SCSI host adapter is probably installed properly. You can exit the Device Manager and begin using your SCSI adapter. If not, you'll need to check the installation.

CONFIGURING THE SCSI BIOS

Today, the vast majority of SCSI host adapters employ a BIOS (*firmware*) to configure the adapter's various operations. In most cases, the default settings of your SCSI BIOS are adequate, and you should not need to change the default configuration of the host adapter. However, you may decide to alter these

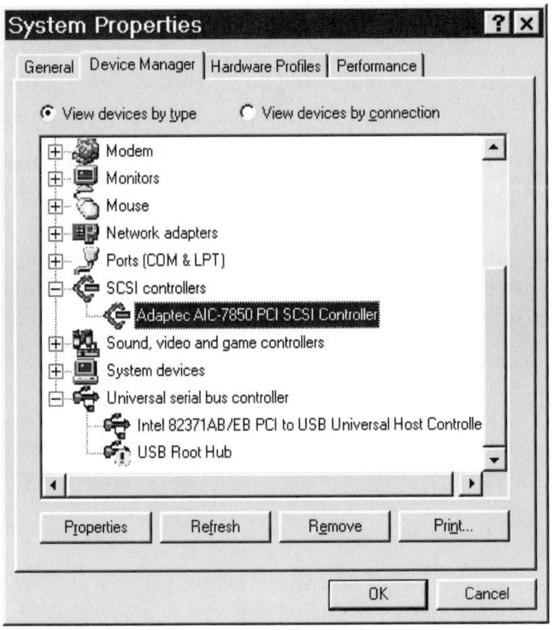

FIGURE 39-1 Checking the SCSI adapter after installation

default values if there is a conflict between device settings, or if you need to optimize the system's performance. This part of the chapter outlines the default settings of a common SCSI host adapter and explains many of the SCSI BIOS settings that you may encounter. Typical default settings are listed in Table 39-8. The "global settings" affect your host adapter and all SCSI devices that are connected to it, but the "device settings" affect only individual SCSI devices.

The version number of your SCSI BIOS appears in a banner displayed on your computer monitor during boot. If a configuration utility is available, a message such as the following also appears on your monitor such as:

```
Press Ctrl-C to start Symbios Configuration Utility...
```

This message remains on your screen for about five seconds, giving you time to start the utility. If you decide to press CTRL+C, the message changes to:

```
Please wait, invoking Symbios Configuration Utility...
```

After a brief pause, your computer monitor displays the *Main Menu* of the Symbios SCSI BIOS Configuration Utility.

> The SCSI BIOS Configuration Utility is a powerful tool. If you somehow disable all of your controllers while using it, pressing CTRL+A (or CTRL+E on version 4.04 or later) after memory initialization during reboot allows you to re-enable the defaults and reconfigure your SCSI BIOS.

> Not all devices detected by the Configuration Utility can be controlled by the BIOS. Devices such as tape drives and scanners require that a device driver specific to that peripheral be loaded. The device manufacturer provides the device drivers.

Main menu When you start the Symbios SCSI BIOS Configuration Utility, the Main Menu appears. This menu displays a list of up to four Symbios PCI to SCSI host adapters in the system and information about each of them. To select an adapter, use only the arrow keys and ENTER key. You can then view or change the current settings for that adapter and the SCSI devices attached to it. Select an adapter only if its

TABLE 39-8 TYPICAL DEFAULT SETTINGS FOR A SCSI HOST ADAPTER

Global default settings	
SCAM Support	Off (applies to BIOS version 4.09 and later)
Parity Checking	Enabled
Host Adapter SCSI ID	7
Scan Order	Low to High (0–Max)
Device default settings	
Synchronous Transfer Rate (MB/s)	40
Data Width	16
Disconnect	On
Read/Write I/O Time-out (seconds)	10
Scan for Devices at Boot Time	Yes
Scan for SCSI LUNs	Yes
Queue Tags	On

Current Status is On. If any settings are altered, the system reboots upon exit from the Configuration Utility when you use the Quit option.

Change adapter status The "Change adapter status" option allows you to activate or deactivate a host adapter and all SCSI devices attached to it. When this option is used to make a change, the change takes place after a reboot once you exit from the utility. To change an adapter's status, select it and press ENTER. Press the ESC key to exit from this menu and return to the Main Menu.

Adapter boot order The "Adapter boot order" option allows you to set the order in which host adapters will boot (when more than one SCSI host adapter is in the system). When this option is selected, the *Boot Order* menu appears. To change an adapter's boot order, select it and press ENTER. The system prompts you to enter the new boot sequence number. To *remove* an adapter from the boot order, press ENTER again rather than entering a new sequence number. Only four adapters can be assigned a boot order, starting with boot sequence number zero (0). If an invalid number is entered, an error message appears. When the adapters are ordered properly, press the ESC key to exit from this menu.

Additional adapter configuration The "Additional adapter configuration" option allows you to configure an adapter that is not assigned a boot order. When this option is selected, the Adapter Configuration menu appears. Highlight the adapter to be configured and press ENTER. The message "Resetting adapter, please wait" appears, and then the system scans for devices. Finally, the Utilities Menu appears and lists the available options.

Display mode The "Display mode" option determines how much information about your host adapter(s) and SCSI devices appear on the computer monitor during boot. For more complete information, choose the "verbose" setting. For a faster boot, choose the "terse" setting.

39

Mono/color The Mono/color option allows a choice between a monochrome or color display for the SCSI BIOS Configuration Utility. Choose the "mono" setting to get a more readable screen on a monochrome monitor (if necessary). In most cases, the "color" option will yield the best results on color displays.

Language When the Language option is enabled, you can select from one of several different languages (English, German, French, Italian, and Spanish).

Utilities menu When you select a host adapter on the Main Menu, the Utilities Menu appears. Choose the Adapter Setup to view and change the selected adapter settings. Choose the Device Selections to view and change settings for the devices attached to the selected adapter. After making changes to the configuration of any host adapter or connected SCSI device, the system returns to the Utilities Menu. Before you exit this menu, you're prompted to save or cancel any changes.

Adapter Setup Menu

The settings in this menu are global settings that affect the selected host adapter and all SCSI devices attached to it. A choice can be selected by highlighting it and pressing ENTER:

- **SCAM Support.** The Symbios BIOS version 4.xx and above supports the SCSI PnP protocol called SCAM (SCSI Configured AutoMatically). SCAM support by default is *off* in versions 4.09 and later for the SYM53C875 controller. You may choose to turn this feature on *only* if the system drivers do not require SCAM to be off.
- **Parity.** The Symbios PCI SCSI host adapters always generate parity, but some older SCSI devices do not. You're offered the option of disabling parity checking. When disabling parity checking, it's also necessary to disable disconnects for all devices, as parity checking for the reselection phase is not dis-

abled. If a device does not generate parity and it disconnects, the I/O cycle never completes because the reselection never finishes.

- **Host SCSI ID.** The host adapter's SCSI ID is a unique number used to identify the device on the SCSI bus. In general, it is suggested that you *not* change the host adapter ID from the default value of 7 (this ID gives the SCSI adapter the highest priority on the SCSI bus). Also, please note that if you have 8-bit SCSI devices (narrow), they *cannot* see host IDs greater than 7.
- **Scan Order.** This option allows the user to tell the SCSI BIOS and device drivers to scan the SCSI bus from low to high (0 to Max) SCSI ID, or from high to low (Max to 0) SCSI ID. If there is more than one device on the SCSI bus, changing the scan order changes the order in which drive letters are assigned by the system. Drive order may be reassigned differently in systems supporting the BIOS Boot Specification (BBS). This scan order option may conflict with operating systems that automatically assign a drive order.
- **Removable Media Support.** This option defines the removable media support for a specific drive. When this option is selected, a window appears with three choices: None, Boot Drive Only, and With Media Installed. "None" indicates there is no removable media support. "Boot Drive Only" provides removable media support for a removable hard drive if it is first in the scan order. "With Media Installed" provides removable media support wherever the drive(s) actually resides. One of these choices can be selected by highlighting it and pressing ENTER.
- **CHS Mapping.** This option defines the "cylinder head sector" (CHS) values that will be mapped onto a disk without preexisting partition information. SCSI PnP Mapping is the default value. To support interchange with noncompatible systems, there is another option that can be selected by choosing CHS Mapping and then selecting Alternate CHS Mapping. Neither of these options will have any effect after the disk has been partitioned with the FDISK command. To remove partitioning, two options are available: "Reformat the disk using the Format Device option" and "Use the FDISK /MBR command at the C:\ prompt," where MBR is the master boot record. After clearing the partitions and data, it is necessary to reboot and clear memory or the old partitioning data will be reused, thus nullifying the previous operation.
- **Spinup Delay (seconds).** This option allows you to stagger spinups for a longer period of time to balance the total current load. The default value is 2 seconds—with choices between 1 and 10 seconds. This is a power management technique designed to accommodate disk devices that may have heavy current loads during power up. If multiple drives are being powered up simultaneously and drawing heavy current, this option staggers the spinups to limit start-up current.

Device Selections Menu

The settings in this menu affect individual SCSI devices attached to the selected host adapter. Changes made from this menu do *not* cause the system to reboot upon exit from the SCSI BIOS Configuration Utility:

- **Sync Rate (MB/s).** This option defines the maximum data transfer rate at which the host adapter will attempt to negotiate. The host adapter and a SCSI device must agree to a rate they can both handle.
- **Width (bits).** This option defines the maximum SCSI data width at which the host adapter will attempt to negotiate. The host adapter and a SCSI device must agree to the data width they can both handle. Only host adapters that can handle 16-bit data transfers have this option enabled.
- **Disconnect.** SCSI devices have the ability to disconnect from the initiator during an I/O transfer. This option frees the SCSI Bus to allow other I/O processes. It also tells the host adapter whether or not to

allow a device to disconnect. Some devices run faster with disconnects enabled (mostly newer devices), while some run faster with disconnects disabled (mostly older devices).

- **Read Write I/O Time-out (seconds).** This option sets the amount of time the host adapter waits for a read, write, or seek command to complete before trying the I/O transfer again. This option is intended to allow the system to recover if an I/O operation fails, and it is recommended that you set the time-out to a value greater than zero. A zero value allows unlimited time for an operation to complete and could result in the system being hung-up.
- **Scan for Device at Boot Time.** Set this option to No if there is a device that you do not want to be available to the system. On a bus with only a few devices attached, you can speed up boot time by changing this setting to No for all unused SCSI IDs.
- **Scan for SCSI Logical Units (LUNs).** Set this option to No if problems arise with a device that responds to all LUNs whether they are occupied or not. For example, if a SCSI device with multiple LUNs is present on your system, but you do not want all of those LUNs to be available to the system, then set this option to No. This will limit the scan to LUN 0 only.
- **Queue Tags.** If the device driver supports this capability, the option will allow you to enable or disable the issuing of queue tags during I/O requests.
- **Initial Boot.** This option allows any device attached to the first adapter to become the boot device. It provides the users of non-BBS personal computers with some of the flexibility of a BBS machine.
- **Format Device.** If enabled, this option allows the user to low-level format a magnetic disk drive. Low-level formatting will completely and irreversibly erase all data on the drive. Formatting will default the drive to a 512-byte sector size even if the drive had previously been formatted to another sector size.
- **Verify.** This option allows the user to read all the sectors on a disk looking for errors. When selected, this option displays the following message: "Verify all sectors on the device. Press ESC to abort. Press any key to continue."
- **Restore Default Setup.** This option resets all device selections back to their default settings. Select this option to restore all manufacturing defaults for the specified adapter. Note that all user-customized options will be lost upon saving after restoring default setup.

39

Exiting the SCSI BIOS

Since some changes take effect only after the system reboots, it is important that you exit this Configuration Utility properly. Return to the Main Menu and exit using the Quit option. Rebooting the system without properly exiting from this utility may cause some changes to *not* take effect.

SCSI considerations Whether you're considering adding SCSI support to your own computer or planning an upgrade for a customer, there are four essential elements that you must consider: the SCSI peripheral(s), the SCSI host adapter, the SCSI cable assembly, and the SCSI software driver(s). If any one of these four elements is missing or ill-planned, your installation is going to run into problems.

SCSI PERIPHERALS

The first items to be considered are the SCSI peripheral(s) themselves. You first need to know what type of device(s) are needed (such as a SCSI hard drive or CD-ROM). The peripheral should be compatible with the architecture of your controller (for instance, SCSI-3 or SCSI-4). You may also find a growing base of Ultra160/m-compliant adapters and peripherals. Each SCSI peripheral device should also have a wide range of available SCSI ID settings. SCSI typically handles eight IDs (0 to 7), and the peripheral should have the flexibility to run on virtually any ID. If only a few IDs are available, you may be limited when it comes time to add other SCSI devices. Peripherals should support SCSI parity.

Ideally, a SCSI-4 host adapter should support SCSI-3 and SCSI-2 devices. If you have any intention of employing SCSI-4 devices, be sure to use a SCSI-4 adapter.

SCSI devices are available in both internal and external versions. If you consider an internal peripheral, make sure that there is adequate drive space in the PC to accommodate the new peripheral. (Either there is a drive bay available, or an existing device may be removed to make room.) If the peripheral is to be an external device (such as a printer or scanner), there should be *two* SCSI connectors on the device to allow for daisy-chaining additional devices later. All SCSI peripherals other than hard drives will require device drivers. Make sure that the device driver is compatible with the same standard protocol used by the adapter (ASPI, CAM, or LADDR). Compatibility is a serious consideration since peripherals using incompatible device driver standards will not work properly. Finally, try to choose SCSI peripherals that offer built-in cable termination.

SCSI HOST ADAPTER

The next item to be considered is the SCSI host adapter (often just called a "host" or "HA"), which fits in the PC expansion bus. Make sure to choose an adapter that is compatible with the PC bus in use (for example, ISA or PCI). Bus-mastering 32/64-bit PCI SCSI adapters will provide superior performance if your system supports them. Like the peripheral itself, the adapter should also be designed to support the SCSI-3 standard (or SCSI-4 if possible). Although most adapters are assigned a SCSI ID of 7, the adapter should be flexible enough to work with any ID from 0 to 7. The host adapter will also require a device driver for using devices other than hard drives. Make sure that the host device driver uses the same standard as the peripheral(s) (ASPI, CAM, or LADDR). It is important to note here that the driver standard has nothing to do with the choice of SCSI-2, SCSI-3, or SCSI-4. It is important only that the peripherals and the adapter use the *same* driver standard.

SCSI CABLES AND TERMINATORS

Check that you select the proper cabling for the SCSI level you are using. Although SCSI cabling is now highly standardized, some older cables may use slight modifications for particular peripherals (typical with SCSI-1 devices). Be certain that you know of any specialized cabling requirements when choosing peripherals. Try to avoid specialized cabling if at all possible, but if you *must* use specialized cabling, you should determine what impact the cabling will have on any other SCSI peripherals that may be installed (or may be installed later). Use good-quality SCSI cables specifically intended for the SCSI level you are using (probably SCSI-3/4), and keep the cables short to minimize signal degradation.

SCSI cables must be terminated at the *beginning* (host adapter) and *end* (after the last device) of the SCSI chain. Try to choose internal peripherals that have built-in terminators. Also try to select a host adapter and peripherals that use the same type of terminator resistor network. SCSI-2 and later systems use active terminator networks. You will see much more about cabling and termination a bit later in this chapter.

SCSI DRIVERS

Device drivers provide the instructions that allow the SCSI host adapter to communicate with the PC, as well as with the peripherals in the SCSI chain (or the SCSI *bus*). The host adapter itself will require a device driver, as will every peripheral that is added. For example, a SCSI system with one CD-ROM will need a driver for the host adapter and a driver for the CD-ROM. Make sure that driver standards (ASPI, CAM, or

LADDR) are the *same* for the host adapter and peripherals. The only exception to the device driver requirement (at this time) is the SCSI hard drive which may be supported by the SCSI adapter's BIOS ROM.

Real-mode device drivers are added by including them in your PC's CONFIG.SYS and AUTOEXEC.BAT files. One issue to keep in mind when adding device drivers is that drivers use *conventional* memory (unless you successfully load the drivers into high memory). The more drivers that are added, the more memory that will be consumed. It is possible that a large number of device drivers may prevent certain memory-demanding DOS applications from running. To keep as much conventional memory (the first 640KB in RAM) free as possible, use the DOS *devicehigh* and *loadhigh* features to load the drivers into upper memory (from 640KB to 1MB in RAM). Windows 95/98 uses protected-mode drivers for the host adapter and devices.

TIPS FOR A SMOOTH INSTALLATION

SCSI is not a terribly difficult technology to implement properly, but the subtle considerations and inconsistencies that have always been a part of SCSI implementations can result in confusion and serious delays for you and your customer. The following tips should help to ease your upgrades:

- ***Add only add one SCSI device at a time.*** By adding one device at a time and testing the system after each installation, it becomes much easier to determine the point where problems occur. Imagine what happens when you add an adapter, hard drive, and CD-ROM without performing checks. If the system fails to function, you will have to isolate and check each item to locate the fault. On the other hand, by adding the adapter and testing it, then adding the hard drive and testing it, then adding the CD-ROM and testing it, installation troubleshooting becomes a much simpler matter (although it may take a bit more time overall).
- ***Record the host adapter's resources.*** One of the most difficult aspects of troubleshooting is determining the configuration of a system. This determination is especially important during an upgrade since you *must* know the interrupts (IRQs), DMA channel(s), and I/O ranges used by other expansion devices in the PC. Any overlap in the use of these system resources will eventually result in a hardware conflict. When you install a SCSI host adapter, make it a point to record its IRQ, DMA, and I/O settings along with the SCSI ID settings of all devices that are installed. Tape the record to the inside of the PC's cover—next time the PC returns for service or upgrade, you'll have the information right at your fingertips.
- ***Use good-quality cabling.*** Using the correct terminators and cables can have a profound effect on the performance of your SCSI installation. Good-quality cables and terminators provide electrical characteristics that support good signal transfer, resulting in good data reliability between the host controller and peripherals. If cable quality is sub-standard or if terminator networks are not correct for the SCSI level being used, the cable's electrical characteristics and data transfer will be degraded.

CABLING AND TERMINATION

Once the host adapter and peripheral are configured and installed, you must connect them with a cable. Internal devices are typically connected with a 50-pin IDC (insulation displacement connector) ribbon cable (an A-cable). By placing multiple connectors along the length of cable, daisy-chaining can be achieved with a single connector on each internal device. External devices typically connect to an external 50-pin connector on the rear of the SCSI adapter, and each device offers two connectors to allow daisy-chaining to additional devices. Most commercial adapter and drive "kits" are packed with an appropriate cable.

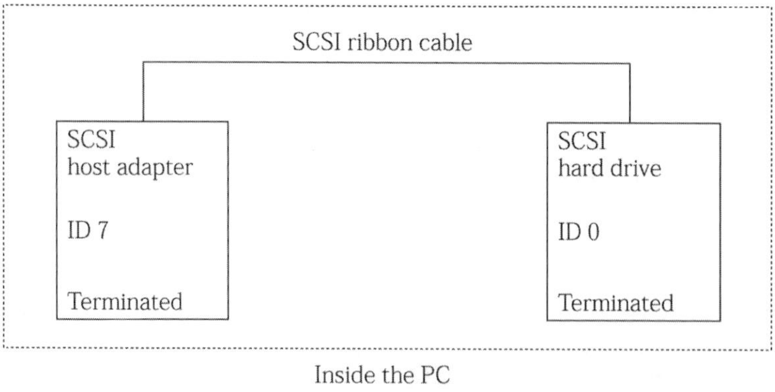

FIGURE 39-2 Terminating an internal SCSI adapter and hard drive

The cable(s) must be *terminated*. There are internal and external SCSI cable terminators, along with SCSI devices that have terminating resistor networks already built in. The concept of termination is reasonably simple—achieve the desired signal cable characteristics by *loading* each end of the SCSI "chain" with resistors. If the chain is not terminated properly, signals will not be carried reliably (which invariably results in system errors). For technicians and end-users alike, the trouble usually arises in determining there the "ends" are. A number of examples will help to clarify how to determine the chain "ends."

For a single SCSI drive and adapter as shown in Figure 39-2, the "ends" are easy to see. One end should be terminated at the host adapter (which usually has terminating resistors built in). The other end should be terminated at the SCSI hard drive (which also usually has terminating resistors built in). In this type of situation, you need only connect the cable between both devices and verify that the terminators are in place.

When a second SCSI peripheral is added, as shown in Figure 39-3, termination becomes a bit more complex. Suppose a CD-ROM is added with a SCSI ID of 6. The terminator on the existing SCSI hard drive is no longer appropriate—it should be removed, and the termination should be made on the CD-ROM, which is now the *last device* in the SCSI chain. In most cases, a terminator network can be deactivated by flipping a DIP switch or changing a jumper on the peripheral itself. If the terminator can

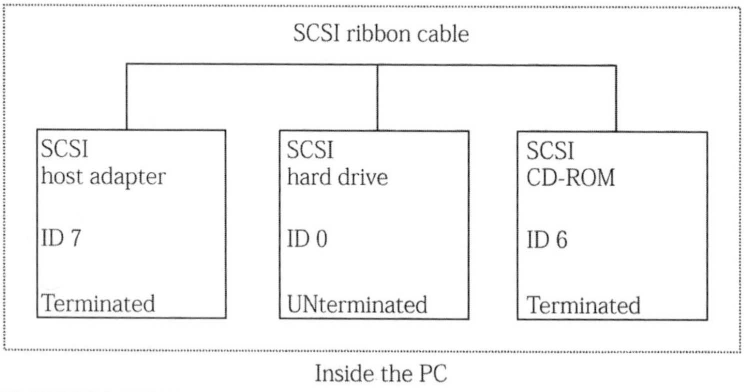

FIGURE 39-3 Terminating an internal SCSI adapter, HDD, and CD-ROM

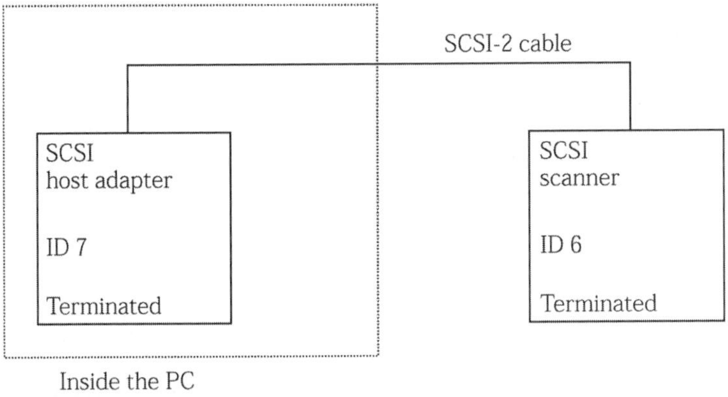

FIGURE 39-4 Terminating an external SCSI device

not be "shut off," it can almost always be removed by gently easing the resistor network out of its holder using needle nose pliers. If you remove a terminator, place it in an envelope and tape it to the inside of the PC enclosure. If it is simply impossible to remove the existing terminator on the hard drive, place the CD-ROM between the adapter and hard drive and remove the CD-ROM's terminator (rearrange the chain). The SCSI host adapter must remain terminated.

So what happens if an *external* device is used (such as a scanner) as in Figure 39-4? An external cable connects the adapter to the scanner. Since the scanner (ID 6) and adapter (ID 7) are the only two points in the chain, both are terminated. Most external devices designed for SCSI-2 compatibility allow the active terminator built into the peripheral to be switched off if necessary.

Suppose both an internal *and* an external SCSI device are being used, as shown in Figure 39-5. The SCSI host adapter (ID 7) is no longer at an end of the chain, so its terminator should be switched off or removed. It is the internal hard drive (ID 0) and external scanner (ID 6) that now form the ends, so both devices should be terminated. Since both peripherals should ideally support internal termination, nothing needs to be done except to confirm that the terminators are in place and switched on.

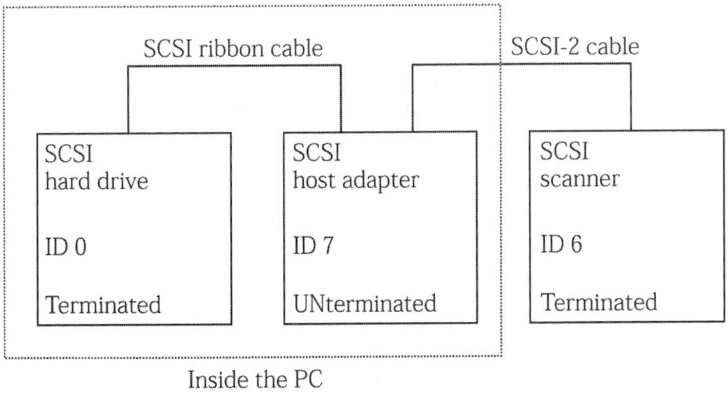

FIGURE 39-5 Terminating mixed internal and external SCSI devices

REAL-MODE SCSI DRIVER ISSUES

Hardware configuration and installation is only one part of the SCSI installation. Software needs to be installed in order to allow the hardware to interact with your system. The problem with SCSI drivers is that, prior to 1991, various drivers were rarely compatible. For example, an adapter and hard drive may have worked fine, but adding a CD-ROM would create havoc since the CD-ROM driver was not compatible with the hard drive or the host adapter driver (or both). After 1991, a set of "universal" driver standards appeared and created a "buffer" between the operating system and hardware that isolated drivers from one another. Drivers can now be written for each peripheral without worry of incompatibility so long as the drivers are written to be compatible with the standard.

There are typically three competing SCSI standards: ASPI (Advanced SCSI Programming Interface), CAM (Common Access Method), and LADDR (Layered Device Driver Architecture). ASPI is certainly the most popular of the three standards. The object of compatibility is to select a host adapter and peripherals that support the *same* standard. For example, if you select a host adapter that uses an ASPI driver, each of the peripherals that you choose must also use ASPI drivers. If you upgrade the host adapter later, you should also upgrade the host's ASPI driver—full compatibility *should* be maintained.

The actual installation process varies little from other software installations. The real-mode driver files for your adapter and peripheral(s) are copied to a subdirectory on the hard drive, then the CONFIG.SYS and AUTOEXEC.BAT files are updated to load the appropriate drivers on system startup. If your particular system commits too much conventional memory to drivers, you can manually optimize your startup files later to load as many drivers as possible into upper memory.

TIPS FOR WINDOWS 95/98 SCSI DRIVERS

If you intend to use your SCSI system under Windows 95/98, you'll need to install protected-mode drivers for the host adapter and devices. Contemporary SCSI host adapters (and many SCSI devices) are compliant with plug-and-play operation under Windows 95/98—this means Windows 95/98 should typically be able to identify the SCSI adapter (or newly installed devices) and install the appropriate protected-mode drivers for it. Ordinarily, this process should be automatic, but the following tips may help you handle Windows 95/98 installations:

- Verify the SCSI adapter and devices in DOS first with its real-mode drivers.
- If Windows 95/98 does *not* automatically identify the SCSI hardware, you should run the Add New Hardware wizard to register the device(s) and install the protected-mode drivers (remember *not* to let Windows 95/98 detect devices itself).
- You can use the Add New Hardware wizard to update existing SCSI drivers if new versions become available.
- If your SCSI hardware is not listed in the Add New Hardware wizard, you'll need to contact the hardware manufacturer(s) and download the correct INF file and protected-mode drivers. If there are no protected-mode drivers for your SCSI hardware (that would be rare today), you'll need to use the real-mode (DOS) drivers—doing this may result in all system drives running in "DOS Compatibility mode" and impair system performance.

Troubleshooting the SCSI System

As far as the *bus* is concerned, there is very little that can go "wrong"—wires and connectors do not fail spontaneously. However, it never hurts to examine the wiring, connectors, and terminator network(s) to ensure that the physical connections are intact (especially after installing or configuring new devices). The most likely areas of trouble are in the installation, setup, and operation of the devices residing on the bus.

ISOLATING TROUBLE SPOTS

Assuming that your SCSI devices have been installed correctly, certain problem scenarios can occur during normal operation. The first indication of a problem usually comes in the form of an error message from your operating system or application program. For example, your SCSI hard drive may not be responding, or the host PC may not be able to identify the SCSI host controller board, and so on.

The advantage to SCSI architecture is that it is reasonably easy to determine problem locations using intuitive deduction. Consider a typical SCSI system with one initiator (a host controller) and one target (a hard drive). If the hard drive fails to function, the trouble is either in the host controller or the drive itself. When you see drive access being attempted and generating an error, the trouble is probably in the drive. If no drive access is attempted before an error is generated, the error is likely in the host controller. As another example, consider a setup with one initiator and two or more targets (hard drive and CD-ROM). If *both* the hard drive *and* CD-ROM become inoperative, the problem is likely in the host controller card since the host adapter controls both targets. If only *one* of the devices becomes inoperative (and the other device works just fine) the trouble is likely in the particular device itself.

Of course, these are only common isolation methods and their effectiveness will depend on the sophistication of the particular system you are working with. There is always some amount of uncertainty in the intuitive approach because it is not *quantitative*. You can suspect where the trouble is coming from, but you cannot *prove* it. Given the great expense of many SCSI peripherals, it is often unwise to purchase replacement parts based solely on intuitive techniques. To "prove" the problem's source, you can track communication along the SCSI bus using a specialized SCSI tester. If you perform extensive SCSI testing on a professional level, you may wish to invest in an SCSI bus tester (such as Ancot's DSC-216 portable SCSI bus analyzer). An analyzer lets you track the communication process along the SCSI bus and provides bus speed calculations and command profiling. Once you have located the problem device, you can deal with that device specifically through replacement or repair.

However, specialized test equipment carries a significant price tag—a worthy investment if you have the service volume to justify it, but hardly a reasonable outlay for the casual PC hobbyist. Fortunately, a growing number of contemporary diagnostic software packages are being upgraded with SCSI test capabilities. For example, the *PC Technician* software by Windsor Technologies can test a limited number of SCSI adapters (such as Western Digital, Adaptec, and NCR) and associated peripherals. *SCSIDiag* by AMI is a diagnostic specifically designed for SCSI system testing. Note that almost every current SCSI adapter provides built-in diagnostic capability.

The reason for the lack of broad diagnostic software support is simple—SCSI is not supported by the PC motherboard BIOS (where IDE and EIDE *are* supported). As a result, the diagnostic must be written to handle specific SCSI controllers. The issue to keep in mind when selecting a diagnostic for SCSI testing is that the software *must* be compatible with the SCSI adapter in your system—just because a diagnostic says "SCSI-compatible" does not necessarily make it so for the PC setup you are faced with. As an alternative to commercial diagnostics, you may be able to find small controller diagnostics right on the software disks that accompany the SCSI adapter. You would normally run the test routine after installation to see that the controller is working, but you can also use it in a pinch for "as-needed" troubleshooting for that particular controller. Check with the manufacturer's BBS or CompuServe forum to find up-to-date test routines for various controllers.

GENERAL TROUBLESHOOTING TIPS

No matter how many precautions you take, you cannot always prevent problems from striking during a SCSI installations or replacements. Fortunately, if you are installing devices one-by-one, as suggested, you will have far fewer problem areas to check. Your first diagnostic for a SCSI installation should be the host adapter's SCSI BIOS initialization message. If you see no initialization message when the system powers up, any problem is likely with the adapter itself. Either it is not installed properly or it is defective. Make sure that the adapter is set to the desired ID (usually 7). Try a new or alternate SCSI adapter. If the adapter provides its initialization message as expected, a problem is probably related to driver installation. Check the installation and any command line switches for each device driver. When installing a SCSI hard drive instead of IDE/EIDE hard drives, you must ensure that any previous hard drive references are "mapped out" of the CMOS setup by entering "none" or "not installed." If preexisting drive references are not removed, the system will try to boot from IDE/EIDE drives that aren't there.

Be aware that faulty SCSI ID settings can result in system problems such as "ghost" disks—disks that the system says are there but that cannot be read from or written to. Some peripherals may also not work properly with the ID that has been assigned. If you have problems interacting with an installed device, try the device with a different ID and make sure that there are no two devices using the *same* ID. Don't be surprised to find that certain types of cables don't work properly with SCSI installations. Make sure that everything is terminated correctly. Also be sure that any external SCSI devices are powered up (if possible) before the PC is initialized. If problems persist, try different cables. An quick-reference checklist is shown below:

- Check the power to all SCSI devices—make sure that the power supply has enough capacity to handle all of your attached SCSI devices.
- Check the 50/68-pin signal cable to all SCSI devices. It should be a good quality cable that is attached securely to each device.
- Check the orientation of each connector on the SCSI cable. Pin 1 must always be in the proper orientation.
- Check the SCSI ID of each device. Duplicate IDs are not allowed.
- Check that both ends of the SCSI cable are properly terminated and that the terminators are active.
- Check the SCSI controller configuration (IRQ, I/O, BIOS addresses, and so on). Verify that the SCSI controller is not conflicting with other devices in the system.
- Check SCSI host adapter BIOS. If you're not booting from SCSI hard drives, you can often leave the SCSI BIOS disabled. This will also simplify the device configuration.
- Check the CMOS Setup for drive configurations. When SCSI drives are in the system and IDE/EIDE drives are not, be sure that the drive entries under CMOS are set for "none" or "not installed."

- Check the PCI bus configuration in the CMOS Setup. See that the PCI slot containing the SCSI host adapter is active and is using a unique IRQ (usually named IRQ A).
- Check for the real-mode drivers under DOS. If you're working under DOS, see that any needed driver(s) for the host adapter and non-HDD device(s) are installed in the CONFIG.SYS and AUTOEXEC.BAT files.
- Check for the protected-mode drivers under Windows 95/98. If you're working under Windows 95/98, see that any needed protected-mode drivers for the host adapter and SCSI devices are installed. The SCSI host adapter should be properly identified in the Device Manager.
- Try remarking-out real-mode drivers if problems occur only under Windows 95/98. Real-mode SCSI drivers can sometimes interfere with protected-mode SCSI drivers. If the SCSI system works fine in DOS, but not in Windows 95/98, try temporarily disabling the DOS drivers in your startup files.

SYMPTOMS

Even the best-planned SCSI setups go wrong from time to time, and SCSI systems already in the field will not run forever. Sooner or later, you will have to deal with a SCSI problem. This part of the chapter is intended to show you a variety of symptoms and solutions for many of the problems that you will likely encounter.

SYMPTOM 39-1 **After initial SCSI installation, the system will not boot from the floppy drive** You may or may not see an error code corresponding to this problem. Suspect the SCSI host adapter first. There may be an internal fault with the adapter that is interfering with system operation. Check that all of the adapter's settings are correct and that all jumpers are intact. If the adapter is equipped with any diagnostic LEDs, check for any problem indications. When adapter problems are indicated, replace the adapter board. If a SCSI hard drive has been installed and the drive light is always on, the SCSI signal cable has probably been reversed between the drive and adapter. Make sure to install the drive cable properly.

Check for the SCSI adapter BIOS message generated when the system starts. If the message does not appear, check for the presence of a ROM address conflict between the SCSI adapter and ROMs on other expansion boards. Try a new address setting for the SCSI adapter. If there is a BIOS wait state jumper on the adapter, try changing its setting. If you see an error message indicating that the SCSI host adapter was not found at a particular address, check the I/O setting for the adapter.

Some more recent SCSI host adapters incorporate a floppy controller. This can cause a conflict with an existing floppy controller. If you choose to continue using the existing floppy controller, be sure to disable the host adapter's floppy controller. If you prefer to use the host adapter's floppy controller, remember to disable the preexisting floppy controller port.

39

SYMPTOM 39-2 **The system will not boot from the SCSI hard drive** Start by checking the system's CMOS setup. When SCSI drives are installed in a PC, the corresponding hard drive reference in the CMOS setup must be changed to "none" or "not installed" (assuming that you will *not* be using IDE/EIDE hard drives in the system). If you have not "mapped out" previous hard drive references, do so now; then save the CMOS Setup and reboot the PC. If the problem persists, check that the SCSI boot drive is set to ID 0. You will need to refer to the user manual for your particular drive to find how the ID is set.

Next, check the SCSI parity to be sure that it is selected consistently among all SCSI devices. Remember that *all* SCSI devices must have SCSI parity enabled or disabled—if even one device in the SCSI chain does not support parity, it must be disabled on *all* devices. Check the SCSI cabling to be sure that all cables are installed and terminated properly. Finally, be sure that the hard drive has been partitioned and formatted properly. If it hasn't, boot from a floppy disk and prepare the hard drive as required using FDISK and FORMAT.

SYMPTOM 39-3 **The SCSI drive fails to respond with an alternate HDD as the boot drive** Technically, you should be able to use a SCSI drive as a non-boot drive (such as drive D:) while using an IDE/EIDE drive as the boot device. If the SCSI drive fails to respond in this kind of arrangement, check the CMOS setting to be sure that drive 1 (the SCSI drive) is "mapped out" (or set to "none" or "not installed"). Save the CMOS Setup and reboot the PC. If the problem persists, check that the SCSI drive is set to SCSI ID 1 (the non-boot ID). Next, make sure that the SCSI parity is enabled or disabled consistently throughout the SCSI installation. If the SCSI parity is enabled for some devices and disabled for others, the SCSI system may function erratically. Finally, check that the SCSI cabling is installed and terminated properly. Faulty cables or termination can easily interrupt a SCSI system. If the problem persists, try another hard drive.

> Later SCSI host adapters use BIOS that allows SCSI drives to boot even with IDE/EIDE drives in the system. In such a configuration, the Boot Order entry in CMOS Setup will determine whether A:, C:, or SCSI will be the boot device.

SYMPTOM 39-4 **The SCSI drive fails to respond with another SCSI drive as the boot drive** This typically occurs in a dual-drive system using two SCSI drives. Check the CMOS Setup and make sure that both drive entries in the setup are set to "none" or "not installed." Save the CMOS Setup. The boot drive should be set to SCSI ID 0, while the supplemental drive should be set to SCSI ID 1 (you will probably have to refer to the manual for the drives to determine how to select a SCSI ID). The hard drives should have a DOS partition and format. If they do not, create the partitions (FDISK) and format the drives (FORMAT) as required. Check to be sure that SCSI parity is enabled or disabled consistently throughout the SCSI system. If some devices use parity and other devices do not, the SCSI system may not function properly. Make sure that all SCSI cables are installed and terminated properly. If the problem persists, try systematically exchanging each hard drive.

SYMPTOM 39-5. **The system works erratically. The PC hangs or the SCSI adapter cannot find the drive(s)** Such intermittent operation can be the result of several different SCSI factors. Before taking any action, be sure that the application software you were running when the fault occurred did not cause the problem. Unstable or buggy software can seriously interfere with system operation. Try different applications and see if the system still hangs up (you might also try any DOS diagnostic utilities that accompanied the host adapter). Check each SCSI device and make sure that parity is enabled or disabled consistently throughout the SCSI system. If parity is enabled in some devices and disabled in others, erratic operation can result. Make sure that no two SCSI devices are using the same ID. Cabling problems are another common source of erratic behavior. Make sure that all SCSI cables are attached correctly and completely. Also check that the cabling is properly terminated.

Next, suspect a possible resource conflict between the SCSI host adapter and another board in the system. Check each expansion board in the system to be sure that nothing is using the same IRQ, DMA, or I/O address as the host adapter (or check the Device Manager under Windows 95/98). If you find a conflict, you should alter the *most recently installed* adapter board. If problems persist, try a new drive adapter board.

SYMPTOM 39-6 **You see an 096xxxx error code** This is a diagnostic error code that indicates a problem in a 32-bit SCSI host adapter board. Check the board to be sure that it is installed correctly and completely. The board should not be shorted against any other board or cable. Try disabling one SCSI device at a time. If normal operation returns, the last device to be removed is responsible for the problem (you may need to disable drivers and reconfigure termination when isolating problems in this fashion). If the problem persists, remove and reinstall all SCSI devices from scratch or try a new SCSI adapter board.

SYMPTOM 39-7 **You see a 112xxxx error code** This diagnostic error code indicates a problem in a 16-bit SCSI adapter board. Check the board to be sure that it is installed correctly and completely. The board should not be shorted against any other board or cable. Try disabling one SCSI device at a time. If normal operation returns, the last device to be removed is responsible for the problem (you may need to disable drivers and reconfigure termination when isolating problems in this fashion). Try a new SCSI host adapter board.

SYMPTOM 39-8 **You see a 113xxxx error code** This is a diagnostic code that indicates a problem in a system (motherboard) SCSI adapter configuration. If there is a SCSI BIOS ROM installed on the motherboard, be sure that it is up-to-date and installed correctly and completely. If problems persist, try replacing the motherboard's SCSI controller IC or replacing the system board. It may be possible to circumvent a damaged motherboard SCSI controller by disabling the motherboard's controller, then installing a SCSI host adapter card.

SYMPTOM 39-9 **You see a 210xxxx error code** There is a fault in a SCSI hard disk. Check that the power and signal cables to the disk are connected properly. Make sure the SCSI cable is correctly terminated. Try repartitioning and reformatting the SCSI hard disk. Finally, try a new SCSI hard disk.

SYMPTOM 39-10 **A SCSI device refuses to function with the SCSI adapter even though both the adapter and device check properly** This is often a classic case of basic incompatibility between the device and host adapter. Even though SCSI-2 and later standards help to streamline compatibility between devices and controllers, there are still situations when the two just don't work together. Check the literature included with the finicky device and see if there are any notices of compatibility problems with the controller (perhaps the particular controller brand) you are using. If there are warnings, there may also be alternative jumper or DIP switch settings to compensate for the problem and allow you to use the device after all. A call to technical support at the device's manufacturer may help shed light on any recently discovered bugs or fixes (such as an updated SCSI BIOS, SCSI device driver, or host adapter driver). If problems remain, try using a similar device from a different manufacturer (for example, try a Connor tape drive instead of a Mountain tape drive).

39

SYMPTOM 39-11 **You see a "No SCSI Controller Present" error message** Immediately suspect that the controller is defective or installed improperly. Check the host adapter installation (including IRQ, DMA, and I/O settings), and see that the proper suite of device drivers has been installed correctly. If the system still refuses to recognize the controller, try installing it in a different PC. If the controller also fails in a different PC, the controller is probably bad and should be replaced. However, if the controller *works* in a different PC, your original PC may not support all the functions under the interrupt 15h call required to configure SCSI adapters (such as an AMI SCSI host adapter). Consider upgrading the PC BIOS ROM to a new version—especially if the PC BIOS is older. There may also be an upgraded SCSI BIOS or host adapter driver to compensate for this problem.

SYMPTOM 39-12 **The PCI SCSI host adapter is not recognized, and the SCSI BIOS banner is not displayed** This often occurs when installing new PCI SCSI host adapters. The host computer must be PCI REV. 2.0 compliant, and the motherboard BIOS must support PCI-to-PCI Bridges (PPB) and bus mastering; this is typically a problem (or limitation) with some older PCI motherboard chipsets, and you'll probably find that the PCI SCSI adapter board works just fine on newer systems. If the system *doesn't* support PPB, it may not be possible to use the PCI SCSI adapter. You can try an ISA SCSI adapter instead or upgrade the motherboard to one with a more recent chipset.

If the system hardware *does* offer PPB support and the problem persists, the motherboard BIOS may still not support PPB features as required by the PCI 2.0 standard. In this case, try a motherboard BIOS upgrade if one is available. If the problem continues, either the board is not in a bus mastering slot, or the PCI slot is not enabled for bus mastering. Configure the PCI slot for bus mastering through CMOS Setup or through a jumper on the motherboard (check your system's documentation to see exactly how).

SYMPTOM 39-13 During boot-up, you see a "Host Adapter Configuration Error" message In virtually all cases, there is a problem with the PCI slot configuration for the SCSI host adapter. Try enabling an IRQ for the SCSI adapter's PCI slot (usually accomplished through the CMOS Setup). Make sure that any IRQ being assigned to the SCSI adapter PCI slot is not conflicting with other devices in the system.

SYMPTOM 39-14 You see an error message such as "No SCSI Functions in Use" Even when a SCSI adapter and devices are installed and configured properly, there are several possible causes for this kind of an error. First, make sure that there are no hard disk drivers installed when there are no physical SCSI hard disks in the system. Also make sure that there are no hard disk drivers installed (in CONFIG.SYS) when the SCSI host adapter BIOS is enabled. HDD drivers aren't needed then, but you could leave the drivers in place and disable the SCSI BIOS. Finally, this error can occur if the HDD was formatted on another SCSI controller that does not support ASPI or uses a specialized format. For example, Western Digital controllers only work with Western Digital HDDs. In such cases, you should try a more generic controller.

SYMPTOM 39-15 You see an error message such as "No Boot Record Found" This is generally a simple problem that can be traced to several possible causes. First, chances are that the drive has never been partitioned (FDISK) or formatted as a bootable drive (FORMAT). Repartition and reformat the hard drive. If you partitioned and formatted the drive with a third-party utility (for instance, TFORMAT), be sure to answer "Y" if asked to make the disk bootable. A third possibility can occur if the disk was formatted on another manufacturer's controller. If this is the case, there may be little alternative but to repartition and reformat the drive again on your current controller.

SYMPTOM 39-16 You see an error such as "Device fails to respond—No devices in use. Driver load aborted" In most cases, the problem is something simple, such as the SCSI device not being turned on or cabled correctly. Verify that the SCSI devices are on and connected correctly. In other cases, the SCSI device is on, but fails the INQUIRY command—this happens when the SCSI device is defective or not supported by the host adapter. The device may need default jumper settings changed (the drive should Spin up and Come Ready on its own). You may find that the SCSI device is sharing the same SCSI ID with another device. Check all SCSI devices to verify that each device has a separate SCSI ID. You may have the wrong device driver loaded for your particular device type. Check CONFIG.SYS to make sure the correct driver is loaded for the drive type (that is, TSCSI.SYS for a hard disk, not a CD-ROM).

SYMPTOM 39-17 You see an error such as "Unknown SCSI Device" or "Waiting for SCSI Device" The SCSI hard disk has failed to boot as the primary drive—check that the primary hard disk is set at SCSI ID 0. Make sure that the drive is partitioned and formatted as the primary drive. If necessary, boot from a floppy with just the ASPI manager loaded in CONFIG.SYS and no other drivers, *then* format drive. It may also be that the SCSI cable termination is not correct (or TERMPWR is not provided by the HARD DISK for the host adapter). Verify the cable terminations and TERMPWR signal.

SYMPTOM 39-18 **You see an error such as "CMD Failure XX"** This typically occurs during the FORMAT process—the "XX" is a vendor-specific code (and you'll need to contact the vendor to determine what the error means). The most *common* problem is trying to partition a drive that is *not* low-level formatted. If this is the case, run the low-level format utility that accompanied the SCSI drive, then try partitioning again. If you're experiencing a different error, you may need to take other action.

SYMPTOM 39-19 **After the SCSI adapter BIOS header appears, you see a message like "Checking for SCSI target 0 LUN 0"** The system pauses about 30 seconds, then reports "BIOS not installed, no INT 13h device found"; the system then boots normally. In most cases, the BIOS is trying to find a hard drive at SCSI ID 0 or 1, but there is no hard drive available. If you do not have a SCSI hard drive attached to the host adapter, then it is recommended that the SCSI BIOS be disabled.

SYMPTOM 39-20 **The system hangs up when the SCSI BIOS header appears** This is usually caused by a terminator problem. Make sure that the SCSI devices at the end of the SCSI chain (either internally or externally) are terminated. Check all device IDs to make sure that they are unique and also check for system resource conflicts (such as BIOS address, I/O address, and interrupts). You may also need to disable the Shadow RAM feature in the CMOS Setup.

SYMPTOM 39-21 **The SCSI BIOS header is displayed during system startup, then you get the message "Host Adapter Diagnostic Error"** The card either has a port address conflict with another card, or the card has been changed to port address 140h and the BIOS is enabled. Some SCSI host adapters are able to use the BIOS under port address 140h, so check for I/O conflicts. You may need to reconfigure the SCSI host adapter.

SYMPTOM 39-22 **When a VL bus SCSI adapter is installed, the system hangs at startup** Chances are that the VL SCSI adapter is a bus mastering device and requires that the VL slot support full 32-bit bus mastering. Most VL bus systems have "slave" slots and/or "master" slots. The SCSI adapter must be inserted into a "master" slot. If you are not sure if the system supports bus mastering or if you have a master slot, contact the system manufacturer.

Also, the slot that the SCSI VL card is inserted into must be a 5 Vdc slot that operates at 33MHz or less. The VL bus speed is typically set through a jumper on the motherboard. It should be set in the <=33MHz position. The motherboard may also need to be set for write-through caching. This setting may be made in the motherboard's CMOS setup utility, or it may be configured via a jumper on the motherboard (if there is both a CMOS setting and a jumper, be sure they are both set the same way).

SYMPTOM 39-23 **When upgrading a VL bus system CPU to a faster model, the system locks up with a SCSI VL card installed, or won't boot from the SCSI HDD** Most likely there is a DMA or other timing discrepancy between the SCSI adapter and the VL local bus. The SCSI adapter probably works fine on VL bus systems running up to 33MHz. Faster CPUs can increase the VL bus speed beyond 33MHz. Above this 33MHz speed, variations in motherboard, chipset, or CPU design may cause the SCSI adapter to function intermittently or to fail. In some cases this problem can be resolved:

- The motherboard may have jumpers that govern the VL bus speed—be sure that the VL bus speed jumper is set in the <=33 MHz position. This setting may also be made in the motherboard's CMOS setup.

- In the CMOS setup, you can disable the CPU external cache or change the caching method to write-through instead of write-back.
- The internal cache on some CPUs may cause the VL SCSI adapter to hang as well. Try disabling the CPU's internal cache.
- Reducing the CPU speed may be necessary to allow the SCSI adapter to function reliably.
- Try disabling the system's "turbo setting" during the boot-up sequence, then re-enable the turbo setting after the system has booted.

SYMPTOM 39-24 **The VL SCSI adapter won't work with an "SLC" type CPU** VL SCSI adapters often refuse to run with "SLC" type CPUs because the SLC uses 16-bit architecture rather than 32-bit at the VL bus. Some VL SCSI adapters *will* run in this configuration, but this is rarely the case. Use an ISA SCSI adapter instead of an VL adapter in this circumstance.

SYMPTOM 39-25 **When running the Qualitas 386MAX memory manager software on ISA or VL systems with an SCSI host adapter, the system crashes when booting** 386MAX is known to cause problems with SCSI systems, and you'll need to adjust the 386MAX command line. Do not allow 386MAX to load during boot up, then include the key NOIOWRAP on the 386MAX command line. Doing this will allow you to boot with 386MAX loaded.

SYMPTOM 39-26 **When installing an EISA SCSI adapter and running the EISA configuration utility, you see an "EISA configuration slot mismatch" or "board not found in slot x" error** This error is caused by your board not being completely seated in the EISA slot. You can verify this by booting to a floppy diskette and running the DOS Debug command. After typing **Debug**, you will receive the debug prompt (a dash). Then type **i** (space) **Xc80**, where "X" is the EISA slot where your board is physically installed. If "04" is returned, the board is correctly seated and the problem lies elsewhere. If "FF" is returned, the board needs to be pushed down further. Power down your system before re-seating your board.

SYMPTOM 39-27 **You can't configure an EISA SCSI adapter in enhanced mode** You get the error "Unable to initialize Host Adapter" or the system hangs after the SCSI BIOS scans the SCSI devices. These errors are usually limited to motherboards that do *not* support LEVEL INT triggering. These chipsets (such as the Hint and SIS) require that a few modifications be made to the host adapter's EISA configuration (.CFG) file. Make the following changes to the !ADP000X.CFG file:

```
CHOICE = "Enhanced Mode"
FREE
INT=IOPORT(1) LOC (7 6 2 1 0) 10000B
LINK
IRQ=11|12|10|15|14|9
SHARE = "AHA-1740"       (Change to: SHARE = NO)
TRIGGER = LEVEL          (Change to: TRIGGER = EDGE)
INIT=IOPORT(3) LOC(4 3 2 1 0) 10010B | 10011B | 10001B | 1010B | 10101B | 10000B
(Change first zero in each binary number to a one; Example: 10010B = 11010B)
```

Another option is to download the latest .CFG file for your SCSI adapter card (ASWC174.EXE). Reconfigure the card with the new .CFG file and select edge triggered IRQ.

SYMPTOM 39-28 **Adaptec EasySCSI software causes an invalid page fault error under Windows 95/98** When you reinstall the Adaptec EZ-SCSI version 4.0x software, you may receive the following error message:

```
ADPST32 caused an invalid page fault in module MSCUISTF.dll at 015f:007d1bf7.
```

After you receive this error message, the computer may hang up. This problem can be caused when an Adaptec 3940UW Dual Channel SCSI adapter is installed on your computer, when you previously set the Write and Read Cache settings to Enable in SCSI Explorer (included with EZ-SCSI 4.0x), or when you uninstalled the EZ-SCSI software and then restarted the computer before attempting to reinstall the EZ-SCSI software. You should restore the firmware defaults for the SCSI BIOS:

1. Reboot the computer. When you see the SCSI BIOS banner, press CTRL+A to start the SCSI BIOS Setup program.
2. In the SCSI BIOS Setup program, press the F6 (or other appropriate) key to restore the factory default settings. You must do this for both channels if you're using a dual channel SCSI host adapter.
3. Turn your computer off and back on.
4. Uninstall and then reinstall the EZ-SCSI software.

SYMPTOM 39-29 **You encounter problems with a BusLogic PCI SCSI controller** If your computer includes a PCI BusLogic SCSI controller, the Windows 95/98 Device Manager displays an exclamation point in a yellow circle next to the "PCI BusLogic SCSI controller," or the system performance is not a good as you expect with the PCI BusLogic SCSI controller. This fault can occur if the BusLogic card is not configured as a "true" PCI device.

To configure the BusLogic card as a "true" PCI device, remove the jumpers in the bottom-right corner of the card. If you remove the jumpers, the card can be enumerated. If you leave the jumpers on the card, the card is detected as a "legacy" device and is *not* enumerated by the PnP system. Also, if you leave the jumpers on, the I/O range is set to a standard address (such as 330h, 334h, 130h, or 134h) instead of a high PCI address. As a rule, if the version number in the top-right corner of the BusLogic card is -01-4.23K or later, the card is supported in true PCI mode and you should remove the jumpers. If the version is earlier than -01-4.23K, leave the jumpers on the card.

SYMPTOM 39-30 **You encounter problems with an Adaptec SCSI controller and CD-RW drive** Your computer may hang up when you start your Windows 98 computer, or your computer may run slowly when you try to access drives in your computer. This problem can occur if you're using an Adaptec AHA-2940U2W SCSI host adapter with a SCSI CD-RW drive. The AIC78U2.MPD driver file included with the Adaptec AHA-2940U2W SCSI adapter is *not* completely compatible with Windows 98. To correct this problem, download the 7800W9X.EXE file from Adaptec's Web site. This self-extracting file contains updated drivers for the Adaptec AHA-2940U2W SCSI adapter.

SYMPTOM 39-31 **Windows 98 cannot locate the SCSI CD-ROM after upgrading** When Windows 98 Setup restarts your computer for the first time, Setup may be unable to access your SCSI CD-ROM drive, and you may receive error messages stating that files cannot be found (the file names vary depending on your computer's hardware). Once Setup is completed and you attempt to start Windows 98, your computer may hang up, and only a blinking cursor may be displayed on a black screen. In virtually every case, this problem will occur if the HIDE120.COM file (a file related to an LS120 drive) is being loaded from the Autoexec.bat file. Open your AUTOEXEC.BAT file and disable (that is, REM-out) the HIDE120 command line, such as:

```
d:\ls1120\hide120.com
```

Further Study

Adaptec: **http://www.adaptec.com**

AMI: **http://www.megatrends.com**

Ancot: **http://www.ancot.com/**

Fibre Channel Association: **http://www.Amdahl.com/ext/CARP/FCA/FCA.html**

Quantum: **http://www.quantum.com/src/**

SCSI FAQ at **http://www.cis.ohio-state.edu/hypertext/faq/usenet/scsi-faq/top.html**

SCSI guide: **http://www.delec.com/guide/scsi/**

SCSI Trade Association: **http://www.scsita.org/**

SCSI-2 spec: **http://abekas.com:8080/SCSI2/**

Symbios articles: **http://www.lsilogic.com/**

Symbios specs: **http://www.symbios.com/x3t10**

Western Digital: **http://www.wdc.com**

40

SERIAL AND INFRARED PORT TROUBLESHOOTING

CHAPTER AT A GLANCE

Every PC needs a means of communicating with external devices. While today's computers make use of USB and IEEE 1394 (a.k.a. Fire-Wire) connections, early PCs relied solely on serial and parallel ports for their device communication. The parallel port was generally considered to be a "printer port," so another port was needed to communicate with simple low-bandwidth devices like modems and mice. The Electronics Industry Association (or EIA) responded to this early need by developing a standard for *serial* communication. Instead of sending 8 bits at a time over a set of data lines (as a parallel port does), only two data lines were used—one to transmit data, and one to receive data. The EIA denoted its serial standard as *RS-232* (or simply the "serial port"). A serial port offers several distinct advantages over early parallel ports. First, the serial port was designed to be bidirectional right from the start. This made "serial" the preferred method for interactive devices such as modems, mice, tablets, and so on. Second, the serial port used fewer physical signal lines than the parallel port. This made cabling less expensive and reduced potential connector problems. Where a printer cable is generally limited to 2 meters, a serial cable can easily exceed 60 meters, which opened the way for basic local networking.

The one problem with serial communication has traditionally been the need to physically connect devices. This often required you to shut down the system, make physical connections, install drivers, and make other changes to the system before the two devices would communicate. With the advent of Windows 95/98, designers have introduced a means of infrared serial communication (based on the same technology used for TV remote controls) that avoids troublesome connection and configuration problems. By employing infrared serial ports adhering to Infrared Device Association (or IrDA) standards, you can conveniently print or exchange files with other IrDA-compliant systems. This chapter shows you the essential concepts of serial communication and port operation, explains the setup and workings of IrDA devices, and then guides you through a series of troubleshooting procedures.

Understanding Asynchronous Communication

The serial port is not terribly difficult to grasp, but its operation is a bit more involved than that of a parallel port. In order to appreciate the operations and signals of a typical serial port, there are a variety of concepts that you should be familiar with. When a parallel port strobes a printer, the printer "knows" that all 8 bits of data are available and valid. However, a serial port must send or receive 8 data bits—one at a time—over a single data line. As you might imagine, this presents some serious challenges for the receiving device, which must determine where the data stream starts and ends—hardly a simple task. It is certainly possible to send a synchronizing clock signal along with the data wire. The receiving device could easily use the clock to detect each data bit. This technique is known as *synchronous* serial communication. It is reliable, but rarely used in PCs (other than the keyboard interface).

Instead of using a discrete clock signal to accompany the data, it is possible to eliminate the clock by embedding synchronization information along with the data bits. Thus, when a data stream reaches a receiving device, it can strip away the synchronization bits, leaving the original data. As a result, serial communication is not constrained by a clock. This is *asynchronous* communication—a popular and inexpensive serial technique. The remainder of this chapter deals with asynchronous communication.

THE DATA FRAME

Asynchronous communication requires that data bits be combined with *synchronization bits* before transmission. Synchronization bits provide three important pieces of information to the receiving device: where the data starts, where the data ends, and if the data is correct. These bits, combined with the data byte, form the *data frame*, as illustrated in Figure 40-1. The first thing you should notice about serial data is that it is bipolar—that is, there are both positive and negative voltages. Contrary to what you might guess, a + voltage represents a logical 0 (called a *space*), and a -voltage represents a logical 1 (called a *mark*). The next thing you should note is that the serial signal line is normally idle in the logic 0 (space) state.

The first element of all asynchronous data frames is a single *start bit*, which is always a logic 1 (mark). When the receiver detects a logic 1, it "knows" the data frame has started. The next 5 to 8 bits are always

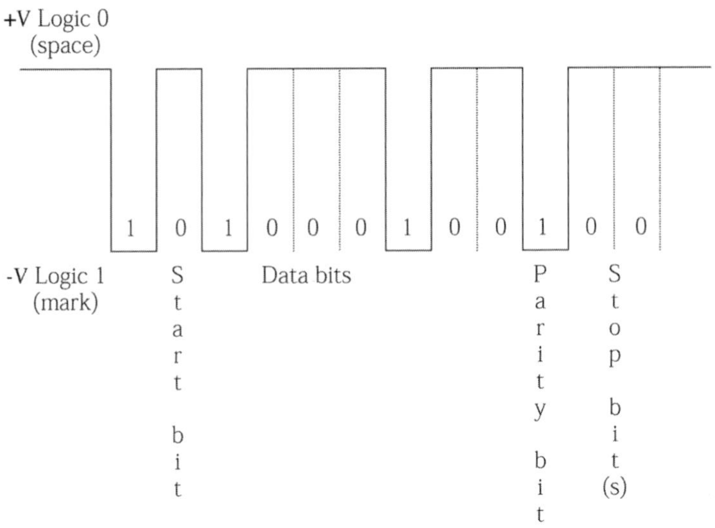

FIGURE 40-1 A typical data frame

the *data bits*. The exact number of bits (usually 8) can be set by the communication software, but must be the same at both the transmitting and receiving ends. After data, a single error-checking bit (called a *parity bit*) can be included if desired. Parity is calculated at the sending device and sent with the word. Parity is also calculated at the receiving device and checked against the received parity bit. If the two match, the data is assumed to be correct. If the two do not match, an error is flagged. There are five classes of parity in serial communication:

- None—no parity bit is added to the word. This is typical for much of today's serial communication.
- Even—if the number of 1's in the data word is odd, parity is set to 1 to make the number of 1's even.
- Odd—if the number of 1's in the data word is even, parity is set to 1 to make the number of 1's odd.
- Mark—parity is always set to 1.
- Space—parity is always set to 0.

Many communication connections today abandon the use of parity in favor of the more reliable and sophisticated cyclical redundancy check (CRC). A CRC has the same effect as a parity check, but instead of checking one byte at a time, an entire block of data is checked.

The last part of a data frame is the *stop bit(s)*—typically only one, but two can be used. Stop bits are always logic 0 (space). After the receiving device detects the stop bit(s), the line remains idle in the space condition awaiting the next subsequent start bit. Framing is usually denoted as data/parity/stop. For example, the connection to a BBS typically uses 8/N/1 framing (8 data bits/no parity bit/1 stop bit).

One of the most important aspects of serial communication is that both the receiving and transmitting ends must be configured for the same data frame. If both ends are not configured identically, serial data will be misinterpreted as meaningless garbage.

SIGNAL LEVELS

Where the parallel port uses TTL-compatible logic signals in its communication, a serial port uses bi-polar signaling (both positive and negative voltages). The advantage of bipolar signaling is that it supports very long cabling with minimum noise. A logic 0 (space) condition is represented by a positive voltage between +3 Vdc and +15 Vdc. A logic 1 (mark) condition is represented by a negative voltage between -3 Vdc and -15 Vdc. On the average, you can expect to see serial ports using +/-5 Vdc or +/-12 Vdc since those voltages are already produced by the PC power supply.

BAUD VS. BPS

Another key concept of asynchronous communication is the idea of *rate*. Since data is traveling across a serial link versus time, the rate at which that data passes becomes an important variable. Although rate is not a literal part of the data frame, it is every bit as important. Simply stated, serial data rates are measured in *bits per second* (or bps). This is a simple and intuitive measurement. If the serial port is delivering 2400 bits in one second, it is working at 2400bps. At that rate, the average bit is (1/2400bps) 417µs. When you're dealing with a serial port, you're dealing with bits and bps.

Traditionally, when the bits from a serial port are processed through a modem, a modem will modulate the data through a series of phase, frequency, or amplitude transitions. A *transition* is referred to as a *baud* (named for French mathematician J. M. E. Baudot). Older modems designed to operate with signal rates of 2400bps or less could modulate the telephone line *at* the bit rate—thus baud would be the same as bps. However, this is a faulty comparison. Since later modems were restricted by the limited bandwidth of a telephone line, modems had to encode more than one bit in every transition. As a result, the effective bps of a modern modem usually exceeds its baud rate by several times. For example, a modem that can encode 4 bits in every transition can work at 2400 baud—yet be sending the equivalent of 9600bps. See the difference? As modems evolved to encompass data compression standards, effective bps has been increased even more (yet the modem still only works at a relatively low baud rate). When you're dealing with modems, you are usually talking about baud rates.

There's another catch you need to be aware of. Since baud refers to any transition (Baudot never said a word about modems), it is *technically* valid to measure a serial port speed in baud, although it can be terribly confusing. For example, today's serial port circuits can sustain data rates of 115200bps. Now, since every bit from the serial port is treated as a "transition" by local devices such as printers, it becomes just as correct to say 115200 baud. The thing to remember here is that most modems don't operate over 2400 baud (though advanced modem modulation techniques can transfer 56Kbps). The telephone line just cannot handle faster signal transition rates. So if you see high baud rates quoted in books or specifications, it probably refers to the performance of the serial port, not the modem.

Understanding the Serial Port

A serial port must be capable of several important operations. It must convert parallel data from the PC system bus into a sequence of serial bits, add the appropriate framing bits (which may be changed for different serial connections), then provide each of those bits to the data line at the proper rate. The serial port must also work in reverse, accepting serial data at a known rate, stripping off the framing bits, converting the serial data bits back into bus form, and checking blocks of data for accuracy. The heart of the serial port is a single chip—the *universal asynchronous receiver/transmitter* (UART). A simplified block diagram for a serial port is illustrated in Figure 40-2.

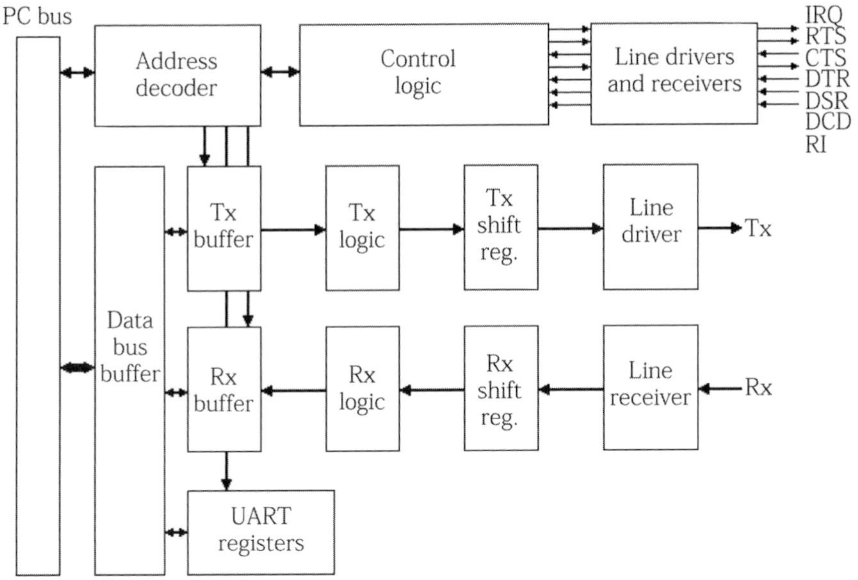

FIGURE 40-2 Block diagram of a UART

The UART connects directly to the PC bus architecture—either added to the motherboard, or incorporated on an expansion board. A UART chip contains all of the internal circuitry necessary to process, transmit, and receive data between the serial line and the PC bus. Since the UART is programmable, its configuration (its framing format and baud rate) can be set through DOS or Windows communication software. All data output, data input, and handshaking signals needed by the serial port are generated within the UART itself. It is interesting to note that the UART is powered by +5 Vdc only—just like any other ASIC in the system. This means data and handshaking signals entering and leaving the UART are all TTL compatible. Transmitted data is converted to bipolar signals through a line driver IC. Bipolar data that appears on the receive line is converted back to TTL levels through a line receiver IC. All that remains is the port connector itself. The original serial port design used a 25-pin male subminiature D-type connector, but newer ports have abandoned the extra handshaking signals to accommodate a 9-pin male subminiature D-type connector.

ADDRESSES AND INTERRUPTS

The UART is controlled through a series of important registers that allow the serial port characteristics to be programmed. They also shuttle the transmitted and received data as required. Older BIOS versions supported only two serial (or COM) ports, but newer BIOS releases support four COM ports (designated COM1, COM2, COM3, and COM4). MicroChannel (MCA) bus systems can support up to eight COM ports (COM1 through COM8). The typical base addresses for the COM ports are shown in Table 40-1. When a new COM port is installed in the system, it must be assigned to a valid base address and interrupt (IRQ). During actual operation, communication software deals with each port register individually. Table 40-2 lists the standard base address offsets for UART registers. Note that with no offset, both transmit and receive registers are available.

TABLE 40-1 TYPICAL SERIAL PORT ADDRESSES AND IRQ ASSIGNMENTS

BUS ARCHITECTURE	PORT	ADDRESS	IRQ
All Systems	COM1	03F8h	IRQ4
All Systems	COM2	02F8h	IRQ3
ISA*	COM3	03E8h	IRQ4
ISA	COM4	02E8h	IRQ3
ISA	COM3	03E0h	IRQ4
ISA	COM4	02E0h	IRQ3
ISA	COM3	0338h	IRQ4
ISA	COM4	0238h	IRQ3
MCA	COM3	3220h	IRQ3
MCA	COM4	3228h	IRQ3
MCA	COM5	4220h	IRQ3
MCA	COM6	4228h	IRQ3
MCA	COM7	5220h	IRQ3
MCA	COM8	5228h	IRQ3

* Systems with DOS 3.3 and later

During system initialization, COM ports are checked in the following order: 03F8h, 02F8h, 03E8h, 02E8h, 03E0h, 02E0h, 0338h, and 0238h. (MCA systems use a different order.) COM designations are assigned depending on what ports are actually found, so keep in mind that the COM addresses may be exchanged depending on your particular system. In virtually all cases, COM1 is available at 03F8h. The specific I/O addresses for each COM port are kept in the BIOS data area of RAM starting at 0400h. As you might expect, only one COM port can be assigned to a base address. If more than one COM port is assigned to the same base address, system problems will almost certainly occur.

The use of interrupts in conjunction with COM ports can easily be confusing. Unlike parallel ports, which can be polled by BIOS, a serial port *demands* the use of interrupts. Since early PCs allocated space for two COM ports, only two IRQ lines were reserved (IRQ4 for COM1 and IRQ3 for COM2). Unfortu-

TABLE 40-2 TYPICAL UART REGISTER ADDRESS OFFSETS

REGISTER	OFFSET
Receive Register	00h
Transmit Register	00h
Interrupt Enable Register	01h
Interrupt ID Register	02h
Data Frame Register	03h
UART Control Register	04h
Serialization Status Register	05h
UART Status Register	06h
General-Purpose Register	07h

nately, when PC BIOS expanded its support for additional COM ports, there were no extra IRQ lines available to assign. Thus, COM ports had to "share" interrupts. For example, COM1 and COM3 must share IRQ4, while COM2 and COM4 must share IRQ3. The problem is that no two devices can use the same IRQ at the same time—otherwise a system conflict will result. Ultimately, though a typical PC can use four COM ports, only *two* of the four can be used at any one time (for example, COM1 and COM2, COM3 and COM4, COM1 and COM4, or COM2 and COM3). Further, the assignment of COM port address and IRQ lines must match. While COM3 and COM4 *can* be polled by BIOS, the speed and asynchronous nature of contemporary data transmission make polling very unreliable for serial ports.

Always begin a service examination by checking the number of serial ports in your system. Serial ports are so simple and easy to add to various expansion cards that you might exceed the maximum number of ports, or allow two ports to conflict, without even realizing it. Be sure to remove or disable any unused or conflicting COM ports by removing the offending port, or disabling it through jumpers or DIP switches. A common oversight is to add an internal modem as COM2 while hardware support for COM2 is still enabled on the motherboard. When you encounter conflicting COM ports, you will need to disable unneeded ports to prevent conflicts.

DTE VS. DCE

As you work with serial ports and peripherals, you will see the acronyms DTE and DCE used frequently. DTE stands for *data terminal equipment*, which is typically the computer containing the serial port. The modem, serial printer, or other serial peripheral is referred to as the *data carrier equipment* (or DCE). The distinction becomes important because the data and handshaking signals are swapped at the DCE end. For example, the Tx pin ("transmit"—usually on pin 3 of a 9-pin DTE) cannot connect directly to the same pin on the DCE; it must route to the Rx ("receive") pin instead. The DCE connector makes those swaps, so pin 3 of the DCE would be the Rx pin, and a straight-through cable can be used without difficulty.

However, suppose that two DTEs had to be connected. Since both devices carry the same signals on the same pins, a straight-through cable would cause confusion (the Tx line would connect to the Tx line on the other device, Rx would connect to Rx, etc.). As you can imagine, two DTEs cannot be connected with a straight-through cable. Of course, a specialized cable can be built that contains the proper wire swaps, but an easier alternative is simply to use a *null-modem*, which plugs into one end of the straight-through cable. The null-modem is little more than a jumper box that contains all of the proper swaps. This allows two DTEs to work as if one were a DTE and one were a DCE.

40

Serial Port Signals

IBM and compatible PCs implement a serial port as either a 25-pin or 9-pin subminiature D-type connector similar to the ones shown in Figure 40-3. Both ends of the serial cable are identical. There are three type of signals to be concerned with in a serial connection: data lines, control (or handshaking) lines, and ground lines. Table 40-3 identifies the name and description of each conductor for both 25-pin and 9-pin serial connections. Keep in mind that all data and control signals on the serial port are bipolar.

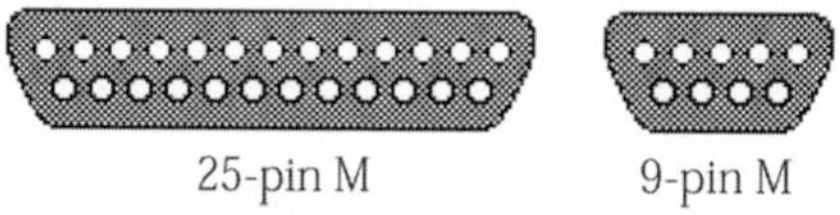

FIGURE 40-3 Serial port connectors

TABLE 40-3 SERIAL PORT CONNECTOR PINOUTS (AT THE PC END)

25-PIN CONNECTOR	9-PIN CONNECTOR	SIGNAL NAME	SIGNAL DIRECTION
1	n/a	Protective Ground	n/a
2	3	Tx—Transmit Data	Output
3	2	Rx—Receive Data	Input
4	7	RTS—Request to Send	Output
5	8	CTS—Clear to Send	Input
6	6	DSR—Data Set Ready	Input
7	5	Signal Ground	n/a
8	1	DCD—Data Carrier Detect	Input
9	n/a	+ Transmit Current Loop	Output
11	n/a	- Transmit Current Loop	Output
18	n/a	+ Receive Current Loop	Input
20	4	DTR—Data Terminal Ready	Output
22	9	RI—Ring Indicator	Input
23	n/a	DSRD—Data Signal Rate Indicator	I/O
25	n/a	- Receive Current Loop	Input

TX AND RX

Tx and Rx are simply the data lines into and out of the port. Tx is the transmit line, which outputs serial data from the PC, and Rx is the receive line, which accepts serial data from the serial peripheral.

RTS AND CTS

The RTS (Request to Send) signal is generated by the DTE. When asserted, it tells the DCE (such as the modem) to expect to receive data. However, the DTE can't just dump data to the DCE. The DCE must be ready to receive the data; so after the RTS line is asserted, the DTE waits for the CTS (Clear to Send) signal back from the DCE. Once the DTE receives a valid CTS signal, it can begin transferring data. It is this RTS/CTS handshake that forms the basis for data flow control via the system hardware.

DTR AND DSR

When the DTE is turned on or initialized and ready to begin serial operation, the DTR (Data Terminal Ready) line is asserted. This tells the DCE (such as the modem) that the DTE (such as the computer) is ready to establish a connection. When the DCE has initialized and is ready for a connection, it will assert the DSR (Data Set Ready) line back to the DTE. Once the DTE is ready and recognizes the DSR signal, a connection is established. This DTR/DSR handshake is established only once when the DTE and DCE devices are first initialized, and must remain active throughout the connection. If either the DTR or DSR signal should fail, the communication channel will be interrupted (and the RTS/CTS handshake will no longer have any effect).

DCD

The DCD (Data Carrier Detect) signal is particularly useful with modems. It is produced by the DCE when a carrier is detected from a remote target and the DCE is ready to establish a communications pathway. The DCD signal is then sent back to the DTE. Once the DCD line is asserted, it will remain as long as a connection is established.

RI

The RI (Ring Indicator) signal is asserted by the DCE and is also particularly useful with modems. It is produced by the DCE when a telephone ring is detected. This becomes a vital signal if it is necessary for a remote user to call in and access your computer for remote diagnostics or other purposes. This is also an important signal when the system's power management is configured to "wake on ring."

IrDA Port Issues

A growing number of desktop and laptop PCs (and their peripherals) are being equipped with infrared serial ports (dubbed "IrDA" by the Infrared Desktop Association). IrDA ports allow PCs and peripherals to communicate serially over an infrared link rather than going through the hassle of using cables. For example, you can type a document on a laptop, then move the laptop into the vicinity of an IrDA printer, and print the document without ever attaching a cable. You can also share files between two IrDA-compliant PCs. Although IrDA ports offer some real connectivity benefits to PC users, they also present some problems with installation and configuration. This part of the chapter outlines the essential techniques to install and use IrDA devices, and offers some solid guidelines for testing and troubleshooting.

INSTALLING THE IRDA DRIVER(S)

The Infrared Communications Driver supports hardware devices that enable networking and communications over infrared media up to 115.2Kbps. The "hardware device" can be an infrared port built into the PC or an infrared adapter connected to one of the PC's serial or parallel ports. IrDA lets you use wireless infrared links instead of serial and parallel cables. For example, you can exchange files between two computers that are equipped with an infrared device and Infrared Communications Driver 2.0 (or later), or you can print to IrDA-capable printers without the need for cable. You can also access your local area network (LAN) using IrLAN. IrLAN currently supports Access Point Mode, which enables a computer with an IrDA adapter to attach to a local area network through an "access point device" that acts as the network adapter for the computer. An "access point device" is hardware supporting both a LAN network interface controller (NIC) and an infrared (IrDA) transceiver.

If you already have a PC fitted with IrDA support, you simply need to use the Add New Hardware wizard to install a new set of drivers, or use the Add Infrared Device wizard from the IR icon in the Control Panel. If you'll be installing IrDA support for the first time, download the newest IR drivers from the Microsoft Web site (**www.microsoft.com**), and run SETUP.EXE:

1. When the Add Infrared Device wizard prompts to choose a manufacturer's name for the IR device, choose "Standard Infrared Devices" if the computer has a built-in device, or choose the name of the manufacturer and the model of the adapter if an IR adapter is attached to the computer. Click the Next button.
2. When the Add Infrared Device wizard prompts to choose the communications port that the IR device is physically connected to, click the port from the list. If you're uncertain which physical communications port the IR device is using, select the first COM port in the list (for example, COM1); then click the Next button.

3. When the Add Infrared Device wizard prompts to select the virtual COM and LPT ports, accept the default values by clicking the Next button. After the wizard copies the IR communications driver files to the hard disk, watch for the wizard to display two "New Hardware Found" messages.
4. When prompted by the Add Infrared Device wizard, click the Finish button to complete the IR device installation. (If the wizard did not display "New Hardware Found" messages, restart the computer.)
5. Activate the IR device by double-clicking the Infrared icon in the Control Panel. If there is no Infrared icon in the Control Panel, select the Refresh option from the Control Panel View menu (or press F5) to make the Infrared icon appear.

TESTING AN IRDA LINK

The next step is to test the IR device. The easiest and quickest way to do this is to print over an IrDA link to an IR-capable printer, or exchange data between two computers using the IR link (and a communications application like LapLink).

> You must always remove any previously installed version of the IrDA communications driver before installing a new driver. For example, if an early beta release of the version 2.0 driver is installed, it must be removed before installing the current version 2.0 release.

Testing an IR Link to a Printer

If you're testing an IR link to an IrDA-compliant printer (such as the HP 5P), you must first install the IR communications driver on your computer, then try the Print option in your printing application. Make sure that you have the correct printer driver installed for your IR-capable printer, and see that you've selected the infrared printing port (the "virtual LPT port") as the printer port. If the application prints correctly to your IR-capable printer, you have validated the link successfully.

Testing an IR Link Between Computers

To test a link between two computers, you must install the IR communications driver on both computers. One way to test an IR link is to use HyperTerminal on both computers, and send characters from the keyboard of each computer over the IR link:

1. On both computers, click Start, highlight Settings, and then click Control Panel.
2. Double-click the Infrared icon.
3. Move the IR devices within three feet of each other, and make sure they're pointing at each other.
4. When the two IR devices discover each other, the message "Available infrared devices in range" will appear on the Status tab of your Infrared Monitor interface.
5. Make sure Infrared Monitor reports that both IR devices have the appropriate infrared device within range before you proceed. You might have to realign the IR devices so they point right at each other, move them closer together, or change the batteries in an IR adapter (or connect AC power to an IR adapter).
6. On one of the computers, click the Options tab in the Infrared Monitor interface and locate the information that starts with "Providing application support on..." Write down the name of the COM port you find there. This is the name of the simulated serial port that the IR link is using. In practice, the name of this virtual serial port might be COM4 or COM5, and it will differ from the

name of the physical communications port that your IR device is running on (which is typically COM1 or COM2).

7. Run HyperTerminal by clicking the Start button, pointing to Programs, selecting Accessories, clicking HyperTerminal, and then double-clicking the HYPERTRM.EXE icon.
8. In the Connection Description dialog box, type a descriptive name (such as **Direct IR**) for the new connection, and then click OK.
9. In the Phone Number dialog box, use the Connect Using drop-down list to select the "Direct to Com*x*" entry (where *x* is the number of the virtual COM port that you wrote down before). Click OK, and you're ready to start using HyperTerminal on one of the computers.
10. Repeat the last four steps on the other computer so that both systems are running HyperTerminal on their correct virtual COM port.
11. Select HyperTerminal on either computer and type any characters at the keyboard. If the characters you type appear in the HyperTerminal window on the other computer, then you've confirmed that the IR link works in that direction. Try the other computer. If the IR link works in both directions using HyperTerminal, you've confirmed successful installation of the IR driver on the two computers.
12. Disconnect the HyperTerminal direct IR connection by exiting HyperTerminal on both computers. When you are prompted to save the session, click Yes. This saves the direct IR connection setup information as an icon in the HyperTerminal main folder. You can double-click this icon to restart one side of the HyperTerminal direct IR connection at any time in the future.

> The IR transceivers on the two computers do not have to be made by the same manufacturer, but both transceivers must be IrDA compliant. For example, you could have a JetEye PC Infrared PC interface (ESI-9680) attached to one desktop system, and an Adaptec AIRport (APA-9320) External Infrared Adapter attached to the other desktop, and the IR link should work.

> Most applications that can communicate over a null-modem cable connecting serial ports on two Windows 95/98 computers should also be able to communicate over an IR link.

RUNNING DCC OVER AN IRDA LINK

With a Direct Cable Connection (or DCC), you can establish a direct serial or parallel cable connection between two computers, and this allows you to share the resources of the computer designated as the host. DCC can also be used over an IR link. The computer that contains the information you want to share is the host, and the other computer is the guest. You can share folder(s) on the host and grant access rights to anyone using the guest computer by following the Windows 95 procedure below:

1. Double-click the My Computer icon.
2. Double-click the icon of the drive that contains the file(s) you want to share (for example, double-click on the icon for your C: drive).
3. Right-click on the icon of the folder you want to share, and then select Properties.
4. In the folder's Properties dialog, select the Sharing tab (Figure 40-4), and then select the Shared As option. Enter a "share name," enter a comment, and add user access rights (Full or Read-Only). The picture of a hand is added to the folder icon to indicate the selected folder is now a shared resource.

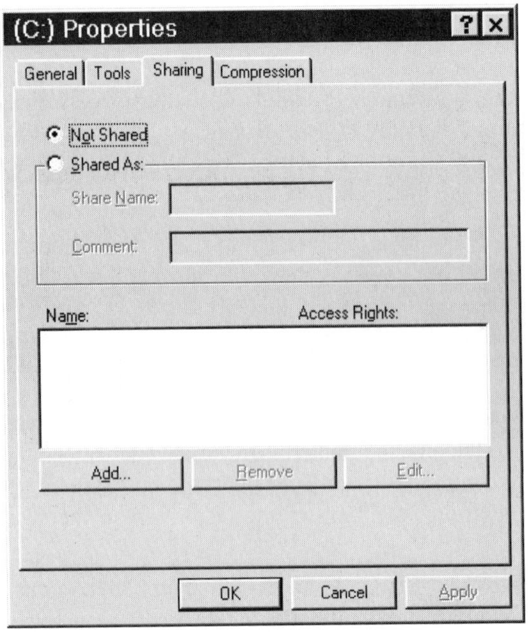

FIGURE 40-4 Sharing files through a drive Properties dialog

Check for the presence of DCC, and install it on both PCs if necessary:

1. Click Start, select Programs, and then point to Accessories. A "Direct Cable Connection" entry appears in this menu if it's installed on your computer. Under Windows 98, DCC is listed in the Communications submenu under Accessories. If DCC is installed, skip these steps. Otherwise, you'll need to install DCC. Be sure to check both computers, and install DCC on both systems if necessary.
2. Click Start, highlight Settings, and then click Control Panel.
3. Double-click the Add/Remove Programs icon.
4. In the Add/Remove Program Properties dialog, click the Windows Setup tab.
5. In the Components list, click Communications, and then click the Details button.
6. In the Communications dialog box, make sure Direct Cable Connection is checked, and then click OK. Windows will install the DCC components.

Now configure and test the DCC IR link between the two computers:

1. Make sure the IR communications driver is properly installed and the IR devices are enabled. Keep in mind that you might want to limit the IR connection speed to 9600bps for the first test of DCC over the IR link, then increase the speed later.
2. On the host computer, click Start, point to Accessories, and then click Direct Cable Connection. Under Windows 98, select the Communications submenu under Accessories, and then click Direct Cable Connection.

3 Follow the steps in the Direct Cable Connection wizard to set up the host computer. When the wizard prompts you, select the Host option. When the wizard prompts you to choose a port, use the same virtual port that you used in the "Testing an IR Link Between Computers" discussion above.

4 The wizard will also offer password protection. You do not need to establish password protection on the host for this test, but you may wish to use password protection for normal use of the IR link. When you're done with the wizard, click the Finish button. DCC will start running on the IR link and display the message "Waiting to connect via serial cable on Com*x*" (where *x* is the name of the virtual port that the IR link is using).

5 Repeat the four steps for the guest computer, but when the wizard prompts you, you must select the Guest option instead of the Host option. When you're done with the wizard, click the Finish button. The DCC connection is automatically made over the IR link, and all the shared folders on the host are displayed on the guest's screen.

6 To copy a shared folder from the host to the guest over the IR link, select the folder's icon in the window that displays all the shared folders that are on the host, and drag the icon to the desktop. To work on a shared folder on the host without copying it to the guest, just double-click on the folder in the display on the guest.

> If the host is connected to a network, the guest can reach shared resources on the network through a DCC connection to the host.

> If infrared communication is interrupted, it's usually because something has moved between the infrared devices, or one device has been moved out of range. Remove the obstruction, or move the device back into range. If there's no obstruction and the devices are in range, check to see if a non-infrared device is interfering with the infrared communication. If communication is restored *before* the Status properties countdown ends, no data will be lost.

REMOVING THE IRDA DRIVER(S)

There are some instances when it may be necessary to remove the IR communication drivers (most often when upgrading the drivers or IR adapter hardware). The IR communication drivers can be removed either by using Add/Remove Programs in the Control Panel or by using the Device Manager. To use Add/Remove Programs in the Control Panel:

1 Click the Start button and select the Settings option; then select Control Panel.

2 Double-click Add/Remove Programs in the Control Panel.

3 When a list of software components is displayed, select the "Infrared Support for Windows 95" entry and click the Add/Remove button.

4 Restart the system when prompted to do so.

To use the Device Manager:

1 Right-click on the My Computer icon, select the Properties option from the pop-up menu, and then click the Device Manager tab in the System Properties dialog.

2 To display the name of the infrared device installed on the computer, make sure the "View devices by type" option is selected in the System Properties dialog. Then click the plus sign to the left of the "Infrared device" class label. Select the infrared device name, and click the Remove button.

3 Click OK to confirm the device removal. After the Device Manager has successfully removed the infrared device installation from the computer, the "Infrared device" class label will disappear from the System Properties dialog. Click the Close button.

The Infrared Monitor icon may still be displayed in the Windows 95 status bar (even after the infrared device is removed). Ignore it—the Infrared Monitor cannot be used to establish an IR link after the infrared device is removed.

MAKING THE MOST OF IRDA

Infrared links are handy and efficient tools that allow you to print and exchange files without the hassle of physical connections between devices. Still, IR communication can be plagued by numerous factors, including data transfer efficiency, device range, and device detection. The tips below can help you deal with efficiency, range, and detection issues.

If you find that your IR communication is not efficient:

- Check for partial obstructions of infrared activity.
- Move the infrared devices closer together.
- Clean the infrared windows.
- Shade the devices, or turn off bright lights.
- Make sure the devices are not moving or vibrating.

If you find that IR devices frequently/intermittently go out of range:

- Check for partial obstructions of infrared activity.
- Move the infrared devices closer together.
- Clean the infrared windows.
- Shade the devices, or turn off bright lights.
- Make sure the devices are not moving or vibrating.
- Recharge/replace the batteries for the IR device, or check its power supply connections.

If you find that the system cannot detect devices that should be in range:

- Verify that the system's infrared support is turned on.
- Verify that the infrared "searching" option is turned on.
- Make sure that the IR search interval is not too high.
- Move the devices closer together.
- Verify that the device is fully IrDA compliant (there should be no non-IrDA devices).
- Double check that the IrDA device is turned on (and that its batteries are fully charged).
- Verify that the infrared device on your PC is turned on.
- Make sure nothing is blocking the infrared activity.
- Check that there is no dirt or grease on the infrared windows.
- Shield the IR windows so that direct sunlight is not shining on the infrared receiver.

IRDA TIPS

Although IR support is reasonably automatic under Windows 95/98, there are a number of tips that can make your troubleshooting much easier. Be sure to review the checklist below carefully before attempting to isolate IR problems on your system.

- Always remove the existing IR drivers before installing new IR drivers (or upgrading the IR adapter hardware). Preexisting drivers can sometimes interfere with new IR drivers.
- If you upgrade the IR adapter hardware on your system, you must remove the IR drivers and install new drivers.
- Be sure to select the proper "virtual COM port" for the IR adapter. If you select the wrong COM port during installation, the system will be unable to use the IR adapter.
- IR communication problems may require you to realign the IR devices so that they are closer together (usually three feet or less) and in a direct line of sight. You may need to try new batteries in the IR adapter.
- If an IR adapter is attached to a COM port that is using an older 8250 UART instead of a 16550A UART (or if an IR adapter is connected to a relatively slow computer such as a 386 running at 20MHz), you might need to use the "Limit Connection Speed To..." option in the Infrared Monitor Options tab to limit the connection speed to 19.2Kbps. After establishing a successful IR connection at this speed, you can use the "Limit Connection Speed To..." option to experiment with higher speed connections.
- Communication over a virtual COM port link between two computers may not be reliable if a printer's IR adapter is also within range. Be sure to move the printer's IR adapter (or any other nonessential IR adapter) out of range.
- Do not suspend a Windows 95/98 computer while an IR connection is established. Wait until the IR link is disconnected (or force a disconnection) before putting the computer in suspend mode. For example, if an IrLAN connection is established on a laptop, you must always move the laptop out of range of the IrLAN "access point" before suspending the system (or closing the laptop lid). Otherwise, the connection remains active and can drain the battery over time.
- Connecting and disconnecting over a low-speed IR link (or over a poor-quality link) can take a few seconds, during which time the screen will appear to be frozen. To work around this, you should use a higher-speed connection and take steps to improve the quality of the connection.
- If you use the Windows 95 version of HyperTerminal to transfer files, you will not be able to transfer files successfully over an IR link using the Zmodem protocol as it's implemented by HyperTerminal.
- When you run the Windows 95 version of Direct Cable Connection (DCC) and establish the connection between the host and guest computers, the guest computer may display the message: "Direct Cable Connection was unable to display shared folders of the host computer" and prompt you to enter the host computer's name. A simple place to find the host computer's name is on the Status tab of the Infrared Monitor dialog.
- For IR adapters that can be powered by either the serial port, AA batteries, or an external power supply, the serial port may not provide sufficient power for the adapter in some cases. This can cause reduced operating range and/or a failure to find another IR device that is nearby and aligned correctly. If you suspect such a problem, connect an AC adapter or add fresh batteries to the battery compartment in the infrared adapter.

- If you have an ACTiSYS 220L IR adapter attached to your computer, and print to a printer that is using an Extended Systems ESI-9580 printer IR adapter (or you're printing to the HP DeskJet 340), you must use the Options tab in Infrared Monitor to limit the connection speed to 19.2Kbps in order to print successfully. If you allow the IR devices to automatically negotiate the connection speed without setting this limit, they'll negotiate a higher connection speed, and your application will not be able to print.
- The TI TravelMate 5000 and Sharp PC 3050 may communicate over an IR link only at very low speeds (such as 9600 baud).
- If you have an HP Omnibook 4000C or an HP Omnibook 600CT, you must install a special echo-canceling serial driver in addition to the components that make up the IR communications driver. The echo-canceling driver is available from Hewlett-Packard.
- If you use the Infrared Monitor Options tab to change the port that the IR adapter is attached to while IR communications are in progress, the IR connection is lost without prompting you to verify that it's OK to disconnect.
- If there's a problem establishing an IR link to an IrLAN "access point device" when the network is also connected to a network interface card in the computer, try disconnecting the LAN from the network interface card. Restart the computer and make sure that the computer's IR device and the LAN access point's IR port are within range. Then use the Infrared icon in the Control Panel to activate the IR link between the computer and the LAN "access point device."
- The IPX protocol may not communicate over an IrLAN access point. This can be caused by the dial-up adapter becoming the primary IPX adapter, and no other adapter (such as the IrLAN adapter) can take over. To work around this fault, you can create a profile that does not contain the dial-up adapter, and use it when accessing the network through IrLAN.
- If the IR connection between the computer and the IrLAN access point is disconnected during a file copy to a NetWare server running burst mode (that is, the IR beam is blocked), the file transfer cannot recover, and the computer will freeze. Turn off burst mode to recover from a disconnection. There will be performance degradation with the burst mode off.
- Using the virtual parallel port connection to an Extended Systems ESI-9910 JetEye Net Plus IrLAN access point in order to send data to a printer may result in a program fault. To work around this problem, use the virtual serial port on the IrLAN access point to reach the printer.

Troubleshooting Serial and Infrared Ports

Although the typical serial port is a rather simple I/O device, it presents some special challenges for the technician. Older PCs provided their serial ports in the form of 8-bit expansion boards—when a port failed, it was a simple matter to replace the board outright. Today, however, virtually all PCs provide at least one serial port directly on the motherboard—usually integrated into a component of the main chipset. When a problem is detected with a motherboard serial port, a technician often has three choices:

- Replace the UART (responsible for virtually all serial port failures) on the motherboard. This requires access to surface-mount soldering tools and replacement ICs, and can be quite economical in volume.

- Set the motherboard jumpers (if possible) to disable the defective serial port, and install an expansion board (such as a "multi-I/O" board) to take the place of the defective port. This assumes there is an available expansion slot.
- Replace the motherboard outright. This is a simple tactic that requires little overhead equipment, but can be rather expensive.

Virtually all commercial diagnostics are capable of locating any installed serial ports and testing the ports thoroughly through a loopback plug. Now that you have reviewed the layout, signals, and operation of a typical serial port, you can take a clear look at port troubleshooting procedures.

USING MODE TO CONFIGURE A SERIAL PORT

On some systems, it may be necessary for you to make changes to the serial port's configuration while in the real mode (DOS). You can use the MODE command to make your changes. From a command line prompt, type

```
mode comX: /<parameters>
```

where X: is the COM port that you need to tweak (for example, COM2), and <parameters> represents the serial port features that are being altered (including baud rate, parity, data bits, and stop bits). For example:

```
MODE COM1: BAUD=2400 PARITY=N DATA=5 STOP=1 TO=OFF XON=ON ODSR=OFF OCTS=ON
DTR=OFF RTS=OFF IDSR=OFF
```

Table 40-4 lists the complete suite of serial port parameters that you can change with the MODE command.

SERIAL PORT CONFLICTS

Hardware and software conflicts with a system's serial ports are some of the most recurring and perplexing problems in PC troubleshooting. Although PC purists are pleased with the fact that current operating sys-

TABLE 40-4 MODE COMMAND PARAMETERS

<table>
<tr><th>PARAMETER</th><th>DESCRIPTION</th></tr>
<tr><td>BAUD=</td><td>Sets the data transmission rate in bits per second.</td></tr>
<tr><td>PARITY=</td><td>Sets how the system checks for transmission errors using the parity bit. The value can be one of the following: N (None), E (Even), O (Odd), M (Mark), or S (Space).</td></tr>
<tr><td>DATA=</td><td>Sets the number of data bits in a frame (5 through 8).</td></tr>
<tr><td>STOP=</td><td>Sets the number of stop bits that define the end of a frame (1, 1.5, or 2).</td></tr>
<tr><td>TO=ON|OFF</td><td>Turns the "infinite timeout processing" option on or off.</td></tr>
<tr><td>X=ON|OFF</td><td>Turns the XON/XOFF (software handshaking) protocol on or off.</td></tr>
<tr><td>ODSR=ON|OFF</td><td>Turns the output handshaking using Data Set Ready (DSR) circuit on or off.</td></tr>
<tr><td>OCTS=ON|OFF</td><td>Turns the output handshaking using Clear to Send (CTS) circuit on or off.</td></tr>
<tr><td>DTR=ON|OFF</td><td>Turns the DTR circuit on or off.</td></tr>
<tr><td>RTS=ON|OFF|HS|TG</td><td>Specifies the settings for the RTS circuit to on, off, handshake, or toggle.</td></tr>
<tr><td>IDSR=ON|OFF</td><td>Turns the DSR circuit sensitivity on or off.</td></tr>
</table>

tems and BIOS support four COM ports, they cannot overcome the fact that there are still only *two* interrupts available to run the ports from. Technicians trying to upgrade a PC often encounter problems adding I/O adapters since many current PC motherboards already provide two COM ports right out of the factory. If a PC offers only one COM port (COM1) and another serial port is placed in the system (by accident or on purpose), be aware that you must choose a port and IRQ that does not conflict with the existing port (such as COM 2 or COM4). If the PC already provides two COM ports (COM1 and COM2), adding a third COM port to the system will cause a hardware conflict. You can rectify the conflict by disabling the new COM port, or by disabling one of the two existing COM ports, and jumpering the new COM port to those settings.

Serial device drivers can also be a source of problems for COM ports. Incorrectly written mouse drivers, printer drivers, or third-party interrupt handlers can leave a port inoperative or erratic. If problems develop after a new driver is installed, disable the driver's reference in CONFIG.SYS, or install an updated protected-mode driver under Windows 95/98 using the Add New Hardware wizard. TSRs (often loaded in AUTOEXEC.BAT) can cause problems as well. If problems develop after a new TSR is installed, disable the offending TSR and try the system again. Remember that drivers and TSRs can easily be disabled by adding the REM statement before the command line in CONFIG.SYS or AUTOEXEC.BAT. If the communication trouble is under Windows 95/98, strongly suspect the Windows communication package, or the registry may need to be adjusted for an optimum modem initialization string.

MATCH THE SETTINGS

It's bad enough that you can only (practically) use two COM ports, but you also have to make sure that the port addresses and IRQ assignments *match*, as shown in Table 40-1. For example, suppose that there is no COM1 at 03F8h, but there *is* a COM port at 02F8h. During system initialization, BIOS locates each available port and assigns a COM designation, so since there is no port at 03F8h, the port at 02F8h (normally COM2) is the first port detected, and assigned as COM1. However, DOS and BIOS expect COM1 to use IRQ4, but the port at 02F8h uses IRQ3. If you attempt to use BASIC or DOS for COM1, the standard interrupt handlers will not work. You would have to use communication software that talks to the port directly (and thus avoids using DOS interrupt handlers) and can be assigned with the address and IRQ setting of your choosing. As an alternative, you can switch the COM port to 03F8h and set the interrupt to IRQ4. That should restore normal COM1 operation through DOS.

FRAME IT RIGHT

The data frame and rate play very important roles in serial communication. The sending and receiving ends of the serial link must be set to the *same configuration*—otherwise, the received data will be interpreted as garbage. If you encounter such troubles, be sure to check the settings for data bits, parity bit, stop bits, and baud rate. Change the data frame at either end of the serial link such that all devices are running with the same parameters. You may need to use the MODE command to make changes to the serial port setup.

FINDING A PORT ADDRESS WITH DEBUG

You can use the DOS Debug utility to determine the I/O addresses of a serial port. Make sure that you boot the computer in the DOS mode, and then switch to the directory containing the Debug utility (such as C:\DOS). Type

```
C:\DOS\> debug
```

A hyphen will appear. This is the Debug prompt. At the debug prompt, type the following:

```
D 40:00 09
```

A single line of text appears, such as:

```
0040:0000 F8 03 F8 02 00 00 00 00-78 03
```

To exit Debug, press Q (to quit), and then press ENTER to leave Debug and return to the DOS prompt. The line of interest begins 0040:0000. In this example, the F8 03 (read 03F8h) and F8 02 (read 02F8h) indicate two serial ports (COM1 and COM2). Other possibilities include E8 03 (read 03E8) and E8 02 (read 02E8). These are COM3 and COM4, respectively. A machine with four serial ports should read

```
0040:0000 F8 03 F8 02 E8 03 E8 02-78 03
```

A machine with no serial ports should read

```
0040:0000 00 00 00 00 00 00 00 00-78 03
```

The -78 03 entry is the address of the first parallel port (read 0378h).

GENERAL SYMPTOMS

Your companion CD contains a variety of tools for identifying and diagnosing COM ports, including EasyCom 2.0.

SYMPTOM 40-1 You hear a beep code or see a POST error indicating a serial port fault The system initialization may or may not halt, depending on how the BIOS is written. Low-level initialization problems generally indicate trouble in the computer's hardware. If the computer's beep code sequence is indistinct, you could try rebooting the computer with a POST analyzer card installed. The BIOS POST code displayed on the card could be matched to a specific error explanation in the POST card's documentation. Once you have clearly identified the error as a serial port fault, you can proceed with troubleshooting.

Start with the system as a whole and remove any expansion boards that have serial ports available. Retest the computer after removing each board. If the error disappears after removing a particular card, then that card is likely at fault. You can simply replace the card with a new one, or attempt to repair the card to the component level. If there is only one serial port in the system, it is most likely built into the motherboard. Again, you can replace the defective UART, replace the motherboard, or disable the defective motherboard port.

SYMPTOM 40-2 You see an 11xx or 12xx serial adapter error displayed on your system A hardware fault has been detected in one of the COM ports. The 11xx errors typically indicate a fault in COM1, while 12xx errors suggest a problem with COM2, COM3, or COM4. In most cases, the fault is in the UART. You have the option whether to replace the UART IC, replace the motherboard, or disable the defective COM port and replace it with an expansion board.

SYMPTOM 40-3 The computer initializes properly, but the serial peripheral does not work Your applications software may indicate that no device is connected. Before you even open your tool kit, you must determine whether the trouble lies in your computer or your peripheral. When your modem or printer stops working, run a self-test to ensure the device is at least operational. Check all cables and connectors (perhaps try a different cable). Also be sure to check the software package being used to operate the serial port. Ensure that the software is configured properly to use the appropriate COM port and that any necessary drivers are selected.

Disconnect the peripheral at the computer and install a serial loopback plug. Run a diagnostic to inspect each available serial port. Take note of any port(s) that register as defective. Locate the corresponding serial port. If the port is installed as an expansion board, replace the defective expansion board. If the port is on the motherboard, you can replace the defective UART IC, install an alternate expansion board, or replace the motherboard outright.

SYMPTOM 40-4 **Data is randomly lost or garbled** Your first step should be to check the communication cable. Make sure the cable is intact and properly secured at both ends. Try a different cable. If the cable checks properly, either the port or peripheral is at fault. Start by suspecting the serial port. Make sure that the DTE and DCE are both set to use the same data frame and data rate. Incorrect settings can easily garble data. If problems persist, disconnect the printer at the computer and install a serial loopback plug. Run a diagnostic to inspect each available serial port. Take note of any port(s) that register as defective. Locate the corresponding serial port(s). If the port is installed as an expansion board, replace the defective expansion board. If the port is on the motherboard, you can replace the defective port controller IC, install an alternate expansion board, or replace the motherboard outright.

If you cannot test the computer's serial port directly, test the port indirectly by trying the peripheral on another known-good computer. If the peripheral works properly on another computer, the trouble is probably in the original computer's serial port circuitry. Replace any defective circuitry or replace the motherboard. If the peripheral remains defective on another computer, the peripheral itself (such as a printer or modem) is probably faulty.

IRDA SYMPTOMS

SYMPTOM 40-5 **LapLink does not recognize the IR COM port** When you attempt to use LapLink with virtual COM ports created by an infrared adapter, you may receive the following error message:

```
This port is unavailable: it may not be physically present in this computer.
If no other communications program is currently running, check for a mouse
or other serial device on this port.
```

This problem occurs because LapLink accesses the hardware directly to determine the status of the COM port and does not recognize virtual COM ports created using the infrared adapter. To work around this problem, you'll need to contact Traveling Software for a possible patch for LapLink, or discard the use of LapLink in favor of the Direct Cable Connection (DCC) tool included with Windows 95/98.

SYMPTOM 40-6 **You encounter problems maintaining an IR connection in the daylight** This is a common problem with all infrared devices, and is usually caused by "interference" from the natural IR component of ordinary sunlight. Try shortening the transmission distance between the transmitter and receiver (move the devices closer together), and make sure the path between the two is as straight as possible.

SYMPTOM 40-7 **You see an error message indicating that there's an "internal error on the IrDA device"** When you double-click the Infrared icon in Control Panel, you may receive the following error message:

```
ERROR 1: There is an internal error on the IRDA device...
```

This error can occur if the infrared port is disabled in the computer's CMOS settings. Enable the Infrared port in the computer's CMOS settings.

SYMPTOM 40-8 **You receive an "internal error 45" when using the IrDA device under Windows 98** When you double-click the Infrared tool in Control Panel, you may receive an error message such as:

```
Internal Error 45: Your infrared software has encountered an error, check
infrared software settings under network properties.
```

This error can crop up when the Fast Infrared Protocol is missing or damaged. If you install an infrared device in Windows 98, the Fast Infrared Protocol is not installed by default. You must manually add the protocol in Network Properties. To resolve this problem, remove and then reinstall the Fast Infrared Protocol:

1. Click Start, point to Settings, and then click Control Panel.
2. Double-click the Network icon.
3. In the list of installed network components, click Fast Infrared Protocol, and then click Remove.
4. Restart your computer when you are prompted to do so.
5. Click Start, point to Settings, and then click Control Panel.
6. Double-click Network.
7. On the Configuration tab, click Add.
8. Click Protocol, and then click Add.
9. In the Manufacturers box, click Microsoft, click Fast Infrared Protocol in the Network Protocols box, and then click OK.
10. Click OK, and then restart your computer when you're prompted to do so.

40

SYMPTOM 40-9 **You receive a Windows 98 error indicating that the "recipient device is not ready to receive"** When you try to transfer a file from one computer to another computer using an IrDA connection, you receive an error message such as:

```
The recipient device is not ready to receive. Please make sure infrared
transfer is enabled on the receiving device.
```

This error message may occur even though infrared transfer *is* enabled on the receiving computer. This fault usually means that the minimum transmission speed for the IR device on one computer is lower than the minimum transmission speed for the IR device on the other computer. For example, you may receive the error if the minimum IR transmission speed on one computer is 2400bps, but the minimum IR transmission speed on the other computer is 9600bps. Reconfigure your IR devices so that they are both using the same speed settings.

SYMPTOM 40-10 **Your infrared system does not search when it's enabled under Windows 98** When you enable or disable infrared searching, you may find several possible symptoms. When you click the "Search for and provide status for devices within range" check box to select it after IR communication is already enabled, searching does not *start*. When you click that same check box to clear it when IR communication is enabled, searching does not *stop*. Also when you click that same check box, you receive an error message such as:

```
Cannot search for devices because other infrared devices are operating nearby
```

To get around these problems, enable or disable IR communication and the "Search for and provide status for devices within range" check boxes at the same time:

1. Click Start, highlight Settings, and then click Control Panel.
2. Double-click Infrared Monitor, and then click the Options tab.
3. Click the Enable Infrared Communication check box to select it, click the "Search for and provide status for devices within range" check box to select it, and then click Apply.
4. Click OK.

Further Study

ActiSys: **http://www.actisys.com**

Adaptec: **http://www.adaptec.com**

HP: **http://www.hp.com**

Sharp: **http://www.sharp.com**

TI: **http://www.ti.com**

41

SOUND CARDS

CHAPTER AT A GLANCE

Sound is an area of the PC that has been largely overlooked in early systems. Aside from a simple oscillator-driven speaker, the early PCs were mute. Driven largely by the demand for better PC games, designers developed stand-alone sound boards that could read sound data recorded in separate files, then reconstruct those files into basic sound, music, and speech. Since the beginning of the 1990s, those early sound boards have blossomed into an array of powerful high-fidelity sound products capable of duplicating voice, orchestral soundtracks, and real-life sounds with uncanny realism (Figure 41-1). Not only have sound products helped the game industry to mature, but they have been instrumental in the development of *multimedia* technology (the integration of sound and picture), as well as Internet Web phones and other powerful communication tools. This chapter is intended to explain the essential ideas and operations of a contemporary sound board, and show you how to isolate a defective sound board when problems arise.

Understanding Sound Boards

Before you attempt to troubleshoot a problem with a sound board, you should have an understanding of how the board works and what it must accomplish. This type of background helps you when recommending a sound board to a customer, or choosing a compatible card as a replacement. If you already have a strong background in digital sound concepts and software, feel free to skip directly to the troubleshooting portion of this chapter.

THE RECORDING PROCESS

All sound starts as *pressure variations* traveling through the air. Sound can come from almost anywhere—a barking dog, a laughing child, a fire engine's siren, a person speaking—you get the idea. The process of recording sound to a hard drive requires sound to be carried through several manipulations (as shown in Figure 41-2). First, sound must be translated from pressure variations in the air to analog electrical signals. This is accomplished by a *microphone*. These analog signals are amplified by the sound card, then digitized (converted to a series of representative digital words, each taken at a fixed time interval). The resulting stream of data is processed and organized through the use of software, which places the data (as well as any overhead or housekeeping data) into a standard file format (such as the WAV format). The file is saved to the drive of choice—typically a hard drive.

THE PLAYBACK PROCESS

Simply speaking, the playback process is virtually the reverse of recording (Figure 41-3). A software application opens a sound file on the hard drive, then passes the digital data back to the sound card. Data is

FIGURE 41-1 Logitech SoundMan Wave sound board (Copyright © 1995 Logitech Corporation)

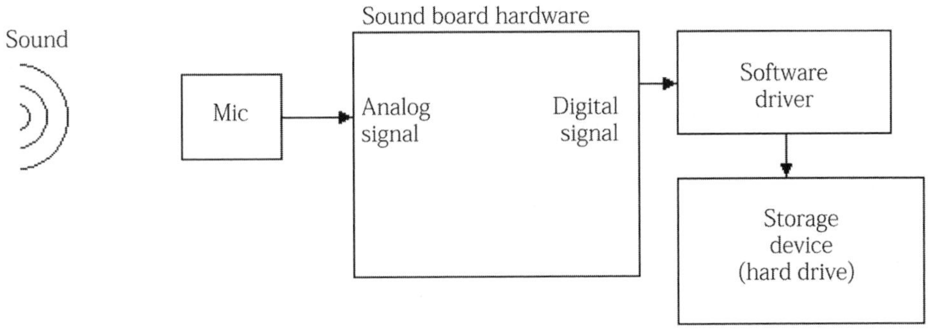

FIGURE 41-2 The sound board recording process

translated back into equivalent analog levels. Ideally, the reconstructed shape of the analog signal closely mimics the original digitized signal. The analog signal is amplified, then passed to a speaker. If the sound was recorded in stereo, the data is divided into two channels that are separately converted back to analog signals, amplified, and sent to their corresponding speakers. Speakers convert the analog signal back into traveling pressure waves that you can hear.

THE CONCEPT OF SAMPLING

To appreciate the intricacies of a sound card's operation, you must understand the concept of *digitization*, otherwise known as *sampling*. In principle, sampling is a straightforward concept: an analog signal is measured periodically, and its voltage at each point in time is converted to a digital number. The device that performs this conversion is known as an *analog-to-digital converter* (ADC). It sounds simple enough in principle, but there are some important wrinkles.

The problem with sampling is that a digitizer circuit has to capture enough points of an analog waveform to reproduce it faithfully. The example in Figure 41-4 illustrates the importance of sampling rate. Waveforms A and B represent the *same* original signal. Waveform A is sampled at a relatively slow rate—only a few samples are taken. The problem comes when the signal is reconstructed with a *digi-*

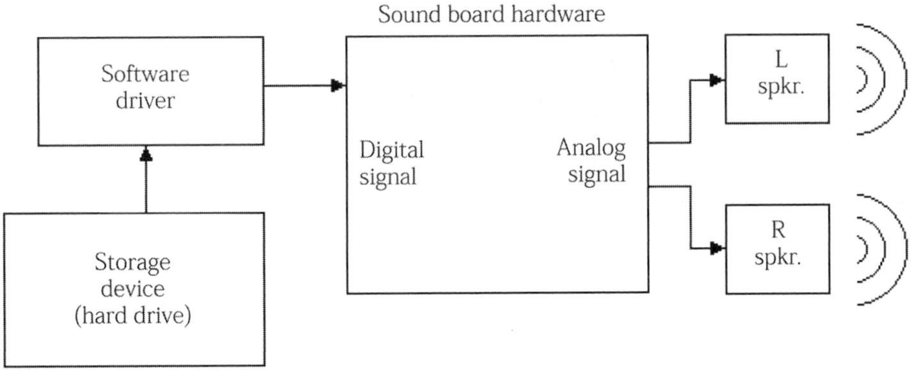

FIGURE 41-3 The sound board playback process

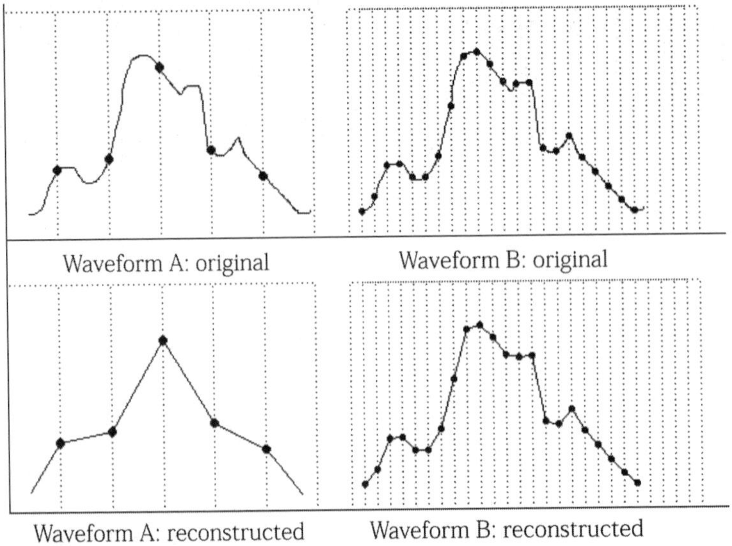

FIGURE 41-4 The concept of sampling rate

tal-to-analog converter (DAC). As you see, there are not enough sample points to reconstruct the original signal. As a result, some of the information in the original signal is lost. This is a form of distortion known as *aliasing*. Waveform B is the same signal, but it is sampled at a much higher rate. When that data is reconstructed, the resulting signal is a much more faithful reproduction of the original.

As a rule, a signal should be sampled at least twice as fast as the highest frequency contained in the signal. This is known as Nyquist's Sampling Theorem. The lowest standard sampling rate used with today's sound boards is 11kHz, which allows fair reproduction of normal speech and vocalization (up to about 5.5kHz). However, most low-end sound boards can digitize signals up to 22kHz. Unfortunately, the human range of hearing is about 22kHz. To capture sounds reasonably well throughout the entire range of hearing, you would need a sampling rate of 44kHz. This is often known as CD-quality sampling since it is the same rate used to record audio on CDs. The disadvantage to high sampling rates is disk space (and sound file size). Each sample is a piece of data, so the more samples taken each second, the larger and faster a file grows.

DATA BITS VS. SOUND QUALITY

Not only does the number of samples affect sound quality, but also the precision (or number of bits) of each sample. Suppose that each sample is converted to a 4-bit number. That means each point can be represented by a number from 0 to 15—not much precision there. If 8 bits are used for each sample, 256 discrete levels can be supported. But the most popular configuration is 16-bit conversion, which allows a sample to be represented by one of 65,536 levels. At that level of resolution, samples will form a very close replica of the original signal. Many common sound boards will capture audio as 16-bit data.

THE ROLE OF MIDI

Although the majority of a sound card is geared toward handling the recording and playback of sound files, the *musical instrument digital interface* (MIDI) port has become an inexpensive and popular addition to most sound card designs. MIDI is a standard protocol that is defined by hardware, software, and electrical interconnections. At the core of a MIDI interface is a *synthesizer* IC. Unlike a sound file, which basically contains the digital equivalent of an analog waveform, a MIDI file is a set of instructions for playing musical notes. Each note is sent to the synthesizer, along with duration, pitch, and timing specifications. The synthesizer can be made to replicate a variety of musical instruments, such as a piano, guitar, harmonica, flute—you name it. The high-end sound boards are capable of synthesizing a small orchestra. Since most synthesizers can process several channels simultaneously, the MIDI standard supports playing a number of "instruments" (or *voices*) at the same time. Thus, very high quality music can be produced with MIDI on a PC. The two most common synthesizer types are FM and Wavetable.

Figure 41-5 illustrates the kinds of things MIDI is capable of. Prerecorded MIDI files can be read from a storage device like a hard drive file, or from CD-ROM. (Many games include an orchestral-quality MIDI soundtrack on the CD.) The MIDI data is passed through to the sound board's synthesizer, which reproduces the sound, and out to the amplified speakers. If you plan on composing music yourself, you can interface a MIDI instrument to the sound board's MIDI port. Using MIDI sequencer software, the notes played on the instrument will be heard through the speaker, as well as recorded to the MIDI file on the hard drive. Note that you do not need a MIDI instrument to play back a MIDI file, but you need an instrument and sequencer software to *create* a MIDI file. Also, since MIDI is not sound (but rather sound "blueprints"), the same MIDI composition entered on a keyboard can be played back as a harp, or a guitar, or a flute.

INSIDE A SOUND BOARD

Now that you're aware of the major functions a sound board must perform, you can see those functions in the context of a complete board. Figure 41-6 shows a simplified block diagram of a sound board. It is important to note that your own particular sound board may differ somewhat, but all contemporary boards should contain these subsections.

The core element of a sound board is the digital signal processor (DSP). A DSP is a variation of a microprocessor that is specially designed to manipulate large volumes of digital data. Like all processor components, the DSP requires memory. A ROM contains all of the instructions needed to operate the DSP and direct the board's major operations. A small quantity of RAM serves two purposes: it provides a "scratch pad" area for the DSP's calculations, and it serves as a buffer for data traveling to or from the PC bus.

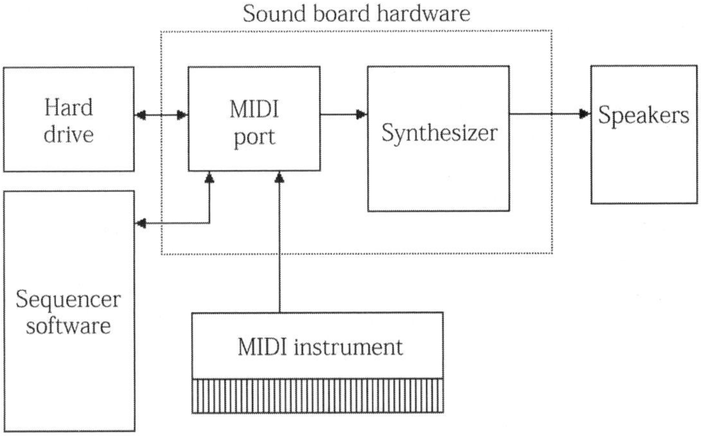

FIGURE 41-5 The path of MIDI signals through the PC

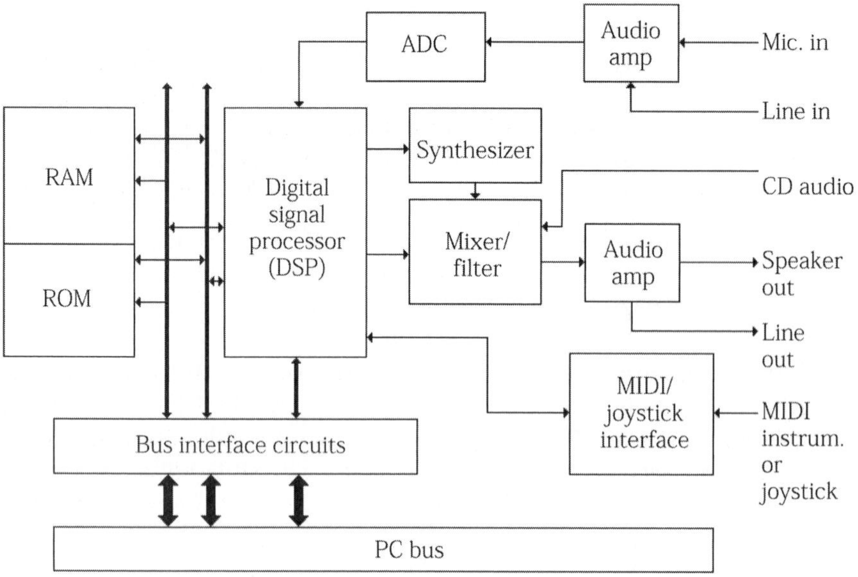

FIGURE 41-6 Simplified block diagram of a sound card

Signals entering the sound board are passed through an amplifier stage and provided to an A/D converter. When recording takes place, the DSP runs the A/D converter and accepts the resulting conversions for processing and storage. Signals delivered by a microphone are typically quite faint, so they are amplified significantly. Signals delivered to the "line" input are often much stronger (such as the output from a CD player or stereo preamp), so they receive less amplification.

For signals leaving the sound board, the first (and often most important) stop is the mixer. It is the mixer that combines CD audio, DSP sound output, and synthesizer output into a single analog channel. Since most sound boards now operate in a stereo mode, there will usually be two mixer channels and amplifier stages. The audio amplifier stage(s) boost the analog signal for delivery to stereo speakers. If the sound will be driving a stereo system, a "line" output provides a separate output. Amplifier output can be adjusted by a single master volume control located on the rear of the board.

Finally, a MIDI controller is provided to accommodate the interface of a MIDI instrument to the sound board. In many cases, the interface can be jumpered to switch the controller to serve as a joystick port. That way, the sound board can support a single joystick if a MIDI instrument will not be used. MIDI information processed by the DSP will be output to the onboard synthesizer.

Knowing the Benchmarks

An important aspect of sound boards is their audio benchmarks. Unlike logic and processing circuitry, which is measured in terms of millions of operations per second, the benchmarks that define a sound card are very much analog. If you are an audiophile, many of the following terms may already be familiar. If most of your experience has been with logic systems, however, these concepts will appear very different from many of the other discussions in this book.

DECIBELS

No discussion of sound concepts is complete without an understanding of the *decibel* (or dB). Decibels are used because they are logarithmic. You see, human hearing is not a linear response. If you increase the power of your stereo output from 4W to 16W, the sound is not four times louder—in fact, it is only twice as loud. If you increase the power from 4W to 64W, the sound is only three times as loud. In human terms, amplitude perception is measured logarithmically. As a result, very small decibel values actually relate to substantial amounts of power. The accepted formula for decibels is as follows:

$$\textit{gain (in dB)} = 10 \log 10 \frac{Pout}{P_{in}}$$

Don't worry if this formula looks intimidating. Chances are that you will not need to use it, but consider what happens when output power is greater than input power. Suppose a 1mW signal is applied to a circuit, and a 2mW signal leaves—the circuit provides a gain of +3dB. Suppose the situation was reversed, where a 2mW signal is applied to the circuit, and a 1mW signal leaves. The circuit would then have a gain of -3dB. Negative gain is a loss, also called *attenuation*. As you see, a small dB number represents a large change in signal levels.

FREQUENCY RESPONSE

Expressed simply, the *frequency response* of a sound board is the range of frequencies that the board will handle uniformly. Examine the sample graph of Figure 41-7. Ideally, a sound board should be able to produce the same amount of power (0dB) across the entire working frequency range (usually 20Hz to 20kHz). This would show up as a flat line across the graph. In actual sound cards, however, this is not practical, and there will invariably be a *rolloff* of signal strength at both ends of the operating range. A good-quality sound board will demonstrate sharp, steep rolloffs. As the rolloffs get longer and more shallow at high and low frequencies, the board has difficulty producing sound power at those frequencies. The result is that bass and treble ranges may sound weak, and this affects the sound's overall fidelity. By looking at a frequency response curve, you can anticipate the frequency ranges where a sound board may sound weak.

41

SIGNAL-TO-NOISE RATIO

The *signal-to-noise ratio* (or SNR) of a sound board is basically the ratio of maximum undistorted signal power to the accompanying electronic noise being generated by the board (primarily hum and hiss) expressed in decibels. Ideally, this will be a very large dB number, which would indicate that the output signal is *so much stronger* than the noise signal, that for all intents and purposes, the noise is imperceptible. In actual practice, a good-quality sound board will enjoy an SNR of 85dB or higher, but these are difficult to find. For most current sound boards with SNR levels below 75dB, there may be audible hum and hiss present during silent periods, as well as a certain amount of sound "grit" underlying sound and music reproduction. Some very inexpensive sound boards are on the market with SNR levels as low as 41dB (noise may be noticeable and actually annoying).

You may also find the SNR value expressed as an *A-weighted* decibel number. The reason for this is that human hearing is not equal at all frequencies, so we cannot hear all noise equally. The process of A-weighting emphasizes the noise levels at frequencies we are most sensitive to. Resulting SNR values are often several dB higher (better) than nonweighted SNR values. Be careful here—a sound board with a low SNR may use the A-weighted value in the specification sheet. If this is the case, subtract about 3dB or 4dB for the actual SNR figure.

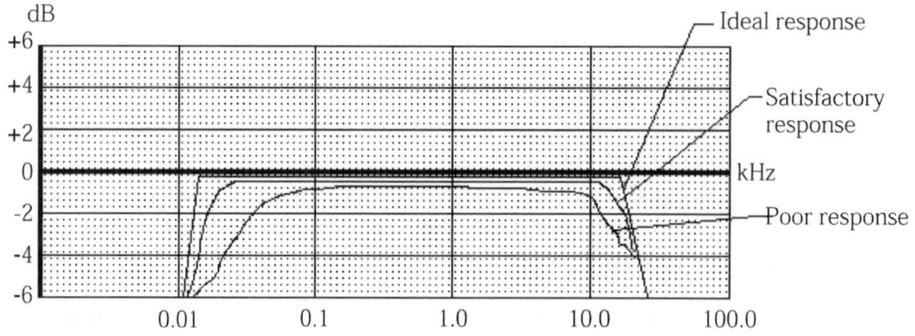

FIGURE 41-7 A sample sound board frequency-response curve

TOTAL HARMONIC DISTORTION

Sound and music are rich in harmonics (overtones) that are basically integer multiples of an original frequency signal (although at much lower levels). As a consequence, harmonics are a valuable attribute of sound. The number and amplitude of harmonics provide the sound characteristics that allow you to distinguish between a guitar, flute, piano, or any other musical instrument played at the same note. Without harmonics, every instrument would produce only flat tones, and every instrument would sound the same.

However, when sound is produced in an electronic circuit, other unwanted harmonics are generated that can alter the sound of the music being produced (thus the term *harmonic distortion*). The *total harmonic distortion* (or THD) of a sound board is the root-mean squared (RMS) sum of all unwanted harmonic frequencies produced, expressed as a percentage of the total undistorted output signal level. In many cases, the RMS value of noise is added to THD (expressed as THD+N). The lower this percentage is, the *better*. THD+N values over 0.1 percent can often be heard, and suggest a less than adequate sound board design.

INTERMODULATION DISTORTION

This form of distortion is related to harmonics. When two or more tones are generated together, amplifiers create harmonics, as well as tone combinations. For example, if a 1kHz and 60Hz tone are mixed, *intermodulation harmonics* will be generated (940Hz, 880Hz, 1060Hz, 1120Hz, etc.). It is this inter-mod ulation that gives sound a harsh overtone. Since intermodulation is not related to sound quality, it is a form of distortion that should be kept to a very low level. Like THD, intermodulation distortion (or IMD) is the RMS sum of all unwanted harmonic frequencies expressed as a percentage of the total undistorted output signal level. IMD should be under 0.1 percent on a well-designed board.

SENSITIVITY

Although it does not directly affect the fidelity of sound reproduction, sensitivity can be an important specification. *Sensitivity* is basically the amplitude of an input signal (such as a microphone signal) that will produce the maximum undistorted signal at the output(s) with volume at maximum.

GAIN

By itself, sensitivity is hard to apply to a sound board, but if you consider the board's output power versus its input signal power and express the ratio as a decibel, you would have the *gain* of the sound board. Many sound boards offer a potential gain of up to 6dB. However, it is important to note that not all sound boards provide positive gain; some boards actually attenuate the signal even with the volume at maximum. In practical terms, this usually forces you to keep the volume control at maximum.

3D AUDIO (A3D)

The A3D audio technology in your sound card (part of your Diamond Multimedia Sonic Impact A3D audio system) was developed by Aureal Semiconductor, and is the result of many years of research into human hearing and digital audio reproduction. In the real world, we can close our eyes, listen to a sound, and pinpoint its direction, distance, and motion. Our ears allow us to hear 360 degrees in all directions, while our eyes cover only about 140 degrees in the direction we're facing. The eyes and ears work in close cooperation to provide us with a seamless perception of reality. When the ears hear a sound from behind, we decide to turn our head and look at an object.

A3D is based on the following premise: we can hear sounds in three dimensions by using only our ears, so it's possible to create sounds from two speakers (or a set of headphones) that have the same effect. There are several listening cues that allow us to hear sounds three-dimensionally. There are split-second differences between what each ear hears when listening to a sound. Sound waves usually appear earlier and louder at the ear closest to the sound source. That same sound (originating from various locations around a listener) will sound different because of the changes in the way it gets reflected and filtered by the shoulders, face, and the outer ear before reaching the eardrum. These listening effects can be summarized in a set of audio filters called Head Related Transfer Functions (or HRTFs).

A3D technology uses advanced signal-processing algorithms and HRTF measurement techniques. This digitally re-creates these "hearing cues" along with the absorption, reflection, and Doppler shift effects, which affect sound waves as they travel from a sound source, through an environment, to the listener's ears. The result is a lifelike audio experience that "surrounds" the listener with sound that seems as if it's in three dimensions, using only a single pair of ordinary speakers or headphones.

Using Microphones

An ever-growing number of sound card owners are using their sound cards to record sound, or broadcast sound over the Internet through such applications as WebPhone. Sound recording demands the use of microphones, and not all microphones work properly with every sound board. Often, the user mistakes a poor microphone response as being a problem with the sound card. This part of the chapter looks at some important considerations for choosing and using a microphone.

MICROPHONE TYPES

There are three types of microphones: dynamic, condenser, and electret condenser. You will find all three microphone types available for sound boards.

- **Dynamic** Dynamic microphones are typically handheld or desktop units. They have a larger response range and typically sound better than condenser microphones. A dynamic microphone does not require phantom power because the diaphragm element in the microphone can create enough electric current for the sound board to use.
- **Condenser** Condenser microphones are the small multimedia microphones that typically come with computers. When you open a new sound board and take the microphone out of the box, it is

almost always a condenser microphone. Their response range is not as good as dynamic microphones, and they also have a smaller diaphragm. This demands phantom power for the sound board.

- **Electret condenser** Electret condenser microphones are basically condenser microphones with a built-in battery for power. They have the same response as a condenser microphone, but they do not require phantom power to operate. Some electret condenser microphones will allow you to remove this internal battery. With the battery not installed, phantom power *would* be required.

PHANTOM POWER

So the next question is "what is phantom power?" Phantom power is simply a small low-current power supply on the sound board that is used to power some microphones. Devices like dynamic microphones can produce enough current on their own to avoid the use of phantom power, but condenser microphones demand phantom power as a current source.

Here's the main problem with today's sound boards: not all of them provide switchable phantom power. Ideally, sound boards (like the Ensoniq Soundscape) would provide phantom power and allow you to jumper the phantom power on or off depending on which microphone you plan to use. If you use a dynamic microphone, you switch phantom power off. If you use a condenser microphone, you switch phantom power on. When a sound board does not provide phantom power at all, you're stuck using a dynamic microphone or a powered electret condenser microphone. If a sound board provides full-time phantom power (and you cannot turn it off), you'll need to stay with a condenser microphone.

You can probably see the potential for trouble here. If you use a condenser microphone on an unpowered sound board, the microphone will not work at all (or generate little more than faint noise). On the other hand, plugging a dynamic or electret microphone into a powered sound board will usually result in severe clipping. Once again, you'll capture little more than noise.

CHOOSING A MICROPHONE

Whether you're choosing a microphone for yourself or recommending one to someone else, there are some considerations to keep in mind. Perhaps the most important issue is the application. If you just need a basic, inexpensive microphone to record a few simple voice notes, a condenser or electret microphone would work just fine, and your sound board will require a phantom power supply. If you want to record more professional vocals, or prepare a presentation, a dynamic microphone will generally provide the best results, and no phantom power is needed.

Installing/Upgrading a Sound Card

Fortunately, adding a sound card to a system is a remarkably straightforward procedure. The only real problem areas are in hardware conflicts and software installation. This part of the chapter covers the essential steps and precautions that you will need to remember when installing a sound card. Although the chances of a system failure during the upgrade are extremely remote, it is always a wise policy to back up any vital files or programs before opening the system.

> If you're replacing an existing sound card, be sure to uninstall all of the sound card's application software, and remove the existing sound card's entry in your Device Manager. Then shut down the system directly.

STATIC DISCHARGE PRECAUTIONS

Most of the chips used in today's expansion boards are fabricated with technologies that make them extremely sensitive to electrostatic discharge (ESD). To ensure the safe handling of sound boards and other system components during the upgrade, make it a point to take the following precautions. First, use an antistatic wrist strap whenever handling components or tools inside the PC. Cable the wrist strap to another reliable earth ground. Next, always try to handle expansion boards by their *edges*—avoid touching the individual IC pins or printed wiring. Third, if you will be removing an old sound board, have a good-quality antistatic bag on hand to store it in. Under no circumstances should you allow a sound board (or any expansion board) to rest on a synthetic or static-prone surface. Finally, excessively dry environments tend to allow substantial buildups of static charges in objects, clothing, and bodies. If possible, try to work in an environment with at least 40 percent humidity.

PREPARE THE SYSTEM

At this point, you can prepare the system for its upgrade. A word of caution is in order here: *be especially careful of screwdriver blades when working inside the PC.* If you should slip, the blade can easily gouge the motherboard (or an expansion board) and result in broken traces. It pays to be careful and gentle when upgrading a expansion device. Before you even consider opening the PC cover, turn the system off, and unplug it from the AC receptacle. This helps to ensure your safety by preventing the PC from being powered accidentally while you are working on it.

Remove the screws holding down the outer cover, and place those screws aside in a safe place. Gently remove the PC's outer cover and set it aside (out of the path of normal floor traffic). You should now be able to look into the PC and observe the motherboard, along with any expansion boards and drives that are installed. If you will be replacing an existing sound board, now is the time for you to label any cables connected to it. Labels need not be fancy—a roll of masking tape and an indelible marker are all that is required.

REMOVE THE OLD BOARD

If there is no sound board already in the PC, feel free to skip right down and continue with the next step. Otherwise, start by disconnecting any cables that are attached to the current sound board. (Make sure each cable is labeled.) You can then remove the screw that attaches the board bracket to the chassis, and gently ease the board from its expansion slot. Be sure to handle the board by its edges. When the old board is removed, seal it in an antistatic bag and set it aside. There are several important cables to look for:

- Speaker output cable
- Microphone input cable (if a microphone is attached)
- Line input cable (if you're mixing in a source from outside of the sound board)
- CD audio cable between the CD-ROM drive and sound board
- CD-ROM drive interface cable (if there's a CD-ROM in the system using that interface)
- The 15-pin joystick or MIDI interface cable

INSTALL THE NEW BOARD

Find an open expansion slot for the new sound board. Virtually all sound boards today are 16-bit devices, so you will need a full ISA slot or a PCI slot. The card slot should also accommodate a "full-length" board. For legacy-type sound boards, check each jumper on the new sound board and see that none of the IRQ,

DMA, or I/O settings conflict with other devices in the system. If problems arise, this list will help isolate conflicts. Ease the new board into its expansion slot, and be careful to avoid flexing the motherboard too much in the process. Once the sound card is installed properly, secure the board bracket to the PC chassis with the single screw.

CONNECT THE CABLES

Now that the new sound card is in place, reconnect the cables as required. As a minimum, you will need to connect speakers, but you may also have to connect a CD audio cable, CD-ROM drive interface cable, microphone, MIDI or joystick cable, and so on. After each of the cables is secured, you can reconnect AC to the computer and reboot the system.

INSTALL THE DOS SOFTWARE

Sound boards require the installation of DOS driver software to set up and configure the board each time the PC is initialized. Other sound board–specific software is usually needed to operate the CD-ROM drive (if the sound board contains a drive controller). Where configuration utilities are loaded, executed, then discarded during initialization, "drive controller" software typically takes the form of device drivers that stay resident in memory after initialization. If you are also installing a CD-ROM, you will need the DOS extension MSCDEX.EXE.

When installing a new sound board to replace an old board, you will need to *replace* the software already configured in CONFIG.SYS and AUTOEXEC.BAT. Before installing the new software, open CONFIG.SYS and AUTOEXEC.BAT into a text editor, and place a REM statement before each command line that references any old sound board software. This effectively disables those lines without removing them. Be sure to save each of the changes you make. You can then proceed to install the new sound board's software (usually from an installation disk). Most current installation routines will automatically add the new command-line references to CONFIG.SYS and AUTOEXEC.BAT.

> Be sure to make a backup copy of your CONFIG.SYS and AUTOEXEC.BAT files before you attempt to edit them.

> These alterations to the CONFIG.SYS and AUTOEXEC.BAT files are needed only if you're using the sound board under DOS or Windows 3.1x. If you work exclusively under Windows 95/98, you do not have to provide DOS support.

INSTALL THE WINDOWS 95/98 SOFTWARE

Once Windows 95/98 starts, you'll need to install the proper drivers and utilities for the sound card. If the sound card is plug-and-play ready (as virtually all are now), Windows 95/98 will probably identify the new sound hardware automatically and attempt to install drivers for it. If your sound board has a Windows 95/98 driver disk or CD, be sure to use the drivers from that media (otherwise, Windows 95/98 may install older or incompatible native drivers).

> Even if Windows 95/98 correctly identifies and installs the new sound card, you may need to manually remove the old sound card (if one was installed) from the Windows 95/98 Device Manager yourself before the new sound card will function.

If the sound card is an older legacy device (or does not fully support plug-and-play), Windows 95/98 may not identify the new sound card automatically. Instead, you'll need to remove the old sound board references in the Windows 95/98 Device Manager (if you haven't already), and use the Add New Hardware wizard under the Windows 95/98 Control Panel to identify the sound board and install its drivers. Once again, you should have a Windows 95/98 driver disk or CD handy to ensure that the latest drivers are installed for your specific sound board.

TEST THE SOUND BOARD

Many different sound boards include a small test routine on the accompanying software disk. You can usually run such a routine directly from the floppy disk, or install it on the hard drive and run it from there. Typically, the test routine will check sound (such as a WAV file) and MIDI (music) operation. If both features work as expected, you can be confident that the speakers are connected and the sound board is installed properly. If either (or both) features fail to work, reexamine the installation, check that all necessary software was installed correctly, and check for any hardware conflicts between the sound board and other devices in the system.

Troubleshooting a Sound Board

Traditionally, sound boards use many of the same chipsets and basic components, but since each board is designed a bit differently, it is very difficult for commercial diagnostic products to identify failed IC functions. For the most part, commercial and shareware diagnostics can only identify whether or not a brand-compatible board is responding. As a result, this chapter will take the subassembly replacement approach. When a sound board is judged to be defective, it should be replaced outright. This part of the chapter reviews the problems and solutions for sound boards under both DOS and Windows 95/98. The following tips may help you nail down a sound problem most efficiently:

- Check to see that your speakers are connected, powered, and turned on.
- Check that the speaker volume and sound card master volume are turned up.
- Check to see that the mixer volume and master volume are set properly.
- Make sure that the music or sound file(s) are installed properly.
- Check that all sound card and multimedia drivers are installed.
- Make sure that the drivers are up-to-date.
- Check for resource conflicts between the sound card and other devices in the system.
- Make sure that the sound card is selected and configured properly (especially for DOS apps).
- The sound device should be enabled and configured under CMOS (for sound functions incorporated on the motherboard).

DRIVERS AND DRIVER ORDER

Unlike most other expansion devices that are driven by system or supplemental BIOS, sound boards make use of small device drivers to set up their operations. These drivers are generally included in CONFIG.SYS and AUTOEXEC.BAT, and are called when the system is first initialized. Most sound board drivers are only used to initialize and set up the board, so they do not remain resident. This is good since it reduces the load on conventional and upper memory. However, these initialization routines vary from board to board. For example, the files installed for a Creative Labs Sound Blaster will not support a Turtle Beach MultiSound board. When you elect to replace a sound board, you must also disable any current sound board drivers, and include any new supporting driver files. The process is not difficult—just follow the installation instructions for the board—but the software consideration does add another wrinkle to the replacement process.

When there are problems installing or upgrading a sound board, one of the first issues to suspect is the driver loading order. Sound boards are typically multifunction devices that require several drivers in CONFIG.SYS and AUTOEXEC.BAT. If the drivers are installed in the wrong order, the sound board (or other features of the board) may not function. As a rule, the drivers should be loaded in the following order *after* your memory managers:

- The sound board's device driver:

```
DEVICE=C:\SB16\DRV\SB16.SYS /A:220
```

- The CD-ROM port setup driver (if the sound board is equipped):

```
DEVICE=C:\SB16\DRV\CDSETUP.SYS /P:340
```

- The CD-ROM driver (if the sound board is equipped):

```
DEVICE=C:\SB16\DRV\MTMCDAE.SYS /D:MSCD001 /P:340 /A:0 /T:5 /I:11
```

FULL-DUPLEX DRIVERS

Many current sound board designs are compatible with "multimedia communication" technologies such as Internet Phone, WebPhone, and communication tools. These tools require full-duplex operation—that is, sound is digitized with the microphone, and received sound is played through the speakers simultaneously. This demands full-duplex drivers. If you plan to use communication tools, you'll need to install full-duplex sound card drivers that are appropriate for your particular sound board and operating system. For example, the Creative Labs SB32, AWE32, and AWE64 require the Windows 95 full-duplex driver file (SBW95UP.EXE) available from the Creative Labs Web site (**http://www.creaf.com**). To use those same devices for full duplex under Windows NT 4.0, you'd need the AWENT40.EXE driver file. As a rule, always check with the sound board maker for current full-duplex drivers.

> You may find that full-duplex drivers are not available for older sound boards, or sound boards running under OS/2 and Windows NT. In that case, you cannot support full-duplex applications.

WAV PLAYBACK PROBLEMS UNDER WINDOWS 95/98

Of all the sound board problems reported, perhaps the most common is the failure to play wave files (ordinary sound files with the WAV extension) under Windows 95/98. This problem usually manifests itself during the Windows startup or shutdown, when the accompanying sounds are not played. There are a variety of issues that can prevent WAV files from playing.

Program-Specific Problems

If you cannot play WAV files from a specific program that you use in Windows 95/98, check to see if the same problem occurs when you play the file from another program. If the problem occurs only with one particular program, the files associated with that program may be damaged, or that program may not be configured correctly under Windows 95/98. If you cannot get WAV files to play under any application, chances are that another issue is responsible.

Sound Device is not Configured properly

If you cannot play any WAV files in Windows 95/98 (or if WAV files are not played at the proper volume), you may not have a sound device selected, or the sound device that you have selected may not be configured properly. To select and configure a sound device in Windows 95/98:

1. Open the Control Panel and double-click the Multimedia icon.
2. In the Playback area under the Audio tab (Figure 41-8), click the playback device that you want to use in the Preferred device list, and then move the Volume slider to the value you want (usually 50 percent to 75 percent volume is adequate).
3. In the Recording area under the Audio tab, click the playback device that you want to use in the Preferred device list, and then move the Volume slider to the value you want.
4. Make sure that the speakers are properly connected to the sound card and that they are turned on.

Mixer Settings are not configured properly

If you cannot play any WAV files under Windows 95/98 (or if WAV files are not played at the proper volume), the mixer control settings may not be configured properly. You can use the mixer control program included with Windows 95/98 to adjust the volume for playback, recording, and voice commands. To configure mixer control settings for Windows 95:

1. Click the Start button, point to Programs, point to Accessories, point to Multimedia, and then click Volume Control (Figure 41-9).
2. Make sure that the Mute all check box below the Volume Control slider and the Mute check box below the Wave slider are not selected, and that the Balance sliders for Volume Control and Wave are in the center of the scale.
3. Move the Volume Control and Wave sliders at least halfway to the top of the scale. You may need to adjust the current Volume Control or Wave settings to play WAV files at the volume level you want.

> If the Volume Control and Wave sliders do not appear, click Properties on the Options menu, and then click the Volume Control and Wave check boxes in the "Show the following volume controls" box to select them.

The Sound Hardware is not configured properly

It is possible that your sound card may not be compatible with the type of WAV file you are attempting to play, or there may be a resource conflict between your sound card and another device installed in your computer. Check the Device Manager to see if there are any resource conflicts with your sound board. To determine whether your sound card supports the WAV file format you are attempting to play, contact the sound card's manufacturer.

Damaged Sound Files

If you cannot play certain WAV files in Windows 95/98 (or if the WAV files are not played properly), the WAV files themselves may be damaged. To check whether a WAV file is damaged, use the right mouse button to click the WAV file in Windows Explorer, click Properties on the menu, and then click the Details tab. The Audio Format line should contain information about the type of compression used to compress the file, the sound quality of the file, and whether or not the file is in stereo. If this information is missing, the WAV file is probably damaged, and it should be reinstalled or recopied to the drive.

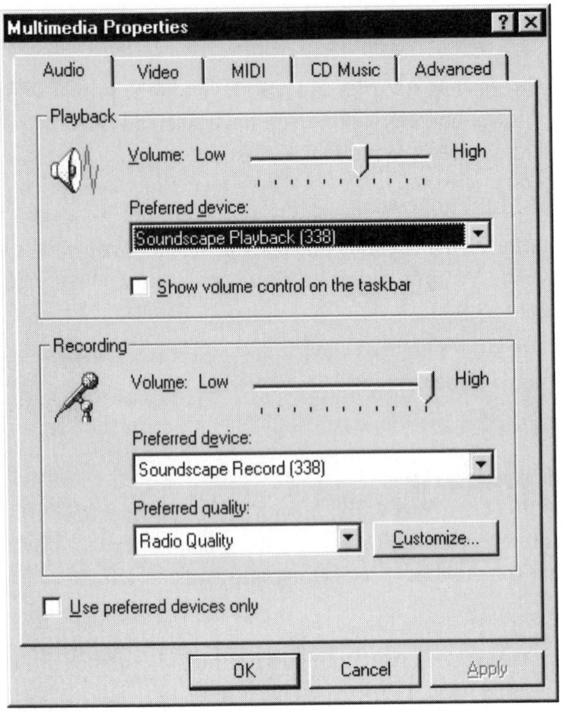

FIGURE 41-8 The Audio tab under the Multimedia Properties dialog

If you can play other WAV files of a similar format, chances are good that the suspect file is indeed damaged. If you can play WAV files of different formats, but not WAV files of a particular format, it may be that your sound board does not support the particular format.

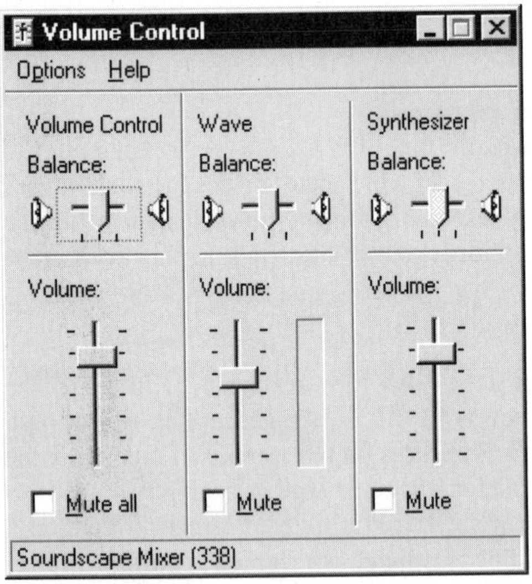

FIGURE 41-9 The multimedia Volume Control applet

Compression-Related Problems

Windows 95/98 includes 32-bit versions of several common CODECS, including Adaptive Delta Pulse Code Modulation (ADPCM), Interactive Multimedia Association (IMA) ADPCM, Group Special Mobile (GSM) 6.10, Consultative Committee for International Telephone and Telegraph (CCITT) G.711 A-Law and u-Law, and Truespeech from DSP. These 32-bit CODECS are installed by default during Windows 95/98 setup, and are used by multimedia programs even if a 16-bit version of the same CODEC is available. Make sure that WAV file format is supported by an available CODEC. Otherwise, you may need to install an appropriate CODEC.

HARDWARE SYMPTOMS

SYMPTOM 41-1 **A noticeable buzz or hum is produced in one or both speakers** Low-cost speakers use unshielded cables. Unfortunately, strong signals from AC cords and other signal-carrying conductors can easily induce interference in the speaker wires. Try rerouting speaker cables clear of other cables in the system. If problems persist, try using higher-quality speakers with shielded cables and enclosures. In most cases, that should resolve everyday noise problems. If the noise continues regardless of what you do, there may be a fault in the sound board amplifier. Try moving the sound board to another bus slot away from other boards or the power supply. If that does not resolve the problem, try a new sound board.

SYMPTOM 41-2 **There is no sound from the speaker(s)** The lack of sound from a sound board can be due to any one of a wide range of potential problems. If the sound board works with some applications, but not with others, it is likely that the problem is due to an improperly installed or configured application. See that the offending application is set up properly (and make sure it is capable of using the sound card). Also check that the proper sound driver files (if any) are loaded into CONFIG.SYS and AUTOEXEC.BAT as required. In many cases, there are one or two sound-related environment variables that are set in AUTOEXEC.BAT. Make sure your startup files are configured properly.

Check your speakers next. See that they are turned on and set to a normal volume level. The speakers should be receiving adequate power and should be plugged properly into the correct output jack. If speakers have been plugged into the wrong jack, no sound will be produced. If the cable is broken or questionable, try a new set of speakers. Also see that the master volume control on the sound board is turned up most (or all) of the way.

If problems continue, there may be a resource conflict between the sound board and another device in the system. Examine the IRQ, DMA, and I/O settings of each device in the system. Make sure that no two devices are using the same resources. You might like to use the PC Configuration Form at the end of this book to record your settings. If problems persist, and no conflict is present, try another sound board.

SYMPTOM 41-3 **CD audio will not play through the sound card** This problem can occur under both DOS and Windows 95/98. First, make sure the sound board is actually capable of playing CD audio. (Older boards may not be compatible.) If the sound card is playing sound files, but is not playing CD audio, there are several things for you to check. First, open the PC and make sure the CD audio cable (a thin, four-wire cable) is attached from the CD-ROM drive to the sound board. If this cable is broken, disconnected, or absent, CD audio will not be passed to the sound board. If the cable is intact, make sure the CD audio player is configured properly for the sound board you are using, and check the startup files to see that any drivers and environment variable needed by CONFIG.SYS and AUTOEXEC.BAT are available. If the CD audio fails to play under Windows 95/98, make sure that an MCI (multimedia control interface) CD audio driver is included in the Drivers dialog box under your Windows Control Panel.

SYMPTOM 41-4 **You see an error such as "No interrupt vector available"** The DOS interrupt vectors used by the sound board's setup drivers (usually INT 80h to BFh) are being used by one or more other drivers in the system. As a consequence, there is a software conflict. Try disabling other drivers in the system one at a time until you see the conflict disappear. Once you have isolated the offending driver(s), you can leave them disabled, or (if possible) alter their command-line settings so that they no longer conflict with the sound board's software.

SYMPTOM 41-5 **There is no MIDI output** Make sure that the file you are trying to play is a valid MIDI file (usually with a .MID extension). In most cases, you will find that the MIDI Mapper under Windows is not set up properly for the sound board. Load the Windows MIDI Mapper applet from the Control Panel, and set it properly to accommodate your sound board.

SYMPTOM 41-6 **Sound play is jerky** Choppy or jerky sound playback is typically the result of a hard drive problem—more specifically, the drive cannot read the sound file to a buffer fast enough. In most cases, the reason for this slow drive performance is excessive disk fragmentation. Under DOS, the sound file(s) may be highly fragmented. Under Windows, the permanent or temporary swap files may be highly fragmented. In either case, use a reliable DOS defragmenter such as PC Tools or Norton Utilities (leave Windows before defragmenting the disk), and defragment the disk thoroughly.

SYMPTOM 41-7 **You see an error such as "Out of environment space"** The system is out of environment space. You will need to increase the system's environment space by adding the following line to your CONFIG.SYS file:

```
shell=c:\command.com /E:512 /P
```

This command line sets the environment space to 512 bytes. If you still encounter the error message, change the E entry to 1024.

SYMPTOM 41-8 **Regular "clicks," "stutters," or "hiccups" occur during the playback of speech** This may also be heard as a "garbled" sound in speech or sound effects. In virtually all cases, the system CPU is simply not fast enough to permit buffering without dropping sound data. Systems with i286 and slow i386 CPUs typically suffer from this kind of problem. This is often compounded by insufficient memory (especially under Windows), which automatically resorts to virtual memory. Since virtual memory is delivered by the hard drive, and the hard drive is much slower than RAM anyway, the hard drive simply can't provide data fast enough. Unfortunately, there is little to be done in this kind of situation (aside from adding RAM, upgrading the CPU, or changing the motherboard). If it is possible to shut off various sound features (music, voice, effects, etc.), try shutting down any extra sound features that you can live without. Make sure that there are no TSRs or other applications running in the background.

SYMPTOM 41-9 **The joystick is not working, or not working properly on all systems** This problem only applies to sound boards with a multifunction MIDI/joystick port being used in the joystick mode. Chances are that the joystick is conflicting with another joystick port in the system. Disable the original joystick port or the new joystick port. Only one joystick port (game adapter) can be active at any one time in the system. Since joystick performance is dependent on CPU speed, the CPU may actually be too *fast* for the joystick port. Disable the joystick port, or try slowing down the CPU.

SYMPTOM 41-10 **You install a sound board and everything works properly, but now the printer does not seem to work** There is an interrupt conflict between the sound board and an IRQ line used by the printer. Although parallel printers are often polled, they can also be driven by an IRQ line (IRQ5 or IRQ7). If the sound board is using either one of these interrupts, try changing to an alternate

IRQ line. When changing an IRQ line, be sure to reflect the changes in any sound board files called by CONFIG.SYS or AUTOEXEC.BAT.

SYMPTOM 41-11 You see the message "Error MMSYSTEM 337: The specified MIDI device is already in use" This problem often occurs with high-end sound boards such as the Creative Labs AWE64. This error is often caused by having the sound board's mixer display on with the wavetable synthesizer selected (for example, the LED display in the Creative Mixer turned on and Creative Wave Synthesizer selected as the MIDI playback device). You can usually correct the problem by turning the mixer display off.

SYMPTOM 41-12 You see the message "Error: Wave device already in use when trying to play wave files while a MIDI file is playing" This problem often occurs with high-end sound boards such as the Creative Labs AWE64, and is usually the result of a device configuration problem. If full duplex is turned on, and you try to play a WAV file and a MIDI file at the same time with the wavetable synthesizer (such as the Creative Wave Synthesizer) selected as the MIDI playback device, an error will occur. To resolve this problem, you need to turn off the full-duplex mode:

1. Hold down the ALT key and double-click My Computer.
2. Select the Device Manager tab. There should be a listing for "Sound, Video, Game Controllers" in the Device Manager. Double-click on the listing to expand it.
3. You should now see a listing for sound boards (such as Creative AWE32 16-Bit Audio). Double-click on the listing, and then select the Settings tab. Uncheck the box labeled "Allow full-duplex operation." Click OK until you are back to the Control Panel.
4. Now try to play a WAV and MIDI file at the same time.

SYMPTOM 41-13 You hear pops and clicks when recording sound under Windows 95/98 There is insufficient cache to adequately support the recording process (or cache is improperly configured). Try the following procedure to alter the way cache is allocated:

1. Open Notepad and load SYSTEM.INI.
2. Locate the area of SYSTEM.INI labeled [vcache].
3. Add the following line below [vcache]:

```
maxfilecache=2048
```

4. Save your changes to the SYSTEM.INI file.
5. From the desktop, right-click on My Computer, and then select Properties.
6. Select the Performance page, and then click on File System.
7. Find the slider marked "Read-ahead optimization," and then pull the slider to None.
8. Save your changes and restart Windows 95/98.

SYMPTOM 41-14 You notice high-frequency distortion in one or possibly both channels In many cases, the AT Bus Clock is set over 8MHz, and data is being randomly lost. This problem usually occurs in very fast systems using an ISA sound board. Enter the system's CMOS setup and check the AT Bus Clock under the Advanced Chipset Setup area. See that the bus clock is set as close as possible to 8MHz. If the bus clock is derived as a divisor of the CPU clock, you may see an entry such as /4. Make sure that divisor results in a clock speed as close to 8MHz as possible. If problems persist, try increasing the divisor to drop the bus speed below 8MHz. (Note that this may have an adverse effect on other ISA peripherals.)

41

SYMPTOM 41-15 You hear pops and clicks when playing back prerecorded files under Windows 95/98 There is an excessive processing load on the system, which is often caused by virtual memory and/or 32-bit access. Start by disabling virtual memory: open the Control Panel and double-click on the System icon. Select the Performance page and click on Virtual Memory. Set the swap file to None and save your changes. Try the file playback again. If problems persist, try disabling 32-bit file access. If that still does not resolve the problem, try disabling 32-bit disk access.

SYMPTOM 41-16 You hear pops and clicks on new recordings only; preexisting files sound clean This is often due to issues with software caching. If you are using DOS or Windows 3.1, disable SmartDrive from both CONFIG.SYS and AUTOEXEC.BAT, and then restart the computer for your changes to take effect. If problems continue (or you are using Windows 95/98), there may be an excessive processing load on the system due to virtual memory or 32-bit access. Follow the recommendations under Symptom 41-15.

SYMPTOM 41-17 You hear pops and clicks when playing back or recording any sound file In most cases, there is a wiring problem with the speaker system. Check all of your cabling between the sound board and speakers. If the speakers are powered by AC, make sure the power jack is inserted properly. If the speakers are powered by battery, make sure the batteries are fresh. Check for loose connections. If you cannot resolve the problem, try some new speakers. If the problem persists, replace the sound board.

SYMPTOM 41-18 The sound board will play back fine, but it will not record The board probably records fine in DOS, but not in Windows. If the sound board is using 16-bit DMA transfer (typical under Windows), there are two DMA channels in use. Chances are that one of those two DMA channels is conflicting with another device in the system. Determine the DMA channels being used under Windows, and then check other devices for DMA conflicts. If you are using Windows 95/98, check the Device Manager and look for entries marked with a yellow icon.

SYMPTOM 41-19 A DMA error is produced when using a sound board with an Adaptec 2842 controller in the system This is a known problem with the Digital Audio Labs "DOC" product and the Adaptec 2842. You will need to alter the controller's FIFO buffer. Go to the controller's setup by pressing CTRL-A when prompted during system startup. Select the advanced configuration option, and then select the FIFO threshold. Chances are that it will be set to 100 percent. Try setting the FIFO threshold to 0 percent, and see if this makes a difference.

SYMPTOM 41-20 A DMA error is produced when using a sound board with an Adaptec 1542 controller in the system This is a known problem with the Digital Audio Labs "DOC" sound product and the Adaptec 1542. The problem can usually be resolved by rearranging the DMA channels. Place the Adaptec controller on DMA 7, and then place the sound board on DMA 5 for playback and DMA 6 for recording.

SYMPTOM 41-21 The sound card will not play or record—the system locks up when either is attempted The board will probably not play in either DOS or Windows, but may run fine on other systems. This is a problem that has been identified with some sound boards and ATI video boards. ATI video boards use unusual address ranges that sometimes overlap the I/O address used by the sound board. Change the sound board to another I/O address.

SYMPTOM 41-22 The sound card will record, but will not playback Assuming that the sound board and its drivers are installed and configured properly, chances are that a playback oscillator on the sound board has failed. Try replacing the sound board outright.

SYMPTOM 41-23 The sound application or editor produces a significant number of DMA errors This type of problem is known to occur frequently when using the standard VGA driver that accompanies Windows. The driver is poorly written and cannot keep up with screen draws. Try updating your video driver to a later, more efficient version. If the driver is known to contain bugs, try using a generic video driver written for the video board's chipset.

SYMPTOM 41-24 The sound board will not record in DOS Several possible problems can account for this behavior. First, suspect a hardware conflict between the sound board and other devices in the system. Make sure the IRQs, DMA channels, and I/O port addresses used by the sound board are not used by other devices.

If the hardware setup appears correct, suspect a problem between DOS drivers. Try a clean boot of the system (with no CONFIG.SYS or AUTOEXEC.BAT). If sound can be run properly now, there is a driver conflict. Examine your entries in CONFIG.SYS or AUTOEXEC.BAT for possible conflicts, or for older drivers that may still be loading to support hardware that is no longer in the system.

Finally, suspect the hard drive controller. Try setting up a RAM drive with RAMDRIVE.SYS. You can install a RAM drive on your system by adding the line

```
device=c:\dos\ramdrive.sys /e 8000
```

The 8000 is for 8MB worth of RAM. Make sure there is enough RAM in the PC. Once the RAM drive is set up, try recording and playing from the RAM drive. (You may have to specify a new path in the sound recorder program.) If that works, the hard drive controller may simply be too slow to support the sound board, and you may need to consider upgrading the drive system.

SYMPTOM 41-25 When recording sound, the system locks up if a key other than the recorder's "hot keys" are pushed This is a frequent problem under Windows 3.1x. The system sounds (generated under Windows) may be interfering with the sound recorder. Try turning off system sounds. Go to the Main icon, choose the Control Panel, and then select Sounds. There will be a box in the lower-left corner marked "Enable system sounds." Click on this box to remove the check mark, and then click OK.

SYMPTOM 41-26 After the sound board driver is loaded, Windows locks up when starting or exiting In virtually all cases, you have a hardware conflict between the sound board and another device in the system. Make sure the IRQs, DMA channels, and I/O port addresses used by the sound board are not used by other devices.

SYMPTOM 41-27 When using Windows sound-editing software, the sound board refuses to enter the digital mode—always switching back to the analog mode Generally speaking, this is a software configuration issue. Make sure that your editing (or other sound) software is set for the correct type of sound board (for example, an AWE32 instead of a Sound Blaster 16/Pro). If problems persist, the issue is with your sound drivers. Check the [drivers] section of the Windows SYSTEM.INI file for your sound board driver entries. If there is more than one entry, you may need to disable the competing driver. This is a known problem with the Digital Audio Labs CardDplus, and is caused by incorrect driver listings. For example, the proper CardDplus driver must be entered as

```
Wave=cardp.drv
```

and the companion driver must be listed as

```
Wave1=tahiti.drv
```

You will need to make sure that the proper driver(s) for your sound board are entered in SYSTEM.INI. You may also need to restart the system after making any changes.

SYMPTOM 41-28 **The microphone records at very low levels (or not at all)** Suspect your microphone itself. Most sound boards demand the use of a good-quality dynamic microphone. Also, Creative Labs and Labtec microphones are not always compatible with sound boards from other manufacturers. Try a generic dynamic microphone. If problems persist, chances are that your recording software is not configured properly for microphone input. Try the following procedure to set up the recording application properly under Windows 95:

1. Open your Control Panel and double-click on the Multimedia icon.
2. The Multimedia Properties dialog will open. Select the Audio page.
3. In the Recording area, make sure to set the Volume slider all the way up.
4. Also see that the Preferred device and Preferred quality settings are correct.
5. Save your changes and try the microphone again.

SYMPTOM 41-29 **The sound card isn't working in full-duplex mode** Virtually all current sound boards are capable of full-duplex operation for such applications as Internet phones. Check the specifications for your sound board and see that the board is in fact capable of full-duplex operation. If it is, and full-duplex isn't working, your audio properties may be set up incorrectly:

1. Open your Control Panel and double-click on the Multimedia icon.
2. The Multimedia Properties dialog will open. Select the Audio page.
3. If the Playback device and the Record device are set to the same I/O address, this is only half duplex.
4. Change the playback device I/O address so it is different from that of the record device.
5. Click the Apply button, then the OK button.
6. You should now be in full-duplex mode.

> Some of the very latest sound boards (such as the Ensoniq SoundscapeVIVO 90) will carry full-duplex operation with the same playback and record device selected.

SYMPTOM 41-30 **You encounter DMA errors using an older sound board and an Adaptec 1542** In many cases, you can clear DMA issues by slowing down the 1542 using the /n switch. Add the /n switch to the ASPI4DOS command line in CONFIG.SYS, such as:

```
device=c:\aspi4dos.sys /n2
```

If slowing the 1542 down with an /n2 switch doesn't fix the problem, you should strongly consider upgrading the sound board. This is a known problem with the older Digital Audio Labs CardD sound board.

SYMPTOM 41-31 **You encounter hard disk recording problems under Windows 95/98** Recorded audio is saved to your hard drive. For most systems, sound data can be transferred to the HDD fast enough to avoid any problems, but if data transfer is interrupted, your recorded sound may pop or break up. There are many factors that affect HDD data transfer speed. The following series of instructions outline a number of procedures that might help you optimize a system for sound recording. First, try disabling the CD Auto Insert Notification feature:

1. Go to the Device Manager and open the CD-ROM entry.
2. Select your CD-ROM drive and click Properties.
3. Go to the Settings page and uncheck the "Auto insert notification" box.
4. Select OK.

Next, try turning down the level of graphics acceleration:

1. Right-click on the My Computer icon and click on Properties.
2. Select the Performance page, and then select the button labeled Graphics.
3. Start by turning down the acceleration one notch. (You can return later to turn it down farther if more performance is required.)
4. Select OK.

It may also be necessary to adjust the size of your virtual memory swap file:

1. Right-click on the My Computer icon and click on Properties.
2. Select the Performance page, and then select the button labeled Virtual Memory.
3. Choose "Let me specify my own virtual memory settings."
4. If your PC has 16MB of RAM, set the minimum and maximum at 40MB. If you have 32MB of RAM, set the minimum and maximum at 64MB.
5. Select OK.

Try removing any active items from your Startup group:

1. Click Start, then Programs, and then select Startup. If you see anything here, it may be hurting your system performance. Eliminate anything that is not absolutely necessary.
2. To remove items, click the Start button, go to Settings, and then select Taskbar.
3. Choose the page labeled Start Menu Programs, and click the Remove button.
4. Open the Startup group by double-clicking it.
5. Remove any items that you feel are not necessary and are wasting resources.
6. Select the Close button when finished.

Clear any indexes of the Find Fast utility:

1. Click Start, then Settings, and then choose the Control Panel.
2. Open the Find Fast utility.
3. Go to the Index menu and select Delete Index.
4. Select an index in the In and Below drop box.
5. Select the OK button.
6. Repeat steps 3 and 4 until all indexes are removed.

Try defragmenting the hard drive:

1. Click Start, then Programs, Accessories, and System Tools.
2. Choose Disk Defragmenter.
3. Select the drive to defragment and click OK.
4. Click the Start button to begin defragmentation.

Finally, you may want to suspend the System Agent (if installed):

1. If System Agent is installed, open it by double-clicking its icon in the task bar.
2. Go to the Advanced menu and choose Suspend System Agent.
3. Close the System Agent window.

SYMPTOM 41-32 The microphone records only at very low levels, or not at all Check your phantom power settings first. In many cases, the microphone's gain is set too low in the sound board's mixer applet. Start the sound board's mixer, make sure that the microphone input is turned on, and then raise the microphone's level control. Remember to save the mixer settings before exiting the mixer. You should not have to restart the system.

SYMPTOM 41-33 Your dynamic microphone clips terribly, and recordings are noisy and faint This is probably due to phantom power being switched on in your sound board. Try turning the phantom power off. If you cannot turn phantom power off, try plugging the dynamic microphone into the sound board's Line Input jack. Remember to start the sound board's mixer applet and set the Line Input level properly.

SYMPTOM 41-34 You have trouble using Creative Labs or Labtec microphones with your (non-Creative Labs) sound board This is a common complaint among Ensoniq sound board users. It turns out that Ensoniq sound boards are not compatible with Creative Labs or Labtec microphones. Try a generic microphone instead.

SYMPTOM 41-35 There is static at the remote end when talking through a voice application such as WebPhone Noise is occurring at the Line Input or Microphone Input and is being transmitted to the remote listener. Check the Line Input signal. You might try reducing or turning off the Line Input mixer level. If the problem persists, check your phantom power setting and your microphone. Try reducing the microphone level in the sound board's mixer. Try a different microphone.

SYMPTOM 41-36 You encounter pops and cracks during recording or playback This is a known problem with SoundBlaster Live and Windows 98 on a VIA motherboard using either an Apollo VP3(VT82C597) or Apollo MVP3(VT82C598) system controller chipset and a VIA IDE bus master driver version 2.1.33 update. Follow these steps to remove the popping/cracking sound:

1. Run SETUP.EXE of the VIA IDE bus master driver version 2.1.33 again.
2. Select the Enable/Disable (Ultra) DMA option instead, and then click the Next button.
3. Unselect/uncheck the available devices, and then click the Next button.
4. Reboot the system.

Please check the VIA Web site at **http://www.viatech.com** for updates on your motherboard.

SYMPTOM 41-37 You encounter short bursts of sound when playing a WAV file This problem happens when you're using a SoundBlaster Live card on a VIA motherboard with the Apollo VP3 (VT82C597) or Apollo MVP3 (VT82C598) system controller chipset. This combination causes repeated buffering during a WAV playback on Windows 98 (Version 4.10.1998). To resolve this problem, download and install the VIA PCI IRQ Miniport driver version 1.3a Setup program. This program can be obtained from the VIA Web site **http://www.via.com.tw/**. Reboot the system after installing the update.

SYMPTOM 41-38 The sound card's SB16 emulation is causing IRQ conflicts on the PC You'll need to disable this device:

1. Click Start, highlight Settings, and click Control Panel.
2. Double-click the System icon, and then click the Device Manager tab.
3. Click the plus sign (+) next to Creative Miscellaneous Devices.
4. Click the sound card's "SB16 Emulation" to highlight it, and then click Properties.
5. Put a check mark in the box labeled Disable This Device In This Hardware Profile.
6. Click OK, click OK again, and then click Close.

This will disable your sound device in DOS mode.

SYMPTOM 41-39 You stop hearing sounds after the system resumes from suspend mode under Windows 98/SE If your computer enters the suspend mode while a program using DirectSound is running, you may no longer hear sounds from the program after you resume the computer. This problem can occur if the DirectSound components of your platform (such as an older version of DirectX) do not resume properly. To correct the issue permanently, download and install the latest version of DirectX from Microsoft at **http://windowsupdate.microsoft.com/**. You can work around the problem and restore sound to the program by rebooting the system.

SYMPTOM 41-40 No WAV sounds are played with Ensoniq PCI sound cards under Windows 98/SE When you're using an Ensoniq PCI sound card, WAV files may not be played properly (or at all), even though MIDI files can be heard normally. This problem occurs if the preferred audio playback device is set to "Use any device." To hear WAV file playback, set the Ensoniq card as the preferred device:

1. Click Start, highlight Settings, and then click Control Panel.
2. Double-click the Multimedia icon.
3. Click the Audio tab.
4. In the Playback section, click Ensoniq in the Preferred Device box.
5. Click OK and reboot the PC if necessary.

SYMPTOM 41-41 Your USB speakers don't work after upgrading to Windows 98/SE This trouble will occur if *another* sound card was detected as the "preferred" audio playback device during the installation of Windows 98/SE. To correct this problem, select the USB audio device as the preferred playback device:

1. Click Start, highlight Settings, and then click Control Panel.

2 Double-click the Multimedia icon.
3 Click the Audio tab.
4 In the Playback section, click your USB audio device in the Preferred Device box.
5 Click OK and reboot the PC if necessary.

SYMPTOM 41-42 **You get no volume from Yamaha USB speakers** This is a known problem for the Yamaha YSTMS55D USB speakers under Windows 98/SE. After you install the Yamaha USB speakers, the speakers may produce little (or no) volume when you use the volume control knob on the speakers. This problem is almost always caused by an incompatible Yamaha driver. You'll need to reinstall or update the device drivers and applications software for your speakers. For the Yamaha speakers, reinstall the Windows 95/98 driver for the Yamaha USB device, the Yamaha Human Interface Device, and the Yamaha Sound Recorder from the original installation media:

1 Click Start, highlight Settings, click Control Panel, and then double-click the System icon.
2 On the Device Manager tab, double-click the "Sound, video and game controllers" branch, and then double-click the "Yamaha USB device."
3 On the Driver tab, click the Update Driver button, click Next, click "Display a list of all the drivers in a specific location, so you can select the driver you want," and then click Next.
4 Click the appropriate Yamaha driver, click Next, click Next, click Finish, and then click Yes to restart your computer.
5 After you change the drivers, open the Volume Control tool and move the volume settings to the highest level. You can then use the volume knob on the speakers to control the sound level.

SYMPTOM 41-43 **An Aztech 2316 sound card is mistakenly identified as a SoundBlaster Pro** When you use the Add New Hardware wizard under Windows 98/SE to detect your Aztech 2316 sound card, it may be incorrectly identified as a SoundBlaster Pro sound card. To fix this error, use the Device Manager to install your Aztech 2316 sound card manually:

1 Click Start, highlight Settings, click Control Panel, and then double-click the System icon.
2 Click the Device Manager tab, double-click the "Sound, video and game controllers" entry, and then double-click Sound Blaster Pro.
3 Click the Driver tab, click Update Driver, and then click Next.
4 Click "Display a list of all the drivers in a specific location," and then click Next.
5 Click "Show all hardware," click Aztech Labs, and click "Aztech 2316 Compatible Legacy Audio (WDM)."
6 Click Next, and then click Finish.
7 Restart your computer.

SYMPTOM 41-44 **Your sound card delivers a "DSP timeout"** This often happens on 440GX motherboards under Windows 98, and you'll find this happens even though you switch card slots and reinstall/update the sound card's drivers. The problem is with the motherboard's 440GX chipset. You must download the INF update utility for the GX chipset from your system or motherboard manufacturer. This motherboard is newer than Windows 98 and must have this patch installed for PCI and AGP devices to function correctly.

SYMPTOM 41-45 **You replace a legacy ISA sound card with a PCI sound card, and now you get a "virtual device driver (VxD)" error at boot time** The problem is almost always caused by the old sound card drivers (not the new sound card drivers). Chances are that you did not remove or uninstall the old sound card's drivers and application software, and they are still trying to load when the system boots. Since the old card is no longer installed, the drivers show an error and refuse to load. You'll need to remove the old sound card's drivers and uninstall the old application software.

SYMPTOM 41-46 **You find that your speakers "sleep" or the bass is too low** This is a known problem with Cambridge 4 Point surround speakers and is almost always caused by a driver problem. Aureal has released a set of drivers (2030_22rc or later) that should address this issue. Go to **http://www.a3d.com/html/download/drivers/** and download the complete drivers for the Vortex 2 chipset. These drivers will allow the bass to function normally in both stereo and quad modes.

SOUND APPLICATION SYMPTOMS

SYMPTOM 41-47 **You cannot install a sound card's software before installing the sound card** This is a known problem with Phoenix BIOS and LiveWare 2.0 when you're installing a SoundBlaster Live card. To install the sound software, you should install the sound card and its drivers first. Install the sound card and reboot your PC. After the PC has restarted, Windows 95/98 will attempt to detect your audio card and install drivers for it. Insert the original installation disc that comes with your sound card into the CD-ROM drive. When prompted to install the drivers:

1. Choose to install the drivers provided by your hardware manufacturer (found in the installation disc).
2. Specify the location and path where the driver software is located.
3. Now run the software setup program.

SYMPTOM 41-48 **You encounter an error such as "Setup cannot detect the sound card on your system"** The sound application's setup program cannot detect the sound card hardware, so you'll need to make a few quick checks to isolate the problem:

1. Check that the sound card is listed and enabled under your Device Manager.
2. Use another mouse device, or disconnect it entirely.
3. Restart the system to your CMOS setup and see that your "PNP OS INSTALLED" option is set to YES.
4. Try moving the card to another PCI slot.

SYMPTOM 41-49 **Your sound card's application software will not install on a Cyrix-based system** This is a known issue with LiveWare 2.0 software on Cyrix 6x86 266MHz (and slower) systems. Check the software's maker to see if there's a patch or update that will work around this problem. Otherwise, you may not be able to use the software on that particular system.

SYMPTOM 41-50 **You try to play back more than one source (for example, a microphone and CD audio), but you cannot keep the sources unmuted at the same time in the mixer** In the sound card's application software (a.k.a. mixer), make sure the What You Hear option is not chosen as the Record source. Choosing another recording source will enable you to unmute multiple analog sources at the same time. However, note that "environment" audio effects can only be applied to the analog source specified as the recording source.

SYMPTOM 41-51 **You find that the mixer settings change every time you switch to an "environment preset" in the surround (A3D) mixer** You're probably trying to maintain the same mixer settings all the time. You can achieve this by dissociating the mixer from the "environment preset." To do this with software like LiveWare 2.0, click the Surround Mixer title in the upper-left corner in the Preset Deck of the Surround Mixer. The system menu appears with Dissociate Mixer Settings. To dissociate mixer settings, make sure the command is checked. To associate mixer settings, make sure the command is not checked.

SYMPTOM 41-52 **You've associated an application to the "environment presets," but the "environmental audio" preset is not activated when the application is launched** Chances are that the AutoEA feature is not working—it must be running. This means the AutoEA icon must appear in the System Tray, or the AutoEA applet must be open. Remember that the AutoEA feature will not work if your current speaker configuration doesn't conform to the one specified in AutoEA. For example, if you specified "2 speakers" in AutoEA, it won't work if your current speaker configuration is "4 speakers."

SYMPTOM 41-53 **The game's acoustics don't seem any different whether "environmental audio effects" (EAX) is enabled or not** Chances are that your EAX system is not initialized properly. For EAX to initialize correctly, you should verify that the current "environmental audio" setting is No Effects.

SYMPTOM 41-54 **You notice slower frame rates with some games when using "environmental audio effects" (EAX) with your sound card's application software** This is a problem with the sound card's application software and not the game itself. Download and install the latest update to your sound card's drivers and application software. This should optimize the game's frame rate by streamlining its audio effect performance.

SYMPTOM 41-55 **You encounter numerous problems with the sound card's application software** These problems may take several forms:

- You hear popping or clicking sounds when using certain features in a given game (for example, using the "RazorJack" weapon in Unreal Tournament).
- You can't use an in-game volume slider in some games after installing the application software.
- You cannot import game presets for your audio setup.

In all cases, the sound card's application software (for example, LiveWare 2.0) is buggy or corrupted. Download and install the newest version of your sound card drivers and application software.

SYMPTOM 41-56 **Your sound card's application software locks up when trying to play audio CDs** This is a known issue with software like Creative PlayCenter. The IDE bus mastering hard disk controllers on your system must support the DMA option for high-speed access to your CD-ROM drive correctly. If the hard disk controllers do not properly support this option, your software may lock up. To determine whether your hard disk controller drivers need updating:

1. Click Start, highlight Settings, and click Control Panel.
2. Double-click the System icon, and then click the Device Manager tab.
3. Click the plus sign (+) next to the CD-ROM entry.
4. Click the first device listed under CD-ROM to highlight it, and then click Properties.
5. Click the Settings tab. If there's a check box labeled "DMA," take the check out of that box.
6. Repeat these steps for any other devices listed under CD-ROM.
7. Click OK.

> If this does not solve the difficulty, you'll need to contact your motherboard manufacturer for updated bus mastering IDE hard disk controller drivers.

SYMPTOM 41-57 **When using a four-speaker system, you notice that the sound seems unbalanced in the four-speaker mode** Ensure that your speakers are properly placed so that the sound output is balanced. There is a chance that one or more of the audio devices (WAV, CD audio, or MIDI) are being positioned within the speaker environment in the Speaker applet, which will result in the imbalance. This could happen if your previous setting was for a Game Environment found in the Environments tab, and you continue to use this same setting for other media playback. Go to the Environments tab and set this to No Effects (or use another neutral preset such as Multi-speaker Normal). Alternately, you can go to the Speaker applet and choose another appropriate setting.

SYMPTOM 41-58 **CD audio is not loud, even with the volume turned all the way up** If your CD audio signal is not loud enough, it is most likely because you're using the A3D reference drivers for your sound card. The A3D drivers add a new feature that allows you to pass the CD audio through an equalizer (or EQ), and your EQ is affecting the volume. Either change the EQ settings, bypass the EQ, or go to A3D settings and remove "CD Audio" from the analog EQ pass-through list.

SOUND CARD UPGRADE SYMPTOMS

SYMPTOM 41-59 **After a new sound board is installed, the system locks up when trying to play sound and/or MIDI files** This is typical of a system hardware conflict between a legacy sound board and one or more other devices in the PC. Unfortunately, the only way to resolve this type of problem is to remove the sound board and check its IRQ, DMA, and I/O settings against other boards in the PC. This is often a cumbersome and time-consuming process. As an alternative, try checking the Device Manager. You can compare the "active" resources against the sound board settings, then adjust any settings that overlap. Also check the sound board software that is called by CONFIG.SYS and AUTOEXEC.BAT. If you have replaced an older sound board, make sure that any command-line references to the older software have been properly disabled with the REM statement.

If you're trying to use a PnP sound board under DOS, you'll need to add a DOS PnP configuration utility to your CONFIG.SYS file. The driver disk that accompanied the PnP sound board should include an appropriate version of this driver. You may need to use this configuration utility to "reserve" the IRQ, DMA, and I/O resources being used by other legacy devices in the system. This will prevent the PnP BIOS from accidentally assigning the sound board to resources that are in use elsewhere.

SYMPTOM 41-60 **The system does not lock up during use, but there is no sound provided by the board** Start with the basics. Make sure the speakers are turned on and powered properly; then check that the speaker cable is properly plugged into the Speaker Out jack. Speakers inadvertently plugged into the Microphone In jack will not produce any sound. Next, check the sound board's volume control and make sure it is turned up at least 75 percent.

Under DOS, check the sound board software that is called by CONFIG.SYS and AUTOEXEC.BAT. See that the sound board software is installed properly. If you have replaced an older sound board, make sure that any command-line references to the older software have been properly disabled with the REM statement. Under Windows 95/98, see that there are no conflicts listed in the Device Manager, and verify that the correct sound board drivers are installed.

SYMPTOM 41-61 **The sound board works, but there is no CD audio under DOS** In almost all cases there is no CD audio cable between the CD-ROM drive and sound board, or the cable is damaged. Check the cable and try a new one. Some CD audio cables are wired a bit differently and will not work with generic CD-ROM and sound board combinations. Also verify that the correct complement of DOS sound card and CD-ROM drivers are installed to support CD audio playback. (Check to see if there is a patch or update driver available.)

SYMPTOM 41-62 **The sound board works, but there is no CD audio under Windows 95/98** The first thing you should suspect is that the CD audio cable between the CD-ROM and sound board is absent, disconnected, or damaged. Check the cable and try a new one. If the cable checks properly, check the Device Manager to verify that the correct complement of Windows 95/98 sound card and CD-ROM drivers are installed to support CD audio playback. (Check to see if there is a patch or update driver available.)

SYMPTOM 41-63 **There is no sound during Windows events** Windows sounds are selected through the Sounds dialog under the Control Panel. If there are no sounds assigned, there will be no sounds generated during Windows events. Check the Sounds dialog and make sure the desired sounds are assigned. If the proper sounds are assigned (but there are still no event sounds), check for the presence of sound board drivers in the Device Manager.

Further Study

Altec-Lansing: **http://www.altecmm.com**

Aztech Labs: **http://www.aztechca.com**

Creative Labs: **http://www.creaf.com**

Diamond Multimedia: **http://www.diamondmm.com**

Ensoniq: **http://www.ensoniq.com**

Frontier Design Group: **http://www.frontierdesign.com/**

SIC Resource: **http://www.sicresource.com/**

Sony Multimedia: **http://www.sel.sony.com/SEL/ccpg/index.html**

Star Multimedia: **http://www.starusa.com/**

Turtle Beach: **http://www.tbeach.com/**

See next page for

Appendix A: Using the Companion Disc

The following chapters are on the accompanying CD:

A

USING THE COMPANION DISC

CHAPTER AT A GLANCE

The key to a successful PC repair rests in a fast and decisive diagnosis of the problem. Determining the source of the problem as quickly and accurately as possible is often the line that separates successful and profitable repair houses from those that are not. *Diagnostics* are the tools technicians use to "look inside" the behavior of ailing PCs. There are many different kinds of diagnostic tools—some are hardware-based test instruments (such as digital multimeters, POST reader cards, and high-voltage probes), while others are software-based programs that probe the PC as it runs and report their findings to the display. Your book comes with the DLS Diagnostic CD III—a CD with over 120 shareware diagnostics and utilities designed to help you identify installed hardware and track down pesky PC problems. In fact, you'll see some references to the "Companion CD" throughout the book. This appendix explains how to use the CD, and it highlights the various software tools you'll find here.

The Shareware Concept

You've seen the word "shareware" used before. At this point, we should discuss exactly what shareware is, and how it relates to commercial software. If you already understand the shareware concept, feel free to skip this section. Otherwise, the following discussion will probably be very helpful to you.

AN ISSUE OF DISTRIBUTION

When we think of diagnostic software, we tend to think of fancy shrink-wrapped boxes lining store shelves. This is *commercial* software sold through distributors. Here's how commercial software works: a bright group of programmers start a small company to write software, but they don't have the marketing or merchandising know-how to get their product into the retail channel. Instead, they will sell (more specifically "license") their brilliant product to a major software publishing house that will put *their own* name on it, put it in *their own* fancy boxes, and use their clout to get it into the hands of retailers. Retail distributors will buy a volume of those products from the publisher (usually at a deep discount) and put them on their store shelves. The publisher then pays the original author(s) a royalty from the volume sales to distributors.

As you might imagine from the scenario above, the people who actually *develop* the software you buy in stores only receive a fraction of the price you actually pay at the store. It's usually the software publishers and retailers that are making the real money. An even more important problem with commercial distribution is that there is only a finite amount of store shelf space to go around, and no distributor is going to stock *everything*. For example, a distributor may choose to carry 2 or 3 diagnostics—not 25 or 30. As a result, a lot of very good products never really get the attention they deserve because the people pushing the product just don't have enough clout with the distributor to gain a foothold on their shelves. As a technician, this means you're denied a broad selection of products.

A

Another serious problem with commercial distribution is that you rarely (if ever) have an opportunity to try a diagnostic (or any other program) *before* you buy it. The back of the box may look pretty, but it hardly ever reveals the "true" product. How many times have you stood in a store trying to decide between two or three similar products, then gotten home with your choice, only to be disappointed? Trying to bring the product back is another challenge entirely. Many software retailers simply will not accept a product return once the box has been opened, and you find yourself out a bundle of money you can barely afford for a product that you can hardly use (if at all). It is a system that is simply not fair to the software buyer.

THE IDEA OF SHAREWARE

The shareware concept is a means of product distribution that allows a vast number of software products to be offered on a "try-before-you-buy" basis. Software writers develop a shareware version of their product that is then distributed freely through bulletin boards, online services (such as CompuServe or the Internet), or even on disks passed between friends. If you like the software and plan to use it, you register (a.k.a. buy) the software with the author. Registration usually involves sending a fee to the author. Some shareware variations only require that you send in your name and mailing address (often referred to as *postcard-ware*); others are complete in the shareware form, and no exchange of money is needed (known as *$0 shareware* or *freeware*). When you register a product, you will typically receive benefits such as an updated version of the product, a printed manual, free technical support, or some other combination of benefits. The advantage of shareware is that *anyone* can put his or her program into distribution, and be assured of a huge distribution network, for virtually no cost.

The important things to remember about shareware are that it is *not* free, it is *not* public domain, and it is *not* a demo version of some shrink-wrapped product. It is fully functional copyrighted software that commands a purchase price. Once you have a shareware product, you may try the product for a certain period of time (typically 30 days). After that time, you *must* register the product (which is the purchase price), or cease using it. When you get a shareware product, it will always be marked as such in the startup screen and disk documentation.

THE PROBLEMS WITH SHAREWARE

Shareware is largely regarded as one of the most important developments in the software industry, and many relatively new companies such as Netscape, Id Software, Apogee Games, PKWARE, and McAfee Associates have gone "commercial" from their product's growth as shareware. Vast numbers of other smaller software makers, like MVP Software, are marketing their products quite successfully where they would never have had a chance through commercial channels. As you venture into the shareware world, however, you should be aware of some potential pitfalls.

First, there is a strong potential for shareware abuse—people who make productive use of the shareware, but refuse to pay for it. This is the great "gray area" of shareware because there is no way to regulate distribution. Shareware only works when the authors receive their registration fees. In turn, this allows them to pay the bills and develop even better software. Software authors have several tactics available to encourage registrations. The most common tool is limited functionality, which means a program may be functional, but limited in its capability. For example, a shareware strategy game I recently found would only allow you to use small and medium-sized play fields with no customized features in the shareware version, but played exactly like as the registered version, which included the added features. In other words, a shareware author will provide you with enough functionality to make the product useful and productive, but not enough functionality to do *everything*. Other incentives for registering the software include the offer of a printed manual—which can be very important for lengthy documentation—and technical support if you need help getting the most from the registered version.

Another issue that some people have with shareware is the inconsistent use of benefits. No two products are alike, and there is no established standard of what you get when you register a product. Some shareware authors provide a wealth of benefits, while others simply send you a registered version on disk or CD. When you decide to register a product, always look at the shareware documentation to see what the benefits are.

Finally, many people become frustrated with the way some shareware authors seem to come and go. Remember that most shareware authors work from home, or from a small office where they've hung out their shingle. If the registrations don't come in, they wind up rocketing into oblivion—leaving their shareware product(s) unsupported on BBS libraries and online forums all over the world. It is certainly disappointing to find a handy shareware product, spend time evaluating it, fill out the registration form, send in your money, and get the registration back unopened a few weeks later because the address listed in the documentation has expired or is undeliverable as addressed. As a rule, if you find a shareware product you like, you should look for the most recent shareware version available before registering it.

The DLS Diagnostic CD III

Now that you understand the idea of shareware, we can finally turn our attention to the CD that accompanies this book. The DLS Diagnostic CD III contains over 120 demo, shareware, $0 shareware (freeware), and public domain diagnostic programs and PC utilities that have been assembled from some of the finest shareware authors in the world. Whether you are a novice attempting to check your PC's configuration for the first time, or an experienced technician trying to manipulate a partition on your customer's hard drive, you'll find an extensive selection of software for testing, troubleshooting, and mastering the PC.

The DLS Diagnostic CD III is arranged as a series of subdirectories, each of which holds an entire product compressed as a single file. Each product resides in its own subdirectory; so once you know the product you are interested in, you can quickly locate the product and install it on your hard drive or floppy disk.

There is no autorun file on the CD, and it will not automatically install or launch any product. The CD is intended to serve as an archive (or library) of shareware products. You can pick and choose the product(s) that you wish to try, then install them individually as required.

The CD and File Compression

The DLS Diagnostic CD III is intended to serve as an archive rather than a working medium, so each of the programs has been compressed as a ZIP file or self-extracting EXE file. To use a program on the CD, you must decompress and install it on your hard drive or a floppy disk. This part of the chapter covers some general guidelines for using the programs on your CD. You might wonder why the programs have been compressed, when they could just as easily been expanded to work (in many cases) directly from the CD itself. Well, there are several important reasons for this decision:

- *Programs generally run very poorly from slow media such as a CD.* Most of the programs on this CD run much better from a floppy disk, or even better from a hard drive.
- *Data files can't be written to the CD.* Some of the diagnostic programs on this CD require that data files be written while the program is running. Since you can't write to an ordinary CD, those programs would not be usable from the CD anyway.
- *Compression conserves space.* Compressed files are smaller and easier to work with than the individual files of an uncompressed product. Using compression allows us to use a minimum amount of space on the CD, and allows the most expansion in future editions of this book.
- *Many authors prohibit the distribution of their products in an uncompressed form.* Gathering up all of the program files into a single compressed file helps us ensure that the original shareware program package has not been tampered with.
- *Some products need to be "installed."* Even if the individual program files were uncompressed, some of the products on the CD need to have an installation routine run in order to organize, sort, and initialize the program files properly; so those programs would still not be executable from the CD.
- *You won't always have a working CD-ROM drive available.* Even if we designed the DLS Diagnostic CD III to run each product directly (and successfully) from the CD itself, it means you would need a working CD-ROM drive on the PC you intend to troubleshoot. You understand that this is not always possible.

INSTALLING THE SOFTWARE

Installing software from the CD to your hard disk or floppy drive is not a difficult process, but you need to pay attention to detail. The process typically involves copying, decompressing, virus checking, and installing.

> Please do not contact Dynamic Learning Systems or McGraw-Hill for information on these programs. We cannot provide support for the installation and use of these programs. For documentation and contact information for each developer, refer to the README file that usually accompanies each program.

- **Step 1**—*Insert the CD in your CD-ROM drive.* Obviously, you will need a PC with a working CD-ROM drive in order to install any files from the CD.
- **Step 2**—*Decide whether you intend to install the CD program to your hard drive or a floppy disk.* Keep in mind that many of the utilities on your CD are too big to fit on a floppy disk in their fully expanded form. You can decompress to a hard drive, then copy to a floppy disk if there is sufficient space on the disk.
- **Step 2a**—*Prepare a subdirectory on your hard disk.* You should never install new software to your hard drive's root directory, so prepare a new directory for the program using the DOS MD command. For example, suppose you want to use the IRQ Diagnostic utility from CTS, Inc., called IRQINFO.ZIP, and install it to your hard drive. You can create a new directory from your DOS prompt such as:

  ```
  C:\> md irqinfo
  ```

  Then switch to the newly created directory using the DOS CD command:

  ```
  C:\> cd\irqinfo
  ```

  The computer will respond with your *new* directory as part of the command prompt:

  ```
  C:\IRQINFO\> _
  ```

- **Step 2b**—*Prepare a subdirectory on your floppy disk.* In most cases, you will be installing only a single product to any one floppy disk, so you generally do not need to concern yourself with creating subdirectories on a floppy disk unless you intend to place more than one product on the disk. Insert a blank floppy disk into drive A: and switch to the A: drive, such as:

  ```
  C:\> A:
  ```

  The floppy drive LED will light for a moment, and the computer will respond with a new prompt:

  ```
  A:\> _
  ```

  Now use the DOS MD command to make a new directory for your product, such as:

  ```
  A:\> md irqinfo
  ```

  Next, switch to the subdirectory you just created using the DOS CD command:

  ```
  A:\> cd\irqinfo
  ```

  The computer will respond with your *new* directory as part of the command prompt:

  ```
  A:\IRQINFO\> _
  ```

- **Step 3—***Copy the desired program to your hard drive or floppy disk.* Now is the time for you to copy the compressed program file from the CD to the media you intend to use. For example, suppose you still want to use that IRQ Diagnostic utility from CTS, Inc., called IRQINFO.ZIP.
- **Step 3a—***Copying from the CD to the hard drive.* If you are copying from the CD to a directory on the hard drive, make sure you are in the desired directory on the hard drive, and type

  ```
  C:\IRQINFO\> copy d:\irqinfo\irqinfo.zip c:
  ```

  This copies the IRQINFO.ZIP file from the CD in drive D: to your current directory (the IRQINFO directory), which you just created on drive C:. Of course, if your CD-ROM and hard drive use different drive letters, be sure to substitute those letters in place of D: and C:.
- **Step 3b—***Copying from the CD to the floppy disk.* If you are copying from the CD to the floppy disk, make sure you are in the desired directory on the floppy disk, and type

  ```
  A:\IRQINFO\> copy d:\irqinfo\irqinfo.zip a:
  ```

  Or if there is no subdirectory on the floppy disk, simply use

  ```
  A:\> copy d:\irqinfo\irqinfo.zip a:
  ```

  This copies the IRQINFO.ZIP file from the CD in drive D: to your current directory (the IRQINFO directory), which you just created on drive A:. If you did not create a subdirectory on drive A:, just copy the compressed file to the root directory of A:. Of course, if your CD-ROM and floppy drive use different drive letters, be sure to substitute those letters in place of D: and A:.
- **Step 4—***Decompress the software.* Now that you have copied the program to wherever you need it, you must decompress the file. Compressed software usually occurs in two forms, an "archive" file (such as a ZIP or ARJ file), or a "self-extracting" file (with an EXE extension). The type of file will slightly affect the process of decompression. An archive file must be decompressed using a utility such as PKUNZIP.EXE, while a self-extracting file will decompress itself when it is executed.
- **Step 4a—***Use PKUNZIP for archive files.* If you must decompress an archive file, use the PKUNZIP.EXE utility (in the root directory of the CD). To use PKUNZIP from the CD directly, try a command such as:

  ```
  C:\IRQINFO\> d:\pkunzip irqinfo
  ```

  This will use PKUNZIP from the root directory of your CD to decompress the IRQINFO file into the current (IRQINFO) subdirectory. If your CD-ROM drive uses a drive letter other than D:, be sure to substitute that letter. If you have trouble running PKUNZIP from the CD directly, copy it to the root directory of your hard drive first, and then run it like the command above—just replace D: with the drive letter of your hard drive.
- **Step 4b—***Execute the self-extracting file.* For compressed files with the .EXE extension, you need only type the name of the file to start the decompression process. Suppose that the IRQINFO.ZIP file was actually named IRQINFO.EXE. Once you're in the right subdirectory, all you need to type is

  ```
  C:\IRQINFO\> irqinfo
  ```

  The file will then decompress (or *extract*) into its constituent files.

A

- **Step 5**—*Check the files for viruses.* Although all of the files on your DLS Diagnostic CD III have been checked for viruses before going to press, you should always make it a point to inspect the decompressed files before executing any new program for the first time. This is a standard operating precaution that you should employ with any program you get regardless of the source. Use tools such as Norton Anti-Virus, Microsoft's MSAV, or any of the virus tools from McAfee Associates (**http://www.mcafee.com/**) to check your program files. If you are placing the diagnostics on floppy disks in order to take them from PC to PC, be sure to write protect the floppy to inhibit the transfer of viruses from other machines.
- **Step 6**—*Install the program files if necessary.* Once you decompress the program files and check for viruses, you should then be able to run the diagnostic or utility from that point. However, many programs need to be configured through an "installation" or "setup" routine before the program can actually be used. You can tell if this is the case by looking at the files you just decompressed. If any of the files are named INSTALL.EXE (or SETUP.EXE), you may need to execute that program first to prepare the diagnostic or utility. The use of installation routines is especially common for programs designed to operate under Windows or Windows 95/98.

REGISTERING YOUR SHAREWARE

Most of the shareware products on your CD carry some sort of registration fee. These fees range from $0 (essentially "free"), to a voluntary contribution of a few dollars, to fees of $40 or more. Now, I am hardly suggesting that you run right out and register everything on the CD. The whole point of shareware is that you can try these products for free to see if they will serve your needs. Chances are that you will try most (if not all) of these programs at one time or another, but you may find only a few programs that you can really use—and these are the ones that you should consider registering. Don't panic; you have plenty of time to try everything!

MONITORS and PRINTERS Diagnostics

In addition to over 120 shareware and public domain products, The DLS Diagnostic CD III also contains two commercial diagnostics from Dynamic Learning Systems: **MONITORS**, a video board/computer monitor diagnostic and alignment program; and **PRINTERS**, a comprehensive diagnostic designed to aid the test of impact, ink-jet, and laser printers. These commercial products are complete, and are compressed on the CD using a password. When you call, fax, or mail your order to Dynamic Learning Systems, you will get a serial number that will unlock the programs. Each program is $30. Check the order form at the back of this book for more information.

Contents of the DLS Diagnostic CD III

The DLS Diagnostic CD III disc contains well over 120 Windows 95/98 utilities that will help you handle tasks ranging from Internet connections to device analysis. This part of the appendix outlines the various shareware products that you'll find on this CD. Table A-1 indexes the products that you'll find on the CD.

TABLE A-1 DLS DIAGNOSTIC CD III SHAREWARE INDEX

PROGRAM	VERSION	DESCRIPTION	PLATFORM	MANUFACTURER	FILE NAME
1-Zip	3.00.071	Make Self-Extracting Files	Win95	Boon Docks, Inc.	1ZIP.ZIP
Access Denied	1.0	Password System	Win95/98	Ivan Mayrakov	AccessDenied10.exe
AccuSet	5.0b	Time Adjusting	Win95	Retsik Software	A32_50.EXE
Adding FreeRAM	1.02	System RAM Manager	Win95	Alexandru Dimitriev	FREERAM.ZIP
AllClear 2000 Pro	2.7e	Year 2000 Testing	Win3.x	SIMCOM Software	AC2000X.EXE
AriTech INI File Editor	1.50	.INI File Editor	Win95/NT	AriTech Development	AINIFE.ZIP
Auto Maintenance	3.03	PC Maintenance Scheduler	Win95/NT	Comp Time	AMWSETUP.EXE
Backup Registry	1.25	Registry Backup Utility	Win95	Mark A. Sowards	RGBKU125.EXE
BCM Diagnostics	1.01.02	PC Diagnostics	Win95	BCM Adv. Res. Inc.	WINDIAG.ZIP
BCWipe	2.13	File Shredder	Win95	Jetico, Inc.	BCWIPE.EXE
Belarc Advisor	---	Upgrade Advisor	Win95/Inter.	Belarc, Inc.	ADVISOR.ZIP
BIOS Finder	1.2	BIOS Upgrade Assistant	Win95	Abstract Concepts	BIOSFIND.ZIP
Boot Locker	5.01	Password System	Win95/98	Steven Eppler	LOCK45.ZIP
BootLog Anal.	1.2	Checks BOOTLOG.TXT	Win95/98	Vision 4 Ltd.	BLA.ZIP
BootManager	4.24	OS Selector	Win95	Nils Hoyer	BOOTMENU.ZIP
Cacheman	3.60	Virtual Memory Manager	Win95	Ultimatum Productions	cacheman.zip
CDCheck	1.1	CD Disc Checker	Win95/98/NT	Mitja Perko	CDCHECK.ZIP
CDLock	1.0	CD Drawer Lock	Win95/NT	Stefan Luyten	CDLOCK.ZIP
CD-R Diagnostic	1.4.1	CD-ROM/CD-R Diagnostic	Win95	CD-ROM Productions	CDRDIAG.EXE
CD-ROM Analyzer	2.1.1	CD-ROM Drive Tester	Win95	Filippof Alex	cdanalyz.zip
CDSpeed 32	1.01	CD Speed Tester	Win95/98/NT	---	CDSPEED.ZIP
ChildProof	2.1	Prevent System Changes	Win95	George Robertson	CHILDPRF.EXE
Clean Floppy	1.1	Floppy Erase/Re-label utility	Win95	Jason Hollet	CLNFLP.ZIP
CliBench MKII	1.0.0	CPU and HDD Benchmark	Win95/98/NT	Marcel Marcus Weber	CLIBENCH.ZIP
ConfigSafe 95	1.05.03	Config. Safe and Restore	Win95	Artisoft, Inc.	CONFGS32.ZIP
Cool Info 99	2.5	Win9x System Information	Win95	Luke Richey	COLINFO.EXE
CPUIdle	5.1	CPU Power-down Utility	Win95	Andreas Goetz	CPUIDLE56.ZIP
CPU Indicator	1.12	CPU Usage Meter	Win95	PY Software, Inc.	CPUSETUP.ZIP
Create a Working DUN	1.0	DUN Setup and Tutorial	Win95	Julian Maytum	DUNANI95.ZIP
Data Advisor	4.04	Drive Data Diagnostic	Win3.1x	Ontrack Data Int'l.	ADV404.ZIP
Dialup Constructor	3.02	Setup DUN Files	Win95	GRV Consulting	SETUP.EXE

TABLE A-1 DLS DIAGNOSTIC CD III SHAREWARE INDEX *(CONTINUED)*

PROGRAM	VERSION	DESCRIPTION	PLATFORM	MANUFACTURER	FILE NAME
Dial-Up Magic	1.8	Setup DUN Files	Win95	TechMagic, LLC	DUNMAG18.EXE
Disk Editor	3.0	Disk Editing Utility (FAT 12/16)	DOS 3.0	Jim Webster	DISKEDIT.ZIP
DiskSpeed 32	1.04	Disk Speed Tester	Win95/98/NT	---	DISKSPEED32.ZIP
DiskState	1.14	Drive Usage Analyzer	Win95	Sveinar Rasmussen	DSKSTATE.ZIP
DLL Show	4.0	Display DLLs	Win95/98	Software Design	DLLSHOW.0
Dr. Hardware	2.5	PC Hardware Analyzer	Win95	Gebhard Peter	DRHW25E.EXE
EasyCom	2.0	Serial Device Tester	Win95	BT Avance Systems	EASYCOM.EXE
Emerg. Recovery Sys.	8.5	Recover System Crashes	Win95	Theodore Fattaleh	ERS98.ZIP
Envite	1.0	Environment Variable Editor	Win95	McMahon Software	ENVITE32.ZIP
ErgoTimer	3.1	Ergonomic Manager	Win95/98/NT	Silvio Kuczynski	ERGT32.EXE
ErrorScan	2.5	Remove Error Files	Win95	Lifestyles Technologies	ESCAN32.EXE
File Rescue	1.0	Undelete from Recycle Bin	Win95/98	Software Shelf	FRDEMO95.ZIP
Floppy	1.8	Floppy Disk Eraser	Win95	Peter Pearson	FLOPPY.ZIP
FreeMem Pro	4.1	System RAM Manager	Win95	Meikel Weber	fmempro.zip
GodeZIP	3.0	Archiving Program	Win95	David Gode	GODEZI32.ZIP
Graphical Memory	1.1	Memory Status Indicator	Win95	Jeff Parker	MEMSTAT.ZIP
GRDuw	3.1	Disk Duplicator	Win95	GR Software	GRDUW31.ZIP
Hagi's Boot Editor	1.1	System Boot Manager	Win95	Hagai Pipko	HAGBOOTE.ZIP
HAL	1.01	File Browser	Win95/98	Robert J. Dykman	HAL.ZIP
Hard Info Pro	1.05	System Info/Benchmark Tool	Win95/98	Ultimate Systems	HISHW105.ZIP
Header Hunter	1.01	File Header Reader	Win95	Dan Zentgraf	HEADERHUNTER.EXE
HeavyLoad	1.0	System Load/Stress Tester	Win95/98/NT	JAM Software	HLOAD.ZIP
Hz Tool	1.2	Video Refresh Rate Adjuster	Win95	Stefan Berglind	HZTOOL.ZIP
InfoPro	2.01	System Information Utility	Win95	EASTern DiGiTAL	IP20SHW.ZIP
InfoTray	1.04	System Information Monitor	Win95/98	Markus Schmidt	INFOTRAY.ZIP
Internet FW2000	1.0	Internet Firewall for PCs	Win95/98	Digital Robotics	IFW2K2.ZIP
Internet Support Diags.	1.2	Internet Connect Testing	Win95	Ken A.	intchdgn.zip
IRQInfo	1.6	IRQ Detection and Mapping	DOS	CTS, Inc.	IRQINFO.ZIP
Keyboard Layout Mgr.	1.121	Keyboard Layout Control	Win95	Milan Vidakovic	KLMLITE.zip
KeyGO	2.2C	Keyboard Management	Win95/98/NT	GDG Systems Inc.	KEYGO22C.EXE
Look RS232	3.0	Serial Debugging Tool	Win95/98/NT	fCoder Programming	LOOKRS232.ZIP
MasterBooter	2.7	Multi-Boot Utility	...	Daniel Nagy	MRBOOT27.ZIP

TABLE A-1 DLS DIAGNOSTIC CD III SHAREWARE INDEX *(CONTINUED)*

PROGRAM	VERSION	DESCRIPTION	PLATFORM	MANUFACTURER	FILE NAME
MemTurbo	1.0	RAM Optimizer	Win95	Silicon Prairie Software	MEMTURBO.ZIP
Modem Doctor	1.0	Modem Diagnostic	Win95	Modem Doctor	MDRW9510.ZIP
ModemHelp Diagnostic	1.0	Modem Info Tool	Win95	BVRP Software	MODDIAGU.ZIP
ModemStatus	2.2	Modem Status Monitor	Win95	TeddyWare	MDMSTA32.ZIP
MSDOS Editor	2.0	MSDOS File Editor	Win95	Alternative Productions	MSDOSED.ZIP
Netmon	2.0a	Dialup Performance Monitor	Win95	Charles Turano	NETMON20.ZIP
OnMark 2000	2.1	Y2K Test/Fix Utility	Win3.1	Viasoft	BTestFix.EXE
PACT ProfileCopy	99.2b	Save/Restore Win Profile	Win95	PACT Software	PACT_PROFILECOPY.EXE
Partition Manager	2.38	Analyze/Manage Partitions	Win95	Mikhail Ranish	PARTBETA.ZIP
Partition Resizer	1.0.2	Partition Management	DOS 5.0	Zofware	PRESZ120.ZIP
PC-Config	9.15	System Information Monitor	DOS 5.0	Holin Datentechnik	CONF915E.ZIP
Performance 95	2.03	Performance Monitor	Win95	BonAmi Software	PERFORMN.ZIP
PortInfo/SPU	5.0	Port Mgmt. and Testing	DOS/Windows	CTS, Inc.	CTSSPU.EXE
PORTS	2.0	UART Identifier	DOS 3.0	MarshallSoft Computing	PORTSX.ZIP
Powertweak	1.03a	Hardware Optimization	Win95/98/NT	Powertweak	POWRT03A.ZIP
PrintDirect	3.0	Print Drive and Directory Tree	Win95	Brad Prendergast	PRINTDIR.ZIP
Procode TrailBlazer	3.0	System Protection	Win95	Procode Dev. Pty.	TB3001B.EXE
ProtectX	1.01	Online Protection	Win95/98/NT	JoFBoF Software	PROTECTX.ZIP
Real Uninstall	1.2	Registry Cleaner	Win95/NT	D++ Software	DRU.ZIP
RegMedic	1.0.03	Analyze/Repair Registry	Win95	Wolf Agency	REGMED.ZIP
RegRepair 2000	3.3	Registry Repair	Win95/98	Wolf Agency	REGREP.ZIP
Resplendent Registrar	0.97	Registry Editor and Manager	Win95	Resplendence Sp	RRPRE.EXE
Rosenthal Utils.	1.0	Utility Suite	Win95/98/NT	Doren Rosenthal	R-UTIL.EXE
SANDRA Std.	2000.3.6.4	PC Diag. and Benchmarking	Win95	3B Software	SAN600.ZIP
ScanBin	6.0	Binary File Scanner	Win95	Jean-Claude Bellamy	SCANB6.EXE
Serial	2.0	Serial Port Reporter	DOS 3.0	Bret Johnson	SERAIL.ZIP
Shortcut Doctor	1.00	Remove Invalid Shortcuts	Win95/98/NT	CronoSoft	DRSHORTCUT.ZIP
Shredder95	1.14	File Eradicator	Win95	Gale-force	SETUP.ZIP
Smart Cleaner	2.1	Remove Problem Files	Win95	PaxWare	SCSETUP.EXE
SmartFormat	1.1	Format Bad Floppy Disks	DOS 4.0	Tecnolec Software	smrtfrmt.zip
SOHO Backup	2.0	Backup to Removable Media	Win95	Sandy Grant	95SOHO20.ZIP

TABLE A-1 DLS DIAGNOSTIC CD III SHAREWARE INDEX *(CONTINUED)*

PROGRAM	VERSION	DESCRIPTION	PLATFORM	MANUFACTURER	FILE NAME
SpeedNet	2.0	Modem Speed Booster	Win95	Brock Debenham	SPEEDFULL.ZIP
StartEd	3.65	Monitor System Boot	Win95	Thomas Reimann	STARTED.ZIP
StartPro	1.32	Control StartUp Folder	Win95	Daedalus Software	START13.EXE
StayAlive	2.0c	Crash Prevention/Recovery	Win95	TFI Technology, Ltd.	SA20C.EXE
Super Disk Scanner 98	2.00.3	Test defective disks	Win95	Christian Kassler	SSDS98!.EXE
SwapMon	1.6	Swap File Analyzer	Win95	FlipTECH	SWAPM.ZIP
System Analyzer	5.1L	PC Hardware Analyzer	DOS	Hans Niekus	SA51SLE.ZIP
System Info.	1.8	System Information Monitor	Win95	Stevens Systems	SYSINF.ZIP
Tasks Manager 98	1.1	Manage Running Applications	Win95	Idyle Software	TSKSMANG.ZIP
TechFacts 98	2.10	System Analyzer Utility	Win95	Dean Software Design	TEKFCT98.ZIP
Terminal Overdrive	2.0	Modem Booster	Win95	Digital Robotics	termovdr.zip
Transfer 95	2.09.03	Create Windows Backup	Win95	ITA Systems	TRANSX95.EXE
TuneDUN	2.1	DUN Manager Utility	Win95	Philip Tang & Sons	TUNEDUN210.ZIP
TweakDUN	2.22	DUN Manager Utility	Win95	Patterson Design	TD_22S.EXE
TweakEzy	1.52	Correct Drifting PC Time	Win95	RealEzy PC Utilities	TWEAK152.ZIP
Tweaki	1.2.506	Windows Optimizing Utility	Win95	JerMar Software	TEWAKI.ZIP
Uninstall Editor	1.0	Manage Uninstall Strings	Win95/98	Jacob Degeling	UNINSTEDIT.ZIP
Waterfall Pro	2.01	CPU Power-down Utility	Win95	Leading WinTech	WFP.ZIP
WinConfig	2.0	Optimize/Clean Windows	Win95	TD Software	WCONFIG.EXE
WinHex	8.0	Hex Editor	Win95/98/NT	Stefan Fleischmann	WINHEX.ZIP
WinImage	4.0.4011	Disk Image Tool	Win95/98/NT	Gilles Vollant	WIMBTA.ZIP
WinRescue 95	8.07	Windows Backup/Restore	Win95	Super Win Software	wrescu.zip
WinSafe 98	2.0	System Setup Protector	Win95	Wolf Agency	WINSD3.ZIIP
WinSystem 98	3.2	System Information Monitor	Win95	NewTech Software	WINSYSTM.ZIP
WinTune 98	1.0.32	PC Hardware Analyzer	Win95	CMP Publications	WT98_32.EXE
Zip Backup	1.90	Compress/Backup Utility	Win95	Gooch Computer Scvs.	BACKUP.EXE
Zip/Jaz Disk Tst.	97-9-9-9	Disk Testing Utility	Win95/98	Walayat Software	ZIP_JAZ.ZIP
Zip Office 98	---	Compresses File Manager	Win95	Atypie Software	ZIPAU.ZIP

ADDITIONAL CHAPTERS

The CD-ROM also contains additional chapters providing even more troubleshooting information. They're contained in the folder titled More Chapters. The additional chapters are

42. Tape Drives
43. Video Adapters and Accelerators
44. USB Troubleshooting
45. Windows 95/98 Issues
46. Removable Media Drives
47. Video Capture Cards
48. Virus Symptoms and Countermeasures
49. PC Cards and Peripherals
50. PC TV/Radio Cards
51. Pen Systems and Touchpads

Appendix B. PC 99 System-Compliance Standards
Appendix C. PC Standards Chart
Appendix D. Index of Filename Extensions
Appendix E. Standard ASCII Chart (0 to 127)
Appendix F. DOS Error Messages
Appendix G. Windows 95/98 Shortcut Keys
Appendix H. PC-Related FAQs and Newsgroups
Appendix I. Preparing for A+
Appendix J. The DLS Technician's Certificate III

These chapters are in Adobe's PDF format. They require the use of Adobe's Acrobat 4 Reader, which is included on the CD in the same folder as the chapters.

BASIC PC MAINTENANCE VIDEO

Also included on the CD-ROM is Dynamic Learning Systems' 41-minute basic maintenance video. This video clearly explains how to clean your system and peripherals, check the PC inside and out, clean your drives, and even optimize your hard drive(s) for peak performance. The video can be found in the Basic PC Maintenance folder and requires an MPEG viewer to run, such as Windows Media Player.

INDEX

B

J

K

L

4th Edition Order Form

Use this form when subscribing to ***The PC Toolbox***™ or when ordering the unlock codes for MONITORS and/or PRINTERS. You may tear out or photocopy this order form.

YES! Please accept my order as shown below: (check any one)

_____ Send me the unlock code for the commercial version of **MONITORS** for **$30** (US)
Massachusetts residents please add $1 sales tax.

_____ Send me the unlock code for the commercial version of **PRINTERS** for **$30** (US)
Massachusetts residents please add $1 sales tax.

_____ Start my 1 year subscription (6 issues) to *The PC Toolbox*™ for **$42** (US). I understand that I have an unconditional 90 day money-back guarantee with the newsletter.

_____ **A special offer! Give me a 1 year subscription to *The PC Toolbox*™, as well as the unlock codes for MONITORS and PRINTERS for just $73 (US).** I understand that I have an unconditional 90 day money-back guarantee with the newsletter.
Massachusetts residents please add $2 sales tax.

PRINT YOUR MAILING INFORMATION HERE:

Name: Company:

Address:

City, State, Zip:

Country:

Telephone: ( ) Fax: ( )

PLACING YOUR ORDER:

*(check our site at **http://www.dlspubs.com**)*

By FAX: Fax this completed order form (24 hrs/day, 7 days/week) to **508-892-1482**

By Phone: Phone in your order (Mon-Fri; 9am-4pm EST) to **508-892-1475**

___ MasterCard Card: ___ ___ ___ ___ ___ ___ ___ ___ ___ ___ ___ ___ ___ ___ ___ ___

___ VISA Exp: ___/___ Sig: ______________________________

Or by Mail: Mail this completed form, along with your check, money order, PO, or credit card info to:

***Dynamic Learning Systems*, P.O. Box 402, Leicester, MA 01524-0402 USA**

Please allow 2-4 weeks for order processing. Returned checks are subject to a $20 charge.

DLS Technician's Certificate III

Information Cover Sheet

Please print clearly

Name: ____

Address: ____

____

City: ____

State: ___ Zip or Postal Code: ________________

Country (other than USA): ______________________________

Telephone: ____________________________

Fax: ____________________________

- the above information is required for proper graing, and to receive proper credit. Tests with incomplete information **cannot** be processed.

Method of Payment

Please Check One

___ Personal or Business *check* for **$50** (US)‡

___ MasterCard *charge* of $50 (US). Card: ______________________________

___ VISA *charge* of $50 (US). Exp: __/__/__ Sig: ______________________

Mail to: **Dynamic Learning Systems, P.O. Box 402, Leicester, MA 01524 USA**

Fax to: **508-892-1482** (24 hrs/day, 7 days/week)

‡ mail *only* - tests without payment cannot be processed. No Purchase Orders.

Please see Appendix J on the CD for further instructions.

WARNING: BEFORE OPENING THE DISC PACKAGE, CAREFULLY READ THE TERMS AND CONDITIONS OF THE FOLLOWING COPYRIGHT STATEMENT AND LIMITED CD-ROM WARRANTY.

Copyright Statement

This software is protected by both United States copyright law and international copyright treaty provision. Except as noted in the contents of the CD-ROM, you must treat this software just like a book. However, you may copy it into a computer to be used and you may make archival copies of the software for the sole purpose of backing up the software and protecting your investment from loss. By saying, "just like a book," The McGraw-Hill Companies, Inc. ("Osborne/McGraw-Hill") means, for example, that this software may be used by any number of people and may be freely moved from one computer location to another, so long as there is no possibility of its being used at one location or on one computer while it is being used at another. Just as a book cannot be read by two different people in two different places at the same time, neither can the software be used by two different people in two different places at the same time.

Limited Warranty

Osborne/McGraw-Hill warrants the physical compact disc enclosed herein to be free of defects in materials and workmanship for a period of sixty days from the purchase date. If the CD included in your book has defects in materials or workmanship, please call McGraw-Hill at 1-800-217-0059, 9am to 5pm, Monday through Friday, Eastern Standard Time, and McGraw-Hill will replace the defective disc.

The entire and exclusive liability and remedy for breach of this Limited Warranty shall be limited to replacement of the defective disc, and shall not include or extend to any claim for or right to cover any other damages, including but not limited to, loss of profit, data, or use of the software, or special incidental, or consequential damages or other similar claims, even if Osborne/McGraw-Hill has been specifically advised of the possibility of such damages. In no event will Osborne/McGraw-Hill's liability for any damages to you or any other person ever exceed the lower of the suggested list price or actual price paid for the license to use the software, regardless of any form of the claim.

OSBORNE/McGRAW-HILL SPECIFICALLY DISCLAIMS ALL OTHER WARRANTIES, EXPRESS OR IMPLIED, INCLUDING BUT NOT LIMITED TO, ANY IMPLIED WARRANTY OF MERCHANTABILITY OR FITNESS FOR A PARTICULAR PURPOSE. Specifically, Osborne/McGraw-Hill makes no representation or warranty that the software is fit for any particular purpose, and any implied warranty of merchantability is limited to the sixty-day duration of the Limited Warranty covering the physical disc only (and not the software), and is otherwise expressly and specifically disclaimed.

This limited warranty gives you specific legal rights; you may have others which may vary from state to state. Some states do not allow the exclusion of incidental or consequential damages, or the limitation on how long an implied warranty lasts, so some of the above may not apply to you.

This agreement constitutes the entire agreement between the parties relating to use of the Product. The terms of any purchase order shall have no effect on the terms of this Agreement. Failure of Osborne/McGraw-Hill to insist at any time on strict compliance with this Agreement shall not constitute a waiver of any rights under this Agreement. This Agreement shall be construed and governed in accordance with the laws of New York. If any provision of this Agreement is held to be contrary to law, that provision will be enforced to the maximum extent permissible, and the remaining provisions will remain in force and effect.

NO TECHNICAL SUPPORT IS PROVIDED WITH THIS CD-ROM.